# COLLINS
# FRENCH
# DICTIONARY

## FRENCH·ENGLISH ENGLISH·FRENCH

### Pierre-Henri Cousin

ZIA FILM DISTRIBUTION COMPANY

8306 WILSHIRE BLVD., SUITE 690
BEVERLY HILLS, CALIFORNIA 90211

First published in this edition 1992

© William Collins Sons & Co. Ltd. 1979, 1982

**Latest reprint 1992**

---

*contributors*
Claude Nimmo, Lorna Sinclair,
Philippe Patry, Hélène Lewis, Elisabeth Campbell,
Renée Birks

*editorial staff*
Catherine Love, Lesley Robertson

---

*Printed in Great Britain*

# INTRODUCTION

**L'usager** qui désire comprendre l'anglais – qui déchiffre – trouvera dans ce dictionnaire un vocabulaire moderne et très complet, comprenant de nombreux composés et locutions appartenant à la langue contemporaine. Il trouvera aussi dans l'ordre alphabétique les principales formes irrégulières, avec un renvoi à la forme de base où figure la traduction, ainsi qu'abréviations, sigles et noms géographiques choisis parmi les plus courants.

L'usager qui veut s'exprimer – communiquer – dans la langue étrangère trouvera un traitement détaillé du vocabulaire fondamental, avec de nombreuses indications le guidant vers la traduction juste, et lui montrant comment l'utiliser correctement.

**The user** whose aim is to read and understand French will find in this dictionary a comprehensive and up-to-date wordlist including numerous phrases in current use. He will also find listed alphabetically the main irregular forms with a cross-reference to the basic form where a translation is given, as well as some of the most common abbreviations, acronyms and geographical names.

The user who wishes to communicate and to express himself in the foreign language will find clear and detailed treatment of all the basic words, with numerous indications pointing to the appropriate translation, and helping him to use it correctly.

# CONTENTS

# ABRÉVIATIONS

# ABBREVIATIONS

| | | |
|---|---|---|
| adjectif, locution adjective | a | adjective, adjectival phrase |
| abréviation | ab(b)r | abbreviation |
| adverbe, locution adverbiale | ad | adverb, adverbial phrase |
| administration | ADMIN | administration |
| agriculture | AGR | agriculture |
| anatomie | ANAT | anatomy |
| architecture | ARCHIT | architecture |
| l'automobile | AUT(O) | the motor car and motoring |
| aviation, voyages aériens | AVIAT | flying, air travel |
| biologie | BIO(L) | biology |
| botanique | BOT | botany |
| anglais de Grande-Bretagne | Brit | British English |
| conjonction | cj | conjunction |
| langue familière (! emploi vulgaire) | col (!) | colloquial usage (! particularly offensive) |
| commerce, finance, banque | COMM | commerce, finance, banking |
| construction | CONSTR | building |
| nom utilisé comme adjectif, ne peut s'employer ni comme attribut, ni après le nom qualifié | cpd | compound element: noun used as an adjective and which cannot follow the noun it qualifies |
| cuisine, art culinaire | CULIN | cookery |
| déterminant: article, adjectif démonstratif ou indéfini etc | dét, det | determiner: article, demonstrative etc. |
| économie | ECON | economics |
| électricité, électronique | ELEC | electricity, electronics |
| exclamation, interjection | excl | exclamation, interjection |
| féminin | f | feminine |
| langue familière (! emploi vulgaire) | fam (!) | colloquial usage (! particularly offensive) |
| emploi figuré | fig | figurative use |
| (verbe anglais) dont la particule est inséparable du verbe | fus | (phrasal verb) where the particle cannot be separated from main verb |
| dans la plupart des sens; généralement | gén, gen | in most or all senses; generally |
| géographie, géologie | GEO | geography, geology |
| géométrie | GEOM | geometry |
| invariable | inv | invariable |
| irrégulier | irg | irregular |
| domaine juridique | JUR | law |
| grammaire, linguistique | LING | grammar, linguistics |
| masculin | m | masculine |
| mathématiques, algèbre | MATH | mathematics, calculus |
| médecine | MED | medical term, medicine |
| masculin ou féminin, suivant le sexe | m/f | either masculine or feminine depending on sex |
| domaine militaire, armée | MIL | military matters |
| musique | MUS | music |
| nom | n | noun |
| navigation, nautisme | NAVIG, NAUT | sailing, navigation |
| adjectif ou nom numérique | num | numeral adjective or noun |
| | o.s. | oneself |
| péjoratif | péj, pej | derogatory, pejorative |
| photographie | PHOT(O) | photography |
| physiologie | PHYSIOL | physiology |
| pluriel | pl | plural |
| politique | POL | politics |
| participe passé | pp | past participle |
| préposition | prép, prep | preposition |
| psychologie, psychiatrie | PSYCH | psychology, psychiatry |

| | | |
|---|---|---|
| temps du passé | **pt** | past tense |
| nom non comptable: ne peut s'utiliser au pluriel | **q** | collective (uncountable) noun: is not used in the plural |
| quelque chose | **qch** | |
| quelqu'un | **qn** | |
| religions, domaine ecclésiastique | **REL** | religions, church service |
| | **sb** | somebody |
| enseignement, système scolaire et universitaire | **SCOL** | schooling, schools and universities |
| singulier | **sg** | singular |
| | **sth** | something |
| subjonctif | **sub** | subjunctive |
| sujet (grammatical) | **su(b)j** | (grammatical) subject |
| techniques, technologie | **TECH** | technical term, technology |
| télécommunications | **TEL** | telecommunications |
| télévision | **TV** | television |
| typographie | **TYP(O)** | typography, printing |
| anglais des USA | **US** | American English |
| verbe | **vb** | verb |
| verbe ou groupe verbal à fonction intransitive | **vi** | verb or phrasal verb used intransitively |
| verbe ou groupe verbal à fonction transitive | **vt** | verb or phrasal verb used transitively |
| zoologie | **ZOOL** | zoology |
| marque déposée | **®** | registered trademark |
| indique une équivalence culturelle | **≈** | introduces a cultural equivalent |

# FRANÇAIS-ANGLAIS
# FRENCH-ENGLISH

# A

**a** *vb voir* **avoir.**

**à** (*à + le* = **au**, *à + les* = **aux**) [a, o] *prép* (*situation*) at, in ; (*direction, attribution*) to ; (*provenance*) from ; (*moyen*) with, by ; **payé au mois** paid by the month ; **100 km/unités à l'heure** 100 km/units per hour ; **à 3 heures/minuit** at 3 c'clock/midnight ; **au mois de juin** in the month of June ; **se chauffer au gaz** to heat one's house with gas ; **à bicyclette** by bicycle *ou* on a bicycle ; **l'homme aux yeux bleus** the man with the blue eyes ; **à la semaine prochaine!** see you next week! ; **à la russe** the Russian way, in the Russian fashion.

**abaisser** [abese] *vt* to lower, bring down ; (*manette*) to pull down ; (*fig*) to debase ; to humiliate ; **s'~** *vi* to go down ; (*fig*) to demean o.s. ; **s'~ à faire/à qch** to stoop *ou* descend to doing/to sth.

**abandon** [abɑ̃dɔ̃] *nm* abandoning ; deserting ; giving up ; relinquishing ; (SPORT) withdrawal ; (*fig*) lack of constraint ; relaxed pose *ou* mood ; **être à l'~** to be in a state of neglect.

**abandonné, e** [abɑ̃dɔne] *a* (*solitaire*) deserted.

**abandonner** [abɑ̃dɔne] *vt* to leave, abandon, desert ; (*projet, activité*) to abandon, give up ; (SPORT) to retire *ou* withdraw from ; (*céder*) to surrender, relinquish ; **s'~** *vi* to let o.s. go ; **s'~ à** (*paresse, plaisirs*) to give o.s. up to.

**abasourdir** [abazuRdiR] *vt* to stun, stagger.

**abat-jour** [abaʒuR] *nm inv* lampshade.

**abats** [aba] *nmpl* (*de bœuf, porc*) offal *sg* ; (*de volaille*) giblets.

**abattage** [abataʒ] *nm* cutting down, felling ; (*entrain*) go, dynamism.

**abattement** [abatmɑ̃] *nm* enfeeblement ; dejection, despondency ; (*déduction*) reduction ; **~ fiscal** ≈ tax allowance.

**abattis** [abati] *nmpl* giblets.

**abattoir** [abatwaR] *nm* abattoir, slaughterhouse.

**abattre** [abatR(ə)] *vt* (*arbre*) to cut down, fell ; (*mur, maison*) to pull down ; (*avion, personne*) to shoot down ; (*animal*) to shoot, kill ; (*fig*) to wear out, tire out ; to demoralize ; **s'~** *vi* to crash down ; **s'~ sur** to beat down on ; to rain down on.

**abbaye** [abei] *nf* abbey.

**abbé** [abe] *nm* priest ; (*d'une abbaye*) abbot ; **M. l'~** Father.

**abc, ABC** [abese] *nm* alphabet primer ; (*fig*) rudiments *pl*.

**abcès** [apsɛ] *nm* abscess.

**abdication** [abdikɑsjɔ̃] *nf* abdication.

**abdiquer** [abdike] *vi* to abdicate // *vt* to renounce, give up.

**abdomen** [abdɔmɛn] *nm* abdomen ; **abdominal, e, aux** *a* abdominal // *nmpl*: **faire des abdominaux** to do exercises for the stomach muscles.

**abécédaire** [abesedɛR] *nm* alphabet primer.

**abeille** [abɛj] *nf* bee.

**aberrant, e** [abɛRɑ̃, -ɑ̃t] *a* absurd.

**abêtir** [abetiR] *vt* to turn into a half-wit.

**abhorrer** [abɔRe] *vt* to abhor, loathe.

**abîme** [abim] *nm* abyss, gulf.

**abîmer** [abime] *vt* to spoil, damage ; **s'~** *vi* to get spoilt *ou* damaged ; (*tomber*) to sink, founder.

**abject, e** [abʒɛkt] *a* abject, despicable.

**abjurer** [abʒyRe] *vt* to abjure, renounce.

**ablation** [ablɑsjɔ̃] *nf* removal.

**ablutions** [ablysjɔ̃] *nfpl*: **faire ses ~** to perform one's ablutions.

**abnégation** [abnegɑsjɔ̃] *nf* (self-) abnegation.

**aboiement** [abwamɑ̃] *nm* bark, barking *q*.

**abois** [abwa] *nmpl*: **aux ~** at bay.

**abolir** [abɔliR] *vt* to abolish ; **abolition** *nf* abolition.

**abominable** [abɔminabl(ə)] *a* abominable.

**abondance** [abɔ̃dɑ̃s] *nf* abundance ; (*richesse*) affluence.

**abondant, e** [abɔ̃dɑ̃, -ɑ̃t] *a* plentiful, abundant, copious.

**abonder** [abɔ̃de] *vi* to abound, be plentiful ; **~ en** to be full of, abound in ; **~ dans le sens de qn** to concur with sb.

**abonné, e** [abɔne] *nm/f* subscriber ; season ticket holder.

**abonnement** [abɔnmɑ̃] *nm* subscription ; (*pour transports en commun, concerts*) season ticket.

**abonner** [abɔne] *vt*: **s'~ à** to subscribe to, take out a subscription to.

**abord** [abɔR] *nm*: **être d'un ~ facile** to be approachable ; **~s** *nmpl* surroundings ; **au premier ~** at first sight, initially ; **d'~** *ad* first.

**abordable** [abɔRdabl(ə)] *a* approachable ; reasonably priced.

**abordage** [abɔRdaʒ] *nm* boarding.

**aborder** [abɔRde] *vi* to land // *vt* (*sujet, difficulté*) to tackle ; (*personne*) to approach ; (*rivage etc*) to reach ; (NAVIG: *attaquer*) to board ; (: *heurter*) to collide with.

**aborigène** [abɔRiʒɛn] *nm* aborigine, native.

**aboulique** [abulik] *a* totally lacking in willpower.

**aboutir** [abutiR] *vi* (*négociations etc*) to succeed ; **~ à/dans/sur** to end up at/in/on ; **aboutissants** *nmpl voir* **tenants.**

**aboyer** [abwaje] *vi* to bark.

**abracadabrant, e** [abRakadabRɑ̃, -ɑ̃t] *a* incredible, preposterous.

**abrasif, ive** [abRazif, -iv] *a, nm* abrasive.

**abrégé** [abReʒe] *nm* summary.

**abréger** [abReʒe] *vt* (*texte*) to shorten, abridge ; (*mot*) to shorten, abbreviate ; (*réunion, voyage*) to cut short, shorten.

**abreuver** [abʀœve] *vt* to water ; (*fig*): ~ **qn de** to shower *ou* swamp sb with ; **s'~** *vi* to drink ; **abreuvoir** *nm* watering place.

**abréviation** [abʀevjɑsjɔ̃] *nf* abbreviation.

**abri** [abʀi] *nm* shelter ; **à l'~** under cover ; **à l'~ de** sheltered from ; (*fig*) safe from.

**abricot** [abʀiko] *nm* apricot ; **abricotier** *nm* apricot tree.

**abriter** [abʀite] *vt* to shelter ; (*loger*) to accommodate ; **s'~** to shelter, take cover.

**abroger** [abʀɔʒe] *vt* to repeal, abrogate.

**abrupt, e** [abʀypt] *a* sheer, steep ; (*ton*) abrupt.

**abruti, e** [abʀyti] *nm/f* (*fam*) idiot, moron.

**abrutir** [abʀytiʀ] *vt* to daze ; to exhaust ; to stupefy.

**abscisse** [apsis] *nf* abscissa, X axis.

**absence** [apsɑ̃s] *nf* absence ; (MÉD) blackout ; mental blank.

**absent, e** [apsɑ̃, -ɑ̃t] *a* absent ; (*chose*) missing, lacking ; (*distrait*: *air*) vacant, faraway // *nm/f* absentee ; **absentéisme** *nm* absenteeism ; **s'absenter** *vi* to take time off work ; (*sortir*) to leave, go out.

**absinthe** [apsɛ̃t] *nf* (*boisson*) absinth(e) ; (BOT) wormwood, absinth(e).

**absolu, e** [apsɔly] *a* absolute ; (*caractère*) rigid, uncompromising ; **~ment** *ad* absolutely.

**absolution** [apsɔlysjɔ̃] *nf* absolution.

**absolutisme** [apsɔlytism(ə)] *nm* absolutism.

**absolve** *etc vb voir* **absoudre**.

**absorbant, e** [apsɔʀbɑ̃, -ɑ̃t] *a* absorbent.

**absorbé, e** [apsɔʀbe] *a* engrossed, absorbed.

**absorber** [apsɔʀbe] *vt* to absorb ; (*gén* MÉD: *manger, boire*) to take.

**absoudre** [apsudʀ(ə)] *vt* to absolve.

**abstenir** [apstəniʀ]: **s'~** *vi* (POL) to abstain ; **s'~ de qch/de faire** to refrain from sth/from doing ; **abstention** *nf* abstention ; **abstentionnisme** *nm* abstentionism.

**abstinence** [apstinɑ̃s] *nf* abstinence.

**abstraction** [apstʀaksjɔ̃] *nf* abstraction ; **faire ~ de** to set *ou* leave aside.

**abstraire** [apstʀɛʀ] *vt* to abstract ; **abstrait, e** *a* abstract.

**absurde** [apsyʀd(ə)] *a* absurd // *nm* absurdity ; absurd ; **par l'~** *ad* absurdio ; **absurdité** *nf* absurdity.

**abus** [aby] *nm* (*excès*) abuse, misuse ; (*injustice*) usage ; **~ de confiance** breach of trust ; embezzlement.

**abuser** [abyze] *vi* to go too far, overstep the mark // *vt* to deceive, mislead ; **~ de** *vt* (*force, droit*) to misuse ; (*alcool*) to take to excess ; (*violer, duper*) to take advantage of ; **s'~** (*se méprendre*) to be mistaken ; **abusif, ive** *a* exorbitant ; excessive ; improper.

**acabit** [akabi] *nm*: **de cet ~** of that type.

**académicien, ne** [akademisjɛ̃, -jɛn] *nm/f* academician.

**académie** [akademi] *nf* (*société*) learned society ; (*école*: *d'art, de danse*) academy ; (ART: *nu*) nude ; (SCOL: *circonscription*) ≈ regional education authority ; **l'A~ (française)** the French Academy ; **académique** *a* academic.

**acajou** [akaʒu] *nm* mahogany.

**acariâtre** [akaʀjɑtʀ(ə)] *a* sour(-tempered).

**accablement** [akɑbləmɑ̃] *nm* despondency, depression.

**accabler** [akɑble] *vt* to overwhelm, overcome ; (*suj*: *témoignage*) to condemn, damn ; **~ qn d'injures** to heap *ou* shower abuse on sb ; **~ qn de travail** to overburden sb with work ; **accablé de dettes/soucis** weighed down with debts/cares.

**accalmie** [akalmi] *nf* lull.

**accaparer** [akapaʀe] *vt* to monopolize ; (*sujet*: *travail etc*) to take up (all) the time *ou* attention of.

**accéder** [aksede] : **~ à** *vt* (*lieu*) to reach ; (*fig*: *pouvoir*) to accede to ; (: *poste*) to attain ; (*accorder*: *requête*) to grant, accede to.

**accélérateur** [akseleʀatœʀ] *nm* accelerator.

**accélération** [akseleʀɑsjɔ̃] *nf* speeding up ; acceleration.

**accélérer** [akseleʀe] *vt* (*mouvement, travaux*) to speed up // *vi* (AUTO) to accelerate.

**accent** [aksɑ̃] *nm* accent ; (*inflexions expressives*) tone (of voice) ; (PHONÉTIQUE, *fig*) stress ; **aux ~s de** (*musique*) to the strains of ; **mettre l'~ sur** (*fig*) to stress ; **~ aigu/grave** acute/grave accent.

**accentuation** [aksɑ̃tyɑsjɔ̃] *nf* accenting ; stressing.

**accentuer** [aksɑ̃tye] *vt* (LING: *orthographe*) to accent ; (: *phonétique*) to stress, accent ; (*fig*) to accentuate, emphasize ; to increase ; **s'~** *vi* to become more marked *ou* pronounced.

**acceptable** [aksɛptabl(ə)] *a* satisfactory, acceptable.

**acceptation** [aksɛptɑsjɔ̃] *nf* acceptance.

**accepter** [aksɛpte] *vt* to accept ; **~ de faire** to agree to do ; (*tolérer*): **~ que qn fasse** to agree to sb doing, let sb do.

**acception** [aksɛpsjɔ̃] *nf* meaning, sense.

**accès** [aksɛ] *nm* (*à un lieu*) access ; (MÉD) attack ; fit, bout ; outbreak // *nmpl* (*routes etc*) means of access, approaches ; **d'~ facile** easily accessible ; **~ de colère** fit of anger ; **~ de joie** burst of joy ; **donner ~ à** (*lieu*) to give access to ; (*carrière*) to open the door to ; **avoir ~ auprès de qn** to have access to sb.

**accessible** [aksesibl(ə)] *a* accessible ; (*livre, sujet*): **~ à qn** within the reach of sb ; (*sensible*): **~ à la pitié/l'amour** open to pity/love.

**accession** [aksɛsjɔ̃] *nf*: **~ à** accession to ; attainment of.

**accessit** [aksesit] *nm* (SCOL) ≈ certificate of merit.

**accessoire** [akseswaʀ] *a* secondary, of secondary importance ; incidental // *nm* accessory ; (THÉÂTRE) prop ; **accessoiriste** *nm/f* (TV, CINÉMA) property man/girl.

**accident** [aksidɑ̃] *nm* accident ; **par ~** by chance ; **~ de la route** road accident ; **accidenté e** *a* damaged *ou* injured (in an accident) ; (*relief, terrain*) uneven ; hilly ; **accidentel, le** *a* accidental.

**acclamation** [aklamɑsjɔ̃] *nf*: **par ~**

(*vote*) by acclamation ; ~s *nfpl* cheers, cheering *sg.*

**acclamer** [aklame] *vt* to cheer, acclaim.

**acclimatation** [aklimatɑsjɔ̃] *nf* acclimatization.

**acclimater** [aklimate] *vt* to acclimatize ; **s'~** *vi* to become acclimatized.

**accointances** [akwɛ̃tɑ̃s] *nfpl*: **avoir des ~ avec** to have contacts with.

**accolade** [akɔlad] *nf* (*amicale*) embrace ; (*signe*) brace ; **donner l'~ à qn** to embrace sb.

**accoler** [akɔle] *vt* to place side by side.

**accommodant, e** [akɔmɔdɑ̃, -ɑ̃t] *a* accommodating.

**accommodement** [akɔmɔdmɑ̃] *nm* compromise.

**accommoder** [akɔmɔde] *vt* (*CULIN*) to prepare ; (*points de vue*) to reconcile ; **s'~ de** to put up with ; to make do with.

**accompagnateur, trice** [akɔ̃paɲatœʀ, -tʀis] *nm/f* (*MUS*) accompanist ; (*de voyage: guide*) guide ; (: *d'enfants*) accompanying adult ; (: *de voyage organisé*) courier.

**accompagnement** [akɔ̃paɲmɑ̃] *nm* (*MUS*) accompaniment.

**accompagner** [akɔ̃paɲe] *vt* to accompany, be *ou* go *ou* come with ; (*MUS*) to accompany.

**accompli, e** [akɔ̃pli] *a* accomplished.

**accomplir** [akɔ̃pliʀ] *vt* (*tâche, projet*) to carry out ; (*souhait*) to fulfil ; **s'~** *vi* to be fulfilled ; **accomplissement** *nm* carrying out ; fulfilment.

**accord** [akɔʀ] *nm* (*entente, convention, LING*) agreement ; (*entre des styles, tons etc*) harmony ; (*consentement*) agreement, consent ; (*MUS*) chord ; **se mettre d'~** to come to an agreement (with each other) ; **être d'~** to agree ; **~ parfait** (*MUS*) tonic chord.

**accordéon** [akɔʀdeɔ̃] *nm* (*MUS*) accordion ; **accordéoniste** *nm/f* accordionist.

**accorder** [akɔʀde] *vt* (*faveur, délai*) to grant ; (*harmoniser*) to match ; (*MUS*) to tune ; **s'~** to get on together ; to agree ; (*LING*) to agree ; **accordeur** *nm* (*MUS*) tuner.

**accoster** [akɔste] *vt* (*NAVIG*) to draw alongside ; (*personne*) to accost // *vi* (*NAVIG*) to berth.

**accotement** [akɔtmɑ̃] *nm* (*de route*) verge, shoulder ; ~s **non stabilisés** soft verges.

**accoter** [akɔte] *vt*: ~ **qch contre/à** to lean *ou* rest sth against/on ; **s'~ contre/à** to lean against/on.

**accouchement** [akuʃmɑ̃] *nm* delivery, (child)birth ; labour.

**accoucher** [akuʃe] *vi* to give birth, have a baby ; (*être en travail*) to be in labour // *vt* to deliver ; ~ **d'un garçon** to give birth to a boy ; **accoucheur** *nm*: (**médecin**) **accoucheur** obstetrician ; **accoucheuse** *nf* midwife.

**accouder** [akude] : **s'~** *vi*: **s'~ à/contre** to rest one's elbows on/against ; **accoudoir** *nm* armrest.

**accouplement** [akupləmɑ̃] *nm* mating ; coupling.

**accoupler** [akuple] *vt* to couple ; (*pour la reproduction*) to mate ; **s'~** to mate.

**accourir** [akuʀiʀ] *vi* to rush *ou* run up.

**accoutrement** [akutʀəmɑ̃] *nm* (*péj*) getup, rig-out.

**accoutumance** [akutymɑ̃s] *nf* (*gén*) adaptation ; (*MÉD*) addiction.

**accoutumé, e** [akutyme] *a* (*habituel*) customary, usual.

**accoutumer** [akutyme] *vt*: ~ **qn à qch/faire** to accustom sb to sth/to doing ; **s'~ à** to get accustomed *ou* used to.

**accréditer** [akʀedite] *vt* (*nouvelle*) to substantiate ; ~ **qn (auprès de)** to accredit sb (to).

**accroc** [akʀo] *nm* (*déchirure*) tear ; (*fig*) hitch, snag.

**accrochage** [akʀɔʃaʒ] *nm* hanging (up) ; hitching (up) ; (*AUTO*) (minor) collision, bump ; (*MIL*) encounter, engagement ; (*dispute*) clash, brush.

**accroche-cœur** [akʀɔʃkœʀ] *nm* kiss-curl.

**accrocher** [akʀɔʃe] *vt* (*suspendre*): ~ **qch à** to hang sth (up) on ; (*attacher: remorque*): ~ **qch à** to hitch sth (up) to ; (*heurter*) to catch ; to catch on ; to hit ; (*déchirer*): ~ **qch (à)** to catch sth (on) ; (*MIL*) to engage ; (*fig*) to catch, attract ; **s'~ à** (*se disputer*) to have a clash *ou* brush ; **s'~ à** (*rester pris à*) to catch on ; (*agripper, fig*) to hang on *ou* cling to.

**accroissement** [akʀwasmɑ̃] *nm* increase.

**accroître** [akʀwatʀ(ə)] *vt* to increase ; **s'~** *vi* to increase.

**accroupi, e** [akʀupi] *a* squatting, crouching (down).

**accroupir** [akʀupiʀ] : **s'~** *vi* to squat, crouch (down).

**accru, e** [akʀy] *pp de* **accroître.**

**accu** [aky] *nm abr de* **accumulateur.**

**accueil** [akœj] *nm* welcome ; **comité d'~** reception committee.

**accueillir** [akœjiʀ] *vt* to welcome ; (*loger*) to accommodate.

**acculer** [akyle] *vt*: ~ **qn à** *ou* **contre** to drive sb back against ; ~ **qn dans** to corner sb in ; ~ **qn à** (*faillite*) to drive sb to the brink of.

**accumulateur** [akymylatœʀ] *nm* accumulator.

**accumulation** [akymylɑsjɔ̃] *nf* accumulation ; **chauffage/radiateur à ~** (night-)storage heating/heater.

**accumuler** [akymyle] *vt* to accumulate, amass ; **s'~** *vi* to accumulate ; to pile up.

**accusateur, trice** [akyzatœʀ, -tʀis] *nm/f* accuser // *a* accusing ; (*document, preuve*) incriminating.

**accusatif** [akyzatif] *nm* (*LING*) accusative.

**accusation** [akyzɑsjɔ̃] *nf* (*gén*) accusation ; (*JUR*) charge ; (*partie*): **l'~** the prosecution ; **mettre en ~** to indict.

**accusé, e** [akyze] *nm/f* accused ; defendant ; ~ **de réception** acknowledgement of receipt.

**accuser** [akyze] *vt* to accuse ; (*fig*) to emphasize, bring out ; to show ; ~ **qn de** to accuse sb of ; (*JUR*) to charge sb with ; ~ **qch de** (*rendre responsable*) to blame sth for ; ~ **réception de** to acknowledge receipt of.

**acerbe** [asɛʀb(ə)] *a* caustic, acid.

**acéré, e** [aseʀe] a sharp.

**achalandé, e** [aʃalɑ̃de] ɔ: **bien ~** well-stocked ; well-patronized.

**acharné, e** [aʃaʀne] a (lutte, adversaire) fierce, bitter ; (travail) relentless, unremitting.

**acharnement** [aʃaʀnəmɑ̃] nm fierceness ; relentlessness.

**acharner** [aʃaʀne]: **s'~** vi: **s'~ sur** to go at fiercely, hound ; **s'~ contre** to set o.s. against ; to dog, pursue ; **s'~ à faire** to try doggedly to do ; to persist in doing.

**achat** [aʃa] nm buying q ; purchase ; **faire l'~ de** to buy, purchase ; **faire des ~s** to do some shopping, buy a few things.

**acheminer** [aʃmine] vt (courrier) to forward, dispatch ; (troupes) to convey, transport ; (train) to route ; **s'~ vers** to head for.

**acheter** [aʃte] vt to buy, purchase ; (soudoyer) to buy ; **~ qch à** (marchand) to buy ou purchase sth from ; (ami etc: offrir) to buy sth for ; **acheteur, euse** nm/f buyer ; shopper ; (COMM) buyer ; (JUR) vendee, purchaser.

**achevé, e** [aʃve] a: **d'un ridicule ~** thoroughly ou absolutely ridiculous.

**achèvement** [aʃɛvmɑ̃] nm completion ; finishing.

**achever** [aʃve] vt to complete, finish ; to end ; (blessé) to finish off ; **s'~** vi to end.

**achoppement** [aʃɔpmɑ̃] nm: **pierre d'~** stumbling block.

**acide** [asid] a acid, sharp ; (CHIMIE) acid(ic) // nm (CHIMIE) acid ; **acidifier** vt to acidify ; **acidité** nf acidity ; sharpness ; **acidulé, e** a slightly acid ; **bonbons acidulés** acid drops.

**acier** [asje] nm steel ; **aciérie** nf steelworks sg.

**acné** [akne] nf acne.

**acolyte** [akɔlit] nm (péj) confederate.

**acompte** [akɔ̃t] nm deposit ; (versement régulier) instalment ; (sur somme due) payment on account ; **un ~ de 100 F** 100 F on account.

**acoquiner** [akɔkine]: **s'~ avec** vt (péj) to team up with.

**à-côté** [akote] nm side-issue ; (argent) extra.

**à-coup** [aku] nm (du moteur) (hic)cough ; (fig) jolt ; **sans ~s** smoothly ; **par ~s** by fits and starts.

**acoustique** [akustik] nf (d'une salle) acoustics pl ; (science) acoustics sg // a acoustic.

**acquéreur** [akeʀœʀ] nm buyer, purchaser.

**acquérir** [akeʀiʀ] vt to acquire ; (par achat) to purchase, acquire ; (valeur) to gain ; **ce que ses efforts lui ont acquis** what his efforts have won ou gained (for) him.

**acquiescer** [akjese] vi (opiner) to agree ; (consentir): **~ (à qch)** to acquiesce ou assent (to sth).

**acquis, e** [aki, -iz] pp de **acquérir** // nm (accumulated) experience ; **être ~ à** (plan, idée) to fully agree with ; **son aide nous est ~e** we can count on ou be sure of her help.

**acquisition** [akizisjɔ̃] nf acquisition ; purchase ; **faire l'~ de** to acquire ; to purchase.

**acquit** [aki] vb voir **acquérir** // nm (quittance) receipt ; **pour ~** received ; **par ~ de conscience** to set one's mind at rest.

**acquittement** [akitmɑ̃] nm acquittal ; payment, settlement.

**acquitter** [akite] vt (JUR) to acquit ; (facture) to pay, settle ; **s'~ de** to discharge ; to fulfil, carry out.

**âcre** [ɑkʀ(ə)] a acrid, pungent.

**acrobate** [akʀɔbat] nm/f acrobat.

**acrobatie** [akʀɔbasi] nf (art) acrobatics sg ; (exercice) acrobatic feat ; **~ aérienne** aerobatics sg ; **acrobatique** a acrobatic.

**acte** [akt(ə)] nm act, action ; (THÉÂTRE) act ; **~s** nmpl (compte-rendu) proceedings ; **prendre ~ de** to note, take note of ; **faire ~ de présence** to put in an appearance ; **l'~ d'accusation** the charges ; the bill of indictment ; **~ de naissance** birth certificate.

**acteur, trice** [aktœʀ, -tʀis] nm/f actor/actress.

**actif, ive** [aktif, -iv] a active // nm (COMM) assets pl ; (fig): **avoir à son ~** to have to one's credit ; **mettre à son ~** to add to one's list of achievements.

**action** [aksjɔ̃] nf (gén) action ; (COMM) share ; **une bonne ~** a good deed ; **~ en diffamation** libel action ; **actionnaire** nm/f shareholder ; **actionner** vt to work ; to activate.

**active** [aktiv] a voir **actif** ; **~ment** ad actively.

**activer** [aktive] vt to speed up ; **s'~** vi to bustle about ; to hurry up.

**activiste** [aktivist(ə)] nm/f activist.

**activité** [aktivite] nf activity ; **volcan en ~** active volcano.

**actrice** [aktʀis] nf voir **acteur**.

**actualiser** [aktɥalize] vt to actualize ; to bring up to date.

**actualité** [aktɥalite] nf (d'un problème) topicality ; (événements): **l'~** current events ; **les ~s** (CINÉMA, TV) the news.

**actuel, le** [aktɥɛl] a (présent) present ; (d'actualité) topical ; (non virtuel) actual ; **~lement** ad at present ; at the present time.

**acuité** [akɥite] nf acuteness.

**acuponcteur, acupuncteur** [akypɔ̃ktœʀ] nm acupuncturist.

**acuponcture, acupuncture** [akypɔ̃ktyʀ] nf acupuncture.

**adage** [adaʒ] nm adage.

**adagio** [adadʒjo] nm adagio.

**adaptateur, trice** [adaptatœʀ, -tʀis] nm/f adapter // nm (ÉLEC) adapter.

**adaptation** [adaptɑsjɔ̃] nf adaptation.

**adapter** [adapte] vt to adapt ; **~ qch à** (approprier) to adapt sth to (fit) ; **~ qch sur/dans/à** (fixer) to fit sth on/into/to ; **s'~ (à)** (suj: personne) to adapt (to).

**additif** [aditif] nm additional clause ; (CHIMIE) additive.

**addition** [adisjɔ̃] nf addition ; (au café) bill ; **additionnel, le** a additional.

**additionner** [adisjɔne] vt to add (up) ; **~**

**un produit d'eau** to add water to a product.

**adepte** [adɛpt(ə)] *nm/f* follower.

**adéquat, e** [adekwa, -at] *a* appropriate, suitable.

**adhérence** [adeRɑ̃s] *nf* adhesion.

**adhérent, e** [adeRɑ̃, -ɑ̃t] *nm/f* (*de club*) member.

**adhérer** [adeRe] *vi* (*coller*) to adhere, stick; ~ à *vt* (*coller*) to adhere *ou* stick to; (*se rallier à: parti, club*) to join; to be a member of; (: *opinion, mouvement*) to support; **adhésif, ive** *a* adhesive, sticky // *nm* adhesive; **adhésion** *nf* joining; membership; support.

**ad hoc** [adɔk] *a* ad hoc.

**adieu, x** [adjø] *excl* goodbye // *nm* farewell; **dire** ~ **à qn** to say goodbye *ou* farewell to sb.

**adipeux, euse** [adipø, -øz] *a* bloated, fat; (ANAT) adipose.

**adjacent, e** [adʒasɑ̃, -ɑ̃t] *a* adjacent.

**adjectif** [adʒɛktif] *nm* adjective; ~ **attribut** adjectival complement; ~ **épithète** attributive adjective.

**adjoindre** [adʒwɛ̃dR(ə)] *vt*: ~ **qch à** to attach sth to; to add sth to; ~ **qn à** (*personne*) to appoint sb as an assistant to; (*comité*) to appoint sb to, attach sb to; **s'**~ (*collaborateur etc*) to take on, appoint; **adjoint, e** *nm/f* assistant; **adjoint au maire** deputy mayor; **directeur adjoint** assistant manager; **adjonction** *nf* attaching; addition; appointment.

**adjudant** [adʒydɑ̃] *nm* (MIL) warrant officer.

**adjudicataire** [adʒydikatɛR] *nm/f* successful bidder, purchaser; successful tenderer.

**adjudication** [adʒydikɑsjɔ̃] *nf* sale by auction; (*pour travaux*) invitation to tender.

**adjuger** [adʒyʒe] *vt* (*prix, récompense*) to award; (*lors d'une vente*) to auction (off); **s'**~ *vt* to take for o.s.

**adjurer** [adʒyRe] *vt*: ~ **qn de faire** to implore *ou* beg sb to do.

**adjuvant** [adʒyvɑ̃] *nm* adjuvant; additive; stimulant.

**admettre** [admɛtR(ə)] *vt* (*visiteur, nouveau-venu*) to admit, let in; (*candidat:* SCOL) to pass; (TECH: *gaz, eau, air*) to admit; (*tolérer*) to allow, accept; (*reconnaître*) to admit, acknowledge.

**administrateur, trice** [administRatœR, -tRis] *nm/f* (COMM) director; (ADMIN) administrator.

**administratif, ive** [administRatif, -iv] *a* administrative.

**administration** [administRɑsjɔ̃] *nf* administration; **l'A**~ ≈ the Civil Service.

**administré, e** [administRe] *nm/f:* **ses** ~**s** the citizens in his care.

**administrer** [administRe] *vt* (*firme*) to manage, run; (*biens, remède, sacrement etc*) to administer.

**admirable** [admiRabl(ə)] *a* admirable, wonderful.

**admirateur, trice** [admiRatœR, -tRis] *nm/f* admirer.

**admiratif, ive** [admiRatif, -iv] *a* admiring.

**admiration** [admiRɑsjɔ̃] *nf* admiration.

**admirer** [admiRe] *vt* to admire.

**admis, e** *pp de* **admettre**.

**admissible** [admisibl(ə)] *a* (*candidat*) eligible; (*comportement*) admissible, acceptable.

**admission** [admisjɔ̃] *nf* admission; acknowledgement; **tuyau d'**~ intake pipe; **demande d'**~ application for membership.

**admonester** [admɔnɛste] *vt* to admonish.

**adolescence** [adɔlesɑ̃s] *nf* adolescence.

**adolescent, e** [adɔlesɑ̃, -ɑ̃t] *nm/f* adolescent.

**adonner** [adɔne]: **s'**~ **à** *vt* (*sport*) to devote o.s. to; (*boisson*) to give o.s. over to.

**adopter** [adɔpte] *vt* to adopt; (*projet de loi etc*) to pass; **adoptif, ive** *a* (*parents*) adoptive; (*fils, patrie*) adopted; **adoption** *nf* adoption.

**adoration** [adɔRɑsjɔ̃] *nf* adoration; worship.

**adorer** [adɔRe] *vt* to adore; (REL) to worship, adore.

**adosser** [adose] *vt*: ~ **qch à** *ou* **contre** to stand sth against; **s'**~ **à** *ou* **contre** to lean with one's back against.

**adoucir** [adusiR] *vt* (*goût, température*) to make milder; (*avec du sucre*) to sweeten; (*peau, voix*) to soften; (*caractère, personne*) to mellow; (*peine*) to soothe, allay; **s'**~ *vi* to become milder; to soften; to mellow.

**adresse** [adRɛs] *nf* (*voir adroit*) skill, dexterity; (*domicile*) address; **à l'**~ **de** (*pour*) for the benefit of.

**adresser** [adRese] *vt* (*lettre: expédier*) to send; (: *écrire l'adresse sur*) to address; (*injure, compliments*) to address; ~ **qn à un docteur/bureau** to refer *ou* send sb to a doctor/an office; ~ **la parole à qn** to speak to *ou* address sb; **s'**~ **à** (*parler à*) to speak to, address; (*s'informer auprès de*) to go and see, go and speak to; (: *bureau*) to enquire at; (*suj: livre, conseil*) to be aimed at.

**Adriatique** [adRiatik] *nf:* **l'**~ the Adriatic.

**adroit, e** [adRwa, -wat] *a* (*joueur, mécanicien*) skilful, dext(e)rous; (*politicien etc*) shrewd, skilled; **adroitement** *ad* skilfully; dext(e)rously.

**aduler** [adyle] *vt* to adulate.

**adulte** [adylt(ə)] *nm/f* adult, grown-up // *a* (*chien, arbre*) fully-grown, mature; (*attitude*) adult, grown-up; **l'âge** ~ adulthood.

**adultère** [adyltɛR] *a* adulterous // *nm/f* adulterer/adulteress // *nm* (*acte*) adultery; **adultérin, e** *a* born of adultery.

**advenir** [advəniR] *vi* to happen; **qu'est-il advenu de** what has become of.

**adverbe** [advɛRb(ə)] *nm* adverb.

**adversaire** [advɛRsɛR] *nm/f* (SPORT, *gén*) opponent, adversary; (MIL) adversary, enemy; (*non partisan*): ~ **de** opponent of.

**adverse** [advɛRs(ə)] *a* opposing.

**adversité** [advɛRsite] *nf* adversity.

**aérateur** [aeRatœR] *nm* ventilator.

**aération** [aeRɑsjɔ̃] *nf* airing; ventilation;

**conduit d'~** ventilation shaft; **bouche d'~** air-vent.

**aéré, e** [aeʀe] *a* (*pièce, local*) airy, well-ventilated; (*tissu*) loose-woven.

**aérer** [aeʀe] *vt* to air; (*fig*) to lighten; **s'~** *vi* to get some (fresh) air.

**aérien, ne** [aeʀjɛ̃ -jɛn] *a* (*AVIAT*) air *cpd*, aerial; (*câble, métro*) overhead; (*fig*) light.

**aéro...** [aeʀɔ] *préfixe:* **~-club** *nm* flying club; **~drome** *nm* aerodrome; **~dynamique** *a* aerodynamic, streamlined // *nf* aerodynamics *sg*; **~gare** *nf* airport (buildings); (*en ville*) air terminal; **~glisseur** *nm* hovercraft; **~nautique** *a* aeronautical // *nf* aeronautics *sg*; **~naval, e** *a* air and sea *cpd* // *nf* the Fleet Air Arm; **~phagie** *nf* aerophagy; **~port** *nm* airport; **~porté, e** *a* airborne, airlifted; **~sol** *nm* aerosol; **~spatial, e, aux** *a* aerospace; **~train** *nm* hovertrain.

**affable** [afabl(ə)] *a* affable.

**affadir** [afadiʀ] *vt* to make insipid *ou* tasteless.

**affaiblir** [afebliʀ] *vt* to weaken; **s'~** *vi* to weaken, grow weaker; **affaiblissement** *nm* weakening.

**affaire** [afɛʀ] *nf* (*problème, question*) matter; (*criminelle, judiciaire*) case; (*scandaleuse etc*) affair; (*entreprise*) business; (*marché, transaction*) (business) deal; (*piece of*) business *q*; (*occasion intéressante*) good deal, bargain; **~s** *nfpl* affairs; (*activité commerciale*) business *sg*; (*effets personnels*) things, belongings; **ce sont mes ~s** (*cela me concerne*) that's my business; **ceci fera l'~** this will do (nicely); **avoir ~ à** to be faced with; to be dealing with; **les A~s étrangères** (*POL*) Foreign Affairs; **s'affairer** *vi* to busy o.s., bustle about; **affairisme** *nm* (political) racketeering.

**affaisser** [afese]: **s'~** *vi* (*terrain, immeuble*) to subside, sink; (*personne*) to collapse.

**affaler** [afale]: **s'~** *vi*: **s'~ dans/sur** to collapse *ou* slump into/onto.

**affamer** [afame] *vt* to starve.

**affectation** [afɛktasjɔ̃] *nf* allotment; appointment; posting; (*voir affecté*) affectedness.

**affecté, e** [afɛkte] *a* affected.

**affecter** [afɛkte] *vt* (*émouvoir*) to affect, move; (*feindre*) to affect, feign; (*telle ou telle forme etc*) to take on, assume; **~ qch à** to allocate *ou* allot sth to; **~ qn à** to appoint sb to; (*diplomate*) to post sb to; **~ qch d'un coefficient** *etc* to modify sth by a coefficient *etc*, tag a coefficient *etc* onto sth.

**affectif, ive** [afɛktif, -iv] *a* emotional, affective.

**affection** [afɛksjɔ̃] *nf* affection; (*mal*) ailment; **affectionner** *vt* to be fond of.

**affectueux, euse** [afɛktɥ̦ø, -øz] *a* affectionate.

**afférent, e** [aferɑ̃, -ɑ̃t] *a*: **~ à** pertaining *ou* relating to.

**affermir** [afɛʀmiʀ] *vt* to consolidate, strengthen.

**affichage** [afiʃaʒ] *nm* billposting; (*électronique*) display; **~ numérique** *ou* **digital** digital display.

**affiche** [afiʃ] *nf* poster; (*officielle*) (public) notice; (*THÉÂTRE*) bill.

**afficher** [afiʃe] *vt* (*affiche*) to put up, post up; (*réunion*) to announce by (means of) posters *ou* public notices; (*électroniquement*) to display; (*fig*) to exhibit, display; **s'~** (*péj*) to flaunt o.s.

**affilée** [afile]: **d'~** *ad* at a stretch.

**affiler** [afile] *vt* to sharpen.

**affilier** [afilje] *vt*: **s'~ à** to become affiliated to.

**affiner** [afine] *vt* to refine; **s'~** *vi* to become (more) refined.

**affinité** [afinite] *nf* affinity.

**affirmatif, ive** [afiʀmatif, -iv] *a* affirmative // *nf*: **répondre par l'affirmative** to reply yes *ou* in the affirmative; **dans l'affirmative** if (the answer is) yes, if he does (*ou* you do *etc*).

**affirmation** [afiʀmasjɔ̃] *nf* assertion.

**affirmer** [afiʀme] *vt* (*prétendre*) to maintain, assert; (*autorité etc*) to assert.

**affleurer** [aflœʀe] *vi* to show on the surface.

**affliction** [afliksjɔ̃] *nf* affliction.

**affligé, e** [afliʒe] *a* distressed, grieved; **~ de** (*maladie, ta̱re*) afflicted with.

**affliger** [afliʒe] *vt* (*peiner*) to distress, grieve.

**affluence** [aflyɑ̃s] *nf* crowds *pl*; **heures d'~** rush hours; **jours d'~** busiest days.

**affluent** [aflyɑ̃] *nm* tributary.

**affluer** [aflye] *vi* (*secours, biens*) to flood in, pour in; (*sang*) to rush, flow; **afflux** *nm* flood, influx; rush.

**affoler** [afɔle] *vt* to throw into a panic; **s'~** *vi* to panic.

**affranchir** [afʀɑ̃ʃiʀ] *vt* to put a stamp *ou* stamps on; (*à la machine*) to frank; (*esclave*) to enfranchise, emancipate; (*fig*) to free, liberate; **affranchissement** *nm* franking; freeing; **tarifs d'affranchissement** postal rates; **affranchissement insuffisant** insufficient postage.

**affres** [afʀ(ə)] *nfpl*: **dans les ~ de** in the throes of.

**affréter** [afʀete] *vt* to charter.

**affreux, euse** [afʀø, -øz] *a* (*laid*) hideous, ghastly; (*épouvantable*) dreadful, awful.

**affriolant, e** [afʀijɔlɑ̃, -ɑ̃t] *a* tempting, arousing.

**affront** [afʀɔ̃] *nm* affront.

**affronter** [afʀɔ̃te] *vt* to confront, face.

**affubler** [afyble] *vt* (*péj*): **~ qn de** to rig *ou* deck sb out in; (*surnom*) to attach to sb.

**affût** [afy] *nm* (*de canon*) gun carriage; **à l'~ (de)** (*gibier*) lying in wait (for); (*fig*) on the look-out (for).

**affûter** [afyte] *vt* to sharpen, grind.

**afin** [afɛ̃]: **~ que** *cj* so that, in order that; **~ de faire** in order to do, so as to do.

**a fortiori** [afɔʀsjɔʀi] *ad* all the more, a fortiori.

**A.F.P.** *sigle f* = *Agence France Presse*.

**africain, e** [afʀikɛ̃, -ɛn] *a*, *nm/f* African.

**Afrique** [afʀik] *nf*: **l'~** Africa; **l'~ du Sud** South Africa.

**agacer** [agase] *vt* to pester, tease; (*involontairement*) to irritate, aggravate; (*aguicher*) to excite, lead on.

**âge** [ɑʒ] *nm* age ; **quel ~ as-tu?** how old are you? ; **prendre de l'~** to be getting on (in years), grow older ; **l'~ ingrat** the awkward *ou* difficult age ; **l'~ mûr** maturity, middle age ; **âgé, e** *a* old, elderly ; **âgé de 10 ans** 10 years old.

**agence** [aʒɑ̃s] *nf* agency, office ; *(succursale)* branch ; **~ immobilière** estate agent's (office) ; **~ matrimoniale** marriage bureau ; **~ de voyages** travel agency.

**agencer** [aʒɑ̃se] *vt* to put together ; to arrange, lay out.

**agenda** [aʒɛ̃da] *nm* diary.

**agenouiller** [aʒnuje]: **s'~** *vi* to kneel (down).

**agent** [aʒɑ̃] *nm (aussi:* **~ de police)** policeman ; *(ADMIN)* official, officer ; *(fig: élément, facteur)* agent ; **~ d'assurances** insurance broker ; **~ de change** stock-broker ; **~ (secret)** (secret) agent.

**agglomération** [aglɔmeRɑsjɔ̃] *nf* town ; built-up area ; **l'~ parisienne** the urban area of Paris.

**aggloméré** [aglɔmeRe] *nm (bois)* chip-board ; *(pierre)* conglomerate.

**agglomérer** [aglɔmeRe] *vt* to pile up ; *(TECH: bois, pierre)* to compress.

**agglutiner** [aglytine] *vt* to stick together ; **s'~** *vi* to congregate.

**aggraver** [agRave] *vt* to worsen, aggravate ; *(JUR: peine)* to increase ; **s'~** *vi* to worsen.

**agile** [aʒil] *a* agile, nimble ; **agilité** *nf* agility, nimbleness.

**agir** [aʒiR] *vi (se comporter)* to behave, act ; *(faire quelque chose)* to act, take action ; *(avoir de l'effet)* to act ; **il s'agit de** it's a matter *ou* question of ; it is about ; *(il importe que)* **il s'agit de faire** we *(ou* you etc) must do ; **agissements** *nmpl (gén péj)* schemes, intrigues.

**agitateur, trice** [aʒitatœR, -tRis] *nm/f* agitator.

**agitation** [aʒitɑsjɔ̃] *nf* (hustle and) bustle ; agitation, excitement ; *(politique)* unrest, agitation.

**agité, e** [aʒite] *a* fidgety, restless ; agitated, perturbed ; *(journée)* hectic ; **une mer ~e** a rough *ou* choppy sea ; **un sommeil ~** (a) disturbed *ou* broken sleep.

**agiter** [aʒite] *vt (bouteille, chiffon)* to shake ; *(bras, mains)* to wave ; *(préoccuper, exciter)* to trouble, perturb ; **s'~** *vi* to bustle about ; *(dormeur)* to toss and turn ; *(enfant)* to fidget ; *(POL)* to grow restless.

**agneau, x** [aɲo] *nm* lamb.

**agonie** [agɔni] *nf* mortal agony, pangs *pl* of death ; *(fig)* death throes *pl*.

**agonir** [agɔniR] *vt:* **~ qn d'injures** to hurl abuse at sb.

**agoniser** [agɔnize] *vi* to be dying.

**agrafe** [agRaf] *nf (de vêtement)* hook, fastener ; *(de bureau)* staple ; **agrafer** *vt* to fasten ; to staple ; **agrafeuse** *nf* stapler.

**agraire** [agRɛR] *a* agrarian ; *(mesure, surface)* land *cpd*.

**agrandir** [agRɑ̃diR] *vt (magasin, domaine)* to extend, enlarge ; *(trou)* to enlarge, make bigger ; *(PHOTO)* to enlarge, blow up ; **s'~** *vi* to be extended ; to be enlarged ; **agrandissement** *nm* extension ; enlarge-

ment ; **agrandisseur** *nm (PHOTO)* enlarger.

**agréable** [agReabl(ə)] *a* pleasant, nice.

**agréé, e** [agRee] *a:* **concessionnaire ~** registered dealer.

**agréer** [agRee] *vt (requête)* to accept ; **~ à** *vt* to please, suit ; **veuillez ~ ...** *(formule épistolaire)* yours faithfully.

**agrégation** [agRegɑsjɔ̃] *nf* highest teaching diploma in France *(competitive examination)* ; **agrégé, e** *nm/f* holder of the *agrégation*.

**agréger** [agReʒe]: **s'~** *vi* to aggregate.

**agrément** [agRemɑ̃] *nm (accord)* consent, approval ; *(attraits)* charm, attractiveness ; *(plaisir)* pleasure.

**agrémenter** [agRemɑ̃te] *vt* to embellish, adorn.

**agrès** [agRɛ] *nmpl* (gymnastics) apparatus *sg*.

**agresser** [agRese] *vt* to attack.

**agresseur** [agRɛsœR] *nm* aggressor, attacker ; *(POL, MIL)* aggressor.

**agressif, ive** [agRɛsif, -iv] *a* aggressive.

**agression** [agRɛsjɔ̃] *nf* attack ; *(POL, MIL, PSYCH)* aggression.

**agressivité** [agRɛsivite] *nf* aggressiveness.

**agreste** [agRɛst(ə)] *a* rustic.

**agricole** [agRikɔl] *a* agricultural, farm *cpd*.

**agriculteur** [agRikyltœR] *nm* farmer.

**agriculture** [agRikyltyR] *nf* agriculture, farming.

**agripper** [agRipe] *vt* to grab, clutch ; *(pour arracher)* to snatch, grab ; **s'~ à** to cling (on) to, clutch, grip.

**agronome** [agRɔnɔm] *nm/f* agronomist.

**agronomie** [agRɔnɔmi] *nf* agronomy, agronomics *sg*.

**agrumes** [agRym] *nmpl* citrus fruit(s).

**aguerrir** [ageRiR] *vt* to harden.

**aguets** [agɛ]: **aux ~** *ad:* **être aux ~** to be on the look-out.

**aguicher** [agiʃe] *vt* to entice.

**ahurissement** [ayRismɑ̃] *nm* stupefaction.

**ai** *vb voir* **avoir**.

**aide** [ɛd] *nm/f* assistant // *nf* assistance, help ; *(secours financier)* aid ; **à l'~ de** *(avec)* with the help *ou* aid of ; **aller à l'~ de qn** to go to sb's aid *ou* to help sb ; **venir en ~ à qn** to help sb, come to sb's assistance ; **appeler (qn) à l'~** to call for help (from sb) ; **~ comptable** *nm* accountant's assistant ; **~ électricien** *nm* electrician's mate ; **~ familiale** *nf* mother's help, home help ; **~ de laboratoire** *nm/f* laboratory assistant ; **~ sociale** *(assistance)* ≈ social security ; **~ soignant, e** *nm/f* auxiliary nurse ; **~ mémoire** *nm inv* memoranda pages *pl* ; (key facts) handbook.

**aider** [ede] *vt* to help ; **~ à qch** *(faciliter)* to help (towards) sth ; **s'~ de** *(se servir de)* to use, make use of.

**aie** *etc vb voir* **avoir**.

**aïe** [aj] *excl* ouch.

**aïeul, e** [ajœl] *nm/f* grandparent, grandfather/grandmother ; forbear.

**aïeux** [ajø] *nmpl* grandparents ; forbears, forefathers.

**aigle** [ɛgl(ə)] *nm* eagle.

**aigre** [ɛgʀ(ə)] *a* sour, sharp ; *(fig)* sharp, cutting ; **~-doux, douce** *a* bitter-sweet ; **~let, te** *a* sourish, sharpish ; **aigreur** *nf* sourness ; sharpness ; **aigreurs d'estomac** heartburn *sg* ; **aigrir** *vt* *(personne)* to embitter ; *(caractère)* to sour ; **s'aigrir** *vi* to become embittered ; to sour ; *(lait etc)* to turn sour.

**aigu, ë** [egy] *a* *(objet, arête)* sharp, pointed ; *(son, voix)* high-pitched, shrill ; *(note)* high(-pitched) ; *(douleur, intelligence)* acute, sharp.

**aigue-marine** [ɛgmaʀin] *nf* aquamarine.

**aiguillage** [eguijaʒ] *nm* (RAIL) points *pl*.

**aiguille** [eguij] *nf* needle ; *(de montre)* hand ; **~ à tricoter** knitting needle.

**aiguiller** [eguije] *vt* *(orienter)* to direct ; (RAIL) to shunt ; **aiguilleur** *nm* (RAIL) points-man ; **aiguilleur du ciel** air traffic controller.

**aiguillon** [eguijɔ̃] *nm* *(d'abeille)* sting ; *(fig)* spur, stimulus ; **aiguillonner** *vt* to spur *ou* goad on.

**aiguiser** [egize] *vt* to sharpen, grind ; *(fig)* to stimulate ; to sharpen ; to excite.

**ail** [aj] *nm* garlic.

**aile** [ɛl] *nf* wing ; **ailé, e** *a* winged ; **aileron** *nm* *(de requin)* fin ; *(d'avion)* aileron ; *(de voiture)* aerofoil ; **ailette** *nf* (TECH) fin ; blade ; wing ; **ailier** *nm* winger.

**aille** *etc vb voir* **aller.**

**ailleurs** [ajœʀ] *ad* elsewhere, somewhere else ; **partout/nulle part ~** every-where/nowhere else ; **d'~** *ad* *(du reste)* moreover, besides ; **par ~** *ad* *(d'autre part)* moreover, furthermore.

**aimable** [ɛmabl(ə)] *a* kind, nice ; **~ment** *ad* kindly.

**aimant** [ɛmɑ̃] *nm* magnet.

**aimant, e** [ɛmɑ̃, -ɑ̃t] *a* loving, affectionate.

**aimanter** [ɛmɑ̃te] *vt* to magnetize.

**aimer** [eme] *vt* to love ; *(d'amitié, affection, par goût)* to like ; *(souhait)*: **j'aimerais...** I would like... ; **bien ~ qn/qch** to quite like sb/sth ; **j'aime mieux** *ou* **autant vous dire que** I may as well tell you that ; **j'aimerais autant y aller maintenant** I'd sooner *ou* rather go now ; **j'aimerais mieux y aller maintenant** I'd much rather go now.

**aine** [ɛn] *nf* groin.

**aîné, e** [ene] *a* elder, older ; *(le plus âgé)* eldest, oldest // *nm/f* oldest child *ou* one, oldest boy *ou* son/girl *ou* daughter ; **il est mon ~ (de 2 ans)** *(rapports non familiaux)* he's (2 years) older than me, he's 2 years my senior ; **~s** *nmpl* *(fig: anciens)* elders ; **aînesse** *nf*: **droit d'aînesse** birthright.

**ainsi** [ɛ̃si] *ad* *(de cette façon)* like this, in this way, thus ; *(ce faisant)* thus // *cj* thus, so ; **~ que** *(comme)* (just) as ; *(et aussi)* as well as ; **pour ~ dire** so to speak, as it were ; **et ~ de suite** and so on (and so forth).

**air** [ɛʀ] *nm* air ; *(mélodie)* tune ; *(expression)* look, air ; **en l'~** (up) into the air ; **tirer en l'~** to fire shots in the air ; **prendre l'~** to get some (fresh) air ; *(avion)* to take off ; **avoir l'~** *(sembler)* to look, appear ; **avoir l'~ de** to look like ; **avoir l'~ de faire** to look as though one is doing, appear to be doing.

**aire** [ɛʀ] *nf* *(zone, fig, MATH)* area ; *(nid)* eyrie ; **~ d'atterrissage** landing strip ; landing patch ; **~ de jeu** play area ; **~ de lancement** launching site ; **~ de stationnement** parking area ; *(d'autoroute)* lay-by.

**aisance** [ɛzɑ̃s] *nf* ease ; *(richesse)* affluence ; **être dans l'~** to be well-off, be affluent.

**aise** [ɛz] *nf* comfort // *a*: **être bien ~ que** to be delighted that ; **~s** *nfpl*: **aimer ses ~s** to like one's (creature) comforts ; **prendre ses ~s** to make o.s. comfortable ; **frémir d'~** to shudder with pleasure ; **être à l'~** *ou* **à son ~** to be comfortable ; *(pas embarrassé)* to be at ease ; *(financièrement)* to be comfortably off ; **se mettre à l'~** to make o.s. comfortable ; **être mal à l'~** *ou* **à son ~** to be un-comfortable ; to be ill at ease ; **mettre qn mal à l'~** to make sb feel ill at ease ; **à votre ~** please yourself, just as you like ; **en faire à son ~** to do as one likes ; **aisé, e** *a* easy ; *(assez riche)* well-to-do, well-off ; **aisément** *ad* easily.

**aisselle** [ɛsɛl] *nf* armpit.

**ait** *vb voir* **avoir.**

**ajonc** [aʒɔ̃] *nm* gorse *q*.

**ajouré, e** [aʒuʀe] *a* openwork *cpd*.

**ajournement** [aʒuʀnəmɑ̃] *nm* adjourn-ment ; deferment ; postponement.

**ajourner** [aʒuʀne] *vt* *(réunion)* to ad-journ ; *(décision)* to defer, postpone ; *(candidat)* to refer ; *(conscrit)* to defer.

**ajout** [aʒu] *nm* addition.

**ajouter** [aʒute] *vt* to add ; **~ à** *vt* *(accroître)* to add to ; **s'~ à** to add to ; **~ foi à** to lend *ou* give credence to.

**ajustage** [aʒystaʒ] *nm* fitting.

**ajusté, e** [aʒyste] *a*: **bien ~** *(robe etc)* close-fitting.

**ajustement** [aʒystəmɑ̃] *nm* adjustment.

**ajuster** [aʒyste] *vt* *(régler)* to adjust ; *(vêtement)* to alter ; *(coup de fusil)* to aim ; *(cible)* to aim at ; *(TECH, gén: adapter)*: **~ qch à** to fit sth to ; **ajusteur** *nm* metal worker.

**alambic** [alɑ̃bik] *nm* still.

**alanguir** [alɑ̃giʀ]: **s'~** *vi* to grow languid.

**alarme** [alaʀm(ə)] *nf* alarm ; **donner l'~** to give *ou* raise the alarm ; **alarmer** *vt* to alarm ; **s'alarmer** *vi* to become alarmed.

**Albanie** [albani] *nf*: **l'~** Albania.

**albâtre** [albɑtʀ(ə)] *nm* alabaster.

**albatros** [albatʀos] *nm* albatross.

**albinos** [albinos] *nm/f* albino.

**album** [albɔm] *nm* album.

**albumen** [albymɛn] *nm* albumen.

**albumine** [albymin] *nf* albumin ; **avoir** *ou* **faire de l'~** to suffer from albuminuria.

**alcalin, e** [alkalɛ̃, -in] *a* alkaline.

**alchimie** [alʃimi] *nf* alchemy ; **alchimiste** *nm* alchemist.

**alcool** [alkɔl] *nm*: **l'~** alcohol ; **un ~** a spirit, a brandy ; **~ à brûler** methylated spirits ; **~ à 90°** surgical spirit ; **~ique** *a*, *nm/f* alcoholic ; **~isé, e** *a* alcoholic ; **~isme** *nm* alcoholism ; **alco(o)test** ® *nm* breathalyser ; *(test)* breath-test.

**alcôve** [alkov] *nf* alcove, recess.

**aléas** [alea] *nmpl* hazards ; **aléatoire** *a* uncertain.

**alentour** [alɑ̃tuR] *ad* around (about) ; ~s *nmpl* surroundings ; **aux** ~s **de** in the vicinity *ou* neighbourhood of, around about ; (*temps*) (a)round about.

**alerte** [alɛRt(ə)] *a* agile, nimble ; brisk, lively // *nf* alert ; warning ; **donner l'** ~ to give the alert ; **alerter** *vt* to alert.

**alèse** [alɛz] *nf* (*drap*) undersheet, drawsheet.

**aléser** [aleze] *vt* to ream.

**alevin** [alvɛ̃] *nm* alevin, young fish.

**algarade** [algaRad] *nf* row, dispute.

**algèbre** [alʒɛbR(ə)] *nf* algebra ; **algébrique** *a* algebraic.

**Alger** [alʒe] *n* Algiers.

**Algérie** [alʒeRi] *nf* Algeria ; **algérien, ne** *a, nm/f* Algerian.

**Algérois, e** [alʒeRwa, -waz] *nm/f* inhabitant *ou* native of Algiers // *nm*: **l'** ~ the Algiers region.

**algorithme** [algɔRitm(ə)] *nm* algorithm.

**algue** [alg(ə)] *nf* (*gén*) seaweed *q* ; (*BOT*) alga (*pl* algae).

**alibi** [alibi] *nm* alibi.

**aliénation** [aljenɑsjɔ̃] *nf* alienation.

**aliéné, e** [aljene] *nm/f* insane person, lunatic (*péj*).

**aliéner** [aljene] *vt* to alienate ; (*bien, liberté*) to give up ; **s'** ~ *vt* to alienate.

**alignement** [aliɲmɑ̃] *nm* alignment ; lining up ; **à l'** ~ in line.

**aligner** [aliɲe] *vt* to align, line up ; (*idées, chiffres*) to string together ; (*adapter*): ~ **qch sur** to bring sth into alignment with ; **s'** ~ (*soldats etc*) to line up ; **s'** ~ **sur** (*POL*) to align o.s. on.

**aliment** [alimɑ̃] *nm* food ; **alimentaire** *a* food *cpd* ; (*péj: besogne*) done merely to earn a living, done as a potboiler ; **produits alimentaires** foodstuffs, foods.

**alimentation** [alimɑ̃tɑsjɔ̃] *nf* feeding ; supplying ; (*commerce*) food trade ; (*produits*) groceries *pl* ; (*régime*) diet.

**alimenter** [alimɑ̃te] *vt* to feed ; (*TECH*): ~ (**en**) to supply (with) ; to feed (with) ; (*fig*) to sustain, keep going.

**alinéa** [alinea] *nm* paragraph ; **'nouvel** ~' new line.

**aliter** [alite] : **s'** ~ *vi* to take to one's bed.

**alizé** [alize] *a, nm*: (**vent**) ~ trade wind.

**allaiter** [alete] *vt* to (breast-)feed, nurse ; (*suj: animal*) to suckle.

**allant** [alɑ̃] *nm* drive, go.

**allécher** [aleʃe] *vt*: ~ **qn** to make sb's mouth water ; to tempt sb, entice sb.

**allée** [ale] *nf* (*de jardin*) path ; (*en ville*) avenue, drive. ~**s et venues** *nfpl* comings and goings.

**allégation** [alegɑsjɔ̃] *nf* allegation.

**alléger** [aleʒe] *vt* (*voiture*) to make lighter ; (*chargement*) to lighten ; (*souffrance*) to alleviate, soothe.

**allégorie** [alegɔRi] *nf* allegory.

**allègre** [alɛgR(ə)] *a* lively, jaunty ; gay, cheerful.

**allégresse** [alegRɛs] *nf* (*joie*) elation, gaiety.

**alléguer** [alege] *vt* to put forward (as proof *ou* an excuse).

**Allemagne** [aləmaɲ] *nf*: **l'** ~ Germany ; **l'** ~ **de l'Est/Ouest** East/West Germany ; **allemand, e** *a, nm/f, nm* (*langue*) German.

**aller** [ale] *nm* (*trajet*) outward journey ; (*billet*) single *ou* one-way ticket // *vi* (*gén*) to go ; ~ **à** (*convenir*) to suit ; (*suj: forme, pointure etc*) to fit ; ~ **avec** (*couleurs, style etc*) to go (well) with ; **je vais y aller/me fâcher** I'm going to go/to get angry ; ~ **voir** to go and see, go to see ; **comment allez-vous** *ou* **ça va?** how are you? ; **comment ça va?** (*affaires etc*) how are things? ; **il va bien/mal** he's well/not well, he's fine/ill ; **ça va bien/mal** (*affaires etc*) it's going well/not going well ; **il y va de leur vie** their lives are at stake ; **s'en** ~ *vi* (*partir*) to be off, go, leave ; (*disparaître*) to go away ; ~ **et retour** *nm* (*trajet*) return trip *ou* journey ; (*billet*) return (ticket).

**allergie** [alɛRʒi] *nf* allergy ; **allergique** *a* allergic ; **allergique à** allergic to.

**alliage** [aljaʒ] *nm* alloy.

**alliance** [aljɑ̃s] *nf* (*MIL, POL*) alliance ; (*mariage*) marriage ; (*bague*) wedding ring ; **neveu par** ~ nephew by marriage.

**allié, e** [alje] *nm/f* ally ; **parents et** ~**s** relatives and relatives by marriage.

**allier** [alje] *vt* (*métaux*) to alloy ; (*POL, gén*) to ally ; (*fig*) to combine ; **s'** ~ to become allies ; (*éléments, caractéristiques*) to combine ; **s'** ~ **à** to become allied to *ou* with.

**allô** [alo] *excl* hullo, hallo.

**allocataire** [alɔkatɛR] *nm/f* beneficiary.

**allocation** [alɔkɑsjɔ̃] *nf* allowance ; ~ **(de) chômage** unemployment benefit ; ~ **(de) logement** rent allowance *ou* subsidy ; ~**s familiales** family allowance(s).

**allocution** [alɔkysjɔ̃] *nf* short speech.

**allonger** [alɔ̃ʒe] *vt* to lengthen, make longer ; (*étendre: bras, jambe*) to stretch (out) ; **s'** ~ *vi* to get longer ; (*se coucher*) to lie down, stretch out ; ~ **le pas** to hasten one's step(s).

**allouer** [alwe] *vt*: ~ **qch à** to allocate sth to, allot sth to.

**allumage** [alymaʒ] *nm* (*AUTO*) ignition.

**allume...** [alym] *préfixe*: ~**-cigare** *nm inv* cigar lighter ; ~**-gaz** *nm inv* gas lighter.

**allumer** [alyme] *vt* (*lampe, phare, radio*) to put *ou* switch on ; (*pièce*) to put *ou* switch the light(s) on in ; (*feu*) to light ; **s'** ~ *vi* (*lumière, lampe*) to come *ou* go on.

**allumette** [alymɛt] *nf* match.

**allumeuse** [alymøz] *nf* (*péj*) teaser, vamp.

**allure** [alyR] *nf* (*vitesse*) speed ; pace ; (*démarche*) walk ; (*maintien*) bearing ; (*aspect, air*) look ; **avoir de l'** ~ to have style *ou* a certain elegance ; **à toute** ~ at top *ou* full speed.

**allusion** [alyzjɔ̃] *nf* allusion ; (*sous-entendu*) hint ; **faire** ~ **à** to allude *ou* refer to ; to hint at.

**alluvions** [alyvjɔ̃] *nfpl* alluvial deposits, alluvium *sg*.

**almanach** [almana] *nm* almanac.

**aloi** [alwa] *nm*: **de bon** ~ of genuine worth *ou* quality.

**alors** [alɔR] *ad* then, at that time // *cj* then, so ; ~ **que** *cj* (*au moment où*) when, as ; (*pendant que*) while, when ; (*tandis que*) whereas, while.

**alouette** [alwɛt] *nf* (sky)lark.
**alourdir** [aluʀdiʀ] *vt* to weigh down, make heavy.
**aloyau** [alwajo] *nm* sirloin.
**alpage** [alpaʒ] *nm* high mountain pasture.
**Alpes** [alp(ə)] *nfpl*: **les** ~ the Alps; **alpestre** *a* alpine.
**alphabet** [alfabɛ] *nm* alphabet; (*livre*) ABC (book), primer; **alphabétique** *a* alphabetic(al); **alphabétiser** *vt* to teach to read and write; to eliminate illiteracy in.
**alpin, e** [alpɛ̃, -in] *a* alpine; **alpinisme** *nm* mountaineering, climbing; **alpiniste** *nm/f* mountaineer, climber.
**Alsace** [alzas] *nf* Alsace; **alsacien, ne** *a, nm/f* Alsatian.
**altérer** [alteʀe] *vt* to falsify; to distort; to debase; to impair; (*donner soif à*) to make thirsty; **s'**~ *vi* to deteriorate; to spoil.
**alternance** [altɛʀnɑ̃s] *nf* alternation; **en** ~ alternately.
**alternateur** [altɛʀnatœʀ] *nm* alternator.
**alternatif, ive** [altɛʀnatif, -iv] *a* alternating // *nf* (*choix*) alternative; **alternativement** *ad* alternately.
**alterner** [altɛʀne] *vt* to alternate // *vi*: ~ (**avec**) to alternate (with); (**faire**) ~ **qch avec qch** to alternate sth with sth.
**Altesse** [altɛs] *nf* Highness.
**altier, ière** [altje, -jɛʀ] *a* haughty.
**altimètre** [altimɛtʀ(ə)] *nm* altimeter.
**altiste** [altist(ə)] *nm/f* viola player, violist.
**altitude** [altityd] *nf* altitude, height; **à 1000 m d'**~ at a height ou an altitude of 1000 m; **en** ~ at high altitudes.
**alto** [alto] *nm* (*instrument*) viola // *nf* (contr)alto.
**altruisme** [altʀɥism(ə)] *nm* altruism.
**aluminium** [alyminjɔm] *nm* aluminium.
**alunir** [alyniʀ] *vi* to land on the moon.
**alvéole** [alveɔl] *nf* (*de ruche*) alveolus; **alvéolé, e** *a* honeycombed.
**amabilité** [amabilite] *nf* kindness, amiability; **il a eu l'**~ **de** he was kind ou good enough to.
**amadou** [amadu] *nm* touchwood, amadou.
**amadouer** [amadwe] *vt* to coax, cajole; to mollify, soothe.
**amaigrir** [amegʀiʀ] *vt* to make thin ou thinner; **régime amaigrissant** slimming diet.
**amalgamer** [amalgame] *vt* to amalgamate.
**amande** [amɑ̃d] *nf* (*de l'amandier*) almond; (*de noyau de fruit*) kernel; **amandier** *nm* almond (tree).
**amant** [amɑ̃] *nm* lover.
**amarre** [amaʀ] *nf* (NAVIG) (mooring) rope ou line; ~**s** moorings; **amarrer** *vt* (NAVIG) to moor; (*gén*) to make fast.
**amas** [amɑ] *nm* heap, pile.
**amasser** [amɑse] *vt* to amass; **s'**~ *vi* to pile up; to accumulate; to gather.
**amateur** [amatœʀ] *nm* amateur; **en** ~ (*péj*) amateurishly; **musicien/sportif** ~ amateur musician/sportsman; ~ **de musique/sport** *etc* music/sport *etc* lover; ~**isme** *nm* amateurism; (*péj*) amateurishness.

**amazone** [amazon] *nf*: **en** ~ sidesaddle.
**ambages** [ɑ̃baʒ]: **sans** ~ *ad* without beating about the bush, plainly.
**ambassade** [ɑ̃basad] *nf* embassy; (*mission*): **en** ~ on a mission; **ambassadeur, drice** *nm/f* ambassador/ambassadress.
**ambiance** [ɑ̃bjɑ̃s] *nf* atmosphere.
**ambiant, e** [ɑ̃bjɑ̃, -ɑ̃t] *a* (*air, milieu*) surrounding; (*température*) ambient.
**ambidextre** [ɑ̃bidɛkstʀ(ə)] *a* ambidextrous.
**ambigu, ë** [ɑ̃bigy] *a* ambiguous; **ambiguïté** *nf* ambiguousness *q*, ambiguity.
**ambitieux, euse** [ɑ̃bisjø, -øz] *a* ambitious.
**ambition** [ɑ̃bisjɔ̃] *nf* ambition; **ambitionner** *vt* to have as one's aim ou ambition.
**ambivalent, e** [ɑ̃bivalɑ̃, -ɑ̃t] *a* ambivalent.
**ambre** [ɑ̃bʀ(ə)] *nm*: ~ (**jaune**) amber; ~ **gris** ambergris.
**ambulance** [ɑ̃bylɑ̃s] *nf* ambulance; **ambulancier, ière** *nm/f* ambulance man/woman.
**ambulant, e** [ɑ̃bylɑ̃, -ɑ̃t] *a* travelling, itinerant.
**âme** [ɑm] *nf* soul; ~ **sœur** kindred spirit.
**améliorer** [ameljɔʀe] *vt* to improve; **s'**~ *vi* to improve, get better.
**aménagement** [amenaʒmɑ̃] *nm* fitting out; laying out; developing; ~**s** *nmpl* developments; **l'**~ **du territoire** ≈ town and country planning; ~**s fiscaux** tax adjustments.
**aménager** [amenaʒe] *vt* (*agencer, transformer*) to fit out; to lay out; (: *quartier, territoire*) to develop; (*installer*) to fix up, put in; **ferme aménagée** converted farmhouse.
**amende** [amɑ̃d] *nf* fine; **mettre à l'**~ to penalize; **faire** ~ **honorable** to make amends.
**amender** [amɑ̃de] *vt* (*loi*) to amend; (*terre*) to enrich; **s'**~ *vi* to mend one's ways.
**amène** [amɛn] *a* affable; **peu** ~ unkind.
**amener** [amne] *vt* to bring; (*causer*) to bring about; (*baisser: drapeau, voiles*) to strike; **s'**~ *vi* (*fam*) to show up, turn up.
**amenuiser** [amənɥize]: **s'**~ *vi* to grow slimmer, lessen; to dwindle.
**amer, amère** [amɛʀ] *a* bitter.
**américain, e** [ameʀikɛ̃, -ɛn] *a, nm/f* American.
**Amérique** [ameʀik] *nf* America; **l'**~ **centrale** Central America; **l'**~ **latine** Latin America; **l'**~ **du Nord** North America; **l'**~ **du Sud** South America.
**amerrir** [ameʀiʀ] *vi* to land (on the sea).
**amertume** [amɛʀtym] *nf* bitterness.
**améthyste** [ametist(ə)] *nf* amethyst.
**ameublement** [amœbləmɑ̃] *nm* furnishing; (*meubles*) furniture; **articles d'**~ furnishings; **tissus d'**~ soft furnishings, fabrics.
**ameuter** [amøte] *vt* (*badauds*) to draw a crowd of; (*peuple*) to rouse, stir up.
**ami, e** [ami] *nm/f* friend; (*amant/maîtresse*) boyfriend/girlfriend // *a*: **pays/groupe** ~ friendly country/group; **être (très)** ~ **avec qn** to be (very)

good friends with sb ; **être ~ de l'ordre** to be a lover of order ; **un ~ des arts** a patron of the arts ; **un ~ des chiens** a dog lover.

**amiable** [amjabl(ə)]: **à l'~** ad (JUR) out of court ; (gén) amicably.

**amiante** [amjɑ̃t] nm asbestos.

**amibe** [amib] nf amoeba (pl ae).

**amical, e, aux** [amikal, -o] a friendly // nf (club) association.

**amidon** [amidɔ̃] nm starch ; **amidonner** vt to starch.

**amincir** [amɛ̃siʀ] vt (objet) to thin (down) ; **~ qn** to make sb thinner ou slimmer ; **s'~** vi to get thinner ; to get slimmer.

**amiral, aux** [amiʀal, -o] nm admiral ; **amirauté** nf admiralty.

**amitié** [amitje] nf friendship ; **prendre en ~** to take a liking to, befriend ; **faire** ou **présenter ses ~s à qn** to send sb one's best wishes ou kind regards.

**ammoniac** [amɔnjak] nm: **(gaz) ~** ammonia.

**ammoniaque** [amɔnjak] nf ammonia (water).

**amnésie** [amnezi] nf amnesia ; **amnésique** a amnesic.

**amnistie** [amnisti] nf amnesty ; **amnistier** vt to amnesty.

**amoindrir** [amwɛ̃dʀiʀ] vt to reduce.

**amollir** [amɔliʀ] vt to soften.

**amonceler** [amɔ̃sle] vt, **s'~** vi to pile ou heap up ; (fig) to accumulate.

**amont** [amɔ̃]: **en ~** ad upstream ; (sur une pente) uphill ; **en ~ de** prép upstream from ; uphill from, above.

**amorce** [amɔʀs(ə)] nf (sur un hameçon) bait ; (explosif) cap ; primer ; priming ; (fig: début) beginning(s), start ; **amorcer** vt to bait ; to prime ; to begin, start.

**amorphe** [amɔʀf(ə)] a passive, lifeless.

**amortir** [amɔʀtiʀ] vt (atténuer: choc) to absorb, cushion ; (bruit, douleur) to deaden ; (COMM: dette) to pay off, amortize ; (: mise de fonds) to write off ; (: matériel) to write off, depreciate ; **~ un abonnement** to make a season ticket pay (for itself).

**amour** [amuʀ] nm love ; (liaison) love affair, love ; (statuette etc) cupid ; **faire l'~** to make love ; **s'~acher de** (péj) to become infatuated with ; **~ette** nf passing fancy ; **~eux, euse** a (regard, tempérament) amorous ; (vie, problèmes) love cpd ; (personne): **~eux (de qn)** in love (with sb) // nm/f lover // nmpl courting couple(s) ; **être ~eux de qch** to be passionately fond of sth ; **un ~eux de la nature** a nature lover ; **~-propre** nm self-esteem, pride.

**amovible** [amɔvibl(ə)] a removable, detachable.

**ampère** [ɑ̃pɛʀ] nm amp(ere) ; **~mètre** nm ammeter.

**amphibie** [ɑ̃fibi] a amphibious.

**amphithéâtre** [ɑ̃fiteɑtʀ(ə)] nm amphitheatre ; (d'université) lecture hall ou theatre.

**amphore** [ɑ̃fɔʀ] nf amphora.

**ample** [ɑ̃pl(ə)] a (vêtement) roomy, ample ; (gestes, mouvement) broad ; (ressources) ample ; **~ment** ad amply ; **~ment**

**suffisant** ample, more than enough ; **ampleur** nf (importance) scale, size ; extent, magnitude.

**amplificateur** [ɑ̃plifikatœʀ] nm amplifier.

**amplifier** [ɑ̃plifje] vt (son, oscillation) to amplify ; (fig) to expand, increase.

**amplitude** [ɑ̃plityd] nf amplitude ; (des températures) range.

**ampoule** [ɑ̃pul] nf (électrique) bulb ; (de médicament) phial ; (aux mains, pieds) blister.

**ampoulé, e** [ɑ̃pule] a (péj) turgid, pompous.

**amputation** [ɑ̃pytɑsjɔ̃] nf amputation.

**amputer** [ɑ̃pyte] vt (MÉD) to amputate ; (fig) to cut ou reduce drastically ; **~ qn d'un bras/pied** to amputate sb's arm/foot.

**amulette** [amylɛt] nf amulet.

**amusant, e** [amyzɑ̃, -ɑ̃t] a (divertissant, spirituel) entertaining, amusing ; (comique) funny, amusing.

**amusé, e** [amyze] a amused.

**amuse-gueule** [amyzgœl] nm inv appetizer, snack.

**amusement** [amyzmɑ̃] nm (voir amusé) amusement ; (voir amuser) entertaining, amusing ; (jeu etc) pastime, diversion.

**amuser** [amyze] vt (divertir) to entertain, amuse ; (égayer, faire rire) to amuse ; (détourner l'attention de) to distract ; **s'~** vi (jouer) to amuse o.s., play ; (se divertir) to enjoy o.s., have fun ; (fig) to mess about ; **s'~ de qch** (trouver comique) to find sth amusing ; **s'~ avec ou de qn** (duper) to make a fool of sb ; **amusette** nf idle pleasure, trivial pastime ; **amuseur** nm entertainer ; (péj) clown.

**amygdale** [amidal] nf tonsil ; **opérer qn des ~s** to take sb's tonsils out.

**an** [ɑ̃] nm year.

**anachronique** [anakʀɔnik] a anachronistic ; **anachronisme** nm anachronism.

**anagramme** [anagʀam] nf anagram.

**anal, e, aux** [anal, -o] a anal.

**analgésique** [analʒezik] nm analgesic.

**analogie** [analɔʒi] nf analogy.

**analogue** [analɔg] a: **~ (à)** analogous (to), similar (to).

**analphabète** [analfabɛt] nm/f illiterate.

**analyse** [analiz] nf (gén) analysis ; (MÉD) test ; **faire l'~ de** to analyse ; **~ grammaticale** grammatical analysis, parsing (SCOL) ; **analyser** vt to analyse ; (MÉD) to test ; **analyste** nm/f analyst ; (psychanalyste) (psycho)analyst ; **analytique** a analytical.

**ananas** [anana] nm pineapple.

**anarchie** [anaʀʃi] nf (gén, POL) anarchy ; **anarchisme** nm anarchism ; **anarchiste** a anarchistic // nm/f anarchist.

**anathème** [anatɛm] nm: **jeter l'~ sur, lancer l'~ contre** to anathematize, curse.

**anatomie** [anatɔmi] nf anatomy ; **anatomique** a anatomical.

**ancestral, e, aux** [ɑ̃sɛstʀal, -o] a ancestral.

**ancêtre** [ɑ̃sɛtʀ(ə)] nm/f ancestor ; (fig): **l'~ de** the forerunner of ; **~s** nmpl (aïeux) ancestors, forefathers.

**anche** [ɑ̃ʃ] *nf* reed.

**anchois** [ɑ̃ʃwa] *nm* anchovy.

**ancien, ne** [ɑ̃sjɛ̃, -jɛn] *a* old ; (*de jadis, de l'antiquité*) ancient ; (*précédent, ex-*) former, old // *nm/f* (*dans une tribu*) elder ; **un ~ ministre** a former minister ; **être plus ~ que qn dans une maison** to have been in a firm longer than sb ; to be senior to sb (in a firm) ; **anciennement** *ad* formerly ; **ancienneté** *nf* oldness ; antiquity ; (ADMIN) (length of) service ; seniority.

**ancrage** [ɑ̃kRaʒ] *nm* anchoring ; (NAVIG) anchorage ; (CONSTR) cramp(-iron), anchor.

**ancre** [ɑ̃kR(ə)] *nf* anchor ; **jeter/lever l'~** to cast/weigh anchor ; **à l'~** at anchor.

**ancrer** [ɑ̃kRe] *vt* (CONSTR) *câble etc*) to anchor ; (*fig*) to fix firmly ; **s'~** *vi* (NAVIG) to (cast) anchor.

**Andorre** [ɑ̃dɔR] *n* Andorra.

**andouille** [ɑ̃duj] *nf* (CULIN) *sausage made of chitterlings* ; (*fam*) clot, nit.

**âne** [ɑn] *nm* donkey, ass ; (*péj*) dunce, fool.

**anéantir** [aneɑ̃tiR] *vt* to annihilate, wipe out ; (*fig*) to obliterate, destroy ; to overwhelm.

**anecdote** [anɛkdɔt] *nf* anecdote ; **anecdotique** *a* anecdotal.

**anémie** [anemi] *nf* anaemia ; **anémié, e** *a* anaemic ; (*fig*) enfeebled ; **anémique** *a* anaemic.

**anémone** [anemɔn] *nf* anemone ; **~ de mer** sea anemone.

**ânerie** [ɑnRi] *nf* stupidity ; stupid *ou* idiotic comment *etc.*

**ânesse** [ɑnɛs] *nf* she-ass.

**anesthésie** [anɛstezi] *nf* anaesthesia ; **faire une ~ locale à qn** to give sb a local anaesthetic ; **anesthésier** *vt* to anaesthetize ; **anesthésique** *a* anaesthetic ; **anesthésiste** *nm/f* anaesthetist.

**anfractuosité** [ɑ̃fRaktɥozite] *nf* crevice.

**ange** [ɑ̃ʒ] *nm* angel ; **être aux ~s** to be over the moon ; **~ gardien** guardian angel ; **angélique** *a* angelic(al).

**angélus** [ɑ̃ʒelys] *nm* angelus.

**angine** [ɑ̃ʒin] *nf* sore throat, throat infection (*tonsillitis or pharyngitis*) ; **~ de poitrine** angina (pectoris).

**anglais, e** [ɑ̃glɛ, -ɛz] *a* English // *nm/f*: **A~, e** Englishman/woman // *nm* (*langue*) English ; **les A~** the English ; **~es** *nfpl* (*cheveux*) ringlets ; **filer à l'~e** to take French leave.

**angle** [ɑ̃gl(ə)] *nm* angle ; (*coin*) corner ; **~ droit/obtus/aigu** right/obtuse/acute angle.

**Angleterre** [ɑ̃glətɛR] *nf*: **l'~** England.

**anglican, e** [ɑ̃glikɑ̃, -an] *a* Anglican.

**anglicisme** [ɑ̃glisism(ə)] *nm* anglicism.

**angliciste** [ɑ̃glisist(ə)] *nm/f* English scholar ; student of English.

**anglo...** [ɑ̃glɔ] *préfixe* Anglo-, anglo(-) ; **~phile** *a* anglophilic ; **~phobe** *a* anglophobic ; **~phone** *a* English-speaking ; **~-saxon, ne** *a* Anglo-Saxon.

**angoisse** [ɑ̃gwas] *nf*: **l'~** anguish *q* ; **angoisser** *vt* to harrow, cause anguish to.

**anguille** [ɑ̃gij] *nf* eel ; **~ de mer** conger (eel).

**angulaire** [ɑ̃gylɛR] *a* angular.

**anguleux, euse** [ɑ̃gylø, -øz] *a* angular.

**anicroche** [anikRɔʃ] *nf* hitch, snag.

**animal, e, aux** [animal, -o] *a, nm* animal ; **~ier** *a*: **peintre ~ier** animal painter.

**animateur, trice** [animatœR, -tRis] *nm/f* (*de télévision, music-hall*) compère ; (*de maison de jeunes*) leader, organizer.

**animation** [animɑsjɔ̃] *nf* (*voir animé*) business ['bɪznɪs] ; liveliness ; (CINÉMA: *technique*) animation.

**animé, e** [anime] *a* (*rue, lieu*) busy, lively ; (*conversation, réunion*) lively, animated ; (*opposé à inanimé, aussi* LING) animate.

**animer** [anime] *vt* (*ville, soirée*) to liven up, enliven ; (*mettre en mouvement*) to drive ; (*stimuler*) to drive, impel ; **s'~** *vi* to liven up, come to life.

**animosité** [animozite] *nf* animosity.

**anis** [ani] *nm* (CULIN) aniseed ; (BOT) anise.

**ankyloser** [ɑ̃kiloze]: **s'~** *vi* to get stiff, to ankylose.

**annales** [anal] *nfpl* annals.

**anneau, x** [ano] *nm* (*de rideau, bague*) ring ; (*de chaîne*) link.

**année** [ane] *nf* year ; **l'~ scolaire/fiscale** the school/tax year ; **~-lumière** *nf* light year.

**annexe** [anɛks(ə)] *a* (*problème*) related ; (*document*) appended ; (*salle*) adjoining // *nf* (*bâtiment*) annex(e) ; (*de document, ouvrage*) annex, appendix ; (*jointe à une lettre, un dossier*) enclosure.

**annexer** [anɛkse] *vt* (*pays, biens*) to annex ; **~ qch à** (*joindre*) to append sth to ; **annexion** *nf* annexation.

**annihiler** [aniile] *vt* to annihilate.

**anniversaire** [anivɛRsɛR] *nm* birthday ; (*d'un événement, bâtiment*) anniversary // *a*: **jour ~** anniversary.

**annonce** [anɔ̃s] *nf* announcement ; (*signe, indice*) sign ; (*aussi*: **~ publicitaire**) advertisement ; (CARTES) declaration ; **les petites ~s** the classified advertisements, the small ads.

**annoncer** [anɔ̃se] *vt* to announce ; (*être le signe de*) to herald ; **s'~ bien/difficile** to look promising/difficult ; **annonceur, euse** *nm/f* (TV, RADIO: *speaker*) announcer ; (*publicitaire*) advertiser ; **l'Annonciation** *nf* the Annunciation.

**annotation** [anɔtɑsjɔ̃] *nf* annotation.

**annoter** [anɔte] *vt* to annotate.

**annuaire** [anɥɛR] *nm* yearbook, annual ; **~ téléphonique** (telephone) directory, phone book.

**annuel, le** [anɥɛl] *a* annual, yearly ; **~lement** *ad* annually, yearly.

**annuité** [anɥite] *nf* annual instalment.

**annulaire** [anylɛR] *nm* ring *ou* third finger.

**annulation** [anylɑsjɔ̃] *nf* cancellation ; annulment ; quashing.

**annuler** [anyle] *vt* (*rendez-vous, voyage*) to cancel, call off ; (*mariage*) to annul ; (*jugement*) to quash ; (*résultats*) to declare void ; (MATH, PHYSIQUE) to cancel out.

**anoblir** [anɔbliR] *vt* to ennoble.

**anode** [anɔd] *nf* anode.

**anodin, e** [anɔdɛ̃, -in] *a* harmless ; insignificant, trivial.

**anomalie** [anɔmali] *nf* anomaly.

**ânonner** [unɔne] *vi, vt* to read in a drone ; to read in a fumbling manner.

**anonymat** [anɔnima] *nm* anonymity.

**anonyme** [anɔnim] *a* anonymous ; *(fig)* impersonal.

**anorak** [anɔRak] *nm* anorak.

**anormal, e, aux** [anɔRmal, -o] *a* abnormal ; *(insolite)* unusual, abnormal.

**anse** [ɑ̃s] *nf (de panier, tasse)* handle ; *(GÉO)* cove.

**antagoniste** [ɑ̃tagɔnist(ə)] *a* antagonistic // *nm* antagonist.

**antan** [ɑ̃tɑ̃]: **d'** ~ *a* of yesteryear, of long ago.

**antarctique** [ɑ̃taRktik] *a* Antarctic // *nm*: **l'A** ~ the Antarctic.

**antécédent** [ɑ̃tesedɑ̃] *nm* (*LING*) antecedent ; ~ **s** *nmpl* (*MÉD etc*) past history *sg*.

**antédiluvien, ne** [ɑ̃tedilyvjɛ̃, -jɛn] *a (fig)* ancient, antediluvian.

**antenne** [ɑ̃tɛn] *nf (de radio, télévision)* aerial ; *(d'insecte)* antenna (*pl* ae), feeler ; *(poste avancé)* outpost ; *(petite succursale)* sub-branch ; **passer à l'** ~ to go on the air ; **prendre l'** ~ to tune in ; **2 heures d'** ~ 2 hours' broadcasting time.

**antépénultième** [ɑ̃tepenyltjɛm] *a* antepenultimate, last but two.

**antérieur, e** [ɑ̃teRjœR] *a (d'avant)* previous, earlier ; *(de devant)* front ; ~ **à** prior *ou* previous to ; **passé/futur** ~ (*LING*) past/future anterior ; ~ **ement** *ad* earlier ; previously ; ~ **ement à** prior *ou* previous to ; **antériorité** *nf* precedence (*in time*).

**anthologie** [ɑ̃tɔlɔʒi] *nf* anthology.

**anthracite** [ɑ̃tRasit] *nm* anthracite.

**anthropo...** [ɑ̃tRɔpɔ] *préfixe*: ~ **centrisme** *nm* anthropocentrism ; ~ **logie** *nf* anthropology ; ~ **logue** *nm/f* anthropologist ; ~ **métrie** *nf* anthropometry ; ~ **morphisme** *nm* anthropomorphism ; ~ **phage** *a* cannibalistic, anthropophagous.

**anti...** [ɑ̃ti] *préfixe* anti... ; ~ **aérien, ne** *a* anti-aircraft ; **abri** ~ **aérien** air-raid shelter ; ~ **alcoolique** *a* against alcohol ; **ligue** ~ **alcoolique** temperance league ; ~ **atomique** *a*: **abri** ~ **atomique** fallout shelter ; ~ **biotique** *nm* antibiotic ; ~ **brouillard** *a*: **phare** ~ **brouillard** fog lamp ; ~ **cancéreux, euse** *a* cancer *cpd*.

**antichambre** [ɑ̃tiʃɑ̃bR(ə)] *nf* antechamber, anteroom ; **faire** ~ to wait (for an audience).

**antichar** [ɑ̃tiʃaR] *a* anti-tank.

**anticipation** [ɑ̃tisipɑsjɔ̃] *nf* anticipation ; payment in advance ; **livre/film d'** ~ science fiction book/film.

**anticipé, e** [ɑ̃tisipe] *a (règlement, paiement)* early, in advance ; *(joie etc)* anticipated, early ; **avec mes remerciements** ~ **s** thanking you in advance *ou* anticipation.

**anticiper** [ɑ̃tisipe] *vt (événement, coup)* to anticipate, foresee ; *(paiement)* to pay *ou* make in advance // *vi* to look *ou* think ahead ; to jump ahead ; to anticipate ; ~ **sur** to anticipate.

**anticlérical, e, aux** [ɑ̃tikleRikal, -o] *a* anticlerical.

**anticonceptionnel, le** [ɑ̃tikɔ̃sɛpsjɔnɛl] *a* contraceptive.

**anticorps** [ɑ̃tikɔR] *nm* antibody.

**anticyclone** [ɑ̃tisiklon] *nm* anticyclone.

**antidater** [ɑ̃tidate] *vt* to backdate, predate.

**antidérapant, e** [ɑ̃tideRapɑ̃, -ɑ̃t] *a* non-skid.

**antidote** [ɑ̃tidɔt] *nm* antidote.

**antienne** [ɑ̃tjɛn] *nf (fig)* chant, refrain.

**antigel** [ɑ̃tiʒɛl] *nm* antifreeze.

**Antilles** [ɑ̃tij] *nfpl*: **les** ~ the West Indies.

**antilope** [ɑ̃tilɔp] *nf* antelope.

**antimilitariste** [ɑ̃timilitaRist(ə)] *a* antimilitarist.

**antimite(s)** [ɑ̃timit] *a, nm*: **(produit)** ~ mothproofer ; moth repellent.

**antiparasite** [ɑ̃tipaRazit] *a (RADIO, TV)* anti-interference ; **dispositif** ~ suppressor.

**antipathie** [ɑ̃tipati] *nf* antipathy ; **antipathique** *a* unpleasant, disagreeable.

**antiphrase** [ɑ̃tifRɑz] *nf*: **par** ~ ironically.

**antipodes** [ɑ̃tipɔd] *nmpl (GÉO)*: **les** ~ the antipodes ; *(fig)*: **être aux** ~ **de** to be the opposite extreme of.

**antiquaire** [ɑ̃tikɛR] *nm/f* antique dealer.

**antique** [ɑ̃tik] *a* antique ; *(très vieux)* ancient, antiquated.

**antiquité** [ɑ̃tikite] *nf (objet)* antique ; **l'A** ~ Antiquity ; **magasin d'** ~ **s** antique shop.

**antirabique** [ɑ̃tiRabik] *a* rabies *cpd*.

**antiraciste** [ɑ̃tiRasist(ə)] *a* antiracist, antiracialist.

**antirides** [ɑ̃tiRid] *a (crème)* anti-wrinkle.

**antirouille** [ɑ̃tiRuj] *a inv*: **peinture** ~ anti-rust paint ; **traitement** ~ rustproofing.

**antisémite** [ɑ̃tisemit] *a* anti-semitic ; **antisémitisme** *nm* anti-semitism.

**antiseptique** [ɑ̃tisɛptik] *a, nm* antiseptic.

**antitétanique** [ɑ̃titetanik] *a* tetanus *cpd*.

**antithèse** [ɑ̃titɛz] *nf* antithesis.

**antituberculeux, euse** [ɑ̃titybɛRkylø, -øz] *a* tuberculosis *cpd*.

**antivol** [ɑ̃tivɔl] *a, nm*: **(dispositif)** ~ anti-theft device.

**antre** [ɑ̃tR(ə)] *nm* den, lair.

**anus** [anys] *nm* anus.

**anxiété** [ɑ̃ksjete] *nf* anxiety.

**anxieux, euse** [ɑ̃ksjø, -øz] *a* anxious, worried.

**aorte** [aɔRt(ə)] *nf* aorta.

**août** [u] *nm* August.

**apaisement** [apɛzmɑ̃] *nm* calming ; soothing ; appeasement ; ~ **s** *nmpl* soothing reassurances ; pacifying words.

**apaiser** [apeze] *vt (colère)* to calm, quell, soothe ; *(faim)* to appease, assuage ; *(douleur)* to soothe ; *(personne)* to calm (down), pacify ; **s'** ~ *vi (tempête, bruit)* to die down, subside.

**apanage** [apanaʒ] *nm*: **être l'** ~ **de** to be the privilege *ou* prerogative of.

**aparté** [apaRte] *nm (THÉÂTRE)* aside ; *(entretien)* private conversation ; **en** ~ *ad* in an aside ; in private.

**apathie** [apati] *nf* apathy ; **apathique** *a* apathetic.

**apatride** [apatRid] *nm/f* stateless person.

**apercevoir** [apɛRsəvwaR] *vt* to see ; **s'** ~ **de** *vt* to notice ; **s'** ~ **que** to notice that.

**aperçu** [apɛʀsy] *nm* (*vue d'ensemble*) general survey; (*intuition*) insight.

**apéritif, ive** [apeʀitif, -iv] *nm* (*boisson*) aperitif; (*réunion*) pre-lunch (*ou* -dinner) drinks *pl* // *a* which stimulates the appetite; **prendre l'~** to have drinks (before lunch *ou* dinner) *ou* an aperitif.

**apesanteur** [apəzɑ̃tœʀ] *nf* weightlessness.

**à-peu-près** [apøpʀɛ] *nm inv* (*péj*) vague approximation.

**apeuré, e** [apœʀe] *a* frightened, scared.

**aphone** [afɔn] *a* voiceless.

**aphrodisiaque** [afʀɔdizjak] *a, nm* aphrodisiac.

**aphte** [aft(ə)] *nm* mouth ulcer.

**aphteuse** [aftøz] *af*: **fièvre ~** foot-and-mouth disease.

**apiculteur** [apikyltœʀ] *nm* beekeeper.

**apiculture** [apikyltyʀ] *nf* beekeeping, apiculture.

**apitoyer** [apitwaje] *vt* to move to pity; **~ qn sur** to move sb to pity for, make sb feel sorry for; **s'~ (sur)** to feel pity *ou* compassion (for).

**aplanir** [aplaniʀ] *vt* to level; (*fig*) to smooth away, iron out.

**aplati, e** [aplati] *a* flat, flattened.

**aplatir** [aplatiʀ] *vt* to flatten; **s'~** *vi* to become flatter; to be flattened; (*fig*) to lie flat on the ground; (: *fam*) to fall flat on one's face; (: *péj*) to grovel.

**aplomb** [aplɔ̃] *nm* (*équilibre*) balance, equilibrium; (*fig*) self-assurance; nerve; **d'~** *ad* steady; (*CONSTR*) plumb.

**apocalypse** [apɔkalips(ə)] *nf* apocalypse.

**apogée** [apɔʒe] *nm* (*fig*) peak, apogee.

**apolitique** [apɔlitik] *a* apolitical.

**apologie** [apɔlɔʒi] *nf* vindication, praise.

**apoplexie** [apɔplɛksi] *nf* apoplexy.

**a posteriori** [apɔsteʀjɔʀi] *ad* after the event, with hindsight, a posteriori.

**apostolat** [apɔstɔla] *nm* (*REL*) apostolate, discipleship; (*gén*) proselytism, preaching; **apostolique** *a* apostolic.

**apostrophe** [apɔstʀɔf] *nf* (*signe*) apostrophe; (*appel*) interpellation.

**apostropher** [apɔstʀɔfe] *vt* (*interpeller*) to shout at, address sharply.

**apothéose** [apɔteoz] *nf* pinnacle (of achievement); grand finale.

**apôtre** [apotʀ(ə)] *nm* apostle, disciple.

**apparaître** [apaʀɛtʀ(ə)] *vi* to appear // *vb avec attribut* to appear, seem; **il apparaît que** it appears that.

**apparat** [apaʀa] *nm*: **tenue/dîner d'~** ceremonial dress/dinner; **~ critique** (*d'un texte*) critical apparatus.

**appareil** [apaʀɛj] *nm* piece of apparatus, device; appliance; (*politique, syndical*) machinery; (*avion*) (aero)plane, aircraft *inv*; (*téléphonique*) phone; (*dentier*) brace; **~ digestif/reproducteur** digestive/reproductive system *ou* apparatus; **qui est à l'~?** who's speaking?; **dans le plus simple ~** in one's birthday suit; **~ de photographie, ~(-photo)** *nm* camera; **~ 24 x 36** *ou* **petit format** 35mm. camera.

**appareillage** [apaʀɛjaʒ] *nm* (*appareils*) equipment; (*NAVIG*) casting off, getting under way.

**appareiller** [apaʀeje] *vi* (*NAVIG*) to cast off, get under way // *vt* (*assortir*) to match up.

**apparemment** [apaʀamɑ̃] *ad* apparently.

**apparence** [apaʀɑ̃s] *nf* appearance; **en ~** apparently, seemingly.

**apparent, e** [apaʀɑ̃, -ɑ̃t] *a* visible; obvious; (*superficiel*) apparent; **coutures ~es** topstitched seams; **poutres ~es** exposed beams.

**apparenté, e** [apaʀɑ̃te] *a*: **~ à** related to; (*fig*) similar to.

**appariteur** [apaʀitœʀ] *nm* attendant, porter (*in French universities*).

**apparition** [apaʀisjɔ̃] *nf* appearance; (*surnaturelle*) apparition.

**appartement** [apaʀtəmɑ̃] *nm* flat.

**appartenance** [apaʀtənɑ̃s] *nf*: **~ à** belonging to, membership of.

**appartenir** [apaʀtəniʀ]: **~ à** *vt* to belong to; (*faire partie de*) to belong to, be a member of; **il lui appartient de** it is up to him to, it is his duty to.

**apparu, e** *pp de* **apparaître**.

**appas** [apɑ] *nmpl* (*d'une femme*) charms.

**appât** [apɑ] *nm* (*PÊCHE*) bait; (*fig*) lure, bait; **appâter** *vt* (*hameçon*) to bait; (*poisson, fig*) to lure, entice.

**appauvrir** [apovʀiʀ] *vt* to impoverish; **s'~** *vi* to grow poorer, become impoverished.

**appel** [apɛl] *nm* call; (*nominal*) roll call; (: *SCOL*) register; (*MIL: recrutement*) call up; (*JUR*) appeal; **faire ~ à** (*invoquer*) to appeal to; (*avoir recours à*) to call on; (*nécessiter*) to call for, require; **faire ou interjeter ~** (*JUR*) to appeal, lodge an appeal; **faire l'~** to call the roll; to call the register; **sans ~** (*fig*) final, irrevocable; **~ d'air** in-draught; **~ d'offres** (*COMM*) invitation to tender; **faire un ~ de phares** to flash one's headlights; **~ (téléphonique)** (tele)phone call.

**appelé** [aple] *nm* (*MIL*) conscript.

**appeler** [aple] *vt* to call; (*faire venir: médecin etc*) to call, send for; (*fig: nécessiter*) to call for, demand; **être appelé à** (*fig*) to be destined to; **~ qn à comparaître** (*JUR*) to summon sb to appear; **en ~ à** to appeal to; **s'~**: **elle s'appelle Gabrielle** her name is Gabrielle, she's called Gabrielle; **comment ça s'appelle?** what is it called?

**appellation** [apelɑsjɔ̃] *nf* designation, appellation.

**appendice** [apɛ̃dis] *nm* appendix; **appendicite** *nf* appendicitis.

**appentis** [apɑ̃ti] *nm* lean-to.

**appesantir** [apzɑ̃tiʀ]: **s'~** *vi* to grow heavier; **s'~ sur** (*fig*) to dwell at length on.

**appétissant, e** [apetisɑ̃, -ɑ̃t] *a* appetizing, mouth-watering.

**appétit** [apeti] *nm* appetite; **avoir un gros/petit ~** to have a big/small appetite; **bon ~!** enjoy your meal!

**applaudir** [aplodiʀ] *vt* to applaud // *vi* to applaud, clap; **~ à** *vt* (*décision*) to applaud, commend; **applaudissements** *nmpl* applause *sg*, clapping *sg*.

**application** [aplikɑsjɔ̃] *nf* application.

**applique** [aplik] *nf* wall lamp.
**appliqué, e** [aplike] *a* (*élève etc*) industrious, assiduous ; (*science*) applied.
**appliquer** [aplike] *vt* to apply ; (*loi*) to enforce ; **s'~** *vi* (*élève etc*) to apply o.s. ; **s'~ à faire qch** to apply o.s. to doing sth, take pains to do sth.
**appoint** [apwɛ̃] *nm* (extra) contribution *ou* help ; **avoir/faire l'~** (*en payant*) to have/give the right change *ou* money ; **chauffage d'~** extra heating.
**appointements** [apwɛ̃tmɑ̃] *nmpl* salary.
**appontement** [apɔ̃tmɑ̃] *nm* landing stage, wharf.
**apport** [apɔʀ] *nm* supply ; contribution.
**apporter** [apɔʀte] *vt* to bring.
**apposer** [apoze] *vt* to append ; to affix.
**apposition** [apozisjɔ̃] *nf* appending ; affixing ; (LING): **en ~** in apposition.
**appréciable** [apʀesjabl(ə)] *a* (*important*) appreciable, significant.
**appréciation** [apʀesjusjɔ̃] *nf* appreciation ; estimation, assessment ; **~s** (*avis*) assessment *sg*, appraisal *sg*.
**apprécier** [apʀesje] *vt* to appreciate ; (*évaluer*) to estimate, assess.
**appréhender** [apʀeɑ̃de] *vt* (*craindre*) to dread ; (*arrêter*) to apprehend ; **~ que** to fear that ; **~ de faire** to dread doing.
**appréhension** [apʀeɑ̃sjɔ̃] *nf* apprehension.
**apprendre** [apʀɑ̃dʀ(ə)] *vt* to learn ; (*événement, résultats*) to learn of, hear of ; **~ qch à qn** (*informer*) to tell sb (of) sth ; (*enseigner*) to teach sb sth ; **~ à faire qch** to learn to do sth ; **~ à qn à faire qch** to teach sb to do sth ; **apprenti, e** *nm/f* apprentice ; (*fig*) novice, beginner ; **apprentissage** *nm* learning ; (COMM. SCOL: *période*) apprenticeship.
**apprêt** [apʀɛ] *nm* (*sur un cuir, une étoffe*) dressing ; (*sur un mur*) size ; (*sur un papier*) finish.
**apprêté, e** [apʀete] *a* (*fig*) affected.
**apprêter** [apʀete] *vt* to dress, finish.
**appris, e** *pp de* **apprendre**.
**apprivoiser** [apʀivwaze] *vt* to tame.
**approbateur, trice** [apʀɔbatœʀ, -tʀis] *a* approving.
**approbation** [apʀɔbɑsjɔ̃] *nf* approval.
**approche** [apʀɔʃ] *nf* approaching ; approach ; **à l'~ du bateau/de l'ennemi** as the ship/enemy approached *ou* drew near.
**approché, e** [apʀɔʃe] *a* approximate.
**approcher** [apʀɔʃe] *vi* to approach, come near // *vt* (*vedette, artiste*) to come close to, approach ; (*rapprocher*): **~ qch (de qch)** to bring *ou* put *ou* move sth near (to sth) ; **~ de** *vt* to draw near to ; (*quantité, moment*) to approach ; **s'~ de** *vt* to approach, go *ou* come *ou* move near to.
**approfondi, e** [apʀɔfɔ̃di] *a* thorough, detailed.
**approfondir** [apʀɔfɔ̃diʀ] *vt* to deepen, make deeper ; (*fig*) to go (deeper *ou* further) into.
**approprié, e** [apʀɔpʀije] *a*: **~ (à)** appropriate (to), suited to.
**approprier** [apʀɔpʀije]: **s'~** *vt* to appropriate, take over.

**approuver** [apʀuve] *vt* to agree with ; (*autoriser: loi, projet*) to approve, pass ; (*trouver louable*) to approve of.
**approvisionnement** [apʀɔvizjɔnmɑ̃] *nm* supplying ; (*provisions*) supply, stock.
**approvisionner** [apʀɔvizjɔne] *vt* to supply ; (*compte bancaire*) to pay funds into ; **~ qn en** to supply sb with ; **s'~ en** to stock up with.
**approximatif, ive** [apʀɔksimatif, -iv] *a* approximate, rough ; (*fig*) vague ; **approximativement** *ad* approximately, roughly ; vaguely.
**Appt** *abr de* **appartement**.
**appui** [apɥi] *nm* support ; **prendre ~ sur** to lean on ; to rest on ; **à l'~ de** (*pour prouver*) in support of ; **l'~ de la fenêtre** the windowsill, the window ledge ; **appui-tête** *nm*, **appuie-tête** *nm inv* headrest.
**appuyer** [apɥije] *vt* (*poser*): **~ qch sur/contre** to lean *ou* rest sth on/against ; (*soutenir: personne, demande*) to support, back (up) ; **~ sur** (*bouton*) to press, push ; (*frein*) to press on, push down ; (*mot, détail*) to stress, emphasize ; (*suj: chose: peser sur*) to rest (heavily) on, press against ; **s'~ sur** *vt* to lean on ; to rely on ; **~ à droite** to bear (to the) right.
**âpre** [ɑpʀ(ə)] *a* acrid, pungent ; (*fig*) harsh ; bitter ; **~ au gain** grasping, greedy.
**après** [apʀɛ] *prép* after // ad afterwards ; **2 heures ~** 2 hours later ; **~ qu'il est ou soit parti/avoir fait** after he left/having done ; **d'~** *prép* (*selon*) according to ; **~ coup** *ad* after the event, afterwards ; **~ tout** *ad* (*au fond*) after all ; **et (puis) ~?** so what? ; **~-demain** *ad* the day after tomorrow ; **~-guerre** *nm* postwar years *pl* ; **~-midi** *nm ou nf inv* afternoon ; **~-ski** *nm inv* (*chaussure*) snow boot ; (*moment*) après-ski.
**à-propos** [apʀopo] *nm* (*d'une remarque*) aptness ; **faire preuve d'~** to show presence of mind, do the right thing.
**apte** [apt(ə)] *a*: **~ à qch/faire qch** capable of sth/doing sth ; **~ (au service)** (MIL) fit (for service) ; **aptitude** *nf* ability, aptitude.
**aquarelle** [akwaʀɛl] *nf* (*tableau*) watercolour ; (*genre*) watercolours *pl*, aquarelle.
**aquarium** [akwaʀjɔm] *nm* aquarium.
**aquatique** [akwatik] *a* aquatic, water *cpd*.
**aqueduc** [akdyk] *nm* aqueduct.
**aqueux, euse** [akø, -øz] *a* aqueous.
**arabe** [aʀab] *a* Arabic ; (*désert, cheval*) Arabian ; (*nation, peuple*) Arab // *nm/f*: **A~** Arab // *nm* (*langue*) Arabic.
**arabesque** [aʀabɛsk(ə)] *nf* arabesque.
**Arabie** [aʀabi] *nf*: **l'~ (Séoudite)** Saudi Arabia.
**arable** [aʀabl(ə)] *a* arable.
**arachide** [aʀaʃid] *nf* (*plante*) groundnut (plant) ; (*graine*) peanut, groundnut.
**araignée** [aʀeɲe] *nf* spider ; **~ de mer** spider crab.
**araser** [aʀaze] *vt* to level ; to plane (down).
**aratoire** [aʀatwaʀ] *a*: **instrument ~** ploughing implement.
**arbalète** [aʀbalɛt] *nf* crossbow.
**arbitrage** [aʀbitʀaʒ] *nm* refereeing ; umpiring ; arbitration.

**arbitraire** [aʀbitʀɛʀ] a arbitrary.

**arbitre** [aʀbitʀ(ə)] nm (SPORT) referee; (: TENNIS, CRICKET) umpire; (fig) arbiter, judge; (JUR) arbitrator; **arbitrer** vt to referee; to umpire; to arbitrate.

**arborer** [aʀbɔʀe] vt to bear, display; to sport.

**arboriculture** [aʀbɔʀikyltyʀ] nf arboriculture.

**arbre** [aʀbʀ(ə)] nm tree; (TECH) shaft; ~ **généalogique** family tree; ~ **de transmission** (AUTO) driveshaft; **arbrisseau, x** nm shrub.

**arbuste** [aʀbyst(ə)] nm small shrub, bush.

**arc** [aʀk] nm (arme) bow; (GÉOM) arc; (ARCHIT) arch; ~ **de cercle** arc of a circle; **en ~ de cercle** a semi-circular; **A~ de triomphe** Triumphal Arch.

**arcade** [aʀkad] nf arch(way); ~s arcade sg, arches; ~ **sourcilière** arch of the eyebrows.

**arcanes** [aʀkan] nmpl mysteries.

**arc-boutant** [aʀkbutɑ̃] nm flying buttress.

**arc-bouter** [aʀkbute]: **s'~** vi: **s'~ contre** to lean ou press against.

**arceau, x** [aʀso] nm (métallique etc) hoop.

**arc-en-ciel** [aʀkɑ̃sjɛl] nm rainbow.

**archaïque** [aʀkaik] a archaic; **archaïsme** nm archaism.

**arche** [aʀʃ(ə)] nf arch; ~ **de Noé** Noah's Ark.

**archéologie** [aʀkeɔlɔʒi] nf archeology; **archéologique** a archeological; **archéologue** nm/f archeologist.

**archer** [aʀʃe] nm archer.

**archet** [aʀʃɛ] nm bow.

**archevêché** [aʀʃəveʃe] nm archbishopric; archbishop's palace.

**archevêque** [aʀʃəvɛk] nm archbishop.

**archi...** [aʀʃi] préfixe (très) dead, extra; ~**simple** dead simple; ~**bondé** chocka-block, packed solid.

**archipel** [aʀʃipɛl] nm archipelago.

**architecte** [aʀʃitɛkt(ə)] nm architect.

**architecture** [aʀʃitɛktyʀ] nf architecture.

**archives** [aʀʃiv] nfpl archives; **archiviste** r.m/f archivist.

**arçon** [aʀsɔ̃] nm voir **cheval**.

**arctique** [aʀktik] a Arctic // nm: **l'A~** the Arctic; **l'océan A~** the Arctic Ocean.

**ardemment** [aʀdamɑ̃] ad ardently, fervently.

**ardent, e** [aʀdɑ̃, -ɑ̃t] a (soleil) blazing; (fièvre) raging; (amour) ardent, passionate; (prière) fervent; **ardeur** nf blazing heat; fervour, ardour.

**ardoise** [aʀdwaz] nf slate.

**Ardt** abr de **arrondissement**.

**ardu, e** [aʀdy] a arduous, difficult.

**are** [aʀ] nm are, 100 square metres.

**arène** [aʀɛn] nf arena; ~s nfpl bull-ring sg.

**arête** [aʀɛt] nf (de poisson) bone; (d'une montagne) ridge; (GÉOM, gén) edge (where two faces meet).

**argent** [aʀʒɑ̃] nm (métal) silver; (monnaie) money; ~ **liquide** ready money, (ready) cash; ~ **de poche** pocket money; **argenté, e** a silver(y); (métal) silverplated; **argenter** vt to silver(-plate); **argenterie** nf silverware; silver plate.

**argentin, e** [aʀʒɑ̃tɛ̃, -in] a (son) silvery; (d'Argentine) Argentinian, Argentine // nm/f Argentinian, Argentine.

**Argentine** [aʀʒɑ̃tin] nf: **l'~** Argentina, the Argentine.

**argile** [aʀʒil] nf clay; **argileux, euse** a clayey.

**argot** [aʀgo] nm slang; **argotique** a slang cpd; slangy.

**arguer** [aʀgɥe]: ~ **de** vt to put forward as a pretext ou reason.

**argument** [aʀgymɑ̃] nm argument.

**argumenter** [aʀgymɑ̃te] vi to argue.

**argus** [aʀgys] nm guide to second-hand car prices.

**arguties** [aʀgysi] nfpl pettifoggery sg, quibbles.

**aride** [aʀid] a arid.

**aristocrate** [aʀistɔkʀat] nm/f aristocrat.

**aristocratie** [aʀistɔkʀasi] nf aristocracy; **aristocratique** a aristocratic.

**arithmétique** [aʀitmetik] a arithmetic(al) // nf arithmetic.

**armateur** [aʀmatœʀ] nm shipowner.

**armature** [aʀmatyʀ] nf framework; (de tente etc) frame; (de soutien-gorge) bone, wiring.

**arme** [aʀm(ə)] nf weapon; (section de l'armée) arm; ~s nfpl (blason) (coat of) arms; **les ~s** (profession) soldiering sg; **passer par les ~s** to execute (by firing squad); **en ~s** up in arms; **prendre/présenter les ~s** to take up/present arms; **se battre à l'~ blanche** to fight with blades; ~ **à feu** firearm.

**armée** [aʀme] nf army; ~ **de l'air** Air Force; **l'~ du Salut** the Salvation Army; ~ **de terre** Army.

**armement** [aʀməmɑ̃] nm (matériel) arms pl, weapons pl; (: d'un pays) arms pl, armament.

**armer** [aʀme] vt to arm; (arme à feu) to cock; (appareil-photo) to wind on; ~ **qch de** to fit sth with; to reinforce sth with; ~ **qn de** to arm ou equip sb with.

**armistice** [aʀmistis] nm armistice.

**armoire** [aʀmwaʀ] nf (tall) cupboard; (penderie) wardrobe.

**armoiries** [aʀmwaʀi] nfpl coat sg of arms.

**armure** [aʀmyʀ] nf armour q, suit of armour.

**armurier** [aʀmyʀje] nm gunsmith; armourer.

**aromates** [aʀɔmat] nmpl seasoning sg, herbs (and spices).

**aromatisé, e** [aʀɔmatize] a flavoured.

**arôme** [aʀom] nm aroma; fragrance.

**arpège** [aʀpɛʒ] nm arpeggio.

**arpentage** [aʀpɑ̃taʒ] nm (land) surveying.

**arpenter** [aʀpɑ̃te] vt (salle, couloir) to pace up and down.

**arpenteur** [aʀpɑ̃tœʀ] nm land surveyor.

**arqué, e** [aʀke] a bow, bandy; arched.

**arrachage** [aʀaʃaʒ] nm: ~ **des mauvaises herbes** weeding.

**arrache-pied** [aʀaʃpje]: **d'~** ad relentlessly.

**arracher** [aʀaʃe] vt to pull out; (page etc) to tear out, tear out; (légume, souche) to lift; (: herbe, souche) to pull up; (bras etc: par explosion) to blow off; (: par accident) to tear off ; ~ **qch à qn** to snatch sth from sb ; (fig) to wring sth out of sb, wrest sth from sb ; ~ **qn à** (solitude, rêverie) to drag sb out of ; (famille etc) to tear ou wrench sb away from ; **s'~** vt (article très recherché) to fight over.

**arraisonner** [aRɛzɔne] vt (bateau) to board and search.

**arrangeant, e** [aRɑ̃ʒɑ̃, -ɑ̃t] a accommodating, obliging.

**arrangement** [aRɑ̃ʒmɑ̃] nm arrangement.

**arranger** [aRɑ̃ʒe] vt (gén) to arrange ; (réparer) to fix, put right ; (régler) to settle, sort out ; (convenir à) to suit, be convenient for ; **s'~** (se mettre d'accord) to come to an agreement ou arrangement ; **je vais m'~** I'll try and manage ; **ça va s'~** it'll sort itself out ; **s'~ pour faire** to manage so that one can do ; **arrangeur** nm (MUS) arranger.

**arrestation** [aRɛstɑsjɔ̃] nf arrest.

**arrêt** [aRɛ] nm stopping ; (de bus etc) stop ; (JUR) judgment, decision ; (FOOTBALL) save ; **~s** nmpl (MIL) arrest sg ; **être à l'~** to be stopped, have come to a halt ; **rester** ou **tomber en ~ devant** to stop short in front of ; **sans ~** without stopping, non-stop ; continually ; **~ de travail** stoppage (of work).

**arrêté** [aRete] nm order, decree.

**arrêter** [aRete] vt to stop ; (chauffage etc) to turn off, switch off ; (fixer: date etc) to appoint, decide on ; (criminel, suspect) to arrest ; **~ de faire** to stop doing ; **s'~** vi to stop.

**arrhes** [aR] nfpl deposit sg.

**arrière** [aRjɛR] nm back ; (SPORT) fullback // a inv: **siège/roue ~** back ou rear seat/wheel ; **à l'~** ad behind, at the back ; **en ~** ad behind ; (regarder) back, behind ; (tomber, aller) backwards ; **en ~ de** prép behind ; **arriéré, e** a (péj) backward // nm (d'argent) arrears pl ; **~-boutique** nf back shop ; **~-garde** nf rearguard ; **~-goût** nm aftertaste ; **~-grand-mère** nf great-grandmother ; nm great-grandfather ; **~-pays** nm inv hinterland ; **~-pensée** nf ulterior motive ; mental reservation ; **~-petits-enfants** nmpl great-grandchildren ; **~-plan** nm background ; **~-saison** nf late autumn ; **~-train** nm hindquarters pl.

**arrimer** [aRime] vt to stow ; to secure, fasten securely.

**arrivage** [aRivaʒ] nm arrival.

**arrivée** [aRive] nf arrival ; (ligne d'arrivée) finish ; **~ d'air/de gaz** air/gas inlet ; **à mon ~** when I arrived.

**arriver** [aRive] vi to arrive ; (survenir) to happen, occur ; **il arrive à Paris à 8h** he gets to ou arrives at Paris at 8 ; **~ à** (atteindre) to reach ; **~ à faire qch** to succeed in doing sth ; **il arrive que** it happens that ; **il lui arrive de faire** he sometimes does ; **arriviste** nm/f go-getter.

**arrogance** [aRɔgɑ̃s] nf arrogance.

**arrogant, e** [aRɔgɑ̃, -ɑ̃t] a arrogant.

**arroger** [aRɔʒe]: **s'~** vt to assume (without right).

**arrondi, e** [aRɔ̃di] a round // nm roundness.

**arrondir** [aRɔ̃diR] vt (forme, objet) to

round ; (somme) to round off ; **s'~** vi to become round(ed).

**arrondissement** [aRɔ̃dismɑ̃] nm (ADMIN) ≈ district.

**arrosage** [aRozaʒ] nm watering ; **tuyau d'~** hose(pipe).

**arroser** [aRoze] vt to water ; (victoire) to celebrate (over a drink) ; (CULIN) to baste ; **arroseuse** nf water cart ; **arrosoir** nm watering can.

**arsenal, aux** [aRsənal, -o] nm (NAVIG) naval dockyard ; (MIL) arsenal ; (fig) gear, paraphernalia.

**arsenic** [aRsənik] nm arsenic.

**art** [aR] nm art ; **~s et métiers** applied arts and crafts ; **~s ménagers** homecraft sg, domestic science sg.

**artère** [aRtɛR] nf (ANAT) artery ; (rue) main road ; **artériel, le** a arterial ; **artériosclérose** nf arteriosclerosis.

**arthrite** [aRtRit] nf arthritis.

**arthrose** [aRtRoz] nf (degenerative) osteoarthritis.

**artichaut** [aRtiʃo] nm artichoke.

**article** [aRtikl(ə)] nm article ; (COMM) item, article ; **à l'~ de la mort** at the point of death ; **~ de fond** (PRESSE) feature article.

**articulaire** [aRtikylɛR] a of the joints, articular.

**articulation** [aRtikylɑsjɔ̃] nf articulation ; (ANAT) joint.

**articuler** [aRtikyle] vt to articulate ; **s'~ (sur)** (ANAT, TECH) to articulate (to).

**artifice** [aRtifis] nm device, trick.

**artificiel, le** [aRtifisjɛl] a artificial ; **~lement** ad artificially.

**artificier** [aRtifisje] nm pyrotechnist.

**artificieux, euse** [aRtifisjø, -øz] a guileful, deceitful.

**artillerie** [aRtijRi] nf artillery, ordnance ; **artilleur** nm artilleryman, gunner.

**artisan** [aRtizɑ̃] nm artisan, (self-employed) craftsman ; **l'~ de la victoire** the architect of victory ; **artisanal, e, aux** a of ou made by craftsmen ; (péj) cottage industry cpd, unsophisticated ; **artisanat** nm arts and crafts pl.

**artiste** [aRtist(ə)] nm/f artist ; (de variétés) entertainer ; performer ; singer ; actor/actress ; **artistique** a artistic.

**aryen, ne** [aRjɛ̃, -jɛn] a Aryan.

**as** vb [a] voir **avoir** // nm [us] ace.

**ascendance** [asɑ̃dɑ̃s] nf (origine) ancestry.

**ascendant, e** [asɑ̃dɑ̃, -ɑ̃t] a upward // nm ascendancy ; **~s** nmpl ascendants.

**ascenseur** [asɑ̃sœR] nm lift.

**ascension** [asɑ̃sjɔ̃] nf ascent ; climb ; **l'A~** (REL) the Ascension.

**ascète** [asɛt] nm/f ascetic ; **ascétique** a ascetic.

**asepsie** [asɛpsi] nf asepsis ; **aseptique** a aseptic ; **aseptiser** vt to sterilize ; to disinfect.

**asiatique** [azjatik] a, nm/f Asiatic, Asian.

**Asie** [azi] nf Asia.

**asile** [azil] nm (refuge) refuge, sanctuary ; (POL): **droit d'~** (political) asylum ; (pour malades mentaux) home, asylum ; (pour vieillards) home.

**aspect** [aspɛ] *nm* appearance, look ; *(fig)* aspect, side ; *(LING)* aspect ; **à l'~ de** at the sight of.

**asperge** [aspɛRʒ(ə)] *nf* asparagus *q.*

**asperger** [aspɛRʒe] *vt* to spray, sprinkle.

**aspérité** [aspeRite] *nf* excrescence, protruding bit (of rock *etc*).

**aspersion** [aspɛRsjɔ̃] *nf* spraying, sprinkling.

**asphalte** [asfalt(ə)] *nm* asphalt ; **asphalter** *vt* to asphalt.

**asphyxie** [asfiksi] *nf* suffocation, asphyxia, asphyxiation ; **asphyxier** *vt* to suffocate, asphyxiate ; *(fig)* to stifle.

**aspic** [aspik] *nm* (*ZOOL*) asp ; (*CULIN*) aspic.

**aspirant, e** [aspiRɑ̃, -ɑ̃t] *a*: **pompe ~e** suction pump // *nm* (*NAVIG*) midshipman.

**aspirateur** [aspiRatœR] *nm* vacuum cleaner, hoover.

**aspiration** [aspiRasjɔ̃] *nf* inhalation ; sucking (up) ; drawing up ; **~s** *nfpl* (*ambitions*) aspirations.

**aspirer** [aspiRe] *vt* (*air*) to inhale ; (*liquide*) to suck (up) ; (*suj: appareil*) to suck *ou* draw up ; **~ à** *vt* to aspire to.

**aspirine** [aspiRin] *nf* aspirin.

**assagir** [asaʒiR] *vt*, **s'~** *vi* to quieten down, sober down.

**assaillant, e** [asajɑ̃, -ɑ̃t] *nm/f* assailant, attacker.

**assaillir** [asajiR] *vt* to assail, attack ; **~ qn de** (*questions*) to assail *ou* bombard sb with.

**assainir** [aseniR] *vt* to clean up ; to purify.

**assaisonnement** [asɛzɔnmɑ̃] *nm* seasoning.

**assaisonner** [asɛzɔne] *vt* to season.

**assassin** [asasɛ̃] *nm* murderer ; assassin.

**assassinat** [asasina] *nm* murder ; assassination.

**assassiner** [asasine] *vt* to murder ; to assassinate.

**assaut** [aso] *nm* assault, attack ; **prendre d'~** to (take by) storm, assault ; **donner l'~** to attack ; **faire ~ de** (*rivaliser*) to vie with *ou* rival each other in.

**assécher** [aseʃe] *vt* to drain.

**assemblage** [asɑ̃blaʒ] *nm* assembling ; (*MENUISERIE*) joint ; **un ~ de** (*fig*) a collection of.

**assemblée** [asɑ̃ble] *nf* (*réunion*) meeting ; (*public, assistance*) gathering ; assembled people ; (*POL*) assembly ; **l'A~ Nationale** the (French) National Assembly.

**assembler** [asɑ̃ble] *vt* (*joindre, monter*) to assemble, put together ; (*amasser*) to gather (together), collect (together) ; **s'~** *vi* to gather, collect.

**assener, asséner** [asene] *vt*: **~ un coup à qn** to deal sb a blow.

**assentiment** [asɑ̃timɑ̃] *nm* assent, consent ; approval.

**asseoir** [aswaR] *vt* (*malade, bébé*) to sit up ; to sit down ; (*autorité, réputation*) to establish ; **~ qch sur** to build sth on ; to base sth on ; **s'~** *vi* to sit (o.s.) down.

**assermenté, e** [asɛRmɑ̃te] *a* sworn, on oath.

**asservir** [asɛRviR] *vt* to subjugate, enslave.

**assesseur** [asesœR] *nm* (*JUR*) assessor.

**asseye** *etc vb voir* **asseoir.**

**assez** [ase] *ad* (*suffisamment*) enough, sufficiently ; (*passablement*) rather, quite, fairly ; **est-il ~ fort/rapide?** is he strong/fast enough *ou* sufficiently strong/fast? ; **il est passé ~ vite** he went past rather *ou* quite *ou* fairly fast ; **~ de pain/livres** enough *ou* sufficient bread/books ; **travailler ~** to work sufficiently (hard), work (hard) enough.

**assidu, e** [asidy] *a* assiduous, painstaking ; regular ; **assiduités** *nfpl* assiduous attentions.

**assied** *etc vb voir* **asseoir.**

**assiéger** [asjeʒe] *vt* to besiege, lay siege to ; (*suj: foule, touristes*) to mob, besiege.

**assiérai** *etc vb voir* **asseoir.**

**assiette** [asjɛt] *nf* plate ; (*contenu*) plate(ful) ; (*équilibre*) seat ; seating ; trim ; **~ anglaise** assorted cold meats ; **~ creuse** (soup) dish, soup plate ; **~ à dessert** dessert plate ; **~ de l'impôt** basis of (tax) assessment ; **~ plate** (dinner) plate.

**assigner** [asiɲe] *vt*: **~ qch à** (*poste, part, travail*) to assign *ou* allot sth to ; (*limites*) to set *ou* fix sth to ; (*cause, effet*) to ascribe *ou* attribute sth to ; **~ qn à** (*affecter*) to assign sb to ; **~ qn à résidence** (*JUR*) to assign a forced residence to sb.

**assimiler** [asimile] *vt* to assimilate, absorb ; (*comparer*): **~ qch/qn à** to liken *ou* compare sth/sb to ; **ils sont assimilés aux infirmières** (*ADMIN*) they are classed as nurses ; **s'~** *vi* (*s'intégrer*) to be assimilated *ou* absorbed.

**assis, e** [asi, -iz] *pp de* **asseoir** // *a* sitting (down), seated // *nf* (*CONSTR*) course ; (*GÉO*) stratum (*pl* a) ; (*fig*) basis (*pl* bases), foundation ; **~es** *nfpl* (*JUR*) assizes ; (*congrès*) (annual) conference.

**assistance** [asistɑ̃s] *nf* (*public*) audience ; (*aide*) assistance ; **porter ~ à qn** to give sb assistance ; **l'A~ (publique)** (*-1953*) ≈ National Assistance ; Child Care.

**assistant, e** [asistɑ̃, -ɑ̃t] *nm/f* assistant ; (*d'université*) probationary lecturer ; **les ~s** *nmpl* (*auditeurs etc*) those present ; **~e sociale** social worker.

**assisté, e** [asiste] *a* (*AUTO*) power assisted.

**assister** [asiste] *vt* to assist ; **~ à** *vt* (*scène, événement*) to witness ; (*conférence, séminaire*) to attend, be (present) at ; (*spectacle, match*) to be at, see.

**association** [asɔsjasjɔ̃] *nf* association.

**associé, e** [asɔsje] *nm/f* associate ; partner.

**associer** [asɔsje] *vt* to associate ; **~ qn à** (*profits*) to give sb a share of ; (*affaire*) to make sb a partner in ; (*joie, triomphe*) to include sb in ; **~ qch à** (*joindre, allier*) to combine sth with ; **s'~** (*suj pl*) to join together ; (*COMM*) to form a partnership ; **s'~** *vt* (*collaborateur*) to take on (as a partner) ; **s'~ à qn pour faire** to join (forces) *ou* join together with sb to do ; **s'~ à** to be combined with ; (*opinions, joie de qn*) to share in.

**assoiffé, e** [aswafe] *a* thirsty.

**assolement** [asɔlmɑ̃] *nm* (systematic) rotation of crops.

**assombrir** [asɔ̃bʀiʀ] *vt* to darken ; (*fig*) to fill with gloom ; **s'**~ *vi* to darken ; to cloud over ; to become gloomy.

**assommer** [asɔme] *vt* to batter to death ; (*étourdir, abrutir*) to knock out ; to stun ; (*fam: ennuyer*) to bore stiff.

**Assomption** [asɔ̃psjɔ̃] *nf*: **l'**~ the Assumption.

**assorti, e** [asɔʀti] *a* matched, matching ; **fromages/légumes** ~**s** assorted cheeses/vegetables ; ~ **à** matching.

**assortiment** [asɔʀtimɑ̃] *nm* assortment, selection.

**assortir** [asɔʀtiʀ] *vt* to match ; ~ **qch à** to match sth with ; ~ **qch de** to accompany sth with ; **s'**~ **de** to be accompanied by.

**assoupi, e** [asupi] *a* dozing, sleeping ; (*fig*) (be)numbed ; dulled ; stilled.

**assoupir** [asupiʀ]: **s'**~ *vi* to doze off.

**assouplir** [asupliʀ] *vt* to make supple ; (*fig*) to relax.

**assourdir** [asuʀdiʀ] *vt* (*bruit*) to deaden, muffle ; (*suj: bruit*) to deafen.

**assouvir** [asuviʀ] *vt* to satisfy, appease.

**assujettir** [asyʒetiʀ] *vt* to subject, subjugate ; ~ **qn à** (*règle, impôt*) to subject sb to.

**assumer** [asyme] *vt* (*fonction, emploi*) to assume, take on.

**assurance** [asyʀɑ̃s] *nf* (*certitude*) assurance ; (*confiance en soi*) (self-)confidence ; (*contrat*) insurance (policy) ; (*secteur commercial*) insurance ; ~ **maladie** health insurance ; ~ **tous risques** (*AUTO*) comprehensive insurance ; ~**s sociales** ≈ National Insurance ; ~-**vie** *nf* life assurance *ou* insurance.

**assuré, e** [asyʀe] *a* (*victoire etc*) certain, sure ; (*démarche, voix*) assured, (self-)confident ; (*certain*): ~ **de** confident of // *nm/f* insured (person) ; ~ **social** ≈ member of the National Insurance scheme ; ~**ment** *ad* assuredly, most certainly.

**assurer** [asyʀe] *vt* (*COMM*) to insure ; (*stabiliser*) to steady ; to stabilize ; (*victoire etc*) to ensure, make certain ; (*frontières, pouvoir*) to make secure ; (*service, garde*) to provide ; to operate ; (*garantir*): ~ **qch à qn** to secure *ou* guarantee sth for sb ; (*certifier*) to assure sb of sth ; ~ **à qn que** to assure sb that ; ~ **qn de** to assure sb of ; **s'**~ (**contre**) (*COMM*) to insure o.s. (against) ; **s'**~ **de/que** (*vérifier*) to make sure of/that ; **s'**~ (**de**) (*aide de qn*) to secure (for o.s.) ; **assureur** *nm* insurance agent ; insurers *pl*.

**astérisque** [asteʀisk(ə)] *nm* asterisk.

**asthmatique** [asmatik] *a* asthmatic.

**asthme** [asm(ə)] *nm* asthma.

**asticot** [astiko] *nm* maggot.

**astiquer** [astike] *vt* to polish, shine.

**astre** [astʀ(ə)] *nm* star.

**astreignant, e** [astʀɛɲɑ̃, -ɑ̃t] *a* demanding.

**astreindre** [astʀɛ̃dʀ(ə)] *vt*: ~ **qn à qch** to force sth upon sb ; ~ **qn à faire** to compel *ou* force sb to do.

**astringent, e** [astʀɛ̃ʒɑ̃, -ɑ̃t]·*a* astringent.

**astrologie** [astʀɔlɔʒi] *nf* astrology ; **astrologue** *nm/f* astrologer.

**astronaute** [astʀɔnot] *nm/f* astronaut.

**astronautique** [astʀɔnotik] *nf* astronautics *sg*.

**astronome** [astʀɔnɔm] *nm/f* astronomer.

**astronomie** [astʀɔnɔmi] *nf* astronomy ; **astronomique** *a* astronomic(al).

**astuce** [astys] *nf* shrewdness, astuteness ; (*truc*) trick, clever way ; (*plaisanterie*) wisecrack ; **astucieux, euse** *a* shrewd, clever, astute.

**asymétrique** [asimetʀik] *a* asymmetric(al).

**atelier** [atəlje] *nm* workshop ; (*de peintre*) studio.

**athée** [ate] *a* atheistic // *nm/f* atheist.

**Athènes** [atɛn] *n* Athens.

**athlète** [atlɛt] *nm/f* (*SPORT*) athlete ; (*costaud*) muscleman ; **athlétique** *a* athletic ; **athlétisme** *nm* athletics *sg*.

**atlantique** [atlɑ̃tik] *a* Atlantic // *nm*: **l'(océan) A**~ the Atlantic (Ocean).

**atlas** [atlɑs] *nm* atlas.

**atmosphère** [atmɔsfɛʀ] *nf* atmosphere ; **atmosphérique** *a* atmospheric.

**atome** [atom] *nm* atom ; **atomique** *a* (*bombe, pile*) atomic, nuclear ; (*usine*) nuclear ; (*nombre, masse*) atomic.

**atomiseur** [atɔmizœʀ] *nm* atomiser.

**atone** [atɔn] *a* lifeless.

**atours** [atuʀ] *nmpl* attire *sg*, finery *sg*.

**atout** [atu] *nm* trump ; (*fig*) asset ; trump card ; '~ **pique/trèfle**' spades/clubs are trumps.

**âtre** [ɑtʀ(ə)] *nm* hearth.

**atroce** [atʀɔs] *a* atrocious ; dreadful ; **atrocité** *nf* atrocity.

**atrophie** [atʀɔfi] *nf* atrophy.

**atrophier** [atʀɔfje]: **s'**~ *vi* to atrophy.

**attabler** [atable]: **s'**~ *vi* to sit down at (the) table.

**attachant, e** [ataʃɑ̃, -ɑ̃t] *a* engaging, lovable, likeable.

**attache** [ataʃ] *nf* clip, fastener ; (*fig*) tie ; **à l'**~ (*chien*) tied up.

**attaché, e** [ataʃe] *a*: **être** ~ **à** (*aimer*) to be attached to // *nm* (*ADMIN*) attaché ; ~-**case** *nm inv* attaché case.

**attachement** [ataʃmɑ̃] *nm* attachment.

**attacher** [ataʃe] *vt* to tie up ; (*étiquette*) to attach, tie on ; (*souliers*) to do up // *vi* (*poêle, riz*) to stick ; **s'**~ **à** (*par affection*) to become attached to ; **s'**~ **à faire qch** to endeavour to do sth ; ~ **qch à** to tie *ou* fasten *ou* attach sth to.

**attaquant** [atakɑ̃] *nm* (*MIL*) attacker ; (*SPORT*) striker, forward.

**attaque** [atak] *nf* attack ; (*cérébrale*) stroke ; (*d'épilepsie*) fit.

**attaquer** [atake] *vt* to attack ; (*en justice*) to bring an action against, sue ; (*travail*) to tackle, set about // *vi* to attack ; **s'**~ **à** to attack ; (*épidémie, misère*) to tackle, attack.

**attardé, e** [ataʀde] *a* (*passants*) late ; (*enfant*) backward ; (*conceptions*) old-fashioned.

**attarder** [ataʀde]: **s'**~ *vi* to linger ; to stay on.

**atteindre** [atɛ̃dR(ə)] *vt* to reach; (*blesser*) to hit; (*contacter*) to reach, contact, get in touch with; (*émouvoir*) to affect.

**atteint, e** [atɛ̃, -ɛ̃t] *a* (MÉD): être ~ de to be suffering from // *nf* attack; **hors d'**~e out of reach; **porter** ~e à to strike a blow at; to undermine.

**attelage** [atlaʒ] *nm* (*de remorque etc*) coupling; (*animaux*) team; (*harnachement*) harness; yoke.

**atteler** [atle] *vt* (*cheval, bœufs*) to hitch up; (*wagons*) to couple; **s'**~ à (*travail*) to buckle down to.

**attelle** [atɛl] *nf* splint.

**attenant, e** [atnɑ̃, -ɑ̃t] *a*: ~ (à) adjoining.

**attendre** [atɑ̃dR(ə)] *vt* (*gén*) to wait for; (*être destiné ou réservé à*) to await, be in store for // *vi* to wait; **s'**~ à (ce que) (*escompter*) to expect (that); ~ **un enfant** to be expecting (a baby); ~ de faire/d'être to wait until one does/is; ~ que to wait until; ~ qch de to expect sth of; **en attendant** *ad* meanwhile, in the meantime; be that as it may.

**attendri, e** [atɑ̃dRi] *a* tender.

**attendrir** [atɑ̃dRiR] *vt* to move (to pity); (*viande*) to tenderize; **s'**~ (sur) to be moved *ou* touched (by); **attendrissant, e** *a* moving, touching; **attendrissement** *nm* emotion; pity.

**attendu** [atɑ̃dy] *nm*: ~s reasons adduced for a judgment; ~ **que** *cj* considering that, since.

**attentat** [atɑ̃ta] *nm* assassination attempt; ~ **à la bombe** bomb attack; ~ **à la pudeur** indecent exposure *q*; indecent assault *q*.

**attente** [atɑ̃t] *nf* wait; (*espérance*) expectation.

**attenter** [atɑ̃te]: ~ à *vt* (*liberté*) to violate; ~ **à la vie de qn** to make an attempt on sb's life.

**attentif, ive** [atɑ̃tif, -iv] *a* (*auditeur*) attentive; (*travail*) scrupulous; careful; ~ à paying attention to; mindful of; careful to.

**attention** [atɑ̃sjɔ̃] *nf* attention; (*prévenance*) attention, thoughtfulness *q*; à l'~ de for the attention of; **faire** ~ (à) to be careful (of); **faire** ~ (à ce) **que** to be *ou* make sure that; ~! careful!, watch *ou* mind (out)!; **attentionné, e** *a* thoughtful, considerate.

**attentisme** [atɑ̃tism(ə)] *nm* wait-and-see policy.

**attentivement** [atɑ̃tivmɑ̃] *ad* attentively.

**atténuer** [atenɥe] *vt* to alleviate, ease; to lessen; to mitigate the effects of; **s'**~ *vi* to ease; to abate.

**atterrer** [ateRe] *vt* to dismay, appal.

**atterrir** [ateRiR] *vi* to land; **atterrissage** *nm* landing; **atterrissage sur le ventre** belly landing.

**attestation** [atɛstasjɔ̃] *nf* certificate; ~ **médicale** doctor's certificate.

**attester** [atɛste] *vt* to testify to, vouch for; (*démontrer*) to attest, testify to; ~ **que** to testify that.

**attiédir** [atjediR]: **s'**~ *vi* to become lukewarm; (*fig*) to cool down.

**attifé, e** [atife] *a* (*fam*) got up, rigged out.

**attique** [atik] *nm*: **appartement en** ~ penthouse (flat).

**attirail** [atiRaj] *nm* gear; (*péj*) paraphernalia.

**attirance** [atiRɑ̃s] *nf* attraction; (*séduction*) lure.

**attirant, e** [atiRɑ̃, -ɑ̃t] *a* attractive, appealing.

**attirer** [atiRe] *vt* to attract; (*appâter*) to lure, entice; ~ **qn dans un coin/vers soi** to draw sb into a corner/towards one; ~ **l'attention de qn (sur)** to attract sb's attention (to); to draw sb's attention (to); **s'**~ **des ennuis** to bring trouble upon o.s., get into trouble.

**attiser** [atize] *vt* (*feu*) to poke (up), stir up; (*fig*) to fan the flame of, stir up.

**attitré, e** [atitRe] *a* qualified; accredited; appointed.

**attitude** [atityd] *nf* attitude; (*position du corps*) bearing.

**attouchements** [atuʃmɑ̃] *nmpl* touching *sg*; (*sexuels*) fondling *sg*, stroking *sg*.

**attraction** [atRaksjɔ̃] *nf* (*gén*) attraction; (*de cabaret, cirque*) number.

**attrait** [atRɛ] *nm* appeal, attraction; lure; **éprouver de l'**~ **pour** to be attracted to; ~**s** *nmpl* attractions.

**attrape** [atRap] *nf voir* **farce** // *préfixe*: ~-**nigaud** *nm* con.

**attraper** [atRape] *vt* (*gén*) to catch; (*habitude, amende*) to get, pick up; (*fam*: *duper*) to take in.

**attrayant, e** [atRɛjɑ̃, -ɑ̃t] *a* attractive.

**attribuer** [atRibɥe] *vt* (*prix*) to award; (*rôle, tâche*) to allocate, assign; (*imputer*): ~ **qch à** to attribute sth to, ascribe sth to, put sth down to; **s'**~ *vt* (*s'approprier*) to claim for o.s.

**attribut** [atRiby] *nm* attribute; (LING) complement.

**attribution** [atRibysjɔ̃] *nf* awarding; allocation, assignment; attribution; ~**s** *nfpl* (*compétence*) attributions.

**attrister** [atRiste] *vt* to sadden.

**attroupement** [atRupmɑ̃] *nm* crowd, mob.

**attrouper** [atRupe]: **s'**~ *vi* to gather.

**au** [o] *prép* + *dét voir* **à.**

**aubade** [obad] *nf* dawn serenade.

**aubaine** [obɛn] *nf* godsend; (*financière*) windfall.

**aube** [ob] *nf* dawn, daybreak; **à l'**~ at dawn *ou* daybreak; **à l'**~ **de** (*fig*) at the dawn of.

**aubépine** [obepin] *nf* hawthorn.

**auberge** [obɛRʒ(ə)] *nf* inn; ~ **de jeunesse** youth hostel.

**aubergine** [obɛRʒin] *nf* aubergine.

**aubergiste** [obɛRʒist(ə)] *nm/f* inn-keeper, hotel-keeper.

**aucun, e** [okœ̃, -yn] *dét* no, *tournure négative* + any; (*positif*) any // *pronom* none, *tournure négative* + any; any(one); **il n'y a** ~ **livre** there isn't any book, there is no book; **je n'en vois** ~ **qui** I can't see any which, I (can) see none which; **sans** ~ **doute** without any doubt; **plus qu'**~ **autre** more than any other; ~ **des deux** neither of the two; ~ **d'entre eux** none of them; **d'**~**s** (*certains*) some;

**aucunement** ad in no way, not in the least.
**audace** [odas] nf daring, boldness ; (péj)
audacity ; **audacieux, euse** a daring, bold.
**au-delà** [odla] ad beyond // nm: **l'~** the
beyond ; **~ de** prép beyond.
**au-dessous** [odsu] ad underneath ;
below ; **~ de** prép under(neath), below ;
(limite, somme etc) below, under ; (dignité,
condition) below.
**au-dessus** [odsy] ad above ; **~ de** prép
above.
**au-devant** [odvɑ̃]: **~ de** prép: aller **~ de**
(personne, danger) to go (out) and meet ;
(souhaits de qn) to anticipate.
**audience** [odjɑ̃s] nf audience ; (JUR:
séance) hearing ; **trouver ~ auprès de** to
arouse much interest among, get the (interested) attention of.
**audio-visuel, le** [odjovizɥɛl] a audio-
visual.
**auditeur, trice** [oditœR, -tRis] nm/f (à la
radio) listener ; (à une conférence) member
of the audience, listener ; **~ libre** unregis-
tered student (attending lectures).
**audition** [odisjɔ̃] nf (ouïe, écoute) hearing ;
(JUR: de témoins) examination ; (MUS,
THÉÂTRE: épreuve) audition ; **auditionner** vt,
vi to audition.
**auditoire** [oditwaR] nm audience.
**auditorium** [oditɔRjɔm] nm (public)
studio.
**auge** [oʒ] nf trough.
**augmentation** [ɔgmɑ̃tɑsjɔ̃] nf increasing ; raising ; increase ; **~ (de salaire)** rise
(in salary).
**augmenter** [ɔgmɑ̃te] vt (gén) to increase ;
(salaire, prix) to increase, raise, put up ;
(employé) to increase the salary of, give
a (salary) rise to // vi to increase.
**augure** [ɔgyR] nm soothsayer, oracle ; **de
bon/mauvais ~** of good/ill omen.
**augurer** [ɔgyRe] vt: **~ qch de** to foresee
sth (coming) out of ; **~ bien de** to augur
well for.
**auguste** [ɔgyst(ə)] a august, noble,
majestic.
**aujourd'hui** [oʒuRdɥi] ad today.
**aumône** [omon] nf alms sg (pl inv) ; **faire
l'~ (à qn)** to give alms (to sb) ; **faire l'~
de qch à qn** (fig) to favour sb with sth.
**aumônerie** [omonRi] nf chaplaincy.
**aumônier** [omonje] nm chaplain.
**auparavant** [oparavɑ̃] ad before(hand).
**auprès** [opRɛ]: **~ de** prép next to, close
to ; (recourir, s'adresser) to ; (en
comparaison de) compared with, next to.
**auquel** [okɛl] prép + pronom voir **lequel**.
**aurai** etc vb voir **avoir**.
**auréole** [ɔReɔl] nf halo ; (tache) ring.
**auriculaire** [ɔRikylɛR] nm little finger.
**aurons** etc vb voir **avoir**.
**aurore** [ɔRɔR] nf dawn, daybreak ; **~
boréale** northern lights pl.
**ausculter** [oskylte] vt to auscultate.
**auspices** [ɔspis] nmpl: **sous les ~ de**
under the patronage ou auspices of ; **sous
de bons/mauvais ~** under fa-
vourable/unfavourable auspices.
**aussi** [osi] ad (également) also, too ; (de
comparaison) as // cj therefore, consequently ; **~ fort que** as strong as ; **moi**

**~ me too**, so do I ; **~ bien que** (de même
que) as well as.
**aussitôt** [osito] ad straight away, immediately ; **~ que** as soon as ; **~ envoyé**
as soon as it is (ou was) sent.
**austère** [ɔstɛR] a austere ; **austérité** nf
austerity.
**austral, e** [ɔstRal] a southern.
**Australie** [ɔstRali] nf Australia ;
**australien, ne** a, nm/f Australian.
**autant** [otɑ̃] ad so much ; (comparatif): **~
(que)** as much (as) ; (nombre) as many
(as) ; **~ (de)** so much (ou many) ; as much
(ou many) ; **~ partir** we (ou you etc) had
better leave ; **y en a-t-il ~ (qu'avant)?**
are there as many (as before)? ; **is there
as much (as before)?** ; **il n'est pas
découragé pour ~** he isn't discouraged
for all that ; **pour ~ que** cj assuming, as
long as ; **d'~ plus/mieux (que)** all the
more/the better (since).
**autarcie** [otaRsi] nf autarchy.
**autel** [ɔtɛl] nm altar.
**auteur** [otœR] nm author ; **l'~ de cette
remarque** the person who said that ; **~-
compositeur** nm composer-songwriter.
**authentifier** [ɔtɑ̃tifje] vt to authenticate.
**authentique** [ɔtɑ̃tik] a authentic, genuine.
**auto** [oto] nf car.
**auto...** [oto] préfixe auto..., self- ;
**~biographie** nf autobiography.
**autobus** [otobys] nm bus.
**autocar** [otokaR] nm coach.
**autochtone** [otokton] nm/f native.
**auto-collant, e** [otokolɑ̃, -ɑ̃t] a self-
adhesive ; (enveloppe) self-seal // nm
sticker.
**auto-couchettes** [otokuʃɛt] a: **train ~**
car sleeper train.
**autocratique** [otokRatik] a autocratic.
**autocritique** [otokRitik] nf self-criticism.
**autodéfense** [otodefɑ̃s] nf self-defence ;
**groupe d'~** vigilance committee.
**autodidacte** [otodidakt(ə)] nm/f self-
taught person.
**auto-école** [otoekɔl] nf driving school.
**autofinancement** [otofinɑ̃smɑ̃] nm self-
financing.
**autogestion** [otoʒɛstjɔ̃] nf self-
management.
**autographe** [otogRaf] nm autograph.
**automate** [otomat] nm automaton.
**automatique** [otomatik] a automatic //
nm: **l'~** ≈ subscriber trunk dialling ;
**~ment** ad automatically ; **automatiser** vt
to automate ; **automatisme** nm
automatism.
**automne** [oton] nm autumn.
**automobile** [otomobil] a motor cpd // nf
(motor) car ; **l'~** motoring ; the car
industry ; **automobiliste** nm/f motorist.
**autonome** [otonom] a autonomous ;
**autonomie** nf autonomy ; (POL) self-
government, autonomy ; **autonomie de
vol** range.
**autopsie** [otopsi] nf post mortem
(examination), autopsy.
**autorisation** [otoRizɑsjɔ̃] nf permission,
authorization ; (papiers) permit ; **avoir l'~
de faire** to be allowed ou have permission
to do, be authorized to do.

**autorisé, e** [ɔtɔRize] a (*opinion, sources*) authoritative.
**autoriser** [ɔtɔRize] vt to give permission for, authorize ; (*fig*) to allow (of), sanction ; ~ qn à faire to give permission to sb to do, authorize sb to do.
**autoritaire** [ɔtɔRitɛR] a authoritarian.
**autorité** [ɔtɔRite] nf authority ; faire ~ to be authoritative.
**autoroute** [ɔtɔRut] nf motorway.
**auto-stop** [ɔtɔstɔp] nm: l'~ hitch-hiking ; faire de l'~ to hitch-hike ; prendre qn en ~ to give sb a lift ; ~peur, euse nm/f hitch-hiker, hitcher.
**autour** [otuR] ad around ; ~ de prép around ; (*environ*) around, about ; tout ~ ad all around.
**autre** [otR(ə)] a other ; un ~ verre (*supplémentaire*) one more glass, another glass ; (*différent*) another glass, a different glass ; un ~ another (one) ; l'~ the other (one) ; les ~s (*autrui*) others ; l'un et l'~ both (of them) ; se détester etc l'un l'~/les uns les ~s to hate etc each other/one another ; se sentir ~ to feel different ; d'une semaine à l'~ from one week to the next ; (*incessamment*) any week now ; ~ chose something else ; ~ part ad somewhere else ; d'~ part ad on the other hand ; entre ~s among others ; among other things ; nous/vous ~s us/you (lot).
**autrefois** [otRəfwa] ad in the past.
**autrement** [otRəmã] ad differently ; in another way ; (*sinon*) otherwise ; ~ dit in other words.
**Autriche** [otRiʃ] nf Austria ; autrichien, ne a, nm/f Austrian.
**autruche** [otRyʃ] nf ostrich.
**autrui** [otRɥi] pronom others.
**auvent** [ovã] nm canopy.
**aux** [o] prép + dét voir à.
**auxiliaire** [ɔksiljɛR] a, nm, nf auxiliary.
**auxquels, auxquelles** [okɛl] prép + pronom voir lequel.
**av.** abr de avenue.
**avachi, e** [avaʃi] a limp, flabby.
**aval** [aval] nm (*accord*) endorsement, backing ; (*GÉO*): en ~ downstream, downriver ; (*sur une pente*) downhill ; en ~ de downstream ou downriver from ; downhill from.
**avalanche** [avalɑ̃ʃ] nf avalanche ; ~ poudreuse powder snow avalanche.
**avaler** [avale] vt to swallow.
**avance** [avɑ̃s] nf (*de troupes etc*) advance ; progress ; (*d'argent*) advance ; (*opposé à retard*) lead ; being ahead of schedule ; ~s nfpl overtures ; (*amoureuses*) advances ; une ~ de 300 m/4 h (*SPORT*) a 300 m/4 hour lead ; (être) en ~ (to be) early ; (*sur un programme*) (to be) ahead of schedule ; payer d'~ to pay in advance ; à l'~ in advance, beforehand.
**avancé, e** [avɑ̃se] a advanced ; well on ou under way // nf projection ; overhang ; jutting part.
**avancement** [avɑ̃smɑ̃] nm (*professionnel*) promotion.
**avancer** [avɑ̃se] vi to move forward, advance ; (*projet, travail*) to make progress ; (*être en saillie*) to overhang ; to project ; to

jut out ; (*montre, réveil*) to be fast ; to gain // vt to move forward, advance ; (*argent*) to advance ; s'~ vi to move forward, advance ; (*fig*) to commit o.s. ; to overhang ; to project ; to jut out ; j'avance (d'une heure) I'm (an hour) fast.
**avanies** [avani] nfpl snubs.
**avant** [avɑ̃] prép before // ad: trop/plus ~ too far/further forward // a inv: siège/roue ~ front seat/wheel // nm (*d'un véhicule, bâtiment*) front ; (*SPORT: joueur*) forward ; ~ qu'il parte/de faire before he leaves/doing ; ~ tout (*surtout*) above all ; à l'~ (*dans un véhicule*) in (the) front ; en ~ ad forward(s) ; en ~ de prép in front of.
**avantage** [avɑ̃taʒ] nm advantage ; (*TENNIS*): ~ service/dehors advantage ou van in/out ; ~s sociaux fringe benefits ; **avantager** vt (*favoriser*) to favour ; (*embellir*) to flatter ; avantageux, euse a attractive ; attractively priced.
**avant-bras** [avɑ̃bRa] nm inv forearm.
**avant-centre** [avɑ̃sɑ̃tR(ə)] nm centre-forward.
**avant-coureur** [avɑ̃kuRœR] a: signe ~ forerunner.
**avant-dernier, ère** [avɑ̃dɛRnje, -jɛR] a, nm/f next to last, last but one.
**avant-garde** [avɑ̃gaRd(ə)] nf (*MIL*) vanguard ; (*fig*) avant-garde.
**avant-goût** [avɑ̃gu] nm foretaste.
**avant-hier** [avɑ̃tjɛR] ad the day before yesterday.
**avant-poste** [avɑ̃pɔst(ə)] nm outpost.
**avant-première** [avɑ̃pRəmjɛR] nf (*de film*) preview.
**avant-projet** [avɑ̃pRɔʒɛ] nm pilot study.
**avant-propos** [avɑ̃pRɔpo] nm foreword.
**avant-veille** [avɑ̃vɛj] nf: l'~ two days before.
**avare** [avaR] a miserly, avaricious // nm/f miser ; ~ de (*compliments etc*) sparing of ; **avarice** nf avarice, miserliness ; **avaricieux, euse** a miserly, niggardly.
**avarié, e** [avaRje] a rotting, going off.
**avaries** [avaRi] nfpl (*NAVIG*) damage sg.
**avatar** [avataR] nm misadventure ; metamorphosis (*pl* phoses).
**avec** [avɛk] prép with ; (*à l'égard de*) to(wards), with.
**avenant, e** [avnɑ̃, -ɑ̃t] a pleasant ; à l'~ ad in keeping.
**avènement** [avɛnmɑ̃] nm (*d'un roi*) accession, succession ; (*d'un changement*) advent, coming.
**avenir** [avniR] nm future ; à l'~ in future ; politicien d'~ politician with prospects ou a future.
**Avent** [avɑ̃] nm: l'~ Advent.
**aventure** [avɑ̃tyR] nf adventure ; (*amoureuse*) affair ; s'aventurer vi to venture ; aventureux, euse a adventurous, venturesome ; (*projet*) risky, chancy ; aventurier, ère nm/f adventurer // nf (*péj*) adventuress.
**avenu, e** [avny] a: nul et non ~ null and void.
**avenue** [avny] nf avenue.
**avérer** [aveRe]: s'~ vb avec attribut to prove (to be).

**averse** [avɛRs(ə)] *nf* shower.
**aversion** [avɛRsjɔ̃] *nf* aversion, loathing.
**averti, e** [avɛRti] *a* (well-)informed.
**avertir** [avɛRtiR] *vt*: ~ **qn (de qch/que)** to warn sb (of sth/that); *(renseigner)* to inform sb (of sth/that); **avertissement** *nm* warning; **avertisseur** *nm* horn, hooter.
**aveu, x** [avø] *nm* confession.
**aveugle** [avœgl(ə)] *a* blind; ~**ment** *nm* blindness; **aveuglément** *ad* blindly; **aveugler** *vt* to blind; **à l'aveuglette** *ad* groping one's way along; *(fig)* in the dark, blindly.
**aviateur, trice** [avjatœR, -tRis] *nm/f* aviator, pilot.
**aviation** [avjɑsjɔ̃] *nf* aviation; *(sport)* flying; *(MIL)* air force.
**avide** [avid] *a* eager; *(péj)* greedy, grasping; **avidité** *nf* eagerness; greed.
**avilir** [aviliR] *vt* to debase.
**aviné, e** [avine] *a* intoxicated, drunken.
**avion** [avjɔ̃] *nm* aeroplane; **aller (quelque part) en** ~ to go (somewhere) by plane, fly (somewhere); **par** ~ by airmail; ~ **à réaction** jet (aeroplane).
**aviron** [aviRɔ̃] *nm* oar; *(sport)*: **l'**~ rowing.
**avis** [avi] *nm* opinion; *(notification)* notice; **être d'**~ **que** to be of the opinion that; **changer d'**~ to change one's mind; **jusqu'à nouvel** ~ until further notice.
**avisé, e** [avize] *a* sensible, wise; **être bien/mal** ~ **de faire** to be well-/ill-advised to do.
**aviser** [avize] *vt (voir)* to notice, catch sight of; *(informer)*: ~ **qn de/que** to advise *ou* inform sb of/that // .*vi* to think about things, assess the situation; **s'**~ **de qch/que** to become suddenly aware of sth/that; **s'**~ **de faire** to take it into one's head to do.
**avocat, e** [avɔka, -at] *nm/f (JUR)* barrister; *(fig)* advocate, champion // *nm (CULIN)* avocado (pear); **l'**~ **de la défense/partie civile** the counsel for the defence/plaintiff; ~ **d'affaires** business lawyer; ~ **général** assistant public prosecutor; ~**-stagiaire** *nm* ≈ barrister doing his articles.
**avoine** [avwan] *nf* oats *pl.*
**avoir** [avwaR] *nm* assets *pl,* resources *pl* // *vt (gén)* to have; *(fam: duper)* to do // *vb auxiliaire* to have; ~ **à faire qch** to have to do sth; **il a 3 ans** he is 3 (years old); *voir* **faim, peur** *etc*; ~ **3 mètres de haut** to be 3 metres high; **il y a there is** + *sg,* there are + *pl*; *(temporel)*: **il y a 10 ans** 10 years ago; **il y a 10 ans/longtemps que je le sais** I've known it for 10 years/a long time; **il y a 10 ans qu'il est arrivé** it's 10 years since he arrived; **il ne peut y en** ~ **qu'un** there can only be one; **il n'y a qu'à** we (*ou* you *etc*) will just have to; **qu'est-ce qu'il y a?** what's the matter?, what is it?; **en** ~ **à** *ou* **contre qn** to have a down on sb.
**avoisinant, e** [avwazinɑ̃, -ɑ̃t] *a* neighbouring.
**avoisiner** [avwazine] *vt* to be near *ou* close to; *(fig)* to border *ou* verge on.
**avortement** [avɔRtəmɑ̃] *nm* abortion.
**avorter** [avɔRte] *vi (MÉD)* to have an abortion; *(fig)* to fail.

**avorton** [avɔRtɔ̃] *nm (péj)* little runt.
**avoué, e** [avwe] *a* avowed // *nm (JUR)* ≈ solicitor.
**avouer** [avwe] *vt (crime, défaut)* to confess (to); ~ **avoir fait/que** to admit *ou* confess to having done/that.
**avril** [avRil] *nm* April.
**axe** [aks(ə)] *nm* axis (*pl* axes); *(de roue etc)* axle; *(fig)* main line; ~ **routier** trunk road, main road; ~ **de symétrie** symmetry axis; **axer** *vt*: **axer qch sur** to centre sth on.
**ayant droit** [ɛjɑ̃dRwa] *nm* assignee; ~ **à** *(pension etc)* person eligible for *ou* entitled to.
**ayons** *etc vb voir* **avoir**.
**azalée** [azale] *nf* azalea.
**azimut** [azimyt] *nm* azimuth; **tous** ~**s** *a (fig)* omnidirectional.
**azote** [azɔt] *nm* nitrogen; **azoté, e** *a* nitrogenous.
**azur** [azyR] *nm (couleur)* azure, sky blue; *(ciel)* sky, skies *pl.*
**azyme** [azim] *a*: **pain** ~ unleavened bread.

## B

**B.A.** *sigle f* (= *bonne action*) good deed (for the day).
**babiller** [babije] *vi* to prattle, chatter; *(bébé)* to babble.
**babines** [babin] *nfpl* chops.
**babiole** [babjɔl] *nf (bibelot)* trinket; *(vétille)* trifle.
**bâbord** [babɔR] *nm*: **à** *ou* **par** ~ to port, on the port side.
**babouin** [babwɛ̃] *nm* baboon.
**bac** [bak] *nm (SCOL) abr de* **baccalauréat**; *(bateau)* ferry; *(récipient)* tub; tray; tank; ~ **à glace** ice-tray.
**baccalauréat** [bakalɔRea] *nm* ≈ **GCE A-levels**.
**bâche** [baʃ] *nf* tarpaulin, canvas sheet.
**bachelier, ère** [baʃəlje, -ljɛR] *nm/f holder of the baccalauréat.*
**bâcher** [baʃe] *vt* to cover (with a canvas sheet *ou* a tarpaulin).
**bachot** [baʃo] *nm abr de* **baccalauréat**.
**bacille** [basil] *nm* bacillus (*pl* i).
**bâcler** [bɑkle] *vt* to botch (up).
**bactérie** [bakteRi] *nf* bacterium (*pl* ia); **bactériologie** *nf* bacteriology.
**badaud, e** [bado, -od] *nm/f* idle onlooker, stroller.
**baderne** [badɛRn(ə)] *nf (péj)*: **(vieille)** ~ old fossil.
**badigeon** [badiʒɔ̃] *nm* distemper; colour-wash; **badigeonner** *vt* to distemper; to colourwash; *(barbouiller)* to daub.
**badin, e** [badɛ̃, -in] *a* light-hearted, playful.
**badinage** [badinaʒ] *nm* banter.
**badine** [badin] *nf* switch (*stick*).
**badiner** [badine] *vi*: ~ **avec qch** to treat sth lightly.
**badminton** [badmintɔn] *nm* badminton.
**baffe** [baf] *nf (fam)* slap, clout.
**bafouer** [bafwe] *vt* to deride, ridicule.
**bafouiller** [bafuje] *vi, vt* to stammer.

**bâfrer** [bɑfʀe] vi, vt (fam) to guzzle, gobble.

**bagage** [bagaʒ] nm: ~s luggage sg; ~ littéraire (stock of) literary knowledge; ~s à main hand-luggage.

**bagarre** [bagaʀ] nf fight, brawl; **il aime la** ~ he loves a fight, he likes fighting; **se bagarrer** vi to have a fight ou scuffle, fight.

**bagatelle** [bagatɛl] nf trifle, trifling sum ou matter.

**bagnard** [baɲaʀ] nm convict.

**bagne** [baɲ] nm penal colony.

**bagnole** [baɲɔl] nf (fam) car, motor.

**bagout** [bagu] nm glibness; **avoir du** ~ to have the gift of the gab.

**bague** [bag] nf ring; ~ **de fiançailles** engagement ring; ~ **de serrage** clip.

**baguenauder** [bagnode]: **se** ~ vi to trail around, loaf around.

**baguer** [bage] vt to ring.

**baguette** [bagɛt] nf stick; (cuisine chinoise) chopstick; (de chef d'orchestre) baton; (pain) stick of (French) bread; ~ **magique** magic wand; ~ **de tambour** drumstick.

**bahut** [bay] nm chest.

**baie** [bɛ] nf (GÉO) bay; (fruit) berry; ~ (vitrée) picture window.

**baignade** [bɛɲad] nf bathing.

**baigné, e** [beɲe] a: ~ **de** bathed in; soaked with; flooded with.

**baigner** [beɲe] vt (bébé) to bath // vi: ~ **dans son sang** to lie in a pool of blood; ~ **dans la brume** to be shrouded in mist; **se** ~ vi to have a swim, go swimming ou bathing; **baigneur, euse** nm/f bather; **baignoire** nf bath(tub).

**bail, baux** [baj, bo] nm lease.

**bâillement** [bɑjmɑ̃] nm yawn.

**bâiller** [bɑje] vi to yawn; (être ouvert) to gape.

**bailleur** [bajœʀ] nm: ~ **de fonds** sponsor, backer.

**bâillon** [bɑjɔ̃] nm gag; **bâillonner** vt to gag.

**bain** [bɛ̃] nm bath; **prendre un** ~ to have a bath; ~ **de foule** walkabout; ~ **de soleil** sunbathing q; **prendre un** ~ **de soleil** to sunbathe; ~**s de mer** sea bathing sg; ~**-marie** nm double boiler; **faire chauffer au** ~**-marie** (boîte etc) to immerse in boiling water.

**baïonnette** [bajɔnɛt] nf bayonet.

**baisemain** [bɛzmɛ̃] nm kissing a lady's hand.

**baiser** [beze] nm kiss // vt (main, front) to kiss; (fam!) to screw (!).

**baisse** [bɛs] nf fall, drop; '~ **sur la viande**' 'meat prices down'.

**baisser** [bese] vt to lower; (radio, chauffage) to turn down; (AUTO: phares) to dip // vi to fall, drop, go down; **se** ~ vi to bend down.

**bajoues** [baʒu] nfpl chaps, chops.

**bal** [bal] nm dance; (grande soirée) ball; ~ **costumé** fancy-dress ball; ~ **musette** dance (with accordion accompaniment).

**balade** [balad] nf walk, stroll; (en voiture) drive.

**balader** [balade] vt (traîner) to trail round; **se** ~ vi to go for a walk ou stroll; to go for a drive.

**baladeuse** [baladøz] nf inspection lamp.

**baladin** [baladɛ̃] nm wandering entertainer.

**balafre** [balafʀ(ə)] nf gash, slash; (cicatrice) scar; **balafrer** vt to gash, slash.

**balai** [balɛ] nm broom, brush; ~**-brosse** nm deck scrubber.

**balance** [balɑ̃s] nf scales pl; (de précision) balance; (signe): **la B**~ Libra, the Scales; **être de la B**~ to be Libra; ~ **des comptes/forces** balance of payments/power; ~ **romaine** steelyard.

**balancer** [balɑ̃se] vt to swing; (lancer) to fling, chuck; (renvoyer, jeter) to chuck out // vi to swing; **se** ~ vi to swing; to rock; to sway; **se** ~ **de** (fam) not to care about; **balancier** nm (de pendule) pendulum; (de montre) balance wheel; (perche) (balancing) pole; **balançoire** nf swing; (sur pivot) seesaw.

**balayer** [baleje] vt (feuilles etc) to sweep up, brush up; (pièce) to sweep; (chasser) to sweep away; to sweep aside; (suj: radar) to scan; (: phares) to sweep across; **balayeur, euse** nm/f roadsweeper // nf (engin) roadsweeper; **balayures** nfpl sweepings.

**balbutier** [balbysje] vi, vt to stammer.

**balcon** [balkɔ̃] nm balcony; (THÉÂTRE) dress circle.

**baldaquin** [baldakɛ̃] nm canopy.

**baleine** [balɛn] nf whale; (de parapluie, corset) rib; **baleinière** nf whaleboat.

**balise** [baliz] nf (NAVIG) beacon; (marker) buoy; (AVIAT) runway light, beacon; (AUTO, SKI) sign, marker; **baliser** vt to mark out (with beacons ou lights etc).

**balistique** [balistik] nf ballistics sg.

**balivernes** [balivɛʀn(ə)] nfpl twaddle sg, nonsense sg.

**ballade** [balad] nf ballad.

**ballant, e** [balɑ̃, -ɑ̃t] a dangling.

**ballast** [balast] nm ballast.

**balle** [bal] nf (de fusil) bullet; (de sport) ball; (du blé) chaff; (paquet) bale; ~ **perdue** stray bullet.

**ballerine** [balʀin] nf ballet dancer; ballet shoe.

**ballet** [balɛ] nm ballet.

**ballon** [balɔ̃] nm (de sport) ball; (jouet, AVIAT) balloon; (de vin) glass; ~ **de football** football.

**ballonner** [balɔne] vt: **j'ai le ventre ballonné** I feel bloated.

**ballon-sonde** [balɔ̃sɔ̃d] nm sounding balloon.

**ballot** [balo] nm bundle; (péj) nitwit.

**ballottage** [balɔtaʒ] nm (POL) second ballot.

**ballotter** [balɔte] vi to roll around; to toss // vt to shake ou throw about; to toss.

**balluchon** [balyʃɔ̃] nm bundle (of clothes).

**balnéaire** [balneɛʀ] a seaside cpd.

**balourd, e** [baluʀ, -uʀd(ə)] a clumsy, doltish; **balourdise** nf clumsiness, doltishness; blunder.

**balte** [balt] a Baltic.

**Baltique** [baltik] *nf*: **la (mer)** ~ the Baltic (Sea).

**baluchon** [balyʃɔ̃] *nm* = **balluchon.**

**balustrade** [balystʀad] *nf* railings *pl*, handrail.

**bambin** [bɑ̃bɛ̃] *nm* little child.

**bambou** [bɑ̃bu] *nm* bamboo.

**ban** [bɑ̃] *nm* round of applause, cheer; ~s *nmpl* (*de mariage*) banns; **être/mettre au** ~ **de** to be outlawed/to outlaw from; **le** ~ **et l'arrière-**~ **de sa famille** every last one of his relatives.

**banal, e** [banal] *a* banal, commonplace; (*péj*) trite; **four/moulin** ~ village oven/mill; ~**ité** *nf* banality; truism, trite remark.

**banane** [banan] *nf* banana; ~**raie** *nf* banana plantation; **bananier** *nm* banana tree; banana boat.

**banc** [bɑ̃] *nm* seat, bench; (*de poissons*) shoal; ~ **des accusés** dock; ~ **d'essai** (*fig*) testing ground; ~ **de sable** sandbank; ~ **des témoins** witness box.

**bancaire** [bɑ̃kɛʀ] *a* banking, bank *cpd.*

**bancal, e** [bɑ̃kal] *a* wobbly; bandy-legged.

**bandage** [bɑ̃daʒ] *nm* bandaging; bandage; ~ **herniaire** truss.

**bande** [bɑ̃d] *nf* (*de tissu etc*) strip; (*MÉD*) bandage; (*motif*) stripe; (*magnétique etc*) tape; (*groupe*) band; (*péj*): ~ bunch *ou* crowd of; **par la** ~ in a roundabout way; **donner de la** ~ to list; **faire** ~ **à part** to keep to o.s.; ~ **dessinée** strip cartoon; ~ **perforée** punched tape; ~ **de roulement** (*de pneu*) tread; ~ **sonore** sound track.

**bandeau, x** [bɑ̃do] *nm* headband; (*sur les yeux*) blindfold; (*MÉD*) head bandage.

**bander** [bɑ̃de] *vt* (*blessure*) to bandage; (*muscle*) to tense; ~ **les yeux à qn** to blindfold sb.

**banderole** [bɑ̃dʀɔl] *nf* banner, streamer.

**bandit** [bɑ̃di] *nm* bandit; **banditisme** *nm* violent crime, armed robberies *pl*

**bandoulière** [bɑ̃duljɛʀ] *nf*: **en** ~ (slung *ou* worn) across the shoulder.

**banjo** [bɑ̃(d)ʒo] *nm* banjo.

**banlieue** [bɑ̃ljø] *nf* suburbs *pl*; **lignes/quartiers de** ~ suburban lines/areas; **trains de** ~ commuter trains.

**bannière** [banjɛʀ] *nf* banner.

**bannir** [baniʀ] *vt* to banish.

**banque** [bɑ̃k] *nf* bank; (*activités*) banking; ~ **d'affaires** merchant bank.

**banqueroute** [bɑ̃kʀut] *nf* bankruptcy.

**banquet** [bɑ̃kɛ] *nm* dinner; (*d'apparat*) banquet.

**banquette** [bɑ̃kɛt] *nf* seat.

**banquier** [bɑ̃kje] *nm* banker.

**banquise** [bɑ̃kiz] *nf* ice field.

**baptême** [batɛm] *nm* christening; baptism; ~ **de l'air** first flight; **baptiser** *vt* to christen.

**baquet** [bakɛ] *nm* tub, bucket.

**bar** [baʀ] *nm* bar.

**baragouin** [baʀagwɛ̃] *nm* gibberish.

**baraque** [baʀak] *nf* shed; (*fam*) house; ~ **foraine** fairground stand.

**baraqué, e** [baʀake] *a* well-built, hefty.

**baraquements** [baʀakmɑ̃] *nmpl* huts (*for refugees, workers etc*).

**baratin** [baʀatɛ̃] *nm* (*fam*) smooth talk, patter; **baratiner** *vt* to chat up.

**barbare** [baʀbaʀ] *a* barbaric // *nm/f* barbarian.

**barbe** [baʀb(ə)] *nf* beard; **quelle** ~ (*fam*) what a drag *ou* bore; ~ **à papa** candy-floss.

**barbelé** [baʀbəle] *nm* barbed wire *q.*

**barbiche** [baʀbiʃ] *nf* goatee.

**barbiturique** [baʀbityʀik] *nm* barbiturate.

**barboter** [baʀbɔte] *vi* to paddle, dabble // *vt* (*fam*) to filch.

**barboteuse** [baʀbɔtøz] *nf* rompers *pl.*

**barbouiller** [baʀbuje] *vt* to daub; **avoir l'estomac barbouillé** to feel queasy *ou* sick.

**barbu, e** [baʀby] *a* bearded.

**barda** [baʀda] *nm* (*fam*) kit, gear.

**barde** [baʀd(ə)] *nf* (*CULIN*) sliver of fat bacon.

**bardé, e** [baʀde] *a*: ~ **de médailles** *etc* bedecked with medals *etc.*

**barder** [baʀde] *vi* (*fam*): **ça va** ~ sparks will fly, things are going to get hot.

**barème** [baʀɛm] *nm* scale; table; ~ **des salaires** salary scale.

**barguigner** [baʀgiɲe] *vi*: **sans** ~ without (any) humming and hawing *ou* shilly-shallying.

**baril** [baʀil] *nm* barrel; keg.

**barillet** [baʀijɛ] *nm* (*de revolver*) cylinder.

**bariolé, e** [baʀjɔle] *a* many-coloured, rainbow-coloured.

**baromètre** [baʀɔmɛtʀ(ə)] *nm* barometer.

**baron** [baʀɔ̃] *nm* baron; **baronne** *nf* baroness.

**baroque** [baʀɔk] *a* (*ART*) baroque; (*fig*) weird.

**baroud** [baʀud] *nm*: ~ **d'honneur** gallant last stand.

**barque** [baʀk(ə)] *nf* small boat.

**barrage** [baʀaʒ] *nm* dam; (*sur route*) roadblock, barricade.

**barre** [baʀ] *nf* bar; (*NAVIG*) helm; (*écrite*) line, stroke; (*JUR*): **comparaître à la** ~ to appear as a witness; ~ **fixe** (*GYM*) horizontal bar; ~ **à mine** crowbar; ~**s parallèles** (*GYM*) parallel bars.

**barreau, x** [baʀo] *nm* bar; (*JUR*): **le** ~ the Bar.

**barrer** [baʀe] *vt* (*route etc*) to block; (*mot*) to cross out; (*chèque*) to cross; (*NAVIG*) to steer; **se** ~ *vi* (*fam*) to clear off.

**barrette** [baʀɛt] *nf* (*pour cheveux*) (hair) slide.

**barreur** [baʀœʀ] *nm* helmsman; (*aviron*) coxswain.

**barricade** [baʀikad] *nf* barricade; **barricader** *vt* to barricade; **se barricader chez soi** (*fig*) to lock o.s. in.

**barrière** [baʀjɛʀ] *nf* fence; (*obstacle*) barrier.

**barrique** [baʀik] *nf* barrel, cask.

**baryton** [baʀitɔ̃] *nm* baritone.

**bas, basse** [bɑ, bɑs] *a* low // *nm* bottom, lower part; (*chaussette*) stocking // *nf* (*MUS*) bass // *ad* low; **plus** ~ lower down; (*dans un texte*) further on, below; (*parler*) more softly; **au** ~ **mot** at the lowest estimate; **enfant en** ~ **âge** infant, young child; **en** ~ down below; at (*ou* to) the bottom; (*dans une maison*) downstairs; **en** ~ **de** at the bottom of; **mettre** ~ *vi* to give birth; **à** ~ ...! 'down with ...!'; ~ **morceaux** *nmpl* (*viande*) cheap cuts.

**basalte** [bazalt(ə)] *nm* basalt.

**basané, e** [bazane] *a* tanned, bronzed.

**bas-côté** [bakote] *nm* (*de route*) verge; (*d'église*) (side) aisle.

**bascule** [baskyl] *nf*: (**jeu de**) ~ seesaw; (**balance à**) ~ scales *pl*; **fauteuil à** ~ rocking chair; **système à** ~ tip-over device; rocker device.

**basculer** [baskyle] *vi* to fall over, topple (over); (*benne*) to tip up // *vt* (*gén*: **faire** ~) to topple over; to tip out, tip up.

**base** [baz] *nf* base; (*POL*) rank and file; (*fondement, principe*) basis (*pl* bases); **de** ~ basic; **à** ~ **de café** *etc* coffee *etc*-based; **baser** *vt* to base; **se baser sur** (*données, preuves*) to base one's argument on.

**bas-fond** [baf5] *nm* (*NAVIG*) shallow; ~**s** (*fig*) dregs.

**basilic** [bazilik] *nm* (*CULIN*) basil.

**basilique** [bazilik] *nf* basilica.

**basket(-ball)** [baskɛt(bol)] *nm* basketball.

**basque** [bask(ə)] *a, nm/f* Basque.

**bas-relief** [bʊrəljɛf] *nm* bas relief.

**basse** [bɑs] *a, nf voir* **bas**; ~**-cour** *nf* farmyard.

**bassin** [basɛ̃] *nm* (*cuvette*) bowl; (*pièce d'eau*) pond, pool; (*de fontaine, GÉO*) basin; (*ANAT*) pelvis; (*portuaire*) dock.

**bassiste** [basist(ə)] *nm/f* (double) bass player.

**bastingage** [bastɛ̃gaʒ] *nm* (ship's) rail.

**bastion** [bastj5] *nm* bastion.

**bas-ventre** [bʊvɑ̃tR(ə)] *nm* (lower part of the) stomach.

**bat** *vb voir* **battre**.

**bât** [bɑ] *nm* packsaddle.

**bataille** [batɑj] *nf* battle; fight.

**bataillon** [bataj5] *nm* battalion.

**bâtard, e** [bɑtaR, -aRd(ə)] *nm/f* illegitimate child, bastard (*péj*).

**bateau, x** [bato] *nm* boat, ship.

**batelier, -ière** [batəlje, -jɛR] *nm/f* (*de bac*) ferryman.

**bat-flanc** [baflɑ̃] *nm inv* raised boards for sleeping, in cells, army huts etc.

**bâti, e** [bati] *a*: **bien** ~ well-built // *nm* (*armature*) frame.

**batifoler** [batifɔle] *vi* to frolic *ou* lark about.

**bâtiment** [batimɑ̃] *nm* building; (*NAVIG*) ship, vessel; (*industrie*) building trade.

**bâtir** [batiR] *vt* to build.

**bâtisse** [batis] *nf* building.

**bâton** [bat5] *nm* stick; **à** ~**s rompus** informally.

**bâtonnier** [batɔnje] *nm* ≈ president of the Bar.

**batraciens** [batRasjɛ̃] *nmpl* amphibians.

**bats** *vb voir* **battre**.

**battage** [bataʒ] *nm* (*publicité*) (hard) plugging.

**battant** [batɑ̃] *nm* (*de cloche*) clapper; (*de volets*) shutter, flap; (*de porte*) side; **porte à double** ~ double door.

**battement** [batmɑ̃] *nm* (*de cœur*) beat; (*intervalle*) interval (*between classes, trains etc*); ~ **de paupières** blinking *q* (of eyelids); **10 minutes de** ~ 10 minutes to spare.

**batterie** [batRi] *nf* (*MIL, ÉLEC*) battery; (*MUS*) drums *pl*, drum kit; ~ **de cuisine** pots and pans *pl*, kitchen utensils *pl*.

**batteur** [batœR] *nm* (*MUS*) drummer; (*appareil*) whisk; **batteuse** *nf* (*AGR*) threshing machine.

**battre** [batR(ə)] *vt* to beat; (*suj: pluie, vagues*) to beat *ou* lash against; (*œufs etc*) to beat up, whisk; (*blé*) to thresh; (*passer au peigne fin*) to scour // *vi* (*cœur*) to beat; (*volets etc*) to bang, rattle; **se** ~ *vi* to fight; ~ **la mesure** to beat time; ~ **en brèche** to demolish; ~ **son plein** to be at its height, be going full swing; ~ **pavillon britannique** to fly the British flag; ~ **des mains** to clap one's hands; ~ **des ailes** to flap its wings; ~ **en retraite** to beat a retreat.

**battue** [baty] *nf* (*chasse*) beat; (*policière etc*) search, hunt.

**baume** [bom] *nm* balm.

**bauxite** [boksit] *nf* bauxite.

**bavard, e** [bavaR, -aRd(ə)] *a* (very) talkative; gossipy; **bavardage** *nm* chatter *q*; gossip *q*; **bavarder** *vi* to chatter; (*indiscrètement*) to gossip; to blab.

**bave** [bav] *nf* dribble; (*de chien etc*) slobber, slaver; (*d'escargot*) slime; **baver** *vi* to dribble; to slobber, slaver; **bavette** *nf* bib; **baveux, euse** *a* dribbling; (*omelette*) runny.

**bavure** [bavyR] *nf* smudge; (*fig*) hitch, flaw.

**bayer** [baje] *vi*: ~ **aux corneilles** to stand gaping.

**bazar** [bazaR] *nm* general store; (*fam*) jumble; **bazarder** *vt* (*fam*) to chuck out.

**B.C.G.** *sigle m* (= *bacille Calmette-Guérin*) BCG.

**bd.** *abr de* **boulevard**.

**B.D.** *sigle f* = **bande dessinée**.

**béant, e** [beɑ̃, -ɑ̃t] *a* gaping.

**béat, e** [bea, -at] *a* showing open-eyed wonder; blissful; **béatitude** *nf* bliss.

**beau(bel), belle, beaux** [bo, bɛl] *a* beautiful, fine, lovely; (*homme*) handsome // *nf* (*SPORT*) decider // *ad*: **il fait** ~ the weather's fine *ou* fair; **un** ~ **jour** one (fine) day; **de plus belle** more than ever, even more; **on a** ~ **essayer** however hard *ou* no matter how hard we try; **faire le** ~ (*chien*) to sit up and beg.

**beaucoup** [boku] *ad* a lot; much (*gén en tournure négative*); **il ne boit pas** ~ he doesn't drink much *ou* a lot; ~ **de** (*nombre*) many, a lot of; (*quantité*) a lot of, much; ~ **plus/trop** *etc* far *ou* much more/too much; **de** ~ by far.

**beau-fils** [bofis] *nm* son-in-law; (*remariage*) stepson.

**beau-frère** [bofRɛR] *nm* brother-in-law.

**beau-père** [bopɛR] *nm* father-in-law; stepfather.

**beauté** [bote] *nf* beauty; **de toute** ~ beautiful; **en** ~ with a flourish, brilliantly.

**beaux-arts** [bozaR] *nmpl* fine arts.

**beaux-parents** [boparɑ̃] *nmpl* wife's/husband's family *sg ou pl*, in-laws.
**bébé** [bebe] *nm* baby.
**bec** [bɛk] *nm* beak, bill; (*de plume*) nib; (*de récipient*) spout; lip; (*fam*) mouth; ~ **de gaz** (street) gaslamp; ~ **verseur** pouring lip.
**bécane** [bekan] *nf* bike.
**bécasse** [bekas] *nf* (*ZOOL*) woodcock; (*fam*) silly goose.
**bec-de-lièvre** [bɛkdəljɛvʀ(ə)] *nm* harelip.
**bêche** [bɛʃ] *nf* spade; **bêcher** *vt* to dig.
**bécoter** [bekɔte]: **se** ~ *vi* to smooch.
**becquée** [beke] *nf*: **donner la** ~ **à** to feed.
**becqueter** [bɛkte] *vt* to peck (at).
**bedaine** [bədɛn] *nf* paunch.
**bedeau, x** [bədo] *nm* beadle.
**bedonnant, e** [bədɔnɑ̃, -ɑ̃t] *a* paunchy, potbellied.
**bée** [be] *a*: **bouche** ~ gaping.
**beffroi** [befʀwa] *nm* belfry.
**bégayer** [begeje] *vt, vi* to stammer.
**bègue** [bɛg] *nm/f*: **être** ~ to have a stammer.
**bégueule** [begœl] *a* prudish.
**béguin** [begɛ̃] *nm*: **avoir le** ~ **de** *ou* **pour** to have a crush on.
**beige** [bɛʒ] *a* beige.
**beignet** [bɛɲɛ] *nm* fritter.
**bel** [bɛl] *a voir* **beau.**
**bêler** [bele] *vi* to bleat.
**belette** [bəlɛt] *nf* weasel.
**belge** [bɛlʒ(ə)] *a, nm/f* Belgian.
**Belgique** [bɛlʒik] *nf* Belgium.
**bélier** [belje] *nm* ram; (*engin*) (battering) ram; (*signe*): **le B~** Aries, the Ram; **être du B~** to be Aries.
**belle** [bɛl] *af, nf voir* **beau; ~-fille** *nf* daughter-in-law; (*remariage*) stepdaughter; **~-mère** *nf* mother-in-law; stepmother; **~-sœur** *nf* sister-in-law.
**belligérant, e** [beliʒeʀɑ̃, -ɑ̃t] *a* belligerent.
**belliqueux, euse** [belikø, -øz] *a* aggressive, warlike.
**belvédère** [bɛlvedɛʀ] *nm* panoramic viewpoint (*or small building at such a place*).
**bémol** [bemɔl] *nm* (*MUS*) flat.
**bénédiction** [benediksjɔ̃] *nf* blessing.
**bénéfice** [benefis] *nm* (*COMM*) profit; (*avantage*) benefit; **bénéficiaire** *nm/f* beneficiary; **bénéficier de** *vt* to enjoy; to benefit by *ou* from; to get, be given; **bénéfique** *a* beneficial.
**benêt** [bənɛ] *nm* simpleton.
**bénévole** [benevɔl] *a* voluntary, unpaid.
**bénin, igne** [benɛ̃, -iɲ] *a* minor, mild; (*tumeur*) benign.
**bénir** [beniʀ] *vt* to bless; **bénit, e** *a* consecrated; **eau bénite** holy water; **bénitier** *nm* stoup, font (*for holy water*).
**benjamin, e** [bɛ̃ʒamɛ̃, -in] *nm/f* youngest child.
**benne** [bɛn] *nf* skip; (*de téléphérique*) (cable) car; ~ **basculante** tipper.
**benzine** [bɛ̃zin] *nf* benzine.
**béotien, ne** [beɔsjɛ̃, -jɛn] *nm/f* philistine.
**B.E.P.C.** *sigle m voir* **brevet.**
**béquille** [bekij] *nf* crutch; (*de bicyclette*) stand.

**bercail** [bɛʀkaj] *nm* fold.
**berceau, x** [bɛʀso] *nm* cradle, crib.
**bercer** [bɛʀse] *vt* to rock, cradle; (*suj: musique etc*) to lull; ~ **qn de** (*promesses etc*) to delude sb with; **berceuse** *nf* lullaby.
**béret (basque)** [beʀɛ(bask(ə))] *nm* beret.
**berge** [bɛʀʒ(ə)] *nf* bank.
**berger, ère** [bɛʀʒe, -ɛʀ] *nm/f* shepherd/shepherdess; **bergerie** *nf* sheep pen.
**berline** [bɛʀlin] *nf* (*AUTO*) saloon (car).
**berlingot** [bɛʀlɛ̃go] *nm* (*emballage*) carton (*pyramid shaped*).
**berlue** [bɛʀly] *nf*: **j'ai la** ~ I must be seeing things.
**berne** [bɛʀn(ə)] *nf*: **en** ~ at half-mast.
**berner** [bɛʀne] *vt* to fool.
**besogne** [bəzɔɲ] *nf* work *q*, job; **besogneux, euse** *a* hard-working.
**besoin** [bəzwɛ̃] *nm* need; (*pauvreté*): **le** ~ need, want; ~**s (naturels)** nature's needs; **faire ses** ~**s** to relieve o.s.; **avoir** ~ **de qch/faire qch** to need sth/to do sth; **au** ~ if need be; **pour les** ~**s de la cause** for the purpose in hand.
**bestial, e, aux** [bɛstjal, -o] *a* bestial, brutish.
**bestiaux** [bɛstjo] *nmpl* cattle.
**bestiole** [bɛstjɔl] *nf* (tiny) creature.
**bétail** [betaj] *nm* livestock, cattle *pl*.
**bête** [bɛt] *nf* animal; (*bestiole*) insect, creature // *a* stupid, silly; **il cherche la petite** ~ he's being pernickety *ou* over-fussy; ~ **noire** pet hate, bugbear; ~ **sauvage** wild beast; ~ **de somme** beast of burden.
**bêtise** [betiz] *nf* stupidity; stupid thing (to say *ou* do).
**béton** [betɔ̃] *nm* concrete; ~ **armé** reinforced concrete; **bétonner** *vt* to concrete (over); **bétonnière** *nf* cement mixer.
**betterave** [bɛtʀav] *nf* (*rouge*) beetroot; ~ **fourragère** mangel-wurzel; ~ **sucrière** sugar beet.
**beugler** [bøgle] *vi* to low; (*radio etc*) to blare // *vt* (*chanson etc*) to bawl out.
**beurre** [bœʀ] *nm* butter; **beurrer** *vt* to butter; **beurrier** *nm* butter dish.
**beuverie** [bœvʀi] *nf* drinking session.
**bévue** [bevy] *nf* blunder.
**bi...** [bi] *préfixe* bi..., two-.
**biais** [bjɛ] *nm* (*moyen*) device, expedient; (*aspect*) angle; **en** ~, **de** ~ (*obliquement*) at an angle; (*fig*) indirectly; **biaiser** *vi* (*fig*) to sidestep the issue.
**bibelot** [biblo] *nm* trinket, curio.
**biberon** [bibʀɔ̃] *nm* (feeding) bottle; **nourrir au** ~ to bottle-feed.
**bible** [bibl(ə)] *nf* bible.
**biblio...** [biblijo] *préfixe*: ~**bus** *nm* mobile library van; ~**graphie** *nf* bibliography; ~**phile** *nm/f* booklover; ~**thécaire** *nm/f* librarian; ~**thèque** *nf* library; (*meuble*) bookcase.
**biblique** [biblik] *a* biblical.
**bicarbonate** [bikaʀbɔnat] *nm*: ~ **(de soude)** bicarbonate of soda.
**biceps** [bisɛps] *nm* biceps.
**biche** [biʃ] *nf* doe.

**bichonner** [biʃɔne] vt to groom.
**bicolore** [bikɔlɔʀ] a two-coloured.
**bicoque** [bikɔk] nf (péj) shack.
**bicorne** [bikɔʀn(ə)] nm cocked hat.
**bicyclette** [bisiklɛt] nf bicycle.
**bide** [bid] nm (fam: ventre) belly ; (THÉÂTRE) flop.
**bidet** [bidɛ] nm bidet.
**bidon** [bidɔ̃] nm can // a inv (fam) phoney.
**bidonville** [bidɔ̃vil] nm shanty town.
**bielle** [bjɛl] nf connecting rod.
**bien** [bjɛ̃] nm good ; (patrimoine) property q ; **faire du ~ à qn** to do sb good ; **dire du ~ de** to speak well of ; **changer en ~** to turn to the good ; **~s de consommation** consumer goods // ad (travailler) well ; **~ jeune** rather young ; **~ assez** quite enough ; **~ mieux** very much better ; **~ du temps/ des gens** quite a time/a number of people ; **j'espère ~ y aller** I do hope to go ; **je veux ~ le faire** (concession) I'm (quite) willing to do it ; **il faut ~ le faire** it has to be done ; **~ sûr** certainly ; **c'est ~ fait** (mérité) it serves him (ou her etc) right ; **croyant ~ faire** thinking he was doing the right thing // a inv (à l'aise): **être ~** to be fine ; **ce n'est pas ~ de** it's not right to ; **cette maison est ~** this house is (very) good ; **elle est ~** (jolie) she's good-looking ; **des gens ~** (parfois péj) respectable people ; **être ~ avec qn** to be on good terms with sb ; **~ que** cj although ; **~-aimé, e** a, nm/f beloved ; **~-être** nm well-being ; **~faisance** nf charity ; **~faisant, e** a (chose) beneficial ; **~fait** nm act of generosity, benefaction ; (de la science etc) benefit ; **~faiteur, trice** nm/f benefactor/benefactress ; **~-fondé** nm soundness ; **~-fonds** nm property ; **~heureux, euse** a happy ; (REL) blessed, blest.
**biennal, e, aux** [bjenal, -o] a biennial.
**bienséance** [bjɛ̃seɑ̃s] nf propriety, decorum q.
**bienséant, e** [bjɛ̃seɑ̃, -ɑ̃t] a proper, seemly.
**bientôt** [bjɛ̃to] ad soon ; **à ~** see you soon.
**bienveillance** [bjɛ̃vɛjɑ̃s] nf kindness.
**bienveillant, e** [bjɛ̃vɛjɑ̃, -ɑ̃t] a kindly.
**bienvenu, e** [bjɛ̃vny] a welcome // nm/f: **être le ~/la ~e** to be welcome // nf: **souhaiter la ~e à** to welcome ; **~e à** welcome to.
**bière** [bjɛʀ] nf (boisson) beer ; (cercueil) bier ; **~ blonde** lager ; **~ brune** brown ale ; **~ (à la) pression** draught beer.
**biffer** [bife] vt to cross out.
**bifteck** [biftɛk] nm steak.
**bifurcation** [bifyʀkɑsjɔ̃] nf fork (in road).
**bifurquer** [bifyʀke] vi (route) to fork ; (véhicule) to turn off.
**bigame** [bigam] a bigamous ; **bigamie** nf bigamy.
**bigarré, e** [bigaʀe] a multicoloured ; (disparate) motley.
**bigorneau, x** [bigɔʀno] nm winkle.
**bigot, e** [bigo, -ɔt] (péj) a churchy // nm/f church fiend.
**bigoudi** [bigudi] nm curler.
**bijou, x** [biʒu] nm jewel ; **~terie** nf jeweller's (shop) ; jewellery ; **~tier, ière** nm/f jeweller.
**bikini** [bikini] nm bikini.
**bilan** [bilɑ̃] nm (COMM) balance sheet(s) ; end of year statement ; (fig) (net) outcome ; (: de victimes) toll ; **faire le ~ de** to assess ; to review ; **déposer son ~** to file a bankruptcy statement.
**bilatéral, e, aux** [bilateʀal, -o] a bilateral.
**bile** [bil] nf bile ; **se faire de la ~** (fam) to worry o.s. sick.
**biliaire** [biljɛʀ] a biliary.
**bilieux, euse** [bilj∅, -j∅z] a bilious ; (fig: colérique) testy.
**bilingue** [bilɛ̃g] a bilingual.
**billard** [bijaʀ] nm billiards sg ; billiard table.
**bille** [bij] nf (gén) ball ; (du jeu de billes) marble ; (de bois) log.
**billet** [bijɛ] nm (aussi: **~ de banque**) (bank)note ; (de cinéma, de bus etc) ticket ; (courte lettre) note ; **~ circulaire** round-trip ticket ; **~ de faveur** complimentary ticket ; **~ de loterie** lottery ticket ; **~ de quai** platform ticket.
**billion** [biljɔ̃] nm billion.
**billot** [bijo] nm block.
**bimensuel, le** [bimɑ̃sɥɛl] a bimonthly, two-monthly.
**bimoteur** [bimɔtœʀ] a twin-engined.
**binaire** [binɛʀ] a binary.
**binocle** [binɔkl(ə)] nm pince-nez.
**binôme** [binom] nm binomial.
**bio...** [bjɔ] préfixe bio... ; **~-dégradable** a biodegradable ; **~graphe** nm/f biographer ; **~graphie** nf biography ; **~graphique** a biographical ; **~logie** nf biology ; **~logique** a biological ; **~logiste** nm/f biologist.
**bipède** [bipɛd] nm biped, two-footed creature.
**biplan** [biplɑ̃] nm biplane.
**biréacteur** [biʀeaktœʀ] nm twin- engined jet.
**bis, e** [bi, biz] a (couleur) greyish brown // ad [bis]: **12 ~** 12a ou A // excl, nm [bis] encore // nf (baiser) kiss ; (vent) North wind.
**bisannuel, le** [bizanɥɛl] a biennial.
**bisbille** [bisbij] nf: **être en ~ avec qn** to be at loggerheads with sb.
**biscornu, e** [biskɔʀny] a crooked, weird(-looking).
**biscotte** [biskɔt] nf rusk.
**biscuit** [biskɥi] nm biscuit ; sponge cake.
**bise** [biz] a, nf voir **bis.**
**biseau, x** [bizo] nm bevelled edge ; **en ~** bevelled ; **~ter** vt to bevel.
**bison** [bizɔ̃] nm bison.
**bisque** [bisk(ə)] nf: **~ d'écrevisses** shrimp bisque.
**bissectrice** [bisɛktʀis] nf bisector.
**bisser** [bise] vt to encore.
**bissextile** [bisɛkstil] a: **année ~** leap year.
**bissexué, e** [bisɛksɥe] a bisexual.
**bistouri** [bisturi] nm lancet.
**bistre** [bistʀ(ə)] a bistre.
**bistro(t)** [bistʀo] nm bistrot, café.

**bitte** [bit] nf: ~ **d'amarrage** bollard (NAUT).
**bitume** [bitym] nm asphalt.
**bivouac** [bivwak] nm bivouac; **bivouaquer** vi to bivouac.
**bizarre** [bizaR] a strange, odd.
**blafard, e** [blafaR, -aRd(ə)] a wan.
**blague** [blag] nf (propos) joke; (farce) trick; **sans** ~! no kidding!; ~ **à tabac** tobacco pouch.
**blaguer** [blage] vi to joke // vt to tease; **blagueur, euse** a teasing // nm/f joker.
**blaireau, x** [blɛRo] nm (ZOOL) badger; (brosse) shaving brush.
**blâmable** [blɑmabl(ə)] a blameworthy.
**blâme** [blɑm] nm blame; (sanction) reprimand.
**blâmer** [blɑme] vt to blame.
**blanc, blanche** [blɑ̃, blɑ̃ʃ] a white; (non imprimé) blank; (innocent) pure // nm/f white, white man/woman // nm (couleur) white; (linge): **le** ~ whites pl; (espace non écrit) blank; (aussi: ~ **d'œuf**) (egg-)white; (aussi: ~ **de poulet**) breast, white meat; (aussi: **vin** ~) white wine // nf (MUS) minim; **chèque en** ~ blank cheque; **à** ~ ad (chauffer) white-hot; (tirer, charger) with blanks; ~**bec** nm greenhorn; **blancheur** nf whiteness.
**blanchir** [blɑ̃ʃiR] vt (gén) to whiten; (linge) to launder; (CULIN) to blanch; (fig: disculper) to clear // vi to grow white; (cheveux) to go white; **blanchissage** nm (du linge) laundering; **blanchisserie** nf laundry; **blanchisseur, euse** nm/f launderer.
**blanc-seing** [blɑ̃sɛ̃] nm signed blank paper.
**blaser** [blɑze] vt to make blasé.
**blason** [blazɔ̃] nm coat of arms.
**blasphème** [blasfɛm] nm blasphemy; **blasphémer** vi to blaspheme // vt to blaspheme against.
**blatte** [blat] nf cockroach.
**blazer** [blazɛR] nm blazer.
**blé** [ble] nm wheat; ~ **en herbe** wheat on the ear.
**bled** [blɛd] nm (péj) hole; (en Afrique du nord): **le** ~ the interior.
**blême** [blɛm] a pale.
**blennoragie** [blenɔRaʒi] nf blennorrhoea.
**blessant, e** [blɛsɑ̃, -ɑ̃t] a hurtful.
**blessé, e** [blese] a injured // nm/f injured person; casualty.
**blesser** [blese] vt to injure; (délibérément: MIL etc) to wound; (suj: souliers etc, offenser) to hurt; **se** ~ to injure o.s.; **se** ~ **au pied** etc to injure one's foot etc.
**blessure** [blesyR] nf injury; wound.
**blet, te** [blɛ, blɛt] a overripe.
**bleu** [blø] a blue; (bifteck) very rare // nm (couleur) blue; (novice) greenhorn; (contusion) bruise; (vêtement: aussi: ~**s**) overalls pl; **au** ~ (CULIN) au bleu.
**bleuet** [bløɛ] nm cornflower.
**bleuir** [bløiR] vt, vi to turn blue.
**bleuté, e** [bløte] a blue-shaded.
**blindage** [blɛ̃daʒ] nm armour-plating.
**blinder** [blɛ̃de] vt to armour; (fig) to harden.
**blizzard** [blizaR] nm blizzard.

**bloc** [blɔk] nm (de pierre etc) block; (de papier à lettres) pad; (ensemble) group, block; **serré à** ~ tightened right down; **en** ~ as a whole; wholesale; ~ **opératoire** operating theatre suite.
**blocage** [blɔkaʒ] nm blocking; jamming; freezing; (PSYCH) hang-up.
**bloc-moteur** [blɔkmɔtœR] nm engine block.
**bloc-notes** [blɔknɔt] nm note pad.
**blocus** [blɔkys] nm blockade.
**blond, e** [blɔ̃, -ɔ̃d] a fair, blond; (sable, blés) golden // nm/f fair-haired ou blond man/woman; ~ **cendré** ash blond; **blondeur** nf fairness.
**bloquer** [blɔke] vt (passage) to block; (pièce mobile) to jam; (crédits, compte) to freeze; (regrouper) to group; ~ **les freins** to jam on the brakes.
**blottir** [blɔtiR]: **se** ~ vi to huddle up.
**blouse** [bluz] nf overall.
**blouson** [bluzɔ̃] nm lumber jacket; ~ **noir** (fig) ≈ teddy boy.
**blues** [bluz] nm blues pl.
**bluet** [blyɛ] nm = **bleuet**.
**bluff** [blœf] nm bluff; ~**er** vi, vt to bluff.
**boa** [bɔa] nm boa.
**bobard** [bɔbaR] nm (fam) tall story.
**bobèche** [bɔbɛʃ] nf candle-ring.
**bobine** [bɔbin] nf reel; (machine à coudre) spool; (ÉLEC) coil.
**bocage** [bɔkaʒ] nm grove, copse.
**bocal, aux** [bɔkal, -o] nm jar.
**bock** [bɔk] nm (beer) glass; glass of beer.
**bœuf** [bœf, pl bø] nm ox (pl oxen), steer; (CULIN) beef.
**bohème** [bɔɛm] a happy-go-lucky, unconventional.
**bohémien, ne** [bɔemjɛ̃, -jɛn] nm/f gipsy.
**boire** [bwaR] vt to drink; (s'imprégner de) to soak up; ~ **un verre** to have a drink.
**bois** [bwa] nm wood; **de** ~, **en** ~ wooden; ~ **de lit** bedstead.
**boisé, e** [bwaze] a wooded.
**boiser** [bwaze] vt (galerie de mine) to timber; (chambre) to panel; (terrain) to plant with trees.
**boiseries** [bwazRi] nfpl panelling sg.
**boisson** [bwasɔ̃] nf drink; **pris de** ~ drunk, intoxicated; ~**s alcoolisées** alcoholic beverages ou drinks; ~**s gazeuses** fizzy drinks.
**boîte** [bwat] nf box; **aliments en** ~ canned ou tinned foods; ~ **de sardines/petits pois** can ou tin of sardines/peas; ~ **d'allumettes** box of matches; (vide) matchbox; ~ **de conserves** can ou tin (of food); ~ **crânienne** cranium, brainpan; ~ **à gants** glove compartment; ~ **aux lettres** letterbox; ~ **de nuit** night club; ~ **postale (B.P.)** P.O. Box; ~ **de vitesses** gear box.
**boiter** [bwate] vi to limp; (fig) to wobble; to be shaky; **boiteux, euse** a lame; wobbly; shaky.
**boîtier** [bwatje] nm case; ~ **de montre** watch case.
**boive** etc vb voir **boire**.
**bol** [bɔl] nm bowl; **un** ~ **d'air** a dose of fresh air.

**bolet** [bɔlɛ] *nm* boletus (mushroom).
**bolide** [bɔlid] *nm* racing car; **comme un ~** at top speed, like a rocket.
**bombance** [bɔ̃bãs] *nf*: **faire ~** to have a feast, revel.
**bombardement** [bɔ̃baʀdəmã] *nm* bombing.
**bombarder** [bɔ̃baʀde] *vt* to bomb; **~ qn de** (*cailloux, lettres*) to bombard sb with; **~ qn directeur** to thrust sb into the director's seat; **bombardier** *nm* bomber.
**bombe** [bɔ̃b] *nf* bomb; (*atomiseur*) (aerosol) spray; **faire la ~** (*fam*) to go on a binge.
**bombé, e** [bɔ̃be] *a* rounded; bulging; cambered.
**bomber** [bɔ̃be] *vi* to bulge; to camber // *vt*: **~ le torse** to swell out one's chest.
**bon, bonne** [bɔ̃, bɔn] *a* good; (*charitable*): **~ (envers)** good (to), kind (to); (*juste*): **le ~ numéro/moment** the right number/moment; (*approprié*): **~ à/pour** fit to/for // *nm* (*billet*) voucher; (*aussi*: **~ cadeau**) gift coupon *ou* voucher // *nf* (*domestique*) maid // *ad*: **il fait ~** it's *ou* the weather's fine; **sentir ~** to smell good; **tenir ~** to stand firm, hold out; **pour de ~** for good; **de bonne heure** early; **~ anniversaire!** happy birthday!; **~ voyage!** have a good journey!, enjoy your trip!; **bonne chance!** good luck!; **bonne année!** happy New Year!; **bonne nuit!** good night!; **~ enfant** *a inv* accommodating, easy-going; **d'essence** *nm* petrol coupon; **~ marché** *a inv, ad* cheap; **~ mot** *nm* witticism; **~ sens** *nm* common sense; **~ à tirer** *nm* pass for press; **~ du Trésor** *nm* Treasury bond; **~ vivant** *nm* jovial chap; **bonne d'enfant** *nf* nanny; **bonne femme** *nf* (*péj*) woman; female; **bonne à tout faire** *nf* general help; **bonnes œuvres** *nfpl* charitable works; charities.
**bonasse** [bɔnas] *a* soft, meek.
**bonbon** [bɔ̃bɔ̃] *nm* (boiled) sweet.
**bonbonne** [bɔ̃bɔn] *nf* demijohn; carboy.
**bonbonnière** [bɔ̃bɔnjɛʀ] *nf* sweet box, bonbonnière.
**bond** [bɔ̃] *nm* leap; **faire un ~** to leap in the air.
**bonde** [bɔ̃d] *nf* (*d'évier etc*) plug; (: *trou*) plughole; (*de tonneau*) bung; bunghole.
**bondé, e** [bɔ̃de] *a* packed (full).
**bondir** [bɔ̃diʀ] *vi* to leap.
**bonheur** [bɔnœʀ] *nm* happiness; **porter ~ (à qn)** to bring (sb) luck; **au petit ~** haphazardly; **par ~** fortunately.
**bonhomie** [bɔnɔmi] *nf* goodnaturedness.
**bonhomme** [bɔnɔm] *nm* (*pl* **bonshommes** [bɔ̃zɔm]) fellow // *a* goodnatured; **aller son ~ de chemin** to carry on in one's own sweet way; **.~ de neige** snowman.
**boni** [bɔni] *nm* profit.
**bonification** [bɔnifikɑsjɔ̃] *nf* bonus.
**bonifier** [bɔnifje] *vt* to improve.
**boniment** [bɔnimã] *nm* patter *q*.
**bonjour** [bɔ̃ʒuʀ] *excl, nm* good morning (*ou* afternoon); hello; **dire ~ à qn** to say hello *ou* good morning/afternoon to sb.

**bonne** [bɔn] *a, nf voir* **bon**; **~ment** *ad*: **tout ~ment** quite simply.
**bonnet** [bɔnɛ] *nm* bonnet, hat; (*de soutiengorge*) cup; **~ d'âne** dunce's cap; **~ de bain** bathing cap; **~ de nuit** nightcap.
**bonneterie** [bɔnɛtʀi] *nf* hosiery.
**bon-papa** [bɔ̃papa] *nm* grandpa, grandad.
**bonsoir** [bɔ̃swaʀ] *excl* good evening.
**bonté** [bɔ̃te] *nf* kindness *q*; **avoir la ~ de** to be kind *ou* good enough to.
**borborygme** [bɔʀbɔʀigm] *nm* rumbling noise.
**bord** [bɔʀ] *nm* (*de table, verre, falaise*) edge; (*de rivière, lac*) bank; (*de route*) side; (*monter*) **à ~** (to go) on board; **jeter par-dessus ~** to throw overboard; **le commandant/les hommes du ~** the ship's master/crew; **au ~ de la mer** at the seaside; **être au ~ des larmes** to be on the verge of tears.
**bordage** [bɔʀdaʒ] *nm* planking *q*, plating *q*.
**bordeaux** [bɔʀdo] *nm* Bordeaux (wine) // *a inv* maroon.
**bordée** [bɔʀde] *nf* broadside; **une ~ d'injures** a volley of abuse.
**bordel** [bɔʀdɛl] *nm* brothel.
**border** [bɔʀde] *vt* (*être le long de*) to border; to line; (*garnir*): **~ qch de** to line sth with; to trim sth with; (*qn dans son lit*) to tuck up.
**bordereau, x** [bɔʀdəʀo] *nm* docket; slip; statement, invoice.
**bordure** [bɔʀdyʀ] *nf* border; (*sur un vêtement*) trim(ming), border; **en ~ de** on the edge of.
**borgne** [bɔʀɲ(ə)] *a* one-eyed; **hôtel ~** shady hotel.
**borne** [bɔʀn(ə)] *nf* boundary stone; (*gén*: **~ kilométrique**) kilometre-marker, ≈ milestone; **~s** *nfpl* (*fig*) limits; **dépasser les ~s** to go too far; **sans ~(s)** boundless.
**borné, e** [bɔʀne] *a* narrow; narrowminded.
**borner** [bɔʀne] *vt* to limit; to confine; **se ~ à faire** to content o.s. with doing; to limit o.s. to doing.
**bosquet** [bɔskɛ] *nm* copse, grove.
**bosse** [bɔs] *nf* (*de terrain etc*) bump; (*enflure*) lump; (*du bossu, du chameau*) hump; **avoir la ~ des maths** *etc* to have a gift for maths *etc*; **il a roulé sa ~** he's been around.
**bosseler** [bɔsle] *vt* (*ouvrer*) to emboss; (*abîmer*) to dent.
**bosser** [bɔse] *vi* (*fam*) to work; to slog (hard).
**bossu, e** [bɔsy] *nm/f* hunchback.
**bot** [bo] *am*: **pied ~** club foot.
**botanique** [bɔtanik] *nf*: **la ~** botany // *a* botanic(al).
**botaniste** [bɔtanist(ə)] *nm/f* botanist.
**botte** [bɔt] *nf* (*soulier*) (high) boot; (*ESCRIME*) thrust; (*gerbe*): **~ de paille** bundle of straw; **~ de radis/d'asperges** bunch of radishes/asparagus; **~s de caoutchouc** wellington boots.
**botter** [bɔte] *vt* to put boots on; to kick; (*fam*): **ça me botte** I fancy that.

**bottier** [bɔtje] *nm* bootmaker.
**bottin** [bɔtɛ̃] *nm* directory.
**bottine** [bɔtin] *nf* ankle boot, bootee.
**bouc** [buk] *nm* goat; (*barbe*) goatee; ~ **émissaire** scapegoat.
**boucan** [bukɑ̃] *nm* din, racket.
**bouche** [buʃ] *nf* mouth; **faire le ~ à ~ à qn** to give sb the kiss of life, to practise mouth-to-mouth resuscitation on sb; ~ **de chaleur** hot air vent; ~ **d'égout** manhole; ~ **d'incendie** fire hydrant; ~ **de métro** métro entrance.
**bouché, e** [buʃe] *a* (*temps, ciel*) overcast; (*péj: personne*) thick; (*JAZZ: trompette*) muted; **avoir le nez** ~ to have a blocked (-up) nose.
**bouchée** [buʃe] *nf* mouthful; ~**s à la reine** chicken vol-au-vents.
**boucher** [buʃe] *nm* butcher // *vt* (*pour colmater*) to stop up; to fill up; (*obstruer*) to block (up); **se** ~ **le nez** to hold one's nose; **se** ~ (*tuyau etc*) to block up, get blocked up.
**bouchère** [buʃɛR] *nf* (woman) butcher; butcher's wife.
**boucherie** [buʃRi] *nf* butcher's (shop); butchery; (*fig*) slaughter.
**bouche-trou** [buʃtRu] *nm* (*fig*) stop-gap.
**bouchon** [buʃɔ̃] *nm* (*en liège*) cork; (*autre matière*) stopper; (*fig: embouteillage*) holdup; (*PÊCHE*) float; ~ **doseur** measuring cap.
**bouchonner** [buʃɔne] *vt* to rub down.
**boucle** [bukl(ə)] *nf* (*forme, figure*) loop; (*objet*) buckle; ~ (**de cheveux**) curl; ~ **d'oreilles** earring.
**bouclé, e** [bukle] *a* curly; (*tapis*) uncut.
**boucler** [bukle] *vt* (*fermer: ceinture etc*) to fasten up; (: *magasin*) to shut; (*terminer*) to finish off; to complete; (: *budget*) to balance; (*enfermer*) to shut away; to lock up; (: *quartier*) to seal off // *vi* to curl.
**bouclier** [buklije] *nm* shield.
**bouddhiste** [budist(ə)] *nm/f* Buddhist.
**bouder** [bude] *vi* to sulk // *vt* to turn one's nose up at; to refuse to have anything to do with; **bouderie** *nf* sulking *q*; **boudeur, euse** *a* sullen, sulky.
**boudin** [budɛ̃] *nm* (*CULIN*) black pudding; (*TECH*) roll.
**boudoir** [budwaR] *nm* boudoir.
**boue** [bu] *nf* mud.
**bouée** [bwe] *nf* buoy; ~ (**de sauvetage**) lifebuoy.
**boueux, euse** [bwø, -øz] *a* muddy // *nm* refuse collector.
**bouffe** [buf] *nf* (*fam*) grub, food.
**bouffée** [bufe] *nf* puff; ~ **de fièvre/de honte** flush of fever/shame; ~ **d'orgueil** fit of pride.
**bouffer** [bufe] *vi* (*fam*) to eat; (*COUTURE*) to puff out // *vt* (*fam*) to eat.
**bouffi, e** [bufi] *a* swollen.
**bouffon, ne** [bufɔ̃, -ɔn] *a* farcical, comical // *nm* jester.
**bouge** [buʒ] *nm* (low) dive; hovel.
**bougeoir** [buʒwaR] *nm* candlestick.
**bougeotte** [buʒɔt] *nf*: **avoir la** ~ to have the fidgets.
**bouger** [buʒe] *vi* to move; (*dent etc*) to

be loose; (*changer*) to alter; (*agir*) to stir // *vt* to move.
**bougie** [buʒi] *nf* candle; (*AUTO*) sparking plug.
**bougon, ne** [bugɔ̃, -ɔn] *a* grumpy.
**bougonner** [bugɔne] *vi, vt* to grumble.
**bougre** [bugR(ə)] *nm* chap; (*fam*): **ce** ~ **de** that confounded.
**bouillabaisse** [bujabɛs] *nf* bouillabaisse.
**bouillant, e** [bujɑ̃, -ɑ̃t] *a* (*qui bout*) boiling; (*très chaud*) boiling (hot); (*fig: ardent*) hot-headed.
**bouilleur de cru** [bujœRdəkRy] *nm* (home) distiller.
**bouillie** [buji] *nf* gruel; (*de bébé*) cereal; **en** ~ (*fig*) crushed.
**bouillir** [bujiR] *vi, vt* to boil; ~ **de colère** *etc* to seethe with anger *etc*.
**bouilloire** [bujwaR] *nf* kettle.
**bouillon** [bujɔ̃] *nm* (*CULIN*) stock *q*; (*bulles, écume*) bubble; ~ **de culture** culture medium.
**bouillonner** [bujɔne] *vi* to bubble; (*fig*) to bubble up; to foam.
**bouillotte** [bujɔt] *nf* hot-water bottle.
**boulanger, ère** [bulɑ̃ʒe, -ɛR] *nm/f* baker // *nf* (woman) baker; baker's wife.
**boulangerie** [bulɑ̃ʒRi] *nf* bakery, baker's (shop); (*commerce*) bakery; ~ **industrielle** bakery; ~-**pâtisserie** *nf* baker's and confectioner's (shop).
**boule** [bul] *nf* (*gén*) ball; (*pour jouer*) bowl; ~ **de neige** snowball; **faire** ~ **de neige** to snowball.
**bouleau, x** [bulo] *nm* (silver) birch.
**bouledogue** [buldɔg] *nm* bulldog.
**boulet** [bulɛ] *nm* (*aussi*: ~ **de canon**) cannonball; (*de bagnard*) ball and chain; (*charbon*) (coal) nut.
**boulette** [bulɛt] *nf* ball.
**boulevard** [bulvaR] *nm* boulevard.
**bouleversement** [bulvɛRsəmɑ̃] *nm* (*politique, social*) upheaval.
**bouleverser** [bulvɛRse] *vt* (*émouvoir*) to overwhelm; (*causer du chagrin*) to distress; (*pays, vie*) to disrupt; (*papiers, objets*) to turn upside down, upset.
**boulier** [bulje] *nm* abacus; (*de jeu*) scoring board.
**boulimie** [bulimi] *nf* compulsive eating, bulimia.
**boulon** [bulɔ̃] *nm* bolt; **boulonner** *vt* to bolt.
**boulot** [bulo] *nm* (*fam: travail*) work.
**boulot, te** [bulo, -ɔt] *a* plump, tubby.
**bouquet** [bukɛ] *nm* (*de fleurs*) bunch (of flowers), bouquet; (*de persil etc*) bunch; (*parfum*) bouquet; (*fig*) crowning piece.
**bouquetin** [buktɛ̃] *nm* ibex.
**bouquin** [bukɛ̃] *nm* book; **bouquiner** *vi* to read; to browse around (in a bookshop); **bouquiniste** *nm/f* bookseller.
**bourbeux, euse** [buRbø, -øz] *a* muddy.
**bourbier** [buRbje] *nm* (quag)mire.
**bourde** [buRd(ə)] *nf* (*erreur*) howler; (*gaffe*) blunder.
**bourdon** [buRdɔ̃] *nm* bumblebee.
**bourdonnement** [buRdɔnmɑ̃] *nm* buzzing.

**bourdonner** [buʀdɔne] *vi* to buzz.

**bourg** [buʀ] *nm* town.

**bourgade** [buʀgad] *nf* township.

**bourgeois, e** [buʀʒwa, -waz] *a* (*souvent péj*) ≈ (upper) middle class; bourgeois // *nm/f* (*autrefois*) burgher.

**bourgeoisie** [buʀʒwazi] *nf* ≈ upper middle classes *pl*; bourgeoisie; **petite** ~ middle classes.

**bourgeon** [buʀʒɔ̃] *nm* bud; **bourgeonner** *vi* to bud.

**Bourgogne** [buʀgɔɲ] *nf*: **la** ~ Burgundy // *nm*: **b**~ burgundy (wine).

**bourguignon, ne** [buʀgiɲɔ̃, -ɔn] *a* of *ou* from Burgundy, Burgundian; **bœuf** ~ bœuf bourguignon.

**bourlinguer** [buʀlɛ̃ge] *vi* to knock about a lot, get around a lot.

**bourrade** [buʀad] *nf* shove, thump.

**bourrage** [buʀaʒ] *nm*: ~ **de crâne** brainwashing; (*SCOL*) cramming.

**bourrasque** [buʀask(ə)] *nf* squall.

**bourratif, ive** [buʀatif, -iv] *a* filling, stodgy.

**bourreau, x** [buʀo] *nm* executioner; (*fig*) torturer; ~ **de travail** glutton for work.

**bourreler** [buʀle] *vt*: **être bourrelé de remords** to be racked by remorse.

**bourrelet** [buʀlɛ] *nm* draught excluder; (*de peau*) fold *ou* roll (of flesh).

**bourrer** [buʀe] *vt* (*pipe*) to fill; (*poêle*) to pack; (*valise*) to cram (full); ~ **de** to cram (full) with; to stuff with; ~ **de coups** to hammer blows on, pummel.

**bourrique** [buʀik] *nf* (*âne*) ass.

**bourru, e** [buʀy] *a* surly, gruff.

**bourse** [buʀs(ə)] *nf* (*subvention*) grant; (*porte-monnaie*) purse; **la B**~ the Stock Exchange; **boursier, ière** *a* (*COMM*) Stock Market *cpd* // *nm/f* (*SCOL*) grant-holder.

**boursouflé, e** [buʀsufle] *a* swollen, puffy; (*fig*) bombastic, turgid.

**boursoufler** [buʀsufle] *vt* to puff up, bloat; **se** ~ *vi* (*visage*) to swell *ou* puff up; (*peinture*) to blister.

**bous** *vb voir* **bouillir**.

**bousculade** [buskylad] *nf* rush; crush.

**bousculer** [buskyle] *vt* to knock over; to knock into; (*fig*) to push, rush.

**bouse** [buz] *nf*: ~ **(de vache)** (cow) dung *q*.

**bousiller** [buzije] *vt* (*fam*) to wreck.

**boussole** [busɔl] *nf* compass.

**bout** [bu] *vb voir* **bouillir** // *nm* bit; (*extrémité*: . *d'un bâton etc*) tip; (: *d'une ficelle, table, rue, période*) end; **au** ~ **de** (*après*) at the end of, after; **pousser qn à** ~ to push sb to the limit (of his patience); **venir à** ~ **de** to manage to overcome *ou* finish (off); **à** ~ **portant** at point-blank range; ~ **filtre** filter tip.

**boutade** [butad] *nf* quip, sally.

**boute-en-train** [butɑ̃tʀɛ̃] *nm inv* live wire.

**bouteille** [butɛj] *nf* bottle; (*de gaz butane*) cylinder.

**boutique** [butik] *nf* shop; **boutiquier, ière** *nm/f* shopkeeper.

**bouton** [butɔ̃] *nm* (*BOT*) bud; (*MÉD*) spot; (*électrique etc*) button; (*de porte*) knob; ~ **de manchette** cuff-link; ~ **d'or** butter-

cup; **boutonner** *vt* to button up, do up; **boutonneux, euse** *a* spotty; **boutonnière** *nf* buttonhole; ~**-pression** *nm* press stud, snap fastener.

**bouture** [butyʀ] *nf* cutting.

**bouvreuil** [buvʀœj] *nm* bullfinch.

**bovidé** [bɔvide] *nm* bovine.

**bovin, e** [bɔvɛ̃, -in] *a* bovine; ~**s** *nmpl* cattle.

**bowling** [bɔliŋ] *nm* (tenpin) bowling; (*salle*) bowling alley.

**box** [bɔks] *nm* lock-up (garage); cubicle; (*d'écurie*) loose-box; **le** ~ **des accusés** the dock.

**boxe** [bɔks(ə)] *nf* boxing; **boxer** *vi* to box; **boxeur** *nm* boxer.

**boyau, x** [bwajo] *nm* (*corde de raquette etc*) (cat) gut; (*galerie*) passage(way); (narrow) gallery; (*pneu de bicyclette*) tubeless tyre // *nmpl* (*viscères*) entrails, guts.

**boycotter** [bɔjkɔte] *vt* to boycott.

**B.P.** *sigle de* **boîte postale**.

**bracelet** [bʀaslɛ] *nm* bracelet; ~**-montre** *nm* wristwatch.

**braconner** [bʀakɔne] *vi* to poach; **braconnier** *nm* poacher.

**brader** [bʀade] *vt* to sell off, sell cheaply.

**braguette** [bʀagɛt] *nf* fly, flies *pl*.

**brailler** [bʀaje] *vi* to bawl, yell // *vt* to bawl out, yell out.

**braire** [bʀɛʀ] *vi* to bray.

**braise** [bʀɛz] *nf* embers *pl*.

**braiser** [bʀeze] *vt* to braise.

**bramer** [bʀame] *vi* to bell; (*fig*) to wail.

**brancard** [bʀɑ̃kaʀ] *nm* (*civière*) stretcher; (*bras, perche*) shaft; **brancardier** *nm* stretcher-bearer.

**branchages** [bʀɑ̃ʃaʒ] *nmpl* branches, boughs.

**branche** [bʀɑ̃ʃ] *nf* branch; (*de lunettes*) side-piece.

**brancher** [bʀɑ̃ʃe] *vt* to connect (up); (*en mettant la prise*) to plug in.

**branchies** [bʀɑ̃ʃi] *nfpl* gills.

**brandir** [bʀɑ̃diʀ] *vt* to brandish, wield.

**brandon** [bʀɑ̃dɔ̃] *nm* firebrand.

**branle** [bʀɑ̃l] *nm*: **donner le** ~ **à** to set in motion.

**branle-bas** [bʀɑ̃lba] *nm inv* commotion.

**branler** [bʀɑ̃le] *vi* to be shaky, be loose // *vt*: **la tête** to shake one's head.

**braquage** [bʀakaʒ] *nm* (*fam*) stick-up; (*AUTO*): **rayon de** ~ turning circle.

**braquer** [bʀake] *vi* (*AUTO*) to turn (the wheel) // *vt* (*revolver etc*): ~ **qch sur** to aim sth at, point sth at; (*mettre en colère*): ~ **qn** to antagonize sb, put sb's back up.

**bras** [bʀa] *nm* arm // *nmpl* (*fig*: *travailleurs*) labour *sg*, hands; **saisir qn à** ~**-le-corps** to take hold of sb (a)round the waist; **à** ~ **raccourcis** with fists flying; ~ **droit** (*fig*) right-hand man; ~ **de levier** lever arm; ~ **de mer** arm of the sea, sound.

**brasero** [bʀazeʀo] *nm* brazier.

**brasier** [bʀazje] *nm* blaze, (blazing) inferno.

**brassage** [bʀasaʒ] *nm* mixing.

**brassard** [bʀasaʀ] *nm* armband.

**brasse** [bʀas] *nf* (*nage*) breast-stroke;

(*mesure*) fathom ; ~ **papillon** butterfly (-stroke).
**brassée** [bRase] *nf* armful.
**brasser** [bRase] *vt* to mix ; ~ **l'argent/les affaires** to handle a lot of money/business.
**brasserie** [bRasRi] *nf* (*restaurant*) brasserie ; (*usine*) brewery.
**brasseur** [bRasœR]̈ *nm* (*de bière*) brewer ; ~ **d'affaires** big businessman.
**brassière** [bRasjɛR] *nf* (baby's) vest.
**bravache** [bRavaʃ] *nm* blusterer, braggart.
**bravade** [bRavad] *nf*: **par** ~ out of bravado.
**brave** [bRav] *a* (*courageux*) brave ; (*bon, gentil*) good, kind.
**braver** [bRave] *vt* to defy.
**bravo** [bRavo] *excl* bravo // *nm* cheer.
**bravoure** [bRavuR] *nf* bravery.
**break** [bRɛk] *nm* (*AUTO*) estate car.
**brebis** [bRəbi] *nf* ewe ; ~ **galeuse** black sheep.
**brèche** [bRɛʃ] *nf* breach, gap ; **être sur la** ~ (*fig*) to be on the go.
**bredouille** [bRəduj] *a* empty-handed.
**bredouiller** [bRəduje] *vi, vt* to mumble, stammer.
**bref, brève** [bRɛf, bRɛv] *a* short, brief // *ad* in short // *nf*: **(voyelle) brève** short vowel ; **d'un ton** ~ sharply, curtly ; **en** ~ in short, in brief.
**brelan** [bRəlɑ̃] *nm* three of a kind ; ~ **d'as** three aces.
**brème** [bRɛm] *nf* bream.
**Brésil** [bRezil] *nm* Brazil ; **b~ien, ne** *a, nm/f* Brazilian.
**Bretagne** [bRətaɲ] *nf* Brittany.
**bretelle** [bRətɛl] *nf* (*de fusil etc*) sling ; (*de combinaison, soutien-gorge*) strap ; (*autoroute*) slip road ; ~**s** *nfpl* (*pour pantalon*) braces.
**breton, ne** [bRətɔ̃, -ɔn] *a, nm/f* Breton.
**breuvage** [bRœvaʒ] *nm* beverage, drink.
**brève** [bRɛv] *a, nf voir* **bref**.
**brevet** [bRəvɛ] *nm* diploma, certificate ; ~ (**d'invention**) patent ; ~ **d'apprentissage** certificate of apprenticeship ; ~ **d'études du premier cycle (B.E.P.C.)** ≈ O levels ; **breveté, e** *a* patented ; (*diplômé*) qualified ; **breveter** *vt* to patent.
**bréviaire** [bRevjɛR] *nm* breviary.
**bribes** [bRib] *nfpl* bits, scraps ; snatches ; **par** ~ piecemeal.
**bric-à-brac** [bRikabRak] *nm inv* bric-a-brac, jumble.
**bricolage** [bRikɔlaʒ] *nm*: **le** ~ do-it-yourself (jobs).
**bricole** [bRikɔl] *nf* trifle ; small job.
**bricoler** [bRikɔle] *vi* to do D.I.Y. jobs ; to potter about ; to do odd jobs // *vt* to fix up ; to tinker with ; **bricoleur, euse** *nm/f* handyman, D.I.Y. enthusiast.
**bride** [bRid] *nf* bridle ; (*d'un bonnet*) string, tie ; **à** ~ **abattue** flat out, hell for leather ; **tenir en** ~ to keep in check ; **lâcher la** ~ **à**, **laisser la** ~ **sur le cou à** to give free rein to.
**bridé, e** [bRide] *a*: **yeux** ~**s** slit eyes.
**brider** [bRide] *vt* (*réprimer*) to keep in check ; (*cheval*) to bridle ; (*CULIN: volaille*) to truss.

**bridge** [bRidʒ(ə)] *nm* bridge.
**brièvement** [bRijɛvmɑ̃] *ad* briefly.
**brièveté** [bRijɛvte] *nf* brevity.
**brigade** [bRigad] *nf* (*POLICE*) squad ; (*MIL*) brigade ; (*gén*) team.
**brigand** [bRigɑ̃] *nm* brigand.
**brigandage** [bRigɑ̃daʒ] *nm* robbery.
**briguer** [bRige] *vt* to aspire to.
**brillamment** [bRijamɑ̃] *ad* brilliantly.
**brillant, e** [bRijɑ̃, -ɑ̃t] *a* brilliant ; bright ; (*luisant*) shiny, shining // *nm* (*diamant*) brilliant.
**briller** [bRije] *vi* to shine.
**brimade** [bRimad] *nf* vexation, harassment *q* ; bullying *q*.
**brimbaler** [bRɛ̃bale] *vb* = **bringuebaler**.
**brimer** [bRime] *vt* to harass ; to bully.
**brin** [bRɛ̃] *nm* (*de laine, ficelle etc*) strand ; (*fig*): **un** ~ **de** a bit of ; ~ **d'herbe** blade of grass ; ~ **de muguet** sprig of lily of the valley ; ~ **de paille** wisp of straw.
**brindille** [bRɛ̃dij] *nf* twig.
**bringuebaler** [bRɛ̃gbale] *vi* to shake (about) // *vt* to cart about.
**brio** [bRijo] *nm* brilliance ; (*MUS*) brio ; **avec** ~ brilliantly, with panache.
**brioche** [bRijɔʃ] *nf* brioche (bun) ; (*fam: ventre*) paunch.
**brique** [bRik] *nf* brick // *a inv* brick red.
**briquer** [bRike] *vt* to polish up.
**briquet** [bRikɛ] *nm* (cigarette) lighter.
**brisant** [bRizɑ̃] *nm* reef ; (*vague*) breaker.
**brise** [bRiz] *nf* breeze.
**brise-glace** [bRizglas] *nm inv* icebreaker.
**brise-jet** [bRizʒɛ] *nm inv* tap swirl.
**brise-lames** [bRizlam] *nm inv* breakwater.
**briser** [bRize] *vt* to break ; **se** ~ *vi* to break ; **briseur, euse de grève** *nm/f* strikebreaker.
**britannique** [bRitanik] *a* British // *nm/f* British person ; **les B~s** the British.
**broc** [bRo] *nm* pitcher.
**brocanteur, euse** [bRɔkɑ̃tœR, -øz] *nm/f* junkshop owner ; junk dealer.
**broche** [bRɔʃ] *nf* brooch ; (*CULIN*) spit ; (*fiche*) spike, peg ; **à la** ~ spit-roast, roasted on a spit.
**broché, e** [bRɔʃe] *a* (*livre*) paper-backed.
**brochet** [bRɔʃɛ] *nm* pike *inv*.
**brochette** [bRɔʃɛt] *nf* skewer ; ~ **de décorations** row of medals.
**brochure** [bRɔʃyR] *nf* pamphlet, brochure, booklet.
**broder** [bRɔde] *vt* to embroider // *vi* to embroider the facts ; **broderie** *nf* embroidery.
**bromure** [bRɔmyR] *nm* bromide.
**broncher** [bRɔ̃ʃe] *vi*: **sans** ~ without flinching ; without turning a hair.
**bronches** [bRɔ̃ʃ] *nfpl* bronchial tubes ; **bronchite** *nf* bronchitis ; **bronchopneumonie** [bRɔ̃kɔ-] *nf* bronco-pneumonia *q*.
**bronze** [bRɔ̃z] *nm* bronze.
**bronzé, e** [bRɔ̃ze] *a* tanned.
**bronzer** [bRɔ̃ze] *vt* to tan // *vi* to get a tan ; **se** ~ to sunbathe.
**brosse** [bRos] *nf* brush ; **donner un coup de** ~ **à qch** to give sth a brush ; **coiffé**

en ~ with a crewcut ; ~ **à cheveux** hairbrush ; ~ **à dents** toothbrush ; ~ **à habits** clothesbrush ; **brosser** *vt* (*nettoyer*) to brush ; (*fig: tableau etc*) to paint ; to draw.

**brouette** [bʀuɛt] *nf* wheelbarrow.

**brouhaha** [bʀuaa] *nm* hubbub.

**brouillard** [bʀujaʀ] *nm* fog.

**brouille** [bʀuj] *nf* quarrel.

**brouiller** [bʀuje] *vt* to mix up ; to confuse ; (*RADIO*) to cause interference to ; to jam ; (*rendre trouble*) to cloud ; (*désunir: amis*) to set at odds ; **se** ~ *vi* (*ciel, vue*) to cloud over ; (*détails*) to become confused ; **se** ~ (**avec**) to fall out (with).

**brouillon, ne** [bʀujɔ̃, -ɔn] *a* disorganised ; unmethodical // *nm* draft.

**broussailles** [bʀusɑj] *nfpl* undergrowth *sg*: **broussailleux, euse** *a* bushy.

**brousse** [bʀus] *nf*: **la** ~ the bush.

**brouter** [bʀute] *vt* to graze on // *vi* to graze ; (*AUTO*) to judder.

**broutille** [bʀutij] *nf* trifle.

**broyer** [bʀwaje] *vt* to crush ; ~ **du noir** to be down in the dumps.

**bru** [bʀy] *nf* daughter-in-law.

**brucelles** [bʀysɛl] *nfpl*: (**pinces**) ~ tweezers.

**bruine** [bʀɥin] *nf* drizzle.

**bruiner** [bʀɥine] *vb impersonnel*: **il bruine** it's drizzling, there's a drizzle.

**bruire** [bʀɥiʀ] *vi* to murmur ; to rustle.

**bruit** [bʀɥi] *nm*: **un** ~ a noise, a sound ; (*fig: rumeur*) a rumour ; **le** ~ noise ; **pas/trop de** ~ no/too much noise ; **sans** ~ without a sound, noiselessly ; ~ **de fond** background noise.

**bruitage** [bʀɥitaʒ] *nm* sound effects *pl* ; **bruiteur, euse** *nm/f* sound-effects engineer.

**brûlant, e** [bʀylɑ̃, -ɑ̃t] *a* burning (hot) ; (*liquide*) boiling (hot) ; (*regard*) fiery ; (*sujet*) red-hot.

**brûlé, e** [bʀyle] *a* (*fig: démasqué*) blown // *nm*: **odeur de** ~ smell of burning.

**brûle-pourpoint** [bʀylpuʀpwɛ̃]: **à** ~ *ad* point-blank.

**brûler** [bʀyle] *vt* to burn ; (*suj: eau bouillante*) to scald ; (*consommer: électricité, essence*) to use ; (*feu rouge, signal*) to go through (without stopping) // *vi* to burn ; (*jeu*) to be warm ; **se** ~ to burn o.s. ; to scald o.s. ; **se** ~ **la cervelle** to blow one's brains out ; ~ (**d'impatience**) **de faire qch** to burn with impatience *ou* be dying to do sth.

**brûleur** [bʀylœʀ] *nm* burner.

**brûlure** [bʀylyʀ] *nf* (*lésion*) burn ; (*sensation*) burning (sensation) ; ~**s d'estomac** heartburn *sg*.

**brume** [bʀym] *nf* mist ; **brumeux, euse** *a* misty ; (*fig*) hazy.

**brun, e** [bʀœ̃, -yn] *a* brown ; (*cheveux, personne*) dark // *nm* (*couleur*) brown ; **brunir** *vi* to get a tan // *vt* to tan.

**brusque** [bʀysk(ə)] *a* (*soudain*) abrupt, sudden ; (*rude*) abrupt, brusque ; ~**ment** *ad* (*soudainement*) abruptly ; suddenly ; **brusquer** *vt* to rush ; **brusquerie** *nf* abruptness, brusqueness.

**brut, e** [bʀyt] *a* raw, crude, rough ; (*COMM*) gross // *nf* brute ; (**champagne**) ~ brut

champagne ; (**pétrole**) ~ crude (oil).

**brutal, e, aux** [bʀytal, -o] *a* brutal ; ~**iser** *vt* to handle roughly, manhandle ; ~**ité** *nf* brutality *q*.

**brute** [bʀyt] *a, nf voir* **brut.**

**Bruxelles** [bʀysɛl] *n* Brussels.

**bruyamment** [bʀɥijamɑ̃] *ad* noisily.

**bruyant, e** [bʀɥijɑ̃, -ɑ̃t] *a* noisy.

**bruyère** [bʀyjɛʀ] *nf* heather.

**bu, e** *pp de* **boire.**

**buanderie** [bɥɑ̃dʀi] *nf* laundry.

**buccal, e, aux** [bykal, -o] *a*: **par voie** ~**e** orally.

**bûche** [byʃ] *nf* log ; **prendre une** ~ (*fig*) to come a cropper ; ~ **de Noël** Yule log.

**bûcher** [byʃe] *nm* pyre ; bonfire // *vb* (*fam*) *vi* to swot, slog away // *vt* to swot up.

**bûcheron** [byʃʀɔ̃] *nm* woodcutter.

**bucolique** [bykɔlik] *a* bucolic, pastoral.

**budget** [bydʒɛ] *nm* budget ; **budgétaire** [bydʒetɛʀ] *a* budgetary, budget *cpd*.

**buée** [bɥe] *nf* (*sur une vitre*) mist ; (*de l'haleine*) steam.

**buffet** [byfɛ] *nm* (*meuble*) sideboard ; (*de réception*) buffet ; ~ (**de gare**) station buffet.

**buffle** [byfl(ə)] *nm* buffalo.

**buis** [bɥi] *nm* box tree ; (*bois*) box(wood).

**buisson** [bɥisɔ̃] *nm* bush.

**buissonnière** [bɥisɔnjɛʀ] *af*: **faire l'école** ~ to play truant.

**bulbe** [bylb(ə)] *nm* (*BOT, ANAT*) bulb ; (*coupole*) onion-shaped dome.

**bulgare** [bylgaʀ] *a, nm/f* Bulgarian.

**Bulgarie** [bylgaʀi] *nf* Bulgaria.

**bulldozer** [buldozœʀ] *nm* bulldozer.

**bulle** [byl] *nf* bubble ; (*papale*) bull ; ~ **de savon** soap bubble.

**bulletin** [byltɛ̃] *nm* (*communiqué, journal*) bulletin ; (*papier*) form ; ticket ; (*SCOL*) report ; ~ **d'informations** news bulletin ; ~ **météorologique** weather report ; ~ **de santé** medical bulletin ; ~ (**de vote**) ballot paper.

**buraliste** [byʀalist(ə)] *nm/f* tobacconist ; clerk.

**bure** [byʀ] *nf* homespun ; frock.

**bureau, x** [byʀo] *nm* (*meuble*) desk ; (*pièce, service*) office ; ~ **de change** (foreign) exchange office *ou* bureau ; ~ **de location** box office ; ~ **de poste** post office ; ~ **de tabac** tobacconist's (shop) ; ~ **de vote** polling station ; ~**cratie** *nm* bureaucrat ; ~**cratie** [-kʀasi] *nf* bureaucracy ; ~**cratique** *a* bureaucratic.

**burette** [byʀɛt] *nf* (*de mécanicien*) oilcan ; (*de chimiste*) burette.

**burin** [byʀɛ̃] *nm* cold chisel ; (*ART*) burin.

**buriné, e** [byʀine] *a* (*fig: visage*) craggy, seamed.

**burlesque** [byʀlɛsk(ə)] *a* ridiculous ; (*LITTÉRATURE*) burlesque.

**burnous** [byʀnu(s)] *nm* burnous.

**bus** *vb* [by] *voir* **boire** // *nm* [bys] bus.

**buse** [byz] *nf* buzzard.

**busqué, e** [byske] *a*: **nez** ~ hook(ed) nose.

**buste** [byst(ə)] *nm* (*ANAT*) chest ; bust ; (*sculpture*) bust.

**but** [by] *vb voir* **boire** // *nm* [*parfois* byt] (*cible*) target; (*fig*) goal; aim; (*FOOTBALL etc*) goal; **de ~ en blanc** point-blank; **avoir pour ~ de faire** to aim to do; **dans le ~ de** with the intention of.
**butane** [bytan] *nm* butane; calor gas.
**buté, e** [byte] *a* stubborn, obstinate // *nf* (*TECH*) stop; (*ARCHIT*) abutment.
**buter** [byte] *vi*: **~ contre/sur** to bump into; to stumble against // *vt* to antagonize; **se ~** *vi* to get obstinate; to dig in one's heels.
**buteur** [bytœR] *nm* striker.
**butin** [bytɛ̃] *nm* booty, spoils *pl*; (*d'un vol*) loot.
**butiner** [bytine] *vi* to gather nectar.
**butor** [bytɔR] *nm* (*fig*) lout.
**butte** [byt] *nf* mound, hillock; **être en ~ à** to be exposed to.
**buvais** *etc vb voir* **boire**.
**buvard** [byvaR] *nm* blotter.
**buvette** [byvɛt] *nf* refreshment room; refreshment stall.
**buveur, euse** [byvœR, -øz] *nm/f* drinker.
**byzantin, e** [bizɑ̃tɛ̃, -in] *a* Byzantine.

## C

**c'** [s] *dét voir* **ce**.
**ça** [sa] *pronom* (*pour désigner*) this; (: *plus loin*) that; (*comme sujet indéfini*) it; **~ m'étonne que** it surprises me that; **~ va?** how are you?; how are things?; (*d'accord?*) OK?, all right?; **c'est ~** that's right.
**çà** [sa] *ad*: **~ et là** here and there.
**caban** [kabɑ̃] *nm* reefer jacket, donkey jacket.
**cabane** [kaban] *nf* hut, cabin.
**cabanon** [kabanɔ̃] *nm* chalet; (country) cottage.
**cabaret** [kabaRɛ] *nm* night club.
**cabas** [kaba] *nm* shopping bag.
**cabestan** [kabɛstɑ̃] *nm* capstan.
**cabillaud** [kabijo] *nm* cod *inv*.
**cabine** [kabin] *nf* (*de bateau*) cabin; (*de plage*) (beach) hut; (*de piscine etc*) cubicle; (*de camion, train*) cab; (*d'avion*) cockpit; **~ (d'ascenseur)** lift cage; **~ d'essayage** fitting room; **~ spatiale** space capsule; **~ (téléphonique)** call *ou* (tele)phone box, (tele)phone booth.
**cabinet** [kabinɛ] *nm* (*petite pièce*) closet; (*de médecin*) surgery; (*de notaire etc*) office; (: *clientèle*) practice; (*POL*) Cabinet; (*d'un ministre*) advisers *pl*; **~s** *nmpl* (*w.-c.*) toilet *sg*, loo *sg*; **~ d'affaires** business consultants' (bureau), business partnership; **~ de toilette** toilet; **~ de travail** study.
**câble** [kɑbl(ə)] *nm* cable.
**câbler** [kɑble] *vt* to cable.
**cabosser** [kabɔse] *vt* to dent.
**cabotage** [kabɔtaʒ] *nm* coastal navigation; **caboteur** *nm* coaster.
**cabotinage** [kabɔtinaʒ] *nm* playacting; third-rate acting, ham acting.
**cabrer** [kabRe]: **se ~** *vi* (*cheval*) to rear up; (*avion*) to nose up; (*fig*) to revolt, rebel; to jib.

**cabri** [kabRi] *nm* kid.
**cabriole** [kabRijɔl] *nf* caper; somersault.
**cabriolet** [kabRijɔlɛ] *nm* convertible.
**cacahuète** [kakayɛt] *nf* peanut.
**cacao** [kakao] *nm* cocoa (powder); (*boisson*) cocoa.
**cachalot** [kaʃalo] *nm* sperm whale.
**cache** [kaʃ] *nm* mask, card (for masking) // *nf* hiding place.
**cache-cache** [kaʃkaʃ] *nm*: **jouer à ~** to play hide-and-seek.
**cachemire** [kaʃmiR] *nm* cashmere // *a*: **dessin ~** paisley pattern.
**cache-nez** [kaʃne] *nm inv* scarf, muffler.
**cache-pot** [kaʃpo] *nm inv* flower-pot holder.
**cacher** [kaʃe] *vt* to hide, conceal; **~ qch à qn** to hide *ou* conceal sth from sb; **se ~** to hide; to be hidden *ou* concealed; **il ne s'en cache pas** he makes no secret of it.
**cachet** [kaʃɛ] *nm* (*comprimé*) tablet; (*sceau: du roi*) seal; (: *de la poste*) postmark; (*rétribution*) fee; (*fig*) style, character; **cacheter** *vt* to seal.
**cachette** [kaʃɛt] *nf* hiding place; **en ~** on the sly, secretly.
**cachot** [kaʃo] *nm* dungeon.
**cachotterie** [kaʃɔtRi] *nf* mystery; **faire des ~s** to be secretive.
**cactus** [kaktys] *nm* cactus.
**cadastre** [kadastR(ə)] *nm* cadastre, land register.
**cadavérique** [kadaveRik] *a* deathly (pale), deadly pale.
**cadavre** [kadavR(ə)] *nm* corpse, (dead) body.
**cadeau, x** [kado] *nm* present, gift; **faire un ~ à qn** to give sb a present *ou* gift; **faire ~ de qch à qn** to make a present of sth to sb, give sb sth as a present.
**cadenas** [kadna] *nm* padlock; **cadenasser** *vt* to padlock.
**cadence** [kadɑ̃s] *nf* (*MUS*) cadence; rhythm; (*de travail etc*) rate; **~s** *nfpl* (*en usine*) production rate *sg*; **en ~** rhythmically; in time; **cadencé, e** *a* rhythmic(al).
**cadet, te** [kadɛ, -ɛt] *a* younger; (*le plus jeune*) youngest // *nm/f* youngest child *ou* one, youngest boy *ou* son/girl *ou* daughter; **il est mon ~ (de deux ans)** (*rapports non familiaux*) he's (2 years) younger than me, he's 2 years my junior; **les ~s** (*SPORT*) the minors (*15 - 17 years*).
**cadran** [kadRɑ̃] *nm* dial; **~ solaire** sundial.
**cadre** [kadR(ə)] *nm* frame; (*environnement*) surroundings *pl*; (*limites*) scope // *nm/f* (*ADMIN*) managerial employee, executive // *a*: **loi ~** outline *ou* blueprint law; **~ moyen/supérieur** (*ADMIN*) middle/senior management employee, junior/senior executive; **rayer qn des ~s** to discharge sb; to dismiss sb; **dans le ~ de** (*fig*) within the framework *ou* context of.
**cadrer** [kadRe] *vi*: **~ avec** to tally *ou* correspond with // *vt* (*CINÉMA*) to centre.
**caduc, uque** [kadyk] *a* obsolete; (*BOT*) deciduous.

**cafard** [kafaʀ] *nm* cockroach ; **avoir le** ~ to be down in the dumps, be feeling low.
**café** [kafe] *nm* coffee ; (*bistro*) café // *a inv* coffee-coloured ; ~ **au lait** white coffee ; ~ **noir** black coffee ; ~ **tabac** *tobacconist's or newsagent's also serving coffee and spirits* ; ~**ine** *nf* caffeine ; **cafetier, ière** *nm/f* café-owner // *nf* (*pot*) coffee-pot.
**cafouiller** [kafuje] *vi* to get in a shambles ; to work in fits and starts.
**cage** [kaʒ] *nf* cage ; ~ **(des buts)** goal ; **en** ~ in a cage, caged up *ou* in ; ~ **d'ascenseur** lift shaft ; ~ **d'escalier** (stair)well ; ~ **thoracique** rib cage.
**cageot** [kaʒo] *nm* crate.
**cagibi** [kaʒibi] *nm* shed.
**cagneux, euse** [kaɲø, -øz] *a* knock-kneed.
**cagnotte** [kaɲɔt] *nf* kitty.
**cagoule** [kagul] *nf* cowl ; hood ; (*SKI etc*) cagoule.
**cahier** [kaje] *nm* notebook ; (*TYPO*) signature ; ~ **de revendications/doléances** list of claims/grievances ; ~ **de brouillons** roughbook, jotter ; ~ **des charges** schedule (of conditions) ; ~ **d'exercices** exercise book.
**cahin-caha** [kaɛ̃kaa] *ad*: **aller** ~ to jog along ; (*fig*) to be so-so.
**cahot** [kao] *nm* jolt, bump ; **cahoter** *vi* to bump along, jog along.
**cahute** [kayt] *nf* shack, hut.
**caïd** [kaid] *nm* big chief, boss.
**caille** [kɑj] *nf* quail.
**caillé, e** [kɑje] *a*: **lait** ~ curdled milk, curds *pl*.
**cailler** [kɑje] *vi* (*lait*) to curdle ; (*sang*) to clot.
**caillot** [kɑjo] *nm* (blood) clot.
**caillou, x** [kaju] *nm* (little) stone ; ~**ter** *vt* (*chemin*) to metal ; ~**teux, euse** *a* stony ; pebbly.
**Caire** [kɛʀ] *nm*: **le** ~ Cairo.
**caisse** [kɛs] *nf* box ; (*où l'on met la recette*) cashbox ; till ; (*où l'on paye*) cash desk ; check-out ; (*de banque*) cashier's desk ; teller's desk ; (*TECH*) case, casing ; ~ **enregistreuse** cash register ; ~ **d'épargne** savings bank ; ~ **de retraite** pension fund ; **caissier, ière** *nm/f* cashier.
**caisson** [kɛsɔ̃] *nm* box, case.
**cajoler** [kaʒɔle] *vt* to wheedle, coax ; to surround with love and care, make a fuss of.
**cake** [kɛk] *nm* fruit cake.
**calaminé, e** [kalamine] *a* (*AUTO*) coked up.
**calamité** [kalamite] *nf* calamity, disaster.
**calandre** [kalɑ̃dʀ(ə)] *nf* radiator grill ; (*machine*) calender, mangle.
**calanque** [kalɑ̃k] *nf* rocky inlet.
**calcaire** [kalkɛʀ] *nm* limestone // *a* (*eau*) hard ; (*GÉO*) limestone *cpd*.
**calciné, e** [kalsine] *a* burnt to ashes.
**calcium** [kalsjɔm] *nm* calcium.
**calcul** [kalkyl] *nm* calculation ; **le** ~ (*SCOL*) arithmetic ; ~ **différentiel/intégral** differential/integral calculus ; ~ **(biliaire)** (gall)stone ; ~ **(rénal)** (kidney) stone ; ~**ateur** *nm*, ~**atrice** *nf* calculator.
**calculer** [kalkyle] *vt* to calculate, work out, reckon ; (*combiner*) to calculate.

**cale** [kal] *nf* (*de bateau*) hold ; (*en bois*) wedge, chock ; ~ **sèche** dry dock.
**calé, e** [kale] *a* (*fam*) clever, bright.
**calebasse** [kalbɑs] *nf* calabash, gourd.
**caleçon** [kalsɔ̃] *nm* pair of underpants, trunks *pl* ; ~ **de bain** bathing trunks *pl*.
**calembour** [kalɑ̃buʀ] *nm* pun.
**calendes** [kalɑ̃d] *nfpl*: **renvoyer aux** ~ **grecques** to postpone indefinitely.
**calendrier** [kalɑ̃dʀije] *nm* calendar ; (*fig*) timetable.
**cale-pied** [kalpje] *nm inv* toe clip.
**calepin** [kalpɛ̃] *nm* notebook.
**caler** [kale] *vt* to wedge, chock up ; ~ **(son moteur/véhicule)** to stall (one's engine/vehicle).
**calfater** [kalfate] *vt* to caulk.
**calfeutrer** [kalføtʀe] *vt* to (make) draughtproof ; **se** ~ to make o.s. snug and comfortable.
**calibre** [kalibʀ(ə)] *nm* (*d'un fruit*) grade ; (*d'une arme*) bore, calibre ; (*fig*) calibre ; **calibrer** *vt* to grade.
**calice** [kalis] *nm* (*REL*) chalice ; (*BOT*) calyx.
**califourchon** [kalifuʀʃɔ̃]: **à** ~ *ad* astride ; **à** ~ **sur** astride, straddling.
**câlin, e** [kɑlɛ̃, -in] *a* cuddly, cuddlesome ; tender.
**câliner** [kɑline] *vt* to fondle, cuddle.
**calleux, euse** [kalø, -øz] *a* horny, callous.
**calligraphie** [kaligʀafi] *nf* calligraphy.
**calmant** [kalmɑ̃] *nm* tranquillizer, sedative ; painkiller.
**calme** [kalm(ə)] *a* calm, quiet // *nm* calm(ness), quietness ; ~ **plat** (*NAVIG*) dead calm.
**calmer** [kalme] *vt* to calm (down) ; (*douleur, inquiétude*) to ease, soothe ; **se** ~ to calm down.
**calomnie** [kalɔmni] *nf* slander ; (*écrite*) libel ; **calomnier** *vt* to slander ; to libel ; **calomnieux, euse** *a* slanderous ; libellous.
**calorie** [kalɔʀi] *nf* calorie.
**calorifère** [kalɔʀifɛʀ] *nm* stove.
**calorifique** [kalɔʀifik] *a* calorific.
**calorifuge** [kalɔʀifyʒ] *a* (heat-) insulating, heat-retaining.
**calot** [kalo] *nm* forage cap.
**calotte** [kalɔt] *nf* (*coiffure*) skullcap ; (*gifle*) slap ; ~ **glaciaire** icecap.
**calque** [kalk(ə)] *nm* (*dessin*) tracing ; (*fig*) carbon copy.
**calquer** [kalke] *vt* to trace ; (*fig*) to copy exactly.
**calvaire** [kalvɛʀ] *nm* (*croix*) wayside cross, calvary ; (*souffrances*) suffering, martyrdom.
**calvitie** [kalvisi] *nf* baldness.
**camaïeu** [kamajø] *nm*: **(motif en)** ~ monochrome motif.
**camarade** [kamaʀad] *nm/f* friend, pal ; (*POL*) comrade ; ~**rie** *nf* friendship.
**cambouis** [kɑ̃bwi] *nm* engine oil.
**cambrer** [kɑ̃bʀe] *vt* to arch ; **se** ~ to arch one's back ; **pied très cambré** foot with high arches *ou* insteps.
**cambriolage** [kɑ̃bʀijɔlaʒ] *nm* burglary.
**cambrioler** [kɑ̃bʀijɔle] *vt* to burgle ; **cambrioleur, euse** *nm/f* burglar.

**cambrure** [kãbRyR] nf (de la route) camber.

**cambuse** [kãbyz] nf storeroom.

**came** [kam] nf: **arbre à ~s** camshaft; **arbre à ~s en tête** overhead camshaft.

**camée** [kame] nm cameo.

**caméléon** [kameleɔ̃] nm chameleon.

**camelot** [kamlo] nm street pedlar.

**camelote** [kamlɔt] nf rubbish, trash, junk.

**caméra** [kameRa] nf camera; (d'amateur) cine-camera.

**camion** [kamjɔ̃] nm lorry, truck; (plus petit, fermé) van; **~-citerne** nm tanker; **camionnage** nm haulage; **camionnette** nf (small) van; **camionneur** nm (entrepreneur) haulage contractor; (chauffeur) lorry ou truck driver; van driver.

**camisole** [kamizɔl] nf: **~ (de force)** strait jacket.

**camomille** [kamɔmij] nf camomile; (boisson) camomile tea.

**camouflage** [kamufla3] nm camouflage.

**camoufler** [kamufle] vt to camouflage; (fig) to conceal, cover up.

**camouflet** [kamuflɛ] nm snub.

**camp** [kã] nm camp; (fig) side; **~ de nudistes/vacances** nudist/holiday camp; **~ de concentration** concentration camp.

**campagnard, e** [kãpaɲaR, -aRd(ə)] a country cpd // nm/f countryman/woman.

**campagne** [kãpaɲ] nf country, countryside; (MIL, POL, COMM) campaign; **à la ~** in the country; **faire ~ pour** to campaign for.

**campement** [kãpmã] nm camp, encampment.

**camper** [kãpe] vi to camp // vt to pull ou put on firmly; to sketch; **se ~ devant** to plant o.s. in front of; **campeur, euse** nm/f camper.

**camphre** [kãfR(ə)] nm camphor.

**camping** [kãpiŋ] nm camping; **(terrain de) ~** campsite, camping site; **faire du ~** to go camping.

**camus, e** [kamy, -yz] a: **nez ~** pug nose.

**Canada** [kanada] nm: **le ~** Canada; **canadien, ne** a, nm/f Canadian // nf (veste) fur-lined jacket.

**canaille** [kanaj] nf (péj) scoundrel // a raffish, rakish.

**canal, aux** [kanal, -o] nm canal; (naturel) channel; (ADMIN): **par le ~ de** through (the medium of), via.

**canalisation** [kanalizasjɔ̃] nf (tuyau) pipe.

**canaliser** [kanalize] vt to canalize; (fig) to channel.

**canapé** [kanape] nm settee, sofa; (CULIN) canapé, open sandwich.

**canard** [kanaR] nm duck.

**canari** [kanaRi] nm canary.

**cancans** [kãkã] nmpl (malicious) gossip sg.

**cancer** [kãsɛR] nm cancer; (signe): **le C~** Cancer, the Crab; **être du C~** to be Cancer; **cancéreux, euse** a cancerous; suffering from cancer; **cancérigène** a carcinogenic.

**cancre** [kãkR(ə)] nm dunce.

**cancrelat** [kãkRəla] nm cockroach.

**candélabre** [kãdelabR(ə)] nm candelabrum; street lamp, lamppost.

**candeur** [kãdœR] nf ingenuousness, guilelessness.

**candi** [kãdi] a inv: **sucre ~** (sugar-)candy.

**candidat, e** [kãdida, -at] nm/f candidate; (à un poste) applicant, candidate; **candidature** nf candidature; application; **poser sa candidature** to submit an application, apply.

**candide** [kãdid] a ingenuous, guileless, naïve.

**cane** [kan] nf (female) duck.

**caneton** [kantɔ̃] nm duckling.

**canette** [kanɛt] nf (de bière) (flip-top) bottle; (de machine à coudre) spool.

**canevas** [kanva] nm (COUTURE) canvas (for tapestry work); (fig) framework, structure.

**caniche** [kaniʃ] nm poodle.

**canicule** [kanikyl] nf scorching heat; midsummer heat, dog days pl.

**canif** [kanif] nm penknife, pocket knife.

**canin, e** [kanɛ̃, -in] a canine // nf canine (tooth), eye tooth; **exposition ~e** dog show.

**caniveau, x** [kanivo] nm gutter.

**canne** [kan] nf (walking) stick; **~ à pêche** fishing rod; **~ à sucre** sugar cane.

**canné, e** [kane] a (chaise) cane cpd.

**cannelle** [kanɛl] nf cinnamon.

**cannelure** [kanlyR] nf flute, fluting q.

**cannibale** [kanibal] nm/f cannibal.

**canoë** [kanɔe] nm canoe; (sport) canoeing.

**canon** [kanɔ̃] nm (arme) gun; (d'une arme: tube) barrel; (fig) model; canon // a: **droit ~** canon law; **~ rayé** rifled barrel.

**cañon** [kaɲɔ̃] nm canyon.

**canoniser** [kanɔnize] vt to canonize.

**canonnade** [kanɔnad] nf cannonade.

**canonnier** [kanɔnje] nm gunner.

**canonnière** [kanɔnjɛR] nf gunboat.

**canot** [kano] nm boat, ding(h)y; **~ pneumatique** rubber ou inflatable ding(h)y; **~ de sauvetage** lifeboat; **canoter** vi to go rowing.

**canotier** [kanɔtje] nm boater.

**cantate** [kãtat] nf cantata.

**cantatrice** [kãtatRis] nf (opera) singer.

**cantine** [kãtin] nf canteen.

**cantique** [kãtik] nm hymn.

**canton** [kãtɔ̃] nm district regrouping several communes; (en Suisse) canton.

**cantonade** [kãtɔnad]: **à la ~** ad to everyone in general; from the rooftops.

**cantonner** [kãtɔne] vt (MIL) to billet; to station; **se ~ dans** to confine o.s. to.

**cantonnier** [kãtɔnje] nm roadmender, roadman.

**canular** [kanylaR] nm hoax.

**caoutchouc** [kautʃu] nm rubber; **~ mousse** foam rubber; **caoutchouté, e** a rubberized; **caoutchouteux, euse** a rubbery.

**cap** [kap] nm (GÉO) cape; headland; (fig) hurdle; watershed; (NAVIG): **changer de ~** to change course; **mettre le ~ sur** to head ou steer for.

**C.A.P.** sigle m = Certificat d'aptitude professionnelle (obtained after trade apprenticeship).

**capable** [kapabl(ə)] a able, capable ; ~ de qch/faire capable of sth/doing ; **livre** ~ **d'intéresser** book liable ou likely to be of interest.

**capacité** [kapasite] nf (compétence) ability ; (JUR, contenance) capacity ; ~ **(en droit)** basic legal qualification.

**cape** [kap] nf cape, cloak ; **rire sous** ~ to laugh up one's sleeve.

**C.A.P.E.S.** [kapɛs] sigle m = Certificat d'aptitude au professorat de l'enseignement du second degré.

**capharnaüm** [kafaʀnaɔm] nm shambles sg.

**capillaire** [kapilɛʀ] a (soins, lotion) hair cpd ; (vaisseau etc) capillary ; **capillarité** nf capillarity.

**capilotade** [kapilɔtad]: **en** ~ ad crushed to a pulp ; smashed to pieces.

**capitaine** [kapitɛn] nm captain ; ~ **des pompiers** fire chief, firemaster ; ~**rie** nf (du port) harbour master's (office).

**capital, e, aux** [kapital -o] a major ; of paramount importance ; fundamental ; (JUR) capital // nm capital ; (fig) stock ; asset // nf (ville) capital ; (lettre) capital (letter) ; // nmpl (fonds) capital sg, money sg ; ~ **(social)** authorized capital ; ~**iser** vt to amass, build up ; (COMM) to capitalize ; ~**isme** nm capitalism ; ~**iste** a, nm/f capitalist.

**capiteux, euse** [kapitø, -øz] a heady ; sensuous, alluring.

**capitonner** [kapitɔne] vt to pad.

**capitulation** [kapitylɑsjɔ̃] nf capitulation.

**capituler** [kapityle] vi to capitulate.

**caporal, aux** [kapɔʀal, -o] nm lance corporal.

**capot** [kapo] nm (AUTO) bonnet.

**capote** [kapɔt] nf (de voiture) hood ; (de soldat) greatcoat.

**capoter** [kapɔte] vi to overturn.

**câpre** [kɑpʀ(ə)] nf caper.

**caprice** [kapʀis] nm whim, caprice ; passing fancy ; ~**s** (de la mode etc) vagaries ; **capricieux, euse** a capricious ; whimsical ; temperamental.

**Capricorne** [kapʀikɔʀn] nm: **le** ~ Capricorn, the Goat ; **être du** ~ to be Capricorn.

**capsule** [kapsyl] nf (de bouteille) cap ; (amorce) primer ; cap ; (BOT etc, spatiale) capsule.

**capter** [kapte] vt (ondes radio) to pick up ; (eau) to harness ; (fig) to win, capture.

**captieux, euse** [kapsjø, -øz] a specious.

**captif, ive** [kaptif, -iv] a captive // nm/f captive, prisoner.

**captiver** [kaptive] vt to captivate.

**captivité** [kaptivite] nf captivity ; **en** ~ in captivity.

**capture** [kaptyʀ] nf capture, catching q ; catch.

**capturer** [kaptyʀe] vt to capture, catch.

**capuche** [kapyʃ] nf hood.

**capuchon** [kapyʃɔ̃] nm hood ; (de stylo) cap, top.

**capucin** [kapysɛ̃] nm Capuchin monk.

**capucine** [kapysin] nf (BOT) nasturtium.

**caquet** [kakɛ] nm: **rabattre le** ~ **à qn** to bring sb down a peg or two.

**caqueter** [kakte] vi (poule) to cackle ; (fig) to prattle, blether.

**car** [kaʀ] nm coach // cj because, for ; ~ **de reportage** broadcasting ou radio van.

**carabine** [kaʀabin] nf carbine, rifle.

**caracoler** [kaʀakɔle] vi to caracole, prance.

**caractère** [kaʀaktɛʀ] nm (gén) character ; **en** ~**s gras** in bold type ; **en petits** ~**s** in small print ; **avoir du** ~ to have character ; **avoir bon/mauvais** ~ to be good-/ill-natured ou -tempered ; **caractériel, le** a (of) character // nm/f emotionally disturbed child.

**caractérisé, e** [kaʀakteʀize] a: **c'est une grippe/de l'insubordination** ~**e** it is a clear(-cut) case of flu/insubordination.

**caractériser** [kaʀakteʀize] vt to characterize ; **se** ~ **par** to be characterized ou distinguished by.

**caractéristique** [kaʀakteʀistik] a, nf characteristic.

**carafe** [kaʀaf] nf decanter ; carafe.

**carambolage** [kaʀɑ̃bɔlaʒ] nm multiple crash, pileup.

**caramel** [kaʀamɛl] nm (bonbon) caramel, toffee ; (substance) caramel ; **caraméliser** vt to caramelize.

**carapace** [kaʀapas] nf shell.

**carat** [kaʀa] nm carat ; **or à 18** ~**s** 18-carat gold.

**caravane** [kaʀavan] nf caravan ; **caravanier** nm caravanner ; **caravaning** nm caravanning ; (emplacement) caravan site.

**carbone** [kaʀbɔn] nm carbon ; (feuille) carbon, sheet of carbon paper ; (double) carbon (copy).

**carbonique** [kaʀbɔnik] a: **gaz** ~ carbonic acid gas ; **neige** ~ dry ice.

**carbonisé, e** [kaʀbɔnize] a charred.

**carboniser** [kaʀbɔnize] vt to carbonize ; to burn down, reduce to ashes.

**carburant** [kaʀbyʀɑ̃] nm (motor) fuel.

**carburateur** [kaʀbyʀatœʀ] nm carburettor.

**carburation** [kaʀbyʀɑsjɔ̃] nf carburation.

**carcan** [kaʀkɑ̃] nm (fig) yoke, shackles pl.

**carcasse** [kaʀkas] nf carcass ; (de véhicule etc) shell.

**carder** [kaʀde] vt to card.

**cardiaque** [kaʀdjak] a cardiac, heart cpd // nm/f heart patient.

**cardigan** [kaʀdigɑ̃] nm cardigan.

**cardinal, e, aux** [kaʀdinal, -o] a cardinal // nm (REL) cardinal.

**cardiologie** [kaʀdjɔlɔʒi] nf cardiology ; **cardiologue** nm/f cardiologist, heart specialist.

**carême** [kaʀɛm] nm: **le C**~ Lent.

**carence** [kaʀɑ̃s] nf incompetence, inadequacy ; (manque) deficiency ; ~ **vitaminique** vitamin deficiency.

**carène** [kaʀɛn] nf hull.

**caréner** [kaʀene] vt (NAVIG) to careen ; (carrosserie) to streamline.

**caressant, e** [karɛsɑ̃, -ɑ̃t] *a* affectionate; caressing, tender.
**caresse** [karɛs] *nf* caress.
**caresser** [karese] *vt* to caress, stroke, fondle; (*fig: projet, espoir*) to toy with.
**cargaison** [kargɛzɔ̃] *nf* cargo, freight.
**cargo** [kargo] *nm* cargo boat, freighter.
**caricatural, e, aux** [karikatyral, -o] *a* caricatural, caricature-like.
**caricature** [karikatyr] *nf* caricature; (*politique etc*) (satirical) cartoon; **caricaturiste** *nm/f* caricaturist; (satirical) cartoonist.
**carie** [kari] *nf*: **la ~ (dentaire)** tooth decay; **une ~** a hole (in a tooth); **carié, e** *a*: **dent cariée** bad *ou* decayed tooth.
**carillon** [karijɔ̃] *nm* (*d'église*) bells *pl*; (*pendule*) chimes *pl*; (*de porte*): **~ (électrique)** (electric) door chime *ou* bell; **carillonner** *vi* to ring, chime, peal.
**carlingue** [karlɛ̃g] *nf* cabin.
**carnage** [karnaʒ] *nm* carnage, slaughter.
**carnassier, ière** [karnasje, -jɛr] *a* carnivorous // *nm* carnivore.
**carnation** [karnɑsjɔ̃] *nf* complexion; **~s** (*PEINTURE*) flesh tones.
**carnaval** [karnaval] *nm* carnival.
**carné, e** [karne] *a* meat *cpd*, meat-based.
**carnet** [karnɛ] *nm* (*calepin*) notebook; (*de tickets, timbres etc*) book; (*d'école*) school report; (*journal intime*) diary; **~ de chèques** cheque book; **~ de commandes** order book; **~ à souches** counterfoil book.
**carnier** [karnje] *nm* gamebag.
**carnivore** [karnivɔr] *a* carnivorous // *nm* carnivore.
**carotide** [karɔtid] *nf* carotid (artery).
**carotte** [karɔt] *nf* carrot.
**carpe** [karp(ə)] *nf* carp.
**carpette** [karpɛt] *nf* rug.
**carquois** [karkwa] *nm* quiver.
**carre** [kar] *nf* (*de ski*) edge.
**carré, e** [kare] *a* square; (*fig: franc*) straightforward // *nm* (*de terrain, jardin*) patch, plot; (*NAVIG: salle*) wardroom; (*MATH*) square; **élever un nombre au ~** to square a number; **mètre/kilomètre ~** square metre/kilometre; (*CARTES*): **~ d'as/de rois** four aces/kings.
**carreau, x** [karo] *nm* (*en faïence etc*) (floor) tile; (*wall*) tile; (*de fenêtre*) (window) pane; (*motif*) check, square; (*CARTES: couleur*) diamonds *pl*; (: *carte*) diamond; **tissu à ~x** checked fabric.
**carrefour** [karfur] *nm* crossroads *sg*.
**carrelage** [karlaʒ] *nm* tiling.
**carreler** [karle] *vt* to tile.
**carrelet** [karlɛ] *nm* (*poisson*) plaice.
**carreleur** [karlœr] *nm* (floor) tiler.
**carrément** [karemɑ̃] *ad* straight out, bluntly; straight; definitely.
**carrer** [kare]: **se ~** *vi*: **se ~ dans un fauteuil** to settle o.s. comfortably *ou* ensconce o.s. in an armchair.
**carrier** [karje] *nm*: **(ouvrier) ~** quarryman, quarrier.
**carrière** [karjɛr] *nf* (*de roches*) quarry; (*métier*) career; **militaire de ~** professional soldier; **faire ~ dans** to make one's career in.

**carriole** [karjɔl] *nf* (*péj*) old cart.
**carrossable** [karɔsabl(ə)] *a* suitable for (motor) vehicles.
**carrosse** [karɔs] *nm* (horse-drawn) coach.
**carrosserie** [karɔsri] *nf* body, coachwork *q*; (*activité, commerce*) coachbuilding; **atelier de ~** coachbuilder's workshop; (*pour réparations*) body repairs shop, panel beaters' (yard); **carrossier** *nm* coachbuilder; (*dessinateur*) car designer.
**carrousel** [karuzɛl] *nm* (*ÉQUITATION*) carousel; (*fig*) merry-go-round.
**carrure** [karyr] *nf* build; (*fig*) stature, calibre.
**cartable** [kartabl(ə)] *nm* (*d'écolier*) satchel, (school)bag.
**carte** [kart(ə)] *nf* (*de géographie*) map; (*marine, du ciel*) chart; (*de fichier, d'abonnement etc, à jouer*) card; (*au restaurant*) menu; (*aussi*: **~ postale**) (post)card; (*aussi*: **~ de visite**) (visiting) card; **avoir/donner ~ blanche** to have/give carte blanche *ou* a free hand; **à la ~** (*au restaurant*) à la carte; **~ de crédit** credit card; **~ d'état-major** ≈ Ordnance Survey map; **la ~ grise** (*AUTO*) the (car) registration book; **~ d'identité** identity card; **~ perforée** punch(ed) card; **la ~ verte** (*AUTO*) the green card; **la ~ des vins** the wine list; **~-lettre** *nf* letter-card.
**carter** [kartɛr] *nm* (*AUTO: d'huile*) sump; (: *de la boîte de vitesses*) casing; (*de bicyclette*) chain guard.
**cartilage** [kartilaʒ] *nm* (*ANAT*) cartilage.
**cartographe** [kartɔgraf] *nm/f* cartographer.
**cartographie** [kartɔgrafi] *nf* cartography, map-making.
**cartomancien, ne** [kartɔmɑ̃sjɛ̃, -ɛn] *nm/f* fortune-teller (*with cards*).
**carton** [kartɔ̃] *nm* (*matériau*) cardboard; (*boîte*) (cardboard) box; (*d'invitation*) invitation card; (*ART*) sketch; cartoon; **faire un ~** (*au tir*) to have a go at the rifle range; to score a hit; **~ (à dessin)** portfolio; **cartonnage** *nm* cardboard (packing); **cartonné, e** *a* (*livre*) hardback, cased; **~-pâte** *nm* pasteboard; **de ~-pâte** (*fig*) cardboard *cpd*.
**cartouche** [kartuʃ] *nf* cartridge; (*de cigarettes*) carton; **cartouchière** *nf* cartridge belt.
**cas** [ka] *nm* case; **faire peu de ~/grand ~ de** to attach little/great importance to; **en aucun ~** on no account, under no circumstances (whatsoever); **au ~ où** in case; **en ~ de** in case of, in the event of; **en ~ de besoin** if need be; **en tout ~** in any case, at any rate; **~ de conscience** matter of conscience.
**casanier, ière** [kazanje, -jɛr] *a* stay-at-home.
**casaque** [kazak] *nf* (*de jockey*) blouse.
**cascade** [kaskad] *nf* waterfall, cascade; (*fig*) stream, torrent.
**cascadeur, euse** [kaskadœr, -øz] *nm/f* stuntman/girl.
**case** [kaz] *nf* (*hutte*) hut; (*compartiment*) compartment; (*pour le courrier*)

pigeonhole ; (*sur un formulaire, de mots croisés, d'échiquier*) square.

**casemate** [kazmat] *nf* blockhouse.

**caser** [kaze] *vt* to put ; to tuck ; to put up ; (*péj*) to find a job for ; to find a husband for.

**caserne** [kazɛʀn(ə)] *nf* barracks *sg ou pl* ; ~ment *nm* barrack buildings *pl*.

**cash** [kaʃ] *ad*: **payer** ~ to pay cash down.

**casier** [kɑzje] *nm* (*à journaux etc*) rack ; (*de bureau*) filing cabinet ; (: *à cases*) set of pigeonholes ; (*case*) compartment ; pigeonhole ; (: *à clef*) locker ; (*PÊCHE*) lobster pot ; ~ **à bouteilles** bottle rack ; ~ **judiciaire** police record.

**casino** [kazino] *nm* casino.

**casque** [kask(ə)] *nm* helmet ; (*chez le coiffeur*) (hair-)drier ; (*pour audition*) (head-)phones *pl*, headset.

**casquette** [kaskɛt] *nf* cap.

**cassant, e** [kɑsɑ̃, -ɑ̃t] *a* brittle ; (*fig*) brusque, abrupt.

**cassate** [kasat] *nf*: (**glace**) ~ cassata.

**cassation** [kɑsasjɔ̃] *nf*: **recours en** ~ appeal to the Supreme Court.

**casse** [kɑs] *nf* (*pour voitures*): **mettre à la** ~ to scrap, send to the breakers ; (*dégâts*): **il y a eu de la** ~ there were a lot of breakages.

**casse...** [kɑs] *préfixe*: ~-**cou** *a inv* daredevil, reckless ; **crier** ~-**cou à qn** to warn sb (*against a risky undertaking*) ; ~-**croûte** *nm inv* snack ; ~-**noisette(s)**, ~-**noix** *nm inv* nutcrackers *pl* ; ~-**pieds** *a, nm/f inv* (*fam*): **il est** ~-**pieds, c'est un** ~-**pieds** he's a pain (in the neck).

**casser** [kɑse] *vt* to break ; (*ADMIN*: *gradé*) to demote ; (*JUR*) to quash // *vi*, **se** ~ to break.

**casserole** [kasʀɔl] *nf* saucepan ; **à la** ~ (*CULIN*) braised.

**casse-tête** [kɑstɛt] *nm inv* (*fig*) brain teaser ; headache (*fig*).

**cassette** [kasɛt] *nf* (*bande magnétique*) cassette ; (*coffret*) casket.

**cassis** [kasis] *nm* blackcurrant ; (*de la route*) dip, bump.

**cassonade** [kasɔnad] *nf* brown sugar.

**cassoulet** [kasulɛ] *nm* cassoulet.

**cassure** [kɑsyʀ] *nf* break, crack.

**castagnettes** [kastaɲɛt] *nfpl* castanets.

**caste** [kast(ə)] *nf* caste.

**castor** [kastɔʀ] *nm* beaver.

**castrer** [kastʀe] *vt* to castrate ; to geld ; to doctor.

**cataclysme** [kataklism(ə)] *nm* cataclysm.

**catacombes** [katakɔ̃b] *nfpl* catacombs.

**catadioptre** [katadjɔptʀ(ə)] *nm* = **cataphote**.

**catafalque** [katafalk(ə)] *nm* catafalque.

**catalogue** [katalɔg] *nm* catalogue.

**cataloguer** [katalɔge] *vt* to catalogue, to list ; (*péj*) to put a label on.

**catalyse** [kataliz] *nf* catalysis ; **catalyseur** *nm* catalyst.

**cataphote** [katafɔt] *nm* reflector.

**cataplasme** [kataplasm(ə)] *nm* poultice.

**catapulte** [katapylt(ə)] *nf* catapult ; **catapulter** *vt* to catapult.

**cataracte** [kataʀakt(ə)] *nf* cataract ;

**opérer qn de la** ~ to operate on sb for (a) cataract.

**catarrhe** [kataʀ] *nm* catarrh.

**catastrophe** [katastʀɔf] *nf* catastrophe, disaster ; **catastrophique** *a* catastrophic, disastrous.

**catch** [katʃ] *nm* (all-in) wrestling ; ~**eur, euse** *nm/f* (all-in) wrestler.

**catéchiser** [kateʃize] *vt* to catechize ; to indoctrinate ; to lecture ; **catéchisme** *nm* catechism ; **catéchumène** [katekymɛn] *nm/f* catechumen (*trainee convert*).

**catégorie** [kategɔʀi] *nf* category.

**catégorique** [kategɔʀik] *a* categorical.

**cathédrale** [katedʀal] *nf* cathedral.

**cathode** [katɔd] *nf* cathode.

**catholicisme** [katɔlisism(ə)] *nm* (Roman) Catholicism.

**catholique** [katɔlik] *a, nm/f* (Roman) Catholic ; **pas très** ~ a bit shady *ou* fishy.

**catimini** [katimini]: **en** ~ *ad* on the sly, on the quiet.

**cauchemar** [koʃmaʀ] *nm* nightmare ; ~**desque** *a* nightmarish.

**caudal, e, aux** [kodal, -o] *a* caudal, tail *cpd*.

**causal, e** [kozal] *a* causal ; ~**ité** *nf* causality.

**cause** [koz] *nf* cause ; (*JUR*) lawsuit, case ; brief ; **à** ~ **de** because of, owing to ; **pour** ~ **de** on account of ; owing to ; (**et**) **pour** ~ and for a (very) good reason ; **être en** ~ to be at stake ; to be involved ; to be in question ; **mettre en** ~ to implicate ; to call into question ; **remettre en** ~ to challenge, call into question.

**causer** [koze] *vt* to cause // *vi* to chat, talk.

**causerie** [kozʀi] *nf* talk.

**caustique** [kostik] *a* caustic.

**cauteleux, euse** [kotlø, -øz] *a* wily.

**cautériser** [koteʀize] *vt* to cauterize.

**caution** [kosjɔ̃] *nf* guarantee, security ; (*JUR*) bail (bond) ; (*fig*) backing, support ; **payer la** ~ **de qn** to stand bail for sb ; **libéré sous** ~ released on bail.

**cautionnement** [kosjɔnmɑ̃] *nm* (*somme*) guarantee, security.

**cautionner** [kosjɔne] *vt* to guarantee ; (*soutenir*) to support.

**cavalcade** [kavalkad] *nf* (*fig*) stampede.

**cavalerie** [kavalʀi] *nf* cavalry.

**cavalier, ière** [kavalje, -jɛʀ] *a* (*désinvolte*) offhand // *nm/f* rider ; (*au bal*) partner // *nm* (*ÉCHECS*) knight ; **faire** ~ **seul** to go it alone.

**cave** [kav] *nf* cellar ; (*cabaret*) (cellar) nightclub // *a*: **yeux** ~**s** sunken eyes.

**caveau, x** [kavo] *nm* vault.

**caverne** [kavɛʀn(ə)] *nf* cave.

**caverneux, euse** [kavɛʀnø, -øz] *a* cavernous.

**caviar** [kavjaʀ] *nm* caviar(e).

**cavité** [kavite] *nf* cavity.

**CC** *sigle voir* **corps**.

**C.C.P.** *sigle m voir* **compte**.

**CD** *sigle voir* **corps**.

**ce(c'), cet, cette, ces** [sə, sɛt, se] *dét* (*gén*) this ; these *pl* ; (*non-proximité*) that ; those *pl* ; **cette nuit** (*qui vient*) tonight ; (*passée*) last night // *pronom*: ~ **qui**, ~

que what ; (*chose qui* ...): **il est bête,** ~ **qui me chagrine** he's stupid, which saddens me ; **tout** ~ **qui bouge** everything that *ou* which moves ; **tout** ~ **que je sais** all I know ; ~ **dont j'ai parlé** what I talked about ; **ce que c'est grand** how big it is!, what a size it is! ; **c'est petit/grand** it's *ou* it is small/big ; **c'est un peintre, ce sont des peintres** he's *ou* he is a painter, they are painters ; **c'est le facteur** *etc* (*à la porte*) it's the postman *etc* ; **c'est une voiture** it's a car ; **qui est-ce?** who is it? ; (*en désignant*) who is he/she? ; **qu'est-ce?** what is it? ; *voir aussi* **-ci, est-ce que, n'est-ce pas, c'est-à-dire.**

**ceci** [səsi] *pronom* this.

**cécité** [sesite] *nf* blindness.

**céder** [sede] *vt* to give up // *vi* (*pont, barrage*) to give way ; (*personne*) to give in ; ~ **à** to yield to, give in to.

**cédille** [sedij] *nf* cedilla.

**cèdre** [sɛdʀ(ə)] *nm* cedar.

**C.E.E.** *sigle f* (= *Communauté économique européenne*) EEC (European Economic Community).

**ceindre** [sɛ̃dʀ(ə)] *vt* (*mettre*) to put on, don ; (*entourer*): ~ **qch de qch** to put sth round sth.

**ceinture** [sɛ̃tyʀ] *nf* belt ; (*taille*) waist ; (*fig*) ring ; belt ; circle ; ~ **de sécurité** safety *ou* seat belt ; ~ (**de sécurité) à enrouleur** inertia reel seat belt ; **ceinturer** *vt* (*saisir*) to grasp (round the waist) ; (*entourer*) to surround ; **ceinturon** *nm* belt.

**cela** [səla] *pronom* that ; (*comme sujet indéfini*) it ; ~ **m'étonne que** it surprises me that ; **quand/où** ~? when/where (was that)?

**célèbre** [selɛbʀ(ə)] *a* famous.

**célébrer** [selebʀe] *vt* to celebrate ; (*louer*) to extol.

**célébrité** [selebʀite] *nf* fame ; (*star*) celebrity.

**céleri** [sɛlʀi] *nm*: ~**-(-rave)** celeriac ; ~ (**en branche**) celery.

**célérité** [seleʀite] *nf* speed, swiftness.

**céleste** [selɛst(ə)] *a* celestial ; heavenly.

**célibat** [seliba] *nm* celibacy ; bachelor/spinsterhood.

**célibataire** [selibatɛʀ] *a* single, unmarried // *nm/f* bachelor/unmarried *ou* single woman.

**celle, celles** [sɛl] *pronom voir* **celui.**

**cellier** [selje] *nm* storeroom.

**cellophane** [selɔfan] *nf* cellophane.

**cellulaire** [selylɛʀ] *a* (*BIO*) cell *cpd*, cellular ; **voiture** *ou* **fourgon** ~ prison *ou* police van.

**cellule** [selyl] *nf* (*gén*) cell.

**cellulite** [selylit] *nf* excess fat, cellulitis.

**cellulose** [selyloz] *nf* cellulose.

**celui, celle, ceux, celles** [səlɥi, sɛl, sø] *pronom* the one ; ~ **qui bouge** the one which *ou* that moves ; (*personne*) the one who moves ; ~ **que je vois** the one (which *ou* that) I see ; the one (whom) I see ; ~ **dont je parle** the one I'm talking about ; ~ **qui veut** (*valeur indéfinie*) whoever wants, the man *ou* person who wants ; ~ **du salon/du dessous** the one in (*ou* from) the lounge/below ; ~ **de mon frère** my brother's ; **celui-ci/-là, celle-ci/-là** this/that one ; **ceux-ci, celles-ci** these ones ; **ceux-là, celles-là** those (ones).

**cénacle** [senakl(ə)] *nm* (literary) coterie *ou* set.

**cendre** [sɑ̃dʀ(ə)] *nf* ash ; ~**s** (*d'un foyer*) ash(es), cinders ; (*volcaniques*) ash *sg* ; (*d'un défunt*) ashes ; **sous la** ~ (*CULIN*) in (the) embers ; **cendré, e** *a* (*couleur*) ashen ; (*piste*) **cendrée** cinder track ; **cendrier** *nm* ashtray.

**cène** [sɛn] *nf*: **la** ~ (Holy) Communion ; (*ART*) the Last Supper.

**censé, e** [sɑ̃se] *a*: **être** ~ **faire** to be supposed to do.

**censeur** [sɑ̃sœʀ] *nm* (*SCOL*) vice-principal, deputy-head ; (*CINÉMA, POL*) censor.

**censure** [sɑ̃syʀ] *nf* censorship.

**censurer** [sɑ̃syʀe] *vt* (*CINÉMA, PRESSE*) to censor ; (*POL*) to censure.

**cent** [sɑ̃] *num* a hundred, one hundred ; **centaine** *nf*: **une centaine (de)** about a hundred, a hundred or so ; (*COMM*) a hundred ; **plusieurs centaines (de)** several hundred ; **des centaines (de)** hundreds (of) ; **centenaire** a hundred-year-old // *nm/f* centenarian // *nm* (*anniversaire*) centenary ; **centième** *num* hundredth ; **centigrade** *nm* centigrade ; **centigramme** *nm* centigramme ; **centilitre** *nm* centilitre ; **centime** *nm* centime ; **centimètre** *nm* centimetre ; (*ruban*) tape measure, measuring tape.

**central, e, aux** [sɑ̃tʀal, -o] *a* central // *nm*: ~ (**téléphonique**) (telephone) exchange // *nf*: ~**e électrique/nucléaire** electric/nuclear power-station ; ~**e syndicale** group of affiliated trade unions.

**centraliser** [sɑ̃tʀalize] *vt* to centralize.

**centre** [sɑ̃tʀ(ə)] *nm* centre ; ~ **de gravité** centre of gravity ; ~ **de tri** (*POSTES*) sorting office ; **le** ~**-ville** the town centre ; **centrer** *vt* to centre // *vi* (*FOOTBALL*) to centre the ball.

**centrifuge** [sɑ̃tʀifyʒ] *a*: **force** ~ centrifugal force ; **centrifuger** *vt* to centrifuge.

**centripète** [sɑ̃tʀipɛt] *a*: **force** ~ centripetal force.

**centuple** [sɑ̃typl(ə)] *nm*: **le** ~ **de qch** a hundred times sth ; **au** ~ a hundredfold ; **centupler** *vi, vt* to increase a hundredfold.

**cep** [sɛp] *nm* (vine) stock ; **cépage** *nm* (type of) vine.

**cèpe** [sɛp] *nm* (edible) boletus.

**cependant** [səpɑ̃dɑ̃] *ad* however, nevertheless.

**céramique** [seʀamik] *nf* ceramic ; (*art*) ceramics *sg*.

**cercle** [sɛʀkl(ə)] *nm* circle ; (*objet*) band, hoop ; ~ **vicieux** vicious circle.

**cercueil** [sɛʀkœj] *nm* coffin.

**céréale** [seʀeal] *nf* cereal.

**cérébral, e, aux** [seʀebʀal, -o] *a* (*ANAT*) cerebral, brain *cpd* ; (*fig*) mental, cerebral.

**cérémonial** [seʀemɔnjal] *nm* ceremonial.

**cérémonie** [seʀemɔni] *nf* ceremony ; ~**s** (*péj*) fuss *sg*, to-do *sg* ; **cérémonieux, euse** *a* ceremonious, formal.

**cerf** [sɛʀ] *nm* stag.

**cerfeuil** [sɛRfœj] *nm* chervil.

**cerf-volant** [sɛRvɔlɑ̃] *nm* kite.

**cerise** [səRiz] *nf* cherry; **cerisier** *nm* cherry (tree).

**cerné, e** [sɛRne] *a*: **les yeux** ~**s** with dark rings *ou* shadows under the eyes.

**cerner** [sɛRne] *vt* (*MIL etc*) to surround; (*fig: problème*) to delimit, define.

**cernes** [sɛRn(ə)] *nfpl* (dark) rings, shadows (under the eyes).

**certain, e** [sɛRtɛ̃, -ɛn] *a* certain; (*sûr*): ~ **(de/que)** certain *ou* sure (of/ that) // *dét* certain; **d'un** ~ **âge** past one's prime, not so young; **un** ~ **temps** (quite) some time; ~**s** *pronom* some; **certainement** *ad* (*probablement*) most probably *ou* likely; (*bien sûr*) certainly, of course.

**certes** [sɛRt(ə)] *ad* admittedly; of course; indeed (yes).

**certificat** [sɛRtifika] *nm* certificate; **le** ~ **d'études** the school leaving certificate.

**certifié, e** [sɛRtifje] *a*: **professeur** ~ qualified teacher.

**certifier** [sɛRtifje] *vt* to certify, guarantee; ~ **à qn que** to assure sb that, guarantee to sb that.

**certitude** [sɛRtityd] *nf* certainty.

**cerveau, x** [sɛRvo] *nm* brain.

**cervelas** [sɛRvəla] *nm* saveloy.

**cervelle** [sɛRvɛl] *nf* (*ANAT*) brain; (*CULIN*) brain(s).

**cervical, e, aux** [sɛRvikal, -o] *a* cervical.

**ces** [se] *dét voir* **ce**.

**césarienne** [sezaRjɛn] *nf* caesarean (section), section.

**cessantes** [sɛsɑ̃t] *afpl*: **toutes affaires** ~ forthwith.

**cessation** [sɛsɑsjɔ̃] *nf*: ~ **des hostilités** cessation of hostilities: ~ **de paiements/commerce** suspension of payments/trading.

**cesse** [sɛs] : **sans** ~ *ad* continually, constantly; continuously; **il n'avait de** ~ **que** he would not rest until.

**cesser** [sese] *vt* to stop // *vi* to stop, cease; ~ **de faire** to stop doing.

**cessez-le-feu** [seselfø] *nm inv* ceasefire.

**cession** [sɛsjɔ̃] *nf* transfer.

**c'est-à-dire** [sɛtadiR] *ad* that is (to say).

**cet** [sɛt] *dét voir* **ce**.

**cétacé** [setase] *nm* cetacean.

**cette** [sɛt] *dét voir* **ce**.

**ceux** [sø] *pronom voir* **celui**.

**C.F.D.T.** *sigle f* = *Confédération française et démocratique du travail (a major association of French trade unions)*.

**C.G.C.** *sigle f* = *Confédération générale des cadres (union of managerial employees)*.

**C.G.T.** *sigle f* = *Confédération générale du travail (a major association of French trade unions)*.

**chacal** [ʃakal] *nm* jackal.

**chacun, e** [ʃakœ̃, -yn] *pronom* each; (*indéfini*) everyone, everybody.

**chagrin, e** [ʃagRɛ̃, -gRin] *a* ill-humoured, morose // *nm* grief, sorrow; **avoir du** ~ to be grieved *ou* sorrowful; **chagriner** *vt* to grieve, distress; (*contrarier*) to bother, worry.

**chahut** [ʃay] *nm* uproar; **chahuter** *vt* to rag, bait // *vi* to make an uproar; **chahuteur, euse** *nm/f* rowdy.

**chai** [ʃɛ] *nm* wine and spirit store(house).

**chaîne** [ʃɛn] *nf* chain; (*RADIO, TV: stations*) channel; **travail à la** ~ production line work; **faire la** ~ to form a (human) chain; ~ **(haute-fidélité** *ou* **hi-fi)** hi-fi system; ~ **(de montage** *ou* **de fabrication**) production *ou* assembly line; ~ **(de montagnes**) (mountain) range; **chaînette** *nf* (small) chain; **chaînon** *nm* link.

**chair** [ʃɛR] *nf* flesh // *a*: **(couleur)** ~ flesh-coloured; **avoir la** ~ **de poule** to have goosepimples *ou* gooseflesh; **bien en** ~ plump, well-padded; ~ **à saucisses** sausage meat.

**chaire** [ʃɛR] *nf* (*d'église*) pulpit; (*d'université*) chair.

**chaise** [ʃɛz] *nf* chair; ~ **de bébé** high chair; ~ **longue** deckchair.

**chaland** [ʃalɑ̃] *nm* (*bateau*) barge.

**châle** [ʃɑl] *nm* shawl.

**chalet** [ʃalɛ] *nm* chalet.

**chaleur** [ʃalœR] *nf* heat; (*fig*) warmth; fire, fervour; heat.

**chaleureux, euse** [ʃalœRø, -øz] *a* warm.

**challenge** [ʃalɑ̃ʒ] *nm* contest, tournament.

**chaloupe** [ʃalup] *nf* launch; (*de sauvetage*) lifeboat.

**chalumeau, x** [ʃalymo] *nm* blowlamp, blowtorch.

**chalut** [ʃaly] *nm* trawl (net); **chalutier** *nm* trawler; (*pêcheur*) trawlerman.

**chamailler** [ʃamaje]: **se** ~ *vi* to squabble, bicker.

**chamarré, e** [ʃamaRe] *a* richly coloured *ou* brocaded.

**chambarder** [ʃɑ̃baRde] *vt* to turn upside down, upset.

**chambranle** [ʃɑ̃bRɑ̃l] *nm* (door) frame.

**chambre** [ʃɑ̃bR(ə)] *nf* bedroom; (*TECH*) chamber; (*POL*) chamber, house; (*JUR*) court; (*COMM*) chamber; federation; **faire** ~ **à part** to sleep in separate rooms; **stratège en** ~ armchair strategist; ~ **à un lit/deux lits** (*à l'hôtel*) single-/double- *ou* twin-bedded room; ~ **d'accusation** court of criminal appeal; ~ **à air** (*de pneu*) (inner) tube; ~ **d'amis** spare *ou* guest room; ~ **à coucher** bedroom; **la C**~ **des députés** the Chamber of Deputies, ≈ the House (of Commons); ~ **forte** strongroom; ~ **froide** *ou* **frigorifique** cold room; ~ **des machines** engine-room; ~ **meublée** bed-sitter, furnished room; ~ **noire** (*PHOTO*) dark room.

**chambrée** [ʃɑ̃bRe] *nf* room.

**chambrer** [ʃɑ̃bRe] *vt* (*vin*) to bring to room temperature.

**chameau, x** [ʃamo] *nm* camel.

**chamois** [ʃamwa] *nm* chamois // *a*: **(couleur)** ~ fawn, buff (-coloured).

**champ** [ʃɑ̃] *nm* field; (*PHOTO*): **dans le** ~ in the picture; **prendre du** ~ to draw back; ~ **de bataille** battlefield; ~ **de courses** racecourse; ~ **de mines** minefield.

**champagne** [ʃɑ̃paɲ] *nm* champagne.

**champêtre** [ʃɑ̃pɛtR(ə)] *a* country *cpd*, rural.

**champignon** [ʃɑ̃piɲɔ̃] *nm* mushroom ; (*terme générique*) fungus (*pl* i) ; ~ **de couche** *ou* **de Paris** cultivated mushroom ; ~ **vénéneux** toadstool, poisonous mushroom.

**champion, ne** [ʃɑ̃pjɔ̃, -jɔn] *a, nm/f* champion ; **championnat** *nm* championship.

**chance** [ʃɑ̃s] *nf*: **la** ~ luck ; **une** ~ a stroke *ou* piece of luck *ou* good fortune ; (*occasion*) a lucky break ; ~**s** *nfpl* (*probabilités*) chances ; **avoir de la** ~ to be lucky ; **il a des** ~**s de gagner** he has a chance of winning.

**chanceler** [ʃɑ̃sle] *vi* to totter.

**chancelier** [ʃɑ̃səlje] *nm* (*allemand*) chancellor ; (*d'ambassade*) secretary.

**chanceux, euse** [ʃɑ̃sø, -øz] *a* lucky, fortunate.

**chancre** [ʃɑ̃kʀ(ə)] *nm* canker.

**chandail** [ʃɑ̃daj] *nm* (thick) jumper *ou* sweater.

**Chandeleur** [ʃɑ̃dlœʀ] *nf*: **la** ~ Candlemas.

**chandelier** [ʃɑ̃dəlje] *nm* candlestick ; (*à plusieurs branches*) candelabra, candlestick.

**chandelle** [ʃɑ̃dɛl] *nf* (tallow) candle ; **dîner aux** ~**s** candlelight dinner.

**change** [ʃɑ̃ʒ] *nm* (*COMM*) exchange ; **opérations de** ~ (foreign) exchange transactions ; **contrôle des** ~**s** exchange control.

**changeant, e** [ʃɑ̃ʒɑ̃, -ɑ̃t] *a* changeable, fickle.

**changement** [ʃɑ̃ʒmɑ̃] *nm* change ; ~ **de vitesses** gears ; gear change.

**changer** [ʃɑ̃ʒe] *vt* (*modifier*) to change, alter ; (*remplacer, COMM, rhabiller*) to change // *vi* to change, alter ; **se** ~ to change (o.s.) ; ~ **de** (*remplacer: adresse, nom, voiture etc*) to change one's ; (*échanger, alterner: côté, place, train etc*) to change + *npl* ; ~ **de couleur/direction** to change colour/direction ; ~ **d'idée** to change one's mind, ~ **de place avec qn** to change places with sb ; ~ **(de train** *etc***)** to change (trains *etc*) ; ~ **qch en** to change sth into.

**changeur** [ʃɑ̃ʒœʀ] *nm* (*personne*) moneychanger ; ~ **automatique** change machine ; ~ **de disques** record changer, autochange.

**chanoine** [ʃanwan] *nm* canon.

**chanson** [ʃɑ̃sɔ̃] *nf* song.

**chansonnier** [ʃɑ̃sɔnje] *nm* cabaret artist (*specializing in political satire*) ; song book.

**chant** [ʃɑ̃] *nm* song ; (*art vocal*) singing ; (*d'église*) hymn ; (*de poème*) canto ; (*TECH*): **de** ~ on edge.

**chantage** [ʃɑ̃taʒ] *nm* blackmail ; **faire du** ~ to use blackmail ; **soumettre qn à un** ~ to blackmail sb.

**chanter** [ʃɑ̃te] *vt, vi* to sing ; **si cela lui chante** (*fam*) if he feels like it *ou* fancies it.

**chanterelle** [ʃɑ̃tʀɛl] *nf* chanterelle (*edible mushroom*).

**chanteur, euse** [ʃɑ̃tœʀ, -øz] *nm/f* singer.

**chantier** [ʃɑ̃tje] *nm* (building) site ; (*sur une route*) roadworks *pl* ; **mettre en** ~ to put in hand, start work on ; ~ **naval** shipyard.

**chantonner** [ʃɑ̃tɔne] *vi, vt* to sing to oneself, hum.

**chanvre** [ʃɑ̃vʀ(ə)] *nm* hemp.

**chaos** [kao] *nm* chaos ; **chaotique** *a* chaotic.

**chaparder** [ʃapaʀde] *vt* to pinch, pilfer.

**chapeau, x** [ʃapo] *nm* hat ; ~ **mou** trilby ; ~**x de roues** hub caps.

**chapeauter** [ʃapote] *vt* (*ADMIN*) to head, oversee.

**chapelet** [ʃaplɛ] *nm* (*REL*) rosary ; (*fig*): **un** ~ **de** a string of ; **dire son** ~ to tell one's beads.

**chapelle** [ʃapɛl] *nf* chapel ; ~ **ardente** chapel of rest.

**chapelure** [ʃaplyʀ] *nf* (dried) breadcrumbs *pl*.

**chaperon** [ʃapʀɔ̃] *nm* chaperon ; **chaperonner** *vt* to chaperon.

**chapiteau, x** [ʃapito] *nm* (*ARCHIT*) capital ; (*de cirque*) marquee, big top.

**chapitre** [ʃapitʀ(ə)] *nm* chapter ; (*fig*) subject, matter ; **avoir voix au** ~ to have a say in the matter.

**chapitrer** [ʃapitʀe] *vt* to lecture.

**chaque** [ʃak] *dét* each, every ; (*indéfini*) every.

**char** [ʃaʀ] *nm* (*à foin etc*) cart, waggon ; (*de carnaval*) float ; ~ **(d'assaut)** tank.

**charabia** [ʃaʀabja] *nm* (*péj*) gibberish, gobbledygook.

**charade** [ʃaʀad] *nf* riddle ; (*mimée*) charade.

**charbon** [ʃaʀbɔ̃] *nm* coal ; ~ **de bois** charcoal ; **charbonnage** *nm*: **les charbonnages de France** the (French) Coal Board *sg* ; **charbonnier** *nm* coalman.

**charcuterie** [ʃaʀkytʀi] *nf* (*magasin*) pork butcher's shop and delicatessen ; (*produits*) cooked pork meats *pl* ; **charcutier, ière** *nm/f* pork butcher.

**chardon** [ʃaʀdɔ̃] *nm* thistle.

**charge** [ʃaʀʒ(ə)] *nf* (*fardeau*) load, burden ; (*explosif, ÉLEC, MIL, JUR*) charge ; (*rôle, mission*) responsibility ; ~**s** *nfpl* (*du loyer*) service charges ; **à la** ~ **de** (*dépendant de*) dependent upon, supported by ; (*aux frais de*) chargeable to, payable by ; **j'accepte, à** ~ **de revanche** I accept, provided I can do the same for you (in return) one day ; **prendre en** ~ to take charge of ; (*suj: véhicule*) to take on ; (*dépenses*) to take care of ; ~ **utile** (*AUTO*) live load ; ~**s sociales** social security contributions.

**chargé** [ʃaʀʒe] *nm*: ~ **d'affaires** chargé d'affaires ; ~ **de cours** ≈ senior lecturer.

**chargement** [ʃaʀʒəmɑ̃] *nm* (*action*) loading ; charging ; (*objets*) load.

**charger** [ʃaʀʒe] *vt* (*voiture, fusil, caméra*) to load ; (*batterie*) to charge // *vi* (*MIL etc*) to charge ; **se** ~ **de** to see to, take care ou charge of ; ~ **qn de qch/faire qch** to give sb the responsibility for sth/of doing sth ; to put sb in charge of sth/doing sth.

**chariot** [ʃaʀjo] *nm* trolley ; (*charrette*) waggon ; (*de machine à écrire*) carriage ; ~ **élévateur** fork-lift truck.

**charitable** [ʃaʀitabl(ə)] *a* charitable ; kind.

**charité** [ʃaʀite] *nf* charity ; **faire la** ~ to

give to charity; to do charitable works;
**faire la** ~ **à** to give (something) to.
**charlatan** [ʃaʀlatɑ̃] *nm* charlatan.
**charmant, e** [ʃaʀmɑ̃, -ɑ̃t] *a* charming.
**charme** [ʃaʀm(ə)] *nm* charm; **charmer** *vt*
to charm; **je suis charmé de** I'm delighted
to; **charmeur, euse** *nm/f* charmer;
**charmeur de serpents** snake charmer.
**charnel, le** [ʃaʀnɛl] *a* carnal.
**charnier** [ʃaʀnje] *nm* mass grave.
**charnière** [ʃaʀnjɛʀ] *nf* hinge; (*fig*)
turning-point.
**charnu, e** [ʃaʀny] *a* fleshy.
**charogne** [ʃaʀɔɲ] *nf* carrion *q*; (*fam!*)
bastard (!).
**charpente** [ʃaʀpɑ̃t] *nf* frame(work); (*fig*)
structure, framework; build, frame; **charpentier** *nm* carpenter.
**charpie** [ʃaʀpi] *nf:* **en** ~ (*fig*) in shreds
*ou* ribbons.
**charretier** [ʃaʀtje] *nm* carter.
**charrette** [ʃaʀɛt] *nf* cart.
**charrier** [ʃaʀje] *vt* to carry (along); to
cart, carry.
**charrue** [ʃaʀy] *nf* plough.
**charte** [ʃaʀt(ə)] *nf* charter.
**chas** [ʃa] *nm* eye (*of needle*).
**chasse** [ʃas] *nf* hunting; (*au fusil*)
shooting; (*poursuite*) chase; (*aussi:* ~
**d'eau**) flush; **la** ~ **est ouverte** the
hunting season is open; ~ **gardée** private
hunting grounds *pl*; **prendre en** ~,
**donner la** ~ **à** to give chase to; **tirer la**
~ (**d'eau**) to flush the toilet, pull the
chain; ~ **à courre** hunting; ~ **à l'homme**
manhunt; ~ **sous-marine** underwater
fishing.
**châsse** [ʃas] *nf* reliquary, shrine.
**chassé-croisé** [ʃasekʀwaze] *nm* (*DANSE*)
chassé-croisé; (*fig*) mix-up *where people
miss each other in turn.*
**chasse-neige** [ʃasnɛʒ] *nm inv*
snowplough.
**chasser** [ʃase] *vt* to hunt; (*expulser*) to
chase away *ou* out, drive away *ou* out;
(*dissiper*) to chase *ou* sweep away; to
dispel, drive away; **chasseur, euse** *nm/f*
hunter // *nm* (*avion*) fighter; (*domestique*)
page (boy), messenger (boy); **chasseurs
alpins** mountain infantry *sg ou pl.*
**chassieux, ieuse** [ʃasjø, -øz] *a* sticky,
gummy.
**châssis** [ʃasi] *nm* (*AUTO*) chassis; (*cadre*)
frame; (*de jardin*) cold frame.
**chaste** [ʃast(ə)] *a* chaste; ~**té** *nf* chastity.
**chasuble** [ʃazybl(ə)] *nf* chasuble.
**chat** [ʃa] *nm* cat; ~ **sauvage** wildcat.
**châtaigne** [ʃatɛɲ] *nf* chestnut;
**châtaignier** *nm* chestnut (tree).
**châtain** [ʃatɛ̃] *a inv* chestnut (brown);
chestnut-haired.
**château, x** [ʃato] *nm* castle; ~ **d'eau**
water tower; ~ **fort** stronghold, fortified
castle; ~ **de sable** sandcastle.
**châtier** [ʃatje] *vt* to punish, castigate;
(*fig: style*) to polish, refine; **châtiment** *nm*
punishment, castigation.
**chatoiement** [ʃatwamɑ̃] *nm*
shimmer(ing).
**chaton** [ʃatɔ̃] *nm* (*ZOOL*) kitten; (*BOT*)
catkin; (*de bague*) bezel; stone.

**chatouiller** [ʃatuje] *vt* to tickle; (*l'odorat,
le palais*) to titillate; **chatouilleux, euse**
*a* ticklish; (*fig*) touchy, over-sensitive.
**chatoyer** [ʃatwaje] *vi* to shimmer.
**châtrer** [ʃatʀe] *vt* to castrate; to geld; to
doctor.
**chatte** [ʃat] *nf* (she-)cat.
**chaud, e** [ʃo, -od] *a* (*gén*) warm; (*très
chaud*) hot; (*fig*) hearty; keen; heated; **il
fait** ~ it's warm; it's hot; **manger** ~ to
have something hot to eat; **avoir** ~ to
be warm; to be hot; **ça me tient** ~ it
keeps me warm; **rester au** ~ to stay in
the warmth; **chaudement** *ad* warmly;
(*fig*) hotly.
**chaudière** [ʃodjɛʀ] *nf* boiler.
**chaudron** [ʃodʀɔ̃] *nm* cauldron.
**chaudronnerie** [ʃodʀɔnʀi] *nf* (*usine*)
boilerworks; (*activité*) boilermaking;
(*boutique*) coppersmith's workshop.
**chauffage** [ʃofaʒ] *nm* heating; ~ **central**
central heating.
**chauffant, e** [ʃofɑ̃, -ɑ̃t] *a:* **couverture** ~**e**
electric blanket; **plaque** ~**e** hotplate.
**chauffard** [ʃofaʀ] *nm* (*péj*) reckless
driver; roadhog; hit-and-run driver.
**chauffe-bain** [ʃofbɛ̃] *nm,* **chauffe-eau**
[ʃofo] *nm inv* water-heater.
**chauffer** [ʃofe] *vt* to heat // *vi* to heat
up, warm up; (*trop chauffer: moteur*) to
overheat; **se** ~ (*se mettre en train*) to
warm up; (*au soleil*) to warm o.s.
**chaufferie** [ʃofʀi] *nf* boiler room.
**chauffeur** [ʃofœʀ] *nm* driver; (*privé*)
chauffeur.
**chaume** [ʃom] *nm* (*du toit*) thatch; (*tiges*)
stubble.
**chaumière** [ʃomjɛʀ] *nf* (thatched)
cottage.
**chaussée** [ʃose] *nf* road(way); (*digue*)
causeway.
**chausse-pied** [ʃospje] *nm* shoe-horn.
**chausser** [ʃose] *vt* (*bottes, skis*) to put on;
(*enfant*) to put shoes on; (*suj: soulier*) to
fit; ~ **du 38/42** to take size 38/42; ~
**grand/bien** to be big-/well-fitting; **se** ~
to put one's shoes on.
**chaussette** [ʃosɛt] *nf* sock.
**chausseur** [ʃosœʀ] *nm* (*marchand*)
footwear specialist, shoemaker.
**chausson** [ʃosɔ̃] *nm* slipper; ~ (**aux
pommes**) (apple) turnover.
**chaussure** [ʃosyʀ] *nf* shoe; (*commerce*)
shoe industry *ou* trade; ~**s montantes**
ankle boots; ~**s de ski** ski boots.
**chaut** [ʃo] *vb:* **peu me** ~ it matters little
to me.
**chauve** [ʃov] *a* bald.
**chauve-souris** [ʃovsuʀi] *nf* bat.
**chauvin, e** [ʃovɛ̃, -in] *a* chauvinistic,
jingoistic; **chauvinisme** *nm* chauvinism;
jingoism.
**chaux** [ʃo] *nf* lime; **blanchi à la** ~
whitewashed.
**chavirer** [ʃaviʀe] *vi* to capsize, overturn.
**chef** [ʃɛf] *nm* head, leader; (*de cuisine*)
chef; **en** ~ (*MIL etc*) in chief; ~
**d'accusation** charge, count (of
indictment); ~ **d'atelier** (shop) foreman;
~ **de bureau** head clerk; ~ **de clinique**
senior hospital lecturer; ~ **d'entreprise**

company head ; ~ **d'équipe** team leader ; ~ **d'état** head of state ; ~ **de famille** head of the family ; ~ **de file** (*de parti etc*) leader ; ~ **de gare** station master ; ~ **d'orchestre** conductor ; ~ **de rayon** department(al) supervisor ; ~ **de service** departmental head.

**chef-d'œuvre** [ʃɛdœvʀ(ə)] *nm* masterpiece.

**chef-lieu** [ʃɛfljø] *nm* county town.

**cheftaine** [ʃɛftɛn] *nf* (guide) captain.

**cheik** [ʃɛk] *nm* sheik.

**chemin** [ʃəmɛ̃] *nm* path ; (*itinéraire, direction, trajet*) way ; **en** ~ on the way ; ~ **de fer** railway ; **par** ~ **de fer** by rail ; **les** ~**s de fer** the railways.

**cheminée** [ʃəmine] *nf* chimney ; (*à l'intérieur*) chimney piece, fireplace ; (*de bateau*) funnel.

**cheminement** [ʃəminmɑ̃] *nm* progress ; course.

**cheminer** [ʃəmine] *vi* to walk (along).

**cheminot** [ʃəmino] *nm* railwayman.

**chemise** [ʃəmiz] *nf* shirt ; (*dossier*) folder ; ~ **de nuit** nightdress ; ~**rie** *nf* (gentlemen's) outfitters' ; **chemisette** *nf* short-sleeved shirt.

**chemisier** [ʃəmizje] *nm* blouse.

**chenal, aux** [ʃənal, -o] *nm* channel.

**chêne** [ʃɛn] *nm* oak (tree) ; (*bois*) oak.

**chenet** [ʃənɛ] *nm* fire-dog, andiron.

**chenil** [ʃənil] *nm* kennels *pl*.

**chenille** [ʃənij] *nf* (*ZOOL*) caterpillar ; (*AUTO*) caterpillar track ; **véhicule à** ~**s** tracked vehicle, caterpillar ; **chenillette** *nf* tracked vehicle.

**cheptel** [ʃɛptɛl] *nm* livestock.

**chèque** [ʃɛk] *nm* cheque ; ~ **barré/sans provision** crossed/bad cheque ; ~ **au porteur** cheque to bearer ; **chéquier** *nm* cheque book.

**cher, ère** [ʃɛʀ] *a* (*aimé*) dear ; (*coûteux*) expensive, dear // *ad*: **cela coûte** ~ it's expensive, it costs a lot of money // *nf*: **la bonne chère** good food ; **mon** ~, **ma chère** my dear.

**chercher** [ʃɛʀʃe] *vt* to look for ; (*gloire etc*) to seek ; **aller** ~ to go for, go and fetch ; ~ **à faire** to try to do.

**chercheur, euse** [ʃɛʀʃœʀ, -øz] *nm/f* researcher, research worker ; ~ **de** seeker of ; hunter of ; ~ **d'or** gold digger.

**chère** [ʃɛʀ] *a,nf voir* **cher**.

**chéri, e** [ʃeʀi] *a* beloved, dear ; (**mon**) ~ darling.

**chérir** [ʃeʀiʀ] *vt* to cherish.

**cherté** [ʃɛʀte] *nf*: **la** ~ **de la vie** the high cost of living.

**chérubin** [ʃeʀybɛ̃] *nm* cherub.

**chétif, ive** [ʃetif, -iv] *a* puny, stunted.

**cheval, aux** [ʃəval, -o] *nm* horse ; (*AUTO*): ~ (**vapeur**) (**C.V.**) horsepower *q* ; **50 chevaux (au frein)** 50 brake horsepower, 50 b.h.p. ; **10 chevaux (fiscaux)** 10 horsepower (*for tax purposes*) ; **faire du** ~ to ride ; **à** ~ on horseback ; **à** ~ **sur** astride, straddling ; (*fig*) overlapping ; ~ **d'arçons** vaulting horse.

**chevaleresque** [ʃəvalʀɛsk(ə)] *a* chivalrous.

**chevalerie** [ʃəvalʀi] *nf* chivalry ; knighthood.

**chevalet** [ʃəvalɛ] *nm* easel.

**chevalier** [ʃəvalje] *nm* knight ; ~ **servant** escort.

**chevalière** [ʃəvaljɛʀ] *nf* signet ring.

**chevalin, e** [ʃəvalɛ̃, -in] *a* of horses, equine ; (*péj*) horsy ; **boucherie** ~**e** horse-meat butcher's.

**cheval-vapeur** [ʃəvalvapœʀ] *nm voir* **cheval.**

**chevauchée** [ʃəvoʃe] *nf* ride ; cavalcade.

**chevaucher** [ʃəvoʃe] *vi* (*aussi*: **se** ~) to overlap (each other) // *vt* to be astride, straddle.

**chevelu, e** [ʃəvly] *a* with a good head of hair, hairy (*péj*).

**chevelure** [ʃəvlyʀ] *nf* hair *q*.

**chevet** [ʃəvɛ] *nm*: **au** ~ **de qn** at sb's bedside ; **lampe de** ~ bedside lamp.

**cheveu, x** [ʃəvø] *nm* hair ; // *nmpl* (*chevelure*) hair *sg* ; **avoir les** ~**x courts** to have short hair.

**cheville** [ʃəvij] *nf* (*ANAT*) ankle ; (*de bois*) peg ; (*pour enfoncer un clou*) plug ; ~ **ouvrière** (*fig*) kingpin.

**chèvre** [ʃɛvʀ(ə)] *nf* (she-)goat.

**chevreau, x** [ʃəvʀo] *nm* kid.

**chèvrefeuille** [ʃɛvʀəfœj] *nm* honeysuckle.

**chevreuil** [ʃəvʀœj] *nm* roe deer *inv* ; (*CULIN*) venison.

**chevron** [ʃəvʀɔ̃] *nm* (*poutre*) rafter ; (*motif*) chevron, v(-shape) ; **à** ~**s** chevron-patterned ; herringbone.

**chevronné, e** [ʃəvʀɔne] *a* seasoned, experienced.

**chevrotant, e** [ʃəvʀɔtɑ̃, -ɑ̃t] *a* quavering.

**chevrotine** [ʃəvʀɔtin] *nf* buckshot *q*.

**chewing-gum** [ʃwiŋɔm] *nm* chewing gum.

**chez** [ʃe] *prép* (*à la demeure de*): ~ **qn** at (*ou* to) sb's house *ou* place ; (*parmi*) among ; ~ **moi** at home ; (*avec direction*) home ; ~ **le boulanger** (*à la boulangerie*) at the baker's ; ~ **ce musicien** (*dans ses œuvres*) in this musician ; ~-**soi** *nm inv* home.

**chic** [ʃik] *a inv* chic, smart ; (*généreux*) nice, decent // *nm* stylishness ; **avoir le** ~ **de** to have the knack of ; **de** ~ *ad* off the cuff ; ~! great!, terrific!

**chicane** [ʃikan] *nf* (*obstacle*) zigzag ; (*querelle*) squabble.

**chiche** [ʃiʃ] *a* a niggardly, mean // *excl* (*à un défi*) you're on!

**chicorée** [ʃikɔʀe] *nf* (*café*) chicory ; (*salade*) endive.

**chicot** [ʃiko] *nm* stump.

**chien** [ʃjɛ̃] *nm* dog ; (*de pistolet*) hammer ; **en** ~ **de fusil** curled up ; ~ **de garde** guard dog.

**chiendent** [ʃjɛ̃dɑ̃] *nm* couch grass.

**chien-loup** [ʃjɛ̃lu] *nm* wolfhound.

**chienne** [ʃjɛn] *nf* dog, bitch.

**chier** [ʃje] *vi* (*fam!*) to crap (!).

**chiffe** [ʃif] *nf*: **il est mou comme une** ~, **c'est une** ~ **molle** he's spineless *ou* wet.

**chiffon** [ʃifɔ̃] *nm* (*de ménage*) (piece of) rag.

**chiffonner** [ʃifɔne] *vt* to crumple, crease.
**chiffonnier** [ʃifɔnje] *nm* ragman, rag-and-bone man ; (*meuble*) chiffonier.
**chiffre** [ʃifʀ(ə)] *nm* (*représentant un nombre*) figure ; numeral ; (*montant, total*) total, sum ; (*d'un code*) code, cipher ; ~s **romains/arabes** roman/arabic figures *ou* numerals ; **en** ~s **ronds** in round figures ; **écrire un nombre en** ~s to write a number in figures ; ~ **d'affaires** turnover ; **chiffrer** *vt* (*dépense*) to put a figure to, assess ; (*message*) to (en)code, cipher.
**chignole** [ʃiɲɔl] *nf* drill.
**chignon** [ʃiɲɔ̃] *nm* chignon, bun.
**Chili** [ʃili] *nm*: **le** ~ Chile ; **chilien, ne** *a*, *nm/f* Chilean.
**chimère** [ʃimɛʀ] *nf* (wild) dream, chimera ; pipe dream, idle fancy.
**chimie** [ʃimi] *nf*: **la** ~ chemistry ; **chimique** *a* chemical ; **produits chimiques** chemicals ; **chimiste** *nm/f* chemist.
**Chine** [ʃin] *nf*: **la** ~ China.
**chiné, e** [ʃine] *a* flecked.
**chinois, e** [ʃinwa, -waz] *a* Chinese ; (*fig*: *péj*) pernickety, fussy // *nm/f* Chinese // *nm* (*langue*): **le** ~ Chinese.
**chiot** [ʃjo] *nm* pup(py).
**chipoter** [ʃipɔte] *vi* to nibble ; to quibble ; to haggle.
**chips** [ʃips] *nfpl* (*aussi*: **pommes** ~) crisps.
**chique** [ʃik] *nf* quid, chew.
**chiquenaude** [ʃiknod] *nf* flick, flip.
**chiquer** [ʃike] *vi* to chew tobacco.
**chiromancien, ne** [kiʀɔmɑ̃sjɛ̃, -ɛn] *nm/f* palmist.
**chirurgical, e, aux** [ʃiʀyʀʒikal, -o] *a* surgical.
**chirurgie** [ʃiʀyʀʒi] *nf* surgery ; ~ **esthétique** plastic surgery ; **chirurgien, ne** *nm/f* surgeon.
**chiure** [ʃjyʀ] *nf*: ~s **de mouche** fly specks.
**chlore** [klɔʀ] *nm* chlorine.
**chloroforme** [klɔʀɔfɔʀm(ə)] *nm* chloroform.
**chlorophylle** [klɔʀɔfil] *nf* chlorophyll.
**choc** [ʃɔk] *nm* impact ; shock ; crash ; (*moral*) shock ; (*affrontement*) clash ; ~ **opératoire/nerveux** post-operative/(nervous) shock.
**chocolat** [ʃɔkɔla] *nm* chocolate ; (*boisson*) (hot) chocolate ; ~ **à croquer** plain chocolate ; ~ **au lait** milk chocolate.
**chœur** [kœʀ] *nm* (*chorale*) choir ; (*OPÉRA, THÉÂTRE*) chorus ; (*ARCHIT*) choir, chancel ; **en** ~ in chorus.
**choir** [ʃwaʀ] *vi* to fall.
**choisi, e** [ʃwazi] *a* (*de premier choix*) carefully chosen ; select ; **textes** ~s selected writings.
**choisir** [ʃwaziʀ] *vt* to choose, select.
**choix** [ʃwa] *nm* choice ; selection ; **avoir le** ~ to have the choice ; **premier** ~ (*COMM*) class *ou* grade one ; **de** ~ choice, selected ; **au** ~ as you wish *ou* prefer.
**choléra** [kɔleʀa] *nm* cholera.
**chômage** [ʃomaʒ] *nm* unemployment ; **mettre au** ~ to make redundant, put out of work ; **être au** ~ to be unemployed *ou*

out of work ; ~ **partiel** short-time working ; ~ **technique** lay-offs *pl* ; **chômer** *vi* to be unemployed, be idle ; **jour chômé** public holiday ; **chômeur, euse** *nm/f* unemployed person, person out of work.
**chope** [ʃɔp] *nf* tankard.
**choquer** [ʃɔke] *vt* (*offenser*) to shock ; (*commotionner*) to shake (up).
**choral, e** [kɔʀal] *a* choral // *nf* choral society, choir.
**chorégraphe** [kɔʀegʀaf] *nm/f* choreographer.
**chorégraphie** [kɔʀegʀafi] *nf* choreography.
**choriste** [kɔʀist(ə)] *nm/f* choir member ; (*OPÉRA*) chorus member.
**chorus** [kɔʀys] *nm*: **faire** ~ (**avec**) to voice one's agreement (with).
**chose** [ʃoz] *nf* thing ; **c'est peu de** ~ it's nothing (really) ; it's not much.
**chou, x** [ʃu] *nm* cabbage // *a inv* cute ; **mon petit** ~ (my) sweetheart ; ~ **à la crème** cream bun (*made of choux pastry*).
**choucas** [ʃuka] *nm* jackdaw.
**chouchou, te** [ʃuʃu, -ut] *nm/f* (*SCOL*) teacher's pet.
**choucroute** [ʃukʀut] *nf* sauerkraut.
**chouette** [ʃwɛt] *nf* owl // *a* (*fam*) great, smashing.
**chou-fleur** [ʃuflœʀ] *nm* cauliflower.
**chou-rave** [ʃuʀav] *nm* kohlrabi.
**choyer** [ʃwaje] *vt* to cherish ; to pamper.
**chrétien, ne** [kʀetjɛ̃, -ɛn] *a*, *nm/f* Christian ; **chrétiennement** *ad* in a Christian way *ou* spirit ; **chrétienté** *nf* Christendom.
**Christ** [kʀist] *nm*: **le** ~ Christ ; **c**~ (*crucifix etc*) figure of Christ ; **christianiser** *vt* to convert to Christianity ; **christianisme** *nm* Christianity.
**chromatique** [kʀɔmatik] *a* chromatic.
**chrome** [kʀom] *nm* chromium ; **chromé, e** *a* chromium-plated.
**chromosome** [kʀɔmozom] *nm* chromosome.
**chronique** [kʀɔnik] *a* chronic // *nf* (*de journal*) column, page ; (*historique*) chronicle ; (*RADIO, TV*): **la** ~ **sportive/théâtrale** the sports/theatre review ; **la** ~ **locale** local news and gossip ; **chroniqueur** *nm* columnist ; chronicler.
**chronologie** [kʀɔnɔlɔʒi] *nf* chronology ; **chronologique** *a* chronological.
**chronomètre** [kʀɔnɔmɛtʀ(ə)] *nm* stopwatch ; **chronométrer** *vt* to time.
**chrysalide** [kʀizalid] *nf* chrysalis.
**chrysanthème** [kʀizɑ̃tɛm] *nm* chrysanthemum.
**chu, e** [ʃy] *pp de* **choir**.
**chuchoter** [ʃyʃɔte] *vt, vi* to whisper.
**chuinter** [ʃɥɛ̃te] *vi* to hiss.
**chut** [ʃyt] *excl* sh!
**chute** [ʃyt] *nf* fall ; (*de bois, papier: déchet*) scrap ; **la** ~ **des cheveux** hair loss ; **faire une** ~ (**de 10 m**) to fall (10 m) ; ~s **de pluie/neige** rain/snowfalls ; ~ (**d'eau**) waterfall ; ~ **libre** free fall.

**Chypre** [ʃipʀ] n Cyprus ; **chypriote** a, nm/f = **cypriote**.
**-ci, ci-** [si] ad voir **par, ci-contre, ci-joint** etc // dét: **ce garçon-ci/-là** this/that boy ; **ces femmes-ci/-là** these/those women.
**ci-après** [siapʀɛ] ad hereafter.
**cible** [sibl(ə)] nf target.
**ciboire** [sibwaʀ] nm ciborium (vessel).
**ciboule** [sibul] nf (large) chive ; **ciboulette** nf (smaller) chive.
**cicatrice** [sikatʀis] nf scar.
**cicatriser** [sikatʀize] vt to heal ; **se** ~ to heal (up), form a scar.
**ci-contre** [sikɔ̃tʀ(ə)] ad opposite.
**ci-dessous** [sidəsu] ad below.
**ci-dessus** [sidəsy] ad above.
**ci-devant** [sidəvɑ̃] nm/f aristocrat who lost his/her title in the French Revolution.
**cidre** [sidʀ(ə)] nm cider.
**Cie** abr de **compagnie**.
**ciel** [sjɛl] nm sky ; (REL) heaven ; ~**s** nmpl (PEINTURE etc) skies ; **cieux** nmpl sky sg, skies ; (REL) heaven sg ; **à** ~ **ouvert** open-air ; (mine) opencast ; ~ **de lit** canopy.
**cierge** [sjɛʀʒ(ə)] nm candle.
**cigale** [sigal] nf cicada.
**cigare** [sigaʀ] nm cigar.
**cigarette** [sigaʀɛt] nf cigarette.
**ci-gît** [siʒi] ad + vb here lies.
**cigogne** [sigɔɲ] nf stork.
**ciguë** [sigy] nf hemlock.
**ci-inclus, e** [siɛ̃kly, -yz] a, ad enclosed.
**ci-joint, e** [siʒwɛ̃, -ɛt] a, ad enclosed.
**cil** [sil] nm (eye)lash.
**ciller** [sije] vi to blink.
**cimaise** [simɛz] nf picture rail.
**cime** [sim] nf top ; (montagne) peak.
**ciment** [simɑ̃] nm cement ; ~ **armé** reinforced concrete ; **cimenter** vt to cement ; **cimenterie** nf cement works sg.
**cimetière** [simtjɛʀ] nm cemetery ; (d'église) churchyard ; ~ **de voitures** scrapyard.
**cinéaste** [sineast(ə)] nm/f film-maker.
**ciné-club** [sineklœb] nm film club ; film society.
**cinéma** [sinema] nm cinema ; ~**scope** nm cinemascope ; ~**thèque** nf film archives pl ou library ; ~**tographique** a film cpd, cinema cpd.
**cinéphile** [sinefil] nm/f film ou cinema enthusiast.
**cinétique** [sinetik] a kinetic.
**cinglé, e** [sɛ̃gle] a (fam) barmy.
**cingler** [sɛ̃gle] vt to lash ; (fig) to sting // vi (NAVIG): ~ **vers** to make ou head for.
**cinq** [sɛ̃k] num five.
**cinquantaine** [sɛ̃kɑ̃tɛn] nf: **une** ~ **(de)** about fifty.
**cinquante** [sɛ̃kɑ̃t] num fifty ; ~**naire** a, nm/f fifty-year-old ; **cinquantième** num fiftieth.
**cinquième** [sɛ̃kjɛm] num fifth.
**cintre** [sɛ̃tʀ(ə)] nm coat-hanger ; (ARCHIT) arch ; ~**s** nmpl (THÉÂTRE) flies.
**cintré, e** [sɛ̃tʀe] a curved ; (chemise) fitted, slim-fitting.
**cirage** [siʀaʒ] nm (shoe) polish.
**circoncision** [siʀkɔ̃sizjɔ̃] nf circumcision.

**circonférence** [siʀkɔ̃feʀɑ̃s] nf circumference.
**circonflexe** [siʀkɔ̃flɛks(ə)] a: **accent** ~ circumflex accent.
**circonscription** [siʀkɔ̃skʀipsjɔ̃] nf district ; ~ **électorale** (d'un député) constituency.
**circonscrire** [siʀkɔ̃skʀiʀ] vt to define, delimit ; (incendie) to contain.
**circonspect, e** [siʀkɔ̃spɛkt] a circumspect, cautious.
**circonstance** [siʀkɔ̃stɑ̃s] nf circumstance ; (occasion) occasion ; ~**s atténuantes** attenuating circumstances.
**circonstancié, e** [siʀkɔ̃stɑ̃sje] a detailed.
**circonstanciel, le** [ siʀkɔ̃stɑ̃sjɛl] a: **complément/proposition** ~**(le)** adverbial phrase/clause.
**circonvenir** [siʀkɔ̃vniʀ] vt to circumvent.
**circonvolutions** [siʀkɔ̃vɔlysjɔ̃] nfpl twists, convolutions.
**circuit** [siʀkɥi] nm (trajet) tour, (round) trip ; (ÉLEC, TECH) circuit ; ~ **automobile** motor circuit ; ~ **de distribution** distribution network.
**circulaire** [siʀkylɛʀ] a, nf circular.
**circulation** [siʀkylasjɔ̃] nf circulation ; (AUTO): **la** ~ (the) traffic ; **mettre en** ~ to put into circulation.
**circuler** [siʀkyle] vi to drive (along) ; to walk along ; (train etc) to run ; (sang, devises) to circulate ; **faire** ~ (nouvelle) to spread (about), circulate ; (badauds) to move on.
**cire** [siʀ] nf wax.
**ciré** [siʀe] nm oilskin.
**cirer** [siʀe] vt to wax, polish ; **cireur** nm shoeshine-boy ; **cireuse** nf floor polisher.
**cirque** [siʀk(ə)] nm circus ; (arène) amphitheatre ; (GÉO) cirque ; (fig) chaos, bedlam ; carry-on.
**cirrhose** [siʀoz] nf: ~ **du foie** cirrhosis of the liver.
**cisaille(s)** [sizɑj] nf(pl) (gardening) shears pl ; **cisailler** vt to clip.
**ciseau, x** [sizo] nm: ~ **(à bois)** chisel ; // nmpl (pair of) scissors ; **sauter en** ~**x** to do a scissors jump ; ~ **à froid** cold chisel.
**ciseler** [sizle] vt to chisel, carve.
**citadelle** [sitadɛl] nf citadel.
**citadin, e** [sitadɛ̃, -in] nm/f city dweller // a town cpd, city cpd, urban.
**citation** [sitasjɔ̃] nf (d'auteur) quotation ; (JUR) summons sg ; (MIL) récompense) mention.
**cité** [site] nf town ; (plus grande) city ; ~ **ouvrière** (workers') housing estate ; ~ **universitaire** students' residences pl.
**citer** [site] vt (un auteur) to quote (from) ; (nommer) to name ; (JUR) to summon.
**citerne** [sitɛʀn(ə)] nf tank.
**cithare** [sitaʀ] nf zither.
**citoyen, ne** [sitwajɛ̃, -ɛn] nm/f citizen ; **citoyenneté** nf citizenship.
**citron** [sitʀɔ̃] nm lemon ; ~ **vert** lime ; **citronnade** nf lemonade ; **citronnier** nm lemon tree.
**citrouille** [sitʀuj] nf pumpkin.
**civet** [sivɛ] nm stew ; ~ **de lièvre** jugged hare.

**civette** [sivɛt] *nf* (*BOT*) chives *pl*; (*ZOOL*) civet (cat).

**civière** [sivjɛʀ] *nf* stretcher.

**civil, e** [sivil] *a* (*JUR, ADMIN, poli*) civil; (*non militaire*) civilian // *nm* civilian; **en** ~ in civilian clothes; **dans le** ~ in civilian life.

**civilisation** [sivilizɑsjɔ̃] *nf* civilization.

**civiliser** [sivilize] *vt* to civilize.

**civique** [sivik] *a* civic.

**civisme** [sivism(ə)] *nm* public-spiritedness.

**claie** [klɛ] *nf* grid, riddle.

**clair, e** [klɛʀ] *a* light; (*chambre*) light, bright; (*eau, son, fig*) clear // *ad*: **voir** ~ to see clearly; **bleu** ~ light blue; **tirer qch au** ~ to clear sth up, clarify sth; **mettre au** ~ (*notes etc*) to tidy up; **le plus** ~ **de son temps/argent** the better part of his time/money; **en** ~ (*non codé*) in clear; ~ **de lune** *nm* moonlight; ~**ement** *ad* clearly.

**claire-voie** [klɛʀvwa]: **à** ~ *ad* letting the light through; openwork *cpd*.

**clairière** [klɛʀjɛʀ] *nf* clearing.

**clairon** [klɛʀɔ̃] *nm* bugle; **claironner** *vt* (*fig*) to trumpet, shout from the rooftops.

**clairsemé, e** [klɛʀsəme] *a* sparse.

**clairvoyant, e** [klɛʀvwajɑ̃, -ɑ̃t] *a* perceptive, clear-sighted.

**clameur** [klamœʀ] *nf* clamour.

**clandestin, e** [klɑ̃dɛstɛ̃, -in] *a* clandestine; (*POL*) underground, clandestine.

**clapier** [klapje] *nm* (rabbit) hutch.

**clapoter** [klapɔte] *vi* to lap; **clapotis** *nm* lap(ping).

**claquage** [klakaʒ] *nm* pulled *ou* strained muscle.

**claque** [klak] *nf* (*gifle*) slap.

**claquer** [klake] *vi* (*drapeau*) to flap; (*porte*) to bang, slam; (*coup de feu*) to ring out // *vt* (*porte*) to slam, bang; (*doigts*) to snap; **se** ~ **un muscle** to pull *ou* strain a muscle.

**claquettes** [klakɛt] *nfpl* tap-dancing *sg*.

**clarifier** [klaʀifje] *vt* (*fig*) to clarify.

**clarinette** [klaʀinɛt] *nf* clarinet.

**clarté** [klaʀte] *nf* lightness; brightness; (*d'un son, de l'eau*) clearness; (*d'une explication*) clarity.

**classe** [klɑs] *nf* class; (*SCOL: local*) class(room); (: *leçon*) class; (: *élèves*) class, form; ~ **touriste** economy class; **faire ses** ~**s** (*MIL*) to do one's (recruit's) training; **faire la** ~ (*SCOL*) to be a *ou* the teacher; to teach; **aller en** ~ to go to school.

**classement** [klɑsmɑ̃] *nm* classifying; filing; grading; closing; (*rang: SCOL*) place; (: *SPORT*) placing; (*liste: SCOL*) class list (in order of merit); (: *SPORT*) placings *pl*; **premier au** ~ **général** (*SPORT*) first overall.

**classer** [klɑse] *vt* (*idées, livres*) to classify; (*papiers*) to file; (*candidat, concurrent*) to grade; (*JUR: affaire*) to close; **se** ~ **premier/dernier** to come first/last; (*SPORT*) to finish first/last.

**classeur** [klɑsœʀ] *nm* (*cahier*) file; (*meuble*) filing cabinet.

**classification** [klasifikɑsjɔ̃] *nf* classification.

**classifier** [klɑsifje] *vt* to classify.

**classique** [klɑsik] *a* classical; (*sobre: coupe etc*) classic(al); (*habituel*) standard, classic // *nm* classic; classical author.

**claudication** [klodikɑsjɔ̃] *nf* limp.

**clause** [kloz] *nf* clause.

**claustrer** [klostʀe] *vt* to confine.

**claustrophobie** [klostʀɔfɔbi] *nf* claustrophobia.

**clavecin** [klavsɛ̃] *nm* harpsichord.

**clavicule** [klavikyl] *nf* clavicle, collarbone.

**clavier** [klavje] *nm* keyboard.

**clé** *ou* **clef** [kle] *nf* key; (*MUS*) clef; (*de mécanicien*) spanner // *a*: **problème** ~ key problem; ~ **de sol/de fa** treble/bass clef; ~ **anglaise** (monkey) wrench; ~ **de contact** ignition key; ~ **à molette** adjustable spanner; ~ **de voûte** keystone.

**clémence** [klemɑ̃s] *nf* mildness; leniency.

**clément, e** [klemɑ̃, -ɑ̃t] *a* (*temps*) mild; (*indulgent*) lenient.

**cleptomane** [klɛptɔman] *nm/f* = **kleptomane.**

**clerc** [klɛʀ] *nm*: ~ **de notaire** solicitor's clerk.

**clergé** [klɛʀʒe] *nm* clergy.

**clérical, e, aux** [kleʀikal, -o] *a* clerical.

**cliché** [kliʃe] *nm* (*PHOTO*) negative; print; (*TYPO*) (printing) plate; (*LING*) cliché.

**client, e** [klijɑ̃, -ɑ̃t] *nm/f* (*acheteur*) customer, client; (*d'hôtel*) guest, patron; (*du docteur*) patient; (*de l'avocat*) client; **clientèle** *nf* (*du magasin*) customers *pl*, clientèle; (*du docteur, de l'avocat*) practice; **accorder sa clientèle à** to give one's custom to.

**cligner** [kliɲe] *vi*: ~ **des yeux** to blink (one's eyes); ~ **de l'œil** to wink.

**clignotant** [kliɲɔtɑ̃] *nm* (*AUTO*) indicator.

**clignoter** [kliɲɔte] *vi* (*étoiles etc*) to twinkle; (*lumière: à intervalles réguliers*) to flash; (: *vaciller*) to flicker.

**climat** [klima] *nm* climate; **climatique** *a* climatic.

**climatisation** [klimatizɑsjɔ̃] *nf* air conditioning; **climatisé, e** *a* air-conditioned..

**clin d'œil** [klɛ̃dœj] *nm* wink; **en un** ~ in a flash.

**clinique** [klinik] *a* clinical // *nf* nursing home, (private) clinic.

**clinquant, e** [klɛ̃kɑ̃, -ɑ̃t] *a* flashy.

**cliqueter** [klikte] *vi* to clash; to jangle, jingle; to chink.

**clitoris** [klitɔʀis] *nm* clitoris.

**clivage** [klivaʒ] *nm* cleavage.

**clochard, e** [klɔʃaʀ, -aʀd(ə)] *nm/f* tramp.

**cloche** [klɔʃ] *nf* (*d'église*) bell; (*fam*) clot; ~ **à fromage** cheese-cover.

**cloche-pied** [klɔʃpje]: **à** ~ *ad* on one leg, hopping (along).

**clocher** [klɔʃe] *nm* church tower; (*en pointe*) steeple // *vi* (*fam*) to be *ou* go wrong; **de** ~ (*péj*) parochial.

**clocheton** [klɔʃtɔ̃] *nm* pinnacle.

**clochette** [klɔʃɛt] *nf* bell.

**cloison** [klwazɔ̃] *nf* partition (wall); **cloisonner** *vt* to partition (off); to divide up; (*fig*) to compartmentalize.

**cloître** [klwatʀ(ə)] *nm* cloister.
**cloîtrer** [klwatʀe] *vt*: **se** ~ to shut o.s. up *ou* away ; (*REL*) to enter a convent *ou* monastery.
**clopin-clopant** [klɔpɛ̃klɔpɑ̃] *ad* hobbling along ; (*fig*) so-so.
**cloporte** [klɔpɔʀt(ə)] *nm* woodlouse (*pl* lice).
**cloque** [klɔk] *nf* blister.
**clore** [klɔʀ] *vt* to close ; **clos, e** *a voir* **maison, huis, vase** // *nm* (enclosed) field.
**clôture** [klotyʀ] *nf* closure, closing ; (*barrière*) enclosure, fence ; **clôturer** *vt* (*terrain*) to enclose, close off ; (*festival, débats*) to close.
**clou** [klu] *nm* nail ; (*MÉD*) boil ; ~s *nmpl* = **passage clouté** ; **pneus à** ~s studded tyres ; **le** ~ **du spectacle** the highlight of the show ; ~ **de girofle** clove ; ~**er** *vt* to nail down *ou* up ; (*fig*): ~**er sur/contre** to pin to/against ; ~**té, e** *a* studded.
**clown** [klun] *nm* clown ; **faire le** ~ (*fig*) to clown (about), play the fool.
**club** [klœb] *nm* club.
**C.N.R.S.** *sigle m* = *Centre national de la recherche scientifique.*
**coaguler** [kɔagyle] *vi, vt*, **se** ~ to coagulate.
**coaliser** [kɔalize]: **se** ~ *vi* to unite, join forces.
**coalition** [kɔalisjɔ̃] *nf* coalition.
**coasser** [kɔase] *vi* to croak.
**cobaye** [kɔbaj] *nm* guinea-pig.
**cocagne** [kɔkaɲ] *nf*: **pays de** ~ land of plenty ; **mât de** ~ greasy pole (*fig*).
**cocaïne** [kɔkain] *nf* cocaine.
**cocarde** [kɔkaʀd(ə)] *nf* rosette.
**cocardier, ère** [kɔkaʀdje, -ɛʀ] *a* jingoistic, chauvinistic.
**cocasse** [kɔkas] *a* comical, funny.
**coccinelle** [kɔksinɛl] *nf* ladybird.
**coccyx** [kɔksis] *nm* coccyx.
**cocher** [kɔʃe] *nm* coachman // *vt* to tick off ; (*entailler*) to notch.
**cochère** [kɔʃɛʀ] *af*: **porte** ~ carriage entrance.
**cochon, ne** [kɔʃɔ̃, -ɔn] *nm* pig // *nm/f* (*péj*) (filthy) pig ; beast ; swine // *a* (*fam*) dirty, smutty ; **cochonnerie** *nf* (*fam*) filth ; rubbish, trash.
**cochonnet** [kɔʃɔnɛ] *nm* (*BOULES*) jack.
**cocktail** [kɔktɛl] *nm* cocktail ; (*réception*) cocktail party.
**coco** [kɔko] *nm voir* **noix** ; (*fam*) bloke, geezer.
**cocon** [kɔkɔ̃] *nm* cocoon.
**cocorico** [kɔkɔʀiko] *excl, nm* cock-a-doodle-do.
**cocotier** [kɔkɔtje] *nm* coconut palm.
**cocotte** [kɔkɔt] *nf* (*en fonte*) casserole ; ~ **(minute)** pressure cooker ; ~ **en papier** paper shape ; **ma** ~ (*fam*) sweetie (pie).
**cocu** [kɔky] *nm* cuckold.
**code** [kɔd] *nm* code // *a*: **éclairage** ~, **phares** ~ dipped lights ; **se mettre en** ~(**s**) to dip one's (head)lights ; ~ **civil** Common Law ; ~ **pénal** penal code ; ~ **postal** (*numéro*) postal code ; ~ **de la route** highway code ; **coder** *vt* to (en)code ; **codifier** *vt* to codify.

**coefficient** [kɔefisjɑ̃] *nm* coefficient.
**coercition** [kɔɛʀsisjɔ̃] *nf* coercion.
**cœur** [kœʀ] *nm* heart ; (*CARTES: couleur*) hearts *pl* ; (*: carte*) heart ; **avoir bon** ~ to be kind-hearted ; **avoir mal au** ~ to feel sick ; ~ **de laitue/d'artichaut** lettuce/artichoke heart ; **de tout son** ~ with all one's heart ; **en avoir le** ~ **net** to be clear in one's own mind (about it) ; **par** ~ by heart ; **de bon** ~ willingly ; **avoir à** ~ **de faire** to make a point of doing ; **cela lui tient à** ~ that's (very) close to his heart.
**coffrage** [kɔfʀaʒ] *nm* (*CONSTR: action*) coffering ; (: *dispositif*) form(work).
**coffre** [kɔfʀ(ə)] *nm* (*meuble*) chest ; (*d'auto*) boot ; **avoir du** ~ (*fam*) to have a lot of puff ; ~(**-fort**) *nm* safe.
**coffrer** [kɔfʀe] *vt* (*fam*) to put inside, lock up.
**coffret** [kɔfʀɛ] *nm* casket ; ~ **à bijoux** jewel box.
**cogner** [kɔɲe] *vi* to knock.
**cohabiter** [kɔabite] *vi* to live together.
**cohérent, e** [kɔeʀɑ̃, -ɑ̃t] *a* coherent, consistent.
**cohésion** [kɔezjɔ̃] *nf* cohesion.
**cohorte** [kɔɔʀt(ə)] *nf* troop.
**cohue** [kɔy] *nf* crowd.
**coi, coite** [kwa, kwat] *a*: **rester** ~ to remain silent.
**coiffe** [kwaf] *nf* headdress.
**coiffé, e** [kwafe] *a*: **bien/mal** ~ with tidy/untidy hair ; ~ **d'un béret** wearing a beret ; ~ **en arrière** with one's hair brushed *ou* combed back.
**coiffer** [kwafe] *vt* (*fig*) to cover, top ; ~ **qn** to do sb's hair ; ~ **qn d'un béret** to put a beret on sb ; **se** ~ to do one's hair ; to put on a *ou* one's hat.
**coiffeur, euse** [kwafœʀ, -øz] *nm/f* hairdresser // *nf* (*table*) dressing table.
**coiffure** [kwafyʀ] *nf* (*cheveux*) hairstyle, hairdo ; (*chapeau*) hat, headgear *q* ; (*art*): **la** ~ hairdressing.
**coin** [kwɛ̃] *nm* corner ; (*pour graver*) die ; (*pour coincer*) wedge ; (*poinçon*) hallmark ; **l'épicerie du** ~ the local grocer ; **dans le** ~ (*les alentours*) in the area, around about ; locally ; **au** ~ **du feu** by the fireside ; **regard en** ~ side(ways) glance.
**coincer** [kwɛ̃se] *vt* to jam ; (*fam*) to catch (out) ; to nab.
**coïncidence** [kɔɛ̃sidɑ̃s] *nf* coincidence.
**coïncider** [kɔɛ̃side] *vi*: ~ **(avec)** to coincide (with).
**coing** [kwɛ̃] *nm* quince.
**coït** [kɔit] *nm* coitus.
**coite** [kwat] *af voir* **coi**.
**coke** [kɔk] *nm* coke.
**col** [kɔl] *nm* (*de chemise*) collar ; (*encolure, cou*) neck ; (*de montagne*) pass ; ~ **du fémur** neck of the thighbone ; ~ **roulé** polo-neck ; ~ **de l'utérus** cervix.
**coléoptère** [kɔleɔptɛʀ] *nm* beetle.
**colère** [kɔlɛʀ] *nf* anger ; **une** ~ a fit of anger ; **coléreux, euse** *a*, **colérique** *a* quick-tempered, irascible.
**colifichet** [kɔlifiʃɛ] *nm* trinket.
**colimaçon** [kɔlimasɔ̃] *nm*: **escalier en** ~ spiral staircase.

**colin** [kɔlɛ̃] *nm* hake.

**colique** [kɔlik] *nf* diarrhoea ; colic (pains).

**colis** [kɔli] *nm* parcel.

**collaborateur, trice** [kɔlabɔRatœR, -tRis] *nm/f (aussi POL)* collaborator ; *(d'une revue)* contributor.

**collaboration** [kɔlabɔRɑsjɔ̃] *nf* collaboration.

**collaborer** [kɔlabɔRe] *vi* to collaborate ; ~ **à** to collaborate on ; *(revue)* to contribute to.

**collant, e** [kɔlɑ̃, -ɑ̃t] *a* sticky ; *(robe etc)* clinging, skintight ; *(péj)* clinging // *nm (bas)* tights *pl* ; *(de danseur)* leotard.

**collation** [kɔlɑsjɔ̃] *nf* light meal.

**colle** [kɔl] *nf* glue ; *(à papiers peints)* (wallpaper) paste ; *(devinette)* teaser, poser.

**collecte** [kɔlɛkt(ə)] *nf* collection.

**collecter** [kɔlɛkte] *vt* to collect ; **collecteur** *nm (égout)* main sewer.

**collectif, ive** [kɔlɛktif, -iv] *a* collective ; *(visite, billet etc)* group *cpd*.

**collection** [kɔlɛksjɔ̃] *nf* collection ; *(ÉDITION)* series ; **pièce de** ~ collector's item ; **faire (la)** ~ **de** to collect ; **collectionner** *vt (tableaux, timbres)* to collect ; **collectionneur, euse** *nm/f* collector.

**collectivité** [kɔlɛktivite] *nf* group ; **la** ~ the community, the collectivity ; **les** ~**s locales** local communities.

**collège** [kɔlɛʒ] *nm (école)* (secondary) school ; *(assemblée)* body ; **collégial, e, aux** *a* collegiate ; **collégien, ne** *nm/f* schoolboy/girl.

**collègue** [kɔlɛg] *nm/f* colleague.

**coller** [kɔle] *vt (papier, timbre)* to stick (on) ; *(affiche)* to stick up ; *(enveloppe)* to stick down ; *(morceaux)* to stick *ou* glue together ; *(fam: mettre, fourrer)* to stick, shove ; *(SCOL: fam)* to keep in, give detention to // *vi (être collant)* to be sticky ; *(adhérer)* to stick ; ~ **qch sur** to stick *(ou* paste *ou* glue) sth on(to) ; ~ **à** to stick to ; *(fig)* to cling to.

**collerette** [kɔlRɛt] *nf* ruff ; *(TECH)* flange.

**collet** [kɔlɛ] *nm (piège)* snare, noose ; *(cou):* **prendre qn au** ~ to grab sb by the throat ; ~ **monté** *a inv* straight-laced.

**collier** [kɔlje] *nm (bijou)* necklace ; *(de chien, TECH)* collar ; ~ **(de barbe), barbe en** ~ narrow beard along the line of the jaw.

**colline** [kɔlin] *nf* hill.

**collision** [kɔlizjɔ̃] *nf* collision, crash ; **entrer en** ~ **(avec)** to collide (with).

**colloque** [kɔlɔk] *nm* colloquium, symposium.

**colmater** [kɔlmate] *vt (fuite)* to seal off ; *(brèche)* to plug, fill in.

**colombe** [kɔlɔ̃b] *nf* dove.

**colon** [kɔlɔ̃] *nm* settler ; *(enfant)* boarder *(in children's holiday camp).*

**côlon** [kolɔ̃] *nm* colon.

**colonel** [kɔlɔnɛl] *nm* colonel ; *(armée de l'air)* group captain.

**colonial, e, aux** [kɔlɔnjal, -o] *a* colonial ; ~**isme** *nm* colonialism.

**colonie** [kɔlɔni] *nf* colony ; ~ **(de vacances)** holiday camp *(for children).*

**colonisation** [kɔlɔnizɑsjɔ̃] *nf* colonization.

**coloniser** [kɔlɔnize] *vt* to colonize.

**colonne** [kɔlɔn] *nf* column ; **se mettre en** ~ **par deux/quatre** to get into twos/fours ; **en** ~ **par deux** in double file ; ~ **de secours** rescue party ; ~ **(vertébrale)** spine, spinal column.

**colophane** [kɔlɔfan] *nf* rosin.

**colorant** [kɔlɔRɑ̃] *nm* colouring.

**coloration** [kɔlɔRɑsjɔ̃] *nf* colour(ing).

**colorer** [kɔlɔRe] *vt* to colour.

**colorier** [kɔlɔRje] *vt* to colour (in) ; **album à** ~ colouring book.

**coloris** [kɔlɔRi] *nm* colour, shade.

**colossal, e, aux** [kɔlɔsal, -o] *a* colossal, huge.

**colporter** [kɔlpɔRte] *vt* to hawk, peddle ; **colporteur, euse** *nm/f* hawker, pedlar.

**colza** [kɔlza] *nm* rape(seed).

**coma** [kɔma] *nm* coma ; **être dans le** ~ to be in a coma ; ~**teux, euse** *a* comatose.

**combat** [kɔ̃ba] *nm* fight ; fighting *q* ; ~ **de boxe** boxing match ; ~ **de rues** street fighting *q*.

**combatif, ive** [kɔ̃batif, -iv] *a* of a fighting spirit.

**combattant** [kɔ̃batɑ̃] *nm* combatant ; *(d'une rixe)* brawler ; **ancien** ~ war veteran.

**combattre** [kɔ̃batR(ə)] *vt* to fight ; *(épidémie, ignorance)* to combat, fight against.

**combien** [kɔ̃bjɛ̃] *ad (quantité)* how much ; *(nombre)* how many ; *(exclamatif)* how ; ~ **de** how much ; how many ; ~ **de temps** how long, how much time ; ~ **coûte/pèse ceci?** how much does this cost/weigh?

**combinaison** [kɔ̃binɛzɔ̃] *nf* combination ; *(astuce)* device, scheme ; *(de femme)* slip ; *(d'aviateur)* flying suit ; *(d'homme-grenouille)* wetsuit ; *(bleu de travail)* boilersuit.

**combine** [kɔ̃bin] *nf* trick ; *(péj)* scheme, fiddle.

**combiné** [kɔ̃bine] *nm (aussi:* ~ **téléphonique)** receiver.

**combiner** [kɔ̃bine] *vt* to combine ; *(plan, horaire)* to work out, devise.

**comble** [kɔ̃bl(ə)] *a (salle)* packed (full) // *nm (du bonheur, plaisir)* height ; ~**s** *nmpl (CONSTR)* attic *sg*, loft *sg* ; **c'est le** ~**!** that beats everything!, that takes the biscuit!

**combler** [kɔ̃ble] *vt (trou)* to fill in ; *(besoin, lacune)* to fill ; *(déficit)* to make good ; *(satisfaire)* to gratify, fulfil ; ~ **qn de joie** to fill sb with joy ; ~ **qn d'honneurs** to shower sb with honours.

**combustible** [kɔ̃bystibl(ə)] *a* combustible // *nm* fuel.

**combustion** [kɔ̃bystjɔ̃] *nf* combustion.

**comédie** [kɔmedi] *nf* comedy ; *(fig)* playacting *q* ; ~ **musicale** musical ; **comédien, ne** *nm/f* actor/actress ; *(comique)* comedy actor/actress, comedian/comedienne ; *(fig)* sham.

**comestible** [kɔmɛstibl(ə)] *a* edible.

**comète** [kɔmɛt] *nf* comet.

**comique** [kɔmik] *a (drôle)* comical ; *(THÉÂTRE)* comic // *nm (artiste)* comic,

comedian; **le ~ de qch** the funny *ou* comical side of sth.
**comité** [kɔmite] *nm* committee; **~ d'entreprise** work's council.
**commandant** [kɔmãdã] *nm* (*gén*) commander, commandant; (*MIL*: *grade*) major; (*armée de l'air*) squadron leader; (*NAVIG*, *AVIAT*) captain.
**commande** [kɔmãd] *nf* (*COMM*) order; **~s** *nfpl* (*AVIAT etc*) controls; **passer une ~ (de)** to put in an order (for); **sur ~** to order; **~ à distance** remote control.
**commandement** [kɔmãdmã] *nm* command; (*ordre*) command, order; (*REL*) commandment.
**commander** [kɔmãde] *vt* (*COMM*) to order; (*diriger, ordonner*) to command; **~ à** (*MIL*) to command; (*contrôler, maîtriser*) to have control over; **~ à qn de faire** to command *ou* order sb to do.
**commanditaire** [kɔmãditɛR] *nm* sleeping partner.
**commandite** [kɔmãdit] *nf*: (**société en**) **~** limited partnership.
**commando** [kɔmãdo] *nm* commando (squad).
**comme** [kɔm] *prép* like; (*en tant que*) as // *cj* as; (*parce que, puisque*) as, since // *ad*: **~ il est fort/c'est bon!** how strong he is/good it is!; **faites-le ~ cela** *ou* **ça** do it like this *ou* this way; **~ ci ~ ça** so-so, middling; **joli ~ tout** ever so pretty.
**commémoration** [kɔmemɔRasjɔ̃] *nf* commemoration.
**commémorer** [kɔmemɔRe] *vt* to commemorate.
**commencement** [kɔmãsmã] *nm* beginning; start; commencement; **~s** (*débuts*) beginnings.
**commencer** [kɔmãse] *vt* to begin, start, commence; (*être placé au début de*) to begin // *vi* to begin, start, commence; **~ à** *ou* **de faire** to begin *ou* start doing.
**commensal, e, aux** [kɔmãsal, -o] *nm/f* companion at table.
**comment** [kɔmã] *ad* how; **~?** (*que dites-vous*) (I beg your) pardon?
**commentaire** [kɔmãtɛR] *nm* comment; remark; **~ (de texte)** (*SCOL*) commentary.
**commentateur, trice** [kɔmãtatœR, -tRis] *nm/f* commentator.
**commenter** [kɔmãte] *vt* (*jugement, événement*) to comment (up)on; (*RADIO, TV*: *match, manifestation*) to cover, give a commentary on.
**commérages** [kɔmeRaʒ] *nmpl* gossip *sg*.
**commerçant, e** [kɔmɛRsã, -ãt] *a* commercial; shopping; trading; commercially shrewd // *nm/f* shopkeeper, trader.
**commerce** [kɔmɛRs(ə)] *nm* (*activité*) trade, commerce; (*boutique*) business; **le petit ~** small shopowners *pl*, small traders *pl*; **faire ~ de** to trade in; (*fig*: *péj*) to trade on; **vendu dans le ~** sold in the shops; **vendu hors-~** sold directly to the public; **commercial, e, aux** *a* commercial, trading; (*péj*) commercial; **commercialiser** *vt* to market.
**commère** [kɔmɛR] *nf* gossip.
**commettre** [kɔmɛtR(ə)] *vt* to commit.

**commis** [kɔmi] *nm* (*de magasin*) (shop) assistant; (*de banque*) clerk; **~ voyageur** commercial traveller.
**commisération** [kɔmizeRasjɔ̃] *nf* commiseration.
**commissaire** [kɔmisɛR] *nm* (*de police*) ≈ (police) superintendent; (*de rencontre sportive etc*) steward; **~-priseur** *nm* auctioneer.
**commissariat** [kɔmisaRja] *nm* police station; (*ADMIN*) commissionership.
**commission** [kɔmisjɔ̃] *nf* (*comité, pourcentage*) commission; (*message*) message; (*course*) errand; **~s** *nfpl* (*achats*) shopping *sg*; **commissionnaire** *nm* delivery boy (*ou* man); messenger.
**commissure** [kɔmisyR] *nf*: **les ~s des lèvres** the corners of the mouth.
**commode** [kɔmɔd] *a* (*pratique*) convenient, handy; (*facile*) easy; (*air, personne*) easy-going; (*personne*): **pas ~** awkward (to deal with) // *nf* chest of drawers; **commodité** *nf* convenience.
**commotion** [kɔmosjɔ̃] *nf*: **~ (cérébrale)** concussion; **commotionné, e** *a* shocked, shaken.
**commuer** [kɔmɥe] *vt* to commute.
**commun, e** [kɔmœ̃, -yn] *a* common; (*pièce*) communal, shared; (*réunion, effort*) joint // *nf* (*ADMIN*) commune, ≈ district; (: *urbaine*) ≈ borough; **~s** *nmpl* (*bâtiments*) outbuildings; **cela sort du ~** it's out of the ordinary; **le ~ des mortels** the common run of people; **en ~ (faire)** jointly; **mettre en ~** to pool, share; **communal, e, aux** *a* (*ADMIN*) of the commune, ≈ (district *ou* borough) council *cpd*.
**communauté** [kɔmynote] *nf* community; (*JUR*): **régime de la ~** communal estate settlement.
**commune** [kɔmyn] *a, nf voir* **commun**.
**communiant, e** [kɔmynjã, -ãt] *nm/f* communicant; **premier ~** child taking his first communion.
**communicatif, ive** [kɔmynikatif, -iv] *a* (*personne*) communicative; (*rire*) infectious.
**communication** [kɔmynikasjɔ̃] *nf* communication; **~ (téléphonique)** (telephone) call; **vous avez la ~** this is your call, you're through; **donnez-moi la ~ avec** put me through to; **~ interurbaine** trunk call; **~ en PCV** reverse charge call.
**communier** [kɔmynje] *vi* (*REL*) to receive communion; (*fig*) to be united.
**communion** [kɔmynjɔ̃] *nf* communion.
**communiqué** [kɔmynike] *nm* communiqué.
**communiquer** [kɔmynike] *vt* (*nouvelle, dossier*) to pass on, convey; (*maladie*) to pass on; (*peur etc*) to communicate; (*chaleur, mouvement*) to transmit // *vi* to communicate; **se ~ à** (*se propager*) to spread to.
**communisme** [kɔmynism(ə)] *nm* communism; **communiste** *a, nm/f* communist.
**commutateur** [kɔmytatœR] *nm* (*ÉLEC*) (change-over) switch, commutator.

**compact, e** [kɔ̃pakt] *a* dense ; compact.
**compagne** [kɔ̃paɲ] *nf* companion.
**compagnie** [kɔ̃paɲi] *nf* (*firme*, MIL) company ; (*groupe*) gathering ; (*présence*): **la ~ de qn** sb's company ; **tenir ~ à qn** to keep sb company ; **fausser ~ à** to give sb the slip, slip *ou* sneak away from sb ; **en ~ de** in the company of ; **Dupont et ~, Dupont et Cie** Dupont and Company, Dupont and Co.
**compagnon** [kɔ̃paɲɔ̃] *nm* companion ; (*autrefois: ouvrier*) craftsman ; journeyman.
**comparable** [kɔ̃paʀabl(ə)] *a*: **~ (à)** comparable (to).
**comparaison** [kɔ̃paʀɛzɔ̃] *nf* comparison ; (*métaphore*) simile.
**comparaître** [kɔ̃paʀɛtʀ(ə)] *vi*: **~ (devant)** to appear (before).
**comparatif, ive** [kɔ̃paʀatif, -iv] *a* comparative.
**comparé, e** [kɔ̃paʀe] *a*: **littérature** *etc* **~e** comparative literature *etc*.
**comparer** [kɔ̃paʀe] *vt* to compare ; **~ qch/qn à** *ou* **et** (*pour choisir*) to compare sth/sb with *ou* and ; (*pour établir une similitude*) to compare sth/sb to.
**comparse** [kɔ̃paʀs(ə)] *nm/f* (*péj*) associate, stooge.
**compartiment** [kɔ̃paʀtimɑ̃] *nm* compartment ; **compartimenté, e** *a* partitioned ; (*fig*) compartmentalized.
**comparution** [kɔ̃paʀysjɔ̃] *nf* appearance.
**compas** [kɔ̃pa] *nm* (GÉOM) (pair of) compasses *pl* ; (NAVIG) compass.
**compassé, e** [kɔ̃pase] *a* starchy, formal.
**compassion** [kɔ̃pasjɔ̃] *nf* compassion.
**compatible** [kɔ̃patibl(ə)] *a* compatible.
**compatir** [kɔ̃patiʀ] *vi*: **~ (à)** to sympathize (with).
**compatriote** [kɔ̃patʀijɔt] *nm/f* compatriot.
**compensation** [kɔ̃pɑ̃sasjɔ̃] *nf* compensation ; (BANQUE) clearing.
**compenser** [kɔ̃pɑ̃se] *vt* to compensate for, make up for.
**compère** [kɔ̃pɛʀ] *nm* accomplice.
**compétence** [kɔ̃petɑ̃s] *nf* competence.
**compétent, e** [kɔ̃petɑ̃, -ɑ̃t] *a* (*apte*) competent, capable ; (JUR) competent.
**compétition** [kɔ̃petisjɔ̃] *nf* (*gén*) competition ; (SPORT: *épreuve*) event ; **la ~ competitive sport** ; **la ~ automobile** motor racing.
**compiler** [kɔ̃pile] *vt* to compile.
**complainte** [kɔ̃plɛ̃t] *nf* lament.
**complaire** [kɔ̃plɛʀ]: **se ~** *vi*: **se ~ dans/parmi** to take pleasure in/in being among.
**complaisance** [kɔ̃plɛzɑ̃s] *nf* kindness ; (*péj*) indulgence ; **attestation de ~** *certificate produced to oblige a patient etc* ; **pavillon de ~** flag of convenience.
**complaisant, e** [kɔ̃plɛzɑ̃, -ɑ̃t] *a* (*aimable*) kind ; obliging ; (*péj*) over-obliging, indulgent.
**complément** [kɔ̃plemɑ̃] *nm* complement ; supplement ; remainder ; (LING) complement ; **~ d'information** (ADMIN) supplementary *ou* further information ; **~ d'agent** agent ; **~ (d'objet) direct/indirect** direct/indirect object ; **~**

(*circonstanciel*) **de lieu/temps** adverbial phrase of place/time ; **~ de nom** possessive phrase ; **complémentaire** *a* complementary ; (*additionnel*) supplementary.
**complet, ète** [kɔ̃plɛ, -ɛt] *a* complete ; (*plein: hôtel etc*) full // *nm* (*aussi*: **~-veston**) suit ; **compléter** *vt* (*porter à la quantité voulue*) to complete ; (*augmenter*) to complement, supplement ; to add to ; **se compléter** *vt réciproque* (*personnes*) to complement one another // *vi* (*collection etc*) to be building up.
**complexe** [kɔ̃plɛks(ə)] *a* complex // *nm* (PSYCH) complex, hang-up ; (*bâtiments*): **~ hospitalier** hospital complex ; **complexé, e** *a* mixed-up, hung-up ; **complexité** *nf* complexity.
**complication** [kɔ̃plikasjɔ̃] *nf* complexity, intricacy ; (*difficulté, ennui*) complication.
**complice** [kɔ̃plis] *nm* accomplice ; **complicité** *nf* complicity.
**compliment** [kɔ̃plimɑ̃] *nm* (*louange*) compliment ; **~s** *nmpl* (*félicitations*) congratulations ; **complimenter qn (sur** *ou* **de)** to congratulate *ou* compliment sb (on).
**compliqué, e** [kɔ̃plike] *a* complicated, complex, intricate ; (*personne*) complicated.
**compliquer** [kɔ̃plike] *vt* to complicate ; **se ~** *vi* (*situation*) to become complicated ; **se ~ la vie** to make life difficult *ou* complicated for o.s.
**complot** [kɔ̃plo] *nm* plot ; **comploter** *vi*, *vt* to plot.
**comportement** [kɔ̃pɔʀtəmɑ̃] *nm* behaviour ; (TECH: *d'une pièce, d'un véhicule*) behaviour, performance.
**comporter** [kɔ̃pɔʀte] *vt* to be composed of, consist of, comprise ; (*être équipé de*) to have ; (*impliquer*) to entail, involve ; **se ~** *vi* to behave ; (TECH) to behave, perform.
**composant** [kɔ̃pozɑ̃] *nm* component, constituent.
**composante** [kɔ̃pozɑ̃t] *nf* component.
**composé, e** [kɔ̃poze] *a* (*visage, air*) studied ; (BIO, CHIMIE, LING) compound // *nm* (CHIMIE, LING) compound.
**composer** [kɔ̃poze] *vt* (*musique, texte*) to compose ; (*mélange, équipe*) to make up ; (*faire partie de*) to make up, form ; (TYPO) to set // *vi* (SCOL) to sit *ou* do a test ; (*transiger*) to come to terms ; **se ~ de** to be composed of, be made up of ; **~ un numéro** (*au téléphone*) to dial a number.
**composite** [kɔ̃pozit] *a* heterogeneous.
**compositeur, trice** [kɔ̃pozitœʀ, -tʀis] *nm/f* (MUS) composer ; (TYPO) compositor, typesetter.
**composition** [kɔ̃pozisjɔ̃] *nf* composition ; (SCOL) test ; (TYPO) typesetting, composition ; **de bonne ~** (*accommodant*) easy to deal with ; **amener qn à ~** to get sb to come to terms.
**composter** [kɔ̃pɔste] *vt* to date stamp ; to punch ; **composteur** *nm* date stamp ; punch ; (TYPO) composing stick.
**compote** [kɔ̃pɔt] *nf* stewed fruit *q* ; **~ de pommes** stewed apples ; **compotier** *nm* fruit dish *ou* bowl.
**compréhensible** [kɔ̃pʀeɑ̃sibl(ə)] *a* comprehensible ; (*attitude*) understandable.

**compréhensif, ive** [kɔ̃pReɑ̃sif, -iv] *a* understanding.

**compréhension** [kɔ̃pReɑ̃sjɔ̃] *nf* understanding ; comprehension.

**comprendre** [kɔ̃pRɑ̃dR(ə)] *vt* to understand ; (*se composer de*) to comprise, consist of.

**compresse** [kɔ̃pRɛs] *nf* compress.

**compresseur** [kɔ̃pRɛsœR] *am voir* **rouleau.**

**compression** [kɔ̃pRɛsjɔ̃] *nf* compression ; reduction.

**comprimé, e** [kɔ̃pRime] *a:* **air** ~ compressed air // *nm* tablet.

**comprimer** [kɔ̃pRime] *vt* to compress ; (*fig: crédit etc*) to reduce, cut down.

**compris, e** [kɔ̃pRi, -iz] *pp de* **comprendre** // *a* (*inclus*) included ; ~ **entre** (*situé*) contained between ; **la maison** ~**e**/**non** ~**e, y/non** ~ **la maison** including/excluding the house ; **service** ~ service (charge) included ; **100 F tout** ~ 100 F all inclusive *ou* all-in.

**compromettre** [kɔ̃pRɔmɛtR(ə)] *vt* to compromise.

**compromis** [kɔ̃pRɔmi] *nm* compromise.

**compromission** [kɔ̃pRɔmisjɔ̃] *nf* compromise, deal.

**comptabilité** [kɔ̃tabilite] *nf* (*activité, technique*) accounting, accountancy ; (*d'une société: comptes*) accounts *pl*, books *pl* ; (: *service*) accounts office *ou* department.

**comptable** [kɔ̃tabl(ə)] *nm/f* accountant // *a* accounts *cpd*, accounting.

**comptant** [kɔ̃tɑ̃] *ad:* **payer** ~ to pay cash ; **acheter** ~ to buy for cash.

**compte** [kɔ̃t] *nm* count, counting ; (*total, montant*) count, (right) number ; (*bancaire, facture*) account ; ~**s** *nmpl* accounts, books ; (*fig*) explanation *sg* ; **faire le** ~ **de** to count up, make a count of ; **en fin de** ~ (*fig*) all things considered, weighing it all up ; **à bon** ~ at a favourable price ; (*fig*) lightly ; **avoir son** ~ (*fig: fam*) to have had it ; **pour le** ~ **de** on behalf of ; **travailler à son** ~ to work for oneself ; **rendre** ~ (**à qn**) **de qch** to give (sb) an account of sth ; ~ **chèques postaux** (**C.C.P.**) ≈ (Post Office) Giro account ; ~ **courant** current account ; ~ **de dépôt** deposit account ; ~ **à rebours** countdown.

**compte-gouttes** [kɔ̃tgut] *nm inv* dropper.

**compter** [kɔ̃te] *vt* to count ; (*facturer*) to charge for ; (*avoir à son actif, comporter*) to have ; (*prévoir*) to allow, reckon ; (*espérer*): ~ **réussir/revenir** to expect to succeed/return // *vi* to count ; (*être économe*) to economize ; (*être non négligeable*) to count, matter ; (*valoir*): ~ **pour** to count for ; (*figurer*): ~ **parmi** to be *ou* rank among ; ~ **sur** *vt* to count (up)on ; ~ **avec qch/qn** to reckon with *ou* take account of sth/sb ; **sans** ~ **que** besides which ; **à** ~ **du 10 janvier** (*COMM*) (as) from 10th January.

**compte-rendu** [kɔ̃tRɑ̃dy] *nm* account, report ; (*de film, livre*) review.

**compte-tours** [kɔ̃ttuR] *nm inv* rev(olution) counter.

**compteur** [kɔ̃tœR] *nm* meter ; ~ **de vitesse** speedometer.

**comptine** [kɔ̃tin] *nf* nursery rhyme.

**comptoir** [kɔ̃twaR] *nm* (*de magasin*) counter ; (*de café*) counter, bar ; (*colonial*) trading post.

**compulser** [kɔ̃pylse] *vt* to consult.

**comte, comtesse** [kɔ̃t, kɔ̃tɛs] *nm/f* count/countess.

**con, ne** [kɔ̃, kɔn] *a* (*fam!*) bloody stupid (!).

**concave** [kɔ̃kav] *a* concave.

**concéder** [kɔ̃sede] *vt* to grant ; (*défaite, point*) to concede ; ~ **que** to concede that.

**concentration** [kɔ̃sɑ̃tRɑsjɔ̃] *nf* concentration.

**concentrationnaire** [kɔ̃sɑ̃tRɑsjɔnɛR] *a* of *ou* in concentration camps.

**concentré** [kɔ̃sɑ̃tRe] *nm* concentrate.

**concentrer** [kɔ̃sɑ̃tRe] *vt* to concentrate ; **se** ~ to concentrate.

**concentrique** [kɔ̃sɑ̃tRik] *a* concentric.

**concept** [kɔ̃sɛpt] *nm* concept.

**conception** [kɔ̃sɛpsjɔ̃] *nf* conception.

**concerner** [kɔ̃sɛRne] *vt* to concern ; **en ce qui me concerne** as far as I am concerned ; **en ce qui concerne ceci** as far as this is concerned, with regard to this.

**concert** [kɔ̃sɛR] *nm* concert ; **de** ~ *ad* in unison ; together.

**concerter** [kɔ̃sɛRte] *vt* to devise ; **se** ~ (*collaborateurs etc*) to put one's heads together, consult (each other).

**concertiste** [kɔ̃sɛRtist(ə)] *nm/f* concert artist.

**concerto** [kɔ̃sɛRto] *nm* concerto.

**concession** [kɔ̃sesjɔ̃] *nf* concession.

**concessionnaire** [kɔ̃sesjɔnɛR] *nm/f* agent, dealer.

**concevoir** [kɔ̃svwaR] *vt* (*idée, projet*) to conceive (of) ; (*méthode, plan d'appartement, décoration etc*) to plan, devise ; (*enfant*) to conceive ; **appartement bien/mal conçu** well-/badly-designed *ou* -planned flat.

**concierge** [kɔ̃sjɛRʒ(ə)] *nm/f* caretaker.

**concile** [kɔ̃sil] *nm* council, synod.

**conciliabules** [kɔ̃siljabyl] *nmpl* (private) discussions, confabulations.

**conciliation** [kɔ̃siljɑsjɔ̃] *nf* conciliation.

**concilier** [kɔ̃silje] *vt* to reconcile ; **se** ~ **qn/l'appui de qn** to win sb over/sb's support.

**concis, e** [kɔ̃si, -iz] *a* concise ; **concision** *nf* concision, conciseness.

**concitoyen, ne** [kɔ̃sitwajɛ̃, -jɛn] *nm/f* fellow citizen.

**conclave** [kɔ̃klav] *nm* conclave.

**concluant, e** [kɔ̃klyɑ̃, -ɑ̃t] *a* conclusive.

**conclure** [kɔ̃klyR] *vt* to conclude ; ~ **à l'acquittement** to decide in favour of an acquittal ; ~ **au suicide** to come to the conclusion (*ou JUR*) to pronounce) that it is *a* case of suicide.

**conclusion** [kɔ̃klyzjɔ̃] *nf* conclusion ; ~**s** *nfpl* (*JUR*) submissions ; findings.

**conçois** *etc vb voir* **concevoir.**

**concombre** [kɔ̃kɔ̃bR(ə)] *nm* cucumber.

**concordance** [kɔ̃kɔRdɑ̃s] *nf* concordance ; **la** ~ **des temps** (*LING*) the sequence of tenses.

**concorde** [kɔ̃kɔRd(ə)] *nf* concord.

**concorder** [kɔkɔrde] *vi* to tally, agree.
**concourir** [kɔkuRiR] *vi* (*SPORT*) to compete ; ~ **à** *vt* (*effet etc*) to work towards.
**concours** [kɔkuR] *nm* competition ; (*SCOL*) competitive examination ; (*assistance*) aid, help ; **recrutement par voie de** ~ recruitment by (competitive) examination ; ~ **de circonstances** combination of circumstances ; ~ **hippique** horse show.
**concret, ète** [kɔkRɛ, -ɛt] *a* concrete.
**concrétiser** [kɔkRetize] *vt* (*plan, projet*) to put in concrete form ; **se** ~ *vi* to materialize.
**conçu, e** [kɔsy] *pp de* **concevoir**.
**concubinage** [kɔkybinaʒ] *nm* (*JUR*) cohabitation.
**concupiscence** [kɔkypisɑs] *nf* concupiscence.
**concurremment** [kɔkyRamɑ] *ad* concurrently ; jointly.
**concurrence** [kɔkyRɑs] *nf* competition ; **jusqu'à** ~ **de** up to ; ~ **déloyale** unfair competition.
**concurrent, e** [kɔkyRɑ, -ɑt] *a* competing // *nm/f* (*SPORT, ÉCON etc*) competitor ; (*SCOL*) candidate.
**condamnation** [kɔdanasjɔ] *nf* condemnation ; sentencing ; sentence ; conviction ; ~ **à mort** death sentence.
**condamner** [kɔdane] *vt* (*blâmer*) to condemn ; (*JUR*) to sentence ; (*porte, ouverture*) to fill in, block up ; (*obliger*): ~ **qn à qch/faire** to condemn sb to sth/to do ; ~ **qn à 2 ans de prison** to sentence sb to 2 years' imprisonment ; ~ **qn à une amende** to impose a fine on sb, request sb to pay a fine.
**condensateur** [kɔdɑsatœR] *nm* condenser.
**condensation** [kɔdɑsasjɔ] *nf* condensation.
**condensé** [kɔdɑse] *nm* digest.
**condenser** [kɔdɑse] *vt*, **se** ~ *vi* to condense.
**condescendre** [kɔdesɑdR(ə)] *vi*: ~ **à** to condescend to.
**condiment** [kɔdimɑ] *nm* condiment.
**condisciple** [kɔdisipl(ə)] *nm/f* school fellow, fellow student.
**condition** [kɔdisjɔ] *nf* condition ; ~**s** *nfpl* (*tarif, prix*) terms ; (*circonstances*) conditions ; **sans** ~ *a* unconditional // *ad* unconditionally ; **sous** ~ **que** on condition that ; **à** ~ **de/que** provided that ; **conditionnel, le** *a* conditional // *nm* conditional (tense) ; **conditionner** *vt* (*déterminer*) to determine ; (*COMM: produit*) to package ; (*fig: personne*) to condition ; **air conditionné** air conditioning ; **réflexe conditionné** conditioned reflex.
**condoléances** [kɔdɔleɑs] *nfpl* condolences.
**conducteur, trice** [kɔdyktœR, -tRis] *a* (*ÉLEC*) conducting // *nm/f* driver // *nm* (*ÉLEC etc*) conductor.
**conduire** [kɔdɥiR] *vt* (*véhicule, passager*) to drive ; (*délégation, troupeau*) to lead ; **se** ~ *vi* to behave ; ~ **vers/à** to lead towards/to ; ~ **qn quelque part** to take sb somewhere ; to drive sb somewhere.

**conduit** [kɔdɥi] *nm* (*TECH*) conduit, pipe ; (*ANAT*) duct, canal.
**conduite** [kɔdɥit] *nf* (*en auto*) driving ; (*comportement*) behaviour ; (*d'eau, de gaz*) pipe ; **sous la** ~ **de** led by ; ~ **forcée** pressure pipe ; ~ **à gauche** left-hand drive ; ~ **intérieure** saloon (car).
**cône** [kon] *nm* cone.
**confection** [kɔfɛksjɔ] *nf* (*fabrication*) making ; (*COUTURE*): **la** ~ the clothing industry, the rag trade ; **vêtement de** ~ ready-to-wear *ou* off-the-peg garment.
**confectionner** [kɔfɛksjɔne] *vt* to make.
**confédération** [kɔfedeRɑsjɔ] *nf* confederation.
**conférence** [kɔfeRɑs] *nf* (*exposé*) lecture ; (*pourparlers*) conference ; ~ **de presse** press conference ; **conférencier, ère** *nm/f* lecturer.
**conférer** [kɔfeRe] *vt*: ~ **à qn** (*titre, grade*) to confer on sb ; ~ **à qch/qn** (*aspect etc*) to endow sth/sb with, give (to) sth/sb.
**confesser** [kɔfese] *vt* to confess ; **se** ~ (*REL*) to go to confession ; **confesseur** *nm* confessor.
**confession** [kɔfɛsjɔ] *nf* confession ; (*culte: catholique etc*) denomination ; **confessionnal, aux** *nm* confessional ; **confessionnel, le** *a* denominational.
**confetti** [kɔfeti] *nm* confetti *q*.
**confiance** [kɔfjɑs] *nf* confidence, trust ; faith ; **avoir** ~ **en** to have confidence *ou* faith in, trust ; **mettre qn en** ~ to win sb's trust ; ~ **en soi** self-confidence.
**confiant, e** [kɔfjɑ, -ɑt] *a* confident ; trusting.
**confidence** [kɔfidɑs] *nf* confidence.
**confident, e** [kɔfidɑ, -ɑt] *nm/f* confidant/confidante.
**confidentiel, le** [kɔfidɑsjɛl] *a* confidential.
**confier** [kɔfje] *vt*: ~ **à qn** (*objet en dépôt, travail etc*) to entrust to sb ; (*secret, pensée*) to confide to sb ; **se** ~ **à qn** to confide in sb.
**configuration** [kɔfigyRɑsjɔ] *nf* configuration, layout.
**confiné, e** [kɔfine] *a* enclosed ; stale.
**confiner** [kɔfine] *vt*: **se** ~ **dans** *ou* **à** to confine o.s. to ; ~ **à** *vt* to confine to.
**confins** [kɔfɛ] *nmpl*: **aux** ~ **de** on the borders of.
**confirmation** [kɔfiRmɑsjɔ] *nf* confirmation.
**confirmer** [kɔfiRme] *vt* to confirm.
**confiscation** [kɔfiskɑsjɔ] *nf* confiscation.
**confiserie** [kɔfizRi] *nf* (*magasin*) confectioner's *ou* sweet shop ; ~**s** *nfpl* (*bonbons*) confectionery *sg*, sweets ; **confiseur, euse** *nm/f* confectioner.
**confisquer** [kɔfiske] *vt* to confiscate.
**confit, e** [kɔfi, -it] *a*: **fruits** ~**s** crystallized fruits // *nm*: ~ **d'oie** conserve of goose.
**confiture** [kɔfityR] *nf* jam ; ~ **d'oranges** (orange) marmalade.
**conflit** [kɔfli] *nm* conflict.
**confluent** [kɔflyɑ] *nm* confluence.
**confondre** [kɔfɔdR(ə)] *vt* (*jumeaux, faits*) to confuse, mix up ; (*témoin, menteur*) to confound ; **se** ~ *vi* to merge ; **se** ~ **en**

**excuses** to offer profuse apologies, apologize profusely.
**confondu, e** [kɔ̃fɔdy] a (*stupéfait*) speechless, overcome.
**conformation** [kɔ̃fɔRmɑsjɔ̃] nf conformation.
**conforme, e** [kɔ̃fɔRm(ə)] a: ~ à in accordance with ; in keeping with ; true to.
**conformé, e** [kɔ̃fɔRme] a: **bien** ~ well-formed.
**conformer** [kɔ̃fɔRme] vt: ~ **qch à** to model sth on ; **se** ~ **à** to conform to ; **conformisme** nm conformity ; **conformiste** a, nm/f conformist.
**conformité** [kɔ̃fɔRmite] nf conformity ; agreement ; **en** ~ **avec** in accordance with ; in keeping with.
**confort** [kɔ̃fɔR] nm comfort ; **tout** ~ (*COMM*) with all mod cons ; **confortable** a comfortable.
**confrère** [kɔ̃fRɛR] nm colleague ; fellow member ; **confrérie** nf brotherhood.
**confrontation** [kɔ̃fRɔ̃tɑsjɔ̃] nf confrontation.
**confronté, e** [kɔ̃fRɔ̃te] a: ~ à confronted by, facing.
**confronter** [kɔ̃fRɔ̃te] vt to confront ; (*textes*) to compare, collate.
**confus, e** [kɔ̃fy, -yz] a (*vague*) confused ; (*embarrassé*) embarrassed.
**confusion** [kɔ̃fyzjɔ̃] nf (*voir confus*) confusion ; embarrassment ; (*voir confondre*) confusion ; mixing up ; (*erreur*) confusion.
**congé** [kɔ̃ʒe] nm (*vacances*) holiday ; (*arrêt de travail*) time off q ; leave q ; (*MIL*) leave q ; (*avis de départ*) notice ; **en** ~ on holiday ; off (work) ; on leave ; **semaine/jour de** ~ week/day off ; **prendre** ~ **de qn** to take one's leave of sb ; **donner son** ~ **à** to hand ou give in one's notice to ; ~ **de maladie** sick leave ; ~**s payés** paid holiday.
**congédier** [kɔ̃ʒedje] vt to dismiss.
**congélateur** [kɔ̃ʒelatœR] nm freezer, deep freeze.
**congeler** [kɔ̃ʒle] vt to freeze.
**congénère** [kɔ̃ʒenɛR] nm/f fellow (bear ou lion etc), fellow creature.
**congénital, e, aux** [kɔ̃ʒenital, -o] a congenital.
**congère** [kɔ̃ʒɛR] nf snowdrift.
**congestion** [kɔ̃ʒɛstjɔ̃] nf congestion ; ~ **cérébrale** stroke ; ~ **pulmonaire** congestion of the lungs.
**congestionner** [kɔ̃ʒɛstjɔne] vt to congest ; (*MED*) to flush.
**congratuler** [kɔ̃gRatyle] vt to congratulate.
**congre** [kɔ̃gR(ə)] nm conger (eel).
**congrégation** [kɔ̃gRegɑsjɔ̃] nf (*REL*) congregation ; (*gén*) assembly ; gathering.
**congrès** [kɔ̃gRɛ] nm congress.
**congru, e** [kɔ̃gRy] a: **la portion** ~**e** the smallest ou meanest share.
**conifère** [kɔnifɛR] nm conifer.
**conique** [kɔnik] a conical.
**conjecture** [kɔ̃ʒɛktyR] nf conjecture, speculation q.
**conjecturer** [kɔ̃ʒɛktyRe] vt, vi to conjecture.

**conjoint, e** [kɔ̃ʒwɛ̃, -wɛ̃t] a joint // nm/f spouse.
**conjonctif, ive** [kɔ̃ʒɔ̃ktif, -iv] a: **tissu** ~ connective tissue.
**conjonction** [kɔ̃ʒɔ̃ksjɔ̃] nf (*LING*) conjunction.
**conjonctivite** [kɔ̃ʒɔ̃ktivit] nf conjunctivitis.
**conjoncture** [kɔ̃ʒɔ̃ktyR] nf circumstances pl ; **la** ~ (**économique**) the economic climate ou circumstances.
**conjugaison** [kɔ̃ʒygɛzɔ̃] nf (*LING*) conjugation.
**conjugal, e, aux** [kɔ̃ʒygal, -o] a conjugal ; married.
**conjuguer** [kɔ̃ʒyge] vt (*LING*) to conjugate ; (*efforts etc*) to combine.
**conjuration** [kɔ̃ʒyRɑsjɔ̃] nf conspiracy.
**conjuré, e** [kɔ̃ʒyRe] nm/f conspirator.
**conjurer** [kɔ̃ʒyRe] vt (*sort, maladie*) to avert ; ~ **qn de faire qch** to beseech ou entreat sb to do sth.
**connaissance** [kɔnɛsɑ̃s] nf (*savoir*) knowledge q ; (*personne connue*) acquaintance ; (*conscience, perception*) consciousness ; **être sans** ~ to be unconscious ; **perdre** ~ to lose consciousness ; **à ma/sa** ~ to (the best of) my/his knowledge ; **avoir** ~ **de** to be aware of ; **prendre** ~ **de** (*document etc*) to peruse ; **en** ~ **de cause** with full knowledge of the facts.
**connaisseur, euse** [kɔnɛsœR, -øz] nm/f connoisseur // a expert.
**connaître** [kɔnɛtR(ə)] vt to know ; (*éprouver*) to experience ; (*avoir*) to have ; to enjoy ; ~ **de nom/vue** to know by name/sight ; **ils se sont connus à Genève** they (first) met in Geneva.
**connecter** [kɔnɛkte] vt to connect.
**connexe** [kɔnɛks(ə)] a closely related.
**connexion** [kɔnɛksjɔ̃] nf connection.
**connu, e** [kɔny] a (*célèbre*) well-known.
**conquérant, e** [kɔ̃keRɑ̃, -ɑ̃t] nm/f conqueror.
**conquérir** [kɔ̃keRiR] vt to conquer, win ; **conquête** nf conquest.
**consacrer** [kɔ̃sakRe] vt (*REL*): ~ **qch (à)** to consecrate sth (to) ; (*fig: usage etc*) to sanction, establish ; (*employer*): ~ **qch à** to devote ou dedicate sth to ; **se** ~ **à qch/faire** to dedicate ou devote o.s. to/to doing.
**consanguin, e** [kɔ̃sɑ̃gɛ̃, -in] a between blood relations.
**conscience** [kɔ̃sjɑ̃s] nf conscience ; (*perception*) consciousness ; **avoir/prendre** ~ **de** to be/become aware of ; **perdre** ~ to lose consciousness ; **avoir bonne/mauvaise** ~ to have a clear/guilty conscience ; ~ **professionnelle** professional conscience ; **consciencieux, euse** a conscientious ; **conscient, e** a conscious ; **conscient de** aware ou conscious of.
**conscription** [kɔ̃skRipsjɔ̃] nf conscription.
**conscrit** [kɔ̃skRi] nm conscript.
**consécration** [kɔ̃sekRɑsjɔ̃] nf consecration.

**consécutif, ive** [kɔ̃sekytif, -iv] *a* consecutive ; ~ à following upon.

**conseil** [kɔ̃sɛj] *nm* (*avis*) piece of advice, advice *q* ; (*assemblée*) council ; (*expert*): ~ **en recrutement** recruitment consultant // *a*: **ingénieur-**~ consulting engineer, engineering consultant ; **tenir** ~ to hold a meeting ; to deliberate ; **prendre** ~ **(auprès de qn)** to take advice (from sb) ; ~ **d'administration** board (of directors) ; ~ **de discipline** disciplinary committee ; ~ **de guerre** court-martial ; **le** ~ **des ministres** ≈ the Cabinet ; ~ **municipal** town council.

**conseiller** [kɔ̃seje] *vt* (*personne*) to advise ; (*méthode, action*) to recommend, advise.

**conseiller, ère** [kɔ̃seje, kɔ̃sɛjɛR] *nm/f* adviser ; ~ **matrimonial** marriage guidance counsellor ; ~ **municipal** town councillor.

**consentement** [kɔ̃sɑ̃tmɑ̃] *nm* consent.

**consentir** [kɔ̃sɑ̃tiR] *vt*: ~ **(à qch/faire)** to agree *ou* consent (to sth/to doing) ; ~ **qch à qn** to grant sb sth.

**conséquence** [kɔ̃sekɑ̃s] *nf* consequence, outcome ; ~**s** *nfpl* consequences, repercussions ; **en** ~ (*donc*) consequently ; (*de façon appropriée*) accordingly ; **ne pas tirer à** ~ to be unlikely to have any repercussions.

**conséquent, e** [kɔ̃sekɑ̃, -ɑ̃t] *a* logical, rational ; **par** ~ consequently.

**conservateur, trice** [kɔ̃sɛRvatœR, -tRis] *a* conservative // *nm/f* (*POL*) conservative ; (*de musée*) curator.

**conservation** [kɔ̃sɛRvɑsjɔ̃] *nf* preserving ; preservation ; retention ; keeping.

**conservatoire** [kɔ̃sɛRvatwaR] *nm* academy.

**conserve** [kɔ̃sɛRv(ə)] *nf* (*gén pl*) canned *ou* tinned food ; ~**s de poisson** canned *ou* tinned fish ; **en** ~ canned, tinned ; **de** ~ (*ensemble*) in convoy ; in concert.

**conserver** [kɔ̃sɛRve] *vt* (*faculté*) to retain, keep ; (*amis, livres*) to keep ; (*maintenir en bon état, aussi CULIN*) to preserve ; **conserverie** *nf* canning factory.

**considérable** [kɔ̃sideRabl(ə)] *a* considerable, significant, extensive.

**considération** [kɔ̃sideRɑsjɔ̃] *nf* consideration ; (*estime*) esteem, respect ; ~**s** *nfpl* (*remarques*) reflections ; **prendre en** ~ to take into consideration *ou* account ; **en** ~ **de** given, because of.

**considéré, e** [kɔ̃sideRe] *a* respected.

**considérer** [kɔ̃sideRe] *vt* to consider ; (*regarder*) to consider, study ; ~ **qch comme** to regard sth as.

**consigne** [kɔ̃siɲ] *nf* (*COMM*) deposit ; (*de gare*) left luggage (office) ; (*punition: SCOL*) detention ; (: *MIL*) confinement to barracks ; (*ordre, instruction*) orders *pl*.

**consigner** [kɔ̃siɲe] *vt* (*note, pensée*) to record ; (*punir*) to confine to barracks ; to put in detention ; (*COMM*) to put a deposit on.

**consistance** [kɔ̃sistɑ̃s] *nf* consistency.

**consistant, e** [kɔ̃sistɑ̃, -ɑ̃t] *a* thick ; solid.

**consister** [kɔ̃siste] *vi*: ~ **en/dans/à faire** to consist of/in/in doing.

**consœur** [kɔ̃sœR] *nf* (lady) colleague ; fellow member.

**consolation** [kɔ̃sɔlɑsjɔ̃] *nf* consolation *q*, comfort *q*.

**console** [kɔ̃sɔl] *nf* console.

**consoler** [kɔ̃sɔle] *vt* to console ; **se** ~ **(de qch)** to console o.s. (for sth).

**consolider** [kɔ̃sɔlide] *vt* to strengthen, reinforce ; (*fig*) to consolidate.

**consommateur, trice** [kɔ̃sɔmatœR, -tRis] *nm/f* (*ÉCON*) consumer ; (*dans un café*) customer.

**consommation** [kɔ̃sɔmɑsjɔ̃] *nf* consumption ; (*JUR*) consummation ; (*boisson*) drink ; ~ **aux 100 km** (*AUTO*) (fuel) consumption per 100 km, ≈ miles per gallon (m.p.g.).

**consommé, e** [kɔ̃sɔme] *a* consummate // *nm* consommé.

**consommer** [kɔ̃sɔme] *vt* (*suj: personne*) to eat *ou* drink, consume ; (*suj: voiture, usine, poêle*) to use (up), consume ; (*JUR*) to consummate // *vi* (*dans un café*) to (have a) drink.

**consonance** [kɔ̃sɔnɑ̃s] *nf* consonance ; **nom à** ~ **étrangère** foreign-sounding name.

**consonne** [kɔ̃sɔn] *nf* consonant.

**consorts** [kɔ̃sɔR] *nmpl*: **et** ~ (*péj*) and company, and his bunch *ou* like.

**conspirateur, trice** [kɔ̃spiRatœR, -tRis] *nm/f* conspirator, plotter.

**conspiration** [kɔ̃spiRɑsjɔ̃] *nf* conspiracy.

**conspirer** [kɔ̃spiRe] *vi* to conspire, plot.

**conspuer** [kɔ̃spɥe] *vt* to boo, shout down.

**constamment** [kɔ̃stamɑ̃] *ad* constantly.

**constant, e** [kɔ̃stɑ̃, -ɑ̃t] *a* constant ; (*personne*) steadfast.

**constat** [kɔ̃sta] *nm* (*d'huissier*) certified report (*by bailiff*) ; (*de police*) report.

**constatation** [kɔ̃statɑsjɔ̃] *nf* noticing ; certifying ; (*remarque*) observation.

**constater** [kɔ̃state] *vt* (*remarquer*) to note, notice ; (*ADMIN, JUR*: *attester*) to certify ; (*dégâts*) to note ; ~ **que** (*dire*) to state that.

**constellation** [kɔ̃stelɑsjɔ̃] *nf* constellation.

**constellé, e** [kɔ̃stele] *a*: ~ **de** studded *ou* spangled with ; spotted with.

**consternation** [kɔ̃stɛRnɑsjɔ̃] *nf* consternation, dismay.

**constipation** [kɔ̃stipɑsjɔ̃] *nf* constipation.

**constipé, e** [kɔ̃stipe] *a* constipated ; (*fig*) stiff.

**constitué, e** [kɔ̃stitɥe] *a*: ~ **de** made up *ou* composed of ; **bien** ~ of sound constitution ; well-formed.

**constituer** [kɔ̃stitɥe] *vt* (*comité, équipe*) to set up, form ; (*dossier, collection*) to put together, build up ; (*suj: éléments, parties: composer*) to make up, constitute ; (*représenter, être*) to constitute ; **se** ~ **prisonnier** to give o.s. up.

**constitution** [kɔ̃stitysjɔ̃] *nf* setting up ; building up ; (*composition*) composition, make-up ; (*santé, POL*) constitution ; **constitutionnel, le** *a* constitutional.

**constructeur** [kɔ̃stRyktœR] *nm* manufacturer, builder.

**construction** [kɔ̃stRyksjɔ̃] *nf* construction, building.

**construire** [kɔ̃stʀɥiʀ] *vt* to build, construct.
**consul** [kɔ̃syl] *nm* consul; ~aire *a* consular; ~at *nm* consulate.
**consultation** [kɔ̃syltɑsjɔ̃] *nf* consultation; ~s *nfpl* (POL) talks; **aller à la** ~ (MÉD) to go to the surgery; **heures de** ~ (MÉD) surgery hours.
**consulter** [kɔ̃sylte] *vt* to consult // *vi* (*médecin*) to hold surgery.
**consumer** [kɔ̃syme] *vt* to consume; **se** ~ *vi* to burn; **se** ~ **de chagrin/douleur** to be consumed with sorrow/grief.
**contact** [kɔ̃takt] *nm* contact; **au** ~ **de** (*air, peau*) on contact with; (*gens*) through contact with; **mettre/couper le** ~ (AUTO) to switch on/off the ignition; **entrer en** ~ (*fils, objets*) to come into contact, make contact; **se mettre en** ~ **avec** (RADIO) to make contact with; **prendre** ~ **avec** (*relation d'affaires, connaissance*) to get in touch *ou* contact with; ~**er** *vt* to contact, get in touch with.
**contagieux, euse** [kɔ̃taʒjø, -øz] *a* contagious, infectious.
**contagion** [kɔ̃taʒjɔ̃] *nf* contagion.
**container** [kɔ̃tɛnɛʀ] *nm* container.
**contaminer** [kɔ̃tamine] *vt* to contaminate.
**conte** [kɔ̃t] *nm* tale; ~ **de fées** fairy tale.
**contempler** [kɔ̃tɑ̃ple] *vt* to contemplate, gaze at.
**contemporain, e** [kɔ̃tɑ̃pɔʀɛ̃, -ɛn] *a, nm/f* contemporary.
**contenance** [kɔ̃tnɑ̃s] *nf* (*d'un récipient*) capacity; (*attitude*) bearing, attitude; **perdre** ~ to lose one's composure; **se donner une** ~ to give the impression of composure.
**contenir** [kɔ̃tniʀ] *vt* to contain; (*avoir une capacité de*) to hold.
**content, e** [kɔ̃tɑ̃, -ɑ̃t] *a* pleased, glad; ~ **de** pleased with; **contentement** *nm* contentment, satisfaction; **contenter** *vt* to satisfy, please; (*envie*) to satisfy; **se contenter de** to content o.s. with.
**contentieux** [kɔ̃tɑ̃sjø] *nm* (COMM) litigation; litigation department; (POL *etc*) contentious issues *pl*.
**contenu** [kɔ̃tny] *nm* (*d'un bol*) contents *pl*; (*d'un texte*) content.
**conter** [kɔ̃te] *vt* to recount, relate.
**contestable** [kɔ̃tɛstabl(ə)] *a* questionable.
**contestation** [kɔ̃tɛstɑsjɔ̃] *nf* questioning, contesting; (POL): **la** ~ anti-establishment activity, protest.
**conteste** [kɔ̃tɛst(ə)]: **sans** ~ *ad* unquestionably, indisputably.
**contester** [kɔ̃tɛste] *vt* to question, contest // *vi* (POL, *gén*) to protest, rebel (against established authority).
**conteur, euse** [kɔ̃tœʀ, -øz] *nm/f* storyteller.
**contexte** [kɔ̃tɛkst(ə)] *nm* context.
**contigu, ë** [kɔ̃tigy] *a*: ~ (**à**) adjacent (to).
**continent** [kɔ̃tinɑ̃] *nm* continent; **continental, e, aux** *a* continental.
**contingences** [kɔ̃tɛ̃ʒɑ̃s] *nfpl* contingencies.
**contingent** [kɔ̃tɛ̃ʒɑ̃] *nm* (MIL) contingent; (COMM) quota; **contingenter** *vt* (COMM) to fix a quota on.

**continu, e** [kɔ̃tiny] *a* continuous; (*courant*) ~ direct current, DC.
**continuation** [kɔ̃tinɥasjɔ̃] *nf* continuation.
**continuel, le** [kɔ̃tinɥɛl] *a* (*qui se répète*) constant, continual; (*continu*) continuous.
**continuer** [kɔ̃tinɥe] *vt* (*travail, voyage etc*) to continue (with), carry on (with), go on (with); (*prolonger: alignement, rue*) to continue // *vi* (*pluie, vie, bruit*) to continue, go on; (*voyageur*) to go on; ~ **à** *ou* **de faire** to go on *ou* continue doing.
**continuité** [kɔ̃tinɥite] *nf* continuity; continuation.
**contorsion** [kɔ̃tɔʀsjɔ̃] *nf* contortion; **se contorsionner** *vi* to contort o.s., writhe about.
**contour** [kɔ̃tuʀ] *nm* outline, contour; ~s *nmpl* (*d'une rivière etc*) windings.
**contourner** [kɔ̃tuʀne] *vt* to bypass, walk (*ou* drive) round.
**contraceptif, ive** [kɔ̃tʀasɛptif, -iv] *a, nm* contraceptive.
**contraception** [kɔ̃tʀasɛpsjɔ̃] *nf* contraception.
**contracté, e** [kɔ̃tʀakte] *a* (*muscle*) tense, contracted; (*personne: tendu*) tense, tensed up.
**contracter** [kɔ̃tʀakte] *vt* (*muscle etc*) to tense, contract; (*maladie, dette, obligation*) to contract; (*assurance*) to take out; **se** ~ *vi* (*métal, muscles*) to contract; **contraction** *nf* contraction.
**contractuel, le** [kɔ̃tʀaktɥɛl] *a* contractual // *nm/f* (*agent*) traffic warden; (*employé*) contract employee.
**contradiction** [kɔ̃tʀadiksjɔ̃] *nf* contradiction; **contradictoire** *a* contradictory, conflicting; **débat contradictoire** (open) debate.
**contraignant, e** [kɔ̃tʀɛɲɑ̃, -ɑ̃t] *a* restricting.
**contraindre** [kɔ̃tʀɛ̃dʀ(ə)] *vt*: ~ **qn à faire** to force *ou* compel sb to do.
**contraint, e** [kɔ̃tʀɛ̃, -ɛ̃t] *a* (*mine, air*) constrained, forced // *nf* constraint; **sans** ~e unrestrainedly, unconstrainedly.
**contraire** [kɔ̃tʀɛʀ] *a, nm* opposite; ~ **à** contrary to; **au** ~ *ad* on the contrary.
**contrarier** [kɔ̃tʀaʀje] *vt* (*personne*) to annoy, bother; (*fig*) to impede; to thwart, frustrate; **contrariété** *nf* annoyance.
**contraste** [kɔ̃tʀast(ə)] *nm* contrast; **contraster** *vi* to contrast.
**contrat** [kɔ̃tʀa] *nm* contract.
**contravention** [kɔ̃tʀavɑ̃sjɔ̃] *nf* (*infraction*): ~ **à** contravention of; (*amende*) fine; (P.V. *pour stationnement interdit*) parking ticket; **dresser** ~ **à** (*automobiliste*) to book; to write out a parking ticket for.
**contre** [kɔ̃tʀ(ə)] *prép* against; (*en échange*) (in exchange) for // *préfixe*: ~-**amiral, aux** *nm* rear admiral; ~-**attaque** *nf* counter-attack; ~-**attaquer** *vi* to counter-attack; ~-**balancer** *vt* to counter-balance; (*fig*) to offset.
**contrebande** [kɔ̃tʀəbɑ̃d] *nf* (*trafic*) contraband, smuggling; (*marchandise*) contraband, smuggled goods *pl*; **faire la** ~ **de** to smuggle; **contrebandier** *nm* smuggler.

**contrebas** [kɔ̃trəba]: **en** ~ *ad* (down) below.

**contrebasse** [kɔ̃trəbas] *nf* (double) bass ; **contrebassiste** *nm/f* (double) bass player.

**contrecarrer** [kɔ̃trəkare] *vt* to thwart.

**contrecœur** [kɔ̃trəkœr]: **à** ~ *ad* (be)grudgingly, reluctantly.

**contrecoup** [kɔ̃trəku] *nm* repercussions *pl.*

**contre-courant** [kɔ̃trəkurɑ̃]: **à** ~ *ad* against the current.

**contredire** [kɔ̃trədir] *vt* (*personne*) to contradict ; (*témoignage, assertion, faits*) to refute.

**contrée** [kɔ̃tre] *nf* region ; land.

**contre-écrou** [kɔ̃trekru] *nm* lock nut.

**contre-espionnage** [kɔ̃trɛspjɔnaʒ] *nm* counter-espionage.

**contre-expertise** [kɔ̃trɛkspɛrtiz] *nf* second (expert) assessment.

**contrefaçon** [kɔ̃trəfasɔ̃] *nf* forgery.

**contrefaire** [kɔ̃trəfɛr] *vt* (*document, signature*) to forge, counterfeit ; (*personne, démarche*) to mimic ; (*dénaturer: sa voix etc*) to disguise.

**contrefait, e** [kɔ̃trəfɛ, -ɛt] *a* misshapen, deformed.

**contreforts** [kɔ̃trəfɔr] *nmpl* foothills.

**contre-indication** [kɔ̃trɛ̃dikasjɔ̃] *nf* contra-indication.

**contre-jour** [kɔ̃trəʒur]: **à** ~ *ad* against the sunlight.

**contremaître** [kɔ̃trəmɛtr(ə)] *nm* foreman.

**contre-manifestation** [kɔ̃trəmanifɛstasjɔ̃] *nf* counter-demonstration.

**contremarque** [kɔ̃trəmark(ə)] *nf* (*ticket*) pass-out ticket.

**contre-offensive** [kɔ̃trɔfɑ̃siv] *nf* counter-offensive.

**contrepartie** [kɔ̃trəparti] *nf* compensation ; **en** ~ in compensation ; in return.

**contre-performance** [kɔ̃trəpɛrfɔrmɑ̃s] *nf* below-average performance.

**contrepèterie** [kɔ̃trəpetri] *nf* spoonerism.

**contre-pied** [kɔ̃trəpje] *nm*: **prendre le** ~ **de** to take the opposing view of ; to take the opposite course to ; **prendre qn à** ~ (*SPORT*) to wrong-foot sb.

**contre-plaqué** [kɔ̃trəplake] *nm* plywood.

**contre-plongée** [kɔ̃trəplɔ̃ʒe] *nf* low-angle shot.

**contrepoids** [kɔ̃trəpwa] *nm* counterweight, counterbalance ; **faire** ~ to act as a counterbalance.

**contrepoint** [kɔ̃trəpwɛ̃] *nm* counter point.

**contrer** [kɔ̃tre] *vt* to counter.

**contresens** [kɔ̃trəsɑ̃s] *nm* misinterpretation ; mistranslation ; nonsense *q* ; **à** ~ *ad* the wrong way.

**contresigner** [kɔ̃trəsiɲe] *vt* to countersign.

**contretemps** [kɔ̃trətɑ̃] *nm* hitch, contretemps ; **à** ~ *ad* (*MUS*) out of time ; (*fig*) at an inopportune moment.

**contre-terrorisme** [kɔ̃trətɛrɔrism(ə)] *nm* counter-terrorism.

**contre-torpilleur** [kɔ̃trətɔrpijœr] *nm* destroyer.

**contrevenir** [kɔ̃trəvnir]: ~ **à** *vt* to contravene.

**contribuable** [kɔ̃tribɥabl(ə)] *nm/f* taxpayer.

**contribuer** [kɔ̃tribɥe]: ~ **à** *vt* to contribute towards ; **contribution** *nf* contribution ; **les contributions** (*bureaux*) ≈ the Tax Office, the Inland Revenue ; **contributions directes/indirectes** (*impôts*) direct/indirect taxation ; **mettre à contribution** to call upon.

**contrit, e** [kɔ̃tri, -it] *a* contrite.

**contrôle** [kɔ̃trol] *nm* checking *q*, check ; supervision ; monitoring ; **perdre le** ~ **de son véhicule** to lose control of one's vehicle ; ~ **d'identité** identity check ; ~ **des naissances** birth control.

**contrôler** [kɔ̃trole] *vt* (*vérifier*) to check ; (*surveiller*) to supervise ; to monitor, control ; (*maîtriser, COMM: firme*) to control ; **contrôleur, euse** *nm/f* (*de train*) (ticket) inspector ; (*de bus*) (bus) conductor/tress.

**contrordre** [kɔ̃trɔrdr(ə)] *nm* counter-order, countermand ; **sauf** ~ unless otherwise directed.

**controverse** [kɔ̃trɔvɛrs(ə)] *nf* controversy ; **controversé, e** *a* much debated.

**contumace** [kɔ̃tymas]: **par** ~ *ad* in absentia.

**contusion** [kɔ̃tyzjɔ̃] *nf* bruise, contusion.

**convaincre** [kɔ̃vɛ̃kr(ə)] *vt*: ~ **qn (de qch)** to convince sb (of sth) ; ~ **qn (de faire)** to persuade sb (to do) ; ~ **qn de** (*JUR*: *délit*) to convict sb of.

**convalescence** [kɔ̃valesɑ̃s] *nf* convalescence ; **maison de** ~ convalescent home.

**convalescent, e** [kɔ̃valesɑ̃, -ɑ̃t] *a, nm/f* convalescent.

**convenable** [kɔ̃vnabl(ə)] *a* (*décent*) acceptable, proper ; (*assez bon*) decent, acceptable ; adequate, passable.

**convenance** [kɔ̃vnɑ̃s] *nf*: **à ma/votre** ~ to my/your liking ; ~**s** *nfpl* proprieties.

**convenir** [kɔ̃vnir] *vi* to be suitable ; ~ **à** to suit ; **il convient de** it is advisable to ; (*bienséant*) it is right *ou* proper to ; ~ **de** *vt* (*bien-fondé de qch*) to admit (to), acknowledge ; (*date, somme etc*) to agree upon ; ~ **que** (*admettre*) to admit that, acknowledge the fact that ; ~ **de faire qch** to agree to do sth ; **il a été convenu que** it has been agreed that ; **comme convenu** as agreed.

**convention** [kɔ̃vɑ̃sjɔ̃] *nf* convention ; ~**s** *nfpl* (*convenances*) convention *sg*, social conventions ; **de** ~ conventional ; ~ **collective** (*ÉCON*) collective agreement ; **conventionné, e** *a* (*ADMIN*) ≈ National Health *cpd* ; **conventionnel, le** *a* conventional.

**conventuel, le** [kɔ̃vɑ̃tɥɛl] *a* monastic ; monastery *cpd* ; conventual, convent *cpd*.

**convenu, e** *pp de* **convenir**.

**convergent, e** [kɔ̃vɛrʒɑ̃, -ɑ̃t] *a* convergent.

**converger** [kɔ̃vɛrʒe] *vi* to converge.

**conversation** [kɔ̃vɛrsasjɔ̃] *nf* conversation ; **avoir de la** ~ to be a good conversationalist.

**converser** [kɔ̃vɛRse] *vi* to converse.
**conversion** [kɔ̃vɛRsjɔ̃] *nf* conversion; (*SKI*) kick turn.
**convertir** [kɔ̃vɛRtiR] *vt*: ~ **qn (à)** to convert sb (to); ~ **qch en** to convert sth into; **se** ~ **(à)** to be converted (to).
**convexe** [kɔ̃vɛks(ə)] *a* convex.
**conviction** [kɔ̃viksjɔ̃] *nf* conviction.
**convienne** *etc vb voir* **convenir.**
**convier** [kɔ̃vje] *vt*: ~ **qn à** (*dîner etc*) to (cordially) invite sb to; ~ **qn à faire** to urge sb to do.
**convive** [kɔ̃viv] *nm/f* guest (*at table*).
**convocation** [kɔ̃vɔkasjɔ̃] *nf* convening, convoking; invitation; summoning; (*document*) notification to attend; summons *sg*.
**convoi** [kɔ̃vwa] *nm* (*de voitures, prisonniers*) convoy; (*train*) train; ~ (*funèbre*) funeral procession.
**convoiter** [kɔ̃vwate] *vt* to covet; **convoitise** *nf* covetousness; (*sexuelle*) lust, desire.
**convoler** [kɔ̃vɔle] *vi*: ~ (**en justes noces**) to be wed.
**convoquer** [kɔ̃vɔke] *vt* (*assemblée*) to convene, convoke; (*subordonné, témoin*) to summon; ~ **qn (à)** (*réunion*) to invite sb (to attend).
**convoyer** [kɔ̃vwaje] *vt* to escort; **convoyeur** *nm* (*NAVIG*) escort ship; **convoyeur de fonds** security guard.
**convulsions** [kɔ̃vylsjɔ̃] *nfpl* convulsions.
**coopératif, ive** [kɔɔpeRatif, -iv] *a, nf* cooperative.
**coopération** [kɔɔpeRasjɔ̃] *nf* cooperation; (*ADMIN*): **la C~** ≈ Voluntary Service Overseas (*sometimes done in place of Military Service*).
**coopérer** [kɔɔpeRe] *vi*: ~ (**à**) to cooperate (in).
**coordination** [kɔɔRdinasjɔ̃] *nf* coordination.
**coordonné, e** [kɔɔRdɔne] *a* coordinated // *nf* (*LING*) coordinate clause; ~**s** *nmpl* (*vêtements*) coordinates; ~**es** *nfpl* (*MATH*) coordinates.
**coordonner** [kɔɔRdɔne] *vt* to coordinate.
**copain, copine** [kɔpɛ̃, kɔpin] *nm/f* mate, pal // *a*: **être** ~ **avec** to be pally with.
**copeau, x** [kɔpo] *nm* shaving; (*de métal*) turning.
**copie** [kɔpi] *nf* copy; (*SCOL*) script, paper; exercise.
**copier** [kɔpje] *vt* to copy; **copieuse** *nf* photo-copier.
**copieux, euse** [kɔpjø, -øz] *a* copious, hearty.
**copilote** [kɔpilɔt] *nm* (*AVIAT*) co-pilot; (*AUTO*) co-driver, navigator.
**copine** [kɔpin] *nf voir* **copain.**
**copiste** [kɔpist(ə)] *nm/f* copyist, transcriber.
**coproduction** [kɔpRɔdyksjɔ̃] *nf* coproduction, joint production.
**copropriété** [kɔpRɔpRijete] *nf* coownership, joint ownership; **acheter en** ~ to buy on a co-ownership basis.
**copulation** [kɔpylasjɔ̃] *nf* copulation.
**coq** [kɔk] *nm* cock, rooster.

**coq-à-l'âne** [kɔkalɑn] *nm inv* abrupt change of subject.
**coque** [kɔk] *nf* (*de noix, mollusque*) shell; (*de bateau*) hull; **à la** ~ (*CULIN*) boiled.
**coquelicot** [kɔkliko] *nm* poppy.
**coqueluche** [kɔklyʃ] *nf* whooping-cough.
**coquet, te** [kɔkɛ, -ɛt] *a* flirtatious; appearance-conscious; pretty.
**coquetier** [kɔktje] *nm* egg-cup.
**coquillage** [kɔkijaʒ] *nm* (*mollusque*) shellfish *inv*; (*coquille*) shell.
**coquille** [kɔkij] *nf* shell; (*TYPO*) misprint; ~ **de beurre** shell of butter; ~ **de noix** nutshell; ~ **St Jacques** scallop.
**coquin, e** [kɔkɛ̃, -in] *a* mischievous, roguish; (*polisson*) naughty // *nm/f* (*péj*) rascal.
**cor** [kɔR] *nm* (*MUS*) horn; (*MÉD*): ~ (**au pied**) corn; **réclamer à** ~ **et à cri** (*fig*) to clamour for; ~ **anglais** cor anglais; ~ **de chasse** hunting horn.
**corail, aux** [kɔRaj, -o] *nm* coral *q*.
**Coran** [kɔRɑ̃] *nm*: **le** ~ the Koran.
**corbeau, x** [kɔRbo] *nm* crow.
**corbeille** [kɔRbɛj] *nf* basket; (*à la Bourse*): **la** ~ the stockbrokers' central enclosure; ~ **de mariage** (*fig*) wedding presents *pl*; ~ **à ouvrage** work-basket; ~ **à pain** bread-basket; ~ **à papier** waste paper basket *ou* bin.
**corbillard** [kɔRbijaR] *nm* hearse.
**cordage** [kɔRdaʒ] *nm* rope; ~**s** *nmpl* (*de voilure*) rigging *sg*.
**corde** [kɔRd(ə)] *nf* rope; (*de violon, raquette, d'arc*) string; (*trame*): **la** ~ the thread; (*ATHLÉTISME, AUTO*): **la** ~ the rails *pl*; **semelles de** ~ rope soles; ~ **à linge** washing *ou* clothes line; ~ **lisse** (*climbing*) rope; ~ **à nœuds** knotted climbing rope; ~ **raide** tight-rope; ~ **à sauter** skipping rope; ~**s vocales** vocal cords.
**cordeau, x** [kɔRdo] *nm* string, line; **tracé au** ~ as straight as a die.
**cordée** [kɔRde] *nf* (*d'alpinistes*) rope, roped party.
**cordial, e, aux** [kɔRdjal, -jo] *a* warm, cordial; ~**ité** *nf* warmth, cordiality.
**cordon** [kɔRdɔ̃] *nm* cord, string; ~ **sanitaire/de police** sanitary/police cordon; ~ **bleu** cordon bleu; ~ **ombilical** umbilical cord.
**cordonnerie** [kɔRdɔnRi] *nf* shoe repairer's *ou* mender's (shop).
**cordonnier** [kɔRdɔnje] *nm* shoe repairer *ou* mender, cobbler.
**coreligionnaire** [kɔRəliʒjɔnɛR] *nm/f* (*d'un musulman, juif etc*) fellow Mahometan/Jew *etc.*
**coriace** [kɔRjas] *a* tough.
**cormoran** [kɔRmɔRɑ̃] *nm* cormorant.
**cornac** [kɔRnak] *nm* elephant driver.
**corne** [kɔRn(ə)] *nf* horn; (*de cerf*) antler; ~ **d'abondance** horn of plenty; ~ **de brume** (*NAVIG*) foghorn.
**cornée** [kɔRne] *nf* cornea.
**corneille** [kɔRnɛj] *nf* crow.
**cornélien, ne** [kɔRneljɛ̃, -jɛn] *a* (*débat etc*) where love and duty conflict.
**cornemuse** [kɔRnəmyz] *nf* bagpipes *pl.*

**corner** nm [kɔRnɛR] (FOOTBALL) corner (kick) // vb [kɔRne] vt (pages) to make dog-eared // vi (klaxonner) to blare out.

**cornet** [kɔRnɛ] nm (paper) cone ; (de glace) cornet, cone ; ~ à piston cornet.

**cornette** [kɔRnɛt] nf cornet (headgear).

**corniaud** [kɔRnjo] nm (chien) mongrel ; (péj) twit, clot.

**corniche** [kɔRniʃ] nf cornice.

**cornichon** [kɔRniʃɔ̃] nm gherkin.

**cornue** [kɔRny] nf retort.

**corollaire** [kɔRɔlɛR] nm corollary.

**corolle** [kɔRɔl] nf corolla.

**coron** [kɔRɔ̃] nm mining cottage ; mining village.

**coronaire** [kɔRɔnɛR] a coronary.

**corporation** [kɔRpɔRɑsjɔ̃] nf corporate body ; (au moyen-âge) guild.

**corporel, le** [kɔRpɔRɛl] a bodily ; (punition) corporal ; soins ~s care sg of the body.

**corps** [kɔR] nm (gén) body ; (cadavre) (dead) body ; à son ~ défendant against one's will ; à ~ perdu headlong ; prendre ~ et biens lost with all hands ; prendre ~ to take shape ; faire ~ avec to be joined to ; to form one body with ; ~ d'armée army corps ; ~ de ballet corps de ballet ; le ~ consulaire (CC) the consular corps ; ~ à ~ ad hand-to-hand // nm clinch ; le ~ du délit (JUR) corpus delicti ; le ~ diplomatique (CD) the diplomatic corps ; le ~ électoral the electorate ; le ~ enseignant the teaching profession ; ~ étranger (MÉD) foreign body ; ~ de garde guardroom.

**corpulent, e** [kɔRpylɑ̃, -ɑ̃t] a stout, corpulent.

**correct, e** [kɔRɛkt] a (exact) accurate, correct ; (bienséant, honnête) correct ; (passable) adequate ; ~ement ad accurately ; correctly.

**correcteur, trice** [kɔRɛktœR, -tRis] nm/f (SCOL) examiner, marker ; (TYPO) proof-reader.

**correction** [kɔRɛksjɔ̃] nf (voir corriger) correction ; marking ; (voir correct) correctness ; (rature, surcharge) correction, emendation ; (coups) thrashing ; ~ (des épreuves) proofreading.

**correctionnel, le** [kɔRɛksjɔnɛl] a (JUR): chambre ~le ≈ police magistrate's court.

**corrélation** [kɔRelasjɔ̃] nf correlation.

**correspondance** [kɔRɛspɔ̃dɑ̃s] nf correspondence ; (de train, d'avion) connection ; ce train assure la ~ avec l'avion de 10 heures this train connects with the 10 o'clock plane ; cours par ~ correspondence course ; vente par ~ mail-order business ; correspondancier, ère nm/f correspondence clerk.

**correspondant, e** [kɔRɛspɔ̃dɑ̃, -ɑ̃t] nm/f correspondent.

**correspondre** [kɔRɛspɔ̃dR(ə)] vi (données, témoignages) to correspond, tally ; (chambres) to communicate ; ~ à to correspond to ; ~ avec qn to correspond with sb.

**corrida** [kɔRida] nf bullfight.

**corridor** [kɔRidɔR] nm corridor, passage.

**corrigé** [kɔRiʒe] nm (SCOL) correct version ; fair copy.

**corriger** [kɔRiʒe] vt (devoir) to correct, mark ; (texte) to correct, emend ; (erreur, défaut) to correct, put right ; (punir) to thrash ; ~ qn de (défaut) to cure sb of.

**corroborer** [kɔRɔbɔRe] vt to corroborate.

**corroder** [kɔRɔde] vt to corrode.

**corrompre** [kɔRɔ̃pR(ə)] vt (soudoyer) to bribe ; (dépraver) to corrupt.

**corrosion** [kɔRozjɔ̃] nf corrosion.

**corruption** [kɔRypsjɔ̃] nf bribery ; corruption.

**corsage** [kɔRsaʒ] nm bodice ; blouse.

**corsaire** [kɔRsɛR] nm pirate, corsair ; privateer.

**corse** [kɔRs(ə)] a, nm/f Corsican // nf: la C~ Corsica.

**corsé, e** [kɔRse] a vigorous ; full-flavoured ; (fig) spicy ; tricky.

**corselet** [kɔRsəlɛ] nm corselet.

**corset** [kɔRsɛ] nm corset ; bodice.

**corso** [kɔRso] nm: ~ fleuri procession of floral floats.

**cortège** [kɔRtɛʒ] nm procession.

**corvée** [kɔRve] nf chore, drudgery q ; (MIL) fatigue (duty).

**cosmétique** [kɔsmetik] nm hair-oil ; beauty care product.

**cosmique** [kɔsmik] a cosmic.

**cosmonaute** [kɔsmɔnot] nm/f cosmonaut, astronaut.

**cosmopolite** [kɔsmɔpɔlit] a cosmopolitan.

**cosmos** [kɔsmɔs] nm outer space ; cosmos.

**cosse** [kɔs] nf (BOT) pod, hull.

**cossu, e** [kɔsy] a opulent-looking ; well-to-do.

**costaud, e** [kɔsto, -od] a strong, sturdy.

**costume** [kɔstym] nm (d'homme) suit ; (de théâtre) costume ; costumé, e a dressed up.

**cote** [kɔt] nf (en Bourse etc) quotation ; quoted value ; (d'un cheval): la ~ de the odds pl on ; (d'un candidat etc) rating ; (mesure: sur une carte) spot height ; (: sur un croquis) dimension ; (de classement) (classification) mark ; reference number ; inscrit à la ~ quoted on the Stock Exchange ; ~ d'alerte danger ou flood level.

**côte** [kɔt] nf (rivage) coast(line) ; (pente) slope ; (: sur une route) hill ; (ANAT) rib ; (d'un tricot, tissu) rib, ribbing q ; ~ à ~ ad side by side ; la C~ (d'Azur) the (French) Riviera.

**côté** [kote] nm (gén) side ; (direction) way, direction ; de tous les ~s from all directions ; de quel ~ est-il parti? which way ou in which direction did he go? ; de ce/de l'autre ~ this/the other way ; du ~ de (provenance) from ; (direction) towards ; du ~ de Lyon (proximité) the Lyons way, near Lyons ; de ~ ad side-ways ; on one side ; to one side ; aside ; laisser de ~ to leave on one side ; mettre de ~ to put on one side, put aside ; à ~ ad (right) nearby ; beside ; next door ; (d'autre part) besides ; à ~ de beside, next to ; (fig) in comparison to ; à ~ (de la cible) off target, wide (of the mark) ; être aux ~s de to be by the side of.

**coteau, x** [kɔto] *nm* hill.
**côtelé, e** [kotle] *a* ribbed ; **pantalon en velours** ~ corduroy trousers *pl.*
**côtelette** [kotlɛt] *nf* chop.
**coter** [kɔte] *vt* (*en Bourse*) to quote.
**coterie** [kɔtʀi] *nf* set.
**côtier, ière** [kotje, -jɛʀ] *a* coastal.
**cotisation** [kɔtizɑsjɔ̃] *nf* subscription, dues *pl* ; (*pour une pension*) contributions *pl.*
**cotiser** [kɔtize] *vi*: ~ (à) to pay contributions (to) ; **se** ~ to club together.
**coton** [kɔtɔ̃] *nm* cotton ; ~ **hydrophile** (absorbent) cotton-wool.
**côtoyer** [kotwaje] *vt* to be close to ; to rub shoulders with ; to run alongside ; to be bordering *ou* verging on.
**cotte** [kɔt] *nf*: ~ **de mailles** coat of mail.
**cou** [ku] *nm* neck.
**couard, e** [kwaʀ, -aʀd] *a* cowardly.
**couchage** [kuʃaʒ] *nm voir* **sac.**
**couchant** [kuʃɑ̃] *a*: **soleil** ~ setting sun.
**couche** [kuʃ] *nf* (*strate: gén, GÉO*) layer, stratum (*pl* a) ; (*de peinture, vernis*) coat ; (*de poussière, crème*) layer ; (*de bébé*) nappy, napkin ; ~**s** *nfpl*, (*MÉD*) confinement *sg* ; ~**s sociales** social levels *ou* strata ; ~**-culotte** *nf* disposable nappy and waterproof pants in one.
**coucher** [kuʃe] *nm* (*du soleil*) setting // *vt* (*personne*) to put to bed ; (: *loger*) to put up ; (*objet*) to lay on its side ; (*écrire*) to inscribe, couch // *vi* (*dormir*) to sleep, spend the night ; (*fam*): ∙~ **avec qn** to sleep with sb, go to bed with sb ; **se** ~ *vi* (*pour dormir*) to go to bed ; (*pour se reposer*) to lie down ; (*soleil*) to set, go down ; **à prendre avant le** ~ (*MÉD*) take at night *ou* before going to bed ; ~ **de soleil** sunset.
**couchette** [kuʃɛt] *nf* couchette ; (*de marin*) bunk.
**coucou** [kuku] *nm* cuckoo // *excl* peek-a-boo.
**coude** [kud] *nm* (*ANAT*) elbow ; (*de tuyau, de la route*) bend ; ~ **à** ~ *ad* shoulder to shoulder, side by side.
**cou-de-pied** [kudpje] *nm* instep.
**coudre** [kudʀ(ə)] *vt* (*bouton*) to sew on ; (*robe*) to sew (up) // *vi* to sew.
**couenne** [kwan] *nf* (*de lard*) rind.
**couettes** [kwɛt] *nfpl* bunches.
**couffin** [kufɛ̃] *nm* Moses basket ; (straw) basket.
**couiner** [kwine] *vi* to squeal.
**coulant, e** [kulɑ̃, -ɑ̃t] *a* (*indulgent*) easy-going ; (*fromage etc*) runny.
**coulée** [kule] *nf* (*de lave, métal en fusion*) flow ; ~ **de neige** snowslide.
**couler** [kule] *vi* to flow, run ; (*fuir: stylo, récipient*) to leak ; (*sombrer: bateau*) to sink // *vt* (*cloche, sculpture*) to cast ; (*bateau*) to sink ; (*fig*) to ruin, bring down ; **se** ~ **dans** (*interstice etc*) to slip into ; **il a coulé une bielle** (*AUTO*) his big-end went.
**couleur** [kulœʀ] *nf* colour ; (*CARTES*) suit.
**couleuvre** [kulœvʀ(ə)] *nf* grass snake.
**coulisse** [kulis] *nf* (*TECH*) runner ; ~**s** *nfpl* (*THÉÂTRE*) wings ; (*fig*): **dans les** ~**s** behind the scenes ; **porte à** ~ sliding door ; **coulisser** *vi* to slide, run.

**couloir** [kulwaʀ] *nm* corridor, passage ; (*de bus*) gangway ; (*SPORT: de piste*) lane ; (*GÉO*) gully ; ~ **de navigation** shipping lane.
**coulpe** [kulp(ə)] *nf*: **battre sa** ~ to repent openly.
**coup** [ku] *nm* (*heurt, choc*) knock ; (*affectif*) blow, shock ; (*agressif*) blow ; (*avec arme à feu*) shot ; (*de l'horloge*) chime ; stroke ; (*SPORT*) stroke ; shot ; blow ; (*ÉCHECS*) move ; ~ **de coude/genou** nudge (with the elbow)/with the knee ; **à** ~**s de hache/marteau** (hitting) with an axe/a hammer ; ~ **de tonnerre** clap of thunder ; ~ **de sonnette** ring of the bell ; ~ **de crayon/pinceau** stroke of the pencil/brush ; **donner un** ~ **de balai** to sweep up, give the floor a sweep ; **donner un** ~ **de chiffon** to go round with the duster ; **avoir le** ~ (*fig*) to have the knack ; **boire un** ~ to have a drink ; **d'un seul** ~ (*subitement*) suddenly ; (*à la fois*) at one go ; in one blow ; **du premier** ~ first time *ou* go, at the first attempt ; **du même** ~ at the same time ; **à** ~ **sûr** definitely, without fail ; ~ **sur** ~ in quick succession ; **sur le** ~ outright ; **sous le** ~ **de** (*surprise etc*) under the influence of ; **tomber sous le** ~ **de la loi** to constitute a statutory offence ; ~ **de chance** stroke of luck ; ~ **de couteau** stab (of a knife) ; ~ **dur** hard blow ; ~ **d'envoi** kick-off ; ~ **d'essai** first attempt ; ~ **d'état** coup d'état ; ~ **de feu** shot ; ~ **de filet** (*POLICE*) haul ; ~ **franc** free kick ; ~ **de frein** (sharp) braking *q* ; ~ **de fusil** rifle shot ; ~ **de grâce** coup de grâce ; ~ **de main**: **donner un** ~ **de main à qn** to give sb a (helping) hand ; ~ **d'œil** glance ; ~ **de pied** kick ; ~ **de poing** punch ; ~ **de soleil** sunburn ; ~ **de téléphone** phone call ; ~ **de tête** (*fig*) (sudden) impulse ; ~ **de théâtre** (*fig*) dramatic turn of events ; ~ **de vent** gust of wind.
**coupable** [kupabl(ə)] *a* guilty ; (*pensée*) guilty, culpable // *nm/f* (*gén*) culprit ; (*JUR*) guilty party ; ~ **de** guilty of.
**coupe** [kup] *nf* (*verre*) goblet ; (*à fruits*) dish ; (*SPORT*) cup ; (*de cheveux, de vêtement*) cut ; (*graphique, plan*) (cross) section ; **être sous la** ~ **de** to be under the control of ; **faire des** ~**s sombres dans** to make drastic cuts in.
**coupé** [kupe] *nm* (*AUTO*) coupé.
**coupe-circuit** [kupsiʀkɥi] *nm inv* cutout, circuit breaker.
**coupée** [kupe] *nf* (*NAVIG*) gangway.
**coupe-papier** [kuppapje] *nm inv* paper knife.
**couper** [kupe] *vt* to cut ; (*retrancher*) to cut (out), take out ; (*route, courant*) to cut off ; (*appétit*) to take away ; (*fièvre*) to take down, reduce ; (*vin, cidre*) to blend ; (: à table) to dilute (with water) // *vi* to cut ; (*prendre un raccourci*) to take a short-cut ; (*CARTES: diviser le paquet*) to cut ; (: *avec l'atout*) to trump ; **se** ~ (*se blesser*) to cut o.s. ; (*en témoignant etc*) to give o.s. away ; ~ **la parole à qn** to cut sb short.
**couperet** [kupʀɛ] *nm* cleaver, chopper.
**couperosé, e** [kupʀoze] *a* blotchy.
**couple** [kupl(ə)] *nm* couple ; ~ **de torsion** torque.

**coupler** [kuple] *vt* to couple (together).
**couplet** [kuplɛ] *nm* verse.
**coupole** [kupɔl] *nf* dome ; cupola.
**coupon** [kupɔ̃] *nm* (*ticket*) coupon ; (*de tissu*) remnant ; roll ; ~-**réponse international** international reply coupon.
**coupure** [kupyR] *nf* cut ; (*billet de banque*) note ; (*de journal*) cutting ; ~ **de courant** power cut.
**cour** [kuR] *nf* (*de ferme, jardin*) (court)yard ; (*d'immeuble*) back yard ; (*JUR, royale*) court ; **faire la** ~ **à qn** to court sb ; ~ **d'assises** court of assizes, ≈ Crown Court ; ~ **de cassation** Court of Cassation ; ~ **martiale** court-martial.
**courage** [kuRaʒ] *nm* courage, bravery ; **courageux, euse** *a* brave, courageous.
**couramment** [kuRamɑ̃] *ad* commonly ; (*avec aisance: parler*) fluently.
**courant, e** [kuRɑ̃, -ɑ̃t] *a* (*fréquent*) common ; (*COMM, gén: normal*) standard ; (*en cours*) current // *nm* current ; (*fig*) movement ; trend ; **être au** ~ (**de**) (*fait, nouvelle*) to know (about) ; **mettre qn au** ~ (**de**) (*fait, nouvelle*) to tell sb (about) ; (*nouveau travail etc*) to teach sb the basics (of) ; **se tenir au** ~ (**de**) (*techniques etc*) to keep o.s. up-to-date (on) ; **dans le** ~ **de** (*pendant*) in the course of ; **le 10** ~ (*COMM*) the 10th inst ; ~ **d'air** draught ; ~ **électrique** (electric) current, power.
**courbature** [kuRbatyR] *nf* ache ; **courbaturé, e** *a* aching.
**courbe** [kuRb(ə)] *a* curved // *nf* curve ; ~ **de niveau** contour line.
**courber** [kuRbe] *vt* to bend ; ~ **la tête** to bow one's head ; **se** ~ *vi* (*branche etc*) to bend, curve ; (*personne*) to bend (down).
**courbette** [kuRbɛt] *nf* low bow.
**coureur, euse** [kuRœR, -øz] *nm/f* (*SPORT*) runner (*ou* driver) ; (*péj*) womaniser/ manhunter ; ~ **cycliste/automobile** racing cyclist/driver.
**courge** [kuRʒ(ə)] *nf* (*BOT*) gourd ; (*CULIN*) marrow.
**courgette** [kuRʒɛt] *nf* courgette, zucchini.
**courir** [kuRiR] *vi* (*gén*) to run ; (*se dépêcher*) to rush ; (*fig: rumeurs*) to go round ; (*COMM: intérêt*) to accrue // *vt* (*SPORT: épreuve*) to compete in ; (*risque*) to run ; (*danger*) to face ; ~ **les cafés/bals** to do the rounds of the cafés/dances ; **le bruit court que** the rumour is going round that ; ~ **après qn** to run after sb, chase (after) sb.
**couronne** [kuRɔn] *nf* crown ; (*de fleurs*) wreath, circlet.
**couronnement** [kuRɔnmɑ̃] *nm* coronation, crowning ; (*fig*) crowning achievement.
**couronner** [kuRɔne] *vt* to crown.
**courons** *etc vb voir* **courir.**
**courre** [kuR] *vb voir* **chasse.**
**courrier** [kuRje] *nm* mail, post ; (*lettres à écrire*) letters *pl* ; (*rubrique*) column ; **long/moyen** ~ *a* (*AVIAT*) long-/medium- haul ; ~ **du cœur** problem page.
**courroie** [kuRwa] *nf* strap ; (*TECH*) belt ; ~ **de transmission/de ventilateur** driving/fan belt.
**courrons** *etc vb voir* **courir.**

**courroucé, e** [kuRuse] *a* wrathful.
**cours** [kuR] *nm* (*leçon*) lesson ; class ; (*série de leçons*) course ; (*cheminement*) course ; (*écoulement*) flow ; (*avenue*) walk ; (*COMM*) rate ; price ; **donner libre** ~ **à** to give free expression to ; **avoir** ~ (*monnaie*) to be legal tender ; (*fig*) to be current ; (*SCOL*) to have a class *ou* lecture ; **en** ~ (*année*) current ; (*travaux*) in progress ; **en** ~ **de route** on the way ; **au** ~ **de** in the course of, during ; **le** ~ **du change** the exchange rate ; ~ **d'eau** water course, generic term for streams, rivers ; ~ **du soir** night school.
**course** [kuRs(ə)] *nf* running ; (*SPORT: épreuve*) race ; (*trajet: du soleil*) course ; (: *d'un projectile*) flight ; (: *d'une pièce mécanique*) travel ; (*excursion*) outing ; climb ; (*d'un taxi, autocar*) journey, trip ; (*petite mission*) errand ; ~s *nfpl* (*achats*) shopping *sg* ; (*HIPPISME*) races.
**court, e** [kuR, kuRt(ə)] *a* short // *ad* short // *nm*: ~ (**de tennis**) (tennis) court ; **tourner** ~ to come to a sudden end ; **à** ~ **de short of** ; **prendre qn de** ~ to catch sb unawares ; **tirer à la** ~e **paille** to draw lots ; ~-**bouillon** *nm* court-bouillon ; ~- **circuit** *nm* short-circuit.
**courtier, ère** [kuRtje, -jɛR] *nm/f* broker.
**courtisan** [kuRtizɑ̃] *nm* courtier.
**courtisane** [kuRtizan] *nf* courtesan.
**courtiser** [kuRtize] *vt* to court, woo.
**courtois, e** [kuRtwa, -waz] *a* courteous ; **courtoisie** *nf* courtesy.
**couru, e** *pp de* **courir.**
**cousais** *etc vb voir* **coudre.**
**cousin, e** [kuzɛ̃, -in] *nm/f* cousin.
**coussin** [kusɛ̃] *nm* cushion.
**cousu, e** [kuzy] *pp de* **coudre** // *a*: ~ **d'or** rolling in riches.
**coût** [ku] *nm* cost ; **le** ~ **de la vie** the cost of living.
**coûtant** [kutɑ̃] *am*: **au prix** ~ at cost price.
**couteau, x** [kuto] *nm* knife ; ~ **à cran d'arrêt** flick-knife ; ~ **de poche** pocket knife ; ~-**scie** *nm* serrated-edged knife.
**coutellerie** [kutɛlRi] *nf* cutlery shop ; cutlery.
**coûter** [kute] *vt, vi* to cost ; **combien ça coûte?** how much is it?, what does it cost? ; **coûte que coûte** at all costs ; **coûteux, euse** *a* costly, expensive.
**coutume** [kutym] *nf* custom ; **coutumier, ère** *a* customary.
**couture** [kutyR] *nf* sewing ; dress- making ; (*points*) seam.
**couturier** [kutyRje] *nm* fashion designer, couturier.
**couturière** [kutyRjɛR] *nf* dressmaker.
**couvée** [kuve] *nf* brood, clutch.
**couvent** [kuvɑ̃] *nm* (*de sœurs*) convent ; (*de frères*) monastery ; (*établissement scolaire*) convent (school).
**couver** [kuve] *vt* to hatch ; (*maladie*) to be sickening for // *vi* (*feu*) to smoulder ; (*révolte*) to be brewing ; ~ **qn/qch des yeux** to look lovingly at ; to look longingly at.
**couvercle** [kuvɛRkl(ə)] *nm* lid ; (*de bombe aérosol etc, qui se visse*) cap, top.

**couvert, e** [kuvɛʀ, -ɛʀt(ə)] *pp de* **couvrir** // *a* (*ciel*) overcast; (*coiffé d'un chapeau*) wearing a hat // *nm* place setting; (*place à table*) place; (*au restaurant*) cover charge; ~**s** *nmpl* place settings; cutlery *sg*; ~ **de** covered with *ou* in; **bien** ~ (*habillé*) well wrapped up; **mettre le** ~ to lay the table; **à** ~ under cover; **sous le** ~ **de** under the shelter of; (*fig*) under cover of.

**couverture** [kuvɛʀtyʀ] *nf* (*de lit*) blanket; (*de bâtiment*) roofing; (*de livre, fig: d'un espion etc*) cover.

**couveuse** [kuvøz] *nf* (*à poules*) sitter, brooder; (*de maternité*) incubator.

**couvre...** [kuvʀ(ə)] *préfixe:* ~**-chef** *nm* hat; ~**-feu** *nm* curfew; ~**-lit** *nm* bedspread.

**couvreur** [kuvʀœʀ] *nm* roofer.

**couvrir** [kuvʀiʀ] *vt* to cover; **se** ~ (*ciel*) to cloud over; (*s'habiller*) to cover up, wrap up; (*se coiffer*) to put on one's hat; (*par une assurance*) to cover o.s.; **se** ~ **de** (*fleurs, boutons*) to become covered in.

**crabe** [kʀɑb] *nm* crab.

**crachat** [kʀaʃa] *nm* spittle *q*, spit *q*.

**cracher** [kʀaʃe] *vi* to spit // *vt* to spit out; (*fig: lave etc*) to belch (out); ~ **du sang** to spit blood.

**crachin** [kʀaʃɛ̃] *nm* drizzle.

**crachoir** [kʀaʃwaʀ] *nm* spittoon; (*de dentiste*) bowl.

**craie** [kʀɛ] *nf* chalk.

**craindre** [kʀɛ̃dʀ(ə)] *vt* to fear, be afraid of; (*être sensible à: chaleur, froid*) to be easily damaged by; ~ **de/que** to be afraid of/that.

**crainte** [kʀɛ̃t] *nf* fear; **de** ~ **de/que** for fear of/that; **craintif, ive** *a* timid.

**cramoisi, e** [kʀamwazi] *a* crimson.

**crampe** [kʀɑ̃p] *nf* cramp; ~ **d'estomac** stomach cramp.

**crampon** [kʀɑ̃pɔ̃] *nm* (*de semelle*) stud; (*ALPINISME*) crampon.

**cramponner** [kʀɑ̃pɔne]: **se** ~ *vi:* **se** ~ (**à**) to hang *ou* cling on (to).

**cran** [kʀɑ̃] *nm* (*entaille*) notch; (*de courroie*) hole; (*courage*) guts *pl*; ~ **d'arrêt** safety catch; ~ **de mire** bead.

**crâne** [kʀɑn] *nm* skull.

**crâner** [kʀɑne] *vi* (*fam*) to swank, show off.

**crânien, ne** [kʀɑnjɛ̃, -jɛn] *a* cranial, skull *cpd*, brain *cpd*.

**crapaud** [kʀapo] *nm* toad.

**crapule** [kʀapyl] *nf* villain.

**craquelure** [kʀaklyʀ] *nf* crack; crackle *q*.

**craquement** [kʀakmɑ̃] *nm* crack, snap; (*du plancher*) creak, creaking *q*.

**craquer** [kʀake] *vi* (*bois, plancher*) to creak; (*fil, branche*) to snap; (*couture*) to come apart, burst; (*fig*) to break down // *vt:* ~ **une allumette** to strike a match.

**crasse** [kʀas] *nf* grime, filth.

**crassier** [kʀasje] *nm* slag heap.

**cratère** [kʀatɛʀ] *nm* crater.

**cravache** [kʀavaʃ] *nf* (riding) crop; **cravacher** *vt* to use the crop on.

**cravate** [kʀavat] *nf* tie; **cravater** *vt* to put a tie on; (*fig*) to grab round the neck.

**crawl** [kʀol] *nm* crawl; **dos crawlé** backstroke.

**crayeux, euse** [kʀɛjø, -øz] *a* chalky.

**crayon** [kʀɛjɔ̃] *nm* pencil; (*de rouge à lèvres etc*) stick, pencil; **écrire au** ~ to write in pencil; ~ **à bille** ball-point pen; ~ **de couleur** crayon, colouring pencil.

**créance** [kʀeɑ̃s] *nf* (*COMM*) (financial) claim, (recoverable) debt; **créancier, ière** *nm/f* creditor.

**créateur, trice** [kʀeatœʀ, -tʀis] *a* creative // *nm/f* creator.

**création** [kʀeasjɔ̃] *nf* creation.

**créature** [kʀeatyʀ] *nf* creature.

**crécelle** [kʀesɛl] *nf* rattle.

**crèche** [kʀɛʃ] *nf* (*de Noël*) crib; (*garderie*) crèche, day nursery.

**crédence** [kʀedɑ̃s] *nf* (small) sideboard.

**crédit** [kʀedi] *nm* (*gén*) credit; ~**s** *nmpl* funds; **payer/acheter à** ~ to pay/buy on credit *ou* on easy terms; **faire** ~ **à qn** to give sb credit; **créditer** *vt:* **créditer un compte (de)** to credit an account (with); **créditeur, trice** *a* in credit, credit *cpd* // *nm/f* customer in credit.

**crédule** [kʀedyl] *a* credulous, gullible; **crédulité** *nf* credulity, gullibility.

**créer** [kʀee] *vt* to create; (*THÉÀTRE*) to produce (for the first time).

**crémaillère** [kʀemajɛʀ] *nf* (*RAIL*) rack; (*tige crantée*) trammel; **direction à** ~ (*AUTO*) rack and pinion steering; **pendre la** ~ to have a house-warming party.

**crémation** [kʀemasjɔ̃] *nf* cremation.

**crématoire** [kʀematwaʀ] *a:* **four** ~ crematorium.

**crème** [kʀɛm] *nf* cream; (*entremets*) cream dessert // *a inv* cream(-coloured); **un (café)** ~ ≈ a white coffee; ~ **fouettée** whipped cream; ~ **à raser** shaving cream; **crémerie** *nf* dairy; (*tearoom*) teashop; **crémeux, euse** *a* creamy; **crémier, ière** *nm/f* dairyman/woman.

**créneau, x** [kʀeno] *nm* (*de fortification*) crenel(le); (*fig*) gap; slot; (*AUTO*): **faire un** ~ to reverse into a parking space (*between cars alongside the kerb*).

**créole** [kʀeol] *a, nm, nf* Creole.

**crêpe** [kʀɛp] *nf* (*galette*) pancake // *nm* (*tissu*) crêpe; (*de deuil*) black mourning crêpe; black armband (*ou* hatband *ou* ribbon); **semelle (de)** ~ crêpe sole; **crêpé, e** *a* (*cheveux*) backcombed; ~**rie** *nf* pancake shop *ou* restaurant.

**crépi** [kʀepi] *nm* roughcast; **crépir** *vt* to roughcast.

**crépiter** [kʀepite] *vi* to sputter, splutter; to crackle; to rattle out; to patter.

**crépon** [kʀepɔ̃] *nm* seersucker.

**crépu, e** [kʀepy] *a* frizzy, fuzzy.

**crépuscule** [kʀepyskyl] *nm* twilight, dusk.

**crescendo** [kʀeʃɛndo] *nm, ad* (*MUS*) crescendo; **aller** ~ (*fig*) to rise higher and higher, grow ever greater.

**cresson** [kʀesɔ̃] *nm* watercress.

**crête** [kʀɛt] *nf* (*de coq*) comb; (*de vague, montagne*) crest.

**crétin, e** [kʀetɛ̃, -in] *nm/f* cretin.

**cretonne** [kʀətɔn] *nf* cretonne.

**creuser** [kʀøze] vt (trou, tunnel) to dig ; (sol) to dig a hole in ; (bois) to hollow out ; (fig) to go (deeply) into ; **cela creuse** (l'estomac) that gives you a real appetite ; **se ~ (la cervelle)** to rack one's brains.

**creuset** [kʀøzɛ] nm crucible ; (fig) melting pot ; (severe) test.

**creux, euse** [kʀø, -øz] a hollow // nm hollow ; (fig: sur graphique etc) trough ; **heures creuses** slack periods ; off-peak periods ; **le ~ de l'estomac** the pit of the stomach.

**crevaison** [kʀəvɛzɔ̃] nf puncture.

**crevasse** [kʀəvas] nf (dans le sol) crack, fissure ; (de glacier) crevasse ; (de la peau) crack.

**crevé, e** [kʀəve] a (fatigué) fagged out, worn out.

**crève-cœur** [kʀɛvkœʀ] nm inv heartbreak.

**crever** [kʀəve] vt (papier) to tear, break ; (tambour, ballon) to burst // vi (pneu) to burst ; (automobiliste) to have a puncture ; (abcès, outre, nuage) to burst (open) ; (fam) to die ; **cela lui a crevé un œil** it blinded him in one eye.

**crevette** [kʀəvɛt] nf: ~ (rose) prawn ; ~ **grise** shrimp.

**cri** [kʀi] nm cry, shout ; (d'animal: spécifique) cry, call ; **c'est le dernier ~** (fig) it's the latest fashion.

**criant, e** [kʀijɑ̃, -ɑ̃t] a (injustice) glaring.

**criard, e** [kʀijaʀ, -aʀd(ə)] a (couleur) garish, loud ; yelling.

**crible** [kʀibl(ə)] nm riddle ; (mécanique) screen, jig ; **passer qch au ~** to put sth through a riddle ; (fig) to go over sth with a fine-tooth comb.

**criblé, e** [kʀible] a: ~ **de** riddled with.

**cric** [kʀik] nm (AUTO) jack.

**crier** [kʀije] vi (pour appeler) to shout, cry (out) ; (de peur, de douleur etc) to scream, yell ; (fig: grincer) to squeal, screech // vt (ordre, injure) to shout (out), yell (out) ; **crieur de journaux** nm newspaper seller.

**crime** [kʀim] nm crime ; (meurtre) murder ; **criminaliste** nm/f specialist in criminal law ; **criminalité** nf criminality, crime ; **criminel, le** a criminal // nm/f criminal ; murderer ; **criminel de guerre** war criminal ; **criminologiste** nm/f criminologist.

**crin** [kʀɛ̃] nm hair q ; (fibre) horsehair ; **à tous ~s, à tout ~** diehard, out-and-out.

**crinière** [kʀinjɛʀ] nf mane.

**crique** [kʀik] nf creek, inlet.

**criquet** [kʀikɛ] nm locust ; grasshopper.

**crise** [kʀiz] nf crisis (pl crises) ; (MÉD) attack ; fit ; ~ **cardiaque** heart attack ; ~ **de foi** crisis of belief ; ~ **de foie** bilious attack ; ~ **de nerfs** attack of nerves.

**crispation** [kʀispɑsjɔ̃] nf twitch ; contraction ; tenseness.

**crisper** [kʀispe] vt to tense ; (poings) to clench ; **se** ~ to tense ; to clench ; (personne) to get tense.

**crisser** [kʀise] vi (neige) to crunch ; (tissu) to rustle ; (pneu) to screech.

**cristal, aux** [kʀistal, -o] nm crystal // nmpl (objets) crystal(ware) sg ; ~ **de plomb** (lead) crystal ; ~ **de roche** rock-

crystal ; **cristaux de soude** washing soda sg.

**cristallin, e** [kʀistalɛ̃, -in] a crystal-clear // nm (ANAT) crystalline lens.

**cristalliser** [kʀistalize] vi, vt, se ~ vi to crystallize.

**critère** [kʀitɛʀ] nm criterion (pl ia).

**critique** [kʀitik] a critical // nm/f (de théâtre, musique) critic // nf criticism ; (THÉÂTRE etc: article) review ; **la ~** (activité) criticism ; (personnes) the critics pl.

**critiquer** [kʀitike] vt (dénigrer) to criticize ; (évaluer, juger) to assess, examine (critically).

**croasser** [kʀɔase] vi to caw.

**croc** [kʀo] nm (dent) fang ; (de boucher) hook.

**croc-en-jambe** [kʀɔkɑ̃ʒɑ̃b] nm: **faire un ~ à qn** to trip sb up.

**croche** [kʀɔʃ] nf (MUS) quaver ; **double ~** sémiquaver.

**crochet** [kʀɔʃɛ] nm hook ; (clef) picklock ; (détour) detour ; (BOXE): ~ **du gauche** left hook ; (TRICOT: aiguille) crochet-hook ; (: technique) crochet ; ~**s** nmpl (TYPO) square brackets ; **vivre aux ~s de qn** to live ou sponge off sb ; **crocheter** vt (serrure) to pick.

**crochu, e** [kʀɔʃy] a hooked ; claw-like.

**crocodile** [kʀɔkɔdil] nm crocodile.

**crocus** [kʀɔkys] nm crocus.

**croire** [kʀwaʀ] vt to believe ; ~ **qn honnête** to believe sb (to be) honest ; **se ~ fort** to think one is strong ; ~ **que** to believe ou think that ; ~ **à,** ~ **en** to believe in.

**crois** vb voir **croître**.

**croisade** [kʀwazad] nf crusade.

**croisé, e** [kʀwaze] a (veston) double-breasted // nm (guerrier) crusader // nf (fenêtre) window, casement ; ~**e d'ogives** intersecting ribs ; **à la ~e des chemins** at the crossroads.

**croisement** [kʀwazmɑ̃] nm (carrefour) crossroads sg ; (BIO) crossing ; crossbreed.

**croiser** [kʀwaze] vt (personne, voiture) to pass ; (route) to cross, cut across ; (BIO) to cross // vi (NAVIG) to cruise ; ~ **les jambes/bras** to cross one's legs/fold one's arms ; **se ~** (personnes, véhicules) to pass each other ; (routes) to cross, intersect ; (lettres) to cross (in the post) ; (regards) to meet.

**croiseur** [kʀwazœʀ] nm cruiser (warship).

**croisière** [kʀwazjɛʀ] nf cruise ; **vitesse de ~** (AUTO etc) cruising speed.

**croisillon** [kʀwazijɔ̃] nm: **motif/fenêtre à ~s** lattice pattern/window.

**croissance** [kʀwasɑ̃s] nf growing, growth ; **maladie de ~** growth disease ; ~ **économique** economic growth.

**croissant, e** [kʀwasɑ̃, -ɑ̃t] a growing ; rising // nm (à manger) croissant ; (motif) crescent.

**croître** [kʀwɑtʀ(ə)] vi to grow ; (lune) to wax.

**croix** [kʀwa] nf cross ; **en ~** a, ad in the form of a cross ; **la C~ Rouge** the Red Cross.

**croquant, e** [kʀɔkɑ̃, -ɑ̃t] a crisp, crunchy // nm/f (péj) yokel, (country) bumpkin.

**croque...** [kRɔk] *préfixe*: **~-mitaine** *nm* bog(e)y-man ; **~-monsieur** *nm inv* toasted ham and cheese sandwich ; **~-mort** *nm* (*péj*) pallbearer.

**croquer** [kRɔke] *vt* (*manger*) to crunch ; to munch ; (*dessiner*) to sketch // *vi* to be crisp *ou* crunchy.

**croquet** [kRɔkɛ] *nm* croquet.

**croquette** [kRɔkɛt] *nf* croquette.

**croquis** [kRɔki] *nm* sketch.

**cross(-country)** [kRɔs(kuntRi)] *nm* cross-country race *ou* run ; cross-country racing *ou* running.

**crosse** [kRɔs] *nf* (*de fusil*) butt ; (*de revolver*) grip ; (*d'évêque*) crook, crosier ; (*de hockey*) hockey stick.

**crotte** [kRɔt] *nf* droppings *pl*.

**crotté, e** [kRɔte] *a* muddy, mucky.

**crottin** [kRɔtɛ̃] *nm*: **~ (de cheval)** (horse) dung *ou* manure.

**crouler** [kRule] *vi* (*s'effondrer*) to collapse ; (*être délabré*) to be crumbling.

**croupe** [kRup] *nf* croup, rump ; **en ~** pillion.

**croupier** [kRupje] *nm* croupier.

**croupir** [kRupiR] *vi* to stagnate.

**croustillant, e** [kRustijɑ̃, -ɑ̃t] *a* crisp ; (*fig*) spicy.

**croustiller** [kRustije] *vi* to be crisp *ou* crusty.

**croûte** [kRut] *nf* crust ; (*du fromage*) rind ; (*de vol-au-vent*) case ; (*MÉD*) scab ; **en ~** (*CULIN*) in pastry, in a pie ; **~ aux champignons** mushrooms on toast ; **~ au fromage** cheese on toast *q* ; **~ de pain** (*morceau*) crust (of bread) ; **~ terrestre** earth's crust.

**croûton** [kRutɔ̃] *nm* (*CULIN*) crouton ; (*bout du pain*) crust, heel.

**croyance** [kRwajɑ̃s] *nf* belief.

**croyant, e** [kRwajɑ̃, -ɑ̃t] *nm/f* believer.

**C.R.S.** *sigle fpl* = *Compagnies républicaines de sécurité* (a state security police force) // *sigle m* member of the C.R.S..

**cru, e** [kRy] *pp de* **croire** // *a* (*non cuit*) raw ; (*lumière, couleur*) harsh ; (*paroles, description*) crude // *nm* (*vignoble*) vineyard ; (*vin*) wine // *nf* (*d'un cours d'eau*) swelling, rising ; **de son (propre) ~** (*fig*) of his own devising ; **du ~** local ; **en ~e** in spate.

**crû** *pp de* **croître**.

**cruauté** [kRyote] *nf* cruelty.

**cruche** [kRyʃ] *nf* pitcher, (earthenware) jug.

**crucial, e, aux** [kRysjal, -o] *a* crucial.

**crucifier** [kRysifje] *vt* to crucify.

**crucifix** [kRysifi] *nm* crucifix.

**cruciforme** [kRysifɔRm(ə)] *a* cruciform, cross-shaped.

**cruciverbiste** [kRysivɛRbist(ə)] *nm/f* crossword puzzle enthusiast.

**crudité** [kRydite] *nf* crudeness *q* ; harshness *q* ; **~s** *nfpl* (*CULIN*) salads.

**crue** [kRy] *nf voir* **cru**.

**cruel, le** [kRyɛl] *a* cruel.

**crus** *etc*, **crûs** *etc vb voir* **croire, croître**.

**crustacés** [kRystase] *nmpl* shellfish.

**crypte** [kRipt(ə)] *nf* crypt.

**cubage** [kybaʒ] *nm* cubage, cubic content.

**cube** [kyb] *nm* cube ; (*jouet*) brick, building block ; **mètre ~** cubic metre ; **2 au ~ =** **8** 2 cubed is 8 ; **élever au ~** to cube ; **cubique** *a* cubic.

**cueillette** [kœjɛt] *nf* picking, gathering ; harvest *ou* crop (of fruit).

**cueillir** [kœjiR] *vt* (*fruits, fleurs*) to pick, gather ; (*fig*) to catch.

**cuiller** *ou* **cuillère** [kɥijɛR] *nf* spoon ; **~ à café** coffee spoon ; (*CULIN*) ≈ teaspoonful ; **~ à soupe** soup-spoon ; (*CULIN*) ≈ tablespoonful ; **cuillerée** *nf* spoonful.

**cuir** [kɥiR] *nm* leather ; (*avant tannage*) hide ; **~ chevelu** scalp.

**cuirasse** [kɥiRas] *nf* breastplate ; **cuirassé** *nm* (*NAVIG*) battleship.

**cuire** [kɥiR] *vt* (*aliments*) to cook ; (*poterie*) to fire // *vi* to cook ; (*picoter*) to smart, sting, burn ; **bien cuit** (*viande*) well done ; **trop cuit** overdone.

**cuisine** [kɥizin] *nf* (*pièce*) kitchen ; (*art culinaire*) cookery, cooking ; (*nourriture*) cooking, food ; **faire la ~** to cook, make a *ou* the meal ; **cuisiner** *vt* to cook ; (*fam*) to grill // *vi* to cook ; **cuisinier, ière** *nm/f* cook // *nf* (*poêle*) cooker.

**cuisse** [kɥis] *nf* (*ANAT*) thigh ; (*CULIN*) leg.

**cuisson** [kɥisɔ̃] *nf* cooking ; firing.

**cuistre** [kɥistR(ə)] *nm* prig.

**cuit, e** *pp de* **cuire**.

**cuivre** [kɥivR(ə)] *nm* copper ; **les ~s** (*MUS*) the brass ; **cuivré, e** *a* coppery ; bronzed.

**cul** [ky] *nm* (*fam*!) arse (!), bum ; **~ de bouteille** bottom of a bottle.

**culasse** [kylas] *nf* (*AUTO*) cylinder-head ; (*de fusil*) breech.

**culbute** [kylbyt] *nf* somersault ; (*accidentelle*) tumble, fall ; **culbuter** *vi* to (take a) tumble, fall (head over heels) ; **culbuteur** *nm* (*AUTO*) rocker arm.

**cul-de-jatte** [kydʒat] *nm/f* legless cripple.

**cul-de-sac** [kydsak] *nm* cul-de-sac.

**culinaire** [kylinɛR] *a* culinary.

**culminant, e** [kylminɑ̃, -ɑ̃t] *a*: **point ~** highest point.

**culminer** [kylmine] *vi* to reach its highest point ; to tower.

**culot** [kylo] *nm* (*d'ampoule*) cap ; (*effronterie*) cheek, nerve.

**culotte** [kylɔt] *nf* (*pantalon*) pants *pl*, trousers *pl* ; (*de femme*): **(petite) ~** knickers *pl* ; **~ de cheval** riding breeches *pl*.

**culotté, e** [kylɔte] *a* (*pipe*) seasoned ; (*cuir*) mellowed ; (*effronté*) cheeky.

**culpabilité** [kylpabilite] *nf* guilt.

**culte** [kylt(ə)] *nm* (*religion*) religion ; (*hommage, vénération*) worship ; (*protestant*) service.

**cultivateur, trice** [kyltivatœR, -tRis] *nm/f* farmer.

**cultivé, e** [kyltive] *a* (*personne*) cultured, cultivated.

**cultiver** [kyltive] *vt* to cultivate ; (*légumes*) to grow, cultivate.

**culture** [kyltyR] *nf* cultivation ; growing ; (*connaissances etc*) culture ; **(champs de) ~s** land(s) under cultivation ; **~ physique** physical training ; **culturel, le** *a* cultural ; **culturisme** *nm* body-building.

**cumin** [kymɛ̃] *nm* (*CULIN*) caraway seeds *pl*, cumin.

**cumul** [kymyl] *nm* (*voir* cumuler) holding (*ou* drawing) concurrently; ~ **de peines** sentences to run consecutively.

**cumuler** [kymyle] *vt* (*emplois, honneurs*) to hold concurrently; (*salaires*) to draw concurrently; (*JUR: droits*) to accumulate.

**cupide** [kypid] *a* greedy, grasping.

**curatif, ive** [kyʀatif, -iv] *a* curative.

**cure** [kyʀ] *nf* (*MÉD*) course of treatment; (*REL*) cure, ≈ living; presbytery, ≈ vicarage; **faire une** ~ **de fruits** to go on a fruit cure *ou* diet; **n'avoir** ~ **de** to pay no attention to; ~ **de sommeil** sleep therapy *q*.

**curé** [kyʀe] *nm* parish priest; **M. le** ~ ≈ Vicar.

**cure-dent** [kyʀdɑ̃] *nm* toothpick.

**cure-pipe** [kyʀpip] *nm* pipe cleaner.

**curer** [kyʀe] *vt* to clean out.

**curieux, euse** [kyʀjø, -øz] *a* (*étrange*) strange, curious; (*indiscret*) curious, inquisitive; (*intéressé*) inquiring, curious // *nmpl* (*badauds*) onlookers, bystanders; **curiosité** *nf* curiosity, inquisitiveness; (*objet*) curio(sity); (*site*) unusual feature *ou* sight.

**curiste** [kyʀist(ə)] *nm/f* person taking the waters at a spa.

**curriculum vitae** [kyʀikylɔmvite] *nm inv* (*abr* **C.V.**) curriculum vitae.

**curry** [kyʀi] *nm* curry; **poulet au** ~ curried chicken, chicken curry.

**curseur** [kyʀsœʀ] *nm* (*de règle*) slide; (*de fermeture-éclair*) slider.

**cursif, ive** [kyʀsif, -iv] *a*: **écriture cursive** cursive script.

**cutané, e** [kytane] *a* cutaneous, skin *cpd*.

**cuti-réaction** [kytiʀeaksjɔ̃] *nf* (*MÉD*) skin-test.

**cuve** [kyv] *nf* vat; (*à mazout etc*) tank.

**cuvée** [kyve] *nf* vintage.

**cuvette** [kyvɛt] *nf* (*récipient*) bowl, basin; (*du lavabo*) (wash)basin; (*des w.-c.*) pan; (*GÉO*) basin.

**C.V.** *sigle m* (*AUTO*) *voir* **cheval**; (*COMM*) = **curriculum vitae**.

**cyanure** [sjanyʀ] *nm* cyanide.

**cybernétique** [sibɛʀnetik] *nf* cybernetics *sg*.

**cyclable** [siklabl(ə)] *a*: **piste** ~ **cycle** track.

**cyclamen** [siklamɛn] *nm* cyclamen.

**cycle** [sikl(ə)] *nm* cycle.

**cyclique** [siklik] *a* cyclic(al).

**cyclisme** [siklism(ə)] *nm* cycling.

**cycliste** [siklist(ə)] *nm/f* cyclist // *a* cycle *cpd*.

**cyclomoteur** [siklɔmɔtœʀ] *nm* moped; **cyclomotoriste** *nm/f* moped-rider.

**cyclone** [siklon] *nm* hurricane.

**cygne** [siɲ] *nm* swan.

**cylindre** [silɛ̃dʀ(ə)] *nm* cylinder; **moteur à 4** ~**s en ligne** straight-4 engine; **cylindrée** *nf* (*AUTO*) (cubic) capacity; une (**voiture de**) **grosse cylindrée** a big-engined car; **cylindrique** *a* cylindrical.

**cymbale** [sɛ̃bal] *nf* cymbal.

**cynique** [sinik] *a* cynical; **cynisme** *nm* cynicism.

**cyprès** [sipʀɛ] *nm* cypress.

**cypriote** [sipʀjɔt] *a*, *nm/f* Cypriot.

**cyrillique** [siʀilik] *a* Cyrillic.

**cystite** [sistit] *nf* cystitis.

**cytise** [sitiz] *nm* laburnum.

## D

**d'** *prép*, *dét voir* **de**.

**dactylo** [daktilo] *nf* (*aussi*: ~**graphe**) typist; (*aussi*: ~**graphie**) typing, typewriting; ~**graphier** *vt* to type (out).

**dada** [dada] *nm* hobby-horse.

**daigner** [deɲe] *vt* to deign.

**daim** [dɛ̃] *nm* (fallow) deer *inv*; (*peau*) buckskin; (*imitation*) suede.

**dallage** [dalaʒ] *nm* paving.

**dalle** [dal] *nf* paving stone, flag(stone); slab.

**daltonien, ne** [daltɔnjɛ̃, -jɛn] *a* colour-blind.

**dam** [dam] *nm*: **au grand** ~ **de** much to the detriment *ou* annoyance of.

**dame** [dam] *nf* lady; (*CARTES, ÉCHECS*) queen; ~**s** *nfpl* (*jeu*) draughts *sg*.

**damer** [dame] *vt* to ram *ou* pack down; ~ **le pion à** (*fig*) to get the better of.

**damier** [damje] *nm* draughtboard; (*dessin*) check (pattern).

**damner** [dane] *vt* to damn.

**dancing** [dɑ̃siŋ] *nm* dance hall.

**dandiner** [dɑ̃dine]: **se** ~ *vi* to sway about; to waddle along.

**Danemark** [danmaʀk] *nm* Denmark.

**danger** [dɑ̃ʒe] *nm* danger; **mettre en** ~ to endanger, put in danger; **dangereux, euse** *a* dangerous.

**danois, e** [danwa, -waz] *a* Danish // *nm/f*: **D**~, **e** Dane // *nm* (*langue*) Danish.

**dans** [dɑ̃] *prép* in; (*direction*) into, to; (*à l'intérieur de*) in, inside; **je l'ai pris** ~ **le tiroir/salon** I took it out of *ou* from the drawer/lounge; **boire** ~ **un verre** to drink out of *ou* from a glass; ~ **2 mois** in 2 months, in 2 months' time, 2 months from now; ~ **les 20 F** about 20 F.

**dansant, e** [dɑ̃sɑ̃, -ɑ̃t] *a*: **soirée** ~**e** evening of dancing; dinner dance.

**danse** [dɑ̃s] *nf*: **la** ~ dancing; (*classique*) (ballet) dancing; **une** ~ a dance; **danser** *vi*, *vt* to dance; **danseur, euse** *nm/f* ballet dancer/ballerina; (*au bal etc*) dancer; partner; **en danseuse** (*à vélo*) standing on the pedals.

**dard** [daʀ] *nm* sting (*organ*).

**darder** [daʀde] *vt* to shoot, send forth.

**date** [dat] *nf* date; **faire** ~ to mark a milestone; ~ **de naissance** date of birth; **dater** *vt*, *vi* to date; **dater de** to date from, go back to; **à dater de** (as) from.

**datif** [datif] *nm* dative.

**datte** [dat] *nf* date; **dattier** *nm* date palm.

**dauphin** [dofɛ̃] *nm* (*ZOOL*) dolphin; (*du roi*) dauphin; (*fig*) heir apparent.

**daurade** [dɔʀad] *nf* gilt-head.

**davantage** [davɑ̃taʒ] *ad* more; (*plus longtemps*) longer; ~ **de** more.

**DCA** [desea] *sigle f* (= *défense contre avions*): **la** ~ anti-aircraft defence.

**de** (*de* + *le* = **du**, *de* + *les* = **des**) [də, dy, de] *prép* of; (*provenance*) from; (*moyen*) with; **la voiture d'Élisabeth/de mes parents** Elizabeth's/my parents' car; **un mur de brique/bureau d'acajou** a brick wall/mahogany desk; **augmenter** *etc* **de 10F** to increase by 10F; **une pièce de 2 m de large** *ou* **large de 2 m** a room 2 m wide *ou* in width, a 2 m wide room; **un bébé de 10 mois** a 10-month-old baby; **un séjour de 2 ans** a 2-year stay; **12 mois de crédit/travail** 12 months' credit/work // *dét*: **du vin, de l'eau, des pommes** (some) wine, (some) water, (some) apples; **des enfants sont venus** some children came; **a-t-il du vin?** has he got any wine?; **il ne veut pas de pommes** he doesn't want any apples; **il n'a pas d'enfants** he has no children, he hasn't got any children; **pendant des mois** for months.

**dé** [de] *nm* (*à jouer*) die *ou* dice (*pl* dice); (*aussi*: ~ **à coudre**) thimble; ~**s** *nmpl* (*jeu*) (game of) dice; **un coup de** ~**s** a throw of the dice.

**déambuler** [deãbyle] *vi* to stroll about.

**débâcle** [debɑkl(ə)] *nf* rout.

**déballer** [debale] *vt* to unpack.

**débandade** [debãdad] *nf* rout; scattering.

**débarbouiller** [debaʀbuje] *vt* to wash; **se** ~ to wash (one's face).

**débarcadère** [debaʀkadɛʀ] *nm* landing stage.

**débardeur** [debaʀdœʀ] *nm* docker, stevedore; (*maillot*) slipover, tank top.

**débarquement** [debaʀkəmã] *nm* unloading; landing; disembarcation; (*MIL*) landing.

**débarquer** [debaʀke] *vt* to unload, land // *vi* to disembark; (*fig*) to turn up.

**débarras** [debaʀa] *nm* lumber room; junk cupboard; outhouse; **bon** ~! good riddance!

**débarrasser** [debaʀase] *vt* to clear; ~ **qn de** (*vêtements, paquets*) to relieve sb of; (*habitude, ennemi*) to rid sb of; ~ **qch de** (*fouillis etc*) to clear sth of; **se** ~ **de** *vt* to get rid of; to rid o.s. of.

**débat** [deba] *nm* discussion, debate; ~**s** (*POL*) proceedings, debates.

**débattre** [debatʀ(ə)] *vt* to discuss, debate; **se** ~ *vi* to struggle.

**débauche** [deboʃ] *nf* debauchery; **une** ~ **de** (*fig*) a profusion of; a riot of.

**débaucher** [deboʃe] *vt* (*licencier*) to lay off, dismiss; (*entraîner*) to lead astray, debauch.

**débile** [debil] *a* weak, feeble; ~ **mental, e** *nm/f* mental defective.

**débit** [debi] *nm* (*d'un liquide, fleuve*) (rate of) flow; (*d'un magasin*) turnover (of goods); (*élocution*) delivery; (*bancaire*) debit; **avoir un** ~ **de 10 F** to be 10 F in debit; ~ **de boissons** drinking establishment; ~ **de tabac** tobacconist's (shop); **débiter** *vt* (*compte*) to debit; (*liquide, gaz*) to yield, produce, give out; (*couper: bois, viande*) to cut up; (*vendre*) to retail; (*péj: paroles etc*) to come out with, churn out; **débiteur, trice** *nm/f* debtor // *a* in debit.

**déblai** [deblɛ] *nm* earth (moved).

**déblaiement** [deblɛmã] *nm* clearing; **travaux de** ~ earth moving *sg*.

**déblayer** [debleje] *vt* to clear.

**débloquer** [debloke] *vt* (*frein*) to release; (*prix, crédits*) to free.

**déboires** [debwaʀ] *nmpl* setbacks.

**déboiser** [debwaze] *vt* to clear of trees; to deforest.

**déboîter** [debwate] *vt* (*AUTO*) to pull out; **se** ~ **le genou** *etc* to dislocate one's knee *etc*.

**débonnaire** [debonɛʀ] *a* easy-going, good-natured.

**débordé, e** [debɔʀde] *a*: **être** ~ **de** (*travail, demandes*) to be snowed under with.

**débordement** [debɔʀdəmã] *nm* overflowing.

**déborder** [debɔʀde] *vi* to overflow; (*lait etc*) to boil over // *vt* (*MIL, SPORT*) to outflank; ~ **(de) qch** (*dépasser*) to extend beyond sth; ~ **de** (*joie, zèle*) to be brimming over with *ou* bursting with.

**débouché** [debuʃe] *nm* (*pour vendre*) outlet; (*perspective d'emploi*) opening; (*sortie*): **au** ~ **de la vallée** where the valley opens out (onto the plain); **au** ~ **de la rue Dupont (sur le boulevard)** where the rue Dupont meets the boulevard.

**déboucher** [debuʃe] *vt* (*évier, tuyau etc*) to unblock; (*bouteille*) to uncork, open // *vi*: ~ **de** to emerge from, come out of; ~ **sur** to come out onto; to open out onto; (*fig*) to arrive at, lead up to.

**débourser** [debuʀse] *vt* to pay out, lay out.

**debout** [dəbu] *ad*: **être** ~ (*personne*) to be standing, stand; (: *levé, éveillé*) to be up (and about); (*chose*) to be upright; **être encore** ~ (*fig: en état*) to be still going; to be still standing; **se mettre** ~ to get up (on one's feet); **se tenir** ~ to stand; ~! stand up!; (*du lit*) get up!; **cette histoire ne tient pas** ~ this story doesn't hold water.

**déboutonner** [debutɔne] *vt* to undo, unbutton; **se** ~ *vi* to come undone *ou* unbuttoned.

**débraillé, e** [debʀɑje] *a* slovenly, untidy.

**débrayage** [debʀɛjaʒ] *nm* (*AUTO*) clutch; (: *action*) disengaging the clutch; (*grève*) stoppage; **faire un double** ~ to double-declutch.

**débrayer** [debʀeje] *vi* (*AUTO*) to declutch, disengage the clutch; (*cesser le travail*) to stop work.

**débridé, e** [debʀide] *a* unbridled, unrestrained.

**débris** [debʀi] *nm* (*fragment*) fragment // *nmpl* (*déchets*) pieces; rubbish *sg*; debris *sg*.

**débrouillard, e** [debʀujaʀ, -aʀd(ə)] *a* smart, resourceful.

**débrouiller** [debʀuje] *vt* to disentangle, untangle; (*fig*) to sort out, unravel; **se** ~ *vi* to manage.

**débroussailler** [debʀusɑje] *vt* to clear (of brushwood).

**débusquer** [debyske] *vt* to drive out (from cover).

**début** [deby] *nm* beginning, start ; ~**s** *nmpl* beginnings ; **début** *sg.*

**débutant, e** [debytɑ̃, -ɑ̃t] *nm/f* beginner, novice.

**débuter** [debyte] *vi* to begin, start ; *(faire ses débuts)* to start out.

**deçà** [dəsa]: **en** ~ **de** *prép* this side of.

**décacheter** [dekaʃte] *vt* to unseal, open.

**décade** [dekad] *nf (10 jours)* (period of) ten days ; *(10 ans)* decade.

**décadence** [dekadɑ̃s] *nf* decadence ; decline.

**décaféiné, e** [dekafeine] *a* decaffeinated, caffeine-free.

**décalage** [dekalaʒ] *nm* gap ; discrepancy ; move forward *ou* back ; shift forward *ou* back ; ~ **horaire** time difference (between time zones) ; time-lag.

**décalcomanie** [dekalkɔmani] *nf* transfer.

**décaler** [dekale] *vt (dans le temps: avancer)* to bring forward ; *(: retarder)* to put back ; *(changer de position)* to shift forward *ou* back ; ~ **de 2 h** to bring *ou* move forward 2 hours ; to put back 2 hours.

**décalquer** [dekalke] *vt* to trace ; *(par pression)* to transfer.

**décamper** [dekɑ̃pe] *vi* to clear out *ou* off.

**décanter** [dekɑ̃te] *vt* to (allow to) settle (and decant) ; **se** ~ to settle.

**décapant** [dekapɑ̃] *nm* acid solution ; scouring agent ; paint stripper.

**décaper** [dekape] *vt* to clean ; *(avec abrasif)* to scour ; *(avec papier de verre)* to sand.

**décapiter** [dekapite] *vt* to behead ; *(par accident)* to decapitate ; *(fig)* to cut the top off ; to remove the top men from.

**décapotable** [dekapɔtabl(ə)] *a* convertible.

**décapoter** [dekapɔte] *vt* to put down the top of.

**décapsuler** [dekapsyle] *vt* to take the cap *ou* top off ; **décapsuleur** *nm* bottle-opener.

**décathlon** [dekatlɔ̃] *nm* decathlon.

**décédé, e** [desede] *a* deceased.

**décéder** [desede] *vi* to die.

**déceler** [desle] *vt* to discover, detect ; to indicate, reveal.

**décélération** [deseleRasjɔ̃] *nf* deceleration.

**décembre** [desɑ̃bR(ə)] *nm* December.

**décemment** [desamɑ̃] *ad* decently.

**décence** [desɑ̃s] *nf* decency.

**décennie** [desni] *nf* decade.

**décent, e** [desɑ̃, -ɑ̃t] *a* decent.

**décentraliser** [desɑ̃tRalize] *vt* to decentralize.

**décentrer** [desɑ̃tRe] *vt* to decentre ; **se** ~ to move off-centre.

**déception** [desɛpsjɔ̃] *nf* disappointment.

**décerner** [desɛRne] *vt* to award.

**décès** [desɛ] *nm* death, decease.

**décevoir** [dɛsvwaR] *vt* to disappoint.

**déchaîner** [deʃene] *vt (passions, colère)* to unleash ; *(rires etc)* to give rise to, arouse ; **se** ~ *vi* to rage ; to burst out, explode ; *(se mettre en colère)* to fly into a rage, loose one's fury.

**déchanter** [deʃɑ̃te] *vi* to become disillusioned.

**décharge** [deʃaRʒ(ə)] *nf (dépôt d'ordures)* rubbish tip *ou* dump ; *(électrique)* electrical discharge ; *(salve)* volley of shots ; **à la** ~ **de** in defence of.

**déchargement** [deʃaRʒəmɑ̃] *nm* unloading.

**décharger** [deʃaRʒe] *vt (marchandise, véhicule)* to unload ; *(ÉLEC)* to discharge ; *(arme: neutraliser)* to unload ; *(: faire feu)* to discharge, fire ; ~ **qn de** *(responsabilité)* to relieve sb of, release sb from.

**décharné, e** [deʃaRne] *a* bony, emaciated, fleshless.

**déchausser** [deʃose] *vt (personne)* to take the shoes off ; *(skis)* to take off ; **se** ~ to take off one's shoes ; *(dent)* to come *ou* work loose.

**déchéance** [deʃeɑ̃s] *nf* degeneration ; decay, decline ; fall.

**déchet** [deʃɛ] *nm (de bois, tissu etc)* scrap ; *(perte: gén COMM)* wastage, waste ; ~**s** *nmpl (ordures)* refuse *sg*, rubbish *sg*.

**déchiffrer** [deʃifRe] *vt* to decipher.

**déchiqueter** [deʃikte] *vt* to tear *ou* pull to pieces.

**déchirant, e** [deʃiRɑ̃, -ɑ̃t] *a* heart-breaking, heart-rending.

**déchirement** [deʃiRmɑ̃] *nm (chagrin)* wrench, heartbreak ; *(gén pl: conflit)* rift, split.

**déchirer** [deʃiRe] *vt* to tear ; *(mettre en morceaux)* to tear up ; *(pour ouvrir)* to tear off ; *(arracher)* to tear out ; *(fig)* to rack ; to tear ; to tear apart ; **se** ~ *vi* to tear, rip ; **se** ~ **un muscle** to tear a muscle.

**déchirure** [deʃiRyR] *nf (accroc)* tear, rip ; ~ **musculaire** torn muscle.

**déchoir** [deʃwaR] *vi (personne)* to lower o.s., demean o.s.

**déchu, e** [deʃy] *a* fallen ; deposed.

**décibel** [desibɛl] *nm* decibel.

**décidé, e** [deside] *a (personne, air)* determined ; **c'est** ~ it's decided ; **être** ~ **à faire** to be determined to do.

**décidément** [desidemɑ̃] *ad* undoubtedly ; really.

**décider** [deside] *vt:* ~ **qch** to decide on sth ; ~ **de faire/que** to decide to do/that ; ~ **qn (à faire qch)** to persuade *ou* induce sb (to do sth) ; ~ **de qch** to decide upon sth ; *(suj: chose)* to determine sth ; **se** ~ **(à faire)** to decide (to do), make up one's mind (to do) ; **se** ~ **pour** to decide on *ou* in favour of.

**décilitre** [desilitR(ə)] *nm* decilitre.

**décimal, e, aux** [desimal, -o] *a, nf* decimal.

**décimer** [desime] *vt* to decimate.

**décimètre** [desimɛtR(ə)] *nm* decimetre ; **double** ~ (20 cm) ruler.

**décisif, ive** [desizif, -iv] *a* decisive ; *(qui l'emporte)*: **le facteur/ l'argument** ~ the deciding factor/ argument.

**décision** [desizjɔ̃] *nf* decision ; *(fermeté)* decisiveness, decision ; **emporter** *ou* **faire la** ~ to be decisive.

**déclamation** [deklamasjɔ̃] *nf* declamation ; *(péj)* ranting, spouting.

**déclaration** [deklaRasjɔ̃] *nf* declaration ; registration ; *(discours: POL etc)* statement ; ~ **(d'amour)** declaration ; ~ **de décès**

registration of death; ∼ **de guerre** declaration of war; ∼ **(d'impôts)** statement of income, tax declaration, ≈ tax return; ∼ **(de sinistre)** (insurance) claim.

**déclarer** [deklaRe] *vt* to declare, announce; *(revenus, marchandises)* to declare; *(décès, naissance)* to register; **se** ∼ *(feu, maladie)* to break out; ∼ **que** to declare that.

**déclassement** [deklasmɑ̃] *nm* (RAIL *etc*) change of class.

**déclasser** [deklase] *vt* to relegate; to downgrade; to lower in status.

**déclenchement** [deklɑ̃ʃmɑ̃] *nm* release; setting off.

**déclencher** [deklɑ̃ʃe] *vt* (*mécanisme etc*) to release; (*sonnerie*) to set off, activate; (*attaque, grève*) to launch; (*provoquer*) to trigger off; **se** ∼ *vi* to release itself; to go off.

**déclic** [deklik] *nm* trigger mechanism; (*bruit*) click.

**déclin** [deklɛ̃] *nm* decline.

**déclinaison** [deklinɛzɔ̃] *nf* declension.

**décliner** [dekline] *vi* to decline // *vt* (*invitation*) to decline, refuse; (*responsabilité*) to refuse to accept; (*nom, adresse*) to state; (LING) to decline.

**déclivité** [deklivite] *nf* slope, incline; **en** ∼ sloping, on the incline.

**décocher** [dekɔʃe] *vt* to throw; to shoot.

**décoder** [dekɔde] *vt* to decipher, decode.

**décoiffer** [dekwafe] *vt*: ∼ **qn** to disarrange *ou* mess up sb's hair; to take sb's hat off; **se** ∼ to take off one's hat.

**décoincer** [dekwɛ̃se] *vt* to unjam, loosen.

**déçois** *etc vb voir* **décevoir.**

**décolérer** [dekɔleRe] *vi*: **il ne décolère pas** he's still angry, he hasn't calmed down.

**décollage** [dekɔlaʒ] *nm* (AVIAT) takeoff.

**décoller** [dekɔle] *vt* to unstick // *vi* (*avion*) to take off; **se** ∼ to come unstuck.

**décolletage** [dekɔltaʒ] *nm* (TECH) cutting.

**décolleté, e** [dekɔlte] *a* low-necked, low-cut; wearing a low-cut dress // *nm* low neck(line); (*bare*) neck and shoulders; (*plongeant*) cleavage.

**décolorant** [dekɔlɔRɑ̃] *nm* decolorant, bleaching agent.

**décoloration** [dekɔlɔRasjɔ̃] *nf*: **se faire une** ∼ (*chez le coiffeur*) to have one's hair bleached *ou* lightened.

**décolorer** [dekɔlɔRe] *vt* (*tissu*) to fade; (*cheveux*) to bleach, lighten; **se** ∼ *vi* to fade.

**décombres** [dekɔ̃bR(ə)] *nmpl* rubble *sg*, debris *sg*.

**décommander** [dekɔmɑ̃de] *vt* to cancel; (*invités*) to put off; **se** ∼ to cancel one's appointment *etc*, cry off.

**décomposé, e** [dekɔ̃poze] *a* (*visage*) haggard, distorted.

**décomposer** [dekɔ̃poze] *vt* to break up; (CHIMIE) to decompose; (MATH) to factorize; **se** ∼ *vi* (*pourrir*) to decompose; **décomposition** *nf* breaking up; decomposition; factorization; **en décomposition** (*organisme*) in a state of decay, decomposing.

**décompression** [dekɔ̃pREsjɔ̃] *nf* decompression.

**décompte** [dekɔ̃t] *nm* deduction; (*facture*) breakdown (of an account), detailed account.

**déconcentration** [dekɔ̃sɑ̃tRasjɔ̃] *nf* (*des industries etc*) dispersal.

**déconcentré, e** [dekɔ̃sɑ̃tRe] *a* (*sportif etc*) who has lost (his/her) concentration.

**déconcerter** [dekɔ̃sɛRte] *vt* to disconcert, confound.

**déconfit, e** [dekɔ̃fi, -it] *a* crestfallen, downcast.

**déconfiture** [dekɔ̃fityR] *nf* failure, defeat; collapse, ruin.

**décongeler** [dekɔ̃ʒle] *vt* to thaw (out).

**décongestionner** [dekɔ̃ʒɛstjɔne] *vt* (MÉD) to decongest; (*rues*) to relieve congestion in.

**déconnecter** [dekɔnɛkte] *vt* to disconnect.

**déconseiller** [dekɔ̃seje] *vt*: ∼ **qch (à qn)** to advise (sb) against sth; ∼ **à qn de faire** to advise sb against doing.

**déconsidérer** [dekɔ̃sideRe] *vt* to discredit.

**déconsigner** [dekɔ̃siɲe] *vt* (*valise*) to collect (*from left luggage*); (*bouteille*) to return the deposit on.

**décontenancer** [dekɔ̃tnɑ̃se] *vt* to disconcert, discountenance.

**décontracter** [dekɔ̃tRakte] *vt*, **se** ∼ to relax.

**déconvenue** [dekɔ̃vny] *nf* disappointment.

**décor** [dekɔR] *nm* décor; (*paysage*) scenery; ∼**s** *nmpl* (THÉÂTRE) scenery *sg*, décor *sg*; (CINÉMA) set *sg*.

**décorateur** [dekɔRatœR] *nm* (interior) decorator; (CINÉMA) set designer.

**décoratif, ive** [dekɔRatif, -iv] *a* decorative.

**décoration** [dekɔRasjɔ̃] *nf* decoration.

**décorer** [dekɔRe] *vt* to decorate.

**décortiquer** [dekɔRtike] *vt* to shell; (*riz*) to hull; (*fig*) to dissect.

**décorum** [dekɔRɔm] *nm* decorum; etiquette.

**découcher** [dekuʃe] *vi* to spend the night away from home.

**découdre** [dekudR(ə)] *vt* to unpick, take the stitching out of; **se** ∼ to come unstitched; **en** ∼ (*fig*) to fight, do battle.

**découler** [dekule] *vi*: ∼ **de** to ensue *ou* follow from.

**découpage** [dekupaʒ] *nm* cutting up; carving; (*image*) cut-out (figure); ∼ **électoral** division into constituencies.

**découper** [dekupe] *vt* (*papier, tissu etc*) to cut up; (*volaille, viande*) to carve; (*détacher: manche, article*) to cut out; **se** ∼ **sur** (*ciel, fond*) to stand out against.

**découplé, e** [dekuple] *a*: **bien** ∼ well-built, well-proportioned.

**découpure** [dekupyR] *nf*: ∼**s** (*morceaux*) cut-out bits; (*d'une côte, arête*) indentations, jagged outline *sg*.

**découragement** [dekuRaʒmɑ̃] *nm* discouragement, despondency.

**décourager** [dekuRaʒe] *vt* to discourage, dishearten; (*dissuader*) to discourage, put off; **se** ∼ to lose heart, become discouraged; ~ **qn de faire/de qch** to discourage sb from doing/from sth, put sb off doing/sth.

**décousu, e** [dekuzy] *a* unstitched; (*fig*) disjointed, disconnected.

**découvert, e** [dekuvɛʀ, -ɛʀt(ə)] *a* (*tête*) bare, uncovered; (*lieu*) open, exposed // *nm* (*bancaire*) overdraft // *nf* discovery; **à ~ ad** (*MIL*) exposed, without cover; (*fig*) openly // *a* (*COMM*) overdrawn; **aller à la ~e de** to go in search of.

**découvrir** [dekuvʀiʀ] *vt* to discover; (*apercevoir*) to see; (*enlever ce qui couvre ou protège*) to uncover; (*montrer, dévoiler*) to reveal; **se ~** to take off one's hat; to take off some clothes; (*au lit*) to uncover o.s.; (*ciel*) to clear; **~ que** to discover that, find out that.

**décrasser** [dekʀase] *vt* to clean.

**décrépi, e** [dekʀepi] *a* peeling; with roughcast rendering removed.

**décrépit, e** [dekʀepi, -it] *a* decrepit; **décrépitude** *nf* decrepitude; decay.

**decrescendo** [dekʀeʃɛndo] *nm* (*MUS*) decrescendo; **aller ~** (*fig*) to decline, be on the wane.

**décret** [dekʀɛ] *nm* decree; **décréter** *vt* to decree; to order; to declare; **~-loi** *nm* statutory order.

**décrié, e** [dekʀije] *a* disparaged.

**décrire** [dekʀiʀ] *vt* to describe; (*courbe, cercle*) to follow, describe.

**décrochement** [dekʀɔʃmɑ̃] *nm* (*d'un mur etc*) recess.

**décrocher** [dekʀɔʃe] *vt* (*dépendre*) to take down; (*téléphone*) to take off the hook; (: *pour répondre*): ~ **(le téléphone)** to pick up *ou* lift the receiver; (*fig: contrat etc*) to get, land // *vi* to drop out; to switch off.

**décroître** [dekʀwatʀ(ə)] *vi* to decrease, decline, diminish.

**décrue** [dekʀy] *nf* drop in level (of the waters).

**décrypter** [dekʀipte] *vt* to decipher.

**déçu, e** [desy] *pp de* **décevoir.**

**déculotter** [dekylɔte] *vt*: ~ **qn** to take off *ou* down sb's trousers.

**décuple** [dekypl(ə)] *nm*: **le ~ de** ten times; **au ~** tenfold; **décupler** *vt, vi* to increase tenfold.

**dédaigner** [dedeɲe] *vt* to despise, scorn; (*négliger*) to disregard, spurn; ~ **de faire** to consider it beneath one to do; not to deign to do; **dédaigneux, euse** *a* scornful, disdainful.

**dédain** [dedɛ̃] *nm* scorn, disdain.

**dédale** [dedal] *nm* maze.

**dedans** [dədɑ̃] *ad* inside; (*pas en plein air*) indoors, inside // *nm* inside; **au ~** on the inside; inside; **en ~** (*vers l'intérieur*) inwards; *voir aussi* **là.**

**dédicace** [dedikas] *nf* dedication; (*manuscrite, sur une photo etc*) inscription; **dédicacer** [dedikase] *vt*: ~ **(à qn)** to sign (for sb), autograph (for sb), inscribe (to sb).

**dédier** [dedje] *vt* to dedicate.

**dédire** [dediʀ]: **se ~** *vi* to go back on one's word; to retract, recant.

**dédit** [dedi] *nm* (*COMM*) forfeit, penalty.

**dédommagement** [dedɔmaʒmɑ̃] *nm* compensation.

**dédommager** [dedɔmaʒe] *vt*: ~ **qn (de)** to compensate sb (for); (*fig*) to repay sb (for).

**dédouaner** [dedwane] *vt* to clear through customs.

**dédoublement** [dedubləmɑ̃] *nm* splitting; (*PSYCH*): ~ **de la personnalité** split *ou* dual personality.

**dédoubler** [deduble] *vt* (*classe, effectifs*) to split (into two); (*couverture etc*) to unfold; (*manteau*) to remove the lining of; ~ **un train/les trains** to run a relief train/additional trains.

**déduction** [dedyksjɔ̃] *nf* (*d'argent*) deduction; (*raisonnement*) deduction, inference.

**déduire** [dedɥiʀ] *vt*: ~ **qch (de)** (*ôter*) to deduct sth (from); (*conclure*) to deduce *ou* infer sth (from).

**déesse** [deɛs] *nf* goddess.

**défaillance** [defajɑ̃s] *nf* (*syncope*) blackout; (*fatigue*) (sudden) weakness *q*; (*technique*) fault, failure; (*morale etc*) weakness; ~ **cardiaque** heart failure.

**défaillant, e** [defajɑ̃, -ɑ̃t] *a* (*JUR*: *témoin*) defaulting.

**défaillir** [defajiʀ] *vi* to faint; to feel faint; (*mémoire etc*) to fail.

**défaire** [defɛʀ] *vt* (*installation, échafaudage*) to take down, dismantle; (*paquet etc, nœud, vêtement*) to undo; **se ~** *vi* to come undone; **se ~ de** *vt* (*se débarrasser de*) to get rid of; (*se séparer de*) to part with.

**défait, e** [defɛ, -ɛt] *a* (*visage*) haggard, ravaged // *nf* defeat.

**défaitiste** [defetist(ə)] *a, nm/f* defeatist.

**défalquer** [defalke] *vt* to deduct.

**défaut** [defo] *nm* (*moral*) fault, failing, defect; (*d'étoffe, métal*) fault, flaw, defect; (*manque, carence*): ~ **de** lack of; shortage of; **en ~** at fault; in the wrong; **faire ~** (*manquer*) to be lacking; **à ~ de** failing that; **à ~ de** for lack *ou* want of; **par ~** (*JUR*) in his (*ou* her *etc*) absence.

**défaveur** [defavœʀ] *nf* disfavour.

**défavorable** [defavɔʀabl(ə)] *a* unfavourable.

**défavoriser** [defavɔʀize] *vt* to put at a disadvantage.

**défectif, ive** [defɛktif, -iv] *a*: **verbe ~** defective verb.

**défection** [defɛksjɔ̃] *nf* defection, failure to give support *ou* assistance; failure to appear; **faire ~** (*d'un parti etc*) to withdraw one's support, leave.

**défectueux, euse** [defɛktɥø, -øz] *a* faulty, defective; **défectuosité** *nf* defectiveness *q*; defect, fault.

**défendre** [defɑ̃dʀ(ə)] *vt* to defend; (*interdire*) to forbid; ~ **à qn qch/de faire** to forbid sb sth/to do; **se ~** to defend o.s.; **il se défend** (*fig*) he can hold his own; **ça se défend** (*fig*) it holds together; **se ~ de/contre** (*se protéger*) to protect o.s. from/against; **se ~ de** (*se garder de*) to refrain from; (*nier*): **se ~ de vouloir** to deny wanting.

**défense** [defɑ̃s] *nf* defence; (*d'éléphant etc*) tusk; **'~ de fumer/cracher'** 'no smoking/ spitting', 'smoking/spitting prohibited' ; **défenseur** nm defender ; (JUR) counsel for the defence ; **défensif, ive** a, nf defensive.

**déférent, e** [deferɑ̃, -ɑ̃t] a (poli) deferential, deferent.

**déférer** [defeRe] vt (JUR) to refer ; ~ à vt (requête, décision) to defer to ; ~ qn à la justice to hand sb over to justice.

**déferlement** [defɛRləmɑ̃] nm breaking ; surge.

**déferler** [defɛRle] vi (vagues) to break ; (fig) to surge.

**défi** [defi] nm (provocation) challenge ; (bravade) defiance.

**défiance** [defjɑ̃s] nf mistrust, distrust.

**déficience** [defisjɑ̃s] nf deficiency.

**déficit** [defisit] nm (COMM) deficit ; (PSYCH etc: manque) defect ; être en ~ to be in deficit, be in the red.

**défier** [defje] vt (provoquer) to challenge ; (fig) to defy, brave ; se ~ de (se méfier de) to distrust, mistrust ; ~ qn de faire to challenge ou defy sb to do ; ~ qn à (jeu etc) to challenge sb to.

**défigurer** [defigyRe] vt to disfigure ; (suj: boutons etc) to mar ou spoil (the looks of) ; (fig: œuvre) to mutilate, deface.

**défilé** [defile] nm (GÉO) (narrow) gorge ou pass ; (soldats) parade ; (manifestants) procession, march ; **un ~ de** (voitures, visiteurs etc) a stream of.

**défiler** [defile] vi (troupes) to march past ; (sportifs) to parade ; (manifestants) to march ; (visiteurs) to pour, stream ; **se ~** vi (se dérober) to slip away, sneak off.

**défini, e** [defini] a definite.

**définir** [definiR] vt to define.

**définitif, ive** [definitif, -iv] a (final) final, definitive ; (pour longtemps) permanent, definitive ; (sans appel) final, definite // nf: **en définitive** eventually ; (somme toute) when all is said and done.

**définition** [definisjɔ̃] nf definition ; (de mots croisés) clue ; (TV) (picture) resolution.

**définitivement** [definitivmɑ̃] ad definitively ; permanently ; definitely.

**déflagration** [deflagRɑsjɔ̃] nf explosion.

**déflation** [deflɑsjɔ̃] nf deflation ; **déflationniste** a deflationist, deflationary.

**déflecteur** [deflɛktœR] nm (AUTO) quarter-light.

**déflorer** [deflɔRe] vt (jeune fille) to deflower ; (fig) to spoil the charm of.

**défoncer** [defɔ̃se] vt (caisse) to stave in ; (porte) to smash in ou down ; (lit, fauteuil) to burst (the springs of) ; (terrain, route) to rip ou plough up.

**déformant, e** [defɔRmɑ̃, -ɑ̃t] a: glace ou miroir ~(e) distorting mirror.

**déformation** [defɔRmɑsjɔ̃] nf loss of shape ; deformation ; distortion ; ~ professionnelle conditioning by one's job.

**déformer** [defɔRme] vt to put out of shape ; (corps) to deform ; (pensée, fait) to distort ; **se ~** vi to lose its shape.

**défouler** [defule]: **se ~** vi (PSYCH) to work off one's tensions, release one's pent-up feelings ; (gén) to unwind, let off steam.

**défraîchir** [defreʃiR]: **se ~** vi to fade ; to become worn.

**défrayer** [defReje] vt: ~ qn to pay sb's expenses ; ~ **la chronique** to be in the news, be the main topic of conversation.

**défricher** [defRiʃe] vt to clear (for cultivation).

**défroquer** [defRɔke] vi (gén: **se ~**) to give up the cloth, renounce one's vows.

**défunt, e** [defœ̃, -œ̃t] a: **son ~ père** his late father // nm/f deceased.

**dégagé, e** [degaʒe] a clear ; (ton, air) casual, jaunty.

**dégagement** [degaʒmɑ̃] nm emission ; freeing ; clearing ; (espace libre) clearing ; passage ; clearance ; (FOOTBALL) clearance ; **voie de ~** itinéraire de ~ alternative route (to relieve traffic congestion).

**dégager** [degaʒe] vt (exhaler) to give off, emit ; (délivrer) to free, extricate ; (MIL: troupes) to relieve ; (désencombrer) to clear ; (isoler: idée, aspect) to bring out ; ~ qn de (engagement, parole etc) to release ou free sb from ; **se ~** vi (odeur) to emanate, be given off ; (passage, ciel) to clear ; **se ~ de** (fig: engagement etc) to get out of ; to go back on.

**dégainer** [degene] vt to draw.

**dégarnir** [degaRniR] vt (vider) to empty, clear ; **se ~** vi to empty ; to be cleaned out ou cleared ; (tempes, crâne) to go bald.

**dégâts** [degu] nmpl damage sg.

**dégazer** [degɑze] vi (pétrolier) to clean its tanks.

**dégel** [deʒɛl] nm thaw.

**dégeler** [deʒle] vt to thaw (out) ; (fig) to unfreeze // vi to thaw (out).

**dégénéré, e** [deʒeneRe] a, nm/f degenerate.

**dégénérer** [deʒeneRe] vi to degenerate ; (empirer) to go from bad to worse.

**dégingandé, e** [deʒɛ̃gɑ̃de] a gangling, lanky.

**dégivrage** [deʒivRaʒ] nm defrosting ; de-icing.

**dégivrer** [deʒivRe] vt (frigo) to defrost ; (vitres) to de-ice ; **dégivreur** nm defroster de-icer.

**déglutir** [deglytiR] vi to swallow.

**dégonflé, e** [degɔ̃fle] a (pneu) flat.

**dégonfler** [degɔ̃fle] vt (pneu, ballon) to let down, deflate ; **se ~** vi (fam) to chicken out.

**dégouliner** [deguline] vi to trickle, drip ; ~ **de** to be dripping with.

**dégoupiller** [degupije] vt (grenade) to take the pin out of.

**dégourdi, e** [deguRdi] a smart, resourceful.

**dégourdir** [deguRdiR] vt to warm (up) ; **se ~ (les jambes)** to stretch one's legs (fig).

**dégoût** [degu] nm disgust, distaste.

**dégoûtant, e** [degutɑ̃, -ɑ̃t] a disgusting.

**dégoûter** [degute] vt to disgust ; **cela me dégoûte** I find this disgusting ou revolting ; ~ **qn de qch** to put sb off sth.

**dégoutter** [degute] vi to drip ; ~ **de** to be dripping with.

**dégradé, e** [degRade] a (couleur) shaded off // nm (PEINTURE) gradation.

**dégrader** [degRade] vt (MIL: officier) to degrade ; (abîmer) to damage, deface ;

(avilir) to degrade, debase ; **se** ~ (*relations, situation*) to deteriorate.

**dégrafer** [degRafe] *vt* to unclip, unhook, unfasten.

**dégraissage** [degRɛsaʒ] *nm*: ~ **et nettoyage à sec** dry cleaning.

**dégraisser** [degRese] *vt* (*soupe*) to skim ; (*vêtement*) to take the grease marks out of.

**degré** [dəgRe] *nm* degree ; (*d'escalier*) step ; **brûlure au 1er/2ème** ~ 1st/2nd degree burn ; **équation du 1er/2ème** ~ linear/quadratic equation ; **alcool à 90** ~**s** 90% proof alcohol (*on Gay-Lussac scale*) ; **vin de 10** ~**s** 10° wine (*on Gay-Lussac scale*) ; **par** ~**(s)** *ad* by degrees, gradually.

**dégressif, ive** [degResif, -iv] *a* on a decreasing sliding scale, degressive.

**dégrever** [degRave] *vt* to grant tax relief to ; to reduce the tax burden on.

**dégringoler** [degRɛ̃gɔle] *vi* to tumble (down).

**dégriser** [degRize] *vt* to sober up.

**dégrossir** [degRosiR] *vt* (*bois*) to trim ; (*fig*) to work out roughly ; to knock the rough edges off.

**déguenillé, e** [dəgnije] *a* ragged, tattered.

**déguerpir** [degɛRpiR] *vi* to clear off, scarper.

**déguisement** [degizmɑ̃] *nm* disguise.

**déguiser** [degize] *vt* to disguise ; **se** ~ (*se costumer*) to dress up ; (*pour tromper*) to disguise o.s.

**dégustation** [degystasjɔ̃] *nf* tasting ; sampling ; savouring ; (*séance*): ~ **de vin(s)** wine-tasting session.

**déguster** [degyste] *vt* (*vins*) to taste ; (*fromages etc*) to sample ; (*savourer*) to enjoy, savour.

**déhancher** [deɑ̃ʃe]: **se** ~ *vi* to sway one's hips ; to lean (one's weight) on one hip.

**dehors** [dəɔR] *ad* outside ; (*en plein air*) outdoors, outside // *nm* outside // *nmpl* (*apparences*) appearances, exterior *sg* ; **mettre** *ou* **jeter** ~ (*expulser*) to throw out ; **au** ~ outside ; outwardly ; **au** ~ **de** outside ; **en** ~ (*vers l'extérieur*) outside ; outwards ; **en** ~ **de** (*hormis*) apart from.

**déjà** [deʒa] *ad* already ; (*auparavant*) before, already ; **quel nom,** ~? what was the name again?

**déjanter** [deʒɑ̃te]: **se** ~ *vi* (*pneu*) to come off the rim.

**déjeté, e** [deʒte] *a* lop-sided, crooked.

**déjeuner** [deʒœne] *vi* to (have) lunch ; (*le matin*) to have breakfast // *nm* lunch ; (*petit déjeuner*) breakfast.

**déjouer** [deʒwe] *vt* to elude ; to foil, thwart.

**delà** [dəla] *ad*: **par** ~, **en** ~ **(de), au** ~ **(de)** beyond.

**délabrer** [delabRe]: **se** ~ *vi* to fall into decay, become dilapidated.

**délacer** [delase] *vt* to unlace, undo.

**délai** [delɛ] *nm* (*attente*) waiting period ; (*sursis*) extension (of time) ; (*temps accordé*) time limit ; **sans** ~ without delay ; **à bref** ~ shortly, very soon ; at short notice ; **dans les** ~**s** within the time limit ; **comptez un** ~ **de livraison de 10 jours** allow 10 days for delivery.

**délaisser** [delese] *vt* to abandon, desert.

**délasser** [delase] *vt* (*reposer*) to relax ; (*divertir*) to divert, entertain ; **se** ~ to relax.

**délateur, trice** [delatœR, -tRis] *nm/f* informer.

**délation** [delasjɔ̃] *nf* denouncement, informing.

**délavé, e** [delave] *a* faded.

**délayer** [deleje] *vt* (*CULIN*) to mix (with water *etc*) ; (*peinture*) to thin down ; (*fig*) to pad out, spin out.

**delco** [dɛlko] *nm* (*AUTO*) distributor.

**délecter** [delɛkte]: **se** ~ *vi*: **se** ~ **de** to revel *ou* delight in.

**délégation** [delegasjɔ̃] *nf* delegation.

**délégué, e** [delege] *a* delegated // *nm/f* delegate ; representative.

**déléguer** [delege] *vt* to delegate.

**délester** [delɛste] *vt* (*navire*) to unballast.

**délibération** [delibeRasjɔ̃] *nf* deliberation.

**délibéré, e** [delibeRe] *a* (*conscient*) deliberate ; (*déterminé*) determined, resolute.

**délibérément** [delibeRemɑ̃] *ad* deliberately.

**délibérer** [delibeRe] *vi* to deliberate.

**délicat, e** [delika, -at] *a* delicate ; (*plein de tact*) tactful ; (*attentionné*) thoughtful ; (*exigeant*) fussy, particular ; **procédés peu** ~ unscrupulous methods ; **délicatement** *ad* delicately ; (*avec douceur*) gently ; **délicatesse** *nf* delicacy, delicate nature ; tactfulness ; thoughtfulness ; **délicatesses** *nfpl* attentions, consideration *sg*.

**délice** [delis] *nm* delight.

**délicieux, euse** [delisjø, -jøz] *a* (*au goût*) delicious ; (*sensation, impression*) delightful.

**délictueux, euse** [deliktɥø, -ɥøz] *a* criminal.

**délié, e** [delje] *a* nimble, agile ; slender, fine // *nm*: **les** ~**s** the upstrokes (*in handwriting*).

**délier** [delje] *vt* to untie ; ~ **qn de** (*serment etc*) to free *ou* release sb from.

**délimitation** [delimitasjɔ̃] *nf* delimitation, demarcation.

**délimiter** [delimite] *vt* to delimit, demarcate ; to determine ; to define.

**délinquance** [delɛ̃kɑ̃s] *nf* criminality ; ~ **juvénile** juvenile delinquency.

**délinquant, e** [delɛ̃kɑ̃, -ɑ̃t] *a, nm/f* delinquent.

**déliquescence** [delikesɑ̃s] *nf*: **en** ~ **in a** state of decay.

**délire** [deliR] *nm* (*fièvre*) delirium ; (*fig*) frenzy ; lunacy.

**délirer** [deliRe] *vi* to be delirious ; (*fig*) to be raving, be going wild.

**délit** [deli] *nm* (*criminal*) offence ; ~ **de droit commun** violation of common law ; ~ **politique** political offence ; ~ **de presse** violation of the press laws.

**délivrance** [delivRɑ̃s] *nf* freeing, release ; (*sentiment*) relief.

**délivrer** [delivRe] *vt* (*prisonnier*) to (set) free, release ; (*passeport, certificat*) to issue ; ~ **qn de** (*ennemis*) to set sb free from, deliver *ou* free sb from ; (*fig*) to relieve sb of ; to rid sb of.

**déloger** [delɔʒe] *vt* (*locataire*) to turn out ; (*objet coincé, ennemi*) to dislodge.

**déloyal, e, aux** [delwajal, -o] a disloyal; unfair.

**delta** [dɛlta] nm (GÉO) delta.

**déluge** [delyʒ] nm (biblique) Flood, Deluge; (grosse pluie) downpour, deluge; (grand nombre): ~ **de** flood of.

**déluré, e** [delyʀe] a smart, resourceful; (péj) forward, pert.

**démagnétiser** [demaɲetize] vt to demagnetize.

**démagogie** [demagɔʒi] nf demagogy, demagoguery; **démagogique** a demagogic, popularity-seeking; vote-catching; **démagogue** a demagogic // nm demagogue.

**démaillé, e** [demaje] a (bas) laddered, with a run, with runs.

**demain** [dəmɛ̃] ad tomorrow.

**demande** [dəmɑ̃d] nf (requête) request; (revendication) demand; (ADMIN, formulaire) application; (ÉCON): **la** ~ demand; '~s **d'emploi**' situations wanted; ~ **en mariage** (marriage) proposal; ~ **de naturalisation** application for naturalization; ~ **de poste** job application.

**demandé, e** [dəmɑ̃de] a (article etc): **très** ~ (very) much in demand.

**demander** [dəmɑ̃de] vt to ask for; (question: date, heure etc) to ask; (requérir, nécessiter) to require, demand; ~ **qch à qn** to ask sb for sth; **to ask sb sth**; ~ **à qn de faire** to ask sb to do; ~ **que/pourquoi** to ask that/why; **se** ~ **si/pourquoi** etc to wonder if/why etc; (sens purement réfléchi) to ask o.s. if/why etc; **on vous demande au téléphone** you're wanted on the phone, someone's asking for you on the phone.

**demandeur, euse** [dəmɑ̃dœʀ, -øz] nm/f: ~ **d'emploi** job-seeker; (job) applicant.

**démangeaison** [demɑ̃ʒɛzɔ̃] nf itching.

**démanger** [demɑ̃ʒe] vi to itch; **la main me démange** my hand is itching; **l'envie me démange de** I'm itching to.

**démanteler** [demɑ̃tle] vt to break up; to demolish.

**démaquillant** [demakijɑ̃] nm make-up remover.

**démaquiller** [demakije] vt: **se** ~ to remove one's make-up.

**démarcage** [demaʀkaʒ] nm = **démarquage.**

**démarcation** [demaʀkasjɔ̃] nf demarcation.

**démarchage** [demaʀʃaʒ] nm (COMM) door-to-door selling.

**démarche** [demaʀʃ(ə)] nf (allure) gait, walk; (intervention) step; approach; (fig: intellectuelle) thought processes pl; approach; **faire des** ~s **auprès de qn** to approach sb.

**démarcheur, euse** [demaʀʃœʀ, -øz] nm/f (COMM) door-to-door salesman/woman.

**démarquage** [demaʀkaʒ] nm mark-down.

**démarqué, e** [demaʀke] a (FOOTBALL) unmarked.

**démarquer** [demaʀke] vt (prix) to mark down; (joueur) to stop marking.

**démarrage** [demaʀaʒ] nm starting q, start; ~ **en côte** hill start.

**démarrer** [demaʀe] vi (conducteur) to start (up); (véhicule) to move off; (travaux) to get moving; (coureur: accélérer) to pull away; **démarreur** nm (AUTO) starter.

**démasquer** [demaske] vt to unmask.

**démâter** [demɑte] vt to dismast // vi to be dismasted.

**démêler** [demele] vt to untangle, disentangle.

**démêlés** [demele] nmpl problems.

**démembrer** [demɑ̃bʀe] vt to slice up, tear apart.

**déménagement** [demenaʒmɑ̃] nm (du point de vue du locataire) move; (: du déménageur) removal; **entreprise/camion de** ~ removal firm/van.

**déménager** [demenaʒe] vt (meubles) to (re)move // vi to move (house); **déménageur** nm removal man; (entrepreneur) furniture remover.

**démence** [demɑ̃s] nf dementia; madness, insanity.

**démener** [demne] : **se** ~ vi to thrash about; (fig) to exert o.s.

**démenti** [demɑ̃ti] nm denial, refutation.

**démentiel, le** [demɑ̃sjɛl] a insane.

**démentir** [demɑ̃tiʀ] vt (nouvelle) to refute; (suj: faits etc) to belie, refute; ~ **que** to deny that; **ne pas se** ~ not to fail; to keep up.

**démériter** [demeʀite] vi: ~ **auprès de qn** to come down in sb's esteem.

**démesure** [deməzyʀ] nf immoderation, immoderateness; **démesuré, e** a immoderate, disproportionate.

**démettre** [demɛtʀ(ə)] vt: ~ **qn de** (fonction, poste) to dismiss sb from; **se** ~ (de ses fonctions) to resign (from) one's duties; **se** ~ **l'épaule** etc to dislocate one's shoulder etc.

**demeurant** [dəmœʀɑ̃]: **au** ~ ad for all that.

**demeure** [dəmœʀ] nf residence; **mettre qn en** ~ **de faire** to enjoin ou order sb to do; **à** ~ ad permanently.

**demeurer** [dəmœʀe] vi (habiter) to live; (séjourner) to stay; (rester) to remain.

**demi, e** [dəmi] a: **et** ~: **trois heures/bouteilles et** ~es three and a half hours/bottles, three hours/bottles and a half; **il est 2 heures/midi et** ~e it's half past 2/12 // nm (bière) ≈ half-pint (.25 litre); (FOOTBALL) half-back; **à** ~ ad half-; **ouvrir à** ~ to half-open; **à** ~ **fini** half-completed; **à la** ~e (heure) on the half-hour.

**demi...** [dəmi] préfixe half-, semi..., demi-; ~**-cercle** nm semicircle; **en** ~**-cercle** a semicircular // ad in a half circle; ~**-douzaine** nf half-dozen, half a dozen; ~**-finale** nf semifinal; ~**-fond** nm (SPORT) medium-distance running; ~**-frère** nm half-brother; ~**-gros** nm wholesale trade; ~**-heure** nf half-hour, half an hour; ~**-jour** nm half-light; ~**-journée** nf half-day, half a day.

**démilitariser** [demilitaʀize] vt to demilitarize.

**demi-litre** [dəmilitʀ(ə)] nm half-litre, half a litre.

**demi-livre** [dəmilivʀ(ə)] *nf* half-pound, half a pound.
**demi-longueur** [dəmilɔ̃gœʀ] *nf* (*SPORT*) half-length, half a length.
**demi-lune** [dəmilyn] *ad*: **en** ~ semicircular.
**demi-mesure** [dəmimzyʀ] *nf* half-measure.
**demi-mot** [dəmimo]: **à** ~ *ad* without having to spell things out.
**déminer** [demine] *vt* to clear of mines; **démineur** *nm* bomb disposal expert.
**demi-pension** [dəmipɑ̃sjɔ̃] *nf* (*à l'hôtel*) half-board.
**demi-pensionnaire** [dəmipɑ̃sjɔnɛʀ] *nm/f* (*au lycée*) half-boarder.
**demi-place** [dəmiplas] *nf* half-fare.
**démis, e** [demi, -iz] *a* (*épaule etc*) dislocated.
**demi-saison** [dəmisɛzɔ̃] *nf*: **vêtements de** ~ spring *ou* autumn clothing.
**demi-sel** [dəmisɛl] *a inv* (*beurre, fromage*) slightly salted.
**demi-sœur** [dəmisœʀ] *nf* half-sister.
**démission** [demisjɔ̃] *nf* resignation; **donner sa** ~ to give *ou* hand in one's notice, hand in one's resignation; **démissionner** *vi* (*de son poste*) to resign, give *ou* hand in one's notice.
**demi-tarif** [dəmitaʀif] *nm* half-price; (*TRANSPORTS*) half-fare.
**demi-tour** [dəmituʀ] *nm* about-turn; **faire un** ~ (*MIL etc*) to make an about-turn; **faire** ~ to turn (and go) back; (*AUTO*) to do a U-turn.
**démobilisation** [demɔbilizasjɔ̃] *nf* demobilization.
**démocrate** [demɔkʀat] *a* democratic // *nm/f* democrat.
**démocratie** [demɔkʀasi] *nf* democracy; ~ **populaire/libérale** people's/liberal democracy.
**démocratique** [demɔkʀatik] *a* democratic.
**démocratiser** [demɔkʀatize] *vt* to democratize.
**démodé, e** [demode] *a* old-fashioned.
**démographie** [demɔgʀafi] *nf* demography.
**démographique** [demɔgʀafik] *a* demographic; **poussée** ~ increase in population.
**demoiselle** [dəmwazɛl] *nf* (*jeune fille*) young lady; (*célibataire*) single lady, maiden lady; ~ **d'honneur** bridesmaid.
**démolir** [demɔliʀ] *vt* to demolish.
**démolisseur** [demɔlisœʀ] *nm* demolition worker.
**démolition** [demɔlisjɔ̃] *nf* demolition.
**démon** [demɔ̃] *nm* demon, fiend; (*enfant turbulent*) devil, demon; **le D**~ the Devil.
**démoniaque** [demɔnjak] *a* fiendish.
**démonstrateur, trice** [demɔ̃stʀatœʀ, -tʀis] *nm/f* demonstrator.
**démonstratif, ive** [demɔ̃stʀatif, -iv] *a* (*aussi LING*) demonstrative.
**démonstration** [demɔ̃stʀɑsjɔ̃] *nf* demonstration; (*aérienne, navale*) display.
**démonté, e** [demɔ̃te] *a* (*fig*) raging, wild.

**démonter** [demɔ̃te] *vt* (*machine etc*) to take down, dismantle; (*fig: personne*) to disconcert; **se** ~ *vi* (*personne*) to lose countenance.
**démontrer** [demɔ̃tʀe] *vt* to demonstrate, show.
**démoraliser** [demɔʀalize] *vt* to demoralize.
**démordre** [demɔʀdʀ(ə)] *vi*: **ne pas** ~ **de** to refuse to give up, stick to.
**démouler** [demule] *vt* (*gâteau*) to turn out.
**démoustiquer** [demustike] *vt* to clear of mosquitoes.
**démultiplication** [demyltiplikɑsjɔ̃] *nf* reduction; reduction ratio.
**démuni, e** [demyni] *a* (*sans argent*) impoverished; ~ **de** without, lacking in.
**démunir** [demyniʀ] *vt*: ~ **qn de** to deprive sb of; **se** ~ **de** to part with, give up.
**dénatalité** [denatalite] *nf* fall in the birth rate.
**dénaturer** [denatyʀe] *vt* (*goût*) to alter (completely); (*pensée, fait*) to distort, misrepresent.
**dénégations** [denegɑsjɔ̃] *nfpl* denials.
**dénicher** [denife] *vt* to unearth; to track *ou* hunt down.
**dénier** [denje] *vt* to deny.
**dénigrer** [denigʀe] *vt* to denigrate, run down.
**dénivellation** [denivɛlɑsjɔ̃] *nf,* **dénivellement** [denivɛlmɑ̃] *nm* ramp; dip; difference in level.
**dénombrer** [denɔ̃bʀe] *vt* (*compter*) to count; (*énumérer*) to enumerate, list.
**dénominateur** [denɔminatœʀ] *nm* denominator; ~ **commun** common denominator.
**dénomination** [denɔminɑsjɔ̃] *nf* designation, appellation.
**dénommer** [denɔme] *vt* to name.
**dénoncer** [denɔ̃se] *vt* to denounce; **se** ~ to give o.s. up, come forward; **dénonciation** *nf* denunciation.
**dénoter** [denɔte] *vt* to denote.
**dénouement** [denumɑ̃] *nm* outcome, conclusion; (*THÉÂTRE*) dénouement.
**dénouer** [denwe] *vt* to unknot, undo.
**dénoyauter** [denwajote] *vt* to stone; **appareil à** ~, **dénoyauteur** *nm* stoner.
**denrée** [dɑ̃ʀe] *nf* food(stuff); ~**s alimentaires** foodstuffs.
**dense** [dɑ̃s] *a* dense.
**densité** [dɑ̃site] *nf* denseness; density; (*PHYSIQUE*) density.
**dent** [dɑ̃] *nf* tooth (*pl* teeth); **faire ses** ~**s** to teethe, cut (one's) teeth; **en** ~**s de scie** serrated; jagged; ~ **de lait/sagesse** milk/wisdom tooth; **dentaire** *a* dental; **denté, e** *a*: **roue dentée** cog wheel.
**dentelé, e** [dɑ̃tle] *a* jagged, indented.
**dentelle** [dɑ̃tɛl] *nf* lace *q*.
**dentier** [dɑ̃tje] *nm* denture.
**dentifrice** [dɑ̃tifʀis] *nm, a*: (**pâte**) ~ toothpaste.
**dentiste** [dɑ̃tist(ə)] *nm/f* dentist.
**dentition** [dɑ̃tisjɔ̃] *nf* teeth *pl*; dentition.
**dénudé, e** [denyde] *a* bare.
**dénuder** [denyde] *vt* to bare.

**dénué, e** [denɥe] *a*: ~ **de** devoid of ; lacking in.

**dénuement** [denymã] *nm* destitution.

**déodorant** [deɔdɔrã] *nm* deodorant.

**dépannage** [depanaʒ] *nm*: **service de** ~ (AUTO) breakdown service.

**dépanner** [depane] *vt* (*voiture, télévision*) to fix, repair ; (*fig*) to bail out, help out ; **dépanneuse** *nf* breakdown lorry.

**déparer** [depaRe] *vt* to spoil, mar.

**départ** [depaR] *nm* leaving *q*, departure ; (SPORT) start ; (*sur un horaire*) departure ; **à son** ~ when he left.

**départager** [depaRtaʒe] *vt* to decide between.

**département** [depaRtəmã] *nm* department.

**départir** [depaRtiR]: **se** ~ **de** *vt* to abandon, depart from.

**dépassé, e** [depase] *a* superseded, outmoded.

**dépassement** [depasmã] *nm* (AUTO) overtaking *q*.

**dépasser** [depase] *vt* (*véhicule, concurrent*) to overtake ; (*endroit*) to pass, go past ; (*somme, limite*) to exceed ; (*fig*: *en beauté etc*) to surpass, outshine ; (*être en saillie sur*) to jut out above (*ou* in front of) // *vi* (AUTO) to overtake ; (*jupon*) to show.

**dépaysement** [depeizmã] *nm* disorientation ; change of scenery.

**dépayser** [depeize] *vt* to disorientate.

**dépecer** [depase] *vt* to joint, cut up ; to dismember.

**dépêche** [depɛʃ] *nf* dispatch ; ~ (**télégraphique**) wire.

**dépêcher** [depeʃe] *vt* to dispatch ; **se** ~ *vi* to hurry.

**dépeindre** [depɛ̃dR(ə)] *vt* to depict.

**dépendance** [depãdãs] *nf* dependence, dependency.

**dépendre** [depãdR(ə)] *vt* (*tableau*) to take down ; ~ **de** *vt* to depend on ; (*financièrement etc*) to be dependent on.

**dépens** [depã] *nmpl*: **aux** ~ **de** at the expense of.

**dépense** [depãs] *nf* spending *q*, expense, expenditure *q* ; (*fig*) consumption ; expenditure ; **une** ~ **de 100 F** an outlay *ou* expenditure of 100 F ; ~ **physique** (physical) exertion ; ~**s publiques** public expenditure.

**dépenser** [depãse] *vt* to spend ; (*gaz, eau*) to use ; (*fig*) to expend, use up ; **se** ~ (*se fatiguer*) to exert o.s.

**dépensier, ière** [depãsje, -jɛR] *a*: **il est** ~ he's a spendthrift.

**déperdition** [depɛRdisjɔ̃] *nf* loss.

**dépérir** [deperiR] *vi* to waste away ; to wither.

**dépêtrer** [depetRe] *vt*: **se** ~ **de** to extricate o.s. from.

**dépeupler** [depœple] *vt* to depopulate ; **se** ~ to be depopulated ; (*rivière, forêt*) to empty of wildlife *etc*.

**déphasé, e** [defaze] *a* (ÉLEC) out of phase ; (*fig*) out of touch.

**dépilatoire** [depilatwaR] *a* depilatory, hair removing.

**dépistage** [depistaʒ] *nm* (MÉD) detection.

**dépister** [depiste] *vt* to detect ; (*voleur*) to track down ; (*poursuivants*) to throw off the scent.

**dépit** [depi] *nm* vexation, frustration ; **en** ~ **de** *prép* in spite of ; **en** ~ **du bon sens** contrary to all good sense ; **dépité, e** *a* vexed, frustrated.

**déplacé, e** [deplase] *a* (*propos*) out of place, uncalled-for.

**déplacement** [deplasmã] *nm* moving ; shifting ; transfer ; trip, travelling *q* ; ~ **d'air** displacement of air ; ~ **de vertèbre** slipped disc.

**déplacer** [deplase] *vt* (*table, voiture*) to move, shift ; (*employé*) to transfer, move ; **se** ~ *vi* to move ; (*organe*) to be displaced ; (*voyager*) to travel // *vt* (*vertèbre etc*) to displace.

**déplaire** [deplɛR] *vi*: **ceci me déplaît** I don't like this, I dislike this ; **il cherche à nous** ~ he's trying to displease us *ou* be disagreeable to us ; **se** ~ **quelque part** to dislike it somewhere ; **déplaisant, e** *a* disagreeable, unpleasant.

**déplaisir** [depleziR] *nm* displeasure, annoyance.

**dépliant** [deplijã] *nm* leaflet.

**déplier** [deplije] *vt* to unfold.

**déplisser** [deplise] *vt* to smooth out.

**déploiement** [deplwamã] *nm* deployment ; display.

**déplorer** [deplɔRe] *vt* to deplore ; to lament.

**déployer** [deplwaje] *vt* to open out, spread ; to deploy ; to display, exhibit.

**dépoli, e** [depɔli] *a*: **verre** ~ frosted glass.

**déportation** [depɔRtasjɔ̃] *nf* deportation.

**déporté, e** [depɔRte] *nm/f* deportee ; (39-45) concentration camp prisoner.

**déporter** [depɔRte] *vt* (POL) to deport ; (*dévier*) to carry off course.

**déposant, e** [depozã, -ãt] *nm/f* (*épargnant*) depositor.

**dépose** [depoz] *nf* taking out ; taking down.

**déposer** [depoze] *vt* (*gén*: *mettre, poser*) to lay down, put down, set down ; (*à la banque, à la consigne*) to deposit ; (*passager*) to drop (off), set down ; (*démonter*: *serrure, moteur*) to take out ; (: *rideau*) to take down ; (*roi*) to depose ; (ADMIN: *faire enregistrer*) to file ; to lodge ; to submit ; to register // *vi* to form a sediment *ou* deposit ; (JUR): ~ (**contre**) to testify *ou* give evidence (against) ; **se** ~ *vi* to settle ; **dépositaire** *nm/f* (JUR) depository ; (COMM) agent ; **déposition** *nf* (JUR) deposition.

**déposséder** [deposede] *vt* to dispossess.

**dépôt** [depo] *nm* (*à la banque, sédiment*) deposit ; (*entrepôt, réserve*) warehouse, store ; (*gare*) depot ; (*prison*) cells *pl* ; ~ **légal** registration of copyright.

**dépotoir** [depɔtwaR] *nm* dumping ground, rubbish dump.

**dépouille** [depuj] *nf* (*d'animal*) skin, hide ; (*humaine*): ~ (**mortelle**) mortal remains *pl*.

**dépouillé, e** [depuje] *a* (*fig*) bare, bald ; ~ **de** stripped of ; lacking in.

**dépouiller** [depuje] *vt* (*animal*) to skin ; (*spolier*) to deprive of one's possessions ; (*documents*) to go through, peruse ; ~

qn/qch de to strip sb/sth of ; ~ le scrutin to count the votes.
**dépourvu, e** [depuRvy] a: ~ de lacking in, without ; au ~ ad unprepared.
**dépoussiérer** [depusjeRe] vt to remove dust from.
**dépravation** [depRavɑsjɔ̃] nf depravity.
**dépraver** [depRave] vt to deprave.
**dépréciation** [depResjɑsjɔ̃] nf depreciation.
**déprécier** [depResje] vt, se ~ vi to depreciate.
**déprédations** [depRedɑsjɔ̃] nfpl damage sg.
**dépression** [depREsjɔ̃] nf depression ; ~ (nerveuse) (nervous) breakdown.
**déprimer** [depRime] vt to depress.
**dépuceler** [depysle] vt (fam) to take the virginity of.
**depuis** [dəpɥi] prép (temps: date) since ; (: période) for ; (espace) since, from ; (quantité, rang: à partir de) from // ad (ever) since ; ~ que (ever) since ; ~ quand le connaissez-vous? how long have you known him? ; je le connais ~ 3 ans I've known him for 3 years ; ~ lors since then.
**députation** [depytɑsjɔ̃] nf deputation ; (fonction) position of deputy, ≈ Parliamentary seat.
**député, e** [depyte] nm/f (POL) deputy, ≈ Member of Parliament.
**députer** [depyte] vt to delegate ; ~ qn auprès de to send sb (as a representative) to.
**déraciner** [deRasine] vt to uproot.
**déraillement** [deRɑjmɑ̃] nm derailment.
**dérailler** [deRɑje] vi (train) to be derailed ; faire ~ to derail.
**dérailleur** [deRɑjœR] nm (de vélo) dérailleur gears pl.
**déraisonnable** [deREzɔnabl(ə)] a unreasonable.
**déraisonner** [deREzɔne] vi to talk nonsense, rave.
**dérangement** [deRɑ̃ʒmɑ̃] nm (gêne) trouble ; (gastrique etc) disorder ; (mécanique) breakdown ; en ~ (téléphone) out of order.
**déranger** [deRɑ̃ʒe] vt (personne) to trouble, bother ; to disturb ; (projets) to disrupt, upset ; (objets, vêtements) to disarrange ; se ~ to put o.s. out ; to (take the trouble to) come ou go out ; est-ce que cela vous dérange si do you mind if.
**dérapage** [deRapaʒ] nm skid, skidding q.
**déraper** [deRape] vi (voiture) to skid ; (personne, semelles, couteau) to slip ; (fig) to go out of control.
**dératiser** [deRatize] vt to rid of rats.
**déréglé, e** [deRegle] a (mœurs) dissolute.
**dérégler** [deRegle] vt (mécanisme) to put out of order, cause to break down ; (estomac) to upset ; se ~ vi to break down, go wrong.
**dérider** [deRide] vt, se ~ vi to brighten up.
**dérision** [deRizjɔ̃] nf: tourner en ~ to deride.
**dérisoire** [deRizwaR] a derisory.

**dérivatif** [deRivatif] nm distraction.
**dérivation** [deRivɑsjɔ̃] nf derivation ; diversion.
**dérive** [deRiv] nf (de dériveur) centre-board ; aller à la ~ (NAVIG, fig) to drift.
**dérivé, e** [deRive] a derived // nm (LING) derivative ; (TECH) by-product // nf (MATH) derivative.
**dériver** [deRive] vt (MATH) to derive ; (cours d'eau etc) to divert // vi (bateau) to drift ; ~ de to derive from ; **dériveur** nm sailing dinghy.
**dermatologie** [dɛRmatɔlɔʒi] nf dermatology ; **dermatologue** nm/f dermatologist.
**dernier, ière** [dɛRnje, -jɛR] a last ; (le plus récent) latest, last ; lundi/le mois ~ last Monday/month ; du ~ chic extremely smart ; les ~s honneurs the last tribute ; en ~ ad last ; ce ~ the latter ; **dernièrement** ad recently ; ~-né, **dernière-née** nm/f (enfant) last-born.
**dérobade** [deRɔbad] nf side-stepping q.
**dérobé, e** [deRɔbe] a (porte) secret, hidden ; à la ~e surreptitiously.
**dérober** [deRɔbe] vt to steal ; ~ qch à (la vue de) qn to conceal ou hide sth from sb('s view) ; se ~ vi (s'esquiver) to slip away ; to shy away ; se ~ sous (s'effondrer) to give way beneath ; se ~ à (justice, regards) to hide from ; (obligation) to shirk.
**dérogation** [deRɔgɑsjɔ̃] nf (special) dispensation.
**déroger** [deRɔʒe]: ~ à vt to go against, depart from.
**dérouiller** [deRuje] vt: se ~ les jambes to stretch one's legs (fig).
**déroulement** [deRulmɑ̃] nm (d'une opération etc) progress.
**dérouler** [deRule] vt (ficelle) to unwind ; (papier) to unroll ; se ~ vi to unwind ; to unroll, come unrolled ; (avoir lieu) to take place ; (se passer) to go on ; to go (off) ; to unfold.
**déroute** [deRut] nf rout ; total collapse ; mettre en ~ to rout.
**dérouter** [deRute] vt (avion, train) to reroute, divert ; (étonner) to disconcert, throw (out).
**derrière** [dɛRjɛR] ad behind // prép behind // nm (d'une maison) back ; (postérieur) behind, bottom ; les pattes de ~ the back legs, the hind legs ; par ~ from behind ; (fig) in an underhand way, behind one's back.
**des** [de] dét, prép + dét voir de.
**dès** [dɛ] prép from ; ~ que cj as soon as ; ~ son retour as soon as he was (ou is) back ; ~ lors ad from then on ; ~ lors que cj from the moment (that).
**D.E.S.** sigle m = diplôme d'études supérieures.
**désabusé, e** [dezabyze] a disillusioned.
**désaccord** [dezakɔR] nm disagreement.
**désaccordé, e** [dezakɔRde] a (MUS) out of tune.
**désaffecté, e** [dezafɛkte] a disused.
**désaffection** [dezafɛksjɔ̃] nf: ~ pour estrangement from.

**désagréable** [dezagʀeable(ə)] a unpleasant, disagreeable.
**désagréger** [dezagʀeʒe]: **se** ~ vi to disintegrate, break up.
**désagrément** [dezagʀemɑ̃] nm annoyance, trouble q.
**désaltérer** [dezalteʀe] vt: **se** ~ to quench one's thirst; **ça désaltère** it's thirst-quenching, it takes your thirst away.
**désamorcer** [dezamɔʀse] vt to remove the primer from; (fig) to defuse; to forestall.
**désappointé, e** [dezapwɛ̃te] a disappointed.
**désapprobation** [dezapʀɔbɑsjɔ̃] nf disapproval.
**désapprouver** [dezapʀuve] vt to disapprove of.
**désarçonner** [dezaʀsɔne] vt to unseat, throw; (fig) to throw, nonplus.
**désarmement** [dezaʀməmɑ̃] nm disarmament.
**désarmer** [dezaʀme] vt (MIL, aussi fig) to disarm; (NAVIG) to lay up.
**désarroi** [dezaʀwa] nm helplessness, disarray.
**désarticulé, e** [dezaʀtikyle] a (pantin, corps) dislocated.
**désarticuler** [dezaʀtikyle] vt: **se** ~ (acrobate) to contort (o.s.).
**désassorti, e** [dezasɔʀti] a unmatching, unmatched.
**désastre** [dezastʀ(ə)] nm disaster; **désastreux, euse** a disastrous.
**désavantage** [dezavɑ̃taʒ] nm disadvantage; (inconvénient) drawback, disadvantage; **désavantager** vt to put at a disadvantage; **désavantageux, euse** a unfavourable, disadvantageous.
**désavouer** [dezavwe] vt to disown, repudiate, disclaim.
**désaxé, e** [dezakse] a (fig) unbalanced.
**désaxer** [dezakse] vt (roue) to put out of true.
**desceller** [desele] vt (pierre) to pull free.
**descendance** [desɑ̃dɑ̃s] nf (famille) descendants pl, issue; (origine) descent.
**descendant, e** [desɑ̃dɑ̃, -ɑ̃t] nm/f descendant.
**descendre** [desɑ̃dʀ(ə)] vt (escalier, montagne) to go (ou come) down; (valise, paquet) to take ou get down; (étagère etc) to lower; (fam: abattre) to shoot down // vi to go (ou come) down; (chemin) to go down; (passager: s'arrêter) to get out, alight; (niveau, température) to go ou come down, fall, drop; ~ **à pied/en voiture** to walk/drive down, to go down on foot/by car; ~ **de** (famille) to be descended from; ~ **du train** to get out of ou off the train; ~ **d'un arbre** to climb down from a tree; ~ **de cheval** to dismount, get off one's horse.
**descente** [desɑ̃t] nf descent, going down; (chemin) way down; (SKI) downhill (race); **au milieu de la** ~ halfway down; **freinez dans les** ~s use the brakes going downhill; ~ **de lit** bedside rug; ~ **(de police)** (police) raid.
**description** [dɛskʀipsjɔ̃] nf description.

**désembuer** [dezɑ̃bɥe] vt to demist.
**désemparé, e** [dezɑ̃paʀe] a bewildered, distraught; (véhicule) crippled.
**désemparer** [dezɑ̃paʀe] vi: **sans** ~ without stopping.
**désemplir** [dezɑ̃pliʀ] vi: **ne pas** ~ to be always full.
**désenchantement** [dezɑ̃ʃɑ̃tmɑ̃] nm disenchantment; disillusion.
**désenfler** [dezɑ̃fle] vi to become less swollen.
**désengagement** [dezɑ̃gaʒmɑ̃] nm (POL) disengagement.
**désensibiliser** [desɑ̃sibilize] vt (MÉD) to desensitize.
**déséquilibre** [dezekilibʀ(ə)] nm (position): **être en** ~ to be unsteady; (fig: des forces, du budget) imbalance; (PSYCH) unbalance.
**déséquilibré, e** [dezekilibʀe] nm/f (PSYCH) unbalanced person.
**déséquilibrer** [dezekilibʀe] vt to throw off balance.
**désert, e** [dezɛʀ, -ɛʀt(ə)] a deserted // nm desert.
**déserter** [dezɛʀte] vi, vt to desert; **déserteur** nm deserter; **désertion** nf desertion.
**désertique** [dezɛʀtik] a desert cpd: barren, empty.
**désescalade** [dezɛskalad] nf (MIL) de-escalation.
**désespéré, e** [dezɛspeʀe] a desperate; ~**ment** ad desperately.
**désespérer** [dezɛspeʀe] vt to drive to despair // vi, **se** ~ vi to despair; ~ **de** to despair of.
**désespoir** [dezɛspwaʀ] nm despair; **faire le** ~ **de qn** to be the despair of sb; **en** ~ **de cause** in desperation.
**déshabillé, e** [dezabije] a undressed // nm négligée.
**déshabiller** [dezabije] vt to undress; **se** ~ to undress (o.s.).
**déshabituer** [dezabitɥe] vt: **se** ~ **de** to get out of the habit of.
**désherbant** [dezɛʀbɑ̃] nm weed-killer.
**déshériter** [dezeʀite] vt to disinherit.
**déshérités** [dezeʀite] nmpl: **les** ~ the underprivileged.
**déshonneur** [dezɔnœʀ] nm dishonour, disgrace.
**déshonorer** [dezɔnɔʀe] vt to dishonour, bring disgrace upon.
**déshydraté, e** [dezidʀate] a dehydrated.
**desiderata** [dezideʀata] nmpl requirements.
**désignation** [deziɲasjɔ̃] nf naming, appointment; (signe, mot) name, designation.
**désigner** [deziɲe] vt (montrer) to point out, indicate; (dénommer) to denote, refer to; (nommer: candidat etc) to name, appoint.
**désillusion** [dezilyzjɔ̃] nf disillusion(ment).
**désinence** [dezinɑ̃s] nf ending, inflexion.
**désinfectant, e** [dezɛ̃fɛktɑ̃, -ɑ̃t] a, nm disinfectant.
**désinfecter** [dezɛ̃fɛkte] vt to disinfect.

**désinfection** [dezɛ̃fɛksjɔ̃] *nf* disinfection.
**désintégrer** [dezɛ̃tegʀe] *vt*, **se** ~ *vi* to disintegrate.
**désintéressé, e** [dezɛ̃teʀese] *a* disinterested, unselfish.
**désintéresser** [dezɛ̃teʀese] *vt*: **se** ~ **(de)** to lose interest (in).
**désintoxication** [dezɛ̃tɔksikɑsjɔ̃] *nf* treatment for alcoholism.
**désinvolte** [dezɛ̃vɔlt(ə)] *a* casual, offhand; **désinvolture** *nf* casualness.
**désir** [deziʀ] *nm* wish; (*fort, sensuel*) desire.
**désirer** [deziʀe] *vt* to want, wish for; (*sexuellement*) to desire; **je désire ...** (*formule de politesse*) I would like ...; **il désire que tu l'aides** he would like *ou* he wants you to help him; ~ **faire** to want *ou* wish to do.
**désireux, euse** [deziʀø, -øz] *a*: ~ **de faire** anxious to do.
**désistement** [dezistəmɑ̃] *nm* withdrawal.
**désister** [deziste] : **se** ~ *vi* to stand down, withdraw.
**désobéir** [dezɔbeiʀ] *vi*: ~ **(à qn/qch)** to disobey (sb/sth); **désobéissance** *nf* disobedience; **désobéissant, e** *a* disobedient.
**désobligeant, e** [dezɔbliʒɑ̃, -ɑ̃t] *a* disagreeable, unpleasant.
**désodorisant** [dezɔdɔʀizɑ̃] *nm* air freshener, deodorizer.
**désœuvré, e** [dezœvʀe] *a* idle; **désœuvrement** *nm* idleness.
**désolation** [dezɔlɑsjɔ̃] *nf* distress, grief; desolation, devastation.
**désolé, e** [dezɔle] *a* (*paysage*) desolate; **je suis** ~ I'm sorry.
**désoler** [dezɔle] *vt* to distress, grieve.
**désolidariser** [desɔlidaʀize] *vt*: **se** ~ **de** *ou* **d'avec** to dissociate o.s. from.
**désopilant, e** [dezɔpilɑ̃, -ɑ̃t] *a* screamingly funny, hilarious.
**désordonné, e** [dezɔʀdɔne] *a* untidy, disorderly.
**désordre** [dezɔʀdʀ(ə)] *nm* disorder(liness), untidiness; (*anarchie*) disorder; ~**s** *nmpl* (*POL*) disturbances, disorder *sg*; **en** ~ in a mess, untidy.
**désorganiser** [dezɔʀganize] *vt* to disorganize.
**désorienté, e** [dezɔʀjɑ̃te] *a* disorientated; (*fig*) bewildered.
**désormais** [dezɔʀmɛ] *ad* in future, from now on.
**désosser** [dezɔse] *vt* to bone.
**despote** [dɛspɔt] *nm* despot; tyrant; **despotisme** *nm* despotism.
**desquels, desquelles** [dekɛl] *prép* + *pronom voir* **lequel**.
**dessaisir** [deseziʀ]: **se** ~ **de** *vt* to give up, part with.
**dessaler** [desale] *vt* (*eau de mer*) to desalinate; (*CULIN*) to soak.
**desséché, e** [deseʃe] *a* dried up.
**dessécher** [deseʃe] *vt* to dry out, parch; **se** ~ *vi* to dry out.
**dessein** [desɛ̃] *nm* design; **dans le** ~ **de** with the intention of; **à** ~ intentionally, deliberately.
**desserrer** [deseʀe] *vt* to loosen; (*frein*) to

release; (*poing, dents*) to unclench; (*objets alignés*) to space out.
**dessert** [desɛʀ] *nm* dessert, pudding.
**desserte** [desɛʀt(ə)] *nf* (*table*) sideboard table; (*transport*): **la** ~ **du village est assurée par autocar** there is a coach service to the village.
**desservir** [desɛʀviʀ] *vt* (*ville, quartier*) to serve; (*nuire à*) to go against, put at a disadvantage; ~ **(la table)** to clear the table.
**dessin** [desɛ̃] *nm* (*œuvre, art*) drawing; (*motif*) pattern, design; (*contour*) (out)line; ~ **animé** cartoon (film); ~ **humoristique** cartoon.
**dessinateur, trice** [desinatœʀ, -tʀis] *nm/f* drawer; (*de bandes dessinées*) cartoonist; (*industriel*) draughtsman.
**dessiner** [desine] *vt* to draw; (*concevoir: carrosserie, maison*) to design.
**dessoûler** [desule] *vt*, *vi* to sober up.
**dessous** [dəsu] *ad* underneath, beneath // *nm* underside // *nmpl* (*sous-vêtements*) underwear *sg*; **en** ~, **par** ~ underneath; **below**; **au-**~ below; **de** ~ **le lit** from under the bed; **au-**~ **de** below; (*peu digne de*) beneath; **avoir le** ~ to get the worst of it; ~**-de-plat** *nm inv* tablemat.
**dessus** [dəsy] *ad* on top; (*collé, écrit*) on it // *nm* top; **en** ~ above; **par** ~ *ad* over it // *prép* over; **au-**~ above; **au-**~ **de** above; **avoir le** ~ to get the upper hand; ~**-de-lit** *nm inv* bedspread.
**destin** [dɛstɛ̃] *nm* fate; (*avenir*) destiny.
**destinataire** [dɛstinatɛʀ] *nm/f* (*POSTES*) addressee; (*d'un colis*) consignee.
**destination** [dɛstinɑsjɔ̃] *nf* (*lieu*) destination; (*usage*) purpose; **à** ~ **de** bound for, travelling to.
**destinée** [dɛstine] *nf* fate; (*existence, avenir*) destiny.
**destiner** [dɛstine] *vt*: ~ **qn à** (*poste, sort*) to destine sb for, intend sb to + *verbe*; ~ **qn/qch à** (*prédestiner*) to mark sb/sth out for, destine sb/sth to + *verbe*; ~ **qch à** (*envisager d'affecter*) to intend to use sth for; ~ **qch à qn** (*envisager de donner*) to intend to give sth to sb, intend sb to have sth; (*adresser*) to intend sth for sb; to aim sth at sb; **se** ~ **à l'enseignement** to intend to become a teacher; **être destiné à** (*sort*) to be destined to + *verbe*; (*usage*) to be intended *ou* meant for; (*suj: sort*) to be in store for.
**destituer** [dɛstitɥe] *vt* to depose.
**destructeur, trice** [dɛstʀyktœʀ, -tʀis] *a* destructive.
**destruction** [dɛstʀyksjɔ̃] *nf* destruction.
**désuet, ète** [desɥɛ, -ɛt] *a* outdated, outmoded; **désuétude** *nf*: **tomber en désuétude** to fall into disuse, become obsolete.
**désuni, e** [dezyni] *a* divided, disunited.
**détachant** [detaʃɑ̃] *nm* stain remover.
**détachement** [detaʃmɑ̃] *nm* detachment.
**détacher** [detaʃe] *vt* (*enlever*) to detach, remove; (*délier*) to untie; (*ADMIN*): ~ **qn (auprès de/à)** to send sb on secondment (to); (*MIL*) to detail; **se** ~ *vi* (*tomber*) to come off; to come out; (*se défaire*) to come undone; (*SPORT*) to pull *ou* break away; **se**

~ **sur** to stand out against; **se** ~ **de** (*se désintéresser*) to grow away from.

**détail** [detaj] *nm* detail; (*COMM*): **le** ~ retail; **au** ~ **ad** (*COMM*) retail; separately; **donner le** ~ **de** to give a detailed account of; (*compte*) to give a breakdown of; **en** ~ in detail.

**détaillant** [detajã] *nm* retailer.

**détaillé, e** [detaje] *a* (*récit*) detailed.

**détailler** [detaje] *vt* (*COMM*) to sell retail; to sell separately; (*expliquer*) to explain in detail; to detail; (*examiner*) to look over, examine.

**détartrant** [detaRtRã] *nm* descaling agent.

**détaxer** [detakse] *vt* to reduce the tax on; to remove the tax from.

**détecter** [detɛkte] *vt* to detect; **détecteur** *nm* detector; **détection** *nf* detection.

**détective** [detɛktiv] *nm* (*Brit: policier*) detective; ~ (**privé**) private detective *ou* investigator.

**déteindre** [detɛdR(ə)] *vi* (*tissu*) to lose its colour; (*fig*): ~ **sur** to rub off on.

**dételer** [detle] *vt* to unharness; to unhitch.

**détendre** [detãdR(ə)] *vt* (*fil*) to slacken, loosen; (*relaxer*) to relax; **se** ~ to lose its tension; to relax.

**détenir** [detniR] *vt* (*fortune, objet, secret*) to be in possession of, have (in one's possession); (*prisonnier*) to detain, hold; (*record*) to hold; ~ **le pouvoir** to be in power.

**détente** [detãt] *nf* relaxation; (*POL*) détente; (*d'une arme*) trigger; (*d'un athlète qui saute*) spring.

**détenteur, trice** [detãtœR, -tRis] *nm/f* holder.

**détention** [detãsjɔ̃] *nf* possession; detention; holding; ~ **préventive** (pre-trial) custody.

**détenu, e** [detny] *nm/f* prisoner.

**détergent** [detɛRʒã] *nm* detergent.

**détérioration** [deteRjɔRasjɔ̃] *nf* damaging; deterioration, worsening.

**détériorer** [deteRjɔRe] *vt* to damage; **se** ~ *vi* to deteriorate.

**déterminant** [detɛRminã] *nm* (*LING*) determiner.

**détermination** [detɛRminasjɔ̃] *nf* determining; (*résolution*) determination.

**déterminé, e** [detɛRmine] *a* (*résolu*) determined; (*précis*) specific, definite.

**déterminer** [detɛRmine] *vt* (*fixer*) to determine; (*décider*): ~ **qn à faire** to decide sb to do; **se** ~ **à faire** to make up one's mind to do.

**déterrer** [detɛRe] *vt* to dig up.

**détersif** [detɛRsif] *nm* detergent.

**détestable** [detɛstabl(ə)] *a* foul, ghastly; detestable, odious.

**détester** [detɛste] *vt* to hate, detest.

**détonant, e** [detɔnã, -ãt] *a*: **mélange** ~ explosive mixture.

**détonateur** [detɔnatœR] *nm* detonator.

**détonation** [detɔnasjɔ̃] *nf* detonation, bang, report (of a gun).

**détoner** [detɔne] *vi* to detonate, explode.

**détonner** [detɔne] *vi* (*MUS*) to go out of tune; (*fig*) to clash.

**détour** [detuR] *nm* detour; (*tournant*) bend, curve; **sans** ~ (*fig*) without beating

about the bush, in a straightforward manner.

**détourné, e** [detuRne] *a* (*moyen*) roundabout.

**détournement** [detuRnəmã] *nm* diversion, rerouting; ~ **d'avion** hijacking; ~ (**de fonds**) embezzlement *ou* misappropriation (of funds); ~ **de mineur** corruption of a minor.

**détourner** [detuRne] *vt* to divert; (*avion*) to divert, reroute; (: *par la force*) to hijack; (*yeux, tête*) to turn away; (*de l'argent*) to embezzle, misappropriate; **se** ~ to turn away.

**détracteur, trice** [detRaktœR, -tRis] *nm/f* disparager, critic.

**détraquer** [detRake] *vt* to put out of order; (*estomac*) to upset; **se** ~ *vi* to go wrong.

**détrempe** [detRãp] *nf* (*ART*) tempera.

**détrempé, e** [detRãpe] *a* (*sol*) sodden, waterlogged.

**détresse** [detRɛs] *nf* distress.

**détriment** [detRimã] *nm*: **au** ~ **de** to the detriment of.

**détritus** [detRitys] *nmpl* rubbish *sg*, refuse *sg*.

**détroit** [detRwa] *nm* strait.

**détromper** [detRɔ̃pe] *vt* to disabuse.

**détrôner** [detRone] *vt* to dethrone, depose; (*fig*) to oust, dethrone.

**détrousser** [detRuse] *vt* to rob.

**détruire** [detRчiR] *vt* to destroy.

**dette** [dɛt] *nf* debt.

**D.E.U.G.** [dœg] *sigle m* = *diplôme d'études universitaires générales*.

**deuil** [dœj] *nm* (*perte*) bereavement; (*période*) mourning; (*chagrin*) grief; **porter le/être en** ~ to wear/be in mourning.

**deux** [dø] *num* two; **les** ~ both; **ses** ~ **mains** both his hands, his two hands; **les** ~ **points** the colon *sg*; **deuxième** *num* second; ~-**pièces** *nm inv* (*tailleur*) two-piece suit; (*de bain*) two-piece (swimsuit); (*appartement*) two-roomed flat; ~-**roues** *nm inv* two-wheeled vehicle; ~-**temps** *a* two-stroke.

**devais** *etc vb voir* **devoir**.

**dévaler** [devale] *vt* to hurtle down.

**dévaliser** [devalize] *vt* to rob, burgle.

**dévaloriser** [devalɔRize] *vt*, **se** ~ *vi* to depreciate.

**dévaluation** [devalчasjɔ̃] *nf* depreciation; (*ÉCON: mesure*) devaluation.

**dévaluer** [devalчe] *vt* to devalue.

**devancer** [dəvãse] *vt* to be ahead of; to get ahead of; to arrive before; (*prévenir*) to anticipate; ~ **l'appel** (*MIL*) to enlist before call-up; **devancier, ière** *nm/f* precursor.

**devant** [dəvã] *ad* in front; (*à distance: en avant*) ahead // *prép* in front of; ahead of; (*avec mouvement: passer*) past; (*fig*) before, in front of; faced with, in the face of; in view of // *nm* front; **prendre les** ~**s** to make the first move; **les pattes de** ~ the front legs, the forelegs; **par** ~ (*boutonner*) at the front; (*entrer*) the front way; **aller au-**~ **de qn** to go out to meet sb ; **aller au-~ de** (*désirs de qn*) to anticipate.

**devanture** [dəvɑ̃tyʀ] *nf* (*façade*) (shop) front ; (*étalage*) display ; (shop) window.

**dévastation** [devastɑsjɔ̃] *nf* devastation.

**dévaster** [devaste] *vt* to devastate.

**déveine** [devɛn] *nf* rotten luck *q*.

**développement** [devlɔpmɑ̃] *nm* development.

**développer** [devlɔpe] *vt* to develop ; **se ~** *vi* to develop.

**devenir** [dəvniʀ] *vb avec attribut* to become ; **~ instituteur** to become a teacher ; **que sont-ils devenus?** what has become of them?

**dévergondé, e** [devɛʀgɔ̃de] *a* wild, shameless.

**devers** [dəvɛʀ] *ad*: **par ~ soi** to oneself.

**déverser** [devɛʀse] *vt* (*liquide*) to pour (out) ; (*ordures*) to tip (out) ; **se ~ dans** (*fleuve, mer*) to flow into ; **déversoir** *nm* overflow.

**dévêtir** [devetiʀ] *vt, se ~* to undress.

**devez** *etc vb voir* **devoir**.

**déviation** [devjɑsjɔ̃] *nf* (*aussi* AUTO) diversion ; **~ de la colonne (vertébrale)** curvature of the spine.

**dévider** [devide] *vt* to unwind ; **dévidoir** *nm* reel.

**devienne** *etc vb voir* **devenir**.

**dévier** [devje] *vt* (*fleuve, circulation*) to divert ; (*coup*) to deflect // *vi* to veer (off course) ; (**faire**) **~** (*projectile*) to deflect ; (*véhicule*) to push off course.

**devin** [dəvɛ̃] *nm* soothsayer, seer.

**deviner** [dəvine] *vt* to guess ; (*prévoir*) to foretell ; to foresee ; (*apercevoir*) to distinguish.

**devinette** [dəvinɛt] *nf* riddle.

**devins** *etc vb voir* **devenir**.

**devis** [dəvi] *nm* estimate, quotation.

**dévisager** [devizaʒe] *vt* to stare at.

**devise** [dəviz] *nf* (*formule*) motto, watchword ; (*ÉCON: monnaie*) currency ; **~s** *nfpl* (*argent*) currency *sg*.

**deviser** [dəvize] *vi* to converse.

**dévisser** [devise] *vt* to unscrew, undo ; **se ~** *vi* to come unscrewed.

**dévoiler** [devwale] *vt* to unveil.

**devoir** [dəvwaʀ] *nm* duty ; (SCOL) piece of homework, homework *q* ; (: *en classe*) exercise // *vt* (*argent, respect*): **~** (à qn) to owe (sb) sth ; (*suivi de l'infinitif: obligation*): **il doit le faire** he has to do it, he must do it ; (: *intention*): **il doit partir demain** he is (due) to leave tomorrow ; (: *probabilité*): **il doit être tard** it must be late.

**dévolu, e** [devɔly] *a*: **~ à** allotted to // *nm*: **jeter son ~ sur** to fix one's choice on.

**dévorant, e** [devɔʀɑ̃, -ɑ̃t] *a* (*faim, passion*) raging.

**dévorer** [devɔʀe] *vt* to devour ; (*suj: feu, soucis*) to consume.

**dévot, e** [devo, -ɔt] *a* devout, pious.

**dévotion** [devɔsjɔ̃] *nf* devoutness ; **être à la ~ de qn** to be totally devoted to sb.

**dévoué, e** [devwe] *a* devoted.

**dévouement** [devumɑ̃] *nm* devotion, dedication.

**dévouer** [devwe]: **se ~** *vi* (*se sacrifier*): **se ~ (pour)** to sacrifice o.s. (for) ; (*se consacrer*): **se ~ à** to devote *ou* dedicate o.s. to.

**dévoyé, e** [devwaje] *a* delinquent.

**devrai** *etc vb voir* **devoir**.

**dextérité** [dɛksteʀite] *nf* skill, dexterity.

**diabète** [djabɛt] *nm* diabetes *sg* ; **diabétique** *nm/f* diabetic.

**diable** [djɑbl(ə)] *nm* devil ; **diabolique** *a* diabolical.

**diabolo** [djabɔlo] *nm* (*boisson*) lemonade and fruit (*ou* mint *etc*) cordial.

**diacre** [djakʀ(ə)] *nm* deacon.

**diadème** [djadɛm] *nm* diadem.

**diagnostic** [djagnɔstik] *nm* diagnosis *sg* ; **diagnostiquer** *vt* to diagnose.

**diagonal, e aux** [djagɔnal, -o] *a, nf* diagonal ; **en ~e** diagonally ; **lire en ~e** to skim through.

**diagramme** [djagʀam] *nm* chart, graph.

**dialecte** [djalɛkt(ə)] *nm* dialect.

**dialogue** [djalɔg] *nm* dialogue ; **dialoguer** *vi* to converse ; (POL) to have a dialogue.

**diamant** [djamɑ̃] *nm* diamond ; **diamantaire** *nm* diamond dealer.

**diamètre** [djamɛtʀ(ə)] *nm* diameter.

**diapason** [djapazɔ̃] *nm* tuning fork.

**diaphragme** [djafʀagm] *nm* (ANAT, PHOTO) diaphragm ; (*contraceptif*) diaphragm, cap ; **ouverture du ~** (PHOTO) aperture.

**diapositive** [djapozitiv] *nf* transparency, slide.

**diapré, e** [djapʀe] *a* many-coloured.

**diarrhée** [djaʀe] *nf* diarrhoea.

**diatribe** [djatʀib] *nf* diatribe.

**dictaphone** [diktafɔn] *nm* Dictaphone.

**dictateur** [diktatœʀ] *nm* dictator ; **dictatorial, e, aux** *a* dictatorial ; **dictature** *nf* dictatorship.

**dictée** [dikte] *nf* dictation ; **prendre sous ~** to take down (*sth dictated*).

**dicter** [dikte] *vt* to dictate.

**diction** [diksjɔ̃] *nf* diction, delivery ; **cours de ~** speech production lesson.

**dictionnaire** [diksjɔnɛʀ] *nm* dictionary ; **~ bilingue/encyclopédique** bilingual/encyclopaedic dictionary.

**dicton** [diktɔ̃] *nm* saying, dictum.

**didactique** [didaktik] *a* technical ; didactic.

**dièse** [djɛz] *nm* sharp.

**diesel** [djezɛl] *nm, a inv* diesel.

**diète** [djɛt] *nf* (*jeûne*) starvation diet ; (*régime*) diet ; **être à la ~** to be on a starvation diet.

**diététicien, ne** [djetetisjɛ̃, -jɛn] *nm/f* dietician.

**diététique** [djetetik] *nf* dietetics *sg* ; **magasin ~** health food shop.

**dieu, x** [djø] *nm* god ; **D~** God ; **le bon D~** the good Lord.

**diffamation** [difamɑsjɔ̃] *nf* slander ; (*écrite*) libel ; **attaquer qn en ~** to sue sb for libel (*ou* slander).

**diffamer** [difame] *vt* to slander ; to libel.

**différé** [difeʀe] *nm* (TV): **en ~** (pre-)recorded.

**différence** [difeʀɑ̃s] *nf* difference ; **à la ~ de** unlike.

**différencier** [difeʀɑ̃sje] *vt* to differentiate ; **se ~** *vi* (*organisme*) to become differentiated ; **se ~ de** to differentiate o.s. from ; to differ from.

**différend** [difeʀɑ̃] *nm* difference (of opinion), disagreement.

**différent, e** [difeʀɑ̃, -ɑ̃t] *a*: **~ (de)** different (from) ; **~s objets** different *ou* various objects.

**différentiel, le** [difeʀɑ̃sjɛl] *a, nm* differential.

**différer** [difeʀe] *vt* to postpone, put off // *vi*: **~ (de)** to differ (from) ; **~ de faire** to delay doing.

**difficile** [difisil] *a* difficult ; (*exigeant*) hard to please, difficult (to please) ; **~ment** *ad* with difficulty ; **~ment lisible** difficult *ou* hard to read.

**difficulté** [difikylte] *nf* difficulty ; **en ~** (*bateau, alpiniste*) in trouble *ou* difficulties ; **avoir de la ~ à faire** to have difficulty (in) doing.

**difforme** [difɔʀm(ə)] *a* deformed, misshapen ; **difformité** *nf* deformity.

**diffracter** [difʀakte] *vt* to diffract.

**diffus, e** [dify, -yz] *a* diffuse.

**diffuser** [difyze] *vt* (*chaleur, bruit*) to diffuse ; (*émission, musique*) to broadcast ; (*nouvelle, idée*) to circulate ; (*COMM*) to distribute ; **diffuseur** *nm* diffuser ; distributor ; **diffusion** *nf* diffusion ; broadcast(ing) ; circulation ; distribution.

**digérer** [diʒeʀe] *vt* to digest ; (*fig: accepter*) to stomach, put up with ; **digestible** *a* digestible ; **digestif, ive** *a* digestive // *nm* (after-dinner) liqueur ; **digestion** *nf* digestion.

**digital, e, aux** [diʒital, -o] *a* digital.

**digne** [diɲ] *a* dignified ; **~ de** worthy of ; **~ de foi** trustworthy.

**dignitaire** [diɲitɛʀ] *nm* dignitary.

**dignité** [diɲite] *nf* dignity.

**digue** [dig] *nf* dike, dyke.

**dilapider** [dilapide] *vt* to squander, waste.

**dilater** [dilate] *vt* to dilate ; (*gaz, métal*) to cause to expand ; (*ballon*) to distend ; **se ~** *vi* to expand.

**dilemme** [dilɛm] *nm* dilemma.

**diligence** [diliʒɑ̃s] *nf* stagecoach, diligence ; (*empressement*) despatch.

**diligent, e** [diliʒɑ̃, -ɑ̃t] *a* prompt and efficient, diligent.

**diluer** [dilɥe] *vt* to dilute.

**diluvien, ne** [dilyvjɛ̃, -jɛn] *a*: **pluie ~ne** torrential rain.

**dimanche** [dimɑ̃ʃ] *nm* Sunday.

**dimension** [dimɑ̃sjɔ̃] *nf* (*grandeur*) size ; (*cote, de l'espace*) dimension.

**diminuer** [diminɥe] *vt* to reduce, decrease ; (*ardeur etc*) to lessen ; (*personne: physiquement*) to undermine ; (*dénigrer*) to belittle // *vi* to decrease, diminish ; **diminutif** *nm* (*LING*) diminutive ; (*surnom*) pet name ; **diminution** *nf* decreasing, diminishing.

**dinde** [dɛ̃d] *nf* turkey.

**dindon** [dɛ̃dɔ̃] *nm* turkey.

**dîner** [dine] *nm* dinner // *vi* to have dinner.

**dingue** [dɛ̃g] *a* (*fam*) crazy.

**diode** [djɔd] *nf* diode.

**diphtérie** [difteʀi] *nf* diphtheria.

**diphtongue** [diftɔ̃g] *nf* diphthong.

**diplomate** [diplɔmat] *a* diplomatic // *nm* diplomat ; (*fig*) diplomatist.

**diplomatie** [diplɔmasi] *nf* diplomacy ; **diplomatique** *a* diplomatic.

**diplôme** [diplom] *nm* diploma, certificate ; (*diploma*) examination ; **diplômé, e** *a* qualified.

**dire** [diʀ] *nm*: **au ~ de** according to ; **leur ~s** what they say // *vt* to say ; (*secret, mensonge*) to tell ; **~ l'heure/la vérité** to tell the time/the truth ; **~ qch à qn** to tell sb sth ; **~ que** to say that ; **~ à qn que** to tell sb that ; **~ à qn qu'il fasse** *ou* **de faire** to tell sb to do ; **on dit que** they say that ; **si cela lui dit** (*plaire*) if he fancies it ; **que dites-vous de** (*penser*) what do you think of ; **on dirait que** it looks (*ou* sounds *etc*) as though.

**direct, e** [diʀɛkt] *a* direct // *nm* (*TV*): **en ~** live ; **~ement** *ad* directly.

**directeur, trice** [diʀɛktœʀ, -tʀis] *nm/f* (*d'entreprise*) director ; (*de service*) manager/eress ; (*d'école*) headmaster/mistress ; **~ de thèse** (*SCOL*) supervisor.

**direction** [diʀɛksjɔ̃] *nf* management ; conducting ; supervision ; (*AUTO*) steering ; (*sens*) direction ; **sous la ~ de** (*MUS*) conducted by.

**directive** [diʀɛktiv] *nf* directive, instruction.

**dirent** *vb voir* **dire**.

**dirigeable** [diʀiʒabl(ə)] *a, nm*: **(ballon) ~** dirigible.

**dirigeant, e** [diʀiʒɑ̃, -ɑ̃t] *a* managerial ; ruling // *nm/f* (*d'un parti etc*) leader ; (*d'entreprise*) manager, member of the management.

**diriger** [diʀiʒe] *vt* (*entreprise*) to manage, run ; (*véhicule*) to steer ; (*orchestre*) to conduct ; (*recherches, travaux*) to supervise, be in charge of ; (*braquer: regard, arme*): **~ sur** to point *ou* level *ou* aim at, (*fig: critiques*): **~ contre** to aim at ; **se ~** (*s'orienter*) to find one's way ; **se ~ vers** *ou* **sur** to make *ou* head for.

**dirigisme** [diʀiʒism(ə)] *nm* (*ÉCON*) state intervention, interventionism.

**dis** *etc vb voir* **dire**.

**discernement** [disɛʀnəmɑ̃] *nm* discernment, judgment.

**discerner** [disɛʀne] *vt* to discern, make out.

**disciple** [disipl(ə)] *nm/f* disciple.

**disciplinaire** [disiplinɛʀ] *a* disciplinary.

**discipline** [disiplin] *nf* discipline ; **discipliné, e** *a* (well-)disciplined ; **discipliner** *vt* to discipline ; to control.

**discontinu, e** [diskɔ̃tiny] *a* intermittent.

**discontinuer** [diskɔ̃tinɥe] *vi*: **sans ~** without stopping, without a break.

**disconvenir** [diskɔ̃vniʀ] *vi*: **ne pas ~ de qch/que** not to deny sth/that.

**discordance** [diskɔʀdɑ̃s] *nf* discordance ; conflict.

**discordant, e** [diskɔʀdɑ̃, -ɑ̃t] *a* discordant ; conflicting.

**discorde** [diskɔʀd(ə)] *nf* discord, dissension.

**discothèque** [diskɔtɛk] *nf* (*disques*) record collection ; (: *dans une bibliothèque*) record library ; (*boîte de nuit*) disco(thèque).

**discourir** [diskuʀiʀ] *vi* to discourse, hold forth.

**discours** [diskuʀ] *nm* speech.

**discréditer** [diskʀedite] *vt* to discredit.

**discret, ète** [diskʀɛ, -ɛt] *a* discreet ; (*fig*) unobtrusive ; quiet ; **discrètement** *ad* discreetly.

**discrétion** [diskʀesjɔ̃] *nf* discretion ; **être à la ∼ de qn** to be in sb's hands ; **à ∼** unlimited ; as much as one wants.

**discrimination** [diskʀiminasjɔ̃] *nf* discrimination ; **sans ∼** indiscriminately ; **discriminatoire** *a* discriminatory.

**disculper** [diskylpe] *vt* to exonerate.

**discussion** [diskysjɔ̃] *nf* discussion.

**discuté, e** [diskyte] *a* controversial.

**discuter** [diskyte] *vt* (*contester*) to question, dispute ; (*débattre: prix*) to discuss // *vi* to talk ; (*ergoter*) to argue ; **∼ de** to discuss.

**dise** *etc vb voir* **dire.**

**disert, e** [dizɛʀ, -ɛʀt(ə)] *a* loquacious.

**disette** [dizɛt] *nf* food shortage.

**diseuse** [dizøz] *nf:* **∼ de bonne aventure** fortuneteller.

**disgrâce** [disgʀɑs] *nf* disgrace.

**disgracieux, euse** [disgʀasjø, -jøz] *a* ungainly, awkward.

**disjoindre** [disʒwɛ̃dʀ(ə)] *vt* to take apart ; **se ∼** *vi* to come apart.

**disjoncteur** [disʒɔ̃ktœʀ] *nm* (*ÉLEC*) circuit breaker, cutout.

**dislocation** [dislɔkasjɔ̃] *nf* dislocation.

**disloquer** [dislɔke] *vt* (*membre*) to dislocate ; (*chaise*) to dismantle ; (*troupe*) to disperse ; **se ∼** *vi* (*parti, empire*) to break up ; **se ∼ l'épaule** to dislocate one's shoulder.

**disons** *vb voir* **dire.**

**disparaître** [dispaʀɛtʀ(ə)] *vi* to disappear ; (*à la vue*) to vanish, disappear ; to be hidden *ou* concealed ; (*être manquant*) to go missing, disappear ; (*se perdre: traditions etc*) to die out ; **faire ∼** to remove ; to get rid of.

**disparate** [dispaʀat] *a* disparate ; ill-assorted.

**disparité** [dispaʀite] *nf* disparity.

**disparition** [dispaʀisjɔ̃] *nf* disappearance.

**disparu, e** [dispaʀy] *nm/f* missing person ; (*défunt*) departed.

**dispendieux, euse** [dispɑ̃djø, -jøz] *a* extravagant, expensive.

**dispensaire** [dispɑ̃sɛʀ] *nm* community clinic.

**dispense** [dispɑ̃s] *nf* exemption ; **∼ d'âge** special exemption from age limit.

**dispenser** [dispɑ̃se] *vt* (*donner*) to lavish, bestow ; (*exempter*): **∼ qn de** to exempt sb from ; **se ∼ de** to avoid ; to get out of.

**disperser** [dispɛʀse] *vt* to scatter ; (*fig: son attention*) to dissipate ; **se ∼** *vi* to scatter ; (*fig*) to dissipate one's efforts.

**disponibilité** [dispɔnibilite] *nf* availability ; (*ADMIN*): **être en ∼** to be on leave of absence.

**disponible** [dispɔnibl(ə)] *a* available.

**dispos** [dispo] *am:* (**frais et**) **∼** fresh (as a daisy).

**disposé, e** [dispoze] *a* (*d'une certaine manière*) arranged, laid-out ; **bien/mal ∼** (*humeur*) in a good/bad mood ; **∼ à** (*prêt à*) willing *ou* prepared to.

**disposer** [dispoze] *vt* (*arranger, placer*) to arrange ; (*inciter*): **∼ qn à qch/faire qch** to dispose *ou* incline sb towards sth/to do sth // *vi*: **vous pouvez ∼** you may leave ; **∼ de** *vt* to have (at one's disposal) ; to use ; **se ∼ à faire** to prepare to do, be about to do.

**dispositif** [dispozitif] *nm* device ; (*fig*) system, plan of action ; set-up.

**disposition** [dispozisjɔ̃] *nf* (*arrangement*) arrangement, layout ; (*humeur*) mood ; (*tendance*) tendency ; **∼s** *nfpl* (*mesures*) steps, measures ; (*préparatifs*) arrangements ; (*testamentaires*) provisions ; (*aptitudes*) bent *sg*, aptitude *sg* ; **à la ∼ de qn** at sb's disposal.

**disproportion** [dispʀopɔʀsjɔ̃] *nf* disproportion ; **disproportionné, e** *a* disproportionate, out of all proportion.

**dispute** [dispyt] *nf* quarrel, argument.

**disputer** [dispyte] *vt* (*match*) to play ; (*combat*) to fight ; (*course*) to run, fight ; **se ∼** *vi* to quarrel, have a quarrel ; **∼ qch à qn** to fight with sb for *ou* over sth.

**disquaire** [diskɛʀ] *nm/f* record dealer.

**disqualification** [diskalifikasjɔ̃] *nf* disqualification.

**disqualifier** [diskalifje] *vt* to disqualify.

**disque** [disk(ə)] *nm* (*MUS*) record ; (*forme, pièce*) disc ; (*SPORT*) discus ; **∼ d'embrayage** (*AUTO*) clutch plate.

**dissection** [disɛksjɔ̃] *nf* dissection.

**dissemblable** [disɑ̃blabl(ə)] *a* dissimilar.

**disséminer** [disemine] *vt* to scatter.

**disséquer** [diseke] *vt* to dissect.

**dissertation** [disɛʀtasjɔ̃] *nf* (*SCOL*) essay.

**disserter** [disɛʀte] *vi:* **∼ sur** to discourse upon.

**dissident, e** [disidɑ̃, -ɑ̃t] *a, nm/f* dissident.

**dissimulation** [disimylasjɔ̃] *nf* concealing ; (*duplicité*) dissimulation.

**dissimuler** [disimyle] *vt* to conceal ; **se ∼** to conceal o.s. ; to be concealed.

**dissipation** [disipasjɔ̃] *nf* squandering ; unruliness ; (*débauche*) dissipation.

**dissiper** [disipe] *vt* to dissipate ; (*fortune*) to squander, fritter away ; **se ∼** *vi* (*brouillard*) to clear, disperse ; (*doutes*) to disappear, melt away ; (*élève*) to become undisciplined *ou* unruly.

**dissolu, e** [disɔly] *a* dissolute.

**dissolution** [disɔlysjɔ̃] *nf* dissolving ; (*POL, JUR*) dissolution.

**dissolvant, e** [disɔlvɑ̃, -ɑ̃t] *a* (*fig*) debilitating // *nm* (*CHIMIE*) solvent ; **∼ (gras)** nail varnish remover.

**dissonant, e** [disɔnɑ̃, -ɑ̃t] *a* discordant.

**dissoudre** [disudʀ(ə)] *vt* to dissolve ; **se ∼** *vi* to dissolve.

**dissuader** [disɥade] *vt:* **∼ qn de faire/de qch** to dissuade sb from doing/from sth.

**dissuasion** [disчɑzjɔ̃] *nf* dissuasion ; **force de** ~ deterrent power.

**dissymétrique** [disimetʀik] *a* dissymmetrical.

**distance** [distɑ̃s] *nf* distance ; (*fig: écart*) gap ; **à** ~ at *ou* from a distance ; **à une** ~ **de 10 km, à 10 km de** ~ 10 km away, at a distance of 10 km ; **à 2 ans de** ~ with a gap of 2 years ; **garder ses** ~**s** to keep one's distance ; **tenir la** ~ (*SPORT*) to cover the distance, last the course ; **distancer** *vt* to outdistance, leave behind.

**distant, e** [distɑ̃, -ɑ̃t] *a* (*réservé*) distant, aloof ; (*éloigné*) distant, far away ; ~ **de** (*lieu*) far away *ou* a long way from ; ~ **de 5 km (d'un lieu)** 5 km away (from a place).

**distendre** [distɑ̃dʀ(ə)] *vt*, **se** ~ *vi* to distend.

**distillation** [distilɑsjɔ̃] *nf* distillation, distilling.

**distillé, e** [distile] *a:* **eau** ~**e** distilled water.

**distiller** [distile] *vt* to distil ; (*fig*) to exude, to elaborate ; **distillerie** *nf* distillery.

**distinct, e** [distɛ̃(kt), distɛ̃kt(ə)] *a* distinct ; **distinctement** *ad* distinctly ; **distinctif, ive** *a* distinctive.

**distinction** [distɛ̃ksjɔ̃] *nf* distinction.

**distingué, e** [distɛ̃ge] *a* distinguished.

**distinguer** [distɛ̃ge] *vt* to distinguish.

**distraction** [distʀaksjɔ̃] *nf* (*manque d'attention*) absent-mindedness ; (*oubli*) lapse (in concentration *ou* attention) ; (*détente*) diversion, recreation ; (*passe-temps*) distraction, entertainment.

**distraire** [distʀɛʀ] *vt* (*déranger*) to distract ; (*divertir*) to entertain, divert ; (*détourner: somme d'argent*) to divert, misappropriate ; **se** ~ to amuse *ou* enjoy o.s.

**distrait, e** [distʀɛ, -ɛt] *a* absent-minded.

**distribuer** [distʀibye] *vt* to distribute ; to hand out ; (*CARTES*) to deal (out) ; (*courrier*) to deliver ; **distributeur** *nm* (*COMM*) distributor ; (*automatique*) (vending *ou* slot) machine ; **distribution** *nf* distribution ; (*postale*) delivery ; (*choix d'acteurs*) casting, cast ; **distribution des prix** (*SCOL*) prize giving.

**district** [distʀikt] *nm* district.

**dit, e** [di, dit] *pp de* **dire** // *a* (*fixé*): **le jour** ~ the arranged day ; (*surnommé*): **X,** ~ **Pierrot X,** known as *ou* called Pierrot.

**dites** *vb voir* **dire**.

**dithyrambique** [ditiʀɑ̃bik] *a* eulogistic.

**diurétique** [djyʀetik] *a* a diuretic.

**diurne** [djyʀn(ə)] *a* diurnal, daytime *cpd*.

**divagations** [divagɑsjɔ̃] *nfpl* wanderings, ramblings ; ravings.

**divaguer** [divage] *vi* to ramble ; to rave.

**divan** [divɑ̃] *nm* divan ; ~**-lit** *nm* divan (bed).

**divergence** [divɛʀʒɑ̃s] *nf* divergence.

**divergent, e** [divɛʀʒɑ̃, -ɑ] *a* divergent.

**diverger** [divɛʀʒe] *vi* to diverge.

**divers, e** [divɛʀ, -ɛʀs(ə)] *a* (*varié*) diverse, varied ; (*différent*) different, various, // *dét* (*plusieurs*) various, several ; (*frais*) ~ sundries, miscellaneous (expenses) ;

**diversement** *ad* in various *ou* diverse ways ; **diversifier** *vt* to diversify.

**diversion** [divɛʀsjɔ̃] *nf* diversion ; **faire** ~ to create a diversion.

**diversité** [divɛʀsite] *nf* diversity ; variety.

**divertir** [divɛʀtiʀ] *vt* to amuse, entertain ; **se** ~ to amuse *ou* enjoy o.s. ; **divertissement** *nm* entertainment ; (*MUS*) divertimento, divertissement.

**dividende** [dividɑ̃d] *nm* (*MATH. COMM*) dividend.

**divin, e** [divɛ̃, -in] *a* divine ; **diviniser** *vt* to deify ; **divinité** *nf* divinity.

**diviser** [divize] *vt* (*gén, MATH*) to divide ; (*morceler, subdiviser*) to divide (up), split (up) ; **diviseur** *nm* (*MATH*) divisor ; **division** *nf* (*gén*) division.

**divorce** [divɔʀs(ə)] *nm* divorce ; **divorcé, e** *nm/f* divorcee ; **divorcer** *vi* to get a divorce, get divorced ; **divorcer de** *ou* **d'avec qn** to divorce sb.

**divulgation** [divylgɑsjɔ̃] *nf* disclosure.

**divulguer** [divylge] *vt* to divulge, disclose.

**dix** [dis] *num* ten ; **dixième** *num* tenth.

**dizaine** [dizɛn] *nf* (*10*) ten ; (*environ 10*): **une** ~ **(de)** about ten, ten or so.

**do** [do] *nm* (*note*) C ; (*en chantant la gamme*) do(h).

**docile** [dɔsil] *a* docile ; **docilité** *nf* docility.

**dock** [dɔk] *nm* dock.

**docker** [dɔkɛʀ] *nm* docker.

**docte** [dɔkt(ə)] *a* learned.

**docteur** [dɔktœʀ] *nm* doctor.

**doctoral, e, aux** [dɔktɔʀal, -o] *a* pompous, bombastic.

**doctorat** [dɔktɔʀa] *nm*: ~ **d'Université** ≈ Ph.D. ; ~ **d'état** ≈ Higher Doctorate.

**doctoresse** [dɔktɔʀɛs] *nf* lady doctor.

**doctrinaire** [dɔktʀinɛʀ] *a* doctrinaire ; pompous, sententious.

**doctrine** [dɔktʀin] *nf* doctrine.

**document** [dɔkymɑ̃] *nm* document.

**documentaire** [dɔkymɑ̃tɛʀ] *a, nm* documentary.

**documentaliste** [dɔkymɑ̃talist(ə)] *nm/f* archivist ; researcher.

**documentation** [dɔkymɑ̃tɑsjɔ̃] *nf* documentation, literature ; (*PRESSE, TV: service*) research.

**documenté, e** [dɔkymɑ̃te] *a* well-informed, well-documented ; well-researched.

**documenter** [dɔkymɑ̃te] *vt*: **se** ~ **(sur)** to gather information *ou* material (on *ou* about).

**dodeliner** [dɔdline] *vi*: ~ **de la tête** to nod one's head gently.

**dodo** [dɔdo] *nm*: **aller faire** ~ to go to bye-byes.

**dodu, e** [dɔdy] *a* plump.

**dogmatique** [dɔgmatik] *a* dogmatic.

**dogme** [dɔgm(ə)] *nm* dogma.

**dogue** [dɔg] *nm* mastiff.

**doigt** [dwa] *nm* finger ; **à deux** ~**s de** within an ace *ou* an inch of ; **un** ~ **de lait/whisky** a drop of milk/whisky ; ~ **de pied** toe.

**doigté** [dwate] *nm* (*MUS*) fingering ; fingering technique ; (*fig: habileté*) diplomacy, tact.

**doigtier** [dwatje] *nm* fingerstall.
**doit** *etc vb voir* **devoir**.
**doléances** [dɔleɑ̃s] *nfpl* complaints; grievances.
**dolent, e** [dɔlɑ̃, -ɑ̃t] *a* doleful, mournful.
**dollar** [dɔlaʀ] *nm* dollar.
**D.O.M.** [parfois dɔm] *sigle m ou mpl* = *département(s) d'outre-mer.*
**domaine** [dɔmɛn] *nm* estate, property; (*fig*) domain, field; **tomber dans le ~ public** (*JUR*) to be out of copyright.
**domanial, e, aux** [dɔmanjal, -jo] *a* (*forêt, biens*) national, state *cpd.*
**dôme** [dom] *nm* dome.
**domesticité** [dɔmɛstisite] *nf* (domestic) staff.
**domestique** [dɔmɛstik] *a* domestic // *nm/f* servant, domestic.
**domestiquer** [dɔmɛstike] *vt* to domesticate.
**domicile** [dɔmisil] *nm* home, place of residence; **à ~** at home; **domicilié, e** *a*: **être domicilié à** to have one's home in ou at.
**dominant, e** [dɔminɑ̃, -ɑ̃t] *a* dominant; predominant.
**dominateur, trice** [dɔminatœʀ, -tʀis] *a* dominating; domineering.
**domination** [dɔminɑsjɔ̃] *nf* domination.
**dominer** [dɔmine] *vt* to dominate; (*passions etc*) to control, master; (*surpasser*) to outclass, surpass; (*surplomber*) to tower above, dominate // *vi* to be in the dominant position; **se ~** to control o.s.
**dominical, e, aux** [dɔminikal, -o] *a* Sunday *cpd*, dominical.
**domino** [dɔmino] *nm* domino; **~s** *nmpl* (*jeu*) dominoes *sg.*
**dommage** [dɔmaʒ] *nm* (*préjudice*) harm, injury; (*dégâts, pertes*) damage *q*; **c'est ~ de faire/que** it's a shame ou pity to do/that; **~s-intérêts** *nmpl* damages.
**dompter** [dɔ̃te] *vt* to tame; **dompteur, euse** *nm/f* trainer; liontamer.
**don** [dɔ̃] *nm* (*cadeau*) gift; (*charité*) donation; (*aptitude*) gift, talent; **avoir des ~s pour** to have a gift ou talent for.
**donateur, trice** [dɔnatœʀ, -tʀis] *nm/f* donor.
**donation** [dɔnɑsjɔ̃] *nf* donation.
**donc** [dɔ̃k] *cj* therefore, so; ( après une digression) so, then.
**donjon** [dɔ̃ʒɔ̃] *nm* keep, donjon.
**donné, e** [dɔne] *a* (*convenu*) given // *nf* (*MATH, gén*) datum (*pl* data); **étant ~ ...** given ... .
**donner** [dɔne] *vt* to give; (*vieux habits etc*) to give away; (*spectacle*) to show; to put on; **~ qch à qn** to give sb sth, give sth to sb; **~ sur** (*suj: fenêtre, chambre*) to look (out) onto; **~ dans** (*piège etc*) to fall into; **se ~ à fond (à son travail)** to give one's all (to one's work); **s'en ~ à cœur joie** (*fam*) to have a great time (of it).
**donneur, euse** [dɔnœʀ, -øz] *nm/f* (*MÉD*) donor; (*CARTES*) dealer; **~ de sang** blood donor.
**dont** [dɔ̃] *pronom relatif*: **la maison ~ je vois le toit** the house whose roof I can see, the house I can see the roof of; **la**

**maison ~ le toit est rouge** the house whose roof is red ou the roof of which is red; **l'homme ~ je connais la sœur** the man whose sister I know; **10 blessés, ~ 2 grièvement** 10 injured, 2 of them seriously; **2 livres, ~ l'un est** 2 books, one of which is; **il y avait plusieurs personnes, ~ Gabrielle** there were several people, among whom was Gabrielle; **le fils ~ il est si fier** the son he's so proud of; **ce ~ je parle** what I'm talking about; *voir adjectifs et verbes à complément prépositionnel*: **responsable de, souffrir de** *etc.*
**dorade** [dɔʀad] *nf* = **daurade.**
**doré, e** [dɔʀe] *a* golden; (*avec dorure*) gilt, gilded.
**dorénavant** [dɔʀenavɑ̃] *ad* from now on, henceforth.
**dorer** [dɔʀe] *vt* (*cadre*) to gild; (**faire**) **~** (*CULIN*) to brown (in the oven).
**dorloter** [dɔʀlɔte] *vt* to pamper, cosset.
**dormant, e** [dɔʀmɑ̃, -ɑ̃t] *a*: **eau ~e** still water.
**dormeur, euse** [dɔʀmœʀ, -øz] *nm/f* sleeper.
**dormir** [dɔʀmiʀ] *vi* to sleep; (*être endormi*) to be asleep.
**dorsal, e, aux** [dɔʀsal, -o] *a* dorsal.
**dortoir** [dɔʀtwaʀ] *nm* dormitory.
**dorure** [dɔʀyʀ] *nf* gilding.
**doryphore** [dɔʀifɔʀ] *nm* Colorado beetle.
**dos** [do] *nm* back; (*de livre*) spine; **'voir au ~'** 'see over'; **de ~** from the back, from behind; **à ~ de chameau** riding on a camel.
**dosage** [dozaʒ] *nm* mixture.
**dos-d'âne** [dodɑn] *nm* humpback.
**dose** [doz] *nf* dose.
**doser** [doze] *vt* to measure out; to mix in the correct proportions; (*fig*) to expend in the right amounts ou proportion; to strike a balance between; **doseur** *nm* measure.
**dossard** [dosaʀ] *nm* number (*worn by competitor*).
**dossier** [dosje] *nm* (*renseignements, fichier*) file; (*enveloppe*) folder, file; (*de chaise*) back.
**dot** [dɔt] *nf* dowry.
**doter** [dɔte] *vt*: **~ qn/qch de** to equip sb/sth with.
**douairière** [dwɛʀjɛʀ] *nf* dowager.
**douane** [dwan] *nf* (*poste, bureau*) customs *pl*; (*taxes*) (customs) duty; **passer la ~** to go through customs; **douanier, ière** *a* customs *cpd* // *nm* customs officer.
**doublage** [dublaʒ] *nm* (*CINÉMA*) dubbing.
**double** [dubl(ə)] *a, ad* double // *nm* (2 fois plus): **le ~ (de)** twice as much (ou many) (as), double the amount (ou number) (of); (*autre exemplaire*) duplicate, copy; (*sosie*) double; **en ~ (exemplaire)** in duplicate; **faire ~ emploi** to be redundant; **~ carburateur** twin carburettor; **à ~s commandes** dual-control; **~ messieurs/mixte** men's/mixed doubles *sg*; **~ toit** (*de tente*) fly sheet.
**doublé, e** [duble] *a* (*vêtement*): **~ (de)** lined (with).
**doublement** [dubləmɑ̃] *nm* doubling;

twofold increase // ad doubly; in two ways, on two counts.
**doubler** [duble] vt (multiplier par 2) to double; (vêtement) to line; (dépasser) to overtake, pass; (film) to dub; (acteur) to stand in for // vi to double, increase twofold; ~ (la classe) (SCOL) to repeat a year.
**doublure** [dublyʀ] nf lining; (CINÉMA) stand-in.
**douce** [dus] a voir doux; ~âtre a sickly sweet; ~ment ad gently; slowly; ~reux, euse a (péj) sugary, suave; douceur nf mildness; gentleness; softness; sweetness; douceurs nfpl (friandises) sweets.
**douche** [duʃ] nf shower; ~s nfpl (salle) shower room sg; se doucher to have ou take a shower.
**doué, e** [dwe] a gifted, talented; ~ de endowed with.
**douille** [duj] nf (ÉLEC) socket; (de projectile) case.
**douillet, te** [dujɛ, -ɛt] a cosy; (péj) soft.
**douleur** [dulœʀ] nf pain; (chagrin) grief, distress; il a eu la ~ de perdre son père he suffered the grief of losing his father; douloureux, euse a painful.
**doute** [dut] nm doubt; sans ~ ad no doubt.
**douter** [dute] vt to doubt; ~ de vt (allié) to doubt, have (one's) doubts about; (résultat) to be doubtful of; se ~ de qch/que to suspect sth/that; je m'en doutais I suspected as much.
**douteux, euse** [dutø, -øz] a (incertain) doubtful; (discutable) dubious, questionable; (péj) dubious-looking.
**douve** [duv] nf (de château) moat; (de tonneau) stave.
**Douvres** [duvʀ(ə)] n Dover.
**doux, douce** [du, dus] a (lisse, moelleux, pas vif: couleur, non calcaire: eau) soft; (sucré, agréable) sweet; (peu fort: moutarde etc, clément: climat) mild; (pas brusque) gentle.
**douzaine** [duzɛn] nf (12) dozen; (environ 12): une ~ (de) a dozen or so, twelve or so.
**douze** [duz] num twelve; douzième num twelfth.
**doyen, ne** [dwajɛ̃, -ɛn] nm/f (en âge, ancienneté) most senior member; (de faculté) dean.
**draconien, ne** [dʀakɔnjɛ̃, -jɛn] a draconian; stringent.
**dragage** [dʀagaʒ] nm dredging.
**dragée** [dʀaʒe] nf sugared almond; (MÉD) (sugar-coated) pill.
**dragon** [dʀagɔ̃] nm dragon.
**drague** [dʀag] nf (filet) dragnet; (bateau) dredger; draguer vt (rivière) to dredge; to drag // vi (fam) to try and pick up girls; to chat up birds; dragueur de mines nm minesweeper.
**drainage** [dʀɛnaʒ] nm drainage.
**drainer** [dʀene] vt to drain.
**dramatique** [dʀamatik] a dramatic; (tragique) tragic // nf (TV) (television) drama.
**dramatiser** [dʀamatize] vt to dramatize.

**dramaturge** [dʀamatyʀʒ(ə)] nm dramatist, playwright.
**drame** [dʀam] nm (THÉÂTRE) drama; (catastrophe) drama, tragedy.
**drap** [dʀa] nm (de lit) sheet; (tissu) woollen fabric.
**drapeau, x** [dʀapo] nm flag; sous les ~x with the colours, in the army.
**draper** [dʀape] vt to drape.
**draperies** [dʀapʀi] nfpl hangings.
**drapier** [dʀapje] nm (woollen) cloth manufacturer; (marchand) clothier.
**dresser** [dʀese] vt (mettre vertical, monter: tente) to put up, erect; (fig: liste, bilan, contrat) to draw up; (animal) to train; se ~ vi (falaise, obstacle) to stand; to tower (up); (personne) to draw o.s. up; ~ qn contre qn d'autre to set sb against sb else.
**dresseur, euse** [dʀɛsœʀ, -øz] nm/f trainer.
**dressoir** [dʀeswaʀ] nm dresser.
**dribbler** [dʀible] vt, vi (SPORT) to dribble.
**drogue** [dʀɔg] nf drug; la ~ drugs pl.
**drogué, e** [dʀɔge] nm/f drug addict.
**droguer** [dʀɔge] vt (victime) to drug; (malade) to give drugs to; se ~ (aux stupéfiants) to take drugs; (péj: de médicaments) to dose o.s. up.
**droguerie** [dʀɔgʀi] nf hardware shop.
**droguiste** [dʀɔgist(ə)] nm keeper (ou owner) of a hardware shop.
**droit, e** [dʀwa, dʀwat] a (non courbe) straight; (vertical) upright, straight; (fig: loyal, franc) upright, straight(forward); (opposé à gauche) right, right-hand // ad straight // nm (prérogative) right; (taxe) duty, tax; (: d'inscription) fee; (lois, branche): le ~ law // nf (ligne) straight line; avoir le ~ de to be allowed to; avoir ~ à to be entitled to; être en ~ de to have a ou the right to; faire ~ à to grant, accede to; être dans son ~ to be within one's rights; à ~e on the right; (direction) (to the) right; de ~e (POL) right-wing; ~ d'auteur copyright; ~s d'auteur royalties; le ~ de vote the (right to) vote.
**droitier, ière** [dʀwatje, -jɛʀ] nm/f right-handed person.
**droiture** [dʀwatyʀ] nf uprightness, straightness.
**drôle** [dʀol] a (amusant) funny, amusing; (bizarre) funny, peculiar.
**dromadaire** [dʀɔmadɛʀ] nm dromedary.
**dru, e** [dʀy] a (cheveux) thick, bushy; (pluie) heavy.
**drugstore** [dʀœgstɔʀ] nm drugstore.
**D.S.T.** sigle f = direction de la surveillance du territoire (the French internal security service).
**du** [dy] prép + dét, dét voir de.
**dû, due** [dy] vb voir devoir // a (somme) owing, owed; (: venant à échéance) due; (causé par): ~ à due to // nm due; (somme) dues pl.
**dubitatif, ive** [dybitatif, -iv] a doubtful, dubious.
**duc** [dyk] nm duke; duché nm dukedom; duchesse nf duchess.
**duel** [dyɛl] nm duel.
**dûment** [dymã] ad duly.

**dune** [dyn] *nf* dune.
**Dunkerque** [dœkɛʀk] *n* Dunkirk.
**duo** [dʮo] *nm* (*MUS*) duet ; (*fig: couple*) duo, pair.
**dupe** [dyp] *nf* dupe // *a*: **(ne pas) être ~ de** (not) to be taken in by.
**duper** [dype] *vt* to dupe, deceive.
**duperie** [dypʀi] *nf* deception, dupery.
**duplex** [dyplɛks] *nm* (*appartement*) split-level appartment, duplex.
**duplicata** [dyplikata] *nm* duplicate.
**duplicateur** [dyplikatœʀ] *nm* duplicator.
**duplicité** [dyplisite] *nf* duplicity.
**duquel** [dykɛl] *prép + pronom voir* **lequel**.
**dur, e** [dyʀ] *a* (*pierre, siège, travail, problème*) hard ; (*lumière, voix, climat*) harsh ; (*sévère*) hard, harsh ; (*cruel*) hard-(-hearted) ; (*porte, col*) stiff ; (*viande*) tough // *ad* hard ; **~ d'oreille** hard of hearing.
**durable** [dyʀabl(ə)] *a* lasting.
**durant** [dyʀɑ̃] *prép* (*au cours de*) during ; (*pendant*) for ; **~ des mois, des mois ~** for months.
**durcir** [dyʀsiʀ] *vt, vi,* **se ~** *vi* to harden.
**durcissement** [dyʀsismɑ̃] *nm* hardening.
**durée** [dyʀe] *nf* length ; (*d'une pile etc*) life ; (*déroulement: des opérations etc*) duration ; **pour une ~ illimitée** for an unlimited length of time.
**durement** [dyʀmɑ̃] *ad* harshly.
**durer** [dyʀe] *vi* to last.
**dureté** [dyʀte] *nf* hardness ; harshness ; stiffness ; toughness.
**durit** [dyʀit] *nf* ® (radiator) hose (*for car*).
**dus** *etc vb voir* **devoir**.
**duvet** [dyvɛ] *nm* down ; **(sac de couchage en) ~** down-filled sleeping bag.
**dynamique** [dinamik] *a* dynamic.
**dynamisme** [dinamism(ə)] *nm* dynamism.
**dynamite** [dinamit] *nf* dynamite.
**dynamiter** [dinamite] *vt* to (blow up with) dynamite.
**dynamo** [dinamo] *nf* dynamo.
**dynastie** [dinasti] *nf* dynasty.
**dysenterie** [disɑ̃tʀi] *nf* dysentery.
**dyslexie** [dislɛksi] *nf* dyslexia, word-blindness.
**dyspepsie** [dispɛpsi] *nf* dyspepsia.

## E

**eau, x** [o] *nf* water // *nfpl* waters ; **prendre l'~** to leak, let in water ; **faire ~** to leak ; **tomber à l'~** (*fig*) to fall through ; **~ de Cologne** Eau de Cologne ; **~ courante** running water ; **~ douce** fresh water ; **~ de Javel** bleach ; **~ minérale** mineral water ; **~ salée** salt water ; **~ de toilette** toilet water ; **les E~x et Forêts** (*ADMIN*) ≈ the National Forestry Commission ; **~-de-vie** *nf* brandy ; **~-forte** *nf* etching.
**ébahi, e** [ebai] *a* dumbfounded, flabbergasted.
**ébats** [eba] *nmpl* frolics, gambols.
**ébattre** [ebatʀ(ə)]: **s'~** *vi* to frolic.
**ébauche** [eboʃ] *nf* (rough) outline, sketch.
**ébaucher** [eboʃe] *vt* to sketch out, outline ; **s'~** *vi* to take shape.

**ébène** [ebɛn] *nf* ebony.
**ébéniste** [ebenist(ə)] *nm* cabinetmaker ; **ébénisterie** *nf* cabinetmaking ; (*bâti*) cabinetwork.
**éberlué, e** [ebɛʀlʮe] *a* astounded, flabbergasted.
**éblouir** [ebluiʀ] *vt* to dazzle.
**éblouissement** [ebluismɑ̃] *nm* dazzle ; (*faiblesse*) dizzy turn.
**éborgner** [ebɔʀɲe] *vt*: **~ qn** to blind sb in one eye.
**éboueur** [ebwœʀ] *nm* dustman.
**ébouillanter** [ebujɑ̃te] *vt* to scald ; (*CULIN*) to blanch.
**éboulement** [ebulmɑ̃] *nm* falling rocks *pl*, rock fall.
**ébouler** [ebule]: **s'~** *vi* to crumble, collapse.
**éboulis** [ebuli] *nmpl* fallen rocks.
**ébouriffé, e** [ebuʀife] *a* tousled, ruffled.
**ébranler** [ebʀɑ̃le] *vt* to shake ; (*rendre instable: mur*) to weaken ; **s'~** *vi* (*partir*) to move off.
**ébrécher** [ebʀeʃe] *vt* to chip.
**ébriété** [ebʀijete] *nf*: **en état d'~** in a state of intoxication.
**ébrouer** [ebʀue]: **s'~** *vi* to shake o.s. ; to snort.
**ébruiter** [ebʀʮite] *vt* to spread, disclose.
**ébullition** [ebylisjɔ̃] *nf* boiling point ; **en ~** boiling ; (*fig*) in an uproar.
**écaille** [ekɑj] *nf* (*de poisson*) scale ; (*de coquil'age*) shell ; (*matière*) tortoiseshell ; (*de roc etc*) flake.
**écailler** [ekɑje] *vt* (*poisson*) to scale ; (*huître*) to open ; **s'~** *vi* to flake ou peel (off).
**écarlate** [ekaʀlat] *a* scarlet.
**écarquiller** [ekaʀkije] *vt*: **~ les yeux** to stare wide-eyed.
**écart** [ekaʀ] *nm* gap ; (*embardée*) swerve ; sideways leap ; (*fig*) departure, deviation ; **à l'~** *ad* out of the way ; **à l'~ de** *prép* away from ; (*fig*) out of ; **~ de conduite** misdemeanour.
**écarté, e** [ekaʀte] *a* (*maison, route*) out-of-the-way, remote ; (*ouvert*): **les jambes ~es** legs apart ; **les bras ~s** arms outstretched.
**écarteler** [ekaʀtəle] *vt* to quarter ; (*fig*) to tear.
**écartement** [ekaʀtəmɑ̃] *nm* space, gap ; (*RAIL*) gauge.
**écarter** [ekaʀte] *vt* (*séparer*) to move apart, separate ; (*éloigner*) to push back, move away ; (*ouvrir: bras, jambes*) to spread, open ; (*: rideau*) to draw (back) ; (*éliminer: candidat, possibilité*) to dismiss ; **s'~** *vi* to part ; to move away ; **s'~ de** to wander from.
**ecchymose** [ekimoz] *nf* bruise.
**ecclésiastique** [eklezjastik] *a* ecclesiastical // *nm* ecclesiastic.
**écervelé, e** [esɛʀvəle] *a* scatterbrained, featherbrained.
**échafaud** [eʃafo] *nm* scaffold.
**échafaudage** [eʃafodaʒ] *nm* scaffolding ; (*fig*) heap, pile.
**échafauder** [eʃafode] *vt* (*plan*) to construct.

**échalas** [eʃala] *nm* stake, pole.

**échalote** [eʃalɔt] *nf* shallot.

**échancrure** [eʃɑ̃kRyR] *nf* (*de robe*) scoop neckline; (*de côte, arête rocheuse*) indentation.

**échange** [eʃɑ̃ʒ] *nm* exchange; **en ~ de** in exchange *ou* return for.

**échanger** [eʃɑ̃ʒe] *vt*: **~ qch (contre)** to exchange sth (for); **échangeur** *nm* (AUTO) interchange.

**échantillon** [eʃɑ̃tijɔ̃] *nm* sample; **échantillonnage** *nm* selection of samples.

**échappatoire** [eʃapatwaR] *nf* way out.

**échappée** [eʃape] *nf* (*vue*) vista; (CYCLISME) breakaway.

**échappement** [eʃapmɑ̃] *nm* (AUTO) exhaust.

**échapper** [eʃape]: **~ à** *vt* (*gardien*) to escape (from); (*punition, péril*) to escape; **~ à qn** (*détail, sens*) to escape sb; (*objet qu'on tient*) to slip out of sb's hands; **s'~** *vi* to escape; **l'~ belle** to have a narrow escape.

**écharde** [eʃaRd(ə)] *nf* splinter (of wood).

**écharpe** [eʃaRp(ə)] *nf* scarf (*pl* scarves); (*de maire*) sash; **avoir un bras en ~** to have one's arm in a sling; **prendre en ~** (*dans une collision*) to hit sideways on.

**écharper** [eʃaRpe] *vt* to tear to pieces.

**échasse** [eʃas] *nf* stilt.

**échassier** [eʃasje] *nm* wader.

**échauffement** [eʃofmɑ̃] *nm* overheating.

**échauffer** [eʃofe] *vt* (*métal, moteur*) to overheat; (*fig: exciter*) to fire, excite; **s'~** (SPORT) to warm up; (*dans la discussion*) to become heated.

**échauffourée** [eʃofuRe] *nf* clash, brawl.

**échéance** [eʃeɑ̃s] *nf* (*d'un paiement: date*) settlement date; (: *somme due*) financial commitment(s); (*fig*) deadline; **à brève/longue ~** a short-/long-term // *ad* in the short/long run.

**échéant** [eʃeɑ̃]: **le cas ~** *ad* if the case arises.

**échec** [eʃɛk] *nm* failure; (ÉCHECS): **~ et mat/au roi** checkmate/check; **~s** *nmpl* (*jeu*) chess *sg*; **tenir en ~** to hold in check; **faire ~ à** to foil *ou* thwart.

**échelle** [eʃɛl] *nf* ladder; (*fig, d'une carte*) scale; **à l'~ de** on the scale of; **sur une grande ~** on a large scale; **faire la courte ~ à qn** to give sb a leg up.

**échelon** [eʃlɔ̃] *nm* (*d'échelle*) rung; (ADMIN) grade.

**échelonner** [eʃlɔne] *vt* to space out, spread out.

**écheveau, x** [ɛʃvo] *nm* skein, hank.

**échevelé, e** [eʃəvle] *a* tousled, dishevelled; wild, frenzied.

**échine** [eʃin] *nf* backbone, spine.

**échiquier** [eʃikje] *nm* chessboard.

**écho** [eko] *nm* echo; **~s** *nmpl* (*potins*) gossip *sg*, rumours.

**échoir** [eʃwaR] *vi* (*dette*) to fall due; (*délais*) to expire; **~ à** *vt* to fall to.

**échoppe** [eʃɔp] *nf* stall, booth.

**échouer** [eʃwe] *vi* to fail // *vt* (*bateau*) to ground; **s'~** *vi* to run aground.

**échu, e** [eʃy] *pp voir* **échoir.**

**éclabousser** [eklabuse] *vt* to splash.

**éclair** [eklɛR] *nm* (*d'orage*) flash of lightning, lightning *q*; (*fig*) flash, spark; (*gâteau*) éclair.

**éclairage** [eklɛRaʒ] *nm* lighting.

**éclaircie** [eklɛRsi] *nf* bright *ou* sunny interval.

**éclaircir** [eklɛRsiR] *vt* to lighten; (*fig*) to clear up; to clarify; (CULIN) to thin (down); **s'~ la voix** to clear one's throat; **éclaircissement** *nm* clearing up; clarification.

**éclairer** [ekleRe] *vt* (*lieu*) to light (up); (*personne: avec une lampe de poche etc*) to light the way for; (*fig*) to enlighten; to shed light on // *vi*: **~ mal/bien** to give a poor/good light; **s'~ à la bougie/l'électricité** to use candlelight/have electric lighting.

**éclaireur, euse** [eklɛRœR, -øz] *nm/f* (*scout*) (boy) scout/(girl) guide // *nm* (MIL) scout; **partir en ~** to go off to reconnoitre.

**éclat** [ekla] *nm* (*de bombe, de verre*) fragment; (*du soleil, d'une couleur etc*) brightness, brilliance; (*d'une cérémonie*) splendour; (*scandale*): **faire un ~** to cause a commotion; **des ~s de verre** broken glass; **flying glass**; **~ de rire** burst *ou* roar of laughter; **~ de voix** shout.

**éclatant, e** [eklatɑ̃, -ɑ̃t] *a* brilliant, bright.

**éclater** [eklate] *vi* (*pneu*) to burst; (*bombe*) to explode; (*guerre, épidémie*) to break out; (*groupe, parti*) to break up; **~ de rire** to burst out laughing.

**éclipse** [eklips(ə)] *nf* eclipse.

**éclipser** [eklipse] *vt* to eclipse; **s'~** *vi* to slip away.

**éclopé, e** [eklɔpe] *a* lame.

**éclore** [eklɔR] *vi* (*œuf*) to hatch; (*fleur*) to open (out).

**écluse** [eklyz] *nf* lock; **éclusier** *nm* lock keeper.

**écœurer** [ekœRe] *vt*: **~ qn** to make sb feel sick.

**école** [ekɔl] *nf* school; **aller à l'~** to go to school; **faire ~** to collect a following; **~ de dessin/danse** art/dancing school; **~ hôtelière** catering college; **~ normale (d'instituteurs)** teachers' training college; **~ de secrétariat** secretarial college; **écolier, ière** *nm/f* schoolboy/girl.

**écologie** [ekɔlɔʒi] *nf* ecology; environmental studies *pl*; **écologique** *a* ecological; environmental; **écologiste** *nm/f* ecologist; environmentalist.

**éconduire** [ekɔ̃duiR] *vt* to dismiss.

**économat** [ekɔnɔma] *nm* bursar's office.

**économe** [ekɔnɔm] *a* thrifty // *nm/f* (*de lycée etc*) bursar.

**économie** [ekɔnɔmi] *nf* (*vertu*) economy, thrift; (*gain: d'argent, de temps etc*) saving; (*science*) economics *sg*; (*situation économique*) economy; **~s** *nfpl* (*pécule*) savings; **économique** *a* (*avantageux*) economical; (ÉCON) economic.

**économiser** [ekɔnɔmize] *vt, vi* to save.

**économiste** [ekɔnɔmist(ə)] *nm/f* economist.

**écoper** [ekɔpe] *vi* to bale out; (*fig*) to cop it; **~ (de)** *vt* to get.

**écorce** [ekɔRs(ə)] *nf* bark; (*de fruit*) peel; **écorcer** *vt* to bark.

**écorché** [ekɔRʃe] *nm* cut-away drawing.
**écorcher** [ekɔRʃe] *vt* (*animal*) to skin;
(*égratigner*) to graze; **écorchure** *nf* graze.
**écossais, e** [ekɔsɛ, -ɛz] *a* Scottish //
*nm/f*: E~, e Scot.
**Écosse** [ekɔs] *nf* Scotland.
**écosser** [ekɔse] *vt* to shell.
**écot** [eko] *nm*: **payer son** ~ to pay one's
share.
**écouler** [ekule] *vt* to sell; to dispose of;
**s'**~ *vi* (*eau*) to flow (out); (*jours, temps*)
to pass (by).
**écourter** [ekuRte] *vt* to curtail, cut short.
**écoute** [ekut] *nf* (*RADIO, TV*): **temps/heure**
**d'**~ listening (*ou* viewing) time/hour;
**prendre l'**~ to tune in; **rester à l'**~ (**de**)
to stay listening (to) *ou* tuned in (to); ~**s**
**téléphoniques** phone tapping *sg*.
**écouter** [ekute] *vt* to listen to; **écouteur**
*nm* (*TÉL*) receiver; (*RADIO*) headphones *pl*,
headset.
**écoutille** [ekutij] *nf* hatch.
**écran** [ekRɑ̃] *nm* screen.
**écrasant, e** [ekRazɑ̃, -ɑ̃t] *a* overwhelming.
**écraser** [ekRaze] *vt* to crush; (*piéton*) to
run over; **s'**~ (**au sol**) to crash; **s'**~
**contre** to crash into.
**écrémer** [ekReme] *vt* to skim.
**écrevisse** [ekRəvis] *nf* crayfish *inv*.
**écrier** [ekRije]: **s'**~ *vi* to exclaim.
**écrin** [ekRɛ̃] *nm* case, box.
**écrire** [ekRiR] *vt* to write; **ça s'écrit**
**comment?** how is it spelt?, how do you
write that?; **écrit** *nm* document; (*examen*)
written paper; **par écrit** in writing.
**écriteau, x** [ekRito] *nm* notice, sign.
**écritoire** [ekRitwaR] *nf* writing case.
**écriture** [ekRityR] *nf* writing; (*COMM*)
entry; ~**s** *nfpl* (*COMM*) accounts, books;
**l'É**~ (**sainte**), **les É**~**s** the Scriptures.
**écrivain** [ekRivɛ̃] *nm* writer.
**écrou** [ekRu] *nm* nut.
**écrouer** [ekRue] *vt* to imprison; to
remand in custody.
**écrouler** [ekRule]: **s'**~ *vi* to collapse.
**écru, e** [ekry] *a* (*toile*) raw, unbleached.
**écueil** [ekœj] *nm* reef; (*fig*) pitfall;
stumbling block.
**écuelle** [ekɥɛl] *nf* bowl.
**éculé, e** [ekyle] *a* (*chaussure*) down-
at-heel; (*fig: péj*) hackneyed.
**écume** [ekym] *nf* foam; (*CULIN*) scum;
**écumer** *vt* (*CULIN*) to skim; (*fig*) to plunder
// *vi* (*mer*) to foam; (*fig*) to boil with rage;
**écumoire** *nf* skimmer.
**écureuil** [ekyRœj] *nm* squirrel.
**écurie** [ekyRi] *nf* stable.
**écusson** [ekysɔ̃] *nm* badge.
**écuyer, ère** [ekɥije, -ɛR] *nm/f* rider.
**eczéma** [ɛgzema] *nm* eczema.
**édenté, e** [edɑ̃te] *a* toothless.
**E.D.F.** *sigle f* = *Électricité de France*, ≈
Electricity Board.
**édifice** [edifis] *nm* building, edifice.
**édifier** [edifje] *vt* to build, erect; (*fig*) to
edify.
**édiles** [edil] *nmpl* city fathers.
**édit** [edi] *nm* edict.
**éditer** [edite] *vt* (*publier*) to publish;
(: *disque*) to produce; (*préparer: texte*) to

edit; **éditeur, trice** *nm/f* editor;
publisher; **édition** *nf* editing *q*; edition;
(*industrie du livre*) publishing.
**éditorial, aux** [editɔRjal, -o] *nm* editorial,
leader; ~**iste** *nm/f* editorial *ou* leader
writer.
**édredon** [edRədɔ̃] *nm* eiderdown.
**éducatif, ive** [edykatif, -iv] *a* educational.
**éducation** [edykasjɔ̃] *nf* education;
(*familiale*) upbringing; (*manières*) (good)
manners *pl*; **l'É**~ (**Nationale**) ≈ The
Department of Education; ~ **physique**
physical education.
**édulcorer** [edylkɔRe] *vt* to sweeten; (*fig*)
to tone down.
**éduquer** [edyke] *vt* to educate; (*élever*) to
bring up; (*faculté*) to train.
**effacer** [efase] *vt* to erase, rub out; **s'**~
*vi* (*inscription etc*) to wear off; (*pour laisser
passer*) to step aside; ~ **le ventre** to pull
one's stomach in.
**effarement** [efaRmɑ̃] *nm* alarm.
**effarer** [efaRe] *vt* to alarm.
**effaroucher** [efaRuʃe] *vt* to frighten *ou*
scare away; to alarm.
**effectif, ive** [efɛktif, -iv] *a* real; effective
// *nm* (*MIL*) strength; (*SCOL*) total number
of pupils, size; ~**s** *nmpl* numbers,
strength *sg*; **effectivement** *ad* effectively;
(*réellement*) actually, really; (*en effet*)
indeed.
**effectuer** [efɛktɥe] *vt* (*opération, mission*)
to carry out; (*déplacement, trajet*) to make,
complete; (*mouvement*) to execute, make.
**efféminé, e** [efemine] *a* effeminate.
**effervescent, e** [efɛRvesɑ̃, -ɑ̃t] *a* (*cachet,
boisson*) effervescent; (*fig*) agitated, in a
turmoil.
**effet** [efɛ] *nm* (*résultat, artifice*) effect;
(*impression*) impression; ~**s** *nmpl*
(*vêtements etc*) things; **faire de l'**~
(*médicament, menace*) to have an effect, be
effective; **en** ~ *ad* indeed.
**effeuiller** [efœje] *vt* to remove the leaves
(*ou* petals) from.
**efficace** [efikas] *a* (*personne*) efficient;
(*action, médicament*) effective; **efficacité**
*nf* efficiency; effectiveness.
**effigie** [efiʒi] *nf* effigy.
**effilé, e** [efile] *a* slender; sharp;
streamlined.
**effiler** [efile] *vt* (*cheveux*) to thin (out);
(*tissu*) to fray.
**effilocher** [efilɔʃe]: **s'**~ *vi* to fray.
**efflanqué, e** [eflɑ̃ke] *a* emaciated.
**effleurer** [eflœRe] *vt* to brush (against);
(*sujet, idée*) to touch upon; (*suj: idée,
pensée*): ~ **qn** to cross sb's mind.
**effluves** [eflyv] *nmpl* exhalation(s).
**effondrement** [efɔ̃dRəmɑ̃] *nm* collapse.
**effondrer** [efɔ̃dRe]: **s'**~ *vi* to collapse.
**efforcer** [efɔRse]: **s'**~ **de** *vt*: **s'**~ **de faire**
to try hard to do.
**effort** [efɔR] *nm* effort; **faire un** ~ to
make an effort.
**effraction** [efRaksjɔ̃] *nf* breaking-in;
**s'introduire par** ~ **dans** to break into.
**effrangé, e** [efRɑ̃ʒe] *a* fringed; (*effiloché*)
frayed.
**effrayant, e** [efRɛjɑ̃, -ɑ̃t] *a* frightening,
fearsome; (*sens affaibli*) dreadful.

**effrayer** [efʀeje] *vt* to frighten, scare ; (*rebuter*) to put off ; **s'~ (de)** to be frightened *ou* scared (by).
**effréné, e** [efʀene] *a* wild.
**effriter** [efʀite]: **s'~** *vi* to crumble.
**effroi** [efʀwɑ] *nm* terror, dread *q*.
**effronté, e** [efʀɔ̃te] *a* insolent, brazen.
**effroyable** [efʀwajabl(ə)] *a* horrifying, appalling.
**effusion** [efyzjɔ̃] *nf* effusion ; **sans ~ de sang** without bloodshed.
**égailler** [egaje]: **s'~** *vi* to scatter, disperse.
**égal, e, aux** [egal, -o] *a* (*identique, ayant les mêmes droits*) equal ; (*plan: surface*) even, level ; (*constant: vitesse*) steady ; (*équitable*) even // *nm/f* equal ; **être ~ à** (*prix, nombre*) to be equal to ; **ça lui est ~** it's all the same to him, it doesn't matter to him ; he doesn't mind ; **sans ~** matchless, unequalled ; **à l'~ de** (*comme*) just like ; **d'~ à ~** as equals ; **~ement** *ad* equally ; evenly ; steadily ; (*aussi*) too, as well ; **~er** *vt* to equal ; **~iser** *vt* (*sol, salaires*) to level (out) ; (*chances*) to equalize // *vi* (*SPORT*) to equalize ; **~itaire** *a* egalitarian ; **~ité** *nf* equality ; evenness ; steadiness ; (*MATH*) identity ; **être à ~ité (de points)** to be level ; **~ité de droits** equality of rights ; **~ité d'humeur** evenness of temper.
**égard** [egaʀ] *nm*: **~s** *nmpl* consideration *sg* ; **à cet ~** in this respect ; **eu ~ à** in view of ; **par ~ pour** out of consideration for ; **sans ~ pour** without regard for ; **à l'~ de** *prép* towards ; concerning.
**égarement** [egaʀmɑ̃] *nm* distraction ; aberration.
**égarer** [egaʀe] *vt* (*objet*) to mislay ; (*moralement*) to lead astray ; **s'~** *vi* to get lost, lose one's way ; (*objet*) to go astray ; (*fig: dans une discussion*) to wander.
**égayer** [egeje] *vt* (*personne*) to amuse ; to cheer up ; (*récit, endroit*) to brighten up, liven up.
**égide** [eʒid] *nf*: **sous l'~ de** under the aegis of.
**églantier** [eglɑ̃tje] *nm* wild *ou* dog rose-(-bush).
**églantine** [eglɑ̃tin] *nf* wild *ou* dog rose.
**églefin** [egləfɛ̃] *nm* haddock.
**église** [egliz] *nf* church ; **aller à l'~** (*être pratiquant*) to go to church, be a churchgoer.
**égocentrique** [egɔsɑ̃tʀik] *a* egocentric, self-centred.
**égoïsme** [egɔism(ə)] *nm* selfishness, egoism ; **égoïste** *a* selfish, egoistic // *nm/f* egoist.
**égorger** [egɔʀʒe] *vt* to cut the throat of.
**égosiller** [egozije]: **s'~** *vi* to shout o.s. hoarse.
**égout** [egu] *nm* sewer ; **égoutier** *nm* sewer worker.
**égoutter** [egute] *vt* (*linge*) to wring out ; (*vaisselle*) to drain // *vi*, **s'~** *vi* to drip ; **égouttoir** *nm* draining board ; (*mobile*) draining rack.
**égratigner** [egʀatiɲe] *vt* to scratch ; **égratignure** *nf* scratch.
**égrener** [egʀəne] *vt*: **~ une grappe, ~ des raisins** to pick grapes off a bunch.

**égrillard, e** [egʀijaʀ, -aʀd(ə)] *a* ribald, bawdy.
**Égypte** [eʒipt(ə)] *nf* Egypt ; **égyptien, ne** *a, nm/f* Egyptian ; **égyptologie** *nf* Egyptology.
**eh** [e] *excl* hey! ; **~ bien** well.
**éhonté, e** [eɔ̃te] *a* shameless, brazen.
**éjaculation** [eʒakylɑsjɔ̃] *nf* ejaculation.
**éjaculer** [eʒakyle] *vi* to ejaculate.
**éjectable** [eʒɛktabl(ə)] *a*: **siège ~** ejector seat.
**éjecter** [eʒɛkte] *vt* (*TECH*) to eject ; (*fam*) to kick *ou* chuck out.
**élaboration** [elabɔʀɑsjɔ̃] *nf* elaboration.
**élaborer** [elabɔʀe] *vt* to elaborate.
**élaguer** [elage] *vt* to prune.
**élan** [elɑ̃] *nm* (*ZOOL*) elk, moose ; (*SPORT: avant le saut*) run up ; (*de véhicule ou objet en mouvement*) momentum ; (*fig: de tendresse etc*) surge ; **prendre son ~ / de l'~** to take a run up/gather speed.
**élancé, e** [elɑ̃se] *a* slender.
**élancement** [elɑ̃smɑ̃] *nm* shooting pain.
**élancer** [elɑ̃se]: **s'~** *vi* to dash, hurl o.s. ; (*fig: arbre, clocher*) to soar (upwards).
**élargir** [elaʀʒiʀ] *vt* to widen ; (*vêtement*) to let out ; (*JUR*) to release ; **s'~** *vi* to widen ; (*vêtement*) to stretch.
**élasticité** [elastisite] *nf* (*aussi ÉCON*) elasticity.
**élastique** [elastik] *a* elastic // *nm* (*de bureau*) rubber band ; (*pour la couture*) elastic *q*.
**électeur, trice** [elɛktœʀ, -tʀis] *nm/f* elector, voter.
**élection** [elɛksjɔ̃] *nf* election ; **~s** *nfpl* (*POL*) election(s) ; **~ partielle** ≈ by-election.
**électoral, e, aux** [elɛktɔʀal, -o] *a* electoral, election *cpd*.
**électorat** [elɛktɔʀa] *nm* electorate.
**électricien, ne** [elɛktʀisjɛ̃, -jɛn] *nm/f* electrician.
**électricité** [elɛktʀisite] *nf* electricity ; **allumer/éteindre l'~** to put on/off the light ; **~ statique** static electricity.
**électrifier** [elɛktʀifje] *vt* (*RAIL*) to electrify.
**électrique** [elɛktʀik] *a* electric(al).
**électriser** [elɛktʀize] *vt* to electrify.
**électro...** [elɛktʀɔ] *préfixe*: **~-aimant** *nm* electromagnet ; **~cardiogramme** *nm* electrocardiogram ; **~choc** *nm* electric shock treatment ; **~cuter** *vt* to electrocute ; **~cution** *nf* electrocution ; **électrode** *nf* electrode ; **~-encéphalogramme** *nm* electroencephalogram ; **~gène** *a*: **groupe ~gène** generating set ; **~lyse** *nf* electrolysis *sg* ; **~magnétique** *a* electromagnetic ; **~ménager** *a*: **appareils ~ménagers** domestic (electrical) appliances.
**électron** [elɛktʀɔ̃] *nm* electron.
**électronicien, ne** [elɛktʀɔnisjɛ̃, -jɛn] *nm/f* electronics engineer.
**électronique** [elɛktʀɔnik] *a* electronic // *nf* electronics *sg*.
**électrophone** [elɛktʀɔfɔn] *nm* record player.
**élégance** [elegɑ̃s] *nf* elegance.
**élégant, e** [elegɑ̃, -ɑ̃t] *a* elegant ; (*solution*)

neat, elegant; (attitude, procédé) courteous, civilized.
**élément** [elemɑ̃] nm element; (pièce) component, part; ~s nmpl (aussi: rudiments) elements; **élémentaire** a elementary; (CHIMIE) elemental.
**éléphant** [elefɑ̃] nm elephant.
**élevage** [ɛlvaʒ] nm breeding; (de bovins) cattle breeding ou rearing.
**élévateur** [elevatœʀ] nm elevator.
**élévation** [elevɑsjɔ̃] nf (gén) elevation; (voir élever) raising; (voir s'élever) rise.
**élève** [elɛv] nm/f pupil; ~ **infirmière** nf student nurse.
**élevé, e** [ɛlve] a (prix, sommet) high; (fig: noble) elevated; **bien/mal** ~ well-/ill-mannered.
**élever** [ɛlve] vt (enfant) to bring up, raise; (bétail, volaille) to breed; (abeilles) to keep; (hausser: immeuble, taux, niveau) to raise; (fig: âme, esprit) to elevate; (édifier: monument) to put up, erect; **s'**~ vi (avion, alpiniste) to go up; (niveau, température, aussi: cri etc) to rise; survenir: difficultés) to arise; **s'**~ **à** (suj: frais, dégâts) to amount to, add up to; **s'**~ **contre qch** to rise up against sth; ~ **une pro-testation/critique** to raise a protest/make a criticism; ~ **la voix** to raise one's voice; ~ **qn au rang de** to raise ou elevate sb to the rank of; **éleveur, euse** nm/f cattle breeder.
**élidé, e** [elide] a elided.
**éligible** [eliʒibl(ə)] a eligible.
**élimé, e** [elime] a worn (thin), threadbare.
**élimination** [eliminɑsjɔ̃] nf elimination.
**éliminatoire** [eliminatwaʀ] a eliminatory; disqualifying // nf (SPORT) heat.
**éliminer** [elimine] vt to eliminate.
**élire** [eliʀ] vt to elect; ~ **domicile à** to take up residence in ou at.
**élision** [elizjɔ̃] nf elision.
**élite** [elit] nf elite.
**elle** [ɛl] pronom (sujet) she; (: chose) it; (complément) her; it; ~**s** (sujet) they; (complément) them; ~**-même** herself; it-self; ~**s-mêmes** themselves; voir note sous **il**.
**ellipse** [elips(ə)] nf ellipse; (LING) ellipsis sg; **elliptique** a elliptical.
**élocution** [elɔkysjɔ̃] nf delivery; **défaut d'**~ speech impediment.
**éloge** [elɔʒ] nm praise (gén q); **faire l'**~ **de** to praise; **élogieux, euse** a laudatory, full of praise.
**éloigné, e** [elwaɲe] a distant, far-off.
**éloignement** [elwaɲmɑ̃] nm removal; putting off; estrangement; distance.
**éloigner** [elwaɲe] vt (objet): ~ **qch (de)** to move ou take sth away (from); (personne): ~ **qn (de)** to take sb away ou remove sb (from); (échéance) to put off, postpone; (soupçons, danger) to ward off; **s'**~ **(de)** (personne) to go away (from); (véhicule) to move away (from); (affectivement) to become estranged (from).
**élongation** [elɔ̃gɑsjɔ̃] nf strained muscle.
**éloquence** [elɔkɑ̃s] nf eloquence.

**éloquent, e** [elɔkɑ̃, -ɑ̃t] a eloquent.
**élu, e** [ely] pp de **élire** // nm/f (POL) elected representative.
**élucider** [elyside] vt to elucidate.
**élucubrations** [elykybʀasjɔ̃] nfpl wild imaginings.
**éluder** [elyde] vt to evade.
**émacié, e** [emasje] a emaciated.
**émail, aux** [emaj, -o] nm enamel.
**émaillé, e** [emaje] a enamelled; (fig): ~ **de** dotted with.
**émanation** [emanɑsjɔ̃] nf emanation, exhalation.
**émanciper** [emɑ̃sipe] vt to emancipate; **s'**~ (fig) to become emancipated ou liberated.
**émaner** [emane]: ~ **de** vt to come from; (ADMIN) to proceed from.
**émarger** [emaʀʒe] vt to sign; ~ **de 1000 F à un budget** to receive 1000 F out of a budget.
**émasculer** [emaskyle] vt to emasculate.
**emballage** [ɑ̃balaʒ] nm wrapping; packaging.
**emballer** [ɑ̃bale] vt to wrap (up); (dans un carton) to pack (up); (fig: fam) to thrill (to bits); **s'**~ vi (moteur) to race; (cheval) to bolt; (fig: personne) to get carried away.
**embarcadère** [ɑ̃baʀkadɛʀ] nm landing stage, pier.
**embarcation** [ɑ̃baʀkɑsjɔ̃] nf (small) boat, (small) craft inv.
**embardée** [ɑ̃baʀde] nf swerve; **faire une** ~ to swerve.
**embargo** [ɑ̃baʀgo] nm embargo; **mettre l'**~ **sur** to put an embargo on, embargo.
**embarquement** [ɑ̃baʀkəmɑ̃] nm embarkation; loading; boarding.
**embarquer** [ɑ̃baʀke] vt (personne) to embark; (marchandise) to load; (fam) to cart off; to nick // vi (passager) to board; (NAVIG) to ship water; **s'**~ vi to board; **s'**~ **dans** (affaire, aventure) to embark upon.
**embarras** [ɑ̃baʀa] nm (obstacle) hindrance; (confusion) embarrassment; (ennuis): **être dans l'**~ to be in a predicament ou an awkward position; ~ **gastrique** stomach upset.
**embarrasser** [ɑ̃baʀase] vt (encombrer) to clutter (up); (gêner) to hinder, hamper; (fig) to cause embarrassment to; to put in an awkward position; **s'**~ **de** to burden o.s. with.
**embauche** [ɑ̃boʃ] nf hiring; **bureau d'**~ labour office.
**embaucher** [ɑ̃boʃe] vt to take on, hire; **s'**~ to get o.s. hired.
**embauchoir** [ɑ̃boʃwaʀ] nm shoetree.
**embaumer** [ɑ̃bome] vt to embalm; to fill with its fragrance; ~ **la lavande** to be fragrant with (the scent of) lavender.
**embellir** [ɑ̃beliʀ] vt to make more attractive; (une histoire) to embellish // vi to grow lovelier ou more attractive.
**embêtements** [ɑ̃bɛtmɑ̃] nmpl trouble sg.
**embêter** [ɑ̃bete] vt to bother; **s'**~ vi (s'ennuyer) to be bored; **il ne s'embête pas!** (ironique) he does all right for himself!
**emblée** [ɑ̃ble]: **d'**~ ad straightaway.

**emblème** [ãblɛm] *nm* emblem.
**emboîter** [ãbwate] *vt* to fit together ; s'~ dans to fit into ; s'~ (l'un dans l'autre) to fit together ; ~ le pas à qn to follow in sb's footsteps.
**embolie** [ãbɔli] *nf* embolism.
**embonpoint** [ãbɔ̃pwɛ̃] *nm* stoutness.
**embouché, e** [ãbuʃe] *a*: mal ~ foul-mouthed.
**embouchure** [ãbuʃyʀ] *nf* (GÉO) mouth ; (MUS) mouthpiece.
**embourber** [ãbuʀbe]: s'~ *vi* to get stuck in the mud.
**embourgeoiser** [ãbuʀʒwaze]: s'~ *vi* to adopt a middle-class outlook.
**embout** [ãbu] *nm* (de canne) tip ; (de tuyau) nozzle.
**embouteillage** [ãbutɛjaʒ] *nm* traffic jam, (traffic) holdup.
**emboutir** [ãbutiʀ] *vt* (TECH) to stamp ; (heurter) to crash into, ram.
**embranchement** [ãbʀãʃmã] *nm* (routier) junction ; (classification) branch.
**embraser** [ãbʀaze]: s'~ *vi* to flare up.
**embrassades** [ãbʀasad] *nfpl* hugging and kissing *sg*.
**embrasser** [ãbʀase] *vt* to kiss ; (sujet, période) to embrace, encompass ; (carrière, métier) to take up, enter upon.
**embrasure** [ãbʀazyʀ] *nf*: dans l'~ de la porte in the door(way).
**embrayage** [ãbʀɛjaʒ] *nm* (mécanisme) clutch.
**embrayer** [ãbʀeje] *vi* (AUTO) to let in the clutch.
**embrigader** [ãbʀigade] *vt* to recruit.
**embrocher** [ãbʀɔʃe] *vt* to (put on a) spit.
**embrouillamini** [ãbʀujamini] *nm* (fam) muddle.
**embrouiller** [ãbʀuje] *vt* (fils) to tangle (up) ; (fiches, idées, personne) to muddle up ; s'~ *vi* (personne) to get in a muddle.
**embroussaillé, e** [ãbʀusaje] *a* overgrown, bushy.
**embruns** [ãbʀœ̃] *nmpl* sea spray *sg*.
**embryon** [ãbʀijɔ̃] *nm* embryo ; **embryonnaire** *a* embryonic.
**embûches** [ãbyʃ] *nfpl* pitfalls, traps.
**embué, e** [ãbɥe] *a* misted up.
**embuscade** [ãbyskad] *nf* ambush ; tendre une ~ à to lay an ambush for.
**embusquer** [ãbyske] *vt* to put in ambush ; s'~ *vi* to take up position (for an ambush).
**éméché, e** [emeʃe] *a* tipsy, merry.
**émeraude** [ɛmʀod] *nf* emerald // *a inv* emerald-green.
**émerger** [emɛʀʒe] *vi* to emerge ; (faire saillie, aussi fig) to stand out.
**émeri** [ɛmʀi] *nm*: toile *ou* papier ~ emery paper.
**émérite** [emeʀit] *a* highly skilled.
**émerveiller** [emɛʀveje] *vt* to fill with wonder ; s'~ de to marvel at.
**émetteur, trice** [emɛtœʀ, -tʀis] *a* transmitting ; (poste) ~ transmitter.
**émettre** [emɛtʀ(ə)] *vt* (son, lumière) to give out, emit ; (message etc: RADIO) to transmit ; (billet, timbre, emprunt) to issue ; (hypothèse, avis) to voice, put forward //

*vi*: ~ sur ondes courtes to broadcast on short wave.
**émeus** etc *vb voir* **émouvoir**.
**émeute** [emøt] *nf* riot ; **émeutier, ère** *nm/f* rioter.
**émietter** [emjete] *vt* to crumble ; (fig) to split up, to disperse.
**émigrant, e** [emigʀã, -ãt] *nm/f* emigrant.
**émigré, e** [emigʀe] *nm/f* expatriate.
**émigrer** [emigʀe] *vi* to emigrate.
**éminemment** [eminamã] *ad* eminently.
**éminence** [eminãs] *nf* distinction ; (colline) knoll, hill ; Son É~ his (ou her) Eminence.
**éminent, e** [eminã, -ãt] *a* distinguished.
**émir** [emiʀ] *nm* emir ; ~at *nm* emirate.
**émissaire** [emisɛʀ] *nm* emissary.
**émission** [emisjɔ̃] *nf* emission ; transmission ; issue ; (RADIO, TV) programme, broadcast.
**emmagasiner** [ãmagazine] *vt* to (put into) store ; (fig) to store up.
**emmailloter** [ãmajote] *vt* to wrap up.
**emmanchure** [ãmãʃyʀ] *nf* armhole.
**emmêler** [ãmele] *vt* to tangle (up) ; (fig) to muddle up ; s'~ to get into a tangle.
**emménager** [ãmenaʒe] *vi* to move in ; ~ dans to move into.
**emmener** [ãmne] *vt* to take (with one) ; (comme otage, capture) to take away ; (SPORT, MIL: joueurs, soldats) to lead ; ~ qn au cinéma to take sb to the cinema.
**emmerder** [ãmɛʀde] (fam!) *vt* to bug, bother ; s'~ (s'ennuyer) to be bored stiff.
**emmitoufler** [ãmitufle] *vt* to wrap up (warmly).
**emmurer** [ãmyʀe] *vt* to wall up, immure.
**émoi** [emwa] *nm* (agitation, effervescence) commotion ; (trouble) agitation.
**émoluments** [emɔlymã] *nmpl* remuneration *sg*, fee *sg*.
**émonder** [emɔ̃de] *vt* to prune.
**émotif, ive** [emɔtif, -iv] *a* emotional.
**émotion** [emɔsjɔ̃] *nf* emotion ; avoir des ~s (fig) to get a fright ; **émotionnel, le** *a* emotional.
**émoulu, e** [emuly] *a*: frais ~ de fresh from, just out of.
**émousser** [emuse] *vt* to blunt ; (fig) to dull.
**émouvoir** [emuvwaʀ] *vt* (troubler) to stir, affect ; (toucher, attendrir) to move ; (indigner) to rouse ; (effrayer) to disturb, worry ; s'~ *vi* to be affected ; to be moved ; to be roused ; to be disturbed *ou* worried.
**empailler** [ãpaje] *vt* to stuff.
**empaler** [ãpale] *vt* to impale.
**empaqueter** [ãpakte] *vt* to pack up.
**emparer** [ãpaʀe]: s'~ de *vt* (objet) to seize, grab ; (comme otage, MIL) to seize ; (suj: peur, doute) to take hold of.
**empâter** [ãpate]: s'~ *vi* to thicken out.
**empattement** [ãpatmã] *nm* (AUTO) wheelbase ; (TYPO) serif.
**empêchement** [ãpɛʃmã] *nm* (unexpected) obstacle, hitch.
**empêcher** [ãpeʃe] *vt* to prevent ; ~ qn de faire to prevent ou stop sb (from) doing ; ~ que qch (n')arrive/qn (ne)

**fasse** to prevent sth from happening/sb from doing; **il n'empêche que** nevertheless, be that as it may; **il n'a pas pu s'~ de rire** he couldn't help laughing.
**empêcheur** [ɑ̃pɛʃœʀ] *nm*: ~ **de danser en rond** spoilsport, killjoy.
**empeigne** [ɑ̃pɛɲ] *nf* upper(s).
**empereur** [ɑ̃pʀœʀ] *nm* emperor.
**empesé, e** [ɑ̃pəze] *a* (*fig*) stiff, starchy.
**empeser** [ɑ̃pəze] *vt* to starch.
**empester** [ɑ̃pɛste] *vt* (*lieu*) to stink out // *vi* to stink, reek; ~ **le tabac/le vin** to stink *ou* reek of tobacco/wine.
**empêtrer** [ɑ̃petʀe] *vt*: **s'~ dans** (*fils etc*) to get tangled up in.
**emphase** [ɑ̃fɑz] *nf* pomposity, bombast.
**empierrer** [ɑ̃pjeʀe] *vt* (*route*) to metal.
**empiéter** [ɑ̃pjete]: ~ **sur** *vt* to encroach upon.
**empiffrer** [ɑ̃pifʀe]: **s'~** *vi* (*péj*) to stuff o.s.
**empiler** [ɑ̃pile] *vt* to pile (up), stack (up).
**empire** [ɑ̃piʀ] *nm* empire; (*fig*) influence.
**empirer** [ɑ̃piʀe] *vi* to worsen, deteriorate.
**empirique** [ɑ̃piʀik] *a* empirical.
**emplacement** [ɑ̃plasmɑ̃] *nm* site.
**emplâtre** [ɑ̃plɑtʀ(ə)] *nm* plaster; (*fam*) twit.
**emplette** [ɑ̃plɛt] *nf*: **faire l'~ de** to purchase; ~**s** *nfpl* shopping *sg*.
**emplir** [ɑ̃pliʀ] *vt* to fill; **s'~ (de)** to fill (with).
**emploi** [ɑ̃plwa] *nm* use; (*COMM, ÉCON*) employment; (*poste*) job, situation; **d'~ facile** easy to use; ~ **du temps** timetable, schedule.
**employé, e** [ɑ̃plwaje] *nm/f* employee; ~ **de bureau/banque** office/bank employee *ou* clerk.
**employer** [ɑ̃plwaje] *vt* (*outil, moyen, méthode, mot*) to use; (*ouvrier, main-d'œuvre*) to employ; **s'~ à faire** to apply *ou* devote o.s. to doing; **employeur, euse** *nm/f* employer.
**empocher** [ɑ̃pɔʃe] *vt* to pocket.
**empoignade** [ɑ̃pwaɲad] *nf* row, set-to.
**empoigne** [ɑ̃pwaɲ] *nf*: **foire d'~** free-for-all.
**empoigner** [ɑ̃pwaɲe] *vt* to grab; **s'~** (*fig*) to have a row *ou* set-to.
**empoisonnement** [ɑ̃pwazɔnmɑ̃] *nm* poisoning.
**empoisonner** [ɑ̃pwazɔne] *vt* to poison; (*empester: air, pièce*) to stink out; (*fam*): ~ **qn** to drive sb mad.
**emportement** [ɑ̃pɔʀtəmɑ̃] *nm* fit of rage, anger *q*.
**emporte-pièce** [ɑ̃pɔʀtəpjɛs] *nm inv* (*TECH*) punch; **à l'~** *a* (*fig*) incisive.
**emporter** [ɑ̃pɔʀte] *vt* to take (with one); (*en dérobant ou enlevant, emmener: blessés, voyageurs*) to take away; (*entraîner*) to carry away *ou* along; (*arracher*) to tear off; to carry away; (*MIL: position*) to take; (*avantage, approbation*) to win; **s'~** *vi* (*de colère*) to fly into a rage, lose one's temper; **l'~ (sur)** to get the upper hand (of); (*méthode etc*) to prevail (over); **boissons à (l')~** take-away drinks.
**empourpré, e** [ɑ̃puʀpʀe] *a* crimson.

**empreint, e** [ɑ̃pʀɛ̃, -ɛ̃t] *a*: ~ **de** marked with; tinged with // *nf* (*de pied, main*) print; (*fig*) stamp, mark; ~**e (digitale)** fingerprint.
**empressé, e** [ɑ̃pʀese] *a* attentive; (*péj*) overanxious to please, overattentive.
**empressement** [ɑ̃pʀɛsmɑ̃] *nm* (*hâte*) eagerness.
**empresser** [ɑ̃pʀese]: **s'~** *vi* to bustle about; **s'~ auprès de qn** to surround sb with attentions; **s'~ de faire** (*se hâter*) to hasten to do.
**emprise** [ɑ̃pʀiz] *nf* hold, ascendancy; **sous l'~ de** under the influence of.
**emprisonnement** [ɑ̃pʀizɔnmɑ̃] *nm* imprisonment.
**emprisonner** [ɑ̃pʀizɔne] *vt* to imprison, jail.
**emprunt** [ɑ̃pʀœ̃] *nm* borrowing *q*, loan (*from debtor's point of view*); (*LING etc*) borrowing; ~ **public à 5%** 5% public loan.
**emprunté, e** [ɑ̃pʀœ̃te] *a* (*fig*) ill-at-ease, awkward.
**emprunter** [ɑ̃pʀœ̃te] *vt* to borrow; (*itinéraire*) to take, follow; (*style, manière*) to adopt, assume; **emprunteur, euse** *nm/f* borrower.
**empuantir** [ɑ̃pɥɑ̃tiʀ] *vt* to stink out.
**ému, e** [emy] *pp de* **émouvoir** // *a* excited; touched; moved.
**émulation** [emylasjɔ̃] *nf* emulation.
**émule** [emyl] *nm/f* imitator.
**émulsion** [emylsjɔ̃] *nf* emulsion.
**en** [ɑ̃] *prép* in; (*avec direction*) to; (*moyen*): ~ **avion/taxi** by plane/taxi; (*composition*): ~ **verre** made of glass, glass *cpd*; **se casser** ~ **plusieurs morceaux** to break into several pieces; ~ **dormant** while sleeping, as one sleeps; ~ **sortant** on going out, as he went out; ~ **réparation** being repaired, under repair; ~ **T/étoile** T-/star-shaped; ~ **chemise/chaussettes** in one's shirt/socks; **peindre qch** ~ **rouge** to paint sth red; ~ **soldat** as a soldier; **le même** ~ **plus grand** the same only *ou* but bigger // *pronom* (*provenance*): **j'~ viens** I've come from there; (*cause*): **il** ~ **est malade** he's ill because of it; (*complément de nom*): **j'~ connais les dangers** I know its dangers; (*indéfini*): **j'~ ai/veux** I have/want some; ~ **as-tu?** have you got any?; **je n'~ veux pas** I don't want any; **j'~ ai assez** I've got enough (of it *ou* them); (*fig*) I've had enough; **j'~ ai 2** I've got 2 (of them); **combien y** ~ **a-t-il?** how many (of them) are there?; **j'~ suis fier/ai besoin** I am proud of it/need it; *voir le verbe ou l'adjectif lorsque 'en' correspond à 'de' introduisant un complément prépositionnel.*
**E.N.A.** [ena] *sigle f* = École Nationale d'Administration: *one of the Grandes Écoles*; **énarque** *nm/f* former E.N.A. student.
**encablure** [ɑ̃kablyʀ] *nf* (*NAVIG*) cable's length.
**encadrement** [ɑ̃kadʀəmɑ̃] *nm* framing; training; (*de porte*) frame.
**encadrer** [ɑ̃kadʀe] *vt* (*tableau, image*) to frame; (*fig: entourer*) to surround; to

flank ; (personnel, soldats etc) to train ;
**encadreur** nm (picture) framer.
**encaisse** [ɑ̃kɛs] nf cash in hand ; ~
or/métallique gold/gold and silver
reserves.
**encaissé, e** [ɑ̃kese] a steep-sided ; with
steep banks.
**encaisser** [ɑ̃kese] vt (chèque) to cash ;
(argent) to collect ; (fig: coup, défaite) to
take ; **encaisseur** nm collector (of debts
etc).
**encan** [ɑ̃kɑ̃]: **à l'~** ad by auction.
**encanailler** [ɑ̃kanɑje]: **s'~** vi to become
vulgar ou common ; to mix with the riffraff.
**encart** [ɑ̃kaʀ] nm insert.
**encastrer** [ɑ̃kastʀe] vt: ~ **qch dans** (mur)
to embed sth in(to) ; (boîtier) to fit sth into ;
**s'~ dans** to fit into ; (heurter) to crash into.
**encaustique** [ɑ̃kɔstik] nf polish, wax ;
**encaustiquer** vt to polish, wax.
**enceinte** [ɑ̃sɛ̃t] af: ~ **(de 6 mois)** (6
months) pregnant // nf (mur) wall ;
(espace) enclosure ; ~ **(acoustique)**
speaker system.
**encens** [ɑ̃sɑ̃] nm incense ; **encenser** vt to
(in)cense ; (fig) to praise to the skies ;
**encensoir** nm thurible.
**encercler** [ɑ̃sɛʀkle] vt to surround.
**enchaîner** [ɑ̃ʃene] vt to chain up ;
(mouvements, séquences) to link (together)
// vi to carry on.
**enchanté, e** [ɑ̃ʃɑ̃te] a delighted ;
enchanted ; ~ **(de faire votre
connaissance)** pleased to meet you, how
do you do?.
**enchantement** [ɑ̃ʃɑ̃tmɑ̃] nm delight ;
(magie) enchantment ; **comme par ~ as**
if by magic.
**enchanter** [ɑ̃ʃɑ̃te] vt to delight.
**enchâsser** [ɑ̃ʃɑse] vt: ~ **qch (dans)** to
set sth (in).
**enchère** [ɑ̃ʃɛʀ] nf bid ; **faire une ~** to
(make a) bid ; **mettre/vendre aux ~s** to
put up for (sale by)/sell by auction.
**enchevêtrer** [ɑ̃ʃvetʀe] vt to tangle (up).
**enclave** [ɑ̃klav] nf enclave ; **enclaver** vt
to enclose, hem in.
**enclencher** [ɑ̃klɑ̃ʃe] vt (mécanisme) to
engage ; **s'~** vi to engage.
**enclin, e** [ɑ̃klɛ̃, -in] a: ~ **à** inclined ou
prone to.
**enclore** [ɑ̃klɔʀ] vt to enclose.
**enclos** [ɑ̃klo] nm enclosure.
**enclume** [ɑ̃klym] nf anvil.
**encoche** [ɑ̃kɔʃ] nf notch.
**encoignure** [ɑ̃kɔɲyʀ] nf corner.
**encoller** [ɑ̃kɔle] vt to paste.
**encolure** [ɑ̃kɔlyʀ] nf (tour de cou) collar
size ; (col, cou) neck.
**encombrant, e** [ɑ̃kɔ̃bʀɑ̃, -ɑ̃t] a
cumbersome, bulky.
**encombre** [ɑ̃kɔ̃bʀ(ə)]: **sans ~** ad without
mishap ou incident.
**encombrement** [ɑ̃kɔ̃bʀəmɑ̃] nm (d'un
lieu) cluttering (up) ; (d'un objet:
dimensions) bulk.
**encombrer** [ɑ̃kɔ̃bʀe] vt to clutter (up) ;
(gêner) to hamper ; **s'~ de** (bagages etc)
to load ou burden o.s. with ; ~ **le passage**
to block ou obstruct the way.

**encontre** [ɑ̃kɔ̃tʀ(ə)]: **à l'~ de** prép
against, counter to.
**encorbellement** [ɑ̃kɔʀbɛlmɑ̃] nm
corbelled construction ; **fenêtre en~** oriel
window.
**encore** [ɑ̃kɔʀ] ad (continuation) still ; (de
nouveau) again ; (restriction) even then ou
so ; (intensif): ~ **plus fort/mieux** even
louder/better ; **pas ~** not yet ; ~ **une fois**
(once) again ; ~ **deux jours** still two days,
two more days ; **si ~** if only.
**encouragement** [ɑ̃kuʀaʒmɑ̃] nm
encouragement.
**encourager** [ɑ̃kuʀaʒe] vt to encourage.
**encourir** [ɑ̃kuʀiʀ] vt to incur.
**encrasser** [ɑ̃kʀase] vt to foul up ; to soot
up.
**encre** [ɑ̃kʀ(ə)] nf ink ; ~ **de Chine** Indian
ink ; ~ **sympathique** invisible ink ;
**encrer** vt to ink ; **encreur** am: **rouleau
encreur** inking roller ; **encrier** nm inkwell.
**encroûter** [ɑ̃kʀute]: **s'~** vi (fig) to get
into a rut, get set in one's ways.
**encyclique** [ɑ̃siklik] nf encyclical.
**encyclopédie** [ɑ̃siklɔpedi] nf
encyclopaedia ; **encyclopédique** a
encyclopaedic.
**endémique** [ɑ̃demik] a endemic.
**endetter** [ɑ̃dete] vt, **s'~** vi to get into debt.
**endeuiller** [ɑ̃dœje] vt to plunge into
mourning ; **manifestation endeuillée par**
event over which a tragic shadow was cast
by.
**endiablé, e** [ɑ̃djɑble] a furious ;
boisterous.
**endiguer** [ɑ̃dige] vt to dyke (up) ; (fig) to
check, hold back.
**endimancher** [ɑ̃dimɑ̃ʃe] vt: **s'~** to put
on one's Sunday best.
**endive** [ɑ̃div] nf chicory q.
**endocrine** [ɑ̃dɔkʀin] af: **glande ~**
endocrine (gland).
**endoctriner** [ɑ̃dɔktʀine] vt to
indoctrinate.
**endommager** [ɑ̃dɔmaʒe] vt to damage.
**endormi, e** [ɑ̃dɔʀmi] a asleep ; (fig)
sleepy, drowsy ; sluggish.
**endormir** [ɑ̃dɔʀmiʀ] vt to put to sleep ;
(MÉD: dent, nerf) to anaesthetize ; (fig:
soupçons) to allay ; **s'~** vi to fall asleep,
go to sleep.
**endosser** [ɑ̃dose] vt (responsabilité) to
take, shoulder ; (chèque) to endorse ;
(uniforme, tenue) to put on, don.
**endroit** [ɑ̃dʀwa] nm place ; (opposé à
l'envers) right side ; **à l'~** right side out ;
the right way up ; (vêtement) the right way
out ; **à l'~ de** prép regarding, with regard
to.
**enduire** [ɑ̃dɥiʀ] vt to coat ; ~ **qch de** to
coat sth with ; **enduit** nm coating.
**endurance** [ɑ̃dyʀɑ̃s] nf endurance.
**endurant, e** [ɑ̃dyʀɑ̃, -ɑ̃t] a tough, hardy.
**endurcir** [ɑ̃dyʀsiʀ] vt (physiquement) to
toughen ; (moralement) to harden ; **s'~** vi
to become tougher ; to become hardened.
**endurer** [ɑ̃dyʀe] vt to endure, bear.
**énergétique** [enɛʀʒetik] a (ressources etc)
energy cpd.
**énergie** [enɛʀʒi] nf (PHYSIQUE) energy ;
(TECH) power ; (fig: physique) energy ;

(: *morale*) vigour, spirit; **énergique** *a* energetic; vigorous; (*mesures*) drastic, stringent.

**énergumène** [enɛRgymɛn] *nm* rowdy character *ou* customer.

**énerver** [enɛRve] *vt* to irritate, annoy; **s'~** *vi* to get excited, get worked up.

**enfance** [ɑ̃fɑ̃s] *nf* (*âge*) childhood; (*fig*) infancy; (*enfants*) children *pl*; **petite ~** infancy.

**enfant** [ɑ̃fɑ̃] *nm/f* child (*pl* children); **~ de chœur** *nm* (*REL*) altar boy; **~ prodige** child prodigy; **enfanter** *vi* to give birth // *vt* to give birth to; **enfantillage** *nm* (*péj*) childish behaviour *q*; **enfantin, e** *a* childlike; child *cpd*.

**enfer** [ɑ̃fɛR] *nm* hell.

**enfermer** [ɑ̃fɛRme] *vt* to shut up; (*à clef, interner*) to lock up.

**enferrer** [ɑ̃feRe]: **s'~** *vi*: **s'~ dans** to tangle o.s. up in.

**enfiévré, e** [ɑ̃fjevRe] *a* (*fig*) feverish.

**enfilade** [ɑ̃filad] *nf*: **une ~ de** a series *ou* line of (interconnecting).

**enfiler** [ɑ̃file] *vt* (*vêtement*): **~ qch** to slip sth on, slip into sth; (*insérer*): **~ qch dans** to stick sth into; (*rue, couloir*) to take; (*perles*) to string; (*aiguille*) to thread; **s'~ dans** to disappear into.

**enfin** [ɑ̃fɛ̃] *ad* at last; (*en énumérant*) lastly; (*de restriction, résignation*) still; well; (*pour conclure*) in a word.

**enflammer** [ɑ̃flame] *vt* to set fire to; (*MÉD*) to inflame; **s'~** to catch fire; to become inflamed.

**enflé, e** [ɑ̃fle] *a* swollen; (*péj: style*) bombastic, turgid.

**enfler** [ɑ̃fle] *vi* to swell (up); **s'~** *vi* to swell; **enflure** *nf* swelling.

**enfoncer** [ɑ̃fɔ̃se] *vt* (*clou*) to drive in; (*faire pénétrer*): **~ qch dans** to push *ou* knock *ou* drive sth into; (*forcer: porte*) to break open; (: *plancher*) to cause to cave in; (*fam: surpasser*) to lick // *vi* (*dans la vase etc*) to sink in; (*sol, surface porteuse*) to give way; **s'~** *vi* to sink; **s'~ dans** to sink into; (*forêt, ville*) to disappear into.

**enfouir** [ɑ̃fwiR] *vt* (*dans le sol*) to bury; (*dans un tiroir etc*) to tuck away; **s'~ dans/sous** to bury o.s. in/under.

**enfourcher** [ɑ̃fuRʃe] *vt* to mount.

**enfourner** [ɑ̃fuRne] *vt*: **~ qch dans** to shove *ou* stuff sth into.

**enfreindre** [ɑ̃fRɛ̃dR(ə)] *vt* to infringe, break.

**enfuir** [ɑ̃fɥiR]: **s'~** *vi* to run away *ou* off.

**enfumer** [ɑ̃fyme] *vt* to smoke out.

**engagé, e** [ɑ̃gaʒe] *a* (*littérature etc*) engagé, committed.

**engageant, e** [ɑ̃gaʒɑ̃, -ɑ̃t] *a* attractive, appealing.

**engagement** [ɑ̃gaʒmɑ̃] *nm* taking on, engaging; starting; investing; (*d'un écrivain etc, professionnel, financier*) commitment; (*promesse*) agreement, promise; (*MIL: combat*) engagement; **prendre l'~ de faire** to undertake to do; **sans ~** (*COMM*) without obligation.

**engager** [ɑ̃gaʒe] *vt* (*embaucher*) to take on, engage; (*commencer*) to start; (*lier*) to bind, commit; (*impliquer, entraîner*) to

involve; (*investir*) to invest, lay out; (*faire intervenir*) to engage; (*inciter*): **~ qn à faire** to urge sb to do; (*faire pénétrer*): **~ qch dans** to insert sth into; **s'~** (*s'embaucher*) to hire o.s., get taken on; (*MIL*) to enlist; (*promettre, politiquement*) to commit o.s.; (*débuter*) to start (up); **s'~ à faire** to undertake to do; **s'~ dans** (*rue, passage*) to enter, turn into; (*s'emboîter*) to engage *ou* fit into; (*fig: affaire, discussion*) to enter into, embark on.

**engelures** [ɑ̃ʒlyR] *nfpl* chilblains.

**engendrer** [ɑ̃ʒɑ̃dRe] *vt* to father; (*fig*) to create, breed.

**engin** [ɑ̃ʒɛ̃] *nm* machine; instrument; vehicle; (*AVIAT*) aircraft *inv*; missile; **~ (explosif)** (explosive) device.

**englober** [ɑ̃glɔbe] *vt* to include.

**engloutir** [ɑ̃glutiR] *vt* to swallow up; **s'~** to be engulfed.

**engoncé, e** [ɑ̃gɔ̃se] *a*: **~ dans** cramped in.

**engorger** [ɑ̃gɔRʒe] *vt* to obstruct, block; **s'~** *vi* to become blocked.

**engouement** [ɑ̃gumɑ̃] *nm* (sudden) passion.

**engouffrer** [ɑ̃gufRe] *vt* to swallow up, devour; **s'~ dans** to rush into.

**engourdi, e** [ɑ̃guRdi] *a* numb.

**engourdir** [ɑ̃guRdiR] *vt* to numb; (*fig*) to dull, blunt; **s'~** *vi* to go numb.

**engrais** [ɑ̃gRɛ] *nm* manure; **~ (chimique)** (chemical) fertilizer.

**engraisser** [ɑ̃gRese] *vt* to fatten (up) // *vi* (*péj*) to get fat(ter).

**engrenage** [ɑ̃gRənaʒ] *nm* gears *pl*, gearing; (*fig*) chain.

**engueuler** [ɑ̃gœle] *vt* (*fam*) to bawl out.

**enhardir** [ɑ̃aRdiR]: **s'~** *vi* to grow bolder.

**énigmatique** [enigmatik] *a* enigmatic.

**énigme** [enigm(ə)] *nf* riddle.

**enivrer** [ɑ̃nivRe] *vt*: **s'~** to get drunk; **s'~ de** (*fig*) to become intoxicated with.

**enjambée** [ɑ̃ʒɑ̃be] *nf* stride.

**enjamber** [ɑ̃ʒɑ̃be] *vt* to stride over; (*suj: pont etc*) to span, straddle.

**enjeu, x** [ɑ̃ʒø] *nm* stakes *pl*.

**enjoindre** [ɑ̃ʒwɛ̃dR(ə)] *vt*: **~ à qn de faire** to enjoin *ou* order sb to do.

**enjôler** [ɑ̃ʒole] *vt* to coax, wheedle.

**enjoliver** [ɑ̃ʒolive] *vt* to embellish; **enjoliveur** *nm* (*AUTO*) hub cap.

**enjoué, e** [ɑ̃ʒwe] *a* playful.

**enlacer** [ɑ̃lase] *vt* (*étreindre*) to embrace, hug; (*suj: lianes*) to wind round, entwine.

**enlaidir** [ɑ̃lediR] *vt* to make ugly // *vi* to become ugly.

**enlèvement** [ɑ̃lɛvmɑ̃] *nm* removal; abduction, kidnapping; **l'~ des ordures ménagères** refuse collection.

**enlever** [ɑ̃lve] *vt* (*ôter: gén*) to remove; (: *vêtement, lunettes*) to take off; (: *MÉD: organe*) to remove, take out; (*emporter: ordures etc*) to collect, take away; (*prendre*): **~ qch à qn** to take sth (away) from sb; (*kidnapper*) to abduct, kidnap; (*obtenir: prix, contrat*) to win; (*MIL: position*) to take; (*morceau de piano etc*) to execute with spirit *ou* brio.

**enliser** [ɑ̃lize]: **s'~** *vi* to sink, get stuck.

**enluminure** [ɑ̃lyminyʀ] *nf* illumination.
**enneigé, e** [ɑ̃neʒe] *a* snowy ; snowed-up.
**enneigement** [ɑ̃nɛʒmɑ̃] *nm* depth of snow, snowfall ; **bulletin d'**~ snow report.
**ennemi, e** [ɛnmi] *a* hostile ; (MIL) enemy *cpd* // *nm, nf* enemy ; **être** ~ **de** to be strongly averse *ou* opposed to.
**ennoblir** [ɑ̃nɔbliʀ] *vt* to ennoble.
**ennui** [ɑ̃ɥi] *nm* (*lassitude*) boredom ; (*difficulté*) trouble *q* ; **avoir des** ~**s** to be in trouble ; **ennuyer** *vt* to bother ; (*lasser*) to bore ; **s'ennuyer** to be bored ; **s'ennuyer de** (*regretter*) to miss ; **ennuyeux, euse** *a* boring, tedious ; annoying.
**énoncé** [enɔ̃se] *nm* terms *pl* ; wording ; (LING) utterance.
**énoncer** [enɔ̃se] *vt* to say, express ; (*conditions*) to set out, state.
**enorgueillir** [ɑ̃nɔʀɡœjiʀ]: **s'**~ **de** *vt* to pride o.s. on ; to boast.
**énorme** [enɔʀm(ə)] *a* enormous, huge ; **énormément** *ad* enormously, tremendously ; **énormément de neige/gens** an enormous amount of snow/number of people ; **énormité** *nf* enormity, hugeness ; outrageous remark.
**enquérir** [ɑ̃keʀiʀ]: **s'**~ **de** *vt* to inquire about.
**enquête** [ɑ̃kɛt] *nf* (*de journaliste, de police*) investigation ; (*judiciaire, administrative*) inquiry ; (*sondage d'opinion*) survey ; **enquêter** *vi* to investigate ; to hold an inquiry ; to conduct a survey ; **enquêteur, euse** *ou* **trice** *nm/f* officer in charge of the investigation ; person conducting a survey.
**enquiers** *etc vb voir* **enquérir**.
**enraciné, e** [ɑ̃ʀasine] *a* deep-rooted.
**enragé, e** [ɑ̃ʀaʒe] *a* (MÉD) rabid, with rabies ; (*fig*) fanatical.
**enrageant, e** [ɑ̃ʀaʒɑ̃, -ɑ̃t] *a* infuriating.
**enrager** [ɑ̃ʀaʒe] *vi* to be furious, be in a rage.
**enrayer** [ɑ̃ʀeje] *vt* to check, stop ; **s'**~ *vi* (*arme à feu*) to jam.
**enregistrement** [ɑ̃ʀʒistʀəmɑ̃] *nm* recording ; (ADMIN) registration ; ~ **des bagages** (*à l'aéroport*) luggage check-in.
**enregistrer** [ɑ̃ʀʒistʀe] *vt* (MUS *etc*) to record ; (*remarquer, noter*) to note, record ; (*fig: mémoriser*) to make a mental note of ; (ADMIN) to register ; (*bagages: par train*) to register ; (: *à l'aéroport*) to check in.
**enrhumer** [ɑ̃ʀyme]: **s'**~ *vi* to catch a cold.
**enrichir** [ɑ̃ʀiʃiʀ] *vt* to make rich(er) ; (*fig*) to enrich ; **s'**~ to get rich(er).
**enrober** [ɑ̃ʀɔbe] *vt*: ~ **qch de** to coat sth with ; (*fig*) to wrap sth up in.
**enrôler** [ɑ̃ʀole] *vt* to enlist ; **s'**~ **(dans)** to enlist (in).
**enrouer** [ɑ̃ʀwe]: **s'**~ *vi* to go hoarse.
**enrouler** [ɑ̃ʀule] *vt* (*fil, corde*) to wind (up) ; ~ **qch autour de** to wind sth (a)round ; **s'**~ to coil up ; to wind ; **enrouleur** *nm voir* **ceinture**.
**enrubanné, e** [ɑ̃ʀybane] *a* trimmed with ribbon.
**ensabler** [ɑ̃sɑble] *vt* (*port, canal*) to silt up, sand up ; (*embarcation*) to strand (on a sandbank) ; **s'**~ *vi* to silt up ; to get stranded.

**ensanglanté, e** [ɑ̃sɑ̃ɡlɑ̃te] *a* covered with blood.
**enseignant, e** [ɑ̃sɛɲɑ̃, -ɑ̃t] *a* teaching // *nm/f* teacher.
**enseigne** [ɑ̃sɛɲ] *nf* sign // *nm*: ~ **de vaisseau** lieutenant ; **à telle** ~ **que** so much so that ; ~ **lumineuse** neon sign.
**enseignement** [ɑ̃sɛɲmɑ̃] *nm* teaching ; (ADMIN): ~ **primaire/ secondaire** primary/secondary education.
**enseigner** [ɑ̃seɲe] *vt, vi* to teach ; ~ **qch à qn/à qn que** to teach sb sth/sb that.
**ensemble** [ɑ̃sɑ̃bl(ə)] *ad* together // *nm* (*assemblage*, MATH) set ; (*totalité*): **l'**~ **du/de la** the whole *ou* entire ; (*vêtement féminin*) ensemble, suit ; (*unité, harmonie*) unity ; (*résidentiel*) housing development ; **impression/idée d'**~ overall *ou* general impression/ idea ; **dans l'**~ (*en gros*) on the whole ; ~ **vocal/musical** vocal/musical ensemble.
**ensemblier** [ɑ̃sɑ̃blije] *nm* interior designer.
**ensemencer** [ɑ̃smɑ̃se] *vt* to sow.
**enserrer** [ɑ̃seʀe] *vt* to hug (tightly).
**ensevelir** [ɑ̃səvliʀ] *vt* to bury.
**ensoleillé, e** [ɑ̃sɔleje] *a* sunny.
**ensoleillement** [ɑ̃sɔlɛjmɑ̃] *nm* period *ou* hours of sunshine.
**ensommeillé, e** [ɑ̃sɔmeje] *a* sleepy, drowsy.
**ensorceler** [ɑ̃sɔʀsəle] *vt* to enchant, bewitch.
**ensuite** [ɑ̃sɥit] *ad* then, next ; (*plus tard*) afterwards, later ; ~ **de quoi** after which.
**ensuivre** [ɑ̃sɥivʀ(ə)]: **s'**~ *vi* to follow, ensue.
**entaille** [ɑ̃taj] *nf* (*encoche*) notch ; (*blessure*) cut.
**entailler** [ɑ̃taje] *vt* to notch ; to cut ; **s'**~ **le doigt** to cut one's finger.
**entamer** [ɑ̃tame] *vt* (*pain, bouteille*) to start ; (*hostilités, pourparlers*) to open ; (*fig: ultérer*) to make a dent in ; to shake ; to damage.
**entartrer** [ɑ̃taʀtʀe]: **s'**~ *vi* to fur up ; (*dents*) to scale.
**entassement** [ɑ̃tɑsmɑ̃] *nm* (*tas*) pile, heap.
**entasser** [ɑ̃tɑse] *vt* (*empiler*) to pile up, heap up ; (*tenir à l'étroit*) to cram together ; **s'**~ *vi* to pile up ; to cram.
**entendement** [ɑ̃tɑ̃dmɑ̃] *nm* understanding.
**entendre** [ɑ̃tɑ̃dʀ(ə)] *vt* to hear ; (*comprendre*) to understand ; (*vouloir dire*) to mean ; (*vouloir*): ~ **être obéi/que** to intend *ou* mean to be obeyed/that ; **j'ai entendu dire que** I've heard (it said) that ; ~ **raison** to see sense ; **s'**~ *vi* (*sympathiser*) to get on ; (*se mettre d'accord*) to agree ; **s'**~ **à qch/à faire** (*être compétent*) to be good at sth/doing.
**entendu, e** [ɑ̃tɑ̃dy] *a* (*réglé*) agreed ; (*au courant: air*) knowing ; **(c'est)** ~! all right, agreed ; **c'est** ~ (*concession*) all right, granted ; **bien** ~! of course!
**entente** [ɑ̃tɑ̃t] *nf* (*entre amis, pays*) understanding, harmony ; (*accord, traité*) agreement, understanding ; **à double** ~ (*sens*) with a double meaning.

**entériner** [ɑ̃teRine] *vt* to ratify, confirm.
**entérite** [ɑ̃teRit] *nf* enteritis *q.*
**enterrement** [ɑ̃tɛRmɑ̃] *nm* burying; (*cérémonie*) funeral, burial.
**enterrer** [ɑ̃teRe] *vt* to bury.
**entêtant, e** [ɑ̃tɛtɑ̃, -ɑ̃t] *a* heady.
**en-tête** [ɑ̃tɛt] *nm* heading; **papier à ~** headed notepaper.
**entêté, e** [ɑ̃tete] *a* stubborn.
**entêter** [ɑ̃tete]: **s'~** *vi*: **s'~ (à faire)** to persist (in doing).
**enthousiasme** [ɑ̃tuzjasm(ə)] *nm* enthusiasm; **enthousiasmer** *vt* to fill with enthusiasm; **s'enthousiasmer (pour qch)** to get enthusiastic (about sth); **enthousiaste** *a* enthusiastic.
**enticher** [ɑ̃tiʃe]: **s'~ de** *vt* to become infatuated with.
**entier, ère** [ɑ̃tje, -jɛR] *a* (*non entamé, en totalité*) whole; (*total, complet*) complete; (*fig: caractère*) unbending, averse to compromise // *nm* (MATH) whole; **en ~** totally; **in its entirety; lait ~** full-cream milk; **pain ~** wholemeal bread; **entièrement** *ad* entirely, completely, wholly.
**entité** [ɑ̃tite] *nf* entity.
**entonner** [ɑ̃tɔne] *vt* (*chanson*) to strike up.
**entonnoir** [ɑ̃tɔnwaR] *nm* (*ustensile*) funnel; (*trou*) shell-hole, crater.
**entorse** [ɑ̃tɔRs(ə)] *nf* (MÉD) sprain; (*fig*): **~ à la loi/au règlement** infringement of the law/rule.
**entortiller** [ɑ̃tɔRtije] *vt* (*envelopper*): **~ qch dans/avec** to wrap sth in/with; (*enrouler*): **~ qch autour de** to twist *ou* wind sth (a)round; (*fam*): **~ qn** to get round sb; to hoodwink sb.
**entourage** [ɑ̃tuRaʒ] *nm* circle; family (circle); entourage; (*ce qui enclôt*) surround.
**entourer** [ɑ̃tuRe] *vt* to surround; (*apporter son soutien à*) to rally round; **~ de** to surround with; (*trait*) to encircle with.
**entourloupettes** [ɑ̃tuRlupɛt] *nfpl* mean tricks.
**entracte** [ɑ̃tRakt(ə)] *nm* interval.
**entraide** [ɑ̃tRɛd] *nf* mutual aid *ou* assistance; **s'entraider** to help each other.
**entrailles** [ɑ̃tRɑj] *nfpl* entrails; bowels.
**entrain** [ɑ̃tRɛ̃] *nm* spirit; **avec/sans ~** spiritedly/half-heartedly.
**entraînant, e** [ɑ̃tRɛnɑ̃, -ɑ̃t] *a* (*musique*) stirring, rousing.
**entraînement** [ɑ̃tRɛnmɑ̃] *nm* training; (TECH): **~ à chaîne/galet** chain/wheel drive.
**entraîner** [ɑ̃tRene] *vt* (*tirer: wagons*) to pull; (*charrier*) to carry *ou* drag along; (TECH) to drive; (*emmener: personne*) to take (off); (*mener à l'assaut, influencer*) to lead; (SPORT) to train; (*impliquer*) to entail; (*causer*) to lead to, bring about; **~ qn à faire** (*inciter*) to lead sb to do; **s'~** (SPORT) to train; **s'~ à qch/à faire** to train o.s. for sth/to do; **entraîneur, euse** *nm/f* (SPORT) coach, trainer // *nm* (HIPPISME) trainer // *nf* (*de bar*) hostess.
**entrave** [ɑ̃tRav] *nf* hindrance.
**entraver** [ɑ̃tRave] *vt* (*circulation*) to hold up; (*action, progrès*) to hinder, hamper.

**entre** [ɑ̃tR(ə)] *prép* between; (*parmi*) among(st); **l'un d'~ eux/nous** one of them/us; **ils se battent ~ eux** they are fighting among(st) themselves.
**entrebâillé, e** [ɑ̃tRəbaje] a half-open, ajar.
**entrechoquer** [ɑ̃tRəʃɔke]: **s'~** *vi* to knock *ou* bang together.
**entrecôte** [ɑ̃tRəkot] *nf* entrecôte *ou* rib steak.
**entrecouper** [ɑ̃tRəkupe ] *vt*: **~ qch de** to intersperse sth with.
**entrecroiser** [ɑ̃tRəkRwaze] *vt*, **s'~** *vi* intertwine.
**entrée** [ɑ̃tRe] *nf* entrance; (*accès: au cinéma etc*) admission; (*billet*) (admission) ticket; (CULIN) first course; **d'~** *ad* from the outset; **'~ interdite'** 'no admittance *ou* entry'; **'~ libre'** 'admission free'; **~ des artistes** stage door; **~ en matière** introduction; **~ de service** service entrance.
**entrefaites** [ɑ̃tRəfɛt]: **sur ces ~** *ad* at this juncture.
**entrefilet** [ɑ̃tRəfilɛ] *nm* paragraph (*short article*).
**entregent** [ɑ̃tRəʒɑ̃] *nm*: **avoir de l'~** to have an easy manner.
**entrejambes** [ɑ̃tRəʒɑ̃b] *nm* crotch.
**entrelacer** [ɑ̃tRəlase] *vt*, **s'~** *vi* to intertwine.
**entrelarder** [ɑ̃tRəlaRde] *vt* to lard.
**entremêler** [ɑ̃tRəmele] *vt*: **~ qch de** to (inter)mingle sth with.
**entremets** [ɑ̃tRəmɛ] *nm* cream dessert.
**entremetteur, euse** [ɑ̃tRəmɛtœR, -øz] *nm/f* go-between.
**entremettre** [ɑ̃tRəmɛtR(ə)]: **s'~** *vi* to intervene.
**entremise** [ɑ̃tRəmiz] *nf* intervention; **par l'~ de** through.
**entrepont** [ɑ̃tRəpɔ̃] *nm* steerage.
**entreposer** [ɑ̃tRəpoze] *vt* to store, put into storage.
**entrepôt** [ɑ̃tRəpo] *nm* warehouse.
**entreprenant, e** [ɑ̃tRəpRənɑ̃, -ɑ̃t] *a* (*actif*) enterprising; (*trop galant*) forward.
**entreprendre** [ɑ̃tRəpRɑ̃dR(ə)] *vt* (*se lancer dans*) to undertake; (*commencer*) to begin *ou* start (upon); (*personne*) to buttonhole; to tackle; **~ de faire** to undertake to do.
**entrepreneur** [ɑ̃tRəpRənœR] *nm*: **~ (en bâtiment)** (building) contractor; **~ de pompes funèbres** (funeral) undertaker.
**entreprise** [ɑ̃tRəpRiz] *nf* (*société*) firm, concern; (*action*) undertaking, venture.
**entrer** [ɑ̃tRe] *vi* to go (*ou* come) in, enter; **(faire) ~ qch dans** to get sth into; **~ dans** (*gén*) to enter; (*pièce*) to go (*ou* come) into, enter; (*club*) to join; (*heurter*) to run into; (*partager: vues, craintes de qn*) to share; (*être une composante de*) to go into; to form part of; **~ à l'hôpital** to go into hospital; **laisser ~ qn/qch** to let sb/sth in; **faire ~** (*visiteur*) to show in.
**entresol** [ɑ̃tRəsɔl] *nm* entresol, mezzanine.
**entre-temps** [ɑ̃tRətɑ̃] *ad* meanwhile, (in the) meantime.
**entretenir** [ɑ̃tRətniR] *vt* to maintain; (*amitié*) to keep alive; (*famille, maîtresse*) to support, keep; **~ qn (de)** to speak to sb (about); **s'~ (de)** to converse (about).

**entretien** [ɑ̃tRətjẽ] *nm* maintenance ; (*discussion*) discussion, talk ; (*audience*) interview.
**entrevoir** [ɑ̃tRəvwaR] *vt* (*à peine*) to make out ; (*brièvement*) to catch a glimpse of.
**entrevue** [ɑ̃tRəvy] *nf* meeting ; (*audience*) interview.
**entr'ouvert, e** [ɑ̃tRuvɛR, -ɛRt(ə)] *a* half-open.
**énumérer** [enymeRe] *vt* to list, enumerate.
**envahir** [ɑ̃vaiR] *vt* to invade ; (*suj: inquiétude, peur*) to come over ; **envahissant, e** *a* (*péj: personne*) interfering, intrusive ; **envahisseur** *nm* (*MIL*) invader.
**enveloppe** [ɑ̃vlɔp] *nf* (*de lettre*) envelope ; (*TECH*) casing ; outer layer ; **mettre sous ~** to put in an envelope.
**envelopper** [ɑ̃vlɔpe] *vt* to wrap ; (*fig*) to envelop, shroud.
**envenimer** [ɑ̃vnime] *vt* to aggravate.
**envergure** [ɑ̃vɛRgyR] *nf* (*d'un oiseau, avion*) wingspan ; (*fig*) scope ; calibre.
**enverrai** *etc vb voir* **envoyer**.
**envers** [ɑ̃vɛR] *prép* towards, to // *nm* other side ; (*d'une étoffe*) wrong side ; **à l'~** upside down ; back to front ; (*vêtement*) inside out.
**envie** [ɑ̃vi] *nf* (*sentiment*) envy ; (*souhait*) desire, wish ; (*tache sur la peau*) birthmark ; (*filet de peau*) hangnail ; **avoir ~ de** to feel like ; (*désir plus fort*) to want ; **avoir ~ de faire** to feel like doing ; to want to do ; **avoir ~ que** to wish that ; **donner à qn l'~ de faire** to make sb want to do ; **ça lui fait ~** he would like that ; **envier** *vt* to envy ; **envieux, euse** *a* envious.
**environ** [ɑ̃viRɔ̃] *ad*: **~ 3 h/2 km, 3 h/2 km ~** (around) about 3 o'clock/2 km, 3 o'clock/2 km or so ; **~s** *nmpl* surroundings ; **aux ~s de** around.
**environnement** [ɑ̃viRɔnmɑ̃] *nm* environment.
**environner** [ɑ̃viRɔne] *vt* to surround.
**envisager** [ɑ̃vizaʒe] *vt* (*examiner, considérer*) to view, contemplate ; (*avoir en vue*) to envisage ; **~ de faire** to consider *ou* contemplate doing.
**envoi** [ɑ̃vwa] *nm* sending ; (*paquet*) parcel, consignment.
**envol** [ɑ̃vɔl] *nm* takeoff.
**envolée** [ɑ̃vɔle] *nf* (*fig*) flight.
**envoler** [ɑ̃vɔle]: **s'~** *vi* (*oiseau*) to fly away *ou* off ; (*avion*) to take off ; (*papier, feuille*) to blow away ; (*fig*) to vanish (into thin air).
**envoûter** [ɑ̃vute] *vt* to bewitch.
**envoyé, e** [ɑ̃vwaje] *nm/f* (*POL*) envoy ; (*PRESSE*) correspondent.
**envoyer** [ɑ̃vwaje] *vt* to send ; (*lancer*) to hurl, throw ; **~ chercher** to send for ; **envoyeur, euse** *nm/f* sender.
**éolien, ne** [eɔljẽ, -jɛn] *a* wind *cpd*.
**épagneul** [epaɲœl] *nm/f* spaniel.
**épais, se** [epɛ, -ɛs] *a* thick ; **épaisseur** *nf* thickness ; **épaissir** *vt*, **s'épaissir** *vi* to thicken.
**épanchement** [epɑ̃ʃmɑ̃] *nm*: **un ~ de sinovie** water on the knee ; **~s** *nmpl* (*fig*) (sentimental) outpourings.

**épancher** [epɑ̃ʃe] *vt* to give vent to ; **s'~** *vi* to open one's heart ; (*liquide*) to pour out.
**épandage** [epɑ̃daʒ] *nm* manure spreading.
**épanouir** [epanwiR]: **s'~** *vi* (*fleur*) to bloom, open out ; (*visage*) to light up ; (*fig*) to blossom (out), bloom ; to open up ; **épanouissement** *nm* blossoming ; opening up.
**épargnant, e** [epaRɲɑ̃, -ɑ̃t] *nm/f* saver, investor.
**épargne** [epaRɲ(ə)] *nf* saving.
**épargner** [epaRɲe] *vt* to save ; (*ne pas tuer ou endommager*) to spare // *vi* to save ; **~ qch à qn** to spare sb sth.
**éparpiller** [epaRpije] *vt* to scatter ; (*pour répartir*) to disperse ; (*fig: efforts*) to dissipate ; **s'~** *vi* to scatter ; (*fig*) to dissipate one's efforts.
**épars, e** [epaR, -aRs(ə)] *a* scattered.
**épatant, e** [epatɑ̃, -ɑ̃t] *a* (*fam*) super, splendid.
**épaté, e** [epate] *a*: **nez ~** flat nose (with wide nostrils).
**épater** [epate] *vt* to amaze ; to impress.
**épaule** [epol] *nf* shoulder.
**épaulement** [epolmɑ̃] *nm* escarpment ; retaining wall.
**épauler** [epole] *vt* (*aider*) to back up, support ; (*arme*) to raise (to one's shoulder) // *vi* to (take) aim.
**épaulette** [epolɛt] *nf* (*MIL*) epaulette ; (*de combinaison*) shoulder strap.
**épave** [epav] *nf* wreck.
**épée** [epe] *nf* sword.
**épeler** [eple] *vt* to spell.
**éperdu, e** [epɛRdy] *a* distraught, overcome ; passionate ; frantic.
**éperon** [epRɔ̃] *nm* spur ; **éperonner** *vt* to spur (on) ; (*navire*) to ram.
**épervier** [epɛRvje] *nm* (*ZOOL*) sparrowhawk ; (*PÊCHE*) casting net.
**éphèbe** [efɛb] *nm* beautiful young man.
**éphémère** [efemɛR] *a* ephemeral, fleeting.
**éphéméride** [efemeRid] *nf* block *ou* tear-off calendar.
**épi** [epi] *nm* (*de blé, d'orge*) ear ; **stationnement en ~** angled parking.
**épice** [epis] *nf* spice ; **épicé, e** *a* highly spiced, spicy ; (*fig*) spicy.
**épicéa** [episea] *nm* spruce.
**épicer** [epise] *vt* to spice ; (*fig*) to add spice to.
**épicerie** [episRi] *nf* (*magasin*) grocer's shop ; (*denrées*) groceries *pl* ; **~ fine** delicatessen (shop) ; **épicier, ière** *nm/f* grocer.
**épidémie** [epidemi] *nf* epidemic.
**épiderme** [epidɛRm(ə)] *nm* skin, epidermis ; **épidermique** *a* skin *cpd* ; epidermic.
**épier** [epje] *vt* to spy on, watch closely ; (*occasion*) to look out for.
**épieu, x** [epjø] *nm* (hunting-)spear.
**épilatoire** [epilatwaR] *a* depilatory, hair-removing.
**épilepsie** [epilɛpsi] *nf* epilepsy ; **épileptique** *a*, *nm/f* epileptic.
**épiler** [epile] *vt* (*jambes*) to remove the hair from ; (*sourcils*) to pluck ; **se faire ~** to get unwanted hair removed.

**épilogue** [epilɔg] *nm* (*fig*) conclusion, dénouement.

**épiloguer** [epilɔge] *vi*: ~ **sur** to hold forth on.

**épinard** [epinaʀ] *nm* spinach *q*.

**épine** [epin] *nf* thorn, prickle; (*d'oursin etc*) spine, prickle; ~ **dorsale** backbone; **épineux, euse** *a* thorny, prickly.

**épingle** [epɛ̃gl(ə)] *nf* pin; **virage en ~ à cheveux** hairpin bend; ~ **de cravate** tie pin; ~ **de nourrice** *ou* **de sûreté** *ou* **double** safety pin.

**épingler** [epɛ̃gle] *vt* (*badge, décoration*): ~ **qch sur** to pin sth on(to); (*fam*) to catch, nick.

**épinière** [epinjɛʀ] *af voir* **moelle**.

**Épiphanie** [epifani] *nf* Epiphany.

**épique** [epik] *a* epic.

**épiscopal, e, aux** [episkɔpal, -o] *a* episcopal.

**épiscopat** [episkɔpa] *nm* bishopric, épiscopate.

**épisode** [epizɔd] *nm* episode; **film/roman à ~s** serialized film/novel, serial; **épisodique** *a* occasional.

**épissure** [episyʀ] *nf* splice.

**épistolaire** [epistɔlɛʀ] *a* epistolary.

**épitaphe** [epitaf] *nf* epitaph.

**épithète** [epitɛt] *nf* (*nom, surnom*) epithet; **adjectif** ~ attributive adjective.

**épître** [epitʀ(ə)] *nf* epistle.

**éploré, e** [eplɔʀe] *a* in tears, tearful.

**épluche-légumes** [eplyʃlegym] *nm inv* potato peeler.

**éplucher** [eplyʃe] *vt* (*fruit, légumes*) to peel; (*comptes, dossier*) to go over with a fine-tooth comb; **éplucheur** *nm* (automatic) peeler; **épluchures** *nfpl* peelings.

**épointer** [epwɛ̃te] *vt* to blunt.

**éponge** [epɔ̃ʒ] *nf* sponge; **éponger** *vt* (*liquide*) to mop *ou* sponge up; (*surface*) to sponge; (*fig: déficit*) to soak up, absorb; **s' éponger le front** to mop one's brow.

**épopée** [epɔpe] *nf* epic.

**époque** [epɔk] *nf* (*de l'histoire*) age, era; (*de l'année, la vie*) time; **d' ~** *a* (*meuble*) period *cpd*.

**épouiller** [epuje] *vt* to pick lice off; to delouse.

**époumoner** [epumɔne]: **s' ~** *vi* to shout o.s. hoarse.

**épouse** [epuz] *nf* wife (*pl* wives).

**épouser** [epuze] *vt* to marry; (*fig: idées*) to espouse; (: *forme*) to fit.

**épousseter** [epuste] *vt* to dust.

**époustouflant, e** [epustuflɑ̃, -ɑ̃t] *a* staggering, mind-boggling.

**épouvantable** [epuvɑ̃tabl(ə)] *a* appalling, dreadful.

**épouvantail** [epuvɑ̃taj] *nm* (*à moineaux*) scarecrow; (*fig*) bog(e)y; bugbear.

**épouvante** [epuvɑ̃t] *nf* terror; **film d' ~** horror film; **épouvanter** *vt* to terrify.

**époux** [epu] *nm* husband // *nmpl* (married) couple.

**éprendre** [epʀɑ̃dʀ(ə)]: **s' ~ de** *vt* to fall in love with.

**épreuve** [epʀœv] *nf* (*d'examen*) test; (*malheur, difficulté*) trial, ordeal; (PHOTO) print; (*d'imprimerie*) proof; (SPORT) event;

à l' ~ **des balles** bulletproof; à **toute** ~ unfailing; **mettre à l' ~** to put to the test.

**épris, e** [epʀi, -iz] *vb voir* **éprendre**.

**éprouver** [epʀuve] *vt* (*tester*) to test; (*mettre à l'épreuve*) to put to the test; (*marquer, faire souffrir*) to afflict, distress; (*ressentir*) to feel.

**éprouvette** [epʀuvɛt] *nf* test tube.

**épuisé, e** [epɥize] *a* exhausted; (*livre*) out of print.

**épuisement** [epɥizmɑ̃] *nm* exhaustion; **jusqu'à ~ des stocks** while stocks last.

**épuiser** [epɥize] *vt* (*fatiguer*) to exhaust, wear *ou* tire out; (*stock, sujet*) to exhaust; **s' ~** *vi* to wear *ou* tire o.s. out, exhaust o.s. (*stock*) to run out.

**épuisette** [epɥizɛt] *nf* landing net; shrimping net.

**épurer** [epyʀe] *vt* (*liquide*) to purify; (*parti, administration*) to purge; (*langue, texte*) to refine.

**équarrir** [ekaʀiʀ] *vt* (*pierre, arbre*) to square (off); (*animal*) to quarter.

**équateur** [ekwatœʀ] *nm* equator; (**la république de) l'É~** Ecuador.

**équation** [ekwasjɔ̃] *nf* equation; **mettre en ~** to equate.

**équatorial, e, aux** [ekwatɔʀjal, -o] *a* equatorial.

**équerre** [ekɛʀ] *nf* (*à dessin*) (set) square; (*pour fixer*) brace; **en ~** at right angles; **à l' ~, d' ~** straight.

**équestre** [ekɛstʀ(ə)] *a* equestrian.

**équidistant, e** [ekɥidistɑ̃, -ɑ̃t] *a*: ~ (**de**) equidistant (from).

**équilatéral, e, aux** [ekɥilateʀal, -o] *a* equilateral.

**équilibrage** [ekilibʀaʒ] *nm* (AUTO): ~ **des roues** wheel balancing.

**équilibre** [ekilibʀ(ə)] *nm* balance; (*d'une balance*) equilibrium; **garder/perdre l' ~** to keep/lose one's balance; **être en ~** to be balanced; **équilibré, e** *a* (*fig*) well-balanced, stable; **équilibrer** *vt* to balance; **s'équilibrer** (*poids*) to balance; (*fig: défauts etc*) to balance each other out; **équilibriste** *nm/f* tightrope walker.

**équinoxe** [ekinɔks] *nm* equinox.

**équipage** [ekipaʒ] *nm* crew.

**équipe** [ekip] *nf* team; (*bande: parfois péj*) bunch.

**équipée** [ekipe] *nf* escapade.

**équipement** [ekipmɑ̃] *nm* equipment; ~s *nmpl* amenities, facilities; installations.

**équiper** [ekipe] *vt* to equip; (*voiture, cuisine*) to equip, fit out; ~ **qn/qch de** to equip sb/sth with; **s' ~** (*sportif*) to equip o.s., kit o.s. out.

**équipier, ière** [ekipje, -jɛʀ] *nm/f* team member.

**équitable** [ekitabl(ə)] *a* fair.

**équitation** [ekitasjɔ̃] *nf* (horse-)riding.

**équité** [ekite] *nf* equity.

**équivalence** [ekivalɑ̃s] *nf* equivalence.

**équivalent, e** [ekivalɑ̃, -ɑ̃t] *a, nm* equivalent.

**équivaloir** [ekivalwaʀ]: ~ **à** *vt* to be equivalent to; (*représenter*) to amount to.

**équivoque** [ekivɔk] *a* equivocal, ambiguous; (*louche*) dubious // *nf* ambiguity.

**érable** [eRabl(ə)] nm maple.
**érafler** [eRafle] vt to scratch ; **éraflure** nf scratch.
**éraillé, e** [eRɑje] a (voix) rasping, hoarse.
**ère** [ɛR] nf era ; **en l'an 1050 de notre ~** in the year 1050 A.D.
**érection** [eRɛksjɔ̃] nf erection.
**éreinter** [eRɛ̃te] vt to exhaust, wear out ; (fig: critiquer) to slate.
**ergot** [ɛRgo] nm (de coq) spur ; (TECH) lug.
**ériger** [eRiʒe] vt (monument) to erect ; **s'~ en critique** to set o.s. up as a critic.
**ermitage** [ɛRmitaʒ] nm retreat.
**ermite** [ɛRmit] nm hermit.
**éroder** [eRɔde] vt to erode ; **érosion** nf erosion.
**érotique** [eRɔtik] a erotic ; **érotisme** nm eroticism.
**erratum, a** [ɛRatɔm, -a] nm erratum (pl a).
**errer** [ɛRe] vi to wander.
**erreur** [eRœR] nf mistake, error ; (morale) error ; **être dans l'~** to be mistaken ; **par ~** by mistake ; **~ judiciaire** miscarriage of justice ; **~ de jugement** error of judgment.
**erroné, e** [eRɔne] a wrong, erroneous.
**éructer** [eRykte] vt belch, eructate.
**érudit, e** [eRydi,-it] a erudite, learned // nm/f scholar ; **érudition** nf erudition, scholarship.
**éruptif, ive** [eRyptif, -iv] a eruptive.
**éruption** [eRypsjɔ̃] nf eruption ; (cutanée) outbreak.
**es** vb voir **être**.
**ès** [ɛs] prép: **licencié ~ lettres/sciences** ≈ Bachelor of Arts/Science.
**escabeau, x** [ɛskabo] nm (tabouret) stool ; (échelle) stepladder.
**escadre** [ɛskadR(ə)] nf (NAVIG) squadron ; (AVIAT) wing.
**escadrille** [ɛskadRij] nf (AVIAT) flight.
**escadron** [ɛskadRɔ̃] nm squadron.
**escalade** [ɛskalad] nf climbing q ; (POL etc) escalation.
**escalader** [ɛskalade] vt to climb, scale.
**escale** [ɛskal] nf (NAVIG) call ; port of call ; (AVIAT) stop(over) ; **faire ~ à** to put in at, call in at ; to stop over at.
**escalier** [ɛskalje] nm stairs pl ; **dans l'~** ou **les ~s** on the stairs ; **~ roulant** escalator ; **~ de service** backstairs.
**escalope** [ɛskalɔp] nf escalope.
**escamotable** [ɛskamɔtabl(ə)] a retractable ; fold-away.
**escamoter** [ɛskamɔte] vt (esquiver) to get round, evade ; (faire disparaître) to conjure away.
**escapade** [ɛskapad] nf: **faire une ~** to go on a jaunt ; to run away ou off.
**escargot** [ɛskaRgo] nm snail.
**escarmouche** [ɛskaRmuʃ] nf skirmish.
**escarpé, e** [ɛskaRpe] a steep.
**escarpement** [ɛskaRpəmɑ̃] nm steep slope.
**escarpin** [ɛskaRpɛ̃] nm flat(-heeled) shoe.
**escarre** [ɛskaR] nf bedsore.
**escient** [esjɑ̃] nm: **à bon ~** advisedly.
**esclaffer** [ɛsklafe]: **s'~** vi to guffaw.

**esclandre** [ɛsklɑ̃dR(ə)] nm scene, fracas.
**esclavage** [ɛsklavaʒ] nm slavery.
**esclave** [ɛsklav] nm/f slave ; **être ~ de** (fig) to be a slave of.
**escompte** [ɛskɔ̃t] nm discount.
**escompter** [ɛskɔ̃te] vt (COMM) to discount ; (espérer) to expect, reckon upon ; **~ que** to reckon ou expect that.
**escorte** [ɛskɔRt(ə)] nf escort ; **escorter** vt to escort ; **escorteur** nm (NAVIG) escort (ship).
**escouade** [ɛskwad] nf squad.
**escrime** [ɛskRim] nf fencing ; **escrimeur, euse** nm/f fencer.
**escrimer** [ɛskRime]: **s'~** vi: **s'~ à faire** to wear o.s. out doing.
**escroc** [ɛskRo] nm swindler, conman.
**escroquer** [ɛskRɔke] vt: **~ qn (de qch)/qch (à qn)** to swindle sb (out of sth)/sth (out of sb) ; **escroquerie** nf swindle.
**espace** [ɛspas] nm space ; **~ vital** living space.
**espacer** [ɛspase] vt to space out ; **s'~** vi (visites etc) to become less frequent.
**espadon** [ɛspadɔ̃] nm swordfish inv.
**espadrille** [ɛspadRij] nf rope-soled sandal.
**Espagne** [ɛspaɲ(ə)] nf: **l'~** Spain ; **espagnol, e** a Spanish // nm/f: **Espagnol, e** Spaniard // nm (langue) Spanish.
**espagnolette** [ɛspaɲɔlɛt] nf (window) catch ; **fermé à l'~** resting on the catch.
**espèce** [ɛspɛs] nf (BIO, BOT, ZOOL) species inv ; (gén: sorte) sort, kind, type ; (péj): **~ de maladroit/de brute!** you clumsy oaf/brute! ; **~s** nfpl (COMM) cash sg ; (REL) species ; **en l'~** ad in the case in point.
**espérance** [ɛspeRɑ̃s] nf hope ; **~ de vie** (DÉMOGRAPHIE) life expectancy.
**espérer** [ɛspeRe] vt to hope for ; **j'espère (bien)** I hope so ; **~ que/faire** to hope that/to do ; **~ en** to trust in.
**espiègle** [ɛspjɛgl(ə)] a mischievous ; **~rie** nf mischievousness ; piece of mischief.
**espion, ne** [ɛspjɔ̃, -ɔn] nm/f spy ; **avion ~** spy plane.
**espionnage** [ɛspjɔnaʒ] nm espionage, spying.
**espionner** [ɛspjɔne] vt to spy (up)on.
**esplanade** [ɛsplanad] nf esplanade.
**espoir** [ɛspwaR] nm hope.
**esprit** [ɛspRi] nm (pensée, intellect) mind ; (humour, ironie) wit ; (mentalité, d'une loi etc, fantôme etc) spirit ; **l'~ d'équipe/de compétition** team/competitive spirit ; **faire de l'~** to try to be witty ; **reprendre ses ~s** to come to ; **perdre l'~** to lose one's mind ; **~s chagrins** faultfinders.
**esquif** [ɛskif] nm skiff.
**esquimau, de, x** [ɛskimo, -od] a, nm/f Eskimo.
**esquinter** [ɛskɛ̃te] vt (fam) to mess up.
**esquisse** [ɛskis] nf sketch ; **l'~ d'un sourire/changement** the suggestion of a smile/of change.
**esquisser** [ɛskise] vt to sketch ; **s'~** vi (amélioration) to begin to be detectable ; **~ un sourire** to give a vague smile.
**esquive** [ɛskiv] nf (BOXE) dodging ; (fig) side-stepping.

**esquiver** [ɛskive] *vt* to dodge ; **s'~** *vi* to slip away.

**essai** [esɛ] *nm* testing ; trying ; *(tentative)* attempt, try, *(RUGBY)* try ; *(LITTÉRATURE)* essay ; **~s** *(AUTO)* trials ; **~ gratuit** *(COMM)* free trial ; **à l'~** on a trial basis.

**essaim** [esɛ̃] *nm* swarm ; **essaimer** *vi* to swarm ; *(fig)* to spread, expand.

**essayage** [esɛjaʒ] *nm (d'un vêtement)* trying on, fitting.

**essayer** [eseje] *vt (gén)* to try ; *(vêtement, chaussures)* to try (on) ; *(tester: ski, voiture)* to test ; *(restaurant, méthode)* to try (out) // *vi* to try ; **~ de faire** to try *ou* attempt to do ; **s'~ à faire** to try one's hand at doing.

**essence** [esɑ̃s] *nf (de voiture)* petrol ; *(extrait de plante, PHILOSOPHIE)* essence ; *(espèce: d'arbre)* species *inv* ; **prendre de l'~** to get petrol ; **~ de citron/rose** lemon/rose oil.

**essentiel, le** [esɑ̃sjɛl] *a* essential ; **emporter l'~** to take the essentials ; **c'est l'~** *(ce qui importe)* that's the main thing ; **l'~ de** *(la majeure partie)* the main part of.

**esseulé, e** [esœle] *a* forlorn.

**essieu, x** [esjø] *nm* axle.

**essor** [esɔʀ] *nm (de l'économie etc)* rapid expansion ; **prendre son ~** *(oiseau)* to fly off.

**essorer** [esɔʀe] *vt (en tordant)* to wring (out) ; *(par la force centrifuge)* to spin-dry ; **essoreuse** *nf* mangle, wringer ; spin-dryer.

**essouffler** [esufle] *vt* to make breathless ; **s'~** *vi* to get out of breath.

**essuie-glace** [esɥiglas] *nm inv* windscreen wiper.

**essuie-mains** [esɥimɛ̃] *nm inv* hand towel.

**essuyer** [esɥije] *vt* to wipe ; *(fig: subir)* to suffer ; **s'~** *(après le bain)* to dry o.s. ; **~ la vaisselle** to dry up, dry the dishes.

**est** [ɛst] *vb* [ɛ] *voir* **être** // *nm:* **l'~** the east // *a east* ; *(côte)* east(ern) ; **à l'~** in the east ; *(direction)* to the east, east(wards) ; **à l'~ de** (to the) east of.

**estafette** [ɛstafɛt] *nf (MIL)* dispatch rider.

**estafilade** [ɛstafilad] *nf* gash, slash.

**est-allemand, e** [ɛstalmɑ̃, -ɑ̃d] *a* East German.

**estaminet** [ɛstaminɛ] *nm* tavern.

**estampe** [ɛstɑ̃p] *nf* print, engraving.

**estampille** [ɛstɑ̃pij] *nf* stamp.

**est-ce que** [ɛskə] *ad:* **~ c'est cher/c'était bon?** is it expensive/was it good? ; **quand est-ce qu'il part?** when does he leave?, when is he leaving? ; **qui est-ce qui le connaît/a fait ça?** who knows him/did that? ; *voir aussi* **que**.

**esthète** [ɛstɛt] *nm/f* aesthete.

**esthéticienne** [ɛstetisjɛn] *nf* beautician.

**esthétique** [ɛstetik] *a* attractive ; aesthetically pleasing // *nf* aesthetics *sg.*

**estimation** [ɛstimasjɔ̃] *nf* valuation ; assessment.

**estime** [ɛstim] *nf* esteem, regard.

**estimer** [ɛstime] *vt (respecter)* to esteem, hold in high regard ; *(expertiser)* to value ; *(évaluer)* to assess, estimate ; *(penser):* **~ que/être** to consider that/o.s. to be ;

**j'estime la distance à 10 km** I reckon the distance to be 10 km.

**estival, e, aux** [ɛstival, -o] *a* summer *cpd.*

**estivant, e** [ɛstivɑ̃, -ɑ̃t] *nm/f* (summer) holiday-maker.

**estocade** [ɛstɔkad] *nf* death-blow.

**estomac** [ɛstɔma] *nm* stomach.

**estomaqué, e** [ɛstɔmake] *a* flabbergasted.

**estompe** [ɛstɔ̃p] *nf* stump ; stump-drawing.

**estomper** [ɛstɔ̃pe] *vt (ART)* to shade off ; *(fig)* to blur, dim ; **s'~** *vi* to soften ; to become blurred.

**estrade** [ɛstrad] *nf* platform, rostrum.

**estragon** [ɛstragɔ̃] *nm* tarragon.

**estropié, e** [ɛstrɔpje] *nm/f* cripple.

**estropier** [ɛstrɔpje] *vt* to cripple, maim ; *(fig)* to twist, distort.

**estuaire** [ɛstɥɛr] *nm* estuary.

**estudiantin, e** [ɛstydjɑ̃tɛ̃, -in] *a* student *cpd.*

**esturgeon** [ɛstyrʒɔ̃] *nm* sturgeon.

**et** [e] *cj* and ; **~ lui?** what about him? ; **~ alors!** so what!

**étable** [etabl(ə)] *nf* cowshed.

**établi** [etabli] *nm* (work)bench.

**établir** [etablir] *vt (papiers d'identité, facture)* to make out ; *(liste, programme)* to draw up ; *(gouvernement, artisan etc: aider à s'installer)* to set up, establish ; *(entreprise, atelier, camp)* to set up ; *(réputation, usage, fait, culpabilité)* to establish ; **s'~** *vi (se faire: entente etc)* to be established ; **s'~** **(à son compte)** to set up one's own business ; **s'~ à/près de** to settle in/near.

**établissement** [etablismɑ̃] *nm* making out ; drawing up ; setting up, establishing ; *(entreprise, institution)* establishment ; **~ de crédit** credit institution ; **~ industriel** industrial plant, factory ; **~ scolaire** school, educational establishment.

**étage** [etaʒ] *nm (d'immeuble)* storey, floor ; *(de fusée)* stage ; *(GÉO: de culture, végétation)* level ; **au 2ème ~** on the 2nd floor ; **de bas ~** a low ; **étager** *vt (cultures)* to lay out in tiers ; **s'étager** *vi (prix)* to range ; *(zones, cultures)* to lie on different levels.

**étagère** [etaʒɛr] *nf (rayon)* shelf ; *(meuble)* shelves *pl,* set of shelves.

**étai** [etɛ] *nm* stay, prop.

**étain** [etɛ̃] *nm* tin ; *(ORFÈVRERIE)* pewter *q.*

**étais** *etc vb voir* **être.**

**étal** [etal] *nm* stall.

**étalage** [etalaʒ] *nm* display ; display window ; **faire ~ de** to show off, parade ; **étalagiste** *nm/f* window-dresser.

**étale** [etal] *a (mer)* slack.

**étalement** [etalmɑ̃] *nm* spreading, staggering.

**étaler** [etale] *vt (carte, nappe)* to spread (out) ; *(peinture, liquide)* to spread ; *(échelonner: paiements, dates, vacances)* to spread, stagger ; *(exposer: marchandises)* to display ; *(richesses, connaissances)* to parade ; **s'~** *vi (liquide)* to spread out ; *(fam)* to come a cropper ; **s'~ sur** *(suj: paiements etc)* to be spread out over.

**étalon** [etalɔ̃] *nm (mesure)* standard ; *(cheval)* stallion ; **étalonner** *vt* to calibrate.

**étamer** [etame] vt (casserole) to tin(plate) ; (glace) to silver.

**étamine** [etamin] nf (BOT) stamen ; (tissu) butter muslin.

**étanche** [etɑ̃ʃ] a (récipient) watertight ; (montre, vêtement) waterproof.

**étancher** [etɑ̃ʃe] vt (liquide) to stop (flowing) ; ~ sa soif to quench ou slake one's thirst.

**étang** [etɑ̃] nm pond.

**étant** [etɑ̃] vb voir être, donné.

**étape** [etap] nf stage ; (lieu d'arrivée) stopping place ; (: CYCLISME) staging point ; faire ~ à to stop off at.

**état** [eta] nm (POL, condition) state ; (d'un article d'occasion etc) condition, state ; (liste) inventory, statement ; (condition professionnelle) profession, trade ; (: sociale) status ; en mauvais ~ in poor condition ; en ~ (de marche) in (working) order ; remettre en ~ to repair ; hors d'~ out of order ; être en ~/hors d'~ de faire to be in a/in no fit state to do ; en tout ~ de cause in any event ; être dans tous ses ~s to be in a state ; faire ~ de (alléguer) to put forward ; en ~ d'arrestation under arrest ; en ~ de grâce (REL) in a state of grace ; (fig) inspired ; ~ civil civil status ; ~ des lieux inventory of fixtures ; ~ de santé state of health ; ~ de siège/d'urgence state of siege/emergency ; ~s d'âme moods ; ~s de service service record sg ; étatiser vt to bring under state control.

**état-major** [etamaʒɔR] nm (MIL) staff ; (d'un parti etc) top advisers pl ; top management.

**États-Unis** [etazyni] nmpl: les ~ (d'Amérique) the United States (of America).

**étau, x** [eto] nm vice.

**étayer** [eteje] vt to prop ou shore up ; (fig) to back up.

**et c(a)etera** [ɛtseteRa], **etc.** ad et cetera, and so on, etc.

**été** [ete] pp de être // nm summer.

**éteignoir** [etɛɲwaR] nm (candle) extinguisher ; (péj) killjoy, wet blanket.

**éteindre** [etɛ̃dR(ə)] vt (lampe, lumière, radio) to turn ou switch off ; (cigarette, incendie, bougie) to put out, extinguish ; (JUR: dette) to extinguish ; s'~ vi to go out ; to go off ; (mourir) to pass away ; **éteint,** e a (fig) lacklustre, dull ; (volcan) extinct.

**étendard** [etɑ̃daR] nm standard.

**étendre** [etɑ̃dR(ə)] vt (appliquer: pâte, liquide) to spread ; (déployer: carte etc) to spread out ; (sur un fil: lessive, linge) to hang up ou out ; (bras, jambes, par terre: blessé) to stretch out ; (diluer) to dilute, thin ; (fig: agrandir) to extend ; (fam: adversaire) to floor ; s'~ vi (augmenter, se propager) to spread ; (terrain, forêt etc): s'~ jusqu'à/de ... à to stretch as far as/from ... to ; s'~ (sur) (s'allonger) to stretch out (upon) ; (se reposer) to lie down (on) ; (fig: expliquer) to elaborate ou enlarge (upon).

**étendu, e** [etɑ̃dy] a extensive // nf (d'eau, de sable) stretch, expanse ; (importance) extent.

**éternel, le** [etɛRnɛl] a eternal ; **les neiges** ~les perpetual snow.

**éterniser** [etɛRnize]: s'~ vi to last for ages ; to stay for ages.

**éternité** [etɛRnite] nf eternity ; de toute ~ from time immemorial.

**éternuer** [etɛRnɥe] vi to sneeze.

**êtes** vb voir être.

**étêter** [etete] vt (arbre) to poll(ard) ; (clou, poisson) to cut the head off.

**éther** [etɛR] nm ether.

**éthique** [etik] a ethical // nf ethics sg.

**ethnie** [ɛtni] nf ethnic group.

**ethnographie** [ɛtnɔgRafi] nf ethnography.

**ethnologie** [ɛtnɔlɔʒi] nf ethnology ; **ethnologue** nm/f ethnologist.

**éthylisme** [etilism(ə)] nm alcoholism.

**étiage** [etjaʒ] nm low water.

**étiez** vb voir être.

**étinceler** [etɛ̃sle] vi to sparkle.

**étincelle** [etɛ̃sɛl] nf spark.

**étioler** [etjɔle]: s'~ vi to wilt.

**étique** [etik] a skinny, bony.

**étiqueter** [etikte] vt to label.

**étiquette** [etikɛt] nf label ; (protocole): l'~ etiquette.

**étirer** [etiRe] vt to stretch ; (ressort) to stretch out ; s'~ vi (personne) to stretch ; (convoi, route): s'~ sur to stretch out over.

**étoffe** [etɔf] nf material, fabric.

**étoffer** [etɔfe] vt, s'~ vi to fill out.

**étoile** [etwal] nf star ; à la belle ~ in the open ; ~ filante shooting star ; ~ de mer starfish ; **étoilé, e** a starry.

**étole** [etɔl] nf stole.

**étonnant, e** [etɔnɑ̃, -ɑ̃t] a amazing.

**étonnement** [etɔnmɑ̃] nm surprise, amazement.

**étonner** [etɔne] vt to surprise, amaze ; s'~ que/de to be amazed that/at ; cela m'étonnerait (que) (j'en doute) I'd be very surprised (if).

**étouffant, e** [etufɑ̃, -ɑ̃t] a stifling.

**étouffée** [etufe]: à l'~ ad (CULIN) steamed ; braised.

**étouffer** [etufe] vt to suffocate ; (bruit) to muffle ; (scandale) to hush up // vi to suffocate ; (avoir trop chaud) to feel stifled ; s'~ vi (en mangeant etc) to choke.

**étourderie** [etuRdəRi] nf heedlessness ; thoughtless blunder.

**étourdi, e** [etuRdi] a (distrait) scatterbrained, heedless.

**étourdir** [etuRdiR] vt (assommer) to stun, daze ; (griser) to make dizzy ou giddy ; **étourdissant, e** a staggering ; **étourdissement** nm dizzy spell.

**étourneau, x** [etuRno] nm starling.

**étrange** [etRɑ̃ʒ] a strange.

**étranger, ère** [etRɑ̃ʒe, -ɛR] a foreign ; (pas de la famille, non familier) strange // nm/f foreigner ; stranger // nm: à l'~ abroad ; de l'~ from abroad ; ~ à (fig) unfamiliar to ; irrelevant to.

**étranglement** [etRɑ̃gləmɑ̃] nm (d'une vallée etc) constriction, narrow passage.

**étrangler** [etRɑ̃gle] vt to strangle ; s'~ vi (en mangeant etc) to choke ; (se resserrer) to make a bottleneck.

étrave [etʀav] nf stem.

être [ɛtʀ(ə)] nm being // vb avec attribut, vi to be // vb auxiliaire to have (ou parfois be); il est instituteur he is a teacher; ~ à qn (appartenir) to be sb's, to belong to sb; c'est à moi/eux it is ou it's mine/theirs; c'est à lui de le faire it's up to him to do it; ~ de (provenance, origine) to be from; (appartenance) to belong to; nous sommes le 10 janvier it's the 10th of January (today); il est 10 heures, c'est 10 heures it is ou it's 10 o'clock; c'est à réparer it needs repairing; c'est à essayer it should be tried; ~ humain human being; voir aussi est-ce que, n'est-ce pas, c'est-à-dire, ce.

étreindre [etʀɛ̃dʀ(ə)] vt to clutch, grip; (amoureusement, amicalement) to embrace; s'~ to embrace; étreinte nf clutch, grip; embrace.

étrenner [etʀene] vt to use (ou wear) for the first time.

étrennes [etʀɛn] nfpl Christmas box sg (fig).

étrier [etʀije] nm stirrup.

étriller [etʀije] vt (cheval) to curry; (fam: battre) to trounce.

étriper [etʀipe] vt to gut; (fam): ~ qn to tear sb's guts out.

étriqué, e [etʀike] a skimpy.

étroit, e [etʀwa, -wat] a narrow; (vêtement) tight; (fig: serré) close, tight; à l'~ ad cramped; ~ d'esprit narrow-minded; étroitesse nf narrowness.

étude [etyd] nf studying; (ouvrage, rapport) study; (de notaire: bureau) office; (: charge) practice; (scol: salle de travail) study room; ~s nfpl (scol) studies; être à l'~ (projet etc) to be under consideration; faires des ~s de droit/médecine to study ou read law/medicine.

étudiant, e [etydjɑ̃, -ɑ̃t] nm/f student.

étudié, e [etydje] a (démarche) studied; (système) carefully designed.

étudier [etydje] vt, vi to study.

étui [etɥi] nm case.

étuve [etyv] nf steamroom; (appareil) sterilizer.

étuvée [etyve]: à l'~ ad braised.

étymologie [etimɔlɔʒi] nf etymology; étymologique a etymological.

eu, eue [y] pp voir avoir.

eucalyptus [økaliptys] nm eucalyptus.

eugénique [øʒenik] a eugenic // nf eugenics sg.

euh [ø] excl er.

eunuque [ønyk] nm eunuch.

euphémisme [øfemism(ə)] nm euphemism.

euphonie [øfɔni] nf euphony.

euphorie [øfɔʀi] nf euphoria; euphorique a euphoric.

eurasien, ne [øʀazjɛ̃, -ɛn] a, nm/f Eurasian.

Europe [øʀɔp] nf Europe; européen, ne a, nm/f European.

eus etc vb voir avoir.

euthanasie [øtanazi] nf euthanasia.

eux [ø] pronom (sujet) they; (objet) them.

évacuation [evakɥasjɔ̃] nf evacuation.

évacuer [evakɥe] vt (salle, région) to evacuate, clear; (occupants, population) to evacuate; (toxine etc) to evacuate, discharge.

évadé, e [evade] a escaped // nm/f escapee.

évader [evade]: s'~ vi to escape.

évaluation [evalɥasjɔ̃] nf assessment, evaluation.

évaluer [evalɥe] vt to assess, evaluate.

évangélique [evɑ̃ʒelik] a evangelical.

évangéliser [evɑ̃ʒelize] vt to evangelize.

évangile [evɑ̃ʒil] nm gospel.

évanouir [evanwiʀ]: s'~ vi to faint, pass out; (disparaître) to vanish, disappear.

évanouissement [evanwismɑ̃] nm (syncope) fainting fit; (dans un accident) loss of consciousness.

évaporation [evapɔʀasjɔ̃] nf evaporation.

évaporé, e [evapɔʀe] a giddy, scatterbrained.

évaporer [evapɔʀe]: s'~ vi to evaporate.

évaser [evɑze] vt (tuyau) to widen, open out; (jupe, pantalon) to flare; s'~ vi to widen, open out.

évasif, ive [evazif, -iv] a evasive.

évasion [evazjɔ̃] nf escape; littérature d'~ escapist literature.

évêché [eveʃe] nm bishopric; bishop's palace.

éveil [evɛj] nm awakening; être en ~ to be alert.

éveillé, e [eveje] a awake; (vif) alert, sharp.

éveiller [eveje] vt to (a)waken; s'~ vi to (a)waken; (fig) to be aroused.

événement [evɛnmɑ̃] nm event.

éventail [evɑ̃taj] nm fan; (choix) range; en ~ fanned out; fan-shaped.

éventaire [evɑ̃tɛʀ] nm stall, stand.

éventer [evɑ̃te] vt (secret) to discover, lay open; (avec un éventail) to fan; s'~ vi (parfum) to go stale.

éventrer [evɑ̃tʀe] vt to disembowel; (fig) to tear ou rip open.

éventualité [evɑ̃tɥalite] nf eventuality; possibility; dans l'~ de in the event of.

éventuel, le [evɑ̃tɥɛl] a possible; ~lement ad possibly.

évêque [evɛk] nm bishop.

évertuer [evɛʀtɥe]: s'~ vi: s'~ à faire to try very hard to do.

éviction [eviksjɔ̃] nf ousting, supplanting; (de locataire) eviction.

évidemment [evidamɑ̃] ad obviously.

évidence [evidɑ̃s] nf obviousness; obvious fact; de toute ~ quite obviously ou evidently; en ~ conspicuous; mettre en ~ to highlight; to bring to the fore.

évident, e [evidɑ̃, -ɑ̃t] a obvious, evident.

évider [evide] vt to scoop out.

évier [evje] nm (kitchen) sink.

évincer [evɛ̃se] vt to oust, supplant.

évitement [evitmɑ̃] nm: place d'~ (AUTO) passing place.

éviter [evite] vt to avoid; ~ de faire/que qch ne se passe to avoid doing/sth happening; ~ qch à qn to spare sb sth.

**évocateur, trice** [evɔkatœʀ, -tʀis] *a* evocative, suggestive.

**évocation** [evɔkɑsjɔ̃] *nf* evocation.

**évolué, e** [evɔlɥe] *a* advanced.

**évoluer** [evɔlɥe] *vi* (*enfant, maladie*) to develop ; (*situation, moralement*) to evolve, develop ; (*aller et venir*: *danseur etc*) to move about, circle ; **évolution** *nf* development ; evolution ; **évolutions** *nfpl* movements.

**évoquer** [evɔke] *vt* to call to mind, evoke ; (*mentionner*) to mention.

**ex...** [ɛks] *préfixe* ex-.

**exacerber** [ɛgzasɛʀbe] *vt* to exacerbate.

**exact, e** [ɛgzakt] *a* (*précis*) exact, accurate, precise ; (*correct*) correct ; (*ponctuel*) punctual ; **l'heure ~e** the right *ou* exact time ; **~ement** *ad* exactly, accurately, precisely ; correctly ; (*c'est cela même*) exactly.

**exactions** [ɛgzaksjɔ̃] *nfpl* exactions.

**exactitude** [ɛgzaktityd] *nf* exactitude, accurateness, precision.

**ex aequo** [ɛgzeko] *a* equally placed ; **classé 1er ~** placed equal first.

**exagération** [ɛgzaʒeʀɑsjɔ̃] *nf* exaggeration.

**exagéré, e** [ɛgzaʒeʀe] *a* (*prix etc*) excessive.

**exagérer** [ɛgzaʒeʀe] *vt* to exaggerate // *vi* (*abuser*) to go too far ; overstep the mark ; (*déformer les faits*) to exaggerate.

**exaltation** [ɛgzaltɑsjɔ̃] *nf* exaltation.

**exalté, e** [ɛgzalte] *a* (over)excited // *nm/f* (*péj*) fanatic.

**exalter** [ɛgzalte] *vt* (*enthousiasmer*) to excite, elate ; (*glorifier*) to exalt.

**examen** [ɛgzamɛ̃] *nm* examination ; (*SCOL*) exam, examination ; **à l'~** under consideration ; (*COMM*) on approval ; **~ blanc** mock exam(ination) ; **~ de la vue** sight test.

**examinateur, trice** [ɛgzaminatœʀ, -tʀis] *nm/f* examiner.

**examiner** [ɛgzamine] *vt* to examine.

**exaspération** [ɛgzaspeʀɑsjɔ̃] *nf* exasperation.

**exaspérer** [ɛgzaspeʀe] *vt* to exasperate ; to exacerbate.

**exaucer** [ɛgzose] *vt* (*vœu*) to grant, fulfil ; **~ qn** to grant sb's wishes.

**excavateur** [ɛkskavatœʀ] *nm* excavator, mechanical digger.

**excavation** [ɛkskavɑsjɔ̃] *nf* excavation.

**excavatrice** [ɛkskavatʀis] *nf* = **excavateur**.

**excédent** [ɛksedɑ̃] *nm* surplus ; **en ~** surplus ; **~ de bagages** excess luggage ; **excédentaire** *a* surplus, excess.

**excéder** [ɛksede] *vt* (*dépasser*) to exceed ; (*agacer*) to exasperate.

**excellence** [ɛksɛlɑ̃s] *nf* excellence ; (*titre*) Excellency.

**excellent, e** [ɛksɛlɑ̃, -ɑ̃t] *a* excellent.

**exceller** [ɛksele] *vi:* **~ (dans)** to excel (in).

**excentricité** [ɛksɑ̃tʀisite] *nf* eccentricity ; **excentrique** *a* eccentric ; (*quartier*) outlying.

**excepté, e** [ɛksɛpte] *a, prép:* **les élèves ~s, ~ les élèves** except for *ou* apart from the pupils ; **~ si** except if.

**excepter** [ɛksɛpte] *vt* to except.

**exception** [ɛksɛpsjɔ̃] *nf* exception ; **à l'~ de** except for, with the exception of ; **d'~** (*mesure, loi*) special, exceptional ; **exceptionnel, le** *a* exceptional.

**excès** [ɛksɛ] *nm* surplus // *nmpl* excesses ; **à l'~** (*méticuleux, généreux*) to excess ; **~ de vitesse** speeding *q*, exceeding the speed limit ; **~ de zèle** overzealousness *q* ; **excessif, ive** *a* excessive.

**exciper** [ɛksipe]: **~ de** *vt* to plead.

**excitant** [ɛksitɑ̃] *nm* stimulant.

**excitation** [ɛksitɑsjɔ̃] *nf* (*état*) excitement.

**exciter** [ɛksite] *vt* to excite ; (*suj: café etc*) to stimulate ; **s'~** *vi* to get excited ; **~ qn à** (*révolte etc*) to incite sb to.

**exclamation** [ɛksklamɑsjɔ̃] *nf* exclamation.

**exclamer** [ɛksklame]: **s'~** *vi* to exclaim.

**exclure** [ɛksklyʀ] *vt* (*faire sortir*) to expel ; (*ne pas compter*) to exclude, leave out ; (*rendre impossible*) to exclude, rule out ; **exclusif, ive** *a* exclusive ; **exclusion** *nf* expulsion ; **à l'exclusion de** with the exclusion *ou* exception of ; **exclusivement** *ad* exclusively ; **exclusivité** *nf* exclusiveness ; (*COMM*) exclusive rights *pl* ; **film passant en exclusivité à** film showing only at.

**excommunier** [ɛkskɔmynje] *vt* to excommunicate.

**excréments** [ɛkskʀemɑ̃] *nmpl* excrement *sg*, faeces.

**excroissance** [ɛkskʀwasɑ̃s] *nf* excrescence, outgrowth.

**excursion** [ɛkskyʀsjɔ̃] *nf* (*en autocar*) excursion, trip ; (*à pied*) walk, hike ; **faire une ~** to go on an excursion *ou* a trip ; to go on a walk *ou* hike ; **excursionniste** *nm/f* tripper ; hiker.

**excuse** [ɛkskyz] *nf* excuse ; **~s** *nfpl* apology *sg*, apologies.

**excuser** [ɛkskyze] *vt* to excuse ; **s'~ (de)** to apologize (for) ; **'excusez-moi'** 'I'm sorry' ; (*pour attirer l'attention*) 'excuse me'.

**exécrable** [ɛgzekʀabl(ə)] *a* atrocious.

**exécrer** [ɛgzekʀe] *vt* to loathe, abhor.

**exécutant, e** [ɛgzekytɑ̃, -ɑ̃t] *nm/f* performer.

**exécuter** [ɛgzekyte] *vt* (*prisonnier*) to execute ; (*tâche etc*) to execute, carry out ; (*MUS: jouer*) to perform, execute ; **s'~** *vi* to comply ; **exécuteur, trice** *nm/f* (*testamentaire*) executor // *nm* (*bourreau*) executioner ; **exécutif, ive** *a, nm* (*POL*) executive ; **exécution** *nf* execution ; carrying out ; **mettre à exécution** to carry out.

**exégèse** [ɛgzeʒɛz] *nf* exegesis.

**exemplaire** [ɛgzɑ̃plɛʀ] *a* exemplary // *nm* copy.

**exemple** [ɛgzɑ̃pl(ə)] *nm* example ; **par ~** for instance, for example ; **donner l'~** to set an example ; **prendre ~ sur** to take as a model ; **à l'~ de** just like.

**exempt, e** [ɛgzɑ̃, -ɑ̃t] *a:* **~ de** (*dispensé de*) exempt from ; (*ne comportant pas de*) free from.

**exempter** [ɛgzɑ̃te] *vt:* **~ de** to exempt from.

**exercé, e** [εgzεRse] *a* trained.

**exercer** [εgzεRse] *vt (pratiquer)* to exercise, practise ; *(faire usage de: prérogative)* to exercise ; *(effectuer: influence, contrôle, pression)* to exert ; *(former)* to exercise, train // *vi (médecin)* to be in practice ; **s'~** *(sportif, musicien)* to practise ; *(se faire sentir: pression etc)* to be exerted.

**exercice** [εgzεRsis] *nm* practice ; exercising ; *(tâche, travail)* exercise ; *(activité, sportive, physique)*: **l'~** exercise ; *(MIL)*: **l'~** drill ; *(COMM, ADMIN: période)* accounting period ; **en ~** *(juge)* in office ; *(médecin)* practising ; **dans l'~ de ses fonctions** in the discharge of his duties.

**exhaler** [εgzale] *vt* to exhale ; to utter, breathe ; **s'~** *vi* to rise (up).

**exhaustif, ive** [εgzostif, -iv] *a* exhaustive.

**exhiber** [εgzibe] *vt (montrer: papiers, certificat)* to present, produce ; *(péj)* to display, flaunt **s'~** to parade ; *(suj: exhibitionniste)* to expose o.s ; **exhibitionnisme** *nm* exhibitionism.

**exhorter** [εgzɔRte] *vt:* **~ qn à faire** to urge sb to do.

**exhumer** [εgzyme] *vt* to exhume.

**exigeant, e** [εgziʒã, -ãt] *a* demanding ; *(péj)* hard to please.

**exigence** [εgziʒãs] *nf* demand, requirement.

**exiger** [εgziʒe] *vt* to demand, require.

**exigu, ë** [εgzigy] *a (lieu)* cramped, tiny.

**exil** [εgzil] *nm* exile ; **en ~** in exile ; **~é, e** *nm/f* exile ; **~er** *vt* to exile ; **s'~er** to go into exile.

**existence** [εgzistãs] *nf* existence.

**exister** [εgziste] *vi* to exist ; **il existe un/des** there is a/are (some).

**exode** [εgzɔd] *nm* exodus.

**exonérer** [εgzɔneRe] *vt:* **~ de** to exempt from.

**exorbitant, e** [εgzɔrbitã, -ãt] *a* exorbitant.

**exorbité, e** [εgzɔrbite] *a:* **yeux ~s** bulging eyes.

**exorciser** [εgzɔRsize] *vt* to exorcize.

**exotique** [εgzɔtik] *a* exótic ; **exotisme** *nm* exoticism ; exotic flavour *ou* atmosphere.

**expansif, ive** [εkspãsif, -iv] *a* expansive, communicative.

**expansion** [εkspãsjɔ̃] *nf* expansion.

**expatrier** [εkspatRije] *vt:* **s'~** to leave one's country, expatriate o.s.

**expectative** [εkspεktativ] *nf:* **être dans l'~** to be still waiting.

**expectorer** [εkspεktɔRe] *vi* to expectorate.

**expédient** [εkspedjã] *nm (péj)* expedient ; **vivre d'~s** to live by one's wits.

**expédier** [εkspedje] *vt (lettre, paquet)* to send ; *(troupes)* to dispatch ; *(péj: travail etc)* to dispose of, dispatch ; **expéditeur, trice** *nm/f* sender.

**expéditif, ive** [εkspeditif, -iv] *a* quick, expeditious.

**expédition** [εkspedisjɔ̃] *nf* sending ; *(scientifique, sportive, MIL)* expedition.

**expéditionnaire** [εkspedisjɔnεR] *a:* **corps ~** task force.

**expérience** [εksperjãs] *nf (de la vie)* experience ; *(scientifique)* experiment ; **avoir de l'~** to have experience, be experienced ; **avoir l'~ de** to have experience of.

**expérimental, e, aux** [εksperimãtal, -o] *a* experimental.

**expérimenté, e** [εksperimãte] *a* experienced.

**expérimenter** [εksperimãte] *vt (technique)* to test out, experiment with.

**expert, e** [εkspεR, -εRt(ə)] *a, nm* expert ; **~ en assurances** insurance valuer ; **~-comptable** *nm* ≈ chartered accountant.

**expertise** [εkspεRtiz] *nf* valuation ; assessment ; valuer's *(ou* assessor's) report ; *(JUR)* (forensic) examination.

**expertiser** [εkspεRtize] *vt (objet de valeur)* to value ; *(voiture accidentée etc)* to assess damage to.

**expier** [εkspje] *vt* to expiate, atone for.

**expiration** [εkspiRasjɔ̃] *nf* expiry ; breathing out *q.*

**expirer** [εkspiRe] *vi (venir à échéance, mourir)* to expire ; *(respirer)* to breathe out.

**explétif, ive** [εkspletif, -iv] *a* expletive.

**explicatif, ive** [εksplikatif, -iv] *a* explanatory.

**explication** [εksplikasjɔ̃] *nf* explanation ; *(discussion)* discussion ; argument ; **~ de texte** *(SCOL)* critical analysis (of a text).

**explicite** [εksplisit] *a* explicit ; **expliciter** *vt* to make explicit.

**expliquer** [εksplike] *vt* to explain ; **s'~** *(discuter)* to discuss things ; to have it out ; **son erreur s'explique** one can understand his mistake.

**exploit** [εksplwa] *nm* exploit, feat.

**exploitant** [εksplwatã] *nm* farmer.

**exploitation** [εksplwatasjɔ̃] *nf* exploitation ; running ; **~ agricole** farming concern.

**exploiter** [εksplwate] *vt (mine)* to exploit, work ; *(entreprise, ferme)* to run, operate ; *(clients, ouvriers, erreur, don)* to exploit ; **exploiteur, euse** *nm/f* exploiter.

**explorateur, trice** [εksplɔRatœR, -tRis] *nm/f* explorer.

**exploration** [εksplɔRasjɔ̃] *nf* exploration.

**explorer** [εksplɔRe] *vt* to explore.

**exploser** [εksploze] *vi* to explode, blow up ; *(engin explosif)* to go off ; *(fig: joie, colère)* to burst out, explode ; *(personne: de colère)* to explode, flare up ; **explosif, ive** *a, nm* explosive ; **explosion** *nf* explosion.

**exportateur, trice** [εkspɔRtatœR, -tRis] *a* export *cpd*, exporting // *nm* exporter.

**exportation** [εkspɔRtasjɔ̃] *nf* exportation ; export.

**exporter** [εkspɔRte] *vt* to export.

**exposant** [εkspozã] *nm* exhibitor ; *(MATH)* exponent.

**exposé, e** [εkspoze] *nm* talk // *a:* **~ au sud** facing south, with a southern aspect ; **bien ~** well situated ; **très ~** very exposed.

**exposer** [εkspoze] *vt (marchandise)* to display ; *(peinture)* to exhibit, show ; *(parler de: problème, situation)* to explain, set out ; *(mettre en danger, orienter, PHOTO)* to expose ; **~ qn/qch à** to expose sb/sth to ; **exposition** nf displaying ; exhibiting ; setting out ; (voir exposé) aspect, situation ; (manifestation) exhibition ; (PHOTO) exposure.

**exprès** [ɛkspRɛ] ad (délibérément) on purpose ; (spécialement) specially ; **faire ∼ de faire qch** to do sth on purpose.

**exprès, esse** [ɛkspRɛs] a (ordre, défense) express, formal // a inv, ad (PTT) express.

**express** [ɛkspRɛs] a, nm: **(café) ∼** espresso ; **(train) ∼** fast train.

**expressément** [ɛkspRɛsemɑ̃] ad expressly ; specifically.

**expressif, ive** [ɛkspResif, -iv] a expressive.

**expression** [ɛkspRɛsjɔ̃] nf expression.

**exprimer** [ɛkspRime] vt (sentiment, idée) to express ; (jus, liquide) to press out ; **s'∼ vi** (personne) to express o.s.

**expropriation** [ɛkspRɔpRijɑsjɔ̃] nf expropriation ; **frapper d'∼** to put a compulsory purchase order on.

**exproprier** [ɛkspRɔpRije] vt to buy up (ou buy the property of) by compulsory purchase, expropriate.

**expulser** [ɛkspylse] vt to expel ; (locataire) to evict ; (FOOTBALL) to send off ; **expulsion** nf expulsion ; eviction ; sending off.

**expurger** [ɛkspyRʒe] vt to expurgate, bowdlerize.

**exquis, e** [ɛkski, -iz] a exquisite ; delightful.

**exsangue** [ɛksɑ̃g] a bloodless, drained of blood.

**extase** [ɛkstɑz] nf ecstasy ; **s'extasier sur** to go into ecstasies ou raptures over.

**extenseur** [ɛkstɑ̃sœR] nm (SPORT) chest expander.

**extensible** [ɛkstɑ̃sibl(ə)] a extensible.

**extensif, ive** [ɛkstɑ̃sif, -iv] a extensive.

**extension** [ɛkstɑ̃sjɔ̃] nf (d'un muscle, ressort) stretching ; (MÉD) à l'∼ in traction ; (fig) extension ; expansion.

**exténuer** [ɛkstenɥe] vt to exhaust.

**extérieur, e** [ɛksteRjœR] a (porte, mur etc) outer, outside ; (au dehors: escalier, w.-c.) outside ; (commerce) foreign ; (influences) external ; (apparent: calme, gaieté etc) surface cpd // nm (d'une maison, d'un récipient etc) outside, exterior ; (d'une personne: apparence) exterior ; (d'un groupe social): l'∼ the outside world ; à l'∼ outside ; (à l'étranger) abroad ; ∼ement ad on the outside ; (en apparence) on the surface ; **extérioriser** vt to show ; to exteriorize.

**exterminer** [ɛkstɛRmine] vt to exterminate, wipe out.

**externat** [ɛkstɛRna] nm day school.

**externe** [ɛkstɛRn(ə)] a external, outer // nm/f (MÉD) non-resident medical student ; (SCOL) day pupil.

**extincteur** [ɛkstɛ̃ktœR] nm (fire) extinguisher.

**extinction** [ɛkstɛ̃ksjɔ̃] nf extinction ; (JUR: d'une dette) extinguishment ; ∼ **de voix** loss of voice.

**extirper** [ɛkstiRpe] vt (tumeur) to extirpate ; (plante) to root out, pull up.

**extorquer** [ɛkstɔRke] vt: ∼ **qch à qn** to extort sth from sb.

**extra** [ɛkstRa] a inv first-rate ; top-quality // nm inv extra help.

**extraction** [ɛkstRaksjɔ̃] nf extraction.

**extrader** [ɛkstRade] vt to extradite ; **extradition** nf extradition.

**extraire** [ɛkstRɛR] vt to extract ; **extrait** nm (de plante) extract ; (de film, livre) extract, excerpt.

**extra-lucide** [ɛkstRalysid] a: **voyante ∼** clairvoyant.

**extraordinaire** [ɛkstRaɔRdinɛR] a extraordinary ; (POL: mesures) special ; **ambassadeur ∼** ambassador extraordinary.

**extravagance** [ɛkstRavagɑ̃s] nf extravagance q ; extravagant behaviour q.

**extravagant, e** [ɛkstRavagɑ̃, -ɑ̃t] a extravagant ; wild.

**extraverti, e** [ɛkstRavɛRti] a extrovert.

**extrême** [ɛkstRɛm] a, nm extreme ; ∼**ment** ad extremely ; ∼-**onction** nf last rites pl, Extreme Unction ; **E∼-Orient** nm Far East ; **extrémiste** a, nm/f extremist.

**extrémité** [ɛkstRemite] nf end ; (situation) straits pl, plight ; (geste désespéré) extreme action ; ∼**s** nfpl (pieds et mains) extremities ; **à la dernière ∼** (à l'agonie) on the point of death.

**exubérant, e** [ɛgzybeRɑ̃, -ɑ̃t] a exuberant.

**exulter** [ɛgzylte] vi to exult.

**exutoire** [ɛgzytwaR] nm outlet, release.

**ex-voto** [ɛksvɔto] nm inv ex-voto.

# F

**F** abr de **franc.**

**fa** [fɑ] nm inv (MUS) F ; (en chantant la gamme) fa.

**fable** [fɑbl(ə)] nf fable ; (mensonge) story, tale.

**fabricant** [fabRikɑ̃] nm manufacturer, maker.

**fabrication** [fabRikɑsjɔ̃] nf manufacture, making.

**fabrique** [fabRik] nf factory.

**fabriquer** [fabRike] vt to make ; (industriellement) to manufacture, make ; (fig): **qu'est-ce qu'il fabrique?** what is he doing?

**fabulation** [fabylɑsjɔ̃] nf fantasizing.

**fabuleux, euse** [fabylø, -øz] a fabulous, fantastic.

**façade** [fasad] nf front, façade ; (fig) façade.

**face** [fas] nf face ; (fig: aspect) side // a: **le côté ∼** heads ; **perdre la ∼** to lose face ; **en ∼ de** prép opposite ; (fig) in front of ; **de ∼** ad from the front ; face on ; ∼ **à** prép facing ; (fig) faced with, in the face of ; **faire ∼ à** to face ; ∼ **à ∼** ad facing each other // nm inv encounter ; ∼-**à-main** nm lorgnette.

**facéties** [fasesi] nfpl jokes, pranks.

**facétieux, euse** [fasesjø, -øz] a mischievous.

**facette** [fasɛt] nf facet.

**fâché, e** [fɑʃe] a angry ; (désolé) sorry.

**fâcher** [fɑʃe] vt to anger ; **se ∼ vi** to get angry ; **se ∼ avec** (se brouiller) to fall out with.

**fâcheux, euse** [faʃø, -øz] a unfortunate, regrettable.
**facial, e, aux** [fasjal, -o] a facial.
**faciès** [fasjɛs] nm features pl, facies.
**facile** [fasil] a easy ; (accommodant) easy-going ; **~ment** ad easily ; **facilité** nf easiness ; (disposition, don) aptitude ; **facilités** nfpl facilities ; **facilités de paiement** easy terms ; **faciliter** vt to make easier.
**façon** [fasɔ̃] nf (manière) way ; (d'une robe etc) making-up ; cut ; **~s** nfpl (péj) fuss sg ; **de quelle ~?** (in) what way? ; **de ~ à** so as to ; **de ~ à ce que** so that ; **de toute ~** anyway, in any case.
**faconde** [fakɔ̃d] nf loquaciousness, volubility.
**façonner** [fasɔne] vt (fabriquer) to manufacture ; (travailler: matière) to shape, fashion ; (fig) to mould, shape.
**fac-similé** [faksimile] nm facsimile.
**facteur, trice** [faktœʀ, -tʀis] nm/f postman/woman // nm (MATH, fig: élément) factor ; **~ d'orgues** organ builder ; **~ de pianos** piano maker.
**factice** [faktis] a artificial.
**faction** [faksjɔ̃] nf (groupe) faction ; (surveillance) guard ou sentry (duty) ; watch ; **en ~** on guard ; standing watch ; **factionnaire** nm guard, sentry.
**factoriel, le** [faktɔʀjɛl] a factorial.
**factotum** [faktɔtɔm] nm odd-job man, dogsbody.
**facture** [faktyʀ] nf (à payer: gén) bill ; (: COMM) invoice ; (d'un artisan, artiste) technique, workmanship ; **facturer** vt to invoice.
**facultatif, ive** [fakyltatif, -iv] a optional ; (arrêt de bus) request cpd.
**faculté** [fakylte] nf (intellectuelle, d'université) faculty ; (pouvoir, possibilité) power.
**fadaises** [fadɛz] nfpl twaddle sg.
**fade** [fad] a insipid.
**fading** [fadiŋ] nm (RADIO) fading.
**fagot** [fago] nm (de bois) bundle of sticks.
**fagoté, e** [fagote] a (fam): drôlement **~** in a peculiar getup.
**faible** [fɛbl(ə)] a weak ; (voix, lumière, vent) faint ; (rendement, intensité, revenu etc) low // nm weak point ; weakness, soft spot ; **~ d'esprit** feeble-minded ; **faiblesse** nf weakness ; **faiblir** vi to weaken ; (lumière) to dim ; (vent) to drop.
**faïence** [fajɑ̃s] nf earthenware q ; piece of earthenware.
**faignant, e** [fɛɲɑ̃, -ɑ̃t] nm/f = **fainéant, e.**
**faille** [faj] vb voir **falloir** // nf (GÉO) fault ; (fig) flaw, weakness.
**faillible** [fajibl(ə)] a fallible.
**faim** [fɛ̃] nf hunger ; **avoir ~** to be hungry ; **rester sur sa ~** (aussi fig) to be left wanting more.
**fainéant, e** [fɛneɑ̃, -ɑ̃t] nm/f idler, loafer.
**faire** [fɛʀ] vt to make ; (effectuer: travail, opération) to do ; **vraiment? fit-il** really? he said ; **fait à la main/machine** hand-/machine-made ; **~ du bruit/des taches** to make a noise/marks ; **~ du rugby/piano** to play rugby/play the piano ; **~ le malade/l'ignorant** to act the

invalid/the fool ; **~ de qn un frustré/avocat** to make sb a frustrated person/a lawyer ; **cela ne me fait rien** (m'est égal) I don't care ou mind ; (me laisse froid) it has no effect on me ; **cela ne fait rien** it doesn't matter ; **je vous le fais 10 F** (j'en demande 10 F) I'll let you have it for 10 F ; **que faites-vous?** (quel métier etc) what do you do? ; (quelle activité: au moment de la question) what are you doing? ; **comment a-t-il fait pour** how did he manage to ; **qu'a-t-il fait de sa valise?** what has he done with his case? ; **2 et 2 font 4** 2 and 2 are ou make 4 // vb avec attribut: **ça fait 10 m/15 F** it's 10 m/15 F // vb substitut: **ne le casse pas comme je l'ai fait** don't break it as I did // vb impersonnel voir **jour, froid** etc ; **ça fait 2 ans qu'il est parti** it's 2 years since he left ; **ça fait 2 ans qu'il y est** he's been there for 2 years ; **faites!** please do! ; **il ne fait que critiquer** (sans cesse) all he (ever) does is criticize ; (seulement) he's only criticizing ; **~ vieux/démodé** to look old/old-fashioned // **~ faire: ~ réparer qch** to get ou have sth repaired ; **~ tomber/bouger qch** to make sth fall/move ; **cela fait dormir** it makes you sleep ; **~ travailler les enfants** to make the children work, get the children to work ; **~ punir les enfants** to have the children punished ; **~ démarrer un moteur/chauffer de l'eau** to start up an engine/heat some water ; **se ~ examiner la vue/opérer** to have one's eyes tested/have an operation ; **il s'est fait aider (par qn)** he got sb to help him ; **il va se ~ tuer/punir** he's going to get himself killed/get (himself) punished ; **se ~ faire un vêtement** to get a garment made for o.s. // **se ~ vi** (fromage, vin) to mature ; **se ~ à** (s'habituer) to get used to ; **cela se fait beaucoup/ne se fait pas** it's done a lot/not done ; **comment se fait-il/faisait-il que** how is it/was it that ; **se ~ vieux** to be getting old ; **se ~ des amis** to make friends ; **il ne s'en fait pas** he doesn't worry.
**faisable** [fəzabl(ə)] a feasible.
**faisan, e** [fəzɑ̃, -an] nm/f pheasant.
**faisandé, e** [fəzɑ̃de] a high.
**faisceau, x** [fɛso] nm (de lumière etc) beam ; (de branches etc) bundle.
**faiseur, euse** [fəzœʀ, -øz] nm/f (gén:péj): **~ de** maker of // nm (bespoke) tailor.
**faisons** vb voir **faire.**
**fait** [fɛ] nm (événement) event, occurrence ; (réalité, donnée: s'oppose à hypothèse) fact ; **le ~ que/de manger** the fact that/of eating ; **être le ~ de** (causé par) to be the work of ; **être au ~ (de)** to be informed (of) ; **au ~** (à propos) by the way ; **en venir au ~** to get to the point ; **de ~ a** (opposé à: de droit) de facto // ad in fact ; **du ~ de ceci/qu'il a menti** because of ou on account of this/his having lied ; **de ce ~** therefore, for this reason ; **en ~** in fact ; **en ~ de repas** by way of a meal ; **prendre ~ et cause pour qn** to support sb, side with sb ; **prendre qn sur le ~** to catch sb in the act ; **~ d'armes** feat of arms ; **~ divers** (short) news item ; **les ~s et gestes de qn** sb's actions ou doings.

**fait, e** [fε, fεt] *a* (*mûr: fromage, melon*) ripe ; **un homme** ~ a grown man ; **c'en est** ~ **de notre tranquillité** that's the end of our peace.
**faîte** [fεt] *nm* top ; (*fig*) pinnacle, height.
**faites** *vb voir* **faire**.
**faîtière** [fεtjεR] *nf* (*de tente*) ridge pole.
**fait-tout** *nm inv*, **faitout** *nm* [fεtu] stewpot.
**fakir** [fakiR] *nm* wizard.
**falaise** [falεz] *nf* cliff.
**fallacieux, euse** [falasjø, -øz] *a* fallacious ; deceptive ; illusory.
**falloir** [falwaR] *vb impersonnel*: **il va** ~ **100 F** we'll (*ou* I'll) need 100 F ; **il doit** ~ **du temps** that must take time ; **il me faudrait 100 F** I would need 100 F ; **il vous faut tourner à gauche après l'église** you have to *ou* want to turn left past the church ; **nous avons ce qu'il (nous) faut** we have what we need ; **il faut qu'il parte/a fallu qu'il parte** (*obligation*) he has to *ou* must leave/had to leave ; **il a fallu le faire** it had to be done // **s'en** ~ : **il s'en est fallu de 100 F/5 minutes** we (*ou* they) were 100 F short/5 minutes late (*ou* early) ; **il s'en faut de beaucoup qu'il soit** he is far from being ; **il s'en est fallu de peu que cela n'arrive** it very nearly happened.
**falot, e** [falo, -ɔt] *a* dreary, colourless // *nm* lantern.
**falsifier** [falsifje] *vt* to falsify ; to doctor.
**famé, e** [fame] *a*: **mal** ~ disreputable, of ill repute.
**famélique** [famelik] *a* half-starved.
**fameux, euse** [famø, -øz] *a* (*illustre*) famous ; (*bon: repas, plat etc*) first-rate, first-class.
**familial, e, aux** [familjal, -o] *a* family *cpd* // *nf* (AUTO) estate car.
**familiariser** [familjaRize] *vt*: ~ **qn avec** to familiarize sb with.
**familiarité** [familjaRite] *nf* informality ; familiarity ; ~ **avec** (*sujet, science*) familiarity with ; ~**s** *nfpl* familiarities.
**familier, ière** [familje, -jεR] *a* (*connu, impertinent*) familiar ; (*dénotant une certaine intimité*) informal, friendly ; (LING) informal, colloquial // *nm* regular (visitor).
**famille** [famij] *nf* family ; **il a de la** ~ **à Paris** he has relatives in Paris.
**famine** [famin] *nf* famine.
**fan** [fan] *nm/f* fan.
**fanal, aux** [fanal, -o] *nm* beacon ; lantern.
**fanatique** [fanatik] *a* fanatical // *nm/f* fanatic ; **fanatisme** *nm* fanaticism.
**faner** [fane]: **se** ~ *vi* to fade.
**faneur, euse** [fanœR, -øz] *nm/f* haymaker.
**fanfare** [fɑ̃faR] *nf* (*orchestre*) brass band ; (*musique*) fanfare.
**fanfaron, ne** [fɑ̃faRɔ̃, -ɔn] *nm/f* braggart.
**fange** [fɑ̃ʒ] *nf* mire.
**fanion** [fanjɔ̃] *nm* pennant.
**fanon** [fanɔ̃] *nm* (*de baleine*) plate of baleen ; (*repli de peau*) dewlap, wattle.
**fantaisie** [fɑ̃tezi] *nf* (*spontanéité*) fancy, imagination ; (*caprice*) whim ; extravagance ; (MUS) fantasia // *a*: **bijou/pain** ~ fancy jewellery/bread.

**fantaisiste** *a* (*péj*) unorthodox, eccentric // *nm/f* (*de music-hall*) variety artist *ou* entertainer.
**fantasme** [fɑ̃tasm(ə)] *nm* fantasy.
**fantasque** [fɑ̃task(ə)] *a* whimsical, capricious ; fantastic.
**fantassin** [fɑ̃tasɛ̃] *nm* infantryman.
**fantastique** [fɑ̃tastik] *a* fantastic.
**fantoche** [fɑ̃tɔʃ] *nm* (*péj*) puppet.
**fantomatique** [fɑ̃tɔmatik] *a* ghostly.
**fantôme** [fɑ̃tom] *nm* ghost, phantom.
**faon** [fɑ̃] *nm* fawn.
**farce** [faRs(ə)] *nf* (*viande*) stuffing ; (*blague*) (practical) joke ; (THÉÂTRE) farce ; ~**s et attrapes** jokes and novelties ; **farceur, euse** *nm/f* practical joker ; **farcir** *vt* (*viande*) to stuff ; (*fig*): **farcir qch de** to stuff sth with.
**fard** [faR] *nm* make-up.
**fardeau, x** [faRdo] *nm* burden.
**farder** [faRde] *vt* to make up.
**farfelu, e** [faRfəly] *a* cranky, hare-brained.
**farfouiller** [faRfuje] *vi* (*péj*) to rummage around.
**farine** [faRin] *nf* flour ; **farineux, euse** *a* (*sauce, pomme*) floury // *nmpl* (*aliments*) starchy foods.
**farouche** [faRuʃ] *a* shy, timid ; savage, wild ; fierce.
**fart** [faR(t)] *nm* (ski) wax ; **farter** *vt* to wax.
**fascicule** [fasikyl] *nm* volume.
**fascination** [fasinɑsjɔ̃] *nf* fascination.
**fasciner** [fasine] *vt* to fascinate.
**fascisme** [faʃism(ə)] *nm* fascism ; **fasciste** *a, nm/f* fascist.
**fasse** *etc vb voir* **faire**.
**faste** [fast(ə)] *nm* splendour // *a*: **c'est un jour** ~ it's his (*ou* our) lucky day.
**fastidieux, euse** [fastidjø, -øz] *a* tedious, tiresome.
**fastueux, euse** [fastɥø, -øz] *a* sumptuous, luxurious.
**fat** [fa] *am* conceited, smug.
**fatal, e** [fatal] *a* fatal ; (*inévitable*) inevitable ; ~**isme** *nm* fatalism ; fatalistic outlook ; ~**ité** *nf* fate ; fateful coincidence ; inevitability.
**fatidique** [fatidik] *a* fateful.
**fatigant, e** [fatigɑ̃, -ɑ̃t] *a* tiring ; (*agaçant*) tiresome.
**fatigue** [fatig] *nf* tiredness, fatigue.
**fatiguer** [fatige] *vt* to tire, make tired ; (TECH) to put a strain on, strain ; (*fig: importuner*) to wear out // *vi* (*moteur*) to labour, strain ; **se** ~ to get tired ; to tire o.s. (out).
**fatras** [fatRa] *nm* jumble, hotchpotch.
**fatuité** [fatɥite] *nf* conceitedness, smugness.
**faubourg** [fobuR] *nm* suburb.
**fauché, e** [foʃe] *a* (*fam*) broke.
**faucher** [foʃe] *vt* (*herbe*) to cut ; (*champs, blés*) to reap ; (*fig*) to cut down ; to mow down ; **faucheur, euse** *nm/f, nf* (*machine*) reaper, mower.
**faucille** [fosij] *nf* sickle.
**faucon** [fokɔ̃] *nm* falcon, hawk.
**faudra** *vb voir* **falloir**.
**faufiler** [fofile] *vt* to tack, baste ; **se** ~ *vi*: **se** ~ **dans** to edge one's way into ; **se** ~

**parmi/entre** to thread one's way among/between.

**faune** [fon] nf (ZOOL) wildlife, fauna // nm faun.

**faussaire** [fosɛʀ] nm forger.

**fausse** [fos] a voir **faux**.

**faussement** [fosmɑ̃] ad (accuser) wrongly, wrongfully; (croire) falsely, erroneously.

**fausser** [fose] vt (objet) to bend, buckle; (fig) to distort.

**fausset** [fosɛ] nm: **voix de** ~ falsetto voice.

**faussete** [foste] nf wrongness; falseness.

**faut** vb voir **falloir**.

**faute** [fot] nf (erreur) mistake, error; (péché, manquement) misdemeanour; (FOOTBALL etc) offence; (TENNIS) fault; (responsabilité): **par la** ~ **de** through the fault of, because of; **c'est de sa/ma** ~ it's his/my fault; **être en** ~ to be in the wrong; ~ **de** (temps, argent) for ou through lack of; **sans** ~ ad without fail; ~ **de frappe** typing error; ~ **d'orthographe** spelling mistake; ~ **professionnelle** professional misconduct q.

**fauteuil** [fotœj] nm armchair; ~ **club** (big) easy chair; ~ **d'orchestre** seat in the front stalls; ~ **roulant** wheelchair.

**fauteur** [fotœʀ] nm: ~ **de troubles** trouble-maker.

**fautif, ive** [fotif, -iv] a (incorrect) incorrect, inaccurate; (responsable) at fault, in the wrong; guilty // nm/f culprit.

**fauve** [fov] nm wildcat // a (couleur) fawn.

**faux** [fo] nf scythe.

**faux, fausse** [fo, fos] a (inexact) wrong; (falsifié) fake; forged; (sournois, postiche) false // ad (MUS) out of tune // nm (copie) fake, forgery; (opposé au vrai): **le** ~ falsehood; **le** ~ **numéro/la fausse clef** the wrong number/key; **faire** ~ **bond à qn** to stand sb up; ~ **col** detachable collar; ~ **frais** nmpl extras, incidental expenses; ~ **mouvement** awkward movement; ~ **nez** funny nose; ~ **pas** tripping q; (fig) faux pas; ~ **témoignage** (délit) perjury; **fausse alerte** false alarm; **fausse couche** miscarriage; ~**-filet** nm sirloin; ~**-fuyant** nm equivocation; ~**-monnayeur** nm counterfeiter, forger.

**faveur** [favœʀ] nf favour; (ruban) ribbon; **traitement de** ~ preferential treatment; **à la** ~ **de** under cover of; thanks to; **en** ~ **de** in favour of.

**favorable** [favɔʀabl(ə)] a favourable.

**favori, te** [favɔʀi, -it] a, nm/f favourite; ~**s** nmpl (barbe) sideboards, sideburns.

**favoriser** [favɔʀize] vt to favour.

**favoritisme** [favɔʀitism(ə)] nm (péj) favouritism.

**FB** sigle = franc belge.

**fébrile** [febʀil] a feverish, febrile.

**fécal, e, aux** [fekal, -o] a voir **matière**.

**fécond, e** [fekɔ̃, -ɔ̃d] a fertile; **féconder** vt to fertilize; **fécondité** nf fertility.

**fécule** [fekyl] nf potato flour.

**fédéral, e, aux** [fedeʀal, -o] a federal; **fédéralisme** nm federalism.

**fédération** [fedeʀasjɔ̃] nf federation.

**fée** [fe] nf fairy; ~**rie** nf enchantment; ~**rique** a magical, fairytale cpd.

**feignant, e** [fɛɲɑ̃, -ɑ̃t] nm/f = **fainéant, e**.

**feindre** [fɛ̃dʀ(ə)] vt to feign // vi to dissemble; ~ **de faire** to pretend to do.

**feinte** [fɛ̃t] nf (SPORT) dummy.

**fêler** [fele] vt to crack.

**félicitations** [felisitasjɔ̃] nfpl congratulations.

**félicité** [felisite] nf bliss.

**féliciter** [felisite] vt: ~ **qn (de)** to congratulate sb (on).

**félin, e** [felɛ̃, -in] a feline // nm (big) cat.

**félon, ne** [felɔ̃, -ɔn] a perfidious, treacherous.

**fêlure** [felyʀ] nf crack.

**femelle** [fəmɛl] a (aussi ÉLEC, TECH) female // nf female; **souris** ~ female mouse, she-mouse.

**féminin, e** [feminɛ̃, -in] a feminine; (sexe) female; (équipe, vêtements etc) women's // nm feminine; **féministe** a feminist; **féminité** nf femininity.

**femme** [fam] nf woman; (épouse) wife (pl wives); **devenir** ~ to attain womanhood; ~ **de chambre** cleaning lady; ~ **de ménage** domestic help, cleaning lady.

**fémur** [femyʀ] nm femur, thighbone.

**fenaison** [fənɛzɔ̃] nf haymaking.

**fendre** [fɑ̃dʀ(ə)] vt (couper en deux) to split; (fissurer) to crack; (fig: traverser) to cut through; to cleave through; **se** ~ vi to crack; **fendu, e** a (sol, mur) cracked; (jupe) slit.

**fenêtre** [fənɛtʀ(ə)] nf window.

**fenouil** [fənuj] nm fennel.

**fente** [fɑ̃t] nf (fissure) crack; (de boîte à lettres etc) slit.

**féodal, e, aux** [feɔdal, -o] a feudal; **féodalité** nf feudality.

**fer** [fɛʀ] nm iron; (de cheval) shoe; **au** ~ **rouge** with a red-hot iron; ~ **à cheval** horseshoe; ~ **forgé** wrought iron; ~ **de lance** spearhead; ~ **(à repasser)** iron; ~ **à souder** soldering iron.

**ferai** etc vb voir **faire**.

**fer-blanc** [fɛʀblɑ̃] nm tin(plate); **ferblanterie** nf tinplate making; tinware; **ferblantier** nm tinsmith.

**férié, e** [feʀje] a: **jour** ~ public holiday.

**ferions** etc vb voir **faire**.

**férir** [feʀiʀ]: **sans coup** ~ ad without meeting any opposition.

**ferme** [fɛʀm(ə)] a firm // ad (travailler etc) hard // nf (exploitation) farm; (maison) farmhouse.

**fermé, e** [fɛʀme] a closed, shut; (gaz, eau etc) off; (fig: personne) uncommunicative; (: milieu) exclusive.

**ferment** [fɛʀmɑ̃] nm ferment.

**fermentation** [fɛʀmɑ̃tasjɔ̃] nf fermentation.

**fermenter** [fɛʀmɑ̃te] vi to ferment.

**fermer** [fɛʀme] vt to close, shut; (cesser l'exploitation de) to close down, shut down; (eau, lumière, électricité, robinet) to put off, turn off; (aéroport, route) to close // vi to close, shut; to close down, shut down; **se**

~ vi (yeux) to close, shut ; (fleur, blessure) to close up.

**fermeté** [fɛʀməte] nf firmness.

**fermeture** [fɛʀmətyʀ] nf closing ; shutting ; closing ou shutting down ; putting ou turning off ; (dispositif) catch ; fastening, fastener ; **heure de** ~ (COMM) closing time ; **jour de** ~ (COMM) day on which the shop (etc) is closed ; ~ **éclair** ® ou **à glissière** zip (fastener), zipper.

**fermier, ière** [fɛʀmje, -jɛʀ] nm farmer // nf woman farmer ; farmer's wife // a: **beurre/cidre** ~ farm butter/cider.

**fermoir** [fɛʀmwaʀ] nm clasp.

**féroce** [feʀɔs] a ferocious, fierce.

**ferons** vb voir **faire**.

**ferraille** [fɛʀɑj] nf scrap iron ; **mettre à la** ~ to scrap ; **ferrailleur** nm scrap merchant.

**ferré, e** [feʀe] a hobnailed ; steel-tipped ; (fam): ~ **en** well up on, hot at.

**ferrer** [feʀe] vt (cheval) to shoe ; (chaussure) to nail ; (canne) to tip ; (poisson) to strike.

**ferreux, euse** [fɛʀø, -øz] a ferrous.

**ferronnerie** [fɛʀɔnʀi] nf ironwork ; ~ **d'art** wrought iron work ; **ferronnier** nm craftsman in wrought iron ; ironware merchant.

**ferroviaire** [fɛʀɔvjɛʀ] a rail(way) cpd.

**ferrure** [fɛʀyʀ] nf (ornamental) hinge.

**ferry-boat** [fɛʀebot] nm ferry.

**fertile** [fɛʀtil] a fertile ; ~ **en incidents** eventful, packed with incidents ; **fertiliser** vt to fertilize ; **fertilité** nf fertility.

**féru, e** [feʀy] a: ~ **de** with a keen interest in.

**férule** [feʀyl] nf: **être sous la** ~ **de qn** to be under sb's (iron) rule.

**fervent, e** [fɛʀvɑ̃, -ɑ̃t] a fervent.

**ferveur** [fɛʀvœʀ] nf fervour.

**fesse** [fɛs] nf buttock ; **fessée** nf spanking.

**festin** [fɛstɛ̃] nm feast.

**festival** [fɛstival] nm festival ; ~**ier** nm festival-goer.

**festivités** [fɛstivite] nfpl festivities, merry-making sg.

**feston** [fɛstɔ̃] nm (ARCHIT) festoon ; (COUTURE) scallop.

**festoyer** [fɛstwaje] vi to feast.

**fêtard** [fɛtaʀ] nm (péj) high liver, merry-maker.

**fête** [fɛt] nf (religieuse) feast ; (publique) holiday ; (en famille etc) celebration ; (kermesse) fête, fair, festival ; (du nom) feast day, name day ; **faire la** ~ to live it up ; **faire** ~ **à qn** to give sb a warm welcome ; **les** ~**s (de fin d'année)** the Christmas and New Year holidays, the festive season ; **la salle/le comité des** ~**s** the village hall/ festival committee ; ~ **foraine** (fun) fair ; ~ **mobile** movable feast (day) ; **la F**~ **Nationale** the national holiday ; **la Fête-Dieu** Corpus Christi ; **fêter** vt to celebrate ; (personne) to have a celebration for.

**fétiche** [fetiʃ] nm fetish ; **fétichisme** nm fetishism.

**fétide** [fetid] a fetid.

**fétu** [fety] nm: ~ **de paille** wisp of straw.

**feu** [fø] a inv: ~ **son père** his late father.

**feu, x** [fø] nm (gén) fire ; (signal lumineux) light ; (de cuisinière) ring ; (sensation de brûlure) burning (sensation) // nmpl (éclat, lumière) fire sg ; (AUTO) (traffic) lights ; **à** ~ **doux/vif** over a slow/brisk heat ; **à petit** ~ (CULIN) over a gentle heat ; **faire** ~ to fire ; **tué au** ~ killed in action ; **mettre à** ~ (fusée) to fire off ; **prendre** ~ to catch fire ; **mettre le** ~ **à** to set fire to, set on fire ; **faire du** ~ to make a fire ; **avez-vous du** ~? (pour cigarette) have you (got) a light? ; ~ **rouge/vert/orange** red/green/ amber light ; ~ **arrière** rear light ; ~ **d'artifice** firework ; (spectacle) fireworks pl ; ~ **de camp** campfire ; ~ **de cheminée** chimney fire ; ~ **de joie** bonfire ; ~ **de paille** (fig) flash in the pan ; ~**x de brouillard** fog-lamps ; ~**x de croisement** dipped headlights ; ~**x de position** sidelights ; ~**x de route** headlights, headlamps.

**feuillage** [fœjaʒ] nm foliage, leaves pl.

**feuille** [fœj] nf (d'arbre) leaf (pl leaves) ; ~ **(de papier)** sheet (of paper) ; ~ **d'or/de métal** gold/metal leaf ; ~ **d'impôts** tax form ; ~ **morte** dead leaf ; ~ **de température** temperature chart ; ~ **de vigne** (BOT) vine leaf ; (sur statue) fig leaf ; ~ **volante** loose sheet.

**feuillet** [fœjɛ] nm leaf (pl leaves), page.

**feuilleté, e** [fœjte] a (CULIN) flaky.

**feuilleter** [fœjte] vt (livre) to leaf through.

**feuilleton** [fœjtɔ̃] nm serial.

**feuillu, e** [fœjy] a leafy ; ~**s** nmpl (BOT) broad-leaved trees.

**feulement** [følmɑ̃] nm growl.

**feutre** [føtʀ(ə)] nm felt ; (chapeau) felt hat ; **feutré, e** a feltlike ; (pas, voix) muffled ; **feutrer** vt to felt ; (fig) to muffle // vi, **se feutrer** vi to felt ; **feutrine** nf (lightweight) felt.

**fève** [fɛv] nf broad bean.

**février** [fevʀije] nm February.

**FF** sigle = franc français.

**F.F.I.** sigle fpl = Forces françaises de l'intérieur (1942-45) // sigle m member of the F.F.I.

**fi** [fi] excl: **faire** ~ **de** to snap one's fingers at.

**fiacre** [fjakʀ(ə)] nm (hackney) cab ou carriage.

**fiançailles** [fjɑ̃saj] nfpl engagement sg.

**fiancé, e** [fjɑ̃se] nm/f fiancé/fiancée // a: **être** ~ **(à)** to be engaged (to).

**fiancer** [fjɑ̃se]: **se** ~ vi: **se** ~**(avec)** to become engaged (to).

**fibre** [fibʀ(ə)] nf fibre ; ~ **de verre** fibre-glass, glass fibre ; **fibreux, euse** a fibrous ; (viande) stringy.

**ficeler** [fisle] vt to tie up.

**ficelle** [fisɛl] nf string q ; piece ou length of string.

**fiche** [fiʃ] nf (pour fichier) (index) card ; (formulaire) form ; (ÉLEC) plug.

**ficher** [fiʃe] vt (pour un fichier) to file ; (POLICE) to put on file ; (planter): ~ **qch dans** to stick ou drive sth into ; (fam) to do ; to give ; to stick ou shove ; **fiche(-moi) le camp** (fam) clear off ; **fiche-moi la paix** (fam) leave me alone ; **se** ~ **dans** (s'enfoncer) to get stuck in, embed itself in ; **se ~ de** (*fam*) to make fun of ; not to care about.

**fichier** [fiʃje] *nm* file ; card index.

**fichu, e** [fiʃy] *pp de* **ficher** (*fam*) // *a* (*fam*: *fini, inutilisable*) bust, done for ; (: *intensif*) wretched, darned // *nm* (*foulard*) (head)scarf (*pl* scarves) ; **mal ~** (*fam*) feeling lousy ; useless.

**fictif, ive** [fiktif, -iv] *a* fictitious.

**fiction** [fiksjɔ̃] *nf* fiction ; (*fait imaginé*) invention.

**fidèle** [fidɛl] *a*: **~ (à)** faithful (to) // *nm/f* (*REL*): **les ~s** the faithful ; (*à l'église*) the congregation ; **fidélité** *nf* faithfulness ; **fidélité conjugale** marital fidelity.

**fief** [fjɛf] *nm* fief ; (*fig*) preserve ; stronghold.

**fiel** [fjɛl] *nm* gall.

**fiente** [fjɑ̃t] *nf* (bird) droppings *pl*.

**fier** [fje]: **se ~ à** *vt* to trust.

**fier, fière** [fjɛR] *a* proud ; **~ de** proud of ; **avoir fière allure** to cut a fine figure ; **~té** *nf* pride.

**fièvre** [fjɛvR(ə)] *nf* fever ; **avoir de la ~/39 de ~** to have a high temperature/a temperature of 39°C ; **~ typhoïde** typhoid fever ; **fiévreux, euse** *a* feverish.

**fifre** [fifR(ə)] *nm* fife ; fife-player.

**figer** [fiʒe] *vt* to congeal ; (*fig: personne*) to freeze, root to the spot ; **se ~** *vi* to congeal ; to freeze ; (*institutions etc*) to become set, stop evolving.

**figue** [fig] *nf* fig ; **figuier** *nm* fig tree.

**figurant, e** [figyRɑ̃, -ɑ̃t] *nm/f* ; (*THÉÂTRE*) walk-on ; (*CINÉMA*) extra.

**figuratif, ive** [figyRatif, -iv] *a* representational, figurative.

**figuration** [figyRɑsjɔ̃] *nf* walk-on parts *pl* ; extras *pl*.

**figure** [figyR] *nf* (*visage*) face ; (*image, tracé, forme, personnage*) figure ; (*illustration*) picture, diagram ; **faire ~ de** to look like.

**figuré, e** [figyRe] *a* (*sens*) figurative.

**figurer** [figyRe] *vi* to appear // *vt* to represent ; **se ~ que** to imagine that.

**figurine** [figyRin] *nf* figurine.

**fil** [fil] *nm* (*brin, fig: d'une histoire*) thread ; (*du téléphone*) cable, wire ; (*textile de lin*) linen ; (*d'un couteau: tranchant*) edge ; **au ~ des années** with the passing of the years ; **au ~ de l'eau** with the stream *ou* current ; **donner/recevoir un coup de ~** to make/get a phone call ; **~ à coudre** (sewing) thread *ou* yarn ; **~ électrique** electric wire ; **~ de fer** wire ; **~ de fer barbelé** barbed wire ; **~ à pêche** fishing line ; **~ à plomb** plumbline ; **~ à souder** soldering wire.

**filament** [filamɑ̃] *nm* (*ÉLEC*) filament ; (*de liquide*) trickle, thread.

**filandreux, euse** [filɑ̃dRø, -øz] *a* stringy.

**filasse** [filas] *a inv* white blond.

**filature** [filatyR] *nf* (*fabrique*) mill ; (*policière*) shadowing *q*, tailing *q*.

**file** [fil] *nf* line ; **~ (d'attente)** queue ; **prendre la ~** to join the (end of the) queue ; **prendre la ~ de droite** (*AUTO*) to move into the right-hand lane ; **se mettre en ~** to form a line ; (*AUTO*) to get into

lane ; **en ~ indienne** in single file ; **à la ~** *ad* (*d'affilée*) in succession.

**filer** [file] *vt* (*tissu, toile, verre*) to spin ; (*dérouler: câble etc*) to pay *ou* let out ; to veer out ; (*prendre en filature*) to shadow, tail ; (*fam: donner*): **~ qch à qn** to slip sb sth // *vi* (*bas, maille, liquide, pâte*) to run ; (*aller vite*) to fly past *ou* by ; (*fam: partir*) to make off ; **~ doux** to behave o.s., toe the line.

**filet** [filɛ] *nm* net ; (*CULIN*) fillet ; (*d'eau, de sang*) trickle ; **~ (à provisions)** string bag.

**filetage** [filtaʒ] *nm* threading ; thread.

**fileter** [filte] *vt* to thread.

**filial, e, aux** [filjal, -o] *a* filial // *nf* (*COMM*) subsidiary.

**filiation** [filjɑsjɔ̃] *nf* filiation.

**filière** [filjɛR] *nf*: **passer par la ~** to go through the (administrative) channels ; **suivre la ~** (*dans sa carrière*) to work one's way up (through the hierarchy).

**filiforme** [filifɔRm(ə)] *a* spindly ; threadlike.

**filigrane** [filigRan] *nm* (*d'un billet, timbre*) watermark ; **en ~** (*fig*) showing just beneath the surface.

**filin** [filɛ̃] *nm* rope.

**fille** [fij] *nf* girl ; (*opposé à fils*) daughter ; **~ de joie** prostitute ; **~ de salle** waitress ; **~-mère** (*péj*) unmarried mother ; **fillette** *nf* (little) girl.

**filleul, e** [fijœl] *nm/f* godchild, godson/daughter.

**film** [film] *nm* (*pour photo*) (roll of) film ; (*œuvre*) film, picture, movie ; (*couche*) film ; **~ muet/parlant** silent/talking picture *ou* movie ; **~ d'animation** animated film ; **filmer** *vt* to film.

**filon** [filɔ̃] *nm* vein, lode ; (*fig*) lucrative line, money spinner.

**fils** [fis] *nm* son ; **~ de famille** moneyed young man.

**filtre** [filtR(ə)] *nm* filter ; '**~ ou sans ~?**' 'tipped or plain?' ; **~ à air** (*AUTO*) air filter ; **filtrer** *vt* to filter ; (*fig: candidats, visiteurs*) to screen // *vi* to filter (through).

**fin** [fɛ̃] *nf* end ; **~s** *nfpl* (*but*) ends ; **à (la) ~ mai** at the end of May ; **en ~ de semaine** at the end of the week ; **prendre ~** to come to an end ; **mettre ~ à** to put an end to ; **à la ~** *ad* in the end, eventually ; **sans ~** *a* endless // *ad* endlessly.

**fin, e** [fɛ̃, fin] *a* (*papier, couche, fil*) thin ; (*cheveux, poudre, pointe, visage*) fine ; (*taille*) neat, slim ; (*esprit, remarque*) subtle ; shrewd // *ad* (*moudre, couper*) finely // *nf* (*alcool*) liqueur brandy ; **~ prêt/soûl** quite ready/drunk ; **un ~ tireur** a crack shot ; **avoir la vue/l'ouïe ~e** to have sharp eyes/ears, have keen eyesight/hearing ; **or/linge/vin ~** fine gold/linen/wine ; **repas ~** gourmet meal ; **une ~e mouche** (*fig*) a sharp customer ; **~es herbes** mixed herbs.

**final, e** [final] *a, nf* final ; **quarts de ~e** quarter finals ; **8èmes/16èmes de ~e** 2nd/1st round (*in 5 round knock-out competition*) ; **~ement** *ad* finally, in the end ; (*après tout*) after all ; **~iste** *nm/f* finalist.

**finance** [finɑ̃s] *nf* finance ; ~s *nfpl* (*situation financière*) finances ; (*activités financières*) finance *sg* ; **moyennant** ~ for a fee *ou* consideration ; **financer** *vt* to finance ; **financier, ière** *a* financial // *nm* financier.

**finaud, e** [fino, -od] *a* wily.

**finesse** [finɛs] *nf* thinness ; fineness ; neatness, slimness ; subtlety ; shrewdness ; ~s *nfpl* (*subtilités*) niceties ; finer points.

**fini, e** [fini] *a* finished ; (*MATH*) finite ; (*intensif*): **un égoïste** ~ an egotist through and through // *nm* (*d'un objet manufacturé*) finish.

**finir** [finiʀ] *vt* to finish // *vi* to finish, end ; ~ **quelque part** to end *ou* finish up somewhere ; ~ **de faire** to finish doing ; (*cesser*) to stop doing ; ~ **par faire** to end *ou* finish up doing ; **il finit par m'agacer** he's beginning to get on my nerves ; ~ **en pointe/tragédie** to end in a point/in tragedy ; **en** ~ **avec** to be *ou* have done with ; **il va mal** ~ he will come to a bad end.

**finish** [finiʃ] *nm* (*SPORT*) finish.

**finissage** [finisaʒ] *nm* finishing.

**finition** [finisjɔ̃] *nf* finishing ; finish.

**finlandais, e** [fɛ̃lɑ̃dɛ, -ɛz] *a* Finnish // *nm/f* Finn.

**Finlande** [fɛ̃lɑ̃d] *nf*: **la** ~ Finland ; **finnois** *nm* Finnish.

**fiole** [fjɔl] *nf* phial.

**fiord** [fjɔʀ(d)] *nm* = **fjord**.

**fioriture** [fjɔʀityʀ] *nf* embellishment, flourish.

**firmament** [fiʀmamɑ̃] *nm* firmament, skies *pl*.

**firme** [fiʀm(ə)] *nf* firm.

**fis** *vb voir* **faire**.

**fisc** [fisk] *nm* tax authorities *pl*, ≈ Inland Revenue ; ~**al, e, aux** *a* tax *cpd*, fiscal ; ~**alité** *nf* tax system ; (*charges*) taxation.

**fission** [fisjɔ̃] *nf* fission.

**fissure** [fisyʀ] *nf* crack.

**fissurer** [fisyʀe] *vt*, **se** ~ *vi* to crack.

**fiston** [fistɔ̃] *nm* (*fam*) son, lad.

**fit** *vb voir* **faire**.

**fixateur** [fiksatœʀ] *nm* (*PHOTO*) fixer ; (*pour cheveux*) hair cream.

**fixatif** [fiksatif] *nm* fixative.

**fixation** [fiksasjɔ̃] *nf* fixing ; fastening ; setting ; (*de ski*) binding ; (*PSYCH*) fixation.

**fixe** [fiks(ə)] *a* fixed ; (*emploi*) steady, regular // *nm* (*salaire*) basic salary ; **à heure** ~ at a set time ; **menu à prix** ~ set menu.

**fixé, e** [fikse] *a*: **être** ~ (**sur**) (*savoir à quoi s'en tenir*) to have made up one's mind (about) ; to know for certain (about).

**fixement** [fiksəmɑ̃] *ad* (*regarder*) fixedly, steadily.

**fixer** [fikse] *vt* (*attacher*): ~ **qch (à/sur)** to fix *ou* fasten sth (to/onto) ; (*déterminer*) to fix, set ; (*CHIMIE, PHOTO*) to fix ; (*poser son regard sur*) to look hard at, stare at ; **se** ~ (*s'établir*) to settle down ; **se** ~ **sur** (*suj: attention*) to focus on.

**fjord** [fjɔʀ(d)] *nm* fjord, fiord.

**flacon** [flakɔ̃] *nm* bottle.

**flageller** [flaʒele] *vt* to flog, scourge.

**flageoler** [flaʒɔle] *vi* (*jambes*) to sag.

**flageolet** [flaʒɔlɛ] *nm* (*MUS*) flageolet ; (*CULIN*) dwarf kidney bean.

**flagorneur, euse** [flagɔʀnœʀ, -øz] *nm/f* toady, fawner.

**flagrant, e** [flagʀɑ̃, -ɑ̃t] *a* flagrant, blatant ; **en** ~ **délit** in the act, in flagrante delicto.

**flair** [flɛʀ] *nm* sense of smell ; (*fig*) intuition ; **flairer** *vt* (*humer*) to sniff (at) ; (*détecter*) to scent.

**flamand, e** [flamɑ̃, -ɑ̃d] *a, nm* (*langue*) Flemish // *nm/f* Fleming ; **les F**~**s** the Flemish.

**flamant** [flamɑ̃] *nm* flamingo.

**flambant** [flɑ̃bɑ̃] *ad*: ~ **neuf** brand new.

**flambé, e** [flɑ̃be] *a* (*CULIN*) flambé // *nf* blaze ; (*fig*) flaring-up, explosion.

**flambeau, x** [flɑ̃bo] *nm* (flaming) torch.

**flamber** [flɑ̃be] *vi* to blaze (up) // *vt* (*poulet*) to singe ; (*aiguille*) to sterilize.

**flamboyant, e** [flɑ̃bwajɑ̃, -ɑ̃t] *a* flashing, blazing ; flaming.

**flamboyer** [flɑ̃bwaje] *vi* to blaze (up) ; to flame.

**flamingant, e** [flamɛ̃gɑ̃, -ɑ̃t] *a* Flemish-speaking.

**flamme** [flam] *nf* flame ; (*fig*) fire, fervour ; **en** ~**s** on fire, ablaze.

**flammèche** [flamɛʃ] *nf* (flying) spark.

**flan** [flɑ̃] *nm* (*CULIN*) custard tart *ou* pie.

**flanc** [flɑ̃] *nm* side ; (*MIL*) flank ; **à** ~ **de colline** on the hillside ; **prêter le** ~ **à** (*fig*) to lay o.s. open to.

**flancher** [flɑ̃ʃe] *vi* to fail, pack up.

**flanelle** [flanɛl] *nf* flannel.

**flâner** [flɑne] *vi* to stroll ; **flânerie** *nf* stroll.

**flanquer** [flɑ̃ke] *vt* to flank ; (*fam: mettre*): ~ **qch sur/dans** to bung *ou* shove sth on/into ; (: *jeter*): ~ **par terre/à la porte** to fling to the ground/chuck out.

**flapi, e** [flapi] *a* dog-tired.

**flaque** [flak] *nf* (*d'eau*) puddle ; (*d'huile, de sang etc*) pool.

**flash, *pl* flashes** [flaʃ] *nm* (*PHOTO*) flash ; ~ (**d'information**) newsflash.

**flasque** [flask(ə)] *a* flabby.

**flatter** [flate] *vt* to flatter ; (*caresser*) to stroke ; **se** ~ **de qch** to pride o.s. on sth ; **flatterie** *nf* flattery *q* ; **flatteur, euse** *a* flattering // *nm/f* flatterer.

**fléau, x** [fleo] *nm* scourge, curse ; (*de balance*) beam ; (*pour le blé*) flail.

**flèche** [flɛʃ] *nf* arrow ; (*de clocher*) spire ; (*de grue*) jib ; **monter en** ~ (*fig*) to soar, rocket ; **flécher** *vt* to arrow, mark with arrows ; **fléchette** *nf* dart ; **fléchettes** *nfpl* (*jeu*) darts *sg*.

**fléchir** [fleʃiʀ] *vt* (*corps, genou*) to bend ; (*fig*) to sway, weaken // *vi* (*poutre*) to sag, bend ; (*fig*) to weaken, flag ; **fléchissement** *nm* bending ; sagging ; flagging.

**flegmatique** [flɛgmatik] *a* phlegmatic.

**flegme** [flɛgm(ə)] *nm* composure.

**flemmard, e** [flemaʀ, -aʀd(ə)] *nm/f* lazybones *sg*, loafer.

**flétrir** [fletʀiʀ] *vt* to wither ; (*stigmatiser*) to condemn (in the most severe terms) ; **se** ~ *vi* to wither.

**fleur** [flœR] *nf* flower ; (*d'un arbre*) blossom, bloom ; **être en ~** (*arbre*) to be in blossom *ou* bloom ; **tissu à ~s** flowered *ou* flowery fabric ; **à ~ de terre** just above the ground ; **~ de lis** fleur-de-lis.

**fleurer** [flœRe] *vt*: **~ la lavande** to be fragrant with the scent of lavender.

**fleuret** [flœRɛ] *nm* (*arme*) foil ; (*sport*) fencing.

**fleuri, e** [flœRi] *a* in flower *ou* bloom ; surrounded by flowers ; (*fig*) flowery ; florid.

**fleurir** [flœRiR] *vi* (*rose*) to flower ; (*arbre*) to blossom ; (*fig*) to flourish ; / *vt* (*tombe*) to put flowers on ; (*chambre*) to decorate with flowers.

**fleuriste** [flœRist(ə)] *nm/f* florist.

**fleuron** [flœRɔ̃] *nm* jewel (*fig*).

**fleuve** [flœv] *nm* river.

**flexible** [flɛksibl(ə)] *a* flexible.

**flexion** [flɛksjɔ̃] *nf* flexing, bending ; (*LING*) inflection.

**flibustier** [flibystje] *nm* buccaneer.

**flic** [flik] *nm* (*fam: péj*) cop.

**flirter** [flœRte] *vi* to flirt.

**F.L.N.** *sigle m* = *Front de libération nationale* (*during the Algerian war*).

**flocon** [flɔkɔ̃] *nm* flake ; (*de laine etc*: *boulette*) flock ; **~s d'avoine** oatflakes.

**flonflons** [flɔ̃flɔ̃] *nmpl* blare *sg*.

**floraison** [flɔRɛzɔ̃] *nf* flowering ; blossoming ; flourishing.

**floral, e, aux** [flɔRal, -o] *a* floral, flower *cpd*.

**floralies** [flɔRali] *nfpl* flower show *sg*.

**flore** [flɔR] *nf* flora.

**florissant, e** [flɔRisɑ̃, -ɑ̃t] *vb voir* **fleurir** // *a* flourishing.

**flot** [flo] *nm* flood, stream ; (*marée*) flood tide ; **~s** *nmpl* (*de la mer*) waves ; **être à ~** (*NAVIG*) to be afloat ; (*fig*) to be on an even keel ; **entrer à ~s** to be streaming *ou* pouring in.

**flottage** [flɔtaʒ] *nm* (*du bois*) floating.

**flottaison** [flɔtɛzɔ̃] *nf*: **ligne de ~** waterline.

**flottant, e** [flɔtɑ̃, -ɑ̃t] *a* (*vêtement*) loose (-fitting) ; (*cours, barème*) floating.

**flotte** [flɔt] *nf* (*NAVIG*) fleet ; (*fam*) water ; rain.

**flottement** [flɔtmɑ̃] *nm* (*fig*) wavering, hesitation.

**flotter** [flɔte] *vi* to float ; (*nuage, odeur*) to drift ; (*drapeau*) to fly ; (*vêtements*) to hang loose ; (*monnaie*) to float // *vt* to float ; **faire ~** to float ; **flotteur** *nm* float.

**flottille** [flɔtij] *nf* flotilla.

**flou, e** [flu] *a* fuzzy, blurred ; (*fig*) woolly, vague.

**flouer** [flue] *vt* to swindle.

**fluctuation** [flyktɥasjɔ̃] *nf* fluctuation.

**fluet, te** [flyɛ, -ɛt] *a* thin, slight.

**fluide** [flɥid] *a* fluid ; (*circulation etc*) flowing freely // *nm* fluid ; (*force*) (*mysterious*) power ; **fluidité** *nf* fluidity ; free flow.

**fluor** [flyɔR] *nm* fluorine.

**fluorescent, e** [flyɔResɑ̃, -ɑ̃t] *a* fluorescent.

**flûte** [flyt] *nf* flute ; (*verre*) flute glass ; (*pain*) long loaf (*pl* loaves) ; **~!** drat it! ;

**petite ~** piccolo (*pl* s) ; **~ à bec** recorder ; **~ de Pan** panpipes *pl* ; **flûtiste** *nm/f* flautist, flute player.

**fluvial, e, aux** [flyvjal, -o] *a* river *cpd*, fluvial.

**flux** [fly] *nm* incoming tide ; (*écoulement*) flow ; **le ~ et le reflux** the ebb and flow.

**fluxion** [flyksjɔ̃] *nf*: **~ de poitrine** pneumonia.

**FM** *sigle voir* **modulation**.

**F.M.I.** *sigle m voir* **fonds**.

**foc** [fɔk] *nm* jib.

**focal, e, aux** [fɔkal, -o] *a* focal // *nf* focal length.

**fœtal, e, aux** [fetal, -o] *a* foetal, fetal.

**fœtus** [fetys] *nm* foetus, fetus.

**foi** [fwa] *nf* faith ; **sous la ~ du serment** under *ou* on oath ; **ajouter ~ à** to lend credence to ; **digne de ~** reliable ; **sur la ~ de** on the word *ou* strength of ; **être de bonne/mauvaise ~** to be sincere/insincere.

**foie** [fwa] *nm* liver ; **~ gras** foie gras.

**foin** [fwɛ̃] *nm* hay ; **faire les ~s** to make hay ; **faire du ~** (*fig: fam*) to kick up a row.

**foire** [fwaR] *nf* fair ; (*fête foraine*) (fun) fair ; **faire la ~** (*fig: fam*) to whoop it up ; **~ (exposition)** trade fair.

**fois** [fwa] *nf*: **une/deux ~** once/twice ; **trois/vingt ~** three/twenty times ; **2 ~ 2** twice 2, 2 times 2 ; **deux/quatre ~ plus grand (que)** twice/four times as large (as) ; **une ~** (*dans le passé*) once ; (*dans le futur*) sometime ; **une ~ pour toutes** once and for all ; **une ~ que c'est fait** once it's done ; **une ~ parti** once he had left ; **des ~** (*parfois*) sometimes ; **cette ~** this (*ou* that) time ; **à la ~** (*ensemble*) (all) at once ; **à la ~ grand et beau** both tall and handsome.

**foison** [fwazɔ̃] *nf*: **une ~ de** an abundance of ; **à ~** *ad* in plenty.

**foisonner** [fwazɔne] *vi* to abound ; **~ en** *ou* **de** to abound in.

**fol** [fɔl] *a voir* **fou**.

**folâtre** [fɔlɑtR(ə)] *a* playful.

**folâtrer** [fɔlɑtRe] *vi* to frolic (about).

**folie** [fɔli] *nf* (*d'une décision, d'un acte*) madness, folly ; (*état*) madness, insanity ; (*acte*) folly ; **la ~ des grandeurs** delusions of grandeur ; **faire des ~s** (*en dépenses*) to be extravagant.

**folklore** [fɔlklɔR] *nm* folklore ; **folklorique** *a* folk *cpd* ; (*fam*) weird.

**folle** [fɔl] *a, nf voir* **fou** ; **~ment** *ad* (*très*) madly, wildly.

**follet** [fɔlɛ] *am*: **feu ~** will-o'-the-wisp.

**fomenter** [fɔmɑ̃te] *vt* to stir up, foment.

**foncé, e** [fɔ̃se] *a* dark ; **bleu ~** dark blue.

**foncer** [fɔ̃se] *vt* to make darker // *vi* to go darker ; (*fam: aller vite*) to tear *ou* belt along ; **~ sur** to charge at.

**foncier, ière** [fɔ̃sje, -jɛR] *a* (*honnêteté etc*) basic, fundamental ; (*malhonnêteté*) deep-rooted, (*COMM*) real estate *cpd* ; **foncièrement** *ad* basically ; thoroughly.

**fonction** [fɔ̃ksjɔ̃] *nf* (*rôle*, MATH, LING) function ; (*emploi, poste*) post, position ; **~s** (*professionnelles*) duties ; **entrer en ~s** to take up one's post *ou* duties ; to take up office ; **voiture de** ~ car provided with the post ; **être** ~ **de** (*dépendre de*) to depend on ; **en** ~ **de** (*par rapport à*) according to ; **faire** ~ **de** to serve as ; **la** ~ **publique** the public *ou* state service.

**fonctionnaire** [fɔksjɔnɛR] *nm/f* state employee, local authority employee ; (*dans l'administration*) ≈ civil servant.

**fonctionnel, le** [fɔksjɔnɛl] *a* functional.

**fonctionnement** [fɔksjɔnmɑ̃] *nm* functioning.

**fonctionner** [fɔksjɔne] *vi* to work, function ; (*entreprise*) to operate, function ; **faire** ~ to work, operate.

**fond** [fɔ̃] *nm voir aussi* **fonds** ; (*d'un récipient, trou*) bottom ; (*d'une salle, scène*) back ; (*d'un tableau, décor*) background ; (*opposé à la forme*) content ; (*SPORT*): **le** ~ long distance (running) ; **au** ~ **de** at the bottom of ; at the back of ; **à** ~ *ad* (*connaître, soutenir*) thoroughly ; (*appuyer, visser*) right down *ou* home ; **à** ~ **(de train)** *ad* (*fam*) full tilt ; **dans le** ~**, au** ~ *ad* (*en somme*) basically, really ; **de** ~ **en comble** *ad* from top to bottom ; ~ **sonore** background noise ; ~ **de teint** make-up base.

**fondamental, e, aux** [fɔ̃damɑ̃tal, -o] *a* fundamental.

**fondant, e** [fɔ̃dɑ̃, -ɑ̃t] *a* (*neige*) melting ; (*poire*) that melts in the mouth ; (*chocolat*) fondant.

**fondateur, trice** [fɔ̃datœR, -tRis] *nm/f* founder ; **membre** ~ founder member.

**fondation** [fɔ̃dasjɔ̃] *nf* founding ; (*établissement*) foundation ; ~**s** *nfpl* (*d'une maison*) foundations ; **travaux de** ~ foundation works.

**fondé, e** [fɔ̃de] *a* (*accusation etc*) well-founded ; **mal** ~ unfounded ; **être** ~ **à croire** to have grounds for believing *ou* good reason to believe ; ~ **de pouvoir** *nm* authorized representative ; (*banking*) executive (*having the signature*).

**fondement** [fɔ̃dmɑ̃] *nm* (*derrière*) behind ; ~**s** *nmpl* foundations ; **sans** ~ *a* (*rumeur etc*) groundless, unfounded.

**fonder** [fɔ̃de] *vt* to found ; (*fig*): ~ **qch sur** to base sth on ; **se** ~ **sur** (*suj: personne*) to base o.s. on.

**fonderie** [fɔ̃dRi] *nf* smelting works *sg*.

**fondeur** [fɔ̃dœR] *nm*: **(ouvrier)** ~ caster.

**fondre** [fɔ̃dR(ə)] *vt* to melt ; (*dans l'eau: sucre, sel*) to dissolve ; (*fig: mélanger*) to merge, blend // *vi* to melt ; to dissolve ; (*fig*) to melt away ; (*se précipiter*): ~ **sur** to swoop down on ; **faire** ~ to melt ; to dissolve ; ~ **en larmes** to burst into tears.

**fondrière** [fɔ̃dRijɛR] *nf* rut.

**fonds** [fɔ̃] *nm* (*de bibliothèque*) collection ; (*COMM*): ~ **(de commerce)** business ; (*fig*): ~ **de probité** *etc* fund of integrity *etc* // *nmpl* (*argent*) funds ; **à** ~ **perdus** *ad* with little or no hope of getting the money back ; **F**~ **Monétaire International (FMI)** International Monetary Fund (IMF) ; ~ **de roulement** *nm* float.

**fondu, e** [fɔ̃dy] *a* (*beurre, neige*) melted ; (*métal*) molten // *nm* (*CINÉMA*): ~ **(enchaîné)** dissolve // *nf* (*CULIN*) fondue.

**font** *vb voir* **faire**.

**fontaine** [fɔ̃tɛn] *nf* fountain ; (*source*) spring.

**fonte** [fɔ̃t] *nf* melting ; (*métal*) cast iron ; **la** ~ **des neiges** the (spring) thaw.

**fonts baptismaux** [fɔ̃batismo] *nmpl* (baptismal) font *sg*.

**football** [futbol] *nm* football, soccer ; ~ **de table** table football ; ~**eur** *nm* footballer, football *ou* soccer player.

**footing** [futiŋ] *nm* jogging.

**for** [fɔR] *nm*: **dans son** ~ **intérieur** in one's heart of hearts.

**forage** [fɔRaʒ] *nm* drilling, boring.

**forain, e** [fɔRɛ̃, -ɛn] *a* fairground *cpd* // *nm* stallholder ; fairground entertainer.

**forçat** [fɔRsa] *nm* convict.

**force** [fɔR(ə)] *nf* strength ; (*puissance: surnaturelle etc*) power ; (*PHYSIQUE, MÉCANIQUE*) force ; ~**s** *nfpl* (*physiques*) strength *sg* ; (*MIL*) forces ; (*effectifs*): **d'importantes** ~**s de police** big contingents of police ; **à** ~ **d'insister** by dint of insisting ; **as he** (*ou* **I**) **kept on insisting** ; **de** ~ *ad* forcibly, by force ; **par la** ~ using force ; **faire** ~ **de rames/voiles** to ply the oars/cram on sail ; **être de** ~ **à faire** to be up to doing ; **de première** ~ first class ; ~ **d'âme** fortitude ; ~ **de frappe** strike force ; ~ **d'inertie** force of inertia ; **la** ~ **publique** the authorities responsible for public order ; ~**s d'intervention** peace-keeping force *sg* ; **les** ~**s de l'ordre** the police.

**forcé, e** [fɔRse] *a* forced ; unintended ; inevitable.

**forcément** [fɔRsemɑ̃] *ad* necessarily ; inevitably ; (*bien sûr*) of course.

**forcené, e** [fɔRsəne] *a* frenzied // *nm/f* maniac.

**forceps** [fɔRsɛps] *nm* forceps *pl*.

**forcer** [fɔRse] *vt* (*contraindre*): ~ **qn à faire** to force sb to do ; (*porte, serrure, plante*) to force ; (*moteur, voix*) to strain // *vi* (*SPORT*) to overtax o.s. ; ~ **la dose/l'allure** to overdo it/increase the pace ; ~ **l'attention/le respect** to command attention/respect.

**forcing** [fɔRsiŋ] *nm*: **faire le** ~ to pile on the pressure.

**forcir** [fɔRsiR] *vi* (*grossir*) to broaden out ; (*vent*) to freshen.

**forer** [fɔRe] *vt* to drill, bore.

**forestier, ière** [fɔRɛstje, -jɛR] *a* forest *cpd*.

**foret** [fɔRɛ] *nm* drill.

**forêt** [fɔRɛ] *nf* forest.

**foreuse** [fɔRøz] *nf* (electric) drill.

**forfait** [fɔRfɛ] *nm* (*COMM*) fixed *ou* set price ; all-in deal *ou* price ; (*crime*) infamy ; **déclarer** ~ to withdraw ; **gagner par** ~ to win by a walkover ; **travailler à** ~ to work for a lump sum ; **forfaitaire** *a* inclusive ; set ; ~**-vacances** *nm* (all-inclusive) holiday package.

**forfanterie** [fɔRfɑ̃tRi] *nf* boastfulness *q*.

**forge** [fɔRʒ(ə)] *nf* forge, smithy.

**forger** [fɔRʒe] *vt* to forge ; (*fig: personnalité*) to form ; (: *prétexte*) to contrive, make up ; **être forgé de toutes pièces** to be a complete fabrication.

**forgeron** [fɔRʒərɔ̃] *nm* (black)smith.

**formaliser** [fɔʀmalize]: **se ~** vi: **se ~ (de)** to take offence (at).

**formalité** [fɔʀmalite] nf formality.

**format** [fɔʀma] nm size; **petit ~** small size; (PHOTO) 35 mm (film).

**formation** [fɔʀmɑsjɔ̃] nf forming; training; (MUS) group; (MIL, AVIAT, GÉO) formation; **la ~ professionnelle** professional training.

**forme** [fɔʀm(ə)] nf (gén) form; (d'un objet) shape, form; **~s** nfpl (bonnes manières) proprieties; (d'une femme) figure sg; **en ~ de poire** pear-shaped, in the shape of a pear; **être en ~** (SPORT etc) to be on form; **en bonne et due ~** in due form; **prendre ~** to take shape.

**formel, le** [fɔʀmɛl] a (preuve, décision) definite, positive; (logique) formal; **~lement** ad (absolument) positively.

**former** [fɔʀme] vt (gén) to form; (éduquer: soldat, ingénieur etc) to train; **se ~** vi to form.

**formidable** [fɔʀmidabl(ə)] a tremendous.

**formol** [fɔʀmɔl] nm formalin, formol.

**formulaire** [fɔʀmylɛʀ] nm form.

**formule** [fɔʀmyl] nf (gén) formula; (formulaire) form; **~ de politesse** polite phrase; letter ending.

**formuler** [fɔʀmyle] vt (émettre: réponse, vœux) to formulate; (expliciter: sa pensée) to express.

**fort, e** [fɔʀ, fɔʀt(ə)] a strong; (intensité, rendement) high, great; (corpulent) stout // ad (serrer, frapper) hard; (sonner) loud(ly); (beaucoup) greatly, very much; (très) most // nm (édifice) fort; (point fort) strong point, forte; **c'est un peu ~!** it's a bit much!; **avoir ~ à faire pour faire** to have a hard job doing; **se faire ~ de ... to claim one can ...**; **~ bien/peu** very well/few; **au plus ~ de** (au milieu de) in the thick of, at the height of.

**forteresse** [fɔʀtəʀɛs] nf fortress.

**fortifiant** [fɔʀtifjɑ̃] nm tonic.

**fortifications** [fɔʀtifikɑsjɔ̃] nfpl fortifications.

**fortifier** [fɔʀtifje] vt to strengthen, fortify; (MIL) to fortify.

**fortin** [fɔʀtɛ̃] nm (small) fort.

**fortiori** [fɔʀtjɔʀi]: **à ~** ad all the more so.

**fortuit, e** [fɔʀtɥi, -it] a fortuitous, chance cpd.

**fortune** [fɔʀtyn] nf fortune; **faire ~** to make one's fortune; **de ~** a makeshift; chance cpd.

**fortuné, e** [fɔʀtyne] a wealthy, well-off.

**forum** [fɔʀɔm] nm forum.

**fosse** [fos] nf (grand trou) pit; (tombe) grave; **la ~ aux lions/ours** the lions' den/bear pit; **~ commune** common ou communal grave; **~** (d'orchestre) (orchestra) pit; **~ à purin** cesspit; **~s nasales** nasal fossae pl.

**fossé** [fose] nm ditch; (fig) gulf, gap.

**fossette** [fosɛt] nf dimple.

**fossile** [fosil] nm fossil // a fossilized, fossil.

**fossoyeur** [foswajœʀ] nm gravedigger.

**fou(fol), folle** [fu, fɔl] a mad; (déréglé etc) wild, erratic; (fam: extrême, très grand) terrific, tremendous // nm/f mad-man/woman // nm (du roi) jester, fool; (ÉCHECS) bishop; **être ~ de** to be mad ou crazy about; **faire le ~** (enfant etc) to play ou act the fool; **avoir le ~ rire** to have the giggles.

**foudre** [fudʀ(ə)] nf lightning; **~s** nfpl (colère) wrath sg.

**foudroyant, e** [fudʀwajɑ̃, -ɑ̃t] a lightning cpd, stunning.

**foudroyer** [fudʀwaje] vt to strike down; **il a été foudroyé** he was struck by lightning.

**fouet** [fwɛ] nm whip; (CULIN) whisk; **de plein ~** ad (se heurter) head on; **~ter** vt to whip; to whisk.

**fougère** [fuʒɛʀ] nf fern.

**fougue** [fug] nf ardour, spirit; **fougueux, euse** a fiery, ardent.

**fouille** [fuj] nf search; **~s** nfpl (archéologiques) excavations; **passer à la ~** to be searched.

**fouiller** [fuje] vt to search; (creuser) to dig // vi: **~ dans/parmi** to rummage in/among.

**fouillis** [fuji] nm jumble, muddle.

**fouine** [fwin] nf stone marten.

**fouiner** [fwine] vi (péj): **~ dans** to nose around ou about in.

**fouisseur, euse** [fwisœʀ, -øz] a burrowing.

**foulante** [fulɑ̃t] af: **pompe ~** force pump.

**foulard** [fulaʀ] nm scarf (pl scarves).

**foule** [ful] nf crowd; **la ~** crowds pl; **les ~s** the masses; **une ~ de** masses of.

**foulée** [fule] nf stride.

**fouler** [fule] vt to press; (sol) to tread upon; **se ~** (fam) to overexert o.s.; **se ~ la cheville** to sprain one's ankle; **~ aux pieds** to trample underfoot.

**foulure** [fulyʀ] nf sprain.

**four** [fuʀ] nm oven; (de potier) kiln; (THÉÂTRE: échec) flop.

**fourbe** [fuʀb(ə)] a deceitful; **~rie** nf deceitfulness; deceit.

**fourbi** [fuʀbi] nm (fam) gear, clobber.

**fourbir** [fuʀbiʀ] vt: **~ ses armes** (fig) to get ready for the fray.

**fourbu, e** [fuʀby] a exhausted.

**fourche** [fuʀʃ(ə)] nf pitchfork; (de bicyclette) fork.

**fourchette** [fuʀʃɛt] nf fork; (STATISTIQUE) bracket, margin.

**fourchu, e** [fuʀʃy] a split; forked.

**fourgon** [fuʀgɔ̃] nm van; (RAIL) wag(g)on; **~ mortuaire** hearse.

**fourgonnette** [fuʀgɔnɛt] nf (delivery) van.

**fourmi** [fuʀmi] nf ant; **~s** nfpl (fig) pins and needles; **~lière** nf ant-hill.

**fourmiller** [fuʀmije] vi to swarm; **~ de** to be teeming with; to be swarming with.

**fournaise** [fuʀnɛz] nf blaze; (fig) furnace, oven.

**fourneau, x** [fuʀno] nm stove.

**fournée** [fuʀne] nf batch.

**fourni, e** [fuʀni] a (barbe, cheveux) thick; (magasin): **bien ~ (en)** well stocked (with).

**fournir** [fuʀniʀ] vt to supply; (preuve, exemple) to provide, supply; (effort) to put in; **~ qch à qn** to supply sth to sb, to supply ou provide sb with sth; **~ qn en**

(*COMM*) to supply sb with; **fournisseur, euse** *nm/f* supplier.

**fourniture** [furnityʀ] *nf* supply(ing); ∼s *nfpl* supplies; ∼s **de bureau** office supplies, stationery; ∼s **scolaires** school stationery.

**fourrage** [fuʀaʒ] *nm* fodder, forage.

**fourrager** [fuʀaʒe] *vi:* ∼ **dans/ parmi** to rummage through/among.

**fourrager, ère** [fuʀaʒe, -ɛʀ] a fodder *cpd.*

**fourré, e** [fuʀe] a (*bonbon, chocolat*) filled; (*manteau, botte*) fur-lined // *nm* thicket.

**fourreau, x** [fuʀo] *nm* sheath; (*de parapluie*) cover.

**fourrer** [fuʀe] *vt (fam):* ∼ **qch dans** to stick *ou* shove sth into; **se** ∼ **dans/sous** to ʒet into/under.

**fourre-tout** [fuʀtu] *nm inv* (*sac*) holdall; (*péj*) junk room *ou* cupboard; (*fig*) rag-bag.

**fourreur** [fuʀœʀ] *nm* f ‾ier.

**fourrière** [fuʀjɛʀ] *nf* pound.

**fourrure** [fuʀyʀ] *nf* fur; (*sur l'animal*) coat; **manteau/col de** ∼ fur coat/collar.

**fourvoyer** [fuʀvwaje]: **se** ∼ *vi* to go astray, stray; **se** ∼ **dans** to stray into.

**foutre** [futʀ(ə)] *vt (fam!)* = **ficher** (*fam*); **foutu, e** a (*fam!*) = **fichu, e** a.

**foyer** [fwaje] *nm* (*de cheminée*) hearth; (*fig*) seat, centre; family; home; (social) club; hostel; (*salon*) foyer; (*OPTIQUE, PHOTO*) focus *sg*; **lunettes à double** ∼ bi-focal glasses.

**fracas** [fʀaka] *nm* din; crash; roar.

**fracassant, e** [fʀakasɑ̃, -ɑ̃t] a sensational, staggering.

**fracasser** [fʀakase] *vt* to smash.

**fraction** [fʀaksjɔ̃] *nf* fraction; **fractionner** *vt* to divide (up), split (up).

**fracture** [fʀaktyʀ] *nf* fracture; ∼ **du crâne** fractured skull; ∼ **de la jambe** broken leg.

**fracturer** [fʀaktyʀe] *vt* (*coffre, serrure*) to break open; (*os, membre*) to fracture.

**fragile** [fʀaʒil] a fragile, delicate; (*fig*) frail; **fragilité** *nf* fragility.

**fragment** [fʀagmɑ̃] *nm* (*d'un objet*) fragment, piece; (*d'un texte*) passage, extract; **fragmentaire** a sketchy; **fragmenter** *vt* to split up.

**frai** [fʀɛ] *nm* spawn; spawning.

**fraîche** [fʀɛʃ] a voir **frais**; ∼**ment** ad coolly; freshly, newly; **fraîcheur** *nf* coolness; freshness; **fraîchir** *vi* to get cooler; (*vent*) to freshen.

**frais, fraîche** [fʀɛ, fʀɛʃ] a (*air, eau, accueil*) cool; (*petit pois, œufs, souvenir, couleur, troupes*) fresh // ad (*récemment*) newly, fresh(ly); **il fait** ∼ it's cool; **servir** ∼ chill before serving, serve chilled // *nm:* **mettre au** ∼ to put in a cool place; **prendre le** ∼ to take a breath of cool air // *nmpl* (*débours*) expenses; (*COMM*) costs; charges; **faire des** ∼ to spend; to go to a lot of expense; ∼ **de déplacement** travel(ling) expenses; ∼**généraux** overheads; ∼ **de scolarité** school fees.

**fraise** [fʀɛz] *nf* strawberry; (*TECH*) countersink (bit); (*de dentiste*) drill; ∼ **des bois** wild strawberry; **fraiser** *vt* to countersink; **fraisier** *nm* strawberry plant.

**framboise** [fʀɑ̃bwaz] *nf* raspberry; **framboisier** *nm* raspberry bush.

**franc, franche** [fʀɑ̃, fʀɑ̃ʃ] a (*personne*) frank, straightforward; (*visage, rire*) open; (*net: refus, couleur*) clear; (: *coupure*) clean; (*intensif*) downright; (*exempt*): ∼ **de port** free, postage paid, carriage paid // ad: **parler** ∼ to be frank ou candid // *nm* franc.

**français, e** [fʀɑ̃sɛ, -ɛz] a French // *nm/f:* **F**∼, e Frenchman/woman // *nm* (*langue*) French; **les F**∼ the French.

**France** [fʀɑ̃s] *nf:* **la** ∼ France.

**franche** [fʀɑ̃ʃ] a voir **franc**; ∼**ment** ad frankly; clearly; (*tout à fait*) downright.

**franchir** [fʀɑ̃ʃiʀ] *vt* (*obstacle*) to clear, get over; (*seuil, ligne, rivière*) to cross; (*distance*) to cover.

**franchise** [fʀɑ̃ʃiz] *nf* frankness; (*douanière, d'impôt*) exemption; (*ASSURANCES*) excess.

**franciser** [fʀɑ̃size] *vt* to gallicize, Frenchify.

**franc-maçon** [fʀɑ̃masɔ̃] *nm* freemason; **franc-maçonnerie** *nf* freemasonry.

**franco** [fʀɑ̃ko] ad (*COMM*) carriage paid, postage paid.

**franco...** [fʀɑ̃ko] préfixe: ∼**phile** a francophile; ∼**phone** a French-speaking // *nm/f* French speaker; ∼**phonie** *nf* French-speaking communities.

**franc-parler** [fʀɑ̃paʀle] *nm inv* outspokenness.

**franc-tireur** [fʀɑ̃tiʀœʀ] *nm* (*MIL*) irregular; (*fig*) freelance.

**frange** [fʀɑ̃ʒ] *nf* fringe.

**frangipane** [fʀɑ̃ʒipan] *nf* almond paste.

**franquette** [fʀɑ̃kɛt]: **à la bonne** ∼ ad without (any) fuss.

**frappe** [fʀap] *nf* (*d'une dactylo, pianiste, machine à écrire*) touch; (*BOXE*) punch; (*péj*) hood, thug.

**frappé, e** [fʀape] a iced.

**frapper** [fʀape] *vt* to hit, strike; (*étonner*) to strike; (*monnaie*) to strike, stamp; **se** ∼ (*s'inquiéter*) to get worked up; ∼ **à la porte** to knock (at) the door; ∼ **dans ses mains** to clap one's hands; ∼ **du poing sur** to bang one's fist on; **frappé de stupeur** dumbfounded.

**frasques** [fʀask(ə)] *nfpl* escapades.

**fraternel, le** [fʀatɛʀnɛl] a brotherly, fraternal.

**fraterniser** [fʀatɛʀnize] *vi* to fraternize.

**fraternité** [fʀatɛʀnite] *nf* brotherhood.

**fratricide** [fʀatʀisid] a fratricidal.

**fraude** [fʀod] *nf* fraud; (*SCOL*) cheating; **passer qch en** ∼ to smuggle sth in (*ou* out); ∼ **fiscale** tax evasion; **frauder** *vi, vt* to cheat; **fraudeur, euse** *nm/f* person guilty of fraud; candidate who cheats; tax evader; **frauduleux, euse** a fraudulent.

**frayer** [fʀeje] *vt* to open up, clear // *vi* to spawn; (*fréquenter*) ∼ **avec** to mix ou associate with; **se** ∼ **un passage dans** to clear o.s. a path through, force one's way through.

**frayeur** [fʀejœʀ] *nf* fright.

**fredaines** [fʀədɛn] *nfpl* mischief *sg*, escapades.

**fredonner** [fʀədɔne] *vt* to hum.
**freezer** [fʀizœʀ] *nm* freezing compartment.
**frégate** [fʀegat] *nf* frigate.
**frein** [fʀɛ̃] *nm* brake ; **mettre un ~ à** (*fig*) to put a brake on, check ; **~ à main** handbrake ; **~ moteur** engine braking ; **~s à disques** disc brakes ; **~s à tambour** drum brakes.
**freinage** [fʀɛnaʒ] *nm* braking ; **distance de ~** braking distance ; **traces de ~** tyre marks.
**freiner** [fʀene] *vi* to brake // *vt* (*progrès etc*) to check.
**frelaté, e** [fʀəlate] *a* adulterated ; (*fig*) tainted.
**frêle** [fʀɛl] *a* frail, fragile.
**frelon** [fʀəlɔ̃] *nm* hornet.
**frémir** [fʀemiʀ] *vi* to tremble, shudder ; to shiver ; to quiver.
**frêne** [fʀɛn] *nm* ash.
**frénésie** [fʀenezi] *nf* frenzy ; **frénétique** *a* frenzied, frenetic.
**fréquemment** [fʀekamɑ̃] *ad* frequently.
**fréquence** [fʀekɑ̃s] *nf* frequency.
**fréquent, e** [fʀekɑ̃, -ɑ̃t] *a* frequent.
**fréquentation** [fʀekɑ̃tasjɔ̃] *nf* frequenting ; seeing ; **~s** *nfpl* company *sg*.
**fréquenté, e** [fʀekɑ̃te] *a*: **très ~** (very) busy ; **mal ~** patronized by disreputable elements.
**fréquenter** [fʀekɑ̃te] *vt* (*lieu*) to frequent ; (*personne*) to see (frequently).
**frère** [fʀɛʀ] *nm* brother.
**fresque** [fʀɛsk(ə)] *nf* (*ART*) fresco.
**fret** [fʀɛ] *nm* freight.
**fréter** [fʀete] *vt* to charter.
**frétiller** [fʀetije] *vi* to wriggle.
**fretin** [fʀətɛ̃] *nm*: **le menu ~** the small fry.
**friable** [fʀijabl(ə)] *a* crumbly, friable.
**friand, e** [fʀijɑ̃, -ɑ̃d] *a*: **~ de** very fond of.
**friandise** [fʀijɑ̃diz] *nf* sweet.
**fric** [fʀik] *nm* (*fam*) cash.
**fric-frac** [fʀikfʀak] *nm* break-in.
**friche** [fʀiʃ] *nf*: **en ~** *a*, *ad* (lying) fallow.
**friction** [fʀiksjɔ̃] *nf* (*massage*) rub, rub-down ; (*chez le coiffeur*) scalp massage ; (*TECH*, *fig*) friction ; **frictionner** *vt* to rub (down) ; to massage.
**frigidaire** [fʀiʒidɛʀ] *nm* ® refrigerator.
**frigide** [fʀiʒid] *a* frigid ; **frigidité** *nf* frigidity.
**frigo** [fʀigo] *nm* fridge.
**frigorifier** [fʀigɔʀifje] *vt* to refrigerate ; **frigorifique** *a* refrigerating.
**frileux, euse** [fʀilø, -øz] *a* sensitive to (the) cold.
**frimas** [fʀima] *nmpl* wintry weather *sg*.
**frimousse** [fʀimus] *nf* (sweet) little face.
**fringale** [fʀɛ̃gal] *nf*: **avoir la ~** to be ravenous.
**fringant, e** [fʀɛ̃gɑ̃, -ɑ̃t] *a* dashing.
**fripé, e** [fʀipe] *a* crumpled.
**fripier, ère** [fʀipje, -jɛʀ] *nm/f* secondhand clothes dealer.
**fripon, ne** [fʀipɔ̃, -ɔn] *a* roguish, mischievous // *nm/f* rascal, rogue.

**fripouille** [fʀipuj] *nf* scoundrel.
**frire** [fʀiʀ] *vt*, *vi*, **faire ~** to fry.
**frise** [fʀiz] *nf* frieze.
**frisé, e** [fʀize] *a* curly, curly-haired ; (**chicorée**) **~e** curly endive.
**friser** [fʀize] *vt*, *vi* to curl ; **se faire ~** to have one's hair curled.
**frisson** [fʀisɔ̃] *nm* shudder, shiver ; quiver ; **frissonner** *vi* to shudder, shiver ; to quiver.
**frit, e** [fʀi, fʀit] *pp de* **frire** // *a* fried // *nf*: (**pommes**) **~es** chips, French fried potatoes ; **friteuse** *nf* chip pan ; **friture** *nf* (*huile*) (deep) fat ; (*plat*): **friture (de poissons)** fried fish ; (*RADIO*) crackle, crackling *q*.
**frivole** [fʀivɔl] *a* frivolous.
**froid, e** [fʀwa, fʀwad] *a*, *nm* cold ; **il fait ~** it's cold ; **avoir ~** to be cold ; **prendre ~** to catch a chill *ou* cold ; **jeter un ~** (*fig*) to cast a chill ; **être en ~ avec** to be on bad terms with ; **froidement** *ad* (*accueillir*) coldly ; (*décider*) coolly.
**froisser** [fʀwase] *vt* to crumple (up), crease ; (*fig*) to hurt, offend ; **se ~** *vi* to crumple, crease ; to take offence *ou* umbrage ; **se ~ un muscle** to strain a muscle.
**frôler** [fʀole] *vt* to brush against ; (*suj*: *projectile*) to skim past ; (*fig*) to come within a hair's breadth of ; to come very close to.
**fromage** [fʀɔmaʒ] *nm* cheese ; **~ blanc** soft white cheese ; **~ de tête** pork brawn ; **fromager, ère** *nm/f* cheesemonger ; **fromagerie** *nf* cheese dairy.
**froment** [fʀɔmɑ̃] *nm* wheat.
**froncer** [fʀɔ̃se] *vt* to gather ; **~ les sourcils** to frown.
**frondaisons** [fʀɔ̃dɛzɔ̃] *nfpl* foliage *sg*.
**fronde** [fʀɔ̃d] *nf* sling ; (*fig*) rebellion, rebelliousness.
**front** [fʀɔ̃] *nm* forehead, brow ; (*MIL*) front ; **avoir le ~ de faire** to have the effrontery *ou* front to do ; **de ~** *ad* (*se heurter*) head-on ; (*rouler*) together (*i.e. 2 or 3 abreast*) ; (*simultanément*) at once ; **faire ~ à** to face up to ; **~ de mer** (sea) front ; **frontal, e, aux** *a* frontal.
**frontalier, ière** [fʀɔ̃talje, -jɛʀ] *a* border *cpd*, frontier *cpd* // *nm/f*: (**travailleurs**) **~s** workers who cross the border to go to work, commuters from across the border.
**frontière** [fʀɔ̃tjɛʀ] *nf* (*GÉO*, *POL*) frontier, border ; (*fig*) frontier, boundary.
**frontispice** [fʀɔ̃tispis] *nm* frontispiece.
**fronton** [fʀɔ̃tɔ̃] *nm* pediment ; (*de pelote basque*) (front) wall.
**frottement** [fʀɔtmɑ̃] *nm* rubbing, scraping ; rubbing *ou* scraping noise.
**frotter** [fʀɔte] *vi* to rub, scrape // *vt* to rub ; (*pour nettoyer*) to rub (up) ; to scrub ; **~ une allumette** to strike a match.
**frottoir** [fʀɔtwaʀ] *nm* (*d'allumettes*) friction strip ; (*pour encaustiquer*) (long-handled) brush.
**fructifier** [fʀyktifje] *vi* to yield a profit ; **faire ~** to turn to good account.
**fructueux, euse** [fʀyktɥø, -øz] *a* fruitful ; profitable.

**frugal, e, aux** [fʀygal, -o] *a* frugal.

**fruit** [fʀɥi] *nm* fruit (*gén q*); ~**s de mer** seafood(s); ~**s secs** dried fruit *sg*; **fruité, e** *a* fruity; **fruitier, ière** *a*: **arbre fruitier** fruit tree // *nm/f* fruiterer, greengrocer.

**fruste** [fʀyst(ə)] *a* unpolished. uncultivated.

**frustration** [fʀystʀɑsjɔ̃] *nf* frustration.

**frustrer** [fʀystʀe] *vt* to frustrate.

**FS** *sigle = franc suisse*.

**fugace** [fygas] *a* fleeting.

**fugitif, ive** [fyʒitif, -iv] *a* (*lueur, amour*) fleeting; (*prisonnier etc*) fugitive, runaway // *nm/f* fugitive.

**fugue** [fyg] *nf* (*d'un enfant*) running away *q*; (*MUS*) fugue; **faire une** ~ to run away, abscond.

**fuir** [fɥiʀ] *vt* to flee from; (*éviter*) to shun // *vi* to run away; (*gaz, robinet*) to leak.

**fuite** [fɥit] *nf* flight; (*écoulement*) leak, leakage; (*divulgation*) leak; **être en** ~ to be on the run; **mettre en** ~ to put to flight; **prendre la** ~ to take flight.

**fulgurant, e** [fylgyʀɑ̃, -ɑ̃t] *a* a lightning *cpd*, dazzling.

**fulminer** [fylmine] *vi*: ~ (**contre**) to thunder forth (against).

**fume-cigarette** [fymsigaʀɛt] *nm inv* cigarette holder.

**fumé, e** [fyme] *a* (*CULIN*) smoked; (*verres*) (grey-)tinted // *nf* smoke.

**fumer** [fyme] *vi* to smoke; (*soupe*) to steam // *vt* to smoke; (*terre, champ*) to manure.

**fumerie** [fymʀi] *nf*: ~ **d'opium** opium den.

**fumerolles** [fymʀɔl] *nfpl* gas and smoke (*from volcano*).

**fûmes** *vb voir* **être**.

**fumet** [fymɛ] *nm* aroma.

**fumeur, euse** [fymœʀ, -øz] *nm/f* smoker.

**fumeux, euse** [fymø, -øz] *a* (*péj*) woolly.

**fumier** [fymje] *nm* manure.

**fumigation** [fymigɑsjɔ̃] *nf* fumigation.

**fumigène** [fymiʒɛn] *a* smoke *cpd*.

**fumiste** [fymist(ə)] *nm* (*ramoneur*) chimney sweep // *nm/f* (*péj*) shirker; phoney.

**fumisterie** [fymistəʀi] *nf* (*péj*) fraud, con.

**fumoir** [fymwaʀ] *nm* smoking room.

**funambule** [fynɑ̃byl] *nm* tightrope walker.

**funèbre** [fynɛbʀ(ə)] *a* funeral *cpd*; (*fig*) doleful; funereal.

**funérailles** [fyneʀɑj] *nfpl* funeral *sg*.

**funéraire** [fyneʀɛʀ] *a* funeral *cpd*, funerary.

**funeste** [fynɛst(ə)] *a* disastrous; deathly.

**funiculaire** [fynikylɛʀ] *nm* funicular (railway).

**fur** [fyʀ]: **au** ~ **et à mesure** *ad* as one goes along; **au** ~ **et à mesure que** as, as soon as; **au** ~ **et à mesure de leur progression** as they advance (*ou* advanced).

**furet** [fyʀɛ] *nm* ferret.

**fureter** [fyʀte] *vi* (*péj*) to nose about.

**fureur** [fyʀœʀ] *nf* fury; (*passion*): ~ **de** passion for; **faire** ~ to be all the rage.

**furibond, e** [fyʀibɔ̃, -ɔ̃d] *a* furious.

**furie** [fyʀi] *nf* fury; (*femme*) shrew, vixen; **en** ~ (*mer*) raging; **furieux, euse** *a* furious.

**furoncle** [fyʀɔ̃kl(ə)] *nm* boil, furuncle.

**furtif, ive** [fyʀtif, -iv] *a* furtive.

**fus** *vb voir* **être**.

**fusain** [fyzɛ̃] *nm* (*BOT*) spindle-tree; (*ART*) charcoal.

**fuseau, x** [fyzo] *nm* (*pour filer*) spindle; ~ **horaire** time zone.

**fusée** [fyze] *nf* rocket; ~ **éclairante** flare.

**fuselage** [fyzlaʒ] *nm* fuselage.

**fuselé, e** [fyzle] *a* slender; tapering.

**fuser** [fyze] *vi* (*rires etc*) to burst forth.

**fusible** [fyzibl(ə)] *nm* (*ÉLEC: fil*) fuse wire; (: *fiche*) fuse.

**fusil** [fyzi] *nm* (*de guerre, à canon rayé*) rifle, gun; (*de chasse, à canon lisse*) shotgun, gun; **fusilier** [-lje] *nm* rifleman; **fusillade** [-jad] *nf* gunfire *q*, shooting *q*; shooting battle; **fusiller** *vt* to shoot; ~-**mitrailleur** *nm* machine gun.

**fusion** [fyzjɔ̃] *nf* fusion, melting; (*fig*) merging; (*COMM*) merger; **en** ~ (*métal, roches*) molten; **fusionner** *vi* to merge.

**fustiger** [fystiʒe] *vt* to denounce.

**fut** *vb voir* **être**.

**fût** [fy] *nm* (*tonneau*) barrel, cask; (*de canon*) stock; (*d'arbre*) bole, trunk; (*de colonne*) shaft.

**futaie** [fytɛ] *nf* forest, plantation.

**futile** [fytil] *a* futile; frivolous.

**futur, e** [fytyʀ] *a, nm* future; **au** ~ (*LING*) in the future; ~**iste** *a* futuristic.

**fuyant, e** [fɥijɑ̃, -ɑ̃t] *vb voir* **fuir** // *a* (*regard etc*) evasive; (*lignes etc*) receding; (*perspective*) vanishing.

**fuyard, e** [fɥijaʀ, -aʀd(ə)] *nm/f* runaway.

# G

**gabardine** [gabaʀdin] *nf* gabardine.

**gabarit** [gabaʀi] *nm* (*fig*) size; calibre; (*TECH*) template.

**gabegie** [gabʒi] *nf* (*péj*) chaos.

**gâcher** [gɑʃe] *vt* (*gâter*) to spoil, ruin; (*gaspiller*) to waste; (*plâtre*) to temper; (*mortier*) to mix.

**gâchette** [gɑʃɛt] *nf* trigger.

**gâchis** [gɑʃi] *nm* waste *q*.

**gadoue** [gadu] *nf* sludge.

**gaffe** [gaf] *nf* (*instrument*) boat hook; (*erreur*) blunder; **faire** ~ (*fam*) to be careful; **gaffer** *vi* to blunder.

**gag** [gag] *nm*. gag.

**gage** [gaʒ] *nm* (*dans un jeu*) forfeit; (*fig: de fidélité*) token; ~**s** *nmpl* (*salaire*) wages; (*garantie*) guarantee *sg*; **mettre en** ~ to pawn; **laisser en** ~ to leave as a security.

**gager** [gaʒe] *vt*: ~ **que** to bet *ou* wager that.

**gageure** [gaʒyʀ] *nf*: **c'est une** ~ it's attempting the impossible.

**gagnant, e** [gaɲɑ̃, -ɑ̃t] *a*: **billet/ numéro** ~ winning ticket/number // *nm/f* winner.

**gagne-pain** [gaɲpɛ̃] *nm inv* job.

**gagner** [gaɲe] *vt* to win; (*somme d'argent, revenu*) to earn; (*aller vers, atteindre*) to reach // *vi* to win ; (*fig*) to gain ; ~ **du temps/de la place** to gain time/save space ; ~ **sa vie** to earn one's living ; ~ **du terrain** to gain ground ; ~ **à faire** (*s'en trouver bien*) to be better off doing.

**gai, e** [ge] *a* gay, cheerful ; (*un peu ivre*) merry.

**gaieté** [gete] *nf* cheerfulness ; ~**s** *nfpl* (*souvent ironique*) delights ; **de** ~ **de cœur** with a light heart.

**gaillard, e** [gajaʀ, -aʀd(ə)] *a* (*robuste*) sprightly ; (*grivois*) bawdy, ribald // *nm/f* (*strapping*) fellow/wench.

**gain** [gɛ̃] *nm* (*revenu*) earnings *pl* ; (*bénéfice: gén pl*) profits *pl* ; (*au jeu: gén pl*) winnings *pl* ; (*fig: de temps, place*) saving ; **avoir** ~ **de cause** to win the case ; (*fig*) to be proved right.

**gaine** [gɛn] *nf* (*corset*) girdle ; (*fourreau*) sheath ; (*de fil électrique etc*) outer covering ; ~**-culotte** *nf* pantie girdle ; **gainer** *vt* to cover.

**gala** [gala] *nm* official reception ; **soirée de** ~ gala evening.

**galant, e** [galɑ̃, -ɑ̃t] *a* (*courtois*) courteous, gentlemanly ; (*entreprenant*) flirtatious, gallant ; (*aventure, poésie*) amorous ; **en** ~**e compagnie** with a lady friend/gentleman friend.

**galaxie** [galaksi] *nf* galaxy.

**galbe** [galb(ə)] *nm* curve(s) ; shapeliness.

**gale** [gal] *nf* scabies *sg*.

**galéjade** [galeʒad] *nf* tall story.

**galère** [galɛʀ] *nf* galley.

**galerie** [galʀi] *nf* gallery ; (*THÉÂTRE*) circle ; (*de voiture*) roof rack ; (*fig: spectateurs*) audience ; ~ **marchande** shopping arcade ; ~ **de peinture** (*private*) art gallery.

**galérien** [galeʀjɛ̃] *nm* galley slave.

**galet** [galɛ] *nm* pebble ; (*TECH*) wheel ; ~**s** *nmpl* pebbles, shingle *sg*.

**galette** [galɛt] *nf* flat cake.

**galeux, euse** [galø, -øz] *a*: **un chien** ~ a mangy dog.

**galimatias** [galimatja] *nm* (*péj*) gibberish.

**Galles** [gal] *n*: **le pays de** ~ Wales.

**gallicisme** [galisism(ə)] *nm* French idiom ; (*tournure fautive*) gallicism.

**gallois, e** [galwa, -waz] *a, nm* (*langue*) Welsh // *nm/f*: **G**~, **e** Welshman/woman.

**galon** [galɔ̃] *nm* (*MIL*) stripe ; (*décoratif*) piece of braid.

**galop** [galo] *nm* gallop ; **au** ~ at a gallop.

**galopade** [galɔpad] *nf* stampede.

**galoper** [galɔpe] *vi* to gallop.

**galopin** [galɔpɛ̃] *nm* urchin, ragamuffin.

**galvaniser** [galvanize] *vt* to galvanize.

**galvauder** [galvode] *vt* to debase.

**gambader** [gɑ̃bade] *vi* (*animal, enfant*) to leap about.

**gamelle** [gamɛl] *nf* mess tin ; billy can ; (*fam*): **ramasser une** ~ to come a cropper.

**gamin, e** [gamɛ̃, -in] *nm/f* kid // *a* mischievous, playful.

**gamme** [gam] *nf* (*MUS*) scale ; (*fig*) range.

**gammé, e** [game] *a*: **croix** ~**e** swastika.

**gang** [gɑ̃g] *nm* gang.

**ganglion** [gɑ̃glijɔ̃] *nm* ganglion.

**gangrène** [gɑ̃gʀɛn] *nf* gangrene.

**gangue** [gɑ̃g] *nf* coating.

**ganse** [gɑ̃s] *nf* braid.

**gant** [gɑ̃] *nm* glove ; ~ **de toilette** (face) flannel ; ~**s de boxe** boxing gloves ; **ganté, e** *a*: **ganté de blanc** wearing white gloves ; **ganterie** *nf* glove trade ; glove shop.

**garage** [gaʀaʒ] *nm* garage ; ~ **à vélos** bicycle shed ; **garagiste** *nm/f* garage owner ; garage mechanic *ou* man.

**garant, e** [gaʀɑ̃, -ɑ̃t] *nm/f* guarantor // *nm* guarantee ; **se porter** ~ **de** to vouch for ; to be answerable for.

**garantie** [gaʀɑ̃ti] *nf* guarantee ; (*gage*) security, surety ; **(bon de)** ~ guarantee *ou* warranty slip.

**garantir** [gaʀɑ̃tiʀ] *vt* to guarantee ; (*protéger*): ~ **de** to protect from ; **je vous garantis que** I can assure you that ; **garanti 2 ans/pure laine** guaranteed for 2 years/pure wool.

**garçon** [gaʀsɔ̃] *nm* boy ; (*célibataire*) bachelor ; (*jeune homme*) boy, lad ; ~ **boucher/coiffeur** butcher's/hairdresser's assistant ; ~ **de courses** messenger ; ~ **d'écurie** stable lad ; **garçonnet** *nm* small boy ; **garçonnière** *nf* bachelor flat.

**garde** [gaʀd(ə)] *nm* (*de prisonnier*) guard ; (*de domaine etc*) warden ; (*soldat, sentinelle*) guardsman // *nf* guarding ; looking after ; (*soldats, BOXE, ESCRIME*) guard ; (*faction*) watch ; (*d'une arme*) hilt ; (*TYPO*): **(page de)** ~ endpaper ; flyleaf ; **de** ~ *a, ad* on duty ; **monter la** ~ to stand guard ; **être sur ses** ~**s** to be on one's guard ; **mettre en** ~ to warn ; **prendre** ~ **(à)** to be careful (of) ; ~ **champêtre** rural policeman ; ~ **du corps** *nm* bodyguard ; ~ **d'enfants** *nf* child minder ; ~ **des enfants** *nf* (*après divorce*) custody of the children ; ~ **forestier** *nm* forest warden ; ~ **mobile** *nm, nf* mobile guard ; ~ **des Sceaux** *nm* ≈ Lord Chancellor ; ~ **à vue** *nf* (*JUR*) ≈ police custody ; ~**-à-vous** *nm inv*: **être/se mettre au** ~**-à-vous** to be at/stand to attention.

**garde...** [gaʀd(ə)] *préfixe*: ~**-barrière** *nm/f* level-crossing keeper ; ~**-boue** *nm inv* mudguard ; ~**-chasse** *nm* gamekeeper ; ~**-fou** *nm* railing, parapet ; ~**-malade** *nf* home nurse ; ~**-manger** *nm inv* meat safe ; pantry, larder ; ~**-meuble** *nm* furniture depository ; ~**-pêche** *nm inv* water bailiff ; fisheries protection ship.

**garder** [gaʀde] *vt* (*conserver*) to keep ; (*surveiller: prisonnier, enfants*) to look after ; (: *immeuble, lieu*) to guard ; ~ **le lit/la chambre** to stay in bed/indoors ; **se** ~ (*aliment: se conserver*) to keep ; **se** ~ **de faire** to be careful not to do ; **pêche/chasse gardée** private fishing/hunting (ground).

**garderie** [gaʀdəʀi] *nf* day nursery, crèche.

**garde-robe** [gaʀdəʀɔb] *nf* wardrobe.

**gardeur, euse** [gaʀdœʀ, -øz] *nm/f* (*d'animaux*) cowherd ; goatherd.

**gardien, ne** [gaʀdjɛ̃, -jɛn] *nm/f* (*garde*) guard ; (*de prison*) warder ; (*de domaine, réserve*) warden ; (*de musée etc*) attendant ; (*de phare, cimetière*) keeper ; (*d'immeuble*) caretaker ; (*fig*) guardian ; ~ **de but**

goalkeeper ; ~ **de nuit** night watchman ; ~ **de la paix** policeman.
**gare** [gaʀ] *nf* (railway) station // *excl* watch out! ; ~ **à ne pas ... mind you don't** ... ; ~ **maritime** harbour station ; ~ **routière** coach station.
**garenne** [gaʀɛn] *nf voir* **lapin.**
**garer** [gaʀe] *vt* to park ; **se** ~ to park ; (*pour laisser passer*) to draw into the side.
**gargariser** [gaʀgaʀize]: **se** ~ *vi* to gargle ; **gargarisme** *nm* gargling *q* ; gargle.
**gargote** [gaʀgɔt] *nf* cheap restaurant.
**gargouille** [gaʀguj] *nf* gargoyle.
**gargouiller** [gaʀguje] *vi* to gurgle.
**garnement** [gaʀnəmã] *nm* tearaway, scallywag.
**garni, e** [gaʀni] *a* (*plat*) served with vegetables (and chips or pasta or rice) // *nm* furnished accommodation *q*.
**garnir** [gaʀniʀ] *vt* to decorate ; to fill ; to cover ; ~ **qch de** (*orner*) to decorate sth with ; to trim sth with ; (*approvisionner*) to fill *ou* stock sth with ; (*protéger*) to fit sth with ; (*CULIN*) to garnish sth with.
**garnison** [gaʀnizɔ̃] *nf* garrison.
**garniture** [gaʀnityʀ] *nf* (*CULIN*) vegetables *pl* ; trimmings *pl* ; filling ; (*décoration*) trimming ; (*protection*) fittings *pl* ; ~ **de frein** brake lining ; ~ **intérieure** (*AUTO*) interior trim.
**garrot** [gaʀo] *nm* (*MÉD*) tourniquet ; (*torture*) garrotte.
**garrotter** [gaʀote] *vt* to tie up ; (*fig*) to muzzle.
**gars** [ga] *nm* lad ; guy.
**gas-oil** [gazɔjl] *nm* diesel oil.
**gaspillage** [gaspijaʒ] *nm* waste.
**gaspiller** [gaspije] *vt* to waste.
**gastrique** [gastʀik] *a* gastric, stomach *cpd*.
**gastronome** [gastʀɔnɔm] *nm/f* gourmet.
**gastronomie** [gastʀɔnɔmi] *nf* gastronomy.
**gâteau, x** [gato] *nm* cake ; ~ **sec** biscuit.
**gâter** [gate] *vt* to spoil ; **se** ~ *vi* (*dent, fruit*) to go bad ; (*temps, situation*) to change for the worse.
**gâterie** [gatʀi] *nf* little treat.
**gâteux, euse** [gatø, -øz] *a* senile.
**gauche** [goʃ] *a* left, left-hand ; (*maladroit*) awkward, clumsy // *nf* (*POL*) left (wing) ; **à** ~ on the left ; (*direction*) (to the) left ; **à** ~ **de** (on *ou* to the) left of ; **à la** ~ **de** to the left of ; **gaucher, ère** *a* left-handed ; ~**rie** *nf* awkwardness, clumsiness ; **gauchir** *vt* to warp ; **gauchisant, e** *a* with left-wing tendencies ; **gauchiste** *nm/f* leftist.
**gaufre** [gofʀ(ə)] *nf* waffle.
**gaufrer** [gofʀe] *vt* (*papier*) to emboss ; (*tissu*) to goffer.
**gaufrette** [gofʀɛt] *nf* wafer.
**gaule** [gol] *nf* (long) pole.
**gaulois, e** [golwa, -waz] *a* Gallic ; (*grivois*) bawdy // *nm/f*: **G~, e** Gaul.
**gausser** [gose]: **se** ~ **de** *vt* to deride.
**gaver** [gave] *vt* to force-feed ; (*fig*): ~ **de** to cram with, fill up with.
**gaz** [gaz] *nm inv* gas ; **mettre les** ~ (*AUTO*) to put one's foot down ; ~ **lacrymogène** tear gas ; ~ **de ville** town gas.

**gaze** [gaz] *nf* gauze.
**gazéifié, e** [gazeifje] *a* aerated.
**gazelle** [gazɛl] *nf* gazelle.
**gazer** [gaze] *vt* to gas // *vi* (*fam*) to be going *ou* working well.
**gazette** [gazɛt] *nf* news sheet.
**gazeux, euse** [gazø, -øz] *a* gaseous ; **eau gazeuse** soda water.
**gazoduc** [gazɔdyk] *nm* gas pipeline.
**gazomètre** [gazɔmɛtʀ(ə)] *nm* gasometer.
**gazon** [gazɔ̃] *nm* (*herbe*) turf ; grass ; (*pelouse*) lawn.
**gazouiller** [gazuje] *vi* to chirp ; (*enfant*) to babble.
**geai** [ʒɛ] *nm* jay.
**géant, e** [ʒeã, -ãt] *a* gigantic, giant ; (*COMM*) giant-size // *nm/f* giant.
**geindre** [ʒɛ̃dʀ(ə)] *vi* to groan, moan.
**gel** [ʒɛl] *nm* frost ; freezing.
**gélatine** [ʒelatin] *nf* gelatine ; **gélatineux, euse** *a* jelly-like, gelatinous.
**gelé, e** [ʒəle] *a* frozen.
**gelée** [ʒəle] *nf* jelly ; (*gel*) frost ; ~ **blanche** hoarfrost, white frost.
**geler** [ʒəle] *vt, vi* to freeze ; **il gèle** it's freezing ; **gelures** *nfpl* frostbite *sg*.
**Gémeaux** [ʒemo] *nmpl*: **les** ~ Gemini, the Twins ; **être des** ~ to be Gemini.
**gémir** [ʒemiʀ] *vi* to groan, moan ; **gémissement** *nm* groan, moan.
**gemme** [ʒɛm] *nf* gem(stone).
**gênant, e** [ʒɛnã, -ãt] *a* annoying ; embarrassing.
**gencive** [ʒãsiv] *nf* gum.
**gendarme** [ʒãdaʀm(ə)] *nm* gendarme ; ~**rie** *nf* military police force in countryside and small towns ; their police station or barracks.
**gendre** [ʒãdʀ(ə)] *nm* son-in-law.
**gêne** [ʒɛn] *nf* (*à respirer, bouger*) discomfort, difficulty ; (*dérangement*) bother, trouble ; (*manque d'argent*) financial difficulties *pl ou* straits *pl* ; (*confusion*) embarrassment.
**gêné, e** [ʒene] *a* embarrassed.
**généalogie** [ʒenealɔʒi] *nf* genealogy ; **généalogique** *a* genealogical.
**gêner** [ʒene] *vt* (*incommoder*) to bother ; (*encombrer*) to hamper ; to be in the way ; (*déranger*) to bother ; (*embarrasser*): ~ **qn** to make sb feel ill-at-ease ; **se** ~ to put o.s. out.
**général, e, aux** [ʒeneʀal, -o] *a, nm* general // *nf*: (*répétition*) ~**e** final dress rehearsal ; **en** ~ usually, in general ; ~**ement** *ad* generally.
**généralisation** [ʒeneʀalizasjɔ̃] *nf* generalization.
**généralisé, e** [ʒeneʀalize] *a* general.
**généraliser** [ʒeneʀalize] *vt, vi* to generalize ; **se** ~ *vi* to become widespread.
**généraliste** [ʒeneʀalist(ə)] *nm/f* general practitioner, G.P.
**généralités** [ʒeneʀalite] *nfpl* generalities ; (*introduction*) general points.
**générateur, trice** [ʒeneʀatœʀ, -tʀis] *a*: ~ **de** which causes *ou* brings about // *nf* generator.
**génération** [ʒeneʀasjɔ̃] *nf* generation.

**généreusement** [ʒenerøzmɑ̃] *ad* generously.

**généreux, euse** [ʒenerø, -øz] *a* generous.

**générique** [ʒenerik] *a* generic // *nm* (*CINÉMA*) credits *pl*, credit titles *pl*.

**générosité** [ʒenerozite] *nf* generosity.

**genèse** [ʒənɛz] *nf* genesis.

**genêt** [ʒənɛ] *nm* broom *q*.

**génétique** [ʒenetik] *a* genetic // *nf* genetics *sg*.

**Genève** [ʒənɛv] *n* Geneva ; **genevois, e** *a, nm/f* Genevan.

**génial, e, aux** [ʒenjal, -o] *a* of genius.

**génie** [ʒeni] *nm* genius ; (*MIL*): **le ~** the Engineers *pl* ; **~ civil** civil engineering.

**genièvre** [ʒənjɛvr(ə)] *nm* juniper (tree) ; (*boisson*) geneva ; **grain de ~** juniper berry.

**génisse** [ʒenis] *nf* heifer.

**génital, e, aux** [ʒenital, -o] *a* genital.

**génitif** [ʒenitif] *nm* genitive.

**genou, x** [ʒnu] *nm* knee ; **à ~x** on one's knees ; **se mettre à ~x** to kneel down ; **genouillère** *nf* (*SPORT*) kneepad.

**genre** [ʒɑ̃r] *nm* kind, type, sort ; (*allure*) manner ; (*LING*) gender ; (*ART*) genre ; (*ZOOL etc*) genus.

**gens** [ʒɑ̃] *nmpl* (*f in some phrases*) people *pl*.

**gentil, le** [ʒɑ̃ti, -ij] *a* kind ; (*enfant: sage*) good ; (*sympa: endroit etc*) nice ; **gentillesse** *nf* kindness ; **gentiment** *ad* kindly.

**génuflexion** [ʒenyflɛksjɔ̃] *nf* genuflexion.

**géographe** [ʒeɔgraf] *nm/f* geographer.

**géographie** [ʒeɔgrafi] *nf* geography ; **géographique** *a* geographical.

**geôlier** [ʒolje] *nm* jailer.

**géologie** [ʒeɔlɔʒi] *nf* geology ; **géologique** *a* geological ; **géologue** *nm/f* geologist.

**géomètre** [ʒeɔmɛtr(ə)] *nm/f*: **(arpenteur-)~** (land) surveyor.

**géométrie** [ʒeɔmetri] *nf* geometry ; **à ~ variable** (*AVIAT*) swing-wing ; **géométrique** *a* geometric.

**gérance** [ʒerɑ̃s] *nf* management ; **mettre en ~** to appoint a manager for.

**géranium** [ʒeranjɔm] *nm* geranium.

**gérant, e** [ʒerɑ̃, -ɑ̃t] *nm/f* manager/manageress ; **~ d'immeuble** managing agent.

**gerbe** [ʒɛrb(ə)] *nf* (*de fleurs*) spray ; (*de blé*) sheaf (*pl* sheaves) ; (*fig*) shower, burst.

**gercé, e** [ʒɛrse] *a* chapped.

**gerçure** [ʒɛrsyr] *nf* crack.

**gérer** [ʒere] *vt* to manage.

**gériatrie** [ʒerjatri] *nf* geriatrics *sg* ; **gériatrique** *a* geriatric.

**germain, e** [ʒɛrmɛ̃, -ɛn] *a*: **cousin ~** first cousin.

**germanique** [ʒɛrmanik] *a* Germanic.

**germe** [ʒɛrm(ə)] *nm* germ.

**germer** [ʒɛrme] *vi* to sprout ; to germinate.

**gésier** [ʒezje] *nm* gizzard.

**gésir** [ʒezir] *vi* to be lying (down) ; *voir aussi* **ci-gît**.

**gestation** [ʒɛstasjɔ̃] *nf* gestation.

**geste** [ʒɛst(ə)] *nm* gesture ; move ; motion.

**gesticuler** [ʒɛstikyle] *vi* to gesticulate.

**gestion** [ʒɛstjɔ̃] *nf* management.

**gibecière** [ʒibsjɛr] *nf* gamebag.

**gibet** [ʒibɛ] *nm* gallows *pl*.

**gibier** [ʒibje] *nm* (*animaux*) game ; (*fig*) prey.

**giboulée** [ʒibule] *nf* sudden shower.

**giboyeux, euse** [ʒibwajø, -øz] *a* well-stocked with game.

**gicler** [ʒikle] *vi* to spurt, squirt.

**gicleur** [ʒiklœr] *nm* (*AUTO*) jet.

**gifle** [ʒifl(ə)] *nf* slap (in the face) ; **gifler** *vt* to slap (in the face).

**gigantesque** [ʒigɑ̃tɛsk(ə)] *a* gigantic.

**gigogne** [ʒigɔɲ] *a*: **lits ~s** pull-out *ou* stowaway beds ; **tables/poupées ~s** nest of tables/dolls.

**gigot** [ʒigo] *nm* leg (of mutton *ou* lamb).

**gigoter** [ʒigɔte] *vi* to wriggle (about).

**gilet** [ʒilɛ] *nm* waistcoat ; (*pull*) cardigan ; (*de corps*) vest ; **~ pare-balles** bulletproof jacket ; **~ de sauvetage** life jacket.

**gin** [dʒin] *nm* gin.

**gingembre** [ʒɛ̃ʒɑ̃br(ə)] *nm* ginger.

**girafe** [ʒiraf] *nf* giraffe.

**giratoire** [ʒiratwar] *a*: **sens ~** roundabout.

**girofle** [ʒirɔfl(ə)] *nm*: **clou de ~** clove.

**girouette** [ʒirwɛt] *nf* weather vane *ou* cock.

**gisait** *etc vb voir* **gésir**.

**gisement** [ʒizmɑ̃] *nm* deposit.

**gît** *vb voir* **gésir**.

**gitan, e** [ʒitɑ̃, -an] *nm/f* gipsy.

**gîte** [ʒit] *nm* home ; shelter ; **~ rural** farmhouse accommodation *q* (for tourists).

**givrage** [ʒivraʒ] *nm* icing.

**givre** [ʒivr(ə)] *nm* (hoar) frost.

**glabre** [glabr(ə)] *a* hairless ; clean-shaven.

**glace** [glas] *nf* ice ; (*crème glacée*) ice cream ; (*verre*) sheet of glass ; (*miroir*) mirror ; (*de voiture*) window ; **~s** *nfpl* (*GÉO*) ice sheets, ice *sg*.

**glacé, e** [glase] *a* icy ; (*boisson*) iced.

**glacer** [glase] *vt* to freeze ; (*boisson*) to chill, ice ; (*gâteau*) to ice ; (*papier, tissu*) to glaze ; (*fig*): **~ qn** to chill sb ; to make sb's blood run cold.

**glaciaire** [glasjɛr] *a* ice *cpd* ; glacial.

**glacial, e** [glasjal] *a* icy.

**glacier** [glasje] *nm* (*GÉO*) glacier ; (*marchand*) ice-cream maker.

**glacière** [glasjɛr] *nf* icebox.

**glaçon** [glasɔ̃] *nm* icicle ; (*pour boisson*) ice cube.

**glaïeul** [glajœl] *nm* gladiola.

**glaire** [glɛr] *nf* (*MÉD*) phlegm *q*.

**glaise** [glɛz] *nf* clay.

**gland** [glɑ̃] *nm* acorn ; (*décoration*) tassel ; (*ANAT*) glans.

**glande** [glɑ̃d] *nf* gland.

**glaner** [glane] *vt, vi* to glean.

**glapir** [glapir] *vi* to yelp.

**glas** [glɑ] *nm* knell, toll.

**glauque** [glok] *a* dull blue-green.

**glissade** [glisad] *nf* (*par jeu*) slide ; (*chute*) slip ; (*dérapage*) skid.

**glissant, e** [glisɑ̃, -ɑ̃t] *a* slippery.

**glissement** [glismɑ̃] *nm* sliding ; (*fig*) shift ; **~ de terrain** landslide.

**glisser** [glise] *vi* (*avancer*) to glide *ou* slide along; (*coulisser, tomber*) to slide; (*déraper*) to slip; (*être glissant*) to be slippery // *vt*: ~ **qch sous/dans/à** to slip sth under/into/to; ~ **sur** (*fig: détail etc*) to skate over; **se** ~ **dans/entre** to slip into/between; **glissière** *nf* slide channel; **à glissière** sliding; **glissoire** *nf* slide.

**global, e, aux** [glɔbal, -o] *a* overall.

**globe** [glɔb] *nm* globe; **sous** ~ under glass; ~ **oculaire** eyeball; **le** ~ **terrestre** the globe.

**globule** [glɔbyl] *nm* (*du sang*): ~ **blanc/rouge** white/red corpuscle.

**globuleux, euse** [glɔbylø, -øz] *a*: **yeux** ~ protruding eyes.

**gloire** [glwaR] *nf* glory; (*mérite*) distinction, credit; (*personne*) celebrity; **glorieux, euse** *a* glorious; **glorifier** *vt* to glorify, extol.

**glossaire** [glɔsɛR] *nm* glossary.

**glousser** [gluse] *vi* to cluck; (*rire*) to chuckle.

**glouton, ne** [glutɔ̃, -ɔn] *a* gluttonous, greedy.

**glu** [gly] *nf* birdlime.

**gluant, e** [glyɑ̃, -ɑ̃t] *a* sticky, gummy.

**glycine** [glisin] *nf* wisteria.

**go** [go]: **tout de** ~ *ad* straight out.

**G.O.** *sigle* = **grandes ondes**.

**gobelet** [gɔblɛ] *nm* tumbler; beaker; (*à dés*) cup.

**gober** [gɔbe] *vt* to swallow.

**godet** [gɔdɛ] *nm* pot.

**godiller** [gɔdije] *vi* to scull.

**goéland** [gɔelɑ̃] *nm* (sea)gull.

**goélette** [gɔelɛt] *nf* schooner.

**goémon** [gɔemɔ̃] *nm* wrack.

**gogo** [gɔgo] *nm* (*péj*) mug, sucker; **à** ~ *ad* galore.

**goguenard, e** [gɔgnaR, -aRd(ə)] *a* mocking.

**goguette** [gɔgɛt] *nf*: **en** ~ on the binge.

**goinfre** [gwɛ̃fR(ə)] *nm* glutton; **se goinfrer** *vi* to make a pig of o.s.; **se goinfrer de** to guzzle.

**goitre** [gwatR(ə)] *nm* goitre.

**golf** [gɔlf] *nm* golf; golf course; ~ **miniature** crazy *ou* miniature golf.

**golfe** [gɔlf(ə)] *nm* gulf; bay.

**gomme** [gɔm] *nf* (*à effacer*) rubber, eraser; (*résine*) gum; **gommer** *vt* to erase; to gum.

**gond** [gɔ̃] *nm* hinge; **sortir de ses** ~**s** (*fig*) to fly off the handle.

**gondole** [gɔ̃dɔl] *nf* gondola.

**gondoler** [gɔ̃dɔle] *vi*, **se** ~ *vi* to warp; to buckle.

**gondolier** [gɔ̃dɔlje] *nm* gondolier.

**gonflage** [gɔ̃flaʒ] *nm* inflating, blowing up.

**gonflé, e** [gɔ̃fle] *a* swollen; bloated.

**gonfler** [gɔ̃fle] *vt* (*pneu, ballon*) to inflate, blow up; (*nombre, importance*) to inflate // *vi* to swell (up); (*CULIN*: pâte) to rise; **gonfleur** *nm* air pump.

**gong** [gɔ̃g] *nm* gong.

**goret** [gɔRɛ] *nm* piglet.

**gorge** [gɔRʒ(ə)] *nf* (*ANAT*) throat; (*poitrine*) breast; (*GÉO*) gorge; (*rainure*) groove.

**gorgé, e** [gɔRʒe] *a*: ~ **de** filled with; (*eau*) saturated with // *nf* mouthful; sip; gulp.

**gorille** [gɔRij] *nm* gorilla; (*fam*) bodyguard.

**gosier** [gozje] *nm* throat.

**gosse** [gɔs] *nm/f* kid.

**gothique** [gɔtik] *a* gothic.

**goudron** [gudRɔ̃] *nm* tar; **goudronner** *vt* to tarmac.

**gouffre** [gufR(ə)] *nm* abyss, gulf.

**goujat** [guʒa] *nm* boor.

**goujon** [guʒɔ̃] *nm* gudgeon.

**goulée** [gule] *nf* gulp.

**goulet** [gulɛ] *nm* bottleneck.

**goulot** [gulo] *nm* neck; **boire au** ~ to drink from the bottle.

**goulu, e** [guly] *a* greedy.

**goupillon** [gupijɔ̃] *nm* (*REL*) sprinkler.

**gourd, e** [guR, guRd(ə)] *a* numb (with cold).

**gourde** [guRd(ə)] *nf* (*récipient*) flask.

**gourdin** [guRdɛ̃] *nm* club, bludgeon.

**gourmand, e** [guRmɑ̃, -ɑ̃d] *a* greedy; **gourmandise** *nf* greed; (*bonbon*) sweet.

**gourmet** [guRmɛ] *nm* epicure.

**gourmette** [guRmɛt] *nf* chain bracelet.

**gousse** [gus] *nf*: ~ **d'ail** clove of garlic.

**gousset** [gusɛ] *nm* (*de gilet*) fob.

**goût** [gu] *nm* taste; **prendre** ~ **à** to develop a taste *ou* a liking for.

**goûter** [gute] *vt* (*essayer*) to taste; (*apprécier*) to enjoy // *vi* to have (afternoon) tea // *nm* (afternoon) tea; ~ **à** to taste, sample; ~ **de** to have a taste of.

**goutte** [gut] *nf* drop; (*MÉD*) gout; (*alcool*) brandy; ~**s** *nfpl* (*MÉD*) (nose) drops.

**goutte-à-goutte** [gutagut] *nm* (*MÉD*) drip; **alimenter au** ~ to drip-feed.

**gouttelette** [gutlɛt] *nf* droplet.

**gouttière** [gutjɛR] *nf* gutter.

**gouvernail** [guvɛRnaj] *nm* rudder; (*barre*) helm, tiller.

**gouvernante** [guvɛRnɑ̃t] *nf* governess.

**gouverne** [guvɛRn(ə)] *nf*: **pour sa** ~ for his guidance.

**gouvernement** [guvɛRnəmɑ̃] *nm* government; **membre du** ~ ≈ Cabinet member; **gouvernemental, e, aux** *a* government *cpd*; pro-government.

**gouverner** [guvɛRne] *vt* to govern; **gouverneur** *nm* governor; commanding officer.

**grâce** [gRas] *nf* grace; favour; (*JUR*) pardon; ~**s** *nfpl* (*REL*) grace *sg*; **dans les bonnes** ~**s de qn** in favour with sb; **faire** ~ **à qn de qch** to spare sb sth; **rendre** ~**(s) à** to give thanks to; **demander** ~ to beg for mercy; **droit de** ~ right of reprieve; ~ **à** *prép* thanks to; **gracier** *vt* to pardon; **gracieux, euse** *a* graceful.

**gracile** [gRasil] *a* slender.

**gradation** [gRadɑsjɔ̃] *nf* gradation.

**grade** [gRad] *nm* rank; **monter en** ~ to be promoted.

**gradé** [gRade] *nm* officer.

**gradin** [gRadɛ̃] *nm* tier; step; ~**s** *nmpl* (*de stade*) terracing *sg*.

**graduation** [gRadɥɑsjɔ̃] *nf* graduation.

**graduel, le** [gRadɥɛl] *a* gradual; progressive.

**graduer** [gradɥe] *vt* (*effort etc*) to increase gradually ; (*règle, verre*) to graduate ; **exercices gradués** exercises graded for difficulty.

**graffiti** [grafiti] *nmpl* graffiti.

**grain** [grɛ̃] *nm* (*gén*) grain ; (NAVIG) squall ; ~ **de beauté** beauty spot ; ~ **de café** coffee bean ; ~ **de poivre** peppercorn ; ~ **de poussière** speck of dust ; ~ **de raisin** grape.

**graine** [grɛn] *nf* seed ; ~**tier** *nm* seed merchant.

**graissage** [grɛsaʒ] *nm* lubrication, greasing.

**graisse** [grɛs] *nf* fat ; (*lubrifiant*) grease ; **graisser** *vt* to lubricate, grease ; (*tacher*) to make greasy ; **graisseux, euse** *a* greasy ; (ANAT) fatty.

**grammaire** [gramɛr] *nf* grammar ; **grammatical, e, aux** *a* grammatical.

**gramme** [gram] *nm* gramme.

**grand, e** [grɑ̃, grɑ̃d] *a* (*haut*) tall ; (*gros, vaste, large*) big, large ; (*long*) long ; (*sens abstraits*) great // *ad*: ~ **ouvert** wide open ; **son** ~ **frère** his older brother ; **il est assez** ~ **pour** he's old enough to ; **au** ~ **air** in the open (air) ; ~**s blessés/brûlés** casualties with severe injuries/burns ; ~ **angle** *nm* (PHOTO) wide-angle lens *sg* ; ~ **écart** splits *pl* ; ~ **ensemble** housing scheme ; ~ **magasin** department store ; ~**e personne** grown-up ; ~**es écoles** *prestige schools of university level, with competitive entrance examination* ; ~**es lignes** (RAIL) main lines ; ~**es vacances** summer holidays ; **grand-chose** *nm/f inv*: **pas grand-chose** not much ; **Grande-Bretagne** *nf*: **la Grande-Bretagne** (Great) Britain ; **grandeur** *nf* (*dimension*) size ; magnitude ; (*fig*) greatness ; **grandeur nature** life-size ; **grandir** *vi* (*enfant, arbre*) to grow ; (*bruit, hostilité*) to increase, grow // *vt*: **grandir qn** (*suj: vêtement, chaussure*) to make sb look taller ; (*fig*) to make sb grow in stature ; ~**mère** *nf* grandmother ; ~**messe** *nf* high mass ; ~**père** *nm* grandfather ; ~**route** *nf* main road ; ~**rue** *nf* high street ; ~**s-parents** *nmpl* grandparents.

**grange** [grɑ̃ʒ] *nf* barn.

**granit** [granit] *nm* granite.

**granulé** [granyle] *nm* granule.

**granuleux, euse** [granylø, -øz] *a* granular.

**graphie** [grafi] *nf* written form.

**graphique** [grafik] *a* graphic // *nm* graph.

**graphisme** [grafism(ə)] *nm* graphic arts *pl* ; graphics *sg*.

**graphologie** [grafɔlɔʒi] *nf* graphology ; **graphologue** *nm/f* graphologist.

**grappe** [grap] *nf* cluster ; ~ **de raisin** bunch of grapes.

**grappiller** [grapije] *vt* to glean.

**grappin** [grapɛ̃] *nm* grapnel ; **mettre le** ~ **sur** (*fig*) to get one's claws on.

**gras, se** [grɑ, grɑs] *a* (*viande, soupe*) fatty ; (*personne*) fat ; (*surface, main*) greasy ; (*toux*) loose, phlegmy ; (*rire*) throaty ; (*plaisanterie*) coarse ; (*crayon*) soft-lead ; (TYPO) bold // *nm* (CULIN) fat ; **faire la** ~**se matinée** to have a lie-in ;

~**sement** *ad*: ~**sement payé** handsomely paid ; ~**souillet, te** *a* podgy, plump.

**gratification** [gratifikasjɔ̃] *nf* bonus.

**gratifier** [gratifje] *vt*: ~ **qn de** to favour sb with, reward sb with ; (*sourire etc*) to favour sb with.

**gratin** [gratɛ̃] *nm* (CULIN) cheese-topped dish ; cheese topping.

**gratiné, e** [gratine] *a* (CULIN) au gratin ; (*fam*) hellish.

**gratis** [gratis] *ad* free.

**gratitude** [gratityd] *nf* gratitude.

**gratte-ciel** [gratsjɛl] *nm inv* skyscraper.

**grattement** [gratmɑ̃] *nm* (*bruit*) scratching (noise).

**gratte-papier** [gratpapje] *nm inv* (*péj*) penpusher.

**gratter** [grate] *vt* (*frotter*) to scrape ; (*enlever*) to scrape off ; (*bras, bouton*) to scratch ; **grattoir** *nm* scraper.

**gratuit, e** [gratɥi, -ɥit] *a* (*entrée, billet*) free ; (*fig*) gratuitous.

**gratuitement** [gratɥitmɑ̃] *ad* free.

**gravats** [grava] *nmpl* rubble *sg*.

**grave** [grav] *a* (*maladie, accident*) serious, bad ; (*sujet, problème*) serious, grave ; (*air*) grave, solemn ; (*voix, son*) deep, low-pitched // *nm* (MUS) low register ; **blessé** ~ seriously injured person ; ~**ment** *ad* seriously ; gravely.

**graver** [grave] *vt* to engrave ; **graveur** *nm* engraver.

**gravier** [gravje] *nm* gravel *q* ; **gravillons** *nmpl* gravel *sg*, loose chippings *ou* gravel.

**gravir** [gravir] *vt* to climb (up).

**gravitation** [gravitasjɔ̃] *nf* gravitation.

**gravité** [gravite] *nf* seriousness ; gravity ; (PHYSIQUE) gravity.

**graviter** [gravite] *vi*: ~ **autour de** to revolve around.

**gravure** [gravyr] *nf* engraving ; (*reproduction*) print ; plate.

**gré** [gre] *nm*: **à son** ~ to his liking ; as he pleases ; **au** ~ **de** according to, following ; **contre le** ~ **de qn** against sb's will ; **de son (plein)** ~ of one's own free will ; **de** ~ **ou de force** whether one likes it or not ; **de bon** ~ willingly ; **de** ~ **à** ~ (COMM) by mutual agreement ; **savoir** ~ **à qn de qch** to be grateful to sb for sth.

**grec, grecque** [grɛk] *a* a Greek ; (*classique*) vase etc) Grecian // *nm/f* Greek.

**Grèce** [grɛs] *nf*: **la** ~ Greece.

**gréement** [gremɑ̃] *nm* rigging.

**greffe** [grɛf] *nf* grafting *q*, graft ; transplanting *q*, transplant // *nm* (JUR) office.

**greffer** [grefe] *vt* (BOT, MÉD: *tissu*) to graft ; (MÉD: *organe*) to transplant.

**greffier** [grefje] *nm* clerk of the court.

**grégaire** [gregɛr] *a* gregarious.

**grège** [grɛʒ] *a*: **soie** ~ raw silk.

**grêle** [grɛl] *a* (*very*) thin // *nf* hail.

**grêlé, e** [grele] *a* pockmarked.

**grêler** [grele] *vb impersonnel*: **il grêle** it's hailing.

**grêlon** [grɛlɔ̃] *nm* hailstone.

**grelot** [grəlo] *nm* little bell.

**grelotter** [grəlɔte] *vi* (*trembler*) to shiver.

**grenade** [grənad] *nf* (*explosive*) grenade ; (*BOT*) pomegranate ; ~ **lacrymogène** teargas grenade.
**grenadier** [grənadje] *nm* (*MIL*) grenadier ; (*BOT*) pomegranate tree.
**grenat** [grəna] *a inv* dark red.
**grenier** [grənje] *nm* attic ; (*de ferme*) loft.
**grenouille** [grənuj] *nf* frog.
**grenu, e** [grəny] *a* grainy, grained.
**grès** [grɛ] *nm* sandstone ; (*poterie*) stoneware.
**grésiller** [grezije] *vi* to sizzle ; (*RADIO*) to crackle.
**grève** [grɛv] *nf* (*d'ouvriers*) strike ; (*plage*) shore ; **se mettre en/faire** ~ to go on/be on strike ; ~ **de la faim** hunger strike ; ~ **sauvage** wildcat strike ; ~ **sur le tas** sit down strike ; ~ **tournante** strike by rota ; ~ **du zèle** work-to-rule *q.*
**grever** [grəve] *vt* to put a strain on ; **grevé d'impôts** crippled by taxes.
**gréviste** [grevist(ə)] *nm/f* striker.
**gribouiller** [gribuje] *vt* to scribble, scrawl // *vi* to doodle.
**grief** [grijɛf] *nm* grievance ; **faire** ~ **à qn de** to reproach sb for.
**grièvement** [grijɛvmɑ̃] *ad* seriously.
**griffe** [grif] *nf* claw ; (*fig*) signature.
**griffer** [grife] *vt* to scratch.
**griffonner** [grifɔne] *vt* to scribble.
**grignoter** [griɲɔte] *vt* to nibble *ou* gnaw at.
**gril** [gril] *nm* steak *ou* grill pan.
**grillade** [grijad] *nf* grill.
**grillage** [grijaʒ] *nm* (*treillis*) wire netting ; wire fencing.
**grille** [grij] *nf* (*portail*) (metal) gate ; (*d'égout*) (metal) grate ; (*fig*) grid.
**grille-pain** [grijpɛ̃] *nm inv* toaster.
**griller** [grije] *vt* (*aussi*: **faire** ~: *pain*) to toast ; (: *viande*) to grill ; (*fig*: *ampoule etc*) to burn out, blow.
**grillon** [grijɔ̃] *nm* cricket.
**grimace** [grimas] *nf* grimace ; (*pour faire rire*): **faire des** ~s to pull *ou* make faces.
**grimer** [grime] *vt* to make up.
**grimper** [grɛ̃pe] *vi, vt* to climb.
**grincement** [grɛ̃smɑ̃] *nm* grating (noise) ; creaking (noise).
**grincer** [grɛ̃se] *vi* (*porte, roue*) to grate ; (*plancher*) to creak ; ~ **des dents** to grind one's teeth.
**grincheux, euse** [grɛ̃ʃ∅, -∅z] *a* grumpy.
**grippe** [grip] *nf* flu, influenza ; **grippé, e** *a*: **être grippé** to have flu.
**gripper** [gripe] *vt, vi* to jam.
**gris, e** [gri, griz] *a* grey ; (*ivre*) tipsy.
**grisaille** [grizaj] *nf* greyness, dullness.
**grisant, e** [grizɑ̃, -ɑ̃t] *a* intoxicating, exhilarating.
**griser** [grize] *vt* to intoxicate.
**grisonner** [grizɔne] *vi* to be going grey.
**grisou** [grizu] *nm* firedamp.
**grive** [griv] *nf* thrush.
**grivois, e** [grivwa, -waz] *a* saucy.
**grog** [grɔg] *nm* grog.
**grogner** [grɔɲe] *vi* to growl ; (*fig*) to grumble.
**groin** [grwɛ̃] *nm* snout.

**grommeler** [grɔmle] *vi* to mutter to o.s.
**grondement** [grɔ̃dmɑ̃] *nm* rumble.
**gronder** [grɔ̃de] *vi* to rumble ; (*fig*: *révolte*) to be brewing // *vt* to scold.
**gros, se** [gro, gros] *a* big, large ; (*obèse*) fat ; (*travaux, dégâts*) extensive ; (*large*: *trait, fil*) thick, heavy // *ad*: **risquer/gagner** ~ to risk/win a lot // *nm* (*COMM*): **le** ~ the wholesale business ; **prix de** ~ wholesale price ; **par** ~ **temps/~se mer** in rough weather/heavy seas ; **le** ~ **de** the main body of ; the bulk of ; **en** ~ roughly ; (*COMM*) wholesale ; ~ **intestin** large intestine ; ~ **lot** jackpot ; ~ **mot** coarse word, vulgarity ; ~ **plan** (*PHOTO*) close-up ; ~ **sel** cooking salt ; ~**se caisse** big drum.
**groseille** [grozɛj] *nf*: ~ (**rouge**)/(**blanche**) red/white currant ; ~ **à maquereau** gooseberry ; **groseillier** *nm* red *ou* white currant bush ; gooseberry bush.
**grosse** [gros] *a voir* **gros.**
**grossesse** [grosɛs] *nf* pregnancy.
**grosseur** [grosœr] *nf* size ; fatness ; (*tumeur*) lump.
**grossier, ière** [grosje, -jɛr] *a* coarse ; (*travail*) rough ; **çrude** ; (*évident*: *erreur*) gross ; **grossièrement** *ad* coarsely ; roughly ; crudely ; (*en gros*) roughly.
**grossir** [grosir] *vi* (*personne*) to put on weight ; (*fig*) to grow, get bigger ; (*rivière*) to swell // *vt* to increase ; to exaggerate ; (*au microscope*) to magnify ; (*suj*: *vêtement*): ~ **qn** to make sb look fatter ; **grossissement** *nm* (*optique*) magnification.
**grossiste** [grosist(ə)] *nm/f* wholesaler.
**grosso modo** [grosomɔdo] *ad* roughly.
**grotte** [grɔt] *nf* cave.
**grouiller** [gruje] *vi* to mill about ; to swarm about ; ~ **de** to be swarming with.
**groupe** [grup] *nm* group ; ~ **sanguin** blood group.
**groupement** [grupmɑ̃] *nm* grouping ; group.
**grouper** [grupe] *vt* to group ; **se** ~ to get together.
**gruau** [gryo] *nm*: **pain de** ~ wheaten bread.
**grue** [gry] *nf* crane.
**grumeaux** [grymo] *nmpl* lumps.
**grutier** [grytje] *nm* crane driver.
**Guadeloupe** [gwadlup] *nf*: **la** ~ Guadeloupe.
**gué** [ge] *nm* ford ; **passer à** ~ to ford.
**guenilles** [gənij] *nfpl* rags.
**guenon** [gənɔ̃] *nf* female monkey.
**guépard** [gepar] *nm* cheetah.
**guêpe** [gɛp] *nf* wasp.
**guêpier** [gepje] *nm* (*fig*) trap.
**guère** [gɛr] *ad* (*avec adjectif, adverbe*): **ne ...** ~ hardly ; (*avec verbe*): **ne ...** ~ **tournure** *négative* + much ; hardly ever ; *tournure négative* + (very) long ; **il n'y a** ~ **que/de** there's hardly anybody (*ou* anything) but/hardly any.
**guéridon** [geridɔ̃] *nm* pedestal table.
**guérilla** [gerija] *nf* guerrilla warfare.
**guérillero** [gerijero] *nm* guerrilla.
**guérir** [gerir] *vt* (*personne, maladie*) to cure ; (*membre, plaie*) to heal // *vi*

(*personne*) to recover, be cured; (*plaie, chagrin*) to heal; ~ **de** to be cured of, recover from; ~ **qn de** to cure sb of; **guérison** *nf* curing; healing; recovery; **guérissable** *a* curable; **guérisseur, euse** *nm/f* healer.

**guérite** [geʀit] *nf* sentry box.

**guerre** [gɛʀ] *nf* war; (*méthode*): ~ **atomique/de tranchées** atomic/ trench warfare *q*; **en** ~ at war; **faire la** ~ **à** to wage war against; **de** ~ **lasse** finally; ~ **civile/ mondiale** civil/world war; ~ **d'usure** war of attrition; **guerrier, ière** *a* warlike // *nm/f* warrior; **guerroyer** *vi* to wage war.

**guet** [gɛ] *nm*: **faire le** ~ to be on the watch *ou* look-out.

**guet-apens** [gɛtapã] *nm* ambush.

**guêtre** [gɛtʀ(ə)] *nf* gaiter.

**guetter** [gete] *vt* (*épier*) to watch (intently); (*attendre*) to watch (out) for; to be lying in wait for; **guetteur** *nm* look-out.

**gueule** [gœl] *nf* mouth; (*fam*) face; mouth; ~ **de bois** (*fam*) hangover.

**gueuler** [gœle] *vi* (*fam*) to bawl.

**gueux** [gø] *nm* beggar; rogue.

**gui** [gi] *nm* mistletoe.

**guichet** [giʃɛ] *nm* (*de bureau, banque*) counter, window; (*d'une porte*) wicket, hatch; **les** ~**s** (*à la gare, au théâtre*) the ticket office; **guichetier, ière** *nm/f* counter clerk.

**guide** [gid] *nm* guide.

**guider** [gide] *vt* to guide.

**guidon** [gidɔ̃] *nm* handlebars *pl*.

**guignol** [giɲɔl] *nm* ≈ Punch and Judy show; (*fig*) clown.

**guillemets** [gijmɛ] *nmpl*: **entre** ~ in inverted commas *ou* quotation marks; ~ **de répétition** ditto marks.

**guilleret, te** [gijʀɛ, -ɛt] *a* perky, bright.

**guillotine** [gijɔtin] *nf* guillotine; **guillotiner** *vt* to guillotine.

**guindé, e** [gɛ̃de] *a* stiff, starchy.

**guirlande** [giʀlɑ̃d] *nf* garland; (*de papier*) paper chain.

**guise** [giz] *nf*: **à votre** ~ as you wish *ou* please; **en** ~ **de** by way of.

**guitare** [gitaʀ] *nf* guitar; **guitariste** *nm/f* guitarist, guitar player.

**gustatif, ive** [gystatif, -iv] *a* gustatory; *voir* **papille.**

**guttural, e, aux** [gytyʀal, -o] *a* guttural.

**Guyane** [gɥijan] *n*: **la** ~ Guiana.

**gymkhana** [ʒimkana] *nm* rally.

**gymnase** [ʒimnɑz] *nm* gym(nasium).

**gymnaste** [ʒimnast(ə)] *nm/f* gymnast.

**gymnastique** [ʒimnastik] *nf* gymnastics *sg*; (*au réveil etc*) keep fit exercises *pl*.

**gynécologie** [ʒinekɔlɔʒi] *nf* gynaecology; **gynécologue** *nm/f* gynaecologist.

**gypse** [ʒips(ə)] *nm* gypsum.

# H

**h.** *abr de* **heure.**

**habile** [abil] *a* skilful; (*malin*) clever; ~**té** *nf* skill, skilfulness; cleverness.

**habilité, e** [abilite] *a*: ~ **à faire** entitled to do, empowered to do.

**habillé, e** [abije] *a* dressed; (*chic*) dressy; (*TECH*): ~ **de** covered with; encased in.

**habillement** [abijmã] *nm* clothes *pl*; (*profession*) clothing industry.

**habiller** [abije] *vt* to dress; (*fournir en vêtements*) to clothe; **s'**~ to dress (o.s.); (*se déguiser, mettre des vêtements chic*) to dress up; **s'**~ **de/en** to dress in/dress up as; **s'**~ **chez/à** to buy one's clothes from/at.

**habit** [abi] *nm* outfit; ~**s** *nmpl* (*vêtements*) clothes; ~ **(de soirée)** tails *pl*; evening dress.

**habitable** [abitabl(ə)] *a* (in)habitable.

**habitacle** [abitakl(ə)] *nm* cockpit; (*AUTO*) passenger cell.

**habitant, e** [abitã, -ãt] *nm/f* inhabitant; (*d'une maison*) occupant, occupier; **loger chez l'**~ to stay with the locals.

**habitat** [abita] *nm* housing conditions *pl*; (*BOT, ZOOL*) habitat.

**habitation** [abitasjɔ̃] *nf* living; residence, home; house; ~**s à loyer modéré (HLM)** low-rent housing *sg*, ≈ council flats.

**habité, e** [abite] *a* inhabited; lived in.

**habiter** [abite] *vt* to live in; (*suj: sentiment*) to dwell in // *vi*: ~ **à/dans** to live in *ou* at/in.

**habitude** [abityd] *nf* habit; **avoir l'**~ **de faire** to be in the habit of doing; (*expérience*) to be used to doing; **d'**~ usually; **comme d'**~ as usual.

**habitué, e** [abitɥe] *a*: **être** ~ **à** to be used *ou* accustomed to // *nm/f* regular visitor; regular (customer).

**habituel, le** [abitɥɛl] *a* usual.

**habituer** [abitɥe] *vt*: ~ **qn à** to get sb used to; **s'**~ **à** to get used to.

***hâbleur, euse** ['ɑblœʀ, -øz] *a* boastful.

***hache** ['aʃ] *nf* axe.

***haché, e** ['aʃe] *a* minced; (*fig*) jerky.

***hacher** ['aʃe] *vt* (*viande*) to mince; (*persil*) to chop.

***hachis** ['aʃi] *nm* mince *q*.

***hachisch** ['aʃiʃ] *nm* hashish.

***hachoir** ['aʃwaʀ] *nm* chopper; (meat) mincer; chopping board.

***hachures** ['aʃyʀ] *nfpl* hatching *sg*.

***hagard, e** ['agaʀ, -aʀd(ə)] *a* wild, distraught.

***haie** ['ɛ] *nf* hedge; (*SPORT*) hurdle; (*fig: rang*) line, row; **200 m** ~**s** 200 m hurdles; ~ **d'honneur** guard of honour.

***haillons** ['ajɔ̃] *nmpl* rags.

***haine** ['ɛn] *nf* hatred; **haineux, euse** *a* full of hatred.

***haïr** ['aiʀ] *vt* to detest, hate.

***halage** ['alaʒ] *nm*: **chemin de** ~ towpath.

***hâle** ['ɑl] *nm* (sun)tan; ***hâlé, e** *a* (sun)tanned, sunburnt.

**haleine** [alɛn] *nf* breath; **tenir en** ~ to hold spellbound; to keep in suspense; **de longue** ~ *a* long-term.

***haleter** ['alte] *vi* to pant.

***hall** ['ol] *nm* hall.

**hallali** [alali] *nm* kill.

***halle** ['al] *nf* (covered) market; ~**s** *nfpl* central food market *sg*.

**hallucinant, e** [alysinɑ̃, -ɑ̃t] *a* staggering.
**hallucination** [alysinɑsjɔ̃] *nf* hallucination.
**halluciné, e** [alysine] *nm/f* person suffering from hallucinations ; (raving) lunatic.
*****halo** ['alo] *nm* halo.
*****halte** ['alt(ə)] *nf* stop, break ; stopping place ; (*RAIL*) halt // *excl* stop! ; **faire ~** to stop.
**haltère** [altɛR] *nm* dumbbell, barbell ; **~s** *nmpl* (*activité*) weight lifting *sg* ; **haltérophile** *nm/f* weight lifter.
*****hamac** ['amak] *nm* hammock.
*****hameau, x** ['amo] *nm* hamlet.
**hameçon** [amsɔ̃] *nm* (fish) hook.
*****hampe** ['ɑ̃p] *nf* shaft.
*****hamster** ['amstɛR] *nm* hamster.
*****hanche** ['ɑ̃ʃ] *nf* hip.
*****hand-ball** ['ɑ̃dbal] *nm* handball.
*****handicap** ['ɑ̃dikap] *nm* handicap ; *****~é, e** *a* handicapped // *nm/f* physically (*ou* mentally) handicapped person ; **~é moteur** spastic ; *****~er** *vt* to handicap.
*****hangar** ['ɑ̃gaR] *nm* shed.
*****hanneton** ['antɔ̃] *nm* cockchafer.
*****hanter** ['ɑ̃te] *vt* to haunt.
*****hantise** ['ɑ̃tiz] *nf* obsessive fear.
*****happer** ['ape] *vt* to snatch ; (*suj: train etc*) to hit.
*****haranguer** [aRɑ̃ge] *vt* to harangue.
*****haras** ['aRɑ] *nm* stud farm.
**harassant, e** [aRasɑ̃, -ɑ̃t] *a* exhausting.
*****harceler** ['aRsəle] *vt* (*MIL, CHASSE*) to harass, harry ; (*importuner*) to plague.
*****hardes** ['aRd(ə)] *nfpl* rags.
*****hardi, e** ['aRdi] *a* bold, daring.
*****hareng** ['aRɑ̃] *nm* herring.
*****hargne** ['aRɲ(ə)] *nf* aggressiveness.
*****haricot** ['aRiko] *nm* bean ; **~ vert/blanc** French/haricot bean.
**harmonica** [aRmɔnika] *nm* mouth organ.
**harmonie** [aRmɔni] *nf* harmony ; **harmonieux, euse** *a* harmonious ; **harmonique** *nm ou nf* harmonic ; **harmoniser** *vt* to harmonize.
*****harnaché, e** ['aRnaʃe] *a* (*fig*) rigged out.
*****harnacher** ['aRnaʃe] *vt* to harness.
*****harnais** ['aRnɛ] *nm* harness.
*****harpe** ['aRp(ə)] *nf* harp ; *****harpiste** *nm/f* harpist.
*****harpon** ['aRpɔ̃] *nm* harpoon ; *****harponner** *vt* to harpoon ; (*fam*) to collar.
*****hasard** ['azaR] *nm:* **le ~** chance, fate ; **un ~** a coincidence ; a stroke of luck ; **au ~** aimlessly ; at random ; haphazardly ; **par ~** by chance ; **à tout ~** just in case ; on the off chance.
*****hasarder** ['azaRde] *vt* (*mot*) to venture ; (*fortune*) to risk ; **se ~ à faire** to risk doing, venture to do.
*****hasardeux, euse** ['azaRdø, øz] *a* hazardous, risky ; (*hypothèse*) rash.
*****haschisch** ['aʃiʃ] *nm* hashish.
*****hâte** ['ɑt] *nf* haste ; **à la ~** hurriedly, hastily ; **en ~** posthaste, with all possible speed ; **avoir ~ de** to be eager *ou* anxious to ; *****hâter** *vt* to hasten ; **se hâter** to hurry ; **se hâter de** to hurry *ou* hasten to.

*****hâtif, ive** ['ɑtif, -iv] *a* hurried ; hasty ; (*légume*) early.
*****hausse** ['os] *nf* rise, increase ; (*de fusil*) backsight adjuster ; **en ~** rising.
*****hausser** ['ose] *vt* to raise ; **~ les épaules** to shrug (one's shoulders).
*****haut, e** ['o, 'ot] *a* high ; (*grand*) tall ; (*son, voix*) high(-pitched) // *ad* high // *nm* top (part) ; **de 3 m de ~** 3 m high, 3 m in height ; **des ~s et des bas** ups and downs ; **en ~ lieu** in high places ; **à ~e voix** aloud, out loud ; **du ~ de** from the top of ; **de ~ en bas** up and down ; downwards ; **plus ~** higher up, further up ; (*dans un texte*) above ; (*parler*) louder ; **en ~** up above ; at (*ou* tc) the top ; (*dans une maison*) upstairs ; **en ~ de** at the top of ; **la ~e couture/coiffure** haute couture/coiffure ; **~e fidélité** hi-fi, high fidelity.
*****hautain, e** ['otɛ̃, -ɛn] *a* (*personne, regard*) haughty.
*****hautbois** ['obwa] *nm* oboe.
*****haut-de-forme** ['odfɔRm(ə)] *nm* top hat.
*****hautement** ['otmɑ̃] *ad* highly.
*****hauteur** ['otœR] *nf* height ; (*GÉO*) height, hill ; (*fig*) loftiness ; haughtiness ; **à ~ des yeux** at eye level ; **à la ~ de** (*sur la même ligne*) level with ; by ; (*fig*) equal to ; **à la ~** (*fig*) up to it, equal to the task.
*****haut-fond** ['ofɔ̃] *nm* shallow, shoal.
*****haut-fourneau** ['ofuRno] *nm* blast *ou* smelting furnace.
*****haut-le-cœur** ['olkœR] *nm inv* retch, heave.
*****haut-parleur** ['opaRlœR] *nm* (loud)speaker.
*****hâve** ['ɑv] *a* gaunt.
*****havre** ['ɑvR(ə)] *nm* haven.
*****Haye** ['ɛ] *n:* **la ~** the Hague.
*****hayon** ['ɛjɔ̃] *nm* tailgate.
**hebdomadaire** [ɛdbɔmadɛR] *a*, *nm* weekly.
**héberger** [ebɛRʒe] *vt* to accommodate, lodge ; (*réfugiés*) to take in.
**hébété, e** [ebete] *a* dazed.
**hébraïque** [ebRaik] *a* Hebrew, Hebraic.
**hébreu, x** [ebRø] *am, nm* Hebrew.
**H.E.C.** *sigle fpl* = Hautes études commerciales.
**hécatombe** [ekatɔ̃b] *nf* slaughter.
**hectare** [ɛktaR] *nm* hectare, 10,000 square metres.
**hectolitre** [ɛktolitR] *nm* hectolitre.
**hégémonie** [eʒemɔni] *nf* hegemony.
*****hein** ['ɛ̃] *excl* eh?
**hélas** ['elɑs] *excl* alas! // *ad* unfortunately.
*****héler** ['ele] *vt* to hail.
**hélice** [elis] *nf* propeller.
**hélicoïdal, e, aux** [elikɔidal, -o] *a* helical ; helicoid.
**hélicoptère** [elikɔptɛR] *nm* helicopter.
**héliogravure** [eljɔgRavyR] *nf* heliogravure.
**héliport** [elipɔR] *nm* heliport.
**héliporté, e** [elipɔRte] *a* transported by helicopter.
**hellénique** [elenik] *a* Hellenic.
**helvétique** [ɛlvetik] *a* Swiss.

**hématome** [ematɔm] nm haematoma.
**hémicycle** [emisikl(ə)] nm semicircle; (POL): l'~ ≈ the benches (of the Commons).
**hémiplégie** [emipleʒi] nf paralysis of one side, hemiplegia.
**hémisphère** [emisfɛʀ] nf: ~ nord/sud northern/southern hemisphere.
**hémophile** [emɔfil] a haemophiliac.
**hémorragie** [emɔʀaʒi] nf bleeding q, haemorrhage.
**hémorroïdes** [emɔʀɔid] nfpl piles, haemorrhoids.
*__hennir__ ['eniʀ] vi to neigh, whinny.
**hépatite** [epatit] nf hepatitis, liver infection.
**herbe** [ɛʀb(ə)] nf grass; (CULIN, MÉD) herb; en ~ unripe; (fig) budding; **herbeux, euse** a grassy; **herbicide** nm weed-killer; **herbier** nm herbarium; **herboriser** vi to collect plants, botanize; **herboriste** nm/f herbalist; **herboristerie** nf herbalist's shop; herb trade.
*__hère__ ['ɛʀ] nm: **pauvre** ~ poor wretch.
**héréditaire** [eʀeditɛʀ] a hereditary.
**hérédité** [eʀedite] nf heredity.
**hérésie** [eʀezi] nf heresy; **hérétique** nm/f heretic.
*__hérissé, e__ ['eʀise] a bristling; ~ **de** spiked with; (fig) bristling with.
*__hérisser__ ['eʀise] vt: ~ **qn** (fig) to ruffle sb; **se** ~ vi to bristle, bristle up.
*__hérisson__ ['eʀisɔ̃] nm hedgehog.
**héritage** [eʀitaʒ] nm inheritance; (fig) heritage; legacy; **faire un (petit)** ~ to come into (a little) money.
**hériter** [eʀite] vi: ~ **de qch (de qn)** to inherit sth (from sb); ~ **de qn** to inherit sb's property; **héritier, ière** nm/f heir/heiress.
**hermétique** [ɛʀmetik] a airtight; watertight; (fig) abstruse; impenetrable; ~**ment** ad tightly, hermetically.
**hermine** [ɛʀmin] nf ermine.
*__hernie__ ['ɛʀni] nf hernia.
**héroïne** [eʀɔin] nf heroine; (drogue) heroin.
**héroïque** [eʀɔik] a heroic.
**héroïsme** [eʀɔism(ə)] nm heroism.
*__héron__ ['eʀɔ̃] nm heron.
*__héros__ ['eʀo] nm hero.
*__herse__ ['ɛʀs(ə)] nf harrow; (de château) portcullis.
**hésitant, e** [ezitɑ̃, -ɑ̃t] a hesitant.
**hésitation** [ezitɑsjɔ̃] nf hesitation.
**hésiter** [ezite] vi: ~ **(à faire)** to hesitate (to do).
**hétéroclite** [eteʀɔklit] a heterogeneous; (objets) sundry.
*__hêtre__ ['ɛtʀ(ə)] nm beech.
**heure** [œʀ] nf hour; (SCOL) period; (moment, moment fixé) time; **c'est l'**~ it's time; **quelle** ~ **est-il?** what time is it?; **être à l'**~ to be on time; (montre) to be right; **mettre à l'**~ to set right; **à toute** ~ at any time; **24** ~**s sur 24** round the clock, 24 hours a day; **à l'**~ **qu'il est** at this time (of day); **by now**; **sur l'**~ at once; ~ **locale/d'été** local/summer time; ~**s de bureau** office hours; ~**s supplémentaires** overtime sg.

**heureusement** [œʀøzmɑ̃] ad (par bonheur) fortunately, luckily.
**heureux, euse** [œʀø, -øz] a happy; (chanceux) lucky, fortunate; (judicieux) felicitous, fortunate.
*__heurt__ ['œʀ] nm (choc) collision; ~**s** nmpl (fig) clashes.
*__heurté, e__ ['œʀte] a (fig) jerky, uneven.
*__heurter__ ['œʀte] vt (mur) to strike, hit; (personne) to collide with; (fig) to go against, upset; **se** ~ **à** vt to collide with; (fig) to come up against; **heurtoir** nm door knocker.
**hexagone** [ɛgzagɔn] nm hexagon.
*__hiatus__ ['jatys] nm hiatus.
*__hiberner__ [ibɛʀne] vi to hibernate.
*__hibou, x__ ['ibu] nm owl.
*__hideux, euse__ ['idø, -øz] a hideous.
**hier** [jɛʀ] ad yesterday; ~ **matin/soir** yesterday morning/evening; **toute la journée d'**~ all day yesterday; **toute la matinée d'**~ all yesterday morning.
*__hiérarchie__ ['jeʀaʀ ʃi] nf hierarchy; *__hiérarchique__ a hierarchic; *__hiérarchiser__ vt to organize into a hierarchy.
**hiéroglyphe** [jeʀɔglif] nm hieroglyphic.
**hilare** [ilaʀ] a mirthful; **hilarité** nf hilarity, mirth.
**hindou, e** [ɛ̃du] a, nm/f Hindu; Indian.
**hippique** [ipik] a equestrian, horse cpd.
**hippisme** [ipism(ə)] nm (horse) riding.
**hippodrome** [ipɔdʀom] nm racecourse.
**hippopotame** [ipɔpɔtam] nm hippopotamus.
**hirondelle** [iʀɔ̃dɛl] nf swallow.
**hirsute** [iʀsyt] a hairy; shaggy; tousled.
**hispanique** [ispanik] a Hispanic.
*__hisser__ ['ise] vt to hoist, haul up; **se** ~ **sur** to haul o.s. up onto.
**histoire** [istwaʀ] nf (science, événements) history; (anecdote, récit, mensonge) story; (affaire) business q; (chichis: gén pl) fuss q; ~**s** nfpl (ennuis) trouble sg; **historien, ne** nm/f historian; **historique** a historic.
**hiver** [ivɛʀ] nm winter; ~**nal, e, aux** a winter cpd; wintry; ~**ner** vi to winter.
**H.L.M.** sigle m ou f voir **habitation**.
*__hocher__ ['ɔʃe] vt: ~ **la tête** to nod; (signe négatif ou dubitatif) to shake one's head.
*__hochet__ ['ɔʃɛ] nm rattle.
*__hockey__ ['ɔkɛ] nm: ~ **(sur glace/gazon)** (ice/field) hockey; *__hockeyeur__ nm hockey player.
**holding** ['ɔldiŋ] nm holding company.
**hold-up** ['ɔldœp] nm inv hold-up.
*__hollandais, e__ ['ɔlɑ̃dɛ, -ɛz] a, nm (langue) Dutch // nm/f: **H**~, e Dutchman/woman; **les H**~ the Dutch.
*__Hollande__ ['ɔlɑ̃d] nf Holland.
*__homard__ ['ɔmaʀ] nm lobster.
**homéopathie** [ɔmeɔpati] nf homoeopathy; **homéopathique** a homoeopathic.
**homérique** [ɔmeʀik] a Homeric.
**homicide** [ɔmisid] nm murder // nm/f murderer/eress; ~ **involontaire** manslaughter.
**hommage** [ɔmaʒ] nm tribute; ~**s** nmpl: **présenter ses** ~**s** to pay one's respects;

**rendre** ~ **à** to pay tribute *ou* homage to ; **faire** ~ **de qch à qn** to present sb with sth.

**homme** [ɔm] *nm* man ; ~ **d'affaires** businessman ; ~ **d'État** statesman ; ~ **de main** hired man ; ~ **de paille** stooge ; ~-**grenouille** *nm* frogman ; ~-**orchestre** *nm* one-man band.

**homogène** [ɔmɔʒɛn] *a* homogeneous ; **homogénéité** *nf* homogeneity.

**homologue** [ɔmɔlɔg] *nm/f* counterpart, opposite number.

**homologué, e** [ɔmɔlɔge] *a* (SPORT) officially recognized, ratified ; (*tarif*) authorized.

**homonyme** [ɔmɔnim] *nm* (LING) homonym ; (*d'une personne*) namesake.

**homosexualité** [ɔmɔsɛksɥalite] *nf* homosexuality.

**homosexuel, le** [ɔmɔsɛksɥɛl] *a* homosexual.

\*****Hongrie** ['ɔ̃gri] *nf:* **la** ~ Hungary ; \*****hongrois, e** *a*, *nm/f*, *nm* (*langue*) Hungarian.

**honnête** [ɔnɛt] *a* (*intègre*) honest ; (*juste, satisfaisant*) fair ; ~**ment** *ad* honestly ; ~**té** *nf* honesty.

**honneur** [ɔnœR] *nm* honour ; (*mérite*): **l'**~ **lui revient** the credit is his ; **en l'**~ **de** in honour of ; (*événement*) on the occasion of ; **faire** ~ **à** (*engagements*) to honour ; (*famille*) to be a credit to ; (*fig: repas etc*) to do justice to ; **être à l'**~ to be in the place of honour ; **être en** ~ to be in favour ; **membre d'**~ honorary member ; **table d'**~ top table.

**honorable** [ɔnɔRabl(ə)] *a* worthy, honourable ; (*suffisant*) decent ; ~**ment** *ad* honorably ; decently.

**honoraire** [ɔnɔRER] *a* honorary ; ~**s** *nmpl* fees *pl* ; **professeur** ~ professor emeritus.

**honorer** [ɔnɔRe] *vt* to honour ; (*estimer*) to hold in high regard ; (*faire honneur à*) to do credit to ; **s'**~ **de** to pride o.s. upon ; **honorifique** *a* honorary.

\*****honte** ['ɔ̃t] *nf* shame ; **avoir** ~ **de** to be ashamed of ; **faire** ~ **à qn** to make sb (feel) ashamed ; \*****honteux, euse** *a* ashamed ; (*conduite, acte*) shameful, disgraceful.

**hôpital, aux** [ɔpital, -o] *nm* hospital.

\*****hoquet** ['ɔkɛ] *nm* hiccough ; **avoir le** ~ to have (the) hiccoughs ; **hoqueter** *vi* to hiccough.

**horaire** [ɔRER] *a* hourly // *nm* timetable, schedule.

\*****horions** ['ɔRjɔ̃] *nmpl* blows.

**horizon** [ɔRizɔ̃] *nm* horizon ; (*paysage*) landscape, view ; **sur l'**~ on the skyline *ou* horizon.

**horizontal, e, aux** [ɔRizɔ̃tal, -o] *a* horizontal ; ~**ement** *ad* horizontally.

**horloge** [ɔRlɔʒ] *nf* clock ; **l'**~ **parlante** the speaking clock ; **horloger, ère** *nm/f* watchmaker ; clockmaker ; ~**rie** *nf* watchmaking ; watchmaker's (shop) ; clockmaker's (shop) ; **pièces d'**~**rie** watch parts *ou* components.

\*****hormis** ['ɔRmi] *prép* save.

**hormonal, e, aux** [ɔRmɔnal, -o] *a* hormonal.

**hormone** [ɔRmɔn] *nf* hormone.

**horoscope** [ɔRɔskɔp] *nm* horoscope.

**horreur** [ɔRœR] *nf* horror ; **avoir** ~ **de** to loathe *ou* detest ; **horrible** *a* horrible ; **horrifier** *vt* to horrify.

**horripiler** [ɔRipile] *vt* to exasperate.

\*****hors** ['ɔR] *prép* except (for) ; ~ **de** out of ; ~ **pair** outstanding ; ~ **de propos** inopportune ; **être** ~ **de soi** to be beside o.s. ; ~-**bord** *nm inv* speedboat (with outboard motor) ; ~-**concours** *a* ineligible to compete ; (*fig*) in a class of one's own ; ~-**d'œuvre** *nm inv* hors d'œuvre ; ~-**jeu** *nm inv* offside ; ~-**la-loi** *nm inv* outlaw ; ~-**taxe** *a* duty-free ; ~-**texte** *nm inv* plate.

**hortensia** [ɔRtɑ̃sja] *nm* hydrangea.

**horticulteur, trice** [ɔRtikyltœR, -tRis] *nm/f* horticulturalist.

**horticulture** [ɔRtikyltyR] *nf* horticulture.

**hospice** [ɔspis] *nm* (*de vieillards*) home.

**hospitalier, ière** [ɔspitalje, -jɛR] *a* (*accueillant*) hospitable ; (MÉD: *service, centre*) hospital *cpd*.

**hospitaliser** [ɔspitalize] *vt* to take (*ou* send) to hospital, hospitalize.

**hospitalité** [ɔspitalite] *nf* hospitality.

**hostie** ['ɔsti] *nf* host.

**hostile** [ɔstil] *a* hostile ; **hostilité** *nf* hostility ; **hostilités** *nfpl* hostilities.

**hôte** [ot] *nm* (*maître de maison*) host ; (*invité*) guest ; (*client*) patron ; (*fig*) inhabitant, occupant.

**hôtel** [otɛl] *nm* hotel ; ~ **(particulier)** (private) mansion ; ~ **de ville** town hall ; **hôtelier, ière** *a* hotel *cpd* // *nm/f* hotelier, hotel-keeper ; ~**lerie** *nf* hotel business ; (*auberge*) inn.

**hôtesse** [otɛs] *nf* hostess ; ~ **de l'air** air hostess *ou* stewardess.

\*****hotte** ['ɔt] *nf* (*panier*) basket (carried on the back) ; (*de cheminée*) hood ; ~ **aspirante** cooker hood.

\*****houblon** ['ublɔ̃] *nm* (BOT) hop ; (*pour la bière*) hops *pl*.

\*****houille** ['uj] *nf* coal ; ~ **blanche** hydroelectric power ; \*****houiller, ère** *a* coal *cpd* ; coal-bearing.

\*****houle** ['ul] *nf* swell.

\*****houlette** ['ulɛt] *nf:* **sous la** ~ **de** under the guidance of.

\*****houleux, euse** ['ulø, -øz] *a* heavy, swelling ; (*fig*) stormy, turbulent.

\*****houppe** ['up] *nf*, \*****houppette** ['upɛt] *nf* powder puff.

\*****hourra** ['uRa] *nm* cheer // *excl* hurrah!

\*****houspiller** ['uspije] *vt* to scold.

\*****housse** ['us] *nf* cover ; dust cover ; loose *ou* stretch cover ; ~ **(penderie)** hanging wardrobe.

\*****houx** ['u] *nm* holly.

\*****hublot** ['yblo] *nm* porthole.

\*****huche** ['yʃ] *nf:* ~ **à pain** bread bin.

\*****huées** ['ɥe] *nfpl* boos.

\*****huer** ['ɥe] *vt* to boo.

**huile** [ɥil] *nf* oil ; (ART) oil painting ; (*fam*) bigwig ; ~ **de foie de morue** cod-liver oil ; ~ **de table** salad oil ; **huiler** *vt* to oil ; **huileux, euse** *a* oily.

**huis** [ɥi] *nm:* **à** ~ **clos** in camera.

**huissier** [ɥisje] *nm* usher ; *(JUR)* ≈ bailiff.
***huit** ['ɥit] *num* eight ; **samedi en** ~ **a**
week on Saturday ; **dans** ~ **jours** in a
week('s time) ; **une huitaine de jours** a
week or so ; ***huitième** *num* eighth.
**huître** [ɥitʀ(ə)] *nf* oyster.
**humain, e** [ymɛ̃, -ɛn] *a* human ;
*(compatissant)* humane // *nm* human
(being) ; **humaniser** *vt* to humanize ;
**humanitaire** *a* humanitarian ; **humanité**
*nf* humanity.
**humble** [œ̃bl(ə)] *a* humble.
**humecter** [ymɛkte] *vt* to dampen ; **s'**~
**les lèvres** to moisten one's lips.
***humer** ['yme] *vt* to smell ; to inhale.
**humeur** [ymœʀ] *nf* mood ; *(tempérament)*
temper ; *(irritation)* bad temper ; **de**
**bonne/mauvaise** ~ in a good/bad mood.
**humide** [ymid] *a* damp ; *(main, yeux)*
moist ; *(climat, chaleur)* humid ; *(route)*
wet ; **humidificateur** *nm* humidifier ;
**humidifier** *vt* to humidify ; **humidité** *nf*
humidity ; dampness ; **traces d'humidité**
traces of moisture ou damp.
**humiliation** [ymiljɑsjɔ̃] *nf* humiliation.
**humilier** [ymilje] *vt* to humiliate.
**humilité** [ymilite] *nf* humility,
humbleness.
**humoriste** [ymɔʀist(ə)] *nm/f* humorist.
**humoristique** [ymɔʀistik] *a* humorous ;
humoristic.
**humour** [ymuʀ] *nm* humour ; **avoir de**
**l'**~ to have a sense of humour ; ~ **noir**
sick humour.
***huppé, e** ['ype] *a* crested ; *(fam)* posh.
***hurlement** ['yʀləmɑ̃] *nm* howling *q*,
howl, yelling *q*, yell.
***hurler** ['yʀle] *vi* to howl, yell.
**hurluberlu** [yʀlybɛʀly] *nm* *(péj)* crank.
***hutte** ['yt] *nf* hut.
**hybride** [ibʀid] *a* hybrid.
**hydratant, e** [idʀatɑ̃, -ɑ̃t] *a* *(crème)*
moisturizing.
**hydrate** [idʀat] *nm:* ~**s de carbone** carbohydrates.
**hydraulique** [idʀolik] *a* hydraulic.
**hydravion** [idʀavjɔ̃] *nm* seaplane,
hydroplane.
**hydro...** [idʀɔ] *préfixe:* ~**carbures** *nmpl*
hydrocarbon oils ; ~**cution** *nf* immersion
syncope ; ~**électrique** a hydroelectric ;
~**gène** *nm* hydrogen ; ~**glisseur** *nm*
hydroplane ; ~**graphie** *nf* *(fleuves)* hydro-
graphy ; ~**phile** *a voir* coton.
**hyène** [jɛn] *nf* hyena.
**hygiène** [iʒjɛn] *nf* hygiene ; ~ **intime**
personal hygiene ; **hygiénique** *a* hygienic.
**hymne** [imn(ə)] *nm* hymn ; ~ **national**
national anthem.
**hypermarché** [ipɛʀmaʀʃe] *nm* hyper-
market.
**hypermétrope** [ipɛʀmetʀɔp] *a* long-
sighted, hypermetropic.
**hypertension** [ipɛʀtɑ̃sjɔ̃] *nf* high blood
pressure, hypertension.
**hypnose** [ipnoz] *nf* hypnosis ;
**hypnotique** *a* hypnotic ; **hypnotiser** *vt* to
hypnotize.
**hypocrisie** [ipɔkʀizi] *nf* hypocrisy.
**hypocrite** [ipɔkʀit] *a* hypocritical // *nm/f*
hypocrite.

**hypotension** [ipɔtɑ̃sjɔ̃] *nf* low blood
pressure, hypotension.
**hypothécaire** [ipɔtekɛʀ] *a* hypothecary ;
**garantie/prêt** ~ mortgage security/loan.
**hypothèque** [ipɔtɛk] *nf* mortgage ;
**hypothéquer** *vt* to mortgage.
**hypothèse** [ipɔtɛz] *nf* hypothesis ;
**hypothétique** *a* hypothetical.
**hystérie** [isteʀi] *nf* hysteria ; **hystérique**
*a* hysterical.

# I

**ibérique** [ibeʀik] *a:* **la péninsule** ~ the
Iberian peninsula.
**iceberg** [isbɛʀg] *nm* iceberg.
**ici** [isi] *ad* here ; **jusqu'**~ as far as this ;
until now ; **d'**~ **là** by then ; in the
meantime ; **d'**~ **peu** before long.
**icône** [ikon] *nf* icon.
**iconographie** [ikɔnɔgʀafi] *nf*
iconography ; (collection of) illustrations.
**idéal, e, aux** [ideal, -o] *a* ideal // *nm*
ideal ; ideals *pl;* ~**iser** *vt* to idealize ;
~**iste** *a* idealistic // *nm/f* idealist.
**idée** [ide] *nf* idea ; **avoir dans l'**~ **que** to
have an idea that ; ~ **fixe** idée fixe,
obsession ; ~**s noires** black *ou* dark
thoughts ; ~**s reçues** accepted ideas.
**identification** [idɑ̃tifikɑsjɔ̃] *nf*
identification.
**identifier** [idɑ̃tifje] *vt* to identify ; ~
**qch/qn à** to identify sth/sb with ; **s'**~ **à**
*(héros etc)* to identify with.
**identique** [idɑ̃tik] *a:* ~ **(à)** identical (to).
**identité** [idɑ̃tite] *nf* identity.
**idéologie** [ideɔlɔʒi] *nf* ideology.
**idiomatique** [idjɔmatik] *a:* **expression** ~
idiom, idiomatic expression.
**idiot, e** [idjo, idjɔt] *a* idiotic // *nm/f* idiot ;
**idiotie** [-si] *nf* idiocy ; idiotic remark *etc.*
**idiotisme** [idjɔtism(ə)] *nm* idiom,
idiomatic phrase.
**idolâtrer** [idɔlɑtʀe] *vt* to idolize.
**idole** [idɔl] *nf* idol.
**idylle** [idil] *nf* idyll ; **idyllique** *a* idyllic.
**if** [if] *nm* yew.
**I.F.O.P.** [ifɔp] *sigle m* = *Institut français*
*d'opinion publique.*
**igloo** [iglu] *nm* igloo.
**ignare** [iɲaʀ] *a* ignorant.
**ignifugé, e** [iɲifyʒe] *a* fireproof(ed).
**ignoble** [iɲɔbl(ə)] *a* vile.
**ignominie** [iɲɔmini] *nf* ignominy ;
ignominious *ou* base act.
**ignorance** [iɲɔʀɑ̃s] *nf* ignorance.
**ignorant, e** [iɲɔʀɑ̃, -ɑ̃t] *a* ignorant.
**ignorer** [iɲɔʀe] *vt* *(ne pas connaître)* not
to know, be unaware *ou* ignorant of ; *(être*
*sans expérience de: plaisir, guerre etc)* not
to know about ; have no experience of ;
*(bouder: personne)* to ignore ; **j'ignore**
**comment/si** I do not know how/if ; ~
**que** to be unaware that, not to know that.
**il** [il] *pronom* he ; *(animal, chose, en tournure*
*impersonnelle)* it ; NB: *en anglais les navires*
*et les pays sont en général assimilés aux*
*femelles, et les bébés aux choses, si le sexe*
*n'est pas spécifié ;* ~**s** they ; **il neige** it's
snowing ; *voir aussi* **avoir.**

**île** [il] *nf* island ; **les ~s anglo-normandes** the Channel Islands ; **les ~s Britanniques** the British Isles.

**illégal, e, aux** [ilegal, -o] *a* illegal, unlawful ; **~ité** *nf* illegality, unlawfulness ; **être dans l'~ité** to be outside the law.

**illégitime** [ileʒitim] *a* illegitimate ; *(optimisme, sévérité)* unjustified ; unwarranted ; **illégitimité** *nf* illegitimacy ; **gouverner dans l'illégitimité** to rule illegally.

**illettré, e** [iletRe] *a, nm/f* illiterate.

**illicite** [ilisit] *a* illicit.

**illimité, e** [ilimite] *a (immense)* boundless, unlimited ; *(congé, durée)* indefinite, unlimited.

**illisible** [ilizibl(ə)] *a* illegible ; *(roman)* unreadable.

**illogique** [ilɔʒik] *a* illogical.

**illumination** [ilyminɑsjɔ̃] *nf* illumination, floodlighting ; flash of inspiration ; **~s** *nfpl* illuminations, lights.

**illuminer** [ilymine] *vt* to light up ; *(monument, rue: pour une fête)* to illuminate, floodlight ; **s'~** *vi* to light up.

**illusion** [ilyzjɔ̃] *nf* illusion ; **se faire des ~s** to delude o.s. ; **faire ~** to delude *ou* fool people ; **~ d'optique** optical illusion ; **illusionniste** *nm/f* conjuror ; **illusoire** *a* illusory, illusive.

**illustrateur** [ilystRatœR] *nm* illustrator.

**illustration** [ilystRɑsjɔ̃] *nf* illustration ; *(d'un ouvrage: photos)* illustrations *pl.*

**illustre** [ilystR(ə)] *a* illustrious, renowned.

**illustré, e** [ilystRe] *a* illustrated // *nm* illustrated magazine ; comic.

**illustrer** [ilystRe] *vt* to illustrate ; **s'~** to become famous, win fame.

**îlot** [ilo] *nm* small island, islet ; *(de maisons)* block.

**image** [imaʒ] *nf (gén)* picture ; *(comparaison, ressemblance, OPTIQUE)* image ; **~ de marque** brand image ; *(d'un politicien)* public image ; **~ pieuse** holy picture ; **imagé, e** *a* full of imagery.

**imaginaire** [imaʒinɛR] *a* imaginary.

**imagination** [imaʒinɑsjɔ̃] *nf* imagination ; *(chimère)* fancy ; **avoir de l'~** to be imaginative, have a good imagination.

**imaginer** [imaʒine] *vt* to imagine ; *(inventer: expédient, mesure)* to devise, think up ; **s'~** *vt (se figurer: scène etc)* to imagine, picture ; **s'~ que** to imagine that ; **~ de faire** *(se mettre dans l'idée de)* to dream up the idea of doing.

**imbattable** [ɛ̃batabl(ə)] *a* unbeatable.

**imbécile** [ɛ̃besil] *a* idiotic // *nm/f* idiot ; *(MÉD)* imbecile ; **imbécillité** *nf* idiocy ; imbecility ; idiotic action *(ou* remark *etc).*

**imberbe** [ɛ̃bɛRb(ə)] *a* beardless.

**imbiber** [ɛ̃bibe] *vt*: **~ qch de** to moisten *ou* wet sth with ; **s'~ de** to become saturated with.

**imbriquer** [ɛ̃bRike]: **s'~** *vi* to overlap (each other) ; *(fig)* to become interlinked *ou* interwoven.

**imbu, e** [ɛ̃by] *a*: **~ de** full of.

**imbuvable** [ɛ̃byvabl(ə)] *a* undrinkable.

**imitateur, trice** [imitatoeR, -tRis] *nm/f (gén)* imitator ; *(MUSIC-HALL*: **d'une personnalité**) impersonator.

**imitation** [imitɑsjɔ̃] *nf* imitation ; *(sketch)* imitation, impression ; impersonation ; **sac ~ cuir** bag in imitation *ou* simulated leather.

**imiter** [imite] *vt* to imitate ; *(contrefaire: signature, document)* to forge, copy ; *(avoir l'aspect de)* to look like ; **il se leva et je l'imitai** he got up and I did likewise.

**immaculé, e** [imakyle] *a* spotless ; immaculate.

**immangeable** [ɛ̃mɑ̃ʒabl(ə)] *a* inedible, uneatable.

**immanquable** [ɛ̃mɑ̃kabl(ə)] *a (cible)* impossible to miss.

**immatriculation** [imatRikylɑsjɔ̃] *nf* registration.

**immatriculer** [imatRikyle] *vt* to register ; **faire/se faire ~** to register ; **voiture immatriculée dans la Seine** car with a Seine registration (number).

**immédiat, e** [imedja, -at] *a* immediate // *nm*: **dans l'~** for the time being ; **immédiatement** *ad* immediately.

**immense** [imɑ̃s] *a* immense.

**immergé, e** [imɛRʒe] *a* submerged.

**immerger** [imɛRʒe] *vt* to immerse, submerge ; to lay under water ; **s'~** *vi (sous-marin)* to dive, submerge.

**immérité, e** [imeRite] *a* undeserved.

**immeuble** [imœbl(ə)] *nm* building // *a (JUR)* immovable, real ; **~ locatif** block of rented flats.

**immigrant, e** [imigRɑ̃, -ɑ̃t] *nm/f* immigrant.

**immigration** [imigRɑsjɔ̃] *nf* immigration.

**immigré, e** [imigRe] *nm/f* immigrant.

**immigrer** [imigRe] *vi* to immigrate.

**imminent, e** [iminɑ̃, -ɑ̃t] *a* imminent, impending.

**immiscer** [imise]: **s'~** *vi*: **s'~ dans** to interfere in *ou* with.

**immobile** [imɔbil] *a* still, motionless ; *(pièce de machine)* fixed ; *(fig)* unchanging.

**immobilier, ière** [imɔbilje, -jɛR] *a* property *cpd*, in real property // *nm*: **l'~** the property *ou* the real estate business.

**immobilisation** [imɔbilizɑsjɔ̃] *nf* immobilization ; **~s** *nfpl (COMM)* fixed assets.

**immobiliser** [imɔbilize] *vt (gén)* to immobilize ; *(circulation, véhicule, affaires)* to bring to a standstill ; **s'~** *(personne)* to stand still ; *(machine, véhicule)* to come to a halt *ou* standstill.

**immobilité** [imɔbilite] *nf* stillness ; immobility.

**immodéré, e** [imɔdeRe] *a* immoderate, inordinate.

**immoler** [imɔle] *vt* to immolate, sacrifice.

**immonde** [imɔ̃d] *a* foul.

**immondices** [imɔ̃dis] *nmpl* refuse *sg* ; filth *sg.*

**immoral, e, aux** [imɔRal, -o] *a* immoral.

**immortaliser** [imɔRtalize] *vt* to immortalize.

**immortel, le** [imɔRtɛl] *a* immortal.

**immuable** [imɥabl(ə)] *a* immutable ; unchanging.

**immunisé, e** [imynize] a: ~ **contre** immune to.

**immuniser** [imynize] vt to immunize.

**immunité** [imynite] nf immunity ; ~ **diplomatique** diplomatic immunity ; ~ **parlementaire** parliamentary privilege.

**impact** [ɛ̃pakt] nm impact.

**impair, e** [ɛ̃pɛR] a odd // nm faux pas, blunder.

**imparable** [ɛ̃paRabl(ə)] a unstoppable.

**impardonnable** [ɛ̃paRdɔnabl(ə)] a unpardonable, unforgivable.

**imparfait, e** [ɛ̃paRfɛ, -ɛt] a imperfect // nm imperfect (tense).

**impartial, e, aux** [ɛ̃paRsjal, -o] a impartial, unbiased ; ~ité nf impartiality.

**impartir** [ɛ̃paRtiR] vt: ~ **qch à qn** to assign sth to sb ; to bestow sth upon sb.

**impasse** [ɛ̃pɑs] nf dead-end, cul-de-sac ; (fig) deadlock.

**impassible** [ɛ̃pasibl(ə)] a impassive.

**impatience** [ɛ̃pasjɑ̃s] nf impatience.

**impatient, e** [ɛ̃pasjɑ̃, -ɑ̃t] a impatient ; **impatienter** vt to irritate, annoy ; **s'impatienter** to get impatient ; **s'impatienter de/contre** to lose patience at/with, grow impatient at/with.

**impayable** [ɛ̃pɛjabl(ə)] a (drôle) priceless.

**impayé, e** [ɛ̃peje] a unpaid.

**impeccable** [ɛ̃pekabl(ə)] a faultless, impeccable ; spotlessly clean ; impeccably dressed ; (fam) smashing.

**impénétrable** [ɛ̃penetRabl(ə)] a impenetrable.

**impénitent, e** [ɛ̃penitɑ̃, -ɑ̃t] a unrepentant.

**impensable** [ɛ̃pɑ̃sabl(ə)] a unthinkable ; unbelievable.

**impératif, ive** [ɛ̃peRatif, -iv] a imperative ; (JUR) mandatory // nm (LING) imperative ; ~s nmpl requirements ; demands.

**impératrice** [ɛ̃peRatRis] nf empress.

**imperceptible** [ɛ̃pɛRsɛptibl(ə)] a imperceptible.

**imperfection** [ɛ̃pɛRfɛksjɔ̃] nf imperfection.

**impérial, e, aux** [ɛ̃peRjal, -o] a imperial // nf upper deck ; **autobus à** ~e double-decker bus.

**impérialiste** [ɛ̃peRjalist(ə)] a imperialist.

**impérieux, euse** [ɛ̃peRjø, -øz] a (caractère, ton) imperious ; (obligation, besoin) pressing, urgent.

**impérissable** [ɛ̃peRisabl(ə)] a undying ; imperishable.

**imperméabiliser** [ɛ̃pɛRmeabilize] vt to waterproof.

**imperméable** [ɛ̃pɛRmeabl(ə)] a waterproof ; (GÉO) impermeable ; (fig): ~ **à** impervious to // nm raincoat ; ~ **à l'air** airtight.

**impersonnel, le** [ɛ̃pɛRsɔnɛl] a impersonal.

**impertinence** [ɛ̃pɛRtinɑ̃s] nf impertinence.

**impertinent, e** [ɛ̃pɛRtinɑ̃, -ɑ̃t] a impertinent.

**imperturbable** [ɛ̃pɛRtyRbabl(ə)] a imperturbable ; unruffled ; unshakeable.

**impétrant, e** [ɛ̃petRɑ̃, -ɑ̃t] nm/f (JUR) applicant.

**impétueux, euse** [ɛ̃petɥø, -øz] a fiery.

**impie** [ɛ̃pi] a impious, ungodly ; **impiété** nf impiety.

**impitoyable** [ɛ̃pitwajabl(ə)] a pitiless, merciless.

**implacable** [ɛ̃plakabl(ə)] a implacable.

**implanter** [ɛ̃plɑ̃te] vt (usine, industrie, usage) to establish ; (colons etc) to settle ; (idée, préjugé) to implant ; **s'**~ **dans** to be established in ; to settle in ; to become implanted in.

**implication** [ɛ̃plikɑsjɔ̃] nf implication.

**implicite** [ɛ̃plisit] a implicit.

**impliquer** [ɛ̃plike] vt to imply ; ~ **qn** (dans) to implicate sb (in).

**implorer** [ɛ̃plɔRe] vt to implore.

**implosion** [ɛ̃plozjɔ̃] nf implosion.

**impoli, e** [ɛ̃pɔli] a impolite, rude ; ~**tesse** nf impoliteness, rudeness ; impolite ou rude remark.

**impondérable** [ɛ̃pɔ̃deRabl(ə)] nm imponderable.

**impopulaire** [ɛ̃pɔpylɛR] a unpopular.

**importance** [ɛ̃pɔRtɑ̃s] nf importance ; **avoir de l'**~ to be important ; **sans** ~ unimportant.

**important, e** [ɛ̃pɔRtɑ̃, -ɑ̃t] a important ; (en quantité) considerable, sizeable ; extensive ; (péj: airs, ton) self-important // nm: **l'**~ the important thing.

**importateur, trice** [ɛ̃pɔRtatœR, -tRis] a importing // nm importer ; **pays** ~ **de blé** wheat-importing country.

**importation** [ɛ̃pɔRtɑsjɔ̃] nf importation ; introduction ; (produit) import.

**importer** [ɛ̃pɔRte] vt (COMM) to import ; (maladies, plantes) to introduce // vi (être important) to matter ; ~ **à qn** to matter to sb ; **il importe qu'il fasse** he must do, it is important that he should do ; **peu m'importe** I don't mind ; I don't care ; **peu importe (que)** it doesn't matter (if) ; voir aussi **n'importe**.

**import-export** [ɛ̃pɔRɛkspɔR] nm import-export business.

**importun, e** [ɛ̃pɔRtœ̃, -yn] a irksome, importunate ; (arrivée, visite) inopportune, ill-timed // nm intruder ; **importuner** vt to bother.

**imposable** [ɛ̃pozabl(ə)] a taxable.

**imposant, e** [ɛ̃pozɑ̃, -ɑ̃t] a imposing.

**imposer** [ɛ̃poze] vt (taxer) to tax ; ~ **qch à qn** to impose sth on sb ; **s'**~ (être nécessaire) to be imperative ; (montrer sa prominence) to stand out, emerge ; (artiste: se faire connaître) to win recognition, come to the fore ; **en** ~ **à** to impress.

**imposition** [ɛ̃pozisjɔ̃] nf (ADMIN) taxation.

**impossibilité** [ɛ̃pɔsibilite] nf impossibility ; **être dans l'**~ **de faire** to be unable to do, find it impossible to do.

**impossible** [ɛ̃pɔsibl(ə)] a impossible ; **il m'est** ~ **de le faire** it is impossible for me to do it, I can't possibly do it ; **faire l'**~ **(pour que)** to do one's utmost (so that).

**imposteur** [ɛ̃pɔstœR] nm impostor.

**imposture** [ɛ̃pɔstyR] nf ~ **imposture**, deception.

**impôt** [ɛpo] *nm* tax ; *(taxes)* taxation ; taxes *pl* ; ~s *nmpl (contributions)* (income) tax *sg* ; **payer 1000 F d'**~s to pay 1,000 F in tax ; ~ **sur le chiffre d'affaires** corporation tax ; ~ **foncier** land tax ; ~ **sur les plus-values** capital gains tax ; ~ **sur le revenu** income tax.

**impotent, e** [ɛpɔtɑ̃, -ɑ̃t] *a* disabled.

**impraticable** [ɛpratikabl(ə)] *a (projet)* impracticable, unworkable ; *(piste)* impassable.

**imprécation** [ɛprekasjɔ̃] *nf* imprecation.

**imprécis, e** [ɛpresi, -iz] *a (contours, souvenir)* imprecise, vague ; *(tir)* inaccurate, imprecise.

**imprégner** [ɛpreɲe] *vt (tissu, tampon)*: ~ **(de)** to soak *ou* impregnate (with); *(lieu, air)*: ~ **(de)** to fill (with) ; *(suj: amertume, ironie)* to pervade ; **s'**~ **de** to become impregnated with ; to be filled with ; *(fig)* to absorb.

**imprenable** [ɛprənabl(ə)] *a (forteresse)* impregnable ; **vue** ~ unimpeded outlook.

**impresario** [ɛpresarjo] *nm* manager, impresario.

**impression** [ɛpresjɔ̃] *nf* impression ; *(d'un ouvrage, tissu)* printing ; *(PHOTO)* exposure ; **faire bonne** ~ to make a good impression.

**impressionnant, e** [ɛpresjɔnɑ̃, -ɑ̃t] *a* impressive ; upsetting.

**impressionner** [ɛpresjɔne] *vt (frapper)* to impress ; *(troubler)* to upset ; *(PHOTO)* to expose.

**impressionnisme** [ɛpresjɔnism(ə)] *nm* impressionism.

**imprévisible** [ɛprevizibl(ə)] *a* unforeseeable.

**imprévoyant, e** [ɛprevwajɑ̃, -ɑ̃t] *a* lacking in foresight ; *(en matière d'argent)* improvident.

**imprévu, e** [ɛprevy] *a* unforeseen, unexpected // *nm* unexpected incident ; **en cas d'**~ if anything unexpected happens.

**imprimé** [ɛprime] *nm (formulaire)* printed form ; *(POSTES)* printed matter *q* ; *(tissu)* printed fabric.

**imprimer** [ɛprime] *vt* to print ; *(apposer: visa, cachet)* to stamp ; *(empreinte etc)* to imprint ; *(publier)* to publish ; *(communiquer: mouvement, impulsion)* to impart, transmit ; **imprimerie** *nf* printing ; *(établissement)* printing works *sg* ; *(atelier)* printing house, printery ; **imprimeur** *nm* printer ; **imprimeur-éditeur/-libraire** printer and publisher/bookseller.

**improbable** [ɛprɔbabl(ə)] *a* unlikely, improbable.

**improductif, ive** [ɛprɔdyktif, -iv] *a* unproductive.

**impromptu, e** [ɛprɔ̃pty] *a* impromptu ; sudden.

**impropre** [ɛprɔpr(ə)] *a* inappropriate ; ~ **à** unsuitable for ; **impropriété** *nf (de langage)* incorrect usage *q*.

**improvisé, e** [ɛprɔvize] *a* makeshift, improvised ; *(jeu etc)* scratch, improvised.

**improviser** [ɛprɔvize] *vt, vi.* to improvise ; **s'**~ *(secours, réunion)* to be improvised ; **s'**~ **cuisinier** to (decide to) act as cook.

**improviste** [ɛprɔvist(ə)]: **à l'**~ *ad* unexpectedly, without warning.

**imprudemment** [ɛprydamɑ̃] *ad* carelessly ; unwisely, imprudently.

**imprudence** [ɛprydɑ̃s] *nf* carelessness ; imprudence ; act of carelessness ; foolish *ou* unwise action.

**imprudent, e** [ɛprydɑ̃, -ɑ̃t] *a (conducteur, geste, action)* careless ; *(remarque)* unwise, imprudent ; *(projet)* foolhardy.

**impubère** [ɛpybɛr] *a* below the age of puberty.

**impudent, e** [ɛpydɑ̃, -ɑ̃t] *a* impudent ; brazen.

**impudique** [ɛpydik] *a* shameless.

**impuissance** [ɛpɥisɑ̃s] *nf* helplessness ; ineffectiveness ; impotence.

**impuissant, e** [ɛpɥisɑ̃, -ɑ̃t] *a* helpless ; *(sans effet)* ineffectual ; *(sexuellement)* impotent // *nm* impotent man ; ~ **à faire** powerless to do.

**impulsif, ive** [ɛpylsif, -iv] *a* impulsive.

**impulsion** [ɛpylsjɔ̃] *nf (ÉLEC, instinct)* impulse ; *(élan, influence)* impetus.

**impunément** [ɛpynemɑ̃] *ad* with impunity.

**impur, e** [ɛpyr] *a* impure ; ~**eté** *nf* impurity.

**imputation** [ɛpytasjɔ̃] *nf* imputation, charge.

**imputer** [ɛpyte] *vt (attribuer)*: ~ **qch à** to ascribe *ou* impute sth to ; *(COMM)*: ~ **à** *ou* **sur** to charge to.

**imputrescible** [ɛpytresibl(ə)] *a* which does not rot.

**inabordable** [inabɔrdabl(ə)] *a (lieu)* inaccessible ; *(cher)* prohibitive.

**inaccentué, e** [inaksɑ̃tɥe] *a (LING)* unstressed.

**inacceptable** [inaksɛptabl(ə)] *a* unacceptable ; inadmissible.

**inaccessible** [inaksesibl(ə)] *a* inaccessible ; unattainable ; *(insensible)*: ~ **à** impervious to.

**inaccoutumé, e** [inakutyme] *a* unaccustomed.

**inachevé, e** [inaʃve] *a* unfinished.

**inactif, ive** [inaktif, -iv] *a* inactive, idle.

**inaction** [inaksjɔ̃] *nf* inactivity.

**inactivité** [inaktivite] *nf (ADMIN)*: **en** ~ out of active service.

**inadapté, e** [inadapte] *a (gén)*: ~ **à** not adapted to, unsuited to ; *(PSYCH)* maladjusted.

**inadmissible** [inadmisibl(ə)] *a* inadmissible.

**inadvertance** [inadvɛrtɑ̃s]: **par** ~ *ad* inadvertently.

**inaliénable** [inaljenabl(ə)] *a* inalienable.

**inaltérable** [inalterabl(ə)] *a (matière)* stable ; *(fig)* unchanging ; ~ **à** unaffected by ; **couleur** ~ **(au lavage/à la lumière)** fast colour/fade-resistant colour.

**inamovible** [inamɔvibl(ə)] *a* fixed ; *(JUR)* irremovable.

**inanimé, e** [inanime] *a (matière)* inanimate ; *(évanoui)* unconscious ; *(sans vie)* lifeless.

**inanité** [inanite] *nf* futility.

**inanition** [inanisjɔ̃] *nf*: **tomber d'**~ to faint with hunger (and exhaustion).

**inaperçu, e** [inapɛʀsy] *a*: **passer** ~ to go unnoticed.
**inappliqué, e** [inaplike] *a* lacking in application.
**inappréciable** [inapʀesjabl(ə)] *a* (*service*) invaluable ; (*différence, nuance*) inappreciable.
**inapte** [inapt(ə)] *a*: ~ **à** incapable of ; (MIL) unfit for.
**inattaquable** [inatakabl(ə)] *a* (MIL) unassailable ; (*texte, preuve*) irrefutable.
**inattendu, e** [inatɑ̃dy] *a* unexpected.
**inattentif, ive** [inatɑ̃tif, -iv] *a* inattentive ; ~ **à** (*dangers, détails*) heedless of ; **inattention** *nf* inattention ; **faute d'inattention** careless mistake.
**inaugural, e, aux** [inɔgyʀal, -o] *a* (*cérémonie*) inaugural, opening ; (*vol, voyage*) maiden.
**inauguration** [inɔgyʀasjɔ̃] *nf* opening ; unveiling.
**inaugurer** [inɔgyʀe] *vt* (*monument*) to unveil ; (*exposition, usine*) to open ; (*fig*) to inaugurate.
**inavouable** [inavwabl(ə)] *a* shameful ; undisclosable.
**inavoué, e** [inavwe] *a* unavowed.
**incalculable** [ɛ̃kalkylabl(ə)] *a* incalculable.
**incandescence** [ɛ̃kɑ̃desɑ̃s] *nf* incandescence ; **porter à** ~ to heat white-hot.
**incantation** [ɛ̃kɑ̃tasjɔ̃] *nf* incantation.
**incapable** [ɛ̃kapabl(ə)] *a* incapable ; ~ **de faire** incapable of doing ; (*empêché*) unable to do.
**incapacité** [ɛ̃kapasite] *nf* incapability ; (JUR) incapacity ; **être dans l'**~ **de faire** to be unable to do ; ~ **permantente/de travail** permanent/industrial disablement ; ~ **électorale** ineligibility to vote.
**incarcérer** [ɛ̃kaʀseʀe] *vt* to incarcerate.
**incarnation** [ɛ̃kaʀnasjɔ̃] *nf* incarnation.
**incarné, e** [ɛ̃kaʀne] *a* incarnate ; (*ongle*) ingrown.
**incarner** [ɛ̃kaʀne] *vt* to embody, personify ; (THÉÂTRE) to play ; (REL) to incarnate.
**incartade** [ɛ̃kaʀtad] *nf* prank, escapade.
**incassable** [ɛ̃kɑsabl(ə)] *a* unbreakable.
**incendiaire** [ɛ̃sɑ̃djɛʀ] *a* incendiary ; (*fig: discours*) inflammatory // *nm/f* fire-raiser, arsonist.
**incendie** [ɛ̃sɑ̃di] *nm* fire ; ~ **criminel** arson *q* ; ~ **de forêt** forest fire.
**incendier** [ɛ̃sɑ̃dje] *vt* (*mettre le feu à*) to set fire to, set alight ; (*brûler complètement*) to burn down.
**incertain, e** [ɛ̃sɛʀtɛ̃, -ɛn] *a* uncertain ; (*temps*) uncertain, unsettled ; (*imprécis: contours*) indistinct, blurred ; **incertitude** *nf* uncertainty.
**incessamment** [ɛ̃sesamɑ̃] *a* very shortly.
**incessant, e** [ɛ̃sesɑ̃, -ɑ̃t] *a* incessant, unceasing.
**inceste** [ɛ̃sɛst(ə)] *nm* incest.
**inchangé, e** [ɛ̃ʃɑ̃ʒe] *a* unchanged, unaltered.
**incidemment** [ɛ̃sidamɑ̃] *ad* in passing.

**incidence** [ɛ̃sidɑ̃s] *nf* (*effet, influence*) effect ; (PHYSIQUE) incidence.
**incident** [ɛ̃sidɑ̃] *nm* incident ; ~ **de parcours** minor hitch *ou* setback ; ~ **technique** technical difficulties *pl*.
**incinérateur** [ɛ̃sineʀatœʀ] *nm* incinerator.
**incinérer** [ɛ̃sineʀe] *vt* (*ordures*) to incinerate ; (*mort*) to cremate.
**incise** [ɛ̃siz] *nf* (LING) interpolated clause.
**incisif, ive** [ɛ̃sizif, -iv] *a* incisive, cutting // *nf* incisor.
**incision** [ɛ̃sizjɔ̃] *nf* incision ; (*d'un abcès*) lancing.
**inciter** [ɛ̃site] *vt*: ~ **qn à faire** to incite *ou* prompt sb to do.
**inclinaison** [ɛ̃klinɛzɔ̃] *nf* (*déclivité: d'une route etc*) incline ; (: *d'un toit*) slope ; (*état penché: d'un mur*) lean ; (: *de la tête*) tilt ; (: *d'un navire*) list.
**inclination** [ɛ̃klinasjɔ̃] *nf* (*penchant*) inclination, tendency ; ~ **de (la) tête** nod (of the head) ; ~ **(de buste)** bow.
**incliner** [ɛ̃kline] *vt* (*tête, bouteille*) to tilt ; (*inciter*): ~ **qn à qch/à faire** to encourage sb towards sth/to do // *vi*: ~ **à qch/à faire** to incline towards sth/doing ; to tend towards sth/to do ; **s'**~ (*route*) to slope ; **s'**~ (*devant*) to bow (before) ; (*céder*) to give in *ou* yield (to) ; ~ **la tête** *ou* **le front** to give a slight bow.
**inclure** [ɛ̃klyʀ] *vt* to include ; (*joindre à un envoi*) to enclose ; **jusqu'au 10 mars inclus** until 10th March inclusive.
**incoercible** [ɛ̃kɔɛʀsibl(ə)] *a* uncontrollable.
**incognito** [ɛ̃kɔɲito] *ad* incognito.
**incohérence** [ɛ̃kɔeʀɑ̃s] *nf* inconsistency.
**incohérent, e** [ɛ̃kɔeʀɑ̃, -ɑ̃t] *a* inconsistent ; incoherent.
**incollable** [ɛ̃kɔlabl(ə)] *a*: **il est** ~ he's got all the answers.
**incolore** [ɛ̃kɔlɔʀ] *a* colourless.
**incomber** [ɛ̃kɔbe]: ~ **à** *vt* (*suj: devoirs, responsabilité*) to rest *ou* be incumbent upon ; (: *frais, travail*) to be the responsibility of.
**incombustible** [ɛ̃kɔbystibl(ə)] *a* incombustible.
**incommensurable** [ɛ̃kɔmɑ̃syʀabl(ə)] *a* immeasurable.
**incommode** [ɛ̃kɔmɔd] *a* inconvenient ; (*posture, siège*) uncomfortable.
**incommoder** [ɛ̃kɔmɔde] *vt*: ~ **qn** to bother *ou* inconvenience sb ; (*embarrasser*) to make sb feel uncomfortable *ou* ill at ease.
**incomparable** [ɛ̃kɔpaʀabl(ə)] *a* not comparable ; (*inégalable*) incomparable, matchless.
**incompatibilité** [ɛ̃kɔpatibilite] *nf* incompatibility ; ~ **d'humeur** (mutual) incompatibility.
**incompatible** [ɛ̃kɔpatibl(ə)] *a* incompatible.
**incompétent, e** [ɛ̃kɔpetɑ̃, -ɑ̃t] *a* (*ignorant*) inexpert ; (JUR) incompetent, not competent.
**incomplet, ète** [ɛ̃kɔplɛ, -ɛt] *a* incomplete.
**incompréhensible** [ɛ̃kɔpʀeɑ̃sibl(ə)] *a* incomprehensible.

**incompréhensif, ive** [ɛ̃kɔ̃pReɑ̃sif, -iv] a lacking in understanding ; unsympathetic.

**incompris, e** [ɛ̃kɔ̃pRi, -iz] a misunderstood.

**inconcevable** [ɛ̃kɔ̃svabl(ə)] a inconceivable.

**inconciliable** [ɛ̃kɔ̃siljabl(ə)] a irreconcilable.

**inconditionnel, le** [ɛ̃kɔ̃disjɔnɛl] a unconditional ; (partisan) unquestioning.

**inconduite** [ɛ̃kɔ̃dɥit] nf wild behaviour q.

**inconfortable** [ɛ̃kɔ̃fɔRtabl(ə)] a uncomfortable.

**incongru, e** [ɛ̃kɔ̃gRy] a unseemly.

**inconnu, e** [ɛ̃kɔny] a unknown ; new, strange // nm/f stranger ; unknown person (ou artist etc) // nm: l'~ the unknown // nf (MATH) unknown ; (fig) unknown factor.

**inconsciemment** [ɛ̃kɔ̃sjamɑ̃] ad unconsciously ; thoughtlessly.

**inconscience** [ɛ̃kɔ̃sjɑ̃s] nf unconsciousness ; thoughtlessness, recklessness.

**inconscient, e** [ɛ̃kɔ̃sjɑ̃, -ɑ̃t] a unconscious ; (irréfléchi) thoughtless, reckless // nm (PSYCH): l'~ the subconscious, the unconscious ; ~ de unaware of.

**inconsidéré, e** [ɛ̃kɔ̃sideRe] a illconsidered.

**inconsistant, e** [ɛ̃kɔ̃sistɑ̃, -ɑ̃t] a flimsy, weak ; runny.

**inconstant, e** [ɛ̃kɔ̃stɑ̃, -ɑ̃t] a inconstant, fickle.

**incontestable** [ɛ̃kɔ̃tɛstabl(ə)] a indisputable.

**incontesté, e** [ɛ̃kɔ̃tɛste] a undisputed.

**incontinence** [ɛ̃kɔ̃tinɑ̃s] nf incontinence.

**incontinent, e** [ɛ̃kɔ̃tinɑ̃, -ɑ̃t] a incontinent // ad forthwith.

**incontrôlable** [ɛ̃kɔ̃tRolabl(ə)] a unverifiable.

**inconvenant, e** [ɛ̃kɔ̃vnɑ̃, -ɑ̃t] a unseemly, improper.

**inconvénient** [ɛ̃kɔ̃venjɑ̃] nm (d'une situation, d'un projet) disadvantage, drawback ; (d'un remède, changement etc) risk, inconvenience ; si vous n'y voyez pas d'~ if you have no objections.

**incorporation** [ɛ̃kɔRpɔRasj̃ɔ] nf (MIL) call-up.

**incorporer** [ɛ̃kɔRpɔRe] vt ~ (à) to mix in (with) ; (paragraphe etc): ~ (dans) to incorporate (in) ; (territoire, immigrants): ~ (à) to incorporate (into) ; (MIL: appeler) to recruit, call up ; (: affecter): ~ qn dans to enlist sb into.

**incorrect, e** [ɛ̃kɔRɛkt] a (impropre, inconvenant) improper ; (défectueux) faulty ; (inexact) incorrect ; (impoli) impolite ; (déloyal) underhand.

**incorrigible** [ɛ̃kɔRiʒibl(ə)] a incorrigible.

**incorruptible** [ɛ̃kɔRyptibl(ə)] a incorruptible.

**incrédule** [ɛ̃kRedyl] a incredulous ; (REL) unbelieving.

**increvable** [ɛ̃kRəvabl(ə)] a (pneu) puncture-proof ; (fam) tireless.

**incriminer** [ɛ̃kRimine] vt (personne) to incriminate ; (action, conduite) to bring

under attack ; (bonne foi, honnêteté) to call into question.

**incroyable** [ɛ̃kRwajabl(ə)] a incredible ; unbelievable.

**incroyant, e** [ɛ̃kRwajɑ̃, -ɑ̃t] nm/f nonbeliever.

**incrustation** [ɛ̃kRystasj̃ɔ] nf inlaying q ; inlay ; (dans une chaudière etc) fur q, scale q.

**incruster** [ɛ̃kRyste] vt (ART): ~ qch dans/qch de to inlay sth into/sth with ; (radiateur etc) to coat with scale ou fur ; s'~ vi (invité) to take root ; (radiateur etc) to become coated with fur ou scale ; s'~ dans (suj: corps étranger, caillou) to become embedded in.

**incubateur** [ɛ̃kybatœR] nm incubator.

**incubation** [ɛ̃kybasj̃ɔ] nf incubation.

**inculpation** [ɛ̃kylpasj̃ɔ] nf charging q ; charge.

**inculpé, e** [ɛ̃kylpe] nm/f accused.

**inculper** [ɛ̃kylpe] vt: ~ (de) to charge (with).

**inculquer** [ɛ̃kylke] vt: ~ qch à to inculcate sth in ou instil sth into.

**inculte** [ɛ̃kylt(ə)] a uncultivated ; (esprit, peuple) uncultured ; (barbe) unkempt.

**incurable** [ɛ̃kyRabl(ə)] a incurable.

**incurie** [ɛ̃kyRi] nf carelessness.

**incursion** [ɛ̃kyRsj̃ɔ] nf incursion, foray.

**incurvé, e** [ɛ̃kyRve] a curved.

**Inde** [ɛ̃d] nf: l'~ India.

**indécence** [ɛ̃desɑ̃s] nf indecency ; indecent remark (ou act etc).

**indécent, e** [ɛ̃desɑ̃, -ɑ̃t] a indecent.

**indéchiffrable** [ɛ̃deʃifRabl(ə)] a indecipherable.

**indécis, e** [ɛ̃desi, -iz] a indecisive ; (perplexe) undecided ; **indécision** nf indecision ; indecisiveness.

**indéfendable** [ɛ̃defɑ̃dabl(ə)] a indefensible.

**indéfini, e** [ɛ̃defini] a (imprécis, incertain) undefined ; (illimité, LING) indefinite ; ~ment ad indefinitely ; ~ssable a indefinable.

**indéformable** [ɛ̃defɔRmabl(ə)] a that keeps its shape.

**indélébile** [ɛ̃delebil] a indelible.

**indélicat, e** [ɛ̃delika, -at] a tactless ; dishonest.

**indémaillable** [ɛ̃demɑjabl(ə)] a run-resist.

**indemne** [ɛ̃dɛmn(ə)] a unharmed.

**indemniser** [ɛ̃dɛmnize] vt: ~ qn (de) to compensate sb (for).

**indemnité** [ɛ̃dɛmnite] nf (dédommagement) compensation q ; (allocation) allowance ; ~ de licenciement redundancy payment ; ~ de logement housing allowance ; ~ parlementaire ≈ M.P.'s salary.

**indéniable** [ɛ̃denjabl(ə)] a undeniable, indisputable.

**indépendamment** [ɛ̃depɑ̃damɑ̃] ad independently ; ~ de (abstraction faite de) irrespective of ; (en plus de) over and above.

**indépendance** [ɛ̃depɑ̃dɑ̃s] nf independence.

**indépendant, e** [ɛ̃depɑ̃dɑ̃, -ɑ̃t] a independent ; ~ de indépendent of ;

chambre ~e room with private entrance.
**indescriptible** [ɛ̃dɛskʀiptibl(ə)] *a* indescribable.

**indésirable** [ɛ̃deziʀabl(ə)] *a* undesirable.

**indestructible** [ɛ̃dɛstʀyktibl(ə)] *a* indestructible ; (*marque, impression*) indelible.

**indétermination** [ɛ̃detɛʀminɑsjɔ̃] *nf* indecision ; indecisiveness.

**indéterminé, e** [ɛ̃detɛʀmine] *a* unspecified ; indeterminate ; indeterminable.

**index** [ɛ̃dɛks] *nm* (*doigt*) index finger ; (*d'un livre etc*) index ; **mettre à l'**~ to blacklist.

**indexé, e** [ɛ̃dɛkse] *a* (*ÉCON*): ~ **(sur)** index-linked (to).

**indicateur** [ɛ̃dikatœʀ] *nm* (*POLICE*) informer ; (*livre*) guide ; directory ; (*TECH*) gauge ; indicator ; ~ **des chemins de fer** railway timetable ; ~ **de direction** (*AUTO*) indicator ; ~ **immobilier** property gazette ; ~ **de rues** street directory ; ~ **de vitesse** speedometer.

**indicatif, ive** [ɛ̃dikatif, -iv] *a*: **à titre** ~ for (your) information // *nm* (*LING*) indicative ; (*d'une émission*) theme *ou* signature tune ; (*téléphonique*) dialling code ; ~ **d'appel** (*RADIO*) call sign.

**indication** [ɛ̃dikɑsjɔ̃] *nf* indication ; (*renseignement*) information *q* ; ~**s** *nfpl* (*directives*) instructions.

**indice** [ɛ̃dis] *nm* (*marque, signe*) indication, sign ; (*POLICE*: *lors d'une enquête*) clue ; (*JUR*: *présomption*) piece of evidence ; (*SCIENCE, TECH*) index ; (*ADMIN*) grading ; rating ; ~ **d'octane** octane rating ; ~ **des prix** price index ; ~ **de traitement** salary grading.

**indicible** [ɛ̃disibl(ə)] *a* inexpressible.

**indien, ne** [ɛ̃djɛ̃, -jɛn] *a* Indian // *nm/f*: **I**~, **ne** (*d'Amérique*) Red Indian ; (*d'Inde*) Indian.

**indifféremment** [ɛ̃difeʀamɑ̃] *ad* (*sans distinction*) equally (well) ; indiscriminately.

**indifférence** [ɛ̃difeʀɑ̃s] *nf* indifference.

**indifférent, e** [ɛ̃difeʀɑ̃, -ɑ̃t] *a* (*peu intéressé*) indifferent ; ~ **à** (*insensible à*) indifferent to, unconcerned about ; (*peu intéressant pour*) indifferent to ; immaterial to.

**indigence** [ɛ̃diʒɑ̃s] *nf* poverty.

**indigène** [ɛ̃diʒɛn] *a* native, indigenous ; local // *nm/f* native.

**indigent, e** [ɛ̃diʒɑ̃, -ɑ̃t] *a* destitute, poverty-stricken ; (*fig*) poor.

**indigeste** [ɛ̃diʒɛst(ə)] *a* indigestible.

**indigestion** [ɛ̃diʒɛstjɔ̃] *nf* indigestion *q*.

**indignation** [ɛ̃diɲɑsjɔ̃] *nf* indignation.

**indigne** [ɛ̃diɲ] *a* unworthy.

**indigner** [ɛ̃diɲe] *vt* to make indignant ; **s'**~ **(de/contre)** to be (*ou* become) indignant (at).

**indignité** [ɛ̃diɲite] *nf* unworthiness *q* ; shameful act.

**indiqué, e** [ɛ̃dike] *a* (*adéquat*) appropriate, suitable ; (*conseillé*) suitable, advisable.

**indiquer** [ɛ̃dike] *vt* (*désigner*): ~ **qch/qn à qn** to point sth/sb out to sb ; (*suj: pendule, aiguille*) to show ; (*suj: étiquette, plan*) to show, indicate ; (*faire connaître*:

*médecin, restaurant*): ~ **qch/qn à qn** to tell sb of sth/sb ; (*renseigner sur*) to point out, tell ; (*déterminer: date, lieu*) to give, state ; (*dénoter*) to indicate, point to ; **pourriez-vous m'**~ **les toilettes/l'heure?** could you direct me to the toilets/tell me the time?

**indirect, e** [ɛ̃diʀɛkt] *a* indirect.

**indiscipline** [ɛ̃disiplin] *nf* lack of discipline ; **indiscipliné, e** *a* undisciplined ; (*fig*) unmanageable.

**indiscret, ète** [ɛ̃diskʀɛ, -ɛt] *a* indiscreet ; **indiscrétion** *nf* indiscretion.

**indiscutable** [ɛ̃diskytabl(ə)] *a* indisputable.

**indispensable** [ɛ̃dispɑ̃sabl(ə)] *a* indispensable ; essential.

**indisponible** [ɛ̃dispɔnibl(ə)] *a* unavailable.

**indisposé, e** [ɛ̃dispoze] *a* indisposed, unwell.

**indisposer** [ɛ̃dispoze] *vt* (*incommoder*) to upset ; (*déplaire à*) to antagonize.

**indistinct, e** [ɛ̃distɛ̃, -ɛ̃kt(ə)] *a* indistinct ; **indistinctement** *ad* (*voir, prononcer*) indistinctly ; (*sans distinction*) without distinction, indiscriminately.

**individu** [ɛ̃dividy] *nm* individual ; ~**aliser** *vt* to individualize ; (*personnaliser*) to tailor to individual requirements ; ~**aliste** *nm/f* individualist.

**individuel, le** [ɛ̃dividɥɛl] *a* (*gén*) individual ; (*opinion, livret, contrôle, avantages*) personal ; **chambre** ~**le** single room ; **maison** ~**le** detached house ; **propriété** ~**le** personal *ou* private property.

**indocile** [ɛ̃dɔsil] *a* unruly.

**indolent, e** [ɛ̃dɔlɑ̃, -ɑ̃t] *a* indolent.

**indolore** [ɛ̃dɔlɔʀ] *a* painless.

**indomptable** [ɛ̃dɔ̃tabl(ə)] *a* untameable ; (*fig*) invincible, indomitable.

**Indonésie** [ɛ̃donezi] *nf* Indonesia ; **indonésien, ne** *a*, *nm/f* Indonesian.

**indu, e** [ɛ̃dy] *a*: **à des heures** ~**es** at some ungodly hour.

**indubitable** [ɛ̃dybitabl(ə)] *a* indubitable.

**induire** [ɛ̃dɥiʀ] *vt*: ~ **qch de** to induce sth from ; ~ **qn en erreur** to lead sb astray, mislead sb.

**indulgence** [ɛ̃dylʒɑ̃s] *nf* indulgence ; leniency.

**indulgent, e** [ɛ̃dylʒɑ̃, -ɑ̃t] *a* (*parent, regard*) indulgent ; (*juge, examinateur*) lenient.

**indûment** [ɛ̃dymɑ̃] *ad* wrongfully ; without due cause.

**industrialiser** [ɛ̃dystʀijalize] *vt* to industrialize ; **s'**~ to become industrialized.

**industrie** [ɛ̃dystʀi] *nf* industry ; ~ **du spectacle** entertainment business ; **industriel, le** *a* industrial // *nm* industrialist ; manufacturer.

**industrieux, euse** [ɛ̃dystʀijø, -øz] *a* industrious.

**inébranlable** [inebʀɑ̃labl(ə)] *a* (*masse, colonne*) solid ; (*personne, certitude, foi*) steadfast, unwavering.

**inédit, e** [inedi, -it] *a* (*correspondance etc*)

hitherto unpublished ; (spectacle, moyen) novel, original.

**ineffable** [inefabl(ə)] a inexpressible, ineffable.

**ineffaçable** [inefasabl(ə)] a indelible.

**inefficace** [inefikas] a (remède, moyen) ineffective ; (machine, employé) inefficient ; **inefficacité** nf ineffectiveness ; inefficiency.

**inégal, e, aux** [inegal, -o] a unequal ; uneven.

**inégalable** [inegalabl(e)] a matchless.

**inégalé, e** [inegale] a unmatched, unequalled.

**inégalité** [inegalite] nf inequality ; unevenness q ; ~ **de 2 hauteurs** difference ou disparity between 2 heights.

**inélégant, e** [inelegɑ̃, -ɑ̃t] a inelegant ; (indélicat) discourteous.

**inéligible** [ineliʒibl(ə)] a ineligible.

**inéluctable** [inelyktabl(ə)] a inescapable, ineluctable.

**inemployé, e** [inɑ̃plwaje] a unused.

**inénarrable** [inenaRabl(ə)] a hilarious.

**inepte** [inɛpt(ə)] a inept ; **ineptie** [-si] nf ineptitude ; nonsense q.

**inépuisable** [inepɥizabl(ə)] a inexhaustible.

**inerte** [inɛRt(ə)] a lifeless ; (apathique) passive, inert ; (PHYSIQUE, CHIMIE) inert.

**inertie** [inɛRsi] nf inertia.

**inespéré, e** [inɛspeRe] a unhoped-for.

**inesthétique** [inɛstetik] a unsightly.

**inestimable** [inɛstimabl(e)] a priceless ; (fig: bienfait) invaluable.

**inévitable** [inevitabl(ə)] a unavoidable ; (fatal, habituel) inevitable.

**inexact, e** [inɛgzakt] a inaccurate, inexact ; unpunctual ; ~**itude** nf inaccuracy.

**inexcusable** [inɛkskyzabl(ə)] a inexcusable, unforgivable.

**inexécutable** [inɛgzekytabl(ə)] a impracticable, unworkable ; (MUS) unplayable.

**inexistant, e** [inɛgzistɑ̃, -ɑ̃t] a non-existent.

**inexorable** [inɛgzɔRabl(ə)] a inexorable.

**inexpérience** [inɛkspeRjɑ̃s] nf inexperience, lack of experience.

**inexplicable** [inɛksplikabl(ə)] a inexplicable.

**inexpliqué, e** [inɛksplike] a unexplained.

**inexploité, e** [inɛksplwate] a unexploited, untapped.

**inexpressif, ive** [inɛkspResif, -iv] a inexpressive ; expressionless.

**inexprimable** [inɛkspRimabl(ə)] a inexpressible.

**inexprimé, e** [inɛkspRime] a unspoken, unexpressed.

**inextensible** [inɛkstɑ̃sibl(ə)] a (tissu) non-stretch.

**in extenso** [inɛkstɛso] ad in full.

**inextricable** [inɛkstRikabl(ə)] a inextricable.

**in extremis** [inɛkstRemis] ad at the last minute // a last-minute ; (testament) death bed cpd.

**infaillibilité** [ɛ̃fajibilite] nf infallibility.

**infaillible** [ɛ̃fajibl(ə)] a infallible ; (instinct) infallible, unerring.

**infâme** [ɛ̃fɑm] a vile.

**infanterie** [ɛ̃fɑ̃tRi] nf infantry.

**infanticide** [ɛ̃fɑ̃tisid] nm/f child-murderer/eress // nm (meurtre) infanticide.

**infantile** [ɛ̃fɑ̃til] a (MÉD) infantile, child cpd ; (ton, réaction, péj) infantile, childish.

**infarctus** [ɛ̃faRktys] nm: ~ **(du myocarde)** coronary (thrombosis).

**infatigable** [ɛ̃fatigabl(ə)] a tireless, indefatigable.

**infatué, e** [ɛ̃fatɥe] a conceited ; ~ **de** full of.

**infécond, e** [ɛ̃fekɔ̃, -ɔ̃d] a infertile, barren.

**infect, e** [ɛ̃fɛkt] a vile, foul ; (repas, vin) revolting, foul.

**infecter** [ɛ̃fɛkte] vt (atmosphère, eau) to contaminate ; (MÉD) to infect ; **s'**~ to become infected ou septic ; **infectieux, euse** [-sjø, -øz] a infectious ; **infection** [-sjɔ̃] nf infection.

**inféoder** [ɛ̃feɔde] vt: **s'**~ **à** to pledge allegiance to.

**inférer** [ɛ̃feRe] vt: ~ **qch de** to infer sth from.

**inférieur, e** [ɛ̃feRjœR] a lower ; (en qualité, intelligence) inferior // nm/f inferior ; ~ **à** (somme, quantité) less ou smaller than ; (moins bon que) inferior to ; (tâche: pas à la hauteur de) unequal to ; **infériorité** nf inferiority.

**infernal, e, aux** [ɛ̃fɛRnal, -o] a (chaleur, rythme) infernal ; (méchanceté, complot) diabolical.

**infester** [ɛ̃fɛste] vt to infest ; **infesté de moustiques** infested with mosquitoes, mosquito-ridden.

**infidèle** [ɛ̃fidɛl] a unfaithful ; (REL) infidel ; **infidélité** nf unfaithfulness q.

**infiltration** [ɛ̃filtRasjɔ̃] nf infiltration.

**infiltrer** [ɛ̃filtRe]: **s'**~ vi: **s'**~ **dans** to penetrate into ; (liquide) to seep into ; (fig: noyauter) to infiltrate.

**infime** [ɛ̃fim] a minute, tiny ; (inférieur) lowly.

**infini, e** [ɛ̃fini] a infinite // nm infinity ; **à l'**~ (MATH) to infinity ; (discourir) ad infinitum, endlessly ; (agrandir, varier) infinitely ; (à perte de vue) endlessly (into the distance) ; ~**ment** ad infinitely ; **infinité** nf: **une infinité de** an infinite number of.

**infinitif, ive** [ɛ̃finitif, -iv] a, nm infinitive.

**infirme** [ɛ̃fiRm(ə)] a disabled // nm/f disabled person ; ~ **de guerre** war cripple ; ~ **du travail** industrially disabled person.

**infirmer** [ɛ̃fiRme] vt to invalidate.

**infirmerie** [ɛ̃fiRməRi] nf sick bay.

**infirmier, ière** [ɛ̃fiRmje, -jɛR] nm/f nurse ; **infirmière chef** sister ; **infirmière diplômée** registered nurse ; **infirmière visiteuse** ≈ district nurse.

**infirmité** [ɛ̃fiRmite] nf disability.

**inflammable** [ɛ̃flamabl(ə)] a (in)flammable.

**inflammation** [ɛ̃flamɑsjɔ̃] nf inflammation.

**inflation** [ɛflɑsjɔ̃] *nf* inflation ; **inflationniste** *a* inflationist.
**infléchir** [ɛfleʃiʀ] *vt* (*fig: politique*) to reorientate, redirect.
**inflexible** [ɛflɛksibl(ə)] *a* inflexible.
**inflexion** [ɛflɛksjɔ̃] *nf* inflexion ; ~ **de la tête** slight nod (of the head).
**infliger** [ɛfliʒe] *vt:* ~ **qch (à qn)** to inflict sth (on sb) ; (*amende, sanction*) to impose sth (on sb).
**influençable** [ɛflyɑ̃sabl(ə)] *a* easily influenced.
**influence** [ɛflyɑ̃s] *nf* influence ; (*d'un médicament*) effect ; **influencer** *vt* to influence ; **influent, e** *a* influential.
**influer** [ɛflye]: ~ **sur** *vt* to have an influence upon.
**influx** [ɛfly] *nm:* ~ **nerveux** (nervous) impulse.
**informaticien, ne** [ɛfɔʀmatisjɛ̃, -jɛn] *nm/f* computer scientist.
**information** [ɛfɔʀmɑsjɔ̃] *nf* (*renseignement*) piece of information ; (*PRESSE, TV: nouvelle*) news *sg* ; (*diffusion de renseignements, INFORMATIQUE*) information ; (*JUR*) inquiry, investigation ; **voyage d'**~ fact-finding trip ; **agence d'**~ news agency ; **journal d'**~ quality newspaper.
**informatique** [ɛfɔʀmatik] *nf* (*techniques*) data processing ; (*science*) computer science ; **informatiser** *vt* to computerize.
**informe** [ɛfɔʀm(ə)] *a* shapeless.
**informer** [ɛfɔʀme] *vt:* ~ **qn (de)** to inform sb (of) // *vi* (*JUR*): ~ **contre/sur** to initiate inquiries about ; **s'**~ **(sur)** to inform o.s. (about) ; **s'**~ **(de/si)** to inquire *ou* find out (about/whether *ou* if).
**infortune** [ɛfɔʀtyn] *nf* misfortune.
**infraction** [ɛfʀaksjɔ̃] *nf* offence ; ~ **à** violation *ou* breach of ; **être en** ~ to be in breach of the law.
**infranchissable** [ɛfʀɑ̃ʃisabl(ə)] *a* impassable ; (*fig*) insuperable.
**infrarouge** [ɛfʀaʀuʒ] *a, nm* infrared.
**infrastructure** [ɛfʀastʀyktyʀ] *nf* (*d'une route etc*) substructure ; (*AVIAT, MIL*) ground installations *pl* ; (*ÉCON: touristique etc*) infrastructure.
**infroissable** [ɛfʀwasabl(ə)] *a* crease-resistant.
**infructueux, euse** [ɛfʀyktɥø, -øz] *a* fruitless, unfruitful.
**infus, e** [ɛfy, -yz] *a:* **avoir la science** ~**e** to have innate knowledge.
**infuser** [ɛfyze] *vt* (*thé*) to brew ; (*tisane*) to infuse // *vi* to brew ; to infuse ; **infusion** *nf* (*tisane*) infusion, herb tea.
**ingambe** [ɛgɑ̃b] *a* spry, nimble.
**ingénier** [ɛʒenje]: **s'**~ *vi:* **s'**~ **à faire** to strive to do.
**ingénieur** [ɛʒenjœʀ] *nm* engineer ; ~ **agronome/chimiste** agricultural/chemical engineer ; ~ **du son** sound engineer.
**ingénieux, euse** [ɛʒenjø, -øz] *a* ingenious, clever ; **ingéniosité** *nf* ingenuity.
**ingénu, e** [ɛʒeny] *a* ingenuous, artless // *nf* (*THÉÂTRE*) ingénue.
**ingérer** [ɛʒeʀe]: **s'**~ *vi:* **s'**~ **dans** to interfere in.

**ingrat, e** [ɛgʀa, -at] *a* (*personne*) ungrateful ; (*sol*) barren, arid ; (*travail, sujet*) arid, thankless ; (*visage*) unprepossessing ; **ingratitude** *nf* ingratitude.
**ingrédient** [ɛgʀedjɑ̃] *nm* ingredient.
**inguérissable** [ɛgeʀisabl(ə)] *a* incurable.
**ingurgiter** [ɛgyʀʒite] *vt* to swallow.
**inhabile** [inabil] *a* clumsy ; (*fig*) inept.
**inhabitable** [inabitabl(ə)] *a* uninhabitable.
**inhabité, e** [inabite] *a* (*régions*) uninhabited ; (*maison*) unoccupied.
**inhabituel, le** [inabitɥɛl] *a* unusual.
**inhalateur** [inalatœʀ] *nm* inhaler ; ~ **d'oxygène** oxygen mask.
**inhalation** [inalɑsjɔ̃] *nf* (*MÉD*) inhalation ; **faire des** ~**s** to use an inhalation bath.
**inhérent, e** [ineʀɑ̃, -ɑ̃t] *a:* ~ **à** inherent in.
**inhibition** [inibisjɔ̃] *nf* inhibition.
**inhospitalier, ière** [inɔspitalje, -jɛʀ] *a* inhospitable.
**inhumain, e** [inymɛ̃, -ɛn] *a* inhuman.
**inhumation** [inymɑsjɔ̃] *nf* interment, burial.
**inhumer** [inyme] *vt* to inter, bury.
**inimaginable** [inimaʒinabl(ə)] *a* unimaginable.
**inimitable** [inimitabl(ə)] *a* inimitable.
**inimitié** [inimitje] *nf* enmity.
**ininflammable** [inɛflamabl(ə)] *a* non-flammable.
**inintelligent, e** [inɛteliʒɑ̃, -ɑ̃t] *a* unintelligent.
**inintelligible** [inɛteliʒibl(ə)] *a* unintelligible.
**inintéressant, e** [inɛteʀɛsɑ̃, -ɑ̃t] *a* uninteresting.
**ininterrompu, e** [inɛtɛʀɔ̃py] *a* (*file, série*) unbroken ; (*flot, vacarme*) uninterrupted, non-stop ; (*effort*) unremitting, continuous.
**iniquité** [inikite] *nf* iniquity.
**initial, e, aux** [inisjal, -o] *a, nf* initial.
**initiateur, trice** [inisjatœʀ, -tʀis] *nm/f* initiator ; (*d'une mode, technique*) innovator, pioneer.
**initiative** [inisjativ] *nf* initiative ; **prendre l'**~ **de qch/de faire** to take the initiative for sth/of *ou* in doing ; **avoir de l'**~ to have initiative, show enterprise.
**initier** [inisje] *vt:* ~ **qn à** to initiate sb into ; (*faire découvrir: art, jeu*) to introduce sb to.
**injecté, e** [ɛʒɛkte] *a:* **yeux** ~**s de sang** bloodshot eyes.
**injecter** [ɛʒɛkte] *vt* to inject ; **injection** [-sjɔ̃] *nf* injection ; **à injection** *a* (*AUTO*) fuel injection *cpd*.
**injonction** [ɛʒɔ̃ksjɔ̃] *nf* injunction, order.
**injure** [ɛʒyʀ] *nf* insult, abuse *q.*
**injurier** [ɛʒyʀje] *vt* to insult, abuse ; **injurieux, euse** *a* abusive, insulting.
**injuste** [ɛʒyst(ə)] *a* unjust, unfair ; **injustice** *nf* injustice.
**inlassable** [ɛlɑsabl(ə)] *a* tireless, indefatigable.
**inné, e** [ine] *a* innate, inborn.
**innocence** [inɔsɑ̃s] *nf* innocence.
**innocent, e** [inɔsɑ̃, -ɑ̃t] *a* innocent // *nm/f*

innocent person; **innocenter** vt to clear, prove innocent.

**innombrable** [inɔ̃bʀabl(ə)] a innumerable.

**innommable** [inɔmabl(ə)] a unspeakable.

**innover** [inɔve] vi to break new ground.

**inobservation** [inɔpsɛʀvɑsjɔ̃] nf non-observation, inobservance.

**inoccupé, e** [inɔkype] a unoccupied.

**inoculer** [inɔkyle] vt: ~ qch à qn (volontairement) to inoculate sb with sth; (accidentellement) to infect sb with sth; ~ qn contre to inoculate sb against.

**inodore** [inɔdɔʀ] a (gaz) odourless; (fleur) scentless.

**inoffensif, ive** [inɔfɑsif, -iv] a harmless, innocuous.

**inondation** [inɔ̃dɑsjɔ̃] nf flooding q; flood.

**inonder** [inɔ̃de] vt to flood; (fig) to inundate, overrun; ~ de (fig) to flood ou swamp with.

**inopérable** [inɔpeʀabl(ə)] a inoperable.

**inopérant, e** [inɔpeʀɑ̃, -ɑ̃t] a inoperative, ineffective.

**inopiné, e** [inɔpine] a unexpected, sudden.

**inopportun, e** [inɔpɔʀtœ̃, -yn] a ill-timed, untimely; inappropriate; (moment) inopportune.

**inoubliable** [inublijabl(ə)] a unforgettable.

**inouï, e** [inwi] a unheard-of, extraordinary.

**inoxydable** [inɔksidabl(ə)] a stainless; (couverts) stainless steel cpd.

**inqualifiable** [ɛ̃kalifjabl(ə)] a unspeakable.

**inquiet, ète** [ɛ̃kjɛ, -ɛt] a (par nature) anxious; (momentanément) worried.

**inquiétant, e** [ɛ̃kjetɑ̃, -ɑ̃t] a worrying, disturbing.

**inquiéter** [ɛ̃kjete] vt to worry, disturb; (harceler) to harass; s'~ to worry, become anxious; s'~ de to worry about; (s'enquérir de) to inquire about.

**inquiétude** [ɛ̃kjetyd] nf anxiety; donner de l'~ ou des ~s à to worry; avoir de l'~ ou des ~s au sujet de to feel anxious ou worried about.

**inquisition** [ɛ̃kizisjɔ̃] nf inquisition.

**insaisissable** [ɛ̃sezisabl(ə)] a elusive.

**insalubre** [ɛ̃salybʀ(ə)] a insalubrious, unhealthy.

**insanité** [ɛ̃sanite] nf madness q, insanity q.

**insatiable** [ɛ̃sasjabl(ə)] a insatiable.

**insatisfait, e** [ɛ̃satisfɛ, -ɛt] a (non comblé) unsatisfied; unfulfilled; (mécontent) dissatisfied.

**inscription** [ɛ̃skʀipsjɔ̃] nf (sur un mur, écriteau etc) inscription; (à une institution: voir s'inscrire) enrolment; registration.

**inscrire** [ɛ̃skʀiʀ] vt (marquer: sur son calepin etc) to note ou write down; (: sur un mur, une affiche etc) to write; (: dans la pierre, le métal) to inscribe; (mettre: sur une liste, un budget etc) to put down; ~ qn à (club, école etc) to enrol sb at; s'~ (pour une excursion etc) to put one's name down; s'~ (à) (club, parti) to join; (université) to register ou enrol (at); (examen, concours) to register ou enter (for); s'~ en faux contre to challenge.

**insecte** [ɛ̃sɛkt(ə)] nm insect; **insecticide** nm insecticide.

**insécurité** [ɛ̃sekyʀite] nf insecurity, lack of security.

**I.N.S.E.E.** [inse] sigle m = Institut national de la statistique et des études économiques.

**insémination** [ɛ̃seminɑsjɔ̃] nf insemination.

**insensé, e** [ɛ̃sɑ̃se] a insane.

**insensibiliser** [ɛ̃sɑ̃sibilize] vt to anaesthetize.

**insensible** [ɛ̃sɑ̃sibl(ə)] a (nerf, membre) numb; (dur, indifférent) insensitive; (imperceptible) imperceptible.

**inséparable** [ɛ̃sepaʀabl(ə)] a inseparable.

**insérer** [ɛ̃seʀe] vt to insert; s'~ dans to fit into; to come within.

**insidieux, euse** [ɛ̃sidjø, -øz] a insidious.

**insigne** [ɛ̃siɲ] nm (d'un parti, club) badge // a distinguished; ~s nmpl (d'une fonction) insignia pl.

**insignifiant, e** [ɛ̃siɲifjɑ̃, -ɑ̃t] a insignificant; trivial.

**insinuation** [ɛ̃sinɥɑsjɔ̃] nf innuendo, insinuation.

**insinuer** [ɛ̃sinɥe] vt to insinuate, imply; s'~ dans to seep into; (fig) to worm one's way into; to creep into.

**insipide** [ɛ̃sipid] a insipid.

**insistance** [ɛ̃sistɑ̃s] nf insistence; avec ~ insistently.

**insister** [ɛ̃siste] vi to insist; (s'obstiner) to keep trying; ~ sur (détail, note) to stress.

**insociable** [ɛ̃sɔsjabl(ə)] a unsociable.

**insolation** [ɛ̃sɔlɑsjɔ̃] nf (MÉD) sunstroke q; (ensoleillement) period of sunshine.

**insolence** [ɛ̃sɔlɑ̃s] nf insolence q.

**insolent, e** [ɛ̃sɔlɑ̃, -ɑ̃t] a insolent.

**insolite** [ɛ̃sɔlit] a strange, unusual.

**insoluble** [ɛ̃sɔlybl(ə)] a insoluble.

**insolvable** [ɛ̃sɔlvabl(ə)] a insolvent.

**insomnie** [ɛ̃sɔmni] nf insomnia q, sleeplessness q.

**insondable** [ɛ̃sɔ̃dabl(ə)] a unfathomable.

**insonore** [ɛ̃sɔnɔʀ] a soundproof; **insonoriser** vt to soundproof.

**insouciance** [ɛ̃susjɑ̃s] nf carefree attitude; heedless attitude.

**insouciant, e** [ɛ̃susjɑ̃, -ɑ̃t] a carefree; (imprévoyant) heedless.

**insoumis, e** [ɛ̃sumi, -iz] a (caractère, enfant) rebellious, refractory; (contrée, tribu) unsubdued.

**insoumission** [ɛ̃sumisjɔ̃] nf rebelliousness; (MIL) absence without leave.

**insoupçonnable** [ɛ̃supsɔnabl(ə)] a above suspicion.

**insoupçonné, e** [ɛ̃supsɔne] a unsuspected.

**insoutenable** [ɛ̃sutnabl(ə)] a (argument) untenable; (chaleur) unbearable.

**inspecter** [ɛ̃spɛkte] vt to inspect.

**inspecteur, trice** [ɛ̃spɛktœʀ, -tʀis] nm/f inspector; ~ d'Académie ≈ Chief Education Officer; ~ des finances ≈ Treasury Inspector.

**inspection** [ɛ̃spɛksjɔ̃] nf inspection.

**inspiration** [ɛ̃spiʀɑsjɔ̃] nf inspiration; breathing in q; sous l'~ de prompted by.

**inspirer** [ɛ̃spiʀe] *vt* (*gén*) to inspire // *vi* (*aspirer*) to breathe in ; **s'~ de** (*suj: artiste*) to draw one's inspiration from ; (*suj: tableau*) to be inspired by ; ~ **à qn** (*œuvre, action*) to inspire sb with ; (*dégoût, crainte*) to fill sb with ; **ça ne m'inspire pas** I'm not keen on the idea.

**instable** [ɛ̃stabl(ə)] *a* (*meuble, équilibre*) unsteady ; (*population, temps*) unsettled ; (*paix, régime, caractère*) unstable.

**installation** [ɛ̃stalasjɔ̃] *nf* installation ; putting in *ou* up ; fitting out ; settling in ; (*appareils etc*) fittings *pl*, installations *pl* ; **~s** *nfpl* installations, plant *sg* ; facilities.

**installer** [ɛ̃stale] *vt* (*loger*): ~ **qn** to get sb settled, install sb ; (*placer*) to put, place ; (*meuble*) to put in ; (*rideau, étagère, tente*) to put up ; (*gaz, électricité etc*) to put in, install ; (*appartement*) to fit out ; **s'~** (*s'établir: artisan, dentiste etc*) to set o.s. up ; (*se loger*) to settle (o.s.) ; (*emménager*) to settle in ; (*sur un siège, à un emplacement*) to settle (down) ; (*fig: maladie, grève*) to take a firm hold *ou* grip.

**instamment** [ɛ̃stamɑ̃] *ad* urgently.

**instance** [ɛ̃stɑ̃s] *nf* (*JUR: procédure*) (legal) proceedings *pl* ; (*ADMIN: autorité*) authority ; **~s** *nfpl* (*prières*) entreaties ; **affaire en ~** matter pending ; **être en ~ de divorce** to be awaiting a divorce ; **en seconde ~** on appeal.

**instant** [ɛ̃stɑ̃] *nm* moment, instant ; **dans un ~** in a moment ; **à l'~** this instant ; **à tout ~** at any moment ; constantly ; **pour l'~** for the moment, for the time being ; **par ~s** at times ; **de tous les ~s** perpetual.

**instantané, e** [ɛ̃stɑ̃tane] *a* (*lait, café*) instant ; (*explosion, mort*) instantaneous // *nm* snapshot.

**instar** [ɛ̃staʀ]: **à l'~ de** *prép* following the example of, like.

**instaurer** [ɛ̃stɔʀe] *vt* to institute.

**instigateur, trice** [ɛ̃stigatœʀ, -tʀis] *nm/f* instigator.

**instigation** [ɛ̃stigasjɔ̃] *nf*: **à l'~ de qn** at sb's instigation.

**instinct** [ɛ̃stɛ̃] *nm* instinct ; ~ **de conservation** instinct of self-preservation ; **instinctif, ive** *a* instinctive.

**instituer** [ɛ̃stitɥe] *vt* to institute, set up.

**institut** [ɛ̃stity] *nm* institute ; ~ **de beauté** beauty salon ; **I~ Universitaire de Technologie (IUT)** ≈ Polytechnic.

**instituteur, trice** [ɛ̃stitytœʀ, -tʀis] *nm/f* (primary school) teacher.

**institution** [ɛ̃stitysjɔ̃] *nf* institution ; (*collège*) private school.

**instructeur, trice** [ɛ̃stʀyktœʀ, -tʀis] *a* (*MIL*): **sergent ~** drill sergeant ; (*JUR*): **juge ~** examining magistrate // *nm/f* instructor.

**instructif, ive** [ɛ̃stʀyktif, -iv] *a* instructive.

**instruction** [ɛ̃stʀyksjɔ̃] *nf* (*enseignement, savoir*) education ; (*JUR*) (preliminary) investigation and hearing ; (*directive*) instruction ; **~s** *nfpl* (*mode d'emploi*) directions, instructions ; ~ **civique** civics *sg* ; ~ **religieuse** religious instruction ; ~ **professionnelle** vocational training.

**instruire** [ɛ̃stʀɥiʀ] *vt* (*élèves*) to teach ; (*recrues*) to train ; (*JUR: affaire*) to conduct the investigation for ; **s'~** to educate o.s. ; ~ **qn de qch** (*informer*) to inform *ou* advise sb of sth ; **instruit, e** *a* educated.

**instrument** [ɛ̃stʀymɑ̃] *nm* instrument ; ~ **à cordes/vent** stringed/wind instrument ; ~ **de mesure** measuring instrument ; ~ **de musique** musical instrument ; ~ **de travail** (working) tool.

**insu** [ɛ̃sy] *nm*: **à l'~ de qn** without sb knowing (it).

**insubmersible** [ɛ̃sybmɛʀsibl(ə)] *a* unsinkable.

**insubordination** [ɛ̃sybɔʀdinasjɔ̃] *nf* rebelliousness ; (*MIL*) insubordination.

**insuccès** [ɛ̃syksɛ] *nm* failure.

**insuffisance** [ɛ̃syfizɑ̃s] *nf* insufficiency ; inadequacy ; **~s** *nfpl* (*lacunes*) inadequacies ; ~ **cardiaque** cardiac insufficiency *q*.

**insuffisant, e** [ɛ̃syfizɑ̃, -ɑ̃t] *a* insufficient ; (*élève, travail*) inadequate.

**insuffler** [ɛ̃syfle] *vt*: ~ **qch dans** to blow sth into ; ~ **qch à qn** to inspire sb with sth.

**insulaire** [ɛ̃sylɛʀ] *a* island *cpd* ; (*attitude*) insular.

**insulte** [ɛ̃sylt(ə)] *nf* insult ; **insulter** *vt* to insult.

**insupportable** [ɛ̃sypɔʀtabl(ə)] *a* unbearable.

**insurgé, e** [ɛ̃syʀʒe] *a*, *nm/f* insurgent, rebel.

**insurger** [ɛ̃syʀʒe]: **s'~** *vi*: **s'~ (contre)** to rise up *ou* rebel (against).

**insurmontable** [ɛ̃syʀmɔ̃tabl(ə)] *a* (*difficulté*) insuperable ; (*aversion*) unconquerable.

**insurrection** [ɛ̃syʀɛksjɔ̃] *nf* insurrection, revolt.

**intact, e** [ɛ̃takt] *a* intact.

**intangible** [ɛ̃tɑ̃ʒibl(ə)] *a* intangible ; (*principe*) inviolable.

**intarissable** [ɛ̃taʀisabl(ə)] *a* inexhaustible.

**intégral, e, aux** [ɛ̃tegʀal, -o] *a* complete // *nf* (*MATH*) integral ; **~ement** *ad* in full.

**intégrant, e** [ɛ̃tegʀɑ̃, -ɑ̃t] *a*: **faire partie ~e de** to be an integral part of, be part and parcel of.

**intègre** [ɛ̃tɛgʀ(ə)] *a* upright.

**intégrer** [ɛ̃tegʀe] *vt*: ~ **qch à/dans** to integrate sth into ; **s'~ à/dans** to become integrated into.

**intégrité** [ɛ̃tegʀite] *nf* integrity.

**intellect** [ɛ̃telɛkt] *nm* intellect.

**intellectuel, le** [ɛ̃telɛktɥɛl] *a* intellectual // *nm/f* intellectual ; (*péj*) highbrow.

**intelligence** [ɛ̃teliʒɑ̃s] *nf* intelligence ; (*compréhension*): **l'~ de** the understanding of ; (*complicité*): **regard d'~** glance of complicity ; (*accord*): **vivre en bonne ~ avec qn** to be on good terms with sb ; **~s** *nfpl* (*MIL, fig*) secret contacts.

**intelligent, e** [ɛ̃teliʒɑ̃, -ɑ̃t] *a* intelligent.

**intelligible** [ɛ̃teliʒibl(ə)] *a* intelligible.

**intempérance** [ɛ̃tɑ̃peʀɑ̃s] *nf* intemperance *q* ; overindulgence *q*.

**intempéries** [ɛ̃tɑ̃peʀi] *nfpl* bad weather *sg*.

**intempestif, ive** [ɛ̃tɑ̃pɛstif, -iv] *a* untimely.

**intenable** [ɛ̃tnabl(ə)] *a* (*chaleur*) unbearable.

**intendance** [ɛ̃tɑ̃dɑ̃s] *nf* (MIL) supply corps; supplies office; (SCOL: *bureau*) bursar's office.

**intendant, e** [ɛ̃tɑ̃dɑ̃, -ɑ̃t] *nm/f* (MIL) quartermaster; (SCOL) bursar; (*d'une propriété*) steward.

**intense** [ɛ̃tɑ̃s] *a* intense; **intensif, ive** *a* intensive; **intensifier** *vt*, **s'intensifier** to intensify; **intensité** *nf* intensity.

**intenter** [ɛ̃tɑ̃te] *vt*: ~ **un procès contre** *ou* **à** to start proceedings against.

**intention** [ɛ̃tɑ̃sjɔ̃] *nf* intention; (JUR) intent; **avoir l'~ de faire** to intend to do, have the intention of doing; **à l'~ de** *prép* for; (*renseignement*) for the benefit *ou* information of; (*film, ouvrage*) aimed at; **à cette** ~ with this aim in view; **intentionné, e** *a*: **bien intentionné** well-meaning *ou* -intentioned; **mal intentionné** ill-intentioned; **intentionnel, le** *a* intentional, deliberate.

**inter** [ɛ̃tɛR] *nm* (TÉL) abr de **interurbain**; (SPORT): **~-gauche/ -droit** inside-left/-right.

**intercalaire** [ɛ̃tɛRkalɛR] *a*: **feuillet** ~ insert; **fiche** ~ divider.

**intercaler** [ɛ̃tɛRkale] *vt* to insert; **s'~ entre** to come in between; to slip in between.

**intercéder** [ɛ̃tɛRsede] *vi*: ~ (**pour qn**) to intercede (on behalf of sb).

**intercepter** [ɛ̃tɛRsɛpte] *vt* to intercept; (*lumière, chaleur*) to cut off; **interception** [-sjɔ̃] *nf* interception; **avion d'interception** interceptor.

**interchangeable** [ɛ̃tɛRʃɑ̃ʒabl(ə)] *a* interchangeable.

**interclasse** [ɛ̃tɛRklɑs] *nm* (SCOL) break (between classes).

**interdiction** [ɛ̃tɛRdiksjɔ̃] *nf* ban; ~ **de séjour** (JUR) order banning ex-prisoner from frequenting specified places.

**interdire** [ɛ̃tɛRdiR] *vt* to forbid; (ADMIN: *stationnement, meeting, passage*) to ban, prohibit; (: *journal, livre*) to ban; ~ **qch à qn** to forbid sb sth; ~ **à qn de faire** to forbid sb to do, prohibit sb from doing; (*suj: empêchement*) to prevent *ou* preclude sb from doing.

**interdit, e** [ɛ̃tɛRdi, -it] *a* (*stupéfait*) taken aback // *nm* interdict, prohibition.

**intéressant, e** [ɛ̃teRɛsɑ̃, -ɑ̃t] *a* interesting.

**intéressé, e** [ɛ̃teRese] *a* (*parties*) involved, concerned; (*amitié, motifs*) self-interested; **les ~s** those concerned *ou* involved.

**intéressement** [ɛ̃teRɛsmɑ̃] *nm* (COMM) profit-sharing.

**intéresser** [ɛ̃teRese] *vt* (*captiver*) to interest; (*toucher*) to be of interest *ou* concern to; (ADMIN: *concerner*) to affect, concern; (COMM: *travailleur*) to give a share in the profits to; (: *partenaire*) to interest (in the business); **s'~ à** to take an interest in, be interested in.

**intérêt** [ɛ̃teRɛ] *nm* (*gén, aussi* COMM) interest; (*égoïsme*) self-interest; **avoir des ~s dans** (COMM) to have a financial interest *ou* a stake in; **avoir ~ à faire** to be well-advised to do.

**interférer** [ɛ̃tɛRfeRe] *vi*: ~ (**avec**) to interfere (with).

**intérieur, e** [ɛ̃teRjœR] *a* (*mur, escalier, poche*) inside; (*commerce, politique*) domestic; (*cour, calme, vie*) inner; (*navigation*) inland // *nm* (*d'une maison, d'un récipient etc*) inside; (*d'un pays, aussi: décor, mobilier*) interior; (POL): **l'I~** the Interior, ≈ the Home Office; **à l'~ (de)** inside; (*fig*) within; **en ~** (CINÉMA) in the studio; **vêtement d'~** indoor garment.

**intérim** [ɛ̃teRim] *nm* interim period; **assurer l'~ (de)** to deputize (for); **par ~** *a* interim // *ad* in a temporary capacity; **~aire** *a* temporary, interim.

**intérioriser** [ɛ̃teRjɔRize] *vt* to internalize.

**interjection** [ɛ̃tɛRʒɛksjɔ̃] *nf* interjection.

**interligne** [ɛ̃tɛRliɲ] *nm* space between the lines // *nf* lead; **simple/double** ~ single/double spacing.

**interlocuteur, trice** [ɛ̃tɛRlɔkytœR, -tRis] *nm/f* speaker; **son** ~ the person he was speaking to.

**interlope** [ɛ̃tɛRlɔp] *a* shady.

**interloquer** [ɛ̃tɛRlɔke] *vt* to take aback.

**interlude** [ɛ̃tɛRlyd] *nm* interlude.

**intermède** [ɛ̃tɛRmɛd] *nm* interlude.

**intermédiaire** [ɛ̃tɛRmedjɛR] *a* intermediate; middle; half-way // *nm/f* intermediary; (COMM) middleman; **sans** ~ directly; **par l'~ de** through.

**interminable** [ɛ̃tɛRminabl(ə)] *a* never-ending.

**intermittence** [ɛ̃tɛRmitɑ̃s] *nf*: **par** ~ sporadically, intermittently.

**intermittent, e** [ɛ̃tɛRmitɑ̃, -ɑ̃t] *a* intermittent.

**internat** [ɛ̃tɛRna] *nm* (SCOL) boarding school.

**international, e, aux** [ɛ̃tɛRnasjɔnal, -o] *a* international // *nm/f* (SPORT) international player.

**interne** [ɛ̃tɛRn(ə)] *a* internal // *nm/f* (SCOL) boarder; (MÉD) houseman.

**interner** [ɛ̃tɛRne] *vt* (POL) to intern; (MÉD) to confine to a mental institution.

**interpellation** [ɛ̃tɛRpelasjɔ̃] *nf* interpellation; (POL) question.

**interpeller** [ɛ̃tɛRpele] *vt* (*appeler*) to call out to; (*apostropher*) to shout at; (POLICE) to take a for questioning; (POL) to question.

**interphone** [ɛ̃tɛRfɔn] *nm* intercom.

**interposer** [ɛ̃tɛRpoze] *vt* to interpose; **s'~** *vi* to intervene; **par personnes interposées** through a third party.

**interprétariat** [ɛ̃tɛRpRetaRja] *nm* interpreting.

**interprétation** [ɛ̃tɛRpRetasjɔ̃] *nf* interpretation.

**interprète** [ɛ̃tɛRpRɛt] *nm/f* interpreter; (*porte-parole*) spokesman.

**interpréter** [ɛ̃tɛRpRete] *vt* to interpret.

**interrogateur, trice** [ɛ̃teRɔgatœR, -tRis] *a* questioning, inquiring // *nm/f* (SCOL) (oral) examiner.

**interrogatif, ive** [ɛ̃teRɔgatif, -iv] *a* (LING) interrogative.

**interrogation** [ɛteʀɔgusjɔ̃] *nf* question ; (*scol*) (written *ou* oral) test.
**interrogatoire** [ɛteʀɔgatwaʀ] *nm* (*police*) questioning *q* ; (*jur*) cross-examination.
**interroger** [ɛteʀɔʒe] *vt* to question ; (*données, ordinateur*) to consult ; (*scol*) to test.
**interrompre** [ɛteʀɔ̃pʀ(ə)] *vt* (*gén*) to interrupt ; (*travail, voyage*) to break off, interrupt ; **s'** ~ to break off.
**interrupteur** [ɛteʀyptœʀ] *nm* switch.
**interruption** [ɛteʀypsjɔ̃] *nf* interruption ; **sans** ~ without a break ; ~ **de grossesse** termination of pregnancy.
**intersection** [ɛtɛʀsɛksjɔ̃] *nf* intersection.
**interstice** [ɛtɛʀstis] *nm* crack ; slit.
**interurbain** [ɛteʀyʀbɛ̃] *nm* (*tél*) trunk call service.
**intervalle** [ɛtɛʀval] *nm* (*espace*) space ; (*de temps*) interval ; **dans l'**~ in the meantime.
**intervenir** [ɛtɛʀvəniʀ] *vi* (*gén*) to intervene ; (*survenir*) to take place ; ~ **auprès de** to intervene with ; **la police a dû** ~ police had to be called in ; **les médecins ont dû** ~ the doctors had to operate.
**intervention** [ɛtɛʀvɑ̃sjɔ̃] *nf* intervention ; ~ **chirurgicale** (surgical) operation.
**intervertir** [ɛtɛʀvɛʀtiʀ] *vt* to invert (the order of), reverse.
**interview** [ɛtɛʀvju] *nf* interview ; **interviewer** *vt* [-ve] to interview.
**intestin, e** [ɛtɛstɛ̃, -in] *a* internal // *nm* intestine ; ~ **grêle** small intestine ; **intestinal, e, aux** *a* intestinal.
**intime** [ɛtim] *a* intimate ; (*vie, journal*) private ; (*conviction*) inmost ; (*dîner, cérémonie*) held among friends, quiet // *nm/f* close friend.
**intimer** [ɛtime] *vt* (*jur*) to notify ; ~ **à qn l'ordre de faire** to order sb to do.
**intimider** [ɛtimide] *vt* to intimidate.
**intimité** [ɛtimite] *nf* intimacy ; privacy ; private life ; **dans l'**~ in private ; (*sans formalités*) with only a few friends, quietly.
**intitulé** [ɛtityle] *nm* title.
**intituler** [ɛtityle] *vt*: **comment a-t-il intitulé son livre?** what title did he give his book? ; **s'**~ to be entitled ; (*personne*) to call o.s.
**intolérable** [ɛtɔleʀabl(ə)] *a* intolerable.
**intolérance** [ɛtɔleʀɑ̃s] *nf* intolerance.
**intolérant, e** [ɛtɔleʀɑ̃, -ɑ̃t] *a* intolerant.
**intonation** [ɛtɔnɑsjɔ̃] *nf* intonation.
**intouchable** [ɛtuʃabl(ə)] *a* (*fig*) above the law, sacrosanct ; (*rel*) untouchable.
**intoxication** [ɛtɔksikɑsjɔ̃] *nf* poisoning *q* ; (*fig*) brainwashing ; ~ **alimentaire** food poisoning.
**intoxiquer** [ɛtɔksike] *vt* to poison ; (*fig*) to brainwash.
**intraduisible** [ɛtʀadɥizibl(ə)] *a* untranslatable ; (*fig*) impossible to render.
**intraitable** [ɛtʀɛtabl(ə)] *a* inflexible, uncompromising.
**intransigeance** [ɛtʀɑ̃ziʒɑ̃s] *nf* intransigence.
**intransigeant, e** [ɛtʀɑ̃ziʒɑ̃, -ɑ̃t] *a* intransigent ; (*morale, passion*) uncompromising.

**intransitif, ive** [ɛtʀɑ̃zitif, -iv] *a* (*ling*) intransitive.
**intransportable** [ɛtʀɑ̃spɔʀtabl(ə)] *a* (*blessé*) unable to travel.
**intraveineux, euse** [ɛtʀavɛnø, -øz] *a* intravenous.
**intrépide** [ɛtʀepid] *a* dauntless.
**intrigant, e** [ɛtʀigɑ̃, -ɑ̃t] *nm/f* schemer.
**intrigue** [ɛtʀig] *nf* intrigue.
**intriguer** [ɛtʀige] *vi* to scheme // *vt* to puzzle, intrigue.
**intrinsèque** [ɛtʀɛ̃sɛk] *a* intrinsic.
**introduction** [ɛtʀɔdyksjɔ̃] *nf* introduction.
**introduire** [ɛtʀɔdɥiʀ] *vt* to introduce ; (*visiteur*) to show in ; (*aiguille, clef*): ~ **qch dans** to insert *ou* introduce sth into ; **s'**~ (*techniques, usages*) to be introduced ; **s'**~ **dans** to gain entry into ; to get in ; **s'**~ accepted into ; (*eau, fumée*) to get into.
**introniser** [ɛtʀɔnize] *vt* to enthrone.
**introspection** [ɛtʀɔspɛksjɔ̃] *nf* introspection.
**introuvable** [ɛtʀuvabl(ə)] *a* which cannot be found ; (*comm*) unobtainable.
**introverti, e** [ɛtʀɔvɛʀti] *nm/f* introvert.
**intrus, e** [ɛtʀy, -yz] *nm/f* intruder.
**intrusion** [ɛtʀyzjɔ̃] *nf* intrusion ; interference.
**intuitif, ive** [ɛtɥitif, -iv] *a* intuitive.
**intuition** [ɛtɥisjɔ̃] *nf* intuition.
**inusable** [inyzabl(ə)] *a* hard-wearing.
**inusité, e** [inyzite] *a* not in common use ; unaccustomed.
**inutile** [inytil] *a* useless ; (*superflu*) unnecessary ; **inutilisable** *a* unusable ; **inutilité** *nf* uselessness.
**invaincu, e** [ɛ̃vɛ̃ky] *a* unbeaten ; unconquered.
**invalide** [ɛ̃valid] *a* disabled ; ~ **de guerre** disabled ex-serviceman ; ~ **du travail** industrially disabled person.
**invalider** [ɛ̃valide] *vt* to invalidate.
**invalidité** [ɛ̃validite] *nf* disability.
**invariable** [ɛ̃vaʀjabl(ə)] *a* invariable.
**invasion** [ɛ̃vuzjɔ̃] *nf* invasion.
**invectiver** [ɛ̃vɛktive] *vt* to hurl abuse at // *vi*: ~ **contre** to rail against.
**invendable** [ɛ̃vɑ̃dabl(ə)] *a* unsaleable ; unmarketable ; **invendus** *nmpl* unsold goods.
**inventaire** [ɛ̃vɑ̃tɛʀ] *nm* inventory ; (*comm: liste*) stocklist ; (: *opération* ) stocktaking *q* ; (*fig*) survey.
**inventer** [ɛ̃vɑ̃te] *vt* to invent ; (*subterfuge*) to devise, invent ; (*histoire, excuse*) to make up, invent ; ~ **de faire** to hit on the idea of doing ; **inventeur** *nm* inventor ; **inventif, ive** *a* inventive ; **invention** [-sjɔ̃] *nf* invention.
**inventorier** [ɛ̃vɑ̃tɔʀje] *vt* to make an inventory of.
**inverse** [ɛ̃vɛʀs(ə)] *a* reverse ; opposite ; inverse // *nm* inverse, reverse ; **en proportion** ~ in inverse proportion ; **dans l'ordre** ~ in the reverse order ; **en sens** ~ in (*ou* from) the opposite direction ; ~**ment** *ad* conversely ; **inverser** *vt* to invert, reverse ; (*élec*) to reverse ; **inversion** *nf* inversion ; reversal.

**inverti, e** [ɛ̃vɛʀti] *nm f* homosexual.

**investigation** [ɛ̃vɛstigɑsjɔ̃] *nf* investigation, inquiry

**investir** [ɛ̃vɛstiʀ] *vt* to invest ; **investissement** *nm* investment ; **investiture** *nf* investiture ; (*à une élection*) nomination.

**invétéré, e** [ɛ̃veteʀe] *a* (*habitude*) ingrained ; (*bavard, buveur*) inveterate.

**invincible** [ɛ̃vɛ̃sibl(ə)] *a* invincible, unconquerable.

**invisible** [ɛ̃vizibl(ə)] *a* invisible.

**invitation** [ɛ̃vitɑsjɔ̃] *nf* invitation.

**invité, e** [ɛ̃vite] *nm/f* guest.

**inviter** [ɛ̃vite] *vt* to invite ; ~ **qn à faire** to invite sb to do ; (*suj: chose*) to induce *ou* tempt sb to do.

**involontaire** [ɛ̃vɔlɔ̃tɛʀ] *a* (*mouvement*) involuntary ; (*insulte*) unintentional ; (*complice*) unwitting.

**invoquer** [ɛ̃vɔke] *vt* (*Dieu, muse*) to call upon, invoke ; (*prétexte*) to put forward (as an excuse) ; (*témoignage*) to call upon ; (*loi, texte*) to refer to ; ~ **la clémence de qn** to beg sb *ou* appeal to sb for clemency.

**invraisemblable** [ɛ̃vʀɛsɑ̃blabl(ə)] *a* unlikely, improbable ; incredible.

**invulnérable** [ɛ̃vylneʀabl(ə)] *a* invulnerable.

**iode** [jɔd] *nm* iodine.

**ion** [jɔ̃] *nm* ion.

**ionique** [jɔnik] *a* (ARCHIT) Ionic ; (SCIENCE) ionic.

**irai** *etc vb voir* **aller.**

**Irak** [iʀuk] *nm* Iraq ; **irakien, ne** *a, nm/f* Iraqi

**Iran** [iʀɑ̃] *nm* Iran ; **Iranien, ne** *nm/f* Iranian.

**irascible** [iʀasibl(ə)] *a* short-tempered, irascible.

**irions** *etc vb voir* **aller.**

**iris** [iʀis] *nm* iris.

**irisé, e** [iʀize] *a* iridescent.

**irlandais, e** [iʀlɑ̃dɛ, -ɛz] *a, nm* (*langue*) Irish // *nm/f* : **I~, e** Irishman/woman ; **les I~** the Irish

**Irlande** [iʀlɑ̃d] *nf* Ireland ; ~ **du Nord** Northern Ireland.

**ironie** [iʀɔni] *nf* irony ; **ironique** *a* ironical ; **ironiser** *vi* to be ironical.

**irons** *etc vb voir* **aller.**

**irradier** [iʀadje] *vi* to radiate // *vt* to irradiate.

**irraisonné, e** [iʀɛzɔne] *a* irrational, unreasoned.

**irrationnel, le** [iʀasjɔnɛl] *a* irrational.

**irréalisable** [iʀealizabl(ə)] *a* unrealizable ; impracticable.

**irréconciliable** [iʀekɔ̃siljabl(ə)] *a* irreconcilable.

**irrécupérable** [iʀekypeʀabl(ə)] *a* unreclaimable, beyond repair ; (*personne*) beyond redemption *ou* recall.

**irrécusable** [iʀekyzabl(ə)] *a* unimpeachable.

**irréductible** [iʀedyktibl(ə)] *a* indomitable, implacable ; (MATH) irreducible.

**irréel, le** [iʀeɛl] *a* unreal.

**irréfléchi, e** [iʀefleʃi] *a* thoughtless.

**irréfutable** [iʀefytabl(ə)] *a* irre-futable.

**irrégularité** [iʀegylaʀite] *nf* irregularity ; unevenness *q.*

**irrégulier, ière** [iʀegylje, -jɛʀ] *a* irregular ; uneven ; (*élève, athlète*) erratic.

**irrémédiable** [iʀemedjabl(ə)] *a* irreparable.

**irremplaçable** [iʀɑ̃plasabl(ə)] *a* irreplaceable.

**irréparable** [iʀepaʀabl(ə)] *a* beyond repair ; (*fig*) irreparable.

**irrépressible** [iʀepʀesibl(ə)] *a* irrepressible, uncontrollable.

**irréprochable** [iʀepʀɔʃabl(ə)] *a* irreproachable, beyond reproach ; (*tenue, toilette*) impeccable.

**irrésistible** [iʀezistibl(ə)] *a* irresistible ; (*preuve, logique*) compelling.

**irrésolu, e** [iʀezɔly] *a* irresolute.

**irrespectueux, euse** [iʀɛspɛktyø, -øz] *a* disrespectful.

**irrespirable** [iʀɛspiʀabl(ə)] *a* unbreathable ; (*fig*) oppressive, stifling.

**irresponsable** [iʀɛspɔ̃sabl(ə)] *a* irresponsible.

**irrévérencieux, euse** [iʀeveʀɑ̃sjø, -øz] *a* irreverent.

**irréversible** [iʀevɛʀsibl(ə)] *a* irreversible.

**irrévocable** [iʀevɔkabl(ə)] *a* irrevocable.

**irrigation** [iʀigɑsjɔ̃] *nf* irrigation.

**irriguer** [iʀige] *vt* to irrigate.

**irritable** [iʀitabl(ə)] *a* irritable.

**irritation** [iʀitɑsjɔ̃] *nf* irritation.

**irriter** [iʀite] *vt* (*agacer*) to irritate, annoy ; (MÉD: *enflammer*) to irritate ; **s'~ contre/de** to get annoyed *ou* irritated at/with.

**irruption** [iʀypsjɔ̃] *nf* irruption *q* ; **faire** ~ **dans** to burst into.

**Islam** [islam] *nm* Islam ; **islamique** *a* Islamic.

**islandais, e** [islɑ̃dɛ, -ɛz] *a, nm* (*langue*) Icelandic // *nm/f* Icelander.

**Islande** [islɑ̃d] *nf* Iceland.

**isocèle** [izɔsɛl] *a* isoceles.

**isolant, e** [izɔlɑ̃, -ɑ̃t] *a* insulating ; (*insonorisant*) soundproofing.

**isolation** [izɔlɑsjɔ̃] *nf* insulation.

**isolé, e** [izɔle] *a* isolated ; insulated.

**isolement** [izɔlmɑ̃] *nm* isolation ; solitary confinement.

**isoler** [izɔle] *vt* to isolate ; (*prisonnier*) to put in solitary confinement ; (*ville*) to cut off, isolate ; (ÉLEC) to insulate ; **isoloir** *nm* polling booth.

**Israël** [isʀaɛl] *nm* Israel ; **israélien, ne** *a, nm/f* Israeli ; **israélite** *a* Jewish // *nm/f* Jew/Jewess.

**issu, e** [isy] *a:* ~ **de** descended from ; (*fig*) stemming from // *nf* (*ouverture, sortie*) exit ; (*solution*) way out, solution ; (*dénouement*) outcome ; **à l'~e de** at the conclusion *ou* close of ; **rue sans ~e** dead end, no through road.

**isthme** [ism(ə)] *nm* isthmus.

**Italie** [itali] *nf* Italy ; **Italien, ne** *a, nm, nf* Italian.

**italique** [italik] *nm:* **en** ~ in italics.

**itinéraire** [itineʀɛʀ] *nm* itinerary, route.

**itinérant, e** [itineRɑ̃, -ɑ̃t] *a* itinerant, travelling.
**I.U.T.** *sigle m voir* **institut.**
**ivoire** [ivwaR] *nm* ivory.
**ivre** [ivR(ə)] *a* drunk ; ~ **de** (*colère, bonheur*) wild with ; **ivresse** *nf* drunkenness ; **ivrogne** *nm/f* drunkard.

**J**

**j'** [ʒ] *pronom voir* **je.**
**jabot** [ʒabo] *nm* (ZOOL) crop ; (*de vêtement*) jabot.
**jacasser** [ʒakase] *vi* to chatter.
**jachère** [ʒaʃɛR] *nf:* (être) **en** ~ (to lie) fallow.
**jacinthe** [ʒasɛ̃t] *nf* hyacinth.
**jade** [ʒad] *nm* jade.
**jadis** [ʒadis] *ad* in times past, formerly.
**jaillir** [ʒajiR] *vi* (*liquide*) to spurt out, gush out ; (*fig*) to rear up ; to burst out ; to flood out.
**jais** [ʒɛ] *nm* jet ; (**d'un noir**) **de** ~ jet-black.
**jalon** [ʒalɔ̃] *nm* range pole ; (*fig*) milestone ; **jalonner** *vt* to mark out ; (*fig*) to mark, punctuate.
**jalouser** [ʒaluze] *vt* to be jealous of.
**jalousie** [ʒaluzi] *nf* jealousy ; (*store*) (venetian) blind.
**jaloux, se** [ʒalu, -uz] *a* jealous.
**jamais** [ʒamɛ] *ad* never ; (*sans négation*) ever ; **ne ...** ~ never.
**jambage** [ʒɑ̃baʒ] *nm* (*de lettre*) downstroke ; (*de porte*) jamb.
**jambe** [ʒɑ̃b] *nf* leg ; **jambières** *nfpl* leggings ; (SPORT) shin pads.
**jambon** [ʒɑ̃bɔ̃] *nm* ham.
**jante** [ʒɑ̃t] *nf* (wheel) rim.
**janvier** [ʒɑ̃vje] *nm* January.
**Japon** [ʒapɔ̃] *nm* Japan ; **japonais, e** *a, nm, nf* Japanese.
**japper** [ʒape] *vi* to yap, yelp.
**jaquette** [ʒakɛt] *nf* (*de cérémonie*) morning coat ; (*de livre*) dust cover, dust jacket.
**jardin** [ʒaRdɛ̃] *nm* garden ; ~ **d'acclimatation** zoological gardens *pl* ; ~ **d'enfants** nursery school ; ~ **public** (public) park, public gardens *pl* ; **jardinage** *nm* gardening ; **jardinier, ière** *nm/f* gardener // *nf* (*de fenêtre*) window box ; **jardinière d'enfants** nursery school teacher.
**jargon** [ʒaRgɔ̃] *nm* jargon.
**jarre** [ʒaR] *nf* (earthenware) jar.
**jarret** [ʒaRɛ] *nm* back of knee, ham ; (CULIN) knuckle, shin.
**jarretelle** [ʒaRtɛl] *nf* suspender.
**jarretière** [ʒaRtjɛR] *nf* garter.
**jaser** [ʒaze] *vi* to chatter, prattle ; (*indiscrètement*) to gossip.
**jasmin** [ʒasmɛ̃] *nm* jasmin.
**jaspe** [ʒasp(ə)] *nm* jasper.
**jatte** [ʒat] *nf* basin, bowl.
**jauge** [ʒoʒ] *nf* (*capacité*) capacity, tonnage ; (*instrument*) gauge ; **jauger** *vt* to gauge the capacity of ; (*fig*) to size up ; **jauger 3000 tonneaux** to measure 3,000 tons.

**jaune** [ʒon] *a, nm* yellow // *nm/f* Asiatic // *ad* (*fam*): **rire** ~ to laugh on the other side of one's face ; ~ **d'œuf** (egg) yolk ; **jaunir** *vi, vt* to turn yellow.
**jaunisse** [ʒonis] *nf* jaundice.
**javel** [ʒavɛl] *nf voir* **eau.**
**javelot** [ʒavlo] *nm* javelin.
**jazz** [dʒaz] *nm* jazz.
**J.-C.** *sigle voir* **Jésus-Christ.**
**je, j'** [ʒ(ə)] *pronom* I.
**jean** [dʒin] *nm* jeans *pl.*
**jérémiades** [ʒeRemjad] *nfpl* moaning *sg.*
**jerrycan** [ʒeRikan] *nm* jerrycan.
**jersey** [ʒɛRzɛ] *nm* jersey.
**Jésus-Christ** [ʒezykRi(st)] *n* Jesus Christ ; **600 avant/après** ~ *ou* **J.-C.** 600 B.C./A.D.
**jet** [ʒɛ] *nm* (*lancer*) throwing *q*, throw ; (*jaillissement*) jet ; spurt ; (*de tuyau*) nozzle ; (*avion*) [dʒɛt] jet ; **arroser au** ~ to hose ; **du premier** ~ at the first attempt *or* shot ; ~ **d'eau** fountain ; spray.
**jetée** [ʒəte] *nf* jetty ; pier.
**jeter** [ʒəte] *vt* (*gén*) to throw ; (*se défaire de*) to throw away *ou* out ; (*son, lueur etc*) to give out ; ~ **qch à qn** to throw sth to sb ; (*de façon agressive*) to throw *ou* hurl sth at sb ; ~ **un coup d'œil (à)** to take a look (at) ; ~ **l'effroi parmi** to spread fear among ; ~ **un sort à qn** to cast a spell on sb ; **se** ~ **dans** (*fleuve*) to flow into.
**jeton** [ʒətɔ̃] *nm* (*au jeu*) counter ; (*de téléphone*) token ; ~**s de présence** (director's) fees.
**jette** *etc vb voir* **jeter.**
**jeu, x** [ʒø] *nm* (*divertissement*, TECH: *d'une pièce*) play ; (*défini par des règles*, TENNIS: *partie*, FOOTBALL *etc:* *façon de jouer*) game ; (THÉÂTRE *etc*) acting ; (*au casino*): **le** ~ gambling ; (*fonctionnement*) working, interplay ; (*série d'objets, jouet*) set ; (*CARTES*) hand ; **en** ~ at stake ; at work ; (*FOOTBALL*) in play ; **remettre en** ~ to throw in ; **entrer/mettre en** ~ to come/bring into play ; ~ **de boules** game of bowls ; (*endroit*) bowling pitch ; (*boules*) set of bowls ; ~ **de cartes** card game ; (*paquet*) pack of cards ; ~ **de construction** building set ; ~ **d'échecs** chess set ; ~ **de hasard** game of chance ; ~ **de mots** pun ; **le** ~ **de l'oie** snakes and ladders *sg* ; ~ **d'orgue(s)** organ stop ; ~ **de société** parlour game ; **J**~**x olympiques** (J.O.) Olympic Games.
**jeudi** [ʒødi] *nm* Thursday.
**jeûn** [ʒœ̃]: **à** ~ *ad* on an empty stomach.
**jeune** [ʒœn] *a* young ; **les** ~**s** young people, the young ; ~ **fille** *nf* girl ; ~ **homme** *nm* young man ; ~ **premier** leading man ; ~**s gens** *nmpl* young people.
**jeûne** [ʒøn] *nm* fast.
**jeunesse** [ʒœnɛs] *nf* youth ; (*aspect*) youthfulness ; youngness ; (*jeunes*) young people *pl*, youth.
**J. O.** *sigle mpl voir* **jeu.**
**joaillerie** [ʒɔajRi] *nf* jewel trade ; jewellery ; **joaillier, ière** *nm/f* jeweller.
**jobard** [ʒɔbaR] *nm* (*péj*) sucker, mug.
**jockey** [ʒɔkɛ] *nm* jockey.

**joie** [ʒwa] *nf* joy.

**joindre** [ʒwɛ̃dR(ə)] *vt* to join ; (*à une lettre*): ~ **qch à** to enclose sth with ; (*contacter*) to contact, get in touch with ; ~ **les mains/talons** to put one's hands/heels together ; **se** ~ **à** to join.

**joint** [ʒwɛ̃] *nm* joint ; (*ligne*) join ; (*de ciment etc*) pointing *q* ; ~ **de cardan** cardan joint ; ~ **de culasse** cylinder head gasket ; ~ **de robinet** washer.

**joli** [ʒɔli] *a* pretty, attractive ; **c'est du** ~ ! (*ironique*) that's very nice! ; ~**ment** *ad* prettily, attractively ; (*fam: très*) pretty.

**jonc** [ʒɔ̃] *nm* (bul)rush.

**joncher** [ʒɔ̃ʃe] *vt* (*suj: choses*) to be strewed on ; **jonché de** strewn with.

**jonction** [ʒɔ̃ksjɔ̃] *nf* joining ; (**point de**) ~ junction ; **opérer une** ~ (*MIL etc*) to rendez-vous.

**jongler** [ʒɔ̃gle] *vi* to juggle ; **jongleur, euse** *nm/f* juggler.

**jonquille** [ʒɔ̃kij] *nf* daffodil.

**Jordanie** [ʒɔRdani] *nf*: **la** ~ Jordan.

**joue** [ʒu] *nf* cheek ; **mettre en** ~ to take aim at.

**jouer** [ʒwe] *vt* (*partie, carte, coup,* MUS: *morceau*) to play ; (*somme d'argent, réputation*) to stake, wager ; (*pièce, rôle*) to perform ; (*film*) to show ; (*simuler: sentiment*) to affect, feign // *vi* to play ; (THÉÂTRE, CINÉMA) to act, perform ; (*bois, porte: se voiler*) to warp ; (*clef, pièce: avoir du jeu*) to be loose ; ~ **sur** (*miser*) to gamble on ; ~ **de** (*MUS*) to play ; ~ **du couteau/des coudes** to use knives/one's elbows ; ~ **à** (*jeu, sport, roulette*) to play ; ~ **au héros** to play the hero ; ~ **avec** (*risquer*) to gamble with ; **se** ~ **de** (*difficultés*) to make light of ; **se** ~ **de qn** to deceive *ou* dupe sb ; ~ **un tour à qn** to play a trick on sb ; ~ **serré** to play a close game ; ~ **de malchance** to be dogged with ill-luck.

**jouet** [ʒwɛ] *nm* toy ; **être le** ~ **de** (*illusion etc*) to be the victim of.

**joueur, euse** [ʒwœR, -øz] *nm/f* player ; **être beau/mauvais** ~ to be a good/bad loser.

**joufflu, e** [ʒufly] *a* chubby-cheeked, chubby.

**joug** [ʒu] *nm* yoke.

**jouir** [ʒwiR] : ~ **de** *vt* to enjoy ; **jouissance** *nf* pleasure ; (*JUR*) use ; **jouisseur, euse** *nm/f* sensualist.

**joujou** [ʒuʒu] *nm* (*fam*) toy.

**jour** [ʒuR] *nm* day ; (*opposé à la nuit*) day, daytime ; (*clarté*) daylight ; (*fig: aspect*) light ; (*ouverture*) opening ; openwork *q* ; **au** ~ **le** ~ from day to day ; **de nos** ~**s** these days, nowadays ; **il fait** ~ it's daylight ; **au** ~ in daylight ; **au grand** ~ (*fig*) in the open ; **mettre au** ~ to uncover, disclose ; **mettre à** ~ to bring up to date, update ; **donner le** ~ **à** to give birth to ; **voir le** ~ to be born ; **se faire** ~ to become clear.

**journal, aux** [ʒuRnal, -o] *nm* (news)paper ; (*personnel*) journal, diary ; ~ **parlé/télévisé** radio/ television news *sg* ; ~ **de bord** log.

**journalier, ière** [ʒuRnalje, -jɛR] *a* daily ; (*banal*) everyday // *nm* day labourer.

**journalisme** [ʒuRnalism(ə)] *nm* journalism ; **journaliste** *nm/f* journalist.

**journée** [ʒuRne] *nf* day ; **la** ~ **continue** the 9 to 5 working day (with short lunch break).

**journellement** [ʒuRnɛlmã] *ad* daily.

**joute** [ʒut] *nf* duel.

**jouvence** [ʒuvãs] *nf*: **bain de** ~ rejuvenating experience.

**jovial** [ʒɔvjal] *a* jovial, jolly.

**joyau, x** [ʒwajo] *nm* gem, jewel.

**joyeux, euse** [ʒwajø, -øz] *a* joyful, merry ; ~ **Noël!** merry *ou* happy Christmas! ; ~ **anniversaire!** many happy returns!

**jubilé** [ʒybile] *nm* jubilee.

**jubiler** [ʒybile] *vi* to be jubilant, exult.

**jucher** [ʒyʃe] *vt*: ~ **qch sur** to perch sth (up)on // *vi* (*oiseau*): ~ **sur** to perch (up)on ; **se** ~ **sur** to perch o.s. (up)on.

**judaïque** [ʒydaik] *a* (*loi*) Judaic ; (*religion*) Jewish.

**judaïsme** [ʒydaism(ə)] *nm* Judaism.

**judas** [ʒyda] *nm* (*trou*) spy-hole.

**judiciaire** [ʒydisjɛR] *a* judicial.

**judicieux, euse** [ʒydisjø, -øz] *a* judicious.

**judo** [ʒydo] *nm* judo ; ~**ka** *nm/f* judoka.

**juge** [ʒyʒ] *nm* judge ; ~ **d'instruction** examining magis-trate ; ~ **de paix** justice of the peace ; ~ **de touche** linesman.

**jugé** [ʒyʒe]: **au** ~ *ad* by guesswork.

**jugement** [ʒyʒmã] *nm* judgment ; (*JUR: au criminel*) sentence ; (: *au civil*) decision ; ~ **de valeur** value judgment.

**jugeote** [ʒyʒɔt] *nf* (*fam*) gumption.

**juger** [ʒyʒe] *vt* to judge ; ~ **qn/qch satisfaisant** to consider sb/sth (to be) satisfactory ; ~ **que** to think *ou* consider that ; ~ **bon de faire** to consider it a good idea to do, see fit to do ; ~ **de** *vt* to appreciate.

**jugulaire** [ʒygylɛR] *a* jugular // *nf* (MIL) chinstrap.

**juif, ive** [ʒɥif, -iv] *a* Jewish // *nm/f* Jew/Jewess.

**juillet** [ʒɥijɛ] *nm* July.

**juin** [ʒɥɛ̃] *nm* June.

**jumeau, elle, x** [ʒymo, -ɛl] *a, nm/f* twin ; **jumelles** *nfpl* binoculars.

**jumeler** [ʒymle] *vt* to twin ; **roues jumelées** double wheels.

**jumelle** [ʒymɛl] *a, nf voir* **jumeau**.

**jument** [ʒymã] *nf* mare.

**jungle** [ʒœ̃gl(ə)] *nf* jungle.

**jupe** [ʒyp] *nf* skirt ; ~**-culotte** *nf* divided skirt, culotte(s).

**jupon** [ʒypɔ̃] *nm* waist slip *ou* petticoat.

**juré, e** [ʒyRe] *nm/f* juror, juryman/woman // *a*: **ennemi** ~ sworn enemy.

**jurer** [ʒyRe] *vt* (*obéissance etc*) to swear, vow // *vi* (*dire des jurons*) to swear, curse ; (*dissoner*): ~ **(avec)** to clash (with) ; (*s'engager*): ~ **de faire/que** to swear *ou* vow to do/that ; (*affirmer*): ~ **que** to swear *ou* vouch that ; ~ **de qch** (*s'en porter garant*) to swear to sth.

**juridiction** [ʒyRidiksjɔ̃] *nf* jurisdiction ; court(s) of law.

**juridique** [ʒyRidik] *a* legal.

**juriste** [ʒyʀist(ə)] *nm/f* jurist ; lawyer.
**juron** [ʒyʀɔ̃] *nm* curse, swearword.
**jury** [ʒyʀi] *nm* (*JUR*) jury ; (*SCOL*) board (of examiners), jury.
**jus** [ʒy] *nm* juice ; (*de viande*) gravy, (meat) juice ; ~ **de fruits** fruit juice ; ~ **de raisin/tomates** grape/tomato juice.
**jusant** [ʒyzɑ̃] *nm* ebb (tide).
**jusque** [ʒysk(ə)]: **jusqu'à** *prép* (*endroit*) as far as, (up) to ; (*moment*) until, till ; (*limite*) up to ; ~ **sur/dans** up to, as far as ; (*y compris*) even on/in ; **jusqu'à présent** until now, so far.
**juste** [ʒyst(ə)] *a* (*équitable*) just, fair ; (*légitime*) just, justified ; (*exact, vrai*) right ; (*étroit, insuffisant*) tight // *ad* right ; tight ; (*chanter*) in tune ; (*seulement*) just ; ~ **assez/au-dessus** just enough/above ; **pouvoir tout** ~ **faire** to be only just able to do ; **au** ~ exactly, actually ; **le** ~ **milieu** the happy medium ; ~**ment** *ad* rightly ; justly ; (*précisément*): **c'est** ~**ment ce que** that's just *ou* precisely what ; **justesse** *nf* (*précision*) accuracy ; (*d'une remarque*) aptness ; (*d'une opinion*) soundness ; **de justesse** just, by a narrow margin.
**justice** [ʒystis] *nf* (*équité*) fairness, justice ; (*ADMIN*) justice ; **rendre la** ~ to dispense justice ; **obtenir** ~ to obtain justice ; **rendre** ~ **à qn** to do sb justice ; **se faire** ~ to take the law into one's own hands ; (*se suicider*) to take one's life.
**justiciable** [ʒystisjabl(ə)] *a*: ~ **de** (*JUR*) answerable to.
**justicier, ière** [ʒystisje, -jɛʀ] *nm/f* judge, righter of wrongs.
**justifiable** [ʒystifjabl(ə)] *a* justifiable.
**justification** [ʒystifikɑsjɔ̃] *nf* justification.
**justifier** [ʒystifje] *vt* to justify ; ~ **de** *vt* to prove.
**jute** [ʒyt] *nm* jute.
**juteux, euse** [ʒytø, -øz] *a* juicy.
**juvénile** [ʒyvenil] *a* young, youthful.
**juxtaposer** [ʒykstapoze] *vt* to juxtapose.

## K

**kaki** [kaki] *a inv* khaki.
**kaléidoscope** [kaleidɔskɔp] *nm* kaleidoscope.
**kangourou** [kɑ̃guʀu] *nm* kangaroo.
**karaté** [kaʀate] *nm* karate.
**karting** [kaʀtiŋ] *nm* go-carting, karting.
**kayac, kayak** [kajak] *nm* kayak.
**képi** [kepi] *nm* kepi.
**kermesse** [kɛʀmɛs] *nf* bazaar, (charity) fête ; village fair.
**kérosène** [keʀozɛn] *nm* jet fuel ; rocket fuel.
**kibboutz** [kibuts] *nm* kibbutz.
**kidnapper** [kidnape] *vt* to kidnap.
**kilogramme** [kilɔgʀam] *nm*, **kilo** *nm* kilogramme.
**kilométrage** [kilɔmetʀaʒ] *nm* number of kilometres travelled, ≈ mileage.
**kilomètre** [kilɔmɛtʀ(ə)] *nm* kilometre.
**kilométrique** [kilɔmetʀik] *a* (*distance*) in kilometres ; **compteur** ~ ≈ mileage indicator.

**kilowatt** [kilɔwat] *nm* kilowatt.
**kinésithérapeute** [kineziteʀapøt] *nm/f* physiotherapist.
**kiosque** [kjɔsk(ə)] *nm* kiosk, stall.
**kirsch** [kiʀʃ] *nm* kirsch.
**klaxon** [klaksɔn] *nm* horn ; **klaxonner** *vi, vt* to hoot.
**kleptomane** [klɛptɔman] *nm/f* kleptomaniac.
**km.** *abr de* **kilomètre** ; **km./h** (= *kilomètres-heure*) ≈ m.p.h. (miles per hour).
**knock-out** [nɔkawt] *nm* knock-out.
**K.-O.** [kao] *a inv* (knocked) out, out for the count.
**kolkhoze** [kɔlkoz] *nm* kolkhoz.
**kyrielle** [kiʀjɛl] *nf*: **une** ~ **de** a stream of.
**kyste** [kist(ə)] *nm* cyst.

## L

**l'** [l] *dét voir* **le.**
**la** [la] *nm* (*MUS*) A ; (*en chantant la gamme*) la.
**la** [la] *dét voir* **le.**
**là** [la] (*voir aussi* **-ci, celui**) *ad* there ; (*ici*) here ; (*dans le temps*) then ; **est-ce que Catherine est** ~? is Catherine there *ou* in? ; **elle n'est pas** ~ she isn't in *ou* here ; **c'est** ~ **que** this is where ; ~ **où** where ; **de** ~ (*fig*) hence ; **par** ~ (*fig*) by that ; **tout son** ~ (*fig*) that's what it's all about ; ~**-bas** *ad* there.
**label** [labɛl] *nm* stamp, seal.
**labeur** [labœʀ] *nm* toil *q*, toiling *q*.
**labo** [labo] *nm* (*abr de* **laboratoire**) lab.
**laborantin, e** [labɔʀɑ̃tɛ̃, -in] *nm/f* laboratory assistant.
**laboratoire** [labɔʀatwaʀ] *nm* laboratory ; ~ **de langues/d'analyses** language/(medical) analysis laboratory.
**laborieux, euse** [labɔʀjø, -øz] *a* (*tâche*) laborious ; (*personne*) hard-working, industrious.
**labour** [labuʀ] *nm* ploughing *q* ; ~**s** *nmpl* ploughed fields ; **cheval de** ~ plough- *ou* cart-horse ; **bœuf de** ~ ox (*pl* oxen).
**labourer** [labuʀe] *vt* to plough ; (*fig*) to make deep gashes *ou* furrows in ; **laboureur** *nm* ploughman.
**labyrinthe** [labiʀɛ̃t] *nm* labyrinth, maze.
**lac** [lak] *nm* lake.
**lacer** [lase] *vt* to lace *ou* do up.
**lacérer** [laseʀe] *vt* to tear to shreds, lacerate.
**lacet** [lasɛ] *nm* (*de chaussure*) lace ; (*de route*) sharp bend ; (*piège*) snare.
**lâche** [lɑʃ] *a* (*poltron*) cowardly ; (*desserré*) loose, slack // ~ *nm/f* coward.
**lâcher** [lɑʃe] *nm* (*de ballons, oiseaux*) release // *vt* to let go of ; (*ce qui tombe, abandonner*) to drop ; (*oiseau, animal: libérer*) to release, set free ; (*fig: mot, remarque*) to let slip, come out with ; (*SPORT: distancer*) to leave behind // *vi* (*fil, amarres*) to break, give way ; (*freins*) to fail ; ~ **les amarres** (*NAVIG*) to cast off (the moorings) ; ~ **les chiens** to unleash the dogs ; ~ **prise** to let go.

**lâcheté** [lɑʃte] *nf* cowardice ; lowness.
**lacis** [lɑsi] *nm* maze.
**laconique** [lakɔnik] *a* laconic.
**lacrymogène** [lakʀimɔʒɛn] *a voir* **gaz, grenade**.
**lacté, e** [lakte] *a (produit, régime)* milk *cpd*.
**lacune** [lakyn] *nf* gap.
**lacustre** [lakystʀ(ə)] *a* lake *cpd*, lakeside *cpd*.
**lad** [lad] *nm* stable-lad.
**là-dedans** [ladədɑ̃] *ad* inside (there), in it ; *(fig)* in that ; **là-dehors** *ad* out there ; **là-derrière** *ad* behind there ; *(fig)* behind that ; **là-dessous** *ad* underneath, under there ; *(fig)* behind that ; **là-dessus** *ad* on there ; *(fig)* at that point ; about that ; **là-devant** *ad* there (in front).
**ladite** [ladit] *dét voir* **ledit**.
**ladre** [ladʀ(ə)] *a* miserly.
**lagon** [lagɔ̃] *nm* lagoon.
**lagune** [lagyn] *nf* lagoon.
**là-haut** [la'o] *ad* up there.
**laïc** [laik] *a, nm/f* = **laïque**.
**laïciser** [laisize] *vt* to secularize.
**laid, e** [lɛ, lɛd] *a* ugly ; *(fig: acte)* mean, cheap ; **laideron** *nm* ugly girl ; **laideur** *nf* ugliness *q* ; meanness *q*.
**laie** [lɛ] *nf* wild sow.
**lainage** [lɛnaʒ] *nm* woollen garment ; woollen material.
**laine** [lɛn] *nf* wool ; ~ **de verre** glass wool ; **laineux, euse** *a* woolly.
**laïque** [laik] *a* lay, civil ; *(SCOL)* state *cpd (as opposed to private and Roman Catholic)* // *nm/f* layman/woman.
**laisse** [lɛs] *nf (de chien)* lead, leash ; **tenir en** ~ to keep on a lead.
**laisser** [lese] *vt* to leave // *vb auxiliaire:* ~ **qn faire** to 'let sb do ; **se** ~ **exploiter** to let o.s. be exploited ; **se** ~ **aller** to let o.s. go ; **laisse-toi faire** let me *(ou* him) do it ; **cela ne laisse pas de surprendre** nonetheless it is surprising ; ~- **aller** *nm* carelessness, slovenliness ; **laissez-passer** *nm inv* pass.
**lait** [lɛ] *nm* milk ; **frère/sœur de** ~ foster brother/sister ; ~ **écrémé/ concentré** skimmed/evaporated milk ; ~ **démaquillant/de beauté** cleansing/beauty lotion ; **laitage** *nm* milk food ; **laiterie** *nf* dairy ; **laiteux, euse** *a* milky ; **laitier, ière** *a* milk *cpd* // *nm/f* milkman/dairywoman.
**laiton** [lɛtɔ̃] *nm* brass.
**laitue** [lety] *nf* lettuce.
**laïus** [lajys] *nm (péj)* spiel.
**lambeau, x** [lɑ̃bo] *nm* scrap ; **en** ~**x** in tatters, tattered.
**lambin, e** [lɑ̃bɛ̃, -in] *a (péj)* slow.
**lambris** [lɑ̃bʀi] *nm* panelling *q* ; **lambrissé, e** *a* panelled.
**lame** [lam] *nf* blade ; *(vague)* wave ; *(lamelle)* strip ; ~ **de fond** ground swell *q* ; ~ **de rasoir** razor blade.
**lamé** [lame] *nm* lamé.
**lamelle** [lamɛl] *nf* thin strip *ou* blade ; *(de champignon)* gill.
**lamentable** [lamɑ̃tabl(ə)] *a* appalling ; pitiful.
**lamentation** [lamɑ̃tasjɔ̃] *nf* wailing *q*, lamentation ; moaning *q*.

**lamenter** [lamɑ̃te]: **se** ~ *vi:* **se** ~ **(sur)** to moan (over).
**laminer** [lamine] *vt* to laminate ; **laminoir** *nm* rolling mill.
**lampadaire** [lɑ̃padɛʀ] *nm (de salon)* standard lamp.
**lampe** [lɑ̃p(ə)] *nf* lamp ; *(TECH)* valve ; ~ **à pétrole** paraffin lamp ; ~ **de poche** torch ; ~ **à souder** blowlamp.
**lampée** [lɑ̃pe] *nf* gulp, swig.
**lampe-tempête** [lɑ̃ptɑ̃pɛt] *nf* storm lantern.
**lampion** [lɑ̃pjɔ̃] *nm* Chinese lantern.
**lampiste** [lɑ̃pist(ə)] *nm* light *(maintenance)* man ; *(fig)* underling.
**lance** [lɑ̃s] *nf* spear ; ~ **d'incendie** fire hose.
**lancée** [lɑ̃se] *nf:* **être/continuer sur sa** ~ to be under way/keep going.
**lance-flammes** [lɑ̃sflam] *nm inv* flamethrower.
**lance-grenades** [lɑ̃sgʀənad] *nm inv* grenade launcher.
**lancement** [lɑ̃smɑ̃] *nm* launching.
**lance-pierres** [lɑ̃spjɛʀ] *nm inv* catapult.
**lancer** [lɑ̃se] *nm (SPORT)* throwing *q*, throw ; *(PÊCHE)* rod and reel fishing // *vt* to throw ; *(émettre, projeter)* to throw out, send out ; *(produit, fusée, bateau, artiste)* to launch ; *(injure)* to hurl, fling ; *(proclamation, mandat d'arrêt)* to issue ; *(moteur)* to send roaring away ; ~ **qch à qn** to throw sth to sb ; *(de façon aggressive)* to throw *ou* hurl sth at sb ; **se** ~ *vi (prendre de l'élan)* to build up speed ; *(se précipiter):* **se** ~ **sur/contre** to rush at ; **se** ~ **dans** *(discussion)* to launch into ; *(aventure)* to embark on ; ~ **du poids** *nm* putting the shot ; **lance-roquettes** *nm inv* rocket launcher ; **lance-torpilles** *nm inv* torpedo tube.
**lancinant, e** [lɑ̃sinɑ̃, -ɑ̃t] *a (regrets etc)* haunting ; *(douleur)* shooting, throbbing.
**landau** [lɑ̃do] *nm* pram.
**lande** [lɑ̃d] *nf* moor.
**langage** [lɑ̃gaʒ] *nm* language.
**lange** [lɑ̃ʒ] *nm* flannel blanket ; ~**s** swaddling clothes.
**langer** [lɑ̃ʒe] *vt* to change (the nappy of) ; **table à** ~ changing table.
**langoureux, euse** [lɑ̃guʀø, -øz] *a* languorous.
**langouste** [lɑ̃gust(ə)] *nf* crayfish *inv* ; **langoustine** *nf* Dublin Bay prawn.
**langue** [lɑ̃g] *nf (ANAT, CULIN)* tongue ; *(LING)* language ; *(bande):* ~ **de terre** spit of land ; **tirer la** ~ **(à)** to stick out one's tongue (at) ; **de** ~ **française** French-speaking ; ~ **maternelle** native language ; mother tongue ; ~ **verte** slang ; ~ **vivante** living language ; ~**-de-chat** finger biscuit, sponge finger.
**languette** [lɑ̃gɛt] *nf* tongue.
**langueur** [lɑ̃gœʀ] *nf* languidness.
**languir** [lɑ̃giʀ] *vi* to languish, *(conversation)* to flag ; **faire** ~ **qn** to keep sb waiting.
**lanière** [lanjɛʀ] *nf (de fouet)* lash ; *(de valise, bretelle)* strap.
**lanterne** [lɑ̃tɛʀn(ə)] *nf (portable)* lantern ;

(*électrique*) light, lamp; (*de voiture*) (side)light; ~ **rouge** (*fig*) tail-ender.
**lapalissade** [lapalisad] *nf* statement of the obvious.
**laper** [lape] *vt* to lap up.
**lapereau, x** [lapRo] *nm* young rabbit.
**lapidaire** [lapidɛR] *a* (*fig*) terse.
**lapider** [lapide] *vt* to stone.
**lapin** [lapɛ̃] *nm* rabbit; (*peau*) rabbitskin; ~ **de garenne** wild rabbit.
**laps** [laps] *nm:* ~ **de temps** space of time, time *q.*
**lapsus** [lapsys] *nm* slip.
**laquais** [lakɛ] *nm* lackey.
**laque** [lak] *nf* lacquer; (*brute*) lac, shellac // *nm* lacquer; piece of lacquer ware; **laqué, e** *a* lacquered; with lacquer finish.
**laquelle** [lakɛl] *pronom voir* **lequel.**
**larbin** [laRbɛ̃] *nm* (*péj*) flunkey.
**larcin** [laRsɛ̃] *nm* theft.
**lard** [laR] *nm* (*graisse*) fat; (*bacon*) (streaky) bacon.
**larder** [laRde] *vt* (*CULIN*) to lard.
**lardon** [laRdɔ̃] *nm* (*CULIN*) lardon.
**large** [laRʒ(ə)] *a* wide; broad; (*fig*) generous // *ad:* **calculer/voir** ~ to allow extra/think big // *nm* (*largeur*): **5 m de** ~ 5 m wide *ou* in width; (*mer*): **le** ~ **the** open sea; **en** ~ *ad* sideways; **au** ~ **de** off; ~ **d'esprit** broad-minded; ~**ment** *ad* widely; greatly; easily; amply; generously; **largesse** *nf* generosity; **largesses** liberalities; **largeur** *nf* (*qu'on mesure*) width; (*impression visuelle*) wideness, width; breadth; broadness.
**larguer** [laRge] *vt* to drop: ~ **les amarres** to cast off (the moorings).
**larme** [laRm(ə)] *nf* tear; (*fig*): **une** ~ **de** a drop of; **en** ~**s** in tears; **larmoyant, e** *a* tearful; **larmoyer** *vi* (*yeux*) to water; (*se plaindre*) to whimper.
**larron** [laRɔ̃] *nm* thief (*pl* thieves).
**larve** [laRv(ə)] *nf* (*ZOOL*) larva (*pl* ae); (*fig*) worm.
**larvé, e** [laRve] *a* (*fig*) latent.
**laryngite** [laRɛ̃ʒit] *nf* laryngitis.
**laryngologiste** [laRɛ̃gɔlɔʒist(ə)] *nm/f* throat specialist.
**larynx** [laRɛ̃ks] *nm* larynx.
**las, lasse** [lɑ, lɑs] *a* weary.
**lascar** [laskaR] *nm* character; rogue.
**lascif, ive** [lasif, -iv] *a* lascivious.
**laser** [lazɛR] *a, nm:* (**rayon**) ~ laser (beam).
**lasse** [lɑs] *af voir* **las.**
**lasser** [lɑse] *vt* to weary, tire; **se** ~ **de** to grow weary *ou* tired of.
**lassitude** [lɑsityd] *nf* lassitude, weariness.
**lasso** [laso] *nm* lasso.
**latent, e** [latɑ̃, -ɑ̃t] *a* latent.
**latéral, e, aux** [lateRal, -o] *a* side *cpd*, lateral.
**latex** [latɛks] *nm* latex.
**latin, e** [latɛ̃, -in] *a, nm, nf* Latin; **latiniste** *nm/f* Latin scholar (*ou* student); **latino-américain, e** *a* Latin-American.
**latitude** [latityd] *nf* latitude; (*fig*): **avoir la** ~ **de faire** to be left free *ou* be at liberty to do; **à 48'' de** ~ **Nord** at latitude 48" North.

**latrines** [latRin] *nfpl* latrines.
**latte** [lat] *nf* lath, slat; (*de plancher*) board.
**lattis** [lati] *nm* lathwork.
**lauréat, e** [lɔRea, -at] *nm/f* winner.
**laurier** [lɔRje] *nm* (*BOT*) laurel; (*CULIN*) bay leaves *pl*; ~**s** *nmpl* (*fig*) laurels.
**lavable** [lavabl(ə)] *a* washable.
**lavabo** [lavabo] *nm* (*de salle de bains*) washbasin; ~**s** *nmpl* toilet *sg.*
**lavage** [lavaʒ] *nm* washing *q*, wash; ~ **d'estomac/d'intestin** stomach/intestinal wash; ~ **de cerveau** brainwashing *q.*
**lavande** [lavɑ̃d] *nf* lavender.
**lavandière** [lavɑ̃djɛR] *nf* washerwoman.
**lave** [lav] *nf* lava *q.*
**lave-glace** [lavglas] *nm* (*AUTO*) windscreen washer.
**lavement** [lavmɑ̃] *nm* (*MÉD*) enema.
**laver** [lave] *vt* to wash; (*tache*) to wash off; (*fig: affront*) to avenge; **se** ~ to have a wash, wash; **se** ~ **les mains/dents** to wash one's hands/clean one's teeth; ~ **qn de** (*accusation*) to clear sb of; **laverie** *nf:* **laverie (automatique)** launderette.
**lavette** [lavɛt] *nf* dish cloth.
**laveur, euse** [lavœR, -øz] *nm/f* cleaner.
**lave-vaisselle** [lavvɛsɛl] *nm inv* dishwasher.
**lavis** [lavi] *nm* (*technique*) washing; (*dessin*) wash drawing.
**lavoir** [lavwaR] *nm* wash house; washtub.
**laxatif, ive** [laksatif, -iv] *a, nm* laxative.
**laxisme** [laksism(ə)] *nm* laxity.
**layette** [lɛjɛt] *nf* layette.
**le(l'), la, les** [l(ə), la, le] *dét* the // *pronom* (*personne: mâle*) him; (: *femelle*) her; (*animal, chose*) it; (*remplaçant une phrase*) it *ou non traduit*; (*indique la possession*): **se casser la jambe** *etc* to break one's leg *etc*; **voir note sous il**; **les** them; **je ne le savais pas** I don't know (about it); **il était riche et ne l'est plus** he was once rich but no longer is; **levez la main** put your hand up; **avoir les yeux gris/le nez rouge** to have grey eyes/a red nose; **le jeudi** *etc* *ad* (*d'habitude*) on Thursdays *etc*; (*ce jeudi-là*) on the Thursday *etc*; **le matin/soir** *ad* in the morning/evening; mornings/ evenings; **10 F le mètre/kilo** 10 F a *ou* per metre/kilo; **le tiers/quart de** a third/quarter of.
**lécher** [leʃe] *vt* to lick; (*laper: lait, eau*) to lick *ou* lap up; ~ **les vitrines** to go window-shopping.
**leçon** [ləsɔ̃] *nf* lesson; **faire la** ~ to teach; **faire la** ~ **à** (*fig*) to give a lecture to; ~**s de conduite** driving lessons; ~**s particulières** private lessons *ou* tuition *sg.*
**lecteur, trice** [lɛktœR, -tRis] *nm/f* reader; (*d'université*) foreign language assistant // *nm* (*TECH*): ~ **de cassettes** cassette player.
**lecture** [lɛktyR] *nf* reading.
**ledit** [lədi], **ladite** [ladit], *mpl* **lesdits** [ledi], *fpl* **lesdites** [ledit] *dét* the aforesaid.
**légal, e, aux** [legal, -o] *a* legal; ~**ement** *ad* legally; ~**iser** *vt* to legalize; ~**ité** *nf* legality, lawfulness; **être dans/sortir de la** ~**ité** to be within/step outside the law.
**légataire** [legatɛR] *nm:* ~ **universel** sole legatee.

**légation** [legɑsjɔ̃] *nf* legation.
**légendaire** [leʒɑ̃dɛʀ] *a* legendary.
**légende** [leʒɑ̃d] *nf* (*mythe*) legend ; (*de carte, plan*) key, legend ; (*de dessin*) caption, legend.
**léger, ère** [leʒe, -ɛʀ] *a* light ; (*bruit, retard*) slight ; (*superficiel*) thoughtless ; (*volage*) free and easy ; flighty ; **blessé** ~ slightly injured person ; **à la légère** *ad* (*parler, agir*) rashly, thoughtlessly ; **légèrement** *ad* lightly ; thoughtlessly, rashly ; **légèrement plus grand** slightly bigger ; **légèreté** *nf* lightness ; thoughtlessness.
**légiférer** [leʒifeʀe] *vi* to legislate.
**légion** [leʒjɔ̃] *nf* legion ; ~ **étrangère** foreign legion ; ~ **d'honneur** Legion of Honour ; **légionnaire** *nm* legionnaire.
**législateur** [leʒislatœʀ] *nm* legislator, lawmaker.
**législatif, ive** [leʒislatif, -iv] *a* legislative.
**législation** [leʒislɑsjɔ̃] *nf* legislation.
**législature** [leʒislatyʀ] *nf* legislature ; term (of office).
**légiste** [leʒist(ə)] *a*: **médecin** ~ forensic surgeon.
**légitime** [leʒitim] *a* (*JUR*) lawful, legitimate ; (*fig*) justified, rightful, legitimate ; **en état de** ~ **défense** in self-defence ; ~**ment** *ad* justifiably, rightfully ; **légitimité** *nf* (*JUR*) legitimacy.
**legs** [lɛg] *nm* legacy.
**léguer** [lege] *vt*: ~ **qch à qn** (*JUR*) to bequeath sth to sb ; (*fig*) to hand sth down *ou* pass sth on to sb.
**légume** [legym] *nm* vegetable.
**lendemain** [lɑ̃dmɛ̃] *nm*: **le** ~ the next *ou* following day ; **le** ~ **matin/soir** the next *ou* following morning/evening ; **le** ~ **de** the day after ; **au** ~ **de** in the days following ; in the wake of ; **penser au** ~ to think of the future ; **sans** ~ short-lived ; **de beaux** ~**s** bright prospects.
**lénifiant, e** [lenifjɑ̃, -ɑ̃t] *a* soothing.
**lent, e** [lɑ̃, lɑ̃t] *a* slow ; **lentement** *ad* slowly ; **lenteur** *nf* slowness *q*.
**lentille** [lɑ̃tij] *nf* (*OPTIQUE*) lens *sg* ; (*BOT*) lentil.
**léopard** [leɔpaʀ] *nm* leopard.
**lèpre** [lɛpʀ(ə)] *nf* leprosy ; **lépreux, euse** *nm/f* leper // *a* (*fig*) flaking, peeling.
**lequel** [ləkɛl], **laquelle** [lakɛl], *mpl* **lesquels**, *fpl* **lesquelles** [lekɛl] (*avec à, de*: **auquel, duquel** *etc*) *pronom* (*interrogatif*) which, which one ; (*relatif: personne*: sujet) who ; (: objet, après préposition) whom ; (: chose) which // *a*: **auquel cas** in which case.
**les** [le] *dét voir* **le**.
**lesbienne** [lɛsbjɛn] *nf* lesbian.
**lesdits** [ledi], **lesdites** [ledit] *dét voir* **ledit**.
**léser** [leze] *vt* to wrong.
**lésiner** [lezine] *vt*: ~ (**sur**) to skimp (on).
**lésion** [lezjɔ̃] *nf* lesion, damage *q* ; ~**s cérébrales** brain damage.
**lesquels, lesquelles** [lekɛl] *pronom voir* **lequel**.
**lessive** [lesiv] *nf* (*poudre*) washing powder ; (*linge*) washing *q*, wash ; (*opération*) washing *q* ; **faire la** ~ to do the washing.

**lessivé, e** [lesive] *a* (*fam*) washed out ; cleaned out.
**lessiver** [lesive] *vt* to wash.
**lessiveuse** [lesivøz] *nf* (*récipient*) (laundry) boiler.
**lest** [lɛst] *nm* ballast.
**leste** [lɛst(ə)] *a* sprightly, nimble.
**lester** [lɛste] *vt* to ballast.
**léthargie** [letaʀʒi] *nf* lethargy.
**léthargique** [letaʀʒik] *a* lethargic.
**lettre** [lɛtʀ(ə)] *nf* letter ; ~**s** *nfpl* literature *sg* ; (*SCOL*) arts (subjects) ; **à la** ~ literally ; **en toutes** ~**s** in words, in full ; ~ **de change** bill of exchange.
**lettré, e** [letʀe] *a* well-read, scholarly.
**leu** [lø] *voir* **queue**.
**leucémie** [løsemi] *nf* leukaemia.
**leur** [lœʀ] *dét* their // *pronom* them ; **le(la)** ~, **les** ~**s** theirs ; **à** ~ **approche** as they came near ; **à** ~ **vue** at the sight of them.
**leurre** [lœʀ] *nm* (*appât*) lure ; (*fig*) delusion ; snare.
**leurrer** [lœʀe] *vt* to delude, deceive.
**levain** [ləvɛ̃] *nm* leaven.
**levant, e** [ləvɑ̃, -ɑ̃t] *a*: **soleil** ~ rising sun // *nm*: **le L**~ the Levant.
**levé, e** [ləve] *a*: **être** ~ to be up.
**levée** [ləve] *nf* (*POSTES*) collection ; (*CARTES*) trick ; ~ **de boucliers** general outcry ; ~ **du corps** collection of the body from house of the deceased, before funeral ; ~ **d'écrou** release from custody ; ~ **de terre** levee ; ~ **de troupes** levy.
**lever** [ləve] *vt* (*vitre, bras etc*) to raise ; (*soulever de terre, supprimer: interdiction, siège*) to lift ; (*séance*) to close ; (*impôts, armée*) to levy ; (*CHASSE*) to start ; to flush ; (*fam: fille*) to pick up // *vi* (*CULIN*) to rise // *nm*: **au** ~ on getting up ; **se** ~ *vi* to get up ; (*soleil*) to rise ; (*jour*) to break ; (*brouillard*) to lift ; **ça va se** ~ the weather will clear ; ~ **du jour** daybreak ; ~ **du rideau** curtain raiser ; ~ **de soleil** sunrise.
**levier** [ləvje] *nm* lever ; **faire** ~ **sur** to lever up (*ou* off) ; ~ **de changement de vitesse** gear lever.
**lèvre** [lɛvʀ(ə)] *nf* lip ; **petites/grandes** ~**s** (*ANAT*) labia minora/majora.
**lévrier** [levʀije] *nm* greyhound.
**levure** [ləvyʀ] *nf* yeast.
**lexicographie** [lɛksikɔgʀafi] *nf* lexicography, dictionary writing.
**lexique** [lɛksik] *nm* vocabulary ; lexicon.
**lézard** [lezaʀ] *nm* lizard.
**lézarde** [lezaʀd(ə)] *nf* crack ; **lézarder: se lézarder** *vi* to crack.
**liaison** [ljɛzɔ̃] *nf* (*rapport*) connection, link ; (*RAIL, AVIAT etc*) link ; (*amoureuse*) affair ; (*PHONÉTIQUE*) liaison ; **entrer/être en** ~ **avec** to get/be in contact with ; ~ **radio** radio contact.
**liane** [ljan] *nf* creeper.
**liant, e** [ljɑ̃, -ɑ̃t] *a* sociable.
**liasse** [ljas] *nf* wad, bundle.
**Liban** [libɑ̃] *nm*: **le** ~ (the) Lebanon ; **libanais, e** *a*, *nm/f* Lebanese.
**libations** [libɑsjɔ̃] *nfpl* libations.
**libelle** [libɛl] *nm* lampoon.
**libeller** [libele] *vt* (*chèque, mandat*): ~ (**au nom de**) to make out (to) ; (*lettre*) to word.

**libellule** [libelyl] *nf* dragonfly.
**libéral, e, aux** [libeʀal, -o] *a*, *nm/f* liberal ; **~iser** *vt* to liberalize ; **~isme** *nm* liberalism.
**libéralité** [libeʀalite] *nf* liberality *q*, generosity *q*.
**libérateur, trice** [libeʀatœʀ, -tʀis] *a* liberating // *nm/f* liberator.
**libération** [libeʀɑsjɔ̃] *nf* liberation, freeing ; release ; discharge.
**libérer** [libeʀe] *vt* (*délivrer*) to free, liberate ; (: *moralement*, PSYCH) to liberate ; (*relâcher*) to release ; to discharge ; (*dégager: gaz, cran d'arrêt*) to release ; **se ~** (*de rendez-vous*) to try and be free, get out of previous engagements ; **~ qn de** to free sb from ; (*promesse*) to release sb from.
**libertaire** [libɛʀtɛʀ] *a* libertarian.
**liberté** [libɛʀte] *nf* freedom ; (*loisir*) free time ; **~s** *nfpl* (*privautés*) liberties ; **mettre/être en ~** to set/be free ; **en ~ provisoire/surveillée/conditionnelle** on bail/ probation/parole ; **~ d'esprit** independence of mind ; **~ d'opinion** freedom of thought ; **~ de réunion** right to hold meetings ; **~s individuelles** personal freedom *sg*.
**libertin, e** [libɛʀtɛ̃, -in] *a* libertine, licentious ; **libertinage** *nm* licentiousness.
**libidineux, euse** [libidinø, -øz] *a* libidinous, lustful.
**libido** [libido] *nf* libido.
**libraire** [libʀɛʀ] *nm/f* bookseller.
**librairie** [libʀeʀi] *nf* bookshop.
**libre** [libʀ(ə)] *a* free ; (*route*) clear ; (*pas pris ou occupé: place etc*) vacant ; empty ; not engaged ; not taken ; (SCOL) private and Roman Catholic (*as opposed to 'laïque'*) ; **~ de qch/de faire** free from sth/ to do ; **~-échange** *nm* free trade ; **~ment** *ad* freely ; **~-service** *nm* self-service store.
**librettiste** [libʀetist(ə)] *nm/f* librettist.
**Libye** [libi] *nf*: **la ~** Libya ; **libyen, ne** *a*, *nm/f* Libyan.
**licence** [lisɑ̃s] *nf* (*permis*) permit ; (*diplôme*) (first) degree ; (*liberté*) liberty ; licence ; licentiousness ; **licencié, e** *nm/f* (SCOL): **licencié ès lettres/en droit** ≈ Bachelor of Arts/Law ; (SPORT) member of *a sports federation*.
**licenciement** [lisɑ̃simɑ̃] *nm* dismissal ; laying off *q* ; redundancy.
**licencier** [lisɑ̃sje] *vt* (*renvoyer*) to dismiss ; (*débaucher*) to make redundant ; to lay off.
**licencieux, euse** [lisɑ̃sjø, -øz] *a* licentious.
**lichen** [likɛn] *nm* lichen.
**licite** [lisit] *a* lawful.
**licorne** [likɔʀn(ə)] *nf* unicorn.
**licou** [liku] *nm* halter.
**lie** [li] *nf* dregs *pl*, sediment.
**lié, e** [lje] *a*: **très ~ avec** very friendly with *ou* close to ; **~ par** (*serment*) bound by.
**liège** [ljɛʒ] *nm* cork.
**lien** [ljɛ̃] *nm* (*corde, fig: affectif*) bond ; (*rapport*) link, connection ; **~ de parenté** family tie.
**lier** [lje] *vt* (*attacher*) to tie up ; (*joindre*) to link up ; (*fig: unir, engager*) to bind ; (CULIN) to thicken ; **~ qch à** to tie sth to ;

to link sth to ; **~ conversation avec** to strike up a conversation with ; **se ~ avec** to make friends with.
**lierre** [ljɛʀ] *nm* ivy.
**liesse** [ljɛs] *nf*: **être en ~** to be celebrating *ou* jubilant.
**lieu, x** [ljø] *nm* place // *nmpl* (*habitation*) premises ; (*endroit: d'un accident etc*) scene *sg* ; **en ~ sûr** in a safe place ; **en premier ~** in the first place ; **en dernier ~** lastly ; **avoir ~** to take place ; **avoir ~ de faire** to have grounds *ou* good reason for doing ; **tenir ~ de** to take the place of ; to serve as ; **donner ~ à** to give rise to, give cause for ; **au ~ de** instead of ; **au ~ qu'il y aille** instead of him going ; **~ commun** commonplace ; **~ géométrique** locus.
**lieu-dit** *nm*, *pl* **lieux-dits** [ljødi] locality.
**lieue** [ljø] *nf* league.
**lieutenant** [ljøtnɑ̃] *nm* lieutenant.
**lièvre** [ljɛvʀ(ə)] *nm* hare.
**liftier** [liftje] *nm* lift boy.
**ligament** [ligamɑ̃] *nm* ligament.
**ligature** [ligatyʀ] *nf* ligature ; **ligaturer** *vt* to ligature.
**lige** [liʒ] *a*: **homme ~** (*péj*) henchman.
**ligne** [liɲ] *nf* (*gén*) line ; (TRANSPORTS: *liaison*) service ; (: *trajet*) route ; (*silhouette féminine*): **garder la ~** to keep one's figure ; **'à la ~'** 'new paragraph' ; **entrer en ~ de compte** to be taken into account ; to come into it ; **~ de but/médiane** goal/halfway line ; **~ d'horizon** skyline.
**lignée** [liɲe] *nf* line ; lineage ; descendants *pl*.
**ligneux, euse** [liɲø, -øz] *a* ligneous, woody.
**lignite** [liɲit] *nm* lignite.
**ligoter** [ligɔte] *vt* to tie up.
**ligue** [lig] *nf* league ; **liguer: se liguer** *vi* to form a league ; **se liguer contre** (*fig*) to combine against.
**lilas** [lila] *nm* lilac.
**limace** [limas] *nf* slug.
**limaille** [limaj] *nf*: **~ de fer** iron filings *pl*.
**limande** [limɑ̃d] *nf* dab.
**lime** [lim] *nf* file ; **~ à ongles** nail file ; **limer** *vt* to file (down) ; (*ongles*) to file ; (*fig: prix*) to pare down, trim.
**limier** [limje] *nm* bloodhound ; (*détective*) sleuth.
**liminaire** [liminɛʀ] *a* (*propos*) introductory.
**limitation** [limitɑsjɔ̃] *nf* limitation, restriction.
**limite** [limit] *nf* (*de terrain*) boundary ; (*partie ou point extrême*) limit ; **charge/vitesse ~** maximum speed/load ; **cas ~** borderline case ; **date ~** deadline.
**limiter** [limite] *vt* (*restreindre*) to limit, restrict ; (*délimiter*) to border, form the boundary of.
**limitrophe** [limitʀɔf] *a* border *cpd* ; **~ de** bordering on.
**limoger** [limɔʒe] *vt* to dismiss.
**limon** [limɔ̃] *nm* silt.
**limonade** [limɔnad] *nf* (*fizzy*) lemonade.
**limpide** [lɛ̃pid] *a* limpid.
**lin** [lɛ̃] *nm* flax.

**linceul** [lɛ̃sœl] *nm* shroud.
**linéaire** [lineɛR] *a* linear.
**linge** [lɛ̃ʒ] *nm* (*serviettes etc*) linen; (*pièce de tissu*) cloth; (*aussi:* ~ **de corps**) underwear; (*aussi:* ~ **de toilette**) towel; (*lessive*) washing; ~ **sale** dirty linen.
**lingerie** [lɛ̃ʒRi] *nf* lingerie, underwear.
**lingot** [lɛ̃go] *nm* ingot.
**linguiste** [lɛ̃gɥist(ə)] *nm/f* linguist.
**linguistique** [lɛ̃gɥistik] *a* linguistic // *nf* linguistics *sg*.
**lino(léum)** [lino(leɔm)] *nm* lino(leum).
**lion, ne** [ljɔ̃, ljɔn] *nm/f* lion/lioness; (*signe*): **le L**~ Leo, the Lion; **être du L**~ to be Leo; **lionceau, x** *nm* lion cub.
**lippu, e** [lipy] *a* thick-lipped.
**liquéfier** [likefje] *vt*, **se** ~ *vi* to liquefy.
**liqueur** [likœR] *nf* liqueur.
**liquidation** [likidasjɔ̃] *nf* liquidation; (*COMM*) clearance (sale).
**liquide** [likid] *a* liquid // *nm* liquid; (*COMM*): **en** ~ in ready money *ou* cash.
**liquider** [likide] *vt* (*société, biens, témoin gênant*) to liquidate; (*compte, problème*) to settle; (*COMM: articles*) to clear, sell off.
**liquidités** [likidite] *nfpl* (*COMM*) liquid assets.
**liquoreux, euse** [likɔRø, -øz] *a* syrupy.
**lire** [liR] *nf* (*monnaie*) lira // *vt, vi* to read; ~ **qch à qn** to read sth (out) to sb.
**lis** *vb* [li] *voir* **lire** // *nm* [lis] = **lys**.
**liseré** [lizRe] *nm* border, edging.
**liseron** [lizRɔ̃] *nm* bindweed.
**liseuse** [lizøz] *nf* book-cover.
**lisible** [lizibl(ə)] *a* legible.
**lisière** [lizjɛR] *nf* (*de forêt*) edge; (*de tissu*) selvage.
**lisons** *vb voir* **lire**.
**lisse** [lis] *a* smooth; **lisser** *vt* to smooth.
**liste** [list(ə)] *nf* list; **faire la** ~ **de** to list, make out a list of; ~ **électorale** electoral roll.
**lit** [li] *nm* (*gén*) bed; **faire son** ~ to make one's bed; **aller/se mettre au** ~ to go to/get into bed; **prendre le** ~ to take to one's bed; **d'un premier** ~ (*JUR*) of a first marriage; ~ **de camp** campbed.
**litanie** [litani] *nf* litany.
**literie** [litRi] *nf* bedding; bedclothes *pl*.
**lithographie** [litɔgRafi] *nf* lithography; (*épreuve*) lithograph.
**litière** [litjɛR] *nf* litter.
**litige** [litiʒ] *nm* dispute; **litigieux, euse** *a* litigious, contentious.
**litre** [litR(ə)] *nm* litre; (*récipient*) litre measure.
**littéraire** [literɛR] *a* literary.
**littéral, e, aux** [literal, -o] *a* literal.
**littérature** [literatyR] *nf* literature.
**littoral, e, aux** [litɔral, -o] *a* coastal // *nm* coast.
**liturgie** [lityRʒi] *nf* liturgy; **liturgique** *a* liturgical.
**livide** [livid] *a* livid, pallid.
**livraison** [livRezɔ̃] *nf* delivery.
**livre** [livR(ə)] *nm* book // *nf* (*poids, monnaie*) pound; ~ **de bord** logbook; ~ **d'or** visitors' book; ~ **de poche** paperback (*cheap and pocket size*).

**livré, e** [livRe] *a*: ~ **à soi-même** left to o.s. *ou* one's own devices // *nf* livery.
**livrer** [livRe] *vt* (*COMM*) to deliver; (*otage, coupable*) to hand over; (*secret, information*) to give away; **se** ~ **à** (*se confier*) to confide in; (*se rendre*) to give o.s. up to; (*s'abandonner à: débauche etc*) to give o.s. up *ou* over to; (*faire: pratiques, actes*) to indulge in; (: *travail*) to be engaged in, engage in; (: *sport*) to practise; (: *enquête*) to carry out; ~ **bataille** to give battle.
**livresque** [livRɛsk(ə)] *a* bookish.
**livret** [livRɛ] *nm* booklet; (*d'opéra*) libretto (*pl s*); ~ **de caisse d'épargne** (savings) bank-book; ~ **de famille** (official) family record book; ~ **scolaire** (school) report book.
**livreur, euse** [livRœR, -øz] *nm/f* delivery boy *ou* man/girl *ou* woman.
**lobe** [lɔb] *nm*: ~ **de l'oreille** ear lobe.
**lobé, e** [lɔbe] *a* (*ARCHIT*) foiled.
**lober** [lɔbe] *vt* to lob.
**local, e, aux** [lɔkal, -o] *a* local // *nm* (*salle*) premises *pl* // *nmpl* premises.
**localiser** [lɔkalize] *vt* (*repérer*) to locate, place; (*limiter*) to localize, confine.
**localité** [lɔkalite] *nf* locality.
**locataire** [lɔkatɛR] *nm/f* tenant; (*de chambre*) lodger.
**locatif, ive** [lɔkatif, -iv] *a* (*charges, réparations*) incumbent upon the tenant; (*valeur*) rental; (*immeuble*) with rented flats, used as a letting concern.
**location** [lɔkasjɔ̃] *nf* (*par le locataire*) renting; (*par l'usager: de voiture etc*) hiring; (*par le propriétaire*) renting out, letting; hiring out; '~ **de voitures**' 'car hire *ou* rental'; ~-**vente** *nf* form of hire purchase for housing.
**lock-out** [lɔkawt] *nm inv* lockout.
**locomotion** [lɔkɔmosjɔ̃] *nf* locomotion.
**locomotive** [lɔkɔmɔtiv] *nf* locomotive, engine; (*fig*) pacesetter, pacemaker.
**locution** [lɔkysjɔ̃] *nf* phrase, locution.
**logarithme** [lɔgaRitm(ə)] *nm* logarithm.
**loge** [lɔʒ] *nf* (*THÉÂTRE: d'artiste*) dressing room; (*de spectateurs*) box; (*de concierge, franc-maçon*) lodge.
**logement** [lɔʒmɑ̃] *nm* accommodation *q*, flat; housing *q*; **chercher un** ~ to look for a flat *ou* for accommodation; **construire des** ~**s bon marché** to build cheap housing *sg ou* flats; **crise du** ~ housing shortage.
**loger** [lɔʒe] *vt* to accommodate // *vi* to live; **se** ~: **trouver à se** ~ to find accommodation; **se** ~ **dans** (*suj: balle, flèche*) to lodge itself in; **logeur, euse** *nm/f* landlord/landlady.
**loggia** [lɔdʒja] *nf* loggia.
**logiciel** [lɔʒisjɛl] *nm* software.
**logique** [lɔʒik] *a* logical // *nf* logic; ~**ment** *ad* logically.
**logis** [lɔʒi] *nm* home; abode, dwelling.
**logistique** [lɔʒistik] *nf* logistics *sg*.
**loi** [lwa] *nf* law; **faire la** ~ to lay down the law.
**loin** [lwɛ̃] *ad* far; (*dans le temps*) a long way off; a long time ago; **plus** ~ further; **moins** ~ (**que**) not as far (as); ~ **de far**

from ; **pas ~ de 1000 F** not far off a 1000 F ; **au ~** far off ; **de ~** *ad* from a distance ; *(fig: de beaucoup)* by far ; **il vient de ~** he's come a long way ; he comes from a long way away.

**lointain, e** [lwɛ̃tɛ̃, -ɛn] *a* faraway, distant ; *(dans le futur, passé)* distant, far-off ; *(cause, parent)* remote, distant // *nm:* **dans le ~** in the distance.

**loir** [lwaʀ] *nm* dormouse *(pl* mice).

**loisir** [lwaziʀ] *nm:* **heures de ~** spare time ; **~s** *nmpl* leisure *sg* ; leisure activities ; **avoir le ~ de faire** to have the time *ou* opportunity to do ; **à ~** at leisure ; at one's pleasure.

**londonien, ne** [lɔ̃dɔnjɛ̃, -jɛn] *a* London *cpd*, of London // *nm/f:* **L~, ne** Londoner.

**Londres** [lɔ̃dʀ(ə)] *n* London.

**long, longue** [lɔ̃, lɔ̃g] *a* long // *ad:* **en savoir ~** to know a great deal // *nm:* **de 3 m de ~** 3 m long, 3 m in length // *nf:* **à la longue** in the end ; **faire ~ feu** to fizzle out ; **ne pas faire ~ feu** not to last long ; **du ~ cours** (NAVIG) ocean *cpd*, ocean-going ; **être ~ à faire** to take a long time to do ; **en ~** *ad* lengthwise ; **(tout) le ~ de** (all) along ; **tout au ~ de** *(année, vie)* throughout ; **de ~ en large** *(marcher)* to and fro, up and down.

**longanimité** [lɔ̃ganimite] *nf* forbearance.

**longe** [lɔ̃ʒ] *nf (corde)* tether ; lead ; (CULIN) loin.

**longer** [lɔ̃ʒe] *vt* to go *(ou* walk *ou* drive) along(side) ; *(suj: mur, route)* to border.

**longévité** [lɔ̃ʒevite] *nf* longevity.

**longiligne** [lɔ̃ʒiliɲ] *a* long-limbed.

**longitude** [lɔ̃ʒityd] *nf* longitude ; **à 45° de ~ ouest** at 45° longitude west.

**longitudinal, e, aux** [lɔ̃ʒitydinal, -o] *a* longitudinal, lengthways ; running lengthways.

**longtemps** [lɔ̃tɑ̃] *ad* (for) a long time, (for) long ; **avant ~** before long ; **pour/pendant ~** for a long time/long ; **mettre ~ à faire** to take a long time to do.

**longue** [lɔ̃g] *af voir* **long** ; **~ment** *ad* for a long time, at length.

**longueur** [lɔ̃gœʀ] *nf* length ; **~s** *nfpl (fig: d'un film etc)* lengthy *ou* drawn-out parts ; **sur une ~ de 10 km** for *ou* over 10 km ; **en ~** *ad* lengthwise ; **tirer en ~** to drag on ; **à ~ de journée** all day long ; **~ d'onde** wavelength.

**longue-vue** [lɔ̃gvy] *nf* telescope.

**lopin** [lɔpɛ̃] *nm:* **~ de terre** patch of land.

**loquace** [lɔkas] *a* loquacious, talkative.

**loque** [lɔk] *nf (personne)* wreck ; **~s** *nfpl (habits)* rags.

**loquet** [lɔkɛ] *nm* latch.

**lorgner** [lɔʀɲe] *vt* to eye ; to have one's eye on.

**lorgnon** [lɔʀɲɔ̃] *nm* lorgnette.

**loriot** [lɔʀjo] *nm* (golden) oriole.

**lors** [lɔʀ]: **~ de** *prép* at the time of ; during ; **~ même que** even though.

**lorsque** [lɔʀsk(ə)] *cj* when, as.

**losange** [lɔzɑ̃ʒ] *nm* diamond ; (GÉOM) lozenge ; **en ~** diamond-shaped.

**lot** [lo] *nm (part)* share ; *(de loterie)* prize ; *(fig: destin)* fate, lot.

**loterie** [lɔtʀi] *nf* lottery ; raffle.

**loti, e** [lɔti] *a:* **bien/mal ~** well-/badly off *(as regards luck, circumstances)*.

**lotion** [losjɔ̃] *nf* lotion.

**lotir** [lɔtiʀ] *vt (terrain)* to divide into plots ; to sell by lots ; **lotissement** *nm* housing development ; plot, lot.

**loto** [lɔto] *nm* lotto ; numerical lottery.

**louable** [lwabl(ə)] *a* praiseworthy, commendable.

**louage** [lwaʒ] *nm:* **voiture de ~** hired car ; hire car.

**louange** [lwɑ̃ʒ] *nf:* **à la ~ de** in praise of ; **~s** *nfpl* praise *sg*.

**louche** [luʃ] *a* shady, fishy, dubious // *nf* ladle.

**loucher** [luʃe] *vi* to squint ; *(fig):* **~ sur** to have one's eye on.

**louer** [lwe] *vt (maison: suj: propriétaire)* to let, rent (out) ; (: *locataire)* to rent ; *(voiture etc)* to hire out, rent (out) ; to hire, rent ; *(réserver)* to book ; *(faire l'éloge de)* to praise ; **'à louer'** 'to let' ; **~ qn de** to praise sb for ; **se ~ de** to congratulate o.s. on.

**loufoque** [lufɔk] *a* crazy, zany.

**loulou** [lulu] *nm (chien)* spitz.

**loup** [lu] *nm* wolf *(pl* wolves) ; **~ de mer** *(marin)* old seadog.

**loupe** [lup] *nf* magnifying glass ; **~ de noyer** burr walnut.

**louper** [lupe] *vt (manquer)* to miss ; *(gâcher)* to mess up, bungle.

**lourd, e** [luʀ, luʀd(ə)] *a, ad* heavy ; **~ de** *(conséquences, menaces)* charged *ou* fraught with ; **lourdaud, e** *a (péj)* clumsy ; oafish ; **lourdement** *ad* heavily ; **lourdeur** *nf* heaviness ; **lourdeur d'estomac** indigestion *q*.

**loutre** [lutʀ(ə)] *nf* otter.

**louve** [luv] *nf* she-wolf.

**louveteau, x** [luvto] *nm* wolf-cub ; *(scout)* cub.

**louvoyer** [luvwaje] *vi* (NAVIG) to tack ; *(fig)* to hedge, evade the issue.

**lover** [lɔve]: **se ~** *vi* to coil up.

**loyal, e, aux** [lwajal, -o] *a (fidèle)* loyal, faithful ; *(fair-play)* fair ; **loyauté** *nf* loyalty, faithfulness ; fairness.

**loyer** [lwaje] *nm* rent.

**lu, e** [ly] *pp de* **lire**.

**lubie** [lybi] *nf* whim, craze.

**lubrifiant** [lybʀifjɑ̃] *nm* lubricant.

**lubrifier** [lybʀifje] *vt* to lubricate.

**lubrique** [lybʀik] *a* lecherous.

**lucarne** [lykaʀn(ə)] *nf* skylight.

**lucide** [lysid] *a (conscient)* lucid, conscious ; *(perspicace)* clear-headed ; lucid ; **lucidité** *nf* lucidity.

**luciole** [lysjɔl] *nf* firefly.

**lucratif, ive** [lykʀatif, -iv] *a* lucrative ; profitable ; **à but non ~** non profit-making.

**luette** [lɥɛt] *nf* uvula.

**lueur** [lɥœʀ] *nf (chatoyante)* glimmer *q* ; *(métallique, mouillée)* gleam *q* ; *(rougeoyante, chaude)* glow *q* ; *(pâle)* (faint) light ; *(fig)* glimmer ; gleam.

**luge** [lyʒ] *nf* sledge.

**lugubre** [lygybʀ(ə)] *a* gloomy ; dismal.

**lui** [lɥi] _pronom_ (_chose, animal_) it ; (_personne: mâle_) him ; (: _en sujet_) he ; (: _femelle_) her ; _voir note sous_ **il** ; ~-**même** himself ; itself.
**luire** [lɥiʀ] _vi_ to shine ; to glow ; to gleam.
**lumbago** [lɔ̃bago] _nm_ lumbago.
**lumière** [lymjɛʀ] _nf_ light ; ~**s** _nfpl_ (_d'une personne_) knowledge _sg_, wisdom _sg_ ; **à la** ~ **de** by the light of ; (_fig_) in the light of ; **fais de la** ~ let's have some light, give us some light ; **mettre en** ~ (_fig_) to bring out _ou_ to light ; ~ **du jour/soleil** day/sunlight.
**luminaire** [lyminɛʀ] _nm_ lamp, light.
**lumineux, euse** [lyminø, -øz] _a_ (_émettant de la lumière_) luminous ; (_éclairé_) illuminated ; (_ciel, journée, couleur_) bright ; (_relatif à la lumière: rayon etc_) of light, light _cpd_ ; (_fig: regard_) radiant ; **luminosité** _nf_ (_TECH_) luminosity.
**lunaire** [lynɛʀ] _a_ lunar, moon _cpd_.
**lunatique** [lynatik] _a_ whimsical, temperamental.
**lunch** [lœntʃ] _nm_ (_réception_) buffet lunch.
**lundi** [lœdi] _nm_ Monday ; ~ **de Pâques** Easter Monday.
**lune** [lyn] _nf_ moon ; ~ **de miel** honeymoon.
**luné, e** [lyne] _a_: **bien/mal** ~ **in a** good/bad mood.
**lunette** [lynɛt] _nf_: ~**s** _nfpl_ glasses, spectacles ; (_protectrices_) goggles ; ~ **d'approche** telescope ; ~ **arrière** (_AUTO_) rear window ; ~**s noires** dark glasses ; ~**s de soleil** sunglasses.
**lurette** [lyʀɛt] _nf_: **il y a belle** ~ **ages ago**.
**luron, ne** [lyʀɔ̃, -ɔn] _nm/f_ lad/lass ; **joyeux** _ou_ **gai** ~ gay dog.
**lus** _etc vb voir_ **lire**.
**lustre** [lystʀ(ə)] _nm_ (_de plafond_) chandelier ; (_fig: éclat_) lustre.
**lustrer** [lystʀe] _vt_ (_faire briller_) to lustre ; (_poil d'un animal_) to put a sheen on ; (_user_) to make shiny.
**lut** _vb voir_ **lire**.
**luth** [lyt] _nm_ lute ; **luthier** _nm_ (stringed-)instrument maker.
**lutin** [lytɛ̃] _nm_ imp, goblin.
**lutrin** [lytʀɛ̃] _nm_ lectern.
**lutte** [lyt] _nf_ (_conflit_) struggle ; (_sport_) wrestling ; **lutter** _vi_ to fight, struggle ; to wrestle ; **lutteur** _nm_ wrestler ; (_fig_) battler, fighter.
**luxation** [lyksasjɔ̃] _nf_ dislocation.
**luxe** [lyks(ə)] _nm_ luxury ; **de** ~ _a_ luxury _cpd_.
**Luxembourg** [lyksɑ̃buʀ] _nm_: **le** ~ Luxemburg.
**luxer** [lykse] _vt_: **se** ~ **l'épaule** to dislocate one's shoulder.
**luxueux, euse** [lyksɥø, -øz] _a_ luxurious.
**luxure** [lyksyʀ] _nf_ lust.
**luxuriant, e** [lyksyʀjɑ̃, -ɑ̃t] _a_ luxuriant, lush.
**luzerne** [lyzɛʀn(ə)] _nf_ lucerne, alfalfa.
**lycée** [lise] _nm_ (state) secondary school ; **lycéen, ne** _nm/f_ secondary school pupil.
**lymphatique** [lɛ̃fatik] _a_ (_fig_) lethargic, sluggish.
**lymphe** [lɛ̃f] _nf_ lymph.
**lyncher** [lɛ̃ʃe] _vt_ to lynch.

**lynx** [lɛ̃ks] _nm_ lynx.
**lyophilisé, e** [ljɔfilize] _a_ freeze-dried.
**lyre** [liʀ] _nf_ lyre.
**lyrique** [liʀik] _a_ lyrical ; (_OPÉRA_) lyric ; **comédie** ~ comic opera ; **théâtre** ~ opera house (_for light opera_) ; **lyrisme** _nm_ lyricism.
**lys** [lis] _nm_ lily.

# M

**m'** [m] _pronom voir_ **me**.
**M.** [ɛm] _abr de_ **Monsieur**.
**ma** [ma] _dét voir_ **mon**.
**maboul, e** [mabul] _a_ (_fam_) loony.
**macabre** [makɑbʀ(ə)] _a_ macabre, gruesome.
**macadam** [makadam] _nm_ tarmac.
**macaron** [makaʀɔ̃] _nm_ (_gâteau_) macaroon ; (_insigne_) (round) badge.
**macaronis** [makaʀɔni] _nmpl_ macaroni _sg_.
**macédoine** [masedwan] _nf_: ~ **de fruits** fruit salad.
**macérer** [maseʀe] _vi, vt_ to macerate ; (_dans du vinaigre_) to pickle.
**mâchefer** [mɑʃfɛʀ] _nm_ clinker, cinders _pl_.
**mâcher** [mɑʃe] _vt_ to chew ; **ne pas** ~ **ses mots** not to mince one's words.
**machin** [maʃɛ̃] _nm_ (_fam_) thingummy, whatsit ; contraption, thing.
**machinal, e, aux** [maʃinal, -o] _a_ mechanical, automatic.
**machination** [maʃinasjɔ̃] _nf_ scheming, frame-up.
**machine** [maʃin] _nf_ machine ; (_locomotive_) engine ; (_fig: rouages_) machinery ; **faire** ~ **arrière** (_NAVIG_) to astern ; ~ **à laver/coudre/ tricoter** washing/sewing/knitting machine ; ~ **à écrire** typewriter ; ~ **à sous** fruit machine ; ~ **à vapeur** steam engine ; ~-**outil** _nf_ machine tool ; ~**rie** _nf_ machinery, plant ; (_d'un navire_) engine room ; **machinisme** _nm_ mechanization ; **machiniste** _nm_ (_THÉÂTRE_) scene shifter ; (_de bus, métro_) driver.
**mâchoire** [mɑʃwaʀ] _nf_ jaw ; ~ **de frein** brake shoe.
**mâchonner** [mɑʃɔne] _vt_ to chew (at).
**maçon** [masɔ̃] _nm_ bricklayer ; builder.
**maçonner** [masɔne] _vt_ (_revêtir_) to face, render (with cement) ; (_boucher_) to brick up.
**maçonnerie** [masɔnʀi] _nf_ (_murs_) brickwork ; masonry, stonework ; (_activité_) bricklaying ; building.
**maçonnique** [masɔnik] _a_ masonic.
**maculer** [makyle] _vt_ to stain ; (_TYPO_) to mackle.
**Madame** [madam], _pl_ **Mesdames** [medam] _nf_: ~ **X** Mrs ['mɪsɪz] X ; **occupez-vous de** ~/**Monsieur/Mademoiselle** please serve this lady/gentleman/(young) lady ; **bonjour** ~/**Monsieur/Mademoiselle** good morning ; (_ton déféren_t) good morning Madam/Sir/Madam ; (_le nom est connu_) good morning Mrs/Mr/Miss X ; ~/**Monsieur/ Mademoiselle!** (_pour appeler_) Madam/Sir/Miss! ; ~/**Monsieur/Mademoiselle** (_sur lettre_) Dear Madam/Sir/Madam ; **chère** ~/**cher**

**Monsieur/chère Mademoiselle** Dear Mrs/Mr/Miss X.
**Mademoiselle** [madmwazɛl], *pl* **Mesdemoiselles** [medmwazɛl] *nf* Miss; *voir aussi* **Madame**.
**madère** [madɛʀ] *nm* Madeira (wine).
**madone** [madɔn] *nf* madonna.
**madré, e** [madʀe] *a* crafty, wily.
**madrier** [madʀije] *nm* beam.
**madrilène** [madʀilɛn] *a* of *ou* from Madrid.
**maestria** [maɛstʀija] *nf* (masterly) skill.
**maf(f)ia** [mafja] *nf* Maf(f)ia.
**magasin** [magazɛ̃] *nm* (*boutique*) shop; (*entrepôt*) warehouse; (*d'une arme*) magazine; **en** ~ (*COMM*) in stock; **magasinier** *nm* warehouseman.
**magazine** [magazin] *nm* magazine.
**mage** [maʒ] *nm*: **les Rois M**~**s** the Magi, the (Three) Wise Men.
**magicien, ne** [maʒisjɛ̃, -jɛn] *nm/f* magician.
**magie** [maʒi] *nf* magic; **magique** *a* magic; (*enchanteur*) magical.
**magistral, e, aux** [maʒistʀal, -o] *a* (*œuvre, addresse*) masterly; (*ton*) authoritative; (*gifle etc*) sound, resounding; (*ex cathedra*): **enseignement** ~ lecturing, lectures *pl*.
**magistrat** [maʒistʀa] *nm* magistrate.
**magistrature** [maʒistʀatyʀ] *nf* magistracy, magistrature.
**magma** [magma] *nm* (*GÉO*) magma; (*fig*) jumble.
**magnanerie** [maɲanʀi] *nf* silk farm.
**magnanime** [maɲanim] *a* magnanimous.
**magnat** [magna] *nm* tycoon, magnate.
**magnésie** [maɲezi] *nf* magnesia.
**magnésium** [maɲezjɔm] *nm* magnesium.
**magnétique** [maɲetik] *a* magnetic.
**magnétiser** [maɲetize] *vt* to magnetize; (*fig*) to mesmerize, hypnotize.
**magnétisme** [maɲetism(ə)] *nm* magnetism.
**magnéto** [maɲeto] *nf* (*ÉLEC*) magneto.
**magnétophone** [maɲetɔfɔn] *nm* tape recorder; ~ **à cassettes** cassette recorder.
**magnétoscope** [maɲetɔskɔp] *nm* videotape recorder.
**magnificence** [maɲifisɑ̃s] *nf* (*faste*) magnificence, splendour.
**magnifique** [maɲifik] *a* magnificent.
**magnolia** [maɲɔlja] *nm* magnolia.
**magnum** [magnɔm] *nm* magnum.
**magot** [mago] *nm* (*argent*) pile (of money); nest egg.
**mahométan, e** [maɔmetɑ̃, -an] *a* Mohammedan, Mahometan.
**mai** [mɛ] *nm* May.
**maigre** [mɛgʀ(ə)] *a* (very) thin, skinny; (*viande*) lean; (*fromage*) low-fat; (*végétation*) thin, sparse; (*fig*) poor, meagre, skimpy // *ad*: **faire** ~ not to eat meat; **jours** ~**s** days of abstinence, fish days; **maigreur** *nf* thinness; **maigrir** *vi* to get thinner, lose weight.
**maille** [maj] *nf* stitch; **avoir** ~ **à partir avec qn** to have a brush with sb.
**maillet** [majɛ] *nm* mallet.

**maillon** [majɔ̃] *nm* link.
**maillot** [majo] *nm* (*aussi*: ~ **de corps**) vest; (*de danseur*) leotard; (*de sportif*) jersey; ~ **de bain** bathing costume, swimsuit; (*d'homme*) bathing trunks *pl*.
**main** [mɛ̃] *nf* hand; **à la** ~ in one's hand; **se donner la** ~ to hold hands; **donner** *ou* **tendre la** ~ **à qn** to hold out one's hand to sb; **se serrer la** ~ to shake hands; **serrer la** ~ **à qn** to shake hands with sb; **sous la** ~ to *ou* at hand; **à** ~ **levée** (*ART*) freehand; **à** ~**s levées** (*voter*) with a show of hands; **attaque à** ~ **armée** armed attack; **à** ~ **droite/gauche** to the right/left; **à remettre en** ~**s propres** to be delivered personally; **de première** ~ (*renseignement*) first-hand; (*COMM: voiture etc*) second-hand with only one previous owner; **faire** ~ **basse sur** to help o.s. to; **mettre la dernière** ~ **à** to put the finishing touches to; **se faire/perdre la** ~ to get one's hand in/lose one's touch; ~ **courante** handrail.
**mainate** [mɛnat] *nm* myna(h) bird.
**main-d'œuvre** [mɛ̃dœvʀ(ə)] *nf* manpower, labour.
**main-forte** [mɛ̃fɔʀt(ə)] *nf*: **prêter** ~ **à qn** to come to sb's assistance.
**mainmise** [mɛ̃miz] *nf* seizure; (*fig*): ~ **sur** complete hold on.
**maint, e** [mɛ̃, mɛ̃t] *a* many a; ~**s** many; **à** ~**es reprises** time and (time) again.
**maintenant** [mɛ̃tnɑ̃] *ad* now; (*actuellement*) nowadays.
**maintenir** [mɛ̃tniʀ] *vt* (*retenir, soutenir*) to support; (*contenir: foule etc*) to keep in check, hold back; (*conserver*) to maintain, uphold; (*affirmer*) to maintain; **se** ~ *vi* to hold; to keep steady; to persist.
**maintien** [mɛ̃tjɛ̃] *nm* maintaining, upholding; (*attitude*) bearing.
**maire** [mɛʀ] *nm* mayor.
**mairie** [meʀi] *nf* (*résidence*) town hall; (*administration*) town council.
**mais** [mɛ] *cj* but; ~ **non!** of course not!; ~ **enfin** but after all; (*indignation*) look here!
**maïs** [mais] *nm* maize.
**maison** [mɛzɔ̃] *nf* house; (*chez-soi*) home; (*COMM*) firm // *a inv* (*CULIN*) home-made; made by the chef; (*fig*) in-house, own; (*fam*) first-rate; **à la** ~ at home; (*direction*) home; ~ **d'arrêt** ≈ remand home; ~ **close** brothel; ~ **de correction** reformatory; ~ **des jeunes** ≈ youth club; ~ **mère** parent company; ~ **de repos** convalescent home; ~ **de retraite** old people's home; ~ **de santé** mental home; **maisonnée** *nf* household, family; **maisonnette** *nf* small house, cottage.
**maître, esse** [mɛtʀ(ə), mɛtʀɛs] *nm/f* master/mistress; (*SCOL*) teacher, schoolmaster/mistress // *nm* (*peintre etc*) master; (*titre*): **M**~ **(Me)** Maître, *term of address gen for a barrister* // *nf* (*amante*) mistress // *a* (*principal, essentiel*) main; **être** ~ **de** (*soi-même, situation*) to be in control of; **se rendre** ~ **de** (*pays, ville*) to gain control of; (*situation, incendie*) to bring under control; **une maîtresse femme** *a* managing woman; ~ **d'armes** fencing master; ~ **chanteur** blackmailer;

~ **de chapelle** choirmaster; ~ **de conférences** ≈ senior lecturer; ~/**maîtresse d'école** teacher, schoolmaster/ mistress; ~ **d'hôtel** (domestique) butler; (d'hôtel) head waiter; ~ **de maison** host; ~ **nageur** lifeguard; ~ **à penser** intellectual leader; ~ **queux** chef; **maîtresse de maison** hostess; housewife (pl wives); ~**-autel** nm high altar.

**maîtrise** [metʀiz] nf (aussi: ~ **de soi**) self-control, self-possession; (habileté) skill, mastery; (suprématie) mastery, command; (diplôme) ≈ master's degree.

**maîtriser** [metʀize] vt (cheval, incendie) to (bring under) control; (sujet) to master; (émotion) to control, master; **se** ~ vt réfléchi to control o.s.

**majesté** [maʒɛste] nf majesty.

**majestueux, euse** [maʒɛstɥø, -øz] a majestic.

**majeur, e** [maʒœʀ] a (important) major; (JUR) of age; (fig) adult // nm/f person who has come of age ou attained his/her majority // nm (doigt) middle finger; **en** ~**e partie** for the most part.

**major** [maʒɔʀ] nm (SCOL): ~ **de la promotion** first of one's year.

**majordome** [maʒɔʀdɔm] nm majordomo.

**majorer** [maʒɔʀe] vt to increase.

**majorette** [maʒɔʀɛt] nf majorette.

**majoritaire** [maʒɔʀitɛʀ] a majority cpd: **système/scrutin** ~ majority system/ ballot.

**majorité** [maʒɔʀite] nf (gén) majority; (parti) party in power; **en** ~ mainly.

**majuscule** [maʒyskyl] a, nf: (lettre) ~ capital (letter).

**mal, maux** [mal, mo] nm (opposé au bien) evil; (tort, dommage) harm; (douleur physique) pain, ache; (maladie) illness, sickness q // ad badly // a. **c'est** ~ **(de faire)** it's bad ou wrong (to do); **être** ~ to be uncomfortable; **être** ~ **avec qn** to be on bad terms with sb; **il comprend** ~ he has difficulty in understanding; **il a** ~ **compris** he misunderstood; **dire du** ~ **de** to speak ill of; **ne voir aucun** ~ **à** to see no harm in, see nothing wrong in; **craignant** ~ **faire** fearing he was doing the wrong thing; **faire du** ~ **à qn** to hurt sb; to harm sb; **se faire** ~ to hurt o.s.; **se faire** ~ **au pied** to hurt one's foot; **ça fait** ~ it hurts; **j'ai** ~ **(ici)** it hurts (here); **j'ai** ~ **au dos** my back aches, I've got a pain in my back; **avoir** ~ **à la tête/aux dents/au cœur** to have a headache/have toothache/feel sick; **avoir le** ~ **de l'air** to be airsick; **avoir le** ~ **du pays** to be homesick; **prendre** ~ to be taken ill, feel unwell; ~ **de mer** seasickness; ~ **en point** a inv in a bad state; **maux de ventre** stomach ache sg.

**malade** [malad] a ill, sick; (poitrine, jambe) bad; (plante) diseased // nm/f invalid, sick person; (à l'hôpital etc) patient; **tomber** ~ to fall ill; **être** ~ **du cœur** to have heart trouble ou a bad heart; ~ **mental** mentally sick ou ill person.

**maladie** [maladi] nf (spécifique) disease, illness; (mauvaise santé) illness, sickness; (fig: manie) mania; ~ **de peau** skin

disease; **maladif, ive** a sickly; (curiosité, besoin) pathological.

**maladresse** [maladʀɛs] nf clumsiness q; (gaffe) blunder.

**maladroit, e** [maladʀwa, -wat] a clumsy.

**malaise** [malɛz] nm (MÉD) feeling of faintness; feeling of discomfort; (fig) uneasiness, malaise.

**malaisé, e** [maleze] a difficult.

**malappris, e** [malapʀi, -iz] nm/f ill-mannered ou boorish person.

**malaria** [malaʀja] nf malaria.

**malavisé, e** [malavize] a ill-advised, unwise.

**malaxer** [malakse] vt to knead; to mix.

**malchance** [malʃɑ̃s] nf misfortune, ill luck q; **par** ~ unfortunately; **malchanceux, euse** a unlucky.

**malcommode** [malkɔmɔd] a impractical, inconvenient.

**maldonne** [maldɔn] nf (CARTES) misdeal; **il y a** ~ (fig) there's been a misunderstanding.

**mâle** [mɑl] a (aussi ÉLEC, TECH) male; (viril: voix, traits) manly // nm male; **souris** ~ male mouse, he-mouse.

**malédiction** [malediksjɔ̃] nf curse.

**maléfice** [malefis] nm evil spell.

**maléfique** [malefik] a evil, baleful.

**malencontreux, euse** [malɑ̃kɔ̃tʀø, -øz] a unfortunate, untoward.

**malentendu** [malɑ̃tɑ̃dy] nm misunderstanding.

**malfaçon** [malfasɔ̃] nf fault.

**malfaisant, e** [malfəzɑ̃, -ɑ̃t] a evil, harmful.

**malfaiteur** [malfɛtœʀ] nm lawbreaker, criminal; burglar, thief (pl thieves).

**malfamé, e** [malfame] a disreputable, of ill repute.

**malformation** [malfɔʀmasjɔ̃] nf malformation.

**malfrat** [malfʀa] nm villain, crook.

**malgache** [malgaʃ] a, nm/f Madagascan, Malagasy // nm (langue) Malagasy.

**malgré** [malgʀe] prép in spite of, despite; ~ **tout** ad all the same.

**malhabile** [malabil] a clumsy.

**malheur** [malœʀ] nm (situation) adversity, misfortune; (événement) misfortune; disaster, tragedy; **malheureux, euse** a (triste) unhappy, miserable; (infortuné, regrettable) unfortunate; (malchanceux) unlucky; (insignifiant) wretched // nm/f poor soul; unfortunate creature; **les malheureux** the destitute.

**malhonnête** [malɔnɛt] a dishonest; (impoli) rude; ~**té** nf dishonesty; rudeness q.

**malice** [malis] nf mischievousness; (méchanceté): **par** ~ out of malice ou spite; **sans** ~ guileless; **malicieux, euse** a mischievous.

**malin, igne** [malɛ̃, -iɲ] a (futé: f gén: **maline**) smart, shrewd; (MÉD) malignant; **faire le** ~ to show off; **éprouver un** ~ **plaisir à** to take malicious pleasure in.

**malingre** [malɛ̃gʀ(ə)] a puny.

**malle** [mal] nf trunk.

**malléable** [maleabl(ə)] a malleable.

**malle-poste** [malpɔst(ə)] *nf* mail coach.
**mallette** [malɛt] *nf* (small) suitcase; overnight case; attaché case.
**malmener** [malməne] *vt* to manhandle; (*fig*) to give a rough handling to.
**malodorant, e** [malɔdɔRɑ̃, -ɑ̃t] *a* foul- *ou* ill-smelling.
**malotru** [malɔtRy] *nm* lout, boor.
**malpoli, e** [malpɔli] *nm/f* rude individual.
**malpropre** [malpRɔpR(ə)] *a* dirty.
**malsain, e** [malsɛ̃, -ɛn] *a* unhealthy.
**malséant, e** [malseɑ̃, -ɑ̃t] *a* unseemly, unbecoming.
**malsonnant, e** [malsɔnɑ̃, -ɑ̃t] *a* offensive.
**malt** [malt] *nm* malt.
**maltais, e** [maltɛ, -ɛz] *a, nm/f* Maltese.
**Malte** [malt(ə)] *nf* Malta.
**maltraiter** [maltRete] *vt* (*brutaliser*) to manhandle, ill-treat.
**malveillance** [malvɛjɑ̃s] *nf* (*animosité*) ill will; (*intention de nuire*) malevolence; (*JUR*) malicious intent *q*.
**malveillant, e** [malvɛjɑ̃, -ɑ̃t] *a* malevolent, malicious.
**malversation** [malvɛRsɑsjɔ̃] *nf* embezzlement, misappropriation (of funds).
**maman** [mamɑ̃] *nf* mum, mother.
**mamelle** [mamɛl] *nf* teat.
**mamelon** [mamlɔ̃] *nm* (*ANAT*) nipple; (*colline*) knoll, hillock.
**mammifère** [mamifɛR] *nm* mammal.
**mammouth** [mamut] *nm* mammoth.
**manche** [mɑ̃ʃ] *nf* (*de vêtement*) sleeve; (*d'un jeu, tournoi*) round; (*GÉO*): **la M** ~ the Channel // *nm* (*d'outil, casserole*) handle; (*de pelle, pioche etc*) shaft; (*de violon, guitare*) neck; (*fam*) clumsy oaf; ~ **à air** *nf* (*AVIAT*) wind-sock; ~ **à balai** *nm* broomstick; (*AVIAT*) joystick.
**manchette** [mɑ̃ʃɛt] *nf* (*de chemise*) cuff; (*coup*) forearm blow; (*titre*) headline.
**manchon** [mɑ̃ʃɔ̃] *nm* (*de fourrure*) muff; ~ **à incandescence** incandescent (gas) mantle.
**manchot** [mɑ̃ʃo] *nm* one-armed man; armless man; (*ZOOL*) penguin.
**mandarine** [mɑ̃daRin] *nf* mandarin (orange), tangerine.
**mandat** [mɑ̃da] *nm* (*postal*) postal *ou* money order; (*d'un député etc*) mandate; (*procuration*) power of attorney, proxy; (*POLICE*) warrant; ~ **d'amener** summons *sg*; ~ **d'arrêt** warrant for arrest; ~ **de dépôt** committal order; **mandataire** *nm/f* representative; proxy.
**mander** [mɑ̃de] *vt* to summon.
**mandibule** [mɑ̃dibyl] *nf* mandible.
**mandoline** [mɑ̃dɔlin] *nf* mandolin(e).
**manège** [manɛ3] *nm* riding school; (*à la foire*) roundabout, merry-go-round; (*fig*) game, ploy.
**manette** [manɛt] *nf* lever, tap.
**manganèse** [mɑ̃ganɛz] *nm* manganese.
**mangeable** [mɑ̃3abl(ə)] *a* edible, eatable.
**mangeaille** [mɑ̃3aj] *nf* (*péj*) grub.
**mangeoire** [mɑ̃3waR] *nf* trough, manger.
**manger** [mɑ̃3e] *vt* to eat; (*ronger: suj: rouille etc*) to eat into *ou* away // *vi* to eat; **mangeur, euse** *nm/f* eater.

**mangouste** [mɑ̃gust(ə)] *nf* mongoose.
**mangue** [mɑ̃g] *nf* mango.
**maniable** [manjabl(ə)] *a* (*outil*) handy; (*voiture, voilier*) easy to handle.
**maniaque** [manjak] *a* finicky, fussy; suffering from a mania // *nm/f* maniac.
**manie** [mani] *nf* mania; (*tic*) odd habit.
**maniement** [manimɑ̃] *nm* handling; ~ **d'armes** arms drill.
**manier** [manje] *vt* to handle.
**manière** [manjɛR] *nf* (*façon*) way, manner; ~**s** *nfpl* (*attitude*) manners; (*chichis*) fuss *sg*; **de** ~ **à** so as to; **de telle** ~ **que** in such a way that; **de cette** ~ in this way *ou* manner; **d'une** ~ **générale** generally speaking, as a general rule; **de toute** ~ in any case; **adverbe de** ~ adverb of manner.
**maniéré, e** [manjeRe] *a* affected.
**manif** [manif] *nf* demo (*pl* s).
**manifestant, e** [manifɛstɑ̃, -ɑ̃t] *nm/f* demonstrator.
**manifestation** [manifɛstasjɔ̃] *nf* (*de joie, mécontentement*) expression, demonstration; (*symptôme*) outward sign; (*fête etc*) event; (*POL*) demonstration.
**manifeste** [manifɛst(ə)] *a* obvious, evident // *nm* manifesto (*pl* s).
**manifester** [manifɛste] *vt* (*volonté, intentions*) to show, indicate; (*joie, peur*) to express, show // *vi* to demonstrate; **se** ~ *vi* (*émotion*) to show *ou* express itself; (*difficultés*) to arise; (*symptômes*) to appear; (*témoin etc*) to come forward.
**manigance** [manigɑ̃s] *nf* scheme.
**manigancer** [manigɑ̃se] *vt* to plot, devise.
**manioc** [manjɔk] *nm* cassava, manioc.
**manipuler** [manipyle] *vt* to handle; (*fig*) to manipulate.
**manivelle** [manivɛl] *nf* crank.
**manne** [man] *nf* (*REL*) manna; (*fig*) godsend.
**mannequin** [mankɛ̃] *nm* (*COUTURE*) dummy; (*MODE*) model.
**manœuvre** [manœvR(ə)] *nf* (*gén*) manœuvre // *nm* labourer.
**manœuvrer** [manœvRe] *vt* to manœuvre; (*levier, machine*) to operate // *vi* to manœuvre.
**manoir** [manwaR] *nm* manor *ou* country house.
**manomètre** [manɔmɛtR(ə)] *nm* gauge, manometer.
**manquant, e** [mɑ̃kɑ̃, -ɑ̃t] *a* missing.
**manque** [mɑ̃k] *nm* (*insuffisance*): ~ **de** lack of; (*vide*) emptiness, gap; (*MÉD*) withdrawal; ~**s** *nmpl* (*lacunes*) faults, defects; ~ **à gagner** loss of profit *ou* earnings.
**manqué, e** [mɑ̃ke] *a* failed; **garçon** ~ tomboy.
**manquement** [mɑ̃kmɑ̃] *nm:* ~ **à** (*discipline, règle*) breach of.
**manquer** [mɑ̃ke] *vi* (*faire défaut*) to be lacking; (*être absent*) to be missing; (*échouer*) to fail // *vt* to miss // *vb impersonnel:* **il (nous) manque encore 100 F** we are still 100 F short; **il manque des pages (au livre)** there are some pages missing *ou* some pages are missing (from the book); **l'argent qui leur manque** the

money they need *ou* are short of ; **le pied/la voix lui manqua** he missed his footing/his voice failed him ; ~ **à qn** (*absent etc*): **il/cela me manque** I miss him/this ; ~ **à** *vt* (*règles etc*) to be in breach of, fail to observe ; ~ **de** *vt* to lack ; **ne pas** ~ **de faire: il n'a pas manqué de le dire** he sure enough said it, he didn't fail to say it ; ~ (**de**) **faire: il a manqué (de) se tuer** he very nearly got killed.

**mansarde** [mɑ̃saʀd(ə)] *nf* attic ; **mansardé, e** *a* attic *cpd*.

**mansuétude** [mɑ̃sɥetyd] *nf* leniency.

**mante** [mɑ̃t] *nf*: ~ **religieuse** praying mantis.

**manteau, x** [mɑ̃to] *nm* coat ; ~ **de cheminée** mantelpiece.

**mantille** [mɑ̃tij] *nf* mantilla.

**manucure** [manykyʀ] *nf* manicurist.

**manuel, le** [manɥɛl] *a* manual // *nm/f* manually gifted pupil *etc* (*as opposed to intellectually gifted*) // *nm* (*ouvrage*) manual, handbook.

**manufacture** [manyfaktyʀ] *nf* factory.

**manufacturé, e** [manyfaktyʀe] *a* manufactured.

**manuscrit, e** [manyskʀi, -it] *a* handwritten // *nm* manuscript.

**manutention** [manytɑ̃sjɔ̃] *nf* (*COMM*) handling ; **manutentionnaire** *nm/f* warehouseman/woman, packer.

**mappemonde** [mapmɔ̃d] *nf* (*plane*) map of the world ; (*sphère*) globe.

**maquereau, x** [makʀo] *nm* (*ZOOL*) mackerel *inv* ; (*fam*) pimp.

**maquerelle** [makʀɛl] *nf* (*fam*) madam.

**maquette** [makɛt] *nf* (*d'un décor, bâtiment, véhicule*) (scale) model ; (*d'une page illustrée*) paste-up.

**maquignon** [makiɲɔ̃] *nm* horse-dealer.

**maquillage** [makijaʒ] *nm* making up ; faking ; (*crème etc*) make-up.

**maquiller** [makije] *vt* (*personne, visage*) to make up ; (*truquer: passeport, statistique*) to fake ; (*: voiture volée*) to do over (*respray etc*) ; **se** ~ to make up (one's face).

**maquis** [maki] *nm* (*GÉO*) scrub ; (*fig*) tangle ; (*MIL*) maquis, underground fighting *q*.

**marabout** [maʀabu] *nm* (*ZOOL*) marabou(t).

**maraîcher, ère** [maʀeʃe, maʀɛʃɛʀ] *a*: **cultures maraîchères** market gardening *sg* // *nm/f* market gardener.

**marais** [maʀɛ] *nm* marsh, swamp ; ~ **salant** salt pen, saltern.

**marasme** [maʀasm(ə)] *nm* stagnation, slump.

**marathon** [maʀatɔ̃] *nm* marathon.

**marâtre** [maʀɑtʀ(ə)] *nf* cruel mother.

**maraude** [maʀod] *nf* pilfering, thieving (*of poultry, crops*) ; (*dans un verger*) scrumping ; (*vagabondage*) prowling ; **en** ~ on the prowl ; (*taxi*) cruising.

**marbre** [maʀbʀ(ə)] *nm* (*pierre, statue*) marble ; (*d'une table, commode*) marble top ; (*TYPO*) stone, bed ; **rester de** ~ to remain stonily indifferent ; **marbrer** *vt* to mottle, blotch ; (*TECH: papier*) to marble ; ~**rie** *nf* monumental mason's yard ; **marbrier** *nm* monumental mason.

**marc** [maʀ] *nm* (*de raisin, pommes*) marc ; ~ **de café** coffee grounds *pl ou* dregs *pl*.

**marcassin** [maʀkasɛ̃] *nm* young wild boar.

**marchand, e** [maʀʃɑ̃, -ɑ̃d] *nm/f* shopkeeper, tradesman/woman ; (*au marché*) stallholder ; (*spécifique*): ~ **de cycles/tapis** bicycle/carpet dealer ; ~ **de charbon/vins** coal/wine merchant // *a*: **prix/valeur** ~(**e**) market price/value ; ~ **de biens** real estate agent ; ~ **de couleurs** ironmonger ; ~**/e de fruits** fruiterer, fruit merchant ; ~**/e de journaux** newsagent ; ~**/e de légumes** greengrocer ; ~**/e de poisson** fishmonger, fish merchant ; ~**e de quatre saisons** costermonger ; ~ **de tableaux** art dealer.

**marchander** [maʀʃɑ̃de] *vt* (*article*) to bargain *ou* haggle over ; (*éloges*) to be sparing with // *vi* to bargain, haggle.

**marchandise** [maʀʃɑ̃diz] *nf* goods *pl*, merchandise *q*.

**marche** [maʀʃ(ə)] *nf* (*d'escalier*) step ; (*activité*) walking ; (*promenade, trajet, allure*) walk ; (*démarche*) walk, gait ; (*MIL etc, MUS*) march ; (*fonctionnement*) running ; (*progression*) progress ; course ; **ouvrir/fermer la** ~ to lead the way/bring up the rear ; **dans le sens de la** ~ (*RAIL*) facing the engine ; **en** ~ (*monter etc*) while the vehicle is moving *ou* in motion ; **mettre en** ~ to start ; **remettre qch en** ~ to set *ou* start sth going again ; **se mettre en** ~ (*personne*) to get moving ; (*machine*) to start ; ~ **arrière** reverse (gear) ; **faire** ~ **arrière** to reverse ; (*fig*) to backtrack, back-pedal ; ~ **à suivre** (correct) procedure ; (*sur notice*) (step by step) instructions *pl*.

**marché** [maʀʃe] *nm* (*lieu, COMM, ÉCON*) market ; (*ville*) trading centre ; (*transaction*) bargain, deal ; **M**~ **commun** Common Market ; ~ **aux fleurs** flower market ; ~ **noir** black market ; **faire du** ~ **noir** to buy and sell on the black market ; ~ **aux puces** flea market.

**marchepied** [maʀʃəpje] *nm* (*RAIL*) step ; (*AUTO*) running board ; (*fig*) stepping stone.

**marcher** [maʀʃe] *vi* to walk ; (*MIL*) to march ; (*aller: voiture, train, affaires*) to go ; (*prospérer*) to go well ; (*fonctionner*) to work, run ; (*fam*) to go along, agree ; to be taken in ; ~ **sur** to walk on ; (*mettre le pied sur*) to step on *ou* in ; (*MIL*) to march upon ; ~ **dans** (*herbe etc*) to walk in *ou* on ; (*flaque*) to step in ; **faire** ~ **qn** to pull sb's leg ; to lead sb up the garden path ; **marcheur, euse** *nm/f* walker.

**mardi** [maʀdi] *nm* Tuesday ; **M**~ **gras** Shrove Tuesday.

**mare** [maʀ] *nf* pond ; ~ **de sang** pool of blood.

**marécage** [maʀekaʒ] *nm* marsh, swamp ; **marécageux, euse** *a* marshy, swampy.

**maréchal, aux** [maʀeʃal, -o] *nm* marshal ; ~ **des logis** (*MIL*) sergeant.

**maréchal-ferrant** [maʀeʃalfɛʀɑ̃] *nm* blacksmith, farrier.

**maréchaussée** [maʀeʃose] *nf* constabulary.

**marée** [maʀe] *nf* tide ; (*poissons*) fresh (sea) fish ; ~ **haute/basse** high/low tide ;

~ **montante/ descendante** rising/ebb tide.

**marelle** [maʀɛl] *nf*: **(jouer à) la** ~ (to play) hopscotch.

**marémotrice** [maʀemɔtʀis] *af* tidal.

**mareyeur, euse** [maʀɛjœʀ, -øz] *nm/f* wholesale (sea) fish merchant.

**margarine** [maʀgaʀin] *nf* margarine.

**marge** [maʀʒ(ə)] *nf* margin; **en** ~ in the margin; **en** ~ **de** *(fig)* on the fringe of; cut off from; connected with; ~ **bénéficiaire** profit margin.

**margelle** [maʀʒɛl] *nf* coping.

**margeur** [maʀʒœʀ] *nm* margin stop.

**marginal, e, aux** [maʀʒinal, -o] *a* marginal.

**marguerite** [maʀgəʀit] *nf* marguerite, (oxeye) daisy.

**marguillier** [maʀgije] *nm* churchwarden.

**mari** [maʀi] *nm* husband.

**mariage** [maʀjaʒ] *nm* (*union, état, fig*) marriage; (*noce*) wedding; ~ **civil/religieux** civil *ou* registry office/church wedding; **un** ~ **de raison/d'amour** a marriage of convenience/love match; ~ **blanc** unconsummated marriage; ~ **en blanc** white wedding.

**marié, e** [maʀje] *a* married // *nm/f* (bride)groom/bride; **les** ~**s** the bride and groom; **les (jeunes)** ~**s** the newly-weds.

**marier** [maʀje] *vt* to marry; *(fig)* to blend; **se** ~ **(avec)** to marry, get married (to); *(fig)* to blend (with).

**marin, e** [maʀɛ̃, -in] *a* sea *cpd*, marine // *nm* sailor // *nf* navy; *(ART)* seascape; ~**e de guerre** navy; ~**e marchande** merchant navy; ~**e à voiles** sailing ships *pl*.

**marinade** [maʀinad] *nf* marinade.

**marine** [maʀin] *af, nf voir* **marin** // *a inv* navy (blue) // *nm* (*MIL*) marine.

**mariner** [maʀine] *vi, vt* to marinate, marinade.

**marinier** [maʀinje] *nm* bargee.

**marinière** [maʀinjɛʀ] *nf* smock // *a inv*: **moules** ~ mussels in white wine.

**marionnette** [maʀjɔnɛt] *nf* puppet.

**marital, e, aux** [maʀital, -o] *a* marital, husband's; ~**ement** *ad* as husband and wife.

**maritime** [maʀitim] *a* sea *cpd*, maritime.

**marjolaine** [maʀʒɔlɛn] *nf* marjoram.

**mark** [maʀk] *nm* mark.

**marmaille** [maʀmaj] *nf* (*péj*) (gang of) brats *pl*.

**marmelade** [maʀm* əlad] *nf* stewed fruit, compote; **en** ~ *(fig)* crushed (to a pulp).

**marmite** [maʀmit] *nf* (cooking-)pot.

**marmiton** [maʀmitɔ̃] *nm* kitchen boy.

**marmonner** [maʀmɔne] *vt, vi* to mumble, mutter.

**marmot** [maʀmo] *nm* brat.

**marmotte** [maʀmɔt] *nf* marmot.

**marmotter** [maʀmɔte] *vt* (*prière*) to mumble, mutter.

**marne** [maʀn(ə)] *nf* marl.

**Maroc** [maʀɔk] *nm*: **le** ~ Morocco; **marocain, e** *a, nm/f* Moroccan.

**maroquin** [maʀɔkɛ̃] *nm* morocco (leather); *(fig)* (minister's) portfolio.

**maroquinerie** [maʀɔkinʀi] *nf* leather craft; fine leather goods *pl*.

**marotte** [maʀɔt] *nf* fad.

**marquant, e** [maʀkɑ̃, -ɑ̃t] *a* outstanding.

**marque** [maʀk(ə)] *nf* mark; (*SPORT, JEU*: *décompte des points*) score; (*COMM*: *de produits*) brand; make; (: *de disques*) label; **à vos** ~**s!** (*SPORT*) on your marks!; **de** ~ *a* (*COMM*) brand-name *cpd*; proprietary; *(fig)* high-class; distinguished; ~ **déposée** registered trademark; ~ **de fabrique** trademark.

**marqué, e** [maʀke] *a* marked.

**marquer** [maʀke] *vt* to mark; (*inscrire*) to write down; (*bétail*) to brand; (*SPORT*: *but etc*) to score; (: *joueur*) to mark; (*accentuer: taille etc*) to emphasize; (*manifester: refus, intérêt*) to show // *vi* (*événement, personnalité*) to stand out, be outstanding; (*SPORT*) to score; ~ **les points** (*tenir la marque*) to keep the score.

**marqueterie** [maʀkətʀi] *nf* inlaid work, marquetry.

**marquis, e** [maʀki, -iz] *nm/f* marquis *ou* marquess/marchioness // *nf* (*auvent*) glass canopy *ou* awning.

**marraine** [maʀɛn] *nf* godmother.

**marrant, e** [maʀɑ̃, -ɑ̃t] *a* (*fam*) funny.

**marre** [maʀ] *ad* (*fam*): **en avoir** ~ **de** to be fed up with.

**marrer** [maʀe]: **se** ~ *vi* (*fam*) to have a (good) laugh.

**marron** [maʀɔ̃] *nm* (*fruit*) chestnut // *a inv* brown // *am* (*péj*) crooked; bogus; ~**s glacés** marrons glacés; **marronnier** *nm* chestnut (tree).

**mars** [maʀs] *nm* March.

**Mars** [maʀs] *nf ou m* Mars.

**marsouin** [maʀswɛ̃] *nm* porpoise.

**marsupiaux** [maʀsypjo] *nmpl* marsupials.

**marteau, x** [maʀto] *nm* hammer; (*de porte*) knocker; ~**-piqueur** *nm* pneumatic drill.

**martel** [maʀtɛl] *nm*: **se mettre** ~ **en tête** to worry o.s.

**marteler** [maʀtəle] *vt* to hammer.

**martial, e, aux** [maʀsjal, -o] *a* martial.

**martien, ne** [maʀsjɛ̃, -jɛn] *a* Martian, of *ou* from Mars.

**martinet** [maʀtinɛ] *nm* (*fouet*) small whip; (*ZOOL*) swift.

**martingale** [maʀtɛ̃gal] *nf* (*COUTURE*) half-belt; (*JEU*) winning formula.

**Martinique** [maʀtinik] *nf*: **la** ~ Martinique.

**martin-pêcheur** [maʀtɛ̃pɛʃœʀ] *nm* kingfisher.

**martre** [maʀtʀ(ə)] *nf* marten.

**martyr, e** [maʀtiʀ] *nm/f* martyr // *a* martyred; **enfants** ~**s** battered children.

**martyre** [maʀtiʀ] *nm* martyrdom; (*fig: sens affaibli*) agony, torture.

**martyriser** [maʀtiʀize] *vt* (*REL*) to martyr; *(fig)* to bully; to batter.

**marxisme** [maʀksism(ə)] *nm* Marxism.

**mascarade** [maskaʀad] *nf* masquerade.

**mascotte** [maskɔt] *nf* mascot.

**masculin, e** [maskylɛ̃, -in] *a* masculine; (*sexe, population*) male; (*équipe, vêtements*) men's; (*viril*) manly // *nm* masculine.

**masochisme** [mazɔʃism(ə)] *nm* masochism.

**masque** [mask(ə)] *nm* mask ; ~ **à gaz** gas mask.

**masqué, e** [maske] *a* masked.

**masquer** [maske] *vt* (*cacher: paysage, porte*) to hide, conceal ; (*dissimuler: vérité, projet*) to mask, obscure.

**massacrant, e** [masakrɑ̃, -ɑ̃t] *a*: **humeur** ~**e** foul temper.

**massacre** [masakr(ə)] *nm* massacre, slaughter.

**massacrer** [masakre] *vt* to massacre, slaughter ; (*fig: texte etc*) to murder.

**massage** [masaʒ] *nm* massage.

**masse** [mas] *nf* mass ; (*péj*): **la** ~ the masses *pl* ; (*ÉLEC*) earth ; (*maillet*) sledgehammer ; ~**s** *nfpl* masses ; **une** ~ **de, des** ~**s de** (*fam*) masses *ou* loads of ; **en** ~ *ad* (*en bloc*) in bulk ; (*en foule*) en masse // *a* (*exécutions, production*) mass *cpd* ; ~ **salariale** aggregate remuneration (of employees).

**massepain** [maspɛ̃] *nm* marzipan.

**masser** [mase] *vt* (*assembler*) to gather ; (*pétrir*) to massage ; **se** ~ *vi* to gather ; **masseur, euse** *nm/f* masseur/masseuse.

**massicot** [masiko] *nm* guillotine.

**massif, ive** [masif, -iv] *a* (*porte*) solid, massive ; (*visage*) heavy, large ; (*bois, or*) solid ; (*dose*) massive ; (*déportations etc*) mass *cpd* // *nm* (*montagneux*) massif ; (*de fleurs*) clump, bank.

**massue** [masy] *nf* club, bludgeon.

**mastic** [mastik] *nm* (*pour vitres*) putty ; (*pour fentes*) filler.

**mastiquer** [mastike] *vt* (*aliment*) to chew, masticate ; (*fente*) to fill ; (*vitre*) to putty.

**masturbation** [mastyrbasjɔ̃] *nf* masturbation.

**masure** [mɑzyr] *nf* tumbledown cottage.

**mat, e** [mat] *a* (*couleur, métal*) mat(t) ; (*bruit, son*) dull // *a inv* (*ÉCHECS*): **être** ~ to be checkmate.

**mât** [mɑ] *nm* (*NAVIG*) mast ; (*poteau*) pole, post.

**match** [matʃ] *nm* match ; ~ **nul** draw ; **faire** ~ **nul** to draw.

**matelas** [matla] *nm* mattress ; ~ **pneumatique** air bed *ou* mattress ; ~ **à ressorts** spring *ou* interior-sprung mattress.

**matelasser** [matlase] *vt* to pad ; to quilt.

**matelot** [matlo] *nm* sailor, seaman.

**mater** [mate] *vt* (*personne*) to bring to heel, subdue ; (*révolte*) to put down.

**matérialiser** [materjalize]: **se** ~ *vi* to materialize.

**matérialiste** [materjalist(ə)] *a* materialistic.

**matériau, x** [materjo] *nm* material // *nmpl* material(s).

**matériel, le** [materjɛl] *a* material // *nm* equipment *q* ; (*de camping etc*) gear *q* ; ~ **d'exploitation** (*COMM*) plant.

**maternel, le** [matɛrnɛl] *a* (*amour, geste*) motherly, maternal ; (*grand-père, oncle*) maternal // *nf* (*aussi:* **école** ~**le**) (state) nursery school.

**maternité** [matɛrnite] *nf* (*établissement*) maternity hospital ; (*état de mère*)

motherhood, maternity ; (*grossesse*) pregnancy.

**mathématicien, ne** [matematisjɛ̃, -jɛn] *nm/f* mathematician.

**mathématique** [matematik] *a* mathematical ; ~**s** *nfpl* (*science*) mathematics *sg*.

**matière** [matjɛr] *nf* (*PHYSIQUE*) matter ; (*COMM, TECH*) material, matter *q* ; (*fig: d'un livre etc*) subject matter, material ; (*SCOL*) subject ; **en** ~ **de** as regards ; **donner** ~ **à** to give cause to ; ~ **plastique** plastic ; ~**s fécales** faeces ; ~**s grasses** fat content *sg* ; ~**s premières** raw materials.

**matin** [matɛ̃] *nm, ad* morning ; **matinal, e, aux** *a* (*toilette, gymnastique*) morning *cpd* ; (*de bonne heure*) early ; **être matinal** (*personne*) to be up early ; to be an early riser.

**matinée** [matine] *nf* morning ; (*spectacle*) matinée, afternoon performance.

**mâtiner** [mɑtine] *vt* to cross.

**matois, e** [matwa, -waz] *a* wily.

**matou** [matu] *nm* tom(cat).

**matraque** [matrak] *nf* cosh ; (*de policier*) truncheon ; **matraquer** *vt* to beat up (with a truncheon) ; to cosh ; (*fig: disque*) to plug.

**matriarcal, e, aux** [matrijarkal, -o] *a* matriarchal.

**matrice** [matris] *nf* (*ANAT*) womb ; (*TECH*) mould ; (*MATH etc*) matrix.

**matricule** [matrikyl] *nf* (*aussi:* **registre** ~) roll, register // *nm* (*aussi:* **numéro** ~) (*MIL*) regimental number ; (*ADMIN*) reference number.

**matrimonial, e, aux** [matrimɔnjal, -o] *a* marital, marriage *cpd*.

**mâture** [mɑtyr] *nf* masts *pl*.

**maturité** [matyrite] *nf* maturity ; (*d'un fruit*) ripeness, maturity.

**maudire** [modir] *vt* to curse.

**maudit, e** [modi, -it] *a* (*fam: satané*) blasted, confounded.

**maugréer** [mogree] *vi* to grumble.

**Mauresque** [mɔrɛsk] *a* Moorish.

**mausolée** [mozɔle] *nm* mausoleum.

**maussade** [mosad] *a* sullen.

**mauvais, e** [mɔvɛ, -ɛz] *a* bad ; (*faux*): **le** ~ **numéro/moment** the wrong number/moment ; (*méchant, malveillant*) malicious, spiteful // *ad*: **il fait** ~ the weather is bad ; **sentir** ~ to have a nasty smell, smell bad *ou* nasty ; **la mer est** ~**e** the sea is rough ; ~ **coup** (*fig*) criminal venture ; ~ **garçon** tough ; ~ **plaisant** hoaxer ; ~ **traitements** ill treatment *sg* ; ~**e herbe** weed ; ~**e langue** gossip, scandalmonger ; ~**e passe** difficult situation ; bad patch ; ~**e tête** rebellious *ou* headstrong customer.

**mauve** [mov] *a* mauve // *nf* mallow.

**mauviette** [movjɛt] *nf* (*péj*) weakling.

**maux** [mo] *nmpl voir* **mal.**

**maximal, e, aux** [maksimal, -o] *a* maximal.

**maxime** [maksim] *nf* maxim.

**maximum** [maksimɔm] *a, nm* maximum ; **au** ~ *ad* (*le plus possible*) to the full ; as much as one can ; (*tout au plus*) at the (very) most *ou* maximum.

**mayonnaise** [majɔnɛz] *nf* mayonnaise.
**mazout** [mazut] *nm* (fuel) oil.
**me, m'** [m(ə)] *pronom* me ; (*réfléchi*) myself.
**Me** *abr de* **Maître.**
**méandres** [meɑ̃dʀ(ə)] *nmpl* meanderings.
**mec** [mɛk] *nm* (*fam*) bloke.
**mécanicien, ne** [mekanisjɛ̃, -jɛn] *nm/f*
mechanic ; (*RAIL*) (train *ou* engine) driver ;
~-**dentiste** *nm/f* dental technician.
**mécanique** [mekanik] *a* mechanical // *nf*
(*science*) mechanics *sg*; (*technologie*)
mechanical engineering ; (*AUTO*): **s'y**
**connaître en** ~ to be mechanically
minded ; (*mécanisme*) mechanism ;
engineering ; works *pl*; **ennui** ~ engine
trouble *q*; **mécaniser** *vt* to mechanize.
**mécanisme** [mekanism(ə)] *nm*
mechanism.
**mécanographie** [mekanɔgʀafi] *nf*
(mechanical) data processing.
**mécène** [mesɛn] *nm* patron.
**méchanceté** [meʃɑ̃ste] *nf* nastiness,
maliciousness ; nasty *ou* spiteful *ou*
malicious remark (*ou* action).
**méchant, e** [meʃɑ̃, -ɑ̃t] *a* nasty, malicious,
spiteful ; (*enfant: pas sage*) naughty ;
(*animal*) vicious ; (*avant le nom: valeur*
*péjorative*) nasty ; miserable ; (: *intensive*)
terrific.
**mèche** [mɛʃ] *nf* (*de lampe, bougie*) wick ;
(*d'un explosif*) fuse ; (*de vilebrequin,*
*perceuse*) bit ; (*de fouet*) lash ; (*de cheveux*)
lock ; **vendre la** ~ to give the game away ;
**de** ~ **avec** in league with.
**méchoui** [meʃwi] *nm* whole sheep barbecue.
**mécompte** [mekɔ̃t] *nm* miscalculation ;
(*déception*) disappointment.
**méconnaissable** [mekɔnɛsabl(ə)] *a*
unrecognizable.
**méconnaissance** [mekɔnɛsɑ̃s] *nf*
ignorance.
**méconnaître** [mekɔnɛtʀ(ə)] *vt* (*ignorer*)
to be unaware of ; (*mésestimer*) to
misjudge.
**mécontent, e** [mekɔ̃tɑ̃, -ɑ̃t] *a*: ~ (**de**)
discontented *ou* dissatisfied *ou* displeased
(with) ; (*contrarié*) annoyed (at) ;
**mécontentement** *nm* dissatisfaction,
discontent, displeasure ; annoyance ;
**mécontenter** *vt* to displease.
**médaille** [medaj] *nf* medal ; **médaillé, e**
*nm/f* (*SPORT*) medal-holder.
**médaillon** [medajɔ̃] *nm* (*portrait*)
medallion ; (*bijou*) locket ; (*CULIN*)
médaillon ; **en** ~ *a* (*carte etc*) inset.
**médecin** [medsɛ̃] *nm* doctor ; ~
**généraliste** general practitioner, G.P.
**médecine** [medsin] *nf* medicine ; ~ **légale**
forensic medicine ; ~ **du travail**
occupational *ou* industrial medicine.
**médian, e** [medjɑ̃, -an] *a* (*MATH*) median.
**médiateur, trice** [medjatœʀ, -tʀis] *nm/f*
mediator ; arbitrator.
**médiation** [medjasjɔ̃] *nf* mediation ; (*dans*
*conflit social etc*) arbitration.
**médical, e, aux** [medikal, -o] *a* medical.
**médicament** [medikamɑ̃] *nm* medicine,
drug.
**médicinal, e, aux** [medisinal, -o] *a*
medicinal.

**médico-légal, e, aux** [medikɔlegal, -o]
*a* forensic.
**médiéval, e, aux** [medjeval, -o] *a*
medieval.
**médiocre** [medjɔkʀ(ə)] *a* mediocre, poor ;
**médiocrité** *nf* mediocrity.
**médire** [mediʀ] *vi*: ~ **de** to speak ill of ;
**médisance** *nf* scandalmongering ; piece of
scandal *ou* of malicious gossip.
**méditatif, ive** [meditatif, -iv] *a*
thoughtful.
**méditation** [meditasjɔ̃] *nf* meditation.
**méditer** [medite] *vt* (*approfondir*) to
meditate on, ponder (over) ; (*combiner*) to
meditate // *vi* to meditate ; ~ **de faire** to
contemplate doing, plan to do.
**Méditerranée** [mediteʀane] *nf*: **la (mer)**
~ the Mediterranean (Sea) ;
**méditerranéen, ne** *a, nm/f* Mediterranean.
**médium** [medjɔm] *nm* medium (*person*).
**médius** [medjys] *nm* middle finger.
**méduse** [medyz] *nf* jellyfish.
**méduser** [medyze] *vt* to dumbfound.
**meeting** [mitiŋ] *nm* (*POL, SPORT*) rally ; ~
**d'aviation** air show.
**méfait** [mefɛ] *nm* (*faute*) misdemeanour,
wrongdoing ; ~**s** *nmpl* (*ravages*) ravages,
damage *sg*.
**méfiance** [mefjɑ̃s] *nf* mistrust, distrust.
**méfiant, e** [mefjɑ̃, -ɑ̃t] *a* mistrustful,
distrustful.
**méfier** [mefje]: **se** ~ *vi* to be wary ; to
be careful ; **se** ~ **de** *vt* to mistrust,
distrust, be wary of ; (*faire attention*) to be
careful about.
**mégarde** [megaʀd(ə)] *nf*: **par** ~
accidentally ; by mistake.
**mégère** [meʒɛʀ] *nf* shrew.
**mégot** [mego] *nm* cigarette end.
**meilleur, e** [mɛjœʀ] *a, ad* better ; (*valeur*
*superlative*) best // *nm*: **le** ~ (*celui qui ...*)
the best (one) ; (*ce qui ...*) the best // *nf*:
**la** ~**e** the best (one) ; **le** ~ **des deux** the
better of the two ; ~ **marché** cheaper.
**mélancolie** [melɑ̃kɔli] *nf* melancholy,
gloom ; **mélancolique** *a* melancholic,
melancholy.
**mélange** [melɑ̃ʒ] *nm* mixture.
**mélanger** [melɑ̃ʒe] *vt* (*substances*) to
mix ; (*vins, couleurs*) to blend ; (*mettre en*
*désordre*) to mix up, muddle (up).
**mélasse** [melas] *nf* treacle, molasses *sg*.
**mêlée** [mele] *nf* mêlée, scramble ; (*RUGBY*)
scrum(mage).
**mêler** [mele] *vt* (*substances, odeurs, races*)
to mix ; (*embrouiller*) to muddle (up), mix
up ; **se** ~ to mix ; to mingle ; **se** ~ **à** (*suj:*
*personne*) to join ; to mix with ; (: *odeurs*
*etc*) to mingle with ; **se** ~ **de** (*suj:*
*personne*) to meddle with, interfere in ; ~
**qn à** (*affaire*) to get sb mixed up *ou*
involved in.
**mélodie** [melɔdi] *nf* melody ; **mélodieux,**
**euse** *a* melodious, tuneful ; **mélodique** *a*
melodic.
**mélodrame** [melɔdʀam] *nm* melodrama.
**mélomane** [melɔmɑn] *nm/f* music lover.
**melon** [mɔlɔ̃] *nm* (*BOT*) (honeydew) melon ;
(*aussi: chapeau* ~) bowler (hat) ; ~ **d'eau**
watermelon.

**mélopée** [melɔpe] *nf* monotonous chant.
**membrane** [mɑ̃bRɑ̃] *nf* membrane.
**membre** [mɑ̃bR(ə)] *nm* (ANAT) limb ; (*personne, pays, élément*) member // a member ; ~ (**viril**) (male) organ.
**même** [mɛm] *a* same // *pronom*: **le(la)** ~ the same (one) // *ad* even ; **en** ~ **temps** at the same time ; **ce sont ses paroles/celles-là** ~**s** they are his very words/the very ones ; **il n'a** ~ **pas pleuré** he didn't even cry ; **ici** ~ at this very place ; **à** ~ **la bouteille** straight from the bottle ; **à** ~ **la peau** next to the skin ; **être à** ~ **de faire** to be in a position *ou* be able to do ; **mettre qn à** ~ **de faire** to enable sb to do ; **faire de** ~ to do likewise ; **lui de** ~ so does (*ou* did *ou* is) he ; **de** ~ **que** just as ; **il en va/est allé de** ~ **pour** the same goes/happened for.
**mémento** [memɛ̃to] *nm* (*agenda*) engagement diary ; (*ouvrage*) summary.
**mémoire** [memwaR] *nf* memory // *nm* (ADMIN, JUR) memorandum (*pl* a) ; (SCOL) dissertation, paper ; ~**s** *nmpl* memoirs ; **avoir la** ~ **des chiffres** to have a good memory for figures ; **à la** ~ **de** to the *ou* in memory of ; **pour** ~ *ad* for the record ; **de** ~ **d'homme** in living memory ; **de** ~ *ad* from memory.
**mémorable** [memɔRabl(ə)] *a* memorable.
**mémorandum** [memɔRɑ̃dɔm] *nm* memorandum (*pl* a).
**mémorial, aux** [memɔRjal, -o] *nm* memorial.
**menaçant, e** [mənasɑ̃, -ɑ̃t] *a* threatening, menacing.
**menace** [mənas] *nf* threat.
**menacer** [mənase] *vt* to threaten.
**ménage** [menaʒ] *nm* (*travail*) housekeeping, housework ; (*couple*) (married) couple ; (*famille*, ADMIN) household ; **faire le** ~ to do the housework ; **faire des** ~**s** to go out charring ; **monter son** ~ to set up house ; **se mettre en** ~ (**avec**) to set up house (with) ; **heureux en** ~ happily married ; **faire bon** ~ **avec** to get on well with ; ~ **de poupée** doll's kitchen set ; ~ **à trois** love triangle.
**ménagement** [menaʒmɑ̃] *nm* care and attention ; ~**s** *nmpl* (*égards*) consideration *sg*, attention *sg*.
**ménager** [menaʒe] *vt* (*traiter*) to handle with tact ; to treat considerately ; (*utiliser*) to use sparingly ; to use with care ; (*prendre soin de*) to take (great) care of, look after ; (*organiser*) to arrange ; (*installer*) to put in ; to make ; ~ **qch à qn** (*réserver*) to have sth in store for sb.
**ménager, ère** [menaʒe, -ɛR] *a* household *cpd*, domestic // *nf* housewife (*pl* wives).
**ménagerie** [menaʒRi] *nf* menagerie.
**mendiant, e** [mɑ̃djɑ̃, -ɑ̃t] *nm/f* beggar.
**mendicité** [mɑ̃disite] *nf* begging.
**mendier** [mɑ̃dje] *vi* to beg // *vt* to beg (for).
**menées** [məne] *nfpl* intrigues, manœuvres.
**mener** [məne] *vt* to lead ; (*enquête*) to conduct ; (*affaires*) to manage // *vi*: ~ **à** (**à la marque**) to lead, be in the lead ; ~ **à/dans** (*emmener*) to take to/into ; ~ **qch à terme** *ou* **à bien** to see sth through (to

a successful conclusion), complete sth successfully.
**meneur, euse** [mənœR, -øz] *nm/f* leader ; (*péj*) agitator ; ~ **d'hommes** born leader ; ~ **de jeu** compère ; quizmaster.
**méningite** [menɛ̃ʒit] *nf* meningitis *q*.
**ménopause** [menɔpoz] *nf* menopause.
**menotte** [mənɔt] *nf* (*main*) mitt, tiny hand ; ~**s** *nfpl* handcuffs ; **passer les** ~**s à** to handcuff.
**mensonge** [mɑ̃sɔ̃ʒ] *nm* lie ; lying *q* ; **mensonger, ère** *a* false.
**mensualité** [mɑ̃sɥalite] *nf* monthly payment ; monthly salary.
**mensuel, le** [mɑ̃sɥɛl] *a* monthly.
**mensurations** [mɑ̃syRɑsjɔ̃] *nfpl* measurements.
**mental, e, aux** [mɑ̃tal, -o] *a* mental.
**mentalité** [mɑ̃talite] *nf* mentality.
**menteur, euse** [mɑ̃tœR, -øz] *nm/f* liar.
**menthe** [mɑ̃t] *nf* mint ; ~ (**à l'eau**) peppermint cordial.
**mention** [mɑ̃sjɔ̃] *nf* (*note*) note, comment ; (SCOL): ~ **bien** *etc* ≈ grade B *etc* (*ou* upper 2nd class *etc*) pass ; **faire** ~ **de** to mention ; **mentionner** *vt* to mention.
**mentir** [mɑ̃tiR] *vi* to lie ; to be lying.
**menton** [mɑ̃tɔ̃] *nm* chin.
**menu, e** [məny] *a* slim, slight ; tiny ; (*frais, difficulté*) minor // *ad* (*couper, hacher*) very fine // *nm* menu ; **par le** ~ (*raconter*) in minute detail ; ~**e monnaie** small change.
**menuet** [mənɥɛ] *nm* minuet.
**menuiserie** [mənɥizRi] *nf* (*travail*) joinery, carpentry ; woodwork ; (*local*) joiner's workshop ; (*ouvrage*) woodwork *q*.
**menuisier** [mənɥizje] *nm* joiner, carpenter.
**méprendre** [mepRɑ̃dR(ə)]: **se** ~ *vi*: **se** ~ **sur** to be mistaken (about).
**mépris** [mepRi] *nm* (*dédain*) contempt, scorn ; (*indifférence*): **le** ~ **de** contempt *ou* disregard for ; **au** ~ **de** regardless of, in defiance of.
**méprisable** [mepRizabl(ə)] *a* contemptible, despicable.
**méprisant, e** [mepRizɑ̃, -ɑ̃t] *a* contemptuous, scornful.
**méprise** [mepRiz] *nf* mistake, error ; misunderstanding.
**mépriser** [mepRize] *vt* to scorn, despise ; (*gloire, danger*) to scorn, spurn.
**mer** [mɛR] *nf* sea ; (*marée*) tide ; **en** ~ at sea ; **prendre la** ~ to put out to sea ; **en haute** ~ off shore, on the open sea ; **la** ~ **du Nord/Rouge** the North/Red Sea.
**mercantile** [mɛRkɑ̃til] *a* (*péj*) mercenary.
**mercenaire** [mɛRsənɛR] *nm* mercenary, hired soldier.
**mercerie** [mɛRsəRi] *nf* haberdashery ; haberdasher's shop.
**merci** [mɛRsi] *excl* thank you // *nf*: **à la** ~ **de qn/qch** at sb's mercy/the mercy of sth ; ~ **beaucoup** thank you very much ; ~ **de** thank you for ; **sans** ~ merciless.
**mercier, ière** [mɛRsje, -jɛR] *nm/f* haberdasher.
**mercredi** [mɛRkRədi] *nm* Wednesday ; ~ **des Cendres** Ash Wednesday.
**mercure** [mɛRkyR] *nm* mercury.

**merde** [mɛʀd(ə)] (*fam!*) *nf* shit (!) // *excl* bloody hell (!).

**mère** [mɛʀ] *nf* mother ; ~ **célibataire** unmarried mother.

**méridien** [meʀidjɛ̃] *nm* meridian.

**méridional, e, aux** [meʀidjɔnal, -o] *a* southern // *nm/f* Southerner.

**meringue** [məʀɛ̃g] *nf* meringue.

**merisier** [məʀizje] *nm* wild cherry (tree).

**méritant, e** [meʀitɑ̃, -ɑ̃t] *a* deserving.

**mérite** [meʀit] *nm* merit ; **le** ~ **(de ceci) lui revient** the credit (for this) is his.

**mériter** [meʀite] *vt* to deserve.

**méritoire** [meʀitwaʀ] *a* praiseworthy, commendable.

**merlan** [mɛʀlɑ̃] *nm* whiting.

**merle** [mɛʀl(ə)] *nm* blackbird.

**merveille** [mɛʀvɛj] *nf* marvel, wonder ; **faire** ~ to work wonders ; **à** ~ perfectly, wonderfully.

**merveilleux, euse** [mɛʀvɛjø, -øz] *a* marvellous, wonderful.

**mes** [me] *dét voir* **mon.**

**mésalliance** [mezaljɑ̃s] *nf* misalliance, mismatch.

**mésange** [mezɑ̃ʒ] *nf* tit(mouse) (*pl* mice) ; ~ **bleue** blue tit.

**mésaventure** [mezavɑ̃tyʀ] *nf* misadventure, misfortune.

**Mesdames** [medam] *nfpl voir* **Madame.**

**Mesdemoiselles** [medmwazɛl] *nfpl voir* **Mademoiselle.**

**mésentente** [mezɑ̃tɑ̃t] *nf* dissension, disagreement.

**mésestimer** [mezɛstime] *vt* to underestimate, underrate ; to have low regard for.

**mesquin, e** [mɛskɛ̃, -in] *a* mean, petty ; **mesquinerie** *nf* pettiness *q*, meanness *q*.

**mess** [mɛs] *nm* mess.

**message** [mesaʒ] *nm* message ; ~ **téléphoné** telegram dictated by telephone ; **messager, ère** *nm/f* messenger ; **messageries** *nfpl* parcels service *sg* ; distribution service *sg*.

**messe** [mɛs] *nf* mass ; **aller à la** ~ to go to mass ; ~ **de minuit** midnight mass.

**messie** [mesi] *nm*: **le M**~ the Messiah.

**Messieurs** [mesjø] *nmpl* (*abr* **Messrs**) *voir* **Monsieur.**

**mesure** [məzyʀ] *nf* (*évaluation, dimension*) measurement ; (*étalon, récipient, contenu*) measure ; (*MUS: cadence*) time, tempo ; (*: division*) bar ; (*retenue*) moderation ; (*disposition*) measure, step ; **sur** ~ (*costume*) made-to-measure ; **à la** ~ **de** (*fig*) worthy of ; on the same scale as ; **dans la** ~ **où** insofar as, inasmuch as ; **à** ~ **que** as ; **en** ~ (*MUS*) in time *ou* tempo ; **être en** ~ **de** to be in a position to ; **dépasser la** ~ (*fig*) to overstep the mark.

**mesurer** [məzyʀe] *vt* to measure ; (*juger*) to weigh up, assess ; (*limiter*) to limit, ration ; (*modérer*) to moderate ; (*proportionner*): ~ **qch à** to match sth to, gear sth to ; **se** ~ **avec** to have a confrontation with ; to tackle ; **il mesure 1 m 80** he's 1 m 80 tall.

**met** *vb voir* **mettre.**

**métairie** [meteʀi] *nf* smallholding.

**métal, aux** [metal, -o] *nm* metal ; ~**lique** *a* metallic ; ~**lisé, e** *a* (*peinture*) metallic ; ~**lurgie** *nf* metallurgy ; ~**lurgiste** *nm/f* steel *ou* metal worker ; metallurgist.

**métamorphose** [metamɔʀfoz] *nf* metamorphosis (*pl* oses).

**métaphore** [metafɔʀ] *nf* metaphor.

**métaphysique** [metafizik] *nf* metaphysics *sg* // *a* metaphysical.

**métayer, ère** [meteje, metɛjɛʀ] *nm/f* (tenant) farmer.

**météo** [meteo] *nf* weather report ; ≈ Met Office.

**météore** [meteɔʀ] *nm* meteor.

**météorologie** [meteɔʀɔlɔʒi] *nf* meteorology ; **météorologique** *a* meteorological, weather *cpd.*

**métèque** [metɛk] *nm* (*péj*) wop.

**méthode** [metɔd] *nf* method ; (*livre, ouvrage*) manual, tutor ; **méthodique** *a* methodical.

**méticuleux, euse** [metikylø, -øz] *a* meticulous.

**métier** [metje] *nm* (*profession: gén*) job ; (*: manuel*) trade ; (*: artisanal*) craft ; (*technique, expérience*) (acquired) skill *ou* technique ; (*aussi*: ~ **à tisser**) (weaving) loom ; **être du** ~ to be in the trade *ou* profession.

**métis, se** [metis] *a, nm/f* half-caste, half-breed.

**métisser** [metise] *vt* to cross.

**métrage** [metʀaʒ] *nm* (*de tissu*) length, ≈ yardage ; (*CINÉMA*) footage, length ; **long/moyen/court** ~ full-length/medium-length/short film.

**mètre** [mɛtʀ(ə)] *nm* metre ; (*règle*) (metre) rule ; (*ruban*) tape measure ; **métrique** *a* metric // *nf* metrics *sg.*

**métro** [metʀo] *nm* underground, subway.

**métropole** [metʀɔpɔl] *nf* (*capitale*) metropolis ; (*pays*) home country ; **métropolitain, e** *a* metropolitan.

**mets** [mɛ] *nm* dish.

**metteur** [metœʀ] *nm*: ~ **en scène** (*THÉÂTRE*) producer ; (*CINÉMA*) director ; ~ **en ondes** producer.

**mettre** [mɛtʀ(ə)] *vt* (*placer*) to put ; (*vêtement: revêtir*) to put on ; (*: porter*) to wear ; (*installer: gaz, l'électricité*) to put in ; (*faire fonctionner: chauffage, électricité*) to put on ; (*noter, écrire*) to say, put down ; **mettons que** let's suppose *ou* say that ; ~ **en bouteille/en sac** to bottle/put in bags *ou* sacks ; **y** ~ **du sien** to pull one's weight ; ~ **du temps/2 heures à faire** to take time/2 hours doing ; **se** ~: **n'avoir rien à se** ~ to have nothing to wear ; **se** ~ **de l'encre sur les doigts** to get ink on one's fingers ; **se** ~ **au lit** to get into bed ; **se** ~ **au piano** (*s'asseoir*) to sit down at the piano ; (*apprendre*) to start learning the piano ; **se** ~ **à faire** to begin *ou* start doing *ou* to ao ; **se** ~ **au travail/à l'étude** to get down to work/one's studies.

**meublant, e** [mœblɑ̃, -ɑ̃t] *a* (*tissus etc*) effective (in the room), decorative.

**meuble** [mœbl(ə)] *nm* piece of furniture ; furniture *q* // *a* (*terre*) loose, friable ; (*JUR*): **biens** ~**s** movables ; **meublé** *nm* furnished room (*ou* flatlet) ; **meubler** *vt* to furnish ;

(fig): **meubler qch (de)** to fill sth (with) ;
se **meubler** to furnish one's house.
**meugler** [møgle] *vi* to low, moo.
**meule** [møl] *nf* (*à broyer*) millstone ; (*à
aiguiser*) grindstone ; (*à polir*) buffwheel ;
(*de foin, blé*) stack ; (*de fromage*) round.
**meunerie** [mønRi] *nf* flour trade ; milling ;
**meunier, ière** *nm* miller // *nf* miller's wife
// *af inv* (*CULIN*) meunière.
**meure** *etc vb voir* **mourir**.
**meurtre** [mœRtR(ə)] *nm* murder ;
**meurtrier, ière** *a* (*arme etc*) deadly ;
(*fureur, instincts*) murderous // *nm/f*
murderer/eress // *nf* (*ouverture*) loophole.
**meurtrir** [mœRtRiR] *vt* to bruise ; (*fig*) to
wound ; **meurtrissure** *nf* bruise ; (*fig*) scar.
**meus** *etc vb voir* **mouvoir**.
**meute** [møt] *nf* pack.
**mexicain, e** [mɛksikɛ̃, -ɛn] *a*, *nm/f*
Mexican.
**Mexico** [mɛksiko] *n* Mexico City.
**Mexique** [mɛksik] *nm:* **le** ~ Mexico.
**MF** *sigle f voir* **modulation**.
**Mgr** *abr de* **Monseigneur**.
**mi** [mi] *nm* (*MUS*) E ; (*en chantant la gamme*)
mi.
**mi...** [mi] *préfixe* half(-) ; mid- ; **à la
~-janvier** in mid-January ; **~-bureau,
~-chambre** half office, half bedroom ; **à
~-jambes/-corps** (up *ou* down) to the
knees/waist ; **à ~-hauteur/-pente**
halfway up *ou* down/up *ou* down the hill.
**miauler** [mijole] *vi* to mew.
**mica** [mika] *nm* mica.
**mi-carême** [mikaRɛm] *nf:* **la** ~ the third
Thursday in Lent.
**miche** [miʃ] *nf* round *ou* cob loaf.
**mi-chemin** [miʃmɛ̃]: **à** ~ *ad* halfway,
midway.
**mi-clos, e** [miklo, -kloz] *a* half-closed.
**micmac** [mikmak] *nm* (*péj*) carry-on.
**micro** [mikRo] *nm* mike, microphone.
**microbe** [mikRɔb] *nm* germ, microbe.
**microfiche** [mikRɔfiʃ] *nf* microfiche.
**microfilm** [mikRɔfilm] *nm* microfilm.
**microphone** [mikRɔfɔn] *nm* microphone.
**microscope** [mikRɔskɔp] *nm*
microscope ; **au** ~ under *ou* through the
microscope.
**midi** [midi] *nm* midday, noon ; (*moment du
déjeuner*) lunchtime ; **à** ~ at 12 (o'clock)
*ou* midday *ou* noon ; (*sud*) south ; **en plein
~** (right) in the middle of the day ; facing
south.
**mie** [mi] *nf* crumb (of the loaf).
**miel** [mjɛl] *nm* honey.
**mielleux, euse** [mjɛlø, -øz] *a* (*péj*)
sugary, honeyed.
**mien, ne** [mjɛ̃, mjɛn] *pronom:* **le(la)
~(ne), les ~s** mine ; **les ~s** my family.
**miette** [mjɛt] *nf* (*de pain, gâteau*) crumb ;
(*fig: de la conversation etc*) scrap ; **en ~s**
(*fig*) in pieces *ou* bits.
**mieux** [mjø] *ad* better // *a* better ; (*plus
joli*) better-looking // *nm* (*progrès*)
improvement ; **le** ~ the best (thing) ; **le(la)
~, les** ~ the best ; **le** ~ **des deux** the
better of the two ; **les livres les** ~ **faits**
the best made books ; **de mon/ton** ~ as
best I/you can (*ou* could) ; **de** ~ **en** ~
better and better ; **pour le** ~ for the best ;

**au** ~ at best ; **au** ~ **avec** on the best of
terms with.
**mièvre** [mjɛvR(ə)] *a* mawkish, sickly
sentimental.
**mignon, ne** [miɲɔ̃, -ɔn] *a* sweet, cute.
**migraine** [migRɛn] *nf* headache ; migraine.
**migrateur, trice** [migRatœR, -tRis] *a*
migratory.
**migration** [migRɑsjɔ̃] *nf* migration.
**mijaurée** [miʒɔRe] *nf* pretentious girl.
**mijoter** [miʒɔte] *vt* to simmer ; (*préparer
avec soin*) to cook lovingly ; (*affaire, projet*)
to plot, cook up // *vi* to simmer.
**mil** [mil] *num* = **mille**.
**mildiou** [mildju] *nm* mildew.
**milice** [milis] *nf* militia ; **milicien, ne** *nm/f*
militia man/woman.
**milieu, x** [miljø] *nm* (*centre*) middle ; (*fig*)
middle course *ou* way ; happy medium ;
(*BIO, GÉO*) environment ; (*entourage social*)
milieu ; background ; circle ; (*pègre*): **le** ~
the underworld ; **au** ~ **de** in the middle
of.
**militaire** [militɛR] *a* military, army *cpd* //
*nm* serviceman.
**militant, e** [militɑ̃, -ɑ̃t] *a*, *nm/f* militant.
**militer** [milite] *vi* to be a militant ; ~
**pour/contre** (*suj: faits, raisons etc*) to
militate in favour of/against.
**mille** [mil] *num* a *ou* one thousand // *nm*
(*mesure*): ~ (**marin**) nautical mile ;
**mettre dans le** ~ to hit the bull's-eye ;
to be bang on target ; **~-feuille** *nm* cream
*ou* vanilla slice ; **millénaire** *nm* millennium
// *a* thousand-year-old ; (*fig*) ancient ; **~-
pattes** *nm inv* centipede.
**millésime** [milezim] *nm* year ; **millésimé,
e** *a* vintage *cpd*.
**millet** [mijɛ] *nm* millet.
**milliard** [miljaR] *nm* milliard, thousand
million ; **milliardaire** *nm/f* multi-
millionaire.
**millier** [milje] *nm* thousand ; **un** ~ (**de**)
a thousand or so, about a thousand ; **par
~s** in (their) thousands, by the thousand.
**milligramme** [miligRam] *nm*
milligramme.
**millimètre** [milimɛtR(ə)] *nm* millimetre ;
**millimétré, e** *a:* **papier millimétré** graph
paper.
**million** [miljɔ̃] *nm* million ; **deux ~s de**
two million ; **toucher cinq ~s** to get five
million ; **riche à ~s** worth millions ;
**millionnaire** *nm/f* millionaire.
**mime** [mim] *nm/f* (*acteur*) mime(r) // *nm*
(*art*) mime, miming.
**mimer** [mime] *vt* to mime ; (*singer*) to
mimic, take off.
**mimétisme** [mimetism(ə)] *nm* (*BIO*)
mimicry.
**mimique** [mimik] *nf* (funny) face ; (*signes*)
gesticulations *pl*, sign language *q*.
**mimosa** [mimoza] *nm* mimosa.
**minable** [minabl(ə)] *a* shabby (-looking) ;
pathetic.
**minauder** [minode] *vi* to mince, simper.
**mince** [mɛ̃s] *a* thin ; (*personne, taille*) slim,
slender ; (*fig: profit, connaissances*) slight,
small // *excl* drat it! ; **minceur** *nf*
thinness ; slimness, slenderness.

**mine** [min] nf (physionomie) expression, look ; (extérieur) exterior, appearance ; (de crayon) lead ; (gisement, exploitation, explosif) mine ; ~s nfpl (péj) simpering airs ; **avoir bonne** ~ (personne) to look well ; (ironique) to look an utter idiot ; **avoir mauvaise** ~ to look unwell ou poorly ; **faire** ~ **de faire** to make a pretence of doing ; to make as if to do ; ~ **de rien** ad with a casual air ; although you wouldn't think so ; ~ **de charbon** coalmine ; ~ **à ciel ouvert** opencast mine.

**miner** [mine] vt (saper) to undermine, erode ; (MIL) to mine.

**minerai** [minʀɛ] nm ore.

**minéral, e, aux** [mineʀal, -o] a mineral ; (CHIMIE) inorganic // nm mineral.

**minéralogie** [mineʀalɔʒi] nf mineralogy.

**minéralogique** [mineʀalɔʒik] a mineralogical ; **plaque** ~ number plate ; **numéro** ~ registration number.

**minet, te** [minɛ, -ɛt] nm/f (chat) pussycat ; (péj) young trendy/dollybird.

**mineur, e** [minœʀ] a minor // nm/f (JUR) minor, person under age // nm (travailleur) miner ; ~ **de fond** face worker.

**miniature** [minjatyʀ] a, nf miniature ; **miniaturiser** vt to miniaturize.

**minibus** [minibys] nm minibus.

**mini-cassette** [minikasɛt] nf cassette (recorder).

**minier, ière** [minje, -jɛʀ] a mining.

**mini-jupe** [miniʒyp] nf mini-skirt.

**minimal, e, aux** [minimal, -o] a minimum.

**minime** [minim] a minor, minimal // nm/f (SPORT) junior.

**minimiser** [minimize] vt to minimize ; (fig) to play down.

**minimum** [minimɔm] a, nm minimum ; **au** ~ (au moins) at the very least ; ~ **vital** living wage ; subsistance level.

**ministère** [ministɛʀ] nm (aussi REL) ministry ; (cabinet) government ; ~ **public** (JUR) Prosecution, State Prosecutor ; **ministériel, le** a cabinet cpd ; ministerial.

**ministre** [ministʀ(ə)] nm (aussi REL) minister ; ~ **d'État** senior minister (of the Interior or of Justice).

**minium** [minjɔm] nm red lead paint.

**minois** [minwa] nm little face.

**minoritaire** [minɔʀitɛʀ] a minority cpd.

**minorité** [minɔʀite] nf minority ; **être en** ~ to be in the ou a minority ; **mettre en** ~ (POL) to defeat.

**minoterie** [minɔtʀi] nf flour-mill.

**minuit** [minɥi] nm midnight.

**minuscule** [minyskyl] a minute, tiny // nf: (lettre) ~ small letter.

**minute** [minyt] nf minute ; (JUR: original) minute, draft ; **à la** ~ (just) this instant ; there and then ; **steak** ~ minute steak ; **minuter** vt to time ; **minuterie** nf time switch.

**minutieux, euse** [minysjø, -øz] a meticulous ; minutely detailed ; requiring painstaking attention to detail.

**mioche** [mjɔʃ] nm (fam) nipper, brat.

**mirabelle** [miʀabɛl] nf (cherry) plum ; (eau-de-vie) plum brandy.

**miracle** [miʀakl(ə)] nm miracle ; **miraculé, e** a who has been miraculously cured (ou rescued) ; **miraculeux, euse** a miraculous.

**mirador** [miʀadɔʀ] nm (MIL) watchtower.

**mirage** [miʀaʒ] nm mirage.

**mire** [miʀ] nf: **point de** ~ target ; (fig) focal point ; **ligne de** ~ line of sight.

**mirer** [miʀe] vt (œufs) to candle ; **se** ~ vi: **se** ~ **dans** to gaze at one's reflection in ; to be mirrored in.

**mirifique** [miʀifik] a wonderful.

**mirobolant, e** [miʀɔbɔlɑ̃, -ɑ̃t] a fantastic.

**miroir** [miʀwaʀ] nm mirror.

**miroiter** [miʀwate] vi to sparkle, shimmer ; **faire** ~ **qch à qn** to paint sth in glowing colours for sb, dangle sth in front of sb's eyes.

**miroiterie** [miʀwatʀi] nf mirror factory ; mirror dealer's (shop).

**mis, e** [mi, miz] pp de **mettre** // a: **bien** ~ well dressed // nf (argent: au jeu) stake ; (tenue) clothing ; attire ; **être de** ~e to be acceptable ou in season ; ~**e de fonds** capital outlay ; ~**e à mort** kill ; ~**e en plis** set ; ~**e au point** (fig) clarification (voir aussi **point**) ; ~**e en scène** production.

**misaine** [mizɛn] nf: **mât de** ~ foremast.

**misanthrope** [mizɑ̃tʀɔp] nm/f misanthropist.

**mise** [miz] a, nf voir **mis**.

**miser** [mize] vt (enjeu) to stake, bet ; ~ **sur** vt (cheval, numéro) to bet on ; (fig) to bank ou count on.

**misérable** [mizeʀabl(ə)] a (lamentable, malheureux) pitiful, wretched ; (pauvre) poverty-stricken ; (insignifiant, mesquin) miserable // nm/f wretch ; (miséreux) poor wretch.

**misère** [mizɛʀ] nf (extreme) poverty, destitution ; ~**s** nfpl woes, miseries ; little troubles ; **être dans la** ~ to be destitute ou poverty-stricken ; **salaire de** ~ starvation wage ; **miséreux, euse** nm/f down-and-out.

**miséricorde** [mizeʀikɔʀd(ə)] nf mercy, forgiveness ; **miséricordieux, euse** a merciful, forgiving.

**misogyne** [mizɔʒin] a misogynous // nm/f misogynist.

**missel** [misɛl] nm missal.

**missile** [misil] nm missile.

**mission** [misjɔ̃] nf mission ; **partir en** ~ (ADMIN, POL) to go on an assignment ; **missionnaire** nm/f missionary.

**missive** [misiv] nf missive.

**mit** vb voir **mettre**.

**mitaine** [mitɛn] nf mitt(en).

**mite** [mit] nf clothes moth ; **mité, e** a motheaten.

**mi-temps** [mitɑ̃] nf inv (SPORT: période) half (pl halves) ; (: pause) half-time ; **à** ~ a, ad part-time.

**miteux, euse** [mitø, -øz] a seedy, shabby.

**mitigé, e** [mitiʒe] a lukewarm ; mixed.

**mitonner** [mitɔne] vt to cook with loving care ; (fig) to cook up quietly.

**mitoyen, ne** [mitwajɛ̃, -ɛn] a common, party cpd ; **maisons** ~**nes** semi-detached houses ; (plus de deux) terraced houses.

**mitraille** [mitʀɑj] *nf* grapeshot ; shellfire.
**mitrailler** [mitʀɑje] *vt* to machine-gun ;
(*fig: photographier*) to take shot after shot
of ; ~ **qn de** to pelt sb with, bombard sb
with ; **mitraillette** *nf* submachine gun ;
**mitrailleur** *nm* machine gunner ;
**mitrailleuse** *nf* machine gun.
**mitre** [mitʀ(ə)] *nf* mitre.
**mitron** [mitʀɔ̃] *nm* baker's boy.
**mi-voix** [mivwa]: **à** ~ *ad* in a low *ou*
hushed voice.
**mixage** [miksaʒ] *nm* (*CINÉMA*) (sound)
mixing.
**mixer** [miksœʀ] *nm* (food) mixer.
**mixité** [miksite] *nf* (*SCOL*) coeducation.
**mixte** [mikst(ə)] *a* (*gén*) mixed ; (*SCOL*)
mixed, coeducational ; **à usage** ~ dual-
purpose ; **cuisinière** ~ gas and electric
cooker ; **équipe** ~ combined team.
**mixture** [mikstyʀ] *nf* mixture ; (*fig*)
concoction.
**M.L.F.** *sigle m* = *mouvement de libération
de la femme*, ≈ Women's Lib.
**Mlle**, *pl* **Mlles** *abr de* **Mademoiselle**.
**MM** *abr de* **Messieurs**.
**Mme**, *pl* **Mmes** *abr de* **Madame**.
**mnémotechnique** [mnemɔtɛknik] *a*
mnemonic.
**Mo** *abr de* **métro**.
**mobile** [mɔbil] *a* mobile ; (*pièce de
machine*) moving ; (*élément de meuble etc*)
movable // *nm* (*motif*) motive ; (*œuvre
d'art*) mobile ; (*PHYSIQUE*) moving object *ou*
body.
**mobilier, ière** [mɔbilje, -jɛʀ] *a* (*JUR*)
personal // *nm* furniture ; **valeurs
mobilières** transferable securities ; **vente
mobilière** sale of personal property *ou*
chattels.
**mobilisation** [mɔbilizɑsjɔ̃] *nf*
mobilization.
**mobiliser** [mɔbilize] *vt* (*MIL*, *gén*) to
mobilize.
**mobilité** [mɔbilite] *nf* mobility.
**mocassin** [mɔkasɛ̃] *nm* moccasin.
**moche** [mɔʃ] *a* (*fam*) ugly ; rotten.
**modalité** [mɔdalite] *nf* form, mode ; ~**s**
*nfpl* (*d'un accord etc*) clauses, terms.
**mode** [mɔd] *nf* fashion ; (*commerce*)
fashion trade *ou* industry // *nm* (*manière*)
form, mode ; (*LING*) mood ; (*MUS*) mode ; **à
la** ~ fashionable, in fashion ; ~ **d'emploi**
directions *pl* (for use) ; ~ **de vie** way of
life.
**modèle** [mɔdɛl] *a*, *nm* model ; (*qui pose:
de peintre*) sitter ; ~ **déposé** registered
design ; ~ **réduit** small-scale model ; ~
**de série** production model.
**modelé** [mɔdle] *nm* relief ; contours *pl*.
**modeler** [mɔdle] *vt* (*ART*) to model, mould ;
(*suj: vêtement, érosion*) to mould, shape ;
~ **qch sur/d'après** to model sth on.
**modérateur, trice** [mɔdeʀatœʀ, -tʀis] *a*
moderating // *nm/f* moderator.
**modération** [mɔdeʀasjɔ̃] *nf* moderation.
**modéré, e** [mɔdeʀe] *a*, *nm/f* moderate.
**modérer** [mɔdeʀe] *vt* to moderate ; **se** ~
*vi* to restrain o.s.
**moderne** [mɔdɛʀn(ə)] *a* modern // *nm*
modern style ; modern furniture ;
**moderniser** *vt* to modernize.

**modeste** [mɔdɛst(ə)] *a* modest ; **modestie**
*nf* modesty.
**modicité** [mɔdisite] *nf*: **la** ~ **des prix** *etc*
the low prices *etc*.
**modification** [mɔdifikɑsjɔ̃] *nf*
modification.
**modifier** [mɔdifje] *vt* to modify, alter ;
(*LING*) to modify ; **se** ~ *vi* to alter.
**modique** [mɔdik] *a* modest.
**modiste** [mɔdist(ə)] *nf* milliner.
**modulation** [mɔdylɑsjɔ̃] *nf* modulation ;
~ **de fréquence (FM** *ou* **MF)** frequency
modulation.
**module** [mɔdyl] *nm* module.
**moduler** [mɔdyle] *vt* to modulate ; (*air*) to
warble.
**moelle** [mwal] *nf* marrow ; (*fig*) pith, core ;
~ **épinière** spinal chord.
**moelleux, euse** [mwalø, -øz] *a* soft ; (*au
goût, à l'ouïe*) mellow.
**moellon** [mwalɔ̃] *nm* rubble stone.
**mœurs** [mœʀ] *nfpl* (*conduite*) morals ;
(*manières*) manners ; (*pratiques sociales,
mode de vie*) habits ; **passer dans les** ~
to become the custom ; **contraire aux
bonnes** ~ contrary to proprieties.
**mohair** [mɔɛʀ] *nm* mohair.
**moi** [mwa] *pronom me* ; (*emphatique*): ~,
je for my part, I, I myself.
**moignon** [mwaɲɔ̃] *nm* stump.
**moi-même** [mwamɛm] *pronom* myself ;
(*emphatique*) I myself.
**moindre** [mwɛ̃dʀ(ə)] *a* lesser ; lower ;
**le(la)** ~, **les** ~**s** the least, the slightest.
**moine** [mwan] *nm* monk, friar.
**moineau, x** [mwano] *nm* sparrow.
**moins** [mwɛ̃] *ad* less // *cj*: ~ **2** minus 2 ;
~ **je travaille, mieux je me porte** the less
I work the better I feel ; ~ **grand que** not
as tall as, less tall than ; **le(la)** ~ **doué(e)**
the least gifted ; **le** ~ the least ; ~ **de**
(*sable, eau*) less ; (*livres, gens*) fewer ; ~
**de 2 ans/100 F** less than 2 years/100 F ;
~ **de midi** not yet midday ; **100 F/3 jours
de** ~ 100 F/3 days less ; **3 livres en** ~
3 books fewer ; 3 books too few ; **de
l'argent en** ~ less money, **le soleil en**
~ but for the sun, minus the sun ; **à** ~
**que** *cj* unless ; **à** ~ **de faire** unless we do
(*ou* he does) ; **à** ~ **de** (*imprévu, accident*)
barring any ; **au** ~ at least ; **de** ~ **en** ~
less and less ; **pour le** ~ at the very least ;
**du** ~ at least ; **il est** ~ **cinq** it's five to ;
**il fait** ~ **cinq** it's five below (freezing) *ou*
minus five.
**moiré, e** [mwaʀe] *a* (*tissu, papier*) moiré,
watered ; (*reflets*) shimmering.
**mois** [mwa] *nm* month ; ~ **double** (*COMM*)
extra month's salary.
**moïse** [mɔiz] *nm* Moses basket.
**moisi, e** [mwazi] *a* mouldy, mildewed //
*nm* mould, mildew ; **odeur de** ~ musty
smell.
**moisir** [mwaziʀ] *vi* to go mouldy ; (*fig*) to
rot ; to hang about.
**moisissure** [mwazisyʀ] *nf* mould q.
**moisson** [mwasɔ̃] *nf* harvest ; (*fig*): **faire
une** ~ **de** to gather a wealth of ;
**moissonner** *vt* to harvest, reap ; (*fig*) to
collect ; **moissonneur, euse** *nm/f*
harvester, reaper // *nf* (*machine*)

harvester ; **moissonneuse-batteuse** *nf* combine harvester.

**moite** [mwat] *a* sweaty, sticky.

**moitié** [mwatje] *nf* half (*pl* halves) ; (*épouse*): **sa** ~ his loving wife, his better half ; **la** ~ half ; **la** ~ **de** half (of), half the amount (*ou* number) of ; **la** ~ **du temps/des gens** half the time/the people ; **à la** ~ **de** halfway through ; ~ **moins grand** half as tall ; ~ **plus long** half as long again, longer by half ; **à** ~ half (*avant le verbe*) ; half- (*avant l'adjectif*) ; **de** ~ by half ; ~ ~ half-and-half.

**moka** [mɔka] *nm* mocha coffee ; mocha cake.

**mol** [mɔl] *a voir* **mou.**

**molaire** [mɔlɛR] *nf* molar.

**molécule** [mɔlekyl] *nf* molecule.

**moleskine** [mɔlɛskin] *nf* imitation leather.

**molester** [mɔlɛste] *vt* to manhandle, maul (about).

**molette** [mɔlɛt] *nf* toothed *ou* cutting wheel.

**molle** [mɔl] *af voir* **mou** ; ~**ment** *ad* softly ; (*péj*) sluggishly ; (*protester*) feebly ; **mollesse** *nf* softness ; flabbiness ; limpness ; sluggishness.

**mollet** [mɔlɛ] *nm* calf (*pl* calves) // *am*: **œuf** ~ soft-boiled egg ; **molletière** *af*: **bande molletière** puttee.

**molletonné, e** [mɔltɔne] *a* fleece-lined, flannelette-lined.

**mollir** [mɔliR] *vi* to give way ; to relent ; to go soft.

**mollusque** [mɔlysk(ə)] *nm* (*ZOOL*) mollusc.

**molosse** [mɔlɔs] *nm* big ferocious dog.

**môme** [mom] *nm/f* (*fam: enfant*) brat ; (: *fille*) bird.

**moment** [mɔmɑ̃] *nm* moment ; **ce n'est pas le** ~ this is not the (right) time ; **à un certain** ~ at some point ; **pour un bon** ~ for a good while ; **pour le** ~ for the moment, for the time being ; **au** ~ **de** at the time of ; **au** ~ **où** as ; at a time when ; **à tout** ~ at any time *ou* moment ; constantly, continually ; **en ce** ~ at the moment ; at present ; **sur le** ~ at the time ; **par** ~**s** now and then, at times ; **du** ~ **où** *ou* **que** seeing that, since ; **momentané, e** a temporary, momentary.

**momie** [mɔmi] *nf* mummy.

**mon** [mɔ̃], **ma** [ma], *pl* **mes** [me] *dét* my.

**monacal, e, aux** [mɔnakal, -o] *a* monastic.

**monarchie** [mɔnaRʃi] *nf* monarchy ; **monarchiste** *a*, *nm/f* monarchist.

**monarque** [mɔnaRk(ə)] *nm* monarch.

**monastère** [mɔnastɛR] *nm* monastery.

**monastique** [mɔnastik] *a* monastic.

**monceau, x** [mɔ̃so] *nm* heap.

**mondain, e** [mɔ̃dɛ̃, -ɛn] *a* society *cpd* ; social ; fashionable // *nm/f* society man/woman, socialite // *nf*: **la M**~**e, la police** ~**e** ≈ the vice squad ; **mondanités** *nfpl* society life *sg* ; (*society*) small talk *sg* ; (*society*) gossip column *sg*.

**monde** [mɔ̃d] *nm* world ; (*haute société*): **le** ~ (high) society ; (*milieu*): **être du même** ~ to move in the same circles ; (*gens*): **il y a du** ~ (*beaucoup de gens*) there are many people ; (*quelques personnes*) there

are some people ; **y a-t-il du** ~ **dans le salon?** is there anybody in the lounge? ; **beaucoup/peu de** ~ many/few people ; **le meilleur** *etc* **du** ~ the best *etc* in the world *ou* on earth ; **mettre au** ~ to bring into the world ; **pas le moins du** ~ not in the least ; **se faire un** ~ **de qch** to make a great deal of fuss about sth ; **mondial, e, aux** *a* (*population*) world *cpd* ; (*influence*) world-wide ; **mondialement** *ad* throughout the world ; **mondovision** *nf* world coverage by satellite.

**monégasque** [mɔnegask(ə)] *a* Monegasque, of *ou* from Monaco.

**monétaire** [mɔnetɛR] *a* monetary.

**mongolien, ne** [mɔ̃gɔljɛ̃, -jɛn] *a*, *nm/f* mongol.

**mongolisme** [mɔ̃gɔlism(ə)] *nm* mongolism.

**moniteur, trice** [mɔnitœR, -tRis] *nm/f* (*SPORT*) instructor/instructress ; (*de colonie de vacances*) supervisor // *nm*: ~ **cardiaque** cardiac monitor ; ~ **d'auto-école** driving instructor.

**monnaie** [mɔnɛ] *nf* (*pièce*) coin ; (*ÉCON, gén: moyen d'échange*) currency ; (*petites pièces*): **avoir de la** ~ to have (some) change ; **faire de la** ~ to get (some) change ; **avoir/faire la** ~ **de 20 F** to have change of/get change for 20 F ; **faire à qn la** ~ **de 20 F** to give sb change for 20 F, change 20 F for sb ; **rendre à qn la** ~ (**sur 20 F**) to give sb the change (out of *ou* from 20 F) ; **c'est** ~ **courante** it's a common occurrence ; **monnayer** *vt* to convert into cash ; (*talent*) to capitalize on ; **monnayeur** *nm voir* **faux.**

**monocle** [mɔnɔkl(ə)] *nm* monocle, eyeglass.

**monocorde** [mɔnɔkɔRd(ə)] *a* monotonous.

**monoculture** [mɔnɔkyltyR] *nf* single-crop farming, monoculture.

**monogramme** [mɔnɔgRam] *nm* monogram.

**monolingue** [mɔnɔlɛ̃g] *a* monolingual.

**monologue** [mɔnɔlɔg] *nm* monologue, soliloquy ; **monologuer** *vi* to soliloquize.

**monôme** [mɔnom] *nm* (*MATH*) monomial ; (*d'étudiants*) students' rag procession.

**monoplace** [mɔnɔplas] *a*, *nm*, *nf* single-seater, one-seater.

**monopole** [mɔnɔpɔl] *nm* monopoly ; **monopoliser** *vt* to monopolize.

**monorail** [mɔnɔRaj] *nm* monorail, monorail train.

**monosyllabe** [mɔnɔsilab] *nm* monosyllable, word of one syllable.

**monotone** [mɔnɔtɔn] *a* monotonous ; **monotonie** *nf* monotony.

**monseigneur** [mɔ̃sɛɲœR] *nm* (*archevêque, évêque*) Your (*ou* His) Grace ; (*cardinal*) Your (*ou* His) Eminence ; **Mgr Thomas** Bishop Thomas ; Cardinal Thomas.

**Monsieur** [məsjø], *pl* **Messieurs** [mesjø] *titre* Mr ['mistə*] // *nm* (*homme quelconque*): **un/le m**~ a/the gentleman ; *voir aussi* **Madame.**

**monstre** [mɔ̃stR(ə)] *nm* monster // *a*: **un travail** ~ a fantastic amount of work ; an enormous job ; **monstrueux, euse** *a* monstrous ; **monstruosité** *nf* monstrosity.

**mont** [mɔ̃] *nm*: **par ~s et par vaux** up hill and down dale ; **le M~ Blanc** Mont Blanc ; **le ~ de Vénus** mons veneris.

**montage** [mɔ̃taʒ] *nm* putting up ; mounting, setting ; assembly ; (PHOTO) photomontage ; (CINÉMA) editing ; **~ sonore** sound editing.

**montagnard, e** [mɔ̃taɲaʀ, -aʀd(ə)] *a* mountain *cpd* // *nm/f* mountain-dweller.

**montagne** [mɔ̃taɲ] *nf* (*cime*) mountain ; (*région*): **la ~** the mountains *pl* ; **~s russes** big dipper *sg*, switchback *sg*.

**montant, e** [mɔ̃tɑ̃, -ɑ̃t] *a* rising ; (*robe, corsage*) high-necked // *nm* (*somme, total*), (sum) total, (total) amount ; (*de fenêtre*) upright ; (*de lit*) post.

**mont-de-piété** [mɔ̃dpjete] *nm* pawnshop.

**monte-charge** [mɔ̃tʃaʀʒ(ə)] *nm inv* goods lift, hoist.

**montée** [mɔ̃te] *nf* rising, rise ; ascent, climb ; (*chemin*) way up ; (*côte*) hill ; **au milieu de la ~** halfway up ; **le moteur chauffe dans les ~s** the engine overheats going uphill.

**monte-plats** [mɔ̃tpla] *nm inv* service lift.

**monter** [mɔ̃te] *vt* (*escalier, côte*) to go (*ou* come) up ; (*valise, paquet*) to take (*ou* bring) up ; (*cheval*) to mount ; (*femelle*) to cover, serve ; (*étagère*) to raise ; (*tente, échafaudage*) to put up ; (*machine*) to assemble ; (*bijou*) to mount, set ; (COUTURE) to set in ; to sew on ; (CINÉMA) to edit ; (THÉÂTRE) to put on, stage ; (*société etc*) to set up // *vi* to go (*ou come*) up ; (*avion etc*) to climb, go up ; (*chemin, niveau, température*) to go up, rise ; (*passager*) to get on ; (*à cheval*): **~ bien/mal** to ride well/badly ; **~ à pied/en voiture** to walk/drive up, go up on foot/by car ; **~ dans le train/l'avion** to get into the train/plane, board the train/plane ; **~ sur** to climb up onto ; **~ à cheval** to get on *ou* mount a horse ; **se ~** (*s'équiper*) to equip o.s., get kitted up ; **se ~ à** (*frais etc*) to add up to, come to ; **~ qn contre qn** to set sb against sb ; **~ la tête à qn** to give sb ideas ; **monteur, euse** *nm/f* (TECH) fitter ; (CINÉMA) (film) editor.

**monticule** [mɔ̃tikyl] *nm* mound.

**montre** [mɔ̃tʀ(ə)] *nf* watch ; (*ostentation*): **pour la ~** for show ; **faire ~ de** to show, display ; **contre la ~** (SPORT) against the clock ; **~-bracelet** *nf* wrist watch.

**montrer** [mɔ̃tʀe] *vt* to show ; **~ qch à qn** to show sb sth ; **montreur de marionnettes** *nm* puppeteer.

**monture** [mɔ̃tyʀ] *nf* (*bête*) mount ; (*d'une bague*) setting ; (*de lunettes*) frame.

**monument** [mɔnymɑ̃] *nm* monument ; **~ aux morts** war memorial ; **monumental, e, aux** *a* monumental.

**moquer** [mɔke]: **se ~ de** *vt* to make fun of, laugh at ; (*fam: se désintéresser de*) not to care about ; (*tromper*): **se ~ de qn** to take sb for a ride.

**moquerie** [mɔkʀi] *nf* mockery *q*.

**moquette** [mɔkɛt] *nf* fitted carpet, wall-to-wall carpeting *q*.

**moqueur, euse** [mɔkœʀ, -øz] *a* mocking.

**moral, e, aux** [mɔʀal, -o] *a* moral // *nm* morale // *nf* (*conduite*) morals *pl* ; (*règles*) moral code, ethic ; (*valeurs*) moral

standards *pl*, morality ; (*science*) ethics *sg*, moral philosophy ; (*conclusion: d'une fable etc*) moral ; **au ~, sur le plan ~** morally ; **faire la ~e à** to lecture, preach at ; **~isateur, trice** *a* moralizing, sanctimonious ; **~iser** *vt* (*sermonner*) to lecture, preach at ; **~iste** *nm/f* moralist // *a* moralistic ; **~ité** *nf* morality ; (*conduite*) morals *pl* ; (*conclusion, enseignement*) moral.

**morbide** [mɔʀbid] *a* morbid.

**morceau, x** [mɔʀso] *nm* piece, bit ; (*d'une œuvre*) passage, extract ; (MUS) piece ; (CULIN: *de viande*) cut ; **mettre en ~x** to pull to pieces *ou* bits.

**morceler** [mɔʀsəle] *vt* to break up, divide up.

**mordant, e** [mɔʀdɑ̃, -ɑ̃t] *a* scathing, cutting ; biting // *nm* spirit ; bite, punch.

**mordicus** [mɔʀdikys] *ad* (*affirmer etc*) obstinately, stubbornly.

**mordiller** [mɔʀdije] *vt* to nibble at, chew at.

**mordoré, e** [mɔʀdɔʀe] *a* lustrous bronze.

**mordre** [mɔʀdʀ(ə)] *vt* to bite ; (*suj: lime, vis*) to bite into // *vi* (*poisson*) to bite ; **~ dans** (*fruit*) to bite into ; **~ sur** (*fig*) to go over into, overlap into ; **~ à l'hameçon** to bite, rise to the bait.

**mordu, e** [mɔʀdy] *pp de* **mordre** // *a* (*amoureux*) smitten // *nm/f*: **un ~ du jazz/de la voile** a jazz/sailing fanatic *ou* buff.

**morfondre** [mɔʀfɔ̃dʀ(ə)]: **se ~** *vi* to fret.

**morgue** [mɔʀg(ə)] *nf* (*arrogance*) haughtiness ; (*lieu: de la police*) morgue ; (: à *l'hôpital*) mortuary.

**moribond, e** [mɔʀibɔ̃, -ɔ̃d] *a* dying, moribund.

**morille** [mɔʀij] *nf* morel.

**morne** [mɔʀn(ə)] *a* dismal, dreary.

**morose** [mɔʀoz] *a* sullen, morose.

**morphine** [mɔʀfin] *nf* morphine ; **morphinomane** *nm/f* morphine addict.

**morphologie** [mɔʀfɔlɔʒi] *nf* morphology.

**mors** [mɔʀ] *nm* bit.

**morse** [mɔʀs(ə)] *nm* (ZOOL) walrus ; (TEL) Morse (code).

**morsure** [mɔʀsyʀ] *nf* bite.

**mort** [mɔʀ] *nf* death ; **se donner la ~** to take one's life.

**mort, e** [mɔʀ, mɔʀt(ə)] *pp de* **mourir** // *a* dead // *nm/f* (*défunt*) dead man/woman ; (*victime*): **il y a eu plusieurs ~s** several people were killed, there were several killed // *nm* (CARTES) dummy ; **~ ou vif** dead or alive ; **~ de peur/fatigue** frightened to death/dead tired.

**mortadelle** [mɔʀtadɛl] *nf* mortadella (*type of luncheon meat*).

**mortalité** [mɔʀtalite] *nf* mortality, death rate.

**mortel, le** [mɔʀtɛl] *a* (*poison etc*) deadly, lethal ; (*accident, blessure*) fatal ; (REL) mortal ; (*fig*) deathly ; deadly boring // *nm/f* mortal.

**morte-saison** [mɔʀtəsɛzɔ̃] *nf* slack *ou* off season.

**mortier** [mɔʀtje] *nm* (*gén*) mortar.

**mortifier** [mɔʀtifje] vt to mortify.

**mort-né, e** [mɔʀne] a (enfant) stillborn; (fig) abortive.

**mortuaire** [mɔʀtɥɛʀ] a funeral cpd; **avis ~s** death announcements, intimations; **chapelle ~** mortuary chapel; **couronne ~** (funeral) wreath; **domicile ~** house of the deceased; **drap ~** pall.

**morue** [mɔʀy] nf (ZOOL) cod inv; (CULIN: salée) salt-cod; **morutier** nm cod fisherman; cod fishing boat.

**morveux, euse** [mɔʀvø, -øz] a (fam) snotty-nosed.

**mosaïque** [mɔzaik] nf (ART) mosaic; (fig) patchwork.

**Moscou** [mɔsku] n Moscow; **moscovite** a of ou from Moscow // nm/f Muscovite.

**mosquée** [mɔske] nf mosque.

**mot** [mo] nm word; (message) line, note; (bon mot etc) saying; sally; **~ à ~ a**, ad word for word; **~ pour ~** word for word, verbatim; **prendre qn au ~** to take sb at his word; **avoir son ~ à dire** to have a say; **~s croisés** crossword (puzzle) sg; **~ d'ordre** watchword; **~ de passe** password.

**motard** [mɔtaʀ] nm motorcycle cop.

**motel** [mɔtɛl] nm motel.

**moteur, trice** [mɔtœʀ, -tʀis] a (ANAT, PHYSIOL) motor; (troubles) motory; (TECH) driving; (AUTO): **à 4 roues motrices** 4-wheel drive // nm engine, motor; (fig) mover, mainspring; **à ~** power-driven, motor cpd; **~ à deux temps** two-stroke engine; **~ à explosion** internal combustion engine.

**motif** [mɔtif] nm (cause) motive; (décoratif) design, pattern, motif; (d'un tableau) subject, motif; (MUS) figure, motif; **~s** nmpl (JUR) grounds pl; **sans ~** a groundless.

**motion** [mɔsjɔ̃] nf motion; **~ de censure** motion of censure, vote of no confidence.

**motivation** [mɔtivɥsjɔ̃] nf motivation.

**motivé, e** [mɔtive] a (acte) justified; (personne) motivated.

**motiver** [mɔtive] vt (justifier) to justify, account for; (ADMIN, JUR, PSYCH) to motivate.

**moto** [mɔto] nf (motor)bike; **~-cross** nm motocross; **~cyclette** nf motorbike, motorcycle; **~cyclisme** nm motorcycle racing; **~cycliste** nm/f motorcyclist.

**motorisé, e** [mɔtɔʀize] a (troupe) motorized; (personne) having transport ou a car.

**motrice** [mɔtʀis] a voir **moteur**; **motricité** nf motor functions.

**motte** [mɔt] nf: **~ de terre** lump of earth, clod (of earth); **~ de gazon** turf, sod; **~ de beurre** lump of butter.

**motus** [mɔtys] excl: **~ (et bouche cousue)!** mum's the word!

**mou(mol), molle** [mu, mɔl] a soft; (péj) flabby; limp; sluggish; feeble // nm (abats) lights pl, lungs pl; (de la corde): **avoir du ~** to be slack.

**mouchard, e** [muʃaʀ, -aʀd(ə)] nm/f grass // nm (appareil) control device.

**mouche** [muʃ] nf fly; (ESCRIME) button; (de taffetas) patch; **prendre la ~** to take the huff; **faire ~** to score a bull's-eye.

**moucher** [muʃe] vt (enfant) to blow the nose of; (chandelle) to snuff (out); **se ~** vi to blow one's nose.

**moucheron** [muʃʀɔ̃] nm midge.

**moucheté, e** [muʃte] a dappled; flecked; (ESCRIME) buttoned.

**mouchoir** [muʃwaʀ] nm handkerchief, hanky; **~ en papier** tissue, paper hanky.

**moudre** [mudʀ(ə)] vt to grind.

**moue** [mu] nf pout; **faire la ~** to pout; (fig) to pull a face.

**mouette** [mwɛt] nf (sea)gull.

**moufle** [mufl(ə)] nf (gant) mitt(en); (TECH) pulley block.

**mouflon** [muflɔ̃] nm mouf(f)lon.

**mouillage** [muja3] nm (NAVIG: lieu) anchorage, moorings pl.

**mouillé, e** [muje] a wet.

**mouiller** [muje] vt (humecter) to wet, moisten; (tremper): **~ qn/qch** to make sb/sth wet; (couper, diluer) to water down; (mine etc) to lay // vi (NAVIG) to lie ou be at anchor; **se ~** to get wet; (fam) to commit o.s.; to get o.s. involved; **~ l'ancre** to drop ou cast anchor; **mouillure** nf wet q; wet patch.

**moulage** [mula3] nm moulding, casting; (objet) cast.

**moule** [mul] nf mussel // nm (creux, CULIN) mould; (modèle plein) cast; **~ à gâteaux** nm cake tin.

**moulent** vb voir aussi **moudre**.

**mouler** [mule] vt (brique) to mould; (statue) to cast; (visage, bas-relief) to make a cast of; (lettre) to shape with care; (suj: vêtement) to hug, fit closely round; **~ qch sur** (fig) to model sth on.

**moulin** [mulɛ̃] nm mill; (fam) engine; **~ à café/à poivre** coffee/pepper mill; **~ à légumes** (vegetable) shredder; **~ à paroles** (fig) chatterbox; **~ à prières** prayer wheel; **~ à vent** windmill.

**moulinet** [mulinɛ] nm (de treuil) winch; (de canne à pêche) reel; (mouvement): **faire des ~s avec qch** to whirl sth around.

**moulinette** [mulinɛt] nf (vegetable) shredder.

**moulu, e** [muly] pp de **moudre**.

**moulure** [mulyʀ] nf (ornement) moulding.

**mourant, e** [muʀɑ̃, -ɑ̃t] a dying // nm/f dying man/woman.

**mourir** [muʀiʀ] vi to die; (civilisation) to die out; **~ de froid/faim** to die of exposure/hunger; **~ de faim/d'ennui** (fig) to be starving/be bored to death; **~ d'envie de faire** to be dying to do.

**mousquetaire** [muskətɛʀ] nm musketeer.

**mousqueton** [muskətɔ̃] nm (fusil) carbine; (anneau) snap-link, karabiner.

**mousse** [mus] nf (BOT) moss; (écume: sur eau, bière) froth, foam; (: shampooing) lather; (CULIN) mousse // nm (NAVIG) ship's boy; **bain de ~** bubble bath; **bas ~** stretch stockings; **balle ~** rubber ball; **~ carbonique** (fire-fighting) foam; **~ de nylon** stretch nylon; foam; **~ à raser** shaving foam.

**mousseline** [muslin] nf muslin; chiffon; **pommes ~** creamed potatoes.

**mousser** [muse] vi to foam; to lather.

**mousseux, euse** [musø, -øz] a frothy // nm: **(vin)** ~ sparkling wine.
**mousson** [musɔ̃] nf monsoon.
**moussu, e** [musy] a mossy.
**moustache** [mustaʃ] nf moustache; ~s nfpl (du chat) whiskers pl; **moustachu, e** a wearing a moustache.
**moustiquaire** [mustikɛʀ] nf mosquito net (ou screen).
**moustique** [mustik] nm mosquito.
**moutarde** [mutaʀd(ə)] nf mustard.
**mouton** [mutɔ̃] nm (ZOOL, péj) sheep inv; (peau) sheepskin; (CULIN) mutton; ~s nmpl (fig) white horses; fluffy ou fleecy clouds; bits of fluff.
**mouture** [mutyʀ] nf grinding; (péj) rehash.
**mouvant, e** [muvɑ̃, -ɑ̃t] a unsettled; changing; shifting.
**mouvement** [muvmɑ̃] nm (gén, aussi: mécanisme) movement; (fig) activity; impulse; reaction; gesture; (MUS: rythme) tempo (pl s); **en** ~ in motion; on the move; **mettre qch en** ~ to set sth in motion, set sth going; ~ **d'humeur** fit ou burst of temper; ~ **d'opinion** trend of (public) opinion; **le** ~ **perpétuel** perpetual, motion; **mouvementé, e** a (vie, poursuite) eventful; (réunion) turbulent.
**mouvoir** [muvwaʀ] vt (levier, membre) to move; (machine) to drive; **se** ~ to move.
**moyen, ne** [mwajɛ̃, -ɛn] a average; (tailles, prix) medium; (de grandeur moyenne) medium-sized // nm (façon) means sg, way // nf average; (MATH) mean; (SCOL: à l'examen) pass mark; (AUTO) average speed; ~s nmpl (capacités) means; **au** ~ **de** by means of; **y a-t-il** ~ **de ...?** is it possible to ...?, can one ...?; **par quel** ~? how?, which way?, by which means?; **par tous les** ~s by every possible means, every possible way; **employer les grands** ~s to resort to drastic measures; **par ses propres** ~s ali by oneself; **en** ~ne on (an) average; ~ **de locomotion/d'expression** means of transport/expression; ~ **âge** Middle Ages; ~**ne d'âge** average age.
**moyennant** [mwajɛnɑ̃] prép (somme) for; (service, conditions) in return for; (travail, effort) with.
**Moyen-Orient** [mwajɛnɔʀjɑ̃] nm: **le** ~ the Middle East.
**moyeu, x** [mwajø] nm hub.
**mû, mue** [my] pp de **mouvoir.**
**mucosité** [mykozite] nf mucus q.
**mucus** [mykys] nm mucus q.
**mue** [my] pp voir **mouvoir** // nf moulting; sloughing; breaking of the voice.
**muer** [mɥe] vi (oiseau, mammifère) to moult; (serpent) to slough; (jeune garçon): **il mue** his voice is breaking; **se** ~ **en** to transform into.
**muet, te** [mɥɛ, -ɛt] a dumb; (fig): ~ **d'admiration** etc speechless with admiration etc; (joie, douleur, CINÉMA) silent; (LING: lettre) silent, mute; (carte) blank // nm/f mute.
**mufle** [myfl(ə)] nm muzzle; (goujat) boor // a boorish.
**mugir** [myʒiʀ] vi to bellow; to low; (fig) to howl.

**muguet** [mygɛ] nm lily of the valley.
**mulâtre, tresse** [mylɑtʀ(ə), -tʀɛs] nm/f mulatto.
**mule** [myl] nf (ZOOL) (she-)mule; ~s nfpl (pantoufles) mules.
**mulet** [mylɛ] nm (ZOOL) (he-)mule; **muletier, ière** a: **chemin muletier** mule track.
**mulot** [mylo] nm field mouse (pl mice).
**multicolore** [myltikɔlɔʀ] a multicoloured.
**multinational, e, aux** [myltinasjɔnal, -o] a multinational.
**multiple** [myltipl(ə)] a multiple, numerous; (varié) many, manifold // nm (MATH) multiple.
**multiplicateur** [myltiplikatœʀ] nm multiplier.
**multiplication** [myltiplikɑsjɔ̃] nf multiplication.
**multiplicité** [myltiplisite] nf multiplicity.
**multiplier** [myltiplije] vt to multiply; **se** ~ vi to multiply; to increase in number.
**multitude** [myltityd] nf multitude; mass; **une** ~ **de** a vast number of, a multitude of.
**municipal, e, aux** [mynisipal, -o] a municipal; town cpd, ≈ borough cpd.
**municipalité** [mynisipalite] nf (corps municipal) town council, corporation; (commune) town, municipality.
**munir** [myniʀ] vt: ~ **qn/qch de** to equip sb/sth with.
**munitions** [mynisjɔ̃] nfpl ammunition sg.
**muqueuse** [mykøz] nf mucous membrane.
**mur** [myʀ] nm wall; ~ **du son** sound barrier.
**mûr, e** [myʀ] a ripe; (personne) mature // nf blackberry; mulberry.
**muraille** [myʀaj] nf (high) wall.
**mural, e, aux** [myʀal, -o] a wall cpd; mural.
**mûrement** [myʀmɑ̃] ad: **ayant** ~ **réfléchi** having given the matter much thought.
**murène** [myʀɛn] nf moray (eel).
**murer** [myʀe] vt (enclos) to wall (in); (porte, issue) to wall up; (personne) to wall up ou in.
**muret** [myʀɛ] nm low wall.
**mûrier** [myʀje] nm blackberry bush; mulberry tree.
**mûrir** [myʀiʀ] vi (fruit, blé) to ripen; (abcès, furoncle) to come to a head; (fig: idée, personne) to mature // vt to ripen; to (make) mature.
**murmure** [myʀmyʀ] nm murmur; ~s nmpl (plaintes) murmurings, mutterings; **murmurer** vi to murmur; (se plaindre) to mutter, grumble.
**musaraigne** [myzaʀɛɲ] nf shrew.
**musarder** [myzaʀde] vi to dawdle (along); to idle (about).
**musc** [mysk] nm musk.
**muscade** [myskad] nf nutmeg.
**muscat** [myska] nm muscat grape; muscatel (wine).
**muscle** [myskl(ə)] nm muscle; **musclé, e** a muscular; **musculation** nf: **exercices de musculation** muscle-developing exercises; **musculature** nf muscle structure, muscles pl.

**museau, x** [myzo] nm muzzle.

**musée** [myze] nm museum ; art gallery.

**museler** [myzle] vt to muzzle ; **muselière** nf muzzle.

**musette** [myzɛt] nf (sac) lunchbag // a inv (orchestre etc) accordion cpd.

**muséum** [myzeɔm] nm museum.

**musical, e, aux** [myzikal, -o] a musical.

**music-hall** [myzikol] nm variety theatre ; (genre) variety.

**musicien, ne** [myzisjɛ̃, -jɛn] nm/f musician.

**musique** [myzik] nf music ; (fanfare) band ; **faire de la** ~ to make some music ; to play an instrument ; ~ **de chambre** chamber music ; ~ **de fond** background music.

**musqué, e** [myske] a musky.

**musulman, e** [myzylmɑ̃, -an] a, nm/f Moslem, Muslim.

**mutation** [mytɑsjɔ̃] nf (ADMIN) transfer ; (BIO) mutation.

**muter** [myte] vt (ADMIN) to transfer.

**mutilation** [mytilɑsjɔ̃] nf mutilation.

**mutilé, e** [mytile] nm/f disabled person (through loss of limbs).

**mutiler** [mytile] vt to mutilate, maim ; (fig) to mutilate, deface.

**mutin, e** [mytɛ̃, -in] a (air, ton) mischievous, impish // nm/f (MIL, NAVIG) mutineer.

**mutiner** [mytine]: **se** ~ vi to mutiny ; **mutinerie** nf mutiny.

**mutisme** [mytism(ə)] nm silence.

**mutuel, le** [mytɥɛl] a mutual // nf mutual benefit society.

**myocarde** [mjɔkaʀd(ə)] nm voir **infarctus.**

**myope** [mjɔp] a short-sighted ; **myopie** nf short-sightedness, myopia.

**myosotis** [mjozɔtis] nm forget-me-not.

**myriade** [miʀjad] nf myriad.

**myrtille** [miʀtij] nf bilberry, whortleberry.

**mystère** [mistɛʀ] nm mystery ; **mystérieux, euse** a mysterious.

**mysticisme** [mistisism(ə)] nm mysticism.

**mystification** [mistifikɑsjɔ̃] nf hoax ; mystification.

**mystifier** [mistifje] vt to fool ; to mystify.

**mystique** [mistik] a mystic, mystical // nm/f mystic.

**mythe** [mit] nm myth ; **mythique** a mythical.

**mythologie** [mitɔlɔʒi] nf mythology ; **mythologique** a mythological.

**mythomane** [mitɔman] nm/f mythomaniac.

## N

**n'** [n] ad voir **ne.**

**nacelle** [nasɛl] nf (de ballon) basket.

**nacre** [nakʀ(ə)] nf mother of pearl ; **nacré, e** a pearly.

**nage** [naʒ] nf swimming ; style of swimming, stroke ; **tra-verser/s'éloigner à la** ~ to swim across/away ; **en** ~ bathed in perspiration.

**nageoire** [naʒwaʀ] nf fin.

**nager** [naʒe] vi to swim ; **nageur, euse** nm/f swimmer.

**naguère** [nagɛʀ] ad formerly.

**naïf, ïve** [naif, naiv] a naïve.

**nain, e** [nɛ̃, nɛn] nm/f dwarf.

**naissance** [nɛsɑ̃s] nf birth ; **donner** ~ **à** to give birth to ; (fig) to give rise to ; **aveugle de** ~ born blind ; **Français de** ~ French by birth ; **à la** ~ **des cheveux** at the roots of the hair.

**naissant, e** [nɛsɑ̃, -ɑ̃t] a budding, incipient ; dawning.

**naître** [nɛtʀ(ə)] vi to be born ; (conflit, complications): ~ **de** to arise from, be born out of ; ~ **à** (amour, poésie) to awaken to ; **il est né ,en 1960** he was born in 1960 ; **il naît plus de filles que de garçons** there are more girls born than boys ; **faire** ~ (fig) to give rise to, arouse.

**naïveté** [naivte] nf naïvety.

**nantir** [nɑ̃tiʀ] vt: ~ **qn de** to provide sb with ; **les nantis** (péj) the well-to-do.

**napalm** [napalm] nm napalm.

**nappe** [nap] nf tablecloth ; (fig) sheet ; layer ; ~**ron** nm table-mat.

**naquit** etc vb voir **naître.**

**narcisse** [naʀsis] nm narcissus.

**narcissisme** [naʀsisism(ə)] narcissism.

**narcotique** [naʀkɔtik] a, nm narcotic.

**narguer** [naʀge] vt to taunt.

**narine** [naʀin] nf nostril.

**narquois, e** [naʀkwa, -waz] a derisive, mocking.

**narrateur, trice** [naʀatœʀ, -tʀis] nm/f narrator.

**narrer** [naʀe] vt to tell the story of, recount.

**nasal, e, aux** [nazal, -o] a nasal.

**naseau, x** [nazo] nm nostril.

**nasiller** [nazije] vi to speak with a (nasal) twang.

**nasse** [nas] nf fish-trap.

**natal, e** [natal] a native.

**nataliste** [natalist(ə)] a supporting a rising birth rate.

**natalité** [natalite] nf birth rate.

**natation** [natɑsjɔ̃] nf swimming.

**natif, ive** [natif, -iv] a native.

**nation** [nɑsjɔ̃] nf nation ; **les N~s Unies** the United Nations.

**national, e, aux** [nasjɔnal, -o] a national // nf: (route) ~**e** trunk road, ≈ A road ; **obsèques** ~**es** state funeral ; ~**iser** vt to nationalize ; ~**isme** nm nationalism ; ~**ité** nf nationality.

**natte** [nat] nf (tapis) mat ; (cheveux) plait.

**naturaliser** [natyʀalize] vt to naturalize.

**naturaliste** [natyʀalist(ə)] nm/f naturalist.

**nature** [natyʀ] nf nature // a, ad (CULIN) plain, without seasoning or sweetening ; (café, thé) black, without sugar ; **payer en** ~ to pay in kind ; **peint d'après** ~ painted from life ; ~ **morte** still-life ; **naturel, le** a (gén, aussi: enfant) natural // nm naturalness ; disposition, nature ; (autochtone) native ; **naturellement** ad naturally ; (bien sûr) of course ; **naturisme** nm naturism ; **naturiste** nm/f naturist.

**naufrage** [nofʀaʒ] nm (ship)wreck ; (fig) wreck ; **faire** ~ to be shipwrecked ;

**naufragé, e** *nm/f* shipwreck victim, castaway.

**nauséabond, e** [nozeabɔ̃, -ɔ̃d] *a* foul, nauseous.

**nausée** [noze] *nf* nausea.

**nautique** [notik] *a* nautical, water *cpd.*

**nautisme** [notism] *nm* water sports.

**naval, e** [naval] *a* naval.

**navet** [navɛ] *nm* turnip; (*péj*) third-rate film.

**navette** [navɛt] *nf* shuttle; (*en car etc*) shuttle (service); **faire la ~ (entre)** to go to and fro *ou* shuttle (between).

**navigable** [navigabl(ə)] *a* navigable.

**navigateur** [navigatœR] *nm* (*NAVIG*) seafarer, sailor; (*AVIAT*) navigator.

**navigation** [navigɑsjɔ̃] *nf* navigation, sailing; shipping.

**naviguer** [navige] *vi* to navigate, sail.

**navire** [naviR] *nm* ship.

**navrer** [navRe] *vt* to upset, distress; **je suis navré** I'm so sorry.

**N.B.** *sigle* (= *nota bene*) NB.

**ne, n'** [n(ə)] *ad voir* **pas, plus, jamais** *etc*; (*explétif*) *non traduit.*

**né, e** [ne] *pp* (*voir* **naître**): **~ en 1960** born in 1960; **~e Scott** née Scott // *a:* **un comédien ~** a born comedian.

**néanmoins** [neɑ̃mwɛ̃] *ad* nevertheless, yet.

**néant** [neɑ̃] *nm* nothingness; **réduire à ~** to bring to nought; to dash.

**nébuleux, euse** [nebylø, -øz] *a* nebulous.

**nébulosité** [nebylozite] *nf* cloud cover; **~ variable** cloudy *ou* some cloud in places.

**nécessaire** [nesesɛR] *a* necessary // *nm* necessary; (*sac*) kit; **~ de couture** sewing kit; **~ de toilette** toilet bag; **nécessité** *nf* necessity; **nécessiter** *vt* to require; **nécessiteux, euse** *a* needy.

**nec plus ultra** [nekplysyltRa] *nm:* **le ~ de** the last word in.

**nécrologique** [nekRɔlɔʒik] *a:* **article ~** obituary; **rubrique ~** obituary column.

**nécromancien, ne** [nekRɔmɑ̃sjɛ̃, -jɛn] *nm/f* necromancer.

**nécrose** [nekRoz] *nf* necrosis.

**néerlandais, e** [neɛRlɑ̃dɛ, -ɛz] *a* Dutch.

**nef** [nɛf] *nf* (*d'église*) nave.

**néfaste** [nefast(ə)] *a* baneful; ill-fated.

**négatif, ive** [negatif, iv] *a* negative // *nm* (*PHOTO*) negative.

**négligé, e** [negliʒe] *a* (*en désordre*) slovenly // *nm* (*tenue*) negligee.

**négligence** [negliʒɑ̃s] *nf* carelessness *q*; careless omission.

**négligent, e** [negliʒɑ̃, -ɑ̃t] *a* careless.

**négliger** [negliʒe] *vt* (*épouse, jardin*) to neglect; (*tenue*) to be careless about; (*avis, précautions*) to disregard; **~ de faire** to fail to do, not bother to do; **se ~** to neglect o.s.

**négoce** [negɔs] *nm* trade.

**négociant** [negɔsjɑ̃] *nm* merchant.

**négociateur** [negɔsjatœR] *nm* negotiator.

**négociation** [negɔsjɑsjɔ̃] *nf* negotiation.

**négocier** [negɔsje] *vi, vt* to negotiate.

**nègre** [nɛgR(ə)] *nm* Negro; hack(writer) // *a* Negro.

**négresse** [negRɛs] *nf* Negro woman.

**neige** [nɛʒ] *nf* snow; **~ carbonique** dry ice; **neiger** *vi* to snow; **neigeux, euse** *a* snowy, snow-covered.

**nénuphar** [nenyfaR] *nm* water-lily.

**néologisme** [neɔlɔʒism(ə)] *nm* neologism.

**néon** [neɔ̃] *nm* neon.

**néophyte** [neɔfit] *nm/f* novice.

**néo-zélandais, e** [neɔzelɑ̃dɛ, -ɛz] *a* New Zealand *cpd* // *nm/f* New Zealander.

**nerf** [nɛR] *nm* nerve; (*fig*) vim, stamina; **nerveux, euse** *a* nervous; (*voiture*) nippy, responsive; (*tendineux*) sinewy; **nervosité** *nf* excitability; state of agitation; nervousness.

**nervure** [nɛRvyR] *nf* vein; (*ARCHIT, TECH*) rib.

**n'est-ce pas** [nɛspɑ] *ad* isn't it?, won't you? *etc, selon le verbe qui précède*; **~ que c'est bon?** it's good, don't you think?

**net, nette** [nɛt] *a* (*sans équivoque, distinct*) clear; (*évident*) definite; (*propre*) neat, clean; (*COMM: prix, salaire*) net // *ad* (*refuser*) flatly; **s'arrêter ~** to stop dead; **la lame a cassé ~** the blade snapped clean through; **mettre au ~** to copy out, tidy up; **~teté** *nf* clearness.

**nettoyage** [nɛtwajaʒ] *nm* cleaning; **~ à sec** dry cleaning.

**nettoyer** [nɛtwaje] *vi* to clean; (*fig*) to clean out.

**neuf** [nœf] *num* nine.

**neuf, neuve** [nœf, nœv] *a* new // *nm:* **repeindre à ~** to redecorate; **remettre à ~** to do up (as good as new), refurbish.

**neurasthénique** [nøRastenik] *a* neurasthenic.

**neurologie** [nøRɔlɔʒi] *nf* neurology.

**neutraliser** [nøtRalize] *vt* to neutralize.

**neutralité** [nøtRalite] *nf* neutrality.

**neutre** [nøtR(ə)] *a* neutral; (*LING*) neuter // *nm* (*LING*) neuter.

**neutron** [nøtRɔ̃] *nm* neutron.

**neuve** [nœv] *a voir* **neuf.**

**neuvième** [nœvjɛm] *num* ninth.

**névé** [neve] *nm* permanent snowpatch.

**neveu, x** [nəvø] *nm* nephew.

**névralgie** [nevRalʒi] *nf* neuralgia.

**névrite** [nevRit] *nf* neuritis.

**névrose** [nevRoz] *nf* neurosis; **névrosé, e** *a*, *nm/f* neurotic.

**nez** [ne] *nm* nose; **~ à ~ avec** face to face with.

**ni** [ni] *cj:* **~ l'un ~ l'autre ne sont** neither one nor the other are; **il n'a rien dit ~ fait** he hasn't said or done anything.

**niais, e** [njɛ, -ɛz] *a* silly, thick.

**niche** [niʃ] *nf* (*du chien*) kennel; (*de mur*) recess, niche.

**nichée** [niʃe] *nf* brood, nest.

**nicher** [niʃe] *vi* to nest; **se ~ dans** to lodge o.s. in; to hide in.

**nickel** [nikɛl] *nm* nickel.

**nicotine** [nikɔtin] *nf* nicotine.

**nid** [ni] *nm* nest; **~ de poule** pothole.

**nièce** [njɛs] *nf* niece.

**nième** [ɛnjɛm] *a:* **la ~ fois** the nth time.

**nier** [nje] *vt* to deny.

**nigaud, e** [nigo, -od] *nm/f* booby, fool.

**n'importe** [nɛ̃pɔʀt(ə)] *ad*: ~ **qui/quoi/où** anybody/anything/ anywhere ; ~ **quand** any time ; ~ **quel** any ; ~ **lequel/laquelle** any (one) ; ~ **comment** (*sans soin*) carelessly.

**nippes** [nip] *nfpl* togs.

**nippon, e** [nipɔ̃, -ɔn] *a* Japanese.

**nique** [nik] *nf*: **faire la** ~ **à** to thumb one's nose at (*fig*).

**nitouche** [nituʃ] *nf* (*péj*): **c'est une sainte** ~ she looks as if butter wouldn't melt in her mouth, she's a little hypocrite.

**nitrate** [nitʀat] *nm* nitrate.

**nitroglycérine** [nitʀogliseʀin] *nf* nitroglycerin(e).

**niveau, x** [nivo] *nm* level ; (*des élèves, études*) standard ; **de** ~ **(avec)** level (with) ; ~ **(à bulle)** spirit level ; **le** ~ **de la mer** sea level ; ~ **de vie** standard of living.

**niveler** [nivle] *vt* to level ; **nivellement** *nm* levelling.

**nobiliaire** [nɔbiljɛʀ] *a voir* **particule**.

**noble** [nɔbl(ə)] *a* noble // *nm/f* noble (man/woman) ; **noblesse** *nf* nobility ; (*d'une action etc*) nobleness.

**noce** [nɔs] *nf* wedding ; (*gens*) wedding party (*ou* guests *pl*) ; **faire la** ~ (*fam*) to go on a binge ; ~**s d'or/d'argent** golden/silver wedding.

**nocif, ive** [nɔsif, -iv] *a* harmful, noxious.

**noctambule** [nɔktɑ̃byl] *nm* night-bird, late-nighter.

**nocturne** [nɔktyʀn(ə)] *a* nocturnal // *nf* (*SPORT*) floodlit fixture.

**Noël** [nɔɛl] *nm* Christmas.

**nœud** [nø] *nm* (*de corde, du bois*, NAVIG) knot ; (*ruban*) bow ; (*fig: liens*) bond, tie ; ~ **coulant** noose ; ~ **papillon** bow tie.

**noir, e** [nwaʀ] *a* black ; (*obscur, sombre*) dark // *nm/f* black man/woman, Negro/Negro woman // *nm*: **dans le** ~ in the dark // *nf* (MUS) crotchet ; ~**ceur** *nf* blackness ; darkness ; ~**cir** *vt, vi* to blacken.

**noise** [nwaz] *nf*: **chercher** ~ **à** to try and pick a quarrel with.

**noisetier** [nwaztje] *nm* hazel.

**noisette** [nwazɛt] *nf* hazelnut.

**noix** [nwa] *nf* walnut ; (*fam*) twit ; (CULIN): **une** ~ **de beurre** a knob of butter ; **à la** ~ (*fam*) worthless ; ~ **de cajou** cashew nut ; ~ **de coco** coconut ; ~ **muscade** nutmeg.

**nom** [nɔ̃] *nm* name ; (LING) noun ; ~ **commun/propre** common/proper noun ; ~ **d'emprunt** assumed name ; ~ **de famille** surname ; ~ **de jeune fille** maiden name.

**nomade** [nɔmad] *a* nomadic // *nm/f* nomad.

**nombre** [nɔ̃bʀ(ə)] *nm* number ; **venir en** ~ to come in large numbers ; **depuis** ~ **d'années** for many years ; **ils sont au** ~ **de 3** there are 3 of them ; **au** ~ **de mes amis** among my friends ; ~ **premier/entier** prime/whole number.

**nombreux, euse** [nɔ̃bʀø, -øz] *a* many, numerous ; (*avec nom sg: foule etc*) large ; **peu** ~ few ; small

**nombril** [nɔ̃bʀi] *nm* navel.

**nomenclature** [nɔmɑ̃klatyʀ] *nf* wordlist ; list of items.

**nominal, e, aux** [nɔminal, -o] *a* nominal.

**nominatif** [nɔminatif] *nm* nominative.

**nomination** [nɔminɑsjɔ̃] *nf* nomination.

**nommément** [nɔmemɑ̃] *ad* (*désigner*) by name.

**nommer** [nɔme] *vt* (*baptiser*) to name, give a name to ; (*qualifier*) to call ; (*mentionner*) to name, give the name of ; (*élire*) to appoint, nominate ; **se** ~ : **il se nomme Pascal** his name's Pascal, he's called Pascal.

**non** [nɔ̃] *ad* (*réponse*) no ; (*avec loin, sans, seulement*) not ; ~ **que** not that ; ~ **plus** : **moi** ~ **plus** neither do I, I don't either.

**nonagénaire** [nɔnaʒenɛʀ] *nm/f* man/woman in his/her nineties.

**non-alcoolisé, e** [nɔnalkɔlize] *a* non-alcoholic.

**nonchalance** [nɔ̃ʃalɑ̃s] *nf* nonchalance, casualness.

**non-fumeur** [nɔ̃fymœʀ] *nm* non-smoker.

**non-lieu** [nɔ̃ljø] *nm*: **il y a eu** ~ the case was dismissed.

**nonne** [nɔn] *nf* nun.

**nonobstant** [nɔnɔpstɑ̃] *prép* notwithstanding.

**non-sens** [nɔ̃sɑ̃s] *nm* absurdity.

**nord** [nɔʀ] *nm* North // *a* northern ; north ; ~**-africain, e** *a, nm/f* North-African ; ~**-est** *nm* North-East ; **nordique** *a* nordic, northern European ; ~**-ouest** *nm* North-West.

**normal, e, aux** [nɔʀmal, -o] *a* normal // *nf*: **la** ~**e** the norm, the average ; ~**ement** *ad* normally ; ~**iser** *vi* (COMM, TECH) to standardize ; (POL) to normalize.

**normand, e** [nɔʀmɑ̃, -ɑ̃d] *a* of Normandy.

**Normandie** [nɔʀmɑ̃di] *nf* Normandy.

**norme** [nɔʀm(ə)] *nf* norm ; (TECH) standard.

**Norvège** [nɔʀvɛʒ] *nf* Norway ; **norvégien, ne** *a, nm, nf* Norwegian.

**nos** [no] *dét voir* **notre.**

**nostalgie** [nɔstalʒi] *nf* nostalgia.

**notable** [nɔtabl(ə)] *a* notable, noteworthy ; (*marqué*) noticeable, marked // *nm* prominent citizen.

**notaire** [nɔtɛʀ] *nm* notary ; solicitor.

**notamment** [nɔtamɑ̃] *ad* in particular, among others.

**notarié, e** [nɔtaʀje] *a*: **acte** ~ deed drawn up by a notary.

**note** [nɔt] *nf* (*écrite*, MUS) note ; (SCOL) mark ; (*facture*) bill ; **prendre** ~ **de** to write down ; to note ; ~ **de service** memorandum.

**noté, e** [nɔte] *a*: **être bien/mal** ~ (*employé etc*) to have a good/bad record.

**noter** [nɔte] *vt* (*écrire*) to write down ; (*remarquer*) to note, notice.

**notice** [nɔtis] *nf* summary, short article ; (*brochure*) leaflet, instruction book.

**notifier** [nɔtifje] *vt*: ~ **qch à qn** to notify sb of sth, notify sth to sb.

**notion** [nosjɔ̃] *nf* notion, idea.

**notoire** [nɔtwaʀ] *a* a widely known ; (*en mal*) notorious ; **le fait est** ~ **ou de notoriété publique** the fact is common knowledge.

**notre, nos** [nɔtʀ(ə), no] *dét* our.
**nôtre** [notʀ(ə)] *pronom*: **le/la** ~ ours ; **les** ~**s** ours ; *(alliés etc)* our own people ; **soyez des** ~**s** join us // ~ ours.
**nouer** [nwe] *vt* to tie, knot ; *(fig: alliance etc)* to strike up ; **sa gorge se noua** a lump came to her throat.
**noueux, euse** [nwø, -øz] *a* gnarled.
**nougat** [nuga] *nm* nougat.
**nouilles** [nuj] *nfpl* noodles ; pasta *sg*.
**nourri, e** [nuʀi] *a (feu etc)* sustained.
**nourrice** [nuʀis] *nf* wet-nurse.
**nourrir** [nuʀiʀ] *vt* to feed ; *(fig: espoir)* to harbour, nurse ; **logé nourri** with board and lodging ; ~ **au sein** to breast-feed ; **nourrissant, e** *a* nourishing, nutritious.
**nourrisson** [nuʀisɔ̃] *nm* (unweaned) infant.
**nourriture** [nuʀityʀ] *nf* food.
**nous** [nu] *pronom (sujet)* we ; *(objet)* us ; ~-**mêmes** ourselves.
**nouveau(nouvel), elle, x** [nuvo, -ɛl] *a* new // *nm/f* new pupil *(ou employee)* // *nf* (piece of) news *sg* ; *(LITTÉRATURE)* short story ; **de** ~, **à** ~ again ; **je suis sans nouvelles de lui** I haven't heard from him ; ~ **venu, nouvelle venue** *nm/f* newcomer ; **Nouvel An** New Year ; ~-**né, e** *nm/f* newborn baby ; **Nouvelle-Zélande** *nf* New Zealand ; ~**té** *nf* novelty ; *(COMM)* new film *(ou book ou creation etc)*.
**nouvel** *am*, **nouvelle** *af*, *nf* [nuvɛl] *voir* **nouveau.**
**novateur, trice** [nɔvatœʀ, -tʀis] *nm/f* innovator.
**novembre** [nɔvɑ̃bʀ(ə)] *nm* November.
**novice** [nɔvis] *a* inexperienced // *nm/f* novice.
**noyade** [nwajad] *nf* drowning *q*.
**noyau, x** [nwajo] *nm (de fruit)* stone ; *(BIO, PHYSIQUE)* nucleus ; *(ÉLEC, GÉO, fig: centre)* core ; ~**ter** *vt (POL)* to infiltrate
**noyé, e** [nwaje] *nm/f* drowning *(ou* drowned) man/woman.
**noyer** [nwaje] *nm* walnut (tree) ; *(bois)* walnut // *vt* to drown ; *(fig)* to flood ; to submerge ; **se** ~ to be drowned, drown ; *(suicide)* to drown o.s.
**nu, e** [ny] *a* naked ; *(membres)* naked, bare ; *(chambre, fil, plaine)* bare // *nm (ART)* nude ; **le** ~ **intégral** total nudity ; ~-**pieds** barefoot ; ~-**tête**, bareheaded ; **à mains** ~**es** with one's bare hands ; **se mettre** ~ to strip ; **mettre à** ~ to bare.
**nuage** [nɥaʒ] *nm* cloud ; **nuageux, euse** *a* cloudy.
**nuance** [nɥɑ̃s] *nf (de couleur, sens)* shade ; **il y a une** ~ **(entre)** there's a slight difference (between) ; **une** ~ **de tristesse** a tinge of sadness ; **nuancer** *vt (opinion)* to bring some reservations *ou* qualifications to.
**nubile** [nybil] *a* nubile.
**nucléaire** [nykleɛʀ] *a* nuclear.
**nudisme** [nydism] *nm* nudism ; **nudiste** *nm/f* nudist.
**nudité** [nydite] *nf* nudity, nakedness ; bareness.
**nuée** [nɥe] *nf*: **une** ~ **de** a cloud *ou* host *ou* swarm of.
**nues** [ny] *nfpl*: **tomber des** ~ to be taken aback ; **porter qn aux** ~ to praise sb to the skies.
**nuire** [nɥiʀ] *vi* to be harmful ; ~ **à** to harm, do damage to ; **nuisible** *a* harmful ; **animal nuisible** pest.
**nuit** [nɥi] *nf* night ; **il fait** ~ it's dark ; **cette** ~ last night ; tonight ; ~ **blanche** sleepless night ; ~ **de noces** wedding night ; **nuitamment** *ad* by night ; **nuitées** *nfpl* overnight stays, beds occupied *(in statistics)*.
**nul, nulle** [nyl] *a (aucun)* no ; *(minime)* nil, non-existent ; *(non valable)* null ; *(péj)* useless, hopeless // *pronom* none, no one ; **résultat** ~, **match** ~ draw ; ~**le part** *ad* nowhere ; ~**lement** *ad* by no means ; ~**lité** *nf* nullity ; hopelessness ; hopeless individual, nonentity.
**numéraire** [nymeʀɛʀ] *nm* cash ; metal currency.
**numération** [nymeʀasjɔ̃] *nf*: ~ **décimale/binaire** decimal/binary notation.
**numérique** [nymeʀik] *a* numerical.
**numéro** [nymeʀo] *nm* number ; *(spectacle)* act, turn ; ~**ter** *vt* to number.
**numismate** [nymismat] *nm/f* numismatist, coin collector.
**nuptial, e, aux** [nypsjal, -o] *a* nuptial ; wedding *cpd*.
**nuque** [nyk] *nf* nape of the neck.
**nutritif, ive** [nytʀitif, -iv] *a* nutritional ; *(aliment)* nutritious.
**nylon** [nilɔ̃] *nm* nylon.
**nymphomane** [nɛ̃fɔman] *nf* nymphomaniac.

## O

**oasis** [ɔazis] *nf* oasis *(pl* oases).
**obédience** [ɔbedjɑ̃s] *nf* allegiance.
**obéir** [ɔbeiʀ] *vi* to obey ; ~ **à** to obey ; *(suj: moteur, véhicule)* to respond to ; **obéissance** *nf* obedience ; **obéissant, e** *a* obedient.
**obélisque** [ɔbelisk(ə)] *nm* obelisk.
**obèse** [ɔbɛz] *a* obese ; **obésité** *nf* obesity.
**objecter** [ɔbʒɛkte] *vt (prétexter)* to plead, put forward as an excuse ; ~ **qch à** *(argument)* to put forward sth against ; ~ **(à qn) que** to object (to sb) that.
**objecteur** [ɔbʒɛktœʀ] *nm*: ~ **de conscience** conscientious objector.
**objectif, ive** [ɔbʒɛktif, -iv] *a* objective // *nm (OPTIQUE, PHOTO)* lens *sg*, objective ; *(MIL, fig)* objective ; ~ **à focale variable** zoom lens.
**objection** [ɔbʒɛksjɔ̃] *nf* objection ; ~ **de conscience** conscientious objection.
**objectivité** [ɔbʒɛktivite] *nf* objectivity.
**objet** [ɔbʒɛ] *nm* object ; *(d'une discussion, recherche)* subject ; **être** *ou* **faire l'**~ **de** *(discussion)* to be the subject of ; *(soins)* to be given *ou* shown ; **sans** ~ *a* purposeless ; groundless ; ~ **d'art** objet d'art ; ~ **personnels** personal items ; ~**s de toilette** toilet requisites ; ~**s trouvés** lost property *sg*.
**objurgations** [ɔbʒyʀgasjɔ̃] *nfpl* objurgations ; entreaties.
**obligation** [ɔbligasjɔ̃] *nf* obligation ; *(COMM)* bond, debenture ; **être dans l'**~ **de**

**faire** to be obliged to do ; **avoir l'~ de faire** to be under an obligation to do ; **obligatoire** *a* compulsory, obligatory.

**obligé, e** [ɔbliʒe] *a* (*redevable*): **être très ~ à qn** to be most obliged to sb ; **obligeance** *nf*: **avoir l'obligeance de** to be kind *ou* good enough to ; **obligeant, e** *a* obliging ; kind.

**obliger** [ɔbliʒe] *vt* (*contraindre*): **~ qn à faire** to force *ou* oblige sb to do ; (*JUR*: *engager*) to bind ; (*rendre service à*) to oblige ; **je suis bien obligé** I have to.

**oblique** [ɔblik] *a* oblique ; **regard ~** sidelong glance ; **en ~** *ad* diagonally ; **obliquer** *vi*: **obliquer vers** to turn off towards.

**oblitération** [ɔbliterɑsjɔ̃] *nf* cancelling *q*, cancellation.

**oblitérer** [ɔblitere] *vt* (*timbre-poste*) to cancel.

**oblong, oblongue** [ɔblɔ̃, -ɔ̃g] *a* oblong.

**obnubiler** [ɔbnybile] *vt* to obsess.

**obole** [ɔbɔl] *nf* offering.

**obscène** [ɔpsɛn] *a* obscene ; **obscénité** *nf* obscenity.

**obscur, e** [ɔpskyʀ] *a* dark ; (*fig*) obscure ; vague ; humble, lowly ; **~cir** *vt* to darken ; (*fig*) to obscure ; **s'~cir** *vi* to grow dark ; **~ité** *nf* darkness ; **dans l'~ité** in the dark, in darkness.

**obsédé, e** [ɔpsede] *nm/f*: **~(e) sexuel(le)** sex maniac.

**obséder** [ɔpsede] *vt* to obsess, haunt.

**obsèques** [ɔpsɛk] *nfpl* funeral *sg*.

**obséquieux, euse** [ɔpsekjø, -øz] *a* obsequious.

**observateur, trice** [ɔpsɛʀvatœʀ, -tʀis] *a* observant, perceptive // *nm/f* observer.

**observation** [ɔpsɛʀvɑsjɔ̃] *nf* observation ; (*d'un règlement etc*) observance ; (*commentaire*) observation, remark ; (*reproche*) reproof ; **en ~** (*MÉD*) under observation.

**observatoire** [ɔpsɛʀvatwaʀ] *nm* observatory ; (*lieu élevé*) observation post, vantage point.

**observer** [ɔpsɛʀve] *vt* (*regarder*) to observe, watch ; (*examiner*) to examine ; (*scientifiquement, aussi*: *règlement, jeûne etc*) to observe ; (*surveiller*) to watch ; (*remarquer*) to observe, notice ; **faire ~ qch à qn** (*dire*) to point out sth to sb.

**obsession** [ɔpsesjɔ̃] *nf* obsession ; **avoir l'~ de** to have an obsession with.

**obstacle** [ɔpstakl(ə)] *nm* obstacle ; (*ÉQUITATION*) jump, hurdle ; **faire ~ à** (*lumière*) to block out ; (*projet*) to hinder, put obstacles in the path of ; **~s antichars** tank defences.

**obstétrique** [ɔpstetʀik] *nf* obstetrics *sg*.

**obstination** [ɔpstinɑsjɔ̃] *nf* obstinacy.

**obstiné, e** [ɔpstine] *a* obstinate.

**obstiner** [ɔpstine]: **s'~** *vi* to insist, dig one's heels in ; **s'~ à faire** to persist (obstinately) in doing ; **s'~ sur qch** to keep working at sth, labour away at sth.

**obstruction** [ɔpstʀyksjɔ̃] *nf* obstruction, blockage ; (*SPORT*) obstruction ; **faire de l'~** (*fig*) to be obstructive.

**obstruer** [ɔpstʀye] *vt* to block, obstruct ; **s'~** *vi* to become blocked.

**obtempérer** [ɔptɑ̃peʀe] *vi* to obey ; **~ à** to obey, comply with.

**obtenir** [ɔptəniʀ] *vt* to obtain, get ; (*total, résultat*) to arrive at, reach ; to achieve, obtain ; **~ de pouvoir faire** to obtain permission to do ; **~ de qn qu'il fasse** to get sb to agree to do ; **obtention** *nf* obtaining.

**obturateur** [ɔptyʀatœʀ] *nm* (*PHOTO*) shutter ; **~ à rideau** focal plane shutter.

**obturation** [ɔptyʀɑsjɔ̃] *nf* closing (up) ; **~ (dentaire)** filling ; **vitesse d'~** (*PHOTO*) shutter speed.

**obturer** [ɔptyʀe] *vt* to close (up) ; (*dent*) to fill.

**obtus, e** [ɔpty, -yz] *a* obtuse.

**obus** [ɔby] *nm* shell.

**obvier** [ɔbvje]: **~ à** *vt* to obviate.

**O.C.** *sigle voir* **onde**.

**occasion** [ɔkɑzjɔ̃] *nf* (*aubaine, possibilité*) opportunity ; (*circonstance*) occasion ; (*COMM*: *article non neuf*) secondhand buy ; (: *acquisition avantageuse*) bargain ; **à plusieurs ~s** on several occasions ; **avoir l'~ de faire** to have the opportunity to do ; **être l'~ de** to occasion, give rise to ; **à l'~** *ad* sometimes, on occasions ; some time ; **d'~** *a*, *ad* secondhand ; **occasionnel, le** *a* (*fortuit*) chance *cpd*: (*non régulier*) occasional ; casual.

**occasionner** [ɔkazjone] *vt* to cause, bring about ; **~ qch à qn** to cause sb sth.

**occident** [ɔksidɑ̃] *nm*: **l'~** the west ; **occidental, e, aux** western ; (*POL*) Western // *nm/f* Westerner.

**occiput** [ɔksipyt] *nm* back of the head, occiput.

**occire** [ɔksiʀ] *vt* to slay.

**occitan, e** [ɔksitɑ̃, -an] *a* of the langue d'oc, of Provençal French.

**occlusion** [ɔklyzjɔ̃] *nf*: **~ intestinale** obstruction of the bowels.

**occulte** [ɔkylt(ə)] *a* occult, supernatural.

**occulter** [ɔkylte] *vt* (*fig*) to overshadow.

**occupant, e** [ɔkypɑ̃, -ɑ̃t] *a* occupying // *nm/f* (*d'un appartement*) occupier, occupant // *nm* (*MIL*) occupying forces *pl* ; (*POL*: *d'usine etc*) occupier.

**occupation** [ɔkypɑsjɔ̃] *nf* occupation.

**occupé, e** [ɔkype] *a* (*MIL, POL*) occupied ; (*personne*: *affairé, pris*) busy ; (*place, sièges*) taken ; (*toilettes, ligne*) engaged.

**occuper** [ɔkype] *vt* to occupy ; (*main-d'œuvre*) to employ ; **s'~** to occupy o.s., keep o.s. busy ; **s'~ de** (*être responsable de*) to be in charge of ; (*se charger de*: *affaire*) to take charge of, deal with ; (: *clients etc*) to attend to ; (*s'intéresser à, pratiquer*) to be involved in ; **ça occupe trop de place** it takes up too much room.

**occurrence** [ɔkyʀɑ̃s] *nf*: **en l'~** in this case.

**océan** [ɔseɑ̃] *nm* ocean ; **l'~ Indien** the Indian Ocean ; **l'Océanie** *nf* Oceania ; **océanique** *a* oceanic ; **océanographie** *nf* oceanography.

**ocelot** [ɔslo] *nm* ocelot ; (*fourrure*) ocelot fur.

**ocre** [ɔkʀ(ə)] *a inv* ochre.

**octane** [ɔktan] *nm* octane.

**octave** [ɔktav] *nf* octave.
**octobre** [ɔktɔbʀ(ə)] *nm* October.
**octogénaire** [ɔktɔʒenɛʀ] *a*, *nm/f* octogenarian.
**octogone** [ɔktɔgɔn] *nm* octagon.
**octroi** [ɔktʀwa] *nm* granting.
**octroyer** [ɔktʀwaje] *vt*: ~ qch à qn to grant sth to sb, grant sb sth.
**oculaire** [ɔkylɛʀ] *a* ocular, eye *cpd* // *nm* (*de microscope*) eyepiece.
**oculiste** [ɔkylist(ə)] *nm/f* eye specialist, oculist.
**ode** [ɔd] *nf* ode.
**odeur** [ɔdœʀ] *nf* smell.
**odieux, euse** [ɔdjø, -øz] *a* odious, hateful.
**odorant, e** [ɔdɔʀɑ̃, -ɑ̃t] *a* sweet-smelling, fragrant.
**odorat** [ɔdɔʀa] *nm* (sense of) smell.
**odoriférant, e** [ɔdɔʀifeʀɑ̃, -ɑ̃t] *a* sweet-smelling, fragrant.
**odyssée** [ɔdise] *nf* odyssey.
**œcuménique** [ekymenik] *a* oecumenical.
**œil** [œj], *pl* **yeux** [jø] *nm* eye ; à l' ~ (*fam*) for free ; à l' ~ **nu** with the naked eye ; **tenir qn à l'** ~ to keep an eye *ou* a watch on sb ; **avoir l'** ~ à to keep an eye on ; **faire de l'** ~ à qn to make eyes at sb ; **à l'** ~ **vif** with a lively expression ; **fermer les yeux (sur)** (*fig*) to turn a blind eye (to) ; **fermer l'** ~ to get a moment's sleep ; ~ **de verre** glass eye.
**œillade** [œjad] *nf*: **lancer une** ~ à qn to wink at sb, give sb a wink ; **faire des** ~s à to make eyes at.
**œillères** [œjɛʀ] *nfpl* blinkers.
**œillet** [œjɛ] *nm* (*BOT*) carnation ; (*trou*) eyelet.
**œnologue** [enɔlɔg] *nm/f* oenologist, wine expert.
**œsophage** [ezɔfaʒ] *nm* oesophagus.
**œuf** [œf, *pl* ø] *nm* egg ; **étouffer dans l'** ~ to nip in the bud ; ~ **à la coque/dur** boiled/hard-boiled egg ; ~ **au plat** fried egg ; ~**s brouillés** scrambled eggs ; ~ **de Pâques** Easter egg ; ~ **à repriser** darning egg.
**œuvre** [œvʀ(ə)] *nf* (*tâche*) task, undertaking ; (*ouvrage achevé, livre, tableau etc*) work ; (*ensemble de la production artistique*) works *pl* ; (*organisation charitable*) charity // *nm* (*d'un artiste*) works *pl* ; (*CONSTR*): **le gros** ~ the shell ; **être à l'** ~ to be at work ; **mettre en** ~ (*moyens*) to make use of ; ~ **d'art** work of art.
**offense** [ɔfɑ̃s] *nf* insult ; (*REL*: *péché*) transgression, trespass.
**offenser** [ɔfɑ̃se] *vt* to offend, hurt ; (*principes, Dieu*) to offend against ; **s'** ~ **de** to take offence at.
**offensif, ive** [ɔfɑ̃sif, -iv] *a*, *nf* offensive ; **passer à l'offensive** to go into the attack *ou* offensive.
**offert, e** [ɔfɛʀ, -ɛʀt(ə)] *pp de* **offrir**.
**offertoire** [ɔfɛʀtwaʀ] *nm* offertory.
**office** [ɔfis] *nm* (*charge*): office ; (*agence*) bureau, agency ; (*REL*) service // *nm ou nf* (*pièce*) pantry ; **faire** ~ **de** to act as ; to do duty as ; **d'** ~ *ad* automatically ; **bons** ~**s** (*POL*) good offices ; ~ **du tourisme** tourist bureau.

**officialiser** [ɔfisjalize] *vt* to make official.
**officiel, le** [ɔfisjɛl] *a*, *nm/f* official.
**officier** [ɔfisje] *nm* officer // *vi* to officiate ; ~ **de l'état-civil** registrar ; ~ **ministériel** member of the legal profession ; ~ **de police** ≈ police officer.
**officieux, euse** [ɔfisjø, -øz] *a* unofficial.
**officinal, e, aux** [ɔfisinal, -o] *a*: **plantes** ~**es** medicinal plants.
**officine** [ɔfisin] *nf* (*de pharmacie*) dispensary ; (*pharmacie*) pharmacy ; (*gén péj*: *bureau*) agency, office.
**offrande** [ɔfʀɑ̃d] *nf* offering.
**offrant** [ɔfʀɑ̃] *nm*: **au plus** ~ to the highest bidder.
**offre** [ɔfʀ(ə)] *nf* offer ; (*aux enchères*) bid ; (*ADMIN*: *soumission*) tender ; (*ÉCON*): **l'** ~ supply ; ~ **d'emploi** job advertised ; '~**s d'emploi'** situations vacant ; ~ **publique d'achat** (**O.P.A.**) takeover bid ; ~**s de service** offer of service.
**offrir** [ɔfʀiʀ] *vt* to offer ; (*faire cadeau de*): ~ **(à qn)** to give (to sb) ; **s'** ~ *vi* (*occasion, paysage*) to present itself // *vt* (*vacances, voiture*) to treat o.s. to ; ~ **(à qn) de faire** qch to offer to do sth (for sb) ; ~ **à boire à qn** to offer sb a drink ; **s'** ~ **comme guide/en otage** to offer one's services as (a) guide/offer o.s. as hostage ; **s'** ~ **aux regards** (*suj*: *personne*) to expose o.s. to the public gaze.
**offset** [ɔfsɛt] *nm* offset (printing).
**offusquer** [ɔfyske] *vt* to offend ; **s'** ~ **de** to take offence at, be offended by.
**ogive** [ɔʒiv] *nf* (*ARCHIT*) diagonal rib ; (*d'obus, de missile*) nose cone ; **voûte en** ~ rib vault ; **arc en** ~ lancet arch ; ~ **nucléaire** nuclear warhead.
**ogre** [ɔgʀ(ə)] *nm* ogre.
**oie** [wa] *nf* (*ZOOL*) goose (*pl* geese).
**oignon** [ɔɲɔ̃] *nm* (*BOT, CULIN*) onion ; (*de tulipe etc*: *bulbe*) bulb ; (*MÉD*) bunion ; **petits** ~**s** pickling onions.
**oindre** [wɛ̃dʀ(ə)] *vt* to anoint.
**oiseau, x** [wazo] *nm* bird ; ~ **de proie** bird of prey ; ~-**mouche** *nm* hummingbird.
**oiselier** [wazəlje] *nm* bird shop.
**oiseux, euse** [wazø, -øz] *a* pointless ; trivial.
**oisif, ive** [wazif, -iv] *a* idle // *nm/f* (*péj*) man/woman of leisure ; **oisiveté** *nf* idleness.
**O.K.** [ɔkɛ] *excl* O.K., all right.
**oléagineux, euse** [ɔleaʒinø, -øz] *a* oleaginous, oil-producing.
**oléoduc** [ɔleɔdyk] *nm* (oil) pipeline.
**olfactif, ive** [ɔlfaktif, -iv] *a* olfactory.
**oligarchie** [ɔligaʀʃi] *nf* oligarchy.
**olivâtre** [ɔlivɑtʀ(ə)] *a* olive-greenish ; (*teint*) sallow.
**olive** [ɔliv] *nf* (*BOT*) olive // *a inv* olive(-green) ; ~**raie** *nf* olive grove ; **olivier** *nm* olive tree ; (*bois*) olive wood.
**olympiade** [ɔlɛ̃pjad] *nf* (*période*) Olympiad ; **les** ~**s** (*jeux*) the Olympiad *sg*.
**olympien, ne** [ɔlɛ̃pjɛ̃, -jɛn] *a* Olympian, of Olympian aloofness.
**olympique** [ɔlɛ̃pik] *a* Olympic.
**ombilical, e, aux** [ɔ̃bilikal, -o] *a* umbilical.

**ombrage** [ɔ̃bʀaʒ] *nm* (*ombre*) (leafy) shade; (*fig*): **prendre** ~ **de** to take umbrage *ou* offence at; **ombragé, e** *a* shaded, shady; **ombrageux, euse** *a* (*cheval*) skittish, nervous; (*personne*) touchy, easily offended.

**ombre** [ɔ̃bʀ(ə)] *nf* (*espace non ensoleillé*) shade; (*ombre portée, tache*) shadow; **à l'**~ in the shade; (*fam*) behind bars; **à l'**~ **de** in the shade of; (*tout près de, fig*) in the shadow of; **tu me fais de l'**~ you're in my light; **ça nous donne de l'**~ it gives us (some) shade; **vivre dans l'**~ (*fig*) to live in obscurity; **laisser dans l'**~ (*fig*) to leave in the dark; ~ **à paupières** eyeshadow; ~ **portée** shadow; ~**s chinoises** (*spectacle*) shadow show *sg.*

**ombrelle** [ɔ̃bʀɛl] *nf* parasol, sunshade.

**omelette** [ɔmlɛt] *nf* omelette; ~ **au fromage/au jambon** cheese/ham omelette; ~ **aux herbes** omelette with herbs.

**omettre** [ɔmɛtʀ(ə)] *vt* to omit, leave out; ~ **de faire** to fail *ou* omit to do; **omission** *nf* omission.

**omni...** [ɔmni] *préfixe*: ~**bus** *nm* slow *ou* stopping train; ~**potent, e** *a* omnipotent; ~**scient, e** *a* omniscient; ~**vore** *a* omnivorous.

**omoplate** [ɔmɔplat] *nf* shoulder blade.

**O.M.S.** *sigle f voir* **organisation.**

**on** [ɔ̃] *pronom* (*indéterminé*): ~ **peut le faire ainsi** you *ou* one can do it like this, it can be done like this; (*quelqu'un*): ~ **les a attaqués** they were attacked; (*nous*): ~ **va y aller demain** we're going tomorrow; (*les gens*): **autrefois,** ~ **croyait aux fantômes** they used to believe in ghosts years ago; ~ **vous demande au téléphone** there's a phone call for you, there's somebody on the phone for you; ~ **ne peut plus** *ad*: ~ **ne peut plus stupide** as stupid as can be.

**oncle** [ɔ̃kl(ə)] *nm* uncle.

**onctueux, euse** [ɔ̃ktɥø, -øz] *a* creamy, smooth; (*fig*) smooth, unctuous.

**onde** [ɔ̃d] *nf* (*PHYSIQUE*) wave; **sur l'**~ on the waters; **sur les** ~**s** on the radio; **mettre en** ~**s** to produce for the radio; **sur** ~**s courtes (o.c.)** on short wave *sg*; **moyennes/ longues** ~**s** medium/long wave *sg.*

**ondée** [ɔ̃de] *nf* shower.

**on-dit** [ɔ̃di] *nm inv* rumour.

**ondoyer** [ɔ̃dwaje] *vi* to ripple, wave.

**ondulant, e** [ɔ̃dylɑ̃, -ɑ̃t] *a* swaying; undulating.

**ondulation** [ɔ̃dylɑsjɔ̃] *nf* undulation.

**onduler** [ɔ̃dyle] *vi* to undulate; (*cheveux*) to wave.

**onéreux, euse** [ɔneʀø, -øz] *a* costly; **à titre** ~ in return for payment.

**ongle** [ɔ̃gl(ə)] *nm* (*ANAT*) nail; **se faire les** ~ **s** to do one's nails.

**onglet** [ɔ̃glɛ] *nm* (*rainure*) (thumbnail) groove; (*bande de papier*) tab.

**onguent** [ɔ̃gɑ̃] *nm* ointment.

**onomatopée** [ɔnɔmatɔpe] *nf* onomatopoeia.

**ont** *vb voir* **avoir.**

**O.N.U.** [ɔny] *sigle f voir* **organisation.**

**onyx** [ɔniks] *nm* onyx.

**onze** [ɔ̃z] *num* eleven; **onzième** *num* eleventh.

**O.P.A.** *sigle f voir* **offre.**

**opacité** [ɔpasite] *nf* opaqueness.

**opale** [ɔpal] *nf* opal.

**opalin, e** [ɔpalɛ̃, -in] *a*, *nf* opaline.

**opaque** [ɔpak] *a* opaque.

**O.P.E.P.** [ɔpɛp] *sigle f* (= *organisation des pays exportateurs de pétrole*) O.P.E.C. (organization of petroleum exporting countries).

**opéra** [ɔpeʀa] *nm* opera; (*édifice*) opera house; ~**-comique** *nm* light opera, opéra comique.

**opérateur, trice** [ɔpeʀatœʀ, -tʀis] *nm/f* operator; ~ **(de prise de vues)** cameraman.

**opération** [ɔpeʀɑsjɔ̃] *nf* operation; (*COMM*) dealing.

**opératoire** [ɔpeʀatwaʀ] *a* operating; (*choc etc*) post-operative.

**opéré, e** [ɔpeʀe] *nm/f* patient (*having undergone an operation*).

**opérer** [ɔpeʀe] *vt* (*MÉD*) to operate on; (*faire, exécuter*) to carry out, make // *vi* (*remède: faire effet*) to act, work; (*procéder*) to proceed; (*MÉD*) to operate; **s'**~ *vi* (*avoir lieu*) to occur, take place; **se faire** ~ to have an operation; **se faire** ~ **des amygdales/du cœur** to have one's tonsils out/have a heart operation.

**opérette** [ɔpeʀɛt] *nf* operetta, light opera.

**ophtalmologie** [ɔftalmɔlɔʒi] *nf* ophthalmology; **ophtalmologue** *nm/f* ophthalmologist.

**opiner** [ɔpine] *vi*: ~ **de la tête** to nod assent.

**opiniâtre** [ɔpinjɑtʀ(ə)] *a* stubborn.

**opinion** [ɔpinjɔ̃] *nf* opinion; **l'**~ **(publique)** public opinion.

**opium** [ɔpjɔm] *nm* opium.

**opportun, e** [ɔpɔʀtœ̃, -yn] *a* timely, opportune; **en temps** ~ **at** the appropriate time; **opportunisme** *nm* opportunism; **opportuniste** *a*, *nm/f* opportunist; **opportunité** *nf* timeliness, opportuneness.

**opposant, e** [ɔpozɑ̃, -ɑ̃t] *a* opposing; ~**s** *nmpl* opponents.

**opposé, e** [ɔpoze] *a* (*direction, rive*) opposite; (*faction*) opposing; (*couleurs*) contrasting; (*opinions, intérêts*) conflicting; (*contre*): ~ **à** opposed to, against // *nm*: **l'**~ the other *ou* opposite side (*ou* direction); (*contraire*) the opposite; **à l'**~ (*fig*) on the other hand; **à l'**~ **de** on the other *ou* opposite side from; (*fig*) contrary to, unlike.

**opposer** [ɔpoze] *vt* (*meubles, objets*) to place opposite each other; (*personnes, armées, équipes*) to oppose; (*couleurs, termes, tons*) to contrast; ~ **qch à** (*comme obstacle, défense*) to set sth against; (*comme objection*) to put sth forward against; to put up sth to; (*en contraste*) to set sth opposite; to match sth with; **s'**~ (*sens réciproque*) to conflict; to clash; to face each other; to contrast; **s'**~ **à** (*interdire, empêcher*) to oppose; (*tenir tête à*) to rebel against; **sa religion s'y oppose**

it's against his religion ; **s'~ à ce que qn fasse** to be opposed to sb's doing.

**opposition** [ɔpozisjɔ̃] *nf* opposition ; **par ~ à** as opposed to, in contrast with ; **entrer en ~ avec** to come into conflict with ; **être en ~ avec** (*idées, conduite*) to be at variance with ; **faire ~ à un chèque** to stop a cheque.

**oppresser** [ɔprese] *vt* to oppress ; **oppresseur** *nm* oppressor ; **oppressif, ive** *a* oppressive ; **oppression** *nf* oppression ; (*malaise*) feeling of suffocation.

**opprimer** [ɔprime] *vt* to oppress ; (*liberté, opinion*) to suppress, stifle ; (*suj: chaleur etc*) to suffocate, oppress.

**opprobre** [ɔprɔbr(ə)] *nm* disgrace.

**opter** [ɔpte] *vi* : **~ pour** to opt for ; **~ entre** to choose between.

**opticien, ne** [ɔptisjɛ̃, -ɛn] *nm/f* optician.

**optimal, e, aux** [ɔptimal, -o] *a* optimal.

**optimisme** [ɔptimism(ə)] *nm* optimism ; **optimiste** *nm/f* optimist.

**optimum** [ɔptimɔm] *a* optimum.

**option** [ɔpsjɔ̃] *nf* option ; **matière à ~** (*scol*) optional subject ; **prendre une ~ sur** to take (out) an option on.

**optique** [ɔptik] *a* (*nerf*) optic ; (*verres*) optical // *nf* (*photo: lentilles etc*) optics *pl* ; (*science, industrie*) optics *sg* ; (*fig: manière de voir*) perspective.

**opulence** [ɔpylɑ̃s] *nf* wealth, opulence.

**opulent, e** [ɔpylɑ̃, -ɑ̃t] *a* wealthy, opulent ; (*formes, poitrine*) ample, generous.

**or** [ɔr] *nm* gold // *cj* now, but ; **en ~** gold *cpd* ; (*fig*) golden, marvellous ; **d'~** (*fig*) golden.

**oracle** [ɔrɑkl(ə)] *nm* oracle.

**orage** [ɔraʒ] *nm* (thunder)storm ; **orageux, euse** *a* stormy.

**oraison** [ɔrɛzɔ̃] *nf* orison, prayer ; **~ funèbre** funeral oration.

**oral, e, aux** [ɔral, -o] *a, nm* oral ; **~ement** *ad* orally.

**orange** [ɔrɑ̃ʒ] *nf, a inv* orange ; **orangé, e** *a* orangey, orange-coloured ; **orangeade** *nf* orangeade ; **oranger** *nm* orange tree ; **~raie** *nf* orange grove ; **~rie** *nf* orangery.

**orateur** [ɔratœr] *nm* speaker ; orator.

**oratoire** [ɔratwar] *nm* oratory ; wayside shrine // *a* oratorical.

**orbital, e, aux** [ɔrbital, -o] *a* orbital.

**orbite** [ɔrbit] *nf* (*anat*) (eye-)socket ; (*physique*) orbit ; **mettre sur ~** to put into orbit ; (*fig*) to launch ; **dans l'~ de** (*fig*) within the sphere of influence of.

**orchestration** [ɔrkɛstrasjɔ̃] *nf* orchestration.

**orchestre** [ɔrkɛstr(ə)] *nm* orchestra ; (*de jazz, danse*) band ; (*places*) stalls *pl* ; **orchestrer** *vt* (*mus*) to orchestrate ; (*fig*) to mount, stage-manage.

**orchidée** [ɔrkide] *nf* orchid.

**ordinaire** [ɔrdinɛr] *a* ordinary ; everyday ; standard // *nm* ordinary ; (*menus*) everyday fare // *nf* (*essence*) ≈ two-star (petrol) ; **d'~** usually, normally ; **à l'~** usually, ordinarily.

**ordinal, e, aux** [ɔrdinal, -o] *a* ordinal.

**ordinateur** [ɔrdinatœr] *nm* computer.

**ordination** [ɔrdinasjɔ̃] *nf* ordination.

**ordonnance** [ɔrdɔnɑ̃s] *nf* organization ; layout ; (*méd*) prescription ; (*jur*) order ; (*mil*) orderly, batman ; **d'~** (*mil*) regulation *cpd*.

**ordonné, e** [ɔrdɔne] *a* tidy, orderly ; (*math*) ordered // *nf* (*math*) ordinate, Y-axis.

**ordonner** [ɔrdɔne] *vt* (*agencer*) to organize, arrange ; (: *meubles, appartement*) to lay out, arrange ; (*donner un ordre*): **~ à qn de faire** to order sb to do ; (*math*) to (arrange in) order ; (*rel*) to ordain ; (*méd*) to prescribe ; (*jur*) to order.

**ordre** [ɔrdr(ə)] *nm* (*gén*) order ; (*propreté et soin*) orderliness, tidiness ; (*nature*): **d'~ pratique** of a practical nature ; **~s** *nmpl* (*rel*) holy orders ; **mettre en ~** to tidy (up), put in order ; **avoir de l'~** to be tidy ou orderly ; **mettre bon ~ à** to put to rights, sort out ; **être aux ~s de qn/sous les ~s de qn** to be at sb's disposal/under sb's command ; **jusqu'à nouvel ~** until further notice ; **dans le même ~ d'idées** in this connection ; **donnez-nous un ~ de grandeur** give us some idea as regards size (*ou* the amount) ; **de premier ~** first-rate ; **~ du jour** (*d'une réunion*) agenda ; (*mil*) order of the day ; **à l'~ du jour** on the agenda ; (*fig*) topical ; (*mil: citer*) in dispatches ; **~ de route** marching orders *pl*.

**ordure** [ɔrdyr] *nf* filth *q* ; **~s** (*balayures, déchets*) rubbish *sg*, refuse *sg* ; **~s ménagères** household refuse ; **ordurier, ière** *a* lewd, filthy.

**oreille** [ɔrɛj] *nf* (*anat*) ear ; (*de marmite, tasse*) handle ; **avoir de l'~** to have a good ear (for music).

**oreiller** [ɔreje] *nm* pillow.

**oreillette** [ɔrɛjɛt] *nf* (*anat*) auricle.

**oreillons** [ɔrɛjɔ̃] *nmpl* mumps *sg*.

**ores** [ɔr]: **d'~ et déjà** *ad* already.

**orfèvre** [ɔrfɛvr(ə)] *nm* goldsmith ; silversmith ; **orfèvrerie** *nf* goldsmith's (*ou* silversmith's) trade ; (*ouvrage*) gold (*ou* silver) plate.

**orfraie** [ɔrfrɛ] *nm* white-tailed eagle ; **pousser des cris d'** to yell at the top of one's voice.

**organe** [ɔrgan] *nm* organ ; (*porte-parole*) representative, mouthpiece ; **~s de commande** (*tech*) controls ; **~s de transmission** (*tech*) transmission system *sg*.

**organigramme** [ɔrganigram] *nm* organization chart ; flow chart.

**organique** [ɔrganik] *a* organic.

**organisateur, trice** [ɔrganizatœr, -tris] *nm/f* organizer.

**organisation** [ɔrganizasjɔ̃] *nf* organization ; **O~ des Nations Unies (O.N.U.)** United Nations (Organization) (U.N., U.N.O.) ; **O~ mondiale de la santé (O.M.S.)** World Health Organization (W.H.O.) ; **O~ du traité de l'Atlantique Nord (O.T.A.N.)** North Atlantic Treaty Organization (N.A.T.O.).

**organiser** [ɔrganize] *vt* to organize ; (*mettre sur pied: service etc*) to set up ; **s'~** to get organized.

**organisme** [ɔrganism(ə)] *nm* (*bio*)

organism ; (*corps humain*) body ; (*ADMIN, POL etc*) body, organism.

**organiste** [ɔʀganist(ə)] *nm/f* organist.

**orgasme** [ɔʀgasm(ə)] *nm* orgasm, climax.

**orge** [ɔʀʒ(ə)] *nf* barley.

**orgelet** [ɔʀʒəlɛ] *nm* sty(e).

**orgie** [ɔʀʒi] *nf* orgy.

**orgue** [ɔʀg(ə)] *nm* organ ; ~s *nfpl* organ *sg* ; ~ **de Barbarie** barrel *ou* street organ.

**orgueil** [ɔʀɡœj] *nm* pride ; **orgueilleux, euse** *a* proud.

**Orient** [ɔʀjɑ̃] *nm*: l'~ the East, the Orient.

**orientable** [ɔʀjɑ̃tabl(ə)] *a* adjustable.

**oriental, e, aux** [ɔʀjɑ̃tal, -o] *a* oriental, eastern ; (*frontière*) eastern // *nm/f*: O~, e Oriental.

**orientation** [ɔʀjɑ̃tasjɔ̃] *nf* positioning ; adjustment ; orientation ; direction ; (*d'un journal*) leanings *pl* ; **avoir le sens de l'**~ to have a (good) sense of direction ; ~ **professionnelle** careers advising ; careers advisory service.

**orienté, e** [ɔʀjɑ̃te] *a* (*fig: article, journal*) slanted ; **bien/mal** ~ (*appartement*) well/badly positioned ; ~ **au sud** facing south *ou* with a southern aspect.

**orienter** [ɔʀjɑ̃te] *vt* (*situer*) to position ; (*placer, disposer: pièce mobile*) to adjust, position ; (*tourner*) to direct, turn ; (*voyageur, touriste, recherches*) to direct ; (*fig: élève*) to orientate ; **s'**~ (*se repérer*) to find one's bearings ; **s'**~ **vers** (*fig*) to turn towards ; **orienteur** *nm* (*SCOL*) careers adviser.

**orifice** [ɔʀifis] *nm* opening, orifice.

**oriflamme** [ɔʀiflam] *nf* banner, standard.

**origan** [ɔʀigɑ̃] *nm* (*CULIN*) oregano.

**originaire** [ɔʀiʒinɛʀ] *a* original ; **être** ~ **de** to be a native of ; (*provenir de*) to originate from ; to be native to.

**original, e, aux** [ɔʀiʒinal, -o] *a* original ; (*bizarre*) eccentric // *nm/f* eccentric // *nm* (*document etc, ART*) original ; (*dactylographie*) top copy ; ~**ité** *nf* originality *q* ; eccentricity.

**origine** [ɔʀiʒin] *nf* origin ; **d'**~ of origin ; (*pneus etc*) original ; (*bureau postal*) dispatching ; **dès l'**~ at *ou* from the outset ; **à l'**~ originally ; **avoir son** ~ **dans** to have its origins in, originate in ; **originel, le** *a* original.

**oripeaux** [ɔʀipo] *nmpl* rags.

**O.R.L.** *nm/f ou titre* = **oto-rhino-laryngologiste**.

**orme** [ɔʀm(ə)] *nm* elm.

**orné, e** [ɔʀne] *a* ornate.

**ornement** [ɔʀnəmɑ̃] *nm* ornament ; (*fig*) embellishment, adornment ; ~**s sacerdotaux** vestments ; **ornemental, e, aux** *a* ornamental ; **ornementer** *vt* to ornament.

**orner** [ɔʀne] *vt* to decorate, adorn ; ~ **qch de** to decorate sth with.

**ornière** [ɔʀnjɛʀ] *nf* rut.

**ornithologie** [ɔʀnitɔlɔʒi] *nf* ornithology.

**orphelin, e** [ɔʀfəlɛ̃, -in] *a* orphan(ed) // *nm/f* orphan ; ~ **de père/mère** fatherless/motherless ; **orphelinat** *nm* orphanage.

**O.R.S.E.C.** [ɔʀsɛk] *sigle* (= *organisation*

*des secours*): **le plan** ~ disaster contingency plan.

**orteil** [ɔʀtɛj] *nm* toe ; **gros** ~ big toe.

**O.R.T.F.** *sigle m* = *Office de la radiodiffusion et télévision française* (*the French broadcasting corporation*).

**orthodoxe** [ɔʀtɔdɔks(ə)] *a* orthodox ; **orthodoxie** *nf* orthodoxy.

**orthographe** [ɔʀtɔgʀaf] *nf* spelling ; **orthographier** *vt* to spell ; **mal orthographié** misspelt.

**orthopédie** [ɔʀtɔpedi] *nf* orthopaedics *sg* ; **orthopédique** *a* orthopaedic ; **orthopédiste** *nm/f* orthopaedic specialist.

**ortie** [ɔʀti] *nf* (stinging) nettle.

**os** [ɔs, *pl* o] *nm* bone ; **sans** ~ (*BOUCHERIE*) off the bone, boned ; ~ **à moelle** marrowbone.

**O.S.** *sigle m voir* **ouvrier**.

**oscillation** [ɔsilɑsjɔ̃] *nf* oscillation ; ~**s** *nfpl* (*fig*) fluctuations.

**osciller** [ɔsile] *vi* (*pendule*) to swing ; (*au vent etc*) to rock ; (*TECH*) to oscillate ; (*fig*): ~ **entre** to waver *ou* fluctuate between.

**osé, e** [oze] *a* daring, bold.

**oseille** [ozɛj] *nf* sorrel.

**oser** [oze] *vi, vt* to dare ; ~ **faire** to dare (to) do.

**osier** [ozje] *nm* willow ; **d'**~, **en** ~ wicker(work).

**ossature** [osatyʀ] *nf* (*ANAT*) frame, skeletal structure ; (: *du visage*) bone structure ; (*fig*) framework.

**osselet** [ɔslɛ] *nm* (*ANAT*) ossicle ; **jouer aux** ~**s** to play knucklebones.

**ossements** [ɔsmɑ̃] *nmpl* bones.

**osseux, euse** [ɔsø, -øz] *a* bony ; (*tissu, maladie, greffe*) bone *cpd*.

**ossifier** [ɔsifje]: **s'**~ *vi* to ossify.

**ossuaire** [ɔsɥɛʀ] *nm* ossuary.

**ostensible** [ɔstɑ̃sibl(ə)] *a* conspicuous.

**ostensoir** [ɔstɑ̃swaʀ] *nm* monstrance.

**ostentation** [ɔstɑ̃tɑsjɔ̃] *nf* ostentation ; **faire** ~ **de** to parade, make a display of.

**ostracisme** [ɔstʀasism(ə)] *nm* ostracism ; **frapper d'**~ to ostracize.

**ostréiculture** [ɔstʀeikyltyʀ] *nf* oyster-farming.

**otage** [ɔtaʒ] *nm* hostage ; **prendre qn comme** ~ to take sb hostage.

**O.T.A.N.** [ɔtɑ̃] *sigle f voir* **organisation**.

**otarie** [ɔtaʀi] *nf* sea-lion.

**ôter** [ote] *vt* to remove ; (*soustraire*) to take away ; ~ **qch à qn** to take sth (away) from sb ; ~ **qch de** to remove sth from.

**otite** [ɔtit] *nf* ear infection.

**oto-rhino(-laryngologiste)** [ɔtɔʀinɔ-(laʀɛ̃gɔlɔʒist(ə))] *nm/f* ear nose and throat specialist.

**ou** [u] *cj* or ; ~ ... ~ either ... or ; ~ **bien** or (else).

**où** [u] *ad, pronom* where ; (*dans lequel*) in which, into which ; from which, out of which ; (*sur lequel*) on which ; (*sens de 'que'*): **au train** ~ **ça va/prix** ~ **c'est** at the rate it's going/price it is ; **le jour** ~ **il est parti** the day (that) he left ; **par** ~ **passer?** which way should we go? ; **les villes par** ~ **il est passé** the towns he went through ; **le village d'**~ **je viens** the village I come from ; **la chambre** ~ **il était**

the room he was in; **d'~ vient qu'il est parti?** how come he left?

**ouate** [wat] *nf* cotton wool; (*bourre*) padding, wadding; **ouaté, e** *a* cotton-wool; (*doublé*) quilted; (*fig*) cocoon-like; muffled.

**oubli** [ubli] *nm* (*acte*): **l'~ de** forgetting; (*étourderie*) forgetfulness *q*; (*négligence*) omission, oversight; (*absence de souvenirs*) oblivion; **~ de soi** self-effacement, self-negation.

**oublier** [ublije] *vt* (*gén*) to forget; (*ne pas voir: erreurs etc*) to miss; (*ne pas mettre: virgule, nom*) to leave out; (*laisser quelque part: chapeau etc*) to leave behind; **s'~** to forget o.s.

**oubliettes** [ublijɛt] *nfpl* dungeon *sg*.

**oublieux, euse** [ublijø, -øz] *a* forgetful.

**oued** [wɛd] *nm* wadi.

**ouest** [wɛst] *nm* west // *a inv* west; (*région*) western; **à l'~** in the west; (*to the*) west, westwards; **à l'~ de** (to the) west of; **vent d'~** westerly wind; **~-allemand, e** *a*, *nm/f* West German.

**ouf** [uf] *excl* phew!

**oui** [wi] *ad* yes; **répondre (par) ~** to answer yes.

**ouï-dire** [widiʀ] *nm inv*: **par ~** by hearsay.

**ouïe** [wi] *nf* hearing; **~s** *nfpl* (*de poisson*) gills; (*de violon*) sound-hole.

**ouïr** [wiʀ] *vt* to hear; **avoir ouï dire que** to have heard it said that.

**ouistiti** [wistiti] *nm* marmoset.

**ouragan** [uʀagɑ̃] *nm* hurricane; (*fig*) storm.

**ourlé, e** [uʀle] *a* hemmed; (*fig*) rimmed.

**ourler** [uʀle] *vt* to hem.

**ourlet** [uʀlɛ] *nm* hem; (*de l'oreille*) rim.

**ours** [uʀs] *nm* bear; **~ brun/blanc** brown/polar bear; **~ mal léché** uncouth fellow; **~ (en peluche)** teddy (bear).

**ourse** [uʀs(ə)] *nf* (*ZOOL*) she-bear; **la Grande/Petite O~** the Great/Little Bear, Ursa Major/ Minor.

**oursin** [uʀsɛ̃] *nm* sea urchin.

**ourson** [uʀsɔ̃] *nm* (bear-)cub.

**ouste** [ust(ə)] *excl* hop it!

**outil** [uti] *nm* tool.

**outillage** [utijaʒ] *nm* set of tools; (*d'atelier*) equipment *q*.

**outiller** [utije] *vt* (*ouvrier, usine*) to equip.

**outrage** [utʀaʒ] *nm* insult; **faire subir les derniers ~s à** (*femme*) to ravish; **~ aux bonnes mœurs** outrage to public decency; **~ à magistrat** contempt of court; **~ à la pudeur** indecent behaviour *q*.

**outrageant, e** [utʀaʒɑ̃, -ɑ̃t] *a* offensive.

**outrager** [utʀaʒe] *vt* to offend gravely; (*fig: contrevenir à*) to outrage, insult.

**outrance** [utʀɑ̃s] *nf* excessiveness *q*, excess; **à ~** excessively, to excess; **outrancier, ière** *a* extreme.

**outre** [utʀ(ə)] *nf* goatskin, water skin // *prép* besides // *ad*: **passer ~ à** to disregard, take no notice of; **en ~** besides, moreover; **~ que** apart from the fact that; **~ mesure** immoderately; unduly.

**outré, e** [utʀe] *a* excessive, exaggerated; outraged.

**outre-Atlantique** [utʀəatlɑ̃tik] *ad* across the Atlantic.

**outrecuidance** [utʀəkɥidɑ̃s] *nf* presumptuousness *q*.

**outre-Manche** [utʀəmɑ̃ʃ] *ad* across the Channel.

**outremer** [utʀəmɛʀ] *a* ultramarine.

**outre-mer** [utʀəmɛʀ] *ad* overseas.

**outrepasser** [utʀəpɑse] *vt* to go beyond, exceed.

**outrer** [utʀe] *vt* to exaggerate; to outrage.

**outsider** [awtsajdœʀ] *nm* outsider.

**ouvert, e** [uvɛʀ, -ɛʀt(ə)] *pp de* **ouvrir** // *a* open; (*robinet, gaz etc*) on; **ouvertement** *ad* openly.

**ouverture** [uvɛʀtyʀ] *nf* opening; (*MUS*) overture; (*POL*): **l'~** the widening of the political spectrum; (*PHOTO*): **~ (du diaphragme)** aperture; **~s** *nfpl* (*propositions*) overtures; **~ d'esprit** open-mindedness; **heures d'~** (*COMM*) opening hours; **jours d'~** (*COMM*) days of opening.

**ouvrable** [uvʀabl(ə)] *a*: **jour ~** working day, weekday.

**ouvrage** [uvʀaʒ] *nm* (*tâche, de tricot etc, MIL*) work *q*; (*texte, livre*) work; **corbeille à ~** work basket; **~ d'art** (*GÉNIE CIVIL*) bridge or tunnel etc.

**ouvragé, e** [uvʀaʒe] *a* finely embroidered (*ou* worked *ou* carved).

**ouvrant, e** [uvʀɑ̃, -ɑ̃t] *a*: **toit ~** (*AUTO*) sunshine roof.

**ouvre-boîte(s)** [uvʀəbwat] *nm inv* tin *ou* can opener.

**ouvre-bouteille(s)** [uvʀəbutɛj] *nm inv* bottle-opener.

**ouvreuse** [uvʀøz] *nf* usherette.

**ouvrier, ière** [uvʀje, -jɛʀ] *nm/f* worker // *nf* (*ZOOL*) worker (bee) // *a* working-class; industrial, labour *cpd*; workers'; **classe ouvrière** working class; **~ qualifié** skilled worker; **~ spécialisé (O.S.)** semiskilled worker; **~ d'usine** factory worker.

**ouvrir** [uvʀiʀ] *vt* (*gén*) to open; (*brèche, passage*) to open up; (*commencer l'exploitation de, créer*) to open (up); (*eau, électricité, chauffage, robinet*) to turn on; (*MÉD: abcès*) to open up, cut open // *vi* to open; to open up; **s'~** *vi* to open; **s'~ à** (*art etc*) to open one's mind to; **s'~ à qn (de qch)** to open one's heart to sb (about sth); **s'~ les veines** to slash *ou* cut one's wrists; **~ l'appétit à qn** to whet sb's appetite.

**ouvroir** [uvʀwaʀ] *nm* workroom; sewing room.

**ovaire** [ɔvɛʀ] *nm* ovary.

**ovale** [ɔval] *a* oval.

**ovation** [ɔvɑsjɔ̃] *nf* ovation; **ovationner** *vt*: **ovationner qn** to give sb an ovation.

**O.V.N.I.** [ɔvni] *sigle m* (= *objet volant non identifié*) U.F.O. (unidentified flying object).

**ovule** [ɔvyl] *nm* (*PHYSIOL*) ovum (*pl* ova); (*MÉD*) pessary.

**oxydable** [ɔksidabl(ə)] *a* liable to rust.

**oxyde** [ɔksid] *nm* oxide; **~ de carbone** carbon monoxide.

**oxyder** [ɔkside]: **s'~** *vi* to become oxidized.

**oxygène** [ɔksiʒɛn] *nm* oxygen ; *(fig):* **cure d'~** fresh air cure.
**oxygéné, e** [ɔksiʒene] *a:* **eau ~e** hydrogen peroxide.
**ozone** [ozɔn] *nm* ozone.

# P

**pacage** [pakaʒ] *nm* grazing, pasture.
**pachyderme** [paʃidɛʀm(ə)] *nm* pachyderm ; elephant.
**pacifier** [pasifje] *vt* to pacify.
**pacifique** [pasifik] *a* *(personne)* peaceable ; *(intentions, coexistence)* peaceful // *nm:* **le P~, l'océan P~** the Pacific (Ocean).
**pacotille** [pakɔtij] *nf (péj)* cheap goods *pl* ; **de ~** cheap.
**pacte** [pakt(ə)] *nm* pact, treaty.
**pactiser** [paktize] *vi:* **~ avec** to come to terms with.
**pagaie** [pagɛ] *nf* paddle.
**pagaille** [pagaj] *nf* mess, shambles *sg.*
**pagayer** [pageje] *vi* to paddle.
**page** [paʒ] *nf* page // *nm* page ; **mettre en ~s** to make up (into pages) ; **à la ~** *(fig)* up-to-date.
**pagne** [paɲ] *nm* loincloth.
**pagode** [pagɔd] *nf* pagoda.
**paie** [pɛ] *nf* **= paye.**
**paiement** [pɛmɑ̃] *nm* **= payement.**
**païen, ne** [pajɛ̃, -jɛn] *a, nm/f* pagan, heathen.
**paillard, e** [pajaʀ, -aʀd(ə)] *a* bawdy.
**paillasse** [pajas] *nf* straw mattress.
**paillasson** [pajasɔ̃] *nm* doormat.
**paille** [pɑj] *nf* straw ; *(défaut)* flaw ; **~ de fer** steel wool.
**pailleté, e** [pajte] *a* sequined.
**paillette** [pajɛt] *nf* speck, flake ; **~s** *nfpl (décoratives)* sequins, spangles ; **lessive en ~s** soapflakes *pl.*
**pain** [pɛ̃] *nm (substance)* bread ; *(unité)* loaf *(pl* loaves) (of bread) ; *(morceau):* **~ de cire** *etc* bar of wax *etc* ; **~ bis/complet** brown/ wholemeal bread ; **~ d'épice** gingerbread ; **~ grillé** toast ; **~ de mie** sandwich loaf ; **~ de seigle** rye bread ; **~ de sucre** sugar loaf.
**pair, e** [pɛʀ] *a (nombre)* even // *nm* peer ; **aller de ~ (avec)** to go hand in hand *ou* together (with) ; **au ~** *(FINANCE)* at par ; **jeune fille au ~** au pair girl.
**paire** [pɛʀ] *nf* pair ; **une ~ de lunettes/tenailles** a pair of glasses/pincers.
**paisible** [pezibl(ə)] *a* peaceful, quiet.
**paitre** [pɛtʀ(ə)] *vi* to graze.
**paix** [pɛ] *nf* peace ; *(fig)* peacefulness ; peace ; **faire la ~ avec** to make peace with ; **avoir la ~** to have peace (and quiet).
**palabrer** [palabʀe] *vi* to argue endlessly.
**palace** [palas] *nm* luxury hotel.
**palais** [palɛ] *nm* palace ; *(ANAT)* palate ; **le P~ Bourbon** *the National Assembly buildings* ; **~ des expositions** exhibition hall ; **le P~ de Justice** the Law Courts *pl.*
**palan** [palɑ̃] *nm* hoist.

**pale** [pal] *nf (d'hélice, de rame)* blade ; *(de roue)* paddle.
**pâle** [pɑl] *a* pale ; **bleu ~** pale blue.
**paléontologie** [paleɔ̃tɔlɔʒi] *nf* paleontology.
**Palestine** [palɛstin] *nf:* **la ~** Palestine ; **palestinien, ne** *a, nm/f* Palestinian.
**palet** [palɛ] *nm* disc ; *(HOCKEY)* puck.
**paletot** [palto] *nm* (short) coat.
**palette** [palɛt] *nf (de peintre)* palette.
**palétuvier** [paletyvje] *nm* mangrove.
**pâleur** [palœʀ] *nf* paleness.
**palier** [palje] *nm (d'escalier)* landing ; *(fig)* level, plateau ; *(TECH)* bearing ; **nos voisins de ~** our neighbours across the landing ; **en ~** *ad* level ; **par ~s** in stages ; **palière** *af* landing *cpd.*
**pâlir** [pɑliʀ] *vi* to turn *ou* go pale ; *(couleur)* to fade.
**palissade** [palisad] *nf* fence.
**palissandre** [palisɑ̃dʀ(ə)] *nm* rosewood.
**palliatif** [paljatif] *nm* palliative ; *(expédient)* stopgap measure.
**pallier** [palje] *vt,* **~ à** *vt* to offset, make up for.
**palmarès** [palmaʀɛs] *nm* record (of achievements) ; *(SCOL)* prize list ; *(SPORT)* list of winners.
**palme** [palm(ə)] *nf (BOT)* palm leaf *(pl* leaves) ; *(symbole)* palm ; *(en caoutchouc)* flipper ; **~s (académiques)** *decoration for services to education* ; **palmé, e** *a (pattes)* webbed.
**palmeraie** [palməʀɛ] *nf* palm grove.
**palmier** [palmje] *nm* palm tree.
**palmipède** [palmipɛd] *nm* palmiped, webfooted bird.
**palombe** [palɔ̃b] *nf* woodpigeon, ringdove.
**pâlot, te** [palo, -ɔt] *a* pale, peaky.
**palourde** [paluʀd(ə)] *nf* clam.
**palper** [palpe] *vt* to feel, finger.
**palpitant, e** [palpitɑ̃, -ɑ̃t] *a* thrilling.
**palpitation** [palpitasjɔ̃] *nf* palpitation.
**palpiter** [palpite] *vi (cœur, pouls)* to beat ; *(: plus fort)* to pound, throb ; *(narines, chair)* to quiver.
**paludisme** [palydism(ə)] *nm* paludism, malaria.
**pâmer** [pame]: **se ~** *vi* to swoon ; *(fig):* **se ~ devant** to go into raptures over ; **pâmoison** *nf:* **tomber en pâmoison** to swoon.
**pampa** [pɑ̃pa] *nf* pampas *pl.*
**pamphlet** [pɑ̃flɛ] *nm* lampoon, satirical tract.
**pamplemousse** [pɑ̃pləmus] *nm* grapefruit.
**pan** [pɑ̃] *nm* section, piece // *excl* bang! ; **~ de chemise** shirt tail.
**panacée** [panase] *nf* panacea.
**panachage** [panaʃaʒ] *nm* blend, mix.
**panache** [panaʃ] *nm* plume ; *(fig)* spirit, panache.
**panaché, e** [panaʃe] *a:* **œillet ~** variegated carnation ; **glace ~e** mixed-flavour ice cream ; **salade ~e** mixed salad ; **bière ~e** shandy.
**panaris** [panaʀi] *nm* whitlow.
**pancarte** [pɑ̃kaʀt(ə)] *nf* sign, notice ; *(dans un défilé)* placard.

**pancréas** [pãkReɑs] *nm* pancreas.
**pané, e** [pane] *a* fried in breadcrumbs.
**panier** [panje] *nm* basket; **mettre au** ∼ to chuck away; ∼ **à provisions** shopping basket; ∼ **à salade** Black Maria, police van; ∼-**repas** *nm* packed lunch.
**panification** [panifikasjɔ̃] *nf* bread-making.
**panique** [panik] *nf, a* panic; **paniquer** *vi* to panic.
**panne** [pan] *nf* (*d'un mécanisme, moteur*) breakdown; **être/tomber en** ∼ to have broken down/break down; **être en** ∼ **d'essence** *ou* **sèche** to have run out of petrol; ∼ **d'électricité** *ou* **de courant** power *ou* electrical failure.
**panneau, x** [pano] *nm* (*écriteau*) sign, notice; (*de boiserie, de tapisserie etc*) panel; **tomber dans le** ∼ (*fig*) to walk into the trap; ∼ **d'affichage** notice board; ∼ **de signalisation** roadsign; ∼-**réclame** *nm* hoarding.
**panonceau, x** [panɔ̃so] *nm* sign.
**panoplie** [panɔpli] *nf* (*jouet*) outfit; (*d'armes*) display; (*fig*) array.
**panorama** [panɔRama] *nm* panorama; **panoramique** *a* panoramic; (*carrosserie*) with panoramic windows.
**panse** [pãs] *nf* paunch.
**pansement** [pãsmã] *nm* dressing, bandage; ∼ **adhésif** sticking plaster.
**panser** [pãse] *vt* (*plaie*) to dress, bandage; (*bras*) to put a dressing on, bandage; (*cheval*) to groom.
**pantalon** [pãtalɔ̃] *nm* (*aussi*: ∼**s, paire de** ∼**s**) trousers *pl*, pair of trousers; ∼ **de ski** ski pants *pl*.
**pantelant, e** [pãtlã, -ãt] *a* gasping for breath, panting.
**panthère** [pãtɛR] *nf* panther.
**pantin** [pãtɛ̃] *nm* jumping jack; (*péj*) puppet.
**pantois** [pãtwa] *am*: **rester** ∼ to be flabbergasted.
**pantomime** [pãtɔmim] *nf* mime; (*pièce*) mime show.
**pantouflard, e** [pãtuflaR, -aRd(ə)] *a* (*péj*) stay-at-home.
**pantoufle** [pãtufl(ə)] *nf* slipper.
**panure** [panyR] *nf* breadcrumbs *pl*.
**paon** [pã] *nm* peacock.
**papa** [papa] *nm* dad(dy).
**papauté** [papote] *nf* papacy.
**pape** [pap] *nm* pope.
**paperasse** [papRas] *nf* (*péj*) bumf *q*, papers *pl*; forms *pl*; ∼**rie** *nf* (*péj*) red tape *q*; paperwork *q*.
**papeterie** [papetRi] *nf* (*usine*) paper mill; (*magasin*) stationer's (shop).
**papetier, ière** [paptje, -jɛR] *nm/f* paper-maker; stationer; ∼-**libraire** *nm* bookseller and stationer.
**papier** [papje] *nm* paper; (*article*) article; ∼**s** *nmpl* (*aussi*: ∼**s d'identité**) (identity) papers; ∼ **couché/glacé** art/glazed paper; ∼ (**d')aluminium** aluminium foil, tinfoil; ∼ **d'Arménie** incense paper; ∼ **bible** India *ou* bible paper; ∼ **buvard** blotting paper; ∼ **calque** tracing paper; ∼ **carbone** carbon paper; ∼ **collant** sellotape ®, sticky tape; ∼ **hygiénique**

toilet paper; ∼ **journal** newsprint; (*pour emballer*) newspaper; ∼ **à lettres** writing paper, notepaper; ∼ **mâché** papier-mâché; ∼ **machine** typing paper; ∼ **peint** wallpaper; ∼ **pelure** India paper; ∼ **de soie** tissue paper; ∼ **de tournesol** litmus paper; ∼ **de verre** sandpaper.
**papille** [papij] *nf*: ∼**s gustatives** taste buds.
**papillon** [papijɔ̃] *nm* butterfly; (*fam: contravention*) (parking) ticket; (*TECH: écrou*) wing *ou* butterfly nut; ∼ **de nuit** moth.
**papillote** [papijɔt] *nf* curlpaper.
**papilloter** [papijɔte] *vi* to blink, flicker.
**papoter** [papɔte] *vi* to chatter.
**paprika** [papRika] *nm* paprika.
**paquebot** [pakbo] *nm* liner.
**pâquerette** [pakRɛt] *nf* daisy.
**Pâques** [pak] *nm, nfpl* Easter; **faire ses** ∼ to do one's Easter duties.
**paquet** [pakɛ] *nm* packet; (*colis*) parcel; (*fig: tas*): ∼ **de** pile *ou* heap of; **mettre le** ∼ (*fam*) to give one's all; ∼ **de mer** big wave; **paquetage** *nm* (MIL) kit, pack; ∼-**cadeau** *nm* gift-wrapped parcel.
**par** [paR] *prép* by; **finir** *etc* ∼ **to end** *etc* **with**; ∼ **amour** out of love; **passer** ∼ **Lyon/la côte** to go via *ou* through Lyons/along by the coast; ∼ **la fenêtre** (*jeter, regarder*) out of the window; **3** ∼ **jour/personne** 3 a *ou* per day/head; **2** ∼ **2** two at a time; in twos; ∼ **où?** which way?; ∼ **ici** this way; (*dans le coin*) round here; ∼-**ci**, ∼-**là** here and there.
**para** [paRa] *nm* (*abr de* **parachutiste**) para.
**parabole** [paRabɔl] *nf* (REL) parable; (GÉOM) parabola; **parabolique** *a* parabolic.
**parachever** [paRaʃve] *vt* to perfect.
**parachute** [paRaʃyt] *nm* parachute.
**parachutiste** [paRaʃytist(ə)] *nm/f* parachutist; (MIL) paratrooper.
**parade** [paRad] *nf* (*spectacle, défilé*) parade; (ESCRIME, BOXE) parry; (*ostentation*): **faire** ∼ **de** to display, show off.
**paradis** [paRadi] *nm* heaven, paradise.
**paradoxal, e, aux** [paRadɔksal, -o] *a* paradoxical.
**paradoxe** [paRadɔks(ə)] *nm* paradox.
**parafe** [paRaf] *nm*, **parafer** [paRafe] *vt voir* **paraphe, parapher**.
**paraffine** [paRafin] *nf* paraffin; **paraffin wax**.
**parages** [paRaʒ] *nmpl*: **dans les** ∼ (**de**) in the area *ou* vicinity (of).
**paragraphe** [paRagRaf] *nm* paragraph.
**paraître** [paRɛtR(ə)] *vb avec attribut* to seem, look, appear // *vi* to appear; (*être visible*) to show; (PRESSE, ÉDITION) to be published, come out, be out; (*briller*) to show off // *vb impersonnel*: **il paraît que** it seems *ou* appears that, they say that; **il me paraît que** it seems to me that.
**parallèle** [paRalɛl] *a* parallel; (*police, marché*) unofficial // *nm* (*comparaison*): **faire un** ∼ **entre** to draw a parallel between; (GÉO) parallel // *nf* parallel (line); **parallélisme** *nm* parallelism; (AUTO) wheel alignment; **parallélogramme** *nm* parallelogram.

**paralyser** [paralize] *vt* to paralyze.
**paralysie** [paralizi] *nf* paralysis.
**paralytique** [paralitik] *a, nm/f* paralytic.
**paramédical, e, aux** [paramedikal, -o] *a* paramedical.
**paranoïaque** [paranɔjak] *nm/f* paranoiac.
**parapet** [parapɛ] *nm* parapet.
**paraphe** [paraf] *nm* flourish; initials *pl*; signature; **parapher** *vt* to initial; to sign.
**paraphrase** [parafrɑz] *nf* paraphrase.
**parapluie** [paraplɥi] *nm* umbrella; ~ **pliant** telescopic umbrella.
**parasite** [parazit] *nm* parasite // *a* (*BOT, BIO*) parasitic(al); ~**s** (*TEL*) interference *sg*.
**parasol** [parasɔl] *nm* parasol, sunshade.
**paratonnerre** [paratɔnɛr] *nm* lightning conductor.
**paravent** [paravɑ̃] *nm* folding screen.
**parc** [park] *nm* (public) park, gardens *pl*; (*de château etc*) grounds *pl*; (*pour le bétail*) pen, enclosure; (*d'enfant*) playpen; (*MIL: entrepôt*) depot; (*ensemble d'unités*) stock; fleet; ~ **automobile** (*d'un pays*) number of cars on the roads; (*d'une société*) car fleet; ~ **à huîtres** oyster bed; ~ **national** national park; ~ **de stationnement** car park.
**parcelle** [parsɛl] *nf* fragment, scrap; (*de terrain*) plot, parcel.
**parce que** [parsk(ə)] *cj* because.
**parchemin** [parʃəmɛ̃] *nm* parchment.
**parcimonie** [parsimɔni] *nf* parsimony, parsimoniousness.
**parc(o)mètre** [park(ɔ)mɛtr(ə)] *nm* parking meter.
**parcourir** [parkurir] *vt* (*trajet, distance*) to cover; (*article, livre*) to skim *ou* glance through; (*lieu*) to go all over, travel up and down; (*suj: frisson, vibration*) to run through; ~ **des yeux** to run one's eye over.
**parcours** [parkur] *nm* (*trajet*) journey; (*itinéraire*) route; (*SPORT: de golf etc*) course; (: *accompli par un concurrent*) round; run; lap.
**par-delà** [pardəla] *prép* beyond.
**par-dessous** [pardəsu] *prép, ad* under(neath).
**pardessus** [pardəsy] *nm* overcoat.
**par-dessus** [pardəsy] *prép* over (the top of) // *ad* over (the top); ~ **le marché** on top of all that.
**par-devant** [pardəvɑ̃] *prép* in the presence of, before // *ad* at the front; round the front.
**pardon** [pardɔ̃] *nm* forgiveness *q* // *excl* sorry; (*pour interpeller etc*) excuse me; **demander** ~ **à qn (de)** to apologize to sb (for); **je vous demande** ~ I'm sorry; excuse me.
**pardonner** [pardɔne] *vt* to forgive; ~ **qch à qn** to forgive sb for sth.
**paré, e** [pare] *a* ready, prepared.
**pare-balles** [parbal] *a inv* bulletproof.
**pare-boue** [parbu] *nm inv* mudguard.
**pare-brise** [parbriz] *nm inv* windscreen.
**pare-chocs** [parʃɔk] *nm inv* bumper.
**pareil, le** [parɛj] *a* (*identique*) the same, alike; (*similaire*) similar; (*tel*): **un courage/livre** ~ such courage/a book,

courage/a book like this; **de** ~**s livres** such books; **j'en veux un** ~ I'd like one just like it; **rien de** ~ no (*ou* any) such thing, nothing (*ou* anything) like it; **ses** ~**s** one's fellow men; one's peers; **ne pas avoir son(sa)** ~**(le)** to be second to none; ~ **à** the same as; similar to; **sans** ~ unparalleled, unequalled; ~**lement** *ad* the same, alike; in such a way; (*également*) likewise.
**parement** [parmɑ̃] *nm* (*CONSTR*) facing; (*REL*): ~ **d'autel** antependium.
**parent, e** [parɑ̃, -ɑ̃t] *nm/f*: **un/une** ~/**e** a relative *ou* relation // *a*: **être** ~ **de** to be related to; ~**s** *nmpl* (*père et mère*) parents; **parenté** *nf* (*lien*) relationship; (*personnes*) relatives *pl*, relations *pl*.
**parenthèse** [parɑ̃tɛz] *nf* (*ponctuation*) bracket, parenthesis; (*MATH*) bracket; (*digression*) parenthesis, digression; **ouvrir/ fermer la** ~ to open/close the brackets; **entre** ~**s** in brackets; (*fig*) incidentally.
**parer** [pare] *vt* to adorn; (*CULIN*) to dress, trim; (*éviter*) to ward off; ~ **à** (*danger*) to ward off; (*inconvénient*) to deal with; ~ **au plus pressé** to attend to what's most urgent.
**pare-soleil** [parsɔlɛj] *nm inv* sun visor.
**paresse** [parɛs] *nf* laziness; **paresser** *vi* to laze around; **paresseux, euse** *a* lazy; (*fig*) slow, sluggish // *nm* (*ZOOL*) sloth.
**parfaire** [parfɛr] *vt* to perfect; to complete.
**parfait, e** [parfɛ, -ɛt] *a* perfect // *nm* (*LING*) perfect (tense); (*CULIN*) parfait // *excl* fine, excellent; **parfaitement** *ad* perfectly // *excl* (most) certainly.
**parfois** [parfwa] *ad* sometimes.
**parfum** [parfœ̃] *nm* (*produit*) perfume, scent; (*odeur: de fleur*) scent, fragrance; (: *de tabac, vin*) aroma; (*à choisir: de glace, milk-shake*) flavour; **parfumé, e** *a* (*fleur, fruit*) fragrant; (*papier à lettres etc*) scented; (*femme*) wearing perfume *ou* scent, perfumed; **parfumé au café** coffee-flavoured, flavoured with coffee; **parfumer** *vt* (*suj: odeur, bouquet*) to perfume; (*mouchoir*) to put scent *ou* perfume on; (*crème, gâteau*) to flavour; **se parfumer** to put on (some) perfume *ou* scent; to use perfume *ou* scent; **parfumerie** *nf* (*commerce*) perfumery; (*produits*) perfumes *pl*; (*boutique*) perfume shop.
**pari** [pari] *nm* bet, wager; (*SPORT*) bet; **P~ Mutuel urbain (P.M.U.)** (*State-controlled*) organisation for forecast betting on horse-racing.
**paria** [parja] *nm* outcast.
**parier** [parje] *vt* to bet; **parieur** *nm* (*turfiste etc*) punter.
**Paris** [pari] *n* Paris; **parisien, ne** *a* Parisian; (*GÉO, ADMIN*) Paris *cpd* // *nm/f*: **Parisien, ne** Parisian.
**paritaire** [paritɛr] *a*: **commission** ~ joint commission.
**parité** [parite] *nf* parity.
**parjure** [parʒyr] *nm* (*acte*) false oath, perjury; breach of oath, perjury // *nm/f* perjurer; **se parjurer** to forswear *ou* perjure o.s.

**parking** [paʀkiŋ] *nm* (*lieu*) car park.
**parlant, e** [paʀlɑ̃, -ɑ̃t] *a* (*fig*) graphic,
vivid ; eloquent ; (*CINÉMA*) talking // *ad*:
**généralement ~** generally speaking.
**parlement** [paʀləmɑ̃] *nm* parliament ;
**parlementaire** *a* parliamentary // *nm/f*
member of parliament ; parliamentarian ;
negotiator, mediator.
**parlementer** [paʀləmɑ̃te] *vi* to negotiate,
parley.
**parler** [paʀle] *nm* speech ; dialect // *vi* to
speak, talk ; (*avouer*) to talk ; **~ (à qn) de**
to talk *ou* speak (to sb) about ; **~ pour**
**qn** (*intercéder*) to speak for sb ; **~ le/en**
**français** to speak French/in French ; **~**
**affaires** to talk business ; **~ en**
**dormant/du nez** to talk in one's
sleep/through one's nose ; **sans ~ de** (*fig*)
not to mention, to say nothing of ; **tu**
**parles!** you must be joking.
**parloir** [paʀlwaʀ] *nm* (*d'une prison, d'un*
*hôpital*) visiting room ; (*REL*) parlour.
**parmi** [paʀmi] *prép* among(st).
**parodie** [paʀɔdi] *nf* parody ; **parodier** *vt*
(*œuvre, auteur*) to parody.
**paroi** [paʀwa] *nf* wall ; (*cloison*) partition ;
**~ rocheuse** rock face.
**paroisse** [paʀwas] *nf* parish ; **paroissial,**
**e, aux** *a* parish *cpd* ; **paroissien, ne** *nm/f*
parishioner // *nm* prayer book.
**parole** [paʀɔl] *nf* (*faculté*): **la ~** speech ;
(*mot, promesse*) word ; **~s** *nfpl* (*MUS*)
words, lyrics ; **tenir ~** to keep one's
word ; **prendre la ~** to speak ; **demander**
**la ~** to ask for permission to speak ; **je**
**le crois sur ~** I'll take his word for it.
**paroxysme** [paʀɔksism(ə)] *nm* height,
paroxysm.
**parpaing** [paʀpɛ̃] *nm* bond-stone, parpen.
**parquer** [paʀke] *vt* (*voiture, matériel*) to
park ; (*bestiaux*) to pen (in *ou* up) ;
(*prisonniers*) to pack in.
**parquet** [paʀkɛ] *nm* (*parquet*) floor ; (*JUR*):
**le ~** the Public Prosecutor's department ;
**parqueter** *vt* to lay a parquet floor in.
**parrain** [paʀɛ̃] *nm* godfather ; (*d'un nouvel*
*adhérent*) sponsor, proposer ; **parrainer** *vt*
(*nouvel adhérent*) to sponsor, propose ;
(*entreprise*) to promote, sponsor.
**parricide** [paʀisid] *nm, nf* parricide.
**pars** *vb voir* **partir**.
**parsemer** [paʀsəme] *vt* (*suj: feuilles,*
*papiers*) to be scattered over ; **~ qch de**
to scatter sth with.
**part** [paʀ] *nf* (*qui revient à qn*) share ;
(*fraction, partie*) part ; (*FINANCE*) (non-
voting) share ; **prendre ~ à** (*débat etc*) to
take part in ; (*soucis, douleur de qn*) to
share in ; **faire ~ de qch à qn** to announce
sth to sb, inform sb of sth ; **pour ma ~**
as for me, as far as I'm concerned ; **à ~**
**entière** a full ; **de la ~ de** (*au nom de*)
on behalf of ; (*donné par*) from ; **de**
**toute(s) ~(s)** from all sides *ou* quarters ;
**de ~ et d'autre** on both sides, on either
side ; **de ~ en ~** right through ; **d'une ~**
**... d'autre ~** on the one hand ... on the
other hand ; **à ~** *ad* separately ; (*de côté*)
aside // *prép* apart from, except for // *a*
exceptional, special ; **faire la ~ des**
**choses** to make allowances.

**partage** [paʀtaʒ] *nm* dividing up ; sharing
(out) *q*, share-out ; sharing ; **recevoir qch**
**en ~** to receive sth as one's share (*ou* lot) ;
**sans ~** undivided.
**partagé, e** [paʀtaʒe] *a* (*opinions etc*)
divided.
**partager** [paʀtaʒe] *vt* to share ;
(*distribuer, répartir*) to share (out) ;
(*morceler, diviser*) to divide (up) ; **se ~** *vt*
(*héritage etc*) to share between themselves
(*ou* ourselves).
**partance** [paʀtɑ̃s]: **en ~** *ad* outbound,
due to leave ; **en ~ pour** (bound) for.
**partant** [paʀtɑ̃] *vb voir* **partir** // *nm*
(*SPORT*) starter ; (*HIPPISME*) runner.
**partenaire** [paʀtənɛʀ] *nm/f* partner.
**parterre** [paʀtɛʀ] *nm* (*de fleurs*) (flower)
bed, border ; (*THÉÀTRE*) stalls *pl*.
**parti** [paʀti] *nm* (*POL*) party ; (*décision*)
course of action ; (*personne à marier*)
match ; **tirer ~ de** to take advantage of,
turn to good account ; **prendre le ~ de**
**faire** to make up one's mind to do, resolve
to do ; **prendre le ~ de qn** to stand up
for sb, side with sb ; **prendre ~**
**(pour/contre)** to take sides *ou* a stand
(for/against) ; **prendre son ~ de** to come
to terms with ; **~ pris** bias.
**partial, e, aux** [paʀsjal, -o] *a* biased,
partial.
**participant, e** [paʀtisipɑ̃, -ɑ̃t] *nm/f*
participant ; (*à un concours*) entrant ;
(*d'une société*) member.
**participation** [paʀtisipɑsjɔ̃] *nf*
participation ; sharing ; (*COMM*) interest ; **la**
**~ aux bénéfices** profit-sharing ; **la ~**
**ouvrière** worker participation.
**participe** [paʀtisip] *nm* participle ; **~**
**passé/présent** past/present participle.
**participer** [paʀtisipe]: **~ à** *vt* (*course,*
*réunion*) to take part in ; (*profits etc*) to
share in ; (*frais etc*) to contribute to ;
(*entreprise: financièrement*) to cooperate
in ; (*chagrin, succès de qn*) to share (in) ;
**~ de** *vt* to partake of.
**particularisme** [paʀtikylaʀism(ə)] *nm*
sense of identity ; specific characteristic.
**particularité** [paʀtikylaʀite] *nf*
particularity ; (*distinctive*) characteristic,
feature.
**particule** [paʀtikyl] *nf* particle ; **~**
**(nobiliaire)** nobiliary particle.
**particulier, ière** [paʀtikylje, -jɛʀ] *a*
(*personnel, privé*) private ; (*spécial*) special,
particular ; (*caractéristique*) characteristic,
distinctive ; (*spécifique*) particular // *nm*
(*individu: ADMIN*) private individual ; '**~**
**vend ...**' (*COMM*) 'for sale privately ...' ; **~**
**à** peculiar to ; **en ~** *ad* (*surtout*) in
particular, particularly ; (*en privé*) in
private ; **particulièrement** *ad* particularly.
**partie** [paʀti] *nf* (*gén*) part ; (*profession,*
*spécialité*) field, subject ; (*JUR etc:*
*protagonistes*) party ; (*de cartes, tennis etc*)
game ; **une ~ de campagne/de pêche** an
outing in the country/a fishing party *ou*
trip ; **en ~** *ad* partly, in part ; **faire ~ de**
to belong to ; (*suj: chose*) to be part of ;
**prendre qn à ~** to take sb to task ;
(*malmener*) to set on sb ; **en grande ~**
largely, in the main ; **~ civile** (*JUR*) private

*party associating in action with public prosecutor.*
**partiel, le** [paʀsjɛl] *a* partial // *nm* (SCOL) class exam.
**partir** [paʀtiʀ] *vi* (*gén*) to go ; (*quitter*) to go, leave ; (*s'éloigner*) to go (*ou* drive *etc*) away *ou* off ; (*moteur*) to start ; (*pétard*) to go off ; ~ **de** (*lieu: quitter*) to leave ; (: *commencer à*) to start from ; (*date*) to run *ou* start from ; **à** ~ **de** from.
**partisan, e** [paʀtizɑ̃, -an] *nm/f* partisan // *a*: **être** ~ **de qch/faire** to be in favour of sth/doing.
**partitif, ive** [paʀtitif, -iv] *a*: **article** ~ article used in the partitive genitive.
**partition** [paʀtisjɔ̃] *nf* (MUS) score.
**partout** [paʀtu] *ad* everywhere ; ~ **où il allait** everywhere *ou* wherever he went ; **trente** ~ (TENNIS) thirty all.
**paru, e** *pp de* **paraître.**
**parure** [paʀyʀ] *nf* (*toilette, bijoux*) finery *q* ; jewellery *q* ; (*assortiment*) set.
**parution** [paʀysjɔ̃] *nf* publication, appearance.
**parvenir** [paʀvəniʀ]: ~ **à** *vt* (*atteindre*) to reach ; (*réussir*): ~ **à faire** to manage to do, succeed in doing ; **faire** ~ **qch à qn** to have sth sent to sb.
**parvenu, e** [paʀvəny] *nm/f* (*péj*) parvenu, upstart.
**parvis** [paʀvi] *nm* square (*in front of a church*).
**pas** [pɑ] *nm voir le mot suivant* // *ad* not ; ~ **de** no ; **ne ...** ~: **il ne le voit** ~/**ne l'a** ~ **vu/ne le verra** ~ he doesn't see it/hasn't seen it *ou* didn't see it/won't see it ; **ils n'ont** ~ **de voiture/d'enfants** they haven't got a car/any children, they have no car/children ; **il m'a dit de ne** ~ **le faire** he told me not to do it ; **il n'est** ~ **plus grand** he isn't bigger, he's no bigger ; **... lui** ~ *ou* ~ **lui** he doesn't (*ou* isn't *etc*) ; **non** ~ **que ...** not that ... ; **une pomme** ~ **mûre** an apple which isn't ripe ; ~ **du tout** not at all ; ~ **plus tard qu'hier** only yesterday ; ~ **mal** *a* not bad, quite good (*ou* pretty *ou* nice) // *ad* quite well ; (*beaucoup*) quite a lot ; ~ **mal de** quite a lot of.
**pas** [pɑ] *ad voir le mot précédent* // *nm* (*allure, mesure*) pace ; (*démarche*) tread ; (*enjambée,* DANSE) step ; (*bruit*) (foot)step ; (*trace*) footprint ; (TECH: *de vis, d'écrou*) thread ; ~ **à** ~ step by step ; **au** ~ at walking pace ; **mettre qn au** ~ to bring sb to heel ; **au** ~ **de gymnastique/de course** at a jog trot/at a run ; **à** ~ **de loup** stealthily ; **faire les cent** ~ to pace up and down ; **faire les premiers** ~ to make the first move ; **sur le** ~ **de la porte** on the doorstep ; **le** ~ **de Calais** (*détroit*) the Straits of Dover ; ~ **de porte** (COMM) key money.
**pascal, e, aux** [paskal, -o] *a* Easter *cpd.*
**passable** [pɑsabl(ə)] *a* (*travail*) passable, tolerable.
**passage** [pɑsaʒ] *nm* (*fait de passer*) *voir* **passer** ; (*lieu, prix de la traversée, extrait de livre etc*) passage ; (*chemin*) way ; **de** ~ (*touristes*) passing through ; (*amants etc*) casual ; ~ **clouté** pedestrian crossing ; '~ **interdit**' 'no entry' ; ~ **à niveau** level

crossing ; '~ **protégé**' right of way over secondary road(s) on your right ; ~ **souterrain** subway, underground passage ; ~ **à tabac** beating-up.
**passager, ère** [pɑsaʒe, -ɛʀ] *a* passing // *nm/f* passenger ; ~ **clandestin** stowaway.
**passant, e** [pɑsɑ̃, -ɑ̃t] *a* (*rue, endroit*) busy // *nm/f* passer-by // *nm* (*pour ceinture etc*) loop.
**passe** [pɑs] *nf* (SPORT, *magnétique,* NAVIG) pass // *nm* (*passe-partout*) master *ou* skeleton key ; **être en** ~ **de faire** to be on the way to doing.
**passé, e** [pɑse] *a* (*événement, temps*) past ; (*couleur, tapisserie*) faded // *prép* after // *nm* past ; (LING) past (tense) ; **il est** ~ **midi** *ou* **midi** ~ it's gone twelve ; ~ **de mode** out of fashion ; ~ **composé** perfect (tense) ; ~ **simple** past historic.
**passe-droit** [pɑsdʀwa] *nm* special privilege.
**passéiste** [pɑseist] *a* backward-looking.
**passementerie** [pɑsmɑ̃tʀi] *nf* trimmings *pl.*
**passe-montagne** [pɑsmɔ̃taɲ] *nm* balaclava.
**passe-partout** [pɑspaʀtu] *nm inv* master *ou* skeleton key // *a inv* all-purpose.
**passe-passe** [pɑspɑs] *nm*: **tour de** ~ trick, sleight of hand *q.*
**passe-plats** [pɑspla] *nm inv* serving hatch.
**passeport** [pɑspɔʀ] *nm* passport.
**passer** [pɑse] *vi* (*se rendre, aller*) to go ; (*voiture, piétons: défiler*) to pass (by), go by ; (*faire une halte rapide: facteur, laitier etc*) to come, call ; (: *pour rendre visite*) to call *ou* drop in ; (*courant, air, lumière, franchir un obstacle etc*) to get through ; (*accusé, projet de loi*): ~ **devant** to come before ; (*film, émission*) to be on ; (*temps, jours*) to pass, go by ; (*couleur, papier*) to fade ; (*douleur*) to pass, go away ; (CARTES) to pass ; (SCOL) to go up (to the next class) // *vt* (*frontière, rivière etc*) to cross ; (*douane*) to go through ; (*examen*) to sit, take ; (*visite médicale etc*) to have ; (*journée, temps*) to spend ; (*donner*): ~ **qch à qn** to pass sth to sb ; to give sb sth ; (*transmettre*): ~ **qch à qn** to pass sth on to sb ; (*enfiler: vêtement*) to slip on ; (*faire entrer, mettre*): **(faire)** ~ **qch dans/par** to get sth into/through ; (*café*) to pour the water on ; (*thé, soupe*) to strain ; (*film, pièce*) to show, put on ; (*disque*) to play, put on ; (*marché, accord*) to agree on ; (*tolérer*): ~ **qch à qn** to let sb get away with sth ; **se** ~ *vi* (*avoir lieu: scène, action*) to take place ; (*se dérouler: entretien etc*) to go ; (*arriver*): **que s'est-il passé?** what happened? ; (*s'écouler: semaine etc*) to pass, go by ; **se** ~ **de** *vt* to go *ou* do without ; **se** ~ **les mains sous l'eau/de l'eau sur le visage** to put one's hands under the tap/run water over one's face ; ~ **par** to go through ; **passe devant/par ici** go in front/this way ; ~ **sur** *vt* (*faute, détail inutile*) to pass over ; ~ **avant qch/qn** (*fig*) to come before sth/sb ; **laisser** ~ (*air, lumière, personne*) to let through ; (*occasion*) to let slip, miss ; (*erreur*) to overlook ; ~ **à la radio/fouille** to be

X-rayed/searched; ~ à la **radio/télévision** to be on the radio/on television; ~ **pour riche** to be taken for a rich man; **il passait pour avoir** he was said to have; ~ **à l'opposition** to go over to the opposition; **passons!** let's say no more (about it); ~ **en seconde,** ~ **la seconde** (*AUTO*) to change into second; ~ **qch en fraude** to smuggle sth in (*ou* out); ~ **la main par la portière** to stick one's hand out of the door; ~ **le balai/l'aspirateur** to sweep up/hoover; **je vous passe M. X** (*je vous mets en communication avec lui*) I'm putting you through to Mr X; (*je lui passe l'appareil*) here is Mr X, I'll hand you over to Mr X.

**passerelle** [pɑsRɛl] *nf* footbridge; (*de navire, avion*) gangway.

**passe-temps** [pɑstɑ̃] *nm inv* pastime.

**passeur, euse** [pɑsœR, -øz] *nm/f* smuggler.

**passible** [pasibl(ə)] *a*: ~ **de** liable to.

**passif, ive** [pasif, -iv] *a* passive // *nm* (*LING*) passive; (*COMM*) liabilities *pl*.

**passion** [pɑsjɔ̃] *nf* passion; **avoir la** ~ **de** to have a passion for; **passionné, e** *a* passionate; impassioned; **passionnel, le** *a* of passion; **passionner** *vt* (*personne*) to fascinate, grip; **se passionner pour** to take an avid interest in; to have a passion for.

**passoire** [pɑswaR] *nf* sieve; (*à légumes*) colander; (*à thé*) strainer.

**pastel** [pastɛl] *nm, a inv* (*ART*) pastel.

**pastèque** [pastɛk] *nf* watermelon.

**pasteur** [pastœR] *nm* (*protestant*) minister, pastor.

**pasteuriser** [pastœRize] *vt* to pasteurize.

**pastiche** [pastiʃ] *nm* pastiche.

**pastille** [pastij] *nf* (*à sucer*) lozenge, pastille; (*de papier etc*) (small) disc; ~s **pour la toux** throat lozenges.

**pastis** [pastis] *nm* pastis.

**patate** [patat] *nf* spud; ~ **douce** sweet potato.

**patauger** [patoʒe] *vi* (*pour s'amuser*) to splash about; (*avec effort*) to wade about; ~ **dans** (*en marchant*) to wade through.

**pâte** [pɑt] *nf* (*à tarte*) pastry; (*à pain*) dough; (*à frire*) batter; (*substance molle*) paste; cream; ~s *nfpl* (*macaroni etc*) pasta *sg*; **fromage à** ~ **dure/molle** hard/soft cheese; ~ **d'amandes** almond paste; ~ **brisée** shortcrust pastry; ~ **de fruits** crystallized fruit *q*; ~ **à modeler** modelling clay, Plasticine ®; ~ **à papier** paper pulp.

**pâté** [pɑte] *nm* (*charcuterie*) pâté; (*tache*) ink blot; (*de sable*) sandcastle, sandpie; ~ **en croûte** ≈ pork pie; ~ **de maisons** block (of houses).

**pâtée** [pɑte] *nf* mash, feed.

**patente** [patɑ̃t] *nf* (*COMM*) trading licence.

**patère** [patɛR] *nf* (coat-)peg.

**paternel, le** [patɛRnɛl] *a* (*amour, soins*) fatherly; (*ligne, autorité*) paternal.

**paternité** [patɛRnite] *nf* paternity, fatherhood.

**pâteux, euse** [pɑtø, -øz] *a* thick; pasty.

**pathétique** [patetik] *a* moving, pathetic.

**pathologie** [patɔlɔʒi] *nf* pathology.

**patibulaire** [patibylɛR] *a* sinister.

**patience** [pasjɑ̃s] *nf* patience.

**patient, e** [pasjɑ̃, -ɑ̃t] *a, nm/f* patient.

**patienter** [pasjɑ̃te] *vi* to wait.

**patin** [patɛ̃] *nm* skate; (*sport*) skating; (*de traîneau, luge*) runner; (*pièce de tissu*) cloth pad (*used as slippers to protect polished floor*); ~s **(à glace)** (ice) skates; ~s **à roulettes** roller skates.

**patinage** [patinaʒ] *nm* skating; ~ **artistique/de vitesse** figure/speed skating.

**patine** [patin] *nf* sheen.

**patiner** [patine] *vi* to skate; (*embrayage*) to slip; (*roue, voiture*) to spin; **se** ~ *vi* (*meuble, cuir*) to acquire a sheen, become polished; **patineur, euse** *nm/f* skater; **patinoire** *nf* skating rink, (ice) rink.

**pâtir** [pɑtiR]: ~ **de** *vt* to suffer because of.

**pâtisserie** [pɑtisRi] *nf* (*boutique*) cake shop; (*métier*) confectionery; (*à la maison*) pastry- *ou* cake-making, baking; ~s *nfpl* (*gâteaux*) pastries, cakes; **pâtissier, ière** *nm/f* pastrycook; confectioner.

**patois** [patwa] *nm* dialect, patois.

**patriarche** [patRijaRʃ(ə)] *nm* patriarch.

**patrie** [patRi] *nf* homeland.

**patrimoine** [patRimwan] *nm* inheritance, patrimony.

**patriote** [patRijɔt] *a* patriotic // *nm/f* patriot; **patriotique** *a* patriotic.

**patron, ne** [patRɔ̃, -ɔn] *nm/f* (*chef*) boss, manager/eress; (*propriétaire*) owner, proprietor/tress; (*employeur*) employer; (*MED*) ≈ senior consultant; (*REL*) patron saint // *nm* (*COUTURE*) pattern; ~ **de thèse** supervisor (of postgraduate thesis); **patronal, e, aux** *a* (*syndicat, intérêts*) employers'.

**patronage** [patRɔnaʒ] *nm* patronage; (parish) youth club.

**patronat** [patRɔna] *nm* employers *pl*.

**patronner** [patRɔne] *vt* to sponsor, support.

**patrouille** [patRuj] *nf* patrol; **patrouiller** *vi* to patrol, be on patrol.

**patte** [pat] *nf* (*jambe*) leg; (*pied: de chien, chat*) paw; (: *d'oiseau*) foot; (*languette*) strap; (: *de poche*) flap; **à** ~s **d'éléphant** a bell-bottomed; ~s **d'oie** (*fig*) crow's feet.

**pattemouille** [patmuj] *nf* damp cloth (*for ironing*).

**pâturage** [pɑtyRaʒ] *nm* pasture.

**pâture** [pɑtyR] *nf* food.

**paume** [pom] *nf* palm.

**paumer** [pome] *vt* (*fam*) to lose.

**paupière** [popjɛR] *nf* eyelid.

**paupiette** [popjɛt] *nf*: ~s **de veau** veal olives.

**pause** [poz] *nf* (*arrêt*) break; (*en parlant, MUS*) pause.

**pauvre** [povR(ə)] *a* poor // *nm/f* poor man/woman; **les** ~s the poor; ~ **en calcium** with a low calcium content; ~**té** *nf* (*état*) poverty.

**pavaner** [pavane]: **se** ~ *vi* to strut about.

**pavé, e** [pave] *a* paved; cobbled // *nm* (*bloc*) paving stone; cobblestone; (*pavage*) paving.

**pavillon** [pavijɔ̃] *nm* (*de banlieue*) small (detached) house; (*kiosque*) lodge; pavilion; (*d'hôpital*) ward; (*MUS: de cor etc*) bell; (*ANAT: de l'oreille*) pavilion, pinna; (*drapeau*) flag; ~ **de complaisance** flag of convenience.

**pavoiser** [pavwaze] *vt* to deck with flags // *vi* to put out flags; (*fig*) to rejoice, exult.

**pavot** [pavo] *nm* poppy.

**payant, e** [pɛjɑ̃, -ɑ̃t] *a* (*spectateurs etc*) paying; (*fig: entreprise*) profitable; **c'est** ~ you have to pay, there is a charge.

**paye** [pɛj] *nf* pay, wages *pl*.

**payement** [pɛjmɑ̃] *nm* payment.

**payer** [peje] *vt* (*créancier, employé, loyer*) to pay; (*achat, réparations, fig: faute*) to pay for // *vi* to pay; (*métier*) to be well-paid; (*tactique etc*) to pay off; **il me l'a fait** ~ **10 F** he charged me 10 F for it; ~ **qch à qn** to buy sth for sb, buy sb sth; **ils nous ont payé le voyage** they paid for our trip; ~ **de sa personne** to give of o.s.; ~ **d'audace** to act with great daring; **cela ne paie pas de mine** it doesn't look much; **se** ~ **la tête de qn** to take the mickey out of sb; to take sb for a ride.

**pays** [pei] *nm* country; land; region; village; **du** ~ *a* local.

**paysage** [peizaʒ] *nm* landscape; **paysagiste** *nm/f* landscape gardener; landscape painter.

**paysan, ne** [peizɑ̃, -an] *nm/f* countryman/woman; farmer; (*péj*) peasant // *a* country *cpd*; farming, farmers'.

**Pays-Bas** [peiba] *nmpl*: **les** ~ the Netherlands.

**P.C.V.** *sigle voir* **communication.**

**P.D.G.** *sigle m voir* **président.**

**péage** [peaʒ] *nm* toll; (*endroit*) tollgate; **pont à** ~ toll bridge.

**peau, x** [po] *nf* skin; **gants de** ~ fine leather gloves; ~ **de chamois** (*chiffon*) chamois leather, shammy; **P**~**-Rouge** *nm/f* Red Indian, redskin.

**peccadille** [pekadij] *nf* trifle; peccadillo.

**pêche** [pɛʃ] *nf* (*sport, activité*) fishing; (*poissons pêchés*) catch; (*fruit*) peach; ~ **à la ligne** (*en rivière*) angling.

**péché** [peʃe] *nm* sin; ~ **mignon** weakness.

**pêche-abricot** [pɛʃabriko] *nf* yellow peach.

**pécher** [peʃe] *vi* (*REL*) to sin; (*fig*) to err; to be flawed.

**pêcher** [peʃe] *nm* peach tree // *vi* to go fishing; (*en rivière*) to go angling // *vt* to catch, land; to fish for; ~ **au chalut** to trawl.

**pêcheur, eresse** [peʃœR, peʃRɛs] *nm/f* sinner.

**pêcheur** [peʃœR] *nm* fisherman; angler; ~ **de perles** pearl diver.

**pectoraux** [pɛktɔRo] *nmpl* pectoral muscles.

**pécule** [pekyl] *nm* savings *pl*, nest egg; (*d'un détenu*) earnings *pl* (*paid on release*).

**pécuniaire** [pekynjɛR] *a* financial.

**pédagogie** [pedagɔʒi] *nf* educational methods *pl*, pedagogy; **pédagogique** *a* educational; **formation pédagogique**

teacher training; **pédagogue** *nm/f* teacher; educationalist.

**pédale** [pedal] *nf* pedal; **pédaler** *vi* to pedal; **pédalier** *nm* pedal and gear mechanism.

**pédalo** [pedalo] *nm* pedalo, pedal-boat.

**pédant, e** [pedɑ̃, -ɑ̃t] *a* (*péj*) pedantic.

**pédéraste** [pederast(ə)] *nm* homosexual, pederast.

**pédestre** [pedɛstR(ə)] *a*: **tourisme** ~ hiking.

**pédiatre** [pedjatR(ə)] *nm/f* paediatrician, child specialist.

**pédiatrie** [pedjatRi] *nf* paediatrics *sg*.

**pédicure** [pedikyR] *nm/f* chiropodist.

**pègre** [pɛgR(ə)] *nf* underworld.

**peignais** *etc vb voir* **peindre.**

**peigne** [pɛɲ] *nm* comb.

**peigné, e** [peɲe] *a*: **laine** ~**e** wool worsted; combed wool.

**peigner** [peɲe] *vt* to comb (the hair of); **se** ~ to comb one's hair.

**peignis** *etc vb voir* **peindre.**

**peignoir** [pɛɲwaR] *nm* dressing gown; ~ **de bain** bathrobe.

**peindre** [pɛ̃dR(ə)] *vt* to paint; (*fig*) to portray, depict.

**peine** [pɛn] *nf* (*affliction*) sorrow, sadness *q*; (*mal, effort*) trouble *q*, effort; (*difficulté*) difficulty; (*punition*, *châtiment*) punishment; (*JUR*) sentence; **faire de la** ~ **à qn** to distress *ou* upset sb; **prendre la** ~ **de faire** to go to the trouble of doing; **se donner de la** ~ to make an effort; **ce n'est pas la** ~ **de faire** there's no point in doing, it's not worth doing; **avoir de la** ~ **à faire** to have difficulty doing; **à** ~ *ad* scarcely, hardly, barely; **à** ~ **... que** hardly ... than; **sous** ~: **sous** ~ **d'être puni** for fear of being punished; **défense d'afficher sous** ~ **d'amende** billposters will be fined; **peiner** *vi* to work hard; to struggle; (*moteur, voiture*) to labour // *vt* to grieve, sadden.

**peintre** [pɛ̃tR(ə)] *nm* painter; ~ **en bâtiment** house painter, painter and decorator; ~ **d'enseignes** signwriter.

**peinture** [pɛ̃tyR] *nf* painting; (*couche de couleur, couleur*) paint; (*surfaces peintes: aussi:* ~**s**) paintwork; ~ **mate/brillante** matt/gloss paint; '~ **fraîche**' 'wet paint'.

**péjoratif, ive** [peʒɔRatif, -iv] *a* pejorative, derogatory.

**pelage** [pəlaʒ] *nm* coat, fur.

**pêle-mêle** [pɛlmɛl] *ad* higgledy-piggledy.

**peler** [pəle] *vt*, *vi* to peel.

**pèlerin** [pɛlRɛ̃] *nm* pilgrim; **pèlerinage** *nm* pilgrimage; place of pilgrimage, shrine.

**pélican** [pelikɑ̃] *nm* pelican.

**pelle** [pɛl] *nf* shovel; (*d'enfant, de terrassier*) spade; ~ **à gâteau** cake slice; ~ **mécanique** mechanical digger; ~**ter** *vt* to shovel (up).

**pelletier** [pɛltje] *nm* furrier.

**pellicule** [pelikyl] *nf* film; ~**s** *nfpl* (*MÉD*) dandruff *sg*.

**pelote** [pəlɔt] *nf* (*de fil, laine*) ball; (*d'épingles*) pin cushion; ~ **basque** pelota.

**peloter** [pəlɔte] *vt* (*fam*) to feel (up); **se** ~ to pet.

**peloton** [pəlɔtɔ̃] *nm* group, squad; (*CYCLISME*) pack; ~ **d'exécution** firing squad.

**pelotonner** [pəlɔtɔne]: **se** ~ *vi* to curl (o.s.) up.

**pelouse** [pəluz] *nf* lawn.

**peluche** [pəlyʃ] *nf*: **animal en** ~ fluffy animal, soft toy; **pelucher** *vi* to become fluffy, fluff up.

**pelure** [pəlyʀ] *nf* peeling, peel *q*; ~ **d'oignon** onion skin.

**pénal, e, aux** [penal, -o] *a* penal.

**pénaliser** [penalize] *vt* to penalize.

**pénalité** [penalite] *nf* penalty.

**penalty, ies** [penalti, -z] *nm* (*SPORT*) penalty (kick).

**penaud, e** [pəno, -od] *a* sheepish, contrite.

**penchant** [pɑ̃ʃɑ̃] *nm* tendency, propensity; liking, fondness.

**penché, e** [pɑ̃ʃe] *a* slanting.

**pencher** [pɑ̃ʃe] *vi* to tilt, lean over // *vt* to tilt; **se** ~ *vi* to lean over; (*se baisser*) to bend down; **se** ~ **sur** to bend over; (*fig*: *problème*) to look into; **se** ~ **au dehors** to lean out; ~ **pour** to be inclined to favour.

**pendaison** [pɑ̃dɛzɔ̃] *nf* hanging.

**pendant, e** [pɑ̃dɑ̃, -ɑ̃t] *a* hanging (out); (*ADMIN, JUR*) pending // *nm* counterpart; matching piece // *prép* during; **faire** ~ **à** to match; to be the counterpart of; ~**s d'oreilles** drop *ou* pendant earrings.

**pendeloque** [pɑ̃dlɔk] *nf* pendant.

**pendentif** [pɑ̃dɑ̃tif] *nm* pendant.

**penderie** [pɑ̃dʀi] *nf* wardrobe; (*placard*) walk-in cupboard.

**pendre** [pɑ̃dʀ(ə)] *vt*, *vi* to hang; **se** ~ **(à)** (*se suicider*) to hang o.s. (on); **se** ~ **à** (*se suspendre*) to hang from; ~ **à** to hang (down) from; ~ **qch à** (*mur*) to hang sth (up) on; (*plafond*) to hang sth (up) from.

**pendule** [pɑ̃dyl] *nf* clock // *nm* pendulum.

**pendulette** [pɑ̃dylɛt] *nf* small clock.

**pêne** [pɛn] *nm* bolt.

**pénétrer** [penetʀe] *vi* to come *ou* get in // *vt* to penetrate; ~ **dans** to enter; (*suj*: *projectile*) to penetrate; (: *air, eau*) to come into, get into; **se** ~ **de qch** to get sth firmly set in one's mind.

**pénible** [penibl(ə)] *a* (*astreignant*) hard; (*affligeant*) painful; (*personne, caractère*) tiresome; ~**ment** *ad* with difficulty.

**péniche** [peniʃ] *nf* barge; ~ **de débarquement** landing craft *inv*.

**pénicilline** [penisilin] *nf* penicillin.

**péninsule** [penɛ̃syl] *nf* peninsula.

**pénis** [penis] *nm* penis.

**pénitence** [penitɑ̃s] *nf* (*repentir*) penitence; (*peine*) penance.

**pénitencier** [penitɑ̃sje] *nm* penitentiary.

**pénombre** [penɔ̃bʀ(ə)] *nf* half-light; darkness.

**pense-bête** [pɑ̃sbɛt] *nm* aide-mémoire.

**pensée** [pɑ̃se] *nf* thought; (*démarche, doctrine*) thinking *q*; (*BOT*) pansy; **en** ~ in one's mind.

**penser** [pɑ̃se] *vi* to think // *vt* to think; (*concevoir*: *problème, machine*) to think out; ~ **à** to think of; (*songer à*: *ami, vacances*) to think of *ou* about; (*réfléchir à*: *problème, offre*): ~ **à qch** to think about

sth *ou* sth over; ~ **à faire qch** to think of doing sth; ~ **faire qch** to be thinking of doing sth, intend to do sth; **penseur** *nm* thinker; **pensif, ive** *a* pensive, thoughtful.

**pension** [pɑ̃sjɔ̃] *nf* (*allocation*) pension; (*prix du logement*) board and lodgings, bed and board; (*maison particulière*) boarding house; (*hôtel*) guesthouse, hotel; (*école*) boarding school; **prendre** ~ **chez** to take board and lodging at; **prendre qn en** ~ to take sb (in) as a lodger; **mettre en** ~ to send to boarding school; ~ **alimentaire** (*d'étudiant*) living allowance; (*de divorcée*) maintenance allowance; alimony; ~ **complète** full board; ~ **de famille** boarding house, guesthouse; **pensionnaire** *nm/f* boarder; guest; **pensionnat** *nm* boarding school.

**pentagone** [pɛ̃tagɔn] *nm* pentagon.

**pente** [pɑ̃t] *nf* slope; **en** ~ *a* sloping.

**Pentecôte** [pɑ̃tkot] *nf*: **la** ~ Whitsun; (*dimanche*) Whitsunday; **lundi de** ~ Whit Monday.

**pénurie** [penyʀi] *nf* shortage.

**pépier** [pepje] *vi* to chirp, tweet.

**pépin** [pepɛ̃] *nm* (*BOT*: *graine*) pip; (*ennui*) snag, hitch; (*fam*) brolly.

**pépinière** [pepinjɛʀ] *nf* tree nursery; (*fig*) nest, breeding-ground.

**pépite** [pepit] *nf* nugget.

**perçant, e** [pɛʀsɑ̃, -ɑ̃t] *a* sharp, keen; piercing, shrill.

**percée** [pɛʀse] *nf* (*trouée*) opening; (*MIL*) breakthrough; (*SPORT*) break.

**perce-neige** [pɛʀsənɛʒ] *nf inv* snowdrop.

**percepteur** [pɛʀsɛptœʀ] *nm* tax collector.

**perceptible** [pɛʀsɛptibl(ə)] *a* perceptible.

**perception** [pɛʀsɛpsjɔ̃] *nf* perception; (*d'impôts etc*) collection.

**percer** [pɛʀse] *vt* to pierce; (*ouverture etc*) to make; (*mystère, énigme*) to penetrate // *vi* to come through; to break through; ~ **une dent** to cut a tooth.

**perceuse** [pɛʀsøz] *nf* drill.

**percevoir** [pɛʀsəvwaʀ] *vt* (*distinguer*) to perceive, detect; (*taxe, impôt*) to collect; (*revenu, indemnité*) to receive.

**perche** [pɛʀʃ(ə)] *nf* (*ZOOL*) perch; (*bâton*) pole.

**percher** [pɛʀʃe] *vt*: ~ **qch sur** to perch sth on // *vi*, **se** ~ *vi* (*oiseau*) to perch; **perchoir** *nm* perch.

**perclus, e** [pɛʀkly, -yz] *a*: ~ **de** (*rhumatismes*) crippled with.

**perçois** *etc vb voir* **percevoir.**

**perçu, e** *pp de* **percevoir.**

**percussion** [pɛʀkysjɔ̃] *nf* percussion.

**percuter** [pɛʀkyte] *vt* to strike; (*suj*: *véhicule*) to crash into.

**perdant, e** [pɛʀdɑ̃, -ɑ̃t] *nm/f* loser.

**perdition** [pɛʀdisjɔ̃] *nf*: **en** ~ (*NAVIG*) in distress; **lieu de** ~ den of vice.

**perdre** [pɛʀdʀ(ə)] *vt* to lose; (*gaspiller*: *temps, argent*) to waste; (*personne*: *moralement etc*) to ruin // *vi* to lose; (*sur une vente etc*) to lose out; (*récipient*) to leak; **se** ~ *vi* (*s'égarer*) to get lost, lose one's way; (*fig*) to go to waste; to disappear, vanish.

**perdreau, x** [pɛʀdʀo] *nm* (young) partridge.

**perdrix** [pɛʀdʀi] *nf* partridge.

**perdu, e** [pɛʀdy] *pp de* **perdre** // *a* (*isolé*) out-of-the-way, godforsaken; (*COMM: emballage*) non-returnable; (*malade*): **il est ~** there's no hope left for him; **à vos moments ~s** in your spare time.

**père** [pɛʀ] *nm* father; **~s** *nmpl* (*ancêtres*) forefathers; **de ~ en fils** from father to son; **~ de famille** man with a family; family man; **le ~ Noël** Father Christmas.

**péremptoire** [peʀɑ̃ptwaʀ] *a* peremptory.

**perfection** [pɛʀfɛksjɔ̃] *nf* perfection.

**perfectionné, e** [pɛʀfɛksjone] *a* sophisticated.

**perfectionnement** [pɛʀfɛksjɔnmɑ̃] *nm* improvement.

**perfectionner** [pɛʀfɛksjone] *vt* to improve, perfect; **se ~ en anglais** to improve one's English.

**perfide** [pɛʀfid] *a* perfidious, treacherous.

**perforant, e** [pɛʀfɔʀɑ̃, -ɑ̃t] *a* (*balle*) armour-piercing.

**perforateur, trice** [pɛʀfɔʀatœʀ, -tʀis] *nm/f* punch-card operator // *nm* (*perceuse*) borer; drill // *nf* (*perceuse*) borer; drill; (*pour cartes*) card-punch; (*de bureau*) punch.

**perforation** [pɛʀfɔʀasjɔ̃] *nf* perforation; punching; (*trou*) hole.

**perforatrice** [pɛʀfɔʀatʀis] *nf voir* **perforateur.**

**perforer** [pɛʀfɔʀe] *vt* to perforate; to punch a hole (*ou* holes) in; (*ticket, bande, carte*) to punch.

**performance** [pɛʀfɔʀmɑ̃s] *nf* performance.

**perfusion** [pɛʀfyzjɔ̃] *nf* perfusion; **faire une ~ à qn** to put sb on a drip.

**péricliter** [peʀiklite] *vi* to go downhill.

**péril** [peʀil] *nm* peril; **périlleux, euse** [-jø, -øz] *a* perilous.

**périmé, e** [peʀime] *a* (out)dated; (*ADMIN*) out-of-date, expired.

**périmètre** [peʀimɛtʀ(ə)] *nm* perimeter.

**période** [peʀjɔd] *nf* period; **périodique** *a* (*phases*) periodic; (*publication*) periodical; (*MATH: fraction*) recurring // *nm* periodical; **garniture** *ou* **serviette périodique** sanitary towel.

**péripéties** [peʀipesi] *nfpl* events, episodes.

**périphérie** [peʀifeʀi] *nf* periphery; (*d'une ville*) outskirts *pl*; **périphérique** *a* (*quartiers*) outlying; (*ANAT, TECH*) peripheral; (*station de radio*) operating from outside France // *nm* (*AUTO*) ring road.

**périphrase** [peʀifʀɑz] *nf* circumlocution.

**périple** [peʀipl(ə)] *nm* journey.

**périr** [peʀiʀ] *vi* to die, perish.

**périscope** [peʀiskɔp] *nm* periscope.

**périssable** [peʀisabl(ə)] *a* perishable.

**péritonite** [peʀitɔnit] *nf* peritonitis.

**perle** [pɛʀl(ə)] *nf* pearl; (*de plastique, métal, sueur*) bead.

**perlé, e** [pɛʀle] *a*: **grève ~e** go-slow.

**perler** [pɛʀle] *vi* to form in droplets.

**perlier, ière** [pɛʀlje, -jɛʀ] *a* pearl *cpd*.

**permanence** [pɛʀmanɑ̃s] *nf* permanence; (*local*) (duty) office; strike headquarters; emergency service; **assurer une ~** (*service public, bureaux*) to operate *ou* maintain a basic service; **être de ~** to be on call *ou* duty; **en ~** *ad* permanently; continuously.

**permanent, e** [pɛʀmanɑ̃, -ɑ̃t] *a* permanent; (*spectacle*) continuous // *nf* perm, permanent wave.

**perméable** [pɛʀmeabl(ə)] *a* (*terrain*) permeable; **~ à** (*fig*) receptive *ou* open to.

**permettre** [pɛʀmɛtʀ(ə)] *vt* to allow, permit; **~ à qn de faire/qch** to allow sb to do/sth.

**permis** [pɛʀmi] *nm* permit, licence; **~ de chasse** hunting permit; **~ (de conduire)** (driving) licence; **~ de construire** planning permission; **~ d'inhumer** burial certificate; **~ poids lourds** HGV (driving) licence; **~ de séjour** residence permit.

**permission** [pɛʀmisjɔ̃] *nf* permission; (*MIL*) leave; (: *papier*) pass; **en ~** on leave; **avoir la ~ de faire** to have permission to do, be allowed to do; **permissionnaire** *nm* soldier on leave.

**permuter** [pɛʀmyte] *vt* to change around, permutate // *vi* to change, swap.

**pernicieux, euse** [pɛʀnisjø, -øz] *a* pernicious.

**pérorer** [peʀɔʀe] *vi* to hold forth.

**perpendiculaire** [pɛʀpɑ̃dikylɛʀ] *a, nf* perpendicular.

**perpétrer** [pɛʀpetʀe] *vt* to perpetrate.

**perpétuel, le** [pɛʀpetɥɛl] *a* perpetual; (*ADMIN etc*) permanent; for life.

**perpétuer** [pɛʀpetɥe] *vt* to perpetuate.

**perpétuité** [pɛʀpetɥite] *nf*: **à ~** *a, ad* for life; **être condamné à ~** to be sentenced to life imprisonment, receive a life sentence.

**perplexe** [pɛʀplɛks(ə)] *a* perplexed, puzzled.

**perquisition** [pɛʀkizisjɔ̃] *nf* (police) search; **perquisitionner** *vi* to carry out a search.

**perron** [pɛʀɔ̃] *nm* steps *pl* (*in front of mansion etc*).

**perroquet** [pɛʀɔkɛ] *nm* parrot.

**perruche** [pɛʀyʃ] *nf* budgerigar, budgie.

**perruque** [pɛʀyk] *nf* wig.

**persan, e** [pɛʀsɑ̃, -an] *a* Persian.

**persécuter** [pɛʀsekyte] *vt* to persecute; **persécution** *nf* persecution.

**persévérant, e** [pɛʀseveʀɑ̃, -ɑ̃t] *a* persevering.

**persévérer** [pɛʀseveʀe] *vi* to persevere.

**persiennes** [pɛʀsjɛn] *nfpl* (metal) shutters.

**persiflage** [pɛʀsiflaʒ] *nm* mockery *q*.

**persil** [pɛʀsi] *nm* parsley.

**Persique** [pɛʀsik] *a*: **le golfe ~** the (Persian) Gulf.

**persistant, e** [pɛʀsistɑ̃, -ɑ̃t] *a* persistent; (*feuilles*) evergreen; **à feuillage ~** evergreen.

**persister** [pɛʀsiste] *vi* to persist; **~ à faire qch** to persist in doing sth.

**personnage** [pɛʀsɔnaʒ] *nm* (*notable*) personality; figure; (*individu*) character, individual; (*THÉÂTRE*) character; (*PEINTURE*) figure.

**personnaliser** [pɛʀsɔnalize] *vt* to personalize.

**personnalité** [pɛʀsɔnalite] *nf* personality.

**personne** [pɛʀsɔn] *nf* person // *pronom* nobody, no one ; (*quelqu'un*) anybody, anyone ; ~s people *pl* ; **il n'y a** ~ there's nobody in, there isn't anybody in ; **10 F par** ~ 10 F per person *ou* a head ; ~ **âgée** elderly person ; **personnel, le** *a* personal // *nm* staff ; personnel ; **personnellement** *ad* personally ; **personnifier** *vt* to personify ; to typify.

**perspective** [pɛʀspɛktiv] *nf* (*ART*) perspective ; (*vue, coup d'œil*) view ; (*point de vue*) viewpoint, angle ; (*chose escomptée, envisagée*) prospect ; **en** ~ in prospect ; in the offing.

**perspicace** [pɛʀspikas] *a* clear-sighted, gifted with (*ou* showing) insight.

**persuader** [pɛʀsɥade] *vt*: ~ **qn (de/de faire)** to persuade sb (of/to do); **persuasif, ive** *a* persuasive ; **persuasion** *nf* persuasion.

**perte** [pɛʀt(ə)] *nf* loss ; (*de temps*) waste ; (*fig: morale*) ruin ; **à** ~ (*COMM*) at a loss ; **à** ~ **de vue** as far as the eye can (*ou* could) see ; (*fig*) interminably ; ~ **sèche** dead loss ; ~**s blanches** (vaginal) discharge *sg*.

**pertinent, e** [pɛʀtinɑ̃, -ɑ̃t] *a* apt, pertinent ; discerning, judicious.

**perturbation** [pɛʀtyʀbɑsjɔ̃] *nf* disruption ; perturbation ; ~ **(atmosphérique)** atmospheric disturbance.

**perturber** [pɛʀtyʀbe] *vt* to disrupt ; (*PSYCH*) to perturb, disturb.

**pervenche** [pɛʀvɑ̃ʃ] *nf* periwinkle.

**pervers, e** [pɛʀvɛʀ, -ɛʀs(ə)] *a* perverted, depraved ; perverse.

**perversion** [pɛʀvɛʀsjɔ̃] *nf* perversion.

**perverti, e** [pɛʀvɛʀti] *nm/f* pervert.

**pervertir** [pɛʀvɛʀtiʀ] *vt* to pervert.

**pesage** [pəzaʒ] *nm* weighing ; (*HIPPISME*) weigh-in ; weighing room ; enclosure.

**pesamment** [pəzamɑ̃] *ad* heavily.

**pesant, e** [pəzɑ̃, -ɑ̃t] *a* heavy, (*fig*) burdensome // *nm*: **valoir son** ~ **de** to be worth one's weight in.

**pesanteur** [pəzɑ̃tœʀ] *nf* gravity.

**pèse-bébé** [pɛzbebe] *nm* (baby) scales *pl*.

**pesée** [pəze] *nf* weighing ; (*BOXE*) weigh-in ; (*pression*) pressure.

**pèse-lettre** [pɛzlɛtʀ(ə)] *nm* letter scales *pl*.

**pèse-personne** [pɛzpɛʀsɔn] *nm* (bathroom) scales *pl*.

**peser** [pəze] *vt, vb avec attribut* to weigh // *vi* to be heavy ; (*fig*) to carry weight ; ~ **sur** (*levier, bouton*) to press, push ; (*fig*) to lie heavy on ; to influence ; ~ **à qn** to weigh heavy on sb.

**pessaire** [pesɛʀ] *nm* pessary.

**pessimisme** [pesimism(ə)] *nm* pessimism ; **pessimiste** *a* pessimistic // *nm/f* pessimist.

**peste** [pɛst(ə)] *nf* plague.

**pester** [pɛste] *vi*: ~ **contre** to curse.

**pestiféré, e** [pɛstifeʀe] *nm/f* plague victim.

**pestilentiel, le** [pɛstilɑ̃sjɛl] *a* foul.

**pet** [pɛ] *nm* (*fam!*) fart (!).

**pétale** [petal] *nm* petal.

**pétanque** [petɑ̃k] *nf* petanque (bowls).

**pétarader** [petaʀade] *vi* to backfire.

**pétard** [petaʀ] *nm* banger ; cracker ; (*RAIL*) detonator.

**péter** [pete] *vi* (*fam: casser, sauter*) to burst ; to bust ; (*fam!*) to fart (!).

**pétiller** [petije] *vi* (*flamme, bois*) to crackle ; (*mousse, champagne*) to bubble ; (*yeux*) to sparkle.

**petit, e** [pəti, -it] *a* (*gén*) small ; (*main, objet, colline, en âge: enfant*) small, little (*avant le nom*) ; (*voyage*) short, little ; (*bruit etc*) faint, slight ; (*mesquin*) mean // *nm* (*d'un animal*) young *pl* ; **faire des** ~**s** to have kittens (*ou* puppies *etc*) ; **en** ~ in miniature ; **mon** ~ son ; little one ; **ma** ~**e** dear ; little one ; **pauvre** ~ poor little thing ; **la classe des** ~**s** the infant class ; **pour** ~**s et grands** for children and adults ; **les tout-petits** the little ones, the tiny tots ; ~ **à** ~ bit by bit, gradually ; ~**/e ami/e** boyfriend/girlfriend ; ~ **déjeuner** breakfast ; ~ **doigt** little finger, pinkie ; ~ **four** petit four ; ~**e vérole** smallpox ; ~**s pois** petit pois *pl*, garden pea(s) ; ~**-bourgeois**, ~**e-bourgeoise** *a* (*péj*) petit-bourgeois(e), middle-class ; ~**e-fille** *nf* granddaughter ; ~**-fils** *nm* grandson.

**pétition** [petisjɔ̃] *nf* petition.

**petit-lait** [pətilɛ] *nm* whey.

**petit-nègre** [ptinɛgʀ(ə)] *nm* (*péj*) pidgin French.

**petits-enfants** [pətizɑ̃fɑ̃] *nmpl* grandchildren.

**pétrifier** [petʀifje] *vt* to petrify ; (*fig*) to paralyze, transfix.

**pétrin** [petʀɛ̃] *nm* kneading-trough ; (*fig*): **dans le** ~ in a jam *ou* fix.

**pétrir** [petʀiʀ] *vt* to knead.

**pétrole** [petʀɔl] *nm* oil ; (*pour lampe, réchaud etc*) paraffin (oil) ; **pétrolier, ière** *a* oil *cpd* // *nm* oil tanker ; **pétrolifère** *a* oil(-bearing).

**peu** [pø] *ad* little, tournure négative + much ; (*avec adjectif*) tournure négative + very // *pronom* few // *nm* little ; ~ **avant/après** shortly before/afterwards ; ~ **de** (*nombre*) few, négation + (very) many ; (*quantité*) little, négation + (very) much ; **pour** ~ **de temps** for (only) a short while ; **le** ~ **de gens qui** the few people who ; **le** ~ **de sable qui** what little sand, the little sand which ; **un (petit)** ~ a little (bit) ; **un** ~ **de** a little ; **un** ~ **plus/moins de** slightly more/less (*ou* fewer) ; **de** ~ (only) just ; ~ **à** ~ little by little ; **à** ~ **près** *ad* just about, more or less ; **à** ~ **près 10 kg/10 F** approximately 10 kg/10 F ; **avant** ~ before long.

**peuplade** [pœplad] *nf* (*horde, tribu*) tribe, people.

**peuple** [pœpl(ə)] *nm* people.

**peupler** [pœple] *vt* (*pays, région*) to populate ; (*étang*) to stock ; (*suj: hommes, poissons*) to inhabit ; (*fig: imagination, rêves*) to fill.

**peuplier** [pøplije] *nm* poplar (tree).

**peur** [pœʀ] *nf* fear ; **avoir** ~ **(de/de faire/que)** to be frightened *ou* afraid (of/of doing/that) ; **faire** ~ **à** to frighten ;

**de ~ de/que** for fear of/that; **~eux, euse** a fearful, timorous.
**peut** vb voir **pouvoir**.
**peut-être** [pøtɛtʀ(ə)] ad perhaps, maybe; **~ que** perhaps, maybe; **~ bien qu'il fera/est** he may well do/be.
**peux** etc vb voir **pouvoir**.
**phalange** [falɑ̃ʒ] nf (ANAT) phalanx (pl phalanges); (MIL) phalanx (pl es).
**phallocrate** [falɔkʀat] nm male chauvinist.
**phallus** [falys] nm phallus.
**phare** [faʀ] nm (en mer) lighthouse; (d'aéroport) beacon; (de véhicule) headlamp; **mettre ses ~s** to put on the full beam; **~s de recul** reversing lights.
**pharmaceutique** [faʀmasøtik] a pharmaceutic(al).
**pharmacie** [faʀmasi] nf (science) pharmacology; (magasin) chemist's, pharmacy; (officine) dispensary; (produits) pharmaceuticals pl; **pharmacien, ne** nm/f pharmacist, chemist.
**pharyngite** [faʀɛ̃ʒit] nf pharyngitis q.
**pharynx** [faʀɛ̃ks] nm pharynx.
**phase** [faz] nf phase.
**phénomène** [fenɔmɛn] nm phenomenon (pl a); (monstre) freak.
**philanthrope** [filɑ̃tʀɔp] nm/f philanthropist.
**philanthropie** [filɑ̃tʀɔpi] nf philanthropy.
**philatélie** [filateli] nf philately, stamp collecting; **philatéliste** nm/f philatelist, stamp collector.
**philharmonique** [filaʀmɔnik] a philharmonic.
**philo** [filo] nf abr de **philosophie**.
**philosophe** [filɔzɔf] nm/f philosopher // a philosophical.
**philosophie** [filɔzɔfi] nf philosophy; **philosophique** a philosophical.
**phobie** [fɔbi] nf phobia.
**phonétique** [fɔnetik] a phonetic // nf phonetics sg.
**phonographe** [fɔnɔgʀaf] nm (wind-up) gramophone.
**phoque** [fɔk] nm seal; (fourrure) sealskin.
**phosphate** [fɔsfat] nm phosphate.
**phosphore** [fɔsfɔʀ] nm phosphorus.
**phosphorescent, e** [fɔsfɔʀesɑ̃, -ɑ̃t] a luminous.
**photo** [fɔto] nf photo(graph); **en ~** in ou on a photograph; **prendre en ~** to take a photo of; **aimer la/faire de la ~** to like taking/take photos; **~ d'identité** passport photograph.
**photo...** [fɔto] préfixe: **~copie** nf photocopying, photostatting; photocopy, photostat (copy); **~copier** vt to photocopy, photostat; **~-électrique** a photoelectric; **~génique** a photogenic; **~graphe** nm/f photographer; **~graphie** nf (procédé, technique) photography; (cliché) photograph; **faire de la ~graphie** to have photography as a hobby; to be a photographer; **~graphier** vt to photograph, take; **~graphique** a photographic; **~maton** nm photo-booth, photomat; **~-robot** nf identikit (picture).

**phrase** [fʀɑz] nf (LING) sentence; (propos, MUS) phrase; **~s** (péj) flowery language sg.
**phtisie** [ftizi] nf consumption.
**physicien, ne** [fizisjɛ̃, -ɛn] nm/f physicist.
**physiologie** [fizjɔlɔʒi] nf physiology; **physiologique** a physiological.
**physionomie** [fizjɔnɔmi] nf face; **physionomiste** nm/f good judge of faces; person who has a good memory for faces.
**physique** [fizik] a physical // nm physique // nf physics sg; **au ~** physically; **~ment** ad physically.
**piaffer** [pjafe] vi to stamp.
**piailler** [pjaje] vi to squawk.
**pianiste** [pjanist(ə)] nm/f pianist.
**piano** [pjano] nm piano.
**pianoter** [pjanɔte] vi to tinkle away (at the piano); (tapoter): **~ sur** to drum one's fingers on.
**piaule** [pjol] nf (fam) pad.
**piauler** [pjole] vi to whimper; to cheep.
**pic** [pik] nm (instrument) pick(axe); (montagne) peak; (ZOOL) woodpecker; **à ~** ad vertically; (fig) just at the right time.
**pichenette** [piʃnɛt] nf flick.
**pichet** [piʃɛ] nm jug.
**pickpocket** [pikpɔkɛt] nm pickpocket.
**pick-up** [pikœp] nm record player.
**picorer** [pikɔʀe] vt to peck.
**picotement** [pikɔtmɑ̃] nm tickle q; smarting q; prickling q.
**picoter** [pikɔte] vt (suj: oiseau) to peck // vi (irriter) to smart, prickle.
**pie** [pi] nf magpie; (fig) chatterbox.
**pièce** [pjɛs] nf (d'un logement) room; (THÉÂTRE) play; (de mécanisme, machine) part; (de monnaie) coin; (COUTURE) patch; (document) document; (de drap, fragment, de bétail, de collection) piece; **dix francs ~** ten francs each; **vendre à la ~** to sell separately ou individually; **travailler/payer à la ~** to do piecework/pay piece rate; **un maillot une ~** a one-piece swimsuit; **un deux-~s cuisine** a two-room(ed) flat with kitchen; **~ à conviction** exhibit; **~ d'eau** ornamental lake ou pond; **~ d'identité: avez-vous une ~ d'identité?** have you got any (means of) identification?; **~ montée** tiered cake; **~s détachées** spares, (spare) parts; **en ~s détachées** (à monter) in kit form.
**pied** [pje] nm foot (pl feet); (de verre) stem; (de table) leg; (de lampe) base; **~s nus** barefoot; **à ~** on foot; **à ~ sec** without getting one's feet wet; **au ~ de la lettre** literally; **au ~ levé** at a moment's notice; **de ~ en cap** from head to foot; **en ~** (portrait) full-length; **avoir ~** to be able to touch the bottom, not to be out of one's depth; **avoir le ~ marin** to be a good sailor; **perdre ~** to lose one's footing; **sur ~** (AGR) on the stalk, uncut; (debout, rétabli) up and about; **mettre sur ~** (entreprise) to set up; **mettre à ~** to dismiss; to lay off; **sur le ~ de guerre** ready for action; **sur ~ d'intervention** on stand-by; **faire du ~ à qn** to give sb a (warning) kick; to play footsy with sb; **~ de lit** footboard; **~ de nez: faire un ~ de nez à** to thumb one's nose at; **~ de salade** lettuce plant; **~ de vigne** vine;

**~-à-terre** nm inv pied-à-terre ; **~-de-biche** nm claw ; (COUTURE) presser foot ; **~-de-poule** a inv hound's-tooth.

**piédestal, aux** [pjedɛstal, -o] nm pedestal.

**pied-noir** [pjenwaR] nm Algerian-born Frenchman.

**piège** [pjɛʒ] nm trap ; **prendre au ~** to trap ; **piéger** vt (avec une mine) to booby-trap ; **lettre/voiture piégée** letter-/car-bomb.

**pierraille** [pjɛRɑj] nf loose stones pl.

**pierre** [pjɛR] nf stone ; **~ à briquet** flint ; **~ fine** semiprecious stone ; **~ de taille** freestone q ; **~ de touche** touchstone ; **mur de ~s sèches** drystone wall.

**pierreries** [pjɛRRi] nfpl gems, precious stones.

**piété** [pjete] nf piety.

**piétiner** [pjetine] vi (trépigner) to stamp (one's foot) ; (marquer le pas) to stand about ; (fig) to be at a standstill // vt to trample on.

**piéton, ne** [pjetɔ̃, -ɔn] nm/f pedestrian ; **piétonnier, ière** a pedestrian cpd.

**piètre** [pjɛtR(ə)] a poor, mediocre.

**pieu, x** [pjø] nm post ; (pointu) stake.

**pieuvre** [pjœvR(ə)] nf octopus.

**pieux, euse** [pjø, -øz] a pious.

**pigeon** [piʒɔ̃] nm pigeon ; **~ voyageur** homing pigeon ; **pigeonnier** nm pigeon house.

**piger** [piʒe] vi, vt (fam) to understand.

**pigment** [pigmɑ̃] nm pigment.

**pignon** [piɲɔ̃] nm (de mur) gable ; (d'engrenage) cog(wheel), gearwheel ; (graine) pine kernel ; **avoir ~ sur rue** (fig) to have a prosperous business.

**pile** [pil] nf (tas) pile ; (ÉLEC) battery // a: **le côté ~** tails // ad (s'arrêter etc) dead ; **à deux heures ~** at two on the dot ; **jouer à ~ ou face** to toss up (for it) ; **~ ou face?** heads or tails?

**piler** [pile] vt to crush, pound.

**pileux, euse** [pilø, -øz] a: **système ~** (body) hair.

**pilier** [pilje] nm pillar.

**pillard, e** [pijaR, -aRd(ə)] nm/f looter ; plunderer.

**piller** [pije] vt to pillage, plunder, loot.

**pilon** [pilɔ̃] nm pestle.

**pilonner** [pilɔne] vt to pound.

**pilori** [pilɔRi] nm: **mettre ou clouer au ~** to pillory.

**pilotage** [pilɔtaʒ] nm piloting ; flying ; **~ sans visibilité** blind flying.

**pilote** [pilɔt] nm pilot ; (de char, voiture) driver // a pilot cpd ; **~ de ligne/d'essai/de chasse** airline/test/fighter pilot.

**piloter** [pilɔte] vt to pilot ; to fly ; to drive ; (fig) : **~ qn** to guide sb round.

**pilotis** [pilɔti] nm pile ; stilt.

**pilule** [pilyl] nf pill ; **prendre la ~** to be on the pill.

**pimbêche** [pɛ̃bɛʃ] nf (péj) stuck-up girl.

**piment** [pimɑ̃] nm (BOT) pepper, capsicum ; (fig) spice, piquancy ; **~ rouge** (CULIN) chilli.

**pimpant, e** [pɛ̃pɑ̃, -ɑ̃t] a trim and fresh-looking.

**pin** [pɛ̃] nm pine (tree) ; (bois) pine(wood).

**pince** [pɛ̃s] nf (outil) pliers pl ; (de homard, crabe) pincer, claw ; (COUTURE: pli) dart ; **~ à sucre/glace** sugar/ice tongs pl ; **~ à épiler** tweezers pl ; **~ à linge** clothes peg ; **~s de cycliste** bicycle clips.

**pinceau, x** [pɛ̃so] nm (paint)brush.

**pincé, e** [pɛ̃se] a (air) stiff // nf: **une ~e de** a pinch of.

**pincer** [pɛ̃se] vt to pinch ; (MUS: cordes) to pluck ; (COUTURE) to dart, put darts in ; (fam) to nab ; **se ~ le nez** to hold one's nose.

**pince-sans-rire** [pɛ̃ssɑ̃Rir] a inv deadpan.

**pincettes** [pɛ̃sɛt] nfpl (pour le feu) (fire) tongs.

**pinède** [pinɛd] nf pinewood, pine forest.

**pingouin** [pɛ̃gwɛ̃] nm penguin.

**ping-pong** [piŋpɔ̃g] nm table tennis.

**pingre** [pɛ̃gR(ə)] a niggardly.

**pinson** [pɛ̃sɔ̃] nm chaffinch.

**pintade** [pɛ̃tad] nf guinea-fowl.

**pin-up** [pinœp] nf inv pinup (girl).

**pioche** [pjɔʃ] nf pickaxe ; **piocher** vt to dig up (with a pickaxe) ; (fam) to swot at ; **piocher dans** to dig into.

**piolet** [pjɔlɛ] nm ice axe.

**pion, ne** [pjɔ̃, pjɔn] nm/f (SCOL: péj) student paid to supervise schoolchildren // nm (ÉCHECS) pawn ; (DAMES) piece, draught.

**pionnier** [pjɔnje] nm pioneer.

**pipe** [pip] nf pipe ; **~ de bruyère** briar pipe.

**pipeau, x** [pipo] nm (reed-)pipe.

**pipe-line** [pajplajn] nm pipeline.

**pipi** [pipi] nm (fam): **faire ~** to have a wee.

**piquant, e** [pikɑ̃, -ɑ̃t] a (barbe, rosier etc) prickly ; (saveur, sauce) hot, pungent ; (fig) racy ; biting // nm (épine) thorn, prickle ; (de hérisson) quill, spine ; (fig) spiciness, spice.

**pique** [pik] nf pike ; (fig) cutting remark // nm (CARTES: couleur) spades pl ; (: carte) spade.

**piqué, e** [pike] a (COUTURE) (machine-)stitched, quilted ; (fam) barmy // nm (AVIAT) dive ; (TEXTILE) piqué.

**pique-assiette** [pikasjɛt] nm/f inv (péj) scrounger, sponger.

**pique-nique** [piknik] nm picnic.

**piquer** [pike] vt (percer) to prick ; (planter) : **~ qch dans** to stick sth into ; (fixer) : **~ qch à/sur** to pin sth onto ; (MÉD) to give a jab to ; (: animal blessé) to put to sleep ; (suj: insecte, fumée, ortie) to sting ; (suj: poivre) to burn ; (: froid) to bite ; (COUTURE) to machine (stitch) ; (intérêt etc) to arouse ; (fam) to pick up ; to pinch ; to nab // vi (avion) to go into a dive ; (saveur) to be pungent ; to be sour ; **~ sur** to swoop down on ; to head straight for ; **se ~ de faire** to pride o.s. on one's ability to do ; **~ du nez** (avion) to go into a nose-dive ; **~ un galop/un cent mètres** to break into a gallop/put on a sprint ; **~ une crise** to throw a fit.

**piquet** [pikɛ] nm (pieu) post, stake ; (de tente) peg ; **mettre un élève au ~** to make a pupil stand in the corner ; **~ de grève** (strike-)picket ; **~ d'incendie** fire-fighting squad.

**piqueté, e** [pikte] a: ~ **de** dotted with.
**piqûre** [pikyʀ] nf (d'épingle) prick; (d'ortie) sting; (de moustique) bite; (MÉD) injection; (COUTURE) (straight) stitch; straight stitching; **faire une** ~ **à qn** to give sb an injection.
**pirate** [piʀat] nm, a pirate; ~ **de l'air** hijacker.
**pire** [piʀ] a worse; (superlatif): **le(la)** ~ ... the worst ... // nm: **le** ~ **(de)** the worst (of).
**pirogue** [piʀɔg] nf dugout canoe.
**pirouette** [piʀwɛt] nf pirouette.
**pis** [pi] nm (de vache) udder; (pire): **le** ~ the worst // a, ad worse; **pis-aller** nm inv stopgap.
**pisciculture** [pisikyltyʀ] nf fish farming.
**piscine** [pisin] nf (swimming) pool; ~ **couverte** indoor (swimming) pool.
**pissenlit** [pisɑ̃li] nm dandelion.
**pisser** [pise] vi (fam!) to pee (!); **pissotière** nf (fam) public urinal.
**pistache** [pistaʃ] nf pistachio (nut).
**piste** [pist(ə)] nf (d'un animal, sentier) track, trail; (indice) lead; (de stade, de magnétophone) track; (de cirque) ring; (de danse) floor; (de patinage) rink; (de ski) run; (AVIAT) runway.
**pistil** [pistil] nm pistil.
**pistolet** [pistɔlɛ] nm (arme) pistol, gun; (à peinture) spray gun; ~ **à bouchon/air comprimé** popgun/ airgun; ~**-mitrailleur** nm submachine gun.
**piston** [pistɔ̃] nm (TECH) piston; (MUS) valve; (fig) string-pulling; **pistonner** vt (candidat) to pull strings for.
**pitance** [pitɑ̃s] nf (péj) (means of) sustenance.
**piteux, euse** [pitø, -øz] a pitiful, sorry (avant le nom).
**pitié** [pitje] nf pity; **sans** ~ a pitiless, merciless; **faire** ~ to inspire pity; **il me fait** ~ I pity him, I feel sorry for him; **avoir** ~ **de** (compassion) to pity, feel sorry for; (merci) to have pity ou mercy on.
**piton** [pitɔ̃] nm (clou) peg, bolt; ~ **rocheux** rocky outcrop.
**pitoyable** [pitwajabl(ə)] a pitiful.
**pitre** [pitʀ(ə)] nm clown; **pitrerie** nf tomfoolery q.
**pittoresque** [pitɔʀɛsk(ə)] a picturesque.
**pivot** [pivo] nm pivot; **pivoter** vi to swivel; to revolve.
**pizza** [pidza] nf pizza.
**P.J.** sigle f voir **police**.
**Pl.** abr de **place**.
**placage** [plakaʒ] nm (bois) veneer.
**placard** [plakaʀ] nm (armoire) cupboard; (affiche) poster, notice; (TYPO) galley; ~ **publicitaire** display advertisement; **placarder** vt (affiche) to put up.
**place** [plas] nf (emplacement, situation, classement) place; (de ville, village) square; (espace libre) room, space; (de parking) space; (siège: de train, cinéma, voiture) seat; (emploi) job; **en** ~ (mettre) in its place; **sur** ~ on the spot; **faire** ~ **à** to give way to; **faire de la** ~ **à** to make room for; **ça prend de la** ~ it takes up a lot of room ou space; **à la** ~ **de** in place of, instead of; **une quatre** ~**s** (AUTO) a four-

seater; **il y a 20** ~**s assises/debout** there are 20 seats/is standing room for 20; ~ **forte** fortified town.
**placé, e** [plase] a (HIPPISME) placed; **haut** ~ (fig) high-ranking.
**placement** [plasmɑ̃] nm placing; investment; **bureau de** ~ employment agency.
**placenta** [plasɑ̃ta] nm placenta.
**placer** [plase] vt to place; (convive, spectateur) to seat; (capital, argent) to place, invest; (dans la conversation) to put ou get in; ~ **qn chez** to get sb a job at (ou with); **se** ~ **au premier rang** to go and stand (ou sit) in the first row.
**placide** [plasid] a placid.
**plafond** [plafɔ̃] nm ceiling.
**plafonner** [plafɔne] vi to reach one's (ou a) ceiling.
**plage** [plaʒ] nf beach; (station) (seaside) resort; (fig) band, bracket; (de disque) track, band; ~ **arrière** (AUTO) parcel ou back shelf.
**plagiat** [plaʒja] nm plagiarism.
**plagier** [plaʒje] vt to plagiarize.
**plaider** [plede] vi (avocat) to plead; (plaignant) to go to court, litigate // vt to plead; ~ **pour** (fig) to speak for; **plaideur, euse** nm/f litigant; **plaidoirie** nf (JUR) speech for the defence; **plaidoyer** nm (JUR) speech for the defence; (fig) plea.
**plaie** [plɛ] nf wound.
**plaignant, e** [plɛɲɑ̃, -ɑ̃t] nm/f plaintiff.
**plaindre** [plɛ̃dʀ(ə)] vt to pity, feel sorry for; **se** ~ (gémir) to moan; (protester, rouspéter): **se** ~ (à qn) (de) to complain (to sb) (about); (souffrir): **se** ~ **de** to complain of.
**plaine** [plɛn] nf plain.
**plain-pied** [plɛ̃pje]: **de** ~ ad at street-level; (fig) straight; **de** ~ **avec** on the same level as.
**plainte** [plɛ̃t] nf (gémissement) moan, groan; (doléance) complaint; **porter** ~ to lodge a complaint; **plaintif, ive** a plaintive.
**plaire** [plɛʀ] vi to be a success, be successful; to please; ~ **à: cela me plaît** I like it; **essayer de** ~ **à qn** (en étant serviable etc) to try and please sb; **elle plaît aux hommes** she's a success with men, men like her; **se** ~ **quelque part** to like being somewhere ou like it somewhere; **se** ~ **à faire** to take pleasure in doing; **ce qu'il vous plaira** what(ever) you like ou wish; **s'il vous plaît** please.
**plaisamment** [plɛzamɑ̃] ad pleasantly.
**plaisance** [plɛzɑ̃s] nf (aussi: navigation de ~) (pleasure) sailing, yachting; **plaisancier** nm amateur sailor, yachting enthusiast.
**plaisant, e** [plɛzɑ̃, -ɑ̃t] a pleasant; (histoire, anecdote) amusing.
**plaisanter** [plɛzɑ̃te] vi to joke; **pour** ~ for a joke; **on ne plaisante pas avec cela** that's no joking matter; **plaisanterie** nf joke; joking q; **plaisantin** nm joker.
**plaise** etc vb voir **plaire**.
**plaisir** [pleziʀ] nm pleasure; **faire** ~ **à qn** (délibérément) to be nice to sb, please sb; (suj: cadeau, nouvelle etc): **ceci me fait** ~ I'm delighted ou very pleased with this; **prendre** ~ **à/faire** to take pleasure in/in

doing; **à** ~ freely; for the sake of it; **au ~ (de vous revoir)** (I hope to) see you again; **pour le ou par** ~ for pleasure.

**plan, e** [plɑ̃, -an] *a* flat // *nm* plan; (*GÉOM*) plane; (*fig*) level, plane; (*CINÉMA*) shot; **au premier/second** ~ in the foreground/middle distance; **à l'arrière** ~ in the background; **mettre qch au premier** ~ (*fig*) to consider sth to be of primary importance; **sur le** ~ **sexuel** sexually, as far as sex is concerned; ~ **d'eau** stretch of water; ~ **de travail** work programme *ou* schedule.

**planche** [plɑ̃ʃ] *nf* (*pièce de bois*) plank, (wooden) board; (*illustration*) plate; **les** ~**s** (*THÉÂTRE*) the stage *sg*, the boards; **faire la** ~ (*dans l'eau*) to float on one's back; ~ **à dessin** drawing board; ~ **à pain** breadboard; ~ **à repasser** ironing board; ~ **de salut** (*fig*) sheet anchor.

**plancher** [plɑ̃ʃe] *nm* floor; floorboards *pl*; (*fig*) minimum level.

**plancton** [plɑ̃ktɔ̃] *nm* plankton.

**planer** [plane] *vi* to glide; ~ **sur** (*fig*) to hang over; to hover above.

**planétaire** [planetɛʀ] *a* planetary.

**planète** [planɛt] *nf* planet.

**planeur** [plancœʀ] *nm* glider.

**planification** [planifikasjɔ̃] *nf* (economic) planning.

**planifier** [planifje] *vt* to plan.

**planning** [planiŋ] *nm* programme, schedule; ~ **familial** family planning.

**planque** [plɑ̃k] *nf* (*fam*) cushy number; hideout; stash.

**plant** [plɑ̃] *nm* seedling, young plant.

**plantaire** [plɑ̃tɛʀ] *a voir* **voûte**.

**plantation** [plɑ̃tasjɔ̃] *nf* plantation.

**plante** [plɑ̃t] *nf* plant; ~ **d'appartement** house *ou* pot plant; ~ **du pied** sole (of the foot).

**planter** [plɑ̃te] *vt* (*plante*) to plant; (*enfoncer*) to hammer *ou* drive in; (*tente*) to put up, pitch; (*fam*) to dump; to ditch; ~ **qch dans** to hammer *ou* drive sth into; to stick sth into; **se** ~ **dans** to sink into; to get stuck in; **se** ~ **devant** to plant o.s. in front of; **planteur** *nm* planter.

**planton** [plɑ̃tɔ̃] *nm* orderly.

**plantureux, euse** [plɑ̃tyʀø, -øz] *a* copious, lavish; buxom.

**plaquage** [plakaʒ] *nm* (*RUGBY*) tackle.

**plaque** [plak] *nf* plate; (*de verglas, d'eczéma*) patch; (*avec inscription*) plaque; ~**s** (**minéralogiques** *ou* **de police** *ou* **d'immatriculation**) number plates; ~ **de beurre** tablet of butter; ~ **chauffante** hotplate; ~ **de chocolat** bar of chocolate; ~ **d'identité** identity disc; ~ **tournante** (*fig*) centre.

**plaqué, e** [plake] *a*: ~ **or/argent** gold-/silver-plated; ~ **acajou** veneered in mahogany.

**plaquer** [plake] *vt* (*bijou*) to plate; (*bois*) to veneer; (*aplatir*): ~ **qch sur/contre** to make sth stick *ou* cling to; (*RUGBY*) to bring down; (*fam*) to ditch; **se** ~ **contre** to flatten o.s. against; ~ **qn contre** to pin sb to.

**plaquette** [plakɛt] *nf* tablet; bar; (*livre*) small volume.

**plasma** [plasma] *nm* plasma.

**plastic** [plastik] *nm* plastic explosive.

**plastifié, e** [plastifje] *a* plastic-coated.

**plastique** [plastik] *a* plastic // *nm* plastic // *nf* plastic arts *pl*; modelling.

**plastiquer** [plastike] *vt* to blow up (*with a plastic bomb*).

**plastron** [plastʀɔ̃] *nm* shirt front.

**plastronner** [plastʀɔne] *vi* to swagger.

**plat, e** [pla, -at] *a* flat; (*cheveux*) straight; (*personne, livre*) dull // *nm* (*récipient, CULIN*) dish; (*d'un repas*): **le premier** ~ the first course; (*partie plate*): **le** ~ **de la main** the flat of the hand; **à** ~ **ventre** *ad* face down; (*tomber*) flat on one's face; **à** ~ **ad**, **a** (*aussi: pneu, batterie*) flat; ~ **du jour** day's special (menu); ~ **de résistance** main course.

**platane** [platan] *nm* plane tree.

**plateau, x** [plato] *nm* (*support*) tray; (*GÉO*) plateau; (*de tourne-disques*) turntable; (*CINÉMA*) set; ~ **à fromages** cheeseboard.

**plate-bande** [platbɑ̃d] *nf* flower bed.

**platée** [plate] *nf* dish(ful).

**plate-forme** [platfɔʀm(ə)] *nf* platform; ~ **de forage/pétrolière** drilling/oil rig.

**platine** [platin] *nm* platinum // *nf* (*d'un tourne-disque*) turntable.

**plâtras** [plɑtʀa] *nm* rubble *q*.

**plâtre** [plɑtʀ(ə)] *nm* (*matériau*) plaster; (*statue*) plaster statue; (*MÉD*) (plaster) cast; **avoir un bras dans le** ~ to have an arm in plaster; **plâtrer** *vt* to plaster; (*MÉD*) to set *ou* put in a (plaster) cast.

**plausible** [plozibl(ə)] *a* plausible.

**plébiscite** [plebisit] *nm* plebiscite.

**plein, e** [plɛ̃, -ɛn] *a* full; (*porte, roue*) solid; (*chienne, jument*) big (with young) // *nm*: **faire le** ~ (**d'essence**) to fill up (with petrol); **les** ~**s** the downstrokes (*in handwriting*); ~ **de** full of; **à** ~**es mains** (*ramasser*) in handfuls; (*empoigner*) firmly; **à** ~ **régime** at maximum revs; (*fig*) full steam; **à** ~ **temps** full-time; **en** ~ **air/~e mer** in the open air/on the open sea; **en** ~ **soleil** right out in the sun; **en** ~**e nuit/rue** in the middle of the night/street; **en** ~ **milieu** right in the middle; **en** ~ **jour** in broad daylight; **en** ~ **sur** right on; ~**-emploi** *nm* full employment.

**plénière** [plenjɛʀ] *af*: **assemblée** ~ plenary assembly.

**plénitude** [plenityd] *nf* fullness.

**pléthore** [pletɔʀ] *nf*: ~ **de** overabundance *ou* plethora of.

**pleurer** [plœʀe] *vi* to cry; (*yeux*) to water // *vt* to mourn (for); ~ **sur** *vt* to lament (over); to bemoan.

**pleurésie** [plœʀezi] *nf* pleurisy.

**pleurnicher** [plœʀniʃe] *vi* to grizzle, whine.

**pleurs** [plœʀ] *nmpl*: **en** ~ in tears.

**pleutre** [pløtʀ(ə)] *a* cowardly.

**pleuvoir** [pløvwaʀ] *vb impersonnel* to rain // *vi* (*fig*): ~ (**sur**) to shower down (upon); to be showered upon.

**plexiglas** [plɛksiglɑs] *nm* plexiglass.

**pli** [pli] *nm* fold; (*de jupe*) pleat; (*de pantalon*) crease; (*aussi:* **faux** ~) crease; (*enveloppe*) envelope; (*lettre*) letter;

(*CARTES*) trick ; **prendre le ~ de faire** to get into the habit of doing ; **~ d'aisance** inverted pleat.

**pliage** [plijaʒ] *nm* folding ; (*ART*) origami.

**pliant, e** [plijã, -ãt] *a* folding // *nm* folding stool, campstool.

**plier** [plije] *vt* to fold ; (*pour ranger*) to fold up ; (*table pliante*) to fold down ; (*genou, bras*) to bend // *vi* to bend ; (*fig*) to yield ; **se ~ à** to submit to ; **~ bagages** to pack up (and go).

**plinthe** [plɛ̃t] *nf* skirting board.

**plissé, e** [plise] *a* (*GÉO*) folded // *nm* (*COUTURE*) pleats *pl*.

**plissement** [plismã] *nm* (*GÉO*) fold.

**plisser** [plise] *vt* (*rider, chiffonner*) to crease ; (*jupe*) to put pleats in.

**plomb** [plɔ̃] *nm* (*métal*) lead ; (*d'une cartouche*) (lead) shot ; (*PÊCHE*) sinker ; (*sceau*) (lead) seal ; (*ÉLEC*) fuse ; **mettre à ~** to plumb.

**plombage** [plɔ̃baʒ] *nm* (*de dent*) filling.

**plomber** [plɔ̃be] *vt* (*canne, ligne*) to weight (with lead) ; (*colis, wagon*) to put a lead seal on ; (*dent*) to fill.

**plomberie** [plɔ̃bʀi] *nf* plumbing.

**plombier** [plɔ̃bje] *nm* plumber.

**plonge** [plɔ̃ʒ] *nf*: **faire la ~** to be a washer-up.

**plongeant, e** [plɔ̃ʒã, -ãt] *a* (*vue*) from above ; (*tir, décolleté*) plunging.

**plongée** [plɔ̃ʒe] *nf* diving *q* ; (*de sous-marin*) submersion, dive ; **en ~** (*sous-marin*) submerged ; (*prise de vue*) high angle.

**plongeoir** [plɔ̃ʒwaʀ] *nm* diving board.

**plongeon** [plɔ̃ʒɔ̃] *nm* dive.

**plonger** [plɔ̃ʒe] *vi* to dive // *vt*: **~ qch dans** (*immerger*) to plunge *ou* dip sth into ; (*planter*) to thrust sth into ; (*fig*) to plunge sth into ; **plongeur, euse** *nm/f* diver ; (*de café*) washer-up.

**ployer** [plwaje] *vt* to bend // *vi* to sag ; to bend.

**plu** *pp de* **plaire, pleuvoir**.

**pluie** [plɥi] *nf* rain ; (*fig*): **~ de** shower of ; **retomber en ~** to shower down ; **sous la ~** in the rain.

**plume** [plym] *nf* feather ; (*pour écrire*) (pen) nib ; (*fig*) pen.

**plumeau, x** [plymo] *nm* feather duster.

**plumer** [plyme] *vt* to pluck.

**plumet** [plymɛ] *nm* plume.

**plumier** [plymje] *nm* pencil box.

**plupart** [plypaʀ]: **la ~** *pronom* the majority, most (of them) ; **la ~ des** most, the majority of ; **la ~ du temps/d'entre nous** most of the time/of us ; **pour la ~** *ad* for the most part, mostly.

**pluriel** [plyʀjɛl] *nm* plural ; **au ~** in the plural.

**plus** *vb* [ply] *voir* **plaire** // *ad* [ply, plyz + *voyelle*] (*comparatif*) more, *adjectif court* + ...*er* ; (*davantage*) [plys] more ; (*négatif*): **ne ... ~** no more, *tournure négative* + any more ; no longer // *cj* [plys]: **~ 2** plus 2 ; **~ que** more than ; **~ grand que** bigger than ; **~ de 10 personnes** more than 10 people, over 10 people ; **~ de pain** more bread ; **~ il travaille, ~ il est heureux** the more he works, the happier he is ; **le ~**

**~ intelligent/grand** the most intelligent/biggest ; **3 heures/kilos de ~ que** 3 hours/kilos more than ; **de ~** what's more, moreover ; **3 kilos en ~** 3 kilos more, 3 extra kilos ; **en ~ de** in addition to ; **de ~ en ~** more and more ; **(tout) au ~** at the (very) most ; **~ ou moins** more or less ; **ni ~ ni moins** no more, no less.

**plusieurs** [plyzjœʀ] *dét, pronom* several ; **ils sont ~** there are several of them.

**plus-que-parfait** [plyskəpaʀfɛ] *nm* pluperfect, past perfect.

**plus-value** [plyvaly] *nf* appreciation ; capital gain ; surplus.

**plut** *vb voir* **plaire**.

**plûtot** [plyto] *ad* rather ; **je ferais ~ ceci** I'd rather *ou* sooner do this ; **fais ~ comme ça** try this way instead, you'd better try this way ; **~ que (de) faire** rather than *ou* instead of doing.

**pluvieux, euse** [plyvjø, -øz] *a* rainy, wet.

**P.M.U.** *sigle m voir* **pari**.

**pneu, x** [pnø] *nm* tyre ; letter sent by pneumatic tube.

**pneumatique** [pnømatik] *a* pneumatic ; rubber *cpd* // *nm* tyre.

**pneumonie** [pnømɔni] *nf* pneumonia.

**P.O.** *sigle* = *petites ondes*.

**poche** [pɔʃ] *nf* pocket ; (*déformation*): **faire une/des ~(s)** to bag ; (*sous les yeux*) bag, pouch // *nm* (*abr de* **livre de ~**) (pocket-size) paperback ; **de ~** pocket *cpd*.

**poché, e** [pɔʃe] *a*: **œuf ~** poached egg ; **œil ~** black eye.

**poche-revolver** [pɔʃʀevɔlvɛʀ] *nf* hip pocket.

**pochette** [pɔʃɛt] *nf* (*de timbres*) wallet, envelope ; (*d'aiguilles etc*) case ; (*sur veston*) breast pocket ; (*mouchoir*) breast pocket handkerchief ; **~ d'allumettes** book of matches ; **~ de disque** record sleeve.

**pochoir** [pɔʃwaʀ] *nm* (*ART*) stencil ; transfer.

**podium** [pɔdjɔm] *nm* podium (*pl* ia).

**poêle** [pwɑl] *nm* stove // *nf*: **~ (à frire)** frying pan.

**poêlon** [pwɑlɔ̃] *nm* casserole.

**poème** [pɔɛm] *nm* poem.

**poésie** [pɔezi] *nf* (*poème*) poem ; (*art*): **la ~** poetry.

**poète** [pɔɛt] *nm* poet.

**poétique** [pɔetik] *a* poetic.

**pognon** [pɔɲɔ̃] *nm* (*fam*) dough.

**poids** [pwa] *nm* weight ; (*SPORT*) shot ; **vendre au ~** to sell by weight ; **prendre du ~** to put on weight ; **~ plume/mouche/coq/ moyen** (*BOXE*) feather/fly/bantam/ middleweight ; **~ et haltères** *nmpl* weight lifting *sg* ; **~ lourd** (*BOXE*) heavyweight ; (*camion*) (big) lorry ; (: *ADMIN*) heavy goods vehicle (HGV) ; **~ mort** dead load.

**poignant, e** [pwaɲã, -ãt] *a* poignant, harrowing.

**poignard** [pwaɲaʀ] *nm* dagger ; **poignarder** *vt* to stab, knife.

**poigne** [pwaɲ] *nf* grip ; (*fig*) firm-handedness.

**poignée** [pwaɲe] *nf* (*de sel etc, fig*) handful; (*de couvercle, porte*) handle; ~ **de main** handshake.

**poignet** [pwaɲɛ] *nm* (ANAT) wrist; (*de chemise*) cuff.

**poil** [pwal] *nm* (ANAT) hair; (*de pinceau, brosse*) bristle; (*de tapis*) strand; (*pelage*) coat; (*ensemble des poils*): **avoir du ~ sur la poitrine** to have hair(s) on one's chest, have a hairy chest; **à ~ a** (*fam*) starkers; **au ~ a** (*fam*) hunky-dory; **poilu, e** *a* hairy.

**poinçon** [pwɛ̃sɔ̃] *nm* awl; bodkin; style; die; (*marque*) hallmark; **poinçonner** *vt* to stamp; to hallmark; (*billet, ticket*) to clip, punch; **poinçonneuse** *nf* (*outil*) punch.

**poing** [pwɛ̃] *nm* fist.

**point** [pwɛ̃] *nm* (*marque, signe*) dot; (: *de ponctuation*) full stop; (*moment, de score etc, fig: question*) point; (*endroit*) spot; (COUTURE, TRICOT) stitch // **ad = pas; faire le ~** (NAVIG) to take a bearing; (*fig*) to take stock (of the situation); **en tout ~ in** every respect; **sur le ~ de faire** (just) about to do; **à tel ~ que** so much so that; **mettre au ~** (*mécanisme, procédé*) to perfect; (*appareil-photo*) to focus; (*affaire*) to settle; **à ~** (CULIN) medium; just right; **à ~ (nommé)** just at the right time; **~ (de côté)** stitch (*pain*); **~ culminant** summit; (*fig*) height, climax; **~ d'eau** spring; water point; **~ d'exclamation** exclamation mark; **~ faible** weak point; **~ final** full stop, period; **~ d'interrogation** question mark; **~ mort** (AUTO): **au ~ mort** in neutral; **~ noir** (*sur le visage*) blackhead; (AUTO) accident spot; **~ de repère** landmark; (*dans le temps*) point of reference; **~ de vente** retail outlet; **~ de vue** viewpoint; (*fig: opinion*) point of view; **du ~ de vue de** from the point of view of; **~s cardinaux** points of the compass, cardinal points; **~s de suspension** suspension points.

**pointe** [pwɛ̃t] *nf* point; (*d'une île*) headland; (*allusion*) dig; sally; (*fig*): **une ~ d'ail/d'accent** a touch ou hint of garlic/of an accent; **être à la ~ de** (*fig*) to be in the forefront of; **sur la ~ des pieds** on tip-toe; **en ~** *ad* (*tailler*) into a point // **a** pointed, tapered; **de ~ a** (*technique etc*) leading; **heures/jours de ~** peak hours/days; **faire du 180 en ~** (AUTO) to have a top ou maximum speed of 180; **faire des ~s** (DANSE) to dance on points; **~ de vitesse** burst of speed.

**pointer** [pwɛ̃te] *vt* (*cocher*) to tick off; (*employés etc*) to check in (ou out); (*diriger: canon, longue-vue, doigt*): **~ vers qch** to point at sth // *vi* (*employé*) to clock in (ou out); **pointeuse** *nf* timeclock.

**pointillé** [pwɛ̃tije] *nm* (*trait*) dotted line; (ART) stippling *q*.

**pointilleux, euse** [pwɛ̃tijø, -øz] *a* particular, pernickety.

**pointu, e** [pwɛ̃ty] *a* pointed; (*clou*) sharp; (*voix*) shrill.

**pointure** [pwɛ̃tyR] *nf* size.

**point-virgule** [pwɛ̃viRgyl] *nm* semi-colon.

**poire** [pwaR] *nf* pear; (*fam: péj*) mug; **~ à injections** syringe.

**poireau, x** [pwaRo] *nm* leek.

**poirier** [pwaRje] *nm* pear tree.

**pois** [pwa] *nm* (BOT) pea; (*sur une étoffe*) dot, spot; **à ~** (*cravate etc*) dotted, polka-dot *cpd*; **~ chiche** chickpea; **~ de senteur** sweet pea.

**poison** [pwazɔ̃] *nm* poison.

**poisse** [pwas] *nf* rotten luck.

**poisseux, euse** [pwasø, -øz] *a* sticky.

**poisson** [pwasɔ̃] *nm* fish *gén inv*; **les P~s** (*signe*) Pisces, the Fishes; **être des P~s** to be Pisces; **~ d'avril!** April fool!; **poissonnerie** *nf* fish-shop; **poissonneux, euse** *a* abounding in fish; **poissonnier, ière** *nm/f* fishmonger.

**poitrail** [pwatRaj] *nm* breast.

**poitrine** [pwatRin] *nf* chest; (*seins*) bust, bosom; (CULIN) breast; **~ de bœuf** brisket.

**poivre** [pwavR(ə)] *nm* pepper; **~ en grains/moulu** whole/ground pepper; **poivré, e a** peppery; **poivrier** *nm* (BOT) pepper plant; (*ustensile*) pepperpot.

**poivron** [pwavRɔ̃] *nm* pepper, capsicum; **~ vert/rouge** green/red pepper.

**poker** [pɔkɛR] *nm*: **le ~** poker; **~ d'as** four aces.

**polaire** [pɔlɛR] *a* polar.

**polariser** [pɔlaRize] *vt* to polarize; (*fig*) to attract; to focus.

**pôle** [pol] *nm* (GÉO, ÉLEC) pole; **le ~ Nord/Sud** the North/South Pole.

**polémique** [pɔlemik] *a* controversial, polemic(al) // *nf* controversy; **polémiste** *nm/f* polemist, polemicist.

**poli, e** [pɔli] *a* polite; (*lisse*) smooth; polished.

**police** [pɔlis] *nf* police; (*discipline*): **assurer la ~ de** ou **dans** to keep order in; **peine de simple ~** sentence imposed by a magistrates' ou police court; **~ d'assurance** insurance policy; **~ judiciaire, P.J.** ≈ Criminal Investigation Department, C.I.D.; **~ des mœurs** ≈ vice squad; **~ secours** ≈ emergency services *pl*.

**polichinelle** [pɔliʃinɛl] *nm* Punch; (*péj*) buffoon.

**policier, ière** [pɔlisje, -jɛR] *a* police *cpd* // *nm* policeman; (*aussi*: **roman ~**) detective novel.

**policlinique** [pɔliklinik] *nf* ≈ outpatients (department).

**polio(myélite)** [pɔljo(mjelit)] *nf* polio(myelitis); **poliomyélitique** *nm/f* polio patient ou case.

**polir** [pɔliR] *vt* to polish.

**polisson, ne** [pɔlisɔ̃, -ɔn] *a* naughty.

**politesse** [pɔlitɛs] *nf* politeness; **~s** (*exchange of*) courtesies, polite gestures; **rendre une ~ à qn** to return sb's favour.

**politicien, ne** [pɔlitisjɛ̃, -ɛn] *nm/f* politician.

**politique** [pɔlitik] *a* political // *nf* (*science, pratique, activité*) politics *sg*; (*mesures, méthode*) policies *pl*; **politiser** *vt* to politicize; **politiser qn** to make sb politically aware.

**pollen** [pɔlɛn] *nm* pollen.

**polluer** [pɔlɥe] *vt* to pollute; **pollution** *nf* pollution.

**polo** [pɔlo] *nm* (*sport*) polo; (*tricot*) sweat shirt.

**Pologne** [pɔlɔɲ] *nf*: la ~ Poland; **polonais, e** *a*, *nm* (*langue*) Polish // *nm/f* Pole.

**poltron, ne** [pɔltRɔ̃, -ɔn] *a* cowardly.

**poly...** [pɔli] *préfixe*: ~**clinique** *nf* polyclinic; ~**copier** *vt* to duplicate; ~**gamie** *nf* polygamy; ~**glotte** *a* polyglot; ~**gone** *nm* polygon.

**Polynésie** [pɔlinezi] *nf*: la ~ Polynesia.

**polytechnicien, ne** [pɔlitɛknisjɛ̃, -ɛn] *nm/f* student (*or former student*) of the École Polytechnique.

**polyvalent, e** [pɔlivalɑ̃, -ɑ̃t] *a* polyvalent; versatile, multi-purpose // *nm* ≈ tax inspector.

**pommade** [pɔmad] *nf* ointment, cream.

**pomme** [pɔm] *nf* (BOT) apple; (*boule décorative*) knob; (*pomme de terre*): steak ~s (frites) steak and chips; **tomber dans les** ~s (*fam*) to pass out; ~ **d'Adam** Adam's apple; ~ **d'arrosoir** (sprinkler) rose; ~ **de pin** pine *ou* fir cone; ~ **de terre** potato; ~s **vapeur** boiled potatoes.

**pommé, e** [pɔme] *a* (*chou etc*) firm, with a good heart.

**pommeau, x** [pɔmo] *nm* (*boule*) knob; (*de selle*) pommel.

**pommette** [pɔmɛt] *nf* cheekbone.

**pommier** [pɔmje] *nm* apple tree.

**pompe** [pɔ̃p] *nf* pump; (*faste*) pomp (and ceremony); ~ **de bicyclette** bicycle pump; ~ **à essence** petrol pump; ~ **à incendie** fire engine (*apparatus*); ~s **funèbres** funeral parlour *sg*, undertaker's *sg*.

**pomper** [pɔ̃pe] *vt* to pump; (*évacuer*) to pump out; (*aspirer*) to pump up; (*absorber*) to soak up // *vi* to pump.

**pompeux, euse** [pɔ̃pø, -øz] *a* pompous.

**pompier** [pɔ̃pje] *nm* fireman // *am* (*style*) pretentious, pompous.

**pompon** [pɔ̃pɔ̃] *nm* pompom, bobble.

**pomponner** [pɔ̃pɔne] *vt* to titivate, dress up.

**ponce** [pɔ̃s] *nf*: **pierre** ~ pumice stone.

**poncer** [pɔ̃se] *vt* to sand (down); **ponceuse** *nf* sander.

**poncif** [pɔ̃sif] *nm* cliché.

**ponction** [pɔ̃ksjɔ̃] *nf*: ~ **lombaire** lumbar puncture.

**ponctualité** [pɔ̃ktɥalite] *nf* punctuality.

**ponctuation** [pɔ̃ktɥasjɔ̃] *nf* punctuation.

**ponctuel, le** [pɔ̃ktɥɛl] *a* (*à l'heure, aussi* TECH) punctual; (*fig: opération etc*) one-off, single; (*scrupuleux*) punctilious, meticulous.

**ponctuer** [pɔ̃ktɥe] *vt* to punctuate; (MUS) to phrase.

**pondéré, e** [pɔ̃deRe] *a* level-headed, composed.

**pondre** [pɔ̃dR(ə)] *vt* to lay; (*fig*) to produce // *vi* to lay.

**poney** [pɔnɛ] *nm* pony.

**pongiste** [pɔ̃ʒist] *nm/f* table tennis player.

**pont** [pɔ̃] *nm* bridge; (AUTO): ~ **arrière/avant** rear/front axle; (NAVIG) deck; **faire le** ~ to take the extra day off; ~ **aérien** airlift; ~ **d'envol** flight deck; ~ **de graissage** ramp (*in garage*); ~ **roulant** travelling crane; ~ **suspendu** suspension bridge; ~ **tournant** swing bridge; **P**~s **et Chaussées** highways department.

**ponte** [pɔ̃t] *nf* laying // *nm* (*fam*) big shot.

**pontife** [pɔ̃tif] *nm* pontiff.

**pontifier** [pɔ̃tifje] *vi* to pontificate.

**pont-levis** [pɔ̃lvi] *nm* drawbridge.

**pop** [pɔp] *a inv* pop.

**populace** [pɔpylas] *nf* (*péj*) rabble.

**populaire** [pɔpylɛR] *a* popular; (*manifestation*) mass *cpd*, of the people; (*milieux, clientèle*) working-class; **populariser** *vt* to popularize; **popularité** *nf* popularity.

**population** [pɔpylasjɔ̃] *nf* population.

**populeux, euse** [pɔpylø, -øz] *a* densely populated.

**porc** [pɔR] *nm* (ZOOL) pig; (CULIN) pork; (*peau*) pigskin.

**porcelaine** [pɔRsəlɛn] *nf* porcelain, china; piece of china(ware).

**porcelet** [pɔRsəlɛ] *nm* piglet.

**porc-épic** [pɔRkepik] *nm* porcupine.

**porche** [pɔRʃ(ə)] *nm* porch.

**porcherie** [pɔRʃəRi] *nf* pigsty.

**porcin, e** [pɔRsɛ̃, -in] *a* porcine; (*fig*) piglike.

**pore** [pɔR] *nm* pore; **poreux, euse** *a* porous.

**pornographie** [pɔRnɔgRafi] *nf* pornography; **pornographique** *a* (*abr* **porno**) pornographic.

**port** [pɔR] *nm* (NAVIG) harbour, port; (*ville*) port; (*de l'uniforme etc*) wearing; (*pour lettre*) postage; (*pour colis, aussi: posture*) carriage; ~ **d'arme** (JUR) carrying of a firearm; ~ **d'attache** (NAVIG) port of registry; ~ **franc** free port.

**portail** [pɔRtaj] *nm* gate; (*de cathédrale*) portal.

**portant, e** [pɔRtɑ̃, -ɑ̃t] *a* (*murs*) structural, weight-bearing; **bien/ mal** ~ in good/poor health.

**portatif, ive** [pɔRtatif, -iv] *a* portable.

**porte** [pɔRt(ə)] *nf* door; (*de ville, forteresse*, SKI) gate; **mettre à la** ~ to throw out; ~ **d'entrée** front door; ~ **à** ~ *nm* door-to-door selling.

**porte...** [pɔRt(ə)] *préfixe*: ~**-à-faux** *nm*: **en** ~**-à-faux** cantilevered; precariously balanced; ~**-avions** *nm inv* aircraft carrier; ~**-bagages** *nm inv* luggage rack; ~**-bonheur** *nm inv* lucky charm; ~**-cartes** *nm inv* card holder; map wallet; ~**-cigarettes** *nm inv* cigarette case; ~**-clefs** *nm inv* keyring; ~**-crayon** *nm* pencil holder; ~**-documents** *nm inv* attaché *ou* document case.

**portée** [pɔRte] *nf* (*d'une arme*) range; (*fig*) impact, import; scope, capability; (*de chatte etc*) litter; (MUS) stave, staff (*pl* staves); **à/hors de** ~ (**de**) within/out of reach (of); **à** ~ **de (la) main** within (arm's) reach; **à** ~ **de voix** within earshot; **à la** ~ **de qn** (*fig*) at sb's level, within sb's capabilities.

**porte-fenêtre** [pɔRtfənɛtR(ə)] *nf* French window.

**portefeuille** [pɔRtəfœj] *nm* wallet; (POL, BOURSE) portfolio.

**porte-jarretelles** [pɔRtʒaRtɛl] *nm inv* suspender belt.

**portemanteau, x** [pɔRtmɑ̃to] *nm* coat hanger ; coat rack.
**porte-mine** [pɔRtəmin] *nm* propelling pencil.
**porte-monnaie** [pɔRtmɔnɛ] *nm inv* purse.
**porte-parole** [pɔRtpaRɔl] *nm inv* spokesman.
**porte-plume** [pɔRtəplym] *nm inv* penholder.
**porter** [pɔRte] *vt* (*charge ou sac etc, aussi: fœtus*) to carry ; (*sur soi: vêtement, barbe, bague*) to wear ; (*fig: responsabilité etc*) to bear, carry ; (*inscription, marque, titre, patronyme, suj: arbre: fruits, fleurs*) to bear ; (*apporter*): ~ **qch quelque part/à qn** to take sth somewhere/to sb ; (*inscrire*): ~ **qch sur** to put sth down on ; to enter sth in // *vi* (*voix, regard, canon*) to carry ; (*coup, argument*) to hit home ; ~ **sur** (*peser*) to rest on ; (*accent*) to fall on ; (*conférence etc*) to concern ; (*heurter*) to strike ; **se** ~ *vi* (*se sentir*): **se** ~ **bien/mal** to be well/unwell ; (*aller*): **se** ~ **vers** to go towards ; **être porté à faire** to be apt *ou* inclined to do ; **elle portait le nom de Rosalie** she was called Rosalie ; ~ **qn au pouvoir** to bring sb to power ; ~ **son âge** to look one's age ; **se faire** ~ **malade** to report sick ; ~ **la main à son chapeau** to raise one's hand to one's hat ; ~ **son effort sur** to direct one's efforts towards.
**porte-savon** [pɔRtsavɔ̃] *nm* soapdish.
**porte-serviettes** [pɔRtsɛRvjɛt] *nm inv* towel rail.
**porteur, euse** [pɔRtœR, -øz] *a*: **être** ~ **de** (*nouvelle*) to be the bearer of // *nm* (*de bagages*) porter ; (COMM: *de chèque*) bearer.
**porte-voix** [pɔRtəvwa] *nm inv* loudhailer.
**portier** [pɔRtje] *nm* commissionnaire, porter.
**portière** [pɔRtjɛR] *nf* door.
**portillon** [pɔRtijɔ̃] *nm* gate.
**portion** [pɔRsjɔ̃] *nf* (*part*) portion, share ; (*partie*) portion, section.
**portique** [pɔRtik] *nm* (GYM) crossbar ; (ARCHIT) portico ; (RAIL) gantry.
**porto** [pɔRto] *nm* port (wine).
**portrait** [pɔRtRɛ] *nm* portrait ; photograph ; **portraitiste** *nm/f* portrait painter ; ~**-robot** *nm* Identikit *ou* photofit picture.
**portuaire** [pɔRtɥɛR] *a* port *cpd*, harbour *cpd*.
**portugais, e** [pɔRtygɛ, -ɛz] *a, nm, nf* Portuguese.
**Portugal** [pɔRtygal] *nm*: **le** ~ Portugal.
**pose** [poz] *nf* laying ; hanging ; (*attitude, d'un modèle*) pose ; (PHOTO) exposure.
**posé, e** [poze] *a* serious.
**posemètre** [pozmɛtR(ə)] *nm* exposure meter.
**poser** [poze] *vt* (*déposer*): ~ **qch (sur)/qn à** to put sth down (on)/drop sb at ; (*placer*): ~ **qch sur/quelque part** to put sth on/somewhere ; (*installer: moquette, carrelage*) to lay ; (: *rideaux, papier peint*) to hang ; (*question*) to ask ; (*principe, conditions*) to lay *ou* set down ; (*problème*) to formulate ; (*difficulté*) to pose // *vi* (*modèle*) to pose ; to sit ; **se** ~ (*oiseau, avion*) to land ; (*question*) to arise.

**poseur, euse** [pozœR, -øz] *nm/f* (*péj*) show-off, poseur ; ~ **de parquets/ carrelages** floor/tile layer.
**positif, ive** [pozitif, -iv] *a* positive.
**position** [pozisjɔ̃] *nf* position ; **prendre** ~ (*fig*) to take a stand.
**posologie** [pozɔlɔʒi] *nf* directions *pl* for use, dosage.
**posséder** [pɔsede] *vt* to own, possess ; (*qualité, talent*) to have, possess ; (*bien connaître: métier, langue*) to master, have a thorough knowledge of ; (*sexuellement, aussi: suj: colère etc*) to possess ; (*fam: duper*) to take in ; **possesseur** *nm* owner ; **possessif, ive** *a, nm* possessive ; **possession** *nf* ownership *q* ; possession ; **être/entrer en possession de qch** to be in/take possession of sth.
**possibilité** [pɔsibilite] *nf* possibility ; ~**s** *nfpl* (*moyens*) means ; (*potentiel*) potential *sg* ; **avoir la** ~ **de faire** to be in a position to do ; to have the opportunity to do.
**possible** [pɔsibl(ə)] *a* possible ; (*projet, entreprise*) feasible // *nm*: **faire son** ~ to do all one can, do one's utmost ; **le plus/moins de livres** ~ as many/few books as possible ; **le plus/moins d'eau** ~ as much/little water as possible ; **dès que** ~ as soon as possible ; **gentil** *etc* **au** ~ as nice *etc* as it is possible to be.
**postal, e, aux** [pɔstal, -o] *a* postal, post office *cpd* ; **sac** ~ mailbag, postbag.
**poste** [pɔst(ə)] *nf* (*service*) post, postal service ; (*administration, bureau*) post office // *nm* (*fonction, MIL*) post ; (*de radio etc*) set ; (*de budget*) item ; ~**s** *nfpl* post office *sg* ; **P**~**s et Télécommunications** (P.T.T.): *abr de* Postes, Télégraphes, Téléphones) ≈ General Post Office (G.P.O.) ; ~ (**de radio/télévision**) *nm* (radio/television) set ; ~ **émetteur** *nm* transmitting set ; ~ **d'essence** *nm* petrol *ou* filling station ; ~ **d'incendie** *nm* fire point ; ~ **de péage** *nm* tollgate ; ~ **de pilotage** *nm* cockpit ; ~ (**de police**) *nm* police station ; ~ **restante** *nf* poste restante ; ~ **de secours** *nm* firstaid post.
**poster** *vt* [pɔste] to post // *nm* [pɔstɛR] poster.
**postérieur, e** [pɔsteRjœR] *a* (*date*) later ; (*partie*) back // *nm* (*fam*) behind.
**posteriori** [pɔsteRjɔRi]: **a** ~ *ad* with hindsight, a posteriori.
**postérité** [pɔsteRite] *nf* posterity.
**posthume** [pɔstym] *a* posthumous.
**postiche** [pɔstiʃ] *a* false // *nm* hairpiece.
**postillonner** [pɔstijɔne] *vi* to sp(l)utter.
**post-scriptum** [pɔstskRiptɔm] *nm inv* postscript.
**postulant, e** [pɔstylɑ̃, -ɑ̃t] *nm/f* applicant.
**postulat** [pɔstyla] *nm* postulate.
**postuler** [pɔstyle] *vt* (*emploi*) to apply for, put in for.
**posture** [pɔstyR] *nf* posture, position ; (*fig*) position.
**pot** [po] *nm* jar, pot ; carton ; (*en métal*) tin ; **boire un** ~ (*fam*) to have a drink ; ~ (**de chambre**) (chamber)pot ; ~ **d'échappement** exhaust pipe ; ~ **de fleurs** plant pot, flowerpot ; (*fleurs*) pot plant ; ~ **à tabac** tobacco jar.

**potable** [pɔtabl(ə)] *a* (*fig*) drinkable ; decent ; **eau** ~ drinking water.
**potache** [pɔtaʃ] *nm* schoolboy.
**potage** [pɔtaʒ] *nm* soup ; soup course.
**potager, ère** [pɔtaʒe, -ɛʀ] *a* (*plante*) edible, vegetable *cpd* ; **(jardin)** ~ kitchen *ou* vegetable garden.
**potasse** [pɔtas] *nf* potassium hydroxide ; (*engrais*) potash.
**potasser** [pɔtase] *vt* (*fam*) to swot up.
**pot-au-feu** [pɔtofø] *nm inv* (beef) stew ; (*viande*) stewing beef.
**pot-de-vin** [podvɛ̃] *nm* bribe.
**poteau, x** [pɔto] *nm* post ; ~ **(d'exécution)** execution post, stake ; ~ **indicateur** signpost ; ~ **télégraphique** telegraph pole ; ~**x (de but)** goal-posts.
**potelé, e** [pɔtle] *a* plump, chubby.
**potence** [pɔtɑ̃s] *nf* gallows *sg*.
**potentiel, le** [pɔtɑ̃sjɛl] *a, nm* potential.
**poterie** [pɔtʀi] *nf* pottery ; piece of pottery.
**potiche** [pɔtiʃ] *nf* large vase.
**potier** [pɔtje] *nm* potter.
**potins** [pɔtɛ̃] *nmpl* gossip *sg*.
**potion** [posjɔ̃] *nf* potion.
**potiron** [pɔtiʀɔ̃] *nm* pumpkin.
**pot-pourri** [popuʀi] *nm* potpourri, medley.
**pou, x** [pu] *nm* louse (*pl* lice).
**poubelle** [pubɛl] *nf* (dust)bin.
**pouce** [pus] *nm* thumb.
**poudre** [pudʀ(ə)] *nf* powder ; (*fard*) (face) powder ; (*explosif*) gunpowder ; **en** ~ : **café en** ~ instant coffee ; **savon en** ~ soap powder ; **lait en** ~ dried *ou* powdered milk ; **poudrer** *vt* to powder ; ~**rie** *nf* gunpowder factory ; **poudreux, euse** *a* dusty ; powdery ; **neige poudreuse** powder snow ; **poudrier** *nm* (powder) compact ; **poudrière** *nf* powder magazine ; (*fig*) powder keg.
**poudroyer** [pudʀwaje] *vi* to rise in clouds *ou* a flurry.
**pouf** [puf] *nm* pouffe.
**pouffer** [pufe] *vi*: ~ **(de rire)** to snigger ; to giggle.
**pouilleux, euse** [pujø, -øz] *a* flea-ridden ; (*fig*) grubby ; seedy.
**poulailler** [pulaje] *nm* henhouse ; (THÉÂTRE): **le** ~ the gods *sg*.
**poulain** [pulɛ̃] *nm* foal ; (*fig*) protégé.
**poularde** [pulaʀd(ə)] *nf* fatted chicken.
**poule** [pul] *nf* (ZOOL) hen ; (CULIN) (boiling) fowl ; (*fam*) tart ; broad ; ~ **d'eau** moorhen ; ~ **mouillée** coward ; ~ **pondeuse** layer ; ~ **au riz** chicken and rice.
**poulet** [pulɛ] *nm* chicken ; (*fam*) cop.
**pouliche** [puliʃ] *nf* filly.
**poulie** [puli] *nf* pulley ; block.
**poulpe** [pulp(ə)] *nm* octopus.
**pouls** [pu] *nm* pulse ; **prendre le** ~ **de qn** to feel sb's pulse.
**poumon** [pumɔ̃] *nm* lung ; ~ **d'acier** iron lung.
**poupe** [pup] *nf* stern ; **en** ~ astern.
**poupée** [pupe] *nf* doll ; **jouer à la** ~ to play with one's doll *ou* dolls.
**poupon** [pupɔ̃] *nm* babe-in-arms ; **pouponnière** *nf* crèche, day nursery.

**pour** [puʀ] *prép* for ; ~ **faire** (so as) to do, in order to do ; ~ **avoir fait** for having done ; ~ **que** so that, in order that ; ~ **riche qu'il soit** rich though he may be ; ~ **10 F d'essence** 10 francs' worth of petrol ; ~ **cent** per cent ; ~ **ce qui est de** as for ; **le** ~ **et le contre** the pros and cons.
**pourboire** [puʀbwaʀ] *nm* tip.
**pourcentage** [puʀsɑ̃taʒ] *nm* percentage.
**pourchasser** [puʀʃase] *vt* to pursue.
**pourlécher** [puʀleʃe]: **se** ~ *vi* to lick one's lips.
**pourparlers** [puʀpaʀle] *nmpl* talks, negotiations ; **être en** ~ **avec** to be having talks with.
**pourpre** [puʀpʀ(ə)] *a* crimson.
**pourquoi** [puʀkwa] *ad, cj* why // *nm inv*: **le** ~ **(de)** the reason (for).
**pourrai** *etc vb voir* **pouvoir**.
**pourri, e** [puʀi] *a* rotten.
**pourrir** [puʀiʀ] *vi* to rot ; (*fruit*) to go rotten *ou* bad // *vt* to rot ; (*fig*) to corrupt ; to spoil thoroughly ; **pourriture** *nf* rot.
**pourrons** *etc vb voir* **pouvoir**.
**poursuite** [puʀsɥit] *nf* pursuit, chase ; ~**s** *nfpl* (JUR) legal proceedings ; **(course)** ~ track race ; (*fig*) chase.
**poursuivant, e** [puʀsɥivɑ̃, -ɑ̃t] *nm/f* pursuer.
**poursuivre** [puʀsɥivʀ(ə)] *vt* to pursue, chase (after) ; (*relancer*) to hound, harry ; (*obséder*) to haunt ; (JUR) to bring proceedings against, prosecute ; (: *au civil*) to sue ; (*but*) to strive towards ; (*voyage, études*) to carry on with, continue // *vi* to carry on, go on ; **se** ~ *vi* to go on, continue.
**pourtant** [puʀtɑ̃] *ad* yet ; **c'est** ~ **facile** (and) yet it's easy.
**pourtour** [puʀtuʀ] *nm* perimeter.
**pourvoi** [puʀvwa] *nm* appeal.
**pourvoir** [puʀvwaʀ] *vt*: ~ **qch/qn de** to equip sth/sb with // *vi*: ~ **à** to provide for ; (*emploi*) to fill ; **se** ~ (JUR): **se** ~ **en cassation** to take one's case to the Court of Appeal.
**pourvu, e** [puʀvy] *a*: ~ **de** equipped with ; ~ **que** *cj* (*si*) provided that, so long as ; (*espérons que*) let's hope (that).
**pousse** [pus] *nf* growth ; (*bourgeon*) shoot.
**poussé, e** [puse] *a* sophisticated, advanced ; (*moteur*) souped-up.
**pousse-café** [puskafe] *nm inv* (after-dinner) liqueur.
**poussée** [puse] *nf* thrust ; (*coup*) push ; (MÉD) eruption ; (*fig*) upsurge.
**pousse-pousse** [puspus] *nm inv* rickshaw.
**pousser** [puse] *vt* to push ; (*inciter*): ~ **qn à** to urge *ou* press sb to + *infinitif* ; (*acculer*): ~ **qn à** to drive sb to ; (*émettre*: *cri etc*) to give ; (*stimuler*) to urge on ; to drive hard ; (*poursuivre*) to carry on (further) // *vi* to push ; (*croître*) to grow ; (*aller*): ~ **plus loin** to push on a bit further ; **se** ~ *vi* to move over ; **faire** ~ (*plante*) to grow.
**poussette** [pusɛt] *nf* (*voiture d'enfant*) push chair.

**poussière** [pusjɛʀ] *nf* dust; (*grain*) speck of dust; **et des ~s** (*fig*) and a bit; **~ de charbon** coaldust; **poussiéreux, euse** *a* dusty.

**poussif, ive** [pusif, -iv] *a* wheezy, wheezing.

**poussin** [pusɛ̃] *nm* chick.

**poutre** [putʀ(ə)] *nf* beam; (*en fer, ciment armé*) girder; **poutrelle** *nf* girder.

**pouvoir** [puvwaʀ] *nm* power; (*POL*: *dirigeants*): **le ~** those in power, the government // *vb + infinitif* can; (*suj*: *personne*) can, to be able to; (*permission*) can, may; (*probabilité, hypothèse*) may; **il peut arriver que** it may happen that; **il pourrait pleuvoir** it might rain; **déçu de ne pas ~ le faire** disappointed not to be able to do it *ou* that he couldn't do it; **il aurait pu le dire!** he could *ou* might have said!; **il se peut que** it may be that; **je n'en peux plus** I'm exhausted; I can't take any more; **~ d'achat** purchasing power; **les ~s publics** the authorities.

**prairie** [pʀeʀi] *nf* meadow.

**praline, e** [pʀaline] *a* sugared; praline-flavoured.

**praticable** [pʀatikabl(ə)] *a* passable, practicable.

**praticien, ne** [pʀatisjɛ̃, -jɛn] *nm/f* practitioner.

**pratiquant, e** [pʀatikɑ̃, -ɑ̃t] *a* practising.

**pratique** [pʀatik] *nf* practice // *a* practical; **dans la ~** in (actual) practice; **mettre en ~** to put into practice.

**pratiquement** [pʀatikmɑ̃] *ad* (*pour ainsi dire*) practically, virtually.

**pratiquer** [pʀatike] *vt* to practise; (*intervention, opération*) to carry out; (*ouverture, abri*) to make // *vi* (*REL*) to be a churchgoer.

**pré** [pʀe] *nm* meadow.

**préalable** [pʀealabl(ə)] *a* preliminary; **condition ~ (de)** precondition (for), prerequisite (for); **sans avis ~** without prior *ou* previous notice; **au ~** first, beforehand.

**préambule** [pʀeɑ̃byl] *nm* preamble; (*fig*) prelude; **sans ~** straight away.

**préau, x** [pʀeo] *nm* playground; inner courtyard.

**préavis** [pʀeavi] *nm* notice; **~ de congé** notice; **communication avec ~** (*TÉL*) personal *ou* person to person call.

**précaire** [pʀekɛʀ] *a* precarious.

**précaution** [pʀekosjɔ̃] *nf* precaution; **avec ~** cautiously; **par ~** as a precaution.

**précédemment** [pʀesedamɑ̃] *ad* before, previously.

**précédent, e** [pʀesedɑ̃, -ɑ̃t] *a* previous // *nm* precedent; **sans ~** unprecedented; **le jour ~** the day before, the previous day.

**précéder** [pʀesede] *vt* to precede; (*marcher ou rouler devant*) to be in front of; (*arriver avant*) to get ahead of.

**précepte** [pʀesɛpt(ə)] *nm* precept.

**précepteur, trice** [pʀesɛptœʀ, tʀis] *nm/f* (private) tutor.

**prêcher** [pʀeʃe] *vt* to preach.

**précieux, euse** [pʀesjø, -øz] *a* precious; invaluable; (*style, écrivain*) précieux, precious.

**précipice** [pʀesipis] *nm* drop, chasm; (*fig*) abyss; **au bord du ~** at the edge of the precipice.

**précipitamment** [pʀesipitamɑ̃] *ad* hurriedly, hastily.

**précipitation** [pʀesipitasjɔ̃] *nf* (*hâte*) haste; **~s (atmosphériques)** (atmospheric) precipitation *sg*.

**précipité, e** [pʀesipite] *a* fast; hurried; hasty.

**précipiter** [pʀesipite] *vt* (*faire tomber*): **~ qn/qch du haut de** to throw *or* hurl sb/sth off *ou* from; (*hâter: marche*) to quicken; (: *depart* (*événements*) to move faster; **se ~ sur/vers** to rush at/towards.

**précis, e** [pʀesi, -iz] *a* precise; (*tir, mesures*) accurate, precise // *nm* handbook; **précisément** *ad* precisely; **préciser** *vt* (*expliquer*) to be more specific about, clarify; (*spécifier*) to state, specify; **se préciser** *vi* to become clear(er); **précision** *nf* precision; accuracy; point *ou* detail (*made clear or to be clarified*); **précisions** *nfpl* further details.

**précoce** [pʀekɔs] *a* early; (*enfant*) precocious; (*calvitie*) premature.

**préconçu, e** [pʀekɔ̃sy] *a* preconceived.

**préconiser** [pʀekɔnize] *vt* to advocate.

**précurseur** [pʀekyʀsœʀ] *am* precursory // *nm* forerunner, precursor.

**prédécesseur** [pʀedesesœʀ] *nm* predecessor.

**prédestiner** [pʀedɛstine] *vt*: **~ qn à qch/faire** to predestine sb for sth/to do.

**prédicateur** [pʀedikatœʀ] *nm* preacher.

**prédiction** [pʀediksjɔ̃] *nf* prediction.

**prédilection** [pʀedilɛksjɔ̃] *nf*: **avoir une ~ pour** to be partial to; **de ~** favourite.

**prédire** [pʀediʀ] *vt* to predict.

**prédisposer** [pʀedispoze] *vt*: **~ qn à qch/faire** to predispose sb to sth/to do.

**prédominer** [pʀedɔmine] *vi* to predominate; (*avis*) to prevail.

**préfabriqué, e** [pʀefabʀike] *a* prefabricated // *nm* prefabricated material.

**préface** [pʀefas] *nf* preface; **préfacer** *vt* to write a preface for.

**préfectoral, e, aux** [pʀefɛktɔʀal, -o] *a* prefectorial.

**préfecture** [pʀefɛktyʀ] *nf* prefecture; **~ de police** police headquarters.

**préférable** [pʀefeʀabl(ə)] *a* preferable.

**préféré, e** [pʀefeʀe] *a, nm/f* favourite.

**préférence** [pʀefeʀɑ̃s] *nf* preference; **de ~** preferably; **de ~ à** in preference to, rather than; **obtenir la ~ sur** to have preference over; **préférentiel, le** *a* preferential.

**préférer** [pʀefeʀe] *vt*: **~ qn/qch (à)** to prefer sb/sth (to), like sb/sth better (than); **~ faire** to prefer to do; **je préférerais du thé** I would rather have tea, I'd prefer tea.

**préfet** [pʀefɛ] *nm* prefect; **~ de police** prefect of police, ≈ Metropolitan Commissioner.

**préfixe** [pʀefiks(ə)] *nm* prefix.

**préhistoire** [pʀeistwaʀ] *nf* prehistory; **préhistorique** *a* prehistoric.

**préjudice** [pʀeʒydis] *nm* (*matériel*) loss ; (*moral*) harm *q* ; **porter ~ à** to harm, be detrimental to ; **au ~ de** at the expense of.

**préjugé** [pʀeʒyʒe] *nm* prejudice ; **avoir un ~ contre** to be prejudiced *ou* biased against.

**préjuger** [pʀeʒyʒe]: **~ de** *vt* to prejudge.

**prélasser** [pʀelɑse]: **se ~** *vi* to lounge.

**prélat** [pʀela] *nm* prelate.

**prélavage** [pʀelavaʒ] *nm* pre-wash.

**prélèvement** [pʀelɛvmɑ̃] *nm* deduction ; withdrawal ; **faire un ~ de sang** to take a blood sample.

**prélever** [pʀɛlve] *vt* (*échantillon*) to take ; (*argent*): **~ (sur)** to deduct (from) ; (: *sur son compte*): **~ (sur)** to withdraw (from).

**préliminaire** [pʀeliminɛʀ] *a* preliminary ; **~s** *nmpl* preliminary talks ; preliminaries.

**prélude** [pʀelyd] *nm* prelude ; (*avant le concert*) warm-up.

**prématuré, e** [pʀematyʀe] *a* a premature ; (*retraite*) early // *nm* premature baby.

**préméditation** [pʀemeditɑsjɔ̃] *nf*: **avec ~** a premeditated // *ad* with intent ; **préméditer** *vt* to premeditate, plan.

**premier, ière** [pʀəmje, -jɛʀ] *a* first ; (*branche, marche, grade*) bottom ; (*fig*) basic ; prime ; initial // *nf* (*THÉÂTRE*) first night ; (*CINÉMA*) première ; (*exploit*) first ; **le ~ venu** the first person to come along ; **P~ Ministre** Prime Minister ; **premièrement** *ad* firstly.

**prémisse** [pʀemis] *nf* premise.

**prémonition** [pʀemɔnisjɔ̃] *nf* premonition ; **prémonitoire** *a* premonitory.

**prémunir** [pʀemyniʀ]: **se ~** *vi*: **se ~ contre** to protect o.s. from, guard o.s. against.

**prénatal, e** [pʀenatal] *a* (*MÉD*) antenatal.

**prendre** [pʀɑ̃dʀ(ə)] *vt* to take ; (*ôter*): **~ qch à** to take sth from ; (*aller chercher*) to get, fetch ; (*se procurer*) to get ; (*malfaiteur, poisson*) to catch ; (*passager*) to pick up ; (*personnel, aussi: couleur, goût*) to take on ; (*locataire*) to take in ; (*élève etc: traiter*) to handle ; (*voix, ton*) to put on ; (*coincer*): **se ~ les doigts dans** to get one's fingers caught in // *vi* (*liquide, ciment*) to set ; (*greffe, vaccin*) to take ; (*mensonge*) to be successful ; (*feu: foyer*) to go ; (: *incendie*) to start ; (*allumette*) to light ; (*se diriger*): **~ à gauche** to turn (to the) left ; **~ qn pour** to take sb for ; **se ~ pour** to think one is ; **s'en ~ à** (*agresser*) to set about ; (*critiquer*) to attack ; **se ~ d'amitié/d'affection pour** to befriend/become fond of ; **s'y ~** (*procéder*) to set about it ; **s'y ~ à l'avance** to see to it in advance ; **s'y ~ à deux fois** to try twice, make two attemps.

**preneur** [pʀənœʀ] *nm*: **être/trouver ~** to be willing to buy/find a buyer.

**preniez, prenne** etc *vb voir* **prendre**.

**prénom** [pʀenɔ̃] *nm* first *ou* Christian name ; **prénommer** *vt*: **elle se prénomme Claude** her (first) name is Claude.

**prénuptial, e, aux** [pʀenypsjal, -o] *a* premarital.

**préoccupation** [pʀeɔkypɑsjɔ̃] *nf* (*souci*) worry, anxiety ; (*idée fixe*) preoccupation.

**préoccuper** [pʀeɔkype] *vt* to worry ; to preoccupy ; **se ~ de qch** to be concerned about sth ; to show concern about sth.

**préparatifs** [pʀepaʀatif] *nmpl* preparations.

**préparation** [pʀepaʀɑsjɔ̃] *nf* preparation ; (*SCOL*) piece of homework.

**préparatoire** [pʀepaʀatwaʀ] *a* preparatory.

**préparer** [pʀepaʀe] *vt* to prepare ; (*café*) to make ; (*examen*) to prepare for ; (*voyage, entreprise*) to plan ; **se ~** *vi* (*orage, tragédie*) to brew, be in the air ; **se ~ (à qch/faire)** to prepare (o.s.) *ou* get ready (for sth/to do) ; **~ qch à qn** (*surprise etc*) to have sth in store for sb.

**prépondérant, e** [pʀepɔ̃deʀɑ̃, -ɑ̃t] *a* major, dominating.

**préposé, e** [pʀepoze] *a*: **~ à** in charge of // *nm/f* employee ; official ; attendant ; postman/woman.

**préposition** [pʀepozisjɔ̃] *nf* preposition.

**prérogative** [pʀeʀɔgativ] *nf* prerogative.

**près** [pʀɛ] *ad* near, close ; **~ de** *prép* near (to), close to ; (*environ*) nearly, almost ; **de ~ ad** closely ; **à 5 kg ~** to within about 5 kg ; **à cela ~ que** apart from the fact that.

**présage** [pʀezaʒ] *nm* omen.

**présager** [pʀezaʒe] *vt* to foresee.

**presbyte** [pʀɛsbit] *a* long-sighted.

**presbytère** [pʀɛsbitɛʀ] *nm* presbytery.

**presbytérien, ne** [pʀɛsbiteʀjɛ̃, -jɛn] *a*, *nm/f* Presbyterian.

**prescription** [pʀɛskʀipsjɔ̃] *nf* (*instruction*) order, instruction ; (*MÉD, JUR*) prescription.

**prescrire** [pʀɛskʀiʀ] *vt* to prescribe ; **se ~** *vi* (*JUR*) to lapse ; **prescrit, e** *a* (*date etc*) stipulated.

**préséance** [pʀeseɑ̃s] *nf* precedence *q*.

**présence** [pʀezɑ̃s] *nf* presence ; (*au bureau etc*) attendance ; **en ~ de** in (the) presence of ; (*fig*) in the face of ; **~ d'esprit** presence of mind.

**présent, e** [pʀezɑ̃, -ɑ̃t] *a*, *nm* present ; **à ~ (que)** now (that).

**présentateur, trice** [pʀezɑ̃tatœʀ, -tʀis] *nm/f* presenter.

**présentation** [pʀezɑ̃tɑsjɔ̃] *nf* introduction ; presentation ; (*allure*) appearance.

**présenter** [pʀezɑ̃te] *vt* to present ; (*soumettre*) to submit ; (*invité, conférencier*): **~ qn (à)** to introduce sb (to) // *vi*: **~ mal/bien** to have an unattractive/a pleasing appearance ; **se ~** *vi* (*sur convocation*) to report, come ; (*à une élection*) to stand ; (*occasion*) to arise ; **se ~ bien/mal** to look good/not too good ; **présentoir** *nm* display shelf (*pl* shelves).

**préservatif** [pʀezɛʀvatif] *nm* sheath, condom.

**préserver** [pʀezɛʀve] *vt*: **~ de** to protect from ; to save from.

**présidence** [pʀezidɑ̃s] *nf* presidency ; office of President ; chairmanship.

**président** [pʀezidɑ̃] *nm* (*POL*) president ; (*d'une assemblée, COMM*) chairman ; **~ directeur général (P.D.G.)** chairman and managing director ; **~ du jury** (*JUR*) foreman of the jury; (*d'examen*) chief examiner; **présidente** *nf* president; president's wife; chairwoman; **présidentiel, le** [-sjɛl] *a* presidential.

**présider** [pʀezide] *vt* to preside over; (*dîner*) to be the guest of honour at; ~ à *vt* to direct; to govern.

**présomption** [pʀezɔ̃psjɔ̃] *nf* presumption.

**présomptueux, euse** [pʀezɔ̃ptɥø, -øz] *a* presumptuous.

**presque** [pʀɛsk(ə)] *ad* almost, nearly; ~ **rien** hardly anything; ~ **pas** hardly (at all).

**presqu'île** [pʀɛskil] *nf* peninsula.

**pressant, e** [pʀesɑ̃, -ɑ̃t] *a* urgent.

**presse** [pʀɛs] *nf* press; (*affluence*): **heures de** ~ busy times; **sous** ~ a in press, being printed; ~ **féminine** women's magazines *pl*; ~ **d'information** quality newspapers *pl.*

**pressé, e** [pʀese] *a* in a hurry; (*air*) hurried; (*besogne*) urgent; **orange** ~e fresh orange juice.

**presse-citron** [pʀɛssitʀɔ̃] *nm inv* lemon squeezer.

**pressentiment** [pʀesɑ̃timɑ̃] *nm* foreboding, premonition.

**pressentir** [pʀesɑ̃tiʀ] *vt* to sense; (*prendre contact avec*) to approach.

**presse-papiers** [pʀɛspapje] *nm inv* paperweight.

**presser** [pʀese] *vt* (*fruit, éponge*) to squeeze; (*interrupteur, bouton*) to press, push; (*allure, affaire*) to speed up; (*débiteur etc*) to press; (*inciter*): ~ **qn de faire** to urge *ou* press sb to do // *vi* to be urgent; **rien ne presse** there's no hurry; **se** ~ (*se hâter*) to hurry (up); (*se grouper*) to crowd; **se** ~ **contre qn** to squeeze up against sb; ~ **qn entre ses bras** to hug sb (tight).

**pressing** [pʀesiŋ] *nm* steam-pressing; (*magasin*) dry-cleaner's.

**pression** [pʀesjɔ̃] *nf* pressure; **faire** ~ **sur** to put pressure on; **sous** ~ pressurized, under pressure; (*fig*) keyed up; ~ **artérielle** blood pressure.

**pressoir** [pʀeswaʀ] *nm* (wine *ou* oil *etc*) press.

**pressurer** [pʀesyʀe] *vt* (*fig*) to squeeze.

**pressurisé, e** [pʀesyʀize] *a* pressurized.

**prestance** [pʀɛstɑ̃s] *nf* presence, imposing bearing.

**prestataire** [pʀɛstatɛʀ] *nm/f* person receiving benefits.

**prestation** [pʀɛstɑsjɔ̃] *nf* (*allocation*) benefit; (*d'une assurance*) cover *q*; (*d'une entreprise*) service provided; (*d'un joueur, artiste*) performance; ~ **de serment** taking the oath; ~ **de service** provision of a service.

**preste** [pʀɛst(ə)] *a* nimble; swift; ~**ment** *ad* swiftly.

**prestidigitateur, trice** [pʀɛstidiʒitatœʀ, -tʀis] *nm/f* conjurer.

**prestidigitation** [pʀɛstidiʒitɑsjɔ̃] *nf* conjuring.

**prestige** [pʀɛstiʒ] *nm* prestige; **prestigieux, euse** *a* prestigious.

**présumer** [pʀezyme] *vt*: ~ **que** to presume *ou* assume that; ~ **de** to

overrate; ~ **qn coupable** to presume sb guilty.

**prêt, e** [pʀɛ, pʀɛt] *a* ready // *nm* lending *q*; loan; ~ **sur gages** pawnbroking *q*; **prêt-à-porter** *nm* ready-to-wear *ou* off-the-peg clothes *pl.*

**prétendant** [pʀetɑ̃dɑ̃] *nm* pretender; (*d'une femme*) suitor.

**prétendre** [pʀetɑ̃dʀ(ə)] *vt* (*affirmer*): ~ **que** to claim that; (*avoir l'intention de*): ~ **faire qch** to mean *ou* intend to do sth; ~ **à** *vt* (*droit, titre*) to lay claim to; **prétendu, e** *a* (*supposé*) so-called.

**prête-nom** [pʀɛtnɔ̃] *nm* (*péj*) figurehead.

**prétentieux, euse** [pʀetɑ̃sjø, -øz] *a* pretentious.

**prétention** [pʀetɑ̃sjɔ̃] *nf* claim; pretentiousness.

**prêter** [pʀete] *vt* (*livres, argent*): ~ **qch (à)** to lend sth (to); (*supposer*): ~ **à qn** (*caractère, propos*) to attribute to sb // *vi* (*aussi*: **se** ~: *tissu, cuir*) to give; ~ **à** (*commentaires etc*) to be open to, give rise to; **se** ~ **à** to lend o.s. (*ou* itself) to; (*manigances etc*) to go along with; ~ **assistance à** to give help to; ~ **serment** to take the oath; ~ **l'oreille** to listen; **prêteur** *nm* moneylender; **prêteur sur gages** pawnbroker.

**prétexte** [pʀetɛkst(ə)] *nm* pretext, excuse; **sous aucun** ~ on no account; **prétexter** *vt* to give as a pretext *ou* an excuse.

**prêtre** [pʀetʀ(ə)] *nm* priest; **prêtrise** *nf* priesthood.

**preuve** [pʀœv] *nf* proof; (*indice*) proof, evidence *q*; **faire** ~ **de** to show; **faire ses** ~s to prove o.s. (*ou* itself).

**prévaloir** [pʀevalwaʀ] *vi* to prevail; **se** ~ **de** *vt* to take advantage of; to pride o.s. on

**prévenances** [pʀevnɑ̃s] *nfpl* thoughtfulness *sg*, kindness *sg.*

**prévenant, e** [pʀevnɑ̃, -ɑ̃t] *a* thoughtful, kind.

**prévenir** [pʀevniʀ] *vt* (*avertir*): ~ **qn (de)** to warn sb (about); (*informer*): ~ **qn (de)** to tell *ou* inform sb (about); (*éviter*) to avoid, prevent; (*anticiper*) to forestall; to anticipate; (*influencer*): ~ **qn contre** to prejudice sb against.

**préventif, ive** [pʀevɑ̃tif, -iv] *a* preventive.

**prévention** [pʀevɑ̃sjɔ̃] *nf* prevention; ~ **routière** road safety.

**prévenu, e** [pʀevny] *nm/f* (*JUR*) defendant, accused.

**prévision** [pʀevizjɔ̃] *nf*: ~s predictions; forecast *sg*; **en** ~ **de** in anticipation of; ~s **météorologiques** *ou* **du temps** weather forecast *sg.*

**prévoir** [pʀevwaʀ] *vt* (*deviner*) to foresee; (*s'attendre à*) to expect, reckon on; (*prévenir*) to anticipate; (*organiser*) to plan; (*préparer, réserver*) to allow; **prévu pour 4 personnes** designed for 4 people; **prévu pour 10h** scheduled for 10 o'clock.

**prévoyance** [pʀevwajɑ̃s] *nf* foresight; **une société/caisse de** ~ a provident society/contingency fund.

**prévoyant, e** [pʀevwajɑ̃, -ɑ̃t] *a* a gifted with (*ou* showing) foresight.

**prier** [pʀije] *vi* to pray // *vt* (*Dieu*) to pray to; (*implorer*) to beg; (*demander*): ~ **qn de faire** to ask sb to do; **se faire** ~ to need coaxing *ou* persuading; **je vous en prie** please do; don't mention it.

**prière** [pʀijɛʀ] *nf* prayer; '~ **de faire ...**' 'please do ...'.

**primaire** [pʀimɛʀ] *a* primary; (*péj*) simple-minded; simplistic // *nm* (*SCOL*) primary education.

**primauté** [pʀimote] *nf* (*fig*) primacy.

**prime** [pʀim] *nf* (*bonification*) bonus; (*subside*) premium; allowance; (*COMM*: *cadeau*) free gift; (*ASSURANCES*, *BOURSE*) premium // *a*: **de** ~ **abord** at first glance; ~ **de risque** danger money *q*.

**primer** [pʀime] *vt* (*l'emporter sur*) to prevail over; (*récompenser*) to award a prize to // *vi* to dominate; to prevail.

**primesautier, ère** [pʀimsotje, -jɛʀ] *a* impulsive.

**primeur** [pʀimœʀ] *nf*: **avoir la** ~ **de** to be the first to hear (*ou* see *etc*); ~**s** *nfpl* (*fruits*, *légumes*) early fruits and vegetables; **marchand de** ~**s** greengrocer.

**primevère** [pʀimvɛʀ] *nf* primrose.

**primitif, ive** [pʀimitif, -iv] *a* primitive; (*originel*) original // *nm/f* primitive.

**primordial, e, aux** [pʀimɔʀdjal, -o] *a* essential, primordial.

**prince, esse** [pʀɛ̃s, pʀɛ̃sɛs] *nm/f* prince/princess; ~ **de Galles** *nm inv* check cloth; ~ **héritier** crown prince; **princier, ière** *a* princely.

**principal, e, aux** [pʀɛ̃sipal, -o] *a* principal, main // *nm* (*SCOL*) principal, head(master) // *nf*: (**proposition**) ~**e** main clause.

**principauté** [pʀɛ̃sipote] *nf* Principality.

**principe** [pʀɛ̃sip] *nm* principle; **partir du** ~ **que** to work on the principle *ou* assumption that; **pour le** ~ on principle, for the sake of it; **de** ~ *a* (*accord*, *hostilité*) automatic; **par** ~ on principle; **en** ~ (*habituellement*) as a rule; (*théoriquement*) in principle.

**printanier, ère** [pʀɛ̃tanje, -jɛʀ] *a* spring *cpd*; spring-like.

**printemps** [pʀɛ̃tɑ̃] *nm* spring.

**priori** [pʀijɔʀi]: **a** ~ *ad* without the benefit of hindsight; a priori; initially.

**prioritaire** [pʀijɔʀitɛʀ] *a* having priority; (*AUTO*) having right of way.

**priorité** [pʀijɔʀite] *nf* (*AUTO*): **avoir la** ~ (**sur**) to have right of way (over); ~ **à droite** right of way to vehicles coming from the right; **en** ~ as a (matter of) priority.

**pris, e** [pʀi, pʀiz] *pp de* **prendre** // *a* (*place*) taken; (*journée, mains*) full; (*billets*) sold; (*personne*) busy; (*MÉD*: *enflammé*): **avoir le nez/la gorge** ~(**e**) to have a stuffy nose/a hoarse throat; (*saisi*): **être** ~ **de peur/de fatigue** to be stricken with fear/overcome with fatigue.

**prise** [pʀiz] *nf* (*d'une ville*) capture; (*PÊCHE*, *CHASSE*) catch; (*de judo ou catch*, *point d'appui ou pour empoigner*) hold; (*ÉLEC*: *fiche*) plug; (: *femelle*) socket; (: *au mur*) point; **en** ~ (*AUTO*) in gear; **être aux** ~**s avec** to be grappling with; to be battling

with; **lâcher** ~ to let go; ~ **en charge** (*taxe*) pick-up charge; ~ **de courant** power point; ~ **d'eau** water (supply) point; tap; ~ **multiple** adaptor; ~ **de sang** blood test; ~ **de son** sound recording; ~ **de tabac** pinch of snuff; ~ **de terre** earth; ~ **de vue** (*photo*) shot; (*action*): ~ **de vue(s)** filming, shooting.

**priser** [pʀize] *vt* (*tabac, héroïne*) to take; (*estimer*) to prize, value // *vi* to take snuff.

**prisme** [pʀism(ə)] *nm* prism.

**prison** [pʀizɔ̃] *nf* prison; **aller/être en** ~ to go to/be in prison *ou* jail; **faire de la** ~ to serve time; **prisonnier, ière** *nm/f* prisoner // *a* captive; **faire qn prisonnier** to take sb prisoner.

**prit** *vb voir* **prendre**.

**privations** [pʀivasjɔ̃] *nfpl* privations, hardships.

**privé, e** [pʀive] *a* private; (*dépourvu*): ~ **de** without, lacking; **en** ~ in private.

**priver** [pʀive] *vt*: ~ **qn de** to deprive sb of; **se** ~ **de** to go *ou* do without; **ne pas se** ~ **de faire** not to refrain from doing.

**privilège** [pʀivilɛʒ] *nm* privilege; **privilégié, e** *a* privileged.

**prix** [pʀi] *nm* (*valeur*) price; (*récompense*, *SCOL*) prize; **hors de** ~ exorbitantly priced; **à aucun** ~ not at any price; **à tout** ~ at all costs; ~ **d'achat/de vente** purchasing/selling price.

**probabilité** [pʀɔbabilite] *nf* probability.

**probable** [pʀɔbabl(ə)] *a* likely, probable; ~**ment** *ad* probably.

**probant, e** [pʀɔbɑ̃, -ɑ̃t] *a* convincing.

**probité** [pʀɔbite] *nf* integrity, probity.

**problème** [pʀɔblɛm] *nm* problem.

**procédé** [pʀɔsede] *nm* (*méthode*) process; (*comportement*) behaviour *q*.

**procéder** [pʀɔsede] *vi* to proceed; to behave; ~ **à** *vt* to carry out.

**procédure** [pʀɔsedyʀ] *nf* (*ADMIN*, *JUR*) procedure.

**procès** [pʀɔsɛ] *nm* trial; (*poursuites*) proceedings *pl*; **être en** ~ **avec** to be involved in a lawsuit with.

**procession** [pʀɔsesjɔ̃] *nf* procession.

**processus** [pʀɔsesys] *nm* process.

**procès-verbal, aux** [pʀɔsɛvɛʀbal, -o] *nm* (*constat*) statement; (*aussi*: **P.V.**): **avoir un** ~ to get a parking ticket; to be booked; (*de réunion*) minutes *pl*.

**prochain, e** [pʀɔʃɛ̃, -ɛn] *a* next; (*proche*) impending; near // *nm* fellow man; **la** ~**e fois/semaine** ~**e** next time/week; **prochainement** *ad* soon, shortly.

**proche** [pʀɔʃ] *a* nearby; (*dans le temps*) imminent; close at hand; (*parent, ami*) close; ~**s** *nmpl* close relatives, next of kin; **être** ~ (**de**) to be near, be close (to); **de** ~ **en** ~ gradually; **le P**~ **Orient** the Middle East, the Near East.

**proclamation** [pʀɔklamasjɔ̃] *nf* proclamation.

**proclamer** [pʀɔklame] *vt* to proclaim.

**procréer** [pʀɔkʀee] *vt* to procreate.

**procuration** [pʀɔkyʀasjɔ̃] *nf* proxy; power of attorney.

**procurer** [pʀɔkyʀe] *vt* (*fournir*): ~ **qch à qn** to get *ou* obtain sth for sb; (*causer*:

*plaisir etc)*: ~ qch à qn to bring *ou* give sb sth ; se ~ *vt* to get.

**procureur** [pʀɔkyʀœʀ] *nm* public prosecutor.

**prodige** [pʀɔdiʒ] *nm* marvel, wonder ; *(personne)* prodigy ; **prodigieux, euse** *a* prodigious ; phenomenal.

**prodigue** [pʀɔdig] *a* generous ; extravagant, wasteful ; **fils** ~ prodigal son.

**prodiguer** [pʀɔdige] *vt (argent, biens)* to be lavish with ; *(soins, attentions)*: ~ qch à qn to give sb sth ; to lavish sth on sb.

**producteur, trice** [pʀɔdyktœʀ, -tʀis] *a*: ~ **de blé** wheat-producing // *nm/f* producer.

**productif, ive** [pʀɔdyktif, -iv] *a* productive.

**production** [pʀɔdyksjɔ̃] *nf (gén)* production ; *(rendement)* output ; *(produits)* products *pl*, goods *pl*.

**productivité** [pʀɔdyktivite] *nf* productivity.

**produire** [pʀɔdɥiʀ] *vt* to produce ; se ~ *vi (acteur)* to perform, appear ; *(événement)* to happen, occur.

**produit** [pʀɔdɥi] *nm (gén)* product ; ~s **agricoles** farm produce *sg* ; ~ **d'entretien** cleaning product.

**proéminent, e** [pʀɔeminɑ̃, -ɑ̃t] *a* prominent.

**profane** [pʀɔfan] *a (REL)* secular // *nm/f* layman.

**profaner** [pʀɔfane] *vt* to desecrate.

**proférer** [pʀɔfeʀe] *vt* to utter.

**professer** [pʀɔfese] *vt (déclarer)* to profess // *vi* to teach.

**professeur** [pʀɔfɛsœʀ] *nm* teacher ; *(titulaire d'une chaire)* professor ; ~ **(de faculté)** (university) lecturer.

**profession** [pʀɔfɛsjɔ̃] *nf* profession ; **sans** ~ unemployed ; **professionnel, le** *a, nm/f* professional.

**professorat** [pʀɔfɛsɔʀa] *nm*: **le** ~ the teaching profession.

**profil** [pʀɔfil] *nm* profile ; *(d'une voiture)* line, contour ; **de** ~ in profile ; ~**er** *vt* to streamline ; se ~**er** *vi (arbre, tour)* to stand out, be silhouetted.

**profit** [pʀɔfi] *nm (avantage)* benefit, advantage ; *(COMM, FINANCE)* profit ; **au** ~ **de** in aid of ; **tirer** ~ **de** to profit from ; **mettre à** ~ to take advantage of ; to turn to good account.

**profitable** [pʀɔfitabl(ə)] *a* beneficial ; profitable.

**profiter** [pʀɔfite] *vi*: ~ **de** to take advantage of ; to make the most of ; ~ **à** to be of benefit to, benefit ; to be profitable to.

**profond, e** [pʀɔfɔ̃, -ɔ̃d] *a* deep ; *(méditation, mépris)* profound ; **profondeur** *nf* depth.

**profusion** [pʀɔfyzjɔ̃] *nf* profusion ; **à** ~ in plenty.

**progéniture** [pʀɔʒenityʀ] *nf* offspring *inv*.

**programmation** [pʀɔgʀamɑsjɔ̃] *nf* programming.

**programme** [pʀɔgʀam] *nm* programme ; *(TV, RADIO)* programmes *pl* ; *(SCOL)* syllabus, curriculum ; *(INFORMATIQUE)* program ; **au** ~ **de ce soir** *(TV)* among tonight's

programmes ; **programmer** *vt (TV, RADIO)* to put on, show ; *(INFORMATIQUE)* to program ; **programmeur, euse** *nm/f* computer programmer.

**progrès** [pʀɔgʀɛ] *nm* progress *q* ; **faire des/être** .**en** ~ to make/be making progress.

**progresser** [pʀɔgʀese] *vi* to progress ; *(troupes etc)* to make headway *ou* progress ; **progressif, ive** *a* progressive ; **progression** *nf* progression ; *(d'une troupe etc)* advance, progress.

**prohiber** [pʀɔibe] *vt* to prohibit, ban.

**proie** [pʀwa] *nf* prey *q* ; **être la** ~ **de** to fall prey to ; **être en** ~ **à** to be prey to ; to be suffering.

**projecteur** [pʀɔʒɛktœʀ] *nm* projector ; *(de théâtre, cirque)* spotlight.

**projectile** [pʀɔʒɛktil] *nm* missile ; *(d'arme)* projectile, bullet *(ou* shell *etc)*.

**projection** [pʀɔʒɛksjɔ̃] *nf* projection ; showing ; **conférence avec** ~s lecture with slides *(ou* a film).

**projet** [pʀɔʒɛ] *nm* plan ; *(ébauche)* draft ; **faire des** ~s to make plans ; ~ **de loi** bill.

**projeter** [pʀɔʒte] *vt (envisager)* to plan ; *(film, photos)* to project ; *(: passer)* to show ; *(ombre, lueur)* to throw, cast, project ; *(jeter)* to throw up *(ou* off *ou* out).

**prolétaire** [pʀɔletɛʀ] *nm* proletarian ; **prolétariat** *nm* proletariat.

**proliférer** [pʀɔlifeʀe] *vi* to proliferate.

**prolifique** [pʀɔlifik] *a* prolific.

**prolixe** [pʀɔliks(ə)] *a* verbose.

**prologue** [pʀɔlɔg] *nm* prologue.

**prolongation** [pʀɔlɔ̃gɑsjɔ̃] *nf* prolongation ; extension ; ~s *nfpl (FOOTBALL)* extra time *sg*.

**prolongement** [pʀɔlɔ̃ʒmɑ̃] *nm* extension ; ~s *nmpl (fig)* repercussions, effects ; **dans le** ~ **de** running on from.

**prolonger** [pʀɔlɔ̃ʒe] *vt (débat, séjour)* to prolong ; *(délai, billet, rue)* to extend ; *(suj: chose)* to be a continuation *ou* an extension of ; se ~ *vi* to go on.

**promenade** [pʀɔmnad] *nf* walk *(ou* drive *ou* ride) ; **faire une** ~ to go for a walk ; **une** ~ **en voiture/à vélo** a drive/(bicycle) ride.

**promener** [pʀɔmne] *vt (chien)* to take out for a walk ; *(fig)* to carry around ; to trail round ; *(doigts, regard)*: ~ **qch sur** to run sth over ; se ~ *vi* to go for *(ou* be out for) a walk ; *(fig)*: se ~ **sur** to wander over ; **promeneur, euse** *nm/f* walker, stroller.

**promesse** [pʀɔmɛs] *nf* promise ; ~ **d'achat** commitment to buy.

**prometteur, euse** [pʀɔmɛtœʀ, -øz] *a* promising.

**promettre** [pʀɔmɛtʀ(ə)] *vt* to promise // *vi* to be *ou* look promising ; se ~ **de faire** to resolve *ou* mean to do ; ~ **à qn de faire** to promise sb that one will do.

**promiscuité** [pʀɔmiskɥite] *nf* crowding ; lack of privacy.

**promontoire** [pʀɔmɔ̃twaʀ] *nm* headland.

**promoteur, trice** [pʀɔmɔtœʀ, -tʀis] *nm/f (instigateur)* instigator, promoter ; ~ **(immobilier)** property developer.

**promotion** [pʀɔmosjɔ̃] *nf* promotion.
**promouvoir** [pʀɔmuvwaʀ] *vt* to promote.
**prompt, e** [pʀɔ̃, pʀɔ̃t] *a* swift, rapid.
**promulguer** [pʀɔmylge] *vt* to promulgate.
**prôner** [pʀone] *vt* (*louer*) to laud, extol ; (*préconiser*) to advocate, commend.
**pronom** [pʀɔnɔ̃] *nm* pronoun ; **pronominal, e, aux** *a* pronominal ; reflexive.
**prononcé, e** [pʀɔnɔ̃se] *a* pronounced, marked.
**prononcer** [pʀɔnɔ̃se] *vt* (*son, mot, jugement*) to pronounce ; (*dire*) to utter ; (*allocution*) to deliver // *vi*: ~ **bien/mal** to have a good/poor pronunciation ; **se** ~ *vi* to reach a decision, give a verdict ; **se** ~ **sur** to give an opinion on ; **se** ~ **contre** to come down against ; **prononciation** *nf* pronunciation.
**pronostic** [pʀɔnɔstik] *nm* (*MÉD*) prognosis (*pl* oses) ; (*fig: aussi:* ~**s**) forecast.
**propagande** [pʀɔpagɑ̃d] *nf* propaganda.
**propager** [pʀɔpaʒe] *vt* to spread ; **se** ~ *vi* to spread ; (*PHYSIQUE*) to be propagated.
**prophète** [pʀɔfɛt] *nm* prophet.
**prophétie** [pʀɔfesi] *nf* prophecy ; **prophétiser** *vt* to prophesy.
**propice** [pʀɔpis] *a* favourable.
**proportion** [pʀɔpɔʀsjɔ̃] *nf* proportion ; **en** ~ **de** in proportion to ; **toute(s)** ~**(s) gardée(s)** making due allowance(s) ; **proportionnel, le** *a* proportional ; **proportionner** *vt*: **proportionner qch à** to proportion *ou* adjust sth to.
**propos** [pʀɔpo] *nm* (*paroles*) talk *q*, remark ; (*intention*) intention, aim ; (*sujet*): **à quel** ~? what about? ; **à** ~ **de** about, regarding ; **à tout** ~ for no reason at all ; **à** ~ *ad* by the way ; (*opportunément*) (just) at the right moment.
**proposer** [pʀɔpoze] *vt* (*suggérer*): ~ **qch (à qn)/de faire** to suggest sth (to sb)/doing, propose to do ; (*offrir*): ~ **qch à qn/de faire** to offer sb sth/to do ; (*candidat*) to nominate, put forward ; (*loi, motion*) to propose ; **se** ~ **(pour faire)** to offer one's services (to do) ; **se** ~ **de faire** to intend *ou* propose to do ; **proposition** *nf* suggestion ; proposal ; offer ; (*LING*) clause.
**propre** [pʀɔpʀ(ə)] *a* clean ; (*net*) neat, tidy ; (*possessif*) own ; (*sens*) literal ; (*particulier*): ~ **à** peculiar to, characteristic of ; (*approprié*): ~ **à** suitable *ou* appropriate for ; (*de nature à*): ~ **à faire** likely to do, that will do // *nm*: **recopier au** ~ to make a fair copy of ; ~**ment** *ad* cleanly ; neatly, tidily ; **à** ~**ment parler** strictly speaking ; ~**té** *nf* cleanliness, cleanness ; neatness ; tidiness.
**propriétaire** [pʀɔpʀijetɛʀ] *nm/f* owner ; (*d'hôtel etc*) proprietor/ tress, owner ; (*pour le locataire*) landlord/lady ; ~ **(immobilier)** house-owner ; householder ; ~ **récoltant** grower ; ~ **(terrien)** landowner.
**propriété** [pʀɔpʀijete] *nf* (*droit*) ownership ; (*objet, immeuble etc*) property *gén q* ; (*villa*) residence, property ; (*terres*) property *gén q*, land *gén q* ; (*qualité, CHIMIE, MATH*) property ; (*correction*) appropriateness, suitability.

**propulser** [pʀɔpylse] *vt* (*missile*) to propel ; (*projeter*) to hurl, fling.
**prorata** [pʀɔʀata] *nm inv*: **au** ~ **de** in proportion to, on the basis of.
**proroger** [pʀɔʀɔʒe] *vt* to put back, defer ; (*assemblée*) to adjourn, prorogue.
**prosaïque** [pʀɔzaik] *a* mundane, prosaic.
**proscrire** [pʀɔskʀiʀ] *vt* (*bannir*) to banish ; (*interdire*) to ban, prohibit.
**prose** [pʀoz] *nf* prose (*style*).
**prospecter** [pʀɔspɛkte] *vt* to prospect ; (*COMM*) to canvass.
**prospectus** [pʀɔspɛktys] *nm* (*feuille*) leaflet ; (*dépliant*) brochure, leaflet.
**prospère** [pʀɔspɛʀ] *a* prosperous ; (*entreprise*) thriving, flourishing ; **prospérer** *vi* to thrive ; **prospérité** *nf* prosperity.
**prosterner** [pʀɔstɛʀne]: **se** ~ *vi* to bow low, prostrate o.s.
**prostituée** [pʀɔstitɥe] *nf* prostitute.
**prostitution** [pʀɔstitysjɔ̃] *nf* prostitution.
**prostré, e** [pʀɔstʀe] *a* prostrate.
**protagoniste** [pʀɔtagɔnist(ə)] *nm* protagonist.
**protecteur, trice** [pʀɔtɛktœʀ, -tʀis] *a* protective ; (*air, ton: péj*) patronizing // *nm/f* protector.
**protection** [pʀɔtɛksjɔ̃] *nf* protection ; (*d'un personnage influent: aide*) patronage.
**protégé, e** [pʀɔteʒe] *nm/f* protégé/e.
**protège-cahier** [pʀɔtɛʒkaje] *nm* exercise-book cover.
**protéger** [pʀɔteʒe] *vt* to protect ; **se** ~ **de/contre** to protect o.s. from.
**protéine** [pʀɔtein] *nf* protein.
**protestant, e** [pʀɔtɛstɑ̃, -ɑ̃t] *a, nm/f* Protestant ; **protestantisme** *nm* Protestantism.
**protestation** [pʀɔtɛstɑsjɔ̃] *nf* (*plainte*) protest ; (*déclaration*) protestation, profession.
**protester** [pʀɔtɛste] *vi*: ~ **(contre)** to protest (against *ou* about) ; ~ **de** (*son innocence, sa loyauté*) to protest.
**prothèse** [pʀɔtɛz] *nf* artificial limb, prosthesis ; ~ **dentaire** denture ; dental engineering.
**protocolaire** [pʀɔtɔkɔlɛʀ] *a* formal ; of protocol.
**protocole** [pʀɔtɔkɔl] *nm* protocol ; (*fig*) etiquette ; ~ **d'accord** draft treaty.
**prototype** [pʀɔtɔtip] *nm* prototype.
**protubérance** [pʀɔtybeʀɑ̃s] *nf* bulge, protuberance ; **protubérant, e** *a* protruding, bulging, protuberant.
**proue** [pʀu] *nf* bow(s *pl*), prow.
**prouesse** [pʀuɛs] *nf* feat.
**prouver** [pʀuve] *vt* to prove.
**provenance** [pʀɔvnɑ̃s] *nf* origin ; (*de mot, coutume*) source ; **avion en** ~ **de** plane (arriving) from.
**provenir** [pʀɔvniʀ]: ~ **de** *vt* to come from ; (*résulter de*) to be due to, be the result of.
**proverbe** [pʀɔvɛʀb(ə)] *nm* proverb ; **proverbial, e, aux** *a* proverbial.
**providence** [pʀɔvidɑ̃s] *nf*: **la** ~ providence ; **providentiel, le** *a* providential.

**province** [pʀɔvɛ̃s] *nf* province; **provincial, e, aux** *a* provincial.
**proviseur** [pʀɔvizœʀ] *nm* ≈ head(master).
**provision** [pʀɔvizjɔ̃] *nf* (*réserve*) stock, supply; (*avance: à un avocat, avoué*) retainer, retaining fee; (*COMM*) funds *pl* (in account); reserve; ~**s** *nfpl* (*vivres*) provisions, food *q*; **faire** ~ **de** to stock up with; **armoire à** ~**s** food cupboard.
**provisoire** [pʀɔvizwaʀ] *a* temporary; (*JUR*) provisional; ~**ment** *ad* temporarily, for the time being.
**provocant, e** [pʀɔvɔkɑ̃, -ɑ̃t] *a* provocative.
**provocation** [pʀɔvɔkɑsjɔ̃] *nf* provocation.
**provoquer** [pʀɔvɔke] *vt* (*défier*) to provoke; (*causer*) to cause, bring about; (: *curiosité*) to arouse, give rise to; (: *aveux*) to prompt, elicit.
**proxénète** [pʀɔksenɛt] *nm* procurer.
**proximité** [pʀɔksimite] *nf* nearness, closeness, proximity; (*dans le temps*) imminence, closeness; **à** ~ near *ou* close by; **à** ~ **de** near (to), close to.
**prude** [pʀyd] *a* prudish.
**prudence** [pʀydɑ̃s] *nf* carefulness; caution; prudence; **avec** ~ carefully; cautiously; wisely; **par (mesure de)** ~ as a precaution.
**prudent, e** [pʀydɑ̃, -ɑ̃t] *a* (*pas téméraire*) careful, cautious, prudent; (: *en général*) safety-conscious; (*sage, conseillé*) wise, sensible; (*réservé*) cautious; **ce n'est pas** ~ it's risky; it's not sensible; **soyez** ~ take care, be careful.
**prune** [pʀyn] *nf* plum.
**pruneau, x** [pʀyno] *nm* prune.
**prunelle** [pʀynɛl] *nf* pupil; eye.
**prunier** [pʀynje] *nm* plum tree.
**psalmodier** [psalmɔdje] *vt* to chant; (*fig*) to drone out.
**psaume** [psom] *nm* psalm.
**pseudonyme** [psødɔnim] *nm* (*gén*) fictitious name; (*d'écrivain*) pseudonym, pen name; (*de comédien*) stage name.
**psychanalyse** [psikanaliz] *nf* psychoanalysis; **psychanalyser** *vt* to psychoanalyze; **se faire psychanalyser** to undergo (psycho)analysis; **psychanalyste** *nm/f* psychoanalyst.
**psychiatre** [psikjatʀ(ə)] *nm/f* psychiatrist.
**psychiatrie** [psikjatʀi] *nf* psychiatry; **psychiatrique** *a* psychiatric; (*hôpital*) mental, psychiatric.
**psychique** [psiʃik] *a* psychological.
**psychologie** [psikɔlɔʒi] *nf* psychology; **psychologique** *a* psychological; **psychologue** *nm/f* psychologist; **être psychologue** (*fig*) to be a good psychologist.
**psychose** [psikoz] *nf* psychosis; obsessive fear.
**Pte** *abr de* **porte.**
**P.T.T.** *sigle fpl voir* **poste.**
**pu** *pp de* **pouvoir.**
**puanteur** [pɥɑ̃tœʀ] *nf* stink, stench.
**pubère** [pybɛʀ] *a* pubescent; **puberté** *nf* puberty.

**pubis** [pybis] *nm* (*bas-ventre*) pubes *pl*; (*os*) pubis.
**public, ique** [pyblik] *a* public; (*école, instruction*) state *cpd* // *nm* public; (*assistance*) audience; **en** ~ in public.
**publication** [pyblikɑsjɔ̃] *nf* publication.
**publiciste** [pyblisist(ə)] *nm/f* adman.
**publicitaire** [pyblisitɛʀ] *a* advertising *cpd*; (*film, voiture*) publicity *cpd*.
**publicité** [pyblisite] *nf* (*méthode, profession*) advertising; (*annonce*) advertisement; (*révélations*) publicity.
**publier** [pyblije] *vt* to publish.
**publique** [pyblik] *af voir* **public.**
**puce** [pys] *nf* flea; ~**s** *nfpl* (*marché*) flea market *sg*.
**puceau, x** [pyso] *am*: **être** ~ to be a virgin.
**pucelle** [pysɛl] *af*: **être** ~ to be a virgin.
**pudeur** [pydœʀ] *nf* modesty.
**pudibond, e** [pydibɔ̃, -ɔ̃d] *a* prudish.
**pudique** [pydik] *a* (*chaste*) modest; (*discret*) discreet.
**puer** [pɥe] (*péj*) *vi* to stink // *vt* to stink of, reek of.
**puéricultrice** [pɥeʀikyltʀis] *nf* paediatric nurse.
**puériculture** [pɥeʀikyltyʀ] *nf* paediatric nursing; infant care.
**puéril, e** [pɥeʀil] *a* childish.
**pugilat** [pyʒila] *nm* (fist) fight.
**puis** [pɥi] *vb voir* **pouvoir** // *ad* then; **et** ~ and (then).
**puiser** [pɥize] *vt* (*eau*): ~ (**dans**) to draw (from); ~ **dans qch** to dip into sth.
**puisque** [pɥisk(ə)] *cj* since.
**puissance** [pɥisɑ̃s] *nf* power; **en** ~ *a* potential; **2 (à la)** ~ **5** 2 to the power of 5.
**puissant, e** [pɥisɑ̃, -ɑ̃t] *a* powerful.
**puisse** *etc vb voir* **pouvoir.**
**puits** [pɥi] *nm* well; ~ **de mine** mine shaft.
**pull(-over)** [pul(ɔvœʀ)] *nm* sweater, jumper.
**pulluler** [pylyle] *vi* to swarm.
**pulmonaire** [pylmɔnɛʀ] *a* lung *cpd*; (*artère*) pulmonary.
**pulpe** [pylp(ə)] *nf* pulp.
**pulsation** [pylsɑsjɔ̃] *nf* beat.
**pulsion** [pylsjɔ̃] *nf* drive, urge.
**pulvérisateur** [pylveʀizatœʀ] *nm* spray.
**pulvériser** [pylveʀize] *vt* (*solide*) to pulverize; (*liquide*) to spray; (*fig*) to pulverize; to smash.
**punaise** [pynɛz] *nf* (*ZOOL*) bug; (*clou*) drawing pin.
**punch** [pɔ̃ʃ] *nm* (*boisson*) punch; [pœnʃ] (*BOXE*) punching ability; (*fig*) punch; **punching-ball** *nm* punchball.
**punir** [pyniʀ] *vt* to punish; **punition** *nf* punishment.
**pupille** [pypij] *nf* (*ANAT*) pupil // *nm/f* (*enfant*) ward; ~ **de l'État** child in care; ~ **de la Nation** war orphan.
**pupitre** [pypitʀ(ə)] *nm* (*SCOL*) desk; (*REL*) lectern; (*de chef d'orchestre*) rostrum; ~ **de commande** panel.
**pur, e** [pyʀ] *a* pure; (*vin*) undiluted; (*whisky*) neat; **en** ~**e perte** fruitlessly, to no avail.

**purée** [pyʀe] *nf:* ~ **(de pommes de terre)** mashed potatoes *pl*; ~ **de marrons** chestnut purée.

**pureté** [pyʀte] *nf* purity.

**purgatif** [pyʀgatif] *nm* purgative, purge.

**purgatoire** [pyʀgatwaʀ] *nm* purgatory.

**purge** [pyʀʒ(ə)] *nf* (*POL*) purge; (*MÉD*) purging *q*; purge.

**purger** [pyʀʒe] *vt* (*radiateur*) to flush (out), drain; (*circuit hydraulique*) to bleed; (*MÉD, POL*) to purge; (*JUR: peine*) to serve.

**purifier** [pyʀifje] *vt* to purify; (*TECH: métal*) to refine.

**purin** [pyʀɛ̃] *nm* liquid manure.

**puritain, e** [pyʀitɛ̃, -ɛn] *a, nm/f* Puritan; **puritanisme** *nm* Puritanism.

**pur-sang** [pyʀsɑ̃] *nm inv* thoroughbred, purebred.

**purulent, e** [pyʀylɑ̃, -ɑ̃t] *a* purulent.

**pus** [py] *nm* pus.

**pusillanime** [pyzilanim] *a* fainthearted.

**putain** [pytɛ̃] *nf* (*fam!*) whore(!); **ce/cette** ~ **de ...** this bloody ...(!).

**putréfier** [pytʀefje] *vt, se* ~ *vi* to putrefy, rot.

**puzzle** [pœzl(ə)] *nm* jigsaw (puzzle).

**P.V.** *sigle m* = **procès-verbal.**

**pygmée** [pigme] *nm* pygmy.

**pyjama** [piʒama] *nm* pyjamas *pl*, pair of pyjamas.

**pylône** [pilon] *nm* pylon.

**pyramide** [piʀamid] *nf* pyramid.

**pyromane** [piʀɔman] *nm/f* fire bug, arsonist.

**python** [pitɔ̃] *nm* python.

## Q

**QG** [kyʒe] *voir* **quartier.**

**QI** [kyi] *voir* **quotient.**

**quadragénaire** [kadʀaʒenɛʀ] *nm/f* man/woman in his/her forties.

**quadrangulaire** [kwadʀɑ̃gylɛʀ] *a* quadrangular.

**quadrilatère** [k(w)adʀilatɛʀ] *nm* quadrilateral; four-sided area.

**quadrillage** [kadʀijaʒ] *nm* (*lignes etc*) square pattern, criss-cross pattern.

**quadrillé, e** [kadʀije] *a* (*papier*) squared.

**quadriller** [kadʀije] *vt* (*papier*) to mark out in squares; (*POLICE*) to keep under tight control, be positioned throughout.

**quadrimoteur** [k(w)adʀimɔtœʀ] *nm* four-engined plane.

**quadripartite** [kwadʀipaʀtit] *a* four-power; four-party.

**quadriphonie** [kadʀifɔni] *nf* quadraphony.

**quadriréacteur** [k(w)adʀiʀeaktœʀ] *nm* four-engined jet.

**quadrupède** [k(w)adʀypɛd] *nm* quadruped.

**quadruple** [k(w)adʀypl(ə)] *nm:* **le** ~ **de** four times as much as; **quadrupler** *vt, vi* to increase fourfold; **quadruplés, ées** *nm/fpl* quadruplets, quads.

**quai** [ke] *nm* (*de port*) quay; (*de gare*) platform; (*de cours d'eau, canal*) embankment; **être à** ~ (*navire*) to be alongside; (*train*) to be in the station.

**qualificatif, ive** [kalifikatif, -iv] *a* (*LING*) qualifying // *nm* (*terme*) term; (*LING*) qualifier.

**qualification** [kalifikasjɔ̃] *nf* qualification.

**qualifier** [kalifje] *vt* to qualify; (*appeler*): ~ **qch/qn de** to describe sth/sb as; **se** ~ *vi* (*SPORT*) to qualify; **être qualifié pour** to be qualified for.

**qualité** [kalite] *nf* quality; (*titre, fonction*) position; **en** ~ **de** in one's capacity as; **avoir** ~ **pour** to have authority to.

**quand** [kɑ̃] *cj, ad* when; ~ **je serai riche** when I'm rich; ~ **même** nevertheless; all the same; really; ~ **bien même** even though.

**quant** [kɑ̃]: ~ **à** *prép* as for, as to; regarding.

**quant-à-soi** [kɑ̃taswa] *nm:* **rester sur son** ~ to remain aloof.

**quantième** [kɑ̃tjɛm] *nm* day (of the month).

**quantifier** [kɑ̃tifje] *vt* to quantify.

**quantitatif, ive** [kɑ̃titatif, -iv] *a* quantitative.

**quantité** [kɑ̃tite] *nf* quantity, amount; (*SCIENCE*) quantity; (*grand nombre*): **une** *ou* **des** ~**(s) de** a great deal of; a lot of; **en grande** ~ in large quantities; **du travail en** ~ a great deal of work; ~ **de** many.

**quarantaine** [kaʀɑ̃tɛn] *nf* (*MÉD*) quarantine; **la** ~ forty, the forty mark; (*âge*) forty, the forties *pl*; **une** ~ **(de)** forty or so, about forty; **mettre en** ~ to put into quarantine; (*fig*) to send to Coventry.

**quarante** [kaʀɑ̃t] *num* forty.

**quart** [kaʀ] *nm* (*fraction*) quarter; (*surveillance*) watch; (*partie*): **un** ~ **de poulet/fromage** a chicken quarter/a quarter of a cheese; **un** ~ **de beurre** a quarter kilo of butter, ≈ a half pound of butter; **un** ~ **de vin** a quarter litre of wine; **une livre un** ~ *ou* **et** ~ one and a quarter pounds; **le** ~ **de** a quarter of; ~ **d'heure** quarter of an hour; **être de/prendre le** ~ to keep/take the watch; ~ **de tour** quarter turn.

**quarteron** [kaʀtəʀɔ̃] *nm* (*péj*) small bunch, handful.

**quartette** [kwaʀtɛt] *nm* quartet(te).

**quartier** [kaʀtje] *nm* (*de ville*) district, area; (*de bœuf*) quarter; (*de fruit, fromage*) piece; ~**s** *nmpl* (*MIL, BLASON*) quarters; **cinéma de** ~ local cinema; **avoir** ~ **libre** (*MIL*) to have leave from barracks; **ne pas faire de** ~ to spare no-one, give no quarter; ~ **général (QG)** headquarters (HQ).

**quartier-maître** [kaʀtjemɛtʀ(ə)] *nm* ≈ leading seaman.

**quartz** [kwaʀts] *nm* quartz.

**quasi** [kazi] *ad* almost, nearly // *préfixe:* ~**-certitude** near certainty; ~**ment** *ad* almost, nearly.

**quatorze** [katɔʀz(ə)] *num* fourteen.

**quatrain** [katʀɛ̃] *nm* quatrain.

**quatre** [katʀ(ə)] *num* four; **à** ~ **pattes** on all fours; **tiré à** ~ **épingles** dressed up to the nines; **faire les** ~ **cent coups** to get a bit wild; **se mettre en** ~ **pour qn** to go out of one's way for sb; ~ **à** ~ (*monter, descendre*) four at a time; ~-

**vingt-dix** *num* ninety ; **~-vingts** *num* eighty ; **quatrième** *num* fourth.

**quatuor** [kwatyɔR] *nm* quartet(te).

**que** [kə] *cj* (*gén*) that ; (*après comparatif*) than ; as: *voir* **plus, autant** *etc* ; **il sait ~ tu es là** he knows (that) you're here ; **je veux ~ tu acceptes** I want you to accept ; **il a dit ~ oui** he said he would (*ou* it was *etc, suivant le contexte*) ; **si vous y allez ou ~ vous lui téléphoniez** if you go there or (if you) phone him ; **quand il rentrera et qu'il aura mangé** when he gets back and (when he) has eaten ; **qu'il le veuille ou non** whether he likes it or not ; **tenez-le qu'il ne tombe pas** hold it so (that) it doesn't fall ; **qu'il fasse ce qu'il voudra** let him do as he pleases ; *voir* **avant, pour, tel** *etc* // *ad*: **qu'il ou qu'est-ce qu'il est bête/court vite** he is so silly/runs so fast ; **~ de** what a lot of // *pronom*: **l'homme ~ je vois** the man (whom) I see ; **le livre ~ tu vois** the book (that *ou* which) you see ; **un jour ~ j'étais** a day when I was ; **c'est une erreur ~ de croire** it's a mistake to believe ; **~ fais-tu?, qu'est-ce que tu fais?** what are you doing? ; **~ préfères-tu, celui-ci ou celui-là?** which do you prefer, this one or that one?

**Québec** [kebɛk] *nm*: **le ~** Quebec.

**quel, quelle** [kɛl] *a*: **~ livre/ homme?** what book/man? ; (*parmi un certain choix*) which book/man? ; **~ est cet homme/ce livre?** who/what is this man/ book? ; **~ est le plus grand?** which is the tallest (*ou* biggest *etc*)? ; **~s acteurs préférez-vous?** which actors do you prefer? ; **dans ~s pays êtes-vous allé?** which *ou* what countries did you go to? ; **~le surprise!** what a surprise! ; **~ que soit le coupable** whoever is guilty ; **~ que soit votre avis** whatever your opinion ; whichever is your opinion.

**quelconque** [kɛlkɔ̃k] *a* (*médiocre*) indifferent, poor ; (*sans attrait*) ordinary, plain ; (*indéfini*) **un ami/ prétexte ~** some friend/pretext or other ; **un livre ~ suffira** any book will do.

**quelque** [kɛlk(ə)] *dét* some ; **~s** a few, some, *tournure interrogative* + any ; **les ~s livres qui** the few books which // *ad* (*environ*): **~ 100 mètres** some 100 metres ; **~ livre qu'il choisisse** whatever (*ou* whichever) book he chooses ; **20 kg et ~(s)** a bit over 20 kg ; **~ chose** something, *tournure interrogative* + anything ; **~ chose d'autre** something else ; anything else ; **~ part** somewhere ; **~ peu** rather, somewhat ; **en ~ sorte** as it were ; **quelquefois** *ad* sometimes ; **quelques-uns, -unes** [-zœ̃] *pronom* some, a few.

**quelqu'un, une** [kɛlkœ̃, -yn] *pronom* someone, somebody, *tournure interrogative* + anyone *ou* anybody ; **~ d'autre** someone *ou* somebody else ; anybody else.

**quémander** [kemɑ̃de] *vt* to beg for.

**qu'en dira-t-on** [kɑ̃diratɔ̃] *nm inv*: **le ~** gossip, what people say.

**quenelle** [kənɛl] *nf* quenelle.

**quenouille** [kənuj] *nf* distaff.

**querelle** [kəRɛl] *nf* quarrel.

**quereller** [kəRele]: **se ~** *vi* to quarrel ; **querelleur, euse** *a* quarrelsome.

**qu'est-ce que** (*ou* **qui**) [kɛskə(ki)] *voir* **que, qui**.

**question** [kɛstjɔ̃] *nf* (*gén*) question ; (*fig*) matter ; issue ; **il a été ~ de** we (*ou* they) spoke about ; **il est ~ de les emprisonner** there's talk of them being jailed ; **de quoi est-il ~?** what is it about? ; **il n'en est pas ~** there's no question of it ; **en ~** in question ; **hors de ~** out of the question ; **remettre en ~** to question ; **poser la ~ de confiance** (*POL*) to ask for a vote of confidence.

**questionnaire** [kɛstjɔnɛR] *nm* questionnaire ; **questionner** *vt* to question.

**quête** [kɛt] *nf* collection ; (*recherche*) quest, search ; **faire la ~** (*à l'église*) to take the collection ; (*artiste*) to pass the hat round ; **en ~ de qch** in search of sth ; **quêter** *vi* (*à l'église*) to take the collection ; (*dans la rue*) to collect money (for charity) // *vt* to seek.

**quetsche** [kwɛtʃ(ə)] *nf* damson.

**queue** [kø] *nf* tail ; (*fig: du classement*) bottom ; (: *de poêle*) handle ; (: *de fruit, feuille*) stalk ; (: *de train, colonne, file*) rear ; **en ~ (de train)** at the rear (of the train) ; **faire la ~** to queue (up) ; **se mettre à la ~** to join the queue ; **à la ~ leu leu** in single file ; (*fig*) one after the other ; **~ de cheval** ponytail ; **~ de poisson: faire une ~ de poisson à qn** (*AUTO*) to cut in front of sb ; **~-de-pie** *nf* (*habit*) tails *pl*, tail coat.

**queux** [kø] *am voir* **maître**.

**qui** [ki] *pronom* (*personne*) who, *prép* + whom ; (*chose, animal*) which, that ; **qu'est-ce ~ est sur la table?** what is on the table? ; **à ~ est ce sac?** whose bag is this? ; **à ~ parlais-tu?** who were you talking to?, to whom were you talking? ; **amenez ~ vous voulez** bring who you like ; **~ que ce soit** whoever it may be.

**quiche** [kiʃ] *nf*: **~ lorraine** quiche Lorraine.

**quiconque** [kikɔ̃k] *pronom* (*celui qui*) whoever, anyone who ; (*personne*) anyone, anybody.

**quidam** [kɥidam] *nm* fellow.

**quiétude** [kjetyd] *nf* (*d'un lieu*) quiet, tranquillity ; **en toute ~** in complete peace ; (*mentale*) with complete peace of mind.

**quignon** [kiɲɔ̃] *nm*: **~ de pain** crust of bread ; hunk of bread.

**quille** [kij] *nf* skittle ; (**jeu de**) **~s** ninepins *sg*, skittles *sg*.

**quincaillerie** [kɛ̃kajRi] *nf* (*ustensiles*) hardware, ironmongery ; (*magasin*) hardware shop, ironmonger's ; **quincaillier, ère** *nm/f* ironmonger.

**quinconce** [kɛ̃kɔ̃s] *nm*: **en ~** in staggered rows.

**quinine** [kinin] *nf* quinine.

**quinquagénaire** [kɛ̃kaʒenɛR] *nm/f* man/woman in his/her fifties.

**quinquennal, e, aux** [kɛ̃kenal, -o] *a* five-year, quinquennial.

**quintal, aux** [kɛ̃tal, -o] *nm* quintal (*100 kg*).

**quinte** [kɛ̃t] *nf*: **~ (de toux)** coughing fit.

**quintette** [kɛ̃tɛt] *nm* quintet(te).
**quintuple** [kɛ̃typl(ə)] *nm*: **le ~ de** five times as much as; **quintupler** *vt, vi* to increase fivefold; **quintuplés, ées** *nm/fpl* quintuplets, quins.
**quinzaine** [kɛ̃zɛn] *nf*: **une ~ (de)** about fifteen, fifteen or so; **une ~ (de jours)** a fortnight, two weeks.
**quinze** [kɛ̃z] *num* fifteen; **demain en ~** a fortnight *ou* two weeks tomorrow; **dans ~ jours** in a fortnight('s time), in two weeks(' time).
**quiproquo** [kiprɔko] *nm* misunderstanding; (*THÉÂTRE*) (case of) mistaken identity.
**quittance** [kitãs] *nf* (*reçu*) receipt; (*facture*) bill.
**quitte** [kit] *a*: **être ~ envers qn** to be no longer in sb's debt; (*fig*) to be quits with sb; **être ~ de** (*obligation*) to be clear of; **en être ~ à bon compte** to get off lightly; **~ à faire** even if it means doing; **~ ou double** (*jeu*) double your money.
**quitter** [kite] *vt* to leave; (*espoir, illusion*) to give up; (*vêtement*) to take off; **se ~** (*couples, interlocuteurs*) to part; **ne quittez pas** (*au téléphone*) hold the line.
**qui-vive** [kiviv] *nm*: **être sur le ~** to be on the alert.
**quoi** [kwa] *pronom* (*interrogatif*) what; **~ de neuf?** what's the news?; **as-tu de ~ écrire?** have you anything to write with?; **il n'a pas de ~ se l'acheter** he can't afford it, he hasn't got the money to buy it; **~ qu'il arrive** whatever happens; **~ qu'il en soit** be that as it may; **~ que ce soit** anything at all; **'il n'y a pas de ~'** '(please) don't mention it'; **en ~ puis-je vous aider?** how can I help you?
**quoique** [kwak(ə)] *cj* (al)though.
**quolibet** [kɔlibɛ] *nm* gibe, jeer.
**quorum** [kɔrɔm] *nm* quorum.
**quota** [kwɔta] *nm* quota.
**quote-part** [kɔtpar] *nf* share.
**quotidien, ne** [kɔtidjɛ̃, -ɛn] *a* daily; (*banal*) everyday // *nm* (*journal*) daily (paper).
**quotient** [kɔsjã] *nm* (*MATH*) quotient; **~ intellectuel (QI)** intelligence quotient (IQ).
**quotité** [kɔtite] *nf* (*FINANCE*) quota.

## R

**r.** *abr de* **route, rue.**
**rabâcher** [rabɑʃe] *vt* to harp on, keep on repeating.
**rabais** [rabɛ] *nm* reduction, discount; **au ~** at a reduction *ou* discount.
**rabaisser** [rabese] *vt* (*rabattre*) to reduce; (*dénigrer*) to belittle.
**rabat** [raba] *nm* flap.
**rabat-joie** [rabaʒwa] *nm/f inv* killjoy, spoilsport.
**rabatteur, euse** [rabatœr, -øz] *nm/f* (*de gibier*) beater; (*péj*) tout.
**rabattre** [rabatr(ə)] *vt* (*couvercle, siège*) to pull *ou* close down; (*col*) to turn down; (*gibier*) to drive; (*somme d'un prix*) to deduct, take off; **se ~** *vi* (*bords, couvercle*) to fall shut; (*véhicule, coureur*) to cut in; **se ~ sur** *vt* to fall back on.

**rabbin** [rabɛ̃] *nm* rabbi.
**rabique** [rabik] *a* rabies *cpd.*
**râble** [rɑbl(ə)] *nm* back; (*CULIN*) saddle.
**râblé, e** [rɑble] *a* broad-backed, stocky.
**rabot** [rabo] *nm* plane; **raboter** *vt* to plane (down).
**raboteux, euse** [rabotø, -øz] *a* uneven, rough.
**rabougri, e** [rabugri] *a* stunted.
**rabrouer** [rabrue] *vt* to snub, rebuff.
**racaille** [rakɑj] *nf* (*péj*) rabble, riffraff.
**raccommodage** [rakɔmɔdaʒ] *nm* mending *q*, repairing *q*; darning *q*.
**raccommoder** [rakɔmɔde] *vt* to mend, repair; (*chaussette*) to darn.
**raccompagner** [rakɔ̃paɲe] *vt* to take *ou* see back.
**raccord** [rakɔr] *nm* link; **~ de maçonnerie** pointing *q*; **~ de peinture** join; touch up.
**raccordement** [rakɔrdəmã] *nm* joining up.
**raccorder** [rakɔrde] *vt* to join (up), link up; (*suj: pont etc*) to connect, link; **~ au réseau du téléphone** to connect to the telephone service.
**raccourci** [rakursi] *nm* short cut.
**raccourcir** [rakursir] *vt* to shorten // *vi* (*vêtement*) to shrink.
**raccroc** [rakro]: **par ~** *ad* by chance.
**raccrocher** [rakroʃe] *vt* (*tableau, vêtement*) to hang back up; (*récepteur*) to put down // *vi* (*TÉL*) to hang up, ring off; **se ~ à** *vt* to cling to, hang on to.
**race** [ras] *nf* race; (*d'animaux, fig: espèce*) breed; (*ascendance, origine*) stock, race; **de ~** a purebred, pedigree; **racé, e** *a* thoroughbred.
**rachat** [raʃa] *nm* buying; buying back; redemption; atonement.
**racheter** [raʃte] *vt* (*article perdu*) to buy another; (*davantage*): **~ du lait/3 œufs** to buy more milk/another 3 eggs *ou* 3 more eggs; (*après avoir vendu*) to buy back; (*d'occasion*) to buy; (*COMM: part, firme*) to buy up; (: *pension, rente*) to redeem; (*REL: pécheur*) to redeem; (: *péché*) to atone for, expiate; (*mauvaise conduite, oubli, défaut*) to make up for; **se ~** (*REL*) to redeem o.s.; (*gén*) to make amends, make up for it.
**rachitique** [raʃitik] *a* suffering from rickets; (*fig*) scraggy, scrawny.
**racial, e, aux** [rasjal, -o] *a* racial.
**racine** [rasin] *nf* root; **~ carrée/cubique** square/cube root; **prendre ~** (*fig*) to take root; to put down roots.
**racisme** [rasism(ə)] *nm* racism, racialism; **raciste** *a, nm/f* racist, racialist.
**racket** [rakɛt] *nm* racketeering *q.*
**raclée** [rakle] *nf* (*fam*) hiding, thrashing.
**racler** [rakle] *vt* (*os, plat*) to scrape; (*tache, boue*) to scrape off; (*suj: chose: frotter contre*) to scrape (against).
**raclette** [raklɛt] *nf* (*CULIN*) raclette (*Swiss cheese dish*).
**racoler** [rakole] *vt* (*attirer: suj: prostituée*) to solicit; (: *parti, marchand*) to solicit for; (*attraper*) to pick up; **racoleur, euse** *a* (*péj: publicité*) cheap and alluring // *nf* streetwalker.

**racontars** [ʀakɔ̃taʀ] *nmpl* stories, gossip *sg.*
**raconter** [ʀakɔ̃te] *vt*: ~ **(à qn)** (*décrire*) to relate (to sb), tell (sb) about; (*dire*) to tell (sb).
**racorni, e** [ʀakɔʀni] *a* hard(ened).
**radar** [ʀadaʀ] *nm* radar.
**rade** [ʀad] *nf* (natural) harbour; **en ~ de** Toulon in Toulon harbour; **rester en ~** (*fig*) to be left stranded.
**radeau, x** [ʀado] *nm* raft.
**radial, e, aux** [ʀadjal, -o] *a* radial; **pneu à carcasse ~e** radial tyre.
**radiateur** [ʀadjatœʀ] *nm* radiator, heater; (*AUTO*) radiator; ~ **électrique/à gaz** electric/gas heater *ou* fire.
**radiation** [ʀadjɑsjɔ̃] *nf* (*voir radier*) striking off *q*; (*PHYSIQUE*) radiation.
**radical, e, aux** [ʀadikal, -o] *a* radical // *nm* (*LING*) stem.
**radier** [ʀadje] *vt* to strike off.
**radieux, euse** [ʀadjø, -øz] *a* radiant; brilliant, glorious.
**radin, e** [ʀadɛ̃, -in] *a* (*fam*) stingy.
**radio** [ʀadjo] *nf* radio; (*MÉD*) X-ray // *nm* radiogram, radiotelegram; radio operator; **à la ~** on the radio; **se faire faire une ~ (des poumons)** to have an X-ray taken (of one's lungs).
**radio...** [ʀadjo] *préfixe*: ~**actif, ive** a radioactive; ~**activité** *nf* radioactivity; **radiodiffuser** *vt* to broadcast (by radio); ~**graphie** *nf* radiography; (*photo*) X-ray photograph, radiograph; ~**graphier** *vt* to X-ray; ~**logue** *nm/f* radiologist; ~**phonique** *a* radio *cpd*; ~**reportage** *nm* radio report; ~**scopie** *nf* radioscopy; ~**télégraphie** *nf* radiotelegraphy; ~**télévisé, e** *a* broadcast on radio and television.
**radis** [ʀadi] *nm* radish; ~ **noir** horseradish *q*.
**radium** [ʀadjɔm] *nm* radium.
**radoter** [ʀadɔte] *vi* to ramble on.
**radoub** [ʀadu] *nm*: **bassin de ~** dry dock.
**radoucir** [ʀadusiʀ]: **se ~** *vi* (*se réchauffer*) to become milder; (*se calmer*) to calm down; to soften.
**rafale** [ʀafal] *nf* (*vent*) gust (of wind); (*tir*) burst of gunfire; ~ **de mitrailleuse** burst of machine-gun fire.
**raffermir** [ʀafɛʀmiʀ] *vt*, **se ~** *vi* (*tissus, muscle*) to firm up; (*fig*) to strengthen.
**raffinage** [ʀafinaʒ] *nm* refining.
**raffiné, e** [ʀafine] *a* refined.
**raffinement** [ʀafinmɑ̃] *nm* refinement.
**raffiner** [ʀafine] *vt* to refine; **raffinerie** *nf* refinery.
**raffoler** [ʀafɔle]: ~ **de** *vt* to be very keen on.
**raffut** [ʀafy] *nm* (*fam*) row, racket.
**rafistoler** [ʀafistɔle] *vt* (*fam*) to patch up.
**rafle** [ʀafl(ə)] *nf* (*de police*) roundup, raid.
**rafler** [ʀufle] *vt* (*fam*) to swipe, run off with.
**rafraîchir** [ʀafʀeʃiʀ] *vt* (*atmosphère, température*) to cool (down); (*aussi: mettre à ~*) to chill; (*suj: air, eau*) to freshen up; (: *boisson*) to refresh; (*fig: rénover*) to brighten up; **se ~** to grow cooler; to freshen up; to refresh o.s.;

**rafraîchissant, e** *a* refreshing; **rafraîchissement** *nm* cooling; (*boisson etc*) cool drink, refreshment.
**ragaillardir** [ʀagajaʀdiʀ] *vt* (*fam*) to perk *ou* buck up.
**rage** [ʀaʒ] *nf* (*MÉD*): **la ~** rabies; (*fureur*) rage, fury; **faire ~** to rage; ~ **de dents** (raging) toothache; **rager** *vi* to fume (with rage); **rageur, euse** *a* snarling; illtempered.
**raglan** [ʀaglɑ̃] *a inv* raglan.
**ragot** [ʀago] *nm* (*fam*) malicious gossip *q*.
**ragoût** [ʀagu] *nm* (*plat*) stew.
**rai** [ʀɛ] *nm*: **un ~ de soleil/lumière** a sunray/ray of light.
**raid** [ʀɛd] *nm* (*MIL*) raid; (*SPORT*) longdistance trek.
**raide** [ʀɛd] *a* (*tendu*) taut, tight; (*escarpé*) steep; (*droit: cheveux*) straight; (*ankylosé, dur, guindé*) stiff; (*fam*) steep, stiff; stony broke // *ad* (*en pente*) steeply; ~ **mort** stone dead; **raideur** *nf* steepness; stiffness; **raidir** *vt* (*muscles*) to stiffen; (*câble*) to pull taut, tighten; **se raidir** *vi* to stiffen; to become taut; (*personne*) to tense up; to brace o.s.; to harden.
**raie** [ʀɛ] *nf* (*ZOOL*) skate, ray; (*rayure*) stripe; (*des cheveux*) parting.
**raifort** [ʀɛfɔʀ] *nm* horseradish.
**rail** [ʀɑj] *nm* (*barre d'acier*) rail; (*chemins de fer*) railways *pl*; **les ~s** (*la voie ferrée*) the rails, the track *sg*; **par ~** by rail; ~ **conducteur** live *ou* conductor rail.
**railler** [ʀɑje] *vt* to scoff at, jeer at.
**rainure** [ʀenyʀ] *nf* groove; slot.
**rais** [ʀɛ] *nm* = **rai.**
**raisin** [ʀɛzɛ̃] *nm* (*aussi*: ~**s**) grapes *pl*; (*variété*): ~ **muscat** muscat grape; ~**s secs** raisins, currants.
**raison** [ʀɛzɔ̃] *nf* reason; **avoir ~** to be right; **donner ~ à qn** to agree with sb; to prove sb right; **avoir ~ de qn/qch** to get the better of sb/sth; **se faire une ~** to learn to live with it; **perdre la ~** to become insane; to take leave of one's senses; **demander ~ à qn de** (*affront etc*) to demand satisfaction from sb for; ~ **de plus** all the more reason; **à plus forte ~** all the more so; **en ~ de** because of; according to; in proportion to; **à ~ de** at the rate of; ~ **sociale** corporate name; **raisonnable** *a* reasonable, sensible.
**raisonnement** [ʀɛzɔnmɑ̃] *nm* reasoning; arguing; argument.
**raisonner** [ʀɛzɔne] *vi* (*penser*) to reason; (*argumenter, discuter*) to argue // *vt* (*personne*) to reason with; (*attitude: justifier*) to reason out.
**rajeunir** [ʀaʒœniʀ] *vt* (*suj: coiffure, robe*): ~ **qn** to make sb look younger; (*suj: cure etc*) to rejuvenate; (*fig*) to brighten up; to give a new look to; to inject new blood into // *vi* to become (*ou* look) younger.
**rajouter** [ʀaʒute] *vt*: ~ **du sel/un œuf** to add some more salt/another egg; ~ **que** to add that.
**rajuster** [ʀaʒyste] *vt* (*vêtement*) to straighten, tidy; (*salaires*) to adjust; (*machine*) to readjust; **se ~** to tidy *ou* straighten o.s. up.
**râle** [ʀɑl] *nm* groan; ~ **d'agonie** death rattle.

**ralenti** [Ralãti] *nm*: **au ~** (*AUTO*): **tourner au ~** to tick over, idle ; (*CINÉMA*) in slow motion ; (*fig*) at a slower pace.

**ralentir** [Ralãtiʀ] *vt, vi*, **se ~** *vi* to slow down.

**râler** [Rɑle] *vi* to groan ; (*fam*) to grouse, moan (and groan).

**ralliement** [Ralimã] *nm* rallying.

**rallier** [Ralje] *vt* (*rassembler*) to rally ; (*rejoindre*) to rejoin ; (*gagner à sa cause*) to win over ; **se ~ à** (*avis*) to come over *ou* round to.

**rallonge** [Ralɔ̃ʒ] *nf* (*de table*) (extra) leaf (*pl* leaves) ; (*de vêtement etc*) extra piece.

**rallonger** [Ralɔ̃ʒe] *vt* to lengthen.

**rallumer** [Ralyme] *vt* to light up again ; (*fig*) to revive ; **se ~** *vi* (*lumière*) to come on again.

**rallye** [Rali] *nm* rally ; (*POL*) march.

**ramages** [Ramaʒ] *nmpl* leaf pattern *sg* ; songs.

**ramassage** [Ramɑsaʒ] *nm*: **~ scolaire** school bus service.

**ramassé, e** [Ramɑse] *a* (*trapu*) squat, stocky.

**ramasse-miettes** [Ramɑsmjɛt] *nm inv* table-tidy.

**ramasse-monnaie** [Ramɑsmɔnɛ] *nm inv* change-tray.

**ramasser** [Ramɑse] *vt* (*objet tombé ou par terre, fam*) to pick up ; (*recueillir*) to collect ; (*récolter*) to gather ; (: *pommes de terre*) to lift ; **se ~** *vi* (*sur soi-même*) to huddle up ; to crouch ; **ramasseur, euse de balles** *nm/f* ballboy/girl ; **ramassis** *nm* (*péj*) bunch ; jumble.

**rambarde** [Rãbaʀd(ə)] *nf* guardrail.

**rame** [Ram] *nf* (*aviron*) oar ; (*de métro*) train ; (*de papier*) ream ; **~ de haricots** bean support.

**rameau, x** [Ramo] *nm* (small) branch ; **les R~x** (*REL*) Palm Sunday *sg*.

**ramener** [Ramne] *vt* to bring back ; (*reconduire*) to take back ; (*rabattre: couverture, visière*): **~ qch sur** to pull sth back over ; **~ qch à** (*réduire à, aussi MATH*) to reduce sth to ; **se ~** *vi* (*fam*) to roll *ou* turn up ; **se ~ à** (*se réduire à*) to come *ou* boil down to.

**ramer** [Rame] *vi* to row ; **rameur, euse** *nm/f* rower.

**ramier** [Ramje] *nm*: **(pigeon) ~** woodpigeon.

**ramification** [Ramifikɑsjɔ̃] *nf* ramification.

**ramifier** [Ramifje]: **se ~** *vi* (*tige, secte, réseau*): **se ~ (en)** to branch out (into) ; (*veines, nerfs*) to ramify.

**ramollir** [Ramɔliʀ] *vt* to soften ; **se ~** *vi* to go soft.

**ramoner** [Ramɔne] *vt* to sweep ; **ramoneur** *nm* (chimney) sweep.

**rampe** [Rãp] *nf* (*d'escalier*) banister(s *pl*) ; (*dans un garage, d'un terrain*) ramp ; (*THÉÂTRE*): **la ~** the footlights *pl* ; **~ de lancement** launching pad.

**ramper** [Rãpe] *vi* to crawl.

**rancard** [Rãkaʀ] *nm* (*fam*) date ; tip.

**rancart** [Rãkaʀ] *nm*: **mettre au ~** to scrap.

**rance** [Rãs] *a* rancid.

**rancœur** [Rãkœʀ] *nf* rancour, resentment.

**rançon** [Rãsɔ̃] *nf* ransom ; (*fig*) price.

**rancune** [Rãkyn] *nf* grudge, rancour ; **garder ~ à qn (de qch)** to bear sb a grudge (for sth) ; **sans ~!** no hard feelings! ; **rancunier, ière** *a* vindictive, spiteful.

**randonnée** [Rãdɔne] *nf* ride ; (*à pied*) walk, ramble ; hike, hiking *q*.

**rang** [Rã] *nm* (*rangée*) row ; (*grade, condition sociale, classement*) rank ; **~s** (*MIL*) ranks ; **se mettre en ~s/sur un ~** to get into *ou* form rows/a line ; **sur 3 ~s** (lined up) 3 deep ; **se mettre en ~s par 4** to form fours *ou* rows of 4 ; **se mettre sur les ~s** (*fig*) to get into the running ; **au premier ~** in the first row ; (*fig*) ranking first ; **avoir ~ de** to hold the rank of.

**rangé, e** [Rãʒe] *a* (*sérieux*) orderly, steady.

**rangée** [Rãʒe] *nf* row.

**ranger** [Rãʒe] *vt* (*classer, grouper*) to order, arrange ; (*mettre à sa place*) to put away ; (*mettre de l'ordre dans*) to tidy up ; (*arranger, disposer: en cercle etc*) to arrange ; (*fig: classer*): **~ qn/qch parmi** to rank sb/sth among ; **se ~** *vi* (*véhicule, conducteur: s'écarter*) to pull over ; (: *s'arrêter*) to pull in ; (*piéton*) to step aside ; (*s'assagir*) to settle down ; **se ~ à** (*avis*) to come round to, fall in with.

**ranimer** [Ranime] *vt* (*personne évanouie*) to bring round ; (*revigorer: forces, courage*) to restore ; (*réconforter: troupes etc*) to kindle new life in ; (*douleur, souvenir*) to revive ; (*feu*) to rekindle.

**rapace** [Rapas] *nm* bird of prey // *a* (*péj*) rapacious, grasping.

**rapatrier** [Rapatʀije] *vt* to repatriate ; (*capitaux*) to bring (back) home.

**râpe** [Rɑp] *nf* (*CULIN*) grater ; (*à bois*) rasp.

**râpé, e** [Rɑpe] *a* (*tissu*) threadbare ; (*CULIN*) grated.

**râper** [Rɑpe] *vt* (*CULIN*) to grate ; (*gratter, râcler*) to rasp.

**rapetasser** [Raptase] *vt* (*fam*) to patch up.

**rapetisser** [Raptise] *vt*: **~ qch** to shorten sth ; to make sth look smaller // *vi*, **se ~** *vi* to shrink.

**rapide** [Rapid] *a* fast ; (*prompt*) quick // *nm* express (train) ; (*de cours d'eau*) rapid ; **~ment** *ad* fast ; quickly ; **rapidité** *nf* speed ; quickness.

**rapiécer** [Rapjese] *vt* to patch.

**rappel** [Rapɛl] *nm* (*d'un ambassadeur, MIL*) recall ; (*THÉÂTRE*) curtain call ; (*MÉD: vaccination*) booster ; (*ADMIN: de salaire*) back pay *q* ; (*d'une aventure, d'un nom*) reminder ; (*TECH*) return ; (*NAVIG*) sitting out ; (*ALPINISME: aussi:* **~ de corde**) abseiling *q*, roping down *q*, abseil ; **~ à l'ordre** call to order.

**rappeler** [Raple] *vt* (*pour faire revenir, retéléphoner*) to call back ; (*ambassadeur, MIL*) to recall ; (*faire se souvenir*): **~ qch à qn** to remind sb of sth ; **se ~** *vt* (*se souvenir de*) to remember, recall ; **~ qn à la vie** to bring sb back to life ; **ça rappelle la Provence** it's reminiscent of Provence, it reminds you of Provence.

**rappliquer** [Raplike] *vi* (*fam*) to turn up.

**rapport** [RapɔR] *nm* (*compte rendu*) report ; (*profit*) yield, return ; revenue ; (*lien, analogie*) relationship ; (*proportion:* MATH, TECH) ratio (*pl* s) ; ~s *nmpl* (*entre personnes, pays*) relations ; **avoir ~ à** to have something to do with, concern ; **être en ~ avec** (*idée de corrélation*) to be in keeping with ; **être/se mettre en ~ avec qn** to have dealings with sb/get in touch with sb ; **par ~ à** in relation to ; with regard to ; **sous le ~ de** from the point of view of ; ~s **(sexuels)** (sexual) intercourse *sg.*

**rapporter** [RapɔRte] *vt* (*rendre, ramener*) to bring back ; (*apporter davantage*) to bring more ; (COUTURE) to sew on ; (*suj: investissement*) to yield ; (: *activité*) to bring in ; (*relater*) to report ; (JUR: *annuler*) to revoke // *vi* (*investissement*) to give a good return *ou* yield ; (: *activité*) to be very profitable ; ~ **qch à** (*fig: rattacher*) to relate sth to ; **se ~ à** (*correspondre à*) to relate to ; **s'en ~ à** to rely on ; **rapporteur, euse** *nm/f* (*de procès, commission*) reporter ; (*péj*) telltale // *nm* (GÉOM) protractor.

**rapproché, e** [RapRɔʃe] *a* (*proche*) near, close at hand ; ~s (*l'un de l'autre*) at close intervals.

**rapprochement** [RapRɔʃmɑ̃] *nm* (*reconciliation: de nations, familles*) reconciliation ; (*analogie, rapport*) parallel.

**rapprocher** [RapRɔʃe] *vt* (*chaise d'une table*): ~ **qch (de)** to bring sth closer (to) ; (*deux tuyaux*) to bring closer together ; (*réunir*) to bring together ; (*établir une analogie entre*) to establish a parallel between ; **se ~** *vi* to draw closer *ou* nearer ; (*fig: familles, pays*) to come together ; to come closer together ; **se ~ de** to come closer to ; (*présenter une analogie avec*) to be close to.

**rapt** [Rapt] *nm* abduction.

**raquette** [Rakɛt] *nf* (*de tennis*) racket ; (*de ping-pong*) bat ; (*à neige*) snowshoe.

**rare** [RaR] *a* rare ; (*main-d'œuvre, denrées*) scarce ; (*cheveux, herbe*) sparse.

**raréfier** [RaRefje]: **se ~** *vi* to grow scarce ; (*air*) to rarefy.

**rarement** [RaRmɑ̃] *ad* rarely, seldom.

**rareté** [RaRte] *nf* rarity ; scarcity.

**ras, e** [Rɑ, Rɑz] *a* (*tête, cheveux*) close-cropped ; (*poil, herbe*) short // *ad* short ; **en ~e campagne** in open country ; **à ~ bords** to the brim ; **au ~ de** level with ; **en avoir ~ le bol** (*fam*) to be fed up ; ~ **du cou** *a* (*pull, robe*) crew-neck.

**rasade** [Razad] *nf* glassful.

**rasé, e** [Raze] *a*: ~ **de frais** freshly shaven ; ~ **de près** close-shaven.

**rase-mottes** [Razmɔt] *nm inv*: **faire du ~** to hedgehop.

**raser** [Raze] *vt* (*barbe, cheveux*) to shave off ; (*menton, personne*) to shave ; (*fam: ennuyer*) to bore ; (*démolir*) to raze (to the ground) ; (*frôler*) to graze ; to skim ; **se ~** to shave ; (*fam*) to be bored (to tears) ; **rasoir** *nm* razor ; **rasoir électrique** electric shaver *ou* razor ; **rasoir de sûreté** safety razor.

**rassasier** [Rasazje] *vt* to satisfy ; **être rassasié** (*dégoûté*) to be sated ; to have had more than enough.

**rassemblement** [Rasɑ̃bləmɑ̃] *nm* (*groupe*) gathering ; (POL) union ; association ; (MIL): **le ~** parade.

**rassembler** [Rasɑ̃ble] *vt* (*réunir*) to assemble, gather ; (*regrouper, amasser*) to gather together, collect ; **se ~** *vi* to gather.

**rasseoir** [RaswaR]: **se ~** *vi* to sit down again.

**rasséréner** [RaseRene]: **se ~** *vi* to recover one's serenity.

**rassis, e** [Rasi, -iz] *a* (*pain*) stale.

**rassurer** [RasyRe] *vt* to reassure ; **se ~** to feel reassured ; **rassure-toi** put your mind at rest *ou* at ease.

**rat** [Ra] *nm* rat ; ~ **d'hôtel** hotel thief (*pl* thieves) ; ~ **musqué** muskrat.

**ratatiné, e** [Ratatine] *a* shrivelled (up), wrinkled.

**rate** [Rat] *nf* spleen.

**raté, e** [Rate] *a* (*tentative*) unsuccessful, failed // *nm/f* failure // *nm* misfiring *q.*

**râteau, x** [Rɑto] *nm* rake.

**râtelier** [Rɑtəlje] *nm* rack ; (*fam*) false teeth *pl.*

**rater** [Rate] *vi* (*affaire, projet etc*) to go wrong, fail // *vt* (*cible, train, occasion*) to miss ; (*démonstration, plat*) to spoil ; (*examen*) to fail.

**ratifier** [Ratifje] *vt* to ratify.

**ration** [Rɑsjɔ̃] *nf* ration ; (*fig*) share.

**rationnel, le** [Rasjɔnɛl] *a* rational.

**rationnement** [Rasjɔnmɑ̃] *nm* rationing ; **ticket de ~** ration coupon.

**rationner** [Rasjɔne] *vt* to ration.

**ratisser** [Ratise] *vt* (*allée*) to rake ; (*feuiller*) to rake up ; (*suj: armée, police*) to comb.

**raton** [Ratɔ̃] *nm*: ~ **laveur** raccoon.

**R.A.T.P.** *sigle f* (= *Régie autonome des transports parisiens*) *Paris transport authority.*

**rattacher** [Rataʃe] *vt* (*animal, cheveux*) to tie up again ; (*incorporer:* ADMIN *etc*): ~ **qch à** to join sth to, unite sth with ; (*fig: relier*): ~ **qch à** to link sth with, relate sth to ; (: *lier*): ~ **qn à** to bind *ou* tie sb to.

**rattrapage** [RatRapaʒ] *nm* (SCOL) remedial classes *pl.*

**rattraper** [RatRape] *vt* (*fugitif*) to recapture ; (*retenir, empêcher de tomber*) to catch (hold of) ; (*atteindre, rejoindre*) to catch up with ; (*réparer: imprudence, erreur*) to make up for ; **se ~** *vi* to make up for lost time ; to make good one's losses ; to make up for it ; **se ~ (à)** (*se raccrocher*) to stop o.s. falling (by catching hold of).

**rature** [RatyR] *nf* deletion, erasure ; **raturer** *vt* to cross out, delete, erase.

**rauque** [Rok] *a* raucous ; hoarse.

**ravagé, e** [Ravaʒe] *a* (*visage*) harrowed.

**ravager** [Ravaʒe] *vt* to devastate, ravage.

**ravages** [Ravaʒ] *nmpl* ravages ; **faire des ~** to wreak havoc.

**ravaler** [Ravale] *vt* (*mur, façade*) to restore ; (*déprécier*) to lower ; ~ **sa colère/son dégoût** to stifle one's anger/distaste.

**ravauder** [Ravode] *vt* to repair, mend.

**rave** [Rav] *nf* (BOT) rape.

**ravi, e** [Ravi] *a* delighted ; **être ~ de/que** to be delighted with/that.

**ravier** [Ravje] *nm* hors d'œuvre dish.

**ravigote** [Ravigɔt] *a*: **sauce** ~ oil and vinegar dressing with shallots.

**ravigoter** [Ravigɔte] *vt (fam)* to buck up.

**ravin** [Ravɛ̃] *nm* gully, ravine.

**raviner** [Ravine] *vt* to furrow, gully.

**ravir** [RaviR] *vt (enchanter)* to delight; *(enlever)*: ~ **qch à qn** to rob sb of sth; **à** ~ *ad* beautifully.

**raviser** [Ravize]: **se** ~ *vi* to change one's mind.

**ravissant, e** [Ravisɑ̃, -ɑ̃t] *a* delightful; ravishing.

**ravisseur, euse** [RavisœR, -øz] *nm/f* abductor.

**ravitaillement** [Ravitɑjmɑ̃] *nm* resupplying; refuelling; *(provisions)* supplies *pl*; **aller au** ~ to go for fresh supplies.

**ravitailler** [Ravitɑje] *vt* to resupply; *(véhicule)* to refuel; **se** ~ *vi* to get fresh supplies.

**raviver** [Ravive] *vt (feu, douleur)* to revive; *(couleurs)* to brighten up.

**ravoir** [RavwaR] *vt* to get back.

**rayé, e** [Reje] *a (à rayures)* striped; *(éraflé)* scratched.

**rayer** [Reje] *vt (érafler)* to scratch; *(barrer)* to cross *ou* score out; *(d'une liste: radier)* to cross *ou* strike off.

**rayon** [Rɛjɔ̃] *nm (de soleil etc)* ray; *(GÉOM)* radius; *(de roue)* spoke; *(étagère)* shelf *(pl* shelves); *(de grand magasin)* department; *(de ruche)* (honey)comb; **dans un** ~ **de** within a radius of; ~ **d'action** range; ~ **de soleil** sunbeam, ray of sunlight; ~**s X** X-rays.

**rayonnage** [Rɛjɔnaʒ] *nm* set of shelves.

**rayonnement** [Rɛjɔnmɑ̃] *nm* radiation; *(fig)* radiance; influence.

**rayonner** [Rɛjɔne] *vi (chaleur, énergie)* to radiate; *(fig)* to shine forth; to be radiant; *(avenues, axes etc)* to radiate; *(touriste)* to go touring *(from one base)*.

**rayure** [RejyR] *nf (motif)* stripe; *(éraflure)* scratch; *(rainure, d'un fusil)* groove; **à** ~**s** striped.

**raz-de-marée** [RɑdmaRe] *nm inv* tidal wave.

**razzia** [Razja] *nf* raid, foray.

**ré** [Re] *nm (MUS)* D; *(en chantant la gamme)* re.

**réacteur** [ReaktœR] *nm* jet engine.

**réaction** [Reaksjɔ̃] *nf* reaction; **moteur à** ~ jet engine; ~ **en chaîne** chain reaction; **réactionnaire** *a* reactionary.

**réadapter** [Readapte] *vt* to readjust; *(MÉD)* to rehabilitate; **se** ~ **(à)** to readjust (to).

**réaffirmer** [ReafiRme] *vt* to reaffirm, reassert.

**réagir** [ReaʒiR] *vi* to react.

**réalisateur, trice** [RealizatœR, -tRis] *nm/f (TV, CINÉMA)* director.

**réalisation** [Realizasjɔ̃] *nf* carrying out; realization; fulfilment; achievement; production; *(œuvre)* production; creation; work.

**réaliser** [Realize] *vt (projet, opération)* to carry out, realize; *(rêve, souhait)* to realize, fulfil; *(exploit)* to achieve; *(achat, vente)*

to make; *(film)* to produce; *(se rendre compte de, COMM: bien, capital)* to realize; **se** ~ *vi* to be realized.

**réaliste** [Realist(ə)] *a* realistic; *(peintre, roman)* realist // *nm/f* realist.

**réalité** [Realite] *nf* reality; **en** ~ in (actual) fact; **dans la** ~ in reality.

**réanimation** [Reanimasjɔ̃] *nf* resuscitation; **service de** ~ intensive care unit.

**réarmer** [ReaRme] *vt (arme)* to reload // *vi (état)* to rearm.

**réassurance** [ReasyRɑs] *nf* reinsurance.

**rébarbatif, ive** [RebaRbatif, -iv] *a* forbidding, off-putting.

**rebattre** [RəbatR(ə)] *vt*: ~ **les oreilles à qn de qch** to keep harping on to sb about sth; **rebattu, e** *a* hackneyed.

**rebelle** [Rəbɛl] *nm/f* rebel // *a (troupes)* rebel; *(enfant)* rebellious; *(mèche etc)* unruly; ~ **à** unamenable to; unwilling to + *verbe*.

**rebeller** [Rəbele]: **se** ~ *vi* to rebel.

**rébellion** [Rebeljɔ̃] *nf* rebellion; *(rebelles)* rebel forces *pl*.

**reboiser** [Rəbwaze] *vt* to replant with trees, reafforest.

**rebondi, e** [Rəbɔ̃di] *a* rounded; chubby, well-rounded.

**rebondir** [Rəbɔ̃diR] *vi (ballon: au sol)* to bounce; *(: contre un mur)* to rebound; *(fig: procès, action, conversation)* to get moving again, be suddenly revived; **rebondissements** *nmpl (fig)* twists and turns, sudden revivals.

**rebord** [RəbɔR] *nm* edge.

**rebours** [RəbuR]: **à** ~ *ad* the wrong way.

**rebouteux, euse** [Rəbutø, -øz] *nm/f (péj)* bonesetter.

**rebrousse-poil** [Rbruspwal]: **à** ~ *ad* the wrong way.

**rebrousser** [RəbRuse] *vt*: ~ **chemin** to turn back.

**rebuffade** [Rəbyfad] *nf* rebuff.

**rébus** [Rebys] *nm inv* rebus.

**rebut** [Rəby] *nm*: **mettre au** ~ to scrap, discard.

**rebuter** [Rəbyte] *vt* to put off.

**récalcitrant, e** [RekalsitRɑ̃, -ɑ̃t] *a* refractory.

**recaler** [Rəkale] *vt (SCOL)* to fail.

**récapituler** [Rekapityle] *vt* to recapitulate; to sum up.

**recel** [Rəsɛl] *nm* receiving (stolen goods).

**receler** [Rəsəle] *vt (produit d'un vol)* to receive; *(malfaiteur)* to harbour; *(fig)* to conceal; **receleur, euse** *nm/f* receiver.

**récemment** [Resamɑ̃] *ad* recently.

**recensement** [Rəsɑ̃smɑ̃] *nm* census; inventory.

**recenser** [Rəsɑ̃se] *vt (population)* to take a census of; *(inventorier)* to make an inventory of; *(dénombrer)* to list.

**récent, e** [Resɑ̃, -ɑ̃t] *a* recent.

**récépissé** [Resepise] *nm* receipt.

**récepteur, trice** [ReseptœR, -tRis] *a* receiving // *nm* receiver; ~ **(de radio)** radio set *ou* receiver.

**réception** [Resɛpsjɔ̃] *nf* receiving q; *(accueil)* reception, welcome; *(bureau)* reception desk; *(réunion mondaine)* reception, party; (*pièces*) reception rooms *pl*; (*SPORT*: *après un saut*) landing; (: *du ballon*) catching *q*; **jour/heures de** ∼ day/hours for receiving visitors (*ou* students *etc*); (*MÉD*) surgery day/hours; **réceptionnaire** *nm/f* receiving clerk; **réceptionner** *vt* (*COMM*) to take delivery of; (*SPORT*: *ballon*) to catch (and control); **réceptionniste** *nm/f* receptionist.

**récession** [Resesjɔ̃] *nf* recession.

**recette** [Rəsɛt] *nf* (*CULIN*) recipe; (*fig*) formula, recipe; (*COMM*) takings *pl*; (*ADMIN*: *bureau*) tax *ou* revenue office; ∼**s** *nfpl* (*COMM*: *rentrées*) receipts.

**receveur, euse** [Rəsvœr, -øz] *nm/f* (*des contributions*) tax collector; (*des postes*) postmaster/mistress; (*d'autobus*) conductor/conductress.

**recevoir** [Rəsvwar] *vt* to receive; (*lettre, prime*) to receive, get; (*client, patient, représentant*) to see; (*SCOL*: *candidat*) to pass // *vi* to receive visitors; to give parties; to see patients *etc*; **se** ∼ *vi* (*athlète*) to land; **être reçu** (*à un examen*) to pass.

**rechange** [Rəʃɑ̃ʒ]: **de** ∼ *a* (*pièces, roue*) spare; (*fig*: *plan*) alternative; **des vêtements de** ∼ a change of clothes.

**rechaper** [Rəʃape] *vt* to remould, retread.

**réchapper** [Reʃape]: ∼ **de** *ou* **à** *vt* (*accident, maladie*) to come through.

**recharge** [Rəʃarʒ(ə)] *nf* refill.

**recharger** [Rəʃarʒe] *vt* (*camion, fusil, appareil-photo*) to reload; (*briquet, stylo*) to refill; (*batterie*) to recharge.

**réchaud** [Reʃo] *nm* (portable) stove; plate-warmer.

**réchauffer** [Reʃofe] *vt* (*plat*) to reheat; (*mains, personne*) to warm; **se** ∼ *vi* (*température*) to get warmer.

**rêche** [Rɛʃ] *a* rough.

**recherche** [Rəʃɛrʃ(ə)] *nf* (*action*): **la** ∼ **de** the search for; (*raffinement*) affectedness, studied elegance; (*scientifique etc*): **la** ∼ research; ∼**s** *nfpl* (*de la police*) investigations; (*scientifiques*) research *sg*; **être/se mettre à la** ∼ **de** to be/go in search of.

**recherché, e** [Rəʃɛrʃe] *a* (*rare, demandé*) much sought-after; (*raffiné*) studied, affected.

**rechercher** [Rəʃɛrʃe] *vt* (*objet égaré, fugitif*) to look for, search for; (*témoins, main-d'œuvre*) to look for; (*causes d'un phénomène, nouveau procédé*) to try to find; (*bonheur etc, l'amitié de qn*) to seek.

**rechigner** [Rəʃiɲe] *vi*: ∼ (**à**) to balk (at).

**rechute** [Rəʃyt] *nf* (*MÉD*) relapse; (*dans le péché, le vice*) lapse; **faire une** ∼ to have a relapse.

**récidiver** [Residive] *vi* to commit a second (*ou* subsequent) offence; (*fig*) to do it again; **récidiviste** *nm/f* second (*ou* habitual) offender, recidivist.

**récif** [Resif] *nm* reef.

**récipient** [Resipjɑ̃] *nm* container.

**réciproque** [Resiprɔk] *a* reciprocal; ∼**ment** *ad* reciprocally; **et** ∼**ment** and vice versa.

**récit** [Resi] *nm* story.

**récital** [Resital] *nm* recital.

**récitation** [Resitɑsjɔ̃] *nf* recitation.

**réciter** [Resite] *vt* to recite.

**réclamation** [Reklamɑsjɔ̃] *nf* complaint; ∼**s** (*bureau*) complaints department *sg*.

**réclame** [Reklam] *nf*: **la** ∼ advertising; **une** ∼ an advert(isement); **article en** ∼ special offer.

**réclamer** [Reklame] *vt* (*aide, nourriture etc*) to ask for; (*revendiquer*: *dû, part, indemnité*) to claim, demand; (*nécessiter*) to demand, require // *vi* to complain; **se** ∼ **de** to give as one's authority; to claim filiation with.

**reclasser** [Rəklɑse] *vt* (*fig*: *fonctionnaire etc*) to regrade.

**reclus, e** [Rəkly, -yz] *nm/f* recluse.

**réclusion** [Reklyzjɔ̃] *nf* imprisonment.

**recoin** [Rəkwɛ̃] *nm* nook, corner; (*fig*) hidden recess.

**reçois** *etc vb voir* **recevoir**.

**récolte** [Rekɔlt(ə)] *nf* harvesting; gathering; (*produits*) harvest, crop; (*fig*) crop, collection.

**récolter** [Rekɔlte] *vt* to harvest, gather (in); (*fig*) to collect; to get.

**recommandable** [Rəkɔmɑ̃dabl(ə)] *a* commendable.

**recommandation** [Rəkɔmɑ̃dɑsjɔ̃] *nf* recommendation.

**recommandé** [Rəkɔmɑ̃de] *nm* (*POSTES*): **en** ∼ by registered mail.

**recommander** [Rəkɔmɑ̃de] *vt* to recommend; (*suj*: *qualités etc*) to commend; (*POSTES*) to register; ∼ **à qn de faire** to recommend sb to do; **se** ∼ **à qn** to commend o.s. to sb; **se** ∼ **de qn** to give sb's name as a reference.

**recommencer** [Rəkɔmɑ̃se] *vt* (*reprendre*: *lutte, séance*) to resume, start again; (*refaire*: *travail, explications*) to start afresh, start (over) again; (*récidiver*: *erreur*) to make again // *vi* to start again; (*récidiver*) to do it again.

**récompense** [Rekɔ̃pɑ̃s] *nf* reward; (*prix*) award; **récompenser** *vt*: **récompenser qn** (**de** *ou* **pour**) to reward sb for.

**réconciliation** [Rekɔ̃siljɑsjɔ̃] *nf* reconciliation.

**réconcilier** [Rekɔ̃silje] *vt* to reconcile; ∼ **qn avec qch** to reconcile sb to sth; **se** ∼ (**avec**) to be reconciled (with).

**reconduction** [Rəkɔ̃dyksjɔ̃] *nf* renewal.

**reconduire** [Rəkɔ̃dɥir] *vt* (*raccompagner*) to take *ou* see back; (*JUR, POL*: *renouveler*) to renew.

**réconfort** [Rekɔ̃fɔr] *nm* comfort.

**réconforter** [Rekɔ̃fɔrte] *vt* (*consoler*) to comfort; (*revigorer*) to fortify.

**reconnaissance** [Rəkɔnɛsɑ̃s] *nf* recognition; acknowledgement; (*gratitude*) gratitude, gratefulness; (*MIL*) reconnaissance, recce; ∼ **de dette** acknowledgement of a debt, IOU.

**reconnaissant, e** [Rəkɔnɛsɑ̃, -ɑ̃t] *a* grateful; **je vous serais** ∼ **de bien vouloir** I should be most grateful if you would (kindly).

**reconnaître** [Rəkɔnɛtr(ə)] *vt* to recognize; (*MIL*: *lieu*) to reconnoitre; (*JUR*: *enfant, dette, droit*) to acknowledge; ∼ **que** to admit *ou* acknowledge that; ∼ **qn/qch**

**à** (*l'identifier grâce à*) to recognize sb/sth by.

**reconstituant, e** [Rəkɔ̃stityɑ̃, -ɑ̃t] *a* (*régime*) strength-building // *nm* tonic, pick-me-up.

**reconstituer** [Rəkɔ̃stitɥe] *vt* (*monument ancien*) to recreate, build a replica of; (*fresque, vase brisé*) to piece together, reconstitute; (*événement, accident*) to reconstruct; (*fortune, patrimoine*) to rebuild; (*BIO: tissus etc*) to regenerate; **reconstitution** *nf* (*JUR: d'accident etc*) reconstruction.

**reconstruire** [Rəkɔ̃stRɥiR] *vt* to rebuild.

**record** [RəkɔR] *nm, a* record.

**recoupement** [Rəkupmɑ̃] *nm*: **par** ~ by cross-checking.

**recouper** [Rəkupe]: **se** ~ *vi* (*témoignages*) to tie *ou* match up.

**recourbé, e** [RəkuRbe] *a* curved; hooked; bent.

**recourir** [RəkuRiR]: ~ **à** *vt* (*ami, agence*) to turn *ou* appeal to; (*force, ruse, emprunt*) to resort *ou* have recourse to.

**recours** [RəkuR] *nm* (*JUR*) appeal; **avoir** ~ **à** = **recourir à**; **en dernier** ~ as a last resort; **sans** ~ final; with no way out; ~ **en grâce** plea for clemency (*ou* pardon).

**recouvrer** [RəkuvRe] *vt* (*vue, santé etc*) to recover, regain; (*impôts*) to collect; (*créance*) to recover.

**recouvrir** [RəkuvRiR] *vt* (*couvrir à nouveau*) to re-cover; (*couvrir entièrement, aussi fig*) to cover; (*cacher, masquer*) to conceal, hide; **se** ~ (*se superposer*) to overlap.

**recracher** [RəkRaʃe[ *vt* to spit out.

**récréatif, ive** [RekReatif, -iv] *a* of entertainment; recreational.

**récréation** [RekReasjɔ̃] *nf* recreation, entertainment; (*SCOL*) break.

**récrier** [RekRije]: **se** ~ *vi* to exclaim.

**récriminations** [RekRiminasjɔ̃] *nfpl* remonstrations, complaints.

**recroqueviller** [RəkRɔkvije]: **se** ~ *vi* (*feuilles*) to curl *ou* shrivel up; (*personne*) to huddle up.

**recru, e** [RəkRy] *a*: ~ **de fatigue** exhausted // *nf* recruit.

**recrudescence** [RəkRydesɑ̃s] *nf* fresh outbreak.

**recrue** [RəkRy] *a, nf voir* **recru**.

**recruter** [RəkRyte] *vt* to recruit.

**rectal, e, aux** [Rɛktal, -o] *a*: **par voie** ~**e** rectally.

**rectangle** [Rɛktɑ̃gl(ə)] *nm* rectangle; **rectangulaire** *a* rectangular.

**recteur** [RɛktœR] *nm* ≈ (regional) director of education.

**rectificatif, ive** [Rɛktifikatif, -iv] *a* corrected // *nm* correction.

**rectification** [Rɛktifikasjɔ̃] *nf* correction.

**rectifier** [Rɛktifje] *vt* (*tracé, virage*) to straighten; (*calcul, adresse*) to correct; (*erreur, faute*) to rectify, put right.

**rectiligne** [Rɛktiliɲ] *a* straight; (*GÉOM*) rectilinear.

**rectitude** [Rɛktityd] *nf* rectitude, uprightness.

**reçu, e** [Rəsy] *pp de* **recevoir** // *a* (*admis, consacré*) accepted // *nm* (*COMM*) receipt.

**recueil** [Rəkœj] *nm* collection.

**recueillement** [Rəkœjmɑ̃] *nm* meditation, contemplation.

**recueillir** [RəkœjiR] *vt* to collect; (*voix, suffrages*) to win; (*accueillir: réfugiés, chat*) to take in; **se** ~ *vi* to gather one's thoughts; to meditate.

**recul** [Rəkyl] *nm* retreat; recession; decline; (*d'arme à feu*) recoil, kick; **avoir un mouvement de** ~ to recoil, start back; **prendre du** ~ to stand back; **avec le** ~ with the passing of time, in retrospect.

**reculade** [Rəkylad] *nf* (*péj*) climb-down.

**reculé, e** [Rəkyle] *a* remote.

**reculer** [Rəkyle] *vi* to move back, back away; (*AUTO*) to reverse, back (up); (*fig*) to (be on the) decline; to be losing ground; (: *se dérober*) to shrink back // *vt* to move back; to reverse, back (up); (*fig: possibilités, limites*) to extend; (: *date, décision*) to postpone.

**reculons** [Rəkylɔ̃]: **à** ~ *ad* backwards.

**récupérer** [RekypeRe] *vt* (*rentrer en possession de*) to recover, get back; (*recueillir: ferraille etc*) to salvage (for reprocessing); (*délinquant etc*) to rehabilitate // *vi* to recover.

**récurer** [RekyRe] *vt* to scour.

**récuser** [Rekyze] *vt* to challenge; **se** ~ to decline to give an opinion.

**reçut** *vb voir* **recevoir**.

**recycler** [Rəsikle] *vt* (*SCOL*) to reorientate; (*employés*) to retrain.

**rédacteur, trice** [RedaktœR, -tRis] *nm/f* (*journaliste*) writer; subeditor; (*d'ouvrage de référence*) editor, compiler; ~ **en chef** chief editor; ~ **publicitaire** copywriter.

**rédaction** [Redaksjɔ̃] *nf* writing; (*rédacteurs*) editorial staff; (*bureau*) editorial office(s); (*SCOL: devoir*) essay, composition.

**reddition** [Redisjɔ̃] *nf* surrender.

**rédemption** [Redɑ̃psjɔ̃] *nf* redemption.

**redescendre** [Rədesɑ̃dR(ə)] *vi* (*à nouveau*) to go back down; (*après la montée*) to go down (again) // *vt* (*pente etc*) to go down.

**redevable** [Rədvable(ə)] *a*: **être** ~ **de qch à qn** (*somme*) to owe sb sth; (*fig*) to be indebted to sb for sth.

**redevance** [Rədvɑ̃s] *nf* (*téléphonique*) rental charge; (*radiophonique*) licence fee.

**rédhibitoire** [RedibitwaR] *a*: **vice** ~ (*fig*) irretrievable flaw.

**rédiger** [Rediʒe] *vt* to write; (*contrat*) to draw up.

**redire** [RədiR] *vt* to repeat; **trouver à** ~ **à** to find fault with; **redite** *nf* (needless) repetition.

**redondance** [Rədɔ̃dɑ̃s] *nf* redundancy.

**redoublé, e** [Rəduble] *a*: **à coups** ~**s** even harder, twice as hard.

**redoubler** [Rəduble] *vi* (*tempête, violence*) to intensify, get even stronger *ou* fiercer etc; (*SCOL*) to repeat a year; ~ **de** *vt* to be twice as + *adjectif*; **le vent redouble de violence** the wind is blowing twice as hard.

**redoutable** [ʀədutabl(ə)] *a* formidable, fearsome.

**redouter** [ʀədute] *vt* to fear ; (*appréhender*) to dread.

**redressement** [ʀədʀɛsmɑ̃] *nm*: **maison de** ~ reformatory.

**redresser** [ʀədʀese] *vt* (*arbre, mât*) to set upright, right ; (*pièce tordue*) to straighten out ; (*AVIAT, AUTO*) to straighten up ; (*situation, économie*) to put right ; **se** ~ *vi* (*objet penché*) to right itself ; to straighten up ; (*personne*) to sit (*ou* stand) up ; to sit (*ou* stand) up straight.

**redresseur** [ʀədʀɛsœʀ] *nm*: ~ **de torts** righter of wrongs.

**réduction** [ʀedyksjɔ̃] *nf* reduction.

**réduire** [ʀedɥiʀ] *vt* (*gén, aussi CULIN, MATH*) to reduce ; (*prix, dépenses*) to cut, reduce ; (*carte*) to scale down, reduce ; (*MÉD*: *fracture*) to set ; (*rebelles*) to put down ; **se** ~ **à** (*revenir à*) to boil down to ; **se** ~ **en** (*se transformer en*) to be reduced to.

**réduit** [ʀedɥi] *nm* tiny room, recess.

**rééducation** [ʀeedykɑsjɔ̃] *nf* (*d'un membre*) re-education ; (*de délinquants, d'un blessé*) rehabilitation ; ~ **de la parole** speech therapy.

**réel, le** [ʀeɛl] *a* real // *nm*: **le** ~ reality.

**réélection** [ʀeelɛksjɔ̃] *nf* re-election.

**réélire** [ʀeeliʀ] *vt* to re-elect.

**réellement** [ʀeɛlmɑ̃] *ad* really.

**réemploi** [ʀeɑ̃plwa] *nm* = **remploi**.

**réescompte** [ʀeɛskɔ̃t] *nm* rediscount.

**réévaluation** [ʀeevalɥasjɔ̃] *nf* revaluation.

**réévaluer** [ʀeevalɥe] *vt* to revalue.

**réexpédier** [ʀeɛkspedje] *vt* (*à l'envoyeur*) to return, send back ; (*au destinataire*) to send on, forward.

**ref.** *abr de* **référence**.

**refaire** [ʀəfɛʀ] *vt* (*faire de nouveau, recommencer*) to do again ; (*réparer, restaurer*) to do up ; **se** ~ *vi* (*en santé*) to recover ; (*en argent*) to make up one's losses ; **être refait** (*fam: dupé*) to be had.

**réfection** [ʀefɛksjɔ̃] *nf* repair.

**réfectoire** [ʀefɛktwaʀ] *nm* (*de collège, couvent, caserne*) refectory.

**référence** [ʀefeʀɑ̃s] *nf* reference ; ~**s** *nfpl* (*recommandations*) reference *sg* ; **faire** ~ **à** to refer to ; **ouvrage de** ~ reference work.

**référendum** [ʀefeʀɑ̃dɔm] *nm* referendum.

**référer** [ʀefeʀe] : **se** ~ **à** *vt* to refer to ; **en** ~ **à qn** to refer the matter to sb.

**refiler** [ʀəfile] *vt* (*fam*): ~ **qch à** *qn* to palm sth off on sb ; to pass sth on to sb.

**réfléchi, e** [ʀefleʃi] *a* (*caractère*) thoughtful ; (*action*) well-thought-out ; (*LING*) reflexive.

**réfléchir** [ʀefleʃiʀ] *vt* to reflect // *vi* to think ; ~ **à** *ou* **sur** to think about.

**reflet** [ʀəflɛ] *nm* reflection ; (*sur l'eau etc*) sheen *q*, glint.

**refléter** [ʀəflete] *vt* to reflect ; **se** ~ *vi* to be reflected.

**réflex** [ʀeflɛks] *a inv* (*PHOTO*) reflex.

**réflexe** [ʀeflɛks(ə)] *nm, a* reflex ; **avoir de bons** ~**s** to have good reactions *ou* reflexes.

**réflexion** [ʀeflɛksjɔ̃] *nf* (*de la lumière etc, pensée*) reflection ; (*fait de penser*)

thought ; (*remarque*) remark ; ~**s** *nfpl* (*méditations*) thought *sg*, reflection *sg* ; **sans** ~ without thinking ; ~ **faite, à la** ~ on reflection.

**refluer** [ʀəflye] *vi* to flow back ; (*foule*) to surge back.

**reflux** [ʀəfly] *nm* (*de la mer*) ebb.

**refondre** [ʀəfɔ̃dʀ(ə)] *vt* (*texte*) to recast.

**réformateur, trice** [ʀefɔʀmatœʀ, -tʀis] *nm/f* reformer.

**Réformation** [ʀefɔʀmɑsjɔ̃] *nf*: **la** ~ **the** Reformation.

**réforme** [ʀefɔʀm(ə)] *nf* reform ; (*MIL*) declaration of unfitness for service ; discharge (*on health grounds*) ; (*REL*): **la R** ~ the Reformation.

**réformé, e** [ʀefɔʀme] *a, nm/f* (*REL*) Protestant.

**réformer** [ʀefɔʀme] *vt* to reform ; (*MIL*: *recrue*) to declare unfit for service ; (*: soldat*) to discharge, invalid out.

**réformisme** [ʀefɔʀmism(ə)] *nm* reformism, policy of reform.

**refoulé, e** [ʀəfule] *a* (*PSYCH*) frustrated, repressed.

**refoulement** [ʀəfulmɑ̃] *nm* (*PSYCH*) repression.

**refouler** [ʀəfule] *vt* (*envahisseurs*) to drive back, repulse ; (*liquide*) to force back ; (*fig*) to suppress ; (*PSYCH*) to repress.

**réfractaire** [ʀefʀaktɛʀ] *a* (*minerai*) refractory ; (*brique*) fire *cpd* ; (*prêtre*) non-juring ; **soldat** ~ draft evader ; **être** ~ **à** to resist.

**réfracter** [ʀefʀakte] *vt* to refract.

**refrain** [ʀəfʀɛ̃] *nm* (*MUS*) refrain, chorus ; (*air, fig*) tune.

**refréner, réfréner** [ʀəfʀene, ʀefʀene] *vt* to curb, check.

**réfrigérant, e** [ʀefʀiʒeʀɑ̃, -ɑ̃t] *a* refrigerant, cooling.

**réfrigérer** [ʀefʀiʒeʀe] *vt* to refrigerate.

**refroidir** [ʀəfʀwadiʀ] *vt* to cool ; (*fig*) to have a cooling effect on // *vi* to cool (down) ; **se** ~ *vi* (*prendre froid*) to catch a chill ; (*temps*) to get cooler *ou* colder ; (*fig*) to cool (off) ; **refroidissement** *nm* cooling ; (*grippe etc*) chill.

**refuge** [ʀəfyʒ] *nm* refuge ; (*pour piétons*) (traffic) island.

**réfugié, e** [ʀefyʒje] *a, nm/f* refugee.

**réfugier** [ʀefyʒje] : **se** ~ *vi* to take refuge.

**refus** [ʀəfy] *nm* refusal ; **ce n'est pas de** ~ I won't say no, it's welcome.

**refuser** [ʀəfyze] *vt* to refuse ; (*SCOL*: *candidat*) to fail ; ~ **qch à qn/de faire** to refuse sb sth/to do ; ~ **du monde** to have to turn customers away ; **se** ~ **à qch/à faire** to refuse to do.

**réfuter** [ʀefyte] *vt* to refute.

**regagner** [ʀəgaɲe] *vt* (*argent, faveur*) to win back ; (*lieu*) to get back to ; ~ **le temps perdu** to make up (for) lost time ; ~ **du terrain** to regain ground.

**regain** [ʀəgɛ̃] *nm* (*herbe*) second crop of hay ; (*renouveau*): **un** ~ **de** renewed + *nom*.

**régal** [ʀegal] *nm* treat.

**régalade** [ʀegalad] *ad*: **à la** ~ from the bottle (held away from the lips).

**régaler** [Regale] *vt*: ~ **qn** to treat sb to a delicious meal; ~ **qn de** to treat sb to; **se** ~ *vi* to have a delicious meal; (*fig*) to enjoy o.s.

**regard** [RəgaR] *nm* (*coup d'œil*) look, glance; (*expression*) look (in one's eye); **parcourir/menacer du** ~ to cast an eye over/look threateningly at; **au** ~ **de** (*loi, morale*) from the point of view of; **en** ~ (*vis à vis*) opposite; **en** ~ **de** in comparison with.

**regardant, e** [RəgaRdã, -ãt] *a*: **très/peu** ~ **(sur)** quite fussy/very free (about); (*économe*) very tight-fisted/quite generous (with).

**regarder** [RəgaRde] *vt* (*examiner, observer, lire*) to look at; (*film, télévision, match*) to watch; (*envisager: situation, avenir*) to view; (*considérer: son intérêt etc*) to be concerned with; (*être orienté vers*): ~ **(vers)** to face; (*concerner*) to concern // *vi* to look; ~ **à** *vt* (*dépense, qualité, détails*) to be fussy with *ou* over; ~ **à faire** to hesitate to do; **dépenser sans** ~ to spend freely; ~ **qn/qch comme** to regard sb/sth as; ~ **(qch) dans le dictionnaire/l'annuaire** to look (sth up) in the dictionary/directory; **cela me regarde** it concerns me, it's my business.

**régate(s)** [Regat] *nf(pl)* regatta.

**régénérer** [ReʒeneRe] *vt* to regenerate; (*fig*) to revive.

**régent** [Reʒã] *nm* regent.

**régenter** [Reʒãte] *vt* to rule over; to dictate to.

**régie** [Reʒi] *nf* (*COMM, INDUSTRIE*) state-owned company; (*THÉÂTRE, CINÉMA*) production; **la** ~ **de l'État** state control.

**regimber** [Rəʒɛ̃be] *vi* to balk, jib.

**régime** [Reʒim] *nm* (*POL*) régime; (*ADMIN: des prisons, fiscal etc*) system; (*GÉO*) régime; (*TECH*) (*engine*) speed; (*fig*) rate, pace; (*de bananes, dattes*) bunch; **se mettre au/suivre un** ~ to go on/be on a diet; ~ **sans sel** salt-free diet; **à bas/haut** ~ (*AUTO*) at low/high revs; ~ **matrimonial** marriage settlement.

**régiment** [Reʒimã] *nm* (*MIL: unité*) regiment; (*fig: fam*): **un** ~ **de** an army of; **un copain de** ~ a pal from military service *ou* (one's) army days.

**région** [Reʒjɔ̃] *nf* region; **la** ~ **parisienne** the Paris area; **régional, e, aux** *a* regional; **régionalisme** *nm* regionalism.

**régir** [ReʒiR] *vt* to govern.

**régisseur** [ReʒisœR] *nm* (*d'un domaine*) steward; (*CINÉMA, TV*) assistant director; (*THÉÂTRE*) stage manager.

**registre** [RəʒistR(ə)] *nm* (*livre*) register; logbook; ledger; (*MUS, LING*) register; (*d'orgue*) stop.

**réglage** [Reglaʒ] *nm* adjustment; tuning.

**règle** [Rɛgl(ə)] *nf* (*instrument*) ruler; (*loi, prescription*) rule; ~**s** *nfpl* (*PHYSIOL*) period *sg*; **en** ~ (*papiers d'identité*) in order; **être/se mettre en** ~ to be/put o.s. straight with the authorities; **en** ~ **générale** as a (general) rule; ~ **à calcul** slide rule.

**réglé, e** [Regle] *a* well-ordered; stable, steady; (*papier*) ruled; (*femme*): **bien** ~**e** whose periods are regular.

**règlement** [Rɛgləmã] *nm* settling; (*arrêté*) regulation; (*règles, statuts*) regulations *pl*, rules *pl*; ~ **de compte(s)** settling of scores; **réglementaire** *a* conforming to the regulations; (*tenue, uniforme*) regulation *cpd*.

**réglementation** [Rɛgləmãtɑsjɔ̃] *nf* regulation, control; regulations *pl*.

**réglementer** [Rɛgləmãte] *vt* to regulate, control.

**régler** [Regle] *vt* (*mécanisme, machine*) to regulate, adjust; (*moteur*) to tune; (*thermostat etc*) to set, adjust; (*emploi du temps etc*) to organize, plan; (*question, conflit, facture, dette*) to settle; (*fournisseur*) to settle up with, pay; (*papier*) to rule; ~ **son compte à qn** to sort sb out, settle sb; ~ **un compte avec qn** to settle a score with sb.

**réglisse** [Reglis] *nf* liquorice.

**règne** [Rɛɲ] *nm* (*d'un roi etc, fig*) reign; (*BIO*): **le** ~ **végétal/animal** the vegetable/animal kingdom.

**régner** [Reɲe] *vi* (*roi*) to rule, reign; (*fig*) to reign.

**regorger** [RəgɔRʒe] *vi* to overflow; ~ **de** to overflow with, be bursting with.

**régression** [RegRɛsjɔ̃] *nf* regression, decline.

**regret** [RəgRɛ] *nm* regret; **à** ~ with regret; **avec** ~ regretfully; **être au** ~ **de devoir faire** to regret having to do.

**regrettable** [RəgRɛtabl(ə)] *a* regrettable.

**regretter** [RəgRete] *vt* to regret; (*personne*) to miss; ~ **que** to regret that, be sorry that; **je regrette** I'm sorry.

**regrouper** [RəgRupe] *vt* (*grouper*) to group together; (*contenir*) to include, comprise; **se** ~ *vi* to gather (together).

**régulariser** [RegylaRize] *vt* (*fonctionnement, trafic*) to regulate; (*passeport, papiers*) to put in order; (*sa situation*) to straighten out, regularize.

**régularité** [RegylaRite] *nf* regularity.

**régulateur, trice** [RegylatœR, -tRis] *a* regulating.

**régulier, ière** [Regylje, -jɛR] *a* (*gén*) regular; (*vitesse, qualité*) steady; (*répartition, pression, paysage*) even; (*TRANSPORTS: ligne, service*) scheduled, regular; (*légal, réglementaire*) lawful, in order; (*fam: correct*) straight, on the level; **régulièrement** *ad* regularly; steadily; evenly; normally.

**réhabiliter** [Reabilite] *vt* to rehabilitate; (*fig*) to restore to favour.

**rehausser** [Rəose] *vt* to heighten, raise; (*fig*) to set off, enhance.

**rein** [Rɛ̃] *nm* kidney; ~**s** *nmpl* (*dos*) back *sg*; **avoir mal aux** ~**s** to have backache.

**reine** [Rɛn] *nf* queen.

**reine-claude** [Rɛnklod] *nf* greengage.

**reinette** [Rɛnɛt] *nf* rennet, pippin.

**réintégrer** [Reɛ̃tegRe] *vt* (*lieu*) to return to; (*fonctionnaire*) to reinstate.

**réitérer** [Reitere] *vt* to repeat, reiterate.

**rejaillir** [RəʒajiR] *vi* to splash up; ~ **sur** to splash up onto; (*fig*) to rebound on; to fall upon.

**rejet** [Rəʒɛ] *nm* (*action, aussi MÉD*)

rejection ; (*POÉSIE*) enjambement, rejet ; (*BOT*) shoot.

**rejeter** [rəʒte] *vt* (*relancer*) to throw back ; (*vomir*) to bring *ou* throw up ; (*écarter*) to reject ; (*déverser*) to throw out, discharge ; ~ **la tête/les épaules en arrière** to throw one's head/pull one's shoulders back ; ~ **la responsabilité de qch sur qn** to lay the responsibility for sth at sb's door.

**rejeton** [rəʒtɔ̃] *nm* offspring.

**rejoindre** [rəʒwɛ̃dR(ə)] *vt* (*famille, régiment*) to rejoin, return to ; (*lieu*) to get (back) to ; (*suj: route etc*) to meet, join ; (*rattraper*) to catch up (with) ; **se** ~ *vi* to meet ; **je te rejoins au café** I'll see *ou* meet you at the café.

**réjoui, e** [Reʒwi] *a* (*mine*) joyous.

**réjouir** [ReʒwiR] *vt* to delight ; **se** ~ *vi* to be delighted ; to rejoice ; **se** ~ **de qch/faire** to be delighted about sth/to do ; **se réjouir** ; **réjouissances** *nfpl* (*joie*) rejoicing *sg* ; (*fête*) festivities, merry-making *sg*.

**relâche** [Rəlaʃ]: **faire** ~ *vi* (*navire*) to put into port ; (*CINÉMA*) to be closed ; **sans** ~ *ad* without respite *ou* a break.

**relâché, e** [Rəlaʃe] *a* loose, lax.

**relâcher** [Rəlaʃe] *vt* (*ressort, prisonnier*) to release ; (*étreinte, cordes*) to loosen // *vi* (*NAVIG*) to put into port ; **se** ~ *vi* to loosen ; (*discipline*) to become slack *ou* lax ; (*élève etc*) to slacken off.

**relais** [Rəlɛ] *nm* (*SPORT*): **(course de)** ~ relay (race) ; (*RADIO, TV*) relay ; **équipe de** ~ shift team ; relay team ; **prendre le** ~ **(de)** to take over (from) ; ~ **de poste** post house, coaching inn ; ~ **routier** ≈ transport café.

**relance** [Rəlɑ̃s] *nf* boosting, revival.

**relancer** [Rəlɑ̃se] *vt* (*balle*) to throw back (again) ; (*moteur*) to restart ; (*fig*) to boost, revive ; (*personne*): ~ **qn** to pester sb ; to get on to sb again.

**relater** [Rəlate] *vt* to relate, recount.

**relatif, ive** [Rəlatif, -iv] *a* relative.

**relation** [Rəlasjɔ̃] *nf* (*récit*) account, report ; (*rapport*) relation(ship) ; ~**s** *nfpl* (*rapports*) relations ; relationship *sg* ; (*connaissances*) connections ; **être/entrer en** ~(s) **avec** to be in contact *ou* be dealing/get in contact with ; ~**s publiques** public relations.

**relativement** [Rəlativmɑ̃] *ad* relatively ; ~ **à** in relation to.

**relativité** [Rəlativite] *nf* relativity.

**relax** [Rəlaks] *a inv*, **relaxe** [Rəlaks(ə)] *a* informal, casual ; easy-going.

**relaxer** [Rəlakse] *vt* to relax ; (*JUR*) to discharge ; **se** ~ *vi* to relax.

**relayer** [Rəleje] *vt* (*collaborateur, coureur etc*) to relieve, take over from ; (*RADIO, TV*) to relay ; **se** ~ (*dans une activité*) to take it in turns.

**relégation** [Rəlegɑsjɔ̃] *nf* (*SPORT*) relegation.

**reléguer** [Rəlege] *vt* to relegate.

**relent(s)** [Rəlɑ̃] *nm(pl)* (foul) smell.

**relève** [Rəlɛv] *nf* relief ; relief team (*ou* troops *pl*) ; **prendre la** ~ to take over.

**relevé, e** [Rəlve] *a* (*bord de chapeau*) turned-up ; (*manches*) rolled-up ; (*virage*) banked ; (*fig: style*) elevated ; (: *sauce*) highly-seasoned // *nm* (*lecture*) reading ;

(*de cotes*) plotting ; (*liste*) statement ; list ; (*facture*) account ; ~ **de compte** bank statement.

**relever** [Rəlve] *vt* (*statue, meuble*) to stand up again ; (*personne tombée*) to help up ; (*vitre, plafond, niveau de vie*) to raise ; (*col*) to turn up ; (*style, conversation*) to elevate ; (*plat, sauce*) to season ; (*sentinelle, équipe*) to relieve ; (*souligner: fautes, points*) to pick out ; (*constater: traces etc*) to find, pick up ; (*répliquer à: remarque*) to react to, reply to ; (: *défi*) to accept, take up ; (*noter: adresse etc*) to take down, note ; (: *plan*) to sketch ; (: *cotes etc*) to plot ; (*compteur*) to read ; (*ramasser: cahiers, copies*) to collect, take in ; ~ **de** *vt* (*maladie*) to be recovering from ; (*être du ressort de*) to be a matter for ; (*ADMIN: dépendre de*) to come under ; (*fig*) to pertain to ; **se** ~ *vi* (*se remettre debout*) to get up ; ~ **qn de** (*vœux*) to release sb from ; (*fonctions*) to relieve sb of ; ~ **la tête** to look up ; to hold up one's head.

**relief** [Rəljɛf] *nm* relief ; (*de pneu*) tread pattern ; ~**s** *nmpl* (*restes*) remains ; **en** ~ in relief ; (*photographie*) three-dimensional ; **mettre en** ~ (*fig*) to bring out, highlight.

**relier** [Rəlje] *vt* to link up ; (*livre*) to bind ; ~ **qch à** to link sth to ; **livre relié cuir** leather-bound book ; **relieur, euse** *nm/f* (book)binder.

**religieux, euse** [Rəliʒjø, -øz] *a* religious // *nm* monk // *nf* nun ; (*gâteau*) cream bun.

**religion** [Rəliʒjɔ̃] *nf* religion ; (*piété, dévotion*) faith ; **entrer en** ~ to take one's vows.

**reliquaire** [RəlikɛR] *nm* reliquary.

**reliquat** [Rəlika] *nm* balance ; remainder.

**relique** [Rəlik] *nf* relic.

**relire** [RəliR] *vt* (*à nouveau*) to reread, read again ; (*vérifier*) to read over.

**reliure** [RəljyR] *nf* binding.

**reluire** [RəlɥiR] *vi* to gleam ; **reluisant, e** *a* gleaming ; **peu reluisant** (*fig*) unattractive ; unsavoury.

**remâcher** [Rəmaʃe] *vt* to chew or ruminate over.

**remailler** [Rəmaje] *vt* to darn ; to mend.

**remaniement** [Rəmanimɑ̃] *nm*: ~ **ministériel** Cabinet reshuffle.

**remanier** [Rəmanje] *vt* to reshape, recast ; (*POL*) to reshuffle.

**remarquable** [RəmaRkabl(ə)] *a* remarkable.

**remarque** [RəmaRk(ə)] *nf* remark ; (*écrite*) note.

**remarquer** [RəmaRke] *vt* (*voir*) to notice ; (*dire*): ~ **que** to remark that ; **se** ~ to be noticeable ; **se faire** ~ to draw attention to o.s. ; **faire** ~ (**à qn**) **que** to point out (to sb) that ; **faire** ~ **qch (à qn)** to point sth out (to sb) ; **remarquez que** mark you, mind you.

**rembarrer** [Rɑ̃baRe] *vt*: ~ **qn** to rebuff sb ; to put sb in his/her place.

**remblai** [Rɑ̃blɛ] *nm* embankment.

**remblayer** [Rɑ̃bleje] *vt* to bank up ; (*fossé*) to fill in.

**rembourrage** [Rɑ̃buRaʒ] *nm* stuffing ; padding.

**rembourré, e** [Rɑ̃buRe] *a* padded.
**rembourrer** [Rɑ̃buRe] *vt* to stuff; (*dossier, vêtement, souliers*) to pad.
**remboursement** [Rɑ̃buRsəmɑ̃] *nm* repayment; **envoi contre** ~ cash on delivery.
**rembourser** [Rɑ̃buRse] *vt* to pay back, repay.
**rembrunir** [Rɑ̃bRyniR]: **se** ~ *vi* to darken; to grow sombre.
**remède** [Rəmɛd] *nm* (*médicament*) medicine; (*traitement, fig*) remedy, cure.
**remédier** [Rəmedje]: ~ **à** *vt* to remedy.
**remembrement** [Rəmɑ̃bRəmɑ̃] *nm* (*AGR*) regrouping of lands.
**remémorer** [RəmemɔRe]: **se** ~ *vt* to recall, recollect.
**remerciements** [RəmɛRsimɑ̃] *nmpl* thanks.
**remercier** [RəmɛRsje] *vt* to thank; (*congédier*) to dismiss; ~ **qn de/d'avoir fait** to thank sb for/for having done; **non, je vous remercie** no thank you.
**remettre** [RəmɛtR(ə)] *vt* (*vêtement*): ~ **qch** to put sth back on, put sth on again; (*replacer*): ~ **qch quelque part** to put sth back somewhere; (*ajouter*): ~ **du sel/un sucre** to add more salt/another lump of sugar; (*rétablir: personne*): ~ **qn** to set sb back on his/her feet; (*rendre, restituer*): ~ **qch à qn** to give sth back to sb, return sth to sb; (*donner, confier: paquet, argent*): ~ **qch à qn** to hand over sth to sb, deliver sth to sb; (*prix, décoration*): ~ **qch à qn** to present sb with sth; (*ajourner*): ~ **qch (à)** to postpone sth *ou* put sth off (until); **se** ~ *vi* to get better, recover; **se** ~ **de** to recover from, get over; **s'en** ~ **à** to leave it (up) to.
**remise** [Rəmiz] *nf* delivery; presentation; (*rabais*) discount; (*local*) shed; ~ **en jeu** (*FOOTBALL*) throw-in; ~ **de peine** reduction of sentence.
**rémission** [Remisjɔ̃]: **sans** ~ *a* irremediable // *ad* unremittingly.
**remontant** [Rəmɔ̃tɑ̃] *nm* tonic, pick-me-up.
**remontée** [Rəmɔ̃te] *nf* rising; ascent; ~**s mécaniques** (*SKI*) towing equipment *sg ou* facilities.
**remonte-pente** [Rəmɔ̃tpɑ̃t] *nm* skilift, (ski) tow.
**remonter** [Rəmɔ̃te] *vi* (*à nouveau*) to go back up; (*après une descente*) to go up (again); (*jupe*) to pull *ou* ride up // *vt* (*pente*) to go up; (*fleuve*) to sail (ou swim etc) up; (*manches, pantalon*) to roll up; (*col*) to turn up; (*rayon, limite*) to raise; (*fig: personne*) to buck up; (*moteur, meuble*) to put back together, reassemble; (*garde-robe etc*) to renew, replenish; (*montre, mécanisme*) to wind up; ~ **à** (*dater de*) to date *ou* go back to; ~ **en voiture** to get back into the car.
**remontoir** [Rəmɔ̃twaR] *nm* winding mechanism, winder.
**remontrance** [Rəmɔ̃tRɑ̃s] *nf* reproof, reprimand.
**remontrer** [Rəmɔ̃tRe] *vt* (*fig*): **en** ~ **à** to prove one's superiority over.
**remords** [RəmɔR] *nm* remorse *q*; **avoir des** ~ to feel remorse, be conscience-stricken.
**remorque** [RəmɔRk(ə)] *nf* trailer; **prendre/être en** ~ to tow/be on tow; **remorquer** *vt* to tow; **remorqueur** *nm* tug(boat).
**rémoulade** [Remulad] *nf* dressing with mustard and herbs.
**rémouleur** [RemulœR] *nm* (knife- *ou* scissor-)grinder.
**remous** [Rəmu] *nm* (*d'un navire*) (back)wash *q*; (*de rivière*) swirl, eddy // *nmpl* (*fig*) stir *sg*.
**rempailler** [Rɑ̃pɑje] *vt* to reseat (*with straw*).
**remparts** [Rɑ̃paR] *nmpl* walls, ramparts.
**rempiler** [Rɑ̃pile] *vi* (*MIL: fam*) to join up again.
**remplaçant, e** [Rɑ̃plasɑ̃, -ɑ̃t] *nm/f* replacement, substitute, stand-in; (*THÉÂTRE*) understudy; (*SCOL*) supply teacher.
**remplacement** [Rɑ̃plasmɑ̃] *nm* replacement; (*job*) replacement work *q*; **assurer le** ~ **de qn** (*suj: remplaçant*) to stand in *ou* substitute for sb.
**remplacer** [Rɑ̃plase] *vt* to replace; (*prendre temporairement la place de*) to stand in for; (*tenir lieu de*) to take the place of, act as a substitute for; ~ **qch/qn par** to replace sth/sb with.
**rempli, e** [Rɑ̃pli] *a* (*emploi du temps*) full, busy; ~ **de** full of, filled with.
**remplir** [Rɑ̃pliR] *vt* to fill (up); (*questionnaire*) to fill out *ou* up; (*obligations, fonction, condition*) to fulfil; **se** ~ *vi* to fill up.
**remplissage** [Rɑ̃plisaʒ] *nm* (*fig: péj*) padding.
**remploi** [Rɑ̃plwa] *nm* re-use.
**remporter** [Rɑ̃pɔRte] *vt* (*marchandise*) to take away; (*fig*) to win, achieve.
**remuant, e** [Rəmɥɑ̃, -ɑ̃t] *a* restless.
**remue-ménage** [Rəmymenaʒ] *nm inv* commotion.
**remuer** [Rəmɥe] *vt* to move; (*café, sauce*) to stir // *vi* to move; (*fig: opposants*) to show signs of unrest; **se** ~ *vi* to move; (*se démener*) to stir o.s.; (*fam*) to get a move on.
**rémunération** [RemyneRɑsjɔ̃] *nf* remuneration.
**rémunérer** [RemyneRe] *vt* to remunerate, pay.
**renâcler** [Rənɑkle] *vi* to snort; (*fig*) to grumble, balk.
**renaissance** [Rənɛsɑ̃s] *nf* rebirth, revival; **la R**~ the Renaissance.
**renaître** [RənɛtR(ə)] *vi* to be revived.
**rénal, e, aux** [Renal, -o] *a* renal, kidney *cpd*.
**renard** [RənaR] *nm* fox.
**rencard** [Rɑ̃kaR] *nm* = **rancard**.
**rencart** [Rɑ̃kaR] *nm* = **rancart**.
**renchérir** [Rɑ̃ʃeRiR] *vi* to become more expensive; (*fig*): ~ **(sur)** to add something (to).
**rencontre** [Rɑ̃kɔ̃tR(ə)] *nf* (*entrevue, congrès, match etc*) meeting; (*imprévue*) encounter; **faire la** ~ **de qn** to meet sb;

**aller à la** ~ **de qn** to go and meet sb ; **amours de** ~ casual love affairs.

**rencontrer** [Rãkõtʀe] *vt* to meet ; (*mot, expression*) to come across ; (*difficultés*) to meet with ; **se** ~ *vi* to meet ; (*véhicules*) to collide.

**rendement** [Rãdmã] *nm* (*d'un travailleur, d'une machine*) output ; (*d'une culture*) yield ; (*d'un investissement*) return ; **à plein** ~ at full capacity.

**rendez-vous** [Rãdevu] *nm* (*rencontre*) appointment ; (: *d'amoureux*) date ; (*lieu*) meeting place ; **donner** ~ **à qn** to arrange to meet sb ; **fixer un** ~ **à qn** to give sb an appointment ; **avoir/prendre** ~ **(avec)** to have/make an appointment (with).

**rendre** [Rãdʀ(ə)] *vt* (*livre, argent etc*) to give back, return ; (*otages, visite etc*) to return ; (*sang, aliments*) to bring up ; (*sons: suj: instrument*) to produce, make ; (*exprimer, traduire*) to render ; (*faire devenir*): ~ **qn célèbre/qch possible** to make sb famous/sth possible ; **se** ~ *vi* (*capituler*) to surrender, give o.s. up ; (*aller*): **se** ~ **quelque part** to go somewhere ; **se** ~ **à** (*arguments etc*) to bow to ; (*ordres*) to comply with ; ~ **la vue/la santé à qn** to restore sb's sight/health ; ~ **la liberté à qn** to set sb free.

**renégat, e** [Rənega, -at] *nm/f* renegade.

**rênes** [Rɛn] *nfpl* reins.

**renfermé, e** [Rãfɛrme] *a* (*fig*) withdrawn // *nm*: **sentir le** ~ to smell stuffy.

**renfermer** [Rãfɛrme] *vt* to contain ; **se** ~ **(sur soi-même)** to withdraw into o.s.

**renflé, e** [Rãfle] *a* bulging, bulbous.

**renflement** [Rãfləmã] *nm* bulge.

**renflouer** [Rãflue] *vt* to refloat ; (*fig*) to set back on its (*ou* his/her) feet (again).

**renfoncement** [Rãfõsmã] *nm* recess.

**renforcer** [Rãfɔrse] *vt* to reinforce.

**renfort** [Rãfɔr] : ~**s** *nmpl* reinforcements ; **en** ~ as a back-up ; **à grand** ~ **de** with a great deal of.

**renfrogner** [Rãfrɔɲe] : **se** ~ *vi* to scowl.

**rengaine** [Rãgɛn] *nf* (*péj*) old tune.

**rengainer** [Rãgene] *vt* (*revolver*) to put back in its holster.

**rengorger** [Rãgɔrʒe] : **se** ~ *vi* (*fig*) to puff o.s. up.

**renier** [Rənje] *vt* (*parents*) to disown, repudiate ; (*foi*) to renounce.

**renifler** [Rənifle] *vi* to sniff // *vt* (*tabac*) to sniff up ; (*odeur*) to sniff.

**renne** [Rɛn] *nm* reindeer *inv.*

**renom** [Rənõ] *nm* reputation ; renown ; **renommé, e** *a* celebrated, renowned // *nf* fame.

**renoncement** [Rənõsmã] *nm* abnegation, renunciation.

**renoncer** [Rənõse] *vi* : ~ **à** *vt* to give up ; ~ **à faire** to give up all idea of doing ; to give up trying to do.

**renouer** [Rənwe] *vt* (*cravate etc*) to retie ; ~ **avec** (*tradition*) to revive ; (*habitude*) to take up again ; ~ **avec qn** to take up with sb again.

**renouveau, x** [Rənuvo] *nm*: ~ **de succès** renewed success ; **le** ~ **printanier** springtide.

**renouveler** [Rənuvle] *vt* to renew ; (*exploit, méfait*) to repeat ; **se** ~ *vi* (*incident*) to recur, happen again, be repeated ; (*cellules etc*) to be renewed *ou* replaced ; **renouvellement** *nm* renewal ; recurrence.

**rénovation** [Renɔvasjõ] *nf* renovation ; restoration.

**rénover** [Renɔve] *vt* (*immeuble*) to renovate, do up ; (*meuble*) to restore ; (*enseignement*) to reform.

**renseignement** [Rãsɛɲmã] *nm* information *q*, piece of information ; **prendre des** ~**s sur** to make inquiries about, ask for information about ; **(guichet des)** ~**s** information desk.

**renseigner** [Rãseɲe] *vt*: ~ **qn (sur)** to give information to sb (about) ; **se** ~ *vi* to ask for information, make inquiries.

**rentable** [Rãtabl(ə)] *a* profitable.

**rente** [Rãt] *nf* income ; pension ; government stock *ou* bond ; ~ **viagère** life annuity ; **rentier, ière** *nm/f* person of private means.

**rentrée** [Rãtre] *nf*: ~ **(d'argent)** cash *q* coming in ; **la** ~ **(des classes)** the start of the new school year ; **la** ~ **(parlementaire)** the reopening *ou* reassembly of parliament ; **faire sa** ~ (*artiste, acteur*) to make a comeback.

**rentrer** [Rãtre] *vi* (*entrer de nouveau*) to go (*ou* come) back in ; (*entrer*) to go (*ou* come) in ; (*revenir chez soi*) to go (*ou* come) (back) home ; (*air, clou: pénétrer*) to go in ; (*revenu, argent*) to come in // *vt* (*foins*) to bring in ; (*véhicule*) to put away ; (*chemise dans pantalon etc*) to tuck in ; (*griffes*) to draw in ; (*train d'atterrissage*) to raise ; (*fig: larmes, colère etc*) to hold back ; ~ **le ventre** to pull in one's stomach ; ~ **dans** to go (*ou* come) back into ; to go (*ou* come) into ; (*famille, patrie*) to go back *ou* return to ; (*heurter*) to crash into ; ~ **dans l'ordre** to be back to normal ; ~ **dans ses frais** to recover one's expenses (*ou* initial outlay).

**renversant, e** [Rãvɛrsã, -ãt] *a* amazing.

**renverse** [Rãvɛrs(ə)]: **à la** ~ *ad* backwards.

**renverser** [Rãvɛrse] *vt* (*faire tomber*: *chaise, verre*) to knock over, overturn ; (*piéton*) to knock down ; (*liquide, contenu*) to spill, upset ; (*retourner: verre, image*) to turn upside down, invert ; (: *ordre des mots etc*) to reverse ; (*fig: gouvernement etc*) to overthrow ; (*stupéfier*) to bowl over, stagger ; **se** ~ *vi* to fall over ; to overturn ; to spill ; ~ **la tête/le corps (en arrière)** to tip one's head back/throw one's body back.

**renvoi** [Rãvwa] *nm* dismissal ; return ; reflection ; postponement ; (*référence*) cross-reference ; (*éructation*) belch.

**renvoyer** [Rãvwaje] *vt* to send back ; (*congédier*) to dismiss ; (*lumière*) to reflect ; (*son*) to echo ; (*ajourner*): ~ **qch (à)** to put sth off *ou* postpone sth (until) ; ~ **qn à** (*fig*) to refer sb to.

**réorganiser** [Reɔrganize] *vt* to reorganize.

**réouverture** [Reuvɛrtyr] *nf* reopening.

**repaire** [Rəpɛʀ] *nm* den.
**repaître** [RəpɛtR(ə)] *vt* to feast; to feed;
**se ~ de** *vt* to feed on; to wallow *ou* revel
in.
**répandre** [Repɑ̃dR(ə)] *vt* (*renverser*) to
spill; (*étaler, diffuser*) to spread; (*lumière*)
to shed; (*chaleur, odeur*) to give off; **se ~**
*vi* to spill; to spread; **se ~ en** (*injures etc*)
to pour out; **répandu, e** *a* (*opinion, usage*)
widespread.
**réparation** [Repaʀɑsjɔ̃] *nf* repairing *q*,
repair.
**réparer** [RepaRe] *vt* to repair; (*fig:
offense*) to make up for, atone for; (: *oubli,
erreur*) to put right.
**repartie** [Rəpaʀti] *nf* retort; **avoir de la
~** to be quick at repartee.
**repartir** [RəpaʀtiR] *vi* to set off again; to
leave again; (*fig*) to get going again, pick
up again; **~ à zéro** to start from scratch
(again).
**répartir** [RepaʀtiR] *vt* (*pour attribuer*) to
share out; (*pour disperser, disposer*) to
divide up; (*poids, chaleur*) to distribute; **se
~** *vt* (*travail, rôles*) to share out between
themselves; **répartition** *nf* sharing out;
dividing up; distribution.
**repas** [Rəpɑ] *nm* meal.
**repasser** [Rəpɑse] *vi* to come (*ou* go) back
// *vt* (*vêtement, tissu*) to iron; to retake,
resit; to show again; (*leçon, rôle: revoir*)
to go over (again).
**repêchage** [Rəpɛʃaʒ] *nm* (*SCOL*): **question
de ~** question to give candidates a second
chance.
**repêcher** [Rəpɛʃe] *vt* (*noyé*) to recover the
body of, fish out.
**repentir** [RəpɑtiR] *nm* repentance; **se ~**
*vi* to repent; **se ~ de** to repent (of).
**répercussions** [Repɛʀkysjɔ̃] *nfpl*
repercussions.
**répercuter** [Repɛʀkyte]: **se ~** *vi* (*bruit*)
to reverberate; (*fig*): **se ~ sur** to have
repercussions on.
**repère** [Rəpɛʀ] *nm* mark; (*monument etc*)
landmark.
**repérer** [RəpeRe] *vt* (*erreur, connaissance*)
to spot; (*abri, ennemi*) to locate; **se ~** *vi*
to find one's way about; **se faire ~** to
be spotted.
**répertoire** [RepɛʀtwaR] *nm* (*liste*)
(alphabetical) list; (*carnet*) index
notebook; (*de carnet*) thumb index;
(*indicateur*) directory, index; (*d'un théâtre,
artiste*) repertoire; **répertorier** *vt* to
itemize, list.
**répéter** [Repete] *vt* to repeat; (*préparer:
leçon: aussi vi*) to learn, go over; (*THÉÂTRE*)
to rehearse; **se ~** (*redire*) to repeat o.s.;
(*se reproduire*) to be repeated, recur.
**répétition** [Repetisjɔ̃] *nf* repetition;
rehearsal; **~s** *nfpl* (*leçons*) private
coaching *sg*; **armes à ~** repeater
weapons; **~ générale** final dress
rehearsal.
**repeupler** [Rəpœple] *vt* to repopulate; to
restock.
**répit** [Repi] *nm* respite; **sans ~** without
letting up.
**replet, ète** [Rəplɛ, -ɛt] *a* chubby, fat.
**repli** [Rəpli] *nm* (*d'une étoffe*) fold; (*MIL. fig*)
withdrawal.

**replier** [Rəplije] *vt* (*rabattre*) to fold down
*ou* over; **se ~** *vi* (*troupes, armée*) to
withdraw, fall back.
**réplique** [Replik] *nf* (*repartie, fig*) reply;
(*THÉÂTRE*) line; (*copie*) replica; **donner la
~ à** to play opposite; to match; **sans ~**
no-nonsense; irrefutable.
**répliquer** [Replike] *vi* to reply; (*riposter*)
to retaliate.
**répondre** [RepɔdR(ə)] *vi* to answer, reply;
(*freins, mécanisme*) to respond; **~ à** *vt* to
reply to, answer; (*avec impertinence*): **~
à qn** to answer sb back; (*invitation,
convocation*) to reply to; (*affection, salut*)
to return; (*provocation, suj: mécanisme etc*)
to respond to; (*correspondre à: besoin*) to
answer; (: *conditions*) to meet; (: *description*) to match; **~ que** to answer *ou* reply
that; **~ de** to answer for.
**réponse** [Repɔs] *nf* answer, reply; **avec
~ payée** (*POSTES*) reply-paid; **en ~ à** in
reply to.
**report** [RəpɔR] *nm* transfer;
postponement.
**reportage** [RəpɔRtaʒ] *nm* (*bref*) report;
(*écrit: documentaire*) story; article; (*en
direct*) commentary; (*genre, activité*): **le ~**
reporting.
**reporter** *nm* [RəpɔRtɛR] reporter // *vt*
[RəpɔRte] (*total*): **~ qch sur** to carry sth
forward *ou* over to; (*ajourner*): **~ qch (à)**
to postpone sth (until); (*transférer*): **~ qch
sur** to transfer sth to; **se ~ à** (*époque*)
to think back to; (*document*) to refer to.
**repos** [Rəpo] *nm* rest; (*fig*) peace (and
quiet); peace of mind; (*MIL*): **~!** stand at
ease!; **en ~** at rest; **de tout ~** safe.
**reposer** [Rəpoz] *vt* refitting.
**reposé, e** [Rəpoze] *a* fresh, rested.
**reposer** [Rəpoze] *vt* (*verre, livre*) to put
down; (*délasser*) to rest; (*problème*) to
reformulate // *vi* (*liquide, pâte*) to settle,
rest; **~ sur** to be built on; (*fig*) to rest
on; **~ vi** to rest; **se ~ sur qn** to rely
on sb.
**repoussant, e** [Rəpusɑ̃, -ɑ̃t] *a* repulsive.
**repoussé, e** [Rəpuse] *a* (*cuir*) embossed
(by hand).
**repousser** [Rəpuse] *vi* to grow again //
*vt* to repel, repulse; (*offre*) to turn down,
reject; (*tiroir, personne*) to push back;
(*différer*) to put back.
**répréhensible** [RepReɑ̃sibl(ə)] *a*
reprehensible.
**reprendre** [RəpRɑ̃dR(ə)] *vt* (*prisonnier,
ville*) to recapture; (*objet prêté, donné*) to
take back; (*chercher*): **je viendrai te ~
à 4h** I'll come and fetch you *ou* I'll come
back for you at 4; (*se resservir de*): **~ du
pain/un œuf** to take (*ou* eat) more
bread/another egg; (*COMM: article usagé*) to
take back; to take in part exchange;
(*firme, entreprise*) to take over; (*travail,
promenade*) to resume; (*emprunter:
argument, idée*) to take up, use; (*refaire:
article etc*) to go over again; (*jupe etc*) to
alter; to take in (*ou* up); to let out (*ou*
down); (*émission, pièce*) to put on again;
(*réprimander*) to tell off; (*corriger*) to
correct // *vi* (*classes, pluie*) to start (up)
again; (*activités, travaux, combats*) to
resume, start (up) again; (*affaires,

*industrie*) to pick up ; (*dire*): **reprit-il** he went on ; **se** ~ (*se ressaisir*) to recover, pull o.s. together ; **s'y** ~ to make another attempt ; ~ **des forces** to recover one's strength ; ~ **courage** to take new heart ; ~ **ses habitudes/sa liberté** to get back into one's old habits/regain one's freedom ; ~ **la route** to resume one's journey, set off again ; ~ **haleine** *ou* **son souffle** to get one's breath back.

**représailles** [RəpRezɑj] *nfpl* reprisals, retaliation *sg.*

**représentant, e** [RəpRezɑ̃tɑ̃, -ɑ̃t] *nm/f* representative.

**représentatif, ive** [RəpRezɑ̃tatif, -iv] *a* representative.

**représentation** [RəpRezɑ̃tɑsjɔ̃] *nf* representation ; performing ; (*symbole, image*) representation ; (*spectacle*) performance ; (*COMM*): **la** ~ commercial travelling ; sales representation ; **frais de** ~ (*d'un diplomate*) entertainment allowance.

**représenter** [RəpRezɑ̃te] *vt* to represent ; (*donner: pièce, opéra*) to perform ; **se** ~ *vt* (*se figurer*) to imagine ; to visualize.

**répression** [RepResjɔ̃] *nf* suppression ; repression ; (*POL*): **la** ~ repression.

**réprimande** [RepRimɑ̃d] *nf* reprimand, rebuke ; **réprimander** *vt* to reprimand, rebuke.

**réprimer** [RepRime] *vt* to suppress, repress.

**repris** [RəpRi] *nm:* ~ **de justice** ex-prisoner, ex-convict.

**reprise** [RəpRiz] *nf* (*TV*) repeat ; (*CINÉMA*) rerun ; (*AUTO*) acceleration *q* ; (*COMM*) trade-in, part exchange ; (*de location*) sum asked *for any extras or improvements made to the property* ; (*raccommodage*) darn ; mend ; **à plusieurs** ~**s** on several occasions, several times.

**repriser** [RəpRize] *vt* to darn ; to mend.

**réprobateur, trice** [RepRɔbatœR, -tRis] *a* reproving.

**réprobation** [RepRɔbɑsjɔ̃] *nf* reprobation.

**reproche** [RəpRɔʃ] *nm* (*remontrance*) reproach ; **faire des** ~**s à qn** to reproach sb ; **sans** ~**(s)** beyond *ou* above reproach.

**reprocher** [RəpRɔʃe] *vt:* ~ **qch à qn** to reproach *ou* blame sb for sth ; ~ **qch à** (*machine, théorie*) to have sth against.

**reproducteur, trice** [RəpRɔdyktœR, -tRis] *a* reproductive.

**reproduction** [RəpRɔdyksjɔ̃] *nf* reproduction ; ~ **interdite** all rights (of reproduction) reserved.

**reproduire** [RəpRɔdɥiR] *vt* to reproduce ; **se** ~ *vi* (*BIO*) to reproduce ; (*recommencer*) to recur, re-occur.

**réprouvé, e** [RepRuve] *nm/f* reprobate.

**réprouver** [RepRuve] *vt* to reprove.

**reptation** [Reptɑsjɔ̃] *nf* crawling.

**reptile** [Reptil] *nm* reptile.

**repu, e** [Rəpy] *a* satisfied, sated.

**républicain, e** [Repyblikɛ̃, -ɛn] *a, nm/f* republican.

**république** [Repyblik] *nf* republic ; **la R**~ **fédérale allemande** the Federal Republic of Germany.

**répudier** [Repydje] *vt* (*femme*) to repudiate ; (*doctrine*) to renounce.

**répugnance** [Repyɲɑ̃s] *nf* repugnance, loathing.

**répugnant, e** [Repyɲɑ̃, -ɑ̃t] *a* repulsive ; loathsome.

**répugner** [Repyɲe]: ~ **à** *vt:* ~ **à qn** to repel *ou* disgust sb ; ~ **à faire** to be loath *ou* reluctant to do.

**répulsion** [Repylsjɔ̃] *nf* repulsion.

**réputation** [Repytɑsjɔ̃] *nf* reputation ; **réputé, e** *a* renowned.

**requérir** [RəkeRiR] *vt* (*nécessiter*) to require, call for ; (*au nom de la loi*) to call upon ; (*JUR: peine*) to call for, demand.

**requête** [Rəkɛt] *nf* request, petition ; (*JUR*) petition.

**requiem** [Rekɥijɛm] *nm* requiem.

**requin** [Rəkɛ̃] *nm* shark.

**requis, e** [Rəki, -iz] *pp de* **requérir** // *a* required.

**réquisition** [Rekizisjɔ̃] *nf* requisition ; **réquisitionner** *vt* to requisition.

**réquisitoire** [RekizitwaR] *nm* (*JUR*) closing speech for the prosecution ; (*fig*): ~ **contre** indictment of.

**R.E.R.** *sigle m* (= *réseau express régional*) *Greater Paris high speed commuter train.*

**rescapé, e** [Rɛskape] *nm/f* survivor.

**rescousse** [Rɛskus] *nf:* **aller à la** ~ **de qn** to go to sb's aid *ou* rescue ; **appeler qn à la** ~ to call on sb for help.

**réseau, x** [Rezo] *nm* network.

**réservation** [RezɛRvɑsjɔ̃] *nf* booking, reservation.

**réserve** [RezɛRv(ə)] *nf* (*gén*) reserve ; (*entrepôt*) storeroom ; (*restriction, aussi: d'Indiens*) reservation ; (*de pêche, chasse*) preserve ; **sous** ~ **de** subject to ; **sans** ~ *ad* unreservedly ; **de** ~ (*provisions etc*) in reserve.

**réservé, e** [RezɛRve] *a* (*discret*) reserved ; (*chasse, pêche*) private ; ~ **à/pour** reserved for.

**réserver** [RezɛRve] *vt* (*gén*) to reserve ; (*retenir: par une agence, au guichet*) to book, reserve ; (*mettre de côté, garder*): ~ **qch pour/à** to keep *ou* save sth for ; ~ **qch à qn** to reserve (*ou* book) sth for sb ; (*fig: destiner*) to have sth in store for sb ; **se** ~ **le droit de faire** to reserve the right to do.

**réserviste** [RezɛRvist(ə)] *nm* reservist.

**réservoir** [RezɛRvwaR] *nm* tank ; (*plan d'eau*) reservoir.

**résidence** [Rezidɑ̃s] *nf* residence ; ~ **secondaire** second home ; **(en)** ~ **surveillée** (under) house arrest ; **résidentiel, le** *a* residential.

**résider** [Rezide] *vi:* ~ **à/dans/en** to reside in ; ~ **dans** (*fig*) to lie in.

**résidu** [Rezidy] *nm* residue *q.*

**résignation** [Reziɲɑsjɔ̃] *nf* resignation.

**résigner** [Reziɲe] *vt* to relinquish, resign ; **se** ~ *vi:* **se** ~ (**à qch/faire**) to resign o.s. (to sth/to doing).

**résilier** [Rezilje] *vt* to terminate.

**résille** [Rezij] *nf* (hair)net.

**résine** [Rezin] *nf* resin ; **résiné, e** *a:* **vin résiné** retsina ; **résineux, euse** *a* resinous // *nm* coniferous tree.

**résistance** [Rezistɑ̃s] *nf* resistance ; (*de réchaud, bouilloire:* fil) element.

**résistant, e** [Rezistɑ̃, -ɑ̃t] *a* (*personne*) robust, tough ; (*matériau*) strong, hardwearing // *nm/f* (*patriote*) Resistance worker *ou* fighter.

**résister** [Reziste] *vi* to resist ; ~ à *vt* (*assaut, tentation*) to resist ; (*effort, souffrance*) to withstand ; (*suj: matériau, plante*) to stand up to, withstand ; (*personne: désobéir à*) to stand up to, oppose.

**résolu, e** [Rezɔly] *pp de* **résoudre** // *a* (*ferme*) resolute ; **être** ~ **à qch/faire** to be set upon sth/doing.

**résolution** [Rezɔlysjɔ̃] *nf* solving ; (*fermeté, décision*) resolution.

**résolve** *etc vb voir* **résoudre**.

**résonance** [Rezɔnɑ̃s] *nf* resonance.

**résonner** [Rezɔne] *vi* (*cloche, pas*) to reverberate, resound ; (*salle*) to be resonant ; ~ **de** to resound with.

**résorber** [RezɔRbe]: **se** ~ *vi* (*MÉD*) to be resorbed ; (*fig*) to be reduced ; to be absorbed.

**résoudre** [RezudR(ə)] *vt* to solve ; ~ **de faire** to resolve to do ; **se** ~ **à faire** to bring o.s. to do.

**respect** [Rɛspɛ] *nm* respect ; **tenir en** ~ to keep at bay.

**respectable** [Rɛspɛktabl(ə)] *a* respectable.

**respecter** [Rɛspɛkte] *vt* to respect ; **le lexicographe qui se respecte** (*fig*) any self-respecting lexicographer.

**respectif, ive** [Rɛspɛktif, -iv] *a* respective ; **respectivement** *ad* respectively.

**respectueux, euse** [Rɛspɛktɥø, -øz] *a* respectful ; ~ **de** respectful of.

**respiration** [RɛspiRɑsjɔ̃] *nf* breathing *q* ; **faire une** ~ **complète** to breathe in and out ; ~ **artificielle** artificial respiration.

**respirer** [RɛspiRe] *vi* to breathe ; (*fig*) to get one's breath, have a break ; to breathe again // *vt* to breathe (in), inhale ; (*manifester: santé, calme etc*) to exude.

**resplendir** [Rɛsplɑ̃diR] *vi* to shine ; (*fig*): ~ **(de)** to be radiant (with).

**responsabilité** [Rɛspɔ̃sabilite] *nf* responsibility ; (*légale*) liability ; **refuser la** ~ **de** to deny responsibility (*ou* liability) for ; **prendre ses** ~**s** to assume responsibility for one's actions.

**responsable** [Rɛspɔ̃sabl(ə)] *a* responsible // *nm/f* (*du ravitaillement etc*) person in charge ; (*de parti, syndicat*) official ; ~ **de** responsible for ; (*légalement: de dégâts etc*) liable for ; (*chargé de*) in charge of, responsible for.

**resquiller** [Rɛskije] *vi* (*au cinéma, au stade*) to get in on the sly ; (*dans le train*) to fiddle a free ride ; **resquilleur, euse** *nm/f* gatecrasher ; fare dodger.

**ressac** [Rəsak] *nm* backwash.

**ressaisir** [RəseziR]: **se** ~ *vi* to regain one's self-control ; (*équipe sportive*) to rally.

**ressasser** [Rəsɑse] *vt* (*remâcher*) to keep turning over ; (*redire*) to keep trotting out.

**ressemblance** [Rəsɑ̃blɑ̃s] *nf* (*visuelle*) resemblance, similarity, likeness ; (: *ART*) likeness ; (*analogie, trait commun*) similarity.

**ressemblant, e** [Rəsɑ̃blɑ̃, -ɑ̃t] *a* (*portrait*) lifelike, true to life.

**ressembler** [Rəsɑ̃ble]: ~ **à** *vt* to be like ; to resemble ; (*visuellement*) to look like ; **se** ~ to be (*ou* look) alike.

**ressemeler** [Rəsəmle] *vt* to (re)sole.

**ressentiment** [Rəsɑ̃timɑ̃] *nm* resentment.

**ressentir** [Rəsɑ̃tiR] *vt* to feel ; **se** ~ **de** to feel (*ou* show) the effects of.

**resserre** [RəsɛR] *nf* shed.

**resserrer** [RəseRe] *vt* (*pores*) to close ; (*nœud, boulon*) to tighten (up) ; (*fig:* liens) to strengthen ; **se** ~ *vi* (*route, vallée*) to narrow ; (*liens*) to strengthen ; **se** ~ (**autour de**) to draw closer (around) ; to close in (on).

**resservir** [RəseRviR] *vi* to do *ou* serve again // *vt*: ~ **qch (à qn)** to serve sth up again (to sb) ; ~ **de qch (à qn)** to give (sb) a second helping of sth ; ~ **qn (d'un plat)** to give sb a second helping (of a dish).

**ressort** [RəsɔR] *nm* (*pièce*) spring ; (*force morale*) spirit ; (*recours*): **en dernier** ~ as a last resort ; (*compétence*): **être du** ~ **de** to fall within the competence of.

**ressortir** [RəsɔRtiR] *vi* to go (*ou* come) out (again) ; (*contraster*) to stand out ; ~ **de** (*résulter de*): **il ressort de ceci que** it emerges from this that ; ~ **à** (*JUR*) to come under the jurisdiction of ; (*ADMIN*) to be the concern of ; **faire** ~ (*fig: souligner*) to bring out.

**ressortissant, e** [RəsɔRtisɑ̃, -ɑ̃t] *nm/f* national.

**ressource** [RəsuRs(ə)] *nf*: **avoir la** ~ **de** to have the possibility of ; **leur seule** ~ **était de** the only course open to them was to ; ~**s** *nfpl* resources ; (*fig*) possibilities.

**ressusciter** [Resysite] *vt* to resuscitate, restore to life ; (*fig*) to revive, bring back // *vi* to rise (from the dead).

**restant, e** [Rɛstɑ̃, -ɑ̃t] *a* remaining // *nm*: **le** ~ **(de)** the remainder (of) ; **un** ~ **de** (*de trop*) some left-over ; (*fig: vestige*) a remnant *ou* last trace of.

**restaurant** [RɛstɔRɑ̃] *nm* restaurant ; **manger au** ~ to eat out ; ~ **d'entreprise** staff canteen ; ~ **universitaire** university refectory.

**restaurateur, trice** [RɛstɔRatœR, -tris] *nm/f* restaurant owner, restaurateur ; (*de tableaux*) restorer.

**restauration** [RɛstɔRɑsjɔ̃] *nf* restoration ; (*hôtellerie*) catering.

**restaurer** [RɛstɔRe] *vt* to restore ; **se** ~ *vi* to have something to eat.

**restauroute** [RɛstɔRut] *nm* = **restoroute**.

**reste** [Rɛst(ə)] *nm* (*restant*): **le** ~ **(de)** the rest (of) ; (*de trop*): **un** ~ **(de)** some left-over ; (*vestige*): **un** ~ **de** a remnant *ou* last trace of ; (*MATH*) remainder ; ~**s** *nmpl* left-overs ; (*d'une cité etc, dépouille mortelle*) remains ; **avoir du temps de** ~ to have time to spare ; **ne voulant pas être en** ~ not wishing to be outdone ; **sans demander son** ~ without waiting to hear more ; **du** ~, **au** ~ *ad* besides, moreover.

**rester** [Rɛste] *vi* (*dans un lieu, un état, une position*) to stay, remain ; (*subsister*) to remain, be left ; (*durer*) to last, live on //

*vb impersonnel*: **il reste du pain/2 œufs** there's some bread/there are 2 eggs left (over); **il reste du temps/10 minutes** there's some time/there are 10 minutes left; **il me reste assez de temps** I have enough time left; **ce qui reste à faire** what remains to be done; **ce qui me reste à faire** what remains for me to do; **en ~ à** (*stade, menaces*) to go no further than, only go as far as; **restons-en là** let's leave it at that; **y ~**: **il a failli y ~** he nearly met his end.

**restituer** [Rɛstitɥe] *vt* (*objet, somme*): **~ qch (à qn)** to return sth (to sb); (*TECH*) to release; to reproduce.

**restoroute** [Rɛstɔrut] *nm* motorway restaurant.

**restreindre** [Rɛstrɛ̃dr(ə)] *vt* to restrict, limit; **se ~** *vi* (*champ de recherches*) to narrow.

**restriction** [Rɛstriksjɔ̃] *nf* restriction; **~s** (*mentales*) reservations.

**résultat** [Rezylta] *nm* result; (*conséquence*) outcome *q*, result; (*d'élection etc*) results *pl*; **~s sportifs** sports results.

**résulter** [Rezylte]: **~ de** *vt* to result from, be the result of.

**résumé** [Rezyme] *nm* summary, résumé; **en ~** *ad* in brief; to sum up.

**résumer** [Rezyme] *vt* (*texte*) to summarize; (*récapituler*) to sum up; (*fig*) to epitomize, typify; **se ~ à** to come down to.

**résurrection** [Rezyrɛksjɔ̃] *nf* resurrection; (*fig*) revival.

**rétablir** [Retablir] *vt* to restore, re-establish; (*personne: suj: traitement*): **~ qn** to restore sb to health, help sb recover; (*ADMIN*): **~ qn dans son emploi** to reinstate sb in his post; **se ~** *vi* (*guérir*) to recover; (*silence, calme*) to return, be restored; (*GYM etc*): **se ~ (sur)** to pull o.s. up (onto); **rétablissement** *nm* restoring; recovery; pull-up.

**rétamer** [Retame] *vt* to re-coat, re-tin.

**retaper** [Rətape] *vt* (*maison, voiture etc*) to do up; (*fam: revigorer*) to buck up; (*redactylographier*) to retype.

**retard** [Rətar] *nm* (*d'une personne attendue*) lateness *q*; (*sur l'horaire, un programme, une échéance*) delay; (*fig: scolaire, mental etc*) backwardness; **en ~ (de 2 heures)** (2 hours) late; **avoir un ~ de 2 km** (*SPORT*) to be 2 km behind; **avoir du ~** to be late; (*sur un programme*) to be behind (schedule); **prendre du ~** (*train, avion*) to be delayed; (*montre*) to lose (time); **sans ~** *ad* without delay; **~ à l'allumage** (*AUTO*) retarded spark.

**retardataire** [Rətardatɛr] *nm/f* latecomer.

**retardement** [Rətardəmɑ̃]: **à ~** *a* delayed action *cpd*; **bombe à ~** time bomb.

**retarder** [Rətarde] *vt* (*sur un horaire*): **~ qn (d'une heure)** to delay sb (an hour); (*sur un programme*): **~ qn (de 3 mois)** to set sb back *ou* delay sb (3 months); (*départ, date*): **~ qch (de 2 jours)** to put sth back (2 days), delay sth (for *ou* by 2 days) // *vi* (*montre*) to be slow; to lose (time); **je retarde (d'une heure)** I'm (an hour) slow.

**retenir** [Rətnir] *vt* (*garder, retarder*) to keep, detain; (*maintenir: objet qui glisse, fig: colère, larmes*) to hold back; (: *objet suspendu*) to hold; (: *chaleur, odeur*) to retain; (*fig: empêcher d'agir*): **~ qn (de faire)** to hold sb back (from doing); (*se rappeler*) to remember; (*réserver*) to reserve; (*accepter*) to accept; (*prélever*): **~ qch (sur)** to deduct sth (from); **se ~** (*se raccrocher*): **se ~ à** to hold onto; (*se contenir*): **se ~ de faire** to restrain o.s. from doing; **~ son souffle** *ou* **haleine** to hold one's breath; **je pose 3 et je retiens 2** put down 3 and carry 2.

**retentir** [Rətɑ̃tir] *vi* to ring out; (*salle*): **~ de** to ring *ou* resound with; **~ sur** *vt* (*fig*) to have an effect upon.

**retentissant, e** [Rətɑ̃tisɑ̃, -ɑ̃t] *a* resounding; (*fig*) impact-making.

**retentissement** [Rətɑ̃tismɑ̃] *nm* repercussion; effect, impact; stir.

**retenue** [Rətny] *nf* (*prélèvement*) deduction; (*SCOL*) detention; (*modération*) (self-)restraint; (*réserve*) reserve, reticence.

**réticence** [Retisɑ̃s] *nf* hesitation, reluctance *q*.

**rétif, ive** [Retif, -iv] *a* restive.

**rétine** [Retin] *nf* retina.

**retiré, e** [Rətire] *a* secluded.

**retirer** [Rətire] *vt* to withdraw; (*vêtement, lunettes*) to take off, remove; (*extraire*): **~ qch de** to take sth out of, remove sth from; (*reprendre: bagages, billets*) to collect, pick up; **~ des avantages de** to derive advantages from; **se ~** *vi* (*partir, reculer*) to withdraw; (*prendre sa retraite*) to retire; **se ~ de** to withdraw from; to retire from.

**retombées** [Rətɔ̃be] *nfpl* (*radioactives*) fallout *sg*; (*fig*) fallout; spin-offs.

**retomber** [Rətɔ̃be] *vi* (*à nouveau*) to fall again; (*atterrir: après un saut etc*) to land; (*tomber, redescendre*) to fall back; (*pendre*) to fall, hang (down); (*échoir*): **~ sur qn** to fall on sb.

**rétorquer** [Retɔrke] *vt*: **~ (à qn) que** to retort (to sb) that.

**retors, e** [Rətɔr, -ɔrs(ə)] *a* wily.

**rétorsion** [Retɔrsjɔ̃] *nf*: **mesures de ~** reprisals.

**retouche** [Rətuʃ] *nf* touching up *q*; alteration.

**retoucher** [Rətuʃe] *vt* (*photographie, tableau*) to touch up; (*texte, vêtement*) to alter.

**retour** [Rətur] *nm* return; **au ~** when we (*ou* they *etc*) get (*ou* got) back; on the way back; **être de ~ (de)** to be back (from); **par ~ du courrier** by return of post; **~ en arrière** (*CINÉMA*) flashback; (*mesure*) backward step; **~ offensif** renewed attack.

**retourner** [Rəturne] *vt* (*dans l'autre sens: matelas, crêpe*) to turn (over); (: *caisse*) to turn upside down; (: *sac, vêtement*) to turn inside out; (*fig: argument*) to turn back; (*e remuant: terre, sol, foin*) to turn over; (*émouvoir: personne*) to shake; (*renvoyer, restituer*): **~ qch à qn** to return sth to sb // *vi* (*aller, revenir*): **~ quelque part/à** to go back *ou* return somewhere/to; **~ à**

(*état, activité*) to return to, go back to ; se
~ vi to turn over ; (*tourner la tête*) to turn
round ; se ~ **contre** (*fig*) to turn against ;
**savoir de quoi il retourne** to know what
it is all about ; ~ **en arrière** *ou* **sur ses
pas** to turn back, retrace one's steps.
**retracer** [RətRase] *vt* to relate, recount.
**rétracter** [Retrakte] *vt*, **se** ~ *vi* to retract.
**retraduire** [RətRadɥiR] *vt* to translate
again ; (*dans la langue de départ*) to
translate back.
**retrait** [RətRɛ] *nm* (*voir retirer*)
withdrawal ; collection ; redemption ; (*voir
se retirer*) withdrawal ; (*rétrécissement*)
shrinkage ; **en** ~ *a* set back ; ~ **du permis
(de conduire)** disqualification from
driving.
**retraite** [RətRɛt] *nf* (*d'une armée,* REL,
*refuge*) retreat ; (*d'un employé*) retirement ;
(retirement) pension ; **être / mettre à la** ~
to be retired *ou* in retirement / pension off
*ou* retire ; **prendre sa** ~ to retire ; ~
**anticipée** early retirement ; ~ **aux
flambeaux** torchlight tattoo ; **retraité, e**
*a* retired // *nm / f* (old age) pensioner.
**retranchement** [RətRɑ̃ʃmɑ̃] *nm*
entrenchment.
**retrancher** [RətRɑ̃ʃe] *vt* (*passage, détails*)
to take out, remove ; (*nombre, somme*): ~
**qch de** to take *ou* deduct sth from ;
(*couper*) to cut off ; **se** ~ **derrière / dans**
to entrench o.s. behind / in ; (*fig*) to take
refuge behind / in.
**retransmettre** [RətRɑ̃smɛtR(ə)] *vt* (RADIO)
to broadcast, relay ; (*TV*) to show ;
**retransmission** *nf* broadcast ; showing.
**retraverser** [RətRavɛRse] *vt* (*dans l'autre
sens*) to cross back over.
**rétrécir** [RetResiR] *vt* (*vêtement*) to take in
// to shrink ; **se** ~ *vi* to narrow.
**retremper** [RətRɑ̃pe] *vt*: **se** ~ **dans** (*fig*)
to reimmerse o.s. in.
**rétribuer** [RetRibɥe] *vt* (*travail*) to pay
for ; (*personne*) to pay ; **rétribution** *nf*
payment.
**rétro** [RetRo] *a inv*: **la mode** ~ the
nostalgia vogue.
**rétroactif, ive** [RetRoaktif, -iv] *a*
retroactive.
**rétrograde** [RetRogRad] *a* reactionary,
backward-looking.
**rétrograder** [RetRogRade] *vi* (*élève*) to fall
back ; (*économie*) to regress ; (AUTO) to
change down.
**rétrospective** [RetRospɛktiv] *nf*
retrospective exhibition ; season showing
old films ; ~**ment** *ad* in retrospect.
**retrousser** [RətRuse] *vt* to roll up.
**retrouvailles** [RətRuvaj] *nfpl* reunion *sg*.
**retrouver** [RətRuve] *vt* (*fugitif, objet
perdu*) to find ; (*occasion*) to find again ;
(*calme, santé*) to regain ; (*revoir*) to see
again ; (*rejoindre*) to meet (again), join ; **se**
~ *vi* to meet ; (*s'orienter*) to find one's
way ; **se** ~ **quelque part** to find o.s.
somewhere ; to end up somewhere ; **s'y** ~
(*rentrer dans ses frais*) to break even.
**rétroviseur** [RetRovizœR] *nm* (rear-view
*ou* driving) mirror.
**réunion** [Reynjɔ̃] *nf* bringing together ;
joining ; (*séance*) meeting ; **l'île de la R~,
la R~** Réunion.

**réunir** [ReyniR] *vt* (*convoquer*) to call
together ; (*rassembler*) to gather together ;
(*cumuler*) to combine ; (*rapprocher*) to
bring together (again), reunite ; (*rattacher*)
to join (together) ; **se** ~ *vi* (*se rencontrer*)
to meet ; (*s'allier*) to unite.
**réussi, e** [Reysi] *a* successful.
**réussir** [ReysiR] *vi* to succeed, be
successful ; (*à un examen*) to pass ; (*plante,
culture*) to thrive, do well // *vt* to make
a success of ; to bring off ; ~ **à faire** to
succeed in doing ; ~ **à qn** to go right for
sb ; to agree with sb.
**réussite** [Reysit] *nf* success ; (CARTES)
patience.
**revaloir** [RəvalwaR] *vt*: **je vous revaudrai
cela** I'll repay you some day ; (*en mal*) I'll
pay you back for this.
**revaloriser** [RəvaloRize] *vt* (*monnaie*) to
revalue ; (*salaires, pensions*) to raise the
level of ; (*institution, tradition*) to reassert
the value of.
**revanche** [Rəvɑ̃ʃ] *nf* revenge ; **prendre sa**
~ **(sur)** to take one's revenge (on) ; **en**
~ on the other hand.
**rêvasser** [Rɛvase] *vi* to daydream.
**rêve** [Rɛv] *nm* dream ; (*activité psychique*):
**le** ~ dreaming ; ~ **éveillé** daydreaming
q, daydream.
**revêche** [Rəvɛʃ] *a* surly, sour-tempered.
**réveil** [Revɛj] *nm* (*d'un dormeur*) waking up
q ; (*fig*) awakening ; (*pendule*) alarm
(clock) ; **au** ~ when I (*ou* he) woke up,
on waking (up) ; **sonner le** ~ (MIL) to
sound the reveille.
**réveille-matin** [Revɛjmatɛ̃] *nm inv* alarm
clock.
**réveiller** [Reveje] *vt* (*personne*) to wake
up ; (*fig*) to awaken, revive ; **se** ~ *vi* to
wake up ; (*fig*) to be revived, reawaken.
**réveillon** [Revɛjɔ̃] *nm* Christmas Eve ; (*de
la Saint-Sylvestre*) New Year's Eve ;
Christmas Eve (*ou* New Year's Eve) party
*ou* dinner ; **réveillonner** *vi* to celebrate
Christmas Eve (*ou* New Year's Eve).
**révélateur, trice** [Revelatœr, -tris] *a*: ~
**(de qch)** revealing (sth) // *nm* (PHOTO)
developer.
**révélation** [Revelasjɔ̃] *nf* revelation.
**révéler** [Revele] *vt* (*gén*) to reveal ;
(*divulguer*) to disclose, reveal ; (*dénoter*) to
reveal, show ; (*faire connaître au public*): ~
**qn / qch** to make sb / sth widely known,
bring sb / sth to the public's notice ; **se** ~
*vi* to be revealed, reveal itself // *vb avec
attribut* to prove (to be).
**revenant, e** [Rəvnɑ̃, -ɑ̃t] *nm / f* ghost.
**revendeur, euse** [Rəvɑ̃dœR, -øz] *nm / f*
(*détaillant*) retailer ; (*d'occasions*)
secondhand dealer.
**revendication** [Rəvɑ̃dikasjɔ̃] *nf* claim,
demand ; **journée de** ~ day of action (in
support of one's claims).
**revendiquer** [Rəvɑ̃dike] *vt* to claim,
demand ; (*responsabilité*) to claim // *vi* to
agitate in favour of one's claims.
**revendre** [Rəvɑ̃dR(ə)] *vt* (*d'occasion*) to
resell ; (*détailler*) to sell ; (*vendre davantage
de*): ~ **du sucre / un foulard / deux
bagues** to sell more sugar / another scarf /
another two rings ; **à** ~ *ad* (*en abondance*)
to spare, aplenty.

revenir [Rǝvniʀ] vi to come back ; (CULIN): faire ~ to brown ; (coûter): ~ cher/à 100 F (à qn) to cost (sb) a lot/100 F ; ~ à (études, projet) to return to, go back to ; (équivaloir à) to amount to ; ~ à qn (rumeur, nouvelle) to get back to sb, reach sb's ears ; (part, honneur) to go to sb, be sb's ; (souvenir, nom) to come back to sb ; ~ de (fig: maladie, étonnement) to recover from ; ~ sur (question, sujet) to go back over ; (engagement) to go back on ; ~ à la charge to return to the attack ; ~ à soi to come round ; n'en pas ~ : je n'en reviens pas I can't get over it ; ~ sur ses pas to retrace one's steps ; cela revient à dire que it amounts to saying that.
revente [Rǝvãt] nf resale.
revenu [Rǝvny] nm income ; (de l'État) revenue ; (d'un capital) yield ; ~s nmpl income sg.
rêver [Reve] vi, vt to dream ; ~ de qch/faire to dream of sth/doing ; ~ à to dream of.
réverbération [Reverberɑsjɔ̃] nf reflection.
réverbère [Reverbɛr] nm street lamp ou light.
réverbérer [Reverbere] vt to reflect.
révérence [Reverãs] nf (vénération) reverence ; (salut) bow ; curtsey.
révérend, e [Reverã, -ãd] a: le ~ père Pascal the Reverend Father Pascal.
révérer [Revere] vt to revere.
rêverie [Rɛvri] nf daydreaming q, daydream.
revers [Rǝvɛr] nm (de feuille, main) back ; (d'étoffe) wrong side ; (de pièce, médaille) back, reverse ; (TENNIS, PING-PONG) backhand ; (de veston) lapel ; (de pantalon) turn-up ; (fig: échec) setback ; le ~ de la médaille (fig) the other side of the coin ; prendre à ~ (MIL) to take from the rear.
réversible [Reversibl(ǝ)] a reversible.
revêtement [Rǝvɛtmã] nm (de paroi) facing ; (des sols) flooring ; (de chaussée) surface ; (de tuyau etc: enduit) coating.
revêtir [Rǝvetir] vt (habit) to don, put on ; (fig) to take on ; ~ qn de to dress sb in ; (fig) to endow ou invest sb with ; ~ qch de to cover sth with ; (fig) to cloak sth in ; ~ d'un visa to append a visa to.
rêveur, euse [Rɛvœr, -øz] a dreamy // nm/f dreamer.
revient [Rǝvjɛ̃] vb voir revenir // nm: prix de ~ cost price.
revigorer [Rǝvigore] vt to invigorate, brace up ; to revive, buck up.
revirement [Rǝvirmã] nm change of mind ; (d'une situation) reversal.
réviser [Revize] vt (texte, SCOL: matière) to revise ; (comptes) to audit ; (machine, installation, moteur) to overhaul, service ; (JUR: procès) to review.
révision [Revizjɔ̃] nf revision ; auditing q ; overhaul ; servicing q ; review ; conseil de ~ (MIL) recruiting board ; faire ses ~s (SCOL) to do one's revision, revise ; la ~ des 10000 km (AUTO) the 10,000 km service.
revisser [Rǝvise] vt to screw back again.
revivifier [Rǝvivifje] vt to revitalize.

revivre [Rǝvivr(ǝ)] vi (reprendre des forces) to come alive again ; (traditions) to be revived // vt (épreuve, moment) to relive.
révocation [Revokasjɔ̃] nf dismissal ; revocation.
revoir [Rǝvwar] vt to see again ; (réviser) to revise // nm: au ~ goodbye ; dire au ~ à qn to say goodbye to sb.
révolte [Revolt(ǝ)] nf rebellion, revolt.
révolter [Revolte] vt to revolt ; to outrage, appal ; se ~ vi: se ~ (contre) to rebel (against) ; se ~ (à) to be outraged (by).
révolu, e [Revoly] a past ; (ADMIN): âgé de 18 ans ~s over 18 years of age ; après 3 ans ~s when 3 full years have passed.
révolution [Revolysjɔ̃] nf revolution ; révolutionnaire a, nm/f revolutionary ; révolutionner vt to revolutionize ; (fig) to stir up.
revolver [Revolvɛr] nm gun ; (à barillet) revolver.
révoquer [Revoke] vt (fonctionnaire) to dismiss, remove from office ; (arrêt, contrat) to revoke.
revue [Rǝvy] nf (inventaire, examen) review ; (MIL: défilé) review, march-past ; (: inspection) inspection, review ; (périodique) review, magazine ; (pièce satirique) revue ; (de music-hall) variety show ; passer en ~ to review, inspect ; (fig) to review, survey ; to go through.
révulsé, e [Revylse] a (yeux) rolled upwards ; (visage) contorted.
rez-de-chaussée [Redʃose] nm inv ground floor.
RF sigle = République Française.
rhabiller [Rabije] vt: se ~ to get dressed again, put one's clothes on again.
rhapsodie [Rapsodi] nf rhapsody.
rhénan, e [Renã, -an] a Rhine cpd.
Rhénanie [Renani] nf: la ~ the Rhineland.
rhésus [Rezys] a, nm rhesus.
rhétorique [Retorik] nf rhetoric.
rhéto-roman, e [Retoromã, -an] a Rhaeto-Romanic.
Rhin [Rɛ̃] nm: le ~ the Rhine.
rhinocéros [Rinoseros] nm rhinoceros.
rhodanien, ne [Rodanjɛ̃, -jɛn] a Rhone cpd.
Rhodésie [Rodezi] nf: la ~ Rhodesia ; rhodésien, ne a Rhodesian.
rhododendron [Rododɛ̃drɔ̃] nm rhododendron.
Rhône [Ron] nm: le ~ the Rhone.
rhubarbe [Rybarb(ǝ)] nf rhubarb.
rhum [Rɔm] nm rum.
rhumatisant, e [Rymatizã, -ãt] nm/f rheumatic.
rhumatismal, e, aux [Rymatismal, -o] a rheumatic.
rhumatisme [Rymatism(ǝ)] nm rheumatism q.
rhume [Rym] nm cold ; ~ de cerveau head cold ; le ~ des foins hay fever.
ri [Ri] pp de rire.
riant, e [Rjã, -ãt] a smiling, cheerful.
ribambelle [Ribãbɛl] nf: une ~ de a herd ou swarm of.
ricaner [Rikane] vi (avec méchanceté) to snigger ; (bêtement, avec gêne) to giggle.

**riche** [Riʃ] *a* (*gén*) rich; (*personne, pays*) rich, wealthy; ~ **en** rich in; ~ **de** full of; rich in; **richesse** *nf* wealth; (*fig*) richness; **richesses** *nfpl* wealth *sg*; treasures; **richesse en vitamines** high vitamin content.

**ricin** [Risɛ̃] *nm:* **huile de** ~ castor oil.

**ricocher** [Rikɔʃe] *vi:* ~ **(sur)** to rebound (off); (*sur l'eau*) to bounce (on *ou* off); **faire** ~ (*galet*) to skim.

**ricochet** [Rikɔʃɛ] *nm* rebound; bounce; **faire des** ~s to skim pebbles; **par** ~ *ad* on the rebound; (*fig*) as an indirect result.

**rictus** [Riktys] *nm* grin; (snarling) grimace.

**ride** [Rid] *nf* wrinkle; (*fig*) ripple.

**ridé, e** [Ride] *a* wrinkled.

**rideau, x** [Rido] *nm* curtain; ~ **de fer** metal shutter; (*POL*): **le** ~ **de fer** the Iron Curtain.

**ridelle** [Ridɛl] *nf* slatted side.

**rider** [Ride] *vt* to wrinkle; (*fig*) to ripple; to ruffle the surface of; **se** ~ *vi* (*avec l'âge*) to become wrinkled; (*de contrariété*) to wrinkle.

**ridicule** [Ridikyl] *a* ridiculous // *nm* ridiculousness *q*; **le** ~ ridicule; **tourner en** ~ to ridicule; **ridiculiser** *vt* to ridicule; **se ridiculiser** to make a fool of o.s.

**rie** *vb voir* **rire**.

**rien** [Rjɛ̃] *pronom* nothing; (*quelque chose*) anything; **ne ...** ~ nothing, *tournure négative* + anything // *nm* nothing; ~ **d'autre** nothing else; ~ **du tout** nothing at all; ~ **que** just, only; nothing but; **il n'a** ~ (*n'est pas blessé*) he's all right; **un petit** ~ (*cadeau*) a little something; **des** ~s trivia *pl*.

**rieur, euse** [Rjœr, -øz] *a* cheerful, merry.

**rigide** [Riʒid] *a* stiff; (*fig*) rigid; strict; **rigidité** *nf* stiffness; **la rigidité cadavérique** rigor mortis.

**rigolade** [Rigɔlad] *nf:* **la** ~ fun; (*fig*): **c'est de la** ~ it's a cinch; it's a big farce.

**rigole** [Rigɔl] *nf* (*conduit*) channel; (*filet d'eau*) rivulet.

**rigoler** [Rigɔle] *vi* (*rire*) to laugh; (*s'amuser*) to have (some) fun; (*plaisanter*) to be joking *ou* kidding.

**rigolo, ote** [Rigɔlo, -ɔt] *a* (*fam*) funny // *nm/f* comic; (*péj*) fraud, phoney.

**rigoureux, euse** [Rigurø, -øz] *a* (*morale*) rigorous, strict; (*personne*) stern, strict; (*climat, châtiment*) rigorous, harsh, severe; (*interdiction, neutralité*) strict; (*preuves, analyse, méthode*) rigorous.

**rigueur** [Rigœr] *nf* rigour; strictness; harshness; **'tenue de soirée de** ~' 'evening dress (to be worn)'; **être de** ~ to be the usual thing *ou* be the rule; **à la** ~ at a pinch; possibly; **tenir** ~ **à qn de qch** to hold sth against sb.

**rillettes** [Rijɛt] *nfpl* potted meat *sg*.

**rime** [Rim] *nf* rhyme; **rimer** *vi:* **rimer (avec)** to rhyme (with); **ne rimer à rien** not to make sense.

**rinçage** [Rɛ̃saʒ] *nm* rinsing (out); (*opération*) rinse.

**rince-doigts** [Rɛ̃sdwa] *nm inv* finger-bowl.

**rincer** [Rɛ̃se] *vt* to rinse; (*récipient*) to rinse out.

**ring** [Riŋ] *nm* (boxing) ring.

**rions** *vb voir* **rire**.

**ripaille** [Ripɑj] *nf:* **faire** ~ to feast.

**ripoliné, e** [Ripɔline] *a* enamel-painted.

**riposte** [Ripɔst(ə)] *nf* retort, riposte; (*fig*) counter-attack, reprisal.

**riposter** [Ripɔste] *vi* to retaliate // *vt:* ~ **que** to retort that; ~ **à** *vt* to counter; to reply to.

**rire** [Rir] *vi* to laugh; (*se divertir*) to have fun // *nm* laugh; **le** ~ laughter; ~ **de** *vt* to laugh at; **se** ~ **de** to make light of; **pour** ~ (*pas sérieusement*) for a joke *ou* a laugh.

**ris** [Ri] *vb voir* **rire** // *nm:* ~ **de veau** (calf) sweetbread.

**risée** [Rize] *nf:* **être la** ~ **de** to be the laughing stock of.

**risette** [Rizɛt] *nf:* **faire** ~ **(à)** to give a nice little smile (to).

**risible** [Rizibl(ə)] *a* laughable, ridiculous.

**risque** [Risk(ə)] *nm* risk; ~ **danger**; **prendre des** ~s to take risks; **à ses** ~s **et périls** at his own risk; **au** ~ **de** at the risk of.

**risqué, e** [Riske] *a* risky; (*plaisanterie*) risqué, daring.

**risquer** [Riske] *vt* to risk; (*allusion, question*) to venture, hazard; **tu risques qu'on te renvoie** you risk being dismissed; **ça ne risque rien** it's quite safe; ~ **de: il risque de se tuer** he could get *ou* risks getting himself killed; **il a risqué de se tuer** he almost got himself killed; **ce qui risque de se produire** what might *ou* could well happen; **il ne risque pas de recommencer** there's no chance of him doing that again; **se** ~ **dans** (*s'aventurer*) to venture into; **se** ~ **à faire** (*tenter*) to venture *ou* dare to do; **risque-tout** *nm/f inv* daredevil.

**rissoler** [Risɔle] *vi, vt:* **(faire)** ~ to brown.

**ristourne** [Risturn(ə)] *nf* rebate.

**rite** [Rit] *nm* rite; (*fig*) ritual.

**ritournelle** [Riturnɛl] *nf* (*fig*) tune.

**rituel, le** [Rityɛl] *a, nm* ritual.

**rivage** [Rivaʒ] *nm* shore.

**rival, e, aux** [Rival, -o] *a, nm/f* rival.

**rivaliser** [Rivalize] *vi:* ~ **avec** to rival, vie with; (*être comparable*) to hold its own against, compare with; ~ **avec qn de** (*élégance etc*) to vie with *ou* rival sb in.

**rivalité** [Rivalite] *nf* rivalry.

**rive** [Riv] *nf* shore; (*de fleuve*) bank.

**river** [Rive] *vt* (*clou, pointe*) to clinch; (*plaques*) to rivet together; **être rivé sur/à** to be riveted on/to.

**riverain, e** [Rivrɛ̃, -ɛn] *a* riverside *cpd*; lakeside *cpd*; roadside *cpd* // *nm/f* riverside (*ou* lakeside) resident; local *ou* roadside resident.

**rivet** [Rivɛ] *nm* rivet; **riveter** *vt* to rivet (together).

**rivière** [Rivjɛr] *nf* river; ~ **de diamants** diamond rivière.

**rixe** [Riks(ə)] *nf* brawl, scuffle.

**riz** [Ri] *nm* rice; ~ **au lait** rice pudding; **rizière** *nf* paddy-field.

**R.N.** *sigle f* = *route nationale, voir* **national**.

**robe** [Rɔb] *nf* dress; (*de juge, d'ecclésiastique*) robe; (*de professeur*) gown; (*pelage*) coat; ~ **de soirée/de mariée** evening/ wedding dress; ~ **de baptême** christening robe; ~ **de chambre** dressing gown; ~ **de grossesse** maternity dress.

**robinet** [Rɔbinɛ] *nm* tap; ~ **du gaz** gas tap; ~ **mélangeur** mixer tap; **robinetterie** *nf* taps *pl*, plumbing.

**roboratif, ive** [Rɔbɔratif, -iv] *a* bracing, invigorating.

**robot** [Rɔbo] *nm* robot.

**robuste** [Rɔbyst(ə)] *a* robust, sturdy.

**roc** [Rɔk] *nm* rock.

**rocade** [Rɔkad] *nf* (*AUTO*) by-road, bypass.

**rocaille** [Rɔkɑj] *nf* loose stones *pl*; rocky *ou* stony ground; (*jardin*) rockery, rock garden // *a* (*style*) rocaille; **rocailleux, euse** *a* rocky, stony; (*voix*) harsh.

**rocambolesque** [Rɔkɑ̃bɔlɛsk(ə)] *a* fantastic, incredible.

**roche** [Rɔʃ] *nf* rock.

**rocher** [Rɔʃe] *nm* rock; (*ANAT*) petrosal bone.

**rochet** [Rɔʃɛ] *nm*: **roue à** ~ rachet wheel.

**rocheux, euse** [Rɔʃø, -øz] *a* rocky.

**rock (and roll)** [Rɔk(ɛnRɔl)] *nm* (*musique*) rock(-'n'-roll); (*danse*) jive.

**rodage** [Rɔdaʒ] *nm* running in; **en** ~ (*AUTO*) running in.

**rodéo** [Rɔdeo] *nm* rodeo (*pl* s).

**roder** [Rɔde] *vt* (*moteur, voiture*) to run in.

**rôder** [Rode] *vi* to roam *ou* wander about; (*de façon suspecte*) to lurk *ou* loiter (about *ou* around); **rôdeur, euse** *nm/f* prowler.

**rodomontades** [Rɔdɔmɔ̃tad] *nfpl* bragging *sg*; sabre rattling *sg*.

**rogatoire** [RɔgatwaR] *a*: **commission** ~ letters rogatory.

**rogne** [Rɔɲ] *nf*: **être en** ~ to be ratty *ou* in a temper.

**rogner** [Rɔɲe] *vt* to trim; to clip; (*fig*) to whittle down; ~ **sur** (*fig*) to cut down *ou* back on.

**rognons** [Rɔɲɔ̃] *nmpl* kidneys.

**rognures** [RɔɲyR] *nfpl* trimmings; clippings.

**rogue** [Rɔg] *a* arrogant.

**roi** [Rwa] *nm* king; **le jour** *ou* **la fête des R**~**s, les** ~**s** Twelfth Night.

**roitelet** [Rwatlɛ] *nm* wren; (*péj*) kinglet.

**rôle** [Rol] *nm* role; (*contribution*) part.

**rollmops** [Rɔlmɔps] *nm* rollmop.

**romain, e** [Rɔmɛ̃, -ɛn] *a, nm/f* Roman // *nf* (*BOT*) cos (lettuce).

**roman, e** [Rɔmɑ̃, -an] *a* (*ARCHIT*) Romanesque; (*LING*) Romance, Romanic // *nm* novel; ~ **d'espionnage** spy novel *ou* story; ~ **photo** romantic picture story.

**romance** [Rɔmɑ̃s] *nf* ballad.

**romancer** [Rɔmɑ̃se] *vt* to make into a novel; to romanticize.

**romanche** [Rɔmɑ̃ʃ] *a, nm* Romansh.

**romancier, ière** [Rɔmɑ̃sje, -jɛR] *nm/f* novelist.

**romand, e** [Rɔmɑ̃, -ɑ̃d] *a* of *ou* from French-speaking Switzerland.

**romanesque** [Rɔmanɛsk(ə)] *a* (*fantastique*) fantastic; storybook *cpd*;

(*sentimental*) romantic; (*LITTÉRATURE*) novelistic.

**roman-feuilleton** [Rɔmɑ̃fœjtɔ̃] *nm* serialized novel.

**romanichel, le** [Rɔmaniʃɛl] *nm/f* gipsy.

**romantique** [Rɔmɑ̃tik] *a* romantic.

**romantisme** [Rɔmɑ̃tism(ə)] *nm* romanticism.

**romarin** [RɔmaRɛ̃] *nm* rosemary.

**Rome** [Rɔm] *nf* Rome.

**rompre** [Rɔ̃pR(ə)] *vt* to break; (*entretien, fiançailles*) to break off // *vi* (*fiancés*) to break it off; **se** ~ *vi* to break; (*MÉD*) to burst, rupture; **se** ~ **les os** *ou* **le cou** to break one's neck; ~ **avec** to break with; **rompez (les rangs)!** (*MIL*) dismiss!, fall out!

**rompu, e** [Rɔ̃py] *a* (*fourbu*) exhausted, worn out; ~ **à** with wide experience of; inured to.

**romsteak** [Rɔ̃mstɛk] *nm* rumpsteak *q*.

**ronce** [Rɔ̃s] *nf* (*BOT*) bramble branch; (*MENUISERIE*): ~ **de noyer** burr walnut; ~**s** *nfpl* brambles, thorns.

**ronchonner** [Rɔ̃ʃɔne] *vi* (*fam*) to grouse, grouch.

**rond, e** [Rɔ̃, Rɔ̃d] *a* a round; (*joues, mollets*) well-rounded; (*fam: ivre*) tight // *nm* (*cercle*) ring; (*fam: sou*) **je n'ai plus un** ~ I haven't a penny left // *nf* (*gén: de surveillance*) rounds *pl*, patrol; (*danse*) round (dance); (*MUS*) semibreve; **en** ~ (*s'asseoir, danser*) in a ring; **à la** ~**e** (*alentour*): **à 10 km à la** ~**e** for 10 km round; (*à chacun son tour*): **passer qch à la** ~**e** to pass sth (a)round; **faire des** ~**s de jambe** to bow and scrape; ~ **de serviette** serviette ring; ~-**de-cuir** *nm* (*péj*) penpusher; **rondelet, e** *a* plump.

**rondelle** [Rɔ̃dɛl] *nf* (*TECH*) washer; (*tranche*) slice, round.

**rondement** [Rɔ̃dmɑ̃] *ad* briskly; frankly.

**rondeur** [Rɔ̃dœR] *nf* (*d'un bras, des formes*) plumpness; (*bonhomie*) friendly straightforwardness; ~**s** *nfpl* (*d'une femme*) curves.

**rondin** [Rɔ̃dɛ̃] *nm* log.

**rond-point** [Rɔ̃pwɛ̃] *nm* roundabout.

**ronéotyper** [Rɔneɔtipe] *vt* to duplicate, roneo.

**ronflant, e** [Rɔ̃flɑ̃, -ɑ̃t] *a* (*péj*) high-flown, grand.

**ronflement** [Rɔ̃flǝmɑ̃] *nm* snore, snoring *q*.

**ronfler** [Rɔ̃fle] *vi* to snore; (*moteur, poêle*) to hum; to roar.

**ronger** [Rɔ̃ʒe] *vt* to gnaw (at); (*suj: vers, rouille*) to eat into; ~ **son frein** to champ (at) the bit; **se** ~ **de souci**, **se** ~ **les sangs** to worry o.s. sick, fret; **se** ~ **les ongles** to bite one's nails; **rongeur, euse** *nm/f* rodent.

**ronronner** [Rɔ̃Rɔne] *vi* to purr.

**roque** [Rɔk] *nm* (*ÉCHECS*) castling; **roquer** *vi* to castle.

**roquet** [Rɔkɛ] *nm* nasty little lap-dog.

**roquette** [Rɔkɛt] *nf* rocket.

**rosace** [Rozas] *nf* (*vitrail*) rose window, rosace; (*motif: de plafond etc*) rose.

**rosaire** [RozɛR] *nm* rosary.

**rosbif** [Rɔsbif] *nm*: **du** ~ roasting beef; (*cuit*) roast beef; **un** ~ a joint of beef.

**rose** [ʀoz] *nf* rose ; (*vitrail*) rose window // *a* pink ; ~ **bonbon** *a inv* candy pink ; ~ **des vents** compass card.

**rosé, e** [ʀoze] *a* pinkish ; **(vin)** ~ rosé (wine).

**roseau, x** [ʀozo] *nm* reed.

**rosée** [ʀoze] *nf* dew ; **goutte de** ~ dewdrop.

**roseraie** [ʀozʀɛ] *nf* rose garden ; (*plantation*) rose nursery.

**rosette** [ʀozɛt] *nf* rosette (*gen of the Légion d'honneur*).

**rosier** [ʀozje] *nm* rosebush, rose tree.

**rosir** [ʀoziʀ] *vi* to go pink.

**rosse** [ʀos] *nf* (*péj: cheval*) nag // *a* nasty, vicious.

**rosser** [ʀose] *vt* (*fam*) to thrash.

**rossignol** [ʀosiɲɔl] *nm* (*ZOOL*) nightingale ; (*crochet*) picklock.

**rot** [ʀo] *nm* belch ; (*de bébé*) burp.

**rotatif, ive** [ʀotatif, -iv] *a* rotary // *nf* rotary press.

**rotation** [ʀotɑsjɔ̃] *nf* rotation ; (*fig*) rotation, swap-around ; turnover ; **par** ~ on a rota basis ; ~ **des cultures** rotation of crops ; ~ **des stocks** stock turnover.

**roter** [ʀote] *vi* (*fam*) to burp, belch.

**rôti** [ʀoti] *nm*: **du** ~ roasting meat ; (*cuit*) roast meat ; **un** ~ **de bœuf/porc** a joint of beef/pork.

**rotin** [ʀotɛ̃] *nm* rattan (cane) ; **fauteuil en** ~ **cane** (arm)chair.

**rôtir** [ʀotiʀ] *vt* (*aussi*: **faire** ~) to roast // *vi* to roast ; **se** ~ **au soleil** to bask in the sun ; **rôtisserie** *nf* steakhouse ; roast meat counter (*ou* shop) ; **rôtissoire** *nf* (roasting) spit.

**rotonde** [ʀotɔ̃d] *nf* (*ARCHIT*) rotunda ; (*RAIL*) engine shed.

**rotondité** [ʀotɔ̃dite] *nf* roundness.

**rotor** [ʀotɔʀ] *nm* rotor.

**rotule** [ʀotyl] *nf* kneecap, patella.

**roturier, ière** [ʀotyʀje, -jɛʀ] *nm/f* commoner.

**rouage** [ʀwaʒ] *nm* cog(wheel), gearwheel ; (*de montre*) part ; (*fig*) cog ; ~**s** (*fig*) internal structure *sg*.

**roublard, e** [ʀublaʀ, -aʀd(ə)] *a* (*péj*) crafty, wily.

**rouble** [ʀubl(ə)] *nm* rouble.

**roucouler** [ʀukule] *vi* to coo ; (*fig: péj*) to warble.

**roue** [ʀu] *nf* wheel ; **faire la** ~ (*paon*) to spread *ou* fan its tail ; (*GYM*) to do a cartwheel ; **descendre en** ~ **libre** to freewheel *ou* coast down ; ~ **à aubes** paddle wheel ; ~ **dentée** cogwheel ; ~ **de secours** spare wheel.

**roué, e** [ʀwe] *a* wily.

**rouer** [ʀwe] *vt*: ~ **qn de coups** to give sb a thrashing.

**rouet** [ʀwɛ] *nm* spinning wheel.

**rouge** [ʀuʒ] *a, nm/f* red // *nm* red ; (*fard*) rouge ; **(vin)** ~ red wine ; **passer au** ~ (*signal*) to go red ; (*automobiliste*) to go through the red lights ; **porter au** ~ (*métal*) to bring to red heat ; ~ **(à lèvres)** lipstick ; **rougeâtre** *a* reddish ; ~**-gorge** *nm* robin (redbreast).

**rougeole** [ʀuʒɔl] *nf* measles *sg*.

**rougeoyer** [ʀuʒwaje] *vi* to glow red.

**rouget** [ʀuʒɛ] *nm* mullet.

**rougeur** [ʀuʒœʀ] *nf* redness ; (*du visage*) red face ; ~**s** *nfpl* (*MÉD*) red blotches.

**rougir** [ʀuʒiʀ] *vi* (*de hònte, timidité*) to blush, flush ; (*de plaisir, colère*) to flush ; (*fraise, tomate*) to go *ou* turn red ; (*ciel*) to redden.

**rouille** [ʀuj] *nf* rust // *a inv* rust-coloured, rusty.

**rouillé, e** [ʀuje] *a* rusty.

**rouiller** [ʀuje] *vt* to rust // *vi* to rust, go rusty ; **se** ~ *vi* to rust ; (*fig*) to become rusty ; to grow stiff.

**roulade** [ʀulad] *nf* (*GYM*) roll ; (*CULIN*) rolled meat *q* ; (*MUS*) roulade, run.

**roulant, e** [ʀulɑ̃, -ɑ̃t] *a* (*meuble*) on wheels ; (*surface, trottoir*) moving ; **matériel** ~ (*RAIL*) rolling stock ; **personnel** ~ (*RAIL*) train crews *pl*.

**rouleau, x** [ʀulo] *nm* (*de papier, tissu, pièces de monnaie, SPORT*) roll ; (*de machine à écrire*) roller, platen ; (*à mise en plis, à peinture, vague*) roller ; ~ **compresseur** steamroller ; ~ **à pâtisserie** rolling pin ; ~ **de pellicule** roll of film.

**roulement** [ʀulmɑ̃] *nm* (*bruit*) rumbling *q*, rumble ; (*rotation*) rotation ; turnover ; **par** ~ on a rota basis ; ~ **(à billes)** ball bearings *pl* ; ~ **de tambour** drum roll.

**rouler** [ʀule] *vt* to roll ; (*papier, tapis*) to roll up ; (*CULIN: pâte*) to roll out ; (*fam*) to do, con // *vi* (*bille, boule*) to roll ; (*voiture, train*) to go, run ; (*automobiliste*) to drive ; (*cycliste*) to ride ; (*bateau*) to roll ; (*tonnerre*) to rumble, roll ; (*dégringoler*): ~ **en bas de** to roll down ; ~ **sur** (*suj: conversation*) to turn on ; **se** ~ **dans** (*boue*) to roll in ; (*couverture*) to roll o.s. (up) in ; ~ **les épaules/hanches** to sway one's shoulders/wiggle one's hips.

**roulette** [ʀulɛt] *nf* (*de table, fauteuil*) castor ; (*de pâtissier*) pastry wheel ; (*jeu*): **la** ~ roulette ; **à** ~**s** on castors.

**roulis** [ʀuli] *nm* roll(ing).

**roulotte** [ʀulɔt] *nf* caravan.

**roumain, e** [ʀumɛ̃, -ɛn] *a, nm/f* Romanian.

**Roumanie** [ʀumani] *nf* Romania.

**roupiller** [ʀupije] *vi* (*fam*) to sleep.

**rouquin, e** [ʀukɛ̃, -in] *nm/f* (*péj*) redhead.

**rouspéter** [ʀuspete] *vi* (*fam*) to moan, grouse.

**rousse** [ʀus] *a voir* **roux**.

**rousseur** [ʀusœʀ] *nf*: **tache de** ~ freckle.

**roussi** [ʀusi] *nm*: **ça sent le** ~ there's a smell of burning ; (*fig*) I can smell trouble.

**roussir** [ʀusiʀ] *vt* to scorch // *vi* (*feuilles*) to go *ou* turn brown ; (*CULIN*): **faire** ~ to brown.

**route** [ʀut] *nf* road ; (*fig: chemin*) way ; (*itinéraire, parcours*) route ; (*fig: voie*) road, path ; **par (la)** ~ by road ; **il y a 3h de** ~ it's a 3-hour ride *ou* journey ; **en** ~ *ad* on the way ; **mettre en** ~ to start up ; **se mettre en** ~ to set off ; **faire** ~ **vers** to head towards ; **routier, ière** *a* road *cpd* // *nm* (*camionneur*) (long-distance) lorry *ou* truck driver ; (*restaurant*) ≈ transport café ; (*scout*) ≈ rover // *nf* (*voiture*) touring car.

**routine** [Rutin] *nf* routine ; **routinier, ière** *a* (*péj*) humdrum ; addicted to routine.

**rouvrir** [RuvRiR] *vt*, *vi* to reopen, open again ; **se ~** *vi* (*blessure*) to open up again.

**roux, rousse** [Ru, Rus] *a* red ; (*personne*) red-haired // *nm/f* redhead // *nm* (CULIN) roux.

**royal, e, aux** [Rwajal, -o] *a* royal ; (*fig*) fit for a king, princely ; blissful ; thorough.

**royaliste** [Rwajalist(ə)] *a*, *nm/f* royalist.

**royaume** [Rwajom] *nm* kingdom ; (*fig*) realm ; **le R~ Uni** the United Kingdom.

**royauté** [Rwajote] *nf* (*dignité*) kingship ; (*régime*) monarchy.

**R.S.V.P.** *sigle* (= *répondez s'il vous plaît*) R.S.V.P.

**Rte** *abr de* **route.**

**ruade** [Ryad] *nf* kick.

**ruban** [Rybã] *nm* (*gén*) ribbon ; (*pour ourlet, couture*) binding ; (*de téléscripteur etc*) tape ; (*d'acier*) strip ; **~ adhésif** adhesive tape.

**rubéole** [Rybeɔl] *nf* German measles *sg*, rubella.

**rubicond, e** [Rybikɔ̃, -ɔ̃d] *a* rubicund, ruddy.

**rubis** [Rybi] *nm* ruby ; (HORLOGERIE) jewel.

**rubrique** [RybRik] *nf* (*titre, catégorie*) heading, rubric ; (PRESSE: *article*) column.

**ruche** [Ryʃ] *nf* hive.

**rude** [Ryd] *a* (*barbe, toile*) rough ; (*métier, tâche*) hard, tough ; (*climat*) severe, harsh ; (*bourru*) harsh, rough ; (*fruste*) rugged, tough ; (*fam*) jolly good ; **~ment** *ad* (*tomber, frapper*) hard ; (*traiter, reprocher*) harshly ; (*fam: très*) terribly, jolly ; (*: beaucoup*) jolly hard.

**rudimentaire** [RydimãtɛR] *a* rudimentary, basic.

**rudiments** [Rydimã] *nmpl* rudiments ; basic knowledge *sg* ; basic principles.

**rudoyer** [Rydwaje] *vt* to treat harshly.

**rue** [Ry] *nf* street.

**ruée** [Rɥe] *nf* rush.

**ruelle** [Rɥɛl] *nf* alley(-way).

**ruer** [Rɥe] *vi* (*cheval*) to kick out ; **se ~ vi: se ~ sur** to pounce on ; **se ~ vers/dans/hors de** to rush *ou* dash towards/into/out of ; **~ dans les brancards** to become rebellious.

**rugby** [Rygbi] *nm* Rugby (football) ; **~ à treize/quinze** Rugby League/Union.

**rugir** [RyʒiR] *vi* to roar ; **rugissement** *nm* roar, roaring *q*.

**rugosité** [Rygozite] *nf* roughness ; (*aspérité*) rough patch.

**rugueux, euse** [Rygø, -øz] *a* rough.

**ruine** [Rɥin] *nf* ruin ; **~s** *nfpl* ruins.

**ruiner** [Rɥine] *vt* to ruin ; **ruineux, euse** *a* terribly expensive to buy (*ou* run), ruinous ; extravagant.

**ruisseau, x** [Rɥiso] *nm* stream, brook ; (*caniveau*) gutter ; (*fig*): **~x de** floods of, streams of.

**ruisseler** [Rɥisle] *vi* to stream ; **~ (d'eau)** to be streaming (with water).

**rumeur** [RymœR] *nf* (*bruit confus*) rumbling ; hubbub *q* ; murmur(ing) ; (*nouvelle*) rumour.

**ruminer** [Rymine] *vt* (*herbe*) to ruminate ; (*fig*) to ruminate on *ou* over, chew over

// *vi* (*vache*) to chew the cud, ruminate.

**rumsteak** [Rɔmstɛk] *nm* = **romsteak.**

**rupture** [RyptyR] *nf* (*de câble, digue*) breaking ; (*de tendon*) rupture, tearing ; (*de négociations etc*) breakdown ; (*de contrat*) breach ; (*séparation, désunion*) break-up, split ; **en ~ de ban** at odds with authority.

**rural, e, aux** [RyRal, -o] *a* rural, country *cpd* // *nmpl*: **les ruraux** country people.

**ruse** [Ryz] *nf*: **la ~** cunning, craftiness ; trickery ; **une ~** a trick, a ruse ; **rusé, e** *a* cunning, crafty.

**russe** [Rys] *a*, *nm*, *nf* Russian.

**Russie** [Rysi] *nf*: **la ~** Russia.

**rustique** [Rystik] *a* rustic.

**rustre** [RystR(ə)] *nm* boor.

**rut** [Ryt] *nm*: **être en ~** to be in *ou* on heat, be rutting.

**rutabaga** [Rytabaga] *nm* swede.

**rutilant, e** [Rytilã, -ãt] *a* gleaming.

**rythme** [Ritm(ə)] *nm* rhythm ; (*vitesse*) rate ; (*: de la vie*) pace, tempo ; **au ~ de 10 par jour** at the rate of 10 a day ; **rythmé, e** *a* rhythmic(al) ; **rythmique** *a* rhythmic(al) // *nf* rhythmics *sg*.

# S

**s'** [s] *pronom voir* **se.**

**sa** [sa] *dét voir* **son.**

**S.A.** *sigle voir* **société.**

**sable** [sabl(ə)] *nm* sand ; **~s mouvants** quicksand(s).

**sablé** [sable] *nm* shortbread biscuit.

**sabler** [sable] *vt* to sand ; (*contre le verglas*) to grit ; **~ le champagne** to drink champagne.

**sableux, euse** [sablø, -øz] *a* sandy.

**sablier** [sablije] *nm* hourglass ; (*de cuisine*) egg timer.

**sablière** [sablijɛR] *nf* sand quarry.

**sablonneux, euse** [sablɔnø, -øz] *a* sandy.

**saborder** [sabɔRde] *vt* (*navire*) to scuttle ; (*fig*) to wind up, shut down.

**sabot** [sabo] *nm* clog ; (*de cheval, bœuf*) hoof ; **~ de frein** brake shoe.

**sabotage** [sabotaʒ] *nm* sabotage.

**saboter** [sabɔte] *vt* to sabotage ; **saboteur, euse** *nm/f* saboteur.

**sabre** [sabR(ə)] *nm* sabre.

**sac** [sak] *nm* bag ; (*à charbon etc*) sack ; (*pillage*) sack(ing) ; **mettre à ~** to sack ; **~ à provisions/de voyage** shopping/travelling bag ; **~ de couchage** sleeping bag ; **~ à dos** rucksack ; **~ à main** handbag.

**saccade** [sakad] *nf* jerk ; **par ~s** jerkily ; haltingly.

**saccager** [sakaʒe] *vt* (*piller*) to sack, lay waste ; (*dévaster*) to create havoc in, wreck.

**saccharine** [sakaRin] *nf* saccharin(e).

**sacerdoce** [sasɛRdɔs] *nm* priesthood ; (*fig*) calling, vocation ; **sacerdotal, e, aux** *a* priestly, sacerdotal.

**sache** *etc vb voir* **savoir.**

**sachet** [saʃɛ] *nm* (small) bag ; (*de lavande, poudre, shampooing*) sachet ; **~ de thé** tea bag.

**sacoche** [sakɔʃ] nf (gén) bag; (de bicyclette) saddlebag; (du facteur) (post-)bag; (d'outils) toolbag.
**sacre** [sakʀ(ə)] nm coronation; consecration.
**sacré, e** [sakʀe] a sacred; (fam: satané) blasted; (: fameux): **un ~ ...** a heck of a ...; (ANAT) sacral.
**sacrement** [sakʀəmɑ̃] nm sacrament; **les derniers ~s** the last rites.
**sacrer** [sakʀe] vt (roi) to crown; (évêque) to consecrate // vi to curse, swear.
**sacrifice** [sakʀifis] nm sacrifice.
**sacrifier** [sakʀifje] vt to sacrifice; **~ à** vt to conform to; **articles sacrifiés** (COMM) items given away at knock-down prices.
**sacrilège** [sakʀilɛʒ] nm sacrilege // a sacrilegious.
**sacristain** [sakʀistɛ̃] nm sexton; sacristan.
**sacristie** [sakʀisti] nf sacristy; (culte protestant) vestry.
**sacro-saint, e** [sakʀɔsɛ̃, -sɛ̃t] a sacrosanct.
**sadique** [sadik] a sadistic // nm/f sadist.
**sadisme** [sadism(ə)] nm sadism.
**safari** [safaʀi] nm safari; **faire un ~** to go on safari; **~-photo** nm photographic safari.
**safran** [safʀɑ̃] nm saffron.
**sagace** [sagas] a sagacious, shrewd.
**sagaie** [sagɛ] nf assegai.
**sage** [saʒ] a wise; (enfant) good // nm wise man; sage.
**sage-femme** [saʒfam] nf midwife (pl wives).
**sagesse** [saʒɛs] nf wisdom.
**Sagittaire** [saʒitɛʀ] nm: **le ~** Sagittarius, the Archer; **être du ~** to be Sagittarius.
**Sahara** [saaʀa] nm: **le ~** the Sahara (desert).
**saharienne** [saaʀjɛn] nf safari jacket.
**saignant, e** [sɛɲɑ̃, -ɑ̃t] a (viande) rare; (blessure, plaie) bleeding.
**saignée** [seɲe] nf (MÉD) bleeding q, bloodletting q; (ANAT): **la ~ du bras** the bend of the arm; (fig) heavy losses pl; savage cut.
**saignement** [sɛɲmɑ̃] nm bleeding; **~ de nez** nosebleed.
**saigner** [seɲe] vi to bleed // vt to bleed; (animal) to kill (by bleeding); **~ du nez** to have a nosebleed.
**saillant, e** [sajɑ̃, -ɑ̃t] a (pommettes, menton) prominent; (corniche etc) projecting; (fig) salient, outstanding.
**saillie** [saji] nf (sur un mur etc) projection; (trait d'esprit) witticism; (accouplement) covering, serving; **faire ~** to project, stick out.
**saillir** [sajiʀ] vi to project, stick out; (veine, muscle) to bulge // vt (ÉLEVAGE) to cover, serve.
**sain, e** [sɛ̃, sɛn] a healthy; (dents, constitution) healthy, sound; (lectures) wholesome; **~ et sauf** safe and sound, unharmed; **~ d'esprit** sound in mind, sane.
**saindoux** [sɛ̃du] nm lard.
**saint, e** [sɛ̃, sɛ̃t] a holy; (fig) saintly // nm/f saint; **le S~ Esprit** the Holy Spirit ou Ghost; **la S~e Vierge** the Blessed Vir-

gin; **sainteté** nf holiness; **le S~-Père** the Holy Father, the Pontiff; **le S~-Siège** the Holy See; **la S~-Sylvestre** New Year's Eve.
**sais** etc vb voir **savoir**.
**saisie** [sezi] nf seizure.
**saisir** [seziʀ] vt to take hold of, grab; (fig: occasion) to seize; (comprendre) to grasp; (entendre) to get, catch; (suj: émotions) to take hold of, come over; (CULIN) to fry quickly; (JUR: biens, publication) to seize; (: juridiction): **~ un tribunal d'une affaire** to submit ou refer a case to a court; **se ~ de** vt to seize; **saisissant, e** a startling, striking; **saisissement** nm emotion.
**saison** [sɛzɔ̃] nf season; **la belle ~** the summer months; **en/hors ~** in/out of season; **haute/morte ~** high/slack season; **la ~ des pluies/des amours** the rainy/ mating season; **saisonnier, ière** a seasonal // nm (travailleur) seasonal worker.
**sait** vb voir **savoir**.
**salace** [salas] a salacious.
**salade** [salad] nf (BOT) lettuce etc (generic term); (CULIN) (green) salad; (fam) tangle, muddle; **haricots en ~** bean salad; **~ de concombres** cucumber salad; **~ de fruits** fruit salad; **~ russe** Russian salad; **saladier** nm salad bowl.
**salaire** [salɛʀ] nm (annuel, mensuel) salary; (hebdomadaire, journalier) pay, wages pl; (fig) reward; **~ de base** basic salary/wage; **~ minimum interprofessionnel garanti (SMIG)/de croissance (SMIC)** index-linked guaranteed minimum wage.
**salaison** [salɛzɔ̃] nf salting; **~s** nfpl salt meat sg.
**salami** [salami] nm salami q, salami sausage.
**salant** [salɑ̃] am: **marais ~** salt pan.
**salarial, e, aux** [salaʀjal, -o] a salary cpd, wage(s) cpd.
**salarié, e** [salaʀje] a salaried; wage-earning // nm/f salaried employee; wage-earner.
**salaud** [salo] nm (fam!) sod (!), bastard (!).
**sale** [sal] a dirty, filthy.
**salé, e** [sale] a (liquide, saveur) salty; (CULIN) salted, salt cpd; (fig) spicy, juicy; steep, stiff.
**saler** [sale] vt to salt.
**saleté** [salte] nf (état) dirtiness; (crasse) dirt, filth; (tache etc) dirt q, something dirty; (fig) filthy trick; rubbish q; filth q; infection, bug.
**salière** [saljɛʀ] nf saltcellar.
**saligaud** [saligo] nm (fam!) sod (!).
**salin, e** [salɛ̃, -in] a saline // nf saltworks sg; salt marsh.
**salinité** [salinite] nf salinity, salt-content.
**salir** [saliʀ] vt to (make) dirty; (fig) to soil the reputation of; **se ~** to get dirty; **salissant, e** a (tissu) which shows the dirt; (métier) dirty, messy.
**salive** [saliv] nf saliva; **saliver** vi to salivate.
**salle** [sal] nf room; (d'hôpital) ward; (de restaurant) dining room; (d'un cinéma) auditorium; (: public) audience; **faire ~**

**comble** to have a full house ; ~ **d'attente** waiting room ; ~ **de bain(s)** bathroom ; ~ **de bal** ballroom ; ~ **de cinéma** cinema ; ~ **de classe** classroom ; ~ **commune** (*d'hôpital*) ward ; ~ **de concert** concert hall ; ~ **de douches** shower-room ; ~ **d'eau** shower-room ; ~ **d'embarquement** (*à l'aéroport*) departure lounge ; ~ **des machines** engine room ; ~ **à manger** dining room ; ~ **d'opération** (*d'hôpital*) operating theatre ; ~ **de projection** film theatre ; ~ **de séjour** living room ; ~ **de spectacle** theatre ; cinema ; ~ **des ventes** saleroom.

**salon** [salɔ̃] *nm* lounge, sitting room ; (*mobilier*) lounge suite ; (*exposition*) exhibition, show ; (*mondain, littéraire*) salon ; ~ **de coiffure** hairdressing salon ; ~ **de thé** tearoom.

**salopard** [salɔpaʀ] *nm* (*fam!*) bastard (!).

**salope** [salɔp] *nf* (*fam!*) bitch(!).

**saloperie** [salɔpʀi] *nf* (*fam!*) filth *q* ; dirty trick ; rubbish *q*.

**salopette** [salɔpɛt] *nf* overall(s).

**salpêtre** [salpɛtʀ(ə)] *nm* saltpetre.

**salsifis** [salsifi] *nm* salsify, oyster-plant.

**saltimbanque** [saltɛ̃bɑ̃k] *nm/f* (travelling) acrobat.

**salubre** [salybʀ(ə)] *a* healthy, salubrious ; **salubrité** *nf* healthiness, salubrity ; **salubrité publique** public health.

**saluer** [salɥe] *vt* (*pour dire bonjour, fig*) to greet ; (*pour dire au revoir*) to take one's leave ; (*MIL*) to salute.

**salut** [saly] *nm* (*sauvegarde*) safety ; (*REL*) salvation ; (*geste*) wave ; (*parole*) greeting ; (*MIL*) salute // *excl* (*fam*) hi (there) ; (*style relevé*) (all) hail.

**salutaire** [salytɛʀ] *a* beneficial ; salutary.

**salutations** [salytɑsjɔ̃] *nfpl* greetings ; **recevez mes ~ distinguées** *ou* **respectueuses** yours faithfully.

**salutiste** [salytist(ə)] *nm/f* Salvationist.

**salve** [salv(ə)] *nf* salvo ; volley of shots.

**samaritain** [samaʀitɛ̃] *nm*: **le bon S~** the Good Samaritan.

**samedi** [samdi] *nm* Saturday.

**sanatorium** [sanatɔʀjɔm] *nm* sanatorium (*pl* a).

**sanctifier** [sɑ̃ktifje] *vt* to sanctify.

**sanction** [sɑ̃ksjɔ̃] *nf* sanction ; (*fig*) penalty ; **prendre des ~s contre** to impose sanctions on ; **sanctionner** *vt* (*loi, usage*) to sanction ; (*punir*) to punish.

**sanctuaire** [sɑ̃ktɥɛʀ] *nm* sanctuary.

**sandale** [sɑ̃dal] *nf* sandal.

**sandalette** [sɑ̃dalɛt] *nf* sandal.

**sandwich** [sɑ̃dwitʃ] *nm* sandwich ; **pris en ~** sandwiched.

**sang** [sɑ̃] *nm* blood ; **en ~** covered in blood ; **se faire du mauvais ~** to fret, get in a state.

**sang-froid** [sɑ̃fʀwa] *nm* calm, sangfroid ; **de ~** in cold blood.

**sanglant, e** [sɑ̃glɑ̃, -ɑ̃t] *a* bloody, covered in blood ; (*combat*) bloody.

**sangle** [sɑ̃gl(ə)] *nf* strap ; ~**s** (*pour lit etc*) webbing *sg* ; **sangler** *vt* to strap up ; (*animal*) to girth.

**sanglier** [sɑ̃glije] *nm* (wild) boar.

**sanglot** [sɑ̃glo] *nm* sob ; **sangloter** *vi* to sob.

**sangsue** [sɑ̃sy] *nf* leech.

**sanguin, e** [sɑ̃gɛ̃, -in] *a* blood *cpd* ; (*fig*) fiery // *nf* blood orange ; (*ART*) red pencil drawing.

**sanguinaire** [sɑ̃ginɛʀ] *a* bloodthirsty ; bloody.

**sanguinolent, e** [sɑ̃ginɔlɑ̃, -ɑ̃t] *a* streaked with blood.

**sanitaire** [sanitɛʀ] *a* health *cpd* ; **installation/appareil ~** bathroom plumbing/appliance ; ~**s** *nmpl* (*salle de bain et w.-c.*) bathroom *sg*.

**sans** [sɑ̃] *prép* without ; ~ **qu'il s'en aperçoive** without him *ou* his noticing ; ~ **scrupules** unscrupulous ; ~ **manches** sleeveless ; ~**-abri** *nmpl* homeless (*after a flood etc*) ; ~**-emploi** *nmpl* jobless ; ~**-façon** *a inv* fuss-free ; free and easy ; ~**-gêne** *a inv* inconsiderate ; ~**-logis** *nmpl* homeless (*through poverty*) ; ~**-travail** *nmpl* unemployed, jobless.

**santal** [sɑ̃tal] *nm* sandal(wood).

**santé** [sɑ̃te] *nf* health ; **en bonne ~** in good health ; **boire à la ~ de qn** to drink (to) sb's health ; **'à la ~ de'** 'here's to' ; **à ta/votre ~!** cheers!

**santon** [sɑ̃tɔ̃] *nm* ornamental figure at a Christmas crib.

**saoul, e** [su, sul] *a* = **soûl, e**.

**sape** [sap] *nf*: **travail de ~** (*MIL*) sap ; (*fig*) insidious undermining process *ou* work.

**saper** [sape] *vt* to undermine, sap.

**sapeur** [sapœʀ] *nm* sapper ; ~**-pompier** *nm* fireman.

**saphir** [safiʀ] *nm* sapphire.

**sapin** [sapɛ̃] *nm* fir (tree) ; (*bois*) fir ; ~ **de Noël** Christmas tree ; **sapinière** *nf* fir plantation *ou* forest.

**sarabande** [saʀabɑ̃d] *nf* saraband ; (*fig*) hullabaloo ; whirl.

**sarbacane** [saʀbakan] *nf* blowpipe, blowgun ; (*jouet*) peashooter.

**sarcasme** [saʀkasm(ə)] *nm* sarcasm *q* ; piece of sarcasm ; **sarcastique** *a* sarcastic.

**sarcler** [saʀkle] *vt* to weed ; **sarcloir** *nm* (weeding) hoe, spud.

**sarcophage** [saʀkɔfaʒ] *nm* sarcophagus (*pl* i).

**Sardaigne** [saʀdɛɲ] *nf*: **la ~** Sardinia ; **sarde** *a, nm/f* Sardinian.

**sardine** [saʀdin] *nf* sardine ; ~**s à l'huile** sardines in oil.

**sardonique** [saʀdɔnik] *a* sardonic.

**S.A.R.L.** *sigle voir* **société**.

**sarment** [saʀmɑ̃] *nm*: ~ **(de vigne)** vine shoot.

**sarrasin** [saʀazɛ̃] *nm* buckwheat.

**sarrau** [saʀo] *nm* smock.

**Sarre** [saʀ] *nf*: **la ~** the Saar.

**sarriette** [saʀjɛt] *nf* savory.

**sarrois, e** [saʀwa, -waz] *a* Saar *cpd* // *nm/f*: **S~, e** inhabitant *ou* native of the Saar.

**sas** [sɑ] *nm* (*de sous-marin, d'engin spatial*) airlock ; (*d'écluse*) lock.

**satané, e** [satane] *a* confounded.

**satanique** [satanik] *a* satanic, fiendish.

**satelliser** [satelize] *vt* (*fusée*) to put into orbit ; (*fig: pays*) to make into a satellite.

**satellite** [satelit] *nm* satellite ; **pays ~** satellite country ; **~-espion** *nm* spy satellite.

**satiété** [sasjete]: **à ~** *ad* to satiety *ou* satiation ; (*répéter*) ad nauseam.

**satin** [satɛ̃] *nm* satin ; **satiné, e** *a* satiny ; (*peau*) satin-smooth.

**satire** [satiʀ] *nf* satire ; **satirique** *a* satirical ; **satiriser** *vt* to satirize.

**satisfaction** [satisfaksjɔ̃] *nf* satisfaction.

**satisfaire** [satisfɛʀ] *vt* to satisfy ; **~ à** *vt* (*engagement*) to fulfil ; (*revendications, conditions*) to satisfy, meet ; to comply with ; **satisfaisant, e** *a* satisfactory ; (*qui fait plaisir*) satisfying ; **satisfait, e** *a* satisfied ; **satisfait de** happy *ou* satisfied with ; pleased with.

**saturation** [satyʀɑsjɔ̃] *nf* saturation.

**saturer** [satyʀe] *vt* to saturate.

**satyre** [satiʀ] *nm* satyr ; (*péj*) lecher.

**sauce** [sos] *nf* sauce ; (*avec un rôti*) gravy ; **~ tomate** tomato sauce ; **saucière** *nf* sauceboat ; gravy boat.

**saucisse** [sosis] *nf* sausage.

**saucisson** [sosisɔ̃] *nm* (slicing) sausage ; **~ à l'ail** garlic sausage.

**sauf** [sof] *prép* except ; **~ si** (*à moins que*) unless ; **~ erreur** if I'm not mistaken ; **~ avis contraire** unless you hear to the contrary.

**sauf, sauve** [sof, sov] *a* unharmed, unhurt ; (*fig: honneur*) intact, saved ; **laisser la vie sauve à qn** to spare sb's life.

**sauf-conduit** [sofkɔ̃dɥi] *nm* safe-conduct.

**sauge** [soʒ] *nf* sage.

**saugrenu, e** [sogʀəny] *a* preposterous, ludicrous.

**saule** [sol] *nm* willow (tree) ; **~ pleureur** weeping willow.

**saumâtre** [somɑtʀ(ə)] *a* briny.

**saumon** [somɔ̃] *nm* salmon *inv* // *a inv* salmon (pink) ; **saumoné, e** *a*: **truite saumonée** salmon trout.

**saumure** [somyʀ] *nf* brine.

**sauna** [sona] *nm* sauna.

**saupoudrer** [sopudʀe] *vt*: **~ qch de** to sprinkle sth with.

**saur** [sɔʀ] *am*: **hareng ~** smoked *ou* red herring, kipper.

**saurai** *etc vb voir* **savoir**.

**saut** [so] *nm* jump ; (*discipline sportive*) jumping ; **faire un ~** to (make a) jump *ou* leap ; **faire un ~ chez qn** to pop over to sb's (place) ; **au ~ du lit** on getting out of bed ; **~ en hauteur/longueur** high/long jump ; **~ à la corde** skipping ; **~ à la perche** pole vaulting ; **~ périlleux** somersault.

**saute** [sot] *nf*: **~ de vent/température** sudden change of wind direction/in the temperature.

**sauté, e** [sote] *a* (*CULIN*) sauté // *nm*: **~ de veau** sauté of veal.

**saute-mouton** [sotmutɔ̃] *nm*: **jouer à ~** to play leapfrog.

**sauter** [sote] *vi* to jump, leap ; (*exploser*) to blow up, explode ; (*: fusibles*) to blow ; (*se rompre*) to snap, burst ; (*se détacher*) to pop out (*ou* off) // *vt* to jump (over), leap (over) ; (*fig: omettre*) to skip, miss

(out) ; **faire ~** to blow up ; to burst open ; (*CULIN*) to sauté ; **~ à pieds joints** to make a standing jump ; **~ en parachute** to make a parachute jump ; **~ au cou de qn** to fly into sb's arms ; **~ aux yeux** to be quite obvious.

**sauterelle** [sotʀɛl] *nf* grasshopper.

**sauteur, euse** [sotœʀ, -øz] *nm/f* (*athlète*) jumper // *nf* (*casserole*) shallow casserole ; **~ à la perche** pole vaulter ; **~ à skis** skijumper.

**sautiller** [sotije] *vi* to hop ; to skip.

**sautoir** [sotwaʀ] *nm* chain ; **~ (de perles)** string of pearls.

**sauvage** [sovaʒ] *a* (*gén*) wild ; (*peuplade*) savage ; (*farouche*) unsociable ; (*barbare*) wild, savage ; (*non officiel*) unauthorized, unofficial // *nm/f* savage ; (*timide*) unsociable type, recluse ; **~rie** *nf* wildness ; savagery ; unsociability.

**sauve** [sov] *af voir* **sauf**.

**sauvegarde** [sovgaʀd(ə)] *nf* safeguard ; **sous la ~ de** under the protection of ; **sauvegarder** *vt* to safeguard.

**sauve-qui-peut** [sovkipø] *nm inv* stampede, mad rush // *excl* run for your life!

**sauver** [sove] *vt* to save ; (*porter secours à*) to rescue ; (*récupérer*) to salvage, rescue ; (*fig: racheter*) to save, redeem ; **se ~** *vi* (*s'enfuir*) to run away ; (*fam: partir*) to be off ; **~ la vie à qn** to save sb's life ; **sauvetage** *nm* rescue ; **sauveteur** *nm* rescuer ; **sauvette**: **à la sauvette** *ad* (*vendre*) without authorization ; (*se marier etc*) hastily, hurriedly ; **sauveur** *nm* saviour.

**savais** *etc vb voir* **savoir**.

**savamment** [savamɑ̃] *ad* (*avec érudition*) learnedly ; (*habilement*) skilfully, cleverly.

**savane** [savan] *nf* savannah.

**savant, e** [savɑ̃, -ɑ̃t] *a* scholarly, learned ; (*calé*) clever // *nm* scientist.

**saveur** [savœʀ] *nf* flavour ; (*fig*) savour.

**savoir** [savwaʀ] *vt* to know ; (*être capable de*): **il sait nager** he knows how to swim, he can swim // *nm* knowledge ; **se ~** (*être connu*) to be known ; **à ~** *ad* that is, namely ; **faire ~ qch à qn** to inform sb about sth, to let sb know sth ; **pas que je sache** not as far as I know ; **~-faire** *nm inv* savoir-faire, know-how.

**savon** [savɔ̃] *nm* (*produit*) soap ; (*morceau*) bar *ou* tablet of soap ; (*fam*): **passer un ~ à qn** to give sb a good dressing-down ; **savonner** *vt* to soap ; **savonnette** *nf* bar *ou* tablet of soap ; **savonneux, euse** *a* soapy.

**savons** *vb voir* **savoir**.

**savourer** [savuʀe] *vt* to savour.

**savoureux, euse** [savuʀø, -øz] *a* tasty ; (*fig*) spicy, juicy.

**saxo(phone)** [saksɔ(fɔn)] *nm* sax(ophone) ; **saxophoniste** *nm/f* saxophonist, sax(ophone) player.

**saynète** [sɛnɛt] *nf* playlet.

**sbire** [sbiʀ] *nm* (*péj*) henchman.

**scabreux, euse** [skabʀø, -øz] *a* risky ; (*indécent*) improper, shocking.

**scalpel** [skalpɛl] *nm* scalpel.

**scalper** [skalpe] vt to scalp.

**scandale** [skɑ̃dal] nm scandal ; (tapage): **faire du** ~ to make a scene, create a disturbance ; **faire** ~ to scandalize people ; **scandaleux, euse** a scandalous, outrageous ; **scandaliser** vt to scandalize ; **se scandaliser (de)** to be scandalized (by).

**scander** [skɑ̃de] vt (vers) to scan ; (slogans) to chant ; **en scandant les mots** stressing each word.

**scandinave** [skɑ̃dinav] a, nm/f Scandinavian.

**Scandinavie** [skɑ̃dinavi] nf Scandinavia.

**scaphandre** [skafɑ̃dʀ(ə)] nm (de plongeur) diving suit ; (de cosmonaute) space-suit ; ~ **autonome** aqualung.

**scarabée** [skaʀabe] nm beetle.

**scarlatine** [skaʀlatin] nf scarlet fever.

**scarole** [skaʀɔl] nf endive.

**scatologique** [skatɔlɔʒik] a scatological, lavatorial.

**sceau, x** [so] nm seal ; (fig) stamp, mark.

**scélérat, e** [seleʀa, -at] nm/f villain, blackguard.

**sceller** [sele] vt to seal.

**scellés** [sele] nmpl seals.

**scénario** [senaʀjo] nm (CINÉMA) scenario ; screenplay, script ; (fig) pattern ; scenario ; **scénariste** nm/f scriptwriter.

**scène** [sɛn] nf (gén) scene ; (estrade, fig: théâtre) stage ; **entrer en** ~ to come on stage ; **mettre en** ~ (THÉÂTRE) to stage ; (CINÉMA) to direct ; (fig) to present, introduce ; **porter à la** ~ to adapt for the stage ; **faire une** ~ (à qn) to make a scene (with sb) ; ~ **de ménage** domestic fight ou scene ; **scénique** a theatrical ; scenic.

**scepticisme** [sɛptisism(ə)] nm scepticism.

**sceptique** [sɛptik] a sceptical // nm/f sceptic.

**sceptre** [sɛptʀ(ə)] nm sceptre.

**schéma** [ʃema] nm (diagramme) diagram, sketch ; (fig) outline ; pattern ; **schématique** a diagrammatic(al), schematic ; (fig) oversimplified.

**schisme** [ʃism(ə)] nm schism ; rift, split.

**schiste** [ʃist(ə)] nm schist.

**schizophrène** [skizɔfʀɛn] nm/f schizophrenic.

**schizophrénie** [skizɔfʀeni] nf schizophrenia.

**sciatique** [sjatik] a: **nerf** ~ sciatic nerve // nf sciatica.

**scie** [si] nf saw ; (fam) catch-tune ; ~ **à bois** wood saw ; ~ **circulaire** circular saw ; ~ **à découper** fretsaw ; ~ **à métaux** hacksaw.

**sciemment** [sjamɑ̃] ad knowingly, wittingly.

**science** [sjɑ̃s] nf science ; (savoir) knowledge ; (savoir-faire) art, skill ; ~**s naturelles** (SCOL) natural science sg, biology sg ; ~**-fiction** nf science fiction ; **scientifique** a scientific // nm/f scientist ; science student.

**scier** [sje] vt to saw ; (retrancher) to saw off ; **scierie** nf sawmill ; **scieur de long** nm pit sawyer.

**scinder** [sɛ̃de] vt, **se** ~ vi to split (up).

**scintillement** [sɛ̃tijmɑ̃] nm sparkling q.

**scintiller** [sɛ̃tije] vi to sparkle.

**scission** [sisjɔ̃] nf split.

**sciure** [sjyʀ] nf: ~ **(de bois)** sawdust.

**sclérose** [skleʀoz] nf sclerosis ; (fig) ossification ; ~ **en plaques** multiple sclerosis ; **sclérosé, e** a sclerosed, sclerotic ; ossified.

**scolaire** [skɔlɛʀ] a school cpd ; (péj) schoolish ; **scolariser** vt to provide with schooling (ou schools) ; **scolarité** nf schooling ; **frais de scolarité** school fees.

**scooter** [skutœʀ] nm (motor) scooter.

**scorbut** [skɔʀbyt] nm scurvy.

**score** [skɔʀ] nm score.

**scories** [skɔʀi] nfpl scoria pl.

**scorpion** [skɔʀpjɔ̃] nm (signe): **le S**~ Scorpio, the Scorpion ; **être du S**~ to be Scorpio.

**scout, e** [skut] a, nm scout ; **scoutisme** nm (boy) scout movement ; (activités) scouting.

**scribe** [skʀib] nm scribe ; (péj) penpusher.

**script** [skʀipt] nm printing ; (CINÉMA) (shooting) script ; ~**-girl** [-gœʀl] nf continuity girl.

**scrupule** [skʀypyl] nm scruple ; **scrupuleux, euse** a scrupulous.

**scrutateur, trice** [skʀytatœʀ, -tʀis] a searching.

**scruter** [skʀyte] vt to search, scrutinize ; (l'obscurité) to peer into ; (motifs, comportement) to examine, scrutinize.

**scrutin** [skʀytɛ̃] nm (vote) ballot ; (ensemble des opérations) poll ; ~ **à deux tours** poll with two ballots ou rounds ; ~ **de liste** list system.

**sculpter** [skylte] vt to sculpt ; (suj: érosion) to carve ; **sculpteur** nm sculptor.

**sculptural, e, aux** [skyltyʀal, -o] a sculptural ; (fig) statuesque.

**sculpture** [skyltyʀ] nf sculpture ; ~ **sur bois** wood carving.

**S.D.E.C.E.** [zdɛk] sigle m = service de documentation extérieure et de contre-espionnage, ≈ Intelligence Service.

**se, s'** [s(ə)] pronom (emploi réfléchi) oneself, m himself, f herself, sujet non humain itself ; pl themselves ; (: réciproque) one another, each other ; (: passif): **cela se répare facilement** it is easily repaired ; (: possessif): ~ **casser la jambe/laver les mains** to break one's leg/wash one's hands ; autres emplois pronominaux: voir le verbe en question.

**séance** [seɑ̃s] nf (d'assemblée, récréative) meeting, session ; (de tribunal) sitting, session ; (musicale, CINÉMA, THÉÂTRE) performance ; ~ **tenante** forthwith.

**séant, e** [seɑ̃, -ɑ̃t] a seemly, fitting // nm posterior.

**seau, x** [so] nm bucket, pail ; ~ **à glace** ice-bucket.

**sec, sèche** [sɛk, sɛʃ] a dry ; (raisins, figues) dried ; (cœur, personne: insensible) hard, cold // nm: **tenir au** ~ to keep in a dry place // ad hard ; **je le bois** ~ I drink it straight ou neat ; **à** ~ a dried up.

**sécateur** [sekatœʀ] nm secateurs pl, shears pl, pair of shears ou secateurs.

**sécession** [sesesjɔ̃] nf: **faire** ~ to secede ; **la guerre de S**~ the American Civil War.

**séchage** [seʃaʒ] *nm* drying ; seasoning.
**sèche** [sɛʃ] *af voir* **sec**.
**sèche-cheveux** [sɛʃʃəvø] *nm inv* hairdrier.
**sécher** [seʃe] *vt* to dry ; (*dessécher: peau, blé*) to dry (out) ; (: *étang*) to dry up ; (*bois*) to season ; (*fam: classe, cours*) to skip // *vi* to dry ; to dry out ; to dry up ; (*fam: candidat*) to be stumped ; **se** ~ (*après le bain*) to dry o.s.
**sécheresse** [seʃRɛs] *nf* dryness ; (*absence de pluie*) drought.
**séchoir** [seʃwaR] *nm* drier.
**second, e** [səgɔ̃, -ɔd] *a* second // *nm* (*assistant*) second in command ; (NAVIG) first mate .// *nf* second ; **voyager en** ~**e** to travel second-class ; **de** ~**e main** second-hand ; **secondaire** *a* secondary ; **seconder** *vt* to assist.
**secouer** [səkwe] *vt* to shake ; (*passagers*) to rock ; (*traumatiser*) to shake (up) ; **se** ~ (*chien*) to shake itself ; (*fam: se démener*) to shake o.s. up ; ~ **la poussière d'un tapis** to shake off the dust from a carpet.
**secourable** [səkuRabl(ə)] *a* helpful.
**secourir** [səkuRiR] *vt* (*aller sauver*) to (go and) rescue ; (*prodiguer des soins à*) to help, assist ; (*venir en aide à*) to assist, aid ; **secourisme** *nm* first aid ; life saving ; **secouriste** *nm/f* first-aid worker.
**secours** [səkuR] *nm* help, aid, assistance // *nmpl* aid *sg* ; **cela lui a été d'un grand** ~ this was a great help to him ; **au** ~! help! **appeler au** ~ to shout *ou* call for help ; **appeler qn à son** ~ to call sb to one's assistance ; **porter** ~ **à qn** to give sb assistance, help sb ; **les premiers** ~ first aid *sg* ; **le** ~ **en montagne** mountain rescue.
**secousse** [səkus] *nf* jolt, bump ; (*électrique*) shock ; (*fig: psychologique*) jolt, shock ; ~ **sismique** *ou* **tellurique** earth tremor.
**secret, ète** [səkRɛ, -ɛt] *a* secret ; (*fig: renfermé*) reticent, reserved // *nm* secret ; (*discrétion absolue*): **le** ~ secrecy ; **en** ~ in secret, secretly ; **au** ~ in solitary confinement ; ~ **de fabrication** trade secret ; ~ **professionnel** professional secrecy.
**secrétaire** [səkRetɛR] *nm/f* secretary // *nm* (*meuble*) writing desk, secretaire ; ~ **d'ambassade** embassy secretary ; ~ **de direction** private *ou* personal secretary ; ~ **d'État** Secretary of State ; ~ **général** Secretary-General ; ~ **de mairie** town clerk ; ~ **de rédaction** sub-editor ; **secrétariat** *nm* (*profession*) secretarial work ; (*bureau: d'entreprise, d'école*) (secretary's) office ; (: *d'organisation internationale*) secretariat ; (POL *etc*: *fonction*) secretaryship, office of Secretary.
**sécréter** [sekRete] *vt* to secrete ; **sécrétion** [-sjɔ̃] *nf* secretion.
**sectaire** [sɛktɛR] *a* sectarian, bigoted.
**secte** [sɛkt(ə)] *nf* sect.
**secteur** [sɛktœR] *nm* sector ; (ADMIN) district ; (ÉLEC): **branché sur le** ~ plugged into the mains (supply) ; **fonctionne sur pile et** ~ battery or mains operated ; **le** ~ **privé** the private sector ; **le** ~

**primaire/tertiaire** primary/tertiary industry.
**section** [sɛksjɔ̃] *nf* section ; (*de parcours d'autobus*) fare stage ; (MIL: *unité*) platoon ; **tube de** ~ **6,5 mm** tube with a 6.5 mm bore ; ~ **rythmique** rhythm section ; **sectionner** *vt* to sever.
**sectoriel, le** [sɛktɔRjɛl] *a* sector-based.
**séculaire** [sekylɛR] *a* secular ; (*très vieux*) age-old.
**séculariser** [sekylaRize] *vt* to give (a feeling of) security to.
**séculier, ière** [sekylje, -jɛR] *a* secular.
**sécurité** [sekyRite] *nf* safety ; security ; **impression de** ~ sense of security ; **la** ~ **internationale** international security ; **système de** ~ safety system ; **être en** ~ to be safe ; **la** ~ **de l'emploi** job security ; **la** ~ **routière** road safety ; **la** ~ **sociale** ≈ (the) Social Security.
**sédatif, ive** [sedatif, -iv] *a, nm* sedative.
**sédentaire** [sedɑ̃tɛR] *a* sedentary.
**sédiment** [sedimɑ̃] *nm* sediment ; ~**s** *nmpl* (*alluvions*) sediment *sg*.
**séditieux, euse** [sedisjø, -øz] *a* insurgent ; seditious.
**sédition** [sedisjɔ̃] *nf* insurrection ; sedition.
**séducteur, trice** [sedyktœR, -tRis] *a* seductive // *nm/f* seducer/seductress.
**séduction** [sedyksjɔ̃] *nf* seduction ; (*charme, attrait*) appeal, charm.
**séduire** [seduiR] *vt* to charm ; (*femme: abuser de*) to seduce ; **séduisant, e** *a* (*femme*) seductive ; (*homme, offre*) very attractive.
**segment** [sɛgmɑ̃] *nm* segment ; (AUTO): ~ (**de piston**) piston ring ; **segmenter** *vt* to segment.
**ségrégation** [segRegasjɔ̃] *nf* segregation.
**seiche** [sɛʃ] *nf* cuttlefish.
**séide** [seid] *nm* (*péj*) henchman.
**seigle** [sɛgl(ə)] *nm* rye.
**seigneur** [sɛɲœR] *nm* lord ; **le S**~ the Lord ; ~**ial, e, aux** *a* lordly, stately.
**sein** [sɛ̃] *nm* breast ; (*entrailles*) womb ; **au** ~ **de** *prép* (*équipe, institution*) within ; (*flots, bonheur*) in the midst of ; **donner le** ~ **à** (*bébé*) to feed (at the breast) ; to breast-feed.
**séisme** [seism(ə)] *nm* earthquake.
**séismique** [seismik] *etc voir* **sismique** etc.
**seize** [sɛz] *num* sixteen ; **seizième** *num* sixteenth.
**séjour** [seʒuR] *nm* stay ; (*pièce*) living room ; ~**ner** *vi* to stay.
**sel** [sɛl] *nm* salt ; (*fig*) wit ; spice ; ~ **de cuisine/de table** cooking/table salt ; ~ **gemme** rock salt.
**sélection** [selɛksjɔ̃] *nf* selection ; ~ **professionnelle** professional recruitment ; **sélectionner** *vt* to select.
**self-service** [sɛlfsɛRvis] *a, nm* self-service.
**selle** [sɛl] *nf* saddle ; ~**s** *nfpl* (MÉD) stools ; **aller à la** ~ (MÉD) to pass a motion ; **se mettre en** ~ to mount, get into the saddle ; **seller** *vt* to saddle.
**sellette** [sɛlɛt] *nf*: **être sur la** ~ to be on the carpet.
**sellier** [selje] *nm* saddler.

**selon** [səlɔ̃] *prép* according to; (*en se conformant à*) in accordance with.

**semailles** [səmɑj] *nfpl* sowing *sg.*

**semaine** [səmɛn] *nf* week; **en ~** during the week, on weekdays.

**sémantique** [semɑ̃tik] *a* semantic // *nf* semantics *sg.*

**sémaphore** [semafɔR] *nm* semaphore signal.

**semblable** [sɑ̃blabl(ə)] *a* similar; (*de ce genre*): **de ~s mésaventures** such mishaps // *nm* fellow creature *ou* man; **~ à** similar to, like.

**semblant** [sɑ̃blɑ̃] *nm*: **un ~ de vérité** a semblance of truth; **faire ~ (de faire)** to pretend (to do).

**sembler** [sɑ̃ble] *vb avec attribut* to seem // *vb impersonnel*: **il semble que/inutile de** it seems *ou* appears that/useless to; **il me semble que** it seems to me that; I think (that); **~ être** to seem to be; **comme bon lui semble** as he sees fit.

**semelle** [səmɛl] *nf* sole; (*intérieure*) insole, inner sole; **~s compensées** platform soles.

**semence** [səmɑ̃s] *nf* (*graine*) seed; (*clou*) tack.

**semer** [səme] *vt* to sow; (*fig: éparpiller*) to scatter; (: *poursuivants*) to lose, shake off; **semé de** (*difficultés*) riddled with.

**semestre** [səmɛstR(ə)] *nm* half-year; (*SCOL*) semester; **semestriel, le** *a* half-yearly; semestral.

**semeur, euse** [səmœR, -øz] *nm/f* sower.

**sémillant, e** [semijɑ̃, -ɑ̃t] *a* vivacious; dashing.

**séminaire** [seminɛR] *nm* seminar; (*REL*) seminary; **séminariste** *nm* seminarist.

**semi-remorque** [səmiRəmɔRk(ə)] *nf* trailer // *nm* articulated lorry.

**semis** [səmi] *nm* (*terrain*) seedbed, seed plot; (*plante*) seedling.

**sémite** [semit] *a* Semitic.

**sémitique** [semitik] *a* Semitic.

**semoir** [səmwaR] *nm* seed-bag; seeder.

**semonce** [səmɔ̃s] *nf* reprimand; **coup de ~** warning shot across the bows.

**semoule** [səmul] *nf* semolina.

**sempiternel, le** [sɛpitɛRnɛl] *a* eternal, never-ending.

**sénat** [sena] *nm* Senate; **sénateur** *nm* Senator.

**sénile** [senil] *a* senile; **sénilité** *nf* senility.

**sens** [sɑ̃s] *nm* (*PHYSIOL, instinct*) sense; (*signification*) meaning, sense; (*direction*) direction // *nmpl* (*sensualité*) senses; **reprendre ses ~** to regain consciousness; **avoir le ~ des affaires/de la mesure** to have business sense/a sense of moderation; **ça n'a pas de ~** that doesn't make (any) sense; **dans le ~ des aiguilles d'une montre** clockwise; **~ commun** common sense; **~ dessus dessous** upside down; **~ interdit, ~ unique** one-way street.

**sensation** [sɑ̃sɑsjɔ̃] *nf* sensation; **faire ~** to cause a sensation, create a stir; **à ~** (*péj*) sensational; **sensationnel, le** *a* sensational; (*fig*) terrific.

**sensé, e** [sɑ̃se] *a* sensible.

**sensibiliser** [sɑ̃sibilize] *vt*: **~ qn à** to make sb sensitive to.

**sensibilité** [sɑ̃sibilite] *nf* sensitivity; (*affectivité, émotivité*) sensitivity, sensibility.

**sensible** [sɑ̃sibl(ə)] *a* sensitive; (*aux sens*) perceptible; (*appréciable*: différence, progrès) appreciable, noticeable; **~ à** sensitive to; **~ment** *ad* (*notablement*) appreciably, noticeably; (*à peu près*): **ils ont ~ment le même poids** they weigh approximately the same; **~rie** *nf* sentimentality, mawkishness; squeamishness.

**sensitif, ive** [sɑ̃sitif, -iv] *a* (*nerf*) sensory; (*personne*) oversensitive.

**sensoriel, le** [sɑ̃sɔRjɛl] *a* sensory, sensorial.

**sensualité** [sɑ̃sɥalite] *nf* sensuality; sensuousness.

**sensuel, le** [sɑ̃sɥɛl] *a* sensual; sensuous.

**sente** [sɑ̃t] *nf* path.

**sentence** [sɑ̃tɑ̃s] *nf* (*jugement*) sentence; (*adage*) maxim; **sentencieux, euse** *a* sententious.

**senteur** [sɑ̃tœR] *nf* scent, perfume.

**sentier** [sɑ̃tje] *nm* path.

**sentiment** [sɑ̃timɑ̃] *nm* feeling; **recevez mes ~s respectueux** yours faithfully; **faire du ~** (*péj*) to be sentimental; **sentimental, e, aux** *a* sentimental; (*vie, aventure*) love *cpd.*

**sentinelle** [sɑ̃tinɛl] *nf* sentry; **en ~** on sentry duty; standing guard.

**sentir** [sɑ̃tiR] *vt* (*par l'odorat*) to smell; (*par le goût*) to taste; (*au toucher, fig*) to feel; (*répandre une odeur de*) to smell of; (: *ressemblance*) to smell like; (*avoir la saveur de*) to taste of; (*à taste like; (fig: dénoter, annoncer*) to be indicative of; to smack of; to foreshadow // *vi* to smell; **~ mauvais** to smell bad; **se ~ bien** to feel good; **se ~ mal** (*être indisposé*) to feel unwell *ou* ill; **se ~ le courage/la force de faire** to feel brave/strong enough to do; **ne plus se ~ de joie** to be beside o.s. with joy; **il ne peut pas le ~** (*fam*) he can't stand him.

**seoir** [swaR]: **~ à** *vt* to become.

**séparation** [sepaRɑsjɔ̃] *nf* separation; (*cloison*) division, partition; **~ de biens** division of property (*in marriage settlement*); **~ de corps** legal separation.

**séparatisme** [sepaRatism(ə)] *nm* separatism.

**séparé, e** [sepaRe] *a* (*appartements, pouvoirs*) separate; (*époux*) separated; **~ de** separate from; separated from; **~ment** *ad* separately.

**séparer** [sepaRe] *vt* (*gén*) to separate; (*suj: divergences etc*) to divide; to drive apart; (: *différences, obstacles*) to stand between; (*détacher*): **~ qch de** to pull sth (off) from; (*dissocier*) to distinguish between; (*diviser*): **~ qch par** to divide sth (up) with; **~ une pièce en deux** to divide a room into two; **se ~** (*époux*) to separate, part; (*prendre congé: amis etc*) to part, leave each other; (*adversaires*) to separate; (*se diviser: route, tige etc*) to divide; (*se détacher*): **se ~ (de)** to split off (from); to come off; **se ~ de** (*époux*)

to separate *ou* part from ; (*employé, objet personnel*) to part with.
**sept** [sɛt] *num* seven.
**septembre** [sɛptɑ̃bʀ(ə)] *nm* September.
**septennat** [sɛpetena] *nm* seven-year term (of office) ; seven-year reign.
**septentrional, e, aux** [sɛptɑ̃tʀijɔnal, -o] *a* northern.
**septicémie** [sɛptisemi] *nf* blood poisoning, septicaemia.
**septième** [sɛtjɛm] *num* seventh.
**septique** [sɛptik] *a* : **fosse** ~ septic tank.
**septuagénaire** [sɛptɥaʒenɛʀ] *a, nm/f* septuagenarian.
**sépulcre** [sepylkʀ(ə)] *nm* sepulchre.
**sépulture** [sepyltyʀ] *nf* burial ; burial place, grave.
**séquelles** [sekɛl] *nfpl* after-effects ; (*fig*) aftermath *sg* ; consequences.
**séquence** [sekɑ̃s] *nf* sequence.
**séquestre** [sekɛstʀ(ə)] *nm* impoundment ; **mettre sous** ~ to impound.
**séquestrer** [sekɛstʀe] *vt* (*personne*) to confine illegally ; (*biens*) to impound.
**serai** *etc vb voir* **être**.
**serein, e** [səʀɛ̃, -ɛn] *a* serene ; (*jugement*) dispassionate.
**sérénade** [seʀenad] *nf* serenade ; (*fam*) hullabaloo.
**sérénité** [seʀenite] *nf* serenity.
**serez** *vb voir* **être**.
**serf, serve** [sɛʀ, sɛʀv(ə)] *nm/f* serf.
**serge** [sɛʀʒ(ə)] *nf* serge.
**sergent** [sɛʀʒɑ̃] *nm* sergeant ; ~**-chef** *nm* staff sergeant ; ~**-major** *nm* ≈ quartermaster sergeant.
**sériciculture** [seʀisikyltyʀ] *nf* silkworm breeding, sericulture.
**série** [seʀi] *nf* (*de questions, d'accidents*) series *inv* ; (*de clés, casseroles, outils*) set ; (*catégorie: SPORT*) rank ; class ; **en** ~ in quick succession ; (*COMM*) mass *cpd* ; **de** ~ *a* standard ; **hors** ~ (*COMM*) custom-built ; (*fig*) outstanding ; ~ **noire** *nm* (crime) thriller ; **sérier** *vt* to classify, sort out.
**sérieusement** [seʀjøzmɑ̃] *ad* seriously ; reliably ; responsibly ; ~? do you mean it?, are you talking in earnest?
**sérieux, euse** [seʀjø, -øz] *a* serious ; (*élève, employé*) reliable, responsible ; (*client, maison*) reliable, dependable ; (*offre, proposition*) genuine, serious ; (*grave, sévère*) serious, solemn ; (*maladie, situation*) serious, grave // *nm* seriousness ; reliability ; **garder son** ~ to keep a straight face ; **manquer de** ~ not to be very responsible (*ou* reliable) ; **prendre qch/qn au** ~ to take sth/sb seriously.
**serin** [səʀɛ̃] *nm* canary.
**seriner** [səʀine] *vt* : ~ **qch à qn** to drum sth into sb.
**seringue** [səʀɛ̃g] *nf* syringe.
**serions** *vb voir* **être**.
**serment** [sɛʀmɑ̃] *nm* (*juré*) oath ; (*promesse*) pledge, vow ; **faire le** ~ **de** to take a vow to, swear to ; **sous** ~ on *ou* under oath.
**sermon** [sɛʀmɔ̃] *nm* sermon ; (*péj*) sermon, lecture.

**serpe** [sɛʀp(ə)] *nf* billhook.
**serpent** [sɛʀpɑ̃] *nm* snake ; ~ **à sonnettes** rattlesnake.
**serpenter** [sɛʀpɑ̃te] *vi* to wind.
**serpentin** [sɛʀpɑ̃tɛ̃] *nm* (*tube*) coil ; (*ruban*) streamer.
**serpillière** [sɛʀpijɛʀ] *nf* floorcloth.
**serrage** [sɛʀaʒ] *nm* tightening ; **collier de** ~ clamp.
**serre** [sɛʀ] *nf* (*AGR*) greenhouse ; ~**s** *nfpl* (*griffes*) claws, talons ; ~ **chaude** hothouse.
**serré, e** [seʀe] *a* (*tissu*) closely woven ; (*réseau*) dense ; (*écriture*) close ; (*habits*) tight ; (*fig: lutte, match*) tight, close-fought ; (*passagers etc*) (tightly) packed.
**serre-livres** [sɛʀlivʀ(ə)] *nm inv* book ends *pl*.
**serrement** [sɛʀmɑ̃] *nm* : ~ **de main** handshake ; ~ **de cœur** pang of anguish.
**serrer** [seʀe] *vt* (*tenir*) to grip *ou* hold tight ; (*comprimer, coincer*) to squeeze ; (*poings, mâchoires*) to clench ; (*suj: vêtement*) to be too tight for ; to fit tightly ; (*rapprocher*) to close up, move closer together ; (*ceinture, nœud, frein, vis*) to tighten // *vi* : ~ **à droite** to keep to the right ; to move into the right-hand lane ; **se** ~ (*se rapprocher*) to squeeze up ; **se** ~ **contre qn** to huddle up to sb ; **se** ~ **les coudes** to stick together, back one another up ; ~ **la main à qn** to shake sb's hand ; ~ **qn dans ses bras** to hug sb, clasp sb in one's arms ; ~ **la gorge à qn** (*suj: chagrin*) to bring a lump to sb's throat ; ~ **qn de près** to follow close behind sb ; ~ **le trottoir** to hug the kerb ; ~ **sa droite** to keep well to the right ; ~ **la vis à qn** to crack down harder on sb.
**serre-tête** [sɛʀtɛt] *nm inv* (*bandeau*) headband ; (*bonnet*) skullcap.
**serrure** [seʀyʀ] *nf* lock.
**serrurerie** [seʀyʀʀi] *nf* (*métier*) locksmith's trade ; ~ **d'art** ornamental ironwork.
**serrurier** [seʀyʀje] *nm* locksmith.
**sert** *etc vb voir* **servir**.
**sertir** [sɛʀtiʀ] *vt* (*pierre*) to set ; (*pièces métalliques*) to crimp.
**sérum** [seʀɔm] *nm* serum ; ~ **antivenimeux** snakebite serum ; ~ **sanguin** (blood) serum ; ~ **de vérité** truth drug.
**servage** [sɛʀvaʒ] *nm* serfdom.
**servant** [sɛʀvɑ̃] *nm* server.
**servante** [sɛʀvɑ̃t] *nf* (maid)servant.
**serve** [sɛʀv] *nf voir* **serf**.
**serveur, euse** [sɛʀvœʀ, -øz] *nm/f* waiter/waitress.
**serviable** [sɛʀvjabl(ə)] *a* obliging, willing to help.
**service** [sɛʀvis] *nm* (*gén*) service ; (*série de repas*) : **premier** ~ first sitting ; (*pourboire*) service (charge) ; (*assortiment de vaisselle*) set, service ; (*bureau: de la vente etc*) department, section ; (*travail*) : **pendant le** ~ on duty ; ~**s** *nmpl* (*travail, ÉCON*) services ; **faire le** ~ to serve ; **être en chez qn** (*domestique*) to be in sb's service ; **être au** ~ **de** (*patron, patrie*) to be in the service of ; **être au** ~ **de qn** (*collaborateur, voiture*) to be at sb's service ; **rendre** ~

à to help ; **il aime rendre** ~ he likes to help ; **rendre un** ~ **à qn** to do sb a favour ; **heures de** ~ hours of duty ; **être de** ~ to be on duty ; **avoir 25 ans de** ~ to have completed 25 years' service ; **être/mettre en** ~ to be in/put into service *ou* operation ; ~ **à thé/café** tea/coffee set *ou* service ; ~ **après vente** after-sales service ; **en** ~ **commandé** on an official assignment ; ~ **funèbre** funeral service ; ~ **militaire** military service ; ~ **d'ordre** police (*ou* stewards) in charge of maintaining order ; ~**s secrets** secret service *sg.*

**serviette** [sɛRvjɛt] *nf* (*de table*) (table) napkin, serviette ; (*de toilette*) towel ; (*porte-documents*) briefcase ; ~ **hygiénique** sanitary towel *ou* pad ; ~**-éponge** *nf* terry towel.

**servile** [sɛRvil] *a* servile.

**servir** [sɛRviR] *vt* (*gén*) to serve ; (*dîneur: au restaurant*) to wait on ; (*client: au magasin*) to serve, attend to ; (*fig: aider*): ~ **qn** to aid sb ; to serve sb's interests ; to stand sb in good stead ; (*COMM: rente*) to pay // *vi* (*TENNIS*) to serve ; (*CARTES*) to deal ; **se** ~ (*prendre d'un plat*) to help o.s. ; **se** ~ **de** (*plat*) to help o.s. to ; (*voiture, outil, relations*) to use ; ~ **à qn** (*diplôme, livre*) to be of use to sb ; **ça m'a servi pour faire** it was useful to me when I did ; I used it to do ; ~ **à qch/faire** (*outil etc*) to be used for sth/doing ; **ça peut** ~ it may come in handy ; **ça peut encore** ~ it can still be used (*ou* of use) ; **à quoi cela sert-il (de faire)?** what's the use (of doing)? ; **cela ne sert à rien** ¦t's no use ; ~ **(à qn) de** to serve as (for sb) ; ~ **la messe** to serve Mass ; ~ **à dîner (à qn)** to serve dinner (to sb).

**serviteur** [sɛRvitœR] *nm* servant.

**servitude** [sɛRvityd] *nf* servitude ; (*fig*) constraint ; (*JUR*) easement.

**servo...** [sɛRvo] *préfixe*: ~**frein** servo (-assisted) brake.

**ses** [se] *dét voir* **son**.

**session** [sesjɔ̃] *nf* session.

**set** [sɛt] *nm* set.

**seuil** [sœj] *nm* doorstep ; (*fig*) threshold ; **sur le** ~ **de sa maison** in the doorway of his house, on his doorstep ; **au** ~ **de** (*fig*) on the threshold *ou* brink *ou* edge of.

**seul, e** [sœl] *a* (*sans compagnie, en isolation*) alone ; (*avec nuance affective: isolé*) lonely ; (*unique*): **un** ~ **livre** only one book, a single book ; **le** ~ **livre** the only book ; ~ **ce livre, ce livre** ~ this book alone, only this book // *ad* (*vivre*) alone, on one's own ; **parler tout** ~ to talk to oneself ; **faire qch (tout)** ~ to do sth (all) on one's own *ou* (all) by oneself // *nm*, **nf il en reste un(e)** ~**(e)** there's only one left ; **à lui (tout)** ~ single-handed, on his own.

**seulement** [sœlmã] *ad* (*pas davantage*): ~ **5, 5** ~ only 5 ; (*exclusivement*): ~ **eux** only them, them alone ; (*pas avant*): ~ **hier/à 10h** only yesterday/at 10 o'clock ; **non** ~ **... mais aussi** *ou* **encore** not only ... but also

**sève** [sɛv] *nf* sap.

**sévère** [sevɛR] *a* severe ; **sévérité** *nf* severity.

**sévices** [sevis] *nmpl* (physical) cruelty *sg*, ill treatment *sg*.

**sévir** [seviR] *vi* (*punir*) to use harsh measures, crack down ; (*suj: fléau*) to rage, be rampant ; ~ **contre** (*abus*) to deal ruthlessly with, crack down on.

**sevrer** [səvRe] *vt* to wean ; (*fig*): ~ **qn de** to deprive sb of.

**sexagénaire** [sɛgzaʒenɛR] *a*, *nm/f* sexagenarian.

**sexe** [sɛks(ə)] *nm* sex ; (*organe mâle*) member ; **sexologue** *nm/f* sexologist, sex specialist.

**sextant** [sɛkstã] *nm* sextant.

**sexualité** [sɛksyalite] *nf* sexuality.

**sexué, e** [sɛksye] *a* sexual.

**sexuel, le** [sɛksyɛl] *a* sexual ; **acte** ~ sex act.

**seyait** *vb voir* **seoir**.

**seyant, e** [sejã, -ãt] *a* becoming.

**shampooing** [ʃãpwɛ̃] *nm* shampoo ; **se faire un** ~ to shampoo one's hair ; ~ **colorant** (colour) rinse.

**short** [ʃɔRt] *nm* (pair of) shorts *pl*.

**si** [si] *nm* (*MUS*) B ; (*en chantant la gamme*) si, se // *ad* (*oui*) yes ; (*tellement*) so // *cj* if ; ~ **seulement** if only ; (**tant et**) ~ **bien que** so much so that ; ~ **rapide qu'il soit** however fast he may be, fast though he is ; **je me demande** ~ I wonder if *ou* whether.

**siamois, e** [sjamwa, -waz] *a* Siamese ; **frères/sœurs siamois/es** Siamese twins.

**Sicile** [sisil] *nf*: **la** ~ Sicily ; **sicilien, ne** *a* Sicilian.

**sidéré, e** [sideRe] *a* staggered.

**sidérurgie** [sideRyRʒi] *nf* iron and steel industry.

**siècle** [sjɛkl(ə)] *nm* century ; (*époque*) age ; (*REL*): **le** ~ the world.

**sied** [sje] *vb voir* **seoir**.

**siège** [sjɛʒ] *nm* seat ; (*d'entreprise*) head office ; (*d'organisation*) headquarters *pl* ; (*MIL*) siege ; **mettre le** ~ **devant** to besiege ; **présentation par le** ~ (*MÉD*) breech presentation ; ~ **baquet** bucket seat ; ~ **social** registered office.

**siéger** [sjeʒe] *vi* to sit.

**sien, ne** [sjɛ̃, sjɛn] *pronom*: **le(la)** ~**(ne)**, **les** ~**s(**~**nes)** his ; hers ; its ; **faire des** ~**nes** (*fam*) to be up to one's (usual) tricks ; **les** ~**s** (*sa famille*) one's family.

**siérait** *etc vb voir* **seoir**.

**sieste** [sjɛst(ə)] *nf* (afternoon) snooze *ou* nap, siesta ; **faire la** ~ to have a snooze *ou* nap.

**sieur** [sjœR] *nm*: **le** ~ **Thomas** Mr Thomas ; (*en plaisantant*) Master Thomas.

**sifflant, e** [siflã, -ãt] *a* (*bruit*) whistling ; (*toux*) wheezing ; (**consonne**) ~**e** sibilant.

**sifflement** [sifləmã] *nm* whistle, whistling *q* ; hissing noise ; whistling noise.

**siffler** [sifle] *vi* (*gén*) to whistle ; (*avec un sifflet*) to blow (on) one's whistle ; (*en parlant, dormant*) to wheeze ; (*serpent, vapeur*) to hiss // *vt* (*chanson*) to whistle ; (*chien etc*) to whistle for ; (*fille*) to whistle at ; (*pièce, orateur*) to hiss, boo ; (*faute*) to blow one's whistle at ; (*fin du match, départ*) to blow one's whistle for ; (*fam: verre, bouteille*) to guzzle, knock back.

**sifflet** [siflɛ] *nm* whistle ; ~s *nmpl* (*de mécontentement*) whistles, boos ; **coup de** ~ whistle.

**siffloter** [siflɔte] *vi, vt* to whistle.

**sigle** [sigl(ə)] *nm* acronym, (set of) initials *pl.*

**signal, aux** [siɲal, -o] *nm* (*signe convenu, appareil*) signal ; (*indice, écriteau*) sign ; **donner le** ~ **de** to give the signal for ; ~ **d'alarme** alarm signal ; ~ **horaire** time signal ; **signaux (lumineux)** (AUTO) traffic signals.

**signalement** [siɲalmɑ̃] *nm* description, particulars *pl.*

**signaler** [siɲale] *vt* to indicate ; to announce ; to report ; (*faire remarquer*): ~ **qch à qn/à qn que** to point out sth to sb/to sb that ; **se** ~ **par** to distinguish o.s. by ; **se** ~ **à l'attention de qn** to attract sb's attention.

**signalétique** [siɲaletik] *a:* **fiche** ~ identification sheet.

**signalisation** [siɲalizasjɔ̃] *nf* signalling, signposting ; signals *pl,* roadsigns *pl ;* **panneau de** ~ roadsign.

**signaliser** [siɲalize] *vt* to put up roadsigns on ; to put signals on.

**signataire** [siɲatɛʀ] *nm/f* signatory.

**signature** [siɲatyʀ] *nf* signing ; signature.

**signe** [siɲ] *nm* sign ; (TYPO) mark ; **c'est bon** ~ it's a good sign ; **faire un** ~ **de la main** to give a sign with one's hand ; **faire** ~ **à qn** (*fig*) to get in touch with sb ; **faire** ~ **à qn d'entrer** to motion (to) sb to come in ; **en** ~ **de** as a sign *ou* mark of ; **le** ~ **de la croix** the sign of the Cross ; ~ **de ponctuation** punctuation mark ; ~ **du zodiaque** sign of the zodiac.

**signer** [siɲe] *vt* to sign , **se** ~ *vi* to cross o.s.

**signet** [siɲɛ] *nm* bookmark.

**significatif, ive** [siɲifikatif, -iv] *a* significant.

**signification** [siɲifikasjɔ̃] *nf* meaning.

**signifier** [siɲifje] *vt* (*vouloir dire*) to mean, signify ; (*faire connaître*): ~ **qch (à qn)** to make sth known (to sb) ; (JUR): ~ **qch à qn** to serve notice of sth on sb.

**silence** [silɑ̃s] *nm* silence ; (MUS) rest ; **garder le** ~ to keep silent, say nothing ; **passer sous** ~ to pass over (in silence) ; **réduire au** ~ to silence ; **silencieux, euse** *a* quiet, silent // *nm* silencer.

**silex** [silɛks] *nm* flint.

**silhouette** [silwɛt] *nf* outline, silhouette ; (*lignes, contour*) outline ; (*figure*) figure.

**silicium** [silisjɔm] *nm* silicon.

**silicone** [silikon] *nf* silicone.

**silicose** [silikoz] *nf* silicosis, dust disease.

**sillage** [sijaʒ] *nm* wake ; (*fig*) trail.

**sillon** [sijɔ̃] *nm* furrow ; (*de disque*) groove ; **sillonner** *vt* to furrow ; to cross, criss-cross.

**silo** [silo] *nm* silo.

**simagrées** [simagʀe] *nfpl* fuss *sg ;* airs and graces.

**simiesque** [simjɛsk(ə)] *a* monkcy-like, ape-like.

**similaire** [similɛʀ] *a* similar ; **similarité** *nf* similarity ; **simili...** *préfixe* imitation *cpd,*

artificial ; **similicuir** *nm* imitation leather ; **similitude** *nf* similarity.

**simple** [sɛ̃pl(ə)] *a* (*gén*) simple ; (*non multiple*) single ; ~s *nmpl* (MÉD) medicinal plants ; ~ **messieurs** (TENNIS) men's singles *sg ;* **un** ~ **particulier** an ordinary citizen ; **cela varie du** ~ **au double** it can double, it can be double the price *etc ;* ~ **course** *a* single ; ~ **d'esprit** *nm/f* simpleton ; ~ **soldat** private ; **simplicité** *nf* simplicity ; **simplifier** *vt* to simplify ; **simpliste** *a* simplistic.

**simulacre** [simylakʀ(ə)] *nm* enactement ; (*péj*): **un** ~ **de** a pretence of, a sham.

**simulateur, trice** [simylatœʀ, -tʀis] *nm/f* shammer, pretender ; (*qui se prétend malade*) malingerer // *nm:* ~ **de vol** flight simulator.

**simulation** [simylasjɔ̃] *nf* shamming, simulation ; malingering.

**simuler** [simyle] *vt* to sham, simulate ; (*suj: substance, revêtement*) to simulate.

**simultané, e** [simyltane] *a* simultaneous ; ~**ment** *ad* simultaneously.

**sincère** [sɛ̃sɛʀ] *a* sincere ; genuine ; heartfelt ; **sincérité** *nf* sincerity.

**sinécure** [sinekyʀ] *nf* sinecure.

**sine die** [sinedje] *ad* sine die, indefinitely.

**sine qua non** [sinekwanɔn] *a:* **condition** ~ indispensable condition.

**singe** [sɛ̃ʒ] *nm* monkey ; (*de grande taille*) ape.

**singer** [sɛ̃ʒe] *vt* to ape, mimic.

**singeries** [sɛ̃ʒʀi] *nfpl* antics ; (*simagrées*) airs and graces.

**singulariser** [sɛ̃gylaʀize] *vt* to mark out ; **se** ~ to call attention to o.s.

**singularité** [sɛ̃gylaʀite] *nf* peculiarity.

**singulier, ière** [sɛ̃gylje, -jɛʀ] *a* remarkable, singular ; (LING) singular // *nm* singular.

**sinistre** [sinistʀ(ə)] *a* sinister // *nm* (*incendie*) blaze ; (*catastrophe*) disaster ; (ASSURANCES) accident (*giving rise to a claim*) ; **sinistré, e** *a* disaster-stricken // *nm/f* disaster victim.

**sino...** [sino] *préfixe:* ~-**indien** Sino-Indian, Chinese-Indian.

**sinon** [sinɔ̃] *cj* (*autrement, sans quoi*) otherwise, or else ; (*sauf*) except, other than ; (*si ce n'est*) if not.

**sinueux, euse** [sinɥø, -øz] *a* winding ; (*fig*) tortuous ; **sinuosités** *nfpl* winding *sg,* curves.

**sinus** [sinys] *nm* (ANAT) sinus ; (GÉOM) sine ; **sinusite** *nf* sinusitis, sinus infection.

**sionisme** [sjɔnism(ə)] *nm* Zionism.

**siphon** [sifɔ̃] *nm* (*tube, d'eau gazeuse*) siphon ; (*d'évier etc*) U-bend ; **siphonner** *vt* to siphon.

**sire** [siʀ] *nm* (*titre*): **S**~ Sire ; **un triste** ~ an unsavoury individual.

**sirène** [siʀɛn] *nf* siren ; ~ **d'alarme** air-raid siren ; fire alarm.

**sirop** [siʀo] *nm* (*à diluer: de fruit etc*) syrup, cordial ; (*boisson*) cordial ; (*pharmaceutique*) syrup, mixture ; ~ **de menthe** mint syrup *ou* cordial ; ~ **contre la toux** cough syrup *ou* mixture.

**siroter** [siʀɔte] *vt* to sip.

**sis, e** [si, siz] *a*: ~ **rue de la Paix** located in the rue de la Paix.
**sismique** [sismik] *a* seismic.
**sismographe** [sismɔgʀaf] *nm* seismograph.
**sismologie** [sismɔlɔʒi] *nf* seismology.
**site** [sit] *nm* (*paysage, environnement*) setting; (*d'une ville etc: emplacement*) site; ~ **(pittoresque)** beauty spot; ~**s touristiques** places of interest; ~**s naturels/historiques** natural/ historic sites.
**sitôt** [sito] *ad*: ~ **parti** as soon as he had left; **pas de** ~ not for a long time.
**situation** [situɑsjɔ̃] *nf* (*gén*) situation; (*d'un édifice, d'une ville*) situation, position; location.
**situé, e** [situe] *a*: **bien** ~ well situated, in a good location; ~ **à/près de** situated at/near.
**situer** [situe] *vt* to site, situate; (*en pensée*) to set, place; **se** ~ *vi*: **se** ~ **à/près de** to be situated at/near.
**six** [sis] *num* six; **sixième** *num* sixth.
**sketch** [skɛtʃ] *nm* (variety) sketch.
**ski** [ski] *nm* (*objet*) ski; (*sport*) skiing; **faire du** ~ to ski; ~ **de fond** lang-lauf; ~ **nautique** water-skiing; ~ **de piste** downhill skiing; ~ **de randonnée** cross-country skiing; **skier** *vi* to ski; **skieur, euse** *nm/f* skier.
**slalom** [slalɔm] *nm* slalom; **faire du** ~ **entre** to slalom between; ~ **géant/spécial** giant/special slalom.
**slave** [slav] *a* Slav(onic), Slavic.
**slip** [slip] *nm* (*sous-vêtement*) pants *pl*, briefs *pl*; (*de bain: d'homme*) (bathing *ou* swimming) trunks *pl*; (: *du bikini*) (bikini) briefs *pl*.
**slogan** [slɔgɑ̃] *nm* slogan.
**S.M.I.C., S.M.I.G.** [smik, smig] *sigle m* voir **salaire**.
**smoking** [smɔkiŋ] *nm* dinner *ou* evening suit.
**snack** [snak] *nm* snack bar.
**S.N.C.F.** *sigle f* = *société nationale des chemins de fer français*, ≈ British Rail.
**snob** [snɔb] *a* snobbish // *nm/f* snob; ~**isme** *nm* snobbery.
**sobre** [sɔbʀ(ə)] *a* temperate, abstemious; (*élégance, style*) sober; ~ **de** (*gestes, compliments*) sparing of; **sobriété** *nf* temperance, abstemiousness; sobriety.
**sobriquet** [sɔbʀikɛ] *nm* nickname.
**soc** [sɔk] *nm* ploughshare.
**sociable** [sɔsjabl(ə)] *a* sociable.
**social, e, aux** [sɔsjal, -o] *a* social.
**socialisme** [sɔsjalism(ə)] *nm* socialism; **socialiste** *nm/f* socialist.
**sociétaire** [sɔsjetɛʀ] *nm/f* member.
**société** [sɔsjete] *nf* society; (*sportive*) club; (*COMM*) company; **la bonne** ~ polite society; **la** ~ **d'abondance/de consommation** the affluent/consumer society; ~ **anonyme (S.A.)** ≈ limited company; ~ **à responsabilité limitée (S.A.R.L.)** *type of limited liability company* (*with non negotiable shares*).
**sociologie** [sɔsjɔlɔʒi] *nf* sociology; **sociologue** *nm/f* sociologist.

**socle** [sɔkl(ə)] *nm* (*de colonne, statue*) plinth, pedestal; (*de lampe*) base.
**socquette** [sɔkɛt] *nf* ankle sock.
**sodium** [sɔdjɔm] *nm* sodium.
**sœur** [sœʀ] *nf* sister; (*religieuse*) nun, sister; ~ **Élisabeth** (*REL*) Sister Elizabeth.
**soi** [swa] *pronom* oneself; **cela va de** ~ that *ou* it goes without saying, it stands to reason; ~**-disant** *a inv* so-called // *ad* supposedly.
**soie** [swa] *nf* silk; (*de porc, sanglier: poil*) bristle; ~**rie** *nf* (*industrie*) silk trade; (*tissu*) silk.
**soif** [swaf] *nf* thirst; (*fig*): ~ **de** thirst *ou* craving for; **avoir** ~ to be thirsty; **donner** ~ **à qn** to make sb thirsty.
**soigné, e** [swaɲe] *a* (*tenue*) well-groomed, neat; (*travail*) careful, meticulous; (*fam*) whopping; stiff.
**soigner** [swaɲe] *vt* (*malade, maladie: suj: docteur*) to treat; (*suj: infirmière, mère*) to nurse, look after; (*blessé*) to tend; (*travail, détails*) to take care over; (*jardin, chevelure, invités*) to look after; **soigneur** *nm* (*CYCLISME, FOOTBALL*) trainer; (*BOXE*) second.
**soigneusement** [swaɲøzmɑ̃] *ad* carefully.
**soigneux, euse** [swaɲø, -øz] *a* (*propre*) tidy, neat; (*méticuleux*) painstaking, careful; ~ **de** careful with.
**soi-même** [swamɛm] *pronom* oneself.
**soin** [swɛ̃] *nm* (*application*) care; (*propreté, ordre*) tidiness, neatness; (*responsabilité*): **le** ~ **de qch** the care of sth; ~**s** *nmpl* (*à un malade, blessé*) treatment *sg*, medical attention *sg*; (*attentions, prévenance*) care and attention *sg*; (*hygiène*) care *sg*; ~**s de la chevelure/de beauté** hair-/beauty care; **les** ~**s du ménage** the care of the home; **avoir** *ou* **prendre** ~ **de** to take care of, look after; **avoir** *ou* **prendre** ~ **de faire** to take care to do; **sans** ~ *a* careless; untidy; **les premiers** ~**s** first aid *sg*; **aux bons** ~**s de** c/o, care of.
**soir** [swaʀ] *nm, ad* evening; **ce** ~ this evening, tonight; **demain** ~ tomorrow evening, tomorrow night.
**soirée** [swaʀe] *nf* evening; (*réception*) party; **donner en** ~ (*film, pièce*) to give an evening performance of.
**soit** [swa] *vb* voir **être**; ~ **un triangle ABC** let ABC be a triangle // *cj* (*à savoir*) namely, to wit; (*ou*): ~ ... ~ either ... or // *ad* so be it, very well; ~ **que** ... ~ **que** *ou* **ou que** whether ... or whether.
**soixantaine** [swasɑ̃tɛn] *nf*: **une** ~ **(de)** sixty or so, about sixty.
**soixante** [swasɑ̃t] *num* sixty.
**soja** [sɔʒa] *nm* soya; (*graines*) soya beans *pl*; **germes de** ~ beansprouts.
**sol** [sɔl] *nm* ground; (*de logement*) floor; (*revêtement*) flooring *q*; (*territoire, AGR, GÉO*) soil; (*MUS*) G; (*en chantant la gamme*) so(h).
**solaire** [sɔlɛʀ] *a* solar, sun *cpd*.
**solarium** [sɔlaʀjɔm] *nm* solarium.
**soldat** [sɔlda] *nm* soldier; **S**~ **inconnu** Unknown Warrior *ou* Soldier; ~ **de plomb** tin *ou* toy soldier.
**solde** [sɔld(ə)] *nf* pay // *nm* (*COMM*) balance; ~**s** *nmpl ou nfpl* (*COMM*) sale goods; sales; **à la** ~ **de qn** (*péj*) in sb's

pay; ~ **à payer** balance outstanding; **en** ~ at sale price; **aux** ~**s** at the sales.

**solder** [sɔlde] *vt* (*compte*) to settle; (*marchandise*) to sell at sale price, sell off; **se** ~ **par** (*fig*) to end in; **article soldé (à) 10 F** item reduced to 10 F.

**sole** [sɔl] *nf* sole *inv*.

**soleil** [sɔlɛj] *nm* sun; (*lumière*) sun(light); (*temps ensoleillé*) sun(shine); (*feu d'artifice*) Catherine wheel; (*acrobatie*) grand circle; (BOT) sunflower; **il y a** *ou* **il fait du** ~ it's sunny; **au** ~ in the sun; **le** ~ **de minuit** the midnight sun.

**solennel, le** [sɔlanɛl] *a* solemn; ceremonial; **solenniser** *vt* to solemnize; **solennité** *nf* (*d'une fête*) solemnity; (*fête*) grand occasion.

**solfège** [sɔlfɛʒ] *nm* rudiments *pl* of music.

**soli** [sɔli] *pl de* **solo**.

**solidaire** [sɔlidɛR] *a* (*personnes*) who stand together, who show solidarity; (*pièces mécaniques*) interdependent; **être** ~ **de** (*collègues*) to stand by; (*mécanisme*) to be bound up with, be dependent on; **se solidariser avec** to show solidarity with; **solidarité** *nf* solidarity; interdependence; **par solidarité (avec)** (*cesser le travail etc*) in sympathy (with).

**solide** [sɔlid] *a* solid; (*mur, maison, meuble*) solid, sturdy; (*connaissances, argument*) sound; (*personne, estomac*) robust, sturdy // *nm* solid; **solidifier** *vt*, **se solidifier** *vi* to solidify; **solidité** *nf* solidity; sturdiness.

**soliloque** [sɔlilɔk] *nm* soliloquy.

**soliste** [sɔlist(ə)] *nm/f* soloist.

**solitaire** [sɔlitɛR] *a* (*sans compagnie*) solitary, lonely; (*isolé*) solitary, isolated, lone; (*désert*) lonely // *nm/f* recluse; loner // *nm* (*diamant, jeu*) solitaire.

**solitude** [sɔlityd] *nf* loneliness; (*paix*) solitude.

**solive** [sɔliv] *nf* joist.

**sollicitations** [sɔlisitɑsjɔ̃] *nfpl* entreaties, appeals; enticements; promptings.

**solliciter** [sɔlisite] *vt* (*personne*) to appeal to; (*emploi, faveur*) to seek; (*moteur*) to prompt; (*suj: occupations, attractions etc*): ~ **qn** to appeal to sb's curiosity *etc*; to entice sb; to make demands on sb's time; ~ **qn de faire** to appeal to *ou* request sb to do.

**sollicitude** [sɔlisityd] *nf* concern.

**solo** [sɔlo] *nm, pl* **soli** [sɔli] (MUS) solo (*pl* s *or* soli).

**solstice** [sɔlstis] *nm* solstice.

**soluble** [sɔlybl(ə)] *a* soluble.

**solution** [sɔlysjɔ̃] *nf* solution; ~ **de continuité** solution of continuity, gap; ~ **de facilité** easy way out.

**solvabilité** [sɔlvabilite] *nf* solvency.

**solvable** [sɔlvabl(ə)] *a* solvent.

**solvant** [sɔlvɑ̃] *nm* solvent.

**sombre** [sɔ̃bR(ə)] *a* dark; (*fig*) sombre, gloomy.

**sombrer** [sɔ̃bRe] *vi* (*bateau*) to sink, go down; ~ **dans** (*misère, désespoir*) to sink into.

**sommaire** [sɔmɛR] *a* (*simple*) basic; (*expéditif*) summary // *nm* summary.

**sommation** [sɔmɑsjɔ̃] *nf* (JUR) summons *sg*; (*avant de faire feu*) warning.

**somme** [sɔm] *nf* (MATH) sum; (*fig*) amount; (*argent*) sum, amount // *nm*: **faire un** ~ to have a (short) nap; **faire la** ~ **de** to add up; **en** ~ *ad* all in all; ~ **toute** *ad* when all's said and done.

**sommeil** [sɔmɛj] *nm* sleep; **avoir** ~ to be sleepy; **avoir le** ~ **léger** to be a light sleeper; **en** ~ (*fig*) dormant; **sommeiller** *vi* to doze; (*fig*) to lie dormant.

**sommelier** [sɔməlje] *nm* wine waiter.

**sommer** [sɔme] *vt*: ~ **qn de faire** to command *ou* order sb to do; (JUR) to summon sb to do.

**sommes** *vb voir aussi* **être**.

**sommet** [sɔmɛ] *nm* top; (*d'une montagne*) summit, top; (*fig: de la perfection, gloire*) height; (GÉOM: *d'angle*) vertex (*pl* vertices).

**sommier** [sɔmje] *nm*: ~ **(à ressorts)** springing *q*; (interior-sprung) divan base; ~ **métallique** mesh-springing; mesh-sprung divan base.

**sommité** [sɔmite] *nf* prominent person, leading light.

**somnambule** [sɔmnɑ̃byl] *nm/f* sleepwalker.

**somnifère** [sɔmnifɛR] *nm* sleeping drug (*ou* pill).

**somnolent, e** [sɔmnɔlɑ̃, -ɑ̃t] *a* sleepy, drowsy.

**somnoler** [sɔmnɔle] *vi* to doze.

**somptuaire** [sɔ̃ptɥɛR] *a*: **lois** ~**s** sumptuary laws; **dépenses** ~**s** extravagant expenditure *sg*.

**somptueux, euse** [sɔ̃ptɥø, -øz] *a* sumptuous; lavish.

**son** [sɔ̃], **sa** [sa], *pl* **ses** [se] *dét* (*antécédent humain mâle*) his; (: *femelle*) her; (: *valeur indéfinie*) one's, his/her; (: *non humain*) its; *voir note sous* **il**.

**son** [sɔ̃] *nm* sound; (*résidu*) bran.

**sonate** [sɔnat] *nf* sonata.

**sondage** [sɔ̃daʒ] *nm* (*de terrain*) boring, drilling; (*mer, atmosphère*) sounding; probe; (*enquête*) survey, sounding out of opinion; ~ **(d'opinion)** (opinion) poll.

**sonde** [sɔ̃d] *nf* (NAVIG) lead *ou* sounding line; (MÉTÉOROLOGIE) sonde; (MÉD) probe; catheter; feeding tube; (TECH) borer, driller; (*pour fouiller etc*) probe; ~ **à avalanche** pole *for probing snow and locating victims*); ~ **spatiale** probe.

**sonder** [sɔ̃de] *vt* (NAVIG) to sound; (*atmosphère, plaie, bagages etc*) to probe; (TECH) to bore, drill; (*fig*) to sound out; to probe.

**songe** [sɔ̃ʒ] *nm* dream.

**songer** [sɔ̃ʒe] *vi* to dream; ~ **à** (*rêver à*) to muse over, think over; (*penser à*) to think of; (*envisager*) to contemplate, think of; to consider; ~ **que** to consider that; to think that; **songerie** *nf* reverie; **songeur, euse** *a* pensive.

**sonnailles** [sɔnaj] *nfpl* jingle of bells.

**sonnant, e** [sɔnɑ̃, -ɑ̃t] *a*: **en espèces** ~**es et trébuchantes** in coin of the realm; **à 8 heures** ~**es** on the stroke of 8.

**sonné, e** [sɔne] *a* (*fam*) cracked; **il est midi** ~ it's gone twelve; **il a quarante ans bien** ~**s** he's well into his forties.

**sonner** [sɔne] *vi* to ring // *vt* (*cloche*) to ring; (*glas, tocsin*) to sound; (*portier,* *infirmière*) to ring for ; (*messe*) to ring the bell for ; (*fam: suj: choc, coup*) to knock out ; ~ **du clairon** to sound the bugle ; ~ **faux** (*instrument*) to sound out of tune ; (*rire*) to ring false ; ~ **les heures** to strike the hours ; **minuit vient de** ~ midnight has just struck ; ~ **chez qn** to ring sb's doorbell, ring at sb's door.

**sonnerie** [sɔnʀi] *nf* (*son*) ringing ; (*sonnette*) bell ; (*mécanisme d'horloge*) striking mechanism ; ~ **d'alarme** alarm bell ; ~ **de clairon** bugle call.

**sonnet** [sɔnɛ] *nm* sonnet.

**sonnette** [sɔnɛt] *nf* bell ; ~ **d'alarme** alarm bell ; ~ **de nuit** night-bell.

**sono** [sɔno] *nf abr de* **sonorisation**.

**sonore** [sɔnɔʀ] *a* (*voix*) sonorous, ringing ; (*salle, métal*) resonant ; (*ondes, film, signal*) sound *cpd* ; (*LING*) voiced.

**sonorisation** [sɔnɔʀizɑsjɔ̃] *nf* (*installations*) public address system, P.A. system.

**sonoriser** [sɔnɔʀize] *vt* (*film, spectacle*) to add the sound track to ; (*salle*) to fit with a public address system.

**sonorité** [sɔnɔʀite] *nf* (*de piano, violon*) tone ; (*de voix, mot*) sonority ; (*d'une salle*) resonance ; acoustics *pl*.

**sont** *vb voir* **être**.

**sophistiqué, e** [sɔfistike] *a* sophisticated.

**soporifique** [sɔpɔʀifik] *a* soporific.

**sorbet** [sɔʀbɛ] *nm* water ice, sorbet.

**sorcellerie** [sɔʀsɛlʀi] *nf* witchcraft *q*, sorcery *q*.

**sorcier, ière** [sɔʀsje, -jɛʀ] *nm/f* sorcerer/witch *ou* sorceress.

**sordide** [sɔʀdid] *a* sordid ; squalid.

**sornettes** [sɔʀnɛt] *nfpl* twaddle *sg*.

**sort** [sɔʀ] *nm* (*fortune, destinée*) fate ; (*condition, situation*) lot ; (*magique*) curse, spell ; **le** ~ **en est jeté** the die is cast ; **tirer au** ~ to draw lots ; **tirer qch au** ~ to draw lots for sth.

**sorte** [sɔʀt(ə)] *nf* sort, kind ; **de la** ~ *ad* in that way ; **de** ~ **à** so as to, in order to ; **de (telle)** ~ **que, en** ~ **que** so that ; so much so that.

**sortie** [sɔʀti] *nf* (*issue*) way out, exit ; (*MIL*) sortie ; (*fig: verbale*) outburst ; sally ; (*promenade*) outing ; (*le soir: au restaurant etc*) night out ; (*COMM: somme*): ~s items of expenditure ; outgoings *sans sg* ; **à sa** ~ as he went out *ou* left ; **à la** ~ **de** **l'école/l'usine** (*moment*) after school/work ; when school/the factory comes out ; (*lieu*) at the school/factory gates ; **à la** ~ **de ce nouveau modèle** when this new model comes out, when they bring out this new model ; ~ **de bain** (*vêtement*) bathrobe ; '~ **de camions**' 'vehicle exit', 'lorries turning', ~ **de secours** emergency exit.

**sortilège** [sɔʀtilɛʒ] *nm* (magic) spell.

**sortir** [sɔʀtiʀ] *vi* (*gén*) to come out ; (*partir, se promener, aller au spectacle etc*) to go out ; (*numéro gagnant*) to come up // *vt* (*gén*) to take out ; (*produit, ouvrage, modèle*) to bring out ; (*boniments, incongruités*) to come out with ; (*fam: expulser*) to throw out ; ~ **qch de** to take sth out of ; ~ **de** (*gén*) to leave ; (*endroit*) to go (*ou* come) out of, leave ; (*rainure etc*)

to come out of ; (*cadre, compétence*) to be outside ; (*provenir de: famille etc*) to come from ; **se** ~ **de** (*affaire, situation*) to get out of ; **s'en** ~ (*malade*) to pull through ; (*d'une difficulté etc*) to come through all right ; to get through, be able to manage.

**S.O.S.** *sigle m* mayday, SOS.

**sosie** [sozi] *nm* double.

**sot, sotte** [so, sɔt] *a* silly, foolish // *nm/f* fool ; **sottise** *nf* silliness, foolishness ; silly *ou* foolish thing (to do *ou* say).

**sou** [su] *nm*: **près de ses** ~s tight-fisted ; **sans le** ~ penniless ; **pas un** ~ **de bon sens** not a scrap *ou* an ounce of good sense.

**soubassement** [subasmɑ̃] *nm* base.

**soubresaut** [subʀəso] *nm* start ; jolt.

**soubrette** [subʀɛt] *nf* soubrette, maidservant.

**souche** [suʃ] *nf* (*d'arbre*) stump ; (*de carnet*) counterfoil, stub ; **de vieille** ~ of old stock.

**souci** [susi] *nm* (*inquiétude*) worry ; (*préoccupation*) concern ; (*BOT*) marigold ; **se faire du** ~ to worry ; **avoir (le)** ~ **de** to have concern for.

**soucier** [susje]: **se** ~ **de** *vt* to care about.

**soucieux, euse** [susjø, -øz] *a* concerned, worried ; ~ **de** concerned about ; **peu** ~ **de/que** caring little about/whether.

**soucoupe** [sukup] *nf* saucer ; ~ **volante** flying saucer.

**soudain, e** [sudɛ̃, -ɛn] *a* (*douleur, mort*) sudden // *ad* suddenly, all of a sudden ; **soudainement** *ad* suddenly ; **soudaineté** *nf* suddenness.

**soude** [sud] *nf* soda.

**soudé, e** [sude] *a* (*fig: pétales, organes*) joined (together).

**souder** [sude] *vt* (*avec fil à souder*) to solder ; (*par soudure autogène*) to weld ; (*fig*) to bind *ou* knit together ; to fuse (together).

**soudoyer** [sudwaje] *vt* (*péj*) to bribe, buy over.

**soudure** [sudyʀ] *nf* soldering ; welding ; (*joint*) soldered joint ; weld.

**souffert, e** [sufɛʀ, -ɛʀt(ə)] *pp de* **souffrir**.

**souffle** [sufl(ə)] *nm* (*en expirant*) breath ; (*en soufflant*) puff, blow ; (*respiration*) breathing ; (*d'explosion, de ventilateur*) blast ; (*du vent*) blowing ; (*fig*) inspiration ; **avoir du/manquer de** ~ to have a lot of/be short of breath ; **être à bout de** ~ to be out of breath ; **avoir le** ~ **court** to be short-winded ; **un** ~ **d'air** *ou* **de vent** a breath of air, a puff of wind.

**soufflé, e** [sufle] *a* (*CULIN*) soufflé ; (*fam: ahuri, stupéfié*) staggered // *nm* (*CULIN*) soufflé.

**souffler** [sufle] *vi* (*gén*) to blow ; (*haleter*) to puff (and blow) // *vt* (*feu, bougie*) to blow out ; (*chasser: poussière etc*) to blow away ; (*TECH: verre*) to blow ; (*suj: explosion*) to destroy (with its blast) ; (*dire*): ~ **qch à qn** to whisper sth to sb ; (*fam: voler*): ~ **qch à qn** to nick sth from sb ; ~ **son rôle à qn** to prompt sb ; **laisser** ~ **qn** (*fig*) to give sb a breather.

**soufflet** [suflɛ] *nm* (*instrument*) bellows *pl* ; (*entre wagons*) vestibule ; (*gifle*) slap (in the face).

**souffleur, euse** [suflœʀ, -øz] *nm/f*
(*THÉÀTRE*) prompter.
**souffrance** [sufʀɑ̃s] *nf* suffering ; **en ~**
(*marchandise*) awaiting delivery ; (*affaire*)
pending.
**souffrant, e** [sufʀɑ̃, -ɑ̃t] *a* unwell.
**souffre-douleur** [sufʀədulœʀ] *nm inv*
whipping boy, underdog.
**souffreteux, euse** [sufʀətø, -øz] *a* sickly.
**souffrir** [sufʀiʀ] *vi* to suffer ; to be in pain
// *vt* to suffer, endure ; (*supporter*) to bear,
stand ; (*admettre: exception etc*) to allow *ou*
admit of ; **~ de** (*maladie, froid*) to suffer
from ; **~ des dents** to have trouble with
one's teeth ; **faire ~ qn** (*suj: personne*) to
make sb suffer ; (: *dents, blessure etc*) to
hurt sb.
**soufre** [sufʀ(ə)] *nm* sulphur.
**souhait** [swɛ] *nm* wish ; **tous nos ~s de**
good wishes *ou* our best wishes for ; **riche**
*etc* **à ~** as rich *etc* as one could wish ;
**à vos ~s!** bless you!
**souhaitable** [swɛtabl(ə)] *a* desirable.
**souhaiter** [swete] *vt* to wish for ; **~ le
bonjour à qn** to bid sb good day ; **~ la
bonne année à qn** to wish sb a happy New
Year.
**souiller** [suje] *vt* to dirty, soil ; (*fig*) to
sully, tarnish ; **souillure** *nf* stain.
**soûl, e** [su, sul] *a* drunk // *nm*: **boire tout
son ~** to drink one's fill.
**soulagement** [sulaʒmɑ̃] *nm* relief.
**soulager** [sulaʒe] *vt* to relieve.
**soûler** [sule] *vt*: **~ qn** to get sb drunk ;
(*suj: boisson*) to make sb drunk ; (*fig*) to
make sb's head spin *ou* reel ; **se ~** to get
drunk ; **se ~ de** (*fig*) to intoxicate o.s.
with ; **soûlerie** *nf* (*péj*) drunken binge.
**soulèvement** [sulɛvmɑ̃] *nm* uprising ;
(*GÉO*) upthrust.
**soulever** [sulve] *vt* to lift ; (*vagues,
poussière*) to send up ; (*peuple*) to stir up
(to revolt) ; (*enthousiasme*) to arouse ;
(*question, débat*) to raise ; **se ~** *vi* (*peuple*)
to rise up ; (*personne couchée*) to lift o.s.
up ; **cela me soulève le cœur** it makes me
feel sick.
**soulier** [sulje] *nm* shoe ; **~s plats/à
talons** flat/heeled shoes.
**souligner** [suliɲe] *vt* to underline ; (*fig*) to
emphasize ; to stress.
**soumettre** [sumɛtʀ] *vt* (*pays*) to subject,
subjugate ; (*rebelle*) to put down, subdue ;
**~ qn/qch à** to subject sb/sth to ; **~ qch
à qn** (*projet etc*) to submit sth to sb ; **se
~** (: *se rendre, obéir*) to submit (to) ; **se
~ à** (*formalités etc*) to submit to ; (*régime
etc*) to submit o.s. to.
**soumis, e** [sumi, -iz] *a* submissive ;
**revenus ~ à l'impôt** taxable income.
**soumission** [sumisjɔ̃] *nf* (*voir se
soumettre*) submission ; (*docilité*)
submissiveness ; (*COMM*) tender.
**soupape** [supap] *nf* valve ; **~ de sûreté**
safety valve.
**soupçon** [supsɔ̃] *nm* suspicion ; (*petite
quantité*): **un ~ de** a hint *ou* touch of ;
**soupçonner** *vt* to suspect ; **soupçonneux,
euse** *a* suspicious.
**soupe** [sup] *nf* soup ; **~ au lait** *a inv* quick-
tempered ; **~ à l'oignon/de poisson**

onion/fish soup ; **~ populaire** soup
kitchen.
**soupente** [supɑ̃t] *nf* cupboard under the
stairs.
**souper** [supe] *vi* to have supper // *nm*
supper ; **avoir soupé de** (*fam*) to be sick
and tired of.
**soupeser** [supəze] *vt* to weigh in one's
hand(s), feel the weight of ; (*fig*) to weigh
up.
**soupière** [supjɛʀ] *nf* (soup) tureen.
**soupir** [supiʀ] *nm* sigh ; (*MUS*) crotchet
rest ; **rendre le dernier ~** to breathe one's
last.
**soupirail, aux** [supiʀaj, -o] *nm* (small)
basement window.
**soupirant** [supiʀɑ̃] *nm* (*péj*) suitor, wooer.
**soupirer** [supiʀe] *vi* to sigh ; **~ après qch**
to yearn for sth.
**souple** [supl(ə)] *a* supple ; (*fig: règlement,
caractère*) flexible ; (: *démarche, taille*) lithe,
supple ; **souplesse** *nf* suppleness ;
flexibility.
**source** [suʀs(ə)] *nf* (*point d'eau*) spring ;
(*d'un cours d'eau, fig*) source ; **prendre sa
~ à/dans** (*suj: cours d'eau*) to have its
source at/in ; **tenir qch de bonne ~/de
~ sûre** to have sth on good
authority/from a reliable source ; **~
thermale/d'eau minérale** hot *ou*
thermal/mineral spring.
**sourcier** [suʀsje] *nm* water diviner.
**sourcil** [suʀsij] *nm* (eye)brow ;
**sourcilière** *af voir* **arcade**.
**sourciller** [suʀsije] *vi*: **sans ~** without
turning a hair *ou* batting an eyelid.
**sourcilleux, euse** [suʀsijø, -øz] *a*
pernickety.
**sourd, e** [suʀ, suʀd(ə)] *a* deaf ; (*bruit, voix*)
muffled ; (*couleur*) muted ; (*douleur*) dull ;
(*lutte*) silent, hidden ; (*LING*) voiceless //
*nm/f* deaf person.
**sourdait** *etc vb voir* **sourdre**.
**sourdine** [suʀdin] *nf* (*MUS*) mute ; **en ~**
*ad* softly, quietly ; **mettre une ~ à** (*fig*)
to tone down.
**sourd-muet, sourde-muette** [suʀmyɛ,
suʀdmyɛt] *a* deaf-and-dumb // *nm/f* deaf-
mute.
**sourdre** [suʀdʀ(ə)] *vi* to rise.
**souriant, e** [suʀjɑ̃, -ɑ̃t] *a* cheerful.
**souricière** [suʀisjɛʀ] *nf* mousetrap ; (*fig*)
trap.
**sourire** [suʀiʀ] *nm* smile // *vi* to smile ;
**~ à qn** to smile at sb ; (*fig*) to appeal to
sb ; to smile on sb ; **faire un ~ à qn** to
give sb a smile ; **garder le ~** to keep
smiling.
**souris** [suʀi] *nf* mouse (*pl* mice).
**sournois, e** [suʀnwa, -waz] *a* deceitful,
underhand.
**sous** [su] *prép* (*gén*) under ; **~ la pluie/le
soleil** in the rain/sunshine ; **~ terre** *a, ad*
underground ; **~ peu** *ad* shortly, before
long.
**sous...** [su, suz + *vowel*] *préfixe* sub- ;
under... ; **~-catégorie** sub-category ; **~-
alimenté/-équipé/-développé** under-
nourished/equipped/developed.
**sous-bois** [subwa] *nm inv* undergrowth.

**sous-chef** [suʃɛf] *nm* deputy chief clerk.
**souscription** [suskʀipsjɔ̃] *nf* subscription ; **offert en** ~ available on subscription.
**souscrire** [suskʀiʀ]: ~ **à** *vt* to subscribe to.
**sous-directeur, trice** [sudiʀɛktœʀ, -tʀis] *nm/f* assistant manager/ manageress, sub-manager/ manageress.
**sous-emploi** [suzɑ̃plwa] *nm* underemployment.
**sous-entendre** [suzɑ̃tɑ̃dʀ(ə)] *vt* to imply, infer ; **sous-entendu, e** *a* implied ; (*verbe, complément*) understood // *nm* innuendo, insinuation.
**sous-estimer** [suzɛstime] *vt* to underestimate.
**sous-exposer** [suzɛkspoze] *vt* to underexpose.
**sous-fifre** [sufifʀ] *nm* (*péj*) underling.
**sous-jacent, e** [suʒasɑ̃, -ɑ̃t] *a* underlying.
**sous-lieutenant** [suljøtnɑ̃] *nm* sub-lieutenant.
**sous-locataire** [sulɔkatɛʀ] *nm/f* subtenant.
**sous-louer** [sulwe] *vt* to sublet.
**sous-main** [sumɛ̃] *nm inv* desk blotter ; **en** ~ *ad* secretly.
**sous-marin, e** [sumaʀɛ̃, -in] *a* (*flore, volcan*) submarine ; (*navigation, pêche, explosif*) underwater // *nm* submarine.
**sous-officier** [suzɔfisje] *nm* ≈ non-comissioned officer (N.C.O.).
**sous-préfecture** [supʀefɛktyʀ] *nf* sub-prefecture.
**sous-préfet** [supʀefɛ] *nm* sub-prefect.
**sous-produit** [supʀɔdɥi] *nm* by-product ; (*fig: péj*) pale imitation.
**sous-secrétaire** [susəkʀetɛʀ] *nm:* ~ **d'État** Under-Secretary of State.
**soussigné, e** [susiɲe] *a:* **je** ~ **I** the undersigned.
**sous-sol** [susɔl] *nm* basement ; (*GÉO*) subsoil.
**sous-titre** [sutitʀ(ə)] *nm* subtitle ; **sous-titré, e** *a* with subtitles.
**soustraction** [sustʀaksjɔ̃] *nf* subtraction.
**soustraire** [sustʀɛʀ] *vt* to subtract, take away ; (*dérober*): ~ **qch à qn** to remove sth from sb ; ~ **qn à** (*danger*) to shield sb from ; **se** ~ **à** (*autorité etc*) to elude, escape from.
**sous-traitance** [sutʀɛtɑ̃s(ə)] *nf* subcontracting.
**sous-verre** [suvɛʀ] *nm inv* glass mount.
**sous-vêtement** [suvɛtmɑ̃] *nm* undergarment, item of underwear ; ~**s** *nmpl* underwear *sg.*
**soutane** [sutan] *nf* cassock, soutane.
**soute** [sut] *nf* hold ; ~ **à bagages** baggage hold.
**soutenable** [sutnabl(ə)] *a* (*opinion*) tenable, defensible.
**soutenance** [sutnɑ̃s] *nf:* ~ **de thèse** ≈ viva voce (examination).
**soutènement** [sutɛnmɑ̃] *nm:* **mur de** ~ retaining wall.
**souteneur** [sutnœʀ] *nm* procurer.
**soutenir** [sutniʀ] *vt* to support ; (*assaut, choc*) to stand up to, withstand ; (*intérêt, effort*) to keep up ; (*assurer*): ~ **que** to

maintain that ; **se** ~ (*dans l'eau etc*) to hold o.s. up ; ~ **la comparaison avec** to bear *ou* stand comparison with ; **soutenu, e** *a* (*efforts*) sustained, unflagging ; (*style*) elevated.
**souterrain, e** [sutɛʀɛ̃, -ɛn] *a* underground // *nm* underground passage.
**soutien** [sutjɛ̃] *nm* support ; ~ **de famille** breadwinner.
**soutien-gorge** [sutjɛ̃gɔʀʒ(ə)] *nm* bra.
**soutirer** [sutiʀe] *vt:* ~ **qch à qn** to squeeze *ou* get sth out of sb.
**souvenance** [suvnɑ̃s] *nf:* **avoir** ~ **de** to recollect.
**souvenir** [suvniʀ] *nm* (*réminiscence*) memory ; (*cadeau*) souvenir, keepsake ; (*de voyage*) souvenir // *vb:* **se** ~ **de** *vt* to remember ; **se** ~ **que** to remember that ; **en** ~ **de** in memory *ou* remembrance of.
**souvent** [suvɑ̃] *ad* often ; **peu** ~ seldom, infrequently.
**souverain, e** [suvʀɛ̃, -ɛn] *a* a sovereign ; (*fig: mépris*) supreme // *nm/f* sovereign, monarch ; **souveraineté** *nf* sovereignty.
**soviétique** [sɔvjetik] *a* Soviet // *nm/f:* **S**~ Soviet citizen.
**soyeux, euse** [swajø, øz] *a* silky.
**soyons** *etc vb voir* **être**.
**S.P.A.** *sigle f* (= *société protectrice des animaux*) ≈ R.S.P.C.A.
**spacieux, euse** [spasjø, -øz] *a* spacious ; roomy.
**spaghettis** [spageti] *nmpl* spaghetti *sg.*
**sparadrap** [spaʀadʀa] *nm* adhesive *ou* sticking plaster.
**spartiate** [spaʀsjat] *a* Spartan ; ~**s** *nfpl* (*sandales*) Roman sandals.
**spasme** [spazm(ə)] *nm* spasm.
**spasmodique** [spazmɔdik] *a* spasmodic.
**spatial, e, aux** [spasjal, -o] *a* (*AVIAT*) space *cpd* ; (*PSYCH*) spatial.
**spatule** [spatyl] *nf* (*ustensile*) slice ; spatula ; (*bout*) tip.
**speaker, ine** [spikœʀ, -kʀin] *nm/f* announcer.
**spécial, e, aux** [spesjal, -o] *a* special ; (*bizarre*) peculiar ; ~**ement** *ad* especially, particularly ; (*tout exprès*) specially.
**spécialisé, e** [spesjalize] *a* specialised.
**spécialiser** [spesjalize] *vt:* **se** ~ to specialize.
**spécialiste** [spesjalist(ə)] *nm/f* specialist.
**spécialité** [spesjalite] *nf* speciality ; (*SCOL*) special field ; ~ **pharmaceutique** patent medicine.
**spécieux, euse** [spesjø, -øz] *a* a specious.
**spécification** [spesifikɑsjɔ̃] *nf* specification.
**spécifier** [spesifje] *vt* to specify, state.
**spécifique** [spesifik] *a* specific.
**spécimen** [spesimɛn] *nm* specimen ; (*revue etc*) specimen *ou* sample copy.
**spectacle** [spɛktakl(ə)] *nm* (*tableau, scène*) sight ; (*représentation*) show ; (*industrie*) show business, entertainment ; **se donner en** ~ (*péj*) to make a spectacle *ou* an exhibition of o.s. ; **spectaculaire** *a* spectacular.
**spectateur, trice** [spɛktatœʀ, -tʀis] *nm/f* (*CINÉMA etc*) member of the audience ;

**(SPORT)** spectator ; **(d'un événement)** onlooker, witness.

**spectre** [spɛktR(ə)] nm (fantôme, fig) spectre ; (PHYSIQUE) spectrum (pl a) ; ~ **solaire** solar spectrum.

**spéculateur, trice** [spekylatœR, -tRis] nm/f speculator.

**spéculation** [spekylɑsjɔ̃] nf speculation.

**spéculer** [spekyle] vi to speculate ; ~ **sur** (COMM) to speculate in ; (réfléchir) to speculate on ; (tabler sur) to bank ou rely on.

**spéléologie** [speleɔlɔʒi] nf (étude) speleology ; (activité) potholing ; **spéléologue** nm/f speleologist ; potholer.

**spermatozoïde** [spɛRmatozɔid] nm sperm, spermatozoon (pl zoa).

**sperme** [spɛRm(ə)] nm semen, sperm.

**sphère** [sfɛR] nf sphere ; **sphérique** a spherical.

**sphincter** [sfɛ̃ktɛR] nm sphincter.

**spiral, aux** [spiRal, -o] nm hairspring.

**spirale** [spiRal] nf spiral ; **en** ~ in a spiral.

**spire** [spiR] nm (single) turn ; whorl.

**spiritisme** [spiRitism(ə)] nm spiritualism, spiritism.

**spirituel, le** [spiRitɥɛl] a spiritual ; (fin, piquant) witty ; **musique** ~**le** sacred music ; **concert** ~ concert of sacred music.

**spiritueux** [spiRitɥø] nm spirit.

**splendeur** [splɑ̃dœR] nf splendour.

**splendide** [splɑ̃did] a splendid ; magnificent.

**spolier** [spɔlje] vt : ~ **qn (de)** to despoil sb (of).

**spongieux, euse** [spɔ̃ʒjø, -øz] a spongy.

**spontané, e** [spɔ̃tane] a spontaneous.

**sporadique** [spɔRadik] a sporadic.

**sport** [spɔR] nm sport // a inv (vêtement) casual ; **faire du** ~ to do sport ; ~**s d'équipe/d'hiver** team/winter sports ; **sportif, ive** a (journal, association, épreuve) sports cpd ; (allure, démarche) athletic ; (attitude, esprit) sporting.

**spot** [spɔt] nm (lampe) spot(light) ; (annonce): ~ **(publicitaire)** commercial (break).

**sprint** [spRint] nm sprint.

**square** [skwaR] nm public garden(s).

**squelette** [skəlɛt] nm skeleton ; **squelettique** a scrawny ; (fig) skimpy.

**stabilisateur, trice** [stabilizatœR, -tRis] a stabilizing // nm stabilizer ; anti-roll device ; tailplane.

**stabiliser** [stabilize] vt to stabilize ; (terrain) to consolidate.

**stabilité** [stabilite] nf stability.

**stable** [stabl(ə)] a stable, steady.

**stade** [stad] nm (SPORT) stadium ; (phase, niveau) stage.

**stage** [staʒ] nm training period ; training course ; (d'avocat stagiaire) articles pl ; **stagiaire** nm/f, a trainee.

**stagnant, e** [stagnɑ̃, -ɑ̃t] a stagnant.

**stalactite** [stalaktit] nf stalactite.

**stalagmite** [stalagmit] nf stalagmite.

**stalle** [stal] nf stall, box.

**stand** [stɑ̃d] nm (d'exposition) stand ; (de foire) stall ; ~ **de tir** (MIL) firing range ;

(à la foire, SPORT) shooting range ; ~ **de ravitaillement** pit.

**standard** [stɑ̃daR] a inv standard // nm switchboard ; **standardiser** vt to standardize ; **standardiste** nm/f switchboard operator.

**standing** [stɑ̃diŋ] nm standing ; **immeuble de grand** ~ block of luxury flats.

**star** [staR] nf star.

**starter** [staRtɛR] nm (AUTO) choke.

**station** [stɑsjɔ̃] nf station ; (de bus) stop ; (de villégiature) resort ; (posture): **la** ~ **debout** standing, an upright posture ; ~ **de ski** ski resort ; ~ **de taxis** taxi rank.

**stationnaire** [stasjɔnɛR] a stationary.

**stationnement** [stasjɔnmɑ̃] nm parking ; **zone de** ~ **interdit** no parking area ; ~ **alterné** parking on alternate sides.

**stationner** [stasjɔne] vi to park.

**station-service** [stasjɔ̃sɛRvis] nf service station.

**statique** [statik] a static.

**statisticien, ne** [statistisjɛ̃, -jɛn] nm/f statistician.

**statistique** [statistik] nf (science) statistics sg ; (rapport, étude) statistic // a statistical ; ~**s** (données) statistics pl.

**statue** [staty] nf statue.

**statuer** [statɥe] vi: ~ **sur** to rule on, give a ruling on.

**statuette** [statɥɛt] nf statuette.

**statu quo** [statykwo] nm status quo.

**stature** [statyR] nf stature.

**statut** [staty] nm status ; ~**s** nmpl (JUR, ADMIN) statutes ; **statutaire** a statutory.

**Sté** abr de **société.**

**steak** [stɛk] nm steak.

**stèle** [stɛl] nf stela, stele.

**stellaire** [stelɛR] a stellar.

**stencil** [stɛnsil] nm stencil.

**sténo...** [stenɔ] préfixe : ~**(dactylo)** nf shorthand typist ; ~**(graphie)** nf shorthand ; ~**graphier** vt to take down in shorthand.

**stentor** [stɑ̃tɔR] nm : **voix de** ~ stentorian voice.

**steppe** [stɛp] nf steppe.

**stère** [stɛR] nm stere.

**stéréo(phonie)** [steReɔ(fɔni)] nf stereo(phony) ; **stéréo(phonique)** a stereo(phonic).

**stéréotype** [steReɔtip] nm stereotype ; **stéréotypé, e** a stereotyped.

**stérile** [steRil] a sterile ; (terre) barren ; (fig) fruitless, futile.

**stérilet** [steRilɛ] nm coil, loop.

**stériliser** [steRilize] vt to sterilize.

**stérilité** [steRilite] nf sterility.

**sternum** [stɛRnɔm] nm breastbone, sternum.

**stéthoscope** [stetɔskɔp] nm stethoscope.

**stigmates** [stigmat] nmpl scars, marks ; (REL) stigmata pl.

**stigmatiser** [stigmatize] vt to denounce, stigmatize.

**stimulant, e** [stimylɑ̃, -ɑ̃t] a stimulating // nm (MÉD) stimulant ; (fig) stimulus (pl i), incentive.

**stimulation** [stimylɑsjɔ̃] *nf* stimulation.
**stimuler** [stimyle] *vt* to stimulate.
**stimulus, i** [stimylys, -i] *nm* stimulus (*pl* i).
**stipulation** [stipylɑsjɔ̃] *nf* stipulation.
**stipuler** [stipyle] *vt* to stipulate, specify.
**stock** [stɔk] *nm* stock ; ~ d'or (*FINANCE*) gold reserves *pl* ; ~er *vt* to stock ; ~iste *nm* stockist.
**stoïque** [stɔik] *a* stoic, stoical.
**stomacal, e, aux** [stɔmakal, -o] *a* gastric, stomach *cpd*.
**stop** [stɔp] *nm* (*AUTO*: écriteau) stop sign ; (: *signal*) brake-light ; (*dans un télégramme*) stop // *excl* stop.
**stoppage** [stɔpaʒ] *nm* invisible mending.
**stopper** [stɔpe] *vt* to stop, halt ; (*COUTURE*) to mend // *vi* to stop, halt.
**store** [stɔʀ] *nm* blind ; (*de magasin*) shade, awning.
**strabisme** [stʀabism(ə)] *nm* squinting.
**strangulation** [stʀɑ̃gylɑsjɔ̃] *nf* strangulation.
**strapontin** [stʀapɔ̃tɛ̃] *nm* jump *ou* foldaway seat.
**strass** [stʀas] *nm* paste, strass.
**stratagème** [stʀataʒɛm] *nm* stratagem.
**stratège** [stʀatɛʒ] *nm* strategist.
**stratégie** [stʀateʒi] *nf* strategy ; **stratégique** *a* strategic.
**stratifié, e** [stʀatifje] *a* (*GÉO*) stratified ; (*TECH*) laminated.
**stratosphère** [stʀatɔsfɛʀ] *nf* stratosphere.
**strict, e** [stʀikt(ə)] *a* strict ; (*tenue, décor*) severe, plain ; **son droit le plus** ~ his most basic right ; **dans la plus** ~**e intimité** strictly in private ; **le** ~ **nécessaire/minimum** the bare essentials/minimum.
**strident, e** [stʀidɑ̃, -ɑ̃t] *a* shrill, strident.
**stridulations** [stʀidylɑsjɔ̃] *nfpl* stridulations, chirrings.
**strie** [stʀi] *nf* streak ; (*ANAT, GÉO*) stria (*pl* ae).
**strier** [stʀije] *vt* to streak ; to striate.
**strip-tease** [stʀiptiz] *nm* striptease ; **strip-teaseuse** *nf* stripper, striptease artist.
**striures** [stʀijyʀ] *nfpl* streaking *sg*.
**strophe** [stʀɔf] *nf* verse, stanza.
**structure** [stʀyktyʀ] *nf* structure ; ~**s d'accueil/touristiques** reception/tourist facilities ; **structurer** *vt* to structure.
**stuc** [styk] *nm* stucco.
**studieux, euse** [stydjø, -øz] *a* studious ; devoted to study.
**studio** [stydjo] *nm* (*logement*) (one-roomed) flatlet ; (*d'artiste, TV etc*) studio (*pl* s).
**stupéfaction** [stypefaksjɔ̃] *nf* stupefaction, amazement.
**stupéfait, e** [stypefɛ, -ɛt] *a* amazed.
**stupéfiant, e** [stypefjɑ̃, -ɑ̃t] *a* stunning, astounding // *nm* (*MÉD*) drug, narcotic.
**stupéfier** [stypefje] *vt* to stupefy ; (*étonner*) to stun, astonish.
**stupeur** [stypœʀ] *nf* (*inertie, insensibilité*) stupor ; (*étonnement*) astonishment, amazement.

**stupide** [stypid] *a* stupid ; **stupidité** *nf* stupidity ; stupid thing (to do *ou* say).
**style** [stil] *nm* style ; **meuble de** ~ period piece of furniture.
**stylé, e** [stile] *a* well-trained.
**stylet** [stilɛ] *nm* stiletto, stylet.
**stylisé, e** [stilize] *a* stylized.
**styliste** [stilist(ə)] *nm/f* designer ; stylist.
**stylistique** [stilistik] *nf* stylistics *sg*.
**stylo** [stilo] *nm*: ~ (**à encre**) (fountain) pen ; ~ (**à**) **bille** ball-point pen ; ~**-feutre** *nm* felt-tip pen.
**su, e** [sy] *pp de* **savoir** // *nm*: **au** ~ **de** with the knowledge of.
**suaire** [sɥɛʀ] *nm* shroud.
**suave** [sɥav] *a* sweet ; suave, smooth ; mellow.
**subalterne** [sybaltɛʀn(ə)] *a* (*employé, officier*) junior ; (*rôle*) subordinate, subsidiary // *nm/f* subordinate, inferior.
**subconscient** [sypkɔ̃sjɑ̃] *nm* subconscious.
**subdiviser** [sybdivize] *vt* to subdivide ; **subdivision** *nf* subdivision.
**subir** [sybiʀ] *vt* (*affront, dégâts, mauvais traitements*) to suffer ; (*influence, charme*) to be under, be subjected to ; (*traitement, opération, châtiment*) to undergo.
**subit, e** [sybi, -it] *a* sudden ; **subitement** *ad* suddenly, all of a sudden.
**subjectif, ive** [sybʒɛktif, -iv] *a* subjective.
**subjonctif** [sybʒɔ̃ktif] *nm* subjunctive.
**subjuguer** [sybʒyge] *vt* to subjugate.
**sublime** [syblim] *a* sublime.
**sublimer** [syblime] *vt* to sublimate.
**submergé, e** [sybmɛʀʒe] *a* submerged ; (*fig*): ~ **de** snowed under with ; overwhelmed with.
**submerger** [sybmɛʀʒe] *vt* to submerge ; (*suj: foule*) to engulf ; (*fig*) to overwhelm.
**submersible** [sybmɛʀsibl(ə)] *nm* submarine.
**subordination** [sybɔʀdinɑsjɔ̃] *nf* subordination.
**subordonné, e** [sybɔʀdɔne] *a, nm/f* subordinate ; ~ **à** subordinate to ; subject to, depending on.
**subordonner** [sybɔʀdɔne] *vt*: ~ **qn/qch à** to subordinate sb/sth to.
**subornation** [sybɔʀnɑsjɔ̃] *nf* bribing.
**subrepticement** [sybʀɛptismɑ̃] *ad* surreptitiously.
**subside** [sypsid] *nm* grant.
**subsidiaire** [sypsidjɛʀ] *a*: **question** ~ deciding question.
**subsistance** [sybzistɑ̃s] *nf* subsistence ; **pourvoir à la** ~ **de qn** to keep sb, provide for sb's subsistence *ou* keep.
**subsister** [sybziste] *vi* (*rester*) to remain, subsist ; (*vivre*) to live ; (*survivre*) to live on.
**substance** [sypstɑ̃s] *nf* substance.
**substantiel, le** [sypstɑ̃sjɛl] *a* substantial.
**substantif** [sypstɑ̃tif] *nm* noun, substantive ; **substantiver** *vt* to nominalize.
**substituer** [sypstitɥe] *vt*: ~ **qn/qch à** to substitute sb/sth for ; **se** ~ **à qn** (*représenter*) to substitute for sb ; (*évincer*) to substitute o.s. for sb.

**substitut** [sypstity] *nm* (*JUR*) deputy public prosecutor ; (*succédané*) substitute.
**substitution** [sypstitysjɔ̃] *nf* substitution.
**subterfuge** [syptɛrfyʒ] *nm* subterfuge.
**subtil, e** [syptil] *a* subtle.
**subtiliser** [syptilize] *vt*: ~ **qch (à qn)** to spirit sth away (from sb).
**subtilité** [syptilite] *nf* subtlety.
**subvenir** [sybvəniʀ]: ~ **à** *vt* to meet.
**subvention** [sybvɑ̃sjɔ̃] *nf* subsidy, grant ; **subventionner** *vt* to subsidize.
**subversif, ive** [sybvɛrsif, -iv] *a* subversive ; **subversion** *nf* subversion.
**suc** [syk] *nm* (*BOT*) sap ; (*de viande, fruit*) juice ; ~**s gastriques** gastric *ou* stomach juices.
**succédané** [syksedane] *nm* substitute.
**succéder** [syksede]: ~ **à** *vt* (*directeur, roi etc*) to succeed ; (*venir après: dans une série*) to follow, succeed ; **se** ~ *vi* (*accidents, années*) to follow one another.
**succès** [syksɛ] *nm* success ; **avoir du** ~ to be a success, be successful ; ~ **de librairie** bestseller ; ~ (**féminins**) conquests.
**successeur** [syksesœr] *nm* successor.
**successif, ive** [syksesif, -iv] *a* successive.
**succession** [syksesjɔ̃] *nf* (*série, POL*) succession ; (*JUR: patrimoine*) estate, inheritance ; **prendre la** ~ **de** (*directeur*) to succeed, take over from ; (*entreprise*) to take over.
**succinct, e** [syksɛ̃, -ɛ̃t] *a* succinct.
**succion** [syksjɔ̃] *nf*: **bruit de** ~ sucking noise.
**succomber** [sykɔ̃be] *vi* to die, succumb ; (*fig*): ~ **à** to give way to, succumb to.
**succulent, e** [sykylɑ̃, -ɑ̃t] *a* succulent.
**succursale** [sykyrsal] *nf* branch ; **magasin à** ~**s multiples** chain *ou* multiple store.
**sucer** [syse] *vt* to suck.
**sucette** [sysɛt] *nf* (*bonbon*) lollipop.
**sucre** [sykr(ə)] *nm* (*substance*) sugar ; (*morceau*) lump of sugar, sugar lump *ou* cube ; ~ **de canne/betterave** cane/beet sugar ; ~ **en morceaux/cristallisé/en poudre** lump/coarse-grained/ granulated sugar ; ~ **d'orge** barley sugar ; **sucré, e** *a* (*produit alimentaire*) sweetened ; (*au goût*) sweet ; (*péj*) sugary, honeyed ; **sucrer** *vt* (*thé, café*) to sweeten, put sugar in ; **sucrer qn** to put sugar in sb's tea (*ou* coffee *etc*) ; **se sucrer** to help o.s. to sugar, have some sugar ; (*fam*) to line one's pocket(s) ; **sucrerie** *nf* (*usine*) sugar refinery ; **sucreries** *nfpl* (*bonbons*) sweets, sweet things ; **sucrier, ière** *a* sugar *cpd* ; sugar-producing // *nm* (*fabricant*) sugar producer ; (*récipient*) sugar bowl *ou* basin.
**sud** [syd] *nm*: **le** ~ the south // *a inv* south ; (*côte*) south, southern ; **au** ~ (*situation*) in the south ; (*direction*) to the south ; **au** ~ **de** (to the) south of ; ~**-africain, e** *a, nm/f* South African ; ~**-américain, e** *a, nm/f* South American.
**sudation** [sydasjɔ̃] *nf* sweating, sudation.
**sud-est** [sydɛst] *nm, a inv* south-east.
**sud-ouest** [sydwɛst] *nm, a inv* south-west.
**Suède** [syɛd] *nf*: **la** ~ Sweden ; **suédois,**

**e** *a* Swedish // *nm/f*: **Suédois, e** Swede // *nm* (*langue*) Swedish.
**suer** [sye] *vi* to sweat ; (*suinter*) to ooze // *vt* (*fig*) to exude ; ~ **à grosses gouttes** to sweat profusely.
**sueur** [sɥœr] *nf* sweat ; **en** ~ sweating, in a sweat ; **avoir des** ~**s froides** to be in a cold sweat.
**suffire** [syfir] *vi* (*être assez*): ~ (**à qn/pour qch/pour faire**) to be enough *ou* sufficient (for sb/for sth/to do) ; (*satisfaire*): **cela lui suffit** he's content with this, this is enough for him ; **se** ~ to be self-sufficient ; **cela suffit pour les irriter/qu'ils se fâchent** it's enough to annoy them/for them to get angry ; **il suffit d'une négligence/qu'on oublie pour que ...** it only takes one act of carelessness/one only needs to forget for
**suffisamment** [syfizamɑ̃] *ad* sufficiently, enough ; ~ **de** sufficient, enough.
**suffisance** [syfizɑ̃s] *nf* (*vanité*) self-importance, bumptiousness ; (*quantité*): **en** ~ in plenty.
**suffisant, e** [syfizɑ̃, -ɑ̃t] *a* (*temps, ressources*) sufficient ; (*résultats*) satisfactory ; (*vaniteux*) self-important, bumptious.
**suffixe** [syfiks(ə)] *nm* suffix.
**suffocation** [syfɔkasjɔ̃] *nf* suffocation.
**suffoquer** [syfɔke] *vt* to choke, suffocate ; (*stupéfier*) to stagger, astound // *vi* to choke, suffocate.
**suffrage** [syfraʒ] *nm* (*POL: voix*) vote ; (: *méthode*): ~ **indirect** indirect suffrage ; (*du peuple etc*) approval *q* ; ~**s exprimés** valid votes.
**suggérer** [syɡʒere] *vt* to suggest ; **suggestif, ive** *a* suggestive ; **suggestion** *nf* suggestion.
**suicidaire** [sɥisidɛr] *a* suicidal.
**suicide** [sɥisid] *nm* suicide.
**suicidé, e** [sɥiside] *nm/f* suicide.
**suicider** [sɥiside]: **se** ~ *vi* to commit suicide.
**suie** [sɥi] *nf* soot.
**suif** [sɥif] *nm* tallow.
**suinter** [sɥɛ̃te] *vi* to ooze.
**suis** *vb voir* **être**.
**suisse** [sɥis] *a, nm/f* Swiss // *nm* (*bedeau*) ≈ verger // *nf*: **la S**~ Switzerland ; **la S**~ **romande/allemande** French-speaking/ German-speaking Switzerland ~ **romand, e** *a, nm/f* Swiss French ; ~**-allemand, e** *a, nm/f* Swiss German ; **Suissesse** *nf* Swiss (woman *ou* girl).
**suite** [sɥit] *nf* (*continuation: d'énumération etc*) rest, remainder ; (: *de feuilleton*) continuation ; (: *second film etc sur le même thème*) sequel ; (*série: de maisons, succès*): **une** ~ **de** a series *ou* succession of ; (*MATH*) series *sg* ; (*conséquence*) result ; (*ordre, liaison logique*) coherence ; (*appartement, MUS*) suite ; (*escorte*) retinue, suite ; ~**s** *nfpl* (*d'une maladie etc*) effects ; **prendre la** ~ **de** (*directeur etc*) to succeed, take over from ; **donner** ~ **à** (*requête, projet*) to follow up ; **faire** ~ **à** to follow ; (**faisant**) ~ **à votre lettre du** further to your letter of the ; **de** ~ *ad* (*d'affilée*) in succession ; (*immédiatement*) at once ; **par la** ~

afterwards, subsequently; **à la ~** *ad* one after the other; **à la ~ de** (*derrière*) behind; (*en conséquence de*) following; **par ~ de** owing to, as a result of; **avoir de la ~ dans les idées** to show great singleness of purpose; **attendre la ~** to wait and see what comes next.

**suivant, e** [sɥivɑ̃, -ɑ̃t] *a* next, following; (*ci-après*): **l'exercice ~** the following exercise // *prép* (*selon*) according to; **au ~!** next!

**suiveur** [sɥivœR] *nm* (CYCLISME) (official) follower.

**suivi, e** [sɥivi] *a* (*régulier*) regular; (COMM: *article*) in general production; (*cohérent*) consistent; coherent; **très/peu ~** (*cours*) well-/poorly-attended; (*feuilleton etc*) widely/not widely followed.

**suivre** [sɥivR(ə)] *vt* (*gén*) to follow; (SCOL: *cours*) to attend; (: *leçon*) to follow, attend to; (: *programme*) to keep up with; (COMM: *article*) to continue to stock // *vi* to follow; (*élève*) to attend, pay attention; to keep up, follow; **se ~** (*accidents etc*) to follow one after the other; (*raisonnement*) to be coherent; **faire ~** (*lettre*) to forward; **~ son cours** (*suj: enquête etc*) to run *ou* take its course; '**à ~**' 'to be continued'.

**sujet, te** [syʒɛ, -ɛt] *a*: **être ~ à** (*vertige etc*) to be liable *ou* subject to // *nm/f* (*d'un souverain*) subject // *nm* subject; (*raison: d'une dispute etc*) cause; **avoir ~ de se plaindre** to have cause for complaint; **au ~ de** *prép* about; **~ à caution** a questionable; **~ de conversation** topic *ou* subject of conversation; **~ d'examen** (SCOL) examination question; examination paper; **~ d'expérience** (BIO etc) experimental subject.

**sujétion** [syʒesjɔ̃] *nf* subjection; (*fig*) constraint.

**sulfater** [sylfate] *vt* to spray with copper sulphate.

**sulfureux, euse** [sylfyRø, -øz] *a* sulphurous.

**sulfurique** [sylfyRik] *a*: **acide ~** sulphuric acid.

**summum** [sɔmɔm] *nm*: **le ~ de** the height of.

**superbe** [sypɛRb(ə)] *a* magnificent, superb.

**super(carburant)** [sypɛR(kaRbyRɑ̃)] *nm* high-octane petrol.

**supercherie** [sypɛRʃəRi] *nf* trick.

**superfétatoire** [sypɛRfetatwaR] *a* superfluous.

**superficie** [sypɛRfisi] *nf* (surface) area; (*fig*) surface.

**superficiel, le** [sypɛRfisjɛl] *a* superficial.

**superflu, e** [sypɛRfly] *a* superfluous.

**supérieur, e** [sypeRjœR] *a* (*lèvre, étages, classes*) upper; (*plus élevé: température, niveau*): **~ (à)** higher (than); (*meilleur: qualité, produit*): **~ (à)** superior (to); (*excellent, hautain*) superior // *nm, nf* superior; **Mère ~e** Mother Superior; **à l'étage ~** on the next floor up; **~ en nombre** superior in number; **supériorité** *nf* superiority.

**superlatif** [sypɛRlatif] *nm* superlative.

**supermarché** [sypɛRmaRʃe] *nm* supermarket.

**superposer** [sypɛRpoze] *vt* to superpose; (*faire chevaucher*) to superimpose; **se ~** *vi* (*images, souvenirs*) to be superimposed; **lits superposés** bunk beds.

**superpréfet** [sypɛRpRefɛ] *nm* prefect in charge of a region.

**superproduction** [sypɛRpRɔdyksjɔ̃] *nf* (*film*) spectacular.

**superpuissance** [sypɛRpɥisɑ̃s] *nf* superpower.

**supersonique** [sypɛRsɔnik] *a* supersonic.

**superstitieux, euse** [sypɛRstisjø, -øz] *a* superstitious.

**superstition** [sypɛRstisjɔ̃] *nf* superstition.

**superstructure** [sypɛRstRyktyR] *nf* superstructure.

**superviser** [sypɛRvize] *vt* to supervise.

**supplanter** [syplɑ̃te] *vt* to supplant.

**suppléance** [sypleɑ̃s] *nf* supply post.

**suppléant, e** [sypleɑ̃, -ɑ̃t] *a* (*juge, fonctionnaire*) deputy *cpd*; (*professeur*) supply *cpd* // *nm/f* deputy; supply teacher; **médecin ~** locum.

**suppléer** [syplee] *vt* (*ajouter: mot manquant etc*) to supply, provide; (*compenser: lacune*) to fill in; (: *défaut*) to make up for; (*remplacer: professeur*) to stand in for; (: *juge*) to deputize for; **~ à** *vt* to make up for; to substitute for.

**supplément** [syplemɑ̃] *nm* supplement; **un ~ de travail** extra *ou* additional work; **un ~ de frites** *etc* an extra portion of chips *etc*; **un ~ de 100 F** a supplement of 100 F, an extra *ou* additional 100 F; **ceci est en ~** (*au menu etc*) this is extra, there is an extra charge for this; **supplémentaire** *a* additional, further; (*train, bus*) relief *cpd*, extra.

**supplétif, ive** [sypletif, -iv] *a* (MIL) auxiliary.

**supplication** [syplikɑsjɔ̃] *nf* (REL) supplication; **~s** *nfpl* (*adjurations*) pleas, entreaties.

**supplice** [syplis] *nm* (*peine corporelle*) torture *q*; form of torture; (*douleur physique, morale*) torture, agony.

**supplier** [syplije] *vt* to implore, beseech.

**supplique** [syplik] *nf* petition.

**support** [sypɔR] *nm* support; (*pour livre, outils*) stand; **~ audio-visuel** audio-visual aid; **~ publicitaire** advertising medium.

**supportable** [sypɔRtabl(ə)] *a* (*douleur*) bearable.

**supporter** *nm* [sypɔRtɛR] supporter, fan // *vt* [sypɔRte] (*poids, poussée*) to support; (*conséquences, épreuve*) to bear, endure; (*défauts, personne*) to tolerate, put up with; (*suj: chose: chaleur etc*) to withstand; (*suj: personne: chaleur, vin*) to take.

**supposé, e** [sypoze] *a* (*nombre*) estimated; (*auteur*) supposed.

**supposer** [sypoze] *vt* to suppose; (*impliquer*) to presuppose; **à ~ que** supposing (that); **supposition** *nf* supposition.

**suppositoire** [sypozitwaR] *nm* suppository.

**suppôt** [sypo] *nm* (*péj*) henchman.

**suppression** [sypResjɔ̃] *nf* removal; deletion; cancellation; suppression.

**supprimer** [sypRime] *vt* (*cloison, cause, anxiété*) to remove ; (*clause, mot*) to delete ; (*congés, service d'autobus etc*) to cancel ; (*publication, article*) to suppress ; (*emplois, privilèges, témoin gênant*) to do away with.
**suppurer** [sypyRe] *vi* to suppurate.
**supputations** [sypytɑsjɔ̃] *nfpl* calculations, reckonings.
**supputer** [sypyte] *vt* to calculate, reckon.
**suprématie** [sypRemasi] *nf* supremacy.
**suprême** [sypRɛm] *a* supreme.
**sur** [syR] *prép* (*gén*) on ; (*par-dessus*) over ; (*au-dessus*) above ; (*direction*) towards ; (*à propos de*) about, on ; **un ~ 10** one out of 10 ; **4m ~ 2** 4m by 2 ; **je n'ai pas d'argent ~ moi** I haven't got any money with *ou* on me ; **~ ce** *ad* hereupon.
**sur, e** [syR] *a* sour.
**sûr, e** [syR] *a* sure, certain ; (*digne de confiance*) reliable ; (*sans danger*) safe ; **peu ~** unreliable ; **~ de qch** sure *ou* certain of sth ; **être ~ de qn** to be sure of sb ; **~ de soi** self-assured, self-confident ; **le plus ~ est de** the safest thing is to.
**surabonder** [syRabɔ̃de] *vi* to be overabundant.
**suraigu, uë** [syRegy] *a* very shrill.
**surajouter** [syRaʒute] *vt*: **~ qch à** to add sth to.
**suralimenté, e** [syRalimɑ̃te] *a* overfed.
**suranné, e** [syRane] *a* outdated, outmoded.
**surbaissé, e** [syRbese] *a* lowered, low.
**surcharge** [syRʃaRʒ(ə)] *nf* (*de passagers, marchandises*) excess load ; (*correction*) alteration ; (*PHILATÉLIE*) surcharge ; **prendre des passagers en ~** to take on excess *ou* extra passengers ; **~ de bagages** excess luggage ; **~ de travail** extra work.
**surcharger** [syRʃaRʒe] *vt* to overload ; (*timbre-poste*) to surcharge.
**surchauffé, e** [syRʃofe] *a* overheated.
**surchoix** [syRʃwa] *a inv* top-quality.
**surclasser** [syRklɑse] *vt* to outclass.
**surcouper** [syRkupe] *vt* to overtrump.
**surcroît** [syRkRwa] *nm*: **un ~ de** additional + *nom* ; **par** *ou* **de ~** moreover ; **en ~** in addition.
**surdi-mutité** [syRdimytite] *nf*: **atteint de ~** deaf and dumb.
**surdité** [syRdite] *nf* deafness.
**sureau, x** [syRo] *nm* elder (tree).
**surélever** [syRɛlve] *vt* to raise, heighten.
**sûrement** [syRmɑ̃] *ad* reliably ; safely, securely ; (*certainement*) certainly.
**surenchère** [syRɑ̃ʃɛR] *nf* (*aux enchères*) higher bid ; (*sur prix fixe*) overbid ; (*fig*) overstatement ; outbidding tactics *pl* ; **surenchérir** *vi* to bid higher ; to raise one's bid ; (*fig*) to try and outbid each other.
**surent** *vb voir* **savoir**.
**surestimer** [syRɛstime] *vt* to overestimate.
**sûreté** [syRte] *nf* (*voir* **sûr**) reliability ; safety ; (*JUR*) guaranty ; surety ; **mettre en ~** to put in a safe place ; **pour plus de ~** as an extra precaution ; **to be on the safe side** ; **la S~ (nationale)** division of the Ministère de l'Intérieur heading all police

forces except the gendarmerie and the Paris préfecture de police.
**surexcité, e** [syRɛksite] *a* overexcited.
**surexposer** [syRɛkspoze] *vt* to overexpose.
**surf** [syRf] *nm* surfing.
**surface** [syRfas] *nf* surface ; (*superficie*) surface area ; **faire ~** to surface ; **en ~** *ad* near the surface ; (*fig*) superficially ; **la pièce fait 100m² de ~** the room has a surface area of 100m² ; **~ de réparation** penalty area.
**surfait, e** [syRfɛ, -ɛt] *a* overrated.
**surfin, e** [syRfɛ̃, -in] *a* superfine.
**surgelé, e** [syRʒəle] *a* (deep-)frozen.
**surgir** [syRʒiR] *vi* (*personne, véhicule*) to appear suddenly ; (*geyser etc: de terre*) to shoot up ; (*fig: problème, conflit*) to arise.
**surhomme** [syRɔm] *nm* superman.
**surhumain, e** [syRymɛ̃, -ɛn] *a* superhuman.
**surimposer** [syRɛ̃poze] *vt* to overtax.
**surimpression** [syRɛ̃pResjɔ̃] *nf* (*PHOTO*) double exposure ; **en ~** superimposed.
**sur-le-champ** [syRləʃɑ̃] *ad* immediately.
**surlendemain** [syRlɑ̃dmɛ̃] *nm*: **le ~ (soir)** two days later (in the evening) ; **le ~ de** two days after.
**surmenage** [syRmənaʒ] *nm* overwork ; **le ~ intellectuel** mental fatigue.
**surmené, e** [syRməne] *a* overworked.
**surmener** [syRməne] *vt*, **se ~** *vi* to overwork.
**surmonter** [syRmɔ̃te] *vt* (*suj: coupole etc*) to surmount, top ; (*vaincre*) to overcome, surmount.
**surmultiplié, e** [syRmyltiplije] *a*, *nf*: **(vitesse) ~e** overdrive.
**surnager** [syRnaʒe] *vi* to float.
**surnaturel, le** [syRnatyRɛl] *a*, *nm* supernatural.
**surnom** [syRnɔ̃] *nm* nickname.
**surnombre** [syRnɔ̃bR(ə)] *nm*: **être en ~** to be too many (*ou* one too many).
**surnommer** [syRnɔme] *vt* to nickname.
**surnuméraire** [syRnymeRɛR] *nm/f* supernumerary.
**suroît** [syRwa] *nm* sou'wester.
**surpasser** [syRpase] *vt* to surpass.
**surpeuplé, e** [syRpœple] *a* overpopulated.
**surplis** [syRpli] *nm* surplice.
**surplomb** [syRplɔ̃] *nm* overhang ; **en ~** overhanging.
**surplomber** [syRplɔ̃be] *vi* to be overhanging // *vt* to overhang ; to tower above.
**surplus** [syRply] *nm* (*COMM*) surplus ; (*reste*): **~ de bois** wood left over ; **~ américains** American army surplus *sg*.
**surprenant, e** [syRpRənɑ̃, -ɑ̃t] *a* surprising.
**surprendre** [syRpRɑ̃dR(ə)] *vt* (*étonner, prendre à l'improviste*) to surprise ; (*tomber sur: intrus etc*) to catch ; (*fig*) to detect ; to chance *ou* happen upon ; to intercept ; to overhear ; **~ la vigilance/bonne foi de qn** to catch sb out/betray sb's good faith ; **se ~ à faire** to catch *ou* find o.s. doing.
**surprime** [syRpRim] *nf* additional premium.

**surpris, e** [syʀpʀi, -iz] *a*: ~ **(de/que)** surprised (at/that).

**surprise** [syʀpʀiz] *nf* surprise ; **faire une** ~ **à qn** to give sb a surprise ; **par** ~ *ad* by surprise.

**surprise-partie** [syʀpʀizpaʀti] *nf* party.

**surproduction** [syʀpʀɔdyksjɔ̃] *nf* overproduction.

**surréaliste** [syʀʀealist(ə)] *a* surrealist.

**sursaut** [syʀso] *nm* start, jump ; ~ **de** (*énergie, indignation*) sudden fit *ou* burst of ; **en** ~ *ad* with a start ; **sursauter** *vi* to (give a) start, jump.

**surseoir** [syʀswaʀ]: ~ **à** *vt* to defer ; (*JUR*) to stay.

**sursis** [syʀsi] *nm* (*JUR*: *gén*) suspended sentence ; (*à l'exécution capitale, aussi fig*) reprieve ; (*MIL*): ~ **(d'appel** *ou* **d'incorporation)** deferment ; **condamné à 5 mois (de prison) avec** ~ given a 5-month suspended (prison) sentence ; **sursitaire** *nm* (*MIL*) deferred conscript.

**sursois** *etc vb voir* **surseoir.**

**surtaxe** [syʀtaks(ə)] *nf* surcharge.

**surtout** [syʀtu] *ad* (*avant tout, d'abord*) above all ; (*spécialement, particulièrement*) especially ; **il aime le sport,** ~ **le football** he likes sport, especially football ; **cet été, il a** ~ **fait de la pêche** this summer he went fishing more than anything (else) ; ~, **ne dites rien!** whatever you do — don't say anything! ; ~ **pas!** certainly *ou* definitely not! ; ~ **que...** especially as ...

**surveillance** [syʀvɛjɑ̃s] *nf* watch ; (*POLICE, MIL*) surveillance ; **sous** ~ **médicale** under medical supervision ; **la** ~ **du territoire** internal security (*voir aussi* **D.S.T.**).

**surveillant, e** [syʀvɛjɑ̃, -ɑ̃t] *nm/f* (*de prison*) warder ; (*SCOL*) monitor ; (*de travaux*) supervisor, overseer.

**surveiller** [syʀveje] *vt* (*enfant, élèves, bagages*) to watch, keep an eye on ; (*malade*) to watch over ; (*prisonnier, suspect*) to keep (a) watch on ; (*territoire, bâtiment*) to (keep) watch over ; (*travaux, cuisson*) to supervise ; (*SCOL*: *examen*) to invigilate ; **se** ~ to keep a check *ou* watch on o.s. ; ~ **son langage/sa ligne** to watch one's language/figure.

**survenir** [syʀvəniʀ] *vi* (*incident, retards*) to occur, arise ; (*événement*) to take place ; (*personne*) to appear, arrive.

**survêtement** [syʀvɛtmɑ̃] *nm* tracksuit.

**survie** [syʀvi] *nf* survival ; (*REL*) afterlife ; **une** ~ **de quelques mois** a few more months of life.

**survivant, e** [syʀvivɑ̃, -ɑ̃t] *nm/f* survivor.

**survivre** [syʀvivʀ(ə)] *vi* to survive ; ~ **à** *vt* (*accident etc*) to survive ; (*personne*) to outlive.

**survol** [syʀvɔl] *nm* flying over.

**survoler** [syʀvɔle] *vt* to fly over ; (*fig: livre*) to skim through.

**survolté, e** [syʀvɔlte] *a* (*ÉLEC*) stepped up, boosted ; (*fig*) worked up.

**sus** [sy(s)]: **en** ~ **de** *prép* in addition to, over and above ; **en** ~ *ad* in addition ; ~ **à** *excl*: ~ **au tyran!** at the tyrant!

**susceptibilité** [sysɛptibilite] *nf* sensitiveness *q*.

**susceptible** [sysɛptibl(ə)] *a* touchy, sensitive ; ~ **d'amélioration** *ou* **d'être amélioré** that can be improved, open to improvement ; ~ **de faire** able to do ; liable to do.

**susciter** [sysite] *vt* (*admiration*) to arouse ; (*obstacles, ennuis*): ~ **(à qn)** to create (for sb).

**susdit, e** [sysdi, -dit] *a* foresaid.

**susmentionné, e** [sysmɑ̃sjɔne] *a* above-mentioned.

**suspect, e** [syspɛ(kt), -ɛkt(ə)] *a* suspicious ; (*témoignage, opinions*) suspect // *nm/f* suspect ; **peu** ~ **de** most unlikely to be suspected of.

**suspecter** [syspɛkte] *vt* to suspect ; (*honnêteté de qn*) to question, have one's suspicions about ; ~ **qn d'être** to suspect sb of being.

**suspendre** [syspɑ̃dʀ(ə)] *vt* (*accrocher*: *vêtement*): ~ **qch (à)** to hang sth up (on) ; (*fixer: lustre etc*): ~ **qch à** to hang sth from ; (*interrompre, démettre*) to suspend ; (*remettre*) to defer ; **se** ~ **à** to hang from.

**suspendu, e** [syspɑ̃dy] *pp de* **suspendre** // *a* (*accroché*): ~ **à** hanging on (*ou* from) ; (*perché*): ~ **au-dessus de** suspended over ; (*AUTO*): **bien/mal** ~ with good/poor suspension.

**suspens** [syspɑ̃]: **en** ~ *ad* (*affaire*) in abeyance ; **tenir en** ~ to keep in suspense.

**suspense** [syspɑ̃s] *nm* suspense.

**suspension** [syspɑ̃sjɔ̃] *nf* suspension ; deferment ; (*AUTO*) suspension ; (*lustre*) pendent light fitting ; **en** ~ in suspension, suspended ; ~ **d'audience** adjournment.

**suspicion** [syspisjɔ̃] *nf* suspicion.

**sustenter** [systɑ̃te]: **se** ~ *vi* to take sustenance.

**susurrer** [sysyʀe] *vt* to whisper.

**sut** *vb voir* **savoir.**

**suture** [sytyʀ] *nf*: **point de** ~ stitch ; **suturer** *vt* to stitch up, suture.

**svelte** [svɛlt(ə)] *a* slender, svelte.

**S.V.P.** *sigle* (= *s'il vous plaît*) please.

**syllabe** [silab] *nf* syllable.

**sylvestre** [silvɛstʀ(ə)] *a*: **pin** ~ Scots pine, Scotch fir.

**sylviculture** [silvikyltyʀ] *nf* forestry, sylviculture.

**symbole** [sɛ̃bɔl] *nm* symbol ; **symbolique** *a* symbolic(al) ; (*geste, offrande*) token *cpd* ; (*salaire, dommage-intérêts*) nominal ; **symboliser** *vt* to symbolize.

**symétrie** [simetʀi] *nf* symmetry ; **symétrique** *a* symmetrical.

**sympa** [sɛ̃pa] *a abr de* **sympathique.**

**sympathie** [sɛ̃pati] *nf* (*inclination*) liking ; (*affinité*) fellow feeling ; (*condoléances*) sympathy ; **accueillir avec** ~ (*projet*) to receive favourably ; **avoir de la** ~ **pour qn** to like sb, have a liking for sb ; **témoignages de** ~ expressions of sympathy ; **croyez à toute ma** ~ you have my deepest sympathy.

**sympathique** [sɛ̃patik] *a* nice, friendly ; likeable ; pleasant.

**sympathisant, e** [sɛ̃patizɑ̃, -ɑ̃t] *nm/f* sympathizer.

**sympathiser** [sɛ̃patize] *vi* (*voisins etc: s'entendre*) to get on (well) ; (: *se fréquenter*) to socialize, see each other ; ~ **avec** to get on (well) with ; to see, socialize with.

**symphonie** [sɛ̃fɔni] *nf* symphony ; **symphonique** *a* (*orchestre, concert*) symphony *cpd* ; (*musique*) symphonic.

**symptomatique** [sɛ̃ptɔmatik] *a* symptomatic.

**symptôme** [sɛ̃ptom] *nm* symptom.

**synagogue** [sinagɔg] *nf* synagogue.

**synchronique** [sɛ̃kRɔnik] *a*: **tableau** ~ synchronic table of events.

**synchroniser** [sɛ̃kRɔnize] *vt* to synchronize.

**syncope** [sɛ̃kɔp] *nf* (MÉD) blackout ; (MUS) syncopation ; **tomber en** ~ to faint, pass out ; **syncopé, e** *a* syncopated.

**syndic** [sɛ̃dik] *nm* managing agent.

**syndical, e, aux** [sɛ̃dikal, -o] *a* (trade-)union *cpd* ; ~**isme** *nm* trade unionism ; union(ist) activities *pl* ; ~**iste** *nm/f* trade unionist.

**syndicat** [sɛ̃dika] *nm* (*d'ouvriers, employés*) (trade) union ; (*autre association d'intérêts*) union, association ; ~ **d'initiative** tourist office *ou* bureau ; ~ **patronal** employers' syndicate, federation of employers ; ~ **de propriétaires** association of property owners.

**syndiqué, e** [sɛ̃dike] *a* belonging to a (trade) union ; **non** ~ non-union.

**syndiquer** [sɛ̃dike]: **se** ~ *vi* to form a trade union ; (*adhérer*) to join a trade union.

**syndrome** [sɛ̃dRom] *nm* syndrome.

**synode** [sinɔd] *nm* synod.

**synonyme** [sinɔnim] *a* synonymous // *nm* synonym ; ~ **de** synonymous with.

**synoptique** [sinɔptik] *a*: **tableau** ~ synoptic table.

**synovie** [sinɔvi] *nf* synovia.

**syntaxe** [sɛ̃taks(ə)] *nf* syntax.

**synthèse** [sɛ̃tɛz] *nf* synthesis (*pl* es) ; **faire la** ~ **de** to synthesize.

**synthétique** [sɛ̃tetik] *a* synthetic.

**synthétiseur** [sɛ̃tetizœR] *nm* (MUS) synthesizer.

**syphilis** [sifilis] *nf* syphilis.

**Syrie** [siRi] *nf*: **la** ~ Syria ; **syrien, ne** *a, nm/f* Syrian.

**systématique** [sistematik] *a* systematic.

**systématiser** [sistematize] *vt* to systematize.

**système** [sistɛm] *nm* system ; **le** ~ **D** resourcefulness ; **le** ~ **solaire** the solar system.

# T

**t'** [t(ə)] *pronom voir* **te**.

**ta** [ta] *dét voir* **ton**.

**tabac** [taba] *nm* tobacco ; tobacconist's (shop) // *a inv*: (**couleur**) ~ buff(-coloured) ; **passer qn à** ~ to beat sb up ; ~ **blond/brun** light/dark tobacco ; ~ **gris** shag ; ~ **à priser** snuff ; **tabagie** *nf* smoke den ; **tabatière** *nf* snuffbox.

**tabernacle** [tabɛRnakl(ə)] *nm* tabernacle.

**table** [tabl(ə)] *nf* table ; **à** ~! dinner *etc* is ready! ; **se mettre à** ~ to sit down to eat ; (*fig: fam*) to come clean ; **mettre la** ~ to lay the table ; **faire** ~ **rase de** to make a clean sweep of ; ~ **basse** coffee table ;

~ **d'écoute** wire-tapping set ; ~ **d'harmonie** sounding board ; ~ **des matières** (table of) contents *pl* ; ~ **de multiplication** multiplication table ; ~ **de nuit** *ou* **de chevet** bedside table ; ~ **ronde** (*débat*) round table ; ~ **de toilette** washstand.

**tableau, x** [tablo] *nm* painting ; (*reproduction, fig*) `picture ; (*panneau*) board ; (*schéma*) table, chart ; ~ **d'affichage** notice board ; ~ **de bord** dashboard ; (AVIAT) instrument panel ; ~ **de chasse** tally ; ~ **noir** blackboard.

**tabler** [table] *vi*: ~ **sur** to count *ou* bank on.

**tablette** [tablɛt] *nf* (*planche*) shelf (*pl* shelves) ; ~ **de chocolat** bar of chocolate.

**tablier** [tablije] *nm* apron ; (*de pont*) roadway.

**tabou** [tabu] *nm, a* taboo.

**tabouret** [tabuRɛ] *nm* stool.

**tabulateur** [tabylatœR] *nm* tabulator.

**tac** [tak] *nm*: **du** ~ **au** ~ tit for tat.

**tache** [taʃ] *nf* (*saleté*) stain, mark ; (ART, *de couleur, lumière*) spot ; splash, patch ; **faire** ~ **d'huile** to spread, gain ground.

**tâche** [taʃ] *nf* task ; **travailler à la** ~ to do general jobbing, work as a jobbing gardener/builder *etc*.

**tacher** [taʃe] *vt* to stain, mark ; (*fig*) to sully, stain.

**tâcher** [taʃe] *vi*: ~ **de faire** to try *ou* endeavour to do.

**tâcheron** [taʃRɔ̃] *nm* (*fig*) drudge.

**tacite** [tasit] *a* tacit.

**taciturne** [tasityRn(ə)] *a* taciturn.

**tacot** [tako] *nm* (*péj*) banger.

**tact** [takt] *nm* tact ; **avoir du** ~ to be tactful, have tact.

**tactile** [taktil] *a* tactile.

**tactique** [taktik] *a* tactical // *nf* (*technique*) tactics *sg* ; (*plan*) tactic.

**taie** [tɛ] *nf*: ~ (**d'oreiller**) pillowslip, pillowcase.

**taille** [taj] *nf* cutting ; pruning ; (*milieu du corps*) waist ; (*hauteur*) height ; (*grandeur*) size ; **de** ~ **à faire** capable of doing ; **de** ~ *a* sizeable.

**taille-crayon(s)** [tajkRɛjɔ̃] *nm* pencil sharpener.

**tailler** [taje] *vt* (*pierre, diamant*) to cut ; (*arbre, plante*) to prune ; (*vêtement*) to cut out ; (*crayon*) to sharpen ; **se** ~ *vt* (*ongles, barbe*) to trim, cut ; (*fig: réputation*) to gain, win // *vi* (*fam*) to beat it ; ~ **dans** (*chair, bois*) to cut into.

**tailleur** [tajœR] *nm* (*couturier*) tailor ; (*vêtement*) suit, costume ; **en** ~ (*assis*) cross-legged ; ~ **de diamants** diamond-cutter.

**taillis** [taji] *nm* copse.

**tain** [tɛ̃] *nm* silvering ; **glace sans** ~ two-way mirror.

**taire** [tɛR] *vt* to keep to o.s., conceal // *vi*: **faire** ~ **qn** to make sb be quiet ; (*fig*) to silence sb ; **se** ~ *vi* (*s'arrêter de parler*) to fall silent, stop talking ; (*ne pas parler*) to be silent *ou* quiet ; to keep quiet ; **tais-toi!, taisez-vous!** be quiet!

**talc** [talk] *nm* talcum powder.

**talé, e** [tale] a (fruit) bruised.

**talent** [talɑ̃] nm talent ; **talentueux, euse** a talented.

**talion** [taljɔ̃] nm: **la loi du** ~ an eye for an eye.

**talisman** [talismɑ̃] nm talisman.

**talon** [talɔ̃] nm heel ; (de chèque, billet) stub, counterfoil ; ~**s plats/aiguilles** flat/stiletto heels.

**talonner** [talɔne] vt to follow hard behind ; (fig) to hound.

**talonnette** [talɔnɛt] nf heelpiece.

**talquer** [talke] vt to put talcum powder on.

**talus** [taly] nm embankment.

**tambour** [tɑ̃buʀ] nm (MUS, aussi TECH) drum ; (musicien) drummer ; (porte) revolving door(s pl).

**tambourin** [tɑ̃buʀɛ̃] nm tambourine.

**tambouriner** [tɑ̃buʀine] vi: ~ **contre** to drum against ou on.

**tambour-major** [tɑ̃buʀmaʒɔʀ] nm drum major.

**tamis** [tami] nm sieve.

**Tamise** [tamiz] nf: **la** ~ the Thames.

**tamisé, e** [tamize] a (fig) subdued, soft.

**tamiser** [tamize] vt to sieve, sift.

**tampon** [tɑ̃pɔ̃] nm (de coton, d'ouate) wad, pad ; (amortisseur) buffer ; (bouchon) plug, stopper ; (cachet, timbre) stamp ; **(hygiénique)** tampon ; **tamponner** vt (timbres) to stamp ; (heurter) to crash ou ram into ; **tamponneuse** a: **autos tamponneuses** dodgems.

**tam-tam** [tamtam] nm tomtom.

**tandem** [tɑ̃dɛm] nm tandem ; (fig) duo, pair.

**tandis** [tɑ̃di]: ~ **que** cj while.

**tangage** [tɑ̃gaʒ] nm pitching (and tossing).

**tangent, e** [tɑ̃ʒɑ̃, -ɑ̃t] a (MATH): ~ **à** tangential to ; (fam) close // nf (MATH) tangent.

**tangible** [tɑ̃ʒibl(ə)] a tangible, concrete.

**tango** [tɑ̃go] nm tango.

**tanguer** [tɑ̃ge] vi to pitch (and toss).

**tanière** [tanjɛʀ] nf lair, den.

**tanin** [tanɛ̃] nm tannin.

**tank** [tɑ̃k] nm tank.

**tanné, e** [tane] a weather-beaten.

**tanner** [tane] vt to tan.

**tannerie** [tanʀi] nf tannery.

**tanneur** [tanœʀ] nm tanner.

**tant** [tɑ̃] ad so much ; ~ **de** (sable, eau) so much ; (gens, livres) so many ; ~ **que** cj as long as ; ~ **que** (comparatif) as much as ; ~ **mieux** that's great ; so much the better ; ~ **pis** never mind ; too bad ; ~ **pis pour lui** too bad for him ; ~ **soit peu** a little bit ; (even) remotely.

**tante** [tɑ̃t] nf aunt.

**tantinet** [tɑ̃tinɛ]: **un** ~ ad a tiny bit.

**tantôt** [tɑ̃to] ad (parfois): ~ ... ~ now ... now ; (cet après-midi) this afternoon.

**taon** [tɑ̃] nm horsefly, gadfly.

**tapage** [tapaʒ] nm uproar, din ; ~ **nocturne** (JUR) disturbance of the peace (at night).

**tapageur, euse** [tapaʒœʀ, -øz] a loud, flashy ; noisy.

**tape** [tap] nf slap.

**tape-à-l'œil** [tapalœj] a inv flashy, showy.

**taper** [tape] vt (porte) to bang, slam ; (dactylographier) to type (out) ; (fam: emprunter): ~ **qn de 10 F** to touch sb for 10 F, cadge 10 F off sb // vi (soleil) to beat down ; ~ **sur qn** to thump sb ; (fig) to run sb down ; ~ **sur qch** to hit sth ; to bang on sth ; ~ **à** (porte etc) to knock on ; ~ **dans** vt (se servir) to dig into ; ~ **des mains/pieds** to clap one's hands/stamp one's feet ; ~ **(à la machine)** to type.

**tapi, e** [tapi] a: ~ **dans/derrière** crouching ou cowering in/behind ; hidden away in/behind.

**tapioca** [tapjɔka] nm tapioca.

**tapis** [tapi] nm carpet ; (de table) cloth ; **mettre sur le** ~ (fig) to bring up for discussion ; ~ **roulant** conveyor belt ; ~ **de sol** (de tente) groundsheet ; ~**-brosse** nm doormat.

**tapisser** [tapise] vt (avec du papier peint) to paper ; (recouvrir): ~ **qch (de)** to cover sth (with).

**tapisserie** [tapisʀi] nf (tenture, broderie) tapestry ; (: travail) tapestry-making ; tapestry work ; (papier peint) wallpaper ; **faire** ~ to sit out, be a wallflower.

**tapissier, ière** [tapisje, -jɛʀ] nm/f: ~ **(-décorateur)** upholsterer (and decorator).

**tapoter** [tapɔte] vt to pat, tap.

**taquet** [takɛ] nm wedge ; peg.

**taquin, e** [takɛ̃, -in] a teasing.

**taquiner** [takine] vt to tease.

**tarabiscoté, e** [taʀabiskɔte] a over-ornate, fussy.

**tarabuster** [taʀabyste] vt to bother, worry.

**tarauder** [taʀode] vt (TECH) to tap ; to thread ; (fig) to pierce.

**tard** [taʀ] ad late ; **au plus** ~ at the latest ; **plus** ~ later (on) ; **sur le** ~ late in life.

**tarder** [taʀde] vi (chose) to be a long time coming ; (personne): ~ **à faire** to delay doing ; **il me tarde d'être** I am longing to be ; **sans (plus)** ~ without (further) delay.

**tardif, ive** [taʀdif, -iv] a late ; **tardivement** ad late.

**tare** [taʀ] nf (COMM) tare ; (fig) defect ; taint, blemish.

**targuer** [taʀge]: **se** ~ **de** vt to boast about.

**tarif** [taʀif] nm (liste) price list ; tariff ; (barème) rates pl ; fares pl ; tariff ; (prix) rate ; fare ; ~**aire** a tariff cpd ; ~**er** vt to fix the price ou rate for ; ~**é 10 F** priced 10 F.

**tarir** [taʀiʀ] vi to dry up, run dry // vt to dry up.

**tarot(s)** [taʀo] nm(pl) tarot cards.

**tartare** [taʀtaʀ] a (CULIN) tartar(e).

**tarte** [taʀt(ə)] nf tart ; ~ **aux pommes/à la crème** apple/custard tart ; ~**lette** nf tartlet.

**tartine** [taʀtin] nf slice of bread and butter (ou jam) ; ~ **au miel** slice of bread and honey ; **tartiner** vt to spread ; **fromage à tartiner** cheese spread.

**tartre** [taʀtʀ(ə)] nm (des dents) tartar ; (de chaudière) fur, scale.

**tas** [tɑ] *nm* heap, pile ; (*fig*): **un ~ de** heaps of, lots of ; **en ~** in a heap *ou* pile ; **dans le ~** (*fig*) in the crowd ; among them ; **formé sur le ~** trained on the job.

**tasse** [tɑs] *nf* cup.

**tassé, e** [tɑse] *a*: **bien ~** (*café etc*) strong.

**tasser** [tɑse] *vt* (*terre, neige*) to pack down ; (*entasser*): **~ qch dans** to cram sth into ; **se ~** *vi* (*terrain*) to settle ; (*fig*) to sort itself out, settle down.

**tâter** [tɑte] *vt* to feel ; (*fig*) to try out ; to test out ; **~ de** (*prison etc*) to have a taste of ; **se ~** (*hésiter*) to be in two minds ; **~ le terrain** (*fig*) to test the ground.

**tatillon, ne** [tatijɔ̃, -ɔn] *a* pernickety.

**tâtonnement** [tɑtɔnmɑ̃] *nm*: **par ~s** (*fig*) by trial and error.

**tâtonner** [tɑtɔne] *vi* to grope one's way along.

**tâtons** [tɑtɔ̃]: **à ~** *ad*: **chercher/avancer à ~** to grope around for/grope one's way forward.

**tatouage** [tatwaʒ] *nm* tattooing ; (*dessin*) tattoo.

**tatouer** [tatwe] *vt* to tattoo.

**taudis** [todi] *nm* hovel, slum.

**taupe** [top] *nf* mole ; **taupinière** *nf* molehill.

**taureau, x** [tɔʀo] *nm* bull ; (*signe*): **le T~** Taurus, the Bull ; **être du T~** to be Taurus.

**tauromachie** [tɔʀɔmaʃi] *nf* bullfighting.

**taux** [to] *nm* rate ; (*d'alcool*) level ; **~ d'intérêt** interest rate.

**tavelé, e** [tavle] *a* marbled.

**taverne** [tavɛʀn(ə)] *nf* inn, tavern.

**taxe** [taks] *nf* tax ; (*douanière*) duty ; **~ de séjour** tourist tax ; **~ à la valeur ajoutée (T.V.A.)** value added tax (V.A.T.).

**taxer** [takse] *vt* (*personne*) to tax ; (*produit*) to put a tax on, tax ; (*fig*): **~ qn de** to call sb + *attribut* ; to accuse sb of, tax sb with.

**taxi** [taksi] *nm* taxi.

**taximètre** [taksimɛtʀ(ə)] *nm* (taxi)meter.

**taxiphone** [taksifɔn] *nm* pay phone.

**T.C.F.** *sigle m* = *Touring Club de France*, ≈ AA *ou* RAC.

**Tchécoslovaquie** [tʃekɔslɔvaki] *nf* Czechoslovakia ; **tchèque** *a, nm, nf* Czech.

**te, t'** [t(ə)] *pronom* you ; (*réfléchi*) yourself.

**té** [te] *nm* T-square.

**technicien, ne** [tɛknisjɛ̃, -jɛn] *nm/f* technician.

**technique** [tɛknik] *a* technical // *nf* technique ; **~ment** *ad* technically.

**technocrate** [tɛknɔkʀat] *nm/f* technocrat.

**technocratie** [tɛknɔkʀasi] *nf* technocracy.

**technologie** [tɛknɔlɔʒi] *nf* technology ; **technologique** *a* technological.

**teck** [tɛk] *nm* teak.

**teckel** [tekɛl] *nm* dachshund.

**teignais** *etc vb voir* **teindre**.

**teigne** [tɛɲ] *nf* (*ZOOL*) moth ; (*MÉD*) ringworm.

**teigneux, euse** [tɛɲø, -øz] *a* (*péj*) nasty, scabby.

**teindre** [tɛ̃dʀ(ə)] *vt* to dye.

**teint, e** [tɛ̃, tɛ̃t] *a* dyed // *nm* (*du visage*)

complexion, colouring ; colour // *nf* shade, colour ; **grand ~** *a inv* colourfast.

**teinté, e** [tɛ̃te] *a* (*verres*) tinted ; (*bois*) stained ; **~ acajou** mahogany-stained ; **~ de** (*fig*) tinged with.

**teinter** [tɛ̃te] *vt* to tint ; (*bois*) to stain ;

**teinture** *nf* dyeing ; (*substance*) dye ; (*MÉD*): **teinture d'iode** tincture of iodine.

**teinturerie** [tɛ̃tyʀʀi] *nf* dry cleaner's.

**teinturier** [tɛ̃tyʀje] *nm* dry cleaner.

**tel, telle** [tɛl] *a* (*pareil*) such ; (*comme*): **~ un/des ...** like a/ like... ; (*indéfini*) such-and-such a, a given ; (*intensif*): **un ~/de ~s ...** such (a)/such ... ; **rien de ~** nothing like it, no such thing ; **~ que** *cj* like, such as ; **~ quel** as it is *ou* stands (*ou* was *etc*).

**tél.** *abr de* **téléphone**.

**télé** [tele] *nf* (*abr de* **télévision**) (*poste*) T.V. (set) ; **à la ~** on the telly, on T.V.

**télé...** [tele] *préfixe*: **~benne** *nf* (*benne*) telecabine, gondola // *nm* telecabine ; **~cabine** *nf* (*benne*) telecabine, gondola // *nm* telecabine ; **~commande** *nf* remote control ; **~commander** *vt* to operate by remote control ; **~communications** *nfpl* telecommunications ; **~férique** *nm* = **~phérique** ; **~gramme** *nm* telegram.

**télégraphe** [telegʀaf] *nm* telegraph ; **télégraphie** *nf* telegraphy ; **télégraphier** *vt* to telegraph, cable ; **télégraphique** *a* telegraph *cpd*, telegraphic ; (*fig*) telegraphic ; **télégraphiste** *nm/f* telegraphist.

**téléguider** [telegide] *vt* to operate by remote control, radio-control.

**téléobjectif** [teleɔbʒɛktif] *nm* telephoto lens *sg*.

**télépathie** [telepati] *nf* telepathy.

**téléphérique** [telefeʀik] *nm* cable-car.

**téléphone** [telefɔn] *nm* telephone ; (*appel*) (telephone) call ; telephone conversation ; **avoir le ~** to be on the (tele)phone ; **au ~** on the phone ; **les T~s** ≈ Post Office Telecommunications ; **~ arabe** bush telephone ; **~ manuel** manually-operated telephone system ; **téléphoner** *vt* to telephone // *vi* to telephone, ring ; to make a phone call ; **téléphoner à** to phone up, ring up, call up ; **téléphonique** *a* telephone *cpd*, phone *cpd* ; **téléphoniste** *nm/f* telephonist, telephone operator ; (*d'entreprise*) switchboard operator.

**télescope** [telɛskɔp] *nm* telescope.

**télescoper** [telɛskɔpe] *vt* to smash up ; **se ~** (*véhicules*) to concertina.

**télescopique** [telɛskɔpik] *a* telescopic.

**téléscripteur** [teleskʀiptœʀ] *nm* teleprinter.

**télésiège** [telesjɛʒ] *nm* chairlift.

**téléski** [teleski] *nm* ski-tow ; **~ à archets** T-bar tow ; **~ à perche** button lift.

**téléspectateur, trice** [telespɛktatœʀ, -tʀis] *nm/f* (television) viewer.

**téléviser** [televize] *vt* to televise.

**téléviseur** [televizœʀ] *nm* television set.

**télévision** [televizjɔ̃] *nf* television ; **avoir la ~** to have a television ; **à la ~** on television.

**télex** [telɛks] *nm* telex.

**telle** [tɛl] *a voir* **tel**.

**tellement** [tɛlmɑ̃] ad (tant) so much ; (si) so ; ~ **plus grand (que)** so much bigger (than) ; ~ **de** (sable, eau) so much ; (gens, livres) so many ; **il s'est endormi ~ il était fatigué** he was so tired (that) he fell asleep ; **pas ~** not (all) that much ; not (all) that + adjectif.

**tellurique** [telyRik] a: **secousse ~** earth tremor.

**téméraire** [temerɛR] a reckless, rash ; **témérité** nf recklessness, rashness.

**témoignage** [temwaɲaʒ] nm (JUR: déclaration) testimony q, evidence q ; (: faits) evidence q ; (rapport, récit) account ; (fig: d'affection etc) token, mark ; expression.

**témoigner** [temwaɲe] vt (intérêt, gratitude) to show // vi (JUR) to testify, give evidence ; ~ **que** to testify that ; (fig) to reveal that, testify to the fact that ; ~ **de** vt to bear witness to, testify to.

**témoin** [temwɛ̃] nm witness ; (fig) testimony ; (SPORT) baton ; (CONSTR) telltale // a control cpd, test cpd ; **appartement ~ show flat** ; **être ~ de** to witness ; to vouch for ; **prendre à ~** to call to witness ; ~ **de moralité** character reference ; ~ **oculaire** eyewitness.

**tempe** [tɑ̃p] nf temple.

**tempérament** [tɑ̃peRamɑ̃] nm temperament, disposition ; (santé) constitution ; **à ~** (vente) on deferred (payment) terms ; (achat) by instalments, hire purchase cpd ; **avoir du ~** to be hot-blooded.

**tempérance** [tɑ̃peRɑ̃s] nf temperance.

**température** [tɑ̃peRatyR] nf temperature ; **prendre la ~ de** to take the temperature of ; (fig) to gauge the feeling of ; **avoir ou faire de la ~** to have ou be running a temperature.

**tempéré, e** [tɑ̃peRe] a temperate.

**tempérer** [tɑ̃peRe] vt to temper.

**tempête** [tɑ̃pɛt] nf storm ; ~ **de sable/neige** sand/snowstorm.

**tempêter** [tɑ̃pete] vi to rant and rave.

**temple** [tɑ̃pl(ə)] nm temple ; (protestant) church.

**tempo** [tɛmpo] nm tempo (pl s).

**temporaire** [tɑ̃pɔRɛR] a temporary ; **~ment** ad temporarily.

**temporel, le** [tɑ̃pɔRɛl] a temporal.

**temporiser** [tɑ̃pɔRize] vi to temporize, play for time.

**temps** [tɑ̃] nm (atmosphérique) weather ; (durée) time ; (époque) time, times pl ; (LING) tense ; (MUS) beat ; (TECH) stroke ; **il fait beau/mauvais ~** the weather is fine/bad ; **avoir le ~/tout le ~/juste le ~** to have time/plenty of time/just enough time ; **avoir fait son ~** (fig) to have had its (ou her etc) day ; **en ~ de paix/guerre** in peacetime/wartime ; **en ~ utile** ou **voulu** in due time ou course ; **de ~ en ~, de ~ à autre** from time to time, now and again ; **à ~** (partir, arriver) in time ; **à ~ partiel** ad, a part-time ; **dans le ~** at one time ; **de tout ~** always ; **du ~ que** at the time when, in the days when ; ~ **d'arrêt** pause, halt ; ~ **mort** (COMM) slack period.

**tenable** [tənabl(ə)] a bearable.

**tenace** [tənas] a tenacious, persistent ; **ténacité** nf tenacity, persistence.

**tenailler** [tənɑje] (fig) vt to torment, torture.

**tenailles** [tənɑj] nfpl pincers.

**tenais** etc vb voir **tenir**.

**tenancier, ière** [tənɑ̃sje, -jɛR] nm/f manager/manageress.

**tenant, e** [tənɑ̃, -ɑ̃t] a voir **séance** // nm/f (SPORT): ~ **du titre** title-holder // nm: **d'un seul ~** in one piece ; **les ~s et les aboutissants** the ins and outs.

**tendance** [tɑ̃dɑ̃s] nf (opinions) leanings pl, sympathies pl ; (inclination) tendency ; (évolution) trend ; ~ **à la hausse** upward trend ; **avoir ~ à** to have a tendency to, tend to ; **tendancieux, euse** a tendentious.

**tendeur** [tɑ̃dœR] nm (de vélo) chain-adjuster ; (de câble) wire-strainer ; (de tente) runner ; (attache) sandow, elastic strap.

**tendon** [tɑ̃dɔ̃] nm tendon, sinew ; ~ **d'Achille** Achilles' tendon.

**tendre** [tɑ̃dR(ə)] a (viande, légumes) tender ; (bois, roche, couleur) soft ; (affectueux) tender, loving // vt (élastique, peau) to stretch, draw tight ; (muscle) to tense ; (donner): ~ **qch à qn** to hold sth out to sb ; to offer sb sth ; (fig: piège) to set, lay ; (tapisserie): **tendu de soie** hung with silk, with silk hangings ; **se ~** vi (corde) to tighten ; (relations) to become strained ; ~ **à qch/à faire** to tend towards sth/to do ; ~ **l'oreille** to prick up one's ears ; ~ **la main/le bras** to hold out one's hand/stretch out one's arm ; **~ment** ad tenderly, lovingly ; **tendresse** nf tenderness.

**tendu, e** [tɑ̃dy] pp de **tendre** // a tight ; tensed ; strained.

**ténèbres** [tenɛbR(ə)] nfpl darkness sg ; **ténébreux, euse** a obscure, mysterious ; (personne) saturnine.

**teneur** [tənœR] nf content, substance ; (d'une lettre) terms pl, content ; ~ **en cuivre** copper content.

**ténia** [tenja] nm tapeworm.

**tenir** [təniR] vt to hold ; (magasin, hôtel) to run ; (promesse) to keep // vi to hold ; (neige, gel) to last ; **se ~** vi (avoir lieu) to be held, take place ; (être: personne) to stand ; **se ~ droit** to stand up (ou sit up) straight ; **bien se ~** to behave well ; **se ~ à qch** to hold on to sth ; **s'en ~ à qch** to confine o.s. to sth ; to stick to sth ; ~ **à** vt to be attached to ; to care about ; to depend on ; to stem from ; ~ **à faire** to want to do, be keen to do ; ~ **de** vt to partake of ; to take after ; **ça ne tient qu'à lui** it is entirely up to him ; ~ **qn pour** to take sb for ; ~ **qch de qn** (histoire) to have heard ou learnt sth from sb ; (qualité, défaut) to have inherited ou got sth from sb ; ~ **les comptes** to keep the books ; ~ **un rôle** to play a part ; ~ **l'alcool** to be able to hold a drink ; ~ **le coup** to hold out ; ~ **3 jours/2 mois** (résister) to hold out ou last 3 days/2 months ; ~ **au chaud/à l'abri** to keep hot/under shelter ou cover ; **tiens/tenez, voilà le stylo!**

there's the pen! ; **tiens, Alain!** look, here's Alain! ; **tiens?** (*surprise*) really?

**tennis** [tenis] *nm* tennis ; (*aussi:* **court de ~**) tennis court // *nm* **ou** *fpl* (*aussi:* **chaussures de ~**) tennis *ou* gym shoes ; **~ de table** table tennis ; **~man** *nm* tennis player.

**ténor** [tenɔʀ] *nm* tenor.

**tension** [tɑ̃sjɔ̃] *nf* tension ; (*fig*) tension ; strain ; (*MÉD*) blood pressure ; **faire** *ou* **avoir de la ~** to have high blood pressure.

**tentaculaire** [tɑ̃takylɛʀ] *a* (*fig*) sprawling.

**tentacule** [tɑ̃takyl] *nm* tentacle.

**tentant, e** [tɑ̃tɑ̃, -ɑ̃t] *a* tempting.

**tentateur, trice** [tɑ̃tatœʀ, -tʀis] *a* tempting // *nm* (*REL*) tempter.

**tentation** [tɑ̃tɑsjɔ̃] *nf* temptation.

**tentative** [tɑ̃tativ] *nf* attempt, bid ; **~ d'évasion** escape bid.

**tente** [tɑ̃t] *nf* tent ; **~ à oxygène** oxygen tent.

**tenter** [tɑ̃te] *vt* (*éprouver, attirer*) to tempt ; (*essayer*): **~ qch/de faire** to attempt *ou* try sth/to do ; **être tenté de** to be tempted to ; **~ sa chance** to try one's luck.

**tenture** [tɑ̃tyʀ] *nf* hanging.

**tenu, e** [tⱥny] *pp de* **tenir** // *a* (*maison, comptes*): **bien ~** well-kept ; (*obligé*): **~ de faire** under an obligation to do // *nf* (*action de tenir*) running ; keeping ; holding ; (*vêtements*) clothes *pl*, gear ; (*allure*) dress *q*, appearance ; (*comportement*) manners *pl*, behaviour ; **en grande ~** in full dress ; **en petite ~e** scantily dressed *ou* clad ; **avoir de la ~e** to have good manners ; (*journal*) to have a high standard ; **une ~e de voyage/sport** travelling/sports clothes *pl ou* gear *q* ; **~e de combat** combat gear *ou* dress ; **~e de route** (*AUTO*) road-holding ; **~e de soirée** evening dress.

**ténu, e** [teny] *a* (*indice, nuance*) tenuous, subtle ; (*fil, objet*) fine ; (*voix*) thin.

**ter** [tɛʀ] *a:* **16 ~** 16b *ou* B.

**térébenthine** [teʀebɑ̃tin] *nf:* (**essence de**) **~** (oil of) turpentine.

**tergiverser** [tɛʀʒivɛʀse] *vi* to shilly-shally.

**terme** [tɛʀm(ə)] *nm* term ; (*fin*) end ; **vente/achat à ~** (*COMM*) forward sale/purchase ; **à court/long ~** *a* short-/long-term *ou* -range // *ad* in the short/long term ; **à ~** (*MÉD*) a full-term // *ad* at term ; **avant ~** (*MÉD*) a premature // *ad* prematurely ; **mettre un ~ à** to put an end *ou* a stop to.

**terminaison** [tɛʀminɛzɔ̃] *nf* (*LING*) ending.

**terminal, e, aux** [tɛʀminal, -o] *a* final // *nm* terminal // *nf* (*SCOL*) ≈ Upper Sixth.

**terminer** [tɛʀmine] *vt* to end ; (*nourriture, repas*) to finish ; **se ~** *vi* to end ; **se ~ par** to end with.

**terminologie** [tɛʀminɔlɔʒi] *nf* terminology.

**terminus** [tɛʀminys] *nm* terminus (*pl* i).

**termite** [tɛʀmit] *nm* termite, white ant.

**terne** [tɛʀn(ə)] *a* dull.

**ternir** [tɛʀniʀ] *vt* to dull ; (*fig*) to sully, tarnish ; **se ~** *vi* to become dull.

**terrain** [teʀɛ̃] *nm* (*sol, fig*) ground ; (*COMM*) land *q*, plot (of land) ; site ; **sur le ~** (*fig*) on the field ; **~ de football/rugby** football/rugby pitch ; **~ d'aviation** airfield ; **~ de camping** camping site ; **un ~ d'entente** an area of agreement ; **~ de golf** golf course ; **~ de jeu** games field ; playground ; **~ de sport** sports ground ; **~ vague** waste ground *q*.

**terrasse** [teʀas] *nf* terrace ; (*de café*) pavement area, terrasse ; **à la ~** (*café*) outside.

**terrassement** [teʀasmɑ̃] *nm* earth-moving, earthworks *pl* ; embankment.

**terrasser** [teʀase] *vt* (*adversaire*) to floor, bring down ; (*suj: maladie etc*) to lay low.

**terrassier** [teʀasje] *nm* navvy, roadworker.

**terre** [tɛʀ] *nf* (*gén, aussi* ÉLEC) earth ; (*substance*) soil, earth ; (*opposé à mer*) land *q* ; (*contrée*) land ; **~s** *nfpl* (*terrains*) lands, land *sg* ; **le travail de la ~** work on the land ; **en ~** (*pipe, poterie*) clay *cpd* ; **à ~ ou par ~** (*mettre, être*) on the ground (*ou* floor) ; (*jeter, tomber*) to the ground, down ; **~ cuite** earthenware ; terracotta ; **la ~ ferme** dry land, terra firma ; **~ glaise** clay ; **la T~ Sainte** the Holy Land ; **~ à ~** *inv* down-to-earth, matter-of-fact.

**terreau** [teʀo] *nm* compost.

**terre-plein** [tɛʀplɛ̃] *nm* platform.

**terrer** [tɛʀe]: **se ~** *vi* to hide away ; to go to ground.

**terrestre** [tɛʀɛstʀ(ə)] *a* (*surface*) earth's, of the earth ; (*BOT, ZOOL, MIL*) land *cpd* ; (*REL*) earthly, worldly.

**terreur** [tɛʀœʀ] *nf* terror *q*, fear.

**terrible** [tɛʀibl(ə)] *a* terrible, dreadful ; (*fam*) terrific ; **~ment** *ad* (*très*) terribly, awfully.

**terrien, ne** [tɛʀjɛ̃, -jɛn] *nm/f* countryman/woman, man/woman of the soil ; (*non martien etc*) earthling.

**terrier** [tɛʀje] *nm* burrow, hole ; (*chien*) terrier.

**terrifier** [tɛʀifje] *vt* to terrify.

**terril** [tɛʀil] *nm* slag heap.

**terrine** [tɛʀin] *nf* (*récipient*) terrine ; (*CULIN*) pâté.

**territoire** [tɛʀitwaʀ] *nm* territory ; **territorial, e, aux** *a* territorial.

**terroir** [tɛʀwaʀ] *nm* (*AGR*) soil ; **accent du ~** country *ou* rural accent.

**terroriser** [tɛʀɔʀize] *vt* to terrorize ; **terrorisme** *nm* terrorism ; **terroriste** *nm/f* terrorist.

**tertiaire** [tɛʀsjɛʀ] *a* tertiary // *nm* (*ÉCON*) tertiary sector, service industries *pl*.

**tertre** [tɛʀtʀ(ə)] *nm* hillock, mound.

**tes** [te] *dét voir* **ton**.

**tesson** [tesɔ̃] *nm:* **~ de bouteille** piece of broken bottle.

**test** [tɛst] *nm* test.

**testament** [tɛstamɑ̃] *nm* (*JUR*) will ; (*REL*) Testament ; **faire son ~** to make out one's will ; **testamentaire** *a* of a will.

**tester** [tɛste] *vt* to test.

**testicule** [tɛstikyl] *nm* testicle.

**tétanos** [tetanos] *nm* tetanus, lockjaw.

**têtard** [tɛtaʀ] *nm* tadpole.

**tête** [tɛt] *nf* head ; (*cheveux*) hair *q* ; (*visage*) face ; (*FOOTBALL*) header ; **de ~** *a* (*wagon etc*) front *cpd* // *ad* (*calculer*) in one's head, mentally ; **perdre la ~** (*fig*) to lose one's

head ; to go off one's head ; **tenir ~ à qn**
to stand up to *ou* defy sb ; **la ~ en bas**
with one's head down ; **la ~ la première**
(*tomber*) headfirst ; **faire une ~** (*FOOTBALL*)
to head the ball ; **faire la ~** (*fig*) to sulk ;
**en ~** (*SPORT*) in the lead ; at the front *ou*
head ; **en ~ à ~** in private, alone
together ; **de la ~ aux pieds** from head
to toe ; **~ d'affiche** (*THÉÂTRE etc*) top of
the bill ; **~ de bétail** head *inv* of cattle ;
**~ chercheuse** homing device ; **~ de**
**lecture** pickup head ; **~ de liste** (*POL*)
chief candidate ; **~ de mort** skull and
crossbones ; **~ de série** (*TENNIS*) seeded
player, seed ; **~ de Turc** (*fig*) whipping
boy ; **~ de veau** (*CULIN*) calf's head ;
**~-à-queue** *nm inv*: **faire un ~-à-queue**
to spin round ; **~-à-~** *nm inv* tête-à-tête ;
**~-bêche** *ad* head to tail.
**tétée** [tete] *nf* (*action*) sucking ; (*repas*)
feed.
**téter** [tete] *vt*: **~ (sa mère)** to suck at
one's mother's breast, feed.
**tétine** [tetin] *nf* teat ; (*sucette*) dummy.
**téton** [tetɔ̃] *nm* (*fam*) breast.
**têtu, e** [tety] *a* stubborn, pigheaded.
**texte** [tɛkst(ə)] *nm* text ; **apprendre son**
**~** (*THÉÂTRE*) to learn one's lines.
**textile** [tɛkstil] *a* textile *cpd* // *nm* textile ;
textile industry.
**textuel, le** [tɛkstyɛl] *a* literal, word for
word.
**texture** [tɛkstyR] *nf* texture.
**thé** [te] *nm* tea ; **prendre le ~** to have tea ;
**faire le ~** to make the tea.
**théâtral, e, aux** [teɑtRal, -o] *a* theatrical.
**théâtre** [teɑtR(ə)] *nm* theatre ; (*techniques,*
*genre*) drama, theatre ; (*activité*) stage,
theatre ; (*œuvres*) plays *pl*, dramatic works
*pl* ; (*fig: lieu*): **le ~ de** the scene of ; (*péj*)
histrionics *pl*, playacting ; **faire du ~** to
be on the stage ; to do some acting ; **~**
**filmé** filmed stage productions *pl*.
**théière** [tejɛR] *nf* teapot.
**thème** [tɛm] *nm* theme ; (*SCOL: traduction*)
prose (composition).
**théologie** [teɔlɔʒi] *nf* theology ;
**théologien** *nm* theologian ; **théologique** *a*
theological.
**théorème** [teɔRɛm] *nm* theorem.
**théoricien, ne** [teɔRisjɛ̃, -jɛn] *nm/f*
theoretician, theorist.
**théorie** [teɔRi] *nf* theory ; **théorique** *a*
theoretical.
**thérapeutique** [teRapøtik] *a* therapeutic
// *nf* therapeutics *sg*.
**thérapie** [teRapi] *nf* therapy.
**thermal, e, aux** [tɛRmal, -o] *a* thermal ;
**station ~e** spa ; **cure ~e** water cure.
**thermes** [tɛRm(ə)] *nmpl* thermal baths ;
(*romains*) thermae *pl*.
**thermique** [tɛRmik] *a* (*énergie*) thermic ;
(*unité*) thermal.
**thermomètre** [tɛRmɔmɛtR(ə)] *nm*
thermometer.
**thermonucléaire** [tɛRmɔnykleɛR] *a*
thermonuclear.
**thermos** ® [tɛRmos] *nm ou nf*: (**bouteille**)
**~** vacuum *ou* Thermos ® flask.
**thermostat** [tɛRmɔsta] *nm* thermostat.

**thésauriser** [tezɔRize] *vi* to hoard money.
**thèse** [tɛz] *nf* thesis (*pl* theses).
**thon** [tɔ̃] *nm* tuna (fish).
**thoracique** [tɔRasik] *a* thoracic.
**thorax** [tɔRaks] *nm* thorax.
**thrombose** [tRɔ̃boz] *nf* thrombosis.
**thym** [tɛ̃] *nm* thyme.
**thyroïde** [tiRɔid] *nf* thyroid (gland).
**tiare** [tjaR] *nf* tiara.
**tibia** [tibja] *nm* shinbone, tibia ; shin.
**tic** [tik] *nm* tic, (nervous) twitch ; (*de*
*langage etc*) mannerism.
**ticket** [tikɛ] *nm* ticket ; **~ de quai**
platform ticket.
**tic-tac** [tiktak] *nm inv* tick-tock ;
**tictaquer** *vi* to tick (away).
**tiède** [tjɛd] *a* lukewarm ; tepid ; (*vent, air*)
mild, warm ; **tiédir** *vi* to cool ; to grow
warmer.
**tien, tienne** [tjɛ̃, tjɛn] *pronom*: **le ~ (la**
**tienne), les ~s (tiennes)** yours ; **à la**
**tienne!** cheers!
**tiens** [tjɛ̃] *vb, excl voir* **tenir**.
**tierce** [tjɛRs(ə)] *a, nf voir* **tiers**.
**tiercé** [tjɛRse] *nm* system of forecast betting
giving first 3 horses.
**tiers, tierce** [tjɛR, tjɛRs(ə)] *a* third // *nm*
(*JUR*) third party ; (*fraction*) third // *nf*
(*MUS*) third ; (*CARTES*) tierce ; **une tierce**
**personne** a third party ; **~ provisionnel**
interim payment of tax.
**tige** [tiʒ] *nf* stem ; (*baguette*) rod.
**tignasse** [tiɲas] *nf* (*péj*) shock *ou* mop of
hair.
**tigre** [tigR(ə)] *nm* tiger.
**tigré, e** [tigre] *a* striped ; spotted.
**tigresse** [tigRɛs] *nf* tigress.
**tilleul** [tijœl] *nm* lime (tree), linden (tree) ;
(*boisson*) lime(-blossom) tea.
**timbale** [tɛ̃bal] *nf* (*metal*) tumbler ; **~s**
*nfpl* (*MUS*) timpani, kettledrums.
**timbre** [tɛ̃bR(ə)] *nm* (*tampon*) stamp ;
(*aussi: ~-poste*) (postage) stamp ; (*cachet*
*de la poste*) postmark ; (*sonnette*) bell ;
(*MUS: de voix, instrument*) timbre, tone.
**timbrer** [tɛ̃bRe] *vt* to stamp.
**timide** [timid] *a* shy ; timid ; (*timoré*) timid,
timorous ; **timidité** *nf* shyness, timidity.
**timonerie** [timɔnRi] *nf* wheelhouse.
**timoré, e** [timɔRe] *a* timorous.
**tins** *etc vb voir* **tenir**.
**tintamarre** [tɛ̃tamaR] *nm* din, uproar.
**tinter** [tɛ̃te] *vi* to ring, chime ; (*argent,*
*clefs*) to jingle.
**tir** [tiR] *nm* (*sport*) shooting ; (*fait ou*
*manière de tirer*) firing *q* ; (*FOOTBALL*) shot ;
(*stand*) shooting gallery ; **~ d'obus/de**
**mitraillette** shell/machine gun fire ; **~ à**
**l'arc** archery ; **~ au pigeon** clay pigeon
shooting.
**tirade** [tiRad] *nf* tirade.
**tirage** [tiRaʒ] *nm* (*action*) printing ; (*de*
*journal*) circulation ; (*de livre*) (print-)run ;
edition ; (*de cheminée*) draught ; (*de loterie*)
draw ; (*désaccord*) friction ; **~ au sort**
drawing lots.
**tirailler** [tiRaje] *vt* to pull at, tug at //
*vi* to fire at random ; **tirailleur** *nm*
skirmisher.

**tirant** [tiʀɑ̃] *nm*: ~ **d'eau** draught.

**tire** [tiʀ] *nf*: **vol à la** ~ pickpocketing.

**tiré** [tiʀe] *nm* (*COMM*) drawee; ~ **à part** off-print.

**tire-au-flanc** [tiʀoflɑ̃] *nm inv* (*péj*) skiver.

**tire-bouchon** [tiʀbuʃɔ̃] *nm* corkscrew.

**tire-d'aile** [tiʀdɛl]: **à** ~ *ad* swiftly.

**tire-fesses** [tiʀfɛs] *nm inv* ski-tow.

**tirelire** [tiʀliʀ] *nf* moneybox.

**tirer** [tiʀe] *vt* (*gén*) to pull; (*extraire*): ~ **qch de** to take *ou* pull sth out of; to get sth out of; to extract sth from; (*tracer*: *ligne, trait*) to draw, trace; (*fermer*: *volet, rideau*) to draw, close; (*choisir*: *carte, conclusion, aussi COMM*: *chèque*) to draw; (*en faisant feu*: *balle, coup*) to fire; (: *animal*) to shoot; (*journal, livre, photo*) to print; (*FOOTBALL*: *corner etc*) to take // *vi* (*faire feu*) to fire; (*faire du tir, FOOTBALL*) to shoot; (*cheminée*) to draw; **se** ~ *vi* (*fam*) to push off; **s'en** ~ to pull through, get off; ~ **sur** to pull on *ou* at; to shoot *ou* fire at; (*pipe*) to draw on; (*fig*: *avoisiner*) to verge on; ~ **son nom de** to take *ou* get its name from; ~ **qn de** (*embarras etc*) to help *ou* get sb out of; ~ **à l'arc/la carabine** to shoot with a bow and arrow/with a rifle.

**tiret** [tiʀɛ] *nm* dash.

**tireur, euse** [tiʀœʀ, -øz] *nm/f* gunman; (*COMM*) drawer; **bon** ~ good shot; ~ **d'élite** marksman; ~**s débutants** beginners at shooting.

**tiroir** [tiʀwaʀ] *nm* drawer; ~-**caisse** *nm* till.

**tisane** [tizan] *nf* herb tea.

**tison** [tizɔ̃] *nm* brand; **tisonner** *vt* to poke; **tisonnier** *nm* poker.

**tissage** [tisaʒ] *nm* weaving *q*.

**tisser** [tise] *vt* to weave; **tisserand** *nm* weaver.

**tissu** [tisy] *nm* fabric, material, cloth *q*; (*ANAT, BIO*) tissue; ~ **de mensonges** web of lies.

**tissu, e** [tisy] *a*: ~ **de** woven through with.

**tissu-éponge** [tisyepɔ̃ʒ] *nm* (terry) towelling *q*.

**titane** [titan] *nm* titanium.

**titanesque** [titanɛsk(ə)] *a* titanic.

**titre** [titʀ(ə)] *nm* (*gén*) title; (*de journal*) headline; (*diplôme*) qualification; (*COMM*) security; (*CHIMIE*) titre; **en** ~ (*champion, responsable*) official, recognised; **à juste** ~ with just cause, rightly; **à quel** ~? on what grounds?; **à aucun** ~ on no account; **au même** ~ (**que**) in the same way (as); **à** ~ **d'exemple** as an *ou* by way of an example; **à** ~ **d'information** for (your) information; **à** ~ **gracieux** free of charge; **à** ~ **d'essai** on a trial basis; **à** ~ **privé** in a private capacity; ~ **de propriété** title deed; ~ **de transport** ticket.

**titré, e** [titʀe] *a* titled.

**titrer** [titʀe] *vt* (*CHIMIE*) to titrate; to assay; (*PRESSE*) to run as a headline; (*suj*: *vin*): ~ **10°** to be 10° proof.

**tituber** [titybe] *vi* to stagger *ou* reel (along).

**titulaire** [titylɛʀ] *a* (*ADMIN*) appointed, with tenure // *nm* (*ADMIN*) incumbent; **être**

~ **de** (*poste*) to hold; (*permis*) to be the holder of.

**toast** [tost] *nm* slice *ou* piece of toast; (*de bienvenue*) (welcoming) toast; **porter un** ~ **à qn** to propose *ou* drink a toast to sb.

**toboggan** [tɔbɔgɑ̃] *nm* toboggan.

**toc** [tɔk] *nm*: **en** ~ imitation *cpd*.

**tocsin** [tɔksɛ̃] *nm* alarm (bell).

**toge** [tɔʒ] *nf* toga; (*de juge*) gown.

**tohu-bohu** [tɔybɔy] *nm* confusion; commotion.

**toi** [twa] *pronom* you.

**toile** [twal] *nf* (*matériau*) cloth *q*; (*bâche*) piece of canvas; (*tableau*) canvas; **grosse** ~ canvas; **tisser sa** ~ (*araignée*) to spin its web; ~ **d'araignée** cobweb; ~ **cirée** oilcloth; ~ **de fond** (*fig*) backdrop; ~ **de jute** hessian; ~ **de lin** linen.

**toilette** [twalɛt] *nf* wash; (*s'habiller et se préparer*) getting ready, washing and dressing; (*habits*) outfit; dress *q*; ~**s** *nfpl* (*w.-c.*) toilet *sg*; **les** ~**s des dames/messieurs** the ladies'/gents' (toilets); **faire sa** ~ to have a wash, get washed; **articles de** ~ toiletries; ~ **intime** personal hygiene.

**toi-même** [twamɛm] *pronom* yourself.

**toise** [twaz] *nf*: **passer à la** ~ to have one's height measured.

**toiser** [twaze] *vt* to eye up and down.

**toison** [twazɔ̃] *nf* (*de mouton*) fleece; (*cheveux*) mane.

**toit** [twa] *nm* roof.

**toiture** [twatyʀ] *nf* roof.

**tôle** [tol] *nf* sheet metal *q*; (*plaque*) steel *ou* iron sheet; ~**s** (*carrosserie*) bodywork *sg*; panels; ~ **d'acier** sheet steel *q*; ~ **ondulée** corrugated iron.

**tolérable** [tɔleʀabl(ə)] *a* tolerable, bearable.

**tolérance** [tɔleʀɑ̃s] *nf* tolerance; (*hors taxe*) allowance.

**tolérant, e** [tɔleʀɑ̃, -ɑ̃t] *a* tolerant.

**tolérer** [tɔleʀe] *vt* to tolerate; (*ADMIN*: *hors taxe etc*) to allow.

**tôlerie** [tolʀi] *nf* sheet metal manufacture; sheet metal workshop.

**tollé** [tɔle] *nm*: **un** ~ (**de protestations**) a general outcry.

**T.O.M.** [*parfois*: tɔm] *sigle m(pl)* = *territoire(s) d'outre-mer*.

**tomate** [tɔmat] *nf* tomato.

**tombal, e** [tɔbal] *a*: **pierre** ~**e** tombstone, gravestone.

**tombant, e** [tɔbɑ̃, -ɑ̃t] *a* (*fig*) drooping, sloping.

**tombe** [tɔb] *nf* (*sépulture*) grave; (*avec monument*) tomb.

**tombeau, x** [tɔbo] *nm* tomb.

**tombée** [tɔbe] *nf*: **à la** ~ **du jour** *ou* **de la nuit** at the close of day, at nightfall.

**tomber** [tɔbe] *vi* to fall // *vt*: ~ **la veste** to slip off one's jacket; **laisser** ~ to drop; ~ **sur** *vt* (*rencontrer*) to come across; (*attaquer*) to set about; ~ **de fatigue/sommeil** to drop from exhaustion/be falling asleep on one's feet; **ça tombe bien** it comes at the right time; **il est bien tombé** he's been lucky.

**tombereau, x** [tɔbʀo] *nm* tipcart.

**tombeur** [tɔ̃bœʀ] *nm* (*péj*) Casanova.
**tombola** [tɔ̃bɔla] *nf* tombola.
**tome** [tɔm] *nm* volume.
**tommette** [tɔmɛt] *nf* hexagonal floor tile.
**ton, ta,** *pl* **tes** [tɔ̃, ta, te] *dét* your.
**ton** [tɔ̃] *nm* (*gén*) tone ; (*MUS*) key ; (*couleur*) shade, tone ; **de bon** ~ in good taste.
**tonal, e** [tɔnal] *a* tonal.
**tonalité** [tɔnalite] *nf* (*au téléphone*) dialling tone ; (*MUS*) tonality ; key ; (*fig*) tone.
**tondeuse** [tɔ̃døz] *nf* (*à gazon*) (lawn)-mower ; (*du coiffeur*) clippers *pl* ; (*pour la tonte*) shears *pl*.
**tondre** [tɔ̃dʀ(ə)] *vt* (*pelouse, herbe*) to mow ; (*haie*) to cut, clip ; (*mouton, toison*) to shear ; (*cheveux*) to crop.
**tonifiant, e** [tɔnifjɑ̃, -ɑ̃t] *a* invigorating, revivifying.
**tonifier** [tɔnifje] *vt* (*peau, organisme*) to tone up.
**tonique** [tɔnik] *a* fortifying // *nm, nf* tonic.
**tonitruant, e** [tɔnitʀyɑ̃, -ɑ̃t] *a*: **voix** ~**e** thundering voice.
**tonnage** [tɔnaʒ] *nm* tonnage.
**tonne** [tɔn] *nf* metric ton, tonne.
**tonneau, x** [tɔno] *nm* (*à vin, cidre*) barrel ; (*NAVIG*) ton ; **faire des** ~**x** (*voiture, avion*) to roll over.
**tonnelier** [tɔnəlje] *nm* cooper.
**tonnelle** [tɔnɛl] *nf* bower, arbour.
**tonner** [tɔne] *vi* to thunder ; **il tonne** it is thundering, there's some thunder.
**tonnerre** [tɔnɛʀ] *nm* thunder ; ~ **d'applaudissements** thunderous applause ; **du** ~ *a* (*fam*) terrific.
**tonsure** [tɔ̃syʀ] *nf* tonsure ; bald patch.
**tonte** [tɔ̃t] *nf* shearing.
**tonus** [tɔnys] *nm* tone.
**top** [tɔp] *nm*: **au 3ème** ~ at the 3rd stroke // *a*: ~ **secret** top secret.
**topaze** [tɔpɑz] *nf* topaz.
**toper** [tɔpe] *vi*: **tope-/topez-là!** it's a deal!, you're on!
**topinambour** [tɔpinɑ̃buʀ] *nm* Jerusalem artichoke.
**topographie** [tɔpɔgʀafi] *nf* topography ; **topographique** *a* topographical.
**toponymie** [tɔpɔnimi] *nf* study of place-names, toponymy.
**toque** [tɔk] *nf* (*de fourrure*) fur hat ; ~ **de jockey/juge** jockey's/judge's cap ; ~ **de cuisinier** chef's hat.
**toqué, e** [tɔke] *a* (*fam*) touched, cracked.
**torche** [tɔʀʃ(ə)] *nf* torch ; **se mettre en** ~ (*parachute*) to candle.
**torcher** [tɔʀʃe] *vt* (*fam*) to wipe.
**torchère** [tɔʀʃɛʀ] *nf* flare.
**torchon** [tɔʀʃɔ̃] *nm* cloth, duster ; (*à vaisselle*) tea towel, dish towel.
**tordre** [tɔʀdʀ(ə)] *vt* (*chiffon*) to wring ; (*barre, fig: visage*) to twist ; **se** ~ *vi* (*barre*) to bend ; (*roue*) to twist, buckle ; (*ver, serpent*) to writhe ; **se** ~ **le pied/bras** to twist *ou* sprain one's foot/arm ; **se** ~ **de douleur/rire** to writhe in pain/be doubled up with laughter.
**tordu, e** [tɔʀdy] *a* (*fig*) warped, twisted.
**torero** [tɔʀeʀo] *nm* bullfighter.
**tornade** [tɔʀnad] *nf* tornado.

**torpeur** [tɔʀpœʀ] *nf* torpor, drowsiness.
**torpille** [tɔʀpij] *nf* torpedo ; **torpiller** *vt* to torpedo.
**torréfier** [tɔʀefje] *vt* to roast.
**torrent** [tɔʀɑ̃] *nm* torrent, mountain stream ; (*fig*): ~ **de** torrent *ou* flood of ; **il pleut à** ~**s** the rain is lashing down ; **torrentiel, le** *a* torrential.
**torride** [tɔʀid] *a* torrid.
**torsade** [tɔʀsad] *nf* twist ; (*ARCHIT*) cable moulding ; **torsader** *vt* to twist.
**torse** [tɔʀs(ə)] *nm* (*ANAT*) torso ; chest.
**torsion** [tɔʀsjɔ̃] *nf* twisting ; torsion.
**tort** [tɔʀ] *nm* (*défaut*) fault ; (*préjudice*) wrong *q* ; ~**s** *nmpl* (*JUR*) fault *sg* ; **avoir** ~ to be wrong ; **être dans son** ~ to be in the wrong ; **donner** ~ **à qn** to lay the blame on sb ; (*fig*) to prove sb wrong ; **causer du** ~ **à** to harm, to be harmful *ou* detrimental to ; **en** ~ in the wrong, at fault ; **à** ~ wrongly ; **à** ~ **et à travers** wildly.
**torticolis** [tɔʀtikɔli] *nm* stiff neck.
**tortiller** [tɔʀtije] *vt* to twist ; to twiddle ; **se** ~ *vi* to wriggle, squirm.
**tortionnaire** [tɔʀsjɔnɛʀ] *nm* torturer.
**tortue** [tɔʀty] *nf* tortoise.
**tortueux, euse** [tɔʀtɥø, -øz] *a* (*rue*) twisting ; (*fig*) tortuous.
**torture** [tɔʀtyʀ] *nf* torture ; **torturer** *vt* to torture ; (*fig*) to torment.
**torve** [tɔʀv(ə)] *a*: **regard** ~ menacing *ou* grim look.
**tôt** [to] *ad* early ; ~ **ou tard** sooner or later ; **si** ~ so early ; (*déjà*) so soon ; **au plus** ~ at the earliest, as soon as possible ; **plus** ~ earlier ; **il eut** ~ **fait de faire** he soon did.
**total, e, aux** [tɔtal, -o] *a, nm* total ; **au** ~ in total *ou* all ; **faire le** ~ to work out the total, add up ; ~**ement** *ad* totally, completely ; ~**iser** *vt* total (up).
**totalitaire** [tɔtalitɛʀ] *a* totalitarian.
**totalité** [tɔtalite] *nf*: **la** ~ **de** all of, the total amount (*ou* number) of ; **the whole** + *sg* ; **en** ~ entirely.
**totem** [tɔtɛm] *nm* totem.
**toubib** [tubib] *nm* (*fam*) doctor.
**touchant, e** [tuʃɑ̃, -ɑ̃t] *a* touching.
**touche** [tuʃ] *nf* (*de piano, de machine à écrire*) key ; (*PEINTURE etc*) stroke, touch ; (*fig: de nostalgie*) touch, hint ; (*RUGBY*) line-out ; (*FOOTBALL: aussi*: **remise en** ~) throw-in ; (: **ligne de** ~) touch-line ; (*ESCRIME*) hit ; **en** ~ in (*ou* into) touch ; **avoir une drôle de** ~ to look a sight.
**touche-à-tout** [tuʃatu] *nm/f inv* (*péj*) meddler ; dabbler.
**toucher** [tuʃe] *nm* touch // *vt* to touch ; (*palper*) to feel ; (*atteindre: d'un coup de feu etc*) to hit ; (*affecter*) to touch, affect ; (*concerner*) to concern, affect ; (*contacter*) to reach, contact ; (*recevoir: récompense*) to receive, get ; (: *salaire*) to draw, get ; **au** ~ to the touch ; **se** ~ (*être en contact*) to touch ; ~ **à** to touch ; (*modifier*) to touch, tamper *ou* meddle with ; (*traiter de, concerner*) to have to do with, concern ; **je vais lui en** ~ **un mot** I'll have a word with him about it ; ~ **à sa fin** to be drawing to a close.

**touffe** [tuf] *nf* tuft.

**touffu, e** [tufy] *a* thick, dense; *(fig)* complex, involved.

**toujours** [tuʒuR] *ad* always; *(encore)* still; *(constamment)* forever; ~ **plus** more and more; **pour** ~ forever; ~ **est-il que** the fact remains that; **essaie** ~ (you can) try anyway.

**toupie** [tupi] *nf* (spinning) top.

**tour** [tuR] *nf* tower; *(immeuble)* high-rise block, tower block; *(ÉCHECS)* castle, rook // *nm* (*excursion*) stroll, walk; run, ride; trip; *(SPORT: aussi:* ~ **de piste)** lap; *(d'être servi ou de jouer etc, tournure, de vis ou clef)* turn; *(de roue etc)* revolution; *(circonférence):* **de 3 m de** ~ 3 m round, with a circumference *ou* girth of 3 m; *(POL: aussi:* ~ **de scrutin)** ballot; *(ruse, de prestidigitation)* trick; *(de potier)* wheel; *(à bois, métaux)* lathe; **faire le** ~ **de** to go round; *(à pied)* to walk round; **faire un** ~ to go for a walk; *(en voiture etc)* to go for a ride; **faire 2** ~s to go round twice; *(hélice etc)* to turn *ou* revolve twice; **fermer à double** ~ *vi* to double-lock the door; **c'est au** ~ **de Renée** it's Renée's turn; **à** ~ **de rôle,** ~ **à** ~ in turn; ~ **de taille/tête** waist/head measurement; ~ **de chant** song recital; ~ **de contrôle** *nf* control tower; ~ **de garde** spell of duty; ~ **d'horizon** *(fig)* general survey; ~ **de lit** valance; ~ **de reins** sprained back.

**tourbe** [tuRb(ə)] *nf* peat; **tourbière** *nf* peat-bog.

**tourbillon** [tuRbijɔ̃] *nm* whirlwind; *(d'eau)* whirlpool; *(fig)* whirl, swirl; **tourbillonner** *vi* to whirl, swirl; to whirl *ou* swirl round.

**tourelle** [tuRɛl] *nf* turret.

**tourisme** [turism(ə)] *nm* tourism; tourist industry; **agence de** ~ tourist agency; **faire du** ~ to do some sightseeing, go touring; **touriste** *nm/f* tourist; **touristique** *a* tourist *cpd*; *(région)* touristic, with tourist appeal.

**tourment** [tuRmɑ̃] *nm* torment.

**tourmente** [tuRmɑ̃t] *nf* storm.

**tourmenté, e** [tuRmɑ̃te] *a* tormented, tortured.

**tourmenter** [tuRmɑ̃te] *vt* to torment; **se** ~ *vi* to fret, worry o.s.

**tournage** [tuRnaʒ] *nm (d'un film)* shooting.

**tournant, e** [tuRnɑ̃, -ɑ̃t] *a:* *voir* **plaque, grève** // *nm (de route)* bend; *(fig)* turning point.

**tournebroche** [tuRnəbRɔʃ] *nm* roasting spit.

**tourne-disque** [tuRnədisk(ə)] *nm* record player.

**tournée** [tuRne] *nf (du facteur etc)* round; *(d'artiste, politicien)* tour; *(au café)* round (of drinks); ~ **musicale** concert tour.

**tourner** [tuRne] *vt* to turn; *(contourner)* to get round; *(CINÉMA)* to shoot; to make // *vi* to turn; *(moteur)* to run; *(compteur)* to tick away; *(lait etc)* to turn (sour); **se** ~ *vi* to turn round; **se** ~ **vers** to turn to; to turn towards; **bien** ~ to turn out well; ~ **autour de** to go round; to revolve round; *(péj)* to hang round; ~ **à/en** to turn into; ~ **à la pluie/au rouge** to turn

rainy/red; ~ **le dos à** to turn one's back on; to have one's back to; **se** ~ **les pouces** to twiddle one's thumbs; ~ **la tête** to look away; ~ **la tête à qn** *(fig)* to go to sb's head; ~ **de l'œil** to pass out.

**tournesol** [tuRnəsɔl] *nm* sunflower.

**tourneur** [tuRnœR] *nm* turner; lathe-operator.

**tournevis** [tuRnəvis] *nm* screwdriver.

**tourniquet** [tuRnikɛ] *nm (pour arroser)* sprinkler; *(portillon)* turnstile; *(présentoir)* revolving stand.

**tournoi** [tuRnwa] *nm* tournament.

**tournoyer** [tuRnwaje] *vi* to whirl round; to swirl round.

**tournure** [tuRnyR] *nf (LING)* turn of phrase; form; phrasing; *(évolution):* **la** ~ **de qch** the way sth is developing; *(aspect):* **la** ~ **de** the look of; ~ **d'esprit** turn *ou* cast of mind; **la** ~ **des événements** the turn of events.

**tourte** [tuRt(ə)] *nf* pie.

**tourteau, x** [tuRto] *nm (AGR)* oilcake, cattle-cake; *(ZOOL)* edible crab.

**tourterelle** [tuRtəRɛl] *nf* turtledove.

**tous** *dét* [tu], *pronom* [tus] *voir* **tout.**

**Toussaint** [tusɛ̃] *nf:* **la** ~ All Saints' Day.

**tousser** [tuse] *vi* to cough; **toussoter** *vi* to have a slight cough; to cough a little; *(pour avertir)* to give a slight cough.

**tout, e,** *pl* **tous, toutes** [tu, tus, tut] *dét* all; ~ **le lait** all the milk, the whole of the milk; ~**e la nuit** all night, the whole night; ~ **le livre** the whole book; ~ **un pain** a whole loaf; **tous les livres** all the books; **toutes les nuits** every night; **à** ~ **âge** at any age; **toutes les fois** every time; **toutes les 3/2 semaines** every third/other *ou* second week; **tous les 2** both *ou* each of us (*ou* them); **toutes les 3** all 3 of us (*ou* them); ~ **le temps** *ad* all the time; the whole time; **c'est** ~ **le contraire** it's quite the opposite; **il avait pour** ~**e nourriture** his only food was // *pronom* everything, all; **tous, toutes** all (of them); **je les vois tous** I can see them all *ou* all of them; **nous y sommes tous allés** all of us went, we all went; **en** ~ in all // *ad* quite; very; ~ **en haut** right at the top; **le** ~ **premier** the very first; **le livre** ~ **entier** the whole book; ~ **seul** all alone; ~ **droit** straight ahead; ~ **en travaillant** while working, as *ou* while he etc works // *nm* whole; **le** ~ all of it (*ou* them), the whole lot; ~ **d'abord** first of all; ~ **à coup** suddenly; ~ **à fait** absolutely; ~ **à l'heure** a short while ago; in a short while, shortly; ~ **de même** all the same; ~ **le monde** everybody; ~ **de suite** immediately, straight away; ~ **terrain** *ou* **tous terrains** *a inv* general-purpose; ~**-à-l'égout** *nm inv* mains drainage.

**toutefois** [tutfwa] *ad* however.

**toutou** [tutu] *nm (fam)* doggie.

**toux** [tu] *nf* cough.

**toxicomane** [tɔksikɔman] *nm/f* drug addict.

**toxine** [tɔksin] *nf* toxin.

**toxique** [tɔksik] *a* toxic, poisonous.

**trac** [tRak] *nm* nerves *pl*; *(THÉÂTRE)* stage

fright; **avoir le** ~ to get an attack of nerves; to have stage fright.

**tracas** [tRaka] *nm* bother *q*, worry *q*; **tracasser** *vt* to worry, bother; to harass; **se tracasser** *vi* to worry o.s., fret; **tracasserie** *nf* annoyance *q*; harassment *q*; **tracassier, ière** *a* irksome.

**trace** [tRas] *nf* (*empreintes*) tracks *pl*; (*marques, aussi fig*) mark; (*restes, vestige*) trace; (*indice*) sign; ~**s de pas** footprints.

**tracé** [tRase] *nm* line; layout.

**tracer** [tRase] *vt* to draw; (*mot*) to trace; (*piste*) to open up.

**trachée(-artère)** [tRaʃe(aRtɛR)] *nf* windpipe, trachea; **trachéite** [tRakeit] *nf* tracheitis.

**tract** [tRakt] *nm* tract, pamphlet.

**tractations** [tRaktɑsjɔ̃] *nfpl* dealings, bargaining *sg*.

**tracteur** [tRaktœR] *nm* tractor.

**traction** [tRaksjɔ̃] *nf* traction; (*GYM*) pull-up; ~ **avant/arrière** front-wheel/rear-wheel drive; ~ **électrique** electric(al) traction *ou* haulage.

**tradition** [tRadisjɔ̃] *nf* tradition; **traditionnel, le** *a* traditional.

**traducteur, trice** [tRadyktœR, -tRis] *nm/f* translator.

**traduction** [tRadyksjɔ̃] *nf* translation.

**traduire** [tRadɥiR] *vt* to translate; (*exprimer*) to render, convey; ~ **en français** to translate into French; ~ **en justice** to bring before the courts.

**trafic** [tRafik] *nm* traffic; ~ **d'armes** arms dealing; **trafiquant, e** *nm/f* trafficker; dealer; **trafiquer** *vt* (*péj*) to doctor, tamper with // *vi* to traffic, be engaged in trafficking.

**tragédie** [tRaʒedi] *nf* tragedy; **tragédien, ne** *nm/f* tragedian/tragedienne.

**tragique** [tRaʒik] *a* tragic; ~**ment** *ad* tragically.

**trahir** [tRaiR] *vt* to betray; (*fig*) to give away, reveal; **trahison** *nf* betrayal; (*MIL*) treason.

**train** [tRɛ̃] *nm* (*RAIL*) train; (*allure*) pace; (*fig: ensemble*) set; **mettre qch en** ~ to get sth under way; **mettre qn en** ~ to put sb in good spirits; **se mettre en** ~ to get started; to warm up; **se sentir en** ~ to feel in good form; ~ **avant/arrière** front-wheel/rear-wheel axle unit; ~ **d'atterrissage** undercarriage; ~ **autos-couchettes** car-sleeper train; ~ **électrique** (*jouet*) (electric) train set; ~ **de pneus** set of tyres; ~ **de vie** style of living.

**traînant, e** [tRɛnɑ̃, -ɑ̃t] *a* (*voix, ton*) drawling.

**traînard, e** [tRɛnaR, -aRd(ə)] *nm/f* (*péj*) slowcoach.

**traîne** [tRɛn] *nf* (*de robe*) train; **être à la** ~ to be in tow; to lag behind.

**traîneau, x** [tRɛno] *nm* sleigh, sledge.

**traînée** [tRɛne] *nf* streak, trail; (*péj*) slut.

**traîner** [tRɛne] *vt* (*remorque*) to pull; (*enfant, chien*) to drag *ou* trail along // *vi* (*être en désordre*) to lie around; (*marcher lentement*) to dawdle (along); (*vagabonder*) to hang about; (*agir lentement*) to idle about; (*durer*) to drag on; **se** ~ *vi* to crawl

along; to drag o.s. along; (*durer*) to drag on; ~ **les pieds** to drag one's feet.

**train-train** [tRɛ̃tRɛ̃] *nm* humdrum routine.

**traire** [tRɛR] *vt* to milk.

**trait** [tRɛ] *nm* (*ligne*) line; (*de dessin*) stroke; (*caractéristique*) feature, trait; (*flèche*) dart, arrow; shaft; ~**s** *nmpl* (*du visage*) features; **d'un** ~ (*boire*) in one gulp; **de** ~ *a* (*animal*) draught; **avoir** ~ **à** to concern; ~ **de caractère** characteristic, trait; ~ **d'esprit** flash of wit; ~ **d'union** hyphen; (*fig*) link.

**traitant** [tRɛtɑ̃] *am*: **votre médecin** ~ your usual *ou* family doctor; **shampooing** ~ medicated shampoo.

**traite** [tRɛt] *nf* (*COMM*) draft; (*AGR*) milking; (*trajet*) stretch; **d'une (seule)** ~ without stopping (once); **la** ~ **des noirs** the slave trade.

**traité** [tRete] *nm* treaty.

**traitement** [tRɛtmɑ̃] *nm* treatment; processing; (*salaire*) salary.

**traiter** [tRete] *vt* (*gén*) to treat; (*TECH: matériaux*) to process, treat; (*affaire*) to deal with, handle; (*qualifier*): ~ **qn d'idiot** to call sb a fool // *vi* to deal; ~ **de** *vt* to deal with; **bien/mal** ~ to treat well/ill-treat.

**traiteur** [tRɛtœR] *nm* caterer.

**traître, esse** [tRɛtR(ə), -tRɛs] *a* (*dangereux*) treacherous // *nm* traitor; **prendre qn en** ~ to make an insidious attack on sb; **traîtrise** *nf* treachery, treacherousness.

**trajectoire** [tRaʒɛktwaR] *nf* trajectory, path.

**trajet** [tRaʒɛ] *nm* journey; (*itinéraire*) route; (*fig*) path, course.

**tralala** [tRalala] *nm* (*péj*) fuss.

**tram** [tRam] *nm abr de* **tramway**.

**trame** [tRam] *nf* (*de tissu*) weft; (*fig*) framework; texture; (*TYPO*) screen.

**tramer** [tRame] *vt* to plot, hatch.

**tramway** [tRamwɛ] *nm* tram(way); tram(car).

**tranchant, e** [tRɑ̃ʃɑ̃, -ɑ̃t] *a* sharp; (*fig*) peremptory // *nm* (*d'un couteau*) cutting edge; (*de la main*) edge.

**tranche** [tRɑ̃ʃ] *nf* (*morceau*) slice; (*arête*) edge; (*partie*) section; (*série*) block; issue; bracket.

**tranché, e** [tRɑ̃ʃe] *a* (*couleurs*) distinct, sharply contrasted; (*opinions*) clear-cut, definite // *nf* trench.

**trancher** [tRɑ̃ʃe] *vt* to cut, sever; (*fig: résoudre*) to settle // *vi*: ~ **avec** to contrast sharply with.

**tranchet** [tRɑ̃ʃɛ] *nm* knife.

**tranchoir** [tRɑ̃ʃwaR] *nm* chopper.

**tranquille** [tRɑ̃kil] *a* calm, quiet; (*enfant, élève*) quiet; (*rassuré*) easy in one's mind, with one's mind at rest; **se tenir** ~ (*enfant*) to be quiet; **avoir la conscience** ~ to have an easy conscience; **laisse-moi/laisse-ça** ~! leave me/it alone; ~**ment** *ad* calmly; **tranquillisant** *nm* tranquillizer; **tranquilliser** *vt* to reassure; **tranquillité** *nf* quietness; peace (and quiet); **tranquillité (d'esprit)** peace of mind.

**transaction** [tʀɑ̃zaksjɔ̃] *nf* (*COMM*) transaction, deal.

**transat** [tʀɑ̃zat] *nm* deckchair.

**transatlantique** [tʀɑ̃zatlɑ̃tik] *a* transatlantic // *nm* transatlantic liner.

**transborder** [tʀɑ̃sbɔʀde] *vt* to tran(s)ship.

**transcendant, e** [tʀɑ̃sɑ̃dɑ̃, -ɑ̃t] *a* transcendent(al).

**transcription** [tʀɑ̃skʀipsjɔ̃] *nf* transcription.

**transcrire** [tʀɑ̃skʀiʀ] *vt* to transcribe.

**transe** [tʀɑ̃s] *nf*: **entrer en ~** to go into a trance ; **~s** agony *sg*.

**transférer** [tʀɑ̃sfeʀe] *vt* to transfer ; **transfert** *nm* transfer.

**transfigurer** [tʀɑ̃sfigyʀe] *vt* to transform.

**transformateur** [tʀɑ̃sfɔʀmatœʀ] *nm* transformer.

**transformation** [tʀɑ̃sfɔʀmɑsjɔ̃] *nf* transformation ; (*RUGBY*) conversion.

**transformer** [tʀɑ̃sfɔʀme] *vt* to transform, alter (*'alter' implique un changement moins radical*) ; (*matière première, appartement, RUGBY*) to convert ; **~ en** to transform into ; to turn into ; to convert into ; **se ~** *vi* to be transformed ; to alter.

**transfuge** [tʀɑ̃sfyʒ] *nm* renegade.

**transfusion** [tʀɑ̃sfyzjɔ̃] *nf*: **~ sanguine** blood transfusion.

**transgresser** [tʀɑ̃sgʀese] *vt* to contravene, disobey.

**transhumance** [tʀɑ̃zymɑ̃s] *nf* transhumance, seasonal move to new pastures.

**transi, e** [tʀɑ̃zi] *a* numb (with cold), chilled to the bone.

**transiger** [tʀɑ̃ziʒe] *vi* to compromise, come to an agreement.

**transistor** [tʀɑ̃zistɔʀ] *nm* transistor.

**transit** [tʀɑ̃zit] *nm* transit ; **~er** *vi* to pass in transit.

**transitif, ive** [tʀɑ̃zitif, -iv] *a* transitive.

**transition** [tʀɑ̃zisjɔ̃] *nf* transition ; **de ~** transitional ; **transitoire** *a* transitional, provisional ; transient.

**translucide** [tʀɑ̃slysid] *a* translucent.

**transmetteur** [tʀɑ̃smɛtœʀ] *nm* transmitter.

**transmettre** [tʀɑ̃smɛtʀ(ə)] *vt* (*passer*): **~ qch à qn** to pass sth on to sb ; (*TECH, TEL, MED*) to transmit ; (*TV, RADIO: retransmettre*) to broadcast ; **transmissible** *a* transmissible.

**transmission** [tʀɑ̃smisjɔ̃] *nf* transmission, passing on ; (*AUTO*) transmission ; **~s** *nfpl* (*MIL*) ≈ signals corps ; **~ de pensée** telepathy.

**transparaître** [tʀɑ̃spaʀɛtʀ(ə)] *vi* to show (through).

**transparence** [tʀɑ̃spaʀɑ̃s] *nf* transparence ; **par ~** (*regarder*) against a source of light ; (*voir*) showing through.

**transparent, e** [tʀɑ̃spaʀɑ̃, -ɑ̃t] *a* transparent.

**transpercer** [tʀɑ̃spɛʀse] *vt* to go through, pierce.

**transpiration** [tʀɑ̃spiʀɑsjɔ̃] *nf* perspiration.

**transpirer** [tʀɑ̃spiʀe] *vi* to perspire.

**transplanter** [tʀɑ̃splɑ̃te] *vt* (*MÉD, BOT*) to transplant ; (*personne*) to uproot, move.

**transport** [tʀɑ̃spɔʀ] *nm* transport ; **~s en commun** public transport *sg*.

**transporter** [tʀɑ̃spɔʀte] *vt* to carry, move ; (*COMM*) to transport, convey ; (*fig*) to send into raptures ; **~ qn à l'hôpital** to take sb to hospital ; **transporteur** *nm* haulier, haulage contractor.

**transposer** [tʀɑ̃spoze] *vt* to transpose ; **transposition** *nf* transposition.

**transvaser** [tʀɑ̃svaze] *vt* to decant.

**transversal, e, aux** [tʀɑ̃svɛʀsal, -o] *a* transverse, cross(-) ; cross-country ; running at right angles.

**trapèze** [tʀapɛz] *nm* (*GÉOM*) trapezium ; (*au cirque*) trapeze ; **trapéziste** *nm/f* trapeze artist.

**trappe** [tʀap] *nf* trap door.

**trappeur** [tʀapœʀ] *nm* trapper, fur trader.

**trapu, e** [tʀapy] *a* squat, stocky.

**traquenard** [tʀaknaʀ] *nm* trap.

**traquer** [tʀake] *vt* to track down ; (*harceler*) to hound.

**traumatiser** [tʀomatize] *vt* to traumatize.

**traumatisme** [tʀomatism(ə)] *nm* traumatism.

**travail, aux** [tʀavaj, -o] *nm* (*gén*) work ; (*tâche, métier*) work *q*, job ; (*ÉCON, MÉD*) labour // *nmpl* (*de réparation, agricoles etc*) work *sg* ; (*sur route*) roadworks *pl* ; (*de construction*) building (work) ; **être/entrer en ~** (*MÉD*) to be in/start labour ; **être sans ~** (*employé*) to be out of work *ou* unemployed ; **~ noir** moonlighting ; **travaux des champs** farmwork *sg* ; **travaux dirigés** (*SCOL*) supervised practical work *sg* ; **travaux forcés** hard labour *sg* ; **travaux manuels** (*SCOL*) handicrafts ; **travaux ménagers** housework *sg* ; **travaux publics** ≈ public works *sg*.

**travaillé, e** [tʀavaje] *a* (*style*) polished.

**travailler** [tʀavaje] *vi* to work ; (*bois*) to warp // *vt* (*bois, métal*) to work ; (*objet d'art, discipline, fig: influencer*) to work on ; **cela le travaille** it is on his mind ; **~ la terre** to till the land ; **~ son piano** to do one's piano practice ; **~ à** to work on ; (*fig: contribuer à*) to work towards ; **travailleur, euse** *a* hard-working // *nm/f* worker ; **travailleur de force** labourer ; **travailliste** *a* Labour.

**travée** [tʀave] *nf* row ; (*ARCHIT*) bay ; span.

**travelling** [tʀavliŋ] *nm* (*chariot*) dolly ; (*technique*) tracking ; **~ optique** zoom shots *pl*.

**travers** [tʀavɛʀ] *nm* fault, failing ; **en ~ (de)** across ; **au ~ (de)** through ; **de ~** a askew // *ad* sideways ; (*fig*) the wrong way ; **à ~** through ; **regarder de ~** (*fig*) to look askance at.

**traverse** [tʀavɛʀs(ə)] *nf* (*RAIL*) sleeper ; **chemin de ~** shortcut.

**traversée** [tʀavɛʀse] *nf* crossing.

**traverser** [tʀavɛʀse] *vt* (*gén*) to cross ; (*ville, tunnel, aussi: percer, fig*) to go through ; (*suj: ligne, trait*) to run across.

**traversin** [tʀavɛʀsɛ̃] *nm* bolster.

**travesti** [tʀavɛsti] nm (costume) fancy dress ; (artiste de cabaret) female impersonator, drag artist ; (pervers) transvestite.

**travestir** [tʀavɛstiʀ] vt (vérité) to misrepresent ; **se** ~ to dress up ; to put on drag ; to dress as a woman.

**trébucher** [tʀebyʃe] vi: ~ **(sur)** to stumble (over), trip (against).

**trèfle** [tʀɛfl(ə)] nm (BOT) clover ; (CARTES: couleur) clubs pl ; (: carte) club ; ~ **à quatre feuilles** four-leaf clover.

**treillage** [tʀɛjaʒ] nm lattice work.

**treille** [tʀɛj] nf vine arbour ; climbing vine.

**treillis** [tʀeji] nm (métallique) wire-mesh ; (toile) canvas ; (uniforme) battle-dress.

**treize** [tʀɛz] num thirteen ; **treizième** num thirteenth.

**tréma** [tʀema] nm diaeresis.

**tremble** [tʀɑ̃bl(ə)] nm (BOT) aspen.

**tremblement** [tʀɑ̃bləmɑ̃] nm trembling q, shaking q, shivering q ; ~ **de terre** earthquake.

**trembler** [tʀɑ̃ble] vi to tremble, shake ; ~ **de** (froid, fièvre) to shiver ou tremble with ; (peur) to shake ou tremble with ; ~ **pour qn** to fear for sb ; **trembloter** vi to tremble ou shake slightly.

**trémolo** [tʀemɔlo] nm (instrument) tremolo ; (voix) quaver.

**trémousser** [tʀemuse]: **se** ~ vi to jig about, wriggle about.

**trempe** [tʀɑ̃p] nf (fig): **de cette/sa** ~ of this/his calibre.

**trempé, e** [tʀɑ̃pe] a soaking (wet), drenched ; (TECH) tempered.

**tremper** [tʀɑ̃pe] vt to soak, drench ; (aussi: **faire** ~, **mettre à** ~) to soak ; (plonger): ~ **qch dans** to dip sth in(to) // vi to soak ; (fig): ~ **dans** to be involved ou have a hand in ; **se** ~ vi to have a quick dip ; **se faire** ~ to get soaked ou drenched ; **trempette** nf: **faire trempette** to have a quick dip.

**tremplin** [tʀɑ̃plɛ̃] nm springboard ; (SKI) ski-jump.

**trentaine** [tʀɑ̃tɛn] nf: **une** ~ **(de)** thirty or so, about thirty.

**trente** [tʀɑ̃t] num thirty ; **trentième** num thirtieth.

**trépaner** [tʀepane] vt to trepan, trephine.

**trépasser** [tʀepase] vi to pass away.

**trépider** [tʀepide] vi to vibrate.

**trépied** [tʀepje] nm (d'appareil) tripod ; (meuble) trivet.

**trépigner** [tʀepiɲe] vi to stamp (one's feet).

**très** [tʀɛ] ad very ; much + pp, highly + pp ; ~ **critiqué** much criticized ; ~ **industrialisé** highly industrialized ; **j'ai** ~ **faim** I'm very hungry.

**trésor** [tʀezɔʀ] nm treasure ; (ADMIN) finances pl ; funds pl ; **T**~ **(public)** public revenue.

**trésorerie** [tʀezɔʀʀi] nf (fonds) funds pl ; (gestion) accounts pl ; (bureaux) accounts department ; (poste) treasurership ; **difficultés de** ~ cash problems, shortage of cash ou funds.

**trésorier, ière** [tʀezɔʀje, -jɛʀ] nm/f treasurer ; ~-**payeur** nm paymaster.

**tressaillir** [tʀesajiʀ] vi to shiver, shudder ; to quiver.

**tressauter** [tʀesote] vi to start, jump.

**tresse** [tʀɛs] nf braid, plait.

**tresser** [tʀese] vi (cheveux) to braid, plait ; (fil, jonc) to plait ; (corbeille) to weave ; (corde) to twist.

**tréteau, x** [tʀeto] nm trestle ; **les** ~**x** (fig) the stage.

**treuil** [tʀœj] nm winch ; **treuiller** vt to winch up.

**trêve** [tʀɛv] nf (MIL, POL) truce ; (fig) respite ; ~ **de** ... enough of this...

**tri** [tʀi] nm sorting out q ; selection ; (POSTES) sorting ; sorting office.

**triage** [tʀijaʒ] nm (RAIL) shunting ; (gare) marshalling yard.

**triangle** [tʀijɑ̃gl(ə)] nm triangle ; ~ **rectangle** right-angled triangle.

**tribal, e, aux** [tʀibal, -o] a tribal.

**tribord** [tʀibɔʀ] nm: **à** ~ to starboard, on the starboard side.

**tribu** [tʀiby] nf tribe.

**tribulations** [tʀibylysjɔ̃] nfpl tribulations, trials.

**tribunal, aux** [tʀibynal, -o] nm (JUR) court ; (MIL) tribunal ; ~ **de police/pour enfants** police/juvenile court ; ~ **d'instance** ≈ magistrates' court ; ~ **de grande instance** ≈ high court.

**tribune** [tʀibyn] nf (estrade) platform, rostrum ; (débat) forum ; (d'église, de tribunal) gallery ; (de stade) stand ; ~ **libre** (PRESSE) opinion column.

**tribut** [tʀiby] nm tribute.

**tributaire** [tʀibytɛʀ] a: **être** ~ **de** to be dependent on ; (GEO) to be a tributary of.

**tricher** [tʀiʃe] vi to cheat ; **tricherie** nf cheating q ; **tricheur, euse** nm/f cheat.

**tricolore** [tʀikɔlɔʀ] a three-coloured ; (français) red, white and blue.

**tricot** [tʀiko] nm (technique, ouvrage) knitting q ; (tissu) knitted fabric ; (vêtement) jersey, sweater.

**tricoter** [tʀikɔte] vt to knit.

**trictrac** [tʀiktʀak] nm backgammon.

**tricycle** [tʀisikl(ə)] nm tricycle.

**triennal, e, aux** [tʀiɛnal, -o] a three-yearly ; three-year.

**trier** [tʀije] vt to sort out ; (POSTES, fruits) to sort.

**trigonométrie** [tʀigɔnɔmetʀi] nf trigonometry.

**trimbaler** [tʀɛ̃bale] vt to cart around, trail along.

**trimer** [tʀime] vi to slave away.

**trimestre** [tʀimɛstʀ(ə)] nm (SCOL) term ; (COMM) quarter ; **trimestriel, le** a quarterly ; (SCOL) end-of-term.

**tringle** [tʀɛ̃gl(ə)] nf rod.

**Trinité** [tʀinite] nf Trinity.

**trinquer** [tʀɛ̃ke] vi to clink glasses ; (fam) to cop it ; ~ **à qch/la santé de qn** to drink to sth/sb.

**trio** [tʀijo] nm trio.

**triomphal, e, aux** [tʀijɔ̃fal, -o] a triumphant, triumphal.

**triomphant, e** [tʀijɔ̃fɑ̃, -ɑ̃t] a triumphant.

**triomphe** [tʀijɔ̃f] nm triumph ; **être reçu/porté en** ~ to be given a triumphant welcome/be carried shoulder-high in triumph.

**triompher** [tʀijɔ̃fe] *vi* to triumph, win; ~ **de** to triumph over, overcome.

**tripes** [tʀip] *nfpl* (*CULIN*) tripe *sg*; (*fam*) guts.

**triple** [tʀipl(ə)] *a* triple; treble // *nm*: **le** ~ **(de)** (*comparaison*) three times as much (as); **en** ~ **exemplaire** in triplicate; ~**ment** *ad* three times over; in three ways, on three counts // *nm* trebling, threefold increase; **tripler** *vi*, *vt* to triple, treble, increase threefold.

**tripot** [tʀipo] *nm* (*péj*) dive.

**tripotage** [tʀipɔtaʒ] *nm* (*péj*) jiggery-pokery.

**tripoter** [tʀipɔte] *vt* to fiddle with, finger.

**trique** [tʀik] *nf* cudgel.

**triste** [tʀist(ə)] *a* sad; (*péj*): ~ **personnage/affaire** sorry individual/affair; **tristesse** *nf* sadness.

**triturer** [tʀityʀe] *vt* (*pâte*) to knead; (*objets*) to manipulate.

**trivial, e, aux** [tʀivjal, -o] *a* coarse, crude; (*commun*) mundane.

**troc** [tʀɔk] *nm* (*ÉCON*) barter; (*transaction*) exchange, swap.

**troglodyte** [tʀɔglɔdit] *nm/f* cave dweller, troglodyte.

**trognon** [tʀɔɲɔ̃] *nm* (*de fruit*) core; (*de légume*) stalk.

**trois** [tʀwɑ] *num* three; **troisième** *num* third; **troisièmement** *ad* thirdly; ~-**quarts** *nmpl*: **les** ~-**quarts de** three-quarters of.

**trolleybus** [tʀɔlɛbys] *nm* trolley bus.

**trombe** [tʀɔ̃b] *nf* waterspout; **des** ~**s d'eau** a downpour; **en** ~ (*arriver, passer*) like a whirlwind.

**trombone** [tʀɔ̃bɔn] *nm* (*MUS*) trombone; (*de bureau*) paper clip; ~ **à coulisse** slide trombone; **tromboniste** *nm/f* trombonist.

**trompe** [tʀɔ̃p] *nf* (*d'éléphant*) trunk; (*MUS*) trumpet, horn; ~ **d'Eustache** Eustachian tube; ~**s utérines** Fallopian tubes.

**trompe-l'œil** [tʀɔ̃plœj] *nm*: **en** ~ in trompe-l'œil style.

**tromper** [tʀɔ̃pe] *vt* to deceive; (*vigilance, poursuivants*) to elude; **se** ~ *vi* to make a mistake, be mistaken; **se** ~ **de voiture/jour** to take the wrong car/get the day wrong; **se** ~ **de 3 cm/20 F** to be out by 3 cm/20 F; **tromperie** *nf* deception, trickery *q*.

**trompette** [tʀɔ̃pɛt] *nf* trumpet; **en** ~ (*nez*) turned-up; **trompettiste** *nm/f* trumpet player.

**trompeur, euse** [tʀɔ̃pœʀ, -øz] *a* deceptive, misleading.

**tronc** [tʀɔ̃] *nm* (*BOT, ANAT*) trunk; (*d'église*) collection box; ~ **d'arbre** tree trunk; ~ **commun** (*SCOL*) common-core syllabus; ~ **de cône** truncated cone.

**tronche** [tʀɔ̃ʃ] *nf* (*fam*) mug, face.

**tronçon** [tʀɔ̃sɔ̃] *nm* section.

**tronçonner** [tʀɔ̃sɔne] *vt* to saw up; **tronçonneuse** *nf* chain saw.

**trône** [tʀon] *nm* throne.

**trôner** [tʀone] *vi* (*fig*) to sit in the place of honour.

**tronquer** [tʀɔ̃ke] *vt* to truncate; (*fig*) to curtail.

**trop** [tʀo] *ad vb* + too much, too + *adjectif, adverbe*; ~ **(nombreux)** too many; ~ **peu (nombreux)** too few; ~ **(souvent)** too often; ~ **(longtemps)** (for) too long; ~ **de** (*nombre*) too many; (*quantité*) too much; **de** ~, **en** ~: **des livres en** ~ a few books too many, a few extra books; **du lait en** ~ some milk over *ou* extra, too much milk; **3 livres/F de** ~ 3 books too many/F too much.

**trophée** [tʀɔfe] *nm* trophy.

**tropical, e, aux** [tʀɔpikal, -o] *a* tropical.

**tropique** [tʀɔpik] *nm* tropic; ~**s** *nmpl* tropics.

**trop-plein** [tʀɔplɛ̃] *nm* (*tuyau*) overflow *ou* outlet (pipe); (*liquide*) overflow.

**troquer** [tʀɔke] *vt*: ~ **qch contre** to barter *ou* trade sth for; (*fig*) to swap sth for.

**trot** [tʀo] *nm* trot; **aller au** ~ to trot along; **partir au** ~ to set off at a trot.

**trotter** [tʀɔte] *vi* to trot; (*fig*) to scamper along (*ou* about).

**trotteuse** [tʀɔtøz] *nf* (*de montre*) second hand.

**trottiner** [tʀɔtine] *vi* (*fig*) to scamper along (*ou* about).

**trottinette** [tʀɔtinɛt] *nf* (child's) scooter.

**trottoir** [tʀɔtwaʀ] *nm* pavement; **faire le** ~ (*péj*) to walk the streets; ~ **roulant** moving walkway, travellator.

**trou** [tʀu] *nm* hole; (*fig*) gap; ~ **d'air** air pocket; ~ **de mémoire** blank, lapse of memory; **le** ~ **de la serrure** the keyhole.

**troublant, e** [tʀublɑ̃, -ɑ̃t] *a* disturbing.

**trouble** [tʀubl(ə)] *a* (*liquide*) cloudy; (*image, mémoire*) indistinct, hazy; (*affaire*) shady, murky // *nm* (*désarroi*) distress, agitation; (*émoi sensuel*) turmoil, agitation; (*embarras*) confusion; (*zizanie*) unrest, discord; ~**s** *nmpl* (*POL*) disturbances, troubles, unrest *sg*; (*MÉD*) trouble *sg*, disorders.

**trouble-fête** [tʀubləfɛt] *nm/f inv* spoilsport.

**troubler** [tʀuble] *vt* (*embarrasser*) to confuse, disconcert; (*émouvoir*) to agitate; to disturb; to perturb; (*perturber: ordre etc*) to disrupt, disturb; (*liquide*) to make cloudy; **se** ~ *vi* (*personne*) to become flustered *ou* confused; ~ **l'ordre public** to cause a breach of the peace.

**troué, e** [tʀue] *a* with a hole (*ou* holes) in it // *nf* gap; (*MIL*) breach.

**trouer** [tʀue] *vt* to make a hole (*ou* holes) in; (*fig*) to pierce.

**trouille** [tʀuj] *nf* (*fam*): **avoir la** ~ to have the jitters, be in a funk.

**troupe** [tʀup] *nf* (*MIL*) troop; (*groupe*) troop, group; **la** ~ (*MIL*) the army; the troops *pl*; ~ **(de théâtre)** (theatrical) company.

**troupeau, x** [tʀupo] *nm* (*de moutons*) flock; (*de vaches*) herd.

**trousse** [tʀus] *nf* case, kit; (*d'écolier*) pencil case; (*de docteur*) instrument case; **aux** ~**s de** (*fig*) on the heels *ou* tail of; ~ **à outils** toolkit; ~ **de toilette** toilet *ou* sponge bag.

**trousseau, x** [tʀuso] *nm* (*de jeune mariée*) trousseau ; ~ **de clefs** bunch of keys.
**trouvaille** [tʀuvaj] *nf* find.
**trouver** [tʀuve] *vt* to find ; (*rendre visite*): **aller/venir** ~ **qn** to go/come and see sb ; **je trouve que** I find *ou* think that ; ~ **à boire/critiquer** to find something to drink/criticize ; **se** ~ *vi* (*être*) to be ; (*être soudain*) to find o.s. ; **se** ~ **être/avoir** to happen to be/have ; **il se trouve que** it happens that, it turns out that ; **se** ~ **bien** to feel well ; **se** ~ **mal** to pass out.
**truand** [tʀyɑ̃] *nm* villain, crook.
**truc** [tʀyk] *nm* (*astuce*) way, device ; (*de cinéma, prestidigitateur*) trick effect ; (*chose*) thing ; (*machin*) thingumajig, whatsit ; **avoir le** ~ to have the knack.
**truchement** [tʀyʃmɑ̃] *nm*: **par le** ~ **de qn** through (the intervention of) sb.
**truculent, e** [tʀykylɑ̃, -ɑ̃t] *a* a colourful.
**truelle** [tʀyɛl] *nf* trowel.
**truffe** [tʀyf] *nf* truffle ; (*nez*) nose.
**truffer** [tʀyfe] *vt* (CULIN) to garnish with truffles ; **truffé de** (*fig*) peppered with ; bristling with.
**truie** [tʀyi] *nf* sow.
**truite** [tʀyit] *nf* trout *inv*.
**truquage** [tʀykaʒ] *nm* fixing ; (CINÉMA) special effects *pl.*
**truquer** [tʀyke] *vt* (*élections, serrure, dés*) to fix ; (CINÉMA) to use special effects in.
**trust** [tʀœst] *nm* (COMM) trust.
**tsar** [dzaʀ] *nm* tsar.
**T.S.F.** [teɛsɛf] *sigle f* (= *télégraphie sans fil*) wireless.
**tsigane** [tsigan] *a*, *nm/f* = **tzigane**.
**T.S.V.P.** *sigle* (= *tournez s.v.p.*) P.T.O. (please turn over).
**T.T.C.** *sigle* = *toutes taxes comprises.*
**tu** [ty] *pronom* you // *nm*: **employer le** ~ to use the 'tu' form.
**tu, e** [ty] *pp de* **taire**.
**tuba** [tyba] *nm* (MUS) tuba ; (SPORT) snorkel.
**tube** [tyb] *nm* tube ; pipe ; (*chanson, disque*) hit song *ou* record ; ~ **digestif** alimentary canal, digestive tract.
**tuberculeux, euse** [tybɛʀkylø, -øz] *a* tubercular // *nm/f* tuberculosis *ou* TB patient.
**tuberculose** [tybɛʀkyloz] *nf* tuberculosis.
**tubulaire** [tybylɛʀ] *a* tubular.
**tubulure** [tybylyʀ] *nf* pipe ; piping *q* ; (AUTO) manifold.
**tué, e** [tɥe] *nm/f*: **5** ~**s** 5 killed *ou* dead.
**tuer** [tɥe] *vt* to kill ; **se** ~ *vi* to be killed ; **se** ~ **au travail** (*fig*) to work o.s. to death ; **tuerie** *nf* slaughter *q.*
**tue-tête** [tytɛt]: **à** ~ *ad* at the top of one's voice.
**tueur** [tɥœʀ] *nm* killer ; ~ **à gages** hired killer.
**tuile** [tɥil] *nf* tile ; (*fam*) spot of bad luck, blow.
**tulipe** [tylip] *nf* tulip.
**tuméfié, e** [tymefje] *a* puffy, swollen.
**tumeur** [tymœʀ] *nf* growth, tumour.
**tumulte** [tymylt(ə)] *nm* commotion, hubbub.
**tumultueux, euse** [tymyltɥø, -øz] *a* stormy, turbulent.

**tunique** [tynik] *nf* tunic ; (*de femme*) smock, tunic.
**Tunisie** [tynizi] *nf*: **la** ~ Tunisia ; **tunisien, ne** *a*, *nm/f* Tunisian.
**tunnel** [tynɛl] *nm* tunnel.
**turban** [tyʀbɑ̃] *nm* turban.
**turbin** [tyʀbɛ̃] *nm* (*fam*) work *q.*
**turbine** [tyʀbin] *nf* turbine.
**turboréacteur** [tyʀbɔʀeaktœʀ] *nm* turbojet.
**turbulences** [tyʀbylɑ̃s] *nfpl* (AVIAT) turbulence *sg.*
**turbulent, e** [tyʀbylɑ̃, -ɑ̃t] *a* boisterous, unruly.
**turc, turque** [tyʀk(ə)] *a* Turkish // *nm/f*: **T**~, **Turque** Turk/Turkish woman // *nm* (*langue*) Turkish ; **à la turque** *ad* crosslegged // *a* (*w.-c.*) seatless.
**turf** [tyʀf] *nm* racing ; ~**iste** *nm/f* racegoer.
**turpitude** [tyʀpityd] *nf* base act, baseness *q.*
**turque** [tyʀk(ə)] *a*, *nf voir* **turc**.
**Turquie** [tyʀki] *nf*: **la** ~ Turkey.
**turquoise** [tyʀkwaz] *nf*, *a inv* turquoise.
**tus** *etc vb voir* **taire**.
**tutelle** [tytɛl] *nf* (JUR) guardianship ; (POL) trusteeship ; **sous la** ~ **de** (*fig*) under the supervision of.
**tuteur** [tytœʀ] *nm* (JUR) guardian ; (*de plante*) stake, support.
**tutoyer** [tytwaje] *vt*: ~ **qn** to address sb as 'tu'.
**tuyau, x** [tɥijo] *nm* pipe ; (*flexible*) tube ; (*fam*) tip ; gen *q* ; ~ **d'arrosage** hosepipe ; ~ **d'échappement** exhaust pipe ; ~**té, e** *a* fluted ; ~**terie** *nf* piping *q.*
**tuyère** [tɥijɛʀ] *nf* nozzle.
**T.V.A.** *sigle f voir* **taxe**.
**tympan** [tɛ̃pɑ̃] *nm* (ANAT) eardrum.
**type** [tip] *nm* type ; (*fam*) chap, bloke // *a* typical, standard ; **avoir le** ~ **nordique** to be Nordic-looking.
**typhoïde** [tifɔid] *nf* typhoid (fever).
**typhon** [tifɔ̃] *nm* typhoon.
**typhus** [tifys] *nm* typhus (fever).
**typique** [tipik] *a* typical.
**typographe** [tipɔgʀaf] *nm/f* typographer.
**typographie** [tipɔgʀafi] *nf* typography ; (*procédé*) letterpress (printing) ; **typographique** *a* typographical ; letterpress *cpd.*
**tyran** [tiʀɑ̃] *nm* tyrant ; **tyrannie** *nf* tyranny ; **tyrannique** *a* tyrannical ; **tyranniser** *vt* to tyrannize.
**tzigane** [dzigan] *a* gipsy, tzigane // *nm/f* (Hungarian) gipsy, Tzigane.

# U

**ubiquité** [ybikɥite] *nf*: **avoir le don d'**~ to be everywhere at once *ou* be ubiquitous.
**ulcère** [ylsɛʀ] *nm* ulcer ; ~ **à l'estomac** stomach ulcer.
**ulcérer** [ylseʀe] *vt* (MÉD) to ulcerate ; (*fig*) to sicken, appal.
**ultérieur, e** [ylteʀjœʀ] *a* later, subsequent ; **remis à une date** ~**e** postponed to a later date ; ~**ement** *ad* later.

**ultimatum** [yltimatɔm] *nm* ultimatum.

**ultime** [yltim] *a* final.

**ultra...** [yltʀa] *préfixe:* ∼**moderne/ -rapide** ultra-modern/-fast ; ∼**-sensible** *a* (PHOTO) high-speed ; ∼**-sons** *nmpl* ultrasonics ; ∼**-violet, te** *a* ultraviolet.

**un, une** [œ̃, yn] *dét* a, an + *voyelle* // *pronom, num, a* one ; **l'un l'autre, les** ∼**s les autres** each other, one another ; **l'** ∼ **..., l'autre** (the) one ..., the other ; **les** ∼**s ..., les autres** some ..., others ; **l'** ∼ **et l'autre** both (of them) ; **l'** ∼ **ou l'autre** either (of them) ; **l'** ∼ **des meilleurs** one of the best.

**unanime** [ynanim] *a* unanimous ; **unanimité** *nf* unanimity ; **à l'unanimité** unanimously.

**uni, e** [yni] *a* (*ton, tissu*) plain ; (*surface*) smooth, even ; (*famille*) close(-knit) ; (*pays*) united.

**unification** [ynifikɑsjɔ̃] *nf* uniting ; unification ; standardization.

**unifier** [ynifje] *vt* to unite, unify ; (*systèmes*) to standardize, unify.

**uniforme** [ynifɔrm(ə)] *a* (*mouvement*) regular, uniform ; (*surface, ton*) even ; (*objets, maisons*) uniform // *nm* uniform ; **être sous l'** ∼ (MIL) to be serving ; **uniformiser** *vt* to make uniform ; (*systèmes*) to standardize ; **uniformité** *nf* regularity ; uniformity ; evenness.

**unijambiste** [yniʒɑ̃bist(ə)] *nm/f* one-legged man/woman.

**unilatéral, e, aux** [ynilateʀal, -o] *a* unilateral ; **stationnement** ∼ parking on one side only.

**union** [ynjɔ̃] *nf* union ; ∼ **conjugale** union of marriage ; ∼ **de consommateurs** consumers' association ; **l'U**∼ **soviétique** the Soviet Union.

**unique** [ynik] *a* (*seul*) only ; (*le même*): **un prix/système** ∼ a single price/system ; (*exceptionnel*) unique ; **ménage à salaire** ∼ one-salary family ; **route à voie** ∼ single-lane road ; **fils/fille** ∼ only son/daughter ; ∼ **en France** the only one of its kind in France ; ∼**ment** *ad* only, solely ; (*juste*) only, merely.

**unir** [yniʀ] *vt* (*nations*) to unite ; (*éléments, couleurs*) to combine ; (*en mariage*) to unite, join together ; ∼ **qch à** to unite sth with ; to combine sth with ; **s'** ∼ to unite ; (*en mariage*) to be joined together.

**unisson** [ynisɔ̃] : **à l'** ∼ *ad* in unison.

**unitaire** [yniteʀ] *a* unitary ; **prix** ∼ price per unit.

**unité** [ynite] *nf* (*harmonie, cohésion*) unity ; (COMM, MIL, *de mesure*, MATH) unit.

**univers** [ynivɛʀ] *nm* universe.

**universel, le** [ynivɛʀsɛl] *a* universal ; (*esprit*) all-embracing.

**universitaire** [ynivɛʀsitɛʀ] *a* university *cpd* ; (*diplôme, études*) academic, university *cpd* // *nm/f* academic.

**université** [ynivɛʀsite] *nf* university.

**uranium** [yʀanjɔm] *nm* uranium.

**urbain, e** [yʀbɛ̃, -ɛn] *a* urban, city *cpd*, town *cpd* ; (*poli*) urbane ; **urbaniser** *vt* to urbanize ; **urbanisme** *nm* town planning ; **urbaniste** *nm/f* town planner.

**urgence** [yʀʒɑ̃s] *nf* urgency ; (MÉD *etc*)

emergency ; **d'** ∼ *a* emergency *cpd* // *ad* as a matter of urgency.

**urgent, e** [yʀʒɑ̃, -ɑ̃t] *a* urgent.

**urinal, aux** [yʀinal, -o] *nm* (bed) urinal.

**urine** [yʀin] *nf* urine ; **uriner** *vi* to urinate ; **urinoir** *nm* (public) urinal.

**urne** [yʀn(ə)] *nf* (*électorale*) ballot box ; (*vase*) urn ; **aller aux** ∼**s** (*voter*) to go to the polls.

**URSS** [*parfois:* yʀs] *sigle f:* **l'** ∼ the USSR.

**urticaire** [yʀtikɛʀ] *nf* nettle rash.

**us** [ys] *nmpl:* ∼ **et coutumes** (habits and) customs.

**U.S.A.** *sigle mpl:* **les** ∼ the U.S.A.

**usage** [yzaʒ] *nm* (*emploi, utilisation*) use ; (*coutume*) custom ; (LING): **l'** ∼ usage ; **faire** ∼ **de** (*pouvoir, droit*) to exercise ; **avoir l'** ∼ **de** to have the use of ; **à l'** ∼ *ad* with use ; **à l'** ∼ **de** (*pour*) for (use of) ; **en** ∼ in use ; **hors d'** ∼ out of service ; wrecked ; **à** ∼ **interne** to be taken ; **à** ∼ **externe** for external use only.

**usagé, e** [yzaʒe] *a* (*usé*) worn ; (*d'occasion*) used.

**usager, ère** [yzaʒe, -ɛʀ] *nm/f* user.

**usé, e** [yze] *a* worn ; (*banal*) hackneyed.

**user** [yze] *vt* (*outil*) to wear down ; (*vêtement*) to wear out ; (*matière*) to wear away ; (*consommer: charbon etc*) to use ; **s'** ∼ *vi* to wear ; to wear out ; (*fig*) to decline ; **s'** ∼ **à la tâche** to wear o.s. out with work ; ∼ **de** *vt* (*moyen, procédé*) to use, employ ; (*droit*) to exercise.

**usine** [yzin] *nf* factory ; ∼ **à gaz** gasworks *sg* ; ∼ **marémotrice** tidal power station.

**usiner** [yzine] *vt* (TECH) to machine.

**usité, e** [yzite] *a* in common use, common ; **peu** ∼ rarely used.

**ustensile** [ystɑ̃sil] *nm* implement ; ∼ **de cuisine** kitchen utensil.

**usuel, le** [yzɥɛl] *a* everyday, common.

**usufruit** [yzyfʀɥi] *nm* usufruct.

**usuraire** [yzyʀɛʀ] *a* usurious.

**usure** [yzyʀ] *nf* wear ; worn state ; (*de l'usurier*) usury ; **avoir qn à l'** ∼ to wear sb down ; **usurier, ière** *nm/f* usurer.

**usurper** [yzyʀpe] *vt* to usurp.

**ut** [yt] *nm* (MUS) C.

**utérin, e** [yteʀɛ̃, -in] *a* uterine.

**utérus** [yteʀys] *nm* uterus, womb.

**utile** [ytil] *a* useful.

**utilisation** [ytilizɑsjɔ̃] *nf* use.

**utiliser** [ytilize] *vt* to use.

**utilitaire** [ytilitɛʀ] *a* utilitarian ; (*objets*) practical.

**utilité** [ytilite] *nf* usefulness *q* ; use ; **jouer les** ∼**s** (THÉÂTRE) to play bit parts ; **reconnu d'** ∼ **publique** state-approved ; **c'est d'une grande** ∼ it's of great use.

**utopie** [ytɔpi] *nf* utopian idea *ou* view ; utopia ; **utopiste** *nm/f* utopian.

**uvule** [yvyl] *nf* uvula.

# V

**va** *vb voir* **aller.**

**vacance** [vakɑ̃s] *nf* (ADMIN) vacancy ; ∼**s** *nfpl* holiday(s *pl*), vacation *sg* ; **prendre des/ses** ∼**s** to take a holiday/one's holiday(s) ; **aller en** ∼**s** to go on holiday ;

**vacancier, ière** *nm/f* holiday-maker.
**vacant, e** [vakã, -ãt] *a* vacant.
**vacarme** [vakaʀm(ə)] *nm* row, din.
**vaccin** [vaksɛ̃] *nm* vaccine ; (*opération*) vaccination ; **vaccination** *nf* vaccination ; **vacciner** *vt* to vaccinate ; (*fig*) to make immune.
**vache** [vaʃ] *nf* (*zool*) cow ; (*cuir*) cowhide // *a* (*fam*) rotten, mean ; ~ **à eau** (canvas) water bag ; ~ **à lait** (*péj*) mug, sucker ; ~ **laitière** dairy cow ; **vachement** *ad* (*fam*) damned, hellish ; **vacher, ère** *nm/f* cowherd ; **vacherie** *nf* (*fam*) meanness *q* ; dirty trick ; nasty remark.
**vaciller** [vasije] *vi* to sway, wobble ; (*bougie, lumière*) to flicker ; (*fig*) to be failing, falter.
**vacuité** [vakɥite] *nf* emptiness, vacuity.
**vade-mecum** [vademekɔm] *nm inv* pocketbook.
**vadrouiller** [vadʀuje] *vi* to rove around *ou* about.
**va-et-vient** [vaevjɛ̃] *nm inv* (*de pièce mobile*) to and fro (*ou* up and down) movement ; (*de personnes, véhicules*) comings and goings *pl*, to-ings and fro-ings *pl*.
**vagabond, e** [vagabɔ̃, -ɔ̃d] *a* wandering ; (*imagination*) roaming, roving // *nm* (*rôdeur*) tramp, vagrant ; (*voyageur*) wanderer.
**vagabondage** [vagabɔ̃daʒ] *nm* roaming, wandering ; (*jur*) vagrancy.
**vagabonder** [vagabɔ̃de] *vi* to roam, wander.
**vagin** [vaʒɛ̃] *nm* vagina.
**vagissement** [vaʒismã] *nm* cry (*of newborn baby*).
**vague** [vag] *nf* wave // *a* vague ; (*regard*) faraway ; (*manteau, robe*) loose(-fitting) ; (*quelconque*): **un ~ bureau/cousin** some office/cousin or other // *nm*: **rester dans le ~** to keep things rather vague ; **regarder dans le ~** to gaze into space ; ~ **à l'âme** *nm* vague melancholy ; ~ **d'assaut** *nf* (*mil*) wave of assault ; ~ **de chaleur** *nf* heatwave ; ~ **de fond** *nf* ground swell ; ~ **de froid** *nf* cold spell ; ~**ment** *ad* vaguely.
**vaillant, e** [vajã, -ãt] *a* (*courageux*) brave, gallant ; (*robuste*) vigorous, hale and hearty ; **n'avoir plus un sou ~** to be penniless.
**vaille** *vb voir* **valoir**.
**vain, e** [vɛ̃, vɛn] *a* vain ; **en ~** *ad* in vain.
**vaincre** [vɛ̃kʀ(ə)] *vt* to defeat ; (*fig*) to conquer, overcome ; **vaincu, e** *nm/f* defeated party ; **vainqueur** *nm* victor ; (*sport*) winner // *am* victorious.
**vais** *vb voir* **aller**.
**vaisseau, x** [vɛso] *nm* (*anat*) vessel ; (*navig*) ship, vessel ; ~ **spatial** spaceship.
**vaisselier** [vɛsəlje] *nm* dresser.
**vaisselle** [vɛsɛl] *nf* (*service*) crockery ; (*plats etc à laver*) (dirty) dishes *pl* ; (*lavage*) washing-up ; **faire la ~** to do the washing-up *ou* the dishes.
**val, vaux** *ou* **vals** [val, vo] *nm* valley.
**valable** [valabl(ə)] *a* valid ; (*acceptable*) decent, worthwhile.

**valent** *etc vb voir* **valoir**.
**valet** [valɛ] *nm* valet ; (*cartes*) jack, knave ; ~ **de chambre** manservant, valet ; ~ **de ferme** farmhand ; ~ **de pied** footman.
**valeur** [valœʀ] *nf* (*gén*) value ; (*mérite*) worth, merit ; (*comm: titre*) security ; **mettre en ~** (*bien*) to exploit ; (*terrain, région*) to develop ; (*fig*) to highlight ; to show off to advantage ; **avoir de la ~** to be valuable ; **prendre de la ~** to go up *ou* gain in value.
**valeureux, euse** [valœʀø, -øz] *a* valorous.
**valide** [valid] *a* (*en bonne santé*) fit, well ; (*indemne*) able-bodied, fit ; (*valable*) valid ; **valider** *vt* to validate ; **validité** *nf* validity.
**valions** *vb voir* **valoir**.
**valise** [valiz] *nf* (suit)case ; **la ~ (diplomatique)** the diplomatic bag.
**vallée** [vale] *nf* valley.
**vallon** [valɔ̃] *nm* small valley.
**vallonné, e** [valɔne] *n* undulating.
**valoir** [valwaʀ] *vi* (*être valable*) to hold, apply // *vt* (*prix, valeur, effort*) to be worth ; (*causer*): ~ **qch à qn** to earn sb sth ; **se ~** to be of equal merit ; (*péj*) to be two of a kind ; **faire ~** (*droits, prérogatives*) to assert ; (*domaine, capitaux*) to exploit ; **faire ~ que** to point out that ; **à ~ on** account ; **à ~ sur** to be deducted from ; **vaille que vaille** somehow or other ; **cela ne me dit rien qui vaille** I don't like the look of it at all ; **ce climat ne me vaut rien** this climate doesn't suit me ; ~ **la peine** to be worth the trouble *ou* worth it ; ~ **mieux: il vaut mieux se taire** it's better to say nothing ; **ça ne vaut rien** it's worthless ; **que vaut ce candidat?** how good is this applicant?
**valoriser** [valɔʀize] *vt* (*écon*) to develop (the economy of) ; (*psych*) to increase the standing of.
**valse** [vals(ə)] *nf* waltz ; **valser** *vi* to waltz ; (*fig*): **aller valser** to go flying.
**valu, e** [valy] *pp de* **valoir**.
**valve** [valv(ə)] *nf* valve.
**vandale** [vãdal] *nm/f* vandal ; **vandalisme** *nm* vandalism.
**vanille** [vanij] *nf* vanilla.
**vanité** [vanite] *nf* vanity ; **vaniteux, euse** *a* vain, conceited.
**vanne** [van] *nf* gate.
**vanner** [vane] *vt* to winnow.
**vannerie** [vanʀi] *nf* basketwork.
**vantail, aux** [vãtaj, -o] *nm* door, leaf (*pl* leaves).
**vantard, e** [vãtaʀ, -aʀd(ə)] *a* boastful ; **vantardise** *nf* boastfulness *q* ; boast.
**vanter** [vãte] *vt* to speak highly of, vaunt ; **se ~** *vi* to boast, brag ; **se ~ de** to boast of.
**va-nu-pieds** [vanypje] *nm/f inv* tramp, beggar.
**vapeur** [vapœʀ] *nf* steam ; (*émanation*) vapour, fumes *pl* ; ~**s** *nfpl* (*bouffées*) vapours ; **à ~** steam-powered, steam *cpd* ; **à toute ~** full steam ahead ; (*fig*) at full tilt ; **renverser la ~** to reverse engines ; (*fig*) to backtrack, backpedal ; **cuit à la ~** steamed.

**vaporeux, euse** [vapɔʀø, -øz] a (flou) hazy, misty ; (léger) filmy, gossamer cpd.
**vaporisateur** [vapɔʀizatœʀ] nm spray.
**vaporiser** [vapɔʀize] vt (CHIMIE) to vaporize ; (parfum etc) to spray.
**vaquer** [vake] vi: ~ à ses occupations to attend to one's affairs, go about one's business.
**varappe** [vaʀap] nf rock climbing ; **varappeur, euse** nm/f (rock) climber.
**varech** [vaʀɛk] nm wrack, varec.
**vareuse** [vaʀøz] nf (blouson) pea jacket ; (d'uniforme) tunic.
**variable** [vaʀjabl(ə)] a variable ; (temps, humeur) changeable, variable ; (TECH: à plusieurs positions etc) adaptable ; (LING) inflectional ; (divers: résultats) varied, various // nf (MATH) variable.
**variante** [vaʀjɑ̃t] nf variant.
**variation** [vaʀjɑsjɔ̃] nf variation ; changing q, change.
**varice** [vaʀis] nf varicose vein.
**varicelle** [vaʀisɛl] nf chickenpox.
**varié, e** [vaʀje] a varied ; (divers) various ; **hors-d'œuvre** ~s selection of hors d'œuvres.
**varier** [vaʀje] vi to vary ; (temps, humeur) to vary, change // vt to vary.
**variété** [vaʀjete] nf variety ; **spectacle de** ~s variety show.
**variole** [vaʀjɔl] nf smallpox.
**variqueux, euse** [vaʀikø, -øz] a varicose.
**vas** vb voir **aller**.
**vase** [vɑz] nm vase // nf silt, mud ; **en** ~ **clos** in isolation ; ~ **de nuit** chamberpot ; ~**s communicants** communicating vessels.
**vaseline** [vazlin] nf vaseline.
**vaseux, euse** [vɑzø, -øz] a silty, muddy ; (fig: confus) woolly, hazy ; (: fatigué) peaky ; woozy.
**vasistas** [vazistɑs] nm fanlight.
**vaste** [vast(ə)] a vast, immense.
**Vatican** [vatikɑ̃] nm: **le** ~ the Vatican.
**vaticiner** [vatisine] vi (péj) to make pompous predictions.
**va-tout** [vatu] nm: **jouer son** ~ to stake one's all.
**vaudeville** [vodvil] nm vaudeville, light comedy.
**vaudrai** etc vb voir **valoir**.
**vau-l'eau** [volo]: **à** ~ ad with the current ; (fig) adrift.
**vaurien, ne** [voʀjɛ̃, -ɛn] nm/f good-for-nothing, guttersnipe.
**vautour** [votuʀ] nm vulture.
**vautrer** [votʀe] : **se** ~ vi: **se** ~ **dans/sur** to wallow in/sprawl on.
**vaux** [vo] pl de **val** // vb voir **valoir**.
**veau, x** [vo] nm (ZOOL) calf (pl calves) ; (CULIN) veal ; (peau) calfskin.
**vecteur** [vɛktœʀ] nm vector ; (MIL) carrier.
**vécu, e** [veky] pp de **vivre** // a (aventure) real(-life).
**vedette** [vədɛt] nf (artiste etc) star ; (canot) patrol boat ; launch ; **avoir la** ~ to top the bill, get star billing.
**végétal, e, aux** [veʒetal, -o] a vegetable // nm vegetable, plant.

**végétarien, ne** [veʒetaʀjɛ̃, -ɛn] a, nm/f vegetarian.
**végétarisme** [veʒetaʀism(ə)] nm vegetarianism.
**végétation** [veʒetɑsjɔ̃] nf vegetation ; ~**s** nfpl (MÉD) adenoids.
**végéter** [veʒete] vi (fig) to vegetate ; to stagnate.
**véhément, e** [veemɑ̃, -ɑ̃t] a vehement.
**véhicule** [veikyl] nm vehicle ; ~ **utilitaire** commercial vehicle.
**veille** [vɛj] nf (garde) watch ; (PSYCH) wakefulness ; (jour): **la** ~ the day before, the previous day ; **la** ~ **au soir** the previous evening ; **la** ~ **de** the day before ; **à la** ~ **de** on the eve of.
**veillée** [veje] nf (soirée) evening ; (réunion) evening gathering ; ~ **d'armes** night before combat ; ~ **(mortuaire)** watch.
**veiller** [veje] vi to stay ou sit up ; to be awake ; to be on watch ; to be watchful // vt (malade, mort) to watch over, sit up with ; ~ **à** vt to attend to, see to ; ~ **à ce que** to make sure that, see to it that ; ~ **sur** vt to keep a watch ou an eye on ; **veilleur de nuit** nm night watchman.
**veilleuse** [vɛjøz] nf (lampe) night light ; (AUTO) sidelight ; (flamme) pilot light ; **en** ~ a, ad (lampe) dimmed.
**veinard, e** [vɛnaʀ, -aʀd(ə)] nm/f (fam) lucky devil.
**veine** [vɛn] nf (ANAT, du bois etc) vein ; (filon) vein, seam ; (fam: chance): **avoir de la** ~ to be lucky ; (inspiration) inspiration ; **veiné, e** a veined ; (bois) grained ; **veineux, euse** a venous.
**vêler** [vele] vi to calve.
**vélin** [velɛ̃] nm vellum (paper).
**velléitaire** [veleitɛʀ] a irresolute, indecisive.
**velléités** [veleite] nfpl vague impulses.
**vélo** [velo] nm bike, cycle ; **faire du** ~ to go cycling.
**véloce** [velɔs] a swift.
**vélodrome** [velɔdʀɔm] nm velodrome.
**vélomoteur** [velɔmɔtœʀ] nm light motorcycle.
**velours** [vəluʀ] nm velvet ; ~ **côtelé** corduroy.
**velouté, e** [vəlute] a (au toucher) velvety ; (à la vue) soft, mellow ; (au goût) smooth, me.low // nm: ~ **d'asperges/de tomates** cream of asparagus/tomato (soup).
**velu, e** [vəly] a hairy.
**venais** etc vb voir **venir**.
**venaison** [vənɛzɔ̃] nf venison.
**vénal, e, aux** [venal, -o] venal ; ~**ité** nf venality.
**venant** [vənɑ̃]: **à tout** ~ ad to all and sundry.
**vendange** [vɑ̃dɑ̃ʒ] nf (opération, période: aussi: ~**s**) grape harvest ; (raisins) grape crop, grapes pl.
**vendanger** [vɑ̃dɑ̃ʒe] vi to harvest the grapes ; **vendangeur, euse** nm/f grape-picker.
**vendeur, euse** [vɑ̃dœʀ, -øz] nm/f (de magasin) shop assistant ; sales assistant ; (COMM) salesman/ woman // nm (JUR) vendor, seller ; ~ **de journaux** newspaper seller.

**vendre** [vɑ̃dR(ə)] *vt* to sell ; ~ qch à qn to sell sb sth ; **cela se vend à la douzaine** these are sold by the dozen ; **cela se vend bien** it's selling well ; **'à ~' 'for sale.'**
**vendredi** [vɑ̃dRədi] *nm* Friday ; **V~ saint** Good Friday.
**vénéneux, euse** [venenø, -øz] *a* poisonous.
**vénérable** [veneRabl(ə)] *a* venerable.
**vénération** [veneRɑsjɔ̃] *nf* veneration.
**vénérer** [veneRe] *vt* to venerate.
**vénérien, ne** [veneRjɛ̃, -ɛn] *a* venereal.
**vengeance** [vɑ̃ʒɑ̃s] *nf* vengeance *q*, revenge *q* ; act of vengeance *ou* revenge
**venger** [vɑ̃ʒe] *vt* to avenge ; **se ~** *vi* to avenge o.s. ; *(par rancune)* to take revenge ; **se ~ de qch** to avenge o.s. for sth ; **se ~ de qn** to take one's revenge for sth ; **se ~ de qn** to take revenge on sb ; **se ~ sur** to wreak vengeance upon ; to take revenge on *ou* through ; to take it out on ; **vengeur, eresse** *a* vengeful // *nm/f* avenger.
**véniel, le** [venjɛl] *a* venial.
**venimeux, euse** [vənimø, -øz] *a* poisonous, venomous ; *(fig: haineux)* venomous, vicious.
**venin** [vənɛ̃] *nm* venom, poison.
**venir** [vəniR] *vi* to come ; ~ **de** to come from ; ~ **de faire: je viens d'y aller/de le voir** I've just been there/seen him ; **s'il vient à pleuvoir** if it should rain, if it happens to rain ; **j'en viens à croire que** I have come to believe that ; **il en est venu à mendier** he has been reduced to begging ; **faire ~** *(docteur, plombier)* to call (out).
**vent** [vɑ̃] *nm* wind ; **il y a du ~** it's windy ; **c'est du ~** it's all hot air ; **au ~** to windward ; **sous le ~** to leeward ; **avoir le ~ debout/arrière** to head into the wind/have the wind astern ; **dans le ~** *(fam)* trendy, with it ; **prendre le ~** *(fig)* to see which way the wind blows ; **avoir ~ de** to get wind of.
**vente** [vɑ̃t] *nf* sale ; **la ~** *(activité)* selling ; *(secteur)* sales *pl* ; **mettre en ~** to put on sale ; *(objets personnels)* to put up for sale ; ~ **de charité** sale in aid of charity ; ~ **aux enchères** auction sale.
**venter** [vɑ̃te] *vb impersonnel*: **il vente** the wind is blowing ; **venteux, euse** *a* windswept, windy.
**ventilateur** [vɑ̃tilatœR] *nm* fan.
**ventilation** [vɑ̃tilɑsjɔ̃] *nf* ventilation.
**ventiler** [vɑ̃tile] *vt* to ventilate ; *(total, statistiques)* to break down.
**ventouse** [vɑ̃tuz] *nf* *(ampoule)* cupping glass ; *(de caoutchouc)* suction pad ; *(ZOOL)* sucker.
**ventre** [vɑ̃tR(ə)] *nm* *(ANAT)* stomach ; *(fig)* belly ; **prendre du ~** to be getting a paunch ; **avoir mal au ~** to have stomach ache.
**ventricule** [vɑ̃tRikyl] *nm* ventricle.
**ventriloque** [vɑ̃tRilɔk] *nm/f* ventriloquist.
**ventripotent, e** [vɑ̃tRipɔtɑ̃, -ɑ̃t] *a* potbellied.
**ventru, e** [vɑ̃tRy] *a* potbellied.
**venu, e** [vəny] *pp de* **venir** // *a*: **être mal ~ à** *ou* **de faire** to have no grounds for doing, be in no position to do // *nf* coming.

**vêpres** [vɛpR(ə)] *nfpl* vespers.
**ver** [vɛR] *nm* *voir aussi* **vers** ; worm ; *(des fruits etc)* maggot ; *(du bois)* woodworm *q* ; ~ **luisant** glow-worm ; ~ **à soie** silkworm ; ~ **solitaire** tapeworm ; ~ **de terre** earthworm.
**véracité** [veRasite] *nf* veracity.
**véranda** [veRɑ̃da] *nf* veranda(h).
**verbal, e, aux** [vɛRbal, -o] *a* verbal.
**verbaliser** [vɛRbalize] *vi* *(POLICE)* to book *ou* report an offender.
**verbe** [vɛRb(ə)] *nm* *(LING)* verb ; *(voix)*: **avoir le ~ sonore** to have a sonorous tone (of voice) ; *(expression)*: **la magie du ~** the magic of language *ou* the word ; *(REL)*: **le V~** the Word.
**verbeux, euse** [vɛRbø, -øz] *a* verbose, wordy.
**verdâtre** [vɛRdɑtR(ə)] *a* greenish.
**verdeur** [vɛRdœR] *nf* *(vigueur)* vigour, vitality ; *(crudité)* forthrightness ; *(défaut de maturité)* tartness, sharpness.
**verdict** [vɛRdik(t)] *nm* verdict.
**verdir** [vɛRdiR] *vi, vt* to turn green.
**verdoyant, e** [vɛRdwajɑ̃, -ɑ̃t] *a* green, verdant.
**verdure** [vɛRdyR] *nf* greenery, verdure.
**véreux, euse** [veRø, -øz] *a* worm-eaten ; *(malhonnête)* shady, corrupt.
**verge** [vɛRʒ(ə)] *nf* *(ANAT)* penis ; *(baguette)* stick, cane.
**verger** [vɛRʒe] *nm* orchard.
**verglacé, e** [vɛRglase] *a* icy, iced-over.
**verglas** [vɛRgla] *nm* (black) ice.
**vergogne** [vɛRgɔɲ]: **sans ~** *ad* shamelessly.
**véridique** [veRidik] *a* truthful, veracious.
**vérification** [veRifikɑsjɔ̃] *nf* checking *q*, check.
**vérifier** [veRifje] *vt* to check ; *(corroborer)* to confirm, bear out.
**vérin** [veRɛ̃] *nm* jack.
**véritable** [veRitabl(ə)] *a* real ; *(ami, amour)* true ; **un ~ désastre** an absolute disaster.
**vérité** [veRite] *nf* truth ; *(d'un portrait romanesque)* lifelikeness ; *(sincérité)* truthfulness, sincerity.
**vermeil, le** [vɛRmɛj] *a* bright red, ruby-red // *nm* *(substance)* vermeil.
**vermicelles** [vɛRmisɛl] *nmpl* vermicelli *sg*.
**vermillon** [vɛRmijɔ̃] *a inv* vermilion, scarlet.
**vermine** [vɛRmin] *nf* vermin *pl*.
**vermoulu, e** [vɛRmuly] *a* worm-eaten, with woodworm.
**vermout(h)** [vɛRmut] *nm* vermouth.
**verni, e** [vɛRni] *a* *(fam)* lucky ; **cuir ~** patent leather.
**vernir** [vɛRniR] *vt* *(bois, tableau, ongles)* to varnish ; *(poterie)* to glaze.
**vernis** [vɛRni] *nm* *(enduit)* varnish ; glaze ; *(fig)* veneer ; ~ **à ongles** nail polish *ou* varnish.
**vernissage** [vɛRnisaʒ] *nm* varnishing ; glazing ; *(d'une exposition)* preview.
**vérole** [veRɔl] *nf* *(variole)* smallpox ; *(fam: syphilis)* pox.
**verrai** *etc vb voir* **voir**.
**verre** [vɛR] *nm* glass ; *(de lunettes)* lens *sg* ; **boire** *ou* **prendre un ~** to have a drink ;

**~ à vin/à liqueur** wine/liqueur glass; **~ à dents** tooth mug; **~ dépoli** frosted glass; **~ de lampe** lamp glass *ou* chimney; **~ de montre** watch glass; **~ à pied** stemmed glass; **~s de contact** contact lenses.

**verrerie** [vɛʀʀi] *nf* (*fabrique*) glassworks *sg*; (*activité*) glass-making; glass-working; (*objets*) glassware.

**verrière** [vɛʀjɛʀ] *nf* (*grand vitrage*) window; (*toit vitré*) glass roof.

**verrons** *etc vb voir* **voir.**

**verroterie** [vɛʀɔtʀi] *nf* glass beads *pl ou* jewellery.

**verrou** [vɛʀu] *nm* (*targette*) bolt; (*fig*) constriction; **mettre le ~** to bolt the door; **mettre qn sous les ~s** to put sb behind bars; **verrouiller** *vt* to bolt; (MIL: *brèche*) to close.

**verrue** [vɛʀy] *nf* wart; (*fig*) eyesore.

**vers** [vɛʀ] *nm* line // *nmpl* (*poésie*) verse *sg* // *prép* (*en direction de*) toward(s); (*près de*) around (about); (*temporel*) about, around.

**versant** [vɛʀsɑ̃] *nm* slopes *pl*, side.

**versatile** [vɛʀsatil] *a* fickle, changeable.

**verse** [vɛʀs(ə)]: **à ~** *ad*: **il pleut à ~** it's pouring (with rain).

**versé, e** [vɛʀse] *a*: **être ~ dans** (*science*) to be (well-)versed in.

**Verseau** [vɛʀso] *nm*: **le ~** Aquarius, the water-carrier; **être du ~** to be Aquarius.

**versement** [vɛʀsəmɑ̃] *nm* payment; **en 3 ~s** in 3 instalments.

**verser** [vɛʀse] *vt* (*liquide, grains*) to pour; (*larmes, sang*) to shed; (*argent*) to pay; (*soldat: affecter*): **~ qn dans** to assign sb to // *vi* (*véhicule*) to overturn; (*fig*): **~ dans** to lapse into.

**verset** [vɛʀsɛ] *nm* verse; versicle.

**verseur** [vɛʀsœʀ] *am voir* **bec.**

**versifier** [vɛʀsifje] *vt* to put into verse // *vi* to versify, write verse.

**version** [vɛʀsjɔ̃] *nf* version; (SCOL) translation (*into the mother tongue*).

**verso** [vɛʀso] *nm* back; **voir au ~** see over(leaf).

**vert, e** [vɛʀ, vɛʀt(ə)] *a* green; (*vin*) young; (*vigoureux*) sprightly; (*cru*) forthright // *nm* green; **~ d'eau** *a inv* sea-green; **~ pomme** *a inv* apple-green; **~-de-gris** *nm* verdigris // *a inv* grey(ish)-green.

**vertébral, e, aux** [vɛʀtebral, -o] *a voir* **colonne.**

**vertèbre** [vɛʀtɛbʀ(ə)] *nf* vertebra (*pl* ae); **vertébré, e** *a, nm/f* vertebrate.

**vertement** [vɛʀtəmɑ̃] *ad* (*réprimander*) sharply.

**vertical, e, aux** [vɛʀtikal, -o] *a, nf* vertical; **à la ~e** *ad*, **~ement** *ad* vertically; **~ité** *nf* verticalness, verticality.

**vertige** [vɛʀtiʒ] *nm* (*peur du vide*) vertigo; (*étourdissement*) dizzy spell; (*fig*) fever; **vertigineux, euse** *a* breathtaking; breathtakingly high (*ou* deep).

**vertu** [vɛʀty] *nf* virtue; **en ~ de** *prép* in accordance with; **~eux, euse** *a* virtuous.

**verve** [vɛʀv(ə)] *nf* witty eloquence; **être en ~** to be in brilliant form.

**verveine** [vɛʀvɛn] *nf* (BOT) verbena, vervain; (*infusion*) verbena tea.

**vésicule** [vezikyl] *nf* vesicle; **~ biliaire** gall-bladder.

**vespasienne** [vɛspazjɛn] *nf* urinal.

**vespéral, e, aux** [vɛspeʀal, -o] *a* vespertine, evening *cpd*.

**vessie** [vesi] *nf* bladder.

**veste** [vɛst(ə)] *nf* jacket; **~ droite/croisée** single-/double-breasted jacket.

**vestiaire** [vɛstjɛʀ] *nm* (*au théâtre etc*) cloakroom; (*de stade etc*) changing-room.

**vestibule** [vɛstibyl] *nm* hall.

**vestige** [vɛstiʒ] *nm* relic; trace; (*fig*) remnant, vestige; **~s** *nmpl* remains; remnants, relics.

**vestimentaire** [vɛstimɑ̃tɛʀ] *a* (*dépenses*) clothing; (*détail*) of dress; (*élégance*) sartorial.

**veston** [vɛstɔ̃] *nm* jacket.

**vêtement** [vɛtmɑ̃] *nm* garment, item of clothing; (COMM): **le ~** the clothing industry; **~s** *nmpl* clothes; **~s de sport** sportswear *sg*, sports clothes.

**vétéran** [veteʀɑ̃] *nm* veteran.

**vétérinaire** [veteʀinɛʀ] *a* veterinary // *nm/f* vet, veterinary surgeon.

**vétille** [vetij] *nf* trifle, triviality.

**vétilleux, euse** [vetijø, -øz] *a* punctilious.

**vêtir** [vetiʀ] *vt* to clothe, dress.

**veto** [veto] *nm* veto; **opposer un ~ à** to veto.

**vêtu, e** [vety] *pp de* **vêtir** // *a*: **~ de** dressed in, wearing; **chaudement ~** warmly dressed.

**vétuste** [vetyst(ə)] *a* ancient, timeworn.

**veuf, veuve** [vœf, vœv] *a* widowed // *nm* widower // *nf* widow.

**veuille** *etc vb voir* **vouloir.**

**veule** [vøl] *a* spineless.

**veuvage** [vœvaʒ] *nm* widowhood.

**veuve** [vœv] *a, nf voir* **veuf.**

**veux** *vb voir* **vouloir.**

**vexations** [vɛksasjɔ̃] *nfpl* humiliations.

**vexatoire** [vɛksatwaʀ] *a*: **mesures ~s** harassment *sg*.

**vexer** [vɛkse] *vt* to hurt, upset; **se ~** *vi* to be hurt, get upset.

**viabiliser** [vjabilize] *vt* to provide with services (*water etc*).

**viabilité** [vjabilite] *nf* viability; (*d'un chemin*) practicability.

**viable** [vjabl(ə)] *a* viable.

**viaduc** [vjadyk] *nm* viaduct.

**viager, ère** [vjaʒe, -ɛʀ] *a*: **rente viagère** life annuity // *nm*: **mettre en ~** to sell in return for a life annuity.

**viande** [vjɑ̃d] *nf* meat.

**viatique** [vjatik] *nm* (REL) viaticum; (*fig*) provisions *pl* (*ou* money) for the journey.

**vibraphone** [vibʀafɔn] *nm* vibraphone, vibes *pl*.

**vibration** [vibʀasjɔ̃] *nf* vibration.

**vibrer** [vibʀe] *vi* to vibrate; (*son, voix*) to be vibrant; (*fig*) to be stirred; **faire ~** to (cause to) vibrate; to stir, thrill; **vibro-masseur** *nm* vibrator.

**vicaire** [vikɛʀ] *nm* curate.

**vice** [vis] *nm* vice; (*défaut*) fault; **~ de forme** legal flaw *ou* irregularity.

**vice...** [vis] *préfixe*: ~-**consul** *nm* vice-consul; ~-**président, e** *nm/f* vice-president; vice-chairman; ~-**roi** *nm* viceroy.

**vice-versa** [visevɛʀsa] *ad* vice versa.

**vichy** [viʃi] *nm* (*toile*) gingham; (*eau*) Vichy water.

**vicié, e** [visje] *a* (*air*) polluted, tainted; (*JUR*) invalidated.

**vicieux, euse** [visjø, -øz] *a* (*pervers*) dirty(-minded); nasty; (*fautif*) incorrect, wrong.

**vicinal, e, aux** [visinal, -o] *a*: **chemin** ~ by-road, byway.

**vicissitudes** [visisityd] *nfpl* (trials and) tribulations.

**vicomte** [vikɔ̃t] *nm* viscount.

**victime** [viktim] *nf* victim; (*d'accident*) casualty; **être (la)** ~ **de** to be the victim of; **être** ~ **d'une attaque/d'un accident** to suffer a stroke/be involved in an accident.

**victoire** [viktwaʀ] *nf* victory; **victorieux, euse** *a* victorious; (*sourire, attitude*) triumphant.

**victuailles** [viktɥɑj] *nfpl* provisions.

**vidange** [vidɑ̃ʒ] *nf* (*d'un fossé, réservoir*) emptying; (*AUTO*) oil change; (*de lavabo: bonde*) waste outlet; ~**s** *nfpl* (*matières*) sewage *sg*; **faire la** ~ (*AUTO*) to change the oil, do an oil change; **vidanger** *vt* to empty.

**vide** [vid] *a* empty // *nm* (*PHYSIQUE*) vacuum; (*solution de continuité*) (empty) space, gap; (*sous soi: dans une falaise etc*) drop; (*futilité, néant*) void; **sous** ~ *ad* in a vacuum; **emballé sous** ~ vacuum packed; **à** ~ *ad* (*sans occupants*) empty; (*sans charge*) unladen; (*TECH*) without gripping *ou* being in gear.

**vide-ordures** [vidɔʀdyʀ] *nm inv* (rubbish) chute.

**vide-poches** [vidpɔʃ] *nm inv* tidy; (*AUTO*) glove compartment.

**vider** [vide] *vt* to empty; (*CULIN: volaille, poisson*) to gut, clean out; (*régler: querelle*) to settle; (*fatiguer*) to wear out; (*fam: expulser*) to throw out, chuck out; **se** ~ *vi* to empty; ~ **les lieux** to quit *ou* vacate the premises; **videur** *nm* (*de boîte de nuit*) bouncer.

**vie** [vi] *nf* life (*pl* lives); **être en** ~ to be alive; **sans** ~ lifeless; **à** ~ for life; **avoir la** ~ **dure** to have nine lives; to die hard; **mener la** ~ **dure à qn** to make life a misery for sb.

**vieil** [vjɛj] *am voir* **vieux**.

**vieillard** [vjɛjaʀ] *nm* old man; **les** ~**s** old people, the elderly.

**vieille** [vjɛj] *a, nf voir* **vieux**.

**vieilleries** [vjɛjʀi] *nfpl* old things *ou* stuff *sg*.

**vieillesse** [vjɛjɛs] *nf* old age; (*vieillards*): **la** ~ the old *pl*, the elderly *pl*.

**vieillir** [vjejiʀ] *vi* (*prendre de l'âge*) to grow old; (*population, vin*) to age; (*doctrine, auteur*) to become dated // *vt* to age; **il a beaucoup vieilli** he has aged a lot; **vieillissement** *nm* growing old; ageing.

**vieillot, te** [vjejo, -ɔt] *a* antiquated, quaint.

**vielle** [vjɛl] *nf* hurdy-gurdy.

**vienne, viens** *etc vb voir* **venir**.

**vierge** [vjɛʀʒ(ə)] *a* virgin; (*jeune fille*): **être** ~ to be a virgin // *nf* virgin; (*signe*): **la V**~ Virgo, the Virgin; **être de la V**~ to be Virgo; ~ **de** (*sans*) free from, unsullied by.

**vieux(vieil), vieille** [vjø, vjɛj] *a* old // *nm/f* old man/woman // *nmpl* old people; **un petit** ~ a little old man; **mon** ~/**ma vieille** (*fam*) old man/girl; **prendre un coup de** ~ to put years on; **un** ~ **de la vieille** one of the old brigade; ~ **garçon** *nm* bachelor; ~ **jeu** *a inv* old-fashioned; ~ **rose** *a inv* old rose; **vieil or** *a inv* old gold; **vieille fille** *nf* spinster.

**vif, vive** [vif, viv] *a* (*animé*) lively; (*alerte*) sharp, quick; (*brusque*) sharp, brusque; (*aigu*) sharp; (*lumière, couleur*) brilliant; (*air*) crisp; (*vent*) keen; (*émotion*) keen, sharp; (*fort: regret, déception*) great, deep; (*vivant*): **brûlé** ~ burnt alive; **de vive voix** personally; **piquer qn au** ~ to cut sb to the quick; **tailler dans le** ~ to cut into the living flesh; **à** ~ (*plaie*) open; **avoir les nerfs à** ~ to be on edge; **sur le** ~ (*ART*) from life; **entrer dans le** ~ **du sujet** to get to the very heart of the matter.

**vif-argent** [vifaʀʒɑ̃] *nm inv* quicksilver.

**vigie** [viʒi] *nf* look-out; look-out post, crow's nest.

**vigilance** [viʒilɑ̃s] *nf* vigilance.

**vigilant, e** [viʒilɑ̃, -ɑ̃t] *a* vigilant.

**vigne** [viɲ] *nf* (*plante*) vine; (*plantation*) vineyard; ~ **vierge** Virginia creeper.

**vigneron** [viɲʀɔ̃] *nm* wine grower.

**vignette** [viɲɛt] *nf* (*motif*) vignette; (*de marque*) manufacturer's label *ou* seal; (*ADMIN*) ≈ (road) tax disc; price label (*on medicines for reimbursement by Social Security*).

**vignoble** [viɲɔbl(ə)] *nm* (*plantation*) vineyard; (*vignes d'une région*) vineyards *pl*.

**vigoureux, euse** [viguʀø, -øz] *a* vigorous, strong, robust.

**vigueur** [vigœʀ] *nf* vigour; **être/entrer en** ~ to be in/come into force; **en** ~ current.

**vil, e** [vil] *a* vile, base; **à** ~ **prix** at a very low price.

**vilain, e** [vilɛ̃, -ɛn] *a* (*laid*) ugly; (*affaire, blessure*) nasty; (*pas sage: enfant*) naughty // *nm* (*paysan*) villein, villain; **ça va tourner au** ~ it's going to turn nasty.

**vilebrequin** [vilbʀəkɛ̃] *nm* (*outil*) (bit-)brace; (*AUTO*) crankshaft.

**vilenie** [vilni] *nf* vileness *q*, baseness *q*.

**vilipender** [vilipɑ̃de] *vt* to revile, vilify.

**villa** [vila] *nf* (detached) house.

**village** [vilaʒ] *nm* village; ~ **de toile** tent village; **villageois, e** *a* village *cpd* // *nm/f* villager.

**ville** [vil] *nf* town; (*importante*) city; (*administration*): **la** ~ ≈ the Corporation; ≈ the (town) council.

**villégiature** [vileʒiatyʀ] *nf* holiday; (holiday) resort.

**vin** [vɛ̃] *nm* wine; **avoir le** ~ **gai** to get happy after a few drinks; ~ **d'honneur** reception (*with wine and snacks*); ~ **de**

**messe** mass wine ; ~ **ordinaire** table wine ; ~ **de pays** local wine.

**vinaigre** [vinɛgʀ(ə)] *nm* vinegar ; **tourner au** ~ *(fig)* to turn sour ; ~ **de vin/d'alcool** wine/spirit vinegar ; **vinaigrette** *nf* vinaigrette, French dressing ; **vinaigrier** *nm* *(fabricant)* vinegar-maker ; *(flacon)* vinegar cruet *ou* bottle.

**vinasse** [vinas] *nf (péj)* cheap wine.

**vindicatif, ive** [vɛ̃dikatif, -iv] *a* vindictive.

**vindicte** [vɛ̃dikt(ə)] *nf*: **désigner qn à la** ~ **publique** to expose sb to public condemnation.

**vineux, euse** [vinø, -øz] *a* win(e)y.

**vingt** [vɛ̃, vɛ̃t + *vowel and in 22 etc*] *num* twenty ; **vingtaine** *nf*: **une vingtaine (de)** around twenty, twenty or so ; **vingtième** *num* twentieth.

**vinicole** [vinikɔl] *a* wine *cpd*, wine-growing.

**vins** *etc vb voir* **venir**.

**viol** [vjɔl] *nm (d'une femme)* rape ; *(d'un lieu sacré)* violation.

**violacé, e** [vjɔlase] *a* purplish, mauvish.

**violation** [vjɔlɑsjɔ̃] *nf* desecration ; violation.

**violemment** [vjɔlamɑ̃] *ad* violently.

**violence** [vjɔlɑ̃s] *nf* violence ; ~**s** *nfpl* acts of violence ; **faire** ~ **à qn** to do violence to sb.

**violent, e** [vjɔlɑ̃, -ɑ̃t] *a* violent ; *(remède)* drastic ; *(besoin, désir)* intense, urgent.

**violenter** [vjɔlɑ̃te] *vt* to assault (sexually).

**violer** [vjɔle] *vt (femme)* to rape ; *(sépulture)* to desecrate, violate ; *(règlement, traité)* to violate.

**violet, te** [vjɔlɛ, -ɛt] *a, nm* purple, mauve // *nf (fleur)* violet.

**violon** [vjɔlɔ̃] *nm* violin ; *(fam: prison)* lock-up ; **premier** ~ *(MUS)* first violin *ou* fiddle ; ~ **d'Ingres** (artistic) hobby.

**violoncelle** [vjɔlɔ̃sɛl] *nm* cello ; **violoncelliste** *nm/f* cellist.

**violoniste** [vjɔlɔnist(ə)] *nm/f* violinist, violin-player.

**vipère** [vipɛʀ] *nf* viper, adder.

**virage** [viʀaʒ] *nm (d'un véhicule)* turn ; *(d'une route, piste)* bend ; *(CHIMIE)* change in colour ; *(de cuti-réaction)* positive reaction ; *(PHOTO)* toning ; *(fig: POL)* change in policy ; **prendre un** ~ to go into a bend, take a bend ; ~ **sans visibilité** blind bend.

**viral, e, aux** [viʀal, -o] *a* viral.

**virée** [viʀe] *nf (courte)* run ; (: *à pied)* walk ; *(longue)* trip ; hike, walking tour.

**virement** [viʀmɑ̃] *nm (COMM)* transfer ; ~ **bancaire/postal** (bank) credit/(National) Giro transfer.

**virent** *vb voir aussi* **voir**.

**virer** [viʀe] *vt (COMM)*: ~ **qch (sur)** to transfer sth (into) ; *(PHOTO)* to tone // *vi* to turn ; *(CHIMIE)* to change colour ; *(cuti-réaction)* to come up positive ; *(PHOTO)* to tone ; ~ **au bleu** to turn blue ; ~ **de bord** to tack ; ~ **sur l'aile** to bank.

**virevolte** [viʀvɔlt(ə)] *nf* twirl ; **virevolter** *vi* to twirl around.

**virginité** [viʀʒinite] *nf* virginity.

**virgule** [viʀgyl] *nf* comma ; *(MATH)* point ;

**4** ~ **2** 4 point 2 ; ~ **flottante** floating decimal.

**viril, e** [viʀil] *a (propre à l'homme)* masculine ; *(énergique, courageux)* manly, virile ; ~**ité** *nf* masculinity ; manliness ; *(sexuelle)* virility.

**virtualité** [viʀtɥalite] *nf* virtuality ; potentiality.

**virtuel, le** [viʀtɥɛl] *a* potential ; *(théorique)* virtual ; ~**lement** *a* potentially ; *(presque)* virtually.

**virtuose** [viʀtɥoz] *nm/f (MUS)* virtuoso ; *(gén)* master ; **virtuosité** *nf* virtuosity ; masterliness, masterful skills *pl*.

**virulent, e** [viʀylɑ̃, -ɑ̃t] *a* virulent.

**virus** [viʀys] *nm* virus.

**vis** *vb* [vi] *voir* **voir, vivre** // *nf* [vis] screw ; ~ **sans fin** worm, endless screw.

**visa** [viza] *nm (sceau)* stamp ; *(validation de passeport)* visa ; ~ **de censure** (censor's) certificate.

**visage** [vizaʒ] *nm* face ; **visagiste** *nm/f* beautician.

**vis-à-vis** [vizavi] *ad* face to face // *nm* person opposite ; house *etc* opposite ; ~ **de** *prép* opposite ; *(fig)* towards, vis-à-vis ; **en** ~ facing *ou* opposite each other, **sans** ~ *(immeuble)* with an open outlook.

**viscéral, e, aux** [viseʀal, -o] *a (fig)* deep-seated, deep-rooted.

**viscères** [visɛʀ] *nmpl* intestines, entrails.

**viscosité** [viskozite] *nf* viscosity.

**visée** [vize] *nf (avec une arme)* aiming ; *(ARPENTAGE)* sighting ; ~**s** *nfpl (intentions)* designs.

**viser** [vize] *vi* to aim // *vt* to aim at ; *(concerner)* to be aimed *ou* directed at ; *(apposer un visa sur)* to stamp, visa ; ~ **à qch/faire** to aim at sth/at doing *ou* to do.

**viseur** [vizœʀ] *nm (d'arme)* sights *pl* ; *(PHOTO)* viewfinder.

**visibilité** [vizibilite] *nf* visibility.

**visible** [vizibl(ə)] *a* visible ; *(disponible)*: **est-il** ~? can he see me?, will he see visitors?

**visière** [vizjɛʀ] *nf (de casquette)* peak ; *(qui s'attache)* eyeshade.

**vision** [vizjɔ̃] *nf* vision ; *(sens)* (eye)sight, vision ; *(fait de voir)*: **la** ~ **de** the sight of ; **première** ~ *(CINÉMA)* first showing ; **visionnaire** *a, nm/f* visionary ; **visionner** *vt* to view ; **visionneuse** *nf* viewer.

**visite** [vizit] *nf* visit ; *(personne qui rend visite)* visitor ; *(médicale, à domicile)* visit, call ; **la** ~ *(MÉD)* (medical) consultations *pl*, surgery ; *(MIL: d'entrée)* medicals *pl* ; (: *quotidienne)* sick parade ; **faire une** ~ **à qn** to call on sb, pay sb a visit ; **rendre** ~ **à qn** to visit sb, pay sb a visit ; **être en** ~ **(chez qn)** to be visiting (sb) ; **heures de** ~ *(hôpital, prison)* visiting hours ; **le droit de** ~ *(JUR: aux enfants)* right of access, access ; ~ **de douane** customs inspection *ou* examination.

**visiter** [vizite] *vt* to visit ; *(musée, ville)* to visit, go round ; **visiteur, euse** *nm/f* visitor ; **visiteur des douanes** customs inspector.

**vison** [vizɔ̃] *nm* mink.

**visqueux, euse** [viskø, -øz] *a* viscous ; *(péj)* gooey ; slimy.

**visser** [vise] vt: ~ **qch** (fixer, serrer) to screw sth on.

**visu** [vizy]: **de** ~ ad with one's own eyes.

**visuel, le** [vizɥɛl] a visual // nm (visual) display.

**vit** vb voir **voir, vivre.**

**vital, e, aux** [vital, -o] a vital.

**vitalité** [vitalite] nf vitality.

**vitamine** [vitamin] nf vitamin; **vitaminique** a vitamin cpd.

**vite** [vit] ad (rapidement) quickly, fast; (sans délai) quickly; soon; **faire** ~ to act quickly; to be quick; **viens** ~ come quick(ly).

**vitesse** [vitɛs] nf speed; (AUTO: dispositif) gear; **faire de la** ~ to drive fast ou at speed; **prendre qn de** ~ to outstrip sb; get ahead of sb; **prendre de la** ~ to pick up ou gather speed; **à toute** ~ at full ou top speed; ~ **acquise** momentum; ~ **du son** speed of sound.

**viticole** [vitikɔl] a wine cpd, wine-growing.

**viticulteur** [vitikyltœr] nm wine grower.

**viticulture** [vitikyltyr] nf wine growing.

**vitrage** [vitraʒ] nm (cloison) glass partition; (toit) glass roof; (rideau) net curtain.

**vitrail, aux** [vitraj, -o] nm stained-glass window.

**vitre** [vitr(ə)] nf (window) pane; (de portière, voiture) window.

**vitré, e** [vitre] a glass ·cpd.

**vitrer** [vitre] vt to glaze.

**vitreux, euse** [vitrø, -øz] a vitreous; (terne) glassy.

**vitrier** [vitrije] nm glazier.

**vitrifier** [vitrifje] vt to vitrify; (parquet) to glaze.

**vitrine** [vitrin] nf (devanture) (shop) window; (étalage) display; (petite armoire) display cabinet; **en** ~ in the window, on display; ~ **publicitaire** display case, showcase.

**vitriol** [vitrijɔl] nm vitriol; **au** ~ (fig) vitriolic.

**vitupérer** [vitypere] vi to rant and rave; ~ **contre** to rail against.

**vivable** [vivabl(ə)] a (personne) livable-with; (endroit) fit to live in.

**vivace** a [vivas] (arbre, plante) hardy; (fig) indestructible, inveterate // ad [vivatʃe] (MUS) vivace.

**vivacité** [vivasite] nf liveliness, vivacity; sharpness; brilliance.

**vivant, e** [vivã, -ãt] a (qui vit) living, alive; (animé) lively; (preuve, exemple) living // nm: **du** ~ **de qn** in sb's lifetime; **les** ~**s et les morts** the living and the dead.

**vivats** [viva] nmpl cheers.

**vive** [viv] af voir **vif** // vb voir **vivre** // excl: ~ **le roi!** long live the king!; ~ **les vacances!** hurrah for the holidays!; ~**ment** ad vivaciously; sharply // excl: ~**ment les vacances!** I can't wait for the holidays!, roll on the holidays!

**viveur** [vivœr] nm (péj) high liver, pleasure-seeker.

**vivier** [vivje] nm fish tank; fishpond.

**vivifiant, e** [vivifjã, -ãt] a invigorating.

**vivions** vb voir **vivre.**

**vivisection** [vivisɛksjɔ̃] nf vivisection.

**vivoter** [vivɔte] vi to rub along, struggle along.

**vivre** [vivr(ə)] vi, vt to live // nm: **le** ~ **et le logement** board and lodging; ~**s** nmpl provisions, food supplies; **il vit encore** he is still alive; **se laisser** ~ to take life as it comes; **ne plus** ~ (être anxieux) to live on one's nerves; **il a vécu** (eu une vie aventureuse) he has seen life; **ce régime a vécu** this regime has had its day; **être facile à** ~ to be easy to get on with; **faire** ~ **qn** (pourvoir à sa subsistance) to provide (a living) for sb; ~ **mal** (chichement) to have a meagre existence; ~ **de** (salaire etc) to live on.

**vlan** [vlã] excl wham!, bang!

**vocable** [vɔkabl(ə)] nm term.

**vocabulaire** [vɔkabylɛr] nm vocabulary.

**vocal, e, aux** [vɔkal, -o] a vocal.

**vocalique** [vɔkalik] a vocalic, vowel cpd.

**vocalise** [vɔkaliz] nf singing exercise.

**vocation** [vɔkasjɔ̃] nf vocation, calling.

**vociférations** [vɔsiferɑsjɔ̃] nfpl cries of rage, screams.

**vociférer** [vɔsifere] vi, vt to scream.

**vodka** [vɔdka] nf vodka.

**vœu, x** [vø] nm wish; (à Dieu) vow; **faire** ~ **de** to take a vow of; ~**x de bonne année** best wishes for the New Year; **avec tous nos** ~**x** with every good wish ou our best wishes.

**vogue** [vɔg] nf fashion, vogue.

**voguer** [vɔge] vi to sail.

**voici** [vwasi] prép (pour introduire, désigner) here is + sg, here are + pl; **et** ~ **que...** and now it (ou he)...; voir aussi **voilà.**

**voie** [vwa] nf way; (RAIL) track, line; (AUTO) lane; **suivre la** ~ **hiérarchique** to go through official channels; **être en bonne** ~ to be shaping ou going well; **mettre qn sur la** ~ to put sb on the right track; **être en** ~ **d'achèvement/de rénovation** to be nearing completion/in the process of renovation; **à** ~ **étroite** narrow-gauge; **route à 2/3** ~**s** 2-/3-lane road; **par la** ~ **aérienne/maritime** by air/sea; ~ **d'eau** (NAVIG) leak; ~ **ferrée** track; railway line; **par** ~ **ferrée** by rail; ~ **de garage** (RAIL) siding; **la** ~ **lactée** the Milky Way; ~ **navigable** waterway; ~ **privée** private road; **la** ~ **publique** the public highway.

**voilà** [vwala] prép (en désignant) there is + sg, there are + pl; **les** ~ ou **voici** here ou there they are; **en** ~ ou **voici un** here's one, there's one; ~ ou **voici deux ans** two years ago; ~ ou **voici deux ans que** it's two years since; **et** ~! there we are!; ~ **tout** that's all; '~ ou **voici**' (en offrant etc) 'there ou here you are'.

**voile** [vwal] nm veil; (tissu léger) net // nf sail; (sport) sailing; **prendre le** ~ to take the veil; **mettre à la** ~ to make way under sail; ~ **du palais** nm soft palate, velum; ~ **au poumon** nm shadow on the lung.

**voiler** [vwale] vt to veil; (fausser: roue) to buckle; (: bois) to warp; **se** ~ vi (lune, regard) to mist over; (ciel) to grow hazy; (voix) to become husky; (roue, disque) to buckle ; *(planche)* to warp ; **se ~ la face** to hide one's face.

**voilette** [vwalɛt] *nf* (hat) veil.

**voilier** [vwalje] *nm* sailing ship ; *(de plaisance)* sailing boat.

**voilure** [vwalyʀ] *nf (de voilier)* sails *pl* ; *(d'avion)* aerofoils *pl* ; *(de parachute)* canopy.

**voir** [vwaʀ] *vi, vt* to see ; **se ~** : **se ~ critiquer/transformer** to be criticized/transformed ; **cela se voit** *(cela arrive)* it happens ; *(c'est visible)* that's obvious, it shows ; **~ venir** *(fig)* to wait and see ; **faire ~ qch à qn** to show sb sth ; **en faire ~ à qn** *(fig)* to give sb a hard time ; **ne pas pouvoir ~ qn** *(fig)* not to be able to stand sb ; **regardez ~** just look ; **dites-~** tell me ; **voyons!** let's see now ; *(indignation etc)* come (along) now! ; **avoir quelque chose à ~ avec** to have something to do with.

**voire** [vwaʀ] *ad* indeed ; nay.

**voirie** [vwaʀi] *nf* highway maintenance ; *(administration)* highways department ; *(enlèvement des ordures)* refuse collection.

**voisin, e** [vwazɛ̃, -in] *a (proche)* neighbouring ; *(contigu)* next ; *(ressemblant)* connected // *nm/f* neighbour ; **voisinage** *nm (proximité)* proximity ; *(environs)* vicinity ; *(quartier, voisins)* neighbourhood ; **relations de bon voisinage** neighbourly terms ; **voisiner** *vi*: **voisiner avec** to be side by side with.

**voiture** [vwatyʀ] *nf* car ; *(wagon)* coach, carriage ; **~ d'enfant** pram ; **~ d'infirme** invalid carriage ; **~ de sport** sports car ; **~-lit** *nf* sleeper.

**voix** [vwa] *nf* voice ; *(POL)* vote ; **à haute ~** aloud ; **à ~ basse** in a low voice ; **à 2/4 ~** *(MUS)* in 2/4 parts ; **avoir ~ au chapitre** to have a say in the matter ; **mettre aux ~** to put to the vote.

**vol** [vɔl] *nm (mode de locomotion)* flying ; *(trajet, voyage, groupe d'oiseaux)* flight ; *(mode d'appropriation)* theft, stealing ; *(larcin)* theft ; **à ~ d'oiseau** as the crow flies ; **au ~** : **attraper qch au ~** to catch sth as it flies past ; **prendre son ~** to take flight ; **en ~** in flight ; **~ avec effraction** breaking and entering *q*, break-in ; **~ libre** *ou* **sur aile delta** hang-gliding ; **~ à main armée** armed robbery ; **~ de nuit** night flight ; **~ à voile** gliding.

**volage** [vɔlaʒ] *a* fickle.

**volaille** [vɔlaj] *nf (oiseaux)* poultry *pl* ; *(viande)* poultry *q* ; *(oiseau)* fowl ; **volailler** *nm* poulterer.

**volant, e** [vɔlɑ̃, -ɑ̃t] *a voir* **feuille** etc // *nm (d'automobile)* (steering) wheel ; *(de commande)* wheel ; *(objet lancé)* shuttlecock ; *(jeu)* battledore and shuttlecock ; *(bande de tissu)* flounce ; *(feuillet détachable)* tear-off portion ; **les ~s** *(AVIAT)* the flight staff.

**volatil, e** [vɔlatil] *a* volatile.

**volatile** [vɔlatil] *nm (volaille)* bird ; *(tout oiseau)* winged creature.

**volatiliser** [vɔlatilize] : **se ~** *vi (CHIMIE)* to volatilize ; *(fig)* to vanish into thin air.

**vol-au-vent** [vɔlovɑ̃] *nm inv* vol-au-vent.

**volcan** [vɔlkɑ̃] *nm* volcano ; **volcanique** *a*

volcanic ; **volcanologue** *nm/f* vulcanologist.

**volée** [vɔle] *nf (groupe d'oiseaux)* flight, flock ; *(TENNIS)* volley ; **~ de coups/de flèches** volley of blows/arrows ; **à la ~** : **rattraper à la ~** to catch in mid air ; **lancer à la ~** to fling about ; **à toute ~** *(sonner les cloches)* vigorously ; *(lancer un projectile)* with full force.

**voler** [vɔle] *vi (avion, oiseau, fig)* to fly ; *(voleur)* to steal // *vt (objet)* to steal ; *(personne)* to rob ; **~ qch à qn** to steal sth from sb.

**volet** [vɔlɛ] *nm (de fenêtre)* shutter ; *(AVIAT)* flap ; *(de feuillet, document)* section ; **trié sur le ~** hand-picked.

**voleter** [vɔlte] *vi* to flutter (about).

**voleur, euse** [vɔlœʀ, -øz] *nm/f* thief *(pl* thieves) // *a* thieving.

**volière** [vɔljɛʀ] *nf* aviary.

**volontaire** [vɔlɔ̃tɛʀ] *a* voluntary ; *(caractère, personne: décidé)* self-willed // *nm/f* volunteer ; **volontariat** *nm* voluntary service.

**volonté** [vɔlɔ̃te] *nf (faculté de vouloir)* will ; *(énergie, fermeté)* will(power) ; *(souhait, désir)* wish ; **se servir/boire à ~** to take/drink as much as one likes ; **bonne ~** goodwill, willingness ; **mauvaise ~** lack of goodwill, unwillingness.

**volontiers** [vɔlɔ̃tje] *ad (de bonne grâce)* willingly ; *(avec plaisir)* willingly, gladly ; *(habituellement, souvent)* readily, willingly ; '**~**' 'with pleasure', 'I'd be glad to'.

**volt** [vɔlt] *nm* volt ; **~age** *nm* voltage.

**volte-face** [vɔltəfas] *nf inv* about-turn.

**voltige** [vɔltiʒ] *nf (EQUITATION)* trick riding ; *(au cirque)* acrobatic feat ; *(AVIAT)* (aerial) acrobatics *sg* ; **numéro de haute ~** acrobatic act.

**voltiger** [vɔltiʒe] *vi* to flutter (about).

**voltigeur, euse** [vɔltiʒœʀ, -øz] *nm/f (au cirque)* acrobat.

**voltmètre** [vɔltmɛtʀ(ə)] *nm* voltmeter.

**volubile** [vɔlybil] *a* voluble.

**volume** [vɔlym] *nm* volume ; *(GEOM: solide)* solid ; **volumineux, euse** *a* voluminous, bulky.

**volupté** [vɔlypte] *nf* sensual delight *ou* pleasure ; **voluptueux, euse** *a* voluptuous.

**volute** [vɔlyt] *nf (ARCHIT)* volute ; **~ de fumée** curl of smoke.

**vomi** [vɔmi] *nm* vomit.

**vomir** [vɔmiʀ] *vi* to vomit, be sick // *vt* to vomit, bring up ; *(fig)* to belch out, spew out ; *(exécrer)* to loathe, abhor ; **vomissement** *nm* vomiting *q* ; **vomissure** *nf* vomit *q* ; **vomitif** *nm* emetic.

**vont** [vɔ̃] *vb voir* **aller.**

**vorace** [vɔʀas] *a* voracious.

**vos** [vo] *dét voir* **votre.**

**votant, e** [vɔtɑ̃, -ɑ̃t] *nm/f* voter.

**vote** [vɔt] *nm* vote ; **~ par correspondance/procuration** postal/proxy vote.

**voter** [vɔte] *vi* to vote // *vt (loi, décision)* to vote for.

**votre** [vɔtʀ(ə)], *pl* **vos** [vo] *dét* your.

**vôtre** [votʀ(ə)] *pronom*: **le ~, la ~, les ~s** yours ; **les ~s** *(fig)* your family *ou* folks ; **à la ~** *(toast)* your (good) health!

**voudrai** *etc vb voir* **vouloir.**

**voué, e** [vwe] *a*: ~ à doomed to, destined for.

**vouer** [vwe] *vt*: ~ **qch à** (*Dieu/un saint*) to dedicate sth to ; ~ **sa vie/son temps à** (*étude, cause etc*) to devote one's life/time to ; ~ **une haine/amitié éternelle à qn** to vow undying hatred/love to sb.

**vouloir** [vulwaʀ] *vi* to show will, have willpower // *vt* to want // *nm*: **le bon ~ de qn** sb's goodwill ; sb's pleasure ; ~ **que qn fasse** to want sb to do ; **je voudrais ceci** I would like this ; **veuillez attendre** please wait ; **je veux bien** (*bonne volonté*) I'll be happy to ; (*concession*) fair enough, that's fine ; **si on veut** (*en quelque sorte*) if you like ; **que me veut-il?** what does he want with me? ; ~ **dire (que)** (*signifier*) to mean (that) ; **sans le ~** (*involontairement*) without meaning to, unintentionally ; **en ~ à qn** to bear sb a grudge ; **en ~ à qch** (*avoir des visées sur*) to be after sth ; **s'en ~ de** to be annoyed with o.s. for ; ~ **de qch/qn** (*accepter*) to want sth/sb.

**voulu, e** [vuly] *a* (*requis*) required, requisite ; (*délibéré*) deliberate, intentional.

**vous** [vu] *pronom* you ; (*objet indirect*) (to) you ; (*réfléchi*) yourself, *pl* yourselves ; (*réciproque*) each other // *nm*: **employer le ~** (*vouvoyer*) to use the 'vous' form ; ~**-même** yourself ; ~**-mêmes** yourselves.

**voûte** [vut] *nf* vault ; ~ **du palais** (*ANAT*) roof of the mouth ; ~ **plantaire** arch (of the foot).

**voûté, e** [vute] *a* vaulted, arched ; (*dos, personne*) bent, stooped.

**voûter** [vute] *vt* (*ARCHIT*) to arch, vault ; **se~** *vi* (*dos, personne*) to become stooped.

**vouvoyer** [vuvwaje] *vt*: ~ **qn** to address sb as 'vous'.

**voyage** [vwajaʒ] *nm* journey, trip ; (*fait de voyager*): **le ~** travel(ling) ; **partir/être en ~** to go off/be away on a journey *ou* trip ; **faire un ~** to go on *ou* make a trip *ou* journey ; **faire bon ~** to have a good journey ; ~ **d'agrément/d'affaires** pleasure/business trip ; ~ **de noces** honeymoon ; ~ **organisé** package tour.

**voyager** [vwajaʒe] *vi* to travel ; **voyageur, euse** *nm/f* traveller ; (*passager*) passenger ; **voyageur (de commerce)** commercial traveller.

**voyant, e** [vwajã, -ãt] *a* (*couleur*) loud, gaudy // *nm* (*signal*) (warning) light // *nf* clairvoyant.

**voyelle** [vwajɛl] *nf* vowel.

**voyeur, euse** [vwajœʀ, -øz] *nm/f* voyeur ; peeping Tom.

**voyou** [vwaju] *nm* lout, hoodlum ; (*enfant*) guttersnipe // *a* loutish.

**vrac** [vʀak]: **en ~** *ad* higgledy-piggledy ; (*COMM*) in bulk.

**vrai, e** [vʀɛ] *a* (*véridique: récit, faits*) true ; (*non factice, authentique*) real ; **à ~ dire** to tell the truth ; **être dans le ~** to be right.

**vraiment** [vʀɛmã] *ad* really.

**vraisemblable** [vʀɛsãblabl(ə)] *a* (*plausible*) likely, plausible ; (*probable*) likely, probable ; ~**ment** *ad* in all likelihood, very likely.

**vraisemblance** [vʀɛsãblãs] *nf* likelihood, plausibility ; (*romanesque*) verisimilitude.

**vrille** [vʀij] *nf* (*de plante*) tendril ; (*outil*) gimlet ; (*spirale*) spiral ; (*AVIAT*) spin.

**vriller** [vʀije] *vt* to bore into, pierce.

**vrombir** [vʀɔ̃biʀ] *vi* to hum.

**vu** [vy] *prép* (*en raison de*) in view of ; ~ **que** in view of the fact that.

**vu, e** [vy] *pp de* **voir** // *a*: **bien/mal ~** (*fig*) well/poorly thought of ; good/bad form // *nm*: **au ~ et au su de tous** openly and publicly.

**vue** [vy] *nf* (*fait de voir*): **la ~ de** the sight of ; (*sens, faculté*) (eye)sight ; (*panorama, image, photo*) view ; (*spectacle*) sight ; ~**s** *nfpl* (*idées*) views ; (*dessein*) designs ; **perdre la ~** to lose one's (eye)sight ; **perdre de ~** to lose sight of ; **à la ~ de tous** in full view of everybody ; **hors de ~** out of sight ; **à première ~** at first sight ; **connaître de ~** to know by sight ; **à ~** (*COMM*) at sight ; **tirer à ~** to shoot on sight ; **à ~ d'œil** *ad* visibly ; at a quick glance ; **en ~** (*visible*) in sight ; (*COMM*) in the public eye ; **avoir qch en ~** (*intentions*) to have one's sights on sth ; **en ~ de** (*arriver, être*) within sight of ; **en ~ de faire** with the intention of doing, with a view to doing ; ~ **de l'esprit** theoretical view.

**vulcaniser** [vylkanize] *vt* to vulcanize.

**vulgaire** [vylgɛʀ] *a* (*grossier*) vulgar, coarse ; (*trivial*) commonplace, mundane ; (*péj: quelconque*): **de ~s touristes/ chaises de cuisine** common tourists/kitchen chairs ; (*BOT, ZOOL: non latin*) common ; ~**ment** *ad* vulgarly, coarsely ; (*communément*) commonly ; **vulgarisation** *nf*: **ouvrage de vulgarisation** popularizing work, popularization ; **vulgariser** *vt* to popularize ; to coarsen ; **vulgarité** *nf* vulgarity, coarseness.

**vulnérable** [vylneʀabl(ə)] *a* vulnerable.

**vulve** [vylv(ə)] *nf* vulva.

## W X Y Z

**wagon** [vagɔ̃] *nm* (*de voyageurs*) carriage ; (*de marchandises*) truck, wagon ; ~**-citerne** *nm* tanker ; ~**-lit** *nm* sleeper, sleeping car ; ~**-poste** *nm* mail van ; ~**-restaurant** *nm* restaurant *ou* dining car.

**wallon, ne** [valɔ̃, -ɔn] *a* Walloon.

**waters** [watɛʀ] *nmpl* toilet *sg*, loo *sg*.

**watt** [wat] *nm* watt.

**w.-c.** [vese] *nmpl* toilet *sg*, lavatory *sg*.

**week-end** [wikɛnd] *nm* weekend.

**western** [wɛstɛʀn] *nm* western.

**whisky,** *pl* **whiskies** [wiski] *nm* whisky.

**x** [iks] *nm*: **plainte contre X** (*JUR*) action against person or persons unknown ; **l'X** the École Polytechnique.

**xénophobe** [ksenɔfɔb] *nm/f* xenophobe.

**xérès** [gzeʀɛs] *nm* sherry.

**xylographie** [ksilɔgʀafi] *nf* xylography ; (*image*) xylograph.

**xylophone** [ksilɔfɔn] *nm* xylophone.

**y** [i] *ad* (*à cet endroit*) there ; (*dessus*) on it (*ou* them) ; (*dedans*) in it (*ou* them) // *pronom* (about *ou* on *ou* of) it: *vérifier la syntaxe du verbe employé*; **j'**~ **pense** I'm thinking about it ; *voir aussi* **aller, avoir.**

**yacht** [jɔt] *nm* yacht.

**yaourt** [jauʀt] *nm* yoghourt.

**yeux** [jø] *pl de* **œil**.

**yoga** [jɔga] *nm* yoga.

**yoghourt** [jɔguʀt] *nm* = **yaourt**.

**yole** [jɔl] *nf* skiff.

**yougoslave** [jugɔslav] *a,* *nm/f* Yugoslav(ian).

**Yougoslavie** [jugɔslavi] *nf* Yugoslavia.

**youyou** [juju] *nm* dinghy.

**yo-yo** [jojo] *nm inv* yo-yo.

**zèbre** [zɛbʀ(ə)] *nm* (*ZOOL*) zebra.

**zébré, e** [zebʀe] *a* striped, streaked ; **zébrure** *nf* stripe, streak.

**zélateur, trice** [zelatœʀ, -tʀis] *nm/f* partisan, zealot.

**zèle** [zɛl] *nm* zeal ; **faire du** ~ (*péj*) to be over-zealous ; **zélé, e** *a* zealous.

**zénith** [zenit] *nm* zenith.

**zéro** [zeʀo] *nm* zero, nought ; **au-dessous de** ~ below zero (Centigrade) *ou* freezing ; **partir de** ~ to start from scratch ; **trois (buts) à** ~ 3 (goals to) nil.

**zeste** [zɛst(ə)] *nm* peel, zest ; **un** ~ **de citron** a piece of lemon peel.

**zézayer** [zezeje] *vi* to have a lisp.

**zibeline** [ziblin] *nf* sable.

**zigzag** [zigzag] *nm* zigzag ; **zigzaguer** *vi* to zigzag (along).

**zinc** [zɛ̃g] *nm* (*CHIMIE*) zinc ; (*comptoir*) bar, counter.

**zizanie** [zizani] *nf*: **semer la** ~ to stir up ill-feeling.

**zizi** [zizi] *nm* (*fam*) willy.

**zodiaque** [zɔdjak] *nm* zodiac.

**zona** [zona] *nm* shingles *sg*.

**zone** [zon] *nf* zone, area ; (*quartiers*): **la** ~ the slum belt ; ~ **bleue** ≈ restricted parking area.

**zoo** [zoo] *nm* zoo.

**zoologie** [zɔɔlɔʒi] *nf* zoology ; **zoologique** *a* zoological ; **zoologiste** *nm/f* zoologist.

**Z.U.P.** [zyp] *sigle f* = *zone à urbaniser en priorité*, ≈ (planned) housing scheme.

**zut** [zyt] *excl* dash (it)!

# ENGLISH-FRENCH
# ANGLAIS-FRANÇAIS

# A

**a, an** [eɪ, ə, æn, ən, n] *det* un(e); **3 a day/week** 3 par jour/semaine; **10 km an hour** 10 km à l'heure.

**A** [eɪ] *n* (*MUS*) la *m*.

**A.A.** *n abbr of Automobile Association*; *Alcoholics Anonymous*.

**aback** [ə'bæk] *ad*: **to be taken ~** être stupéfait(e).

**abacus,** *pl* **abaci** ['æbəkəs, -saɪ] *n* boulier *m*.

**abandon** [ə'bændən] *vt* abandonner // *n* abandon *m*.

**abashed** [ə'bæʃt] *a* confus(e), embarrassé(e).

**abate** [ə'beɪt] *vi* s'apaiser, se calmer.

**abattoir** ['æbətwɑ:*] *n* abattoir *m*.

**abbey** ['æbɪ] *n* abbaye *f*.

**abbot** ['æbət] *n* père supérieur.

**abbreviate** [ə'bri:vɪeɪt] *vt* abréger; **abbreviation** [-'eɪʃən] *n* abréviation *f*.

**abdicate** ['æbdɪkeɪt] *vt,vi* abdiquer; **abdication** [-'keɪʃən] *n* abdication *f*.

**abdomen** ['æbdəmɛn] *n* abdomen *m*; **abdominal** [æb'dɔmɪnl] *a* abdominal(e).

**abduct** [æb'dʌkt] *vt* enlever; **abduction** [-ʃən] *n* enlèvement *m*.

**abet** [ə'bɛt] *vt* encourager; aider.

**abeyance** [ə'beɪəns] *n*: **in ~** (*law*) en désuétude; (*matter*) en suspens.

**abhor** [əb'hɔ:*] *vt* abhorrer, exécrer; **~rent** *a* odieux(euse), exécrable.

**abide,** *pt,pp* **abode** *or* **abided** [ə'baɪd, ə'bəud] *vt* souffrir, supporter; **to ~ by** *vt fus* observer, respecter.

**ability** [ə'bɪlɪtɪ] *n* compétence *f*; capacité *f*; talent *m*.

**ablaze** [ə'bleɪz] *a* en feu, en flammes; **~ with light** resplendissant de lumière.

**able** ['eɪbl] *a* compétent(e); **to be ~ to do sth** pouvoir faire qch, être capable de faire qch; **~-bodied** *a* robuste; **ably** *ad* avec compétence *or* talent, habilement.

**abnormal** [æb'nɔ:məl] *a* anormal(e); **~ity** [-'mælɪtɪ] *n* anomalie *f*.

**aboard** [ə'bɔ:d] *ad* à bord // *prep* à bord de.

**abode** [ə'bəud] *pt,pp of* **abide**.

**abolish** [ə'bɔlɪʃ] *vt* abolir.

**abolition** [æbəu'lɪʃən] *n* abolition *f*.

**abominable** [ə'bɔmɪnəbl] *a* abominable.

**aborigine** [æbə'rɪdʒɪnɪ] *n* aborigène *m/f*.

**abort** [ə'bɔ:t] *vt* faire avorter; **~ion** [ə'bɔ:ʃən] *n* avortement *m*; **~ive** *a* manqué(e).

**abound** [ə'baund] *vi* abonder; **to ~ in** abonder en, regorger de.

**about** [ə'baut] *prep* au sujet de, à propos de // *ad* environ; (*here and there*) de côté et d'autre, çà et là; **it takes ~ 10 hours** ça prend environ *or* à peu près 10 heures; **at ~ 2 o'clock** vers 2 heures; **it's ~ here** c'est par ici, c'est dans les parages; **to walk ~ the town** se promener dans *or* à travers la ville; **to be ~ to**: he was

**~ to cry** il allait pleurer, il était sur le point de pleurer; **what** *or* **how ~ doing this?** et si nous faisions ceci?; **~ turn** *n* demi-tour *m*.

**above** [ə'bʌv] *ad* au-dessus // *prep* au-dessus de; **mentioned ~** mentionné ci-dessus; **costing ~ £10** coûtant plus de 10 livres; **~ all** par-dessus tout, surtout; **~board** *a* franc(franche), loyal(e); honnête.

**abrasion** [ə'breɪʒən] *n* frottement *m*; (*on skin*) écorchure *f*.

**abrasive** [ə'breɪzɪv] *a* abrasif(ive); (*fig*) caustique, agressif(ive).

**abreast** [ə'brɛst] *ad* de front; **to keep ~ of** se tenir au courant de.

**abridge** [ə'brɪdʒ] *vt* abréger.

**abroad** [ə'brɔ:d] *ad* à l'étranger.

**abrupt** [ə'brʌpt] *a* (*steep, blunt*) abrupt(e); (*sudden, gruff*) brusque.

**abscess** ['æbsɪs] *n* abcès *m*.

**abscond** [əb'skɔnd] *vi* disparaître, s'enfuir.

**absence** ['æbsəns] *n* absence *f*.

**absent** ['æbsənt] *a* absent(e); **~ee** [-'ti:] *n* absent/e; **~eeism** [-'ti:ɪzəm] *n* absentéisme *m*; **~-minded** *a* distrait(e); **~-mindedness** *n* distraction *f*.

**absolute** ['æbsəlu:t] *a* absolu(e); **~ly** [-'lu:tlɪ] *ad* absolument.

**absolve** [əb'zɔlv] *vt*: **to ~ sb (from)** (*sin etc*) absoudre qn (de); **to ~ sb from** (*oath*) délier qn de.

**absorb** [əb'zɔ:b] *vt* absorber; **to be ~ed in a book** être plongé dans un livre; **~ent** *a* absorbant(e); **~ent cotton** *n* (*US*) coton *m* hydrophile; **~ing** *a* absorbant(e).

**abstain** [əb'steɪn] *vi*: **to ~ (from)** s'abstenir (de).

**abstemious** [əb'sti:mɪəs] *a* sobre, frugal(e).

**abstention** [əb'stɛnʃən] *n* abstention *f*.

**abstinence** ['æbstɪnəns] *n* abstinence *f*.

**abstract** *a and n* ['æbstrækt] *a* abstrait(e) // *n* (*summary*) résumé *m* // *vt* [æb'strækt] extraire.

**absurd** [əb'sə:d] *a* absurde; **~ity** *n* absurdité *f*.

**abundance** [ə'bʌndəns] *n* abondance *f*; **abundant** *a* abondant(e).

**abuse** *n* [ə'bju:s] abus *m*; insultes *fpl*, injures *fpl* // *vt* [ə'bju:z] abuser de; **abusive** *a* grossier(ère), injurieux(euse).

**abysmal** [ə'bɪzməl] *a* exécrable; (*ignorance etc*) sans bornes.

**abyss** [ə'bɪs] *n* abîme *m*, gouffre *m*.

**academic** [ækə'dɛmɪk] *a* universitaire; (*pej: issue*) oiseux(euse), purement théorique // *n* universitaire *m/f*; **~ freedom** *n* liberté *f* académique.

**academy** [ə'kædəmɪ] *n* (*learned body*) académie *f*; (*school*) collège *m*; **military/naval ~** école militaire/navale; **~ of music** conservatoire *m*.

**accede** [æk'si:d] *vi*: **to ~ to** (*request, throne*) accéder à.
**accelerate** [æk'sɛləreɪt] *vt,vi* accélérer ; **acceleration** [-'reɪʃən] *n* accélération *f*; **accelerator** *n* accélérateur *m*.
**accent** ['æksɛnt] *n* accent *m*.
**accept** [ək'sɛpt] *vt* accepter ; **~able** *a* acceptable ; **~ance** *n* acceptation *f*.
**access** ['æksɛs] *n* accès *m* ; **to have ~ to** (*information, library etc*) avoir accès à, pouvoir utiliser *or* consulter ; (*person*) avoir accès auprès de ; **~ible** [æk'sɛsəbl] *a* accessible ; **~ion** [æk'sɛʃən] *n* accession *f*.
**accessory** [æk'sɛsərɪ] *n* accessoire *m* ; **toilet accessories** *npl* articles *mpl* de toilette.
**accident** ['æksɪdənt] *n* accident *m*; (*chance*) hasard *m*; **by ~** par hasard ; accidentellement ; **~al** [-'dɛntl] *a* accidentel(le) ; **~ally** [-'dɛntəlɪ] *ad* accidentellement ; **~-prone** *a* sujet(te) aux accidents.
**acclaim** [ə'kleɪm] *vt* acclamer // *n* acclamation *f*.
**acclimatize** [ə'klaɪmətaɪz] *vt*: **to become ~d** s'acclimater.
**accommodate** [ə'kɔmədeɪt] *vt* loger, recevoir ; (*oblige, help*) obliger ; (*adapt*): **to ~ one's plans to** adapter ses projets à.
**accommodating** [ə'kɔmədeɪtɪŋ] *a* obligeant(e), arrangeant(e).
**accommodation** [əkɔmə'deɪʃən] *n* logement *m*; **he's found ~** il a trouvé à se loger ; **they have ~ for 500** ils peuvent recevoir 500 personnes, il y a de la place pour 500 personnes.
**accompaniment** [ə'kʌmpənɪmənt] *n* accompagnement *m*.
**accompanist** [ə'kʌmpənɪst] *n* accompagnateur/trice.
**accompany** [ə'kʌmpənɪ] *vt* accompagner.
**accomplice** [ə'kʌmplɪs] *n* complice *m/f*.
**accomplish** [ə'kʌmplɪʃ] *vt* accomplir ; **~ed** *a* accompli(e) ; **~ment** *n* accomplissement *m*; réussite *f*, résultat *m*; **~ments** *npl* talents *mpl*.
**accord** [ə'kɔ:d] *n* accord *m* // *vt* accorder ; **of his own ~** de son plein gré ; **~ance** *n*: **in ~ance with** conformément à ; **~ing** **to** *prep* selon ; **~ingly** *ad* en conséquence.
**accordion** [ə'kɔ:dɪən] *n* accordéon *m*.
**accost** [ə'kɔst] *vt* accoster, aborder.
**account** [ə'kaunt] *n* (*COMM*) compte *m*; (*report*) compte rendu ; récit *m*; **by all ~s** au dire de tous ; **of little ~** de peu d'importance ; **on ~** en acompte ; **on no ~** en aucun cas ; **on ~ of** à cause de ; **to take into ~**, **take ~ of** tenir compte de ; **to ~ for** expliquer, rendre compte de ; **~able** *a* responsable.
**accountancy** [ə'kauntənsɪ] *n* comptabilité *f*.
**accountant** [ə'kauntənt] *n* comptable *m/f*.
**accredited** [ə'krɛdɪtɪd] *a* accrédité(e) ; admis(e).
**accretion** [ə'kri:ʃən] *n* accroissement *m*.
**accrue** [ə'kru:] *vi* s'accroître ; **~d interest** intérêt couru.
**accumulate** [ə'kju:mjuleɪt] *vt* accumuler, amasser // *vi* s'accumuler, s'amasser ; **accumulation** [-'leɪʃən] *n* accumulation *f*.

**accuracy** ['ækjurəsɪ] *n* exactitude *f*, précision *f*.
**accurate** ['ækjurɪt] *a* exact(e), précis(e) ; **~ly** *ad* avec précision.
**accusation** [ækju'zeɪʃən] *n* accusation *f*.
**accusative** [ə'kju:zətɪv] *n* (*LING*) accusatif *m*.
**accuse** [ə'kju:z] *vt* accuser ; **~d** *n* accusé/e.
**accustom** [ə'kʌstəm] *vt* accoutumer, habituer ; **~ed** *a* (*usual*) habituel(le) ; **~ed to** habitué *or* accoutumé à.
**ace** [eɪs] *n* as *m*; **within an ~ of** à deux doigts *or* un cheveu de.
**ache** [eɪk] *n* mal *m*, douleur *f* // *vi* (*be sore*) faire mal, être douloureux(euse) ; **my head ~s** j'ai mal à la tête ; **I'm aching all over** j'ai mal partout.
**achieve** [ə'tʃi:v] *vt* (*aim*) atteindre ; (*victory, success*) remporter, obtenir ; (*task*) accomplir ; **~ment** *n* exploit *m*, réussite *f*.
**acid** ['æsɪd] *a,n* acide (*m*) ; **~ity** [ə'sɪdɪtɪ] *n* acidité *f*.
**acknowledge** [ək'nɔlɪdʒ] *vt* (*letter*) accuser réception de ; (*fact*) reconnaître ; **~ment** *n* accusé *m* de réception.
**acne** ['æknɪ] *n* acné *m*.
**acorn** ['eɪkɔ:n] *n* gland *m*.
**acoustic** [ə'ku:stɪk] *a* acoustique ; **~s** *n,npl* acoustique *f*.
**acquaint** [ə'kweɪnt] *vt*: **to ~ sb with sth** mettre qn au courant de qch ; **to be ~ed with** (*person*) connaître ; **~ance** *n* connaissance *f*.
**acquire** [ə'kwaɪə*] *vt* acquérir.
**acquisition** [ækwɪ'zɪʃən] *n* acquisition *f*.
**acquisitive** [ə'kwɪzɪtɪv] *a* qui a l'instinct de possession *or* le goût de la propriété.
**acquit** [ə'kwɪt] *vt* acquitter ; **to ~ o.s. well** bien se comporter, s'en tirer très honorablement ; **~tal** *n* acquittement *m*.
**acre** ['eɪkə*] *n* acre *f* (= *4047 m²*) ; **~age** *n* superficie *f*.
**acrimonious** [ækrɪ'məunɪəs] *a* acrimonieux(euse), aigre.
**acrobat** ['ækrəbæt] *n* acrobate *m/f*.
**acrobatics** [ækrəu'bætɪks] *n,npl* acrobatie *f*.
**across** [ə'krɔs] *prep* (*on the other side*) de l'autre côté de ; (*crosswise*) en travers de // *ad* de l'autre côté ; en travers ; **to walk ~** (*the road*) traverser (la route) ; **to take sb ~ the road** faire traverser la route à qn ; **a road ~ the wood** une route qui traverse le bois ; **~ from** en face de.
**act** [ækt] *n* acte *m*, action *f*; (*THEATRE*) acte ; (*in music-hall etc*) numéro *m*; (*LAW*) loi *f* // *vi* agir ; (*THEATRE*) jouer ; (*pretend*) jouer la comédie // *vt* (*part*) jouer, tenir ; **to ~ Hamlet** tenir *or* jouer le rôle d'Hamlet ; **to ~ the fool** faire l'idiot ; **to ~ as** servir de ; **~ing** *a* suppléant(e), par intérim // *n* (*of actor*) jeu *m*; (*activity*): **to do some ~ing** faire du théâtre (*or* du cinéma).
**action** ['ækʃən] *n* action *f*; (*MIL*) combat(s) *m(pl)*; (*LAW*) procès *m*, action en justice ; **out of ~** hors de combat ; hors d'usage ; **to take ~** agir, prendre des mesures.
**activate** ['æktɪveɪt] *vt* (*mechanism*)

actionner, faire fonctionner ; (CHEM, PHYSICS) activer.
**active** ['æktɪv] a actif(ive) ; (volcano) en activité ; ~ly ad activement.
**activity** [æk'tɪvɪtɪ] n activité f.
**actor** ['æktə*] n acteur m.
**actress** ['æktrɪs] n actrice f.
**actual** ['æktjuəl] a réel(le), véritable ; ~ly ad réellement, véritablement ; en fait.
**acumen** ['ækjumən] n perspicacité f.
**acupuncture** ['ækjupʌŋktʃə*] n acupuncture f.
**acute** [ə'kju:t] a aigu(ë) ; (mind, observer) pénétrant(e).
**ad** [æd] n abbr of **advertisement**.
**A.D.** ad (abbr of Anno Domini) ap. J.-C.
**Adam** ['ædəm] n Adam m ; ~'s apple n pomme f d'Adam.
**adamant** ['ædəmənt] a inflexible.
**adapt** [ə'dæpt] vt adapter // vi: **to ~ (to)** s'adapter (à) ; ~**able** a (device) adaptable ; (person) qui s'adapte facilement ; ~**ation** [ædæp'teɪʃən] n adaptation f ; ~**er** n (ELEC) adapteur m.
**add** [æd] vt ajouter ; (figures: also: **to ~ up**) additionner // vi: **to ~ to** (increase) ajouter à, accroître.
**adder** ['ædə*] n vipère f.
**addict** ['ædɪkt] n intoxiqué m ; (fig) fanatique m/f ; ~**ed** [ə'dɪktɪd] a: **to be ~ed to** (drink etc) être adonné à ; (fig: football etc) être un fanatique de ; ~**ion** [ə'dɪkʃən] n (MED) dépendance f.
**adding machine** ['ædɪŋməʃi:n] n machine f à calculer.
**addition** [ə'dɪʃən] n addition f ; **in ~** de plus ; de surcroît ; **in ~ to** en plus de ; ~**al** a supplémentaire.
**additive** ['ædɪtɪv] n additif m.
**addled** ['ædld] a (egg) pourri(e).
**address** [ə'drɛs] n adresse f ; (talk) discours m, allocution f // vt adresser ; (speak to) s'adresser à.
**adenoids** ['ædɪnɔɪdz] npl végétations fpl.
**adept** ['ædɛpt] a: ~ **at** expert(e) à or en.
**adequate** ['ædɪkwɪt] a adéquat(e) ; suffisant(e) ; compétent(e) ; ~**ly** ad de façon adéquate.
**adhere** [əd'hɪə*] vi: **to ~ to** adhérer à ; (fig: rule, decision) se tenir à.
**adhesion** [əd'hi:ʒən] n adhésion f.
**adhesive** [əd'hi:zɪv] a adhésif(ive) // n adhésif m.
**adjacent** [ə'dʒeɪsənt] a adjacent(e) ; ~ **to** adjacent à.
**adjective** ['ædʒɛktɪv] n adjectif m.
**adjoining** [ə'dʒɔɪnɪŋ] a voisin(e), adjacent(e), attenant(e) // prep voisin de, adjacent à.
**adjourn** [ə'dʒə:n] vt ajourner // vi suspendre la séance ; lever la séance ; clore la session ; (go) se retirer.
**adjust** [ə'dʒʌst] vt ajuster, régler ; rajuster // vi: **to ~ (to)** s'adapter (à) ; ~**able** a réglable ; ~**ment** n ajustage m, réglage m ; (of prices, wages) rajustement m ; (of person) adaptation f.
**adjutant** ['ædʒətənt] n adjudant m.
**ad-lib** [æd'lɪb] vt,vi improviser // n improvisation f // ad: **ad lib** à volonté, à discrétion.

**administer** [əd'mɪnɪstə*] vt administrer ; (justice) rendre.
**administration** [ədmɪnɪs'treɪʃən] n administration f.
**administrative** [əd'mɪnɪstrətɪv] a administratif(ive).
**administrator** [əd'mɪnɪstreɪtə*] n administrateur/trice.
**admirable** ['ædmərəbl] a admirable.
**admiral** ['ædmərəl] n amiral m ; **A~ty** n amirauté f ; ministère m de la Marine.
**admiration** [ædmə'reɪʃən] n admiration f.
**admire** [əd'maɪə*] vt admirer ; ~**r** n admirateur/trice.
**admission** [əd'mɪʃən] n admission f ; (to exhibition, night club etc) entrée f ; (confession) aveu m.
**admit** [əd'mɪt] vt laisser entrer ; admettre ; (agree) reconnaître, admettre ; **to ~ of** admettre, permettre ; **to ~ to** reconnaître, avouer ; ~**tance** n admission f, (droit m d')entrée f ; ~**tedly** ad il faut en convenir.
**admonish** [əd'mɔnɪʃ] vt donner un avertissement à ; réprimander.
**ado** [ə'du:] n: **without (any) more ~** sans plus de cérémonies.
**adolescence** [ædəu'lɛsns] n adolescence f.
**adolescent** [ædəu'lɛsnt] a,n adolescent(e).
**adopt** [ə'dɔpt] vt adopter ; ~**ed** a adoptif(ive), adopté(e) ; ~**ion** [ə'dɔpʃən] n adoption f.
**adore** [ə'dɔ:*] vt adorer ; **adoringly** ad avec adoration.
**adorn** [ə'dɔ:n] vt orner ; ~**ment** n ornement m.
**adrenalin** [ə'drɛnəlɪn] n adrénaline f.
**Adriatic (Sea)** [eɪdrɪ'ætɪk(si:)] n Adriatique f.
**adrift** [ə'drɪft] ad à la dérive.
**adroit** [ə'drɔɪt] a adroit(e), habile.
**adult** ['ædʌlt] n adulte m/f.
**adulterate** [ə'dʌltəreɪt] vt frelater, falsifier.
**adultery** [ə'dʌltərɪ] n adultère m.
**advance** [əd'vɑ:ns] n avance f // vt avancer // vi s'avancer ; **in ~** en avance, d'avance ; ~**d** a avancé(e) ; (SCOL: studies) supérieur(e) ; ~**ment** n avancement m.
**advantage** [əd'vɑ:ntɪdʒ] n (also TENNIS) avantage m ; **to take ~ of** profiter de ; ~**ous** [ædvən'teɪdʒəs] a avantageux(euse).
**advent** ['ædvənt] n avènement m, venue f ; **A~** Avent m.
**adventure** [əd'vɛntʃə*] n aventure f ; **adventurous** [-tʃərəs] a aventureux(euse).
**adverb** ['ædvə:b] n adverbe m.
**adversary** ['ædvəsərɪ] n adversaire m/f.
**adverse** ['ædvə:s] a contraire, adverse ; **in ~ circumstances** dans l'adversité ; ~ **to** hostile à.
**adversity** [əd'və:sɪtɪ] n adversité f.
**advert** ['ædvə:t] n abbr of **advertisement**.
**advertise** ['ædvətaɪz] vi(vt) faire de la publicité or de la réclame (pour) ; mettre une annonce (pour vendre).
**advertisement** [əd'və:tɪsmənt] n (COMM) réclame f, publicité f ; (in classified ads) annonce f.

**advertising** ['ædvətaızıŋ] n publicité f, réclame f.

**advice** [əd'vaıs] n conseils mpl; (notification) avis m; **piece of** ~ conseil.

**advisable** [əd'vaızəbl] a recommandable, indiqué(e).

**advise** [əd'vaız] vt conseiller; **to** ~ **sb of sth** aviser or informer qn de qch; ~**r** n conseiller/ère; **advisory** [-ərı] a consultatif(ive).

**advocate** vt ['ædvəkeıt] recommander, prôner.

**aegis** ['i:dʒıs] n: **under the** ~ **of** sous l'égide de.

**aerial** ['ɛərıəl] n antenne f // a aérien(ne).

**aeroplane** ['ɛərəpleın] n avion m.

**aerosol** ['ɛərəsɔl] n aérosol m.

**aesthetic** [ıs'θɛtık] a esthétique.

**afar** [ə'fu:*] ad: **from** ~ de loin.

**affable** ['æfəbl] a affable.

**affair** [ə'fɛə*] n affaire f; (also: **love** ~) liaison f; aventure f.

**affect** [ə'fɛkt] vt affecter; ~**ation** [æfɛk'teıʃən] n affectation f; ~**ed** a affecté(e).

**affection** [ə'fɛkʃən] n affection f; ~**ate** a affectueux(euse); ~**ately** ad affectueusement.

**affiliated** [ə'fılıeıtıd] a affilié(e).

**affinity** [ə'fınıtı] n affinité f.

**affirmation** [æfə'meıʃən] n affirmation f, assertion f.

**affirmative** [ə'fə:mətıv] a affirmatif(ive) // n: **in the** ~ dans or par l'affirmative.

**affix** [ə'fıks] vt apposer, ajouter.

**afflict** [ə'flıkt] vt affliger; ~**ion** [ə'flıkʃən] n affliction f, détresse f.

**affluence** ['æfluəns] n abondance f, opulence f.

**affluent** ['æfluənt] a abondant(e); opulent(e); (person) dans l'aisance, riche.

**afford** [ə'fɔ:d] vt se permettre; avoir les moyens d'acheter or d'entretenir; (provide) fournir, procurer; **I can't** ~ **the time** je n'ai vraiment pas le temps.

**affray** [ə'freı] n échauffourée f.

**affront** [ə'frʌnt] n affront m; ~**ed** a insulté(e).

**afield** [ə'fi:ld] ad: **far** ~ loin.

**afloat** [ə'fləut] a à flot // ad: **to stay** ~ surnager; **to keep/get a business** ~ maintenir à flot/lancer une affaire.

**afoot** [ə'fut] ad: **there is something** ~ il se prépare quelque chose.

**aforesaid** [ə'fɔ:sɛd] a susdit(e), susmentionné(e).

**afraid** [ə'freıd] a effrayé(e); **to be** ~ **of** or **to** avoir peur de; **I am** ~ **that** je crains que + sub.

**afresh** [ə'frɛʃ] ad de nouveau.

**Africa** ['æfrıkə] n Afrique f; ~**n** a africain(e) // n Africain/e.

**aft** [ɑ:ft] ad à l'arrière, vers l'arrière.

**after** ['ɑ:ftə*] prep, ad après // cj après que, après avoir or être + pp; **what/who are you** ~? que/qui cherchez-vous?; **ask** ~ **him** demander de ses nouvelles; ~ **all** après tout; ~**effects** npl répercussions fpl; (of illness) séquelles fpl, suites fpl; ~**life** n vie future; ~**math** n conséquences fpl; **in the** ~**math of** dans

les mois or années etc qui suivirent, au lendemain de; ~**noon** n après-midi m or f; ~-**shave (lotion)** n after-shave m; ~**thought** n: **I had an** ~**thought** il m'est venu une idée après coup; ~**wards** ad après.

**again** [ə'gɛn] ad de nouveau; **to begin/see** ~ recommencer/revoir; **not** ... ~ ne ... plus; ~ **and** ~ à plusieurs reprises; **he's opened it** ~ il l'a rouvert, il l'a de nouveau or l'a encore ouvert.

**against** [ə'gɛnst] prep contre; ~ **a blue background** sur un fond bleu.

**age** [eıdʒ] n âge m // vt, vi vieillir; **it's been** ~**s since** ça fait une éternité que; **to come of** ~ atteindre sa majorité; ~**d** a âgé(e); ~**d 10** âgé de 10 ans; **the** ~**d** ['eıdʒıd] les personnes âgées; ~ **group** n tranche f d'âge; ~**less** a sans âge; ~ **limit** n limite f d'âge.

**agency** ['eıdʒənsı] n agence f; **through** or **by the** ~ **of** par l'entremise or l'action de.

**agenda** [ə'dʒɛndə] n ordre m du jour.

**agent** ['eıdʒənt] n agent m.

**aggravate** ['ægrəveıt] vt aggraver; (annoy) exaspérer.

**aggravation** [ægrə'veıʃən] n (of quarrel) envenimement m.

**aggregate** ['ægrıgeıt] n ensemble m, total m; **on** ~ (SPORT) au goal average.

**aggression** [ə'grɛʃən] n agression f.

**aggressive** [ə'grɛsıv] a agressif(ive); ~**ness** n agressivité f.

**aggrieved** [ə'gri:vd] a chagriné(e), affligé(e).

**aghast** [ə'gu:st] a consterné(e), atterré(e).

**agile** ['ædʒaıl] a agile.

**agitate** ['ædʒıteıt] vt rendre inquiet(ète) or agité(e); agiter // vi faire de l'agitation (politique); **to** ~ **for** faire campagne pour; **agitator** n agitateur/trice (politique).

**ago** [ə'gəu] ad: **2 days** ~ il y a deux jours; **not long** ~ il n'y a pas longtemps.

**agonizing** ['ægənaızıŋ] a angoissant(e); déchirant(e).

**agony** ['ægənı] n grande souffrance or angoisse; **to be in** ~ souffrir le martyre.

**agree** [ə'gri:] vt (price) convenir de // vi: **to** ~ (**with**) (person) être d'accord (avec); (statements etc) concorder (avec); (LING) s'accorder (avec); **to** ~ **to do** accepter de or consentir à faire; **to** ~ **to sth** consentir à qch; **to** ~ **that** (admit) convenir or reconnaître que; **they** ~**d on this** ils sont d'accord sur ce point; **they** ~**d on going/a price** ils se mirent d'accord pour y aller/sur un prix; **garlic doesn't** ~ **with me** je ne supporte pas l'ail; ~**able** a agréable; (willing) consentant(e), d'accord; **are you** ~**able to this?** est-ce que cela vous va or convient?; ~**d** a (time, place) convenu(e); **to be** ~**d** être d'accord; ~**ment** n accord m; **in** ~**ment** d'accord.

**agricultural** [ægrı'kʌltʃərəl] a agricole.

**agriculture** ['ægrıkʌltʃə*] n agriculture f.

**aground** [ə'graund] ad: **to run** ~ s'échouer.

**ahead** [ə'hɛd] ad en avant; devant; ~ **of** devant; (fig: schedule etc) en avance sur; ~ **of time** en avance; **go right** or **straight** ~ allez tout droit; **they were (right)** ~

**of us** ils nous précédaient (de peu), ils étaient (juste) devant nous.

**aid** [eɪd] *n* aide *f* // *vt* aider ; **to** ~ **and abet** (*LAW*) se faire le complice de.

**aide** [eɪd] *n* (*person*) collaborateur/trice, assistant/e.

**ailment** ['eɪlmənt] *n* petite maladie, affection *f.*

**aim** [eɪm] *vt*: **to** ~ **sth at** (*such as gun, camera*) braquer *or* pointer qch sur, diriger qch contre ; (*missile*) lancer qch à *or* contre *or* en direction de ; (*remark, blow*) destiner *or* adresser qch à // *vi* (*also*: **to take** ~) viser // *n* but *m*; **to** ~ **at** viser ; (*fig*) viser (à) ; avoir pour but *or* ambition ; **to** ~ **to do** avoir l'intention de faire ; ~**less** *a* sans but ; ~**lessly** *ad* sans but, à l'aventure.

**air** [ɛə*] *n* air *m* // *vt* aérer ; (*grievances, ideas*) exposer (librement) // *cpd* (*currents, attack etc*) aérien(ne) ; ~**bed** *n* matelas *m* pneumatique ; ~**borne** *a* en vol ; aeroporté(e) ; ~**-conditioned** *a* climatisé(e), à air conditionné ; ~ **conditioning** *n* climatisation *f*; ~**-cooled** *a* à refroidissement à air ; ~**craft** *n,pl inv* avion *m*; ~**craft carrier** *n* porte-avions *m inv*; ~ **cushion** *n* coussin *m* d'air ; **A**~ **Force** *n* Armée *f* de l'air ; ~**gun** *n* fusil *m* à air comprimé ; ~ **hostess** *n* hôtesse *f* de l'air ; ~**ily** *ad* d'un air dégagé ; ~**letter** *n* aérogramme *m*; ~**lift** *n* pont aérien ; ~**line** *n* ligne aérienne ; compagnie *f* d'aviation ; ~**liner** *n* avion *m* de ligne ; ~**lock** *n* sas *m*; by ~**mail** par avion ; ~**port** *n* aéroport *m*; ~ **raid** *n* attaque aérienne ; ~**sick** *a* qui a le mal de l'air ; ~**strip** *n* terrain *m* d'atterrissage ; ~**tight** *a* hermétique ; ~**y** *a* bien aéré(e) ; (*manners*) dégagé(e).

**aisle** [aɪl] *n* (*of church*) allée centrale ; nef latérale.

**ajar** [ə'dʒɑ:*] *a* entrouvert(e).

**alarm** [ə'lɑ:m] *n* alarme *f* // *vt* alarmer ; ~ **clock** *n* réveille-matin *m*, réveil *m*; ~**ist** *n* alarmiste *m/f.*

**Albania** [æl'beɪnɪə] *n* Albanie *f.*

**album** ['ælbəm] *n* album *m*; (*L.P.*) 33 tours *m inv.*

**albumen** ['ælbjumɪn] *n* albumine *f*; (*of egg*) albumen *m.*

**alchemy** ['ælkɪmɪ] *n* alchimie *f.*

**alcohol** ['ælkəhɔl] *n* alcool *m*; ~**ic** [-'hɔlɪk] *a,n* alcoolique (*m/f*); ~**ism** *n* alcoolisme *m.*

**alcove** ['ælkəuv] *n* alcôve *f.*

**alderman** ['ɔ:ldəmən] *n* conseiller municipal (*en Angleterre*).

**ale** [eɪl] *n* bière *f.*

**alert** [ə'lə:t] *a* alerte, vif(vive) ; vigilant(e) // *n* alerte *f*; **on the** ~ sur le qui-vive ; (*MIL*) en état d'alerte.

**algebra** ['ældʒɪbrə] *n* algèbre *m.*

**Algeria** [æl'dʒɪərɪə] *n* Algérie *f*; ~**n** *a* algérien(ne) // *n* Algérien/ne.

**Algiers** [æl'dʒɪəz] *n* Alger *m.*

**alias** ['eɪlɪæs] *ad* alias // *n* faux nom, nom d'emprunt.

**alibi** ['ælɪbaɪ] *n* alibi *m.*

**alien** ['eɪlɪən] *n* étranger/ère // *a*: ~ **(to/from)** étranger(ère) (à) ; ~**ate** *vt* aliéner ; s'aliéner ; ~**ation** [-'neɪʃən] *n* aliénation *f.*

**alight** [ə'laɪt] *a,ad* en feu // *vi* mettre pied à terre ; (*passenger*) descendre ; (*bird*) se poser.

**align** [ə'laɪn] *vt* aligner ; ~**ment** *n* alignement *m.*

**alike** [ə'laɪk] *a* semblable, pareil(le) // *ad* de même ; **to look** ~ se ressembler.

**alimony** ['ælɪmənɪ] *n* (*payment*) pension *f* alimentaire.

**alive** [ə'laɪv] *a* vivant(e) ; (*active*) plein(e) de vie ; ~ **with** grouillant(e) de ; ~ **to** sensible à.

**alkali** ['ælkəlaɪ] *n* alcali *m.*

**all** [ɔ:l] *a* tout(e), tous(toutes) *pl* // *pronoun* tout *m*; (*pl*) tous(toutes) // *ad* tout ; ~ **wrong/alone** tout faux/seul ; ~ **the time/his life** tout le temps/toute sa vie ; ~ **five** (tous) les cinq ; ~ **of them** tous, toutes ; ~ **of it** tout ; ~ **of us went** nous y sommes tous allés ; **not as hard** *etc* **as** ~ **that** pas si dur *etc* que ça ; ~ **in** ~ à tout prendre, l'un dans l'autre.

**allay** [ə'leɪ] *vt* (*fears*) apaiser, calmer.

**allegation** [ælɪ'geɪʃən] *n* allégation *f.*

**allege** [ə'lɛdʒ] *vt* alléguer, prétendre ; ~**dly** [ə'lɛdʒɪdlɪ] *ad* à ce que l'on prétend, paraît-il.

**allegiance** [ə'li:dʒəns] *n* fidélité *f*, obéissance *f.*

**allegory** ['ælɪgərɪ] *n* allégorie *f.*

**all-embracing** ['ɔ:lɪm'breɪsɪŋ] *a* universel(le).

**allergic** [ə'lə:dʒɪk] *a*: ~ **to** allergique à.

**allergy** ['ælədʒɪ] *n* allergie *f.*

**alleviate** [ə'li:vɪeɪt] *vt* soulager, adoucir.

**alley** ['ælɪ] *n* ruelle *f*; (*in garden*) allée *f.*

**alliance** [ə'laɪəns] *n* alliance *f.*

**allied** ['ælaɪd] *a* allié(e).

**alligator** ['ælɪgeɪtə*] *n* alligator *m.*

**all-important** ['ɔ:lɪm'pɔ:tənt] *a* capital(e), crucial(e).

**all-in** ['ɔ:lɪn] *a* (*also ad*: *charge*) tout compris ; ~ **wrestling** *n* catch *m.*

**alliteration** [əlɪtə'reɪʃən] *n* allitération *f.*

**all-night** ['ɔ:l'naɪt] *a* ouvert(e) *or* qui dure toute la nuit.

**allocate** ['æləkeɪt] *vt* (*share out*) répartir, distribuer ; (*duties*): **to** ~ **sth to** assigner *or* attribuer qch à ; (*sum, time*): **to** ~ **sth to** allouer qch à ; **to** ~ **sth for** affecter qch à.

**allocation** [æləu'keɪʃən] *n*: ~ **(of money)** crédit(s) *m(pl)*, somme(s) allouée(s).

**allot** [ə'lɔt] *vt* (*share out*) répartir, distribuer ; (*time*): **to** ~ **sth to** allouer qch à ; (*duties*): **to** ~ **sth to** assigner qch à ; ~**ment** *n* (*share*) part *f*; (*garden*) lopin *m* de terre (*loué à la municipalité*).

**all-out** ['ɔ:l'aut] *a* (*effort etc*) total(e) // *ad*: **all out** à fond.

**allow** [ə'lau] *vt* (*practice, behaviour*) permettre, autoriser ; (*sum to spend etc*) accorder ; allouer ; (*sum, time estimated*) compter, prévoir ; (*concede*): **to** ~ **that** convenir que ; **to** ~ **sb to do** permettre à qn de faire, autoriser qn à faire ; **to** ~ **for** *vt fus* tenir compte de ; ~**ance** *n* (*money received*) allocation *f*; subside *m*; indemnité *f*; (*TAX*) somme *f* déductible du revenu imposable, abattement *m*; **to make** ~**ances for** tenir compte de.

**alloy** ['ælɔɪ] *n* alliage *m*.
**all right** ['ɔːl'raɪt] *ad (feel, work)* bien ; *(as answer)* d'accord.
**all-round** ['ɔːl'raund] *a* compétent(e) dans tous les domaines ; *(athlete etc)* complet(ète).
**all-time** ['ɔːl'taɪm] *a (record)* sans précédent, absolu(e).
**allude** [ə'luːd] *vi*: **to ~ to** faire allusion à.
**alluring** [ə'ljuərɪŋ] *a* séduisant(e), alléchant(e).
**allusion** [ə'luːʒən] *n* allusion *f*.
**alluvium** [ə'luːvɪəm] *n* alluvions *fpl*.
**ally** ['ælaɪ] *n* allié *m*.
**almighty** [ɔːl'maɪtɪ] *a* tout-puissant.
**almond** ['ɑːmənd] *n* amande *f*.
**almost** ['ɔːlməust] *ad* presque.
**alms** [ɑːmz] *n* aumône(s) *f(pl)*.
**alone** [ə'ləun] *a* seul(e) ; **to leave sb ~** laisser qn tranquille ; **to leave sth ~** ne pas toucher à qch.
**along** [ə'lɔŋ] *prep* le long de // *ad*: **is he coming ~?** vient-il avec nous? ; **he was hopping/limping ~** il venait *or* avançait en sautillant/boitant ; **~ with** en compagnie de ; avec, en plus de ; **~side** *prep* le long de ; au côté de // *ad* bord à bord ; côte à côte.
**aloof** [ə'luːf] *a,ad* à distance, à l'écart ; **~ness** réserve (hautaine), attitude distante.
**aloud** [ə'laud] *ad* à haute voix.
**alphabet** ['ælfəbɛt] *n* alphabet *m* ; **~ical** [-'bɛtɪkəl] *a* alphabétique.
**alpine** ['ælpaɪn] *a* alpin(e), alpestre.
**Alps** [ælps] *npl*: **the ~** les Alpes *fpl*.
**already** [ɔːl'rɛdɪ] *ad* déjà.
**alright** [ɔːl'raɪt] *ad* = **all right**.
**also** ['ɔːlsəu] *ad* aussi.
**altar** ['ɔltə*] *n* autel *m*.
**alter** ['ɔltə*] *vt,vi* changer, modifier ; **~ation** [ɔltə'reɪʃən] *n* changement *m*, modification *f*.
**alternate** *a* [ɔl'tə:nɪt] alterné(e), alternant(e), alternatif(ive) // *vi* ['ɔltə:neɪt] alterner ; **on ~ days** un jour sur deux, tous les deux jours ; **~ly** *ad* alternativement, en alternant ; **alternating** *a (current)* alternatif(ive).
**alternative** [ɔl'tə:nətɪv] *a (solutions)* interchangeable, possible ; *(solution)* autre, de remplacement // *n (choice)* alternative *f* ; *(other possibility)* solution *f* de remplacement *or* de rechange, autre possibilité *f* ; **~ly** *ad*: **~ly one could** une autre *or* l'autre solution serait de.
**alternator** ['ɔltə:neɪtə*] *n (AUT)* alternateur *m*.
**although** [ɔːl'ðəu] *cj* bien que + *sub*.
**altitude** ['æltɪtjuːd] *n* altitude *f*.
**alto** ['æltəu] *n (female)* contralto *m* ; *(male)* haute-contre *f*.
**altogether** [ɔːltə'gɛðə*] *ad* entièrement, tout à fait ; *(on the whole)* tout compte fait ; *(in all)* en tout.
**altruistic** [æltru'ɪstɪk] *a* altruiste.
**aluminium** [ælju'mɪnɪəm], **aluminum** [ə'luːmɪnəm] *(US) n* aluminium *m*.
**always** ['ɔːlweɪz] *ad* toujours.

**am** [æm] *vb see* **be**.
**a.m.** *ad (abbr of ante meridiem)* du matin.
**amalgamate** [ə'mælgəmeɪt] *vt,vi* fusionner ; **amalgamation** [-'meɪʃən] *n* fusion *f* ; *(COMM)* fusionnement *m* ; amalgame *m*.
**amass** [ə'mæs] *vt* amasser.
**amateur** ['æmətə*] *n* amateur *m* // *a (SPORT)* amateur *inv* ; **~ish** *a (pej)* d'amateur.
**amaze** [ə'meɪz] *vt* stupéfier ; **~ment** *n* stupéfaction *f*, stupeur *f*.
**ambassador** [æm'bæsədə*] *n* ambassadeur *m*.
**amber** ['æmbə*] *n* ambre *m* ; **at ~** *(AUT)* à l'orange.
**ambidextrous** [æmbɪ'dɛkstrəs] *a* ambidextre.
**ambiguity** [æmbɪ'gjuɪtɪ] *n* ambiguïté *f*.
**ambiguous** [æm'bɪgjuəs] *a* ambigu(ë).
**ambition** [æm'bɪʃən] *n* ambition *f*.
**ambitious** [æm'bɪʃəs] *a* ambitieux(euse).
**ambivalent** [æm'bɪvələnt] *a (attitude)* ambivalent(e).
**amble** ['æmbl] *vi (gen*: **to ~ along**) aller d'un pas tranquille.
**ambulance** ['æmbjuləns] *n* ambulance *f*.
**ambush** ['æmbuʃ] *n* embuscade *f* // *vt* tendre une embuscade à.
**ameliorate** [ə'miːlɪəreɪt] *vt* améliorer.
**amenable** [ə'miːnəbl] *a*: **~ to** *(advice etc)* disposé(e) à écouter *or* suivre ; **~ to the law** responsable devant la loi.
**amend** [ə'mɛnd] *vt (law)* amender ; *(text)* corriger ; *(habits)* réformer // *vi* s'amender, se corriger ; **to make ~s** réparer ses torts, faire amende honorable ; **~ment** *n (to law)* amendement *m* ; *(to text)* correction *f*.
**amenities** [ə'miːnɪtɪz] *npl* aménagements *mpl (prévus pour le loisir des habitants)*.
**amenity** [ə'miːnɪtɪ] *n* charme *m*, agrément *m*.
**America** [ə'mɛrɪkə] *n* Amérique *f* ; **~n** *a* américain(e) // *n* Américain/e ; **a~nize** *vt* américaniser.
**amethyst** ['æmɪθɪst] *n* améthyste *f*.
**amiable** ['eɪmɪəbl] *a* aimable, affable.
**amicable** ['æmɪkəbl] *a* amical(e).
**amid(st)** [ə'mɪd(st)] *prep* parmi, au milieu de.
**amiss** [ə'mɪs] *a,ad*: **there's something ~** il y a quelque chose qui ne va pas *or* qui cloche ; **to take sth ~** prendre qch mal *or* de travers.
**ammunition** [æmju'nɪʃən] *n* munitions *fpl*.
**amnesia** [æm'niːzɪə] *n* amnésie *f*.
**amnesty** ['æmnɪstɪ] *n* amnistie *f*.
**amok** [ə'mɔk] *ad*: **to run ~** être pris(e) d'un accès de folie furieuse.
**among(st)** [ə'mʌŋ(st)] *prep* parmi, entre.
**amoral** [æ'mɔrəl] *a* amoral(e).
**amorous** ['æmərəs] *a* amoureux(euse).
**amorphous** [ə'mɔːfəs] *a* amorphe.
**amount** [ə'maunt] *n* somme *f* ; montant *m* ; quantité *f* ; nombre *m* // *vi*: **to ~ to** *(total)* s'élever à ; *(be same as)* équivaloir à, revenir à.

**amp(ère)** ['æmp(εə*)] *n* ampère *m*.
**amphibian** [æm'fɪbɪən] *n* batracien *m*.
**amphibious** [æm'fɪbɪəs] *a* amphibie.
**amphitheatre**          ['æmfɪθɪətə*] *n* amphithéâtre *m*.
**ample** ['æmpl] *a* ample ; spacieux(euse) ; (*enough*): **this is** ~ c'est largement suffisant ; **to have** ~ **time/room** avoir bien assez de temps/place, avoir largement le temps/la place.
**amplifier** ['æmplɪfaɪə*] *n* amplificateur *m*.
**amplify** ['æmplɪfaɪ] *vt* amplifier.
**amply** ['æmplɪ] *ad* amplement, largement.
**amputate** ['æmpjuteɪt] *vt* amputer.
**amuck** [ə'mʌk] *ad* = **amok**.
**amuse** [ə'mjuːz] *vt* amuser ; ~**ment** *n* amusement *m*.
**an** [æn, ən, n] *det see* **a**.
**anaemia** [ə'niːmɪə] *n* anémie *f*.
**anaemic** [ə'niːmɪk] *a* anémique.
**anaesthetic** [ænɪs'θεtɪk] *a,n* anesthésique (*m*) ; **under the** ~ sous anesthésie.
**anaesthetist** [æ'niːsθɪtɪst] *n* anesthésiste *m/f*.
**anagram** ['ænəgræm] *n* anagramme *m*.
**analgesic** [ænæl'dʒiːsɪk] *a,n* analgésique (*m*).
**analogy** [ə'nælədʒɪ] *n* analogie *f*.
**analyse** ['ænəlaɪz] *vt* analyser.
**analysis**, *pl* **analyses** [ə'næləsɪs, -siːz] *n* analyse *f*.
**analyst** ['ænəlɪst] *n* (*US*) psychanalyste *m/f*.
**analytic(al)** [ænə'lɪtɪk(əl)] *a* analytique.
**analyze** ['ænəlaɪz] *vt* (*US*) = **analyse**.
**anarchist** ['ænəkɪst] *a,n* anarchiste (*m/f*).
**anarchy** ['ænəkɪ] *n* anarchie *f*.
**anathema** [ə'næθɪmə] *n*: **it is** ~ **to him** il a cela en abomination.
**anatomical** [ænə'tɔmɪkəl] *a* anatomique.
**anatomy** [ə'nætəmɪ] *n* anatomie *f*.
**ancestor** ['ænsɪstə*] *n* ancêtre *m*, aïeul *m*.
**ancestral** [æn'sεstrəl] *a* ancestral(e).
**ancestry** ['ænsɪstrɪ] *n* ancêtres *mpl* ; ascendance *f*.
**anchor** ['æŋkə*] *n* ancre *f* // *vi* (*also*: **to drop** ~) jeter l'ancre, mouiller // *vt* mettre à l'ancre ; ~**age** *n* mouillage *m*, ancrage *m*.
**anchovy** ['æntʃəvɪ] *n* anchois *m*.
**ancient** ['eɪnʃənt] *a* ancien(ne), antique ; (*fig*) d'un âge vénérable, antique.
**and** [ænd] *cj* et ; ~ **so on** et ainsi de suite ; **try** ~ **come** tâchez de venir ; **come** ~ **sit here** viens t'asseoir ici ; **better** ~ **better** de mieux en mieux ; **more** ~ **more** de plus en plus.
**Andes** ['ændiːz] *npl*: **the** ~ les Andes *fpl*.
**anecdote** ['ænɪkdəut] *n* anecdote *f*.
**anemia** [ə'niːmɪə] *n* = **anaemia**.
**anemic** [ə'niːmɪk] *a* = **anaemic**.
**anesthetic** [ænɪs'θεtɪk] *a,n* = **anaesthetic**.
**anesthetist** [æ'niːsθɪtɪst] *n* = **anaesthetist**.
**anew** [ə'njuː] *ad* à nouveau.
**angel** ['eɪndʒəl] *n* ange *m*.
**anger** ['æŋgə*] *n* colère *f* // *vt* mettre en colère, irriter.

**angina** [æn'dʒaɪnə] *n* angine *f* de poitrine.
**angle** ['æŋgl] *n* angle *m* ; **from their** ~ de leur point de vue // *vi*: **to** ~ **for** (*trout*) pêcher ; (*compliments*) chercher, quêter ; ~**r** *n* pêcheur/euse à la ligne.
**Anglican** ['æŋglɪkən] *a,n* anglican(e).
**anglicize** ['æŋglɪsaɪz] *vt* angliciser.
**angling** ['æŋglɪŋ] *n* pêche *f* à la ligne.
**Anglo-** ['æŋgləu] *prefix* anglo(-) ; ~**Saxon** *a,n* anglo-saxon(ne).
**angrily** ['æŋgrɪlɪ] *ad* avec colère.
**angry** ['æŋgrɪ] *a* en colère, furieux(euse) ; **to be** ~ **with sb/at sth** être furieux contre qn/de qch ; **to get** ~ se fâcher, se mettre en colère ; **to make sb** ~ mettre qn en colère.
**anguish** ['æŋgwɪʃ] *n* angoisse *f*.
**angular** ['æŋgjulə*] *a* anguleux(euse).
**animal** ['ænɪməl] *n* animal *m* // *a* animal(e) ; ~ **spirits** *npl* entrain *m*, vivacité *f*.
**animate** *vt* ['ænɪmeɪt] animer // *a* ['ænɪmɪt] animé(e), vivant(e) ; ~**d** *a* animé(e).
**animosity** [ænɪ'mɔsɪtɪ] *n* animosité *f*.
**aniseed** ['ænɪsiːd] *n* anis *m*.
**ankle** ['æŋkl] *n* cheville *f*.
**annex** *n* ['ænεks] (*also*: **annexe**) annexe *f* // *vt* [ə'nεks] annexer ; ~**ation** [-'eɪʃən] *n* annexion *f*.
**annihilate** [ə'naɪəleɪt] *vt* annihiler, anéantir.
**anniversary** [ænɪ'vəːsərɪ] *n* anniversaire *m* ; ~ **dinner** *n* dîner commémoratif *or* anniversaire.
**annotate** ['ænəuteɪt] *vt* annoter.
**announce** [ə'nauns] *vt* annoncer ; (*birth, death*) faire part de ; ~**ment** *n* annonce *f* ; (*for births etc: in newspaper*) avis *m* de faire-part ; (*:letter, card*) faire-part *m* ; ~**r** *n* (*RADIO, TV*) (*between programmes*) speaker/ine ; (*in a programme*) présentateur/trice.
**annoy** [ə'nɔɪ] *vt* agacer, ennuyer, contrarier ; **don't get** ~**ed!** ne vous fâchez pas! ; ~**ance** *n* mécontentement *m*, contrariété *f* ; ~**ing** *a* ennuyeux(euse), agaçant(e), contrariant(e).
**annual** ['ænjuəl] *a* annuel(le) // *n* (*BOT*) plante annuelle ; (*book*) album *m* ; ~**ly** *ad* annuellement.
**annuity** [ə'njuːɪtɪ] *n* rente *f* ; **life** ~ rente viagère.
**annul** [ə'nʌl] *vt* annuler ; (*law*) abroger ; ~**ment** *n* annulation *f* ; abrogation *f*.
**annum** ['ænəm] *n see* **per**.
**anoint** [ə'nɔɪnt] *vt* oindre.
**anomalous** [ə'nɔmələs] *a* anormal(e).
**anomaly** [ə'nɔməlɪ] *n* anomalie *f*.
**anonymity** [ænə'nɪmɪtɪ] *n* anonymat *m*.
**anonymous** [ə'nɔnɪməs] *a* anonyme.
**anorak** ['ænəræk] *n* anorak *m*.
**another** [ə'nʌðə*] *a*: ~ **book** (*one more*) un autre livre, encore un livre, un livre de plus ; (*a different one*) un autre livre // *pronoun* un(e) autre, encore un(e), un(e) de plus ; *see also* **one**.
**answer** ['ɑːnsə*] *n* réponse *f* ; solution *f* // *vi* répondre // *vt* (*reply to*) répondre à ; (*problem*) résoudre ; (*prayer*) exaucer ; **to** ~ **the phone** répondre (au téléphone) ;

in ~ to your letter suite à or en réponse à votre lettre ; to ~ the bell or the door aller or venir ouvrir (la porte) ; to ~ back vi répondre, répliquer ; to ~ for vt fus répondre de, se porter garant de ; être responsable de ; to ~ to vt fus (description) répondre or correspondre à ; ~able a: ~able (to sb/for sth) responsable (devant qn/de qch) ; I am ~able to no-one je n'ai de comptes à rendre à personne.

**ant** [ænt] n fourmi f.

**antagonism** [æn'tægənɪzəm] n antagonisme m.

**antagonist** [æn'tægənɪst] n antagoniste m/f, adversaire m/f ; ~ic [æntægə'nɪstɪk] a opposé(e) ; antagoniste.

**antagonize** [æn'tægənaɪz] vt éveiller l'hostilité de, contrarier.

**Antarctic** [ænt'ɑːktɪk] n Antarctique m // a antarctique, austral(e).

**anteater** ['ænti:tə*] n fourmilier m, tamanoir m.

**antecedent** [æntɪ'siːdənt] n antécédent m.

**antelope** ['æntɪləup] n antilope f.

**antenatal** ['æntɪ'neɪtl] a prénatal(e) ; ~ clinic n service m de consultation prénatale.

**antenna, pl ~e** [æn'tɛnə, -niː] n antenne f.

**anthem** ['ænθəm] n motet m ; **national ~** hymne national.

**ant-hill** ['ænthɪl] n fourmilière f.

**anthology** [æn'θɒlədʒɪ] n anthologie f.

**anthropologist** [ænθrə'pɒlədʒɪst] n anthropologue m/f.

**anthropology** [ænθrə'pɒlədʒɪ] n anthropologie f.

**anti-** ['æntɪ] prefix anti-.

**anti-aircraft** ['æntɪ'ɛəkrɑːft] a antiaérien(ne) ; ~ **defence** n défense f contre avions, DCA f.

**antibiotic** ['æntɪbaɪ'ɒtɪk] a,n antibiotique (m).

**anticipate** [æn'tɪsɪpeɪt] vt s'attendre à ; prévoir ; (wishes, request) aller au devant de, devancer.

**anticipation** [æntɪsɪ'peɪʃən] n attente f ; thanking you in ~ en vous remerciant d'avance, avec mes remerciements anticipés.

**anticlimax** ['æntɪ'klaɪmæks] n réalisation décevante d'un événement que l'on escomptait important, intéressant etc.

**anticlockwise** ['æntɪ'klɒkwaɪz] a dans le sens inverse des aiguilles d'une montre.

**antics** ['æntɪks] npl singeries fpl.

**anticyclone** ['æntɪ'saɪkləun] n anticyclone m.

**antidote** ['æntɪdəut] n antidote m, contrepoison m.

**antifreeze** ['æntɪ'friːz] n antigel m.

**antipathy** [æn'tɪpəθɪ] n antipathie f.

**antiquarian** [æntɪ'kwɛərɪən] a: ~ **bookshop** librairie f d'ouvrages anciens // n expert m en objets or livres anciens ; amateur m d'antiquités.

**antiquated** ['æntɪkweɪtɪd] a vieilli(e), suranné(e), vieillot(te).

**antique** [æn'tiːk] n objet m d'art ancien, meuble ancien or d'époque, antiquité f //

a ancien(ne) ; (pre-mediaeval) antique ; ~ **dealer** n antiquaire m/f ; ~ **shop** n magasin m d'antiquités.

**antiquity** [æn'tɪkwɪtɪ] n antiquité f.

**antiseptic** [æntɪ'sɛptɪk] a,n antiseptique (m).

**antisocial** ['æntɪ'səuʃəl] a peu liant(e), sauvage, insociable ; (against society) anti-social(e).

**antlers** ['æntləz] npl bois mpl, ramure f.

**anus** ['eɪnəs] n anus m.

**anvil** ['ænvɪl] n enclume f.

**anxiety** [æŋ'zaɪətɪ] n anxiété f ; (keenness): ~ **to do** grand désir or impatience f de faire.

**anxious** ['æŋkʃəs] a anxieux(euse), (très) inquiet(ète) ; (keen): ~ **to do/that** qui tient beaucoup à faire/à ce que ; impatient(e) de faire/que ; ~**ly** ad anxieusement.

**any** ['ɛnɪ] a (in negative and interrogative sentences = some) de, d' ; du, de l', de la, des ; (no matter which) n'importe quel(le), quelconque ; (each and every) tout(e), chaque ; I haven't ~ **money/books** je n'ai pas d'argent/de livres ; have you ~ **butter/children?** avez-vous du beurre/des enfants? ; **without** ~ **difficulty** sans la moindre difficulté ; **come (at)** ~ **time** venez à n'importe quelle heure ; **at** ~ **moment** à tout moment, d'un instant à l'autre ; **in** ~ **case** de toute façon ; en tout cas ; **at** ~ **rate** de toute façon // pronoun n'importe lequel(laquelle) ; (anybody) n'importe qui ; (in negative and interrogative sentences): I haven't ~ je n'en ai pas, je n'en ai aucun ; have you got ~? en avez-vous? ; can ~ of you sing? est-ce que l'un d'entre vous or quelqu'un parmi vous sait chanter? // ad (in negative sentences) nullement, aucunement ; (in interrogative and conditional constructions) un peu ; tant soit peu ; I can't hear him ~ more je ne l'entends plus ; are you feeling ~ better? vous sentez-vous un peu mieux? ; do you want ~ more soup? voulez-vous encore un peu de soupe? ; ~**body** pronoun n'importe qui ; (in interrogative sentences) quelqu'un ; (in negative sentences): I don't see ~**body** je ne vois personne ; ~**how** ad quoi qu'il en soit ; ~**one** = ~**body** ; ~**thing** pronoun (see anybody) n'importe quoi ; quelque chose ; ne ... rien ; ~**time** ad n'importe quand ; ~**way** ad de toute façon ; ~**where** ad (see anybody) n'importe où ; quelque part ; I don't see him ~**where** je ne le vois nulle part.

**apart** [ə'pɑːt] ad (to one side) à part ; de côté ; à l'écart ; (separately) séparément ; 10 **miles/a long way** ~ à 10 milles/très éloignés l'un de l'autre ; they are living ~ ils sont séparés ; ~ **from** prep à part, excepté.

**apartheid** [ə'pɑːteɪt] n apartheid m.

**apartment** [ə'pɑːtmənt] n (US) appartement m, logement m ; ~**s** npl appartement m.

**apathetic** [æpə'θɛtɪk] a apathique, indifférent(e).

**apathy** ['æpəθɪ] n apathie f, indifférence f.

**ape** [eɪp] n (grand) singe // vt singer.
**aperitif** [ə'pɛrɪtɪv] n apéritif m.
**aperture** ['æpətʃjuə*] n orifice m, ouverture f; (PHOT) ouverture (du diaphragme).
**apex** ['eɪpɛks] n sommet m.
**aphrodisiac** [æfrəʊ'dɪzɪæk] a,n aphrodisiaque (m).
**apiece** [ə'piːs] ad (for each person) chacun(e), par tête; (for each item) chacun(e), (la) pièce.
**aplomb** [ə'plɔm] n sang-froid m, assurance f.
**apocalypse** [ə'pɔkəlɪps] n apocalypse f.
**apolitical** [eɪpə'lɪtɪkl] a apolitique.
**apologetic** [əpɔlə'dʒɛtɪk] a (tone, letter) d'excuse; **to be very ~ about** s'excuser vivement de.
**apologize** [ə'pɔlədʒaɪz] vi: **to ~ (for sth to sb)** s'excuser (de qch auprès de qn), présenter des excuses (à qn pour qch).
**apology** [ə'pɔlədʒɪ] n excuses fpl; **to send one's apologies** envoyer une lettre or un mot d'excuse, s'excuser (de ne pas pouvoir venir).
**apoplexy** ['æpəplɛksɪ] n apoplexie f.
**apostle** [ə'pɔsl] n apôtre m.
**apostrophe** [ə'pɔstrəfɪ] n apostrophe f.
**appal** [ə'pɔːl] vt consterner, atterrer; horrifier; **~ling** a épouvantable; (stupidity) consternant(e).
**apparatus** [æpə'reɪtəs] n appareil m, dispositif m.
**apparent** [ə'pærənt] a apparent(e); **~ly** ad apparemment.
**apparition** [æpə'rɪʃən] n apparition f.
**appeal** [ə'piːl] vi (LAW) faire or interjeter appel // n (LAW) appel m; (request) prière f; appel m; (charm) attrait m, charme m; **to ~ for** demander (instamment); implorer; **to ~ to** (subj: person) faire appel à; (subj: thing) plaire à; **to ~ to sb for mercy** implorer la pitié de qn, prier or adjurer qn d'avoir pitié; **it doesn't ~ to me** cela ne m'attire pas; **~ing** a (nice) attrayant(e); (touching) attendrissant(e).
**appear** [ə'pɪə*] vi apparaître, se montrer; (LAW) comparaître; (publication) paraître, sortir, être publié(e); (seem) paraître, sembler; **it would ~ that** il semble que; **to ~ in Hamlet** jouer dans Hamlet; **to ~ on TV** passer à la télé; **~ance** n apparition f; parution f; (look, aspect) apparence f, aspect m; **to put in or make an ~ance** faire acte de présence; (THEATRE): **by order of ~ance** par ordre d'entrée en scène.
**appease** [ə'piːz] vt apaiser, calmer.
**appendage** [ə'pɛndɪdʒ] n appendice m.
**appendicitis** [əpɛndɪ'saɪtɪs] n appendicite f.
**appendix, pl appendices** [ə'pɛndɪks, -siːz] n appendice m.
**appetite** ['æpɪtaɪt] n appétit m.
**appetizing** ['æpɪtaɪzɪŋ] a appétissant(e).
**applaud** [ə'plɔːd] vt,vi applaudir.
**applause** [ə'plɔːz] n applaudissements mpl.
**apple** ['æpl] n pomme f; **it's the ~ of my eye** j'y tiens comme à la prunelle de mes

yeux; **~ tree** n pommier m; **~ turnover** n chausson m aux pommes.
**appliance** [ə'plaɪəns] n appareil m.
**applicable** [ə'plɪkəbl] a applicable.
**applicant** ['æplɪkənt] n candidat/e (for a post à un poste).
**application** [æplɪ'keɪʃən] n application f; (for a job, a grant etc) demande f; candidature f; **on ~** sur demande.
**applied** [ə'plaɪd] a appliqué(e); **~ arts** npl arts décoratifs.
**apply** [ə'plaɪ] vt (paint, ointment): **to ~ (to)** appliquer (sur); (theory, technique): **to ~ (to)** appliquer (à) // vi: **to ~ to** (ask) s'adresser à; (be suitable for, relevant to) s'appliquer à; se rapporter à; être valable pour; **to ~ (for)** (permit, grant) faire une demande (en vue d'obtenir); (job) poser sa candidature (pour), faire une demande d'emploi (concernant); **to ~ the brakes** actionner les freins, freiner; **to ~ o.s. to** s'appliquer à.
**appoint** [ə'pɔɪnt] vt nommer, engager; (date, place) fixer, désigner; **~ment** n nomination f; rendez-vous m; **to make an ~ment (with)** prendre rendez-vous (avec).
**apportion** [ə'pɔːʃən] vt (share out) répartir, distribuer; **to ~ sth to sb** attribuer or assigner or allouer qch à qn.
**appraisal** [ə'preɪzl] n évaluation f.
**appreciable** [ə'priːʃəbl] a appréciable.
**appreciate** [ə'priːʃɪeɪt] vt (like) apprécier, faire cas de; être reconnaissant(e) de; (assess) évaluer; (be aware of) comprendre; se rendre compte de // vi (FINANCE) prendre de la valeur.
**appreciation** [əpriːʃɪ'eɪʃən] n appréciation f; reconnaissance f; (COMM) hausse f, valorisation f.
**appreciative** [ə'priːʃɪətɪv] a (person) sensible; (comment) élogieux(euse).
**apprehend** [æprɪ'hɛnd] vt appréhender, arrêter; (understand) comprendre.
**apprehension** [æprɪ'hɛnʃən] n appréhension f, inquiétude f.
**apprehensive** [æprɪ'hɛnsɪv] a inquiet-(ète), appréhensif(ive).
**apprentice** [ə'prɛntɪs] n apprenti m; **~ship** n apprentissage m.
**approach** [ə'prəʊtʃ] vi approcher // vt (come near) approcher de; (ask, apply to) s'adresser à; (subject, passer-by) aborder // n approche f; accès m, abord m; démarche f (auprès de qn); démarche (intellectuelle); **~able** a accessible.
**approbation** [æprə'beɪʃən] n approbation f.
**appropriate** vt [ə'prəʊprɪeɪt] (take) s'approprier; (allot): **to ~ sth for** affecter qch à // a [ə'prəʊprɪt] opportun(e); qui convient, approprié(e); **~ly** ad pertinemment, avec à-propos.
**approval** [ə'pruːvəl] n approbation f; **on ~** (COMM) à l'examen.
**approve** [ə'pruːv] vt approuver; **to ~ of** vt fus approuver; **~d school** n centre m d'éducation surveillée; **approvingly** ad d'un air approbateur.
**approximate** a [ə'prɔksɪmɪt] approximatif(ive) // vt [ə'prɔksɪmeɪt] se rapprocher de; être proche de;

**approximation** [-'meiʃən] *n* approximation *f*.

**apricot** ['eiprikɔt] *n* abricot *m*.

**April** ['eiprəl] *n* avril *m* ; ~ **fool!** poisson d'avril!

**apron** ['eiprən] *n* tablier *m*.

**apt** [æpt] *a* (*suitable*) approprié(e) ; (*able*): ~ **(at)** doué(e) (pour) ; apte (à) ; (*likely*): ~ **to do** susceptible de faire ; ayant tendance à faire.

**aptitude** ['æptitju:d] *n* aptitude *f*.

**aqualung** ['ækwəlʌŋ] *n* scaphandre *m* autonome.

**aquarium** [ə'kwɛəriəm] *n* aquarium *m*.

**Aquarius** [ə'kwɛəriəs] *n* le Verseau ; **to be** ~ être du Verseau.

**aquatic** [ə'kwætik] *a* aquatique ; (*SPORT*) nautique.

**aqueduct** ['ækwidʌkt] *n* aqueduc *m*.

**Arab** ['ærəb] *n* Arabe *m/f*.

**Arabia** [ə'reibiə] *n* Arabie *f* ; ~**n** *a* arabe.

**Arabic** ['ærəbik] *a*,*n* arabe (*m*).

**arable** ['ærəbl] *a* arable.

**arbiter** ['ɑ:bitə*] *n* arbitre *m*.

**arbitrary** ['ɑ:bitrəri] *a* arbitraire.

**arbitrate** ['ɑ:bitreit] *vi* arbitrer ; trancher ; **arbitration** [-'treiʃən] *n* arbitrage *m*.

**arbitrator** ['ɑ:bitreitə*] *n* arbitre *m*, médiateur/trice.

**arc** [ɑ:k] *n* arc *m*.

**arcade** [ɑ:'keid] *n* arcade *f* ; (*passage with shops*) passage *m*, galerie *f*.

**arch** [ɑ:tʃ] *n* arche *f* ; (*of foot*) cambrure *f*, voûte *f* plantaire // *vt* arquer, cambrer // *a* malicieux(euse) // *prefix*: ~**(-)** achevé(e) ; par excellence ; **pointed** ~ *n* ogive *f*.

**archaeologist** [ɑ:ki'ɔlədʒist] *n* archéologue *m/f*.

**archaeology** [ɑ:ki'ɔlədʒi] *n* archéologie *f*.

**archaic** [ɑ:'keiik] *a* archaïque.

**archbishop** [ɑ:tʃ'biʃəp] *n* archevêque *m*.

**arch-enemy** ['ɑ:tʃ'enimi] *n* ennemi *m* de toujours *or* par excellence.

**archeologist** [ɑ:ki'ɔlədʒist] *n* (*US*) = **archaeologist**.

**archeology** [ɑ:ki'ɔlədʒi] *n* (*US*) = **archaeology**.

**archer** ['ɑ:tʃə*] *n* archer *m* ; ~**y** *n* tir *m* à l'arc.

**archetype** ['ɑ:kitaip] *n* prototype *m*, archétype *m*.

**archipelago** [ɑ:ki'pɛligəu] *n* archipel *m*.

**architect** ['ɑ:kitɛkt] *n* architecte *m* ; ~**ural** [ɑ:ki'tɛktʃərəl] *a* architectural(e) ; ~**ure** ['ɑ:kitɛktʃə*] *n* architecture *f*.

**archives** ['ɑ:kaivz] *npl* archives *fpl* ; **archivist** ['ɑ:kivist] *n* archiviste *m/f*.

**archway** ['ɑ:tʃwei] *n* voûte *f*, porche voûté *or* cintré.

**Arctic** ['ɑ:ktik] *a* arctique // *n*: **the** ~ l'Arctique *m*.

**ardent** ['ɑ:dənt] *a* fervent(e).

**arduous** ['ɑ:djuəs] *a* ardu(e).

**are** [ɑ:*] *vb see* **be**.

**area** ['ɛəriə] *n* (*GEOM*) superficie *f* ; (*zone*) région *f* ; (*:smaller*) secteur *m* ; **dining** ~ *n* coin *m* salle à manger.

**arena** [ə'ri:nə] *n* arène *f*.

**aren't** [ɑ:nt] = **are not**.

**Argentina** [ɑ:dʒən'ti:nə] *n* Argentine *f* ; **Argentinian** [-'tiniən] *a* argentin(e) // *n* Argentin/e.

**arguable** ['ɑ:gjuəbl] *a* discutable.

**argue** ['ɑ:gju:] *vi* (*quarrel*) se disputer ; (*reason*) argumenter ; **to** ~ **that** objecter *or* alléguer que, donner comme argument que.

**argument** ['ɑ:gjumənt] *n* (*reasons*) argument *m* ; (*quarrel*) dispute *f*, discussion *f* ; (*debate*) discussion *f*, controverse *f* ; ~**ative** [ɑ:gju'mɛntətiv] *a* ergoteur(euse), raisonneur(euse).

**arid** ['ærid] *a* aride ; ~**ity** [ə'riditi] *n* aridité *f*.

**Aries** ['ɛəriz] *n* le Bélier ; **to be** ~ être du Bélier.

**arise,** *pt* **arose,** *pp* **arisen** [ə'raiz, -'rəuz, -'rizn] *vi* survenir, se présenter ; **to** ~ **from** résulter de.

**aristocracy** [æris'tɔkrəsi] *n* aristocratie *f*.

**aristocrat** ['æristəkræt] *n* aristocrate *m/f* ; ~**ic** [-'krætik] *a* aristocratique.

**arithmetic** [ə'riθmətik] *n* arithmétique *f*.

**ark** [ɑ:k] *n*: **Noah's A**~ l'Arche *f* de Noé.

**arm** [ɑ:m] *n* bras *m* ; (*MIL: branch*) arme *f* // *vt* armer ; ~**s** *npl* (*weapons, HERALDRY*) armes *fpl* ; ~ **in** ~ bras dessus bras dessous ; ~**band** *n* brassard *m* ; ~**chair** *n* fauteuil *m* ; ~**ed** *a* armé(e) ; ~**ed robbery** *n* vol *m* à main armée ; ~**ful** *n* brassée *f*.

**armistice** ['ɑ:mistis] *n* armistice *m*.

**armour** ['ɑ:mə*] *n* armure *f* ; (*also*: ~-**plating**) blindage *m* ; (*MIL: tanks*) blindés *mpl* ; ~**ed car** *n* véhicule blindé ; ~**y** *n* arsenal *m*.

**armpit** ['ɑ:mpit] *n* aisselle *f*.

**army** ['ɑ:mi] *n* armée *f*.

**aroma** [ə'rəumə] *n* arôme *m* ; ~**tic** [ærə'mætik] *a* aromatique.

**arose** [ə'rəuz] *pt of* **arise**.

**around** [ə'raund] *ad* (tout) autour ; dans les parages // *prep* autour de ; (*fig: about*) environ ; vers ; **is he** ~? est-il dans les parages *or* là?

**arouse** [ə'rauz] *vt* (*sleeper*) éveiller ; (*curiosity, passions*) éveiller, susciter ; exciter.

**arpeggio** [ɑ:'pɛdʒiəu] *n* arpège *m*.

**arrange** [ə'reindʒ] *vt* arranger ; (*programme*) arrêter, convenir de ; ~**ment** *n* arrangement *m* ; (*plans etc*): ~**ments** dispositions *fpl*.

**array** [ə'rei] *n*: ~ **of** déploiement *m* or étalage *m* de.

**arrears** [ə'riəz] *npl* arriéré *m* ; **to be in** ~ **with one's rent** devoir un arriéré de loyer, être en retard pour le paiement de son loyer.

**arrest** [ə'rɛst] *vt* arrêter ; (*sb's attention*) retenir, attirer // *n* arrestation *f* ; **under** ~ en état d'arrestation.

**arrival** [ə'raivəl] *n* arrivée *f* ; (*COMM*) arrivage *m* ; (*person*) arrivant/e.

**arrive** [ə'raiv] *vi* arriver ; **to** ~ **at** *vt fus* (*fig*) parvenir à.

**arrogance** ['ærəgəns] *n* arrogance *f*.

**arrogant** ['ærəgənt] *a* arrogant(e).

**arrow** ['ærəu] *n* flèche *f.*
**arsenal** ['ɑ:sɪnl] *n* arsenal *m.*
**arsenic** ['ɑ:snɪk] *n* arsenic *m.*
**arson** ['ɑ:sn] *n* incendie criminel.
**art** [ɑ:t] *n* art *m* ; (*craft*) métier *m* ; **A~s** *npl* (*SCOL*) les lettres *fpl* ; ~ **gallery** *n* musée *m* d'art ; (*small and private*) galerie *f* de peinture.
**artefact** ['ɑ:tɪfækt] *n* objet fabriqué.
**artery** ['ɑ:tərɪ] *n* artère *f.*
**artful** ['ɑ:tful] *a* rusé(e).
**arthritis** [ɑ:'θraɪtɪs] *n* arthrite *f.*
**artichoke** ['ɑ:tɪtʃəuk] *n* artichaut *m.*
**article** ['ɑ:tɪkl] *n* article *m* ; (*LAW: training*): ~**s** *npl* ≈ stage *m.*
**articulate** *a* [ɑ:'tɪkjulɪt] (*person*) qui s'exprime clairement et aisément ; (*speech*) bien articulé(e), prononcé(e) clairement // *vi* [ɑ:'tɪkjuleɪt] articuler, parler distinctement ; ~**d lorry** *n* (camion *m*) semi-remorque *m.*
**artifice** ['ɑ:tɪfɪs] *n* ruse *f.*
**artificial** [ɑ:tɪ'fɪʃəl] *a* artificiel(le) ; ~ **respiration** *n* respiration artificielle.
**artillery** [ɑ:'tɪlərɪ] *n* artillerie *f.*
**artisan** ['ɑ:tɪzæn] *n* artisan/e.
**artist** ['ɑ:tɪst] *n* artiste *m/f* ; ~**ic** [ɑ:'tɪstɪk] *a* artistique ; ~**ry** *n* art *m*, talent *m.*
**artless** ['ɑ:tlɪs] *a* naïf(ïve), simple, ingénu(e).
**as** [æz, əz] *cj* (*cause*) comme, puisque ; (*time: moment*) alors que, comme ; (*duration*) tandis que ; (*manner*) comme ; (*in the capacity of*) en tant que, en qualité de ; ~ **big** ~ aussi grand que ; **twice** ~ **big** ~ deux fois plus grand que ; **big** ~ **it is** si grand que ce soit ; ~ **she said** comme elle l'avait dit ; ~ **if** *or* **though** comme si ; ~ **for** *or* **to** en ce qui concerne, quant à ; ~ **or so long** ~ *cj* à condition que ; si ; ~ **much/many** (~) autant (que) ; ~ **soon** ~ *cj* aussitôt que, dès que ; ~ **such** *ad* en tant que tel(le) ; ~ **well** *ad* aussi ; ~ **well** ~ *cj* en plus de, en même temps que ; *see also* **so, such**.
**asbestos** [æz'bɛstəs] *n* asbeste *m*, amiante *m.*
**ascend** [ə'sɛnd] *vt* gravir ; ~**ancy** *n* ascendant *m.*
**ascent** [ə'sɛnt] *n* ascension *f.*
**ascertain** [æsə'teɪn] *vt* s'assurer de, vérifier ; établir.
**ascetic** [ə'sɛtɪk] *a* ascétique.
**ascribe** [ə'skraɪb] *vt:* **to** ~ **sth to** attribuer qch à ; (*blame*) imputer qch à.
**ash** [æʃ] *n* (*dust*) cendre *f* ; ~ (**tree**) frêne *m.*
**ashamed** [ə'feɪmd] *a* honteux(euse), confus(e) ; **to be** ~ **of** avoir honte de ; **to be** ~ (**of o.s.**) **for having done** avoir honte d'avoir fait.
**ashen** ['æʃn] *a* (*pale*) cendreux(euse), blême.
**ashore** [ə'ʃɔ:*] *ad* à terre ; **to go** ~ aller à terre, débarquer.
**ashtray** ['æʃtreɪ] *n* cendrier *m.*
**Asia** ['eɪʃə] *n* Asie *f* ; ~ **Minor** *n* Asie Mineure ; ~**n** *n* Asiatique *m/f* // *a* asiatique ; ~**tic** [eɪsɪ'ætɪk] *a* asiatique.
**aside** [ə'saɪd] *ad* de côté ; à l'écart // *n* aparté *m.*

**ask** [ɑ:sk] *vt* demander ; (*invite*) inviter ; **to** ~ **sb sth/to do sth** demander à qn qch/de faire qch ; **to** ~ **sb about sth** questionner qn au sujet de qch ; se renseigner auprès de qn au sujet de qch ; **to** ~ **about the price** s'informer du prix, se renseigner au sujet du prix ; **to** ~ **(sb) a question** poser une question (à qn) ; **to** ~ **sb out to dinner** inviter qn au restaurant ; **to** ~ **for** *vt fus* demander.
**askance** [ə'skɑ:ns] *ad:* **to look** ~ **at sb** regarder qn de travers *or* d'un œil désapprobateur.
**askew** [ə'skju:] *ad* de travers, de guinguois.
**asleep** [ə'sli:p] *a* endormi(e) ; **to be** ~ dormir, être endormi ; **to fall** ~ s'endormir.
**asp** [æsp] *n* aspic *m.*
**asparagus** [əs'pærəgəs] *n* asperges *fpl* ; ~ **tips** *npl* pointes *fpl* d'asperges.
**aspect** ['æspɛkt] *n* aspect *m* ; (*direction in which a building etc faces*) orientation *f*, exposition *f.*
**aspersions** [əs'pə:ʃənz] *npl:* **to cast** ~ **on** dénigrer.
**asphalt** ['æsfælt] *n* asphalte *m.*
**asphyxiate** [æs'fɪksɪeɪt] *vt* asphyxier ; **asphyxiation** [-'eɪʃən] *n* asphyxie *f.*
**aspirate** *vt* ['æspəreɪt] aspirer // *a* ['æspərɪt] aspiré(e).
**aspiration** [æspə'reɪʃən] *n* aspiration *f.*
**aspire** [əs'paɪə*] *vi:* **to** ~ **to** aspirer à.
**aspirin** ['æsprɪn] *n* aspirine *f.*
**ass** [æs] *n* âne *m* ; (*col*) imbécile *m/f.*
**assail** [ə'seɪl] *vt* assaillir ; ~**ant** *n* agresseur *m* ; assaillant *m.*
**assassin** [ə'sæsɪn] *n* assassin *m* ; ~**ate** *vt* assassiner ; ~**ation** [əsæsɪ'neɪʃən] *n* assassinat *m.*
**assault** [ə'sɔ:lt] *n* (*MIL*) assaut *m* ; (*gen: attack*) agression *f* ; (*LAW*): ~ (**and battery**) voies *fpl* de fait, coups *mpl* et blessures *fpl* // *vt* attaquer ; (*sexually*) violenter.
**assemble** [ə'sɛmbl] *vt* assembler // *vi* s'assembler, se rassembler.
**assembly** [ə'sɛmblɪ] *n* (*meeting*) rassemblement *m* ; (*construction*) assemblage *m* ; ~ **line** *n* chaîne *f* de montage.
**assent** [ə'sɛnt] *n* assentiment *m*, consentement *m* // *vi* donner son assentiment, consentir.
**assert** [ə'sə:t] *vt* affirmer, déclarer ; établir ; ~**ion** [ə'sə:ʃən] *n* assertion *f*, affirmation *f* ; ~**ive** *a* assuré(e), péremptoire.
**assess** [ə'sɛs] *vt* évaluer, estimer ; (*tax, damages*) établir *or* fixer le montant de ; (*property etc: for tax*) calculer la valeur imposable de ; ~**ment** *n* évaluation *f*, estimation *f* ; ~**or** *n* expert *m* (*en matière d'impôt et d'assurance*).
**asset** ['æsɛt] *n* avantage *m*, atout *m* ; ~**s** *npl* capital *m* ; avoir(s) *m(pl)* ; actif *m.*
**assiduous** [ə'sɪdjuəs] *a* assidu(e).
**assign** [ə'saɪn] *vt* (*date*) fixer, arrêter ; (*task*): **to** ~ **sth to** assigner qch à ; (*resources*): **to** ~ **sth to** affecter qch à ; (*cause, meaning*): **to** ~ **sth to** attribuer qch à ; ~**ment** *n* tâche *f*, mission *f.*

**assimilate** [ə'sımıleıt] *vt* assimiler ;
**assimilation** [-'leıʃən] *n* assimilation *f*.
**assist** [ə'sıst] *vt* aider, assister ; secourir ;
~**ance** *n* aide *f*, assistance *f* ; secours *mpl* ;
~**ant** *n* assistant/e, adjoint/e ; (*also*: **shop**
~**ant**) vendeur/euse.
**assizes** [ə'saızız] *npl* assises *fpl*.
**associate** *a,n* [ə'səuʃıt] associé(e) // *vb*
[ə'səuʃıeıt] *vt* associer // *vi*: **to** ~ **with**
**sb** fréquenter qn.
**association** [əsəusı'eıʃən] *n* association *f* ;
~ **football** *n* football *m*.
**assorted** [ə'sɔ:tıd] *a* assorti(e).
**assortment** [ə'sɔ:tmənt] *n* assortiment *m*.
**assume** [ə'sju:m] *vt* supposer ;
(*responsibilities etc*) assumer ; (*attitude*,
*name*) prendre, adopter ; ~**d name** *n* nom
*m* d'emprunt.
**assumption** [ə'sʌmpʃən] *n* supposition *f*,
hypothèse *f*.
**assurance** [ə'ʃuərəns] *n* assurance *f*.
**assure** [ə'ʃuə*] *vt* assurer.
**asterisk** ['æstərısk] *n* astérisque *m*.
**astern** [ə'stə:n] *ad* à l'arrière.
**asthma** ['æsmə] *n* asthme *m* ; ~**tic**
[æs'mætık] *a,n* asthmatique (*m/f*).
**astir** [ə'stə:*] *ad* en émoi.
**astonish** [ə'stɔnıʃ] *vt* étonner, stupéfier ;
~**ment** *n* étonnement *m*.
**astound** [ə'staund] *vt* stupéfier, sidérer.
**astray** [ə'streı] *ad*: **to go** ~ s'égarer ; (*fig*)
quitter le droit chemin.
**astride** [ə'straıd] *ad* à cheval // *prep* à
cheval sur.
**astringent** [əs'trındʒənt] *a* astringent(e)
// *n* astringent *m*.
**astrologer** [əs'trɔlədʒə*] *n* astrologue *m*.
**astrology** [əs'trɔlədʒı] *n* astrologie *f*.
**astronaut** ['æstrənɔ:t] *n* astronaute *m/f*.
**astronomer** [əs'trɔnəmə*] *n* astronome *m*.
**astronomical** [æstrə'nɔmıkəl] *a*
astronomique.
**astronomy** [əs'trɔnəmı] *n* astronomie *f*.
**astute** [əs'tju:t] *a* astucieux(euse),
malin(igne).
**asunder** [ə'sʌndə*] *ad*: **to tear** ~ déchirer.
**asylum** [ə'saıləm] *n* asile *m*.
**at** [æt] *prep* à ; (*because of: following surprised, annoyed etc*) de ; par ; ~ **Pierre's**
chez Pierre ; ~ **the baker's** chez le
boulanger, à la boulangerie ; ~ **times**
parfois.
**ate** [eıt] *pt of* **eat**.
**atheism** ['eıθıızəm] *n* athéisme *m*.
**atheist** ['eıθııst] *n* athée *m/f*.
**Athens** ['æθınz] *n* Athènes *m*.
**athlete** ['æθli:t] *n* athlète *m/f*.
**athletic** [æθ'letık] *a* athlétique ; ~**s** *n*
athlétisme *m*.
**Atlantic** [ət'læntık] *a* atlantique // *n*: **the**
~ **(Ocean)** l'Atlantique *m*, l'océan *m*
Atlantique.
**atlas** ['ætləs] *n* atlas *m*.
**atmosphere** ['ætməsfıə*] *n* atmosphère *f*.
**atmospheric** [ætməs'ferık] *a*
atmosphérique ; ~**s** *n* (*RADIO*) parasites
*mpl*.
**atoll** ['ætɔl] *n* atoll *m*.
**atom** ['ætəm] *n* atome *m* ; ~**ic** [ə'tɔmık]
*a* atomique ; ~**(ic) bomb** *n* bombe *f*

atomique ; ~**izer** ['ætəmaızə*] *n*
atomiseur *m*.
**atone** [ə'təun] *vi*: **to** ~ **for** expier, racheter.
**atrocious** [ə'trəuʃəs] *a* (*very bad*) atroce,
exécrable.
**atrocity** [ə'trɔsıtı] *n* atrocité *f*.
**atrophy** ['ætrəfı] *n* atrophie *f* // *vt*
atrophier // *vi* s'atrophier.
**attach** [ə'tætʃ] *vt* (*gen*) attacher ;
(*document, letter*) joindre ; (*MIL*: *troops*)
affecter ; **to be** ~**ed to sb/sth** (*to like*) être
attaché à qn/qch ; ~**é** [ə'tæʃeı] *n* attaché
*m* ; ~**é case** *n* mallette *f*, attaché-case *m* ;
~**ment** *n* (*tool*) accessoire *m* ; (*love*):
~**ment (to)** affection *f* (pour),
attachement *m* (à).
**attack** [ə'tæk] *vt* attaquer ; (*task etc*)
s'attaquer à // *n* attaque *f* ; (*also*: **heart**
~) crise *f* cardiaque ; ~**er** *n* attaquant *m* ;
agresseur *m*.
**attain** [ə'teın] *vt* (*also*: **to** ~ **to**) parvenir
à, atteindre ; acquérir ; ~**ments** *npl*
connaissances *fpl*, résultats *mpl*.
**attempt** [ə'tempt] *n* tentative *f* // *vt*
essayer, tenter ; ~**ed theft** *etc* (*LAW*)
tentative de vol *etc* ; **to make an** ~ **on**
**sb's life** attenter à la vie de qn.
**attend** [ə'tend] *vt* (*course*) suivre ;
(*meeting, talk*) assister à ; (*school, church*)
aller à, fréquenter ; (*patient*) soigner,
s'occuper de ; **to** ~ **(up)on** servir ; être au
service de ; **to** ~ **to** *vt fus* (*needs, affairs*
*etc*) s'occuper de ; (*customer*) s'occuper de,
servir ; ~**ance** *n* (*being present*) présence
*f* ; (*people present*) assistance *f* ; ~**ant** *n*
employé/e ; gardien/ne // *a*
concomitant(e), qui accompagne *or*
s'ensuit.
**attention** [ə'tenʃən] *n* attention *f* ; ~**s**
attentions *fpl*, prévenances *fpl* ; ~**!** (*MIL*)
garde-à-vous! ; **at** ~ (*MIL*) au
garde-à-vous ; **for the** ~ **of** (*ADMIN*) à
l'attention de.
**attentive** [ə'tentıv] *a* attentif(ive) ; (*kind*)
prévenant(e) ; ~**ly** *ad* attentivement, avec
attention.
**attenuate** [ə'tenjueıt] *vt* atténuer // *vi*
s'atténuer.
**attest** [ə'test] *vi*: **to** ~ **to** témoigner de,
attester (de).
**attic** ['ætık] *n* grenier *m*, combles *mpl*.
**attire** [ə'taıə*] *n* habit *m*, atours *mpl*.
**attitude** ['ætıtju:d] *n* attitude *f*, manière
*f* ; pose *f*, maintien *m*.
**attorney** [ə'tə:nı] *n* (*lawyer*) avoué *m* ;
(*having proxy*) mandataire *m* ; **A**~
**General** *n* (*Brit*) ≈ procureur général ;
(*US*) ≈ garde *m* des Sceaux, ministre *m*
de la Justice ; **power of** ~ *n* procuration
*f*.
**attract** [ə'trækt] *vt* attirer ; ~**ion**
[ə'trækʃən] *n* (*gen pl*: *pleasant things*)
attraction *f*, attrait *m* ; (*PHYSICS*) attraction
*f* ; (*fig: towards sth*) attirance *f* ; ~**ive** *a*
séduisant(e), attrayant(e).
**attribute** *n* ['ætrıbju:t] attribut *m* // *vt*
[ə'trıbju:t]: **to** ~ **sth to** attribuer qch à.
**attrition** [ə'trıʃən] *n*: **war of** ~ guerre *f*
d'usure.
**aubergine** ['əubəʒi:n] *n* aubergine *f*.
**auburn** ['ɔ:bən] *a* auburn *inv*, châtain roux
*inv*.

**auction** ['ɔːkʃən] n (also: **sale by** ~) vente f aux enchères // vt (also: **to sell by** ~) vendre aux enchères ; (also: **to put up for** ~) mettre aux enchères ; ~**eer** [-'nɪə*] n commissaire-priseur m.

**audacious** [ɔː'deɪʃəs] a impudent(e) ; audacieux(euse), intrépide.

**audacity** [ɔː'dæsɪtɪ] n impudence f ; audace f.

**audible** ['ɔːdɪbl] a audible.

**audience** ['ɔːdɪəns] n (people) assistance f, auditoire m ; auditeurs mpl ; spectateurs mpl ; (interview) audience f.

**audio-visual** [ɔːdɪəu'vɪzjuəl] a audio-visuel(le).

**audit** ['ɔːdɪt] n vérification f des comptes, apurement m // vt vérifier, apurer.

**audition** [ɔː'dɪʃən] n audition f.

**auditor** ['ɔːdɪtə*] n vérificateur m des comptes.

**auditorium** [ɔːdɪ'tɔːrɪəm] n auditorium m, salle f de concert or de spectacle.

**augment** [ɔːg'mɛnt] vt,vi augmenter.

**augur** ['ɔːgə*] vt (be a sign of) présager, annoncer // vi: **it** ~**s well** c'est bon signe or de bon augure, cela s'annonce bien.

**August** ['ɔːgəst] n août m.

**august** [ɔː'gʌst] a majestueux(euse), imposant(e).

**aunt** [ɑːnt] n tante f ; ~**ie**, ~**y** n diminutive of **aunt**.

**au pair** ['əu'pɛə*] n (also: ~ **girl**) jeune fille f au pair.

**aura** ['ɔːrə] n atmosphère f.

**auspices** ['ɔːspɪsɪz] npl: **under the** ~ **of** sous les auspices de.

**auspicious** [ɔːs'pɪʃəs] a de bon augure, propice.

**austere** [ɔs'tɪə*] a austère.

**Australia** [ɔs'treɪlɪə] n Australie f ; ~**n** a australien(ne) // n Australien/ne.

**Austria** ['ɔstrɪə] n Autriche f ; ~**n** a autrichien(ne) // n Autrichien/ne.

**authentic** [ɔː'θɛntɪk] a authentique ; ~**ate** vt établir l'authenticité de.

**author** ['ɔːθə*] n auteur m.

**authoritarian** [ɔːθɔrɪ'tɛərɪən] a autoritaire.

**authoritative** [ɔː'θɔrɪtətɪv] a (account) digne de foi ; (study, treatise) qui fait autorité ; (manner) autoritaire.

**authority** [ɔː'θɔrɪtɪ] n autorité f ; (permission) autorisation (formelle) ; **the authorities** npl les autorités fpl, l'administration f.

**authorize** ['ɔːθəraɪz] vt autoriser.

**authorship** ['ɔːθəʃɪp] n paternité f (littéraire etc).

**autistic** [ɔː'tɪstɪk] a autistique.

**auto** ['ɔːtəu] n (US) auto f, voiture f.

**autobiography** [ɔːtəbaɪ'ɔgrəfɪ] n autobiographie f.

**autocratic** [ɔːtə'krætɪk] a autocratique.

**autograph** ['ɔːtəgrɑːf] n autographe m // vt signer, dédicacer.

**automatic** [ɔːtə'mætɪk] a automatique // n (gun) automatique m ; ~**ally** ad automatiquement.

**automation** [ɔːtə'meɪʃən] n automatisation f.

**automaton, pl automata** [ɔː'tɔmətən, -tə] n automate m.

**automobile** ['ɔːtəməbiːl] n (US) automobile f.

**autonomous** [ɔː'tɔnəməs] a autonome.

**autonomy** [ɔː'tɔnəmɪ] n autonomie f.

**autopsy** ['ɔːtɔpsɪ] n autopsie f.

**autumn** ['ɔːtəm] n automne m.

**auxiliary** [ɔːg'zɪlɪərɪ] a auxiliaire // n auxiliaire m/f.

**Av.** abbr of **avenue**.

**avail** [ə'veɪl] vt: **to** ~ **o.s. of** user de ; profiter de // n: **to no** ~ sans résultat, en vain, en pure perte.

**availability** [əveɪlə'bɪlɪtɪ] n disponibilité f.

**available** [ə'veɪləbl] a disponible ; **every** ~ **means** tous les moyens possibles or à sa (or notre etc) disposition.

**avalanche** ['ævəlɑːnʃ] n avalanche f.

**avant-garde** ['ævɑ̃'gɑːd] a d'avant-garde.

**avaricious** [ævə'rɪʃəs] a avare.

**Ave.** abbr of **avenue**.

**avenge** [ə'vɛndʒ] vt venger.

**avenue** ['ævənjuː] n avenue f.

**average** ['ævərɪdʒ] n moyenne f // a moyen(ne) // vt (a certain figure) atteindre or faire etc en moyenne ; **on** ~ en moyenne ; **above/below (the)** ~ au-dessus/en-dessous de la moyenne ; **to** ~ **out** vi: **to** ~ **out at** représenter en moyenne, donner une moyenne de.

**averse** [ə'vəːs] a: **to be** ~ **to sth/doing** éprouver une forte répugnance envers qch/à faire ; **I wouldn't be** ~ **to a drink** un petit verre ne serait pas de refus, je ne dirais pas non à un petit verre.

**aversion** [ə'vəːʃən] n aversion f, répugnance f.

**avert** [ə'vəːt] vt prévenir, écarter ; (one's eyes) détourner.

**aviary** ['eɪvɪərɪ] n volière f.

**aviation** [eɪvɪ'eɪʃən] n aviation f.

**avid** ['ævɪd] a avide ; ~**ly** ad avidement, avec avidité.

**avocado** [ævə'kɑːdəu] n (also: ~ **pear**) avocat m.

**avoid** [ə'vɔɪd] vt éviter ; ~**able** a évitable ; ~**ance** n le fait d'éviter.

**await** [ə'weɪt] vt attendre ; ~**ing attention/delivery** (COMM) en souffrance.

**awake** [ə'weɪk] a éveillé(e) ; (fig) en éveil // vb (pt **awoke** [ə'wəuk], pp **awoken** [ə'wəukən] or **awaked**) vt éveiller // vi s'éveiller ; ~ **to** conscient de ; **he was still** ~ il ne dormait pas encore ; ~**ning** [ə'weɪknɪŋ] n réveil m.

**award** [ə'wɔːd] n récompense f, prix m // vt (prize) décerner ; (LAW: damages) accorder.

**aware** [ə'wɛə*] a: ~ **of** (conscious) conscient(e) de ; (informed) au courant de ; **to become** ~ **of** avoir conscience de, prendre conscience de ; se rendre compte de ; **politically/socially** ~ sensibilisé aux or ayant pris conscience des problèmes politiques/sociaux ; ~**ness** n le fait d'être conscient, au courant etc.

**awash** [ə'wɔʃ] a recouvert(e) (d'eau) ; ~ **with** inondé(e) de.

**away** [ə'weɪ] *a,ad* (au) loin; absent(e);
**two kilometres** ~ à (une distance de)
deux kilomètres, à deux kilomètres de
distance; **two hours** ~ **by car** à deux
heures de voiture *or* de route; **the holiday
was two weeks** ~ il restait deux
semaines jusqu'aux vacances; ~ **from**
loin de; **he's** ~ **for a week** il est parti
(pour) une semaine; **to take** ~ *vt*
emporter; **to work/pedal/laugh** *etc* ~ *la
particule indique la constance et l'énergie de
l'action*: il pédalait *etc* tant qu'il pouvait;
**to fade/wither** *etc* ~ *la particule renforce
l'idée de la disparition, l'éloignement*; ~
**match** *n* (SPORT) match *m* à l'extérieur.

**awe** [ɔ:] *n* respect mêlé de crainte, effroi
mêlé d'admiration; ~-**inspiring**, ~**some**
*a* impressionnant(e); ~**struck** *a* frappé(e)
d'effroi.

**awful** ['ɔ:fəl] *a* affreux(euse); ~**ly** *ad*
(*very*) terriblement, vraiment.

**awhile** [ə'waɪl] *ad* un moment, quelque
temps.

**awkward** ['ɔ:kwəd] *a* (*clumsy*) gauche,
maladroit(e); (*inconvenient*) malaisé(e),
d'emploi malaisé, peu pratique;
(*embarrassing*) gênant(e), délicat(e).

**awl** [ɔ:l] *n* alêne *f*.

**awning** ['ɔ:nɪŋ] *n* (*of tent*) auvent *m*; (*of
shop*) store *m*;(*of hotel etc*) marquise *f* (de
toile).

**awoke, awoken** [ə'wəuk, -kən] *pt,pp of*
**awake**.

**awry** [ə'raɪ] *ad,a* de travers; **to go** ~ mal
tourner.

**axe, ax** (*US*) [æks] *n* hache *f* // *vt*
(*employee*) renvoyer; (*project etc*)
abandonner; (*jobs*) supprimer.

**axiom** ['æksɪəm] *n* axiome *m*.

**axis**, *pl* **axes** ['æksɪs, -si:z] *n* axe *m*.

**axle** ['æksl] *n* (*also*: ~-**tree**) essieu *m*.

**ay(e)** [aɪ] *excl* (*yes*) oui; **the ayes** *npl* les
oui.

**azure** ['eɪʒə\*] *a* azuré(e).

# B

**B** [hi:] *n* (MUS) si *m*.

**B.A.** *abbr see* **bachelor**.

**babble** ['bæbl] *vi* babiller // *n* babillage
*m*.

**baboon** [bə'bu:n] *n* babouin *m*.

**baby** ['beɪbɪ] *n* bébé *m*; ~ **carriage** *n* (*US*)
voiture *f* d'enfant; ~**hood** *n* petite
enfance; ~**ish** *a* enfantin(e), de bébé; ~-
**sit** *vi* garder les enfants; ~-**sitter** *n* baby-
sitter *m/f*.

**bachelor** ['bætʃələ\*] *n* célibataire *m*; **B**~
**of Arts/Science** (**B.A./B.Sc.**) ≈
licencié/e ès *or* en lettres/sciences; **B**~
**of Arts/Science degree** (**B.A./B.Sc.**) *n*
≈ licence *f* ès *or* en lettres/ sciences;
~**hood** *n* célibat *m*.

**back** [bæk] *n* (*of person, horse*) dos *m*; (*of
hand*) dos, revers *m*; (*of house*) derrière *m*;
(*of car, train*) arrière *m*; (*of chair*) dossier
*m*; (*of page*) verso *m*; (FOOTBALL) arrière *m*
// *vt* (*candidate: also:* ~ **up**) soutenir,
appuyer; (*horse: at races*) parier *or* miser
sur; (*car*) (faire) reculer // *vi* reculer; (*car
etc*) faire marche arrière // *a* (*in compounds*) de derrière, à l'arrière; ~

**seats/wheels** (AUT) sièges *mpl*/roues *fpl*
arrière; ~ **payments/rent** arriéré *m* de
paiements/loyer // *ad* (*not forward*) en
arrière; (*returned*): **he's** ~ il est rentré, il
est de retour; **he ran** ~ il est revenu en
courant; (*restitution*): **throw the ball** ~
renvoie la balle; **can I have it** ~? puis-
je le ravoir?, peux-tu me le rendre?;
(*again*): **he called** ~ il a rappelé; **to** ~
**down** *vi* rabattre de ses prétentions; **to**
~ **out** *vi* (*of promise*) se dédire; ~**ache**
*n* maux *mpl* de reins; ~**bencher** *n* membre
du parlement sans portefeuille; ~**biting** *n*
médisance(s) *f(pl)*; ~**bone** *n* colonne
vertébrale, épine dorsale; ~-**cloth** *n* toile
*f* de fond; ~**date** *vt* (*letter*) antidater;
~**dated pay rise** augmentation *f* avec
effet rétroactif; ~**er** *n* partisan *m*; (COMM)
commanditaire *m*; ~**fire** *vi* (AUT)
pétarader; (*plans*) mal tourner;
~**gammon** *n* trictrac *m*; ~**ground** *n*
arrière-plan *m*; (*of events*) situation *f*, conjoncture *f*; (*basic knowledge*) éléments *mpl*
de base; (*experience*) formation *f*; **family**
~**ground** milieu familial; ~**ground noise**
*n* bruit *m* de fond; ~**hand** *n* (TENNIS: *also*:
~**hand stroke**) revers *m*; ~**handed** *a*
(*fig*) déloyal(e); équivoque; ~**hander** *n*
(*bribe*) pot-de-vin *m*; ~**ing** *n* (*fig*) soutien
*m*, appui *m*; ~**lash** *n* contre-coup *m*,
répercussion *f*; ~**log** *n*: ~**log of work**
travail *m* en retard; ~ **number** *n* (*of
magazine etc*) vieux numéro; ~ **pay** *n*
rappel *m* de traitement; ~**side** *n* (*col*)
derrière *m*, postérieur *m*; ~**stroke** *n* nage
*f* sur le dos; ~**ward** *a* (*movement*) en
arrière; (*measure*) rétrograde; (*person,
country*) arriéré(e); attardé(e); (*shy*)
hésitant(e); ~**ward and forward movement** mouvement de va-et-vient;
~**wards** *ad* (*move, go*) en arrière; (*read
a list*) à l'envers, à rebours; (*fall*) à la
renverse; (*walk*) à reculons; (*in time*) en
arrière, vers le passé; ~**water** *n* (*fig*) coin
reculé; bled perdu; ~**yard** *n* arrière-cour
*f*.

**bacon** ['beɪkən] *n* bacon *m*, lard *m*.

**bacteria** [bæk'tɪərɪə] *npl* bactéries *fpl*.

**bad** [bæd] *a* mauvais(e); (*child*) vilain(e);
(*meat, food*) gâté(e), avarié(e); **his** ~ **leg**
sa jambe malade.

**bade** [bæd] *pt of* **bid**.

**badge** [bædʒ] *n* insigne *m*; (*of policemen*)
plaque *f*.

**badger** ['bædʒə\*] *n* blaireau *m* // *vt*
harceler.

**badly** ['bædlɪ] *ad* (*work, dress etc*) mal; ~
**wounded** grièvement blessé; **he needs it**
~ il en a absolument besoin; ~ **off** *a,ad*
dans la gêne.

**badminton** ['bædmɪntən] *n* badminton *m*.

**bad-tempered** ['bæd'tɛmpəd] *a* ayant
mauvais caractère; de mauvaise humeur.

**baffle** ['bæfl] *vt* (*puzzle*) déconcerter.

**bag** [bæg] *n* sac *m*; (*of hunter*) gibecière
*f*; chasse *f* // *vt* (*col: take*) empocher;
s'approprier; (TECH) mettre en sacs; ~**s
under the eyes** poches *fpl* sous les yeux;
~**ful** *n* plein sac; ~**gage** *n* bagages *mpl*;
~**gy** *a* avachi(e), qui fait des poches;
~**pipes** *npl* cornemuse *f*.

**Bahamas** [bə'hɑ:məz] *npl*: **the** ~ les
Bahamas *fpl*.

**bail** [beɪl] *n* caution *f* // *vt* (*prisoner: gen*: **to give ~ to**) mettre en liberté sous caution ; (*boat: also*: **~ out**) écoper ; *see* **bale**; **to ~ out** *vt* (*prisoner*) payer la caution de.

**bailiff** ['beɪlɪf] *n* huissier *m*.

**bait** [beɪt] *n* appât *m* // *vt* appâter ; (*fig*) tourmenter.

**bake** [beɪk] *vt* (faire) cuire au four // *vi* cuire (au four) ; faire de la pâtisserie ; **~d beans** *npl* haricots blancs à la sauce tomate ; **~r** *n* boulanger *m* ; **~ry** *n* boulangerie *f* ; boulangerie industrielle ; **baking** *n* cuisson *f* ; **baking powder** *n* levure *f* (chimique).

**balaclava** [bælə'klɑːvə] *n* (*also*: **~ helmet**) passe-montagne *m*.

**balance** ['bæləns] *n* équilibre *m* ; (*COMM*: *sum*) solde *m* ; (*scales*) balance *f* ; (*ECON*: *of trade etc*) balance // *vt* mettre *or* faire tenir en équilibre ; (*pros and cons*) peser ; (*budget*) équilibrer ; (*account*) balancer ; (*compensate*) compenser, contrebalancer ; **~ of trade/payments** balance commerciale/des comptes *or* paiements ; **~d** *a* (*personality, diet*) équilibré(e) ; **~ sheet** *n* bilan *m* ; **~ wheel** *n* balancier *m*.

**balcony** ['bælkənɪ] *n* balcon *m*.

**bald** [bɔːld] *a* chauve ; (*tree, hill*) dénudé(e) ; **~ness** *n* calvitie *f*.

**bale** [beɪl] *n* balle *f*, ballot *m* ; **to ~ out** *vi* (*of a plane*) sauter en parachute.

**baleful** ['beɪlful] *a* funeste, maléfique.

**balk** [bɔːk] *vi*: **to ~ (at)** regimber (contre) ; (*horse*) se dérober (devant).

**ball** [bɔːl] *n* boule *f* ; (*football*) ballon *m* ; (*for tennis, golf*) balle *f* ; (*dance*) bal *m*.

**ballad** ['bæləd] *n* ballade *f*.

**ballast** ['bæləst] *n* lest *m*.

**ballerina** [bælə'riːnə] *n* ballerine *f*.

**ballet** ['bæleɪ] *n* ballet *m* ; (*art*) danse *f* (classique).

**ballistics** [bə'lɪstɪks] *n* balistique *f*.

**balloon** [bə'luːn] *n* ballon *m* ; (*in comic strip*) bulle *f* ; **~ist** *n* aéronaute *m/f*.

**ballot** ['bælət] *n* scrutin *m* ; **~ box** *n* urne (électorale) , **~ paper** *n* bulletin *m* de vote.

**ball-point pen** ['bɔːlpɔɪnt'pɛn] *n* stylo *m* à bille.

**ballroom** ['bɔːlrum] *n* salle *f* de bal.

**balmy** ['bɑːmɪ] *a* (*breeze, air*) doux(douce) ; (*col*) = **barmy**.

**balsam** ['bɔːlsəm] *n* baume *m*.

**Baltic** [bɔːltɪk] *a,n*: **the ~ (Sea)** la (mer) Baltique.

**bamboo** [bæm'buː] *n* bambou *m*.

**bamboozle** [bæm'buːzl] *vt* (*col*) embobiner.

**ban** [bæn] *n* interdiction *f* // *vt* interdire.

**banal** [bə'nɑːl] *a* banal(e).

**banana** [bə'nɑːnə] *n* banane *f*.

**band** [bænd] *n* bande *f* ; (*at a dance*) orchestre *m* ; (*MIL*) musique *f*, fanfare *f* ; **to ~ together** *vi* se liguer.

**bandage** ['bændɪdʒ] *n* bandage *m*, pansement *m*.

**bandit** ['bændɪt] *n* bandit *m*.

**bandwagon** ['bændwægən] *n*: **to jump on the ~** (*fig*) monter dans *or* prendre le train en marche.

**bandy** ['bændɪ] *vt* (*jokes, insults*) échanger ; **to ~ about** *vt* employer à tout bout de champ *or* à tort et à travers.

**bandy-legged** ['bændɪ'lɛgd] *a* aux jambes arquées.

**bang** [bæŋ] *n* détonation *f* ; (*of door*) claquement *m* ; (*blow*) coup (violent) // *vt* frapper (violemment) ; (*door*) claquer // *vi* détoner ; claquer ; **to ~ at the door** cogner à la porte.

**banger** ['bæŋə*] *n* (*car: gen*: **old ~**) (vieux) tacot.

**bangle** ['bæŋgl] *n* bracelet *m*.

**banish** ['bænɪʃ] *vt* bannir.

**banister(s)** ['bænɪstə(z)] *n(pl)* rampe *f* (d'escalier).

**banjo, ~es** *or* **~s** ['bændʒəu] *n* banjo *m*.

**bank** [bæŋk] *n* banque *f* ; (*of river, lake*) bord *m*, rive *f* ; (*of earth*) talus *m*, remblai *m* // *vi* (*AVIAT*) virer sur l'aile ; (*COMM*): **they ~ with Pitt's** leur banque *or* banquier est Pitt's ; **to ~ on** *vt fus* miser *or* tabler sur ; **~ account** *n* compte *m* en banque ; **~er** *n* banquier *m* ; **B~ holiday** *n* jour férié (*où les banques sont fermées*) ; **~ing** *n* opérations *fpl* bancaires ; profession *f* de banquier ; **~ing hours** *npl* heures *fpl* d'ouverture des banques ; **~note** *n* billet *m* de banque ; **~ rate** *n* taux *m* de l'escompte.

**bankrupt** ['bæŋkrʌpt] *n* fàilli/e // *a* en faillite ; **to go ~** faire faillite ; **~cy** *n* faillite *f*.

**banner** ['bænə*] *n* bannière *f*.

**bannister(s)** ['bænɪstə(z)] *n(pl)* = **banister(s)**.

**banns** [bænz] *npl* bans *mpl* (de mariage).

**banquet** ['bæŋkwɪt] *n* banquet *m*, festin *m*.

**bantam-weight** ['bæntəmweɪt] *n* poids *m* coq *inv*.

**banter** ['bæntə*] *n* badinage *m*.

**baptism** ['bæptɪzəm] *n* baptême *m*.

**Baptist** ['bæptɪst] *n* baptiste *m/f*.

**baptize** [bæp'taɪz] *vt* baptiser.

**bar** [bɑː*] *n* barre *f* ; (*of window etc*) barreau *m*, (*of chocolate*) tablette *f*, plaque *f* ; (*fig*) obstacle *m* ; mesure *f* d'exclusion ; (*pub*) bar *m* ; (*counter: in pub*) comptoir *m*, bar ; (*MUS*) mesure *f* // *vt* (*road*) barrer ; (*window*) munir de barreaux ; (*person*) exclure ; (*activity*) interdire ; **~ of soap** savonnette *f* ; **the B~** (*LAW*) le barreau ; **~ none** sans exception.

**Barbados** [bɑː'beɪdɒs] *n* Barbade *f*.

**barbaric** [bɑː'bærɪk] *a* barbare.

**barbarous** [bɑːbərəs] *a* barbare, cruel(le).

**barbecue** ['bɑːbɪkjuː] *n* barbecue *m*.

**barbed wire** ['bɑːbd'waɪə*] *n* fil *m* de fer barbelé.

**barber** ['bɑːbə*] *n* coiffeur *m* (pour hommes).

**barbiturate** [bɑː'bɪtjurɪt] *n* barbiturique *m*.

**bare** [bɛə*] *a* nu(e) // *vt* mettre à nu, dénuder ; (*teeth*) montrer ; **the ~ essentials** le strict nécessaire ; **~back** *ad* à cru, sans selle ; **~faced** *a* impudent(e), effronté(e) ; **~foot** *a,ad* nu-pieds, (les) pieds nus ; **~headed** *a,ad* nu-tête, (la) tête nue ; **~ly** *ad* à peine.

**bargain** ['bɑ:gɪn] n (transaction) marché m; (good buy) affaire f, occasion f // vi (haggle) marchander; (trade) négocier, traiter; **into the** ~ par-dessus le marché.
**barge** [bɑ:dʒ] n péniche f; **to** ~ **in** vi (walk in) faire irruption; (interrupt talk) intervenir mal à propos; **to** ~ **into** vt fus rentrer dans.
**baritone** ['bærɪtəun] n baryton m.
**bark** [bɑ:k] n (of tree) écorce f; (of dog) aboiement m // vi aboyer.
**barley** ['bɑ:lɪ] n orge f.
**barmaid** ['bɑ:meɪd] n serveuse f (de bar), barmaid f.
**barman** ['bɑ:mən] n serveur m (de bar), barman m.
**barmy** ['bɑ:mɪ] a (col) timbré(e), cinglé(e).
**barn** [bɑ:n] n grange f.
**barnacle** ['bɑ:nəkl] n anatife m, bernache f.
**barometer** [bə'rɔmɪtə*] n baromètre m.
**baron** ['bærən] n baron m; ~**ess** baronne f.
**barracks** ['bærəks] npl caserne f.
**barrage** ['bærɑ:ʒ] n (MIL) tir m de barrage; (dam) barrage m.
**barrel** ['bærəl] n tonneau m; (of gun) canon m; ~ **organ** n orgue m de Barbarie.
**barren** ['bærən] a stérile; (hills) aride.
**barricade** [bærɪ'keɪd] n barricade f // vt barricader.
**barrier** ['bærɪə*] n barrière f.
**barring** ['bɑ:rɪŋ] prep sauf.
**barrister** ['bærɪstə*] n avocat (plaidant).
**barrow** ['bærəu] n (cart) charrette f à bras.
**bartender** ['bɑ:tɛndə*] n (US) barman m.
**barter** ['bɑ:tə*] n échange m, troc m // vt: **to** ~ **sth for** échanger qch contre.
**base** [beɪs] n base f // vt: **to** ~ **sth on** baser or fonder qch sur // a vil(e), bas(se); **coffee-**~**d** à base de café; **a Paris-**~**d firm** une maison opérant de Paris or dont le siège est à Paris; ~**ball** n base-ball m; ~**ment** n sous-sol m.
**bases** ['beɪsi:z] npl of **basis**; ['beɪsɪz] npl of **base**.
**bash** [bæʃ] vt (col) frapper, cogner; ~**ed in** a enfoncé(e), défoncé(e).
**bashful** ['bæʃful] a timide; modeste.
**bashing** ['bæʃɪŋ] n (col) raclée f.
**basic** ['beɪsɪk] a fondamental(e), de base; réduit(e) au minimum, rudimentaire; ~**ally** [-lɪ] ad fondamentalement, à la base; en fait, au fond.
**basil** ['bæzl] n basilic m.
**basin** ['beɪsn] n (vessel, also GEO) cuvette f, bassin m; (for food) bol m; (also: **wash**~) lavabo m.
**basis**, pl **bases** ['beɪsɪs, -si:z] n base f.
**bask** [bɑ:sk] vi: **to** ~ **in the sun** se chauffer au soleil.
**basket** ['bɑ:skɪt] n corbeille f; (with handle) panier m; ~**ball** n basket-ball m.
**bass** [beɪs] n (MUS) basse f; ~ **clef** n clé f de fa.
**bassoon** [bə'su:n] n basson m.
**bastard** ['bɑ:stəd] n enfant naturel(le), bâtard/e; (col!) salaud m(!).
**baste** [beɪst] vt (CULIN) arroser; (SEWING) bâtir, faufiler.

**bastion** ['bæstɪən] n bastion m.
**bat** [bæt] n chauve-souris f; (for baseball etc) batte f; (for table tennis) raquette f; **off one's own** ~ de sa propre initiative; **he didn't** ~ **an eyelid** il n'a pas sourcillé or bronché.
**batch** [bætʃ] n (of bread) fournée f; (of papers) liasse f.
**bated** ['beɪtɪd] a: **with** ~ **breath** en retenant son souffle.
**bath** [bɑ:θ, pl bɑ:ðz] n see also **baths**; bain m; (bathtub) baignoire f // vt baigner, donner un bain à; **to have a** ~ prendre un bain; ~**chair** n fauteuil roulant.
**bathe** [beɪð] vi se baigner // vt baigner; ~**r** n baigneur/euse.
**bathing** ['beɪðɪŋ] n baignade f; ~ **cap** n bonnet m de bain; ~ **costume** n maillot m (de bain).
**bath**: ~**mat** n tapis m de bain; ~**room** n salle f de bains; ~**s** npl établissement m de bains(-douches); ~ **towel** n serviette f de bain.
**batman** ['bætmən] n (MIL) ordonnance f.
**baton** ['bætən] n bâton m; (MUS) baguette f; (club) matraque f.
**battalion** [bə'tælɪən] n bataillon m.
**batter** ['bætə*] vt battre // n pâte f à frire; ~**ed** a (hat, pan) cabossé(e); ~**ed wife/child** épouse/enfant maltraité(e) or martyr(e); ~**ing ram** n bélier m (fig).
**battery** ['bætərɪ] n batterie f; (of torch) pile f.
**battle** ['bætl] n bataille f, combat m // vi se battre, lutter; ~ **dress** n tenue f de campagne or d'assaut; ~**field** n champ m de bataille; ~**ments** npl remparts mpl; ~**ship** n cuirassé m.
**baulk** [bɔ:lk] vi = **balk**.
**bawdy** ['bɔ:dɪ] a paillard(e).
**bawl** [bɔ:l] vi hurler, brailler.
**bay** [beɪ] n (of sea) baie f; **to hold sb at** ~ tenir qn à distance or en échec.
**bayonet** ['beɪənɪt] n baïonnette f.
**bay window** ['beɪ'wɪndəu] n baie vitrée.
**bazaar** [bə'zɑ:*] n bazar m; vente f de charité.
**bazooka** [bə'zu:kə] n bazooka m.
**b. & b., B. & B.** abbr see **bed**.
**BBC** n abbr of British Broadcasting Corporation (office de la radiodiffusion et télévision britannique).
**B.C.** ad (abbr of before Christ) av. J.-C.
**BCG** n (abbr of Bacillus Calmette-Guérin) BCG.
**be**, pt **was, were**, pp **been** [bi:, wɔz, wə:*, bi:n] vi être; **how are you?** comment allez-vous?; **I am warm** j'ai chaud; **it is cold** il fait froid; **how much is it?** combien ça coûte?; **he is four (years old)** il a quatre ans; **2 and 2 are 4** 2 et 2 font 4; **where have you been?** où êtes-vous allé(s)?; où étiez-vous?.
**beach** [bi:tʃ] n plage f // vt échouer; ~**wear** n tenues fpl de plage.
**beacon** ['bi:kən] n (lighthouse) fanal m; (marker) balise f.
**bead** [bi:d] n perle f.
**beak** [bi:k] n bec m.
**beaker** ['bi:kə*] n gobelet m.

**beam** [bi:m] *n* poutre *f*; (*of light*) rayon *m* // *vi* rayonner; ~**ing** *a* (*sun, smile*) radieux(euse).

**bean** [bi:n] *n* haricot *m*; (*of coffee*) grain *m*.

**bear** [bɛə*] *n* ours *m* // *vb* (*pt* **bore**, *pp* **borne** [bɔ:*, bɔ:n]) *vt* porter; (*endure*) supporter // *vi*: **to** ~ **right/left** obliquer à droite/gauche, se diriger vers la droite/gauche; **to** ~ **the responsibility of** assumer la responsabilité de; **to** ~ **comparison with** soutenir la comparaison avec; ~**able** *a* supportable.

**beard** [bɪəd] *n* barbe *f*; ~**ed** *a* barbu(e).

**bearer** ['bɛərə*] *n* porteur *m*.

**bearing** ['bɛərɪŋ] *n* maintien *m*, allure *f*; (*connection*) rapport *m*; (**ball**) ~**s** *npl* roulements *mpl* (à billes); **to take a** ~ faire le point; **to find one's** ~**s** s'orienter.

**beast** [bi:st] *n* bête *f*; (*col*): **he's a** ~ c'est une brute; ~**ly** *a* infect(e).

**beat** [bi:t] *n* battement *m*; (MUS) temps *m*; mesure *f*; (*of policeman*) ronde *f* // *vt* (*pt* **beat**, *pp* **beaten**) battre; **off the** ~**en track** hors des chemins *or* sentiers battus; **to** ~ **about the bush** tourner autour du pot; **to** ~ **time** battre la mesure; **to** ~ **off** *vt* repousser; **to** ~ **up** *vt* (*col: person*) tabasser; (*eggs*) battre; ~**er** *n* (*for eggs, cream*) fouet *m*, batteur *m*; ~**ing** *n* raclée *f*.

**beautician** [bju:'tɪʃən] *n* esthéticien/ne.

**beautiful** ['bju:tɪful] *a* beau(belle); ~**ly** *ad* admirablement.

**beautify** ['bju:tɪfaɪ] *vt* embellir.

**beauty** ['bju:tɪ] *n* beauté *f*; ~ **salon** *n* institut *m* de beauté; ~ **spot** *n* grain *m* de beauté; (TOURISM) site naturel (d'une grande beauté).

**beaver** ['bi:və*] *n* castor *m*.

**becalmed** [bɪ'kɑ:md] *a* immobilisé(e) par le calme plat.

**became** [bɪ'keɪm] *pt of* **become**.

**because** [bɪ'kɔz] *cj* parce que; ~ **of** *prep* à cause de.

**beckon** ['bɛkən] *vt* (*also*: ~ **to**) faire signe (de venir) à.

**become** [bɪ'kʌm] *vt* (*irg: like* **come**) devenir; **to** ~ **fat/thin** grossir/maigrir; **what has** ~ **of him?** qu'est-il devenu?

**becoming** [bɪ'kʌmɪŋ] *a* (*behaviour*) convenable, bienséant(e); (*clothes*) seyant(e).

**bed** [bɛd] *n* lit *m*; (*of flowers*) parterre *m*; (*of coal, clay*) couche *f*; **to go to** ~ aller se coucher; ~ **and breakfast (b. & b.)** *n* (*terms*) chambre et petit déjeuner; ~**clothes** *npl* couvertures *fpl* et draps *mpl*; ~**cover** *n* couvre-lit *m*, dessus-de-lit *m*; ~**ding** *n* literie *f*.

**bedlam** ['bɛdləm] *n* chahut *m*, cirque *m*.

**bedpost** ['bɛdpəust] *n* colonne *f* de lit.

**bedraggled** [bɪ'dræɡld] *a* dépenaillé(e), les vêtements en désordre.

**bed**: ~**ridden** *a* cloué(e) au lit; ~**room** *n* chambre *f* (à coucher); ~**side** *n*: **at sb's** ~**side** au chevet de qn; ~**side book** *n* livre *m* de chevet; ~**sit(ter)** *n* chambre meublée, studio *m*; ~**spread** *n* couvre-lit *m*, dessus-de-lit *m*.

**bee** [bi:] *n* abeille *f*.

**beech** [bi:tʃ] *n* hêtre *m*.

**beef** [bi:f] *n* bœuf *m*.

**beehive** ['bi:haɪv] *n* ruche *f*.

**beeline** ['bi:laɪn] *n*: **to make a** ~ **for** se diriger tout droit vers.

**been** [bi:n] *pp of* **be**.

**beer** [bɪə*] *n* bière *f*.

**beetle** ['bi:tl] *n* scarabée *m*; coléoptère *m*.

**beetroot** ['bi:tru:t] *n* betterave *f*.

**befall** [bɪ'fɔ:l] *vi(vt)* (*irg: like* **fall**) advenir (à).

**befit** [bɪ'fɪt] *vt* seoir à.

**before** [bɪ'fɔ:*] *prep* (*of time*) avant; (*of space*) devant // *cj* avant que + *sub*; avant de // *ad* avant; **the week** ~ la semaine précédente *or* d'avant; **I've seen it** ~ je l'ai déjà vu; **I've never seen it** ~ c'est la première fois que je le vois; ~**hand** *ad* au préalable, à l'avance.

**befriend** [bɪ'frɛnd] *vt* venir en aide à; traiter en ami.

**beg** [bɛɡ] *vi* mendier // *vt* mendier; (*favour*) quémander, solliciter; (*entreat*) supplier.

**began** [bɪ'ɡæn] *pt of* **begin**.

**beggar** ['bɛɡə*] *n* (*also*: ~**man**, ~**woman**) mendiant/e.

**begin** [bɪ'ɡɪn], *pt* **began**, *pp* **begun** [bɪ'ɡɪn, -'ɡæn, -'ɡʌn] *vt*, *vi* commencer; ~**ner** *n* débutant/e; ~**ning** *n* commencement *m*, début *m*.

**begrudge** [bɪ'ɡrʌdʒ] *vt*: **to** ~ **sb sth** envier qch à qn; donner qch à contrecœur *or* à regret à qn; **I don't** ~ **doing it** je le fais volontiers.

**begun** [bɪ'ɡʌn] *pp of* **begin**.

**behalf** [bɪ'hɑ:f] *n*: **on** ~ **of** de la part de; au nom de; pour le compte de.

**behave** [bɪ'heɪv] *vi* se conduire, se comporter; (*well: also*: ~ **o.s.**) se conduire bien *or* comme il faut.

**behaviour, behavior** (US) [bɪ'heɪvjə*] *n* comportement *m*, conduite *f* (*the latter often from a moral point of view, the former being more objective*).

**beheld** [bɪ'hɛld] *pt,pp of* **behold**.

**behind** [bɪ'haɪnd] *prep* derrière; (*time*) en retard sur // *ad* derrière; en retard // *n* derrière *m*; ~ **the scenes** dans les coulisses.

**behold** [bɪ'həuld] *vt* (*irg: like* **hold**) apercevoir, voir.

**beige** [beɪʒ] *a* beige.

**being** ['bi:ɪŋ] *n* être *m*; **to come into** ~ prendre naissance.

**belated** [bɪ'leɪtɪd] *a* tardif(ive).

**belch** [bɛltʃ] *vi* avoir un renvoi, roter // *vt* (*gen*: ~ **out**: *smoke etc*) vomir, cracher.

**belfry** ['bɛlfrɪ] *n* beffroi *m*.

**Belgian** ['bɛldʒən] *a* belge, de Belgique // *n* Belge *m/f*.

**Belgium** ['bɛldʒəm] *n* Belgique *f*.

**belie** [bɪ'laɪ] *vt* démentir.

**belief** [bɪ'li:f] *n* (*opinion*) conviction *f*; (*trust, faith*) foi *f*; (*acceptance as true*) croyance *f*.

**believable** [bɪ'li:vəbl] *a* croyable.

**believe** [bɪ'li:v] *vt,vi* croire; ~**r** *n* croyant/e.

**belittle** [bɪ'lɪtl] *vt* déprécier, rabaisser.

**bell** [bɛl] n cloche f; (small) clochette f, grelot m; (on door) sonnette f; (electric) sonnerie f; ~-**bottomed trousers** npl pantalon m à pattes d'éléphant.

**belligerent** [bɪ'lɪdʒərənt] a (at war) belligérant(e); (fig) agressif(ive).

**bellow** ['bɛləu] vi mugir // vt (orders) hurler.

**bellows** ['bɛləuz] npl soufflet m.

**belly** ['bɛlɪ] n ventre m; to ~**ache** vi (col) ronchonner; ~**button** n nombril m.

**belong** [bɪ'lɔŋ] vi: to ~ to appartenir à; (club etc) faire partie de; **this book ~s here** ce livre va ici, la place de ce livre est ici; ~**ings** npl affaires fpl, possessions fpl.

**beloved** [bɪ'lʌvɪd] a (bien-)aimé(e), chéri(e) // n bien-aiméУe.

**below** [bɪ'ləu] prep sous, au-dessous de // ad en dessous; en contre-bas; **see ~** voir plus bas or plus loin or ci-dessous.

**belt** [bɛlt] n ceinture f; (TECH) courroie f // vt (thrash) donner une raclée à // vi (col) filer (à toutes jambes).

**bench** [bɛntʃ] n banc m; (in workshop) établi m; **the B~** (LAW) la magistrature, la Cour.

**bend** [bɛnd] vb (pt,pp bent [bɛnt]) vt courber; (leg, arm) plier // vi se courber // n (in road) virage m, tournant m; (in pipe, river) coude m; to ~ **down** vi se baisser; to ~ **over** vi se pencher.

**beneath** [bɪ'ni:θ] prep sous, au-dessous de; (unworthy of) indigne de // ad dessous, au-dessous, en bas.

**benefactor** ['bɛnɪfæktə*] n bienfaiteur m.

**benefactress** ['bɛnɪfæktrɪs] n bienfaitrice f.

**beneficial** [bɛnɪ'fɪʃəl] a salutaire; avantageux(euse).

**benefit** ['bɛnɪfɪt] n avantage m, profit m; (allowance of money) allocation f // vt faire du bien à, profiter à // vi: **he'll ~ from it** cela lui fera du bien, il y gagnera or s'en trouvera bien; ~ **performance** n représentation f or gala m de bienfaisance.

**Benelux** ['bɛnɪlʌks] n Bénélux m.

**benevolent** [bɪ'nɛvələnt] a bienveillant(e).

**bent** [bɛnt] pt,pp of **bend** // n inclination f, penchant m // a (dishonest) véreux(euse); **to be ~ on** être résolu(e) à.

**bequeath** [bɪ'kwi:ð] vt léguer.

**bequest** [bɪ'kwɛst] n legs m.

**bereaved** [bɪ'ri:vd] n: **the ~** la famille du disparu.

**bereavement** [bɪ'ri:vmənt] n deuil m.

**beret** ['bɛreɪ] n béret m.

**Bermuda** [bə:'mju:də] n Bermudes fpl.

**berry** ['bɛrɪ] n baie f.

**berserk** [bə'sə:k] a: **to go ~** être pris(e) d'une rage incontrôlable; se déchaîner.

**berth** [bə:θ] n (bed) couchette f; (for ship) poste m d'amarrage; mouillage m // vi (in harbour) venir à quai; (at anchor) mouiller.

**beseech**, pt,pp **besought** [bɪ'si:tʃ, -'sɔ:t] vt implorer, supplier.

**beset**, pt,pp **beset** [bɪ'sɛt] vt assaillir.

**beside** [bɪ'saɪd] prep à côté de; **to be ~ o.s. (with anger)** être hors de soi.

**besides** [bɪ'saɪdz] ad en outre, de plus // prep en plus de; excepté.

**besiege** [bɪ'si:dʒ] vt (town) assiéger; (fig) assaillir.

**besought** [bɪ'sɔ:t] pt,pp of **beseech.**

**bespectacled** [bɪ'spɛktɪkld] a à lunettes.

**best** [bɛst] a meilleur(e) // ad le mieux; **the ~ part of** (quantity) le plus clair de, la plus grande partie de; **at ~** au mieux; **to make the ~ of sth** s'accommoder de qch (du mieux que l'on peut); **to the ~ of my knowledge** pour autant que je sache; **to the ~ of my ability** du mieux que je pourrai; ~ **man** n garçon m d'honneur.

**bestow** [bɪ'stəu] vt accorder; (title) conférer.

**bestseller** ['bɛst'sɛlə*] n bestseller m, succès m de librairie.

**bet** [bɛt] n pari m // vt,vi (pt,pp bet or betted) parier.

**betray** [bɪ'treɪ] vt trahir; ~**al** n trahison f.

**better** ['bɛtə*] a meilleur(e) // ad mieux // vt améliorer // n: **to get the ~ of** triompher de, l'emporter sur; **you had ~ do it** vous feriez mieux de le faire; **he thought ~ of it** il s'est ravisé; **to get ~** aller mieux; s'améliorer; ~ **off** a plus à l'aise financièrement; (fig): **you'd be ~ off this way** vous vous en trouveriez mieux ainsi, ce serait mieux or plus pratique ainsi.

**betting** ['bɛtɪŋ] n paris mpl; ~ **shop** n bureau m de paris.

**between** [bɪ'twi:n] prep entre // ad au milieu; dans l'intervalle.

**bevel** ['bɛvəl] n (also: ~ **edge**) biseau m.

**beverage** ['bɛvərɪdʒ] n boisson f (gén sans alcool).

**bevy** ['bɛvɪ] n: **a ~ of** un essaim or une volée de.

**beware** [bɪ'wɛə*] vt,vi: **to ~ (of)** prendre garde (à).

**bewildered** [bɪ'wɪldəd] a dérouté(e), ahuri(e).

**bewitching** [bɪ'wɪtʃɪŋ] a enchanteur-(teresse).

**beyond** [bɪ'jɔnd] prep (in space) au-delà de; (exceeding) au-dessus de // ad au-delà; ~ **doubt** hors de doute; ~ **repair** irréparable.

**bias** ['baɪəs] n (prejudice) préjugé m, parti pris; (preference) prévention f; ~(s)**ed** a partial(e), montrant un parti pris.

**bib** [bɪb] n bavoir m, bavette f.

**Bible** ['baɪbl] n Bible f.

**bibliography** [bɪblɪ'ɔgrəfɪ] n bibliographie f.

**bicker** ['bɪkə*] vi se chamailler.

**bicycle** ['baɪsɪkl] n bicyclette f.

**bid** [bɪd] n offre f; (at auction) enchère f; (attempt) tentative f // vb (pt bade [bæd] or bid, pp bidden ['bɪdn] or bid) vi faire une enchère or offre // vt faire une enchère or offre de; **to ~ sb good day** souhaiter le bonjour à qn; ~**der** n: **the highest ~der** le plus offrant; ~**ding** n enchères fpl.

**bide** [baɪd] vt: **to ~ one's time** attendre son heure.

**bier** [bɪə*] n bière f.
**big** [bɪg] a grand(e) ; gros(se).
**bigamy** ['bɪgəmɪ] n bigamie f.
**bigheaded** ['bɪg'hɛdɪd] a prétentieux(euse).
**big-hearted** ['bɪg'hɑ:tɪd] a au grand cœur.
**bigot** ['bɪgət] n fanatique m/f, sectaire m/f ; ~ed a fanatique, sectaire ; ~ry n fanatisme m, sectarisme m.
**bigwig** ['bɪgwɪg] n (col) grosse légume, huile f.
**bike** [baɪk] n vélo m, bécane f.
**bikini** [bɪ'ki:nɪ] n bikini m.
**bile** [baɪl] n bile f.
**bilingual** [baɪ'lɪŋgwəl] a bilingue.
**bilious** ['bɪlɪəs] a bilieux(euse) ; (fig) maussade, irritable.
**bill** [bɪl] n note f, facture f ; (POL) projet m de loi ; (US: banknote) billet m (de banque) ; (of bird) bec m ; to fit or fill the ~ (fig) faire l'affaire.
**billet** ['bɪlɪt] n cantonnement m (chez l'habitant).
**billfold** ['bɪlfəuld] n (US) portefeuille m.
**billiards** ['bɪlɪədz] n (jeu m de) billard m.
**billion** ['bɪlɪən] n (Brit) billion m (million de millions) ; (US) milliard m.
**billy goat** ['bɪlɪgəut] n bouc m.
**bin** [bɪn] n boîte f ; (also: dust~) poubelle f ; (for coal) coffre m ; bread~ n boîte f or huche f à pain.
**bind**, pt,pp **bound** [baɪnd, baund] vt attacher ; (book) relier ; (oblige) obliger, contraindre ; ~ing n (of book) reliure f // a (contract) constituant une obligation.
**bingo** ['bɪŋgəu] n sorte de jeu de loto pratiqué dans des établissements publics et connaissant une grande vogue en Grande-Bretagne.
**binoculars** [bɪ'nɔkjuləz] npl jumelles fpl.
**bio...** [baɪə'...] prefix : ~chemistry n biochimie f ; ~graphic(al) a biographique ; ~graphy [baɪ'ɔgrəfɪ] n biographie f ; ~logical a biologique ; -logist [baɪ'ɔlədʒɪst] n biologiste m/f, ~logy [baɪ'ɔlədʒɪ] n biologie f.
**birch** [bə:tʃ] n bouleau m.
**bird** [bə:d] n oiseau m ; (col: girl) nana f ; ~'s-eye view n vue f à vol d'oiseau ; (fig) vue d'ensemble or générale ; ~ watcher n ornithologue m/f amateur.
**birth** [bə:θ] n naissance f ; ~ certificate n acte m de naissance ; ~ control n limitation f des naissances ; méthode(s) contraceptive(s) ; ~day n anniversaire m ; ~place n lieu m de naissance ; ~ rate n (taux m de) natalité f.
**biscuit** ['bɪskɪt] n biscuit m.
**bisect** [baɪ'sɛkt] vt couper or diviser en deux.
**bishop** ['bɪʃəp] n évêque m.
**bit** [bɪt] pt of bite // n morceau m ; (of tool) mèche f ; (of horse) mors m ; a ~ of un peu de ; a ~ mad/dangerous un peu fou/risqué.
**bitch** [bɪtʃ] n (dog) chienne f ; (col!) salope f (!), garce f.
**bite** [baɪt] vt,vi (pt bit [bɪt], pp bitten ['bɪtn]) mordre // n morsure f ; (insect ~) piqûre f ; (mouthful) bouchée f ; let's have

a ~ (to eat) mangeons un morceau ; to ~ one's nails se ronger les ongles.
**biting** ['baɪtɪŋ] a mordant(e).
**bitten** ['bɪtn] pp of bite.
**bitter** ['bɪtə*] a amer(ère) ; (wind, criticism) cinglant(e) // n (beer) bière f (à forte teneur en houblon) ; to the ~ end jusqu'au bout ; ~ness n amertume f ; goût amer ; ~sweet a aigre-doux(douce).
**bivouac** ['bɪvuæk] n bivouac m.
**bizarre** [bɪ'zɑ:*] a bizarre.
**blab** [blæb] vi jaser, trop parler // vt (also: ~ out) laisser échapper, aller raconter.
**black** [blæk] a noir(e) // n noir m // vt (shoes) cirer ; (INDUSTRY) boycotter ; to give sb a ~ eye pocher l'œil à qn, faire un œil au beurre noir à qn ; ~ and blue a couvert(e) de bleus ; ~berry n mûre f ; ~bird n merle m ; ~board n tableau noir ; ~currant n cassis m ; ~en vt noircir ; ~leg n briseur m de grève, jaune m ; ~list n liste noire ; ~mail n chantage m // vt faire chanter, soumettre au chantage ; ~mailer n maître-chanteur m ; ~ market n marché noir ; ~out n panne f d'électricité ; (fainting) syncope f ; (in wartime) black-out m ; the B~ Sea n la mer Noire ; ~ sheep n brebis galeuse ; ~smith n forgeron m.
**bladder** ['blædə*] n vessie f.
**blade** [bleɪd] n lame f ; (of oar) plat m ; ~ of grass brin m d'herbe.
**blame** [bleɪm] n faute f, blâme m // vt : to ~ sb/sth for sth attribuer à qn/qch la responsabilité de qch ; reprocher qch à qn/qch ; who's to ~? qui est le fautif or coupable or responsable? ; ~less a irréprochable.
**bland** [blænd] a affable ; (taste) doux(douce), fade.
**blank** [blæŋk] a blanc(blanche) ; (look) sans expression, dénué(e) d'expression // n espace m vide, blanc m ; (cartridge) cartouche f à blanc.
**blanket** ['blæŋkɪt] n couverture f.
**blare** [blɛə*] vi (brass band, horns, radio) beugler.
**blarney** ['blɑ:nɪ] n boniment m.
**blasé** ['blɑ:zeɪ] a blasé(e).
**blasphemous** ['blæsfɪməs] a (words) blasphématoire ; (person) blasphémateur(trice).
**blasphemy** ['blæsfɪmɪ] n blasphème m.
**blast** [blɑ:st] n souffle m ; explosion f // vt faire sauter or exploser ; ~-off n (SPACE) lancement m.
**blatant** ['bleɪtənt] a flagrant(e), criant(e).
**blaze** [bleɪz] n (fire) incendie m ; (fig) flamboiement m // vi (fire) flamber ; (fig) flamboyer, resplendir // vt : to ~ a trail (fig) montrer la voie.
**blazer** ['bleɪzə*] n blazer m.
**bleach** [bli:tʃ] n (also: household ~) eau f de Javel // vt (linen) blanchir ; ~ed a (hair) oxygéné(e), décoloré(e).
**bleak** [bli:k] a morne, désolé(e).
**bleary-eyed** ['blɪərɪ'aɪd] a aux yeux pleins de sommeil.
**bleat** [bli:t] n bêlement m // vi bêler.
**bleed**, pt,pp **bled** [bli:d, blɛd] vt, vi

saigner ; **my nose is** ～**ing** je saigne du nez.

**blemish** ['blɛmɪʃ] n défaut m ; (on reputation) tache f.

**blend** [blɛnd] n mélange m // vt mélanger // vi (colours etc) se mélanger, se fondre, s'allier.

**bless,** pt,pp **blessed** or **blest** [blɛs, blɛst] vt bénir ; **to be** ～**ed with** avoir le bonheur de jouir de or d'avoir ; ～**ing** n bénédiction f ; bienfait m.

**blew** [blu:] pt of **blow**.

**blight** [blaɪt] n (of plants) rouille f // vt (hopes etc) anéantir, briser.

**blimey** ['blaɪmɪ] excl (col) mince alors!

**blind** [blaɪnd] a aveugle // n (for window) store m // vt aveugler ; **to turn a** ～ **eye (on** or **to)** fermer les yeux (sur) ; ～ **alley** n impasse f ; ～ **corner** n virage m sans visibilité ; ～**fold** n bandeau m // a,ad les yeux bandés // vt bander les yeux à ; ～**ly** ad aveuglément ; ～**ness** n cécité f ; (fig) aveuglement m ; ～ **spot** n (AUT etc) angle m aveugle ; (fig) angle mort.

**blink** [blɪŋk] vi cligner des yeux ; (light) clignoter ; ～**ers** npl œillères fpl.

**blinking** ['blɪŋkɪŋ] a (col): **this** ～... ce fichu or sacré ... .

**bliss** [blɪs] n félicité f, bonheur m sans mélange.

**blister** ['blɪstə*] n (on skin) ampoule f, cloque f ; (on paintwork) boursouflure f // vi (paint) se boursoufler, se cloquer.

**blithe** [blaɪð] a joyeux(euse), allègre.

**blithering** ['blɪðərɪŋ] a (col): **this** ～ **idiot** cet espèce d'idiot.

**blitz** [blɪts] n bombardement (aérien).

**blizzard** ['blɪzəd] n blizzard m, tempête f de neige.

**bloated** ['bləʊtɪd] a (face) bouffi(e) ; (stomach) gonflé(e).

**blob** [blɔb] n (drop) goutte f ; (stain, spot) tache f.

**block** [blɔk] n bloc m ; (in pipes) obstruction f ; (toy) cube m ; (of buildings) pâté m (de maisons) // vt bloquer ; ～**ade** [-'keɪd] n blocus m // vt faire le blocus de ; ～**age** n obstruction f ; ～**head** n imbécile m/f ; ～ **of flats** n immeuble (locatif) ; ～ **letters** npl majuscules fpl.

**bloke** [bləʊk] n (col) type m.

**blonde** [blɔnd] a,n blond(e).

**blood** [blʌd] n sang m ; ～ **donor** n donneur/euse de sang ; ～**less** a (victory) sans effusion de sang ; (pale) anémié(e) ; ～ **poisoning** n empoisonnement m du sang ; ～ **pressure** n tension f (artérielle) ; ～**shed** n effusion f de sang, carnage m ; ～**shot** a: ～**shot eyes** yeux injectés de sang ; ～**stained** a taché(e) de sang ; ～**stream** n sang m, système sanguin ; ～**thirsty** a sanguinaire ; ～ **transfusion** n transfusion f de sang ; ～**y** a sanglant(e) ; (col!): **this** ～**y** ... ce foutu..., ce putain de... (!) ; ～**y strong/good** (col!) vachement or sacrément fort/bon ; ～**y-minded** a (col) contrariant(e), obstiné(e).

**bloom** [blu:m] n fleur f ; (fig) épanouissement m // vi être en fleur ; (fig) s'épanouir ; être florissant ; ～**ing** a (col): **this** ～**ing**... ce fichu or sacré... .

**blossom** ['blɔsəm] n fleur(s) f(pl) // vi être en fleurs ; (fig) s'épanouir.

**blot** [blɔt] n tache f // vt tacher ; (ink) sécher ; **to** ～ **out** vt (memories) effacer ; (view) cacher, masquer ; (nation, city) annihiler.

**blotchy** ['blɔtʃɪ] a (complexion) couvert(e) de marbrures.

**blotting paper** ['blɔtɪŋpeɪpə*] n buvard m.

**blouse** [blauz] n (feminine garment) chemisier m, corsage m.

**blow** [bləʊ] n coup m // vb (pt **blew**, pp **blown** [blu:, bləʊn]) vi souffler // vt (glass) souffler ; (fuse) faire sauter ; **to** ～ **one's nose** se moucher ; **to** ～ **a whistle** siffler ; **to** ～ **away** vt chasser, faire s'envoler ; **to** ～ **down** vt faire tomber, renverser ; **to** ～ **off** vt emporter ; **to** ～ **off course** faire dévier ; **to** ～ **out** vi éclater, sauter ; **to** ～ **over** vi s'apaiser ; **to** ～ **up** vi exploser, sauter // vt faire sauter ; (tyre) gonfler ; (PHOT) agrandir ; ～**lamp** n chalumeau m ; ～**-out** n (of tyre) éclatement m.

**blubber** ['blʌbə*] n blanc m de baleine // vi (pej) pleurer comme un veau.

**bludgeon** ['blʌdʒən] n gourdin m, trique f.

**blue** [blu:] a bleu(e) ; ～ **film/joke** film m/histoire f pornographique ; **to have the** ～**s** avoir le cafard ; ～**bell** n jacinthe f des bois ; ～**bottle** n mouche f à viande ; ～**jeans** npl blue-jeans mpl ; ～**print** n (fig) projet m, plan directeur.

**bluff** [blʌf] vi bluffer // n bluff m // a (person) bourru(e), brusque ; **to call sb's** ～ mettre qn au défi d'exécuter ses menaces.

**blunder** ['blʌndə*] n gaffe f, bévue f // vi faire une gaffe or une bévue.

**blunt** [blʌnt] a émoussé(e), peu tranchant(e) ; (person) brusque, ne mâchant pas ses mots // vt émousser ; ～**ly** ad carrément, sans prendre de gants ; ～**ness** n (of person) brusquerie f, franchise brutale.

**blur** [blə:*] n tache or masse floue or confuse // vt brouiller, rendre flou.

**blurt** [blə:t]: **to** ～ **out** vt (reveal) lâcher ; (say) balbutier, dire d'une voix entrecoupée.

**blush** [blʌʃ] vi rougir // n rougeur f.

**blustering** ['blʌstərɪŋ] a fanfaron(ne).

**blustery** ['blʌstərɪ] a (weather) à bourrasques.

**B.O.** n (abbr of body odour) odeurs corporelles.

**boar** [bɔ:*] n sanglier m.

**board** [bɔ:d] n planche f ; (on wall) panneau m ; (committee) conseil m, comité m ; (in firm) conseil d'administration // vt (ship) monter à bord de ; (train) monter dans ; ～ **and lodging** n chambre f avec pension ; **full** ～ pension complète ; **with** ～ **and lodging** (job) logé nourri ; **to go by the** ～ (fig): **which goes by the** ～ (fig) qu'on laisse tomber, qu'on abandonne ; **to** ～ **up** vt (door) condamner (au moyen de planches, de tôle) ; ～**er** n pensionnaire m/f ; (SCOL) interne m/f, pensionnaire m/f ; ～**ing house** n pension f ; ～**ing school** n internat m, pensionnat m ; ~ **room** n salle f du conseil d'administration (souvent symbole de pouvoir décisionnaire).

**boast** [bəust] vi se vanter // vt s'enorgueillir de // n vantardise f; sujet m d'orgueil or de fierté ; ~**ful** a vantard(e) ; ~**fulness** n vantardise f.

**boat** [bəut] n bateau m ; (small) canot m ; barque f; **to be in the same** ~ (fig) être logé à la même enseigne ; ~**er** n (hat) canotier m ; ~**ing** n canotage m ; ~**swain** ['bəusn] n maître m d'équipage.

**bob** [bɔb] vi (boat, cork on water: also: ~ **up and down**) danser, se balancer // n (col) = **shilling** ; **to** ~ **up** vi surgir or apparaître brusquement.

**bobbin** ['bɔbɪn] n bobine f; (of sewing machine) navette f.

**bobby** ['bɔbɪ] n (col) ≈ agent m (de police).

**bobsleigh** ['bɔbsleɪ] n bob m.

**bodice** ['bɔdɪs] n corsage m.

**bodily** ['bɔdɪlɪ] a corporel(le) // ad physiquement ; dans son entier or ensemble ; en personne.

**body** ['bɔdɪ] n corps m ; (of car) carrosserie f; (of plane) fuselage m ; (fig: society) organe m, organisme m ; (fig: quantity) ensemble m, masse f; (of wine) corps m ; **in a** ~ en masse, ensemble ; ~**guard** n garde m du corps ; ~ **repairs** npl travaux mpl de carrosserie ; ~**work** n carrosserie f.

**bog** [bɔg] n tourbière f // vt: **to get** ~**ged down** (fig) s'enliser.

**boggle** ['bɔgl] vi: **the mind** ~**s** c'est incroyable, on en reste sidéré.

**bogie** ['bəugɪ] n bogie m.

**bogus** ['bəugəs] a bidon inv ; fantôme.

**boil** [bɔɪl] vt (faire) bouillir // vi bouillir // n (MED) furoncle m ; **to come to the** ~ bouillir ; **to** ~ **down** vi (fig): **to** ~ **down to** se réduire or ramener à ; ~**er** n chaudière f; ~**er suit** n bleu m de travail, combinaison f; ~**ing hot** a brûlant(e), bouillant(e) ; ~**ing point** n point m d'ébullition.

**boisterous** ['bɔɪstərəs] a bruyant(e), tapageur(euse).

**bold** [bəuld] a hardi(e), audacieux(euse) ; (pej) effronté(e) ; (outline, colour) franc(franche), tranché(e), marqué(e) ; ~**ness** n hardiesse f, audace f; aplomb m, effronterie f; ~ **type** n caractères mpl gras.

**Bolivia** [bə'lɪvɪə] n Bolivie f.

**bollard** ['bɔləd] n (NAUT) bitte f d'amarrage ; (AUT) borne lumineuse or de signalisation.

**bolster** ['bəulstə*] n traversin m ; **to** ~ **up** vt soutenir.

**bolt** [bəult] n verrou m ; (with nut) boulon m // vt verrouiller ; (food) engloutir // vi se sauver, filer (comme une flèche) ; **a** ~ **from the blue** (fig) un coup de tonnerre dans un ciel bleu.

**bomb** [bɔm] n bombe f // vt bombarder ; ~**ard** [bɔm'bɑ:d] vt bombarder ; ~**ardment** [bɔm'bɑ:dmənt] n bombardement m.

**bombastic** ['bɔm'bæstɪk] a grandiloquent(e), pompeux(euse).

**bomb disposal** ['bɔmdɪspəuzl] n: ~ **unit** section f de déminage.

**bomber** ['bɔmə*] n caporal m d'artillerie ; (AVIAT) bombardier m.

**bombing** ['bɔmɪŋ] n bombardement m.

**bombshell** ['bɔmʃɛl] n obus m ; (fig) bombe f.

**bona fide** ['bəunə'faɪdɪ] a de bonne foi ; (offer) sérieux(euse).

**bond** [bɔnd] n lien m ; (binding promise) engagement m, obligation f; (FINANCE) obligation f.

**bone** [bəun] n os m ; (of fish) arête f // vt désosser ; ôter les arêtes de ; ~-**dry** a absolument sec(sèche) ; ~**r** n (US) gaffe f, bourde f.

**bonfire** ['bɔnfaɪə*] n feu m (de joie) ; (for rubbish) feu m.

**bonnet** ['bɔnɪt] n bonnet m ; (Brit: of car) capot m.

**bonus** ['bəunəs] n prime f, gratification f.

**bony** ['bəunɪ] a (arm, face, MED: tissue) osseux(euse) ; (meat) plein(e) d'os ; (fish) plein d'arêtes.

**boo** [bu:] excl hou!, peuh! // vt huer // n huée f.

**booby trap** ['bu:bɪtræp] n engin piégé.

**book** [buk] n livre m ; (of stamps etc) carnet m ; (COMM): ~**s** comptes mpl, comptabilité f // vt (ticket) prendre ; (seat, room) réserver ; (driver) dresser un procès-verbal à ; (football player) prendre le nom de ; ~**able** a: **seats are** ~**able** on peut réserver ses places ; ~**case** n bibliothèque f (meuble) ; ~ **ends** npl serre-livres m inv ; ~**ing office** n bureau m de location ; ~-**keeping** n comptabilité f; ~**let** n brochure f; ~**maker** n bookmaker m ; ~**seller** n libraire m/f; ~**shop** n librairie f; ~**stall** n kiosque m à journaux ; ~**store** n = ~**shop**.

**boom** [bu:m] n (noise) grondement m ; (busy period) boom m, vague f de prospérité // vi gronder ; prospérer.

**boomerang** ['bu:məræŋ] n boomerang m.

**boon** [bu:n] n bénédiction f, grand avantage.

**boorish** ['buərɪʃ] a grossier(ère), rustre.

**boost** [bu:st] n stimulant m, remontant m ; (MED: vaccine) rappel m // vt stimuler.

**boot** [bu:t] n botte f; (for hiking) chaussure f (de marche) ; (for football etc) soulier m ; (Brit: of car) coffre m ; **to** ~ (in addition) par-dessus le marché, en plus.

**booth** [bu:ð] n (at fair) baraque (foraine) ; (of cinema, telephone etc) cabine f; (also: **voting** ~) isoloir m.

**booty** ['bu:tɪ] n butin m.

**booze** [bu:z] (col) n boissons fpl alcooliques, alcool m // vi boire, picoler.

**border** ['bɔ:də*] n bordure f; bord m ; (of a country) frontière f; **the B**~ la frontière entre l'Écosse et l'Angleterre ; **the B**~**s** la région frontière entre l'Écosse et l'Angleterre ; **to** ~ **on** vt fus être voisin(e) de, toucher à ; ~**line** n (fig) ligne f de démarcation ; ~**line case** n cas m limite.

**bore** [bɔ:*] pt of **bear** // vt (hole) percer ; (person) ennuyer, raser // n (person) raseur/euse ; (of gun) calibre m ; ~**dom** n ennui m.

**boring** ['bɔ:rɪŋ] a ennuyeux(euse).
**born** [bɔ:n] a: **to be ~** naître; **I was ~ in 1960** je suis né en 1960; **~ blind** aveugle de naissance; **a ~ comedian** un comédien-né.
**borne** [bɔ:n] pp of **bear**.
**borough** ['bʌrə] n municipalité f.
**borrow** ['bɔrəu] vt: **to ~ sth (from sb)** emprunter qch (à qn).
**borstal** ['bɔ:stl] n ≈ maison f de correction.
**bosom** ['buzəm] n poitrine f; (fig) sein m; **~ friend** n ami/e intime.
**boss** [bɔs] n patron/ne // vt commander; **~y** a autoritaire.
**bosun** ['bəusn] n maître m d'équipage.
**botanical** [bə'tænɪkl] a botanique.
**botanist** ['bɔtənɪst] n botaniste m/f.
**botany** ['bɔtənɪ] n botanique f.
**botch** [bɔtʃ] vt (also: **~ up**) saboter, bâcler.
**both** [bəuθ] a les deux, l'un(e) et l'autre // pronoun: **~ (of them)** les deux, tous(toutes) (les) deux, l'un(e) et l'autre; **~ of us went, we ~ went** nous y sommes allés (tous) les deux // ad: **they sell ~ the fabric and the finished curtains** ils vendent (et) le tissu et les rideaux (finis), ils vendent à la fois le tissu et les rideaux (finis).
**bother** ['bɔðə*] vt (worry) tracasser; (needle, bait) importuner, ennuyer; (disturb) déranger // vi (gen: **~ o.s.**) se tracasser, se faire du souci; **to ~ doing** prendre la peine de faire // n: **it is a ~ to have to do** c'est vraiment ennuyeux d'avoir à faire; **it was no ~** finding it n'y a eu aucun problème pour or ç'a été très facile de trouver.
**bottle** ['bɔtl] n bouteille f; (baby's) biberon m // vt mettre en bouteille(s); **to ~ up** vt refouler, contenir; **~neck** n étranglement m; **~-opener** n ouvre-bouteille m.
**bottom** ['bɔtəm] n (of container, sea etc) fond m; (buttocks) derrière m; (of page, list) bas m; (of chair) siège m // a du fond; du bas; **~less** a sans fond, insondable.
**bough** [bau] n branche f, rameau m.
**bought** [bɔ:t] pt,pp of **buy**.
**boulder** ['bəuldə*] n gros rocher (gén lisse, arrondi).
**bounce** [bauns] vi (ball) rebondir; (cheque) être refusé (étant sans provision); (gen: **to ~ forward/out** etc) bondir, s'élancer // vt faire rebondir // n (rebound) rebond m.
**bound** [baund] pt,pp of **bind** // n (gen pl) limite f; (leap) bond m // vt (leap) bondir; (limit) borner // a: **to be ~ to do sth** (obliged) être obligé(e) or avoir obligation de faire qch; **he's ~ to fail** (likely) il est sûr d'échouer, son échec est inévitable or assuré; **~ for** à destination de.
**boundary** ['baundrɪ] n frontière f.
**boundless** ['baundlɪs] a illimité(e), sans bornes.
**bout** [baut] n période f; (of malaria etc) accès m, crise f, attaque f; (BOXING etc) combat m, match m.

**bow** n [bəu] nœud m; (weapon) arc m; (MUS) archet m; [bau] révérence f, inclination f (du buste or corps) // vi [bau] faire une révérence, s'incliner; (yield): **to ~ to** or **before** s'incliner devant, se soumettre à.
**bowels** [bauəlz] npl intestins mpl; (fig) entrailles fpl.
**bowl** [bəul] n (for eating) bol m; (for washing) cuvette f; (ball) boule f; (of pipe) fourneau m // vi (CRICKET) lancer (la balle); **~s** n (jeu m de) boules fpl; **to ~ over** vt (fig) renverser (fig).
**bow-legged** ['bəulɛgɪd] a aux jambes arquées.
**bowler** ['bəulə*] n joueur m de boules; (CRICKET) lanceur m (de la balle); (also: **~ hat**) (chapeau m) melon m.
**bowling** ['bəulɪŋ] n (game) jeu m de boules; **~ alley** n bowling m; jeu m de quilles; **~ green** n terrain m de boules (gazonné et carré).
**bow tie** ['bəu'taɪ] n nœud m papillon.
**box** [bɔks] n boîte f; (also: **cardboard ~**) carton m; (THEATRE) loge f // vt mettre en boîte; (SPORT) boxer avec // vi boxer, faire de la boxe; **~er** n (person) boxeur m; (dog) boxer m; **~ing** n (SPORT) boxe f; **B~ing Day** n le lendemain de Noël; **~ing gloves** npl gants mpl de boxe; **~ing ring** n ring m; **~ office** n bureau m de location; **~ room** n débarras m; chambrette f.
**boy** [bɔɪ] n garçon m; (servant) boy m.
**boycott** ['bɔɪkɔt] n boycottage m // vt boycotter.
**boyfriend** ['bɔɪfrɛnd] n (petit) ami.
**boyish** ['bɔɪʃ] a d'enfant, de garçon.
**B.R.** abbr of **British Rail.**
**bra** [brɑ:] n soutien-gorge m.
**brace** [breɪs] n attache f, agrafe f; (on teeth) appareil m (dentaire); (tool) vilbrequin m; (TYP: also: **~ bracket**) accolade f // vt consolider, soutenir; **~s** npl bretelles fpl; **to ~ o.s.** (fig) se préparer mentalement.
**bracelet** ['breɪslɪt] n bracelet m.
**bracing** ['breɪsɪŋ] a tonifiant(e), tonique.
**bracken** ['brækən] n fougère f.
**bracket** ['brækɪt] n (TECH) tasseau m, support m; (group) classe f, tranche f; (also: **brace ~**) accolade f; (also: **round ~**) parenthèse f; (gen: **square ~**) crochet m // vt mettre entre parenthèse(s).
**brag** [bræg] vi se vanter.
**braid** [breɪd] n (trimming) galon m; (of hair) tresse f, natte f.
**Braille** [breɪl] n braille m.
**brain** [breɪn] n cerveau m; **~s** npl cervelle f; **he's got ~s** il est intelligent; **~less** a sans cervelle, stupide; **~wash** vt faire subir un lavage de cerveau à; **~wave** n idée géniale; **~y** a intelligent(e), doué(e).
**braise** [breɪz] vt braiser.
**brake** [breɪk] n (on vehicle) frein m // vt,vi freiner.
**bramble** ['bræmbl] n ronces fpl.
**bran** [bræn] n son m.
**branch** [brɑ:ntʃ] n branche f; (COMM) succursale f // vi bifurquer.
**brand** [brænd] n marque (commerciale) // vt (cattle) marquer (au fer rouge); (fig:

*pej*): **to ~ sb a communist** *etc* traiter *or* qualifier qn de communiste *etc*.
**brandish** ['brændɪʃ] *vt* brandir.
**brand-new** ['brænd'nju:] *a* tout(e) neuf(neuve), flambant neuf(neuve).
**brandy** ['brændɪ] *n* cognac *m*, fine *f*.
**brash** [bræʃ] *a* effronté(e).
**brass** [brɑ:s] *n* cuivre *m* (jaune), laiton *m*; **the ~** (MUS) les cuivres; **~ band** *n* fanfare *f*.
**brassière** ['bræsɪə*] *n* soutien-gorge *m*.
**brat** [bræt] *n* (*pej*) mioche *m/f*, môme *m/f*.
**bravado** [brəˈvɑːdəu] *n* bravade *f*.
**brave** [breɪv] *a* courageux(euse), brave // *n* guerrier indien // *vt* braver, affronter; **~ry** *n* bravure *f*, courage *m*.
**brawl** [brɔːl] *n* rixe *f*, bagarre *f* // *vi* se bagarrer.
**brawn** [brɔːn] *n* muscle *m*; (*meat*) fromage *m* de tête; **~y** *a* musclé(e), costaud(e).
**bray** [breɪ] *n* braiement *m* // *vi* braire.
**brazen** ['breɪzn] *a* impudent(e), effronté(e) // *vt*: **to ~ it out** payer d'effronterie, crâner.
**brazier** ['breɪzɪə*] *n* brasero *m*.
**Brazil** [brəˈzɪl] *n* Brésil *m*; **~ian** *a* brésilien(ne) // *n* Brésilien/ne; **~ nut** *n* noix *f* du Brésil.
**breach** [briːtʃ] *vt* ouvrir une brèche dans // *n* (*gap*) brèche *f*; (*breaking*): **~ of confidence** abus *m* de confiance; **~ of contract** rupture *f* de contrat; **~ of the peace** attentat *m* à l'ordre public.
**bread** [brɛd] *n* pain *m*; **~ and butter** *n* tartines *fpl* (beurrées); (*fig*) subsistance *f*; **~crumbs** *npl* miettes *fpl* de pain; (CULIN) chapelure *f*, panure *f*; **~ line** *n*: **to be on the ~ line** être sans le sou *or* dans l'indigence.
**breadth** [brɛtθ] *n* largeur *f*.
**breadwinner** ['brɛdwɪnə*] *n* soutien *m* de famille.
**break** [breɪk] *vb* (*pt* **broke** [brəuk], *pp* **broken** ['brəukən]) *vt* casser, briser; (*promise*) rompre; (*law*) violer // *vi* (se) casser, se briser; (*weather*) tourner // *n* (*gap*) brèche *f*; (*fracture*) cassure *f*; (*rest*) interruption *f*, arrêt *m*; (:*short*) pause *f*; (:*at school*) récréation *f*; (*chance*) chance *f*, occasion *f* favorable; **to ~ one's leg** *etc* se casser la jambe *etc*; **to ~ a record** battre un record; **to ~ the news to sb** annoncer la nouvelle à qn; **to ~ down** *vt* (*figures, data*) décomposer, analyser // *vi* s'effondrer; (MED) faire une dépression (nerveuse); (AUT) tomber en panne; **to ~ even** *vi* rentrer dans ses frais; **to ~ free** *or* **loose** *vi* se dégager, s'échapper; **to ~ in** *vt* (*horse etc*) dresser // *vi* (*burglar*) entrer par effraction; **to ~ into** *vt fus* (*house*) s'introduire *or* pénétrer par effraction dans; **to ~ off** *vi* (*speaker*) s'interrompre; (*branch*) se rompre; **to ~ open** *vt* (*door etc*) forcer, fracturer; **to ~ out** *vi* éclater, se déclarer; **to ~ out in spots** se couvrir de boutons; **to ~ up** *vi* (*partnership*) cesser, prendre fin; (*friends*) se séparer // *vt* fracasser, casser; (*fight etc*) interrompre, faire cesser; **~able** *a* cassable, fragile; **~age** *n* casse *f*; **~down** *n* (AUT) panne *f*; (*in communications*) rupture *f*; (MED: *also:* **nervous ~down**)

dépression (nerveuse); **~down lorry** *n* dépanneuse *f*; **~down service** *n* service *m* de dépannage; **~er** *n* brisant *m*.
**breakfast** ['brɛkfəst] *n* petit déjeuner *m*.
**breakthrough** ['breɪkθru:] *n* percée *f*.
**breakwater** ['breɪkwɔ:tə*] *n* brise-lames *m inv*, digue *f*.
**breast** [brɛst] *n* (*of woman*) sein *m*; (*chest*) poitrine *f*; **~-stroke** *n* brasse *f*.
**breath** [brɛθ] *n* haleine *f*, souffle *m*; **to go out for a ~ of air** sortir prendre l'air; **out of ~** à bout de souffle, essoufflé(e); **~alyser** *n* alcootest *m*.
**breathe** [briːð] *vt,vi* respirer; **~r** *n* moment *m* de repos *or* de répit.
**breathless** ['brɛθlɪs] *a* essoufflé(e), haletant(e); oppressé(e).
**breath-taking** ['brɛθteɪkɪŋ] *a* stupéfiant(e), à vous couper le souffle.
**breed** [briːd] *vb* (*pt,pp* **bred** [brɛd]) *vt* élever, faire l'élevage de // *vi* se reproduire // *n* race *f*, variété *f*; **~er** *n* (*person*) éleveur *m*; **~ing** *n* reproduction *f*; élevage *m*.
**breeze** [briːz] *n* brise *f*.
**breezy** ['briːzɪ] *a* frais(fraîche); aéré(e); désinvolte, jovial(e).
**brevity** ['brevɪtɪ] *n* brièveté *f*.
**brew** [bru:] *vt* (*tea*) faire infuser; (*beer*) brasser; (*plot*) tramer, préparer // *vi* (*tea*) infuser; (*beer*) fermenter; (*fig*) se préparer, couver; **~er** *n* brasseur *m*; **~ery** *n* brasserie *f* (*fabrique*).
**bribe** [braɪb] *n* pot-de-vin *m* // *vt* acheter; soudoyer; **~ry** *n* corruption *f*.
**brick** [brɪk] *n* brique *f*; **~layer** *n* maçon *m*; **~work** *n* briquetage *m*, maçonnerie *f*; **~works** *n* briqueterie *f*.
**bridal** ['braɪdl] *a* nuptial(e); **~ party** *n* noce *f*.
**bride** [braɪd] *n* mariée *f*, épouse *f*; **~groom** *n* marié *m*, époux *m*; **~smaid** *n* demoiselle *f* d'honneur.
**bridge** [brɪdʒ] *n* pont *m*; (NAUT) passerelle *f* (de commandement); (*of nose*) arête *f*; (CARDS, DENTISTRY) bridge *m* // *vt* (*river*) construire un pont sur; (*gap*) combler; **bridging loan** *n* prêt *m* de raccord.
**bridle** ['braɪdl] *n* bride *f* // *vt* refréner, mettre la bride à; (*horse*) brider; **~ path** *n* piste *or* allée cavalière.
**brief** [bri:f] *a* bref(brève) // *n* (LAW) dossier *m*, cause *f* // *vt* donner des instructions à; **~s** *npl* slip *m*; **~case** *n* serviette *f*; porte-documents *m inv*; **~ing** *n* instructions *fpl*; **~ly** *ad* brièvement; **~ness** *n* brièveté *f*.
**brigade** [brɪˈgeɪd] *n* (MIL) brigade *f*.
**brigadier** [brɪgəˈdɪə*] *n* brigadier général.
**bright** [braɪt] *a* brillant(e); (*room, weather*) clair(e); (*person*) intelligent(e), doué(e); (*colour*) vif(vive); **~en** *vt* (*room*) éclaircir; égayer // *vi* s'éclaircir; (*person: gen:* **~en up**) retrouver un peu de sa gaieté; **~ly** *ad* brillamment.
**brilliance** ['brɪljəns] *n* éclat *m*.
**brilliant** ['brɪljənt] *a* brillant(e).
**brim** [brɪm] *n* bord *m*; **~ful** *a* plein(e) à ras bord; (*fig*) débordant(e).
**brine** [braɪn] *n* eau salée; (CULIN) saumure *f*.

**bring,** *pt,pp* **brought** [brɪŋ, brɔ:t] *vt* (*thing*) apporter ; (*person*) amener ; **to ~ about** *vt* provoquer, entraîner ; **to ~ back** *vt* rapporter ; ramener ; **to ~ down** *vt* abaisser ; faire s'effondrer ; **to ~ forward** *vt* avancer ; **to ~ off** *vt* (*task, plan*) réussir, mener à bien ; **to ~ out** *vt* (*meaning*) faire ressortir, mettre en relief ; **to ~ round** *or* **to** *vt* (*unconscious person*) ranimer ; **to ~ up** *vt* élever ; (*question*) soulever.

**brink** [brɪŋk] *n* bord *m*.

**brisk** [brɪsk] *a* vif(vive), alerte.

**bristle** ['brɪsl] *n* poil *m* // *vi* se hérisser ; **bristling with** hérissé(e) de.

**Britain** ['brɪtən] *n* Grande-Bretagne *f*.

**British** ['brɪtɪʃ] *a* britannique ; **the ~** *npl* les Britanniques *mpl* ; **the ~ Isles** *npl* les Îles *fpl* Britanniques.

**Briton** ['brɪtən] *n* Britannique *m/f*.

**Brittany** ['brɪtənɪ] *n* Bretagne *f*.

**brittle** ['brɪtl] *a* cassant(e), fragile.

**broach** [brəutʃ] *vt* (*subject*) aborder.

**broad** [brɔ:d] *a* large ; (*distinction*) général(e) ; (*accent*) prononcé(e) ; **in ~ daylight** en plein jour ; **~ hint** *n* allusion transparente ; **~cast** *n* émission *f* // *vb* (*pt,pp* **broadcast**) *vt* radiodiffuser ; téléviser // *vi* émettre ; **~casting** *n* radiodiffusion *f* ; télévision *f* ; **~en** *vt* élargir // *vi* s'élargir ; **~ly** *ad* en gros, généralement ; **~-minded** *a* large d'esprit.

**brochure** ['brəuʃjuə\*] *n* prospectus *m*, dépliant *m*.

**broil** [brɔɪl] *vt* rôtir ; **~er** *n* (*fowl*) poulet *m* (à rôtir).

**broke** [brəuk] *pt of* **break** // *a* (*col*) fauché(e) ; **~n** *pp of* **break** // *a*: **~n leg** *etc* jambe *etc* cassée ; **in ~n French/English** dans un français/anglais approximatif *or* hésitant ; **~n-hearted** *a* (ayant) le cœur brisé.

**broker** ['brəukə\*] *n* courtier *m*.

**bronchitis** [brɔŋ'kaɪtɪs] *n* bronchite *f*.

**bronze** [brɔnz] *n* bronze *m* ; **~d** *a* bronzé(e), hâlé(e).

**brooch** [brəutʃ] *n* broche *f*.

**brood** [bru:d] *n* couvée *f* // *vi* (*hen, storm*) couver ; (*person*) méditer (sombrement), ruminer ; **~y** *a* (*fig*) taciturne, mélancolique.

**brook** [bruk] *n* ruisseau *m*.

**broom** [brum] *n* balai *m* ; **~stick** *n* manche *m* à balai.

**Bros.** *abbr of* **Brothers**.

**broth** [brɔθ] *n* bouillon *m* de viande et de légumes.

**brothel** ['brɔθl] *n* maison close, bordel *m*.

**brother** ['brʌðə\*] *n* frère *m* ; **~hood** *n* fraternité *f* ; **~-in-law** *n* beau-frère *m* ; **~ly** *a* fraternel(le).

**brought** [brɔ:t] *pt,pp of* **bring**.

**brow** [brau] *n* front *m* ; (*rare, gen:* **eye~**) sourcil *m* ; (*of hill*) sommet *m* ; **~beat** *vt* intimider, brusquer.

**brown** [braun] *a* brun(e) // *n* (*colour*) brun *m* // *vt* brunir ; (*CULIN*) faire dorer, faire roussir ; **~ie** *n* jeannette *f*, éclaireuse (cadette).

**browse** [brauz] *vi* (*among books*) bouquiner, feuilleter les livres.

**bruise** [bru:z] *n* bleu *m*, ecchymose *f*, contusion *f* // *vt* contusionner, meurtrir // *vi* (*fruit*) se taler, se meurtrir ; **to ~ one's arm** se faire un bleu au bras.

**brunette** [bru:'nɛt] *n* (*femme*) brune.

**brunt** [brʌnt] *n*: **the ~ of** (*attack, criticism etc*) le plus gros de.

**brush** [brʌʃ] *n* brosse *f* ; (*quarrel*) accrochage *m*, prise *f* de bec // *vt* brosser ; (*gen:* **~ past**, **~ against**) effleurer, frôler ; **to ~ aside** *vt* écarter, balayer ; **to ~ up** *vt* (*knowledge*) rafraîchir, réviser ; **~-off** *n*: **to give sb the ~-off** envoyer qn promener ; **~wood** *n* broussailles *fpl*, taillis *m*.

**Brussels** ['brʌslz] *n* Bruxelles ; **~ sprout** *n* chou *m* de Bruxelles.

**brutal** ['bru:tl] *a* brutal(e) ; **~ity** [bru:'tælɪtɪ] *n* brutalité *f*.

**brute** [bru:t] *n* brute *f*.

**brutish** ['bru:tɪʃ] *a* grossier(ère), brutal(e).

**B.Sc.** *abbr see* **bachelor**.

**bubble** ['bʌbl] *n* bulle *f* // *vi* bouillonner, faire des bulles ; (*sparkle, fig*) pétiller.

**buck** [bʌk] *n* mâle *m* (*d'un lapin, lièvre, daim etc*) ; (*US: col*) dollar *m* // *vi* ruer, lancer une ruade ; **to pass the ~** (**to sb**) se décharger de la responsabilité (sur qn) ; **to ~ up** *vi* (*cheer up*) reprendre du poil de la bête, se remonter.

**bucket** ['bʌkɪt] *n* seau *m*.

**buckle** ['bʌkl] *n* boucle *f* // *vt* boucler, attacher ; (*warp*) tordre, gauchir ; (: *wheel*) voiler.

**bud** [bʌd] *n* bourgeon *m* ; (*of flower*) bouton *m* // *vi* bourgeonner ; (*flower*) éclore.

**Buddha** ['budə] *n* Bouddha *m* ; **Buddhism** *n* bouddhisme *m* ; **Buddhist** *a* bouddhiste // *n* Bouddhiste *m/f*.

**budding** ['bʌdɪŋ] *a* (*flower*) en bouton ; (*poet etc*) en herbe ; (*passion etc*) naissant(e).

**buddy** ['bʌdɪ] *n* (*US*) copain *m*.

**budge** [bʌdʒ] *vt* faire bouger // *vi* bouger.

**budgerigar** ['bʌdʒərɪgɑ:\*] *n* perruche *f*.

**budget** ['bʌdʒɪt] *n* budget *m* // *vi*: **to ~ for sth** inscrire qch au budget.

**budgie** ['bʌdʒɪ] *n* = **budgerigar**.

**buff** [bʌf] *a* (couleur *f*) chamois *m* // *n* (*enthusiast*) mordu/e.

**buffalo,** *pl* **~** *or* **~es** ['bʌfələu] *n* buffle *m* ; (*US*) bison *m*.

**buffer** ['bʌfə\*] *n* tampon *m* ; **~ state** *n* état *m* tampon.

**buffet** *n* ['bufeɪ] (*bar, food*) buffet *m* // *vt* ['bʌfɪt] gifler, frapper ; secouer, ébranler.

**buffoon** [bə'fu:n] *n* buffon *m*, pitre *m*.

**bug** [bʌg] *n* (*insect*) punaise *f* ; (: *gen*) insecte *m*, bestiole *f* ; (: *fig: germ*) virus *m*, microbe *m* ; (*spy device*) dispositif *m* d'écoute (électronique), micro clandestin // *vt* garnir de dispositifs d'écoute ; **~bear** *n* cauchemar *m*, bête noire.

**bugle** ['bju:gl] *n* clairon *m*.

**build** [bɪld] *n* (*of person*) carrure *f*, charpente *f* // *vt* (*pt,pp* **built** [bɪlt]) construire, bâtir ; **~er** *n* entrepreneur *m* ; **~ing** *n* construction *f* ; bâtiment *m*, construction *f* ; (*habitation, offices*) immeuble *m* ; **~ing society** *n* société *f* de crédit immobilier ; **to ~ up** *vt* accumuler, amasser ; accroître ; **~-up** n (of gas etc) accumulation f.

**built** [bɪlt] pt,pp of **build** ; **well-~** a (person) bien bâti(e) ; **~-in** a (cupboard) encastré(e) ; (device) incorporé(e) ; intégré(e) ; **~-up area** n agglomération (urbaine) ; zone urbanisée.

**bulb** [bʌlb] n (BOT) bulbe m, oignon m ; (ELEC) ampoule f ; **~ous** a bulbeux(euse).

**Bulgaria** [bʌl'gɛərɪə] n Bulgarie f ; **~n** a bulgare // n Bulgare m/f ; (LING) bulgare m.

**bulge** [bʌldʒ] n renflement m, gonflement m // vi faire saillie ; présenter un renflement ; **to be bulging with** être plein(e) à craquer de.

**bulk** [bʌlk] n masse f, volume m ; **in ~** (COMM) en vrac ; **the ~ of** la plus grande or grosse partie de ; **~head** n cloison f (étanche) ; **~y** a volumineux(euse), encombrant(e).

**bull** [bul] n taureau m ; **~dog** n bouledogue m.

**bulldoze** ['buldəuz] vt passer or raser au bulldozer ; **~r** n bulldozer m.

**bullet** ['bulɪt] n balle f (de fusil etc).

**bulletin** ['bulɪtɪn] n bulletin m, communiqué m.

**bullfight** ['bulfaɪt] n corrida f, course f de taureaux ; **~er** n torero m ; **~ing** n tauromachie f.

**bullion** ['buljən] n or m or argent m en lingots.

**bullock** ['bulək] n bœuf m.

**bull's-eye** ['bulzaɪ] n centre m (de la cible).

**bully** ['bulɪ] n brute f, tyran m // vt tyranniser, rudoyer ; (frighten) intimider ; **~ing** n brimades fpl.

**bum** [bʌm] n (col: backside) derrière m ; (tramp) vagabond/e, traine-savates m/f inv ; **to ~ around** vi vagabonder.

**bumblebee** ['bʌmblbi:] n (ZOOL) bourdon m.

**bump** [bʌmp] n (blow) coup m, choc m ; (jolt) cahot m ; (on road etc, on head) bosse f // vt heurter, cogner ; **to ~ along** vi avancer en cahotant ; **to ~ into** vt fus rentrer dans, tamponner ; **~er** n (Brit) pare-chocs m inv // a : **~er crop/harvest** récolte/moisson exceptionnelle.

**bumptious** ['bʌmpʃəs] a suffisant(e), prétentieux(euse).

**bumpy** ['bʌmpɪ] a cahoteux(euse).

**bun** [bʌn] n petit pain au lait ; (of hair) chignon m.

**bunch** [bʌntʃ] n (of flowers) bouquet m ; (of keys) trousseau m ; (of bananas) régime m ; (of people) groupe m ; **~ of grapes** grappe f de raisin.

**bundle** ['bʌndl] n paquet m // vt (also: **~ up**) faire un paquet de ; (put): **to ~ sth/sb into** fourrer or enfourner qch/qn dans ; **to ~ off** vt (person) faire sortir (en toute hâte) ; expédier ; **to ~ out** vt éjecter, sortir (sans ménagements).

**bung** [bʌŋ] n bonde f, bouchon m // vt (throw: gen: **~ into**) flanquer.

**bungalow** ['bʌŋgələu] n bungalow m.

**bungle** ['bʌŋgl] vt bâcler, gâcher.

**bunion** ['bʌnjən] n oignon m (au pied).

**bunk** [bʌŋk] n couchette f ; **~ beds** npl lits superposés.

**bunker** ['bʌŋkə*] n (coal store) soute f à charbon ; (MIL, GOLF) bunker m.

**bunny** ['bʌnɪ] n (also: **~ rabbit**) Jeannot m lapin ; **~ girl** n hôtesse de cabaret.

**bunting** ['bʌntɪŋ] n pavoisement m, drapeaux mpl.

**buoy** [bɔɪ] n bouée f ; **to ~ up** vt faire flotter ; (fig) soutenir, épauler ; **~ancy** n (of ship) flottabilité f ; **~ant** a gai(e), plein(e) d'entrain.

**burden** ['bə:dn] n fardeau m, charge f // vt charger ; (oppress) accabler, surcharger.

**bureau**, pl **~x** [bjuə'rəu, -z] n (furniture) bureau m, secrétaire m ; (office) bureau m, office m.

**bureaucracy** [bjuə'rɔkrəsɪ] n bureaucratie f.

**bureaucrat** ['bjuərəkræt] n bureaucrate m/f, rond-de-cuir m ; **~ic** [-'krætɪk] a bureaucratique.

**burglar** ['bə:glə*] n cambrioleur m ; **~ alarm** n sonnerie f d'alarme ; **~ize** vt (US) cambrioler ; **~y** n cambriolage m.

**burgle** ['bə:gl] vt cambrioler.

**Burgundy** ['bə:gəndɪ] n Bourgogne f.

**burial** ['bɛrɪəl] n enterrement m ; **~ ground** n cimetière m.

**burlesque** [bə:'lɛsk] n caricature f, parodie f.

**burly** ['bə:lɪ] a de forte carrure, costaud(e).

**Burma** ['bə:mə] n Birmanie f ; **Burmese** [-'mi:z] a birman(e), de Birmanie // n, pl inv Birman/e ; (LING) birman m.

**burn** [bə:n] vt,vi (pt,pp **burned** or **burnt** [bə:nt]) brûler // n brûlure f ; **to ~ down** vt incendier, détruire par le feu ; **~er** n brûleur m ; **~ing question** n question brûlante.

**burnish** ['bə:nɪʃ] vt polir.

**burnt** [bə:nt] pt,pp of **burn** ; **~ sugar** n caramel m.

**burp** [bə:p] (col) n rot m // vi roter.

**burrow** ['bʌrəu] n terrier m // vt creuser.

**bursar** ['bə:sə*] n économe m/f ; (student) boursier/ère ; **~y** n bourse f (d'études).

**burst** [bə:st] vb (pt,pp **burst**) vt crever ; faire éclater // vi éclater ; (tyre) crever // n explosion f ; (also: **~ pipe**) rupture f, fuite f ; **~ of energy** déploiement soudain d'énergie, activité soudaine ; **~ of laughter** éclat m de rire ; **~ blood vessel** rupture f de vaisseau sanguin ; **to ~ into flames** s'enflammer soudainement ; **to ~ into laughter** éclater de rire ; **to ~ into tears** fondre en larmes ; **to be ~ing with** être plein (à craquer) de ; regorger de ; **to ~ into** vt fus (room etc) faire irruption dans ; **to ~ open** vi s'ouvrir violemment or soudainement ; **to ~ out of** vt fus sortir précipitamment de.

**bury** ['bɛrɪ] vt enterrer ; **to ~ one's face in one's hands** se couvrir le visage de ses mains ; **to ~ one's head in the sand** (fig) pratiquer la politique de l'autruche ; **to ~ the hatchet** enterrer la hache de guerre.

**bus**, **~es** [bʌs, 'bʌsɪz] n autobus m.

**bush** [buʃ] n buisson m ; (scrub land) brousse f.

**bushel** ['buʃl] *n* boisseau *m*.
**bushy** ['buʃɪ] *a* broussailleux(euse), touffu(e).
**busily** ['bɪzɪlɪ] *ad* activement.
**business** ['bɪznɪs] *n* (*matter, firm*) affaire *f*; (*trading*) affaires *fpl*; (*job, duty*) travail *m*; **to be away on** ~ être en déplacement d'affaires; **it's none of my** ~ cela ne me regarde pas, ce ne sont pas mes affaires; **he means** ~ il ne plaisante pas, il est sérieux; ~**like** *a* sérieux(euse); efficace; ~**man** *n* homme *m* d'affaires.
**bus-stop** ['bʌsstɔp] *n* arrêt *m* d'autobus.
**bust** [bʌst] *n* buste *m* // *a* (*broken*) fichu(e), fini(e); **to go** ~ faire faillite.
**bustle** ['bʌsl] *n* remue-ménage *m*, affairement *m* // *vi* s'affairer, se démener; **bustling** *a* (*person*) affairé(e); (*town*) très animé(e).
**bust-up** ['bʌstʌp] *n* (*col*) engueulade *f*.
**busy** ['bɪzɪ] *a* occupé(e); (*shop, street*) très fréquenté(e) // *vt*: **to** ~ **o.s.** s'occuper; ~**body** *n* mouche *f* du coche, âme *f* charitable.
**but** [bʌt] *cj* mais // *prep* excepté, sauf; **nothing** ~ rien d'autre que; ~ **for** sans, si ce n'était pour; **all** ~ **finished** pratiquement fini; **anything** ~ **finished** tout sauf fini, très loin d'être fini.
**butane** ['bjuːteɪn] *n* butane *m*.
**butcher** ['butʃə*] *n* boucher *m* // *vt* massacrer; (*cattle etc for meat*) tuer.
**butler** ['bʌtlə*] *n* maître *m* d'hôtel.
**butt** [bʌt] *n* (*cask*) gros tonneau; (*thick end*) (gros) bout; (*of gun*) crosse *f*; (*of cigarette*) mégot *m*; (*fig: target*) cible *f* // *vt* donner un coup de tête à.
**butter** ['bʌtə*] *n* beurre *m* // *vt* beurrer; ~ **dish** *n* beurrier *m*.
**butterfly** ['bʌtəflaɪ] *n* papillon *m*.
**buttocks** ['bʌtəks] *npl* fesses *fpl*.
**button** ['bʌtn] *n* bouton *m* // *vt* boutonner // *vi* se boutonner; ~**hole** *n* boutonnière *f* // *vt* accrocher, arrêter, retenir.
**buttress** ['bʌtrɪs] *n* contrefort *m*.
**buxom** ['bʌksəm] *a* aux formes avantageuses *or* épanouies, bien galbé(e).
**buy** [baɪ] *vb* (*pt,pp* **bought** [bɔːt]) *vt* acheter; **to** ~ **sb sth/sth from sb** acheter qch à qn; **to** ~ **sb a drink** offrir un verre *or* à boire à qn; **to** ~ **up** *vt* acheter en bloc, rafler; ~**er** *n* acheteur/euse.
**buzz** [bʌz] *n* bourdonnement *m*; (*col: phone call*) coup *m* de fil // *vi* bourdonner.
**buzzard** ['bʌzəd] *n* buse *f*.
**buzzer** ['bʌzə*] *n* timbre *m* électrique.
**by** [baɪ] *prep* par; (*beside*) à côté de; au bord de; (*before*): ~ **4 o'clock** avant 4 heures, d'ici 4 heures // *ad see* **pass, go** *etc*; ~ **bus/car** en autobus/voiture; **paid** ~ **the hour** payé à l'heure; **to increase** *etc* ~ **the hour** augmenter *etc* d'heure en heure; (**all**) ~ **oneself** tout(e) seul(e); ~ **the way** à propos; ~ **and large** dans l'ensemble; ~ **and** ~ bientôt.
**bye(-bye)** ['baɪ('baɪ)] *excl* au revoir!, salut!
**by(e)-law** ['baɪlɔː] *n* arrêté municipal.
**by-election** ['baɪɪlɛkʃən] *n* élection (législative) partielle.
**bygone** ['baɪgɔn] *a* passé(e) // *n*: **let** ~**s be** ~**s** passons l'éponge, oublions le passé.

**bypass** ['baɪpɑːs] *n* (route *f* de) contournement *m* // *vt* éviter.
**by-product** ['baɪprɔdʌkt] *n* sous-produit *m*, dérivé *m*; (*fig*) conséquence *f* secondaire, retombée *f*.
**byre** ['baɪə*] *n* étable *f* (à vaches).
**bystander** ['baɪstændə*] *n* spectateur/-trice, badaud/e.
**byword** ['baɪwəːd] *n*: **to be a** ~ **for** être synonyme de (*fig*).

## C

**C** [siː] *n* (*MUS*) do *m*.
**C.** *abbr of* **centigrade**.
**C.A.** *abbr of* **chartered accountant**.
**cab** [kæb] *n* taxi *m*; (*of train, truck*) cabine *f*; (*horse-drawn*) fiacre *m*.
**cabaret** ['kæbəreɪ] *n* attractions *fpl*, spectacle *m* de cabaret.
**cabbage** ['kæbɪdʒ] *n* chou *m*.
**cabin** ['kæbɪn] *n* cabane *f*, hutte *f*; (*on ship*) cabine *f*; ~ **cruiser** *n* yacht *m* (à moteur).
**cabinet** ['kæbɪnɪt] *n* (*POL*) cabinet *m*; (*furniture*) petit meuble à tiroirs et rayons; (*also*: **display** ~) vitrine *f*, petite armoire vitrée; **cocktail** ~ *n* meuble-bar *m*; **medicine** ~ *n* armoire *f* à pharmacie; ~-**maker** *n* ébéniste *m*.
**cable** ['keɪbl] *n* câble *m* // *vt* câbler, télégraphier; ~-**car** *n* téléphérique *m*; ~-**gram** *n* câblogramme *m*; ~ **railway** *n* funiculaire *m*.
**cache** [kæʃ] *n* cachette *f*; **a** ~ **of food** *etc* un dépôt secret de provisions *etc*, une cachette contenant des provisions *etc*.
**cackle** ['kækl] *vi* caqueter.
**cactus**, *pl* **cacti** ['kæktəs, -taɪ] *n* cactus *m*.
**caddie** ['kædɪ] *n* caddie *m*.
**cadet** [kə'dɛt] *n* (*MIL*) élève *m* officier.
**cadge** [kædʒ] *vt* se faire donner; **to** ~ **a meal (off sb)** se faire inviter à manger (par qn); ~**r** *n* pique-assiette *m/f inv*, tapeur/euse.
**Caesarean** [siː'zɛərɪən] *a*: ~ (**section**) césarienne *f*.
**café** ['kæfeɪ] *n* ≈ café(-restaurant) *m* (*sans alcool*); **cafeteria** [kæfɪ'tɪərɪə] *n* cafeteria *f*.
**caffein(e)** ['kæfiːn] *n* caféine *f*.
**cage** [keɪdʒ] *n* cage *f* // *vt* mettre en cage.
**cagey** ['keɪdʒɪ] *a* (*col*) réticent(e); méfiant(e).
**Cairo** ['kaɪərəu] *n* le Caire.
**cajole** [kə'dʒəul] *vt* couvrir de flatteries *or* de gentillesses.
**cake** [keɪk] *n* gâteau *m*; ~ **of soap** savonnette *f*; ~**d** *a*: ~**d with** raidi(e) par, couvert(e) d'une croûte de.
**calamitous** [kə'læmɪtəs] *a* catastrophique, désastreux(euse).
**calamity** [kə'læmɪtɪ] *n* calamité *f*, désastre *m*.
**calcium** ['kælsɪəm] *n* calcium *m*.
**calculate** ['kælkjuleɪt] *vt* calculer; **calculating** *a* calculateur(trice); **calculation** [-'leɪʃən] *n* calcul *m*; **calculator** *n* machine *f* à calculer, calculatrice *f*.

**calculus** ['kælkjuləs] *n* analyse *f* (mathématique), calcul infinitésimal ; **integral/differential** ~ calcul intégral/différentiel.

**calendar** ['kæləndə*] *n* calendrier *m* ; ~ **month** *n* mois *m* (de calendrier) ; ~ **year** *n* année civile.

**calf, calves** [kɑ:f, kɑ:vz] *n* (*of cow*) veau *m* ; (*of other animals*) petit *m* ; (*also*: ~**skin**) veau *m*, vachette *f* ; (ANAT) mollet *m*.

**calibre, caliber** (US) ['kælɪbə*] *n* calibre *m*.

**call** [kɔ:l] *vt* (*gen, also* TEL) appeler // *vi* appeler ; (*visit: also*: ~ **in**, ~ **round**): **to** ~ **(for)** passer (prendre) // *n* (*shout*) appel *m*, cri *m* ; (*visit*) visite *f* ; (*also*: **telephone** ~) coup *m* de téléphone ; communication *f* ; **she's** ~**ed Suzanne** elle s'appelle Suzanne ; **to be on** ~ être de permanence ; **to** ~ **for** *vt fus* demander ; **to** ~ **off** *vt* annuler ; **to** ~ **on** *vt fus* (*visit*) rendre visite à, passer voir ; (*request*): **to** ~ **on sb to do** inviter qn à faire ; **to** ~ **up** *vt* (MIL) appeler, mobiliser ; ~**box** *n* cabine *f* téléphonique ; ~**er** *n* personne *f* qui appelle ; visiteur *m* ; ~ **girl** *n* call-girl *f* ; ~**ing** *n* vocation *f* ; (*trade, occupation*) état *m* ; ~**ing card** *n* (US) carte *f* de visite.

**callous** ['kæləs] *a* dur(e), insensible ; ~**ness** *n* dureté *f*, manque *m* de cœur, insensibilité *f*.

**callow** ['kæləu] *a* sans expérience (de la vie).

**calm** [kɑ:m] *n* calme *m* // *vt* calmer, apaiser // *a* calme ; ~**ly** *ad* calmement, avec calme ; ~**ness** *n* calme *m* ; **to** ~ **down** *vi* se calmer, s'apaiser // *vt* calmer, apaiser.

**calorie** ['kælərɪ] *n* calorie *f*.

**calve** [kɑ:v] *vi* vêler, mettre bas.

**calves** [kɑ:vz] *npl of* **calf**.

**camber** ['kæmbə*] *n* (*of road*) bombement *m*.

**Cambodia** [kæm'bəudjə] *n* Cambodge *m*.

**came** [keɪm] *pt of* **come**.

**camel** ['kæməl] *n* chameau *m*.

**cameo** ['kæmɪəu] *n* camée *m*.

**camera** ['kæmərə] *n* appareil-photo *m* ; (*also*: **cine-**~, **movie** ~) caméra *f* ; **35mm** ~ appareil 24 x 36 *or* petit format ; **in** ~ à huis clos, en privé ; ~**man** *n* caméraman *m*.

**camouflage** ['kæməflɑ:ʒ] *n* camouflage *m* // *vt* camoufler.

**camp** [kæmp] *n* camp *m* //. *vi* camper.

**campaign** [kæm'peɪn] *n* (MIL, POL *etc*) campagne *f* // *vi* (*also fig*) faire campagne.

**campbed** ['kæmp'bɛd] *n* lit *m* de camp.

**camper** ['kæmpə*] *n* campeur/euse.

**camping** ['kæmpɪŋ] *n* camping *m* ; ~ **site** *n* (terrain *m* de) camping.

**campsite** ['kæmpsaɪt] *n* campement *m*.

**campus** ['kæmpəs] *n* campus *m*.

**can** [kæn] *auxiliary vb* (*gen*) pouvoir ; (*know how to*) savoir ; **I** ~ **swim** *etc* je sais nager *etc* ; **I** ~ **speak French** je parle français // *n* (*of milk, oil, water*) bidon *m* ; (US: *tin*) boîte *f* (de conserve) // *vt* mettre en conserve.

**Canada** ['kænədə] *n* Canada *m*.

**Canadian** [kə'neɪdɪən] *a* canadien(ne) // *n* Canadien/ne.

**canal** [kə'næl] *n* canal *m*.

**canary** [kə'nɛərɪ] *n* canari *m*, serin *m*.

**cancel** ['kænsəl] *vt* annuler ; (*train*) supprimer ; (*party, appointment*) décommander ; (*cross out*) barrer, rayer ; (*stamp*) oblitérer ; ~**lation** [-'leɪʃən] *n* annulation *f* ; suppression *f* ; oblitération *f* ; (TOURISM) réservation annulée, client *etc* qui s'est décommandé.

**cancer** ['kænsə*] *n* cancer *m* ; **C**~ (*sign*) le Cancer ; **to be C**~ être du Cancer.

**candid** ['kændɪd] *a* (très) franc(franche), sincère.

**candidate** ['kændɪdeɪt] *n* candidat/e.

**candle** ['kændl] *n* bougie *f* ; (*of tallow*) chandelle *f* ; (*in church*) cierge *m* ; **by** ~**light** à la lumière d'une bougie ; (*dinner*) aux chandelles ; ~**stick** *n* (*also*: ~ **holder**) bougeoir *m* ; (*bigger, ornate*) chandelier *m*.

**candour** ['kændə*] *n* (grande) franchise *or* sincérité.

**candy** ['kændɪ] *n* sucre candi ; (US) bonbon *m* ; ~**-floss** *n* barbe *f* à papa.

**cane** [keɪn] *n* canne *f* // *vt* (SCOL) administrer des coups de bâton à.

**canine** ['kænaɪn] *a* canin(e).

**canister** ['kænɪstə*] *n* boîte *f* (*gén en métal*).

**cannabis** ['kænəbɪs] *n* (*drug*) cannabis *m* ; (*also*: ~ **plant**) chanvre indien.

**canned** ['kænd] *a* (*food*) en boîte, en conserve.

**cannibal** ['kænɪbəl] *n* cannibale *m/f*, anthropophage *m/f* ; ~**ism** *n* cannibalisme *m*, anthropophagie *f*.

**cannon**, *pl* ~ *or* ~**s** ['kænən] *n* (*gun*) canon *m* ; ~**ball** *n* boulet *m* de canon.

**cannot** ['kænɔt] = **can not**.

**canny** ['kænɪ] *a* madré(e), finaud(e).

**canoe** [kə'nu:] *n* pirogue *f* ; (SPORT) canoë *m* ; ~**ing** *n* (SPORT) canoë *m* ; ~**ist** *n* canoëiste *m/f*.

**canon** ['kænən] *n* (*clergyman*) chanoine *m* ; (*standard*) canon *m*.

**canonize** ['kænənaɪz] *vt* canoniser.

**can opener** ['kænəupnə*] *n* ouvre-boîte *m*.

**canopy** ['kænəpɪ] *n* baldaquin ; dais *m*.

**cant** [kænt] *n* jargon *m* // *vt, vi* pencher.

**can't** [kænt] = **can not**.

**cantankerous** [kæn'tæŋkərəs] *a* querelleur(euse), acariâtre.

**canteen** [kæn'ti:n] *n* cantine *f* ; (*of cutlery*) ménagère *f*.

**canter** ['kæntə*] *n* petit galop // *vi* aller au petit galop.

**cantilever** ['kæntɪli:və*] *n* porte-à-faux *m inv*.

**canvas** ['kænvəs] *n* (*gen*) toile *f* ; **under** ~ (*camping*) sous la tente ; (NAUT) toutes voiles dehors.

**canvass** ['kænvəs] *vt*: ~**ing** (POL) prospection électorale, démarchage électoral ; (COMM) démarchage, prospection.

**canyon** ['kænjən] *n* cañon *m*, gorge *f* (profonde).

**cap** [kæp] *n* casquette *f* ; (*of pen*) capuchon *m* ; (*of bottle*) capsule *f* ; (*also*: **Dutch** ~)

diaphragme *m*; (*FOOTBALL*) sèlection *f* pour l'équipe nationale // *vt* capsuler; (*outdo*) surpasser; ~**ped with** coiffé(e) de.

**capability** [keɪpə'bɪlɪtɪ] *n* aptitude *f*, capacité *f*.

**capable** ['keɪpəbl] *a* capable; ~ **of** capable de; susceptible de.

**capacity** [kə'pæsɪtɪ] *n* capacité *f*, contenance *f*; aptitude *f*; **in his ~ as** en sa qualité de; **to work at full ~** travailler à plein rendement.

**cape** [keɪp] *n* (*garment*) cape *f*; (*GEO*) cap *m*.

**caper** ['keɪpə*] *n* (*CULIN*: *gen*: ~s) câpre *f*.

**capital** ['kæpɪtl] *n* (*also*: ~ **city**) capitale *f*; (*money*) capital *m*; (*also*: ~ **letter**) majuscule *f*; ~ **gains** *npl* plus-values *fpl*; ~**ism** *n* capitalisme *m*; ~**ist** *a* capitaliste; ~ **punishment** *n* peine capitale.

**capitulate** [kə'pɪtjuleɪt] *vi* capituler; **capitulation** [-'leɪʃən] *n* capitulation *f*.

**capricious** [kə'prɪʃəs] *a* capricieux(euse), fantasque.

**Capricorn** ['kæprɪkɔ:n] *n* le Capricorne; **to be ~** être du Capricorne.

**capsize** [kæp'saɪz] *vt* faire chavirer // *vi* chavirer.

**capstan** ['kæpstən] *n* cabestan *m*.

**capsule** ['kæpsju:l] *n* capsule *f*.

**captain** ['kæptɪn] *n* capitaine *m* // *vt* commander, être le capitaine de.

**caption** ['kæpʃən] *n* légende *f*.

**captivate** ['kæptɪveɪt] *vt* captiver, fasciner.

**captive** ['kæptɪv] *a*, *n* captif(ivc).

**captivity** [kæp'tɪvɪtɪ] *n* captivité *f*.

**capture** ['kæptʃə*] *vt* capturer, prendre; (*attention*) capter // *n* capture *f*.

**car** [kɑ:*] *n* voiture *f*, auto *f*.

**carafe** [kə'ræf] *n* carafe *f*; (*in restaurant*: ~ **wine**) ≈ vin ouvert.

**caramel** ['kærəməl] *n* caramel *m*.

**carat** ['kærət] *n* carat *m*.

**caravan** ['kærəvæn] *n* caravane *f*.

**caraway** ['kærəweɪ] *n*: ~ **seed** graine *f* de cumin, cumin *m*.

**carbohydrates** [kɑ:bəu'haɪdreɪts] *npl* (*foods*) aliments *mpl* riches en hydrate de carbone.

**carbon** ['kɑ:bən] *n* carbone *m*; ~ **copy** *n* carbone *m*; ~ **paper** *n* papier *m* carbone.

**carburettor** [kɑ:bju'rɛtə*] *n* carburateur *m*.

**carcass** ['kɑ:kəs] *n* carcasse *f*.

**card** [kɑ:d] *n* carte *f*; ~**board** *n* carton *m*; ~ **game** *n* jeu *m* de cartes.

**cardiac** ['kɑ:dɪæk] *a* cardiaque.

**cardigan** ['kɑ:dɪgən] *n* cardigan *m*.

**cardinal** ['kɑ:dɪnl] *a* cardinal(e) // *n* cardinal *m*.

**card index** ['kɑ:dɪndɛks] *n* fichier *m* (alphabétique).

**care** [kɛə*] *n* soin *m*, attention *f*; (*worry*) souci *m* // *vi*: **to ~ about** se soucier de, s'intéresser à; **would you ~ to/for . . . ?** voulez-vous ...?; **I wouldn't ~ to do it** je n'aimerais pas le faire; **in sb's ~** à la garde de qn, confié à qn; **to take ~** faire attention, prendre garde; **to take ~ of** *vt* s'occuper de, prendre soin de; **to ~**

**for** *vt fus* s'occuper de; (*like*) aimer; **I don't ~** ça m'est bien égal, peu m'importe; **I couldn't ~ less** cela m'est complètement égal, je m'en fiche complètement.

**career** [kə'rɪə*] *n* carrière *f* // *vi* (*also*: ~ **along**) aller à toute allure.

**carefree** ['kɛəfri:] *a* sans souci, insouciant(e).

**careful** ['kɛəful] *a* soigneux(euse); (*cautious*) prudent(e); **(be) ~!** (fais) attention!; ~**ly** *ad* avec soin, soigneusement; prudemment.

**careless** ['kɛəlɪs] *a* négligent(e); (*heedless*) insouciant(e); ~**ly** *ad* négligemment; avec insouciance; ~**ness** *n* manque *m* de soin, négligence *f*; insouciance *f*.

**caress** [kə'rɛs] *n* caresse *f* // *vt* caresser.

**caretaker** ['kɛəteɪkə*] *n* gardien/ne, concierge *m/f*.

**car-ferry** ['kɑ:fɛrɪ] *n* (*on sea*) ferry (-boat) *m*; (*on river*) bac *m*.

**cargo, ~es** ['kɑ:gəu] *n* cargaison *f*, chargement *m*.

**Caribbean** [kærɪ'bi:ən] *a*: **the ~ (Sea)** la mer des Antilles *or* Caraïbes.

**caricature** ['kærɪkətjuə*] *n* caricature *f*.

**carnal** ['kɑ:nl] *a* charnel(le).

**carnation** [kɑ:'neɪʃən] *n* œillet *m*.

**carnival** ['kɑ:nɪvəl] *n* (*public celebration*) carnaval *m*.

**carol** ['kærəl] *n*: **(Christmas) ~** chant *m* de Noël.

**carp** [kɑ:p] *n* (*fish*) carpe *f*; **to ~ at** *vt fus* critiquer.

**car park** ['kɑ:pɑ:k] *n* parking *m*, parc *m* de stationnement.

**carpenter** ['kɑ:pɪntə*] *n* charpentier *m*.

**carpentry** ['kɑ:pɪntrɪ] *n* charpenterie *f*, métier *m* de charpentier; (*woodwork*: *at school etc*) menuiserie *f*.

**carpet** ['kɑ:pɪt] *n* tapis *m* // *vt* recouvrir (d'un tapis).

**carriage** ['kærɪdʒ] *n* voiture *f*; (*of goods*) transport *m*; (: *taxe*) port *m*; (*of typewriter*) chariot *m*; (*bearing*) maintien *m*, port *m*; ~**way** *n* (*part of road*) chaussée *f*.

**carrier** ['kærɪə*] *n* transporteur *m*, camionneur *m*; ~ **bag** *n* sac *m* en papier *or* en plastique; ~ **pigeon** *n* pigeon voyageur.

**carrot** ['kærət] *n* carotte *f*.

**carry** ['kærɪ] *vt* (*subj*: *person*) porter; (: *vehicle*) transporter; (*a motion*, *bill*) voter, adopter; (*involve*: *responsibilities etc*) comporter, impliquer // *vi* (*sound*) porter; **to be carried away** (*fig*) s'emballer, s'enthousiasmer; **to ~ on** *vi*: **to ~ on with sth/doing** continuer qch/à faire // *vt* entretenir, poursuivre; **to ~ out** *vt* (*orders*) exécuter; (*investigation*) effectuer; ~**cot** *n* porte-bébé *m*.

**cart** [kɑ:t] *n* charrette *f* // *vt* transporter.

**cartilage** ['kɑ:tɪlɪdʒ] *n* cartilage *m*.

**cartographer** [kɑ:'tɔgrəfə*] *n* cartographe *m/f*.

**carton** ['kɑ:tən] *n* (*box*) carton *m*; (*of yogurt*) pot *m* (en carton); (*of cigarettes*) cartouche *f*.

**cartoon** [kɑ:'tu:n] n (PRESS) dessin m (humoristique); (satirical) caricature f; (comic strip) bande dessinée; (CINEMA) dessin animé; **~ist** n dessinateur/trice humoristique; caricaturiste m/f; auteur m de dessins animés; auteur de bandes dessinées.

**cartridge** ['kɑ:trɪdʒ] n (for gun, pen) cartouche f; (for camera) chargeur m; (music tape) cassette f; (of record player) cellule f.

**carve** [kɑ:v] vt (meat) découper; (wood, stone) tailler, sculpter; **carving** n (in wood etc) sculpture f; **carving knife** n couteau m à découper.

**car wash** ['kɑ:wɔʃ] n station f de lavage (de voitures).

**cascade** [kæs'keɪd] n cascade f // vi tomber en cascade.

**case** [keɪs] n cas m; (LAW) affaire f, procès m; (box) caisse f, boîte f, étui m; (also: suit~) valise f; **he hasn't put forward his ~ very well** ses arguments ne sont guère convaincants; **in ~ of** en cas de; **in ~ he** au cas où il; **just in ~** à tout hasard.

**cash** [kæʃ] n argent m; (COMM) argent liquide, numéraire m; liquidités fpl; (COMM: in payment) argent comptant, espèces fpl // vt encaisser; **to pay (in) ~** payer (en argent) comptant; **~ with order/ on delivery** (COMM) payable or paiement à la commande/livraison; **~book** n livre m de caisse; **~desk** n caisse f.

**cashew** [kæ'ʃu:] n (also: ~ nut) noix f de cajou.

**cashier** [kæ'ʃɪə*] n caissier/ère.

**cashmere** [kæʃ'mɪə*] n cachemire m.

**cash payment** ['kæʃ'peɪmənt] n paiement comptant, versement m en espèces.

**cash register** ['kæʃrɛdʒɪstə*] n caisse enregistreuse.

**casing** ['keɪsɪŋ] n revêtement (protecteur), enveloppe (protectrice).

**casino** [kə'si:nəu] n casino m.

**cask** [kɑ:sk] n tonneau m.

**casket** ['kɑ:skɪt] n coffret m; (US: coffin) cercueil m.

**casserole** ['kæsərəul] n cocotte f; (food) ragoût m (en cocotte).

**cassette** [kæ'sɛt] n cassette f, musicassette f; **~player** lecteur m de cassettes; **~recorder** magnétophone m à cassettes.

**cast** [kɑ:st] vt (pt, pp cast) (throw) jeter; (shed) perdre; se dépouiller de; (metal) couler, fondre // n (THEATRE) distribution f; (mould) moule m; (also: plaster ~) plâtre m; (THEATRE): **to ~ sb as Hamlet** attribuer à qn le rôle d'Hamlet; **to ~ one's vote** voter, exprimer son suffrage; **to ~ off** vi (NAUT) larguer les amarres.

**castanets** [kæstə'nɛts] npl castagnettes fpl.

**castaway** ['kɑ:stəwəɪ] n naufragé/e.

**caste** [kɑ:st] n caste f, classe sociale.

**casting** ['kɑ:stɪŋ] a: ~ **vote** voix prépondérante (pour départager).

**cast iron** ['kɑ:st'aɪən] n fonte f.

**castle** ['kɑ:sl] n château-fort m; (manor) château m.

**castor** ['kɑ:stə*] n (wheel) roulette f; ~ **oil** n huile f de ricin; ~ **sugar** n sucre m semoule.

**castrate** [kæs'treɪt] vt châtrer.

**casual** ['kæʒjul] a (by chance) de hasard, fait(e) au hasard, fortuit(e); (irregular: work etc) temporaire; (unconcerned) désinvolte; ~ **wear** n vêtements mpl sport inv; ~ **labour** n main-d'œuvre f temporaire; ~**ly** ad avec désinvolture, négligemment; fortuitement.

**casualty** ['kæʒjultɪ] n accidenté/e, blessé/e; (dead) victime f, mort/e; **heavy casualties** npl lourdes pertes.

**cat** [kæt] n chat m.

**catalogue, catalog** (US) ['kætələg] n catalogue m // vt cataloguer.

**catalyst** ['kætəlɪst] n catalyseur m.

**catapult** ['kætəpʌlt] n lance-pierres m inv, fronde m; (AVIAT, HISTORY) catapulte f.

**cataract** ['kætərækt] n (also MED) cataracte f.

**catarrh** [kə'tɑ:*] n rhume m chronique, catarrhe f.

**catastrophe** [kə'tæstrəfɪ] n catastrophe f; **catastrophic** [kætə'strɔfɪk] a catastrophique.

**catch** [kætʃ] vb (pt,pp caught [cɔ:t]) vt (ball, train, thief, cold) attraper; (person: by surprise) prendre, surprendre; (understand) saisir; (get entangled) accrocher // vi (fire) prendre // n (fish etc caught) prise f; (thief etc caught) capture f; (trick) attrape f; (TECH) loquet m; cliquet m; **to ~ sb's attention** or **eye** attirer l'attention de qn; **to ~ fire** prendre feu; **to ~ sight of** apercevoir; **to ~ up** vi se rattraper, combler son retard // vt (also: ~ up with) rattraper.

**catching** ['kætʃɪŋ] a (MED) contagieux(euse).

**catchment area** ['kætʃmənt'ɛərɪə] n (SCOL) aire f de recrutement; (GEO) bassin m hydrographique.

**catch phrase** ['kætʃfreɪz] n slogan m; expression toute faite.

**catchy** ['kætʃɪ] a (tune) facile à retenir.

**catechism** ['kætɪkɪzəm] n (REL) catéchisme m.

**categoric(al)** [kætɪ'gɔrɪk(əl)] a catégorique.

**categorize** ['kætɪgəraɪz] vt classer par catégories.

**category** ['kætɪgərɪ] n catégorie f.

**cater** ['keɪtə*] vi (gen: ~ for sb) préparer des repas, se charger de la restauration; **to ~ for** vt fus (needs) satisfaire, pourvoir à; (readers, consumers) s'adresser à, pourvoir aux besoins de; ~**er** n traiteur m; fournisseur m; ~**ing** n restauration f; approvisionnement m, ravitaillement m; ~**ing (trade)** restauration f.

**caterpillar** ['kætəpɪlə*] n chenille f; ~ **track** n chenille f; ~ **vehicle** n véhicule m à chenille.

**cathedral** [kə'θi:drəl] n cathédrale f.

**catholic** ['kæθəlɪk] a éclectique; universel(le); libéral(e); **C~** a,n (REL) catholique (m/f).

**cattle** ['kætl] npl bétail m, bestiaux mpl.

**catty** ['kætɪ] *a* méchant(e).
**Caucasus** ['kɔ:kəsəs] *n* Caucase *m*.
**caught** [kɔ:t] *pt,pp of* **catch**.
**cauliflower** ['kɔlɪflauə*] *n* chou-fleur *m*.
**cause** [kɔ:z] *n* cause *f* // *vt* causer ; **there is no ~ for concern** il n'y a pas lieu de s'inquiéter.
**causeway** ['kɔ:zweɪ] *n* chaussée (surélevée).
**caustic** ['kɔ:stɪk] *a* caustique.
**caution** ['kɔ:ʃən] *n* prudence *f*; (*warning*) avertissement *m* // *vt* avertir, donner un avertissement à.
**cautious** ['kɔ:ʃəs] *a* prudent(e) ; **~ly** *ad* prudemment, avec prudence ; **~ness** *n* prudence *f*.
**cavalier** [kævə'lɪə*] *a* cavalier(ère), désinvolte.
**cavalry** ['kævəlrɪ] *n* cavalerie *f*.
**cave** [keɪv] *n* caverne *f*, grotte *f*; **to ~ in** *vi* (*roof etc*) s'effondrer ; **~man** *n* homme *m* des cavernes.
**cavern** ['kævən] *n* caverne *f*.
**caviar(e)** ['kævɪɑ:*] *n* caviar *m*.
**cavity** ['kævɪtɪ] *n* cavité *f*.
**cavort** [kə'vɔ:t] *vi* cabrioler, faire des cabrioles.
**CBI** *n* *abbr of* Confederation of British Industries (*groupement du patronat*).
**cc** *abbr of* cubic centimetres ; carbon copy.
**cease** [si:s] *vt,vi* cesser ; **~fire** *n* cessez-le-feu *m*; **~less** *a* incessant(e), continuel(le).
**cedar** ['si:də*] *n* cèdre *m*.
**cede** [si:d] *vt* céder.
**cedilla** [sɪ'dɪlə] *n* cédille *f*.
**ceiling** ['si:lɪŋ] *n* plafond *m*.
**celebrate** ['sɛlɪbreɪt] *vt,vi* célébrer ; **~d** *a* célèbre ; **celebration** [-'breɪʃən] *n* célébration *f*.
**celebrity** [sɪ'lɛbrɪtɪ] *n* célébrité *f*.
**celery** ['sɛlərɪ] *n* céleri *m* (en branches).
**celestial** [sɪ'lɛstɪəl] *a* céleste.
**celibacy** ['sɛlɪbəsɪ] *n* célibat *m*.
**cell** [sɛl] *n* (*gen*) cellule *f*; (*ELEC*) élément *m* (de pile).
**cellar** ['sɛlə*] *n* cave *f*.
**'cellist** ['tʃɛlɪst] *n* violoncelliste *m/f*.
**'cello** ['tʃɛləu] *n* violoncelle *m*.
**cellophane** ['sɛləfeɪn] *n* ® cellophane *f* ®.
**cellular** ['sɛljulə*] *a* cellulaire.
**cellulose** ['sɛljuləus] *n* cellulose *f*.
**Celtic** ['kɛltɪk, 'sɛltɪk] *a* celte.
**cement** [sə'mɛnt] *n* ciment *m* // *vt* cimenter.
**cemetery** ['sɛmɪtrɪ] *n* cimetière *m*.
**cenotaph** ['sɛnətɑ:f] *n* cénotaphe *m*.
**censor** ['sɛnsə*] *n* censeur *m*; **~ship** *n* censure *f*.
**censure** ['sɛnʃə*] *vt* blâmer, critiquer.
**census** ['sɛnsəs] *n* recensement *m*.
**cent** [sɛnt] *n* (US: coin) cent *m*, = 1:100 du dollar ; see also **per**.
**centenary** [sɛn'ti:nərɪ] *n* centenaire *m*.
**center** ['sɛntə*] *n* (US) = **centre**.
**centi...** ['sɛntɪ] prefix: **~grade** *a* centigrade ; **~litre** *n* centilitre *m*; **~metre** *n* centimètre *m*.
**centipede** ['sɛntɪpi:d] *n* mille-pattes *m inv*.

**central** ['sɛntrəl] *a* central(e) ; **~ heating** *n* chauffage central ; **~ize** *vt* centraliser.
**centre** ['sɛntə*] *n* centre *m*; **~-forward** *n* (SPORT) avant-centre *m* // *vt* centrer ; (PHOT) cadrer **~-half** *n* (SPORT) demi-centre *m*.
**centrifugal** [sɛn'trɪfjugəl] *a* centrifuge.
**century** ['sɛntjurɪ] *n* siècle *m*.
**ceramic** [sɪ'ræmɪk] *a* céramique.
**cereal** ['si:rɪəl] *n* céréale *f*.
**ceremony** ['sɛrɪmənɪ] *n* cérémonie *f*; **to stand on ~** faire des façons.
**certain** ['sə:tən] *a* certain(e) ; **to make ~ of** s'assurer de ; **for ~** certainement, sûrement ; **~ly** *ad* certainement ; **~ty** *n* certitude *f*.
**certificate** [sə'tɪfɪkɪt] *n* certificat *m*.
**certify** ['sə:tɪfaɪ] *vt* certifier // *vi*: **to ~ to** attester.
**cervix** ['sə:vɪks] *n* col *m* de l'utérus.
**cessation** [sə'seɪʃən] *n* cessation *f*, arrêt *m*.
**cesspool** ['sɛspu:l] *n* fosse *f* d'aisance.
**Ceylon** [sɪ'lɔn] *n* Ceylan *m*.
**cf.** (abbr = compare) cf., voir.
**chafe** [tʃeɪf] *vt* irriter, frotter contre.
**chaffinch** ['tʃæfɪntʃ] *n* pinson *m*.
**chagrin** ['ʃægrɪn] *n* contrariété *f*, déception *f*.
**chain** [tʃeɪn] *n* (gen) chaîne *f* // *vt* (also: **~ up**) enchaîner, attacher (avec une chaîne) ; **~ reaction** *n* réaction *f* en chaîne ; **to ~ smoke** *vi* fumer cigarette sur cigarette ; **~ store** *n* magasin *m* à succursales multiples.
**chair** [tʃɛə*] *n* chaise *f*; (armchair) fauteuil *m*; (of university) chaire *f* // *vt* (meeting) présider ; **~lift** *n* télésiège *m*; **~man** *n* président *m*.
**chalet** ['ʃæleɪ] *n* chalet *m*.
**chalice** ['tʃælɪs] *n* calice *m*.
**chalk** [tʃɔ:k] *n* craie *f*.
**challenge** ['tʃælɪndʒ] *n* défi *m* // *vt* défier ; (statement, right) mettre en question, contester ; **to ~ sb to a fight/game** inviter qn à se battre/à jouer (sous forme d'un défi) ; **to ~ sb to do** mettre qn au défi de faire ; **~r** *n* (SPORT) challenger *m*; **challenging** *a* de défi, provocateur(trice).
**chamber** ['tʃeɪmbə*] *n* chambre *f*; **~ of commerce** chambre *f* de commerce ; **~maid** *n* femme *f* de chambre ; **~ music** *n* musique *f* de chambre ; **~pot** *n* pot *m* de chambre.
**chamois** ['ʃæmwɑ:] *n* chamois *m*; **~ leather** ['ʃæmɪlɛðə*] *n* peau *f* de chamois.
**champagne** [ʃæm'peɪn] *n* champagne *m*.
**champion** ['tʃæmpɪən] *n* champion/ne *m*; **~ship** *n* championnat *m*.
**chance** [tʃɑ:ns] *n* hasard *m*; (opportunity) occasion *f*, possibilité *f*; (hope, likelihood) chance *f* // *vt*: **to ~ it** risquer (le coup), essayer // *a* fortuit(e), de hasard ; **there is little ~ of his coming** il est peu probable or il y a peu de chances qu'il vienne ; **to take a ~** prendre un risque ; **by ~** par hasard.
**chancel** ['tʃɑ:nsəl] *n* chœur *m*.
**chancellor** ['tʃɑ:nsələ*] *n* chancelier *m*;

C~ of the Exchequer *n* chancelier *m* de l'Échiquier.

**chandelier** [ʃændə'liə*] *n* lustre *m*.

**change** [tʃeɪndʒ] *vt* (*alter, replace,* COMM: *money*) changer ; (*switch, substitute: gear, hands, trains, clothes, one's name etc*) changer de ; (*transform*): **to ~ sb into** changer *or* transformer qn en // *vi* (*gen*) changer ; (*change clothes*) se changer ; (*be transformed*): **to ~ into** se changer *or* transformer en // *n* changement *m* ; (*money*) monnaie *f* ; **to ~ one's mind** changer d'avis ; **a ~ of clothes** des vêtements de rechange ; **for a ~** pour changer ; **small ~** petite monnaie ; **to give sb ~ for** *or* **of £10** faire à qn la monnaie de 10 livres ; **~able** *a* (*weather*) variable ; **~over** *n* (*to new system*) changement *m*, passage *m*.

**changing** ['tʃeɪndʒɪŋ] *a* changeant(e) ; **~ room** *n* (*in shop*) salon *m* d'essayage ; (SPORT) vestiaire *m*.

**channel** ['tʃænl] *n* (TV) chaîne *f* ; (*waveband, groove, fig: medium*) canal *m* ; (*of river, sea*) chenal *m* // *vt* canaliser ; **through the usual ~s** en suivant la filière habituelle ; **the (English) C~** la Manche ; **the C~ Islands** les îles de la Manche, les îles anglo-normandes.

**chant** [tʃɑːnt] *n* chant *m* ; mélopée *f* ; psalmodie *f* // *vt* chanter, scander ; psalmodier.

**chaos** ['keɪɔs] *n* chaos *m*.

**chaotic** [keɪ'ɔtɪk] *a* chaotique.

**chap** [tʃæp] *n* (col: *man*) type *m* // *vt* (*skin*) gercer, crevasser.

**chapel** ['tʃæpəl] *n* chapelle *f*.

**chaperon** ['ʃæpərəun] *n* chaperon *m* // *vt* chaperonner.

**chaplain** ['tʃæplɪn] *n* aumônier *m*.

**chapter** ['tʃæptə*] *n* chapitre *m*.

**char** [tʃɑː*] *vt* (*burn*) carboniser // *vi* (*cleaner*) faire des ménages // *n* = **charlady**.

**character** ['kærɪktə*] *n* caractère *m* ; (*in novel, film*) personnage *m* ; (*eccentric*) numéro *m*, phénomène *m* ; **~istic** [-'rɪstɪk] *a,n* caractéristique (*f*) ; **~ize** *vt* caractériser.

**charade** [ʃə'rɑːd] *n* charade *f*.

**charcoal** ['tʃɑːkəul] *n* charbon *m* de bois.

**charge** [tʃɑːdʒ] *n* accusation *f* ; (LAW) inculpation *f* ; (*cost*) prix (demandé) ; (*of gun, battery,* MIL: *attack*) charge *f* // *vt* (LAW): **to ~sb (with)** inculper qn (de) ; (*gun, battery,* MIL: *enemy*) charger ; (*customer, sum*) faire payer // *vi* (*gen with: up, along* etc) foncer ; **~s** *npl*: **bank/labour ~s** frais *mpl* de banque/main -d'œuvre ; **to ~ in/out** entrer/sortir en trombe ; **to ~ down/up** dévaler/grimper à toute allure ; **is there a ~?** doit-on payer? ; **there's no ~** c'est gratuit, on ne fait pas payer ; **to take ~ of** se charger de ; **to be in ~ of** être responsable de, s'occuper de ; **to have ~ of sb** avoir la charge de qn ; **they ~d us £10 for the meal** ils nous ont fait payer le repas 10 livres, ils nous ont compté 10 livres pour le repas ; **how much do you ~ for this repair?** combien demandez-vous pour cette réparation? ; **to ~ an**

**expense (up) to sb** mettre une dépense sur le compte de qn.

**charitable** ['tʃærɪtəbl] *a* charitable.

**charity** ['tʃærɪtɪ] *n* charité *f* ; institution *f* charitable *or* de bienfaisance, œuvre *f* (de charité).

**charlady** ['tʃɑːleɪdɪ] *n* femme *f* de ménage.

**charm** [tʃɑːm] *n* charme *m* // *vt* charmer, enchanter ; **~ing** *a* charmant(e).

**chart** [tʃɑːt] *n* tableau *m*, diagramme *m* ; graphique *m* ; (*map*) carte marine // *vt* dresser *or* établir la carte de.

**charter** ['tʃɑːtə*] *vt* (*plane*) affréter // *n* (*document*) charte *f* ; **~ed accountant** *n* expert-comptable *m* ; **~ flight** *n* charter *m*.

**charwoman**    ['tʃɑːwumən]    *n* = **charlady**.

**chase** [tʃeɪs] *vt* poursuivre, pourchasser // *n* poursuite *f*, chasse *f*.

**chasm** ['kæzəm] *n* gouffre *m*, abîme *m*.

**chassis** ['ʃæsɪ] *n* châssis *m*.

**chastity** ['tʃæstɪtɪ] *n* chasteté *f*.

**chat** [tʃæt] *vi* (*also:* **have a ~**) bavarder, causer // *n* conversation *f*.

**chatter** ['tʃætə*] *vi* (*person*) bavarder, papoter // *n* bavardage *m*, papotage *m* ; **my teeth are ~ing** je claque des dents ; **~box** *n* moulin *m* à paroles, babillard/e.

**chatty** ['tʃætɪ] *a* (*style*) familier(ère) ; (*person*) enclin(e) à bavarder *or* au papotage.

**chauffeur** ['ʃəufə*] *n* chauffeur *m* (de maître).

**cheap** [tʃiːp] *a* bon marché *inv*, pas cher(chère) ; (*joke*) facile, d'un goût douteux ; (*poor quality*) à bon marché, de qualité médiocre // *ad* à bon marché, pour pas cher ; **~en** *vt* rabaisser, déprécier ; **~ly** *ad* à bon marché, à bon compte.

**cheat** [tʃiːt] *vi* tricher // *vt* tromper, duper ; (*rob*) escroquer // *n* tricheur/euse ; escroc *m* ; (*trick*) duperie *f*, tromperie *f* ; **~ing** *n* tricherie *f*.

**check** [tʃɛk] *vt* vérifier ; (*passport, ticket*) contrôler ; (*halt*) enrayer ; (*restrain*) maîtriser // *n* vérification *f* ; contrôle *m* ; (*curb*) frein *m* ; (*bill*) addition *f* ; (*pattern: gen pl*) carreaux *mpl* ; (US) = **cheque** ; **to ~ in** *vi* (*in hotel*) remplir sa fiche (d'hôtel) ; (*at airport*) se présenter à l'enregistrement // *vt* (*luggage*) (faire) enregistrer ; **to ~ off** *vt* cocher ; **to ~ out** *vi* (*in hotel*) régler sa note // *vt* (*luggage*) retirer ; **to ~ up** *vi*: **to ~ up on sth** vérifier (qch) ; **to ~ up on sb** se renseigner sur le compte de qn ; **~ers** *n* (US) jeu *m* de dames ; **~mate** *n* échec et mat *m* ; **~point** *n* contrôle *m* ; **~up** *n* (MED) examen médical, check-up *m*.

**cheek** [tʃiːk] *n* joue *f* ; (*impudence*) toupet *m*, culot *m* ; **~bone** *n* pommette *f* ; **~y** *a* effronté(e), culotté(e).

**cheer** [tʃɪə*] *vt* acclamer, applaudir ; (*gladden*) réjouir, réconforter // *vi* applaudir // *n* (*gen pl*) acclamations *fpl*, applaudissements *mpl* ; bravos *mpl*, hourras *mpl* ; **~s!** (à votre) santé! ; **to ~ up** *vi* se dérider, reprendre courage // *vt* remonter le moral *or* de, dérider, égayer ; **~ful** *a* gai(e), joyeux(euse) ; **~fulness** *n* gaieté *f*, bonne humeur ; **~io** *excl* salut!, au revoir! ; **~less** *a* sombre, triste.

**cheese** [tʃiːz] n fromage m ; ~**board** n plateau m à fromages.

**chef** [ʃɛf] n chef (cuisinier).

**chemical** ['kɛmɪkəl] a chimique // n produit m chimique.

**chemist** ['kɛmɪst] n pharmacien/ne ; (scientist) chimiste m/f ; ~**ry** n chimie f ; ~'s (shop) n pharmacie f.

**cheque** [tʃɛk] n chèque m ; ~**book** n chéquier m, carnet m de chèques.

**chequered** ['tʃɛkəd] a (fig) varié(e).

**cherish** ['tʃɛrɪʃ] vt chérir ; (hope etc) entretenir.

**cheroot** [ʃə'ruːt] n cigare m de Manille.

**cherry** ['tʃɛrɪ] n cerise f.

**chess** [tʃɛs] n échecs mpl ; ~**board** n échiquier m ; ~**man** n pièce f (de jeu d'échecs) ; ~**player** n joueur/euse d'échecs.

**chest** [tʃɛst] n poitrine f ; (box) coffre m, caisse f ; ~ of drawers n commode f.

**chestnut** ['tʃɛsnʌt] n châtaigne f ; ~ (tree) n châtaignier m.

**chew** [tʃuː] vt mâcher ; ~**ing gum** n chewing-gum m.

**chic** [ʃiːk] a chic inv, élégant(e).

**chick** [tʃɪk] n poussin m.

**chicken** ['tʃɪkɪn] n poulet m ; ~ feed n (fig) broutilles fpl, bagatelle f ; ~ pox n varicelle f.

**chick pea** ['tʃɪkpiː] n pois m chiche.

**chicory** ['tʃɪkərɪ] n (for coffee) chicorée f ; (salad) endive f.

**chief** [tʃiːf] n chef m // a principal(e) ; ~**ly** ad principalement, surtout.

**chiffon** ['ʃɪfɒn] n mousseline f de soie.

**chilblain** ['tʃɪlblein] n engelure f.

**child**, pl ~**ren** [tʃaild, 'tʃɪldrən] n enfant m/f ; ~**birth** n accouchement m ; ~**hood** n enfance f ; ~**ish** a puéril(e), enfantin(e) ; ~**like** a innocent(e), pur(e) ; ~ **minder** n garde f d'enfants.

**Chile** ['tʃɪlɪ] n Chili m ; ~**an** a chilien(ne) // n Chilien/ne.

**chill** [tʃɪl] n froid m ; (MED) refroidissement m, coup m de froid // a froid(e), glacial(e) // vt faire frissonner ; refroidir ; (CULIN) mettre au frais, rafraîchir ; serve ~ed à servir frais ; ~**y** a froid(e), glacé(e) ; (sensitive to cold) frileux(euse) ; to feel ~y avoir froid.

**chime** [tʃaim] n carillon m // vi carillonner, sonner.

**chimney** ['tʃɪmnɪ] n cheminée f.

**chimpanzee** [tʃɪmpæn'ziː] n chimpanzé m.

**chin** [tʃɪn] n menton m.

**china** ['tʃainə] n porcelaine f ; (vaisselle f en) porcelaine.

**China** ['tʃainə] n Chine f.

**Chinese** [tʃai'niːz] a chinois(e) // n Chinois/e ; (LING) chinois m.

**chink** [tʃɪŋk] n (opening) fente f, fissure f ; (noise) tintement m.

**chip** [tʃɪp] n (gen pl: CULIN) frite f ; (of wood) copeau m ; (of glass, stone) éclat m // vt (cup, plate) ébrécher ; ~**board** n aggloméré m ; ~**pings** npl: loose ~**pings** gravillons mpl.

**chiropodist** [kɪ'rɒpədɪst] n pédicure m/f.

**chirp** [tʃəːp] n pépiement m, gazouillis m // vi pépier, gazouiller.

**chisel** ['tʃɪzl] n ciseau m.

**chit** [tʃɪt] n mot m, note f.

**chitchat** ['tʃɪttʃæt] n bavardage m, papotage m.

**chivalrous** ['ʃɪvəlrəs] a chevaleresque.

**chivalry** ['ʃɪvəlrɪ] n chevalerie f ; esprit m chevaleresque.

**chives** [tʃaivz] npl ciboulette f, civette f.

**chloride** ['klɔːraid] n chlorure m.

**chlorine** ['klɔːriːn] n chlore m.

**chock** [tʃɒk] n cale f ; ~-a-block, ~-full a plein(e) à craquer.

**chocolate** ['tʃɒklɪt] n chocolat m.

**choice** [tʃɔis] n choix m // a de choix.

**choir** ['kwaiə*] n chœur m, chorale f ; ~**boy** n jeune choriste m, petit chanteur.

**choke** [tʃəuk] vi étouffer // vt étrangler ; étouffer ; (block) boucher, obstruer // n (AUT) starter m.

**cholera** ['kɒlərə] n choléra m.

**choose**, pt **chose**, pp **chosen** [tʃuːz, tʃəuz, 'tʃəuzn] vt choisir ; to ~ to do décider de faire, juger bon de faire.

**chop** [tʃɒp] vt (wood) couper (à la hache) ; (CULIN: also: ~ up) couper (fin), émincer, hacher (en morceaux) // n coup m (de hache, du tranchant de la main) ; (CULIN) côtelette f ; ~**s** npl (jaws) mâchoires fpl ; babines fpl ; to ~ down vt (tree) abattre ; ~**py** a (sea) un peu agité(e) ; ~**sticks** npl baguettes fpl.

**choral** ['kɔːrəl] a choral(e), chanté(e) en chœur.

**chord** [kɔːd] n (MUS) accord m.

**chore** [tʃɔː*] n travail m de routine ; **household** ~**s** travaux mpl du ménage.

**choreographer** [kɒri'ɒgrəfə*] n chorégraphe m/f.

**chorister** ['kɒristə*] n choriste m/f.

**chortle** ['tʃɔːtl] vi glousser.

**chorus** ['kɔːrəs] n chœur m ; (repeated part of song, also fig) refrain m.

**chose** [tʃəuz] pt of **choose**.

**chosen** ['tʃəuzn] pp of **choose**.

**chow** [tʃau] n (dog) chow-chow m.

**Christ** [kraist] n Christ m.

**christen** ['krisn] vt baptiser ; ~**ing** n baptême m.

**Christian** ['kristiən] a,n chrétien(ne) ; ~**ity** [-'ænɪtɪ] n christianisme m ; chrétienté f ; ~ **name** n prénom m.

**Christmas** ['krisməs] n Noël m or f ; ~ **card** n carte f de Noël ; ~ **Eve** n la veille de Noël ; la nuit de Noël ; ~ **tree** n arbre m de Noël.

**chrome** [krəum] n = **chromium**.

**chromium** ['krəumiəm] n chrome m ; (also: ~ **plating**) chromage m.

**chromosome** ['krəuməsəum] n chromosome m.

**chronic** ['krɒnɪk] a chronique.

**chronicle** ['krɒnɪkl] n chronique f.

**chronological** [krɒnə'lɒdʒɪkəl] a chronologique.

**chrysanthemum** [krɪ'sænθəməm] n chrysanthème m.

**chubby** ['tʃʌbɪ] a potelé(e), rondelet(te).

**chuck** [tʃʌk] vt lancer, jeter; **to ～ out** vt flanquer dehors or à la porte; **to ～ (up)** vt lâcher, plaquer.
**chuckle** ['tʃʌkl] vi glousser.
**chum** [tʃʌm] n copain/copine.
**chunk** [tʃʌŋk] n gros morceau; (of bread) quignon m.
**church** [tʃəːtʃ] n église f; **～yard** n cimetière m.
**churlish** ['tʃəːlɪʃ] a grossier(ère); hargneux(euse).
**churn** [tʃəːn] n (for butter) baratte f; (for transport: **milk ～**) (grand) bidon à lait.
**chute** [ʃuːt] n glissoire f; (also: **rubbish ～**) vide-ordures m inv; (children's slide) toboggan m.
**chutney** ['tʃʌtnɪ] n condiment m à base de fruits.
**CID** n (abbr of Criminal Investigation Department) ≈ Police f judiciaire (P.J.).
**cider** ['saɪdə*] n cidre m.
**cigar** [sɪ'gɑː*] n cigare m.
**cigarette** [sɪgə'rɛt] n cigarette f; **～ case** n étui m à cigarettes; **～ end** n mégot m; **～ holder** n fume-cigarettes m inv.
**cinch** [sɪntʃ] n (col): **it's a ～** c'est du gâteau, c'est l'enfance de l'art.
**cinder** ['sɪndə*] n cendre f.
**cine** ['sɪnɪ]: **～-camera** n caméra f; **～-film** n film m.
**cinema** ['sɪnəmə] n cinéma m.
**cine-projector** [sɪnɪprə'dʒɛktə*] n projecteur m de cinéma.
**cinnamon** ['sɪnəmən] n cannelle f.
**cipher** ['saɪfə*] n code secret; (fig: faceless employee etc) numéro m.
**circle** ['səːkl] n cercle m; (in cinema) balcon m // vi faire or décrire des cercles // vt (surround) entourer, encercler; (move round) faire le tour de, tourner autour de.
**circuit** ['səːkɪt] n circuit m; **～ous** [səː'kjuɪtəs] a indirect(e), qui fait un détour.
**circular** ['səːkjulə*] a circulaire // n circulaire f.
**circulate** ['səːkjuleɪt] vi circuler // vt faire circuler; **circulation** [-'leɪʃən] n circulation f; (of newspaper) tirage m.
**circumcise** ['səːkəmsaɪz] vt circoncire.
**circumference** [sə'kʌmfərəns] n circonférence f.
**circumspect** ['səːkəmspɛkt] a circonspect(e).
**circumstances** ['səːkəmstənsɪz] npl circonstances fpl; (financial condition) moyens mpl, situation financière.
**circus** ['səːkəs] n cirque m.
**cistern** ['sɪstən] n réservoir m (d'eau); (in toilet) réservoir m de la chasse d'eau.
**cite** [saɪt] vt citer.
**citizen** ['sɪtɪzn] n (POL) citoyen/ne; (resident): **the ～s of this town** les habitants de cette ville; **～ship** n citoyenneté f.
**citrus fruit** ['sɪtrəs'fruːt] n agrume m.
**city** ['sɪtɪ] n ville f, cité f; **the C～** la Cité de Londres (centre des affaires).
**civic** ['sɪvɪk] a civique.
**civil** ['sɪvɪl] a civil(e); poli(e), civil; **～ engineer** n ingénieur civil; **～ engineering** n génie civil, travaux publics; **～ian** [sɪ'vɪlɪən] a,n civil(e).

**civilization** [sɪvɪlaɪ'zeɪʃən] n civilisation f.
**civilized** ['sɪvɪlaɪzd] a civilisé(e); (fig) où règnent les bonnes manières, empreint(e) d'une courtoisie de bon ton.
**civil**: **～ law** n code civil; (study) droit civil; **～ servant** n fonctionnaire m/f; **C～ Service** n fonction publique, administration f; **～ war** n guerre civile.
**claim** [kleɪm] vt revendiquer; demander, prétendre à; déclarer, prétendre // vi (for insurance) faire une déclaration de sinistre // n revendication f; demande f; prétention f, déclaration f; (right) droit m, titre m; **(insurance) ～** demande f d'indemnisation, déclaration f de sinistre; **～ant** n (ADMIN, LAW) requérant/e.
**clam** [klæm] n palourde f.
**clamber** ['klæmbə*] vi grimper, se hisser.
**clammy** ['klæmɪ] a humide et froid(e) (au toucher), moite.
**clamp** [klæmp] n étau m à main; agrafe f, crampon m // vt serrer; cramponner; **to ～ down on** vt fus sévir contre, prendre des mesures draconiennes à l'égard de.
**clan** [klæn] n clan m.
**clang** [klæŋ] n bruit m or fracas m métallique.
**clap** [klæp] vi applaudir // vt: **to ～ (one's hands)** battre des mains // n claquement m; tape f; **～ping** n applaudissements mpl.
**claret** ['klærət] n (vin m de) bordeaux m (rouge).
**clarification** [klærɪfɪ'keɪʃən] n (fig) clarification f, éclaircissement m.
**clarify** ['klærɪfaɪ] vt clarifier.
**clarinet** [klærɪ'nɛt] n clarinette f.
**clarity** ['klærɪtɪ] n clarté f.
**clash** [klæʃ] n choc m; (fig) conflit m // vi se heurter; être or entrer en conflit.
**clasp** [klɑːsp] n fermoir m // vt serrer, étreindre.
**class** [klɑːs] n (gen) classe f // vt classer, classifier.
**classic** ['klæsɪk] a classique // n (author) classique m; (race etc) classique f; **～al** a classique.
**classification** [klæsɪfɪ'keɪʃən] n classification f.
**classified** ['klæsɪfaɪd] a (information) secret(ète); **～ ads** petites annonces.
**classify** ['klæsɪfaɪ] vt classifier, classer.
**classmate** ['klɑːsmeɪt] n camarade m/f de classe.
**classroom** ['klɑːsrum] n (salle f de) classe f.
**clatter** ['klætə*] n cliquetis m; caquetage m // vi cliqueter; (talk) caqueter, jacasser.
**clause** [klɔːz] n clause f; (LING) proposition f.
**claustrophobia** [klɔːstrə'fəubɪə] n claustrophobie f.
**claw** [klɔː] n griffe f; (of bird of prey) serre f; (of lobster) pince f // vt griffer; déchirer.
**clay** [kleɪ] n argile f.
**clean** [kliːn] a propre; (clear, smooth) net(te) // vt nettoyer; **to ～ out** vt nettoyer (à fond); **to ～ up** vt nettoyer; (fig) remettre de l'ordre dans; **～er** n (person) nettoyeur/euse, femme f de ménage; (also: **dry ～er**) teinturier/ière; (product) détachant m; **～ing** n nettoyage

*m* ; ~**liness** ['klɛnlɪnɪs] *n* propreté *f* ; ~**ly** *ad* proprement ; nettement.

**cleanse** [klɛnz] *vt* nettoyer ; purifier ; ~**r** *n* détergent *m* ; (*for face*) démaquillant *m* ; **cleansing department** *n* service *m* de voirie.

**clean-shaven** ['kli:n'ʃeɪvn] *a* rasé(e) de près.

**clean-up** ['kli:n'ʌp] *n* nettoyage *m*.

**clear** [klɪə*] *a* clair(e) ; (*road, way*) libre, dégagé(e) // *vt* dégager, déblayer, débarrasser ; faire évacuer ; (*COMM: goods*) liquider ; (*LAW: suspect*) innocenter ; (*obstacle*) franchir *or* sauter sans heurter // *vi* (*weather*) s'éclaircir ; (*fog*) se dissiper // *ad:* ~ **of** à distance de, à l'écart de ; **to** ~ **one's throat** s'éclaircir la gorge ; **to** ~ **up** *vi* s'éclaircir, se dissiper // *vt* ranger, mettre en ordre ; (*mystery*) éclaircir, résoudre ; ~**ance** *n* (*removal*) déblayage *m* ; (*free space*) dégagement *m* ; (*permission*) autorisation *f* ; ~**ance sale** *n* liquidation *f* ; ~**cut** *a* précise(e), nettement défini(e) ; ~**ing** *n* clairière *f* ; (*BANKING*) compensation *f*, clearing *m* ; ~**ly** *ad* clairement ; de toute évidence ; ~**way** *n* (*Brit*) route *f* à stationnement interdit.

**cleavage** ['kli:vɪdʒ] *n* (*of dress*) décolleté *m*.

**clef** [klɛf] *n* (*MUS*) clé *f*.

**clench** [klɛntʃ] *vt* serrer.

**clergy** ['klə:dʒɪ] *n* clergé *m* ; ~**man** *n* ecclésiastique *m*.

**clerical** ['klɛrɪkəl] *a* de bureau, d'employé de bureau ; (*REL*) clérical(e), du clergé.

**clerk** [klɑ:k, (*US*) klə:rk] *n* employé/e de bureau ; (*US: salesman/woman*) vendeur/-euse.

**clever** ['klɛvə*] *a* (*mentally*) intelligent(e) ; (*deft, crafty*) habile, adroit(e) ; (*device, arrangement*) ingénieux(euse), astucieux-(euse).

**cliché** ['kli:ʃeɪ] *n* cliché *m*.

**click** [klɪk] *vi* faire un bruit sec *or* un déclic.

**client** ['klaɪənt] *n* client/e ; ~**ele** [kli:ɑ̃:n'tɛl] *n* clientèle *f*.

**cliff** [klɪf] *n* falaise *f*.

**climate** ['klaɪmɪt] *n* climat *m*.

**climax** ['klaɪmæks] *n* apogée *m*, point culminant ; (*sexual*) orgasme *m*.

**climb** [klaɪm] *vi* grimper, monter // *vt* gravir, escalader, monter sur // *n* montée *f*, escalade *f* ; **to** ~ **down** *vi* (re)descendre ; ~**er** *n* (*also:* **rock** ~) grimpeur/euse, varappeur/ euse ; ~**ing** *n* (*also:* **rock** ~**ing**) escalade *f*, varappe *f*.

**clinch** [klɪntʃ] *vt* (*deal*) conclure, sceller.

**cling** [klɪŋ], *pt*, *pp* **clung** [klʌŋ, klʌŋ] *vi:* **to** ~ (**to**) se cramponner (à), s'accrocher (à) ; (*of clothes*) coller (à).

**clinic** ['klɪnɪk] *n* centre médical ; ~**al** *a* clinique.

**clink** [klɪŋk] *vi* tinter, cliqueter.

**clip** [klɪp] *n* (*for hair*) barrette *f* ; (*also:* **paper** ~) trombone *m* ; (*also:* **bulldog** ~) pince *f* de bureau ; (*holding hose etc*) collier *m* or bague *f* (métallique) de serrage // *vt* (*also:* ~ **together:** *papers*) attacher ; (*hair, nails*) couper ; (*hedge*) tailler ; ~**pers** *npl* tondeuse *f* ; (*also:* **nail** ~**pers**) coupe-ongles *m* *inv*.

**clique** [kli:k] *n* clique *f*, coterie *f*.

**cloak** [kləuk] *n* grande cape ; ~**room** *n* (*for coats etc*) vestiaire *m* ; (*W.C.*) toilettes *fpl*.

**clock** [klɔk] *n* (*large*) horloge *f* ; (*small*) pendule *f* ; ~**wise** *ad* dans le sens des aiguilles d'une montre ; ~**work** *n* mouvement *m* (d'horlogerie) ; rouages *mpl*, mécanisme *m*.

**clog** [klɔg] *n* sabot *m* // *vt* boucher, encrasser // *vi* se boucher, s'encrasser.

**cloister** ['klɔɪstə*] *n* cloître *m*.

**close** *a, ad and derivatives* [kləus] *a* près, proche ; (*writing, texture*) serré(e) ; (*watch*) étroit(e), strict(e) ; (*examination*) attentif(ive), minutieux(euse) ; (*weather*) lourd(e), étouffant(e) ; (*room*) mal aéré(e) // *ad* près, à proximité ; **a** ~ **friend** un ami intime ; **to have a** ~ **shave** (*fig*) l'échapper belle // *vb and derivatives* [kləuz] *vt* fermer // *vi* (*shop etc*) fermer ; (*lid, door etc*) se fermer ; (*end*) se terminer, se conclure // *n* (*end*) conclusion *f* ; **to** ~ **down** *vt,vi* fermer (*définitivement*) ; ~**d** *a* (*shop etc*) fermé(e) ; (*road*) fermé à la circulation ; ~**d shop** *n* organisation *f* qui n'admet que des travailleurs syndiqués ; ~**ly** *ad* (*examine, watch*) de près.

**closet** ['klɔzɪt] *n* (*cupboard*) placard *m*, réduit *m*.

**close-up** ['kləusʌp] *n* gros plan.

**closure** ['kləuʒə*] *n* fermeture *f*.

**clot** [klɔt] *n* (*gen: blood* ~) caillot *m* // *vi* (*blood*) former des caillots ; (: *external bleeding*) se coaguler ; ~**ted cream** *n* crème caillée.

**cloth** [klɔθ] *n* (*material*) tissu *m*, étoffe *f* ; (*also:* **tea**~) torchon *m* ; lavette *f*.

**clothe** [kləuð] *vt* habiller, vêtir ; ~**s** *npl* vêtements *mpl*, habits *mpl* ; ~**s brush** *n* brosse *f* à habits ; ~**s line** *n* corde *f* (à linge) ; ~**s peg** *n* pince *f* à linge.

**clothing** ['kləuðɪŋ] *n* = **clothes.**

**cloud** [klaud] *n* nuage *m* ; ~**burst** *n* violente averse ; ~**y** *a* nuageux(euse), couvert(e) ; (*liquid*) trouble.

**clout** [klaut] *n* (*blow*) taloche *f* // *vt* flanquer une taloche à.

**clove** [kləuv] *n* clou *m* de girofle ; ~ **of garlic** gousse *f* d'ail.

**clover** ['kləuvə*] *n* trèfle *m* ; ~**leaf** *n* feuille *f* de trèfle ; ~**leaf junction** (*AUT*) *n* croisement *m* en trèfle.

**clown** [klaun] *n* clown *m* // *vi* (*also:* ~ **about,** ~ **around**) faire le clown.

**club** [klʌb] *n* (*society*) club *m* ; (*weapon*) massue *f*, matraque *f* ; (*also:* **golf** ~) club // *vt* matraquer // *vi:* **to** ~ **together** s'associer ; ~**s** *npl* (*CARDS*) trèfle *m* ; ~**house** *n* pavillon *m*.

**cluck** [klʌk] *vi* glousser.

**clue** [klu:] *n* indice *m* ; (*in crosswords*) définition *f* ; **I haven't a** ~ je n'en ai pas la moindre idée.

**clump** [klʌmp] *n:* ~ **of trees** bouquet *m* d'arbres.

**clumsy** ['klʌmzɪ] *a* (*person*) gauche, maladroit(e) ; (*object*) malcommode, peu maniable.

**clung** [klʌŋ] *pt*, *pp of* **cling.**

**cluster** ['klʌstə*] *n* (petit) groupe// *vi* se rassembler.

**clutch** [klʌtʃ] n (grip, grasp) étreinte f, prise f; (AUT) embrayage m // vt agripper, serrer fort; **to ~ at** se cramponner à.
**clutter** ['klʌtə*] vt encombrer.
**Co.** abbr of **county**; **company**.
**c/o** (abbr of care of) c/o, aux bons soins de.
**coach** [kəutʃ] n (bus) autocar m; (horse-drawn) diligence f; (of train) voiture f, wagon m; (SPORT: trainer) entraîneur/euse; (school: tutor) répétiteur/trice // vt entraîner; donner des leçons particulières à.
**coagulate** [kəu'ægjuleɪt] vt coaguler // vi se coaguler.
**coal** [kəul] n charbon m; **~ face** n front m de taille; **(~) face workers** npl mineurs mpl de fond; **~field** n bassin houiller.
**coalition** [kəuə'lɪʃən] n coalition f.
**coalman, coal merchant** ['kəulmən, 'kəulmɑːtʃənt] n charbonnier m, marchand m de charbon.
**coalmine** ['kəulmaɪn] n mine f de charbon.
**coarse** [kɔːs] a grossier(ère), rude.
**coast** [kəust] n côte f // vi (with cycle etc) descendre en roue libre; **~al** a côtier(ère); **~er** n caboteur m; **~guard** n garde-côte m; **~line** n côte f, littoral m.
**coat** [kəut] n manteau m; (of animal) pelage m, poil m; (of paint) couche f // vt couvrir, enduire; **~ of arms** n blason m, armoiries fpl; **~ hanger** n cintre m; **~ing** n couche f, enduit m.
**coax** [kəuks] vt persuader par des cajoleries.
**cob** [kɔb] n see **corn.**
**cobbles, cobblestones** ['kɔblz, 'kɔblstəunz] npl pavés (ronds).
**cobra** ['kəubrə] n cobra m.
**cobweb** ['kɔbwɛb] n toile f d'araignée.
**cocaine** [kɔ'keɪn] n cocaïne f.
**cock** [kɔk] n (rooster) coq m; (male bird) mâle m // vt (gun) armer; **to ~ one's ears** (fig) dresser l'oreille; **~erel** n jeune coq m; **~-eyed** a (fig) de travers; qui louche; qui ne tient pas debout (fig).
**cockle** ['kɔkl] n coque f.
**cockney** ['kɔknɪ] n cockney m/f (habitant des quartiers populaires de l'East End de Londres), ≈ faubourien/ne.
**cockpit** ['kɔkpɪt] n (in aircraft) poste m de pilotage, cockpit m.
**cockroach** ['kɔkrəutʃ] n cafard m, cancrelat m.
**cocktail** ['kɔkteɪl] n cocktail m; **~ cabinet** n (meuble-)bar m; **~ party** n cocktail m; **~ shaker** n shaker m.
**cocoa** ['kəukəu] n cacao m.
**coconut** ['kəukənʌt] n noix f de coco.
**cocoon** [kə'kuːn] n cocon m.
**cod** [kɔd] n morue (fraîche), cabillaud m.
**code** [kəud] n code m.
**codify** ['kəudɪfaɪ] vt codifier.
**coeducational** ['kəuɛdju'keɪʃənl] a mixte.
**ccerce** [kəu'əːs] vt contraindre; **coercion** [-'əːʃən] n contrainte f.
**coexistence** ['kəuɪg'zɪstəns] n coexistence f.
**coffee** ['kɔfɪ] n café m; **~ grounds** npl marc m de café; **~pot** n cafetière f; **~ table** n (petite) table basse.

**coffin** ['kɔfɪn] n cercueil m.
**cog** [kɔg] n dent f (d'engrenage); **~wheel** n roue dentée.
**cogent** ['kəudʒənt] a puissant(e), convaincant(e).
**cognac** ['kɔnjæk] n cognac m.
**coherent** [kəu'hɪərənt] a cohérent(e).
**coil** [kɔɪl] n rouleau m, bobine f; (one loop) anneau m, spire f; (contraceptive) stérilet m // vt enrouler.
**coin** [kɔɪn] n pièce f de monnaie // vt (word) inventer; **~age** n monnaie f, système m monétaire; **~-box** n cabine f téléphonique.
**coincide** [kəuɪn'saɪd] vi coïncider; **~nce** [kəu'ɪnsɪdəns] n coïncidence f.
**coke** [kəuk] n coke m.
**colander** ['kɔləndə*] n passoire f (à légumes).
**cold** [kəuld] a froid(e) // n froid m; (MED) rhume m; **it's ~** il fait froid; **to be ~** avoir froid; **to have ~ feet** avoir froid aux pieds; (fig) avoir la frousse or la trouille; **to give sb the ~ shoulder** battre froid à qn; **~ly** a froidement; **~ sore** n herpès m.
**coleslaw** ['kəulslɔː] n sorte de salade de chou cru.
**colic** ['kɔlɪk] n colique(s) f(pl).
**collaborate** [kə'læbəreɪt] vi collaborer; **collaboration** [-'reɪʃən] n collaboration f; **collaborator** n collaborateur/trice.
**collage** [kɔ'lɑːʒ] n (ART) collage m.
**collapse** [kə'læps] vi s'effondrer, s'écrouler // n effondrement m, écroulement m.
**collapsible** [kə'læpsəbl] a pliant(e); télescopique.
**collar** ['kɔlə*] n (of coat, shirt) col m; **~bone** n clavicule f.
**collate** [kɔ'leɪt] vt collationner.
**colleague** ['kɔliːg] n collègue m/f.
**collect** [kə'lɛkt] vt rassembler; ramasser; (as a hobby) collectionner; (call and pick up) (passer) prendre; (mail) faire la levée de, ramasser; (money owed) encaisser; (donations, subscriptions) recueillir // vi se rassembler; s'amasser; **~ed** a: **~ed works** œuvres complètes; **~ion** [kə'lɛkʃən] n collection f; levée f; (for money) collecte f, quête f.
**collective** [kə'lɛktɪv] a collectif(ive).
**collector** [kə'lɛktə*] n collectionneur m; (of taxes) percepteur m; (of rent, cash) encaisseur m.
**college** ['kɔlɪdʒ] n collège m; **~ of education** ≈ école normale.
**collide** [kə'laɪd] vi: **to ~ (with)** entrer en collision (avec); (fig) entrer en conflit (avec), se heurter (à).
**colliery** ['kɔlɪərɪ] n mine f de charbon, houillère f.
**collision** [kə'lɪʒən] n collision f, heurt m; (fig) conflit m.
**colloquial** [kə'ləukwɪəl] a familier(ère).
**colon** ['kəulən] n (sign) deux-points mpl; (MED) côlon m.
**colonel** ['kəːnl] n colonel m.
**colonial** [kə'ləunɪəl] a colonial(e).
**colonize** ['kɔlənaɪz] vt coloniser.

**colony** ['kɔlənı] *n* colonie *f*.
**color** ['kʌlə*] *n*,*vt* (*US*) = **colour.**
**Colorado** [kɔlə'rɑːdəu]: ~ **beetle** *n* doryphore *m*.
**colossal** [kə'lɔsl] *a* colossal(e).
**colour, color** (*US*) ['kʌlə*] *n* couleur *f* // *vt* colorer ; peindre ; (*with crayons*) colorier ; (*news*) fausser, exagérer ; ~s *npl* (*of party, club*) couleurs *fpl* ; ~ **bar** *n* discrimination raciale (*dans un établissement etc*) ; ~-**blind** *a* daltonien(ne) ; ~**ed** *a* coloré(e) ; (*photo*) en couleur // *n*: ~**eds** personnes *fpl* de couleur ; ~ **film** *n* (*for camera*) pellicule *f* (en) couleur ; ~**ful** *a* coloré(e), vif(vive) ; (*personality*) pittoresque, haut(e) en couleurs ; ~ **scheme** *n* combinaison *f* de(s) couleurs ; ~ **television** *n* télévision *f* en couleur.
**colt** [kəult] *n* poulain *m*.
**column** ['kɔləm] *n* colonne *f* ; ~**ist** ['kɔləmnıst] *n* rédacteur/trice d'une rubrique.
**coma** ['kəumə] *n* coma *m*.
**comb** [kəum] *n* peigne *m* // *vt* (*hair*) peigner ; (*area*) ratisser, passer au peigne fin.
**combat** ['kɔmbæt] *n* combat *m* // *vt* combattre, lutter contre.
**combination** [kɔmbı'neıʃən] *n* (*gen*) combinaison *f*.
**combine** *vb* [kəm'baın] *vt* combiner ; (*one quality with another*) joindre (à), allier (à) // *vi* s'associer ; (*CHEM*) se combiner // *n* ['kɔmbaın] association *f* ; (*ECON*) trust *m* ; ~ (**harvester**) *n* moissonneuse-batteuse(-lieuse) *f*.
**combustible** [kəm'bʌstıbl] *a* combustible.
**combustion** [kəm'bʌstʃən] *n* combustion *f*.
**come**, *pt* **came**, *pp* **come** [kʌm, keım] *vi* venir ; arriver ; **to** ~ **into sight** *or* **view** apparaître ; **to** ~ **to** (*decision etc*) parvenir *or* arriver à ; **to** ~ **undone/loose** se défaire/desserrer ; **to** ~ **about** *vi* se produire, arriver ; **to** ~ **across** *vt fus* rencontrer par hasard, tomber sur ; **to** ~ **along** *vi* = **to come on** ; **to** ~ **apart** *vi* s'en aller en morceaux ; se détacher ; **to** ~ **away** *vi* partir, s'en aller ; se détacher ; **to** ~ **back** *vi* revenir ; **to** ~ **by** *vt fus* (*acquire*) obtenir, se procurer ; **to** ~ **down** *vi* descendre ; (*prices*) baisser ; (*buildings*) s'écrouler ; être démoli(e) ; **to** ~ **forward** *vi* s'avancer ; se présenter, s'annoncer ; **to** ~ **in** *vi* entrer ; **to** ~ **in for** *vt fus* (*criticism etc*) être l'objet de ; **to** ~ **into** *vt fus* (*money*) hériter de ; **to** ~ **off** *vi* (*button*) se détacher ; (*stain*) s'enlever ; (*attempt*) réussir ; **to** ~ **on** *vi* (*pupil, undertaking*) faire des progrès, avancer ; ~ **on!** viens! ; allons!, allez! ; **to** ~ **out** *vi* sortir ; (*book*) paraître ; (*strike*) cesser le travail, se mettre en grève ; **to** ~ **to** *vi* revenir à soi ; **to** ~ **up** *vi* monter ; **to** ~ **up against** *vt fus* (*resistance, difficulties*) rencontrer ; **to** ~ **up with** *vt fus*: **he came up with an idea** il a eu une idée, il a proposé quelque chose ; **to** ~ **upon** *vt fus* tomber sur ; ~**back** *n* (*THEATRE etc*) rentrée *f*.

**comedian** [kə'miːdıən] *n* (*in music hall etc*) comique *m* ; (*THEATRE*) comédien *m*.
**comedienne** [kəmiːdı'ɛn] *n* comédienne *f*.
**comedown** ['kʌmdaun] *n* déchéance *f*.
**comedy** ['kɔmıdı] *n* comédie *f*.
**comet** ['kɔmıt] *n* comète *f*.
**comfort** ['kʌmfət] *n* confort *m*, bien-être *m* ; (*solace*) consolation *f*, réconfort *m* // *vt* consoler, réconforter ; ~s *npl* aises *fpl* ; ~**able** *a* confortable ; ~ **station** *n* (*US*) toilettes *fpl*.
**comic** ['kɔmık] *a* (*also*: ~**al**) comique // *n* comique *m* ; (*magazine*) illustré *m* ; ~ **strip** *n* bande dessinée.
**coming** ['kʌmıŋ] *n* arrivée *f* ; ~(**s**) **and going(s)** *n(pl)* va-et-vient *m inv*.
**comma** ['kɔmə] *n* virgule *f*.
**command** [kə'mɑːnd] *n* ordre *m*, commandement *m* ; (*MIL*: *authority*) commandement *m* ; (*mastery*) maîtrise *f* // *vt* (*troops*) commander ; (*be able to get*) (pouvoir) disposer de, avoir à sa disposition ; (*deserve*) avoir droit à ; **to** ~ **sb to do** donner l'ordre *or* commander à qn de faire ; ~**eer** [kɔmən'dıə*] *vt* réquisitionner (par la force) ; ~**er** *n* chef *m* ; (*MIL*) commandant *m* ; ~**ing officer** *n* commandant *m*.
**commando** [kə'mɑːndəu] *n* commando *m* ; membre *m* d'un commando.
**commemorate** [kə'mɛməreıt] *vt* commémorer ; **commemoration** [-'reıʃən] *n* commémoration *f*.
**commemorative** [kə'mɛmərətıv] *a* commémoratif(ive).
**commence** [kə'mɛns] *vt*,*vi* commencer.
**commend** [kə'mɛnd] *vt* louer ; recommander ; ~**able** *a* louable ; ~**ation** [kɔmɛn'deıʃən] *n* éloge *m* ; recommandation *f*.
**commensurate** [kə'mɛnʃərıt] *a*: ~ **with** en proportion de, proportionné(e) à.
**comment** ['kɔmɛnt] *n* commentaire *m* // *vi* faire des remarques *or* commentaires ; ~**ary** ['kɔməntərı] *n* commentaire *m* ; (*SPORT*) reportage *m* (en direct) ; ~**ator** ['kɔmənteıtə*] *n* commentateur *m* ; reporter *m*.
**commerce** ['kɔməːs] *n* commerce *m*.
**commercial** [kə'məːʃəl] *a* commercial(e) // *n* (*TV*: *also*: ~ **break**) annonce *f* publicitaire, spot *m* (publicitaire) ; ~ **college** *n* école *f* de commerce ; ~**ize** *vt* commercialiser ; ~ **television** *n* la publicité à la télévision, les chaînes indépendantes ; ~ **traveller** *n* voyageur *m* de commerce ; ~ **vehicle** *n* véhicule *m* utilitaire.
**commiserate** [kə'mızəreıt] *vi*: **to** ~ **with** compatir à.
**commission** [kə'mıʃən] *n* (*committee, fee*) commission *f* ; (*order for work of art etc*) commande *f* // *vt* (*MIL*) nommer (à un commandement) ; (*work of art*) commander, charger un artiste de l'exécution de ; **out of** ~ (*NAUT*) hors de service ; ~**aire** [kəmıʃə'nɛə*] *n* (*at shop, cinema etc*) portier *m* (en uniforme) ; ~**er** *n* membre *m* d'une commission ; (*POLICE*) préfet *m* (de police).
**commit** [kə'mıt] *vt* (*act*) commettre ; (*to sb's care*) confier (à) ; **to** ~ **o.s. (to do)** s'engager (à faire) ; **to** ~ **suicide** se

suicider; **to ~ to writing** coucher par écrit; **~ment** n engagement m, responsabilité(s) f(pl).
**committee** [kə'mıtı] n comité m.
**commodity** [kə'mɔdıtı] n produit m, marchandise f, article m; (food) denrée f.
**common** ['kɔmən] a (gen, also pej) commun(e); (usual) courant(e) // n terrain communal; **the C~s** npl la chambre des Communes; **in ~** en commun; **it's ~ knowledge that** il est bien connu or notoire que; **to the ~ good** pour le bien de tous, dans l'intérêt général; **~er** n roturier/ière; **~ ground** n (fig) terrain m d'entente; **~ law** n droit coutumier; **~ly** ad communément, généralement; couramment; **C~ Market** n Marché commun; **~place** a banal(e), ordinaire; **~room** n salle commune; (SCOL) salle des professeurs; **~ sense** n bon sens; **the C~wealth** n le Commonwealth.
**commotion** [kə'məuʃən] n désordre m, tumulte m.
**communal** ['kɔmjuːnl] a (life) communautaire; (for common use) commun(e).
**commune** n ['kɔmjuːn] (group) communauté f // vi [kə'mjuːn]: **to ~ with** converser intimement avec; communier avec.
**communicate** [kə'mjuːnıkeıt] vt communiquer, transmettre // vi: **to ~ (with)** communiquer (avec).
**communication** [kəmjuːnı'keıʃən] n communication f; **~ cord** n sonnette f d'alarme.
**communion** [kə'mjuːnıən] n (also: **Holy C~**) communion f.
**communiqué** [kə'mjuːnıkeı] n communiqué m.
**communism** ['kɔmjunızəm] n communisme m; **communist** a,n communiste (m/f).
**community** [kə'mjuːnıtı] n communauté f; **~ centre** n foyer socio-éducatif, centre m de loisirs; **~ chest** n (US) fonds commun.
**commutation ticket** [kɔmjuː'teıʃəntıkıt] n (US) carte f d'abonnement.
**commute** [kə'mjuːt] vi faire le trajet journalier (de son domicile à un lieu de travail assez éloigné) // vt (LAW) commuer; (MATH: terms etc) opérer la commutation de; **~r** n banlieusard/e (qui ... see vi).
**compact** a [kəm'pækt] compact(e) // n ['kɔmpækt] contrat m, entente f; (also: **powder ~**) poudrier m.
**companion** [kəm'pænıən] n compagnon/-compagne; **~ship** n camaraderie f.
**company** ['kʌmpənı] n (also COMM, MIL, THEATRE) compagnie f; **he's good ~** il est d'une compagnie agréable; **we have ~** nous avons de la visite; **to keep sb ~** tenir compagnie à qn; **to part ~ with** se séparer de; **~ secretary** n (COMM) secrétaire général (d'une société).
**comparable** ['kɔmpərəbl] a comparable.
**comparative** [kəm'pærətıv] a comparatif(ive); (relative) relatif(ive).

**compare** [kəm'pɛə*] vt: **to ~ sth/sb with/to** comparer qch/qn avec or et/à // vi: **to ~ (with)** se comparer (à); être comparable (à); **comparison** [-'pærısn] n comparaison f; **in comparison (with)** en comparaison (de).
**compartment** [kəm'pɑːtmənt] n (also RAIL) compartiment m.
**compass** ['kʌmpəs] n boussole f; **~es** npl compas m.
**compassion** [kəm'pæʃən] n compassion f, humanité f; **~ate** a accessible à la compassion, au cœur charitable et bienveillant; **on ~ate grounds** pour raisons personnelles or de famille.
**compatible** [kəm'pætıbl] a compatible.
**compel** [kəm'pɛl] vt contraindre, obliger; **~ling** a (fig: argument) irrésistible.
**compendium** [kəm'pɛndıəm] n abrégé m.
**compensate** ['kɔmpənseıt] vt indemniser, dédommager // vi: **to ~ for** compenser; **compensation** [-'seıʃən] n compensation f; (money) dédommagement m, indemnité f.
**compère** ['kɔmpɛə*] n présentateur/trice, animateur/trice.
**compete** [kəm'piːt] vi (take part) concourir; (vie): **to ~ (with)** rivaliser (avec), faire concurrence (à).
**competence** ['kɔmpıtəns] n compétence f, aptitude f.
**competent** ['kɔmpıtənt] a compétent(e), capable.
**competition** [kɔmpı'tıʃən] n compétition f, concours m; (ECON) concurrence f.
**competitive** [kəm'pɛtıtıv] a (ECON) concurrentiel(le); **~ examination** n (SCOL) concours m.
**competitor** [kəm'pɛtıtə*] n concurrent/e.
**compile** [kəm'paıl] vt compiler.
**complacency** [kəm'pleısnsı] n contentement m de soi, vaine complaisance.
**complacent** [kəm'pleısənt] a (trop) content(e) de soi; suffisant(e).
**complain** [kəm'pleın] vi: **to ~ (about)** se plaindre (de); (in shop etc) réclamer (au sujet de); **to ~ of** vt fus (MED) se plaindre de; **~t** n plainte f; réclamation f; (MED) affection f.
**complement** ['kɔmplımənt] n complément m; (especially of ship's crew etc) effectif complet; **~ary** [kɔmplı'mɛntərı] a complémentaire.
**complete** [kəm'pliːt] a complet(ète) // vt achever, parachever; (a form) remplir; **~ly** ad complètement; **completion** n achèvement m.
**complex** ['kɔmplɛks] a complexe // n (PSYCH, buildings etc) complexe m.
**complexion** [kəm'plɛkʃən] n (of face) teint m; (of event etc) aspect m, caractère m.
**complexity** [kəm'plɛksıtı] n complexité f.
**compliance** [kəm'plaıəns] n (see compliant) docilité f; (see comply): **~ with** le fait de se conformer à; **in ~ with** en conformité avec, conformément à.
**compliant** [kəm'plaıənt] a docile, très accommodant(e).
**complicate** ['kɔmplıkeıt] vt compliquer;

~**d** *a* compliqué(e) ; **complication** [-'keɪʃən] *n* complication *f.*

**compliment** *n* ['kɔmplɪmənt] compliment *m* // *vt* ['kɔmplɪmɛnt] complimenter ; ~**s** *npl* compliments *mpl*, hommages *mpl* ; vœux *mpl* ; ~**ary** [-'mɛntərɪ] *a* flatteur(euse) ; (*free*) à titre gracieux ; ~**ary ticket** *n* billet *m* de faveur.

**comply** [kəm'plaɪ] *vi* : **to** ~ **with** se soumettre à, se conformer à.

**component** [kəm'pəunənt] *a* composant(e), constituant(e) // *n* composant *m*, élément *m.*

**compose** [kəm'pəuz] *vt* composer ; **to** ~ **o.s.** se calmer, se maîtriser ; prendre une contenance ; ~**d** *a* calme, posé(e) ; ~**r** *n* (*MUS*) compositeur *m.*

**composite** ['kɔmpəzɪt] *a* composite ; (*BOT, MATH*) composé(e).

**composition** [kɔmpə'zɪʃən] *n* composition *f.*

**compost** ['kɔmpɔst] *n* compost *m.*

**composure** [kəm'pəuʒə*] *n* calme *m*, maîtrise *f* de soi.

**compound** ['kɔmpaund] *n* (*CHEM, LING*) composé *m* ; (*enclosure*) enclos *m*, enceinte *f* // *a* composé(e) ; ~ **fracture** *n* fracture compliquée ; ~ **interest** *n* intérêt composé.

**comprehend** [kɔmprɪ'hɛnd] *vt* comprendre ; **comprehension** [-'hɛnʃən] *n* compréhension *f.*

**comprehensive** [kɔmprɪ'hɛnsɪv] *a* (très) complet(ète) ; ~ **policy** *n* (*INSURANCE*) assurance *f* tous risques ; ~ (**school**) *n* école secondaire non sélective, avec libre circulation d'une section à l'autre, ≈ C.E.S. *m.*

**compress** *vt* [kəm'prɛs] comprimer // *n* ['kɔmprɛs] (*MED*) compresse *f* ; ~**ion** [-'prɛʃən] *n* compression *f.*

**comprise** [kəm'praɪz] *vt* (*also* : **be** ~**d of**) comprendre.

**compromise** ['kɔmprəmaɪz] *n* compromis *m* // *vt* compromettre // *vi* transiger, accepter un compromis.

**compulsion** [kəm'pʌlʃən] *n* contrainte *f*, force *f.*

**compulsive** [kəm'pʌlsɪv] *a* (*reason, demand*) coercitif(ive) ; (*PSYCH*) compulsif(ive) ; **he's a** ~ **smoker** c'est un fumeur invétéré.

**compulsory** [kəm'pʌlsərɪ] *a* obligatoire.

**computer** [kəm'pju:tə*] *n* ordinateur *m* ; (*mechanical*) calculatrice *f* ; ~**ize** *vt* traiter *or* automatiser par ordinateur ; ~ **language** *n* langage *m* machine *or* de programmation ; ~ **programming** *n* programmation *f* ; ~ **science** *n* informatique *f* ; ~ **scientist** *n* informaticien/ne.

**comrade** ['kɔmrɪd] *n* camarade *m/f* ; ~**ship** *n* camaraderie *f.*

**con** [kɔn] *vt* duper ; escroquer.

**concave** ['kɔn'keɪv] *a* concave.

**conceal** [kən'si:l] *vt* cacher, dissimuler.

**concede** [kən'si:d] *vt* concéder // *vi* céder.

**conceit** [kən'si:t] *n* vanité *f*, suffisance *f*, prétention *f* ; ~**ed** *a* vaniteux(euse), suffisant(e).

**conceivable** [kən'si:vəbl] *a* concevable, imaginable.

**conceive** [kən'si:v] *vt* concevoir.

**concentrate** ['kɔnsəntreɪt] *vi* se concentrer // *vt* concentrer.

**concentration** [kɔnsən'treɪʃən] *n* concentration *f* ; ~ **camp** *n* camp *m* de concentration.

**concentric** [kɔn'sɛntrɪk] *a* concentrique.

**concept** ['kɔnsɛpt] *n* concept *m.*

**conception** [kən'sɛpʃən] *n* conception *f.*

**concern** [kən'sə:n] *n* affaire *f* ; (*COMM*) entreprise *f*, firme *f* ; (*anxiety*) inquiétude *f*, souci *m* // *vt* concerner ; **to be** ~**ed** (**about**) s'inquiéter (de), être inquiet (au sujet de) ; ~**ing** *prep* en ce qui concerne, à propos de.

**concert** ['kɔnsət] *n* concert *m* ; **in** ~ à l'unisson, en chœur ; ensemble ; ~**ed** [kən'sə:tɪd] *a* concerté(e) ; ~ **hall** *n* salle *f* de concert.

**concertina** [kɔnsə'ti:nə] *n* concertina *m* // *vi* se télescoper, se caramboler.

**concerto** [kən'tʃə:təu] *n* concerto *m.*

**concession** [kən'sɛʃən] *n* concession *f.*

**conciliation** [kənsɪlɪ'eɪʃən] *n* conciliation *f*, apaisement *m.*

**conciliatory** [kən'sɪlɪətrɪ] *a* conciliateur(trice) ; conciliant(e).

**concise** [kən'saɪs] *a* concis(e).

**conclave** ['kɔnkleɪv] *n* assemblée secrète ; (*REL*) conclave *m.*

**conclude** [kən'klu:d] *vt* conclure ; **conclusion** [-'klu:ʒən] *n* conclusion *f* ; **conclusive** [-'klu:sɪv] *a* concluant(e), définitif(ive).

**concoct** [kən'kɔkt] *vt* confectionner, composer.

**concourse** ['kɔŋkɔ:s] *n* (*hall*) hall *m*, salle *f* des pas perdus ; (*crowd*) affluence *f* ; multitude *f.*

**concrete** ['kɔŋkri:t] *n* béton *m* // *a* concret(ète) ; en béton.

**concur** [kən'kə:*] *vi* être d'accord.

**concurrently** [kən'kʌrntlɪ] *ad* simultanément.

**concussion** [kən'kʌʃən] *n* ébranlement *m*, secousse *f* ; (*MED*) commotion (cérébrale).

**condemn** [kən'dɛm] *vt* condamner ; ~**ation** [kɔndɛm'neɪʃən] *n* condamnation *f.*

**condensation** [kɔndɛn'seɪʃən] *n* condensation *f.*

**condense** [kən'dɛns] *vi* se condenser // *vt* condenser ; ~**d milk** *n* lait condensé (sucré).

**condescend** [kɔndɪ'sɛnd] *vi* condescendre, s'abaisser ; ~**ing** *a* condescendant(e).

**condition** [kən'dɪʃən] *n* condition *f* // *vt* déterminer, conditionner ; **on** ~ **that** à condition que + *sub*, à condition de ; ~**al** *a* conditionnel(le) ; **to be** ~**al upon** dépendre de.

**condolences** [kən'dəulənsɪz] *npl* condoléances *fpl.*

**condone** [kən'dəun] *vt* fermer les yeux sur, approuver (tacitement).

**conducive** [kən'dju:sɪv] *a* : ~ **to** favorable à, qui contribue à.

**conduct** *n* ['kɔndʌkt] conduite *f* // *vt* [kən'dʌkt] conduire ; (*manage*) mener, diriger ; (*MUS*) diriger ; **to** ~ **o.s.** se conduire, se comporter ; ~ed tour n voyage organisé, visite guidée ; ~or n (of orchestra) chef m d'orchestre ; (on bus) receveur m ; (ELEC) conducteur m ; ~ress n (on bus) receveuse f.

conduit ['kɔndɪt] n conduit m, tuyau m ; tube m.

cone [kəun] n cône m ; (for ice-cream) cornet m ; (BOT) pomme f de pin, cône.

confectioner [kən'fɛkʃənə*] n (of cakes) pâtissier/ière ; (of sweets) confiseur/euse ; ~y n pâtisserie f ; confiserie f.

confederation [kənfɛdə'reɪʃən] n confédération f.

confer [kən'fə:*] vt: to ~ sth on conférer qch à // vi conférer, s'entretenir.

conference ['kɔnfərns] n conférence f.

confess [kən'fɛs] vt confesser, avouer // vi se confesser ; ~ion [-'fɛʃən] n confession f ; ~ional [-'fɛʃənl] n confessional m ; ~or n confesseur m.

confetti [kən'fɛtɪ] n confettis mpl.

confide [kən'faɪd] vi: to ~ in s'ouvrir à, se confier à.

confidence ['kɔnfɪdns] n confiance f ; (also: self-~) assurance f, confiance en soi ; (secret) confidence f ; ~ trick n escroquerie f ; confident a sûr(e), assuré(e) ; confidential [kɔnfɪ'dɛnʃəl] a confidentiel(le).

confine [kən'faɪn] vt limiter, borner ; (shut up) confiner, enfermer ; ~s ['kɔnfaɪnz] npl confins mpl, bornes fpl ; ~d a (space) restreint(e), réduit(e) ; ~ment n emprisonnement m, détention f ; (MIL) consigne f (au quartier) ; (MED) accouchement m.

confirm [kən'fə:m] vt (report) confirmer ; (appointment) ratifier ; ~ation [kɔnfə'meɪʃən] n confirmation f ; ~ed a invétéré(e), incorrigible.

confiscate ['kɔnfɪskeɪt] vt confisquer ; confiscation [-'keɪʃən] n confiscation f.

conflagration [kɔnflə'greɪʃən] n incendie m.

conflict n ['kɔnflɪkt] conflit m, lutte f // vi [kən'flɪkt] être or entrer en conflit ; (opinions) s'opposer, se heurter ; ~ing a contradictoire.

conform [kən'fɔ:m] vi: to ~ (to) se conformer (à) ; ~ist n conformiste m/f.

confound [kən'faund] vt confondre ; ~ed a maudit(e), sacré(e).

confront [kən'frʌnt] vt confronter, mettre en présence ; (enemy, danger) affronter, faire face à ; ~ation [kɔnfrən'teɪʃən] n confrontation f.

confuse [kən'fju:z] vt embrouiller ; (one thing with another) confondre ; confusing a peu clair(e), déroutant(e) ; confusion [-'fju:ʒən] n confusion f.

congeal [kən'dʒi:l] vi (oil) se figer ; (blood) se coaguler.

congenial [kən'dʒi:nɪəl] a sympathique, agréable.

congenital [kən'dʒɛnɪtl] a congénital(e).

conger eel ['kɔngəri:l] n congre m.

congested [kən'dʒɛstɪd] a (MED) congestionné(e) ; (fig) surpeuplé(e) ; congestionné ; bloqué(e).

congestion [kən'dʒɛstʃən] n congestion f ; (fig) encombrement m.

conglomeration [kənglɔmə'reɪʃən] n groupement m ; agglomération f.

congratulate [kən'grætjuleɪt] vt: to ~ sb (on) féliciter qn (de) ; congratulations [-'leɪʃənz] npl félicitations fpl.

congregate ['kɔngrɪgeɪt] vi se rassembler, se réunir.

congregation [kɔngrɪ'geɪʃən] n assemblée f (des fidèles).

congress ['kɔngrɛs] n congrès m ; ~man n (US) membre m du Congrès.

conical ['kɔnɪkl] a (de forme) conique.

conifer ['kɔnɪfə*] n conifère m ; ~ous [kə'nɪfərəs] a (forest) de conifères.

conjecture [kən'dʒɛktʃə*] n conjecture f // vt, vi conjecturer.

conjugal ['kɔndʒugl] a conjugal(e).

conjugate ['kɔndʒugeɪt] vt conjuguer ; conjugation [-'geɪʃən] n conjugaison f.

conjunction [kən'dʒʌnkʃən] n conjonction f.

conjunctivitis [kəndʒʌnktɪ'vaɪtɪs] n conjonctivite f.

conjure ['kʌndʒə*] vt faire apparaître (par la prestidigitation) ; [kən'dʒuə*] conjurer, supplier ; to ~ up vt (ghost, spirit) faire apparaître ; (memories) évoquer ; ~r n prestidigitateur m, illusionniste m/f ; conjuring trick n tour m de prestidigitation.

conk [kɔnk]: to ~ out vi (col) tomber or rester en panne.

conman ['kɔnmæn] n escroc m.

connect [kə'nɛkt] vt joindre, relier ; (ELEC) connecter ; (fig) établir un rapport entre, faire un rapprochement entre // vi (train): to ~ with assurer la correspondance avec ; to be ~ed with avoir un rapport avec ; avoir des rapports avec, être en relation avec ; ~ion [-ʃən] n relation f, lien m ; (ELEC) connexion f ; (TEL) communication f ; in ~ion with à propos de.

connexion [kə'nɛkʃən] n = connection.

conning tower ['kɔnɪŋtauə*] n kiosque m (de sous-marin).

connive [kə'naɪv] vi: to ~ at se faire le complice de.

connoisseur [kɔnɪ'sə*] n connaisseur m.

connotation [kɔnə'teɪʃən] n connotation f, implication f.

connubial [kɔ'nju:bɪəl] a conjugal(e).

conquer ['kɔnkə*] vt conquérir ; (feelings) vaincre, surmonter ; ~or n conquérant m, vainqueur m.

conquest ['kɔnkwɛst] n conquête f.

cons [kɔnz] npl see pro, convenience.

conscience ['kɔnʃəns] n conscience f.

conscientious [kɔnʃɪ'ɛnʃəs] a consciencieux(euse) ; (scruple, objection) de conscience ; ~ objector n objecteur m de conscience.

conscious ['kɔnʃəs] a conscient(e) ; ~ness n conscience f ; (MED) connaissance f ; to lose/regain ~ness perdre/reprendre connaissance.

conscript ['kɔnskrɪpt] n conscrit m ; ~ion [kən'skrɪpʃən] n conscription f.

**consecrate** ['kɔnsɪkreɪt] *vt* consacrer.
**consecutive** [kən'sɛkjutɪv] *a* consécutif(ive).
**consensus** [kən'sɛnsəs] *n* consensus *m*.
**consent** [kən'sɛnt] *n* consentement *m* // *vi*: **to ~ (to)** consentir (à); **age of ~** âge nubile (légal).
**consequence** ['kɔnsɪkwəns] *n* suites *fpl*, conséquence *f*; importance *f*.
**consequently** ['kɔnsɪkwəntlɪ] *ad* par conséquent, donc.
**conservation** [kɔnsə'veɪʃən] *n* préservation *f*, protection *f*.
**conservative** [kən'sə:vətɪv] *a* conservateur(trice); (*cautious*) prudent(e); **C~** *a,n* conservateur(trice).
**conservatory** [kən'sə:vətrɪ] *n* (*greenhouse*) serre *f*.
**conserve** [kən'sə:v] *vt* conserver, préserver.
**consider** [kən'sɪdə*] *vt* considérer, réfléchir à; (*take into account*) penser à, prendre en considération; (*regard, judge*) considérer, estimer.
**considerable** [kən'sɪdərəbl] *a* considérable.
**considerate** [kən'sɪdərɪt] *a* prévenant(e), plein(e) d'égards.
**consideration** [kənsɪdə'reɪʃən] *n* considération *f*; (*reward*) rétribution *f*, rémunération *f*; **out of ~ for** par égard pour; **under ~** à l'étude.
**considering** [kən'sɪdərɪŋ] *prep* étant donné.
**consign** [kən'saɪn] *vt* expédier, livrer; **~ment** *n* arrivage *m*, envoi *m*.
**consist** [kən'sɪst] *vi*: **to ~ of** consister en, se composer de.
**consistency** [kən'sɪstənsɪ] *n* consistance *f*; (*fig*) cohérence *f*.
**consistent** [kən'sɪstənt] *a* logique, cohérent(e); **~ with** compatible avec, en accord avec.
**consolation** [kɔnsə'leɪʃən] *n* consolation *f*.
**console** *vt* [kən'səul] consoler // *n* ['kɔnsəul] console *f*.
**consolidate** [kən'sɔlɪdeɪt] *vt* consolider.
**consommé** [kən'sɔmeɪ] *n* consommé *m*.
**consonant** ['kɔnsənənt] *n* consonne *f*.
**consortium** [kən'sɔ:tɪəm] *n* consortium *m*, comptoir *m*.
**conspicuous** [kən'spɪkjuəs] *a* voyant(e), qui attire la vue *or* l'attention.
**conspiracy** [kən'spɪrəsɪ] *n* conspiration *f*, complot *m*.
**conspire** [kən'spaɪə*] *vi* conspirer, comploter.
**constable** ['kʌnstəbl] *n* ≈ agent *m* de police, gendarme *m*; **chief ~** *n* ≈ préfet *m* de police.
**constabulary** [kən'stæbjulərɪ] *n* ≈ police *f*, gendarmerie *f*.
**constant** ['kɔnstənt] *a* constant(e); incessant(e); **~ly** *ad* constamment, sans cesse.
**constellation** [kɔnstə'leɪʃən] *n* constellation *f*.
**consternation** [kɔnstə'neɪʃən] *n* consternation *f*.

**constipated** ['kɔnstɪpeɪtəd] *a* constipé(e).
**constipation** [kɔnstɪ'peɪʃən] *n* constipation *f*.
**constituency** [kən'stɪtjuənsɪ] *n* circonscription électorale.
**constituent** [kən'stɪtjuənt] *n* électeur/-trice; (*part*) élément constitutif, composant *m*.
**constitute** ['kɔnstɪtju:t] *vt* constituer.
**constitution** [kɔnstɪ'tju:ʃən] *n* constitution *f*; **~al** *a* constitutionnel(le).
**constrain** [kən'streɪn] *vt* contraindre, forcer; **~ed** *a* contraint(e), gêné(e); **~t** *n* contrainte *f*.
**constrict** [kən'strɪkt] *vt* rétrécir, resserrer; gêner, limiter.
**construct** [kən'strʌkt] *vt* construire; **~ion** [-ʃən] *n* construction *f*; **~ive** *a* constructif(ive).
**construe** [kən'stru:] *vt* analyser, expliquer.
**consul** ['kɔnsl] *n* consul *m*; **~ate** ['kɔnsjulɪt] *n* consulat *m*.
**consult** [kən'sʌlt] *vt* consulter; **~ancy** *n*: **~ancy fee** honoraires *mpl* d'expert; **~ant** *n* (*MED*) médecin consultant; (*other specialist*) consultant *m*, (expert-)conseil *m* // *a*: **~ant engineer** ingénieur-conseil *m*; **legal/management ~ant** conseiller *m* juridique/en gestion; **~ation** [kɔnsəl'teɪʃən] *n* consultation *f*; **~ing room** *n* cabinet *m* de consultation.
**consume** [kən'sju:m] *vt* consommer; **~r** *n* consommateur/ trice; **consumerism** *n* mouvement *m* pour la protection des consommateurs; **~r society** *n* société *f* de consommation.
**consummate** ['kɔnsʌmeɪt] *vt* consommer.
**consumption** [kən'sʌmpʃən] *n* consommation *f*; (*MED*) consomption *f* (pulmonaire).
**cont.** *abbr of* continued.
**contact** ['kɔntækt] *n* contact *m*; (*person*) connaissance *f*, relation *f* // *vt* se mettre en contact *or* en rapport avec; **~ lenses** *npl* verres *mpl* de contact.
**contagious** [kən'teɪdʒəs] *a* contagieux(euse).
**contain** [kən'teɪn] *vt* contenir; **to ~ o.s.** se contenir, se maîtriser; **~er** *n* récipient *m*; (*for shipping etc*) container *m*.
**contaminate** [kən'tæmɪneɪt] *vt* contaminer; **contamination** [-'neɪʃən] *n* contamination *f*.
**cont'd** *abbr of* continued.
**contemplate** ['kɔntəmpleɪt] *vt* contempler; (*consider*) envisager; **contemplation** [-'pleɪʃən] *n* contemplation *f*.
**contemporary** [kən'tɛmpərərɪ] *a* contemporain(e); (*design, wallpaper*) moderne // *n* contemporain/e.
**contempt** [kən'tɛmpt] *n* mépris *m*, dédain *m*; **~ible** *a* méprisable, vil(e); **~uous** *a* dédaigneux(euse), méprisant(e).
**contend** [kən'tɛnd] *vt*: **to ~ that** soutenir *or* prétendre que // *vi*: **to ~ with** rivaliser avec, lutter avec; **~er** *n* prétendant/e; adversaire *m/f*.
**content** [kən'tɛnt] *a* content(e), satisfait(e) // *vt* contenter, satisfaire // *n* ['kɔntɛnt] contenu *m*; teneur *f*; **~s** *npl*

contenu ; (*of barrel etc*: *capacity*) contenance *f* ; **(table of)** ~s table *f* des matières ; **to be ~ with** se contenter de ; ~**ed** *a* content(e), satisfait(e).

**contention** [kən'tɛnʃən] *n* dispute *f*, contestation *f* ; (*argument*) assertion *f*, affirmation *f* ; **contentious** *a* querelleur(euse) ; litigieux(euse).

**contentment** [kən'tɛntmənt] *n* contentement *m*, satisfaction *f*.

**contest** *n* ['kɔntɛst] combat *m*, lutte *f* ; (*competition*) concours *m* // *vt* [kən'tɛst] contester, discuter ; (*compete for*) disputer ; ~**ant** [kən'tɛstənt] *n* concurrent/e ; (*in fight*) adversaire *m/f*.

**context** ['kɔntɛkst] *n* contexte *m*.

**continent** ['kɔntɪnənt] *n* continent *m* ; **the C~** l'Europe continentale ; ~**al** [-'nɛntl] *a* continental(e) // *n* Européen/ne (continental(e)).

**contingency** [kən'tɪndʒənsɪ] *n* éventualité *f*, événement imprévu ; ~ **plan** *n* plan *m* d'urgence.

**contingent** [kən'tɪndʒənt] *a* contingent(e) // *n* contingent *m* ; **to be ~ upon** dépendre de.

**continual** [kən'tɪnjuəl] *a* continuel(le) ; ~**ly** *ad* continuellement, sans cesse.

**continuation** [kəntɪnju'eɪʃən] *n* continuation *f* ; (*after interruption*) reprise *f* ; (*of story*) suite *f*.

**continue** [kən'tɪnju:] *vi* continuer // *vt* continuer ; (*start again*) reprendre ; **to be ~d** (*story*) à suivre.

**continuity** [kɔntɪ'njuɪtɪ] *n* continuité *f* ; ~ **girl** *n* (*CINEMA*) script-girl *f*.

**continuous** [kən'tɪnjuəs] *a* continu(e), permanent(e).

**contort** [kən'tɔ:t] *vt* tordre, crisper ; ~**ion** [-'tɔ:ʃən] *n* crispation *f*, torsion *f* ; (*of acrobat*) contorsion *f* ; ~**ionist** [-'tɔ:ʃənɪst] *n* contorsionniste *m/f*.

**contour** ['kɔntuə*] *n* contour *m*, profil *m* ; (*also*: ~ **line**) courbe *f* de niveau.

**contraband** ['kɔntrəbænd] *n* contrebande *f*.

**contraception** [kɔntrə'sɛpʃən] *n* contraception *f*.

**contraceptive** [kɔntrə'sɛptɪv] *a* contraceptif(ive), anticonceptionnel(le) // *n* contraceptif *m*.

**contract** *n* ['kɔntrækt] contrat *m* // *vb* [kən'trækt] *vi* (*COMM*): **to ~ to do sth** s'engager (par contrat) à faire qch ; (*become smaller*) se contracter, se resserrer // *vt* contracter ; ~**ion** [-ʃən] *n* contraction *f* ; (*LING*) forme contractée ; ~**or** *n* entrepreneur *m*.

**contradict** [kɔntrə'dɪkt] *vt* contredire ; (*be contrary to*) démentir, être en contradiction avec ; ~**ion** [-ʃən] *n* contradiction *f*.

**contralto** [kən'træltəu] *n* contralto *m*.

**contraption** [kən'træpʃən] *n* (*pej*) machin *m*, truc *m*.

**contrary** ['kɔntrərɪ] *a* contraire, opposé(e) ; [kən'trɛərɪ] (*perverse*) contrariant(e), entêté(e) // *n* contraire *m* ; **on the ~** au contraire ; **unless you hear to the ~** sauf avis contraire.

**contrast** *n* ['kɔntrɑ:st] contraste *m* // *vt* [kən'trɑ:st] mettre en contraste,

contraster ; ~**ing** *a* opposé(e), contrasté(e).

**contravene** [kɔntrə'vi:n] *vt* enfreindre, violer, contrevenir à.

**contribute** [kən'trɪbju:t] *vi* contribuer // *vt*: **to ~ £10/an article to** donner 10 livres/un article à ; **to ~ to** (*gen*) contribuer à ; (*newspaper*) collaborer à ; **contribution** [kɔntrɪ'bju:ʃən] *n* contribution *f* ; **contributor** *n* (*to newspaper*) collaborateur/trice.

**contrite** ['kɔntraɪt] *a* contrit(e).

**contrivance** [kən'traɪvəns] *n* invention *f*, combinaison *f* ; mécanisme *m*, dispositif *m*.

**contrive** [kən'traɪv] *vt* combiner, inventer // *vi*: **to ~ to do** s'arranger pour faire, trouver le moyen de faire.

**control** [kən'trəul] *vt* maîtriser ; (*check*) contrôler // *n* contrôle *m*, autorité *f* ; maîtrise *f* ; ~**s** *npl* commandes *fpl* ; **to be in ~ of** être maître de, maîtriser ; **to be responsable de** ; **circumstances beyond our ~** circonstances indépendantes de notre volonté ; ~ **point** *n* (poste *m* de) contrôle ; ~ **tower** *n* (*AVIAT*) tour *f* de contrôle.

**controversial** [kɔntrə'və:ʃl] *a* discutable, controversé(e).

**controversy** ['kɔntrəvə:sɪ] *n* controverse *f*, polémique *f*.

**convalesce** [kɔnvə'lɛs] *vi* relever de maladie, se remettre (d'une maladie).

**convalescence** [kɔnvə'lɛsns] *n* convalescence *f*.

**convalescent** [kɔnvə'lɛsnt] *a*, *n* convalescent(e).

**convector** [kən'vɛktə*] *n* radiateur *m* à convection, appareil *m* de chauffage par convection.

**convene** [kən'vi:n] *vt* convoquer, assembler // *vi* se réunir, s'assembler.

**convenience** [kən'vi:nɪəns] *n* commodité *f* ; **at your ~** quand *or* comme cela vous convient ; **all modern ~s, all mod cons** avec tout le confort moderne, tout confort.

**convenient** [kən'vi:nɪənt] *a* commode.

**convent** ['kɔnvənt] *n* couvent *m* ; ~ **school** *n* couvent *m*.

**convention** [kən'vɛnʃən] *n* convention *f* ; ~**al** *a* conventionnel(le).

**converge** [kən'və:dʒ] *vi* converger.

**conversant** [kən'və:snt] *a*: **to be ~ with** s'y connaître en ; être au courant de.

**conversation** [kɔnvə'seɪʃən] *n* conversation *f* ; ~**al** *a* de la conversation ; ~**alist** *n* brillant/e causeur/euse.

**converse** *n* ['kɔnvə:s] contraire *m*, inverse *m* ; ~**ly** [-'və:slɪ] *ad* inversement, réciproquement.

**conversion** [kən'və:ʃən] *n* conversion *f* ; ~ **table** *n* table *f* de conversion.

**convert** *vt* [kən'və:t] (*REL*, *COMM*) convertir ; (*alter*) transformer, aménager ; (*RUGBY*) transformer // *n* ['kɔnvə:t] converti/e ; ~**ible** *a* (voiture *f*) décapotable *f*.

**convex** ['kɔnvɛks] *a* convexe.

**convey** [kən'veɪ] *vt* transporter ; (*thanks*) transmettre ; (*idea*) communiquer ; ~**or belt** *n* convoyeur *m*, tapis roulant *m*.

**convict** vt [kən'vɪkt] déclarer (or reconnaître) coupable // n ['kɔnvɪkt] forçat m, convict m; **~ion** [-ʃən] n condamnation f; (belief) conviction f.

**convince** [kən'vɪns] vt convaincre, persuader; **convincing** a persuasif(ive), convaincant(e).

**convivial** [kən'vɪvɪəl] a joyeux(euse), plein(e) d'entrain.

**convoy** ['kɔnvɔɪ] n convoi m.

**convulse** [kən'vʌls] vt ébranler; **to be ~d with laughter** se tordre de rire.

**convulsion** [kən'vʌlʃən] n convulsion f.

**coo** [ku:] vi roucouler.

**cook** [kuk] vt (faire) cuire // vi cuire; (person) faire la cuisine // n cuisinier/ière; **~book** n = **~ery book**; **~er** n cuisinière f; **~ery** n cuisine f; **~ery book** n livre m de cuisine; **~ie** n (US) biscuit m, petit gâteau sec; **~ing** n cuisine f.

**cool** [ku:l] a frais(fraîche); (not afraid) calme; (unfriendly) froid(e); (impertinent) effronté(e) // vt, vi rafraîchir, refroidir; **~ing tower** n refroidisseur m; **~ness** n fraîcheur f; sang-froid m, calme m.

**coop** [ku:p] n poulailler m // vt: **to ~ up** (fig) cloîtrer, enfermer.

**co-op** ['kəuɔp] n abbr of Cooperative (Society).

**cooperate** [kəu'ɔpəreɪt] vi coopérer, collaborer; **cooperation** [-'reɪʃən] n coopération f, collaboration f.

**cooperative** [kəu'ɔpərətɪv] a coopératif(ive) // n coopérative f.

**coordinate** [kəu'ɔ:dɪneɪt] vt coordonner; **coordination** [-'neɪʃən] n coordination f.

**coot** [ku:t] n foulque f.

**cop** [kɔp] n (col) flic m.

**cope** [kəup] vi se débrouiller; **to ~ with** faire face à; s'occuper de.

**co-pilot** ['kəu'paɪlət] n copilote m.

**copious** ['kəupɪəs] a copieux(euse), abondant(e).

**copper** ['kɔpə*] n cuivre m; (col: policeman) flic m; **~s** npl petite monnaie.

**coppice** ['kɔpɪs] n taillis m.

**copse** [kɔps] n = **coppice**.

**copulate** ['kɔpjuleɪt] vi copuler.

**copy** ['kɔpɪ] n copie f; (book etc) exemplaire m // vt copier; **~cat** n (pej) copieur/euse; **~right** n droit m d'auteur, copyright m; **~right reserved** tous droits (de reproduction) réservés; **~writer** n rédacteur/trice publicitaire.

**coral** ['kɔrəl] n corail m; **~ reef** n récif m de corail.

**cord** [kɔ:d] n corde f; (fabric) velours côtelé; whipcord m; corde f.

**cordial** ['kɔ:dɪəl] a cordial(e), chaleureux(euse) // n sirop m; cordial m.

**cordon** ['kɔ:dn] n cordon m; **to ~ off** vt boucler (par cordon de police).

**corduroy** ['kɔ:dərɔɪ] n velours côtelé.

**core** [kɔ:*] n (of fruit) trognon m, cœur m; (TECH) noyau m // vt enlever le trognon or le cœur de.

**coriander** [kɔrɪ'ændə*] n coriandre f.

**cork** [kɔ:k] n liège m; (of bottle) bouchon m; **~age** n droit payé par le client qui apporte sa propre bouteille de vin; **~screw** n tire-bouchon m.

**corm** [kɔ:m] n bulbe m.

**cormorant** ['kɔ:mərnt] n cormoran m.

**corn** [kɔ:n] n blé m; (US: maize) maïs m; (on foot) cor m; **~ on the cob** (CULIN) épi m de maïs au naturel.

**cornea** ['kɔ:nɪə] n cornée f.

**corned beef** ['kɔ:nd'bi:f] n corned-beef m.

**corner** ['kɔ:nə*] n coin m; (AUT) tournant m, virage m // vt acculer, mettre au pied du mur; coincer; (COMM: market) accaparer // vi prendre un virage; **~ flag** n (FOOTBALL) piquet m de coin; **~ kick** n corner m; **~stone** n pierre f angulaire.

**cornet** ['kɔ:nɪt] n (MUS) cornet m à pistons; (of ice-cream) cornet (de glace).

**cornflour** ['kɔ:nflauə*] n farine f de maïs, maïzena f.

**cornice** ['kɔ:nɪs] n corniche f.

**Cornish** ['kɔ:nɪʃ] a de Cornouailles, cornouaillais(e).

**cornucopia** [kɔ:nju'kəupɪə] n corne f d'abondance.

**Cornwall** ['kɔ:nwəl] n Cornouailles f.

**corny** ['kɔ:nɪ] a (col) rebattu(e), galvaudé(e).

**corollary** [kə'rɔlərɪ] n corollaire m.

**coronary** ['kɔrənərɪ] n: **~ (thrombosis)** infarctus m (du myocarde), thrombose f coronaire.

**coronation** [kɔrə'neɪʃən] n couronnement m.

**coroner** ['kɔrənə*] n coroner m.

**coronet** ['kɔrənɪt] n couronne f.

**corporal** ['kɔ:pərl] n caporal m, brigadier m // a: **~ punishment** châtiment corporel.

**corporate** ['kɔ:pərɪt] a en commun; constitué(e) (en corporation).

**corporation** [kɔ:pə'reɪʃən] n (of town) municipalité f, conseil municipal; (COMM) société f; **~ tax** n ≈ impôt m sur les bénéfices.

**corps** [kɔ:*], pl **corps** [kɔ:z] n corps m.

**corpse** [kɔ:ps] n cadavre m.

**corpuscle** ['kɔ:pʌsl] n corpuscule m.

**corral** [kə'rɑ:l] n corral m.

**correct** [kə'rɛkt] a (accurate) correct(e), exact(e); (proper) correct(e), convenable // vt corriger; **~ion** [-ʃən] n correction f.

**correlate** ['kɔrɪleɪt] vt mettre en corrélation.

**correspond** [kɔrɪs'pɔnd] vi correspondre; **~ence** n correspondance f; **~ence course** n cours m par correspondance; **~ent** n correspondant/e.

**corridor** ['kɔrɪdɔ:*] n couloir m, corridor m.

**corroborate** [kə'rɔbəreɪt] vt corroborer, confirmer.

**corrode** [kə'rəud] vt corroder, ronger // vi se corroder; **corrosion** [-'rəuʒən] n corrosion f.

**corrugated** ['kɔrəgeɪtɪd] a plissé(e); cannelé(e); ondulé(e); **~ cardboard** n carton ondulé; **~ iron** n tôle ondulée.

**corrupt** [kə'rʌpt] a corrompu(e) // vt corrompre; **~ion** [-ʃən] n corruption f.

**corset** ['kɔːsɪt] *n* corset *m*.

**Corsica** ['kɔːsɪkə] *n* Corse *f*.

**cortège** [kɔː'tɛːʒ] *n* cortège *m* (*gén funèbre*).

**coruscating** ['kɔrəskeɪtɪŋ] *a* scintillant(e).

**cosh** [kɔʃ] *n* matraque *f*.

**cosignatory** ['kəu'sɪgnətərɪ] *n* cosignataire *m/f*.

**cosiness** ['kəuzɪnɪs] *n* atmosphère douillette, confort *m*.

**cos lettuce** [kɔs'lɛtɪs] *n* (laitue *f*) romaine *f*.

**cosmetic** [kɔz'mɛtɪk] *n* produit *m* de beauté, cosmétique *m*.

**cosmic** ['kɔzmɪk] *a* cosmique.

**cosmonaut** ['kɔzmənɔːt] *n* cosmonaute *m/f*.

**cosmopolitan** [kɔzmə'pɔlɪtn] *a* cosmopolite.

**cosmos** ['kɔzmɔs] *n* cosmos *m*.

**cosset** ['kɔsɪt] *vt* choyer, dorloter.

**cost** [kɔst] *n* coût *m* // *vb* (*pt, pp* **cost**) *vi* coûter // *vt* établir *or* calculer le prix de revient de ; **it ~s £5/too much** cela coûte cinq livres/trop cher ; **it ~ him his life/job** ça lui a coûté la vie/son emploi ; **at all ~s** coûte que coûte, à tout prix.

**co-star** ['kəustɑː*] *n* partenaire *m/f*.

**costly** ['kɔstlɪ] *a* coûteux(euse).

**cost price** ['kɔst'praɪs] *n* prix coûtant *or* de revient.

**costume** ['kɔstjuːm] *n* costume *m* ; (*lady's suit*) tailleur *m* ; (*also:* **swimming ~**) maillot *m* (de bain) ; **~ jewellery** *n* bijoux *mpl* de fantaisie.

**cosy** ['kəuzɪ] *a* douillet(te).

**cot** [kɔt] *n* (*child's*) lit *m* d'enfant, petit lit.

**cottage** ['kɔtɪdʒ] *n* petite maison (à la campagne), cottage *m* ; **~ cheese** *n* fromage blanc (*maigre*).

**cotton** ['kɔtn] *n* coton *m* ; **~ dress** *etc* robe *etc* en *or* de coton ; **~ wool** *n* ouate *f*, coton *m* hydrophile.

**couch** [kautʃ] *n* canapé *m* ; divan *m* // *vt* formuler, exprimer.

**cough** [kɔf] *vi* tousser // *n* toux *f* ; **~ drop** *n* pastille *f* pour *or* contre la toux.

**could** [kud] *pt of* **can** ; **~n't = could not.**

**council** ['kaunsl] *n* conseil *m* ; **city** *or* **town ~** conseil municipal ; **~ estate** *n* (quartier *m or* zone *f* de) logements loués à/par la municipalité ; **~ house** *n* maison *f* (à loyer modéré) louée par la municipalité ; **~lor** *n* conseiller/ère.

**counsel** ['kaunsl] *n* avocat/e ; consultation *f*, délibération *f* ; **~lor** *n* conseiller/ère.

**count** [kaunt] *vt, vi* compter // *n* compte *m* ; (*nobleman*) comte *m* ; **~ on** *vt fus* compter sur ; **to ~ up** *vt* compter, additionner ; **~down** *n* compte *m* à rebours.

**countenance** ['kauntɪnəns] *n* expression *f* // *vt* approuver.

**counter** ['kauntə*] *n* comptoir *m* ; (*machine*) compteur *m* // *vt* aller à l'encontre de, opposer ; (*blow*) parer // *ad:* **~ to** à l'encontre de ; contrairement à ; **~act** *vt* neutraliser, contrebalancer ; **~attack** *n* contre-attaque *f* // *vi* contre-attaquer ; **~balance** *vt* contrebalancer,

faire contrepoids à ; **~-clockwise** *ad* en sens inverse des aiguilles d'une montre ; **~-espionage** *n* contre-espionnage *m*.

**counterfeit** ['kauntəfɪt] *n* faux *m*, contrefaçon *f* // *vt* contrefaire // *a* faux(fausse).

**counterfoil** ['kauntəfɔɪl] *n* talon *m*, souche *f*.

**counterpart** ['kauntəpɑːt] *n* (*of document etc*) double *m* ; (*of person*) homologue *m/f*.

**countersink** ['kauntəsɪŋk] *vt* (*hole*) fraiser.

**countess** ['kauntɪs] *n* comtesse *f*.

**countless** ['kauntlɪs] *a* innombrable.

**countrified** ['kʌntrɪfaɪd] *a* rustique, à l'air campagnard.

**country** ['kʌntrɪ] *n* pays *m* ; (*native land*) patrie *f* ; (*as opposed to town*) campagne *f* ; (*region*) région *f*, pays *m* ; **~ dancing** *n* danse *f* folklorique ; **~ house** *n* manoir *m*, (petit) château ; **~man** *n* (*national*) compatriote *m* ; (*rural*) habitant *m* de la campagne, campagnard *m* ; **~side** *n* campagne *f*.

**county** ['kauntɪ] *n* comté *m* ; **~ town** *n* chef-lieu *m*.

**coup, ~s** [kuː, -z] *n* beau coup *m* ; (*also:* **~ d'état**) coup d'État.

**coupé** [kuː'peɪ] *n* coupé *m*.

**couple** ['kʌpl] *n* couple *m* // *vt* (*carriages*) atteler ; (*TECH*) coupler ; (*ideas, names*) associer ; **a ~ of** deux.

**couplet** ['kʌplɪt] *n* distique *m*.

**coupling** ['kʌplɪŋ] *n* (*RAIL*) attelage *m*.

**coupon** ['kuːpɔn] *n* coupon *m*, bon-prime *m*, bon-réclame *m* ; (*COMM*) coupon *m*.

**courage** ['kʌrɪdʒ] *n* courage *m* ; **~ous** [kə'reɪdʒəs] *a* courageux (euse).

**courier** ['kurɪə*] *n* messager *m*, courrier *m* ; (*for tourists*) accompagnateur/trice.

**course** [kɔːs] *n* cours *m* ; (*of ship*) route *f* ; (*CONSTR*) assise *f* ; (*for golf*) terrain *m* ; (*part of meal*) plat *m* ; **first ~** entrée *f* ; **of ~** *ad* bien sûr ; **in due ~** en temps utile *or* voulu ; **~ of action** parti *m*, ligne *f* de conduite , **~ of lectures** série *f* de conférences ; **~ of treatment** (*MED*) traitement *m*.

**court** [kɔːt] *n* cour *f* ; (*LAW*) cour, tribunal *m* ; (*TENNIS*) court *m* // *vt* (*woman*) courtiser, faire la cour à ; **out of ~** (*LAW: settle*) à l'amiable ; **to take to ~** actionner *or* poursuivre en justice.

**courteous** ['kʌːtɪəs] *a* courtois(e), poli(e).

**courtesan** [kɔːtɪ'zæn] *n* courtisane *f*.

**courtesy** ['kəːtəsɪ] *n* courtoisie *f*, politesse *f*.

**court-house** ['kɔːthaus] *n* (*US*) palais *m* de justice.

**courtier** ['kɔːtɪə*] *n* courtisan *m*, dame *f* de cour.

**court-martial,** *pl* **courts-martial** ['kɔːt'mɑːʃəl] *n* cour martiale, conseil *m* de guerre.

**courtroom** ['kɔːtrum] *n* salle *f* de tribunal.

**courtyard** ['kɔːtjɑːd] *n* cour *f*.

**cousin** ['kʌzn] *n* cousin/e.

**cove** [kəuv] *n* petite baie, anse *f*.

**covenant** ['kʌvənənt] *n* contrat *m*, engagement *m*.

**cover** ['kʌvə*] vt couvrir // n (for bed, of book, COMM) couverture f; (of pan) couvercle m; (over furniture) housse f; (shelter) abri m; **under** ~ à l'abri; **~age** n reportage m; (INSURANCE) couverture f; ~ **charge** n couvert m (supplément à payer); **~ing** n couverture f, enveloppe f; **~ing letter** n lettre explicative.

**covet** ['kʌvit] vt convoiter.

**cow** [kau] n vache f // cpd femelle.

**coward** ['kauəd] n lâche m/f; **~ice** [-is] n lâcheté f; **~ly** a lâche.

**cowboy** ['kaubɔi] n cow-boy m.

**cower** ['kauə*] vi se recroqueviller; trembler.

**cowshed** ['kauʃɛd] n étable f.

**coxswain** ['kɔksn] n (abbr: cox) barreur m; (of ship) patron m.

**coy** [kɔi] a faussement effarouché(e) or timide.

**coyote** [kɔi'əuti] n coyote m.

**crab** [kræb] n crabe m; ~ **apple** n pomme f sauvage.

**crack** [kræk] n fente f, fissure f; fêlure f; lézarde f; (noise) craquement m, coup (sec) // vt fendre, fissurer; fêler; lézarder; (whip) faire claquer; (nut) casser // a (athlete) de première classe, d'élite; **to** ~ **up** vi être au bout de son rouleau, flancher; **~ed** a (col) toqué(e), timbré(e); **~er** n pétard m; biscuit (salé), craquelin m.

**crackle** ['krækl] vi crépiter, grésiller // n (of china) craquelure f; **crackling** n crépitement m, grésillement m; (of pork) couenne f.

**cradle** ['kreidl] n berceau m.

**craft** [krɑːft] n métier (artisanal); (cunning) ruse f, astuce f; (boat) embarcation f, barque f; **~sman** n artisan m, ouvrier (qualifié); **~smanship** n métier m, habileté f; **~y** a rusé(e), malin(igne), astucieux(euse).

**crag** [kræg] n rocher escarpé; **~gy** a escarpé(e), rocheux(euse).

**cram** [kræm] vt (fill): **to** ~ **sth with** bourrer qch de; (put): **to** ~ **sth into** fourrer qch dans; **~ming** n (fig: pej) bachotage m.

**cramp** [kræmp] n crampe f // vt gêner, entraver; **~ed** a à l'étroit, très serré(e).

**crampon** [kræmpən] n crampon m.

**cranberry** ['krænbəri] n canneberge f.

**crane** [krein] n grue f.

**cranium**, pl **crania** ['kreiniəm, 'kreiniə] n boîte crânienne.

**crank** [kræŋk] n manivelle f; (person) excentrique m/f; **~shaft** n vilebrequin m.

**cranky** ['kræŋki] a excentrique, loufoque; (bad-tempered) grincheux(euse), revêche.

**cranny** ['kræni] n see **nook**.

**crash** [kræʃ] n fracas m; (of car, plane) collision f // vt (plane) écraser // vi (plane) s'écraser; (two cars) se percuter, s'emboutir; (fig) s'effondrer; **to** ~ **into** se jeter or se fracasser contre; ~ **course** n cours intensif; ~ **helmet** n casque (protecteur); ~ **landing** n atterrissage forcé or en catastrophe.

**crate** [kreit] n cageot m.

**crater** ['kreitə*] n cratère m.

**cravat(e)** [krə'væt] n foulard (noué autour du cou).

**crave** [kreiv] vt: **to** ~ **for** désirer violemment, avoir un besoin physiologique de, avoir une envie irrésistible de.

**crawl** [krɔːl] vi ramper; (vehicle) avancer au pas // n (SWIMMING) crawl m.

**crayfish** ['kreifiʃ] n, pl inv écrevisse f; langoustine f.

**crayon** ['kreiən] n crayon m (de couleur).

**craze** [kreiz] n engouement m.

**crazy** ['kreizi] a fou(folle); ~ **paving** n dallage irrégulier (en pierres plates).

**creak** [kriːk] vi grincer; craquer.

**cream** [kriːm] n crème f // a (colour) crème inv; ~ **cake** n (petit) gâteau à la crème; ~ **cheese** n fromage m à la crème, fromage blanc; **~ery** n (shop) crèmerie f; (factory) laiterie f; **~y** a crémeux(euse).

**crease** [kriːs] n pli m // vt froisser, chiffonner // vi se froisser, se chiffonner.

**create** [kriː'eit] vt créer; **creation** [-ʃən] n création f; **creative** a créateur(trice); **creator** n créateur/trice.

**creature** ['kriːtʃə*] n créature f.

**credence** ['kriːdns] n croyance f, foi f.

**crèche, creche** [krɛʃ] n garderie f, crèche f.

**credentials** [kri'denʃlz] npl (papers) références fpl.

**credibility** [krɛdi'biliti] n crédibilité f.

**credible** ['krɛdibl] a digne de foi, crédible.

**credit** ['krɛdit] n crédit m // vt (COMM) créditer; (believe: also: **give** ~ **to**) ajouter foi à, croire; ~**s** npl (CINEMA) générique m; **to** ~ **sb with** (fig) prêter or attribuer à qn; **to** ~ **£5 to sb** créditer (le compte de) qn de 5 livres; **to one's** ~ à son honneur; à son actif; **to take the** ~ **for** s'attribuer le mérite de; **it does him** ~ cela lui fait honneur; **~able** a honorable, estimable; ~ **card** n carte f de crédit; **~or** n créancier/ière.

**credulity** [kri'djuːliti] n crédulité f.

**creed** [kriːd] n croyance f; credo m, principes mpl.

**creek** [kriːk] n crique f, anse f; (US) ruisseau m, petit cours d'eau.

**creep, pt, pp crept** [kriːp, krɛpt] vi ramper; (fig) se faufiler, se glisser; (plant) grimper; **~er** n plante grimpante; **~y** a (frightening) qui fait frissonner, qui donne la chair de poule.

**cremate** [kri'meit] vt incinérer; **cremation** [-ʃən] n incinération f.

**crematorium**, pl **crematoria** [krɛmə'tɔːriəm, -'tɔːriə] n four m crématoire.

**creosote** ['kriəsaut] n créosote f.

**crêpe** [kreip] n crêpe m; ~ **bandage** n bande f Velpeau ®.

**crept** [krɛpt] pt, pp of **creep**.

**crescendo** [kri'ʃɛndəu] n crescendo m.

**crescent** ['krɛsnt] n croissant m; rue f (en arc de cercle).

**cress** [krɛs] n cresson m.

**crest** [krɛst] n crête f; (of helmet) cimier m; (of coat of arms) timbre m; **~fallen** a déconfit(e), découragé(e).

**Crete** ['kriːt] n Crète f.

**crevasse** [krı'væs] *n* crevasse *f*.
**crevice** ['krɛvıs] *n* fissure *f*, lézarde *f*, fente
*f*.
**crew** [kru:] *n* équipage *m*; **to have a**
~**-cut** avoir les cheveux en brosse; ~-
**neck** *n* col ras.
**crib** [krıb] *n* lit *m* d'enfant // *vt* (*col*) copier.
**cribbage** ['krıbıdʒ] *n* sorte de jeu de cartes.
**crick** [krık] *n* crampe *f*.
**cricket** ['krıkıt] *n* (*insect*) grillon *m*, cri-cri
*m inv*; (*game*) cricket *m*; ~**er** *n* joueur *m*
de cricket.
**crime** [kraım] *n* crime *m*; **criminal**
['krımınl] *a*, *n* criminel(le); **the Criminal**
**Investigation Department (C.I.D.)** ≈ la
police judiciaire (P.J.).
**crimp** [krımp] *vt* friser, frisotter.
**crimson** ['krımzn] *a* cramoisi(e).
**cringe** [krındʒ] *vi* avoir un mouvement de
recul; (*fig*) s'humilier, ramper.
**crinkle** ['krıŋkl] *vt* froisser, chiffonner.
**cripple** ['krıpl] *n* boiteux/euse, infirme
*m/f* // *vt* estropier, paralyser.
**crisis**, *pl* **crises** ['kraısıs, -si:z] *n* crise *f*.
**crisp** [krısp] *a* croquant(e); (*fig*) vif(vive);
brusque; ~**s** *npl* (pommes) chips *fpl*.
**criss-cross** ['krıskrɔs] *a* entrecroisé(e).
**criterion**, *pl* **criteria** [kraı'tıərıən, -'tıərıə]
*n* critère *m*.
**critic** ['krıtık] *n* critique *m/f*; ~**al** *a*
critique; ~**ally** *ad* d'un œil critique;
~**ally ill** gravement malade; ~**ism**
['krıtısızm] *n* critique *f*; ~**ize** ['krıtısaız]
*vt* critiquer.
**croak** [krəuk] *vi* (*frog*) coasser; (*raven*)
croasser.
**crochet** ['krəuʃeı] *n* travail *m* au crochet.
**crockery** ['krɔkərı] *n* vaisselle *f*.
**crocodile** ['krɔkədaıl] *n* crocodile *m*.
**crocus** ['krəukəs] *n* crocus *m*.
**croft** [krɔft] *n* petite ferme; ~**er** *n* fermier
*m*.
**crony** ['krəunı] *n* copain/copine.
**crook** [kruk] *n* escroc *m*; (*of shepherd*)
houlette *f*; ~**ed** ['krukıd] *a* courbé(e),
tordu(e); (*action*) malhonnête.
**crop** [krɔp] *n* récolte *f*; culture *f*; **to** ~
**up** *vi* surgir, se présenter, survenir.
**cropper** ['krɔpə*] *n*: **to come a** ~ (*col*)
faire la culbute, s'étaler.
**croquet** ['krəukeı] *n* croquet *m*.
**croquette** [krə'kɛt] *n* croquette *f*.
**cross** [krɔs] *n* croix *f*; (*BIOL*) croisement
*m* // *vt* (*street etc*) traverser; (*arms, legs,*
*BIOL*) croiser; (*cheque*) barrer // *a* en
colère, fâché(e); **to** ~ **out** *vt* barrer,
biffer; **to** ~ **over** *vi* traverser; ~**bar** *n*
barre transversale; ~**breed** *n* hybride *m*,
métis/se; ~**country (race)** *n* cross(-
country) *m*; ~**-examination** *n* examen *m*
contradictoire (*d'un témoin*); ~**-examine**
*vt* (*LAW*) faire subir un examen
contradictoire à; ~**-eyed** *a* qui louche;
~**ing** *n* croisement *m*, carrefour *m*; (*sea-*
*passage*) traversée *f*; (*also*: **pedestrian**
~**ing**) passage clouté; ~**-reference** *n*
renvoi *m*, référence *f*; ~**roads** *n* carrefour
*m*; ~ **section** *n* (*BIOL*) coupe transversale;
(*in population*) échantillon *m*; ~**wind** *n*
vent *m* de travers; ~**wise** *ad* en travers;
~**word** *n* mots croisés *mpl*.

**crotch** [krɔtʃ] *n* (*of garment*) entre-jambes
*m inv*.
**crotchet** ['krɔtʃıt] *n* (*MUS*) noire *f*.
**crotchety** ['krɔtʃıtı] *a* (*person*)
grognon(ne), grincheux(euse).
**crouch** [krautʃ] *vi* s'accroupir; se tapir;
se ramasser.
**crouton** ['kru:tɔn] *n* croûton *m*.
**crow** [krəu] (*bird*) corneille *f*; (*of cock*)
chant *m* du coq, cocorico *m* // *vi* (*cock*)
chanter; (*fig*) pavoiser, chanter victoire.
**crowbar** ['krəubɑ:*] *n* levier *m*.
**crowd** [kraud] *n* foule *f* // *vt* bourrer,
remplir // *vi* affluer, s'attrouper,
s'entasser; ~**ed** *a* bondé(e), plein(e); ~**ed**
**with** plein(e) de.
**crown** [kraun] *n* couronne *f*; (*of head*)
sommet *m* de la tête, calotte crânienne;
(*of hat*) fond *m*; (*of hill*) sommet *m* // *vt*
couronner; **C**~ **court** *n* ≈ Cour *f*
d'assises; ~ **jewels** *npl* joyaux *mpl* de la
Couronne; ~ **prince** *n* prince héritier.
**crow's-nest** ['krəuznɛst] *n* (*on sailing-ship*)
nid *m* de pie.
**crucial** ['kru:ʃl] *a* crucial(e), décisif(ive).
**crucifix** ['kru:sıfıks] *n* crucifix *m*; ~**ion**
[-'fıkʃən] *n* crucifiement *m*, crucifixion *f*.
**crucify** ['kru:sıfaı] *vt* crucifier, mettre en
croix.
**crude** [kru:d] *a* (*materials*) brut(e); non
raffiné(e); (*fig: basic*) rudimentaire,
sommaire; (: *vulgar*) cru(e), grossier(ère);
~ **(oil)** *n* (pétrole) brut *m*.
**cruel** ['kruəl] *a* cruel(le); ~**ty** *n* cruauté
*f*.
**cruet** ['kru:ıt] *n* huilier *m*; vinaigrier *m*.
**cruise** [kru:z] *n* croisière *f* // *vi* (*ship*)
croiser; (*car*) rouler; (*aircraft*) voler; (*taxi*)
être en maraude; ~**r** *n* croiseur *m*;
**cruising speed** *n* vitesse *f* de croisière.
**crumb** [krʌm] *n* miette *f*.
**crumble** ['krʌmbl] *vt* émietter // *vi*
s'émietter; (*plaster etc*) s'effriter; (*land,*
*earth*) s'ébouler; (*building*) s'écrouler,
crouler; (*fig*) s'effondrer; **crumbly** *a*
friable.
**crumpet** ['krʌmpıt] *n* petite crêpe
(épaisse).
**crumple** ['krʌmpl] *vt* froisser, friper.
**crunch** [krʌntʃ] *vt* croquer; (*underfoot*)
faire craquer, écraser; faire crisser // *n*
(*fig*) instant *m or* moment *m* critique,
moment de vérité; ~**y** *a* croquant(e),
croustillant(e).
**crusade** [kru:'seıd] *n* croisade *f*; ~**r** *n*
croisé *m*.
**crush** [krʌʃ] *n* foule *f*, cohue *f*; (*love*): **to**
**have a** ~ **on sb** avoir le béguin pour qn;
(*drink*): **lemon** ~ citron pressé // *vt*
écraser; (*crumple*) froisser; ~**ing** *a*
écrasant(e).
**crust** [krʌst] *n* croûte *f*.
**crutch** [krʌtʃ] *n* béquille *f*; (*TECH*) support
*m*.
**crux** [krʌks] *n* point crucial.
**cry** [kraı] *vi* pleurer; (*shout*) crier // *n* cri
*m*; **to** ~ **off** *vi* se dédire; se
décommander; ~**ing** *a* (*fig*) criant(e),
flagrant(e).
**crypt** [krıpt] *n* crypte *f*.

**cryptic** ['krıptık] *a* énigmatique.

**crystal** ['krıstl] *n* cristal *m*; ~-**clear** *a* clair(e) comme de l'eau de roche; **crystallize** *vt* cristalliser // *vi* (se) cristalliser.

**cu.** *abbr*: ~ **ft.** = *cubic feet*; ~ **in.** = *cubic inches*.

**cub** [kʌb] *n* petit *m* (d'un *animal*).

**Cuba** ['kju:bə] *n* Cuba *m*; ~**n** *a* cubain(e) // *n* Cubain/e.

**cubbyhole** ['kʌbıhəul] *n* cagibi *m*.

**cube** [kju:b] *n* cube *m* // *vt* (MATH) élever au cube; ~ **root** *n* racine *f* cubique; **cubic** *a* cubique; **cubic metre** *etc* mètre *m* cube *etc*.

**cubicle** ['kju:bıkl] *n* box *m*, cabine *f*.

**cuckoo** ['kuku:] *n* coucou *m*; ~ **clock** *n* (pendule *f* à) coucou *m*.

**cucumber** ['kju:kʌmbə*] *n* concombre *m*.

**cud** [kʌd] *n*: **to chew the** ~ ruminer.

**cuddle** ['kʌdl] *vt* câliner, caresser // *vi* se blottir l'un contre l'autre; **cuddly** *a* câlin(e).

**cudgel** ['kʌdʒl] *n* gourdin *m*.

**cue** [kju:] *n* queue *f* de billard; (THEATRE *etc*) signal *m*.

**cuff** [kʌf] *n* (of *shirt*, *coat etc*) poignet *m*, manchette *f*; (US) = **turn-up**; **off the** ~ *ad* de chic, à l'improviste; ~**link** *n* bouton *m* de manchette.

**cuisine** [kwı'zi:n] *n* cuisine *f*, art *m* culinaire.

**cul-de-sac** ['kʌldəsæk] *n* cul-de-sac *m*, impasse *f*.

**culinary** ['kʌlınərı] *a* culinaire.

**cull** [kʌl] *vt* sélectionner.

**culminate** ['kʌlmıneıt] *vi* culminer; **culmination** [-'neıʃən] *n* point culminant.

**culpable** ['kʌlpəbl] *a* coupable.

**culprit** ['kʌlprıt] *n* coupable *m/f*.

**cult** [kʌlt] *n* culte *m*.

**cultivate** ['kʌltıveıt] *vt* (*also fig*) cultiver; **cultivation** [-'veıʃən] *n* culture *f*.

**cultural** ['kʌltʃərəl] *a* culturel(le).

**culture** ['kʌltʃə*] *n* (*also fig*) culture *f*; ~**d** *a* cultivé(e) (fig).

**cumbersome** ['kʌmbəsəm] *a* encombrant(e), embarrassant(e).

**cumulative** ['kju:mjulətıv] *a* cumulatif(ive).

**cunning** ['kʌnıŋ] *n* ruse *f*, astuce *f* // *a* rusé(e), malin(igne).

**cup** [kʌp] *n* tasse *f*; (*prize*, *event*) coupe *f*; (of *bra*) bonnet *m*.

**cupboard** ['kʌbəd] *n* placard *m*.

**Cupid** ['kju:pıd] *n* Cupidon *m*; (*figurine*) amour *m*.

**cupidity** [kju:'pıdıtı] *n* cupidité *f*.

**cupola** ['kju:pələ] *n* coupole *f*.

**cup-tie** ['kʌptaı] *n* match *m* de coupe.

**curable** ['kjuərəbl] *a* guérissable, curable.

**curate** ['kju:rıt] *n* vicaire *m*.

**curator** [kju'reıtə*] *n* conservateur *m* (d'un *musée etc*).

**curb** [kə:b] *vt* refréner, mettre un frein à // *n* frein *m* (fig); (US) = **kerb**.

**curdle** ['kə:dl] *vi* (se) cailler.

**curds** [kə:ds] *npl* lait caillé.

**cure** [kjuə*] *vt* guérir; (CULIN) saler; fumer; sécher // *n* remède *m*.

**curfew** ['kə:fju:] *n* couvre-feu *m*.

**curio** ['kjuərıəu] *n* bibelot *m*, curiosité *f*.

**curiosity** [kjuərıɔsıtı] *n* curiosité *f*.

**curious** ['kjuərıəs] *a* curieux(euse); ~**ly** *ad* curieusement.

**curl** [kə:l] *n* boucle *f* (de cheveux) // *vt*, *vi* boucler; (*tightly*) friser; **to** ~ **up** *vi* s'enrouler; se pelotonner; ~**er** *n* bigoudi *m*, rouleau *m*; (SPORT) joueur/euse de curling.

**curling** ['kə:lıŋ] *n* (SPORT) curling *m*.

**curly** ['kə:lı] *a* bouclé(e); frisé(e).

**currant** ['kʌrnt] *n* raisin *m* de Corinthe, raisin sec.

**currency** ['kʌrnsı] *n* monnaie *f*; **foreign** ~ devises étrangères, monnaie étrangère; **to gain** ~ (*fig*) s'accréditer.

**current** ['kʌrnt] *n* courant *m* // *a* courant(e); ~ **account** *n* compte courant; ~ **affairs** *npl* (questions *fpl* d')actualité *f*; ~**ly** *ad* actuellement.

**curriculum**, *pl* ~**s** *or* **curricula** [kə'rıkjuləm, -lə] *n* programme *m* d'études; ~ **vitae** *n* curriculum vitae (C.V.) *m*.

**curry** ['kʌrı] *n* curry *m* // *vt*: **to** ~ **favour with** chercher à gagner la faveur *or* à s'attirer les bonnes grâces de; **chicken** ~ curry de poulet, poulet *m* au curry; ~ **powder** *n* poudre *f* de curry.

**curse** [kə:s] *vi* jurer, blasphémer // *vt* maudire // *n* malédiction *f*; fléau *m*; (*swearword*) juron *m*.

**cursory** ['kə:sərı] *a* superficiel(le), hâtif(ive).

**curt** [kə:t] *a* brusque, sec(sèche).

**curtail** [kə:'teıl] *vt* (*visit etc*) écourter; (*expenses etc*) réduire.

**curtain** ['kə:tn] *n* rideau *m*.

**curts(e)y** [kə:tsı] *n* révérence *f* // *vi* faire une révérence.

**curve** [kə:v] *n* courbe *f*; (*in the road*) tournant *m*, virage *m* // *vt* courber // *vi* se courber; (*road*) faire une courbe.

**cushion** ['kuʃən] *n* coussin *m* // *vt* (*seat*) rembourrer; (*shock*) amortir.

**custard** ['kʌstəd] *n* (*for pouring*) crème anglaise.

**custodian** [kʌs'təudıən] *n* gardien/ne; (of *collection etc*) conservateur/trice.

**custody** ['kʌstədı] *n* (of *child*) garde *f*; (for *offenders*) détention préventive.

**custom** ['kʌstəm] *n* coutume *f*, usage *m*; (LAW) droit coutumier, coutume *f*; (COMM) clientèle *f*; ~**ary** *a* habituel(le).

**customer** ['kʌstəmə*] *n* client/e.

**custom-made** ['kʌstəm'meıd] *a* (*clothes*) fait(e) sur mesure; (*other goods*) hors série, fait(e) sur commande.

**customs** ['kʌstəmz] *npl* douane *f*; ~ **duty** *n* droits *mpl* de douane; ~ **officer** *n* douanier *m*.

**cut** [kʌt] *vb* (*pt*, *pp* **cut**) *vt* couper; (*meat*) découper; (*shape*, *make*) tailler; couper; creuser; graver; (*reduce*) réduire // *vi* couper; (*intersect*) se couper // *n* (*gen*) coupure *f*; (of *clothes*) coupe *f*; (of *jewel*) taille *f*; (in *salary etc*) réduction *f*; (of *meat*) morceau *m*; **power** ~ coupure de courant; **to** ~ **teeth** (*baby*) faire ses dents; **to** ~ **a tooth** percer une dent; **to** ~ **down (on)** *vt fus* réduire; **to** ~ **off** *vt* couper; (fig) isoler; **to ～ out** vt ôter; découper; tailler; **～away** a, n: **～away (drawing)** écorché m; **～back** n réductions fpl.

**cute** [kju:t] a mignon(ne), adorable; (clever) rusé(e), astucieux(euse).

**cut glass** [kʌt'glɑ:s] n cristal taillé.

**cuticle** ['kju:tɪkl] n (on nail): **～ remover** n repousse-peaux m inv.

**cutlery** ['kʌtlərɪ] n couverts mpl; (trade) coutellerie f.

**cutlet** ['kʌtlɪt] n côtelette f.

**cut: ～off switch** n interrupteur m; **～out** n coupe-circuit m inv; **～-price** a au rabais, à prix réduit; **～ throat** n assassin m.

**cutting** ['kʌtɪŋ] a tranchant(e), coupant(e); (fig) cinglant(e), mordant(e) // n (PRESS) coupure f (de journal); (RAIL) tranchée f.

**cuttlefish** ['kʌtlfɪʃ] n seiche f.

**cut-up** ['kʌtʌp] a affecté(e), démoralisé(e).

**cwt** abbr of **hundredweight(s)**.

**cyanide** ['saɪənaɪd] n cyanure m.

**cybernetics** [saɪbə'nɛtɪks] n cybernétique f.

**cyclamen** ['sɪkləmən] n cyclamen m.

**cycle** ['saɪkl] n cycle m // vi faire de la bicyclette.

**cycling** ['saɪklɪŋ] n cyclisme m.

**cyclist** ['saɪklɪst] n cycliste m/f.

**cyclone** ['saɪkləun] n cyclone m.

**cygnet** ['sɪgnɪt] n jeune cygne m.

**cylinder** ['sɪlɪndə*] n cylindre m; **～ block** n bloc-cylindres m; **～ capacity** n cylindrée f; **～ head** n culasse f; **～-head gasket** n joint m de culasse.

**cymbals** ['sɪmblz] npl cymbales fpl.

**cynic** ['sɪnɪk] n cynique m/f; **～al** a cynique; **～ism** ['sɪnɪsɪzəm] n cynisme m.

**cypress** ['saɪprɪs] n cyprès m.

**Cypriot** ['sɪprɪət] a cypriote, chypriote // n Cypriote m/f, Chypriote m/f.

**Cyprus** ['saɪprəs] n Chypre f.

**cyst** [sɪst] n kyste m.

**cystitis** [sɪs'taɪtɪs] n cystite f.

**czar** [zɑ:*] n tsar m.

**Czech** [tʃɛk] a tchèque // n Tchèque m/f; (LING) tchèque m.

**Czechoslovakia** [tʃɛkəslə'vækɪə] n la Tchécoslovaquie; **～n** a tchécoslovaque // n Tchécoslovaque m/f.

## D

**D** [di:] n (MUS) ré m; **～-day** n le jour J.

**dab** [dæb] vt (eyes, wound) tamponner; (paint, cream) appliquer (par petites touches or rapidement); **a ～ of paint** un petit coup de peinture.

**dabble** ['dæbl] vi: **to ～ in** faire or se mêler or s'occuper un peu de.

**dad, daddy** [dæd, 'dædɪ] n papa m; **daddy-long-legs** n tipule f; faucheux m.

**daffodil** ['dæfədɪl] n jonquille f.

**daft** [dɑ:ft] a idiot(e), stupide; **to be ～ about** être toqué or mordu de.

**dagger** ['dægə*] n poignard m; **to be at ～s drawn with sb** être à couteaux tirés

avec qn; **to look ～s at sb** foudroyer qn du regard.

**daily** ['deɪlɪ] a quotidien(ne), journalier-(ère) // n quotidien m // ad tous les jours.

**dainty** ['deɪntɪ] a délicat(e), mignon(ne).

**dairy** ['dɛərɪ] n (shop) crémerie f, laiterie f; (on farm) laiterie // a laitier(ère).

**daisy** ['deɪzɪ] n pâquerette f.

**dale** [deɪl] n vallon m.

**dally** ['dælɪ] vi musarder, flâner.

**dam** [dæm] n barrage m // vt endiguer.

**damage** ['dæmɪdʒ] n dégâts mpl, dommages mpl; (fig) tort m // vt endommager, abimer; (fig) faire du tort à; **～s** npl (LAW) dommages-intérêts mpl.

**damn** [dæm] vt condamner; (curse) maudire // n (col): **I don't give a ～** je m'en fous // a (col): **this ～ ...** ce sacré or foutu ...; **～ (it)!** zut!; **～ing** a (evidence) accablant(e).

**damp** [dæmp] a humide // n humidité f // vt (also: **～en**) (cloth, rag) humecter; (enthusiasm etc) refroidir; **～ness** n humidité f.

**damson** ['dæmzən] n prune f de Damas.

**dance** [dɑ:ns] n danse f; (ball) bal m // vi danser; **～ hall** n salle f de bal, dancing m; **～r** n danseur/euse.

**dancing** ['dɑ:nsɪŋ] n danse f.

**dandelion** ['dændɪlaɪən] n pissenlit m.

**dandruff** ['dændrəf] n pellicules fpl.

**Dane** [deɪn] n Danois/e.

**danger** ['deɪndʒə*] n danger m; **there is a ～ of fire** il y a (un) risque d'incendie; **in ～** en danger; **he was in ～ of falling** il risquait de tomber; **～ous** a dangereux(euse); **～ously** ad dangereuse-ment.

**dangle** ['dæŋgl] vt balancer; (fig) faire miroiter // vi pendre, se balancer.

**Danish** ['deɪnɪʃ] a danois(e) // n (LING) danois m.

**dapper** ['dæpə*] a pimpant(e).

**dare** [dɛə*] vt: **to ～ sb to do** défier qn or mettre qn au défi de faire // vi: **to ～ (to) do sth** oser faire qch; **～devil** n casse-cou m inv; **daring** a hardi(e), audacieux(euse).

**dark** [dɑ:k] a (night, room) obscur(e), sombre; (colour, complexion) foncé(e), sombre; (fig) sombre // n: **in the ～** dans le noir; **in the ～ about** (fig) ignorant tout de; **after ～** après la tombée de la nuit; **～en** vt obscurcir, assombrir // vi s'obscurcir, s'assombrir; **～ glasses** npl lunettes noires; **～ness** n obscurité f; **～room** n chambre noire.

**darling** ['dɑ:lɪŋ] a, n chéri(e).

**darn** [dɑ:n] vt repriser.

**dart** [dɑ:t] n fléchette f // vi: **to ～ towards** (also: **make a ～ towards**) se précipiter or s'élancer vers; **to ～ away/along** partir/passer comme une flèche; **～s** n jeu m de fléchettes; **～board** n cible f (de jeu de fléchettes).

**dash** [dæʃ] n (sign) tiret m // vt (missile) jeter or lancer violemment; (hopes) anéantir // vi: **to ～ towards** (also: **make a ～ towards**) se précipiter or se ruer vers; **to ～ away** vi partir à toute allure;

**~board** *n* tableau *m* de bord ; **~ing** *a* fringant(e).

**data** ['deɪtə] *npl* données *fpl* ; **~ processing** *n* traitement *m* (électronique) de l'information.

**date** [deɪt] *n* date *f* ; rendez-vous *m* ; (*fruit*) datte *f* // *vt* dater ; **to ~** *ad* à ce jour ; **out of ~** périmé(e) ; **up to ~** à la page ; mis(e) à jour ; moderne ; **~d the 13th** daté du 13 ; **~d** *a* démodé(e) ; **~line** *n* ligne *f* de changement de date.

**daub** [dɔ:b] *vt* barbouiller.

**daughter** ['dɔ:tə\*] *n* fille *f* ; **~-in-law** *n* belle-fille *f*, bru *f*.

**daunt** [dɔ:nt] *vt* intimider, décourager ; **~less** *a* intrépide.

**dawdle** ['dɔ:dl] *vi* traîner, lambiner.

**dawn** [dɔ:n] *n* aube *f*, aurore *f* // *vi* (*day*) se lever, poindre ; (*fig*) naître, se faire jour.

**day** [deɪ] *n* jour *m* ; (*as duration*) journée *f* ; (*period of time, age*) époque *f*, temps *m* ; **the ~ before** la veille, le jour précédent ; **the following ~** le lendemain, le jour suivant ; **by ~** de jour ; **~ boy/girl** *n* (*SCOL*) externe *m/f* ; **~break** *n* point *m* du jour ; **~dream** *n* rêverie *f* // *vi* rêver (tout éveillé) ; **~light** *n* (lumière *f* du) jour *m* ; **~time** *n* jour *m*, journée *f*.

**daze** [deɪz] *vt* (*subject: drug*) hébéter ; (: *blow*) étourdir // *n*: **in a ~** hébété(e); étourdi(e).

**dazzle** ['dæzl] *vt* éblouir, aveugler.

**dead** [dɛd] *a* mort(e) ; (*numb*) engourdi(e), insensible // *ad* absolument, complètement ; **he was shot ~** il a été tué d'un coup de revolver ; **~ on time** à l'heure pile ; **~ tired** éreinté, complètement fourbu ; **to stop ~** s'arrêter pile *or* net ; **the ~** les morts ; **~en** *vt* (*blow, sound*) amortir ; (*make numb*) endormir, rendre insensible ; **~ end** *n* impasse *f* ; **~ heat** *n* (*SPORT*): **to finish in a ~ heat** terminer ex-æquo ; **~line** *n* date *f* or heure *f* limite ; **~lock** *n* impasse *f* (*fig*) ; **~ly** *a* mortel(le) ; (*weapon*) meurtrier(ère) ; **~pan** *a* impassible ; (*humour*) pince-sans-rire *inv*.

**deaf** [dɛf] *a* sourd(e) ; **~-aid** *n* appareil auditif ; **~en** *vt* rendre sourd ; (*fig*) assourdir ; **~ening** *a* assourdissant(e) ; **~ness** *n* surdité *f* ; **~-mute** *n* sourd/e-muet/te.

**deal** [di:l] *n* affaire *f*, marché *m* // *vt* (*pt, pp* **dealt** [dɛlt]) (*blow*) porter ; (*cards*) donner, distribuer ; **a great ~ (of)** beaucoup (de) ; **to ~ in** faire le commerce de ; **to ~ with** *vt fus* (*COMM*) traiter avec ; (*handle*) s'occuper *or* se charger de ; (*be about: book etc*) traiter de ; **~er** *n* marchand *m* ; **~ings** *npl* (*COMM*) transactions *fpl* ; (*relations*) relations *fpl*, rapports *mpl*.

**dean** [di:n] *n* (*SCOL*) doyen *m*.

**dear** [dɪə\*] *a* cher(chère) ; (*expensive*) cher, coûteux(euse) // *n*: **my ~** mon cher/ma chère ; **~ me!** mon Dieu! ; **D~ Sir/Madam** (*in letter*) Monsieur/Madame ; **D~ Mr/Mrs X** Cher Monsieur/Chère Madame X ; **~ly** *ad* (*love*) tendrement ; (*pay*) cher.

**dearth** [də:θ] *n* disette *f*, pénurie *f*.

**death** [dɛθ] *n* mort *f* ; (*ADMIN*) décès *m* ; **~bed** *n* lit *m* de mort ; **~ certificate** *n* acte *m* de décès ; **~ duties** *npl* (*Brit*) droits *mpl* de succession ; **~ly** *a* de mort ; **~ penalty** *n* peine *f* de mort ; **~ rate** *n* (taux *m* de) mortalité *f*.

**debar** [dɪ'bɑ:\*] *vt*: **to ~ sb from a club** *etc* exclure qn d'un club *etc* ; **to ~ sb from doing** interdire à qn de faire.

**debase** [dɪ'beɪs] *vt* (*currency*) déprécier, dévaloriser ; (*person*) abaisser, avilir.

**debatable** [dɪ'beɪtəbl] *a* discutable, contestable.

**debate** [dɪ'beɪt] *n* discussion *f*, débat *m* // *vt* discuter, débattre // *vi* (*consider*): **to ~ whether** se demander si.

**debauchery** [dɪ'bɔ:tʃərɪ] *n* débauche *f*.

**debit** ['dɛbɪt] *n* débit *m* // *vt*: **to ~ a sum to sb** *or* **to sb's account** porter une somme au débit de qn, débiter qn d'une somme.

**debris** ['dɛbri:] *n* débris *mpl*, décombres *mpl*.

**debt** [dɛt] *n* dette *f* ; **to be in ~** avoir des dettes, être endetté(e) ; **~or** *n* débiteur/trice.

**début** ['deɪbju:] *n* début(s) *m(pl)*.

**decade** ['dɛkeɪd] *n* décennie *f*, décade *f*.

**decadence** ['dɛkədəns] *n* décadence *f*.

**decanter** [dɪ'kæntə\*] *n* carafe *f*.

**decarbonize** [di:'kɑ:bənaɪz] *vt* (*AUT*) décalaminer.

**decay** [dɪ'keɪ] *n* décomposition *f*, pourrissement *m* ; (*fig*) déclin *m*, délabrement *m* ; (*also:* **tooth ~**) carie *f* (dentaire) // *vi* (*rot*) se décomposer, pourrir ; (*fig*) se délabrer ; décliner ; se détériorer.

**decease** [dɪ'si:s] *n* décès *m* ; **~d** *n* défunt/e.

**deceit** [dɪ'si:t] *n* tromperie *f*, supercherie *f* ; **~ful** *a* trompeur(euse).

**deceive** [dɪ'si:v] *vt* tromper ; **to ~ o.s.** s'abuser.

**decelerate** [di:'sɛləreɪt] *vt,vi* ralentir.

**December** [dɪ'sɛmbə\*] *n* décembre *m*.

**decency** ['di:sənsɪ] *n* décence *f*.

**decent** ['di:sənt] *a* décent(e), convenable ; **they were very ~ about it** ils se sont montrés très chics.

**decentralize** [di:'sɛntrəlaɪz] *vt* décentraliser.

**deception** [dɪ'sɛpʃən] *n* tromperie *f*.

**deceptive** [dɪ'sɛptɪv] *a* trompeur(euse).

**decibel** ['dɛsɪbɛl] *n* décibel *m*.

**decide** [dɪ'saɪd] *vt* (*person*) décider ; (*question, argument*) trancher, régler // *vi* se décider, décider ; **to ~ to do/that** décider de faire/que ; **to ~ on** décider, se décider pour ; **to ~ on doing** décider de faire ; **~d** *a* (*resolute*) résolu(e), décidé(e) ; (*clear, definite*) net(te), marqué(e) ; **~dly** [-dɪdlɪ] *ad* résolument ; incontestablement, nettement.

**deciduous** [dɪ'sɪdjuəs] *a* à feuilles caduques.

**decimal** ['dɛsɪməl] *a* décimal(e) // *n* décimale *f* ; **~ point** *n* ≈ virgule *f*.

**decimate** ['dɛsɪmeɪt] *vt* décimer.

**decipher** [dɪ'saɪfə\*] *vt* déchiffrer.

**decision** [dɪ'sɪʒən] *n* décision *f*.
**decisive** [dɪ'saɪsɪv] *a* décisif(ive).
**deck** [dɛk] *n* (*NAUT*) pont *m*; (*of bus*): **top** ~ impériale *f*; (*of cards*) jeu *m*; ~**chair** *n* chaise longue; ~ **hand** *n* matelot *m*.
**declaration** [dɛklə'reɪʃən] *n* déclaration *f*.
**declare** [dɪ'klɛə*] *vt* déclarer.
**decline** [dɪ'klaɪn] *n* (*decay*) déclin *m*; (*lessening*) baisse *f* // *vt* refuser, décliner // *vi* décliner; être en baisse, baisser.
**declutch** ['di:'klʌtʃ] *vi* débrayer.
**decode** ['di:'kəud] *vt* décoder.
**decompose** [di:kəm'pəuz] *vi* se décomposer; **decomposition** [di:kɔmpə'zɪʃən] *n* décomposition *f*.
**decontaminate** [di:kən'tæmɪneɪt] *vt* décontaminer.
**décor** ['deɪkɔ:*] *n* décor *m*.
**decorate** ['dɛkəreɪt] *vt* (*adorn, give a medal to*) décorer; (*paint and paper*) peindre et tapisser; **decoration** [-'reɪʃən] *n* (*medal etc, adornment*) décoration *f*; **decorative** ['dɛkərətɪv] *a* décoratif(ive); **decorator** *n* peintre *m* en bâtiment.
**decoy** ['di:kɔɪ] *n* piège *m*; **they used him as a** ~ **for the enemy** ils se sont servis de lui pour attirer l'ennemi.
**decrease** *n* ['di:kri:s] diminution *f* // *vt, vi* [di:'kri:s] diminuer.
**decree** [dɪ'kri:] *n* (*POL, REL*) décret *m*; (*LAW: of tribunal*) arrêt *m*, jugement *m*; ~ **nisi** *n* jugement *m* provisoire de divorce.
**decrepit** [dɪ'krɛpɪt] *a* décrépit(e); délabré(e).
**dedicate** ['dɛdɪkeɪt] *vt* consacrer; (*book etc*) dédier.
**dedication** [dɛdɪ'keɪʃən] *n* (*devotion*) dévouement *m*.
**deduce** [dɪ'dju:s] *vt* déduire, conclure.
**deduct** [dɪ'dʌkt] *vt*: **to ~ sth** (**from**) déduire qch (de), retrancher qch (de); (*from wage etc*) prélever qch (sur), retenir qch (sur); ~**ion** [dɪ'dʌkʃən] *n* (*deducting*) déduction *f*; (*from wage etc*) prélèvement *m*, retenue *f*; (*deducing*) déduction, conclusion *f*.
**deed** [di:d] *n* action *f*, acte *m*; (*LAW*) acte notarié, contrat *m*.
**deep** [di:p] *a* (*water, sigh, sorrow, thoughts*) profond(e); (*voice*) grave; **he took a ~ breath** il inspira profondément, il prit son souffle; **4 metres** ~ de 4 mètres de profondeur // *ad*: ~ **in snow** recouvert(e) d'une épaisse couche de neige; **spectators stood 20** ~ il y avait 20 rangs de spectateurs; **knee-**~ **in water** dans l'eau jusqu'aux genoux; ~**en** *vt* (*hole*) approfondir // *vi* s'approfondir; (*darkness*) s'épaissir; ~**-freeze** *n* congélateur *m* // *vt* surgeler; ~**-fry** *vt* faire frire (en friteuse); ~**-sea** *a*: ~**-sea diving** *n* plongée sous-marine; ~**-sea fishing** *n* pêche hauturière; ~**-seated** *a* (*beliefs*) profondément enraciné(e); ~**-set** *a* (*eyes*) enfoncé(e).
**deer** [dɪə*] *n, pl inv*: **the** ~ les cervidés *mpl* (*ZOOL*); (**red**) ~ cerf *m*; (**fallow**) ~ daim *m*; (**roe**) ~ chevreuil *m*; ~**skin** *n* peau *f* de daim.
**deface** [dɪ'feɪs] *vt* dégrader; barbouiller; rendre illisible.

**defamation** [dɛfə'meɪʃən] *n* diffamation *f*.
**default** [dɪ'fɔ:lt] *vi* (*LAW*) faire défaut; (*gen*) manquer à ses engagements // *n*: **by** ~ (*LAW*) par défaut, par contumace; (*SPORT*) par forfait; ~**er** *n* (*in debt*) débiteur défaillant.
**defeat** [dɪ'fi:t] *n* défaite *f* // *vt* (*team, opponents*) battre; (*fig: plans, efforts*) faire échouer; ~**ist** *a,n* défaitiste (*m/f*).
**defect** *n* ['di:fɛkt] défaut *m* // *vi* [dɪ'fɛkt]: **to ~ to the enemy/the West** passer à l'ennemi/l'Ouest; ~**ive** [dɪ'fɛktɪv] *a* défectueux(euse).
**defence** [dɪ'fɛns] *n* défense *f*; **in ~ of** pour défendre; ~**less** *a* sans défense.
**defend** [dɪ'fɛnd] *vt* défendre; ~**ant** *n* défendeur/deresse; (*in criminal case*) accusé/e, prévenu/e; ~**er** *n* défenseur *m*.
**defense** [dɪ'fɛns] *n* (*US*) = **defence**.
**defensive** [dɪ'fɛnsɪv] *a* défensif(ive).
**defer** [dɪ'fə:*] *vt* (*postpone*) différer, ajourner.
**deference** ['dɛfərəns] *n* déférence *f*; égards *mpl*.
**defiance** [dɪ'faɪəns] *n* défi *m*; **in ~ of** au mépris de.
**defiant** [dɪ'faɪənt] *a* provocant(e), de défi.
**deficiency** [dɪ'fɪʃənsɪ] *n* insuffisance *f*, déficience *f*; carence *f*; ~ **disease** *n* maladie *f* de carence.
**deficient** [dɪ'fɪʃənt] *a* insuffisant(e); défectueux(euse); déficient(e); ~ **in** manquant de.
**deficit** ['dɛfɪsɪt] *n* déficit *m*.
**defile** *vb* [dɪ'faɪl] *vt* souiller // *vi* défiler // *n* ['di:faɪl] défilé *m*.
**define** [dɪ'faɪn] *vt* définir.
**definite** ['dɛfɪnɪt] *a* (*fixed*) défini(e), (bien) déterminé(e); (*clear, obvious*) net(te), manifeste; (*LING*) défini(e); **he was ~ about it** il a été catégorique; il était sûr de son fait; ~**ly** *ad* sans aucun doute.
**definition** [dɛfɪ'nɪʃən] *n* définition *f*.
**definitive** [dɪ'fɪnɪtɪv] *a* définitif(ive).
**deflate** [di:'fleɪt] *vt* dégonfler.
**deflation** [di:'fleɪʃən] *n* (*COMM*) déflation *f*.
**deflect** [dɪ'flɛkt] *vt* détourner, faire dévier.
**deform** [dɪ'fɔ:m] *vt* déformer; ~**ed** *a* difforme; ~**ity** *n* difformité *f*.
**defraud** [dɪ'frɔ:d] *vt* frauder; **to ~ sb of sth** soutirer qch malhonnêtement à qn; escroquer qch à qn; frustrer qn de qch.
**defray** [dɪ'freɪ] *vt*: **to ~ sb's expenses** défrayer qn (de ses frais), rembourser *or* payer à qn ses frais.
**defrost** [di:'frɔst] *vt* (*fridge*) dégivrer.
**deft** [dɛft] *a* adroit(e), preste.
**defunct** [dɪ'fʌŋkt] *a* défunt(e).
**defuse** [di:'fju:z] *vt* désamorcer.
**defy** [dɪ'faɪ] *vt* défier; (*efforts etc*) résister à.
**degenerate** *vi* [dɪ'dʒɛnəreɪt] dégénérer // *a* [dɪ'dʒɛnərɪt] dégénéré(e).
**degradation** [dɛgrə'deɪʃən] *n* dégradation *f*.
**degrading** [dɪ'greɪdɪŋ] *a* dégradant(e).
**degree** [dɪ'gri:] *n* degré *m*; grade *m* (universitaire); **a** (**first**) ~ **in maths** une licence en maths.
**dehydrated** [di:haɪ'dreɪtɪd] *a* déshydraté(e); (*milk, eggs*) en poudre.

**de-ice** [di:'aɪs] vt (windscreen) dégivrer.
**deign** [deɪn] vi: **to ~ to do** daigner faire.
**deity** ['di:ɪtɪ] n divinité f; dieu m, déesse f.
**dejected** [dɪ'dʒɛktɪd] a abattu(e), déprimé(e).
**dejection** [dɪ'dʒɛkʃən] n abattement m, découragement m.
**delay** [dɪ'leɪ] vt (journey, operation) retarder, différer; (travellers, trains) retarder // n délai m, retard m; **without ~** sans délai; sans tarder; **~ed-action** a à retardement.
**delegate** n ['dɛlɪgɪt] délégué/e // vt ['dɛlɪgeɪt] déléguer.
**delegation** [dɛlɪ'geɪʃən] n délégation f.
**delete** [dɪ'li:t] vt rayer, supprimer.
**deliberate** a [dɪ'lɪbərɪt] (intentional) délibéré(e); (slow) mesuré(e) // vi [dɪ'lɪbəreɪt] délibérer, réfléchir; **~ly** ad (on purpose) exprès, délibérément.
**delicacy** ['dɛlɪkəsɪ] n délicatesse f; (choice food) mets fin or délicat, friandise f.
**delicate** ['dɛlɪkɪt] a délicat(e).
**delicatessen** [dɛlɪkə'tɛsn] n épicerie fine.
**delicious** [dɪ'lɪʃəs] a délicieux(euse), exquis(e).
**delight** [dɪ'laɪt] n (grande) joie, grand plaisir // vt enchanter; **a ~ to the eyes** un régal or plaisir pour les yeux; **to take ~ in** prendre grand plaisir à; **to be the ~ of** faire les délices or la joie de; **~ful** a adorable; merveilleux(euse); délicieux(euse).
**delinquency** [dɪ'lɪŋkwənsɪ] n délinquance f.
**delinquent** [dɪ'lɪŋkwənt] a,n délinquant(e).
**delirium** [dɪ'lɪrɪəm] n délire m.
**deliver** [dɪ'lɪvə*] vt (mail) distribuer; (goods) livrer; (message) remettre; (speech) prononcer; (warning, ultimatum) lancer; (free) délivrer; (MED) accoucher; **to ~ the goods** (fig) tenir ses promesses; **~y** n distribution f; livraison f; (of speaker) élocution f; (MED) accouchement m; **to take ~y of** prendre livraison de.
**delouse** ['di:'laus] vt épouiller, débarrasser de sa (or leur etc) vermine.
**delta** ['dɛltə] n delta m.
**delude** [dɪ'lu:d] vt tromper, leurrer; **to ~ o.s.** se leurrer, se faire des illusions.
**deluge** ['dɛlju:dʒ] n déluge m.
**delusion** [dɪ'lu:ʒən] n illusion f.
**delve** [dɛlv] vi: **to ~ into** fouiller dans.
**demagogue** ['dɛməgɔg] n démagogue m/f.
**demand** [dɪ'mɑ:nd] vt réclamer, exiger // n exigence f; (claim) revendication f; (ECON) demande f; **in ~** demandé(e), recherché(e); **on ~** sur demande; **~ing** a (boss) exigeant(e); (work) astreignant(e).
**demarcation** [di:mɑ:'keɪʃən] n démarcation f.
**demean** [dɪ'mi:n] vt: **to ~ o.s.** s'abaisser.
**demeanour** [dɪ'mi:nə*] n comportement m; maintien m.
**demented** [dɪ'mɛntɪd] a dément(e), fou(folle).
**demise** [dɪ'maɪz] n décès m.
**demister** [di:'mɪstə*] n (AUT) dispositif m anti-buée inv.

**demobilize** [di:'məubɪlaɪz] vt démobiliser.
**democracy** [dɪ'mɔkrəsɪ] n démocratie f.
**democrat** ['dɛməkræt] n démocrate m/f; **~ic** [dɛmə'krætɪk] a démocratique.
**demography** [dɪ'mɔgrəfɪ] n démographie f.
**demolish** [dɪ'mɔlɪʃ] démolir.
**demolition** [dɛmə'lɪʃən] n démolition f.
**demonstrate** ['dɛmənstreɪt] vt démontrer, prouver.
**demonstration** [dɛmən'streɪʃən] n démonstration f, manifestation f.
**demonstrative** [dɪ'mɔnstrətɪv] a démonstratif(ive).
**demonstrator** ['dɛmənstreɪtə*] n (POL) manifestant/e.
**demoralize** [dɪ'mɔrəlaɪz] vt démoraliser.
**demote** [dɪ'məut] vt rétrograder.
**demur** [dɪ'mə:*] vi protester; hésiter.
**demure** [dɪ'mjuə*] a sage, réservé(e); d'une modestie affectée.
**den** [dɛn] n tanière f, antre m.
**denial** [dɪ'naɪəl] n démenti m; dénégation f.
**denigrate** ['dɛnɪgreɪt] vt dénigrer.
**denim** ['dɛnɪm] n coton émerisé; **~s** npl (blue-)jeans mpl.
**Denmark** ['dɛnmɑ:k] n Danemark m.
**denomination** [dɪnɔmɪ'neɪʃən] n (money) valeur f; (REL) confession f; culte m.
**denominator** [dɪ'nɔmɪneɪtə*] n dénominateur m.
**denote** [dɪ'nəut] vt dénoter.
**denounce** [dɪ'nauns] vt dénoncer.
**dense** [dɛns] a dense; (stupid) obtus(e), dur(e) or lent(e) à la comprenette; **~ly** ad: **~ly wooded** couvert d'épaisses forêts; **~ly populated** à forte densité (de population), très peuplé.
**density** ['dɛnsɪtɪ] n densité f.
**dent** [dɛnt] n bosse f // vt (also: **make a ~ in**) cabosser; **to make a ~ in** (fig) entamer.
**dental** ['dɛntl] a dentaire; **~ surgeon** (chirurgien/ne) dentiste.
**dentifrice** ['dɛntɪfrɪs] n dentifrice m.
**dentist** ['dɛntɪst] n dentiste m/f; **~ry** n art m dentaire.
**denture** ['dɛntʃə*] n dentier m.
**deny** [dɪ'naɪ] vt nier; (refuse) refuser; (disown) renier.
**deodorant** [di:'əudərənt] n désodorisant m, déodorant m.
**depart** [dɪ'pɑ:t] vi partir; **to ~ from** (leave) quitter, partir de; (fig: differ from) s'écarter de.
**department** [dɪ'pɑ:tmənt] n (COMM) rayon m; (SCOL) section f; (POL) ministère m, département m; **~ store** n grand magasin.
**departure** [dɪ'pɑ:tʃə*] n départ m; (fig): **~ from** écart m par rapport à.
**depend** [dɪ'pɛnd] vi: **to ~ on** dépendre de; (rely on) compter sur; **it ~s** cela dépend; **~able** a sûr(e), digne de confiance; **~ence** n dépendance f; **~ant, ~ent** n personne f à charge.
**depict** [dɪ'pɪkt] vt (in picture) représenter; (in words) (dé)peindre, décrire.
**depleted** [dɪ'pli:tɪd] a (considérablement) réduit(e) or diminué(e).

**deplorable** [dɪ'plɔ:rəbl] *a* déplorable, lamentable.

**deplore** [dɪ'plɔ:*] *vt* déplorer.

**deploy** [dɪ'plɔɪ] *vt* déployer.

**depopulation** ['di:pɔpju'leɪʃən] *n* dépopulation *f*, dépeuplement *m*.

**deport** [dɪ'pɔ:t] *vt* déporter ; expulser ; ~ation [di:pɔ:'teɪʃən] *n* déportation *f*, expulsion *f* ; ~ment *n* maintien *m*, tenue *f*.

**depose** [dɪ'pəuz] *vt* déposer.

**deposit** [dɪ'pɔzɪt] *n* (CHEM, COMM, GEO) dépôt *m* ; (*of ore, oil*) gisement *m* ; (*part payment*) arrhes *fpl*, acompte *m* ; (*on bottle etc*) consigne *f* ; (*for hired goods etc*) cautionnement *m*, garantie *f* // *vt* déposer ; mettre *or* laisser en dépôt ; fournir *or* donner en acompte ; laisser en garantie ; ~ **account** *n* compte *m* de dépôt ; ~**or** *n* déposant/e.

**depot** ['dɛpəu] *n* dépôt *m*.

**deprave** [dɪ'preɪv] *vt* dépraver, corrompre, pervertir.

**depravity** [dɪ'prævɪtɪ] *n* dépravation *f*.

**deprecate** ['dɛprɪkeɪt] *vt* désapprouver.

**depreciate** [dɪ'pri:ʃɪeɪt] *vt* déprécier // *vi* se déprécier, se dévaloriser ; **depreciation** [-'eɪʃən] *n* dépréciation *f*.

**depress** [dɪ'prɛs] *vt* déprimer ; (*press down*) appuyer sur, abaisser ; ~**ed** *a* (*person*) déprimé(e), abattu(e) ; (*area*) en déclin, touché(e) par le sous-emploi ; ~**ing** *a* déprimant(e) ; ~**ion** [dɪ'prɛʃən] *n* dépression *f*.

**deprivation** [dɛprɪ'veɪʃən] *n* privation *f* ; (*loss*) perte *f*.

**deprive** [dɪ'praɪv] *vt*: **to** ~ **sb of** priver qn de ; enlever à qn ; ~**d** *a* déshérité(e).

**depth** [dɛpθ] *n* profondeur *f* ; **in the** ~**s of** au fond de ; au cœur de ; au plus profond de ; ~ **charge** *n* grenade sous-marine.

**deputation** [dɛpju'teɪʃən] *n* députation *f*, délégation *f*.

**deputize** ['dɛpjutaɪz] *vi*: **to** ~ **for** assurer l'intérim de.

**deputy** ['dɛpjutɪ] *a*: ~ **chairman** vice-président *m* ; ~ **head** directeur adjoint, sous-directeur *m* // *n* (*replacement*) suppléant/e, intérimaire *m/f* ; (*second in command*) adjoint/e.

**derail** [dɪ'reɪl] *vt* faire dérailler ; **to be** ~**ed** dérailler ; ~**ment** *n* déraillement *m*.

**deranged** [dɪ'reɪndʒd] *a* (*machine*) déréglé(e) ; **to be** (**mentally**) ~ avoir le cerveau dérangé.

**derelict** ['dɛrɪlɪkt] *a* abandonné(e), à l'abandon.

**deride** [dɪ'raɪd] *vt* railler.

**derision** [dɪ'rɪʒən] *n* dérision *f*.

**derisive** [dɪ'raɪsɪv] *a* moqueur (euse), railleur(euse).

**derisory** [dɪ'raɪsərɪ] *a* (*sum*) dérisoire ; (*smile, person*) moqueur(euse), railleur(euse).

**derivation** [dɛrɪ'veɪʃən] *n* dérivation *f*.

**derivative** [dɪ'rɪvətɪv] *n* dérivé *m* // *a* dérivé(e).

**derive** [dɪ'raɪv] *vt*: **to** ~ **sth from** tirer qch de ; trouver qch dans // *vi*: **to** ~ **from** provenir de, dériver de.

**dermatology** [də:mə'tɔlədʒɪ] *n* dermatologie *f*.

**derogatory** [dɪ'rɔgətərɪ] *a* désobligeant(e) ; péjoratif(ive).

**derrick** ['dɛrɪk] *n* mât *m* de charge ; derrick *m*.

**desalination** [di:salɪ'neɪʃən] *n* dessalement *m*, dessalage *m*.

**descend** [dɪ'sɛnd] *vt, vi* descendre ; **to** ~ **from** descendre de, être issu de ; ~**ant** *n* descendant/e.

**descent** [dɪ'sɛnt] *n* descente *f* ; (*origin*) origine *f*.

**describe** [dɪs'kraɪb] *vt* décrire ; **description** [-'krɪpʃən] *n* description *f* ; (*sort*) sorte *f*, espèce *f* ; **descriptive** [-'krɪptɪv] *a* descriptif(ive).

**desecrate** ['dɛsɪkreɪt] *vt* profaner.

**desert** *n* ['dɛzət] désert *m* // *vb* [dɪ'zə:t] *vt* déserter, abandonner // *vi* (MIL) déserter ; ~**er** *n* déserteur *m* ; ~**ion** [dɪ'zə:ʃən] *n* désertion *f*.

**deserve** [dɪ'zə:v] *vt* mériter ; **deserving** *a* (*person*) méritant(e) ; (*action, cause*) méritoire.

**design** [dɪ'zaɪn] *n* (*sketch*) plan *m*, dessin *m* ; (*layout, shape*) conception *f*, ligne *f* ; (*pattern*) dessin *m*, motif(s) *m(pl)* ; (COMM) esthétique industrielle ; (*intention*) dessein *m* // *vt* dessiner ; concevoir ; **to have** ~**s on** avoir des visées sur ; **well-**~**ed** *a* bien conçu(e).

**designate** *vt* ['dɛzɪgneɪt] désigner // *a* ['dɛzɪgnɪt] désigné(e) ; **designation** [-'neɪʃən] *n* désignation *f*.

**designer** [dɪ'zaɪnə*] *n* (ART, TECH) dessinateur/trice ; (*fashion*) modéliste *m/f*.

**desirability** [dɪzaɪərə'bɪlɪtɪ] *n* avantage *m* ; attrait *m*.

**desirable** [dɪ'zaɪərəbl] *a* désirable.

**desire** [dɪ'zaɪə*] *n* désir *m* // *vt* désirer, vouloir.

**desirous** [dɪ'zaɪərəs] *a*: ~ **of** désireux-(euse) de.

**desk** [dɛsk] *n* (*in office*) bureau *m* ; (*for pupil*) pupitre *m* ; (*in shop, restaurant*) caisse *f* ; (*in hotel, at airport*) réception *f*.

**desolate** ['dɛsəlɪt] *a* désolé(e).

**desolation** [dɛsə'leɪʃən] *n* désolation *f*.

**despair** [dɪs'pɛə*] *n* désespoir *m* // *vi*: **to** ~ **of** désespérer de.

**despatch** [dɪs'pætʃ] *n,vt* = **dispatch**.

**desperate** ['dɛspərɪt] *a* désespéré(e) ; (*fugitive*) prêt(e) à tout ; ~**ly** *ad* désespérément ; (*very*) terriblement, extrêmement.

**desperation** [dɛspə'reɪʃən] *n* désespoir *m* ; **in** ~ à bout de nerf ; en désespoir de cause.

**despicable** [dɪs'pɪkəbl] *a* méprisable.

**despise** [dɪs'paɪz] *vt* mépriser, dédaigner.

**despite** [dɪs'paɪt] *prep* malgré, en dépit de.

**despondent** [dɪs'pɔndənt] *a* découragé(e), abattu(e).

**dessert** [dɪ'zə:t] *n* dessert *m* ; ~**spoon** *n* cuiller *f* à dessert.

**destination** [dɛstɪ'neɪʃən] *n* destination *f*.

**destine** ['dɛstɪn] *vt* destiner.

**destiny** ['dɛstɪnɪ] *n* destinée *f*, destin *m*.

**destitute** ['dɛstɪtju:t] *a* indigent(e), dans

le dénuement ; ~ of dépourvu or dénué de.

**destroy** [dɪs'trɔɪ] vt détruire ; ~**er** n (NAUT) contre-torpilleur m.

**destruction** [dɪs'trʌkʃən] n destruction f.

**destructive** [dɪs'trʌktɪv] a destructeur(trice).

**detach** [dɪ'tætʃ] vt détacher ; ~**able** a amovible, détachable ; ~**ed** a (attitude) détaché(e) ; ~**ed house** n pavillon m, maison(nette) (individuelle) ; ~**ment** n (MIL) détachement m ; (fig) détachement m, indifférence f.

**detail** ['di:teɪl] n détail m // vt raconter en détail, énumérer ; (MIL): **to** ~ **sb (for)** affecter qn (à), détacher qn (pour) ; **in** ~ en détail ; ~**ed** a détaillé(e).

**detain** [dɪ'teɪn] vt retenir ; (in captivity) détenir ; (in hospital) hospitaliser.

**detect** [dɪ'tɛkt] vt déceler, percevoir ; (MED. POLICE) dépister ; (MIL, RADAR, TECH) détecter ; ~**ion** [dɪ'tɛkʃən] n découverte f ; dépistage m ; détection f ; **to escape** ~**ion** échapper aux recherches, éviter d'être découvert ; **crime** ~**ion** le dépistage des criminels ; ~**ive** n agent m de la sûreté, policier m ; **private** ~**ive** détective privé ; ~**ive story** n roman policier ; ~**or** n détecteur m.

**detention** [dɪ'tɛnʃən] n détention f ; (SCOL) retenue f, consigne f.

**deter** [dɪ'tə:*] vt dissuader.

**detergent** [dɪ'tə:dʒənt] n détersif m, détergent m.

**deteriorate** [dɪ'tɪərɪəreɪt] vi se détériorer, se dégrader ; **deterioration** [-'reɪʃən] n détérioration f.

**determination** [dɪtə:mɪ'neɪʃən] n détermination f.

**determine** [dɪ'tə:mɪn] vt déterminer ; **to** ~ **to do** résoudre de faire, se déterminer à faire ; ~**d** a (person) déterminé(e), décidé(e) ; (quantity) déterminé, établi(e).

**deterrent** [dɪ'tɛrənt] n effet m de dissuasion ; force f de dissuasion.

**detest** [dɪ'tɛst] vt détester, avoir horreur de ; ~**able** a détestable, odieux(euse).

**detonate** ['dɛtəneɪt] vi exploser ; détoner // vt faire exploser or détoner ; **detonator** n détonateur m.

**detour** ['di:tuə*] n détour m.

**detract** [dɪ'trækt] vt: **to** ~ **from** (quality, pleasure) diminuer ; (reputation) porter atteinte à.

**detriment** ['dɛtrɪmənt] n: **to the** ~ **of** au détriment de, au préjudice de ; ~**al** [dɛtrɪ'mɛntl] a: ~**al to** préjudiciable or nuisible à.

**devaluation** [dɪvælju'eɪʃən] n dévaluation f.

**devalue** ['di:'vælju:] vt dévaluer.

**devastate** ['dɛvəsteɪt] vt dévaster.

**devastating** ['dɛvəsteɪtɪŋ] a dévastateur(trice).

**develop** [dɪ'vɛləp] vt (gen) développer ; (habit) contracter ; (resources) mettre en valeur, exploiter // vi se développer ; (situation, disease: evolve) évoluer ; (facts, symptoms: appear) se manifester, se produire ; ~**er** n (PHOT) révélateur m ; (of land) promoteur m ; ~**ing country** pays m en voie de développement ; ~**ment** n développement m ; (of affair, case)

rebondissement m, fait(s) nouveau(x).

**deviate** ['di:vieɪt] vi dévier.

**deviation** [di:vɪ'eɪʃən] n déviation f.

**device** [dɪ'vaɪs] n (scheme) moyen m, expédient m ; (apparatus) engin m, dispositif m.

**devil** ['dɛvl] n diable m ; démon m ; ~**ish** a diabolique.

**devious** ['di:vɪəs] a (means) détourné(e) ; (person) sournois(e), dissimulé(e).

**devise** [dɪ'vaɪz] vt imaginer, concevoir.

**devoid** [dɪ'vɔɪd] a: ~ **of** dépourvu(e) de, dénué(e) de.

**devote** [dɪ'vəut] vt: **to** ~ **sth to** consacrer qch à ; ~**d** a dévoué(e) ; **to be** ~**d to** être dévoué or très attaché à ; ~**e** [dɛvəu'ti:] n (REL) adepte m/f ; (MUS, SPORT) fervent/e.

**devotion** [dɪ'vəuʃən] n dévouement m, attachement m ; (REL) dévotion f, piété f.

**devour** [dɪ'vauə*] vt dévorer.

**devout** [dɪ'vaut] a pieux(euse), dévot(e).

**dew** [dju:] n rosée f.

**dexterity** [dɛks'tɛrɪtɪ] n dextérité f, adresse f.

**diabetes** [daɪə'bi:ti:z] n diabète m ; **diabetic** [-'bɛtɪk] a, n diabétique (m/f).

**diaeresis** [daɪ'ɛrɪsɪs] n tréma m.

**diagnose** [daɪəg'nəuz] vt diagnostiquer.

**diagnosis, pl diagnoses** [daɪəg'nəusɪs, -si:z] n diagnostic m.

**diagonal** [daɪ'ægənl] a diagonal(e) // n diagonale f.

**diagram** ['daɪəgræm] n diagramme m, schéma m ; graphique m.

**dial** ['daɪəl] n cadran m // vt (number) faire, composer ; ~**ling tone** n tonalité f.

**dialect** ['daɪəlɛkt] n dialecte m.

**dialogue** ['daɪələg] n dialogue m.

**diameter** [daɪ'æmɪtə*] n diamètre m.

**diamond** ['daɪəmənd] n diamant m ; (shape) losange m ; ~**s** npl (CARDS) carreau m.

**diaper** ['daɪəpə*] n (US) couche f.

**diaphragm** ['daɪəfræm] n diaphragme m.

**diarrhoea, diarrhea** (US) [daɪə'ri:ə] n diarrhée f.

**diary** ['daɪərɪ] n (daily account) journal m ; (book) agenda m.

**dice** [daɪs] n, pl inv dé m // vt (CULIN) couper en dés or en cubes.

**dictate** vt [dɪk'teɪt] dicter // n ['dɪkteɪt] injonction f.

**dictation** [dɪk'teɪʃən] n dictée f.

**dictator** [dɪk'teɪtə*] n dictateur m ; ~**ship** n dictature f.

**diction** ['dɪkʃən] n diction f, élocution f.

**dictionary** ['dɪkʃənrɪ] n dictionnaire m.

**did** [dɪd] pt of **do**.

**die** [daɪ] n (pl: **dice**) dé m ; (pl: **dies**) coin m ; matrice f ; étampe f // vi mourir ; **to** ~ **away** vi s'éteindre ; **to** ~ **down** vi se calmer, s'apaiser ; **to** ~ **out** vi disparaître, s'éteindre.

**Diesel** ['di:zəl]: ~ **engine** n moteur m diesel.

**diet** ['daɪət] n alimentation f ; (restricted food) régime m // vi (also: **be on a** ~) suivre un régime.

**differ** ['dɪfə*] vi: **to** ~ **from sth** être différent de ; différer de ; **to** ~ **from sb**

**over sth** ne pas être d'accord avec qn au sujet de qch ; ~**ence** n différence f ; (quarrel) différend m, désaccord m ; ~**ent** a différent(e) ; ~**ential** [-'rɛnʃəl] n (AUT. wages) différentiel m ; ~**entiate** [-'rɛnʃieit] vt différencier // vi se différencier ; **to** ~**entiate between** faire une différence entre ; ~**ently** ad différemment.

**difficult** ['dɪfɪkəlt] a difficile ; ~**y** n difficulté f.

**diffidence** ['dɪfɪdəns] n manque m de confiance en soi, manque d'assurance.

**diffident** ['dɪfɪdənt] a qui manque de confiance ɔr d'assurance, peu sûr(e) de soi.

**diffuse** a [dɪ'fju:s] diffus(e) // vt [dɪ'fju:z] diffuser, répandre.

**dig** [dɪg] vt (pt, pp **dug** [dʌg] ) (hole) creuser ; (garden) bêcher // n (prod) coup m de coude ; (fig) coup de griffe or de patte ; **to** ~ **into** (snow, soil) creuser ; **to** ~ **one's nails into** enfoncer ses ongles dans ; **to** ~ **up** vt déterrer.

**digest** vt [daɪ'dʒɛst] digérer // n ['daɪdʒɛst] sommaire m, résumé m ; ~**ible** [dɪ'dʒɛstəbl] a digestible ; ~**ion** [dɪ'dʒɛstʃən] n digestion f.

**digit** ['dɪdʒɪt] n chiffre m (de 0 à 9) ; (finger) doigt m ; ~**al** a digital(e) ; à affichage numérique or digital.

**dignified** ['dɪgnɪfaɪd] a digne.

**dignitary** ['dɪgnɪtərɪ] n dignitaire m.

**dignity** ['dɪgnɪtɪ] n dignité f.

**digress** [daɪ'grɛs] vi: **to** ~ **from** s'écarter de, s'éloigner de ; ~**ion** [daɪ'grɛʃən] n digression f.

**digs** [dɪgz] npl (Brit: col) piaule f, chambre meublée.

**dilapidated** [dɪ'læpɪdeɪtɪd] a délabré(e).

**dilate** [daɪ'leɪt] vt dilater // vi se dilater.

**dilatory** ['dɪlətərɪ] a dilatoire.

**dilemma** [daɪ'lɛmə] n dilemme m.

**diligent** ['dɪlɪdʒənt] a appliqué(e), assidu(e).

**dilute** [daɪ'lu:t] vt diluer // a dilué(e).

**dim** [dɪm] a (light, eyesight) faible ; (memory, outline) vague, indécis(e) ; (stupid) borné(e), obtus(e) // vt (light) réduire, baisser.

**dime** [daɪm] n (US) = 10 cents.

**dimension** [dɪ'mɛnʃən] n dimension f.

**diminish** [dɪ'mɪnɪʃ] vt,vi diminuer.

**diminutive** [dɪ'mɪnjutɪv] a minuscule, tout(e) petit(e) // n (LING) diminutif m.

**dimly** ['dɪmlɪ] ad faiblement ; vaguement.

**dimple** ['dɪmpl] n fossette f.

**dim-witted** ['dɪm'wɪtɪd] a (col) stupide, borné(e).

**din** [dɪn] n vacarme m.

**dine** [daɪn] vi dîner ; ~**r** n (person) dîneur/euse ; (RAIL) = dining car.

**dinghy** ['dɪŋgɪ] n youyou m ; canot m pneumatique ; (also: **sailing** ~) voilier m, dériveur m.

**dingy** ['dɪndʒɪ] a miteux(euse), minable.

**dining** ['daɪnɪŋ] cpd: ~ **car** n wagon-restaurant m ; ~ **room** n salle f à manger.

**dinner** ['dɪnə*] n dîner m ; (public) banquet m ; ~ **jacket** n smoking m ; ~ **party** n dîner m ; ~ **time** n heure f du dîner.

**diocese** ['daɪəsɪs] n diocèse m.

**dip** [dɪp] n déclivité f ; (in sea) baignade f, bain m // vt tremper, plonger ; (AUT: lights) mettre en code, baisser // vi plonger.

**diphtheria** [dɪf'θɪərɪə] n diphtérie f.

**diphthong** ['dɪfθɔŋ] n diphtongue f.

**diploma** [dɪ'pləumə] n diplôme m.

**diplomacy** [dɪ'pləuməsɪ] n diplomatie f.

**diplomat** ['dɪpləmæt] n diplomate m ; ~**ic** [dɪplə'mætɪk] a diplomatique ; ~**ic corps** n corps m diplomatique.

**dipstick** ['dɪpstɪk] n (AUT) jauge f de niveau d'huile.

**dire** [daɪə*] a terrible, extrême, affreux(euse).

**direct** [daɪ'rɛkt] a direct(e) // vt diriger, orienter ; **can you** ~ **me to ...?** pouvez-vous m'indiquer le chemin de ...? ; ~ **current** n courant continu ; ~ **hit** n coup m au but, touché m.

**direction** [dɪ'rɛkʃən] n direction f ; **sense of** ~ sens m de l'orientation ; ~**s** npl (advice) indications fpl ; ~**s for use** mode m d'emploi.

**directly** [dɪ'rɛktlɪ] ad (in straight line) directement, tout droit ; (at once) tout de suite, immédiatement.

**director** [dɪ'rɛktə*] n directeur m ; administrateur m ; (THEATRE) metteur m en scène ; (CINEMA, TV) réalisateur/trice.

**directory** [dɪ'rɛktərɪ] n annuaire m.

**dirt** [də:t] n saleté f ; crasse f ; ~-**cheap** a (ne) coûtant presque rien ; ~ **road** n (US) chemin non macadamisé or non revêtu ; ~**y** a sale // vt salir ; ~**y story** n histoire cochonne ; ~**y trick** n coup tordu.

**disability** [dɪsə'bɪlɪtɪ] n invalidité f, infirmité f.

**disabled** [dɪs'eɪbld] a infirme, invalide ; (maimed) mutilé(e) ; (through illness, old age) impotent(e).

**disadvantage** [dɪsəd'vɑ:ntɪdʒ] n désavantage m, inconvénient m ; ~**ous** [dɪsædvɑ:n'teɪdʒəs] a désavantageux-(euse).

**disagree** [dɪsə'gri:] vi (differ) ne pas concorder ; (be against, think otherwise): **to** ~ **(with)** ne pas être d'accord (avec) ; **garlic** ~**s with me** l'ail ne me convient pas, je ne supporte pas l'ail ; ~**able** a désagréable ; ~**ment** n désaccord m, différend m.

**disallow** ['dɪsə'lau] vt rejeter, désavouer.

**disappear** [dɪsə'pɪə*] vi disparaître ; ~**ance** n disparition f.

**disappoint** [dɪsə'pɔint] vt décevoir ; ~**ment** n déception f.

**disapproval** [dɪsə'pru:vəl] n désapprobation f.

**disapprove** [dɪsə'pru:v] vi: **to** ~ **of** désapprouver.

**disarm** [dɪs'ɑ:m] vt désarmer ; ~**ament** n désarmement m.

**disarray** [dɪsə'reɪ] n désordre m, confusion f.

**disaster** [dɪ'zɑ:stə*] n catastrophe f, désastre m ; **disastrous** a désastreux-(euse).

**disband** [dɪs'bænd] vt démobiliser ; disperser // vi se séparer ; se disperser.

**disbelief** ['dɪsbə'liːf] n incrédulité f.

**disc** [dɪsk] n disque m.

**discard** [dɪs'kɑːd] vt (old things) se défaire de, mettre au rencart or au rebut ; (fig) écarter, renoncer à.

**disc brake** ['dɪskbreɪk] n frein m à disque.

**discern** [dɪ'səːn] vt discerner, distinguer ; ~ing a judicieux(euse), perspicace.

**discharge** vt [dɪs'tʃɑːdʒ] (duties) s'acquitter de ; (waste etc) déverser ; décharger ; (ELEC, MED) émettre ; (patient) renvoyer (chez lui) ; (employee, soldier) congédier, licencier ; (defendant) relaxer, élargir // n ['dɪstʃɑːdʒ] (ELEC, MED) émission f ; (dismissal) renvoi m ; licenciement m ; élargissement m ; to ~ one's gun faire feu.

**disciple** [dɪ'saɪpl] n disciple m.

**disciplinary** ['dɪsɪplɪnərɪ] a disciplinaire.

**discipline** ['dɪsɪplɪn] n discipline f // vt discipliner ; (punish) punir.

**disc jockey** ['dɪskdʒɔkɪ] n disque-jockey m.

**disclaim** [dɪs'kleɪm] vt désavouer, dénier.

**disclose** [dɪs'kləuz] vt révéler, divulguer ; **disclosure** [-'kləuʒə*] n révélation f, divulgation f.

**disco** ['dɪskəu] n abbr of **discothèque**.

**discoloured** [dɪs'kʌləd] a décoloré(e) ; jauni(e).

**discomfort** [dɪs'kʌmfət] n malaise m, gêne f ; (lack of comfort) manque m de confort.

**disconcert** [dɪskən'səːt] vt déconcerter, décontenancer.

**disconnect** [dɪskə'nɛkt] vt détacher ; (ELEC, RADIO) débrancher ; (gas, water) couper ; ~ed a (speech, thought) décousu(e), peu cohérent(e).

**disconsolate** [dɪs'kɔnsəlɪt] a inconsolable.

**discontent** [dɪskən'tɛnt] n mécontentement m ; ~ed a mécontent(e).

**discontinue** [dɪskən'tɪnjuː] vt cesser, interrompre ; '~d' (COMM) 'fin de série'.

**discord** ['dɪskɔːd] n discorde f, dissension f ; (MUS) dissonance f ; ~ant [dɪs'kɔːdənt] a discordant(e), dissonant(e).

**discothèque** ['dɪskəutɛk] n discothèque f.

**discount** n ['dɪskaunt] remise f, rabais m // vt [dɪs'kaunt] ne pas tenir compte de.

**discourage** [dɪs'kʌrɪdʒ] vt décourager ; **discouraging** a décourageant(e).

**discourteous** [dɪs'kəːtɪəs] a incivil(e), discourtois(e).

**discover** [dɪs'kʌvə*] vt découvrir ; ~y n découverte f.

**discredit** [dɪs'krɛdɪt] vt mettre en doute ; discréditer.

**discreet** [dɪ'skriːt] a discret(ète) ; ~ly ad discrètement.

**discrepancy** [dɪ'skrɛpənsɪ] n divergence f, contradiction f.

**discretion** [dɪ'skrɛʃən] n discrétion f.

**discriminate** [dɪ'skrɪmɪneɪt] vi: to ~ between établir une distinction entre, faire la différence entre ; to ~ against pratiquer une discrimination contre ; **discriminating** a qui a du discernement ;

**discrimination** [-'neɪʃən] n discrimination f ; (judgment) discernement m.

**discus** ['dɪskəs] n disque m.

**discuss** [dɪ'skʌs] vt discuter de ; (debate) discuter ; ~ion [dɪ'skʌʃən] n discussion f.

**disdain** [dɪs'deɪn] n dédain m.

**disease** [dɪ'ziːz] n maladie f.

**disembark** [dɪsɪm'bɑːk] vt,vi débarquer.

**disembodied** [dɪsɪm'bɔdɪd] a désincarné(e).

**disembowel** [dɪsɪm'bauəl] vt éviscérer, étriper.

**disenchanted** [dɪsɪn'tʃɑːntɪd] a désenchanté(e), désabusé(e).

**disengage** [dɪsɪn'geɪdʒ] vt dégager ; (TECH) déclencher ; **to ~ the clutch** (AUT) débrayer ; ~ment n (POL) désengagement m.

**disentangle** [dɪsɪn'tæŋgl] vt démêler.

**disfavour** [dɪs'feɪvə*] n défaveur f ; disgrâce f // vt voir d'un mauvais œil, désapprouver.

**disfigure** [dɪs'fɪgə*] vt défigurer.

**disgorge** [dɪs'gɔːdʒ] vt déverser.

**disgrace** [dɪs'greɪs] n honte f ; (disfavour) disgrâce f // vt déshonorer, couvrir de honte ; ~ful a scandaleux(euse), honteux(euse).

**disgruntled** [dɪs'grʌntld] a mécontent(e).

**disguise** [dɪs'gaɪz] n déguisement m // vt déguiser ; **in ~** déguisé(e).

**disgust** [dɪs'gʌst] n dégoût m, aversion f // vt dégoûter, écœurer ; ~ing a dégoûtant(e) ; révoltant(e).

**dish** [dɪʃ] n plat m ; **to do** or **wash the ~es** faire la vaisselle ; **to ~ up** servir ; (facts, statistics) sortir, débiter ; ~cloth n (for drying) torchon m ; (for washing) lavette f.

**dishearten** [dɪs'hɑːtn] vt décourager.

**dishevelled** [dɪ'ʃɛvəld] a ébouriffé(e) ; décoiffé(e) ; débraillé(e).

**dishonest** [dɪs'ɔnɪst] a malhonnête ; ~y n malhonnêteté f.

**dishonour** [dɪs'ɔnə*] n déshonneur m ; ~able a déshonorant(e).

**dishwasher** ['dɪʃwɔʃə*] n lave-vaisselle m ; (person) plongeur/euse.

**disillusion** [dɪsɪ'luːʒən] vt désabuser, désenchanter // n désenchantement m.

**disinfect** [dɪsɪn'fɛkt] vt désinfecter ; ~ant n désinfectant m.

**disintegrate** [dɪs'ɪntɪgreɪt] vi se désintégrer.

**disinterested** [dɪs'ɪntrəstɪd] a désintéressé(e).

**disjointed** [dɪs'dʒɔɪntɪd] a décousu(e), incohérent(e).

**disk** [dɪsk] n = **disc**.

**dislike** [dɪs'laɪk] n aversion f, antipathie f // vt ne pas aimer.

**dislocate** ['dɪsləkeɪt] vt disloquer ; déboîter ; désorganiser.

**dislodge** [dɪs'lɔdʒ] vt déplacer, faire bouger ; (enemy) déloger.

**disloyal** [dɪs'lɔɪəl] a déloyal(e).

**dismal** ['dɪzml] a lugubre, maussade.

**dismantle** [dɪs'mæntl] vt démonter ; (fort, warship) démanteler.

**dismast** [dɪs'mɑːst] vt démâter.

**dismay** [dɪs'meɪ] *n* consternation *f* // *vt* consterner.

**dismiss** [dɪs'mɪs] *vt* congédier, renvoyer ; (*idea*) écarter ; (*LAW*) rejeter ; ~**al** *n* renvoi *m*.

**dismount** [dɪs'maunt] *vi* mettre pied à terre.

**disobedience** [dɪsə'biːdɪəns] *n* désobéissance *f* ; insoumission *f*.

**disobedient** [dɪsə'biːdɪənt] *a* désobéissant(e) ; (*soldier*) indiscipliné(e).

**disobey** [dɪsə'beɪ] *vt* désobéir à.

**disorder** [dɪs'ɔːdə*] *n* désordre *m* ; (*rioting*) désordres *mpl* ; (*MED*) troubles *mpl* ; ~**ly** *a* en désordre ; désordonné(e).

**disorganize** [dɪs'ɔːgənaɪz] *vt* désorganiser.

**disorientate** [dɪs'ɔːrɪɛnteɪt] *vt* désorienter.

**disown** [dɪs'əun] *vt* renier.

**disparaging** [dɪs'pærɪdʒɪŋ] *a* désobligeant(e).

**disparity** [dɪs'pærɪtɪ] *n* disparité *f*.

**dispassionate** [dɪs'pæʃənət] *a* calme, froid(e) ; impartial(e), objectif(ive).

**dispatch** [dɪs'pætʃ] *vt* expédier, envoyer // *n* envoi *m*, expédition *f* ; (*MIL, PRESS*) dépêche *f*.

**dispel** [dɪs'pɛl] *vt* dissiper, chasser.

**dispensary** [dɪs'pɛnsərɪ] *n* pharmacie *f* ; (*in chemist's*) officine *f*.

**dispense** [dɪs'pɛns] *vt* distribuer, administrer ; **to ~ sb from** dispenser qn de ; **to ~ with** *vt fus* se passer de ; ~**r** *n* (*container*) distributeur *m* ; **dispensing chemist** *n* pharmacie *f*.

**dispersal** [dɪs'pəːsl] *n* dispersion *f* ; (*ADMIN*) déconcentration *f*.

**disperse** [dɪs'pəːs] *vt* disperser ; (*knowledge*) disséminer // *vi* se disperser.

**dispirited** [dɪs'pɪrɪtɪd] *a* découragé(e), déprimé(e).

**displace** [dɪs'pleɪs] *vt* déplacer ; ~**d person** *n* (*POL*) personne déplacée ; ~**ment** *n* déplacement *m*.

**display** [dɪs'pleɪ] *n* étalage *m* ; déploiement *m* ; affichage *m* ; (*screen*) écran *m* de visualisation, visuel *m* ; (*of feeling*) manifestation *f* ; (*pej*) ostentation *f* // *vt* montrer ; (*goods*) mettre à l'étalage, exposer ; (*results, departure times*) afficher ; (*troops*) déployer ; (*pej*) faire étalage de.

**displease** [dɪs'pliːz] *vt* mécontenter contrarier ; ~**d with** mécontent(e) de ; **displeasure** [-'plɛʒə*] *n* mécontentement *m*.

**disposable** [dɪs'pəuzəbl] *a* (*pack etc*) à jeter ; (*income*) disponible.

**disposal** [dɪs'pəuzl] *n* (*availability, arrangement*) disposition *f* ; (*of property*) disposition *f*, cession *f* ; (*of rubbish*) évacuation *f*, destruction *f* ; **at one's ~** à sa disposition.

**dispose** [dɪs'pəuz] *vt* disposer ; **to ~ of** *vt* (*time, money*) disposer de ; (*unwanted goods*) se débarrasser de, se défaire de ; (*problem*) expédier ; ~**d** *a*: ~**d to do** disposé(e) à faire ; **disposition** [-'zɪʃən] *n* disposition *f* ; (*temperament*) naturel *m*.

**disproportionate** [dɪsprə'pɔːʃənət] *a* disproportionné(e).

**disprove** [dɪs'pruːv] *vt* réfuter.

**dispute** [dɪs'pjuːt] *n* discussion *f* ; (*also*: **industrial ~**) conflit *m* // *vt* contester ; (*matter*) discuter ; (*victory*) disputer.

**disqualification** [dɪskwɔlɪfɪ'keɪʃən] *n* disqualification *f* ; ~ **(from driving)** retrait *m* du permis (de conduire).

**disqualify** [dɪs'kwɔlɪfaɪ] *vt* (*SPORT*) disqualifier ; **to ~ sb for sth/from doing** rendre qn inapte à qch/à faire ; signifier à qn l'interdiction de faire ; mettre qn dans l'impossibilité de faire ; **to ~ sb (from driving) for speeding** retirer à qn son permis (de conduire) pour excès de vitesse.

**disquiet** [dɪs'kwaɪət] *n* inquiétude *f*, trouble *m*.

**disregard** [dɪsrɪ'gɑːd] *vt* ne pas tenir compte de.

**disrepair** [dɪsrɪ'pɛə*] *n* mauvais état.

**disreputable** [dɪs'rɛpjutəbl] *a* (*person*) de mauvaise réputation, peu recommandable ; (*behaviour*) déshonorant-(e).

**disrespectful** [dɪsrɪ'spɛktful] *a* irrespectueux(euse).

**disrupt** [dɪs'rʌpt] *vt* (*plans*) déranger ; (*conversation*) interrompre ; ~**ion** [-'rʌpʃən] *n* dérangement *m* ; interruption *f*.

**dissatisfaction** [dɪssætɪs'fækʃən] *n* mécontentement *m*, insatisfaction *f*.

**dissatisfied** [dɪs'sætɪsfaɪd] *a*: ~ **(with)** mécontent(e) *or* insatisfait(e) (de).

**dissect** [dɪ'sɛkt] *vt* disséquer.

**disseminate** [dɪ'sɛmɪneɪt] *vt* disséminer.

**dissent** [dɪ'sɛnt] *n* dissentiment *m*, différence *f* d'opinion.

**disservice** [dɪs'səːvɪs] *n*: **to do sb a ~** rendre un mauvais service à qn ; desservir qn.

**dissident** ['dɪsɪdnt] *a* dissident(e).

**dissimilar** [dɪ'sɪmɪlə*] *a*: ~ **(to)** dissemblable (à), différent(e) (de).

**dissipate** ['dɪsɪpeɪt] *vt* dissiper ; (*energy, efforts*) disperser ; ~**d** *a* dissolu(e) ; débauché(e).

**dissociate** [dɪ'səuʃɪeɪt] *vt* dissocier.

**dissolute** ['dɪsəluːt] *a* débauché(e), dissolu(e).

**dissolve** [dɪ'zɔlv] *vt* dissoudre // *vi* se dissoudre, fondre ; (*fig*) disparaître.

**dissuade** [dɪ'sweɪd] *vt*: **to ~ sb (from)** dissuader qn (de).

**distance** ['dɪstns] *n* distance *f* ; **in the ~** au loin.

**distant** ['dɪstnt] *a* lointain(e), éloigné(e) ; (*manner*) distant(e), froid(e).

**distaste** [dɪs'teɪst] *n* dégoût *m* ; ~**ful** *a* déplaisant(e), désagréable.

**distemper** [dɪs'tɛmpə*] *n* (*paint*) détrempe *f*, badigeon *m*.

**distend** [dɪs'tɛnd] *vt* distendre // *vi* se distendre, se ballonner.

**distil** [dɪs'tɪl] *vt* distiller ; ~**lery** *n* distillerie *f*.

**distinct** [dɪs'tɪŋkt] *a* distinct(e) ; (*preference, progress*) marqué(e) ; ~**ion** [dɪs'tɪŋkʃən] *n* distinction *f* ; (*in exam*) mention *f* très bien ; ~**ive** *a* distinctif(ive) ; ~**ly** *ad* distinctement ; expressément.

**distinguish** [dɪs'tɪŋgwɪʃ] vt distinguer; différencier; **~ed** a (eminent) distingué(e); **~ing** a (feature) distinctif(ive), caractéristique.

**distort** [dɪs'tɔ:t] vt déformer; **~ion** [dɪs'tɔ:ʃən] n déformation f.

**distract** [dɪs'trækt] vt distraire, déranger; **~ed** a éperdu(e), égaré(e); **~ion** [dɪs'trækʃən] n distraction f; égarement m; **to drive sb to ~ion** rendre qn fou(folle).

**distraught** [dɪs'trɔ:t] a éperdu(e).

**distress** [dɪs'trɛs] n détresse f; (pain) douleur f // vt affliger; **~ed area** n zone sinistrée; **~ing** a douloureux(euse), pénible; **~ signal** n signal m de détresse.

**distribute** [dɪs'trɪbju:t] vt distribuer; **distribution** [-'bju:ʃən] n distribution f; **distributor** n distributeur m.

**district** ['dɪstrɪkt] n (of country) région f; (of town) quartier m; (ADMIN) district m; **~ attorney** n (US) ≈ procureur m de la République; **~ nurse** n (Brit) infirmière visiteuse.

**distrust** [dɪs'trʌst] n méfiance f, doute m // vt se méfier de.

**disturb** [dɪs'tə:b] vt troubler; (inconvenience) déranger; **~ance** n dérangement m; (political etc) troubles mpl; (by drunks etc) tapage m; **~ing** a troublant(e), inquiétant(e).

**disuse** [dɪs'ju:s] n: **to fall into ~** tomber en désuétude f.

**disused** [dɪs'ju:zd] a désaffecté(e).

**ditch** [dɪtʃ] n fossé m // vt (col) abandonner.

**dither** ['dɪðə*] vi hésiter.

**ditto** ['dɪtəu] ad idem.

**divan** [dɪ'væn] n divan m.

**dive** [daɪv] n plongeon m; (of submarine) plongée f; (AVIAT) piqué m; (pej) bouge m // vi plonger; **~r** n plongeur m.

**diverge** [daɪ'və:dʒ] vi diverger.

**diverse** [daɪ'və:s] a divers(e).

**diversify** [daɪ'və:sɪfaɪ] vt diversifier.

**diversion** [daɪ'və:ʃən] n (AUT) déviation f; (distraction, MIL) diversion f.

**diversity** [daɪ'və:sɪtɪ] n diversité f, variété f.

**divert** [daɪ'və:t] vt (traffic) dévier; (river) détourner; (amuse) divertir.

**divest** [daɪ'vɛst] vt: **to ~ sb of** dépouiller qn de.

**divide** [dɪ'vaɪd] vt diviser; (separate) séparer // vi se diviser; **~d skirt** n jupe-culotte f.

**dividend** ['dɪvɪdɛnd] n dividende m.

**divine** [dɪ'vaɪn] a divin(e).

**diving** ['daɪvɪŋ] n plongée (sous-marine); **~ board** n plongeoir m; **~ suit** n scaphandre m.

**divinity** [dɪ'vɪnɪtɪ] n divinité f; théologie f.

**division** [dɪ'vɪʒən] n division f; séparation f; (Brit POL) vote m.

**divorce** [dɪ'vɔ:s] n divorce m // vt divorcer d'avec; **~d** a divorcé(e); **~e** [-'si:] n divorcé/e.

**divulge** [daɪ'vʌldʒ] vt divulguer, révéler.

**D.I.Y.** a,n abbr of **do-it-yourself**.

**dizziness** ['dɪzɪnɪs] n vertige m, étourdissement m.

**dizzy** ['dɪzɪ] a (height) vertigineux(euse); **to make sb ~** donner le vertige à qn; **to feel ~** avoir la tête qui tourne.

**DJ** n abbr of **disc jockey**.

**do**, pt **did**, pp **done** [du:, dɪd, dʌn] vt, vi faire; **he didn't laugh** il n'a pas ri; **~ you want any?** en voulez-vous?, est-ce que vous en voulez?; **she swims better than I ~** elle nage mieux que moi; **he laughed, didn't he?** il a ri, n'est-ce pas?; **~ they?** ah oui?, vraiment?; **who broke it? - I did** qui l'a cassé? - (c'est) moi; **~ you agree? - I ~** êtes-vous d'accord? - oui; **to ~ one's nails/teeth** se faire les ongles/brosser les dents; **will it ~?** est-ce que ça ira?; **to ~ without sth** se passer de qch; **what did he ~ with the cat?** qu'a-t-il fait du chat?; **to ~ away with** vt fus supprimer, abolir; **to ~ up** vt remettre à neuf.

**docile** ['dəusaɪl] a docile.

**dock** [dɔk] n dock m; (LAW) banc m des accusés // vi se mettre à quai; **~er** n docker m.

**docket** ['dɔkɪt] n bordereau m.

**dockyard** ['dɔkjɑ:d] n chantier m de construction navale.

**doctor** ['dɔktə*] n médecin m, docteur m; (Ph.D. etc) docteur // vt (cat) couper; (fig) falsifier.

**doctrine** ['dɔktrɪn] n doctrine f.

**document** ['dɔkjumənt] n document m; **~ary** [-'mɛntərɪ] a, n documentaire (m); **~ation** [-'teɪʃən] n documentation f.

**doddering** ['dɔdərɪŋ] a (senile) gâteux(euse).

**dodge** [dɔdʒ] n truc m; combine f // vt esquiver, éviter.

**dodgems** ['dɔdʒəmz] npl autos tamponneuses.

**dog** [dɔg] n chien/ne; **~ biscuits** npl biscuits mpl pour chien; **~ collar** n collier m de chien; (fig) faux-col m d'ecclésiastique; **~-eared** a corné(e).

**dogged** ['dɔgɪd] a obstiné(e), opiniâtre.

**dogma** ['dɔgmə] n dogme m; **~tic** [-'mætɪk] a dogmatique.

**doings** ['duɪŋz] npl activités fpl.

**do-it-yourself** [du:ɪtjɔ:'sɛlf] n bricolage m.

**doldrums** ['dɔldrəmz] npl: **to be in the ~** avoir le cafard; être dans le marasme.

**dole** [dəul] n (Brit) allocation f de chômage; **on the ~** au chômage; **to ~ out** vt donner au compte-goutte.

**doleful** ['dəulful] a triste, lugubre.

**doll** [dɔl] n poupée f; **to ~ o.s. up** se faire beau(belle).

**dollar** ['dɔlə*] n dollar m.

**dolphin** ['dɔlfɪn] n dauphin m.

**domain** [də'meɪn] n domaine m.

**dome** [dəum] n dôme m.

**domestic** [də'mɛstɪk] a (duty, happiness) familial(e); (policy, affairs, flights) intérieur(e); (animal) domestique; **~ated** a domestiqué(e); (pej) domestique.

**domicile** ['dɔmɪsaɪl] n domicile m.

**dominant** ['dɔmɪnənt] a dominant(e).

**dominate** ['dɔmɪneɪt] vt dominer; **domination** [-'neɪʃən] n domination f;

**domineering** [-'nɪərɪŋ] *a* dominateur(trice), autoritaire.

**dominion** [də'mɪnɪən] *n* domination *f*; territoire *m*; dominion *m*.

**domino,** ~**es** ['dɔmɪnəu] *n* domino *m*; ~**es** *n* (*game*) dominos *mpl*.

**don** [dɔn] *n* professeur *m* d'université // *vt* revêtir.

**donate** [də'neɪt] *vt* faire don de, donner; **donation** [də'neɪʃən] *n* donation *f*, don *m*.

**done** [dʌn] *pp of* **do**.

**donkey** ['dɔŋkɪ] *n* âne *m*.

**donor** ['dəunə*] *n* (*of blood etc*) donneur/euse; (*to charity*) donateur/trice.

**don't** [dəunt] *vb* = **do not**.

**doom** [du:m] *n* destin *m*; ruine *f* // *vt*: **to be** ~**ed** (**to failure**) être voué(e) à l'échec; ~**sday** *n* le Jugement dernier.

**door** [dɔ:*] *n* porte *f*; ~**bell** *n* sonnette *f*; ~ **handle** *n* poignée *f* de porte; ~**man** *n* (*in hotel*) portier *m*; (*in block of flats*) concierge *m*; ~**mat** *n* paillasson *m*; ~**post** *n* montant *m* de porte; ~**step** *n* pas *m* de (la) porte, seuil *m*.

**dope** [dəup] *n* (*col*) drogue *f* // *vt* (*horse etc*) doper.

**dopey** ['dəupɪ] *a* (*col*) à moitié endormi(e).

**dormant** ['dɔ:mənt] *a* assoupi(e), en veilleuse; (*rule, law*) inappliqué(e).

**dormice** ['dɔ:maɪs] *npl of* **dormouse**.

**dormitory** ['dɔ:mɪtrɪ] *n* dortoir *m*.

**dormouse,** *pl* **dormice** ['dɔ:maus, -maɪs] *n* loir *m*.

**dosage** ['dəusɪdʒ] *n* dose *f*; dosage *m*; (*on label*) posologie *f*.

**dose** [dəus] *n* dose *f*; (*bout*) attaque *f* // *vt*: **to** ~ **o.s.** se bourrer de médicaments.

**doss house** ['dɔshaus] *n* asile *m* de nuit.

**dot** [dɔt] *n* point *m* // *vt*: ~**ted with** parsemé(e) de; **on the** ~ à l'heure tapante.

**dote** [dəut]: **to** ~ **on** *vt fus* être fou(folle) de.

**dotted line** [dɔtɪd'laɪn] *n* ligne pointillée; (AUT) ligne discontinue.

**double** ['dʌbl] *a* double // *ad* (*fold*) en deux; (*twice*): **to cost** ~ (**sth**) coûter le double (de qch) *or* deux fois plus (que qch) // *n* double *m*; (CINEMA) doublure *f* // *vt* doubler; (*fold*) plier en deux // *vi* doubler; **at the** ~ au pas de course; ~**s** *n* (TENNIS) double *m*; ~ **bass** *n* contrebasse *f*; ~ **bed** *n* grand lit; ~ **bend** *n* virage *m* en S; ~**breasted** *a* croisé(e); ~**cross** *vt* doubler, trahir; ~**decker** *n* autobus *m* à impériale; ~ **declutch** *vi* faire un double débrayage; ~ **exposure** *n* surimpression *f*; ~ **parking** *n* stationnement *m* en double file; ~ **room** *n* chambre *f* pour deux; **doubly** *ad* doublement, deux fois plus.

**doubt** [daut] *n* doute *m* // *vt* douter de; **to** ~ **that** douter que; ~**ful** *a* douteux(euse); (*person*) incertain(e); ~**less** *ad* sans doute, sûrement.

**dough** [dəu] *n* pâte *f*; ~**nut** *n* beignet *m*.

**dour** [duə*] *a* austère.

**dove** [dʌv] *n* colombe *f*.

**Dover** ['dəuvə*] *n* Douvres.

**dovetail** ['dʌvteɪl] *n*: ~ **joint** *n* assemblage *m* à queue d'aronde // *vi* (*fig*) concorder.

**dowdy** ['daudɪ] *a* démodé(e); mal fagoté(e).

**down** [daun] *n* (*fluff*) duvet *m* // *ad* en bas // *prep* en bas de // *vt* (*enemy*) abattre; (*col: drink*) vider; **the D**~**s** collines crayeuses du S.-E. de l'Angleterre; ~ **with X!** à bas X!; ~**at-heel** *a* éculé(e); (*fig*) miteux(euse); ~**cast** *a* démoralisé(e); ~**fall** *n* chute *f*; ruine *f*; ~**hearted** *a* découragé(e); ~**hill** *ad*: **to go** ~**hill** descendre; ~ **payment** *n* acompte *m*; ~**pour** *n* pluie torrentielle, déluge *m*; ~**right** *a* franc(franche); (*refusal*) catégorique; ~**stairs** *ad* au rez-de-chaussée; à l'étage inférieur; ~**stream** *ad* en aval; ~**to-earth** *a* terre à terre *inv*; ~**town** *ad* en ville // *a* (US): ~**town Chicago** le centre commerçant de Chicago; ~**ward** ['daunwəd] *a,ad*, ~**wards** ['daunwədz] *ad* vers le bas.

**dowry** ['daurɪ] *n* dot *f*.

**doz.** *abbr of* **dozen**.

**doze** [dəuz] *vi* sommeiller; **to** ~ **off** *vi* s'assoupir.

**dozen** ['dʌzn] *n* douzaine *f*; **a** ~ **books** une douzaine de livres.

**Dr.** *abbr of* **doctor**; **drive** (*n*).

**drab** [dræb] *a* terne, morne.

**draft** [drɑ:ft] *n* brouillon *m*; (COMM) traite *f*; (US: MIL) contingent *m*; (: *call-up*) conscription *f* // *vt* faire le brouillon de; *see also* **draught**.

**drag** [dræg] *vt* traîner; (*river*) draguer // *vi* traîner // *n* (*col*) raseur/euse; corvée *f*; **to** ~ **on** *vi* s'éterniser.

**dragonfly** ['drægənflaɪ] *n* libellule *f*.

**drain** [dreɪn] *n* égout *m*; (*on resources*) saignée *f* // *vt* (*land, marshes*) assécher; (*vegetables*) égoutter; (*reservoir etc*) vider // *vi* (*water*) s'écouler; ~**age** *n* système *m* d'égouts; ~**ing board,** ~**board** (US) *n* égouttoir *m*; ~**pipe** *n* tuyau *m* d'écoulement.

**dram** [dræm] *n* petit verre.

**drama** ['drɑ:mə] *n* (*art*) théâtre *m*, art *m* dramatique; (*play*) pièce *f*; (*event*) drame *m*, ~**tic** [drə'mætɪk] *a* dramatique; spectaculaire; ~**tist** ['dræmətɪst] *n* auteur *m* dramatique.

**drank** [dræŋk] *pt of* **drink**.

**drape** [dreɪp] *vt* draper; ~**s** *npl* (US) rideaux *mpl*; ~**r** *n* marchand/e de nouveautés.

**drastic** ['dræstɪk] *a* sévère; énergique.

**draught** [drɑ:ft] *n* courant *m* d'air; (*of chimney*) tirage *m*; (NAUT) tirant *m* d'eau; ~**s** *n* (*jeu m de*) dames *fpl*; **on** ~ (*beer*) à la pression; ~**board** *n* damier *m*.

**draughtsman** ['drɑ:ftsmən] *n* dessinateur/trice (industriel/le).

**draw** [drɔ:] *vb* (*pt* **drew**, *pp* **drawn** [dru:, drɔ:n]) *vt* tirer; (*attract*) attirer; (*picture*) dessiner; (*line, circle*) tracer; (*money*) retirer // *vi* (SPORT) faire match nul // *n* match nul; tirage *m* au sort; loterie *f*; **to** ~ **to a close** toucher à *or* tirer à sa fin; **to** ~ **near** *vi* s'approcher; approcher; **to** ~ **out** *vi* (*lengthen*) s'allonger // *vt* (*money*) retirer; **to** ~ **up** *vi* (*stop*) s'arrêter // *vt* (*document*) établir, dresser; ~**back** *n* inconvénient *m*, désavantage *m*; ~**bridge** *n* pont-levis *m*.

**drawer** [drɔ:*] *n* tiroir *m*.

**drawing** ['drɔ:ɪŋ] *n* dessin *m* ; ~ **board** *n* planche *f* à dessin ; ~ **pin** *n* punaise *f* ; ~ **room** *n* salon *m*.

**drawl** [drɔ:l] *n* accent traînant.

**drawn** [drɔ:n] *pp of* **draw.**

**dread** [drɛd] *n* épouvante *f*, effroi *m* // *vt* redouter, appréhender ; ~**ful** *a* épouvantable, affreux(euse).

**dream** [dri:m] *n* rêve *m* // *vt, vi* (*pt, pp* **dreamed** *or* **dreamt** [drɛmt]) rêver ; ~**er** *n* rêveur/euse ; ~ **world** *n* monde *m* imaginaire ; ~**y** *a* rêveur(euse).

**dreary** ['drɪərɪ] *a* triste ; monotone.

**dredge** [drɛdʒ] *vt* draguer ; ~**r** *n* (*ship*) dragueur *m* ; (*machine*) drague *f* ; (*also:* **sugar** ~**r**) saupoudreuse *f*.

**dregs** [drɛgz] *npl* lie *f*.

**drench** [drɛntʃ] *vt* tremper.

**dress** [drɛs] *n* robe *f* ; (*clothing*) habillement *m*, tenue *f* // *vt* habiller ; (*wound*) panser ; (*food*) préparer ; **to ~ up** *vi* s'habiller ; (*in fancy dress*) se déguiser ; ~ **circle** *n* premier balcon ; ~ **designer** *n* modéliste *m/f* ; ~**er** *n* (*THEATRE*) habilleur/euse ; (*also:* **window** ~**er**) étalagiste *m/f* ; (*furniture*) buffet *m* ; ~**ing** *n* (*MED*) pansement *m* ; (*CULIN*) sauce *f*, assaisonnement *m* ; ~**ing gown** *n* robe *f* de chambre ; ~**ing room** *n* (*THEATRE*) loge *f* ; (*SPORT*) vestiaire *m* ; ~**ing table** *n* coiffeuse *f* ; ~**maker** *n* couturière *f* ; ~**making** *n* couture *f* ; travaux *mpl* de couture ; ~ **rehearsal** *n* (répétition) générale ; ~ **shirt** *n* chemise *f* à plastron.

**drew** [dru:] *pt of* **draw.**

**dribble** ['drɪbl] *vi* tomber goutte à goutte ; (*baby*) baver ; (*ball*) dribbler.

**dried** [draɪd] *a* (*fruit, beans*) sec(sèche) ; (*eggs, milk*) en poudre.

**drift** [drɪft] *n* (*of current etc*) force *f* ; direction *f* ; (*of sand etc*) amoncellement *m* ; (*of snow*) rafale *f* ; coulée *f* ; (: *on ground*) congère *f* ; (*general meaning*) sens général // *vi* (*boat*) aller à la dérive, dériver ; (*sand, snow*) s'amonceler, s'entasser ; ~**wood** *n* bois flotté.

**drill** [drɪl] *n* perceuse *f* ; (*bit*) foret *m* ; (*of dentist*) roulette *f*, fraise *f* ; (*MIL*) exercice *m* // *vt* percer // *vi* (*for oil*) faire un *or* des forage(s).

**drink** [drɪŋk] *n* boisson *f* // *vt, vi* (*pt* **drank,** *pp* **drunk** [dræŋk, drʌŋk]) boire ; **to have a ~** boire quelque chose, boire un verre ; prendre l'apéritif ; ~**er** *n* buveur/euse ; ~**ing water** *n* eau *f* potable.

**drip** [drɪp] *n* bruit *m* d'égouttement ; goutte *f* ; (*MED*) goutte-à-goutte *m inv* ; perfusion *f* // *vi* tomber goutte à goutte ; (*washing*) s'égoutter ; (*wall*) suinter ; ~**-dry** *a* (*shirt*) sans repassage ; ~**-feed** *vt* alimenter au goutte-à-goutte *or* par perfusion ; ~**ping** *n* graisse *f* de rôti ; ~**ping wet** *a* trempé(e).

**drive** [draɪv] *n* promenade *f or* trajet *m* en voiture ; (*also:* ~**way**) allée *f* ; (*energy*) dynamisme *m*, énergie *f* ; (*PSYCH*) besoin *m* ; pulsion *f* ; (*push*) effort (concerté) ; campagne *f* ; (*SPORT*) drive *m* ; (*TECH*) entraînement *m* ; traction *f* ; transmission *f* // *vb* (*pt* **drove,** *pp* **driven** [drəuv, 'drɪvn]) *vt* conduire ; (*nail*) enfoncer ; (*push*) chasser, pousser ; (*TECH: motor*) actionner ; entraîner // *vi* (*AUT: at controls*) conduire ; (: *travel*) aller en voiture ; **left-/right-hand** ~ conduite *f* à gauche/droite.

**driver** ['draɪvə*] *n* conducteur/trice ; (*of taxi, bus*) chauffeur *m* ; ~**'s license** *n* (*US*) permis *m* de conduire.

**driving** ['draɪvɪŋ] *a*: ~ **rain** *n* pluie battante // *n* conduite *f* ; ~ **belt** *n* courroie *f* de transmission ; ~ **instructor** *n* moniteur *m* d'auto-école ; ~ **lesson** *n* leçon *f* de conduite ; ~ **licence** *n* (*Brit*) permis *m* de conduire ; ~ **school** *n* auto-école *f* ; ~ **test** *n* examen *m* du permis de conduire.

**drizzle** ['drɪzl] *n* bruine *f*, crachin *m* // *vi* bruiner.

**droll** [drəul] *a* drôle.

**dromedary** ['drɔmədərɪ] *n* dromadaire *m*.

**drone** [drəun] *n* bourdonnement *m* ; (*male bee*) faux-bourdon *m*.

**drool** [dru:l] *vi* baver.

**droop** [dru:p] *vi* s'affaisser ; tomber.

**drop** [drɔp] *n* goutte *f* ; (*fall*) baisse *f* ; (*also:* **parachute** ~) saut *m* ; (*of cliff*) dénivellation *f* ; à-pic *m* // *vt* laisser tomber ; (*voice, eyes, price*) baisser ; (*set down from car*) déposer // *vi* tomber ; **to ~ off** *vi* (*sleep*) s'assoupir ; **to ~ out** *vi* (*withdraw*) se retirer ; (*student etc*) abandonner, décrocher ; ~**pings** *npl* crottes *fpl*.

**dross** [drɔs] *n* déchets *mpl* ; rebut *m*.

**drought** [draut] *n* sécheresse *f*.

**drove** [drəuv] *pt of* **drive** // *n*: ~**s of people** une foule de gens.

**drown** [draun] *vt* noyer // *vi* se noyer.

**drowsy** ['drauzɪ] *a* somnolent(e).

**drudge** [drʌdʒ] *n* bête *f* de somme (*fig*) ; ~**ry** ['drʌdʒərɪ] *n* corvée *f*.

**drug** [drʌg] *n* médicament *m* ; (*narcotic*) drogue *f* // *vt* droguer ; ~ **addict** *n* toxicomane *m/f* ; ~**gist** *n* (*US*) pharmacien/ne-droguiste ; ~**store** *n* (*US*) pharmacie-droguerie *f*, drugstore *m*.

**drum** [drʌm] *n* tambour *m* ; (*for oil, petrol*) bidon *m* ; ~**mer** *n* (joueur *m* de tambour *m* ; ~ **roll** *n* roulement *m* de tambour ; ~**stick** *n* (*MUS*) baguette *f* de tambour ; (*of chicken*) pilon *m*.

**drunk** [drʌŋk] *pp of* **drink** // *a* ivre, soûl(e) // *n* soûlard/e ; homme/femme soûl(e) ; ~**ard** ['drʌŋkəd] *n* ivrogne *m/f* ; ~**en** *a* ivre, soûl(e) ; ivrogne, d'ivrogne ; ~**enness** *n* ivresse *f* ; ivrognerie *f*.

**dry** [draɪ] *a* sec(sèche) ; (*day*) sans pluie // *vt* sécher ; (*clothes*) faire sécher // *vi* sécher ; **to ~ up** *vi* se tarir ; ~**-cleaner** *n* teinturier *m* ; ~**-cleaner's** *n* teinturerie *f* ; ~**-cleaning** *n* nettoyage *m* à sec ; ~**er** *n* séchoir *m* ; ~**ness** *n* sécheresse *f* ; ~ **rot** *n* pourriture sèche (*du bois*).

**dual** ['djuəl] *a* double ; ~ **carriageway** *n* route *f* à quatre voies ; ~**-control** *a* à doubles commandes ; ~ **nationality** *n* double nationalité *f* ; ~**-purpose** *a* à double emploi.

**dubbed** [dʌbd] *a* (*CINEMA*) doublé(e) ; (*nicknamed*) surnommé(e).

**dubious** ['dju:bɪəs] *a* hésitant(e), incertain(e) ; (*reputation, company*) douteux(euse).

**duchess** ['dʌtʃɪs] *n* duchesse *f*.
**duck** [dʌk] *n* canard *m* // *vi* se baisser vivement, baisser subitement la tête ; **~ling** *n* caneton *m*.
**duct** [dʌkt] *n* conduite *f*, canalisation *f*; (ANAT) conduit *m*.
**dud** [dʌd] *n* (*shell*) obus non éclaté ; (*object*, *tool*): **it's a ~** c'est de la camelote, ça ne marche pas // *a* (*cheque*) sans provision ; (*note*, *coin*) faux(fausse).
**due** [dju:] *a* dû(due); (*expected*) attendu(e); (*fitting*) qui convient // *n* dû *m* // *ad*: **~ north** droit vers le nord ; **~s** *npl* (*for club*, *union*) cotisation *f*; (*in harbour*) droits *mpl* (de port); **in ~ course** en temps utile *or* voulu ; finalement ; **~ to** dû(due) à ; causé(e) par.
**duel** ['djuəl] *n* duel *m*.
**duet** [dju:'ɛt] *n* duo *m*.
**dug** [dʌg] *pt*, *pp of* **dig**.
**duke** [dju:k] *n* duc *m*.
**dull** [dʌl] *a* ennuyeux(euse); terne ; (*sound*, *pain*) sourd(e); (*weather*, *day*) gris(e), maussade ; (*blade*) émoussé(e) // *vt* (*pain*, *grief*) atténuer ; (*mind*, *senses*) engourdir.
**duly** ['dju:lɪ] *ad* (*on time*) en temps voulu ; (*as expected*) comme il se doit.
**dumb** [dʌm] *a* muet(te); (*stupid*) bête ; **dumbfounded** [dʌm'faundɪd] *a* sidéré(e).
**dummy** ['dʌmɪ] *n* (*tailor's model*) mannequin *m* ; (SPORT) feinte *f*; (*for baby*) tétine *f* // *a* faux(fausse), factice.
**dump** [dʌmp] *n* tas *m* d'ordures ; (*place*) décharge (publique); (MIL) dépôt *m* // *vt* (*put down*) déposer ; déverser ; (*get rid of*) se débarrasser de ; **~ing** *n* (ECON) dumping *m* ; (*of rubbish*): **'no ~ing'** 'décharge interdite'.
**dumpling** ['dʌmplɪŋ] *n* boulette *f* (de pâte).
**dunce** [dʌns] *n* âne *m*, cancre *m*.
**dune** [dju:n] *n* dune *f*.
**dung** [dʌŋ] *n* fumier *m*.
**dungarees** [dʌŋgə'ri:z] *npl* bleu(s) *m*(*pl*) ; salopette *f*.
**dungeon** ['dʌndʒən] *n* cachot *m*.
**Dunkirk** [dʌn'kɔːk] *n* Dunkerque.
**dupe** [dju:p] *n* dupe *f* // *vt* duper, tromper.
**duplicate** *n* ['dju:plɪkət] double *m*, copie exacte // *vt* ['dju:plɪkeɪt] faire un double de ; (*on machine*) polycopier ; **in ~** en deux exemplaires, en double ; **duplicator** *n* duplicateur *m*.
**durable** ['djuərəbl] *a* durable ; (*clothes*, *metal*) résistant(e), solide.
**duration** [djuə'reɪʃən] *n* durée *f*.
**duress** [djuə'rɛs] *n*: **under ~** sous la contrainte.
**during** ['djuərɪŋ] *prep* pendant, au cours de.
**dusk** [dʌsk] *n* crépuscule *m* ; **~y** *a* sombre.
**dust** [dʌst] *n* poussière *f* // *vt* (*furniture*) essuyer, épousseter ; (*cake etc*): **to ~ with** saupoudrer de ; **~bin** *n* (Brit) poubelle *f*; **~er** *n* chiffon *m* ; **~ jacket** *n* jaquette *f*; **~man** *n* (Brit) boueux *m*, éboueur *m* ; **~y** *a* poussiéreux(euse).
**Dutch** [dʌtʃ] *a* hollandais(e), néerlandais(e) // *n* (LING) hollandais *m*; **the ~** les Hollandais ; **~man/woman** *n* Hollandais/e.

**dutiable** ['dju:tɪəbl] *a* taxable ; soumis(e) à des droits de douane.
**duty** ['dju:tɪ] *n* devoir *m*; (*tax*) droit *m*, taxe *f*; **duties** *npl* fonctions *fpl*; **on ~** de service ; (*at night etc*) de garde ; **off ~** libre, pas de service *or* de garde ; **~-free** *a* exempté(e) de douane, hors-taxe.
**dwarf** [dwɔːf] *n* nain/e // *vt* écraser.
**dwell**, *pt*, *pp* **dwelt** [dwɛl, dwɛlt] *vi* demeurer ; **to ~ on** *vt fus* s'étendre sur ; **~ing** *n* habitation *f*, demeure *f*.
**dwindle** ['dwɪndl] *vi* diminuer, décroître.
**dye** [daɪ] *n* teinture *f* // *vt* teindre ; **~stuffs** *npl* colorants *mpl*.
**dying** ['daɪɪŋ] *a* mourant(e), agonisant(e).
**dyke** [daɪk] *n* digue *f*.
**dynamic** [daɪ'næmɪk] *a* dynamique ; **~s** *n or npl* dynamique *f*.
**dynamite** ['daɪnəmaɪt] *n* dynamite *f*.
**dynamo** ['daɪnəməu] *n* dynamo *f*.
**dynasty** ['dɪnəstɪ] *n* dynastie *f*.
**dysentery** ['dɪsntrɪ] *n* dysenterie *f*.

## E

**E** [iː] *n* (MUS) mi *m*.
**each** [iːtʃ] *det* chaque // *pronoun* chacun(e); **~ one** chacun(e); **~ other** se (*or* nous *etc*); **they hate ~ other** ils se détestent (mutuellement); **you are jealous of ~ other** vous êtes jaloux l'un de l'autre.
**eager** ['iːgə*] *a* impatient(e); avide ; ardent(e), passionné(e); **to be ~ to do sth** être impatient de faire qch, brûler de faire qch ; désirer vivement faire qch ; **to be ~ for** désirer vivement, être avide de.
**eagle** ['iːgl] *n* aigle *m*.
**ear** [ɪə*] *n* oreille *f*; (*of corn*) épi *m* ; **~ache** *n* douleurs *fpl* aux oreilles ; **~drum** *n* tympan *m* ; **~ nose and throat specialist** *n* oto-rhino-laryngologiste *m/f*.
**earl** [əːl] *n* comte *m*.
**earlier** ['əːljə] *a* (*date etc*) plus rapproché(e); (*edition etc*) plus ancien(ne), antérieur(e) // *ad* plus tôt.
**early** ['əːlɪ] *ad* tôt, de bonne heure ; (*ahead of time*) en avance // *a* précoce ; anticipé(e); qui se manifeste (*or* se fait) tôt *or* de bonne heure ; **have an ~ night/start** couchez-vous/partez tôt *or* de bonne heure ; **take the ~ train/plane** prenez le premier train/vol ; **in the ~** *or* **~ in the spring/19th century** au début *or* commencement du printemps/ 19ème siècle ; **~ retirement** *n* retraite anticipée.
**earmark** ['ɪəmɑːk] *vt*: **to ~ sth for** réserver *or* destiner qch à.
**earn** [əːn] *vt* gagner ; (COMM: *yield*) rapporter ; **this ~ed him much praise, he ~ed much praise for this** ceci lui a valu de nombreux éloges ; **he's ~ed his rest/reward** il mérite *or* a bien mérité *or* a bien gagné son repos/sa récompense.
**earnest** ['əːnɪst] *a* sérieux(euse); **in ~** *ad* sérieusement, pour de bon.
**earnings** ['əːnɪŋz] *npl* salaire *m*; gains *mpl*.
**earphones** ['ɪəfəunz] *npl* écouteurs *mpl*.
**earring** ['ɪərɪŋ] *n* boucle *f* d'oreille.
**earshot** ['ɪəʃɔt] *n*: **out of/within ~** hors de portée/à portée de la voix.

**earth** [ə:θ] n (gen, also ELEC) terre f; (of fox etc) terrier m / i vt (ELEC) relier à la terre; ~**enware** n poterie f; faïence f // a de or en faïence; ~**quake** n tremblement m de terre, séisme m; ~ **tremor** n secousse f sismique; ~**works** npl travaux mpl de terrassement; ~**y** a (fig) terre à terre inv; truculent(e).

**earwax** ['ɪəwæks] n cérumen m.

**earwig** ['ɪəwɪg] n perce-oreille m.

**ease** [i:z] n facilité f, aisance f // vt (soothe) calmer; (loosen) relâcher, détendre; (help pass): **to** ~ **sth in/out** faire pénétrer/sortir qch délicatement or avec douceur; faciliter la pénétration/la sortie de qch; **life of** ~ vie oisive; **at** ~ à l'aise; (MIL) au repos; **to** ~ **off** or **up** vi diminuer; ralentir; se détendre.

**easel** ['i:zl] n chevalet m.

**easily** ['i:zɪlɪ] ad facilement.

**east** [i:st] n est m // a d'est // ad à l'est, vers l'est; **the E**~ l'Orient m.

**Easter** ['i:stə*] n Pâques fpl.

**easterly** ['i:stəlɪ] a d'est.

**eastern** ['i:stən] a de l'est, oriental(e).

**East Germany** [i:st'dʒə:mənɪ] n Allemagne f de l'Est.

**eastward(s)** ['i:stwəd(z)] ad vers l'est, à l'est.

**easy** ['i:zɪ] a facile; (manner) aisé(e) // ad: **to take it** or **things** ~ ne pas se fatiguer; ne pas (trop) s'en faire; ~ **chair** n fauteuil m; ~ **going** a accommodant(e), facile à vivre.

**eat**, pt **ate**, pp **eaten** [i:t, eɪt, 'i:tn] vt manger; **to** ~ **into**, **to** ~ **away at** vt fus ronger, attaquer; ~**able** a mangeable; (safe to eat) comestible.

**eaves** [i:vz] npl avant-toit m.

**eavesdrop** ['i:vzdrɔp] vi: **to** ~ (**on a conversation**) écouter (une conversation) de façon indiscrète.

**ebb** [ɛb] n reflux m // vi refluer; (fig: also: ~ **away**) décliner.

**ebony** ['ɛbənɪ] n ébène f.

**ebullient** [ɪ'bʌlɪənt] a exubérant(e).

**eccentric** [ɪk'sɛntrɪk] a,n excentrique (m/f).

**ecclesiastic** [ɪkli:zɪ'æstɪk] n ecclésiastique m; ~**al** a ecclésiastique.

**echo**, ~**es** ['ɛkəu] n écho m // vt répéter; faire chorus avec // vi résonner; faire écho.

**eclipse** [ɪ'klɪps] n éclipse f // vt éclipser.

**ecology** [ɪ'kɔlədʒɪ] n écologie f.

**economic** [i:kə'nɔmɪk] a économique; (business etc) rentable; ~**al** a économique; (person) économe; ~**s** n économie f politique.

**economist** [ɪ'kɔnəmɪst] n économiste m/f.

**economize** [ɪ'kɔnəmaɪz] vi économiser, faire des économies.

**economy** [ɪ'kɔnəmɪ] n économie f.

**ecstasy** ['ɛkstəsɪ] n extase f; **to go into ecstasies over** s'extasier sur; **ecstatic** [-'tætɪk] a extatique, en extase.

**ecumenical** [i:kju'mɛnɪkl] a œcuménique.

**eczema** ['ɛksɪmə] n eczéma m.

**eddy** ['ɛdɪ] n tourbillon m.

**edge** [ɛdʒ] n bord m; (of knife etc) tranchant m, fil m // vt border; **on** ~ (fig)

= **edgy**; **to have the** ~ **on** l'emporter (de justesse) sur, être légèrement meilleur que; **to** ~ **away from** s'éloigner furtivement de; ~**ways** ad latéralement; **he couldn't get a word in** ~**ways** il ne pouvait pas placer un mot; **edging** n bordure f.

**edgy** ['ɛdʒɪ] a crispé(e), tendu(e).

**edible** ['ɛdɪbl] a comestible; (meal) mangeable.

**edict** ['i:dɪkt] n décret m.

**edifice** ['ɛdɪfɪs] n édifice m.

**edit** ['ɛdɪt] vt éditer; ~**ion** [ɪ'dɪʃən] n édition f; ~**or** n (in newspaper) rédacteur/trice; rédacteur/trice en chef; (of sb's work) éditeur/trice; ~**orial** [-'tɔ:rɪəl] a de la rédaction, éditorial(e) // n éditorial m.

**educate** ['ɛdjukeɪt] vt instruire; éduquer.

**education** [ɛdju'keɪʃən] n éducation f; (schooling) enseignement m, instruction f; ~**al** a pédagogique; scolaire; instructif(ive).

**EEC** n (abbr of European Economic Community) C.E.E. (Communauté économique européenne).

**eel** [i:l] n anguille f.

**eerie** ['ɪərɪ] a inquiétant(e), spectral(e), surnaturel(le).

**effect** [ɪ'fɛkt] n effet m // vt effectuer; ~**s** npl (THEATRE) effets mpl; **to take** ~ (law) entrer en vigueur, prendre effet; (drug) agir, faire son effet; **in** ~ en fait; ~**ive** a efficace; ~**iveness** n efficacité f.

**effeminate** [ɪ'fɛmɪnɪt] a efféminé(e).

**effervescent** [ɛfə'vɛsnt] a effervescent(e).

**efficacy** ['ɛfɪkəsɪ] n efficacité f.

**efficiency** [ɪ'fɪʃənsɪ] n efficacité f; rendement m.

**efficient** [ɪ'fɪʃənt] a efficace; ~**ly** ad efficacement.

**effigy** ['ɛfɪdʒɪ] n effigie f.

**effort** ['ɛfət] n effort m; ~**less** a sans effort, aisé(e).

**effrontery** [ɪ'frʌntərɪ] n effronterie f.

**e.g.** ad (abbr of exempli gratia) par exemple, p. ex.

**egalitarian** [ɪgælɪ'tɛərɪən] a égalitaire.

**egg** [ɛg] n œuf m; **to** ~ **on** vt pousser; ~**cup** n coquetier m; ~**plant** n aubergine f; ~**shell** n coquille f d'œuf // a (colour) blanc cassé inv.

**ego** ['i:gəu] n moi m.

**egoist** ['ɛgəuɪst] n égoïste m/f.

**egotist** ['ɛgəutɪst] n égocentrique m/f.

**Egypt** ['i:dʒɪpt] n Égypte f; ~**ian** [ɪ'dʒɪpʃən] a égyptien(ne) // n Égyptien/ne.

**eiderdown** ['aɪdədaun] n édredon m.

**eight** [eɪt] num huit; ~**een** num dix-huit; **eighth** num huitième; ~**y** num quatre-vingt(s).

**Eire** ['ɛərə] n République f d'Irlande.

**either** ['aɪðə*] det l'un ou l'autre; (both, each) chaque; **on** ~ **side** de chaque côté // pronoun: ~ (**of them**) l'un ou l'autre; **I don't like** ~ je n'aime ni l'un ni l'autre // ad non plus; **no, I don't** ~ moi non plus // cj: ~ **good or bad** ou bon ou mauvais, soit bon soit mauvais; **I haven't**

**seen** ~ **one or the other** je n'ai vu ni l'un ni l'autre.

**ejaculation** [ıdʒækju'leıʃən] n (PHYSIOL) éjaculation f.

**eject** [ı'dʒɛkt] vt expulser ; éjecter ; ~**or seat** n siège m éjectable.

**eke** [i:k]: **to** ~ **out** vt faire durer ; augmenter.

**elaborate** a [ı'læbərıt] compliqué(e), recherché(e), minutieux (euse) // vb [ı'læbəreıt] vt élaborer // vi entrer dans les détails.

**elapse** [ı'læps] vi s'écouler, passer.

**elastic** [ı'læstık] a, n élastique (m) ; ~ **band** n élastique m ; ~**ity** [-'tısıtı] n élasticité f.

**elated** [ı'leıtıd] a transporté(e) de joie.

**elation** [ı'leıʃən] n (grande) joie, allégresse f.

**elbow** ['ɛlbəu] n coude m.

**elder** ['ɛldə*] a aîné(e) // n (tree) sureau m ; **one's** ~**s** ses aînés ; ~**ly** a âgé(e) // n: **the** ~**ly** les personnes âgées.

**eldest** ['ɛldıst] a,n: **the** ~ **(child)** l'aîné(e) (des enfants).

**elect** [ı'lɛkt] vt élire ; **to** ~ **to do** choisir de faire // a: **the president** ~ le président désigné ; ~**ion** [ı'lɛkʃən] n élection f ; ~**ioneering** [ılɛkʃə'nıərıŋ] n propagande électorale, manœuvres électorales ; ~**or** n électeur/trice ; ~**oral** a électoral(e) ; ~**orate** n électorat m.

**electric** [ı'lɛktrık] a électrique ; ~**al** a électrique ; ~ **blanket** n couverture chauffante ; ~ **chair** n chaise f électrique ; ~ **cooker** n cuisinière f électrique ; ~ **current** n courant m électrique ; ~ **fire** n radiateur m électrique.

**electrician** [ılɛk'trıʃən] n électricien m.

**electricity** [ılɛk'trısıtı] n électricité f.

**electrify** [ı'lɛktrıfaı] vt (RAIL) électrifier ; (audience) électriser.

**electro...** [ı'lɛktrəu] prefix: **electrocute** [-kju:t] vt électrocuter ; **electrode** [ı'lɛktrəud] n électrode f ; **electrolysis** [ılɛk'trɔlısıs] n électrolyse f.

**electron** [ı'lɛktrɔn] n électron m.

**electronic** [ılɛk'trɔnık] a électronique ; ~**s** n électronique f.

**elegance** ['ɛlıgəns] n élégance f.

**elegant** ['ɛlıgənt] a élégant(e).

**element** ['ɛlımənt] n (gen) élément m ; (of heater, kettle etc) résistance f ; ~**ary** [-'mɛntərı] a élémentaire ; (school, education) primaire.

**elephant** ['ɛlıfənt] n éléphant m.

**elevate** ['ɛlıveıt] vt élever ; ~**d railway** n métro aérien.

**elevation** [ɛlı'veıʃən] n élévation f ; (height) altitude f.

**elevator** ['ɛlıveıtə*] n élévateur m, monte-charge m inv ; (US: lift) ascenseur m.

**eleven** [ı'lɛvn] num onze ; ~**ses** npl ≈ pause-café f ; ~**th** a onzième.

**elf, elves** [ɛlf, ɛlvz] n lutin m.

**elicit** [ı'lısıt] vt: **to** ~ **(from)** obtenir (de), arracher (à).

**eligible** ['ɛlıdʒəbl] a éligible ; (for membership) admissible ; ~ **for a pension** ayant droit à la retraite.

**eliminate** [ı'lımıneıt] vt éliminer ; **elimination** n élimination f.

**élite** [eı'li:t] n élite f.

**ellipse** [ı'lıps] n ellipse f.

**elliptical** [ı'lıptıkl] a elliptique.

**elm** [ɛlm] n orme m.

**elocution** [ɛlə'kju:ʃən] n élocution f.

**elongated** ['i:lɔŋgeıtıd] a étiré(e), allongé(e).

**elope** [ı'ləup] vi (lovers) s'enfuir (ensemble) ; ~**ment** n fugue amoureuse.

**eloquence** ['ɛləkwəns] n éloquence f.

**eloquent** ['ɛləkwənt] a éloquent(e).

**else** [ɛls] ad d'autre ; **something** ~ quelque chose d'autre, autre chose ; **somewhere** ~ ailleurs, autre part ; **everywhere** ~ partout ailleurs ; **where** ~? à quel autre endroit? ; **little** ~ pas grand-chose d'autre ; ~**where** ad ailleurs, autre part.

**elucidate** [ı'lu:sıdeıt] vt élucider.

**elude** [ı'lu:d] vt échapper à ; (question) éluder.

**elusive** [ı'lu:sıv] a insaisissable ; (answer) évasif(ive).

**elves** [ɛlvz] npl of elf.

**emaciated** [ı'meısıeıtıd] a émacié(e), décharné(e).

**emanate** ['ɛməneıt] vi: **to** ~ **from** émaner de.

**emancipate** [ı'mænsıpeıt] vt émanciper ; **emancipation** [-'peıʃən] n émancipation f.

**embalm** [ım'bɑ:m] vt embaumer.

**embankment** [ım'bæŋkmənt] n (of road, railway) remblai m, talus m ; (riverside) berge f, quai m ; (dyke) digue f.

**embargo, ~es** [ım'bɑ:gəu] n embargo m // vt frapper d'embargo, mettre l'embargo sur.

**embark** [ım'bɑ:k] vi: **to** ~ **(on)** (s')embarquer (à bord de or sur) // vt embarquer ; **to** ~ **on** (fig) se lancer or s'embarquer dans ; ~**ation** [ɛmbɑ:'keıʃən] n embarquement m.

**embarrass** [ım'bærəs] vt embarrasser, gêner ; ~**ing** a gênant(e), embarrassant(e) ; ~**ment** n embarras m, gêne f.

**embassy** ['ɛmbəsı] n ambassade f.

**embed** [ım'bɛd] vt enfoncer, ficher, sceller.

**embellish** [ım'bɛlıʃ] vt embellir ; enjoliver.

**embers** ['ɛmbəz] npl braise f.

**embezzle** [ım'bɛzl] vt détourner ; ~**ment** n détournement m (de fonds).

**embitter** [ım'bıtə*] vt aigrir ; envenimer.

**emblem** ['ɛmbləm] n emblème m.

**embodiment** [ım'bɔdımənt] n personification f, incarnation f.

**embody** [ım'bɔdı] vt (features) réunir, comprendre ; (ideas) formuler, exprimer.

**embossed** [ım'bɔst] a repoussé(e) ; gaufré(e) ; ~ **with** où figure(nt) en relief.

**embrace** [ım'breıs] vt embrasser, étreindre ; (include) embrasser, couvrir // n étreinte f.

**embroider** [ım'brɔıdə*] vt broder ; (fig: story) enjoliver ; ~**y** n broderie f.

**embryo** ['ɛmbrıəu] n (also fig) embryon m.

**emerald** ['ɛmərəld] n émeraude f.

**emerge** [ɪ'mə:dʒ] *vi* apparaître, surgir.
**emergence** [ɪ'mə:dʒəns] *n* apparition *f*.
**emergency** [ɪ'mə:dʒənsɪ] *n* urgence *f*; **in an ~** en cas d'urgence; **state of ~** état *m* d'urgence; **~ exit** *n* sortie *f* de secours.
**emergent** [ɪ'mə:dʒənt] *a*: **~ nation** pays *m* en voie de développement.
**emery** ['ɛmərɪ] *n*: **~ board** *n* lime *f* à ongles (*en carton émerisé*); **~ paper** *n* papier *m* (d')émeri.
**emetic** [ɪ'mɛtɪk] *n* vomitif *m*, émétique *m*.
**emigrant** ['ɛmɪgrənt] *n* émigrant/e.
**emigrate** ['ɛmɪgreɪt] *vi* émigrer; **emigration** [-'greɪʃən] *n* émigration *f*.
**eminence** ['ɛmɪnəns] *n* éminence *f*.
**eminent** ['ɛmɪnənt] *a* éminent(e).
**emission** [ɪ'mɪʃən] *n* émission *f*.
**emit** [ɪ'mɪt] *vt* émettre.
**emotion** [ɪ'məuʃən] *n* émotion *f*; **~al** *a* (*person*) émotif(ive), très sensible; (*scene*) émouvant(e); (*tone, speech*) qui fait appel aux sentiments; **~ally** *ad*: **~ally disturbed** qui souffre de troubles de l'affectivité.
**emotive** [ɪ'məutɪv] *a* émotif(ive); **~ power** *n* capacité *f* d'émouvoir *or* de toucher.
**emperor** ['ɛmpərə*] *n* empereur *m*.
**emphasis, pl ases** ['ɛmfəsɪs, -siːz] *n* accent *m*; force *f*, insistance *f*.
**emphasize** ['ɛmfəsaɪz] *vt* (*syllable, word, point*) appuyer *or* insister sur; (*feature*) souligner, accentuer.
**emphatic** [ɛm'fætɪk] *a* (*strong*) énergique, vigoureux(euse); (*unambiguous, clear*) catégorique; **~ally** *ad* avec vigueur *or* énergie; catégoriquement.
**empire** ['ɛmpaɪə*] *n* empire *m*.
**empirical** [ɛm'pɪrɪkl] *a* empirique.
**employ** [ɪm'plɔɪ] *vt* employer; **~ee** [-'iː] *n* employé/e; **~er** *n* employeur/euse; **~ment** *n* emploi *m*; **~ment agency** *n* agence *f* or bureau *m* de placement; **~ment exchange** *n* bourse *f* du travail.
**empower** [ɪm'pauə*] *vt*: **to ~ sb to do** autoriser *or* habiliter qn à faire.
**empress** ['ɛmprɪs] *n* impératrice *f*.
**emptiness** ['ɛmptɪnɪs] *n* vide *m*.
**empty** ['ɛmptɪ] *a* vide; (*threat, promise*) en l'air, vain(e) // *vt* vider // *vi* se vider; (*liquid*) s'écouler; **on an ~ stomach** à jeun; **~-handed** *a* les mains vides.
**emulate** ['ɛmjuleɪt] *vt* rivaliser avec, imiter.
**emulsion** [ɪ'mʌlʃən] *n* émulsion *f*; **~ (paint)** *n* peinture mate.
**enable** [ɪ'neɪbl] *vt*: **to ~ sb to do** permettre à qn de faire, donner à qn la possibilité de faire.
**enamel** [ɪ'næməl] *n* émail *m*.
**enamoured** [ɪ'næməd] *a*: **~ of** amoureux(euse) de; (*idea*) enchanté(e) par.
**encased** [ɪn'keɪst] *a*: **~ in** enfermé(e) dans, recouvert(e) de.
**enchant** [ɪn'tʃuːnt] *vt* enchanter; (*subject: magic spell*) ensorceler; **~ing** *a* ravissant(e), enchanteur(eresse).
**encircle** [ɪn'sə:kl] *vt* entourer, encercler.
**encl.** (*abbr of enclosed*) annexe(s).

**enclose** [ɪn'kləuz] *vt* (*land*) clôturer; (*letter etc*): **to ~ (with)** joindre (à); **please find ~d** veuillez trouver ci-joint.
**enclosure** [ɪn'kləuʒə*] *n* enceinte *f*; (*COMM*) annexe *f*.
**encore** [ɔŋ'kɔ:*] *excl, n* bis (*m*).
**encounter** [ɪn'kauntə*] *n* rencontre *f* // *vt* rencontrer.
**encourage** [ɪn'kʌrɪdʒ] *vt* encourager; **~ment** *n* encouragement *m*.
**encroach** [ɪn'krəutʃ] *vi*: **to ~ (up)on** empiéter sur.
**encyclop(a)edia** [ɛnsaɪkləu'pi:dɪə] *n* encyclopédie *f*.
**end** [ɛnd] *n* (*gen, also: aim*) fin *f*; (*of table, street etc*) bout *m*, extrémité *f* // *vt* terminer; (*also*: **bring to an ~, put an ~ to**) mettre fin à // *vi* se terminer, finir; **to come to an ~** prendre fin; **in the ~** finalement; **on ~** (*object*) debout, dressé(e); **for 5 hours on ~** durant 5 heures d'affilée *or* de suite; **for hours on ~** pendant des heures (et des heures); **to ~ up** *vi*: **to ~ up in** finir *or* se terminer par; (*place*) finir *or* aboutir à.
**endanger** [ɪn'deɪndʒə*] *vt* mettre en danger.
**endearing** [ɪn'dɪərɪŋ] *a* attachant(e).
**endeavour** [ɪn'dɛvə*] *n* tentative *f*, effort *m* // *vi*: **to ~ to do** tenter *or* s'efforcer de faire.
**ending** ['ɛndɪŋ] *n* dénouement *m*, conclusion *f*; (*LING*) terminaison *f*.
**endive** ['ɛndaɪv] *n* chicorée *f*.
**endless** ['ɛndlɪs] *a* sans fin, interminable; (*patience, resources*) inépuisable, sans limites.
**endorse** [ɪn'dɔ:s] *vt* (*cheque*) endosser; (*approve*) appuyer, approuver, sanctionner; **~ment** *n* (*on driving licence*) contravention portée au permis de conduire.
**endow** [ɪn'dau] *vt* (*provide with money*) faire une donation à, doter; (*equip*): **to ~ with** gratifier de, doter de.
**end product** ['ɛndprɔdəkt] *n* produit fini; (*fig*) résultat *m*.
**endurable** [ɪn'djuərəbl] *a* supportable.
**endurance** [ɪn'djuərəns] *n* endurance *f*, résistance *f*; patience *f*.
**endure** [ɪn'djuə*] *vt* supporter, endurer // *vi* durer.
**enemy** ['ɛnəmɪ] *a,n* ennemi(e).
**energetic** [ɛnə'dʒɛtɪk] *a* énergique; actif(ive); qui fait se dispenser (physiquement).
**energy** ['ɛnədʒɪ] *n* énergie *f*.
**enervating** ['ɛnə:veɪtɪŋ] *a* débilitant(e), affaiblissant(e).
**enforce** [ɪn'fɔ:s] *vt* (*LAW*) appliquer, faire respecter; **~d** *a* forcé(e).
**engage** [ɪn'geɪdʒ] *vt* engager; (*MIL*) engager le combat avec // *vi* (*TECH*) s'enclencher, s'engrener; **to ~ in** se lancer dans; **~d** *a* (*busy, in use*) occupé(e); (*betrothed*) fiancé(e); **to get ~d** se fiancer; **he is ~d in research/a survey** il fait de la recherche/une enquête; **~ment** *n* obligation *f*, engagement *m*; rendez-vous *m inv*; (*to marry*) fiançailles *fpl*; (*MIL*) combat *m*; **~ment ring** *n* bague *f* de fiançailles.

**engaging** [ɪn'geɪdʒɪŋ] *a* engageant(e), attirant(e).

**engender** [ɪn'dʒɛndə*] *vt* produire, causer.

**engine** ['ɛndʒɪn] *n* (AUT) moteur *m*; (RAIL) locomotive *f*; ~ **failure** *n* panne *f*; ~ **trouble** *n* ennuis *mpl* mécaniques.

**engineer** [ɛndʒɪ'nɪə*] *n* ingénieur *m*; (US: RAIL) mécanicien *m*; ~**ing** *n* engineering *m*, ingénierie *f*; (of bridges, ships) génie *m*; (of machine) mécanique *f*.

**England** ['ɪŋglənd] *n* Angleterre *f*.

**English** ['ɪŋglɪʃ] *a* anglais(e) // *n* (LING) anglais *m*; **the** ~ les Anglais; ~**man/woman** *n* Anglais/e.

**engrave** [ɪn'greɪv] *vt* graver.

**engraving** [ɪn'greɪvɪŋ] *n* gravure *f*.

**engrossed** [ɪn'grəust] *a*: ~ **in** absorbé(e) par, plongé(e) dans.

**engulf** [ɪn'gʌlf] *vt* engloutir.

**enhance** [ɪn'hɑ:ns] *vt* rehausser, mettre en valeur.

**enigma** [ɪ'nɪgmə] *n* énigme *f*; ~**tic** [ɛnɪg'mætɪk] *a* énigmatique.

**enjoy** [ɪn'dʒɔɪ] *vt* aimer, prendre plaisir à; (have: health, fortune) jouir de; (: success) connaître; **to** ~ **oneself** s'amuser; ~**able** *a* agréable; ~**ment** *n* plaisir *m*.

**enlarge** [ɪn'lɑ:dʒ] *vt* accroître; (PHOT) agrandir // *vi*: **to** ~ **on** (subject) s'étendre sur; ~**ment** *n* (PHOT) agrandissement *m*.

**enlighten** [ɪn'laɪtn] *vt* éclairer; ~**ed** *a* éclairé(e); ~**ment** *n* édification *f*; vues éclairées; éclaircissements *mpl*; (HISTORY): **the E**~**ment** ≈ le Siècle des lumières.

**enlist** [ɪn'lɪst] *vt* recruter; (support) s'assurer // *vi* s'engager.

**enmity** ['ɛnmɪtɪ] *n* inimitié *f*.

**enormity** [ɪ'nɔ:mɪtɪ] *n* énormité *f*.

**enormous** [ɪ'nɔ:məs] *a* énorme.

**enough** [ɪ'nʌf] *a, n*: ~ **time/books** assez or suffisamment de temps/livres; **have you got** ~? (en) avez-vous assez? // *ad*: **big** ~ assez or suffisamment grand; **he has not worked** ~ il n'a pas assez or suffisamment travaillé, il n'a pas travaillé assez or suffisamment; ~! assez!, ça suffit! ; **it's hot** ~ **(as it is)!** il fait assez chaud comme ça! ; **... which, funnily** ~ ... qui, chose curieuse.

**enquire** [ɪn'kwaɪə*] *vt,vi* = inquire.

**enrich** [ɪn'rɪtʃ] *vt* enrichir.

**enrol** [ɪn'rəul] *vt* inscrire // *vi* s'inscrire; ~**ment** *n* inscription *f*.

**ensconced** [ɪn'skɒnst] *a*: ~ **in** bien calé(e) dans; plongé(e) dans.

**ensign** *n* (NAUT) ['ɛnsən] enseigne *f*, pavillon *m*; (MIL) ['ɛnsaɪn] porte-étendard *m*.

**enslave** [ɪn'sleɪv] *vt* asservir.

**ensue** [ɪn'sju:] *vi* s'ensuivre, résulter.

**ensure** [ɪn'ʃuə*] *vt* assurer; garantir; **to** ~ **that** s'assurer que.

**entail** [ɪn'teɪl] *vt* entraîner, nécessiter.

**entangle** [ɪn'tæŋgl] *vt* emmêler, embrouiller.

**enter** ['ɛntə*] *vt* (room) entrer dans, pénétrer dans; (club, army) entrer à; (competition) s'inscrire à or pour; (sb for a competition) (faire) inscrire; (write down) inscrire, noter; **to** ~ **for** *vt fus* s'inscrire à, se présenter pour or à; **to** ~ **into** *vt*

*fus* (exploration) se lancer dans; (debate) prendre part à; (agreement) conclure; **to** ~ **up** *vt* inscrire; **to** ~ **(up)on** *vt fus* commencer.

**enterprise** ['ɛntəpraɪz] *n* entreprise *f*; (esprit *m* d')initiative *f*.

**enterprising** ['ɛntəpraɪzɪŋ] *a* entreprenant(e), dynamique.

**entertain** [ɛntə'teɪn] *vt* amuser, distraire; (invite) recevoir (à dîner); (idea, plan) envisager; ~**er** *n* artiste *m/f* de variétés; ~**ing** *a* amusant(e), distrayant(e); ~**ment** *n* (amusement) distraction *f*, divertissement *m*, amusement *m*; (show) spectacle *m*.

**enthralled** [ɪn'θrɔ:ld] *a* captivé(e).

**enthusiasm** [ɪn'θu:zɪæzəm] *n* enthousiasme *m*.

**enthusiast** [ɪn'θu:zɪæst] *n* enthousiaste *m/f*; **a jazz** *etc* ~ un fervent or passionné du jazz *etc*; ~**ic** [-'æstɪk] *a* enthousiaste.

**entice** [ɪn'taɪs] *vt* attirer, séduire.

**entire** [ɪn'taɪə*] *a* (tout) entier(ère); ~**ly** *ad* entièrement, complètement; ~**ty** [ɪn'taɪərətɪ] *n*: **in its** ~**ty** dans sa totalité.

**entitle** [ɪn'taɪtl] *vt* (allow): **to** ~ **sb to do** donner (le) droit à qn de faire; **to** ~ **sb to sth** donner droit à qch à qn; ~**d** *a* (book) intitulé(e); **to be** ~**d to do** avoir le droit de or être habilité à faire.

**entrance** *n* ['ɛntrns] entrée *f* // *vt* [ɪn'trɑ:ns] enchanter, ravir; **to gain** ~ **to** (university etc) être admis à; ~ **examination** *n* examen *m* d'entrée; ~ **fee** *n* droit *m* d'inscription; (to museum etc) prix *m* d'entrée.

**entrant** ['ɛntrnt] *n* participant/e; concurrent/e.

**entreat** [ɛn'tri:t] *vt* supplier; ~**y** *n* supplication *f*, prière *f*.

**entrée** ['ɔntreɪ] *n* (CULIN) entrée *f*.

**entrenched** [ɛn'trɛntʃd] *a* retranché(e).

**entrust** [ɪn'trʌst] *vt*: **to** ~ **sth to** confier qch à.

**entry** ['ɛntrɪ] *n* entrée *f*; (in register) inscription *f*; ~ **form** *n* feuille *f* d'inscription.

**entwine** [ɪn'twaɪn] *vt* entrelacer.

**enumerate** [ɪ'nju:məreɪt] *vt* énumérer.

**enunciate** [ɪ'nʌnsɪeɪt] *vt* énoncer; prononcer.

**envelop** [ɪn'vɛləp] *vt* envelopper.

**envelope** ['ɛnvələup] *n* enveloppe *f*.

**envious** ['ɛnvɪəs] *a* envieux(euse).

**environment** [ɪn'vaɪərnmənt] *n* milieu *m*; environnement *m*; ~**al** [-'mɛntl] *a* écologique; du milieu.

**envisage** [ɪn'vɪzɪdʒ] *vt* envisager; prévoir.

**envoy** ['ɛnvɔɪ] *n* envoyé/e.

**envy** ['ɛnvɪ] *n* envie *f* // *vt* envier.

**enzyme** ['ɛnzaɪm] *n* enzyme *m*.

**ephemeral** [ɪ'fɛmərl] *a* éphémère.

**epic** ['ɛpɪk] *n* épopée *f* // *a* épique.

**epidemic** [ɛpɪ'dɛmɪk] *n* épidémie *f*.

**epilepsy** ['ɛpɪlɛpsɪ] *n* épilepsie *f*; **epileptic** [-'lɛptɪk] *a,n* épileptique (*m/f*).

**epilogue** ['ɛpɪlɒg] *n* épilogue *m*.

**episode** ['ɛpɪsəud] *n* épisode *m*.

**epistle** [ɪ'pɪsl] *n* épître *f*.

**epitaph** ['ɛpɪtɑ:f] *n* épitaphe *f*.

**epitome** [ɪ'pɪtəmɪ] *n* résumé *m*;

quintessence *f*, type *m*; **epitomize** *vt* résumer; illustrer, incarner.

**epoch** ['ɪːpɔk] *n* époque *f*, ère *f*; ~-**making** a qui fait époque.

**equable** ['ɛkwəbl] *a* égal(e); de tempérament égal.

**equal** ['iːkwl] *a* égal(e) // *n* égal/e // *vt* égaler; ~ **to** (*task*) à la hauteur de; ~ **to doing** de taille à *or* capable de faire; ~**ity** [iːˈkwɔlɪtɪ] *n* égalité *f*; ~**ize** *vt,vi* égaliser; ~**izer** *n* but égalisateur; ~**ly** *ad* également; (*just as*) tout aussi; ~(**s**) **sign** *n* signe *m* d'égalité.

**equanimity** [ɛkwəˈnɪmɪtɪ] *n* égalité *f* d'humeur.

**equate** [ɪˈkweɪt] *vt*: **to** ~ **sth with** comparer qch à; assimiler qch à; **to** ~ **sth to** mettre qch en équation avec; égaler qch à; **equation** [ɪˈkweɪʃən] *n* (*MATH*) équation *f*.

**equator** [ɪˈkweɪtə*] *n* équateur *m*; ~**ial** [ɛkwəˈtɔːrɪəl] *a* équatorial(e).

**equilibrium** [iːkwɪˈlɪbrɪəm] *n* équilibre *m*.

**equinox** ['iːkwɪnɔks] *n* équinoxe *m*.

**equip** [ɪˈkwɪp] *vt* équiper; **to** ~ **sb/sth with** équiper *or* munir qn/qch de; ~**ment** *n* équipement *m*; (*electrical etc*) appareillage *m*, installation *f*.

**equitable** ['ɛkwɪtəbl] *a* équitable.

**equity** ['ɛkwɪtɪ] *n* équité *f*; **equities** *npl* (*COMM*) actions cotées en Bourse.

**equivalent** [ɪˈkwɪvələnt] *a* équivalent(e) // *n* équivalent *m*.

**equivocal** [ɪˈkwɪvəkl] *a* équivoque; (*open to suspicion*) douteux(euse).

**era** ['ɪərə] *n* ère *f*, époque *f*.

**eradicate** [ɪˈrædɪkeɪt] *vt* éliminer.

**erase** [ɪˈreɪz] *vt* effacer; ~**r** *n* gomme *f*.

**erect** [ɪˈrɛkt] *a* droit(e) // *vt* construire; (*monument*) ériger; élever; (*tent etc*) dresser.

**erection** [ɪˈrɛkʃən] *n* érection *f*.

**ermine** ['əːmɪn] *n* hermine *f*.

**erode** [ɪˈrəud] *vt* éroder; (*metal*) ronger; **erosion** [ɪˈrəuʒən] *n* érosion *f*.

**erotic** [ɪˈrɔtɪk] *a* érotique; ~**ism** [ɪˈrɔtɪsɪzm] *n* érotisme *m*.

**err** [əː*] *vi* se tromper; (*REL*) pécher.

**errand** ['ɛrnd] *n* course *f*, commission *f*; ~ **boy** *n* garçon *m* de courses.

**erratic** [ɪˈrætɪk] *a* irrégulier(ère); inconstant(e).

**erroneous** [ɪˈrəunɪəs] *a* erroné(e).

**error** ['ɛrə*] *n* erreur *f*.

**erudite** ['ɛrjudaɪt] *a* savant(e).

**erupt** [ɪˈrʌpt] *vi* entrer en éruption; (*fig*) éclater; ~**ion** [ɪˈrʌpʃən] *n* éruption *f*.

**escalate** ['ɛskəleɪt] *vi* s'intensifier; **escalation** [-ˈleɪʃən] *n* escalade *f*.

**escalator** ['ɛskəleɪtə*] *n* escalier roulant.

**escapade** [ɛskəˈpeɪd] *n* fredaine *f*; équipée *f*.

**escape** [ɪˈskeɪp] *n* évasion *f*; fuite *f*; (*of gas etc*) échappement *m*; fuite // *vi* s'échapper, fuir; (*from jail*) s'évader; (*fig*) s'en tirer; (*leak*) s'échapper; fuir // *vt* échapper à; **to** ~ **from sb** échapper à qn; **to** ~ **from** (*place*) s'échapper de; (*fig*) fuir; **escapism** *n* évasion *f* (*fig*).

**escort** *n* ['ɛskɔːt] escorte *f* // *vt* [ɪˈskɔːt]

escorter; ~ **agency** *n* bureau *m* d'hôtesses.

**Eskimo** ['ɛskɪməu] *n* Esquimau/de.

**especially** [ɪˈspɛʃlɪ] *ad* particulièrement; surtout; exprès.

**espionage** ['ɛspɪɑːʒ] *n* espionnage *m*.

**esplanade** [ɛspləˈneɪd] *n* esplanade *f*.

**Esquire** [ɪˈskwaɪə*] *n* (*abbr* **Esq.**): **J. Brown,** ~ **Monsieur J. Brown.**

**essay** ['ɛseɪ] *n* (*SCOL*) dissertation *f*; (*LITERATURE*) essai *m*; (*attempt*) tentative *f*.

**essence** ['ɛsns] *n* essence *f*.

**essential** [ɪˈsɛnʃl] *a* essentiel(le); (*basic*) fondamental(e); ~**ly** *ad* essentiellement.

**establish** [ɪˈstæblɪʃ] *vt* établir; (*business*) fonder, créer; (*one's power etc*) asseoir, affermir; ~**ment** *n* établissement *m*; **the E~ment** les pouvoirs établis; l'ordre établi; les milieux dirigeants.

**estate** [ɪˈsteɪt] *n* domaine *m*, propriété *f*; biens *mpl*, succession *f*; ~ **agent** *n* agent immobilier; ~ **car** *n* (*Brit*) break *m*.

**esteem** [ɪˈstiːm] *n* estime *f*.

**esthetic** [ɪsˈθɛtɪk] *a* (*US*) = **aesthetic**.

**estimate** *n* ['ɛstɪmət] estimation *f*; (*COMM*) devis *m* // *vt* ['ɛstɪmeɪt] estimer; **estimation** [-ˈmeɪʃən] *n* opinion *f*; estime *f*.

**estuary** ['ɛstjuərɪ] *n* estuaire *m*.

**etching** ['ɛtʃɪŋ] *n* eau-forte *f*.

**eternal** [ɪˈtəːnl] *a* éternel(le).

**eternity** [ɪˈtəːnɪtɪ] *n* éternité *f*.

**ether** ['iːθə*] *n* éther *m*.

**ethical** ['ɛθɪkl] *a* moral(e).

**ethics** ['ɛθɪks] *n* éthique *f* // *npl* moralité *f*.

**ethnic** ['ɛθnɪk] *a* ethnique.

**ethnology** [ɛθˈnɔlədʒɪ] *n* ethnologie *f*.

**etiquette** ['ɛtɪkɛt] *n* convenances *fpl*, étiquette *f*.

**etymology** [ɛtɪˈmɔlədʒɪ] *n* étymologie *f*.

**eulogy** ['juːlədʒɪ] *n* éloge *m*.

**euphemism** ['juːfəmɪzm] *n* euphémisme *m*.

**euphoria** [juːˈfɔːrɪə] *n* euphorie *f*.

**Europe** ['juərəp] *n* Europe *f*; ~**an** [-ˈpiːən] *a* européen(ne) // *n* Européen/ne.

**euthanasia** [juːθəˈneɪzɪə] *n* euthanasie *f*.

**evacuate** [ɪˈvækjueɪt] *vt* évacuer; **evacuation** [-ˈeɪʃən] *n* évacuation *f*.

**evade** [ɪˈveɪd] *vt* échapper à; (*question etc*) éluder; (*duties*) se dérober à.

**evaluate** [ɪˈvæljueɪt] *vt* évaluer.

**evangelist** [ɪˈvændʒəlɪst] *n* évangéliste *m*.

**evangelize** [ɪˈvændʒəlaɪz] *vt* évangéliser, prêcher l'Évangile à.

**evaporate** [ɪˈvæpəreɪt] *vi* s'évaporer // *vt* faire évaporer; ~**d milk** *n* lait concentré; **evaporation** [-ˈreɪʃən] *n* évaporation *f*.

**evasion** [ɪˈveɪʒən] *n* dérobade *f*; faux-fuyant *m*.

**evasive** [ɪˈveɪsɪv] *a* évasif(ive).

**eve** [iːv] *n*: **on the** ~ **of** à la veille de.

**even** ['iːvn] *a* régulier(ère), égal(e); (*number*) pair(e) // *ad* même; ~ **more** encore plus; ~ **so** quand même; **to** ~ **out** *vi* s'égaliser; **to get** ~ **with sb** prendre sa revanche sur qn.

**evening** ['iːvnɪŋ] *n* soir *m*; (*as duration, event*) soirée *f*; **in the** ~ le soir; ~ **class**

*n* cours *m* du soir ; ~ **dress** *n* (*man's*) habit *m* de soirée, smoking *m* ; (*woman's*) robe *f* de soirée.

**evensong** ['i:vnsɔŋ] *n* office *m* du soir.

**event** ['ɪ'vɛnt] *n* événement *m* ; (*SPORT*) épreuve *f* ; **in the** ~ **of** en cas de ; ~**ful** *a* mouvementé(e).

**eventual** [ɪ'vɛntʃuəl] *a* final(e) ; ~**ity** [-'æliti] *n* possibilité *f*, éventualité *f* ; ~**ly** *ad* finalement.

**ever** ['ɛvə*] *ad* jamais ; (*at all times*) toujours ; **the best** ~ le meilleur qu'on ait jamais vu ; **have you** ~ **seen it?** l'as-tu déjà vu?, as-tu eu l'occasion *or* t'est-il arrivé de le voir? ; **hardly** ~ ne ... presque jamais ; ~ **since** *ad* depuis // *cj* depuis que ; ~ **so pretty** si joli ; ~**green** *n* arbre *m* à feuilles persistantes ; ~**lasting** *a* éternel(le).

**every** ['ɛvrɪ] *det* chaque ; ~ **day** tous les jours, chaque jour ; ~ **other/third day** tous les deux/trois jours ; ~ **other car** une voiture sur deux ; ~ **now and then** de temps en temps ; ~**body** *pronoun* tout le monde, tous *pl* ; ~**day** *a* quotidien(ne) ; de tous les jours ; ~**one** = ~**body** ; ~**thing** *pronoun* tout ; ~**where** *ad* partout.

**evict** [ɪ'vɪkt] *vt* expulser ; ~**ion** [ɪ'vɪkʃən] *n* expulsion *f*.

**evidence** ['ɛvɪdns] *n* (*proof*) preuve(s) *f(pl)* ; (*of witness*) témoignage *m* ; (*sign*): **to show** ~ **of** donner des signes de ; **to give** ~ témoigner, déposer ; **in** ~ (*obvious*) en évidence ; en vue.

**evident** ['ɛvɪdnt] *a* évident(e) ; ~**ly** *ad* de toute évidence.

**evil** ['i:vl] *a* mauvais(e) // *n* mal *m*.

**evocative** [ɪ'vɔkətɪv] *a* évocateur(trice).

**evoke** [ɪ'vəuk] *vt* évoquer.

**evolution** [i:və'lu:ʃən] *n* évolution *f*.

**evolve** [ɪ'vɔlv] *vt* élaborer // *vi* évoluer, se transformer.

**ewe** [ju:] *n* brebis *f*.

**ewer** ['ju:ə*] *n* broc *m*.

**ex-** [ɛks] *prefix* ex-.

**exact** [ɪg'zækt] *a* exact(e) // *vt*: **to** ~ **sth** (**from**) extorquer qch (à) ; exiger qch (de) ; ~**ing** *a* exigeant(e) ; (*work*) fatigant(e) ; ~**itude** *n* exactitude *f*, précision *f* ; ~**ly** *ad* exactement.

**exaggerate** [ɪg'zædʒəreɪt] *vt,vi* exagérer ; **exaggeration** [-'reɪʃən] *n* exagération *f*.

**exalt** [ɪg'zɔ:lt] *vt* exalter ; élever.

**exam** [ɪg'zæm] *n abbr of* **examination.**

**examination** [ɪgzæmɪ'neɪʃən] *n* (*SCOL, MED*) examen *m*.

**examine** [ɪg'zæmɪn] *vt* (*gen*) examiner ; (*SCOL, LAW: person*) interroger ; (*at customs: luggage*) inspecter ; ~**r** *n* examinateur/trice.

**example** [ɪg'zɑ:mpl] *n* exemple *m* ; **for** ~ par exemple.

**exasperate** [ɪg'zɑ:spəreɪt] *vt* exaspérer, agacer.

**excavate** ['ɛkskəveɪt] *vt* excaver ; (*object*) mettre au jour ; **excavation** [-'veɪʃən] *n* excavation *f* ; **excavator** *n* excavateur *m*, excavatrice *f*.

**exceed** [ɪk'si:d] *vt* dépasser ; (*one's powers*) outrepasser ; ~**ingly** *ad* excessivement.

**excel** [ɪk'sɛl] *vi* exceller // *vt* surpasser.

**excellence** ['ɛksələns] *n* excellence *f*.

**Excellency** ['ɛksələnsɪ] *n*: **His** ~ son Excellence *f*.

**excellent** ['ɛksələnt] *a* excellent(e).

**except** [ɪk'sɛpt] *prep* (*also*: ~ **for,** ~**ing**) sauf, excepté, à l'exception de // *vt* excepter ; ~ **if/when** sauf si/quand ; ~ **that** excepté que, si ce n'est que ; ~**ion** [ɪk'sɛpʃən] *n* exception *f* ; **to take** ~**ion to** s'offusquer de ; ~**ional** [ɪk'sɛpʃənl] *a* exceptionnel(le).

**excerpt** ['ɛksə:pt] *n* extrait *m*.

**excess** [ɪk'sɛs] *n* excès *m* ; ~ **fare** *n* supplément *m* ; ~ **baggage** *n* excédent *m* de bagages ; ~**ive** *a* excessif(ive).

**exchange** [ɪks'tʃeɪndʒ] *n* échange *m* ; (*also*: **telephone** ~) central *m* // *vt* échanger ; ~ **market** *n* marché *m* des changes.

**exchequer** [ɪks'tʃɛkə*] *n* Échiquier *m*, ≈ ministère *m* des Finances.

**excisable** [ɪk'saɪzəbl] *a* taxable.

**excise** *n* ['ɛksaɪz] taxe *f* // *vt* [ɛk'saɪz] exciser ; ~ **duties** *npl* impôts indirects.

**excite** [ɪk'saɪt] *vt* exciter ; **to get** ~**d** s'exciter ; ~**ment** *n* excitation *f* ; **exciting** *a* passionnant(e).

**exclaim** [ɪk'skleɪm] *vi* s'exclamer ; **exclamation** [ɛkskləˈmeɪʃən] *n* exclamation *f* ; **exclamation mark** *n* point *m* d'exclamation.

**exclude** [ɪk'sklu:d] *vt* exclure ; **exclusion** [ɪk'sklu:ʒən] *n* exclusion *f*.

**exclusive** [ɪk'sklu:sɪv] *a* exclusif(ive) ; (*club, district*) sélect(e) ; (*item of news*) en exclusivité // *ad* (*COMM*) exclusivement, non inclus ; ~ **of VAT** TVA non comprise ; ~**ly** *ad* exclusivement ; ~ **rights** *npl* (*COMM*) exclusivité *f*.

**excommunicate** [ɛkskə'mju:nɪkeɪt] *vt* excommunier.

**excrement** ['ɛkskrəmənt] *n* excrément *m*.

**excruciating** [ɪk'skru:ʃɪeɪtɪŋ] *a* atroce, déchirant(e).

**excursion** [ɪk'skə:ʃən] *n* excursion *f*.

**excusable** [ɪk'skju:zəbl] *a* excusable.

**excuse** *n* [ɪk'skju:s] excuse *f* // *vt* [ɪk'skju:z] excuser ; **to** ~ **sb from** (*activity*) dispenser qn de ; ~ **me!** excusez-moi!, pardon!

**execute** ['ɛksɪkju:t] *vt* exécuter.

**execution** [ɛksɪ'kju:ʃən] *n* exécution *f* ; ~**er** *n* bourreau *m*.

**executive** [ɪg'zɛkjutɪv] *n* (*COMM*) cadre *m* ; (*POL*) exécutif *m* // *a* exécutif(ive).

**executor** [ɪg'zɛkjutə*] *n* exécuteur/trice testamentaire.

**exemplary** [ɪg'zɛmplərɪ] *a* exemplaire.

**exemplify** [ɪg'zɛmplɪfaɪ] *vt* illustrer.

**exempt** [ɪg'zɛmpt] *a*: ~ **from** exempté(e) *or* dispensé(e) de // *vt*: **to** ~ **sb from** exempter *or* dispenser qn de ; ~**ion** [ɪg'zɛmpʃən] *n* exemption *f*, dispense *f*.

**exercise** ['ɛksəsaɪz] *n* exercice *m* // *vt* exercer ; (*patience, clemency*) faire preuve de ; (*dog*) promener ; **to take** ~ prendre de l'exercice ; ~ **book** *n* cahier *m*.

**exert** [ɪg'zə:t] *vt* exercer, employer ; **to** ~ **o.s.** se dépenser.

# Ex

**exhaust** [ɪg'zɔ:st] n (also: ~ fumes) gaz mpl d'échappement ; (also: ~ pipe) tuyau m d'échappement // vt épuiser ; ~ed a épuisé(e) ; ~ion [ɪg'zɔ:stʃən] n épuisement m ; ~ive a très complet(ète).

**exhibit** [ɪg'zɪbɪt] n (ART) pièce f or objet m exposé(e) ; (LAW) pièce à conviction // vt exposer ; (courage, skill) faire preuve de ; ~ion [ɛksɪ'bɪʃən] n exposition f ; ~ion of temper n manifestation f de colère ; ~ionist [ɛksɪ'bɪʃənɪst] n exhibitionniste m/f ; ~or n exposant/e.

**exhilarating** [ɪg'zɪləreɪtɪŋ] a grisant(e) ; stimulant(e).

**exhort** [ɪg'zɔ:t] vt exhorter.

**exile** ['ɛksaɪl] n exil m ; exilé/e // vt exiler ; in ~ en exil.

**exist** [ɪg'zɪst] vi exister ; ~ence n existence f ; to be in ~ence exister.

**exit** ['ɛksɪt] n sortie f.

**exonerate** [ɪg'zɔnəreɪt] vt: to ~ from disculper de ; (free) exempter de.

**exorcize** ['ɛksɔ:saɪz] vt exorciser.

**exotic** [ɪg'zɔtɪk] a exotique.

**expand** [ɪk'spænd] vt agrandir ; accroître, étendre // vi (trade etc) se développer, s'accroître ; s'étendre ; (gas, metal) se dilater.

**expanse** [ɪk'spæns] n étendue f.

**expansion** [ɪk'spænʃən] n développement m, accroissement m ; dilatation f.

**expatriate** n [ɛks'pætrɪət] expatrié/e // vt [ɛks'pætrɪeɪt] expatrier, exiler.

**expect** [ɪk'spɛkt] vt (anticipate) s'attendre à, s'attendre à ce que + sub ; (count on) compter sur, escompter ; (hope for) espérer ; (require) demander, exiger ; (suppose) supposer ; (await, also baby) attendre // vi: to be ~ing être enceinte ; to ~ sb to do s'attendre à ce que qn fasse ; attendre de qn qu'il fasse ; ~ant a qui attend (quelque chose) ; ~ant mother n future maman ; ~ation [ɛkspɛk'teɪʃən] n attente f, prévisions fpl ; espérance(s) f(pl).

**expedience, expediency** [ɛk'spi:dɪəns, ɛk'spi:dɪənsɪ] n: for the sake of ~ parce que c'est plus commode.

**expedient** [ɪk'spi:dɪənt] a indiqué(e), opportun(e) ; commode // n expédient m.

**expedite** ['ɛkspədaɪt] vt hâter ; expédier.

**expedition** [ɛkspə'dɪʃən] n expédition f.

**expeditious** [ɛkspə'dɪʃəs] a expéditif(ive), prompt(e).

**expel** [ɪk'spɛl] vt chasser, expulser ; (SCOL) renvoyer, exclure.

**expend** [ɪk'spɛnd] vt consacrer ; (use up) dépenser ; ~able a remplaçable ; ~iture [ɪk'spɛndɪtʃə*] n dépense f ; dépenses fpl.

**expense** [ɪk'spɛns] n dépense f ; frais mpl ; (high cost) coût m ; ~s npl (COMM) frais mpl ; at great/little ~ à grands/peu de frais ; at the ~ of aux dépens de ; ~ account n (note f de) frais mpl.

**expensive** [ɪk'spɛnsɪv] a cher(chère), coûteux(euse) ; to be ~ coûter cher ; ~ tastes npl goûts mpl de luxe.

**experience** [ɪk'spɪərɪəns] n expérience f // vt connaître ; éprouver ; ~d a expérimenté(e).

**experiment** [ɪk'spɛrɪmənt] n expérience f // vi faire une expérience ; to ~ with expérimenter ; ~al [-'mɛntl] a expérimental(e).

**expert** ['ɛkspə:t] a expert(e) // n expert m ; ~ise [-'ti:z] n (grande) compétence.

**expire** [ɪk'spaɪə*] vi expirer ; **expiry** n expiration f.

**explain** [ɪk'spleɪn] vt expliquer ; **explanation** [ɛksplə'neɪʃən] n explication f ; **explanatory** [ɪk'splænətrɪ] a explicatif(ive).

**explicit** [ɪk'splɪsɪt] a explicite ; (definite) formel(le).

**explode** [ɪk'spləud] vi exploser // vt faire exploser.

**exploit** n ['ɛksplɔɪt] exploit m // vt [ɪk'splɔɪt] exploiter ; ~ation [-'teɪʃən] n exploitation f.

**exploration** [ɛksplə'reɪʃən] n exploration f.

**exploratory** [ɪk'splɔrətrɪ] a (fig: talks) préliminaire.

**explore** [ɪk'splɔ:*] vt explorer ; (possibilities) étudier, examiner ; ~r n explorateur/trice.

**explosion** [ɪk'spləuʒən] n explosion f.

**explosive** [ɪk'spləusɪv] a explosif(ive) // n explosif m.

**exponent** [ɪk'spəunənt] n (of school of thought etc) interprète m, représentant m ; (MATH) exposant m.

**export** vt [ɛk'spɔ:t] exporter // n ['ɛkspɔ:t] exportation f // cpd d'exportation ; ~ation [-'teɪʃən] n exportation f ; ~er n exportateur m.

**expose** [ɪk'spəuz] vt exposer ; (unmask) démasquer, dévoiler ; to ~ o.s. (LAW) commettre un outrage à la pudeur.

**exposure** [ɪk'spəuʒə*] n exposition f ; (PHOT) (temps m de) pose f ; (: shot) pose f ; **suffering from** ~ (MED) souffrant des effets du froid et de l'épuisement ; ~ meter n posemètre m.

**expound** [ɪk'spaund] vt exposer, expliquer.

**express** [ɪk'sprɛs] a (definite) formel(le), exprès(esse) ; (letter etc) exprès inv // n (train) rapide m // ad (send) exprès // vt exprimer ; ~ion [ɪk'sprɛʃən] n expression f ; ~ive a expressif(ive) ; ~ly ad expressément, formellement.

**expropriate** [ɛks'prəuprɪeɪt] vt exproprier.

**expulsion** [ɪk'spʌlʃən] n expulsion f ; renvoi m.

**exquisite** [ɛk'skwɪzɪt] a exquis(e).

**extend** [ɪk'stɛnd] vt (visit, street) prolonger ; (building) agrandir ; (offer) présenter, offrir // vi (land) s'étendre.

**extension** [ɪk'stɛnʃən] n prolongation f ; agrandissement m ; (building) annexe f ; (to wire, table) rallonge f ; (telephone: in offices) poste m ; (: in private house) téléphone m supplémentaire.

**extensive** [ɪk'stɛnsɪv] a étendu(e), vaste ; (damage, alterations) considérable ; (inquiries) approfondi(e) ; (use) largement répandu(e) ; **he's travelled** ~ly il a beaucoup voyagé ; ~ **travelling** déplacements fréquents et prolongés.

**extent** [ɪk'stɛnt] *n* étendue *f*; **to some ~**
dans une certaine mesure; **to what ~?**
dans quelle mesure?, jusqu'à quel point?
**exterior** [ɛk'stɪərɪə*] *a* extérieur(e), du
dehors // *n* extérieur *m*; dehors *m*.
**exterminate** [ɪk'stə:mɪneɪt] *vt*
exterminer; **extermination** [-'neɪʃən] *n*
extermination *f*.
**external** [ɛk'stə:nl] *a* externe; **~ly** *ad*
extérieurement.
**extinct** [ɪk'stɪŋkt] *a* éteint(e); **~ion**
[ɪk'stɪŋkʃən] *n* extinction *f*.
**extinguish** [ɪk'stɪŋgwɪʃ] *vt* éteindre; **~er**
*n* extincteur *m*.
**extol** [ɪk'stəul] *vt* porter aux nues, chanter
les louanges de.
**extort** [ɪk'stɔ:t] *vt*: **to ~ sth (from)**
extorquer qch (à); **~ion** [ɪk'stɔ:ʃən] *n*
extorsion *f*; **~ionate** [ɪk'stɔ:ʃnət] *a*
exorbitant(e).
**extra** ['ɛkstrə] *a* supplémentaire, de plus
// *ad* (*in addition*) en plus // *n* supplément
*m*; (THEATRE) figurant/e.
**extra...** ['ɛkstrə] *prefix* extra... .
**extract** *vt* [ɪk'strækt] extraire; (*tooth*)
arracher; (*money, promise*) soutirer // *n*
['ɛkstrækt] extrait *m*; **~ion** [ɪk'strækʃən]
*n* (*also descent*) extraction *f*.
**extradite** ['ɛkstrədaɪt] *vt* extrader;
**extradition** [-'dɪʃən] *n* extradition *f*.
**extramarital** [ɛkstrə'mærɪtl] *a* extra-
conjugal(e).
**extramural** [ɛkstrə'mjuərl] *a* hors-faculté
*inv*.
**extraneous** [ɛk'streɪnɪəs] *a*: **~ to**
étranger(ère) à.
**extraordinary** [ɪk'strɔ:dnrɪ] *a*
extraordinaire.
**extra time** [ɛkstrə'taɪm] *n* (FOOTBALL)
prolongations *fpl*.
**extravagant** [ɪk'strævəgənt] *a*
extravagant(e); (*in spending*) prodigue,
dépensier(ère); dispendieux(euse).
**extreme** [ɪk'stri:m] *a,n* extrême (*m*); **~ly**
*ad* extrêmement; **extremist** *a,n*
extrémiste (*m/f*).
**extremity** [ɪk'strɛmətɪ] *n* extrémité *f*.
**extricate** ['ɛkstrɪkeɪt] *vt*: **to ~ sth (from)**
dégager qch (de).
**extrovert** ['ɛkstrəvə:t] *n* extraverti/e.
**exuberant** [ɪg'zju:bərnt] *a* exubérant(e).
**exude** [ɪg'zju:d] *vt* exsuder; (*fig*) respirer;
**the charm** *etc* **he ~s** le charme *etc* qui
émane de lui.
**exult** [ɪg'zʌlt] *vi* exulter, jubiler.
**eye** [aɪ] *n* œil *m* (*pl* yeux); (*of needle*) trou
*m*, chas *m* // *vt* examiner; **to keep an ~**
**on** surveiller; **in the public ~** en vue;
**~ball** *n* globe *m* oculaire; **~bath** *n* œillère
*f* (*pour bains d'œil*); **~brow** *n* sourcil *m*;
**~-catching** *a* voyant(e),
accrocheur(euse); **~drops** *npl* gouttes *fpl*
pour les yeux; **~glass** *n* monocle *m*;
**~lash** *n* cil *m*; **~let** ['aɪlɪt] *n* œillet *m*;
**~lid** *n* paupière *f*; **~opener** *n* révélation
*f*; **~shadow** *n* ombre *f* à paupières;
**~sight** *n* vue *f*; **~sore** *n* horreur *f*, chose
*f* qui dépare or enlaidit; **~wash** *n* bain
*m* d'œil; (*fig*) frime *f*; **~ witness** *n* témoin
*m* oculaire.

**eyrie** ['ɪərɪ] *n* aire *f*.

**F** [ɛf] *n* (MUS) fa *m*.
**F.** *abbr of* Fahrenheit.
**fable** ['feɪbl] *n* fable *f*.
**fabric** ['fæbrɪk] *n* tissu *m*.
**fabrication** [fæbrɪ'keɪʃən] *n* invention(s)
*f(pl)*, fabulation *f*; fait *m* (*or* preuve *f*)
forgé(e) de toutes pièces.
**fabulous** ['fæbjuləs] *a* fabuleux(euse);
(*col: super*) formidable, sensationnel(le).
**façade** [fə'sɑ:d] *n* façade *f*.
**face** [feɪs] *n* visage *m*, figure *f*; expression
*f*; grimace *f*; (*of clock*) cadran *m*; (*of
building*) façade *f*; (*side, surface*) face *f* //
*vt* faire face à; **to lose ~** perdre la face;
**to pull a ~** faire une grimace; **in the ~**
**of** (*difficulties etc*) face à, devant; **on the**
**~ of it** à première vue; **to ~ up to** *vt*
*fus* faire face à, affronter; **~ cloth** *n* gant
*m* de toilette; **~ cream** *n* crème *f* pour
le visage; **~ lift** *n* lifting *m*; (*of façade etc*)
ravalement *m*, retapage *m*; **~ powder** *n*
poudre *f* (pour le visage).
**facet** ['fæsɪt] *n* facette *f*.
**facetious** [fə'si:ʃəs] *a* facétieux(euse).
**face-to-face** ['feɪstə'feɪs] *ad* face à face.
**face value** ['feɪs'vælju:] *n* (*of coin*) valeur
nominale; **to take sth at ~** (*fig*) prendre
qch pour argent comptant.
**facia** ['feɪʃə] *n* = **fascia**.
**facial** ['feɪʃəl] *a* facial(e).
**facile** ['fæsaɪl] *a* facile.
**facilitate** [fə'sɪlɪteɪt] *vt* faciliter.
**facility** [fə'sɪlɪtɪ] *n* facilité *f*; **facilities** *npl*
installations *fpl*, équipement *m*.
**facing** ['feɪsɪŋ] *n* (*of wall etc*) revêtement
*m*; (SEWING) revers *m*.
**facsimile** [fæk'sɪmɪlɪ] *n* fac-similé *m*.
**fact** [fækt] *n* fait *m*; **in ~** en fait.
**faction** ['fækʃən] *n* faction *f*.
**factor** ['fæktə*] *n* facteur *m*.
**factory** ['fæktərɪ] *n* usine *f*, fabrique *f*.
**factual** ['fæktjuəl] *a* basé(e) sur les faits.
**faculty** ['fækəltɪ] *n* faculté *f*; (*US: teaching
staff*) corps enseignant.
**fad** [fæd] *n* manie *f*; engouement *m*.
**fade** [feɪd] *vi* se décolorer, passer; (*light,
sound, hope*) s'affaiblir, disparaître;
(*flower*) se faner.
**fag** [fæg] *n* (*col: cigarette*) sèche *f*; (: *chore*):
**what a ~!** quelle corvée!; **~ end** *n* mégot
*m*; **~ged out** *a* (*col*) crevé(e).
**fail** [feɪl] *vt* (*exam*) échouer à; (*candidate*)
recaler; (*subj: courage, memory*) faire
défaut à // *vi* échouer; (*supplies*)
manquer; (*eyesight, health, light*) baisser,
s'affaiblir; **to ~ to do sth** (*neglect*)
négliger de faire qch; (*be unable*) ne pas
arriver *or* parvenir à faire qch; **without**
**~** à coup sûr; sans faute; **~ing** *n* défaut
*m* // *prep* faute de; **~ure** ['feɪljə*] *n* échec
*m*; (*person*) raté/e; (*mechanical etc*)
défaillance *f*.
**faint** [feɪnt] *a* faible; (*recollection*) vague;
(*mark*) à peine visible // *n* évanouissement
*m* // *vi* s'évanouir; **to feel ~** défaillir; **~-
hearted** *a* pusillanime; **~ly** *ad*

faiblement ;    vaguement ;    **~ness** *n* faiblesse *f*.

**fair** [fɛə*] *a* blond(e) ; équitable, juste, impartial(e) ; *(skin, complexion)* pâle, blanc(blanche) ; *(weather)* beau(belle) ; *(good enough)* assez bon(ne) ; *(sizeable)* considérable // *ad (play)* franc-jeu // *n* foire *f* ; **~ copy** *n* copie *f* au propre ; corrigé *m* ; **~ly** *ad* équitablement ; *(quite)* assez ; **~ness** *n* justice *f*, équité *f*, impartialité *f*.

**fairy** ['fɛərɪ] *n* fée *f* ; **~ tale** *n* conte *m* de fées.

**faith** [feɪθ] *n* foi *f* ; *(trust)* confiance *f* ; *(sect)* culte *m*, religion *f* ; **~ful** *a* fidèle ; **~fully** *ad* fidèlement.

**fake** [feɪk] *n* *(painting etc)* faux *m* ; *(photo)* trucage *m* ; *(person)* imposteur *m* // *a* faux(fausse) ; simulé(e) // *vt* simuler ; *(photo)* truquer ; *(story)* fabriquer ; **his illness is a ~** sa maladie est une comédie *or* de la simulation.

**falcon** ['fɔːlkən] *n* faucon *m*.

**fall** [fɔːl] *n* chute *f* ; *(US: autumn)* automne *m* // *vi (pt* **fell,** *pp* **fallen** [fɛl, 'fɔːlən]) tomber ; **~s** *npl (waterfall)* chute *f* d'eau, cascade *f* ; **to ~ flat** *vi (on one's face)* tomber de tout son long, s'étaler ; *(joke)* tomber à plat ; *(plan)* échouer ; **to ~ back on** *vt fus* se rabattre sur ; **to ~ behind** *vi* prendre du retard ; **to ~ down** *vi (person)* tomber ; *(building, hopes)* s'effondrer, s'écrouler ; **to ~ for** *vt fus (trick)* se laisser prendre à ; *(person)* tomber amoureux . de ; **to ~ in** *vi* s'effondrer ; (MIL) se mettre en rangs ; **to ~ off** *vi* tomber ; *(diminish)* baisser, diminuer ; **to ~ out** *vi (friends etc)* se brouiller ; **to ~ through** *vi (plan, project)* tomber à l'eau.

**fallacy** ['fæləsɪ] *n* erreur *f*, illusion *f*.

**fallen** ['fɔːlən] *pp of* **fall.**

**fallible** ['fæləbl] *a* faillible.

**fallout**    ['fɔːlaut]    *n*    retombées (radioactives).

**fallow** ['fæləu] *a* en jachère ; en friche.

**false** [fɔːls] *a* faux(fausse) ; **under ~ pretences** sous un faux prétexte ; **~ alarm** *n* fausse alerte ; **~hood** *n* mensonge *m* ; **~ly** *ad (accuse)* à tort ; **~ teeth** *npl* fausses dents.

**falter** ['fɔːltə*] *vi* chanceler, vaciller.

**fame** [feɪm] *n* renommée *f*, renom *m*.

**familiar** [fə'mɪlɪə*] *a* familier(ère) ; **to be ~ with** *(subject)* connaître ; **~ity** [fəmɪlɪ'ærɪtɪ] *n* familiarité *f* ; **~ize** [fə'mɪlɪəraɪz] *vt* familiariser.

**family** ['fæmɪlɪ] *n* famille *f* ; **~ allowance** *n* allocations familiales ; **~ business** *n* entreprise familiale ; **~ doctor** *n* médecin *m* de famille ; **~ life** *n* vie *f* de famille.

**famine** ['fæmɪn] *n* famine *f*.

**famished** ['fæmɪʃt] *a* affamé(e).

**famous** ['feɪməs] *a* célèbre ; **~ly** *ad (get on)* fameusement, à merveille.

**fan** [fæn] *n (folding)* éventail *m* ; (ELEC) ventilateur *m* ; *(person)* fan *m*, admirateur/trice ; supporter *m/f* // *vt* éventer ; *(fire, quarrel)* attiser ; **to ~ out** *vi* se déployer (en éventail).

**fanatic** [fə'nætɪk] *n* fanatique *m/f* ; **~al** *a* fanatique.

**fan belt** ['fænbɛlt] *n* courroie *f* de ventilateur.

**fancied** ['fænsɪd] *a* imaginaire.

**fanciful** ['fænsɪful] *a* fantaisiste.

**fancy** ['fænsɪ] *n* fantaisie *f*, envie *f* ; imagination *f* // *cpd* (de) fantaisie *inv* // *vt (feel like, want)* avoir envie de ; **to take a ~ to** se prendre d'affection pour ; s'enticher de ; **it took** *or* **caught my ~** ça m'a plu ; **to ~ that ...** se figurer *or* s'imaginer que ... ; **he fancies her** elle lui plaît ; **~ dress** *n* déguisement *m*, travesti *m* ; **~-dress ball** *n* bal masqué *or* costumé.

**fang** [fæŋ] *n* croc *m* ; *(of snake)* crochet *m*.

**fanlight** ['fænlaɪt] *n* imposte *f*.

**fantastic** [fæn'tæstɪk] *a* fantastique.

**fantasy** ['fæntəzɪ] *n* imagination *f*, fantaisie *f* ; fantasme *m* ; chimère *f*.

**far** [fɑː*] *a*: **the ~ side/end** l'autre côté/bout // *ad* loin ; **~ away, ~ off** au loin, dans le lointain ; **~ better** beaucoup mieux ; **~ from** loin de ; **by ~** de loin, de beaucoup ; **go as ~ as the farm** allez jusqu'à la ferme ; **as ~ as I know** pour autant que je sache ; **as ~ as possible** dans la mesure du possible ; **~away** *a* lointain(e).

**farce** [fɑːs] *n* farce *f*.

**farcical** ['fɑːsɪkəl] *a* grotesque.

**fare** [fɛə*] *n (on trains, buses)* prix *m* du billet ; *(in taxi)* prix de la course ; *(passenger in taxi)* client *m* ; *(food)* table *f*, chère *f* // *vi* se débrouiller.

**Far East** [fɑː'riːst] *n*: **the ~** l'Extrême-Orient *m*.

**farewell** [fɛə'wɛl] *excl, n* adieu *m* ; **~ party** *n* soirée *f* d'adieux.

**far-fetched** ['fɑː'fɛtʃt] *a* exagéré(e), poussé(e).

**farm** [fɑːm] *n* ferme *f* // *vt* cultiver ; **~er** *n* fermier/ère ; cultivateur/trice ; **~hand** *n* ouvrier/ère agricole ; **~house** *n* (maison *f* de) ferme *f* ; **~ing** *n* agriculture *f* ; **intensive ~ing** culture intensive ; **~land** *n* terres cultivées *or* arables ; **~ worker** *n* = **~hand** ; **~yard** *n* cour *f* de ferme.

**far-reaching** ['fɑː'riːtʃɪŋ] *a* d'une grande portée.

**far-sighted** ['fɑː'saɪtɪd] *a* presbyte ; *(fig)* prévoyant(e), qui voit loin.

**fart** [fɑːt] *(col!)* *n* pet *m* // *vi* péter.

**farther** ['fɑːðə*] *ad* plus loin.

**farthest** ['fɑːðɪst] *superlative of* **far.**

**fascia** ['feɪʃə] *n* (AUT) (garniture *f* du) tableau *m* de bord.

**fascinate** ['fæsɪneɪt] *vt* fasciner, captiver ; **fascination** [-'neɪʃən] *n* fascination *f*.

**fascism** ['fæʃɪzəm] *n* fascisme *m*.

**fascist** ['fæʃɪst] *a,n* fasciste (*m/f*).

**fashion** ['fæʃən] *n* mode *f* ; *(manner)* façon *f*, manière *f* // *vt* façonner ; **in ~** à la mode ; **out of ~** démodé(e) ; **~able** *a* à la mode ; **~ show** *n* défilé *m* de mannequins *or* de mode.

**fast** [fɑːst] *a* rapide ; *(clock)*: **to be ~** avancer ; *(dye, colour)* grand *or* bon teint *inv* // *ad* vite, rapidement ; *(stuck, held)* solidement // *n* jeûne *m* // *vi* jeûner ; **~ asleep** profondément endormi.

**fasten** ['fɑ:sn]. *vt* attacher, fixer ; (*coat*) attacher, fermer // *vi* se fermer, s'attacher ; ~**er**, ~**ing** *n* fermeture *f*, attache *f*.

**fastidious** [fæs'tıdıəs] *a* exigeant(e), difficile.

**fat** [fæt] *a* gros(se) // *n* graisse *f*; (*on meat*) gras *m*.

**fatal** ['feıtl] *a* mortel(le) ; fatal(e) ; désastreux(euse) ; ~**ism** *n* fatalisme *m*; ~**ity** [fə'tælıtı] *n* (*road death etc*) victime *f*, décès *m*; ~**ly** *ad* mortellement.

**fate** [feıt] *n* destin *m*; (*of person*) sort *m*; **to meet one's** ~ trouver la mort ; ~**ful** *a* fatidique.

**father** ['fɑ:ðə*] *n* père *m*; ~**-in-law** *n* beau-père *m*; ~**ly** *a* paternel(le).

**fathom** ['fæðəm] *n* brasse *f* (= *1828 mm*) // *vt* (*mystery*) sonder, pénétrer.

**fatigue** [fə'ti:g] *n* fatigue *f*; (*MIL*) corvée *f*.

**fatness** ['fætnıs] *n* corpulence *f*, grosseur *f*.

**fatten** ['fætn] *vt,vi* engraisser.

**fatty** ['fætı] *a* (*food*) gras(se).

**fatuous** ['fætjuəs] *a* stupide.

**faucet** ['fɔ:sıt] *n* (*US*) robinet *m*.

**fault** [fɔ:lt] *n* faute *f*; (*defect*) défaut *m*; (*GEO*) faille *f* // *vt* trouver des défauts à, prendre en défaut ; **it's my** ~ c'est de ma faute ; **to find** ~ **with** trouver à redire *or* à critiquer à ; **at** ~ fautif(ive), coupable ; **to a** ~ à l'excès ; ~**less** *a* sans fautes ; impeccable ; irréprochable ; ~**y** *a* défectueux(euse).

**fauna** ['fɔ:nə] *n* faune *f*.

**favour, favor** (*US*) ['feıvə*] *n* faveur *f*; (*help*) service *m* // *vt* (*proposition*) être en faveur de ; (*pupil etc*) favoriser ; (*team, horse*) donner gagnant ; **to do sb a** ~ rendre un service à qn ; **in** ~ **of** en faveur de ; ~**able** *a* favorable ; (*price*) avantageux(euse) ; ~**ably** *ad* favorablement ; ~**ite** [-rıt] *a,n* favori(te) ; ~**itism** *n* favoritisme *m*.

**fawn** [fɔ:n] *n* faon *m* // *a* (*also:* ~**-coloured**) fauve // *vi*: **to** ~ (**up**)**on** flatter servilement.

**fear** [fıə*] *n* crainte *f*, peur *f* // *vt* craindre ; **for** ~ **of** de peur que + *sub or* de + *infinitive* ; ~**ful** *a* craintif(ive) ; (*sight, noise*) affreux(euse), épouvantable ; ~**less** *a* intrépide, sans peur.

**feasibility** [fi:zə'bılıtı] *n* (*of plan*) possibilité *f* de réalisation.

**feasible** ['fi:zəbl] *a* faisable, réalisable.

**feast** [fi:st] *n* festin *m*, banquet *m*; (*REL: also:* ~ **day**) fête *f* // *vi* festoyer ; **to** ~ **on** se régaler de.

**feat** [fi:t] *n* exploit *m*, prouesse *f*.

**feather** ['feðə*] *n* plume *f*; ~**-weight** *n* poids *m* plume *inv*.

**feature** ['fi:tʃə*] *n* caractéristique *f*; (*article*) chronique *f*, rubrique *f* // *vt* (*subj: film*) avoir pour vedette(s) // *vi* figurer (en bonne place) ; ~**s** *npl* (*of face*) traits *mpl*; ~ **film** *n* film principal ; ~**less** *a* anonyme, sans traits distinctifs.

**February** ['februərı] *n* février *m*.

**fed** [fɛd] *pt,pp* of **feed** ; **to be** ~ **up** en avoir marre *or* plein le dos.

**federal** ['fɛdərəl] *a* fédéral(e).

**federation** [fɛdə'reıʃən] *n* fédération *f*.

**fee** [fi:] *n* rémunération *f*; (*of doctor, lawyer*) honoraires *mpl*; (*of school, college etc*) frais *mpl* de scolarité ; (*for examination*) droits *mpl*.

**feeble** ['fi:bl] *a* faible ; ~**-minded** *a* faible d'esprit.

**feed** [fi:d] *n* (*of baby*) tétée *f* // *vt* (*pt, pp* **fed** [fɛd]) nourrir ; (*horse etc*) donner à manger à ; (*machine*) alimenter ; (*data, information*): **to** ~ **into** fournir à ; **to** ~ **on** *vt fus* se nourrir de ; ~**back** *n* feedback *m*; ~**ing bottle** *n* biberon *m*.

**feel** [fi:l] *n* sensation *f* // *vt* (*pt, pp* **felt** [fɛlt]) toucher, tâter, palper ; (*cold, pain*) sentir ; (*grief, anger*) ressentir, éprouver ; (*think, believe*): **to** ~ (**that**) trouver que ; **to** ~ **hungry/cold** avoir faim/froid ; **to** ~ **lonely/better** se sentir seul/mieux ; **to** ~ **sorry for** avoir pitié de ; **it** ~**s soft** c'est doux au toucher ; **it** ~**s like velvet** on dirait du velours, ça ressemble au velours ; **to** ~ **like** (*want*) avoir envie de ; **to** ~ **about** *or* **around** fouiller, tâtonner ; ~**er** *n* (*of insect*) antenne *f*; **to put out a** ~**er** tâter le terrain ; ~**ing** *n* sensation *f*; sentiment *m*; **my** ~**ing is that...** j'estime que... .

**feet** [fi:t] *npl* of **foot**.

**feign** [feın] *vt* feindre, simuler.

**felicitous** [fı'lısıtəs] *a* heureux(euse).

**fell** [fɛl] *pt* of **fall** // *vt* (*tree*) abattre ; (*person*) assommer ; ~**-walking** *n* randonnée *f* en montagne.

**fellow** ['fɛləu] *n* type *m*; compagnon *m*; (*of learned society*) membre *m*; **their** ~ **prisoners/students** leurs camarades prisonniers/étudiants ; ~ **citizen** *n* concitoyen/ne ; ~ **countryman** *n* compatriote *m*; ~ **men** *npl* semblables *mpl*; ~**ship** *n* association *f*; amitié *f*, camaraderie *f*; sorte de bourse universitaire.

**felony** ['fɛlənı] *n* crime *m*, forfait *m*.

**felt** [fɛlt] *pt, pp* of **feel** // *n* feutre *m*; ~**-tip pen** *n* stylo-feutre *m*.

**female** ['fi:meıl] *n* (*ZOOL*) femelle *f*; (*pej: woman*) bonne femme // *a* (*BIOL, ELEC*) femelle ; (*sex, character*) féminin(e) ; (*vote etc*) des femmes ; (*child etc*) du sexe féminin ; **male and** ~ **students** étudiants et étudiantes ; ~ **impersonator** *n* travesti *m*.

**feminine** ['fɛmının] *a* féminin(e) // *n* féminin *m*.

**feminist** ['fɛmınıst] *n* féministe *m/f*.

**fence** [fɛns] *n* barrière *f*; (*col: person*) receleur/euse // *vt* (*also:* ~ **in**) clôturer // *vi* faire de l'escrime ; **fencing** *n* escrime *m*.

**fend** [fɛnd] *vi*: **to** ~ **for o.s.** se débrouiller (tout seul).

**fender** ['fɛndə*] *n* garde-feu *m inv*; (*US*) gardeboue *m inv*; pare-chocs *m inv*.

**ferment** *vi* [fə'mɛnt] fermenter // *n* ['fə:mɛnt] agitation *f*, effervescence *f*; ~**ation** [-'teıʃən] *n* fermentation *f*.

**fern** [fə:n] *n* fougère *f*.

**ferocious** [fə'rəuʃəs] *a* féroce.

**ferocity** [fə'rɔsıtı] *n* férocité *f*.

**ferry** ['fɛrı] *n* (*small*) bac *m*; (*large: also:* ~**boat**) ferry(-boat) *m* // *vt* transporter.

**fertile** ['fə:taɪl] *a* fertile ; (*BIOL*) fécond(e) ; **~ period** *n* période *f* de fécondité ; **fertility** [fə'tɪlɪtɪ] *n* fertilité *f* ; fécondité *f* ; **fertilize** ['fə:tɪlaɪz] *vt* fertiliser ; féconder ; **fertilizer** *n* engrais *m*.

**fervent** ['fə:vənt] *a* fervent(e), ardent(e).

**fester** ['fɛstə*] *vi* suppurer.

**festival** ['fɛstɪvəl] *n* (*REL*) fête *f* ; (*ART, MUS*) festival *m*.

**festive** ['fɛstɪv] *a* de fête ; **the ~ season** (*Christmas*) la période des fêtes.

**festivities** [fɛs'tɪvɪtɪz] *npl* réjouissances *fpl*.

**fetch** [fɛtʃ] *vt* aller chercher ; (*sell for*) se vendre.

**fetching** ['fɛtʃɪŋ] *a* charmant(e).

**fête** [feɪt] *n* fête *f*, kermesse *f*.

**fetish** ['fɛtɪʃ] *n* fétiche *m*.

**fetters** ['fɛtəz] *npl* chaînes *fpl*.

**fetus** ['fi:təs] *n* (*US*) = **foetus.**

**feud** [fju:d] *n* dispute *f*, dissension *f* // *vi* se disputer, se quereller ; **~al** *a* féodal(e) ; **~alism** *n* féodalité *f*.

**fever** ['fi:və*] *n* fièvre *f* ; **~ish** *a* fiévreux(euse), fébrile.

**few** [fju:] *a* peu de ; **they were ~** ils étaient peu (nombreux) ; **a ~** *a* quelques // *pronoun* quelques-uns ; **~er** *a* moins de ; moins (nombreux) ; **~est** *a* le moins nombreux.

**fiancé** [fɪ'ɑ̃:ŋseɪ] *n* fiancé *m* ; **~e** *n* fiancée *f*.

**fiasco** [fɪ'æskəu] *n* fiasco *m*.

**fib** [fɪb] *n* bobard *m*.

**fibre, fiber** (*US*) ['faɪbə*] *n* fibre *f* ; **~-glass** *n* fibre de verre.

**fickle** ['fɪkl] *a* inconstant(e), volage, capricieux(euse).

**fiction** ['fɪkʃən] *n* romans *mpl*, littérature *f* romanesque ; fiction *f* ; **~al** *a* fictif(ive).

**fictitious** [fɪk'tɪʃəs] *a* fictif(ive), imaginaire.

**fiddle** ['fɪdl] *n* (*MUS*) violon *m* ; (*cheating*) combine *f* ; escroquerie *f* // *vt* (*accounts*) falsifier, maquiller ; **to ~ with** *vt fus* tripoter ; **~r** *n* violoniste *m/f*.

**fidelity** [fɪ'dɛlɪtɪ] *n* fidélité *f*.

**fidget** ['fɪdʒɪt] *vi* se trémousser, remuer ; **~y** *a* agité(e), qui a la bougeotte.

**field** [fi:ld] *n* champ *m* ; (*fig*) domaine *m*, champ *m* ; (*SPORT: ground*) terrain *m* ; **~ glasses** *npl* jumelles *fpl* ; **~ marshal** *n* maréchal *m* ; **~work** *n* travaux *mpl* pratiques (sur le terrain).

**fiend** [fi:nd] *n* démon *m* ; **~ish** *a* diabolique.

**fierce** [fɪəs] *a* (*look*) féroce, sauvage ; (*wind, attack*) (très) violent(e) ; (*fighting, enemy*) acharné(e).

**fiery** ['faɪərɪ] *a* ardent(e), brûlant(e) ; fougueux(euse).

**fifteen** [fɪf'ti:n] *num* quinze.

**fifth** [fɪfθ] *num* cinquième.

**fiftieth** ['fɪftɪθ] *num* cinquantième.

**fifty** ['fɪftɪ] *num* cinquante.

**fig** [fɪg] *n* figue *f*.

**fight** [faɪt] *n* bagarre *f* ; (*MIL*) combat *m* ; (*against cancer etc*) lutte *f* // *vb* (*pt, pp* **fought** [fɔ:t]) *vt* se battre contre ; (*cancer, alcoholism*) combattre, lutter contre // *vi*
se battre ; **~er** *n* lutteur *m* (*fig*) ; (*plane*) chasseur *m* ; **~ing** *n* combats *mpl*.

**figment** ['fɪgmənt] *n*: **a ~ of the imagination** une invention.

**figurative** ['fɪgjurətɪv] *a* figuré(e).

**figure** ['fɪgə*] *n* (*DRAWING, GEOM*) figure *f* ; (*number, cipher*) chiffre *m* ; (*body, outline*) silhouette *f*, ligne *f*, formes *fpl* // *vt* (*US*) supposer // *vi* (*appear*) figurer ; (*US: make sense*) s'expliquer ; **to ~ out** *vt* arriver à comprendre ; calculer ; **~head** *n* (*NAUT*) figure *f* de proue ; (*pej*) prête-nom *m* ; **figure skating** *n* figures imposées (*en patinage*).

**filament** ['fɪləmənt] *n* filament *m*.

**file** [faɪl] *n* (*tool*) lime *f* ; (*dossier*) dossier *m* ; (*folder*) classeur *m* ; (*row*) file *f* // *vt* (*nails, wood*) limer ; (*papers*) classer ; (*LAW: claim*) faire enregistrer ; déposer ; **to ~ in/out** *vi* entrer/sortir l'un derrière l'autre ; **to ~ past** *vt fus* défiler devant.

**filing** ['faɪlɪŋ] *n* (*travaux mpl* de) classement *m* ; **~s** *npl* limaille *f* ; **~ cabinet** *n* classeur *m* (*meuble*).

**fill** [fɪl] *vt* remplir // *n*: **to eat one's ~** manger à sa faim ; **to ~ in** *vt* (*hole*) boucher ; (*form*) remplir ; **to ~ up** *vt* remplir // *vi* (*AUT*) faire le plein ; **~ it up, please** (*AUT*) le plein, s'il vous plaît.

**fillet** ['fɪlɪt] *n* filet *m* // *vt* préparer en filets.

**filling** ['fɪlɪŋ] *n* (*CULIN*) garniture *f*, farce *f* ; (*for tooth*) plombage *m* ; **~ station** *n* station *f* d'essence.

**fillip** ['fɪlɪp] *n* coup *m* de fouet (*fig*).

**film** [fɪlm] *n* film *m* ; (*PHOT*) pellicule *f*, film *m* // *vt* (*scene*) filmer ; **~ star** *n* vedette *f* de cinéma ; **~strip** *n* (*film* *m* pour) projection *f* fixe.

**filter** ['fɪltə*] *n* filtre *m* // *vt* filtrer ; **~ lane** *n* (*AUT*) voie *f* de sortie ; **~ tip** *n* bout *m* filtre.

**filth** [fɪlθ] *n* saleté *f* ; **~y** *a* sale, dégoûtant(e) ; (*language*) ordurier (ère), grossier(ère).

**fin** [fɪn] *n* (*of fish*) nageoire *f*.

**final** ['faɪnl] *a* final(e), dernier(ère) ; définitif(ive) // *n* (*SPORT*) finale *f* ; **~s** *npl* (*SCOL*) examens *mpl* de dernière année ; **~e** [fɪ'nɑ:lɪ] *n* finale *m* ; **~ist** *n* (*SPORT*) finaliste *m/f* ; **~ize** *vt* mettre au point ; **~ly** *ad* (*lastly*) en dernier lieu ; (*eventually*) enfin, finalement ; (*irrevocably*) définitivement.

**finance** [faɪ'næns] *n* finance *f* ; **~s** *npl* finances *fpl* // *vt* financer.

**financial** [faɪ'nænʃəl] *a* financier (ère) ; **~ly** *ad* financièrement ; **~ year** *n* année *f* budgétaire.

**financier** [faɪ'nænsɪə*] *n* financier *m*.

**find** [faɪnd] *vt* (*pt, pp* **found** [faund]) trouver ; (*lost object*) retrouver // *n* trouvaille *f*, découverte *f* ; **to ~ sb guilty** (*LAW*) déclarer qn coupable ; **to ~ out** *vt* se renseigner sur ; (*truth, secret*) découvrir ; (*person*) démasquer ; **to ~ out about** se renseigner sur ; (*by chance*) apprendre ; **~ings** *npl* (*LAW*) conclusions *fpl*, verdict *m* ; (*of report*) constatations *fpl*.

**fine** [faɪn] *a* beau(belle) ; excellent(e) ; fin(e) // *ad* (*well*) très bien ; (*small*) fin, finement // *n* (*LAW*) amende *f* ; contravention *f* // *vt* (*LAW*) condamner à

une amende ; donner une contravention à ;
~ **arts** npl beaux-arts mpl.
**finery** ['faɪnərɪ] n parure f.
**finesse** [fɪ'nɛs] n finesse f.
**finger** ['fɪŋgə*] n doigt m // vt palper,
toucher ; ~**nail** n ongle m (de la main);
~**print** n empreinte digitale ; ~**stall** n
doigtier m ; ~**tip** n bout m du doigt.
**finicky** ['fɪnɪkɪ] a tatillon(ne),
méticuleux(euse) ; minutieux(euse).
**finish** ['fɪnɪʃ] n fin f; (SPORT) arrivée f;
(polish etc) finition f // vt finir, terminer
// vi finir, se terminer ; (session)
s'achever ; **to** ~ **off** vt finir, terminer ;
(kill) achever ; **to** ~ **up** vi,vt finir ; ~**ing
line** n ligne f d'arrivée ; ~**ing school** n
institution privée (pour jeunes filles).
**finite** ['faɪnaɪt] a fini(e) ; (verb) conju-
gué(e).
**Finland** ['fɪnlənd] n Finlande f.
**Finn** [fɪn] n Finnois/e ; Finlandais/e ;
~**ish** a finnois(e) ; finlandais(e) // n (LING)
finnois m.
**fiord** [fjɔːd] n fjord m.
**fir** [fə:*] n sapin m.
**fire** ['faɪə*] n feu m; incendie m // vt
(discharge): **to** ~ **a gun** tirer un coup de
feu ; (fig) enflammer, animer ; (dismiss)
mettre à la porte, renvoyer // vi tirer, faire
feu ; **on** ~ en feu ; ~ **alarm** n avertisseur
m d'incendie ; ~**arm** n arme f à feu ; ~
**brigade** n (régiment m de
sapeurs-)pompiers mpl ; ~ **engine** n
pompe f à incendie ; ~ **escape** n escalier
m de secours ; ~ **extinguisher** n
extincteur m ; ~**man** n pompier m ; ~
**master** n capitaine m des pompiers ;
~**place** n cheminée f; ~**proof** a ignifuge ;
~**side** n foyer m, coin m du feu ; ~ **station**
n caserne f de pompiers ; ~**wood** n bois
m de chauffage ; ~**work** n feu m
d'artifice ; ~**works** npl (display) feu(x)
d'artifice.
**firing** ['faɪərɪŋ] n (MIL) feu m, tir m ; ~
**squad** n peloton m d'exécution.
**firm** [fə:m] a ferme // n compagnie f, firme
f; ~**ly** ad fermement ; ~**ness** n fermeté
f.
**first** [fə:st] a premier(ère) // ad (before
others) le premier, la première ; (before
other things) en premier, d'abord ; (when
listing reasons etc) en premier lieu,
premièrement // n (person: in race)
premier/ère ; (SCOL) mention f très bien ;
(AUT) première f; **at** ~ au commencement,
au début ; ~ **of all** tout d'abord, pour
commencer ; ~ **aid** premiers secours or
soins ; ~**-aid kit** n trousse f à pharmacie ;
~**-class** a de première classe ; ~**-hand** a
de première main ; ~ **lady** n (US) femme
f du président ; ~**ly** ad premièrement, en
premier lieu ; ~ **name** n prénom m ; ~
**night** n (THEATRE) première f; ~**-rate** a
excellent(e).
**fir tree** ['fə:triː] n sapin m.
**fiscal** ['fɪskəl] a fiscal(e).
**fish** [fɪʃ] n,pl inv poisson m ; poissons mpl
// vt,vi pêcher ; **to** ~ **a river** pêcher dans
une rivière ; **to go** ~**ing** aller à la pêche ;
~**erman** n pêcheur m ; ~**ery** n pêcherie
f; ~ **fingers** npl bâtonnets de poisson
(congelés) ; ~ **hook** n hameçon m ; ~**ing**

**boat** n barque f de pêche ; ~**ing line** n
ligne f (de pêche) ; ~**ing rod** n canne f
à pêche ; ~**ing tackle** n attirail m de
pêche ; ~ **market** n marché m au poisson ;
~**monger** n marchand m de poisson ; ~
**slice** n pelle f à poisson ; ~**y** a (fig)
suspect(e), louche.
**fission** ['fɪʃən] n fission f.
**fissure** ['fɪʃə*] n fissure f.
**fist** [fɪst] n poing m.
**fit** [fɪt] a (MED, SPORT) en (bonne) forme ;
(proper) convenable ; approprié(e) // vt
(subj: clothes) aller à ; (adjust) ajuster ;
(put in, attach) installer, poser ; adapter ;
(equip) équiper, garnir, munir // vi
(clothes) aller ; (parts) s'adapter ; (in space,
gap) entrer, s'adapter // n (of coughing)
quinte f; ~ **to** en
état de ; ~ **for** digne de ; apte à ; **this
dress is a tight/good** ~ cette robe est
un peu juste/(me) va très bien ; **by** ~**s
and starts** par à-coups ; **to** ~ **in** vi
s'accorder ; s'adapter ; **to** ~ **out** (also: ~
**up**) vt équiper ; ~**ful** a intermittent(e) ;
~**ment** n meuble encastré, élément m ;
~**ness** n (MED) forme f physique ; (of
remark) à-propos m, justesse f; ~**ter** n
monteur m ; (DRESSMAKING) essayeur/euse ;
~**ting** a approprié(e) // n (of dress)
essayage m ; (of piece of equipment) pose
f, installation f; ~**tings** npl installations
fpl.
**five** [faɪv] num cinq ; ~**r** n (Brit: col) billet
m de cinq livres.
**fix** [fɪks] vt fixer ; arranger ; (mend) réparer
// n: **to be in a** ~ être dans le pétrin ;
~**ed** [fɪkst] a (prices etc) fixe ; ~**ture**
['fɪkstʃə*] n installation f (fixe) ; (SPORT)
rencontre f (au programme).
**fizz** [fɪz] vi pétiller.
**fizzle** ['fɪzl] vi pétiller ; **to** ~ **out** vi rater.
**fizzy** ['fɪzɪ] a pétillant(e) ; gazeux(euse).
**fjord** [fjɔːd] n = **fiord**.
**flabbergasted** ['flæbəgɑːstɪd] a sidéré(e),
ahuri(e).
**flabby** ['flæbɪ] a mou(molle).
**flag** [flæg] n drapeau m ; (also: ~**stone**)
dalle f // vi faiblir, fléchir ; **to** ~ **down**
vt héler, faire signe (de s'arrêter) à ; ~ **of
convenience** n pavillon m de
complaisance.
**flagon** ['flægən] n bonbonne f.
**flagpole** ['flægpəul] n mât m.
**flagrant** ['fleɪgrənt] a flagrant(e).
**flair** [flɛə*] n flair m.
**flake** [fleɪk] n (of rust, paint) écaille f; (of
snow, soap powder) flocon m // vi (also:
~ **off**) s'écailler.
**flamboyant** [flæm'bɔɪənt] a
flamboyant(e), éclatant(e) ; (person)
haut(e) en couleur.
**flame** [fleɪm] n flamme f.
**flamingo** [flə'mɪŋgəu] n flamant m (rose).
**flammable** ['flæməbl] a inflammable.
**flan** [flæn] n tarte f.
**Flanders** ['flɑːndəz] n Flandre(s) f(pl).
**flange** [flændʒ] n boudin m ; collerette f.
**flank** [flæŋk] n flanc m // vt flanquer.
**flannel** ['flænl] n (also: **face** ~) gant m
de toilette ; (fabric) flanelle f; (col) baratin
m ; ~**s** npl pantalon m de flanelle.

**flap** [flæp] n (of pocket, envelope) rabat m // vt (wings) battre (de) // vi (sail, flag) claquer ; (col: also: **be in a ~**) paniquer.

**flare** [flɛə*] n fusée éclairante ; (in skirt etc) évasement m ; **to ~ up** vi s'embraser ; (fig: person) se mettre en colère, s'emporter ; (: revolt) éclater ; **~d** a (trousers) à jambes évasées.

**flash** [flæʃ] n éclair m ; (also: **news ~**) flash m (d'information) ; (PHOT) flash m // vt (switch on) allumer (brièvement) ; (direct): **to ~ sth at** braquer qch sur ; (display) étaler, exhiber ; (send: message) câbler // vi briller ; jeter des éclairs ; (light on ambulance etc) clignoter ; **in a ~** en un clin d'œil ; **to ~ one's headlights** faire un appel de phares ; **he ~ed by** or **past** il passa (devant nous) comme un éclair ; **~back** n flashback m, retour m en arrière ; **~ bulb** n ampoule f de flash ; **~er** n (AUT) clignotant m.

**flashy** ['flæʃɪ] a (pej) tape-à-l'œil inv, tapageur(euse).

**flask** [flɑːsk] n flacon m, bouteille f ; (CHEM) ballon m ; (also: **vacuum ~**) bouteille f thermos ®.

**flat** [flæt] a plat(e) ; (tyre) dégonflé(e), à plat ; (denial) catégorique ; (MUS) bémolisé(e) // n (rooms) appartement m ; (MUS) bémol m ; (AUT) crevaison f, pneu crevé ; **to be ~-footed** avoir les pieds plats ; **~ly** ad catégoriquement ; **~ness** n (of land) absence f de relief, aspect plat ; **~ten** vt (also: **~ten out**) aplatir.

**flatter** ['flætə*] vt flatter ; **~er** n flatteur m ; **~ing** a flatteur(euse) ; **~y** n flatterie f.

**flatulence** ['flætjuləns] n flatulence f.

**flaunt** [flɔːnt] vt faire étalage de.

**flavour, flavor** (US) ['fleɪvə*] n goût m, saveur f ; (of ice cream etc) parfum m // vt parfumer, aromatiser ; **vanilla—-ed** à l'arôme de vanille, vanillé(e) ; **to give** or **add ~ to** donner du goût à, relever ; **~ing** n arôme m (synthétique).

**flaw** [flɔː] n défaut m ; **~less** a sans défaut.

**flax** [flæks] n lin m ; **~en** a blond(e).

**flea** [fliː] n puce f.

**fledg(e)ling** ['flɛdʒlɪŋ] n oisillon m.

**flee**, pt, pp **fled** [fliː, flɛd] vt fuir, s'enfuir de // vi fuir, s'enfuir.

**fleece** [fliːs] n toison f // vt (col) voler, filouter.

**fleet** [fliːt] n flotte f ; (of lorries etc) parc m ; convoi m.

**fleeting** ['fliːtɪŋ] a fugace, fugitif(ive) ; (visit) très bref(brève).

**Flemish** ['flɛmɪʃ] a flamand(e) // n (LING) flamand m ; **the ~** les Flamands.

**flesh** [flɛʃ] n chair f ; **~ wound** n blessure superficielle.

**flew** [fluː] pt of **fly.**

**flex** [flɛks] n fil m or câble m électrique (souple) // vt fléchir ; (muscles) tendre ; **~ibility** [-'bɪlɪtɪ] n flexibilité f ; **~ible** a flexible.

**flick** [flɪk] n petite tape ; chiquenaude f ; sursaut m ; **~ knife** n couteau m à cran d'arrêt ; **to ~ through** vt fus feuilleter.

**flicker** ['flɪkə*] vi vaciller // n vacillement m ; **a ~ of light** une brève lueur.

**flier** ['flaɪə*] n aviateur m.

**flight** [flaɪt] n vol m ; (escape) fuite f ; (also: **~ of steps**) escalier m ; **to take ~** prendre la fuite ; **to put to ~** mettre en fuite ; **~ deck** n (AVIAT) poste m de pilotage ; (NAUT) pont m d'envol.

**flimsy** ['flɪmzɪ] a (partition, fabric) peu solide, mince ; (excuse) pauvre, mince.

**flinch** [flɪntʃ] vi tressaillir ; **to ~ from** se dérober à, reculer devant.

**fling**, pt, pp **flung** [flɪŋ, flʌŋ] vt jeter, lancer.

**flint** [flɪnt] n silex m ; (in lighter) pierre f (à briquet).

**flip** [flɪp] n chiquenaude f.

**flippant** ['flɪpənt] a désinvolte, irrévérencieux(euse).

**flirt** [fləːt] vi flirter // n flirteuse f ; **~ation** [-'teɪʃən] n flirt m.

**flit** [flɪt] vi voleter.

**float** [fləut] n flotteur m ; (in procession) char m // vi flotter // vt faire flotter ; (loan, business) lancer ; **~ing** a flottant(e).

**flock** [flɔk] n troupeau m ; (of people) foule f.

**flog** [flɔg] vt fouetter.

**flood** [flʌd] n inondation f ; (of words, tears etc) flot m, torrent m // vt inonder ; **in ~** en crue ; **~ing** n inondation f ; **~light** n projecteur m // vt éclairer aux projecteurs, illuminer.

**floor** [flɔː*] n sol m ; (storey) étage m ; (fig: at meeting): **the ~** l'assemblée f, les membres mpl de l'assemblée // vt terrasser ; **on the ~** par terre ; **ground ~** (Brit), **first ~** (US) rez-de-chaussée m ; **first ~** (Brit), **second ~** (US) premier étage ; **~board** n planche f (du plancher) ; **~ show** n spectacle m de variétés.

**flop** [flɔp] n fiasco m // vi (fail) faire fiasco.

**floppy** ['flɔpɪ] a lâche, flottant(e) ; **~ hat** n chapeau m à bords flottants.

**flora** ['flɔːrə] n flore f.

**floral** ['flɔːrl] a floral(e).

**florid** ['flɔrɪd] a (complexion) fleuri(e) ; (style) plein(e) de fioritures.

**florist** ['flɔrɪst] n fleuriste m/f.

**flounce** [flauns] n volant m ; **to ~ out** vi sortir dans un mouvement d'humeur.

**flounder** ['flaundə*] vi patauger.

**flour** ['flauə*] n farine f.

**flourish** ['flʌrɪʃ] vi prospérer // vt brandir // n fioriture f ; (of trumpets) fanfare f ; **~ing** a prospère, florissant(e).

**flout** [flaut] vt se moquer de, faire fi de.

**flow** [fləu] n flot m ; courant m ; circulation f ; (tide) flux m // vi couler ; (traffic) s'écouler ; (robes, hair) flotter ; **~ chart** n organigramme m.

**flower** ['flauə*] n fleur f // vi fleurir ; **~ bed** n plate-bande f ; **~pot** n pot m (à fleurs) ; **~y** a fleuri(e).

**flown** [fləun] pp of **fly.**

**flu** [fluː] n grippe f.

**fluctuate** ['flʌktjueɪt] vi varier, fluctuer ; **fluctuation** [-'eɪʃən] n fluctuation f, variation f.

**fluency** ['fluːənsɪ] n facilité f, aisance f.

**fluent** ['fluːənt] a (speech) coulant(e), aisé(e) ; **he speaks ~ French, he's ~ in French** il parle le français couramment ;

~**ly** ad couramment ; avec aisance or facilité.

**fluff** [flʌf] n duvet m ; peluche f ; ~y a duveteux(euse) ; pelucheux (euse) ; ~y **toy** n jouet m en peluche.

**fluid** ['flu:ɪd] a,n fluide (m) ; ~ **ounce** n = 0.028 l ; 0.05 pints.

**fluke** [flu:k] n (col) coup m de veine or de chance.

**flung** [flʌŋ] pt,pp of **fling**.

**fluorescent** [fluə'rɛsnt] a fluorescent(e).

**fluoride** ['fluəraɪd] n fluor m.

**fluorine** ['fluəri:n] n fluor m.

**flurry** ['flʌrɪ] n (of snow) rafale f, bourrasque f ; ~ **of activity/excitement** affairement m/excitation f soudain(e).

**flush** [flʌʃ] n rougeur f ; excitation f // vt nettoyer à grande eau // vi rougir // a: ~ **with** au ras de, de niveau avec ; ~ **against** tout contre ; **to** ~ **the toilet** tirer la chasse (d'eau) ; ~ed a (tout(e)) rouge.

**fluster** ['flʌstə*] n agitation f, trouble m ; ~ed a énervé(e).

**flute** [flu:t] n flûte f.

**fluted** ['flu:tɪd] a cannelé(e).

**flutter** ['flʌtə*] n agitation f ; (of wings) battement m // vi battre des ailes, voleter ; (person) aller et venir dans une grande agitation.

**flux** [flʌks] n: **in a state of** ~ fluctuant sans cesse.

**fly** [flaɪ] n (insect) mouche f ; (on trousers: also: **flies**) braguette f // vb (pt **flew**, pp **flown** [flu:, fləun]) vt piloter ; (passengers, cargo) transporter (par avion) ; (distances) parcourir // vi voler ; (passengers) aller en avion ; (escape) s'enfuir, fuir ; (flag) se déployer ; **to** ~ **open** vi s'ouvrir brusquement ; ~**ing** n (activity) aviation f // a: ~**ing visit** visite f éclair inv ; **with** ~**ing colours** haut la main ; ~**ing buttress** n arc-boutant m ; ~**ing saucer** n soucoupe volante ; ~**ing start** n: **to get off to a** ~**ing start** faire un excellent départ ; ~**over** n (Brit: bridge) saut-de-mouton m ; ~**past** n défilé aérien ; ~**sheet** n (for tent) double toit m ; ~**wheel** n volant m (de commande).

**F.M.** (abbr of frequency modulation) F.M., M.F. (modulation f de fréquence).

**foal** [fəul] n poulain m.

**foam** [fəum] n écume f ; (on beer) mousse f ; (also: **plastic** ~) mousse cellulaire or de plastique // vi écumer ; (soapy water) mousser ; ~ **rubber** n caoutchouc m mousse.

**fob** [fɔb] vt: **to** ~ **sb off with** refiler à qn ; se débarrasser de qn avec.

**focal** ['fəukəl] a focal(e).

**focus** ['fəukəs] n (pl: ~**es**) foyer m ; (of interest) centre m // vt (field glasses etc) mettre au point ; (light rays) faire converger ; **in** ~ au point ; **out of** ~ pas au point.

**fodder** ['fɔdə*] n fourrage m.

**foe** [fəu] n ennemi m.

**foetus** ['fi:təs] n fœtus m.

**fog** [fɔg] n brouillard m ; ~**gy** a: **it's** ~**gy** il y a du brouillard.

**foible** ['fɔɪbl] n faiblesse f.

**foil** [fɔɪl] vt déjouer, contrecarrer // n feuille f de métal ; (also: **kitchen** ~) papier m d'alu(minium) ; (FENCING) fleuret m ; **to act as a** ~ **to** (fig) servir de repoussoir or de faire-valoir à.

**fold** [fəuld] n (bend, crease) pli m ; (AGR) parc m à moutons ; (fig) bercail m // vt plier ; **to** ~ **up** vi (map etc) se plier, se replier ; (business) fermer boutique // vt (map etc) plier, replier ; ~**er** n (for papers) chemise f ; classeur m ; (brochure) dépliant m ; ~**ing** a (chair, bed) pliant(e).

**foliage** ['fəulɪdʒ] n feuillage m.

**folk** [fəuk] npl gens mpl // a folklorique ; ~**s** npl famille f, parents mpl ; ~**lore** ['fəuklɔ:*] n folklore m ; ~**song** n chanson f folklorique (gén de l'Ouest américain).

**follow** ['fɔləu] vt suivre // vi suivre ; (result) s'ensuivre ; **he** ~**ed suit** il fit de même ; **to** ~ **up** vt (victory) tirer parti de ; (letter, offer) donner suite à ; (case) suivre ; ~**er** n disciple m/f, partisan/e ; ~**ing a** suivant(e) // n partisans mpl, disciples mpl.

**folly** ['fɔlɪ] n inconscience f ; sottise f ; (building) folie f.

**fond** [fɔnd] a (memory, look) tendre, affectueux(euse) ; **to be** ~ **of** aimer beaucoup.

**fondle** ['fɔndl] vt caresser.

**fondness** ['fɔndnɪs] n (for things) attachement m ; (for people) sentiments affectueux ; **a special** ~ **for** une prédilection pour.

**font** [fɔnt] n fonts baptismaux.

**food** [fu:d] n nourriture f ; ~ **mixer** n mixeur m ; ~ **poisoning** n intoxication f alimentaire ; ~**stuffs** npl denrées fpl alimentaires.

**fool** [fu:l] n idiot/e ; (HISTORY: of king) bouffon m, fou m ; (CULIN) purée f de fruits à la crème // vt berner, duper // vi (gen: ~ **around**) faire l'idiot or l'imbécile ; ~**hardy** a téméraire, imprudent(e) ; ~**ish** a idiot(e), stupide ; imprudent(e) ; écervelé(e) ; ~**proof** a (plan etc) infaillible.

**foot** [fut] n (pl: **feet** [fi:t]) pied m ; (measure) pied (= 304 mm, 12 inches) ; (of animal) patte f // vt (bill) casquer, payer ; **on** ~ à pied ; ~ **and mouth (disease)** n fièvre aphteuse ; ~**ball** n ballon m (de football) ; (sport) football m ; ~**baller** m footballeur m ; ~**brake** n frein m à pied ; ~**bridge** n passerelle f ; ~**hills** npl contreforts mpl ; ~**hold** n prise f (de pied) ; ~**ing** n (fig) position f ; **to lose one's** ~**ing** perdre pied ; **on an equal** ~**ing** sur pied d'égalité ; ~**lights** npl rampe f ; ~**man** n laquais m ; ~**note** n note f (en bas de page) ; ~**path** n sentier m ; (in street) trottoir m ; ~**rest** n marchepied m ; ~**sore** a aux pieds endoloris ; ~**step** n pas m ; ~**wear** n chaussure(s) f(pl) (terme générique en anglais).

**for** [fɔ:*] prep pour ; (during) pendant ; (in spite of) malgré // cj car ; **I haven't seen him** ~ **a week** je ne l'ai pas vu depuis une semaine, cela fait une semaine que je ne l'ai pas vu ; **he went down** ~ **the paper** il est descendu chercher le journal ; ~ **sale** à vendre.

**forage** ['fɔrɪdʒ] n fourrage m // vi fourrager, fouiller ; ~ **cap** n calot m.

**foray** ['fɔreɪ] n incursion f.

**forbad(e)** [fə'bæd] pt of **forbid**.

**forbearing** [fɔ:'bɛərɪŋ] a patient(e), tolérant(e).

**forbid,** pt **forbad(e),** pp **forbidden** [fə'bɪd, -'bæd, -'bɪdn] vt défendre, interdire; ~**den** a défendu(e); ~**ding** a d'aspect or d'allure sévère or sombre.

**force** [fɔ:s] n force f // vt forcer; **the F~s** npl l'armée f; **in ~** en force; **to come into ~** entrer en vigueur; ~**d** [fɔ:st] a forcé(e); ~**ful** a énergique, volontaire.

**forceps** ['fɔ:sɛps] npl forceps m.

**forcibly** ['fɔ:səblɪ] ad par la force, de force; (vigorously) énergiquement.

**ford** [fɔ:d] n gué m // vt passer à gué.

**fore** [fɔ:*] n: **to the ~** en évidence.

**forearm** ['fɔ:rɑ:m] n avant-bras m inv.

**foreboding** [fɔ:'bəudɪŋ] n pressentiment m (néfaste).

**forecast** ['fɔ:kɑ:st] n prévision f // vt (irg: like **cast**) prévoir.

**forecourt** ['fɔ:kɔ:t] n (of garage) devant m.

**forefathers** ['fɔ:fɑ:ðəz] npl ancêtres mpl.

**forefinger** ['fɔ:fɪŋgə*] n index m.

**forego,** pt **forewent,** pp **foregone** [fɔ:'gəu, -'wɛnt, -'gɔn] vt = **forgo**.

**foregone** ['fɔ:gɔn] a: **it's a ~ conclusion** c'est à prévoir, c'est couru d'avance.

**foreground** ['fɔ:graund] n premier plan.

**forehead** ['fɔrɪd] n front m.

**foreign** ['fɔrɪn] a étranger(ère); (trade) extérieur(e); ~ **body** n corps étranger; ~**er** n étranger/ère; ~ **exchange market** n marché m des devises; ~ **exchange rate** n cours m des devises; ~ **minister** n ministre m des Affaires étrangères.

**foreleg** ['fɔ:lɛg] n patte f de devant; jambe antérieure.

**foreman** ['fɔ:mən] n contremaître m.

**foremost** ['fɔ:məust] a le(la) plus en vue; premier(ère).

**forensic** [fə'rɛnsɪk] a: ~ **medicine** médecine légale; ~ **expert** expert m de la police, expert légiste.

**forerunner** ['fɔ:rʌnə*] n précurseur m.

**foresee,** pt **foresaw,** pp **foreseen** [fɔ:'si:, -'sɔ:, -'si:n] vt prévoir; ~**able** a prévisible.

**foresight** ['fɔ:saɪt] n prévoyance f.

**forest** ['fɔrɪst] n forêt f.

**forestall** [fɔ:'stɔ:l] vt devancer.

**forestry** ['fɔrɪstrɪ] n sylviculture f.

**foretaste** ['fɔ:teɪst] n avant-goût m.

**foretell,** pt,pp **foretold** [fɔ:'tɛl, -'təuld] vt prédire.

**forever** [fə'rɛvə*] ad pour toujours; (fig) continuellement.

**forewent** [fɔ:'wɛnt] pt of **forego**.

**foreword** ['fɔ:wə:d] n avant-propos m inv.

**forfeit** ['fɔ:fɪt] n prix m, rançon f // vt perdre; (one's life, health) payer de.

**forgave** [fə'geɪv] pt of **forgive**.

**forge** [fɔ:dʒ] n forge f // vt (signature) contrefaire; (wrought iron) forger; **to ~ documents/a will** fabriquer des faux papiers/un faux testament; **to ~ money** fabriquer de la fausse monnaie; **to ~ ahead** vi pousser de l'avant, prendre de l'avance; ~**r** n faussaire m; ~**ry** n faux m, contrefaçon f.

**forget,** pt **forgot,** pp **forgotten** [fə'gɛt, -'gɔt, -'gɔtn] vt,vi oublier; ~**ful** a distrait(e), étourdi(e); ~**ful** of oublieux(euse) de; ~**fulness** n tendance f aux oublis; (oblivion) oubli m.

**forgive,** pt **forgave,** pp **forgiven** [fə'gɪv, -'geɪv, -'gɪvn] vt pardonner; ~**ness** n pardon m.

**forgo,** pt **forwent,** pp **forgone** [fɔ:'gəu, -'wɛnt, -'gɔn] vt renoncer à.

**forgot** [fə'gɔt] pt of **forget**.

**forgotten** [fə'gɔtn] pp of **forget**.

**fork** [fɔ:k] n (for eating) fourchette f; (for gardening) fourche f; (of roads) bifurcation f; (of railways) embranchement m // vi (road) bifurquer; **to ~ out** (col: pay) vt allonger, se fendre de // vi casquer; ~**ed** [fɔ:kt] a (lightning) en zigzags, ramifié(e); ~**-lift truck** n chariot élévateur.

**form** [fɔ:m] n forme f; (SCOL) classe f; (questionnaire) formulaire m // vt former; **in top ~** en pleine forme.

**formal** [fɔ:məl] a (offer, receipt) en bonne et due forme; (person) cérémonieux(euse), à cheval sur les convenances; (occasion, dinner) officiel(le); (ART, PHILOSOPHY) formel(le); ~**ly** ad officiellement; formellement; cérémonieusement.

**format** ['fɔ:mæt] n format m.

**formation** [fɔ:'meɪʃən] n formation f.

**formative** ['fɔ:mətɪv] a: ~ **years** années fpl d'apprentissage (fig) or de formation (d'un enfant, d'un adolescent).

**former** ['fɔ:mə*] a ancien(ne) (before n), précédent(e); **the ~ ... the latter** le premier ... le second, celui-là ... celui-ci; ~**ly** ad autrefois.

**formidable** ['fɔ:mɪdəbl] a redoutable.

**formula** ['fɔ:mjulə] n formule f.

**formulate** ['fɔ:mjuleɪt] vt formuler.

**forsake,** pt **forsook,** pp **forsaken** [fə'seɪk, -'suk, -'seɪkən] vt abandonner.

**fort** [fɔ:t] n fort m.

**forte** ['fɔ:tɪ] n (point) fort m.

**forth** [fɔ:θ] ad en avant; **to go back and ~** aller et venir; **and so ~** et ainsi de suite; ~**coming** a qui va paraître or avoir lieu prochainement; (character) ouvert(e), communicatif(ive); ~**right** a franc(franche), direct(e).

**fortieth** ['fɔ:tɪɪθ] num quarantième.

**fortification** [fɔ:tɪfɪ'keɪʃən] n fortification f.

**fortify** ['fɔ:tɪfaɪ] vt fortifier; **fortified wine** n vin liquoreux or de liqueur.

**fortitude** ['fɔ:tɪtju:d] n courage m, force f d'âme.

**fortnight** ['fɔ:tnaɪt] n quinzaine f, quinze jours mpl; ~**ly** a bimensuel(le) // ad tous les quinze jours.

**fortress** ['fɔ:trɪs] n forteresse f.

**fortuitous** [fɔ:'tju:ɪtəs] a fortuit(e).

**fortunate** ['fɔ:tʃənɪt] a: **to be ~** avoir de la chance; **it is ~ that** c'est une chance que, il est heureux que; ~**ly** ad heureusement, par bonheur.

**fortune** ['fɔ:tʃən] n chance f; (wealth) fortune f; ~**teller** n diseuse f de bonne aventure.

**forty** ['fɔ:tɪ] *num* quarante.

**forum** ['fɔ:rəm] *n* forum *m*, tribune *f*.

**forward** ['fɔ:wəd] *a* (*ahead of schedule*) en avance ; (*movement, position*) en avant, vers l'avant ; (*not shy*) ouvert(e) ; direct(e) ; effronté(e) // *ad* en avant // *n* (*SPORT*) avant *m* // *vt* (*letter*) faire suivre ; (*parcel, goods*) expédier ; (*fig*) promouvoir, contribuer au développement *or* à l'avancement *or* ; **to move** ~ avancer ; ~**s** *ad* en avant.

**forwent** [fɔ:'wɛnt] *pt of* **forgo**.

**fossil** ['fɔsl] *a,n* fossile (*m*).

**foster** ['fɔstə*] *vt* encourager, favoriser ; ~ **brother** *n* frère adoptif ; frère de lait ; ~ **child** *n* enfant adopté ; ~ **mother** *n* mère adoptive ; mère nourricière.

**fought** [fɔ:t] *pt, pp of* **fight**.

**foul** [faul] *a* (*weather, smell, food*) infect(e) ; (*language*) ordurier(ère) ; (*deed*) infâme // *n* (*FOOTBALL*) faute *f* // *vt* salir, encrasser ; (*football player*) commettre une faute sur ; ~ **play** *n* (*SPORT*) jeu déloyal ; ~ **play is not suspected** la mort (*or* l'incendie *etc*) n'a pas de causes suspectes, on écarte l'hypothèse d'un meurtre (*or* d'un acte criminel).

**found** [faund] *pt, pp of* **find** // *vt* (*establish*) fonder ; ~**ation** [-'deɪʃən] *n* (*act*) fondation *f* ; (*base*) fondement *m* ; (*also*: ~**ation cream**) fond *m* de teint ; ~**ations** *npl* (*of building*) fondations *fpl*.

**founder** ['faundə*] *n* fondateur *m* // *vi* couler, sombrer.

**foundry** ['faundrɪ] *n* fonderie *f*.

**fount** [faunt] *n* source *f* ; ~**ain** ['fauntɪn] *n* fontaine *f* ; ~**ain pen** *n* stylo *m* (à encre).

**four** [fɔ:*] *num* quatre ; **on all** ~**s** à quatre pattes ; ~**some** ['fɔ:səm] *n* partie *f* à quatre ; sortie *f* à quatre ; ~**teen** *num* quatorze ; ~**teenth** *num* quatorzième ; ~**th** *num* quatrième.

**fowl** [faul] *n* volaille *f*.

**fox** [fɔks] *n* renard *m* // *vt* mystifier.

**foyer** ['fɔɪeɪ] *n* vestibule *m* ; (*THEATRE*) foyer *m*.

**fraction** ['trækʃən] *n* fraction *f*.

**fracture** ['fræktʃə*] *n* fracture *f* // *vt* fracturer.

**fragile** ['fræudʒaɪl] *a* fragile.

**fragment** ['frægmənt] *n* fragment *m* ; ~**ary** *a* fragmentaire.

**fragrance** ['freɪgrəns] *n* parfum *m*.

**fragrant** ['freɪgrənt] *a* parfumé(e), odorant(e).

**frail** [freɪl] *a* fragile, délicat(e).

**frame** [freɪm] *n* (*of building*) charpente *f* ; (*of human, animal*) charpente, ossature *f* ; (*of picture*) cadre *m* ; (*of door, window*) encadrement *m*, chambranle *m* ; (*of spectacles: also*: ~**s**) monture *f* // *vt* encadrer ; (*theory, plan*) construire, élaborer ; ~ **of mind** *n* disposition *f* d'esprit ; ~**work** *n* structure *f*.

**France** [frɑ:ns] *n* France *f*.

**franchise** ['fræntʃaɪz] *n* (*POL*) droit *m* de vote.

**frank** [fræŋk] *a* franc(franche) // *vt* (*letter*) affranchir ; ~**ly** *ad* franchement ; ~**ness** *n* franchise *f*.

**frantic** ['fræntɪk] *a* frénétique ; ~**ally** *ad* frénétiquement.

**fraternal** [frə'tə:nl] *a* fraternel(le).

**fraternity** [frə'tə:nɪtɪ] *n* (*club*) communauté *f*, confrérie *f* ; (*spirit*) fraternité *f*.

**fraternize** ['frætənaɪz] *vi* fraterniser.

**fraud** [frɔ:d] *n* supercherie *f*, fraude *f*, tromperie *f* ; imposteur *m*.

**fraudulent** ['frɔ:djulənt] *a* frauduleux(euse).

**fraught** [frɔ:t] *a*: ~ **with** chargé(e) de, plein(e) de.

**fray** [freɪ] *n* bagarre *f* // *vt* effilocher // *vi* s'effilocher ; **tempers were** ~**ed** les gens commençaient à s'énerver *or* perdre patience ; **her nerves were** ~**ed** elle était à bout de nerfs.

**freak** [fri:k] *n* (*also cpd*) phénomène *m*, créature ou événement exceptionnel par sa rareté, son caractère d'anomalie.

**freckle** ['frɛkl] *n* tache *f* de rousseur.

**free** [fri:] *a* libre ; (*gratis*) gratuit(e) ; (*liberal*) généreux(euse), large // *vt* (*prisoner etc*) libérer ; (*jammed object or person*) dégager ; ~ (**of charge**) *ad* gratuitement ; ~**dom** ['fri:dəm] *n* liberté *f* ; ~**-for-all** *n* mêlée générale ; ~ **kick** *n* coup franc ; ~**lance** *a* indépendant(e) ; ~**ly** *ad* librement ; (*liberally*) libéralement ; ~**mason** *n* franc-maçon *m* ; ~**masonry** *n* franc-maçonnerie *f* ; ~ **trade** *n* libre-échange *m* ; ~**way** *n* (*US*) autoroute *f* ; ~**wheel** *vi* descendre en roue libre ; ~ **will** *n* libre arbitre *m* ; **of one's own** ~ **will** de son plein gré.

**freeze** [fri:z] *vb* (*pt* **froze**, *pp* **frozen** [frəuz, 'frəuzn]) *vi* geler // *vt* geler ; (*food*) congeler ; (*prices, salaries*) bloquer, geler // *n* gel *m* ; blocage *m* ; ~**-dried** *a* lyophilisé(e) ; ~**r** *n* congélateur *m*.

**freezing** ['fri:zɪŋ] *a*: ~ **cold** *a* glacial(e) ; ~ **point** *n* point *m* de congélation ; **3 degrees below** ~ 3 degrés au-dessous de zéro.

**freight** [freɪt] *n* (*goods*) fret *m*, cargaison *f* ; (*money charged*) fret, prix *m* du transport ; ~ **car** *n* (*US*) wagon *m* de marchandises ; ~**er** *n* (*NAUT*) cargo *m*.

**French** [frɛntʃ] *a* français(e) // *n* (*LING*) français *m* ; **the** ~ les Français ; ~ **fried** (**potatoes**) *npl* (pommes de terre *fpl*) frites *fpl* ; ~**man** *n* Français *m* ; ~ **window** *n* porte-fenêtre *f* ; ~**woman** *n* Française *f*.

**frenzy** ['frɛnzɪ] *n* frénésie *f*.

**frequency** ['fri:kwənsɪ] *n* fréquence *f*.

**frequent** *a* ['fri:kwənt] fréquent(e) // *vt* [frɪ'kwɛnt] fréquenter ; ~**ly** *ad* fréquemment.

**fresco** ['frɛskəu] *n* fresque *f*.

**fresh** [frɛʃ] *a* frais(fraîche) ; (*new*) nouveau(nouvelle) ; (*cheeky*) familier(ère), culotté(e) ; ~**en** *vi* (*wind, air*) fraîchir ; **to** ~**en up** *vi* faire un brin de toilette ; ~**ly** *ad* nouvellement, récemment ; ~**ness** *n* fraîcheur *f* ; ~**water** *a* (*fish*) d'eau douce.

**fret** [frɛt] *vi* s'agiter, se tracasser.

**friar** ['fraɪə*] *n* moine *m*, frère *m*.

**friction** ['frɪkʃən] *n* friction *f*, frottement *m*.

**Friday** ['fraɪdɪ] *n* vendredi *m*.

**fridge** [frɪdʒ] n frigo m, frigidaire m ®.
**fried** [fraɪd] pt, pp of **fry** // a frit(e).
**friend** [frɛnd] n ami/e ; **to make ~s with** se lier (d'amitié) avec ; **~liness** n attitude amicale ; **~ly** a amical(e) ; gentil(le) ; **to be ~ly with** être ami(e) avec ; **~ship** n amitié f.
**frieze** [friːz] n frise f, bordure f.
**frigate** ['frɪgɪt] n (NAUT: modern) frégate f.
**fright** [fraɪt] n peur f, effroi m ; **she looks a ~** elle a l'air d'un épouvantail ; **~en** vt effrayer, faire peur à ; **~ened** a: **to be ~ened (of)** avoir peur (de) ; **~ening** a effrayant(e) ; **~ful** a affreux(euse) ; **~fully** ad affreusement.
**frigid** ['frɪdʒɪd] a (woman) frigide ; **~ity** [frɪ'dʒɪdɪtɪ] n frigidité f.
**frill** [frɪl] n (of dress) volant m ; (of shirt) jabot m.
**fringe** [frɪndʒ] n frange f ; (edge: of forest etc) bordure f ; (fig): **on the ~** en marge ; **~ benefits** npl avantages sociaux or en nature.
**frisk** [frɪsk] vt fouiller.
**frisky** ['frɪskɪ] a vif(vive), sémillant(e).
**fritter** ['frɪtə*] n beignet m ; **to ~ away** vt gaspiller.
**frivolity** [frɪ'vɔlɪtɪ] n frivolité f.
**frivolous** ['frɪvələs] a frivole.
**frizzy** ['frɪzɪ] a crépu(e).
**fro** [frəu] see **to**.
**frock** [frɔk] n robe f.
**frog** [frɔg] n grenouille f ; **~man** n homme-grenouille m.
**frolic** ['frɔlɪk] n ébats mpl // vi folâtrer, batifoler.
**from** [frɔm] prep de ; **~ a pound/January** à partir d'une livre/de janvier ; **~ what he says** d'après ce qu'il dit.
**front** [frʌnt] n (of house, dress) devant m ; (of coach, train) avant m ; (of book) couverture f ; (promenade: also: **sea ~**) bord m de mer ; (MIL, POL, METEOROLOGY) front m ; (fig: appearances) contenance f, façade f // a de devant ; premier(ère) ; **in ~ (of)** devant ; **~age** ['frʌntɪdʒ] n façade f ; **~al** a frontal(e) ; **~ door** n porte f d'entrée ; (of car) portière f avant ; **~ier** ['frʌntɪə*] n frontière f ; **~ page** n première page ; **~ room** n (Brit) pièce f de devant, salon m ; **~-wheel drive** n traction f avant.
**frost** [frɔst] n gel m, gelée f ; **~bite** n gelures fpl ; **~ed** a (glass) dépoli(e) ; **~y** a (window) couvert(e) de givre ; (welcome) glacial(e).
**froth** ['frɔθ] n mousse f ; écume f.
**frown** [fraun] n froncement m de sourcils // vi froncer les sourcils.
**froze** [frəuz] pt of **freeze** ; **~n** pp of **freeze** // a (food) congelé(e).
**frugal** ['fruːgəl] a frugal(e).
**fruit** [fruːt] n, pl inv fruit m ; **~erer** n fruitier m, marchand/e de fruits ; **~ful** a fructueux(euse) ; (plant, soil) fécond(e) ; **~ion** [fruː'ɪʃən] n: **to come to ~ion** se réaliser ; **~ machine** n machine f à sous ; **~ salad** n salade f de fruits.
**frustrate** [frʌs'treɪt] vt frustrer ; (plot, plans) faire échouer ; **~d** a frustré(e) ; **frustration** [-'treɪʃən] n frustration f.

**fry**, pt, pp **fried** [fraɪ, -d] vt (faire) frire ; **the small ~** le menu fretin ; **~ing pan** n poêle f (à frire).
**ft.** abbr of **foot, feet.**
**fuchsia** ['fjuːʃə] n fuchsia m.
**fuddy-duddy** ['fʌdɪdʌdɪ] n (pej) vieux schnock.
**fudge** [fʌdʒ] n (CULIN) sorte de confiserie à base de sucre, de beurre et de lait.
**fuel** [fjuəl] n (for heating) combustible m ; (for propelling) carburant m ; **~ oil** n mazout m ; **~ tank** n cuve f à mazout, citerne f ; (on vehicle) réservoir m de or à carburant.
**fugitive** ['fjuːdʒɪtɪv] n fugitif/ive.
**fulfil** [ful'fɪl] vt (function) remplir ; (order) exécuter ; (wish, desire) satisfaire, réaliser ; **~ment** n (of wishes) réalisation f.
**full** [ful] a plein(e) ; (details, information) complet(ète) ; (skirt) ample, large // ad: **to know ~ well that** savoir fort bien que ; **I'm ~** j'ai bien mangé ; **~ employment/fare** plein emploi/tarif ; **a ~ two hours** deux bonnes heures ; **at ~ speed** à toute vitesse ; **in ~** (reproduce, quote) intégralement ; (write name etc) en toutes lettres ; **~back** n (RUGBY, FOOTBALL) arrière m ; **~-length** a (portrait) en pied ; **~ moon** n pleine lune ; **~-sized** a (portrait etc) grandeur nature inv ; **~ stop** n point m ; **~-time** a (work) à plein temps // n (SPORT) fin f du match ; **~y** ad entièrement, complètement ; **~y-fledged** a (teacher, barrister) diplômé(e) ; (citizen, member) à part entière.
**fumble** ['fʌmbl] vi fouiller, tâtonner // vt (ball) mal réceptionner, cafouiller ; **to ~ with** vt fus tripoter.
**fume** [fjuːm] vi rager ; **~s** npl vapeurs fpl, émanations fpl, gaz mpl.
**fumigate** ['fjuːmɪgeɪt] vt désinfecter (par fumigation).
**fun** [fʌn] n amusement m, divertissement m ; **to have ~** s'amuser ; **for ~** pour rire ; **it's not much ~** ce n'est pas très drôle or amusant ; **to make ~ of** vt fus se moquer de.
**function** ['fʌŋkʃən] n fonction f ; cérémonie f, soirée officielle // vi fonctionner ; **~al** a fonctionnel(le).
**fund** [fʌnd] n caisse f, fonds m ; (source, store) source f, mine f ; **~s** npl fonds mpl.
**fundamental** [fʌndə'mɛntl] a fondamental(e) ; **~s** npl principes mpl de base ; **~ly** ad fondamentalement.
**funeral** ['fjuːnərəl] n enterrement m, obsèques fpl (more formal occasion) ; **~ director** n entrepreneur m des pompes funèbres ; **~ service** n service m funèbre.
**funereal** [fjuː'nɪərɪəl] a lugubre, funèbre.
**fun fair** ['fʌnfɛə*] n fête (foraine).
**fungus**, pl **fungi** ['fʌŋgəs, -gaɪ] n champignon m ; (mould) moisissure f.
**funnel** ['fʌnl] n entonnoir m ; (of ship) cheminée f.
**funnily** ['fʌnɪlɪ] ad drôlement ; curieusement.
**funny** ['fʌnɪ] a amusant(e), drôle ; (strange) curieux(euse), bizarre.
**fur** [fə:*] n fourrure f ; (in kettle etc) (dépôt m de) tartre m ; **~ coat** n manteau m de fourrure.

**furious** ['fjuərɪəs] a furieux(euse) ; (effort) acharné(e) ; ~ly ad furieusement ; avec acharnement.

**furl** [fə:l] vt rouler ; (NAUT) ferler.

**furlong** ['fə:lɔŋ] n = 201.17 m (terme d'hippisme).

**furlough** ['fə:ləu] n (US) permission f, congé m.

**furnace** ['fə:nɪs] n fourneau m.

**furnish** ['fə:nɪʃ] vt meubler ; (supply) fournir ; ~ings npl mobilier m, articles mpl d'ameublement.

**furniture** ['fə:nɪtʃə*] n meubles mpl, mobilier m ; **piece of** ~ meuble m ; ~ **polish** n encaustique f.

**furrier** ['fʌrɪə*] n fourreur m.

**furrow** ['fʌrəu] n sillon m.

**furry** ['fə:rɪ] a (animal) à fcurrure ; (toy) en peluche.

**further** ['fə:ðə*] a supplémentaire, autre ; nouveau(nouvelle) ; plus loin // ad plus loin ; (more) davantage ; (moreover) de plus // vt faire avancer or progresser, promouvoir ; **until** ~ **notice** jusqu'à nouvel ordre or avis ; ~ **education** n enseignement m post-scolaire (recyclage, formation professionnelle) ; ~**more** [fə:ðə'mɔ:*] ad de plus, en outre.

**furthest** ['fə:ðɪst] superlative of **far**.

**furtive** ['fə:tɪv] a furtif(ive) ; ~ly ad furtivement.

**fury** ['fjuərɪ] n fureur f.

**fuse, fuze** (US) [fju:z] n fusible m ; (for bomb etc) amorce f, détonateur m // vt,vi (metal) fondre ; (fig) fusionner ; (ELEC): to ~ **the lights** faire sauter les fusibles or les plombs ; ~ **box** n boîte f à fusibles.

**fuselage** ['fju:zəlɑ:ʒ] n fuselage m.

**fusion** ['fju:ʒən] n fusion f.

**fuss** [fʌs] n chichis mpl, façons fpl, embarras mpl ; (complaining) histoire(s) f(pl) ; **to make a** ~ faire des façons etc ; ~**y** a (person) tatillon(ne), difficile ; chichiteux(euse) ; (dress, style) tarabiscoté(e).

**futile** ['fju:taɪl] a futile.

**futility** [fju:'tɪlɪtɪ] n futilité f.

**future** ['fju:tʃə*] a futur(e) // n avenir m ; (LING) futur m ; **in** (the) ~ à l'avenir ; **futuristic** [ˈrɪstɪk] a futuriste.

**fuze** [fju:z] n, vt, vi (US) = **fuse**.

**fuzzy** ['fʌzɪ] a (PHOT) flou(e) ; (hair) crépu(e).

# G

**g.** abbr of **gram(s)**.

**G** [dʒi:] n (MUS) sol m.

**gabble** ['gæbl] vi bredouiller ; jacasser.

**gable** ['geɪbl] n pignon m.

**gadget** ['gædʒɪt] n gadget m.

**Gaelic** ['geɪlɪk] n (LING) gaélique m.

**gag** [gæg] n bâillon m ; (joke) gag m // vt bâillonner.

**gaiety** ['geɪtɪ] n gaieté f.

**gaily** ['geɪlɪ] ad gaiement.

**gain** [geɪn] n gain m, profit m // vt gagner // vi (watch) avancer ; **to** ~ **in/by** gagner en/à ; **to** ~ **3lbs (in weight)** prendre 3 livres ; ~**ful** a profitable, lucratif(ive).

**gainsay** [geɪn'seɪ] vt irg (like **say**) contredire ; nier.

**gait** [geɪt] n démarche f.

**gal.** abbr of **gallon**.

**gala** ['gɑ:lə] n gala m.

**galaxy** ['gæləksɪ] n galaxie f.

**gale** [geɪl] n rafale f de vent ; coup m de vent.

**gallant** ['gælənt] a vaillant(e), brave ; (towards ladies) empressé(e), galant(e) ; ~**ry** n bravoure f, vaillance f ; empressement m, galanterie f.

**gall-bladder** ['gɔ:lblædə*] n vésicule f biliaire.

**gallery** ['gælərɪ] n galerie f ; (also: **art** ~) musée m ; (: private) galerie.

**galley** ['gælɪ] n (ship's kitchen) cambuse f ; (ship) galère f ; (TYP) placard m, galée f.

**gallon** ['gæln] n gallon m (= 4.543 l ; 8 pints).

**gallop** ['gæləp] n galop m // vi galoper.

**gallows** ['gæləuz] n potence f.

**gallstone** ['gɔ:lstəun] n calcul m (biliaire).

**gambit** ['gæmbɪt] n (fig): (opening) ~ manœuvre f stratégique.

**gamble** ['gæmbl] n pari m, risque calculé // vt, vi jouer ; **to** ~ **on** (fig) miser sur ; ~**r** n joueur m ; **gambling** n jeu m.

**game** [geɪm] n jeu m ; (event) match m ; (HUNTING) gibier m // a brave ; (ready): **to be** ~ **(for sth/to do)** être prêt(e) (à qch/à faire), se sentir de taille (à faire) ; **a** ~ **of football/tennis** une partie de football/tennis ; **big** ~ n gros gibier ; ~**keeper** n garde-chasse m.

**gammon** ['gæmən] n (bacon) quartier m de lard fumé ; (ham) jambon fumé.

**gamut** ['gæmət] n gamme f.

**gang** [gæŋ] n bande f, groupe m // vi: **to** ~ **up on sb** se liguer contre qn.

**gangrene** ['gæŋgri:n] n gangrène f.

**gangster** ['gæŋstə*] n gangster m, bandit m.

**gangway** ['gæŋweɪ] n passerelle f ; (of bus) couloir central ; (THEATRE, CINEMA) allée f.

**gantry** ['gæntrɪ] n portique m.

**gaol** [dʒeɪl] n, vt = **jail**.

**gap** [gæp] n trou m ; (in time) intervalle f ; (fig) lacune f ; vide m.

**gape** [geɪp] vi être or rester bouche bée ; **gaping** a (hole) béant(e).

**garage** ['gærɑ:ʒ] n garage m.

**garb** [gɑ:b] n tenue f, costume m.

**garbage** ['gɑ:bɪdʒ] n ordures fpl, détritus mpl ; ~ **can** n (US) poubelle f, boîte f à ordures.

**garbled** ['gɑ:bld] a déformé(e) ; faussé(e).

**garden** ['gɑ:dn] n jardin m // vi jardiner ; ~**er** n jardinier m ; ~**ing** n jardinage m.

**gargle** ['gɑ:gl] vi se gargariser // n gargarisme m.

**gargoyle** ['gɑ:gɔɪl] n gargouille f.

**garish** ['gɛərɪʃ] a criard(e), voyant(e).

**garland** ['gɑ:lənd] n guirlande f ; couronne f.

**garlic** ['gɑ:lɪk] n ail m.

**garment** ['gɑ:mənt] n vêtement m.

**garnish** ['gɑ:nɪʃ] vt garnir.

**garret** ['gærɪt] n mansarde f.

**garrison** ['gærɪsn] n garnison f // vt mettre en garnison, stationner.

**garrulous** ['gærjuləs] *a* volubile, loquace.
**garter** ['gɑ:tə*] *n* jarretière *f.*
**gas** [gæs] *n* gaz *m* ; (*used as anaesthetic*): **to be given** ~ se faire endormir ; (*US: gasoline*) essence *f //* *vt* asphyxier ; (*MIL*) gazer ; ~ **cooker** *n* cuisinière *f* à gaz ; ~ **cylinder** *n* bouteille *f* de gaz ; ~ **fire** *n* radiateur *m* à gaz.
**gash** [gæʃ] *n* entaille *f* ; (*on face*) balafre *f // vt* taillader ; balafrer.
**gasket** ['gæskɪt] *n* (*AUT*) joint *m* de culasse.
**gasmask** ['gæsmɑ:sk] *n* masque *m* à gaz.
**gas meter** ['gæsmi:tə*] *n* compteur *m* à gaz.
**gasoline** ['gæsəli:n] *n* (*US*) essence *f.*
**gasp** [gɑ:sp] *vi* haleter ; (*fig*) avoir le souffle coupé.
**gas ring** ['gæsrɪŋ] *n* brûleur *m.*
**gas stove** ['gæsstəuv] *n* réchaud *m* à gaz ; (*cooker*) cuisinière *f* à gaz.
**gassy** ['gæsɪ] *a* gazeux(euse).
**gastric** ['gæstrɪk] *a* gastrique ; ~ **ulcer** *n* ulcère *m* de l'estomac.
**gastronomy** [gæs'trɔnəmɪ] *n* gastronomie *f.*
**gasworks** ['gæswə:ks] *n* usine *f* à gaz.
**gate** [geɪt] *n* (*of garden*) portail *m* ; (*of farm*) barrière *f* ; (*of building*) porte *f* ; (*of lock*) vanne *f* ; ~**crash** *vt* s'introduire sans invitation dans ; ~**way** *n* porte *f.*
**gather** ['gæðə*] *vt* (*flowers, fruit*) cueillir ; (*pick up*) ramasser ; (*assemble*) rassembler, réunir ; (*understand*) comprendre // *vi* (*assemble*) se rassembler ; **to** ~ **speed** prendre de la vitesse ; ~**ing** *n* rassemblement *m.*
**gauche** [gəuʃ] *a* gauche, maladroit(e).
**gaudy** ['gɔ:dɪ] *a* voyant(e).
**gauge** [geɪdʒ] *n* (*standard measure*) calibre *m* ; (*RAIL*) écartement *m* ; (*instrument*) jauge *f // vt* jauger.
**gaunt** [gɔ:nt] *a* décharné(e) ; (*grim, desolate*) désolé(e).
**gauntlet** ['gɔ:ntlɪt] *n* (*fig*): **to run the** ~ **through an angry crowd** se frayer un passage à travers une foule hostile *ou* entre deux haies de manifestants *etc* hostiles.
**gauze** [gɔ:z] *n* gaze *f.*
**gave** [geɪv] *pt of* **give.**
**gavel** ['gævl] *n* marteau *m.*
**gawp** [gɔ:p] *vi*: **to** ~ **at** regarder bouche bée.
**gay** [geɪ] *a* (*person*) gai(e), réjoui(e) ; (*colour*) gai, vif(vive) ; (*col*) homosexuel(le).
**gaze** [geɪz] *n* regard *m* fixe ; **to** ~ **at** *vt* fixer du regard.
**gazelle** [gə'zɛl] *n* gazelle *f.*
**gazetteer** [gæzə'tɪə*] *n* dictionnaire *m* géographique.
**gazumping** [gə'zʌmpɪŋ] *n* le fait de revenir sur une promesse de vente pour accepter un prix plus élevé.
**G.B.** *abbr of* **Great Britain.**
**G.C.E.** *n* (*abbr of* **General Certificate of Education**) ≈ baccalauréat *m.*
**Gdns.** *abbr of* **gardens.**
**gear** [gɪə*] *n* matériel *m*, équipement *m* ; attirail *m* ; (*TECH*) engrenage *m* ; (*AUT*) vitesse *f* ; **top/low/bottom** ~ quatrième (*or* cinquième/deuxième/première vi-

tesse ; **in** ~ en prise ; **out of** ~ au point mort ; ~ **box** *n* boîte *f* de vitesse ; ~ **lever,** ~ **shift** (*US*) *n* levier *m* de vitesse.
**geese** [gi:s] *npl of* **goose.**
**gelatin(e)** ['dʒɛləti:n] *n* gélatine *f.*
**gelignite** ['dʒɛlɪgnaɪt] *n* plastic *m.*
**gem** [dʒɛm] *n* pierre précieuse.
**Gemini** ['dʒɛmɪnaɪ] *n* les Gémeaux *mpl* ; **to be** ~ être des Gémeaux.
**gender** ['dʒɛndə*] *n* genre *m.*
**general** ['dʒɛnərl] *n* général *m //* *a* général(e) ; **in** ~ en général ; ~ **election** *n* élection(s) législative(s) ; ~**ization** [-'zeɪʃən] *n* généralisation *f* ; ~**ize** *vi* généraliser ; ~**ly** *ad* généralement ; **G**~ **Post Office** (**GPO**) *n* Postes et Télécommunications *fpl* (**PTT**) ; ~ **practitioner** (**G.P.**) *n* généraliste *m/f* ; **who's your G.P.?** qui est votre médecin traitant?
**generate** ['dʒɛnəreɪt] *vt* engendrer ; (*electricity*) produire.
**generation** [dʒɛnə'reɪʃən] *n* génération *f.*
**generator** ['dʒɛnəreɪtə*] *n* générateur *m.*
**generosity** [dʒɛnə'rɔsɪtɪ] *n* générosité *f.*
**generous** ['dʒɛnərəs] *a* généreux (euse) ; (*copious*) copieux(euse).
**genetics** [dʒɪ'nɛtɪks] *n* génétique *f.*
**Geneva** [dʒɪ'ni:və] *n* Genève.
**genial** ['dʒi:nɪəl] *a* cordial(e), chaleureux(euse) ; (*climate*) clément(e).
**genitals** ['dʒɛnɪtlz] *npl* organes génitaux.
**genitive** ['dʒɛnɪtɪv] *n* génitif *m.*
**genius** ['dʒi:nɪəs] *n* génie *m.*
**gent** [dʒɛnt] *n* abbr of **gentleman.**
**genteel** [dʒɛn'ti:l] *a* de bon ton, distingué(e).
**gentle** ['dʒɛntl] *a* doux(douce).
**gentleman** ['dʒɛntlmən] *n* monsieur *m* ; (*well-bred man*) gentleman *m.*
**gentleness** ['dʒɛntlnɪs] *n* douceur *f.*
**gently** ['dʒɛntlɪ] *ad* doucement.
**gentry** ['dʒɛntrɪ] *n* petite noblesse.
**gents** [dʒɛnts] *n* W.-C. *mpl* (pour hommes).
**genuine** ['dʒɛnjuɪn] *a* véritable, authentique ; sincère.
**geographer** [dʒɪ'ɔgrəfə*] *n* géographe *m/f.*
**geographic(al)** [dʒɪə'græfɪk(l)] *a* géographique.
**geography** [dʒɪ'ɔgrəfɪ] *n* géographie *f.*
**geological** [dʒɪə'lɔdʒɪkl] *a* géologique.
**geologist** [dʒɪ'ɔlədʒɪst] *n* géologue *m/f.*
**geology** [dʒɪ'ɔlədʒɪ] *n* géologie *f.*
**geometric(al)** [dʒɪə'mɛtrɪk(l)] *a* géométrique.
**geometry** [dʒɪ'ɔmətrɪ] *n* géométrie *f.*
**geranium** [dʒɪ'reɪnjəm] *n* géranium *m.*
**germ** [dʒə:m] *n* (*MED*) microbe *m* ; (*BIO, fig*) germe *m.*
**German** ['dʒə:mən] *a* allemand(e) // *n* Allemand/e ; (*LING*) allemand *m* ; ~ **measles** *n* rubéole *f.*
**Germany** ['dʒə:mənɪ] *n* Allemagne *f.*
**germination** [dʒə:mɪ'neɪʃən] *n* germination *f.*
**gerrymandering** ['dʒɛrɪmændərɪŋ] *n* tripotage *m* du découpage électoral.
**gestation** [dʒɛs'teɪʃən] *n* gestation *f.*

**gesticulate** [dʒɛs'tɪkjuleɪt] vi gesticuler.
**gesture** ['dʒɛstjə*] n geste m.
**get**, pt, pp **got**, pp **gotten** (US) [gɛt, gɔt, 'gɔtn] vt (obtain) avoir, obtenir ; (receive) recevoir ; (find) trouver, acheter ; (catch) attraper ; (fetch) aller chercher ; (understand) comprendre, saisir ; (have): **to have got** avoir ; (become): **to ~ rich/old** s'enrichir/vieillir // vi: **to ~ to** (place) aller à ; arriver à ; parvenir à ; **he got across the bridge/under the fence** il a traversé le pont/est passé par-dessous la barrière ; **to ~ ready/washed/shaved** etc se préparer/laver/raser etc ; **to ~ sb to do sth** faire faire qch à qn ; **to ~ sth through/out** faire passer qch par/sortir qch de ; **to ~ about** vi se déplacer ; (news) se répandre ; **to ~ along** vi (agree) s'entendre ; (depart) s'en aller ; (manage) = **to get by**; **to ~ at** vt fus (attack) s'en prendre à ; (reach) attraper, atteindre ; **to ~ away** vi partir, s'en aller ; (escape) s'échapper ; **to ~ away with** vt fus en être quitte pour ; se faire passer or pardonner ; **to ~ back** vi (return) rentrer // vt récupérer, recouvrer ; **to ~ by** vi (pass) passer ; (manage) se débrouiller ; **to ~ down** vi, vt fus descendre // vt descendre ; (depress) déprimer ; **to ~ down to** vt fus (work) se mettre à (faire) ; **to ~ in** vi entrer ; (train) arriver ; (arrive home) rentrer ; **to ~ into** vt fus entrer dans ; **to ~ into bed/a rage** se mettre au lit/en colère ; **to ~ off** vi (from train etc) descendre ; (depart: person, car) s'en aller ; (escape) s'en tirer // vt (remove: clothes, stain) enlever // vt fus (train, bus) descendre de ; **to ~ on** vi (at exam etc) se débrouiller ; (agree): **to ~ on** (with) s'entendre (avec) // vt fus monter dans ; (horse) monter sur ; **to ~ out** vi sortir ; (of vehicle) descendre // vt sortir ; **to ~ out of** vt fus sortir de ; (duty etc) échapper à, se soustraire à ; **to ~ over** vt fus (illness) se remettre de ; **to ~ round** vt fus contourner ; (fig: person) entortiller ; **to ~ through** vi (TEL) avoir la communication ; **to ~ through to** vt fus (TEL) atteindre ; **to ~ together** vi se réunir // vt assembler ; **to ~ up** vi (rise) se lever // vt fus monter ; **to ~ up to** vt fus (reach) arriver à ; (prank etc) faire ; **~away** n fuite f.
**geyser** ['giːzə*] n chauffe-eau m inv ; (GEO) geyser m.
**Ghana** ['gɑːnə] n Ghana m ; **~ian** [-'neɪən] a ghanéen(ne) // n Ghanéen/ne.
**ghastly** ['gɑːstlɪ] a atroce, horrible ; (pale) livide, blême.
**gherkin** ['gəːkɪn] n cornichon m.
**ghetto** ['gɛtəu] n ghetto m.
**ghost** [gəust] n fantôme m, revenant m ; **~ly** a fantomatique.
**giant** ['dʒaɪənt] n géant/e // a géant(e), énorme.
**gibberish** ['dʒɪbərɪʃ] n charabia m.
**gibe** [dʒaɪb] n sarcasme m // vi: **to ~ at** railler.
**giblets** ['dʒɪblɪts] npl abats mpl.
**giddiness** ['gɪdɪnɪs] n vertige m.
**giddy** ['gɪdɪ] a (dizzy): **to be ~** avoir le

vertige ; (height) vertigineux(euse) ; (thoughtless) sot(te), étourdi(e).
**gift** [gɪft] n cadeau m, présent m ; (donation, ability) don m ; **~ed** a doué(e).
**gigantic** [dʒaɪ'gæntɪk] a gigantesque.
**giggle** ['gɪgl] vi pouffer, ricaner sottement // n petit rire sot, ricanement m.
**gild** [gɪld] vt dorer.
**gill** n [dʒɪl] (measure) = 0.14 l; 0.25 pints ; **~s** [gɪlz] npl (of fish) ouïes fpl, branchies fpl.
**gilt** [gɪlt] n dorure f // a doré(e).
**gimlet** ['gɪmlɪt] n vrille f.
**gimmick** ['gɪmɪk] n truc m.
**gin** [dʒɪn] n (liquor) gin m.
**ginger** ['dʒɪndʒə*] n gingembre m ; **to ~ up** vt secouer ; animer ; **~ ale**, **~ beer** n boisson gazeuse au gingembre ; **~bread** n pain m d'épices ; **~ group** n groupe m de pression ; **~-haired** a roux(rousse).
**gingerly** ['dʒɪndʒəlɪ] ad avec précaution.
**gingham** ['gɪŋəm] n vichy m.
**gipsy** ['dʒɪpsɪ] n gitan/e, bohémien/ne.
**giraffe** [dʒɪ'rɑːf] n girafe f.
**girder** ['gəːdə*] n poutrelle f.
**girdle** ['gəːdl] n (corset) gaine f // vt ceindre.
**girl** [gəːl] n fille f, fillette f ; (young unmarried woman) jeune fille ; (daughter) fille ; **an English ~** une jeune Anglaise ; **a little English ~** une petite Anglaise ; **~friend** n (of girl) amie f ; (of boy) petite amie ; **~ish** a de jeune fille.
**Giro** ['dʒaɪrəu] n: **the National ~** ≈ les comptes chèques postaux.
**girth** [gəːθ] n circonférence f ; (of horse) sangle f.
**gist** [dʒɪst] n essentiel m.
**give** [gɪv] n (of fabric) élasticité f // vb (pt **gave**, pp **given** [geɪv, 'gɪvn]) vt donner // vi (break) céder ; (stretch: fabric) se prêter ; **to ~ sb sth**, **~ sth to sb** donner qch à qn ; **to ~ a cry/sigh** pousser un cri/un soupir ; **to ~ away** vt donner ; (give free) faire cadeau de ; (betray) donner, trahir ; (disclose) révéler ; (bride) conduire à l'autel ; **to ~ back** vt rendre ; **to ~ in** vi céder // vt donner ; **to ~ off** vt dégager ; **to ~ out** vt distribuer ; annoncer ; **to ~ up** vi renoncer // vt renoncer à ; **to ~ up smoking** arrêter de fumer ; **to ~ o.s. up** se rendre ; **to ~ way** vi céder ; (AUT) donner la priorité.
**glacier** ['glæsɪə*] n glacier m.
**glad** [glæd] a content(e) ; **~den** vt réjouir.
**gladioli** [glædɪ'əulaɪ] npl glaïeuls mpl.
**gladly** ['glædlɪ] ad volontiers.
**glamorous** ['glæmərəs] a séduisant(e).
**glamour** ['glæmə*] n éclat m, prestige m.
**glance** [glɑːns] n coup m d'œil // vi: **to ~ at** jeter un coup d'œil à ; **to ~ off** (bullet) ricocher sur ; **glancing** a (blow) oblique.
**gland** [glænd] n glande f.
**glandular** ['glændjulə*] a: **~ fever** n mononucléose infectieuse.
**glare** [glɛə*] n lumière éblouissante // vi briller d'un éclat aveuglant ; **to ~ at** lancer un or des regard(s) furieux à ; **glaring** a (mistake) criant(e), qui saute aux yeux.

**glass** [glɑ:s] *n* verre *m*; (*also:* **looking** ~) miroir *m*; ~**es** *npl* lunettes *fpl*; ~**house** *n* serre *f*; ~**ware** *n* verrerie *f*; ~**y** *a* (*eyes*) vitreux(euse).

**glaze** [gleɪz] *vt* (*door*) vitrer; (*pottery*) vernir // *n* vernis *m*; ~**d** *a* (*eye*) vitreux(euse); (*pottery*) verni(e); (*tiles*) vitrifié(e).

**glazier** ['gleɪzɪə*] *n* vitrier *m*.

**gleam** [gli:m] *n* lueur *f*; rayon *m* // *vi* luire, briller; ~**ing** *a* luisant(e).

**glee** [gli:] *n* joie *f*; ~**ful** *a* joyeux(euse).

**glen** [glɛn] *n* vallée *f*.

**glib** [glɪb] *a* qui a du bagou; facile.

**glide** [glaɪd] *vi* glisser; (*AVIAT*, *birds*) planer // *n* glissement *m*; vol plané; ~**r** *n* (*AVIAT*) planeur *m*; **gliding** *n* (*AVIAT*) vol *m* à voile.

**glimmer** ['glɪmə*] *vi* luire // *n* lueur *f*.

**glimpse** [glɪmps] *n* vision passagère, aperçu *m* // *vt* entrevoir, apercevoir.

**glint** [glɪnt] *n* éclair *m* // *vi* étinceler.

**glisten** ['glɪsn] *vi* briller, luire.

**glitter** ['glɪtə*] *vi* scintiller, briller // *n* scintillement *m*.

**gloat** [gləut] *vi:* **to** ~ (**over**) jubiler (à propos de).

**global** ['gləubl] *a* mondial(e).

**globe** [gləub] *n* globe *m*.

**gloom** [glu:m] *n* obscurité *f*; (*sadness*) tristesse *f*, mélancolie *f*; ~**y** *a* sombre, triste, mélancolique.

**glorification** [glɔ:rɪfɪ'keɪʃən] *n* glorification *f*.

**glorify** ['glɔ:rɪfaɪ] *vt* glorifier.

**glorious** ['glɔ:rɪəs] *a* glorieux (euse); splendide.

**glory** ['glɔ:rɪ] *n* gloire *f*; splendeur *f*; **to** ~ **in** se glorifier de.

**gloss** [glɔs] *n* (*shine*) brillant *m*, vernis *m*; **to** ~ **over** *vt fus* glisser sur.

**glossary** ['glɔsərɪ] *n* glossaire *m*, lexique *m*.

**gloss paint** ['glɔspeɪnt] *n* peinture brillante.

**glossy** ['glɔsɪ] *a* brillant(e), luisant(e); ~ (**magazine**) *n* revue *f* de luxe.

**glove** [glʌv] *n* gant *m*; ~ **compartment** *n* (*AUT*) boîte *f* à gants, vide-poches *m inv*.

**glow** [gləu] *vi* rougeoyer; (*face*) rayonner // *n* rougeoiement *m*.

**glower** ['glauə*] *vi* lancer des regards mauvais.

**glucose** ['glu:kəus] *n* glucose *m*.

**glue** [glu:] *n* colle *f* // *vt* coller.

**glum** [glʌm] *a* maussade, morose.

**glut** [glʌt] *n* surabondance *f* // *vt* rassasier; (*market*) encombrer.

**glutton** ['glʌtn] *n* glouton/ne; **a** ~ **for work** un bourreau de travail; ~**ous** *a* glouton(ne); ~**y** *n* gloutonnerie *f*; (*sin*) gourmandise *f*.

**glycerin(e)** ['glɪsəri:n] *n* glycérine *f*.

**gm, gms** *abbr of* **gram(s)**.

**gnarled** [nɑ:ld] *a* noueux(euse).

**gnat** [næt] *n* moucheron *m*.

**gnaw** [nɔ:] *vt* ronger.

**gnome** [nəum] *n* gnome *m*, lutin *m*.

**go** [gəu] *vb* (*pt* **went**, *pp* **gone** [wɛnt, gɔn]) *vi* aller; (*depart*) partir, s'en aller; (*work*) marcher; (*be sold*): **to** ~ **for £10** se vendre 10 livres; (*fit, suit*): **to** ~ **with** aller avec; (*become*): **to** ~ **pale/mouldy** pâlir/moisir; (*break etc*) céder // *n* (*pl*: ~**es**): **to have a** ~ (**at**) essayer (de faire); **to be on the** ~ être en mouvement; **whose** ~ **is it?** à qui est-ce de jouer?; **he's going to do** il va faire, il est sur le point de faire; **to** ~ **for a walk** aller se promener; **to** ~ **dancing/shopping** aller danser/faire les courses; **how is it** ~**ing?** comment ça marche?; **how did it** ~? comment est-ce que ça s'est passé?; **to** ~ **round the back/by the shop** passer par derrière/devant le magasin; **to** ~ **about** *vi* (*rumour*) se répandre // *vt fus*: **how do I** ~ **about this?** comment dois-je m'y prendre (pour faire ceci)?; **to** ~ **ahead** *vi* (*make progress*) avancer; (*get going*) y aller; **to** ~ **along** *vi* aller, avancer // *vt fus* longer, parcourir; **as you** ~ **along** (**with your work**) au fur et à mesure (de votre travail); **to** ~ **away** *vi* partir, s'en aller; **to** ~ **back** *vi* rentrer; revenir; (*go again*) retourner; **to** ~ **back on** *vt fus* (*promise*) revenir sur; **to** ~ **by** *vi* (*years, time*) passer, s'écouler // *vt fus* s'en tenir à; en croire; **to** ~ **down** *vi* descendre; (*ship*) couler; (*sun*) se coucher // *vt fus* descendre; **to** ~ **for** *vt fus* (*fetch*) aller chercher; (*like*) aimer; (*attack*) s'en prendre à; attaquer; **to** ~ **in** *vi* entrer; **to** ~ **in for** *vt fus* (*competition*) se présenter à; (*like*) aimer; **to** ~ **into** *vt fus* entrer dans; (*investigate*) étudier, examiner; (*embark on*) se lancer dans; **to** ~ **off** *vi* partir, s'en aller; (*food*) se gâter; (*explode*) sauter; (*event*) se dérouler // *vt fus* ne plus aimer, ne plus avoir envie de; **the gun went off** le coup est parti; **to** ~ **off to sleep** s'endormir; **to** ~ **on** *vi* continuer; (*happen*) se passer; **to** ~ **on doing** continuer à faire; **to** ~ **on with** *vt fus* poursuivre, continuer; **to** ~ **out** *vi* sortir; (*fire, light*) s'éteindre; **to** ~ **over** *vi* (*ship*) chavirer // *vt fus* (*check*) revoir, vérifier; **to** ~ **through** *vt fus* (*town etc*) traverser; **to** ~ **up** *vi* monter; (*price*) augmenter // *vt fus* gravir; **to** ~ **without** *vt fus* se passer de.

**goad** [gəud] *vt* aiguillonner.

**go-ahead** ['gəuəhɛd] *a* dynamique, entreprenant(e) // *n* feu vert.

**goal** [gəul] *n* but *m*; ~**keeper** *n* gardien *m* de but; ~**-post** *n* poteau *m* de but.

**goat** [gəut] *n* chèvre *f*.

**gobble** ['gɔbl] *vt* (*also:* ~ **down,** ~ **up**) engloutir.

**go-between** ['gəubɪtwi:n] *n* médiateur *m*.

**goblet** ['gɔblɪt] *n* goblet *m*.

**goblin** ['gɔblɪn] *n* lutin *m*.

**go-cart** ['gəukɑ:t] *n* kart *m*; ~ **racing** *n* karting *m*.

**god** [gɔd] *n* dieu *m*; **G**~ *n* Dieu *m*; ~**child** *n* filleul/e; ~**dess** *n* déesse *f*; ~**father** *n* parrain *m*; ~**-forsaken** *a* maudit(e); ~**mother** *n* marraine *f*; ~**send** *n* aubaine *f*; ~**son** *n* filleul *m*.

**goggle** ['gɔgl] *vi:* **to** ~ **at** regarder avec des yeux ronds; ~**s** *npl* lunettes *fpl* (protectrices: *de motocycliste etc*).

**going** ['gəuɪŋ] *n* (*conditions*) état *m* du terrain // *a:* **the** ~ **rate** le tarif (en vigueur) ; **a ~ concern** une affaire prospère.

**go-kart** ['gəukɑːt] *n* = **go-cart**.

**gold** [gəuld] *n* or *m* // *a* en or ; **~en** *a* (*made of gold*) en or ; (*gold in colour*) doré(e) ; **~en rule/age** règle/âge d'or ; **~fish** *n* poisson *m* rouge ; **~mine** *n* mine *f* d'or.

**golf** [gɔlf] *n* golf *m* ; **~ club** *n* club *m* de golf ; (*stick*) club *m*, crosse *f* de golf ; **~ course** *n* terrain *m* de golf ; **~er** *n* joueur/euse de golf.

**gondola** ['gɔndələ] *n* gondole *f*.

**gone** [gɔn] *pp of* **go** // *a* parti(e).

**gong** [gɔŋ] *n* gong *m*.

**good** [gud] *a* bon(ne) ; (*kind*) gentil(le) ; (*child*) sage // *n* bien *m* ; **~s** *npl* marchandise *f* ; articles *mpl* ; **she is ~ with children/her hands** elle sait bien s'occuper des enfants/sait se servir de ses mains ; **would you be ~ enough to ...?** auriez-vous la bonté *or* l'amabilité de ...? ; **a ~ deal (of)** beaucoup (de) ; **a ~ many** beaucoup (de) ; **~ morning/afternoon!** bonjour! ; **~ evening!** bonsoir! ; **~ night!** bonsoir! ; (*on going to bed*) bonne nuit! ; **~bye!** au revoir! ; **G~ Friday** *n* Vendredi saint ; **~-looking** *a* bien *inv* ; **~ness** *n* (*of person*) bonté *f* ; **for ~ness sake!** je vous en prie! ; **~ness gracious!** mon Dieu! ; **~will** *n* bonne volonté *f* ; (*COMM*) réputation *f* (auprès de la clientèle).

**goose**, *pl* **geese** [guːs, giːs] *n* oie *f*.

**gooseberry** ['guzbərɪ] *n* groseille *f* à maquereau ; **to play ~** tenir la chandelle.

**gooseflesh** ['guːsflɛʃ] *n* chair *f* de poule.

**gore** [gɔː*] *vt* encorner // *n* sang *m*.

**gorge** [gɔːdʒ] *n* gorge *f* // *vt*: **to ~ o.s. (on)** se gorger (de).

**gorgeous** ['gɔːdʒəs] *a* splendide, superbe.

**gorilla** [gə'rɪlə] *n* gorille *m*.

**gorse** [gɔːs] *n* ajoncs *mpl*.

**gory** ['gɔːrɪ] *a* sanglant(e).

**go-slow** ['gəu'sləu] *n* grève perlée.

**gospel** ['gɔspl] *n* évangile *m*.

**gossamer** ['gɔsəmə*] *n* (*cobweb*) fils *mpl* de la vierge ; (*light fabric*) étoffe très légère.

**gossip** ['gɔsɪp] *n* bavardages *mpl* ; commérage *m*, cancans *mpl* ; (*person*) commère *f* // *vi* bavarder ; (*maliciously*) cancaner, faire des commérages.

**got** [gɔt] *pt,pp of* **get** ; **~ten** (*US*) *pp of* **get**.

**gout** [gaut] *n* goutte *f*.

**govern** ['gʌvən] *vt* (*gen, LING*) gouverner.

**governess** ['gʌvənɪs] *n* gouvernante *f*.

**government** ['gʌvnmənt] *n* gouvernement *m* ; (*ministers*) ministère *m* // *cpd* de l'État ; **~al** ['mɛntl] *a* gouvernemental(e).

**governor** ['gʌvənə*] *n* (*of state, bank*) gouverneur *m* ; (*of school, hospital*) administrateur *m*.

**Govt** *abbr of* **government**.

**gown** [gaun] *n* robe *f* ; (*of teacher, judge*) toge *f*.

**G.P.** *n abbr see* **general**.

**GPO** *n abbr see* **general**.

**grab** [græb] *vt* saisir, empoigner ; (*property, power*) se saisir de.

**grace** [greɪs] *n* grâce *f* // *vt* honorer ; **5 days' ~** répit *m* de 5 jours ; **to say ~**

dire le bénédicité ; (*after meal*) dire les grâces ; **~ful** *a* gracieux(euse), élégant(e) ; **gracious** ['greɪʃəs] *a* bienveillant(e) ; de bonne grâce ; miséricordieux(euse).

**gradation** [grə'deɪʃən] *n* gradation *f*.

**grade** [greɪd] *n* (*COMM*) qualité *f* ; calibre *m* ; catégorie *f* ; (*in hierarchy*) grade *m*, échelon *m* ; (*US: SCOL*) note *f* ; classe *f* // *vt* classer ; calibrer ; graduer ; **~ crossing** *n* (*US*) passage *m* à niveau.

**gradient** ['greɪdɪənt] *n* inclinaison *f*, pente *f* ; (*GEOM*) gradient *m*.

⟶ **gradual** ['grædjuəl] *a* graduel(le), progressif(ive) ; **~ly** *ad* peu à peu, graduellement.

**graduate** *n* ['grædjuɪt] diplômé/e d'université // *vi* ['grædjueɪt] obtenir un diplôme d'université ; **graduation** [-'eɪʃən] *n* cérémonie *f* de remise des diplômes.

**graft** [grɑːft] *n* (*AGR, MED*) greffe *f* ; (*bribery*) corruption *f* // *vt* greffer ; **hard ~** *n* (*col*) boulot acharné.

**grain** [greɪn] *n* grain *m* ; **it goes against the ~** cela va à l'encontre de sa (*or* ma) nature.

**gram** [græm] *n* gramme *m*.

**grammar** ['græmə*] *n* grammaire *f*.

**grammatical** [grə'mætɪkl] *a* grammatical(e).

**gramme** [græm] *n* = **gram**.

**gramophone** ['græməfəun] *n* gramophone *m*.

**granary** ['grænərɪ] *n* grenier *m*.

**grand** [grænd] *a* magnifique, splendide ; noble ; **~children** *npl* petits-enfants *mpl* ; **~dad** *n* grand-papa *m* ; **~daughter** *n* petite-fille *f* ; **~eur** ['grændjə*] *n* grandeur *f*, noblesse *f* ; **~father** *n* grand-père *m* ; **~iose** ['grændɪəuz] *a* grandiose ; (*pej*) pompeux(euse) ; **~ma** *n* grand-maman *f* ; **~mother** *n* grand-mère *f* ; **~pa** *n* = **~dad** ; **~ piano** *n* piano *m* à queue ; **~son** *n* petit-fils *m* ; **~stand** *n* (*SPORT*) tribune *f*.

**granite** ['grænɪt] *n* granit *m*.

**granny** ['grænɪ] *n* grand-maman *f*.

**grant** [grɑːnt] *vt* accorder ; (*a request*) accéder à ; (*admit*) concéder // *n* (*SCOL*) bourse *f* ; (*ADMIN*) subside *m*, subvention *f* ; **to take sth for ~ed** considérer qch comme acquis *or* allant de soi.

**granulated** ['grænjuleɪtɪd] *a*: **~ sugar** *n* sucre *m* en poudre.

**granule** ['grænjuːl] *n* granule *m*.

**grape** [greɪp] *n* raisin *m*.

**grapefruit** ['greɪpfruːt] *n* pamplemousse *m*.

**graph** [grɑːf] *n* graphique *m*, courbe *f* ; **~ic** *a* graphique ; (*vivid*) vivant(e).

**grapple** ['græpl] *vi*: **to ~ with** être aux prises avec.

**grasp** [grɑːsp] *vt* saisir, empoigner ; (*understand*) saisir, comprendre // *n* (*grip*) prise *f* ; (*fig*) emprise *f*, pouvoir *m* ; compréhension *f*, connaissance *f* ; **~ing** *a* avide.

**grass** [grɑːs] *n* herbe *f* ; gazon *m* ; **~hopper** *n* sauterelle *f* ; **~land** *n* prairie *f* ; **~ snake** *n* couleuvre *f* ; **~y** *a* herbeux(euse).

**grate** [greɪt] *n* grille *f* de cheminée // *vi* grincer // *vt* (*CULIN*) râper.

**grateful** ['greɪtful] a reconnaissant(e) ; **~ly** ad avec reconnaissance.

**grater** ['greɪtə*] n râpe f.

**gratify** ['grætɪfaɪ] vt faire plaisir à ; (whim) satisfaire ; **~ing** a agréable ; satisfaisant(e).

**grating** ['greɪtɪŋ] n (iron bars) grille f // a (noise) grinçant(e).

**gratitude** ['grætɪtjuːd] n gratitude f.

**gratuitous** [grə'tjuːɪtəs] a gratuit(e).

**gratuity** [grə'tjuːɪtɪ] n pourboire m.

**grave** [greɪv] n tombe f // a grave, sérieux(euse) ; **~digger** n fossoyeur m.

**gravel** ['grævl] n gravier m.

**gravestone** ['greɪvstəun] n pierre tombale.

**graveyard** ['greɪvjɑːd] n cimetière m.

**gravitate** ['grævɪteɪt] vi graviter.

**gravity** ['grævɪtɪ] n (PHYSICS) gravité f ; pesanteur f ; (seriousness) gravité f, sérieux m.

**gravy** ['greɪvɪ] n jus m (de viande) ; sauce f.

**gray** [greɪ] a = grey.

**graze** [greɪz] vi paître, brouter // vt (touch lightly) frôler, effleurer ; (scrape) écorcher // n (MED) écorchure f.

**grease** [griːs] n (fat) graisse f ; (lubricant) lubrifiant m // vt graisser ; lubrifier ; **~gun** n graisseur m ; **~proof paper** n papier sulfurisé ; **greasy** a gras(se), graisseux(euse).

**great** [greɪt] a grand(e) ; (col) formidable ; **G~ Britain** n Grande-Bretagne f ; **~-grandfather** n arrière-grand-père m ; **~-grandmother** n arrière-grand-mère f ; **~ly** ad très, grandement ; (with verbs) beaucoup ; **~ness** n grandeur f.

**Grecian** ['griːʃən] a grec(grecque).

**Greece** [griːs] n Grèce f.

**greed** [griːd] n (also: **~iness**) avidité f ; (for food) gourmandise f ; **~ily** ad avidement ; avec gourmandise ; **~y** a avide ; gourmand(e).

**Greek** [griːk] a grec(grecque) // n Grec/Grecque ; (LING) grec m.

**green** [griːn] a vert(e) ; (inexperienced) (bien) jeune, naïf(ïve) // n vert m ; (stretch of grass) pelouse f ; (also: **village ~**) ≈ place f du village ; **~s** npl légumes verts ; **~gage** n reine-claude f ; **~grocer** n marchand m de fruits et légumes ; **~house** n serre f ; **~ish** a verdâtre.

**Greenland** ['griːnlənd] n Groenland m.

**greet** [griːt] vt accueillir ; **~ing** n salutation f ; **Christmas/birthday ~ings** souhaits mpl de Noël/de bon anniversaire ; **~ing(s) card** n carte f de vœux.

**gregarious** [grə'gɛərɪəs] a grégaire ; sociable.

**grenade** [grə'neɪd] n grenade f.

**grew** [gruː] pt of **grow**.

**grey** [greɪ] a gris(e) ; (dismal) sombre ; **~-haired** a aux cheveux gris ; **~hound** n lévrier m.

**grid** [grɪd] n grille f ; (ELEC) réseau m ; **~iron** n gril m.

**grief** [griːf] n chagrin m, douleur f.

**grievance** ['griːvəns] n doléance f, grief m.

**grieve** [griːv] vi avoir du chagrin ; se désoler // vt faire de la peine à, affliger ; **to ~ at** se désoler de ; pleurer.

**grievous** ['griːvəs] a grave ; cruel(le).

**grill** [grɪl] n (on cooker) gril m // vt griller ; (question) interroger longuement, cuisiner.

**grille** [grɪl] n grillage m ; (AUT) calandre f.

**grill(room)** ['grɪl(rum)] n rôtisserie f.

**grim** [grɪm] a sinistre, lugubre.

**grimace** [grɪ'meɪs] n grimace f // vi grimacer, faire une grimace.

**grime** [graɪm] n crasse f.

**grimy** ['graɪmɪ] a crasseux(euse).

**grin** [grɪn] n large sourire m // vi sourire.

**grind** [graɪnd] vt (pt, pp **ground** [graund]) écraser ; (coffee, pepper etc) moudre ; (make sharp) aiguiser // n (work) corvée f ; **to ~ one's teeth** grincer des dents.

**grip** [grɪp] n étreinte f, poigne f ; prise f ; (handle) poignée f ; (holdall) sac m de voyage // vt saisir, empoigner ; étreindre ; **to come to ~s with** en venir aux prises avec ; **to ~ the road** (AUT) adhérer à la route.

**gripe(s)** [graɪp(s)] n(pl) coliques fpl.

**gripping** ['grɪpɪŋ] a prenant(e), palpitant(e).

**grisly** ['grɪzlɪ] a sinistre, macabre.

**gristle** ['grɪsl] n cartilage m (de poulet etc).

**grit** [grɪt] n gravillon m ; (courage) cran m // vt (road) sabler ; **to ~ one's teeth** serrer les dents.

**grizzle** ['grɪzl] vi pleurnicher.

**groan** [grəun] n gémissement m ; grognement m // vi gémir ; grogner.

**grocer** ['grəusə*] n épicier m ; **at the ~'s** à l'épicerie, chez l'épicier ; **~ies** npl provisions fpl.

**grog** [grɔg] n grog m.

**groggy** ['grɔgɪ] a groggy inv.

**groin** [grɔɪn] n aine f.

**groom** [gruːm] n palefrenier m ; (also: **bride~**) marié m // vt (horse) panser ; (fig): **to ~ sb for** former qn pour.

**groove** [gruːv] n sillon m, rainure f.

**grope** [grəup] vi tâtonner ; **to ~ for** vt fus chercher à tâtons.

**gross** [grəus] a grossier(ère) ; (COMM) brut(e) ; **~ly** ad (greatly) très, grandement.

**grotesque** [grə'tɛsk] a grotesque.

**grotto** ['grɔtəu] n grotte f.

**ground** [graund] pt, pp of **grind** // n sol m, terre f ; (land) terrain m, terres fpl ; (SPORT) terrain ; (reason: gen pl) raison f // vt (plane) empêcher de décoller, retenir au sol // vi (ship) s'échouer ; **~s** npl (of coffee etc) marc m ; (gardens etc) parc m, domaine m ; **on the ~, to the ~** par terre ; **~ floor** n rez-de-chaussée m ; **~ing** n (in education) connaissances fpl de base ; **~less** a sans fondement ; **~sheet** n tapis m de sol ; **~ staff** n équipage m au sol ; **~work** n préparation f.

**group** [gruːp] n groupe m // vt (also: **~ together**) grouper // vi (also: **~ together**) se grouper.

**grouse** [graus] n, pl inv (bird) grouse f (sorte de coq de bruyère) // vi (complain) rouspéter, râler.

**grove** [grəuv] n bosquet m.

**grovel** ['grɔvl] vi (fig): **to** ~ **(before)** ramper (devant).

**grow,** pt **grew,** pp **grown** [grəu, gru:, grəun] vi (plant) pousser, croître ; (person) grandir ; (increase) augmenter, se développer ; (become): **to** ~ **rich/weak** s'enrichir/s'affaiblir // vt cultiver, faire pousser ; **to** ~ **up** vi grandir ; ~**er** n producteur m ; ~**ing** a (fear, amount) croissant(e), grandissant(e).

**growl** [graul] vi grogner.

**grown** [grəun] pp of **grow** // a adulte ; ~**-up** n adulte m/f, grande personne.

**growth** [grəuθ] n croissance f, développement m ; (what has grown) pousse f; poussée f; (MED) grosseur f, tumeur f.

**grub** [grʌb] n larve f; (col: food) bouffe f.

**grubby** ['grʌbɪ] a crasseux(euse).

**grudge** [grʌdʒ] n rancune f // vt: **to** ~ **sb sth** donner qch à qn à contre-cœur ; reprocher qch à qn ; **to bear sb a** ~ **(for)** garder rancune or en vouloir à qn (de) ; **he** ~**s spending** il rechigne à dépenser ; **grudgingly** ad à contre-cœur, de mauvaise grâce.

**gruelling** ['gruəlɪŋ] a exténuant(e).

**gruesome** ['gru:səm] a horrible.

**gruff** [grʌf] a bourru(e).

**grumble** ['grʌmbl] vi rouspéter, ronchonner.

**grumpy** ['grʌmpɪ] a grincheux (euse).

**grunt** [grʌnt] vi grogner // n grognement m.

**G-string** ['dʒiːstrɪŋ] n (garment) cache-sexe m inv.

**guarantee** [gærən'tiː] n garantie f // vt garantir.

**guarantor** [gærən'tɔ:*] n garant/e.

**guard** [gɑːd] n garde f, surveillance f; (squad, BOXING, FENCING) garde f; (one man) garde m ; (RAIL) chef m de train // vt garder, surveiller ; ~**ed** a (fig) prudent(e) ; ~**ian** n gardien/ne ; (of minor) tuteur/trice ; ~'**s van** n (RAIL.) fourgon m.

**guerrilla** [gə'rɪlə] n guérillero m ; ~ **warfare** n guérilla f.

**guess** [gɛs] vi deviner // vt deviner ; (US) croire, penser // n supposition f, hypothèse f; **to take/have a** ~ essayer de deviner ; ~**work** n hypothèse f.

**guest** [gɛst] n invité/e ; (in hotel) client/e ; ~**-house** n pension f; ~ **room** n chambre f d'amis.

**guffaw** [gʌ'fɔ:] n gros rire // vi pouffer de rire.

**guidance** ['gaɪdəns] n conseils mpl ; **under the** ~ **of** conseillé(e) or encadré(e) par, sous la conduite de.

**guide** [gaɪd] n (person, book etc) guide m // vt guider ; **(girl)** ~ n guide f; ~**book** n guide m ; ~**d missile** n missile téléguidé ; ~ **dog** n chien m d'aveugle ; ~ **lines** npl (fig) instructions générales, conseils mpl.

**guild** [gɪld] n corporation f; cercle m, association f; ~**hall** n (Brit) hôtel m de ville.

**guile** [gaɪl] n astuce f; ~**less** a candide.

**guillotine** ['gɪləti:n] n guillotine f; (for paper) massicot m.

**guilt** [gɪlt] n culpabilité f; ~**y** a coupable.

**guinea** ['gɪnɪ] n (Brit) guinée f (= 21 shillings: cette monnaie de compte ne s'emploie plus).

**guinea pig** ['gɪnɪpɪg] n cobaye m.

**guise** [gaɪz] n aspect m, apparence f.

**guitar** [gɪ'tɑ:*] n guitare f; ~**ist** n guitariste m/f.

**gulf** [gʌlf] n golfe m ; (abyss) gouffre m.

**gull** [gʌl] n mouette f.

**gullet** ['gʌlɪt] n gosier m.

**gullible** ['gʌlɪbl] a crédule.

**gully** ['gʌlɪ] n ravin m ; ravine f; couloir m.

**gulp** [gʌlp] vi avaler sa salive ; (from emotion) avoir la gorge serrée, s'étrangler // vt (also: ~ **down**) avaler // n: **at one** ~ d'un seul coup.

**gum** [gʌm] n (ANAT) gencive f; (glue) colle f; (sweet) boule f de gomme ; (also: **chewing-**~) chewing-gum m // vt coller ; ~**boil** n abcès m dentaire ; ~**boots** npl bottes fpl en caoutchouc.

**gumption** ['gʌmpʃən] n bon sens, jugeote f.

**gun** [gʌn] n (small) revolver m, pistolet m ; (rifle) fusil m, carabine f; (cannon) canon m ; ~**boat** n canonnière f; ~**fire** n fusillade f; ~**man** n bandit armé ; ~**ner** n artilleur m ; **at** ~**point** sous la menace du pistolet (or fusil) ; ~**powder** n poudre f à canon ; ~**shot** n coup m de feu ; **within** ~**shot** à portée de fusil ; ~**smith** n armurier m.

**gurgle** ['gə:gl] n gargouillis m // vi gargouiller.

**gush** [gʌʃ] n jaillissement m, jet m // vi jaillir ; (fig) se répandre en effusions.

**gusset** ['gʌsɪt] n gousset m, soufflet m.

**gust** [gʌst] n (of wind) rafale f; (of smoke) bouffée f.

**gusto** ['gʌstəu] n enthousiasme m.

**gut** [gʌt] n intestin m, boyau m ; (MUS etc) boyau m ; ~**s** npl (courage) cran m.

**gutter** ['gʌtə*] n (of roof) gouttière f; (in street) caniveau m ; (fig) ruisseau m.

**guttural** ['gʌtərl] a guttural(e).

**guy** [gaɪ] n (also: ~**rope**) corde f; (col: man) type m ; (figure) effigie de Guy Fawkes.

**guzzle** ['gʌzl] vi s'empiffrer // vt avaler gloutonnement.

**gym** [dʒɪm] n (also: **gymnasium**) gymnase m ; (also: **gymnastics**) gym f; ~ **shoes** npl chaussures fpl de gym(nastique) ; ~ **slip** n tunique f (d'écolière).

**gymnast** ['dʒɪmnæst] n gymnaste m/f; ~**ics** [-'næstɪks] n, npl gymnastique f.

**gynaecologist, gynecologist** (US) [gaɪnɪ'kɔlədʒɪst] n gynécologue m/f.

**gynaecology, gynecology** (US) [gaɪnə'kɔlədʒɪ] n gynécologie f.

**gypsy** ['dʒɪpsɪ] n = **gipsy**.

**gyrate** [dʒaɪ'reɪt] vi tournoyer.

## H

**haberdashery** ['hæbə'dæʃərɪ] n mercerie f.

**habit** ['hæbɪt] n habitude f; (costume) habit m, tenue f.

**habitable** ['hæbɪtəbl] a habitable.
**habitation** [hæbɪ'teɪʃən] n habitation f.
**habitual** [hə'bɪtjuəl] a habituel(le); (drinker, liar); invétéré(e); ~**ly** ad habituellement, d'habitude.
**hack** [hæk] vt hacher, tailler // n (cut) entaille f; (blow) coup m; (pej: writer) nègre m.
**hackney cab** ['hæknɪ'kæb] n fiacre m.
**hackneyed** ['hæknɪd] a usé(e), rebattu(e).
**had** [hæd] pt, pp of **have**.
**haddock**, pl ~ or ~s ['hædək] n églefin m; **smoked** ~ haddock m.
**hadn't** ['hædnt] = **had not**.
**haemorrhage**, **hemorrhage** (US) ['hɛmərɪdʒ] n hémorragie f.
**haemorrhoids**, **hemorrhoids** (US) ['hɛmərɔɪdz] npl hémorroïdes fpl.
**haggard** ['hægəd] a hagard(e), égaré(e).
**haggle** ['hægl] vi marchander; **to** ~ **over** chicaner sur; **haggling** n marchandage m.
**Hague** [heɪg] n: **The** ~ La Haye.
**hail** [heɪl] n grêle f // vt (call) héler; (greet) acclamer // vi grêler; ~**stone** n grêlon m.
**hair** [hɛə*] n cheveux mpl; (single hair: on head) cheveu m; (: on body) poil m; **to do one's** ~ se coiffer; ~**brush** n brosse f à cheveux; ~**cut** n coupe f (de cheveux); ~**do** ['hɛədu:] n coiffure f; ~**dresser** n coiffeur/euse; ~**drier** n sèche-cheveux m; ~**net** n résille f; ~ **oil** n huile f capillaire; ~**piece** n postiche m; ~**pin** n épingle f à cheveux; ~**pin bend** n virage m en épingle à cheveux; ~**raising** a à (vous) faire dresser les cheveux sur la tête; ~ **remover** n dépilateur m; ~ **spray** n laque f (pour les cheveux); ~**style** n coiffure f; ~**y** a poilu(e); chevelu(e); (fig) effrayant(e).
**hake** [heɪk] n colin m, merlu m.
**half** [hɑ:f] n (pl: **halves** [hɑ:vz]) moitié f // a demi(e) // ad (à) moitié, à demi; ~-**an-hour** une demi-heure; **two and a** ~ deux et demi; **a week and a** ~ une semaine et demie; ~ (**of it**) la moitié; ~ (**of**) la moitié de; ~ **the amount of** la moitié de; **to cut sth in** ~ couper qch en deux; ~-**back** n (SPORT) demi m; ~-**breed**, ~-**caste** n métis/se; ~-**hearted** a tiède, sans enthousiasme; ~-**hour** n demi-heure f; ~-**penny** ['heɪpnɪ] n demi-penny m; (**at**) ~-**price** à moitié prix; ~-**time** n mi-temps f; ~-**way** ad à mi-chemin.
**halibut** ['hælɪbət] n, pl inv flétan m.
**hall** [hɔ:l] n salle f; (entrance way) hall m, entrée f; (corridor) couloir m; (mansion) château m, manoir m; ~ **of residence** n pavillon m or résidence f universitaire.
**hallmark** ['hɔ:lmɑ:k] n poinçon m; (fig) marque f.
**hallo** [hə'ləu] excl = **hello**.
**hallucination** [həlu:sɪ'neɪʃən] n hallucination f.
**halo** ['heɪləu] n (of saint etc) auréole f; (of sun) halo m.
**halt** [hɔ:lt] n halte f, arrêt m // vt faire arrêter // vi faire halte, s'arrêter.
**halve** [hɑ:v] vt (apple etc) partager or diviser en deux; (expense) réduire de moitié.

**halves** [hɑ:vz] npl of **half**.
**ham** [hæm] n jambon m.
**hamburger** ['hæmbə:gə*] n hamburger m.
**hamstring** ['hæmstrɪŋ] n (ANAT) tendon m du jarret.
**hamlet** ['hæmlɪt] n hameau m.
**hammer** ['hæmə*] n marteau m // vt (fig) éreinter, démolir.
**hammock** ['hæmək] n hamac m.
**hamper** ['hæmpə*] vt gêner // n panier m (d'osier).
**hand** [hænd] n main f; (of clock) aiguille f; (handwriting) écriture f; (at cards) jeu m; (worker) ouvrier/ère // vt passer, donner; **to give sb a** ~ donner un coup de main à qn; **at** ~ à portée de la main; **in** ~ en main; (work) en cours; **on the one** ~ ..., **on the other** ~ d'une part ..., d'autre part; **to** ~ **in** vt remettre; **to** ~ **out** vt distribuer; **to** ~ **over** vt transmettre; céder; ~**bag** n sac m à main; ~**ball** n handball m; ~**basin** n lavabo m; ~**book** n manuel m; ~**brake** n frein m à main; ~ **cream** n crème f pour les mains; ~**cuffs** npl menottes fpl; ~**ful** n poignée f.
**handicap** ['hændɪkæp] n handicap m // vt handicaper.
**handicraft** ['hændɪkrɑ:ft] n travail m d'artisanat, technique artisanale.
**handkerchief** ['hæŋkətʃɪf] n mouchoir m.
**handle** ['hændl] n (of door etc) poignée f; (of cup etc) anse f; (of knife etc) manche m; (of saucepan) queue f; (for winding) manivelle f // vt toucher, manier; (deal with) s'occuper de; (treat: people) prendre; '~ **with care**' 'fragile'; ~**bar(s)** n(pl) guidon m.
**hand-luggage** ['hændlʌgɪdʒ] n bagages mpl à main.
**handmade** ['hændmeɪd] a fait(e) à la main.
**handout** ['hændaut] n documentation f, prospectus m.
**handshake** ['hændʃeɪk] n poignée f de main.
**handsome** ['hænsəm] a beau(belle); généreux(euse); considérable.
**handwriting** ['hændraɪtɪŋ] n écriture f.
**handwritten** ['hændrɪtn] a manuscrit(e), écrit(e) à la main.
**handy** ['hændɪ] a (person) adroit(e); (close at hand) sous la main; (convenient) pratique; **handyman** n bricoleur m; (servant) homme m à tout faire.
**hang**, pt, pp **hung** [hæŋ, hʌŋ] vt accrocher; (criminal: pt,pp **hanged**) pendre // vi pendre; (hair, drapery) tomber; **to** ~ **about** vi flâner, traîner; **to** ~ **on** vi (wait) attendre; **to** ~ **up** vi (TEL) raccrocher // vt accrocher, suspendre.
**hangar** ['hæŋə*] n hangar m.
**hanger** ['hæŋə*] n cintre m, portemanteau m.
**hanger-on** [hæŋər'ɔn] n parasite m.
**hang-gliding** ['hæŋglaɪdɪŋ] n vol m libre or sur aile delta.
**hangover** ['hæŋəuvə*] n (after drinking) gueule f de bois.
**hang-up** ['hæŋʌp] n complexe m.

hank [hæŋk] n écheveau m.
hanker ['hæŋkə*] vi: to ~ after avoir envie de.
hankie, hanky ['hæŋkɪ] n abbr of handkerchief.
haphazard [hæp'hæzəd] a fait(e) au hasard, fait(e) au petit bonheur.
happen ['hæpən] vi arriver; se passer, se produire; as it ~s justement; ~ing n événement m.
happily ['hæpɪlɪ] ad heureusement.
happiness ['hæpɪnɪs] n bonheur m.
happy ['hæpɪ] a heureux(euse); ~ with (arrangements etc) satisfait(e) de; ~-go-lucky a insouciant(e).
harass ['hærəs] vt accabler, tourmenter; ~ment n tracasseries fpl.
harbour, harbor (US) ['hɑːbə*] port m // vt héberger, abriter; ~ master n capitaine m du port.
hard [hɑːd] a dur(e) // ad (work) dur; (think, try) sérieusement; to drink ~ boire sec; ~ luck! pas de veine!; no ~ feelings! sans rancune!; to be ~ of hearing être dur(e) d'oreille; to be ~ done by être traité(e) injustement; ~back n livre relié; ~board n Isorel m ®; ~-boiled egg n œuf dur; ~ cash n espèces fpl; ~en vt durcir; (fig) endurcir // vi durcir; ~ening n durcissement m; ~-headed a réaliste; décidé(e); ~ labour n travaux forcés.
hardly ['hɑːdlɪ] ad (scarcely) à peine; it's ~ the case ce n'est guère le cas; ~ anywhere presque nulle part.
hardness ['hɑːdnɪs] n dureté f.
hard sell ['hɑːd'sɛl] n (COMM) promotion de ventes agressive.
hardship ['hɑːdʃɪp] n épreuves fpl; privations fpl.
hard-up [hɑːd'ʌp] a (col) fauché(e).
hardware ['hɑːdwɛə*] n quincaillerie f; (COMPUTERS) matériel m; ~ shop n quincaillerie f.
hard-wearing [hɑːd'wɛərɪŋ] a solide.
hard-working [hɑːd'wɔːkɪŋ] a travailleur(euse).
hardy ['hɑːdɪ] a robuste; (plant) résistant(e) au gel.
hare [hɛə*] n lièvre m; ~-brained a farfelu(e); écervelé(e); ~lip n (MED) bec-de-lièvre m.
harem [hɑː'riːm] n harem m.
harm [hɑːm] n mal m; (wrong) tort m // vt (person) faire du mal or du tort à; (thing) endommager; to mean no ~ ne pas avoir de mauvaises intentions; out of ~'s way à l'abri du danger, en lieu sûr; ~ful a nuisible; ~less a inoffensif(ive); sans méchanceté.
harmonic [hɑː'mɔnɪk] a harmonique.
harmonica [hɑː'mɔnɪkə] n harmonica m.
harmonics [hɑː'mɔnɪks] npl harmoniques mpl or fpl.
harmonious [hɑː'məunɪəs] a harmonieux-(euse).
harmonium [hɑː'məunɪəm] n harmonium m.
harmonize ['hɑːmənaɪz] vt harmoniser // vi s'harmoniser.

harmony ['hɑːmənɪ] n harmonie f.
harness ['hɑːnɪs] n harnais m // vt (horse) harnacher; (resources) exploiter.
harp [hɑːp] n harpe f // vi: to ~ on about parler tout le temps de; ~ist n harpiste m/f.
harpoon [hɑː'puːn] n harpon m.
harpsichord ['hɑːpsɪkɔːd] n clavecin m.
harrow ['hærəu] n (AGR) herse f.
harrowing ['hærəuɪŋ] a déchirant(e).
harsh [hɑːʃ] a (hard) dur(e); (severe) sévère; (rough: surface) rugueux(euse); (unpleasant: sound) discordant(e); (: colour) criard(e); cru(e); (: wine) âpre; ~ly ad durement; sévèrement; ~ness n dureté f; sévérité f.
harvest ['hɑːvɪst] n (of corn) moisson f; (of fruit) récolte f; (of grapes) vendange f // vi moissonner; récolter; vendanger; ~er n (machine) moissonneuse f.
has [hæz] see have.
hash [hæʃ] n (CULIN) hachis m; (fig: mess) gâchis m; also abbr of hashish.
hashish ['hæʃɪʃ] n haschisch m.
hassle ['hæsl] n chamaillerie f.
haste [heɪst] n hâte f; précipitation f; ~n ['heɪsn] vt hâter, accélérer // vi se hâter, s'empresser; hastily ad à la hâte; précipitamment; hasty a hâtif(ive); précipité(e).
hat [hæt] n chapeau m; ~box n carton m à chapeau.
hatch [hætʃ] n (NAUT: also: ~way) écoutille f; (also: service ~) passe-plats m inv // vi éclore // vt faire éclore; (plot) tramer.
hatchback ['hætʃbæk] n (AUT) modèle m avec hayon arrière.
hatchet ['hætʃɪt] n hachette f.
hate [heɪt] vt haïr, détester // n haine f; to ~ to do or doing détester faire; ~ful a odieux(euse), détestable.
hatred ['heɪtrɪd] n haine f.
hat trick [hæt'trɪk] n (SPORT, also fig) triplé m (3 buts réussis au cours du même match etc).
haughty ['hɔːtɪ] a hautain(e), arrogant(e).
haul [hɔːl] vt traîner, tirer; (by lorry) camionner; (NAUT) haler // n (of fish) prise f; (of stolen goods etc) butin m; ~age n halage m; camionnage m; ~ier n transporteur (routier), camionneur m.
haunch [hɔːntʃ] n hanche f; ~ of venison n cuissot m de chevreuil.
haunt [hɔːnt] vt (subj: ghost, fear) hanter; (: person) fréquenter // n repaire m.
have pt,pp had [hæv, hæd] vt avoir; (meal, shower) prendre; to ~ sth done faire faire qch; he had a suit made il s'est fait faire un costume; she has to do it il faut qu'elle le fasse, elle doit le faire; I had better leave je ferais mieux de partir; to ~ it out with sb s'expliquer (franchement) avec qn; I won't ~ it cela ne se passera pas ainsi; he's been had (col) il s'est fait avoir or rouler.
haven ['heɪvn] n port m; (fig) havre m.
haversack ['hævəsæk] n sac m à dos.
havoc ['hævək] n ravages mpl; to play ~ with (fig) désorganiser; détraquer.

**hawk** [hɔːk] *n* faucon *m*.
**hawker** ['hɔːkə*] *n* colporteur *m*.
**hay** [heɪ] *n* foin *m*; ~ **fever** *n* rhume *m* des foins; ~**stack** *n* meule *f* de foin.
**haywire** ['heɪwaɪə*] *a* (*col*): **to go** ~ perdre la tête; mal tourner.
**hazard** ['hæzəd] *n* hasard *m*, chance *f*; danger *m*, risque *m* // *vt* risquer, hasarder; ~**ous** *a* hasardeux(euse), risqué(e).
**haze** [heɪz] *n* brume *f*.
**hazelnut** ['heɪzlnʌt] *n* noisette *f*.
**hazy** ['heɪzɪ] *a* brumeux(euse); (*idea*) vague; (*photograph*) flou(e).
**he** [hiː] *pronoun* il; **it is** ~ **who ...** c'est lui qui ...; **here** ~ **is** le voici; ~**-bear** *n* ours *m* mâle.
**head** [hɛd] *n* tête *f*; (*leader*) chef *m* // *vt* (*list*) être en tête de; (*group*) être à la tête de; ~**s** (*on coin*) (le côté) face; ~**s or tails** pile ou face; **to** ~ **the ball** faire une tête; **to** ~ **for** *vt fus* se diriger vers; ~**ache** *n* mal *m* de tête; ~ **cold** *n* rhume *m* de cerveau; ~**ing** *n* titre *m*; rubrique *f*; ~**lamp** *n* phare *m*; ~**land** *n* promontoire *m*, cap *m*; ~**light** = ~**lamp**; ~**line** *n* titre *m*; ~**long** *ad* (*fall*) la tête la première; (*rush*) tête baissée; ~**master** *n* directeur *m*, proviseur *m*; ~**mistress** *n* directrice *f*; ~ **office** *n* bureau central; ~**-on** *a* (*collision*) de plein fouet; ~**phones** *npl* casque *m* (à écouteurs); ~**quarters (HQ)** *npl* bureau *or* siège central; (*MIL*) quartier général; ~**-rest** *n* appui-tête *m*; ~**room** *n* (*in car*) hauteur *f* de plafond; (*under bridge*) hauteur limite; dégagement *m*; ~**scarf** *n* foulard *m*; ~**strong** *a* têtu(e), entêté(e); ~ **waiter** *n* maître *m* d'hôtel; ~**way** *n* avance *f*, progrès *m*; ~**wind** *n* vent *m* contraire; ~**y** *a* capiteux(euse) enivrant(e).
**heal** [hiːl] *vt,vi* guérir.
**health** [hɛlθ] *n* santé *f*; ~ **food shop** *n* magasin *m* diététique; **the H**~ **Service** ≈ la Sécurité Sociale; ~**y** *a* (*person*) en bonne santé; (*climate, food, attitude etc*) sain(e).
**heap** [hiːp] *n* tas *m*, monceau *m* // *vt* entasser, amonceler.
**hear,** *pt, pp* **heard** [hɪə*, həːd] *vt* entendre; (*news*) apprendre; (*lecture*) assister à, écouter // *vi* entendre; **to** ~ **about** avoir des nouvelles de; entendre parler de; **did you** ~ **about the move?** tu es au courant du déménagement?; **to** ~ **from sb** recevoir des nouvelles de qn; ~**ing** *n* (*sense*) ouïe *f*; (*of witnesses*) audition *f*; (*of a case*) audience *f*; (*of committee*) séance *f*; ~**ing aid** *n* appareil *m* acoustique; **by** ~**say** *ad* par ouï-dire *m*.
**hearse** [həːs] *n* corbillard *m*.
**heart** [hɑːt] *n* cœur *m*; ~**s** *npl* (*CARDS*) cœur; **at** ~ au fond; **by** ~ (*learn, know*) par cœur; **to lose** ~ perdre courage, se décourager; ~ **attack** *n* crise *f* cardiaque; ~**beat** *n* battement *m* de cœur; ~**breaking** *a* navrant(e), déchirant(e); **to be** ~**broken** avoir beaucoup de chagrin; ~**burn** *n* brûlures *fpl* d'estomac; ~ **failure** *n* arrêt *m* du cœur; ~**felt** *a* sincère.
**hearth** [hɑːθ] *n* foyer *m*, cheminée *f*.

**heartily** ['hɑːtɪlɪ] *ad* chaleureusement; (*laugh*) de bon cœur; (*eat*) de bon appétit; **to agree** ~ être entièrement d'accord.
**heartless** ['hɑːtlɪs] *a* sans cœur, insensible; cruel(le).
**heartwarming** ['hɑːtwɔːmɪŋ] *a* réconfortant(e).
**hearty** ['hɑːtɪ] *a* chaleureux(euse); robuste; vigoureux(euse).
**heat** [hiːt] *n* chaleur *f*; (*fig*) ardeur *f*; feu *m*; (*SPORT: also:* **qualifying** ~) éliminatoire *f* // *vt* chauffer; **to** ~ **up** *vi* (*liquids*) chauffer; (*room*) se réchauffer // *vt* réchauffer; ~**ed** *a* chauffé(e); (*fig*) passionné(e); échauffé(e), excité(e); ~**er** *n* appareil *m* de chauffage; radiateur *m*.
**heath** [hiːθ] *n* (*Brit*) lande *f*.
**heathen** ['hiːðn] *a, n* païen(ne).
**heather** ['hɛðə*] *n* bruyère *f*.
**heating** ['hiːtɪŋ] *n* chauffage *m*.
**heatstroke** ['hiːtstrəuk] *n* coup *m* de chaleur.
**heatwave** ['hiːtweɪv] *n* vague *f* de chaleur.
**heave** [hiːv] *vt* soulever (avec effort) // *vi* se soulever // *n* nausée *f*, haut-le-cœur *m*; (*push*) poussée *f*.
**heaven** ['hɛvn] *n* ciel *m*, paradis *m*; ~ **forbid!** surtout pas!; ~**ly** *a* céleste, divin(e).
**heavily** ['hɛvɪlɪ] *ad* lourdement; (*drink, smoke*) beaucoup; (*sleep, sigh*) profondément.
**heavy** ['hɛvɪ] *a* lourd(e); (*work, sea, rain, eater*) gros(se); (*drinker, smoker*) grand(e); **it's** ~ **going** ça ne va pas tout seul, c'est pénible; ~**weight** *n* (*SPORT*) poids lourd.
**Hebrew** ['hiːbruː] *a* hébraïque // *n* (*LING*) hébreu *m*.
**heckle** ['hɛkl] *vt* interpeller (*un orateur*).
**hectare** ['hɛktɑː*] *n* hectare *m*.
**hectic** ['hɛktɪk] *a* agité(e), trépidant(e).
**he'd** [hiːd] = **he would, he had**.
**hedge** [hɛdʒ] *n* haie *f* // *vi* se défiler; **to** ~ **one's bets** (*fig*) se couvrir; **to** ~ **in** *vt* entourer d'une haie.
**hedgehog** ['hɛdʒhɔg] *n* hérisson *m*.
**heed** [hiːd] *vt* (*also:* **take** ~ **of**) tenir compte de, prendre garde à; ~**less** *a* insouciant(e).
**heel** [hiːl] *n* talon *m* // *vt* (*shoe*) retalonner; **to bring sb to** ~ rappeler qn à l'ordre.
**hefty** ['hɛftɪ] *a* (*person*) costaud(e); (*parcel*) lourd(e); (*piece, price*) gros(se).
**heifer** ['hɛfə*] *n* génisse *f*.
**height** [haɪt] *n* (*of person*) taille *f*, grandeur *f*; (*of object*) hauteur *f*; (*of plane, mountain*) altitude *f*; (*high ground*) hauteur, éminence *f*; (*fig: of glory*) sommet *m*; (: *of stupidity*) comble *m*; ~**en** *vt* hausser, surélever; (*fig*) augmenter.
**heir** [ɛə*] *n* héritier *m*; ~**ess** *n* héritière *f*; ~**loom** *n* meuble *m* (*or* bijou *m or* tableau *m*) de famille.
**held** [hɛld] *pt, pp of* **hold**.
**helicopter** ['hɛlɪkɔptə*] *n* hélicoptère *m*.
**helium** ['hiːlɪəm] *n* hélium *m*.
**hell** [hɛl] *n* enfer *m*; **a** ~ **of a...** (*col*) un(e) sacré(e)... .
**he'll** [hiːl] = **he will, he shall**.

**hellish** ['hɛlıʃ] *a* infernal(e).
**hello** [hə'ləu] *excl* bonjour!; salut! (*to sb one addresses as 'tu'*); (*surprise*) tiens!
**helm** [hɛlm] *n* (*NAUT*) barre *f*.
**helmet** ['hɛlmıt] *n* casque *m*.
**helmsman** ['hɛlmzmən] *n* timonier *m*.
**help** [hɛlp] *n* aide *f*; (*charwoman*) femme *f* de ménage; (*assistant etc*) employé/e // *vt* aider; ~! au secours!; ~ **yourself** (*to bread*) servez-vous (de pain); **I can't** ~ **saying** je ne peux pas m'empêcher de dire; **he can't** ~ **it** il n'y peut rien; ~**er** *n* aide *m/f*, assistant/e; ~**ful** *a* serviable, obligeant(e); (*useful*) utile; ~**ing** *n* portion *f*; ~**less** *a* impuissant(e); faible.
**hem** [hɛm] *n* ourlet *m* // *vt* ourler; **to** ~ **in** *vt* cerner.
**hemisphere** ['hɛmısfıə*] *n* hémisphère *m*.
**hemorrhage** ['hɛmərıdʒ] *n* (*US*) = **haemorrhage**.
**hemorrhoids** ['hɛmərɔıdz] *npl* (*US*) = **haemorrhoids**.
**hemp** [hɛmp] *n* chanvre *m*.
**hen** [hɛn] *n* poule *f*.
**hence** [hɛns] *ad* (*therefore*) d'où, de là; **2 years** ~ d'ici 2 ans; ~**forth** *ad* dorénavant.
**henchman** ['hɛntʃmən] *n* (*pej*) acolyte *m*, séide *m*.
**henpecked** ['hɛnpɛkt] *a* dominé par sa femme.
**her** [hə:*] *pronoun* (*direct*) la, l' + *vowel or h mute*; (*indirect*) lui; (*stressed, after prep*) elle; *see note at* **she** // *a* son(sa), ses *pl*; **I see** ~ je la vois; **give** ~ **a book** donne-lui un livre; **after** ~ après elle.
**herald** ['hɛrəld] *n* héraut *m* // *vt* annoncer.
**heraldry** ['hɛrəldrı] *n* héraldique *f*.
**herb** [hə:b] *n* herbe *f*; ~**s** *npl* (*CULIN*) fines herbes.
**herd** [hə:d] *n* troupeau *m* // *vt*: ~**ed together** parqués (comme du bétail).
**here** [hıə*] *ad* ici // *excl* tiens!, tenez!; ~! présent!; ~**'s my sister** voici ma sœur; ~ **she is** la voici; ~ **she comes** la voici qui vient; ~**after** *ad* après, plus tard; ci-après // *n*: **the** ~**after** l'au-delà *m*; ~**by** *ad* (*in letter*) par la présente.
**hereditary** [hı'rɛdıtrı] *a* héréditaire.
**heredity** [hı'rɛdıtı] *n* hérédité *f*.
**heresy** ['hɛrəsı] *n* hérésie *f*.
**heretic** ['hɛrətık] *n* hérétique *m/f*; ~**al** [hı'rɛtıkl] *a* hérétique.
**herewith** [hıə'wıð] *ad* avec ceci, ci-joint.
**heritage** ['hɛrıtıdʒ] *n* héritage *m*.
**hermetically** [hə:'mɛtıklı] *ad* hermétiquement.
**hermit** ['hə:mıt] *n* ermite *m*.
**hernia** ['hə:nıə] *n* hernie *f*.
**hero, ~es** ['hıərəu] *n* héros *m*; ~**ic** [hı'rəuık] *a* héroïque.
**heroin** ['hɛrəuın] *n* héroïne *f*.
**heroine** ['hɛrəuın] *n* héroïne *f*.
**heroism** ['hɛrəuızm] *n* héroïsme *m*.
**heron** ['hɛrən] *n* héron *m*.
**herring** ['hɛrıŋ] *n* hareng *m*.
**hers** [hə:z] *pronoun* le(la) sien(ne), les siens(siennes).
**herself** [hə:'sɛlf] *pronoun* (*reflexive*) se; (*emphatic*) elle-même; (*after prep*) elle.

**he's** [hi:z] = **he is, he has**.
**hesitant** ['hɛzıtənt] *a* hésitant(e), indécis(e).
**hesitate** ['hɛzıteıt] *vi*: **to** ~ (**about/to do**) hésiter (sur/à faire); **hesitation** ['-teıʃən] *n* hésitation *f*.
**hessian** ['hɛsıən] *n* toile *f* de jute.
**het up** [hɛt'ʌp] *a* agité(e), excité(e).
**hew** [hju:] *vt* tailler (*à la hache*).
**hexagon** ['hɛksəgən] *n* hexagone *m*; ~**al** [-'sægənl] *a* hexagonal(e).
**heyday** ['heıdeı] *n*: **the** ~ **of** l'âge *m* d'or de, les beaux jours de.
**hi** [haı] *excl* salut!
**hibernate** ['haıbəneıt] *vi* hiberner.
**hiccough, hiccup** ['hıkʌp] *vi* hoqueter // *n* hoquet *m*; **to have (the)** ~**s** avoir le hoquet.
**hid** [hıd] *pt of* **hide**.
**hidden** ['hıdn] *pp of* **hide**.
**hide** [haıd] *n* (*skin*) peau *f* // *vb* (*pt* **hid**, *pp* **hidden** [hıd, 'hıdn]) *vt*: **to** ~ **sth** (**from sb**) cacher qch (à qn) // *vi*: **to** ~ (**from sb**) se cacher de qn; ~**-and-seek** *n* cache-cache *m*; ~**away** *n* cachette *f*.
**hideous** ['hıdıəs] *a* hideux(euse); atroce.
**hiding** ['haıdıŋ] *n* (*beating*) correction *f*, volée *f* de coups; **to be in** ~ (*concealed*) se tenir caché(e); ~ **place** *n* cachette *f*.
**hierarchy** ['haıərɑ:kı] *n* hiérarchie *f*.
**high** [haı] *a* haut(e); (*speed, respect, number*) grand(e); (*price*) élevé(e); (*wind*) fort(e), violent(e); (*voice*) aigu(aiguë) // *ad* haut, en haut; **20 m** ~ haut(e) de 20 m; ~**brow** *a,n* intellectuel(le); ~**chair** *n* chaise haute (*pour enfant*); ~**-flying** *a* (*fig*) ambitieux(euse); ~**-handed** *a* très autoritaire; très cavalier(ère); ~**-heeled** *a* à hauts talons; ~**jack** = **hijack**; ~ **jump** *n* (*SPORT*) saut *m* en hauteur; ~**light** *n* (*fig: of event*) point culminant // *vt* faire ressortir, souligner; ~**ly** *ad* très, fort, hautement; ~**ly strung** *a* nerveux(euse), toujours tendu(e); **H**~ **Mass** *n* grand-messe *f*; ~**ness** *n* hauteur *f*; **Her H**~**ness** son Altesse *f*; ~**-pitched** *a* aigu(aiguë); ~**-rise block** *n* tour *f* (d'habitation).
**high school** ['haısku:l] *n* lycée *m*; (*US*) établissement *m* d'enseignement supérieur.
**high street** ['haıstri:t] *n* grand-rue *f*.
**highway** ['haıweı] *n* grand'route *f*, route nationale.
**hijack** ['haıdʒæk] *vt* détourner (*par la force*); ~**er** *n* auteur *m* d'un détournement d'avion, pirate *m* de l'air.
**hike** [haık] *vi* aller à pied // *n* excursion *f* à pied, randonnée *f*; ~**r** *n* promeneur/euse, excursionniste *m/f*; **hiking** *n* excursions *fpl* à pied, randonnée *f*.
**hilarious** [hı'lɛərıəs] *a* (*behaviour, event*) désopilant(e).
**hilarity** [hı'lærıtı] *n* hilarité *f*.
**hill** [hıl] *n* colline *f*; (*fairly high*) montagne *f*; (*on road*) côte *f*; ~**side** *n* (flanc *m* de) coteau *m*; ~ **start** *n* (*AUT*) démarrage *m* en côte; ~**y** *a* vallonné(e); montagneux (euse); (*road*) à fortes côtes.
**hilt** [hılt] *n* (*of sword*) garde *f*.
**him** [hım] *pronoun* (*direct*) le, l' + *vowel or h mute*; (*stressed, indirect, after prep*) lui;

**I** see ~ je le vois ; **give** ~ **a book** donne-lui un livre ; **after** ~ après lui ; ~**self** *pronoun* (*reflexive*) se ; (*emphatic*) lui-même ; (*after prep*) lui.

**hind** [haɪnd] *a* de derrière // *n* biche *f*.

**hinder** ['hɪndə*] *vt* gêner ; (*delay*) retarder ; (*prevent*): **to** ~ **sb from doing** empêcher qn de faire ; **hindrance** ['hɪndrəns] *n* gêne *f*, obstacle *m*.

**Hindu** ['hɪnduː] *n* Hindou/e.

**hinge** [hɪndʒ] *n* charnière *f* // *vi* (*fig*): **to** ~ **on** dépendre de.

**hint** [hɪnt] *n* allusion *f*; (*advice*) conseil *m* // *vt*: **to** ~ **that** insinuer que // *vi*: **to** ~ **at** faire une allusion à.

**hip** [hɪp] *n* hanche *f*; ~ **pocket** *n* poche *f* revolver.

**hippopotamus**, *pl* ~**es** *or* **hippopota-mi** [hɪpə'pɔtəməs, -'pɔtəmaɪ] *n* hippopotame *m*.

**hire** ['haɪə*] *vt* (*car*, *equipment*) louer ; (*worker*) embaucher, engager // *n* location *f*; **for** ~ à louer ; (*taxi*) libre ; ~ **purchase** (**H.P.**) *n* achat *m* (*or* vente *f*) à tempérament *or* crédit.

**his** [hɪz] *pronoun* le(la) sien(ne), les siens(siennes) // *a* son(sa), ses *pl*.

**hiss** [hɪs] *vi* siffler // *n* sifflement *m*.

**historian** [hɪ'stɔːrɪən] *n* historien/ne.

**historic(al)** [hɪ'stɔrɪk(l)] *a* historique.

**history** ['hɪstərɪ] *n* histoire *f*.

**hit** [hɪt] *vt* (*pt*, *pp* **hit**) frapper ; (*knock against*) cogner ; (*reach: target*) atteindre, toucher ; (*collide with: car*) entrer en collision avec, heurter ; (*fig: affect*) toucher ; (*find*) tomber sur // *n* coup *m*; (*success*) coup réussi ; succès *m*; (*song*) chanson *f* à succès, tube *m*; **to** ~ **it off with sb** bien s'entendre avec qn ; ~**-and-run driver** *n* chauffard *m*; ~**-or-miss** *a* fait(e) au petit bonheur.

**hitch** [hɪtʃ] *vt* (*fasten*) accrocher, attacher ; (*also:* ~ **up**) remonter d'une saccade // *n* (*knot*) nœud *m*; (*difficulty*) anicroche *f*, contretemps *m*; **to** ~ **a lift** faire du stop.

**hitch-hike** ['hɪtʃhaɪk] *vi* faire de l'auto-stop ; ~**r** *n* auto-stoppeur/ euse.

**hive** [haɪv] *n* ruche *f*.

**H.M.S.** *abbr of His(Her) Majesty's Ship.*

**hoard** [hɔːd] *n* (*of food*) provisions *fpl*, réserves *fpl*; (*of money*) trésor *m* // *vt* amasser.

**hoarding** ['hɔːdɪŋ] *n* panneau *m* d'affichage *or* publicitaire.

**hoarfrost** ['hɔːfrɔst] *n* givre *m*.

**hoarse** [hɔːs] *a* enroué(e).

**hoax** [həʊks] *n* canular *m*.

**hob** [hɔb] *n* plaque chauffante.

**hobble** ['hɔbl] *vi* boitiller.

**hobby** ['hɔbɪ] *n* passe-temps favori ; ~**-horse** *n* cheval *m* à bascule ; (*fig*) dada *m*.

**hobo** ['həʊbəʊ] *n* (*US*) vagabond *m*.

**hock** [hɔk] *n* vin *m* du Rhin.

**hockey** ['hɔkɪ] *n* hockey *m*.

**hoe** [həʊ] *n* houe *f*, binette *f* // *vt* biner, sarcler.

**hog** [hɔg] *n* sanglier *m* // *vt* (*fig*) accaparer ; **to go the whole** ~ aller jusqu'au bout.

**hoist** [hɔɪst] *n* palan *m* // *vt* hisser.

**hold** [həʊld] *vb* (*pt*, *pp* **held** [hɛld]) *vt* tenir ; (*contain*) contenir ; (*keep back*) retenir ; (*believe*) maintenir ; considérer ; (*possess*) avoir ; détenir // *vi* (*withstand pressure*) tenir (bon) ; (*be valid*) valoir // *n* prise *f*; (*fig*) influence *f*; (*NAUT*) cale *f*; ~ **the line!** (*TEL*) ne quittez pas! ; **to** ~ **one's own** (*fig*) (*bien*) se défendre ; **to catch** *or* **get** (**a**) ~ **of** saisir ; **to get** ~ **of** (*fig*) trouver ; **to get** ~ **of o.s.** se contrôler ; **to** ~ **back** *vt* retenir ; (*secret*) cacher ; **to** ~ **down** *vt* (*person*) maintenir à terre ; (*job*) occuper ; **to** ~ **off** *vt* tenir à distance ; **to** ~ **on** *vi* tenir bon ; (*wait*) attendre ; ~ **on!** (*TEL*) ne quittez pas! ; **to** ~ **on to** *vt fus* se cramponner à ; (*keep*) conserver, garder ; **to** ~ **out** *vt* offrir // *vi* (*resist*) tenir bon ; **to** ~ **up** *vt* (*raise*) lever ; (*support*) soutenir ; (*delay*) retarder ; ~**all** *n* fourre-tout *m inv*; ~**er** *n* (*of ticket, record*) détenteur/trice ; (*of office,* title *etc*) titulaire *m/f*; ~**ing** *n* (*share*) intérêts *mpl*; (*farm*) ferme *f*; ~**ing company** *n* holding *m*; ~**up** *n* (*robbery*) hold-up *m*; (*delay*) retard *m*; (*in traffic*) embouteillage *m*.

**hole** [həʊl] *n* trou *m* // *vt* trouer, faire un trou dans.

**holiday** ['hɔlɪdɪ] *n* vacances *fpl*; (*day off*) jour *m* de congé ; (*public*) jour férié ; ~**-maker** *n* vacancier/ère ; ~ **resort** *n* centre *m* de villégiature *or* de vacances.

**holiness** ['həʊlɪnɪs] *n* sainteté *f*.

**Holland** ['hɔlənd] *n* Hollande *f*.

**hollow** ['hɔləʊ] *a* creux(euse) ; (*fig*) faux(fausse) // *n* creux *m*; (*in land*) dépression *f* (de terrain), cuvette *f* // *vt*: **to** ~ **out** creuser, évider.

**holly** ['hɔlɪ] *n* houx *m*; ~**hock** *n* rose trémière.

**holster** ['həʊlstə*] *n* étui *m* de revolver.

**holy** ['həʊlɪ] *a* saint(e) ; (*bread, water*) bénit(e) ; (*ground*) sacré(e) ; **H**~ **Ghost** *or* **Spirit** *n* Saint-Esprit *m*; ~ **orders** *npl* ordres (majeurs).

**homage** ['hɔmɪdʒ] *n* hommage *m*; **to pay** ~ **to** rendre hommage à.

**home** [həʊm] *n* foyer *m*, maison *f*; (*country*) pays natal, patrie *f*; (*institution*) maison *f* // *a* de famille ; (*ECON, POL*) national(e), intérieur(e) // *ad* chez soi, à la maison ; au pays natal ; (*right in: nail etc*) à fond ; **at** ~ chez soi, à la maison ; **to go** (*or* **come**) ~ rentrer (chez soi), rentrer à la maison (*or* au pays) ; **make yourself at** ~ faites comme chez vous ; **near my** ~ près de chez moi ; ~ **address** *n* domicile permanent ; ~**land** *n* patrie *f*; ~**less** *a* sans foyer ; sans abri ; ~**ly** simple, sans prétention ; accueillant(e) ; ~**-made** *a* fait(e) à la maison ; ~ **rule** *n* autonomie *f*; **H**~ **Secretary** *n* (*Brit*) ministre *m* de l'Intérieur ; ~**sick** *a*: **to be** ~**sick** avoir le mal du pays ; s'ennuyer de sa famille ; ~ **town** *n* ville natale ; ~**ward** ['həʊmwəd] *a* (*journey*) du retour ; ~**work** *n* devoirs *mpl*.

**homicide** ['hɔmɪsaɪd] *n* (*US*) homicide *m*.

**homoeopathy** [həʊmɪ'ɔpəθɪ] *n* homéopathie *f*.

**homogeneous** [hɔməʊ'dʒiːnɪəs] *a* homogène.

**homosexual** [hɔməu'sɛksjuəl] *a,n* homosexuel(le).

**hone** [həun] *n* pierre *f* à aiguiser // *vt* affûter, aiguiser.

**honest** ['ɔnɪst] *a* honnête; (*sincere*) franc(franche); ~**ly** *ad* honnêtement; franchement; ~**y** *n* honnêteté *f*.

**honey** ['hʌnɪ] *n* miel *m*; ~**comb** *n* rayon *m* de miel; (*pattern*) nid *m* d'abeilles, motif alvéolé; ~**moon** *n* lune *f* de miel; (*trip*) voyage *m* de noces.

**honk** [hɔŋk] *n* (*AUT*) coup *m* de klaxon // *vi* klaxonner.

**honorary** ['ɔnərərɪ] *a* honoraire; (*duty, title*) honorifique.

**honour, honor** (*US*) ['ɔnə*] *vt* honorer // *n* honneur *m*; ~**able** *a* honorable; ~**s degree** *n* (*SCOL*) licence avec mention.

**hood** [hud] *n* capuchon *m*; (*Brit*: *AUT*) capote *f*; (*US*: *AUT*) capot *m*; ~**wink** *vt* tromper.

**hoof**, ~**s** *or* **hooves** [hu:f, hu:vz] *n* sabot *m*.

**hook** [huk] *n* crochet *m*; (*on dress*) agrafe *f*; (*for fishing*) hameçon *m* // *vt* accrocher; (*dress*) agrafer.

**hooligan** ['hu:lɪgən] *n* voyou *m*.

**hoop** [hu:p] *n* cerceau *m*; (*of barrel*) cercle *m*.

**hoot** [hu:t] *vi* (*AUT*) klaxonner; (*siren*) mugir // *vt* (*jeer at*) huer // *n* huée *f*; coup *m* de klaxon; mugissement *m*; **to** ~ **with laughter** rire aux éclats; ~**er** *n* (*AUT*) klaxon *m*; (*NAUT*) sirène *f*.

**hooves** [hu:vz] *npl of* **hoof.**

**hop** [hɔp] *vi* sauter; (*on one foot*) sauter à cloche-pied // *n* saut *m*.

**hope** [həup] *vt,vi* espérer // *n* espoir *m*; **I** ~ **so** je l'espère; **I** ~ **not** j'espère que non; ~**ful** *a* (*person*) plein(e) d'espoir; (*situation*) prometteur(euse), encourageant(e); ~**fully** *ad* avec espoir, avec optimisme; ~**less** *a* désespéré(e); (*useless*) nul(le).

**hops** [hɔps] *npl* houblon *m*.

**horde** [hɔ:d] *n* horde *f*.

**horizon** [hə'raɪzn] *n* horizon *m*; ~**tal** [hɔrɪ'zɔntl] *a* horizontal(e).

**hormone** ['hɔ:məun] *n* hormone *f*.

**horn** [hɔ:n] *n* corne *f*; (*MUS*) cor *m*; (*AUT*) klaxon *m*; ~**ed** *a* (*animal*) à cornes.

**hornet** ['hɔ:nɪt] *n* frelon *m*.

**horny** ['hɔ:nɪ] *a* corné(e); (*hands*) calleux(euse).

**horoscope** ['hɔrəskəup] *n* horoscope *m*.

**horrible** ['hɔrɪbl] *a* horrible, affreux(euse).

**horrid** ['hɔrɪd] *a* méchant(e), désagréable.

**horrify** ['hɔrɪfaɪ] *vt* horrifier.

**horror** ['hɔrə*] *n* horreur *f*; ~ **film** *n* film *m* d'épouvante.

**hors d'œuvre** [ɔ:'də:vrə] *n* hors d'œuvre *m*.

**horse** [hɔ:s] *n* cheval *m*; **on** ~**back** à cheval; ~ **chestnut** *n* marron *m* (d'Inde); ~**-drawn** *a* tiré(e) par des chevaux; ~**man** *n* cavalier *m*; ~**power** (**h.p.**) *n* puissance *f* (en chevaux); ~**-racing** *n* courses *fpl* de chevaux; ~**radish** *n* raifort *m*; ~**shoe** *n* fer *m* à cheval.

**horsy** ['hɔ:sɪ] *a* féru(e) d'équitation *or* de cheval; chevalin(e).

**horticulture** ['hɔ:tɪkʌltʃə*] *n* horticulture *f*.

**hose** [həuz] *n* (*also*: ~**pipe**) tuyau *m*; (*also*: **garden** ~) tuyau d'arrosage.

**hosiery** ['həuzɪərɪ] *n* (*in shop*) (rayon *m* des) bas *mpl*.

**hospitable** ['hɔspɪtəbl] *a* hospitalier(ère).

**hospital** ['hɔspɪtl] *n* hôpital *m*; **in** ~ à l'hôpital.

**hospitality** [hɔspɪ'tælɪtɪ] *n* hospitalité *f*.

**host** [həust] *n* hôte *m*; (*in hotel etc*) patron *m*; (*large number*): **a** ~ **of** une foule de; (*REL*) hostie *f*.

**hostage** ['hɔstɪdʒ] *n* otage *m*.

**hostel** ['hɔstl] *n* foyer *m*; (**youth**) ~ *n* auberge *f* de jeunesse.

**hostess** ['həustɪs] *n* hôtesse *f*.

**hostile** ['hɔstaɪl] *a* hostile.

**hostility** [hɔ'stɪlɪtɪ] *n* hostilité *f*.

**hot** [hɔt] *a* chaud(e); (*as opposed to only warm*) très chaud(e); (*spicy*) fort(e); (*fig*) acharné(e); brûlant(e); violent(e), passionné(e); ~ **dog** *n* hot-dog *m*.

**hotel** [həu'tɛl] *n* hôtel *m*; ~**ier** *n* hôtelier/ère.

**hot:** ~**-headed** *a* impétueux(euse); ~**house** *n* serre chaude; ~**ly** *ad* passionnément, violemment; ~**-water bottle** *n* bouillotte *f*.

**hound** [haund] *vt* poursuivre avec acharnement // *n* chien courant; **the** ~**s** la meute.

**hour** ['auə*] *n* heure *f*; ~**ly** *a* toutes les heures; ~**ly paid** *a* payé(e) à l'heure.

**house** *n* [haus] (*pl*: ~**s** ['hauzɪz]) (*also*: *firm*) maison *f*; (*POL*) chambre *f*; (*THEATRE*) salle *f*; auditoire *m* // *vt* [hauz] (*person*) loger, héberger; **the H**~ (*of Commons*) la Chambre des communes; **on the** ~ (*fig*) aux frais de la maison; ~ **arrest** *n* assignation *f* à domicile; ~**boat** *n* bateau (aménagé en habitation); ~**breaking** *n* cambriolage *m* (avec effraction); ~**hold** *n* famille *f*, maisonnée *f*; ménage *m*; ~**keeper** *n* gouvernante *f*; ~**keeping** *n* (*work*) ménage *m*; ~**-warming party** *n* pendaison *f* de crémaillère; ~**wife** *n* ménagère *f*; ~**work** *n* (travaux *mpl* du) ménage *m*.

**housing** ['hauzɪŋ] *n* logement *m*; ~ **estate** *n* cité *f*, lotissement *m*; ~ **shortage** *n* crise *f* du logement.

**hovel** ['hɔvl] *n* taudis *m*.

**hover** ['hɔvə*] *vi* planer; **to** ~ **round sb** rôder *or* tourner autour de qn; ~**craft** *n* aéroglisseur *m*.

**how** [hau] *ad* comment; ~ **are you?** comment allez-vous?; ~ **long have you been here?** depuis combien de temps êtes-vous là?; ~ **lovely!** que *or* comme c'est joli!; ~ **many?** combien?; ~ **many people/much milk** combien de gens/lait; ~ **old are you?** quel âge avez-vous?; ~ **is it that ...?** comment se fait-il que ...? + *sub*; ~**ever** *ad* de quelque façon *or* manière que + *sub*; (+ *adjective*) quelque *or* si ... que + *sub*; (*in questions*) comment // *cj* pourtant, cependant.

**howl** ['haul] *n* hurlement *m* // *vi* hurler.

**howler** ['haulə*] *n* gaffe *f*, bourde *f*.

**h.p., H.P.** *see* **hire**; **horse.**

**HQ** *abbr of* **headquarters**.
**hr(s)** *abbr of* **hour(s)**.
**hub** [hʌb] *n (of wheel)* moyeu *m*; *(fig)* centre *m*, foyer *m*.
**hubbub** ['hʌbʌb] *n* brouhaha *m*.
**hub cap** ['hʌbkæp] *n* enjoliveur *m*.
**huddle** ['hʌdl] *vi*: **to ~ together** se blottir les uns contre les autres.
**hue** [hju:] *n* teinte *f*, nuance *f*; **~ and cry** *n* tollé (général), clameur *f*.
**huff** [hʌf] *n*: **in a ~** fâché(e); **to take the ~** prendre la mouche.
**hug** [hʌg] *vt* serrer dans ses bras; *(shore, kerb)* serrer // *n* étreinte *f*; **to give sb a ~** serrer qn dans ses bras.
**huge** [hju:dʒ] *a* énorme, immense.
**hulk** [hʌlk] *n (ship)* vieux rafiot; *(car etc)* carcasse *f*; **~ing** *a* balourd(e).
**hull** [hʌl] *n (of ship, nuts)* coque *f*; *(of peas)* cosse *f*.
**hullo** [hə'ləu] *excl* = **hello**.
**hum** [hʌm] *vt (tune)* fredonner // *vi* fredonner; *(insect)* bourdonner; *(plane, tool)* vrombir // *n* fredonnement *m*; bourdonnement *m*; vrombissement *m*.
**human** ['hju:mən] *a* humain(e) // *n* être humain.
**humane** [hju:'meɪn] *a* humain(e), humanitaire.
**humanity** [hju:'mænɪtɪ] *n* humanité *f*.
**humble** ['hʌmbl] *a* humble, modeste // *vt* humilier; **humbly** *ad* humblement, modestement.
**humbug** ['hʌmbʌg] *n* fumisterie *f*; *(sweet)* sorte de bonbon à la menthe.
**humdrum** ['hʌmdrʌm] *a* monotone, routinier(ère).
**humid** ['hju:mɪd] *a* humide; **~ity** [-'mɪdɪtɪ] *n* humidité *f*.
**humiliate** [hju:'mɪlɪeɪt] *vt* humilier; **humiliation** [-'eɪʃən] *n* humiliation *f*.
**humility** [hju:'mɪlɪtɪ] *n* humilité *f*.
**humorist** ['hju:mərɪst] *n* humoriste *m/f*.
**humorous** ['hju:mərəs] *a* humoristique; *(person)* plein(e) d'humour.
**humour, humor** *(US)* ['hju:mə*] *n* humour *m*; *(mood)* humeur *f* // *vt (person)* faire plaisir à; se prêter aux caprices de.
**hump** [hʌmp] *n* bosse *f*; **~back** *n* dos-d'âne *m*.
**hunch** [hʌntʃ] *n* bosse *f*; *(premonition)* intuition *f*; **~back** *n* bossu/e; **~ed** *a* arrondi(e), voûté(e).
**hundred** ['hʌndrəd] *num* cent; **~weight** *n (Brit)* = *50.8 kg*; *112 lb*; *(US)* = *45.3 kg*; *100 lb*.
**hung** [hʌŋ] *pt, pp of* **hang**.
**Hungarian** [hʌŋ'gɛərɪən] *a* hongrois(e) // *n* Hongrois/e; *(LING)* hongrois *m*.
**Hungary** ['hʌŋgərɪ] *n* Hongrie *f*.
**hunger** ['hʌŋgə*] *n* faim *f* // *vi*: **to ~ for** avoir faim de, désirer ardemment.
**hungrily** ['hʌŋgrəlɪ] *ad* voracement; *(fig)* avidement.
**hungry** ['hʌŋgrɪ] *a* affamé(e); **to be ~** avoir faim.
**hunt** [hʌnt] *vt (seek)* chercher; *(SPORT)* chasser // *vi* chasser // *n* chasse *f*; **~er** *n* chasseur *m*; **~ing** *n* chasse *f*.
**hurdle** ['hə:dl] *n (for fences)* claie *f*; *(SPORT)* haie *f*; *(fig)* obstacle *m*.

**hurl** [hə:l] *vt* lancer (avec violence).
**hurrah, hurray** [hu'rɑ:, hu'reɪ] *n* hourra *m*.
**hurricane** ['hʌrɪkən] *n* ouragan *m*.
**hurried** ['hʌrɪd] *a* pressé(e), précipité(e); *(work)* fait(e) à la hâte; **~ly** *ad* précipitamment, à la hâte.
**hurry** ['hʌrɪ] *n* hâte *f*, précipitation *f* // *vi* se presser, se dépêcher // *vt (person)* faire presser, faire se dépêcher; *(work)* presser; **to be in a ~** être pressé(e); **to do sth in a ~** faire qch en vitesse; **to ~ in/out** entrer/sortir précipitamment.
**hurt** [hə:t] *vb (pt, pp hurt)* *vt (cause pain to)* faire mal à; *(injure, fig)* blesser // *vi* faire mal // *a* blessé(e); **~ful** *a (remark)* blessant(e).
**hurtle** ['hə:tl] *vt* lancer (de toutes ses forces) // *vi*: **to ~ past** passer en trombe; **to ~ down** dégringoler.
**husband** ['hʌzbənd] *n* mari *m*.
**hush** [hʌʃ] *n* calme *m*, silence *m* // *vt* faire taire; **~!** chut!
**husk** [hʌsk] *n (of wheat)* balle *f*; *(of rice, maize)* enveloppe *f*; *(of peas)* cosse *f*.
**husky** ['hʌskɪ] *a* rauque; *(burly)* costaud(e) // *n* chien m esquimau *or* de traîneau.
**hustle** ['hʌsl] *vt* pousser, bousculer // *n* bousculade *f*; **~ and bustle** *n* tourbillon *m* (d'activité).
**hut** [hʌt] *n* hutte *f*; *(shed)* cabane *f*; *(MIL)* baraquement *m*.
**hutch** [hʌtʃ] *n* clapier *m*.
**hyacinth** ['haɪəsɪnθ] *n* jacinthe *f*.
**hybrid** ['haɪbrɪd] *a, n* hybride *(m)*.
**hydrant** ['haɪdrənt] *n* prise *f* d'eau; *(also:* **fire ~**) bouche *f* d'incendie.
**hydraulic** [haɪ'drɔ:lɪk] *a* hydraulique.
**hydroelectric** [haɪdrəuɪ'lɛktrɪk] *a* hydro-électrique.
**hydrogen** ['haɪdrədʒən] *n* hydrogène *m*.
**hyena** [haɪ'i:nə] *n* hyène *f*.
**hygiene** ['haɪdʒi:n] *n* hygiène *f*.
**hygienic** [haɪ'dʒi:nɪk] *a* hygiénique.
**hymn** [hɪm] *n* hymne *m*; cantique *m*.
**hyphen** ['haɪfn] *n* trait *m* d'union.
**hypnosis** [hɪp'nəusɪs] *n* hypnose *f*.
**hypnotism** ['hɪpnətɪzm] *n* hypnotisme *m*.
**hypnotist** ['hɪpnətɪst] *n* hypnotiseur/euse.
**hypnotize** ['hɪpnətaɪz] *vt* hypnotiser.
**hypocrisy** [hɪ'pɔkrɪsɪ] *n* hypocrisie *f*.
**hypocrite** ['hɪpəkrɪt] *n* hypocrite *m/f*; **hypocritical** [-'krɪtɪkl] *a* hypocrite.
**hypothesis, pl hypotheses** [haɪ'pɔθɪsɪs, -si:z] *n* hypothèse *f*.
**hypothetic(al)** [haɪpəu'θɛtɪk(l)] *a* hypothétique.
**hysteria** [hɪ'stɪərɪə] *n* hystérie *f*.
**hysterical** [hɪ'stɛrɪkl] *a* hystérique; **to become ~** avoir une crise de nerfs.
**hysterics** [hɪ'stɛrɪks] *npl* (violente) crise de nerfs; *(laughter)* crise de rire.

**I**

**I** [aɪ] *pronoun* je; *(before vowel)* j'; *(stressed)* moi.
**ice** [aɪs] *n* glace *f*; *(on road)* verglas *m* // *vt (cake)* glacer; *(drink)* faire rafraîchir //

*vi* (*also*: ~ **over**) geler; (*also*: ~ **up**) se givrer; ~ **axe** *n* piolet *m*; ~**berg** *n* iceberg *m*; ~**box** *n* (*US*) réfrigérateur *m*; (*Brit*) compartiment *m* à glace; (*insulated box*) glacière *f*; ~**cold** *a* glacé(e); ~ **cream** *n* glace *f*; ~ **cube** *n* glaçon *m*; ~ **hockey** *n* hockey *m* sur glace.

**Iceland** ['aɪslənd] *n* Islande *f*; ~**er** *n* Islandais/e; ~**ic** [-'lændɪk] *a* islandais(e) // *n* (*LING*) islandais *m*.

**ice rink** ['aɪsrɪŋk] *n* patinoire *f*.

**icicle** ['aɪsɪkl] *n* glaçon *m* (*naturel*).

**icing** ['aɪsɪŋ] *n* (*AVIAT etc*) givrage *m*; (*CULIN*) glaçage *m*; ~ **sugar** *n* sucre *m* glace.

**icon** ['aɪkɔn] *n* icône *f*.

**icy** ['aɪsɪ] *a* glacé(e); (*road*) verglacé(e); (*weather, temperature*) glacial(e).

**I'd** [aɪd] = **I would, I had**.

**idea** [aɪ'dɪə] *n* idée *f*.

**ideal** [aɪ'dɪəl] *n* idéal *m* // *a* idéal(e); ~**ist** *n* idéaliste *m/f*.

**identical** [aɪ'dɛntɪkl] *a* identique.

**identification** [aɪdɛntɪfɪ'keɪʃən] *n* identification *f*; **means of** ~ pièce *f* d'identité.

**identify** [aɪ'dɛntɪfaɪ] *vt* identifier.

**identity** [aɪ'dɛntɪtɪ] *n* identité *f*.

**ideology** [aɪdɪ'ɔlədʒɪ] *n* idéologie *f*.

**idiocy** ['ɪdɪəsɪ] *n* idiotie *f*, stupidité *f*.

**idiom** ['ɪdɪəm] *n* langue *f*, idiome *m*; (*phrase*) expression *f* idiomatique.

**idiosyncrasy** [ɪdɪəu'sɪŋkrəsɪ] *n* particularité *f*, caractéristique *f*.

**idiot** ['ɪdɪət] *n* idiot/e, imbécile *m/f*; ~**ic** [-'ɔtɪk] *a* idiot(e), bête, stupide.

**idle** ['aɪdl] *a* sans occupation, désœuvré(e); (*lazy*) oisif(ive), paresseux(euse); (*unemployed*) au chômage; (*machinery*) au repos; (*question, pleasures*) vain(e), futile; **to lie** ~ être arrêté, ne pas fonctionner; ~**ness** *n* désœuvrement *m*; oisiveté *f*; ~**r** *n* désœuvré/e; oisif/ive.

**idol** ['aɪdl] *n* idole *f*; ~**ize** *vt* idolâtrer, adorer.

**idyllic** [ɪ'dɪlɪk] *a* idyllique.

**i.e.** *ad* (*abbr of id est*) c'est-à-dire.

**if** [ɪf] *cj* si.

**igloo** ['ɪglu:] *n* igloo *m*.

**ignite** [ɪg'naɪt] *vt* mettre le feu à, enflammer // *vi* s'enflammer.

**ignition** [ɪg'nɪʃən] *n* (*AUT*) allumage *m*; **to switch on/off the** ~ mettre/couper le contact; ~ **key** *n* (*AUT*) clé *f* de contact.

**ignoramus** [ɪgnə'reɪməs] *n* personne *f* ignare.

**ignorance** ['ɪgnərəns] *n* ignorance *f*.

**ignorant** ['ɪgnərənt] *a* ignorant(e).

**ignore** [ɪg'nɔ:*] *vt* ne tenir aucun compte de, ne pas relever; (*person*) faire semblant de ne pas reconnaître, ignorer; (*fact*) méconnaître.

**ikon** ['aɪkɔn] *n* = **icon**.

**I'll** [aɪl] = **I will, I shall**.

**ill** [ɪl] *a* (*sick*) malade; (*bad*) mauvais(e) // *n* mal *m*; **to take** *or* **be taken** ~ tomber malade; ~**-advised** *a* (*decision*) peu judicieux(euse); (*person*) malavisé(e); ~**-at-ease** *a* mal à l'aise.

**illegal** [ɪ'li:gl] *a* illégal(e); ~**ly** *ad* illégalement.

**illegible** [ɪ'lɛdʒɪbl] *a* illisible.

**illegitimate** [ɪlɪ'dʒɪtɪmət] *a* illégitime.

**ill-fated** [ɪl'feɪtɪd] *a* malheureux(euse); (*day*) néfaste.

**ill feeling** [ɪl'fi:lɪŋ] *n* ressentiment *m*, rancune *f*.

**illicit** [ɪ'lɪsɪt] *a* illicite.

**illiterate** [ɪ'lɪtərət] *a* illettré(e); (*letter*) plein(e) de fautes.

**ill-mannered** [ɪl'mænəd] *a* impoli(e), grossier(ère).

**illness** ['ɪlnɪs] *n* maladie *f*.

**illogical** [ɪ'lɔdʒɪkl] *a* illogique.

**ill-treat** [ɪl'tri:t] *vt* maltraiter.

**illuminate** [ɪ'lu:mɪneɪt] *vt* (*room, street*) éclairer; (*building*) illuminer; ~**d sign** *n* enseigne lumineuse; **illumination** [-'neɪʃən] *n* éclairage *m*; illumination *f*.

**illusion** [ɪ'lu:ʒən] *n* illusion *f*; **to be under the** ~ **that** s'imaginer *or* croire que.

**illusive, illusory** [ɪ'lu:sɪv, ɪ'lu:sərɪ] *a* illusoire.

**illustrate** ['ɪləstreɪt] *vt* illustrer; **illustration** [-'streɪʃən] *n* illustration *f*.

**illustrious** [ɪ'lʌstrɪəs] *a* illustre.

**ill will** [ɪl'wɪl] *n* malveillance *f*.

**I'm** [aɪm] = **I am**.

**image** ['ɪmɪdʒ] *n* image *f*; (*public face*) image de marque; ~**ry** *n* images *fpl*.

**imaginary** [ɪ'mædʒɪnərɪ] *a* imaginaire.

**imagination** [ɪmædʒɪ'neɪʃən] *n* imagination *f*.

**imaginative** [ɪ'mædʒɪnətɪv] *a* imaginatif(ive); plein(e) d'imagination.

**imagine** [ɪ'mædʒɪn] *vt* s'imaginer; (*suppose*) imaginer, supposer.

**imbalance** [ɪm'bæləns] *n* déséquilibre *m*.

**imbecile** ['ɪmbəsi:l] *n* imbécile *m/f*.

**imbue** [ɪm'bju:] *vt*: **to** ~ **sth with** imprégner qch de.

**imitate** ['ɪmɪteɪt] *vt* imiter; **imitation** [-'teɪʃən] *n* imitation *f*; **imitator** *n* imitateur/trice.

**immaculate** [ɪ'mækjulət] *a* impeccable; (*REL*) immaculé(e).

**immaterial** [ɪmə'tɪərɪəl] *a* sans importance, insignifiant(e).

**immature** [ɪmə'tjuə*] *a* (*fruit*) qui n'est pas mûr(e); (*person*) qui manque de maturité.

**immediate** [ɪ'mi:dɪət] *a* immédiat(e); ~**ly** *ad* (*at once*) immédiatement; ~**ly next to** juste à côté de.

**immense** [ɪ'mɛns] *a* immense; énorme.

**immerse** [ɪ'mə:s] *vt* immerger, plonger; **to** ~ **sth in** plonger qch dans.

**immersion heater** [ɪ'mə:ʃnhi:tə*] *n* chauffe-eau *m* électrique.

**immigrant** ['ɪmɪgrənt] *n* immigrant/e; immigré/e.

**immigration** [ɪmɪ'greɪʃən] *n* immigration *f*.

**imminent** ['ɪmɪnənt] *a* imminent(e).

**immobilize** [ɪ'məubɪlaɪz] *vt* immobiliser.

**immoderate** [ɪ'mɔdərət] *a* immodéré(e), démesuré(e).

**immoral** [ɪ'mɔrl] *a* immoral(e); ~**ity** [-'rælɪtɪ] *n* immoralité *f*.

**immortal** [ɪ'mɔ:tl] *a, n* immortel(le); ~**ize** *vt* immortaliser.

**immune** [ɪ'mju:n] *a*: ~ (to) immunisé(e) (contre).

**immunization** [ɪmjunaɪ'zeɪʃən] *n* immunisation *f.*

**immunize** ['ɪmjunaɪz] *vt* immuniser.

**impact** ['ɪmpækt] *n* choc *m*, impact *m*; (*fig*) impact.

**impair** [ɪm'pɛə*] *vt* détériorer, diminuer.

**impale** [ɪm'peɪl] *vt* empaler.

**impartial** [ɪm'pɑ:ʃl] *a* impartial(e); ~ity [ɪmpɑ:ʃɪ'ælɪtɪ] *n* impartialité *f.*

**impassable** [ɪm'pɑ:səbl] *a* infranchissable; (*road*) impraticable.

**impassioned** [ɪm'pæʃənd] *a* passionné(e).

**impatience** [ɪm'peɪʃəns] *n* impatience *f.*

**impatient** [ɪm'peɪʃənt] *a* impatient(e).

**impeach** [ɪm'pi:tʃ] *vt* accuser, attaquer; (*public official*) mettre en accusation.

**impeccable** [ɪm'pɛkəbl] *a* impeccable, parfait(e).

**impede** [ɪm'pi:d] *vt* gêner.

**impediment** [ɪm'pɛdɪmənt] *n* obstacle *m*; (*also*: **speech** ~) défaut *m* d'élocution.

**impending** [ɪm'pɛndɪŋ] *a* imminent(e).

**impenetrable** [ɪm'pɛnɪtrəbl] *a* impénétrable.

**imperative** [ɪm'pɛrətɪv] *a* nécessaire; urgent(e), pressant(e); (*voice*) impérieux(euse) // *n* (*LING*) impératif *m.*

**imperceptible** [ɪmpə'sɛptɪbl] *a* imperceptible.

**imperfect** [ɪm'pə:fɪkt] *a* imparfait(e); (*goods etc*) défectueux(euse) // *n* (*LING*: *also*: ~ **tense**) imparfait *m*; ~ion [-'fɛkʃən] *n* imperfection *f*, défectuosité *f.*

**imperial** [ɪm'pɪərɪəl] *a* impérial(e); (*measure*) légal(e); ~ism *n* impérialisme *m.*

**imperil** [ɪm'pɛrɪl] *vt* mettre en péril.

**impersonal** [ɪm'pə:sənl] *a* impersonnel(le).

**impersonate** [ɪm'pə:səneɪt] *vt* se faire passer pour; (*THEATRE*) imiter; **impersonation** [-'neɪʃən] *n* (*LAW*) usurpation *f* d'identité; (*THEATRE*) imitation *f.*

**impertinent** [ɪm'pə:tɪnənt] *a* impertinent(e), insolent(e).

**impervious** [ɪm'pə:vɪəs] *a* imperméable; (*fig*): ~ **to** insensible à; inaccessible à.

**impetuous** [ɪm'pɛtjuəs] *a* impétueux(euse), fougueux(euse).

**impetus** ['ɪmpətəs] *n* impulsion *f*; (*of runner*) élan *m.*

**impinge** [ɪm'pɪndʒ]: **to** ~ **on** *vt fus* (*person*) affecter, toucher; (*rights*) empiéter sur.

**implausible** [ɪm'plɔ:zɪbl] *a* peu plausible.

**implement** *n* ['ɪmplɪmənt] outil *m*, instrument *m*; (*for cooking*) ustensile *m* // *vt* ['ɪmplɪmɛnt] exécuter, mettre à effet.

**implicate** ['ɪmplɪkeɪt] *vt* impliquer, compromettre; **implication** [-'keɪʃən] *n* implication *f.*

**implicit** [ɪm'plɪsɪt] *a* implicite; (*complete*) absolu(e), sans réserve.

**implore** [ɪm'plɔ:*] *vt* implorer, supplier.

**imply** [ɪm'plaɪ] *vt* suggérer, laisser entendre; indiquer, supposer.

**impolite** [ɪmpə'laɪt] *a* impoli(e).

**imponderable** [ɪm'pɒndərəbl] *a* impondérable.

**import** *vt* [ɪm'pɔ:t] importer // *n* ['ɪmpɔ:t] (*COMM*) importation *f*; (*meaning*) portée *f*, signification *f.*

**importance** [ɪm'pɔ:tns] *n* importance *f.*

**important** [ɪm'pɔ:tnt] *a* important(e).

**importation** [ɪmpɔ:'teɪʃən] *n* importation *f.*

**imported** [ɪm'pɔ:tɪd] *a* importé(e), d'importation.

**importer** [ɪm'pɔ:tə*] *n* importateur/trice.

**impose** [ɪm'pəuz] *vt* imposer // *vi*: **to** ~ **on sb** abuser de la gentillesse (*or* crédulité) de qn.

**imposing** [ɪm'pəuzɪŋ] *a* imposant(e), impressionnant(e).

**impossibility** [ɪmpɒsə'bɪlɪtɪ] *n* impossibilité *f.*

**impossible** [ɪm'pɒsɪbl] *a* impossible.

**impostor** [ɪm'pɒstə*] *n* imposteur *m.*

**impotence** ['ɪmpətns] *n* impuissance *f.*

**impotent** ['ɪmpətnt] *a* impuissant(e).

**impound** [ɪm'paund] *vt* confisquer, saisir.

**impoverished** [ɪm'pɒvərɪʃt] *a* pauvre, appauvri(e).

**impracticable** [ɪm'præktɪkəbl] *a* impraticable.

**impractical** [ɪm'præktɪkl] *a* pas pratique; (*person*) qui manque d'esprit pratique.

**imprecise** [ɪmprɪ'saɪs] *a* imprécis(e).

**impregnable** [ɪm'prɛgnəbl] *a* (*fortress*) imprenable; (*fig*) inattaquable; irréfutable.

**impregnate** ['ɪmprɛgneɪt] *vt* imprégner; (*fertilize*) féconder.

**impresario** [ɪmprɪ'sɑ:rɪəu] *n* impresario *m.*

**impress** [ɪm'prɛs] *vt* impressionner, faire impression sur; (*mark*) imprimer, marquer; **to** ~ **sth on sb** faire bien comprendre qch à qn.

**impression** [ɪm'prɛʃən] *n* impression *f*; (*of stamp, seal*) empreinte *f*; **to be under the** ~ **that** avoir l'impression que; ~able *a* impressionnable, sensible; ~ist *n* impressionniste *m/f.*

**impressive** [ɪm'prɛsɪv] *a* impressionnant(e).

**imprinted** [ɪm'prɪntɪd] *a*: ~ **on** imprimé(e) sur; (*fig*) imprimé(e) *or* gravé(e) dans.

**imprison** [ɪm'prɪzn] *vt* emprisonner, mettre en prison; ~ment *n* emprisonnement *m.*

**improbable** [ɪm'prɒbəbl] *a* improbable; (*excuse*) peu plausible.

**impromptu** [ɪm'prɒmptju:] *a* impromptu(e).

**improper** [ɪm'prɒpə*] *a* incorrect(e); (*unsuitable*) déplacé(e), de mauvais goût; indécent(e); **impropriety** [ɪmprə'praɪətɪ] *n* inconvenance *f*; (*of expression*) impropriété *f.*

**improve** [ɪm'pru:v] *vt* améliorer // *vi* s'améliorer; (*pupil etc*) faire des progrès; ~ment *n* amélioration *f*; progrès *m.*

**improvisation** [ɪmprəvaɪ'zeɪʃən] *n* improvisation *f.*

**improvise** ['ɪmprəvaɪz] *vt,vi* improviser.

**imprudence** [ɪm'pru:dns] *n* imprudence *f.*

**imprudent** [ɪm'pru:dnt] *a* imprudent(e).

**impudent** ['ɪmpjudnt] a impudent(e).
**impulse** ['ɪmpʌls] n impulsion f.
**impulsive** [ɪm'pʌlsɪv] a impulsif(ive).
**impunity** [ɪm'pju:nɪtɪ] n impunité f.
**impure** [ɪm'pjuə*] a impur(e).
**impurity** [ɪm'pjuərɪtɪ] n impureté f.
**in** [ɪn] prep dans ; (with time: during, within):
~ **May/2 days** en mai/2 jours ; (: after):
~ **2 weeks** dans 2 semaines ; (with substance) en ; (with town) à ; (with country):
it's ~ **France/Portugal** c'est en
France/au Portugal // ad dedans, à
l'intérieur ; (fashionable) à la mode ; **is he
~?** est-il là? ; ~ **the country** à la
campagne ; ~ **town** en ville ; ~ **the sun**
au soleil ; ~ **the rain** sous la pluie ; ~
**French** en français ; **a man** ~ **10** un
homme sur 10 ; ~ **hundreds** par
centaines ; **the best pupil** ~ **the class** le
meilleur élève de la classe ; ~ **saying this**
en disant ceci ; **their party is** ~ leur parti
est au pouvoir ; **to ask sb** ~ inviter qn
à entrer ; **to run/limp** etc ~ entrer en
courant/boitant etc ; **the** ~**s and outs of**
les tenants et aboutissants de.
**in., ins** abbr of **inch(es)**.
**inability** [ɪnə'bɪlɪtɪ] n incapacité f.
**inaccessible** [ɪnək'sɛsɪbl] a inaccessible.
**inaccuracy** [ɪn'ækjurəsɪ] n inexactitude
f ; manque m de précision.
**inaccurate** [ɪn'ækjurət] a inexact(e) ;
(person) qui manque de précision.
**inaction** [ɪn'ækʃən] n inaction f, inactivité
f.
**inactivity** [ɪnæk'tɪvɪtɪ] n inactivité f.
**inadequacy** [ɪn'ædɪkwəsɪ] n insuffisance
f.
**inadequate** [ɪn'ædɪkwət] a insuffisant(e),
inadéquat(e).
**inadvertently** [ɪnəd'və:tntlɪ] ad par
mégarde.
**inadvisable** [ɪnəd'vaɪzəbl] a à
déconseiller ; **it is** ~ **to** il est déconseillé
de.
**inane** [ɪ'neɪn] a inepte, stupide.
**inanimate** [ɪn'ænɪmət] a inanimé(e).
**inappropriate** [ɪnə'prəuprɪət] a
inopportun(e), mal à propos ; (word,
expression) impropre.
**inapt** [ɪn'æpt] a inapte ; peu approprié(e) ;
~**itude** n inaptitude f.
**inarticulate** [ɪnɑː'tɪkjulət] a (person) qui
s'exprime mal ; (speech) indistinct(e).
**inasmuch as** [ɪnəz'mʌtʃæz] ad dans la
mesure où ; (seeing that) attendu que.
**inattention** [ɪnə'tɛnʃən] n manque m
d'attention.
**inattentive** [ɪnə'tɛntɪv] a inattentif(ive),
distrait(e) ; négligent(e).
**inaudible** [ɪn'ɔːdɪbl] a inaudible.
**inaugural** [ɪ'nɔːgjurəl] a inaugural(e).
**inaugurate** [ɪ'nɔːgjureɪt] vt inaugurer ;
(president, official) investir de ses
fonctions ; **inauguration** [-'reɪʃən] n
inauguration f ; investiture f.
**in-between** [ɪnbɪ'twiːn] a entre les deux.
**inborn** [ɪn'bɔːn] a (feeling) inné(e) ; (defect)
congénital(e).
**inbred** [ɪn'brɛd] a inné(e), naturel(le) ;
(family) consanguin(e).

**inbreeding** [ɪn'briːdɪŋ] n croisement m
d'animaux de même souche ; unions
consanguines.
**Inc.** abbr see **incorporated**.
**incalculable** [ɪn'kælkjuləbl] a
incalculable.
**incapability** [ɪnkeɪpə'bɪlɪtɪ] n incapacité f.
**incapable** [ɪn'keɪpəbl] a incapable.
**incapacitate** [ɪnkə'pæsɪteɪt] vt: **to** ~ **sb
from doing** rendre qn incapable de faire ;
~**d** a (LAW) frappé(e) d'incapacité.
**incapacity** [ɪnkə'pæsɪtɪ] n incapacité f.
**incarcerate** [ɪn'kɑːsəreɪt] vt incarcérer.
**incarnate** a [ɪn'kɑːnɪt] incarné(e) // vt
['ɪnkɑːneɪt] incarner ; **incarnation**
[-'neɪʃən] n incarnation f.
**incendiary** [ɪn'sɛndɪərɪ] a incendiaire.
**incense** n ['ɪnsɛns] encens m // vt [ɪn'sɛns]
(anger) mettre en colère ; ~ **burner** n
encensoir m.
**incentive** [ɪn'sɛntɪv] n encouragement m,
raison f de se donner de la peine ; ~ **bonus**
n prime f d'encouragement.
**incessant** [ɪn'sɛsnt] a incessant(e) ; ~**ly**
ad sans cesse, constamment.
**incest** ['ɪnsɛst] n inceste m.
**inch** [ɪntʃ] n pouce m (= 25 mm ; 12 in a
foot) ; **within an** ~ **of** à deux doigts de ;
~ **tape** n centimètre m (de couturière).
**incidence** ['ɪnsɪdns] n (of crime, disease)
fréquence f.
**incident** ['ɪnsɪdnt] n incident m ; (in book)
péripétie f.
**incidental** [ɪnsɪ'dɛntl] a accessoire ;
(unplanned) accidentel(le) ; ~ **to** qui
accompagne ; ~ **expenses** npl faux frais
mpl ; ~**ly** [-'dɛntəlɪ] ad (by the way) à
propos.
**incinerator** [ɪn'sɪnəreɪtə*] n incinérateur
m.
**incipient** [ɪn'sɪpɪənt] a naissant(e).
**incision** [ɪn'sɪʒən] n incision f.
**incisive** [ɪn'saɪsɪv] a incisif(ive) ;
mordant(e).
**incite** [ɪn'saɪt] vt inciter, pousser.
**inclement** [ɪn'klɛmənt] a inclément(e),
rigoureux(euse).
**inclination** [ɪnklɪ'neɪʃən] n inclination f.
**incline** n ['ɪnklaɪn] pente f, plan incliné //
vb [ɪn'klaɪn] vt incliner // vi: **to** ~ **to** avoir
tendance à ; **to be** ~**d to do** être enclin(e)
à faire ; avoir tendance à faire ; **to be well
~d towards sb** être bien disposé(e) à
l'égard de qn.
**include** [ɪn'kluːd] vt inclure, comprendre ;
**including** prep y compris.
**inclusion** [ɪn'kluːʒən] n inclusion f.
**inclusive** [ɪn'kluːsɪv] a inclus(e),
compris(e) ; ~ **terms** npl prix tout
compris.
**incognito** [ɪnkɔg'niːtəu] ad incognito.
**incoherent** [ɪnkəu'hɪərənt] a
incohérent(e).
**income** ['ɪnkʌm] n revenu m ; ~ **tax** n
impôt m sur le revenu ; ~ **tax inspector**
n inspecteur m des contributions directes ;
~ **tax return** n déclaration f des revenus.
**incoming** ['ɪnkʌmɪŋ] a: ~ **tide** n marée
montante.
**incompatible** [ɪnkəm'pætɪbl] a incompatible.

**incompetence** [ɪn'kɔmpɪtns] *n* incompétence *f*, incapacité *f*.

**incompetent** [ɪn'kɔmpɪtnt] *a* incompétent(e), incapable.

**incomplete** [ɪnkəm'pliːt] *a* incomplet(ète).

**incomprehensible** [ɪnkɔmprɪ'hɛnsɪbl] *a* incompréhensible.

**inconclusive** [ɪnkən'kluːsɪv] *a* peu concluant(e); (*argument*) peu convaincant(e).

**incongruous** [ɪn'kɔŋgruəs] *a* peu approprié(e); (*remark*, *act*) incongru(e), déplacé(e).

**inconsequential** [ɪnkɔnsɪ'kwɛnʃl] *a* sans importance.

**inconsiderate** [ɪnkən'sɪdərət] *a* (*action*) inconsidéré(e); (*person*) qui manque d'égards.

**inconsistent** [ɪnkən'sɪstnt] *a* sans cohérence; peu logique; qui présente des contradictions; ~ **with** en contradiction avec.

**inconspicuous** [ɪnkən'spɪkjuəs] *a* qui passe inaperçu(e); (*colour*, *dress*) discret(ète); **to make o.s.** ~ ne pas se faire remarquer.

**inconstant** [ɪn'kɔnstnt] *a* inconstant(e); variable.

**incontinence** [ɪn'kɔntɪnəns] *n* incontinence *f*.

**incontinent** [ɪn'kɔntɪnənt] *a* incontinent(e).

**inconvenience** [ɪnkən'viːnjəns] *n* inconvénient *m*; (*trouble*) dérangement *m* // *vt* déranger.

**inconvenient** [ɪnkən'viːnjənt] *a* malcommode; (*time*, *place*) mal choisi(e), qui ne convient pas.

**incorporate** [ɪn'kɔːpəreɪt] *vt* incorporer; (*contain*) contenir // *vi* fusionner; (*two firms*) se constituer en société; ~**d** *a*: ~**d company** (*US*, *abbr* **Inc.**) société *f* anonyme (S.A.).

**incorrect** [ɪnkə'rɛkt] *a* incorrect(e); (*opinion*, *statement*) inexact(e).

**incorruptible** [ɪnkə'rʌptɪbl] *a* incorruptible.

**increase** *n* ['ɪnkriːs] augmentation *f* // *vi*, *vt* [ɪn'kriːs] augmenter.

**increasing** [ɪn'kriːsɪŋ] *a* (*number*) croissant(e); ~**ly** *ad* de plus en plus.

**incredible** [ɪn'krɛdɪbl] *a* incroyable.

**incredulous** [ɪn'krɛdjuləs] *a* incrédule.

**increment** ['ɪnkrɪmənt] *n* augmentation *f*.

**incriminate** [ɪn'krɪmɪneɪt] *vt* incriminer, compromettre.

**incubation** [ɪnkju'beɪʃən] *n* incubation *f*.

**incubator** ['ɪnkjubeɪtə\*] *n* incubateur *m*; (*for babies*) couveuse *f*.

**incur** [ɪn'kəː\*] *vt* (*expenses*) encourir; (*anger*, *risk*) s'exposer à; (*debt*) contracter; (*loss*) subir.

**incurable** [ɪn'kjuərəbl] *a* incurable.

**incursion** [ɪn'kəːʃən] *n* incursion *f*.

**indebted** [ɪn'dɛtɪd] *a*: **to be** ~ **to sb** (**for**) être redevable à qn (de).

**indecent** [ɪn'diːsnt] *a* indécent(e), inconvenant(e); ~ **assault** *n* attentat *m* à la pudeur; ~ **exposure** *n* outrage *m* (public) à la pudeur.

**indecision** [ɪndɪ'sɪʒən] *n* indécision *f*.

**indecisive** [ɪndɪ'saɪsɪv] *a* indécis(e); (*discussion*) peu concluant(e).

**indeed** [ɪn'diːd] *ad* en effet; vraiment; **yes** ~! certainement!

**indefinable** [ɪndɪ'faɪnəbl] *a* indéfinissable.

**indefinite** [ɪn'dɛfɪnɪt] *a* indéfini(e); (*answer*) vague; (*period*, *number*) indéterminé(e); ~**ly** *ad* (*wait*) indéfiniment; (*speak*) vaguement, avec imprécision.

**indelible** [ɪn'dɛlɪbl] *a* indélébile.

**indemnify** [ɪn'dɛmnɪfaɪ] *vt* indemniser, dédommager.

**indentation** [ɪndɛn'teɪʃən] *n* découpure *f*; (*TYP*) alinéa *m*; (*on metal*) bosse *f*.

**independence** [ɪndɪ'pɛndns] *n* indépendance *f*.

**independent** [ɪndɪ'pɛndnt] *a* indépendant(e); ~**ly** *ad* de façon indépendante; ~**ly of** indépendamment de.

**indescribable** [ɪndɪ'skraɪbəbl] *a* indescriptible.

**index** ['ɪndɛks] *n* (*pl*: ~**es**: *in book*) index *m*; (: *in library etc*) catalogue *m*; (*pl*: **indices** ['ɪndɪsiːz]: *ratio*, *sign*) indice *m*; ~ **card** *n* fiche *f*; ~ **finger** *n* index *m*; ~-**linked** *a* indexé(e) (sur le coût de la vie etc).

**India** ['ɪndɪə] *n* Inde *f*; ~**n** *a* indien(ne) // *n* Indien/ne; ~**n ink** *n* encre *f* de Chine; ~**n Ocean** *n* océan Indien; ~ **paper** *n* papier *m* bible.

**indicate** ['ɪndɪkeɪt] *vt* indiquer; **indication** [-'keɪʃən] *n* indication *f*, signe *m*.

**indicative** [ɪn'dɪkətɪv] *a* indicatif(ive) // *n* (*LING*) indicatif *m*.

**indicator** ['ɪndɪkeɪtə\*] *n* (*sign*) indicateur *m*; (*AUT*) clignotant *m*.

**indices** ['ɪndɪsiːz] *npl of* **index**.

**indict** [ɪn'daɪt] *vt* accuser; ~**able** *a* (*person*) passible de poursuites; ~**able offence** *n* délit pénal; ~**ment** *n* accusation *f*.

**indifference** [ɪn'dɪfrəns] *n* indifférence *f*.

**indifferent** [ɪn'dɪfrənt] *a* indifférent(e); (*poor*) médiocre, quelconque.

**indigenous** [ɪn'dɪdʒɪnəs] *a* indigène.

**indigestible** [ɪndɪ'dʒɛstɪbl] *a* indigeste.

**indigestion** [ɪndɪ'dʒɛstʃən] *n* indigestion *f*, mauvaise digestion.

**indignant** [ɪn'dɪgnənt] *a*: ~ (**at sth/with sb**) indigné(e) (de qch/contre qn).

**indignation** [ɪndɪg'neɪʃən] *n* indignation *f*.

**indignity** [ɪn'dɪgnɪtɪ] *n* indignité *f*, affront *m*.

**indigo** ['ɪndɪgəu] *a* indigo *inv* // *n* indigo *m*.

**indirect** [ɪndɪ'rɛkt] *a* indirect(e); ~**ly** *ad* indirectement.

**indiscreet** [ɪndɪ'skriːt] *a* indiscret(ète); (*rash*) imprudent(e).

**indiscretion** [ɪndɪ'skrɛʃən] *n* indiscrétion *f*; imprudence *f*.

**indiscriminate** [ɪndɪ'skrɪmɪnət] *a* (*person*) qui manque de discernement; (*admiration*) aveugle; (*killings*) commis(e) au hasard.

**indispensable** [ɪndɪ'spɛnsəbl] *a* indispensable.

**indisposed** [ɪndɪ'spəuzd] *a* (*unwell*) indisposé(e), souffrant(e).

**indisposition** [ɪndɪspə'zɪʃən] *n* (*illness*) indisposition *f*, malaise *m*.

**indisputable** [ɪndɪ'spju:təbl] *a* incontestable, indiscutable.

**indistinct** [ɪndɪ'stɪŋkt] *a* indistinct(e); (*memory, noise*) vague.

**individual** [ɪndɪ'vɪdjuəl] *n* individu *m* // *a* individuel(le); (*characteristic*) particulier(ère), original(e); **~ist** *n* individualiste *m/f*; **~ity** [-'ælɪtɪ] *n* individualité *f*; **~ly** *ad* individuellement.

**indoctrinate** [ɪn'dɔktrɪneɪt] *vt* endoctriner; **indoctrination** [-'neɪʃən] *n* endoctrinement *m*.

**indolent** ['ɪndələnt] *a* indolent(e), nonchalant(e).

**indoor** ['ɪndɔ:*] *a* d'intérieur; (*plant*) d'appartement; (*swimming-pool*) couvert(e); (*sport, games*) pratiqué(e) en salle; **~s** [ɪn'dɔ:z] *ad* à l'intérieur; (*at home*) à la maison.

**indubitable** [ɪn'dju:bɪtəbl] *a* indubitable, incontestable.

**induce** [ɪn'dju:s] *vt* persuader; (*bring about*) provoquer; **~ment** *n* incitation *f*; (*incentive*) but *m*; (*pej: bribe*) pot-de-vin *m*.

**induct** [ɪn'dʌkt] *vt* établir dans ses fonctions; (*fig*) initier.

**induction** [ɪn'dʌkʃən] *n* (MED: *of birth*) accouchement provoqué; **~ course** *n* stage *m* de mise au courant.

**indulge** [ɪn'dʌldʒ] *vt* (*whim*) céder à, satisfaire; (*child*) gâter // *vi*: **to ~ in sth** s'offrir qch, se permettre qch; se livrer à qch; **~nce** *n* fantaisie *f* (que l'on s'offre); (*leniency*) indulgence *f*; **~nt** *a* indulgent(e).

**industrial** [ɪn'dʌstrɪəl] *a* industriel(le); (*injury*) du travail; (*dispute*) ouvrier(ère); **~ action** *n* action revendicative; **~ estate** *n* zone industrielle; **~ist** *n* industriel *m*; **~ize** *vt* industrialiser.

**industrious** [ɪn'dʌstrɪəs] *a* travailleur(euse).

**industry** ['ɪndəstrɪ] *n* industrie *f*; (*diligence*) zèle *m*, application *f*.

**inebriated** [ɪ'ni:brɪeɪtɪd] *a* ivre.

**inedible** [ɪn'ɛdɪbl] *a* immangeable; (*plant etc*) non comestible.

**ineffective** [ɪnɪ'fɛktɪv] *a* inefficace.

**ineffectual** [ɪnɪ'fɛktʃuəl] *a* inefficace; incompétent(e).

**inefficiency** [ɪnɪ'fɪʃənsɪ] *n* inefficacité *f*.

**inefficient** [ɪnɪ'fɪʃənt] *a* inefficace.

**inelegant** [ɪn'ɛlɪgənt] *a* peu élégant(e).

**ineligible** [ɪn'ɛlɪdʒɪbl] *a* (*candidate*) inéligible; **to be ~ for sth** ne pas avoir droit à qch.

**inept** [ɪ'nɛpt] *a* inepte.

**inequality** [ɪnɪ'kwɔlɪtɪ] *n* inégalité *f*.

**ineradicable** [ɪnɪ'rædɪkəbl] *a* indéracinable, tenace.

**inert** [ɪ'nə:t] *a* inerte.

**inertia** [ɪ'nə:ʃə] *n* inertie *f*; **~ reel seat belt** *n* ceinture *f* de sécurité à enrouleur.

**inescapable** [ɪnɪ'skeɪpəbl] *a* inéluctable, inévitable.

**inessential** [ɪnɪ'sɛnʃl] *a* superflu(e).

**inestimable** [ɪn'ɛstɪməbl] *a* inestimable, incalculable.

**inevitable** [ɪn'ɛvɪtəbl] *a* inévitable.

**inexact** [ɪnɪg'zækt] *a* inexact(e).

**inexhaustible** [ɪnɪg'zɔ:stɪbl] *a* inépuisable.

**inexorable** [ɪn'ɛksərəbl] *a* inexorable.

**inexpensive** [ɪnɪk'spɛnsɪv] *a* bon marché *inv*.

**inexperience** [ɪnɪk'spɪərɪəns] *n* inexpérience *f*, manque *m* d'expérience; **~d** *a* inexpérimenté(e).

**inexplicable** [ɪnɪk'splɪkəbl] *a* inexplicable.

**inexpressible** [ɪnɪk'sprɛsɪbl] *a* inexprimable.

**inextricable** [ɪnɪk'strɪkəbl] *a* inextricable.

**infallibility** [ɪnfælə'bɪlɪtɪ] *n* infaillibilité *f*.

**infallible** [ɪn'fælɪbl] *a* infaillible.

**infamous** ['ɪnfəməs] *a* infâme, abominable.

**infamy** ['ɪnfəmɪ] *n* infamie *f*.

**infancy** ['ɪnfənsɪ] *n* petite enfance, bas âge; (*fig*) enfance *f*, débuts *mpl*.

**infant** ['ɪnfənt] *n* (*baby*) nourrisson *m*; (*young child*) petit(e) enfant; **~ile** *a* infantile; **~ school** *n* classes *fpl* préparatoires (*entre 5 et 7 ans*).

**infantry** ['ɪnfəntrɪ] *n* infanterie *f*; **~man** *n* fantassin *m*.

**infatuated** [ɪn'fætjueɪtɪd] *a*: **~ with** entiché(e) de.

**infatuation** [ɪnfætju'eɪʃən] *n* toquade *f*; engouement *m*.

**infect** [ɪn'fɛkt] *vt* infecter, contaminer; (*fig: pej*) corrompre; **~ed with** (*illness*) atteint(e) de; **~ion** [ɪn'fɛkʃən] *n* infection *f*; contagion *f*; **~ious** [ɪn'fɛkʃəs] *a* infectieux(euse); (*also: fig*) contagieux(euse).

**infer** [ɪn'fə:*] *vt* conclure, déduire; **~ence** ['ɪnfərəns] *n* conclusion *f*; déduction *f*.

**inferior** [ɪn'fɪərɪə*] *a* inférieur(e); (*goods*) de qualité inférieure // *n* inférieur/e; (*in rank*) subalterne *m/f*; **~ity** [ɪnfɪərɪ'ɔrətɪ] *n* infériorité *f*; **~ity complex** *n* complexe *m* d'infériorité.

**infernal** [ɪn'fə:nl] *a* infernal(e); **~ly** *ad* abominablement.

**inferno** [ɪn'fə:nəu] *n* enfer *m*; brasier *m*.

**infertile** [ɪn'fə:taɪl] *a* stérile; **infertility** [-'tɪlɪtɪ] *n* infertilité *f*, stérilité *f*.

**infested** [ɪn'fɛstɪd] *a*: **~ (with)** infesté(e) (de).

**infidelity** [ɪnfɪ'dɛlɪtɪ] *n* infidélité *f*.

**in-fighting** ['ɪnfaɪtɪŋ] *n* querelles *fpl* internes.

**infiltrate** ['ɪnfɪltreɪt] *vt* (*troops etc*) faire s'infiltrer; (*enemy line etc*) s'infiltrer dans // *vi* s'infiltrer.

**infinite** ['ɪnfɪnɪt] *a* infini(e).

**infinitive** [ɪn'fɪnɪtɪv] *n* infinitif *m*.

**infinity** [ɪn'fɪnɪtɪ] *n* infinité *f*; (*also* MATH) infini *m*.

**infirm** [ɪn'fə:m] *a* infirme.

**infirmary** [ɪn'fə:mərɪ] *n* hôpital *m*; (*in school, factory*) infirmerie *f*.

**infirmity** [ɪn'fə:mɪtɪ] *n* infirmité *f*.

**inflame** [ɪn'fleɪm] *vt* enflammer.

**inflammable** [ɪn'flæməbl] *a* inflammable.

**inflammation** [ɪnflə'meɪʃən] *n* inflammation *f*.

**inflate** [ɪn'fleɪt] *vt* (*tyre, balloon*) gonfler; (*fig*) grossir; gonfler; faire monter; **to ~ the currency** avoir recours à l'inflation;

~d a (*style*) enflé(e) ; (*value*) exagéré(e) ;
**inflation** [ɪn'fleɪʃən] n (ECON) inflation f.
**inflexible** [ɪn'flɛksɪbl] a inflexible, rigide.
**inflict** [ɪn'flɪkt] vt: **to ~ on** infliger à ;
~**ion** [ɪn'flɪkʃən] n infliction f; affliction
f.
**inflow** ['ɪnfləu] n afflux m.
**influence** ['ɪnfluəns] n influence f // vt
influencer ; **under the ~ of** sous l'effet
de ; **under the ~ of drink** en état d'ébriété.
**influential** [ɪnflu'ɛnʃl] a influent(e).
**influenza** [ɪnflu'ɛnzə] n grippe f.
**influx** ['ɪnflʌks] n afflux m.
**inform** [ɪn'fɔ:m] vt: **to ~ sb (of)** informer
or avertir qn (de) ; **to ~ sb about**
renseigner qn sur, mettre qn au courant
de.
**informal** [ɪn'fɔ:ml] a (*person, manner*)
simple, sans façon ; (*visit, discussion*)
dénué(e) de formalités ; (*announcement,
invitation*) non-officiel(le) ; **'dress ~'**
'tenue de ville' ; ~**ity** [-'mælɪtɪ] n
simplicité f, absence f de cérémonie ;
caractère non-officiel ; **~ language** n
langage m de la conversation.
**information** [ɪnfə'meɪʃən] n information
f; renseignements mpl ; (*knowledge*)
connaissances fpl ; **a piece of ~** un
renseignement.
**informative** [ɪn'fɔ:mətɪv] a instructif(ive).
**informer** [ɪn'fɔ:mə*] n dénonciateur/-
trice ; (*also*: **police ~**) indicateur/trice.
**infra-red** [ɪnfrə'rɛd] a infrarouge.
**infrequent** [ɪn'fri:kwənt] a peu
fréquent(e), rare.
**infringe** [ɪn'frɪndʒ] vt enfreindre // vi: **to
~ on** empiéter sur ; ~**ment** n: ~**ment
(of)** infraction f (à).
**infuriate** [ɪn'fjuərɪeɪt] vt mettre en fureur ;
**infuriating** a exaspérant(e).
**ingenious** [ɪn'dʒi:njəs] a ingénieux(euse).
**ingenuity** [ɪndʒɪ'nju:ɪtɪ] n ingéniosité f.
**ingenuous** [ɪn'dʒɛnjuəs] a naïf(ïve),
ingénu(e).
**ingot** ['ɪŋgət] n lingot m.
**ingrained** [ɪn'greɪnd] a enraciné(e).
**ingratiate** [ɪn'greɪʃɪeɪt] vt: **to ~ o.s. with**
s'insinuer dans les bonnes grâces de, se
faire bien voir de.
**ingratitude** [ɪn'grætɪtju:d] n ingratitude f.
**ingredient** [ɪn'gri:dɪənt] n ingrédient m ;
élément m.
**ingrown** ['ɪngrəun] a: **~ toenail** ougle
incarné.
**inhabit** [ɪn'hæbɪt] vt habiter.
**inhabitant** [ɪn'hæbɪtnt] n habitant/e.
**inhale** [ɪn'heɪl] vt inhaler ; (*perfume*)
respirer // vi (*in smoking*) avaler la fumée.
**inherent** [ɪn'hɪərənt] a: **~ (in** or **to)**
inhérent(e) (à).
**inherit** [ɪn'hɛrɪt] vt hériter (de) ; ~**ance** n
héritage m ; **law of ~ance** n droit m de
la succession.
**inhibit** [ɪn'hɪbɪt] vt (PSYCH) inhiber ; **to ~
sb from doing** empêcher or retenir qn de
faire ; ~**ing** a gênant(e) ; ~**ion** [-'bɪʃən] n
inhibition f.
**inhospitable** [ɪnhɔs'pɪtəbl] a inhospita-
lier(ère).
**inhuman** [ɪn'hju:mən] a inhumain(e).

**inimitable** [ɪ'nɪmɪtəbl] a inimitable.
**iniquity** [ɪ'nɪkwɪtɪ] n iniquité f.
**initial** [ɪ'nɪʃl] a initial(e) // n initiale f //
vt parafer ; ~**s** npl initiales fpl ; (*as
signature*) parafe m ; ~**ly** ad initialement,
au début.
**initiate** [ɪ'nɪʃɪeɪt] vt (*start*) entreprendre ;
amorcer ; lancer ; (*person*) initier ; **to ~ sb
into a secret** initier qn à un secret ; **to
~ proceedings against sb** (LAW) intenter
une action à qn ; **initiation** [-'eɪʃən] n (*into
secret etc*) initiation f.
**initiative** [ɪ'nɪʃətɪv] n initiative f.
**inject** [ɪn'dʒɛkt] vt (*liquid*) injecter ;
(*person*) faire une piqûre à ; ~**ion**
[ɪn'dʒɛkʃən] n injection f, piqûre f.
**injure** ['ɪndʒə*] vt blesser ; (*wrong*) faire
du tort à ; (*damage: reputation etc*)
compromettre.
**injury** ['ɪndʒərɪ] n blessure f; (*wrong*) tort
m ; **~ time** n (SPORT) arrêts mpl de jeu.
**injustice** [ɪn'dʒʌstɪs] n injustice f.
**ink** [ɪŋk] n encre f.
**inkling** ['ɪŋklɪŋ] n soupçon m, vague idée
f.
**inky** ['ɪŋkɪ] a taché(e) d'encre.
**inlaid** ['ɪnleɪd] a incrusté(e) ; (*table etc*)
marqueté(e).
**inland** a ['ɪnlənd] intérieur(e) // ad
[ɪn'lænd] à l'intérieur, dans les terres ; **I~
Revenue** n (*Brit*) fisc m, contributions
directes ; **~ waterways** npl canaux mpl et
rivières fpl.
**in-laws** ['ɪnlɔ:z] npl beaux-parents mpl ;
belle famille.
**inlet** ['ɪnlɛt] n (GEO) crique f; **~ pipe** n
(TECH) tuyau m d'arrivée.
**inmate** ['ɪnmeɪt] n (*in prison*) détenu/e ; (*in
asylum*) interné/e.
**inn** [ɪn] n auberge f.
**innate** [ɪ'neɪt] a inné(e).
**inner** ['ɪnə*] a intérieur(e) ; **~ city** n centre
m de zone urbaine ; **~ tube** n (*of tyre*)
chambre f à air.
**innocence** ['ɪnəsns] n innocence f.
**innocent** ['ɪnəsnt] a innocent(e).
**innocuous** [ɪ'nɔkjuəs] a inoffensif(ive).
**innovation** [ɪnəu'veɪʃən] n innovation f.
**innuendo,** ~**es** [ɪnju'ɛndəu] n
insinuation f, allusion (malveillante).
**innumerable** [ɪ'nju:mrəbl] a innombrable.
**inoculation** [ɪnɔkju'leɪʃən] n inoculation f.
**inopportune** [ɪn'ɔpətju:n] a inoppor-
tun(e).
**inordinately** [ɪ'nɔ:dɪnɪtlɪ] ad démesuré-
ment.
**inorganic** [ɪnɔ:'gænɪk] a inorganique.
**in-patient** ['ɪnpeɪʃənt] n malade
hospitalisé(e).
**input** ['ɪnput] n (ELEC) énergie f, puissance
f; (*of machine*) consommation f; (*of
computer*) information fournie.
**inquest** ['ɪnkwɛst] n enquête (criminelle).
**inquire** [ɪn'kwaɪə*] vi demander // vt
demander, s'informer de ; **to ~ about** vt
fus s'informer de, se renseigner sur ; **to ~
after** vt fus demander des nouvelles de ;
**to ~ into** vt fus faire une enquête sur ;
**inquiring** a (*mind*) curieux(euse),
investigateur(trice) ; **inquiry** n demande f
de renseignements ; (LAW) enquête f,

investigation f; **inquiry office** n bureau m de renseignements.

**inquisitive** [ɪn'kwɪzɪtɪv] a curieux(euse).

**inroad** ['ɪnrəud] n incursion f.

**insane** [ɪn'seɪn] a fou(folle); (MED) aliéné(e).

**insanitary** [ɪn'sænɪtərɪ] a insalubre.

**insanity** [ɪn'sænɪtɪ] n folie f; (MED) aliénation (mentale).

**insatiable** [ɪn'seɪʃəbl] a insatiable.

**inscribe** [ɪn'skraɪb] vt inscrire; (book etc): to ~ (to sb) dédicacer (à qn).

**inscription** [ɪn'skrɪpʃən] n inscription f; dédicace f.

**inscrutable** [ɪn'skru:təbl] a impénétrable.

**insect** ['ɪnsɛkt] n insecte m; ~icide [ɪn'sɛktɪsaɪd] n insecticide m.

**insecure** [ɪnsɪ'kjuə*] a peu solide; peu sûr(e); (person) anxieux (euse); **insecurity** n insécurité f.

**insensible** [ɪn'sɛnsɪbl] a insensible; (unconscious) sans connaissance.

**insensitive** [ɪn'sɛnsɪtɪv] a insensible.

**inseparable** [ɪn'sɛprəbl] a inséparable.

**insert** vt [ɪn'sə:t] insérer // n ['ɪnsə:t] insertion f; ~ion [ɪn'sə:ʃən] n insertion f.

**inshore** [ɪn'ʃɔ:*] a côtier(ère) // ad près de la côte; vers la côte.

**inside** ['ɪn'saɪd] n intérieur m // a intérieur(e) // ad à l'intérieur, dedans // prep à l'intérieur de; (of time): ~ 10 minutes en moins de 10 minutes; ~s npl (col) intestins mpl; ~ forward n (SPORT) intérieur m; ~ lane n (AUT: in Britain) voie f de gauche; ~ out ad à l'envers; (know) à fond; to turn ~ out retourner.

**insidious** [ɪn'sɪdɪəs] a insidieux(euse).

**insight** ['ɪnsaɪt] n perspicacité f; (glimpse, idea) aperçu m.

**insignificant** [ɪnsɪg'nɪfɪknt] a insignifiant(e).

**insincere** [ɪnsɪn'sɪə*] a hypocrite; **insincerity** [-'sɛrɪtɪ] n manque m de sincérité, hypocrisie f.

**insinuate** [ɪn'sɪnjueɪt] vt insinuer; **insinuation** [-'eɪʃən] n insinuation f.

**insipid** [ɪn'sɪpɪd] a insipide, fade.

**insist** [ɪn'sɪst] vi insister; to ~ on doing insister pour faire; to ~ that insister pour que; (claim) maintenir or soutenir que; ~ence n insistance f; ~ent a insistant(e), pressant(e).

**insolence** ['ɪnsələns] n insolence f.

**insolent** ['ɪnsələnt] a insolent(e).

**insoluble** [ɪn'sɔljubl] a insoluble.

**insolvent** [ɪn'sɔlvənt] a insolvable; en faillite.

**insomnia** [ɪn'sɔmnɪə] n insomnie f.

**inspect** [ɪn'spɛkt] vt inspecter; (ticket) contrôler; ~ion [ɪn'spɛkʃən] n inspection f; contrôle m; ~or n inspecteur/trice; contrôleur/euse.

**inspiration** [ɪnspə'reɪʃən] n inspiration f.

**inspire** [ɪn'spaɪə*] vt inspirer; **inspiring** a inspirant(e).

**instability** [ɪnstə'bɪlɪtɪ] n instabilité f.

**install** [ɪn'stɔ:l] vt installer; ~ation [ɪnstə'leɪʃən] n installation f.

**instalment, installment** (US) [ɪn'stɔ:lmənt] n acompte m, versement partiel; (of TV serial etc) épisode m.

**instance** ['ɪnstəns] n exemple m; for ~ par exemple; in many ~s dans bien des cas.

**instant** ['ɪnstənt] n instant m // a immédiat(e); urgent(e); (coffee, food) instantané(e), en poudre; the 10th ~ le 10 courant; ~ly ad immédiatement, tout de suite.

**instead** [ɪn'stɛd] ad au lieu de cela; ~ of au lieu de; ~ of sb à la place de qn.

**instep** ['ɪnstɛp] n cou-de-pied m; (of shoe) cambrure f.

**instigation** [ɪnstɪ'geɪʃən] n instigation f.

**instil** [ɪn'stɪl] vt: to ~ (into) inculquer (à); (courage) insuffler (à).

**instinct** ['ɪnstɪŋkt] n instinct m.

**instinctive** [ɪn'stɪŋktɪv] a instinctif(ive); ~ly ad instinctivement.

**institute** ['ɪnstɪtju:t] n institut m // vt instituer, établir; (inquiry) ouvrir; (proceedings) entamer.

**institution** [ɪnstɪ'tju:ʃən] n institution f; établissement m (scolaire); établissement m (psychiatrique).

**instruct** [ɪn'strʌkt] vt instruire, former; to ~ sb in sth enseigner qch à qn; to ~ sb to do charger qn or ordonner à qn de faire; ~ion [ɪn'strʌkʃən] n instruction f; ~ions npl directives fpl; ~ions (for use) mode m d'emploi; ~ive a instructif(ive); ~or n professeur m; (for skiing, driving) moniteur m.

**instrument** ['ɪnstrumənt] n instrument m; ~al [-'mɛntl] a (MUS) instrumental(e); to be ~al in contribuer à; ~alist [-'mɛntəlɪst] n instrumentiste m/f; ~ panel n tableau m de bord.

**insubordinate** [ɪnsə'bɔ:dənɪt] a insubordonné(e); **insubordination** [-'neɪʃən] n insubordination f.

**insufferable** [ɪn'sʌfrəbl] a insupportable.

**insufficient** [ɪnsə'fɪʃənt] a insuffisant(e); ~ly ad insuffisamment.

**insular** ['ɪnsjulə*] a insulaire; (outlook) étroit(e); (person) aux vues étroites.

**insulate** ['ɪnsjuleɪt] vt isoler; (against sound) insonoriser; **insulating tape** n ruban isolant; **insulation** [-'leɪʃən] n isolation f; insonorisation f.

**insulin** ['ɪnsjulɪn] n insuline f.

**insult** n ['ɪnsʌlt] insulte f, affront m // vt [ɪn'sʌlt] insulter, faire un affront à; ~ing a insultant(e), injurieux(euse).

**insuperable** [ɪn'sju:prəbl] a insurmontable.

**insurance** [ɪn'ʃuərəns] n assurance f; **fire/life** ~ assurance-incendie/-vie; ~ **agent** n agent m d'assurances; ~ **policy** n police f d'assurance.

**insure** [ɪn'ʃuə*] vt assurer.

**insurrection** [ɪnsə'rɛkʃən] n insurrection f.

**intact** [ɪn'tækt] a intact(e).

**intake** ['ɪnteɪk] n (TECH) admission f; adduction f; (of food) consommation f; (SCOL): an ~ of 200 a year 200 admissions fpl par an.

**intangible** [ɪn'tændʒɪbl] a intangible; (assets) immatériel(le).

**integral** ['ɪntɪgrəl] a intégral(e); (part) intégrant(e).

**integrate** ['ɪntɪgreɪt] *vt* intégrer // *vi* s'intégrer.
**integrity** [ɪn'tɛgrɪtɪ] *n* intégrité *f.*
**intellect** ['ɪntəlɛkt] *n* intelligence *f*; ~ual [-'lɛktjuəl] *a, n* intellectuel(le).
**intelligence** [ɪn'tɛlɪdʒəns] *n* intelligence *f*; (*MIL etc*) informations *fpl*, renseignements *mpl*; **I**~ **Service** *n* services *mpl* de renseignements.
**intelligent** [ɪn'tɛlɪdʒənt] *a* intelligent(e); ~ly *ad* intelligemment.
**intelligible** [ɪn'tɛlɪdʒɪbl] *a* intelligible.
**intemperate** [ɪn'tɛmpərət] *a* immodéré(e); (*drinking too much*) adonné(e) à la boisson.
**intend** [ɪn'tɛnd] *vt* (*gift etc*): **to** ~ **sth for** destiner qch à; **to** ~ **to do** avoir l'intention de faire; ~ed *a* (*insult*) intentionnel(le); (*journey*) projeté(e); (*effect*) voulu(e).
**intense** [ɪn'tɛns] *a* intense; (*person*) véhément(e); ~ly *ad* intensément; profondément.
**intensify** [ɪn'tɛnsɪfaɪ] *vt* intensifier.
**intensity** [ɪn'tɛnsɪtɪ] *n* intensité *f.*
**intensive** [ɪn'tɛnsɪv] *a* intensif(ive); ~ **care unit** *n* service *m* de réanimation.
**intent** [ɪn'tɛnt] *n* intention *f* // *a* attentif(ive), absorbé(e); **to all** ~s **and purposes** en fait, pratiquement; **to be** ~ **on doing sth** être (bien) décidé à faire qch.
**intention** [ɪn'tɛnʃən] *n* intention *f*; ~al *a* intentionnel(le), délibéré(e).
**intently** [ɪn'tɛntlɪ] *ad* attentivement.
**inter** [ɪn'tə:*] *vt* enterrer.
**interact** [ɪntər'ækt] *vi* avoir une action réciproque; ~ion [-'ækʃən] *n* interaction *f.*
**intercede** [ɪntə'si:d] *vi*: **to** ~ (**with**) intercéder (auprès de).
**intercept** [ɪntə'sɛpt] *vt* intercepter; (*person*) arrêter au passage; ~ion [-'sɛpʃən] *n* interception *f.*
**interchange** *n* ['ɪntətʃeɪndʒ] (*exchange*) échange *m*; (*on motorway*) échangeur *m* // *vt* [ɪntə'tʃeɪndʒ] échanger; mettre à la place l'un(e) de l'autre; ~able *a* interchangeable.
**intercom** ['ɪntəkɔm] *n* interphone *m.*
**interconnect** [ɪntəkə'nɛkt] *vi* (*rooms*) communiquer.
**intercourse** ['ɪntəkɔ:s] *n* rapports *mpl.*
**interest** ['ɪntrɪst] *n* intérêt *m*; (*COMM: stake, share*) intérêts *mpl* // *vt* intéresser; ~ed *a* intéressé(e); **to be** ~ed **in** s'intéresser à; ~ing *a* intéressant(e).
**interfere** [ɪntə'fɪə*] *vi*: **to** ~ **in** (*quarrel, other people's business*) se mêler à; **to** ~ **with** (*object*) tripoter, toucher à; (*plans*) contrecarrer; (*duty*) être en conflit avec; **don't** ~ mêlez-vous de vos affaires.
**interference** [ɪntə'fɪərəns] *n* (*gen*) intrusion *f*; (*PHYSICS*) interférence *f*; (*RADIO, TV*) parasites *mpl.*
**interim** ['ɪntərɪm] *a* provisoire; (*post*) intérimaire // *n*: **in the** ~ dans l'intérim.
**interior** [ɪn'tɪərɪə*] *n* intérieur *m* // *a* intérieur(e).
**interjection** [ɪntə'dʒɛkʃən] *n* interjection *f.*

**interlock** [ɪntə'lɔk] *vi* s'enclencher // *vt* enclencher.
**interloper** ['ɪntələupə*] *n* intrus/e.
**interlude** ['ɪntəlu:d] *n* intervalle *m*; (*THEATRE*) intermède *m.*
**intermarry** [ɪntə'mærɪ] *vi* former des alliances entre familles (*or* tribus); former des unions consanguines.
**intermediary** [ɪntə'mi:dɪərɪ] *n* intermédiaire *m/f.*
**intermediate** [ɪntə'mi:dɪət] *a* intermédiaire; (*SCOL: course, level*) moyen(ne).
**intermission** [ɪntə'mɪʃən] *n* pause *f*; (*THEATRE, CINEMA*) entracte *m.*
**intermittent** [ɪntə'mɪtnt] *a* intermittent(e); ~ly *ad* par intermittence, par intervalles.
**intern** *vt* [ɪn'tə:n] interner // *n* ['ɪntə:n] (*US*) interne *m/f.*
**internal** [ɪn'tə:nl] *a* interne; (*dispute, reform etc*) intérieur(e); ~ly *ad* intérieurement; '**not to be taken** ~ly' 'pour usage externe'; ~ **revenue** *n* (*US*) fisc *m.*
**international** [ɪntə'næʃənl] *a* international(e) // *n* (*SPORT*) international *m.*
**internment** [ɪn'tə:nmənt] *n* internement *m.*
**interplay** ['ɪntəpleɪ] *n* effet *m* réciproque, jeu *m.*
**interpret** [ɪn'tə:prɪt] *vt* interpréter // *vi* servir d'interprète; ~ation [-'teɪʃən] *n* interprétation *f*; ~er *n* interprète *m/f*; ~ing *n* (*profession*) interprétariat *m.*
**interrelated** [ɪntərɪ'leɪtɪd] *a* en corrélation, en rapport étroit.
**interrogate** [ɪn'tɛrəugeɪt] *vt* interroger; (*suspect etc*) soumettre à un interrogatoire; **interrogation** [-'geɪʃən] *n* interrogation *f*; interrogatoire *m*; **interrogative** [ɪntə'rɔgətɪv] *a* interrogateur(trice) // *n* (*LING*) interrogatif *m*; **interrogator** *n* interrogateur/trice.
**interrupt** [ɪntə'rʌpt] *vt* interrompre; ~ion [-'rʌpʃən] *n* interruption *f.*
**intersect** [ɪntə'sɛkt] *vt* couper, croiser // *vi* (*roads*) se croiser, se couper; ~ion [-'sɛkʃən] *n* intersection *f*; (*of roads*) croisement *m.*
**intersperse** [ɪntə'spə:s] *vt*: **to** ~ **with** parsemer de.
**intertwine** [ɪntə'twaɪn] *vt* entrelacer // *vi* s'entrelacer.
**interval** ['ɪntəvl] *n* intervalle *m*; (*SCOL*) récréation *f*; (*THEATRE*) entracte *m*; (*SPORT*) mi-temps *f*; **bright** ~s (*in weather*) éclaircies *fpl*; **at** ~s par intervalles.
**intervene** [ɪntə'vi:n] *vi* (*time*) s'écouler (entre-temps); (*event*) survenir; (*person*) intervenir; **intervention** [-'vɛnʃən] *n* intervention *f.*
**interview** ['ɪntəvju:] *n* (*RADIO, TV etc*) interview *f*; (*for job*) entrevue *f* // *vt* interviewer; avoir une entrevue avec; ~er *n* interviewer *m.*
**intestate** [ɪn'tɛsteɪt] *a* intestat.
**intestinal** [ɪn'tɛstɪnl] *a* intestinal(e).
**intestine** [ɪn'tɛstɪn] *n* intestin *m.*
**intimacy** ['ɪntɪməsɪ] *n* intimité *f.*
**intimate** *a* ['ɪntɪmət] intime; (*knowledge*) approfondi(e) // *vt* ['ɪntɪmeɪt] suggérer,

laisser entendre ; (*announce*) faire savoir ; ~**ly** *ad* intimement.
**intimation** [ɪntɪ'meɪʃən] *n* annonce *f.*
**intimidate** [ɪn'tɪmɪdeɪt] *vt* intimider ; **intimidation** [-'deɪʃən] *n* intimidation *f.*
**into** ['ɪntu] *prep* dans ; ~ **3 pieces/French** en 3 morceaux/français.
**intolerable** [ɪn'tɔlərəbl] *a* intolérable.
**intolerance** [ɪn'tɔlərns] *n* intolérance *f.*
**intolerant** [ɪn'tɔlərnt] *a* intolérant(e).
**intonation** [ɪntəu'neɪʃən] *n* intonation *f.*
**intoxicate** [ɪn'tɔksɪkeɪt] *vt* enivrer ; ~**d** *a* ivre ; **intoxication** [-'keɪʃən] *n* ivresse *f.*
**intractable** [ɪn'træktəbl] *a* (*child, temper*) indocile, insoumis(e) ; (*problem*) insoluble.
**intransigent** [ɪn'trænsɪdʒənt] *a* intransigeant(e).
**intransitive** [ɪn'trænsɪtɪv] *a* intransitif(ive).
**intra-uterine** [ɪntrə'juːtəraɪn] *a* intra-utérin(e) ; ~ **device (I.U.D.)** *n* moyen de contraception intra-utérin.
**intravenous** [ɪntrə'viːnəs] *a* intraveineux(euse).
**intrepid** [ɪn'trɛpɪd] *a* intrépide.
**intricacy** ['ɪntrɪkəsɪ] *n* complexité *f.*
**intricate** ['ɪntrɪkət] *a* complexe, compliqué(e).
**intrigue** [ɪn'triːg] *n* intrigue *f* // *vt* intriguer ; **intriguing** *a* fascinant(e).
**intrinsic** [ɪn'trɪnsɪk] *a* intrinsèque.
**introduce** [ɪntrə'djuːs] *vt* introduire ; **to** ~ **sb (to sb)** présenter qn (à qn) ; **to** ~ **sb to** (*pastime, technique*) initier qn à ; **introduction** [-'dʌkʃən] *n* introduction *f* ; (*of person*) présentation *f* ; **introductory** *a* préliminaire, d'introduction.
**introspective** [ɪntrəu'spɛktɪv] *a* introspectif(ive).
**introvert** ['ɪntrəuvəːt] *a,n* introverti(e).
**intrude** [ɪn'truːd] *vi* (*person*) être importun(e) ; **to** ~ **on** *or* **into** s'immiscer dans ; **am I intruding?** est-ce que je vous dérange? ; ~**r** *n* intrus/e ; **intrusion** [ ʒən] *n* intrusion *f* ; **intrusive** *a* importun(e), gênant(e).
**intuition** [ɪntjuː'ɪʃən] *n* intuition *f.*
**intuitive** [ɪn'tjuːɪtɪv] *a* intuitif(ive).
**inundate** ['ɪnʌndeɪt] *vt*: **to** ~ **with** inonder de.
**invade** [ɪn'veɪd] *vt* envahir ; ~**r** *n* envahisseur *m.*
**invalid** *n* ['ɪnvəlɪd] malade *m/f* ; (*with disability*) invalide *m/f* // *a* [ɪn'vælɪd] (*not valid*) invalide, non valide ; ~**ate** [ɪn'vælɪdeɪt] *vt* invalider, annuler.
**invaluable** [ɪn'væljuəbl] *a* inestimable, inappréciable.
**invariable** [ɪn'vɛərɪəbl] *a* invariable ; (*fig*) immanquable.
**invasion** [ɪn'veɪʒən] *n* invasion *f.*
**invective** [ɪn'vɛktɪv] *n* invective *f.*
**invent** [ɪn'vɛnt] *vt* inventer ; ~**ion** [ɪn'vɛnʃən] *n* invention *f* ; ~**ive** *a* inventif(ive) ; ~**iveness** *n* esprit inventif *or* d'invention ; ~**or** *n* inventeur/trice.
**inventory** ['ɪnvəntrɪ] *n* inventaire *m.*
**inverse** [ɪn'vəːs] *a* inverse // *n* inverse *m*, contraire *m* ; ~**ly** *ad* inversement.
**invert** [ɪn'vəːt] *vt* intervertir ; (*cup, object*)

retourner ; ~**ed commas** *npl* guillemets *mpl.*
**invertebrate** [ɪn'vəːtɪbrət] *n* invertébré *m.*
**invest** [ɪn'vɛst] *vt* investir // *vi* faire un investissement.
**investigate** [ɪn'vɛstɪgeɪt] *vt* étudier, examiner ; (*crime*) faire une enquête sur ; **investigation** [-'geɪʃən] *n* examen *m* ; (*of crime*) enquête *f*, investigation *f* ; **investigator** *n* investigateur/trice.
**investiture** [ɪn'vɛstɪtʃə*] *n* investiture *f.*
**investment** [ɪn'vɛstmənt] *n* investissement *m*, placement *m.*
**investor** [ɪn'vɛstə*] *n* épargnant/e ; actionnaire *m/f.*
**inveterate** [ɪn'vɛtərət] *a* invétéré(e).
**invidious** [ɪn'vɪdɪəs] *a* injuste ; (*task*) déplaisant(e).
**invigorating** [ɪn'vɪgəreɪtɪŋ] *a* vivifiant(e) ; stimulant(e).
**invincible** [ɪn'vɪnsɪbl] *a* invincible.
**inviolate** [ɪn'vaɪələt] *a* inviolé(e).
**invisible** [ɪn'vɪzɪbl] *a* invisible ; ~ **ink** encre *f* sympathique ; ~ **mending** *n* stoppage *m.*
**invitation** [ɪnvɪ'teɪʃən] *n* invitation *f.*
**invite** [ɪn'vaɪt] *vt* inviter ; (*opinions etc*) demander ; (*trouble*) chercher ; **inviting** *a* engageant(e), attrayant(e) ; (*gesture*) encourageant(e).
**invoice** ['ɪnvɔɪs] *n* facture *f* // *vt* facturer.
**invoke** [ɪn'vəuk] *vt* invoquer.
**involuntary** [ɪn'vɔləntrɪ] *a* involontaire.
**involve** [ɪn'vɔlv] *vt* (*entail*) entraîner, nécessiter ; (*associate*): **to** ~ **sb (in)** impliquer qn (dans), mêler qn à ; faire participer qn (à) ; ~**d** *a* complexe ; **to feel** ~**d** se sentir concerné(e) ; ~**ment** *n* mise *f* en jeu ; implication *f* ; ~**ment (in)** participation *f* (à) ; rôle *m* (dans).
**invulnerable** [ɪn'vʌlnərəbl] *a* invulnérable.
**inward** ['ɪnwəd] *a* (*movement*) vers l'intérieur ; (*thought, feeling*) profond(e), intime ; ~**ly** *ad* (*feel, think etc*) secrètement, en son for intérieur ; ~**(s)** *ad* vers l'intérieur.
**Iodine** ['aɪəudiːn] *n* iode *m.*
**iota** [aɪ'əutə] *n* (*fig*) brin *m*, grain *m.*
**IOU** *n* (*abbr of I owe you*) reconnaissance *f* de dette.
**IQ** *n* (*abbr of intelligence quotient*) Q.I. *m* (quotient intellectuel).
**Iran** [ɪ'rɑːn] *n* Iran *m* ; ~**ian** [ɪ'reɪnɪən] *a* iranien(ne) // *n* Iranien/ne ; (*LING*) iranien *m.*
**Iraq** [ɪ'rɑːk] *n* Irak *m* ; ~**i** *a* irakien(ne) // *n* Irakien/ne ; (*LING*) irakien *m.*
**irascible** [ɪ'ræsɪbl] *a* irascible.
**irate** [aɪ'reɪt] *a* courroucé(e).
**Ireland** ['aɪlənd] *n* Irlande *f.*
**iris**, ~**es** ['aɪrɪs, -ɪz] *n* iris *m.*
**Irish** ['aɪrɪʃ] *a* irlandais(e) // *npl*: **the** ~ les Irlandais ; ~**man** *n* Irlandais *m* ; ~ **Sea** *n* mer *f* d'Irlande ; ~**woman** *n* Irlandaise *f.*
**irk** [əːk] *vt* ennuyer ; ~**some** *a* ennuyeux(euse).
**iron** ['aɪən] *n* fer *m* ; (*for clothes*) fer *m* à repasser // *a* de *or* en fer // *vt* (*clothes*) repasser ; ~**s** *npl* (*chains*) fers *mpl*, chaînes

*fpl*; **to ~ out** *vt* (*crease*) faire disparaître au fer; (*fig*) aplanir; faire disparaître; **the ~ curtain** *n* le rideau de fer.

**ironic(al)** [aɪ'rɔnɪk(l)] *a* ironique.

**ironing** ['aɪənɪŋ] *n* repassage *m*; **~ board** *n* planche *f* à repasser.

**ironmonger** ['aɪənmʌŋgə*] *n* quincailler *m*; **~'s** (**shop**) *n* quincaillerie *f*.

**iron ore** ['aɪən'ɔ:*] *n* minerai *m* de fer.

**ironworks** ['aɪənwə:ks] *n* usine *f* sidérurgique.

**irony** ['aɪrənɪ] *n* ironie *f*.

**irrational** [ɪ'ræʃənl] *a* irrationnel(le); déraisonnable; qui manque de logique.

**irreconcilable** [ɪrɛkən'saɪləbl] *a* irréconciliable; (*opinion*): **~ with** inconciliable avec.

**irredeemable** [ɪrɪ'di:məbl] *a* (*COMM*) non remboursable.

**irrefutable** [ɪrɪ'fju:təbl] *a* irréfutable.

**irregular** [ɪ'rɛgjulə*] *a* irrégulier(ère); **~ity** [-'lærɪtɪ] *n* irrégularité *f*.

**irrelevance** [ɪ'rɛləvəns] *n* manque *m* de rapport *or* d'à-propos.

**irrelevant** [ɪ'rɛləvənt] *a* sans rapport, hors de propos.

**irreligious** [ɪrɪ'lɪdʒəs] *a* irréligieux(euse).

**irreparable** [ɪ'rɛprəbl] *a* irréparable.

**irreplaceable** [ɪrɪ'pleɪsəbl] *a* irremplaçable.

**irrepressible** [ɪrɪ'prɛsəbl] *a* irrépressible.

**irreproachable** [ɪrɪ'prəutʃəbl] *a* irréprochable.

**irresistible** [ɪrɪ'zɪstɪbl] *a* irrésistible.

**irresolute** [ɪ'rɛzəlu:t] *a* irrésolu(e), indécis(e).

**irrespective** [ɪrɪ'spɛktɪv]: **~ of** *prep* sans tenir compte de.

**irresponsible** [ɪrɪ'spɔnsɪbl] *a* (*act*) irréfléchi(e); (*person*) qui n'a pas le sens des responsabilités.

**irretrievable** [ɪrɪ'tri:vəbl] *a* irréparable, irrémédiable.

**irreverent** [ɪ'rɛvərnt] *a* irrévérencieux(euse).

**irrevocable** [ɪ'rɛvəkəbl] *a* irrévocable.

**irrigate** ['ɪrɪgeɪt] *vt* irriguer; **irrigation** [-'geɪʃən] *n* irrigation *f*.

**irritable** ['ɪrɪtəbl] *a* irritable.

**irritate** ['ɪrɪteɪt] *vt* irriter; **irritation** [-'teɪʃən] *n* irritation *f*.

**is** [ɪz] *vb see* **be**.

**Islam** ['ɪzlɑ:m] *n* Islam *m*.

**island** ['aɪlənd] *n* île *f*; (*also*: **traffic ~**) refuge *m* (pour piétons); **~er** *n* habitant/e d'une île, insulaire *m/f*.

**isle** [aɪl] *n* île *f*.

**isn't** ['ɪznt] = **is not**.

**isolate** ['aɪsəleɪt] *vt* isoler; **~d** *a* isolé(e); **isolation** [-'leɪʃən] *n* isolement *m*; **isolationism** [-'leɪʃənɪzm] *n* isolationnisme *m*.

**isotope** ['aɪsəutəup] *n* isotope *m*.

**Israel** ['ɪzreɪl] *n* Israël *m*; **~i** [ɪz'reɪlɪ] *a* israélien(ne) // *n* Israélien/ne.

**issue** ['ɪsju:] *n* question *f*, problème *m*; (*outcome*) résultat *m*, issue *f*; (*of banknotes etc*) émission *f*; (*of newspaper etc*) numéro *m*; (*offspring*) descendance *f* // *vt* (*rations, equipment*) distribuer; (*orders*) donner;

(*book*) faire paraître, publier; (*banknotes, cheques, stamps*) émettre, mettre en circulation; **at ~** en jeu, en cause.

**isthmus** ['ɪsməs] *n* isthme *m*.

**it** [ɪt] *pronoun* (*subject*) il(elle); (*direct object*) le(la), l'; (*indirect object*) lui; (*impersonal*) il; ce, cela, ça; **~'s raining** il pleut; **I've come from ~** j'en viens; **it's on ~** c'est dessus; **he's proud of ~** il en est fier; **he agreed to ~** il y a consenti.

**Italian** [ɪ'tæljən] *a* italien(ne) // *n* Italien/ne; (*LING*) italien *m*.

**italic** [ɪ'tælɪk] *a* italique; **~s** *npl* italique *m*.

**Italy** ['ɪtəlɪ] *n* Italie *f*.

**itch** [ɪtʃ] *n* démangeaison *f* // *vi* (*person*) éprouver des démangeaisons; (*part of body*) démanger; **I'm ~ing to do l'**envie me démange de faire; **~ing** *n* démangeaison *f*; **~y** *a* qui démange.

**it'd** ['ɪtd] = **it would**; **it had**.

**item** ['aɪtəm] *n* (*gen*) article *m*; (*on agenda*) question *f*, point *m*; (*in programme*) numéro *m*; (*also*: **news ~**) nouvelle *f*; **~ize** *vt* détailler, spécifier.

**itinerant** [ɪ'tɪnərənt] *a* itinérant(e); (*musician*) ambulant(e).

**itinerary** [aɪ'tɪnərərɪ] *n* itinéraire *m*.

**it'll** ['ɪtl] = **it will, it shall**.

**its** [ɪts] *a* son(sa), ses *pl* // *pronoun* le(la) sien(ne), les siens(siennes).

**it's** [ɪts] = **it is; it has**.

**itself** [ɪt'sɛlf] *pronoun* (*emphatic*) lui-même(elle-même); (*reflexive*) se.

**ITV** *n abbr of Independent Television* (*chaîne fonctionnant en concurrence avec la BBC*).

**I.U.D.** *n abbr see* **intra-uterine**.

**I've** [aɪv] = **I have**.

**ivory** ['aɪvərɪ] *n* ivoire *m*; **~ tower** *n* (*fig*) tour *f* d'ivoire.

**ivy** ['aɪvɪ] *n* lierre *m*.

## J

**jab** [dʒæb] *vt*: **to ~ sth into** enfoncer *or* planter qch dans // *n* coup *m*; (*MED*: *col*) piqûre *f*.

**jabber** ['dʒæbə*] *vt,vi* bredouiller, baragouiner.

**jack** [dʒæk] *n* (*AUT*) cric *m*; (*BOWLS*) cochonnet *m*; (*CARDS*) valet *m*; **to ~ up** *vt* soulever (au cric).

**jacket** ['dʒækɪt] *n* veste *f*, veston *m*; (*of boiler etc*) enveloppe *f*; (*of book*) couverture *f*, jaquette *f*; **potatoes in their ~s** pommes de terre en robe des champs.

**jack-knife** ['dʒæknaɪf] *n* couteau *m* de poche // *vi*: **the lorry ~d** la remorque (du camion) s'est mise en travers.

**jackpot** ['dʒækpɔt] *n* gros lot.

**jade** [dʒeɪd] *n* (*stone*) jade *m*.

**jaded** ['dʒeɪdɪd] *a* éreinté(e), fatigué(e).

**jagged** ['dʒægɪd] *a* dentelé(e).

**jail** [dʒeɪl] *n* prison *f*; **~break** *n* évasion *f*; **~er** *n* geôlier/ière.

**jam** [dʒæm] *n* confiture *f*; (*of shoppers etc*) cohue *f*; (*also*: **traffic ~**) embouteillage *m* // *vt* (*passage etc*) encombrer, obstruer; (*mechanism, drawer etc*) bloquer, coincer; (*RADIO*) brouiller // *vi* (*mechanism, sliding*

*part)* se coincer, se bloquer; *(gun)* s'enrayer; **to ~ sth into** entasser or comprimer qch dans; enfoncer qch dans.
**Jamaica** [dʒə'meɪkə] *n* Jamaïque *f*.
**jangle** ['dʒæŋgl] *vi* cliqueter.
**janitor** ['dʒænɪtə*] *n (caretaker)* huissier *m*; concierge *m*.
**January** ['dʒænjuərɪ] *n* janvier *m*.
**Japan** [dʒə'pæn] *n* Japon *m*; **~ese** [dʒæpə'niːz] *a* japonais(e) // *n, pl inv* Japonais/e; *(LING)* japonais *m*.
**jar** [dʒɑː*] *n (glass)* pot *m*, bocal *m* // *vi (sound)* produire un son grinçant or discordant; *(colours etc)* détonner, jurer // *vt (subject: shock)* ébranler, secouer.
**jargon** ['dʒɑːgən] *n* jargon *m*.
**jasmin(e)** ['dʒæzmɪn] *n* jasmin *m*.
**jaundice** ['dʒɔːndɪs] *n* jaunisse *f*; **~d** *a (fig)* envieux(euse), désapprobateur(trice).
**jaunt** [dʒɔːnt] *n* balade *f*; **~y** *a* enjoué(e); désinvolte.
**javelin** ['dʒævlɪn] *n* javelot *m*.
**jaw** [dʒɔː] *n* mâchoire *f*.
**jaywalker** ['dʒeɪwɔːkə*] *n* piéton indiscipliné.
**jazz** [dʒæz] *n* jazz *m*; **to ~ up** *vt* animer, égayer; **~ band** *n* orchestre *m* or groupe *m* de jazz; **~y** *a* bariolé(e), tapageur(euse).
**jealous** ['dʒɛləs] *a* jaloux(ouse); **~y** *n* jalousie *f*.
**jeans** [dʒiːnz] *npl* (blue-)jean *m*.
**jeep** [dʒiːp] *n* jeep *f*.
**jeer** [dʒɪə*] *vi*: **to ~ (at)** huer; se moquer cruellement (de), railler; **~s** *npl* huées *fpl*; sarcasmes *mpl*.
**jelly** ['dʒɛlɪ] *n* gelée *f*; **~fish** *n* méduse *f*.
**jeopardize** ['dʒɛpədaɪz] *vt* mettre en danger or péril.
**jeopardy** ['dʒɛpədɪ] *n*: **in ~** en danger or péril.
**jerk** [dʒəːk] *n* secousse *f*; saccade *f*; sursaut *m*, spasme *m* // *vt* donner une secousse à // *vi (vehicles)* cahoter.
**jerkin** ['dʒəːkɪn] *n* blouson *m*.
**jerky** ['dʒəːkɪ] *a* saccadé(e); cahotant(e).
**jersey** ['dʒəːzɪ] *n* tricot *m*.
**jest** [dʒɛst] *n* plaisanterie *f*; **in ~** en plaisantant.
**jet** [dʒɛt] *n (gas, liquid)* jet *m*; *(AVIAT)* gicleur *m*; *(AVIAT)* avion *m* à réaction, jet *m*; **~-black** *a* (d'un noir) de jais; **~ engine** *n* moteur *m* à réaction.
**jetsam** ['dʒɛtsəm] *n* objets jetés à la mer (et rejetés sur la côte).
**jettison** ['dʒɛtɪsn] *vt* jeter par-dessus bord.
**jetty** ['dʒɛtɪ] *n* jetée *f*, digue *f*.
**Jew** [dʒuː] *n* Juif *m*.
**jewel** ['dʒuːəl] *n* bijou *m*, joyau *m*; **~ler** *n* bijoutier/ère, joaillier *m*; **~ler's (shop)** *n* bijouterie *f*, joaillerie *f*; **~lery** *n* bijoux *mpl*.
**Jewess** ['dʒuːɪs] *n* Juive *f*.
**Jewish** ['dʒuːɪʃ] *a* juif(juive).
**jib** [dʒɪb] *n (NAUT)* foc *m*; *(of crane)* flèche *f* // *vi*: **to ~ (at)** renâcler or regimber (devant).
**jibe** [dʒaɪb] *n* sarcasme *m*.
**jiffy** ['dʒɪfɪ] *n (col)*: **in a ~** en un clin d'œil.
**jigsaw** ['dʒɪgsɔː] *n (also: ~ puzzle)* puzzle *m*.

**jilt** [dʒɪlt] *vt* laisser tomber, plaquer.
**jingle** ['dʒɪŋgl] *n (advert)* couplet *m* publicitaire // *vi* cliqueter, tinter.
**jinx** [dʒɪŋks] *n (col)* (mauvais) sort.
**jitters** ['dʒɪtəz] *npl (col)*: **to get the ~** avoir la trouille or la frousse.
**jiujitsu** [dʒuː'dʒɪtsu:] *n* jiu-jitsu *m*.
**job** [dʒɔb] *n* travail *m*; *(employment)* emploi *m*, poste *m*, place *f*; **~bing** *a (workman)* à la tâche, à la journée; **~less** *a* sans travail, au chômage.
**jockey** ['dʒɔkɪ] *n* jockey *m* // *vi*: **to ~ for position** manœuvrer pour être bien placé.
**jocular** ['dʒɔkjulə*] *a* jovial(e), enjoué(e); facétieux(euse).
**jog** [dʒɔg] *vt* secouer // *vi*: **to ~ along** cahoter; trotter; **to ~ sb's memory** rafraîchir la mémoire de qn.
**join** [dʒɔɪn] *vt* unir, assembler; *(become member of)* s'inscrire à; *(meet)* rejoindre, retrouver; se joindre à // *vi (roads, rivers)* se rejoindre, se rencontrer // *n* raccord *m*; **to ~ up** *vi* s'engager.
**joiner** ['dʒɔɪnə*] *n* menuisier *m*; **~y** *n* menuiserie *f*.
**joint** [dʒɔɪnt] *n (TECH)* jointure *f*; joint *m*; *(ANAT)* articulation *f*, jointure; *(CULIN)* rôti *m*; *(col: place)* boîte *f* // *a* commun(e); **~ly** *ad* ensemble, en commun.
**joist** [dʒɔɪst] *n* solive *f*.
**joke** [dʒəuk] *n* plaisanterie *f*; *(also: practical ~)* farce *f* // *vi* plaisanter; **to play a ~ on** jouer un tour à, faire une farce à; **~r** *n* plaisantin *m*, blagueur/euse; *(CARDS)* joker *m*.
**jollity** ['dʒɔlɪtɪ] *n* réjouissances *fpl*, gaieté *f*.
**jolly** ['dʒɔlɪ] *a* gai(e), enjoué(e) // *ad (col)* rudement, drôlement.
**jolt** [dʒəult] *n* cahot *m*, secousse *f* // *vt* cahoter, secouer..
**Jordan** [dʒɔːdən] *n* Jordanie *f*.
**jostle** ['dʒɔsl] *vt* bousculer, pousser // *vi* jouer des coudes.
**jot** [dʒɔt] *n*: **not one ~** pas un brin; **to ~ down** *vt* inscrire rapidement, noter; **~ter** *n* cahier *m* (de brouillon); bloc-notes *m*.
**journal** ['dʒəːnl] *n* journal *m*; **~ese** [-'liːz] *n (pej)* style *m* journalistique; **~ism** *n* journalisme *m*; **~ist** *n* journaliste *m/f*.
**journey** ['dʒəːnɪ] *n* voyage *m*; *(distance covered)* trajet *m*.
**jowl** [dʒaul] *n* mâchoire *f (inférieure)*; bajoue *f*.
**joy** [dʒɔɪ] *n* joie *f*; **~ful, ~ous** *a* joyeux(euse); **~ ride** *n* virée *f (gén avec une voiture volée)*.
**J.P.** *n abbr see* justice.
**Jr, Jun., Junr** *abbr of* junior.
**jubilant** ['dʒuːbɪlnt] *a* triomphant(e); réjoui(e).
**jubilation** [dʒuːbɪ'leɪʃən] *n* jubilation *f*.
**jubilee** ['dʒuːbɪliː] *n* jubilé *m*.
**judge** [dʒʌdʒ] *n* juge *m* // *vt* juger; **judg(e)ment** *n* jugement *m*; *(punishment)* châtiment *m*; **in my judg(e)ment** à mon avis, selon mon opinion.
**judicial** [dʒuː'dɪʃl] *a* judiciaire; *(fair)* impartial(e).

**judicious** [dʒu:'dɪʃəs] a judicieux(euse).
**judo** ['dʒu:dəu] n judo m.
**jug** [dʒʌg] n pot m, cruche f.
**juggernaut** ['dʒʌgənɔ:t] n (huge truck) mastodonte m.
**juggle** ['dʒʌgl] vi jongler ; ~r n jongleur m.
**Jugoslav** ['ju:gəu'slɑ:v] a,n = **Yugoslav.**
**juice** [dʒu:s] n jus m.
**juicy** ['dʒu:sɪ] a juteux(euse).
**jukebox** ['dʒu:kbɔks] n juke-box m.
**July** [dʒu:'laɪ] n juillet m.
**jumble** ['dʒʌmbl] n fouillis m // vt (also: ~ up) mélanger, brouiller ; ~ sale n (Brit) vente f de charité.
**jumbo** ['dʒʌmbəu] a: ~ jet avion géant, gros porteur (à réaction).
**jump** [dʒʌmp] vi sauter, bondir ; (start) sursauter ; (increase) monter en flèche // vt sauter, franchir // n saut m, bond m ; sursaut m ; **to** ~ **the queue** passer avant son tour.
**jumper** ['dʒʌmpə*] n pull-over m.
**jumpy** ['dʒʌmpɪ] a nerveux(euse), agité(e).
**junction** ['dʒʌŋkʃən] n (of roads) carrefour m ; (of rails) embranchement n.
**juncture** ['dʒʌŋktʃə*] n: **at this** ~ à ce moment-là, sur ces entrefaites.
**June** [dʒu:n] n juin m.
**jungle** ['dʒʌŋgl] n jungle f.
**junior** ['dʒu:nɪə*] a, n: **he's** ~ **to me (by 2 years), he's my** ~ **(by 2 years)** il est mon cadet (de 2 ans), il est plus jeune que moi (de 2 ans) ; **he's** ~ **to me** (seniority) il est en dessous de moi (dans la hiérarchie), j'ai plus d'ancienneté que lui ; ~ **executive** n jeune cadre m ; ~ **minister** n ministre m sous tutelle ; ~ **partner** n associé(-adjoint) m ; ~ **school** n école f primaire, cours moyen ; ~ **sizes** npl (COMM) tailles fpl fillettes/garçonnets.
**juniper** ['dʒu:nɪpə*] n: ~ **berry** baie f de genièvre.
**junk** [dʒʌŋk] n (rubbish) bric-à-brac m inv ; (ship) jonque f ; ~**shop** n (boutique f de) brocanteur m.
**junta** ['dʒʌntə] n junte f.
**jurisdiction** [dʒuərɪs'dɪkʃən] n juridiction f.
**jurisprudence** [dʒuərɪs'pru:dəns] n jurisprudence f.
**juror** ['dʒuərə*] n juré m.
**jury** ['dʒuərɪ] n jury m ; ~**man** n = **juror.**
**just** [dʒʌst] a juste // ad: **he's** ~ **done it/left** il vient de le faire/partir ; ~ **as I expected** exactement or précisément comme je m'y attendais ; ~ **right/two o'clock** exactement or juste ce qu'il faut/deux heures ; ~ **as he was leaving** au moment or à l'instant précis où il partait ; ~ **before/enough/here** juste avant/assez/là ; **it's** ~ **me/a mistake** ce n'est que moi/(rien) qu'une erreur ; ~ **missed/caught** manqué/attrapé de justesse ; ~ **listen to this!** écoutez un peu ça!
**justice** ['dʒʌstɪs] n justice f ; **Lord Chief J**~ premier président de la cour d'appel ; **J**~ **of the Peace (J.P.)** n juge m de paix.
**justifiable** [dʒʌstɪ'faɪəbl] a justifiable.

**justifiably** [dʒʌstɪ'faɪəblɪ] ad légitimement.
**justification** [dʒʌstɪfɪ'keɪʃən] n justification f.
**justify** ['dʒʌstɪfaɪ] vt justifier.
**justly** ['dʒʌstlɪ] ad avec raison, justement.
**justness** ['dʒʌstnɪs] n justesse f.
**jut** [dʒʌt] vi (also: ~ out) dépasser, faire saillie.
**juvenile** ['dʒu:vənaɪl] a juvénile ; (court, books) pour enfants // n adolescent/e.
**juxtapose** ['dʒʌkstəpəuz] vt juxtaposer.

## K

**kaleidoscope** [kə'laɪdəskəup] n kaléidoscope m.
**kangaroo** [kæŋgə'ru:] n kangourou m.
**keel** [ki:l] n quille f ; **on an even** ~ (fig) à flot.
**keen** [ki:n] a (interest, desire) vif(vive) ; (eye, intelligence) pénétrant(e) ; (competition) vif, âpre ; (edge) effilé(e) ; (eager) plein(e) d'enthousiasme ; **to be** ~ **to do** or **on doing sth** désirer vivement faire qch, tenir beaucoup à faire qch ; **to be** ~ **on sth/sb** aimer beaucoup qch/qn ; ~**ness** n (eagerness) enthousiasme m ; ~**ness to do** vif désir de faire.
**keep** [ki:p] vb (pt,pp kept [kɛpt]) vt (retain, preserve) garder ; (hold back) retenir ; (a shop, the books, a diary) tenir ; (feed: one's family etc) entretenir, assurer la subsistance de ; (a promise) tenir ; (chickens, bees, pigs etc) élever // vi (food) se conserver ; (remain: in a certain state or place) rester // n (of castle) donjon m ; (food etc): **enough for his** ~ assez pour (assurer) sa subsistance ; **to** ~ **doing sth** continuer à faire qch ; faire qch continuellement ; **to** ~ **sb from doing/sth from happening** empêcher qn de faire or que qn (ne) fasse/que qch (n')arrive ; **to** ~ **sb happy/a place tidy** faire que qn soit content/que qn tienne un endroit reste propre ; **to** ~ **sth to o.s.** garder qch pour soi, tenir qch secret ; **to** ~ **sth (back) from sb** cacher qch à qn ; **to** ~ **time** (clock) être à l'heure, ne pas retarder ; **to** ~ **on** vi continuer ; **to** ~ **on doing** continuer à faire ; **to** ~ **out** vt empêcher d'entrer ; '~ **out**' 'défense d'entrer' ; **to** ~ **up** vi se maintenir // vt continuer, maintenir ; **to** ~ **up with** se maintenir au niveau de ; ~**er** n gardien/ne ; ~**ing** n (care) garde f ; **in** ~**ing with** à l'avenant de ; en accord avec ; ~**sake** n souvenir m.
**keg** [kɛg] n barrique f, tonnelet m.
**kennel** ['kɛnl] n niche f ; ~**s** npl chenil m.
**Kenya** ['kɛnjə] n Kenya m.
**kept** [kɛpt] pt,pp de **keep.**
**kerb** [kə:b] n bordure f du trottoir.
**kernel** ['kə:nl] n amande f ; (fig) noyau m.
**kerosene** ['kɛrəsi:n] n kérosène m.
**ketchup** ['kɛtʃəp] n ketchup m.
**kettle** ['kɛtl] n bouilloire f.
**kettle drums** ['kɛtldrʌmz] npl timbales fpl.
**key** [ki:] n (gen, MUS) clé f ; (of piano, typewriter) touche f // cpd (-)clé ; ~**board** n clavier m ; ~**hole** n trou m de la serrure ;

~**note** *n* (*MUS*) tonique *f*; (*fig*) note dominante; ~ **ring** *n* porte-clés *m*.
**khaki** ['kɑ:kɪ] *a,n* kaki (*m*).
**kibbutz** [kɪ'buːts] *n* kibboutz *m*.
**kick** [kɪk] *vt* donner un coup de pied à // *vi* (*horse*) ruer // *n* coup *m* de pied; (*of rifle*) recul *m*; (*thrill*): **he does it for** ~**s** il le fait parce que ça l'excite, il le fait pour le plaisir; **to** ~ **around** *vi* (*col*) traîner; **to** ~ **off** *vi* (*SPORT*) donner le coup d'envoi; ~**-off** *n* (*SPORT*) coup *m* d'envoi.
**kid** [kɪd] *n* gamin/e, gosse *m/f*; (*animal, leather*) chevreau *m* // *vi* (*col*) plaisanter, blaguer.
**kidnap** ['kɪdnæp] *vt* enlever, kidnapper; ~**per** *n* ravisseur/euse; ~**ping** *n* enlèvement *m*.
**kidney** ['kɪdnɪ] *n* (*ANAT*) rein *m*; (*CULIN*) rognon *m*.
**kill** [kɪl] *vt* tuer; (*fig*) faire échouer; détruire; supprimer // *n* mise *f* à mort; ~**er** *n* tueur/euse; meurtrier/ère; ~**ing** *n* meurtre *m*; tuerie *f*, massacre *m*; (*col*): **to make a** ~**ing** se remplir les poches, réussir un beau coup // *a* (*col*) tordant(e).
**kiln** [kɪln] *n* four *m*.
**kilo** ['kiːləʊ] *n* kilo *m*; ~**gram(me)** ['kɪləʊgræm] *n* kilogramme *m*; ~**metre**, ~**meter** (*US*) ['kɪləmiːtə\*] *n* kilomètre *m*; ~**watt** ['kɪləʊwɔt] *n* kilowatt *m*.
**kilt** [kɪlt] *n* kilt *m*.
**kimono** [kɪ'məʊnəʊ] *n* kimono *m*.
**kin** [kɪn] *n* see **next, kith**.
**kind** [kaɪnd] *a* gentil(le), aimable // *n* sorte *f*, espèce *f*; (*species*) genre *m*; **in** ~ (*COMM*) en nature; (*fig*): **to repay sb in** ~ rendre la pareille à qn.
**kindergarten** ['kɪndəgɑ:tn] *n* jardin *m* d'enfants.
**kind-hearted** [kaɪnd'hɑ:tɪd] *a* bon (bonne).
**kindle** ['kɪndl] *vt* allumer, enflammer.
**kindly** ['kaɪndlɪ] *a* bienveillant(e), plein(e) de gentillesse // *ad* avec bonté; **will you** ~**...** auriez-vous la bonté *or* l'obligation de...; **he didn't take it** ~ il l'a mal pris.
**kindness** ['kaɪndnɪs] *n* bonté *f*, gentillesse *f*.
**kindred** ['kɪndrɪd] *a* apparenté(e); ~ **spirit** *n* âme *f* sœur.
**kinetic** [kɪ'nɛtɪk] *a* cinétique.
**king** [kɪŋ] *n* roi *m*; ~**dom** *n* royaume *m*; ~**fisher** *n* martin-pêcheur *m*; ~**pin** *n* cheville ouvrière; ~**-size** *a* long format *inv*; format géant *inv*.
**kink** [kɪŋk] *n* (*of rope*) entortillement *m*.
**kinky** ['kɪŋkɪ] *a* (*fig*) excentrique; aux goûts spéciaux.
**kiosk** ['kiːɔsk] *n* kiosque *m*; cabine *f* (téléphonique).
**kipper** ['kɪpə\*] *n* hareng fumé et salé.
**kiss** [kɪs] *n* baiser *m* // *vt* embrasser; **to** ~ (**each other**) s'embrasser.
**kit** [kɪt] *n* équipement *m*, matériel *m*; (*set of tools etc*) trousse *f*; (*for assembly*) kit *m*; ~**bag** *n* sac *m* de voyage *or* de marin.
**kitchen** ['kɪtʃɪn] *n* cuisine *f*; ~ **garden** *n* jardin *m* potager; ~ **sink** *n* évier *m*; ~**ware** *n* vaisselle *f*; ustensiles *mpl* de cuisine.

**kite** [kaɪt] *n* (*toy*) cerf-volant *m*; (*ZOOL*) milan *m*.
**kith** [kɪθ] *n*: ~ **and kin** parents et amis *mpl*.
**kitten** ['kɪtn] *n* petit chat, chaton *m*.
**kitty** ['kɪtɪ] *n* (*pool of money*) cagnotte *f*.
**kleptomaniac** [klɛptəʊ'meɪnɪæk] *n* kleptomane *m/f*.
**knack** [næk] *n*: **to have the** ~ (**for doing**) avoir le coup (pour faire); **there's a** ~ il y a un coup à prendre or une combine.
**knapsack** ['næpsæk] *n* musette *f*.
**knave** [neɪv] *n* (*CARDS*) valet *m*.
**knead** [niːd] *vt* pétrir.
**knee** [niː] *n* genou *m*; ~**cap** *n* rotule *f*.
**kneel** [niːl] *vi* (*pt,pp* **knelt** [nɛlt]) s'agenouiller.
**knell** [nɛl] *n* glas *m*.
**knelt** [nɛlt] *pt,pp of* **kneel**.
**knew** [njuː] *pt of* **know**.
**knickers** ['nɪkəz] *npl* culotte *f* (de femme).
**knife, knives** [naɪf, naɪvz] *n* couteau *m* // *vt* poignarder, frapper d'un coup de couteau.
**knight** [naɪt] *n* chevalier *m*; (*CHESS*) cavalier *m*; ~**hood** *n* chevalerie *f*; (*title*): **to get a** ~**hood** être fait chevalier.
**knit** [nɪt] *vt* tricoter; (*fig*): **to** ~ **together** unir // *vi* (*broken bones*) se ressouder; ~**ting** *n* tricot *m*; ~**ting machine** *n* machine *f* à tricoter; ~**ting needle** *n* aiguille *f* à tricoter; ~**wear** *n* tricots *mpl*, lainages *mpl*.
**knives** [naɪvz] *npl of* **knife**.
**knob** [nɔb] *n* bouton *m*; (*fig*): **a** ~ **of butter** une noix de beurre.
**knock** [nɔk] *vt* frapper; heurter; (*fig: col*) dénigrer // *vi* (*engine*) cogner; (*at door etc*): **to** ~ **at/on** frapper à/sur // *n* coup *m*; **to** ~ **down** *vt* renverser; **to** ~ **off** *vi* (*col: finish*) s'arrêter (de travailler); **to** ~ **out** *vt* assommer; (*BOXING*) mettre k.-o.; ~**er** *n* (*on door*) heurtoir *m*; ~**-kneed** *a* aux genoux cagneux; ~**out** *n* (*BOXING*) knock-out *m*, K.-O. *m*; ~**out competition** *n* compétition *f* avec épreuves éliminatoires.
**knot** [nɔt] *n* (*gen*) nœud *m* // *vt* nouer; ~**ty** *a* (*fig*) épineux(euse).
**know** [nəʊ] *vt* (*pt* **knew**, *pp* **known** [njuː, nəʊn]) savoir; (*person, author, place*) connaître; **to** ~ **that...** savoir que...; **to** ~ **how to do** savoir comment faire; ~**-how** *n* savoir-faire *m*, technique *f*, compétence *f*; ~**ing** *a* (*look etc*) entendu(e); ~**ingly** *ad* sciemment; d'un air entendu.
**knowledge** ['nɔlɪdʒ] *n* connaissance *f*; (*learning*) connaissances, savoir *m*; ~**able** *a* bien informé(e).
**known** [nəʊn] *pp of* **know**.
**knuckle** ['nʌkl] *n* articulation *f* (des phalanges), jointure *f*.
**K.O.** *n* (*abbr of* **knockout**) K.-O. *m* // *vt* mettre K.-O.
**Koran** [kɔ'rɑ:n] *n* Coran *m*.
**kudos** ['kjuːdɔs] *n* gloire *f*, lauriers *mpl*.
**kw** *abbr of* **kilowatt(s)**.

# L

**l.** *abbr of* **litre**.
**lab** [læb] *n* (*abbr of* **laboratory**) labo *m*.
**label** ['leɪbl] *n* étiquette *f*; (*brand: of record*) marque *f* // *vt* étiqueter; **to ~ sb a...** qualifier qn de... .
**laboratory** [lə'bɔrətərɪ] *n* laboratoire *m*.
**laborious** [lə'bɔ:rɪəs] *a* laborieux(euse).
**labour** ['leɪbə*] *n* (*task*) travail *m*; (*workmen*) main-d'œuvre *f*; (MED) travail, accouchement *m* // *vi*: **to ~ (at)** travailler dur (à), peiner (sur); **in ~** (MED) en travail; **L~, the L~ party** le parti travailliste, les travaillistes *mpl*; **~ camp** *n* camp *m* de travaux forcés; **~ed** *a* lourd(e), laborieux(euse); **~er** *n* manœuvre *m*; (*on farm*) ouvrier *m* agricole; **~ force** *n* main-d'œuvre *f*; **~ pains** *npl* douleurs *fpl* de l'accouchement.
**labyrinth** ['læbɪrɪnθ] *n* labyrinthe *m*, dédale *m*.
**lace** [leɪs] *n* dentelle *f*; (*of shoe etc*) lacet *m* // *vt* (*shoe*) lacer.
**lack** [læk] *n* manque *m* // *vt* manquer de; **through** *or* **for ~ of** faute de, par manque de; **to be ~ing** manquer, faire défaut; **to be ~ing in** manquer de.
**lackadaisical** [lækə'deɪzɪkl] *a* nonchalant(e), indolent(e).
**laconic** [lə'kɔnɪk] *a* laconique.
**lacquer** ['lækə*] *n* laque *f*.
**lad** [læd] *n* garçon *m*, gars *m*.
**ladder** ['lædə*] *n* échelle *f*; (*in tights*) maille filée // *vt*, *vi* (*tights*) filer.
**laden** ['leɪdn] *a*: **~ (with)** chargé(e) (de).
**ladle** ['leɪdl] *n* louche *f*.
**lady** ['leɪdɪ] *n* dame *f*; dame (du monde); **L~ Smith** lady Smith; **the ladies' (toilets)** les toilettes *fpl* des dames; **~bird**, **~bug** (US) *n* coccinelle *f*; **~-in-waiting** *n* dame *f* d'honneur; **~like** *a* distingué(e).
**lag** [læg] *n* = **time ~** // *vi* (*also*: **~ behind**) rester en arrière, traîner // *vt* (*pipes*) calorifuger.
**lager** ['lɑ:gə*] *n* bière blonde.
**lagging** ['lægɪŋ] *n* enveloppe isolante, calorifuge *m*.
**lagoon** [lə'gu:n] *n* lagune *f*.
**laid** [leɪd] *pt*, *pp of* **lay**.
**lain** [leɪn] *pp of* **lie**.
**lair** [lɛə*] *n* tanière *f*, gîte *m*.
**laity** ['leɪətɪ] *n* laïques *mpl*.
**lake** [leɪk] *n* lac *m*.
**lamb** [læm] *n* agneau *m*; **~ chop** *n* côtelette *f* d'agneau; **~skin** *n* (peau *f* d'agneau *m*; **~swool** *n* laine *f* d'agneau.
**lame** [leɪm] *a* boiteux(euse).
**lament** [lə'mɛnt] *n* lamentation *f* // *vt* pleurer, se lamenter sur; **~able** ['læməntəbl] *a* déplorable, lamentable.
**laminated** ['læmɪneɪtɪd] *a* laminé(e); (*windscreen*) (en verre) feuilleté.
**lamp** [læmp] *n* lampe *f*.
**lampoon** [læm'pu:n] *n* pamphlet *m*.
**lamp**: **~post** *n* réverbère *m*; **~shade** *n* abat-jour *m* *inv*.
**lance** [lɑ:ns] *n* lance *f* // *vt* (MED) inciser;

**~ corporal** *n* (soldat *m* de) première classe *m*.
**lancet** ['lɑ:nsɪt] *n* bistouri *m*.
**land** [lænd] *n* (*as opposed to sea*) terre *f* (ferme); (*country*) pays *m*; (*soil*) terre; terrain *m*; (*estate*) terre(s), domaine(s) *m(pl)* // *vi* (*from ship*) débarquer; (AVIAT) atterrir; (*fig: fall*) (re)tomber // *vt* (*obtain*) décrocher; (*passengers, goods*) débarquer; **to ~ up** *vi* atterrir, (finir par) se retrouver; **~ed gentry** *n* propriétaires terriens *or* fonciers; **~ing** *n* débarquement *m*; atterrissage *m*; (*of staircase*) palier *m*; **~ing craft** *n* chaland *m* de débarquement; **~ing stage** *n* débarcadère *m*, embarcadère *m*; **~ing strip** *n* piste *f* d'atterrissage; **~lady** *n* propriétaire *f*, logeuse *f*; **~locked** *a* entouré(e) de terre(s), sans accès à la mer; **~lord** *n* propriétaire *m*, logeur *m*; (*of pub etc*) patron *m*; **~lubber** *n* terrien/ne; **~mark** *n* (point *m* de) repère *m*; **~owner** *n* propriétaire foncier *or* terrien.
**landscape** ['lænskeɪp] *n* paysage *m*; **~d** *a* aménagé(e) (par un paysagiste).
**landslide** ['lændslaɪd] *n* (GEO) glissement *m* (de terrain); (*fig: POL*) raz-de-marée (électoral).
**lane** [leɪn] *n* (*in country*) chemin *m*; (*in town*) ruelle *f*; (AUT) voie *f*; file *f*; (*in race*) couloir *m*.
**language** ['læŋgwɪdʒ] *n* langue *f*; (*way one speaks*) langage *m*; **bad ~** grossièretés *fpl*, langage grossier.
**languid** ['læŋgwɪd] *a* languissant(e); langoureux(euse).
**languish** ['læŋgwɪʃ] *vi* languir.
**lank** [læŋk] *a* (*hair*) raide et terne.
**lanky** ['læŋkɪ] *a* grand(e) et maigre, efflanqué(e).
**lantern** ['læntn] *n* lanterne *f*.
**lap** [læp] *n* (*of track*) tour *m* (de piste); (*of body*): **in** *or* **on one's ~** sur les genoux // *vt* (*also*: **~ up**) laper // *vi* (*waves*) clapoter; **~dog** *n* chien *m* d'appartement.
**lapel** [lə'pɛl] *n* revers *m*.
**Lapland** ['læplænd] *n* Laponie *f*.
**Lapp** [læp] *a* lapon(ne) // *n* Lapon/ne; (LING) lapon *m*.
**lapse** [læps] *n* défaillance *f* // *vi* (LAW) cesser d'être en vigueur; se périmer; **to ~ into bad habits** prendre de mauvaises habitudes; **~ of time** laps *m* de temps, intervalle *m*.
**larceny** ['lɑ:sənɪ] *n* vol *m*.
**lard** [lɑ:d] *n* saindoux *m*.
**larder** ['lɑ:də*] *n* garde-manger *m* *inv*.
**large** [lɑ:dʒ] *a* grand(e); (*person, animal*) gros(grosse); **at ~** (*free*) en liberté; (*generally*) en général; pour la plupart; **~ly** *ad* en grande partie; **~-scale** *a* (*map*) à grande échelle; (*fig*) important(e).
**lark** [lɑ:k] *n* (*bird*) alouette *f*; (*joke*) blague *f*, farce *f*; **to ~ about** *vi* faire l'idiot, rigoler.
**larva, pl larvae** ['lɑ:və, -i:] *n* larve *f*.
**laryngitis** [lærɪn'dʒaɪtɪs] *n* laryngite *f*.
**larynx** ['lærɪŋks] *n* larynx *m*.
**lascivious** [lə'sɪvɪəs] *a* lascif(ive).
**laser** ['leɪzə*] *n* laser *m*.

**lash** [læʃ] *n* coup *m* de fouet ; (*gen:* **eyelash**) cil *m* // *vt* fouetter ; (*tie*) attacher ; **to ~ out** *vi*: **to ~ out (at** *or* **against** sb/sth) attaquer violemment (qn/qch) ; **to ~ out (on sth)** (*col: spend*) se fendre (de qch).

**lass** [læs] *n* (jeune) fille *f*.

**lasso** [læˈsuː] *n* lasso *m* // *vt* prendre au lasso.

**last** [lɑːst] *a* dernier(ère) // *ad* en dernier // *vi* durer ; **~ week** la semaine dernière ; **~ night** hier soir, la nuit dernière ; **at ~** enfin ; **~ but one** avant-dernier(ère) ; **~ing** a durable ; **~-minute** a de dernière minute.

**latch** [lætʃ] *n* loquet *m* ; **~key** *n* clé *f* (de la porte d'entrée).

**late** [leɪt] *a* (*not on time*) en retard ; (*far on in day etc*) dernier(ère) ; tardif(ive) ; (*recent*) récent(e), (*former*) ancien(ne) ; (*dead*) défunt(e) // *ad* tard ; (*behind time, schedule*) en retard ; **of ~** dernièrement ; **in ~** May vers la fin (du mois) de mai, fin mai ; **the ~ Mr X** feu M. X ; **~comer** *n* retardataire *m/f* ; **~ly** *ad* récemment ; **~ness** *n* (*of person*) retard *m* ; (*of event*) heure tardive.

**latent** ['leɪtnt] *a* latent(e).

**later** ['leɪtə*] *a* (*a date etc*) ultérieur(e) ; (*version etc*) plus récent(e) // *ad* plus tard.

**lateral** ['lætərl] *a* latéral(e).

**latest** ['leɪtɪst] *a* tout(e) dernier(ère) : **at the ~** au plus tard.

**latex** ['leɪtɛks] *n* latex *m*.

**lath,** **~s** [læθ, læðz] *n* latte *f*.

**lathe** [leɪð] *n* tour *m* ; **~ operator** *n* tourneur *m* (*en usine*).

**lather** ['lɑːðə*] *n* mousse *f* (de savon) // *vt* savonner // *vi* mousser.

**Latin** ['lætɪn] *n* latin *m* // *a* latin(e) ; **~ America** *n* Amérique latine ; **~- American** *a* d'Amérique latine.

**latitude** ['lætɪtjuːd] *n* latitude *f*.

**latrine** [lə'triːn] *n* latrines *fpl*.

**latter** ['lætə*] *a* deuxième, dernier(ère) // *n*: **the ~** ce dernier, celui-ci ; **~ly** *ad* dernièrement, récemment.

**lattice** ['lætɪs] *n* treillis *m* ; treillage *m*.

**laudable** ['lɔːdəbl] *a* louable.

**laudatory** ['lɔːdətrɪ] *a* élogieux(euse).

**laugh** [lɑːf] *n* rire *m* // *vi* rire ; **to ~ at** *vt fus* se moquer de ; **to ~ off** *vt* écarter *or* rejeter une plaisanterie *or* par une boutade ; **~able** *a* risible, ridicule ; **~ing** *a* (*face*) rieur(euse) ; **the ~ing stock of** la risée de ; **~ter** *n* rire *m* ; rires *mpl*.

**launch** [lɔːntʃ] *n* lancement *m* ; (*boat*) chaloupe *f* ; (*also:* **motor ~**) vedette *f* // *vt* (*ship, rocket, plan*) lancer ; **~ing** *n* lancement *m* ; **~(ing) pad** *n* rampe *f* de lancement.

**launder** ['lɔːndə*] *vt* blanchir.

**launderette** [lɔːn'drɛt] *n* laverie *f* (automatique).

**laundry** ['lɔːndrɪ] *n* blanchisserie *f* ; (*clothes*) linge *m* ; **to do the ~** faire la lessive.

**laureate** ['lɔːrɪət] *a see* **poet**.

**laurel** ['lɔrl] *n* laurier *m*.

**lava** ['lɑːvə] *n* lave *f*.

**lavatory** ['lævətərɪ] *n* toilettes *fpl*.

**lavender** ['lævəndə*] *n* lavande *f*.

**lavish** ['lævɪʃ] *a* copieux(euse) ; somptueux(euse) ; (*giving freely*): **~ with** prodigue de // *vt*: **to ~ on sb/sth** (*care*) prodiguer à qn/qch ; (*money*) dépenser sans compter pour qn/qch.

**law** [lɔː] *n* loi *f* ; (*science*) droit *m* ; **~-abiding** *a* respectueux(euse) des lois ; **~ and order** *n* l'ordre public ; **~breaker** *n* personne *f* qui transgresse la loi ; **~ court** *n* tribunal *m*, cour *f* de justice ; **~ful** *a* légal(e) ; permis(e) ; **~fully** *ad* légalement ; **~less** *a* sans loi.

**lawn** [lɔːn] *n* pelouse *f* ; **~mower** *n* tondeuse *f* à gazon ; **~ tennis** [-'tɛnɪs] *n* tennis *m*.

**law:** **~ school** *n* faculté *f* de droit ; **~ student** *n* étudiant/e en droit.

**lawsuit** ['lɔːsuːt] *n* procès *m*.

**lawyer** ['lɔːjə*] *n* (*consultant, with company*) juriste *m* ; (*for sales, wills etc*) ≈ notaire *m* ; (*partner, in court*) ≈ avocat *m*.

**lax** [læks] *a* relâché(e).

**laxative** ['læksətɪv] *n* laxatif *m*.

**laxity** ['læksɪtɪ] *n* relâchement *m*.

**lay** [leɪ] *pt of* **lie** // *a* laïque ; profane // *vt* (*pt, pp* **laid** [leɪd] ) poser, mettre ; (*eggs*) pondre ; (*trap*) tendre ; (*plans*) élaborer ; **to ~ the table** mettre la table ; **to ~ aside** *or* **by** *vt* mettre de côté ; **to ~ down** *vt* poser ; **to ~ down the law** faire la loi ; **to ~ off** *vt* (*workers*) licencier ; **to ~ on** *vt* (*water, gas*) mettre, installer ; (*provide*) fournir ; (*paint*) étaler ; **to ~ out** *vt* (*design*) dessiner, concevoir ; (*display*) disposer ; (*spend*) dépenser ; **to ~ up** *vt* (*to store*) amasser ; (*car*) remiser ; (*ship*) désarmer ; (*subj: illness*) forcer à s'aliter ; **~about** *n* fainéant/e ; **~-by** *n* aire *f* de stationnement (sur le bas-côté).

**layer** ['leɪə*] *n* couche *f*.

**layette** [leɪ'ɛt] *n* layette *f*.

**layman** ['leɪmən] *n* laïque *m* ; profane *m*.

**layout** ['leɪaut] *n* disposition *f*, plan *m*, agencement *m* ; (*PRESS*) mise *f* en page.

**laze** [leɪz] *vi* paresser.

**laziness** ['leɪzɪnɪs] *n* paresse *f*.

**lazy** ['leɪzɪ] *a* paresseux(euse).

**lb.** *abbr of* **pound** (*weight*).

**lead** [liːd] *see also next headword* ; *n* (*front position*) tête *f* ; (*distance, time ahead*) avance *f* ; (*clue*) piste *f* ; (*in battery*) raccord *m* ; (*ELEC*) fil *m* ; (*for dog*) laisse *f* ; (*THEATRE*) rôle principal // *vb* (*pt,pp* **led** [lɛd]) *vt* mener, conduire ; (*induce*) amener ; (*be leader of*) être à la tête de ; (*SPORT*) être en tête de // *vi* mener, être en tête ; **to ~ to** mener à ; conduire à ; aboutir à ; **to ~ astray** *vt* détourner du droit chemin ; **to ~ away** *vt* emmener ; **to ~ back to** ramener à ; **to ~ on** *vt* (*tease*) faire marcher ; **to ~ on to** *vt* (*induce*) amener à ; **to ~ up to** conduire à.

**lead** [lɛd] *see also previous headword* ; *n* plomb *m* ; (*in pencil*) mine *f* ; **~en** *a* de *or* en plomb.

**leader** ['liːdə*] *n* chef *m* ; dirigeant/e, leader *m* ; (*of newspaper*) éditorial *m* ; **~ship** *n* direction *f* ; qualités *fpl* de chef.

**leading** ['liːdɪŋ] *a* de premier plan ; principal(e) ; **~ lady** *n* (*THEATRE*) vedette (féminine); ~ **light** n (person) vedette f, sommité f; ~ **man** n (THEATRE) vedette (masculine).

**leaf, leaves** [li:f, li:vz] n feuille f; (of table) rallonge f.

**leaflet** ['li:flɪt] prospectus m, brochure f; (POL. REL) tract m.

**leafy** ['li:fɪ] a feuillu(e).

**league** [li:g] n ligue f; (FOOTBALL) championnat m; (measure) lieue f; **to be in ~ with** avoir partie liée avec, être de mèche avec.

**leak** [li:k] n (out, also fig) fuite f; (in) infiltration f // vi (pipe, liquid etc) fuir; (shoes) prendre l'eau // vt (liquid) répandre; (information) divulguer; **to ~ out** vi fuir; être divulgué(e).

**lean** [li:n] a maigre // n (of meat) maigre m // vb (pt,pp leaned or leant [lɛnt] ) vt: **to ~ sth on** appuyer qch sur // vi (slope) pencher; (rest): **to ~ against** s'appuyer contre; être appuyé(e) contre; **to ~ on** s'appuyer sur; **to ~ back/forward** vi se pencher en arrière/avant; **to ~ over** vi se pencher; **~ing** a penché(e) // n: **~ing (towards)** penchant m (pour); **~-to** n appentis m.

**leap** [li:p] n bond m, saut m // vi (pt,pp leaped or leapt [lɛpt]) bondir, sauter; **~frog** n jeu m de saute-mouton; **~ year** n année f bissextile.

**learn**, pt,pp **learned** or **learnt** [lə:n, -t] vt,vi apprendre; **~ed** ['lə:nɪd] a érudit(e), savant(e); **~er** n débutant/e; **~ing** n savoir m.

**lease** [li:s] n bail m // vt louer à bail.

**leash** [li:ʃ] n laisse f.

**least** [li:st] ad le moins // a: **the ~ + noun** le (la) plus petit(e), le (la) moindre; (smallest amount of) le moins de; **the ~ + adjective** le moins; **the ~ money** le moins d'argent; **the ~ expensive** le moins cher; **at ~** au moins; **not in the ~** pas le moins du monde.

**leather** ['lɛðə*] n cuir m // cpd en or de cuir.

**leave** [li:v] vb (pt,pp left [lɛft]) vt laisser; (go away from) quitter // vi partir, s'en aller; n (time off) congé m; (MIL, also: consent) permission f; **to be left** rester; **there's some milk left over** il reste du lait; **on ~** en permission; **to take one's ~ of** prendre congé de; **to ~ out** vt oublier, omettre.

**leaves** [li:vz] npl of **leaf**.

**Lebanon** ['lɛbənən] n Liban m.

**lecherous** ['lɛtʃərəs] a lubrique.

**lectern** ['lɛktə:n] n lutrin m, pupitre m.

**lecture** ['lɛktʃə*] n conférence f; (SCOL) cours (magistral) // vi donner des cours; enseigner; **to ~ on** faire un cours (or son cours) sur.

**lecturer** ['lɛktʃərə*] n (speaker) conférencier/ère; (at university) professeur m (d'université), ≈ maître assistant, ≈ maître de conférences; **assistant ~** n ≈ assistant/e; **senior ~** n ≈ chargé/e d'enseignement.

**led** [lɛd] pt,pp of **lead**.

**ledge** [lɛdʒ] n (of window, on wall) rebord m; (of mountain) saillie f, corniche f.

**ledger** ['lɛdʒə*] n registre m, grand livre.

**lee** [li:] n côté m sous le vent.

**leech** [li:tʃ] n sangsue f.

**leek** [li:k] n poireau m.

**leer** [lɪə*] vi: **to ~ at sb** regarder qn d'un air mauvais or concupiscent, lorgner qn.

**leeway** ['li:weɪ] n (fig): **to make up ~** rattraper son retard; **to have some ~** avoir une certaine liberté d'action.

**left** [lɛft] pt,pp of **leave** // a gauche // ad à gauche // n gauche f; **the L~** (POL) la gauche; **~-handed** a gaucher(ère); **~-hand side** n gauche f, côté m gauche; **~-luggage (office)** n consigne f; **~-overs** npl restes mpl; **~ wing** n (MIL. SPORT) aile f gauche; (POL) gauche f; **~-wing** a (POL) de gauche.

**leg** [lɛg] n jambe f; (of animal) patte f; (of furniture) pied m; (CULIN: of chicken) cuisse f; **1st/2nd ~** (SPORT) match m aller/retour; (of journey) 1ère/2ème étape; **~ of lamb** n (CULIN) gigot m d'agneau.

**legacy** ['lɛgəsɪ] n héritage m, legs m.

**legal** ['li:gl] a légal(e); **~ize** vt légaliser; **~ly** ad légalement; **~ tender** n monnaie légale.

**legation** [lɪ'geɪʃən] n légation f.

**legend** ['lɛdʒənd] n légende f; **~ary** a légendaire.

**-legged** ['lɛgɪd] suffix: **two~** à deux pattes (or jambes or pieds).

**leggings** ['lɛgɪnz] npl jambières fpl, guêtres fpl.

**legibility** [lɛdʒɪ'bɪlɪtɪ] n lisibilité f.

**legible** ['lɛdʒəbl] a lisible.

**legibly** ['lɛdʒəblɪ] ad lisiblement.

**legion** ['li:dʒən] n légion f.

**legislate** ['lɛdʒɪsleɪt] vi légiférer; **legislation** [-'leɪʃən] n législation f; **legislative** ['lɛdʒɪslətɪv] a législatif(ive); **legislator** n législateur/trice; **legislature** ['lɛdʒɪslətʃə*] n corps législatif.

**legitimacy** [lɪ'dʒɪtɪməsɪ] n légitimité f.

**legitimate** [lɪ'dʒɪtɪmət] a légitime.

**leg-room** ['lɛgru:m] n place f pour les jambes.

**leisure** ['lɛʒə*] n loisir m, temps m libre; loisirs mpl; **at ~** (tout) à loisir; à tête reposée; **~ centre** n centre m de loisirs; **~ly** a tranquille; fait(e) sans se presser.

**lemon** ['lɛmən] n citron m; **~ade** n [-'neɪd] limonade f; **~ squeezer** n presse-citron m inv.

**lend**, pt,pp **lent** [lɛnd, lɛnt] vt: **to ~ sth (to sb)** prêter qch (à qn); **~er** n prêteur/euse; **~ing library** n bibliothèque f de prêt.

**length** [lɛŋθ] n longueur f; (section: of road, pipe etc) morceau m, bout m; **~ of time** durée f; **at ~** (at last) enfin, à la fin; (lengthily) longuement; **~en** vt allonger, prolonger // vi s'allonger; **~ways** ad dans le sens de la longueur, en long; **~y** a (très) long(longue).

**leniency** ['li:nɪənsɪ] n indulgence f, clémence f.

**lenient** ['li:nɪənt] a indulgent(e), clément(e); **~ly** ad avec indulgence or clémence.

**lens** [lɛnz] *n* lentille *f*; (*of spectacles*) verre *m*; (*of camera*) objectif *m*.

**lent** [lɛnt] *pt,pp of* **lend**.

**Lent** [lɛnt] *n* Carême *m*.

**lentil** [ˈlɛntl] *n* lentille *f*.

**Leo** [ˈliːəu] *n* le Lion; **to be** ~ être du Lion.

**leopard** [ˈlɛpəd] *n* léopard *m*.

**leotard** [ˈliːətɑːd] *n* collant *m* (*de danseur etc*).

**leper** [ˈlɛpə*] *n* lépreux/euse.

**leprosy** [ˈlɛprəsɪ] *n* lèpre *f*.

**lesbian** [ˈlɛzbɪən] *n* lesbienne *f*.

**less** [lɛs] *det* moins de // *pronoun, ad* moins; ~ **than that/you** moins que cela/vous; ~ **than half** moins de la moitié; ~ **and** ~ de moins en moins; **the** ~ **he works...** moins il travaille... .

**lessen** [ˈlɛsn] *vi* diminuer, s'amoindrir, s'atténuer // *vt* diminuer, réduire, atténuer.

**lesson** [ˈlɛsn] *n* leçon *f*; **a maths** ~ une leçon or un cours de maths.

**lest** [lɛst] *cj* de peur de + *infinitive*, de peur que + *sub*.

**let**, *pt,pp* **let** [lɛt] *vt* laisser; (*lease*) louer; **he** ~ **me go** il m'a laissé partir; ~ **the water boil and...** faites bouillir l'eau et...; ~**'s go** allons-y; ~ **him come** qu'il vienne; **'to** ~' 'à louer'; **to** ~ **down** *vt* (*lower*) baisser; (*dress*) rallonger; (*hair*) défaire; (*disappoint*) décevoir; **to** ~ **go** *vi* lâcher prise // *vt* lâcher; **to** ~ **in** *vt* laisser entrer; (*visitor etc*) faire entrer; **to** ~ **off** *vt* laisser partir; (*firework etc*) faire partir; (*smell etc*) dégager; **to** ~ **out** *vt* laisser sortir; (*dress*) élargir; (*scream*) laisser échapper; **to** ~ **up** *vi* diminuer, s'arrêter.

**lethal** [ˈliːθl] *a* mortel(le), fatal(e).

**lethargic** [lɛˈθɑːdʒɪk] *a* léthargique.

**lethargy** [ˈlɛθədʒɪ] *n* léthargie *f*.

**letter** [ˈlɛtə*] *n* lettre *f*; ~**s** *npl* (*LITERATURE*) lettres; ~ **bomb** *n* lettre piégée; ~**-box** *n* boîte *f* aux or à lettres; ~**ing** *n* lettres *fpl*; caractères *mpl*.

**lettuce** [ˈlɛtɪs] *n* laitue *f*, salade *f*.

**let-up** [ˈlɛtʌp] *n* répit *m*, détente *f*.

**leukaemia, leukemia** (*US*) [luːˈkiːmɪə] *n* leucémie *f*.

**level** [ˈlɛvl] *a* plat(e), plan(e), uni(e); horizontal(e) // *n* niveau *m*; (*flat place*) terrain plat; (*also*: **spirit** ~) niveau à bulle // *vt* niveler, aplanir; **to be** ~ **with** être au même niveau que; **'A'** ~**s** *npl* ≈ baccalauréat *m*; **'O'** ~**s** *npl* ≈ B.E.P.C.; **on the** ~ à l'horizontale; (*fig: honest*) régulier(ère); **to** ~ **off** or **out** *vi* (*prices etc*) se stabiliser; ~ **crossing** *n* passage *m* à niveau; ~**-headed** *a* équilibré(e).

**lever** [ˈliːvə*] *n* levier *m* // *vt*: **to** ~ **up/out** soulever/extraire au moyen d'un levier; ~**age** *n*: ~**age (on** or **with)** prise *f* (sur).

**levity** [ˈlɛvɪtɪ] *n* manque *m* de sérieux, légèreté *f*.

**levy** [ˈlɛvɪ] *n* taxe *f*, impôt *m* // *vt* prélever, imposer; percevoir.

**lewd** [luːd] *a* obscène, lubrique.

**liability** [laɪəˈbɪlɪtɪ] *n* responsabilité *f*; (*handicap*) handicap *m*; **liabilities** *npl* obligations *fpl*, engagements *mpl*; (*on balance sheet*) passif *m*.

**liable** [ˈlaɪəbl] *a* (*subject*): ~ **to** sujet(te) à; passible de; (*responsible*): ~ **(for)** responsable (de); (*likely*): ~ **to do** susceptible de faire.

**liaison** [liːˈeɪzɔn] *n* liaison *f*.

**liar** [ˈlaɪə*] *n* menteur/euse.

**libel** [ˈlaɪbl] *n* écrit *m* diffamatoire; diffamation *f* // *vt* diffamer.

**liberal** [ˈlɪbərl] *a* libéral(e); (*generous*): ~ **with** prodigue de, généreux(euse) avec.

**liberate** [ˈlɪbəreɪt] *vt* libérer; **liberation** [-ˈreɪʃən] *n* libération *f*.

**liberty** [ˈlɪbətɪ] *n* liberté *f*; **at** ~ **to do** libre de faire; **to take the** ~ **of** prendre la liberté de, se permettre de.

**Libra** [ˈliːbrə] *n* la Balance; **to be** ~ être de la Balance.

**librarian** [laɪˈbrɛərɪən] *n* bibliothécaire *m/f*.

**library** [ˈlaɪbrərɪ] *n* bibliothèque *f*.

**libretto** [lɪˈbrɛtəu] *n* livret *m*.

**Libya** [ˈlɪbɪə] *n* Lybie *f*; ~**n** *a* lybien(ne), de Lybie // *n* Lybien/ne.

**lice** [laɪs] *npl of* **louse**.

**licence, license** (*US*) [ˈlaɪsns] *n* autorisation *f*, permis *m*; (*COMM*) licence *f*; (*RADIO, TV*) redevance *f*; (*also*: **driving** ~) permis *m* (de conduire); (*excessive freedom*) licence; ~ **plate** *n* plaque *f* minéralogique.

**license** [ˈlaɪsns] *n* (*US*) = **licence** // *vt* donner une licence à; ~**d** *a* (*for alcohol*) patenté(e) pour la vente des spiritueux, qui a une patente de débit de boissons.

**licensee** [laɪsənˈsiː] *n* (*in a pub*) patron/ne, gérant/e.

**licentious** [laɪˈsɛnʃəs] *a* licentieux(euse).

**lichen** [ˈlaɪkən] *n* lichen *m*.

**lick** [lɪk] *vt* lécher // *n* coup *m* de langue; **a** ~ **of paint** un petit coup de peinture.

**licorice** [ˈlɪkərɪs] *n* = **liquorice**.

**lid** [lɪd] *n* couvercle *m*.

**lido** [ˈlaɪdəu] *n* piscine *f* en plein air.

**lie** [laɪ] *n* mensonge *m* // *vi* mentir; (*pt* **lay**, *pp* **lain** [leɪ, leɪn]) (*rest*) être étendu(e) or allongé(e) or couché(e); (*in grave*) être enterré(e), reposer; (*of object: be situated*) se trouver, être; **to** ~ **low** (*fig*) se cacher, rester caché(e); **to** ~ **about** *vi* traîner; **to have a** ~**-down** s'allonger, se reposer; **to have a** ~**-in** faire la grasse matinée.

**lieu** [luː]: **in** ~ **of** *prep* au lieu de.

**lieutenant** [lɛfˈtɛnənt] *n* lieutenant *m*.

**life, lives** [laɪf, laɪvz] *n* vie *f* // *cpd* de vie; de la vie; à vie; ~ **assurance** *n* assurance-vie *f*; ~**-belt** *n* bouée *f* de sauvetage; ~**boat** *n* canot *m* or chaloupe *f* de sauvetage; ~**-buoy** *n* bouée *f* de sauvetage; ~ **expectancy** *n* espérance *f* de vie; ~**guard** *n* surveillant *m* de baignade; ~ **jacket** *n* gilet *m* or ceinture *f* de sauvetage; ~**less** *a* sans vie, inanimé(e); (*dull*) qui manque de vie or de vigueur; ~**like** *a* qui semble vrai(e) or vivant(e); ressemblant(e); ~**line** *n* corde *f* de sauvetage; ~**long** *a* de toute une vie, de toujours; ~ **preserver** *n* (*US*) gilet *m* or ceinture *f* de sauvetage; (*Brit: col*) matraque *f*; ~**-raft** *n* radeau *m* de sauvetage; ~**-saver** *n* surveillant *m* de baignade; ~ **sentence** *n* condamnation *f* à vie *or* à perpétuité ; **~-sized** *a* grandeur nature *inv* ; ~ **span** *n* (durée *f* de) vie *f* ; ~ **support system** *n* (*MED*) respirateur artificiel ; **~time** *n*: **in his ~time** de son vivant ; **in a ~time** au cours d'une vie entière ; **dans sa vie**.

**lift** [lɪft] *vt* soulever, lever ; (*steal*) prendre, voler // *vi* (*fog*) se lever // *n* (*elevator*) ascenseur *m* ; **to give sb a ~** emmener *or* prendre qn en voiture ; **~-off** *n* décollage *m*.

**ligament** ['lɪgəmənt] *n* ligament *m*.

**light** [laɪt] *n* lumière *f* ; (*daylight*) lumière, jour *m* ; (*lamp*) lampe *f* ; (*ALT: traffic ~, rear ~*) feu *m* ; (: *headlamp*) phare *m* ; (*for cigarette etc*): **have you got a ~?** avez-vous du feu? // *vt* (*pt, pp* **lighted** *or* **lit** [lɪt]) (*candle, cigarette, fire*) allumer ; (*room*) éclairer // *a* (*room, colour*) clair(e) ; (*not heavy, also fig*) léger(ère) ; **to ~ up** *vi* s'allumer ; (*face*) s'éclairer // *vt* (*illuminate*) éclairer, illuminer ; ~ **bulb** *n* ampoule *f* ; **~en** *vi* s'éclairer // *vt* (*give light to*) éclairer ; (*make lighter*) éclaircir ; (*make less heavy*) alléger ; **~er** *n* (*also*: **cigarette ~**) briquet *m* ; (: *in car*) allume-cigare *m inv* ; (*boat*) péniche *f* ; **~-headed** *a* étourdi(e), écervelé(e) ; **~-hearted** *a* gai(e), joyeux(euse), enjoué(e) ; **~house** *n* phare *m* ; **~ing** *n* (*on road*) éclairage *m* ; (*in theatre*) éclairages ; **~ing-up time** *n* heure officielle de la tombée du jour ; **~ly** *ad* légèrement ; ~ **meter** *n* (*PHOT*) photomètre *m*, cellule *f* ; **~ness** *n* clarté *f* ; (*in weight*) légèreté *f*.

**lightning** ['laɪtnɪŋ] *n* éclair *m*, foudre *f* ; ~ **conductor** *n* paratonnerre *m*.

**lightship** ['laɪtʃɪp] *n* bateau-phare *m*.

**lightweight** ['laɪtweɪt] *a* (*suit*) léger(ère) ; (*boxer*) poids léger *inv*.

**light year** ['laɪtjɪə*] *n* année-lumière *f*.

**lignite** ['lɪgnaɪt] *n* lignite *m*.

**like** [laɪk] *vt* aimer (bien) // *prep* comme // a semblable, pareil(le) // *n*: **the ~** un(e) pareil(le) *or* semblable ; le(la) pareil(le) ; (*pej*) (d')autres du même genre *or* acabit ; **his ~s and dislikes** ses goûts *mpl or* préférences *fpl* ; **I would ~, I'd ~** je voudrais, j'aimerais ; **to be/look ~ sb/sth** ressembler à qn/qch ; **that's just ~ him** c'est bien de lui, ça lui ressemble ; **nothing ~...** rien de tel que... ; **~able** *a* sympathique, agréable.

**likelihood** ['laɪklɪhud] *n* probabilité *f*.

**likely** ['laɪklɪ] *a* probable ; plausible ; **he's ~ to leave** il va sûrement partir, il risque fort de partir.

**like-minded** [laɪk'maɪndɪd] *a* de même opinion.

**liken** ['laɪkən] *vt*: **to ~ sth to** comparer qch à.

**likewise** ['laɪkwaɪz] *ad* de même, pareillement.

**liking** ['laɪkɪŋ] *n*: ~ (**for**) affection *f* (pour), penchant *m* (pour) ; goût *m* (pour).

**lilac** ['laɪlək] *n* lilas *m* // *a* lilas *inv*.

**lilting** ['lɪltɪŋ] *a* aux cadences mélodieuses ; chantant(e).

**lily** ['lɪlɪ] *n* lis *m* ; ~ **of the valley** *n* muguet *m*.

**limb** [lɪm] *n* membre *m*.

**limber** ['lɪmbə*]: **to ~ up** *vi* se dégourdir, se mettre en train.

**limbo** ['lɪmbəu] *n*: **to be in ~** (*fig*) être tombé(e) dans l'oubli.

**lime** [laɪm] *n* (*tree*) tilleul *m* ; (*fruit*) lime *f* ; (*GEO*) chaux *f* ; ~ **juice** *n* jus *m* de citron vert.

**limelight** ['laɪmlaɪt] *n*: **in the ~** (*fig*) en vedette, au premier plan.

**limerick** ['lɪmərɪk] *n* poème *m* humoristique (de 5 vers).

**limestone** ['laɪmstəun] *n* pierre *f* à chaux ; (*GEO*) calcaire *m*.

**limit** ['lɪmɪt] *n* limite *f* // *vt* limiter ; **~ation** [-'teɪʃən] *n* limitation *f*, restriction *f* ; **~ed** *a* limité(e), restreint(e) ; **~ed (liability) company (Ltd)** *n* ≈ société *f* anonyme (S.A.).

**limousine** ['lɪməzi:n] *n* limousine *f*.

**limp** [lɪmp] *n*: **to have a ~** boiter // *vi* boiter // *a* mou(molle).

**limpet** ['lɪmpɪt] *n* patelle *f* ; **like a ~** (*fig*) comme une ventouse.

**line** [laɪn] *n* (*gen*) ligne *f* ; (*rope*) corde *f* ; (*wire*) fil *m* ; (*of poem*) vers *m* ; (*row, series*) rangée *f* ; file *f*, queue *f* ; (*COMM: series of goods*) article(s) *m(pl)* // *vt* (*clothes*): **to ~ (with)** doubler (de) ; (*box*): **to ~ (with)** garnir *or* tapisser (de) ; (*subj: trees, crowd*) border ; **in his ~ of business** dans sa partie, dans son rayon ; **in ~ with** en accord avec ; **to ~ up** *vi* s'aligner, se mettre en rang(s) // *vt* aligner.

**linear** ['lɪnɪə*] *a* linéaire.

**linen** ['lɪnɪn] *n* linge *m* (de corps *or* de maison) ; (*cloth*) lin *m*.

**liner** ['laɪnə*] *n* paquebot *m* de ligne.

**linesman** ['laɪnzmən] *n* (*TENNIS*) juge *m* de ligne ; (*FOOTBALL*) juge de touche.

**line-up** ['laɪnʌp] *n* file *f* ; (*SPORT*) (composition *f* de l')équipe *f*.

**linger** ['lɪŋgə*] *vi* s'attarder ; traîner ; (*smell, tradition*) persister ; **~ing** *a* persistant(e) ; qui subsiste ; (*death*) lent(e).

**lingo, ~es** ['lɪŋgəu] *n* (*pej*) jargon *m*.

**linguist** ['lɪŋgwɪst] *n* linguiste *m/f* ; personne douée pour les langues ; **~ic** *a* linguistique ; **~ics** *n* linguistique *f*.

**lining** ['laɪnɪŋ] *n* doublure *f*.

**link** [lɪŋk] *n* (*of a chain*) maillon *m* ; (*connection*) lien *m*, rapport *m* // *vt* relier, lier, unir ; **~s** *npl* (terrain *m* de) golf *m* ; **to ~ up** *vt* relier // *vi* se rejoindre ; s'associer ; **~-up** *n* liaison *f*.

**linoleum** [lɪ'nəuliəm] *n* linoléum *m*.

**linseed oil** ['lɪnsi:d'ɔɪl] *n* huile *f* de lin.

**lint** [lɪnt] *n* tissu ouaté (*pour pansements*).

**lintel** ['lɪntl] *n* linteau *m*.

**lion** ['laɪən] *n* lion *m* ; ~ **cub** lionceau *m* ; **~ess** *n* lionne *f*.

**lip** [lɪp] *n* lèvre *f* ; (*of cup etc*) rebord *m* ; (*insolence*) insolences *fpl* ; **~read** *vi* lire sur les lèvres ; **to pay ~ service to sth** ne reconnaître le mérite de qch que pour la forme *or* qu'en paroles ; **~stick** *n* rouge *m* à lèvres.

**liquefy** ['lɪkwɪfaɪ] *vt* liquéfier.

**liqueur** [lɪ'kjuə*] *n* liqueur *f*.

**liquid** ['lɪkwɪd] *n* liquide *m* // *a* liquide ; ~ **assets** *npl* liquidités *fpl*, disponibilités *fpl*.

**liquidate** ['lıkwıdeıt] *vt* liquider; **liquidation** [-'deıʃən] *n* liquidation *f*; **liquidator** *n* liquidateur *m*.

**liquidize** ['lıkwıdaız] *vt* (*CULIN*) passer au mixeur.

**liquor** ['lıkə\*] *n* spiritueux *m*, alcool *m*.

**liquorice** ['lıkərıs] *n* réglisse *m*.

**lisp** [lısp] *n* zézaiement *m*.

**list** [lıst] *n* liste *f*; (*of ship*) inclinaison *f* // *vt* (*write down*) inscrire; faire la liste de; (*enumerate*) énumérer // *vi* (*ship*) gîter, donner de la bande.

**listen** ['lısn] *vi* écouter; **to ~ to** écouter; **~er** *n* auditeur/trice.

**listless** ['lıstlıs] *a* indolent(e), apathique; **~ly** *ad* avec indolence *or* apathie.

**lit** [lıt] *pt,pp of* **light**.

**litany** ['lıtənı] *n* litanie *f*.

**literacy** ['lıtərəsı] *n* degré *m* d'alphabétisation, fait *m* de savoir lire et écrire.

**literal** ['lıtərl] *a* littéral(e); (*unimaginative*) prosaïque, sans imagination; **~ly** *ad* littéralement.

**literary** ['lıtərərı] *a* littéraire.

**literate** ['lıtərət] *a* qui sait lire et écrire, instruit(e).

**literature** ['lıtərıtʃə\*] *n* littérature *f*; (*brochures etc*) copie *f* publicitaire, prospectus *mpl*.

**lithe** [laıð] *a* agile, souple.

**lithography** [lı'θɒgrəfı] *n* lithographie *f*.

**litigate** ['lıtıgeıt] *vt* mettre en litige // *vi* plaider; **litigation** [-'geıʃən] *n* litige *m*; contentieux *m*.

**litmus** ['lıtməs] *n*: **~ paper** papier *m* de tournesol.

**litre, liter** (*US*) ['li:tə\*] *n* litre *m*.

**litter** ['lıtə\*] *n* (*rubbish*) détritus *mpl*, ordures *fpl*; (*young animals*) portée *f* // *vt* éparpiller; laisser des détritus dans // *vi* (*ZOOL*) mettre bas; **~ bin** *n* boîte *f* à ordures, poubelle *f*; **~ed with** jonché(e) de, couvert(e) de.

**little** ['lıtl] *a* (*small*) petit(e); (*not much*): **it's ~** c'est peu; **~ milk** peu de lait // *ad* peu; **a ~** un peu (de); **a ~ milk** un peu de lait; **~ by ~** petit à petit, peu à peu; **to make ~ of** faire peu de cas de.

**liturgy** ['lıtədʒı] *n* liturgie *f*.

**live** *vi* [lıv] vivre; (*reside*) vivre, habiter // *a* [laıv] (*animal*) vivant(e), en vie; (*wire*) sous tension; (*broadcast*) (transmis(e)) en direct; **to ~ down** vt faire oublier (avec le temps); **to ~ in** *vi* être logé(e) et nourri(e); être interne; **to ~ on** *vt fus* (*food*) vivre de // *vi* survivre, subsister; **to ~ up to** *vt fus* se montrer à la hauteur de.

**livelihood** ['laıvlıhud] *n* moyens *mpl* d'existence.

**liveliness** ['laıvlınəs] *n* vivacité *f*, entrain *m*.

**lively** ['laıvlı] *a* vif(vive), plein(e) d'entrain.

**liver** ['lıvə\*] *n* (*ANAT*) foie *m*; **~ish** *a* qui a mal au foie; (*fig*) grincheux(euse).

**livery** ['lıvərı] *n* livrée *f*.

**lives** [laıvz] *npl of* **life**.

**livestock** ['laıvstɒk] *n* cheptel *m*, bétail *m*.

**livid** ['lıvıd] *a* livide, blafard(e); (*furious*) furieux(euse), furibond(e).

**living** ['lıvıŋ] *a* vivant(e), en vie // *n*: **to earn** *or* **make a ~** gagner sa vie; **~ room** *n* salle *f* de séjour; **~ standards** *npl* niveau *m* de vie; **~ wage** *n* salaire *m* permettant de vivre (décemment).

**lizard** ['lızəd] *n* lézard *m*.

**llama** ['lɑ:mə] *n* lama *m*.

**load** [ləud] *n* (*weight*) poids *m*; (*thing carried*) chargement *m*, charge *f*; (*ELEC. TECH*) charge // *vt*: **to ~ (with)** (*lorry, ship*) charger (de); (*gun, camera*) charger (avec); **a ~ of, ~s of** (*fig*) un *or* des tas de, des masses de; **~ed** *a* (*dice*) pipé(e); (*question, word*) insidieux(euse); (*col: rich*) bourré(e) de fric; (: *drunk*) bourré.

**loaf, loaves** [ləuf, ləuvz] *n* pain *m*, miche *f* // *vi* (*also:* **~ about, ~ around**) fainéanter, traîner.

**loam** [ləum] *n* terreau *m*.

**loan** [ləun] *n* prêt *m* // *vt* prêter; **on ~** prêté(e), en prêt; **public ~** emprunt public.

**loath** [ləuθ] *a*: **to be ~ to do** répugner à faire.

**loathe** [ləuð] *vt* détester, avoir en horreur; **loathing** *n* dégoût *m*, répugnance *f*.

**loaves** [ləuvz] *npl of* **loaf**.

**lobby** ['lɒbı] *n* hall *m*, entrée *f*; (*POL: pressure group*) groupe *m* de pression, lobby *m* // *vt* faire pression sur.

**lobe** [ləub] *n* lobe *m*.

**lobster** ['lɒbstə\*] *n* homard *m*.

**local** ['ləukl] *a* local(e) // *n* (*pub*) pub *m* *or* café *m* du coin; **the ~s** *npl* les gens *mpl* du pays *or* du coin; **~ call** *n* communication urbaine; **~ government** *n* administration locale *or* municipale.

**locality** [ləu'kælıtı] *n* région *f*, environs *mpl*; (*position*) lieu *m*.

**locally** ['ləukəlı] *ad* localement; dans les environs *or* la région.

**locate** [ləu'keıt] *vt* (*find*) trouver, repérer; (*situate*) situer.

**location** [ləu'keıʃən] *n* emplacement *m*; **on ~** (*CINEMA*) en extérieur.

**loch** [lɒx] *n* lac *m*, loch *m*.

**lock** [lɒk] *n* (*of door, box*) serrure *f*; (*of canal*) écluse *f*; (*of hair*) mèche *f*, boucle *f* // *vt* (*with key*) fermer à clé; (*immobilize*) bloquer // *vi* (*door etc*) fermer à clé; (*wheels*) se bloquer.

**locker** ['lɒkə\*] *n* casier *m*.

**locket** ['lɒkıt] *n* médaillon *m*.

**lockjaw** ['lɒkdʒɔ:] *n* tétanos *m*.

**locomotive** [ləukə'məutıv] *n* locomotive *f*.

**locust** ['ləukəst] *n* locuste *f*, sauterelle *f*.

**lodge** [lɒdʒ] *n* pavillon *m* (de gardien); (*FREEMASONRY*) loge *f* // *vi* (*person*): **to ~ (with)** être logé(e) (chez), être en pension (chez) // *vt* (*appeal etc*) présenter; déposer; **to ~ a complaint** porter plainte; **to ~ (itself) in/between** se loger dans/entre; **~r** *n* locataire *m/f*; (*with room and meals*) pensionnaire *m/f*.

**lodgings** ['lɒdʒıŋz] *npl* chambre *f*; meublé *m*.

**loft** [lɒft] *n* grenier *m*.

**lofty** ['lɒftı] *a* élevé(e); (*haughty*) hautain(e).

**log** [lɒg] *n* (*of wood*) bûche *f*; (*book*) = **logbook**.

**logarithm** ['lɔgərɪðəm] n logarithme m.

**logbook** ['lɔgbuk] n (NAUT) livre m or journal m de bord ; (AVIAT) carnet m de vol ; (of lorry-driver) carnet de route ; (of events, movement of goods etc) registre m ; (of car) ≈ carte grise.

**loggerheads** ['lɔgəhɛdz] npl: at ~ (with) à couteaux tirés (avec).

**logic** ['lɔdʒɪk] n logique f ; ~al a logique ; ~ally ad logiquement.

**logistics** [lɔ'dʒɪstɪks] n logistique f.

**loin** [lɔɪn] n (CULIN) filet m, longe f ; ~s npl reins mpl.

**loiter** ['lɔɪtə*] vi s'attarder ; to ~ (about) traîner, musarder ; (pej) rôder.

**loll** [lɔl] vi (also: ~ about) se prélasser, fainéanter.

**lollipop** ['lɔlɪpɔp] n sucette f ; ~ man/lady n contractuel/le qui fait traverser la rue aux enfants.

**London** ['lʌndən] n Londres m ; ~er n Londonien/ne.

**lone** [ləun] a solitaire.

**loneliness** ['ləunlɪnɪs] n solitude f, isolement m.

**lonely** ['ləunlɪ] a seul(e) ; solitaire, isolé(e) ; to feel ~ se sentir seul.

**loner** ['ləunə*] n solitaire m/f.

**long** [lɔŋ] a long(longue) // ad longtemps // vi: to ~ for sth/to do avoir très envie de qch/de faire ; attendre qch avec impatience/impatience de faire ; he had ~ understood that... il avait compris depuis longtemps que... ; how ~ is this river/course? quelle est la longueur de ce fleuve/la durée de ce cours? ; 6 metres ~ (long) de 6 mètres ; 6 months ~ qui dure 6 mois, de 6 mois ; all night ~ toute la nuit ; ~ before longtemps avant ; before ~ (+ future) avant peu, dans peu de temps ; (+ past) peu de temps après ; at ~ last enfin ; no ~er, any ~er ne...plus ; ~-distance a (race) de fond ; (call) interurbain(e) ; ~-haired a (person) aux cheveux longs ; (animal) aux longs poils ; ~hand n écriture normale or courante ; ~ing n désir m, envie f, nostalgie f // a plein(e) d'envie or de nostalgie.

**longitude** ['lɔŋgɪtjuːd] n longitude f.

**long:** ~ jump n saut m en longueur ; ~-lost a perdu(e) depuis longtemps ; ~-playing a: ~-playing record (L.P.) n (disque m) 33 tours m inv ; ~-range a à longue portée ; ~-sighted a presbyte ; (fig) prévoyant(e) ; ~-standing a de longue date ; ~-suffering a empreint(e) d'une patience résignée ; extrêmement patient(e) ; ~-term a à long terme ; ~ wave n grandes ondes ; ~-winded a intarissable, interminable.

**loo** [luː] n (col) w.-c. mpl, petit coin.

**loofah** ['luːfə] n sorte d'éponge végétale.

**look** [luk] vi regarder ; (seem) sembler, paraître, avoir l'air ; (building etc): to ~ south/on to the sea donner au sud/sur la mer // n regard m ; (appearance) air m, allure f, aspect m ; ~s npl mine f ; physique m ; beauté f ; to ~ like ressembler à ; it ~s like him on dirait que c'est lui ; to ~ after vt fus s'occuper de, prendre soin de ; garder, surveiller ; to ~ at vt fus regarder ; to ~ down on vt fus

(fig) regarder de haut, dédaigner ; to ~ for vt fus chercher ; to ~ forward to vt fus attendre avec impatience ; to ~ on vi regarder (en spectateur) ; to ~ out vi (beware): to ~ out (for) prendre garde (à), faire attention (à) ; to ~ out for vt fus être à la recherche de ; guetter ; to ~ to vt fus veiller à ; (rely on) compter sur ; to ~ up vi lever les yeux ; (improve) s'améliorer // vt (word) chercher ; (friend) passer voir ; to ~ up to vt fus avoir du respect pour ; ~-out n poste m de guet ; guetteur m ; to be on the ~-out (for) guetter.

**loom** [luːm] n métier m à tisser // vi surgir ; (fig) menacer, paraître imminent(e).

**loop** [luːp] n boucle f ; (contraceptive) stérilet m ; ~hole n porte f de sortie (fig) ; échappatoire f.

**loose** [luːs] a (knot, screw) desserré(e) ; (stone) branlant(e) ; (clothes) vague, ample, lâche ; (animal) en liberté, échappé(e) ; (life) dissolu(e) ; (morals, discipline) relâché(e) ; (thinking) peu rigoureux(euse), vague ; (translation) approximatif(ive) ; to be at a ~ end ne pas trop savoir quoi faire ; ~ly ad sans serrer ; approximativement ; ~n vt desserrer, relâcher, défaire.

**loot** [luːt] n butin m // vt piller ; ~ing n pillage m.

**lop** [lɔp]: to ~ off vt couper, trancher.

**lop-sided** ['lɔp'saɪdɪd] a de travers, asymétrique.

**lord** [lɔːd] n seigneur m ; L~ Smith lord Smith ; the L~ le Seigneur ; the (House of) L~s la Chambre des Lords ; ~ly a noble, majestueux(euse) ; (arrogant) hautain(e) ; ~ship n: your L~ship Monsieur le comte (or le baron or le Juge).

**lore** [lɔː*] n tradition(s) f(pl).

**lorry** ['lɔrɪ] n camion m ; ~ driver n camionneur m, routier m.

**lose,** pt,pp **lost** [luːz, lɔst] vt perdre ; (opportunity) manquer, perdre ; (pursuers) distancer, semer // vi perdre ; to ~ (time) (clock) retarder ; to get lost vi se perdre ; ~r n perdant/e.

**loss** [lɔs] n perte f ; to be at a ~ être perplexe or embarrassé(e) ; to be at a ~ to do se trouver incapable de faire.

**lost** [lɔst] pt,pp of **lose** // a perdu(e) ; ~ property n objets trouvés.

**lot** [lɔt] n (at auctions) lot m ; (destiny) sort m, destinée f ; the ~ le tout ; tous mpl, toutes fpl ; a ~ beaucoup ; a ~ of beaucoup de ; ~s of tas de ; to draw ~s (for sth) tirer (qch) au sort.

**lotion** ['ləuʃən] n lotion f.

**lottery** ['lɔtərɪ] n loterie f.

**loud** [laud] a bruyant(e), sonore, fort(e) ; (gaudy) voyant(e), tapageur(euse) // ad (speak etc) fort ; ~hailer n porte-voix m inv ; ~ly ad fort, bruyamment ; ~speaker n haut-parleur m.

**lounge** [laundʒ] n salon m // vi se prélasser, paresser ; ~ suit n complet m ; 'tenue de ville'.

**louse,** pl **lice** [laus, laɪs] n pou m.

**lousy** ['lauzɪ] a (fig) infect(e), moche.

**lout** [laut] *n* rustre *m*, butor *m*.
**lovable** ['lʌvəbl] *a* très sympathique ; adorable.
**love** [lʌv] *n* amour *m* // *vt* aimer ; aimer beaucoup ; **to ~ to do** aimer beaucoup *or* adorer faire ; **to be in ~ with** être amoureux(euse) de ; **to make ~** faire l'amour ; **'15 ~'** (*TENNIS*) '15 à rien *or* zéro' ; **~ at first sight** le coup de foudre ; **~ affair** *n* liaison (amoureuse) ; **~ letter** *n* lettre *f* d'amour ; **~ life** *n* vie sentimentale.
**lovely** ['lʌvlɪ] *a* (très) joli(e) ; ravissant(e), charmant(e) ; agréable.
**lover** ['lʌvə*] *n* amant *m* ; (*amateur*): **a ~ of** un(e) ami(e) de ; un(e) amoureux(euse) de.
**lovesong** ['lʌvsɔŋ] *n* chanson *f* d'amour.
**loving** ['lʌvɪŋ] *a* affectueux(euse), tendre, aimant(e).
**low** [ləu] *a* bas(basse) // *ad* bas // *n* (*METEOROLOGY*) dépression *f* // *vi* (*cow*) mugir ; **to feel ~** se sentir déprimé(e) ; **he's very ~** (*ill*) il est bien bas *or* très affaibli ; **to turn (down) ~** *vt* baisser ; **~-cut** *a* (*dress*) décolleté(e) ; **~er** *vt* abaisser, baisser ; **~ly** *a* humble, modeste ; **~-lying** *a* à faible altitude ; **~-paid** *a* mal payé(e), aux salaires bas.
**loyal** ['lɔɪəl] *a* loyal(e), fidèle ; **~ty** *n* loyauté *f*, fidélité *f*.
**lozenge** ['lɔzɪndʒ] *n* (*MED*) pastille *f* ; (*GEOM*) losange *m*.
**L.P.** *n abbr see* **long-playing**.
**L-plates** ['ɛlpleɪts] *npl* plaques *fpl* d'apprenti conducteur.
**Ltd** *abbr see* **limited**.
**lubricant** ['lu:brɪkənt] *n* lubrifiant *m*.
**lubricate** ['lu:brɪkeɪt] *vt* lubrifier, graisser.
**lucid** ['lu:sɪd] *a* lucide ; **~ity** [-'sɪdɪtɪ] *n* lucidité *f*.
**luck** [lʌk] *n* chance *f* ; **bad ~** malchance *f*, malheur *m* ; **good ~!** bonne chance! **~ily** *ad* heureusement, par bonheur ; **~y** *a* (*person*) qui a de la chance ; (*coincidence*) heureux(euse) ; (*number etc*) qui porte bonheur.
**lucrative** ['lu:krətɪv] *a* lucratif(ive), rentable, qui rapporte.
**ludicrous** ['lu:dɪkrəs] *a* ridicule, absurde.
**ludo** ['lu:dəu] *n* jeu *m* des petits chevaux.
**lug** [lʌg] *vt* traîner, tirer.
**luggage** ['lʌgɪdʒ] *n* bagages *mpl* ; **~ rack** *n* (*in train*) porte-bagages *m inv* ; (: *made of string*) filet *m* à bagages ; (*on car*) galerie *f*.
**lugubrious** [lu'gu:brɪəs] *a* lugubre.
**lukewarm** ['lu:kwɔ:m] *a* tiède.
**lull** [lʌl] *n* accalmie *f* // *vt* (*child*) bercer ; (*person, fear*) apaiser, calmer.
**lullaby** ['lʌləbaɪ] *n* berceuse *f*.
**lumbago** [lʌm'beɪgəu] *n* lumbago *m*.
**lumber** ['lʌmbə*] *n* bric-à-brac *m inv* ; **~jack** *n* bûcheron *m*.
**luminous** ['lu:mɪnəs] *a* lumineux(euse).
**lump** [lʌmp] *n* morceau *m* ; (*in sauce*) grumeau *m* ; (*swelling*) grosseur *f* // *vt* (*also*: **~ together**) réunir, mettre en tas ; **a ~ sum** une somme globale *or* forfaitaire ; **~y** *a* (*sauce*) qui a des grumeaux.

**lunacy** ['lu:nəsɪ] *n* démence *f*, folie *f*.
**lunar** ['lu:nə*] *a* lunaire.
**lunatic** ['lu:nətɪk] *n* fou/folle, dément/e // *a* fou(folle), dément(e).
**lunch** [lʌntʃ] *n* déjeuner *m* ; **it is his ~ hour** c'est l'heure où il déjeune ; **it is ~time** c'est l'heure du déjeuner.
**luncheon** ['lʌntʃən] *n* déjeuner *m* ; **~ meat** *n* sorte de saucisson ; **~ voucher** *n* chèque-déjeuner *m*.
**lung** [lʌŋ] *n* poumon *m* ; **~ cancer** *n* cancer *m* du poumon.
**lunge** [lʌndʒ] *vi* (*also*: **~ forward**) faire un mouvement brusque en avant.
**lupin** ['lu:pɪn] *n* lupin *m*.
**lurch** [lə:tʃ] *vi* vaciller, tituber // *n* écart *m* brusque, embardée *f*.
**lure** [luə*] *n* appât *m*, leurre *m* // *vt* attirer *or* persuader par la ruse.
**lurid** ['luərɪd] *a* affreux(euse), atroce.
**lurk** [lə:k] *vi* se tapir, se cacher.
**luscious** ['lʌʃəs] *a* succulent(e) ; appétissant(e).
**lush** [lʌʃ] *a* luxuriant(e).
**lust** [lʌst] *n* luxure *f* ; lubricité *f* ; désir *m* ; (*fig*): **~ for** soif *f* de ; **to ~ after** *vt fus* convoiter, désirer ; **~ful** *a* lascif(ive).
**lustre, luster** (*US*) ['lʌstə*] *n* lustre *m*, brillant *m*.
**lusty** ['lʌstɪ] *a* vigoureux(euse), robuste.
**lute** [lu:t] *n* luth *m*.
**Luxembourg** ['lʌksəmbə:g] *n* Luxembourg *m*.
**luxuriant** [lʌg'zjuərɪənt] *a* luxuriant(e).
**luxurious** [lʌg'zjuərɪəs] *a* luxueux(euse).
**luxury** ['lʌkʃərɪ] *n* luxe *m* // *cpd* de luxe.
**lying** ['laɪɪŋ] *n* mensonge(s) *m(pl)*.
**lynch** [lɪntʃ] *vt* lyncher.
**lynx** [lɪnks] *n* lynx *m inv*.
**lyre** ['laɪə*] *n* lyre *f*.
**lyric** ['lɪrɪk] *a* lyrique ; **~s** *npl* (*of song*) paroles *fpl* ; **~al** *a* lyrique ; **~ism** ['lɪrɪsɪzəm] *n* lyrisme *m*.

# M

**m.** *abbr of* **metre, mile, million**.
**M.A.** *abbr see* **master**.
**mac** [mæk] *n* imper(méable) *m*.
**macaroni** [mækə'rəunɪ] *n* macaronis *mpl*.
**macaroon** [mækə'ru:n] *n* macaron *m*.
**mace** [meɪs] *n* masse *f* ; (*spice*) macis *m*.
**machine** [mə'ʃi:n] *n* machine *f* // *vt* (*dress etc*) coudre à la machine ; **~ gun** *n* mitrailleuse *f* ; **~ry** *n* machinerie *f*, machines *fpl* ; (*fig*) mécanisme(s) *m(pl)* ; **~ tool** *n* machine-outil *f* ; **machinist** *n* machiniste *m/f*.
**mackerel** ['mækrl] *n, pl inv* maquereau *m*.
**mackintosh** ['mækɪntɔʃ] *n* imperméable *m*.
**mad** [mæd] *a* fou(folle) ; (*foolish*) insensé(e) ; (*angry*) furieux(euse).
**madam** ['mædəm] *n* madame *f* ; **yes ~** oui Madame.
**madden** ['mædn] *vt* exaspérer.
**made** [meɪd] *pt, pp of* **make** ; **~-to-measure** *a* fait(e) sur mesure.
**madly** ['mædlɪ] *ad* follement.

**madman** ['mædmən] n fou m, aliéné m.

**madness** ['mædnɪs] n folie f.

**magazine** [mægə'ziːn] n (PRESS) magazine m, revue f; (MIL: store) dépôt m, arsenal m; (of firearm) magasin m.

**maggot** ['mægət] n ver m, asticot m.

**magic** ['mædʒɪk] n magie f // a magique; ~al a magique; ~ian [mə'dʒɪʃən] n magicien/ne.

**magistrate** ['mædʒɪstreɪt] n magistrat m; juge m.

**magnanimous** [mæg'nænɪməs] a magnanime.

**magnate** ['mægneɪt] n magnat m.

**magnesium** [mæg'niːzɪəm] n magnésium m.

**magnet** ['mægnɪt] n aimant m; ~ic [-'netɪk] a magnétique; ~ism n magnétisme m.

**magnification** [mægnɪfɪ'keɪʃən] n grossissement m.

**magnificence** [mæg'nɪfɪsns] n magnificence f.

**magnificent** [mæg'nɪfɪsnt] a superbe, magnifique.

**magnify** ['mægnɪfaɪ] vt grossir; (sound) amplifier; ~ing glass n loupe f.

**magnitude** ['mægnɪtjuːd] n ampleur f.

**magnolia** [mæg'nəulɪə] n magnolia m.

**magpie** ['mægpaɪ] n pie f.

**mahogany** [mə'hɔgənɪ] n acajou m // cpd en (bois d')acajou.

**maid** [meɪd] n bonne f; old ~ (pej) vieille fille.

**maiden** ['meɪdn] n jeune fille f // a (aunt etc) non mariée; (speech, voyage) inaugural(e); ~ name n nom m de jeune fille.

**mail** [meɪl] n poste f; (letters) courrier m // vt envoyer (par la poste); ~box n (US) boîte f aux lettres; ~ing list n liste f d'adresses; ~-order n vente f or achat m par correspondance.

**maim** [meɪm] vt mutiler.

**main** [meɪn] a principal(e) // n (pipe) conduite principale, canalisation f; the ~s (ELEC) le secteur; in the ~ dans l'ensemble; ~land n continent m; ~stay n (fig) pilier m.

**maintain** [meɪn'teɪn] vt entretenir; (continue) maintenir, préserver; (affirm) soutenir; **maintenance** ['meɪntənəns] n entretien m.

**maisonette** [meɪzə'net] n appartement m en duplex.

**maize** [meɪz] n maïs m.

**majestic** [mə'dʒestɪk] a majestueux(euse).

**majesty** ['mædʒɪstɪ] n majesté f.

**major** ['meɪdʒə*] n (MIL) commandant m // a important(e), principal(e); (MUS) majeur(e).

**majority** [mə'dʒɔrɪtɪ] n majorité f.

**make** [meɪk] vt (pt, pp made [meɪd]) faire; (manufacture) faire, fabriquer; (cause to be): to ~ sb sad etc rendre qn triste etc; (force): to ~ sb do sth obliger qn à faire qch, faire faire qch à qn; (equal): 2 and 2 ~ 4 2 et 2 font 4 // n fabrication f; (brand) marque f; to ~ do with se contenter de; se débrouiller avec; to ~ for vt fus (place) se diriger vers; to ~ out

vt (write out) écrire; (understand) comprendre; (see) distinguer; to ~ up vt (invent) inventer, imaginer; (parcel) faire // vi se réconcilier; (with cosmetics) se maquiller, se farder; to ~ up for vt fus compenser; racheter; ~-believe a feint(e), de fantaisie; ~r n fabricant m; ~shift a provisoire, improvisé(e); ~-up n maquillage m.

**making** ['meɪkɪŋ] n (fig): in the ~ en formation or gestation.

**maladjusted** [mælə'dʒʌstɪd] a inadapté(e).

**malaise** [mæ'leɪz] n malaise m.

**malaria** [mə'lɛərɪə] n malaria f, paludisme m.

**Malay** [mə'leɪ] a malais(e) // n (person) Malais/e; (language) malais m.

**Malaysia** [mə'leɪzɪə] n Malaisie f.

**male** [meɪl] n (BIOL, ELEC) mâle m // a (sex, attitude) masculine(e); mâle; (child etc) du sexe masculin; ~ and female students étudiants et étudiantes.

**malevolence** [mə'lɛvələns] n malveillance f.

**malevolent** [mə'lɛvələnt] a malveillant(e).

**malfunction** [mæl'fʌŋkʃən] n fonctionnement défectueux.

**malice** ['mælɪs] n méchanceté f, malveillance f; **malicious** [mə'lɪʃəs] a méchant(e), malveillant(e); (LAW) avec intention criminelle.

**malign** [mə'laɪn] vt diffamer, calomnier.

**malignant** [mə'lɪɡnənt] a (MED) malin(igne).

**malingerer** [mə'lɪŋɡərə*] n simulateur/trice.

**malleable** ['mælɪəbl] a malléable.

**mallet** ['mælɪt] n maillet m.

**malnutrition** [mælnju:'trɪʃən] n malnutrition f.

**malpractice** [mæl'præktɪs] n faute professionnelle; négligence f.

**malt** [mɔːlt] n malt m // cpd (whisky) pur malt.

**Malta** ['mɔːltə] n Malte f; **Maltese** [-'tiːz] a maltais(e) // n, pl inv Maltais/e.

**maltreat** [mæl'triːt] vt maltraiter.

**mammal** ['mæml] n mammifère m.

**mammoth** ['mæməθ] n mammouth m // a géant(e), monstre.

**man, pl men** [mæn,mɛn] n homme m; (CHESS) pièce f; (DRAUGHTS) pion m // vt garnir d'hommes; servir, assurer le fonctionnement de; être de service à; an old ~ un vieillard.

**manage** ['mænɪdʒ] vi se débrouiller // vt (be in charge of) s'occuper de; gérer; to ~ to do se débrouiller pour faire; réussir à faire; ~able a maniable; faisable; ~ment n administration f, direction f; ~r n directeur m; administrateur m; (of hotel etc) gérant m; (of artist) impresario m; ~ress [-ə'rɛs] n directrice f; gérante f; ~rial [-ə'dʒɪɛrɪəl] a directorial(e); ~rial staff n cadres mpl; **managing** a: **managing director** directeur général.

**mandarin** ['mændərɪn] n (also: ~ orange) mandarine f; (person) mandarin m.

**mandate** ['mændeɪt] *n* mandat *m*.
**mandatory** ['mændətərɪ] *a* obligatoire ; (*powers etc*) mandataire.
**mandolin(e)** ['mændəlɪn] *n* mandoline *f*.
**mane** [meɪn] *n* crinière *f*.
**maneuver** [mə'nu:və*] *etc* (*US*) = **manoeuvre** *etc*.
**manful** ['mænful] *a* courageux(euse), vaillant(e).
**manganese** [mæŋgə'ni:z] *n* manganèse *m*.
**mangle** ['mæŋgl] *vt* déchiqueter ; mutiler // *n* essoreuse *f* ; calandre *f*.
**mango**, ~**es** ['mæŋgəu] *n* mangue *f*.
**mangrove** ['mæŋgrəuv] *n* palétuvier *m*.
**mangy** ['meɪndʒɪ] *a* galeux(euse).
**manhandle** ['mænhændl] *vt* malmener.
**manhole** ['mænhəul] *n* trou *m* d'homme.
**manhood** ['mænhud] *n* âge *m* d'homme ; virilité *f*.
**manhunt** ['mænhʌnt] *n* chasse *f* à l'homme.
**mania** ['meɪnɪə] *n* manie *f* ; ~**c** ['meɪnɪæk] *n* maniaque *m/f*.
**manicure** ['mænɪkjuə*] *n* manucure *f* // *vt* (*person*) faire les mains à ; ~ **set** *n* trousse *f* à ongles.
**manifest** ['mænɪfɛst] *vt* manifester // *a* manifeste, évident(e) ; ~**ation** [-'teɪʃən] *n* manifestation *f*.
**manifesto** [mænɪ'fɛstəu] *n* manifeste *m*.
**manipulate** [mə'nɪpjuleɪt] *vt* manipuler.
**mankind** [mæn'kaɪnd] *n* humanité *f*, genre humain.
**manly** ['mænlɪ] *a* viril(e) ; courageux(euse).
**man-made** ['mæn'meɪd] *a* artificiel(le).
**manner** ['mænə*] *n* manière *f*, façon *f* ; ~**s** *npl* manières ; ~**ism** *n* particularité *f* de langage (*or* de comportement), tic *m*.
**manoeuvre**, **maneuver** (*US*) [mə'nu:və*] *vt,vi* manœuvrer // *n* manœuvre *f*.
**manor** ['mænə*] *n* (*also*: ~ **house**) manoir *m*.
**manpower** ['mænpauə*] *n* main-d'œuvre *f*.
**manservant**, *pl* **menservants** ['mænsə:vənt, 'mɛn-] *n* domestique *m*.
**mansion** ['mænʃən] *n* château *m*, manoir *m*.
**manslaughter** ['mænslɔ:tə*] *n* homicide *m* involontaire.
**mantelpiece** ['mæntlpi:s] *n* cheminée *f*.
**mantle** ['mæntl] *n* cape *f* ; (*fig*) manteau *m*.
**manual** ['mænjuəl] *a* manuel(le) // *n* manuel *m*.
**manufacture** [mænju'fæktʃə*] *vt* fabriquer // *n* fabrication *f* ; ~**r** *n* fabricant *m*.
**manure** [mə'njuə*] *n* fumier *m* ; (*artificial*) engrais *m*.
**manuscript** ['mænjuskrɪpt] *n* manuscrit *m*.
**many** ['mɛnɪ] *det* beaucoup de, de nombreux(euses) // *pronoun* beaucoup, un grand nombre ; **a great** ~ un grand nombre (de) ; ~ **a...** bien des... , plus d'un(e)... .

**map** [mæp] *n* carte *f* // *vt* dresser la carte de ; **to** ~ **out** *vt* tracer.
**maple** ['meɪpl] *n* érable *m*.
**mar** [ma:*] *vt* gâcher, gâter.
**marathon** ['mærəθən] *n* marathon *m*.
**marauder** [mə'rɔ:də*] *n* maraudeur/euse.
**marble** ['ma:bl] *n* marbre *m* ; (*toy*) bille *f* ; ~**s** *n* (*game*) billes.
**March** [ma:tʃ] *n* mars *m*.
**march** [ma:tʃ] *vi* marcher au pas ; défiler // *n* marche *f* ; (*demonstration*) rallye *m* ; ~**-past** *n* défilé *m*.
**mare** [mɛə*] *n* jument *f*.
**margarine** [ma:dʒə'ri:n] *n* margarine *f*.
**margin** ['ma:dʒɪn] *n* marge *f* ; ~**al** *a* marginal(e).
**marigold** ['mærɪgəuld] *n* souci *m*.
**marijuana** [mærɪ'wa:nə] *n* marijuana *f*.
**marina** [mə'ri:nə] *n* marina *f*.
**marine** [mə'ri:n] *a* marin(e) // *n* fusilier marin ; (*US*) marine *m*.
**marital** ['mærɪtl] *a* matrimonial(e).
**maritime** ['mærɪtaɪm] *a* maritime.
**marjoram** ['ma:dʒərəm] *n* marjolaine *f*.
**mark** [ma:k] *n* marque *f* ; (*of skid etc*) trace *f* ; (*SCOL*) note *f* ; (*SPORT*) cible *f* ; (*currency*) mark *m* // *vt* marquer ; (*stain*) tacher ; (*SCOL*) noter ; corriger ; **to** ~ **time** marquer le pas ; **to** ~ **out** *vt* désigner ; ~**ed** *a* marqué(e), net(te) ; ~**er** *n* (*sign*) jalon *m* ; (*bookmark*) signet *m*.
**market** ['ma:kɪt] *n* marché *m* // *vt* (*COMM*) commercialiser ; ~ **day** *n* jour *m* de marché ; ~ **garden** *n* (*Brit*) jardin maraîcher ; ~**ing** *n* marketing *m* ; ~ **place** *n* place *f* du marché.
**marksman** ['ma:ksmən] *n* tireur *m* d'élite ; ~**ship** *n* adresse *f* au tir.
**marmalade** ['ma:məleɪd] *n* confiture *f* d'oranges.
**maroon** [mə'ru:n] *vt* (*fig*): **to be** ~**ed** (**in** *or* **at**) être bloqué(e) (à) // *a* bordeaux *inv*.
**marquee** [ma:'ki:] *n* chapiteau *m*.
**marquess**, **marquis** ['ma:kwɪs] *n* marquis *m*.
**marriage** ['mærɪdʒ] *n* mariage *m* ; ~ **bureau** *n* agence matrimoniale.
**married** ['mærɪd] *a* marié(e) ; (*life, love*) conjugal(e).
**marrow** ['mærəu] *n* moelle *f* ; (*vegetable*) courge *f*.
**marry** ['mærɪ] *vt* épouser, se marier avec ; (*subj: father, priest etc*) marier // *vi* (*also*: **get married**) se marier.
**Mars** [ma:z] *n* (*planet*) Mars *f*.
**marsh** [ma:ʃ] *n* marais *m*, marécage *m*.
**marshal** ['ma:ʃl] *n* maréchal *m* ; (*US: fire, police*) ≈ capitaine *m* // *vt* rassembler ; ~**ing yard** *n* gare *f* de triage.
**marshy** ['ma:ʃɪ] *a* marécageux(euse).
**martial** ['ma:ʃl] *a* martial(e) ; ~ **law** *n* loi martiale.
**Martian** ['ma:ʃɪən] *n* Martien/ne.
**martyr** ['ma:tə*] *n* martyr/e // *vt* martyriser ; ~**dom** *n* martyre *m*.
**marvel** ['ma:vl] *n* merveille *f* // *vi*: **to** ~ (**at**) s'émerveiller (de) ; ~**lous**, ~**ous** (*US*) *a* merveilleux(euse).
**Marxism** ['ma:ksɪzəm] *n* marxisme *m*.

**Marxist** ['mɑ:ksɪst] *a,n* marxiste (*m/f*).
**marzipan** ['mɑ:zɪpæn] *n* pâte *f* d'amandes.
**mascara** [mæs'kɑ:rə] *n* mascara *m*.
**mascot** ['mæskət] *n* mascotte *f*.
**masculine** ['mæskjulɪn] *a* masculin(e) // *n* masculin *m*; **masculinity** [-'lɪnɪtɪ] *n* masculinité *f*.
**mashed** [mæʃt] *a*: ~ **potatoes** purée *f* de pommes de terre.
**mask** [mɑ:sk] *n* masque *m* // *vt* masquer.
**masochist** ['mæsəukɪst] *n* masochiste *m/f*.
**mason** ['meɪsn] *n* (*also*: **stone**~) maçon *m*; (*also*: **free**~) franc-maçon *m*; ~**ic** [mə'sɔnɪk] *a* maçonnique; ~**ry** *n* maçonnerie *f*.
**masquerade** [mæskə'reɪd] *n* bal masqué; (*fig*) mascarade *f* // *vi*: **to** ~ **as** se faire passer pour.
**mass** [mæs] *n* multitude *f*, masse *f*; (*PHYSICS*) masse; (*REL*) messe *f* // *vi* se masser; **the** ~**es** les masses.
**massacre** ['mæsəkə*] *n* massacre *m* // *vt* massacrer.
**massage** ['mæsɑ:ʒ] *n* massage *m* // *vt* masser.
**masseur** [mæ'sə:*] *n* masseur *m*; **masseuse** [-'sə:z] *n* masseuse *f*.
**massive** ['mæsɪv] *a* énorme, massif(ive).
**mass media** ['mæs'mi:dɪə] *npl* mass-media *mpl*.
**mass-produce** ['mæsprə'dju:s] *vt* fabriquer en série.
**mast** [mɑ:st] *n* mât *m*.
**master** ['mɑ:stə*] *n* maître *m*; (*in secondary school*) professeur *m*; (*title for boys*): **M**~ **X** Monsieur X // *vt* maîtriser; (*learn*) apprendre à fond; (*understand*) posséder parfaitement or à fond; **M**~**'s degree** *n* ≈ maîtrise *f*; ~ **key** *n* passe-partout *m inv*; ~**ly** *a* magistral(e); ~**mind** *n* esprit supérieur // *vt* diriger, être le cerveau de; **M**~ **of Arts/Science (M.A./M.Sc.)** *n* ≈ titulaire *m/f* d'une maîtrise (en lettres/science); **M**~ **of Arts/Science degree (M.A./M.Sc.)** *n* ≈ maîtrise *f*; ~**piece** *n* chef-d'œuvre *m*; ~ **plan** *n* stratégie *f* d'ensemble; ~. **stroke** *n* coup *m* de maître; ~**y** *n* maîtrise *f*; connaissance parfaite.
**masturbate** ['mæstəbeɪt] *vi* se masturber; **masturbation** [-'beɪʃən] *n* masturbation *f*.
**mat** [mæt] *n* petit tapis; (*also*: **door**~) paillasson *m* // *a* = **matt**.
**match** [mætʃ] *n* allumette *f*; (*game*) match *m*, partie *f*; (*fig*) égal/e; mariage *m*; parti *m* // *vt* assortir; (*go well with*) aller bien avec, s'assortir à; (*equal*) égaler, valoir // *vi* être assorti(e); **to be a good** ~ être bien assorti(e); **to** ~ **up** *vt* assortir; ~**box** *n* boîte *f* d'allumettes; ~**ing** *a* assorti(e); ~**less** *a* sans égal.
**mate** [meɪt] *n* camarade *m/f* de travail; (*col*) copain/copine; (*animal*) partenaire *m/f*, mâle/femelle; (*in merchant navy*) second *m* // *vi* s'accoupler // *vt* accoupler.
**material** [mə'tɪərɪəl] *n* (*substance*) matière *f*, matériau *m*; (*cloth*) tissu *m*, étoffe *f* // *a* matériel(le); (*important*) essentiel(le); ~**s** *npl* matériaux *mpl*; ~**istic** [-ə'lɪstɪk] *a*

**matérialiste; ~ize** *vi* se matérialiser, se réaliser; ~**ly** *ad* matériellement.
**maternal** [mə'tə:nl] *a* maternel(le).
**maternity** [mə'tə:nɪtɪ] *n* maternité *f* // *cpd* de maternité, de grossesse; ~ **hospital** *n* maternité *f*.
**matey** ['meɪtɪ] *a* (*col*) copain-copain *inv*.
**mathematical** [mæθə'mætɪkl] *a* mathématique.
**mathematician** [mæθəmə'tɪʃən] *n* mathématicien/ne.
**mathematics** [mæθə'mætɪks] *n* mathématiques *fpl*.
**maths** [mæθs] *n* math(s) *fpl*.
**matinée** ['mætɪneɪ] *n* matinée *f*.
**mating** ['meɪtɪŋ] *n* accouplement *m*; ~ **call** *n* appel *m* du mâle; ~ **season** *n* saison *f* des amours.
**matriarchal** [meɪtrɪ'ɑ:kl] *a* matriarcal(e).
**matrices** ['meɪtrɪsi:z] *npl of* **matrix**.
**matriculation** [mətrɪkju'leɪʃən] *n* inscription *f*.
**matrimonial** [mætrɪ'məunɪəl] *a* matrimonial(e), conjugal(e).
**matrimony** ['mætrɪmənɪ] *n* mariage *m*.
**matrix**, *pl* **matrices** ['meɪtrɪks, 'meɪtrɪsi:z] *n* matrice *f*.
**matron** ['meɪtrən] *n* (*in hospital*) infirmière-chef *f*; (*in school*) infirmière; ~**ly** *a* de matrone; imposant(e).
**matt** [mæt] *a* mat(e).
**matted** ['mætɪd] *a* emmêlé(e).
**matter** ['mætə*] *n* question *f*; (*PHYSICS*) matière *f*, substance *f*; (*content*) contenu *m*, fond *m*; (*MED*: *pus*) pus *m* // *vi* importer; **it doesn't** ~ cela n'a pas d'importance; (*I don't mind*) cela ne fait rien; **what's the** ~? qu'est-ce qu'il y a?, qu'est-ce qui ne va pas?; **no** ~ **what** quoiqu'il arrive; **that's another** ~ c'est une autre affaire; **as a** ~ **of course** tout naturellement; **as a** ~ **of fact** en fait; **it's a** ~ **of habit** c'est une question d'habitude; ~**-of-fact** *a* terre à terre, neutre.
**matting** ['mætɪŋ] *n* natte *f*.
**mattress** ['mætrɪs] *n* matelas *m*.
**mature** [mə'tjuə*] *a* mûr(e); (*cheese*) fait(e) // *vi* mûrir; se faire; **maturity** *n* maturité *f*.
**maudlin** ['mɔ:dlɪn] *a* larmoyant(e).
**maul** [mɔ:l] *vt* lacérer.
**Mauritius** [mə'rɪʃəs] *n* l'île *f* Maurice.
**mausoleum** [mɔ:sə'lɪəm] *n* mausolée *m*.
**mauve** [məuv] *a* mauve.
**mawkish** ['mɔ:kɪʃ] *a* mièvre; fade.
**max.** *abbr of* **maximum**.
**maxim** ['mæksɪm] *n* maxime *f*.
**maxima** ['mæksɪmə] *npl of* **maximum**.
**maximum** ['mæksɪməm] *a* maximum // *n* (*pl* **maxima** ['mæksɪmə]) maximum *m*.
**May** [meɪ] *n* mai *m*.
**may** [meɪ] *vi* (*conditional*: **might**) (*indicating possibility*): **he** ~ **come** il se peut qu'il vienne; (*be allowed to*): ~ **I smoke?** puis-je fumer?; (*wishes*): ~ **God bless you!** (que) Dieu vous bénisse!; **he might be there** il pourrait bien y être, il se pourrait qu'il y soit; **I might as well go** je ferais aussi bien d'y aller, autant y

aller ; **you might like to try** vous pourriez (peut-être) essayer.
**maybe** ['meɪbi:] *ad* peut-être ; ~ **he'll...** peut-être qu'il... .
**mayday** ['meɪdeɪ] *n* S.O.S. *m.*
**May Day** ['meɪdeɪ] *n* le Premier mai.
**mayhem** ['meɪhɛm] *n* grabuge *m.*
**mayonnaise** [meɪə'neɪz] *n* mayonnaise *f.*
**mayor** [mɛə*] *n* maire *m* ; ~**ess** *n* maire *m* ; épouse *f* du maire.
**maypole** ['meɪpəʊl] *n* mât enrubanné (*autour duquel on danse*).
**maze** [meɪz] *n* labyrinthe *m,* dédale *m.*
**M.D.** *abbr* = *Doctor of Medicine.*
**me** [mi:] *pronoun* me, m' + *vowel* ; (*stressed, after prep*) moi.
**meadow** ['mɛdəʊ] *n* prairie *f,* pré *m.*
**meagre, meager** (*US*) ['mi:gə*] *a* maigre.
**meal** [mi:l] *n* repas *m* ; (*flour*) farine *f* ; ~**time** *n* l'heure *f* du repas ; ~**y-mouthed** *a* mielleux(euse).
**mean** [mi:n] *a* (*with money*) avare, radin(e) ; (*unkind*) mesquin(e), méchant(e) ; (*average*) moyen(ne) // *vt* (*pt, pp* **meant** [mɛnt]) (*signify*) signifier, vouloir dire ; (*intend*): **to** ~ **to do** avoir l'intention de faire // *n* moyenne *f* ; ~**s** *npl* moyens *mpl* ; **by** ~**s of** par l'intermédiaire de ; au moyen de ; **by all** ~**s** je vous en prie ; **to be meant for** être destiné(e) à ; **what do you** ~**?** que voulez-vous dire?
**meander** [mɪ'ændə*] *vi* faire des méandres ; (*fig*) flâner.
**meaning** ['mi:nɪŋ] *n* signification *f,* sens *m* ; ~**ful** *a* significatif(ive) ; ~**less** *a* dénué(e) de sens.
**meanness** ['mi:nnɪs] *n* avarice *f* ; mesquinerie *f.*
**meant** [mɛnt] *pt, pp of* **mean.**
**meantime** ['mi:ntaɪm] *ad,* **meanwhile** ['mi:nwaɪl] *ad* (*also:* **in the** ~) pendant ce temps.
**measles** ['mi:zlz] *n* rougeole *f.*
**measly** ['mi:zlɪ] *a* (*col*) minable.
**measurable** ['mɛʒərəbl] *a* mesurable.
**measure** ['mɛʒə*] *vt, vi* mesurer // *n* mesure *f* ; (*ruler*) règle (graduée) ; ~**d** *a* mesuré(e) ; ~**ments** *npl* mesures *fpl* ; **chest**/**hip** ~**ment** tour *m* de poitrine/hanches.
**meat** [mi:t] *n* viande *f* ; ~ **pie** *n* pâté *m* en croûte ; ~**y** *a* qui a le goût de la viande ; (*fig*) substantiel(le).
**Mecca** ['mɛkə] *n* la Mecque.
**mechanic** [mɪ'kænɪk] *n* mécanicien *m* ; ~**s** *n* mécanique *f* // *npl* mécanisme *m* ; ~**al** *a* mécanique.
**mechanism** ['mɛkənɪzəm] *n* mécanisme *m.*
**mechanization** [mɛkənaɪ'zeɪʃən] *n* mécanisation *f.*
**medal** ['mɛdl] *n* médaille *f* ; ~**lion** [mɪ'dælɪən] *n* médaillon *m* ; ~**list, ~ist** (*US*) *n* (*SPORT*) médaillé/e.
**meddle** ['mɛdl] *vi*: **to** ~ **in** se mêler de, s'occuper de ; **to** ~ **with** toucher à ; ~**some** *a* indiscret(ète).
**media** ['mi:dɪə] *npl* media *mpl.*
**mediaeval** [mɛdɪ'i:vl] *a* = **medieval.**

**mediate** ['mi:dɪeɪt] *vi* s'interposer ; servir d'intermédiaire ; **mediation** [-'eɪʃən] *n* médiation *f* ; **mediator** *n* médiateur/trice.
**medical** ['mɛdɪkl] *a* médical(e) ; ~ **student** *n* étudiant/e en médecine.
**medicated** ['mɛdɪkeɪtɪd] *a* traitant(e), médicamenteux(euse).
**medicinal** [mɛ'dɪsɪnl] *a* médicinal(e).
**medicine** ['mɛdsɪn] *n* médecine *f* ; (*drug*) médicament *m* ; ~ **chest** *n* pharmacie *f* (*murale ou portative*).
**medieval** [mɛdɪ'i:vl] *a* médiéval(e).
**mediocre** [mi:dɪ'əʊkə*] *a* médiocre ; **mediocrity** [-'ɔkrɪtɪ] *n* médiocrité *f.*
**meditate** ['mɛdɪteɪt] *vi*: **to** ~ **(on)** méditer (sur) ; **meditation** [-'teɪʃən] *n* méditation *f.*
**Mediterranean** [mɛdɪtə'reɪnɪən] *a* méditerranéen(ne) ; **the** ~ **(Sea)** la (mer) Méditerranée.
**medium** ['mi:dɪəm] *a* moyen(ne) // *n* (*pl* **media**: *means*) moyen *m* ; (*pl* **mediums**: *person*) médium *m* ; **the happy** ~ le juste milieu.
**medley** ['mɛdlɪ] *n* mélange *m.*
**meek** [mi:k] *a* doux(douce), humble.
**meet,** *pt,pp* **met** [mi:t, mɛt] *vt* rencontrer ; (*by arrangement*) retrouver, rejoindre ; (*for the first time*) faire la connaissance de ; (*go and fetch*): **I'll** ~ **you at the station** j'irai te chercher à la gare ; (*fig*) faire face à ; satisfaire à ; se joindre à // *vi* se rencontrer ; se retrouver ; (*in session*) se réunir ; (*join*: *objects*) se joindre ; **to** ~ **with** *vt fus* rencontrer ; ~**ing** *n* rencontre *f* ; (*session*: *of club etc*) réunion *f* ; (*interview*) entrevue *f* ; **she's at a** ~**ing** (*COMM*) elle est en conférence.
**megaphone** ['mɛgəfəʊn] *n* porte-voix *m inv.*
**melancholy** ['mɛlənkəlɪ] *n* mélancolie *f* // *a* mélancolique.
**mellow** ['mɛləʊ] *a* velouté(e) ; doux(douce) ; (*colour*) riche et profond(e) ; (*fruit*) mûr(e) // *vi* (*person*) s'adoucir.
**melodious** [mɪ'ləʊdɪəs] *a* mélodieux(euse).
**melodrama** ['mɛləʊdrɑːmə] *n* mélodrame *m.*
**melody** ['mɛlədɪ] *n* mélodie *f.*
**melon** ['mɛlən] *n* melon *m.*
**melt** [mɛlt] *vi* fondre ; (*become soft*) s'amollir ; (*fig*) s'attendrir // *vt* faire fondre ; (*person*) attendrir ; **to** ~ **away** *vi* fondre complètement ; **to** ~ **down** *vt* fondre ; ~**ing point** *n* point *m* de fusion ; ~**ing pot** *n* (*fig*) creuset *m.*
**member** ['mɛmbə*] *n* membre *m* ; ~ **country**/**state** *n* pays *m*/état *m* member ; **M~ of Parliament (M.P.)** député *m* ; ~**ship** *n* adhésion *f* ; statut *m* de membre ; (*nombre m de*) membres *mpl,* adhérents *mpl.*
**membrane** ['mɛmbreɪn] *n* membrane *f.*
**memento** [mə'mɛntəʊ] *n* souvenir *m.*
**memo** ['mɛməʊ] *n* note *f* (de service).
**memoir** ['mɛmwɑ:*] *n* mémoire *m,* étude *f* ; ~**s** *npl* mémoires.
**memorable** ['mɛmərəbl] *a* mémorable.
**memorandum,** *pl* **memoranda** [mɛmə'rændəm, -də] *n* note *f* (de service) ; (*DIPLOMACY*) mémorandum *m.*

**memorial** [mɪ'mɔːrɪəl] n mémorial m // a commémoratif(ive).

**memorize** ['mɛməraɪz] vt apprendre or retenir par cœur.

**memory** ['mɛmərɪ] n mémoire f; (recollection) souvenir m; **in ~ of** à la mémoire de.

**men** [mɛn] npl of **man.**

**menace** ['mɛnəs] n menace f // vt menacer; **menacing** a menaçant(e).

**menagerie** [mɪ'nædʒərɪ] n ménagerie f.

**mend** [mɛnd] vt réparer; (darn) raccommoder, repriser // n reprise f; **on the ~** en voie de guérison; **~ing** n raccommodages mpl.

**menial** ['miːnɪəl] a de domestique, inférieur(e); subalterne.

**meningitis** [mɛnɪn'dʒaɪtɪs] n méningite f.

**menopause** ['mɛnəupɔːz] n ménopause f.

**menservants** npl of **manservant.**

**menstruate** ['mɛnstrueɪt] vi avoir ses règles; **menstruation** [-'eɪʃən] n menstruation f.

**mental** ['mɛntl] a mental(e).

**mentality** [mɛn'tælɪtɪ] n mentalité f.

**mention** ['mɛnʃən] n mention f // vt mentionner, faire mention de; **don't ~ it!** je vous en prie, il n'y a pas de quoi!

**menu** ['mɛnjuː] n (set ~) menu m; (printed) carte f.

**mercantile** ['mɜːkəntaɪl] a marchand(e); (law) commercial(e).

**mercenary** ['mɜːsɪnərɪ] a mercantile // n mercenaire m.

**merchandise** ['mɜːtʃəndaɪz] n marchandises fpl.

**merchant** ['mɜːtʃənt] n négociant m, marchand m; **timber/wine** ~ négociant en bois/vins, marchand de bois/vins; **~ bank** n banque f d'affaires; **~ navy** n marine marchande.

**merciful** ['mɜːsɪful] a miséricordieux(euse), clément(e).

**merciless** ['mɜːsɪlɪs] a impitoyable, sans pitié.

**mercurial** [mɜː'kjuərɪəl] a changeant(e); (lively) vif(vive).

**mercury** ['mɜːkjurɪ] n mercure m.

**mercy** ['mɜːsɪ] n pitié f, merci f; (REL) miséricorde f; **to have ~ on sb** avoir pitié de qn; **at the ~ of** à la merci de.

**mere** [mɪə*] a simple; **~ly** ad simplement, purement.

**merge** [mɜːdʒ] vt unir // vi se fondre; (COMM) fusionner; **~r** n (COMM) fusion f.

**meridian** [mə'rɪdɪən] n méridien m.

**meringue** [mə'ræŋ] n meringue f.

**merit** ['mɛrɪt] n mérite m, valeur f // vt mériter.

**mermaid** ['mɜːmeɪd] n sirène f.

**merrily** ['mɛrɪlɪ] ad joyeusement, gaiement.

**merriment** ['mɛrɪmənt] n gaieté f.

**merry** ['mɛrɪ] a gai(e); **~-go-round** n manège m.

**mesh** [mɛʃ] n maille f; filet m // vi (gears) s'engrener.

**mesmerize** ['mɛzməraɪz] vt hypnotiser; fasciner.

**mess** [mɛs] n désordre m, fouillis m, pagaille f; (MIL) mess m, cantine f; **to ~**

**about** vi (col) perdre son temps; **to ~ about with** vt fus (col) chambarder, tripoter; **to ~ up** vt salir; chambarder; gâcher.

**message** ['mɛsɪdʒ] n message m.

**messenger** ['mɛsɪndʒə*] n messager m.

**messy** ['mɛsɪ] a sale; en désordre.

**met** [mɛt] pt, pp of **meet.**

**metabolism** [mɛ'tæbəlɪzəm] n métabolisme m.

**metal** ['mɛtl] n métal m // vt empierrer; **~lic** [-'tælɪk] a métallique; **~lurgy** [-'tælədʒɪ] n métallurgie f.

**metamorphosis,** pl **phoses** [mɛtə'mɔːfəsɪs, -iːz] n métamorphose f.

**metaphor** ['mɛtəfə*] n métaphore f.

**metaphysics** [mɛtə'fɪzɪks] n métaphysique f.

**mete** [miːt]: **to ~ out** vt fus infliger.

**meteor** ['miːtɪə*] n météore m.

**meteorological** [miːtɪərə'lɔdʒɪkl] a météorologique.

**meteorology** [miːtɪə'rɔlədʒɪ] n météorologie f.

**meter** ['miːtə*] n (instrument) compteur m; (US) = **metre.**

**method** ['mɛθəd] n méthode f; **~ical** [mɪ'θɔdɪkl] a méthodique.

**Methodist** ['mɛθədɪst] a,n méthodiste (m/f).

**methylated spirit** ['mɛθɪleɪtɪd'spɪrɪt] n (also: **meths**) alcool m à brûler.

**meticulous** [mɛ'tɪkjuləs] a méticuleux(euse).

**metre, meter** (US) ['miːtə*] n mètre m.

**metric** ['mɛtrɪk] a métrique; **~al** a métrique; **~ation** [-'keɪʃən] n conversion f au système métrique.

**metronome** ['mɛtrənəum] n métronome m.

**metropolis** [mɪ'trɔpəlɪs] n métropole f.

**mettle** ['mɛtl] n courage m.

**mew** [mjuː] vi (cat) miauler.

**mews** [mjuːz] n: **~ cottage** maisonnette aménagée dans les anciennes écuries d'un hôtel particulier.

**Mexican** ['mɛksɪkən] a mexicain(e) // n Mexicain/e.

**Mexico** ['mɛksɪkəu] n Mexique m; **~ City** Mexico.

**mezzanine** ['mɛtsəniːn] n mezzanine f; (of shops, offices) entresol m.

**miaow** [miː'au] vi miauler.

**mice** [maɪs] npl of **mouse.**

**microbe** ['maɪkrəub] n microbe m.

**microfilm** ['maɪkrəufɪlm] n microfilm m // vt microfilmer.

**microphone** ['maɪkrəfəun] n microphone m.

**microscope** ['maɪkrəskəup] n microscope m; **microscopic** [-'skɔpɪk] a microscopique.

**mid** [mɪd] a: **~ May** la mi-mai; **~ afternoon** le milieu de l'après-midi; **in ~ air** en plein ciel; **~day** midi m.

**middle** ['mɪdl] n milieu m; (waist) ceinture f, taille f // a du milieu; **~-aged** a d'un certain âge; **the M~ Ages** npl le moyen âge; **~-class** a ≈ bourgeois(e); **the ~ class(es)** ≈ les classes moyennes; **M~ East** n Proche-Orient m, Moyen-Orient m;

~man *n* intermédiaire *m*; ~ name *n* deuxième nom *m*.

middling ['mɪdlɪŋ] *a* moyen(ne).

midge [mɪdʒ] *n* moucheron *m*.

midget ['mɪdʒɪt] *n* nain/e // *a* minuscule.

Midlands ['mɪdləndz] *npl* comtés du centre de l'Angleterre.

midnight ['mɪdnaɪt] *n* minuit *m*.

midriff ['mɪdrɪf] *n* estomac *m*, taille *f*.

midst [mɪdst] *n*: in the ~ of au milieu de.

midsummer [mɪd'sʌmə*] *n* milieu *m* de l'été.

midway [mɪd'weɪ] *a*, *ad*: ~ (between) à mi-chemin (entre).

midweek [mɪd'wi:k] *n* milieu *m* de la semaine.

midwife, midwives ['mɪdwaɪf, -vz] *n* sage-femme *f*; ~ry [-wɪfərɪ] *n* obstétrique *f*.

midwinter [mɪd'wɪntə*] *n* milieu *m* de l'hiver.

might [maɪt] *vb see* may // *n* puissance *f*, force *f*; ~y a puissant(e) // *ad* (col) rudement.

migraine ['mi:greɪn] *n* migraine *f*.

migrant ['maɪgrənt] *n* (bird, animal) migrateur *m*; (person) migrant/e; nomade *m/f* // *a* migrateur(trice); migrant(e); nomade; (worker) saisonnier(ère).

migrate [maɪ'greɪt] *vi* émigrer; migration [-'greɪʃən] *n* migration *f*.

mike [maɪk] *n* (abbr of microphone) micro *m*.

mild [maɪld] *a* doux(douce); (reproach) léger(ère); (illness) bénin(bénigne) // *n* bière légère.

mildew ['mɪldju:] *n* mildiou *m*.

mildly ['maɪldlɪ] *ad* doucement; légèrement.

mildness ['maɪldnɪs] *n* douceur *f*.

mile [maɪl] *n* mil(l)e *m* (= 1609 m); ~age *n* distance *f* en milles, ≈ kilométrage *m*;. ~ometer *n* = milometer; ~stone *n* borne *f*; (fig) jalon *m*.

milieu ['mi:ljə:] *n* milieu *m*.

militant ['mɪlɪtnt] *a,n* militant(e).

military ['mɪlɪtərɪ] *a* militaire // *n*: the ~ l'armée *f*, les militaires *mpl*.

militate ['mɪlɪteɪt] *vi*: to ~ against militer contre.

militia [mɪ'lɪʃə] *n* milice *f*.

milk [mɪlk] *n* lait *m* // *vt* (cow) traire; (fig) dépouiller, plumer; ~ chocolate *n* chocolat *m* au lait; ~ing *n* traite *f*; ~man *n* laitier *m*; ~ shake *n* milk-shake *m*; ~y *a* lacté(e); (colour) laiteux(euse); M~y Way *n* Voie lactée.

mill [mɪl] *n* moulin *m*; (factory) usine *f*, fabrique *f*; (spinning) filature *f*; (flour ~) minoterie *f* // *vt* moudre, broyer // *vi* (also: ~ about) grouiller.

millennium, *pl* ~s or millennia [mɪ'lɛnɪəm, -'lɛnɪə] *n* millénaire *m*.

miller ['mɪlə*] *n* meunier *m*.

millet ['mɪlɪt] *n* millet *m*.

milli... ['mɪlɪ] *prefix*: ~gram(me) *n* milligramme *m*; ~litre *n* millilitre *m*; ~metre *n* millimètre *m*.

milliner ['mɪlɪnə*] *n* modiste *f*; ~y *n* modes *fpl*.

million ['mɪljən] *n* million *m*; ~aire *n* millionnaire *m*.

millstone ['mɪlstəun] *n* meule *f*.

millwheel ['mɪlwi:l] *n* roue *f* de moulin.

milometer [maɪ'lɔmɪtə*] *n* ≈ compteur *m* kilométrique.

mime [maɪm] *n* mime *m* // *vt*, *vi* mimer.

mimic ['mɪmɪk] *n* imitateur/trice // *vt*, *vi* imiter, contrefaire; ~ry *n* imitation *f*; (ZOOL) mimétisme *m*.

min. *abbr of* minute(s), minimum.

minaret [mɪnə'rɛt] *n* minaret *m*.

mince [mɪns] *vt* hacher // *vi* (in walking) marcher à petits pas maniérés // *n* (CULIN) viande hachée, hachis *m*; he does not ~ (his) words il ne mâche pas ses mots; ~meat *n* hachis de fruits secs utilisés en pâtisserie; ~ pie *n* sorte de tarte aux fruits secs; ~r *n* hachoir *m*.

mincing ['mɪnsɪŋ] *a* affecté(e).

mind [maɪnd] *n* esprit *m* // *vt* (attend to, look after) s'occuper de; (be careful) faire attention à; (object to): I don't ~ the noise je ne crains pas le bruit, le bruit ne me dérange pas; do you ~ if ...? est-ce que cela vous gêne si ...?; I don't ~ cela ne me dérange pas; it is on my ~ cela me préoccupe; to my ~ à mon avis or sens; to be out of one's ~ ne plus avoir toute sa raison; never ~ peu importe, ça ne fait rien; to keep sth in ~ ne pas oublier qch; to bear sth in ~ tenir compte de qch; to make up one's ~ se décider; '~ the step' 'attention à la marche'; to have in ~ to do avoir l'intention de faire; ~ful a: ~ful of attentif(ive) à, soucieux(euse) de; ~less a irréfléchi(e).

mine [maɪn] *pronoun* le(la) mien(ne), *pl* les miens(miennes) // *a*: this book is ~ ce livre est à moi // *n* mine *f* // *vt* (coal) extraire; (ship, beach) miner; ~ detector *n* détecteur *m* de mines; ~field *n* champ *m* de mines; ~r *n* mineur *m*.

mineral ['mɪnərəl] *a* minéral(e) // *n* minéral *m*; ~s *npl* (soft drinks) boissons gazeuses (sucrées); ~ogy [-'rælədʒɪ] *n* minéralogie *f*; ~ water *n* eau minérale.

minesweeper ['maɪnswi:pə*] *n* dragueur *m* de mines.

mingle ['mɪŋgl] *vt* mêler, mélanger // *vi*: to ~ with se mêler à.

mingy ['mɪndʒɪ] *a* (col) radin(e).

miniature ['mɪnətʃə*] *a* (en) miniature // *n* miniature *f*.

minibus ['mɪnɪbʌs] *n* minibus *m*.

minicab ['mɪnɪkæb] *n* minitaxi *m*.

minim ['mɪnɪm] *n* (MUS) blanche *f*.

minima ['mɪnɪmə] *npl of* minimum.

minimal ['mɪnɪml] *a* minimal(e).

minimize ['mɪnɪmaɪz] *vt* minimiser.

minimum ['mɪnɪməm] *n* (*pl*: minima ['mɪnɪmə]) minimum *m* // *a* minimum.

mining ['maɪnɪŋ] *n* exploitation minière // *a* minier(ère); de mineurs.

minion ['mɪnjən] *n* (pej) laquais *m*; favori/te.

miniskirt ['mɪnɪskə:t] *n* mini-jupe *f*.

minister ['mɪnɪstə*] *n* (POL) ministre *m*; (REL) pasteur *m*; ~ial [-'tɪərɪəl] *a* (POL) ministériel(le).

**ministry** ['mɪnɪstrɪ] n ministère m; (REL): to go into the ~ devenir pasteur.

**mink** [mɪŋk] n vison m; ~ coat n manteau m de vison.

**minnow** ['mɪnəu] n vairon m.

**minor** ['maɪnə*] a petit(e), de peu d'importance; (MUS) mineur(e) // n (LAW) mineur/e.

**minority** [maɪˈnɔrɪtɪ] n minorité f.

**minster** ['mɪnstə*] n église abbatiale.

**minstrel** ['mɪnstrəl] n trouvère m, ménestrel m.

**mint** [mɪnt] n (plant) menthe f; (sweet) bonbon m à la menthe // vt (coins) battre; the (Royal) M~ ≈ l'hôtel m de la Monnaie; in ~ condition à l'état de neuf; ~ sauce n sauce f à la menthe.

**minuet** [mɪnjuˈɛt] n menuet m.

**minus** ['maɪnəs] n (also: ~ sign) signe m moins // prep moins.

**minute** a [maɪˈnjuːt] minuscule; (detail) minutieux(euse) // n ['mɪnɪt] minute f; (official record) procès-verbal m, compte rendu; ~s npl procès-verbal.

**miracle** ['mɪrəkl] n miracle m; **miraculous** [mɪˈrækjuləs] a miraculeux(euse).

**mirage** ['mɪrɑːʒ] n mirage m.

**mirror** ['mɪrə*] n miroir m, glace f // vt refléter.

**mirth** [mə:θ] n gaieté f.

**misadventure** [mɪsədˈvɛntʃə*] n mésaventure f; **death by** ~ décès accidentel.

**misanthropist** [mɪˈzænθrəpɪst] n misanthrope m/f.

**misapprehension** ['mɪsæprɪˈhɛnʃən] n malentendu m, méprise f.

**misappropriate** [mɪsəˈprəuprɪeɪt] vt détourner.

**misbehave** [mɪsbɪˈheɪv] vi se conduire mal; **misbehaviour** n mauvaise conduite.

**miscalculate** [mɪsˈkælkjuleɪt] vt mal calculer; **miscalculation** [-ˈleɪʃən] n erreur f de calcul.

**miscarriage** ['mɪskærɪdʒ] n (MED) fausse couche; ~ of justice erreur f judiciaire.

**miscellaneous** [mɪsɪˈleɪnɪəs] a (items) divers(es); (selection) varié(e).

**miscellany** [mɪˈsɛlənɪ] n recueil m.

**mischance** [mɪsˈtʃɑːns] n malchance f.

**mischief** ['mɪstʃɪf] n (naughtiness) sottises fpl; (harm) mal m, dommage m; (maliciousness) méchanceté f; **mischievous** a (naughty) coquin(e), espiègle; (harmful) méchant(e).

**misconception** ['mɪskənˈsɛpʃən] n idée fausse.

**misconduct** [mɪsˈkɔndʌkt] n inconduite f; **professional** ~ faute professionnelle.

**misconstrue** [mɪskənˈstruː] vt mal interpréter.

**miscount** [mɪsˈkaunt] vt,vi mal compter.

**misdemeanour, misdemeanor** (US) [mɪsdɪˈmiːnə*] n écart m de conduite; infraction f.

**misdirect** [mɪsdɪˈrɛkt] vt (person) mal renseigner; (letter) mal adresser.

**miser** ['maɪzə*] n avare m/f.

**miserable** ['mɪzərəbl] a malheureux(euse); (wretched) misérable.

**miserly** ['maɪzəlɪ] a avare.

**misery** ['mɪzərɪ] n (unhappiness) tristesse f; (pain) souffrances fpl; (wretchedness) misère f.

**misfire** [mɪsˈfaɪə*] vi rater; (car engine) avoir des ratés.

**misfit** ['mɪsfɪt] n (person) inadapté/e.

**misfortune** [mɪsˈfɔːtʃən] n malchance f, malheur m.

**misgiving(s)** [mɪsˈgɪvɪŋ(z)] n(pl) craintes fpl, soupçons mpl.

**misguided** [mɪsˈgaɪdɪd] a malavisé(e).

**mishandle** [mɪsˈhændl] vt (treat roughly) malmener; (mismanage) mal s'y prendre pour faire or résoudre etc.

**mishap** ['mɪshæp] n mésaventure f.

**mishear** [mɪsˈhɪə*] vt irg mal entendre.

**misinform** [mɪsɪnˈfɔːm] vt mal renseigner.

**misinterpret** [mɪsɪnˈtəːprɪt] vt mal interpréter; ~ation [-ˈteɪʃən] n interprétation erronée, contresens m.

**misjudge** [mɪsˈdʒʌdʒ] vt méjuger, se méprendre sur le compte de.

**mislay** [mɪsˈleɪ] vt irg égarer.

**mislead** [mɪsˈliːd] vt irg induire en erreur; ~ing a trompeur(euse).

**mismanage** [mɪsˈmænɪdʒ] vt mal gérer; mal s'y prendre pour faire or résoudre etc; ~ment n mauvaise gestion.

**misnomer** [mɪsˈnəumə*] n terme or qualificatif trompeur or peu approprié.

**misogynist** [mɪˈsɔdʒɪnɪst] n misogyne m/f.

**misplace** [mɪsˈpleɪs] vt égarer.

**misprint** ['mɪsprɪnt] n faute f d'impression.

**mispronounce** [mɪsprəˈnauns] vt mal prononcer.

**misread** [mɪsˈriːd] vt irg mal lire.

**misrepresent** [mɪsrɛprɪˈzɛnt] vt présenter sous un faux jour.

**miss** [mɪs] vt (fail to get) manquer, rater; (regret the absence of): I ~ him/it il/cela me manque // vi manquer // n (shot) coup manqué; (fig): that was a near ~ il s'en est fallu de peu; to ~ out vt oublier.

**Miss** [mɪs] n Mademoiselle.

**missal** ['mɪsl] n missel m.

**misshapen** [mɪsˈʃeɪpən] a difforme.

**missile** ['mɪsaɪl] n (AVIAT) missile m; (object thrown) projectile m.

**missing** ['mɪsɪŋ] a manquant(e); (after escape, disaster: person) disparu(e); to go ~ disparaître.

**mission** ['mɪʃən] n mission f; ~ary n missionnaire m/f.

**missive** ['mɪsɪv] n missive f.

**misspent** ['mɪsˈspɛnt] a: his ~ youth sa folle jeunesse.

**mist** [mɪst] n brume f, brouillard m // vi (also: ~ over, ~ up) devenir brumeux(euse); (windows) s'embuer.

**mistake** [mɪsˈteɪk] n erreur f, faute f // vt (irg: like take) mal comprendre; se méprendre sur; to make a ~ se tromper, faire une erreur; to ~ for prendre pour; ~n a (idea etc) erroné(e); to be ~n faire erreur, se tromper; ~n identity n erreur f d'identité.

**mister** ['mɪstə*] n (col) Monsieur m; see **Mr**.

**mistletoe** ['mɪsltəu] n gui m.
**mistook** [mɪs'tuk] pt of **mistake**.
**mistranslation** [mɪstræns'leɪʃən] n
erreur f de traduction, contresens m.
**mistreat** [mɪs'triːt] vt maltraiter.
**mistress** ['mɪstrɪs] n (also: lover)
maîtresse f; (in primary school) institutrice
f; see **Mrs**.
**mistrust** [mɪs'trʌst] vt se méfier de.
**misty** ['mɪstɪ] a brumeux(euse).
**misunderstand** [mɪsʌndə'stænd] vt, vi
irg mal comprendre; ~ing n méprise f,
malentendu m.
**misuse** n [mɪs'juːs] mauvais emploi; (of
power) abus m // vt [mɪs'juːz] mal
employer; abuser de.
**mitigate** ['mɪtɪgeɪt] vt atténuer.
**mitre, miter** (US) ['maɪtə*] n mitre f;
(CARPENTRY) onglet m.
**mitt(en)** ['mɪt(n)] n mitaine f; moufle f.
**mix** [mɪks] vt mélanger // vi se mélanger
// n mélange m; dosage m; **to ~ up** vt
mélanger; (confuse) confondre; ~**ed** a
(assorted) assortis(ies); (school etc) mixte;
~**ed grill** n assortiment m de grillades;
~**ed-up** a (confused) désorienté(e),
embrouillé(e); ~**er** n (for food) batteur m,
mixeur m; (person): **he is a good** ~**er** il
est très liant; ~**ture** n assortiment m,
mélange m; (MED) préparation f; ~**-up** n
confusion f.
**moan** [məun] n gémissement m // vi
gémir; (col: complain): **to** ~ **(about)** se
plaindre (de); ~**ing** n gémissements mpl.
**moat** [məut] n fossé m, douves fpl.
**mob** [mɔb] n foule f; (disorderly) cohue f;
(pej): **the** ~ la populace // vt assaillir.
**mobile** ['məubaɪl] a mobile // n mobile m;
~ **home** n caravane f.
**mobility** [məu'bɪlɪtɪ] n mobilité f.
**moccasin** ['mɔkəsɪn] n mocassin m.
**mock** [mɔk] vt ridiculiser, se moquer de
// a faux(fausse); ~**ery** n moquerie f,
raillerie f; ~**ing** a moqueur(euse);
~**ingbird** n moqueur m; ~**-up** n maquette
f.
**mod** [mɔd] a see **convenience**.
**mode** [məud] n mode m.
**model** ['mɔdl] n modèle m; (person: for
fashion) mannequin m; (: for artist) modèle
// vt modeler // vi travailler comme
mannequin // a (railway: toy) modèle
réduit inv; (child, factory) modèle; **to** ~
**clothes** présenter des vêtements; ~**ler**,
~**er** (US) n modeleur m; (~ maker)
maquettiste m/f; fabricant m de modèles
réduits.
**moderate** a,n ['mɔdərət] a modéré(e) //
n (POL) modéré/e // vb ['mɔdəreɪt] vi se
modérer, se calmer // vt modérer;
**moderation** [-'reɪʃən] n modération f,
mesure f; **in moderation** à dose
raisonnable, pris(e) or pratiqué(e)
modérément.
**modern** ['mɔdən] a moderne; ~**ize** vt
moderniser.
**modest** ['mɔdɪst] a modeste; ~**y** n
modestie f.
**modicum** ['mɔdɪkəm] n: **a** ~ **of** un
minimum de.

**modification** [mɔdɪfɪ'keɪʃən] n
modification f.
**modify** ['mɔdɪfaɪ] vt modifier.
**modulation** [mɔdju'leɪʃən] n modulation
f.
**module** ['mɔdjuːl] n module m.
**mohair** ['məuhɛə*] n mohair m.
**moist** [mɔɪst] a humide, moite; ~**en**
['mɔɪsn] vt humecter, mouiller
légèrement; ~**ure** ['mɔɪstʃə*] n humidité
f; (on glass) buée f; ~**urizer**
['mɔɪstʃəraɪzə*] n produit hydratant.
**molar** ['məulə*] n molaire f.
**molasses** [məu'læsɪz] n mélasse f.
**mold** [məuld] n, vt (US) = **mould**.
**mole** [məul] n (animal) taupe f; (spot)
grain m de beauté.
**molecule** ['mɔlɪkjuːl] n molécule f.
**molehill** ['məulhɪl] n taupinière f.
**molest** [məu'lɛst] vt tracasser; molester.
**mollusc** ['mɔləsk] n mollusque m.
**mollycoddle** ['mɔlɪkɔdl] vt chouchouter,
couver.
**molt** [meult] vi (US) = **moult**.
**molten** ['meultən] a fondu(e).
**moment** ['məumənt] n moment m, instant
m; importance f; ~**ary** a momentané(e),
passager(ère); ~**ous** [-'mɛntəs] a
important(e), capital(e).
**momentum** [məu'mɛntəm] n élan m,
vitesse acquise; **to gather** ~ prendre de
la vitesse.
**monarch** ['mɔnək] n monarque m; ~**ist**
n monarchiste m/f; ~**y** n monarchie f.
**monastery** ['mɔnəstərɪ] n monastère m.
**monastic** [mə'næstɪk] a monastique.
**Monday** ['mʌndɪ] n lundi m.
**monetary** ['mʌnɪtərɪ] a monétaire.
**money** ['mʌnɪ] n argent m; **to make** ~
gagner de l'argent; faire des bénéfices;
rapporter; **danger** ~ prime f de risque;
~**ed** a riche; ~**lender** n prêteur/euse; ~
**order** n mandat m.
**mongol** ['mɔŋgəl] a,n (MED) mongolien(ne).
**mongoose** ['mɔŋguːs] n mangouste f.
**mongrel** ['mʌŋgrəl] n (dog) bâtard m.
**monitor** ['mɔnɪtə*] n (SCOL) chef m de
classe; (also: **television** ~) moniteur m //
vt contrôler.
**monk** [mʌŋk] n moine m.
**monkey** ['mʌŋkɪ] n singe m; ~ **nut** n
cacahuète f; ~ **wrench** n clé f à molette.
**mono...** ['mɔnəu] prefix: ~**chrome** a
monochrome.
**monocle** ['mɔnəkl] n monocle m.
**monogram** ['mɔnəgræm] n monogramme
m.
**monologue** ['mɔnəlɔg] n monologue m.
**monopolize** [mə'nɔpəlaɪz] vt monopoliser.
**monopoly** [mə'nɔpəlɪ] n monopole m.
**monorail** ['mɔnəureɪl] n monorail m.
**monosyllabic** [mɔnəusɪ'læbɪk] a
monosyllabique; (person) laconique.
**monotone** ['mɔnətəun] n ton m (or voix
f) monocorde.
**monotonous** [mə'nɔtənəs] a monotone.
**monotony** [mə'nɔtənɪ] n monotonie f.
**monsoon** [mɔn'suːn] n mousson f.
**monster** ['mɔnstə*] n monstre m.

**monstrosity** [mɔns'trɔsiti] n monstruosité f, atrocité f.

**monstrous** ['mɔnstrəs] a (huge) gigantesque ; (atrocious) monstrueux(euse), atroce.

**montage** [mɔn'tɑ:ʒ] n montage m.

**month** [mʌnθ] n mois m; ∼ly a mensuel(le) // ad mensuellement // n (magazine) mensuel m, publication mensuelle.

**monument** ['mɔnjumənt] n monument m; ∼al [-'mɛntl] a monumental(e) ; ∼al mason n marbrier m.

**moo** [mu:] vi meugler, beugler.

**mood** [mu:d] n humeur f, disposition f; **to be in a good/bad** ∼ être de bonne/mauvaise humeur ; **to be in the** ∼ **for** être d'humeur à, avoir envie de ; ∼y a (variable) d'humeur changeante, lunatique ; (sullen) morose, maussade.

**moon** [mu:n] n lune f; ∼beam n rayon m de lune ; ∼light n clair m de lune ; ∼lit a éclairé(e) par la lune.

**moor** [muə*] n lande f // vt (ship) amarrer // vi mouiller.

**Moor** [muə*] n Maure/Mauresque.

**moorings** ['muəriŋz] npl (chains) amarres fpl ; (place) mouillage m.

**Moorish** ['muəriʃ] a maure (mauresque).

**moorland** ['muələnd] n lande f.

**moose** [mu:s] n, pl inv élan m.

**moot** [mu:t] vt soulever // a: ∼ **point** point m discutable.

**mop** [mɔp] n balai m à laver // vt éponger, essuyer ; **to** ∼ **up** vt éponger ; ∼ **of hair** n tignasse f.

**mope** [məup] vi avoir le cafard, se morfondre.

**moped** ['məupɛd] n (Brit) cyclomoteur m.

**moquette** [mɔ'kɛt] n moquette f.

**moral** ['mɔrl] a moral(e) // n morale f; ∼s npl moralité f.

**morale** [mɔ'rɑ:l] n moral m.

**morality** [mə'ræliti] n moralité f.

**morally** ['mɔrəli] ad moralement.

**morass** [mə'ræs] n marais m, marécage m.

**morbid** ['mɔ:bid] a morbide.

**more** [mɔ:*] det plus de, davantage de // ad plus ; ∼ **people** plus de gens ; **I want** ∼ j'en veux plus or davantage ; ∼ **dangerous than** plus dangereux que ; ∼ **or less** plus ou moins ; ∼ **than ever** plus que jamais.

**moreover** [mɔ:'rəuvə*] ad de plus.

**morgue** [mɔ:g] n morgue f.

**moribund** ['mɔribʌnd] a moribond(e).

**morning** ['mɔ:niŋ] n matin m; matinée f; **in the** ∼ le matin ; **7 o'clock in the** ∼ 7 heures du matin ; ∼ **sickness** n nausées matinales.

**Moroccan** [mə'rɔkən] a marocain(e) // n Marocain/e.

**Morocco** [mə'rɔkəu] n Maroc m.

**moron** ['mɔ:rɔn] n idiot/e, minus m/f; ∼ic [mə'rɔnik] a idiot(e), imbécile.

**morose** [mə'rəus] a morose, maussade.

**morphine** ['mɔ:fi:n] n morphine f.

**Morse** [mɔ:s] n (also: ∼ **code**) morse m.

**morsel** ['mɔ:sl] n bouchée f.

**mortal** ['mɔ:tl] a, n mortel(le) ; ∼ity [-'tæliti] n mortalité f.

**mortar** ['mɔ:tə*] n mortier m.

**mortgage** ['mɔ:gidʒ] n hypothèque f; (loan) prêt m (or crédit m) hypothécaire // vt hypothéquer.

**mortified** ['mɔ:tifaid] a mortifié(e).

**mortuary** ['mɔ:tjuəri] n morgue f.

**mosaic** [məu'zeiik] n mosaïque f.

**Moscow** ['mɔskəu] n Moscou.

**Moslem** ['mɔzləm] a, n = **Muslim**.

**mosque** [mɔsk] n mosquée f.

**mosquito**, ∼**es** [mɔs'ki:təu] n moustique m; ∼ **net** n moustiquaire f.

**moss** [mɔs] n mousse f; ∼y a moussu(e).

**most** [məust] det la plupart de ; le plus de // pronoun la plupart // ad le plus ; (very) très, extrêmement ; **the** ∼ (also: + adjective) le plus ; ∼ **fish** la plupart des poissons ; ∼ **of** la plus grande partie de ; **I saw** ∼ j'en ai vu la plupart ; c'est moi qui en ai vu le plus ; **at the (very)** ∼ au plus ; **to make the** ∼ **of** profiter au maximum de ; ∼**ly** ad surtout, principalement.

**MOT** n (abbr of Ministry of Transport): **the** ∼ **(test)** la visite technique (annuelle) obligatoire des véhicules à moteur.

**motel** [məu'tɛl] n motel m.

**moth** [mɔθ] n papillon m de nuit ; mite f; ∼**ball** n boule f de naphtaline ; ∼**-eaten** a mité(e).

**mother** ['mʌðə*] n mère f // vt (care for) dorloter ; ∼**hood** n maternité f; ∼**-in-law** n belle-mère f; ∼**ly** a maternel(le) ; ∼**-of-pearl** n nacre f; ∼**-to-be** n future maman ; ∼ **tongue** n langue maternelle.

**mothproof** ['mɔθpru:f] a traité(e) à l'antimite.

**motif** [məu'ti:f] n motif m.

**motion** ['məuʃən] n mouvement m; (gesture) geste m ; (at meeting) motion f // vt, vi: **to** ∼ **(to) sb to do** faire signe à qn de faire ; ∼**less** a immobile, sans mouvement ; ∼ **picture** n film m.

**motivated** ['məutiveitid] a motivé(e).

**motivation** [məuti'veiʃən] n motivation f.

**motive** ['məutiv] n motif m, mobile m // a moteur(trice).

**motley** ['mɔtli] a hétéroclite ; bigarré(e), bariolé(e).

**motor** ['məutə*] n moteur m; (col: vehicle) auto f // a moteur(trice) ; ∼**bike** n moto f; ∼**boat** n bateau m à moteur ; ∼**car** n automobile f; ∼**cycle** n vélomoteur m; ∼**cyclist** n motocycliste m/f; ∼**ing** n tourisme m automobile // a: ∼**ing accident** n accident m de voiture ; ∼**ing holiday** n vacances fpl en voiture ; ∼**ist** n automobiliste m/f; ∼ **oil** n huile f de graissage ; ∼ **racing** n course f automobile ; ∼ **scooter** n scooter m; ∼ **vehicle** n véhicule m automobile ; ∼**way** n (Brit) autoroute f.

**mottled** ['mɔtld] a tacheté(e), marbré(e).

**motto**, ∼**es** ['mɔtəu] n devise f.

**mould, mold** (US) [məuld] n moule m; (mildew) moisissure f // vt mouler, modeler ; (fig) façonner ; ∼**er** vi (decay) moisir ; ∼**ing** n (in plaster) moulage m, moulure f; (in wood) moulure; ~y a moisi(e).

**moult, molt** (US) [məult] vi muer.

**mound** [maund] n monticule m, tertre m.

**mount** [maunt] n mont m, montagne f; (horse) monture f; (for jewel etc) monture // vt monter // vi (also: ~ up) s'élever, monter.

**mountain** ['mauntɪn] n montagne f // cpd de (la) montagne; ~eer [-'nɪə*] n alpiniste m/f; ~eering [-'nɪərɪŋ] n alpinisme m; to go ~eering faire de l'alpinisme; ~ous a montagneux(euse); (very big) gigantesque; ~ side n flanc m or versant m de la montagne.

**mourn** [mɔ:n] vt pleurer // vi: to ~ (for) se lamenter (sur); ~er n parent/e or ami/e du défunt; personne f en deuil or venue rendre hommage au défunt; ~ful a triste, lugubre; ~ing n deuil m // cpd (dress) de deuil; in ~ing en deuil.

**mouse**, pl mice [maus, maɪs] n souris f; ~trap n souricière f.

**moustache** [məs'tɑ:ʃ] n moustache(s) f(pl).

**mousy** ['mausɪ] a (person) effacé(e); (hair) d'un châtain terne.

**mouth**, ~s [mauθ, -ðz] n bouche f; (of dog, cat) gueule f; (of river) embouchure f; (of bottle) goulot m; (opening) orifice m; ~ful n bouchée f; ~ organ n harmonica m; ~piece n (of musical instrument) embouchure f; (spokesman) porte-parole m inv; ~wash n bain m de bouche; ~-watering a qui met l'eau à la bouche.

**movable** ['mu:vəbl] a mobile.

**move** [mu:v] n (movement) mouvement m; (in game) coup m; (: turn to play) tour m; (change of house) déménagement m // vt déplacer. bouger; (emotionally) émouvoir; (POL: resolution etc) proposer // vi (gen) bouger, remuer; (traffic) circuler; (also: ~ house) déménager; to ~ towards se diriger vers; to ~ sb to do sth pousser or inciter qn à faire qch; to get a ~ on se dépêcher, se remuer; to ~ about vi (fidget) remuer; (travel) voyager, se déplacer; to ~ along vi se pousser; to ~ away vi s'en aller, s'éloigner; to ~ back vi revenir, retourner; to ~ forward vi avancer // vt avancer; (people) faire avancer; to ~ in vi (to a house) emménager; to ~ on vi se remettre en route // vt (onlookers) faire circuler; to ~ out vi (of house) déménager; to ~ up vi avancer; (employee) avoir de l'avancement.

**movement** ['mu:vmənt] n mouvement m.

**movie** ['mu:vɪ] n film m; the ~s le cinéma; ~ camera n caméra f.

**moving** ['mu:vɪŋ] a en mouvement; émouvant(e).

**mow**, pt mowed, pp mowed or mown [məu, -n] vt faucher; (lawn) tondre; to ~ down vt faucher; ~er n faucheur/euse.

**M.P.** n abbr see **member**.

**m.p.g.** abbr = miles per gallon (30 m.p.g. = 29.5 l. aux 100 km).

**m.p.h.** abbr = miles per hour (60 m.p.h. = 96 km/h).

**Mr** ['mɪstə*] n: ~ X Monsieur X, M. X.

**Mrs** ['mɪsɪz] n: ~ X Madame X, Mme X.

**Ms** [mɪz] n (= Miss or Mrs): ~ X ≈ Madame X, Mme X.

**M.Sc.** abbr see **master**.

**much** [mʌtʃ] det beaucoup de // ad, n or pronoun beaucoup; ~ milk beaucoup de lait; how ~ is it? combien est-ce que ça coûte?; it's not ~ ce n'est pas beaucoup.

**muck** [mʌk] n (mud) boue f; (dirt) ordures fpl; to ~ about vi (col) faire l'imbécile; (waste time) traînasser; to ~ up vt (col: ruin) gâcher, esquinter; ~y a (dirty) boueux(euse), sale.

**mucus** ['mju:kəs] n mucus m.

**mud** [mʌd] n boue f.

**muddle** ['mʌdl] n pagaille f; désordre m, fouillis m // vt (also: ~ up) brouiller, embrouiller; to be in a ~ (person) ne plus savoir ou l'on en est; to get in a ~ (while explaining etc) s'embrouiller; to ~ through vi se débrouiller.

**mud:** ~dy a boueux(euse); ~ flats npl plage f de vase; ~guard n garde-boue m inv; ~pack n masque m de beauté; ~-slinging n médisance f, dénigrement m.

**muff** [mʌf] n manchon m.

**muffin** ['mʌfɪn] n petit pain rond et plat.

**muffle** ['mʌfl] vt (sound) assourdir, étouffer; (against cold) emmitoufler; ~d a étouffé(e), voilé(e).

**mufti** ['mʌftɪ] n: in ~ en civil.

**mug** [mʌg] n (cup) tasse f (sans soucoupe); (: for beer) chope f; (col: face) bouille f; (: fool) poire f // vt (assault) agresser; ~ging n agression f.

**muggy** ['mʌgɪ] a lourd(e), moite.

**mulatto**, ~es [mju'lætəu] n mulâtre/sse.

**mule** [mju:l] n mule f.

**mull** [mʌl]: to ~ over vt réfléchir à, ruminer.

**mulled** [mʌld] a: ~ wine vin chaud.

**multi...** ['mʌltɪ] prefix multi...; ~coloured, ~colored (US) a multicolore.

**multifarious** [mʌltɪ'fɛərɪəs] a divers(es); varié(e).

**multiple** ['mʌltɪpl] a, n multiple (m); ~ crash n carambolage m; ~ sclerosis n sclérose f en plaques; ~ store n grand magasin (à succursales multiples).

**multiplication** [mʌltɪplɪ'keɪʃən] n multiplication f.

**multiply** ['mʌltɪplaɪ] vt multiplier // vi se multiplier.

**multitude** ['mʌltɪtju:d] n multitude f.

**mum** [mʌm] n maman f // a: to keep ~ ne pas souffler mot; ~'s the word! motus et bouche cousue!

**mumble** ['mʌmbl] vt, vi marmotter, marmonner.

**mummy** ['mʌmɪ] n (mother) maman f; (embalmed) momie f.

**mumps** [mʌmps] n oreillons mpl.

**munch** [mʌntʃ] vt,vi mâcher.

**mundane** [mʌn'deɪn] a banal(e), terre à terre inv.

**municipal** [mju:'nɪsɪpl] a municipal(e); ~ity [-'pælɪtɪ] n municipalité f.

**munitions** [mju:'nɪʃənz] npl munitions fpl.

**mural** ['mjuərl] n peinture murale.

**murder** ['mə:də*] n meurtre m, assassinat m // vt assassiner; ~er n meurtrier m, assassin *m* ; ~**ess** *n* meurtrière *f* ; ~**ous** a meurtrier(ère).

**murk** [mə:k] *n* obscurité *f* ; ~**y** *a* sombre, ténébreux(euse).

**murmur** ['mə:mə*] *n* murmure *m* // *vt, vi* murmurer.

**muscle** ['mʌsl] *n* muscle *m* ; **to ~ in** *vi* s'imposer, s'immiscer.

**muscular** ['mʌskjulə*] *a* musculaire ; (*person, arm*) musclé(e).

**muse** [mju:z] *vi* méditer, songer // *n* muse *f*.

**museum** [mju:'zɪəm] *n* musée *m*.

**mushroom** ['mʌʃrum] *n* champignon *m* // *vi* (*fig*) pousser comme un (*or* des) champignon(s).

**mushy** ['mʌʃɪ] *a* en bouillie ; (*pej*) à l'eau de rose.

**music** ['mju:zɪk] *n* musique *f* ; ~**al** *a* musical(e) ; (*person*) musicien(ne) // *n* (*show*) comédie musicale ; ~**al box** *n* boîte *f* à musique ; ~**al instrument** *n* instrument *m* de musique ; ~ **hall** *n* music-hall *m* ; ~**ian** [-'zɪʃən] *n* musicien/ne ; ~ **stand** *n* pupitre *m* à musique.

**musket** ['mʌskɪt] *n* mousquet *m*.

**Muslim** ['mʌzlɪm] *a, n* musulman(e).

**muslin** ['mʌzlɪn] *n* mousseline *f*.

**musquash** ['mʌskwɔʃ] *n* loutre *f*.

**mussel** ['mʌsl] *n* moule *f*.

**must** [mʌst] *auxiliary vb* (*obligation*): **I ~ do it** je dois le faire, il faut que je le fasse ; (*probability*): **he ~ be there by now** il doit y être maintenant, il y est probablement maintenant, **I ~ have made a mistake** j'ai dû me tromper // *n* nécessité *f*, impératif *m*.

**mustard** ['mʌstəd] *n* moutarde *f*.

**muster** ['mʌstə*] *vt* rassembler.

**mustn't** ['mʌsnt] = **must not**.

**musty** ['mʌstɪ] *a* qui sent le moisi *or* le renfermé.

**mute** [mju:t] *a, n* muet(te).

**muted** ['mju:tɪd] *a* assourdi(e) ; voilé(e) ; (*MUS*) en sourdine ; (: *trumpet*) bouché(e).

**mutilate** ['mju:tɪleɪt] *vt* mutiler ; **mutilation** [-'leɪʃən] *n* mutilation *f*.

**mutinous** ['mju:tɪnəs] *a* (*troops*) mutiné(e) ; (*attitude*) rebelle.

**mutiny** ['mju:tɪnɪ] *n* mutinerie *f* // *vi* se mutiner.

**mutter** ['mʌtə*] *vt, vi* marmonner, marmotter.

**mutton** ['mʌtn] *n* mouton *m*.

**mutual** ['mju:tʃuəl] *a* mutuel(le), réciproque ; ~**ly** *ad* mutuellement, réciproquement.

**muzzle** ['mʌzl] *n* museau *m* ; (*protective device*) muselière *f* ; (*of gun*) gueule *f* // *vt* museler.

**my** [maɪ] *a* mon(ma), mes *pl*.

**myopic** [maɪ'ɔpɪk] *a* myope.

**myself** [maɪ'sɛlf] *pronoun* (*reflexive*) me ; (*emphatic*) moi-même ; (*after prep*) moi.

**mysterious** [mɪs'tɪərɪəs] *a* mystérieux(euse).

**mystery** ['mɪstərɪ] *n* mystère *m* ; ~ **story** *n* roman *m* à suspense.

**mystic** ['mɪstɪk] *n* mystique *m/f* // *a* (*mysterious*) ésotérique ; ~**al** *a* mystique.

**mystify** ['mɪstɪfaɪ] *vt* mystifier ; (*puzzle*) ébahir.

**mystique** [mɪs'ti:k] *n* mystique *f*.

**myth** [mɪθ] *n* mythe *m* ; ~**ical** *a* mythique ; ~**ological** [mɪθə'lɔdʒɪkl] *a* mythologique ; ~**ology** [mɪ'θɔlədʒɪ] *n* mythologie *f*.

# N

**nab** [næb] *vt* pincer, attraper.

**nag** [næg] *n* (*pej: horse*) canasson *m* // *vt* (*person*) être toujours après, reprendre sans arrêt ; ~**ging** *a* (*doubt, pain*) persistant(e) // *n* remarques continuelles.

**nail** [neɪl] *n* (*human*) ongle *m* ; (*metal*) clou *m* // *vt* clouer ; **to ~ sb down to a date/price** contraindre qn à accepter *or* donner une date/un prix ; ~**brush** *n* brosse *f* à ongles ; ~**file** *n* lime *f* à ongles ; ~ **polish** *n* vernis *m* à ongles ; ~ **scissors** *npl* ciseaux *mpl* à ongles.

**naïve** [naɪ'i:v] *a* naïf(ive).

**naked** ['neɪkɪd] *a* nu(e) ; ~**ness** *n* nudité *f*.

**name** [neɪm] *n* nom *m* ; réputation *f* // *vt* nommer ; citer ; (*price, date*) fixer, donner ; **in the ~ of** au nom de ; ~ **dropping** *n* mention *f* (*pour se faire valoir*) du nom de personnalités qu'on connaît (*ou* prétend connaître) ; ~**less** *a* sans nom ; (*witness, contributor*) anonyme ; ~**ly** *ad* à savoir ; ~**sake** *n* homonyme *m*.

**nanny** ['nænɪ] *n* bonne *f* d'enfants ; ~ **goat** *n* chèvre *f*.

**nap** [næp] *n* (*sleep*) (petit) somme ; **to be caught** ~**ping** être pris à l'improviste *or* en défaut.

**napalm** ['neɪpɑ:m] *n* napalm *m*.

**nape** [neɪp] *n* : ~ **of the neck** nuque *f*.

**napkin** ['næpkɪn] *n* serviette *f* (de table) ; (*Brit: for baby*) couche *f* (*gen pl*).

**nappy** ['næpɪ] *n* couche *f* (*gen pl*).

**narcissus**, *pl* **narcissi** [nɑ:'sɪsəs, -saɪ] *n* narcisse *m*.

**narcotic** [nɑ:'kɔtɪk] *n* (*drug*) stupéfiant *m* ; (*MED*) narcotique *m*.

**nark** [nɑ:k] *vt* mettre en rogne.

**narrate** [nə'reɪt] *vt* raconter, narrer.

**narrative** ['nærətɪv] *n* récit *m* // *a* narratif(ive).

**narrator** [nə'reɪtə*] *n* narrateur/trice.

**narrow** ['nærəu] *a* étroit(e) ; (*fig*) restreint(e), limité(e) // *vi* devenir plus étroit, se rétrécir ; **to have a ~ escape** l'échapper belle ; **to ~ sth down to** réduire qch à ; ~ **gauge** *a* à voie étroite ; ~**ly** *ad*: **he ~ly missed injury/the tree** il a failli se blesser/rentrer dans l'arbre ; **he only ~ly missed the target** il a manqué la cible de peu *or* de justesse ; ~-**minded** *a* à l'esprit étroit, borné(e).

**nasal** ['neɪzl] *a* nasal(e).

**nastily** ['nɑ:stɪlɪ] *ad* (*say, act*) méchamment.

**nastiness** ['nɑ:stɪnɪs] *n* (*of remark*) méchanceté *f*.

**nasty** ['nɑ:stɪ] *a* (*person*) méchant(e) ; très désagréable ; (*smell*) dégoûtant(e) ; (*wound, situation*) mauvais(e), vilain(e) ; **it's a ~ business** c'est une sale affaire.

**nation** ['neɪʃən] *n* nation *f*.

**national** ['næʃənl] *a* national(e) // *n* (*abroad*) ressortissant/e ; (*when home*) national/e ; ~ **dress** *n* costume national ; ~**ism** *n* nationalisme *m* ; ~**ist** *a,n* nationaliste (*m/f*) ; ~**ity** [-'nælɪtɪ] *n* nationalité *f* ; ~**ization** [-aɪ'zeɪʃən] *n* nationalisation *f* ; ~**ize** *vt* nationaliser ; ~**ly** *ad* du point de vue national ; dans le pays entier ; ~ **park** *n* parc national.

**nation-wide** ['neɪʃənwaɪd] *a* s'étendant à l'ensemble du pays ; (*problem*) à l'échelle du pays entier // *ad* à travers *or* dans tout le pays.

**native** ['neɪtɪv] *n* habitant/e du pays, autochtone *m/f* ; (*in colonies*) indigène *m/f* // *a* du pays, indigène ; (*country*) natal(e) ; (*language*) maternel(le) ; (*ability*) inné(e) ; **a** ~ **of Russia** une personne originaire de Russie ; **a** ~ **speaker of French** une personne de langue maternelle française.

**NATO** ['neɪtəu] *n* (*abbr of North Atlantic Treaty Organization*) O.T.A.N.

**natter** ['nætə*] *vi* bavarder.

**natural** ['nætʃrəl] *a* naturel(le) ; ~ **gas** *n* gaz naturel ; ~**ist** *n* naturaliste *m/f* ; ~**ize** *vt* naturaliser ; (*plant*) acclimater ; ~**ly** *ad* naturellement ; ~**ness** *n* naturel *m*.

**nature** ['neɪtʃə*] *n* nature *f* ; **by** ~ par tempérament, de nature.

**naught** [nɔ:t] *n* zéro *m*.

**naughty** ['nɔ:tɪ] *a* (*child*) vilain(e), pas sage ; (*story, film*) polisson(ne).

**nausea** ['nɔ:sɪə] *n* nausée *f* ; ~**te** ['nɔ:sɪeɪt] *vt* écœurer, donner la nausée à.

**nautical** ['nɔ:tɪkl] *a* nautique ; ~ **mile** *n* mille marin (= *1853 m*).

**naval** ['neɪvl] *a* naval(e) ; ~ **officer** *n* officier *m* de marine.

**nave** [neɪv] *n* nef *f*.

**navel** ['neɪvl] *n* nombril *m*.

**navigable** ['nævɪgəbl] *a* navigable.

**navigate** ['nævɪgeɪt] *vt* diriger, piloter // *vi* naviguer ; **navigation** [-'geɪʃən] *n* navigation *f* ; **navigator** *n* navigateur *m*.

**navvy** ['nævɪ] *n* terrassier *m*.

**navy** ['neɪvɪ] *n* marine *f* ; ~**-(blue)** *a* bleu marine *inv*.

**neap** [ni:p] *n* (*also*: ~**tide**) mortes- eaux *fpl*.

**near** [nɪə*] *a* proche // *ad* près // *prep* (*also*: ~ **to**) près de // *vt* approcher de ; **to come** ~ *vi* s'approcher ; ~**by** [nɪə'baɪ] *a* proche // *ad* tout près, à proximité ; **N~ East** *n* Proche-Orient *m* ; ~**er** *a* plus proche // *ad* plus près ; ~**ly** *ad* presque ; **I** ~**ly fell** j'ai failli tomber ; ~ **miss** *n* collision évitée de justesse ; (*when aiming*) coup manqué de peu *or* de justesse ; ~**ness** *n* proximité *f* ; ~**side** *n* (AUT: *right-hand drive*) côté *m* gauche ; ~**-sighted** *a* myope.

**neat** [ni:t] *a* (*person, work*) soigné(e) ; (*room etc*) bien tenu(e) *or* rangé(e) ; (*solution, plan*) habile ; (*spirits*) pur(e) ; **I drink it** ~ je le bois sec *or* sans eau ; ~**ly** *ad* avec soin *or* ordre ; habilement.

**nebulous** ['nɛbjuləs] *a* nébuleux(euse).

**necessarily** ['nɛsɪsrɪlɪ] *ad* nécessairement.

**necessary** ['nɛsɪsrɪ] *a* nécessaire.

**necessitate** [nɪ'sɛsɪteɪt] *vt* nécessiter.

**necessity** [nɪ'sɛsɪtɪ] *n* nécessité *f* ; chose nécessaire *or* essentielle.

**neck** [nɛk] *n* cou *m* ; (*of horse, garment*) encolure *f* ; (*of bottle*) goulot *m* ; ~ **and** ~ à égalité.

**necklace** ['nɛklɪs] *n* collier *m*.

**neckline** ['nɛklaɪn] *n* encolure *f*.

**necktie** ['nɛktaɪ] *n* cravate *f*.

**née** [neɪ] *a*: ~ **Scott** née Scott.

**need** [ni:d] *n* besoin *m* // *vt* avoir besoin de ; **to** ~ **to do** devoir faire ; avoir besoin de faire.

**needle** ['ni:dl] *n* aiguille *f* // *vt* asticoter, tourmenter ; ~**cord** *n* velours *m* milleraies.

**needless** ['ni:dlɪs] *a* inutile ; ~**ly** *ad* inutilement.

**needlework** ['ni:dlwə:k] *n* (*activity*) travaux *mpl* d'aiguille ; (*object*) ouvrage *m*.

**needy** ['ni:dɪ] *a* nécessiteux(euse) ; **in** ~ **circumstances** dans le besoin.

**negation** [nɪ'geɪʃən] *n* négation *f*.

**negative** ['nɛgətɪv] *n* (PHOT, ELEC) négatif *m* ; (LING) terme *m* de négation // *a* négatif(ive) ; **to answer in the** ~ répondre par la négative.

**neglect** [nɪ'glɛkt] *vt* négliger // *n* (*of person, duty, garden*) le fait de négliger ; (*state of*) ~ abandon *m*.

**negligee** ['nɛglɪʒeɪ] *n* déshabillé *m*.

**negligence** ['nɛglɪdʒəns] *n* négligence *f*.

**negligent** ['nɛglɪdʒənt] *a* négligent(e) ; ~**ly** *ad* par négligence ; (*offhandedly*) négligemment.

**negligible** ['nɛglɪdʒɪbl] *a* négligeable.

**negotiable** [nɪ'gəuʃɪəbl] *a* négociable.

**negotiate** [nɪ'gəuʃɪeɪt] *vi* négocier // *vt* (COMM) négocier ; (*obstacle*) franchir, négocier ; **negotiation** [-'eɪʃən] *n* négociation *f*, pourparlers *mpl* ; **negotiator** *n* négociateur/trice.

**Negress** ['ni:grɪs] *n* négresse *f*.

**Negro** ['ni:grəu] *a* (*gen*) noir(e) ; (*music, arts*) nègre, noir // *n* (*pl*: ~**es**) Noir/e.

**neighbour**, (US) **neighbor** ['neɪbə*] *n* voisin/e ; ~**hood** *n* quartier *m* ; voisinage *m*, ~**ing** *a* voisin(e), avoisinant(e) ; ~**ly** *a* obligeant(e) ; (*relations*) de bon voisinage.

**neither** ['naɪðə*] *a, pronoun* aucun(e) (des deux), ni l'un(e) ni l'autre // *cj*: **I didn't move and** ~ **did Claude** je n'ai pas bougé, (et) Claude non plus ; ~ ..., ~ **did I refuse** ..., (et *or* mais) je n'ai pas non plus refusé // *ad*: ~ **good nor bad** ni bon ni mauvais.

**neo...** ['ni:əu] *prefix* néo-.

**neon** ['ni:ɔn] *n* néon *m* ; ~ **light** *n* lampe *f* au néon ; ~ **sign** *n* enseigne (lumineuse) au néon.

**nephew** ['nɛvju:] *n* neveu *m*.

**nerve** [nə:v] *n* nerf *m* ; (*fig*) sang-froid *m*, courage *m* ; aplomb *m*, toupet *m* ; **he gets on my** ~**s** il m'énerve ; ~**-racking** *a* éprouvant (pour les nerfs).

**nervous** ['nə:vəs] *a* nerveux(euse) ; inquiet(ète), plein(e) d'appréhension ; ~ **breakdown** *n* dépression nerveuse ; ~**ly** *ad* nerveusement ; ~**ness** *n* nervosité *f* ; inquiétude *f*, appréhension *f*.

**nest** [nɛst] *n* nid *m* ; ~ **of tables** *n* table *f* gigogne.

**nestle** ['nɛsl] *vi* se blottir.
**net** [nɛt] *n* filet *m* // *a* net(te) ; ~**ball** *n* netball *m*.
**Netherlands** ['nɛðələndz] *npl*: the ~ les Pays-Bas *mpl*.
**nett** [nɛt] *a* = **net**.
**netting** ['nɛtɪŋ] *n* (*for fence etc*) treillis *m*, grillage *m*.
**nettle** ['nɛtl] *n* ortie *f*.
**network** ['nɛtwə:k] *n* réseau *m*.
**neurosis, pl neuroses** [njuə'rəusɪs, -si:z] *n* névrose *f*.
**neurotic** [njuə'rɔtɪk] *a*, *n* névrosé(e).
**neuter** ['nju:tə*] *a*, *n* neutre (*m*) // *vt* (*cat etc*) châtrer, couper.
**neutral** ['nju:trəl] *a* neutre // *n* (*AUT*) point mort ; ~**ity** [-'trælɪtɪ] *n* neutralité *f*.
**never** ['nɛvə*] *ad* (ne ...) jamais ; ~ **again** plus jamais ; ~**-ending** *a* interminable ; ~**theless** [nɛvəðə'lɛs] *ad* néanmoins, malgré tout.
**new** [nju:] *a* nouveau(nouvelle) ; (*brand new*) neuf(neuve) ; ~**born** *a* nouveau-né(e) ; ~**comer** ['nju:kʌmə*] *n* nouveau venu/nouvelle venue ; ~**ly** *ad* nouvellement, récemment ; ~ **moon** *n* nouvelle lune ; ~**ness** *n* nouveauté *f*.
**news** [nju:z] *n* nouvelle(s) *f(pl)* ; (*RADIO, TV*) informations *fpl* ; **a piece of** ~ une nouvelle ; ~ **agency** agence *f* de presse ; ~**agent** *n* marchand *m* de journaux ; ~ **flash** *n* flash *m* d'information ; ~**letter** *n* bulletin *m* ; ~**paper** *n* journal *m* ; ~**reel** *n* actualités (filmées) ; ~ **stand** *n* kiosque *m* à journaux.
**New Year** ['nju:'jɪə*] *n* Nouvel An ; ~**'s Day** *n* le jour de l'An ; ~**'s Eve** *n* la Saint-Sylvestre.
**New Zealand** [nju:'zi:lənd] *n* la Nouvelle-Zélande.
**next** [nɛkst] *a* (*seat, room*) voisin(e), d'à côté ; (*meeting, bus stop*) suivant(e) ; prochain(e) // *ad* la fois suivante ; la prochaine fois ; (*afterwards*) ensuite ; **when do we meet** ~? quand nous revoyons-nous? ; ~ **door** *ad* à côté ; ~**of-kin** *n* parent *m* le plus proche ; ~ **time** *ad* la prochaine fois ; ~ **to** *prep* à côté de ; ~ **to nothing** presque rien.
**N.H.S.** *n abbr of* National Health Service.
**nib** [nɪb] *n* (*of pen*) (bec *m* de) plume *f*.
**nibble** ['nɪbl] *vt* grignoter.
**nice** [naɪs] *a* (*holiday, trip*) agréable ; (*flat, picture*) joli(e) ; (*person*) gentil(le) ; (*distinction, point*) subtil(e) ; ~**-looking** *a* joli(e) ; ~**ly** *ad* agréablement ; joliment ; gentiment ; subtilement.
**niceties** ['naɪsɪtɪz] *npl* subtilités *fpl*.
**nick** [nɪk] *n* encoche *f* // *vt* (*col*) faucher, piquer ; **in the** ~ of **time** juste à temps.
**nickel** ['nɪkl] *n* nickel *m* ; (*US*) pièce *f* de 5 cents.
**nickname** ['nɪkneɪm] *n* surnom *m* // *vt* surnommer.
**nicotine** ['nɪkəti:n] *n* nicotine *f*.
**niece** [ni:s] *n* nièce *f*.
**Nigeria** [naɪ'dʒɪərɪə] *n* Nigéria *m or f* ; ~**n** *a* nigérien(ne) // *n* Nigérien/ne.
**niggardly** ['nɪgədlɪ] *a* pingre.
**niggling** ['nɪglɪŋ] *a* tatillon(ne).

**night** [naɪt] *n* nuit *f* ; (*evening*) soir *m* ; **at** ~ la nuit ; **by** ~ de nuit ; ~**cap** *n* boisson prise avant le coucher ; ~ **club** *n* boîte *f* de nuit ; ~**dress** *n* chemise *f* de nuit ; ~**fall** *n* tombée *f* de la nuit ; ~**ie** ['naɪtɪ] *n* chemise *f* de nuit.
**nightingale** ['naɪtɪŋgeɪl] *n* rossignol *m*.
**night life** ['naɪtlaɪf] *n* vie *f* nocturne.
**nightly** ['naɪtlɪ] *a* de chaque nuit *or* soir ; (*by night*) nocturne // *ad* chaque nuit *or* soir ; nuitamment.
**nightmare** ['naɪtmɛə*] *n* cauchemar *m*.
**night school** ['naɪtsku:l] *n* cours *mpl* du soir.
**night-time** ['naɪttaɪm] *n* nuit *f*.
**night watchman** ['naɪt'wɔtʃmən] *n* veilleur *m* de nuit.
**nil** [nɪl] *n* rien *m* ; (*SPORT*) zéro *m*.
**nimble** ['nɪmbl] *a* agile.
**nine** [naɪn] *num* neuf ; ~**teen** *num* dix-neuf ; ~**ty** *num* quatre-vingt-dix.
**ninth** [naɪnθ] *a* neuvième.
**nip** [nɪp] *vt* pincer // *n* pincement *m*.
**nipple** ['nɪpl] *n* (*ANAT*) mamelon *m*, bout *m* du sein.
**nippy** ['nɪpɪ] *a* (*person*) alerte, leste.
**nitrogen** ['naɪtrədʒən] *n* azote *m*.
**no** [nəu] *det* pas de, aucun(e) + *sg* // *ad*, *n* non (*m*) ; ~ **entry** défense d'entrer, entrée interdite ; ~ **dogs** les chiens ne sont pas admis.
**nobility** [nəu'bɪlɪtɪ] *n* noblesse *f*.
**noble** ['nəubl] *a* noble ; ~**man** *n* noble *m* ; **nobly** *ad* noblement.
**nobody** ['nəubədɪ] *pronoun* personne (*with negative*).
**nod** [nɔd] *vi* faire un signe de (la) tête (*affirmatif ou amical*) ; (*sleep*) somnoler // *n* signe *m* de (la) tête ; **to** ~ **off** *vi* s'assoupir.
**noise** [nɔɪz] *n* bruit *m* ; ~**less** *a* silencieux(euse) ; **noisily** *ad* bruyamment ; **noisy** *a* bruyant(e).
**nomad** ['nəumæd] *n* nomade *m/f* ; ~**ic** [-'mædɪk] *a* nomade.
**no man's land** ['nəumænzlænd] *n* no man's land *m*.
**nominal** ['nɔmɪnl] *a* (*rent, fee*) symbolique ; (*value*) nominal(e).
**nominate** ['nɔmɪneɪt] *vt* (*propose*) proposer ; (*elect*) nommer.
**nomination** [nɔmɪ'neɪʃən] *n* nomination *f*.
**nominee** [nɔmɪ'ni:] *n* candidat agréé ; personne nommée.
**non...** [nɔn] *prefix* non- ; ~**alcoholic** *a* non-alcoolisé(e) ; ~**breakable** *a* incassable ; ~**committal** ['nɔnkə'mɪtl] *a* évasif(ive) ; ~**descript** ['nɔndɪskrɪpt] *a* quelconque, indéfinissable.
**none** [nʌn] *pronoun* aucun/e ; **he's** ~ **the worse for it** il ne s'en porte pas plus mal.
**nonentity** [nɔ'nɛntɪtɪ] *n* personne insignifiante.
**non:** ~**-fiction** *n* littérature *f* non-romanesque ; ~**-flammable** *a* ininflammable.
**nonplussed** [nɔn'plʌst] *a* perplexe.
**nonsense** ['nɔnsəns] *n* absurdités *fpl*, idioties *fpl*.
**non:** ~**-smoker** *n* non-fumeur *m* ; ~**-stick** *a* qui n'attache pas ; ~**-stop** *a*

direct(e), sans arrêt (*or* escale) // *ad* sans arrêt.

**noodles** ['nu:dlz] *npl* nouilles *fpl.*

**nook** [nuk] *n*: ~s **and crannies** recoins *mpl.*

**noon** [nu:n] *n* midi *m.*

**no one** ['nəuwʌn] *pronoun* = **nobody.**

**nor** [nɔ:*] *cj* = **neither** // *ad see* **neither.**

**norm** [nɔ:m] *n* norme *f.*

**normal** ['nɔ:ml] *a* normal(e); ~**ly** *ad* normalement.

**Normandy** ['nɔ:məndɪ] *n* Normandie *f.*

**north** [nɔ:θ] *n* nord *m* // *a* du nord, nord (*inv*) // *ad* au *or* vers le nord; **N**~ **America** *n* Amérique *f* du Nord; ~**-east** *n* nord-est *m*; ~**ern** ['nɔ:ðən] *a* du nord, septentrional(e); **N**~**ern Ireland** *n* Irlande *f* du Nord; **N**~ **Pole** *n* pôle *m* Nord; **N**~ **Sea** *n* mer *f* du Nord; ~**ward(s)** ['nɔ:θwəd(z)] *ad* vers le nord; ~**-west** *n* nord-ouest *m.*

**Norway** ['nɔ:weɪ] *n* Norvège *f.*

**Norwegian** [nɔ:'wi:dʒən] *a* norvégien(ne) // *n* Norvégien/ne; (*LING*) norvégien *m.*

**nose** [nəuz] *n* nez *m*; (*fig*) flair *m*; ~**bleed** *n* saignement *m* de nez; ~**-dive** *n* (descente *f* en) piqué *m*; ~**y** *a* curieux(euse).

**nostalgia** [nɔs'tældʒɪə] *n* nostalgie *f*; **nostalgic** *a* nostalgique.

**nostril** ['nɔstrɪl] *n* narine *f*; (*of horse*) naseau *m.*

**nosy** ['nəuzɪ] *a* = **nosey.**

**not** [nɔt] *ad* (ne ...) pas; ~ **at all** pas du tout; **you must** ~ *or* **mustn't do this** tu ne dois pas faire ça; **he isn't...** il n'est pas...

**notable** ['nəutəbl] *a* notable.

**notably** ['nəutəblɪ] *ad* en particulier.

**notch** [nɔtʃ] *n* encoche *f.*

**note** [nəut] *n* note *f*; (*letter*) mot *m*; (*banknote*) billet *m* // *vt* (*also:* ~ **down**) noter; (*notice*) constater; ~**book** *n* carnet *m*; ~**-case** *n* porte-feuille *m*; ~**d** ['nəutɪd] *a* réputé(e); ~**paper** *n* papier *m* à lettres.

**nothing** ['nʌθɪŋ] *n* rien *m*; ~ **new** rien de nouveau; ~ **for** ~ (*free*) pour rien, gratuitement.

**notice** ['nəutɪs] *n* avis *m*; (*of leaving*) congé *m* // *vt* remarquer, s'apercevoir de; **to take** ~ **of** prêter attention à; **to bring sth to sb's** ~ porter qch à la connaissance de qn; **to avoid** ~ éviter de se faire remarquer; ~**able** *a* visible; ~ **board** *n* (*Brit*) panneau *m* d'affichage.

**notify** ['nəutɪfaɪ] *vt*: **to** ~ **sth to sb** notifier qch à qn; **to** ~ **sb of sth** avertir qn de qch.

**notion** ['nəuʃən] *n* idée *f*; (*concept*) notion *f.*

**notorious** [nəu'tɔ:rɪəs] *a* notoire (*souvent en mal*).

**notwithstanding** [nɔtwɪθ'stændɪŋ] *ad* néanmoins // *prep* en dépit de.

**nougat** ['nu:gɑ:] *n* nougat *m.*

**nought** [nɔ:t] *n* zéro *m.*

**noun** [naun] *n* nom *m.*

**nourish** ['nʌrɪʃ] *vt* nourrir; ~**ing** *a* nourrissant(e); ~**ment** *n* nourriture *f.*

**novel** ['nɔvl] *n* roman *m* // *a*

nouveau(nouvelle), original(e); ~**ist** *n* romancier *m*; ~**ty** *n* nouveauté *f.*

**November** [nəu'vɛmbə*] *n* novembre *m.*

**novice** ['nɔvɪs] *n* novice *m/f.*

**now** [nau] *ad* maintenant; ~ **and then,** ~ **and again** de temps en temps; **from** ~ **on** dorénavant; ~**adays** ['nauədeɪz] *ad* de nos jours.

**nowhere** ['nəuwɛə*] *ad* nulle part.

**nozzle** ['nɔzl] *n* (*of hose*) jet *m*, lance *f.*

**nuance** ['nju:ɑ:ns] *n* nuance *f.*

**nuclear** ['nju:klɪə*] *a* nucléaire.

**nucleus**, *pl* **nuclei** ['nju:klɪəs, 'nju:klɪaɪ] *n* noyau *m.*

**nude** [nju:d] *a* nu(e) // *n* (*ART*) nu *m*; **in the** ~ (tout(e)) nu(e).

**nudge** [nʌdʒ] *vt* donner un (petit) coup de coude à.

**nudist** ['nju:dɪst] *n* nudiste *m/f.*

**nudity** ['nju:dɪtɪ] *n* nudité *f.*

**nuisance** ['nju:sns] *n*: **it's a** ~ c'est (très) ennuyeux *or* gênant; **he's a** ~ il est assommant *or* casse-pieds.

**null** [nʌl] *a*: ~ **and void** nul(le) et non avenu(e); ~**ify** ['nʌlɪfaɪ] *vt* invalider.

**numb** [nʌm] *a* engourdi(e) // *vt* engourdir.

**number** ['nʌmbə*] *n* nombre *m*; (*numeral*) chiffre *m*; (*of house, car, telephone, newspaper*) numéro *m* // *vt* numéroter; (*include*) compter; **a** ~ **of** un certain nombre de; **the staff** ~**s 20** le nombre d'employés s'élève à *or* est de 20; ~ **plate** *n* plaque *f* minéralogique *or* d'immatriculation.

**numbness** ['nʌmnɪs] *n* engourdissement *m.*

**numeral** ['nju:mərəl] *n* chiffre *m.*

**numerical** ['nju:'mɛrɪkl] *a* numérique.

**numerous** ['nju:mərəs] *a* nombreux(euse).

**nun** [nʌn] *n* religieuse *f*, sœur *f.*

**nurse** [nə:s] *n* infirmière *f* // *vt* (*patient, cold*) soigner; (*hope*) nourrir; ~(**maid**) *n* bonne *f* d'enfants.

**nursery** ['nə:sərɪ] *n* (*room*) nursery *f*; (*institution*) pouponnière *f*; (*for plants*) pépinière *f*; ~ **rhyme** *n* comptine *f*, chansonnette *f* pour enfants; ~ **school** *n* école maternelle; ~ **slope** *n* (*SKI*) piste *f* pour débutants.

**nursing** ['nə:sɪŋ] *n* (*profession*) profession *f* d'infirmière; ~ **home** *n* clinique *f*; maison *f* de convalescence.

**nut** [nʌt] *n* (*of metal*) écrou *m*; (*fruit*) noix *f*, noisette *f*, cacahuète *f* (*terme générique en anglais*); **he's** ~**s** (*col*) il est dingue; ~**case** *n* (*col*) dingue *m/f*; ~**crackers** *npl* casse-noix *m inv*, casse-noisette(s) *m*; ~**meg** ['nʌtmɛg] *n* (*noix f*) muscade *f.*

**nutrient** ['nju:trɪənt] *n* substance nutritive.

**nutrition** [nju:'trɪʃən] *n* nutrition *f*, alimentation *f.*

**nutritious** [nju:'trɪʃəs] *a* nutritif(ive), nourrissant(e).

**nutshell** ['nʌtʃɛl] *n* coquille *f* de noix; **in a** ~ en un mot.

**nylon** ['naɪlɔn] *n* nylon *m*; ~**s** *npl* bas *mpl* nylon.

# O

**oaf** [əuf] *n* balourd *m.*

**oak** [əuk] n chêne m.

**O.A.P.** abbr see old.

**oar** [ɔ:*] n aviron m, rame f; ~sman/woman rameur/euse.

**oasis,** pl **oases** [əu'eɪsɪs, əu'eɪsi:z] n oasis f.

**oath** [əuθ] n serment m; (swear word) juron m; **to take the** ~ prêter serment; **on** ~ sous serment; assermenté(e).

**oatmeal** ['əutmi:l] n flocons mpl d'avoine.

**oats** [əuts] n avoine f.

**obedience** [ə'bi:dɪəns] n obéissance f; **in** ~ **to** conformément à.

**obedient** [ə'bi:dɪənt] a obéissant(e).

**obelisk** ['ɔbɪlɪsk] n obélisque m.

**obesity** [əu'bi:sɪtɪ] n obésité f.

**obey** [ə'beɪ] vt obéir à; (instructions, regulations) se conformer à // vi obéir.

**obituary** [ə'bɪtjuərɪ] n nécrologie f.

**object** n ['ɔbdʒɪkt] objet m; (purpose) but m, objet m; (LING) complément m d'objet // vi [əb'dʒɛkt]: **to** ~ **to** (attitude) désapprouver; (proposal) protester contre, élever une objection contre; **I** ~**!** je proteste!; **he** ~**ed that ...** il a fait valoir or a objecté que ...; ~**ion** [əb'dʒɛkʃən] n objection f; (drawback) inconvénient m; **if you have no** ~**ion** si vous n'y voyez pas d'inconvénient; ~**ionable** [əb'dʒɛnəbl] a très désagréable; choquant(e); ~**ive** n objectif m // a objectif(ive); ~**ivity** [ɔbdʒɪk'tɪvɪtɪ] n objectivité f; ~**or** n opposant/e.

**obligation** [ɔblɪ'geɪʃən] n obligation f, devoir m; (debt) dette f (de reconnaissance).

**obligatory** [ə'blɪgətərɪ] a obligatoire.

**oblige** [ə'blaɪdʒ] vt (force): **to** ~ **sb to do** obliger or forcer qn à faire; (do a favour) rendre service à, obliger; **to be** ~**d to sb for sth** être obligé(e) à qn de qch; **obliging** a obligeant(e), serviable.

**oblique** [ə'bli:k] a oblique; (allusion) indirect(e).

**obliterate** [ə'blɪtəreɪt] vt effacer.

**oblivion** [ə'blɪvɪən] n oubli m.

**oblivious** [ə'blɪvɪəs] a: ~ **of** oublieux(euse) de.

**oblong** ['ɔblɔŋ] a oblong(ue) // n rectangle m.

**obnoxious** [əb'nɔkʃəs] a odieux (euse); (smell) nauséabond(e).

**oboe** ['əubəu] n hautbois m.

**obscene** [əb'si:n] a obscène.

**obscenity** [əb'sɛnɪtɪ] n obscénité f.

**obscure** [əb'skjuə*] a obscur(e) // vt obscurcir; (hide: sun) cacher; **obscurity** n obscurité f.

**obsequious** [əb'si:kwɪəs] a obséquieux(euse).

**observable** [əb'zə:vəbl] a observable; (appreciable) notable.

**observance** [əb'zə:vns] n observance f, observation f.

**observant** [əb'zə:vnt] a observateur(trice).

**observation** [ɔbzə'veɪʃən] n observation f; (by police etc) surveillance f.

**observatory** [əb'zə:vətrɪ] n observatoire m.

**observe** [əb'zə:v] vt observer; (remark) faire observer or remarquer; ~**r** n observateur/trice.

**obsess** [əb'sɛs] vt obséder; ~**ion** [əb'sɛʃən] n obsession f; ~**ive** a obsédant(e).

**obsolescence** [ɔbsə'lɛsns] n vieillissement m; **built-in** or **planned** ~ (COMM) désuétude calculée.

**obsolete** ['ɔbsəli:t] a dépassé(e); démodé(e).

**obstacle** ['ɔbstəkl] n obstacle m; ~ **race** n course f d'obstacles.

**obstetrics** [ɔb'stɛtrɪks] n obstétrique f.

**obstinacy** ['ɔbstɪnəsɪ] n obstination f.

**obstinate** ['ɔbstɪnɪt] a obstiné(e); (pain, cold) persistant(e).

**obstreperous** [əb'strɛpərəs] a turbulent(e).

**obstruct** [əb'strʌkt] vt (block) boucher, obstruer; (halt) arrêter; (hinder) entraver; ~**ion** [əb'strʌkʃən] n obstruction f; obstacle m; ~**ive** a obstructionniste.

**obtain** [əb'teɪn] vt obtenir // vi avoir cours; ~**able** a qu'on peut obtenir.

**obtrusive** [əb'tru:sɪv] a (person) importun(e); (smell) pénétrant(e); (building etc) trop en évidence.

**obtuse** [əb'tju:s] a obtus(e).

**obviate** ['ɔbvɪeɪt] vt parer à, obvier à.

**obvious** ['ɔbvɪəs] a évident(e), manifeste; ~**ly** ad manifestement; bien sûr.

**occasion** [ə'keɪʒən] n occasion f; (event) événement m // vt occasionner, causer; ~**al** a pris(e) or fait(e) etc de temps en temps; occasionnel(le); ~**al table** n table décorative.

**occupation** [ɔkju'peɪʃən] n occupation f; (job) métier m, profession f; **unfit for** ~ (house) impropre à l'habitation; ~**al disease** n maladie f du travail; ~**al hazard** n risque m du métier.

**occupier** ['ɔkjupaɪə*] n occupant/e.

**occupy** ['ɔkjupaɪ] vt occuper; **to** ~ **o.s. with** or **by doing** s'occuper à faire.

**occur** [ə'kə:*] vi se produire; (difficulty, opportunity) se présenter; (phenomenon, error) se rencontrer; **to** ~ **to sb** venir à l'esprit de qn; ~**rence** n présence f, existence f; cas m, fait m.

**ocean** ['əuʃən] n océan m; ~**-going** a de haute mer; ~ **liner** n paquebot m.

**ochre** ['əukə*] a ocre.

**o'clock** [ə'klɔk] ad: **it is 5** ~ il est 5 heures.

**octagonal** [ɔk'tægənl] a octogonal(e).

**octane** ['ɔkteɪn] n octane m.

**octave** ['ɔktɪv] n octave f.

**October** [ɔk'təubə*] n octobre m.

**octopus** ['ɔktəpəs] n pieuvre f.

**odd** [ɔd] a (strange) bizarre, curieux(euse); (number) impair(e); (left over) qui reste, en plus; (not of a set) dépareillé(e); **60-**~ 60 et quelques; **at** ~ **times** de temps en temps; **the** ~ **one out** l'exception f; ~**ity** n bizarrerie f; (person) excentrique m/f; ~**-job man** n homme m à tout faire; ~ **jobs** npl petits travaux divers; ~**ly** ad bizarrement, curieusement; ~**ments** npl (COMM) fins fpl de série; ~**s** npl (in betting) cote f; **the** ~**s are against his coming** il y a peu de chances qu'il vienne; **it**

**makes no** ~s cela n'a pas d'importance ; **at** ~s en désaccord.
**ode** [əud] n ode f.
**odious** ['əudɪəs] a odieux(euse), détestable.
**odour, odor** (US) ['əudə*] n odeur f ; ~**less** a inodore.
**of** [ɔv, əv] prep de ; **a friend** ~ **ours** un de nos amis ; **3** ~ **them went** 3 d'entre eux y sont allés ; **the 5th** ~ **July** le 5 juillet ; **a boy** ~ **10** un garçon de 10 ans.
**off** [ɔf] a,ad (engine) coupé(e) ; (tap) fermé(e) ; (food: bad) mauvais(e), avancé(e) ; (milk) tourné(e) ; (absent) absent(e) ; (cancelled) annulé(e) // prep de ; sur ; **to be** ~ (to leave) partir, s'en aller ; **to be** ~ **sick** être absent(e) pour cause de maladie ; **a day** ~ un jour de congé ; **to have an** ~ **day** n'être pas en forme ; **he had his coat** ~ il avait enlevé son manteau ; **the hook is** ~ le crochet s'est détaché ; le crochet n'est pas mis ; **10%** ~ (COMM) 10% de rabais ; **5 km** ~ **(the road)** à 5 km (de la route) ; ~ **the coast** au large de la côte ; **a house** ~ **the main road** une maison à l'écart de la grand-route ; **I'm** ~ **meat** je ne mange plus de viande ; je n'aime plus la viande ; **on the** ~ **chance** à tout hasard.
**offal** ['ɔfl] n (CULIN) abats mpl.
**offbeat** ['ɔfbiːt] a excentrique.
**off-colour** ['ɔf'kʌlə*] a (ill) malade, mal fichu(e).
**offence, offense** (US) [ə'fɛns] n (crime) délit m, infraction f ; **to give** ~ **to** blesser, offenser ; **to take** ~ **at** se vexer de, s'offenser de.
**offend** [ə'fɛnd] vt (person) offenser, blesser ; ~**er** n délinquant/e ; (against regulations) contrevenant/e.
**offensive** [ə'fɛnsɪv] a offensant(e), choquant(e) ; (smell etc) très déplaisant(e) ; (weapon) offensif(ive) // n (MIL) offensive f.
**offer** ['ɔfə*] n offre f, proposition f // vt offrir, proposer ; 'on ~' (COMM) 'en promotion' ; ~**ing** n offrande f.
**offhand** [ɔf'hænd] a désinvolte // ad spontanément.
**office** ['ɔfɪs] n (place) bureau m ; (position) charge f, fonction f ; **to take** ~ entrer en fonctions ; ~ **block** n immeuble m de bureaux ; ~ **boy** n garçon m de bureau ; ~**r** n (MIL etc) officier m ; (of organization) membre m du bureau directeur ; (also: **police** ~**r**) agent m (de police) ~ **work** n travail m de bureau ; ~ **worker** n employé/e de bureau.
**official** [ə'fɪʃl] a (authorized) officiel(le) // n officiel m ; (civil servant) fonctionnaire m/f ; employé/e ; ~**ly** ad officiellement.
**officious** [ə'fɪʃəs] a trop empressé(e).
**offing** ['ɔfɪŋ] n: **in the** ~ (fig) en perspective.
**off:** ~-**licence** n (Brit: shop) débit m de vins et de spiritueux ; ~-**peak** a aux heures creuses ; ~-**putting** a rébarbatif(ive) ; rebutant(e), peu engageant(e) ; ~-**season** a, ad hors-saison.
**offset** ['ɔfsɛt] vt irg (counteract) contrebalancer, compenser // n (also: ~ **printing**) offset m.

**offshore** [ɔf'ʃɔː*] a (breeze) de terre ; (island) proche du littoral ; (fishing) côtier(ère).
**offside** ['ɔf'saɪd] a (SPORT) hors jeu // n (AUT: with right-hand drive) côté droit.
**offspring** ['ɔfsprɪŋ] n progéniture f.
**off:** ~-**stage** ad dans les coulisses ; ~-**the-cuff** ad au pied levé ; de chic ; ~-**the-peg** ad en prêt-à-porter ; ~-**white** a blanc cassé inv.
**often** ['ɔfn] ad souvent ; **as** ~ **as not** la plupart du temps.
**ogle** ['əugl] vt lorgner.
**oil** [ɔɪl] n huile f ; (petroleum) pétrole m ; (for central heating) mazout m // vt (machine) graisser ; ~**can** n burette f de graissage ; (for storing) bidon m à huile ; ~ **change** n vidange f ; ~**field** n gisement m de pétrole ; ~-**fired** a au mazout ; ~ **level** n niveau m d'huile ; ~ **painting** n peinture f à l'huile ; ~ **refinery** n raffinerie f de pétrole ; ~ **rig** n derrick m ; (at sea) plate-forme pétrolière ; ~**skins** npl ciré m ; ~ **slick** n nappe f de mazout ; ~ **tanker** n pétrolier m ; ~ **well** n puits m de pétrole ; ~**y** a huileux(euse) ; (food) gras(se).
**ointment** ['ɔɪntmənt] n onguent m.
**O.K., okay** ['əu'keɪ] excl d'accord! // a bien ; en règle ; en bon état ; pas mal // vt approuver, donner son accord à ; **is it** ~?, **are you** ~? ça va?
**old** [əuld] a vieux(vieille) ; (person) vieux, âgé(e) ; (former) ancien(ne), vieux ; **how** ~ **are you?** quel âge avez-vous? ; **he's 10 years** ~ il a 10 ans, il est âgé de 10 ans ; ~ **age** n vieillesse f ; ~-**age pensioner (O.A.P.)** n retraité/e ; ~**er brother**/**sister** frère/sœur aîné(e) ; ~-**fashioned** a démodé(e) ; (person) vieux jeu inv ; ~ **people's home** n maison f de retraite.
**olive** ['ɔlɪv] n (fruit) olive f ; (tree) olivier m // a (also: ~-**green**) (vert) olive inv ; ~ **oil** n huile f d'olive.
**Olympic** [əu'lɪmpɪk] a olympique ; **the** ~ **Games, the** ~s les Jeux mpl olympiques.
**omelet(te)** ['ɔmlɪt] n omelette f ; **ham**/**cheese** ~ omelette au jambon/fromage.
**omen** ['əumən] n présage m.
**ominous** ['ɔmɪnəs] a menaçant(e), inquiétant(e) ; (event) de mauvais augure.
**omission** [əu'mɪʃən] n omission f.
**omit** [əu'mɪt] vt omettre.
**on** [ɔn] prep sur // ad (machine) en marche ; (light, radio) allumé(e) ; (tap) ouvert(e) ; **is the meeting still** ~? est-ce que la réunion a bien lieu? ; la réunion dure-t-elle encore? ; **when is this film** ~? quand passe or passe-t-on ce film? ; ~ **the train** dans le train ; ~ **the wall** sur le or au mur ; ~ **television** à la télévision ; ~ **learning this** en apprenant cela ; ~ **arrival** à l'arrivée ; ~ **the left** à gauche ; ~ **Friday** vendredi ; ~ **Fridays** le vendredi ; **a week** ~ **Friday** vendredi en huit ; **to have one's coat** ~ avoir (mis) son manteau ; **to walk etc** ~ continuer à marcher etc ; **it's not** ~! pas question! ; ~ **and off** de temps à autre.
**once** [wʌns] ad une fois ; (formerly) autrefois // cj une fois que ; **at** ~ tout de suite, immédiatement ; (simultaneously) à la fois ;

**all at** ~ *ad* tout d'un coup ; ~ **a week** une fois par semaine ; ~ **more** encore une fois ; ~ **and for all** une fois pour toutes.

**oncoming** ['ɔnkʌmɪŋ] *a* (*traffic*) venant en sens inverse.

**one** [wʌn] *det, num* un(e) // *pronoun* un(e) ; (*impersonal*) on ; **this** ~ celui-ci/celle-ci ; **that** ~ celui-là/celle-là ; **the** ~ **book which...** l'unique livre que... ; ~ **by** ~ un(e) par un(e) ; ~ **never knows** on ne sait jamais ; ~ **another** l'un(e) l'autre ; ~-**man** *a* (*business*) dirigé(e) *etc* par un seul homme ; ~-**man band** *n* homme-orchestre *m* ; ~-**self** *pronoun* se ; (*after prep, also emphatic*) soi-même ; ~-**way** *a* (*street, traffic*) à sens unique.

**ongoing** ['ɔngəuɪŋ] *a* en cours ; suivi(e).

**onion** ['ʌnjən] *n* oignon *m*.

**onlooker** ['ɔnlukə*] *n* spectateur/trice.

**only** ['əunlɪ] *ad* seulement // *a* seul(e), unique // *cj* seulement, mais ; **an** ~ **child** un enfant unique ; **not** ~ non seulement ; **I** ~ **took one** j'en ai seulement pris un, je n'en ai pris qu'un.

**onset** ['ɔnsɛt] *n* début *m* ; (*of winter, old age*) approche *f*.

**onshore** ['ɔnʃɔ:*] *a* (*wind*) du large.

**onslaught** ['ɔnslɔ:t] *n* attaque *f*, assaut *m*.

**onto** ['ɔntu] *prep* = **on to**.

**onus** ['əunəs] *n* responsabilité *f*.

**onward(s)** ['ɔnwəd(z)] *ad* (*move*) en avant ; **from this time** ~ dorénavant.

**onyx** ['ɔnɪks] *n* onyx *m*.

**ooze** [u:z] *vi* suinter.

**opacity** [əu'pæsɪtɪ] *n* (*of substance*) opacité *f*.

**opal** ['əupl] *n* opale *f*.

**opaque** [əu'peɪk] *a* opaque.

**OPEC** ['əupɛk] *n* (*abbr of Organization of petroleum exporting countries*) O.P.E.P. (*Organisation des pays exportateurs de pétrole*).

**open** ['əupn] *a* ouvert(e) ; (*car*) découvert(e) ; (*road, view*) dégagé(e) ; (*meeting*) public(ique) ; (*admiration*) manifeste ; (*question*) non résolu(e) ; (*enemy*) déclaré(e) // *vt* ouvrir // *vi* (*flower, eyes, door, debate*) s'ouvrir ; (*shop, bank, museum*) ouvrir ;. (*book etc*: *commence*) commencer, débuter ; **to** ~ **on to** *vt fus* (*subj: room, door*) donner sur ; **to** ~ **out** *vt* ouvrir // *vi* s'ouvrir ; **to** ~ **up** *vt* ouvrir ; (*blocked road*) dégager // *vi* s'ouvrir ; **in the** ~ (**air**) en plein air ; ~-**air** *a* en plein air ; ~**ing** *n* ouverture *f* ; (*opportunity*) occasion *f* ; débouché *m* ; (*job*) poste vacant ; ~**ly** *ad* ouvertement ; ~-**minded** *a* à l'esprit ouvert ; ~-**necked** *a* à col ouvert ; ~ **sandwich** *n* canapé *m* ; **the** ~ **sea** *n* le large.

**opera** ['ɔpərə] *n* opéra *m* ; ~ **glasses** *npl* jumelles *fpl* de théâtre ; ~ **house** *n* opéra *m*.

**operate** ['ɔpəreɪt] *vt* (*machine*) faire marcher, faire fonctionner ; (*system*) pratiquer // *vi* fonctionner ; (*drug*) faire effet ; **to** ~ **on sb (for)** (MED) opérer qn (de).

**operatic** [ɔpə'rætɪk] *a* d'opéra.

**operating** ['ɔpəreɪtɪŋ] *a*: ~ **table/theatre** table *f*/salle *f* d'opération.

**operation** [ɔpə'reɪʃən] *n* opération *f* ; **to be in** ~ (*machine*) être en service ;

(*system*) être en vigueur ; ~**al** *a* opérationnel(le).

**operative** ['ɔpərətɪv] *a* (*measure*) en vigueur // *n* (*in factory*) ouvrier/ère.

**operator** ['ɔpəreɪtə*] *n* (*of machine*) opérateur/trice ; (TEL) téléphoniste *m/f*.

**operetta** [ɔpə'rɛtə] *n* opérette *f*.

**opinion** [ə'pɪnɪən] *n* opinion *f*, avis *m* ; **in my** ~ à mon avis ; ~**ated** *a* aux idées bien arrêtées ; ~ **poll** *n* sondage *m* (d'opinion).

**opium** ['əupɪəm] *n* opium *m*.

**opponent** [ə'pəunənt] *n* adversaire *m/f*.

**opportune** ['ɔpətju:n] *a* opportun(e) ; **opportunist** [-'tju:nɪst] *n* opportuniste *m/f*.

**opportunity** [ɔpə'tju:nɪtɪ] *n* occasion *f* ; **to take the** ~ **of doing** profiter de l'occasion pour faire.

**oppose** [ə'pəuz] *vt* s'opposer à ; ~**d to a** opposé(e) à ; **as** ~**d to** par opposition à ; **opposing** *a* (*side*) opposé(e).

**opposite** ['ɔpəzɪt] *a* opposé(e) ; (*house etc*) d'en face // *ad* en face // *prep* en face de // *n* opposé *m*, contraire *m* ; (*of word*) contraire *m* ; '**see** ~ **page**' 'voir ci-contre' ; **his** ~ **number** son homologue *m/f*.

**opposition** [ɔpə'zɪʃən] *n* opposition *f*.

**oppress** [ə'prɛs] *vt* opprimer ; ~**ion** [ə'prɛʃən] *n* oppression *f* ; ~**ive** *a* oppressif(ive).

**opt** [ɔpt] *vi*: **to** ~ **for** opter pour ; **to** ~ **to do** choisir de faire ; **to** ~ **out of** choisir de quitter.

**optical** ['ɔptɪkl] *a* optique ; (*instrument*) d'optique.

**optician** [ɔp'tɪʃən] *n* opticien/ne.

**optimism** ['ɔptɪmɪzəm] *n* optimisme *m*.

**optimist** ['ɔptɪmɪst] *n* optimiste *m/f* ; ~**ic** [-'mɪstɪk] *a* optimiste.

**optimum** ['ɔptɪməm] *a* optimum.

**option** ['ɔpʃən] *n* choix *m*, option *f* ; (SCOL) matière *f* à option ; (COMM) option ; **to keep one's** ~**s open** (*fig*) ne pas s'engager ; ~**al** *a* facultatif(ive) ; (COMM) en option.

**opulence** ['ɔpjuləns] *n* opulence *f* ; abondance *f*.

**opulent** ['ɔpjulənt] *a* opulent(e) ; abondant(e).

**or** [ɔ:*] *cj* ou ; (*with negative*): **he hasn't seen** ~ **heard anything** il n'a rien vu ni entendu ; ~ **else** sinon ; ou bien.

**oracle** ['ɔrəkl] *n* oracle *m*.

**oral** ['ɔ:rəl] *a* oral(e) // *n* oral *m*.

**orange** ['ɔrɪndʒ] *n* (*fruit*) orange *f* // *a* orange *inv*.

**oration** [ɔ:'reɪʃən] *n* discours solennel.

**orator** ['ɔrətə*] *n* orateur/trice.

**oratorio** [ɔrə'tɔ:rɪəu] *n* oratorio *m*.

**orb** [ɔ:b] *n* orbe *m*.

**orbit** ['ɔ:bɪt] *n* orbite *f* // *vt* décrire une *or* des orbite(s) autour de.

**orchard** ['ɔ:tʃəd] *n* verger *m*.

**orchestra** ['ɔ:kɪstrə] *n* orchestre *m* ; ~**l** [-'kɛstrəl] *a* orchestral(e) ; (*concert*) symphonique.

**orchid** ['ɔ:kɪd] *n* orchidée *f*.

**ordain** [ɔ:'deɪn] *vt* (REL) ordonner ; (*decide*) décréter.

**ordeal** [ɔ:'di:l] *n* épreuve *f*.

**order** ['ɔ:də*] *n* ordre *m* ; (COMM) commande *f* // *vt* ordonner ; (COMM) commander ; **in** ~ en ordre ; (*of document*) en règle ; **in ~ of size** par ordre de grandeur ; **in ~ to do/that** pour faire/que + *sub* ; **to ~ sb to do** ordonner à qn de faire ; **the lower ~s** (*pej*) les classes inférieures ; **~ form** *n* bon *m* de commande ; **~ly** *n* (*MIL*) ordonnance *f* // *a* (*room*) en ordre ; (*mind*) méthodique ; (*person*) qui a de l'ordre.

**ordinal** ['ɔ:dɪnl] *a* (*number*) ordinal(e).

**ordinary** ['ɔ:dnrɪ] *a* ordinaire, normal(e) ; (*pej*) ordinaire, quelconque.

**ordination** [ɔ:dɪ'neɪʃən] *n* ordination *f*.

**ordnance** ['ɔ:dnəns] *n* (*MIL: unit*) service *m* du matériel ; **O~ Survey map** *n* ≈ carte *f* d'État-major.

**ore** [ɔ:*] *n* minerai *m*.

**organ** ['ɔ:gən] *n* organe *m* ; (*MUS*) orgue *m*, orgues *fpl* ; **~ic** [ɔ:'gænɪk] *a* organique.

**organism** ['ɔ:gənɪzəm] *n* organisme *m*.

**organist** ['ɔ:gənɪst] *n* organiste *m/f*.

**organization** [ɔ:gənaɪ'zeɪʃən] *n* organisation *f*.

**organize** ['ɔ:gənaɪz] *vt* organiser ; **~d labour** *n* main-d'œuvre syndiquée ; **~r** *n* organisateur/trice.

**orgasm** ['ɔ:gæzəm] *n* orgasme *m*.

**orgy** ['ɔ:dʒɪ] *n* orgie *f*.

**Orient** ['ɔ:rɪənt] *n*: **the ~** l'Orient *m* ; **oriental** [-'ɛntl] *a* oriental(e) // *n* Oriental/e.

**orientate** ['ɔ:rɪənteɪt] *vt* orienter.

**orifice** ['ɔrɪfɪs] *n* orifice *m*.

**origin** ['ɔrɪdʒɪn] *n* origine *f*.

**original** [ə'rɪdʒɪnl] *a* original(e) ; (*earliest*) originel(le) // *n* original *m* ; **~ity** [-'nælɪtɪ] *n* originalité *f* ; **~ly** *ad* (*at first*) à l'origine.

**originate** [ə'rɪdʒɪneɪt] *vi*: **to ~ from** être originaire de ; (*suggestion*) provenir de ; **to ~ in** prendre naissance dans ; avoir son origine dans ; **originator** auteur *m*.

**ornament** ['ɔ:nəmənt] *n* ornement *m* ; (*trinket*) bibelot *m* ; **~al** [-'mɛntl] *a* décoratif(ive) ; (*garden*) d'agrément ; **~ation** [-'teɪʃən] *n* ornementation *f*.

**ornate** [ɔ:'neɪt] *a* très orné(e).

**ornithologist** [ɔ:nɪ'θɔlədʒɪst] *n* ornithologue *m/f*.

**ornithology** [ɔ:nɪ'θɔlədʒɪ] *n* ornithologie *f*.

**orphan** ['ɔ:fn] *n* orphelin/e // *vt*: **to be ~ed** devenir orphelin ; **~age** *n* orphelinat *m*.

**orthodox** ['ɔ:θədɔks] *a* orthodoxe.

**orthopaedic, orthopedic** (*US*) [ɔ:θə'pi:dɪk] *a* orthopédique.

**oscillate** ['ɔsɪleɪt] *vi* osciller.

**ostensible** [ɔs'tɛnsɪbl] *a* prétendu(e) ; apparent(e) ; **ostensibly** *ad* en apparence.

**ostentation** [ɔstɛn'teɪʃən] *n* ostentation *f*.

**ostentatious** [ɔstɛn'teɪʃəs] *a* prétentieux(euse) ; ostentatoire.

**osteopath** ['ɔstɪəpæθ] *n* ostéopathe *m/f*.

**ostracize** ['ɔstrəsaɪz] *vt* frapper d'ostracisme.

**ostrich** ['ɔstrɪtʃ] *n* autruche *f*.

**other** ['ʌðə*] *a* autre ; **~ than** autrement que ; à part ; **~wise** *ad,cj* autrement.

**otter** ['ɔtə*] *n* loutre *f*.

**ought** [ɔ:t], *pt* **ought** *auxiliary vb*: **I ~ to do it** je devrais le faire, il faudrait que je le fasse ; **this ~ to have been corrected**

cela aurait dû être corrigé ; **he ~ to win** il devrait gagner.

**ounce** [auns] *n* once *f* (= *28.35 g* ; *16 in a pound*).

**our** ['auə*] *a* notre, *pl* nos ; **~s** *pronoun* le(la) nôtre, les nôtres ; **~selves** *pronoun pl* (*reflexive, after preposition*) nous ; (*emphatic*) nous-mêmes.

**oust** [aust] *vt* évincer.

**out** [aut] *ad* dehors ; (*published, not at home etc*) sorti(e) ; (*light, fire*) éteint(e) ; **~ here** ici ; **~ there** là-bas ; **he's ~** (*absent*), il est sorti ; (*unconscious*) il est sans connaissance ; **to be ~ in one's calculations** s'être trompé dans ses calculs ; **to run/back** *etc* **~** sortir en courant/en reculant *etc* ; **~ loud** *ad* à haute voix ; **~ of** (*outside*) en dehors de ; (*because of*: *anger etc*) par ; (*from among*): **~ of 10** sur 10 ; (*without*): **~ of petrol** sans essence, à court d'essence ; **made ~ of wood** en or de bois ; **~ of order** (*machine*) en panne ; (*TEL: line*) en dérangement ; **~-of-the-way** écarté(e) ; (*fig*) insolite.

**outback** ['autbæk] *n* campagne isolée ; (*in Australia*) intérieur *m*.

**outboard** ['autbɔ:d] *n*: **~ (motor)** (moteur *m*) hors-bord *m*.

**outbreak** ['autbreɪk] *n* accès *m* ; début *m* ; éruption *f*.

**outbuilding** ['autbɪldɪŋ] *n* dépendance *f*.

**outburst** ['autbə:st] *n* explosion *f*, accès *m*.

**outcast** ['autkɑ:st] *n* exilé/e ; (*socially*) paria *m*.

**outclass** [aut'klɑ:s] *vt* surclasser.

**outcome** ['autkʌm] *n* issue *f*, résultat *m*.

**outcry** ['autkraɪ] *n* tollé *m* (général).

**outdated** [aut'deɪtɪd] *a* démodé(e).

**outdo** [aut'du:] *vt irg* surpasser.

**outdoor** [aut'dɔ:*] *a* de or en plein air ; **~s** *ad* dehors ; au grand air.

**outer** ['autə*] *a* extérieur(e) ; **~ space** *n* espace *m* cosmique ; **~ suburbs** *npl* grande banlieue.

**outfit** ['autfɪt] *n* équipement *m* ; (*clothes*) tenue *f* ; **'~ter's'** 'confection pour hommes'.

**outgoings** ['autgəuɪŋz] *npl* (*expenses*) dépenses *fpl*.

**outgrow** [aut'grəu] *vt irg* (*clothes*) devenir trop grand(e) pour.

**outing** ['autɪŋ] *n* sortie *f* ; excursion *f*.

**outlandish** [aut'lændɪʃ] *a* étrange.

**outlaw** ['autlɔ:] *n* hors-la-loi *m inv* // *vt* (*person*) mettre hors la loi ; (*practice*) proscrire.

**outlay** ['autleɪ] *n* dépenses *fpl* ; (*investment*) mise *f* de fonds.

**outlet** ['autlɛt] *n* (*for liquid etc*) issue *f*, sortie *f* ; (*for emotion*) exutoire *m* ; (*for goods*) débouché *m* ; (*also*: **retail ~**) point *m* de vente.

**outline** ['autlaɪn] *n* (*shape*) contour *m* ; (*summary*) esquisse *f*, grandes lignes.

**outlive** [aut'lɪv] *vt* survivre à.

**outlook** ['autluk] *n* perspective *f*.

**outlying** ['autlaɪɪŋ] *a* écarté(e).

**outmoded** [aut'məudɪd] *a* démodé(e) ; dépassé(e).

**outnumber** [aut'nʌmbə*] vt surpasser en nombre.

**outpatient** ['autpeɪʃənt] n malade m/f en consultation externe.

**outpost** ['autpəust] n avant-poste m.

**output** ['autput] n rendement m, production f.

**outrage** ['autreɪdʒ] n atrocité f, acte m de violence; scandale m // vt outrager; **~ous** [-'reɪdʒəs] a atroce; scandaleux(euse).

**outrider** ['autraɪdə*] n (on motorcycle) motard m.

**outright** ad [aut'raɪt] complètement; catégoriquement; carrément; sur le coup // a ['autraɪt] complet(ète); catégorique.

**outset** ['autsɛt] n début m.

**outside** [aut'saɪd] n extérieur m // a extérieur(e) // ad (au) dehors, à l'extérieur // prep hors de, à l'extérieur de; **at the ~** (fig) au plus or maximum; **~ lane** n (AUT: in Britain) voie f de droite; **~-left/-right** (FOOTBALL) ailier gauche/droit; **~r** n (in race etc) outsider m; (stranger) étranger/ère.

**outsize** ['autsaɪz] a énorme; (clothes) grande taille inv.

**outskirts** ['autskə:ts] npl faubourgs mpl.

**outspoken** [aut'spəukən] a très franc(he).

**outstanding** [aut'stændɪŋ] a remarquable, exceptionnel(le); (unfinished) en suspens; en souffrance; non réglé(e).

**outstay** [aut'steɪ] vt: **to ~ one's welcome** abuser de l'hospitalité de son hôte.

**outstretched** [aut'strɛtʃt] a (hand) tendu(e); (body) étendu(e).

**outward** ['autwəd] a (sign, appearances) extérieur(e); (journey) (d')aller; **~ly** ad extérieurement; en apparence.

**outweigh** [aut'weɪ] vt l'emporter sur.

**outwit** [aut'wɪt] vt se montrer plus malin que.

**oval** ['əuvl] a,n ovale (m).

**ovary** ['əuvəri] n ovaire m.

**ovation** [əu'veɪʃən] n ovation f.

**oven** ['ʌvn] n four m; **~proof** a allant au four.

**over** ['əuvə*] ad (par-)dessus // a (or ad) (finished) fini(e), terminé(e); (too much) en plus // prep sur; par-dessus; (above) au-dessus de; (on the other side of) de l'autre côté de; (during) pendant; **~ here** ici; **~ there** là-bas; **all ~** (everywhere) partout; (finished) fini(e); **~ and (again)** à plusieurs reprises; **~ and above** en plus de; **to ask sb ~** inviter qn (à passer); **to go ~ to sb's** passer chez qn.

**over...** ['əuvə*] prefix: **~abundant** surabondant(e).

**overact** [əuvər'ækt] vi (THEATRE) outrer son rôle.

**overall** a,n ['əuvərɔ:l] a (length) total(e); (study) d'ensemble // n (Brit) blouse f // ad [əuvər'ɔ:l] dans l'ensemble, en général // **~s** npl bleus mpl (de travail).

**overawe** [əuvər'ɔ:] vt impressionner.

**overbalance** [əuvə'bæləns] vi basculer.

**overbearing** [əuvə'bɛərɪŋ] a impérieux(euse), autoritaire.

**overboard** ['əuvəbɔ:d] ad (NAUT) par-dessus bord.

**overcast** ['əuvəkɑ:st] a couvert(e).

**overcharge** [əuvə'tʃɑ:dʒ] vt: **to ~ sb for sth** faire payer qch trop cher à qn.

**overcoat** ['əuvəkəut] n pardessus m.

**overcome** [əuvə'kʌm] vt irg triompher de; surmonter; **to be ~ by** être saisi(e) de; succomber à; être victime de; **~ with grief** accablé(e) de douleur.

**overcrowded** [əuvə'kraudɪd] a bondé(e).

**overcrowding** [əuvə'kraudɪŋ] n surpeuplement m; (in bus) encombrement m.

**overdo** [əuvə'du:] vt irg exagérer; (overcook) trop cuire.

**overdose** ['əuvədəus] n dose excessive.

**overdraft** ['əuvədrɑ:ft] n découvert m.

**overdrawn** [əuvə'drɔ:n] a (account) à découvert.

**overdrive** ['əuvədraɪv] n (AUT) (vitesse) surmultipliée f.

**overdue** [əuvə'dju:] a en retard; (recognition) tardif(ive).

**overestimate** [əuvər'ɛstɪmeɪt] vt surestimer.

**overexcited** [əuvərɪk'saɪtɪd] a surexcité(e).

**overexertion** [əuvərɪg'zə:ʃən] n surmenage m (physique).

**overexpose** [əuvərɪk'spəuz] vt (PHOT) surexposer.

**overflow** vi [əuvə'fləu] déborder // n ['əuvəfləu] trop-plein m; (also: **~ pipe**) tuyau m d'écoulement, trop-plein m.

**overgrown** [əuvə'grəun] a (garden) envahi(e) par la végétation.

**overhaul** vt [əuvə'hɔ:l] réviser // n ['əuvəhɔ:l] révision f.

**overhead** ad [əuvə'hɛd] au-dessus // a ['əuvəhɛd] aérien(ne); (lighting) vertical(e); **~s** npl frais généraux.

**overhear** [əuvə'hɪə*] vt irg entendre (par hasard).

**overjoyed** [əuvə'dʒɔɪd] a ravi(e), enchanté(e).

**overland** ['əuvəlænd] a, ad par voie de terre.

**overlap** vi [əuvə'læp] se chevaucher // n ['əuvəlæp] chevauchement m.

**overleaf** [əuvə'li:f] ad au verso.

**overload** [əuvə'ləud] vt surcharger.

**overlook** [əuvə'luk] vt (have view on) donner sur; (miss) oublier, négliger; (forgive) fermer les yeux sur.

**overlord** ['əuvəlɔ:d] n chef m suprême.

**overnight** [əuvə'naɪt] ad (happen) durant la nuit; (fig) soudain // a d'une (or de) nuit; soudain(e); **he stayed there ~** il y a passé la nuit; **if you travel ~...** si tu fais le voyage de nuit...; **he'll be away ~** il ne rentrera pas ce soir.

**overpass** ['əuvəpɑ:s] n pont autoroutier.

**overpower** [əuvə'pauə*] vt vaincre; (fig) accabler; **~ing** a irrésistible; (heat, stench) suffocant(e).

**overrate** [əuvə'reɪt] vt surestimer.

**overreact** [əuvəri:'ækt] vi réagir de façon excessive.

**override** [əuvə'raɪd] vt (irg: like ride) (order, objection) passer outre à; (decision)

annuler ; **overriding** a prépondérant(e).
**overrule** [əuvə'ru:l] vt (decision) annuler ; (claim) rejeter.
**overseas** [əuvə'si:z] ad outre-mer ; (abroad) à l'étranger // a (trade) extérieur(e) ; (visitor) étranger(ère).
**overseer** ['əuvəsɪə*] n (in factory) contremaître m.
**overshadow** [əuvə'ʃædəu] vt (fig) éclipser.
**overshoot** [əuvə'ʃu:t] vt irg dépasser.
**oversight** ['əuvəsaɪt] n omission f, oubli m.
**oversimplify** [əuve'sɪmplɪfaɪ] vt simplifier à l'excès.
**oversleep** [əuvə'sli:p] vi irg se réveiller (trop) tard.
**overspill** ['əuvəspɪl] n excédent m de population.
**overstate** [əuvə'steɪt] vt exagérer ; **~ment** n exagération f.
**overt** [əu'və:t] a non dissimulé(e).
**overtake** [əuvə'teɪk] vt irg dépasser ; (AUT) dépasser, doubler ; **overtaking** n (AUT) dépassement m.
**overthrow** [əuvə'θrəu] vt irg (government) renverser.
**overtime** ['əuvətaɪm] n heures fpl supplémentaires.
**overtone** ['əuvətəun] n (also: ~s) note f, sous-entendus mpl.
**overture** ['əuvətʃuə*] n (MUS, fig) ouverture f.
**overturn** [əuvə'tə:n] vt renverser // vi se retourner.
**overweight** [əuvə'weɪt] a (person) trop gros(se) ; (luggage) trop lourd(e).
**overwhelm** [əuvə'wɛlm] vt accabler ; submerger ; écraser ; **~ing** a (victory, defeat) écrasant(e) ; (desire) irrésistible.
**overwork** [əuvə'wə:k] n surmenage m // vt surmener // vi se surmener.
**overwrought** [əuvə'rɔ:t] a excédé(e).
**owe** [əu] vt devoir ; to ~ sb sth, to ~ sth to sb devoir qch à qn.
**owing to** ['əuɪŋtu:] prep à cause de, en raison de.
**owl** [aul] n hibou m.
**own** [əun] vt posséder // a propre ; **a room of my** ~ une chambre à moi, ma propre chambre ; **to get one's** ~ **back** prendre sa revanche ; **on one's** ~ tout(e) seul(e) ; to ~ **up** vi avouer ; **~er** n propriétaire m/f ; **~ership** n possession f.
**ox**, pl **oxen** [ɔks, 'ɔksn] n bœuf m.
**oxide** ['ɔksaɪd] n oxyde m.
**oxtail** ['ɔksteɪl] n: ~ **soup** soupe f à la queue de bœuf.
**oxygen** ['ɔksɪdʒən] n oxygène m ; ~ **mask/tent** n masque m/tente f à oxygène.
**oyster** ['ɔɪstə*] n huître f.
**oz.** abbr of **ounce(s)**.
**ozone** ['əuzəun] n ozone m.

## P

**p** [pi:] abbr of **penny, pence**.
**p.a.** abbr of **per annum**.
**P.A.** see **public, personal**.

**pa** [pɑ:] n (col) papa m.
**pace** [peɪs] n pas m ; (speed) allure f ; vitesse f // vi: to ~ **up and down** faire les cent pas ; **to keep** ~ **with** aller à la même vitesse que ; (events) se tenir au courant de ; **~maker** n (MED) stimulateur m cardiaque.
**pacification** [pæsɪfɪ'keɪʃən] n pacification f.
**pacific** [pə'sɪfɪk] a pacifique // n: **the P~ (Ocean)** le Pacifique, l'océan m Pacifique.
**pacifist** ['pæsɪfɪst] n pacifiste m/f.
**pacify** ['pæsɪfaɪ] vt pacifier ; (soothe) calmer.
**pack** [pæk] n paquet m ; ballot m ; (of hounds) meute f ; (of thieves etc) bande f ; (of cards) jeu m // vt (goods) empaqueter, emballer ; (in suitcase etc) emballer ; (box) remplir ; (cram) entasser ; (press down) tasser ; damer ; to ~ **(one's bags)** faire ses bagages ; to ~ **one's case** faire sa valise.
**package** ['pækɪdʒ] n paquet m ; ballot m ; (also: ~ **deal**) marché global ; forfait m ; ~ **tour** n voyage organisé.
**packet** ['pækɪt] n paquet m.
**pack ice** [pækaɪs] n banquise f.
**packing** ['pækɪŋ] n emballage m ; ~ **case** n caisse f (d'emballage).
**pact** [pækt] n pacte m ; traité m.
**pad** [pæd] n bloc(-notes) m ; (for inking) tampon encreur ; (col: flat) piaule f // vt rembourrer ; **~ding** n rembourrage m ; (fig) délayage m.
**paddle** ['pædl] n (oar) pagaie f // vi barboter, faire trempette ; ~ **steamer** n bateau m à aubes ; **paddling pool** n petit bassin.
**paddock** ['pædək] n enclos m ; paddock m.
**paddy** ['pædɪ] n: ~ **field** n rizière f.
**padlock** ['pædlɔk] n cadenas m // vt cadenasser.
**padre** ['pɑ:drɪ] n aumônier m.
**paediatrics, pediatrics** (US) [pi:dɪ'ætrɪks] n pédiatrie f.
**pagan** ['peɪgən] a,n païen(ne).
**page** [peɪdʒ] n (of book) page f ; (also: ~ **boy**) groom m, chasseur m ; (at wedding) garçon m d'honneur // vt (in hotel etc) (faire) appeler.
**pageant** ['pædʒənt] n spectacle m historique ; grande cérémonie ; ~**ry** n apparat m, pompe f.
**pagoda** [pə'gəudə] n pagode f.
**paid** [peɪd] pt, pp of **pay** // a (work, official) rémunéré(e) ; **to put** ~ **to** mettre fin à, régler.
**pail** [peɪl] n seau m.
**pain** [peɪn] n douleur f ; **to be in** ~ souffrir, avoir mal ; **to have a** ~ **in** avoir mal à or une douleur à or dans ; **to take** ~**s to do** se donner du mal pour faire ; ~**ed** a peiné(e), chagrin(e) ; ~**ful** a douloureux(euse) ; difficile, pénible ; ~**fully** ad (fig: very) terriblement ; ~**killer** n calmant m ; ~**less** a indolore ; ~**staking** ['peɪnzteɪkɪŋ] a (person) soigneux(euse) ; (work) soigné(e).
**paint** [peɪnt] n peinture f // vt peindre ; (fig) dépeindre ; **to** ~ **the door blue**

peindre la porte en bleu ; **to ~ in oils** faire de la peinture à l'huile ; **~brush** n pinceau m ; **~er** n peintre m ; **~ing** n peinture f ; (picture) tableau m ; **~-stripper** n décapant m.

**pair** [pɛə*] n (of shoes, gloves etc) paire f ; (of people) couple m ; duo m ; paire ; **~ of scissors** (paire de) ciseaux mpl ; **~ of trousers** pantalon m.

**pajamas** [pɪ'dʒɑ:məz] npl (US) pyjama(s) m(pl).

**Pakistan** [pɑ:kɪ'stɑ:n] n Pakistan m ; **~i** a pakistanais(e) // n Pakistanais/e.

**pal** [pæl] n (col) copain/copine.

**palace** ['pæləs] n palais m.

**palatable** ['pælɪtəbl] a bon(bonne), agréable au goût.

**palate** ['pælɪt] n palais m.

**palaver** [pə'lɑ:və*] n palabres fpl or mpl ; histoire(s) f(pl).

**pale** [peɪl] a pâle ; **to grow ~** pâlir ; **~ blue** a bleu pâle inv ; **~ness** n pâleur f.

**Palestine** ['pælɪstaɪn] n Palestine f ; **Palestinian** [-'tɪnɪən] a palestinien(ne) // n Palestinien/ne.

**palette** ['pælɪt] n palette f.

**palisade** [pælɪ'seɪd] n palissade f.

**pall** [pɔ:l] n (of smoke) voile m// vi: **to ~ (on)** devenir lassant (pour).

**pallid** ['pælɪd] a blême.

**pally** ['pælɪ] a (col) copain(copine).

**palm** [pɑ:m] n (ANAT) paume f ; (also: **~ tree**) palmier m ; (leaf, symbol) palme f // vt: **to ~ sth off on sb** (col) refiler qch à qn ; **~ist** n chiromancien/ne ; **P~ Sunday** n le dimanche des Rameaux.

**palpable** ['pælpəbl] a évident(e), manifeste.

**palpitation** [pælpɪ'teɪʃən] n palpitation(s) f(pl).

**paltry** ['pɔ:ltrɪ] a dérisoire ; piètre.

**pamper** ['pæmpə*] vt gâter, dorloter.

**pamphlet** ['pæmflət] n brochure f.

**pan** [pæn] n (also: **sauce~**) casserole f ; (also: **frying ~**) poêle f ; (of lavatory) cuvette f // vi (CINEMA) faire un panoramique.

**panacea** [pænə'sɪə] n panacée f.

**Panama** ['pænəmɑ:] n Panama m ; **~ canal** n canal m de Panama.

**pancake** ['pænkeɪk] n crêpe f.

**panda** ['pændə] n panda m ; **~ car** n ≈ voiture f pie inv.

**pandemonium** [pændɪ'məunɪəm] n tohu-bohu m.

**pander** ['pændə*] vi: **to ~ to** flatter bassement ; obéir servilement à.

**pane** [peɪn] n carreau m (de fenêtre).

**panel** ['pænl] n (of wood, cloth etc) panneau m ; (RADIO, TV) panel m ; invités mpl, experts mpl ; **~ling, ~ing** (US) n boiseries fpl.

**pang** [pæŋ] n: **~s of remorse** pincements mpl de remords ; **~s of hunger/conscience** tiraillements mpl d'estomac/de la conscience.

**panic** ['pænɪk] n panique f, affolement m // vi s'affoler, paniquer ; **~ky** a (person) qui panique or s'affole facilement.

**pannier** ['pænɪə*] n (on animal) bât m ; (on bicycle) sacoche f.

**panorama** [pænə'rɑ:mə] n panorama m ; **panoramic** a panoramique.

**pansy** ['pænzɪ] n (BOT) pensée f ; (col) tapette f, pédé m.

**pant** [pænt] vi haleter // n: see **pants**.

**pantechnicon** [pæn'tɛknɪkən] n (grand) camion de déménagement.

**panther** ['pænθə*] n panthère f.

**panties** ['pæntɪz] npl slip m, culotte f.

**pantomime** ['pæntəmaɪm] n spectacle m de Noël.

**pantry** ['pæntrɪ] n garde-manger m inv ; (room) office f or m.

**pants** [pænts] n (woman's) culotte f, slip m ; (man's) slip m, caleçon m ; (US: trousers) pantalon m.

**papacy** ['peɪpəsɪ] n papauté f.

**papal** ['peɪpəl] a papal(e), pontifical(e).

**paper** ['peɪpə*] n papier m ; (also: **wall~**) papier peint ; (also: **news~**) journal m ; (study, article) article m ; (exam) épreuve écrite / a en or de papier // vt tapisser (de papier peint) ; **(identity) ~s** npl papiers (d'identité) ; **~back** n livre m de poche ; livre broché or non relié // a: **~back edition** édition brochée ; **~ bag** n sac m en papier ; **~ clip** n trombone m ; **~ hankie** n mouchoir m en papier ; **~ mill** n papeterie f ; **~weight** n presse-papiers m inv ; **~work** n paperasserie f.

**papier-mâché** ['pæpɪeɪ'mæʃeɪ] n papier mâché.

**paprika** ['pæprɪkə] n paprika m.

**par** [pɑ:*] n pair m ; (GOLF) normale f du parcours ; **on a ~ with** à égalité avec, au même niveau que.

**parable** ['pærəbl] n parabole f (REL).

**parabola** [pə'ræbələ] n parabole f (MATH).

**parachute** ['pærəʃu:t] n parachute m // vi sauter en parachute ; **~ jump** n saut m en parachute.

**parade** [pə'reɪd] n défilé m ; (inspection) revue f ; (street) boulevard m // vt (fig) faire étalage de // vi défiler.

**paradise** ['pærədaɪs] n paradis m.

**paradox** ['pærədɔks] n paradoxe m ; **~ical** [-'dɔksɪkl] a paradoxal(e).

**paraffin** ['pærəfɪn] n: (oil) pétrole (lampant) ; **liquid ~** huile f de paraffine.

**paragraph** ['pærəgrɑ:f] n paragraphe m.

**parallel** ['pærəlɛl] a parallèle ; (fig) analogue // n (line) parallèle f ; (fig, GEO) parallèle m.

**paralysis** [pə'rælɪsɪs] n paralysie f.

**paralytic** [pærə'lɪtɪk] a paralysé(e) ; paralysant(e).

**paralyze** ['pærəlaɪz] vt paralyser.

**paramount** ['pærəmaunt] a: **of ~ importance** de la plus haute or grande importance.

**paranoia** [pærə'nɔɪə] n paranoia f.

**paraphernalia** [pærəfə'neɪlɪə] n attirail m, affaires fpl.

**paraphrase** ['pærəfreɪz] vt paraphraser.

**paraplegic** [pærə'pli:dʒɪk] n paraplégique m/f.

**parasite** ['pærəsaɪt] n parasite m.

**paratrooper** ['pærətru:pə*] n parachutiste m (soldat).

**parcel** ['pɑ:sl] n paquet m, colis m // vt

(also: ~ up) empaqueter ; ~ **post** n service m de colis postaux.

**parch** [pɑ:ʃ] vt dessécher ; ~**ed** a (person) asoiffé(e).

**parchment** ['pɑ:tʃmənt] n parchemin m.

**pardon** ['pɑ:dn] n pardon m ; grâce f // vt pardonner à ; (LAW) gracier ; ~! pardon! ; ~ **me**! excusez-moi! ; **I beg your** ~! pardon!, je suis désolé! ; **I beg your** ~? pardon?

**parent** ['pɛərənt] n père m or mère f ; ~**s** npl parents mpl ; ~**al** [pə'rɛntl] a parental(e), des parents.

**parenthesis,**    pl    **parentheses** [pə'rɛnθɪsɪs, -siːz] n parenthèse f.

**Paris** ['pærɪs] n Paris.

**parish** ['pærɪʃ] n paroisse f ; (civil) ≈ commune f // a paroissial(e) ; ~**ioner** [pə'rɪʃənə*] n paroissien/ne.

**Parisian** [pə'rɪzɪən] a parisien(ne) // n Parisien/ne.

**parity** ['pærɪtɪ] n parité f.

**park** [pɑ:k] n parc m, jardin public // vt garer // vi se garer ; ~**ing** n stationnement m ; ~**ing lot** n (US) parking m, parc m de stationnement ; ~**ing meter** n parcomètre m ; ~**ing place** n place f de stationnement.

**parliament** ['pɑ:ləmənt] n parlement m ; ~**ary** [-'mɛntərɪ] parlementaire.

**parlour, parlor** (US) ['pɑ:lə*] n salon m.

**parochial** [pə'rəukɪəl] a paroissial(e) ; (pej) à l'esprit de clocher.

**parody** ['pærədɪ] n parodie f.

**parole** [pə'rəul] n: **on** ~ en liberté conditionnelle.

**parquet** ['pɑ:keɪ] n: ~ **floor(ing)** parquet m.

**parrot** ['pærət] n perroquet m ; ~ **fashion** ad comme un perroquet.

**parry** ['pærɪ] vt esquiver, parer à.

**parsimonious**     [pɑ:sɪ'məunɪəs]     a parcimonieux(euse).

**parsley** ['pɑ:slɪ] n persil m.

**parsnip** ['pɑ:snɪp] n panais m.

**parson** ['pɑ:sn] n ecclésiastique m ; (Church of England) pasteur m.

**part** [pɑ:t] n partie f ; (of machine) pièce f ; (THEATRE etc) rôle m ; (MUS) voix f ; partie // a partiel(le) // ad = **partly** // vt séparer // vi (people) se séparer ; (roads) se diviser ; **to take** ~ **in** participer à, prendre part à ; **on his** ~ de sa part ; **for my** ~ en ce qui me concerne ; **for the most** ~ en grande partie ; dans la plupart des cas ; **to** ~ **with** vt fus se séparer de ; se défaire de ; (take leave) quitter, prendre congé de ; **in** ~ **exchange** en reprise.

**partial** ['pɑ:ʃl] a partiel(le) ; (unjust) partial(e) ; **to be** ~ **to** aimer, avoir un faible pour ; ~**ly** ad en partie, partiellement ; partialement.

**participate** [pɑ:'tɪsɪpeɪt] vi: **to** ~ **(in)** participer (à), prendre part (à) ; **participation** [-'peɪʃən] n participation f.

**participle** ['pɑ:tɪsɪpl] n participe m.

**particle** ['pɑ:tɪkl] n particule f.

**particular** [pə'tɪkjulə*] a particulier(ère) ; spécial(e) ; (detailed) détaillé(e) ; (fussy) difficile ; méticuleux(euse) ; ~**s** npl détails mpl ; (information) renseignements mpl ;

~**ly** ad particulièrement ; en particulier.

**parting** ['pɑ:tɪŋ] n séparation f ; (in hair) raie f // a d'adieu.

**partisan** [pɑ:tɪ'zæn] n partisan/e // a partisan(e) ; de parti.

**partition** [pɑ:'tɪʃən] n (POL) partition f, division f ; (wall) cloison f.

**partly** ['pɑ:tlɪ] ad en partie, partiellement.

**partner** ['pɑ:tnə*] n (COMM) associé/e ; (SPORT) partenaire m/f ; (at dance) cavalier/ère // vt être l'associé or le partenaire or le cavalier de ; ~**ship** n association f.

**partridge** ['pɑ:trɪdʒ] n perdrix f.

**part-time** ['pɑ:t'taɪm] a,ad à mi-temps, à temps partiel.

**party** ['pɑ:tɪ] n (POL) parti m ; (team) équipe f ; groupe m ; (LAW) partie f ; (celebration) réception f ; soirée f ; fête f.

**pass** [pɑ:s] vt (time, object) passer ; (place) passer devant ; (car, friend) croiser ; (exam) être reçu(e) à, réussir ; (candidate) admettre ; (overtake, surpass) dépasser ; (approve) approuver, accepter // vi passer ; (SCOL) être reçu(e) or admis(e), réussir // n (permit) laissez-passer m inv ; carte f d'accès or d'abonnement ; (in mountains) col m ; (SPORT) passe f ; (SCOL: also: ~ **mark**): **to get a** ~ être reçu(e) (sans mention) ; **to** ~ **sth through a ring** etc (faire) passer qch dans un anneau etc ; **could you** ~ **the vegetables round?** pourriez-vous faire passer les légumes? ; **to** ~ **away** vi mourir ; **to** ~ **by** vi passer // vt négliger ; **to** ~ **for** passer pour ; **to** ~ **out** vi s'évanouir ; ~**able** a (road) praticable ; (work) acceptable.

**passage** ['pæsɪdʒ] n (also: ~**way**) couloir m ; (gen, in book) passage m ; (by boat) traversée f.

**passenger** ['pæsɪndʒə*] n passager/ère.

**passer-by** [pɑ:sə'baɪ] n passant/e.

**passing** ['pɑ:sɪŋ] a (fig) passager(ère) ; **in** ~ en passant.

**passion** ['pæʃən] n passion f ; amour m ; **to have a** ~ **for sth** avoir la passion de qch ; ~**ate** a passionné(e).

**passive** ['pæsɪv] a (also LING) passif(ive).

**Passover** ['pɑ:səuvə*] n Pâque (juive).

**passport** ['pɑ:spɔ:t] n passeport m.

**password** ['pɑ:swə:d] n mot m de passe.

**past** [pɑ:st] prep (further than) au delà de, plus loin que ; après ; (later than) après // a passé(e) ; (president etc) ancien(ne) // n passé m ; **he's** ~ **forty** il a dépassé la quarantaine, il a plus de or passé quarante ans ; **it's** ~ **midnight** il est plus de minuit, il est passé minuit ; **for the** ~ **few/3 days** depuis quelques/3 jours ; ces derniers/3 derniers jours ; **to run** ~ passer en courant ; **he ran** ~ **me** il m'a dépassé en courant ; il a passé devant moi en courant.

**pasta** ['pæstə] n pâtes fpl.

**paste** [peɪst] n (glue) colle f (de pâte) ; (jewellery) strass m ; (CULIN) pâté m (à tartiner) ; pâte f // vt coller.

**pastel** ['pæstl] a pastel inv.

**pasteurized** ['pæstəraɪzd] a pasteurisé(e).

**pastille** ['pæstl] n pastille f.

**pastime** ['pɑ:staɪm] n passe-temps m inv, distraction f.

**pastoral** ['pɑ:stərl] a pastoral(e).

**pastry** ['peɪstrɪ] n pâte f; (cake) pâtisserie f.

**pasture** ['pɑ:stʃə*] n pâturage m.

**pasty** n ['pæstɪ] petit pâté (en croûte) // a ['peɪstɪ] pâteux(euse); (complexion) terreux(euse).

**pat** [pæt] vt donner une petite tape à // n: a ~ of butter une noisette de beurre.

**patch** [pætʃ] n (of material) pièce f; (spot) tache f; (of land) parcelle f // vt (clothes) rapiécer; a bad ~ une période difficile; to ~ up vt réparer; ~work n patchwork m; ~y a inégal(e).

**pate** [peɪt] n: a bald ~ un crâne chauve or dégarni.

**pâté** ['pæteɪ] n pâté m, terrine f.

**patent** ['peɪtnt] n brevet m (d'invention) // vt faire breveter // a patent(e), manifeste; ~ leather n cuir verni; ~ medicine n spécialité f pharmaceutique.

**paternal** [pə'tə:nl] a paternel(le).

**paternity** [pə'tə:nɪtɪ] n paternité f.

**path** [pɑ:θ] n chemin m, sentier m; allée f; (of planet) course f; (of missile) trajectoire f.

**pathetic** [pə'θɛtɪk] a (pitiful) pitoyable; (very bad) lamentable, minable; (moving) pathétique.

**pathologist** [pə'θɔlədʒɪst] n pathologiste m/f.

**pathology** [pə'θɔlədʒɪ] n pathologie f.

**pathos** ['peɪθɔs] n pathétique m.

**pathway** ['pɑ:θweɪ] n chemin m, sentier m.

**patience** ['peɪʃns] n patience f; (CARDS) réussite f.

**patient** ['peɪʃnt] n patient/e; malade m/f // a patient(e) // ~ly ad patiemment.

**patio** ['pætɪəu] n patio m.

**patriotic** [pætrɪ'ɔtɪk] a patriotique; (person) patriote.

**patrol** [pə'trəul] n patrouille f // vt patrouiller dans; ~ car n voiture f de police; ~man n (US) agent m de police.

**patron** ['peɪtrən] n (in shop) client/e; (of charity) patron/ne; ~ of the arts mécène m; ~age ['pætrənɪdʒ] n patronage m, appui m; ~ize ['pætrənaɪz] vt être (un) client or un habitué de; (fig) traiter avec condescendance; ~ saint n saint(e) patron(ne).

**patter** ['pætə*] n crépitement m, tapotement m; (sales talk) boniment m // vi crépiter, tapoter.

**pattern** ['pætən] n modèle m; (SEWING) patron m; (design) motif m; (sample) échantillon m.

**paunch** [pɔ:ntʃ] n gros ventre, bedaine f.

**pauper** ['pɔ:pə*] n indigent/e; ~'s grave n fosse commune.

**pause** [pɔ:z] n pause f, arrêt m; (MUS) silence m // vi faire une pause, s'arrêter.

**pave** [peɪv] vt paver, daller; to ~ the way for ouvrir la voie à.

**pavement** ['peɪvmənt] n (Brit) trottoir m.

**pavilion** [pə'vɪlɪən] n pavillon m; tente f.

**paving** ['peɪvɪŋ] n pavage m, dallage m; ~ stone n pavé m.

**paw** [pɔ:] n patte f // vt donner un coup de patte à; (subj: person: pej) tripoter.

**pawn** [pɔ:n] n gage m; (CHESS, also fig) pion m // vt mettre en gage; ~broker n prêteur m sur gages; ~shop n mont-de-piété m.

**pay** [peɪ] n salaire m; paie f // vb (pt, pp **paid** [peɪd]) vt payer // vi payer; (be profitable) être rentable; to ~ attention (to) prêter attention (à); to ~ back vt rembourser; to ~ for vt payer; to ~ in vt verser; to ~ up vt régler; ~able a payable; ~ day n jour m de paie; ~ee n bénéficiaire m/f; ~ing a payant(e); ~ment n paiement m; règlement m; versement m; ~ packet n paie f; ~roll n registre m du personnel; ~ slip n bulletin m de paie.

**p.c.** abbr of per cent.

**pea** [pi:] n (petit) pois.

**peace** [pi:s] n paix f; (calm) calme m, tranquillité f; ~able a paisible; ~ful a paisible, calme; ~-keeping n maintien m de la paix; ~ offering n gage m de réconciliation.

**peach** [pi:tʃ] n pêche f.

**peacock** ['pi:kɔk] n paon m.

**peak** [pi:k] n (mountain) pic m, cime f; (fig: highest level) maximum m; (: of career, fame) apogée m; ~ period n période f de pointe.

**peal** [pi:l] n (of bells) carillon m; ~s of laughter éclats mpl de rire.

**peanut** ['pi:nʌt] n arachide f, cacahuète f; ~ butter n beurre m de cacahuète.

**pear** [pɛə*] n poire f.

**pearl** [pə:l] n perle f.

**peasant** ['pɛznt] n paysan/ne.

**peat** [pi:t] n tourbe f.

**pebble** ['pɛbl] n galet m, caillou m.

**peck** [pɛk] vt (also: ~ at) donner un coup de bec à; (food) picorer // n coup m de bec; (kiss) bécot m; ~ing order n ordre m des préséances; ~ish a (col): I feel ~ish je mangerais bien quelque chose, j'ai la dent.

**peculiar** [pɪ'kju:lɪə*] a étrange, bizarre, curieux(euse); particulier(ère); ~ to particulier à; ~ity [pɪkju:lɪ'ærɪtɪ] n particularité f; (oddity) bizarrerie f.

**pecuniary** [pɪ'kju:nɪərɪ] a pécuniaire.

**pedal** ['pɛdl] n pédale f // vi pédaler.

**pedantic** [pɪ'dæntɪk] a pédant(e).

**peddle** ['pɛdl] vt colporter.

**pedestal** ['pɛdəstl] n piédestal m.

**pedestrian** [pɪ'dɛstrɪən] n piéton m // a piétonnier(ère); (fig) prosaïque, terre à terre inv; ~ crossing n passage clouté m.

**pediatrics** [pi:dɪ'ætrɪks] n (US) = **paediatrics**.

**pedigree** ['pɛdɪgri:] n ascendance f; (of animal) pedigree m // cpd (animal) de race.

**peek** [pi:k] vi jeter un coup d'œil (furtif).

**peel** [pi:l] n pelure f, épluchure f; (of orange, lemon) écorce f // vt peler, éplucher // vi (paint etc) s'écailler; (wallpaper) se décoller; ~ings npl pelures fpl, épluchures fpl.

**peep** [pi:p] n (look) coup d'œil furtif; (sound) pépiement m // vi jeter un coup d'œil (furtif); to ~ out vi se montrer (furtivement); ~hole n judas m.

**peer** [pɪə*] vi: **to ~ at** regarder attentivement, scruter // n (noble) pair m; (equal) pair m, égal/e; **~age** n pairie f; **~less** n incomparable, sans égal.

**peeved** [pi:vd] a irrité(e), ennuyé(e).

**peevish** ['pi:vɪʃ] a grincheux(euse), maussade.

**peg** [pɛg] n cheville f; (for coat etc) patère f; (also: **clothes ~**) pince f à linge; **off the ~** ad en prêt-à-porter.

**pejorative** [pɪ'dʒɔrətɪv] a péjoratif(ive).

**pekingese** [pi:kɪ'ni:z] n pékinois m.

**pelican** ['pɛlɪkən] n pélican m.

**pellet** ['pɛlɪt] n boulette f; (of lead) plomb m.

**pelmet** ['pɛlmɪt] n cantonnière f; lambrequin m.

**pelt** [pɛlt] vt: **to ~ sb (with)** bombarder qn (de) // vi (rain) tomber à seaux // n peau f.

**pelvis** ['pɛlvɪs] n bassin m.

**pen** [pɛn] n (for writing) stylo m; (for sheep) parc m.

**penal** ['pi:nl] a pénal(e); **~ize** vt pénaliser; (fig) désavantager; **~ servitude** n travaux forcés.

**penalty** ['pɛnltɪ] n pénalité f; sanction f; (fine) amende f; (SPORT) pénalisation f; **~ (kick)** n (FOOTBALL) penalty m.

**penance** ['pɛnəns] n pénitence f.

**pence** [pɛns] npl of **penny**.

**pencil** ['pɛnsl] n crayon m // vt: **to ~ sth in** noter qch au crayon; **~ sharpener** n taille-crayon(s) m inv.

**pendant** ['pɛndnt] n pendentif m.

**pending** ['pɛndɪŋ] prep en attendant // a en suspens.

**pendulum** ['pɛndjuləm] n pendule m; (of clock) balancier m.

**penetrate** ['pɛnɪtreɪt] vt pénétrer dans; pénétrer; **penetrating** a pénétrant(e); **penetration** [-'treɪʃən] n pénétration f.

**penfriend** ['pɛnfrɛnd] n correspondant/e.

**penguin** ['pɛŋgwɪn] n pingouin m.

**penicillin** [pɛnɪ'sɪlɪn] n pénicilline f.

**peninsula** [pə'nɪnsjulə] n péninsule f.

**penis** ['pi:nɪs] n pénis m, verge f.

**penitence** ['pɛnɪtns] n repentir m.

**penitent** ['pɛnɪtnt] a repentant(e).

**penitentiary** [pɛnɪ'tɛnʃərɪ] n (US) prison f.

**penknife** ['pɛnnaɪf] n canif m.

**pennant** ['pɛnənt] n flamme f, banderole f.

**penniless** ['pɛnɪlɪs] a sans le sou.

**penny,** pl **pennies** or **pence** ['pɛnɪ, 'pɛnɪz, pɛns] n penny m (pl pennies) (new: 100 in a pound; old: 12 in a shilling; on tend à employer 'pennies' ou 'two-pence piece' etc pour les pièces, 'pence' pour la valeur).

**pension** ['pɛnʃən] n retraite f; (MIL.) pension f; **~able** a qui a droit à une retraite; **~er** n retraité/e; **~ fund** n caisse f de retraite.

**pensive** ['pɛnsɪv] a pensif(ive).

**pentagon** ['pɛntəgən] n pentagone m.

**Pentecost** ['pɛntɪkɔst] n Pentecôte f.

**penthouse** ['pɛnthaus] n appartement m (de luxe) en attique.

**pent-up** ['pɛntʌp] a (feelings) refoulé(e).

**penultimate** [pɛ'nʌltɪmət] a pénultième, avant-dernier(ère).

**people** ['pi:pl] npl gens mpl; personnes fpl; (citizens) peuple m // n (nation, race) peuple m // vt peupler; **4/several ~ came** 4/plusieurs personnes sont venues; **the room was full of ~** la salle était pleine de monde or de gens; **~ say that...** on dit or les gens disent que.

**pep** [pɛp] n (col) entrain m, dynamisme m; **to ~ up** vt remonter.

**pepper** ['pɛpə*] n poivre m; (vegetable) poivron m // vt poivrer; **~mint** n (plant) menthe poivrée; (sweet) pastille f de menthe.

**peptalk** ['pɛptɔ:k] n (col) (petit) discours d'encouragement.

**per** [pə:*] prep par; **~ hour** (miles etc) à l'heure; (fee) (de) l'heure; **~ kilo** etc le kilo etc; **~ day/person** par jour/personne; **~ cent** pour cent; **~ annum** par an.

**perceive** [pə'si:v] vt percevoir; (notice) remarquer, s'apercevoir de.

**percentage** [pə'sɛntɪdʒ] n pourcentage m.

**perceptible** [pə'sɛptɪbl] a perceptible.

**perception** [pə'sɛpʃən] n perception f; sensibilité f; perspicacité f.

**perceptive** [pə'sɛptɪv] a pénétrant(e); perspicace.

**perch** [pə:tʃ] n (fish) perche f; (for bird) perchoir m // vi (se) percher.

**percolator** ['pə:kəleɪtə*] n percolateur m; cafetière f électrique.

**percussion** [pə'kʌʃən] n percussion f.

**peremptory** [pə'rɛmptərɪ] a péremptoire.

**perennial** [pə'rɛnɪəl] a perpétuel(le); (BOT) vivace // n plante f vivace.

**perfect** a,n ['pə:fɪkt] a parfait(e) // n (also: **~ tense**) parfait m // vt [pə'fɛkt] parfaire; mettre au point; **~ion** [-'fɛkʃən] n perfection f; **~ionist** n perfectionniste m/f; **~ly** ad parfaitement.

**perforate** ['pə:fəreɪt] vt perforer, percer; **perforation** [-'reɪʃən] n perforation f; (line of holes) pointillé m.

**perform** [pə'fɔ:m] vt (carry out) exécuter, remplir; (concert etc) jouer, donner // vi jouer; **~ance** n représentation f, spectacle m; (of an artist) interprétation f; (of player etc) prestation f; (of car, engine) performance f; **~er** n artiste m/f; **~ing** a (animal) savant(e).

**perfume** ['pə:fju:m] n parfum m // vt parfumer.

**perfunctory** [pə'fʌŋktərɪ] a négligent(e), pour la forme.

**perhaps** [pə'hæps] ad peut-être; **~ he'll...** peut-être qu'il... .

**peril** ['pɛrɪl] n péril m; **~ous** a périlleux(euse).

**perimeter** [pə'rɪmɪtə*] n périmètre m; **~ wall** n mur m d'enceinte.

**period** ['pɪərɪəd] n période f; (HISTORY) époque f; (SCOL) cours m; (full stop) point m; (MED) règles fpl // a (costume, furniture) d'époque; **~ic** [-'ɔdɪk] a périodique; **~ical** [-'ɔdɪkl] a périodique // n périodique m; **~ically** [-'ɔdɪklɪ] ad périodiquement.

**peripheral** [pə'rıfərəl] a périphérique.
**periphery** [pə'rıfərı] n périphérie f.
**periscope** ['pərıskəup] n périscope m.
**perish** ['pɛrıʃ] vi périr, mourir ; (decay) se détériorer ; ~**able** a périssable ; ~**ing** a (col: cold) glacial(e).
**perjure** ['pə:dʒə*] vt: **to** ~ **o.s.** se parjurer ; **perjury** n (LAW: in court) faux témoignage ; (breach of oath) parjure m.
**perk** [pə:k] n avantage m, à-côté m ; **to** ~ **up** vi (cheer up) se ragaillardir ; ~**y** a (cheerful) guilleret(te), gai(e).
**perm** [pə:m] n (for hair) permanente f.
**permanence** ['pə:mənəns] n permanence f.
**permanent** ['pə:mənənt] a permanent(e) ; ~**ly** ad de façon permanente.
**permeable** ['pə:mıəbl] a perméable.
**permeate** ['pə:mıeıt] vi s'infiltrer // vt s'infiltrer dans ; pénétrer.
**permissible** [pə'mısıbl] a permis(e), acceptable.
**permission** [pə'mıʃən] n permission f, autorisation f.
**permissive** [pə'mısıv] a tolérant(e) ; **the** ~ **society** la société de tolérance.
**permit** n ['pə:mıt] permis m // vt [pə'mıt] permettre ; **to** ~ **sb to do** autoriser qn à faire, permettre à qn de faire.
**permutation** [pə:mju'teıʃən] n permutation f.
**pernicious** [pə:'nıʃəs] a pernicieux(euse), nocif(ive).
**pernickety** [pə'nıkıtı] a pointilleux(euse), tatillon(ne).
**perpendicular** [pə:pən'dıkjulə*] a,n perpendiculaire (f).
**perpetrate** ['pə:pıtreıt] vt perpétrer, commettre.
**perpetual** [pə'pɛtjuəl] a perpétuel(le).
**perpetuate** [pə'pɛtjueıt] vt perpétuer.
**perpetuity** [pə:pı'tju:ıtı] n: **in** ~ à perpétuité.
**perplex** [pə'plɛks] vt rendre perplexe ; (complicate) embrouiller.
**persecute** ['pə:sıkju:t] vt persécuter ; **persecution** [-'kju:ʃən] n persécution f.
**persevere** [pə:sı'vıə*] vi persévérer.
**Persian** ['pə:ʃən] a persan(e) // n (LING) persan m ; **the (**~**) Gulf** n le golfe Persique.
**persist** [pə'sıst] vi: **to** ~ **(in doing)** persister (à faire), s'obstiner (à faire) ; ~**ence** n persistance f, obstination f ; opiniâtreté f ; ~**ent** a persistant(e), tenace.
**person** ['pə:sn] n personne f ; ~**able** a de belle prestance, au physique attrayant ; ~**al** a personnel(le) ; individuel(le) ; ~**al assistant (P.A.)** n secrétaire privé/e ; ~**al call** (TEL) communication f avec préavis ; ~**ality** [-'nælıtı] n personnalité f ; ~**ally** ad personnellement ; ~**ify** [-'sɔnıfaı] vt personnifier.
**personnel** [pə:sə'nɛl] n personnel m ; ~ **manager** n chef m du personnel.
**perspective** [pə'spɛktıv] n perspective f.
**perspex** ['pə:spɛks] n sorte de plexiglas.
**perspicacity** [pə:spı'kæsıtı] n perspicacité f.
**perspiration** [pə:spı'reıʃən] n transpiration f.

**perspire** [pə'spaıə*] vi transpirer.
**persuade** [pə'sweıd] vt persuader.
**persuasion** [pə'sweıʒən] n persuasion f.
**persuasive** [pə'sweısıv] a persuasif(ive).
**pert** [pə:t] a (brisk) sec(sèche), brusque ; (bold) effronté(e), impertinent(e).
**pertaining** [pə:'teınıŋ]: ~ **to** prep relatif(ive) à.
**pertinent** ['pə:tınənt] a pertinent(e).
**perturb** [pə'tə:b] vt perturber ; inquiéter.
**Peru** [pə'ru:] n Pérou m.
**perusal** [pə'ru:zl] n lecture (attentive).
**Peruvian** [pə'ru:vjən] a péruvien(ne) // n Péruvien/ne.
**pervade** [pə'veıd] vt se répandre dans, envahir.
**perverse** [pə'və:s] a pervers(e) ; (stubborn) entêté(e), contrariant(e).
**perversion** [pə'və:ʃn] n perversion f.
**perversity** [pə'və:sıtı] n perversité f.
**pervert** n ['pə:və:t] perverti/e // vt [pə'və:t] pervertir.
**pessimism** ['pɛsımızəm] n pessimisme m.
**pessimist** ['pɛsımıst] n pessimiste m/f ; ~**ic** [-'mıstık] a pessimiste.
**pest** [pɛst] n animal m (or insecte m) nuisible ; (fig) fléau m.
**pester** ['pɛstə*] vt importuner, harceler.
**pesticide** ['pɛstısaıd] n pesticide m.
**pestle** ['pɛsl] n pilon m.
**pet** [pɛt] n animal familier ; (favourite) chouchou m // vt choyer // vi (col) se peloter ; ~ **lion** n lion apprivoisé.
**petal** ['pɛtl] n pétale m.
**peter** ['pi:tə*]: **to** ~ **out** vi s'épuiser ; s'affaiblir.
**petite** [pə'ti:t] a menu(e).
**petition** [pə'tıʃən] n pétition f // vt adresser une pétition à.
**petrified** ['pɛtrıfaıd] a (fig) mort(e) de peur.
**petrify** ['pɛtrıfaı] vt pétrifier.
**petrol** ['pɛtrəl] n (Brit) essence f ; ~ **engine** n moteur m à essence.
**petroleum** [pə'trəulıəm] n pétrole m.
**petrol:** ~ **pump** n (in car, at garage) pompe f à essence ; ~ **station** n station-service f ; ~ **tank** n réservoir m d'essence.
**petticoat** ['pɛtıkəut] n jupon m.
**pettifogging** ['pɛtıfɔgıŋ] a chicanier(ère).
**pettiness** ['pɛtınıs] n mesquinerie f.
**petty** ['pɛtı] a (mean) mesquin(e) ; (unimportant) insignifiant(e), sans importance ; ~ **cash** n menue monnaie ; ~ **officer** n second-maître m.
**petulant** ['pɛtjulənt] a irritable.
**pew** [pju:] n banc m (d'église).
**pewter** ['pju:tə*] n étain m.
**phallic** ['fælık] a phallique.
**phantom** ['fæntəm] n fantôme m ; (vision) fantasme m.
**Pharaoh** ['fɛərəu] n pharaon m.
**pharmacist** ['fɑ:məsıst] n pharmacien/ne.
**pharmacy** ['fɑ:məsı] n pharmacie f.
**phase** [feız] n phase f, période f // vt: **to** ~ **sth in/out** introduire/supprimer qch progressivement.
**Ph.D.** (abbr = Doctor of Philosophy) title ≈ Docteur m en Droit or Lettres etc // n ≈ doctorat m ; titulaire m d'un doctorat.

**pheasant** ['fɛznt] n faisan m.
**phenomenon,** pl **phenomena**
[fə'nɔmɪnən, -nə] n phénomène m.
**phew** [fju:] excl ouf!
**phial** ['faɪəl] n fiole f.
**philanderer** [fɪ'lændərə*] n don Juan m.
**philanthropic** [fɪlən'θrɔpɪk] a philan-
thropique.
**philanthropist** [fɪ'lænθrəpɪst] n philanthrope m/f.
**philatelist** [fɪ'lætəlɪst] n philatéliste m/f.
**philately** [fɪ'lætəlɪ] n philatélie f.
**Philippines** ['fɪlɪpi:nz] npl (also:
Philippine Islands) Philippines fpl.
**philosopher** [fɪ'lɔsəfə*] n philosophe m.
**philosophical** [fɪlə'sɔfɪkl] a philosophique.
**philosophy** [fɪ'lɔsəfɪ] n philosophie f.
**phlegm** [flɛm] n flegme m; ~**atic**
[flɛg'mætɪk] a flegmatique.
**phobia** ['fəubjə] n phobie f.
**phone** [fəun] n téléphone m // vt
téléphoner; **to be on the** ~ avoir le
téléphone; (be calling) être au téléphone;
**to** ~ **back** vt,vi rappeler.
**phonetics** [fə'nɛtɪks] n phonétique f.
**phoney** ['fəunɪ] a faux(fausse), factice //
n (person) charlatan m; fumiste m/f.
**phonograph** ['fəunəgrɑ:f] n (US)
électrophone m.
**phony** ['fəunɪ] a,n = **phoney**.
**phosphate** ['fɔsfeɪt] n phosphate m.
**phosphorus** ['fɔsfərəs] n phosphore m.
**photo** ['fəutəu] n photo f.
**photo...** ['fəutəu] prefix: ~**copier** n
machine f à photocopier; ~**copy** n
photocopie f // vt photocopier; ~**electric**
a photoélectrique; ~**genic** [-'dʒɛnɪk] a
photogénique; ~**graph** n photographie f
// vt photographier; ~**grapher**
[fə'tɔgrəfə*] n photographe m/f;
~**graphic** [-'græfɪk] a photographique;
~**graphy** [fə'tɔgrəfɪ] n photographie f;
~**stat** ['fəutəustæt] n photocopie f,
photostat m.
**phrase** [freɪz] n expression f; (LING)
locution f // vt exprimer; ~**book** n recueil
m d'expressions (pour touristes).
**physical** ['fɪzɪkl] a physique; ~**ly** ad
physiquement.
**physician** [fɪ'zɪʃən] n médecin m.
**physicist** ['fɪzɪsɪst] n physicien/ne.
**physics** ['fɪzɪks] n physique f.
**physiology** [fɪzɪ'ɔlədʒɪ] n physiologie f.
**physiotherapist** [fɪzɪəu'θɛrəpɪst] n
kinésithérapeute m/f.
**physiotherapy** [fɪzɪəu'θɛrəpɪ] n
kinésithérapie f.
**physique** [fɪ'zi:k] n physique m;
constitution f.
**pianist** ['pi:ənɪst] n pianiste m/f.
**piano** [pɪ'ænəu] n piano m.
**piccolo** ['pɪkələu] n piccolo m.
**pick** [pɪk] n (tool: also: ~**-axe**) pic m,
pioche f // vt choisir; (gather) cueillir;
**take your** ~ faites votre choix; **the** ~
of le(la) meilleur(e) de; **to** ~ **a bone**
ronger un os; **to** ~ **one's teeth** se curer
les dents; **to** ~ **pockets** pratiquer le vol
à la tire; **to** ~ **on** vt fus (person) harceler;
**to** ~ **out** vt choisir; (distinguish)

**distinguer; to** ~ **up** vi (improve) remonter,
s'améliorer // vt ramasser; (telephone)
décrocher; (collect) passer prendre;
(learn) apprendre; **to** ~ **up speed** prendre
de la vitesse; **to** ~ **o.s. up** se relever.
**picket** ['pɪkɪt] n (in strike) gréviste m/f
participant à un piquet de grève; piquet
m de grève // vt mettre un piquet de grève
devant; ~ **line** n piquet m de grève.
**pickle** ['pɪkl] n (also: ~**s:** as condiment)
pickles mpl // vt conserver dans du
vinaigre or dans de la saumure.
**pick-me-up** ['pɪkmiːʌp] n remontant m.
**pickpocket** ['pɪkpɔkɪt] n pickpocket m.
**pickup** ['pɪkʌp] n (on record player) bras
m pick-up; (small truck) pick-up m inv.
**picnic** ['pɪknɪk] n pique-nique m // vi
pique-niquer; ~**ker** n pique-niqueur/euse.
**pictorial** [pɪk'tɔ:rɪəl] a illustré(e).
**picture** ['pɪktʃə*] n image f; (painting)
peinture f, tableau m; (photograph)
photo(graphie) f; (drawing) dessin m;
(film) film m // vt se représenter;
(describe) dépeindre, représenter; **the** ~**s**
le cinéma m; ~ **book** n livre m d'images.
**picturesque** [pɪktʃə'rɛsk] a pittoresque.
**picture window** ['pɪktʃəwɪndəu] n baie
vitrée, fenêtre f panoramique.
**piddling** ['pɪdlɪŋ] a (col) insignifiant(e).
**pidgin** ['pɪdʒɪn] a: ~ **English** n pidgin m.
**pie** [paɪ] n tourte f; (of meat) pâté m en
croûte.
**piebald** ['paɪbɔ:ld] a pie inv.
**piece** [pi:s] n morceau m; (of land) parcelle
f; (item): a ~ **of furniture/advice** un
meuble/conseil // vt: **to** ~ **together**
rassembler; **in** ~**s** (broken) en morceaux,
en miettes; (not yet assembled) en pièces
détachées; **to take to** ~**s** démonter;
~**meal** ad par bouts; ~**work** n travail m
aux pièces.
**pier** [pɪə*] n jetée f; (of bridge etc) pile f.
**pierce** [pɪəs] vt percer, transpercer.
**piercing** ['pɪəsɪŋ] a (cry) perçant(e).
**piety** ['paɪətɪ] n piété f.
**piffling** ['pɪflɪŋ] a insignifiant(e).
**pig** [pɪg] n cochon m, porc m.
**pigeon** ['pɪdʒən] n pigeon m; ~**hole** n
casier m; ~**-toed** a marchant les pieds en
dedans.
**piggy bank** ['pɪgɪbæŋk] n tirelire f.
**pigheaded** ['pɪg'hɛdɪd] a entêté(e), têtu(e).
**piglet** ['pɪglɪt] n petit cochon, porcelet m.
**pigment** ['pɪgmənt] n pigment m; ~**ation**
[-'teɪʃən] n pigmentation f.
**pigmy** ['pɪgmɪ] n = **pygmy.**
**pigsty** ['pɪgstaɪ] n porcherie f.
**pigtail** ['pɪgteɪl] n natte f, tresse f.
**pike** [paɪk] n (spear) pique f; (fish) brochet
m.
**pilchard** ['pɪltʃəd] n pilchard m (sorte de
sardine).
**pile** [paɪl] n (pillar, of books) pile f; (heap)
tas m; (of carpet) épaisseur f // vb (also:
~ **up**) vt empiler, entasser // vi s'entasser.
**piles** [paɪlz] n hémorroïdes fpl.
**pileup** ['paɪlʌp] n (AUT) télescopage m,
collision f en série.
**pilfer** ['pɪlfə*] vt chaparder; ~**ing** n
chapardage m.

**pilgrim** ['pɪlgrɪm] *n* pèlerin *m*; ~**age** *n* pèlerinage *m*.

**pill** [pɪl] *n* pilule *f*; **the** ~ la pilule.

**pillage** ['pɪlɪdʒ] *vt* piller.

**pillar** ['pɪlə*] *n* pilier *m*; ~ **box** *n* (*Brit*) boîte *f* aux lettres.

**pillion** ['pɪljən] *n* (*of motor cycle*) siège *m* arrière; **to ride** ~ être derrière; (*on horse*) être en croupe.

**pillory** ['pɪlərɪ] *n* pilori *m* // *vt* mettre au pilori.

**pillow** ['pɪləu] *n* oreiller *m*; ~**case** *n* taie *f* d'oreiller.

**pilot** ['paɪlət] *n* pilote *m* // *cpd* (*scheme etc*) pilote, expérimental(e) // *vt* piloter; ~ **boat** *n* bateau-pilote *m*; ~ **light** *n* veilleuse *f*.

**pimp** [pɪmp] *n* souteneur *m*, maquereau *m*.

**pimple** ['pɪmpl] *n* bouton *m*; **pimply** *a* boutonneux(euse).

**pin** [pɪn] *n* épingle *f*; (*TECH*) cheville *f* // *vt* épingler; ~**s and needles** fourmis *fpl*; **to** ~ **sb against**/**to** clouer qn contre/à; **to** ~ **sb down** (*fig*) obliger qn à répondre.

**pinafore** ['pɪnəfɔ:*] *n* tablier *m*; ~ **dress** *n* robe-chasuble *f*.

**pincers** ['pɪnsəz] *npl* tenailles *fpl*.

**pinch** [pɪntʃ] *n* pincement *m*; (*of salt etc*) pincée *f* // *vt* pincer; (*col*: *steal*) piquer, chiper // *vi* (*shoe*) serrer; **at a** ~ à la rigueur.

**pincushion** ['pɪnkuʃən] *n* pelote *f* à épingles.

**pine** [paɪn] *n* (*also*: ~ **tree**) pin *m* // *vi*: **to** ~ **for** aspirer à, désirer ardemment; **to** ~ **away** *vi* dépérir.

**pineapple** ['paɪnæpl] *n* ananas *m*.

**ping** [pɪŋ] *n* (*noise*) tintement *m*; ~**-pong** *n* ® ping-pong *m* ®.

**pink** [pɪŋk] *a* rose // *n* (*colour*) rose *m*; (*BOT*) œillet *m*, mignardise *f*.

**pin money** ['pɪnmʌnɪ] *n* argent *m* de poche.

**pinnacle** ['pɪnəkl] *n* pinacle *m*.

**pinpoint** ['pɪnpɔɪnt] *n* pointe *f* d'épingle // *vt* indiquer (avec précision).

**pinstripe** ['pɪnstraɪp] *n* rayure très fine.

**pint** [paɪnt] *n* pinte *f* (= *0.56 l*).

**pinup** ['pɪnʌp] *n* pin-up *f inv*.

**pioneer** [paɪə'nɪə*] *n* explorateur/trice; (*early settler*) pionnier *m*; (*fig*) pionnier *m*, précurseur *m*.

**pious** ['paɪəs] *a* pieux(euse).

**pip** [pɪp] *n* (*seed*) pépin *m*; (*time signal on radio*) top *m*.

**pipe** [paɪp] *n* tuyau *m*, conduite *f*; (*for smoking*) pipe *f*; (*MUS*) pipeau *m* // *vt* amener par tuyau; ~**s** *npl* (*also*: **bag**~**s**) cornemuse *f*; **to** ~ **down** *vi* (*col*) se taire; ~ **dream** *n* chimère *f*, utopie *f*; ~**line** *n* pipe-line *m*; ~**r** *n* joueur/euse de pipeau (*or de cornemuse*); ~ **tobacco** *n* tabac *m* pour la pipe.

**piping** ['paɪpɪŋ] *ad*: ~ **hot** très chaud(e).

**piquant** ['pi:kənt] *a* piquant(e).

**pique** ['pi:k] *n* dépit *m*.

**piracy** ['paɪərəsɪ] *n* piraterie *f*.

**pirate** ['paɪərət] *n* pirate *m*; ~ **radio** *n* radio *f* pirate.

**pirouette** [pɪru'ɛt] *n* pirouette *f* // *vi* faire une *or* des pirouette(s).

**Pisces** ['paɪsi:z] *n* les Poissons *mpl*; **to be** ~ être des Poissons.

**pistol** ['pɪstl] *n* pistolet *m*.

**piston** ['pɪstən] *n* piston *m*.

**pit** [pɪt] *n* trou *m*, fosse *f*; (*also*: **coal** ~) puits *m* de mine; (*also*: **orchestra** ~) fosse *f* d'orchestre // *vt*: **to** ~ **sb against** **sb** opposer qn à qn; ~**s** *npl* (*AUT*) aire *f* de service; **to** ~ **o.s. against** se mesurer à.

**pitch** [pɪtʃ] *n* (*throw*) lancement *m*; (*MUS*) ton *m*; (*of voice*) hauteur *f*; (*SPORT*) terrain *m*; (*NAUT*) tangage *m*; (*tar*) poix *f* // *vt* (*throw*) lancer // *vi* (*fall*) tomber; (*NAUT*) tanguer; **to** ~ **a tent** dresser une tente; **to be** ~**ed forward** être projeté en avant; ~**-black** *a* noir(e) comme poix; ~**ed battle** *n* bataille rangée.

**pitcher** ['pɪtʃə*] *n* cruche *f*.

**pitchfork** ['pɪtʃfɔ:k] *n* fourche *f*.

**piteous** ['pɪtɪəs] *a* pitoyable.

**pitfall** ['pɪtfɔ:l] *n* trappe *f*, piège *m*.

**pith** [pɪθ] *n* (*of plant*) moelle *f*; (*of orange*) intérieur *m* de l'écorce; (*fig*) essence *f*; vigueur *f*.

**pithead** ['pɪthɛd] *n* bouche *f* de puits.

**pithy** ['pɪθɪ] *a* piquant(e); vigoureux(euse).

**pitiable** ['pɪtɪəbl] *a* pitoyable.

**pitiful** ['pɪtɪful] *a* (*touching*) pitoyable; (*contemptible*) lamentable.

**pitiless** ['pɪtɪlɪs] *a* impitoyable.

**pittance** ['pɪtns] *n* salaire *m* de misère.

**pity** ['pɪtɪ] *n* pitié *f* // *vt* plaindre; **what a** ~! quel dommage!; ~**ing** *a* compatissant(e).

**pivot** ['pɪvət] *n* pivot *m* // *vi* pivoter.

**pixie** ['pɪksɪ] *n* lutin *m*.

**placard** ['plækɑ:d] *n* affiche *f*.

**placate** [plə'keɪt] *vt* apaiser, calmer.

**place** [pleɪs] *n* endroit *m*, lieu *m*; (*proper position, rank, seat*) place *f*; (*house*) maison *f*, logement *m*; (*home*): **at**/**to his** ~ chez lui // *vt* (*object*) placer, mettre; (*identify*) situer; reconnaître; **to take** ~ avoir lieu; se passer; **to** ~ **an order** passer une commande; **to be** ~**d** (*in race, exam*) se placer; **out of** ~ (*not suitable*) déplacé(e), inopportun(e); **in the first** ~ d'abord, en premier; ~ **mat** *n* set *m* de table.

**placid** ['plæsɪd] *a* placide; ~**ity** [plə'sɪdɪtɪ] *n* placidité *f*.

**plagiarism** ['pleɪdʒjərɪzm] *n* plagiat *m*.

**plagiarize** ['pleɪdʒjəraɪz] *vt* plagier.

**plague** [pleɪg] *n* fléau *m*; (*MED*) peste *f*.

**plaice** [pleɪs] *n*, *pl inv* carrelet *m*.

**plaid** [plæd] *n* tissu écossais.

**plain** [pleɪn] *a* (*clear*) clair(e), évident(e); (*simple*) simple, ordinaire; (*frank*) franc(franche); (*not handsome*) quelconque, ordinaire; (*cigarette*) sans filtre; (*without seasoning etc*) nature *inv*; (*in one colour*) uni(e) // *ad* franchement, carrément // *n* plaine *f*; **in** ~ **clothes** (*police*) en civil; ~**ly** *ad* clairement; (*frankly*) carrément, sans détours; ~**ness** *n* simplicité *f*.

**plaintiff** ['pleɪntɪf] *n* plaignant/e.

**plait** [plæt] *n* tresse *f*, natte *f* // *vt* tresser, natter.

**plan** [plæn] *n* plan *m*; (*scheme*) projet *m* // *vt* (*think in advance*) projeter; (*prepare*) organiser // vi faire des projets ; **to ~ to do** projeter de faire.

**plane** [pleɪn] n (AVIAT) avion m ; (tree) platane m ; (tool) rabot m ; (ART, MATH etc) plan m // a plan(e), plat(e) // vt (with tool) raboter.

**planet** ['plænɪt] n planète f.

**planetarium** [plænɪ'tɛərɪəm] n planétarium m.

**plank** [plæŋk] n planche f ; (POL) point m d'un programme.

**plankton** ['plæŋktən] n plancton m.

**planner** ['plænə*] n planificateur/trice.

**planning** ['plænɪŋ] n planification f ; **family ~** planning familial.

**plant** [plɑ:nt] n plante f ; (machinery) matériel m ; (factory) usine f // vt planter ; (colony) établir ; (bomb) déposer, poser.

**plantation** [plæn'teɪʃən] n plantation f.

**plant pot** ['plɑ:ntpɔt] n pot m (de fleurs).

**plaque** [plæk] n plaque f.

**plasma** ['plæzmə] n plasma m.

**plaster** ['plɑ:stə*] n plâtre m ; (also: **sticking ~**) pansement adhésif // vt plâtrer ; (cover): **to ~ with** couvrir de ; **in ~** (leg etc) dans le plâtre ; **~ed** a (col) soûl(e) ; **~er** n plâtrier m.

**plastic** ['plæstɪk] n plastique m // a (made of plastic) en plastique ; (flexible) plastique, malléable ; (art) plastique.

**plasticine** ['plæstɪsi:n] n ® pâte f à modeler.

**plastic surgery** ['plæstɪk'sə:dʒərɪ] n chirurgie f esthétique.

**plate** [pleɪt] n (dish) assiette f ; (sheet of metal, PHOT) plaque f ; (in book) gravure f ; **gold/silver ~** (dishes) vaisselle f d'or/d'argent.

**plateau, ~s** or **~x** ['plætəu, -z] n plateau m.

**plateful** ['pleɪtful] n assiette f, assiettée f.

**plate glass** [pleɪt'glɑ:s] n verre m (de vitrine).

**platelayer** ['pleɪtleɪə*] n (RAIL) poseur m de rails.

**platform** ['plætfɔ:m] n (at meeting) tribune f ; (stage) estrade f ; (RAIL) quai m ; **~ ticket** n billet m de quai.

**platinum** ['plætɪnəm] n platine m.

**platitude** ['plætɪtju:d] n platitude f, lieu commun.

**platoon** [plə'tu:n] n peloton m.

**platter** ['plætə*] n plat m.

**plausible** ['plɔ:zɪbl] a plausible ; (person) convaincant(e).

**play** [pleɪ] n jeu m ; (THEATRE) pièce f (de théâtre) // vt (game) jouer à ; (team, opponent) jouer contre ; (instrument) jouer de ; (play, part, piece of music, note) jouer // vi jouer ; **to ~ down** vt minimiser ; **to ~ up** vi (cause trouble) faire des siennes ; **to ~act** vi jouer la comédie ; **~ed-out** a épuisé(e) ; **~er** n joueur/euse ; (THEATRE) acteur/trice ; (MUS) musicien/ne ; **~ful** a enjoué(e) ; **~goer** n amateur/trice de théâtre, habitué/e des théâtres ; **~ground** n cour f de récréation ; **~group** n garderie f ; **~ing card** n carte f à jouer ; **~ing field** n terrain m de sport ; **~mate** n camarade m/f, copain/copine ; **~-off** n (SPORT) belle f ; **~ on words** n jeu m de.mots ; **~pen**

n parc m (pour bébé) ; **~thing** n jouet m ; **~wright** n dramaturge m.

**plea** [pli:] n (request) appel m ; (excuse) excuse f ; (LAW) défense f.

**plead** [pli:d] vt plaider ; (give as excuse) invoquer // vi (LAW) plaider ; (beg): **to ~ with sb** implorer qn.

**pleasant** ['plɛznt] a agréable ; **~ly** ad agréablement ; **~ness** n (of person) amabilité f ; (of place) agrément m ; **~ry** n (joke) plaisanterie f ; **~ries** npl (polite remarks) civilités fpl.

**please** [pli:z] vt plaire à // vi (think fit): **do as you ~** faites comme il vous plaira ; **~!** s'il te (or vous) plaît ; **~ my bill, ~** l'addition, s'il vous plaît ; **~ yourself!** à ta (or votre) guise! ; **~d** a: **~d (with)** content(e) (de) ; **~d to meet you** enchanté (de faire votre connaissance) ; **pleasing** a plaisant(e), qui fait plaisir.

**pleasurable** ['plɛʒərəbl] a très agréable.

**pleasure** ['plɛʒə*] n plaisir m ; **'it's a ~'** 'je vous en prie' ; **~ steamer** n vapeur m de plaisance.

**pleat** [pli:t] n pli m.

**plebiscite** ['plɛbɪsɪt] n plébiscite m.

**plebs** [plɛbz] npl (pej) bas peuple.

**plectrum** ['plɛktrəm] n plectre m.

**pledge** [plɛdʒ] n gage m ; (promise) promesse f // vt engager ; promettre.

**plentiful** ['plɛntɪful] a abondant(e), copieux(euse).

**plenty** ['plɛntɪ] n abondance f ; **~ of** beaucoup de ; (bien) assez de.

**pleurisy** ['pluərɪsɪ] n pleurésie f.

**pliable** ['plaɪəbl] a flexible ; (person) malléable.

**pliers** ['plaɪəz] npl pinces fpl.

**plight** [plaɪt] n situation f critique.

**plimsolls** ['plɪmsəlz] npl (chaussures fpl) tennis fpl.

**plinth** [plɪnθ] n socle m.

**plod** [plɔd] vi avancer péniblement ; (fig) peiner ; **~der** n bûcheur/euse ; **~ding** a pesant(e).

**plonk** [plɔŋk] (col) n (wine) pinard m, piquette f // vt: **to ~ sth down** poser brusquement qch.

**plot** [plɔt] n complot m, conspiration f ; (of story, play) intrigue f ; (of land) lot m de terrain, lopin m // vt (mark out) pointer ; relever ; (conspire) comploter // vi comploter ; **~ter** n conspirateur/trice.

**plough, plow** (US) [plau] n charrue f // vt (earth) labourer ; **to ~ back** vt (COMM) réinvestir ; **to ~ through** vt fus (snow etc) avancer péniblement dans ; **~ing** n labourage m.

**ploy** [plɔɪ] n stratagème m.

**pluck** [plʌk] vt (fruit) cueillir ; (musical instrument) pincer ; (bird) plumer // n courage m, cran m ; **to ~ one's eyebrows** s'épiler les sourcils ; **to ~ up courage** prendre son courage à deux mains ; **~y** a courageux(euse).

**plug** [plʌg] n bouchon m, bonde f ; (ELEC) prise f de courant ; (AUT: also: **sparking ~**) bougie f // vt (hole) boucher ; (col: advertise) faire du battage pour, matraquer ; **to ~ in** vt (ELEC) brancher.

**plum** [plʌm] n (*fruit*) prune f // a: ~ **job** n (*col*) travail m en or.

**plumb** [plʌm] a vertical(e) // n plomb m // ad (*exactly*) en plein // vt sonder.

**plumber** ['plʌmə*] n plombier m.

**plumbing** ['plʌmɪŋ] n (*trade*) plomberie f; (*piping*) tuyauterie f.

**plumbline** ['plʌmlaɪn] n fil m à plomb.

**plume** [plu:m] n plume f, plumet m.

**plummet** ['plʌmɪt] vi plonger, dégringoler.

**plump** [plʌmp] a rondelet(te), dodu(e), bien en chair // vt: **to ~ sth (down) on** laisser tomber qch lourdement sur; **to ~ for** (*col: choose*) se décider pour.

**plunder** ['plʌndə*] n pillage m // vt piller.

**plunge** [plʌndʒ] n plongeon m // vt plonger // vi (*fall*) tomber, dégringoler; **to take the ~** se jeter à l'eau; **plunging** a (*neckline*) plongeant(e).

**pluperfect** [plu:'pə:fɪkt] n plus-que-parfait m.

**plural** ['pluərl] a pluriel(le) // n pluriel m.

**plus** [plʌs] n (*also:* ~ **sign**) signe m plus // prep plus; **ten/twenty ~** plus de dix/vingt; **it's a ~** c'est un atout; ~ **fours** npl pantalon m (de) golf.

**plush** [plʌʃ] a somptueux(euse) // n peluche f.

**ply** [plaɪ] n (*of wool*) fil m; (*of wood*) feuille f, épaisseur f // vt (*tool*) manier; (*a trade*) exercer // vi (*ship*) faire la navette; **three ~** (*wool*) n laine f trois fils; **to ~ sb with drink** donner continuellement à boire à qn; ~**wood** n contre-plaqué m.

**P.M.** abbr see **prime**.

**p.m.** ad (*abbr of post meridiem*) de l'après-midi.

**pneumatic** [nju:'mætɪk] a pneumatique.

**pneumonia** [nju:'məunɪə] n pneumonie f.

**P.O.** abbr see **post office**.

**poach** [pəutʃ] vt (*cook*) pocher; (*steal*) pêcher (*or chasser*) sans permis // vi braconner; ~**ed** a (*egg*) poché(e); ~**er** n braconnier m; ~ **ing** n braconnage m.

**pocket** ['pɔkɪt] n poche f // vt empocher; **to be out of ~** en être de sa poche; ~**book** n (*wallet*) portefeuille m; (*notebook*) carnet m; ~ **knife** n canif m; ~ **money** n argent m de poche.

**pockmarked** ['pɔkmɑ:kt] a (*face*) grêlé(e).

**pod** [pɔd] n cosse f // vt écosser.

**podgy** ['pɔdʒɪ] a rondelet(te).

**poem** ['pəuɪm] n poème m.

**poet** ['pəuɪt] n poète m; ~**ic** [-'ɛtɪk] a poétique; ~ **laureate** n poète lauréat (*nommé et appointé par la Cour royale*); ~**ry** n poésie f.

**poignant** ['pɔɪnjənt] a poignant(e); (*sharp*) vif(vive).

**point** [pɔɪnt] n (*tip*) pointe f; (*in time*) moment m; (*in space*) endroit m; (GEOM, SCOL, SPORT. *on scale*) point m; (*subject, idea*) point m, sujet m; (*also:* **decimal ~**): **2 ~ 3 (2.3)** 2 virgule 3 (2,3) // vt (*show*) indiquer; (*wall, window*) jointoyer; (*gun etc*): **to ~ sth at** braquer *or* diriger qch sur // vi montrer du doigt; ~**s** npl (AUT) vis platinées; (RAIL) aiguillage m; **to make a ~** faire une remarque; **to make one's ~** se faire comprendre; **to get the ~** comprendre, saisir; **to come to the ~** en

venir au fait; **there's no ~ (in doing)** cela ne sert à rien (de faire); **good ~s** qualités fpl; **to ~ out** vt faire remarquer, souligner; **to ~ to** montrer du doigt; (*fig*) signaler; ~**-blank** ad (*also:* **at ~-blank range**) à bout portant; (*fig*) catégorique; ~**ed** a (*shape*) pointu(e); (*remark*) plein(e) de sous-entendus; ~**edly** ad d'une manière significative; ~**er** n (*stick*) baguette f; (*needle*) aiguille f; (*dog*) chien m d'arrêt; ~**less** a inutile, vain(e); ~ **of view** n point m de vue.

**poise** [pɔɪz] n (*balance*) équilibre m; (*of head, body*) port m; (*calmness*) calme m // vt placer en équilibre; **to be ~d for** (*fig*) être prêt à.

**poison** ['pɔɪzn] n poison m // vt empoisonner; ~**ing** n empoisonnement m; ~**ous** a (*snake*) venimeux(euse); (*substance etc*) vénéneux(euse).

**poke** [pəuk] vt (*fire*) tisonner; (*jab with finger, stick etc*) piquer; pousser du doigt; (*put*): **to ~ sth in(to)** fourrer *or* enfoncer qch dans // n (*to fire*) coup m de tisonnier; **to ~ about** vi fureter.

**poker** ['pəukə*] n tisonnier m; (CARDS) poker m; ~**-faced** a au visage impassible.

**poky** ['pəukɪ] a exigu(ë).

**Poland** ['pəulənd] n Pologne f.

**polar** ['pəulə*] a polaire; ~ **bear** n ours blanc.

**polarize** ['pəuləraɪz] vt polariser.

**pole** [pəul] n (*of wood*) mât m, perche f; (ELEC) poteau m; (GEO) pôle m.

**Pole** [pəul] n Polonais/e.

**polecat** ['pəulkæt] n (US) putois m.

**polemic** [pɔ'lɛmɪk] n polémique f.

**pole star** ['pəulstɑ:*] n étoile polaire f.

**pole vault** ['pəulvɔ:lt] n saut m à la perche.

**police** [pə'li:s] n police f, (man: pl inv) policier m, homme m; // vt maintenir l'ordre dans; ~ **car** n voiture f de police; ~**man** n agent m de police, policier m; ~ **record** n casier m judiciaire; ~ **state** n état policier; ~ **station** n commissariat m de police; ~**woman** n femme-agent f.

**policy** ['pɔlɪsɪ] n politique f; (*also:* **insurance ~**) police f (d'assurance).

**polio** ['pəulɪəu] n polio f.

**Polish** ['pəulɪʃ] a polonais(e) // n (LING) polonais m.

**polish** ['pɔlɪʃ] n (*for shoes*) cirage m; (*for floor*) cire f, encaustique f; (*for nails*) vernis m; (*shine*) éclat m, poli m; (*fig: refinement*) raffinement m // vt (*put polish on shoes, wood*) cirer; (*make shiny*) astiquer, faire briller; (*fig: improve*) perfectionner; **to ~ off** vt (*work*) expédier; (*food*) liquider; ~**ed** a (*fig*) raffiné(e).

**polite** [pə'laɪt] a poli(e); ~**ly** ad poliment; ~**ness** n politesse f.

**politic** ['pɔlɪtɪk] a diplomatique; ~**al** [pə'lɪtɪkl] a politique; ~**ian** [-'tɪʃən] n homme m politique, politicien m; ~**s** npl politique f.

**polka** ['pɔlkə] n polka f; ~ **dot** n pois m.

**poll** [pəul] n scrutin m, vote m; (*also:* **opinion ~**) sondage m (d'opinion) // vt obtenir.

**pollen** ['pɔlən] n pollen m; ~ **count** n taux m de pollen.

**pollination** [pɔli'neɪʃən] n pollinisation f.
**polling booth** ['pəuliŋbu:ð] n isoloir m.
**polling day** ['pəuliŋdeɪ] n jour m des élections.
**polling station** ['pəliŋsteɪʃən] n bureau m de vote.
**pollute** [pə'lu:t] vt polluer.
**pollution** [pə'lu:ʃən] n pollution f.
**polo** ['pəuləu] n polo m; ~-neck a à col roulé.
**polyester** [pɔli'ɛstə*] n polyester m.
**polygamy** [pə'ligəmɪ] n polygamie f.
**Polynesia** [pɔli'ni:zɪə] n Polynésie f.
**polytechnic** [pɔli'tɛknɪk] n (college) I.U.T. m, Institut m Universitaire de Technologie.
**polythene** ['pɔliθi:n] n polyéthylène m; ~ bag n sac m en plastique.
**pomegranate** ['pɔmɪgrænɪt] n grenade f.
**pommel** ['pɔml] n pommeau m.
**pomp** [pɔmp] n pompe f, faste f, apparat m.
**pompous** ['pɔmpəs] a pompeux(euse).
**pond** [pɔnd] n étang m; mare f.
**ponder** ['pɔndə*] vi réfléchir // vt considérer, peser; ~ous a pesant(e), lourd(e).
**pontiff** ['pɔntɪf] n pontife m.
**pontificate** [pɔn'tɪfɪkeɪt] vi (fig): to ~ (about) pontifier (sur).
**pontoon** [pɔn'tu:n] n ponton m.
**pony** ['pəunɪ] n poney m; ~tail n queue f de cheval; ~ trekking n randonnée f à cheval.
**poodle** ['pu:dl] n caniche m.
**pooh-pooh** [pu:pu:] vt dédaigner.
**pool** [pu:l] n (of rain) flaque f; (pond) mare f; (artificial) bassin m; (also: swimming ~) piscine f; (sth shared) fonds commun; (money at cards) cagnotte f; (billiards) poule f // vt mettre en commun.
**poor** [puə*] a pauvre; (mediocre) médiocre, faible, mauvais(e) // npl: the ~ les pauvres mpl; // ad pauvrement, médiocrement // a souffrant(e), malade.
**pop** [pɔp] n (noise) bruit sec; (MUS) musique f pop; (US: col: father) papa m // vt (put) fourrer, mettre (rapidement) // vi éclater; (cork) sauter; to ~ in vi entrer en passant; to ~ out vi sortir; to ~ up vi apparaître, surgir; ~ concert n concert m pop; ~corn n pop-corn m.
**pope** [pəup] n pape m.
**poplar** ['pɔplə*] n peuplier m.
**poplin** ['pɔplin] n popeline f.
**poppy** ['pɔpɪ] n coquelicot m; pavot m.
**populace** ['pɔpjuləs] n peuple m.
**popular** ['pɔpjulə*] a populaire; (fashionable) à la mode; ~ity [-'lærɪtɪ] n popularité f; ~ize vt populariser; (science) vulgariser.
**populate** ['pɔpjuleɪt] vt peupler.
**population** [pɔpju'leɪʃən] n population f.
**populous** ['pɔpjuləs] a populeux(euse).
**porcelain** ['pɔ:slin] n porcelaine f.
**porch** [pɔ:tʃ] n porche m.
**porcupine** ['pɔ:kjupaɪn] n porc-épic m.
**pore** [pɔ:*] n pore m // vi: to ~ over s'absorber dans, être plongé(e) dans.
**pork** [pɔ:k] n porc m.

**pornographic** [pɔ:nə'græfɪk] a pornographique.
**pornography** [pɔ:'nɔgrəfɪ] n pornographie f.
**porous** ['pɔ:rəs] a poreux(euse).
**porpoise** ['pɔ:pəs] n marsouin m.
**porridge** ['pɔrɪdʒ] n porridge m.
**port** [pɔ:t] n (harbour) port m; (opening in ship) sabord m; (NAUT: left side) bâbord m; (wine) porto m; to ~ (NAUT) à bâbord.
**portable** ['pɔ:təbl] a portatif(ive).
**portal** ['pɔ:tl] n portail m.
**portcullis** [pɔ:t'kʌlɪs] n herse f.
**portend** [pɔ:'tɛnd] vt présager, annoncer.
**portent** ['pɔ:tɛnt] n présage m.
**porter** ['pɔ:tə*] n (for luggage) porteur m; (doorkeeper) gardien/ne; portier m.
**porthole** ['pɔ:thəul] n hublot m.
**portico** ['pɔ:tɪkəu] n portique m.
**portion** ['pɔ:ʃən] n portion f, part f.
**portly** ['pɔ:tlɪ] a corpulent(e).
**portrait** ['pɔ:treɪt] n portrait m.
**portray** [pɔ:'treɪ] vt faire le portrait de; (in writing) dépeindre, représenter; ~al n portrait m, représentation f.
**Portugal** ['pɔ:tjugl] n Portugal m.
**Portuguese** [pɔ:tju'gi:z] a portugais(e) // n, pl inv Portugais/e; (LING) portugais m.
**pose** [pəuz] n pose f; (pej) affectation f // vi poser; (pretend): to ~ as se poser en // vt poser, créer; ~r n question embarrassante.
**posh** [pɔʃ] a (col) chic inv.
**position** [pə'zɪʃən] n position f; (job) situation f // vt mettre en place or en position.
**positive** ['pɔzɪtɪv] a positif(ive); (certain) sûr(e), certain(e); (definite) formel(le), catégorique; indéniable, réel(le).
**posse** ['pɔsɪ] n (US) détachement m.
**possess** [pə'zɛs] vt posséder; ~ion [pə'zɛʃən] n possession f; ~ive a possessif(ive); ~ively ad d'une façon possessive; ~or n possesseur m.
**possibility** [pɔsɪ'bɪlɪtɪ] n possibilité f; éventualité f.
**possible** ['pɔsɪbl] a possible; if ~ si possible; as big as ~ aussi gros que possible.
**possibly** ['pɔsɪblɪ] ad (perhaps) peut-être; if you ~ can si cela vous est possible; I cannot ~ come il m'est impossible de venir.
**post** [pəust] n poste f; (collection) levée f; (letters, delivery) courrier m; (job, situation) poste m; (pole) poteau m // vt (send by post, MIL) poster; (appoint): to ~ to affecter à; (notice) afficher; ~age n affranchissement m; ~al a postal(e); ~al order n mandat(-poste) m; ~box n boîte f aux lettres; ~card n carte postale.
**postdate** [pəust'deɪt] vt (cheque) postdater.
**poster** ['pəustə*] n affiche f.
**poste restante** [pəust'rɛstã:nt] n poste restante.
**posterior** [pɔs'tɪərɪə*] n (col) postérieur m, derrière m.
**posterity** [pɔs'tɛrɪtɪ] n postérité f.
**postgraduate** ['pəust'grædjuət] n ≈ étudiant/e de troisième cycle.

**posthumous** ['pɔstjuməs] a posthume ; ~**ly** ad après la mort de l'auteur, à titre posthume.

**postman** ['pəustmən] n facteur m.

**postmark** ['pəustmɑ:k] n cachet m (de la poste).

**postmaster** ['pəustmɑ:stə*] n receveur m des postes.

**post-mortem** [pəust'mɔ:təm] n autopsie f.

**post office** ['pəustɔfıs] n (building) poste f; (organization) postes fpl; ~ **box (P.O. box)** n boîte postale (B.P.).

**postpone** [pəs'pəun] vt remettre (à plus tard), reculer ; ~**ment** n ajournement m, renvoi m.

**postscript** ['pəustskrıpt] n post-scriptum m.

**postulate** ['pɔstjuleıt] vt postuler.

**posture** ['pɔstʃə*] n posture f, attitude f // vi poser.

**postwar** [pəust'wɔ:*] a d'après-guerre.

**posy** ['pəuzı] n petit bouquet.

**pot** [pɔt] n (for cooking) marmite f; casserole f; (for plants, jam) pot m; (col: marijuana) herbe f // vt (plant) mettre en pot ; **to go to** ~ aller à vau-l'eau.

**potash** ['pɔtæʃ] n potasse f.

**potato,** ~**es** [pə'teıtəu] n pomme f de terre ; ~ **flour** n fécule f.

**potency** ['pəutnsı] n puissance f, force f; (of drink) degré m d'alcool.

**potent** ['pəutnt] a puissant(e) ; (drink) fort(e), très alcoolisé(e).

**potentate** ['pəutnteıt] n potentat m.

**potential** [pə'tɛnʃl] a potentiel(le) // n potentiel m; ~**ly** ad en puissance.

**pothole** ['pɔthəul] n (in road) nid m de poule ; (underground) gouffre m, caverne f; ~**r** n spéléologue m/f; **potholing** n: **to go potholing** faire de la spéléologie.

**potion** ['pəuʃən] n potion f.

**potluck** [pɔt'lʌk] n: **to take** ~ tenter sa chance.

**potpourri** [pəu'puri:] n pot-pourri m.

**potshot** ['pɔtʃɔt] n: **to take** ~**s at** canarder.

**potted** ['pɔtıd] a (food) en conserve ; (plant) en pot.

**potter** ['pɔtə*] n potier m // vt: **to** ~ **around,** ~ **about** bricoler ; ~**y** n poterie f.

**potty** ['pɔtı] a (col: mad) dingue // n (child's) pot m; ~-**training** n apprentissage m de la propreté.

**pouch** [pautʃ] n (ZOOL) poche f; (for tobacco) blague f.

**pouf(fe)** [pu:f] n (stool) pouf m.

**poultice** ['pəultıs] n cataplasme m.

**poultry** ['pəultrı] n volaille f; ~ **farm** n élevage m de volaille.

**pounce** [pauns] vi: **to** ~ **(on)** bondir (sur), fondre sur // n bond m, attaque f.

**pound** [paund] n livre f (weight = 453g, 16 ounces; money = 100 new pence, 20 shillings) ; (for dogs, cars) fourrière f // vt (beat) bourrer de coups, marteler ; (crush) piler, pulvériser ; (with guns) pilonner // vi (beat) battre violemment, taper ; ~ **sterling** n livre f sterling.

**pour** [pɔ:*] vt verser // vi couler à flots ; (rain) pleuvoir à verse ; **to** ~ **away** or **off** vt vider ; **to** ~ **in** vi (people) affluer, se précipiter ; **to** ~ **out** vi (people) sortir en masse // vt vider ; déverser ; (serve: a drink) verser ; ~**ing** a: ~**ing rain** pluie torrentielle.

**pout** [paut] n moue f // vi faire la moue.

**poverty** ['pɔvətı] n pauvreté f, misère f; ~-**stricken** a pauvre, déshérité(e).

**powder** ['paudə*] n poudre f // vt poudrer ; ~ **room** n toilettes fpl (pour dames) ; ~**y** a poudreux(euse).

**power** ['pauə*] n (strength) puissance f, force f; (ability, POL: of party, leader) pouvoir m; (MATH) puissance f; (mental) facultés mentales ; (ELEC) courant m // vt faire marcher ; ~ **cut** n coupure f de courant ; ~**ed** a: ~**ed by** actionné(e) par, fonctionnant à, ~**ful** a puissant(e) ; ~**less** a impuissant(e) ; ~ **line** n ligne f électrique ; ~ **point** n prise f de courant ; ~ **station** n centrale f électrique.

**powwow** ['pauwau] n assemblée f.

**pox** [pɔks] n see **chicken.**

**p.p.** abbr (= per procurationem): ~ **J. Smith** pour M. J. Smith.

**P.R.** abbr of **public relations.**

**practicability** [præktıkə'bılıtı] n possibilité f de réalisation.

**practicable** ['præktıkəbl] a (scheme) réalisable.

**practical** ['præktıkl] a pratique ; ~ **joke** n farce f; ~**ly** ad (almost) pratiquement.

**practice** ['præktıs] n pratique f; (of profession) exercice m; (at football etc) entraînement m; (business) cabinet m; clientèle f // vt,vi (US) = **practise; in** ~ (in reality) en pratique ; **out of** ~ rouillé(e) ; **2 hours' piano** ~ 2 heures de travail or d'exercices au piano ; ~ **match** n match m d'entraînement.

**practise,** (US) **practice** ['præktıs] vt (work at: piano, one's backhand etc) s'exercer à, travailler ; (train for: skiing, running etc) s'entraîner à ; (a sport, religion, method) pratiquer ; (profession) exercer // vi s'exercer, travailler ; (train) s'entraîner ; **to** ~ **for a match** s'entraîner pour un match ; **practising** a (Christian etc) pratiquant(e) ; (lawyer) en exercice.

**practitioner** [præk'tıʃənə*] n praticien/ne.

**pragmatic** [præg'mætık] a pragmatique.

**prairie** ['prɛərı] n savane f; (US): **the** ~**s** la Prairie.

**praise** [preız] n éloge(s) m(pl), louange(s) f(pl) // vt louer, faire l'éloge de ; ~**worthy** a digne de louanges.

**pram** [præm] n landau m, voiture f d'enfant.

**prance** [prɑ:ns] vi (horse) caracoler.

**prank** [præŋk] n farce f.

**prattle** ['prætl] vi jacasser.

**prawn** [prɔ:n] n crevette f (rose).

**pray** [preı] vi prier.

**prayer** [prɛə*] n prière f; ~ **book** n livre m de prières.

**preach** [pri:tʃ] vt,vi prêcher ; **to** ~ **at sb** faire la morale à qn ; ~**er** n prédicateur m.

preamble [prɪ'æmbl] n préambule m.
prearranged [pri:ə'reɪndʒd] a organisé(e) or fixé(e) à l'avance.
precarious [prɪ'kɛərɪəs] a précaire.
precaution [prɪ'kɔ:ʃən] n précaution f; ~ary a (measure) de précaution.
precede [prɪ'si:d] vt,vi précéder.
precedence ['prɛsɪdəns] n préséance f.
precedent ['prɛsɪdənt] n précédent m.
preceding [prɪ'si:dɪŋ] a qui précède (or précédait).
precept ['pri:sɛpt] n précepte m.
precinct ['pri:sɪŋkt] n (round cathedral) pourtour m, enceinte f; pedestrian ~ n zone piétonnière; shopping ~ n centre commerical.
precious ['prɛʃəs] a précieux(euse).
precipice ['prɛsɪpɪs] n précipice m.
precipitate a [prɪ'sɪpɪtɪt] (hasty) précipité(e) // vt [prɪ'sɪpɪteɪt] précipiter; precipitation [-'teɪʃən] n précipitation f.
precipitous [prɪ'sɪpɪtəs] a (steep) abrupt(e), à pic.
précis, pl précis ['preɪsɪ:, -z] n résumé m.
precise [prɪ'saɪs] a précis(e); ~ly ad précisément.
preclude [prɪ'klu:d] vt exclure, empêcher; to ~ sb from doing empêcher qn de faire.
precocious [prɪ'kəuʃəs] a précoce.
preconceived [pri:kən'si:vd] a (idea) préconçu(e).
precondition [pri:kən'dɪʃən] n condition f nécessaire.
precursor [pri:'kə:sə*] n précurseur m.
predator ['prɛdətə*] n prédateur m, rapace m; ~y a rapace.
predecessor ['pri:dɪsɛsə*] n prédécesseur m.
predestination [pri:dɛstɪ'neɪʃən] n prédestination f.
predetermine [pri:dɪ'tə:mɪn] vt déterminer à l'avance.
predicament [prɪ'dɪkəmənt] n situation f difficile.
predicate ['prɛdɪkɪt] n (LING) prédicat m.
predict [prɪ'dɪkt] vt prédire; ~ion [-'dɪkʃən] n prédiction f.
predominance [prɪ'dɒmɪnəns] n prédominance f.
predominant [prɪ'dɒmɪnənt] a prédominant(e); ~ly ad en majeure partie; surtout.
predominate [prɪ'dɒmɪneɪt] vi prédominer.
pre-eminent [pri:'ɛmɪnənt] a prééminent(e).
pre-empt [pri:'ɛmt] vt acquérir par droit de préemption; (fig): to ~ the issue conclure avant même d'ouvrir les débats.
preen [pri:n] vt: to ~ itself (bird) se lisser les plumes; to ~ o.s. s'admirer.
prefab ['pri:fæb] n bâtiment préfabriqué.
prefabricated [pri:'fæbrikeɪtɪd] a préfabriqué(e).
preface ['prɛfəs] n préface f.
prefect ['pri:fɛkt] n (Brit: in school) élève chargé(e) de certaines fonctions de discipline; (in France) préfet m.
prefer [prɪ'fə:*] vt préférer; ~able ['prɛfrəbl] a préférable; ~ably ['prɛfrəblɪ]

ad de préférence; ~ence ['prɛfrəns] n préférence f; ~ential [prɛfə'rɛnʃəl] a préférentiel(le) ~ential treatment traitement m de faveur.
prefix ['pri:fɪks] n préfixe m.
pregnancy ['prɛgnənsɪ] n grossesse f.
pregnant ['prɛgnənt] a enceinte af.
prehistoric ['pri:hɪs'tɒrɪk] a préhistorique.
prehistory [pri:'hɪstərɪ] n préhistoire f.
prejudge [pri:'dʒʌdʒ] vt préjuger de.
prejudice ['prɛdʒudɪs] n préjugé m; (harm) tort m, préjudice m // vt porter préjudice à; ~d a (person) plein(e) de préjugés; (view) préconçu(e), partial(e).
prelate ['prɛlət] n prélat m.
preliminary [prɪ'lɪmɪnərɪ] a préliminaire; preliminaries npl préliminaires mpl.
prelude ['prɛlju:d] n prélude m.
premarital ['pri:'mærɪtl] a avant le mariage.
premature ['prɛmətʃuə*] a prématuré(e).
premeditated [pri:'mɛdɪteɪtɪd] a prémédité(e).
premeditation [pri:mɛdɪ'teɪʃən] n préméditation f.
premier ['prɛmɪə*] a premier(ère), capital(e), primordial(e) // n (POL) premier ministre.
première ['prɛmɪɛə*] n première f.
premise ['prɛmɪs] n prémisse f; ~s npl locaux mpl; on the ~s sur les lieux; sur place.
premium ['pri:mɪəm] n prime f.
premonition [prɛmə'nɪʃən] n prémonition f.
preoccupation [pri:ɔkju'peɪʃən] n préoccupation f.
preoccupied [pri:'ɔkjupaɪd] a préoccupé(e).
prep [prɛp] n (SCOL: study) étude f; ~ school n = preparatory school.
prepackaged [pri:'pækɪdʒd] a préempaqueté(e).
prepaid [pri:'peɪd] a payé(e) d'avance.
preparation [prɛpə'reɪʃən] n préparation f; ~s npl (for trip, war) préparatifs mpl.
preparatory [prɪ'pærətərɪ] a préparatoire; ~ school n école primaire privée.
prepare [prɪ'pɛə*] vt préparer // vi: to ~ for se préparer à; ~d for preparé(e) à; ~d to prêt(e) à.
preponderance [prɪ'pɒndərns] n prépondérance f.
preposition [prɛpə'zɪʃən] n préposition f.
preposterous [prɪ'pɒstərəs] a absurde.
prerequisite [pri:'rɛkwɪzɪt] n condition f préalable.
prerogative [prɪ'rɔgətɪv] n prérogative f.
presbyterian [prɛzbɪ'tɪərɪən] a,n presbytérien(ne).
presbytery ['prɛzbɪtərɪ] n presbytère m.
preschool ['pri:'sku:l] a préscolaire.
prescribe [prɪ'skraɪb] vt prescrire.
prescription [prɪ'skrɪpʃən] n prescription f; (MED) ordonnance f.
prescriptive [prɪ'skrɪptɪv] a normatif(ive).
presence ['prɛzns] n présence f; ~ of mind n présence d'esprit.
present ['prɛznt] a présent(e) // n cadeau m; (also: ~ tense) présent m // vt

[prɪ'zɛnt] présenter ; (*give*): **to ~ sb with sth** offrir qch à qn ; **at ~** en ce moment ; **~able** [prɪ'zɛntəbl] *a* présentable ; **~ation** [-'teɪʃən] *n* présentation *f* ; (*gift*) cadeau *m*, présent *m* ; (*ceremony*) remise *f* du cadeau ; **~-day** *a* contemporain(e), actuel(le) ; **~ly** *ad* (*soon*) tout à l'heure, bientôt ; (*at present*) en ce moment.

**preservation** [prɛzə'veɪʃən] *n* préservation *f*, conservation *f*.

**preservative** [prɪ'zə:vətɪv] *n* agent *m* de conservation.

**preserve** [prɪ'zə:v] *vt* (*keep safe*) préserver, protéger ; (*maintain*) conserver, garder ; (*food*) mettre en conserve // *n* (*for game, fish*) réserve *f* ; (*often pl*: *jam*) confiture *f* ; (: *fruit*) fruits *mpl* en conserve.

**preside** [prɪ'zaɪd] *vi* présider.

**presidency** ['prɛzɪdənsɪ] *n* présidence *f*.

**president** ['prɛzɪdənt] *n* président/e ; **~ial** ['dɛnʃl] *a* présidentiel(le).

**press** [prɛs] *n* (*tool, machine, newspapers*) presse *f* ; (*for wine*) pressoir *m* ; (*crowd*) cohue *f*, foule *f* // *vt* (*push*) appuyer sur ; (*squeeze*) presser, serrer ; (*clothes*: *iron*) repasser ; (*pursue*) talonner ; (*insist*): **to ~ sth on sb** presser qn d'accepter qch // *vi* appuyer, peser ; se presser ; **we are ~ed for time** le temps nous manque ; **to ~ for sth** faire pression pour obtenir qch ; **to ~ on** *vi* continuer ; **~ agency** *n* agence *f* de presse ; **~ conference** *n* conférence *f* de presse ; **~ cutting** *n* coupure *f* de presse ; **~-gang** *n* recruteurs de la marine (*jusqu'au 19ème siècle*) ; **~ing** *a* urgent(e), pressant(e) // *n* repassage *m* ; **~ stud** *n* bouton-pression *m*.

**pressure** ['prɛʃə*] *n* pression *f* ; (*stress*) tension *f* ; **~ cooker** *n* cocotte-minute *f* ; **~ gauge** *n* manomètre *m* ; **~ group** *n* groupe *m* de pression ; **pressurized** *a* pressurisé(e).

**prestige** [prɛs'ti:ʒ] *n* prestige *m*.

**prestigious** [prɛs'tɪdʒəs] *a* prestigieux(euse).

**presumably** [prɪ'zju:məblɪ] *ad* vraisemblablement.

**presume** [prɪ'zju:m] *vt* présumer, supposer ; **to ~ to do** (*dare*) se permettre de faire.

**presumption** [prɪ'zʌmpʃən] *n* supposition *f*, présomption *f* ; (*boldness*) audace *f*.

**presumptuous** [prɪ'zʌmpʃəs] *a* présomptueux(euse).

**presuppose** [pri:sə'pəuz] *vt* présupposer.

**pretence, pretense** (*US*) [prɪ'tɛns] *n* (*claim*) prétention *f* ; **to make a ~ of doing** faire semblant de faire ; **on the ~ of** sous le prétexte de.

**pretend** [prɪ'tɛnd] *vt* (*feign*) feindre, simuler // *vi* (*feign*) faire semblant ; (*claim*): **to ~ to sth** prétendre à qch ; **to ~ to do** faire semblant de faire.

**pretense** [prɪ'tɛns] *n* (*US*) = **pretence**.

**pretentious** [prɪ'tɛnʃəs] *a* prétentieux(euse).

**preterite** ['prɛtərɪt] *n* prétérit *m*.

**pretext** ['pri:tɛkst] *n* prétexte *m*.

**pretty** ['prɪtɪ] *a* joli(e) // *ad* assez.

**prevail** [prɪ'veɪl] *vi* (*win*) l'emporter, prévaloir ; (*be usual*) avoir cours ; (*persuade*): **to ~ (up)on sb to do**

persuader qn de faire ; **~ing** *a* dominant(e).

**prevalent** ['prɛvələnt] *a* répandu(e), courant(e).

**prevarication** [prɪværɪ'keɪʃən] *n* (*usage m de*) faux-fuyants *mpl*.

**prevent** [prɪ'vɛnt] *vt*: **to ~ (from doing)** empêcher (de faire) ; **~able** *a* évitable ; **~ative** *a* préventif(ive) ; **~ion** [-'vɛnʃən] *n* prévention *f* ; **~ive** *a* préventif(ive).

**preview** ['pri:vju:] *n* (*of film*) avant-première *f* ; (*fig*) aperçu *m*.

**previous** ['pri:vɪəs] *a* précédent(e) ; antérieur(e) ; **~ to doing** avant de faire ; **~ly** *ad* précédemment, auparavant.

**prewar** [pri:'wɔ:*] *a* d'avant-guerre.

**prey** [preɪ] *n* proie *f* // *vi*: **to ~ on** s'attaquer à ; **it was ~ing on his mind** ça le rongeait *or* minait.

**price** [praɪs] *n* prix *m* // *vt* (*goods*) fixer le prix de ; tarifer ; **~less** *a* sans prix, inestimable ; **~ list** *n* liste *f* des prix, tarif *m*.

**prick** [prɪk] *n* piqûre *f* // *vt* piquer ; **to ~ up one's ears** dresser *or* tendre l'oreille.

**prickle** ['prɪkl] *n* (*of plant*) épine *f* ; (*sensation*) picotement *m*.

**prickly** ['prɪklɪ] *a* piquant(e), épineux(euse) ; (*fig: person*) irritable ; **~ heat** *n* fièvre *f* miliaire ; **~ pear** *n* figue *f* de Barbarie.

**pride** [praɪd] *n* orgueil *m* ; fierté *f* // *vt*: **to ~ o.s. on** se flatter de ; s'enorgueillir de.

**priest** [pri:st] *n* prêtre *m* ; **~ess** *n* prêtresse *f* ; **~hood** *n* prêtrise *f*, sacerdoce *m*.

**prig** [prɪg] *n* poseur/euse, fat *m*.

**prim** [prɪm] *a* collet monté *inv*, guindé(e).

**primarily** ['praɪmərɪlɪ] *ad* principalement, essentiellement.

**primary** ['praɪmərɪ] *a* primaire ; (*first in importance*) premier(ère), primordial(e) ; **~ colour** *n* couleur fondamentale ; **~ school** *n* école primaire *f*.

**primate** *n* (*REL*) ['praɪmɪt] primat *m* ; (*ZOOL*) ['praɪmeɪt] primate *m*.

**prime** [praɪm] *a* primordial(e), fondamental(e) ; (*excellent*) excellent(e) // *vt* (*gun, pump*) amorcer ; (*fig*) mettre au courant ; **in the ~ of life** dans la fleur de l'âge ; **~ minister (P.M.)** *n* premier ministre ; **~r** *n* (*book*) premier livre, manuel *m* élémentaire ; (*paint*) apprêt *m* ; (*of gun*) amorce *f*.

**primeval** [praɪ'mi:vl] *a* primitif(ive).

**primitive** ['prɪmɪtɪv] *a* primitif(ive).

**primrose** ['prɪmrəuz] *n* primevère *f*.

**primus (stove)** ['praɪməs(stəuv)] *n* ® réchaud *m* de camping.

**prince** [prɪns] *n* prince *m*.

**princess** [prɪn'sɛs] *n* princesse *f*.

**principal** ['prɪnsɪpl] *a* principal(e) // *n* (*headmaster*) directeur *m*, principal *m* ; (*money*) capital *m*, principal *m*.

**principality** [prɪnsɪ'pælɪtɪ] *n* principauté *f*.

**principally** ['prɪnsɪplɪ] *ad* principalement.

**principle** ['prɪnsɪpl] *n* principe *m*.

**print** [prɪnt] *n* (*mark*) empreinte *f* ; (*letters*) caractères *mpl* ; (*fabric*) imprimé *m* ; (*ART*) gravure f, estampe f ; (PHOT) épreuve f // vt imprimer ; (publish) publier ; (write in capitals) écrire en majuscules ; out of ~ épuisé(e) ; ~ed matter n imprimés mpl ; ~er n imprimeur m ; ~ing n impression f ; ~ing press n presse f typographique ; ~out n listage m.

**prior** ['praɪə*] a antérieur(e), précédent(e) // n prieur m ; ~ to doing avant de faire.

**priority** [praɪ'ɔrɪtɪ] n priorité f.

**priory** ['praɪərɪ] n prieuré m.

**prise** [praɪz] vt: to ~ open forcer.

**prism** ['prɪzəm] n prisme m.

**prison** ['prɪzn] n prison f ; ~er n prisonnier/ère.

**prissy** ['prɪsɪ] a bégueule.

**pristine** ['prɪstiːn] a virginal(e).

**privacy** ['prɪvəsɪ] n intimité f, solitude f.

**private** ['praɪvɪt] a privé(e) ; personnel(le) ; (house, car, lesson) particulier(ère) // n soldat m de deuxième classe ; '~' (on envelope) 'personnelle' ; in ~ en privé ; ~ eye n détective privé ; ~ly ad en privé ; (within oneself) intérieurement.

**privet** ['prɪvɪt] n troène m.

**privilege** ['prɪvɪlɪdʒ] n privilège m ; ~d a privilégié(e).

**privy** ['prɪvɪ] a: to be ~ to être au courant de ; P~ council n conseil privé.

**prize** [praɪz] n prix m // a (example, idiot) parfait(e) ; (bull, novel) primé(e) // vt priser, faire grand cas de ; ~ fight n combat professionnel ; ~ giving n distribution f des prix ; ~winner n gagnant/e.

**pro** [prəu] n (SPORT) professionnel/le ; the ~s and cons le pour et le contre.

**probability** [prɔbə'bɪlɪtɪ] n probabilité f.

**probable** ['prɔbəbl] a probable ; **probably** ad probablement.

**probation** [prə'beɪʃən] n (in employment) essai m ; (LAW) liberté surveillée ; (REL) noviciat m, probation f ; on ~ (employee) à l'essai ; (LAW) en liberté surveillée ; ~ary a (period) d'essai.

**probe** [prəub] n (MED, SPACE) sonde f ; (enquiry) enquête f, investigation f // vt sonder, explorer.

**probity** ['prəubɪtɪ] n probité f.

**problem** ['prɔbləm] n problème m ; ~atic [-'mætɪk] a problématique.

**procedure** [prə'siːdʒə*] n (ADMIN, LAW) procédure f ; (method) marche f à suivre, façon f de procéder.

**proceed** [prə'siːd] vi (go forward) avancer ; (go about it) procéder ; (continue): to ~ (with) continuer, poursuivre ; to ~ to aller à ; passer à ; to ~ to do se mettre à faire ; ~ing n procédé m, façon d'agir f ; ~ings npl mesures fpl ; (LAW) poursuites fpl ; (meeting) réunion f, séance f ; (records) compte rendu ; actes mpl ; ~s ['prəusiːdz] npl produit m, recette f.

**process** ['prəusɛs] n processus m ; (method) procédé m // vt traiter ; ~ed cheese fromage fondu ; in ~ en cours ; ~ing n traitement m.

**procession** [prə'sɛʃən] n défilé m, cortège m ; (REL) procession f.

**proclaim** [prə'kleɪm] vt déclarer, proclamer.

**proclamation** [prɔklə'meɪʃən] n proclamation f.

**proclivity** [prə'klɪvɪtɪ] n inclination f.

**procrastination** [prəukræstɪ'neɪʃən] n procrastination f.

**procreation** [prəukrɪ'eɪʃən] n procréation f.

**procure** [prə'kjuə*] vt (for o.s.) se procurer ; (for sb) procurer.

**prod** [prɔd] vt pousser // n (push, jab) petit coup, poussée f.

**prodigal** ['prɔdɪgl] a prodigue.

**prodigious** ['prə'dɪdʒəs] a prodigieux(euse).

**prodigy** ['prɔdɪdʒɪ] n prodige m.

**produce** n ['prɔdjuːs] (AGR) produits mpl // vt [prə'djuːs] produire ; (to show) présenter ; (cause) provoquer, causer ; (THEATRE) monter, mettre en scène ; ~r n (THEATRE) metteur m en scène ; (AGR, CINEMA) producteur m.

**product** ['prɔdʌkt] n produit m.

**production** [prə'dʌkʃən] n production f ; (THEATRE) mise f en scène ; ~ line n chaîne f (de fabrication).

**productive** [prə'dʌktɪv] a productif(ive).

**productivity** [prɔdʌk'tɪvɪtɪ] n productivité f.

**profane** [prə'feɪn] a sacrilège ; (lay) profane.

**profess** [prə'fɛs] vt professer.

**profession** [prə'fɛʃən] n profession f ; ~al n (SPORT) professionnel/le // a professionnel(le) ; (work) de professionnel ; he's a ~al man il exerce une profession libérale ; ~alism n professionnalisme m.

**professor** [prə'fɛsə*] n professeur m (titulaire d'une chaire).

**proficiency** [prə'fɪʃənsɪ] n compétence f, aptitude f.

**proficient** [prə'fɪʃənt] a compétent(e), capable.

**profile** ['prəufaɪl] n profil m.

**profit** ['prɔfɪt] n bénéfice m ; profit m // vi: to ~ (by or from) profiter (de) ; ~ability [-'bɪlɪtɪ] n rentabilité f ; ~able a lucratif(ive), rentable.

**profiteering** [prɔfɪ'tɪərɪŋ] n (pej) mercantilisme m.

**profound** [prə'faund] a profond(e).

**profuse** [prə'fjuːs] a abondant(e) ; (with money) prodigue ; ~ly ad en abondance, profusion ; **profusion** [-'fjuːʒən] n profusion f, abondance f.

**progeny** ['prɔdʒɪnɪ] n progéniture f ; descendants mpl.

**programme**, **program** (US) ['prəugræm] n programme m ; (RADIO, TV) émission f // vt programmer ; **programming**, **programing** (US) n programmation f.

**progress** n ['prəugrɛs] progrès m // vi [prə'grɛs] progresser, avancer ; in ~ en cours ; to make ~ progresser, faire des progrès, être en progrès ; ~ion [-'grɛʃən] n progression f ; ~ive [-'grɛsɪv] a progressif(ive) ; (person) progressiste ; ~ively [-'grɛsɪvlɪ] ad progressivement.

**prohibit** [prə'hɪbɪt] vt interdire, défendre ; **to ~ sb from doing** défendre or interdire à qn de faire ; **~ion** [prəʊɪ'bɪʃən] n (US) prohibition f; **~ive** a (price etc) prohibitif(ive).

**project** n ['prɔdʒɛkt] (plan) projet m, plan m ; (venture) opération f, entreprise f; (gen SCOL: research) étude f, dossier m // vb [prə'dʒɛkt] vt projeter // vi (stick out) faire saillie, s'avancer.

**projectile** [prə'dʒɛktaɪl] n projectile m.

**projection** [prə'dʒɛkʃən] n projection f; saillie f.

**projector** [prə'dʒɛktə*] n projecteur m.

**proletarian** [prəʊlɪ'tɛərɪən] a prolétarien(ne) // n prolétaire m/f.

**proletariat** [prəʊlɪ'tɛərɪət] n prolétariat m.

**proliferate** [prə'lɪfəreɪt] vi proliférer ; **proliferation** [-'reɪʃən] n prolifération f.

**prolific** [prə'lɪfɪk] a prolifique.

**prologue** ['prəʊlɔg] n prologue m.

**prolong** [prə'lɔŋ] vt prolonger.

**prom** [prɔm] n abbr of **promenade** ; (US: ball) bal m d'étudiants.

**promenade** [prɔmə'nɑ:d] n (by sea) esplanade f, promenade f; **~ concert** n concert m (de musique classique) ; **~ deck** n pont m promenade.

**prominence** ['prɔmɪnəns] n proéminence f; importance f.

**prominent** ['prɔmɪnənt] a (standing out) proéminent(e) ; (important) important(e).

**promiscuity** [prɔmɪs'kju:ɪtɪ] n (sexual) légèreté f de mœurs.

**promiscuous** [prə'mɪskjuəs] a (sexually) de mœurs légères.

**promise** ['prɔmɪs] n promesse f // vt,vi promettre ; **promising** a prometteur(euse).

**promontory** ['prɔməntrɪ] n promontoire m.

**promote** [prə'məʊt] vt promouvoir ; (venture, event) organiser, mettre sur pied ; (new product) lancer ; **~r** n (of sporting event) organisateur/trice ; **promotion** [-'məʊʃən] n promotion f.

**prompt** [prɔmpt] a rapide // ad (punctually) à l'heure // vt inciter ; provoquer ; (THEATRE) souffler (son rôle or ses répliques) à ; **to ~ sb to do** inciter or pousser qn à faire ; **~er** n (THEATRE) souffleur m; **~ly** ad rapidement, sans délai ; ponctuellement ; **~ness** n rapidité f; promptitude f; ponctualité f.

**promulgate** ['prɔməlgeɪt] vt promulguer.

**prone** [prəʊn] a (lying) couché(e) (face contre terre) ; **~ to** enclin(e) à.

**prong** [prɔŋ] n pointe f; (of fork) dent f.

**pronoun** ['prəʊnaʊn] n pronom m.

**pronounce** [prə'naʊns] vt prononcer // vi: **to ~ (up)on** se prononcer sur ; **~d** a (marked) prononcé(e) ; **~ment** n déclaration f.

**pronunciation** [prənʌnsɪ'eɪʃən] n prononciation f.

**proof** [pru:f] n preuve f; (test, of book, PHOT) épreuve f; (of alcohol) degré m // a: **~ against** à l'épreuve de ; **to be 70 ~** ≈ titrer 40 degrés ; **~reader** n correcteur/trice (d'épreuves).

**prop** [prɔp] n support m, étai m // vt (also:

**~ up)** étayer, soutenir ; (lean): **to ~ sth against** appuyer qch contre or à.

**propaganda** [prɔpə'gændə] n propagande f.

**propagation** [prɔpə'geɪʃən] n propagation f.

**propel** [prə'pɛl] vt propulser, faire avancer ; **~ler** n hélice f; **~ling pencil** n porte-mine m inv.

**propensity** [prə'pɛnsɪtɪ] n propension f.

**proper** ['prɔpə*] a (suited, right) approprié(e), bon(bonne) ; (seemly) correct(e), convenable ; (authentic) vrai(e), véritable ; (col: real) n + fini(e), vrai(e) ; **~ly** ad correctement, convenablement ; bel et bien ; **~ noun** n nom m propre.

**property** ['prɔpətɪ] n (things owned) biens mpl; propriété(s) f(pl); immeuble m ; terres fpl, domaine m ; (CHEM etc: quality) propriété f; **it's their ~** cela leur appartient, c'est leur propriété ; **~ owner** n propriétaire m.

**prophecy** ['prɔfɪsɪ] n prophétie f.

**prophesy** ['prɔfɪsaɪ] vt prédire // vi prophétiser.

**prophet** ['prɔfɪt] n prophète m; **~ic** [prə'fɛtɪk] a prophétique.

**proportion** [prə'pɔ:ʃən] n proportion f; (share) part f, partie f // vt proportionner ; **~al, ~ate** a proportionnel(le).

**proposal** [prə'pəʊzl] n proposition f, offre f; (plan) projet m ; (of marriage) demande f en mariage.

**propose** [prə'pəʊz] vt proposer, suggérer // vi faire sa demande en mariage ; **to ~ to do** avoir l'intention de faire ; **~r** n (of motion etc) auteur m.

**proposition** [prɔpə'zɪʃən] n proposition f.

**propound** [prə'paʊnd] vt proposer, soumettre.

**proprietary** [prə'praɪətərɪ] a de marque déposée.

**proprietor** [prə'praɪətə*] n propriétaire m/f.

**propulsion** [prə'pʌlʃən] n propulsion f.

**pro rata** [prəʊ'rɑ:tə] ad au prorata.

**prosaic** [prəʊ'zeɪɪk] a prosaïque.

**prose** [prəʊz] n prose f; (SCOL: translation) thème m.

**prosecute** ['prɔsɪkju:t] vt poursuivre ; **prosecution** [-'kju:ʃən] n poursuites fpl judiciaires ; (accusing side) accusation f; **prosecutor** n procureur m; (also: **public ~**) ministère public.

**prospect** n ['prɔspɛkt] perspective f; (hope) espoir m, chances fpl // vt,vi [prə'spɛkt] prospecter ; **~s** npl (for work etc) possibilités fpl d'avenir, débouchés mpl; **prospecting** n prospection f; **prospective** a (possible) éventuel(le) ; (certain) futur(e) ; **prospector** n prospecteur m.

**prospectus** [prə'spɛktəs] n prospectus m.

**prosper** ['prɔspə*] vi prospérer ; **~ity** [-'spɛrɪtɪ] n prospérité f; **~ous** a prospère.

**prostitute** ['prɔstɪtju:t] n prostituée f.

**prostrate** ['prɔstreɪt] a prosterné(e) ; (fig) prostré(e).

**protagonist** [prə'tægənɪst] n protagoniste m.

**protect** [prə'tɛkt] vt protéger ; ~**ion** n protection f ; ~**ive** a protecteur(trice) ; ~**or** n protecteur/trice.
**protégé** ['prəutɛʒeɪ] n protégé m ; ~**e** n protégée f.
**protein** ['prəutiːn] n protéine f.
**protest** n ['prəutɛst] protestation f // vi [prə'tɛst] protester.
**Protestant** ['prɔtɪstənt] a,n protestant(e).
**protocol** ['prəutəkɔl] n protocole m.
**prototype** ['prəutətaɪp] n prototype m.
**protracted** [prə'træktɪd] a prolongé(e).
**protractor** [prə'træktə*] n rapporteur m.
**protrude** [prə'truːd] vi avancer, dépasser.
**protuberance** [prə'tjuːbərəns] n protubérance f.
**proud** [praud] a fier(ère) ; (pej) orgueilleux(euse) ; ~**ly** ad fièrement.
**prove** [pruːv] vt prouver, démontrer // vi: **to ~ correct** etc s'avérer juste etc ; **to ~ o.s.** montrer ce dont on est capable ; **to ~ o.s./itself (to be) useful** etc se montrer or se révéler utile etc.
**proverb** ['prɔvəːb] n proverbe m ; ~**ial** [prə'vəːbɪəl] a proverbial(e).
**provide** [prə'vaɪd] vt fournir ; **to ~ sb with sth** fournir qch à qn ; **to ~ for** vt (person) subvenir aux besoins de ; (emergency) prévoir ; ~**d (that)** cj à condition que + sub.
**Providence** ['prɔvɪdəns] n Providence f.
**providing** [prə'vaɪdɪŋ] cj à condition que + sub.
**province** ['prɔvɪns] n province f ; **provincial** [prə'vɪnʃəl] a provincial(e).
**provision** [prə'vɪʒən] n (supply) provision f ; (supplying) fourniture f ; approvisionnement m ; (stipulation) disposition f ; ~**s** npl (food) provisions fpl ; ~**al** a provisoire ; ~**ally** ad provisoirement.
**proviso** [prə'vaɪzəu] n condition f.
**provocation** [prɔvə'keɪʃən] n provocation f.
**provocative** [prə'vɔkətɪv] a provocateur(trice), provocant(e).
**provoke** [prə'vəuk] vt provoquer ; inciter.
**prow** [prau] n proue f.
**prowess** ['prauɪs] n prouesse f.
**prowl** [praul] vi (also: ~ **about**, ~ **around**) rôder // n: **on the ~** à l'affût ; ~**er** n rôdeur/euse.
**proximity** [prɔk'sɪmɪtɪ] n proximité f.
**proxy** ['prɔksɪ] n procuration f ; **by ~** par procuration.
**prudence** ['pruːdns] n prudence f.
**prudent** ['pruːdnt] a prudent(e).
**prudish** ['pruːdɪʃ] a prude, pudibond(e).
**prune** [pruːn] n pruneau m // vt élaguer.
**pry** [praɪ] vi: **to ~ into** fourrer son nez dans.
**psalm** [sɑːm] n psaume m.
**pseudo-** ['sjuːdəu] prefix pseudo- ; ~**nym** n pseudonyme m.
**psyche** ['saɪkɪ] n psychisme m.
**psychiatric** [saɪk'ætrɪk] a psychiatrique.
**psychiatrist** [saɪ'kaɪətrɪst] n psychiatre m/f.
**psychiatry** [saɪ'kaɪətrɪ] n psychiatrie f.

**psychic** ['saɪkɪk] a (also: ~**al**) (méta)psychique ; (person) doué(e) de télépathie or d'un sixième sens.
**psychoanalyse** [saɪkəu'ænəlaɪz] vt psychanalyser.
**psychoanalysis,** pl **lyses** [saɪkəuə'nælɪsɪs, -siːz] n psychanalyse f.
**psychoanalyst** [saɪkəu'ænəlɪst] n psychanalyste m/f.
**psychological** [saɪkə'lɔdʒɪkl] a psychologique.
**psychologist** [saɪ'kɔlədʒɪst] n psychologue m/f.
**psychology** [saɪ'kɔlədʒɪ] n psychologie f.
**psychopath** ['saɪkəupæθ] n psychopathe m/f.
**psychosomatic** ['saɪkəusə'mætɪk] a psychosomatique.
**psychotic** [saɪ'kɔtɪk] a,n psychotique (m/f).
**P.T.O.** abbr (= please turn over) T.S.V.P. (tournez s'il vous plaît).
**pub** [pʌb] n (abbr of public house) pub m.
**puberty** ['pjuːbətɪ] n puberté f.
**public** ['pʌblɪk] a public(ique) // n public m ; **the general ~** le grand public ; ~ **address system (P.A.)** sonorisation f ; **hauts-parleurs** mpl.
**publican** ['pʌblɪkən] n patron m de pub.
**publication** [pʌblɪ'keɪʃən] n publication f.
**public: ~ company** n société f anonyme (cotée en bourse) ; ~ **convenience** n toilettes fpl ; ~ **house** n pub m.
**publicity** [pʌb'lɪsɪtɪ] n publicité f.
**publicly** ['pʌblɪklɪ] ad publiquement.
**public: ~ opinion** n opinion publique ; ~ **relations (PR)** n relations publiques ; ~ **school** n (Brit) école privée ; ~**-spirited** a qui fait preuve de civisme.
**publish** ['pʌblɪʃ] vt publier ; ~**er** n éditeur m ; ~**ing** n (industry) édition f ; (of a book) publication f.
**puce** [pjuːs] a puce.
**puck** [pʌk] n (elf) lutin m, (ICE HOCKEY) palet m.
**pucker** ['pʌkə*] vt plisser.
**pudding** ['pudɪŋ] n dessert m, entremets m ; (sausage) boudin m.
**puddle** ['pʌdl] n flaque f d'eau.
**puerile** ['pjuəraɪl] a puéril(e).
**puff** [pʌf] n bouffée f ; (also: **powder ~**) houppette f // vt: **to ~ one's pipe** tirer sur sa pipe // vi sortir par bouffées ; (pant) haleter ; **to ~ out smoke** envoyer des bouffées de fumée ; ~**ed** a (col: out of breath) tout(e) essoufflé(e).
**puffin** ['pʌfɪn] n macareux m.
**puff pastry** ['pʌf'peɪstrɪ] n pâte feuilletée.
**puffy** ['pʌfɪ] a bouffi(e), boursouflé(e).
**pugnacious** [pʌg'neɪʃəs] a pugnace, batailleur(euse).
**pull** [pul] n (tug): **to give sth a ~** tirer sur qch ; (fig) influence f // vt tirer ; (muscle) se claquer // vi tirer ; **to ~ a face** faire une grimace ; **to ~ to pieces** mettre en morceaux ; **to ~ one's punches** ménager son adversaire ; **to ~ one's weight** y mettre du sien ; **to ~ o.s. together** se ressaisir ; **to ~ sb's leg** faire marcher qn ; **to ~ apart** vt séparer ; (break) mettre en pièces, démantibuler ; **to**

~ **down** vt baisser, abaisser ; (house) démolir ; (tree) abattre ; **to ~ in** vi (AUT: at the kerb) se ranger ; (RAIL) entrer en gare ; **to ~ off** vt enlever, ôter ; (deal etc) conclure ; **to ~ out** vi démarrer, partir ; se retirer ; (AUT: come out of line) déboîter // vt sortir ; arracher ; (withdraw) retirer ; **to ~ round** vi (unconscious person) revenir à soi ; (sick person) se rétablir ; **to ~ through** vi s'en sortir ; **to ~ up** vi (stop) s'arrêter // vt remonter ; (uproot) déraciner, arracher ; (stop) arrêter.

**pulley** ['pulɪ] n poulie f.

**pull-in** ['pulɪn] n (AUT) parking m.

**pullover** ['puləuvə*] n pull-over m, tricot m.

**pulp** [pʌlp] n (of fruit) pulpe f ; (for paper) pâte f à papier.

**pulpit** ['pulpɪt] n chaire f.

**pulsate** [pʌl'seɪt] vi battre, palpiter ; (music) vibrer.

**pulse** [pʌls] n (of blood) pouls m ; (of heart) battement m ; (of music, engine) vibrations fpl.

**pulverize** ['pʌlvəraɪz] vt pulvériser.

**puma** ['pju:mə] n puma m.

**pummel** ['pʌml] vt rouer de coups.

**pump** [pʌmp] n pompe f ; (shoe) escarpin m // vt pomper ; (fig: col) faire parler ; **to ~ up** vt gonfler.

**pumpkin** ['pʌmpkɪn] n potiron m, citrouille f.

**pun** [pʌn] n jeu m de mots, calembour m.

**punch** [pʌntʃ] n (blow) coup m de poing ; (fig: force) vivacité f, mordant m ; (tool) poinçon m ; (drink) punch m // vt (hit): **to ~ sb/sth** donner un coup de poing à qn/sur qch ; (make a hole) poinçonner, perforer ; **to ~ a hole (in)** faire un trou (dans) ; ~-**drunk** a sonné(e) ; ~-**up** n (col) bagarre f.

**punctual** ['pʌŋktjuəl] a ponctuel(le) ; ~ity [-'ælɪtɪ] n ponctualité f.

**punctuate** ['pʌŋktjueɪt] vt ponctuer ; **punctuation** [-'eɪʃən] n ponctuation f.

**puncture** ['pʌŋktʃə*] n crevaison f // vt crever.

**pundit** ['pʌndɪt] n individu m qui pontifie, pontife m.

**pungent** ['pʌndʒənt] a piquant(e) ; (fig) mordant(e), caustique.

**punish** ['pʌnɪʃ] vt punir ; ~**able** a punissable ; ~**ment** n punition f, châtiment m.

**punt** [pʌnt] n (boat) bachot m ; (FOOTBALL) coup m de volée.

**punter** ['pʌntə*] n (gambler) parieur/euse.

**puny** ['pju:nɪ] a chétif(ive).

**pup** [pʌp] n chiot m.

**pupil** ['pju:pl] n élève m/f.

**puppet** ['pʌpɪt] n marionnette f, pantin m.

**puppy** ['pʌpɪ] n chiot m, petit chien.

**purchase** ['pə:tʃɪs] n achat m // vt acheter ; ~**r** n acheteur/euse.

**pure** [pjuə*] a pur(e).

**purée** ['pjuəreɪ] n purée f.

**purge** [pə:dʒ] n (MED) purge f ; (POL) épuration f, purge // vt purger ; (fig) épurer, purger.

**purification** [pjuərɪfɪ'keɪʃən] n purification f.

**purify** ['pjuərɪfaɪ] vt purifier, épurer.

**purist** ['pjuərɪst] n puriste m/f.

**puritan** ['pjuərɪtən] n puritain/e ; ~**ical** [-'tænɪkl] a puritain(e).

**purity** ['pjuərɪtɪ] n pureté f.

**purl** [pə:l] n maille f à l'envers // vt tricoter à l'envers.

**purple** ['pə:pl] a violet(te) ; cramoisi(e).

**purport** [pə:'pɔ:t] vi: **to ~ to be/do** prétendre être/faire.

**purpose** ['pə:pəs] n intention f, but m ; **on ~** exprès ; ~**ful** a déterminé(e), résolu(e) ; ~**ly** ad exprès.

**purr** [pə:*] n ronronnement m // vi ronronner.

**purse** [pə:s] n porte-monnaie m inv, bourse f // vt serrer, pincer.

**purser** ['pə:sə*] n (NAUT) commissaire m du bord.

**pursue** [pə'sju:] vt poursuivre ; ~**r** n poursuivant/e.

**pursuit** [pə'sju:t] n poursuite f ; (occupation) occupation f, activité f ; **scientific ~s** recherches fpl scientifiques.

**purveyor** [pə'veɪə*] n fournisseur m.

**pus** [pʌs] n pus m.

**push** [puʃ] n poussée f ; (effort) gros effort ; (drive) énergie f // vt pousser ; (button) appuyer sur ; (thrust): **to ~ sth (into)** enfoncer qch (dans) ; (fig) mettre en avant, faire de la publicité pour // vi pousser ; appuyer ; **to ~ aside** vt écarter ; **to ~ off** vi (col) filer, ficher le camp ; **to ~ on** vi (continue) continuer ; **to ~ over** vt renverser ; **to ~ through** vt (measure) faire voter ; **to ~ up** vt (total, prices) faire monter ; ~**chair** n poussette f ; ~**ing** a dynamique ; ~**over** n (col): **it's a ~over** c'est un jeu d'enfant ; ~**y** a (pej) arriviste.

**puss, pussy(-cat)** [pus, 'pusɪ(kæt)] n minet m.

**put**, pt, pp **put** [put] vt mettre, poser, placer ; (say) dire, exprimer ; (a question) poser ; (estimate) estimer ; **to ~ about** vi (NAUT) virer de bord // vt (rumour) faire courir ; **to ~ across** vt (ideas etc) communiquer ; faire comprendre ; **to ~ away** vt (store) ranger ; **to ~ back** vt (replace) remettre, replacer ; (postpone) remettre ; (delay) retarder ; **to ~ by** vt (money) mettre de côté, économiser ; **to ~ down** vt (parcel etc) poser, déposer ; (pay) verser ; (in writing) mettre par écrit, inscrire ; (suppress: revolt etc) réprimer, faire cesser ; (attribute) attribuer ; **to ~ forward** vt (ideas) avancer, proposer ; (date) avancer ; **to ~ in** vt (gas, electricity) installer ; (application, complaint) soumettre ; **to ~ off** vt (light etc) éteindre ; (postpone) remettre à plus tard, ajourner ; (discourage) dissuader ; **to ~ on** vt (clothes, lipstick etc) mettre ; (light etc) allumer ; (play etc) monter ; (food, meal) servir ; (airs, weight) prendre ; (brake) mettre ; **to ~ on the brakes** freiner ; **to ~ out** vt mettre dehors ; (one's hand) tendre ; (news, rumour) faire courir, répandre ; (light etc) éteindre ; (person: inconvenience) déranger, gêner ; **to ~ up** vt (raise) lever, relever, remonter ; (pin up) afficher ; (hang) accrocher ; (build) construire, ériger ; (a tent) monter ; (increase) augmenter ;

(*accommodate*) loger ; **to ~ up with** vt fus supporter.

**putrid** ['pju:trɪd] a putride.

**putt** [pʌt] vt poter (la balle) // n coup roulé ; **~er** n (*GOLF*) putter m ; **~ing green** n green m.

**putty** ['pʌtɪ] n mastic m.

**put-up** ['putʌp] a: ~ **job** n affaire montée.

**puzzle** ['pʌzl] n énigme f, mystère m ; (*jigsaw*) puzzle m ; (*also*: **crossword ~**) problème m de mots croisés // vt intriguer, rendre perplexe // vi se creuser la tête ; **puzzling** a déconcertant(e), inexplicable.

**PVC** abbr of polyvinyl chloride.

**pygmy** ['pɪgmɪ] n pygmée m/f.

**pyjamas** [pɪ'dʒɑ:məz] npl pyjama m.

**pylon** ['paɪlən] n pylône m.

**pyramid** ['pɪrəmɪd] n pyramide f.

**python** ['paɪθən] n python m.

## Q

**quack** [kwæk] n (*of duck*) coin-coin m inv ; (*pej*: *doctor*) charlatan m.

**quad** [kwɔd] abbr of **quadrangle, quadruplet.**

**quadrangle** ['kwɔdræŋgl] n (*MATH*) quadrilatère m ; (*courtyard*: abbr: **quad**) cour f.

**quadruped** ['kwɔdrupɛd] n quadrupède m.

**quadruple** [kwɔ'drupl] a,n quadruple (m) // vt, vi quadrupler ; **~t** [-'dru:plɪt] n quadruplé/e.

**quagmire** ['kwægmaɪə*] n bourbier m.

**quail** [kweɪl] n (*ZOOL*) caille f.

**quaint** [kweɪnt] a bizarre ; (*old-fashioned*) désuet(ète) ; au charme vieillot, pittoresque.

**quake** [kweɪk] vi trembler // n abbr of **earthquake.**

**Quaker** ['kweɪkə*] n quaker/esse.

**qualification** [kwɔlɪfɪ'keɪʃən] n (*degree etc*) diplôme m ; (*ability*) compétence f, qualification f ; (*limitation*) réserve f, restriction f.

**qualified** ['kwɔlɪfaɪd] a diplômé(e) ; (*able*) compétent(e), qualifié(e) ; (*limited*) conditionnel(le).

**qualify** ['kwɔlɪfaɪ] vt qualifier ; (*limit: statement*) apporter des réserves à // vi: **to ~ (as)** obtenir son diplôme (de) ; **to ~ (for)** remplir les conditions requises (pour) ; (*SPORT*) se qualifier (pour).

**qualitative** ['kwɔlɪtətɪv] a qualitatif(ive).

**quality** ['kwɔlɪtɪ] n qualité f // cpd de qualité ; **the ~ papers** la presse d'information.

**qualm** [kwɑ:m] n doute m ; scrupule m.

**quandary** ['kwɔndrɪ] n: **in a ~** devant un dilemme, dans l'embarras.

**quantitative** ['kwɔntɪtətɪv] a quantitatif(ive).

**quantity** ['kwɔntɪtɪ] n quantité f ; **~ surveyor** n métreur m vérificateur.

**quarantine** ['kwɔrntɪːn] n quarantaine f.

**quarrel** ['kwɔrl] n querelle f, dispute f // vi se disputer, se quereller ; **~some** a querelleur(euse).

**quarry** ['kwɔrɪ] n (*for stone*) carrière f ;

(*animal*) proie f, gibier m // vt (*marble etc*) extraire.

**quart** [kwɔ:t] n ≈ litre m (= 2 pints).

**quarter** ['kwɔ:tə*] n quart m ; (*of year*) trimestre m ; (*district*) quartier m // vt partager en quartiers or en quatre ; (*MIL*) caserner, cantonner ; **~s** npl logement m ; (*MIL*) quartiers mpl, cantonnement m ; **a ~ of an hour** un quart d'heure ; **~-deck** n (*NAUT*) plage f arrière ; **~ final** n quart m de finale ; **~ly** a trimestriel(le) // ad tous les trois mois ; **~master** n (*MIL*) intendant m militaire de troisième classe ; (*NAUT*) maître m de manœuvre.

**quartet(te)** [kwɔ:'tɛt] n quatuor m ; (*jazz players*) quartette m.

**quartz** [kwɔ:ts] n quartz m ; **~ watch** n montre f à quartz.

**quash** [kwɔʃ] vt (*verdict*) annuler, casser.

**quasi-** ['kweɪzaɪ] prefix quasi- + noun ; quasi, presque + adjective.

**quaver** ['kweɪvə*] n (*MUS*) croche f // vi trembler.

**quay** [ki:] n (*also*: **~side**) quai m.

**queasy** ['kwi:zɪ] a (*stomach*) délicat(e) ; **to feel ~** avoir mal au cœur.

**queen** [kwi:n] n (*gen*) reine f ; (*CARDS etc*) dame f ; **~ mother** n reine mère f.

**queer** [kwɪə*] a étrange, curieux(euse) ; (*suspicious*) louche ; (*sick*): **I feel ~** je ne me sens pas bien // n (*col*) homosexuel m.

**quell** [kwɛl] vt réprimer, étouffer.

**quench** [kwɛntʃ] vt (*flames*) éteindre ; **to ~ one's thirst** se désaltérer.

**query** ['kwɪərɪ] n question f ; (*doubt*) doute m ; (*question mark*) point m d'interrogation // vt mettre en question or en doute.

**quest** [kwɛst] n recherche f, quête f.

**question** ['kwɛstʃən] n question f // vt (*person*) interroger ; (*plan, idea*) mettre en question or en doute ; **it's a ~ of doing** il s'agit de faire ; **there's some ~ of doing** il est question de faire ; **beyond ~** ad sans aucun doute ; **out of the ~** hors de question ; **~able** a discutable ; **~ing** a interrogateur(trice) // n interrogatoire m ; **~ mark** n point m d'interrogation.

**questionnaire** [kwɛstʃə'nɛə*] n questionnaire m.

**queue** [kju:] n queue f, file f // vi faire la queue.

**quibble** ['kwɪbl] vi ergoter, chicaner.

**quick** [kwɪk] a rapide ; (*reply*) prompt(e), rapide ; (*mind*) vif(vive) // ad vite, rapidement // n: **cut to the ~** (*fig*) touché(e) au vif ; **be ~!** dépêche-toi! ; **~en** vt accélérer, presser ; (*rouse*) stimuler // vi s'accélérer, devenir plus rapide ; **~lime** n chaux vive ; **~ly** ad vite, rapidement ; **~ness** n rapidité f ; promptitude f ; vivacité f ; **~sand** n sables mouvants ; **~step** n (*dance*) fox-trot m ; **~-witted** a à l'esprit vif.

**quid** [kwɪd] n, pl inv (*Brit: col*) livre f.

**quiet** ['kwaɪət] a tranquille, calme ; (*ceremony, colour*) discret(ète) // n tranquillité f, calme m ; **keep ~!** tais-toi! ; **on the ~** en secret, en cachette ; **~en** (*also*: **~en down**) vi se calmer, s'apaiser // vt calmer, apaiser ; **~ly** ad tranquillement, calmement ;

discrètement ; **~ness** n tranquillité f, calme m ; silence m.
**quill** [kwɪl] n plume f (d'oie).
**quilt** [kwɪlt] n édredon m ; **(continental)** ~ n couverture f édredon ; **~ing** n ouatine f ; molletonnage m.
**quin** [kwɪn] abbr of **quintuplet**.
**quince** [kwɪns] n coing m ; (tree) cognassier m.
**quinine** [kwɪ'ni:n] n quinine f.
**quintet(te)** [kwɪn'tɛt] n quintette m.
**quintuplet** [kwɪn'tju:plɪt] n quintuplé/e.
**quip** [kwɪp] n remarque piquante or spirituelle, pointe f // vt: ... **he ~ped** ... lança-t-il.
**quirk** [kwə:k] n bizarrerie f.
**quit**, pt, pp **quit** or **quitted** [kwɪt] vt quitter // vi (give up) abandonner, renoncer ; (resign) démissionner ; **to ~ doing** arrêter de faire ; **notice to ~** congé m (signifié au locataire).
**quite** [kwaɪt] ad (rather) assez, plutôt ; (entirely) complètement, tout à fait ; **I ~ understand** je comprends très bien ; ~ **a few of them** un assez grand nombre d'entre eux ; ~ **(so)!** exactement!
**quits** [kwɪts] a: ~ **(with)** quitte (envers).
**quiver** ['kwɪvə*] vi trembler, frémir // n (for arrows) carquois m.
**quiz** [kwɪz] n (game) jeu-concours m ; test m de connaissances // vt interroger ; **~zical** a narquois(e).
**quoits** [kwɔɪts] npl jeu m du palet.
**quorum** ['kwɔ:rəm] n quorum m.
**quota** ['kwəutə] n quota m.
**quotation** [kwəu'teɪʃən] n citation f ; (of shares etc) cote f, cours m ; (estimate) devis m ; ~ **marks** npl guillemets mpl.
**quote** [kwəut] n citation f // vt (sentence) citer ; (price) donner, fixer ; (shares) coter // vi: **to ~ from** citer ; **to ~ for a job** établir un devis pour des travaux.
**quotient** ['kwəuʃənt] n quotient m.

# R

**rabbi** ['ræbaɪ] n rabbin m.
**rabbit** ['ræbɪt] n lapin m ; ~ **hole** n terrier m (de lapin) ; ~ **hutch** n clapier m.
**rabble** ['ræbl] n (pej) populace f.
**rabid** ['ræbɪd] a enragé(e).
**rabies** ['reɪbi:z] n rage f.
**RAC** n abbr of Royal Automobile Club.
**raccoon** [rə'ku:n] n raton m laveur.
**race** [reɪs] n race f ; (competition, rush) course f // vt (person) faire la course avec ; (horse) faire courir ; (engine) emballer // vi courir ; ~**course** n champ m de courses ; ~**horse** n cheval m de course ; ~ **relations** npl rapports mpl entre les races ; ~**track** n piste f.
**racial** ['reɪʃl] a racial(e) ; ~ **discrimination** n discrimination raciale ; ~**ism** n racisme m ; ~**ist** a, n raciste m/f.
**racing** ['reɪsɪŋ] n courses fpl ; ~ **car** n voiture f de course ; ~ **driver** n pilote m de course.
**racist** ['reɪsɪst] a,n (pej) raciste (m/f).
**rack** [ræk] n (also: **luggage** ~) filet m à bagages ; (also: **roof** ~) galerie f // vt tourmenter ; **magazine** ~ n porte-revues

m inv ; **shoe** ~ n étagère f à chaussures ; **toast** ~ n porte-toast m.
**racket** ['rækɪt] n (for tennis) raquette f ; (noise) tapage m ; vacarme m ; (swindle) escroquerie f ; (organized crime) racket m.
**racoon** [rə'ku:n] n = **raccoon**.
**racquet** ['rækɪt] n raquette f.
**racy** ['reɪsɪ] a plein(e) de verve ; osé(e).
**radar** ['reɪdɑ:*] n radar m // cpd radar inv.
**radiance** ['reɪdɪəns] n éclat m, rayonnement m.
**radiant** ['reɪdɪənt] a rayonnant(e) ; (PHYSICS) radiant(e).
**radiate** ['reɪdɪeɪt] vt (heat) émettre, dégager // vi (lines) rayonner.
**radiation** [reɪdɪ'eɪʃən] n rayonnement m ; (radioactive) radiation f.
**radiator** ['reɪdɪeɪtə*] n radiateur m ; ~ **cap** n bouchon m de radiateur.
**radical** ['rædɪkl] a radical(e).
**radii** ['reɪdɪaɪ] npl of **radius**.
**radio** ['reɪdɪəu] n radio f ; **on the** ~ à la radio ; ~ **station** station f de radio.
**radio...** ['reɪdɪəu] prefix: ~**active** a radioactif(ive) ; ~**activity** n radioactivité f ; ~**grapher** [-'ɔgrəfə*] n radiologue m/f (technicien) ; ~**graphy** [-'ɔgrəfɪ] n radiographie f ; ~**logy** [-'ɔlədʒɪ] n radiologie f ; ~**therapist** n radiothérapeute m/f.
**radish** ['rædɪʃ] n radis m.
**radium** ['reɪdɪəm] n radium m.
**radius**, pl **radii** ['reɪdɪəs, -ɪaɪ] n rayon m ; (ANAT) radius m.
**raffia** ['ræfɪə] n raphia m.
**raffish** ['ræfɪʃ] a dissolu(e) ; canaille.
**raffle** ['ræfl] n tombola f.
**raft** [rɑ:ft] n (also: **life** ~) radeau m ; (logs) train m de flottage.
**rafter** ['rɑ:ftə*] n chevron m.
**rag** [ræg] n chiffon m ; (pej: newspaper) feuille f, torchon m ; (for charity) attractions organisées par les étudiants au profit d'œuvres de charité // vt chahuter, mettre en boîte ; ~**s** npl haillons mpl ; ~**-and-bone man** n chiffonnier m ; ~**bag** n (fig) ramassis m.
**rage** [reɪdʒ] n (fury) rage f, fureur f // vi (person) être fou(folle) de rage ; (storm) faire rage, être déchaîné(e) ; **it's all the** ~ cela fait fureur.
**ragged** ['rægɪd] a (edge) inégal(e), qui accroche ; (cuff) effiloché(e) ; (appearance) déguenillé(e).
**raid** [reɪd] n (MIL) raid m ; (criminal) hold-up m inv ; (by police) descente f, rafle f // vt faire un raid sur or un hold-up dans or une descente dans ; ~**er** n malfaiteur m ; (plane) bombardier m.
**rail** [reɪl] n (on stair) rampe f ; (on bridge, balcony) balustrade f ; (of ship) bastingage m ; (for train) rail m ; ~**s** npl rails mpl, voie ferrée ; **by** ~ par chemin de fer ; ~ **ing(s)** n(pl) grille f ; ~**road** n (US), ~**way** n chemin m de fer ; ~**wayman** n cheminot m ; ~**way station** n gare f.
**rain** [reɪn] n pluie f // vi pleuvoir ; **in the** ~ sous la pluie ; ~**bow** n arc-en-ciel m ; ~**coat** n imperméable m ; ~**drop** n goutte f de pluie ; ~**fall** n chute f de pluie ; (measurement) hauteur f des précipitations ;

**~proof** *a* imperméable ; **~storm** *n* pluie torrentielle ; **~y** *a* pluvieux(euse).

**raise** [reɪz] *n* augmentation *f* // *vt* (*lift*) lever ; hausser ; (*build*) ériger ; (*increase*) augmenter ; (*a protest, doubt*) provoquer, causer ; (*a question*) soulever ; (*cattle, family*) élever ; (*crop*) faire pousser ; (*army, funds*) rassembler ; (*loan*) obtenir ; **to ~ one's voice** élever la voix.

**raisin** ['reɪzn] *n* raisin sec.

**raj** [rɑːdʒ] *n* empire *m* (*aux Indes*).

**rajah** ['rɑːdʒə] *n* radja(h) *m*.

**rake** [reɪk] *n* (*tool*) râteau *m* ; (*person*) débauché *m* // *vt* (*garden*) ratisser ; (*fire*) tisonner ; (*with machine gun*) balayer ; **to ~ through** (*fig: search*) fouiller (dans).

**rakish** ['reɪkɪʃ] *a* dissolu(e) ; cavalier(ère).

**rally** ['rælɪ] *n* (*POL etc*) meeting *m*, rassemblement *m* ; (*AUT*) rallye *m* ; (*TENNIS*) échange *m* // *vt* rassembler, rallier // *vi* se rallier ; (*sick person*) aller mieux ; (*Stock Exchange*) reprendre ; **to ~ round** *vt fus* se rallier à ; venir en aide à.

**ram** [ræm] *n* bélier *m* // *vt* enfoncer ; (*soil*) tasser ; (*crash into*) emboutir ; percuter ; éperonner.

**ramble** ['ræmbl] *n* randonnée *f* // *vi* (*pej: also:* **~ on**) discourir, pérorer ; **~r** *n* promeneur/euse, randonneur/euse ; (*BOT*) rosier grimpant ; **rambling** *a* (*speech*) décousu(e) ; (*BOT*) grimpant(e).

**ramification** [ræmɪfɪ'keɪʃən] *n* ramification *f*.

**ramp** [ræmp] *n* (*incline*) rampe *f* ; dénivellation *f* ; (*in garage*) pont *m*.

**rampage** [ræm'peɪdʒ] *n*: **to be on the ~** se déchaîner // *vi*: **they went rampaging through the town** ils ont envahi les rues et ont tout saccagé sur leur passage.

**rampant** ['ræmpənt] *a* (*disease etc*) qui sévit.

**rampart** ['ræmpɑːt] *n* rempart *m*.

**ramshackle** ['ræmʃækl] *a* (*house*) délabré(e) ; (*car etc*) déglingué(e).

**ran** [ræn] *pt of* **run**.

**ranch** [rɑːntʃ] *n* ranch *m* ; **~er** *n* propriétaire *m* de ranch ; cowboy *m*.

**rancid** ['rænsɪd] *a* rance.

**rancour, rancor** (*US*) ['ræŋkə*] *n* rancune *f*.

**random** ['rændəm] *a* fait(e) *or* établi(e) au hasard // *n*: **at ~** au hasard.

**randy** ['rændɪ] *a* (*col*) excité(e) ; lubrique.

**rang** [ræŋ] *pt of* **ring**.

**range** [reɪndʒ] *n* (*of mountains*) chaîne *f* ; (*of missile, voice*) portée *f* ; (*of products*) choix *m*, gamme *f* ; (*MIL: also:* **shooting ~**) champ *m* de tir ; (*also:* **kitchen ~**) fourneau *m* (de cuisine) // *vt* (*place*) mettre en rang, placer ; (*roam*) parcourir // *vi*: **to ~ over** couvrir ; **to ~ from ... to** aller de ... à ; **~r** *n* garde *m* forestier.

**rank** [ræŋk] *n* rang *m* ; (*MIL*) grade *m* ; (*also:* **taxi ~**) station *f* de taxis // *vi*: **to ~ among** compter *or* se classer parmi // *a* (qui sent) fort(e) ; extrême ; **the ~s** (*MIL*) la troupe ; **the ~ and file** (*fig*) la masse, la base.

**rankle** ['ræŋkl] *vi* (*insult*) rester sur le cœur.

**ransack** ['rænsæk] *vt* fouiller (à fond) ; (*plunder*) piller.

**ransom** ['rænsəm] *n* rançon *f* ; **to hold sb to ~** (*fig*) exercer un chantage sur qn.

**rant** [rænt] *vi* fulminer ; **~ing** *n* invectives *fpl*.

**rap** [ræp] *n* petit coup sec ; tape *f* // *vt* frapper sur *or* à ; taper sur.

**rape** [reɪp] *n* viol *m* // *vt* violer.

**rapid** ['ræpɪd] *a* rapide ; **~s** *npl* (*GEO*) rapides *mpl* ; **~ity** [rə'pɪdɪtɪ] *n* rapidité *f*.

**rapist** ['reɪpɪst] *n* auteur *m* d'un viol.

**rapport** [ræ'pɔː*] *n* entente *f*.

**rapture** ['ræptʃə*] *n* extase *f*, ravissement *m* ; **to go into ~s over** s'extasier sur ; **rapturous** *a* extasié(e) ; frénétique.

**rare** [rɛə*] *a* rare ; (*CULIN: steak*) saignant(e).

**rarebit** ['rɛəbɪt] *n see* **Welsh**.

**rarefied** ['rɛərɪfaɪd] *a* (*air, atmosphere*) raréfié(e).

**rarely** ['rɛəlɪ] *ad* rarement.

**rarity** ['rɛərɪtɪ] *n* rareté *f*.

**rascal** ['rɑːskl] *n* vaurien *m*.

**rash** [ræʃ] *a* imprudent(e), irréfléchi(e) // *n* (*MED*) rougeur *f*, éruption *f*.

**rasher** ['ræʃə*] *n* fine tranche (de lard).

**rasp** [rɑːsp] *n* (*tool*) lime *f*.

**raspberry** ['rɑːzbərɪ] *n* framboise *f* ; **~ bush** *n* framboisier *m*.

**rasping** ['rɑːspɪŋ] *a*: **~ noise** grincement *m*.

**rat** [ræt] *n* rat *m*.

**ratable** ['reɪtəbl] *a* = **rateable**.

**ratchet** ['rætʃɪt] *n*: **~ wheel** roue *f* à rochet.

**rate** [reɪt] *n* (*ratio*) taux *m*, pourcentage *m* ; (*speed*) vitesse *f*, rythme *m* ; (*price*) tarif *m* // *vt* classer ; évaluer ; **to ~ sb/sth as** considérer qn/qch comme ; **to ~ sb/sth among** classer qn/qch parmi ; **~s** *npl* (*Brit*) impôts locaux ; (*fees*) tarifs *mpl* ; **~able value** *n* valeur locative imposable ; **of exchange** « taux *m* *or* cours *m* du change ; **~ of flow** *n* débit *m* ; **~payer** *n* contribuable *m/f* (*payant les impôts locaux*).

**rather** ['rɑːðə*] *ad* plutôt ; **it's ~ expensive** c'est assez cher ; (*too much*) c'est un peu cher ; **I would** *or* **I'd ~ go** j'aimerais mieux *or* je préférerais partir ; **I had ~ go** il vaudrait mieux que je parte.

**ratification** [rætɪfɪ'keɪʃən] *n* ratification *f*.

**ratify** ['rætɪfaɪ] *vt* ratifier.

**rating** ['reɪtɪŋ] *n* classement *m* ; cote *f* ; (*NAUT: category*) classe *f* ; (*: sailor*) matelot *m*.

**ratio** ['reɪʃɪəu] *n* proportion *f* ; **in the ~ of 100 to 1** dans la proportion de 100 contre 1.

**ration** ['ræʃən] *n* (*gen pl*) ration(s) *f(pl)* // *vt* rationner.

**rational** ['ræʃənl] *a* raisonnable, sensé(e) ; (*solution, reasoning*) logique ; (*MED*) lucide ; **~e** [-'nɑːl] *n* raisonnement *m* ; justification *f* ; **~ize** *vt* rationaliser ; (*conduct*) essayer d'expliquer *or* de motiver ; **~ly** *ad* raisonnablement ; logiquement.

**rationing** ['ræʃnɪŋ] *n* rationnement *m*.

**rat poison** ['rætpɔɪzn] *n* mort-aux-rats *f inv*.

**rat race** ['rætreɪs] n foire f d'empoigne.
**rattle** ['rætl] n cliquetis m ; (louder) bruit m de ferraille ; (object: of baby) hochet m ; (: of sports fan) crécelle f // vi cliqueter ; faire un bruit de ferraille or du bruit // vt agiter (bruyamment) ; ~snake n serpent m à sonnettes.
**raucous** ['rɔ:kəs] a rauque ; ~ly ad d'une voix rauque.
**ravage** ['rævɪdʒ] vt ravager ; ~s npl ravages mpl.
**rave** [reɪv] vi (in anger) s'emporter ; (with enthusiasm) s'extasier ; (MED) délirer.
**raven** ['reɪvən] n corbeau m.
**ravenous** ['rævənəs] a affamé(e).
**ravine** [rə'vi:n] n ravin m.
**raving** ['reɪvɪŋ] a: ~ lunatic n fou furieux/folle furieuse.
**ravioli** [rævɪ'əulɪ] n ravioli mpl.
**ravish** ['rævɪʃ] vt ravir ; ~ing a enchanteur(eresse).
**raw** [rɔ:] a (uncooked) cru(e) ; (not processed) brut(e) ; (sore) à vif, irrité(e) ; (inexperienced) inexpérimenté(e) ; ~ material n matière première.
**ray** [reɪ] n rayon m ; ~ of hope n lueur f d'espoir.
**rayon** ['reɪɔn] n rayonne f.
**raze** [reɪz] vt raser, détruire.
**razor** ['reɪzə*] n rasoir m ; ~ blade n lame f de rasoir.
**Rd** abbr of **road**.
**re** [ri:] prep concernant.
**reach** [ri:tʃ] n portée f, atteinte f ; (of river etc) étendue f // vt atteindre ; parvenir à // vi s'étendre ; **out of/within** ~ (object) hors de/à portée ; **within easy** ~ (of) (place) à proximité, proche (de) ; **to** ~ **out** vi: **to** ~ **out for** allonger le bras pour prendre.
**react** [ri:'ækt] vi réagir ; ~ion [-'ækʃən] n réaction f ; ~ionary [-'ækʃənrɪ] a,n réactionnaire (m/f).
**reactor** [ri:'æktə*] n réacteur m.
**read**, pt,pp **read** [ri:d, rɛd] vi lire // vt lire ; (understand) comprendre, interpréter ; (study) étudier ; (subj: instrument etc) indiquer, marquer ; **to** ~ **out** vt lire à haute voix ; ~**able** a facile or agréable à lire ; ~**er** n lecteur/trice ; (book) livre m de lecture ; (at university) maître m de conférences ; ~**ership** n (of paper etc) (nombre m de) lecteurs mpl.
**readily** ['rɛdɪlɪ] ad volontiers, avec empressement ; (easily) facilement.
**readiness** ['rɛdɪnɪs] n empressement m ; **in** ~ (prepared) prêt(e).
**reading** ['ri:dɪŋ] n lecture f ; (understanding) interprétation f ; (on instrument) indications fpl ; ~ **lamp** n lampe f de bureau ; ~ **room** n salle f de lecture.
**readjust** [ri:ə'dʒʌst] vt rajuster ; (instrument) régler de nouveau // vi (person): **to** ~ **(to)** se réadapter (à).
**ready** ['rɛdɪ] a prêt(e) ; (willing) prêt, disposé(e) ; (quick) prompt(e) ; (available) disponible // ad: ~**-cooked** tout(e) cuit(e) (d'avance) // n: **at the** ~ (MIL) prêt à faire feu ; (fig) tout(e) prêt(e) ; ~ **cash** n (argent m) liquide m ; ~**-made** a tout(e) fait(e) ; ~**-mix** n (for cakes etc) préparation f en

sachet ; ~ **reckoner** n barème m ; ~**-to-wear** a en prêt-à-porter.
**real** [rɪəl] a réel(le) ; véritable ; **in** ~ **terms** dans la réalité ; ~ **estate** n biens fonciers or immobiliers ; ~**ism** n (also ART) réalisme m ; ~**ist** n réaliste m/f ; ~**istic** [-'lɪstɪk] a réaliste.
**reality** [ri:'ælɪtɪ] n réalité f ; **in** ~ en réalité, en fait.
**realization** [rɪəlaɪ'zeɪʃən] n prise f de conscience ; réalisation f.
**realize** ['rɪəlaɪz] vt (understand) se rendre compte de ; (a project, COMM: asset) réaliser.
**really** ['rɪəlɪ] ad vraiment.
**realm** [rɛlm] n royaume m.
**ream** [ri:m] n rame f (de papier).
**reap** [ri:p] vt moissonner ; (fig) récolter ; ~**er** n (machine) moissonneuse f.
**reappear** [ri:ə'pɪə*] vi réapparaître, reparaître ; ~**ance** n réapparition f.
**reapply** [ri:ə'plaɪ] vi: **to** ~ **for** faire une nouvelle demande d'emploi concernant ; reposer sa candidature à.
**rear** [rɪə*] a de derrière, arrière inv ; (AUT: wheel etc) arrière // n arrière m, derrière m // vt (cattle, family) élever // vi (also: ~ **up**) (animal) se cabrer ; ~**-engined** a (AUT) avec moteur à l'arrière ; ~**guard** n arrière-garde f.
**rearm** [ri:'ɑ:m] vt, vi réarmer ; ~**ament** n réarmement m.
**rearrange** [ri:ə'reɪndʒ] vt réarranger.
**rear-view** ['rɪəvju:] a: ~ **mirror** n (AUT) rétroviseur m.
**reason** ['ri:zn] n raison f // vi: **to** ~ **with sb** raisonner qn, faire entendre raison à qn ; **to have** ~ **to think** avoir lieu de penser ; **it stands to** ~ **that** il va sans dire que ; ~**able** a raisonnable ; (not bad) acceptable ; ~**ably** ad raisonnablement ; **one can** ~**ably assume that ...** on est fondé à or il est permis de supposer que ... ; ~**ed** a (argument) raisonné(e) ; ~**ing** n raisonnement m.
**reassemble** [ri:ə'sɛmbl] vt rassembler ; (machine) remonter.
**reassert** [ri:ə'sə:t] vt réaffirmer.
**reassure** [ri:ə'ʃuə*] vt rassurer ; **to** ~ **sb of** donner à qn l'assurance répétée de ; **reassuring** a rassurant(e).
**reawakening** [ri:ə'weɪknɪŋ] n réveil m.
**rebate** ['ri:beɪt] n (on product) rabais m ; (on tax etc) dégrèvement m ; (repayment) remboursement m.
**rebel** n ['rɛbl] rebelle m/f // vi [rɪ'bɛl] se rebeller, se révolter ; ~**lion** n rébellion f, révolte f ; ~**lious** a rebelle.
**rebirth** [ri:'bə:θ] n renaissance f.
**rebound** vi [rɪ'baund] (ball) rebondir ; (bullet) ricocher // n ['ri:baund] rebond m ; ricochet m.
**rebuff** [rɪ'bʌf] n rebuffade f // vt repousser.
**rebuild** [ri:'bɪld] vt irg reconstruire.
**rebuke** [rɪ'bju:k] n réprimande f, reproche m // vt réprimander.
**rebut** [rɪ'bʌt] vt réfuter ; ~**tal** n réfutation f.
**recall** [rɪ'kɔ:l] vt rappeler ; (remember) se rappeler, se souvenir de // n rappel m ; **beyond** ~ a irrévocable.

**recant** [rɪ'kænt] *vi* se rétracter ; (REL) abjurer.

**recap** ['ri:kæp] *n* récapitulation *f* // *vt, vi* récapituler.

**recapture** [ri:'kæptʃə*] *vt* reprendre ; (atmosphere) recréer.

**recede** [rɪ'si:d] *vi* s'éloigner ; reculer ; redescendre ; **receding** *a* (forehead, chin) fuyant(e) ; **receding hairline** *n* front dégarni.

**receipt** [rɪ'si:t] *n* (document) reçu *m* ; (for parcel etc) accusé *m* de réception ; (act of receiving) réception *f* ; **~s** *npl* (COMM) recettes *fpl*.

**receive** [rɪ'si:v] *vt* recevoir ; (guest) recevoir, accueillir.

**receiver** [rɪ'si:və*] *n* (TEL) récepteur *m*, combiné *m* ; (of stolen goods) receleur *m* ; (COMM) administrateur *m* judiciaire.

**recent** ['ri:snt] *a* récent(e) ; **~ly** *ad* récemment ; **as ~ly as** pas plus tard que.

**receptacle** [rɪ'sɛptɪkl] *n* récipient *m*.

**reception** [rɪ'sɛpʃən] *n* réception *f* ; (welcome) accueil *m*, réception ; **~ desk** *n* réception ; **~ist** *n* réceptionniste *m/f*.

**receptive** [rɪ'sɛptɪv] *a* réceptif(ive).

**recess** [rɪ'sɛs] *n* (in room) renfoncement *m* ; (for bed) alcôve *f* ; (secret place) recoin *m* ; (POL etc: holiday) vacances *fpl*.

**recharge** [ri:'tʃɑ:dʒ] *vt* (battery) recharger.

**recipe** ['rɛsɪpɪ] *n* recette *f*.

**recipient** [rɪ'sɪpɪənt] *n* bénéficiaire *m/f* ; (of letter) destinataire *m/f*.

**reciprocal** [rɪ'sɪprəkl] *a* réciproque.

**reciprocate** [rɪ'sɪprəkeɪt] *vt* retourner, offrir en retour.

**recital** [rɪ'saɪtl] *n* récital *m*.

**recite** [rɪ'saɪt] *vt* (poem) réciter ; (complaints etc) énumérer.

**reckless** ['rɛkləs] *a* (driver etc) imprudent(e) ; (spender etc) insouciant(e) ; **~ly** *ad* imprudemment ; avec insouciance.

**reckon** ['rɛkən] *vt* (count) calculer, compter ; (consider) considérer, estimer ; (think): **I ~ that ...** je pense que ... ; **to ~ on** *vt fus* compter sur, s'attendre à ; **~ing** *n* compte *m*, calcul *m* ; estimation *f* ; **the day of ~ing** le jour du Jugement.

**reclaim** [rɪ'kleɪm] *vt* (land) amender ; (: from sea) assécher ; (: from forest) défricher ; (demand back) réclamer (le remboursement *or* la restitution de) ; **reclamation** [rɛklə'meɪʃən] *n* amendement *m* ; assèchement *m* ; défrichement *m*.

**recline** [rɪ'klaɪn] *vi* être allongé(e) *or* étendu(e) ; **reclining** *a* (seat) à dossier réglable.

**recluse** [rɪ'klu:s] *n* reclus/e, ermite *m*.

**recognition** [rɛkəg'nɪʃən] *n* reconnaissance *f* ; **to gain ~** être reconnu(e) ; **transformed beyond ~** méconnaissable.

**recognizable** ['rɛkəgnaɪzəbl] *a*: **~ (by)** reconnaissable (à).

**recognize** ['rɛkəgnaɪz] *vt*: **to ~ (by/as)** reconnaître (à/comme étant).

**recoil** [rɪ'kɔɪl] *vi* (gun) reculer ; (spring) se détendre ; (person): **to ~ (from)** reculer (devant) // *n* recul *m* ; détente *f*.

**recollect** [rɛkə'lɛkt] *vt* se rappeler, se souvenir de ; **~ion** [-'lɛkʃən] *n* souvenir *m*.

**recommend** [rɛkə'mɛnd] *vt* recommander ; **~ation** [-'deɪʃən] *n* recommandation *f*.

**recompense** ['rɛkəmpɛns] *vt* récompenser ; (compensate) dédommager.

**reconcilable** ['rɛkənsaɪləbl] *a* (ideas) conciliable.

**reconcile** ['rɛkənsaɪl] *vt* (two people) réconcilier ; (two facts) concilier, accorder ; **to ~ o.s. to** se résigner à ; **reconciliation** [-sɪlɪ'eɪʃən] *n* réconciliation *f* ; conciliation *f*.

**recondition** [ri:kən'dɪʃən] *vt* remettre à neuf ; réviser entièrement.

**reconnaissance** [rɪ'kɔnɪsns] *n* (MIL) reconnaissance *f*.

**reconnoitre, reconnoiter** (US) [rɛkə'nɔɪtə*] (MIL) *vt* reconnaître // *vi* faire une reconnaissance.

**reconsider** [ri:kən'sɪdə*] *vt* reconsidérer.

**reconstitute** [ri:'kɔnstɪtju:t] *vt* reconstituer.

**reconstruct** [ri:kən'strʌkt] *vt* (building) reconstruire ; (crime) reconstituer ; **~ion** [-kʃən] *n* reconstruction *f* ; reconstitution *f*.

**record** *n* ['rɛkɔ:d] rapport *m*, récit *m* ; (of meeting etc) procès-verbal *m* ; (register) registre *m* ; (file) dossier *m* ; (also: **police ~**) casier *m* judiciaire ; (MUS: disc) disque *m* ; (SPORT) record *m* // *vt* [rɪ'kɔ:d] (set down) noter ; (relate) rapporter ; (MUS: song etc) enregistrer ; **in ~ time** dans un temps record *inv* ; **to keep a ~ of** noter ; **off the ~** *a* officieux(euse) ; **to keep the ~ straight** (fig) mettre les choses au point ; **~ card** *n* (in file) fiche *f* ; **~er** *n* (LAW) avocat nommé à la fonction de juge ; (MUS) flûte *f* à bec ; **~ holder** *n* (SPORT) détenteur/trice du record ; **~ing** *n* (MUS) enregistrement *m* ; **~ library** *n* discothèque *f* ; **~ player** *n* électrophone *m*.

**recount** [rɪ'kaunt] *vt* raconter.

**re-count** *n* ['ri:kaunt] (POL: of votes) pointage *m* // *vt* [ri:'kaunt] recompter.

**recoup** [rɪ'ku:p] *vt*: **to ~ one's losses** récupérer ce qu'on a perdu, se refaire.

**recourse** [rɪ'kɔ:s] *n* recours *m* ; expédient *m* ; **to have ~ to** recourir à, avoir recours à.

**recover** [rɪ'kʌvə*] *vt* récupérer // *vi* (from illness) se rétablir ; (from shock) se remettre ; (country) se redresser.

**re-cover** [ri:'kʌvə*] *vt* (chair etc) recouvrir.

**recovery** [rɪ'kʌvərɪ] *n* récupération *f* ; rétablissement *m* ; redressement *m*.

**recreate** [ri:krɪ'eɪt] *vt* recréer.

**recreation** [rɛkrɪ'eɪʃən] *n* récréation *f* ; détente *f* ; **~al** *a* pour la détente, récréatif(ive).

**recrimination** [rɪkrɪmɪ'neɪʃən] *n* récrimination *f*.

**recruit** [rɪ'kru:t] *n* recrue *f* // *vt* recruter ; **~ing office** *n* bureau *m* de recrutement ; **~ment** *n* recrutement *m*.

**rectangle** ['rɛktæŋgl] *n* rectangle *m* ; **rectangular** [-'tæŋgjulə*] *a* rectangulaire.

**rectify** ['rɛktɪfaɪ] *vt* (error) rectifier, corriger ; (omission) réparer.

**rector** ['rɛktə*] *n* (REL) pasteur *m* ; **rectory** *n* presbytère *m*.

**recuperate** [rɪ'kju:pəreɪt] vi récupérer ; (from illness) se rétablir.

**recur** [rɪ'kə:*] vi se reproduire ; (idea, opportunity) se retrouver ; (symptoms) réapparaître ; ~**rence** n répétition f ; réapparition f ; ~**rent** a périodique, fréquent(e) ; ~**ring** a (MATH) périodique.

**red** [rɛd] n rouge m ; (POL: pej) rouge m/f // a rouge ; **in the** ~ (account) à découvert ; (business) en déficit ; ~ **carpet treatment** n réception f en grande pompe ; **R~ Cross** n Croix-Rouge f ; ~ **currant** n groseille f (rouge) ; ~**den** vt,vi rougir ; ~**dish** a rougeâtre ; (hair) plutôt roux(rousse).

**redecorate** [ri:'dɛkəreɪt] vt refaire à neuf, repeindre et retapisser ; **redecoration** [-'reɪʃən] n remise f à neuf.

**redeem** [rɪ'di:m] vt (debt) rembourser ; (sth in pawn) dégager ; (fig, also REL) racheter ; ~**ing** a (feature) qui sauve, qui rachète (le reste).

**redeploy** [ri:dɪ'plɔɪ] vt (resources) réorganiser.

**red-haired** [rɛd'hɛəd] a roux(rousse).

**red-handed** [rɛd'hændɪd] a: **to be caught** ~ être pris(e) en flagrant délit or la main dans le sac.

**redhead** ['rɛdhɛd] n roux/rousse.

**red herring** ['rɛd'hɛrɪŋ] n (fig) diversion f, fausse piste.

**red-hot** [rɛd'hɔt] a chauffé(e) au rouge, brûlant(e).

**redirect** [ri:daɪ'rɛkt] vt (mail) faire suivre.

**redistribute** [ri:dɪ'strɪbju:t] vt redistribuer.

**red-letter day** ['rɛdlɛtə'deɪ] n grand jour, jour mémorable.

**red light** ['rɛd'laɪt] n: **to go through a** ~ (AUT) brûler un feu rouge ; **red-light district** n quartier réservé.

**redness** ['rɛdnɪs] n rougeur f ; (of hair) rousseur f.

**redo** [ri:'du:] vt irg refaire.

**redolent** ['rɛdəulnt] a: ~ **of** qui sent ; (fig) qui évoque.

**redouble** [ri:'dʌbl] vt: **to** ~ **one's efforts** redoubler d'efforts.

**redress** [rɪ'drɛs] n réparation f.

**red tape** ['rɛd'teɪp] n (fig) paperasserie f (administrative).

**reduce** [rɪ'dju:s] vt réduire ; (lower) abaisser ; '~ **speed now'** (AUT) 'ralentir' ; **at a** ~**d price** (of goods) au rabais, en solde ; (of ticket etc) à prix réduit ; **reduction** [rɪ'dʌkʃən] n réduction f ; (of price) baisse f ; (discount) rabais m ; réduction.

**redundancy** [rɪ'dʌndənsɪ] n licenciement m, mise f au chômage.

**redundant** [rɪ'dʌndnt] a (worker) mis(e) au chômage, licencié(e) ; (detail, object) superflu(e) ; **to make** ~ licencier, mettre au chômage.

**reed** [ri:d] n (BOT) roseau m ; (MUS: of clarinet etc) anche f.

**reef** [ri:f] n (at sea) récif m, écueil m.

**reek** [ri:k] vi: **to** ~ **(of)** puer, empester.

**reel** [ri:l] n bobine f ; (TECH) dévidoir m ; (FISHING) moulinet m ; (CINEMA) bande f // vt (TECH) bobiner ; (also: ~ **up**) enrouler // vi (sway) chanceler.

**re-election** [ri:ɪ'lɛkʃən] n réélection f.

**re-engage** [ri:ɪn'geɪdʒ] vt (worker) réembaucher.

**re-enter** [ri:'ɛntə*] vt rentrer dans ; **re-entry** n rentrée f.

**ref** [rɛf] n (col: abbr of referee) arbitre m.

**refectory** [rɪ'fɛktərɪ] n réfectoire m.

**refer** [rɪ'fə:*] vt: **to** ~ **sb** (or **sth**) **to** (dispute, decision) soumettre qch à ; (inquirer: for information) adresser or envoyer qn à ; (reader: to text) renvoyer qn à ; **to** ~ **to** vt fus (allude to) parler de, faire allusion à ; (apply to) s'appliquer à ; (consult) se reporter à ; ~**ring to your letter** (COMM) en réponse à votre lettre.

**referee** [rɛfə'ri:] n arbitre m ; (for job application) répondant/e // vt arbitrer.

**reference** ['rɛfrəns] n référence f, renvoi m ; (mention) allusion f, mention f ; (for job application: letter) références ; lettre f de recommandation ; (: person) répondant/e ; **with** ~ **to** en ce qui concerne ; (COMM: in letter) me référant à ; '**please quote this** ~' (COMM) 'prière de rappeler cette référence' ; ~ **book** n ouvrage m de référence.

**referendum, pl referenda** [rɛfə'rɛndəm, -də] n référendum m.

**refill** vt [ri:'fɪl] remplir à nouveau ; (pen, lighter etc) recharger // n ['ri:fɪl] (for pen etc) recharge f.

**refine** [rɪ'faɪn] vt (sugar, oil) raffiner ; (taste) affiner ; ~**d** a (person, taste) raffiné(e) ; ~**ment** n (of person) raffinement m ; ~**ry** n raffinerie f.

**reflect** [rɪ'flɛkt] vt (light, image) réfléchir, refléter ; (fig) refléter // vi (think) réfléchir, méditer ; **to** ~ **on** vt fus (discredit) porter atteinte à, faire tort à ; ~**ion** [-'flɛkʃən] n réflexion f ; (image) reflet m ; (criticism): ~**ion on** critique f de ; atteinte f à ; **on** ~**ion** réflexion faite ; ~**or** n (also AUT) réflecteur m.

**reflex** ['ri:flɛks] a, n réflexe (m) ; ~**ive** [rɪ'flɛksɪv] a (LING) réfléchi(e).

**reform** [rɪ'fɔ:m] n réforme f // vt réformer ; **the R~ation** [rɛfə'meɪʃən] n la Réforme ; ~**ed** a amendé(e), assagi(e) ; ~**er** n réformateur/trice.

**refrain** [rɪ'freɪn] vi: **to** ~ **from doing** s'abstenir de faire // n refrain m.

**refresh** [rɪ'frɛʃ] vt rafraîchir ; (subj: food) redonner des forces à ; (: sleep) reposer ; ~**er course** n cours m de recyclage ; ~**ment room** n buffet m ; ~**ments** npl rafraîchissements mpl.

**refrigeration** [rɪfrɪdʒə'reɪʃən] n réfrigération f.

**refrigerator** [rɪ'frɪdʒəreɪtə*] n réfrigérateur m, frigidaire m.

**refuel** [ri:'fjuəl] vt ravitailler en carburant // vi se ravitailler en carburant.

**refuge** ['rɛfju:dʒ] n refuge m ; **to take** ~ **in** se réfugier dans.

**refugee** [rɛfju'dʒi:] n réfugié/e.

**refund** n ['ri:fʌnd] remboursement m // vt [rɪ'fʌnd] rembourser.

**refurbish** [ri:'fə:bɪʃ] vt remettre à neuf.

**refurnish** [ri:'fə:nɪʃ] vt remeubler.

**refusal** [rɪ'fju:zəl] n refus m.

**refuse** n ['rɛfjuːs] ordures fpl, détritus mpl // vt, vi [rɪ'fjuːz] refuser ; ~ **collection** n ramassage m d'ordures ; ~ **collector** n éboueur m.

**refute** [rɪ'fjuːt] vt réfuter.

**regain** [rɪ'geɪn] vt regagner ; retrouver.

**regal** ['riːgl] a royal(e) ; ~**ia** [rɪ'geɪlɪə] n insignes mpl de la royauté.

**regard** [rɪ'gɑːd] n respect m, estime f, considération f // vt considérer ; **to give one's** ~**s to** faire ses amitiés à ; '**with kindest** ~**s**' 'bien amicalement' ; ~**ing, as** ~**s, with** ~ **to** en ce qui concerne ; ~**less** ad quand même ; ~**less of** sans se soucier de.

**regatta** [rɪ'gætə] n régate f.

**regency** ['riːdʒənsɪ] n régence f.

**regent** ['riːdʒənt] n régent/e.

**régime** [reɪ'ʒiːm] n régime m.

**regiment** ['rɛdʒɪmənt] n régiment m ; ~**al** [-'mɛntl] a d'un or du régiment ; ~**ation** [-'teɪʃən] n réglementation excessive.

**region** ['riːdʒən] n région f ; **in the** ~ **of** (fig) aux alentours de ; ~**al** a régional(e) ; ~**al development** n aménagement m du territoire.

**register** ['rɛdʒɪstə*] n registre m ; (also: **electoral** ~) liste électorale // vt enregistrer, inscrire ; (birth) déclarer ; (vehicle) immatriculer ; (luggage) enregistrer ; (letter) envoyer en recommandé ; (subj: instrument) marquer // vi se faire inscrire ; (at hotel) signer le registre ; (make impression) être (bien) compris(e) ; ~**ed** a (design) déposé(e) ; (letter) recommandé(e).

**registrar** ['rɛdʒɪstrɑː*] n officier m de l'état civil ; secrétaire (général).

**registration** [rɛdʒɪs'treɪʃən] n (act) enregistrement m ; inscription f ; (AUT: also: ~ **number**) numéro m d'immatriculation.

**registry** ['rɛdʒɪstrɪ] n bureau m de l'enregistrement ; ~ **office** n bureau m de l'état civil ; **to get married in a** ~ **office** ≈ se marier à la mairie.

**regret** [rɪ'grɛt] n regret m // vt regretter ; **to** ~ **that** regretter que + sub ; ~**fully** ad à or avec regret ; ~**table** a regrettable.

**regroup** [riː'gruːp] vt regrouper // vi se regrouper.

**regular** ['rɛgjulə*] a régulier(ère) ; (usual) habituel(le), normal(e) ; (soldier) de métier ; (COMM: size) ordinaire // n (client etc) habitué/e ; ~**ity** [-'lærɪtɪ] n régularité f ; ~**ly** ad régulièrement.

**regulate** ['rɛgjuleɪt] vt régler ; **regulation** [-'leɪʃən] n (rule) règlement m ; (adjustment) réglage m // cpd réglementaire.

**rehabilitation** ['riːhəbɪlɪ'teɪʃən] n (of offender) réhabilitation f ; (of disabled) rééducation f, réadaptation f.

**rehash** [riː'hæʃ] vt (col) remanier.

**rehearsal** [rɪ'həːsəl] n répétition f.

**rehearse** [rɪ'həːs] vt répéter.

**reign** [reɪn] n règne m // vi régner ; ~**ing** a (monarch) régnant(e) ; (champion) actuel(le).

**reimburse** [riːɪm'bəːs] vt rembourser.

**rein** [reɪn] n (for horse) rêne f.

**reincarnation** [riːɪnkɑː'neɪʃən] n réincarnation f.

**reindeer** ['reɪndɪə*] n (pl inv) renne m.

**reinforce** [riːɪn'fɔːs] vt renforcer ; ~**d concrete** n béton armé ; ~**ment** n (action) renforcement m ; ~**ments** npl (MIL) renfort(s) m(pl).

**reinstate** [riːɪn'steɪt] vt rétablir, réintégrer.

**reissue** [riː'ɪʃjuː] vt (book) rééditer ; (film) ressortir.

**reiterate** [riː'ɪtəreɪt] vt réitérer, répéter.

**reject** n ['riːdʒɛkt] (COMM) article m de rebut // vt [rɪ'dʒɛkt] refuser ; (COMM: goods) mettre au rebut ; (idea) rejeter ; ~**ion** [rɪ'dʒɛkʃən] n rejet m, refus m.

**rejoice** [rɪ'dʒɔɪs] vi: **to** ~ (**at** or **over**) se réjouir (de).

**rejuvenate** [rɪ'dʒuːvəneɪt] vt rajeunir.

**rekindle** [riː'kɪndl] vt rallumer ; (fig) raviver.

**relapse** [rɪ'læps] n (MED) rechute f.

**relate** [rɪ'leɪt] vt (tell) raconter ; (connect) établir un rapport entre ; ~**d** a apparenté(e) ; ~**d to** apparenté à ; **relating: relating to** prep concernant.

**relation** [rɪ'leɪʃən] n (person) parent/e ; (link) rapport m, lien m ; ~**ship** n rapport m, lien m ; (personal ties) relations fpl, rapports ; (also: **family** ~**ship**) lien m de parenté ; (affair) liaison f.

**relative** ['rɛlətɪv] n parent/e // a relatif(ive) ; (respective) respectif(ive) ; **all her** ~**s** toute sa famille ; ~**ly** ad relativement.

**relax** [rɪ'læks] vi se relâcher ; (person: unwind) se détendre // vt relâcher ; (mind, person) détendre ; ~**ation** [riːlæk'seɪʃən] n relâchement m ; détente f ; (entertainment) distraction f ; ~**ed** a relâché(e) ; détendu(e) ; ~**ing** a délassant(e).

**relay** ['riːleɪ] n (SPORT) course f de relais // vt (message) retransmettre, relayer.

**release** [rɪ'liːs] n (from prison, obligation) libération f ; (of gas etc) émission f ; (of film etc) sortie f ; (record) disque m ; (device) déclencheur m // vt (prisoner) libérer ; (book, film) sortir ; (report, news) rendre public, publier ; (gas etc) émettre, dégager ; (free: from wreckage etc) dégager ; (TECH: catch, spring etc) déclencher ; (let go) relâcher ; lâcher ; desserrer ; **to** ~ **one's grip** or **hold** lâcher prise ; **to** ~ **the clutch** (AUT) débrayer.

**relegate** ['rɛləgeɪt] vt reléguer.

**relent** [rɪ'lɛnt] vi se laisser fléchir ; ~**less** a implacable.

**relevance** ['rɛləvəns] n pertinence f ; ~ **of sth to sth** rapport m entre qch et qch.

**relevant** ['rɛləvənt] a approprié(e) ; (fact) significatif(ive) ; (information) utile, pertinent(e) ; ~ **to** ayant rapport à, approprié à.

**reliability** [rɪlaɪə'bɪlɪtɪ] n sérieux m ; solidité f.

**reliable** [rɪ'laɪəbl] a (person, firm) sérieux(euse) ; (method) sûr(e) ; (machine) solide ; **reliably** ad: **to be reliably informed** savoir de source sûre.

**reliance** [rɪ'laɪəns] n: ~ (**on**) confiance f (en) ; besoin m de, dépendance f (de).

**relic** ['rɛlɪk] n (REL) relique f ; (of the past) vestige m.

**relief** [rɪ'liːf] n (from pain, anxiety) soulagement m ; (help, supplies) secours m(pl) ; (of *guard*) relève *f* ; (*ART, GEO*) relief *m* ; ~ **road** *n* route *f* de délestage ; ~ **valve** *n* soupape *f* de sûreté.

**relieve** [rɪ'li:v] *vt* (*pain, patient*) soulager ; (*bring help*) secourir ; (*take over from: gen*) relayer ; (*: guard*) relever ; **to ~ sb of sth** débarrasser qn de qch.

**religion** [rɪ'lɪdʒən] *n* religion *f* ; **religious** *a* religieux(euse) ; (*book*) de piété.

**reline** [ri:'laɪn] *vt* (*brakes*) refaire la garniture de.

**relinquish** [rɪ'lɪŋkwɪʃ] *vt* abandonner ; (*plan, habit*) renoncer à.

**relish** ['rɛlɪʃ] *n* (*CULIN*) condiment *m* ; (*enjoyment*) délectation *f* // *vt* (*food etc*) savourer ; **to ~ doing** se délecter à faire.

**relive** [ri:'lɪv] *vt* revivre.

**reload** [ri:'ləud] *vt* recharger.

**reluctance** [rɪ'lʌktəns] *n* répugnance *f*.

**reluctant** [rɪ'lʌktənt] *a* peu disposé(e), qui hésite ; ~**ly** *ad* à contrecœur, sans enthousiasme.

**rely** [rɪ'laɪ] : **to ~ on** *vt fus* compter sur ; (*be dependent*) dépendre de.

**remain** [rɪ'meɪn] *vi* rester ; ~**der** *n* reste *m* ; (*COMM*) fin *f* de série ; ~**ing** *a* qui reste ; ~**s** *npl* restes *mpl*.

**remand** [rɪ'mɑ:nd] *n*: **on ~** en détention préventive // *vt*: **to ~ in custody** écrouer ; renvoyer en détention provisoire ; ~ **home** *n* maison *f* d'arrêt.

**remark** [rɪ'mɑ:k] *n* remarque *f*, observation *f* // *vt* (faire) remarquer, dire ; (*notice*) remarquer ; ~**able** *a* remarquable.

**remarry** [ri:'mærɪ] *vi* se remarier.

**remedial** [rɪ'mi:dɪəl] *a* (*tuition, classes*) de rattrapage.

**remedy** ['rɛmədɪ] *n*: ~ **(for)** remède *m* (contre *or* à) // *vt* remédier à.

**remember** [rɪ'mɛmbə*] *vt* se rappeler, se souvenir de ; ~ **me to** (*in letter*) rappelezmoi au bon souvenir de ; **remembrance** *n* souvenir *m* ; mémoire *f*.

**remind** [rɪ'maɪnd] *vt*: **to ~ sb of sth** rappeler qch à qn ; **to ~ sb to do** faire penser à qn à faire, rappeler à qn qu'il doit faire ; ~**er** *n* rappel *m* ; (*note etc*) pense-bête *m*.

**reminisce** [rɛmɪ'nɪs] *vi*: **to ~ (about)** évoquer ses souvenirs (de).

**reminiscences** [rɛmɪ'nɪsnsɪz] *npl* réminiscences *fpl*, souvenirs *mpl*.

**reminiscent** [rɛmɪ'nɪsnt] *a*: ~ **of** qui rappelle, qui fait penser à.

**remission** [rɪ'mɪʃən] *n* rémission *f* ; (*of debt, sentence*) remise *f* ; (*of fee*) exemption *f*.

**remit** [rɪ'mɪt] *vt* (*send: money*) envoyer ; ~**tance** *n* envoi *m*, paiement *m*.

**remnant** ['rɛmnənt] *n* reste *m*, restant *m* ; ~**s** *npl* (*COMM*) coupons *mpl* ; fins *fpl* de série.

**remorse** [rɪ'mɔ:s] *n* remords *m* ; ~**ful** *a* plein(e) de remords ; ~**less** *a* (*fig*) impitoyable.

**remote** [rɪ'məut] *a* éloigné(e), lointain(e) ; (*person*) distant(e) ; ~ **control** *n* télécommande *f* ; ~**ly** *ad* au loin ; (*slightly*) très vaguement ; ~**ness** *n* éloignement *m*.

**remould** ['ri:məuld] *n* (*tyre*) pneu rechapé.

**removable** [rɪ'mu:vəbl] *a* (*detachable*) amovible.

**removal** [rɪ'mu:vəl] *n* (*taking away*) enlèvement *m* ; suppression *f* ; (*from house*) déménagement *m* ; (*from office: sacking*) renvoi *m* ; (*MED*) ablation *f* ; ~ **man** *n* déménageur *m* ; ~ **van** *n* camion *m* de déménagement.

**remove** [rɪ'mu:v] *vt* enlever, retirer ; (*employee*) renvoyer ; (*stain*) faire partir ; (*doubt, abuse*) supprimer ; ~**r** (*for paint*) décapant *m* ; (*for varnish*) dissolvant *m* ; ~**rs** *npl* (*company*) entreprise *f* de déménagement.

**remuneration** [rɪmju:nə'reɪʃən] *n* rémunération *f*.

**rename** [ri:'neɪm] *vt* rebaptiser.

**rend, ***pt, pp* **rent** [rɛnd, rɛnt] *vt* déchirer.

**render** ['rɛndə*] *vt* rendre ; (*CULIN: fat*) clarifier ; ~**ing** *n* (*MUS etc*) interprétation *f*.

**rendez-vous** ['rɔndɪvu:] *n* rendez-vous *m* *inv* // *vi* opérer une jonction, se rejoindre.

**renegade** ['rɛnɪgeɪd] *n* rénégat/e.

**renew** [rɪ'nju:] *vt* renouveler ; (*negotiations*) reprendre ; (*acquaintance*) renouer ; ~**al** *n* renouvellement *m* ; reprise *f*.

**renounce** [rɪ'nauns] *vt* renoncer à ; (*disown*) renier.

**renovate** ['rɛnəveɪt] *vt* rénover ; (*art work*) restaurer ; **renovation** [-'veɪʃən] *n* rénovation *f* ; restauration *f*.

**renown** [rɪ'naun] *n* renommée *f* ; ~**ed** *a* renommé(e).

**rent** [rɛnt] *pt, pp of* **rend** // *n* loyer *m* // *vt* louer ; ~**al** *n* (*for television, car*) (prix *m* de) location *f*.

**renunciation** [rɪnʌnsɪ'eɪʃən] *n* renonciation *f* ; (*self-denial*) renoncement *m*.

**reopen** [ri:'əupən] *vt* rouvrir ; ~**ing** *n* réouverture *f*.

**reorder** [ri:'ɔ:də*] *vt* commander de nouveau ; (*rearrange*) réorganiser.

**reorganize** [ri:'ɔ:gənaɪz] *vt* réorganiser.

**rep** [rɛp] *n* (*COMM: abbr of* **representative**) représentant *m* (de commerce) ; (*THEATRE: abbr of* **repertory**) théâtre *m* de répertoire.

**repair** [rɪ'pɛə*] *n* réparation *f* // *vt* réparer ; **in good/bad** ~ en bon/mauvais état ; ~ **kit** *n* trousse *f* de réparations ; ~ **man** *n* réparateur *m* ; ~ **shop** *n* (*AUT etc*) atelier *m* de réparations.

**repartee** [rɛpɑ:'ti:] *n* repartie *f*.

**repay** [ri:'peɪ] *vt irg* (*money, creditor*) rembourser ; (*sb's efforts*) récompenser ; ~**ment** *n* remboursement *m* ; récompense *f*.

**repeal** [rɪ'pi:l] *n* (*of law*) abrogation *f* ; (*of sentence*) annulation *f* // *vt* abroger ; annuler.

**repeat** [rɪ'pi:t] *n* (*RADIO, TV*) reprise *f* // *vt* répéter ; (*pattern*) reproduire ; (*promise, attack, also COMM: order*) renouveler ; (*SCOL: a class*) redoubler ; ~**edly** *ad* souvent, à plusieurs reprises.

**repel** [rɪ'pɛl] *vt* (*lit, fig*) repousser ; ~**lent** *a* repoussant(e) // *n*: **insect** ~**lent** insectifuge *m* ; **moth** ~**lent** produit *m* antimite(s).

**repent** [rɪ'pɛnt] *vi*: **to ~ (of)** se repentir (de) ; ~**ance** *n* repentir *m*.

**repercussion** [ri:pə'kʌʃən] *n* (*consequence*) répercussion *f*.

**repertoire** ['rɛpətwɑ:*] n répertoire m.
**repertory** ['rɛpətərɪ] n (also: ~ **theatre**) théâtre m de répertoire.
**repetition** [rɛpɪ'tɪʃən] n répétition f; (of promise, COMM: order etc) renouvellement m.
**repetitive** [rɪ'pɛtɪtɪv] a (movement, work) répétitif(ive); (speech) plein(e) de redites.
**replace** [rɪ'pleɪs] vt (put back) remettre, replacer; (take the place of) remplacer; (TEL): '~ **the receiver**' 'raccrochez'; ~**ment** n replacement m; (person) remplaçant/e; ~**ment part** n pièce f de rechange.
**replenish** [rɪ'plɛnɪʃ] vt (glass) remplir (de nouveau); (stock etc) réapprovisionner.
**replete** [rɪ'pli:t] a rempli(e); (well-fed) rassasié(e).
**replica** ['rɛplɪkə] n réplique f, copie exacte.
**reply** [rɪ'plaɪ] n réponse f // vi répondre.
**report** [rɪ'pɔ:t] n rapport m; (PRESS etc) reportage m; (also: **school** ~) bulletin m (scolaire); (of gun) détonation f // vt rapporter, faire un compte rendu de; (PRESS etc) faire un reportage sur; (bring to notice: occurrence) signaler; (: person) dénoncer // vi (make a report) faire un rapport (or un reportage); (present o.s.): **to** ~ (**to sb**) se présenter (chez qn); **it is** ~**ed that** on dit or annonce que; ~**ed speech** n (LING) discours indirect; ~**er** n reporter m.
**reprehensible** [rɛprɪ'hɛnsɪbl] a répréhensible.
**represent** [rɛprɪ'zɛnt] vt représenter; (explain): **to** ~ **to sb that** expliquer à qn que; ~**ation** [-'teɪʃən] n représentation f; ~**ations** npl (protest) démarche f; ~**ative** n représentant/e; (US: POL) député m // a représentatif(ive), caractéristique.
**repress** [rɪ'prɛs] vt réprimer; ~**ion** [-'prɛʃən] n répression f; ~**ive** a répressif(ive).
**reprieve** [rɪ'pri:v] n (LAW) grâce f; (fig) sursis m, délai m // vt gracier; accorder un sursis or un délai à.
**reprimand** ['rɛprɪmɑ:nd] n réprimande f // vt réprimander.
**reprint** n ['ri:prɪnt] réimpression f // vt [ri:'prɪnt] réimprimer.
**reprisal** [rɪ'praɪzl] n représailles fpl.
**reproach** [rɪ'prəutʃ] n reproche m // vt: **to** ~ **sb with sth** reprocher qch à qn; **beyond** ~ irréprochable; ~**ful** a de reproche.
**reproduce** [ri:prə'dju:s] vt reproduire // vi se reproduire; **reproduction** [-'dʌkʃən] n reproduction f; **reproductive** [-'dʌktɪv] a reproducteur(trice).
**reprove** [rɪ'pru:v] vt (action) réprouver; (person): **to** ~ (**for**) blâmer (de); **reproving** a réprobateur(trice).
**reptile** ['rɛptaɪl] n reptile m.
**republic** [rɪ'pʌblɪk] n république f; ~**an** a,n républicain(e).
**repudiate** [rɪ'pju:dɪeɪt] vt (wife, accusation) répudier; (friend) renier.
**repugnant** [rɪ'pʌgnənt] a répugnant(e).
**repulse** [rɪ'pʌls] vt repousser.
**repulsion** [rɪ'pʌlʃən] n répulsion f.
**repulsive** [rɪ'pʌlsɪv] a repoussant(e), répulsif(ive).

**reputable** ['rɛpjutəbl] a de bonne réputation; (occupation) honorable.
**reputation** [rɛpju'teɪʃən] n réputation f; **to have a** ~ **for** être réputé(e) pour.
**repute** [rɪ'pju:t] n (bonne) réputation; ~**d** a réputé(e); ~**dly** ad d'après ce qu'on dit.
**request** [rɪ'kwɛst] n demande f; (formal) requête f // vt: **to** ~ (**of** or **from sb**) demander (à qn); ~ **stop** n (for bus) arrêt facultatif.
**requiem** ['rɛkwɪəm] n requiem m.
**require** [rɪ'kwaɪə*] vt (need: subj: person) avoir besoin de; (: thing, situation) demander; (want) vouloir; exiger; (order) obliger; ~**d** a requis(e), voulu(e); **if** ~**d** s'il le faut; ~**ment** n exigence f; besoin m; condition requise.
**requisite** ['rɛkwɪzɪt] n chose nécessaire // a requis(e), nécessaire; **toilet** ~**s** accessoires mpl de toilette.
**requisition** [rɛkwɪ'zɪʃən] n: ~ (**for**) demande f (de) // vt (MIL) réquisitionner.
**reroute** [ri:'ru:t] vt (train etc) dérouter.
**resale** ['ri:'seɪl] n revente f.
**rescind** [rɪ'sɪnd] vt annuler; (law) abroger; (judgment) rescinder.
**rescue** ['rɛskju:] n sauvetage m; (help) secours mpl // vt sauver; ~ **party** n équipe f de sauvetage; ~**r** n sauveteur m.
**research** [rɪ'sə:tʃ] n recherche(s) f(pl) // vt faire des recherches sur; ~**er** n chercheur/euse; ~ **work** n recherches fpl; ~ **worker** n chercheur/euse.
**resell** [ri:'sɛl] vt irg revendre.
**resemblance** [rɪ'zɛmbləns] n ressemblance f.
**resemble** [rɪ'zɛmbl] vt ressembler à.
**resent** [rɪ'zɛnt] vt éprouver du ressentiment de, être contrarié(e) par; ~**ful** a irrité(e), plein(e) de ressentiment; ~**ment** n ressentiment m.
**reservation** [rɛzə'veɪʃən] n (booking) réservation f; (doubt) réserve f; (protected area) réserve; (on road: also: **central** ~) bande f médiane; **to make a** ~ (**in an hotel/a restaurant/a plane**) réserver or retenir une chambre/une table/une place.
**reserve** [rɪ'zə:v] n réserve f; (SPORT) remplaçant/e // vt (seats etc) réserver, retenir; ~**s** npl (MIL) réservistes mpl; **in** ~ en réserve; ~**d** a réservé(e); **reservist** n (MIL) réserviste m.
**reservoir** ['rɛzəvwɑ:*] n réservoir m.
**reshape** [ri:'ʃeɪp] vt (policy) réorganiser.
**reshuffle** [ri:'ʃʌfl] n: **Cabinet** ~ (POL) remaniement ministériel.
**reside** [rɪ'zaɪd] vi résider.
**residence** ['rɛzɪdəns] n résidence f; ~ **permit** n permis m de séjour.
**resident** ['rɛzɪdənt] n résident/e // a résidant(e).
**residential** [rɛzɪ'dɛnʃəl] a de résidence; (area) résidentiel(le).
**residue** ['rɛzɪdju:] n reste m; (CHEM, PHYSICS) résidu m.
**resign** [rɪ'zaɪn] vt (one's post) se démettre de // vi démissionner; **to** ~ **o.s. to** (endure) se résigner à; ~**ation** [rɛzɪg'neɪʃən] n démission f; résignation f; ~**ed** a résigné(e).

**resilience** [rɪ'zɪlɪəns] *n* (*of material*) élasticité *f*; (*of person*) ressort *m*.

**resilient** [rɪ'zɪlɪənt] *a* (*person*) qui réagit, qui a du ressort.

**resin** ['rɛzɪn] *n* résine *f*.

**resist** [rɪ'zɪst] *vt* résister à; ~ance *n* résistance *f*.

**resolute** ['rɛzəluːt] *a* résolu(e).

**resolution** [rɛzə'luːʃən] *n* résolution *f*.

**resolve** [rɪ'zɔlv] *n* résolution *f* // *vt* (*decide*): **to ~ to do** résoudre *or* décider de faire; (*problem*) résoudre; ~**d** *a* résolu(e).

**resonant** ['rɛzənənt] *a* résonnant(e).

**resort** [rɪ'zɔːt] *n* (*town*) station *f*; (*recourse*) recours *m* // *vi*: **to ~ to** avoir recours à; **in the last ~** en dernier ressort.

**resound** [rɪ'zaund] *vi*: **to ~ (with)** retentir (de); ~**ing** *a* retentissant(e).

**resource** [rɪ'sɔːs] *n* ressource *f*; ~**s** *npl* ressources; ~**ful** *a* plein(e) de ressource, débrouillard(e); ~**fulness** *n* ressource *f*.

**respect** [rɪs'pɛkt] *n* respect *m* // *vt* respecter; **with ~ to** en ce qui concerne; **in ~ of** sous le rapport de, quant à; **in this ~** sous ce rapport, à cet égard; ~**ability** [-ə'bɪlɪtɪ] *n* respectabilité *f*; ~**able** *a* respectable; ~**ful** *a* respectueux(euse).

**respective** [rɪs'pɛktɪv] *a* respectif(ive); ~**ly** *ad* respectivement.

**respiration** [rɛspɪ'reɪʃən] *n* respiration *f*.

**respirator** ['rɛspɪreɪtə*] *n* respirateur *m*.

**respiratory** [rɛs'pɪrətərɪ] *a* respiratoire.

**respite** ['rɛspaɪt] *n* répit *m*.

**resplendent** [rɪs'plɛndənt] *a* resplendissant(e).

**respond** [rɪs'pɔnd] *vi* répondre; (*to treatment*) réagir.

**response** [rɪs'pɔns] *n* réponse *f*; (*to treatment*) réaction *f*.

**responsibility** [rɪspɔnsɪ'bɪlɪtɪ] *n* responsabilité *f*.

**responsible** [rɪs'pɔnsɪbl] *a* (*liable*): ~ **(for)** responsable (de); (*character*) digne de confiance; (*job*) qui comporte des responsabilités; **responsibly** *ad* avec sérieux.

**responsive** [rɪs'pɔnsɪv] *a* qui n'est pas réservé(e) *or* indifférent(e).

**rest** [rɛst] *n* repos *m*; (*stop*) arrêt *m*, pause *f*; (*MUS*) silence *m*; (*support*) support *m*, appui *m*; (*remainder*) reste *m*, restant *m* // *vi* se reposer; (*be supported*): **to ~ on** appuyer *or* reposer sur; (*remain*) rester // *vt* (*lean*): **to ~ sth on/against** appuyer qch sur/contre; **the ~ of them** les autres; **it ~s with him to** c'est à lui de.

**restart** [riː'stɑːt] *vt* (*engine*) remettre en marche; (*work*) reprendre.

**restaurant** ['rɛstərɔŋ] *n* restaurant *m*; ~ **car** *n* wagon-restaurant *m*.

**rest cure** ['rɛstkjuə*] *n* cure *f* de repos.

**restful** ['rɛstful] *a* reposant(e).

**rest home** ['rɛsthəum] *n* maison *f* de repos.

**restitution** [rɛstɪ'tjuːʃən] *n* (*act*) restitution *f*; (*reparation*) réparation *f*.

**restive** ['rɛstɪv] *a* agité(e), impatient(e); (*horse*) rétif(ive).

**restless** ['rɛstlɪs] *a* agité(e); ~**ly** *ad* avec agitation.

**restock** [riː'stɔk] *vt* réapprovisionner.

**restoration** [rɛstə'reɪʃən] *n* restauration *f*; restitution *f*.

**restore** [rɪ'stɔː*] *vt* (*building*) restaurer; (*sth stolen*) restituer; (*peace, health*) rétablir.

**restrain** [rɪs'treɪn] *vt* (*feeling*) contenir; (*person*): **to ~ (from doing)** retenir (de faire); ~**ed** *a* (*style*) sobre; (*manner*) mesuré(e); ~**t** *n* (*restriction*) contrainte *f*; (*moderation*) retenue *f*; (*of style*) sobriété *f*.

**restrict** [rɪs'trɪkt] *vt* restreindre, limiter; ~**ed area** *n* (*AUT*) zone *f* à vitesse limitée; ~**ion** [-kʃən] *n* restriction *f*, limitation *f*; ~**ive** *a* restrictif(ive).

**rest room** ['rɛstrum] *n* (*US*) toilettes *fpl*.

**result** [rɪ'zʌlt] *n* résultat *m* // *vi*: **to ~ in** aboutir à, se terminer par.

**resume** [rɪ'zjuːm] *vt*, *vi* (*work, journey*) reprendre.

**resumption** [rɪ'zʌmpʃən] *n* reprise *f*.

**resurgence** [rɪ'səːdʒəns] *n* réapparition *f*.

**resurrection** [rɛzə'rɛkʃən] *n* résurrection *f*.

**resuscitate** [rɪ'sʌsɪteɪt] *vt* (*MED*) réanimer; **resuscitation** [-'teɪʃn] *n* réanimation *f*.

**retail** ['riːteɪl] *n* (vente *f* au) détail *m* // *cpd* de *or* au détail // *vt* vendre au détail; ~**er** *n* détaillant/e; ~ **price** *n* prix *m* de détail.

**retain** [rɪ'teɪn] *vt* (*keep*) garder, conserver; (*employ*) engager; ~**er** *n* (*servant*) serviteur *m*; (*fee*) acompte *m*, provision *f*.

**retaliate** [rɪ'tælɪeɪt] *vi*: **to ~ (against)** se venger (de); **to ~ (on sb)** rendre la pareille à qn); **retaliation** [-'eɪʃən] *n* représailles *fpl*, vengeance *f*.

**retarded** [rɪ'tɑːdɪd] *a* retardé(e).

**retch** [rɛtʃ] *vi* avoir des haut-le-coeur.

**retentive** [rɪ'tɛntɪv] *a*: ~ **memory** excellente mémoire.

**rethink** ['riː'θɪŋk] *vt* repenser.

**reticence** ['rɛtɪsns] *n* réticence *f*.

**reticent** ['rɛtɪsnt] *a* réticent(e).

**retina** ['rɛtɪnə] *n* rétine *f*.

**retinue** ['rɛtɪnjuː] *n* suite *f*, cortège *m*.

**retire** [rɪ'taɪə*] *vi* (*give up work*) prendre sa retraite; (*withdraw*) se retirer, partir; (*go to bed*) (aller) se coucher; ~**d** *a* (*person*) retraité(e); ~**ment** *n* retraite *f*; **retiring** *a* (*person*) réservé(e); **retiring age** *n* âge *m* de la retraite.

**retort** [rɪ'tɔːt] *n* (*reply*) riposte *f*; (*container*) cornue *f* // *vi* riposter.

**retrace** [riː'treɪs] *vt* reconstituer; **to ~ one's steps** revenir sur ses pas.

**retract** [rɪ'trækt] *vt* (*statement, claws*) rétracter; (*undercarriage, aerial*) rentrer, escamoter // *vi* se rétracter; rentrer; ~**able** *a* escamotable.

**retrain** [riː'treɪn] *vt* (*worker*) recycler; ~**ing** *n* recyclage *m*.

**retread** [riː'trɛd] *vt* (*AUT: tyre*) rechaper.

**retreat** [rɪ'triːt] *n* retraite *f* // *vi* battre en retraite; (*flood*) reculer.

**retrial** [riː'traɪəl] *n* nouveau procès.

**retribution** [rɛtrɪ'bju:ʃən] *n* châtiment *m*.
**retrieval** [rɪ'tri:vəl] *n* récupération *f*; réparation *f*; recherche *f* et extraction *f*.
**retrieve** [rɪ'tri:v] *vt* (*sth lost*) récupérer; (*situation, honour*) sauver; (*error, loss*) réparer; (*COMPUTERS*) rechercher; ∼**r** *n* chien *m* d'arrêt.
**retrospect** ['rɛtrəspɛkt] *n*: **in** ∼ rétrospectivement, après coup; ∼**ive** [-'spɛktɪv] *a* (*law*) rétroactif(ive).
**return** [rɪ'tə:n] *n* (*going or coming back*) retour *m*; (*of sth stolen etc*) restitution *f*; (*recompense*) récompense *f*; (*FINANCE: from land, shares*) rapport *m*; (*report*) relevé *m*, rapport // *cpd* (*journey*) de retour; (*ticket*) aller et retour; (*match*) retour // *vi* (*person etc: come back*) revenir; (: *go back*) retourner // *vt* rendre; (*bring back*) rapporter; (*send back*) renvoyer; (*put back*) remettre; (*POL: candidate*) élire; ∼**s** *npl* (*COMM*) recettes *fpl*; bénéfices *mpl*; **many happy** ∼**s (of the day)!** bon anniversaire!; ∼**able** *a* (*bottle etc*) consigné(e).
**reunion** [ri:'ju:nɪən] *n* réunion *f*.
**reunite** [ri:ju:'naɪt] *vt* réunir.
**rev** [rɛv] *n* (*abbr of* **revolution**: *AUT*) tour *m* // *vb* (*also*: ∼ **up**) *vt* emballer // *vi* s'emballer.
**revamp** ['ri:væmp] *vt* (*house*) retaper; (*firm*) réorganiser.
**reveal** [rɪ'vi:l] *vt* (*make known*) révéler; (*display*) laisser voir; ∼**ing** *a* révélateur(trice); (*dress*) au décolleté généreux *or* suggestif.
**reveille** [rɪ'vælɪ] *n* (*MIL*) réveil *m*.
**revel** ['rɛvl] *vi*: **to** ∼ **in sth/in doing** délecter de qch/à faire.
**revelation** [rɛvə'leɪʃən] *n* révélation *f*.
**reveller** ['rɛvlə*] *n* fêtard *m*.
**revelry** ['rɛvlrɪ] *n* festivités *fpl*.
**revenge** [rɪ'vɛndʒ] *n* vengeance *f*; (*in game etc*) revanche *f* // *vt* venger; **to take** ∼ se venger; ∼**ful** *a* vengeur(eresse); vindicatif(ive).
**revenue** ['rɛvənju:] *n* revenu *m*.
**reverberate** [rɪ'və:bəreɪt] *vi* (*sound*) retentir, se répercuter; (*light*) se réverbérer; **reverberation** [-'reɪʃən] *n* répercussion *f*; réverbération *f*.
**revere** [rɪ'vɪə*] *vt* vénérer, révérer.
**reverence** ['rɛvərəns] *n* vénération *f*, révérence *f*.
**reverent** ['rɛvərənt] *a* respectueux(euse).
**reverie** ['rɛvərɪ] *n* rêverie *f*.
**reversal** [rɪ'və:sl] *n* (*of opinion*) revirement *m*.
**reverse** [rɪ'və:s] *n* contraire *m*, opposé *m*; (*back*) dos *m*, envers *m*; (*AUT: also*: ∼ **gear**) marche *f* arrière // *a* (*order, direction*) opposé(e), inverse // *vi* (*turn*) renverser, retourner; (*change*) renverser, changer complètement; (*LAW: judgment*) réformer // *vi* (*AUT*) faire marche arrière; ∼**d charge call** *n* (*TEL*) communication *f* en PCV.
**reversion** [rɪ'və:ʃən] *n* retour *m*.
**revert** [rɪ'və:t] *vi*: **to** ∼ **to** revenir à, retourner à.
**review** [rɪ'vju:] *n* revue *f*· (*of book, film*) critique *f* // *vt* passer en revue; faire la critique de; ∼**er** *n* critique *m*.

**revise** [rɪ'vaɪz] *vt* (*manuscript*) revoir, corriger; (*opinion*) réviser, modifier; (*study: subject, notes*) réviser; **revision** [rɪ'vɪʒən] *n* révision *f*.
**revitalize** [ri:'vaɪtəlaɪz] *vt* revitaliser.
**revival** [rɪ'vaɪvəl] *n* reprise *f*; rétablissement *m*; (*of faith*) renouveau *m*.
**revive** [rɪ'vaɪv] *vt* (*person*) ranimer; (*custom*) rétablir; (*hope, courage*) redonner; (*play, fashion*) reprendre // *vi* (*person*) reprendre connaissance; (*hope*) renaître; (*activity*) reprendre.
**revoke** [rɪ'vəuk] *vt* révoquer; (*promise, decision*) revenir sur.
**revolt** [rɪ'vəult] *n* révolte *f* // *vi* se révolter, se rebeller; ∼**ing** *a* dégoûtant(e).
**revolution** [rɛvə'lu:ʃən] *n* révolution *f*; (*of wheel etc*) tour *m*, révolution; ∼**ary** *a, n* révolutionnaire (*m/f*); **rev(olution) counter** *n* compte-tours *m inv*; ∼**ize** *vt* révolutionner.
**revolve** [rɪ'vɔlv] *vi* tourner.
**revolver** [rɪ'vɔlvə*] *n* revolver *m*.
**revolving** [rɪ'vɔlvɪŋ] *a* (*chair*) pivotant(e); (*light*) tournant(e); ∼ **door** *n* (*porte f à*) tambour *m*.
**revue** [rɪ'vju:] *n* (*THEATRE*) revue *f*.
**revulsion** [rɪ'vʌlʃən] *n* dégoût *m*, répugnance *f*.
**reward** [rɪ'wɔ:d] *n* récompense *f* // *vt*: **to** ∼ **(for)** récompenser (de); ∼**ing** *a* (*fig*) qui (en) vaut la peine.
**rewind** [ri:'waɪnd] *vt irg* (*watch*) remonter; (*ribbon etc*) réembobiner.
**rewire** [ri:'waɪə*] *vt* (*house*) refaire l'installation électrique de.
**reword** [ri:'wə:d] *vt* formuler *or* exprimer différemment.
**rewrite** [ri:'raɪt] *vt irg* récrire.
**rhapsody** ['ræpsədɪ] *n* (*MUS*) rhapsodie *f*; (*fig*) éloge délirant.
**rhetoric** ['rɛtərɪk] *n* rhétorique *f*; ∼**al** [rɪ'tɔrɪkl] *a* rhétorique.
**rheumatic** [ru:'mætɪk] *a* rhumatismal(e).
**rheumatism** ['ru:mətɪzəm] *n* rhumatisme *m*.
**Rhine** [raɪn] *n*: **the** ∼ le Rhin.
**rhinoceros** [raɪ'nɔsərəs] *n* rhinocéros *m*.
**Rhodesia** [rəu'di:ʒə] *n* Rhodésie *f*; ∼**n** *a* rhodésien(ne) // *n* Rhodésien/ne.
**rhododendron** [rəudə'dɛndrn] *n* rhododendron *m*.
**Rhone** [rəun] *n*: **the** ∼ le Rhône.
**rhubarb** ['ru:bɑ:b] *n* rhubarbe *f*.
**rhyme** [raɪm] *n* rime *f*; (*verse*) vers *mpl*.
**rhythm** ['rɪðm] *n* rythme *m*; ∼**ic(al)** *a* rythmique; ∼**ically** *ad* avec rythme.
**rib** [rɪb] *n* (*ANAT*) côte *f* // *vt* (*mock*) taquiner.
**ribald** ['rɪbəld] *a* paillard(e).
**ribbed** [rɪbd] *a* (*knitting*) à côtes; (*shell*) strié(e).
**ribbon** ['rɪbən] *n* ruban *m*; **in** ∼**s** (*torn*) en lambeaux.
**rice** [raɪs] *n* riz *m*; ∼**field** *n* rizière *f*; ∼ **pudding** *n* riz *m* au lait.
**rich** [rɪtʃ] *a* riche; (*gift, clothes*) somptueux(euse); **the** ∼ les riches *mpl*; ∼**es** *npl* richesses *fpl*; ∼**ness** *n* richesse *f*.
**rickets** ['rɪkɪts] *n* rachitisme *m*.

**rickety** ['rɪkɪtɪ] *a* branlant(e).

**rickshaw** ['rɪkʃɔ:] *n* pousse(-pousse) *m inv.*

**ricochet** ['rɪkəʃeɪ] *n* ricochet *m* // *vi* ricocher.

**rid**, *pt, pp* **rid** [rɪd] *vt*: **to ~ sb of** débarrasser qn de; **to get ~ of** se débarrasser de; **good riddance!** bon débarras!

**ridden** ['rɪdn] *pp* of **ride**.

**riddle** ['rɪdl] *n* (*puzzle*) énigme *f* // *vt*: **to be ~d with** être criblé(e) de.

**ride** [raɪd] *n* promenade *f*, tour *m*; (*distance covered*) trajet *m* // *vb* (*pt* **rode**, *pp* **ridden** [rəʊd, 'rɪdn]) *vi* (*as sport*) monter (à cheval), faire du cheval; (*go somewhere: on horse, bicycle*) aller (à cheval or bicyclette *etc*); (*journey: on bicycle, motor cycle, bus*) rouler // *vt* (*a certain horse*) monter; (*distance*) parcourir, faire; **we rode all day/all the way** nous sommes restés toute la journée en selle/avons fait tout le chemin en selle or à cheval; **to ~ a horse/bicycle/camel** monter à cheval/à bicyclette/à dos de chameau; **to ~ at anchor** (NAUT) être à l'ancre; **horse/car ~** promenade or tour à cheval/en voiture; **to take sb for a ~** (*fig*) faire marcher qn; rouler qn; **~r** *n* cavalier/ère; (*in race*) jockey *m*; (*on bicycle*) cycliste *m/f*; (*on motorcycle*) motocycliste *m/f*; (*in document*) annexe *f*, clause additionnelle.

**ridge** [rɪdʒ] *n* (*of hill*) faîte *m*; (*of roof, mountain*) arête *f*; (*on object*) strie *f*.

**ridicule** ['rɪdɪkju:l] *n* ridicule *m*; dérision *f* // *vt* ridiculiser, tourner en dérision.

**ridiculous** [rɪ'dɪkjuləs] *a* ridicule.

**riding** ['raɪdɪŋ] *n* équitation *f*; **~ school** *n* manège *m*, école *f* d'équitation.

**rife** [raɪf] *a* répandu(e); **~ with** abondant(e) en.

**riffraff** ['rɪfræf] *n* racaille *f*.

**rifle** ['raɪfl] *n* fusil *m* (à canon rayé) // *vt* vider, dévaliser; **~ range** *n* champ *m* de tir; (*indoor*) stand *m* de tir.

**rift** [rɪft] *n* fente *f*, fissure *f*; (*fig: disagreement*) désaccord *m*.

**rig** [rɪg] *n* (*also: oil ~: on land*) derrick *m*; (: *at sea*) plate-forme pétrolière // *vt* (*election etc*) truquer; **to ~ out** *vt* habiller; (*pej*) fringuer, attifer; **to ~ up** *vt* arranger, faire avec des moyens de fortune; **~ging** *n* (NAUT) gréement *m*.

**right** [raɪt] *a* (*true*) juste, exact(e); (*correctly chosen: answer, road etc*) bon(bonne); (*suitable*) approprié(e), convenable; (*just*) juste, équitable; (*morally good*) bien *inv*; (*not left*) droit(e) // *n* (*title, claim*) droit *m*; (*not left*) droite *f* // *ad* (*answer*) correctement; (*not on the left*) à droite // *vt* redresser // *excl* bon!; **to be ~** (*person*) avoir raison; (*answer*) être juste or correct(e); **~ now** en ce moment même; tout de suite; **~ against the wall** tout contre le mur; **~ ahead** tout droit; droit devant; **~ in the middle** en plein milieu; **~ away** immédiatement; **by ~s** en toute justice; **on the ~** à droite; **~ angle** *n* angle droit; **~eous** ['raɪtʃəs] *a* droit(e), vertueux(euse); (*anger*) justifié(e); **~eousness** ['raɪtʃəsnɪs] *n* droiture *f*, vertu *f*; **~ful** *a* (*heir*) légitime;

**~fully** *ad* à juste titre, légitimement; **~handed** *a* (*person*) droitier(ère); **~-hand man** *n* bras droit (*fig*); **the ~-hand side** le côté droit; **~ly** *ad* bien, correctement; (*with reason*) à juste titre; **~-minded** *a* sensé(e), sain(e) d'esprit; **~ of way** *n* droit *m* de passage; (AUT) priorité *f*; **~ wing** *n* (MIL, SPORT) aile droite; (POL) droite *f*; **~-wing** *a* (POL) de droite.

**rigid** ['rɪdʒɪd] *a* rigide; (*principle*) strict(e); **~ity** [rɪ'dʒɪdɪtɪ] *n* rigidité *f*; **~ly** *ad* rigidement; (*behave*) inflexiblement.

**rigmarole** ['rɪgmərəʊl] *n* galimatias *m*; comédie *f*.

**rigor mortis** ['rɪgə'mɔ:tɪs] *n* rigidité *f* cadavérique.

**rigorous** ['rɪgərəs] *a* rigoureux (euse); **~ly** *ad* rigoureusement.

**rigour, rigor** (US) ['rɪgə*] *n* rigueur *f*.

**rig-out** ['rɪgaʊt] *n* (*col*) tenue *f*.

**rile** [raɪl] *vt* agacer.

**rim** [rɪm] *n* bord *m*; (*of spectacles*) monture *f*; (*of wheel*) jante *f*; **~less** *a* (*spectacles*) à monture invisible; **~med** *a* bordé(e); janté(e).

**rind** [raɪnd] *n* (*of bacon*) couenne *f*; (*of lemon etc*) écorce *f*.

**ring** [rɪŋ] *n* anneau *m*; (*on finger*) bague *f*; (*also:* **wedding ~**) alliance *f*; (*for napkin*) rond *m*; (*of people, objects*) cercle *m*; (*of spies*) réseau *m*; (*of smoke etc*) rond *m*; (*arena*) piste *f*, arène *f*; (*for boxing*) ring *m*; (*sound of bell*) sonnerie *f*; (*telephone call*) coup *m* de téléphone // *vb* (*pt* **rang**, *pp* **rung** [ræŋ, rʌŋ]) *vi* (*person, bell*) sonner; (*also:* **~ out**: *voice, words*) retentir; (TEL) téléphoner // *vt* (TEL: *also:* **~ up**) téléphoner à; **to ~ the bell** sonner; **to ~ back** *vi* (TEL) rappeler; **to ~ off** *vi* (TEL) raccrocher; **~ binder** *n* classeur *m* à anneaux; **~leader** *n* (*of gang*) chef *m*, meneur *m*.

**ringlets** ['rɪŋlɪts] *npl* anglaises *fpl*.

**ring road** ['rɪŋrəʊd] *n* route *f* de ceinture.

**rink** [rɪŋk] *n* (*also:* **ice ~**) patinoire *f*.

**rinse** [rɪns] *n* rinçage *m* // *vt* rincer.

**riot** ['raɪət] *n* émeute *f*, bagarres *fpl* // *vi* faire une émeute, manifester avec violence; **a ~ of colours** une débauche or orgie de couleurs; **to run ~** se déchaîner; **~er** *n* émeutier/ère, manifestant/e; **~ous** *a* tapageur(euse); tordant(e); **~ously funny** tordant(e).

**rip** [rɪp] *n* déchirure *f* // *vt* déchirer // *vi* se déchirer; **~cord** *n* poignée *f* d'ouverture.

**ripe** [raɪp] *a* (*fruit*) mûr(e); (*cheese*) fait(e); **~n** *vt* mûrir // *vi* mûrir; se faire; **~ness** *n* maturité *f*.

**riposte** [rɪ'pɔst] *n* riposte *f*.

**ripple** ['rɪpl] *n* ride *f*, ondulation *f*; égrènement *m*, cascade *f* // *vi* se rider, onduler // *vt* rider, faire onduler.

**rise** [raɪz] *n* (*slope*) côte *f*, pente *f*; (*hill*) élévation *f*; (*increase: in wages*) augmentation *f*; (: *in prices, temperature*) hausse *f*, augmentation *f*; (*fig: to power etc*) essor *m*, ascension *f* // *vi* (*pt* **rose**, *pp* **risen** [rəʊz, 'rɪzn]) s'élever, monter; (*prices*) augmenter, monter; (*waters, river*) monter; (*sun, wind, person: from chair, bed*) se lever; (*also:* **~ up**: *rebel*) se révolter;

se rebeller ; **to give** ~ **to** donner lieu à ; **to** ~ **to the occasion** se montrer à la hauteur.

**risk** [rɪsk] n risque m ; danger m // vt risquer ; **to take** or **run the** ~ **of doing** courir le risque de faire ; **at** ~ en danger ; **at one's own** ~ à ses risques et périls ; ~**y** a risqué(e).

**risqué** ['riːskeɪ] a (joke) risqué(e).

**rissole** ['rɪsəul] n croquette f.

**rite** [raɪt] n rite m.

**ritual** ['rɪtjuəl] a rituel(le) // n rituel m.

**rival** ['raɪvl] n rival/e ; (in business) concurrent/e // a rival(e) ; qui fait concurrence // vt être en concurrence avec ; **to** ~ **sb/sth in** rivaliser avec qn/qch de ; ~**ry** n rivalité f; concurrence f.

**river** ['rɪvə*] n rivière f; (major, also fig) fleuve m ; ~**bank** n rive f, berge f; ~**bed** n lit m (de rivière or de fleuve) ; ~**side** n bord m de la rivière or du fleuve // cpd (port, traffic) fluvial(e).

**rivet** ['rɪvɪt] n rivet m // vt riveter ; (fig) river, fixer.

**Riviera** [rɪvɪ'ɛərə] n: **the (French)** ~ la Côte d'Azur.

**RN** abbr of Royal Navy.

**road** [rəud] n route f; (small) chemin m ; (in town) rue f; (fig) chemin, voie f; '~ **up**' 'attention travaux' ; ~**block** n barrage routier ; ~**hog** n chauffard m ; ~ **map** n carte routière ; ~**side** n bord m de la route, bas-côté m // cpd (situé(e) etc) au bord de la route ; ~**sign** n panneau m de signalisation ; ~ **user** n usager m de la route ; ~**way** n chaussée f; ~**worthy** a en bon état de marche.

**roam** [rəum] vi errer, vagabonder // vt parcourir, errer par.

**roar** [rɔ:*] n rugissement m ; (of crowd) hurlements mpl ; (of vehicle, thunder, storm) grondement m // vi rugir ; hurler ; gronder ; **to** ~ **with laughter** éclater de rire ; **a** ~**ing fire** une belle flambée ; **to do a** ~**ing trade** faire des affaires d'or.

**roast** [rəust] n rôti m // vt (meat) (faire) rôtir.

**rob** [rɔb] vt (person) voler ; (bank) dévaliser ; **to** ~ **sb of sth** voler or dérober qch à qn ; (fig: deprive) priver qn de qch ; ~**ber** n bandit m, voleur m ; ~**bery** n vol m.

**robe** [rəub] n (for ceremony etc) robe f; (also: bath ~) peignoir m // vt revêtir (d'une robe).

**robin** ['rɔbɪn] n rouge-gorge m.

**robot** ['rəubɔt] n robot m.

**robust** [rəu'bʌst] a robuste ; (material, appetite) solide.

**rock** [rɔk] n (substance) roche f, roc m ; (boulder) rocher m ; roche ; (sweet) ≈ sucre m d'orge // vt (swing gently: cradle) balancer ; (: child) bercer ; (shake) ébranler, secouer // vi (se) balancer ; être ébranlé(e) or secoué(e) ; **on the** ~**s** (drink) avec des glaçons ; (ship) sur les écueils ; (marriage etc) en train de craquer ; **to** ~ **the boat** (fig) jouer les trouble-fête ; ~-**bottom** n (fig) niveau le plus bas ; ~**ery** n (jardin m de) rocaille f.

**rocket** ['rɔkɪt] n fusée f; (MIL) fusée, roquette f.

**rock face** ['rɔkfeɪs] n paroi rocheuse.

**rock fall** ['rɔkfɔ:l] n chute f de pierres.

**rocking chair** ['rɔkɪŋtʃɛə*] n fauteuil m à bascule.

**rocking horse** ['rɔkɪŋhɔ:s] n cheval m à bascule.

**rocky** ['rɔkɪ] a (hill) rocheux(euse) ; (path) rocailleux(euse) ; (unsteady: table) branlant(e).

**rod** [rɔd] n (metallic) tringle f; (TECH) tige f; (wooden) baguette f; (also: **fishing** ~) canne f à pêche.

**rode** [rəud] pt of **ride**.

**rodent** ['rəudnt] n rongeur m.

**rodeo** ['rəudɪəu] n rodéo m.

**roe** [rəu] n (species: also: ~ **deer**) chevreuil m ; (of fish) œufs mpl de poisson ; **soft** ~ laitance f; ~ **deer** n chevreuil m ; chevreuil femelle.

**rogue** [rəug] n coquin/e ; **roguish** a coquin(e).

**role** [rəul] n rôle m.

**roll** [rəul] n rouleau m ; (of banknotes) liasse f; (also: **bread** ~) petit pain ; (register) liste f; (sound: of drums etc) roulement m ; (movement: of ship) roulis m // vt rouler ; (also: ~ **up:** string) enrouler ; (also: ~ **out:** pastry) étendre au rouleau // vi rouler ; (wheel) tourner ; (sway: person) se balancer ; **to** ~ **by** vi (time) s'écouler, passer ; **to** ~ **in** vi (mail, cash) affluer ; **to** ~ **over** vi se retourner ; **to** ~ **up** vi (col: arrive) arriver, s'amener // vt (carpet) rouler ; ~ **call** n appel m ; ~**ed gold** a plaqué or inv ; ~**er** n rouleau m ; (wheel) roulette f; ~**er skates** npl patins mpl à roulettes.

**rollicking** ['rɔlɪkɪŋ] a bruyant(e) et joyeux(euse) ; (play) bouffon(ne) ; **to have a** ~ **time** s'amuser follement.

**rolling** ['rəulɪŋ] a (landscape) onduleux(euse) ; ~ **pin** n rouleau m à pâtisserie ; ~ **stock** n (RAIL) matériel roulant.

**roll-on-roll-off** ['rəulɔn'rəulɔf] a (ferry) transroulier(ère).

**roly-poly** ['rəulɪ'pəulɪ] n (CULIN) roulé m à la confiture.

**Roman** ['rəumən] a romain(e) // n Romain/e ; ~ **Catholic** a, n catholique (m/f).

**romance** [rə'mæns] n histoire f (or film m or aventure f) romanesque ; (charm) poésie f; (love affair) idylle f // vi enjoliver (à plaisir), exagérer.

**Romanesque** [rəumə'nɛsk] a roman(e).

**Romania** [rəu'meɪnɪə] n Roumanie f; ~**n** a roumain(e) // n Roumain/e.

**romantic** [rə'mæntɪk] a romantique ; sentimental(e).

**romanticism** [rə'mæntɪsɪzəm] n romantisme m.

**romp** [rɔmp] n jeux bruyants // vi (also: ~ **about**) s'ébattre, jouer bruyamment.

**rompers** ['rɔmpəz] npl barboteuse f.

**rondo** ['rɔndəu] n (MUS) rondeau m.

**roof** [ru:f] n toit m ; (of tunnel, cave) plafond m // vt couvrir (d'un toit) ; **the** ~ **of the mouth** la voûte du palais ; ~ **garden** n toit-terrasse m ; ~**ing** n toiture f; ~ **rack** n (AUT) galerie f.

**rook** [ruk] *n* (*bird*) freux *m*; (*CHESS*) tour *f* // *vt* (*cheat*) rouler, escroquer.

**room** [ru:m] *n* (*in house*) pièce *f*; (*also*: **bed~**) chambre *f* (à coucher); (*in school etc*) salle *f*; (*space*) place *f*; **~s** *npl* (*lodging*) meublé *m*; **'~s to let'** 'chambres à louer'; **~ing house** *n* (*US*) maison *f* de rapport; **~mate** *n* camarade *m/f* de chambre; **~ service** *n* service *m* des chambres (*dans un hôtel*); **~y** *a* spacieux(euse); (*garment*) ample.

**roost** [ru:st] *n* juchoir *m* // *vi* se jucher.

**rooster** ['ru:stə*] *n* coq *m*.

**root** [ru:t] *n* (*BOT, MATH*) racine *f*; (*fig: of problem*) origine *f*, fond *m* // *vt* (*plant, belief*) enraciner; **to ~ about** *vi* (*fig*) fouiller; **to ~ for** *vt fus* applaudir; **to ~ out** *vt* extirper.

**rope** [rəup] *n* corde *f*; (*NAUT*) cordage *m* // *vt* (*box*) corder; (*climbers*) encorder; **to ~ sb in** (*fig*) embringuer qn; **to know the ~s** (*fig*) être au courant, connaître les ficelles; **~ ladder** *n* échelle *f* de corde.

**rosary** ['rəuzərı] *n* chapelet *m*; rosaire *m*.

**rose** [rəuz] *pt of* **rise** // *n* rose *f*; (*also*: **~bush**) rosier *m*; (*on watering can*) pomme *f* // *a* rose.

**rosé** ['rəuzeı] *n* rosé *m*.

**rose**: **~bed** *n* massif *m* de rosiers; **~bud** *n* bouton *m* de rose; **~bush** *n* rosier *m*.

**rosemary** ['rəuzmərı] *n* romarin *m*.

**rosette** [rəu'zɛt] *n* rosette *f*; (*larger*) cocarde *f*.

**roster** ['rɔstə*] *n*: **duty ~** tableau *m* de service.

**rostrum** ['rɔstrəm] *n* tribune *f* (*pour un orateur etc*).

**rosy** ['rəuzı] *a* rose; **a ~ future** un bel avenir.

**rot** [rɔt] *n* (*decay*) pourriture *f*; (*fig: pej*) idioties *fpl*, balivernes *fpl* // *vt, vi* pourrir.

**rota** ['rəutə] *n* liste *f*, tableau *m* de service; **on a ~ basis** par roulement.

**rotary** ['rəutərı] *a* rotatif(ive).

**rotate** [rəu'teıt] *vt* (*revolve*) faire tourner; (*change round: crops*) alterner; (*:jobs*) faire à tour de rôle // *vi* (*revolve*) tourner; **rotating** *a* (*movement*) tournant(e); **rotation** [-'teıʃən] *n* rotation *f*; **in rotation** à tour de rôle.

**rotor** ['rəutə*] *n* rotor *m*.

**rotten** ['rɔtn] *a* (*decayed*) pourri(e); (*dishonest*) corrompu(e); (*col: bad*) mauvais(e), moche; **to feel ~** (*ill*) être mal fichu(e).

**rotting** ['rɔtıŋ] *a* pourrissant(e).

**rotund** [rəu'tʌnd] *a* rondelet(te); arrondi(e).

**rouble, ruble** (*US*) ['ru:bl] *n* rouble *m*.

**rouge** [ru:ʒ] *n* rouge *m* (à joues).

**rough** [rʌf] *a* (*cloth, skin*) rêche, rugueux(euse); (*terrain*) accidenté(e); (*path*) rocailleux(euse); (*voice*) rauque, rude; (*person, manner: coarse*) rude, fruste; (*: violent*) brutal(e); (*district, weather*) mauvais(e); (*plan*) ébauché(e); (*guess*) approximatif(ive) // *n* (*GOLF*) rough *m*; (*person*) voyou *m*; **to ~ it** vivre à la dure; **to play ~** jouer avec brutalité; **to sleep ~** coucher à la dure; **to feel ~** être mal fichu(e); **to ~ out** *vt* (*draft*) ébaucher; **~en** *vt* (*a surface*) rendre rude or rugueux(euse); **~ justice** *n* justice *f* sommaire; **~ly** *ad* (*handle*) rudement, brutalement; (*make*) grossièrement; (*approximately*) à peu près, en gros; **~ness** *n* rugosité *f*; rudesse *f*; brutalité *f*; **~ work** *n* (*at school etc*) brouillon *m*.

**roulette** [ru:'lɛt] *n* roulette *f*.

**Roumania** [ru:'meınıə] *n* = **Romania**.

**round** [raund] *a* rond(e) // *n* rond *m*, cercle *m*; (*of toast*) tranche *f*; (*duty: of policeman, milkman etc*) tournée *f*; (*: of doctor*) visites *fpl*; (*game: of cards, in competition*) partie *f*; (*BOXING*) round *m*; (*of talks*) série *f* // *vt* (*corner*) tourner; (*bend*) prendre; (*cape*) doubler // *prep* autour de // *ad*: **right ~, all ~** tout autour; **the long way ~** (par) le chemin le plus long; **all the year ~** toute l'année; **it's just ~ the corner** c'est juste après le coin; (*fig*) c'est tout près; **to go ~** faire le tour *or* un détour; **to go ~ to sb's (house)** aller chez qn; **to go ~ an obstacle** contourner un obstacle; **go ~ the back** passe par derrière; **to go ~ a house** visiter une maison, faire le tour d'une maison; **to go the ~s** (*disease, story*) circuler; **to ~ off** *vt* (*speech etc*) terminer; **to ~ up** *vt* rassembler; (*criminals*) effectuer une rafle de; (*prices*) arrondir (au chiffre supérieur); **~about** *n* (*AUT*) rond-point *m* (à sens giratoire); (*at fair*) manège *m* (de chevaux de bois) // *a* (*route, means*) détourné(e); **~ of ammunition** *n* cartouche *f*; **~ of applause** *n* ban *m*, applaudissements *mpl*; **~ of drinks** *n* tournée *f*; **~ of sandwiches** *n* sandwich *m*; **~ed** *a* arrondi(e); (*style*) harmonieux(euse); **~ly** *ad* (*fig*) tout net, carrément; **~-shouldered** *a* au dos rond; **~sman** *n* livreur *m*; **~ trip** *n* (*voyage m*) aller et retour *m*; **~up** *n* rassemblement *m*; (*of criminals*) rafle *f*.

**rouse** [rauz] *vt* (*wake up*) réveiller; (*stir up*) susciter; provoquer; éveiller; **rousing** *a* (*welcome*) enthousiaste.

**rout** [raut] *n* (*MIL*) déroute *f* // *vt* mettre en déroute.

**route** [ru:t] *n* itinéraire *m*; (*of bus*) parcours *m*; (*of trade, shipping*) route *f*; **'all ~s'** (*AUT*) 'toutes directions'; **~ map** *n* (*for journey*) croquis *m* d'itinéraire; (*for trains etc*) carte *f* du réseau.

**routine** [ru:'ti:n] *a* (*work*) ordinaire, courant(e); (*procedure*) d'usage // *n* (*pej*) routine *f*; (*THEATRE*) numéro *m*; **daily ~** occupations journalières.

**roving** ['rəuvıŋ] *a* (*life*) vagabond(e); **~ reporter** *n* reporter volant.

**row** [rəu] *n* (*line*) rangée *f*; (*of people, seats, KNITTING*) rang *m*; (*behind one another: of cars, people*) file *f* // *vi* (*in boat*) ramer; (*as sport*) faire de l'aviron // *vt* (*boat*) faire aller à la rame *or* à l'aviron; **in a ~** (*fig*) d'affilée.

**row** [rau] *n* (*noise*) vacarme *m*; (*dispute*) dispute *f*, querelle *f*; (*scolding*) réprimande *f*, savon *m* // *vi* se disputer, se quereller.

**rowdiness** ['raudınıs] *n* tapage *m*, chahut *m*; (*fighting*) bagarre *f*.

**rowdy** ['raudı] *a* chahuteur(euse); bagarreur(euse) // *n* voyou *m*.

**rowing** ['rəuɪŋ] n canotage m; (as sport) aviron m; ~ **boat** n canot m (à rames).

**rowlock** ['rɔlək] n dame f de nage, tolet m.

**royal** ['rɔɪəl] a royal(e); ~**ist** a, n royaliste (m/f).

**royalty** ['rɔɪəltɪ] n (royal persons) (membres mpl de la) famille royale; (payment: to author) droits mpl d'auteur; (: to inventor) royalties fpl.

**r.p.m.** abbr (AUT: = revs per minute) tr/mn (tours/minute).

**R.S.P.C.A.** n (abbr of Royal Society for the Prevention of Cruelty to Animals), ≈ S.P.A..

**R.S.V.P.** abbr (= répondez s'il vous plaît) R.S.V.P.

**Rt Hon.** abbr (= Right Honourable) titre donné aux députés de la Chambre des communes.

**rub** [rʌb] n (with cloth) coup m de chiffon or de torchon; (on person) friction f // vt frotter; frictionner; to ~ **sb up the wrong way** prendre qn à rebrousse-poil; to ~ **off** vi partir; to ~ **off on** déteindre sur.

**rubber** ['rʌbə*] n caoutchouc m; (Brit: eraser) gomme f (à effacer); ~ **band** n élastique m; ~ **plant** n caoutchouc m (plante verte); ~ **stamp** n tampon m; ~-**stamp** vt (fig) approuver sans discussion; ~**y** a caoutchouteux(euse).

**rubbish** ['rʌbɪʃ] n (from household) ordures fpl; (fig:pej) choses fpl sans valeur; camelote f; bêtises fpl, idioties fpl; ~ **bin** n boîte f à ordures, poubelle f; ~ **dump** n (in town) décharge publique, dépotoir m.

**rubble** ['rʌbl] n décombres mpl; (smaller) gravats mpl.

**ruble** ['ru:bl] n (US) = **rouble**.

**ruby** ['ru:bɪ] n rubis m.

**rucksack** ['rʌksæk] n sac m à dos.

**ructions** ['rʌkʃənz] npl grabuge m.

**rudder** ['rʌdə*] n gouvernail m.

**ruddy** ['rʌdɪ] a (face) coloré(e); (sky) rougeoyant(e); (col: damned) sacré(e), fichu(e).

**rude** [ru:d] a (impolite: person) impoli(e); (: word, manners) grossier(ère); (shocking) indécent(e), inconvenant(e); ~**ly** ad impoliment; grossièrement; ~**ness** n impolitesse f; grossièreté f.

**rudiment** ['ru:dɪmənt] n rudiment m; ~**ary** [-'mɛntərɪ] a rudimentaire.

**rueful** ['ru:ful] a triste.

**ruff** [rʌf] n fraise f, collerette f.

**ruffian** ['rʌfɪən] n brute f, voyou m.

**ruffle** ['rʌfl] vt (hair) ébouriffer; (clothes) chiffonner; (water) agiter; (fig: person) émouvoir, faire perdre son flegme à.

**rug** [rʌg] n petit tapis; (for knees) couverture f.

**rugby** ['rʌgbɪ] n (also: ~ **football**) rugby m.

**rugged** ['rʌgɪd] a (landscape) accidenté(e); (tree bark) rugueux(euse); (features, kindness, character) rude; (determination) farouche.

**rugger** ['rʌgə*] n (col) rugby m.

**ruin** ['ru:ɪn] n ruine f // vt ruiner; (spoil: clothes) abîmer; ~**s** npl ruine(s); ~**ation** [-'neɪʃən] n ruine f; ~**ous** a ruineux(euse).

**rule** [ru:l] n règle f; (regulation) règlement m; (government) autorité f, gouvernement m // vt (country) gouverner; (person) dominer; (decide) décider; (draw: lines) tirer à la règle // vi commander; décider; (LAW) statuer; **as a** ~ normalement, en règle générale; ~**d** a (paper) réglé(e); ~**r** n (sovereign) souverain/e; (leader) chef m (d'État); (for measuring) règle f; **ruling** a (party) au pouvoir; (class) dirigeant(e) // n (LAW) décision f.

**rum** [rʌm] n rhum m // a (col) bizarre.

**Rumania** [ru:'meɪnɪə] n = **Romania**.

**rumble** ['rʌmbl] n grondement m; gargouillement m // vi gronder; (stomach, pipe) gargouiller.

**rummage** ['rʌmɪdʒ] vi fouiller.

**rumour, rumor** (US) ['ru:mə*] n rumeur f, bruit m (qui court) // vt: **it is** ~**ed that** le bruit court que.

**rump** [rʌmp] n (of animal) croupe f; ~**steak** n rumsteck m.

**rumpus** ['rʌmpəs] n (col) tapage m, chahut m; (quarrel) prise f de bec.

**run** [rʌn] n (pas m de) course f; (outing) tour m or promenade f (en voiture); parcours m, trajet m; (series) suite f, série f; (THEATRE) série de représentations; (SKI) piste f // vb (pt **ran**, pp **run** [ræn, rʌn]) vt (operate: business) diriger; (: competition, course) organiser; (: hotel, house) tenir; (force through: rope, pipe): to ~ **sth through** faire passer qch à travers; (to pass: hand, finger): to ~ **sth over** promener or passer qch sur; (water, bath) faire couler // vi courir; (pass: road etc) passer; (work: machine, factory) marcher; (bus, train: operate) être en service; (: travel) circuler; (continue: play) se jouer; (: contract) être valide; (slide: drawer etc) glisser; (flow: river, bath) couler; (colours, washing) déteindre; (in election) être candidat, se présenter; **there was a** ~ **on** (meat, tickets) les gens se sont rués sur; **to break into a** ~ se mettre à courir; **in the long** ~ à longue échéance; à la longue; en fin de compte; **in the short** ~ à brève échéance, à court terme; **on the** ~ en fuite; **I'll** ~ **you to the station** je vais vous emmener or conduire à la gare; to ~ **a risk** courir un risque; to ~ **about** vi (children) courir çà et là; to ~ **across** vt fus (find) trouver par hasard; to ~ **away** vi s'enfuir; to ~ **down** vi (clock) s'arrêter (faute d'avoir été remonté) // vt (AUT) renverser; (criticize) critiquer, dénigrer; **to be** ~ **down** être fatigué(e) or à plat; to ~ **off** vi s'enfuir; to ~ **out** vi (person) sortir en courant; (liquid) couler; (lease) expirer; (money) être épuisé(e); to ~ **out of** vt fus se trouver à court de; to ~ **over** vt sep (AUT) écraser // vt fus (revise) revoir, reprendre; to ~ **through** vt fus (instructions) reprendre, revoir; to ~ **up** vt (debt) laisser accumuler; to ~ **up against** (difficulties) se heurter à; ~-**away** a (horse) emballé(e); (truck) fou(folle); (inflation) galopant(e).

**rung** [rʌŋ] pp of **ring** // n (of ladder) barreau m.

**runner** ['rʌnə*] n (in race: person) coureur/euse; (: horse) partant m; (on sledge) patin m; (on curtain) suspendeur m ; (for drawer etc) coulisseau m ; (carpet: in hall etc) chemin m ; ~ **bean** n (BOT) haricot m (à rames) ; **~-up** n second/e.

**running** ['rʌnɪŋ] n course f ; direction f ; organisation f ; marche f, fonctionnement m // a (water) courant(e) ; (commentary) suivi(e) ; **6 days** ~ 6 jours de suite.

**runny** ['rʌnɪ] a qui coule.

**run-of-the-mill** ['rʌnəvðə'mɪl] a ordinaire, banal(e).

**runt** [rʌnt] n (also: pej) avorton m.

**run-through** ['rʌnθruː] n répétition f, essai m.

**runway** ['rʌnweɪ] n (AVIAT) piste f (d'envol cu d'atterrissage).

**rupee** [ruːˈpiː] n roupie f.

**rupture** ['rʌptʃə*] n (MED) hernie f // vt: **to** ~ **o.s.** se donner une hernie.

**rural** ['ruərl] a rural(e).

**ruse** [ruːz] n ruse f.

**rush** [rʌʃ] n course précipitée ; (of crowd) ruée f, bousculade f ; (hurry) hâte f, bousculade ; (current) flot m // vt transporter or envoyer d'urgence ; (attack: town etc) prendre d'assaut ; (col: overcharge) estamper ; faire payer // vi se précipiter ; **don't** ~ **me!** laissez-moi le temps de souffler! ; **~es** npl (BOT) jonc m ; ~ **hour** n heures fpl de pointe or d'affluence.

**rusk** [rʌsk] n biscotte f.

**Russia** ['rʌʃə] n Russie f ; **~n** a russe // n Russe m/f ; (LING) russe m.

**rust** [rʌst] n rouille f // vi rouiller.

**rustic** ['rʌstɪk] a rustique // n (pej) rustaud/e.

**rustle** ['rʌsl] vi bruire, produire un bruissement // vt (paper) froisser ; (US: cattle) voler.

**rustproof** ['rʌstpruːf] a inoxydable ; **~ing** n traitement m antirouille.

**rusty** ['rʌstɪ] a rouillé(e).

**rut** [rʌt] n ornière f ; (ZOOL) rut m.

**ruthless** ['ruːθlɪs] a sans pitié, impitoyable ; **~ness** n dureté f, cruauté f.

**rye** [raɪ] n seigle m ; ~ **bread** n pain m de seigle.

# S

**sabbath** ['sæbəθ] n sabbat m.

**sabbatical** [səˈbætɪkl] a: ~ **year** n année f sabbatique.

**sabotage** ['sæbətɑːʒ] n sabotage m // vt saboter.

**saccharin(e)** ['sækərɪn] n saccharine f.

**sack** [sæk] n (bag) sac m // vt (dismiss) renvoyer, mettre à la porte ; (plunder) piller, mettre à sac ; **to get the** ~ être renvoyé or mis à la porte ; **a ~ful of** un (plein) sac de ; **~ing** n toile f à sac ; renvoi m.

**sacrament** ['sækrəmənt] n sacrement m.

**sacred** ['seɪkrɪd] a sacré(e).

**sacrifice** ['sækrɪfaɪs] n sacrifice m // vt sacrifier.

**sacrilege** ['sækrɪlɪdʒ] n sacrilège m.

**sacrosanct** ['sækrəʊsæŋkt] a sacrosaint(e).

**sad** [sæd] a (unhappy) triste ; (deplorable) triste, fâcheux(euse) ; **~den** vt attrister, affliger.

**saddle** ['sædl] n selle f // vt (horse) seller ; **to be** ~**d with sth** (col) avoir qch sur les bras ; **~bag** n sacoche f.

**sadism** ['seɪdɪzm] n sadisme m ; **sadist** n sadique m/f ; **sadistic** [səˈdɪstɪk] a sadique.

**sadly** ['sædlɪ] ad tristement ; fâcheusement.

**sadness** ['sædnɪs] n tristesse f.

**safari** [səˈfɑːrɪ] n safari m.

**safe** [seɪf] a (out of danger) hors de danger, en sécurité ; (not dangerous) sans danger ; (cautious) prudent(e) ; (sure: bet etc) assuré(e) // n coffre-fort m ; ~ **from** à l'abri de ; ~ **and sound** sain(e) et sauf(sauve) ; **(just) to be on the** ~ **side** pour plus de sûreté, par précaution ; **~guard** n sauvegarde f, protection f // vt sauvegarder, protéger ; **~keeping** n bonne garde ; **~ly** ad sans danger, sans risque ; (without mishap) sans accident.

**safety** ['seɪftɪ] n sécurité f ; ~ **belt** n ceinture f de sécurité ; ~ **curtain** n rideau m de fer ; ~ **first!** la sécurité d'abord! ; ~ **pin** n épingle f de sûreté or de nourrice.

**saffron** ['sæfrən] n safran m.

**sag** [sæg] vi s'affaisser, fléchir ; pendre.

**sage** [seɪdʒ] n (herb) sauge f ; (man) sage m.

**Sagittarius** [sædʒɪˈtɛərɪəs] n le Sagittaire ; **to be** ~ être du Sagittaire.

**sago** ['seɪgəʊ] n sagou m.

**said** [sɛd] pt, pp of **say.**

**sail** [seɪl] n (on boat) voile f ; (trip): **to go for a** ~ faire un tour en bateau // vt (boat) manœuvrer, piloter // vi (travel: ship) avancer, naviguer ; (: passenger) aller or se rendre (en bateau) ; (set off) partir, prendre la mer ; (SPORT) faire de la voile ; **they ~ed into Le Havre** ils sont entrés dans le port du Havre ; **to** ~ **through** vi, vt fus (fig) réussir haut la main ; **~boat** n (US) bateau m à voiles, voilier m ; **~ing** n (SPORT) voile f ; **to go** ~ **ing** faire de la voile ; **~ing boat** n bateau m à voiles, voilier m ; **~ing ship** n grand voilier ; **~or** n marin m, matelot m.

**saint** [seɪnt] n saint/e ; **~ly** a saint(e), plein(e) de bonté.

**sake** [seɪk] n: **for the** ~ **of** pour (l'amour de), dans l'intérêt de ; par égard pour ; **for pity's** ~ par pitié.

**salad** ['sæləd] n salade f ; ~ **bowl** n saladier m ; ~ **cream** n (sorte f de) mayonnaise f ; ~ **dressing** n vinaigrette f ; ~ **oil** n huile f de table.

**salaried** ['sælərɪd] a (staff) salarié(e), qui touche un traitement.

**salary** ['sælərɪ] n salaire m, traitement m.

**sale** [seɪl] n vente f ; (at reduced prices) soldes mpl ; **'for** ~**'** 'à vendre' ; **on** ~ en vente ; **on** ~ **or return** vendu(e) avec faculté de retour ; **~room** n salle f des ventes ; **~sman** n vendeur m ; (representative) représentant m de commerce ; **~smanship** n art m de la vente ; **~swoman** n vendeuse f.

**salient** ['seɪlɪənt] a saillant(e).

**saliva** [səˈlaɪvə] n salive f.

**sallow** ['sæləʊ] a cireux(euse).

**salmon** ['sæmən] n, pl inv saumon m ; ~ **trout** n truite saumonée.

**saloon** [sə'lu:n] *n* (*US*) bar *m*; (*AUT*) berline *f*; (*ship's lounge*) salon *m*.

**salt** [sɔlt] *n* sel *m* // *vt* saler // *cpd* de sel; (*CULIN*) salé(e); ~ **cellar** *n* salière *f*; ~-**free** *a* sans sel; ~-**y** *a* salé.

**salutary** ['sæljutərɪ] *a* salutaire.

**salute** [sə'lu:t] *n* salut *m* // *vt* saluer.

**salvage** ['sælvɪdʒ] *n* (*saving*) sauvetage *m*; (*things saved*) biens sauvés *or* récupérés // *vt* sauver, récupérer.

**salvation** [sæl'veɪʃən] *n* salut *m*; S~ Army *n* Armée *f* du Salut.

**salver** ['sælvə*] *n* plateau *m* de métal.

**salvo** ['sælvəu] *n* salve *f*.

**same** [seɪm] *a* même // *pronoun*: the ~ le(la) même, les mêmes; the ~ book as le même livre que; all *or* just the ~ tout de même, quand même; to do the ~ faire de même, en faire autant; to do the ~ as sb faire comme qn; the ~ again! (*in bar etc*) la même chose!

**sample** ['sɑ:mpl] *n* échantillon *m*; (*MED*) prélèvement *m* // *vt* (*food, wine*) goûter.

**sanatorium**, *pl* **sanatoria** [sænə'tɔ:rɪəm, -rɪə] *n* sanatorium *m*.

**sanctify** ['sæŋktɪfaɪ] *vt* sanctifier.

**sanctimonious** [sæŋktɪ'məunɪəs] *a* moralisateur(trice).

**sanction** ['sæŋkʃən] *n* sanction *f* // *vt* cautionner, sanctionner.

**sanctity** ['sæŋktɪtɪ] *n* sainteté *f*, caractère sacré.

**sanctuary** ['sæŋktjuərɪ] *n* (*holy place*) sanctuaire *m*; (*refuge*) asile *m*; (*for wild life*) réserve *f*.

**sand** [sænd] *n* sable *m* // *vt* sabler; ~**s** *npl* plage *f* (de sable).

**sandal** ['sændl] *n* sandale *f*.

**sandbag** ['sændbæg] *n* sac *m* de sable.

**sandcastle** ['sændkɑ:sl] *n* château *m* de sable.

**sand dune** ['sænddju:n] *n* dune *f* de sable.

**sandpaper** ['sændpeɪpə*] *n* papier *m* de verre.

**sandpit** ['sændpɪt] *n* (*for children*) tas *m* de sable.

**sandstone** ['sændstəun] *n* grès *m*.

**sandwich** ['sændwɪtʃ] *n* sandwich *m* // *vt* (*also*: ~ in) intercaler; ~ed between pris en sandwich entre; cheese/ham ~ sandwich au fromage/jambon; ~ course *n* cours de formation professionnelle.

**sandy** ['sændɪ] *a* sablonneux(euse); couvert(e) de sable; (*colour*) sable *inv*, blond roux *inv*.

**sane** [seɪn] *a* (*person*) sain(e) d'esprit; (*outlook*) sensé(e), sain(e).

**sang** [sæŋ] *pt of* sing.

**sanguine** ['sæŋgwɪn] *a* optimiste.

**sanitarium**, *pl* **sanitaria** [sænɪ'tɛərɪəm, -rɪə] *n* (*US*) = **sanatorium**.

**sanitary** ['sænɪtərɪ] *a* (*system, arrangements*) sanitaire; (*clean*) hygiénique; ~ towel, ~ napkin (*US*) *n* serviette *f* hygiénique.

**sanitation** [sænɪ'teɪʃən] *n* (*in house*) installations *fpl* sanitaires; (*in town*) système *m* sanitaire.

**sanity** ['sænɪtɪ] *n* santé mentale; (*common sense*) bon sens.

**sank** [sæŋk] *pt of* sink.

**Santa Claus** [sæntə'klɔ:z] *n* le Père Noël.

**sap** [sæp] *n* (*of plants*) sève *f* // *vt* (*strength*) saper, miner.

**sapling** ['sæplɪŋ] *n* jeune arbre *m*.

**sapphire** ['sæfaɪə*] *n* saphir *m*.

**sarcasm** ['sɑ:kæzm] *n* sarcasme *m*, raillerie *f*.

**sarcastic** [sɑ:'kæstɪk] *a* sarcastique.

**sarcophagus**, *pl* **sarcophagi** [sɑ:'kɔfəgəs, -gaɪ] *n* sarcophage *m*.

**sardine** [sɑ:'di:n] *n* sardine *f*.

**Sardinia** [sɑ:'dɪnɪə] *n* Sardaigne *f*.

**sardonic** [sɑ:'dɔnɪk] *a* sardonique.

**sartorial** [sɑ:'tɔ:rɪəl] *a* vestimentaire.

**sash** [sæʃ] *n* écharpe *f*; ~ **window** *n* fenêtre *f* à guillotine.

**sat** [sæt] *pt,pp of* sit.

**satanic** [sə'tænɪk] *a* satanique, démoniaque.

**satchel** ['sætʃl] *n* cartable *m*.

**satellite** ['sætəlaɪt] *a, n* satellite (*m*).

**satin** ['sætɪn] *n* satin *m* // *a* en *or* de satin, satiné(e).

**satire** ['sætaɪə*] *n* satire *f*; **satirical** [sə'tɪrɪkl] *a* satirique; **satirize** ['sætɪraɪz] *vt* faire la satire de, satiriser.

**satisfaction** [sætɪs'fækʃən] *n* satisfaction *f*.

**satisfactory** [sætɪs'fæktərɪ] *a* satisfaisant(e).

**satisfy** ['sætɪsfaɪ] *vt* satisfaire, contenter; (*convince*) convaincre, persuader; ~**ing** *a* satisfaisant(e).

**saturate** ['sætʃəreɪt] *vt*: to ~ (with) saturer (de); **saturation** [-'reɪʃən] *n* saturation *f*.

**Saturday** ['sætədɪ] *n* samedi *m*.

**sauce** [sɔ:s] *n* sauce *f*; ~**pan** *n* casserole *f*.

**saucer** ['sɔ:sə*] *n* soucoupe *f*.

**saucy** ['sɔ:sɪ] *a* impertinent(e).

**sauna** ['sɔ:nə] *n* sauna *m*.

**saunter** ['sɔ:ntə*] *vi*: to ~ to aller en flânant *or* se balader jusqu'à.

**sausage** ['sɔsɪdʒ] *n* saucisse *f*; ~ **roll** *n* friand *m*.

**savage** ['sævɪdʒ] *a* (*cruel, fierce*) brutal(e), féroce; (*primitive*) primitif(ive), sauvage // *n* sauvage *m/f* // *vt* attaquer férocement; ~**ry** *n* sauvagerie *f*, brutalité *f*, férocité *f*.

**save** [seɪv] *vt* (*person, belongings*) sauver; (*money*) mettre de côté, économiser; (*time*) (faire) gagner; (*food*) garder; (*avoid: trouble*) éviter // *vi* (*also*: ~ up) mettre de l'argent de côté // *n* (*SPORT*) arrêt *m* (du ballon) // *prep* sauf, à l'exception de.

**saving** ['seɪvɪŋ] *n* économie *f* // *a*: the ~ grace of ce qui rachète; ~**s** *npl* économies *fpl*; ~**s bank** *n* caisse *f* d'épargne.

**saviour, savor** (*US*) ['seɪvjə*] *n* sauveur *m*.

**savour, savor** (*US*) ['seɪvə*] *n* saveur *f*, goût *m* // *vt* savourer; ~**y** *a* savoureux(euse); (*dish: not sweet*) salé(e).

**savvy** ['sævɪ] *n* (*col*) jugeote *f*.

**saw** [sɔ:] *pt of* see // *n* (*tool*) scie *f* // *vt* (*pt* sawed, *pp* sawed *or* sawn [sɔ:n]) scier; ~**dust** *n* sciure *f*; ~**mill** *n* scierie *f*.

**saxophone** ['sæksəfəun] *n* saxophone *m*.
**say** [seɪ] *n*: **to have one's** ~ dire ce qu'on a à dire ; **to have a** ~ avoir voix au chapitre // *vt* (*pt, pp* **said** [sɛd]) dire ; **could you** ~ **that again?** pourriez-vous répéter ceci? ; **that is to** ~ c'est-à-dire ; **to** ~ **nothing of** sans compter ; ~ **that ...** mettons *or* disons que ... ; **that goes without** ~**ing** cela va sans dire, cela va de soi ; ~**ing** *n* dicton *m*, proverbe *m*.
**scab** [skæb] *n* croûte *f* ; (*pej*) jaune *m* ; ~**by** *a* croûteux(euse).
**scaffold** ['skæfəuld] *n* échafaud *m* ; ~**ing** *n* échafaudage *m*.
**scald** [skɔ:ld] *n* brûlure *f* // *vt* ébouillanter ; ~**ing** *a* (*hot*) brûlant(e), bouillant(e).
**scale** [skeɪl] *n* (*of fish*) écaille *f* ; (*MUS*) gamme *f* ; (*of ruler, thermometer etc*) graduation *f*, échelle (graduée) ; (*of salaries, fees etc*) barème *m* ; (*of map, also size, extent*) échelle *f* // *vt* (*mountain*) escalader ; (*fish*) écailler ; ~**s** *npl* balance *f*, (*larger*) bascule *f* ; **on a large** ~ sur une grande échelle, en grand ; ~ **drawing** *n* dessin *m* à l'échelle ; ~ **model** *n* modèle *m* à l'échelle ; **small-**~ **model** modèle réduit.
**scallop** ['skɔləp] *n* coquille *f* Saint-Jacques.
**scalp** [skælp] *n* cuir chevelu // *vt* scalper.
**scalpel** ['skælpl]. *n* scalpel *m*.
**scamp** [skæmp] *vt* bâcler.
**scamper** ['skæmpə*] *vi*: **to** ~ **away, ~ off** détaler.
**scan** [skæn] *vt* scruter, examiner ; (*glance at quickly*) parcourir ; (*poetry*) scander ; (*TV, RADAR*) balayer.
**scandal** ['skændl] *n* scandale *m* ; (*gossip*) ragots *mpl* ; ~**ize** *vt* scandaliser, indigner ; ~**ous** *a* scandaleux(euse).
**Scandinavia** [skændɪ'neɪvɪə] *n* Scandinavie *f* ; ~**n** *a* scandinave // *n* Scandinave *m/f*.
**scant** [skænt] *a* insuffisant(e) ; ~**y** *a* peu abondant(e), insuffisant(e), maigre.
**scapegoat** ['skeɪpgəut] *n* bouc *m* émissaire.
**scar** [skɑ:] *n* cicatrice *f* // *vt* laisser une cicatrice *or* une marque à.
**scarce** [skɛəs] *a* rare, peu abondant(e) ; ~**ly** *ad* à peine, presque pas ; **scarcity** *n* rareté *f*, manque *m*, pénurie *f*.
**scare** [skɛə*] *n* panique *f* // *vt* effrayer, faire peur à ; **to** ~ **sb stiff** faire une peur bleue à qn ; **bomb** ~ alerte *f* à la bombe ; ~**crow** *n* épouvantail *m* ; ~**d** *a*: **to be** ~**d** avoir peur ; ~**monger** *n* alarmiste *m/f*.
**scarf, scarves** [skɑ:f, skɑ:vz] *n* (*long*) écharpe *f* ; (*square*) foulard *m*.
**scarlet** ['skɑ:lɪt] *a* écarlate ; ~ **fever** *n* scarlatine *f*.
**scarves** [skɑ:vz] *npl of* scarf.
**scary** ['skɛərɪ] *a* (*col*) qui fiche la frousse.
**scathing** ['skeɪðɪŋ] *a* cinglant(e), acerbe.
**scatter** ['skætə*] *vt* éparpiller, répandre ; (*crowd*) disperser // *vi* se disperser ; ~**brained** *a* écervelé(e), étourdi(e) ; ~**ed** *a* épars(e), dispersé(e).
**scatty** ['skætɪ] *a* (*col*) loufoque.
**scavenger** ['skævəndʒə*] *n* éboueur *m*.

**scene** [si:n] *n* (*THEATRE, fig etc*) scène *f* ; (*of crime, accident*) lieu(x) *m(pl)*, endroit *m* ; (*sight, view*) spectacle *m*, vue *f* ; **to appear on the** ~ faire son apparition ; ~**ry** *n* (*THEATRE*) décor(s) *m(pl)* ; (*landscape*) paysage *m* ; **scenic** *a* scénique ; offrant de beaux paysages *or* panoramas.
**scent** [sɛnt] *n* parfum *m*, odeur *f* ; (*fig: track*) piste *f* ; (*sense of smell*) odorat *m* // *vt* parfumer ; (*smell, also fig*) flairer.
**sceptic, skeptic** (*US*) ['skɛptɪk] *n* sceptique *m/f* ; ~**al** *a* sceptique ; ~**ism** ['skɛptɪsɪzm] *n* scepticisme *m*.
**sceptre, scepter** (*US*) ['sɛptə*] *n* sceptre *m*.
**schedule** ['ʃɛdju:l] *n* programme *m*, plan *m* ; (*of trains*) horaire *m* ; (*of prices etc*) barème *m*, tarif *m* // *vt* prévoir ; **as** ~**d** comme prévu ; **on** ~ à l'heure (prévue) ; à la date prévue ; **to be ahead of/behind** ~ avoir de l'avance/du retard.
**scheme** [ski:m] *n* plan *m*, projet *m* ; (*method*) procédé *m* ; (*dishonest plan, plot*) complot *m*, combine *f* ; (*arrangement*) arrangement *m*, classification *f* // *vt,vi* comploter, manigancer ; **scheming** *a* rusé(e), intrigant(e) // *n* manigances *fpl*, intrigues *fpl*.
**schism** ['skɪzəm] *n* schisme *m*.
**schizophrenic** [skɪtsə'frɛnɪk] *a* schizophrène.
**scholar** ['skɔlə*] *n* érudit/e ; ~**ly** *a* érudit(e), savant(e) ; ~**ship** *n* érudition *f* ; (*grant*) bourse *f* (d'études).
**school** [sku:l] *n* (*gen*) école *f* ; (*in university*) faculté *f* ; (*secondary school*) collège *m*, lycée *m* // *cpd* scolaire // *vt* (*animal*) dresser ; ~**book** *n* livre *m* scolaire *or* de classe ; ~**boy** *n* écolier *m* ; collégien *m*, lycéen *m* ; ~**days** *npl* années *fpl* de scolarité ; ~**girl** *n* écolière *f* ; collégienne *f*, lycéenne *f* ; ~**ing** *n* instruction *f*, études *fpl* ; ~**-leaving age** *n* âge *m* de fin de scolarité ; ~**master** *n* (*primary*) instituteur *m* ; (*secondary*) professeur *m* ; ~**mistress** *n* institutrice *f* ; professeur *m* ; ~ **report** *n* bulletin *m* (scolaire) ; ~**room** *n* (salle *f* de) classe *f* ; ~**teacher** *n* instituteur/trice ; professeur *m*.
**schooner** ['sku:nə*] *n* (*ship*) schooner *m*, goélette *f* ; (*glass*) grand verre (à xérès).
**sciatica** [saɪ'ætɪkə] *n* sciatique *f*.
**science** ['saɪəns] *n* science *f* ; ~ **fiction** *n* science-fiction *f* ; **scientific** [-'tɪfɪk] *a* scientifique ; **scientist** *n* scientifique *m/f* ; (*eminent*) savant *m*.
**scintillating** ['sɪntɪleɪtɪŋ] *a* scintillant(e), étincelant(e).
**scissors** ['sɪzəz] *npl* ciseaux *mpl* ; **a pair of** ~ une paire de ciseaux.
**sclerosis** [sklɪ'rəusɪs] *n* sclérose *f*.
**scoff** [skɔf] *vt* (*col: eat*) avaler, bouffer // *vi*: **to** ~ (**at**) (*mock*) se moquer (de).
**scold** [skəuld] *vt* gronder, attraper, réprimander.
**scone** [skɔn] *n* sorte de petit pain rond au lait.
**scoop** [sku:p] *n* pelle *f* (à main) ; (*for ice cream*) boule *f* à glace ; (*PRESS*) reportage exclusif *or* à sensation ; **to** ~ **out** *vt* évider, creuser ; **to** ~ **up** *vt* ramasser.
**scooter** ['sku:tə*] *n* (*motor cycle*) scooter *m* ; (*toy*) trottinette *f*.

**scope** [skəup] *n* (*capacity*: *of plan, under-taking*) portée *f*, envergure *f*; (: *of person*) compétence *f*, capacités *fpl*; (*opportunity*) possibilités *fpl*; **within the ~ of** dans les limites de.

**scorch** [skɔ:tʃ] *vt* (*clothes*) brûler (légère-ment), roussir; (*earth, grass*) dessécher, brûler; **~ed earth policy** *n* politique *f* de la terre brûlée; **~er** *n* (*col: hot day*) journée *f* torride; **~ing** *a* torride, brûlant(e).

**score** [skɔ:*] *n* score *m*, décompte *m* des points; (*MUS*) partition *f*; (*twenty*) vingt // *vt* (*goal, point*) marquer; (*success*) rem-porter // *vi* marquer des points; (*FOOTBALL*) marquer un but; (*keep score*) compter les points; **on that ~** sur ce chapitre, à cet égard; **to ~ well/6 out of 10** obtenir un bon résultat/6 sur 10; **~board** *n* tableau *m*; **~card** *n* (*SPORT*) carton *m*; feuille *f* de marque; **~r** *n* auteur *m* du but; marqueur *m* de buts; (*keeping score*) marqueur *m*.

**scorn** [skɔ:n] *n* mépris *m*, dédain *m* // *vt* mépriser, dédaigner; **~ful** *a* méprisant(e), dédaigneux(euse).

**Scorpio** ['skɔ:pɪəu] *n* le Scorpion; **to be ~** être du Scorpion.

**scorpion** ['skɔ:pɪən] *n* scorpion *m*.

**Scot** [skɔt] *n* Écossais/e.

**scotch** [skɔtʃ] *vt* faire échouer; enrayer; étouffer; **S~** *n* whisky *m*, scotch *m*.

**scot-free** ['skɔt'fri:] *a* sans être puni(e); sans payer.

**Scotland** ['skɔtlənd] *n* Écosse *f*.

**Scots** [skɔts] *a* écossais(e); **~man/woman** Écossais/e.

**Scottish** ['skɔtɪʃ] *a* écossais(e).

**scoundrel** ['skaundrl] *n* vaurien *m*; (*child*) coquin *m*.

**scour** ['skauə*] *vt* (*clean*) récurer; frotter; décaper; (*search*) battre, parcourir; **~er** *n* tampon abrasif *or* à récurer.

**scourge** [skə:dʒ] *n* fléau *m*.

**scout** [skaut] *n* (*MIL*) éclaireur *m*; (*also:* **boy ~**) scout *m*; **to ~ around** explorer, chercher.

**scowl** [skaul] *vi* se renfrogner, avoir l'air maussade; **to ~ at** regarder de travers.

**scraggy** ['skrægɪ] *a* décharné(e), ef-flanqué(e), famélique.

**scram** [skræm] *vi* (*col*) ficher le camp.

**scramble** ['skræmbl] *n* bousculade *f*, ruée *f* // *vi* avancer tant bien que mal (à quatre pattes *or* en grimpant); **to ~ for** se bous-culer *or* se disputer pour (avoir); **~d eggs** *npl* œufs brouillés.

**scrap** [skræp] *n* bout *m*, morceau *m*; (*fight*) bagarre *f*; (*also:* **~ iron**) ferraille *f* // *vt* jeter, mettre au rebut; (*fig*) aban-donner, laisser tomber; **~s** *npl* (*waste*) dé-chets *mpl*; **~book** *n* album *m*.

**scrape** [skreɪp] *vt,vi* gratter, racler // *n*: **to get into a ~** s'attirer des ennuis; **~r** *n* grattoir *m*, racloir *m*.

**scrap**: **~ heap** *n* tas *m* de ferraille; (*fig*): **on the ~ heap** au rancart *or* rebut; **~ merchant** *n* marchand *m* de ferraille; **~ paper** *n* papier *m* brouillon; **~py** *a* fragmentaire, décousu(e).

**scratch** [skrætʃ] *n* égratignure *f*, rayure *f*; éraflure *f*; (*from claw*) coup *m* de griffe // *a*: **~ team** *n* équipe de fortune *or* im-provisé(e) // *vt* (*record*) rayer; (*paint etc*) érafler; (*with claw, nail*) griffer // *vi* (se) gratter; **to start from ~** partir de zéro; **to be up to ~** être à la hauteur.

**scrawl** [skrɔ:l] *n* gribouillage *m* // *vi* gribouiller.

**scrawny** ['skrɔ:nɪ] *a* décharné(e).

**scream** [skri:m] *n* cri perçant, hurlement *m* // *vi* crier, hurler; **to be a ~** être im-payable.

**scree** [skri:] *n* éboulis *m*.

**screech** [skri:tʃ] *n* cri strident, hurlement *m*; (*of tyres, brakes*) crissement *m*, grince-ment *m* // *vi* hurler; crisser, grincer.

**screen** [skri:n] *n* écran *m*, paravent *m*; (*CINEMA, TV*) écran; (*fig*) écran, rideau *m* // *vt* masquer, cacher; (*from the wind etc*) abriter, protéger; (*film*) projeter; (*book*) porter à l'écran; (*candidates etc*) filtrer; **~ing** *n* (*MED*) test *m* (*or* tests) de dépistage.

**screw** [skru:] *n* vis *f*; (*propeller*) hélice *f* // *vt* visser; **to have one's head ~ed on** avoir la tête sur les épaules; **~driver** *n* tournevis *m*; **~y** *a* (*col*) dingue, cinglé(e).

**scribble** ['skrɪbl] *n* gribouillage *m* // *vt* gribouiller, griffonner.

**scribe** [skraɪb] *n* scribe *m*.

**script** [skrɪpt] *n* (*CINEMA etc*) scénario *m*, texte *m*; (*in exam*) copie *f*.

**Scripture** ['skrɪptʃə*] *n* Écriture Sainte.

**scriptwriter** ['skrɪptraɪtə*] *n* scénariste *m/f*, dialoguiste *m/f*.

**scroll** [skrəul] *n* rouleau *m*.

**scrounge** [skraundʒ] *vt* (*col*): **to ~ sth (off *or* from sb)** se faire payer qch (par qn), emprunter qch (à qn) // *vi*: **to ~ on sb** vivre aux crochets de qn; **~r** *n* par-asite *m*.

**scrub** [skrʌb] *n* (*clean*) nettoyage *m* (à la brosse); (*land*) broussailles *fpl* // *vt* (*floor*) nettoyer à la brosse; (*pan*) récurer; (*wash-ing*) frotter; (*reject*) annuler.

**scruff** [skrʌf] *n*: **by the ~ of the neck** par la peau du cou.

**scruffy** ['skrʌfɪ] *a* débraillé(e).

**scrum(mage)** ['skrʌm(ɪdʒ)] *n* mêlée *f*.

**scruple** ['skru:pl] *n* scrupule *m*.

**scrupulous** ['skru:pjuləs] *a* scrupu-leux(euse).

**scrutinize** ['skru:tɪnaɪz] *vt* scruter, examiner minutieusement.

**scrutiny** ['skru:tɪnɪ] *n* examen minutieux.

**scuff** [skʌf] *vt* érafler.

**scuffle** ['skʌfl] *n* échauffourée *f*, rixe *f*.

**scull** [skʌl] *n* aviron *m*.

**scullery** ['skʌlərɪ] *n* arrière-cuisine *f*.

**sculptor** ['skʌlptə*] *n* sculpteur *m*.

**sculpture** ['skʌlptʃə*] *n* sculpture *f*.

**scum** [skʌm] *n* écume *f*, mousse *f*; (*pej: people*) rebut *m*, lie *f*.

**scurrilous** ['skʌrɪləs] *a* haineux(euse), virulent(e); calomnieux(euse).

**scurry** ['skʌrɪ] *vi* filer à toute allure.

**scurvy** ['skə:vɪ] *n* scorbut *m*.

**scuttle** ['skʌtl] *n* (*NAUT*) écoutille *f*; (*also:* **coal ~**) seau *m* (à charbon) // *vt* (*ship*) saborder // *vi* (*scamper*): **to ~ away, ~ off** détaler.

**scythe** [saɪð] *n* faux *f*.

**sea** [si:] *n* mer *f* // *cpd* marin(e), de (la) mer, maritime; **on the ~** (*boat*) en mer;

*(town)* au bord de la mer ; **to be all at** ~ *(fig)* nager complètement ; ~ **bird** *n* oiseau *m* de mer ; ~**board** *n* côte *f* ; ~ **breeze** *n* brise *f* de mer ; ~**farer** *n* marin *m* ; ~**food** *n* fruits *mpl* de mer ; ~ **front** *n* bord *m* de mer ; ~**going** *a (ship)* de haute mer ; ~**gull** *n* mouette *f*.

**seal** [si:l] *n (animal)* phoque *m* ; *(stamp)* sceau *m*, cachet *m* ; *(impression)* cachet, estampille *f* // *vt* sceller ; *(envelope)* coller ; (: *with seal)* cacheter.

**sea level** ['si:lɛvl] *n* niveau *m* de la mer.

**sealing wax** ['si:lɪŋwæks] *n* cire *f* à cacheter.

**sea lion** ['si:laɪən] *n* lion *m* de mer.

**seam** [si:m] *n* couture *f* ; *(of coal)* veine *f*, filon *m*.

**seaman** ['si:mən] *n* marin *m*.

**seamless** ['si:mlɪs] *a* sans couture(s).

**seamy** ['si:mɪ] *a* louche, mal famé(e).

**seance** ['seɪɔns] *n* séance *f* de spiritisme.

**seaplane** ['si:pleɪn] *n* hydravion *m*.

**seaport** ['si:pɔ:t] *n* port *m* de mer.

**search** [sə:tʃ] *n (for person, thing)* recherche(s) *f(pl)* ; *(of drawer, pockets)* fouille *f* ; *(LAW: at sb's home)* perquisition *f* // *vt* fouiller ; *(examine)* examiner minutieusement ; scruter // *vi* : **to** ~ **for** chercher ; **to** ~ **through** *vt fus* fouiller ; **in** ~ **of** à la recherche de ; ~**ing** *a* pénétrant(e) ; minutieux(euse) ; ~**light** *n* projecteur *m* ; ~ **party** *n* expédition *f* de secours ; ~ **warrant** *n* mandat *m* de perquisition.

**seashore** ['si:ʃɔ:*] *n* rivage *m*, plage *f*, bord *m* de (la) mer.

**seasick** ['si:sɪk] *a* qui a le mal de mer.

**seaside** ['si:saɪd] *n* bord *m* de la mer ; ~ **resort** *n* station *f* balnéaire.

**season** ['si:zn] *n* saison *f* // *vt* assaisonner, relever ; ~**al** *a* saisonnier(ère) ; ~**ing** *n* assaisonnement *m* ; ~ **ticket** *n* carte *f* d'abonnement.

**seat** [si:t] *n* siège *m* ; *(in bus, train: place)* place *f* ; *(PARLIAMENT)* siège ; *(buttocks)* postérieur *m* ; *(of trousers)* fond *m* // *vt* faire asseoir, placer ; *(have room for)* avoir des places assises pour, pouvoir accueillir ; ~ **belt** *n* ceinture *f* de sécurité ; ~**ing room** *n* places assises.

**sea water** ['si:wɔ:tə*] *n* eau *f* de mer.

**seaweed** ['si:wi:d] *n* algues *fpl*.

**seaworthy** ['si:wə:ðɪ] *a* en état de naviguer.

**sec.** *abbr of* **second(s)**.

**secede** [sɪ'si:d] *vi* faire sécession.

**secluded** [sɪ'klu:dɪd] *a* retiré(e), à l'écart.

**seclusion** [sɪ'klu:ʒən] *n* solitude *f*.

**second** ['sɛkənd] *num* deuxième, second(e) // *ad (in race etc)* en seconde position ; *(RAIL)* en seconde // *n (unit of time)* seconde *f* ; *(in series, position)* deuxième *m/f*, second/e ; *(SCOL)* ≈ licence *f* avec mention bien *or* assez bien ; *(AUT: also:* ~ **gear***)* seconde *f* ; *(COMM: imperfect)* article *m* de second choix // *vt (motion)* appuyer ; ~**ary** *a* secondaire ; ~**ary school** *n* collège *m*, lycée *m* ; ~- **class** *a* de deuxième classe ; ~**er** *n* personne *f* qui appuie une motion ; ~**hand** *a* d'occasion ; de seconde main ; ~ **hand** *n (on clock)* trot-

teuse *f* ; ~**ly** *ad* deuxièmement ; ~**ment** [sɪ'kɔndmənt] *n* détachement *m* ; ~-**rate** *a* de deuxième ordre, de qualité inférieure ; ~ **thoughts** *npl* doutes *mpl* ; **on** ~ **thoughts** à la réflexion.

**secrecy** ['si:krəsɪ] *n* secret *m* ; **in** ~ en secret, dans le secret.

**secret** ['si:krɪt] *a* secret(ète) // *n* secret *m*.

**secretarial** [sɛkrɪ'tɛərɪəl] *a* de secrétaire, de secrétariat.

**secretariat** [sɛkrɪ'tɛərɪət] *n* secrétariat *m*.

**secretary** ['sɛkrətərɪ] *n* secrétaire *m/f* ; *(COMM)* secrétaire général ; **S~ of State (for)** *(Brit: POL)* ministre *m* (de).

**secretive** ['si:krətɪv] *a* réservé(e) ; *(pej)* cachottier(ère), dissimulé(e).

**sect** [sɛkt] *n* secte *f* ; ~**arian** [-'tɛərɪən] *a* sectaire.

**section** ['sɛkʃən] *n* coupe *f*, section *f* ; *(department)* section ; *(COMM)* rayon *m* ; *(of document)* section, article *m*, paragraphe *m* // *vt* sectionner ; ~**al** *a (drawing)* en coupe.

**sector** ['sɛktə*] *n* secteur *m*.

**secular** ['sɛkjulə*] *a* profane ; laïque ; séculier(ère).

**secure** [sɪ'kjuə*] *a (free from anxiety)* sans inquiétude, sécurisé(e) ; *(firmly fixed)* solide, bien attaché(e) (*or* fermé(e) *etc*) ; *(in safe place)* en lieu sûr, en sûreté // *vt (fix)* fixer, attacher ; *(get)* obtenir, se procurer.

**security** [sɪ'kjurɪtɪ] *n* sécurité *f* ; mesures *fpl* de sécurité ; *(for loan)* caution *f*, garantie *f*.

**sedate** [sɪ'deɪt] *a* calme ; posé(e) // *vt* donner des sédatifs à.

**sedation** [sɪ'deɪʃən] *n (MED)* sédation *f*.

**sedative** ['sɛdɪtɪv] *n* calmant *m*, sédatif *m*.

**sedentary** ['sɛdntrɪ] *a* sédentaire.

**sediment** ['sɛdɪmənt] *n* sédiment *m*, dépôt *m*.

**seduce** [sɪ'dju:s] *vt (gen)* séduire ; **seduction** [-'dʌkʃən] *n* séduction *f* ; **seductive** [-'dʌktɪv] *a* séduisant(e), séducteur(trice).

**see** [si:] *vb (pt saw, pp seen* [sɔ:, si:n]) *vt (gen)* voir ; *(accompany)* : **to** ~ **sb to the door** reconduire *or* raccompagner qn jusqu'à la porte // *vi* voir // *n* évêché *m* ; **to** ~ **that** *(ensure)* veiller à ce que + *sub*, faire en sorte que + *sub*, s'assurer que ; **to** ~ **off** *vt* accompagner (à la gare *or* à l'aéroport *etc)* ; **to** ~ **through** *vt* mener à bonne fin // *vt fus* voir clair dans ; **to** ~ **to** *vt fus* s'occuper de, se charger de ; ~ **you!** au revoir!, à bientôt!

**seed** [si:d] *n* graine *f* ; *(fig)* germe *m* ; *(TENNIS)* tête *f* de série ; **to go to** ~ monter en graine ; *(fig)* se laisser aller ; ~**ling** *n* jeune plant *m*, semis *m* ; ~**y** *a (shabby)* minable, miteux(euse).

**seeing** ['si:ɪŋ] *cj* : ~ **(that)** vu que, étant donné que.

**seek**, *pt,pp* **sought** [si:k, sɔ:t] *vt* chercher, rechercher.

**seem** [si:m] *vi* sembler, paraître ; **there seems to be ...** il semble qu'il y a ... ; **on** ~ **dirait qu'il y a ...** ; ~**ingly** *ad* apparemment.

**seen** [si:n] *pp of* **see**.

**seep** [si:p] *vi* suinter, filtrer.

**seer** [sɪə*] *n* prophète/prophétesse, voyant/e.

**seersucker** ['sɪəsʌkə*] *n* cloqué *m*, étoffe cloquée.

**seesaw** ['si:sɔ:] *n* (jeu *m* de) bascule *f*.

**seethe** [si:ð] *vi* être en effervescence; **to ~ with anger** bouillir de colère.

**see-through** ['si:θru:] *a* transparent(e).

**segment** ['sɛgmənt] *n* segment *m*.

**segregate** ['sɛgrɪgeɪt] *vt* séparer, isoler; **segregation** [-'geɪʃən] *n* ségrégation *f*.

**seismic** ['saɪzmɪk] *a* sismique.

**seize** [si:z] *vt* (*grasp*) saisir, attraper; (*take possession of*) s'emparer de; (*LAW*) saisir; **to ~ (up)on** *vt fus* saisir, sauter sur; **to ~ up** *vi* (*TECH*) se gripper.

**seizure** ['si:ʒə*] *n* (*MED*) crise *f*, attaque *f*; (*LAW*) saisie *f*.

**seldom** ['sɛldəm] *ad* rarement.

**select** [sɪ'lɛkt] *a* choisi(e), d'élite; select *inv* // *vt* sélectionner, choisir; **~ion** [-'lɛkʃən] *n* sélection *f*, choix *m*; **~ive** a sélectif(ive); (*school*) à recrutement sélectif; **~or** *n* (*person*) sélectionneur/euse; (*TECH*) sélecteur *m*.

**self** [sɛlf] *n* (*pl* selves [sɛlvz]): **the ~** le moi *inv* // *prefix* auto-; **~-adhesive** *a* auto-collant(e); **~-assertive** *a* autoritaire; **~-assured** *a* sûr(e) de soi, plein(e) d'assurace; **~-catering** *a* avec cuisine, où l'on peut faire sa cuisine; **~-centred** *a* égocentrique; **~-coloured** *a* uni(e); **~-confidence** *n* confiance *f* en soi; **~-conscious** *a* timide, qui manque d'assurance; **~-contained** *a* (*flat*) avec entrée particulière, indépendant(e); **~-control** *n* maîtrise *f* de soi; **~-defeating** *a* qui a un effet contraire à l'effet recherché; **~-defence** *n* légitime défense *f*; **~-discipline** *n* discipline personnelle; **~-employed** *a* qui travaille à son compte; **~-evident** *a* évident(e), qui va de soi; **~-explanatory** *a* qui se passe d'explication; **~-indulgent** *a* qui ne se refuse rien; **~-interest** *n* intérêt personnel; **~-ish** *a* égoïste; **~-ishness** *n* égoïsme *m*; **~-lessly** *ad* sans penser à soi; **~-pity** *n* apitoiement *m* sur soi-même; **~-portrait** *n* autoportrait *m*; **~-possessed** *a* assuré(e); **~-preservation** *n* instinct *m* de conservation; **~-reliant** *a* indépendant(e); **~-respect** *n* respect *m* de soi, amour-propre *m*; **~-respecting** *a* qui se respecte; **~-righteous** *a* satisfait(e) de soi, pharisaïque; **~-sacrifice** *n* abnégation *f*; **~-satisfied** *a* content(e) de soi, suffisant(e); **~-seal** *a* (enveloppe) auto-collant(e); **~-service** *n* libre-service *m*, self-service *m*; **~-sufficient** *a* indépendant(e); **~-supporting** *a* financièrement indépendant(e); **~-taught** *a* autodidacte.

**sell**, *pt,pp* **sold** [sɛl, səuld] *vt* vendre // *vi* se vendre; **to ~ at** *or* **for 10F** se vendre 10F; **to ~ off** *vt* liquider; **~er** *n* vendeur/euse, marchand/e; **~ing price** *n* prix *m* de vente.

**sellotape** ['sɛləuteɪp] *n* ® papier collant, scotch *m* ®.

**sellout** ['sɛlaut] *n* trahison *f*, capitulation *f*; (*of tickets*): **it was a ~** tous les billets ont été vendus.

**selves** [sɛlvz] *npl of* self.

**semantic** [sɪ'mæntɪk] *a* sémantique; **~s** *n* sémantique *f*.

**semaphore** ['sɛməfɔ:*] *n* signaux *mpl* à bras; (*RAIL*) sémaphore *m*.

**semen** ['si:mən] *n* sperme *m*.

**semi** ['sɛmɪ] *prefix* semi-, demi-; à demi, à moitié; **~-breve** ronde *f*; **~-circle** *n* demi-cercle *m*; **~-colon** *n* point-virgule *m*; **~-conscious** *a* à demi conscient(e); **~-detached (house)** *n* maison jumelée *or* jumelle; **~-final** *n* demi-finale *f*.

**seminar** ['sɛmɪnɑ:*] *n* séminaire *m*.

**semiquaver** ['sɛmɪkweɪvə*] *n* double croche *f*.

**semiskilled** ['sɛmɪ'skɪld] *a*: **~ worker** *n* ouvrier/ère spécialisé/e.

**semitone** ['sɛmɪtəun] *n* (*MUS*) demi-ton *m*.

**semolina** [sɛmə'li:nə] *n* semoule *f*.

**senate** ['sɛnɪt] *n* sénat *m*; **senator** *n* sénateur *m*.

**send**, *pt,pp* **sent** [sɛnd, sɛnt] *vt* envoyer; **to ~ sb to Coventry** mettre qn en quarantaine; **to ~ away** *vt* (*letter, goods*) envoyer, expédier; **to ~ away for** *vt fus* commander par correspondance, se faire envoyer; **to ~ back** *vt* renvoyer; **to ~ for** *vt fus* envoyer chercher; faire venir; **to ~ off** *vt* · (*goods*) envoyer, expédier; (*SPORT: player*) expulser *or* renvoyer du terrain; **to ~ out** *vt* (*invitation*) envoyer (par la poste); **to ~ up** *vt* (*person, price*) faire monter; (*parody*) mettre en boîte, parodier; (*blow up*) faire sauter; **~er** *n* expéditeur/trice; **~-off** *n*: **a good ~-off** des adieux chaleureux.

**senile** ['si:naɪl] *a* sénile.

**senility** [sɪ'nɪlɪtɪ] *n* sénilité *f*.

**senior** ['si:nɪə*] *a* (*older*) aîné(e), plus âgé(e); (*of higher rank*) supérieur(e) // *n* aîné/e; (*in service*) personne *f* qui a plus d'ancienneté; **~ity** [-'ɔrɪtɪ] *n* priorité *f* d'âge, ancienneté *f*.

**sensation** [sɛn'seɪʃən] *n* sensation *f*; **to create a ~** faire sensation; **~al** *a* qui fait sensation; (*marvellous*) sensationnel(le).

**sense** [sɛns] *n* sens *m*; (*feeling*) sentiment *m*; (*meaning*) signification *f*; (*wisdom*) bon sens // *vt* sentir, pressentir; **it makes ~** c'est logique; **~s** *npl* raison *f*; **~less** *a* insensé(e), stupide; (*unconscious*) sans connaissance; **anyone in his ~s** tout homme sensé.

**sensibility** [sɛnsɪ'bɪlɪtɪ] *n* sensibilité *f*; **sensibilities** *npl* susceptibilité *f*.

**sensible** ['sɛnsɪbl] *a* sensé(e), raisonnable; sage; pratique.

**sensitive** ['sɛnsɪtɪv] *a*: **~ (to)** sensible (à); **sensitivity** [-'tɪvɪtɪ] *n* sensibilité *f*.

**sensual** ['sɛnsjuəl] *a* sensuel(le).

**sensuous** ['sɛnsjuəs] *a* voluptueux(euse), sensuel(le).

**sent** [sɛnt] *pt,pp of* send.

**sentence** ['sɛntns] *n* (*LING*) phrase *f*; (*LAW: judgment*) condamnation *f*, sentence *f*; (: *punishment*) peine *f* // *vt*: **to ~ sb to death/to 5 years** condamner qn à mort/à 5 ans.

**sentiment** ['sɛntɪmənt] *n* sentiment *m*; (*opinion*) opinion *f*, avis *m*; **~al** [-'mɛntl] *a* sentimental(e); **~ality** [-'tælɪtɪ] *n* sentimentalité *f*, sensiblerie *f*.

**sentry** ['sɛntrɪ] n sentinelle f, factionnaire m.

**separable** ['sɛprəbl] a séparable.

**separate** a ['sɛprɪt] séparé(e), indépendant(e), différent(e) // vb ['sɛpəreɪt] vt séparer // vi se séparer; ~ly ad séparément; ~s npl (clothes) coordonnés mpl; **separation** [-'reɪʃən] n séparation f.

**September** [sɛp'tɛmbə*] n septembre m.

**septic** ['sɛptɪk] a septique; (wound) infecté(e).

**sequel** ['si:kwl] n conséquence f; séquelles fpl; (of story) suite f.

**sequence** ['si:kwəns] n ordre m, suite f; ~ of tenses concordance f des temps.

**sequin** ['si:kwɪn] n paillette f.

**serenade** [sɛrə'neɪd] n sérénade f // vt donner une sérénade à.

**serene** [sɪ'ri:n] a serein(e), calme, paisible; **serenity** [sə'rɛnɪtɪ] n sérénité f, calme m.

**sergeant** ['sa:dʒənt] n sergent m; (POLICE) brigadier m.

**serial** ['sɪərɪəl] n feuilleton m // a (number) de série; ~ize vt publier (or adapter) en feuilleton.

**series** ['sɪəri:s] n série f; (PUBLISHING) collection f.

**serious** ['sɪərɪəs] a sérieux(euse), réfléchi(e); grave; ~ly ad sérieusement, gravement; ~ness n sérieux m, gravité f.

**sermon** ['sə:mən] n sermon m.

**serrated** [sɪ'reɪtɪd] a en dents de scie.

**serum** ['sɪərəm] n sérum m.

**servant** ['sə:vənt] n domestique m/f; (fig) serviteur/servante.

**serve** [sə:v] vt (employer etc) servir, être au service de; (purpose) servir à; (customer, food, meal) servir; (apprenticeship) faire, accomplir; (prison term) faire; purger // vi (also TENNIS) servir; (be useful): **to ~ as/for/to do** servir de/à/faire // n (TENNIS) service m; **it ~s him right** c'est bien fait pour lui; **to ~ out, ~ up** vt (food) servir.

**service** ['sə:vɪs] n (gen) service m; (AUT: maintenance) révision f // vt (car, washing machine) réviser; **the S~s** les forces armées; **to be of ~ to sb, to do sb a ~** rendre service à qn; **to put one's car in for (a) ~** donner sa voiture à réviser; **dinner ~** n service m de table; ~**able** a pratique, commode; ~ **area** n (on motorway) aire f de services; ~**man** n militaire m; ~ **station** n station-service f.

**serviette** [sə:vɪ'ɛt] n serviette f (de table).

**servile** ['sə:vaɪl] a servile.

**session** ['sɛʃən] n (sitting) séance f; (SCOL) année f scolaire (or universitaire); **to be in ~** siéger, être en session or en séance.

**set** [sɛt] n série f, assortiment m; (of tools etc) jeu m; (RADIO, TV) poste m; (TENNIS) set m; (group of people) cercle m, milieu m; (CINEMA) plateau m; (THEATRE: stage) scène f; (: scenery) décor m; (MATH) ensemble m; (HAIRDRESSING) mise f en plis // a (fixed) fixe, déterminé(e); (ready) prêt(e) // vb (pt, pp set) (place) mettre, poser, placer; (fix) fixer; (adjust) régler; (decide: rules etc) fixer, choisir; (TYP) composer // vi (sun) se coucher; (jam, jelly, concrete) prendre; **to be ~ on doing** être résolu à faire; **to be (dead) ~ against** être (totalement) opposé à; **to ~ (to music)** mettre en musique; **to ~ on fire** mettre le feu à; **to ~ free** libérer; **to ~ sth going** déclencher qch; **to ~ sail** partir, prendre la mer; **to ~ about** vt fus (task) entreprendre, se mettre à; **to ~ aside** vt mettre de côté; **to ~ back** vt (in time): **to ~ back (by)** retarder (de); **to ~ off** vi se mettre en route, partir // vt (bomb) faire exploser; (cause to start) déclencher; (show up well) mettre en valeur, faire valoir; **to ~ out** vi: **to ~ out to do** entreprendre de; avoir pour but or intention de // vt (arrange) disposer; (state) présenter, exposer; **to ~ up** vt (organization) fonder, constituer; (record) établir; (monument) ériger; **to ~ up shop** (fig) s'établir, s'installer; ~**back** n (hitch) revers m, contretemps m.

**settee** [sɛ'ti:] n canapé m.

**setting** ['sɛtɪŋ] n cadre m; (of jewel) monture f.

**settle** ['sɛtl] vt (argument, matter) régler; (problem) résoudre; (MED: calm) calmer // vi (bird, dust etc) se poser; (sediment) se déposer; (also: ~ down) s'installer, se fixer; se calmer; se ranger; **to ~ to sth** se mettre sérieusement à qch; **to ~ for sth** accepter qch, se contenter de qch; **to ~ in** vi s'installer; **to ~ on sth** opter or se décider pour qch; **to ~ up with sb** régler (ce que l'on doit à) qn; ~**ment** n (payment) règlement m; (agreement) accord m; (colony) colonie f; (village etc) établissement m; hameau m; ~**r** n colon m.

**setup** ['sɛtʌp] n (arrangement) manière f dont les choses sont organisées; (situation) situation f, allure f des choses.

**seven** ['sɛvn] num sept; ~**teen** num dix-sept; ~**th** num septième; ~**ty** num soixante-dix.

**sever** ['sɛvə*] vt couper, trancher; (relations) rompre.

**several** ['sɛvərl] a,pronoun plusieurs (m/fpl); ~ **of us** plusieurs d'entre nous.

**severance** ['sɛvərəns] n (of relations) rupture f; ~ **pay** n indemnité f de licenciement.

**severe** [sɪ'vɪə*] a sévère, strict(e); (serious) grave, sérieux(euse); (hard) rigoureux(euse), dur(e); (plain) sévère, austère; **severity** [sɪ'vɛrɪtɪ] n sévérité f; gravité f; rigueur f.

**sew,** pt **sewed**, pp **sewn** [səu, səud, səun] vt,vi coudre; **to ~ up** vt (re)coudre; **it is all sewn up** (fig) c'est dans le sac or dans la poche.

**sewage** ['su:ɪdʒ] n vidange(s) f(pl).

**sewer** ['su:ə*] n égout m.

**sewing** ['səuɪŋ] n couture f; ~ **machine** n machine f à coudre.

**sewn** [səun] pp of **sew.**

**sex** [sɛks] n sexe m; **to have ~ with** avoir des rapports (sexuels) avec; ~ **act** n acte sexuel.

**sextet** [sɛks'tɛt] n sextuor m.

**sexual** ['sɛksjuəl] a sexuel(le).

**sexy** ['sɛksɪ] a sexy inv.

**shabby** ['ʃæbɪ] a miteux(euse); (behaviour) mesquin(e), méprisable.

**shack** [ʃæk] n cabane f, hutte f.
**shackles** ['ʃæklz] npl chaînes fpl, entraves fpl.
**shade** [ʃeɪd] n ombre f; (for lamp) abat-jour m inv; (of colour) nuance f, ton m; (small quantity): **a ~ of** un soupçon de // vt abriter du soleil, ombrager; **in the ~** à l'ombre; **a ~ smaller** un tout petit peu plus petit.
**shadow** ['ʃædəu] n ombre f // vt (follow) filer; **~ cabinet** n (POL) cabinet parallèle formé par le parti qui n'est pas au pouvoir; **~y** a ombragé(e); (dim) vague, indistinct(e).
**shady** ['ʃeɪdɪ] a ombragé(e); (fig: dishonest) louche, véreux(euse).
**shaft** [ʃɑːft] n (of arrow, spear) hampe f; (AUT, TECH) arbre m; (of mine) puits m; (of lift) cage f; (of light) rayon m, trait m.
**shaggy** ['ʃægɪ] a hirsute; en broussaille.
**shake** [ʃeɪk] vb (pt **shook**, pp **shaken** [ʃuk, 'ʃeɪkn]) vt secouer; (bottle, cocktail) agiter; (house, confidence) ébranler // vi trembler // n secousse f; **to ~ hands with sb** serrer la main à qn; **to ~ off** vt secouer; (fig) se débarrasser de; **to ~ up** vt secouer; **~-up** n grand remaniement; **shaky** a (hand, voice) tremblant(e); (building) branlant(e), peu solide.
**shale** [ʃeɪl] n schiste argileux.
**shall** [ʃæl] auxiliary vb: **I ~ go** j'irai.
**shallot** [ʃə'lɔt] n échalote f.
**shallow** ['ʃæləu] a peu profond(e); (fig) superficiel(le), qui manque de profondeur.
**sham** [ʃæm] n frime f; (jewellery, furniture) imitation f // a feint(e), simulé(e) // vt feindre, simuler.
**shambles** ['ʃæmblz] n confusion f, pagaïe f, fouillis m.
**shame** [ʃeɪm] n honte f // vt faire honte à; **it is a ~ (that/to do)** c'est dommage (que + sub/de faire); **what a ~!** quel dommage!; **~faced** a honteux(euse), penaud(e); **~ful** a honteux(euse), scandaleux(euse); **~less** a éhonté(e), effronté(e); (immodest) impudique.
**shampoo** [ʃæm'puː] n shampooing m // vt faire un shampooing à.
**shamrock** ['ʃæmrɔk] n trèfle m (emblème national de l'Irlande).
**shandy** ['ʃændɪ] n bière panachée.
**shan't** [ʃɑːnt] = **shall not**.
**shanty** ['ʃæntɪ] n cabane f, baraque f; **~town** n bidonville m.
**shape** [ʃeɪp] n forme f // vt façonner, modeler; (statement) formuler; (sb's ideas) former; (sb's life) déterminer // vi (also: **~ up**) (events) prendre tournure; (person) faire des progrès, s'en sortir; **to take ~** prendre forme or tournure; **-shaped** suffix: **heart-shaped** en forme de cœur; **~less** a informe, sans forme; **~ly** a bien proportionné(e), beau(belle).
**share** [ʃɛə*] n (thing received, contribution) part f; (COMM) action f // vt partager; (have in common) avoir en commun; **to ~ out (among or between)** partager (entre); **~holder** n actionnaire m/f.
**shark** [ʃɑːk] n requin m.
**sharp** [ʃɑːp] a (razor, knife) tranchant(e), bien aiguisé(e); (point) aigu(guë); (nose,

chin) pointu(e); (outline) net(te); (cold, pain) vif(vive); (MUS) dièse; (voice) coupant(e); (person: quick-witted) vif(vive), éveillé(e); (: unscrupulous) malhonnête // n (MUS) dièse m // ad: **at 2 o'clock ~** à 2 heures pile or tapantes; **look ~!** dépêche-toi!; **~en** vt aiguiser; (pencil) tailler; (fig) aviver; **~ener** n (also: **pencil ~ener**) taille-crayon(s) m inv; (also: **knife ~ener**) aiguisoir m; **~-eyed** a à qui rien n'échappe; **~-witted** a à l'esprit vif, malin(igne).
**shatter** ['ʃætə*] vt fracasser, briser, faire voler en éclats; (fig: upset) bouleverser; (: ruin) briser, ruiner // vi voler en éclats, se briser, se fracasser.
**shave** [ʃeɪv] vt raser // vi se raser // n: **to have a ~** se raser; **~n** a (head) rasé(e); **~r** n (also: **electric ~**) rasoir m électrique.
**shaving** ['ʃeɪvɪŋ] n (action) rasage m; **~s** npl (of wood etc) copeaux mpl; **~ brush** n blaireau m; **~ cream** n crème f à raser; **~ soap** n savon m à barbe.
**shawl** [ʃɔːl] n châle m.
**she** [ʃiː] pronoun elle // cpd: **~-** femelle; **~-cat** n chatte f; **~-elephant** n éléphant m femelle; NB: for ships, countries follow the gender of your translation.
**sheaf, sheaves** [ʃiːf, ʃiːvz] n gerbe f.
**shear** [ʃɪə*] vt (pt **~ed**, pp **~ed** or **shorn** [ʃɔːn]) (sheep) tondre; **to ~ off** vt tondre; (branch) élaguer; **~s** npl (for hedge) cisaille(s) f(pl).
**sheath** [ʃiːθ] n gaine f, fourreau m, étui m; (contraceptive) préservatif m; **~e** [ʃiːð] vt gainer; (sword) rengainer.
**sheaves** [ʃiːvz] npl of **sheaf**.
**shed** [ʃɛd] n remise f, resserre f // vt (pt,pp **shed**) (leaves, fur etc) perdre; (tears) verser, répandre.
**she'd** [ʃiːd] = **she had**; **she would**.
**sheep** [ʃiːp] n, pl inv mouton m; **~dog** n chien m de berger; **~ish** a penaud(e), timide; **~skin** n peau f de mouton.
**sheer** [ʃɪə*] a (utter) pur(e), pur et simple; (steep) à pic, abrupt(e); (almost transparent) extrêmement fin(e) // ad à pic, abruptement.
**sheet** [ʃiːt] n (on bed) drap m; (of paper) feuille f; (of glass, metal) feuille, plaque f; **~ lightning** n éclair m en nappe(s); **~ metal** n tôle f.
**sheik(h)** [ʃeɪk] n cheik m.
**shelf, shelves** [ʃɛlf, ʃɛlvz] n étagère f, rayon m; **set of shelves** rayonnage m.
**shell** [ʃɛl] n (on beach) coquillage m; (of egg, nut etc) coquille f; (explosive) obus m; (of building) carcasse f // vt (crab, prawn etc) décortiquer; (peas) écosser; (MIL) bombarder (d'obus).
**she'll** [ʃiːl] = **she will**; **she shall**.
**shellfish** ['ʃɛlfɪʃ] n, pl inv (crab etc) crustacé m; (scallop etc) coquillage m; (pl: as food) crustacés, coquillages.
**shelter** ['ʃɛltə*] n abri m, refuge m // vt abriter, protéger; (give lodging to) donner asile à // vi s'abriter, se mettre à l'abri; **~ed** a (life) retiré(e), à l'abri des soucis; (spot) abrité(e).
**shelve** [ʃɛlv] vt (fig) mettre en suspens or en sommeil; **~s** npl of **shelf**.

**shepherd** ['ʃɛpəd] n berger m // vt (guide) guider, escorter; **~ess** n bergère f; **~'s pie** n ≈ hachis m Parmentier.

**sheriff** ['ʃɛrɪf] n shérif m.

**sherry** ['ʃɛrɪ] n xérès m, sherry m.

**she's** [ʃiːz] = **she is**; **she has**.

**shield** [ʃiːld] n bouclier m // vt: **to ~ (from)** protéger (de or contre).

**shift** [ʃɪft] n (change) changement m; (of workers) équipe f, poste m // vt déplacer, changer de place; (remove) enlever // vi changer de place, bouger; **~ work** n travail m en équipe or par relais or par roulement; **~y** a sournois(e); (eyes) fuyant(e).

**shilling** ['ʃɪlɪŋ] n shilling m (= 12 old pence; 20 in a pound).

**shilly-shally** ['ʃɪlɪʃælɪ] vi tergiverser, atermoyer.

**shimmer** ['ʃɪmə*] n miroitement m, chatoiement m // vi miroiter, chatoyer.

**shin** [ʃɪn] n tibia m.

**shine** [[aɪn] n éclat m, brillant m // vb (pt,pp shone [ʃɔn]) vi briller // vt faire briller or reluire; (torch): **to ~ sth on** braquer qch sur.

**shingle** ['ʃɪŋgl] n (on beach) galets mpl; (on roof) bardeau m; **~s** n (MED) zona m.

**shiny** ['ʃaɪnɪ] a brillant(e).

**ship** [ʃɪp] n bateau m; (large) navire m // vt transporter (par mer); (send) expédier (par mer); (load) charger, embarquer; **~building** n construction navale; **~ canal** n canal m maritime or de navigation; **~ment** n cargaison f; **~per** n affréteur m, expéditeur m; **~ping** n (ships) navires mpl; (traffic) navigation f; **~shape** a en ordre impeccable; **~wreck** n épave f; (event) naufrage m; **~yard** n chantier naval.

**shire** ['ʃaɪə*] n comté m.

**shirk** [ʃəːk] vt esquiver, se dérober à.

**shirt** [ʃəːt] n (man's) chemise f; **in ~ sleeves** en bras de chemise; **~y** a (col) de mauvais poil.

**shiver** ['ʃɪvə*] n frisson m // vi frissonner.

**shoal** [ʃəul] n (of fish) banc m.

**shock** [ʃɔk] n (impact) choc m, heurt m; (ELEC) secousse f; (emotional) choc, secousse f; (MED) commotion f, choc // vt choquer, scandaliser; bouleverser; **~ absorber** n amortisseur m; **~ing** a choquant(e), scandaleux(euse); épouvantable; révoltant(e); **~proof** a anti-choc inv.

**shod** [ʃɔd] pt,pp of **shoe**; **well-~** a bien chaussé(e).

**shoddy** ['ʃɔdɪ] a de mauvaise qualité, mal fait(e).

**shoe** [ʃuː] n chaussure f, soulier m; (also: **horse~**) fer m à cheval // vt (pt,pp shod [ʃɔd]) (horse) ferrer; **~brush** n brosse f à chaussures; **~horn** n chausse-pied m; **~lace** n lacet m (de soulier); **~ polish** n cirage m; **~shop** n magasin m de chaussures; **~tree** n embauchoir m.

**shone** [ʃɔn] pt,pp of **shine**.

**shook** [ʃuk] pt of **shake**.

**shoot** [ʃuːt] n (on branch, seedling) pousse f // vb (pt,pp shot [ʃɔt]) vt (game) chasser; tirer; abattre; (person) blesser (or tuer)

d'un coup de fusil (or de revolver); (execute) fusiller; (film) tourner // vi (with gun, bow): **to ~ (at)** tirer (sur); (FOOTBALL) shooter, tirer; **to ~ down** vt (plane) abattre; **to ~ in/out** vi entrer/sortir comme une flèche; **to ~ up** vi (fig) monter en flèche; **~ing** n (shots) coups mpl de feu, fusillade f; (HUNTING) chasse f; **~ing range** n stand m de tir; **~ing star** n étoile filante.

**shop** [ʃɔp] n magasin m; (workshop) atelier m // vi (also: go **~ping**) faire ses courses or ses achats; **~ assistant** n vendeur/euse; **~ floor** n ateliers mpl; (fig) ouvriers mpl; **~keeper** n marchand/e, commerçant/e; **~lifter** n voleur/euse à l'étalage; **~lifting** n vol m à l'étalage; **~per** n personne f qui fait ses courses, acheteur/euse; **~ping** n (goods) achats mpl, provisions fpl; **~ping bag** n sac m (à provisions); **~ping centre**, **~ping center** (US) n centre commercial; **~-soiled** a défraîchi(e), qui a fait la vitrine; **~ steward** n (INDUSTRY) délégué/e syndical(e); **~ window** n vitrine f.

**shore** [ʃɔː*] n (of sea, lake) rivage m, rive f // vt: **to ~ (up)** étayer.

**shorn** [ʃɔːn] pp of **shear**; **~ of** dépouillé(e) de.

**short** [ʃɔːt] a (not long) court(e); (soon finished) court, bref(brève); (person, step) petit(e); (curt) brusque, sec(sèche); (insufficient) insuffisant(e) // n (also: **~ film**) court métrage; **(a pair of) ~s** un short; **to be ~ of sth** être à court de or manquer de qch; **I'm 3 ~** il m'en manque 3; **in ~** bref; en bref; **~ of doing** à moins de faire; **everything ~ of** tout sauf; **it is ~ for** c'est l'abréviation or le diminutif de; **to cut ~** (speech, visit) abréger, écourter; (person) couper la parole à; **to fall ~ of** ne pas être à la hauteur de; **to stop ~** s'arrêter net; **to stop ~ of** ne pas aller jusqu'à; **~age** n manque m, pénurie f; **~bread** n ≈ sablé m; **~-circuit** n court-circuit m // vt court-circuiter // vi se mettre en court-circuit; **~coming** n défaut m; **~(crust) pastry** pâte brisée; **~cut** n raccourci m; **~en** vt raccourcir; (text, visit) abréger; **~ening** n (CULIN) matière grasse; **~hand** n sténo(graphie) f; **~hand typist** n sténodactylo m/f; **~list** n (for job) liste f des candidats sélectionnés; **~-lived** a de courte durée; **~ly** ad bientôt, sous peu; **~ness** n brièveté f; **~-sighted** a myope; (fig) qui manque de clairvoyance; **~ story** n nouvelle f; **~-tempered** a qui s'emporte facilement; **~-term** a (effect) à court terme; **~wave** n (RADIO) ondes courtes.

**shot** [ʃɔt] pt,pp of **shoot** // n coup m (de feu); (person) tireur m; (try) coup, essai m; (injection) piqûre f; (PHOT) photo f; **like a ~** comme une flèche; (very readily) sans hésiter; **~gun** n fusil m de chasse.

**should** [ʃud] auxiliary vb: **I ~ go now** je devrais partir maintenant; **he ~ be there now** il devrait être arrivé maintenant; **I ~ go if I were you** si j'étais vous j'irais; **I ~ like to** j'aimerais bien, volontiers.

**shoulder** ['ʃəuldə*] n épaule f; (of road): **hard ~** accotement m // vt (fig) endosser, se charger de; **~ bag** n sac m à bandoulière ; ∼ **blade** n omoplate f ; ∼ **strap** n bretelle f.

**shouldn't** ['ʃudnt] = **should not**.

**shout** [ʃaut] n cri m // vt crier // vi crier, pousser des cris ; **to give sb a** ∼ appeler qn ; **to** ∼ **down** vt huer ; ∼**ing** n cris mpl.

**shove** [ʃʌv] vt pousser ; (col: put): **to** ∼ **sth in** fourrer or ficher qch dans ; **to** ∼ **off** vi (NAUT) pousser au large ; (fig: col) ficher le camp.

**shovel** ['ʃʌvl] n pelle f // vt pelleter, enlever (or enfourner) à la pelle.

**show** [ʃəu] n (of emotion) manifestation f, démonstration f ; (semblance) semblant m, apparence f ; (exhibition) exposition f ; salon m ; (THEATRE) spectacle m, représentation f ; (CINEMA) séance f // vb (pt ∼**ed**, pp **shown** [ʃəun]) vt montrer ; (courage etc) faire preuve de, manifester ; (exhibit) exposer // vi se voir, être visible ; **to** ∼ **sb in** faire entrer qn ; **to** ∼ **off** vi (pej) crâner // vt (display) faire valoir ; (pej) faire étalage de ; **to** ∼ **sb out** reconduire qn (jusqu'à la porte) ; **to** ∼ **up** vi (stand out) ressortir ; (col: turn up) se montrer // vt démontrer ; (unmask) démasquer, dénoncer ; ∼ **business** n le monde du spectacle ; ∼**down** n épreuve f de force.

**shower** ['ʃauə*] n (rain) averse f ; (of stones etc) pluie f, grêle f ; (also: ∼**bath**) douche f // vi prendre une douche, se doucher // vt: **to** ∼ **sb with** (gifts etc) combler qn de ; (abuse etc) accabler qn de ; (missiles) bombarder qn de ; ∼**proof** a imperméable ; ∼**y** a (weather) pluvieux(euse).

**showground** ['ʃəugraund] n champ m de foire.

**showing** ['ʃəuiŋ] n (of film) projection f.

**show jumping** ['ʃəudʒʌmpiŋ] n concours m hippique.

**showmanship** ['ʃəumənʃip] n art m de la mise en scène.

**shown** [ʃəun] pp of **show**.

**show-off** ['ʃəuɔf] n (col: person) crâneur/euse, m'as-tu-vu/e.

**showpiece** ['ʃəupi:s] n (of exhibition etc) joyau m, clou m.

**showroom** ['ʃəurum] n magasin m or salle f d'exposition.

**shrank** [ʃræŋk] pt of **shrink**.

**shrapnel** ['ʃræpnl] n éclats mpl d'obus.

**shred** [ʃrɛd] n (gen pl) lambeau m, petit morceau // vt mettre en lambeaux, déchirer ; (CULIN) râper ; couper en lanières.

**shrewd** [ʃru:d] a astucieux(euse), perspicace ; ∼**ness** n perspicacité f.

**shriek** [ʃri:k] n cri perçant or aigu, hurlement m // vt,vi hurler, crier.

**shrift** [ʃrift] n: **to give sb short** ∼ expédier qn sans ménagements.

**shrill** [ʃril] a perçant(e), aigu(guë), strident(e).

**shrimp** [ʃrimp] n crevette grise.

**shrine** [ʃrain] n châsse f ; (place) lieu m de pèlerinage.

**shrink, pt shrank, pp shrunk** [ʃriŋk, ʃræŋk, ʃrʌŋk] vi se réduire ; (fig) se réduire ; se contracter // vt (wool) (faire) rétrécir // n (col: pej) psychanalyste ; ∼**age** n rétrécissement m.

**shrivel** ['ʃrivl] (also: ∼ **up**) vt ratatiner, flétrir // vi se ratatiner, se flétrir.

**shroud** [ʃraud] n linceul m // vt: ∼**ed in mystery** enveloppé(e) de mystère.

**Shrove Tuesday** ['ʃrəuv'tju:zdi] n (le) Mardi gras.

**shrub** [ʃrʌb] n arbuste m ; ∼**bery** n massif m d'arbustes.

**shrug** [ʃrʌg] n haussement m d'épaules // vt,vi: **to** ∼ **(one's shoulders)** hausser les épaules ; **to** ∼ **off** vt faire fi de.

**shrunk** [ʃrʌŋk] pp of **shrink** ; ∼**en** a ratatiné(e).

**shudder** ['ʃʌdə*] n frisson m, frémissement m // vi frissonner, frémir.

**shuffle** ['ʃʌfl] vt (cards) battre ; **to** ∼ **(one's feet)** traîner les pieds.

**shun** [ʃʌn] vt éviter, fuir.

**shunt** [ʃʌnt] vt (RAIL: direct) aiguiller ; (: divert) détourner // vi: **to** ∼ **(to and fro)** faire la navette ; ∼**ing** n (RAIL.) triage m.

**shush** [ʃuʃ] excl chut!

**shut, pt, pp shut** [ʃʌt] vt fermer // vi (se) fermer ; **to** ∼ **down** vt, vi fermer définitivement ; **to** ∼ **off** vt couper, arrêter ; **to** ∼ **up** vi (col: keep quiet) se taire // vt (close) fermer ; (silence) faire taire ; ∼**ter** n volet m ; (PHOT) obturateur m.

**shuttle** ['ʃʌtl] n navette f ; (also: ∼ **service**) (service m de) navette f.

**shuttlecock** ['ʃʌtlkɔk] n volant m (de badminton).

**shy** [ʃai] a timide ; **to fight** ∼ **of** se dérober devant ; ∼**ness** n timidité f.

**Siamese** [saiə'mi:z] a: ∼ **cat** chat siamois.

**Sicily** ['sisili] n Sicile f.

**sick** [sik] a (ill) malade ; (vomiting): **to be** ∼ vomir ; (humour) noir(e), macabre ; **to feel** ∼ avoir envie de vomir, avoir mal au cœur ; **to be** ∼ **of** (fig) en avoir assez de ; ∼ **bay** n infirmerie f ; ∼**en** vt écœurer ; ∼**ening** a (fig) écœurant(e), révoltant(e), répugnant(e).

**sickle** ['sikl] n faucille f.

**sick**: ∼ **leave** n congé m de maladie ; ∼**ly** a maladif(ive), souffreteux(euse) ; (causing nausea) écœurant(e) ; ∼**ness** n maladie f ; (vomiting) vomissement(s) m(pl) ; ∼ **pay** n indemnité f de maladie.

**side** [said] n côté m ; (of lake, road) bord m // cpd (door, entrance) latéral(e) // vi: **to** ∼ **with sb** prendre le parti de qn, se ranger du côté de qn ; **by the** ∼ **of** au bord de ; **by** ∼ côte à côte ; **from all** ∼**s** de tous côtés ; **to take** ∼**s (with)** prendre parti (pour) ; ∼**board** n buffet m ; ∼**boards**, ∼**burns** npl (whiskers) pattes fpl ; ∼ **effect** n (MED) effet m secondaire ; ∼**light** n (AUT) veilleuse f ; ∼**line** n (SPORT) (ligne f de) touche f ; (fig) activité f secondaire ; ∼**long** a oblique, de coin ; ∼ **road** n petite route, route transversale ; ∼**saddle** ad en amazone ; ∼ **show** n attraction f ; ∼**track** vt (fig) faire dévier de son sujet ; ∼**walk** n (US) trottoir m ; ∼**ways** ad de côté.

**siding** ['saidiŋ] n (RAIL) voie f de garage.

**sidle** ['saidl] vi: **to** ∼ **up (to)** s'approcher furtivement (de).

**siege** [si:dʒ] n siège m.

**sieve** [sɪv] *n* tamis *m*, passoire *f* // *vt* tamiser, passer (au tamis).

**sift** [sɪft] *vt* passer au tamis *or* au crible; (*fig*) passer au crible.

**sigh** [saɪ] *n* soupir *m* // *vi* soupirer, pousser un soupir.

**sight** [saɪt] *n* (*faculty*) vue *f*; (*spectacle*) spectacle *m*; (*on gun*) mire *f* // *vt* apercevoir; **in ~** visible; (*fig*) en vue; **out of ~** hors de vue; **~seeing** *n* tourisme *m*; **to go ~seeing** faire du tourisme; **~seer** *n* touriste *m/f*.

**sign** [saɪn] *n* (*gen*) signe *m*; (*with hand etc*) signe, geste *m*; (*notice*) panneau *m*, écriteau *m* // *vt* signer; **to ~ in/out** signer le registre (en arrivant/partant); **to ~ up** (*MIL*) *vt* engager // *vi* s'engager.

**signal** ['sɪgnl] *n* signal *m* // *vt* (*person*) faire signe à; (*message*) communiquer par signaux.

**signature** ['sɪgnətʃə*] *n* signature *f*; **~ tune** *n* indicatif musical.

**signet ring** ['sɪgnətrɪŋ] *n* chevalière *f*.

**significance** [sɪg'nɪfɪkəns] *n* signification *f*; importance *f*.

**significant** [sɪg'nɪfɪkənt] *a* significatif(ive); (*important*) important(e), considérable.

**signify** ['sɪgnɪfaɪ] *vt* signifier.

**sign language** ['saɪnlæŋgwɪdʒ] *n* langage *m* par signes.

**signpost** ['saɪnpəust] *n* poteau indicateur.

**silence** ['saɪlns] *n* silence *m* // *vt* faire taire, réduire au silence; **~r** *n* (*on gun*, *AUT*) silencieux *m*.

**silent** ['saɪlnt] *a* silencieux(euse); (*film*) muet(te); **~ly** *ad* silencieusement.

**silhouette** [sɪlu:'ɛt] *n* silhouette *f* // *vt*: **~d against** se profilant sur, se découpant contre.

**silicon chip** ['sɪlɪkən'tʃɪp] *n* plaquette *f* de silicium.

**silk** [sɪlk] *n* soie *f* // *cpd* de *or* en soie; **~y** *a* soyeux(euse).

**silly** ['sɪlɪ] *a* stupide, sot(te), bête.

**silt** [sɪlt] *n* vase *f*; limon *m*.

**silver** ['sɪlvə*] *n* argent *m*; (*money*) monnaie *f* (en pièces d'argent); (*also*: **~ware**) argenterie *f* // *cpd* d'argent, en argent; **~ paper** *n* papier *m* d'argent *or* d'étain; **~-plated** *a* plaqué(e) argent; **~smith** *n* orfèvre *m/f*; **~y** *a* argenté(e).

**similar** ['sɪmɪlə*] *a*: **~ (to)** semblable (à); **~ity** [-'lærɪtɪ] *n* ressemblance *f*, similarité *f*; **~ly** *ad* de la même façon, de même.

**simile** ['sɪmɪlɪ] *n* comparaison *f*.

**simmer** ['sɪmə*] *vi* cuire à feu doux, mijoter.

**simple** ['sɪmpl] *a* simple; **~-minded** *a* simplet(te), simple d'esprit; **simplicity** [-'plɪsɪtɪ] *n* simplicité *f*; **simplification** [-'keɪʃən] *n* simplification *f*; **simplify** ['sɪmplɪfaɪ] *vt* simplifier; **simply** *ad* simplement; avec simplicité.

**simulate** ['sɪmjuleɪt] *vt* simuler, feindre; **simulation** [-'leɪʃən] *n* simulation *f*.

**simultaneous** [sɪməl'teɪnɪəs] *a* simultané(e); **~ly** *ad* simultanément.

**sin** [sɪn] *n* péché *m* // *vi* pécher.

**since** [sɪns] *ad,prep* depuis // *cj* (*time*) depuis que; (*because*) puisque, étant donné que, comme; **~ then** depuis ce moment-là.

**sincere** [sɪn'sɪə*] *a* sincère; **sincerity** [-'serɪtɪ] *n* sincérité *f*.

**sine** [saɪn] *n* (*MATH*) sinus *m*.

**sinew** ['sɪnju:] *n* tendon *m*; **~s** *npl* muscles *mpl*.

**sinful** ['sɪnful] *a* coupable.

**sing**, *pt* **sang**, *pp* **sung** [sɪŋ, sæŋ, sʌŋ] *vt,vi* chanter.

**singe** [sɪndʒ] *vt* brûler légèrement; (*clothes*) roussir.

**singer** ['sɪŋə*] *n* chanteur/euse.

**singing** ['sɪŋɪŋ] *n* chant *m*.

**single** ['sɪŋgl] *a* seul(e), unique; (*unmarried*) célibataire; (*not double*) simple // *n* (*also*: **~ ticket**) aller *m* (simple); (*record*) 45 tours *m*; **~s** *npl* (*TENNIS*) simple *m*; **to ~ out** *vt* choisir; distinguer; **~ bed** *n* lit à une place; **~-breasted** *a* droit(e); **in ~ file** en file indienne; **~-handed** *ad* tout(e) seul(e), sans (aucune) aide; **~-minded** *a* résolu(e), tenace; **~ room** *n* chambre *f* à un lit *or* pour une personne.

**singlet** ['sɪŋglɪt] *n* tricot *m* de corps.

**singly** ['sɪŋglɪ] *ad* séparément.

**singular** ['sɪŋgjulə*] *a* singulier(ère), étrange; remarquable; (*LING*) (au) singulier, du singulier // *n* (*LING*) singulier *m*; **~ly** *ad* singulièrement; remarquablement; étrangement.

**sinister** ['sɪnɪstə*] *a* sinistre.

**sink** [sɪŋk] *n* évier *m* // *vb* (*pt* **sank**, *pp* **sunk** [sæŋk, sʌŋk]) *vt* (*ship*) (faire) couler, faire sombrer; (*foundations*) creuser; (*piles etc*): **to ~ sth into** enfoncer qch dans // *vi* couler, sombrer; (*ground etc*) s'affaisser; **to ~ in** *vi* s'enfoncer, pénétrer; **a ~ing feeling** un serrement de cœur.

**sinner** ['sɪnə*] *n* pécheur/eresse.

**Sino-** ['saɪnəu] *prefix* sino-.

**sinuous** ['sɪnjuəs] *a* sinueux(euse).

**sinus** ['saɪnəs] *n* (*ANAT*) sinus *m inv*.

**sip** [sɪp] *n* petite gorgée // *vt* boire à petites gorgées.

**siphon** ['saɪfən] *n* siphon *m*; **to ~ off** *vt* siphonner.

**sir** [sə*] *n* monsieur *m*; **S~ John Smith** sir John Smith; **yes ~** oui Monsieur.

**siren** ['saɪərn] *n* sirène *f*.

**sirloin** ['sə:lɔɪn] *n* aloyau *m*.

**sirocco** [sɪ'rɔkəu] *n* sirocco *m*.

**sissy** ['sɪsɪ] *n* (*col*: *coward*) poule mouillée.

**sister** ['sɪstə*] *n* sœur *f*; (*nun*) religieuse *f*, (bonne) sœur; (*nurse*) infirmière *f* en chef; **~-in-law** *n* belle-sœur *f*.

**sit**, *pt,pp* **sat** [sɪt, sæt] *vi* s'asseoir; (*assembly*) être en séance, siéger; (*for painter*) poser // *vt* (*exam*) passer, se présenter à; **to ~ tight** ne pas bouger; **to ~ down** *vi* s'asseoir; **to ~ up** *vi* s'asseoir; (*not go to bed*) rester debout, ne pas se coucher.

**sitcom** ['sɪtkɔm] *n* (*abbr of* **situation comedy**) comédie *f* de situation.

**site** [saɪt] *n* emplacement *m*, site *m*; (*also*: **building ~**) chantier *m* // *vt* placer.

**sit-in** ['sɪtɪn] *n* (*demonstration*) sit-in *m inv*, occupation *f* de locaux.

**siting** ['saɪtɪŋ] *n* (*location*) emplacement *m*.

**sitter** ['sɪtə] *n* (*for painter*) modèle *m*.

**sitting** ['sɪtɪŋ] *n* (*of assembly etc*) séance *f*; (*in canteen*) service *m*; ~ **room** *n* salon *m*.

**situated** ['sɪtjueɪtɪd] *a* situé(e).

**situation** [sɪtju'eɪʃən] *n* situation *f*; '~s vacant/wanted' 'offres/demandes d'emploi'.

**six** [sɪks] *num* six; ~**teen** *num* seize; ~**th** *a* sixième; ~**ty** *num* soixante.

**size** [saɪz] *n* taille *f*; dimensions *fpl*; (*of clothing*) taille; (*of shoes*) pointure *f*; (*glue*) colle *f*; **to ~ up** *vt* juger, jauger; ~**able** *a* assez grand(e) *or* gros(se); assez important(e).

**sizzle** ['sɪzl] *vi* grésiller.

**skate** [skeɪt] *n* patin *m*; (*fish: pl inv*) raie *f // vi* patiner; ~**board** *n* skateboard *m*, planche *f* à roulettes; ~**r** *n* patineur/euse; **skating** *n* patinage *m*; **skating rink** *n* patinoire *f*.

**skeleton** ['skɛlɪtn] *n* squelette *m*; (*outline*) schéma *m*; ~ **staff** *n* effectifs réduits.

**skeptic** ['skɛptɪk] *n* (*US*) = **sceptic**.

**sketch** [skɛtʃ] *n* (*drawing*) croquis *m*, esquisse *f*; (*THEATRE*) sketch *m*, saynète *f // vt* esquisser, faire un croquis *or* une esquisse de; ~ **book** *n* carnet *m* à dessin; ~ **pad** *n* bloc *m* à dessin; ~**y** *a* incomplet(ète), fragmentaire.

**skew** [skju:] *n*: **on the ~** de travers, en biais.

**skewer** ['skju:ə*] *n* brochette *f*.

**ski** [ski:] *n* ski *m // vi* skier, faire du ski; ~ **boot** *n* chaussure *f* de ski.

**skid** [skɪd] *n* dérapage *m // vi* déraper; ~**mark** *n* trace *f* de dérapage.

**skier** ['ski:ə*] *n* skieur/euse.

**skiing** ['ski:ɪŋ] *n* ski *m*.

**ski jump** ['ski:dʒʌmp] *n* saut *m* à skis.

**skilful** ['skɪlful] *a* habile, adroit(e).

**ski lift** ['ski:lɪft] *n* remonte-pente *m inv*.

**skill** [skɪl] *n* habileté *f*, adresse *f*, talent *m*; ~**ed** *a* habile, adroit(e); (*worker*) qualifié(e).

**skim** [skɪm] *vt* (*milk*) écrémer; (*soup*) écumer; (*glide over*) raser, effleurer *// vi*: **to ~ through** (*fig*) parcourir.

**skimp** [skɪmp] *vt* (*work*) bâcler, faire à la va-vite; (*cloth etc*) lésiner sur; ~**y** *a* étriqué(e); maigre.

**skin** [skɪn] *n* peau *f // vt* (*fruit etc*) éplucher; (*animal*) écorcher; ~-**deep** *a* superficiel(le); ~ **diving** *n* plongée sous-marine; ~ **graft** *n* greffe *f* de peau; ~**ny** *a* maigre, maigrichon(ne); ~ **test** *n* cuti-réaction) *f*; ~**tight** *a* (*dress etc*) collant(e), ajusté(e).

**skip** [skɪp] *n* petit bond *or* saut; (*container*) benne *f // vi* gambader, sautiller; (*with rope*) sauter à la corde *// vt* (*pass over*) sauter.

**ski pants** ['ski:pænts] *npl* fuseau *m* (de ski).

**skipper** ['skɪpə*] *n* (*NAUT, SPORT*) capitaine *m // vt* (*boat*) commander; (*team*) être le chef de.

**skipping rope** ['skɪpɪŋrəup] *n* corde *f* à sauter.

**skirmish** ['skə:mɪʃ] *n* escarmouche *f*, accrochage *m*.

**skirt** [skə:t] *n* jupe *f // vt* longer, contourner; ~**ing board** *n* plinthe *f*.

**skit** [skɪt] *n* sketch *m* satirique.

**ski tow** ['ski:təu] *n* = **ski lift**.

**skittle** ['skɪtl] *n* quille *f*; ~**s** *n* (*game*) (jeu *m* de) quilles.

**skive** [skaɪv] (*Brit*) *vi* (*col*) tirer au flanc.

**skulk** [skʌlk] *vi* rôder furtivement.

**skull** [skʌl] *n* crâne *m*.

**skunk** [skʌŋk] *n* mouffette *f*; (*fur*) sconse *m*.

**sky** [skaɪ] *n* ciel *m*; ~-**blue** *a* bleu ciel *inv*; ~**light** *n* lucarne *f*; ~**scraper** *n* gratte-ciel *m inv*.

**slab** [slæb] *n* plaque *f*; dalle *f*.

**slack** [slæk] *a* (*loose*) lâche, desserré(e); (*slow*) stagnant(e); (*careless*) négligent(e), peu sérieux(euse) *or* consciencieux(euse) *// n* (*in rope etc*) mou *m*; ~**s** *npl* pantalon *m*; ~**en** (*also*: ~**en off**) *vi* ralentir, diminuer; (*in one's work, attention*) se relâcher *// vt* relâcher.

**slag** [slæg] *n* scories *fpl*; ~ **heap** *n* crassier *m*.

**slam** [slæm] *vt* (*door*) (faire) claquer; (*throw*) jeter violemment, flanquer; (*criticize*) éreinter, démolir *// vi* claquer.

**slander** ['slɑ:ndə*] *n* calomnie *f*; diffamation *f // vt* calomnier; diffamer; ~**ous** *a* calomnieux(euse); diffamatoire.

**slang** [slæŋ] *n* argot *m*.

**slant** [slɑ:nt] *n* inclinaison *f*; (*fig*) angle *m*, point *m* de vue; ~**ed** *a* tendancieux(euse); ~**ing** *a* en pente, incliné(e); couché(e).

**slap** [slæp] *n* claque *f*, gifle *f*; tape *f // vt* donner une claque *or* une gifle *or* une tape à *// ad* (*directly*) tout droit, en plein; ~**dash** *a* fait(e) sans soin *or* à la va-vite; ~**stick** *n* (*comedy*) grosse farce, style *m* tarte à la crème; **a ~-up meal** un repas extra *or* fameux.

**slash** [slæʃ] *vt* entailler, taillader; (*fig: prices*) casser.

**slate** [sleɪt] *n* ardoise *f // vt* (*fig: criticize*) éreinter, démolir.

**slaughter** ['slɔ:tə*] *n* carnage *m*, massacre *m // vt* (*animal*) abattre; (*people*) massacrer; ~**house** *n* abattoir *m*.

**Slav** [slɑ:v] *a* slave.

**slave** [sleɪv] *n* esclave *m/f // vi* (*also*: ~ **away**) trimer, travailler comme un forçat; ~**ry** *n* esclavage *m*.

**Slavic** ['slævɪk] *a* slave.

**slavish** ['sleɪvɪʃ] *a* servile.

**Slavonic** [slə'vɔnɪk] *a* slave.

**sleazy** ['sli:zɪ] *a* miteux(euse), minable.

**sledge** [slɛdʒ] *n* luge *f*; ~**hammer** *n* marteau *m* de forgeron.

**sleek** [sli:k] *a* (*hair, fur*) brillant(e), luisant(e); (*car, boat*) aux lignes pures *or* élégantes.

**sleep** [sli:p] *n* sommeil *m // vi* (*pt, pp slept* [slɛpt]) dormir; (*spend night*) dormir, coucher; **to go to ~** s'endormir; **to ~ in** *vi* (*lie late*) faire la grasse matinée; (*oversleep*) se réveiller trop tard; ~**er** *n* (*person*) dormeur/euse; (*RAIL: on track*) traverse *f*; (: *train*) train *m* de voitures-lits; ~**ily** *ad* d'un air endormi; ~**ing** *a* qui dort, endormi(e) ; ~ing **bag** *n* sac *m* de couchage ; ~ing **car** *n* wagon-lits *m*, voiture-lits *f* ; ~ing **pill** *n* somnifère *m* ; ~**lessness** *n* insomnie *f* ; **a ~less night** une nuit blanche ; ~**walker** *n* somnambule *m/f* ; ~**y a** qui a envie de dormir ; (*fig*) endormi(e).

**sleet** [sli:t] *n* neige fondue.

**sleeve** [sli:v] *n* manche *f* ; ~**less** *a* (*garment*) sans manches.

**sleigh** [sleɪ] *n* traîneau *m*.

**sleight** [slaɪt] *n*: ~ **of hand** tour *m* de passe-passe.

**slender** ['slɛndə*] *a* svelte, mince ; faible, ténu(e).

**slept** [slɛpt] *pt,pp of* **sleep**.

**slice** [slaɪs] *n* tranche *f* ; (*round*) rondelle *f* // *vt* couper en tranches (*or* en rondelles).

**slick** [slɪk] *a* brillant(e) en apparence ; mielleux(euse) // *n* (*also*: **oil ~**) nappe *f* de pétrole, marée noire.

**slid** [slɪd] *pt,pp of* **slide**.

**slide** [slaɪd] *n* (*in playground*) toboggan *m* ; (*PHOT*) diapositive *f* ; (*also*: **hair ~**) barrette *f* ; (*in prices*) chute *f*, baisse *f* // *vb* (*pt,pp* **slid** [slɪd]) *vt* (faire) glisser // *vi* glisser ; **~ rule** *n* règle *f* à calcul ; **sliding** *a* (*door*) coulissant(e) ; **sliding scale** *n* échelle *f* mobile.

**slight** [slaɪt] *a* (*slim*) mince, menu(e) ; (*frail*) frêle ; (*trivial*) faible, insignifiant(e) ; (*small*) petit(e), léger(ère) (*before n*) // *n* offense *f*, affront *m* // *vt* (*offend*) blesser, offenser ; **the ~est** le (*or* la) moindre ; **not in the ~est** pas le moins du monde, pas du tout ; ~**ly** *ad* légèrement, un peu.

**slim** [slɪm] *a* mince // *vi* maigrir, suivre un régime amaigrissant.

**slime** [slaɪm] *n* vase *f* ; substance visqueuse ; **slimy** *a* visqueux(euse), gluant(e).

**sling** [slɪŋ] *n* (*MED*) écharpe *f* // *vt* (*pt,pp* **slung** [slʌŋ]) lancer, jeter.

**slip** [slɪp] *n* faux pas ; (*mistake*) erreur *f* ; étourderie *f* ; bévue *f* ; (*underskirt*) combinaison *f* ; (*of paper*) petite feuille, fiche *f* // *vt* (*slide*) glisser // *vi* (*slide*) glisser ; (*move smoothly*): **to ~ into/out of** se glisser *or* se faufiler dans/hors de ; (*decline*) baisser ; **to give sb the ~** fausser compagnie à qn ; **a ~ of the tongue** un lapsus ; **to ~ away** *vi* s'esquiver ; **to ~ in** *vt* glisser ; **to ~ out** *vi* sortir ; ~**ped disc** *n* déplacement *m* de vertèbres.

**slipper** ['slɪpə*] *n* pantoufle *f*.

**slippery** ['slɪpərɪ] *a* glissant(e) ; insaisissable.

**slip road** ['slɪprəud] *n* (*to motorway*) bretelle *f* d'accès.

**slipshod** ['slɪpʃɔd] *a* négligé(e), peu soigné(e).

**slip-up** ['slɪpʌp] *n* bévue *f*.

**slipway** ['slɪpweɪ] *n* cale *f* (de construction *or* de lancement).

**slit** [slɪt] *n* fente *f* ; (*cut*) incision *f* ; (*tear*) déchirure *f* // *vt* (*pt,pp* **slit**) fendre ; couper ; inciser ; déchirer.

**slither** ['slɪðə*] *vi* glisser, déraper.

**slob** [slɔb] *n* (*col*) rustaud *m*.

**slog** [slɔg] *n* gros effort ; tâche fastidieuse // *vi* travailler très dur.

**slogan** ['sləugən] *n* slogan *m*.

**slop** [slɔp] *vi* (*also*: ~ **over**) se renverser ; déborder // *vt* répandre ; renverser.

**slope** [sləup] *n* pente *f*, côte *f* ; (*side of mountain*) versant *m* ; (*slant*) inclinaison *f* // *vi*: **to ~ down** être *or* descendre en pente ; **to ~ up** monter ; **sloping** *a* en pente, incliné(e) ; (*handwriting*) penché(e).

**sloppy** ['slɔpɪ] *a* (*work*) peu soigné(e), bâclé(e) ; (*appearance*) négligé(e), débraillé(e) ; (*film etc*) sentimental(e).

**slot** [slɔt] *n* fente *f* // *vt*: **to ~ into** encastrer *or* insérer dans ; ~ **machine** *n* distributeur *m* (automatique), machine *f* à sous.

**slouch** [slautʃ] *vi* avoir le dos rond, être voûté(e).

**slovenly** ['slʌvənlɪ] *a* sale, débraillé(e), négligé(e).

**slow** [sləu] *a* lent(e) ; (*watch*): **to be ~** retarder // *ad* lentement // *vt,vi* (*also*: ~ **down**, ~ **up**) ralentir ; ' ~ ' (*road sign*) 'ralentir' ; ~**ly** *ad* lentement ; **in ~ motion** au ralenti ; ~**ness** *n* lenteur *f*.

**sludge** [slʌdʒ] *n* boue *f*.

**slug** [slʌg] *n* limace *f* ; (*bullet*) balle *f* ; ~**gish** *a* mou(molle), lent(e).

**sluice** [slu:s] *n* vanne *f* ; écluse *f*.

**slum** [slʌm] *n* taudis *m*.

**slumber** ['slʌmbə*] *n* sommeil *m*.

**slump** [slʌmp] *n* baisse soudaine, effondrement *m* ; crise *f* // *vi* s'effondrer, s'affaisser.

**slung** [slʌŋ] *pt,pp of* **sling**.

**slur** [slə:*] *n* bredouillement *m* ; (*smear*): ~ **(on)** atteinte *f* (à) ; insinuation *f* (contre) ; (*MUS*) liaison *f* // *vt* mal articuler ; **to be a ~ on** porter atteinte à.

**slush** [slʌʃ] *n* neige fondue ; ~**y** *a* (*snow*) fondu(e) ; (*street*) couvert(e) de neige fondue ; (*fig*) sentimental(e).

**slut** [slʌt] *n* souillon *f*.

**sly** [slaɪ] *a* rusé(e) ; sournois(e) ; **on the ~** en cachette.

**smack** [smæk] *n* (*slap*) tape *f* ; (*on face*) gifle *f* // *vt* donner une tape à, gifler ; (*child*) donner la fessée à // *vi*: **to ~ of** avoir des relents de, sentir ; **to ~ one's lips** se lécher les babines.

**small** [smɔ:l] *a* petit(e) ; ~ **ads** *npl* petites annonces ; ~**holder** *n* petit cultivateur ; **in the ~ hours** au petit matin ; ~**ish** plutôt *or* assez petit ; ~**pox** *n* variole *f* ; ~ **talk** *n* menus propos.

**smarmy** ['smɑ:mɪ] *a* (*col*) flagorneur(euse), lécheur(euse).

**smart** [smɑ:t] *a* élégant(e), chic *inv* ; (*clever*) intelligent(e), astucieux(euse), futé(e) ; (*quick*) rapide, vif(vive), prompt(e) // *vi* faire mal, brûler ; **to ~en up** *vi* devenir plus élégant(e), se faire beau(belle) // *vt* rendre plus élégant(e).

**smash** [smæʃ] *n* (*also*: ~-**up**) collision *f*, accident *m* // *vt* casser, briser, fracasser ; (*opponent*) écraser ; (*hopes*) ruiner, détruire ; (*SPORT: record*) pulvériser // *vi* se briser, se fracasser ; s'écraser ; ~**ing** *a* (*col*) formidable.

**smattering** ['smætərɪŋ] *n*: **a ~ of** quelques notions de.

**smear** [smɪə\*] *n* tache *f*, salissure *f*; trace *f*; (*MED*) frottis *m* // *vt* enduire; (*fig*) porter atteinte à.

**smell** [smɛl] *n* odeur *f*; (*sense*) odorat *m* // *vb* (*pt,pp* **smelt** *or* **smelled** [smɛlt, smɛld]) *vt* sentir // *vi* (*food etc*): **to ~ (of)** sentir; (*pej*) sentir mauvais; **~y** a qui sent mauvais, malodorant(e).

**smile** [smaɪl] *n* sourire *m* // *vi* sourire; **smiling** *a* souriant(e).

**smirk** [smə:k] *n* petit sourire suffisant *or* affecté.

**smith** [smɪθ] *n* maréchal-ferrant *m*; forgeron *m*; **~y** *n* forge *f*.

**smitten** ['smɪtn] *a*: **~ with** pris(e) de; frappé(e) de.

**smock** [smɔk] *n* blouse *f*, sarrau *m*.

**smog** [smɔg] *n* brouillard mêlé de fumée.

**smoke** [sməuk] *n* fumée *f* // *vt*, *vi* fumer; **to have a ~** fumer une cigarette; **~d** *a* (*bacon*, *glass*) fumé(e); **~r** *n* (*person*) fumeur/euse; (*RAIL*) wagon *m* fumeurs; **smoking** *n*: **'no smoking'** (*sign*) 'défense de fumer'; **smoking room** *n* fumoir *m*; **smoky** *a* enfumé(e); (*surface*) noirci(e) par la fumée.

**smolder** ['sməuldə\*] *vi* (*US*) = **smoulder**.

**smooth** [smu:ð] *a* lisse; (*sauce*) onctueux(euse); (*flavour*, *whisky*) moelleux(euse); (*movement*) régulier(ère), sans à-coups *or* heurts; (*person*) doucereux(euse), mielleux(euse) // *vt* lisser, défroisser; (*also*: **~ out**) (*creases*, *difficulties*) faire disparaître.

**smother** ['smʌðə\*] *vt* étouffer.

**smoulder** ['sməuldə\*] *vi* couver.

**smudge** [smʌdʒ] *n* tache *f*, bavure *f* // *vt* salir, maculer.

**smug** [smʌg] *a* suffisant(e), content(e) de soi.

**smuggle** ['smʌgl] *vt* passer en contrebande *or* en fraude; **~r** *n* contrebandier/ère; **smuggling** *n* contrebande *f*.

**smutty** ['smʌtɪ] *a* (*fig*) grossier(ère), obscène.

**snack** [snæk] *n* casse-croûte *m inv*; **~ bar** *n* snack(-bar) *m*.

**snag** [snæg] *n* inconvénient *m*, difficulté *f*.

**snail** [sneɪl] *n* escargot *m*.

**snake** [sneɪk] *n* serpent *m*.

**snap** [snæp] *n* (*sound*) claquement *m*, bruit sec; (*photograph*) photo *f*, instantané *m*; (*game*) sorte *f* de jeu de bataille // *a* subit(e); fait(e) sans réfléchir // *vt* faire claquer; (*break*) casser net; (*photograph*) prendre un instantané de // *vi* se casser net *or* avec un bruit sec; **to ~ open/shut** s'ouvrir/se refermer brusquement; **to ~ at** *vt fus* (*subj*: *dog*) essayer de mordre; **to ~ off** *vt* (*break*) casser net; **to ~ up** *vt* sauter sur, saisir; **~ fastener** *n* bouton-pression *m*; **~py** *a* prompt(e); **~shot** *n* photo *f*, instantané *m*.

**snare** [snɛə\*] *n* piège *m* // *vt* attraper, prendre au piège.

**snarl** [snɑ:l] *n* grondement *m* *or* grognement *m* féroce // *vi* gronder.

**snatch** [snætʃ] *n* (*fig*) vol *m*; (*small amount*): **~es of** des fragments *mpl* or

bribes *fpl* de // *vt* saisir (*d'un geste vif*); (*steal*) voler.

**sneak** [sni:k] *vi*: **to ~ in/out** entrer/sortir furtivement *or* à la dérobée; **~y** *a* sournois(e).

**sneer** [snɪə\*] *n* ricanement *m* // *vi* ricaner, sourire d'un air sarcastique.

**sneeze** [sni:z] *n* éternuement *m* // *vi* éternuer.

**snide** [snaɪd] *a* sarcastique, narquois(e).

**sniff** [snɪf] *n* reniflement *m* // *vi* renifler // *vt* renifler, flairer.

**snigger** ['snɪgə\*] *n* ricanement *m*; rire moqueur // *vi* ricaner; pouffer de rire.

**snip** [snɪp] *n* petit bout; (*bargain*) (bonne) occasion *or* affaire // *vt* couper.

**sniper** ['snaɪpə\*] *n* (*marksman*) tireur embusqué.

**snippet** ['snɪpɪt] *n* bribes *fpl*.

**snivelling** ['snɪvlɪŋ] *a* (*whimpering*) larmoyant(e), pleurnicheur(euse).

**snob** [snɔb] *n* snob *m/f*; **~bery** *n* snobisme *m*; **~bish** *a* snob *inv*.

**snooker** ['snu:kə\*] *n* sorte de jeu de billard.

**snoop** ['snu:p] *vi*: **to ~ on sb** espionner qn.

**snooty** ['snu:tɪ] *a* snob *inv*, prétentieux(euse).

**snooze** [snu:z] *n* petit somme // *vi* faire un petit somme.

**snore** [snɔ:\*] *vi* ronfler; **snoring** *n* ronflement(s) *m(pl)*.

**snorkel** ['snɔ:kl] *n* (*of swimmer*) tuba *m*.

**snort** [snɔ:t] *n* grognement *m* // *vi* grogner; (*horse*) renâcler.

**snotty** ['snɔtɪ] *a* morveux(euse).

**snout** [snaut] *n* museau *m*.

**snow** [snəu] *n* neige *f* // *vi* neiger; **~ball** *n* boule *f* de neige; **~bound** *a* enneigé(e), bloqué(e) par la neige; **~drift** *n* congère *f*; **~drop** *n* perce-neige *m*; **~fall** *n* chute *f* de neige; **~flake** *n* flocon *m* de neige; **~man** *n* bonhomme *m* de neige; **~plough, ~plow** (*US*) *n* chasse-neige *m inv*; **~storm** *n* tempête *f* de neige.

**snub** [snʌb] *vt* repousser, snober // *n* rebuffade *f*, **~-nosed** *a* au nez retroussé.

**snuff** [snʌf] *n* tabac *m* à priser.

**snug** [snʌg] *a* douillet(te), confortable.

**so** [səu] *ad* (*degree*) si, tellement; (*manner*: *thus*) ainsi, de cette façon // *cj* donc, par conséquent; **~ as to do** afin de *or* pour faire; **~ that** (*purpose*) afin de + *infinitive*, pour que *or* afin que + *sub*; (*result*) si bien que, de (telle) sorte que; **~ do I, ~ am I** *etc* moi *etc* aussi; **if ~** si oui; **I hope ~** je l'espère; **10 or ~** 10 à peu près *or* environ; **~ far** jusqu'ici, jusqu'à maintenant; (*in past*) jusque-là; **~ long!** à bientôt!, au revoir!; **~ many** tant de; **~ much** *ad* tant // *det* tant de; **~ and ~ n** un tel(une telle).

**soak** [səuk] *vt* faire *or* laisser tremper // *vi* tremper; **to be ~ed through** être trempé jusqu'aux os; **to ~ in** *vi* pénétrer, être absorbé(e); **to ~ up** *vt* absorber.

**soap** [səup] *n* savon *m*; **~flakes** *npl* paillettes *fpl* de savon; **~ powder** *n* lessive *f*, détergent *m*; **~y** *a* savonneux(euse).

**soar** [sɔ:*] *vi* monter (en flèche), s'élancer.

**sob** [sɔb] *n* sanglot *m* // *vi* sangloter.

**sober** ['səubə*] *a* qui n'est pas (*or* plus) ivre; (*sedate*) sérieux(euse), sensé(e); (*moderate*) mesuré(e); (*colour, style*) sobre, discret(ète); **to ~ up** *vt* dégriser // *vi* se dégriser.

**Soc.** *abbr of* **society**.

**so-called** ['səu'kɔ:ld] *a* soi-disant *inv*.

**soccer** ['sɔkə*] *n* football *m*.

**sociable** ['səuʃəbl] *a* sociable.

**social** ['səuʃl] *a* social(e) // *n* (petite) fête; **~ club** *n* amicale *f*, foyer *m*; **~ism** *n* socialisme *m*; **~ist** *a,n* socialiste (*m/f*); **~ly** *ad* socialement, en société; **~ science** *n* sciences humaines; **~ security** *n* aide sociale; **~ welfare** *n* sécurité sociale; **~ work** *n* assistance sociale; **~ worker** *n* assistant/e social/e.

**society** [sə'saɪətɪ] *n* société *f*; (*club*) société, association *f*; (*also:* **high ~**) (haute) société, grand monde.

**sociological** [səusɪə'lɔdʒɪkl] *a* sociologique.

**sociologist** [səusɪ'ɔlədʒɪst] *n* sociologue *m/f*.

**sociology** [səusɪ'ɔlədʒɪ] *n* sociologie *f*.

**sock** [sɔk] *n* chaussette *f* // *vt* (*hit*) flanquer un coup à.

**socket** ['sɔkɪt] *n* cavité *f*; (*ELEC: also:* **wall ~**) prise *f* de courant; (: *for light bulb*) douille *f*.

**sod** [sɔd] *n* (*of earth*) motte *f*; (*col!*) con *m* (!); salaud *m* (!).

**soda** ['səudə] *n* (*CHEM*) soude *f*; (*also:* **~ water**) eau *f* de Seltz.

**sodden** ['sɔdn] *a* trempé(e); détrempé(e).

**sodium** ['səudɪəm] *n* sodium *m*.

**sofa** ['səufə] *n* sofa *m*; canapé *m*.

**soft** [sɔft] *a* (*not rough*) doux/(douce); (*not hard*) doux; mou(molle); (*not loud*) doux, léger(ère); (*kind*) doux, gentil(le); (*weak*) indulgent(e); (*stupid*) stupide, débile; **~ drink** *n* boisson non alcoolisée; **~en** ['sɔfn] *vt* (r)amollir; adoucir; atténuer // *vi* se ramollir; s'adoucir; s'atténuer; **~-hearted** *a* au cœur tendre; **~ly** *ad* doucement; gentiment; **~ness** *n* douceur *f*; **~ware** *n* logiciel *m*, software *m*.

**soggy** ['sɔgɪ] *a* trempé(e); détrempé(e).

**soil** [sɔɪl] *n* (*earth*) sol *m*, terre *f* // *vt* salir; (*fig*) souiller; **~ed** *a* sale; (*COMM*) défraîchi(e).

**solar** ['səulə*] *a* solaire.

**sold** [səuld] *pt,pp of* **sell**; **~ out** *a* (*COMM*) épuisé(e).

**solder** ['səuldə*] *vt* souder (*au fil à souder*) // *n* soudure *f*.

**soldier** ['səuldʒə*] *n* soldat *m*, militaire *m*.

**sole** [səul] *n* (*of foot*) plante *f*; (*of shoe*) semelle *f*; (*fish: pl inv*) sole *f* // *a* seul(e), unique; **~ly** *ad* seulement, uniquement.

**solemn** ['sɔləm] *a* solennel(le); sérieux(euse), grave.

**solicitor** [sə'lɪsɪtə*] *n* (*for wills etc*) ≈ notaire *m*; (*in court*) ≈ avocat *m*.

**solid** ['sɔlɪd] *a* (*not hollow*) plein(e), compact(e), massif(ive); (*strong, sound, reliable, not liquid*) solide; (*meal*) consistant(e), substantiel(le) // *n* solide *m*.

**solidarity** [sɔlɪ'dærɪtɪ] *n* solidarité *f*.

**solidify** [sə'lɪdɪfaɪ] *vi* se solidifier // *vt* solidifier.

**solidity** [sə'lɪdɪtɪ] *n* solidité *f*.

**soliloquy** [sə'lɪləkwɪ] *n* monologue *m*.

**solitaire** [sɔlɪ'tɛə*] *n* (*game, gem*) solitaire *m*.

**solitary** ['sɔlɪtərɪ] *a* solitaire; **~ confinement** *n* (*LAW*) isolement *m*.

**solitude** ['sɔlɪtjuːd] *n* solitude *f*.

**solo** ['səuləu] *n* solo *m*; **~ist** *n* soliste *m/f*.

**solstice** ['sɔlstɪs] *n* solstice *m*.

**soluble** ['sɔljubl] *a* soluble.

**solution** [sə'luːʃən] *n* solution *f*.

**solve** [sɔlv] *vt* résoudre.

**solvent** ['sɔlvənt] *a* (*COMM*) solvable // *n* (*CHEM*) (dis)solvant *m*.

**sombre, somber** (*US*) ['sɔmbə*] *a* sombre, morne.

**some** [sʌm] *det* (*a few*) quelques; (*certain*) certains(certaines); (*a certain number or amount*) *see phrases below*; (*unspecified*) un(e)... (quelconque) // *pronoun* quelques uns(unes); un peu // *ad:* **~ 10 people** quelque 10 personnes, 10 personnes environ; **~ children came** des enfants sont venus; **have ~ tea/ice-cream/water** prends du thé/de la glace/de l'eau; **there's ~ milk in the fridge** il y a un peu de lait *or* du lait dans le frigo; **~ (of it) was left** il en est resté un peu; **I've got ~** (*i.e. books etc*) j'en ai (quelques uns); (*i.e. milk, money etc*) j'en ai (un peu); **~body** *pronoun* quelqu'un; **~ day** *ad* un de ces jours, un jour ou l'autre; **~how** *ad* d'une façon ou d'une autre; (*for some reason*) pour une raison ou une autre; **~one** *pronoun* = **somebody**; **~place** *ad* (*US*) = **somewhere**.

**somersault** ['sʌməsɔ:lt] *n* culbute *f*, saut périlleux // *vi* faire la culbute *or* un saut périlleux; (*car*) faire un tonneau.

**something** ['sʌmθɪŋ] *pronoun* quelque chose *m*; **~ interesting** quelque chose d'intéressant.

**sometime** ['sʌmtaɪm] *ad* (*in future*) un de ces jours, un jour ou l'autre; (*in past*): **~ last month** au cours du mois dernier.

**sometimes** ['sʌmtaɪmz] *ad* quelquefois, parfois.

**somewhat** ['sʌmwɔt] *ad* quelque peu, un peu.

**somewhere** ['sʌmwɛə*] *ad* quelque part.

**son** [sʌn] *n* fils *m*.

**sonata** [sə'nɑ:tə] *n* sonate *f*.

**song** [sɔŋ] *n* chanson *f*; **~book** *n* chansonnier *m*; **~writer** *n* auteur-compositeur *m*.

**sonic** ['sɔnɪk] *a* (*boom*) supersonique.

**son-in-law** ['sʌnɪnlɔ:] *n* gendre *m*, beau-fils *m*.

**sonnet** ['sɔnɪt] *n* sonnet *m*.

**sonny** ['sʌnɪ] *n* (*col*) fiston *m*.

**soon** [su:n] *ad* bientôt; (*early*) tôt; **~ afterwards** peu après; *see also* **as**; **~er** *ad* (*time*) plus tôt; (*preference*): **I would ~er do** j'aimerais autant *or* je préférerais faire; **~er or later** tôt ou tard.

**soot** [sut] *n* suie *f*.

**soothe** [su:ð] *vt* calmer, apaiser.
**sop** [sɔp] *n*: **that's only a** ~ c'est pour nous (*or* les *etc*) amadouer.
**sophisticated** [sə'fɪstɪkeɪtɪd] *a* raffiné(e) ; sophistiqué(e) ; hautement perfectionné(e), très complexe.
**sophomore** ['sɔfəmɔ:*] *n* (*US*) étudiant/e de seconde année.
**soporific** [sɔpə'rɪfɪk] *a* soporifique // *n* somnifère *m.*
**sopping** ['sɔpɪŋ] *a* (*also*: ~ **wet**) tout(e) trempé(e).
**soppy** ['sɔpɪ] *a* (*pej*) sentimental(e).
**soprano** [sə'prɑ:nəu] *n* (*voice*) soprano *m* ; (*singer*) soprano *m/f.*
**sorcerer** ['sɔ:sərə*] *n* sorcier *m.*
**sordid** ['sɔ:dɪd] *a* sordide.
**sore** [sɔ:*] *a* (*painful*) douloureux(euse), sensible ; (*offended*) contrarié(e), vexé(e) // *n* plaie *f* ; ~**ly** *ad* (*tempted*) fortement.
**sorrel** ['sɔrəl] *n* oseille *f.*
**sorrow** ['sɔrəu] *n* peine *f*, chagrin *m* ; ~**ful** *a* triste.
**sorry** ['sɔrɪ] *a* désolé(e) ; (*condition, excuse*) triste, déplorable ; ~! pardon!, excusez-moi! ; **to feel** ~ **for sb** plaindre qn.
**sort** [sɔ:t] *n* genre *m*, espèce *f*, sorte *f* // *vt* (*also*: ~ **out**: *papers*) trier ; classer ; ranger ; (: *letters etc*) trier ; (: *problems*) résoudre, régler ; ~**ing office** *n* bureau *m* de tri.
**SOS** *n* (*abbr of save our souls*) S.O.S. *m.*
**so-so** ['səusəu] *ad* comme ci comme ça.
**soufflé** ['su:fleɪ] *n* soufflé *m.*
**sought** [sɔ:t] *pt,pp* of **seek.**
**soul** [səul] *n* âme *f* ; ~**-destroying** *a* démoralisant(e) ; ~**ful** *a* plein(e) de sentiment ; ~**less** *a* sans cœur, inhumain(e).
**sound** [saund] *a* (*healthy*) en bonne santé, sain(e) ; (*safe, not damaged*) solide, en bon état ; (*reliable, not superficial*) sérieux(euse), solide ; (*sensible*) sensé(e) // *ad*: ~ **asleep** dormant d'un profond sommeil // *n* (*noise*) son *m* ; bruit *m* ; (*GEO*) détroit *m*, bras *m* de mer // *vt* (*alarm*) sonner ; (*also*: ~ **out**: *opinions*) sonder // *vi* sonner, retentir ; (*fig*: *seem*) sembler (être) ; **to** ~ **one's horn** (*AUT*) actionner son avertisseur ; **to** ~ **like** ressembler à ; ~ **barrier** *n* mur *m* du son ; ~ **effects** *npl* bruitage *m* ; ~**ing** *n* (*NAUT etc*) sondage *m* ; ~**ly** *ad* (*sleep*) profondément ; (*beat*) complètement, à plate couture ; ~**proof** *vt* insonoriser // *a* insonorisé(e) ; ~**track** *n* (*of film*) bande *f* sonore.
**soup** [su:p] *n* soupe *f*, potage *m* ; **in the** ~ (*fig*) dans le pétrin ; ~ **course** *n* potage *m* ; ~**spoon** *n* cuiller *f* à soupe.
**sour** ['sauə*] *a* aigre, acide ; (*milk*) tourné(e), aigre ; (*fig*) acerbe, aigre ; revêche ; **it's** ~ **grapes** c'est du dépit.
**source** [sɔ:s] *n* source *f.*
**south** [sauθ] *n* sud *m* // *a* sud *inv*, du sud // *ad* au sud, vers le sud ; **S~ Africa** *n* Afrique *f* du Sud ; **S~ African** *a* sud-africain(e) // *n* Sud-Africain/e ; **S~ America** *n* Amérique *f* du Sud ; **S~ American** *a* sud-américain(e) // *n* Sud-Américain/e ; ~**-east** *n* sud-est *m* ; ~**erly** ['sʌðəlɪ] *a* du sud ; au sud ; ~**ern** ['sʌðən] *a* (du) sud ; méridional(e) ; exposé(e) au

sud ; **S~ Pole** *n* Pôle *m* Sud ; ~**ward(s)** *ad* vers le sud ; ~**-west** *n* sud-ouest *m.*
**souvenir** [su:və'nɪə*] *n* souvenir *m* (*objet*).
**sovereign** ['sɔvrɪn] *a,n* souverain(e) ; ~**ty** *n* souveraineté *f.*
**soviet** ['səuvɪət] *a* soviétique ; **the S~ Union** l'Union *f* soviétique.
**sow** *n* [sau] truie *f* // *vt* [səu] (*pt* ~**ed**, *pp* **sown** [səun]) semer.
**soy** [sɔɪ] *n* (*also*: ~ **sauce**) sauce *f* de soja.
**soya bean** ['sɔɪəbi:n] *n* graine *f* de soja.
**spa** [spɑ:] *n* (*spring*) source minérale ; (*town*) station thermale.
**space** [speɪs] *n* (*gen*) espace *m* ; (*room*) place *f* ; espace ; (*length of time*) laps *m* de temps // *cpd* spatial(e) // *vt* (*also*: ~ **out**) espacer ; ~**craft** *n* engin spatial ; ~**man/woman** *n* astronaute *m/f*, cosmonaute *m/f* ; **spacing** *n* espacement *m* ; **single/double spacing** interligne *m* simple/double.
**spacious** ['speɪʃəs] *a* spacieux(euse), grand(e).
**spade** [speɪd] *n* (*tool*) bêche *f*, pelle *f* ; (*child's*) pelle ; ~**s** *npl* (*CARDS*) pique *m* ; ~**work** *n* (*fig*) gros *m* du travail.
**spaghetti** [spə'gɛtɪ] *n* spaghetti *mpl.*
**Spain** [speɪn] *n* Espagne *f.*
**span** [spæn] *pt of* **spin** // *n* (*of bird, plane*) envergure *f* ; (*of arch*) portée *f* ; (*in time*) espace *m* de temps, durée *f* // *vt* enjamber, franchir ; (*fig*) couvrir, embrasser.
**Spaniard** ['spænjəd] *n* Espagnol/e.
**spaniel** ['spænjəl] *n* épagneul *m.*
**Spanish** ['spænɪʃ] *a* espagnol(e), d'Espagne // *n* (*LING*) espagnol *m.*
**spank** [spæŋk] *vt* donner une fessée à.
**spanner** ['spænə*] *n* clé *f* (de mécanicien).
**spare** [spɛə*] *a* de réserve, de rechange ; (*surplus*) de or en trop, de reste // *n* (*part*) pièce *f* de rechange, pièce détachée // *vt* (*do without*) se passer de ; (*afford to give*) donner, accorder, passer ; (*refrain from hurting*) épargner ; (*refrain from using*) ménager ; **to** ~ (*surplus*) en surplus, de trop ; ~ **part** *n* pièce *f* de rechange, pièce détachée ; ~ **time** *n* moments *mpl* de loisir.
**sparing** ['spɛərɪŋ] *a* modéré(e), restreint(e) ; ~ **of** chiche de ; ~**ly** *ad* avec modération.
**spark** [spɑ:k] *n* étincelle *f* ; (*fig*) étincelle, lueur *f* ; ~**(ing) plug** *n* bougie *f.*
**sparkle** ['spɑ:kl] *n* scintillement *m*, étincellement *m*, éclat *m* // *vi* étinceler, scintiller ; (*bubble*) pétiller ; **sparkling** *a* étincelant(e), scintillant(e) ; (*wine*) mousseux (euse), pétillant(e).
**sparrow** ['spærəu] *n* moineau *m.*
**sparse** [spɑ:s] *a* clairsemé(e).
**spasm** ['spæzəm] *n* (*MED*) spasme *m* ; (*fig*) accès *m* ; ~**odic** [-'mɔdɪk] *a* spasmodique ; (*fig*) intermittent(e).
**spastic** ['spæstɪk] *n* handicapé/e moteur.
**spat** [spæt] *pt,pp* of **spit.**
**spate** [speɪt] *n* (*fig*): ~ **of** avalanche *f* or torrent *m* de ; **in** ~ (*river*) en crue.
**spatter** ['spætə*] *n* éclaboussure(s) *f(pl)* // *vt* éclabousser // *vi* gicler.
**spatula** ['spætjulə] *n* spatule *f.*
**spawn** [spɔ:n] *vt* pondre // *vi* frayer // *n* frai *m.*

**speak**, *pt* **spoke**, *pp* **spoken** [spi:k, spəuk, 'spəukn] *vt* (*language*) parler; (*truth*) dire // *vi* parler; (*make a speech*) prendre la parole; **to ~ to sb/of** *or* **about sth** parler à qn/de qch; **it ~s for itself** c'est évident; **~ up!** parle plus fort!; **~er** *n* (*in public*) orateur *m*; (*also*: **loud~er**) haut-parleur *m*; (POL): **the S~er** le président de la chambre des Communes; **to be on ~ing terms** se parler.

**spear** [spɪə*] *n* lance *f* // *vt* transpercer.

**spec** [spɛk] *n* (*col*): **on ~** à tout hasard.

**special** ['spɛʃl] *a* spécial(e); **take ~ care** soyez particulièrement prudents; **today's ~** (*at restaurant*) le menu; **~ist** *n* spécialiste *m/f*; **~ity** [spɛʃɪ'ælɪtɪ] *n* spécialité *f*; **~ize** *vi*: **to ~ize (in)** se spécialiser (dans); **~ly** *ad* spécialement, particulièrement.

**species** ['spi:ʃi:z] *n* espèce *f*.

**specific** [spə'sɪfɪk] *a* précis(e); particulier(ère); (BOT, CHEM *etc*) spécifique; **~ally** *ad* expressément, explicitement; **~ation** [spɛsɪfɪ'keɪʃn] *n* spécification *f*; stipulation *f*.

**specify** ['spɛsɪfaɪ] *vt* spécifier, préciser.

**specimen** ['spɛsɪmən] *n* spécimen *m*, échantillon *m*; (MED) prélèvement *m*.

**speck** [spɛk] *n* petite tache, petit point; (*particle*) grain *m*.

**speckled** ['spɛkld] *a* tacheté(e), moucheté(e).

**specs** [spɛks] *npl* (*col*) lunettes *fpl*.

**spectacle** ['spɛktəkl] *n* spectacle *m*; **~s** *npl* lunettes *fpl*; **spectacular** [-'tækjulə*] *a* spectaculaire // *n* (CINEMA *etc*) superproduction *f*.

**spectator** [spɛk'teɪtə*] *n* spectateur/trice.

**spectra** ['spɛktrə] *npl of* **spectrum**.

**spectre, specter** (US) ['spɛktə*] *n* spectre *m*, fantôme *m*.

**spectrum, pl spectra** ['spɛktrəm, -rə] *n* spectre *m*; (*fig*) gamme *f*.

**speculate** ['spɛkjuleɪt] *vi* spéculer; (*try to guess*): **to ~ about** s'interroger sur; **speculation** [-'leɪʃən] *n* spéculation *f*; conjectures *fpl*; **speculative** *a* spéculatif(ive).

**speech** [spi:tʃ] *n* (*faculty*) parole *f*; (*talk*) discours *m*, allocution *f*; (*manner of speaking*) façon *f* de parler, langage *m*; (*enunciation*) élocution *f*; **~ day** *n* (SCOL) distribution *f* des prix; **~less** *a* muet(te); **~ therapy** *n* orthophonie *f*.

**speed** [spi:d] *n* vitesse *f*; (*promptness*) rapidité *f*; **at full** *or* **top ~** à toute vitesse *or* allure; **to ~ up** *vi* aller plus vite, accélérer // *vt* accélérer; **~boat** *n* vedette *f*; hors-bord *m inv*; **~ily** *ad* rapidement, promptement; **~ing** *n* (AUT) excès *m* de vitesse; **~ limit** *n* limitation *f* de vitesse, vitesse maximale permise; **~ometer** [spɪ'dɔmɪtə*] *n* compteur *m* (de vitesse); **~way** *n* (SPORT) piste *f* de vitesse pour motos; **~y** *a* rapide, prompt(e).

**speleologist** [spɛlɪ'ɔlədʒɪst] *n* spéléologue *m/f*.

**spell** [spɛl] *n* (*also*: **magic ~**) sortilège *m*, charme *m*; (*period of time*) (courte) période // *vt* (*pt,pp* **spelt** *or* **~ed** [spɛlt, spɛld]) (*in writing*) écrire, orthographier; (*aloud*) épeler; (*fig*) signifier; **to cast a ~ on sb**

jeter un sort à qn; **he can't ~** il fait des fautes d'orthographe; **~bound** *a* envoûté(e), subjugué(e); **~ing** *n* orthographe *f*.

**spelt** [spɛlt] *pt,pp of* **spell**.

**spend**, *pt,pp* **spent** [spɛnd, spɛnt] *vt* (*money*) dépenser; (*time, life*) passer; consacrer; **~ing money** *n* argent *m* de poche; **~thrift** *n* dépensier/ère.

**spent** [spɛnt] *pt,pp of* **spend** // *a* (*patience*) épuisé(e), à bout.

**sperm** [spə:m] *n* spermatozoïde *m*; (*semen*) sperme *m*; **~ whale** *n* cachalot *m*.

**spew** [spju:] *vt* vomir.

**sphere** [sfɪə*] *n* sphère *f*; (*fig*) sphère, domaine *m*; **spherical** ['sfɛrɪkl] *a* sphérique.

**sphinx** [sfɪŋks] *n* sphinx *m*.

**spice** [spaɪs] *n* épice *f* // *vt* épicer.

**spick-and-span** ['spɪkən'spæn] *a* impeccable.

**spicy** ['spaɪsɪ] *a* épicé(e), relevé(e); (*fig*) piquant(e).

**spider** ['spaɪdə*] *n* araignée *f*.

**spiel** [spi:l] *n* laïus *m inv*.

**spike** [spaɪk] *n* pointe *f*.

**spill**, *pt,pp* **spilt** *or* **~ed** [spɪl, -t, -d] *vt* renverser; répandre // *vi* se répandre.

**spin** [spɪn] *n* (*revolution of wheel*) tour *m*; (AVIAT) (chute *f* en) vrille *f*; (*trip in car*) petit tour, balade *f* // *vb* (*pt* **spun, span,** *pp* **spun** [spʌn, spæn]) *vt* (*wool etc*) filer; (*wheel*) faire tourner // *vi* tourner, tournoyer; **to ~ a yarn** débiter une longue histoire; **to ~ a coin** jouer à pile ou face; **to ~ out** *vt* faire durer.

**spinach** ['spɪnɪtʃ] *n* épinard *m*; (*as food*) épinards *mpl*.

**spinal** ['spaɪnl] *a* vertébral(e), spinal(e); **~ cord** *n* moelle épinière.

**spindly** ['spɪndlɪ] *a* grêle, filiforme.

**spin-drier** [spɪn'draɪə*] *n* essoreuse *f*.

**spine** [spaɪn] *n* colonne vertébrale; (*thorn*) épine *f*, piquant *m*; **~less** *a* invertébré(e); (*fig*) mou(molle), sans caractère.

**spinner** ['spɪnə*] *n* (*of thread*) fileur/euse.

**spinning** ['spɪnɪŋ] *n* (*of thread*) filage *m*; (*by machine*) filature *f*; **~ top** *n* toupie *f*; **~ wheel** *n* rouet *m*.

**spinster** ['spɪnstə*] *n* célibataire *f*; vieille fille.

**spiral** ['spaɪərl] *n* spirale *f* // *a* en spirale // *vi* (*fig*) monter en flèche; **~ staircase** *n* escalier *m* en colimaçon.

**spire** [spaɪə*] *n* flèche *f*, aiguille *f*.

**spirit** ['spɪrɪt] *n* (*soul*) esprit *m*, âme *f*; (*ghost*) esprit, revenant *m*; (*mood*) esprit, état *m* d'esprit; (*courage*) courage *m*, énergie *f*; **~s** *npl* (*drink*) spiritueux *mpl*, alcool *m*; **in good ~s** de bonne humeur; **in low ~s** démoralisé(e); **~ed** *a* vif(vive), fougueux(euse), plein(e) d'allant; **~ level** *n* niveau *m* à bulle.

**spiritual** ['spɪrɪtjuəl] *a* spirituel(le); religieux(euse) // *n* (*also*: **Negro ~**) spiritual *m*; **~ism** *n* spiritisme *m*.

**spit** [spɪt] *n* (*for roasting*) broche *f* // *vi* (*pt, pp* **spat** [spæt]) cracher; (*sound*) crépiter.

**spite** [spaɪt] n rancune f, dépit m // vt contrarier, vexer ; **in ~ of** en dépit de, malgré ; **~ful** a malveillant(e), rancunier(ère).

**spitroast** ['spɪt'rəust] vt faire rôtir à la broche.

**spittle** ['spɪtl] n salive f ; bave f ; crachat m.

**spiv** [spɪv] n (col) chevalier m d'industrie, aigrefin m.

**splash** [splæʃ] n éclaboussement m ; (sound) plouf ; (of colour) tache f // vt éclabousser ; vi (also: ~ **about**) barboter, patauger.

**splay** [spleɪ] a: **~footed** marchant les pieds en dehors.

**spleen** [spli:n] n (ANAT) rate f.

**splendid** ['splɛndɪd] a splendide, superbe, magnifique.

**splendour, splendor** (US) ['splɛndə*] n splendeur f, magnificence f.

**splice** [splaɪs] vt épisser.

**splint** [splɪnt] n attelle f, éclisse f.

**splinter** ['splɪntə*] n (wood) écharde f ; (metal) éclat m // vi se fragmenter.

**split** [splɪt] n fente f, déchirure f ; (fig: POL) scission f // vb (pt, pp **split**) vt fendre, déchirer ; (party) diviser ; (work, profits) partager, répartir // vi (divide) se diviser ; **to ~ up** vi (couple) se séparer, rompre ; (meeting) se disperser ; **~ting headache** n mal m de tête atroce.

**splutter** ['splʌtə*] vi bafouiller ; postillonner.

**spoil, pt,pp spoilt** or **~ed** [spɔɪl, -t, -d] vt (damage) abîmer ; (mar) gâcher ; (child) gâter ; **~s** npl butin m ; **~sport** n trouble-fête m, rabat-joie m.

**spoke** [spəuk] pt of **speak** // n rayon m.

**spoken** ['spəukn] pp of **speak**.

**spokesman** ['spəuksmən] n porteparole m inv.

**sponge** [spʌndʒ] n éponge f // vt éponger // vi: **to ~ on** vivre aux crochets de ; **~ bag** n sac m de toilette ; **~ cake** n ~ gâteau m de Savoie ; **~r** n (pej) parasite m ; **spongy** a spongieux(euse).

**sponsor** ['spɔnsə*] n (RADIO, TV) personne f (or organisme m) qui assure le patronage // vt patronner ; parrainer ; **~ship** n patronage m ; parrainage m.

**spontaneity** [spɔntə'neɪtɪ] n spontanéité f.

**spontaneous** [spɔn'teɪnɪəs] a spontané(e).

**spooky** ['spu:kɪ] a qui donne la chair de poule.

**spool** [spu:l] n bobine f.

**spoon** [spu:n] n cuiller f ; **~-feed** vt nourrir à la cuiller ; (fig) mâcher le travail à ; **~ful** n cuillerée f.

**sporadic** [spə'rædɪk] a sporadique.

**sport** [spɔ:t] n sport m ; (person) chic type/chic fille // vt arborer ; **~ing** a sportif(ive) ; **to give sb a ~ing chance** donner sa chance à qn ; **~s car** n voiture f de sport ; **~s jacket** n veste f de sport ; **~sman** n sportif m ; **~smanship** n esprit sportif, sportivité f ; **~s page** n page f des sports ; **~swear** n vêtements mpl de sport ; **~swoman** n sportive f ; **~y** a sportif(ive).

**spot** [spɔt] n tache f ; (dot: on pattern) pois m ; (pimple) bouton m ; (place) endroit m, coin m ; (small amount): **a ~ of** un peu de // vt (notice) apercevoir, repérer ; **on the ~** sur place, sur les lieux ; **to come out in ~s** se couvrir de boutons, avoir une éruption de boutons ; **~ check** n sondage m, vérification ponctuelle ; **~less** a immaculé(e) ; **~light** n projecteur m ; (AUT) phare m auxiliaire ; **~ted** a tacheté(e), moucheté(e) ; à pois ; **~ted with** tacheté(e) de ; **~ty** a (face) boutonneux(euse).

**spouse** [spauz] n époux/épouse.

**spout** [spaut] n (of jug) bec m ; (of liquid) jet m // vi jaillir.

**sprain** [spreɪn] n entorse f, foulure f // vt: **to ~ one's ankle** se fouler or se tordre la cheville.

**sprang** [spræŋ] pt of **spring**.

**sprawl** [sprɔ:l] vi s'étaler.

**spray** [spreɪ] n jet m (en fines gouttelettes) ; (container) vaporisateur m, bombe f ; (of flowers) petit bouquet // vt vaporiser, pulvériser ; (crops) traiter.

**spread** [sprɛd] n propagation f ; (distribution) répartition f ; (CULIN) pâte f à tartiner // vb (pt,pp **spread**) vt étendre, étaler ; répandre ; propager // vi s'étendre ; se répandre ; se propager.

**spree** [spri:] n: **to go on a ~** faire la fête.

**sprig** [sprɪg] n rameau m.

**sprightly** ['spraɪtlɪ] a alerte.

**spring** [sprɪŋ] n (leap) bond m, saut m ; (coiled metal) ressort m ; (season) printemps m ; (of water) source f // vi (pt **sprang, pp sprung** [spræŋ, sprʌŋ]) bondir, sauter ; **to ~ from** provenir de ; **to ~ up** vi (problem) se présenter, surgir ; **~board** n tremplin m ; **~-clean** n (also: **~-cleaning**) grand nettoyage de printemps ; **~time** n printemps m ; **~y** a élastique, souple.

**sprinkle** ['sprɪŋkl] vt (pour) répandre ; verser ; **to ~ water etc on, ~ with water** etc asperger d'eau etc ; **to ~ sugar etc on, ~ with sugar** etc saupoudrer de sucre etc ; **~d with** (fig) parsemé(e) de.

**sprint** [sprɪnt] n sprint m // vi sprinter ; **~er** n sprinteur/euse.

**sprite** [spraɪt] n lutin m.

**sprout** [spraut] vi germer, pousser ; **(Brussels) ~s** npl choux mpl de Bruxelles.

**spruce** [spru:s] n épicéa m // a net(te), pimpant(e).

**sprung** [sprʌŋ] pp of **spring**.

**spry** [spraɪ] a alerte, vif(vive).

**spud** [spʌd] n (col: potato) patate f.

**spun** [spʌn] pt, pp of **spin**.

**spur** [spə:*] n éperon m ; (fig) aiguillon m // vt (also: **~ on**) éperonner ; aiguillonner ; **on the ~ of the moment** sous l'impulsion du moment.

**spurious** ['spjuərɪəs] a faux(fausse).

**spurn** [spə:n] vt repousser avec mépris.

**spurt** [spə:t] n jet m ; (of energy) sursaut m // vi jaillir, gicler.

**spy** [spaɪ] n espion/ne // vi: **to ~ on** espionner, épier // vt (see) apercevoir ; **~ing** n espionnage m.

**sq.** (*MATH*), **Sq.** (*in address*) *abbr of* **square**.

**squabble** ['skwɔbl] *n* querelle *f*, chamaillerie *f* // *vi* se chamailler.

**squad** [skwɔd] *n* (*MIL*, *POLICE*) escouade *f*, groupe *m* ; (*FOOTBALL*) contingent *m*.

**squadron** ['skwɔdrn] *n* (*MIL*) escadron *m* ; (*AVIAT*, *NAUT*) escadrille *f*.

**squalid** ['skwɔlɪd] *a* sordide, ignoble.

**squall** [skwɔ:l] *n* rafale *f*, bourrasque *f*.

**squalor** ['skwɔlə*] *n* conditions *fpl* sordides.

**squander** ['skwɔndə*] *vt* gaspiller, dilapider.

**square** [skwɛə*] *n* carré *m* ; (*in town*) place *f* ; (*instrument*) équerre *f* // *a* carré(e) ; (*honest*) honnête, régulier(ère) ; (*col: ideas, tastes*) vieux jeu *inv*, qui retarde // *vt* (*arrange*) régler ; arranger ; (*MATH*) élever au carré // *vi* (*agree*) cadrer, s'accorder ; **all** ~ quitte ; à égalité ; **a** ~ **meal** un repas convenable ; **2 metres** ~ (de) 2 mètres sur 2 ; **1** ~ **metre** 1 mètre carré ; ~**ly** *ad* carrément.

**squash** [skwɔʃ] *n* (*drink*): **lemon / orange** ~ citronnade *f/* orangeade *f* ; (*SPORT*) squash *m* // *vt* écraser.

**squat** [skwɔt] *a* petit(e) et épais(se), ramassé(e) // *vi* s'accroupir ; ~**ter** *n* squatter *m*.

**squawk** [skwɔ:k] *vi* pousser un *or* des gloussement(s).

**squeak** [skwi:k] *n* grincement *m* ; petit cri // *vi* grincer, crier.

**squeal** [skwi:l] *vi* pousser un *or* des cri(s) aigu(s) *or* perçant(s).

**squeamish** ['skwi:mɪʃ] *a* facilement dégoûté(e) ; facilement scandalisé(e).

**squeeze** [skwi:z] *n* pression *f* ; restrictions *fpl* de crédit // *vt* presser ; (*hand, arm*) serrer ; **to** ~ **out** *vt* exprimer ; (*fig*) soutirer.

**squelch** [skwɛltʃ] *vi* faire un bruit de succion ; patauger.

**squib** [skwɪb] *n* pétard *m*.

**squid** [skwɪd] *n* calmar *m*.

**squint** [skwɪnt] *vi* loucher // *n*: **he has a** ~ il louche, il souffre de strabisme.

**squire** ['skwaɪə*] *n* propriétaire terrien.

**squirm** [skwə:m] *vi* se tortiller.

**squirrel** ['skwɪrəl] *n* écureuil *m*.

**squirt** [skwə:t] *n* jet *m* // *vi* jaillir, gicler.

**Sr** *abbr of* **senior**.

**St** *abbr of* **saint**, **street**.

**stab** [stæb] *n* (*with knife etc*) coup *m* (de couteau *etc*) ; (*col: try*): **to have a** ~ **at (doing)** sth s'essayer à (faire) qch // *vt* poignarder.

**stability** [stə'bɪlɪtɪ] *n* stabilité *f*.

**stabilize** ['steɪbəlaɪz] *vt* stabiliser ; ~**r** *n* stabilisateur *m*.

**stable** ['steɪbl] *n* écurie *f* // *a* stable.

**stack** [stæk] *n* tas *m*, pile *f* // *vt* empiler, entasser.

**stadium** ['steɪdɪəm] *n* stade *m*.

**staff** [stɑ:f] *n* (*work force*) personnel *m* ; (: *SCOL*) professeurs *mpl* ; (: *servants*) domestiques *mpl* ; (*MIL*) état-major *m* ; (*stick*) perche *f*, bâton *m* // *vt* pourvoir en personnel.

**stag** [stæg] *n* cerf *m*.

**stage** [steɪdʒ] *n* scène *f* ; (*profession*): **the** ~ le théâtre ; (*point*) étape *f*, stade *m* ; (*platform*) estrade *f* // *vt* (*play*) monter, mettre en scène ; (*demonstration*) organiser ; (*fig: perform: recovery etc*) effectuer ; **in** ~**s** par étapes, par degrés ; ~**coach** *n* diligence *f* ; ~ **door** *n* entrée *f* des artistes ; ~ **fright** *n* trac *m* ; ~ **manager** *n* régisseur *m*.

**stagger** ['stægə*] *vi* chanceler, tituber // *vt* (*person*) stupéfier ; bouleverser ; (*hours, holidays*) étaler, échelonner ; ~**ing** *a* (*amazing*) stupéfiant(e), renversant(e).

**stagnant** ['stægnənt] *a* stagnant(e).

**stagnate** [stæg'neɪt] *vi* stagner, croupir.

**stag party** ['stægpɑ:tɪ] *n* enterrement *m* de vie de garçon.

**staid** [steɪd] *a* posé(e), rassis(e).

**stain** [steɪn] *n* tache *f* ; (*colouring*) colorant *m* // *vt* tacher ; (*wood*) teindre ; ~**ed glass window** *n* vitrail *m* ; ~**less** *a* (*steel*) inoxydable ; ~ **remover** *n* détachant *m*.

**stair** [stɛə*] *n* (*step*) marche *f* ; ~**s** *npl* escalier *m* ; **on the** ~**s** dans l'escalier ; ~**case**, ~**way** *n* escalier *m*.

**stake** [steɪk] *n* pieu *m*, poteau *m* ; (*BETTING*) enjeu *m* // *vt* risquer, jouer ; **to be at** ~ être en jeu.

**stalactite** ['stæləktaɪt] *n* stalactite *f*.

**stalagmite** ['stæləgmaɪt] *n* stalagmite *m*.

**stale** [steɪl] *a* (*bread*) rassis(e) ; (*beer*) éventé(e) ; (*smell*) de renfermé.

**stalemate** ['steɪlmeɪt] *n* pat *m* ; (*fig*) impasse *f*.

**stalk** [stɔ:k] *n* tige *f* // *vt* traquer // *vi* marcher avec raideur.

**stall** [stɔ:l] *n* éventaire *m*, étal *m* ; (*in stable*) stalle *f* // *vt* (*AUT*) caler // *vi* (*AUT*) caler ; (*fig*) essayer de gagner du temps ; ~**s** *npl* (*in cinema, theatre*) orchestre *m*.

**stalwart** ['stɔ:lwət] *n* partisan *m* fidèle.

**stamina** ['stæmɪnə] *n* vigueur *f*, endurance *f*.

**stammer** ['stæmə*] *n* bégaiement *m* // *vi* bégayer.

**stamp** [stæmp] *n* timbre *m* ; (*mark, also fig*) empreinte *f* ; (*on document*) cachet *m* // *vi* taper du pied // *vt* tamponner, estamper ; (*letter*) timbrer ; ~ **album** *n* album *m* de timbres(-poste) ; ~ **collecting** *n* philatélie *f*.

**stampede** [stæm'pi:d] *n* ruée *f*.

**stance** [stæns] *n* position *f*.

**stand** [stænd] *n* (*position*) position *f* ; (*MIL*) résistance *f* ; (*structure*) guéridon *m* ; support *m* ; (*COMM*) étalage *m*, stand *m* ; (*SPORT*) tribune *f* // *vb* (*pt,pp* **stood** [stud]) *vi* être *or* se tenir (debout) ; (*rise*) se lever, se mettre debout ; (*be placed*) se trouver // *vt* (*place*) mettre, poser ; (*tolerate, withstand*) supporter ; **to make a** ~ prendre position ; **to** ~ **for parliament** se présenter aux élections (*comme candidat à la députation*) ; **it** ~**s to reason** c'est logique ; cela va de soi ; **to** ~ **by** *vi* (*be ready*) se tenir prêt // *vt fus* (*opinion*) s'en tenir à ; **to** ~ **for** *vt fus* (*defend*) défendre, être pour ; (*signify*) représenter, signifier ; (*tolerate*) supporter, tolérer ; **to** ~ **in for** *vt fus* remplacer ; **to** ~ **out** *vi* (*be prominent*) ressortir ; **to** ~ **up** *vi* (*rise*) se lever, se mettre debout ; **to** ~ **up for** *vt* *fus* défendre ; **to ~ up to** *vt fus* tenir tête à, résister à.

**standard** ['stændəd] *n* niveau voulu ; (*flag*) étendard *m* // *a* (*size etc*) ordinaire, normal(e) ; courant(e) ; **~s** *npl* (*morals*) morale *f*, principes *mpl* ; **~ization** [-'zeɪʃən] *n* standardisation *f* ; **~ize** *vt* standardiser ; **~ lamp** *n* lampadaire *m* ; **~ of living** *n* niveau *m* de vie.

**stand-by** ['stændbaɪ] *n* remplaçant/e ; **~ ticket** *n* (*AVIAT*) billet *m* sans garantie.

**stand-in** ['stændɪn] *n* remplaçant/e ; (*CINEMA*) doublure *f*.

**standing** ['stændɪŋ] *a* debout *inv* // *n* réputation *f*, rang *m*, standing *m* ; **of many years' ~** qui dure *or* existe depuis longtemps ; **~ committee** *n* commission permanente ; **~ order** *n* (*at bank*) virement *m* automatique, prélèvement *m* bancaire ; **~ orders** *npl* (*MIL*) règlement *m* ; **~ room** places *fpl* debout.

**stand-offish** [stænd'ɔfɪʃ] *a* distant(e), froid(e).

**standpoint** ['stændpɔɪnt] *n* point *m* de vue.

**standstill** ['stændstɪl] *n*: **at a ~** à l'arrêt ; (*fig*) au point mort ; **to come to a ~** s'immobiliser, s'arrêter.

**stank** [stæŋk] *pt of* **stink**.

**stanza** ['stænzə] *n* strophe *f* ; couplet *m*.

**staple** ['steɪpl] *n* (*for papers*) agrafe *f* // *a* (*food etc*) de base, principal(e) // *vt* agrafer ; **~r** *n* agrafeuse *f*.

**star** [stɑ:*] *n* étoile *f* ; (*celebrity*) vedette *f* // *vi*: **to ~ (in)** être la vedette (de) // *vt* (*CINEMA*) avoir pour vedette.

**starboard** ['stɑ:bəd] *n* tribord *m* ; **to ~** à tribord.

**starch** [stɑ:tʃ] *n* amidon *m* ; **~ed** *a* (*collar*) amidonné(e), empesé(e) ; **~y** *a* riche en féculents ; (*person*) guindé(e).

**stardom** ['stɑ:dəm] *n* célébrité *f*.

**stare** [stɛə*] *n* regard *m* fixe // *vt*: **to ~ at** regarder fixement.

**starfish** ['stɑ:fɪʃ] *n* étoile *f* de mer.

**stark** [stɑ:k] *a* (*bleak*) désolé(e), morne // *ad*: **~ naked** complètement nu(e).

**starlight** ['stɑ:laɪt] *n*: **by ~** à la lumière des étoiles.

**starling** ['stɑ:lɪŋ] *n* étourneau *m*.

**starlit** ['stɑ:lɪt] *a* étoilé(e) ; illuminé(e) par les étoiles.

**starry** ['stɑ:rɪ] *a* étoilé(e) ; **~-eyed** *a* (*innocent*) ingénu(e).

**start** [stɑ:t] *n* commencement *m*, début *m* ; (*of race*) départ *m* ; (*sudden movement*) sursaut *m* // *vt* commencer // *vi* partir, se mettre en route ; (*jump*) sursauter ; **to ~ doing sth** se mettre à faire qch ; **to ~ off** *vi* commencer ; (*leave*) partir ; **to ~ up** *vi* commencer ; (*car*) démarrer // *vt* déclencher ; (*car*) mettre en marche ; **~er** *n* (*AUT*) démarreur *m* ; (*SPORT: official*) starter *m* ; (: *runner, horse*) partant *m* ; (*CULIN*) entrée *f* ; **~ing handle** *n* manivelle *f* ; **~ing point** *n* point *m* de départ.

**startle** ['stɑ:tl] *vt* faire sursauter ; donner un choc à ; **startling** *a* surprenant(e), saisissant(e).

**starvation** [stɑ:'veɪʃən] *n* faim *f*, famine *f* ; **to die of ~** mourir de faim *or* d'inanition.

**starve** [stɑ:v] *vi* mourir de faim ; être affamé(e) // *vt* affamer ; **I'm starving** je meurs de faim.

**state** [steɪt] *n* état *m* // *vt* déclarer, affirmer ; formuler ; **the S~s** les États-Unis *mpl* ; **to be in a ~** être dans tous ses états ; **~ control** *n* contrôle *m* de l'État ; **~d** *a* fixé(e), prescrit(e) ; **~ly** *a* majestueux(euse), imposant(e) ; **~ment** *n* déclaration *f* ; (*LAW*) déposition *f* ; **~ secret** *n* secret *m* d'État ; **~sman** *n* homme *m* d'État.

**static** ['stætɪk] *n* (*RADIO*) parasites *mpl* // *a* statique ; **~ electricity** *n* électricité *f* statique.

**station** ['steɪʃən] *n* gare *f* ; poste *m* (militaire *or* de police *etc*) ; (*rank*) condition *f*, rang *m* // *vt* placer, poster.

**stationary** ['steɪʃnərɪ] *a* à l'arrêt, immobile.

**stationer** ['steɪʃənə*] *n* papetier/ère ; **~'s (shop)** *n* papeterie *f* ; **~y** *n* papier *m* à lettres, petit matériel de bureau.

**station master** ['steɪʃənmɑ:stə*] *n* (*RAIL*) chef *m* de gare.

**station wagon** ['steɪʃənwægən] *n* (*US*) break *m*.

**statistic** [stə'tɪstɪk] *n* statistique *f* ; **~s** *npl* (*science*) statistique *f* ; **~al** *a* statistique.

**statue** ['stætju:] *n* statue *f* ; **statuesque** [-'ɛsk] *a* sculptural(e).

**stature** ['stætʃə*] *n* stature *f* ; (*fig*) envergure *f*.

**status** ['steɪtəs] *n* position *f*, situation *f* ; prestige *m* ; statut *m* ; **the ~ quo** le statu quo ; **~ symbol** *n* marque *f* de standing, signe extérieur de richesse.

**statute** ['stætju:t] *n* loi *f* ; **~s** *npl* (*of club etc*) statuts *mpl* ; **statutory** *a* statutaire, prévu(e) par un article de loi.

**staunch** [stɔ:ntʃ] *a* sûr(e), loyal(e).

**stave** [steɪv] *n* (*MUS*) portée *f* // *vt*: **to ~ off** (*attack*) parer ; (*threat*) conjurer.

**stay** [steɪ] *n* (*period of time*) séjour *m* // *vi* rester ; (*reside*) loger ; (*spend some time*) séjourner ; **to ~ put** ne pas bouger ; **to ~ with friends** loger chez des amis ; **to ~ the night** passer la nuit ; **to ~ behind** *vi* rester en arrière ; **to ~ in** *vi* (*at home*) rester à la maison ; **to ~ on** *vi* rester ; **to ~ out** *vi* (*of house*) ne pas rentrer ; **to ~ up** *vi* (*at night*) ne pas se coucher.

**STD** *n* (*abbr of Subscriber Trunk Dialling*) l'automatique *m*.

**steadfast** ['stɛdfɑ:st] *a* ferme, résolu(e).

**steadily** ['stɛdɪlɪ] *ad* progressivement ; sans arrêt ; (*walk*) d'un pas ferme.

**steady** ['stɛdɪ] *a* stable, solide, ferme ; (*regular*) constant(e), régulier(ère) ; (*person*) calme, pondéré(e) // *vt* stabiliser ; assujettir ; calmer ; **to ~ oneself** reprendre son aplomb.

**steak** [steɪk] *n* (*meat*) bifteck *m*, steak *m* ; (*fish*) tranche *f* ; **~house** *n* ≈ grill-room *m*.

**steal**, *pt* **stole**, *pp* **stolen** [sti:l, stəul, 'stəuln] *vt,vi* voler.

**stealth** [stɛlθ] *n*: **by ~** furtivement ; **~y** *a* furtif(ive).

**steam** [sti:m] *n* vapeur *f* // *vt* passer à la vapeur ; (*CULIN*) cuire à la vapeur // *vi* fumer ; (*ship*): **to ~ along** filer // **~ engine**

*n* locomotive *f* à vapeur ; ~**er** *n* (bateau *m* à) vapeur *m* ; ~**roller** *n* rouleau compresseur ; ~**y** *a* embué(e), humide.

**steed** [sti:d] *n* coursier *m*.

**steel** [sti:l] *n* acier *m* // *cpd* d'acier ; ~**works** *n* aciérie *f*.

**steep** [sti:p] *a* raide, escarpé(e) ; (*price*) très élevé(e), excessif(ive) // *vt* (faire) tremper.

**steeple** ['sti:pl] *n* clocher *m* ; ~**chase** *n* steeple(-chase) *m* ; ~**jack** *n* réparateur *m* de clochers et de hautes cheminées.

**steeply** ['sti:plɪ] *ad* en pente raide.

**steer** [stɪə*] *n* bœuf *m* // *vt* diriger, gouverner ; guider // *vi* tenir le gouvernail ; ~**ing** *n* (AUT) conduite *f* ; ~**ing column** *n* colonne *f* de direction ; ~**ing wheel** *n* volant *m*.

**stellar** ['stɛlə*] *a* stellaire.

**stem** [stɛm] *n* tige *f* ; queue *f* ; (NAUT) avant *m*, proue *f* // *vt* contenir, endiguer, juguler ; **to** ~ **from** *vt fus* provenir de, découler de.

**stench** [stɛntʃ] *n* puanteur *f*.

**stencil** ['stɛnsl] *n* stencil *m* ; pochoir *m* // *vt* polycopier.

**step** [stɛp] *n* pas *m* ; (*stair*) marche *f* ; (*action*) mesure *f*, disposition *f* // *vi* : **to** ~ **forward** faire un pas en avant, avancer ; ~**s** *npl* = **stepladder** ; **to** ~ **down** *vi* (fig) se retirer, se désister ; **to** ~ **off** *vt fus* descendre de ; **to** ~ **over** *vt fus* marcher sur ; **to** ~ **up** *vt* augmenter ; intensifier ; ~**brother** *n* demi-frère *m* ; ~**child** *n* beau-fils/belle-fille ; ~**father** *n* beau-père *m* ; ~**ladder** *n* escabeau *m* ; ~**mother** *n* belle-mère *f* ; **stepping stone** *n* pierre *f* de gué ; (fig) tremplin *m* ; ~**sister** *n* demi-sœur *f*.

**stereo** ['stɛrɪəu] *n* (*system*) stéréo *f* ; (*record player*) chaîne *f* stéréo // *a* (*also*: ~**phonic**) *a* stéréophonique.

**stereotype** ['stɪərɪətaɪp] *n* stéréotype *m* // *vt* stéréotyper.

**sterile** ['stɛraɪl] *a* stérile ; **sterility** [-'rɪlɪtɪ] *n* stérilité *f* ; **sterilization** [-'zeɪʃən] *n* stérilisation *f* ; **sterilize** ['stɛrɪlaɪz] *vt* stériliser.

**sterling** ['stə:lɪŋ] *a* sterling *inv* ; (*silver*) de bon aloi, fin(e) ; (fig) à toute épreuve, excellent(e) ; ~ **area** *n* zone *f* sterling *inv*.

**stern** [stə:n] *a* sévère // *n* (NAUT) arrière *m*, poupe *f*.

**stethoscope** ['stɛθəskəup] *n* stéthoscope *m*.

**stevedore** ['sti:vədɔ:*] *n* docker *m*, débardeur *m*.

**stew** [stju:] *n* ragoût *m* // *vt*, *vi* cuire à la casserole ; ~**ed tea** thé trop infusé.

**steward** ['stjuəd] *n* (AVIAT, NAUT, RAIL) steward *m* ; (*in club etc*) intendant *m* ; ~**ess** *n* hôtesse *f*.

**stick** [stɪk] *n* bâton *m* ; morceau *m* // *vb* (*pt, pp* **stuck** [stʌk]) *vt* (*glue*) coller ; (*thrust*): **to** ~ **sth into** piquer or planter or enfoncer qch dans ; (*col: put*) mettre, fourrer ; (*col: tolerate*) supporter // *vi* se planter ; tenir ; (*remain*) rester ; **to** ~ **out**, **to** ~ **up** *vi* dépasser, sortir ; **to** ~ **up for** *vt fus* défendre ; ~**er** *n* auto-collant *m*.

**stickleback** ['stɪklbæk] *n* épinoche *f*.

**stickler** ['stɪklə*] *n* : **to be a** ~ **for** être pointilleux(euse) sur.

**sticky** ['stɪkɪ] *a* poisseux(euse) ; (*label*) adhésif(ive).

**stiff** [stɪf] *a* raide ; rigide ; dur(e) ; (*difficult*) difficile, ardu(e) ; (*cold*) froid(e), distant(e) ; (*strong, high*) fort(e), élevé(e) ; ~**en** *vt* raidir, renforcer // *vi* se raidir ; se durcir ; ~ **neck** *n* torticolis *m* ; ~**ness** *n* raideur *f*.

**stifle** ['staɪfl] *vt* étouffer, réprimer ; **stifling** *a* (*heat*) suffocant(e).

**stigma, *pl*** (BOT, MED, REL) ~**ta**, (fig) ~**s** ['stɪgmə, stɪg'mɑ:tə] *n* stigmate *m*.

**stile** [staɪl] *n* échalier *m*.

**stiletto** [stɪ'lɛtəu] *n* (*also:* ~ **heel**) talon *m* aiguille.

**still** [stɪl] *a* immobile ; calme, tranquille // *ad* (*up to this time*) encore, toujours ; (*even*) encore ; (*nonetheless*) quand même, tout de même ; ~**born** *a* mort-né(e) ; ~ **life** *n* nature morte.

**stilt** [stɪlt] *n* échasse *f* ; (*pile*) pilotis *m*.

**stilted** ['stɪltɪd] *a* guindé(e), emprunté(e).

**stimulant** ['stɪmjulənt] *n* stimulant *m*.

**stimulate** ['stɪmjuleɪt] *vt* stimuler ; **stimulating** *a* stimulant(e) ; **stimulation** [-'leɪʃən] *n* stimulation *f*.

**stimulus, *pl* stimuli** ['stɪmjuləs, 'stɪmjulaɪ] *n* stimulant *m* ; (BIOL, PSYCH) stimulus *m*.

**sting** [stɪŋ] *n* piqûre *f* ; (*organ*) dard *m* // *vt* (*pt,pp* **stung** [stʌŋ]) piquer.

**stingy** ['stɪndʒɪ] *a* avare ; pingre, chiche.

**stink** [stɪŋk] *n* puanteur *f* // *vi* (*pt* **stank**, *pp* **stunk** [stæŋk, stʌŋk]) puer, empester ; ~**er** *n* (col) vacherie *f* ; dégueulasse *m/f* ; ~**ing** *a* (col): **a** ~**ing...** un(e) vache de..., un(e) foutu(e)... .

**stint** [stɪnt] *n* part *f* de travail // *vi* : **to** ~ **on** lésiner sur, être chiche de.

**stipend** ['staɪpɛnd] *n* (*of vicar etc*) traitement *m*.

**stipulate** ['stɪpjuleɪt] *vt* stipuler ; **stipulation** [-'leɪʃən] *n* stipulation *f*, condition *f*.

**stir** [stə:*] *n* agitation *f*, sensation *f* // *vt* remuer // *vi* remuer, bouger ; **to** ~ **up** *vt* exciter ; ~**ring** *a* excitant(e) ; émouvant(e).

**stirrup** ['stɪrəp] *n* étrier *m*.

**stitch** [stɪtʃ] *n* (SEWING) point *m* ; (KNITTING) maille *f* ; (MED) point de suture ; (*pain*) point de côté // *vt* coudre, piquer ; suturer.

**stoat** [stəut] *n* hermine *f* (*avec son pelage d'été*).

**stock** [stɔk] *n* réserve *f*, provision *f* ; (COMM) stock *m* ; (AGR) cheptel *m*, bétail *m* ; (CULIN) bouillon *m* ; (FINANCE) valeurs *fpl*, titres *mpl* // *a* (fig: *reply etc*) courant(e) ; classique // *vt* (*have in stock*) avoir, vendre ; **well-**~**ed** bien approvisionné(e) or fourni(e) ; **to take** ~ (fig) faire le point ; **to** ~ **up** *vt* remplir, garnir // *vi* : **to** ~ **up (with)** s'approvisionner (en).

**stockade** [stɔ'keɪd] *n* palissade *f*.

**stockbroker** ['stɔkbrəukə*] *n* agent *m* de change.

**stock exchange** ['stɔkɪkstʃeɪndʒ] *n* Bourse *f* (des valeurs).

**stocking** ['stɔkɪŋ] *n* bas *m*.

**stockist** ['stɔkɪst] *n* stockiste *m*.
**stock market** ['stɔkmɑːkɪt] *n* Bourse *f*, marché financier.
**stock phrase** ['stɔk'freɪz] *n* cliché *m*.
**stockpile** ['stɔkpaɪl] *n* stock *m*, réserve *f* // *vt* stocker, accumuler.
**stocktaking** ['stɔkteɪkɪŋ] *n* (COMM) inventaire *m*.
**stocky** ['stɔkɪ] *a* trapu(e), râblé(e).
**stodgy** ['stɔdʒɪ] *a* bourratif(ive), lourd(e).
**stoic** ['stəuɪk] *n* stoïque *m/f* ; ~**al** a stoïque.
**stoke** [stəuk] *vt* garnir, entretenir ; chauffer ; ~**r** *n* chauffeur *m*.
**stole** [stəul] *pt of* steal // *n* étole *f*.
**stolen** ['stəuln] *pp of* steal.
**stolid** ['stɔlɪd] *a* impassible, flegmatique.
**stomach** ['stʌmək] *n* estomac *m* ; (*abdomen*) ventre *m* // *vt* supporter, digérer ; ~ **ache** *n* mal *m* à l'estomac *or* au ventre.
**stone** [stəun] *n* pierre *f* ; (*pebble*) caillou *m*, galet *m* ; (*in fruit*) noyau *m* ; (MED) calcul *m* ; (*weight*) mesure de poids = 6.348 kg. ; 14 pounds // *cpd* de *or* en pierre // *vt* dénoyauter ; ~**-cold** *a* complètement froid(e) ; ~**-deaf** *a* sourd(e) comme un pot ; ~**mason** *n* tailleur *m* de pierre(s) ; ~**work** *n* maçonnerie *f* ; **stony** *n* pierreux(euse), rocailleux(euse).
**stood** [stud] *pt,pp of* stand.
**stool** [stuːl] *n* tabouret *m*.
**stoop** [stuːp] *vi* (*also:* **have a** ~) être voûté(e) ; (*bend*) se baisser, se courber.
**stop** [stɔp] *n* arrêt *m* ; halte *f* ; (*in punctuation*) point *m* // *vt* arrêter ; (*break off*) interrompre ; (*also:* **put a** ~ **to**) mettre fin à // *vi* s'arrêter ; (*rain, noise etc*) cesser, s'arrêter ; **to** ~ **doing sth** cesser *or* arrêter de faire qch ; **to** ~ **dead** *vi* s'arrêter net ; **to** ~ **off** *vi* faire une courte halte ; **to** ~ **up** *vt* (*hole*) boucher ; ~**lights** *npl* (AUT) signaux *mpl* de stop, feux *mpl* arrière ; ~**over** *n* halte *f* ; (AVIAT) escale *f*.
**stoppage** ['stɔpɪdʒ] *n* arrêt *m* ; (*of pay*) retenue *f* ; (*strike*) arrêt de travail.
**stopper** ['stɔpə*] *n* bouchon *m*.
**stop-press** ['stɔp'prɛs] *n* nouvelles *fpl* de dernière heure.
**stopwatch** ['stɔpwɔtʃ] *n* chronomètre *m*.
**storage** ['stɔːrɪdʒ] *n* emmagasinage *m* ; (COMPUTERS) mise *f* en mémoire *or* réserve.
**store** [stɔː*] *n* provision *f*, réserve *f* ; (*depot*) entrepôt *m* ; (*large shop*) grand magasin // *vt* emmagasiner ; **to** ~ **up** *vt* mettre en réserve, emmagasiner ; ~**room** *n* réserve *f*, magasin *m*.
**storey, story** (*US*) ['stɔːrɪ] *n* étage *m*.
**stork** [stɔːk] *n* cigogne *f*.
**storm** [stɔːm] *n* orage *m*, tempête *f* ; ouragan *m* // *vi* (*fig*) fulminer // *vt* prendre d'assaut ; ~ **cloud** *n* nuage *m* d'orage ; ~**y** *a* orageux(euse).
**story** ['stɔːrɪ] *n* histoire *f* ; récit *m* ; (*US*) = storey ; ~**book** *n* livre *m* d'histoires *or* de contes ; ~**teller** *n* conteur/euse.
**stout** [staut] *a* solide ; (*brave*) intrépide ; (*fat*) gros(se), corpulent(e) // *n* bière brune.
**stove** [stəuv] *n* (*for cooking*) fourneau *m* ; (: *small*) réchaud *m* ; (*for heating*) poêle *m*.

**stow** [stəu] *vt* ranger ; cacher ; ~**away** *n* passager/ère clandestin(e).
**straddle** ['strædl] *vt* enjamber, être à cheval sur.
**strafe** [strɑːf] *vt* mitrailler.
**straggle** ['strægl] *vi* être (*or* marcher) en désordre ; ~**d along the coast** disséminé(e) tout au long de la côte ; ~**r** *n* traînard/e ; **straggling, straggly** *a* (*hair*) en désordre.
**straight** [streɪt] *a* droit(e) ; (*frank*) honnête, franc(he) *or* (tout) droit ; (*drink*) sec, sans eau // *n*: **the** ~ la ligne droite ; **to put** *or* **get** ~ mettre en ordre, mettre de l'ordre dans ; ~ **away, ~ off** (*at once*) tout de suite ; ~ **off, ~ out** sans hésiter ; ~**en** *vt* (*also:* ~**en out**) redresser ; ~**forward** *a* simple ; honnête, direct(e).
**strain** [streɪn] *n* (TECH) tension *f* ; pression *f* ; (*physical*) effort *m* ; (*mental*) tension (nerveuse) ; (MED) entorse *f* ; (*streak, trace*) tendance *f* ; élément *m* // *vt* tendre fortement ; mettre à l'épreuve ; (*filter*) passer, filtrer // *vi* peiner, fournir un gros effort ; ~**s** *npl* (MUS) accords *mpl*, accents *mpl* ; ~**ed** *a* (*laugh etc*) forcé(e), contraint(e) ; (*relations*) tendu(e) ; ~**er** *n* passoire *f*.
**strait** [streɪt] *n* (GEO) détroit *m* ; ~ **jacket** *n* camisole *f* de force ; ~**-laced** *a* collet monté *inv*.
**strand** [strænd] *n* (*of thread*) fil *m*, brin *m* // *vt* (*boat*) échouer ; ~**ed** *a* en rade, en plan.
**strange** [streɪndʒ] *a* (*not known*) inconnu(e) ; (*odd*) étrange, bizarre ; ~**ly** *ad* étrangement, bizarrement ; ~**r** *n* inconnu/e ; étranger/ère.
**strangle** ['stræŋgl] *vt* étrangler ; ~**hold** *n* (*fig*) emprise totale, mainmise *f* ; **strangulation** [-'leɪʃən] *n* strangulation *f*.
**strap** [stræp] *n* lanière *f*, courroie *f*, sangle *f* ; (*of slip, dress*) bretelle *f* // *vt* attacher (avec une courroie *etc*) ; (*child etc*) administrer une correction à.
**strapping** ['stræpɪŋ] *a* bien découplé(e), costaud(e).
**strata** ['strɑːtə] *npl of* stratum.
**stratagem** ['strætɪdʒəm] *n* stratagème *m*.
**strategic** [strə'tiːdʒɪk] *a* stratégique.
**strategist** ['strætɪdʒɪst] *n* stratège *m*.
**strategy** ['strætɪdʒɪ] *n* stratégie *f*.
**stratosphere** ['strætəsfɪə*] *n* stratosphère *f*.
**stratum, *pl* strata** ['strɑːtəm, 'struːtə] *n* strate *f*, couche *f*.
**straw** [strɔː] *n* paille *f*.
**strawberry** ['strɔːbərɪ] *n* fraise *f* ; (*plant*) fraisier *m*.
**stray** [streɪ] *a* (*animal*) perdu(e), errant(e) // *vi* s'égarer ; ~ **bullet** *n* balle perdue.
**streak** [striːk] *n* raie *f*, bande *f*, filet *m* ; (*fig: of madness etc*): **a** ~ **of** une *or* des tendance(s) à // *vt* zébrer, strier // *vi*: **to** ~ **past** passer à toute allure ; ~**y** *a* zébré(e), strié(e) ; ~**y bacon** *n* ≈ lard *m* (maigre).
**stream** [striːm] *n* ruisseau *m* ; courant *m*, flot *m* ; (*of people*) défilé ininterrompu, flot // *vt* (SCOL) répartir par niveau // *vi*

ruisseler ; **to ~ in/out** entrer/sortir à flots.

**streamer** ['stri:mə*] *n* serpentin *m*, banderole *f*.

**streamlined** ['stri:mlaɪnd] *a* (*AVIAT*) fuselé(e), profilé(e) ; (*AUT*) aérodynamique ; (*fig*) rationalisé(e).

**street** [stri:t] *n* rue *f* ; ~ **car** *n* (*US*) tramway *m* ; ~ **lamp** *n* réverbère *m*.

**strength** [strɛŋθ] *n* force *f* ; (*of girder, knot etc*) solidité *f* ; ~**en** *vt* fortifier ; renforcer ; consolider.

**strenuous** ['strɛnjuəs] *a* vigoureux(euse), énergique ; (*tiring*) ardu(e), fatigant(e).

**stress** [strɛs] *n* (*force, pressure*) pression *f* ; (*mental strain*) tension (nerveuse) ; (*accent*) accent *m* // *vt* insister sur, souligner.

**stretch** [strɛtʃ] *n* (*of sand etc*) étendue *f* // *vi* s'étirer ; (*extend*): **to ~ to/as far as** s'étendre jusqu'à // *vt* tendre, étirer ; (*spread*) étendre ; (*fig*) pousser (au maximum) ; **at a ~** sans discontinuer, sans interruption ; **to ~ a muscle** se distendre un muscle ; **to ~ out** *vi* s'étendre // *vt* (*arm etc*) allonger, tendre ; (*to spread*) étendre ; **to ~ out for something** allonger la main pour prendre qch.

**stretcher** ['strɛtʃə*] *n* brancard *m*, civière *f*.

**strewn** [stru:n] *a*: ~ **with** jonché(e) de.

**stricken** ['strɪkən] *a* très éprouvé(e) ; dévasté(e) ; ~ **with** frappé(e) *or* atteint(e) de.

**strict** [strɪkt] *a* strict(e) ; ~**ly** *ad* strictement ; ~**ness** *n* sévérité *f*.

**stride** [straɪd] *n* grand pas, enjambée *f* // *vi* (*pt* **strode**, *pp* **stridden** [strəud, 'strɪdn]) marcher à grands pas.

**strident** ['straɪdnt] *a* strident(c).

**strife** [straɪf] *n* conflit *m*, dissensions *fpl*.

**strike** [straɪk] *n* grève *f* ; (*of oil etc*) découverte *f* ; (*attack*) raid *m* // *vb* (*pt,pp* **struck** [strʌk]) *vt* frapper ; (*oil etc*) trouver, découvrir // *vi* faire grève ; (*attack*) attaquer ; (*clock*) sonner ; **to ~ a match** frotter une allumette ; **to ~ down** *vt* (*fig*) terrasser ; **to ~ out** *vt* rayer ; **to ~ up** *vt* (*MUS*) se mettre à jouer ; **to ~ up a friendship with** se lier d'amitié avec ; ~**breaker** *n* briseur *m* de grève ; ~**r** *n* gréviste *m/f* ; (*SPORT*) buteur *m* ; **striking** *a* frappant(e), saisissant(e).

**string** [strɪŋ] *n* ficelle *f*, fil *m* ; (*row*) rang *m* ; chapelet *m* ; file *f* ; (*MUS*) corde *f* // *vt* (*pt,pp* **strung** [strʌŋ]): **to ~ out** échelonner ; **the ~s** *npl* (*MUS*) les instruments *mpl* à corde ; ~ **bean** *n* haricot vert ; ~**(ed) instrument** *n* (*MUS*) instrument *m* à cordes.

**stringent** ['strɪndʒənt] *a* rigoureux(euse) ; (*need*) impérieux(euse).

**strip** [strɪp] *n* bande *f* // *vt* déshabiller ; dégarnir, dépouiller ; (*also*: ~ **down**: *machine*) démonter // *vi* se déshabiller ; ~ **cartoon** *n* bande dessinée.

**stripe** [straɪp] *n* raie *f*, rayure *f* ; ~**d** *a* rayé(e), à rayures.

**strip light** ['strɪplaɪt] *n* (tube *m* au) néon *m*.

**stripper** ['strɪpə*] *n* strip-teaseuse *f*.

**striptease** ['strɪpti:z] *n* strip-tease *m*.

**strive, ***pt* **strove,** *pp* **striven** [straɪv, strəuv, 'strɪvn] *vi*: **to ~ to do** s'efforcer de faire.

**strode** [strəud] *pt of* **stride.**

**stroke** [strəuk] *n* coup *m* ; (*MED*) attaque *f* ; (*caress*) caresse *f* // *vt* caresser ; **at a ~** d'un (seul) coup ; **on the ~ of 5** à 5 heures sonnantes ; **a 2-~ engine** un moteur à 2 temps.

**stroll** [strəul] *n* petite promenade // *vi* flâner, se promener nonchalamment.

**strong** [strɔŋ] *a* fort(e) ; vigoureux(euse) ; solide ; vif(vive) ; **they are 50 ~** ils sont au nombre de 50 ; ~**hold** *n* bastion *m* ; ~**ly** *ad* fortement, avec force ; vigoureusement ; solidement ; ~**room** *n* chambre forte.

**strove** [strəuv] *pt of* **strive.**

**struck** [strʌk] *pt,pp of* **strike.**

**structural** ['strʌktʃərəl] *a* structural(e) ; (*CONSTR*) de construction ; affectant les parties portantes ; ~**ly** *ad* du point de vue de la construction.

**structure** ['strʌktʃə*] *n* structure *f* ; (*building*) construction *f* ; édifice *m*.

**struggle** ['strʌgl] *n* lutte *f* // *vi* lutter, se battre.

**strum** [strʌm] *vt* (*guitar*) gratter de.

**strung** [strʌŋ] *pt,pp of* **string.**

**strut** [strʌt] *n* étai *m*, support *m* // *vi* se pavaner.

**stub** [stʌb] *n* bout *m* ; (*of ticket etc*) talon *m* ; **to ~ out** *vt* écraser.

**stubble** ['stʌbl] *n* chaume *m* ; (*on chin*) barbe *f* de plusieurs jours.

**stubborn** ['stʌbən] *a* têtu(e), obstiné(e), opiniâtre.

**stubby** ['stʌbɪ] *a* trapu(e) ; gros(se) et court(e).

**stuck** [stʌk] *pt,pp of* **stick** // *a* (*jammed*) bloqué(e), coincé(e) ; ~-**up** *a* prétentieux(euse).

**stud** [stʌd] *n* clou *m* (à grosse tête) ; bouton *m* de col ; (*of horses*) écurie *f*, haras *m* ; (*also*: ~ **horse**) étalon *m* // *vt* (*fig*): ~**ded with** parsemé(e) *or* criblé(e) de.

**student** ['stju:dənt] *n* étudiant/e // *cpd* estudiantin(e) ; universitaire ; d'étudiant.

**studied** ['stʌdɪd] *a* étudié(e), calculé(e).

**studio** ['stju:dɪəu] *n* studio *m*, atelier *m*.

**studious** ['stju:dɪəs] *a* studieux(euse), appliqué(e) ; (*studied*) étudié(e) ; ~**ly** *ad* (*carefully*) soigneusement.

**study** ['stʌdɪ] *n* étude *f* ; (*room*) bureau *m* // *vt* étudier ; examiner // *vi* étudier, faire ses études.

**stuff** [stʌf] *n* chose(s) *f(pl)*, truc *m* ; affaires *fpl* ; (*substance*) substance *f* // *vt* rembourrer ; (*CULIN*) farcir ; ~**ing** *n* bourre *f*, rembourrage *m* ; (*CULIN*) farce *f* ; ~**y** *a* (*room*) mal ventilé(e) *or* aéré(e) ; (*ideas*) vieux jeu *inv*.

**stumble** ['stʌmbl] *vi* trébucher ; **to ~ across** (*fig*) tomber sur ; **stumbling block** *n* pierre *f* d'achoppement.

**stump** [stʌmp] *n* souche *f* ; (*of limb*) moignon *m* // *vt*: **to be ~ed** sécher, ne pas savoir que répondre.

**stun** [stʌn] *vt* étourdir ; abasourdir.

**stung** [stʌŋ] *pt, pp of* **sting**.

**stunk** [stʌŋk] *pp of* **stink**.

**stunning** ['stʌnɪŋ] *a* étourdissant(e), stupéfiant(e).

**stunt** [stʌnt] *n* tour *m* de force ; truc *m* publicitaire ; (*AVIAT*) acrobatie *f* // *vt* retarder, arrêter ; **~ed** *a* rabougri(e) ; **~man** *n* cascadeur *m*.

**stupefy** ['stju:pɪfaɪ] *vt* étourdir ; abrutir ; (*fig*) stupéfier.

**stupendous** [stju:'pɛndəs] *a* prodigieux(euse), fantastique.

**stupid** ['stju:pɪd] *a* stupide, bête ; **~ity** [-'pɪdɪtɪ] *n* stupidité *f*, bêtise *f* ; **~ly** *ad* stupidement, bêtement.

**stupor** ['stju:pə*] *n* stupeur *f*.

**sturdy** ['stə:dɪ] *a* robuste, vigoureux(euse) ; solide.

**sturgeon** ['stə:dʒən] *n* esturgeon *m*.

**stutter** ['stʌtə*] *n* bégaiement *m* // *vi* bégayer.

**sty** [staɪ] *n* (*of pigs*) porcherie *f*.

**stye** [staɪ] *n* (*MED*) orgelet *m*.

**style** [staɪl] *n* style *m* ; (*distinction*) allure *f*, cachet *m*, style *m* ; **stylish** *a* élégant(e), chic *inv*.

**stylized** ['staɪlaɪzd] *a* stylisé(e).

**stylus** ['staɪləs] *n* (*of record player*) pointe *f* de lecture.

**suave** [swɑ:v] *a* doucereux(euse), onctueux(euse).

**sub...** [sʌb] *prefix* sub..., sous- ; **subconscious** *a* subconscient(e) // *n* subconscient *m* ; **subdivide** *vt* subdiviser ; **subdivision** *n* subdivision *f*.

**subdue** [səb'dju:] *vt* subjuguer, soumettre ; **~d** *a* contenu(e), atténué(e) ; (*light*) tamisé(e) ; (*person*) qui a perdu de son entrain.

**subject** *n* ['sʌbdʒɪkt] sujet *m* ; (*SCOL*) matière *f* // *vt* [səb'dʒɛkt]: **to ~ to** soumettre à ; exposer à ; **to be ~ to** (*law*) être soumis(e) à ; (*disease*) être sujet(te) à ; **~ion** [-'dʒɛkʃən] soumission *f*, sujétion *f* ; **~ive** *a* subjectif(ive) ; (*LING*) sujet(te) ; **~ matter** *n* sujet *m* ; contenu *m*.

**sub judice** [sʌb'dju:dɪsɪ] *a* devant les tribunaux.

**subjunctive** [səb'dʒʌŋktɪv] *a* subjonctif(ive) // *n* subjonctif *m*.

**sublet** [sʌb'lɛt] *vt* sous-louer.

**sublime** [sə'blaɪm] *a* sublime.

**submachine gun** ['sʌbmə'ʃi:ngʌn] *n* fusil-mitrailleur *m*.

**submarine** [sʌbmə'ri:n] *n* sous-marin *m*.

**submerge** [səb'mə:dʒ] *vt* submerger ; immerger // *vi* plonger.

**submission** [səb'mɪʃən] *n* soumission *f*.

**submissive** [səb'mɪsɪv] *a* soumis(e).

**submit** [səb'mɪt] *vt* soumettre // *vi* se soumettre.

**subordinate** [sə'bɔ:dɪnət] *a,n* subordonné(e).

**subpoena** [səb'pi:nə] (*LAW*) *n* citation *f*, assignation *f* // *vt* citer *or* assigner (à comparaître).

**subscribe** [səb'skraɪb] *vi* cotiser ; **to ~ to** (*opinion, fund*) souscrire à ; (*newspaper*) s'abonner à ; être abonné(e) à ; **~r** *n* (*to periodical, telephone*) abonné/e.

**subscription** [səb'skrɪpʃən] *n* souscription *f* ; abonnement *m*.

**subsequent** ['sʌbsɪkwənt] *a* ultérieur(e), suivant(e) ; consécutif(ive) ; **~ly** *ad* par la suite.

**subside** [səb'saɪd] *vi* s'affaisser ; (*flood*) baisser ; (*wind*) tomber ; **~nce** [-'saɪdns] *n* affaissement *m*.

**subsidiary** [səb'sɪdɪərɪ] *a* subsidiaire ; accessoire // *n* filiale *f*.

**subsidize** ['sʌbsɪdaɪz] *vt* subventionner.

**subsidy** ['sʌbsɪdɪ] *n* subvention *f*.

**subsistence** [səb'sɪstəns] *n* existence *f*, subsistance *f*.

**substance** ['sʌbstəns] *n* substance *f* ; (*fig*) essentiel *m* ; **a man of ~** un homme jouissant d'une certaine fortune.

**substandard** [sʌb'stændəd] *a* de qualité inférieure.

**substantial** [səb'stænʃl] *a* substantiel(le) ; (*fig*) important(e) ; **~ly** *ad* considérablement ; en grande partie.

**substantiate** [səb'stænʃɪeɪt] *vt* étayer, fournir des preuves à l'appui de.

**substitute** ['sʌbstɪtju:t] *n* (*person*) remplaçant/e ; (*thing*) succédané *m* // *vt*: **to ~ sth/sb for** substituer qch/qn à, remplacer par qch/qn ; **substitution** [-'tju:ʃən] *n* substitution *f*.

**subterfuge** ['sʌbtəfju:dʒ] *n* subterfuge *m*.

**subterranean** [sʌbtə'reɪnɪən] *a* souterrain(e).

**subtitle** ['sʌbtaɪtl] *n* (*CINEMA*) sous-titre *m*.

**subtle** ['sʌtl] *a* subtil(e) ; **~ty** *n* subtilité *f*.

**subtract** [səb'trækt] *vt* soustraire, retrancher ; **~ion** [-'trækʃən] *n* soustraction *f*.

**subtropical** [sʌb'trɔpɪkl] *a* subtropical(e).

**suburb** ['sʌbə:b] *n* faubourg *m* ; **the ~s** la banlieue ; **~an** [sə'bə:bən] *a* de banlieue, suburbain(e).

**subvention** [səb'vɛnʃən] *n* (*US: subsidy*) subvention *f*.

**subversive** [səb'və:sɪv] *a* subversif(ive).

**subway** ['sʌbweɪ] *n* (*US*) métro *m* ; (*Brit*) passage souterrain.

**sub-zero** [sʌb'zɪərəu] *a* au-dessous de zéro.

**succeed** [sək'si:d] *vi* réussir ; avoir du succès // *vt* succéder à ; **to ~ in doing** réussir à faire ; **~ing** *a* (*following*) suivant(e).

**success** [sək'sɛs] *n* succès *m* ; réussite *f* ; **~ful** *a* (*venture*) couronné(e) de succès ; **to be ~ful (in doing)** réussir (à faire) ; **~fully** *ad* avec succès.

**succession** [sək'sɛʃən] *n* succession *f*.

**successive** [sək'sɛsɪv] *a* successif(ive) ; consécutif(ive).

**successor** [sək'sɛsə*] *n* successeur *m*.

**succinct** [sək'sɪŋkt] *a* succinct(e), bref(brève).

**succulent** ['sʌkjulənt] *a* succulent(e).

**succumb** [sə'kʌm] *vi* succomber.

**such** [sʌtʃ] *a, det* tel(telle) ; (*of that kind*): **~ a book** un livre de ce genre *or* pareil, un tel livre ; **~ books** des livres de ce genre *or* pareils, de tels livres ; (*so much*): **~ courage** un tel courage ; **~ a long trip** un si long voyage ; **~ good books** de si bons livres; ~ **a long trip that** un voyage si *or* tellement long que; ~ **a lot of** tellement *or* tant de; **making** ~ **a noise that** faisant un tel bruit que *or* tellement de bruit que; ~ **as** (*like*) tel(telle) que, comme; **a noise** ~ **as to** un bruit de nature à; **as** ~ *ad* en tant que tel(telle), à proprement parler; ~**-and-**~ *det* tel(telle) ou tel(telle).

**suck** [sʌk] *vt* sucer; (*breast, bottle*) téter; ~**er** *n* (*BOT, ZOOL, TECH*) ventouse *f*; (*col*) naïf/ïve, poire *f*.

**suckle** ['sʌkl] *vt* allaiter.

**suction** ['sʌkʃən] *n* succion *f*.

**sudden** ['sʌdn] *a* soudain(e), subit(e); **all of a** ~ soudain, tout à coup; ~**ly** *ad* brusquement, tout à coup, soudain.

**suds** [sʌdz] *npl* eau savonneuse.

**sue** [su:] *vt* poursuivre en justice, intenter un procès à.

**suede** [sweɪd] *n* daim *m*, cuir suédé // *cpd* de daim.

**suet** ['suɪt] *n* graisse *f* de rognon *or* de bœuf.

**Suez Canal** ['su:ɪzkə'næl] *n* canal *m* de Suez.

**suffer** ['sʌfə*] *vt* souffrir, subir; (*bear*) tolérer, supporter // *vi* souffrir; ~**er** *n* malade *m/f*; victime *m/f*; ~**ing** *n* souffrance(s) *f(pl)*.

**suffice** [sə'faɪs] *vi* suffire.

**sufficient** [sə'fɪʃənt] *a* suffisant(e); ~ **money** suffisamment d'argent; ~**ly** *ad* suffisamment, assez.

**suffix** ['sʌfɪks] *n* suffixe *m*.

**suffocate** ['sʌfəkeɪt] *vi* suffoquer; étouffer; **suffocation** [-'keɪʃən] *n* suffocation *f*; (*MED*) asphyxie *f*.

**sugar** ['ʃugə*] *n* sucre *m* // *vt* sucrer; ~ **beet** *n* betterave sucrière; ~ **cane** *n* canne f à sucre; ~**y** *a* sucré(e).

**suggest** [sə'dʒɛst] *vt* suggérer, proposer; dénoter; ~**ion** [-'dʒɛstʃən] *n* suggestion *f*; ~**ive** *a* suggestif(ive).

**suicidal** [suɪ'saɪdl] *a* suicidaire.

**suicide** ['suɪsaɪd] *n* suicide *m*.

**suit** [su:t] *n* (*man's*) costume *m*, complet *m*; (*woman's*) tailleur *m*, ensemble *m*; (*CARDS*) couleur *f* // *vt* aller à; convenir à; (*adapt*): **to** ~ **sth to** adapter *or* approprier qch à; ~**able** *a* qui convient; approprié(e); ~**ably** *ad* comme il se doit (*or* se devait *etc*), convenablement.

**suitcase** ['su:tkeɪs] *n* valise *f*.

**suite** [swi:t] *n* (*of rooms, also MUS*) suite *f*; (*furniture*): **bedroom/dining room** ~ (ensemble *m* de) chambre *f* à coucher/salle *f* à manger.

**sulfur** ['sʌlfə*] *etc* (*US*) = **sulphur** *etc*.

**sulk** [sʌlk] *vi* bouder; ~**y** *a* boudeur(euse), maussade.

**sullen** ['sʌlən] *a* renfrogné(e), maussade; morne.

**sulphur, sulfur** (*US*) ['sʌlfə*] *n* soufre *m*; ~**ic** [-'fjuərɪk] *a*: ~**ic acid** acide *m* sulfurique.

**sultan** ['sʌltən] *n* sultan *m*.

**sultana** [sʌl'tɑ:nə] *n* (*fruit*) raisin sec de Smyrne.

**sultry** ['sʌltrɪ] *a* étouffant(e).

**sum** [sʌm] *n* somme *f*; (*SCOL etc*) calcul *m*; *f*; **to** ~ **up** *vt,vi* résumer.

**summarize** ['sʌməraɪz] *vt* résumer.

**summary** ['sʌmərɪ] *n* résumé *m* // *a* (*justice*) sommaire.

**summer** ['sʌmə*] *n* été *m* // *cpd* d'été, estival(e); ~**house** *n* (*in garden*) pavillon *m*; ~**time** *n* (*season*) été *m*; ~ **time** *n* (*by clock*) heure *f* d'été.

**summit** ['sʌmɪt] *n* sommet *m*; ~ (**conference**) *n* (conférence *f* au) sommet *m*.

**summon** ['sʌmən] *vt* appeler, convoquer; **to** ~ **up** *vt* rassembler, faire appel à; ~**s** *n* citation *f*, assignation *f* // *vt* citer, assigner.

**sump** [sʌmp] *n* (*AUT*) carter *m*.

**sumptuous** ['sʌmptjuəs] *a* somptueux(euse).

**sun** [sʌn] *n* soleil *m*; **in the** ~ au soleil; ~**bathe** *vi* prendre un bain de soleil; ~**burnt** *a* bronzé(e), hâlé(e); (*painfully*) brûlé(e) par le soleil; ~ **cream** *n* crème *f* (anti-)solaire.

**Sunday** ['sʌndɪ] *n* dimanche *m*.

**sundial** ['sʌndaɪəl] *n* cadran *m* solaire.

**sundry** ['sʌndrɪ] *a* divers(e), différent(e); **all and** ~ tout le monde, n'importe qui; **sundries** *npl* articles divers.

**sunflower** ['sʌnflauə*] *n* tournesol *m*.

**sung** [sʌŋ] *pp of* sing.

**sunglasses** ['sʌnglɑ:sɪz] *npl* lunettes *fpl* de soleil.

**sunk** [sʌŋk] *pp of* sink; ~**en** *a* submergé(e); creux(euse).

**sun:** ~**light** *n* (lumière *f* du) soleil *m*; ~**lit** *a* ensoleillé(e); ~**ny** *a* ensoleillé(e); (*fig*) épanoui(e), radieux(euse); ~**rise** *n* lever *m* du soleil; ~**set** *n* coucher *m* du soleil; ~**shade** *n* (*over table*) parasol *m*; ~**shine** *n* (lumière *f* du) soleil *m*; ~**spot** *n* tache *f* solaire; ~**stroke** *n* insolation *f*, coup *m* de soleil; ~**tan** *n* bronzage *m*; ~**tan oil** *n* huile *f* solaire; ~**trap** *n* coin très ensoleillé.

**super** ['su:pə*] *a* (*col*) formidable.

**superannuation** [su:pərænju'eɪʃən] *n* cotisations *fpl* pour la pension.

**superb** [su:'pə:b] *a* superbe, magnifique.

**supercilious** [su:pə'sɪlɪəs] *a* hautain(e), dédaigneux(euse).

**superficial** [su:pə'fɪʃəl] *a* superficiel(le); ~**ly** *ad* superficiellement.

**superfluous** [su'pə:fluəs] *a* superflu(e).

**superhuman** [su:pə'hju:mən] *a* surhumain(e).

**superimpose** ['su:pərɪm'pəuz] *vt* superposer.

**superintendent** [su:pərɪn'tɛndənt] *n* directeur/trice; (*POLICE*) ≈ commissaire *m*.

**superior** [su'pɪərɪə*] *a,n* supérieur(e); ~**ity** [-'ɔrɪtɪ] *n* supériorité *f*.

**superlative** [su'pə:lətɪv] *a* sans pareil(le), suprême // *n* (*LING*) superlatif *m*.

**superman** ['su:pəmæn] *n* surhomme *m*.

**supermarket** ['su:pəmɑ:kɪt] *n* supermarché *m*.

**supernatural** [su:pə'nætʃərəl] *a* surnaturel(le).

**superpower** ['su:pəpauə*] *n* (*POL*) grande puissance.

**supersede** [su:pə'si:d] *vt* remplacer, supplanter.

**supersonic** ['su:pə'sɔnɪk] a supersonique.
**superstition** [su:pə'stɪʃən] n superstition f.
**superstitious** [su:pə'stɪʃəs] a superstitieux(euse).
**supertanker** ['su:pətæŋkə*] n pétrolier géant, superpétrolier m.
**supervise** ['su:pəvaɪz] vt surveiller; diriger; **supervision** [-'vɪʒən] n surveillance f; contrôle m; **supervisor** n surveillant/e; (in shop) chef m de rayon; **supervisory** a de surveillance.
**supper** ['sʌpə*] n dîner m; (late) souper m.
**supple** ['sʌpl] a souple.
**supplement** n ['sʌplɪmənt] supplément m // vt [sʌplɪ'mɛnt] ajouter à, compléter; ~**ary** [-'mɛntərɪ] a supplémentaire.
**supplier** [sə'plaɪə*] n fournisseur m.
**supply** [sə'plaɪ] vt (provide) fournir; (equip): **to** ~ **(with)** approvisionner or ravitailler (en); fournir (en); alimenter (en) // n provision f, réserve f; (supplying) approvisionnement m; (TECH) alimentation f // cpd (teacher etc) suppléant(e); **supplies** npl (food) vivres mpl; (MIL) subsistances fpl; ~ **and demand** l'offre f et la demande.
**support** [sə'pɔ:t] n (moral, financial etc) soutien m, appui m; (TECH) support m, soutien // vt soutenir, supporter; (financially) subvenir aux besoins de; (uphold) être pour, être partisan de, appuyer; (endure) supporter, tolérer; ~**er** n (POL etc) partisan/e; (SPORT) supporter m.
**suppose** [sə'pəuz] vt, vi supposer; imaginer; **to be** ~**d to do** être censé(e) faire; ~**dly** [sə'pəuzɪdlɪ] ad soi-disant; **supposing** cj si, à supposer que + sub; **supposition** [sʌpə'zɪʃən] n supposition f, hypothèse f.
**suppress** [sə'prɛs] vt réprimer; supprimer; étouffer; refouler; ~**ion** [sə'prɛʃən] n suppression f, répression f; ~**or** n (ELEC etc) dispositif m antiparasite.
**supremacy** [su'prɛməsɪ] n suprématie f.
**supreme** [su'pri:m] a suprême.
**surcharge** ['sə:tʃɑ:dʒ] n surcharge f; (extra tax) surtaxe f.
**sure** [ʃuə*] a (gen) sûr(e); (definite, convinced) sûr(e), certain(e); ~**!** (of course) bien sûr!; ~ **enough** effectivement; **to make** ~ **of** s'assurer de; vérifier; ~**-footed** a au pied sûr; ~**ly** ad sûrement; certainement.
**surety** ['ʃuərətɪ] n caution f.
**surf** [sə:f] n ressac m.
**surface** ['sə:fɪs] n surface f // vt (road) poser le revêtement de // vi remonter à la surface; faire surface; ~ **mail** n courrier m par voie de terre (or maritime).
**surfboard** ['sə:fbɔ:d] n planche f de surf.
**surfeit** ['sə:fɪt] n: **a** ~ **of** un excès de; une indigestion de.
**surfing** ['sə:fɪŋ] n surf m.
**surge** [sə:dʒ] n vague f, montée f // vi déferler.
**surgeon** ['sə:dʒən] n chirurgien m.
**surgery** ['sə:dʒərɪ] n chirurgie f; (room) cabinet m (de consultation); **to undergo**

~ être opéré(e); ~ **hours** npl heures fpl de consultation.
**surgical** ['sə:dʒɪkl] a chirurgical(e); ~ **spirit** n alcool m à 90s.
**surly** ['sə:lɪ] a revêche, maussade.
**surmise** [sə'maɪz] vt présumer, conjecturer.
**surmount** [sə'maunt] vt surmonter.
**surname** ['sə:neɪm] n nom m de famille.
**surpass** [sə:'pɑ:s] vt surpasser, dépasser.
**surplus** ['sə:pləs] n surplus m, excédent m // a en surplus, de trop.
**surprise** [sə'praɪz] n (gen) surprise f; (astonishment) étonnement m // vt surprendre; étonner; **surprising** a surprenant(e), étonnant(e).
**surrealist** [sə'rɪəlɪst] a surréaliste.
**surrender** [sə'rɛndə*] n reddition f, capitulation f // vi se rendre, capituler.
**surreptitious** [sʌrəp'tɪʃəs] a subreptice, furtif(ive).
**surround** [sə'raund] vt entourer; (MIL etc) encercler; ~**ing** a environnant(e); ~**ings** npl environs mpl, alentours mpl.
**surveillance** [sə:'veɪləns] n surveillance f.
**survey** n ['sə:veɪ] enquête f, étude f; (in housebuying etc) inspection f, (rapport m d')expertise f; (of land) levé m // vt [sə:'veɪ] passer en revue; enquêter sur; inspecter; ~**ing** n (of land) arpentage m; ~**or** n expert m; (arpenteur m) géomètre m.
**survival** [sə'vaɪvl] n survie f; (relic) vestige m.
**survive** [sə'vaɪv] vi survivre; (custom etc) subsister // vt survivre à, réchapper de; (person) survivre à; **survivor** n survivant/e.
**susceptible** [sə'sɛptəbl] a: ~ **(to)** sensible (à); (disease) prédisposé(e) (à).
**suspect** a, n ['sʌspɛkt] suspect(e) // vt [səs'pɛkt] soupçonner, suspecter.
**suspend** [səs'pɛnd] vt suspendre; ~**ed sentence** n condamnation f avec sursis; ~**er belt** n porte-jarretelles m inv; ~**ers** npl jarretelles fpl; (US) bretelles fpl.
**suspense** [səs'pɛns] n attente f; (in film etc) suspense m.
**suspension** [səs'pɛnʃən] n (gen AUT) suspension f; (of driving licence) retrait m provisoire; ~ **bridge** n pont suspendu.
**suspicion** [səs'pɪʃən] n soupçon(s) m(pl).
**suspicious** [səs'pɪʃəs] a (suspecting) soupçonneux(euse), méfiant(e); (causing suspicion) suspect(e).
**sustain** [səs'teɪn] vt supporter; soutenir; corroborer; (suffer) subir; recevoir; ~**ed** a (effort) soutenu(e), prolongé(e).
**sustenance** ['sʌstɪnəns] n nourriture f; moyens mpl de subsistance.
**swab** [swɔb] n (MED) tampon m; prélèvement m.
**swagger** ['swægə*] vi plastronner, parader.
**swallow** ['swɔləu] n (bird) hirondelle f; (of food etc) gorgée f // vt avaler; (fig) gober; **to** ~ **up** vt engloutir.
**swam** [swæm] pt of **swim**.
**swamp** [swɔmp] n marais m, marécage m // vt submerger; ~**y** a marécageux(euse).

swan [swɔn] n cygne m.

swap [swɔp] n échange m, troc m // vt: to ~ (for) échanger (contre), troquer (contre).

swarm [swɔ:m] n essaim m // vi fourmiller, grouiller.

swarthy ['swɔ:ðı] a basané(e), bistré(e).

swastika ['swɔstıkə] n croix gammée.

swat [swɔt] vt écraser.

sway [sweı] vi se balancer, osciller; tanguer // vt (influence) influencer.

swear, pt swore, pp sworn [swɛə*, swɔ:*, swɔ:n] vi jurer; to ~ to sth jurer de qch; ~word n gros mot, juron m.

sweat [swɛt] n sueur f, transpiration f // vi suer; in a ~ en sueur.

sweater ['swɛtə*] n tricot m, pull m.

sweaty ['swɛtı] a en sueur, moite or mouillé(e) de sueur.

swede [swi:d] n rutabaga m.

Swede [swi:d] n Suédois/e.

Sweden ['swi:dn] n Suède f.

Swedish ['swi:dıʃ] a suédois(e) // n (LING) suédois m.

sweep [swi:p] n coup m de balai; (curve) grande courbe; (range) champ m; (also: chimney ~) ramoneur m // vb (pt, pp swept [swɛpt]) vt balayer // vi avancer majestueusement or rapidement; s'élancer; s'étendre; to ~ away vt balayer; entraîner; emporter; to ~ past vi passer majestueusement or rapidement; to ~ up vt, vi balayer; ~ing a (gesture) large; circulaire; a ~ing statement une généralisation hâtive.

sweet [swi:t] n dessert m; (candy) bonbon m // a doux(douce); (not savoury) sucré(e); (fresh) frais(fraîche), pur(e); (fig) agréable, doux; gentil(le); mignon(ne); ~bread n ris m de veau; ~corn n maïs sucré; ~en vt sucrer; adoucir; ~heart n amoureux/euse; ~ly ad gentiment; mélodieusement; ~ness n goût sucré; douceur f; ~ pea n pois m de senteur; to have a ~ tooth aimer les sucreries.

swell [swɛl] n (of sea) houle f // a (col: excellent) chouette // vb (pt ~ed, pp swollen, ~ed ['swəulən]) vt augmenter; grossir // vi grossir, augmenter; (sound) s'enfler; (MED) enfler; ~ing n (MED) enflure f; grosseur f.

sweltering ['swɛltərıŋ] a étouffant(e), oppressant(e).

swept [swɛpt] pt,pp of sweep.

swerve [swə:v] vi faire une embardée or un écart; dévier.

swift [swıft] n (bird) martinet m // a rapide, prompt(e); ~ness n rapidité f.

swig [swıg] n (col: drink) lampée f.

swill [swıl] n pâtée f // vt (also: ~ out, ~ down) laver à grande eau.

swim [swım] n: to go for a ~ aller nager or se baigner // vb (pt swam, pp swum [swæm, swʌm]) vi nager; (SPORT) faire de la natation; (head, room) tourner // vt traverser (à la nage); faire (à la nage); ~mer n nageur/euse; ~ming n nage f, natation f; ~ming baths npl piscine f; ~ming cap n bonnet m de bain; ~ming costume n maillot m (de bain); ~ming

pool n piscine f; ~suit n maillot m (de bain).

swindle ['swındl] n escroquerie f // vt escroquer; ~r n escroc m.

swine [swaın] n, pl inv pourceau m, porc m; (col!) salaud m (!).

swing [swıŋ] n balançoire f; (movement) balancement m, oscillations fpl; (MUS) swing m; rythme m // vb (pt, pp swung [swʌŋ]) vt balancer, faire osciller; (also: ~ round) tourner, faire virer // vi se balancer, osciller; (also: ~ round) virer, tourner; to be in full ~ battre son plein; ~ bridge n pont tournant; ~ door n porte battante.

swingeing ['swındʒıŋ] a écrasant(e); considérable.

swinging ['swıŋıŋ] a rythmé(e); entraînant(e).

swipe [swaıp] n grand coup; gifle f // vt (hit) frapper à toute volée; gifler; (col: steal) piquer.

swirl [swə:l] n tourbillon m // vi tourbillonner, tournoyer.

swish [swıʃ] a (col: smart) rupin(e) // vi siffler.

Swiss [swıs] a suisse // n, pl inv Suisse/esse; ~ German a suisse-allemand(e).

switch [swıtʃ] n (for light, radio etc) bouton m; (change) changement m, revirement m // vt (change) changer; intervertir; to ~ off vt éteindre; (engine) arrêter; to ~ on vt allumer; (engine, machine) mettre en marche; ~back n montagnes fpl russes; ~board n (TEL) standard m; ~board operator standardiste m/f.

Switzerland ['swıtsələnd] n Suisse f.

swivel ['swıvl] vi (also: ~ round) pivoter, tourner.

swollen ['swəulən] pp of swell // a (ankle etc) enflé(e).

swoon [swu:n] vi se pâmer.

swoop [swu:p] n (by police etc) rafle f, descente f // vi (also: ~ down) descendre en piqué, piquer.

swop [swɔp] n, vt = swap.

sword [sɔ:d] n épée f; ~fish n espadon m.

swore [swɔ:*] pt of swear.

sworn [swɔ:n] pp of swear.

swot [swɔt] vt, vi bûcher, potasser.

swum [swʌm] pp of swim.

swung [swʌŋ] pt, pp of swing.

sycamore ['sıkəmɔ:*] n sycomore m.

sycophantic [sıkə'fæntık] a flagorneur(euse).

syllable ['sıləbl] n syllabe f.

syllabus ['sıləbəs] n programme m.

symbol ['sımbl] n symbole m; ~ic(al) [-'bɔlık(l)] a symbolique; ~ism n symbolisme m; ~ize vt symboliser.

symmetrical [sı'mɛtrıkl] a symétrique.

symmetry ['sımıtrı] n symétrie f.

sympathetic [sımpə'θɛtık] a compatissant(e); bienveillant(e), compréhensif(ive); ~ towards bien disposé(e) envers; ~ally ad avec compassion (or bienveillance).

sympathize ['sımpəθaız] vi: to ~ with

**sb** plaindre qn ; s'associer à la douleur de qn ; **~r** n (POL) sympathisant/e.

**sympathy** ['sɪmpəθɪ] n compassion f; **in ~ with** en accord avec ; (strike) en or par solidarité avec ; **with our deepest ~** en vous priant d'accepter nos sincères condoléances.

**symphonic** [sɪm'fɔnɪk] a symphonique.

**symphony** ['sɪmfənɪ] n symphonie f; **~ orchestra** n orchestre m symphonique.

**symposium** [sɪm'pəuzɪəm] n symposium m.

**symptom** ['sɪmptəm] n symptôme m; indice m; **~atic** [-'mætɪk] a symptomatique.

**synagogue** ['sɪnəgɔg] n synagogue f.

**synchromesh** [sɪŋkrəu'mɛʃ] n synchronisation f.

**synchronize** ['sɪŋkrənaɪz] vt synchroniser // vi: **to ~ with** se produire en même temps que.

**syncopated** ['sɪŋkəpeɪtɪd] a syncopé(e).

**syndicate** ['sɪndɪkɪt] n syndicat m, coopérative f.

**syndrome** ['sɪndrəum] n syndrome m.

**synonym** ['sɪnənɪm] n synonyme m; **~ous** [sɪ'nɔnɪməs] a: **~ous (with)** synonyme (de).

**synopsis**, pl **synopses** [sɪ'nɔpsɪs, -si:z] n résumé m, synopsis m or f.

**syntax** ['sɪntæks] n syntaxe f.

**synthesis**, pl **syntheses** ['sɪnθəsɪs, -si:z] n synthèse f.

**synthetic** [sɪn'θɛtɪk] a synthétique ; **~s** npl textiles artificiels.

**syphilis** ['sɪfɪlɪs] n syphilis f.

**syphon** ['saɪfən] n, vb = **siphon.**

**Syria** ['sɪrɪə] n Syrie f; **~n** a syrien(ne) // n Syrien/ne.

**syringe** [sɪ'rɪndʒ] n seringue f.

**syrup** ['sɪrəp] n sirop m; (also: **golden ~**) mélasse raffinée ; **~y** a sirupeux(euse).

**system** ['sɪstəm] n système m; (order) méthode f; (ANAT) organisme m; **~atic** [-'mætɪk] a systématique ; méthodique ; **~s analyst** n analyste-programmeur m/f.

# T

**ta** [tɑ:] excl (Brit: col) merci!

**tab** [tæb] n (loop on coat etc) attache f; (label) étiquette f; **to keep ~s on** (fig) surveiller.

**tabby** ['tæbɪ] n (also: **~ cat**) chat/te tigré(e).

**tabernacle** ['tæbənækl] n tabernacle m.

**table** ['teɪbl] n table f // vt (motion etc) présenter ; **to lay** or **set the ~** mettre le couvert or la table ; **~ of contents** n table f des matières ; **~cloth** n nappe f; **~ d'hôte** [tɑ:bl'dəut] a (meal) à prix fixe ; **~ lamp** n lampe f décorative ; **~mat** n (for plate) napperon m, set m ; (for hot dish) dessous-de-plat m inv ; **~ salt** n sel fin or de table ; **~spoon** n cuiller f de service ; (also: **~spoonful**: as measurement) cuillerée f à soupe.

**tablet** ['tæblɪt] n (MED) comprimé m ; (: for sucking) pastille f; (for writing) bloc m ; (of stone) plaque f.

**table**: **~ tennis** n ping-pong m, tennis m de table ; **~ wine** n vin m de table.

**taboo** [tə'bu:] a, n tabou (m).

**tabulate** ['tæbjuleɪt] vt (data, figures) mettre sous forme de table(s) ; **tabulator** n tabulateur m.

**tacit** ['tæsɪt] a tacite.

**taciturn** ['tæsɪtə:n] a taciturne.

**tack** [tæk] n (nail) petit clou ; (stitch) point m de bâti ; (NAUT) bord m, bordée f // vt clouer ; bâtir // vi tirer un or des bord(s) ; **to change ~** virer de bord ; **on the wrong ~** (fig) sur la mauvaise voie.

**tackle** ['tækl] n matériel m, équipement m ; (for lifting) appareil m de levage ; (RUGBY) plaquage m // vt (difficulty) s'attaquer à ; (RUGBY) plaquer.

**tacky** ['tækɪ] a collant(e) ; pas sec(sèche).

**tact** [tækt] n tact m ; **~ful** a plein(e) de tact ; **~fully** ad avec tact.

**tactical** ['tæktɪkl] a tactique ; **~ error** n erreur f de tactique.

**tactics** ['tæktɪks] n,npl tactique f.

**tactless** ['tæktlɪs] a qui manque de tact ; **~ly** ad sans tact.

**tadpole** ['tædpəul] n têtard m.

**taffy** ['tæfɪ] n (US) (bonbon m au) caramel m.

**tag** [tæg] n étiquette f; **to ~ along** vi suivre.

**tail** [teɪl] n queue f; (of shirt) pan m // vt (follow) suivre, filer ; **~s** (on coin) (le côté) pile ; **to ~ away**, **~ off** vi (in size, quality etc) baisser peu à peu ; **~back** n bouchon m ; **~ coat** n habit m ; **~ end** n bout m, fin f; **~gate** hayon m (arrière).

**tailor** ['teɪlə*] n tailleur m (artisan) ; **~ing** n (cut) coupe f; **~-made** a fait(e) sur mesure ; (fig) conçu(e) spécialement.

**tailwind** ['teɪlwɪnd] n vent m arrière inv.

**tainted** ['teɪntɪd] a (food) gâté(e) ; (water, air) infecté(e) ; (fig) souillé(e).

**take**, pt **took**, pp **taken** [teɪk, tuk, 'teɪkn] vt prendre ; (gain: prize) remporter ; (require: effort, courage) demander ; (tolerate) accepter, supporter ; (hold: passengers etc) contenir ; (accompany) emmener, accompagner ; (bring, carry) apporter, emporter ; (exam) passer, se présenter à ; **to ~ sth from** (drawer etc) prendre qch dans ; (person) prendre qch à ; **I ~ it that** je suppose que ; **to ~ for a walk** (child, dog) emmener promener ; **to ~ after** vt fus ressembler à ; **to ~ apart** vt démonter ; **to ~ away** vt emporter ; enlever ; **to ~ back** vt (return) rendre, rapporter ; (one's words) retirer ; **to ~ down** vt (building) démolir ; (letter etc) prendre, écrire ; **to ~ in** vt (deceive) tromper, rouler ; (understand) comprendre, saisir ; (include) couvrir, inclure ; (lodger) prendre ; **to ~ off** vi (AVIAT) décoller // vt (remove) enlever ; (imitate) imiter, pasticher ; **to ~ on** vt (work) accepter, se charger de ; (employee) prendre, embaucher ; (opponent) accepter de se battre contre ; **to ~ out** vt sortir ; (remove) enlever ; (licence) prendre, se procurer ; **to ~ sth out of** enlever qch de ; prendre qch dans ; **to ~ over** vt (business) reprendre // vi: **to ~ over from sb** prendre la relève de qn ; **to ~ to** vt fus (person) se prendre

d'amitié pour ; (*activity*) prendre goût à ;
**to ~ up** *vt* (*one's story, a dress*) reprendre ;
(*occupy: time, space*) prendre, occuper ;
(*engage in: hobby etc*) se mettre à ; **~away**
*a* (*food*) à emporter ; **~-home pay** *n*
salaire net ; **~off** *n* (*AVIAT*) décollage *m* ;
**~over** *n* (*COMM*) rachat *m* ; **~over bid** *n*
offre publique d'achat.

**takings** ['teɪkɪŋz] *npl* (*COMM*) recette *f.*

**talc** [tælk] *n* (*also:* **~um powder**) talc *m.*

**tale** [teɪl] *n* (*story*) conte *m*, histoire *f* ;
(*account*) récit *m* ; (*pej*) histoire.

**talent** ['tælnt] *n* talent *m*, don *m* ; **~ed** *a*
doué(e), plein(e) de talent.

**talk** [tɔ:k] *n* propos *mpl* ; (*gossip*) racontars
*mpl* (*pej*) ; (*conversation*) discussion *f* ;
(*interview*) entretien *m* ; (*a speech*) causerie
*f*, exposé *m* // *vi* (*chatter*) bavarder ; **to**
**~ about** parler de ; (*converse*) s'entretenir
*or* parler de ; **to ~ sb out of/into doing**
persuader qn de ne pas faire/de faire ; **to**
**~ shop** parler métier *or* affaires ; **to ~**
**over** *vt* discuter (de) ; **~ative** *a* bavard(e) ;
**~er** *n* causeur/euse ; (*pej*) bavard/e.

**tall** [tɔ:l] *a* (*person*) grand(e) ; (*building,*
*tree*) haut(e) ; **to be 6 feet ~ ≈** mesurer
1 mètre 80 ; **~boy** *n* grande commode ;
**~ness** *n* grande taille ; hauteur *f* ; **~ story**
*n* histoire *f* invraisemblable.

**tally** ['tælɪ] *n* compte *m* // *vi:* **to ~ (with)**
correspondre (à).

**tambourine** [tæmbə'ri:n] *n* tambourin *m.*

**tame** [teɪm] *a* apprivoisé(e) ; (*fig: story,*
*style*) insipide.

**tamper** ['tæmpə*] *vi:* **to ~ with** toucher
à (*en cachette ou sans permission*).

**tampon** ['tæmpən] *n* tampon *m*
hygiénique *or* périodique.

**tan** [tæn] *n* (*also:* **sun~**) bronzage *m* //
*vt,vi* bronzer, brunir // *a* (*colour*) brun
roux *inv.*

**tandem** ['tændəm] *n* tandem *m.*

**tang** [tæŋ] *n* odeur (*or* saveur) piquante.

**tangent** ['tændʒənt] *n* (*MATH*) tangente *f.*

**tangerine** [tændʒə'ri:n] *n* mandarine *f.*

**tangible** ['tændʒəbl] *a* tangible.

**tangle** ['tæŋgl] *n* enchevêtrement *m* // *vt*
enchevêtrer ; **to get in(to) a ~** s'emmêler.

**tango** ['tæŋgəʊ] *n* tango *m.*

**tank** [tæŋk] *n* (*on sink etc*) réservoir *m* ; (*for processing*)
cuve *f* ; (*for fish*) aquarium *m* ; (*MIL*) char
*m* d'assaut, tank *m.*

**tankard** ['tæŋkəd] *n* chope *f.*

**tanker** ['tæŋkə*] *n* (*ship*) pétrolier *m*,
tanker *m* ; (*truck*) camion-citerne *m.*

**tanned** [tænd] *a* (*skin*) bronzé(e).

**tantalizing** ['tæntəlaɪzɪŋ] *a* (*smell*)
extrêmement appétissant(e) ; (*offer*)
terriblement tentant(e).

**tantamount** ['tæntəmaunt] *a:* **~ to** qui
équivaut à.

**tantrum** ['tæntrəm] *n* accès *m* de colère.

**tap** [tæp] *n* (*on sink etc*) robinet *m* ; (*gentle*
*blow*) petite tape // *vt* frapper *or* taper
légèrement ; (*resources*) exploiter, utiliser ;
**~-dancing** *n* claquettes *fpl.*

**tape** [teɪp] *n* ruban *m* ; (*also:* **magnetic ~**)
bande *f* (magnétique) // *vt* (*record*)
enregistrer (sur bande) ; **~ measure** *n*
mètre *m* à ruban.

**taper** ['teɪpə*] *n* cierge *m* // *vi* s'effiler.

**tape recorder** ['teɪprɪkɔ:də*] *n*
magnétophone *m.*

**tapered** ['teɪpəd], **tapering** ['teɪpərɪŋ] *a*
fuselé(e), effilé(e).

**tapestry** ['tæpɪstrɪ] *n* tapisserie *f.*

**tapioca** [tæpɪ'əʊkə] *n* tapioca *m.*

**tappet** ['tæpɪt] *n* (*AUT*) poussoir *m* (de
soupape).

**tar** [tɑ:] *n* goudron *m.*

**tarantula** [tə'ræntjulə] *n* tarentule *f.*

**tardy** ['tɑ:dɪ] *a* tardif(ive).

**target** ['tɑ:gɪt] *n* cible *f* ; (*fig: objective*)
objectif *m* ; **~ practice** *n* exercices *mpl* de
tir (à la cible).

**tariff** ['tærɪf] *n* (*COMM*) tarif *m* ; (*taxes*) tarif
douanier.

**tarmac** ['tɑ:mæk] *n* macadam *m* ; (*AVIAT*)
aire *f* d'envol // *vt* goudronner.

**tarnish** ['tɑ:nɪʃ] *vt* ternir.

**tarpaulin** [tɑ:'pɔ:lɪn] *n* bâche goudronnée.

**tarragon** ['tærəgən] *n* estragon *m.*

**tart** [tɑ:t] *n* (*CULIN*) tarte *f* ; (*col: pej:*
*woman*) poule *f* // *a* (*flavour*) âpre,
aigrelet(te).

**tartan** ['tɑ:tn] *n* tartan *m* // *a* écossais(e).

**tartar** ['tɑ:tə*] *n* (*on teeth*) tartre *m* ; **~**
**sauce** *n* sauce *f* tartare.

**task** [tɑ:sk] *n* tâche *f* ; **to take to ~**
prendre à partie ; **~ force** *n* (*MIL, POLICE*)
détachement spécial.

**Tasmania** [tæz'meɪnɪə] *n* Tasmanie *f.*

**tassel** ['tæsl] *n* gland *m* ; pompon *m.*

**taste** [teɪst] *n* goût *m* ; (*fig: glimpse, idea*)
idée *f*, aperçu *m* // *vt* goûter // *vi:* **to ~**
**of** (*fish etc*) avoir le *or* un goût de ; **it ~s**
**like fish** ça a un *or* le goût de poisson,
on dirait du poisson ; **what does it ~ like?**
quel goût ça a? ; **you can ~ the garlic**
(**in it**) on sent bien l'ail ; **can I have a ~**
**of this wine?** puis-je goûter un peu de ce
vin? ; **to have a ~ of sth** goûter (à) qch ;
**to have a ~ for sth** aimer qch, avoir un
penchant pour qch ; **~ful** *a* de bon goût ;
**~fully** *ad* avec goût ; **~less** *a* (*food*) qui
n'a aucun goût ; (*remark*) de mauvais
goût ; **tasty** *a* savoureux(euse),
délicieux(euse).

**tattered** ['tætəd] *a see* **tatters.**

**tatters** ['tætəz] *mpl:* **in ~** (*also:* **tattered**)
en lambeaux.

**tattoo** [tə'tu:] *n* tatouage *m* ; (*spectacle*)
parade *f* militaire // *vt* tatouer.

**tatty** ['tætɪ] *a* (*col*) défraîchi(e), en piteux
état.

**taught** [tɔ:t] *pt,pp* of **teach.**

**taunt** [tɔ:nt] *n* raillerie *f* // *vt* railler.

**Taurus** ['tɔ:rəs] *n* le Taureau ; **to be ~**
être du Taureau.

**taut** [tɔ:t] *a* tendu(e).

**tavern** ['tævən] *n* taverne *f.*

**tawdry** ['tɔ:drɪ] *a* (d'un mauvais goût)
criard.

**tawny** ['tɔ:nɪ] *a* fauve (*couleur*).

**tax** [tæks] *n* (*on goods etc*) taxe *f* ; (*on*
*income*) impôts *mpl*, contributions *fpl* // *vt*
taxer ; imposer ; (*fig: strain: patience etc*)
mettre à l'épreuve ; **~ation** [-'seɪʃən] *n*
taxation *f* ; impôts *mpl*, contributions *fpl* ;
**~ avoidance** *n* évasion fiscale ; **~**
**collector** *n* percepteur *m* ; **~ evasion** *n*

fraude fiscale ; ~ **exile** n personne qui s'expatrie pour fuir une fiscalité excessive ; ~-**free** a exempt(e) d'impôts.

**taxi** ['tæksɪ] n taxi m // vi (AVIAT) rouler (lentement) au sol.

**taxidermist** ['tæksɪdəːmɪst] n empailleur/euse (d'animaux).

**taxi:** ~ **driver** n chauffeur m de taxi ; ~ **rank,** ~ **stand** n station f de taxis.

**tax:** ~ **payer** n contribuable m/f ; ~ **return** n déclaration f d'impôts or de revenus.

**TB** abbr of **tuberculosis.**

**tea** [tiː] n thé m ; (snack: for children) goûter m ; **high** ~ collation combinant goûter et dîner ; ~ **bag** n sachet m de thé ; ~ **break** n pause-thé f ; ~**cake** n petit pain brioché.

**teach,** pt, pp **taught** [tiːtʃ, tɔːt] vt: **to** ~ **sb sth,** ~ **sth to sb** apprendre qch à qn ; (in school etc) enseigner qch à qn // vi enseigner ; ~**er** n (in secondary school) professeur m ; (in primary school) instituteur/trice ; ~**ing** n enseignement m ; ~**ing staff** n enseignants mpl.

**tea cosy** ['tiːkəuzɪ] n couvre-théière m.

**teacup** ['tiːkʌp] n tasse f à thé.

**teak** [tiːk] n teck m // a en or de teck.

**tea leaves** ['tiːliːvz] npl feuilles fpl de thé.

**team** [tiːm] n équipe f ; (of animals) attelage m ; ~ **games/work** jeux mpl/travail m d'équipe.

**tea party** ['tiːpɑːtɪ] n thé m (réception).

**teapot** ['tiːpɔt] n théière f.

**tear** n [tɛə*] déchirure f ; [tɪə*] larme f // vb [tɛə*] (pt **tore,** pp **torn** [tɔː*, tɔːn]) vt déchirer // vi se déchirer ; in ~**s** en larmes ; **to burst into** ~**s** fondre en larmes ; **to** ~ **along** vi (rush) aller à toute vitesse ; ~**ful** a larmoyant(e) ; ~ **gas** n gaz m lacrymogène.

**tearoom** ['tiːruːm] n salon m de thé.

**tease** [tiːz] n taquin/e // vt taquiner ; (unkindly) tourmenter.

**tea set** ['tiːsɛt] n service m à thé.

**teashop** ['tiːʃɔp] n pâtisserie-salon de thé f.

**teaspoon** ['tiːspuːn] n petite cuiller ; (also: ~**ful**: as measurement) ≈ cuillerée f à café.

**tea strainer** ['tiːstreɪnə*] n passoire f (à thé).

**teat** [tiːt] n tétine f.

**teatime** ['tiːtaɪm] n l'heure f du thé.

**tea towel** ['tiːtauəl] n torchon m (à vaisselle).

**tea urn** ['tiːəːn] n fontaine f à thé.

**technical** ['tɛknɪkl] a technique ; ~**ity** [-'kælɪtɪ] n technicité f ; (detail) détail m technique ; ~**ly** ad techniquement.

**technician** [tɛk'nɪʃn] n technicien/ne.

**technique** [tɛk'niːk] n technique f.

**technological** [tɛknə'lɔdʒɪkl] a technologique.

**technologist** [tɛk'nɔlədʒɪst] n technologue m/f.

**technology** [tɛk'nɔlədʒɪ] n technologie f.

**teddy (bear)** ['tɛdɪ(bɛə*)] n ours m (en peluche).

**tedious** ['tiːdɪəs] a fastidieux(euse).

**tedium** ['tiːdɪəm] n ennui m.

**tee** [tiː] n (GOLF) tee m.

**teem** [tiːm] vi grouiller, abonder ; **to** ~ **with** grouiller de ; **it is** ~**ing (with rain)** il pleut à torrents.

**teenage** ['tiːneɪdʒ] a (fashions etc) pour jeunes, pour adolescents ; ~**r** n jeune m/f, adolescent/e.

**teens** [tiːnz] npl: **to be in one's** ~ être adolescent(e).

**tee-shirt** ['tiːʃəːt] n = **T-shirt.**

**teeter** ['tiːtə*] vi chanceler, vaciller.

**teeth** [tiːθ] npl of **tooth.**

**teethe** [tiːð] vi percer ses dents.

**teething** ['tiːðɪŋ] a: ~ **ring** n anneau m (pour bébé qui perce ses dents) ; ~ **troubles** npl (fig) difficultés initiales.

**teetotal** ['tiːtəutl] a (person) qui ne boit jamais d'alcool.

**telecommunications** ['tɛlɪkəmjuːnɪ'keɪʃənz] n télécommunications fpl.

**telegram** ['tɛlɪgræm] n télégramme m.

**telegraph** ['tɛlɪgrɑːf] n télégraphe m ; ~**ic** [-'græfɪk] a télégraphique ; ~ **pole** n poteau m télégraphique.

**telepathic** [tɛlɪ'pæθɪk] a télépathique.

**telepathy** [tə'lɛpəθɪ] n télépathie f.

**telephone** ['tɛlɪfəun] n téléphone m // vt (person) téléphoner à ; (message) téléphoner ; ~ **booth,** ~ **box** n cabine f téléphonique ; ~ **call** n coup m de téléphone, appel m téléphonique ; communication f téléphonique ; ~ **directory** n annuaire m (du téléphone) ; ~ **exchange** n central m (téléphonique) ; ~ **number** n numéro m de téléphone ; ~ **operator** téléphoniste m/f, standardiste m/f ; **telephonist** [tə'lɛfənɪst] n téléphoniste m/f.

**telephoto** ['tɛlɪ'fəutəu] a: ~ **lens** n téléobjectif m.

**teleprinter** ['tɛlɪprɪntə*] n téléscripteur m.

**telescope** ['tɛlɪskəup] n télescope m // vt télescoper ; **telescopic** [-'skɔpɪk] a télescopique.

**televiewer** ['tɛlɪvjuːə*] n téléspectateur/trice.

**televise** ['tɛlɪvaɪz] vt téléviser.

**television** ['tɛlɪvɪʒən] n télévision f ; ~ **programme** n émission f de télévision ; ~ **set** n poste m de télévision.

**tell,** pt, pp **told** [tɛl, təuld] vt dire ; (relate: story) raconter ; (distinguish): **to** ~ **sth from** distinguer qch de // vi (have effect) se faire sentir, se voir ; **to** ~ **sb to do** dire à qn de faire ; **to** ~ **on vt fus** (inform against) dénoncer, rapporter contre ; **to** ~ **off** vt réprimander, gronder ; ~**er** n (in bank) caissier/ère ; ~**ing** a (remark, detail) révélateur(trice) ; ~**tale** a (sign) éloquent(e), révélateur(trice) // n (CONSTR) témoin m.

**telly** ['tɛlɪ] n (col: abbr of **television**) télé f.

**temerity** [tə'mɛrɪtɪ] n témérité f.

**temp** [tɛmp] n (abbr of **temporary**) (secrétaire f) intérimaire f.

**temper** ['tɛmpə*] n (nature) caractère m ; (mood) humeur f ; (fit of anger) colère f // vt (moderate) tempérer, adoucir ; **to be in a** ~ être en colère ; **to lose one's** ~ se mettre en colère.

**temperament** ['tɛmprəmənt] n (nature) tempérament m; ~**al** [-'mɛntl] a capricieux(euse).
**temperance** ['tɛmpərns] n modération f; (in drinking) tempérance f.
**temperate** ['tɛmprət] a modéré(e); (climate) tempéré(e).
**temperature** ['tɛmprətʃə*] n température f; **to have** or **run a** ~ avoir de la fièvre; ~ **chart** n (MED) feuille f de température.
**tempered** ['tɛmpəd] a (steel) trempé(e).
**tempest** ['tɛmpɪst] n tempête f.
**tempi** ['tɛmpi:] npl of **tempo.**
**template** ['tɛmplɪt] n patron m.
**temple** ['tɛmpl] n (building) temple m; (ANAT) tempe f.
**tempo,** ~**s** or **tempi** ['tɛmpəu, 'tɛmpi:] n tempo m; (fig: of life etc) rythme m.
**temporal** ['tɛmpərl] a temporel(le).
**temporarily** ['tɛmpərərɪlɪ] ad temporairement; provisoirement.
**temporary** ['tɛmpərərɪ] a temporaire, provisoire; (job, worker) temporaire; ~ **secretary** n (secrétaire f) intérimaire f.
**temporize** ['tɛmpəraɪz] vi atermoyer; transiger.
**tempt** [tɛmpt] vt tenter; **to** ~ **sb into doing** induire qn à faire; ~**ation** [-'teɪʃən] n tentation f; ~**ing** a tentant(e).
**ten** [tɛn] num dix.
**tenable** ['tɛnəbl] a défendable.
**tenacious** [tə'neɪʃəs] a tenace.
**tenacity** [tə'næsɪtɪ] n ténacité f.
**tenancy** ['tɛnənsɪ] n location f; état m de locataire.
**tenant** ['tɛnənt] n locataire m/f.
**tend** [tɛnd] vt s'occuper de // vi: **to** ~ **to do** avoir tendance à faire; (colour): **to** ~ **to** tirer sur.
**tendency** ['tɛndənsɪ] n tendance f.
**tender** ['tɛndə*] a tendre; (delicate) délicat(e); (sore) sensible; (affectionate) tendre, doux(douce) // n (COMM: offer) soumission f; (money): **legal** ~ cours légal // vt offrir; ~**ize** vt (CULIN) attendrir; ~**ly** ad tendrement; ~**ness** n tendresse f; (of meat) tendreté f.
**tendon** ['tɛndən] n tendon m.
**tenement** ['tɛnəmənt] n immeuble m (de rapport).
**tenet** ['tɛnət] n principe m.
**tennis** ['tɛnɪs] n tennis m; ~ **ball** n balle f de tennis; ~ **court** n (court m de) tennis; ~ **racket** n raquette f de tennis.
**tenor** ['tɛnə*] n (MUS) ténor m; (of speech etc) sens général.
**tense** [tɛns] a tendu(e); (person) tendu, crispé(e) // n (LING) temps m; ~**ness** n tension f.
**tension** ['tɛnʃən] n tension f.
**tent** [tɛnt] n tente f.
**tentacle** ['tɛntəkl] n tentacule m.
**tentative** ['tɛntətɪv] a timide, hésitant(e); (conclusion) provisoire.
**tenterhooks** ['tɛntəhuks] npl: **on** ~ sur des charbons ardents.
**tenth** [tɛnθ] num dixième.
**tent:** ~ **peg** n piquet m de tente; ~ **pole** n montant m de tente.

**tenuous** ['tɛnjuəs] a ténu(e).
**tenure** ['tɛnjuə*] n (of property) bail m; (of job) période f de jouissance; statut m de titulaire.
**tepid** ['tɛpɪd] a tiède.
**term** [tə:m] n (limit) terme m; (word) terme, mot m; (SCOL) trimestre m; (LAW) session f // vt appeler; ~**s** npl (conditions) conditions fpl; (COMM) tarif m; ~ **of imprisonment** peine f de prison; **in the short/long** ~ à court/long terme; '**easy** ~**s**' (COMM) 'facilités de paiement'; **to be on good** ~**s with** bien s'entendre avec, être en bons termes avec; **to come to** ~**s with** (person) arriver à un accord avec; (problem) faire face à.
**terminal** ['tə:mɪnl] a terminal(e); (disease) dans sa phase terminale // n (ELEC) borne f; (for oil, ore etc) terminal m; (also: **air** ~) aérogare f; (also: **coach** ~) gare routière.
**terminate** ['tə:mɪneɪt] vt mettre fin à // vi: **to** ~ **in** finir en or par.
**termination** [tə:mɪ'neɪʃən] n fin f; (of contract) résiliation f; ~ **of pregnancy** n (MED) interruption f de grossesse.
**termini** ['tə:mɪnaɪ] npl of **terminus.**
**terminology** [tə:mɪ'nɔlədʒɪ] n terminologie f.
**terminus,** pl **termini** ['tə:mɪnəs, 'tə:mɪnaɪ] n terminus m inv.
**termite** ['tə:maɪt] n termite m.
**terrace** ['tɛrəs] n terrasse f; (row of houses) rangée f de maisons (attenantes les unes aux autres); **the** ~**s** (SPORT) les gradins mpl; ~**ed** a (garden) en terrasses.
**terracotta** ['tɛrə'kɔtə] n terre cuite.
**terrain** [tɛ'reɪn] n terrain m (sol).
**terrible** ['tɛrɪbl] a terrible, atroce; (weather, work) affreux(euse), épouvantable; **terribly** ad terriblement; (very badly) affreusement mal.
**terrier** ['tɛrɪə*] n terrier m (chien).
**terrific** [tə'rɪfɪk] a fantastique, incroyable, terrible; (wonderful) formidable, sensationnel(le).
**terrify** ['tɛrɪfaɪ] vt terrifier.
**territorial** [tɛrɪ'tɔ:rɪəl] a territorial(e).
**territory** ['tɛrɪtərɪ] n territoire m.
**terror** ['tɛrə*] n terreur f; ~**ism** n terrorisme m; ~**ist** n terroriste m/f; ~**ize** vt terroriser.
**terse** [tə:s] a (style) concis(e); (reply) laconique.
**test** [tɛst] n (trial, check) essai m; (: of goods in factory) contrôle m; (of courage etc) épreuve f; (MED) examens mpl; (CHEM) analyses fpl; (exam: of intelligence etc) test m (d'aptitude); (: in school) interrogation f de contrôle; (also: **driving** ~) (examen du) permis m de conduire // vt essayer; contrôler; mettre à l'épreuve; examiner; analyser; tester; faire subir une interrogation (de contrôle) à.
**testament** ['tɛstəmənt] n testament m; **the Old/New T**~ l'Ancien/le Nouveau Testament.
**test:** ~ **case** n (LAW, fig) affaire-test f; ~ **flight** n vol m d'essai.
**testicle** ['tɛstɪkl] n testicule m.

**testify** ['tɛstɪfaɪ] vi (LAW) témoigner, déposer.

**testimonial** [tɛstɪ'məunɪəl] n (reference) recommandation f; (gift) témoignage m d'estime.

**testimony** ['tɛstɪmənɪ] n (LAW) témoignage m, déposition f.

**test**: ~ **match** n (CRICKET, RUGBY) match international; ~ **paper** n (SCOL) interrogation écrite; ~ **pilot** n pilote m d'essai; ~ **tube** n éprouvette f.

**testy** ['tɛstɪ] a irritable.

**tetanus** ['tɛtənəs] n tétanos m.

**tether** ['tɛðə*] vt attacher // n: at the end of one's ~ à bout (de patience).

**text** [tɛkst] n texte m; ~**book** n manuel m.

**textile** ['tɛkstaɪl] n textile m.

**texture** ['tɛkstʃə*] n texture f; (of skin, paper etc) grain m.

**Thai** [taɪ] a thaïlandais(e) // n Thaïlandais/e; (LING) thai m; ~**land** n Thaïlande f.

**Thames** [tɛmz] n: the ~ la Tamise.

**than** [ðæn, ðən] cj que; (with numerals): **more** ~ **10/once** plus de 10/d'une fois; **I have more/less** ~ **you** j'en ai plus/moins que toi; **she has more apples** ~ **pears** elle a plus de pommes que de poires.

**thank** [θæŋk] vt remercier, dire merci à; ~ **you (very much)** merci (beaucoup); ~**s** npl remerciements mpl // excl merci!; ~**s to** prep grâce à; ~**ful** a: ~**ful (for)** reconnaissant(e) (de); ~**less** a ingrat(e); **T**~**sgiving (Day)** n jour m d'action de grâce.

**that** [ðæt, ðət] cj que // det ce(cet + vowel or h mute), f cette; (not 'this'): ~ **book** ce livre-là // pronoun ce; (not 'this one') cela, ça; (the one) celui(celle); (relative: subject) qui; (: object) que, prep + lequel(laquelle); (with time): **on the day** ~ **he came** le jour où il est venu // ad: ~ **high** aussi haut; si haut; **it's about** ~ **high** c'est à peu près de cette hauteur; ~ **one** celui-là(celle-là); **what's** ~? qu'est-ce que c'est?; **who's** ~? qui est-ce?; **is** ~ **you?** c'est toi?; ~**'s what he said** c'est or voilà ce qu'il a dit; ~ **is...** c'est-à-dire..., à savoir...; **all** ~ tout cela, tout ça; **I can't work** ~ **much** je ne peux pas travailler autant que cela.

**thatched** [θætʃt] a (roof) de chaume; ~ **cottage** chaumière f.

**thaw** [θɔ:] n dégel m // vi (ice) fondre; (food) dégeler // vt (food) (faire) dégeler; **it's** ~**ing** (weather) il dégèle.

**the** [ði:, ðə] det le, f la, (l' + vowel or h mute), pl les; (NB: à + le(s) = au(x); de + le = du; de + les = des).

**theatre, theater** (US) ['θɪətə*] n théâtre m; ~-**goer** n habitué/e du théâtre.

**theatrical** [θɪ'ætrɪkl] a théâtral(e); ~ **company** n troupe f de théâtre.

**theft** [θɛft] n vol m (larcin).

**their** [ðɛə*] a leur, pl leurs; ~**s** pronoun le(la) leur, les leurs; **it is** ~**s** c'est à eux; **a friend of** ~**s** un de leurs amis.

**them** [ðɛm, ðəm] pronoun (direct) les; (indirect) leur; (stressed, after prep)

eux(elles); **I see** ~ je les vois; **give** ~ **the book** donne-leur le livre.

**theme** [θi:m] n thème m; ~ **song** n chanson principale.

**themselves** [ðəm'sɛlvz] pl pronoun (reflexive) se; (emphatic) eux-mêmes(elles-mêmes); **between** ~ entre eux(elles).

**then** [ðɛn] ad (at that time) alors, à ce moment-là; (next) puis, ensuite; (and also) et puis // cj (therefore) alors, dans ce cas // a: the ~ **president** le président d'alors or de l'époque; **from** ~ **on** dès lors.

**theologian** [θɪə'ləudʒən] n théologien/ne.

**theological** [θɪə'lɒdʒɪkl] a théologique.

**theology** [θɪ'ɒlədʒɪ] n théologie f.

**theorem** ['θɪərəm] n théorème m.

**theoretical** [θɪə'rɛtɪkl] a théorique.

**theorize** ['θɪəraɪz] vi élaborer une théorie; (pej) faire des théories.

**theory** ['θɪərɪ] n théorie f.

**therapeutic(al)** [θɛrə'pju:tɪk(l)] a thérapeutique.

**therapist** ['θɛrəpɪst] n thérapeute m/f.

**therapy** ['θɛrəpɪ] n thérapie f.

**there** [ðɛə*] ad là, là-bas; ~, ~! allons, allons!; **it's** ~ c'est là; **he went** ~ il y est allé; ~ **is,** ~ **are** il y a; ~ **he is** le voilà; ~ **has been** il y a eu; **on/in** ~ là-dessus/ -dedans; **to go** ~ **and back** faire l'aller et retour; ~**abouts** ad (place) par là, près de là; (amount) environ, à peu près; ~**after** ad par la suite; ~**fore** ad donc, par conséquent; ~**'s** = ~ **is**; ~ **has.**

**thermal** ['θə:ml] a thermique.

**thermometer** [θə'mɒmɪtə*] n thermomètre m.

**thermonuclear** ['θə:məu'nju:klɪə*] a thermonucléaire.

**Thermos** ['θə:məs] n ® (also: ~ **flask**) thermos m or f inv ®.

**thermostat** ['θə:məustæt] n thermostat m.

**thesaurus** [θɪ'sɔ:rəs] n dictionnaire m synonymique.

**these** [ði:z] pl pronoun ceux-ci(celles-ci) // pl det ces; (not 'those'): ~ **books** ces livres-ci.

**thesis,** pl **theses** ['θi:sɪs, 'θi:si:z] n thèse f.

**they** [ðeɪ] pl pronoun ils(elles); (stressed) eux(elles); ~ **say that...** (it is said that) on dit que...; ~**'d** = **they had**; **they would**; ~**'ll** = **they shall**; **they will**; ~**'re** = **they are**; ~**'ve** = **they have.**

**thick** [θɪk] a épais(se); (crowd) dense; (stupid) bête, borné(e) // n: **in the** ~ **of** au beau milieu de, en plein cœur de; **it's 20 cm** ~ ça a 20 cm d'épaisseur; ~**en** vi s'épaissir // vt (sauce etc) épaissir; ~**ness** n épaisseur f; ~**set** a trapu(e), costaud(e); ~**skinned** a (fig) peu sensible.

**thief, thieves** [θi:f, θi:vz] n voleur/euse.

**thieving** ['θi:vɪŋ] n vol m (larcin).

**thigh** [θaɪ] n cuisse f; ~**bone** n fémur m.

**thimble** ['θɪmbl] n dé m (à coudre).

**thin** [θɪn] a mince; (person) maigre; (soup) peu épais(se); (hair, crowd) clairsemé(e); (fog) léger(ère) // vt (hair) éclaircir; **to** ~ (**down**) (sauce, paint) délayer.

**thing** [θɪŋ] *n* chose *f*; (*object*) objet *m*; (*contraption*) truc *m*; ~s *npl* (*belongings*) affaires *fpl*; **for one** ~ d'abord; **the best** ~ **would be to** le mieux serait de; **how are** ~s? comment ça va?

**think**, *pt*, *pp* **thought** [θɪŋk, θɔ:t] *vi* penser, réfléchir // *vt* penser, croire; (*imagine*) s'imaginer; **to** ~ **of** penser à; **what did you** ~ **of them?** qu'as-tu pensé d'eux?; **to** ~ **about sth/sb** penser à qch/qn; **I'll** ~ **about it** je vais y réfléchir; **to** ~ **of doing** avoir l'idée de faire; **I** ~ **so** je crois *or* pense que oui; **to** ~ **well of** avoir une haute opinion de; **to** ~ **over** *vt* bien réfléchir à; **to** ~ **up** *vt* inventer, trouver.

**thinly** ['θɪnlɪ] *ad* (*cut*) en tranches fines; (*spread*) en couche mince.

**thinness** ['θɪnnɪs] *n* minceur *f*; maigreur *f*.

**third** [θə:d] *num* troisième // *n* troisième *m/f*; (*fraction*) tiers *m*; (*SCOL: degree*) ≈ licence *f* avec mention passable; **a** ~ **of** le tiers de; ~**ly** *ad* troisièmement; ~ **party insurance** *n* assurance *f* au tiers; ~**-rate** *a* de qualité médiocre; **the T**~ **World** *n* le Tiers-Monde.

**thirst** [θə:st] *n* soif *f*; ~**y** *a* (*person*) qui a soif, assoiffé(e).

**thirteen** ['θə:'ti:n] *num* treize.

**thirty** ['θə:tɪ] *num* trente.

**this** [ðɪs] *det* ce(cet + *vowel or h mute*), *f* cette; (*not 'that'*): ~ **book** ce livre-ci // *pronoun* ce; ceci; (*not 'that one'*) celui-ci(celle-ci); ~ **is what he said** voici ce qu'il a dit.

**thistle** ['θɪsl] *n* chardon *m*.

**thong** [θɒŋ] *n* lanière *f*.

**thorn** [θɔ:n] *n* épine *f*; ~ **bush** *n* buisson *m* d'épines; ~**y** *a* épineux(euse).

**thorough** ['θʌrə] *a* (*search*) minutieux(euse); (*knowledge*, *research*) approfondi(e); (*work*) consciencieux(euse); (*cleaning*) à fond; ~**bred** *n* (*horse*) pur-sang *m inv*; ~**fare** *n* rue *f*; **'no** ~**fare'** 'passage interdit'; ~**ly** *ad* minutieusement; en profondeur; à fond; **he** ~**ly agreed** il était tout à fait d'accord.

**those** [ðəuz] *pl pronoun* ceux-là(celles-là) // *pl det* ces; (*not 'these'*): ~ **books** ces livres-là.

**though** [ðəu] *cj* bien que + *sub*, quoique + *sub* // *ad* pourtant.

**thought** [θɔ:t] *pt*, *pp of* **think** // *n* pensée *f*; (*opinion*) avis *m*; (*intention*) intention *f*; ~**ful** *a* pensif(ive); réfléchi(e); (*considerate*) prévenant(e); ~**less** *a* étourdi(e); qui manque de considération.

**thousand** ['θauzənd] *num* mille; ~**th** *num* millième; **one** ~ mille; ~**s of** des milliers de.

**thrash** [θræʃ] *vt* rouer de coups; donner une correction à; (*defeat*) battre à plate couture; **to** ~ **about** *vi* se débattre; **to** ~ **out** *vt* débattre de.

**thread** [θrɛd] *n* fil *m*; (*of screw*) pas *m*, filetage *m* // *vt* (*needle*) enfiler; **to** ~ **one's way between** se faufiler entre; ~**bare** *a* râpé(e), élimé(e).

**threat** [θrɛt] *n* menace *f*; ~**en** *vi* (*storm*) menacer // *vt*: **to** ~**en sb with sth/to do** menacer qn de qch/de faire.

**three** [θri:] *num* trois (*m inv*); ~**-dimensional** *a* à trois dimensions; (*film*) en relief; ~**-fold** *ad*: **to increase** ~**fold** tripler; ~**-piece suit** *n* complet *m* (avec gilet); ~**-piece suite** *n* salon *m* comprenant un canapé et deux fauteuils assortis; ~**-ply** *a* (*wood*) à trois épaisseurs; (*wool*) trois fils *inv*; ~**-wheeler** *n* (*car*) voiture *f* à trois roues.

**thresh** [θrɛʃ] *vt* (*AGR*) battre; ~**ing machine** *n* batteuse *f*.

**threshold** ['θrɛʃhəuld] *n* seuil *m*.

**threw** [θru:] *pt of* **throw**.

**thrift** [θrɪft] *n* économie *f*; ~**y** *a* économe.

**thrill** [θrɪl] *n* frisson *m*, émotion *f* // *vi* tressaillir, frissonner // *vt* (*audience*) électriser; **to be** ~**ed** (*with gift etc*) être ravi; ~**er** *n* film *m* (*or* roman *m or* pièce *f*) à suspense.

**thrive**, *pt* **thrived**, **throve** *pp* **thrived**, **thriven** [θraɪv, θrəuv, 'θrɪvn] *vi* pousser *or* se développer bien; (*business*) prospérer; **he** ~**s on it** cela lui réussit; **thriving** *a* vigoureux(euse); prospère.

**throat** [θrəut] *n* gorge *f*; **to have a sore** ~ avoir mal à la gorge.

**throb** [θrɒb] *n* (*of heart*) pulsation *f*; (*of engine*) vibration *f*; (*of pain*) élancement *m* // *vi* (*heart*) palpiter; (*engine*) vibrer; (*pain*) lanciner; (*wound*) causer des élancements.

**throes** [θrəuz] *npl*: **in the** ~ **of** au beau milieu de; en proie à; **in the** ~ **of death** à l'agonie.

**thrombosis** [θrɒm'bəusɪs] *n* thrombose *f*.

**throne** [θrəun] *n* trône *m*.

**throttle** ['θrɒtl] *n* (*AUT*) accélérateur *m* // *vt* étrangler.

**through** [θru:] *prep* à travers; (*time*) pendant, durant; (*by means of*) par, par l'intermédiaire de; (*owing to*) à cause de // *a* (*ticket, train, passage*) direct(e) // *ad* à travers; **to put sb** ~ **to sb** (*TEL*) passer qn à qn; **to be** ~ (*TEL*) avoir la communication; (*have finished*) avoir fini; **'no** ~ **way'** 'impasse'; ~**out** *prep* (*place*) partout dans; (*time*) durant tout(e) le(la) // *ad* partout.

**throve** [θrəuv] *pt of* **thrive**.

**throw** [θrəu] *n* jet *m*; (*SPORT*) lancer *m* // *vt* (*pt* **threw**, *pp* **thrown** [θru:, θrəun]) lancer, jeter; (*SPORT*) lancer; (*rider*) désarçonner; (*fig*) décontenancer; (*pottery*) tourner; **to** ~ **a party** donner une réception; **to** ~ **away** *vt* jeter; **to** ~ **off** *vt* se débarrasser de; **to** ~ **out** *vt* jeter dehors; (*reject*) rejeter; **to** ~ **up** *vi* vomir; ~**away** *a* à jeter; ~**-in** *n* (*SPORT*) remise *f* en jeu.

**thru** [θru:] *prep*, *a*, *ad* (*US*) = **through**.

**thrush** [θrʌʃ] *n* grive *f*.

**thrust** [θrʌst] *n* (*TECH*) poussée *f* // *vt* (*pt*, *pp* **thrust**) pousser brusquement; (*push in*) enfoncer; ~**ing** *a* dynamique; (*fig*) qui se met trop en avant.

**thud** [θʌd] *n* bruit sourd.

**thug** [θʌg] *n* voyou *m*.

**thumb** [θʌm] *n* (*ANAT*) pouce *m* // *vt* (*book*) feuilleter; **to** ~ **a lift** faire de l'auto-stop, arrêter une voiture; ~ **index** *n* répertoire *m* (à onglets); ~**nail** *n* ongle *m* du pouce; ~**tack** *n* (*US*) punaise *f* (*clou*).

**thump** [θʌmp] *n* grand coup ; (*sound*) bruit sourd // *vt* cogner sur // *vi* cogner, frapper.

**thunder** ['θʌndə*] *n* tonnerre *m* // *vi* tonner ; (*train etc*): **to ~ past** passer dans un grondement *or* un bruit de tonnerre ; **~clap** *n* coup *m* de tonnerre ; **~ous** *a* étourdissant(e) ; **~storm** *n* orage *m* ; **~struck** *a* (*fig*) abasourdi(e) ; **~y** *a* orageux(euse).

**Thursday** ['θəːzdɪ] *n* jeudi *m*.

**thus** [ðʌs] *ad* ainsi.

**thwart** [θwɔːt] *vt* contrecarrer.

**thyme** [taɪm] *n* thym *m*.

**thyroid** ['θaɪrɔɪd] *n* thyroïde *f*.

**tiara** [tɪ'ɑːrə] *n* (*woman's*) diadème *m*.

**tic** [tɪk] *n* tic (nerveux).

**tick** [tɪk] *n* (*sound: of clock*) tic-tac *m* ; (*mark*) coche *f* ; (*ZOOL*) tique *f* ; (*col*): **in a ~** dans un instant // *vi* faire tic-tac // *vt* cocher ; **to ~ off** *vt* cocher ; (*person*) réprimander, attraper.

**ticket** ['tɪkɪt] *n* billet *m* ; (*for bus, tube*) ticket *m* ; (*in shop: on goods*) étiquette *f* ; (*: from cash register*) reçu *m*, ticket ; (*for library*) carte *f* ; **~ collector** *n* contrôleur/euse ; **~ holder** *n* personne munie d'un billet ; **~ office** *n* guichet *m*, bureau *m* de vente des billets.

**tickle** ['tɪkl] *n* chatouillement *m* // *vt* chatouiller ; (*fig*) plaire à ; faire rire ; **ticklish** *a* chatouilleux(euse).

**tidal** ['taɪdl] *a* à marée ; **~ wave** *n* raz-de-marée *m inv*.

**tiddlywinks** ['tɪdlɪwɪŋks] *n* jeu *m* de puce.

**tide** [taɪd] *n* marée *f* ; (*fig: of events*) cours *m* // *vt*: **to ~ sb over** dépanner qn.

**tidily** ['taɪdɪlɪ] *ad* avec soin, soigneusement.

**tidiness** ['taɪdɪnɪs] *n* bon ordre ; goût *m* de l'ordre.

**tidy** ['taɪdɪ] *a* (*room*) bien rangé(e) ; (*dress, work*) net(nette), soigné(e) ; (*person*) ordonné(e), qui a de l'ordre // *vt* (*also: ~ up*) ranger ; **to ~ o.s. up** s'arranger.

**tie** [taɪ] *n* (*string etc*) cordon *m* ; (*also: neck~*) cravate *f* ; (*fig: link*) lien *m* ; (*SPORT: draw*) égalité *f* de points ; match nul // *vt* (*parcel*) attacher ; (*ribbon*) nouer // *vi* (*SPORT*) faire match nul ; finir à égalité de points ; **'black/white ~'** 'smoking/habit de rigueur' ; **to ~ sth in a bow** faire un nœud or avec qch ; **to ~ a knot in sth** faire un nœud à qch ; **to ~ down** *vt* attacher ; (*fig*): **to ~ sb down to** contraindre qn à accepter, fixer à qn ; **to ~ up** *vt* (*parcel*) ficeler ; (*dog, boat*) attacher ; (*arrangements*) conclure ; **to be ~d up** (*busy*) être pris *or* occupé.

**tier** [tɪə*] *n* gradin *m* ; (*of cake*) étage *m*.

**tiff** [tɪf] *n* petite querelle.

**tiger** ['taɪgə*] *n* tigre *m*.

**tight** [taɪt] *a* (*rope*) tendu(e), raide ; (*clothes*) étroit(e), très juste ; (*budget, programme, bend*) serré(e) ; (*control*) strict(e), sévère ; (*col: drunk*) ivre, rond(e) // *ad* (*squeeze*) très fort ; (*shut*) à bloc, hermétiquement ; **~s** *npl* collant *m* ; **~en** *vt* (*rope*) tendre ; (*screw*) resserrer ; (*control*) renforcer // *vi* se tendre, se resserrer ; **~-fisted** *a* avare ; **~ly** *ad* (*grasp*) bien, très fort ; **~-rope** *n* corde *f* raide.

**tile** [taɪl] *n* (*on roof*) tuile *f* ; (*on wall or floor*) carreau *m* ; **~d** *a* en tuiles ; carrelé(e).

**till** [tɪl] *n* caisse (enregistreuse) // *vt* (*land*) cultiver // *prep*, *cj* = **until**.

**tiller** ['tɪlə*] *n* (*NAUT*) barre *f* (du gouvernail).

**tilt** [tɪlt] *vt* pencher, incliner // *vi* pencher, être incliné(e).

**timber** ['tɪmbə*] *n* (*material*) bois *m* de construction ; (*trees*) arbres *mpl*.

**time** [taɪm] *n* temps *m* ; (*epoch: often pl*) époque *f*, temps ; (*by clock*) heure *f* ; (*moment*) moment *m* ; (*occasion, also MATH*) fois *f* ; (*MUS*) mesure *f* // *vt* (*race*) chronométrer ; (*programme*) minuter ; (*remark etc*) choisir le moment de ; **a long ~** un long moment, longtemps ; **for the ~ being** pour le moment ; **from ~ to ~** de temps en temps ; **in ~** (*soon enough*) à temps ; (*after some time*) avec le temps, à la longue ; (*MUS*) en mesure ; **in a week's ~** dans une semaine ; **on ~** à l'heure ; **5 ~s 5** 5 fois 5 ; **what ~ is it?** quelle heure est-il? ; **to have a good ~** bien s'amuser ; **~'s up!** c'est l'heure! ; **I've no ~ for it** (*fig*) cela m'agace ; **~ bomb** *n* bombe *f* à retardement ; **~keeper** *n* (*SPORT*) chronomètre *m* ; **~ lag** *n* décalage *m* ; (*in travel*) décalage *m* horaire ; **~less** *a* éternel(le) ; **~ limit** *n* limite *f* de temps, délai *m* ; **~ly** *a* opportun(e) ; **~ off** *n* temps *m* libre ; **~r** *n* (*in kitchen*) compte-minutes *m inv* ; **~-saving** *a* qui fait gagner du temps ; **~ switch** *n* minuteur *m* ; (*for lighting*) minuterie *f* ; **~table** *n* (*RAIL*) (indicateur *m*) horaire *m* ; (*SCOL*) emploi *m* du temps ; **~ zone** *n* fuseau *m* horaire.

**timid** ['tɪmɪd] *a* timide ; (*easily scared*) peureux(euse).

**timing** ['taɪmɪŋ] *n* minutage *m* ; chronométrage *m* ; **the ~ of his resignation** le moment choisi pour sa démission ; **~ device** *n* mécanisme *m* de retardement.

**timpani** ['tɪmpənɪ] *npl* timbales *fpl*.

**tin** [tɪn] *n* étain *m* ; (*also: ~ plate*) fer-blanc *m* ; (*can*) boîte *f* (de conserve) ; (*for baking*) moule *m* (à gâteau) ; **~ foil** *n* papier *m* d'étain.

**tinge** [tɪndʒ] *n* nuance *f* // *vt*: **~d with** teinté(e) de.

**tingle** ['tɪngl] *n* picotement *m* ; frisson *m* // *vi* picoter.

**tinker** ['tɪŋkə*] *n* rétameur ambulant ; (*gipsy*) romanichel *m* ; **to ~ with** *vt* bricoler, rafistoler.

**tinkle** ['tɪŋkl] *vi* tinter // *n* (*col*): **to give sb a ~** passer un coup de fil à qn.

**tinned** [tɪnd] *a* (*food*) en boîte, en conserve.

**tinny** ['tɪnɪ] *a* métallique.

**tin opener** ['tɪnəupnə*] *n* ouvre-boîte(s) *m*.

**tinsel** ['tɪnsl] *n* guirlandes *fpl* de Noël (argentées).

**tint** [tɪnt] *n* teinte *f* ; (*for hair*) shampooing colorant.

**tiny** ['taɪnɪ] *a* minuscule.

**tip** [tɪp] *n* (*end*) bout *m* ; (*protective: on umbrella etc*) embout *m* ; (*gratuity*) pourboire *m* ; (*for coal*) terril *m* ; (*for rubbish*) décharge *f* ; (*advice*) tuyau *m* // *vt* (*waiter*) donner un pourboire à ; (*tilt*) incliner ; (*overturn: also: ~ over*)

renverser ; (*empty: also:* ~ **out**) déverser ;
~-**off** *n* (*hint*) tuyau *m* ; ~**ped** *a* (*cigarette*)
(à bout) filtre *inv* ; **steel-**~**ped** à bout
métallique, à embout de métal.

**tipple** ['tɪpl] *vi* picoler // *n*: **to have a** ~
boire un petit coup.

**tipsy** ['tɪpsɪ] *a* un peu ivre, éméché(e).

**tiptoe** ['tɪptəu] *n*: **on** ~ sur la pointe des
pieds.

**tiptop** ['tɪp'tɔp] *a*: **in** ~ **condition** en
excellent état.

**tire** ['taɪə*] *n* (*US*) = **tyre** // *vt* fatiguer
// *vi* se fatiguer ; ~**d** a fatigué(e) ; **to be**
~**d of** en avoir assez de, être las(lasse)
de ; ~**dness** *n* fatigue *f* ; ~**less** *a*
infatigable, inlassable ; ~**some** *a*
ennuyeux(euse) ; **tiring** *a* fatigant(e).

**tissue** ['tɪʃuː] *n* tissu *m* ; (*paper
handkerchief*) mouchoir *m* en papier,
kleenex *m* ® ; ~ **paper** *n* papier *m* de soie.

**tit** [tɪt] *n* (*bird*) mésange *f* ; **to give** ~ **for
tat** rendre coup pour coup.

**titanium** [tɪ'teɪnɪəm] *n* titane *m*.

**titbit** ['tɪtbɪt] *n* (*food*) friandise *f* ; (*news*)
potin *m*.

**titillate** ['tɪtɪleɪt] *vt* titiller, exciter.

**titivate** ['tɪtɪveɪt] *vt* pomponner.

**title** ['taɪtl] *n* titre *m* ; ~ **deed** *n* (*LAW*) titre
(constitutif) de propriété ; ~ **role** *n* rôle
principal.

**titter** ['tɪtə*] *vi* rire (bêtement).

**tittle-tattle** ['tɪtltætl] *n* bavardages *mpl*.

**titular** ['tɪtjulə*] *a* (*in name only*)
nominal(e).

**tizzy** ['tɪzɪ] *n*: **to be in a** ~ être dans tous
ses états.

**to** [tuː, tə] *prep* à ; (*towards*) vers ; envers ;
**give it** ~ **me** donne-le-moi ; **the key** ~
**the front door** la clé de la porte d'entrée ;
**the main thing is** ~... l'important est
de... ; **to go** ~ **France/Portugal** aller en
France/au Portugal ; **I went** ~ **Claude's**
je suis allé chez Claude ; **to go** ~
**town/school** aller en ville/à l'école ;
**pull/push the door** ~ tire/pousse la
porte ; **to go** ~ **and fro** aller et venir.

**toad** [təud] *n* crapaud *m* ; ~**stool** *n*
champignon (vénéneux) ; ~**y** *vi* flatter
bassement.

**toast** [təust] *n* (*CULIN*) pain grillé, toast *m* ;
(*drink, speech*) toast // *vt* (*CULIN*) faire
griller ; (*drink to*) porter un toast à ; **a
piece** *or* **slice of** ~ un toast ; ~**er** *n* grille-
pain *m inv* ; ~**master** *n* animateur *m* pour
réceptions ; ~**rack** *n* porte-toast *m*.

**tobacco** [tə'bækəu] *n* tabac *m* ; ~**nist** *n*
marchand/e de tabac ; ~**nist's (shop)** *n*
(bureau *m* de) tabac *m*.

**toboggan** [tə'bɔgən] *n* toboggan *m* ;
(*child's*) luge *f*.

**today** [tə'deɪ] *ad,n* (*also fig*) aujourd'hui
(*m*).

**toddler** ['tɔdlə*] *n* enfant *m/f* qui
commence à marcher, bambin *m*.

**toddy** ['tɔdɪ] *n* grog *m*.

**to-do** [tə'duː] *n* (*fuss*) histoire *f*, affaire *f*.

**toe** [təu] *n* doigt *m* de pied, orteil *m* ; (*of
shoe*) bout *m* ; **to** ~ **the line** (*fig*) obéir,
se conformer ; ~**hold** *n* prise *f* ; ~**nail** *n*
ongle *m* de l'orteil.

**toffee** ['tɔfɪ] *n* caramel *m* ; ~ **apple** *n*
pomme caramélisée.

**toga** ['təugə] *n* toge *f*.

**together** [tə'geðə*] *ad* ensemble ; (*at same
time*) en même temps ; ~ **with** *prep* avec ;
~**ness** *n* camaraderie *f* ; intimité *f*.

**toil** [tɔɪl] *n* dur travail, labeur *m* // *vi*
travailler dur ; peiner.

**toilet** ['tɔɪlət] *n* (*lavatory*) toilettes *fpl*,
cabinets *mpl* // *cpd* (*bag, soap etc*) de
toilette ; ~ **bowl** *n* cuvette *f* des W.-C. ;
~ **paper** *n* papier *m* hygiénique ; ~**ries**
*npl* articles *mpl* de toilette ; ~ **roll** *n*
rouleau *m* de papier hygiénique ; ~ **water**
*n* eau *f* de toilette.

**token** ['təukən] *n* (*sign*) marque *f*,
témoignage *m* ; (*voucher*) bon *m*, coupon
*m* ; **book/record** ~ *n* chèque-livre/disque
*m*.

**told** [təuld] *pt, pp* *of* **tell**.

**tolerable** ['tɔlərəbl] *a* (*bearable*) tolérable ;
(*fairly good*) passable.

**tolerance** ['tɔlərns] *n* (*also*: *TECH*)
tolérance *f*.

**tolerant** ['tɔlərnt] *a*: ~ (**of**) tolérant(e) (à
l'égard de).

**tolerate** ['tɔləreɪt] *vt* supporter ; (*MED,
TECH*) tolérer ; **toleration** [-'reɪʃən] *n*
tolérance *f*.

**toll** [təul] *n* (*tax, charge*) péage *m* // *vi* (*bell*)
sonner ; **the accident** ~ **on the roads** le
nombre des victimes de la route ; ~**bridge**
*n* pont *m* à péage.

**tomato,** ~**es** [tə'mɑːtəu] *n* tomate *f*.

**tomb** [tuːm] *n* tombe *f*.

**tombola** [tɔm'bəulə] *n* tombola *f*.

**tomboy** ['tɔmbɔɪ] *n* garçon manqué.

**tombstone** ['tuːmstəun] *n* pierre tombale.

**tomcat** ['tɔmkæt] *n* matou *m*.

**tomorrow** [tə'mɔrəu] *ad,n* (*also fig*)
demain (*m*) ; **the day after** ~ après-
demain ; ~ **morning** demain matin.

**ton** [tʌn] *n* tonne *f* (= *1016 kg* ; *20 cwt*) ;
(*NAUT: also*: **register** ~) tonneau *m* (= *2.83
cu.m* ; *100 cu. ft*) ; ~**s of** (*col*) des tas de.

**tonal** ['təunl] *a* tonal(e).

**tone** [təun] *n* ton *m* ; (*of radio*) tonalité *f*
// *vi* s'harmoniser ; **to** ~ **down** *vt* (*colour,
criticism*) adoucir ; (*sound*) baisser ; **to** ~
**up** *vt* (*muscles*) tonifier ; ~-**deaf** *a* qui n'a
pas d'oreille.

**tongs** [tɔŋz] *npl* pinces *fpl* ; (*for coal*)
pincettes *fpl* ; (*for hair*) fer *m* à friser.

**tongue** [tʌŋ] *n* langue *f* ; ~ **in cheek** *ad*
ironiquement ; ~-**tied** *a* (*fig*) muet(te) ; ~-
**twister** *n* phrase *f* très difficile à
prononcer.

**tonic** ['tɔnɪk] *n* (*MED*) tonique *m* ; (*MUS*)
tonique *f* ; (*also*: ~ **water**) tonic *m*.

**tonight** [tə'naɪt] *ad, n* cette nuit ; (*this
evening*) ce soir.

**tonnage** ['tʌnɪdʒ] *n* (*NAUT*) tonnage *m*.

**tonne** [tʌn] *n* (*metric ton*) tonne *f*.

**tonsil** ['tɔnsl] *n* amygdale *f* ; ~**litis** [-'laɪtɪs]
*n* amygdalite *f*.

**too** [tuː] *ad* (*excessively*) trop ; (*also*) aussi ;
~ **much** *ad* trop // *det* trop de ; ~ **many**
*det* trop de ; ~ **bad!** tant pis!

**took** [tuk] *pt* *of* **take**.

**tool** [tuːl] *n* outil *m* // *vt* travailler,

ouvrager ; ~ **box/kit** n boîte f/trousse f à outils.

**toot** [tu:t] n coup m de sifflet (or de klaxon) // vi siffler ; (with car-horn) klaxonner.

**tooth,** pl **teeth** [tu:θ, ti:θ] n (ANAT. TECH) dent f; ~**ache** n mal m de dents ; ~**brush** n brosse f à dents ; ~**paste** n (pâte f) dentifrice m; ~**pick** n cure-dent m; ~ **powder** n poudre f dentifrice.

**top** [tɔp] n (of mountain, head) sommet m; (of page, ladder) haut m; (of box, cupboard, table) dessus m; (lid: of box, jar) couvercle m; (: of bottle) bouchon m; (toy) toupie f // a du haut ; (in rank) premier(ère) ; (best) meilleur(e) // vt (exceed) dépasser ; (be first in) être en tête de ; **on** ~ **of** sur ; (in addition to) en plus de ; **from** ~ **to toe** de la tête aux pieds ; **at the** ~ **of the list** en tête de liste ; **to** ~ **up** vt remplir ; ~**coat** n pardessus m; ~ **floor** n dernier étage ; ~ **hat** n haut-de-forme m; ~**-heavy** a (object) trop lourd(e) du haut.

**topic** ['tɔpɪk] n sujet m, thème m; ~**al** a d'actualité.

**top**: ~**less** a (bather etc) aux seins nus ; ~**less swimsuit** n monokini m; ~**-level** a (talks) à l'échelon le plus élevé ; ~**most** a le(la) plus haut(e).

**topple** ['tɔpl] vt renverser, faire tomber // vi basculer ; tomber.

**topsy-turvy** ['tɔp si'tə:vɪ] a,ad sens dessus-dessous.

**torch** [tɔ:tʃ] n torche f; (electric) lampe f de poche.

**tore** [tɔ:*] pt of **tear.**

**torment** n ['tɔ:mɛnt] tourment m // vt [tɔ:'mɛnt] tourmenter ; (fig: annoy) agacer.

**torn** [tɔ:n] pp of **tear** // a: ~ **between** (fig) tiraillé(e) entre.

**tornado,** ~**es** [tɔ:'neɪdəu] n tornade f.

**torpedo,** ~**es** [tɔ:'pi:dəu] n torpille f.

**torpor** ['tɔ:pə*] n torpeur f.

**torque** [tɔ:k] n couple m de torsion.

**torrent** ['tɔrnt] n torrent m; ~**ial** [-'rɛnʃl] a torrentiel(le).

**torso** ['tɔ:səu] n torse m.

**tortoise** ['tɔ:təs] n tortue f; ~**shell** ['tɔ:təʃɛl] a en écaille.

**tortuous** ['tɔ:tjuəs] a tortueux(euse).

**torture** ['tɔ:tʃə*] n torture f // vt torturer.

**Tory** ['tɔ:rɪ] a tory (pl tories), conservateur(trice) // n tory m/f, conservateur/trice.

**toss** [tɔs] vt lancer, jeter ; (pancake) faire sauter ; (head) rejeter en arrière ; **to** ~ **a coin** jouer à pile ou face ; **to** ~ **up for sth** jouer qch à pile ou face ; **to** ~ **and turn** (in bed) se tourner et se retourner.

**tot** [tɔt] n (drink) petit verre ; (child) bambin m.

**total** ['təutl] a total(e) // n total m // vt (add up) faire le total de, totaliser ; (amount to) s'élever à.

**totalitarian** [təutælɪ'tɛərɪən] a totalitaire.

**totality** [təu'tælɪtɪ] n totalité f.

**totem pole** ['təutəmpəul] n mât m totémique.

**totter** ['tɔtə*] vi chanceler.

**touch** [tʌtʃ] n contact m, toucher m; (sense, also skill: of pianist etc) toucher ; (fig: note, also: FOOTBALL) touche f // vt

(gen) toucher ; (tamper with) toucher à ; **a** ~ **of** (fig) un petit peu de ; une touche de ; **in** ~ **with** en contact or rapport avec ; **to get in** ~ **with** prendre contact avec ; **to lose** ~ (friends) se perdre de vue ; **to** ~ **on** vt fus (topic) effleurer, toucher ; **to** ~ **up** vt (paint) retoucher ; ~**-and-go** a incertain(e) ; **it was** ~**-and-go whether we did it** nous avons failli ne pas le faire ; ~**down** n atterrissage m; (on sea) amerrissage m; ~**ed** a touché(e) ; (col) cinglé(e) ; ~**ing** a touchant(e), attendrissant(e) ; ~**line** n (SPORT) (ligne f de) touche f; ~**y** a (person) susceptible.

**tough** [tʌf] a dur(e) ; (resistant) résistant(e), solide ; (meat) dur, coriace // n (gangster etc) dur m; (col) **luck!** pas de chance! ; tant pis! ; ~**en** vt rendre plus dur(e) (or plus résistant(e) or plus solide) ; ~**ness** n dureté f; résistance f; solidité f.

**toupee** ['tu:peɪ] n postiche m.

**tour** ['tuə*] n voyage m; (also: **package** ~) voyage organisé ; (of town, museum) tour m, visite f; (by artist) tournée f // vt visiter ; ~**ing** n voyages mpl touristiques, tourisme m.

**tourism** ['tuərɪzm] n tourisme m.

**tourist** ['tuərɪst] n touriste m/f // ad (travel) en classe touriste // cpd touristique ; ~ **office** n syndicat m d'initiative.

**tournament** ['tuənəmənt] n tournoi m.

**tour operator** ['tuər'ɔpəreɪtə*] n organisateur m de voyages.

**tousled** ['tauzld] a (hair) ébouriffé(e).

**tout** [taut] vi: **to** ~ **for** essayer de raccrocher, racoler ; **to** ~ **sth (around)** essayer de placer or (re)vendre qch.

**tow** [təu] vt remorquer ; '**on** ~' (AUT) 'véhicule en remorque'.

**toward(s)** [tə'wɔ:d(z)] prep vers ; (of attitude) envers, à l'égard de ; (of purpose) pour.

**towel** ['tauəl] n serviette f (de toilette) ; (also: **tea** ~) torchon m; ~**ling** n (fabric) tissu-éponge m; ~ **rail** n porte-serviettes m inv.

**tower** ['tauə*] n tour f; ~ **block** n tour f (d'habitation), imposant(e).

**towline** ['təulaɪn] n (câble m de) remorque f.

**town** [taun] n ville f; **to go to** ~ aller en ville ; (fig) y mettre le paquet ; ~ **clerk** n ≈ secrétaire m/f de mairie ; ~ **council** n conseil municipal ; ~ **hall** n ≈ mairie f; ~ **planner** n urbaniste m/f; ~ **planning** n urbanisme m.

**towpath** ['təupɑ:θ] n (chemin m de) halage m.

**towrope** ['təurəup] n (câble m de) remorque f.

**toxic** ['tɔksɪk] a toxique.

**toy** [tɔɪ] n jouet m; **to** ~ **with** vt fus jouer avec ; (idea) caresser ; ~**shop** m magasin m de jouets.

**trace** [treɪs] n trace f // vt (draw) tracer, dessiner ; (follow) suivre la trace de ; (locate) retrouver ; **without** ~ (disappear) sans laisser de traces.

**track** [træk] n (mark) trace f; (path: gen) chemin m, piste f; (: of bullet etc) trajectoire *f*; (: *of suspect, animal*) piste ; (*RAIL*) voie ferrée, rails *mpl*; (*on tape, SPORT*) piste // *vt* suivre la trace *or* la piste de ; **to keep ~ of** suivre ; **to ~ down** *vt* (*prey*) trouver et capturer ; (*sth lost*) finir par retrouver ; **~ed** *a* (*AUT*) à chenille ; **~er dog** *n* chien policier ; **~suit** *n* survêtement *m*.

**tract** [trækt] *n* (*GEO*) étendue *f*, zone *f*; (*pamphlet*) tract *m*; **respiratory ~** (*ANAT*) système *m* respiratoire.

**tractor** ['træktə*] *n* tracteur *m*.

**trade** [treɪd] *n* commerce *m*; (*skill, job*) métier *m* // *vi* faire du commerce ; **to ~ with/in** faire du commerce avec/le commerce de ; **to ~ in** *vt* (*old car etc*) faire reprendre ;**~-in** (**value**) *n* reprise *f*; **~mark** *n* marque *f* de fabrique ; **~name** *n* marque déposée ; **~r** *n* commerçant/e, négociant/e ; **~sman** *n* (*shopkeeper*) commerçant ; **~ union** *n* syndicat *m*; **~ unionist** syndicaliste *m/f*; **trading** *n* affaires *fpl*, commerce *m*; **trading estate** *n* zone industrielle ; **trading stamp** *n* timbre-prime *m*.

**tradition** [trə'dɪʃən] *n* tradition *f*; **~s** *npl* coutumes *fpl*, traditions ; **~al** *a* traditionnel(le).

**traffic** ['træfɪk] *n* trafic *m*; (*cars*) circulation *f* // *vi*: **to ~ in** (*pej: liquor, drugs*) faire le trafic de ; **~ circle** *n* (*US*) rond-point *m*; **~ jam** *n* embouteillage *m*; **~ lights** *npl* feux *mpl* (de signalisation) ; **~ sign** *n* panneau *m* de signalisation ; **~ warden** *n* contractuel/le.

**tragedy** ['trædʒədɪ] *n* tragédie *f*.

**tragic** ['trædʒɪk] *a* tragique.

**trail** [treɪl] *n* (*tracks*) trace *f*, piste *f*; (*path*) chemin *m*, piste ; (*of smoke etc*) traînée *f* // *vt* traîner, tirer ; (*follow*) suivre // *vi* traîner ; **to ~ behind** *vi* traîner, être à la traîne ; **~er** *n* (*AUT*) remorque *f*; (*US*) caravane *f*; (*CINEMA*) court film de lancement ; **~ing plant** *n* plante rampante.

**train** [treɪn] *n* train *m*; (*in underground*) rame *f*; (*of dress*) traîne *f* // *vt* (*apprentice, doctor etc*) former ; (*sportsman*) entraîner ; (*dog*) dresser ; (*memory*) exercer ; (*point: gun etc*): **to ~ sth on** braquer qch sur // *vi* recevoir sa formation ; s'entraîner ; **one's ~ of thought** le fil de sa pensée ; **~ed** *a* qualifié(e), qui a reçu une formation ; dressé(e) ; **~ee** [treɪ'niː] *n* stagiaire *m/f*; (*in trade*) apprenti/e ; **~er** *n* (*SPORT*) entraîneur/euse ; (*of dogs etc*) dresseur/euse ; **~ing** *n* formation *f*; entraînement *m*; dressage *m*; **in ~ing** (*SPORT*) à l'entraînement ; (*fit*) en forme ; **~ing college** *n* école professionnelle ; (*for teachers*) ≈ école normale.

**traipse** [treɪps] *vi* (se) traîner, déambuler.

**trait** [treɪt] *n* trait *m* (de caractère).

**traitor** ['treɪtə*] *n* traître *m*.

**tram** [træm] *n* (*also*: **~car**) tram(way) *m*; **~line** *n* ligne *f* de tram(way).

**tramp** [træmp] *n* (*person*) vagabond/e, clochard/e // *vi* marcher d'un pas lourd // *vt* (*walk through: town, streets*) parcourir à pied.

**trample** ['træmpl] *vt*: **to ~ (underfoot)** piétiner ; (*fig*) bafouer.

**trampoline** ['træmpəliːn] *n* trampolino *m*.

**trance** [trɑːns] *n* transe *f*; (*MED*) catalepsie *f*.

**tranquil** ['træŋkwɪl] *a* tranquille ; **~lity** *n* tranquillité *f*; **~lizer** *n* (*MED*) tranquillisant *m*.

**transact** [træn'zækt] *vt* (*business*) traiter ; **~ion** [-'zækʃən] *n* transaction *f*; **~ions** *npl* (*minutes*) actes *mpl*.

**transatlantic** ['trænzət'læntɪk] *a* transatlantique.

**transcend** [træn'sɛnd] *vt* transcender ; (*excel over*) surpasser.

**transcript** ['trænskrɪpt] *n* transcription *f* (*texte*) ; **~ion** [-'skrɪpʃən] *n* transcription.

**transept** ['trænsɛpt] *n* transept *m*.

**transfer** *n* ['trænsfə*] (*gen, also SPORT*) transfert *m*; (*POL: of power*) passation *f*; (*picture, design*) décalcomanie *f*; (: *stick-on*) autocollant *m* // *vt* [træns'fə:*] transférer ; passer ; décalquer ; **to ~ the charges** (*TEL*) téléphoner en P.C.V. ; **~able** [-'fə:rəbl] *a* transmissible, transférable ; **'not ~able'** 'personnel'.

**transform** [træns'fɔ:m] *vt* transformer ; **~ation** [-'meɪʃən] *n* transformation *f*; **~er** *n* (*ELEC*) transformateur *m*.

**transfusion** [træns'fju:ʒən] *n* transfusion *f*.

**transient** ['trænzɪənt] *a* transitoire, éphémère.

**transistor** [træn'zɪstə*] *n* (*ELEC, also*: **~ radio**) transistor *m*.

**transit** ['trænzɪt] *n*: **in ~** en transit ; **~ lounge** *n* salle *f* de transit.

**transition** [træn'zɪʃən] *n* transition *f*; **~al** *a* transitoire.

**transitive** ['trænzɪtɪv] *a* (*LING*) transitif(ive).

**transitory** ['trænzɪtərɪ] *a* transitoire.

**translate** [trænz'leɪt] *vt* traduire ; **translation** [-'leɪʃən] *n* traduction *f*; (*SCOL: as opposed to prose*) version *f*; **translator** *n* traducteur/trice.

**transmission** [trænz'mɪʃən] *n* transmission *f*.

**transmit** [trænz'mɪt] *vt* transmettre ; (*RADIO, TV*) émettre ; **~ter** *m* émetteur *m*.

**transparency** [træns'pɛərnsɪ] *n* (*PHOT*) diapositive *f*.

**transparent** [træns'pærnt] *a* transparent(e).

**transplant** *vt* [træns'plɑ:nt] transplanter ; (*seedlings*) repiquer // *n* ['trænsplɑ:nt] (*MED*) transplantation *f*.

**transport** *n* ['trænspɔ:t] transport *m* // *vt* [træns'pɔ:t] transporter ; **~ation** [-'teɪʃən] *n* (*moyen m de*) transport *m*; (*of prisoners*) transportation *f*; **~ café** *n* ≈ restaurant *m* de routiers.

**transverse** ['trænzvə:s] *a* transversal(e).

**transvestite** [trænz'vɛstaɪt] *n* travesti/e.

**trap** [træp] *n* (*snare, trick*) piège *m*; (*carriage*) cabriolet *m* // *vt* prendre au piège ; (*immobilize*) bloquer ; (*jam*) coincer ; **to shut one's ~** (*col*) la fermer ; **~ door** *n* trappe *f*.

**trapeze** [trə'pi:z] *n* trapèze *m*.

**trapper** ['træpə*] *n* trappeur *m*.

**trappings** ['træpɪŋz] *npl* ornements *mpl*; attributs *mpl*.

# trash 473 trivial

**trash** [træʃ] *n* (*pej: goods*) camelote *f*; (: *nonsense*) sottises *fpl*; ~ **can** *n* (*US*) boite *f* à ordures.

**trauma** ['trɔ:mə] *n* traumatisme *m*; ~**tic** [-'mætɪk] *a* traumatisant(e).

**travel** ['trævl] *n* voyage(s) *m*(*pl*) // *vi* voyager; (*move*) aller, se déplacer // *vt* (*distance*) parcourir; ~ **agent's** *n* agence *f* de voyages; ~**ler**, ~**er** (*US*) *n* voyageur/euse; ~**ler's cheque** *n* chèque *m* de voyage; ~**ling**, ~**ing** (*US*) *n* voyage(s) *m*(*pl*) // *cpd* (*bag, clock*) de voyage; (*expenses*) de déplacement; ~ **sickness** *n* mal *m* de la route (*or* de mer *or* de l'air).

**traverse** ['trævəs] *vt* traverser.

**travesty** ['trævəstɪ] *n* parodie *f*.

**trawler** ['trɔ:lə*] *n* chalutier *m*.

**tray** [treɪ] *n* (*for carrying*) plateau *m*; (*on desk*) corbeille *f*.

**treacherous** ['trɛtʃərəs] *a* traître(sse).

**treachery** ['trɛtʃərɪ] *n* traîtrise *f*.

**treacle** ['tri:kl] *n* mélasse *f*.

**tread** [trɛd] *n* pas *m*; (*sound*) bruit *m* de pas; (*of tyre*) chape *f*, bande *f* de roulement // *vi* (*pt* trod, *pp* trodden [trɔd, 'trɔdn]) marcher; **to** ~ **on** *vt fus* marcher sur.

**treason** ['tri:zn] *n* trahison *f*.

**treasure** ['trɛʒə*] *n* trésor *m* // *vt* (*value*) tenir beaucoup à; (*store*) conserver précieusement; ~ **hunt** *n* chasse *f* au trésor.

**treasurer** ['trɛʒərə*] *n* trésorier/ère.

**treasury** ['trɛʒərɪ] *n* trésorerie *f*; **the T**~ (*POL*) le ministère des Finances.

**treat** [tri:t] *n* petit cadeau, petite surprise // *vt* traiter; **it was a** ~ ça m'a (*or* nous a *etc*) vraiment fait plaisir; **to** ~ **sb to sth** offrir qch à qn.

**treatise** ['tri:tɪz] *n* traité *m* (*ouvrage*).

**treatment** ['tri:tmənt] *n* traitement *m*.

**treaty** ['tri:tɪ] *n* traité *m*.

**treble** ['trɛbl] *a* triple // *n* (*MUS*) soprano *m* // *vt, vi* tripler; ~ **clef** *n* clé *f* de sol.

**tree** [tri:] *n* arbre *m*; ~-**lined** *a* bordé(e) d'arbres; ~**top** *n* cime *f* d'un arbre; ~ **trunk** *n* tronc *m* d'arbre.

**trek** [trɛk] *n* voyage *m*; randonnée *f*; (*tiring walk*) tirée *f* // *vi* (*as holiday*) faire de la randonnée.

**trellis** ['trɛlɪs] *n* treillis *m*, treillage *m*.

**tremble** ['trɛmbl] *vi* trembler; (*machine*) vibrer; ~**ing** tremblement *m*; vibrations *fpl* // *a* tremblant(e); vibrant(e).

**tremendous** [trɪ'mɛndəs] *a* (*enormous*) énorme, fantastique; (*excellent*) formidable.

**tremor** ['trɛmə*] *n* tremblement *m*; (*also:* **earth** ~) secousse *f* sismique.

**trench** [trɛntʃ] *n* tranchée *f*.

**trend** [trɛnd] *n* (*tendency*) tendance *f*; (*of events*) cours *m*; (*fashion*) mode *f*; ~**y** *a* (*idea*) dans le vent; (*clothes*) dernier cri *inv*.

**trepidation** [trɛpɪ'deɪʃən] *n* vive agitation.

**trespass** ['trɛspəs] *vi*: **to** ~ **on** s'introduire sans permission dans; (*fig*) empiéter sur; **'no** ~**ing'** 'propriété privée', 'défense d'entrer'.

**tress** [trɛs] *n* boucle *f* de cheveux.

**trestle** ['trɛsl] *n* tréteau *m*; ~ **table** *n* table *f* à tréteaux.

**trial** ['traɪəl] *n* (*LAW*) procès *m*, jugement *m*; (*test: of machine etc*) essai *m*; (*hardship*) épreuve *f*; (*worry*) souci *m*; **to be on** ~ passer en jugement; **by** ~ **and error** par tâtonnements.

**triangle** ['traɪæŋgl] *n* (*MATH, MUS*) triangle *m*; **triangular** [-'æŋgjulə*] *a* triangulaire.

**tribal** ['traɪbəl] *a* tribal(e).

**tribe** [traɪb] *n* tribu *f*; ~**sman** *n* membre *m* de la tribu.

**tribulation** [trɪbju'leɪʃən] *n* tribulation *f*, malheur *m*.

**tribunal** [traɪ'bju:nl] *n* tribunal *m*.

**tributary** ['trɪbju:tərɪ] *n* (*river*) affluent *m*.

**tribute** ['trɪbju:t] *n* tribut *m*, hommage *m*; **to pay** ~ **to** rendre hommage à.

**trice** [traɪs] *n*: **in a** ~ en un clin d'œil.

**trick** [trɪk] *n* ruse *f*; (*clever act*) astuce *f*; (*joke*) tour *m*; (*CARDS*) levée *f* // *vt* attraper, rouler; **to play a** ~ **on sb** jouer un tour à qn; ~**ery** *n* ruse *f*.

**trickle** ['trɪkl] *n* (*of water etc*) filet *m* // *vi* couler en un filet *or* goutte à goutte; **to** ~ **in/out** (*people*) entrer/sortir par petits groupes.

**tricky** ['trɪkɪ] *a* difficile, délicat(e).

**tricycle** ['traɪsɪkl] *n* tricycle *m*.

**trifle** ['traɪfl] *n* bagatelle *f*; (*CULIN*) ≈ diplomate *m* // *ad*: **a** ~ **long** un peu long; **trifling** *a* insignifiant(e).

**trigger** ['trɪgə*] *n* (*of gun*) gâchette *f*; **to** ~ **off** *vt* déclencher.

**trigonometry** [trɪgə'nɔmətrɪ] *n* trigonométrie *f*.

**trilby** ['trɪlbɪ] *n* (*chapeau m en*) feutre *m*.

**trim** [trɪm] *a* net(te); (*house, garden*) bien tenu(e); (*figure*) svelte // *n* (*haircut etc*) légère coupe; (*embellishment*) finitions *fpl*; (*on car*) garnitures *fpl* // *vt* couper légèrement; (*decorate*): **to** ~ (**with**) décorer (de); (*NAUT: a sail*) gréer; ~**mings** *npl* décorations *fpl*; (*extras: gen CULIN*) garniture *f*.

**Trinity** ['trɪnɪtɪ] *n*: **the** ~ la Trinité.

**trinket** ['trɪŋkɪt] *n* bibelot *m*; (*piece of jewellery*) colifichet *m*.

**trio** ['tri:əu] *n* trio *m*.

**trip** [trɪp] *n* voyage *m*; (*excursion*) excursion *f*; (*stumble*) faux pas // *vi* faire un faux pas, trébucher; (*go lightly*) marcher d'un pas léger; **on a** ~ en voyage; **to** ~ **up** *vi* trébucher // *vt* faire un croc-en-jambe à.

**tripe** [traɪp] *n* (*CULIN*) tripes *fpl*; (*pej: rubbish*) idioties *fpl*.

**triple** ['trɪpl] *a* triple.

**triplets** ['trɪplɪts] *npl* triplés/ées.

**triplicate** ['trɪplɪkət] *n*: **in** ~ en trois exemplaires.

**tripod** ['traɪpɔd] *n* trépied *m*.

**tripper** ['trɪpə*] *n* touriste *m/f*; excursionniste *m/f*.

**trite** [traɪt] *a* banal(e).

**triumph** ['traɪʌmf] *n* triomphe *m* // *vi*: **to** ~ (**over**) triompher (de); ~**al** [-'ʌmfl] *a* triomphal(e); ~**ant** [-'ʌmfənt] *a* triomphant(e).

**trivia** ['trɪvɪə] *npl* futilités *fpl*.

**trivial** ['trɪvɪəl] *a* insignifiant(e); (*commonplace*) banal(e); ~**ity** [-'ælɪtɪ] *n* caractère insignifiant; banalité *f*.

**trod** [trɔd] *pt of* **tread** ; ~**den** *pp of* **tread**.
**trolley** ['trɔlɪ] *n* chariot *m* ; ~ **bus** *n* trolleybus *m*.
**trollop** ['trɔləp] *n* prostituée *f*.
**trombone** [trɔm'bəun] *n* trombone *m*.
**troop** [tru:p] *n* bande *f*, groupe *m* ; ~**s** *npl* (MIL) troupes *fpl* ; (: *men*) hommes *mpl*, soldats *mpl* ; **to** ~ **in/out** *vi* entrer/sortir en groupe ; ~**er** *n* (MIL) soldat *m* de cavalerie ; ~**ing the colour** (*ceremony*) le salut au drapeau ; ~**ship** *n* (navire *m* de) transport *m*.
**trophy** ['trəufɪ] *n* trophée *m*.
**tropic** ['trɔpɪk] *n* tropique *m* ; **in the** ~**s** sous les tropiques ; **T**~ **of Cancer/Capricorn** *n* tropique du Cancer/Capricorne ; ~**al** *a* tropical(e).
**trot** [trɔt] *n* trot *m* // *vi* trotter ; **on the** ~ (fig: col) d'affilée.
**trouble** ['trʌbl] *n* difficulté(s) *f(pl)*, problème(s) *m(pl)* ; (*worry*) ennuis *mpl*, soucis *mpl* ; (*bother, effort*) peine *f* ; (POL) conflits *mpl*, troubles *mpl* ; (MED): **stomach etc** ~ troubles gastriques *etc* // *vt* déranger, gêner ; (*worry*) inquiéter // *vi*: **to** ~ **to do** prendre la peine de faire ; ~**s** *npl* (POL etc) troubles *mpl* ; **to be in** ~ avoir des ennuis ; (*ship, climber etc*) être en difficulté ; **to go to the** ~ **of doing** se donner le mal de faire ; **it's no** ~! je vous en prie! ; **what's the** ~? qu'est-ce qui ne va pas? ; ~**d** *a* (*person*) inquiet(ète) ; (*epoch, life*) agité(e) ; ~**-free** *a* sans problèmes *or* ennuis ; ~**maker** *n* élément perturbateur, fauteur *m* de troubles ; ~**shooter** *n* (*in conflict*) conciliateur *m* ; ~**some** *a* ennuyeux(euse), gênant(e).
**trough** [trɔf] *n* (*also:* **drinking** ~) abreuvoir *m* ; (*also:* **feeding** ~) auge *f* ; (*channel*) chenal *m* ; ~ **of low pressure** *n* (GEO) dépression *f*.
**trounce** [trauns] *vt* (*defeat*) battre à plates coutures.
**troupe** [tru:p] *n* troupe *f*.
**trousers** ['trauzəz] *npl* pantalon *m* ; **short** ~ *npl* culottes courtes.
**trousseau,** *pl* ~**x** *or* ~**s** ['tru:səu, -z] *n* trousseau *m*.
**trout** [traut] *n*, *pl inv* truite *f*.
**trowel** ['trauəl] *n* truelle *f*.
**truant** ['truənt] *n*: **to play** ~ faire l'école buissonnière.
**truce** [tru:s] *n* trêve *f*.
**truck** [trʌk] *n* camion *m* ; (RAIL) wagon *m* à plate-forme ; (*for luggage*) chariot *m* (à bagages) ; ~ **driver** *n* camionneur *m* ; ~ **farm** *n* (US) jardin maraîcher.
**truculent** ['trʌkjulənt] *a* agressif(ive).
**trudge** [trʌdʒ] *vi* marcher lourdement, se traîner.
**true** [tru:] *a* vrai(e) ; (*accurate*) exact(e) ; (*genuine*) vrai, véritable ; (*faithful*) fidèle.
**truffle** ['trʌfl] *n* truffe *f*.
**truly** ['tru:lɪ] *ad* vraiment, réellement ; (*truthfully*) sans mentir ; (*faithfully*) fidèlement ; '**yours** ~' (*in letter*) 'je vous prie d'agréer l'expression de mes sentiments respectueux.'
**trump** [trʌmp] *n* atout *m* ; ~**ed-up** *a* inventé(e) (de toutes pièces).

**trumpet** ['trʌmpɪt] *n* trompette *f* ; (*player*) trompettiste *m/f*.
**truncated** [trʌŋ'keɪtɪd] *a* tronqué(e).
**truncheon** ['trʌntʃən] *n* bâton *m* (d'agent de police) ; matraque *f*.
**trundle** ['trʌndl] *vt*, *vi*: **to** ~ **along** rouler bruyamment.
**trunk** [trʌŋk] *n* (*of tree, person*) tronc *m* ; (*of elephant*) trompe *f* ; (*case*) malle *f* ; ~**s** *npl* caleçon *m* ; (*also:* **swimming** ~**s**) maillot *m or* slip *m* de bain ; ~ **call** *n* (TEL) communication interurbaine ; ~ **road** ≈ route nationale.
**truss** [trʌs] *n* (MED) bandage *m* herniaire ; **to** ~ (**up**) *vt* (CULIN) brider.
**trust** [trʌst] *n* confiance *f* ; (LAW) fidéicommis *m* ; (COMM) trust *m* // *vt* (*rely on*) avoir confiance en ; (*entrust*): **to** ~ **sth to sb** confier qch à qn ; ~ (**that**) l'on a confiance ; ~**ee** [trʌs'ti:] *n* (LAW) fidéicommissaire *m/f* ; (*of school etc*) administrateur/trice ; ~**ful,** ~**ing** *a* confiant(e) ; ~**worthy** *a* digne de confiance ; ~**y** *a* fidèle.
**truth,** ~**s** [tru:θ, tru:ðz] *n* vérité *f* ; ~**ful** *a* (*person*) qui dit la vérité ; (*description*) exact(e), vrai(e) ; ~**fully** *ad* sincèrement, sans mentir ; ~**fulness** *n* véracité *f*.
**try** [traɪ] *n* essai *m*, tentative *f* ; (RUGBY) essai // *vt* (LAW) juger ; (*test: sth new*) essayer, tester ; (*strain*) éprouver // *vi* essayer ; **to** ~ **to do** essayer de faire ; (*seek*) chercher à faire ; **to** ~ **on** *vt* (*clothes*) essayer ; **to** ~ **it on** (fig) tenter le coup, bluffer ; **to** ~ **out** *vt* essayer, mettre à l'essai ; ~**ing** *a* pénible.
**tsar** [zɑ:*] *n* tsar *m*.
**T-shirt** ['ti:ʃə:t] *n* tee-shirt *m*.
**T-square** ['ti:skwɛə*] *n* équerre *f* en T.
**tub** [tʌb] *n* cuve *f* ; baquet *m* ; (*bath*) baignoire *f*.
**tuba** ['tju:bə] *n* tuba *m*.
**tubby** ['tʌbɪ] *a* rondelet(te).
**tube** [tju:b] *n* tube *m* ; (*underground*) métro *m* ; (*for tyre*) chambre *f* à air.
**tuberculosis** [tjubə:kju'ləusɪs] *n* tuberculose *f*.
**tube station** ['tju:bsteɪʃən] *n* station *f* de métro.
**tubing** ['tju:bɪŋ] *n* tubes *mpl* ; **a piece of** ~ un tube.
**tubular** ['tju:bjulə*] *a* tubulaire.
**TUC** *n* (*abbr of Trades Union Congress*) confédération *f* des syndicats britanniques.
**tuck** [tʌk] *n* (SEWING) pli *m*, rempli *m* // *vt* (*put*) mettre ; **to** ~ **away** *vt* cacher, ranger ; **to** ~ **in** *vt* rentrer ; (*child*) border // *vi* (*eat*) manger de bon appétit ; attaquer le repas ; **to** ~ **up** *vt* (*child*) border ; ~ **shop** *n* boutique *f* à provisions (*dans une école*).
**Tuesday** ['tju:zdɪ] *n* mardi *m*.
**tuft** [tʌft] *n* touffe *f*.
**tug** [tʌg] *n* (*ship*) remorqueur *m* // *vt* tirer (sur) ; ~**-of-war** *n* lutte *f* à la corde.
**tuition** [tju:'ɪʃən] *n* leçons *fpl*.
**tulip** ['tju:lɪp] *n* tulipe *f*.
**tumble** ['tʌmbl] *n* (*fall*) chute *f*, culbute *f* // *vi* tomber, dégringoler ; (*with somersault*) faire une *or* des culbute(s) // *vt* renverser, faire tomber ; ~**down** *a*

délabré(e) ; ~ **dryer** n séchoir m (à linge) à air chaud.
**tumbler** ['tʌmblə*] n verre (droit), gobelet m ; acrobate m/f.
**tummy** ['tʌmɪ] n (col) ventre m.
**tumour** ['tju:mə*] n tumeur f.
**tumult** ['tju:mʌlt] n tumulte m ; ~**uous** [-'mʌltjuəs] a tumultueux(euse).
**tuna** ['tju:nə] n, pl inv (also: ~ **fish**) thon m.
**tune** [tju:n] n (melody) air m // vt (MUS) accorder ; (RADIO, TV, AUT) régler, mettre au point ; **to be in/out of** ~ (instrument) être accordé/désaccordé ; (singer) chanter juste/faux ; **to be in/out of** ~ **with** (fig) être en accord/désaccord avec ; **to** ~ **in (to)** (RADIO, TV) se mettre à l'écoute (de) ; **to** ~ **up** vi (musician) accorder son instrument ; ~**ful** a mélodieux(euse) ; ~**r** n (radio set) radio-préamplificateur m ; **piano** ~**r** accordeur m de pianos ; ~**r amplifier** n radio-ampli m.
**tungsten** ['tʌnstn] n tungstène m.
**tunic** ['tju:nɪk] n tunique f.
**tuning** ['tju:nɪŋ] n réglage m ; ~ **fork** n diapason m.
**Tunisia** [tju:'nɪzɪə] n Tunisie f ; ~**n** a tunisien(ne) // n Tunisien/ne.
**tunnel** ['tʌnl] n tunnel m ; (in mine) galerie f // vi creuser un tunnel (or une galerie).
**tunny** ['tʌnɪ] n thon m.
**turban** ['tə:bən] n turban m.
**turbid** ['tə:bɪd] a boueux(euse).
**turbine** ['tə:baɪn] n turbine f.
**turbojet** ['tə:bəu'dʒɛt] n turboréacteur m.
**turbot** ['tə:bət] n, pl inv turbot m.
**turbulence** ['tə:bjuləns] n (AVIAT) turbulence f.
**turbulent** ['tə:bjulənt] a turbulent(e) ; (sea) agité(e).
**tureen** [təˈri:n] n soupière f.
**turf** [tə:f] n gazon m ; (clod) motte f (de gazon) // vt gazonner ; **the T**~ n le turf, les courses fpl ; **to** ~ **out** vt (col) jeter ; jeter dehors.
**turgid** ['tə:dʒɪd] a (speech) pompeux(euse).
**Turk** [tə:k] n Turc/Turque.
**turkey** ['tə:kɪ] n dindon m, dinde f.
**Turkey** ['tə:kɪ] n Turquie f.
**Turkish** ['tə:kɪʃ] a turc(turque) // n (LING) turc m ; ~ **bath** n bain turc ; ~ **delight** n loukoum m.
**turmoil** ['tə:mɔɪl] n trouble m, bouleversement m.
**turn** [tə:n] n tour m ; (in road) tournant m ; (tendency: of mind, events) tournure f ; (performance) numéro m ; (MED) crise f, attaque f // vt tourner ; (collar, steak) retourner ; (milk) faire tourner ; (change): **to** ~ **sth into** changer qch en // vi tourner ; (person: look back) se (re)tourner ; (reverse direction) faire demi-tour ; (change) changer ; (become) devenir ; **to** ~ **into** se changer en ; **a good** ~ un service ; **a bad** ~ un mauvais tour ; **it gave me quite a** ~ ça m'a fait un coup ; '**no left** ~' (AUT) 'défense de tourner à gauche' ; **it's your** ~ c'est (à) votre tour ; **in** ~ à son tour ; à tour de rôle ; **to take** ~**s** se relayer ; **to take** ~**s at** faire à tour de rôle ; **to** ~ **about** vi faire demi-tour ;

faire un demi-tour ; **to** ~ **away** vi se détourner, tourner la tête ; **to** ~ **back** vi revenir, faire demi-tour ; **to** ~ **down** vt (refuse) rejeter, refuser ; (reduce) baisser ; (fold) rabattre ; **to** ~ **in** vi (col: go to bed) aller se coucher // vt (fold) rentrer ; **to** ~ **off** vi (from road) tourner // vt (light, radio etc) éteindre ; (engine) arrêter ; **to** ~ **on** vt (light, radio etc) allumer ; (engine) mettre en marche ; **to** ~ **out** vt (light, gas) éteindre // vi: **to** ~ **out to be**... s'avérer..., se révéler... ; **to** ~ **up** (person) arriver, se pointer ; (lost object) être retrouvé(e) // vt (collar) remonter ; (increase: sound, volume etc) mettre plus fort ; **to** ~ **around** n volteface f ; ~**ed-up** a (nose) retroussé(e) ; ~**ing** n (in road) tournant m ; ~**ing circle** n rayon m de braquage ; ~**ing point** n (fig) tournant m, moment décisif.
**turnip** ['tə:nɪp] n navet m.
**turnout** ['tə:naut] n (nombre m de personnes dans l') assistance f.
**turnover** ['tə:nəuvə*] n (COMM: amount of money) chiffre m d'affaires ; (: of goods) roulement m ; (CULIN) sorte de chausson.
**turnpike** ['tə:npaɪk] n (US) autoroute f à péage.
**turnstile** ['tə:nstaɪl] n tourniquet m (d'entrée).
**turntable** ['tə:nteɪbl] n (on record player) platine f.
**turn-up** ['tə:nʌp] n (on trousers) revers m.
**turpentine** ['tə:pəntaɪn] n (also: **turps**) (essence f de) térébenthine f.
**turquoise** ['tə:kwɔɪz] n (stone) turquoise f // a turquoise inv.
**turret** ['tʌrɪt] n tourelle f.
**turtle** ['tə:tl] n tortue marine ; ~**neck** (**sweater**) n pullover m à col montant.
**tusk** [tʌsk] n défense f.
**tussle** ['tʌsl] n bagarre f, mêlée f.
**tutor** ['tju:tə*] n (in college) directeur/trice d'études ; (private teacher) précepteur/-trice ; ~**ial** [-'tɔ:rɪəl] (SCOL) (séance f de) travaux mpl pratiques.
**tuxedo** [tʌk'si:dəu] n (US) smoking m.
**T.V.** [ti:'vi:] n (abbr of **television**) télé f.
**twaddle** ['twɔdl] n balivernes fpl.
**twang** [twæŋ] n (of instrument) son vibrant ; (of voice) ton nasillard // vi vibrer // vt (guitar) pincer les cordes de.
**tweed** [twi:d] n tweed m.
**tweezers** ['twi:zəz] npl pince f à épiler.
**twelfth** [twɛlfθ] num douzième ; **T**~ **Night** n la fête des Rois.
**twelve** [twɛlv] num douze ; **at** ~ à midi ; (midnight) à minuit.
**twentieth** ['twɛntɪθ] num vingtième.
**twenty** ['twɛntɪ] num vingt.
**twerp** [twə:p] n (col) imbécile m/f.
**twice** [twaɪs] ad deux fois ; ~ **as much** deux fois plus.
**twig** [twɪg] n brindille f // vt, vi (col) piger.
**twilight** ['twaɪlaɪt] n crépuscule m.
**twill** [twɪl] n serge f.
**twin** [twɪn] a, n jumeau(elle) // vt jumeler.
**twine** [twaɪn] n ficelle f // vi (plant) s'enrouler ; (road) serpenter.
**twinge** [twɪndʒ] n (of pain) élancement m ; (of conscience) remords m.

**twinkle** ['twɪŋkl] n scintillement m; pétillement m // vi scintiller; (eyes) pétiller.

**twin town** [twɪn'taun] n ville jumelée.

**twirl** [twə:l] n tournoiement m // vt faire tournoyer // vi tournoyer.

**twist** [twɪst] n torsion f, tour m; (in wire, flex) tortillon m; (in story) coup m de théâtre // vt tordre; (weave) entortiller; (roll around) enrouler; (fig) déformer // vi s'entortiller; s'enrouler; (road) serpenter.

**twit** [twɪt] n (col) crétin/e.

**twitch** [twɪtʃ] n saccade f; (nervous) tic m // vi se convulser; avoir un tic.

**two** [tu:] num deux; to put ~ and ~ together (fig) faire le rapport; ~-door a (AUT) à deux portes; ~-faced a (pej: person) faux(fausse); ~fold ad: to increase ~fold doubler; ~-piece (suit) n (costume m) deux-pièces m inv; ~-piece (swimsuit) n (maillot m de bain) deux-pièces m inv; ~-seater n (plane) (avion m) biplace m; (car) voiture f à deux places; ~some n (people) couple m; ~-way a (traffic) dans les deux sens.

**tycoon** [taɪ'ku:n] n: (business) ~ gros homme d'affaires.

**type** [taɪp] n (category) genre m, espèce f; (model) modèle m; (example) type m; (TYP) type, caractère m // vt (letter etc) taper (à la machine); ~-cast a (actor) condamné(e) à toujours jouer le même rôle; ~script n texte dactylographié; ~writer n machine f à écrire; ~written a dactylographié(e).

**typhoid** ['taɪfɔɪd] n typhoïde f.

**typhoon** [taɪ'fu:n] n typhon m.

**typhus** ['taɪfəs] n typhus m.

**typical** ['tɪpɪkl] a typique, caractéristique.

**typify** ['tɪpɪfaɪ] vt être caractéristique de.

**typing** ['taɪpɪŋ] n dactylo(graphie) f; ~ error n faute f de frappe; ~ paper n papier m machine.

**typist** ['taɪpɪst] n dactylo m/f.

**tyranny** ['tɪrənɪ] n tyrannie f.

**tyrant** ['taɪərnt] n tyran m.

**tyre, tire** (US) ['taɪə*] n pneu m; ~ pressure n pression f (de gonflage).

**tzar** [zɑ:*] n = **tsar**.

## U

**U-bend** ['ju:'bɛnd] n (AUT) coude m, virage m en épingle à cheveux; (in pipe) coude.

**ubiquitous** [ju:'bɪkwɪtəs] a doué(e) d'ubiquité, omniprésent(e).

**udder** ['ʌdə*] n pis m, mamelle f.

**UFO** ['ju:fəu] n (abbr of unidentified flying object) O.V.N.I. (objet volant non identifié).

**ugh** [ə:h] excl pouah!

**ugliness** ['ʌglɪnɪs] n laideur f.

**ugly** ['ʌglɪ] a laid(e), vilain(e); (fig) répugnant(e).

**UHF** abbr of ultra-high frequency.

**UHT** a (abbr of ultra-heat treated): ~ milk n lait upérisé or longue conservation.

**U.K.** n abbr see **united**.

**ulcer** ['ʌlsə*] n ulcère m; (also: mouth ~) aphte f.

**Ulster** ['ʌlstə*] n Ulster m.

**ulterior** [ʌl'tɪərɪə*] a ultérieur(e); ~ motive n arrière-pensée f.

**ultimate** ['ʌltɪmət] a ultime, final(e); (authority) suprême; ~ly ad en fin de compte; finalement; par la suite.

**ultimatum** [ʌltɪ'meɪtəm] n ultimatum m.

**ultraviolet** ['ʌltrə'vaɪəlɪt] a ultraviolet(te).

**umbilical** [ʌmbɪ'laɪkl] a: ~ cord cordon ombilical.

**umbrage** ['ʌmbrɪdʒ] n: to take ~ prendre ombrage, se froisser.

**umbrella** [ʌm'brɛlə] n parapluie m; (fig): under the ~ of sous les auspices de; chapeauté(e) par.

**umpire** ['ʌmpaɪə*] n arbitre m // vt arbitrer.

**umpteen** [ʌmp'ti:n] a je ne sais combien de; for the ~th time pour la nième fois.

**UN, UNO** abbr see **united**.

**unabashed** [ʌnə'bæʃt] a nullement intimidé(e).

**unabated** [ʌnə'beɪtɪd] a non diminué(e).

**unable** [ʌn'eɪbl] a: to be ~ to ne (pas) pouvoir, être dans l'impossibilité de; être incapable de.

**unaccompanied** [ʌnə'kʌmpənɪd] a (child, lady) non accompagné(e).

**unaccountably** [ʌnə'kauntəblɪ] ad inexplicablement.

**unaccustomed** [ʌnə'kʌstəmd] a inaccoutumé(e), inhabituel(le); to be ~ to sth ne pas avoir l'habitude de qch.

**unadulterated** [ʌnə'dʌltəreɪtɪd] a pur(e), naturel(le).

**unaided** [ʌn'eɪdɪd] a sans aide, tout(e) seul(e).

**unanimity** [ju:nə'nɪmɪtɪ] n unanimité f.

**unanimous** [ju:'nænɪməs] a unanime; ~ly ad à l'unanimité.

**unashamed** [ʌnə'ʃeɪmd] a sans honte; impudent(e).

**unassuming** [ʌnə'sju:mɪŋ] a modeste, sans prétentions.

**unattached** [ʌnə'tætʃt] a libre, sans attaches.

**unattended** [ʌnə'tɛndɪd] a (car, child, luggage) sans surveillance.

**unattractive** [ʌnə'træktɪv] a peu attrayant(e).

**unauthorized** [ʌn'ɔ:θəraɪzd] a non autorisé(e), sans autorisation.

**unavoidable** [ʌnə'vɔɪdəbl] a inévitable.

**unaware** [ʌnə'wɛə*] a: to be ~ of ignorer, ne pas savoir, être inconscient(e) de; ~s ad à l'improviste, au dépourvu.

**unbalanced** [ʌn'bælənst] a déséquilibré(e).

**unbearable** [ʌn'bɛərəbl] a insupportable.

**unbeatable** [ʌn'bi:təbl] a imbattable.

**unbeaten** [ʌn'bi:tn] a invaincu(e).

**unbecoming** [ʌnbɪ'kʌmɪŋ] a malséant(e), inconvenant(e).

**unbeknown(st)** [ʌnbɪ'nəun(st)] ad: ~ to à l'insu de.

**unbelief** [ʌnbɪ'li:f] n incrédulité f.

**unbelievable** [ʌnbɪ'li:vəbl] a incroyable.

**unbend** [ʌn'bɛnd] vb (irg) vi se détendre // vt (wire) redresser, détordre.

**unbounded** [ʌn'baundɪd] a sans bornes, illimité(e).

**unbreakable** [ʌn'breɪkəbl] *a* incassable.
**unbridled** [ʌn'braɪdld] *a* débridé(e), déchaîné(e).
**unbroken** [ʌn'brəukən] *a* intact(e) ; continu(e).
**unburden** [ʌn'bə:dn] *vt*: **to ~ o.s.** s'épancher, se livrer.
**unbutton** [ʌn'bʌtn] *vt* déboutonner.
**uncalled-for** [ʌn'kɔ:ldfɔ:*] *a* déplacé(e), injustifié(e).
**uncanny** [ʌn'kænɪ] *a* étrange, troublant(e).
**unceasing** [ʌn'si:sɪŋ] *a* incessant(e), continu(e).
**uncertain** [ʌn'sə:tn] *a* incertain(e) ; mal assuré(e) ; **~ty** *n* incertitude *f*, doutes *mpl*.
**unchanged** [ʌn'tʃeɪndʒd] *a* inchangé(e).
**uncharitable** [ʌn'tʃærɪtəbl] *a* peu charitable.
**uncharted** [ʌn'tʃɑ:tɪd] *a* inexploré(e).
**unchecked** [ʌn'tʃɛkt] *a* non réprimé(e).
**uncle** ['ʌŋkl] *n* oncle *m*.
**uncomfortable** [ʌn'kʌmfətəbl] *a* inconfortable ; (*uneasy*) mal à l'aise, gêné(e) ; désagréable.
**uncommon** [ʌn'kɔmən] *a* rare, singulier(ère), peu commun(e).
**uncompromising** [ʌn'kɔmprəmaɪzɪŋ] *a* intransigeant(e), inflexible.
**unconditional** [ʌnkən'dɪʃənl] *a* sans conditions.
**uncongenial** [ʌnkən'dʒi:nɪəl] *a* peu agréable.
**unconscious** [ʌn'kɔnʃəs] *a* sans connaissance, évanoui(e) ; (*unaware*) inconscient(e) // *n*: **the ~** l'inconscient *m* ; **~ly** *ad* inconsciemment.
**uncontrollable** [ʌnkən'trəuləbl] *a* irrépressible ; indiscipliné(e).
**uncork** [ʌn'kɔ:k] *vt* déboucher.
**uncouth** [ʌn'ku:θ] *a* grossier(ère), fruste.
**uncover** [ʌn'kʌvə*] *vt* découvrir.
**unctuous** ['ʌŋktjuəs] *a* onctueux(euse), mielleux(euse).
**undaunted** [ʌn'dɔ:ntɪd] *a* non intimidé(e), inébranlable.
**undecided** [ʌndɪ'saɪdɪd] *a* indécis(e), irrésolu(e).
**undeniable** [ʌndɪ'naɪəbl] *a* indéniable, incontestable.
**under** ['ʌndə*] *prep* sous ; (*less than*) (de) moins de ; au-dessous de ; (*according to*) selon, en vertu de // *ad* au-dessous ; en dessous ; **from ~ sth** de dessous *or* de sous qch ; **~ there** là-dessous ; **~ repair** en (cours de) réparation.
**under...** ['ʌndə*] *prefix* sous- ; **~age** *a* qui n'a pas l'âge réglementaire ; **~carriage, ~cart** *n* train *m* d'atterrissage ; **~clothes** *npl* sous-vêtements *mpl* ; (*women's only*) dessous *mpl* ; **~coat** *n* (*paint*) couche *f* de fond ; **~cover** *a* secret(ète), clandestin(e) ; **~current** *n* courant sous-jacent ; **~cut** *n* (*CULIN*) (morceau *m* de) filet *m* // *vt irg* vendre moins cher que ; **~developed** *a* sous-développé(e) ; **~dog** *n* opprimé *m* ; **~done** *a* (*CULIN*) saignant(e) ; (*pej*) pas assez cuit(e) ; **~estimate** *vt* sous-estimer, mésestimer ; **~exposed** *a* (*PHOT*) sous-exposé(e) ; **~fed** *a* sous-alimenté(e) ; **~foot** *ad* sous les pieds ; **~go** *vt irg* subir ; (*treatment*) suivre ; **~graduate** *n*

étudiant/e (qui prépare la licence) ; **~ground** *n* métro *m* ; (*POL*) clandestinité *f* ; **~growth** *n* broussailles *fpl*, sous-bois *m* ; **~hand(ed)** *a* (*fig*) sournois(e), en dessous ; **~lie** *vt irg* être à la base de ; **~line** *vt* souligner ; **~ling** ['ʌndəlɪŋ] *n* (*pej*) sousfifre *m*, subalterne *m* ; **~mine** *vt* saper, miner ; **~neath** [ʌndə'ni:θ] *ad* (en) dessous // *prep* sous, au-dessous de ; **~paid** *a* sous-payé(e) ; **~pants** *npl* (*Brit*) caleçon *m*, slip *m* ; **~pass** *n* passage souterrain ; (*on motorway*) passage inférieur ; **~play** *vt* minimiser ; **~price** *vt* vendre à un prix trop bas ; **~privileged** *a* défavorisé(e), économiquement faible ; **~rate** *vt* sous-estimer, mésestimer ; **~shirt** *n* (*US*) tricot *m* de corps ; **~shorts** *npl* (*US*) caleçon *m*, slip *m* ; **~side** *n* dessous *m* ; **~skirt** *n* jupon *m*.
**understand** [ʌndə'stænd] *vb* (*irg: like* **stand**) *vt, vi* comprendre ; **I ~ that...** je me suis laissé dire que... ; je crois comprendre que... ; **~able** *a* compréhensible ; **~ing** *a* compréhensif(ive) // *n* compréhension *f* ; (*agreement*) accord *m*.
**understatement** [ʌndə'steɪtmənt] *n*: **that's an ~** c'est (bien) peu dire, le terme est faible.
**understood** [ʌndə'stud] *pt, pp of* **understand** // *a* entendu(e) ; (*implied*) sous-entendu(e).
**understudy** ['ʌndəstʌdɪ] *n* doublure *f*.
**undertake** [ʌndə'teɪk] *vt irg* entreprendre ; se charger de.
**undertaker** ['ʌndəteɪkə*] *n* entrepreneur *m* des pompes funèbres, croque-mort *m*.
**undertaking** [ʌndə'teɪkɪŋ] *n* entreprise *f* ; (*promise*) promesse *f*.
**underwater** [ʌndə'wɔ:tə*] *ad* sous l'eau // *a* sous-marin(e).
**underwear** ['ʌndəwɛə*] *n* sous-vêtements *mpl* ; (*women's only*) dessous *mpl*.
**underweight** [ʌndə'weɪt] *a* d'un poids insuffisant ; (*person*) (trop) maigre.
**underworld** ['ʌndəwə:ld] *n* (*of crime*) milieu *m*, pègre *f*.
**underwriter** ['ʌndəraɪtə*] *n* (*INSURANCE*) souscripteur *m*.
**undesirable** [ʌndɪ'zaɪərəbl] *a* peu souhaitable ; indésirable.
**undies** ['ʌndɪz] *npl* (*col*) dessous *mpl*, lingerie *f*.
**undisputed** [ʌndɪ'spju:tɪd] *a* incontesté(e).
**undistinguished** [ʌndɪs'tɪŋgwɪʃt] *a* médiocre, quelconque.
**undo** [ʌn'du:] *vt irg* défaire ; **~ing** *n* ruine *f*, perte *f*.
**undoubted** [ʌn'dautɪd] *a* indubitable, certain(e) ; **~ly** *ad* sans aucun doute.
**undress** [ʌn'drɛs] *vi* se déshabiller.
**undue** [ʌn'dju:] *a* indu(e), excessif(ive).
**undulating** ['ʌndjuleɪtɪŋ] *a* ondoyant(e), onduleux(euse).
**unduly** [ʌn'dju:lɪ] *ad* trop, excessivement.
**unearth** [ʌn'ə:θ] *vt* déterrer ; (*fig*) dénicher.
**unearthly** [ʌn'ə:θlɪ] *a* surnaturel(le) ; (*hour*) indu(e), impossible.
**uneasy** [ʌn'i:zɪ] *a* mal à l'aise, gêné(e) ; (*worried*) inquiet(ète).

**uneconomic(al)** ['ʌniːkə'nɔmɪk(l)] *a* peu économique ; peu rentable.
**uneducated** [ʌn'ɛdjukeɪtɪd] *a* sans éducation.
**unemployed** [ʌnɪm'plɔɪd] *a* sans travail, en chômage // *n*: the ~ les chômeurs *mpl*.
**unemployment** [ʌnɪm'plɔɪmənt] *n* chômage *m*.
**unending** [ʌn'ɛndɪŋ] *a* interminable.
**unenviable** [ʌn'ɛnvɪəbl] *a* peu enviable.
**unerring** [ʌn'əːrɪŋ] *a* infaillible, sûr(e).
**uneven** [ʌn'iːvn] *a* inégal(e) ; irrégulier(ère).
**unexpected** [ʌnɪk'spɛktɪd] *a* inattendu(e), imprévu(e).
**unexploded** [ʌnɪk'spləudɪd] *a* non explosé(e) *or* éclaté(e).
**unfailing** [ʌn'feɪlɪŋ] *a* inépuisable ; infaillible.
**unfair** [ʌn'fɛə*] *a*: ~ (to) injuste (envers) ; ~ly *ad* injustement.
**unfaithful** [ʌn'feɪθful] *a* infidèle.
**unfamiliar** [ʌnfə'mɪlɪə*] *a* étrange, inconnu(e).
**unfasten** [ʌn'fɑːsn] *vt* défaire ; détacher.
**unfathomable** [ʌn'fæðəməbl] *a* insondable.
**unfavourable, unfavorable** (*US*) [ʌn'feɪvərəbl] *a* défavorable.
**unfeeling** [ʌn'fiːlɪŋ] *a* insensible, dur(e).
**unfinished** [ʌn'fɪnɪʃt] *a* inachevé(e).
**unfit** [ʌn'fɪt] *a* en mauvaise santé ; pas en forme ; (*incompetent*): ~ (for) impropre (à) ; (*work, service*) inapte (à).
**unflagging** [ʌn'flægɪŋ] *a* infatigable, inlassable.
**unflappable** [ʌn'flæpəbl] *a* imperturbable.
**unflinching** [ʌn'flɪntʃɪŋ] *a* stoïque.
**unfold** [ʌn'fəuld] *vt* déplier ; (*fig*) révéler, exposer // *vi* se dérouler.
**unforeseen** ['ʌnfɔː'siːn] *a* imprévu(e).
**unforgivable** [ʌnfə'gɪvəbl] *a* impardonnable.
**unfortunate** [ʌn'fɔːtʃnət] *a* malheureux-(euse) ; (*event, remark*) malencontreux-(euse) ; ~ly *ad* malheureusement.
**unfounded** [ʌn'faundɪd] *a* sans fondement.
**unfriendly** [ʌn'frɛndlɪ] *a* froid(e), inamical(e).
**unfurnished** [ʌn'fəːnɪʃt] *a* non meublé(e).
**ungainly** [ʌn'geɪnlɪ] *a* gauche, dégingandé(e).
**ungodly** [ʌn'gɔdlɪ] *a* impie ; at an ~ hour à une heure indue.
**unguarded** [ʌn'gɑːdɪd] *a*: ~ moment *n* moment *m* d'inattention.
**unhappiness** [ʌn'hæpɪnɪs] *n* tristesse *f*, peine *f*.
**unhappy** [ʌn'hæpɪ] *a* triste, malheureux(euse) ; ~ with (*arrangements etc*) mécontent(e) de, peu satisfait(e) de.
**unharmed** [ʌn'hɑːmd] *a* indemne, sain(e) et sauf(sauve).
**unhealthy** [ʌn'hɛlθɪ] *a* (*gen*) malsain(e) ; (*person*) maladif(ive).
**unheard-of** [ʌn'həːdɔv] *a* inouï(e), sans précédent.
**unhook** [ʌn'huk] *vt* décrocher ; dégrafer.

**unhurt** [ʌn'həːt] *a* indemne, sain(e) et sauf(sauve).
**unicorn** ['juːnɪkɔːn] *n* licorne *f*.
**unidentified** [ʌnaɪ'dɛntɪfaɪd] *a* non identifié(e).
**uniform** ['juːnɪfɔːm] *n* uniforme *m* // *a* uniforme ; ~ity [-'fɔːmɪtɪ] *n* uniformité *f*.
**unify** ['juːnɪfaɪ] *vt* unifier.
**unilateral** [juːnɪ'lætərəl] *a* unilatéral(e).
**unimaginable** [ʌnɪ'mædʒɪnəbl] *a* inimaginable, inconcevable.
**unimpaired** [ʌnɪm'pɛəd] *a* intact(e).
**uninhibited** [ʌnɪn'hɪbɪtɪd] *a* sans inhibitions ; sans retenue.
**unintentional** [ʌnɪn'tɛnʃənəl] *a* involontaire.
**union** ['juːnjən] *n* union *f*; (*also*: trade ~) syndicat *m* // *cpd* du syndicat, syndical(e) ; U~ Jack *n* drapeau du Royaume-Uni.
**unique** [juː'niːk] *a* unique.
**unison** ['juːnɪsn] *n*: in ~ à l'unisson, en chœur.
**unit** ['juːnɪt] *n* unité *f*; (*section: of furniture etc*) élément *m*, bloc *m* ; (*team, squad*) groupe *m*, service *m*.
**unite** [juː'naɪt] *vt* unir // *vi* s'unir ; ~d *a* uni(e) ; unifié(e) ; (*efforts*) conjugué(e) ; U~d Kingdom (U.K.) *n* Royaume-Uni *m* ; U~d Nations (Organization) (UN, UNO) *n* (Organisation *f* des) Nations unies (O.N.U.) ; U~d States (of America) (US, USA) *n* États-Unis *mpl*.
**unit trust** ['juːnɪttrʌst] *n* (*Brit*) société *f* d'investissement.
**unity** ['juːnɪtɪ] *n* unité *f*.
**universal** [juːnɪ'vəːsl] *a* universel(le).
**universe** ['juːnɪvəːs] *n* univers *m*.
**university** [juːnɪ'vəːsɪtɪ] *n* université *f*.
**unjust** [ʌn'dʒʌst] *a* injuste.
**unkempt** [ʌn'kɛmpt] *a* mal tenu(e), débraillé(e) ; mal peigné(e).
**unkind** [ʌn'kaɪnd] *a* peu gentil(le), méchant(e).
**unknown** [ʌn'nəun] *a* inconnu(e).
**unladen** [ʌn'leɪdn] *a* (*ship, weight*) à vide.
**unlawful** [ʌn'lɔːful] *a* illégal(e).
**unleash** [ʌn'liːʃ] *vt* détacher ; (*fig*) déchaîner, déclencher.
**unleavened** [ʌn'lɛvnd] *a* sans levain.
**unless** [ʌn'lɛs] *cj*: ~ he leaves à moins qu'il (ne) parte ; ~ we leave à moins de partir, à moins que nous (ne) partions ; ~ otherwise stated sauf indication contraire.
**unlicensed** [ʌn'laɪsənst] *a* non patenté(e) pour la vente des spiritueux.
**unlike** [ʌn'laɪk] *a* dissemblable, différent(e) // *prep* à la différence de, contrairement à.
**unlikely** [ʌn'laɪklɪ] *a* improbable ; invraisemblable.
**unlimited** [ʌn'lɪmɪtɪd] *a* illimité(e).
**unload** [ʌn'ləud] *vt* décharger.
**unlock** [ʌn'lɔk] *vt* ouvrir.
**unlucky** [ʌn'lʌkɪ] *a* malchanceux(euse) ; (*object, number*) qui porte malheur.
**unmannerly** [ʌn'mænəlɪ] *a* mal élevé(e), impoli(e).

unmarried [ʌn'mærɪd] a célibataire.
unmask [ʌn'mɑːsk] vt démasquer.
unmistakable [ʌnmɪs'teɪkəbl] a indubitable ; qu'on ne peut pas ne pas reconnaître.
unmitigated [ʌn'mɪtɪgeɪtɪd] a non mitigé(e), absolu(e), pur(e).
unnatural [ʌn'nætʃrəl] a non naturel(le) ; contre nature.
unnecessary [ʌn'nɛsəsərɪ] a inutile, superflu(e).
unnerve [ʌn'nəːv] vt faire perdre son sang-froid à.
UNO [juːnəu] n see united.
unobtainable [ʌnəb'teɪnəbl] a (TEL) impossible à obtenir.
unoccupied [ʌn'ɔkjupaɪd] a (seat etc) libre.
unofficial [ʌnə'fɪʃl] a non officiel(le) ; (strike) ≈ non sanctionné(e) par la centrale.
unorthodox [ʌn'ɔːθədɔks] a peu orthodoxe.
unpack [ʌn'pæk] vi défaire sa valise, déballer ses affaires.
unpalatable [ʌn'pælətəbl] a (truth) désagréable (à entendre).
unparalleled [ʌn'pærəlɛld] a incomparable, sans égal.
unpleasant [ʌn'plɛznt] a déplaisant(e), désagréable.
unplug [ʌn'plʌg] vt débrancher.
unpopular [ʌn'pɔpjulə*] a impopulaire.
unprecedented [ʌn'prɛsɪdəntɪd] a sans précédent.
unpredictable [ʌnprɪ'dɪktəbl] a imprévisible.
unprepossessing ['ʌnpriːpə'zɛsɪŋ] a peu avenant(e).
unpretentious [ʌnprɪ'tɛnʃəs] a sans prétention(s).
unqualified [ʌn'kwɔlɪfaɪd] a (teacher) non diplômé(e), sans titres, (success) sans réserve, total(e).
unravel [ʌn'rævl] vt démêler.
unreal [ʌn'rɪəl] a irréel(le).
unreasonable [ʌn'riːznəbl] a qui n'est pas raisonnable.
unrelated [ʌnrɪ'leɪtɪd] a sans rapport ; sans lien de parenté.
unrelenting [ʌnrɪ'lɛntɪŋ] a implacable ; acharné(e).
unreliable [ʌnrɪ'laɪəbl] a sur qui (or quoi) on ne peut pas compter, peu fiable.
unrelieved [ʌnrɪ'liːvd] a (monotony) constant(e), uniforme.
unremitting [ʌnrɪ'mɪtɪŋ] a inlassable, infatigable, acharné(e).
unrepeatable [ʌnrɪ'piːtəbl] a (offer) unique, exceptionnel(le).
unrepentant [ʌnrɪ'pɛntənt] a impénitent(e).
unrest [ʌn'rɛst] n agitation f, troubles mpl.
unroll [ʌn'rəul] vt dérouler.
unruly [ʌn'ruːlɪ] a indiscipliné(e).
unsafe [ʌn'seɪf] a dangereux(euse), hasardeux(euse).
unsaid [ʌn'sɛd] a: to leave sth ~ passer qch sous silence.

unsatisfactory ['ʌnsætɪs'fæktərɪ] a qui laisse à désirer.
unsavoury, unsavory (US) [ʌn'seɪvərɪ] a (fig) peu recommandable, répugnant(e).
unscathed [ʌn'skeɪðd] a indemne.
unscrew [ʌn'skruː] vt dévisser.
unscrupulous [ʌn'skruːpjuləs] a sans scrupules, indélicat(e).
unseemly [ʌn'siːmlɪ] a inconvenant(e).
unsettled [ʌn'sɛtld] a perturbé(e) ; instable ; incertain(e).
unshaven [ʌn'ʃeɪvn] a non or mal rasé(e).
unsightly [ʌn'saɪtlɪ] a disgracieux(euse), laid(e).
unskilled [ʌn'skɪld] a: ~ worker n manœuvre m.
unsophisticated [ʌnsə'fɪstɪkeɪtɪd] a simple, naturel(le).
unspeakable [ʌn'spiːkəbl] a indicible ; (bad) innommable.
unsteady [ʌn'stɛdɪ] a mal assuré(e), chancelant(e), instable.
unstuck [ʌn'stʌk] a: to come ~ se décoller ; (fig) faire fiasco.
unsuccessful [ʌnsək'sɛsful] a (attempt) infructueux(euse) ; (writer, proposal) qui n'a pas de succès ; (marriage) malheureux(euse), qui ne réussit pas ; to be ~ (in attempting sth) ne pas réussir ; ne pas avoir de succès ; (application) ne pas être retenu(e) ; ~ly ad en vain.
unsuitable [ʌn'suːtəbl] a qui ne convient pas, peu approprié(e) ; inopportun(e).
unsuspecting [ʌnsə'spɛktɪŋ] a qui ne se méfie pas.
unswerving [ʌn'swəːvɪŋ] a inébranlable.
untangle [ʌn'tæŋgl] vt démêler, débrouiller.
untapped [ʌn'tæpt] a (resources) inexploité(e).
unthinkable [ʌn'θɪŋkəbl] a impensable, inconcevable.
untidy [ʌn'taɪdɪ] a (room) en désordre ; (appearance) désordonné(e), débraillé(e) ; (person) sans ordre, désordonné ; débraillé ; (work) peu soigné(e).
untie [ʌn'taɪ] vt (knot, parcel) défaire ; (prisoner, dog) détacher.
until [ən'tɪl] prep jusqu'à ; (after negative) avant // cj jusqu'à ce que + sub, en attendant que + sub ; (in past, after negative) avant que + sub ; ~ then jusque-là.
untimely [ʌn'taɪmlɪ] a inopportun(e) ; (death) prématuré(e).
untold [ʌn'təuld] a incalculable ; indescriptible.
untoward [ʌntə'wɔːd] a fâcheux (euse), malencontreux(euse).
untranslatable [ʌntrænz'leɪtəbl] a intraduisible.
unused [ʌn'juːzd] a neuf(neuve).
unusual [ʌn'juːʒuəl] a insolite, exceptionnel(le), rare.
unveil [ʌn'veɪl] vt dévoiler.
unwavering [ʌn'weɪvərɪŋ] a inébranlable.
unwell [ʌn'wɛl] a indisposé(e), souffrant(e).
unwieldy [ʌn'wiːldɪ] a difficile à manier.
unwilling [ʌn'wɪlɪŋ] a: to be ~ to do ne pas vouloir faire ; ~ly ad à contrecœur, contre son gré.

**unwind** [ʌn'waɪnd] *vb* (*irg*) *vt* dérouler // *vi* (*relax*) se détendre.

**unwitting** [ʌn'wɪtɪŋ] *a* involontaire.

**unworthy** [ʌn'wə:ðɪ] *a* indigne.

**unwrap** [ʌn'ræp] *vt* défaire ; ouvrir.

**unwritten** [ʌn'rɪtn] *a* (*agreement*) tacite.

**up** [ʌp] *prep*: **to go/be ~ sth** monter/être sur qch // *ad* en haut ; en l'air ; **~ there** là-haut ; **~ above** au-dessus ; **~ to** jusqu'à ; **to be ~** (*out of bed*) être levé(e), être debout *inv* ; **it is ~ to you** c'est à vous de décider, ça ne tient qu'à vous ; **what is he ~ to?** qu'est-ce qu'il peut bien faire? ; **he is not ~ to it** il n'en est pas capable ; **~-and-coming** *a* plein d'avenir *or* de promesses ; **~s and downs** *npl* (*fig*) hauts *mpl* et bas *mpl*.

**upbringing** ['ʌpbrɪŋɪŋ] *n* éducation *f*.

**update** [ʌp'deɪt] *vt* mettre à jour.

**upend** [ʌp'ɛnd] *vt* mettre debout.

**upgrade** [ʌp'greɪd] *vt* promouvoir ; (*job*) revaloriser.

**upheaval** [ʌp'hi:vl] *n* bouleversement *m* ; branle-bas *m* ; crise *f*.

**uphill** [ʌp'hɪl] *a* qui monte ; (*fig: task*) difficile, pénible // *ad*: **to go ~** monter.

**uphold** [ʌp'həuld] *vt irg* maintenir ; soutenir.

**upholstery** [ʌp'həulstərɪ] *n* rembourrage *m* ; (*of car*) garniture *f*.

**upkeep** ['ʌpki:p] *n* entretien *m*.

**upon** [ə'pɔn] *prep* sur.

**upper** ['ʌpə*] *a* supérieur(e) ; du dessus // *n* (*of shoe*) empeigne *f* ; **the ~ class** ≈ la haute bourgeoisie ; **~-class** *a* bourgeois(e) ; **~most** *a* le(la) plus haut(e) ; en dessus.

**upright** ['ʌpraɪt] *a* droit(e) ; vertical(e) ; (*fig*) droit, honnête // *n* montant *m*.

**uprising** ['ʌpraɪzɪŋ] *n* soulèvement *m*, insurrection *f*.

**uproar** ['ʌprɔ:*] *n* tumulte *m*, vacarme *m*.

**uproot** [ʌp'ru:t] *vt* déraciner.

**upset** *n* ['ʌpsɛt] dérangement *m* // *vt* [ʌp'sɛt] (*irg: like set*) (*glass etc*) renverser ; (*plan*) déranger ; (*person: offend*) contrarier ; (: *grieve*) faire de la peine à ; bouleverser // *a* [ʌp'sɛt] contrarié(e) ; peiné(e) ; (*stomach*) détraqué(e), dérangé(e).

**upshot** ['ʌpʃɔt] *n* résultat *m*.

**upside** ['ʌpsaɪd]: **~-down** *ad* à l'envers.

**upstairs** [ʌp'stɛəz] *ad* en haut // *a* (*room*) du dessus, d'en haut // *n*: **there's no ~** il n'y a pas d'étage.

**upstart** ['ʌpstɑ:t] *n* parvenu/e.

**upstream** [ʌp'stri:m] *ad* en amont.

**uptake** ['ʌpteɪk] *n*: **he is quick/slow on the ~** il comprend vite/est lent à comprendre.

**up-to-date** ['ʌptə'deɪt] *a* moderne ; très récent(e).

**upturn** ['ʌptə:n] *n* (*in luck*) retournement *m*.

**upward** ['ʌpwəd] *a* ascendant(e) ; vers le haut ; **~(s)** *ad* vers le haut ; **and ~(s)** et plus, et au-dessus.

**uranium** [juə'reɪnɪəm] *n* uranium *m*.

**urban** ['ə:bən] *a* urbain(e).

**urbane** [ə:'beɪn] *a* urbain(e), courtois(e).

**urchin** ['ə:tʃɪn] *n* gosse *m*, garnement *m* ; **sea ~** *n* oursin *m*.

**urge** [ə:dʒ] *n* besoin *m* ; envie *f* ; forte envie, désir *m* // *vt*: **to ~ sb to do** exhorter qn à faire, pousser qn à faire ; recommander vivement à qn de faire ; **to ~ on** *vt* aiguillonner, talonner.

**urgency** ['ə:dʒənsɪ] *n* urgence *f* ; (*of tone*) insistance *f*.

**urgent** ['ə:dʒənt] *a* urgent(e) ; **~ly** *ad* d'urgence, sans délai.

**urinal** ['juərɪnl] *n* urinoir *m*.

**urinate** ['juərɪneɪt] *vi* uriner.

**urn** [ə:n] *n* urne *f* ; (*also*: **tea ~**) fontaine *f* à thé.

**us** [ʌs] *pronoun* nous.

**US, USA** *n abbr see* **united**.

**usage** ['ju:zɪdʒ] *n* usage *m*.

**use** *n* [ju:s] emploi *m*, utilisation *f* ; usage *m* // *vt* [ju:z] se servir de, utiliser, employer ; **she ~d to do it** elle le faisait (autrefois), elle avait coutume de le faire ; **in ~** en usage ; **out of ~** hors d'usage ; **it's no ~** ça ne sert à rien ; **to have the ~ of** avoir l'usage de ; **to be ~d to** avoir l'habitude de, être habitué(e) à ; **to ~ up** *vt* finir, épuiser ; consommer ; **~d** *a* (*car*) d'occasion ; **~ful** *a* utile ; **~fulness** *n* utilité *f* ; **~less** *a* inutile ; **~r** *n* utilisateur/trice, usager *m*.

**usher** ['ʌʃə*] *n* placeur *m* ; **~ette** [-'rɛt] *n* (*in cinema*) ouvreuse *f*.

**USSR** *n*: **the ~** l'URSS *f*.

**usual** ['ju:ʒuəl] *a* habituel(le) ; **as ~** comme d'habitude ; **~ly** *ad* d'habitude, d'ordinaire.

**usurer** ['ju:ʒərə*] *n* usurier/ère.

**usurp** [ju:'zə:p] *vt* usurper.

**utensil** [ju:'tɛnsl] *n* ustensile *m*.

**uterus** ['ju:tərəs] *n* utérus *m*.

**utilitarian** [ju:tɪlɪ'tɛərɪən] *a* utilitaire.

**utility** [ju:'tɪlɪtɪ] *n* utilité *f* ; (*also*: **public ~**) service public.

**utilization** [ju:tɪlaɪ'zeɪʃn] *n* utilisation *f*.

**utilize** ['ju:tɪlaɪz] *vt* utiliser ; exploiter.

**utmost** ['ʌtməust] *a* extrême, le(la) plus grand(e) // *n*: **to do one's ~** faire tout son possible.

**utter** ['ʌtə*] *a* total(e), complet(ète) // *vt* prononcer, proférer ; émettre ; **~ance** *n* paroles *fpl* ; **~ly** *ad* complètement, totalement.

**U-turn** ['ju:'tə:n] *n* demi-tour *m*.

# V

**v.** *abbr of* **verse, versus, volt** ; (*abbr of* **vide**) voir.

**vacancy** ['veɪkənsɪ] *n* (*job*) poste vacant ; (*room*) chambre *f* disponible ; '**no vacancies**' 'complet'.

**vacant** ['veɪkənt] *a* (*post*) vacant(e) ; (*seat etc*) libre, disponible ; (*expression*) distrait(e).

**vacate** [və'keɪt] *vt* quitter.

**vacation** [və'keɪʃən] *n* vacances *fpl* ; **~ course** *n* cours *mpl* de vacances.

**vaccinate** ['væksɪneɪt] *vt* vacciner ; **vaccination** [-'neɪʃən] *n* vaccination *f*.

**vaccine** ['væksi:n] *n* vaccin *m*.

**vacuum** ['vækjum] *n* vide *m*; ~ **cleaner** *n* aspirateur *m*; ~ **flask** *n* bouteille *f* thermos ®.
**vagary** ['veɪgərɪ] *n* caprice *m*.
**vagina** [və'dʒaɪnə] *n* vagin *m*.
**vagrant** ['veɪgrnt] *n* vagabond/e, mendiant/e.
**vague** [veɪg] *a* vague, imprécis(e); (*blurred: photo, memory*) flou(e); ~**ly** *ad* vaguement.
**vain** [veɪn] *a* (*useless*) vain(e); (*conceited*) vaniteux(euse); **in** ~ en vain.
**valance** ['væləns] *n* (*of bed*) tour *m* de lit.
**valentine** ['væləntaɪn] *n* (*also*: ~ **card**) carte *f* de la Saint-Valentin.
**valeting** ['vælɪtɪŋ] *a*: ~ **service** *n* pressing *m*.
**valiant** ['vælɪənt] *a* vaillant(e), courageux(euse).
**valid** ['vælɪd] *a* valide, valable; (*excuse*) valable; ~**ity** [-'lɪdɪtɪ] *n* validité *f*.
**valise** [və'liːz] *n* sac *m* de voyage.
**valley** ['vælɪ] *n* vallée *f*.
**valuable** ['væljuəbl] *a* (*jewel*) de grande valeur; (*time*) précieux (euse); ~**s** *npl* objets *mpl* de valeur.
**valuation** [vælju'eɪʃən] *n* évaluation *f*, expertise *f*.
**value** ['væljuː] *n* valeur *f* // *vt* (*fix price*) évaluer, expertiser; (*cherish*) tenir à; ~ **added tax (VAT)** *n* taxe *f* à la valeur ajoutée (T.V.A.); ~**d** *a* (*appreciated*) estimé(e); ~**r** *n* expert *m* (en estimations).
**valve** [vælv] *n* (*in machine*) soupape *f*; (*on tyre*) valve *f*; (*in radio*) lampe *f*.
**van** [væn] *n* (AUT) camionnette *f*; (RAIL) fourgon *m*.
**vandal** ['vændl] *n* vandale *m/f*; ~**ism** *n* vandalisme *m*; ~**ize** *vt* saccager.
**vanguard** ['væŋgɑːd] *n* avant-garde *m*.
**vanilla** [və'nɪlə] *n* vanille *f* // *cpd* (*ice cream*) à la vanille.
**vanish** ['vænɪʃ] *vi* disparaître.
**vanity** ['vænɪtɪ] *n* vanité *f*; ~ **case** *n* sac *m* de toilette.
**vantage** ['vɑːntɪdʒ] *n*: ~ **point** bonne position.
**vapour, vapor** (US) ['veɪpə*] *n* vapeur *f*; (*on window*) buée *f*.
**variable** ['vɛərɪəbl] *a* variable; (*mood*) changeant(e).
**variance** ['vɛərɪəns] *n*: **to be at** ~ **(with)** être en désaccord (avec); (*facts*) être en contradiction (avec).
**variant** ['vɛərɪənt] *n* variante *f*.
**variation** [vɛərɪ'eɪʃən] *n* variation *f*; (*in opinion*) changement *m*.
**varicose** ['værɪkəus] *a*: ~ **veins** *npl* varices *fpl*.
**varied** ['vɛərɪd] *a* varié(e), divers(e).
**variety** [və'raɪətɪ] *n* variété *f*; (*quantity*) nombre *m*, quantité *f*; ~ **show** *n* (spectacle *m* de) variétés *fpl*.
**various** ['vɛərɪəs] *a* divers(e), différent(e); (*several*) divers, plusieurs.
**varnish** ['vɑːnɪʃ] *n* vernis *m* // *vt* vernir.
**vary** ['vɛərɪ] *vt*, *vi* varier, changer; ~**ing** *a* variable.
**vase** [vɑːz] *n* vase *m*.
**vast** [vɑːst] *a* vaste, immense; (*amount,*

*success*) énorme; ~**ly** *ad* infiniment, extrêmement; ~**ness** *n* immensité *f*.
**vat** [væt] *n* cuve *f*.
**VAT** [væt] *n abbr see* **value**.
**Vatican** ['vætɪkən] *n*: **the** ~ le Vatican.
**vault** [vɔːlt] *n* (*of roof*) voûte *f*; (*tomb*) caveau *m*; (*in bank*) salle *f* des coffres; chambre forte; (*jump*) saut *m* // *vt* (*also*: ~ **over**) sauter (d'un bond).
**vaunted** ['vɔːntɪd] *a*: **much-**~ tant célébré(e).
**VD** *n abbr see* **venereal**.
**veal** [viːl] *n* veau *m*.
**veer** [vɪə*] *vi* tourner; virer.
**vegetable** ['vɛdʒtəbl] *n* légume *m* // *a* végétal(e); ~ **garden** *n* potager *m*.
**vegetarian** [vɛdʒɪ'tɛərɪən] *a*, *n* végétarien(ne).
**vegetate** ['vɛdʒɪteɪt] *vi* végéter.
**vegetation** [vɛdʒɪ'teɪʃən] *n* végétation *f*.
**vehemence** ['viːɪməns] *n* véhémence *f*, violence *f*.
**vehicle** ['viːɪkl] *n* véhicule *m*.
**vehicular** [vɪ'hɪkjulə*] *a*: '**no** ~ **traffic**' 'interdit à tout véhicule'.
**veil** [veɪl] *n* voile *m* // *vt* voiler.
**vein** [veɪn] *n* veine *f*; (*on leaf*) nervure *f*; (*fig: mood*) esprit *m*.
**velocity** [vɪ'lɒsɪtɪ] *n* vélocité *f*.
**velvet** ['vɛlvɪt] *n* velours *m*.
**vending machine** ['vɛndɪŋməʃiːn] *n* distributeur *m* automatique.
**vendor** ['vɛndə*] *n* vendeur/euse.
**veneer** [və'nɪə*] *n* placage *m* de bois; (*fig*) vernis *m*.
**venerable** ['vɛnərəbl] *a* vénérable.
**venereal** [vɪ'nɪərɪəl] *a*: ~ **disease** (VD) *n* maladie vénérienne.
**Venetian** [vɪ'niːʃən] *a*: ~ **blind** *n* store vénitien.
**Venezuela** [vɛnɛ'zweɪlə] *n* Venezuela *m*; ~**n** *a* vénézuélien(ne) // *n* Vénézuélien/ne.
**vengeance** ['vɛndʒəns] *n* vengeance *f*; **with a** ~ (*fig*) vraiment, pour de bon.
**venison** ['vɛnɪsn] *n* venaison *f*.
**venom** ['vɛnəm] *n* venin *m*; ~**ous** *a* venimeux(euse).
**vent** [vɛnt] *n* orifice *m*, conduit *m*; (*in dress, jacket*) fente *f* // *vt* (*fig: one's feelings*) donner libre cours à.
**ventilate** ['vɛntɪleɪt] *vt* (*room*) ventiler, aérer; **ventilation** [-'leɪʃən] *n* ventilation *f*, aération *f*; **ventilator** *n* ventilateur *m*.
**ventriloquist** [vɛn'trɪləkwɪst] *n* ventriloque *m/f*.
**venture** ['vɛntʃə*] *n* entreprise *f* // *vt* risquer, hasarder // *vi* s'aventurer, se risquer.
**venue** ['vɛnjuː] *n* lieu *m* de rendez-vous *or* rencontre; (SPORT) lieu de la rencontre.
**veranda(h)** [və'rændə] *n* véranda *f*.
**verb** [vəːb] *n* verbe *m*; ~**al** *a* verbal(e); (*translation*) littéral(e).
**verbatim** [vəː'beɪtɪm] *a*, *ad* mot pour mot.
**verbose** [vəː'bəus] *a* verbeux(euse).
**verdict** ['vəːdɪkt] *n* verdict *m*.
**verge** [vəːdʒ] *n* bord *m*; '**soft** ~**s**' 'accotements non stabilisés'; **on the** ~ **of doing** sur le point de faire; **to** ~ **on** *vt fus* approcher de.

**verger** ['və:dʒə*] n (REL) bedeau m.
**verification** [vɛrɪfɪ'keɪʃən] n vérification
f.
**verify** ['vɛrɪfaɪ] vt vérifier.
**vermin** ['və:mɪn] npl animaux mpl
nuisibles; (insects) vermine f.
**vermouth** ['və:məθ] n vermouth m.
**vernacular** [və'nækjulə*] n langue f
vernaculaire, dialecte m.
**versatile** ['və:sətaɪl] a (person) aux talents
variés; (machine, tool etc) aux usages
variés; aux applications variées.
**verse** [və:s] n vers mpl; (stanza) strophe
f; (in bible) verset m.
**versed** [və:st] a: (well-)~ in versé(e)
dans.
**version** ['və:ʃən] n version f.
**versus** ['və:səs] prep contre.
**vertebra**, pl ~e ['və:tɪbrə, -bri:] n
vertèbre f.
**vertebrate** ['və:tɪbrɪt] n vertébré m.
**vertical** ['və:tɪkl] a vertical(e) // n
verticale f; ~ly ad verticalement.
**vertigo** ['və:tɪgəu] n vertige m.
**verve** [və:v] n brio m; enthousiasme m.
**very** ['vɛrɪ] ad très // a: the ~ book
which le livre même que; at the ~ end
tout à la fin; the ~ last le tout dernier;
at the ~ least au moins; ~ much
beaucoup.
**vespers** ['vɛspəz] npl vêpres fpl.
**vessel** ['vɛsl] n (ANAT, NAUT) vaisseau m;
(container) récipient m.
**vest** [vɛst] n tricot m de corps; (US:
waistcoat) gilet m // vt: to ~ sb with sth,
to ~ sth in sb investir qn de qch; ~ed
**interests** npl (COMM) droits acquis.
**vestibule** ['vɛstɪbjuːl] n vestibule m.
**vestige** ['vɛstɪdʒ] n vestige m.
**vestry** ['vɛstrɪ] n sacristie f.
**vet** [vɛt] n (abbr of veterinary surgeon)
vétérinaire m/f // vt examiner
minutieusement; (text) revoir.
**veteran** ['vɛtərn] n vétéran m; (also: war
~) ancien combattant; ~ car n voiture
f d'époque.
**veterinary** ['vɛtrɪnərɪ] a vétérinaire; ~
**surgeon** n vétérinaire m/f.
**veto** ['viːtəu] n, pl ~es veto m // vt
opposer son veto à.
**vex** [vɛks] vt fâcher, contrarier; ~ed a
(question) controversé(e).
**VHF** abbr of very high frequency.
**via** ['vaɪə] prep par, via.
**viable** ['vaɪəbl] a viable.
**viaduct** ['vaɪədʌkt] n viaduc m.
**vibrate** [vaɪ'breɪt] vi: to ~ (with) vibrer
(de); (resound) retentir (de); **vibration**
[-'breɪʃən] n vibration f.
**vicar** ['vɪkə*] n pasteur m (de l'Église
anglicane); ~age n presbytère m.
**vice** [vaɪs] n (evil) vice m; (TECH) étau m.
**vice-** [vaɪs] prefix vice-; ~chairman n
vice-président/e.
**vice squad** ['vaɪsskwɔd] n ≈ brigade
mondaine.
**vice versa** ['vaɪsɪ'və:sə] ad vice versa.
**vicinity** [vɪ'sɪnɪtɪ] n environs mpl,
alentours mpl.

**vicious** ['vɪʃəs] a (remark) cruel(le),
méchant(e); (blow) brutal(e); ~ness n
méchanceté f, cruauté f; brutalité f.
**vicissitudes** [vɪ'sɪsɪtjuːdz] npl
vicissitudes fpl.
**victim** ['vɪktɪm] n victime f; ~ization
[-'zeɪʃən] n brimades fpl; représailles fpl;
~ize vt brimer; exercer des représailles
sur.
**victor** ['vɪktə*] n vainqueur m.
**Victorian** [vɪk'tɔ:rɪən] a victorien(ne).
**victorious** [vɪk'tɔ:rɪəs] a victorieux(euse).
**victory** ['vɪktərɪ] n victoire f.
**video** ['vɪdɪəu] cpd vidéo inv; ~ (-tape)
recorder n magnétoscope m.
**vie** [vaɪ] vi: to ~ with lutter avec, rivaliser
avec.
**Vienna** [vɪ'ɛnə] n Vienne.
**view** [vjuː] n vue f; (opinion) avis m, vue
// vt (situation) considérer; (house)
visiter; on ~ (in museum etc) exposé(e);
in my ~ à mon avis; in ~ of the fact
that étant donné que; to have in ~ avoir
en vue; ~er n (viewfinder) viseur m;
(small projector) visionneuse f; (TV)
téléspectateur/trice; ~finder n viseur m;
~point n point m de vue.
**vigil** ['vɪdʒɪl] n veille f; ~ance n vigilance
f; ~ance committee n comité m
d'autodéfense; ~ant a vigilant(e).
**vigorous** ['vɪgərəs] a vigoureux(euse).
**vigour, vigor** (US) ['vɪgə*] n vigueur f.
**vile** [vaɪl] a (action) vil(e); (smell)
abominable; (temper) massacrant(e).
**vilify** ['vɪlɪfaɪ] vt calomnier.
**villa** ['vɪlə] n villa f.
**village** ['vɪlɪdʒ] n village m; ~r n
villageois/e.
**villain** ['vɪlən] n (scoundrel) scélérat m;
(criminal) bandit m; (in novel etc) traître
m.
**vindicate** ['vɪndɪkeɪt] vt défendre avec
succès; justifier.
**vindictive** [vɪn'dɪktɪv] a vindicatif(ive),
rancunier(ère).
**vine** [vaɪn] n vigne f; (climbing plant)
plante grimpante; ~ grower n viticulteur
m.
**vinegar** ['vɪnɪgə*] n vinaigre m.
**vineyard** ['vɪnjɑːd] n vignoble m.
**vintage** ['vɪntɪdʒ] n (year) année f,
millésime m; ~ wine n vin m de grand
cru.
**vinyl** ['vaɪnl] n vinyle m.
**viola** [vɪ'əulə] n alto m.
**violate** ['vaɪəleɪt] vt violer; **violation**
[-'leɪʃən] n violation f.
**violence** ['vaɪələns] n violence f; (POL etc)
incidents violents.
**violent** ['vaɪələnt] a violent(e); ~ly ad
violemment; extrêmement.
**violet** ['vaɪələt] a (colour) violet(te) // n
(plant) violette f.
**violin** [vaɪə'lɪn] n violon m; ~ist n
violoniste m/f.
**VIP** n (abbr of very important person) V.I.P.
m.
**viper** ['vaɪpə*] n vipère f.
**virgin** ['və:dʒɪn] n vierge f // a vierge; she
is a ~ elle est vierge; the Blessed V~

la Sainte Vierge; ~ity [-'dʒɪnɪtɪ] n virginité f.

**Virgo** ['vɜːgəʊ] n la Vierge; **to be** ~ être de la Vierge.

**virile** ['vɪraɪl] a viril(e).

**virility** [vɪ'rɪlɪtɪ] n virilité f.

**virtually** ['vɜːtjʊəlɪ] ad (almost) pratiquement.

**virtue** ['vɜːtjuː] n vertu f; (advantage) mérite m, avantage m; **by** ~ **of** par le fait de.

**virtuoso** [vɜːtju'əʊzəʊ] n virtuose m/f.

**virtuous** ['vɜːtjuəs] a vertueux(euse).

**virulent** ['vɪrʊlənt] a virulent(e).

**virus** ['vaɪərəs] n virus m.

**visa** ['viːzə] n visa m.

**vis-à-vis** [viːzə'viː] prep vis-à-vis de.

**viscount** ['vaɪkaʊnt] n vicomte m.

**visibility** [vɪzɪ'bɪlɪtɪ] n visibilité f.

**visible** ['vɪzəbl] a visible; **visibly** ad visiblement.

**vision** ['vɪʒən] n (sight) vue f, vision f; (foresight, in dream) vision; ~**ary** n visionnaire m/f.

**visit** ['vɪzɪt] n visite f; (stay) séjour m // vt (person) rendre visite à; (place) visiter; ~**ing card** n carte f de visite; ~**ing professor** n ≈ professeur associé; ~**or** n visiteur/euse; (in hotel) client/e; ~**ors' book** n livre m d'or; (in hotel) registre m.

**visor** ['vaɪzə*] n visière f.

**vista** ['vɪstə] n vue f, perspective f.

**visual** ['vɪzjʊəl] a visuel(le); (nerve) optique; ~ **aid** n support visuel (pour l'enseignement).

**visualize** ['vɪzjʊəlaɪz] vt se représenter; (foresee) prévoir.

**vital** ['vaɪtl] a vital(e); ~**ity** [-'tælɪtɪ] n vitalité f; ~**ly** ad extrêmement; ~ **statistics** npl (fig) mensurations fpl.

**vitamin** ['vɪtəmɪn] n vitamine f.

**vitiate** ['vɪʃɪeɪt] vt vicier.

**vivacious** [vɪ'veɪʃəs] a animé(e), qui a de la vivacité.

**vivacity** [vɪ'væsɪtɪ] n vivacité f.

**vivid** ['vɪvɪd] a (account) frappant(e); (light, imagination) vif(vive); ~**ly** ad (describe) d'une manière vivante; (remember) de façon précise.

**vivisection** [vɪvɪ'sɛkʃən] n vivisection f.

**V-neck** ['viːnɛk] n décolleté m en V.

**vocabulary** [vəʊ'kæbjʊlərɪ] n vocabulaire m.

**vocal** ['vəʊkl] a (MUS) vocal(e); (communication) verbal(e); (noisy) bruyant(e); ~ **chords** npl cordes vocales; ~**ist** n chanteur/euse.

**vocation** [vəʊ'keɪʃən] n vocation f; ~**al** a professionnel(le).

**vociferous** [və'sɪfərəs] a bruyant(e).

**vodka** ['vɒdkə] n vodka f.

**vogue** [vəʊg] n mode f; (popularity) vogue f.

**voice** [vɔɪs] n voix f; (opinion) avis m // vt (opinion) exprimer, formuler.

**void** [vɔɪd] n vide m // a: ~ **of** vide de, dépourvu(e) de.

**voile** [vɔɪl] n voile m (tissu).

**volatile** ['vɒlətaɪl] a volatil(e); (fig) versatile.

**volcanic** [vɒl'kænɪk] a volcanique.

**volcano**, ~**es** [vɒl'keɪnəʊ] n volcan m.

**volition** [və'lɪʃən] n: **of one's own** ~ de son propre gré.

**volley** ['vɒlɪ] n (of gunfire) salve f; (of stones etc) pluie f, volée f; (TENNIS etc) volée f; ~**ball** n volley(-ball) m.

**volt** [vəʊlt] n volt m; ~**age** n tension f, voltage m.

**voluble** ['vɒljʊbl] a volubile.

**volume** ['vɒljuːm] n volume m; ~ **control** n (RADIO, TV) bouton m de réglage du volume.

**voluntarily** ['vɒləntrɪlɪ] ad volontairement; bénévolement.

**voluntary** ['vɒləntərɪ] a volontaire; (unpaid) bénévole.

**volunteer** [vɒlən'tɪə*] n volontaire m/f // vi (MIL) s'engager comme volontaire; **to** ~ **to do** se proposer pour faire.

**voluptuous** [və'lʌptjuəs] a voluptueux(euse).

**vomit** ['vɒmɪt] n vomissure f // vt, vi vomir.

**vote** [vəʊt] n vote m, suffrage m; (cast) voix f, vote; (franchise) droit m de vote // vt (bill) voter; (chairman) élire // vi voter; ~ **of censure** n motion f de censure; ~ **of thanks** n discours m de remerciement; ~**r** n électeur/trice; **voting** n scrutin m.

**vouch** [vaʊtʃ]: **to** ~ **for** vt se porter garant de.

**voucher** ['vaʊtʃə*] n (for meal, petrol) bon m; (receipt) reçu m.

**vow** [vaʊ] n vœu m, serment m // vi jurer.

**vowel** ['vauəl] n voyelle f.

**voyage** ['vɔɪdʒ] n voyage m par mer, traversée f.

**vulgar** ['vʌlgə*] a vulgaire; ~**ity** [-'gærɪtɪ] n vulgarité f.

**vulnerability** [vʌlnərə'bɪlɪtɪ] n vulnérabilité f.

**vulnerable** ['vʌlnərəbl] a vulnérable.

**vulture** ['vʌltʃə*] n vautour m.

# W

**wad** [wɒd] n (of cotton wool, paper) tampon m; (of banknotes etc) liasse f.

**wade** [weɪd] vi: **to** ~ **through** marcher dans, patauger dans // vt passer à gué.

**wafer** ['weɪfə*] n (CULIN) gaufrette f; (REL) pain m d'hostie f.

**waffle** ['wɒfl] n (CULIN) gaufre f; (col) rabâchage m; remplissage m // vi parler pour ne rien dire; faire du remplissage.

**waft** [wɒft] vt porter // vi flotter.

**wag** [wæg] vt agiter, remuer // vi remuer.

**wage** [weɪdʒ] n salaire m, paye f // vt: **to** ~ **war** faire la guerre; ~**s** npl salaire, paye; ~ **claim** n demande f d'augmentation de salaire; ~ **earner** n salarié/e; (breadwinner) soutien m de famille; ~ **freeze** n blocage m des salaires.

**wager** ['weɪdʒə*] n pari m.

**waggle** ['wægl] vt, vi remuer.

**wag(g)on** ['wægən] n (horse-drawn) chariot m; (truck) camion m; (RAIL) wagon m (de marchandises).

**wail** [weɪl] n gémissement m; (of siren) hurlement m // vi gémir; hurler.

**waist** [weɪst] n taille f, ceinture f; ~**coat** n gilet m; ~**line** n (tour m de) taille f.
**wait** [weɪt] n attente f // vi attendre; **to lie in ~ for** guetter; **I can't ~ to** (fig) jè meurs d'envie de; **to ~ behind** vi rester (à attendre); **to ~ for** attendre; **to ~ on** vt fus servir; ~**er** n garçon m (de café), serveur m; **'no ~ing'** (AUT) 'stationnement interdit'; ~**ing list** n liste f d'attente; ~**ing room** n salle f d'attente; ~**ress** n serveuse f.
**waive** [weɪv] vt renoncer à, abandonner.
**wake** [weɪk] vb (pt **woke**, ~**d**, pp **woken**, ~**d** [wəuk, 'wəukn]) vt (also: ~ **up**) réveiller // vi (also: ~ **up**) se réveiller // n (for dead person) veillée f mortuaire; (NAUT) sillage m; ~**n** vt, vi = **wake**.
**Wales** [weɪlz] n pays m de Galles.
**walk** [wɔːk] n promenade f; (short) petit tour; (gait) démarche f; (pace): **at a quick** ~ d'un pas rapide; (path) chemin m; (in park etc) allée f // vi marcher; (for pleasure, exercise) se promener // vt (distance) faire à pied; (dog) promener; **10 minutes' ~ from** à 10 minutes de marche de; **from all ~s of life** de toutes conditions sociales; ~**er** n (person) marcheur/euse; ~**ie-talkie** [wɔːkɪˈtɔːkɪ] n talkie-walkie m; ~**ing** n marche f à pied; ~**ing holiday** n vacances passées à faire de la randonnée; ~**ing shoes** npl chaussures fpl de marche; ~**ing stick** n canne f; ~**out** n (of workers) grève-surprise f; ~**over** n (col) victoire f or examen m etc facile; ~**way** n promenade f.
**wall** [wɔːl] n mur m; (of tunnel, cave) paroi m; ~ **cupboard** n placard mural; ~**ed** a (city) fortifié(e).
**wallet** [ˈwɔlɪt] n portefeuille m.
**wallflower** [ˈwɔːlflauə*] n giroflée f; **to be a ~** (fig) faire tapisserie.
**wallop** [ˈwɔləp] vt (col) taper sur, cogner.
**wallow** [ˈwɔləu] vi se vautrer.
**wallpaper** [ˈwɔːlpeɪpə*] n papier peint.
**walnut** [ˈwɔːlnʌt] n noix f; (tree) noyer m.
**walrus**, pl ~ or ~**es** [ˈwɔːlrəs] n morse m.
**waltz** [wɔːlts] n valse f // vi valser.
**wan** [wɔn] a pâle; triste.
**wand** [wɔnd] n (also: **magic** ~) baguette f (magique).
**wander** [ˈwɔndə*] vi (person) errer, aller sans but; (thoughts) vagabonder; (river) serpenter; ~**er** n vagabond/e.
**wane** [weɪn] vi (moon) décroître; (reputation) décliner.
**wangle** [ˈwæŋgl] vt (col) se débrouiller pour avoir; carotter.
**want** [wɔnt] vt vouloir; (need) avoir besoin de; (lack) manquer de // n: **for ~ of** par manque de, faute de; ~**s** npl (needs) besoins mpl; **to ~ to do** vouloir faire; **to ~ sb to do** vouloir que qn fasse; **to be found ~ing** ne pas être à la hauteur.
**wanton** [ˈwɔntn] a capricieux(euse); dévergondé(e).
**war** [wɔː*] n guerre f; **to go to ~** se mettre en guerre.
**ward** [wɔːd] n (in hospital) salle f; (POL) section électorale; (LAW: child) pupille m/f; **to ~ off** vt parer, éviter.

**warden** [ˈwɔːdn] n (of institution) directeur/trice; (of park, game reserve) gardien/ne; (also: **traffic** ~) contractuel/le.
**warder** [ˈwɔːdə*] n gardien m de prison.
**wardrobe** [ˈwɔːdrəub] n (cupboard) armoire f; (clothes) garde-robe f; (THEATRE) costumes mpl.
**warehouse** [ˈwɛəhaus] n entrepôt m.
**wares** [wɛəz] npl marchandises fpl.
**warfare** [ˈwɔːfɛə*] n guerre f.
**warhead** [ˈwɔːhɛd] n (MIL) ogive f.
**warily** [ˈwɛərɪlɪ] ad avec prudence, avec précaution.
**warlike** [ˈwɔːlaɪk] a guerrier(ère).
**warm** [wɔːm] a chaud(e); (thanks, welcome, applause) chaleureux(euse); **it's** ~ il fait chaud; **I'm** ~ j'ai chaud; **to ~ up** vi (person, room) se réchauffer; (water) chauffer; (athlete, discussion) s'échauffer // vt réchauffer; chauffer; (engine) faire chauffer; ~**-hearted** a affectueux(euse); ~**ly** ad chaudement; vivement; chaleureusement; ~**th** n chaleur f.
**warn** [wɔːn] vt avertir, prévenir; ~**ing** n avertissement m; (notice) avis m; ~**ing light** n avertisseur lumineux.
**warp** [wɔːp] vi travailler, se voiler // vt voiler; (fig) pervertir.
**warrant** [ˈwɔrnt] n (guarantee) garantie f; (LAW: to arrest) mandat m d'arrêt; (: to search) mandat de perquisition.
**warranty** [ˈwɔrəntɪ] n garantie f.
**warrior** [ˈwɔrɪə*] n guerrier/ère.
**warship** [ˈwɔːʃɪp] n navire m de guerre.
**wart** [wɔːt] n verrue f.
**wartime** [ˈwɔːtaɪm] n: **in** ~ en temps de guerre.
**wary** [ˈwɛərɪ] a prudent(e).
**was** [wɔz] pt of **be**.
**wash** [wɔʃ] vt laver // vi se laver // n (paint) badigeon m; (washing programme) lavage m; (of ship) sillage m; **to give sth a** ~ laver qch; **to have a** ~ se laver, faire sa toilette; **to ~ away** vt (stain) enlever au lavage; (subj: river etc) emporter; **to ~ down** vt laver; laver à grande eau; **to ~ off** vi partir au lavage; **to ~ up** vi faire la vaisselle; ~**able** a lavable; ~**basin** n lavabo m; ~**er** n (TECH) rondelle f, joint m; ~**ing** n (linen etc) lessive f; ~**ing machine** n machine f à laver; ~**ing powder** n lessive f (en poudre); ~**ing-up** n vaisselle f; ~**-out** n (col) désastre m; ~**room** n toilettes fpl.
**wasn't** [ˈwɔznt] = **was not**.
**wasp** [wɔsp] n guêpe f.
**wastage** [ˈweɪstɪdʒ] n gaspillage m; (in manufacturing, transport etc) déchet m.
**waste** [weɪst] n gaspillage m; (of time) perte f; (rubbish) déchets mpl; (also: **household** ~) ordures fpl // a (material) de rebut; (heat) perdu(e); (food) inutilisé(e); (land) inculte // vt gaspiller; (time, opportunity) perdre; ~**s** npl étendue f désertique; **to ~ away** vi dépérir; ~**bin** n corbeille f à papier; (in kitchen) boîte f à ordures; ~ **disposal unit** n broyeur m d'ordures; ~**ful** a gaspilleur(euse); (process) peu économique; ~ **ground** n terrain m vague; ~**paper basket** n corbeille f à papier.

**watch** [wɔtʃ] *n* montre *f*; (*act of watching*) surveillance *f*; guet *m*; (*guard*: MIL) sentinelle *f*; (: NAUT) homme *m* de quart; (NAUT: *spell of duty*) quart *m* // *vt* (*look at*) observer; (: *match, programme*) regarder; (*spy on, guard*) surveiller; (*be careful of*) faire attention à // *vi* regarder; (*keep guard*) monter la garde; **to ~ out** *vi* faire attention; **~dog** *n* chien *m* de garde; **~ful** *a* attentif(ive), vigilant(e); **~maker** *n* horloger/ère; **~man** *n* gardien *m*; (*also*: **night ~man**) veilleur *m* de nuit; **~ strap** *n* bracelet *m* de montre.

**water** ['wɔːtə*] *n* eau *f* // *vt* (*plant*) arroser; **in British ~s** dans les eaux territoriales Britanniques; **to ~ down** *vt* (*milk*) couper d'eau; (*fig: story*) édulcorer; **~ closet** *n* w.-c. *mpl*, waters *mpl*; **~colour** *n* aquarelle *f*; **~colours** *npl* couleurs *fpl* pour aquarelle; **~cress** *n* cresson *m* (de fontaine); **~fall** *n* chute *f* d'eau; **~ hole** *n* mare *f*; **~ ice** *n* sorbet *m*; **~ing can** *n* arrosoir *m*; **~ level** *n* niveau *m* de l'eau; (*of flood*) niveau *m* des eaux; **~ lily** *n* nénuphar *m*; **~logged** *a* détrempé(e); imbibé(e) d'eau; **~line** *n* (NAUT) ligne *f* de flottaison; **~ main** *n* canalisation *f* d'eau; **~mark** *n* (*on paper*) filigrane *m*; **~melon** *n* pastèque *f*; **~polo** *n* water-polo *m*; **~proof** *a* imperméable; **~shed** *n* (GEO) ligne *f* de partage des eaux; (*fig*) moment *m* critique, point décisif; **~-skiing** *n* ski *m* nautique; **~ softener** *n* adoucisseur *m* d'eau; **~ tank** *n* réservoir *m* d'eau; **~tight** *a* étanche; **~works** *npl* station *f* hydraulique; **~y** *a* (*colour*) délavé(e); (*coffee*) trop faible.

**watt** [wɔt] *n* watt *m*.

**wave** [weɪv] *n* vague *f*; (*of hand*) geste *m*, signe *m*; (RADIO) onde *f*; (*in hair*) ondulation *f* // *vi* faire signe de la main; (*flag*) flotter au vent // *vt* (*handkerchief*) agiter; (*stick*) brandir; (*hair*) onduler; **~length** *n* longueur *f* d'ondes.

**waver** ['weɪvə*] *vi* vaciller; (*voice*) trembler; (*person*) hésiter.

**wavy** ['weɪvɪ] *a* ondulé(e); onduleux(euse).

**wax** [wæks] *n* cire *f*; (*for skis*) fart *m* // *vt* cirer; (*car*) lustrer // *vi* (*moon*) croître; **~en** *a* cireux(euse); **~works** *npl* personnages *mpl* de cire; musée *m* de cire.

**way** [weɪ] *n* chemin *m*, voie *f*; (*path, access*) passage *m*; (*distance*) distance *f*; (*direction*) chemin, direction *f*; (*manner*) façon *f*, manière *f*; (*habit*) habitude *f*, façon; (*condition*) état *m*; **which ~?** — **this ~** par où *or* de quel côté? — par ici; **to be on one's ~** être en route; **to be in the ~** bloquer le passage; (*fig*) gêner; **to go out of one's ~ to do** (*fig*) se donner du mal pour faire; **in a ~** d'un côté; **in some ~s** à certains égards; d'un côté; **in the ~ of** en fait de, comme; **'~ in'** 'entrée'; **'~ out'** 'sortie'; **the ~ back** le chemin du retour; **this ~ and that** par-ci par-là; **'give ~'** (AUT) 'cédez la priorité'.

**waylay** ['weɪ'leɪ] *vt irg* attaquer; (*fig*) **I got waylaid** quelqu'un m'a accroché.

**wayward** ['weɪwəd] *a* capricieux(euse), entêté(e).

**W.C.** ['dʌblju'siː] *n* w.-c. *mpl*, waters *mpl*.

**we** [wiː] *pl pronoun* nous.

**weak** [wiːk] *a* faible; (*health*) fragile; (*beam etc*) peu solide; **~en** *vi* faiblir // *vt* affaiblir; **~ling** *n* gringalet *m*; faible *m/f*; **~ness** *n* faiblesse *f*; (*fault*) point *m* faible.

**wealth** [wɛlθ] *n* (*money, resources*) richesse(s) *f(pl)*; (*of details*) profusion *f*; **~y** *a* riche.

**wean** [wiːn] *vt* sevrer.

**weapon** ['wɛpən] *n* arme *f*.

**wear** [wɛə*] *n* (*use*) usage *m*; (*deterioration through use*) usure *f*; (*clothing*): **sports/baby~** vêtements *mpl* de sport/pour bébés // *vb* (*pt* **wore**, *pp* **worn** [wɔː*, wɔːn]) *vt* (*clothes*) porter; mettre; (*beard etc*) avoir; (*damage: through use*) user // *vi* (*last*) faire de l'usage; (*rub etc through*) s'user; **town/evening ~** *n* tenue *f* de ville/de soirée; **~ and tear** *n* usure *f*; **to ~ away** *vt* user, ronger // *vi* s'user, être rongé(e); **to ~ down** *vt* user; (*strength*) épuiser; **to ~ off** *vi* disparaître; **to ~ on** *vi* se poursuivre; passer; **to ~ out** *vt* user; (*person, strength*) épuiser.

**wearily** ['wɪərɪlɪ] *ad* avec lassitude.

**weariness** ['wɪərɪnɪs] *n* épuisement *m*, lassitude *f*.

**weary** ['wɪərɪ] *a* (*tired*) épuisé(e); (*dispirited*) las(lasse); abattu(c) // *vt* lasser // *vi*: **to ~ of** se lasser de.

**weasel** ['wiːzl] *n* (ZOOL) belette *f*.

**weather** ['wɛðə*] *n* temps *m* // *vt* (*wood*) faire mûrir; (*tempest, crisis*) essuyer, être pris(e) dans; survivre à, tenir le coup durant; **~-beaten** *a* (*person*) hâlé(e); (*building*) dégradé(e) par les intempéries; **~ cock** *n* girouette *f*; **~ forecast** *n* prévisions *fpl* météorologiques, météo *f*; **~ vane** *n* = **~ cock**.

**weave**, *pt* **wove**, *pp* **woven** [wiːv, wəuv, 'wəuvn] *vt* (*cloth*) tisser; (*basket*) tresser; **~r** *n* tisserand/e; **weaving** *n* tissage *m*.

**web** [wɛb] *n* (*of spider*) toile *f*; (*on foot*) palmure *f*; (*fabric, also fig*) tissu *m*; **~bed** *a* (*foot*) palmé(e); **~bing** *n* (*on chair*) sangles *fpl*.

**wed** [wɛd] *vt* (*pt, pp* **wedded**) épouser // *n*: **the newly-~s** les jeunes mariés.

**we'd** [wiːd] = **we had**, **we would**.

**wedded** ['wɛdɪd] *pt, pp* of **wed**.

**wedding** ['wɛdɪŋ] *n* mariage *m*; **silver/golden ~** *n* noces *fpl* d'argent/d'or; **~ day** *n* jour *m* du mariage; **~ dress** *n* robe *f* de mariage; **~ present** *n* cadeau *m* de mariage; **~ ring** *n* alliance *f*.

**wedge** [wɛdʒ] *n* (*of wood etc*) coin *m*; (*under door etc*) cale *f*; (*of cake*) part *f* // *vt* (*fix*) caler; (*push*) enfoncer, coincer; **~-heeled shoes** *npl* chaussures *fpl* à semelles compensées.

**wedlock** ['wɛdlɔk] *n* (union *f* du) mariage *m*.

**Wednesday** ['wɛdnzdɪ] *n* mercredi *m*.

**wee** [wiː] *a* (*Scottish*) petit(e); tout(e) petit(e).

**weed** [wiːd] *n* mauvaise herbe // *vt* désherber; **~-killer** *n* désherbant *m*.

**week** [wiːk] *n* semaine *f*; **~day** *n* jour *m* de semaine; (COMM) jour ouvrable; **~end** *n* week-end *m*; **~ly** *ad* une fois par

semaine, chaque semaine // *a,n*
hebdomadaire (*m*).

**weep**, *pt, pp* **wept** [wi:p, wɛpt] *vi* (*person*)
pleurer ; ~**ing willow** *n* saule pleureur.

**weigh** [weɪ] *vt,vi* peser ; **to** ~ **anchor**
lever l'ancre ; **to** ~ **down** *vt* (*branch*) faire
plier ; (*fig: with worry*) accabler ; **to** ~ **up**
*vt* examiner ; ~**bridge** *n* pont-bascule *m*.

**weight** [weɪt] *n* poids *m*; **sold by** ~
vendu(e) au poids ; ~**lessness** *n*
apesanteur *f*; ~ **lifter** *n* haltérophile *m*;
~**y** *a* lourd(e).

**weir** [wɪə*] *n* barrage *m*.

**weird** [wɪəd] *a* bizarre ; (*eerie*)
surnaturel(le).

**welcome** ['wɛlkəm] *a* bienvenu(e) // *n*
accueil *m* // *vt* accueillir ; (*also:* **bid** ~)
souhaiter la bienvenue à ; (*be glad of*) se
réjouir de ; **to be** ~ être le(la)
bienvenu(e) ; **welcoming** *a* accueillant(e) ;
(*speech*) d'accueil.

**weld** [wɛld] *n* soudure *f* // *vt* souder ; ~**er**
*n* (*person*) soudeur *m*; ~**ing** *n* soudure *f*
(autogène).

**welfare** ['wɛlfɛə*] *n* bien-être *m*; ~ **state**
*n* État-providence *m*; ~ **work** *n* travail
social.

**well** [wɛl] *n* puits *m* // *ad* bien // *a:* **to**
**be** ~ aller bien // *excl* eh bien! ; bon! ;
enfin! ; ~ **done!** bravo! ; **get** ~ **soon!**
remets-toi vite! ; **to do** ~ **in** sth bien
réussir en *or* dans qch.

**we'll** [wi:l] = **we will, we shall**.

**well:** ~-**behaved** *a* sage, obéissant(e) ;
~-**being** *n* bien-être *m*; ~-**built** *a*
(*building*) bien construit(e) ; (*person*) bien
bâti(e) ; ~-**developed** *a* (*girl*) bien fait(e) ;
~-**earned** *a* (*rest*) bien mérité(e) ; ~-
**groomed** *a* très soigné(e) de sa personne ;
~-**heeled** *a* (*col: wealthy*) fortuné(e), riche.

**wellingtons** ['wɛlɪŋtənz] *npl* (*also:*
**wellington boots**) bottes *fpl* de
caoutchouc.

**well:** ~-**known** *a* (*person*) bien
connu(e) ; ~-**meaning** *a* bien intention-
né(e) ; ~-**off** *a* aisé(e), assez riche ; ~-
**read** *a* cultivé(e) ; ~-**to-do** *a* aisé(e), assez
riche ; ~-**wisher** *n:* scores of ~-**wishers**
**had gathered** de nombreux amis et
admirateurs s'étaient rassemblés ; **letters**
**from** ~-**wishers** des lettres d'encouragement.

**Welsh** [wɛlʃ] *a* gallois(e) // *n* (*LING*) gallois
*m*; ~**man/woman** *n* Gallois/e ; ~
**rarebit** *n* croûte *f* au fromage.

**went** [wɛnt] *pt of* **go.**

**wept** [wɛpt] *pt, pp of* **weep.**

**were** [wə:*] *pt of* **be.**

**we're** [wɪə*] = **we are.**

**weren't** [wə:nt] = **were not.**

**west** [wɛst] *n* ouest *m* // *a* ouest *inv*, de
*or* à l'ouest // *ad* à *or* vers l'ouest ; **the**
**W**~ *n* l'Occident *m*, l'Ouest ; **the W**~
**Country** *n* le sud-ouest de l'Angleterre ;
~**erly** *a* (*situation*) à l'ouest ; (*wind*)
d'ouest ; ~**ern** *a* occidental(e), de *or* à
l'ouest // *n* (*CINEMA*) western *m*; **W**~
**Germany** *n* Allemagne *f* de l'Ouest ; **W**~
**Indies** *npl* Antilles *fpl* ; ~**ward(s)** *ad* vers
l'ouest.

**wet** [wɛt] *a* mouillé(e) ; (*damp*) humide ;
(*soaked*) trempé(e) ; (*rainy*) pluvieux-

(euse) ; **to get** ~ se mouiller ; ~ **blanket**
*n* (*fig*) rabat-joie *m inv*; ~**ness** *n* humidité
*f*; '~ **paint**' 'attention peinture fraîche' ;
~ **suit** *n* combinaison *f* de plongée.

**we've** [wi:v] = **we have.**

**whack** [wæk] *vt* donner un grand coup à ;
~**ed** *a* (*col: tired*) crevé(e).

**whale** [weɪl] *n* (*ZOOL*) baleine *f*.

**wharf, wharves** [wɔ:f, wɔ:vz] *n* quai *m*.

**what** [wɔt] *excl* quoi!, comment! // *det*
quel(le) // *pronoun* (*interrogative*) que, *prep*
+ quoi ; (*relative, indirect: object*) ce que ;
(*: subject*) ce qui ; ~ **are you doing?** que
fais-tu?, qu'est-ce que tu fais? ; ~ **has**
**happened?** que s'est-il passé?, qu'est-ce
qui s'est passé? ; ~**'s in there?** qu'y a-t-
il là-dedans?, qu'est-ce qu'il y a
là-dedans? ; **I saw** ~ **you did/is on the**
**table** j'ai vu ce que vous avez fait/ce qui
est sur la table ; ~ **a mess!** quel désordre! ;
~ **is it called?** comment est-ce que ça
s'appelle? ; ~ **about doing ...?** et si on
faisait ...? ; ~ **about me?** et moi? ; ~**ever**
*det:* ~**ever book** quel que soit le livre que
(*or* qui) +*sub*; n'importe quel livre //
*pronoun:* **do** ~**ever is necessary/you**
**want** faites (tout) ce qui est
nécessaire/(tout) ce que vous voulez ;
~**ever happens** quoi qu'il arrive ; **no**
**reason** ~**ever** *or* ~**soever** pas la moindre
raison.

**wheat** [wi:t] *n* blé *m*, froment *m*.

**wheel** [wi:l] *n* roue *f*; (*AUT: also:* **steering**
~) volant *m*; (*NAUT*) gouvernail *m* // *vt*
pousser, rouler // *vi* (*also:* ~ **round**)
tourner ; ~**barrow** *n* brouette *f*; ~**chair**
*n* fauteuil roulant.

**wheeze** [wi:z] *n* respiration bruyante
(*d'asthmatique*) // *vi* respirer bruyamment.

**when** [wɛn] *ad* quand // *cj* quand,
lorsque ; (*whereas*) alors que ; **on the day**
~ **I met him** le jour où je l'ai rencontré ;
~**ever** *ad* quand donc // *cj* quand ; (*every*
*time that*) chaque fois que.

**where** [wɛə*] *ad,cj* où ; **this is** ~ c'est là
que ; ~**abouts** *ad* où donc // *n:* **sb's**
~**abouts** l'endroit où se trouve qn ; ~**as**
*cj* alors que ; ~**ver** [-'ɛvə*] *ad* où donc //
*cj* où que + *sub*.

**whet** [wɛt] *vt* aiguiser.

**whether** ['wɛðə*] *cj* si ; **I don't know** ~
**to accept or not** je ne sais pas si je dois
accepter ou non ; **it's doubtful** ~ il est
peu probable que ; ~ **you go or not** que
vous y alliez ou non.

**which** [wɪtʃ] *det* (*interrogative*) quel(le), *pl*
quels(quelles) ; ~ **one of you?**
lequel(laquelle) d'entre vous? ; **tell me** ~
**one you want** dis-moi lequel tu veux *or*
celui que tu veux // *pronoun* (*interrogative*)
lequel(laquelle), *pl* lesquels (lesquelles) ;
(*indirect*) celui(celle) qui (*or* que) ; (*relative:*
*subject*) qui ; (*: object*) que, *prep* +
lequel(laquelle) (*NB:* à + *lequel* = auquel ;
*de* + *lequel* = duquel) ; **I don't mind** ~
peu importe lequel ; **the apple** ~ **you**
**ate/**~ **is on the table** la pomme que vous
avez mangée/qui est sur la table ; **the**
**chair on** ~ la chaise sur laquelle ; **the**
**book of** ~ le livre dont *or* duquel ; **he said**
**he knew,** ~ **is true/I feared** il a dit qu'il
le savait, ce qui est vrai/ce que je

craignais ; **after** ~ après quoi ; **in** ~ **case** auquel cas ; ~**ever** det: **take** ~**ever book you prefer** prenez le livre que vous préférez, peu importe lequel ; ~**ever book you take** quel que soit le livre que vous preniez ; ~**ever way you** de quelque façon que vous + sub.

**whiff** [wɪf] n bouffée f.

**while** [waɪl] n moment m // cj pendant que ; (as long as) tant que ; (whereas) alors que ; bien que + sub ; **for a** ~ pendant quelque temps.

**whim** [wɪm] n caprice m.

**whimper** ['wɪmpə*] n geignement m // vi geindre.

**whimsical** ['wɪmzɪkl] a (person) capricieux(euse) ; (look) étrange.

**whine** [waɪn] n gémissement m // vi gémir, geindre ; pleurnicher.

**whip** [wɪp] n fouet m ; (for riding) cravache f ; (Brit: POL: person) chef m de file (assurant la discipline dans son groupe parlementaire) // vt fouetter ; (snatch) enlever (or sortir) brusquement ; ~**ped cream** n crème fouettée ; ~-**round** n collecte f.

**whirl** [wə:l] n tourbillon m // vt faire tourbillonner ; faire tournoyer // vi tourbillonner ; ~**pool** n tourbillon m ; ~**wind** n tornade f.

**whirr** [wə:*] vi bruire ; ronronner ; vrombir.

**whisk** [wɪsk] n (CULIN) fouet m // vt fouetter, battre ; **to** ~ **sb away** or **off** emmener qn rapidement.

**whisker** ['wɪskə*] n: ~**s** (of animal) moustaches fpl ; (of man) favoris mpl.

**whisky, whiskey** (Irlande, US) ['wɪskɪ] n whisky m.

**whisper** ['wɪspə*] n chuchotement m ; (fig: of leaves) bruissement m ; (rumour) rumeur f // vt,vi chuchoter.

**whist** [wɪst] n whist m.

**whistle** ['wɪsl] n (sound) sifflement m ; (object) sifflet m // vi siffler.

**white** [waɪt] a blanc(blanche) ; (with fear) blême // n blanc m ; (person) blanc/blanche ; ~**bait** n blanchaille f ; ~-**collar worker** n employé/e de bureau ; ~ **elephant** n (fig) objet dispendieux et superflu ; ~ **lie** n pieux mensonge ; ~**ness** n blancheur f ; ~ **paper** n (POL) livre blanc ; ~**wash** n (paint) lait m de chaux // vt blanchir à la chaux ; (fig) blanchir.

**whiting** ['waɪtɪŋ] n, pl inv (fish) merlan m.

**Whitsun** ['wɪtsn] n la Pentecôte.

**whittle** ['wɪtl] vt: **to** ~ **away**, ~ **down** (costs) réduire, rogner.

**whizz** [wɪz] vi aller (or passer) à toute vitesse ; ~ **kid** n (col) petit prodige.

**WHO** n (abbr of World Health Organization) O.M.S. f (Organisation mondiale de la Santé).

**who** [hu:] pronoun qui ; ~**dunit** [hu:'dʌnɪt] n (col) roman policier ; ~**ever** pronoun: ~**ever finds it** celui(celle) qui le trouve, (qui que ce soit), quiconque le trouve ; **ask** ~**ever you like** demandez à qui vous voulez ; ~**ever he marries** qui que ce soit or quelle que soit la personne qu'il épouse ; ~**ever told you that?** qui a bien pu vous dire ça?, qui donc vous a dit ça?

**whole** [həul] a (complete) entier(ère) ; tout(e) ; (not broken) intact(e), complet(ète) // n (total) totalité f ; (sth not broken) tout m ; **the** ~ **of the time** tout le temps ; **the** ~ **of the town** la ville tout entière ; **on the** ~, **as a** ~ dans l'ensemble ; ~**hearted** a sans réserve(s), sincère ; ~**sale** n (vente f en) gros m // a de gros ; (destruction) systématique ; ~**saler** n grossiste m/f ; ~**some** a sain(e) ; (advice) salutaire ; **wholly** ad entièrement, tout à fait.

**whom** [hu:m] pronoun que, prep + qui (check syntax of French verb used) ; (interrogative) qui.

**whooping cough** ['hu:pɪŋkɔf] n coqueluche f.

**whopping** ['wɔpɪŋ] a (col: big) énorme.

**whore** [hɔ:*] n (col: pej) putain f.

**whose** [hu:z] det: ~ **book is this?** à qui est ce livre? ; ~ **pencil have you taken?** à qui est le crayon que vous avez pris?, c'est le crayon de qui que vous avez pris? ; **the man** ~ **son you rescued** l'homme dont or de qui vous avez sauvé le fils ; **the girl** ~ **sister you were speaking to** la fille à la sœur de qui or laquelle vous parliez // pronoun: ~ **is this?** à qui est ceci? ; **I know** ~ **it is** je sais à qui c'est.

**Who's Who** ['hu:z'hu:] n ≈ Bottin Mondain.

**why** [waɪ] ad pourquoi // excl eh bien!, tiens! ; **the reason** ~ la raison pour laquelle ; ~**ever** ad pourquoi donc, mais pourquoi.

**wick** [wɪk] n mèche f (de bougie).

**wicked** ['wɪkɪd] a mauvais(e), méchant(e) ; inique ; cruel(le) ; (mischievous) malicieux(euse).

**wicker** ['wɪkə*] n osier m ; (also: ~**work**) vannerie f.

**wicket** ['wɪkɪt] n (CRICKET) guichet m ; espace compris entre les deux guichets.

**wide** [waɪd] a large ; (region, knowledge) vaste, très étendu(e) ; (choice) grand(e) // ad: **to open** ~ ouvrir tout grand ; **to shoot** ~ tirer à côté ; ~-**angle lens** n objectif m grand-angulaire ; ~-**awake** a bien éveillé(e) ; ~**ly** ad (different) radicalement ; (spaced) sur une grande étendue ; (believed) généralement ; ~**n** vt élargir ; ~**ness** n largeur f ; ~ **open** a grand(e) ouvert(e) ; ~**spread** a (belief etc) très répandu(e).

**widow** ['wɪdəu] n veuve f ; ~**ed** a (qui est devenu(e)) veuf(veuve) ; ~**er** n veuf m.

**width** [wɪdθ] n largeur f.

**wield** [wi:ld] vt (sword) manier ; (power) exercer.

**wife, wives** [waɪf, waɪvz] n femme (mariée), épouse f.

**wig** [wɪg] n perruque f.

**wiggle** ['wɪgl] vt agiter remuer // vi (loose screw etc) branler ; (worm) se tortiller.

**wild** [waɪld] a sauvage ; (sea) déchaîné(e) ; (idea, life) fou(folle) ; extravagant(e) ; ~**s** npl régions fpl sauvages ; ~**erness** ['wɪldənɪs] n désert m, région f sauvage ; ~-**goose chase** n (fig) fausse piste ; ~**life** n faune f ; ~**ly** ad (applaud) frénétiquement ; (hit, guess) au hasard ; (happy) follement.

**wilful** ['wɪlful] *a* (*person*) obstiné(e); (*action*) délibéré(e); (*crime*) prémédité(e).

**will** [wɪl] *auxiliary vb*: **he ~ come** il viendra // *vt* (*pt, pp* ~**ed**): **to ~ sb to do** souhaiter ardemment que qn fasse; **he ~ed himself to go on** par un suprême effort de volonté, il continua // *n* volonté *f*; testament *m*; ~**ing** *a* de bonne volonté, serviable; **he's ~ing to do it** il est disposé à le faire, il veut bien le faire; ~**ingly** *ad* volontiers; ~**ingness** *n* bonne volonté.

**willow** ['wɪləu] *n* saule *m*.

**will power** ['wɪlpauə*] *n* volonté *f*.

**wilt** [wɪlt] *vi* dépérir.

**wily** ['waɪlɪ] *a* rusé(e).

**win** [wɪn] *n* (*in sports etc*) victoire *f* // *vb* (*pt, pp* **won** [wʌn]) *vt* (*battle, money*) gagner; (*prize*) remporter; (*popularity*) acquérir // *vi* gagner; **to ~ over, ~ round** *vt* gagner, se concilier.

**wince** [wɪns] *n* tressaillement *m* // *vi* tressaillir.

**winch** [wɪntʃ] *n* treuil *m*.

**wind** *n* [wɪnd] (*also MED*) vent *m* // *vb* [waɪnd] (*pt, pp* **wound** [waund]) *vt* enrouler; (*wrap*) envelopper; (*clock, toy*) remonter; (*take breath away*: [wɪnd]) couper le souffle à // *vi* (*road, river*) serpenter; **the ~(s)** (*MUS*) les instruments *mpl* à vent; **to ~ up** *vt* (*clock*) remonter; (*debate*) terminer, clôturer; ~**break** *n* brise-vent *m inv*; ~**fall** *n* coup *m* de chance; ~**ing** *a* (*road*) sinueux(euse); (*staircase*) tournant(e); ~ **instrument** *n* (*MUS*) instrument *m* à vent; ~**mill** *n* moulin *m* à vent.

**window** ['wɪndəu] *n* fenêtre *f*; (*in car, train, also*: ~ **pane**) vitre *f*; (*in shop etc*) vitrine *f*; ~ **box** *n* jardinière *f*; ~ **cleaner** *n* (*person*) laveur/euse de vitres; ~ **frame** *n* châssis *m* de fenêtre; ~ **ledge** *n* rebord *m* de la fenêtre; ~ **pane** *n* vitre *f*, carreau *m*; ~**sill** *n* (*inside*) appui *m* de la fenêtre; (*outside*) rebord *m* de la fenêtre.

**windpipe** ['wɪndpaɪp] *n* gosier *m*.

**windscreen, windshield** (*US*) ['wɪndskriːn, 'wɪndʃiːld] *n* pare-brise *m inv*; ~ **washer** *n* lave-glace *m inv*; ~ **wiper** *n* essuie-glace *m inv*.

**windswept** ['wɪndswɛpt] *a* balayé(e) par le vent.

**windy** ['wɪndɪ] *a* venté(e), venteux(euse); **it's ~** il y a du vent.

**wine** [waɪn] *n* vin *m*; ~ **cellar** *n* cave *f* à vins; ~ **glass** *n* verre *m* à vin; ~ **list** *n* carte *f* des vins; ~ **merchant** *n* marchand/e de vins; ~ **tasting** *n* dégustation *f* (de vins); ~ **waiter** *n* sommelier *m*.

**wing** [wɪŋ] *n* aile *f*; (*in air force*) groupe *m* d'escadrilles; ~**s** *npl* (*THEATRE*) coulisses *fpl*; ~**er** *n* (*SPORT*) ailier *m*.

**wink** [wɪŋk] *n* clin *m* d'œil // *vi* faire un clin d'œil; (*blink*) cligner des yeux.

**winner** ['wɪnə*] *n* gagnant/e.

**winning** ['wɪnɪŋ] *a* (*team*) gagnant(e); (*goal*) décisif(ive); ~**s** *npl* gains *mpl*; ~ **post** *n* poteau *m* d'arrivée.

**winter** ['wɪntə*] *n* hiver *m* // *vi* hiverner; ~ **sports** *npl* sports *mpl* d'hiver.

**wintry** ['wɪntrɪ] *a* hivernal(e).

**wipe** [waɪp] *n* coup *m* de torchon (*or* de chiffon *or* d'éponge) // *vt* essuyer; **to ~ off** *vt* essuyer; **to ~ out** *vt* (*debt*) régler; (*memory*) oublier; (*destroy*) anéantir; **to ~ up** *vt* essuyer.

**wire** ['waɪə*] *n* fil *m* (de fer); (*ELEC*) fil électrique; (*TEL*) télégramme *m* // *vt* (*fence*) grillager; (*house*) faire l'installation électrique de; (*also*: ~ **up**) brancher; ~ **brush** *n* brosse *f* métallique.

**wireless** ['waɪəlɪs] *n* télégraphie *f* sans fil; (*set*) T.S.F. *f*.

**wiry** ['waɪərɪ] *a* noueux(euse), nerveux(euse).

**wisdom** ['wɪzdəm] *n* sagesse *f*; (*of action*) prudence *f*; ~ **tooth** *n* dent *f* de sagesse.

**wise** [waɪz] *a* sage, prudent(e), judicieux(euse).

**...wise** [waɪz] *suffix*: **time~** en ce qui concerne le temps, question temps.

**wisecrack** ['waɪzkræk] *n* sarcasme *m*.

**wish** [wɪʃ] *n* (*desire,*) désir *m*; (*specific desire*) souhait *m*, vœu *m* // *vt* souhaiter, désirer, vouloir; **best ~es** (*on birthday etc*) meilleurs vœux; **with best ~es** (*in letter*) bien amicalement; **give her my best ~es** faites-lui mes amitiés; **to ~ sb goodbye** dire au revoir à qn; **he ~ed me well** il me souhaitait de réussir; **to ~ to do/sb to do** désirer *or* vouloir faire/que qn fasse; **to ~ for** souhaiter; **it's ~ful thinking** c'est prendre ses désirs pour des réalités.

**wisp** [wɪsp] *n* fine mèche (*de cheveux*); (*of smoke*) mince volute *f*; **a ~ of straw** un fétu de paille.

**wistful** ['wɪstful] *a* mélancolique.

**wit** [wɪt] *n* (*gen pl*) intelligence *f*, esprit *m*; présence *f* d'esprit; (*wittiness*) esprit; (*person*) homme/femme d'esprit; **to be at one's ~s' end** (*fig*) ne plus savoir que faire; **to ~** *ad* à savoir.

**witch** [wɪtʃ] *n* sorcière *f*; ~**craft** *n* sorcellerie *f*.

**with** [wɪð, wɪθ] *prep* avec; **red ~ anger** rouge de colère; **the man ~ the grey hat** l'homme au chapeau gris; **to be ~ it** (*fig*) être dans le vent; **I am ~ you** (*I understand*) je vous suis.

**withdraw** [wɪθ'drɔː] *vb* (*irg*) *vt* retirer // *vi* se retirer; (*go back on promise*) se rétracter; ~**al** *n* retrait *m*; (*MED*) état *m* de manque.

**wither** ['wɪðə*] *vi* se faner; ~**ed** *a* fané(e), flétri(e); (*limb*) atrophié(e).

**withhold** [wɪθ'həuld] *vt irg* (*money*) retenir; (*decision*) remettre; (*permission*): **to ~ (from)** refuser (à); (*information*): **to ~ (from)** cacher (à).

**within** [wɪð'ɪn] *prep* à l'intérieur de // *ad* à l'intérieur; ~ **sight of** en vue de; ~ **a mile of** à moins d'un mille de; ~ **the week** avant la fin de la semaine.

**without** [wɪð'aut] *prep* sans.

**withstand** [wɪθ'stænd] *vt irg* résister à.

**witness** ['wɪtnɪs] *n* (*person*) témoin *m*; (*evidence*) témoignage *m* // *vt* (*event*) être témoin de; (*document*) attester l'authenticité de; **to bear ~ to sth** témoigner de qch; ~ **box**, ~ **stand** (*US*) *n* barre *f* des témoins.

witticism ['wɪtɪsɪzm] n mot m d'esprit.
witty ['wɪtɪ] a spirituel(le), plein(e)
d'esprit.
wives [waɪvz] npl of wife.
wizard ['wɪzəd] n magicien m.
wk abbr of week.
wobble ['wɔbl] vi trembler; (chair)
branler.
woe [wəu] n malheur m.
woke [wəuk] pt of wake; ~n pp of wake.
wolf, wolves [wulf, wulvz] n loup m.
woman, pl women ['wumən, 'wɪmɪn] n
femme f; ~ doctor n femme f médecin;
~ly a féminin(e); ~ teacher n professeur
m femme f.
womb [wu:m] n (ANAT) utérus m.
women ['wɪmɪn] npl of woman.
won [wʌn] pt,pp of win.
wonder ['wʌndə*] n merveille f, miracle
m; (feeling) émerveillement m // vi: to ~
whether se demander si; to ~ at
s'étonner de; s'émerveiller de; to ~
about songer à; it's no ~ that il n'est
pas étonnant que + sub; ~ful a
merveilleux(euse); ~fully ad (+ adjective)
merveilleusement; (+ vb) à merveille.
wonky ['wɔŋkɪ] a (col) qui ne va or ne
marche pas très bien.
won't [wəunt] = will not.
woo [wu:] vt (woman) faire la cour à.
wood [wud] n (timber, forest) bois m; ~
carving n sculpture f en or sur bois; ~ed
a boisé(e); ~en a en bois; (fig) raide;
inexpressif(ive); ~pecker n pic m
(oiseau); ~wind n (MUS) bois m; the
~wind (MUS) les bois; ~work n
menuiserie f; ~worm n ver m du bois.
wool [wul] n laine f; to pull the ~ over
sb's eyes (fig) en faire accroire à qn;
~len, ~en (US) a de laine; (industry)
lainier(ère); ~lens npl lainages mpl; ~ly,
~y (US) a laineux(euse); (fig: ideas)
confus(e).
word [wə:d] n mot m; (spoken) mot, parole
f; (promise) parole; (news) nouvelles fpl //
vt rédiger, formuler; in other ~s en
d'autres termes; to break/keep one's ~
manquer à/tenir sa parole; I'll take your
~ for it je vous crois sur parole; to send
~ of prévenir de; ~ing n termes mpl,
langage m; ~y a verbeux(euse).
wore [wɔ:*] pt of wear.
work [wə:k] n travail m; (ART, LITERATURE)
œuvre f // vi travailler; (mechanism)
marcher, fonctionner; (plan etc) marcher;
(medicine) faire son effet // vt (clay, wood
etc) travailler; (mine etc) exploiter;
(machine) faire marcher or fonctionner; to
be out of ~ être au chômage; ~s n
(factory) usine f // npl (of clock, machine)
mécanisme m; Minister/Ministry of
W~s ministre m/ministère m des
Travaux publics; to ~ loose vi se défaire,
se desserrer; to ~ on vt fus travailler à;
(principle) se baser sur; to ~ out vi (plans
etc) marcher // vt (problem) résoudre;
(plan) élaborer; it ~s out at £100 ça fait
100 livres; to get ~ed up se mettre dans
tous ses états; ~able a (solution)
réalisable; ~er n travailleur/euse,
ouvrier/ère; ~ing class n classe
ouvrière; ~ing-class a ouvrière(ère);

~ing man n travailleur m; in ~ing order
en état de marche; ~man n ouvrier m;
~manship n métier m, habileté f; facture
f; ~shop n atelier m; ~-to-rule n grève
f du zèle.
world [wə:ld] n monde m // cpd
(champion) du monde; (power, war)
mondial(e); to think the ~ of sb (fig) ne
jurer que par qn; out of this ~ a
extraordinaire; ~ly a de ce monde; ~-
wide a universel(le).
worm [wə:m] n ver m.
worn [wɔ:n] pp of wear // a usé(e); ~-
out a (object) complètement usé(e);
(person) épuisé(e).
worried ['wʌrɪd] a inquiet(ète).
worrier ['wʌrɪə*] n inquiet/ète.
worry ['wʌrɪ] n souci m // vt inquiéter //
vi s'inquiéter, se faire du souci; ~ing a
inquiétant(e).
worse [wə:s] a pire, plus mauvais(e) //
ad plus mal // n pire m; a change for
the ~ une détérioration; ~n vt,vi
empirer; ~ off a moins à l'aise
financièrement; (fig): you'll be ~ off this
way ça ira moins bien de cette façon.
worship ['wə:ʃɪp] n culte m // vt (God)
rendre un culte à; (person) adorer; Your
W~ (to mayor) Monsieur le Maire; (to
judge) Monsieur le Juge; ~per n
adorateur/trice; (in church) fidèle m/f.
worst [wə:st] a le(la) pire, le(la) plus
mauvais(e) // ad le plus mal // n pire m;
at ~ au pis aller.
worsted ['wustɪd] n: (wool) ~ laine
peignée.
worth [wə:θ] n valeur f // a: to be ~
valoir; it's ~ it cela en vaut la peine; 50
pence ~ of apples (pour) 50 pence de
pommes; ~less a qui ne vaut rien;
~while a (activity) qui en vaut la peine;
(cause) louable; a ~while book un livre
qui vaut la peine d'être lu.
worthy [wə:ðɪ] a (person) digne; (motive)
louable; ~ of digne de.
would [wud] auxiliary vb: she ~ come elle
viendrait; he ~ have come il serait venu;
~ you like a biscuit? voulez-vous or
voudriez-vous un biscuit?; he ~ go there
on Mondays il y allait le lundi; ~-be a
(pej) soi-disant.
wound vb [waund] pt, pp of wind // n,vt
[wu:nd] n blessure f // vt blesser; ~ed
in the leg blessé à la jambe.
wove [wəuv] pt of weave; ~n pp of
weave.
wrangle ['ræŋgl] n dispute f // vi se
disputer.
wrap [ræp] n (stole) écharpe f; (cape)
pèlerine f // vt (also: ~ up) envelopper;
~per n (of book) couverture f; ~ping
paper n papier m d'emballage; (for gift)
papier cadeau.
wrath [rɔθ] n courroux m.
wreath, ~s [ri:θ, ri:ðz] n couronne f.
wreck [rɛk] n (sea disaster) naufrage m;
(ship) épave f; (pej: person) loque humaine
// vt démolir; (ship) provoquer le
naufrage de; (fig) briser, ruiner; ~age n
débris mpl; (of building) décombres mpl;
(of ship) épave f.

**wren** [rɛn] n (ZOOL) roitelet m.

**wrench** [rɛntʃ] n (TECH) clé f (à écrous) ; (tug) violent mouvement de torsion ; (fig) arrachement m // vt tirer violemment sur, tordre ; **to ~ sth from** arracher qch (violemment) à or de.

**wrestle** ['rɛsl] vi: **to ~ (with sb)** lutter (avec qn) ; **to ~ with** (fig) se débattre avec, lutter contre ; **~r** n lutteur/euse ; **wrestling** n lutte f; (also: **all-in wrestling**) catch m; **wrestling match** n rencontre f de lutte (or de catch).

**wretched** ['rɛtʃɪd] a misérable ; (col) maudit(e).

**wriggle** ['rɪgl] n tortillement m // vi se tortiller.

**wring,** pt, pp **wrung** [rɪŋ, rʌŋ] vt tordre ; (wet clothes) essorer ; (fig): **to ~ sth out of** arracher qch à.

**wrinkle** ['rɪŋkl] n (on skin) ride f; (on paper etc) pli m // vt rider, plisser // vi se plisser.

**wrist** [rɪst] n poignet m; **~ watch** n montre-bracelet f.

**writ** [rɪt] n acte m judiciaire ; **to issue a ~ against sb** assigner qn en justice.

**write,** pt **wrote,** pp **written** [raɪt, rəut, 'rɪtn] vt,vi écrire ; **to ~ down** vt noter ; (put in writing) mettre par écrit ; **to ~ off** vt (debt) passer aux profits et pertes ; (depreciate) amortir ; **to ~ out** vt écrire ; (copy) recopier ; **to ~ up** vt rédiger ; **~-off** n perte totale ; **the car is a ~-off** la voiture est bonne pour la casse ; **~r** n auteur m, écrivain m.

**writhe** [raɪð] vi se tordre.

**writing** ['raɪtɪŋ] n écriture f; (of author) œuvres fpl; **in ~** par écrit ; **~ paper** n papier m à lettres.

**written** ['rɪtn] pp of **write**.

**wrong** [rɔŋ] a faux(fausse) ; (incorrectly chosen: number, road etc) mauvais(e) ; (not suitable) qui ne convient pas ; (wicked) mal ; (unfair) injuste // ad faux // n tort m // vt faire du tort à, léser ; **you are ~ to do it** tu as tort de le faire ; **you are ~ about that, you've got it ~** tu te trompes ; **to be in the ~** avoir tort ; **what's ~?** qu'est-ce qui ne va pas? ; **to go ~** (person) se tromper ; (plan) mal tourner ; (machine) tomber en panne ; **~ful** a injustifié(e) ; **~ly** ad à tort ; **~ side** n (of cloth) envers m.

**wrote** [rəut] pt of **write**.

**wrought** [rɔːt] a: **~ iron** fer forgé.

**wrung** [rʌŋ] pt, pp of **wring**.

**wry** [raɪ] a désabusé(e).

**wt.** abbr of **weight**.

## X Y Z

**Xmas** ['ɛksməs] n abbr of **Christmas**.

**X-ray** [ɛks'reɪ] n rayon m X ; (photograph) radio(graphie) f // vt radiographier.

**xylophone** ['zaɪləfəun] n xylophone m.

**yacht** [jɔt] n yacht m; voilier m; **~ing** n yachting m, navigation f de plaisance ; **~sman** n yacht(s)man m.

**Yank** [jæŋk] n (pej) Amerloque m/f.

**yap** [jæp] vi (dog) japper.

**yard** [jɑːd] n (of house etc) cour f;

(measure) yard m (= 914 mm ; 3 feet) ; **~stick** n (fig) mesure f, critère m.

**yarn** [jɑːn] n fil m; (tale) longue histoire.

**yawn** [jɔːn] n bâillement m // vi bâiller ; **~ing** a (gap) béant(e).

**yd.** abbr of **yard(s)**.

**year** [jɪə*] n an m, année f; **every ~** tous les ans, chaque année ; **to be 8 ~s old** avoir 8 ans ; **~ly** a annuel(le) // ad annuellement.

**yearn** [jəːn] vi: **to ~ for sth/to do** aspirer à qch/à faire, languir après qch ; **~ing** n désir ardent, envie f.

**yeast** [jiːst] n levure f.

**yell** [jɛl] n hurlement m, cri m // vi hurler.

**yellow** ['jɛləu] a,n jaune (m) ; **~ fever** n fièvre f jaune.

**yelp** [jɛlp] n jappement m; glapissement m // vi japper ; glapir.

**yeoman** ['jəumən] n: **Y~ of the Guard** hallebardier m de la garde royale.

**yes** [jɛs] ad oui ; (answering negative question) si // n oui m.

**yesterday** ['jɛstədɪ] ad,n hier (m).

**yet** [jɛt] ad encore ; déjà // cj pourtant, néanmoins ; **it is not finished ~** ce n'est pas encore fini or toujours pas fini ; **must you go just ~?** dois-tu déjà partir? ; **the best ~** le meilleur jusqu'ici or jusque-là ; **as ~** jusqu'ici, encore ; **a few days ~** encore quelques jours.

**yew** [juː] n if m.

**Yiddish** ['jɪdɪʃ] n yiddish m.

**yield** [jiːld] n production f, rendement m; rapport m // vt produire, rendre, rapporter ; (surrender) céder // vi céder.

**yodel** ['jəudl] vi faire des tyroliennes, jodler.

**yoga** ['jəugə] n yoga m.

**yog(h)ourt, yog(h)urt** ['jəugət] n yaourt m.

**yoke** [jəuk] n joug m.

**yolk** [jəuk] n jaune m (d'œuf).

**yonder** ['jɔndə*] ad là(-bas).

**you** [juː] pronoun tu ; (polite form) vous ; (pl) vous ; (complement) te,t' + vowel ; vous ; (stressed) toi ; vous ; (one): **fresh air does ~ good** l'air frais fait du bien ; **~ never know** on ne sait jamais.

**you'd** [juːd] = **you had** ; **you would**.

**you'll** [juːl] = **you will** ; **you shall**.

**young** [jʌŋ] a jeune // npl (of animal) petits mpl; (people): **the ~** les jeunes, la jeunesse ; **~ish** a assez jeune ; **~ster** n jeune m (garçon m) ; (child) enfant m/f.

**your** [jɔː*] a ton(ta), pl tes ; votre, pl vos.

**you're** [juə*] = **you are**.

**yours** [jɔːz] pronoun le(la) tien(ne), les tiens(tiennes) ; le(la) vôtre, les vôtres ; **is it ~?** c'est à toi (or à vous)? ; **yours sincerely/faithfully** je vous prie d'agréer l'expression de mes sentiments les meilleurs/mes sentiments respectueux or dévoués.

**yourself** [jɔː'sɛlf] pronoun (reflexive) te ; vous ; (after prep) toi ; vous ; (emphatic) toi-même ; vous-même ; **yourselves** pl pronoun vous ; (emphatic) vous mêmes.

**youth** [juːθ] n jeunesse f; (young man: pl **~s** [juːðz]) jeune homme m; **~ful** a jeune ; de jeunesse ; juvénile ; ~ **hostel** *n* auberge *f* de jeunesse.

**you've** [ju:v] = **you have**.

**Yugoslav** ['ju:gəu'slɑ:v] *a* yougoslave // *n* Yougoslave *m/f*.

**Yugoslavia** ['ju:gəu'sla:vɪə] *n* Yougoslavie *f*.

**Yule** [ju:l]: ~ **log** *n* bûche *f* de Noël.


**zany** ['zeɪnɪ] *a* farfelu(e), loufoque.

**zeal** [zi:l] *n* zèle *m*, ferveur *f*; empressement *m*; ~**ous** ['zɛləs] *a* zélé(e) ; empressé(e).

**zebra** ['zi:brə] *n* zèbre *m* ; ~ **crossing** *n* passage *m* pour piétons.

**zenith** ['zɛnɪθ] *n* zénith *m*.

**zero** ['zɪərəu] *n* zéro *m* ; ~ **hour** *n* l'heure *f* H.

**zest** [zɛst] *n* entrain *m*, élan *m* ; zeste *m*.

**zigzag** ['zɪgzæg] *n* zigzag *m* // *vi* zigzaguer, faire des zigzags.

**zinc** [zɪŋk] *n* zinc *m*.

**Zionism** ['zaɪənɪzm] *n* sionisme *m*.

**zip** [zip] *n* (*also*: ~ **fastener**, ~**per**) fermeture *f* éclair ® // *vt* (*also*: ~ **up**) fermer avec une fermeture éclair ®.

**zither** ['zɪðə*] *n* cithare *f*.

**zodiac** ['zəudɪæk] *n* zodiaque *m*.

**zombie** ['zɔmbɪ] *n* (*fig*): **like a** ~ l'air complètement dans les vapes, avec l'air d'un mort vivant.

**zone** [zəun] *n* zone *f* ; (*subdivision of town*) secteur *m*.

**zoo** [zu:] *n* zoo *m*.

**zoological** [zuə'lɔdʒɪkl] *a* zoologique.

**zoologist** [zu'ɔlədʒɪst] *n* zoologiste *m/f*.

**zoology** [zu:'ɔlədʒɪ] *n* zoologie *f*.

**zoom** [zu:m] *vi*: **to** ~ **past** passer en trombe ; ~ **lens** *n* zoom *m*, objectif *m* à focale variable.

# NOTES TO THE USER OF THIS DICTIONARY

# I. Using the dictionary

In using this book, you will either want to check the meaning of a French word you don't know, or find the French for an English word. These two operations are quite different, and so are the problems you may face when using one side of the dictionary or the other. In order to help you, we have tried to explain below the main features of this book.

The 'wordlist' is the alphabetical list of all the items in large bold type, ie. all the 'headwords'. Each 'entry', or article, is introduced by a headword, and may contain additional 'references' in smaller bold type, such as phrases, derivatives, and compound words. Section 1. below deals with the way references are listed.

The typography distinguishes between three broad categories of text within the dictionary. All items in bold type, large or smaller, are 'source language' references, for which an equivalence in the other language is provided. All items in standard type are translations. Items in italics are information about the words being translated, ie. either labels, or 'signposts' pinpointing the appropriate translation, or explanations.

## 1. *Where to look for a word*

### 1.1 Derivatives

In order to save space, a number of derivatives have been listed within entries, provided this does not break alphabetical order. Thus, **pensionnaire** and **pensionnat** are listed within the entry for **pension,** or **caller** and **calling** under **call.** You must remember this when looking for a word you don't find listed as a headword. These derivatives are always listed last within an entry (see also I.2 on entry layout).

### 1.2 Homographs

Homographs are words which are spelt in exactly the same way, like French **boucher** (to block) and **boucher** (butcher), or English **fine** (nice etc) and **fine** (penalty). As a rule, in order to save space, such words have been treated as one headword only. In the very few cases where this was not possible, either a cross-reference is given (see **pas,** in the French wordlist), or else the presence of a feminine form helps distinguish between two consecutive homograph entries (**boulot** vs **boulot,-te, vu** vs **vu,-e** vs **vue**).

## 1.3 Phrases

Because of the constraints of space, there can be only a limited number of idiomatic phrases in a pocket dictionary like this one. Particular emphasis is given to verbal phrases like **mettre au point, mettre à jour, prendre feu, faire feu, faire du feu,** etc, and also to basic constructions (see for instance the entries for **apply, agree, apprendre, moment**).

Verbal phrases with the ten or so basic verbs like *faire, mettre, prendre,* etc. are listed under the noun. Other phrases and idioms are listed under the first key word (ie. not a preposition), for instance **filer doux** under **filer, d'emblée** under **emblée.**

## 1.4 Abbreviations and proper names

For easier reference, abbreviations, acronyms and proper names have been listed alphabetically in the wordlist, as opposed to being relegated to the appendices. **M.O.T.** is used in every way like **certificate** or **permit, R.E.R.** like **métro,** and these words are treated like other nouns.

## 1.5 Compounds

**Housewife, bicycle track, pare-chocs** and **pomme de terre** are all compounds. One-word compounds like 'housewife' are no problem as regards consulting the dictionary, since they can appear only in one place and in strict alphabetical order. When it comes to other compounds, however – hyphenated compounds and compounds made up of separate words – each language presents its own peculiar problems.

### 1.5.1 French compounds

There are many compounds made up of two or more 'words'. When it comes to checking a French compound, you might not be aware that you are dealing with a compound and not a string of autonomous words, and there might inevitably be some toing and froing between entries.

As spelling is quite set in French, we have listed French compounds under the first word, and grouped them alphabetically within that entry. For instance, **cour martiale** is within the entry for **cour** and comes before the headword **courage. Fête mobile** is within the entry for **fête,** and comes before **Fête-Dieu** and **fêter** at the end of the same entry (see also section 2.). Remember that the meaning of a phrase or of a compound can be quite different from that of its elements taken separately, so be prepared to check through an entry thoroughly before giving up.

### 1.5.2  French 'verbes pronominaux'

Verbs like **se rappeler, se noyer, se promener, s'arroger** are called 'pronominaux' in French because they are used with a 'pronom personnel': je *me* rappelle, tu *te* promènes etc. They must be distinguished from truly reflexive or reciprocal uses like 'il *se* regarde dans la glace' (he is looking *at himself* in the mirror) and 'ils *se* regardaient sans rien dire' (they were looking *at each other* in silence). The 'verbes pronominaux' are intransitive or transitive verbs in their own right: 'se promener' is intransitive like 'flâner', and 's'arroger' transitive in the same way as 'prendre'.

There are no such verbs in English (which has another type of 'compound verb', the phrasal verb, see 1.5.4), where a verb used with 'oneself' is as a rule truly reflexive. Compare for instance the translations for **se noyer** (accidentellement) and **se noyer** (suicide). These verbs have been listed as phrases under the entry for the key word. See for instance the entries for **rappeler, rapporter, ingénier.**

### 1.5.3  English compounds

Here there is a problem of where to find a compound because of less predictable spelling than is the case with French: is it **airgun, air-gun** or **air gun**? This is why we choose to list them according to strict alphabetical order. Thus **tea set** comes between **tease** and **teashop.** The entries between **tax** and **technical** will provide a good illustration of the system of listing. It has drawbacks, for instance in that **tax-free** and **tax-payer** are separated by **taxi, taxidermist** and three 'taxi' compounds. However, in a short dictionary used by beginners, it has the merit of simplicity and consistency.

### 1.5.4  English 'phrasal verbs'

'Phrasal verbs' are verbs like **go off, blow up, cut down** etc. Here you have the advantage of knowing that these words belong together, whereas it will take the foreign user some time before he can identify these verbs immediately. They have been listed under the entry for the basic verb (eg. **go, blow, cut**), grouped alphabetically before any other derivative or compound – eg. **pull up** comes before **pulley**. For instance, look up **to back out, to look up** (a word), **to look out.**

### 1.6  Irregular forms

When looking up a French word, you may not immediately find the form you are looking for, although the word in question has been duly entered in the dictionary. This is possibly because you are looking up an irregular noun or verb form, and these are not always given as entries in their own right. Obviously we have assumed that you know the basics

496

regarding French verb forms, noun plurals and feminine forms. Thus you will be expected to know that 'chantent' is a form of the verb **chanter,** chevaux the plural of **cheval,** and so on. However, in order to help you, we have included the main irregular forms as entries in their own right, with a cross-reference to the basic form.

Thus, if you come across the word 'buvais' and attempt to look up a verb 'buver', you won't find it but what you will find at that place in the wordlist, between **butte** and **buvard,** is the entry **buvais** *etc vb voir* **boire.**

Similarly, **fausse,** and **fasse** are cross-referred to *faux* and *faire* respectively. With past participles, it sometimes happens that in addition to the purely verbal form there is an adjectival or noun use, for instance **connu** or **meublé.** These usages are translated as autonomous words, but they are also cross-referred to the verb whenever appropriate (see for instance entries for **couvert** or **assis**).

## 2. *Entry layout*

All entries, however long or complex, are arranged in a very systematic manner. But it may be a little difficult at first to find one's way through an entry like **passer, back, round** or **run** because homographs are grouped together (see 1.2) and the text is run on without any breakdown into paragraphs, in order to save space. Ease of reference comes with practice, but the guidelines below will make it easier for you.

### 2.1 'Signposting'

If you look up a French word and find a string of quite different English translations, you are unlikely to have much trouble finding out which is the relevant one for the context, because you know what the English words mean, and the context will almost automatically rule out unsuitable translations.

It is quite a different matter when you want to find the French for, say, **lock,** in the context 'we got to the lock around lunchtime', and are faced with an entry that reads 'lock: serrure (f); écluse (f); mèche (f), boucle (f)'. Obviously you can then go to the other side and check what each translation means. But this is time-consuming, and it doesn't always work. This is why we have provided the user with signposts which pinpoint the relevant translation. For instance with **lock,** the entry reads: ... (*of door, box*) serrure *f*; (*of canal*) écluse *f*; (*of hair*) mèche *f*, boucle *f* ...

For the context suggested above, it is now clear that 'écluse' is the right word.

## 2.2 Grammatical categories and meaning categories

Complex entries are first broken down into grammatical categories, eg.:
**lock** *n // vt // vi*. Be prepared to go through entries like **run** or **back** carefully, and you will find how useful all these 'signposts' are. Each grammatical category is then split where appropriate into the various meanings, eg.:

> **lock** *n* (*of door, box*) serrure *f*; (*of canal*) écluse *f*; (*of hair*) mèche *f*, boucle *f* // *vt* (*with key*) fermer à clé; (*immobilize*) bloquer // *vi* (*door etc*) fermer à clé; (*wheels*) se bloquer.

## 3. *Using the translations*

### 3.1 Gender

All feminine endings for French adjectives have been given on the English-French side. This may appear to duplicate information given on the other side, but we feel it is a useful reminder where and when it matters. The feminine version is given for words like **driver, teacher, research worker** etc. Remember that the French equivalents of **his, her, its** or **the** do not behave like their English counterparts: see section II for more information.

### 3.2 Plural

We have assumed knowledge on the part of the user of plural formation in French (see section II), including the plural of compounds. A form like 'yeux' is given (see entry for **eye**), but in the main, plural forms are not shown.

### 3.3 Verb forms

Irregular French verbs appearing as translations have not been marked as such, and the user should refer to the French verb tables when in doubt (pp. 507–514).

### 3.4 Colloquial language

You should as a rule proceed with great caution when handling foreign language which has a degree of informality. When an English word or phrase has been labelled (*col*), ie. colloquial, you must assume that the translation belongs to a similar level of informality. If the translation is followed by (!) you should handle it with extreme care, or best avoid it unless you are with close friends!

## 3.5 'Grammatical words'

It is exceedingly difficult to give adequate treatment for words like **for, away, whose, which, out, off** etc. in a short dictionary such as this one. We have tried to go some way towards providing as much relevant information as possible regarding the most frequent uses of these words. However, for further information use a good monolingual dictionary of French, especially one for foreign learners, and a good modern French grammar.

## 3.6 'Approximate' translations and cultural equivalents

It is not always possible to give a genuine translation, when for instance an English word denotes a thing or institution which either does not exist in France, or is quite different. Therefore, only an approximate equivalence can be given, or else an explanation. See for instance **whip, shadow cabinet, C.I.D.,** and on the French-English side **hémicycle, R.E.R., rosette.**

## 3.7 Alternative translations

As a rule, translations separated by commas can be regarded as broadly interchangeable for the meaning indicated. Translations separated by a semi-colon are not interchangeable and when in doubt you should consult either a larger bilingual dictionary such as the Collins-Robert French dictionary, or a good monolingual French dictionary. You will find however that there are very few cases of translations separated by a semi-colon without an intervening 'signpost'.

## II. Notes on French grammar

When you are first confronted with French at school, or if you happen to be at a business meeting where you are the only one speaking little or no French, it may seem to you that French is very different from English. On the other hand, if you stand back and consider a wider range of related and unrelated languages, French can look very close to English.

We have tried here to show some of the main differences, especially with the beginner and the dictionary user in mind, without dwelling on subtleties or aspects of French that are broadly similar to English. Among the greatest obstacles for the beginner are gender, verb forms and tenses, the position of adjectives, the use of prepositions and of course the sounds of French.

## 1. *Nouns and 'satellite' words (articles, adjectives)*

### 1.1  Gender

One of the basic differences: 'the table and the knife', but '**la** table et **le** couteau'. Largely unpredictable, this business of gender must be learned as a feature to be remembered with each new word. It is most important to get the article right, and of course the agreement of adjectives and past participles: 'la **vieille** maison et le **vieux** chalet'. See also 1.4 (possessive adjectives).

### 1.2  Articles: le, la, un, du, des etc.

Apart from the problem of gender, there is the question of whether the article is used or not, and French does not always follow the English pattern. For instance you say 'I like wine' but the French say 'j'aime **le** vin'. Conversely, 'my father is **a** publisher' but 'mon père est éditeur'.

### 1.2.1  'le, la, les'

(a)  In almost all cases where 'the' is not used in English, the article must be used in French. For instance:

apples are good for you   **les** pommes sont bonnes pour la santé
salmon is expensive   **le** saumon est cher
love is not enough   l'amour ne suffit pas
he won't stand laziness   il ne tolère pas **la** paresse
France is beautiful   **la** France est belle
he likes skiing   il aime **le** ski

NB. A few names of countries are used without the article in French, like Cuba or Madagascar, Chypre, Malte, Jersey.

(b)  use of 'le/la' with parts of the body

Where the possessive is used in English, 'le/la' tends to be used in French (sometimes together with a pronoun):

I broke **my** leg   je **me** suis cassé **la** jambe
Put up **your** hand   levez **la** main
He trod on **my** foot   il **m'**a marché sur **le** pied

(c)  à + le, de + le

Remember the contracted forms (shown in the dictionary under **à** and **de**): je vais **au** cinéma, le parapet **du** pont.

## 1.2.2 'un, une, des'

(a)   In structures of the type 'with incredible courage', the article 'un/une' is used in French:

He showed incredible coolness   il a fait preuve d'**un** sang-froid incroyable
A film in appallingly bad taste   un film d'**un** mauvais goût désolant

(b)   On the other hand, this article is not used in French in structures equivalent to 'my father is a teacher':

my sister is **a** nurse   ma sœur est infirmière
he is **a** sailor's son   il est fils de marin (or: c'est **un** fils de marin, c'est le fils d'un marin)

But this only applies with names of professions and crafts:

his brother is an idiot   son frère est un imbécile

my sister is a very liberated young lady   ma sœur est une jeune fille très émancipée

(c)   'without a pen', 'without bread': no article in French

Where the English uses the article with a so-called 'countable' noun (like 'hat' as opposed to 'milk' or 'water' or 'bread'), the French doesn't: 'sans plume, on ne peut pas écrire', 'un repas sans pain'.

(d)   'des'

Remember to use 'des' in the plural, although there may be no article in English:

friends from Paris have arrived   **des** amis de Paris sont arrivés

## 1.2.3 'du, de la, des', 'de' = 'some', 'any'

Remember not to confuse 'du' as in 'le titre du livre' and 'du' as in 'j'aimerais du pain' (see entry **de**). Where you have 'some' or 'any' or sometimes nothing in English, the French use 'du' etc., as shown below:

je veux du pain   I want some bread

veux-tu du pain/de la soupe/des cigarettes? Would you like any (or some) bread/soup/cigarettes?

je ne veux pas de pain/soupe/cigarettes   I don't want any bread/soup/
cigarettes

## 1.3   Adjectives

Apart from the question of gender (subtil-subtile *but* utile, etc.), the
main difficulty is the position of adjectives. As a general rule, they follow
the noun (des plantes marines, un repas délicieux, des volets rouges).
Some adjectives or types of adjectives will always go after the noun (une
maison délabrée, des plantes marines, une robe rouge). Some can also
come before the noun for stylistic effect, without any change in meaning
(un délicieux repas). A few others will usually or always go before the
noun.

Among adjectives usually found before the noun are 'petit, grand,
haut, long, gros; vieux, jeune; bon, mauvais, joli; nouveau, ancien'.
Some like 'premier' are not found after the noun (except maybe in the
odd set phrase). Others like 'brave' or 'ancien' will be found in either
position, but with different meanings. The dictionary makes these
different meanings clear.

## 1.4   Possessives

### 1.4.1   Son/sa, mon/ma, ton/ta *vs* his/her/its, my, your

Contrary to what happens in English, the possessive varies according to
the gender of the noun it qualifies. Whether the owner is male or female,
it will be **sa** valise and **son** parapluie. There is no such difference in the
plural: **ses** valises et **ses** parapluies.

### 1.4.2   Le mien, la mienne, les miens, les miennes etc. *vs* mine etc.

Here again, the form of the possessive depends on the gender and
number of the qualified noun (ie. 'hers' will be **la sienne** if a car – la
voiture – is being referred to, and **le sien** if it's a handbag – le sac). In
the plural (ie. several owners) with a plural noun there is no gender
distinction: les nôtres, les vôtres, les leurs.

## 1.5   Demonstratives: *ce, ce ...-ci, celui-ci, ceux-ci* etc.

### 1.5.1   The distinction 'this' vs 'that' is rendered in French by a
demonstrative plus '-ci' or '-là', eg. **ce** garçon-**ci** – this boy; **ce**
garçon-**là** – that boy. However, whereas English always draws the
distinction between 'this' and 'that', the French demonstratives are often
used without the '-ci' and '-là' additions, so that 'ce garçon' may mean
'this boy' or 'that boy'. The main difference is again one of gender:
remember to use 'cette', 'celle' or 'celles' with a feminine noun.

1.6   Comparative and superlative: *plus … que* etc.

1.6.1   The comparative and superlative in French are formed by placing **plus** and **le plus** respectively in front of the adjective or adverb. Eg.: plus grand – bigger; le plus grand – the biggest; plus vite – more quickly; le plus vite – the most quickly.

2.   *Verbs*

This is one of the main areas of difficulty for English-speaking learners. There are four major problems. First the variety of endings (je par*s*, nous part*ons* etc) and the number of irregular or 'semi-irregular' forms. Second, the difference in the formation of negative or interrogative phrases (no equivalent of 'do', 'did' etc. as in 'I didn't go, did you?'). Third, the difference in the use of tenses (eg. no real equivalent of our 'continuous' tense). Fourth the use of 'avoir' or 'être' as auxiliary verbs where English just uses 'to have'.

2.1   Verb forms

The verb tables on pp. 507 to 514 will give you ending patterns for the main regular verbs, plus a list of the most common irregular verbs. There is no substitute for practice on this, but try not to look at these forms as a vast number of separate items to be learnt: there are two basic combining patterns, one relating to the person (a 'nous' form vs a 'vous' form etc), and one relating to the tense. Also, don't learn and practise too many different tenses at once, parrot-fashion. The present, the imperfect, the future, the conditional and the perfect will cater for most of your needs when it comes to expressing yourself in French.

2.2   Negatives and questions

'**ne** (**n'**) + verb form + **pas** ( + past participle)' is the basic pattern of negative verb phrases. 'Je **ne** crois (vraiment) **pas** que …', 'il **n'**est **pas** parti (tout de suite)', il **n'**a **pas** (tout de suite) répondu'. The one place where no adverb can fit is between 'ne' and the verb form. Otherwise, there are various possible combinations, depending on the adverb and the meaning of the whole sentence.

One easy way to form an interrogative phrase is to use the invariable question form **est-ce que/qu'…**, eg. 'il part demain': '**est-ce qu'**il part demain?'. Alternatively, use the inversion of verb and subject (but only when the subject is a pronoun), eg. 'il part demain': 'part-il demain?'. Very often in spoken French (and, whatever they say to the contrary, for most people), intonation only is used to indicate the question form: 'il part demain?' (voice raised on the last syllable).

## 2.3 Tenses

2.3.1 There is no equivalent in French of our 'progressive' -ing form (I am reading). When the English has the sense of 'to be in the process of doing ...' it can be translated with the structure 'être en train de' + infinitive. In other cases, the present tense or the imperfect will convey the same meaning: I was living at Rosalie's: j'habitais chez Rosalie; we are seeing him tomorrow: nous le voyons demain.

2.3.2 The two tenses of the past in English (I went there, he has taken it) do not correspond closely to the French. Of the imperfect (j'habitais), the perfect (j'ai répondu) and the past historic (je partis), the last is hardly ever used in spoken French. The perfect is used much more widely than its counterpart in English and it can be used in many cases when the English would use the preterite (*I went, he gave* etc.).

### 2.3.3 The perfect tense ('passé composé')

The use of 'avoir' as an auxiliary verb is by far the most common, hence it is convenient to concentrate on the few verbs which use 'être'. They are all intransitive and verbs expressing movement or becoming, like *aller, venir; partir, arriver, retourner; descendre, monter, entrer, sortir; naître, mourir, devenir.*

The second thing to remember is that the past participle will occasionally take the marks of gender and/or plural. Thick tomes have been written on the agreement of the past participle, but two basic rules should enable you to cope with most problems. The past participle remains in the form of the masculine singular (j'ai répondu, il a passé) unless: *a.* with a transitive verb, the object precedes the verb — '*les livres* que j'ai lus'; *b.* the auxiliary 'être' is used: '*elle* est partie hier'.

### 2.3.4 The imperfect ('imparfait')

This is used for an action or state without definite limits in time. Compare for instance 'he lived in London during the war: il habitait à Londres pendant la guerre', 'he stood near the window: il se tenait (il était) près de la fenêtre' and 'they lived here from '64 to '68: ils ont habité ici de 64 à 68', 'he stood up: il s'est levé (il se leva)'.

2.4 The subjunctive ('subjonctif'): je veux qu'il fasse ... *vs* je sais qu'il fait ...

Good command of the present tense of the subjunctive is necessary in order to speak reasonably good French. However, as far as basic communication is concerned, in only a very few cases is the use of the subjunctive essential in order to avoid a misunderstanding. In other words, the use of the subjunctive is a constraint which if ignored will identify you as a poor speaker of French without impairing communication in any significant way.

One instance where ignoring the subjunctive might lead to a misunderstanding is with the verb 'dire': 'dites-lui qu'il vienne' means 'tell him to come', but 'dites-lui qu'il vient' means 'tell him (or her) that he's coming'.

It is not possible to give a simple rule showing when the subjunctive should be used. This dictionary will occasionally show you when a particular construction requires the use of the subjunctive (see for instance English **lest**).

It usually follows a verb + *que* construction where the sentence expresses doubt, a hypothesis rather than a fact, a question (tu veux qu'on y aille?), an interdiction.

It is always used after 'vouloir que ...', 'il faut que ...'. There are also a few conjunctions which always take the subjunctive, usually those which express desire or intention (eg. 'afin que ...', 'de sorte que ...' – 'so that ...').

## 2.5 The passive

Broadly speaking, the passive voice is similar in French. 'He was dismissed' or 'he has been dismissed' can both be rendered by 'il a été renvoyé'. Note that impersonal uses such as 'I was told that ...' are often best rendered by the 'on' construction: 'on m'a dit que ...' (see entry for French **on**).

Constructions like 'the road is being repaired' are often best translated without using the passive: 'la route est en réparation', 'on est en train de réparer la route'. In cases like 'the book I was given' or 'the book I was given by my brother', where the subject ('I') would in fact be the indirect object in the active voice, the passive cannot be used in French: 'le livre qu'on m'a donné', 'le livre que m'a donné mon frère'.

## 3. *Personal pronouns*

| | |
|---|---|
| I, me | **je** voyage, **je me** coiffe, il **me** parle, il **me** voit, il **m'**a vu, et **moi**? |
| we, us | **nous** voyageons, **nous nous** coiffons, il **nous** parle, il **nous** voit, il **nous** a vus(vues), et **nous**? |
| he, him | il voyage, **il se** coiffe, je **lui** parle, je **le** vois, je **l'**ai vu, et **lui**? |
| she, her | **elle** voyage, **elle se** coiffe, je **lui** parle, je **la** vois, je **l'**ai vue, et **elle**? |

| | |
|---|---|
| it | **il(elle)** est rouge, **il(elle) se** casse, je **le(la)** vois, je **l'**ai vu(e) |
| they, them | **ils(elles)** voyagent, **ils(elles) se** coiffent, je **leur** parle, je **les** vois, je **les** ai vus(vues), et **eux(elles)**? |
| you (*plural*) | **vous** voyagez, **vous vous** coiffez, coiffez-**vous**, je **vous** parle, je **vous** vois, je **vous** ai vus(vues), et **vous**? |
| you (*singular*) | *familiar form*: **tu** voyages, **tu te** coiffes, coiffe-**toi**, je **te** parle, je **te** vois, je **t'**ai vu(vue), et **toi**? |
| | *polite form*: **vous** voyagez, **vous vous** coiffez, coiffez-**vous**, je **vous** parle, je **vous** vois, et **vous**? |

'Voyager' is an intransitive verb; 'se coiffer' is a reflexive verb ('verbe pronominal'); 'parler' is shown here with an indirect object ('parler à quelqu'un'); 'voir' is shown with a direct object ('voir quelqu'un'); the strong pronoun form is shown last, and is the one used after a preposition ('pour moi', 'après lui', 'devant nous' etc.); the imperative is shown for the 2nd person with the reflexive verb.

When there is a direct and an indirect object, personal pronouns are in the following order (indirect object shown in bold):

| | |
|---|---|
| me | il **me** le(la) donne, il **me** l'a donné(donnée), il ne **me** l'a pas donné(donnée) |
| us | il **nous** le(la) donne, il **nous** l'a donné(donnée), il ne **nous** l'a pas donné(donnée) |
| him, her | je le(la) **lui** donne, je le(la) **lui** ai donné(donnée), je ne le(la) **lui** ai pas donné(donnée) |
| them | je le(la) **leur** donne, je le(la) **leur** ai donné(donnée), je ne le(la) **leur** ai pas donné(donnée) |
| you (*plural*) | je **vous** le(la) donne, je **vous** l'ai donné(donnée), je ne **vous** l'ai pas donné(donnée) |
| you (*singular*) | *familiar form*: je **te** le(la) donne, je **te** l'ai donné(donnée), je ne **te** l'ai pas donné(donnée) |
| | *polite form*: je **vous** le(la) donne, je **vous** l'ai donné(donnée), je ne **vous** l'ai pas donné(donnée) |

# III. French verbs

1. The following tables of irregular verbs are self-explanatory. Unless stated otherwise, if one form only is given, it is the first person singular; if two forms are given, they are the first person singular and the first person plural. If not shown, the second person singular is the same as the first; the second and third person plural are regularly formed on the root of the first person plural (ie. *part*ons, *part*ez, *part*ent).

2. For verbs in '-ir' not appearing in the list of irregular verbs, follow 'finir'. For verbs in '-duire', follow 'conduire'. For verbs in '-andre, -ondre, -perdre, -ordre', follow 'rendre'.

3. Do not forget to use the appropriate pronoun with pronominal verbs: je me rase, il se rase, vous vous êtes coupé.

4. 'Semi-irregular' verbs.

Some verbs are only 'irregular' in a few predictable ways:

4.1 A 'c' will change to a 'ç' before 'o' or 'a' (the corresponding sound remaining [s]): **placer,** nous plaçons, nous plaçâmes.

4.2 A 'g' will change to 'ge' before 'o' or 'a' (the corresponding sound remaining [ʒ]): **bouger,** nous bougeons, nous bougeâmes; **protéger,** nous protégeons, nous protégeâmes.

4.3 An 'l' or a 't' will change to 'll' or 'tt' before 'e(s)' or 'ent', and in the future and conditional tenses (ie. at the end of a syllable): **appeler,** j'appelle, ils appellent, ils appelleront (*but*: nous appelons, j'appelais); **jeter,** je jette, ils jettent, nous jetterons (*but*: nous jetons, je jetais).

4.4 An 'e' will change to 'è' if followed by a consonant sound within the syllable: **geler,** il gèle, ils gèlent, il gèlera (*but*: nous gelons, il gelait); **acheter,** j'achète, ils achètent, ils achèteront (*but*: nous achetons, j'achetais); also: **dépecer, protéger.**

4.5 A 'y' will change to 'i' before 'e(s)', 'ent', and in the future and conditional tenses (ie. at the end of a syllable): **nettoyer,** il nettoie, ils nettoient, ils nettoieront (*but*: vous nettoyez, je nettoyais); also for '-uyer' and '-ayer' verbs (ennuyer, balayer). **Payer** may either retain the 'y' or follow the above changes.

5. The 'temps composés' are formed as follows:

5.1 Perfect ('passé composé'): with 'être' je suis parti, tu es parti etc. (see 'être'); with 'avoir' j'ai couru, tu as couru etc. (see 'avoir')

5.2 Pluperfect ('plus-que-parfait'): j'étais parti etc.; j'avais couru etc.

5.3 Future anterior ('futur antérieur'): je serai parti etc.; j'aurai couru etc.

5.4 Past conditional ('conditionnel passé'): je serais parti etc.; j'aurais couru etc.

5.5 The past anterior ('passé antérieur') – j'eus couru etc. – and the pluperfect subjunctive ('plus-que-parfait du subjonctif') – j'eusse couru etc. – are rarely used.

6. The imperfect subjunctive ('imparfait du subjonctif') is practically obsolete in spoken French and rare in written French. It is recognizable by its 'ss' element – que je fusse, que nous fussions; que j'eusse, que nous eussions etc – and also by the circumflex in the 3rd person singular – qu'il fût, qu'il eût, qu'il allât.

A typical regular verb: 'parler' [paʀle]

| PAST HISTORIC | | | |
|---|---|---|---|
| | ai | | [e] |
| | as | | [a] |
| | a | | |
| parl- | | [paʀl... | |
| | âmes | | [ɑm] |
| | âtes | | [ɑt] |
| | èrent | | [ɛʀ] |

| IMPERFECT | | | |
|---|---|---|---|
| | ais | | [ɛ] |
| | ais | | |
| | ait | | |
| parl- | | [paʀl... | |
| | ions | | [jɔ̃] |
| | iez | | [je] |
| | aient | | [ɛ] |

| PRESENT ( + SUBJUNCTIVE) | | | |
|---|---|---|---|
| parl- | e<br>es<br>e<br>ons (ions)<br>ez (iez)<br>ent | [paʀl…] | not sounded<br>or [ə]<br><br><br>[ɔ̃] ([jɔ̃])<br>[e] ([je])<br>not sounded<br>or [ə] |

| FUTURE ( + CONDITIONAL) | | | |
|---|---|---|---|
| parl-e-r- | ai (ais)<br>as (ais)<br>a (ait)<br>ons (ions)<br>ez (iez)<br>ont (aient) | [paʀləʀ…] | [e] ([ɛ])<br>[a] ([ɛ])<br>[a] ([ɛ])<br>[ɔ̃] ([jɔ̃])<br>[e] ([je])<br>[ɔ̃] ([ɛ]) |

| IMPERATIVE | parle, parlez [paʀl(ə), paʀle] |
|---|---|
| PAST PARTICIPLE | parlé (parlée) [paʀle] |
| PERFECT | j'ai parlé, tu as parlé etc. |

# VERB TABLES

**VERB TABLES:** 1 Participe présent 2 Participe passé 3 Présent
4 Subjonctif présent 5 Imparfait 6 Futur 7 Conditionnel 8 Passé simple

**absoudre** 1 absolvant 2 absout(absoute) 3 absous, absout, absolvons
4 absolve, absolvions 5 absolvais, absolvions 6 absoudrai, absoudrons
7 absoudrais, absoudrions 8 absolus, absolûmes
**acquérir** 1 acquérant 2 acquis(acquise) 3 acquiers, acquiert,
acquérons, acquièrent 4 acquière, acquérions 5 acquérais, acquérions
6 acquerrai, acquerrons 7 acquerrais, acquerrions 8 acquis, acquîmes
**aller** 1 allant 2 allé(allée) 3 vais, vas, va, allons, allez, vont 4 aille, ailles,
aille, allions, alliez, aillent 5 allais, allions 6 irai, irons 7 irais, irions
8 allai, allâmes
**assaillir** 1 assaillant 2 assailli(assaillie) 3 assaille, assaillons 4 assaille,
assaillions 5 assaillais, assaillions 6 assaillirai, assaillirons 7 assaillirais,
assaillirions 8 assaillis, assaillîmes

**asseoir** 1 asseyant 2 assis(assise) 3 assieds, assied, asseyons, asseyez, asseyent 4 asseye, asseyions 5 asseyais, asseyions 6 assiérai, assiérons 7 assiérais, assiérions 8 assis, assîmes

**atteindre** 1 atteignant 2 atteint(atteinte) 3 atteins, atteint, atteignons 4 atteigne, atteignions 5 atteignais, atteignions 6 atteindrai, atteindrons 7 atteindrais, atteindrions 8 atteignis, atteignîmes

**avoir** 1 ayant 2 eu(eue) 3 ai, as, a, avons, avez, ont 4 aie, aies, ait, ayons, ayez, aient 5 avais, avions 6 aurai, aurons 7 aurais, aurions 8 eus, eûmes

**battre** 1 battant 2 battu(battue) 3 bats, bats, bat, battons, battez, battent 4 batte, battions 5 battais, battions 6 battrai, battrons 7 battrais, battrions 8 battis, battîmes

**boire** 1 buvant 2 bu(bue) 3 bois, boit, buvons, buvez, boivent 4 boive, buvions, boivent 5 buvais, buvions 6 boirai, boirons 7 boirais, boirions 8 bus, bûmes

**bouillir** 1 bouillant 2 bouilli(bouillie) 3 bous, bout, bouillons, bouillent 4 bouille, bouillions 5 bouillais, bouillions 6 bouillirai, bouillirons 7 bouillirais, bouillirions 8 bouillis, bouillîmes

**clore** 2 clos(close) 3 clos, clôt, closent 4 close 6 clorai 7 clorais

**conclure** 1 concluant 2 conclu(conclue) 3 conclus, conclut, concluons, concluent 4 conclue, concluions, concluent 5 concluais, concluions 6 conclurai, conclurons 7 conclurais, conclurions 8 conclus, conclûmes

**conduire** 1 conduisant 2 conduit(conduite) 3 conduis, conduit, conduisons 4 conduise, conduisions 5 conduisais, conduisions 6 conduirai, conduirons 7 conduirais, conduirions 8 conduisis, conduisîmes

**connaître** 1 connaissant 2 connu(connue) 3 connais, connaît, connaissons 4 connaisse, connaissions 5 connaissais, connaissions 6 connaîtrai, connaîtrons 7 connaîtrais, connaîtrions 8 connus, connûmes

**coudre** 1 cousant 2 cousu(cousue) 3 couds, coud, cousons 4 couse, cousions 5 cousais, cousions 6 coudrai, coudrons 7 coudrais, coudrions 8 cousis, cousîmes

**courir** 1 courant 2 couru(courue) 3 cours, court, courons 4 coure, courions 5 courais, courions 6 courrai, courrons 7 courrais, courrions 8 courus, courûmes

**couvrir** 1 couvrant 2 couvert(couverte) 3 couvre, couvrons 4 couvre, couvrions 5 couvrais, couvrions 6 couvrirai, couvrirons 7 couvrirais, couvririons 8 couvris, couvrîmes

**craindre** 1 craignant 2 craint(crainte) 3 crains, craint, craignons, craignent 4 craigne, craignions 5 craignais, craignions 6 craindrai, craindrons 7 craindrais, craindrions 8 craignis, craignîmes

**croire** 1 croyant 2 cru(crue) 3 crois, croit, croyons, croient 4 croie, croyions 5 croyais, croyions 6 croirai, croirons 7 croirais, croirions 8 crus, crûmes

**croître** 1 croissant 2 crû(crue) 3 croîs, croît, croissons 4 croisse, croissions **5** croissais, croissions **6** croîtrai, croîtrons **7** croîtrais, croîtrions **8** crûs, crûmes

**cueillir** **1** cueillant **2** cueilli(cueillie) **3** cueille, cueillons, cueillent **4** cueille, cueillions **5** cueillais, cueillions **6** cueillerai, cueillerons **7** cueillerais, cueillerions **8** cueillis, cueillîmes

**devoir** **1** devant **2** dû(due) **3** dois, doit, devons, doivent **4** doive, devions, doivent **5** devais, devions **6** devrai, devrons **7** devrais, devrions **8** dus, dûmes

**dire** **1** disant **2** dit(dite) **3** dis, dit, disons, dites, disent **4** dise, disions **5** disais, disions **6** dirai, dirons **7** dirais, dirions **8** dis, dîmes.

**dormir** **1** dormant **2** dormi **3** dors, dort, dormons **4** dorme, dormions **5** dormais, dormions **6** dormirai, dormirons **7** dormirais, dormirions **8** dormis, dormîmes

**écrire** **1** écrivant **2** écrit(écrite) **3** écris, écrit, écrivons **4** écrive, écrivions **5** écrivais, écrivions **6** écrirai, écrirons **7** écrirais, écririons **8** écrivis, écrivîmes

**être** **1** étant **2** été **3** suis, es, est, sommes, êtes, sont **4** sois, sois, soit, soyons, soyez, soient **5** étais, étions **6** serai, serons **7** serais, serions **8** fus, fûmes

**faire** **1** faisant **2** fait(faite) **3** fais, fais, fait, faisons, faites, font **4** fasse, fassions, fassent **5** faisais, faisions **6** ferai, ferons **7** ferais, ferions **8** fis, fîmes

**falloir** **2** fallu **3** faut **4** faille **5** fallait **6** faudra **7** faudrait **8** fallut

**finir** **1** finissant **2** fini(finie) **3** finis, finis, finit, finissons, finissez, finissent **4** finisse, finissions **5** finissais, finissions **6** finirai, finirons **7** finirais, finirions **8** finis, finîmes

**fuir** **1** fuyant **2** fui **3** fuis, fuit, fuyons, fuient **4** fuie, fuyions, fuient **5** fuyais, fuyions **6** fuirai, fuirons **7** fuirais, fuirions **8** fuis, fuîmes

**haïr** **1** haïssant **2** haï(haïe) **3** hais, hait, haïssons **4** haïsse, haïssions **5** haïssais, haïssions **6** haïrai, haïrons **7** haïrais, haïrions

**joindre** **1** joignant **2** joint(jointe) **3** joins, joint, joignons, joignent **4** joigne, joignions **5** joignais, joignions **6** joindrai, joindrons **7** joindrais, joindrions **8** joignis, joignîmes

**lire** **1** lisant **2** lu(lue) **3** lis, lit, lisons **4** lise, lisions **5** lisais, lisions **6** lirai, lirons **7** lirais, lirions **8** lus, lûmes

**luire** **1** luisant **2** lui **3** luis, luit, luisons **4** luise, luisions **5** luisais, luisions **6** luirai, luirons **7** luirais, luirions

**maudire** **1** maudissant **2** maudit(maudite) **3** maudis, maudit, maudissons **4** maudisse, maudissions **5** maudissais, maudissions **6** maudirai, maudirons **7** maudirais, maudirions **8** maudis, maudîmes

**mentir** **1** mentant **2** menti **3** mens, ment, mentons **4** mente, mentions **5** mentais, mentions **6** mentirai, mentirons **7** mentirais, mentirions **8** mentis, mentîmes

**mettre** **1** mettant **2** mis(mise) **3** mets, met, mettons **4** mette, mettions **5** mettais, mettions **6** mettrai, mettrons **7** mettrais, mettrions **8** mis, mîmes

**moudre** **1** moulant **2** moulu(moulue) **3** mouds, moud, moulons

4 moule, moulions 5 moulais, moulions 6 moudrai, moudrons 7 moudrais, moudrions 8 moulus, moulûmes

**mourir** 1 mourant 2 mort(morte) 3 meurs, meurt, mourons, meurent 4 meure, mourions, meurent 5 mourais, mourions 6 mourrai, mourrons 7 mourrais, mourrions 8 mourus, mourûmes

**mouvoir** 1 mouvant 2 mû(mue) 3 meus, meut, mouvons, meuvent 4 meuve, mouvions, meuvent 5 mouvais, mouvions 6 mouvrai, mouvrons 7 mouvrais, mouvrions 8 mus, mûmes

**naître** 1 naissant 2 né(née) 3 nais, naît, naissons 4 naisse, naissions 5 naissais, naissions 6 naîtrai, naîtrons 7 naîtrais, naîtrions 8 naquis, naquîmes

**nuire** *voir* **luire**

**offrir** 1 offrant 2 offert(offerte) 3 offre, offrons 4 offre, offrions 5 offrais, offrions 6 offrirai, offrirons 7 offrirais, offririons 8 offris, offrîmes

**partir** 1 partant 2 parti(partie) 3 pars, part, partons 4 parte, partions 5 partais, partions 6 partirai, partirons 7 partirais, partirions 8 partis, partîmes

**peindre** 1 peignant 2 peint(peinte) 3 peins, peint, peignons 4 peigne, peignions 5 peignais, peignions 6 peindrai, peindrons 7 peindrais, peindrions 8 peignis, peignîmes

**placer** 'ç' before a vowel other than 'e' or 'i': 'nous plaçons' etc.

**plaire** 1 plaisant 2 plu 3 plais, plaît, plaisons 4 plaise, plaisions 5 plaisais, plaisions 6 plairai, plairons 7 plairais, plairions 8 plus, plûmes

**pleuvoir** 1 pleuvant 2 plu 3 pleut, pleuvent 4 pleuve, pleuvent 5 pleuvait, pleuvaient 6 pleuvra, pleuvront 7 pleuvrait, pleuvraient *NB. 3rd person only*

**pourvoir** 1 pourvoyant 2 pourvu(pourvue) 3 pourvois, pourvoit, pourvoyons, pourvoient 4 pourvoie, pourvoyions 5 pourvoyais, pourvoyions 6 pourvoirai, pourvoirons 7 pourvoirais, pourvoirions 8 pourvus, pourvûmes

**pouvoir** 1 pouvant 2 pu 3 peux, peut, pouvons, peuvent 4 puisse, puissions, puissent 5 pouvais, pouvions 6 pourrai, pourrons 7 pourrais, pourrions 8 pus, pûmes

**prendre** 1 prenant 2 pris(prise) 3 prends, prend, prenons, prennent 4 prenne, prenions, prennent 5 prenais, prenions 6 prendrai, prendrons 7 prendrais, prendrions 8 pris, prîmes

**prévoir** 1 prévoyant 2 prévu(prévue) 3 prévois, prévoit, prévoyons, prévoient 4 prévoie, prévoyions, prévoient 5 prévoyais, prévoyions 6 prévoirai, prévoirons 7 prévoirais, prévoirions 8 prévis, prévîmes

**recevoir** 1 recevant 2 reçu(reçue) 3 reçois, reçoit, recevons, reçoivent 4 reçoive, recevions 5 recevais, recevions 6 recevrai, recevrons 7 recevrais, recevrions 8 reçus, reçûmes

**rendre** 1 rendant 2 rendu(rendue) 3 rends, rend, rendons 4 rende, rendions 5 rendais, rendions 6 rendrai, rendrons 7 rendrais, rendrions 8 rendis, rendîmes

**résoudre** 1 résolvant 2 résolu(résolue) 3 résous, résout, résolvons 4 résolve, résolvions 5 résolvais, résolvions 6 résoudrai, résoudrons 7 résoudrais, résoudrions 8 résolus, résolûmes

**rire** 1 riant 2 ri 3 ris, rit, rions, rient 4 rie, riions, rient 5 riais, riions 6 rirai, rirons 7 rirais, ririons 8 ris, rîmes

**rompre** 1 rompant 2 rompu(rompue) 3 romps, rompt, rompons 4 rompe, rompions 5 rompais, rompions 6 romprai, romprons 7 romprais, romprions 8 rompis, rompîmes

**savoir** 1 sachant 2 su(sue) 3 sais, sait, savons, savent 4 sache, sachions 5 savais, savions 6 saurai, saurons 7 saurais, saurions 8 sus, sûmes

**sentir** 1 sentant 2 senti(sentie) 3 sens, sent, sentons 4 sente, sentions 5 sentais, sentions 6 sentirai, sentirons 7 sentirais, sentirions 8 sentis, sentîmes

**servir** 1 servant 2 servi(servie) 3 sers, sert, servons 4 serve, servions 5 servais, servions 6 servirai, servirons 7 servirais, servirions 8 servis, servîmes

**sortir** 1 sortant 2 sorti(sortie) 3 sors, sort, sortons 4 sorte, sortions 5 sortais, sortions 6 sortirai, sortirons 7 sortirais, sortirions 8 sortis, sortîmes

**souffrir** 1 souffrant 2 souffert(soufferte) 3 souffre, souffrons 4 souffre, souffrions 5 souffrais, souffrions 6 souffrirai, souffrirons 7 souffrirais, souffririons 8 souffris, souffrîmes

**suffire** 1 suffisant 2 suffi 3 suffis, suffit, suffisons 4 suffise, suffisions 5 suffisais, suffisions 6 suffirai, suffirons 7 suffirais, suffirions 8 suffis, suffîmes

**suivre** 1 suivant 2 suivi(suivie) 3 suis, suit, suivons 4 suive, suivions 5 suivais, suivions 6 suivrai, suivrons 7 suivrais, suivrions 8 suivis, suivîmes

**taire** 1 taisant 2 tu(tue) 3 tais, tait, taisons 4 taise, taisions 5 taisais, taisions 6 tairai, tairons 7 tairais, tairions 8 tus, tûmes

**tenir** 1 tenant 2 tenu(tenue) 3 tiens, tient, tenons, tiennent 4 tienne, tenions, tiennent 5 tenais, tenions 6 tiendrai, tiendrons 7 tiendrais, tiendrions 8 tins, tînmes

**traire** 1 trayant 2 trait(traite) 3 trais, trait, trayons, traient 4 traie, trayions, traient 5 trayais, trayions 6 trairai, trairons 7 trairais, trairions

**vaincre** 1 vainquant 2 vaincu(vaincue) 3 vaincs, vainc, vainquons, vainquent 4 vainque, vainquions, vainquent 5 vainquais, vainquions 6 vaincrai, vaincrons 7 vaincrais, vaincrions 8 vainquis, vainquîmes

**valoir** 1 valant 2 valu 3 vaux, vaut, valons 4 vaille, valions, vaillent 5 valais, valions 6 vaudrai, vaudrons 7 vaudrais, vaudrions 8 valus, valûmes

**venir** 1 venant 2 venu(venue) 3 viens, vient, venons, viennent 4 vienne, venions, viennent 5 venais, venions 6 viendrai, viendrons 7 viendrais, viendrions 8 vins, vînmes

**vêtir** 1 vêtant 2 vêtu(vêtue) 3 vêts, vêt, vêtons, vêtent 4 vête, vêtions 5 vêtais, vêtions 6 vêtirai, vêtirons 7 vêtirais, vêtirions 8 vêtis, vêtîmes

**vivre** 1 vivant 2 vécu(vécue) 3 vis, vit, vivons 4 vive, vivions 5 vivais, vivions 6 vivrai, vivrons 7 vivrais, vivrions 8 vécus, vécûmes

**voir** 1 voyant 2 vu(vue) 3 vois, voit, voyons, voient 4 voie, voyions, voient 5 voyais, voyions 6 verrai, verrons 7 verrais, verrions 8 vis, vîmes

**vouloir** 1 voulant 2 voulu(voulue) 3 veux, veut, voulons, veulent 4 veuille, voulions, veuillent 5 voulais, voulions 6 voudrai, voudrons 7 voudrais, voudrions 8 voulus, voulûmes *impératif :* veuille, veuillez

# IV. The sounds of French

Learning to pronounce French well is, as with all foreign languages, largely a matter of adopting different 'speech habits' from those used in speaking English.

A 'foreign accent' results from using the sounds of one's own language to approximate the sounds of the foreign language. This is particularly tempting when the same letter or letters represent similar sounds in each language. For instance the letter 'i' is used in both French and English, but to represent slightly different sounds in each, and many French speakers are unable to pronounce it in the English manner. It is possible that many do not even realize that the English speaker uses a different sound from the French — hence the typical French pronunciation of 'it is' which sounds to the English speaker as if it were written 'eet eese'.

These are the main ways in which French 'speech habits' differ from the English:

## 1. Activity of the lips

The lips play a very important part in French. When a vowel is described as having 'rounded' lips, the lips are slightly drawn together and pursed, as when the English speaker expresses exaggerated surprise with the vowel 'ooh!'. Equally, if the lips are said to be 'spread', the corners are pulled firmly back towards the cheeks, tending to reveal the front teeth.

In English, lip position is not important, and vowel sounds tend to merge because of this. In French, the activity of the lips means that every vowel sound is clearly distinct from every other.

## 2. No diphthongs

A diphthong is a glide between two vowel sounds in the same syllable. In English, there are few 'pure' vowel sounds, but largely diphthongs instead. Although speakers of English may *think* they produce one vowel sound in the word 'day', in fact they use a diphthong, which in this instance is a glide between the vowels [e] and [ɪ]: [deɪ]. In French the tension maintained in the lips, tongue and the mouth in general prevents diphthongs occurring, as the vowel sound is kept constant throughout. Hence the French word corresponding to the above example, 'dé', is pronounced with no final [ɪ] sound, but is phonetically represented thus: [de].

## 3. Consonants
Consonants in French are always given their full value. In English, consonants are often pronounced with a degree of laxness that can result in their practically disappearing altogether although not strictly 'silent'. In a relaxed pronunciation of a word such as 'hat', the 't' is often scarcely heard, or is replaced by a 'glottal stop' (a sort of jerk in the throat). Hence a Frenchman sounds unmistakeably foreign to an English speaker if he pronounces the 't' and 'l' in a word such as 'bottle' as energetically as he would in French.

## 4. Stress
In English, each word has its own particular stress pattern – for instance, the two different stress patterns for the word 'escort' produces two different words, one a noun and one a verb (*an escort bureau, may I escort you*). There is no possibility of this in French, since individual words have no characteristic stress pattern; syllables are stressed only when they occur at the end of the sentence or phrase:

eg. je les ai *vus*
je les ai vus *hier*
je les ai vus hier ma*tin*

The stressed syllable is in italics in each case, and all the other syllables are unstressed. This gives French a peculiarly 'staccato' effect, since all unstressed syllables tend to be of about the same length.

### Pronunciation of the sounds of French

## I. Vowels

| as in: | Hints on pronunciation |
| --- | --- |
| [a] p*a*tte pl*a*t *a*mour | Pronounced more or less as in English 'pat'. |
| [ɑ] b*a*s p*â*te | Longer and further back in the mouth than [a]. This sound resembles the English exclamation of surprise: 'ah!'. Similar to the vowel in English 'car', without the r-sound, but a little shorter. |
| [ɛ] l*ai*t jou*et* m*e*rci | Similar to the sound in English 'pet', but the lips are slightly further apart. Beware of substituting the English diphthong [eɪ] as in 'pay' when the sound [ɛ] comes at the end of a word |

515

| | |
|---|---|
| [e] *été* jou*er* | The tongue is held very tense and quite high in the mouth to pronounce a pure [e] sound. Again quite different from English [eɪ] of 'pay' |
| [ə] *le* pr*e*mier | The lips are slightly rounded for this vowel, and this is what distinguishes it from the sound in 'butt*er*' |
| [i] *ici* v*ie* lyc*ée* | The lips are well spread towards the cheeks and held very tensely while uttering this sound. Try saying English 'see' with your lips in this position. The sound is however shorter in French than the corresponding English vowel |
| [ɔ] m*o*rt h*o*mme | The lips must be well rounded, and the sound is half-way between 'u' and 'o' in the English words 'c*u*t' and 'c*o*t' |
| [o] m*o*t d*ô*me *eau* | A 'pure' vowel with strongly rounded lips. Make sure this sound does not become the diphthong used in English 'bone' and 'low' |
| [u] gen*ou* r*ou*e | Again, a 'pure' vowel with strongly rounded lips. The lip position is like that used at the beginning of the consonant [w] in English |
| [y] r*ue* vêt*u* | This sound is often considered the most difficult for English speakers to produce. Round your lips to say [u] (see above), then try to say [i] instead. Easier for Scots: try this sound in 'muesli' or 'Zürich'. There is no [j] sound (as in English 'pure') before this vowel |
| [œ] s*œu*r b*eu*rre | Similar to the vowel sound in English 'f*i*r' or 'm*u*rmur', but without the 'r' sounded, and with greater lip-rounding |
| [ø] p*eu* d*eux* | To pronounce this vowel, try to say [e] (see above) with strongly rounded lips |

Nasal vowels

These are always spelt with a vowel followed by a 'nasal' consonant – *n* or *m*. The production of nasal vowels can scarcely be explained without the help of a teacher or a recording of the sound quality. As a guide, however, the vowel is pronounced by allowing air to come partly down the nose and partly through the mouth, and the consonant disappears altogether. Best tip: ask a native French speaker to say and repeat for you the words 'mais*on*', 'jard*in*', 'ch*a*mbre', 'br*un*', and try to copy what you hear.

[ā] l*e*nt s*a*ng d*a*ns

[ɛ̃] mat*in* pl*ein*

[ɔ̃] n*on* p*on*t

[œ̃] br*un un*

In each case the vowel shown in the phonetic symbol is pronounced in the normal way, but air is allowed to come down the nose as well as through the mouth

## II. Consonants

Those consonants which are pronounced more or less as in English are represented phonetically as [b, f, g, k, m, p, v, w]. There is no aspiration with the production of [b, p, d, t, g, k] in French. Most other consonants are similar to their English counterparts but slight differences should be noted:

[d] *d*in*d*e

[t] *t*en*t*e

[n] *n*on*n*e

[l] *L*il*l*e

The tip of the tongue touches the upper teeth and not the roof of the mouth as in English

[s] *ç*a tou*s*

[z] *z*éro ro*s*e

As in English, but the tip of the tongue is held low, behind the bottom teeth

[ʃ] *ch*ose ta*ch*e          As in English '*sh*out'

[ʒ] *j*e *g*ilet be*ig*e          As in English 'mea*s*ure', 'bei*g*e'

[j] *y*eux pa*ill*e          As in English '*y*es'

Three consonant sounds are not heard in English:

[ʀ] *r*are veni*r*          For many speakers of English, 'r' is often silent, eg. 'farm'. In French, the 'r' is always pronounced, unless it follows an 'e' at the end of a word (cherch*er*, berg*er*). Its pronunciation in French is similar to the final sound of the Scottish word 'lo*ch*'. If you find this difficult, try thinking of the sound made when gargling, since the French [ʀ] is produced at the back of the mouth in a similar way [ɲ] vi*gne* a*gn*eau      Very similar to [nj] as in 'Spa*ni*ard'

[ɥ] *h*u*ile l*u*eur      Like a very rapid [y] (see above) followed by the next vowel sound in the word

There are two extra symbols used in this dictionary: * and '. See for instance the entry for *haie*. These symbols mean that no liaison is made before the following vowel:

cf. la haie vs l'habitation<br>les haies vs les habitations.

## From spelling to sounds

French spelling can be very confusing since one and the same sound can be represented in many different ways in the written word. Conversely, a given letter or group of letters can have different pronunciations depending on its position in the word. You may therefore be surprised to learn that these differences are governed by fairly precise 'rules' that are not difficult to assimilate.

The most important distinction to be drawn is whether the group of letters comes at the end of a word or syllable, or whether the letters are split between two syllables. Eg. in 'ma-tin' the dash represents the break between syllables and you can see that the word consists of two syllables of which the final one ends in 'in', one of the characteristic spellings of the nasal vowel [ɛ̃]. However in 'ma-ti-née', as the dashes show, the 'i' and the 'n' belong to different syllables, and they no longer constitute a single sound. The 'i' has its usual value (as in 'ici'), and the 'n' is pronounced as part of the next syllable.

This example illustrates how one of several French consonants is silent when it occurs at the end of the word or syllable, but is sounded when it begins a word or syllable. Other consonants which regularly behave in this way at the end of words are:

| | | | |
|---|---|---|---|
| t | éclat [ekla] | BUT | écla-ter [ekla*r*e] |
| d | chaud [ʃo] | BUT | chau-dement [ʃo*d*mɑ̃] |
| s | des [de] | BUT | dé-sir [deziʀ] |
| n | vain [vɛ̃] | BUT | vai-nement [vɛ*n*mɑ̃] |
| | matin [matɛ̃] | BUT | mati-née [mati*n*e] |
| m | parfum [paʀfœ̃] | BUT | parfu-mer [paʀfy*m*e] |
| x | aux [o] | BUT | au-xiliaire [o*ks*iljɛʀ] |
| z | nez [ne] | BUT | zé-zayer [zezeje] |
| r | aider [ede] | BUT | nous parle-rons [paʀlǝʀɔ̃] |

'm' and 'n' at the end of syllables (but not necessarily at the end of words):

m im-perméable

 [ɛpɛʀmeɑbl]  BUT i-magination [imaʒinɑsjɔ̃]

        BUT im-mobile [imɔbil]

n in-cident [ɛ̃sidɑ̃] BUT i-nique [inik]

Typical pronunciation of some French spellings

There are several groups of vowels in French spelling which are regularly pronounced in the same way, and these can easily be learnt:

| spelling | pronunciation | examples |
|---|---|---|
| ai | [ɛ] or [e] | maison, marchai (verb form), faire |
| au | [o] | auberge, landau |
| eau | [o] | eau, beau, tableau |
| ou | [u] | fou, oublier |
| eu | [œ] or [ø] | peur, feu, heureux, feuille |
| œu | [œ] | sœur, cœur |
| ue | [y] | rue |
| | | BUT recueil [ʀəkœj] |

Added to these are the many groups of letters occurring at the end of words, where their pronunciation is predictable, bearing in mind the tendency (see above) of final consonants to remain silent:

| *typical words* | *pronunciation of final syllable* |
|---|---|
| pas, mât, chat | [ɑ] or [a] |
| marcher, marchez,<br>marchais, marchait,<br>baie, valet, mes, fumée | [e] or [ɛ] |
| nid | [i] |
| chaud, vaut, faux,<br>sot, tôt, Pernod, dos, croc | [o] |
| bout, bijoux, sous, boue | [u] |
| fut, fût, crus, crûs | [y] |
| queue, heureux, bleus | [ø] |
| en, vend, vent,<br>an, sang, grand, dans | [ɑ̃] |
| fin, feint, frein, vain | [ɛ̃] |
| on, pont, fond, avons | [ɔ̃] |
| brun, parfum | [œ̃] |

# V. The time

**what time is it?**   quelle heure est-il?

**it is ...**       il est ..., c'est ...
**at what time?**  à quelle heure?
**at ...**      à ...

00.00 minuit
00.10 minuit dix
00.15 minuit et quart
00.30 minuit et demie, minuit trente
00.45 une heure moins (le) quart

01.00 une heure du matin
01.10 une heure dix (du matin)
01.15 une heure et quart, une heure quinze
01.30 une heure et demie, une heure trente
01.45 deux heures moins (le) quart, une heure quarante-cinq, une heure trois quarts
01.50 deux heures moins dix, une heure cinquante
01.59 deux heures moins une, une heure cinquante-neuf

12.00 midi, douze heures
12.30 midi et demie, midi trente

13.00 une heure de l'après-midi, treize heures
01.30 une heure et demic (de l'après-midi), une heure trente, treize heures trente

19.00 sept heures du soir, dix-neuf heures
19.30 sept heures et demie (du soir), sept heures trente, dix-neuf heures trente

23.00 onze heures (du soir), vingt-trois heures
23.45 onze heures trois quarts, onze heures quarante-cinq, vingt-trois heures quarante-cinq, minuit moins quart

**in 20 minutes**     dans vingt minutes

**20 minutes ago**   il y a vingt minutes

**wake me up at 7**  réveillez-moi à sept heures

**1 hour, 20', 45"**   une heure, vingt minutes et quarante-cinq secondes

# Dates and numbers

## 1. The date

**what's the date today?**  quelle est la date d'aujourd'hui?, quel jour sommes-nous?

**it's the ...**  nous sommes le ..., c'est le ...

| | |
|---|---|
| **1st of February** | premier février |
| **2nd of February** | deux février |
| **28th of February** | vingt-huit février |

**he's coming on the 7th (of May)**  il vient le sept (mai)

*NB: use cardinal numbers except for the first day of the month*

**I was born in 1945**
je suis né en dix-neuf cent quarante-cinq
**I was born on the 15th of July 1945**
je suis né le quinze juillet dix-neuf cent quarante-cinq

| | |
|---|---|
| **during the sixties** | dans les années soixante |
| **in the twentieth century** | au vingtième siècle |
| **in May** | en mai |
| **on Monday (the 15th)** | lundi (quinze) |
| **on Mondays** | le lundi |
| **next/last Monday** | lundi prochain/dernier |
| **in 10 days' time** | dans dix jours |

## 2. Telephone numbers

**I would like Paris 334 22 15**
j'aimerais Paris trois cent trente-quatre / vingt-deux / quinze
**give me Paris 302 02 02**
donnez-moi Paris trois cent deux / zéro deux / zéro deux
**could you get me Dijon 22 00 79, extension 2233**
pouvez-vous m'appeler Dijon vingt-deux / zéro zéro / soixante-dix-neuf, poste vingt-deux / trente-trois
**the Geneva prefix is 022**
l'indicatif de Genève est zéro / vingt-deux

## 3. Using numbers

| | |
|---|---|
| **he lives at number 10** | il habite au dix |
| **it's in chapter 7, on page 7** | c'est au chapitre sept, à la page sept |
| **he lives on the 7th floor** | il habite au septième (étage) |
| **he came in 7th** | il est arrivé (le) septième |
| **a share of one seventh** | une part d'un septième |
| **scale 1:25,000** | échelle au vingt-cinq millième |

# Numbers

| | | | | |
|---|---|---|---|---|
| 1 | un(une) | 1st | premier(première), 1er |
| 2 | deux | 2nd | deuxième, 2e *or* 2ème |
| 3 | trois | 3rd | troisième, 3e *or* 3ème |
| 4 | quatre | 4th | quatrième |
| 5 | cinq | 5th | cinquième |
| 6 | six | 6th | sixième |
| 7 | sept | 7th | septième |
| 8 | huit | 8th | huitième |
| 9 | neuf | 9th | neuvième |
| 10 | dix | 10th | dixième |
| 11 | onze | 11th | onzième |
| 12 | douze | 12th | douzième |
| 13 | treize | 13th | treizième |
| 14 | quatorze | 14th | quatorzième |
| 15 | quinze | 15th | quinzième |
| 16 | seize | 16th | seizième |
| 17 | dix-sept | 17th | dix-septième |
| 18 | dix-huit | 18th | dix-huitième |
| 19 | dix-neuf | 19th | dix-neuvième |
| 20 | vingt | 20th | vingtième |
| 21 | vingt et un(une) | 21st | vingt-et-unième |
| 22 | vingt-deux | 22nd | vingt-deuxième |
| 30 | trente | 30th | trentième |
| 40 | quarante | 100th | centième |
| 50 | cinquante | 101st | cent-unième |
| 60 | soixante | 1,000th | millième |
| 70 | soixante-dix | | |
| 71 | soixante et onze | 1/2 | un demi |
| 72 | soixante-douze | 1/3 | un tiers |
| 80 | quatre-vingts | 2/3 | deux tiers |
| 81 | quatre-vingt-un(-une) | 1/4 | un quart |
| 90 | quatre-vingt-dix | 1/5 | un cinquième |
| 91 | quatre-vingt-onze | | |
| 100 | cent | 0.5 | zéro virgule cinq, 0,5 |
| 101 | cent un(une) | 1.5 | un virgule cinq, 1,5 |
| 300 | trois cents | 10% | dix pour cent |
| 301 | trois cent un(une) | | |
| 1,000 | mille, 1 000 | 2 + 2 | deux plus deux |
| 1,001 | mille un(une) | 2 ÷ 2 | deux divisé par deux |
| 5,000 | cinq mille, 5 000 | 2 × 2 | deux fois deux |
| 1,000,000 | un million | 2 − 2 = | deux moins deux égale ... |

$6^2$ six au carré, six à la puissance deux;    20 m$^2$ vingt mètres carrés
$6^3$ six au cube, six à la puissance trois;    20 m$^3$ vingt mètres cubes